A HISTORY of WORLD SOCIETIES

A HISTORY *of* WORLD SOCIETIES

JOHN P. MCKAY

BENNETT D. HILL

JOHN BUCKLER

University of Illinois, Urbana

Editorial Advisers

FRANK F. CONLON

University of Washington
(India, Middle East)

JOHN W. DARDESS

University of Kansas
(East Asia)

LYMAN L. JOHNSON

University of North Carolina at Charlotte
(Latin America)

K. DAVID PATTERSON

University of North Carolina at Charlotte
(Africa)

HOUGHTON MIFFLIN COMPANY

BOSTON   DALLAS   GENEVA, ILLINOIS   LAWRENCEVILLE, NEW JERSEY   PALO ALTO

About the Authors

John P. McKay A native of St. Louis, Missouri, John P. McKay received his B.A. from Wesleyan University (1961), his M.A. from the Fletcher School of Law and Diplomacy (1962), and his Ph.D. from the University of California, Berkeley (1968). He began teaching history at the University of Illinois in 1966 and became a professor there in 1976. John won the Herbert Baxter Adams Prize for his book *Pioneers for Profit: Foreign Entrepreneurship and Russian Industrialization, 1885–1913* (1970). He has also written *Tramways and Trolleys: The Rise of Urban Mass Transport in Europe* (1976) and has translated Jules Michelet's *The People* (1973). His research has been supported by fellowships from the Ford Foundation, the Guggenheim Foundation, and IREX. Recently named general editor of *Industrial Development and the Social Fabric: An International Series of Historical Monographs,* John continues to serve on the editorial board of the *Journal of Economic History.*

Bennett D. Hill A native of Philadelphia, Bennett D. Hill earned an A.B. at Princeton (1956) and advanced degrees from Harvard (A.M., 1958) and Princeton (Ph.D., 1963). He taught history at the University of Illinois at Urbana, where he was department chairman from 1978 to 1981. He has published *English Cistercian Monasteries and Their Patrons in the Twelfth Century* (1968) and *Church and State in the Middle Ages* (1970); and articles in *Analecta Cisterciensia, The New Catholic Encyclopaedia, The American Benedictine Review,* and *The Dictionary of the Middle Ages.* His reviews have appeared in *The American Historical Review, Speculum, The Historian, The Catholic Historical Review,* and *Library Journal.* He has been a fellow of the American Council of Learned Societies, served on committees for the National Endowment for the Humanities and the Woodrow Wilson Foundation, and is now a Benedictine monk at St. Anselm's Abbey, Washington, D.C.

John Buckler Born in Louisville, Ky., John Buckler received his B.A. from the University of Louisville in 1967. Harvard University awarded him the Ph.D. in 1973. He is currently an associate professor at the University of Illinois, and is serving on the Subcommittee on Cartography of the American Philological Association. In 1980 Harvard University Press published his *The Theban Hegemony, 371–362 B.C.* His articles have appeared in journals both here and abroad, like the *American Journal of Ancient History, Classical Philology, Rheinisches Museum für Philologie, Classical Quarterly, Wiener Studien,* and *Symbolae Osloenses.*

Text Credits Excerpts from S. N. Kramer, *The Sumerians* (Chicago: University of Chicago Press, 1964), copyright © by the University of Chicago. Reprinted by permission. Excerpts from "Sumerian Myths and Epic Tales," transl. S. N. Kramer; "Akkadian Myths and Epics," transl. E. A. Speiser; "Laws from Mesopotamia and Asia Minor," transl. S. N. Kramer; "Summarian Wisdom Text," transl. S. N. Kramer; and "Hymn to the Nile," transl. John A. Wilson in *Ancient Near Eastern Texts Relating to the Old Testament,* 3rd edn. with Supplement. Copyright © 1969 by Princeton University Press, pp. 44–590. Reprinted by permission of Princeton University Press. Excerpt reprinted from *The Mahabharata I, The Book of the Beginning,* trans. by J. A. B. van Buitenen, by permission of The University of Chicago Press. Copyright 1973 by the University of Chicago. Excerpts from Juan Mascaro, trans., *The Upanishads* (London: Penguin Classics, 1965), pp. 117–118. Copyright © Juan Mascaro, 1965. Reprinted by permission of Penguin Books Ltd. Excerpts from D. C. Lau, trans., *Tao Tzu Ching* (London: Penguin Classics, 1963), pp. 59, 75, 82. Copyright © D. C. Lau, 1963. Reprinted by permission of Penguin Books Ltd. By kind permission of Sidgwick and Jackson, extracts from *The Wonder That Was India* by A. L. Basham. Excerpts from J. T. McNeil and H. Gamer, trans. *Medieval Handbooks of Penance,* Octagon Books, New York, 1965. Reprinted by permission of Columbia University Press. Excerpts from *More Translations from the Chinese,* translated by Arthur Waley. Copyright 1919 and renewed 1969 by Alfred A.

(Credits continued on page xvii)

Cover: *A Marriage Procession Passing Through a Bazaar.* Bilaspar or Mandi, c. 1680, on loan to the Victoria and Albert Museum from a Private Collector. Victoria and Albert Museum, Crown Copyright.

Printed in the U.S.A.

Library of Congress Catalog Card Number: 83–81878

ISBN: 0-395-34363-1

DEFGHIJ-M-898765

CONTENTS

MAPS

Credits (continued from copyright page):

Knopf, Inc. Reprinted by permission of the publisher and George Allen & Unwin (Publishers) Ltd. Riddle No. 44 from Michael Alexander, trans., *The Earliest English Poems* (London: Penguin Books Ltd, 1966), p. 99. Copyright © Michael Alexander, 1966. Reprinted by permission of Penguin Books Ltd. Excerpts from "The White Man's Burden" by Rudyard Kipling from *Rudyard Kipling's Verse: Definitive Edition.* Reprinted by permission of the National Trust and Doubleday & Company, Inc.

PREFACE

A HISTORY OF WORLD SOCIETIES grew out of the authors' desire to infuse new life into the broad study of human history. Initially, this desire led us to write *A History of Western Society* (1979, second edition 1983); when the response to that work was quite favorable, we were encouraged to extend our basic approach to global history. Although this proved to be an enormous undertaking, we have fond hopes that intense effort, coupled with careful criticism from area specialists and experienced teachers, has achieved the intended result.

As we noted in 1979, the study of history is beset by a disconcerting paradox today. On the one hand, historians have brought many changes to their discipline in recent years, as imaginative questions and research have opened up vast new areas of interest and increased historical knowledge. The pushing back of the frontiers of knowledge has been especially dramatic in social history, where the history of population, women, the family, and popular culture – to name only four important components – have emerged as major fields of inquiry. Similar but less well-publicized advances have characterized economic and intellectual history, while new research and fresh interpretations have been simultaneously revitalizing the traditional mainstream of political, diplomatic, and religious development. Yet, while new discoveries and contro-versies have been stimulating professional historians, both the general public and the intelligentsia often appear to be losing interest in the past. The distinguished mathematical economist of our acquaintance who smugly quips "What's new in history?" – confident that the answer is nothing and that historians are as dead as the events they examine – is not alone.

It was our conviction, based on considerable experience introducing large numbers of students to the broad sweep of historical development, that a book reflecting current trends in scholarship could excite readers and inspire a new interest in history and the gradual making of the modern world. Our strategy was twofold. First, we made social history the core element of our work. Not only did we incorporate recent research by social historians, but we sought to re-create the life of ordinary people in appealing human terms. At the same time we were determined to give the great economic, political, intellectual, and cultural developments the attention they unquestionably deserve. We wanted to give individual readers and instructors a balanced, integrated perspective, so that they could pursue on their own or in the classroom those themes and questions they found particularly exciting and significant.

In writing *A History of World Societies* we

have adhered to our original strategy, while adding a new element — a firm commitment to a global perspective. Thus social history remains at the core of this work, and important research on population and diet, women, the family, popular culture, and similar topics has been integrated into the text. The strong social element is, we believe, especially appropriate in a world history, since identification with ordinary people in past time allows today's reader to pass through a doorway that leads toward the empathetic understanding of different cultures and civilizations. In extending the scope of our work we have also taken great pains to realize the promise of the balanced approach, making certain in particular that major intellectual and cultural developments are treated fully.

The challenge and appeal of this edition for the authors is the expansion of our earlier investigations to encompass the whole world. In the course of this expansion, we have added ten chapters devoted to the history of Asia, Africa, and the Americas to the foundation already laid by the thirty-one chapters of *A History of Western Society*. As North Americans whose scholarly research has focused on Europe, we have been acutely aware of the great drama of our times — the passing of the European era and the simultaneous rise of Asian and African peoples in world affairs. Increasingly, the whole world interacts, and to understand that interaction and what it means for today's citizens we must study the whole world's history.

To do so, we have adopted a comprehensive yet realistic global perspective. We have studied all geographical areas and the world's main civilizations, conscious of their separate identities and unique contributions. Yet we have also stressed the links between civilizations, for these links eventually transformed multicentered world history into a complex interactive process of different continents, peoples, and civilizations in recent times. Finally, it is our place neither to praise nor to vilify our own civilization's major role in the growth of global integration, accepting it rather as part of our heritage and seeking to understand it and the consequences for all concerned.

Our book has other notable features. To help guide the reader toward historical understanding we have posed specific historical questions at the beginning of each chapter. These questions are then answered in the course of the chapter, and each chapter concludes with a concise summary of the chapter's findings. Timelines, which students find useful, have been inserted into many chapters.

We have also tried to suggest how historians actually work and think. We have quoted rather extensively from a wide variety of primary sources and have demonstrated in our use of these quotations how historians sift and weigh evidence. We want the reader to realize that history is neither a list of cut-and-dried facts nor a senseless jumble of conflicting opinions. It is our further hope that the primary quotations, so carefully fitted into their historical context, will give the reader a sense that even in the earliest and most remote periods of human experience history has been shaped by individual men and women, some of them great aristocrats, others ordinary folk.

Each chapter concludes with several carefully selected suggestions for further reading. These suggestions are briefly described, in order to help readers know where to go to continue thinking and learning about world history. The chapter bibliographies are deliberately extensive, in order to keep them current with the vast and complex new work being done in many fields. In a number of areas each new journal or monograph may present fresh perspectives or challenge accepted views, and the best of these recent works have been singled out for citation.

All the illustrations in *A History of World Societies* have been carefully selected to re-enforce both the book's social theme and its balanced treatment of all aspects of global history. Artwork is an integral part of our book, for the past can speak in pictures as well as words. Maps and line drawings are also a fundamental part of the book and, as with illustrations, they carry captions to enhance their value.

World civilization courses differ widely in chronological structure from one campus to another. To accommodate the various divisions of historical time into intervals that fit a two-quarter or two-semester period, *A History of World Societies* is being published in two versions, both formats embracing the complete work:

One-volume hardcover edition, A HISTORY OF WORLD SOCIETIES; and a two-volume paperback, A HISTORY OF WORLD SOCIETIES *Volume I: To 1715* (Chapters 1–21), *Volume II: Since 1500* (Chapters 19–41).

Note that overlapping chapters in the two-volume set permit still wider flexibility in matching the appropriate volume with the opening and closing dates of a course term.

A History of World Societies also has a study guide for students, an excellent aid that has been written primarily by Professor James Schmiechen of Central Michigan University. Professor Schmiechen read all our drafts, from the first prospectus to the final typescript, and he gave us many valuable suggestions in addition to his enthusiastic and warmly appreciated support. His *Study Guide* contains chapter summaries, chapter outlines, study questions, self-check lists of important concepts and events, and a variety of study aids

and suggestions. A feature of the *Study Guide* – one that we feel will be extremely useful to the student – is our step-by-step Reading with Understanding exercises, which take the reader by ostensive example through reading and studying activities like underlining, summarizing, identifying main points, classifying information according to sequence, and making historical comparisons. To enable both students and instructors to use the *Study Guide* with the greatest possible flexibility, the guide is available in two volumes, with the same overlapping of chapters as the text.

In expanding our earlier work to consider all of human history, we have benefited greatly from the expert criticisms and suggestions of the editorial advisers. Their aid, always given in an objective, highly professional manner, certainly improved our efforts, and it is with real gratitude that we warmly thank Frank F. Conlon, University of Washington; John W. Dardess, University of Kansas; Lyman L. Johnson, University of North Carolina at Charlotte; and K. David Patterson, University of North Carolina at Charlotte.

We would like to take this opportunity to express our appreciation to John E. Lane, Long Island University-Brooklyn Center; Charlotte L. Beahan, Murray State University; Robert Burton, California Polytechnic State University, San Luis Obispo; Gregory C. Kozlowski, DePaul University; Marian Nelson, University of Nebraska-Omaha; Frederick Gifrun, Southeastern Massachusetts University; J. Carlton Hayden, Morgan State University; S. D. Ehrenpreis, Bronx Community College-CUNY; Richard Rice, University of Tennessee-Chattanooga; J. Chris Arndt, Florida State University; Jonathan Goldstein, West Georgia College; Max E. Riedlsperger, California Polytechnic State University, San Luis Obispo; Kevin Marchisio, Cuyahoga

Community College-Parma; and Michael Batinski, Southern Illinois University-Carbondale, who read and critiqued the new chapters of this work.

It is also a pleasure to thank Roger Schlesinger, Washington State University; Charles Rearick, University of Massachusetts at Amherst; Donald Buck, DeAnza College; James Powell, Syracuse University; John M. Riddle, North Carolina State University; Laurence Lee Howe, University of Louisville; Archibald Lewis, University of Massachusetts at Amherst; Jack R. Harlan, University of Illinois; Marc Cooper, Southwestern Missouri State University; Lowell L. Blaisdell, Texas Tech University; Kevin K. Carroll, Arizona State University; Robert G. Clouse, Indiana State University; Albert A. Hayden, Wittenberg University; Harry M. Hutson, University of Tennessee at Martin; Dorothy Vogel Krupnik, Indiana University of Pennsylvania; Charles A. Le Guin, Portland State University; Carolyn C. Lougee, Stanford University; Paul J. Pinckney, University of Tennessee-Knoxville; C. Mary Taney, Glassboro State College; William M. Welch, Jr., Troy State University; and John C. White, University of Alabama-Huntsville, who read and critiqued the manuscript of the second edition of *A History of Western Society* through its development.

Many of our colleagues at the University of Illinois kindly provided information and stimulation for our book, often without even knowing it. N. Frederick Nash, Rare Book Librarian, gave freely of his time and made many helpful suggestions for illustrations. Barbara Bohen, Director of the World Heritage Museum at the University, allowed us complete access to the sizable holdings of the museum. James Dengate kindly supplied information on objects from the museum's collection. Caroline Buckler took many excellent photographs of the museum's objects and generously helped us at crucial moments in production. Such wide-ranging expertise was a great asset for which we are very appreciative. Bennett Hill wishes to thank Dr. Manoel Cardozo, Curator of the Oliveira Lima Library at Catholic University, for his most gracious assistance and Dr. Paul McKane, OSB, for his photographic help.

Each of us has benefited from the generous criticism of his co-authors, although each of us assumes responsibility for what he has written. John Buckler has written Chapters 1-8 and 10; Bennett Hill has contributed Chapters 9, 11-20, 25, and 32; and John McKay has written Chapters 21-24, 26-31, and 33-41. Finally, we warmly welcome any comments or suggestions for improvements from our readers.

JOHN P. MCKAY
BENNETT D. HILL
JOHN BUCKLER

A HISTORY of WORLD SOCIETIES

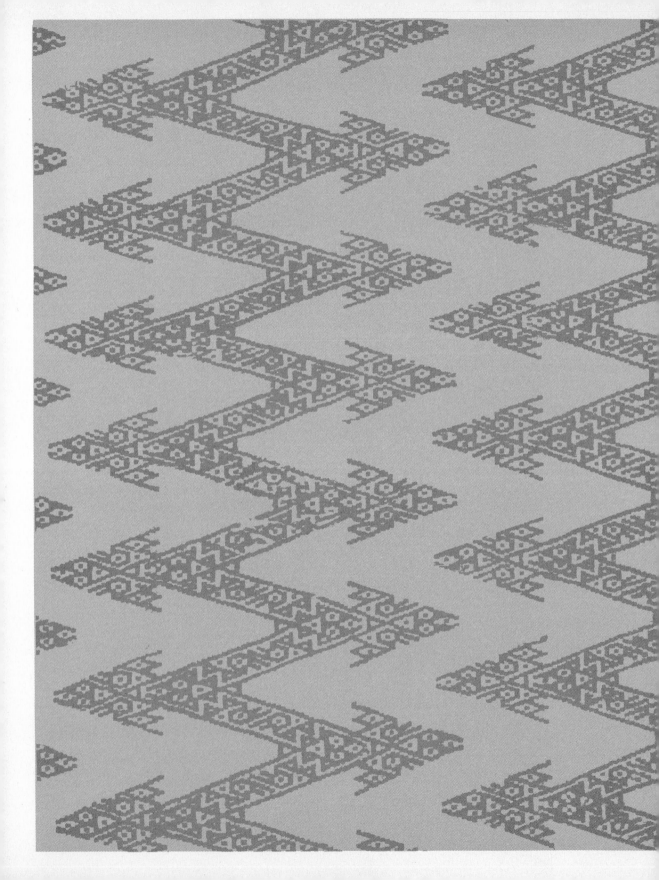

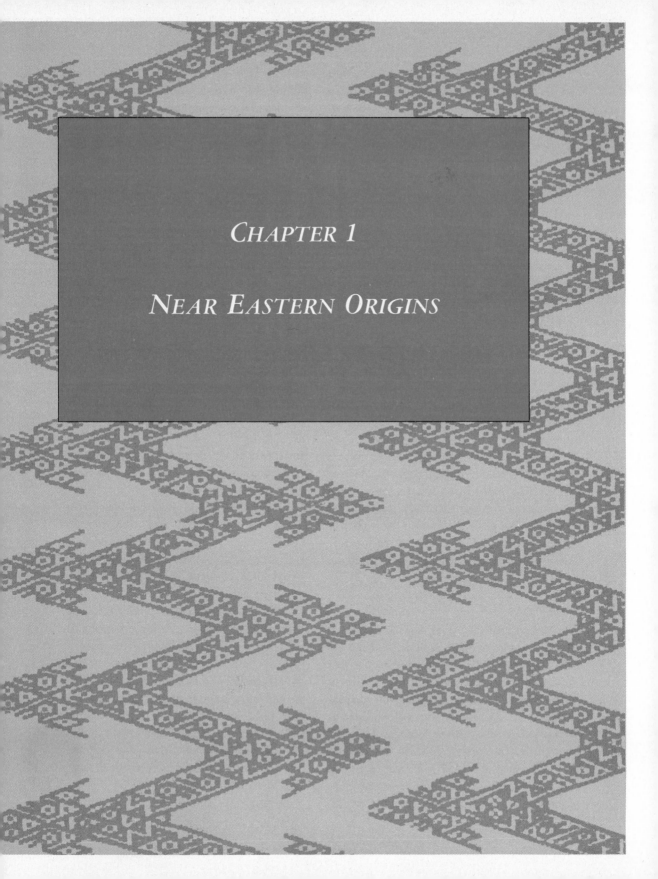

CHAPTER 1

NEAR EASTERN ORIGINS

THE CULTURE of the modern Western world has its origins in places as far away as modern Iraq, Iran, and Egypt. In these areas human beings abandoned their life of roaming and hunting to settle in stable agricultural communities. From these communities grew cities and civilizations, societies that invented concepts and techniques that have become integral parts of contemporary life. Fundamental is the development of writing by the Sumerians in Mesopotamia, an invention that enables knowledge of the past to be preserved and facilitates the spread and accumulation of learning, lore, literature, and science. Mathematics, astronomy, and architecture were all innovations of the ancient Near Eastern civilizations. So too were the first law codes and religious concepts that still permeate daily life.

How did wild hunters become urban dwellers? How did the roots of Western culture establish themselves in far-off Mesopotamia, and what caused Mesopotamian culture to become predominant throughout most of the ancient Near East? What part did the Egyptians play in this vast story? Lastly, what did the arrival of the Hittites on the fringes of Mesopotamia and Egypt mean to the superior cultures of their new neighbors? These are the questions this chapter will explore.

On December 27, 1831, young Charles Darwin stepped aboard the H.M.S. *Beagle* to begin a voyage to South America and the Pacific Ocean. In the course of that five-year voyage he became convinced that species of animals and human beings had evolved from lower forms. At first Darwin was reluctant to make public his theories because they ran counter to the biblical account of creation, which claimed that God had made Adam in one day. Finally, however, in 1859 he published *On the Origin of Species.* In 1871 he fol-

lowed it with *The Descent of Man,* in which he argued that human beings and apes are descended from a common ancestor. Even before Darwin had proclaimed his theories, evidence to support them had come to light. In 1856, the fossilized bones of an early form of man were discovered in the Neander valley of Germany. Called Neanderthal Man after the place of his discovery, he was physically more primitive than and anatomically a bit different from modern man (*Homo sapiens,* or thinking man). But he was clearly a human being and not an ape. He offered proof of Darwin's theory that *Homo sapiens* had evolved from less-developed forms.

The theories of Darwin, supported by the evidence of fossilized remains, ushered in a new scientific era, an era in which scientists and scholars have re-examined the very nature of human beings and their history. Men and women of the twentieth century have made new discoveries, solved some old problems, and raised many new ones. Since 1959, the anthropologists Louis and Mary Leakey and their son Richard, working in the Olduvai Gorge in East Africa, have uncovered fossilized bones of several very early types of human beings as well as species of advanced apes. The work of the Leakeys alone demonstrates how complex the course of human evolution has been.

Why did some human types become extinct while others thrived? More importantly, what are the links among the fossilized remains? The answers to these questions lie in the future. For the moment, perhaps the wisest and most humble answer is the observation of Loren Eiseley, a noted American anthropologist: "The human interminglings of hundreds of thousands of years of prehistory are not to be clarified by a single generation of archaeologists."[1]

Despite the enormous uncertainty surrounding human development, a reasonably clear picture can be had of two important early periods: the Paleolithic or Old Stone Age, and the Neolithic or New Stone Age. The immensely long Paleolithic Age, which lasted from about 400,000 B.C. until about 7000 B.C., takes its name from the crude stone tools the earliest hunters chipped from flint and obsidian, a black volcanic rock. During the much shorter Neolithic Age, which lasted from about 7000 B.C. to about 3000 B.C., human beings began using new types of stone tools and pursuing agriculture.

THE PALEOLITHIC AGE

Life in the Paleolithic Age was perilous and uncertain at best. Survival depended largely on the success of the hunt, but the hunt often brought sudden and violent death. Paleolithic peoples hunted in a variety of ways, depending on the climate and the environment. Often the hunters stationed themselves at river fords and waterholes and waited for their prey to come to them. Paleolithic hunters were thoroughly familiar with the habits of the animals they relied upon, and paid close attention to their migratory habits. Other hunters trapped their quarry, and those who lived in open areas stalked and pursued game. Paleolithic peoples hunted a huge variety of animals, ranging from elephants in Spain to deer in China.

Success in the hunt often depended more on the quality and effectiveness of the hunters' social organization than on their bravery. Paleolithic hunters were organized – they hunted in groups. They used their knowledge of the animal world and their power of thinking to plan how to down their prey. The ability to think and to act as an organized social group meant that Paleolithic hunters could successfully feed on animals that were bigger, faster, and stronger than themselves.

Paleolithic peoples also nourished themselves by gathering nuts, berries, and seeds. Just as they knew the habits of animals, so they had vast knowledge of the plant kingdom. Some Paleolithic peoples even knew how to plant wild seeds to supplement their food supply. Thus, they relied on every part of the environment for their survival.

Home for Paleolithic folk also varied according to climate and environment. Particularly in cold regions, they sought refuge in caves from the weather, predatory animals, and other people. In warmer climates and in open country they built shelters, some of them no more elaborate than temporary huts or sunscreens.

The basic social unit of Paleolithic societies was probably the family, but family bonds were no doubt stronger and more extensive than those of families in modern, urban, and industrialized societies. It is likely that the bonds of kinship were strong not just within the nuclear family of father, mother, and children, but throughout the extended family of uncles, aunts, cousins, nephews, and nieces. People in nomadic societies typically depend on the extended family for cooperative work and mutual protection. The ties of kinship probably also extended beyond the family to the tribe. A *tribe* was a group of families, led by a patriarch, who considered themselves to be descended from a common ancestor. Most tribes probably consisted of from thirty to fifty people.

As in the hunt, so too in other aspects of life – the members of the group had to cooperate in order to survive. The adult males normally hunted, and between hunts made their stone weapons. The realm of the women was probably the camp. There they made utensils, and were probably responsible for the invention of weaving. They fashioned skins into cloths, tents, and footwear. They left the camp to gather nuts, grains, and fruits to supplement the group's diet. Their unique function was the bearing of children, who were essential to the continuation of the group.

Women also had to tend the children, especially in their earliest and most helpless days. Part of women's work was tending the fire, which served for warmth and cooking and also for protection against wild animals.

Paleolithic peoples were also world travelers. Before the dawn of history bands of *Homo sapiens* flourished in Europe, Africa, and Asia, and had crossed into the continents of North and South America and Australia. By the end of the Paleolithic Age, there were very few "undiscovered" areas left in the world.

Some of the most striking accomplishments of Paleolithic peoples were intellectual. The development of the human brain made thought possible. Unlike animals, whose behavior is the result of instinct, Paleolithic peoples used reason to govern their actions. Thought and language permitted the lore and experience of the old to be passed on to the young. An invisible world also opened up to *Homo sapiens*. The Neanderthalers developed the custom of burying their dead and of leaving offerings with the body, perhaps in the belief that in some way life continued after death.

Paleolithic peoples produced the first art. They decorated the walls of their caves with paintings of animals and scenes of the hunt. They also began to fashion clay models of pregnant women and of animals. Many of the surviving paintings, such as those at Altamira in Spain and Lascaux in France, are located deep in the caves, in areas not easily accessible.

These areas were probably places of ritual and initiation, where young men were taken when they joined the ranks of the hunters. They were also places of magic. The animals depicted on the walls were either those hunted for food or those feared as predators. Many are shown wounded by spears or arrows; others are pregnant. The early artists may have been expressing the hope that the hunt would be successful and game plentiful. By portraying the animals as realistically as possible, the artists and hunters may have hoped to gain power over them. The statuettes of pregnant women seem to express a wish for fertile women to have babies and thus ensure the group's survival. The wall paintings and statuettes express human beings' earliest yearnings to control their environment.

Despite their many achievements, Paleolithic peoples were sometimes their own worst enemies. At times they fought each other for control of hunting grounds, and some early hunters wiped out less aggressive peoples. On occasion Paleolithic peoples seem to have preyed on one another, probably under the threat of starvation. One of the grimmest indications that Neanderthal Man was at times cannibalistic comes from a cave in Yugoslavia, where investigators found human bones burned and split open. Even so, cannibalism appears to have been rare. The overriding struggle of the Paleolithic Age was with an uncompromising environment.

THE NEOLITHIC AGE

Hunting is at best a precarious way of life, even when the diet is supplemented with seeds and fruits. If the climate changed even slightly, the all-important herds might move to new areas. As recently as the late 1950s the

Caribou Eskimos of the Canadian Northwest Territories suffered a severe famine when the caribou herds, their only source of food and bone for weapons, changed their migration route. Paleolithic tribes either moved with the herds, and adapted themselves to new circumstances, or – like the Caribou Eskimos – perished. Several long ice ages – periods when huge glaciers covered vast parts of Europe – subjected small bands of Paleolithic hunters to extreme hardship.

Not long after the last Ice Age, around 7000 B.C., some hunters and gatherers began to rely chiefly on agriculture for their sustenance. This development has traditionally been called "the Agricultural Revolution." Yet the work of Jack R. Harlan, a leading scientist in the field of agronomy, has caused scholars to reappraise the origins of agriculture:

Agriculture is not an invention or a discovery and is not as revolutionary as we had thought; furthermore, it was adopted slowly and with reluctance. The current evidence indicates that agriculture evolved through an extension and intensification of what people had already been doing for a long time.[2]

Striking support for Harlan's view came in 1981 from an American archaeological expedition to the Nile valley in Egypt. Investigators found that for thousands of years nomads had planted wheat and barley in the silt left by the flooding of the Nile. These people, however, never shifted to a life of settled farming. Instead, the crops they grew were just another, though important, source of their food. In short, hunters and gatherers apparently long knew how to grow crops, but did not base their existence on them.

The real transformation of human life occurred when hunters and gatherers gave up their nomadic way of life to depend primarily on the grain they grew and the animals they domesticated. Agriculture made for a more stable and secure life. Neolithic peoples thus flourished, fashioning an energetic and creative era. They were responsible for many fundamental inventions and innovations that the modern world takes for granted. First, obviously, is systematic agriculture, the primary economic activity of the entire ancient world and the basis of all modern life. The settled routine of Neolithic farmers led to the evolution of towns and eventually cities. Neolithic farmers usually raised more food than they could consume, and their surpluses permitted larger and healthier populations. Since surpluses of food could also be bartered for other commodities, the Neolithic era witnessed the beginnings of large-scale trade. In time the increasing complexity of Neolithic societies led to the development of writing, prompted by the need to keep records and later by the urge to chronicle experiences, learning, and beliefs.

The transition to settled life also had a profound impact on the family. The shared needs and pressures that make for strong extended-family ties in nomadic societies are less prominent in settled societies. Bonds to the extended family weakened. In towns and cities, the nuclear family – father, mother, and children – was more dependent on its immediate neighbors than on kinfolk.

Meanwhile, however, the nomadic way of life and the family relationships it nurtured continued to flourish alongside settled agriculture. Even nomadic life changed. Neolithic nomads traveled with flocks of domesticated animals, which were their main source of wealth and food. Often farmers and nomads bartered peaceably with one another, each group trading its surpluses for those of the other. Although nomadic peoples continued

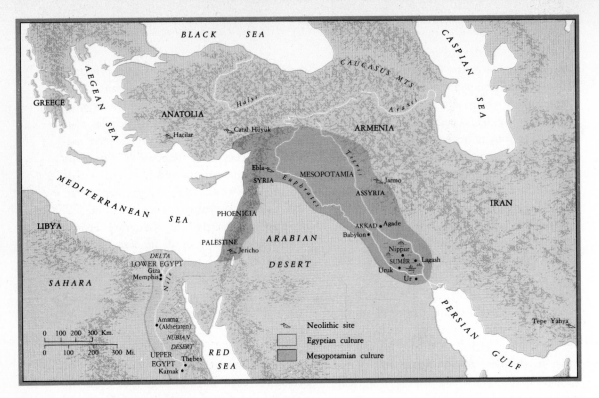

MAP 1.1 SPREAD OF CULTURES *This map illustrates the spread of Mesopotamian and Egyptian culture through a semicircular stretch of land often called the "Fertile Crescent."*

to exist throughout the Neolithic period and into modern times, the future belonged to the Neolithic farmers and their descendants. While the development of agriculture may not have been revolutionary, the changes that it ushered in certainly were.

Until recently, scholars thought that agriculture originated in the ancient Near East and gradually spread elsewhere. Contemporary work, however, points to a more complex pattern of development. For unknown reasons people in various parts of the world all seem to have begun domesticating plants and animals at roughly the same time, around 7000 B.C. Four main points of origin have been identified. In the Near East, sites as far apart as Tepe Yahya in modern Iran, Jarmo in Iraq, Jericho in Palestine, and Hacilar in modern

Turkey (see Map 1.1) raised wheat, barley, peas, and lentils. They also kept herds of sheep, pigs, and possibly goats. In western Africa, Neolithic farmers domesticated many plants, including millet, sorghum, and yams. In northeastern China, peoples of the Yangshao culture developed techniques of field agriculture, animal husbandry, potterymaking, and bronze metallurgy. Innovations in the New World were equally striking. Indians in Central and South America domesticated a host of plants, among them corn, beans, and squash. From these far-flung areas, knowledge of farming techniques spread to still other regions.

The first farmers gathered and planted the seeds of wild wheat, barley, and other plants. Later farmers learned to improve their crops.

The excavators of Tepe Yahya demonstrated in 1976 how specialization in farming could have led to a new species of grain: the Neolithic farmers of Tepe Yahya, preferring a particular species of wheat to others, planted only that species; when nearby wild grasses fertilized the wheat naturally, a new hybrid species resulted.

The deliberate planting of crops itself led to changes in their genetic structure. The plants and animals cultivated by Neolithic farmers gradually evolved to the point where most of them could no longer survive in the wild. Thus human beings and the plants and animals they domesticated depended on each other for survival. Contemporary work on the origins of farming has led to a chilling revelation: the genetic base of most modern domesticated plants, like wheat and corn, is so narrow that a new pest or plant disease could destroy much of it. The result would be widespread famine. Human society is depending on a precarious food base.

Once people began to rely on farming for their livelihood, they settled in permanent villages and built houses. The location of the village was crucial. Early farmers chose places where the water supply was constant and adequate for their crops and flocks. At first, villages were small, consisting of a few households. As the population expanded and prospered, villages usually developed into towns. Between 8000 and 7000 B.C., the community at Jericho grew to at least two thousand people. Jericho's inhabitants lived in mud-brick houses built on stone foundations, and they surrounded their town with a massive fortification wall. The Neolithic site of Catal Hüyük in Anatolia (modern Turkey) covered thirty-two acres. The outer houses of the settlement formed a solid wall of mud brick, which served as a bulwark against attack. At Tepe Yahya, too, the Neolithic farmers surrounded their town with a wall.

Walls offered protection and permitted a more secure and stable way of life than that of the nomad. They also prove that towns grew in size, population, and wealth, for these fortifications were so large that they could have been raised only by a large labor force. They also indicate that towns were developing social and political organization. The fortifications were the work of the whole community, and they would have been impossible without central planning.

One of the major effects of the advent of agriculture and settled life was a dramatic increase in population. No census figures exist for this period, but the number and size of the towns prove that Neolithic society was expanding. Early farmers found that agriculture provided a larger and much more dependable food supply than had hunting and gathering. No longer did the long winter months mean the immediate threat of starvation. Farmers raised more food than they could consume, and they learned to store the surplus for the winter. Because the farming community was better fed than ever before, it was also more resistant to diseases that kill people who are suffering from malnutrition. Thus Neolithic farmers were healthier and longer-lived than their predecessors. All these factors explain the growth of towns like Jericho and Jarmo.

The surplus of food had two other momentous consequences. First, grain became an article of commerce. The farming community traded surplus grain for items it could not produce itself. The community thus obtained raw materials such as precious gems and metals. In Mesopotamia the early towns imported copper from the north, and eventually copper replaced stone for tools and weapons. Trade also brought Neolithic communities

TOWER AT JERICHO *Photographed during excavation, this tower is a good example of the strong fortifications of Neolithic towns. The sheer size of the walls amply illustrates the huge amount of labor and central planning necessary to build them. (Consulate General of Israel)*

into touch with one another, making possible the spread of ideas and techniques.

Second, agricultural surplus made possible the division of labor. It freed some members of the community from the necessity of raising food. Artisans and craftsmen devoted their attention to making the new stone tools farming demanded — hoes and sickles for fieldwork and mortars and pestles for grinding the grain. Other artisans began to shape clay into pottery vessels, which were used to store grain, wine, and oil, and which served as kitchen utensils. Still other artisans wove baskets and cloth. People who could specialize in particular crafts produced more and better goods than any single individual could.

Prosperity and stable conditions nurtured other innovations and discoveries. Neolithic farmers improved their tools and agricultural techniques. They domesticated bigger, stronger animals, such as the bull and the horse, to work for them. To harness the power of these animals they invented tools like the plow, which came into use by 3000 B.C. The first plows had wooden shares and could break only light soils, but they were far more efficient than stone hoes. By 3000 B.C. the wheel had been invented, and farmers devised ways of hitching bulls and horses to wagons. These developments enabled Neolithic farmers to raise more food more efficiently and easily than ever before, simply because animals and machines were doing a greater proportion of the actual work.

In arid regions like Mesopotamia and Egypt, farmers learned to irrigate their land. By diverting water from rivers, they were able to open new land to cultivation. River waters flooding the fields deposited layers of rich mud, which increased the fertility of the soil. Thus the rivers, together with the manure of domesticated animals, kept replenishing the land. One result was a further increase in population and wealth. Irrigation, especially on a large scale, demanded group effort. The entire community had to plan which land to irrigate and how to lay out the canals. Then everyone had to help dig the canals. The demands of irrigation underscored the need for strong central authority within the community. Successful irrigation projects in turn strengthened such central authority by proving it effective and beneficial. Towns evolved corporate spirit and governments, to which individuals were subordinate. Here were the makings of urban life.

The development of systematic agriculture

was a fundamental turning-point in the history of civilization. Farming gave rise to stable settled societies, which enjoyed considerable prosperity. It made possible an enormous increase in population. Some inhabitants of the budding towns turned their attention to the production of goods that made life more comfortable. Settled circumstances and a certain amount of leisure made the accumulation and spread of knowledge easier. Finally, sustained farming prepared the way for urban life.

MESOPOTAMIAN CIVILIZATION

Mesopotamia is the Greek name for the land between the Euphrates and Tigris rivers. Both rivers have their headwaters in the mountains of Armenia in modern Turkey. Both are fed by numerous tributaries, and the entire river system drains a vast mountainous region. Overland routes in Mesopotamia usually follow the Euphrates, because the banks of the Tigris are frequently steep and difficult. North of the ancient city of Babylon, the land levels out into a barren expanse. In 401 B.C., the Greek writer and adventurer Xenophon gave a vivid description of this area:

In this area the land is a level plain just like the sea, full of wormwood. If there was any brush or reed there, it was invariably fragrant, like spices. Trees there were none, but wild animals of all sorts – a great many wild asses and many ostriches. There were also bustards and gazelles.[3]

The desert continues south of Babylon, and in 1857 the English geologist and traveler W. K. Loftus depicted it in grim terms:

There is no life for miles around. No river glides in grandeur at the base of its [the ancient city of

Uruk] mounds; no green date groves flourish near its ruins. The jackal and the hyena appear to shun the dull aspect of its tombs. The king of birds never hovers over the deserted waste. A blade of grass or an insect finds no existence there. The shrivelled lichen alone, clinging to the weathered surface of the broken brick, seems to glory in its universal dominion upon those barren walls.[4]

Farther south the desert gives way to a six-thousand square-mile region of marshes, lagoons, mudflats, and reed banks. At last, in the extreme south the Euphrates and the Tigris unite and empty into the Persian Gulf.

This forbidding area became the home of many folk and the land of the first cities. Bands of Semitic nomads occupied the region around Akkad (modern Baghdad). Into the south came the Sumerians, a people who probably migrated from the east. The Sumerians were farmers and city builders. By 3000 B.C. they had established a number of cities in the southernmost part of Mesopotamia, a region that became known as Sumer. As the Sumerians pushed north, they came into contact with the Semites, who readily adopted Sumerian culture, and turned to urban life. The Sumerians soon changed the face of the land and made Mesopotamia the "cradle of civilization" (see Map 1.1).

ENVIRONMENT AND MESOPOTAMIAN CULTURE

From the outset geography had a profound effect on the evolution of Mesopotamian civilization. In this region agriculture is possible only with irrigation. Consequently, the Sumerians and later the Akkadians built their cities along the Tigris and Euphrates and their branches. The rivers supplied fish, a major element of the city dwellers' diet. The rivers also provided reeds and clay, which they used

MAP OF NIPPUR *The oldest map in the world, dating to ca 1500 B.C., shows the layout of the Mesopotamian city of Nippur. Inscribed on a clay tablet, the map has enabled archaeologists to locate ruined buildings: (A) the ziggurat, (B) canal, (C) enclosure and gardens, (D) city gates, and (E) the Euphrates River. (From the photographic collections of the University Museum, The University of Pennsylvania)*

as building materials. Since this entire area lacks stone, mud-brick became the primary building-block of Mesopotamian architecture.

Although the rivers sustained life, they acted simultaneously as a powerful restraining force, especially on Sumerian political development. They made Sumer a geographical maze. Between the rivers, streams, and irrigation canals stretched open desert or swamp, where nomadic tribes roamed. Communication between cities was difficult and at times dangerous. City was isolated from city, each in its own locale. Thus each Sumerian city became a state, independent of the others and protective of its independence. Any city that tried to unify the country was resisted by the other cities. As a result, the political history of Sumer is one of almost constant warfare.

The experience of the city of Nippur is an example of how bad conditions could become. At one point in its history Nippur was conquered eighteen times in twenty-four years. Although Sumer was eventually unified, unification came late and was always tenuous.

The harsh environment fostered a grim, even pessimistic, spirit among the Mesopotamians. They especially feared the ravages of flood. The Tigris can bring quick devastation, as it did to Baghdad in 1831, when floodwaters destroyed seven thousand homes in a single night. The same tragedy occurred often in antiquity. The chronicle of King Hammurabi recorded years when floods wiped out whole cities. Vulnerability to natural disaster deeply influenced Mesopotamian religious beliefs.

The Mesopotamians considered natural catastrophes the work of the gods. At times the Sumerians described their chief god, Enlil, as "the raging flood which has no rival." The gods, they believed, even used nature to punish the Mesopotamians. According to the myth of the Deluge, which gave rise to the biblical story of Noah, the god Enki warned Ziusudra, the Sumerian Noah:

A flood will sweep over the cult-centers;
To destroy the seed of mankind . . .
Is the decision, the word of the assembly of
*   the gods.*[5]

The myth of Atrahasis describes the gods' annoyance at the prosperity of mankind and tells how Enlil complained to the other gods:

Oppressive has become the clamor of mankind.
By their uproar they prevent sleep.
Let the flour be cut off for the people,
In their bellies let the greens be too few.[6]

Enlil and the other gods decide to send a drought and then a flood to destroy human life. In the face of harsh conditions, the Mesopotamians considered themselves weak and insignificant as compared to the gods. This feeling was particularly strong among the Sumerians.

The Mesopotamians did not worship their deities because the gods were holy. Human beings were too insignificant to pass judgment on the conduct of the gods, and the gods were too superior to honor human morals. Rather, the Mesopotamians worshiped the gods because they were mighty. Likewise, it was not the place of men and women to understand the gods. The Sumerian Job once complained to his god:

The man of deceit has conspired against me,
And you, my god, do not thwart him,
You carry off my understanding.[7]

The motives of the gods were not always clear. In times of affliction one could only pray and offer sacrifices to appease them.

SUMERIAN SOCIETY

The Sumerians sought to please and calm the gods, especially the patron deity of the city. In the center of each city the people erected a shrine and then built their houses around it. The best way to honor the god was to make the shrine as grand and as impressive as possible, for a god who had a splendid temple might think twice about sending floods to destroy the city.

The temple had to be worthy of the god, a symbol of his power, and it had to last. Special skills and materials were needed to build it. Only stone was suitable for its foundations and precious metals for its decoration. Since the Mesopotamians had to import both stone and metals, temple construction encouraged trade. Architects, engineers, craftsmen, and workers had to devote a great deal of thought, effort, and time to build the temple. By 2000

B.C. the result was Mesopotamia's first monumental architecture – the ziggurat, a massive stepped tower that dominated the city.

Once the ziggurat was built, a professional priesthood was needed to run it and to perform the god's rituals. The people of the city met the expenses of building and maintaining the temple and its priesthood by setting aside extensive tracts of land for that purpose. The priests took charge of the produce of the temple lands and the sacred flocks. Part of the yield went to the feeding and clothing of the priests and the temple staff, and for offerings to the gods. Part was sold or bartered to obtain goods, such as precious metals or stone, needed for construction, maintenance, and ritual.

Until recently, the dominant position and wealth of the temple had led historians to consider the Sumerian city-state an absolute theocracy, or government by an established priesthood. According to this view, the temple and its priests owned the city's land and controlled its economy. Newly discovered documents and recent works, however, have resulted in new ideas about the Sumerian city and its society. It is now known that the temple owned a large fraction, but not all, of the city's territory, and did not govern the city. A king, or *lugal*, exercised political power, and most of the city's land was the property of individual citizens.

Sumerian society was a complex arrangement of freedom and dependence and was divided into four categories: nobles, free clients of the nobility, commoners, and slaves. The nobility consisted of the king and his family, the chief priests, and high palace officials. The king originally rose to power as a war leader, elected by the citizenry, who established a regular army, trained it and led it into battle. The might of the king and the frequency of warfare in Mesopotamia quickly made him the supreme figure in the city, and kingship soon became hereditary. The symbol of his status was the palace, which rivaled the temple in grandeur.

The king and the lesser nobility held extensive tracts of land that were, like the estates of the temple, worked by slaves and clients. Clients were free men and women who were dependent on the nobility. In return for their labor the clients received small plots of land to work for themselves. Although this arrangement assured the clients of a livelihood, the land they worked remained the possession of the nobility or the temple. Thus, not only did the nobility control most − and probably the best − land, they also commanded the obedience of a huge segment of society. They were the dominant force in Mesopotamian society.

Commoners were free citizens. They were independent of the nobility; however, they could not rival the nobility in social status and political power. Commoners belonged to large patriarchal families that owned land in their own right. Commoners could sell their land, if the family approved, but even the king could not legally take their land without their approval. Commoners had a voice in the political affairs of the city and full protection under the law.

Until comparatively recent times, slavery has been a fact of life throughout the history of Western society. Some Sumerian slaves were foreigners and prisoners of war. Some were criminals, who had lost their freedom as punishment for their crimes. Still others served as slaves in repayment of debts. These were more fortunate than the others, because the law required that they be freed after three years. But all slaves were subject to whatever treatment their owners might mete out. They could be beaten and even branded. Yet they were not considered dumb beasts. Slaves engaged in trade and made profits. Indeed, many slaves bought their freedom. They could borrow money, and they received at least some protection under the law.

THE SPREAD OF MESOPOTAMIAN CULTURE

The Sumerians established the basic social, economic, and intellectual patterns of Mesopotamia, but the Semites played a large part in spreading Sumerian culture far beyond the boundaries of Mesopotamia. Despite the cultural ascendancy of the Sumerians, their unending wars wasted their strength. In 2331 B.C., the Semitic chieftain Sargon conquered Sumer and created a new empire. The symbol of his triumph was a new capital, the city of Agade. Sargon, the first "world conqueror," led his armies to the Mediterranean Sea. Although his empire lasted only a few generations, it spread Mesopotamian culture throughout the Fertile Crescent, the belt of rich farmland that extends from Mesopotamia in the east up through Syria in the north and down to Egypt in the west (see Map 1.1).

Sargon's impact and the extent of Mesopotamian influence even at this early period have been dramatically revealed at Ebla in modern Syria. In 1964, archaeologists unearthed there a once-flourishing Semitic civilization that had assimilated political, intellectual, and artistic aspects of Mesopotamian culture. In 1975, the excavators uncovered thousands of clay tablets, which proved that the people of Ebla had learned the art of writing from the Mesopotamians. Eblaite artists borrowed heavily from Mesopotamian art but developed their own style, which in turn influenced Mesopotamian artists. The Eblaites transmitted the heritage of Mesopotamia to other Semitic centers in

Syria. In the process, a universal culture developed in the ancient Near East, a culture basically Mesopotamian but fertilized by the traditions, genius, and ways of many other peoples.

When the clay tablets of Ebla were discovered, many scholars confidently predicted that they would shed fresh light on the Bible. Some even claimed to recognize in them biblical names like Jerusalem and the "Five Cities of the Plain," which included Sodom and Gomorrah. Careful study since then suggests that these claims were more often optimistic than accurate: so far the Ebla tablets have added very little to biblical scholarship. Yet they are a goldmine of data on the ancient history of northern Syria. Some of them deal with Ebla's relations with neighboring peoples, while others provide detailed information on local agricultural production and the weaving industry. All confirm the existence and importance of direct contact between Mesopotamia and Syria as early as the third millennium B.C. Moreover, they demonstrate the early and widespread influence of Mesopotamian civilization far beyond its own borders.

SARGON OF AKKAD This bronze head, with elaborately worked hair and beard, portrays the great conqueror Sargon of Akkad. Originally the eyes were probably precious jewels, which have subsequently been gouged out. This head was found in the ruins of the Assyrian capital of Nineveh, where it had been taken as loot. (Directorate General of Antiquities, Baghdad, Iraq)

THE TRIUMPH OF BABYLON

Although the empire of Sargon was extensive, it was also short-lived. It was left to the Babylonians to unite Mesopotamia politically as well as culturally. The Babylonians were Amorites, a Semitic people who had migrated from Arabia and settled in the Sumerian city of Babylon. Babylon enjoyed an excellent geographical position, and it was ideally suited to be the capital of Mesopotamia. It dominated trade on the Tigris and Euphrates rivers: all commerce to and from Sumer and Akkad had to pass by its walls. It also looked beyond Mesopotamia. Babylonian merchants followed the Tigris north to Assyria and Anatolia. The Euphrates led merchants to Syria, Palestine, and the Mediterranean. The city grew great because of its commercial importance and its power being soundly based.

Babylon was also fortunate in its far-seeing and able king Hammurabi (1792–1750 B.C.). Hammurabi set out to do three things: to make Babylon secure, to unify Mesopotamia, and to win for the Babylonians a place in Mesopotamian civilization. The first two he accomplished by conquering Assyria in the north and Sumer and Akkad in the south. Then he turned to his third goal.

Politically, Hammurabi joined in his kingship the Semitic concept of the tribal chieftain

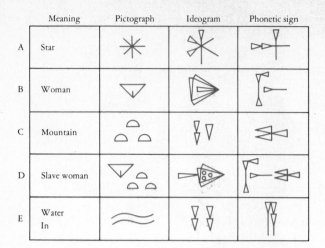

Meaning	Pictograph	Ideogram	Phonetic sign
A	Star			
B	Woman			
C	Mountain			
D	Slave woman			
E	Water In			

FIGURE 1.1 SUMERIAN WRITING (Excerpted from S. N. Kramer, The Sumerians: Their History, Culture and Character, *University of Chicago Press, Chicago, 1963, pp. 302–306)*

and the Sumerian idea of urban kingship. Culturally, he encouraged the spread of myths that explained how Marduk, the god of Babylon, had been elected king of the gods by the other Mesopotamian deities. Hammurabi's success in making Marduk the god of all Mesopotamians made Babylon the religious center of Mesopotamia. Through Hammurabi's genius the Babylonians made their own contribution to Mesopotamian culture — a culture vibrant enough to maintain its identity even while assimilating new influences. Hammurabi's conquests and the activity of Babylonian merchants spread this enriched culture north to Anatolia and west to Syria and Palestine.

THE INVENTION OF WRITING AND THE FIRST SCHOOLS

Mesopotamian culture spread as rapidly as it did largely because of the invention and evolution of writing. Until recently, scholars have credited the Sumerians with the invention of writing. Recent work, however, suggests that the Sumerian achievement, a form of writing called cuneiform – from the Latin for wedge-shaped, which describes the strokes of the stylus – may have been a comparatively late stage in the development of writing. The origins of writing probably go back thousands of years earlier than previously thought. As early as the ninth millennium B.C., Near Eastern peoples used clay tokens as counters for recordkeeping. By the fourth millennium B.C., people had realized that drawing pictures of the tokens on clay was simpler than making tokens. This breakthrough in turn suggested that more information could be conveyed by adding pictures of still other objects. The result was a complex system of pictographs, in which each sign was a picture of an object. Pictographs were the forerunners of cuneiform writing.

How did this pictographic system work and how did it evolve into cuneiform writing? At first, if a scribe wanted to indicate a star, he simply drew a picture of it on a wet clay tablet (see line A of Figure 1.1), which became rock-hard when baked. Anyone looking at the picture would know what it meant and would think of the word for star. This complicated and laborious system had serious limitations. It would not represent abstract ideas or combinations of ideas. For instance, how could it depict a slave woman?

The solution appeared when the scribe discovered that he could combine signs to express meaning. To refer to a slave woman he used the sign for woman (line B) and the sign for mountain (line C) – literally, "mountain woman" (line D). Since the Sumerians regularly obtained their slave women from the mountains, this combination of signs was easily understandable.

The next step was to simplify the system. Instead of drawing pictures, the scribe made conventionalized signs. Thus, the signs became ideograms: they symbolized ideas. The sign for star could also be used to indicate heaven, sky, or even god.

The real breakthrough came when the scribe learned to use signs to represent sounds. For instance, the scribe drew two parallel wavy lines to indicate the word *a*, or "water" (line E). Besides water, the word *a* in Sumerian also meant "in." The word *in* expresses a relationship that is very difficult to represent pictorially. Instead of trying to invent a sign to mean *in*, some clever scribe used the sign for water, because the two words sounded alike. This phonetic use of signs made possible the combining of signs to convey abstract ideas. The use of writing enabled merchants to keep complicated business records, inventories, and bills of lading. More important, the learning, lore, history, and philosophy of a culture could be recorded and preserved for unborn generations.

The Sumerian system of writing was so complicated that only professional scribes mastered it, and even they had to study it for many years. By 2500 B.C., scribal schools flourished throughout Sumer. Most students came from wealthy families, and it was largely a male profession. Each school had a master, teachers, and monitors. Discipline was strict, and students were caned for sloppy work and misbehavior. One graduate of a scribal school had few fond memories of the joy of learning. He described a typical day:

My headmaster read my tablet, said:
"There is something missing," caned me.

. . . .

The fellow in charge of silence said:
"Why did you talk without permission," caned me.
The fellow in charge of the assembly said:
"Why did you stand at ease without permission,"
    caned me.[8]

The boy was so lax at his work that he was expelled. Only when his father wined and dined the headmaster was he allowed to return to school.

The Sumerian system of schooling set the educational standards of Mesopotamian culture, and the Akkadians and Babylonians adopted its practices and techniques. Students began by learning how to prepare clay tablets and make signs. They studied grammar and word lists, and they solved simple mathematical problems. Mesopotamian education always had a practical side, because of the economic and administrative importance of scribes. Most scribes took administrative positions in the temple or palace, where they kept records of business transactions, accounts, and inventories. But scribal schools did not limit their curriculum to business affairs. They were also centers of culture and learning. Topics of study included mathematics, botany, and linguistics. Advanced students copied and studied the classics of Mesopotamian literature. Talented students and learned scribes wrote compositions of their own. As a result of this work many literary, mathematical, and religious texts survive today, giving a surprisingly full picture of Mesopotamian intellectual and spiritual life.

MESOPOTAMIAN THOUGHT AND RELIGION

The Mesopotamians made significant and sophisticated advances in mathematics, using a numerical system based on units of sixty. For practical purposes they also used factors of ten and six. They developed the concept of place value — that the value of a number depends on where it stands in relation to other numbers. Mesopotamian mathematical texts are of two kinds: tables and problems. Scribes compiled tables of squares and square roots, cubes and cube roots, and reciprocals. They wrote texts of problems, which dealt not only with equations and pure mathematics but also with concrete problems, such as how to plan irrigation ditches. The Mesopotamians did not consider mathematics a purely theoretical science. The building of cities, palaces, temples, and canals demanded knowledge of geometry and trigonometry. The Mesopotamians solved the practical problems involved, but they did not turn their knowledge into theories. In this respect, they were quite different from the Greeks, who enjoyed theorizing.

Mesopotamian medicine was a combination of magic, prescriptions, and surgery. Mesopotamians believed that demons and evil spirits caused sickness and that incantations and magic spells could drive them out. Or, they believed, the physician could force the demon out by giving the patient a foul-tasting prescription. As medical knowledge grew, some prescriptions were found to work and thus were true medicines. The physician relied heavily on plants, animals, and minerals for his recipes, and he often mixed them with beer to cover their unpleasant taste. Surgeons practiced a dangerous occupation, and the penalties for failure were severe. One section of Hammurabi's law code decreed: "If a physician performed a major operation on a seignior with a bronze lancet and has caused the seignior's death, or he opened up the eye-socket of a seignior and has destroyed the seignior's eye, they shall cut off his hand."[9] No wonder that one medical text warned physicians to have nothing to do with a dying person.

Mesopotamian thought had its profoundest impact in theology and religion. The Sumerians originated many beliefs, and the Akkadians and Babylonians added to them. The American journalist H. L. Mencken once suggested that "the theory that the universe is run by a single God must be abandoned and . . . in place of it we must set up the theory that it is actually ruled by a board of gods all of equal puissance and authority."[10] The Mesopotamians would have agreed that many gods run the world, but they did not consider all gods and goddesses equal to one another. Some deities had very important jobs, such as taking care of music, law, sex, and victory, while others had lesser tasks, such as overseeing leatherworking and basketweaving. The god in charge of metalworking was hardly the equal of the god of wisdom.

Divine society was a hierarchy. According to the Sumerians the air-god Enlil was the king of the gods, and he laid down the rules by which the universe was to be run. Enki, the god of wisdom, put Enlil's plans into effect. The Babylonians believed that the gods elected Marduk as their king, after which he assigned the lesser gods various duties to perform. Once the gods received their tasks, they carried them out forever.

Mesopotamian gods lived their lives much as human beings lived theirs. The gods were anthropomorphic, or human in form. Unlike men and women, they were powerful and immortal and could make themselves invisible. Otherwise, Mesopotamian gods and goddesses were very human: they celebrated with food and drink, and they raised families. They enjoyed their own "Garden of Eden," a green and fertile place. They could be irritable, and they were not always holy. Even Enlil was punished by other gods because he had once raped the goddess Ninlil.

The Mesopotamians had many myths and epics to account for the creation of the universe. According to one Sumerian myth, only the primeval sea existed at first. Genesis, the first book of the Old Testament, says precisely the same thing. The sea produced heaven and earth, which were united. Heaven and earth gave birth to Enlil, who separated them and made possible the creation of the other gods.

Babylonian beliefs were similar. In the beginning was the primeval sea, the goddess Tiamat, who gave birth to the gods. When Tiamat tried to destroy the gods, Marduk killed her and divided her body:

He split her like a shellfish into two parts:
Half of her he set up and ceiled as sky,
Pulled down the bar and posted guards.
He bade them not to let her waters escape.[11]

These myths are the earliest known attempts to answer the question "how did it all begin?" The Mesopotamians obviously thought about these matters, as about the gods, in human terms. They never organized their beliefs into a philosophy, but their myths offered understandable explanations of natural phenomena. They were emotionally satisfying, and that was their greatest appeal.

Mesopotamian myths also explained the origin of human beings. In one myth the gods decided to make their lives easier by creating servants, whom they wanted made in their own image. Nammu, the goddess of the watery deep, brought the matter to Enki. After some thought, Enki instructed Nammu and the others:

Mix the heart of the clay that is over the abyss.
The good and princely fashioners will thicken the clay.
You, do you bring the limbs into existence.[12]

In Mesopotamian myth, as in Genesis, men and women were made in the divine image. However, human beings lacked godlike powers. The myth "The Creation of the Pickax" gives an excellent idea of their insignificance. According to this myth, Enlil drove his pickax into the ground, and out of the hole crawled the Sumerians, the first people.

As Enlil stood looking at them, some of his fellow gods approached him. They were so pleased with Enlil's work that they asked him to give them some people to serve them. Consequently, the Mesopotamians believed it their duty to supply the gods with sacrifices of food and drink and to house them in fine temples. In return, they hoped that the gods would be kind.

These ideas about the creation of the universe and of human beings are part of the Mesopotamian legacy to Western civilization. They spread throughout the ancient Near East and found a home among the Hebrews, who adopted much of Mesopotamian religious thought and made it part of their own beliefs. Biblical parallels to Mesopotamian literary and religious themes are many. Such stories as the creation of Adam, the Deluge, the Garden of Eden, and the tale of Job can be traced back to Mesopotamian originals. Through the Bible, Mesopotamian as well as Jewish religious concepts influenced Christianity and Islam. Thus these first attempts by women and men to understand themselves and their world are still alive today.

DAILY LIFE IN MESOPOTAMIA

The law code of King Hammurabi offers a wealth of information about daily life in Mesopotamia. Hammurabi issued his code to "establish law and justice in the language of the land, thereby promoting the welfare of the people." His code may seem harsh, but it was no more harsh than the Mosaic law of the Hebrews, which it heavily influenced. Hammurabi's code inflicted such penalties as mutilation, whipping, and burning. Today in parts of the Islamic world these punishments are still in use. Despite its severity, a spirit of justice and a sense of responsibility pervade the code. Hammurabi genuinely felt that his

LAW CODE OF HAMMURABI *Hammurabi ordered his code to be inscribed on a stone pillar and set up in public. At the top of the pillar Hammurabi is depicted receiving the scepter of authority from the god Shamash. (Clichés des Musées Nationaux, Paris)*

duty was to govern the Mesopotamians as righteously as possible. He tried to regulate the relations of his people so that they could live together in harmony.

Hammurabi's code has two striking characteristics. First, the law differed according to the social status of the offender. Aristocrats were not punished as harshly as commoners, nor commoners as harshly as slaves. Even slaves had rights, however, and received some protection under the law. Second, the code demanded that the punishment fit the crime. Like the Mosaic law of the Hebrews, it called for "an eye for an eye, and a tooth for a tooth," at least among equals. However, an aristocrat who destroyed the eye of a commoner or slave could pay a fine instead of los-

ing his own eye. Otherwise, as long as the criminal and the victim shared the same social status, the victim could demand exact vengeance for his injury.

Hammurabi's code began with legal procedure. There were no public prosecutors or district attorneys, so individuals brought their own complaints before the court. Each side had to produce written documents or witnesses to support its case. In cases of murder, the accuser had to prove the defendant guilty: any accuser who failed to do so was put to death. This strict law was designed to prevent people from lodging groundless charges. The Mesopotamians were very worried about witchcraft and sorcery. Anyone accused of witchcraft, even if the charges were not proved, underwent an ordeal by water. The gods themselves would decide the case. The defendant was thrown into the Euphrates, which was considered the instrument of the gods. A defendant who sank was guilty; a defendant who floated was innocent. (In medieval Europe and colonial America accused witches also underwent ordeals by water, but they were considered innocent only if they sank.) Another procedural regulation covered the conduct of judges. Once a judge had rendered a verdict, he could not change it. Any judge who did so was fined heavily and deposed from his position. In short, the code tried to guarantee a fair trial and a just verdict.

Hammurabi expected his officials to do their duty and to protect his subjects. Governors and city officials were required to wipe out crime, and they paid personally for their failures to protect the innocent. If a person was robbed and the robber was not caught, the officials had to repay the victim. This law encouraged officials to keep order. Soldiers either carried out the king's commands or faced dire consequences. Any officer or private who tried to shirk his duty by hiring a substitute was put to death, as was any officer who illegally forced men to serve in the army. The law protected soldiers from abuse by their officers. Any officer who wronged a soldier or stole his property was put to death.

Consumer protection is not a modern idea; it goes back to Hammurabi's day. Merchants and businessmen had to guarantee the quality of their goods and services. A boatbuilder who did sloppy work had to repair the boat at his own expense. A boatman who lost the owner's boat or sank someone else's boat replaced it and its cargo. Housebuilders guaranteed their work with their lives. Careless work could result in the collapse of a house and the death of its inhabitants. If that happened, the builder himself was put to death. A merchant who tried to increase the interest rate on a loan forfeited the entire amount. A farmer who hired an overseer to cultivate his land had the right to order an incompetent overseer to be dragged through the fields. Hammurabi's laws tried to ensure that consumers got what they paid for and paid a just price.

Crime was a feature of Mesopotamian urban life just as it is in modern cities. Burglary was a serious problem, hard to control. Because houses were built of mud-brick, it was easy for an intruder to dig through the walls. Hammurabi's punishment for burglary matched the crime. A burglar caught in the act was put to death on the spot, and his body was walled into the breach he had made. The penalty for looting was also grim: anyone caught looting a burning house was thrown into the fire.

Mesopotamian cities had breeding places of crime. Taverns were notorious for being the haunts of criminals, especially since they often met at taverns to make their plans. Tavernkeepers were expected to keep order and arrest anyone overheard planning a crime.

Taverns were normally run by women, and they also served as houses of prostitution. Prostitution was disreputable but not illegal, and the law did not regulate it. Despite their social stigma, taverns were popular places, for Mesopotamians were fond of beer and wine. Tavernkeepers made a nice profit, but if they were caught increasing their profits by watering drinks, they were drowned.

The aim of all these statutes was to punish the criminal. Exact retribution gave the victim or the victim's family legal satisfaction and was intended to end the matter. To some degree the code protected society by eliminating people who had committed serious crimes. Beyond that it did not go.

Because farming was essential to Mesopotamian life, Hammurabi's code dealt extensively with agriculture. Tenant farming was widespread, and tenants rented land on a yearly basis. Instead of money they paid a proportion of their crops as rent. Unless the land was carefully cultivated, it quickly reverted to wasteland. Therefore tenants faced severe penalties for neglecting the land or not working it at all. Since irrigation was essential to grow crops, tenants had to keep the canals and ditches in good repair. Otherwise, the land would be subject to floods and farmers to crippling losses. Anyone whose neglect of the canals resulted in damaged crops had to bear all the expense of the lost crops. If the tenant could not pay the costs, he was sold into slavery.

The oxen farmers used for plowing and threshing grain were ordinarily allowed to roam the streets. If an ox gored a passer-by, its owner had to pad its horns, tie it up, or else bear the responsibility for future damages. Sheep raising was very lucrative because textile production was a major Mesopotamian industry. (Mesopotamian cloth was famous throughout the Near East.) The shepherd was a hired man with considerable responsibility. He was expected to protect the flock from wild animals, which were a standing problem, and to keep the sheep out of the crops. Since date palms were the only source of wood in Mesopotamia, wanton destruction of trees was a serious offense. This strict regulation of agriculture paid rich dividends. The Mesopotamians often enjoyed bumper crops, which fostered a large and thriving population.

Hammurabi gave careful attention to marriage and the family. As elsewhere in the Near East, marriage had aspects of a business agreement. The prospective groom and the father of the future bride arranged everything. The man offered the father a bridal gift, usually a sum of money. If the man and his bridal gift were acceptable, the father provided his daughter with a dowry. After marriage the dowry belonged to the woman (although the husband normally administered it) and was a means of protecting her rights and status. Once the two men agreed upon financial matters, they drew up a contract; no marriage was considered legal without one. Either party could break off the marriage, but not without paying a stiff penalty. Fathers often contracted marriages while their children were still young. The girl either continued to live in her father's house until she reached maturity or she went to live in the house of her father-in-law. During this time she was legally considered a wife. Once she and her husband became of age, they set up their own house.

The wife was expected to be rigorously faithful. The penalty for adultery was death. According to Hammurabi's code: "If the wife of a man has been caught while lying with another man, they shall bind them and throw them into the water."[13] The husband had the power to spare his wife by obtaining a pardon for her from the king. He could, however, accuse his wife of adultery even if he had not caught her in the act. In such a case she could try to clear herself before the city council, which investigated. If she was found innocent, she could take her dowry and leave her husband. If a woman decided to take the direct approach and kill her husband, she was impaled.

The husband had virtually absolute power over his household. Like the later Roman *paterfamilias* (Chapter 7), he could even sell his wife and children into slavery to pay his debts. Sons did not lightly oppose their fathers, and any son who struck his father could have his hand cut off. A father was free to adopt children and include them in his will. Artisans sometimes adopted children to teach them the family trade. Although the father's power was great, he could not disinherit a son without just cause. Cases of disinheritance became matters for the city to decide, and the code ordered the courts to forgive a son for his first offense. Only if a son wronged his father a second time could he be disinherited.

Law codes are preoccupied with the problems of society, and provide a bleak view of things. Other Mesopotamian documents give a happier glimpse of life. Although Hammurabi's code dealt with marriage shekel by shekel, a Mesopotamian poem tells of two people meeting secretly in the city. Their parting is delightfully modern:

Come now, set me free, I must go home,
Kuli-Enlil . . . set me free, I must go home.
What can I say to deceive my mother?[14]

Countless wills and testaments show that husbands habitually left their estates to their wives, who in turn willed the property to their children. All this suggests happy family life. Hammurabi's code restricted married women from commercial pursuits, but financial documents prove that many women engaged in business without hindrance. Some carried on the family business, while others became wealthy landowners in their own right. Mesopotamians found their lives lightened by holidays and religious festivals. Traveling merchants brought news of the outside world, and swapped marvelous tales. Despite their pessimism, the Mesopotamians enjoyed a vibrant and creative culture, a culture that left its mark on the entire Near East.

EGYPT, THE LAND OF THE PHARAOHS (3100–1200 B.C.)

The Greek historian and traveler Herodotus in the fifth century B.C. called Egypt the gift of the Nile River. No other single geographical factor had such a fundamental and profound impact on the shaping of Egyptian life, society, and history as the Nile. Unlike the rivers of Mesopotamia it rarely brought death and destruction. Its waters, even in flood times, seem almost tame when compared to the rampaging Tigris. The river was primarily a creative force. The Egyptians never feared the Nile in the way the Mesopotamians feared their rivers. Instead, they sang its praises:

Hail to thee, O Nile, that issues from the earth
*   and comes to keep Egypt alive! . . .*
He that waters the meadows which Re created,
He that makes to drink the desert . . .
He who makes barley and brings emmer [wheat]
*   into being . . .*
He who brings grass into being for the cattle . . .
He who makes every beloved tree to grow . . .
O Nile, verdant art thou, who makest man and
*   cattle to live.*[15]

In the mind of the Egyptians the Nile was the supreme fertilizer and renewer of the land. Each September the Nile floods its valley,

transforming it into a huge area of marsh or lagoon. By the end of November the water retreats, leaving behind a thin covering of fertile mud ready to be planted with crops.

The annual flood made the growing of abundant crops almost effortless, especially in southern Egypt. Herodotus, who was used to the rigors of Greek agriculture, was amazed by the ease with which the Egyptians raised their crops:

For indeed without trouble they obtain crops from the land more easily than all other men. . . . They do not labor to dig furrows with the plough or hoe or do the work which other men do to raise grain. But when the river by itself inundates the fields and the water recedes, then each man, having sown his field, sends pigs into it. When the pigs trample down the seed, he waits for the harvest. Then when the pigs thresh the grain, he gets his crop.[16]

As late as 1822, John Burckhardt, an English traveler, watched nomads sowing grain by digging large holes in the mud and throwing in seeds. The extraordinary fertility of the Nile valley made it easy to produce an annual agricultural surplus, which in turn sustained a growing and prosperous population.

Whereas the Tigris and Euphrates and their many tributaries carved up Mesopotamia into isolated areas, the Nile served to unify Egypt. The river was the principal highway, and promoted easy communication throughout the valley. As individual bands of settlers moved into the Nile valley, they created stable agricultural communities. By about 3100 B.C., there were some forty of these communities, which were in constant contact with one another. This contact, encouraged and facilitated by the Nile, virtually assured the early political unification of the country.

Egypt was fortunate in that it was nearly self-sufficient. Besides the fertility of its soil, Egypt possessed enormous quantities of stone,

PERIODS OF EGYPTIAN HISTORY

PERIOD	DATES	SIGNIFICANT EVENTS
Archaic	3100–2660 B.C.	Unification of Egypt
Old Kingdom	2660–2180 B.C.	Construction of the pyramids
First Intermediate	2180–2080 B.C.	Political chaos
Middle Kingdom	2080–1640 B.C.	Recovery and political stability
Second Intermediate	1640–1570 B.C.	Hyksos "invasion"
New Kingdom	1570–1075 B.C.	Creation of an Egyptian empire
		Akhenaten's religious policy

which served as the raw material of architecture and sculpture. Abundant clay was available for pottery, as was gold for jewelry and ornaments. The raw materials that Egypt lacked were close at hand. The Egyptians could obtain copper from Sinai and timber from Lebanon. They had little cause to look to the outside world for their essential needs, which helps to explain the insular quality of Egyptian life.

Geography further encouraged isolation by closing Egypt off from the outside world. To the east and west of the Nile valley stretch grim deserts. The Nubian Desert and the cataracts of the Nile discourage penetration from the south. Only in the north did the Mediterranean Sea leave Egypt exposed. Thus geography shielded Egypt from invasion and from extensive immigration. Unlike the Mesopotamians, the Egyptians enjoyed centuries of peace and tranquillity, during which they could devote most of their resources to peaceful development of their distinctive civilization.

Yet Egypt was not completely sealed off. As early as 3250 B.C. Mesopotamian influences,

notably architectural techniques and materials and perhaps even writing, made themselves felt in Egyptian life. Still later, from 1680 to 1580 B.C., northern Egypt was ruled by foreign invaders, the Hyksos. Infrequent though they were, such periods of foreign influence fertilized Egyptian culture without changing it in any fundamental way.

THE GOD-KING OF EGYPT

The geographic unity of Egypt quickly gave rise to political unification of the country under the authority of a king, whom the Egyptians called pharaoh. The details of this process have been lost, though some archaeologists recently made a startling suggestion. Tomb finds from the ancient region of Nubia, in modern Sudan, indicate that monarchy may have developed there earlier than in Egypt. If so, Egyptians may have developed the concept of kingship from their neighbors to the south.

The Egyptians themselves told of a great king, Menes, who united Egypt into a single kingdom around 3100 B.C. Thereafter the

Egyptians divided their history into dynasties, or families of kings. For modern historical purposes, however, it is more useful to divide Egyptian history into periods. The political unification of Egypt ushered in the period known as the Old Kingdom, an era remarkable for its prosperity and artistic flowering, and for the evolution of religious beliefs.

In the realm of religion, the Egyptians developed complex and often contradictory ideas about an afterlife. These beliefs were all rooted in the environment of Egypt itself. The climate of Egypt is so stable that change is cyclical and dependable: though the heat of summer bakes the land, the Nile always floods and replenishes it. The dry air preserves much that would decay in other climates. Thus there was an air of permanence about Egypt; the old lived on and became part of the present.

This cyclical rhythm permeated Egyptian religious beliefs. According to the Egyptians, the god Osiris, a fertility god associated with the Nile, dies each year, and each year his wife Isis brings him back to life. Osiris eventually became king of the dead, a god who weighed the hearts of human beings to determine whether they had lived justly enough to deserve everlasting life. Osiris's care for the dead was shared by Anubis, the jackal-headed god who annually helped Isis resuscitate Osiris. Anubis was the god of mummification, which was essential to Egyptian funerary rites.

The focal point of religious and political life in the Old Kingdom was the pharaoh, who commanded the wealth, resources, and the people of all Egypt. The pharaoh's power was such that the Egyptians considered him to be the falcon-god Horus in human form. He was a guarantee to his people, a pledge that the gods of Egypt (strikingly unlike those of Mesopotamia) cared for their people. The king's surroundings had to be worthy of

THE PYRAMIDS AT GIZA *Giza was the burial place of the pharaohs of the Old Kingdom and of their aristocracy, whose rectangular tombs are visible behind the middle pyramid. The small pyramids at the foot of the foremost pyramid probably belong to the pharaoh's wives. (Courtesy, Museum of Fine Arts, Boston)*

a god. Only a magnificent palace was suitable for his home; in fact, the very word *pharaoh* means "great house." The king's tomb also had to reflect his might and exalted status. To this day the great pyramids at Giza near Cairo bear silent but magnificent testimony to the god-kings of Egypt. The pharaoh's ability to command the resources and labor necessary to build a huge pyramid amply demonstrates that the god-king was an absolute ruler.

The religious significance of the pyramid is as awesome as the political. The pharaoh as a god was the earthly sun, and the pyramid, which towered to the sky, helped him ascend

EGYPTIAN FARM WORK *This tomb depicts the cycle of the agricultural year from ploughing to reaping. (Metropolitan Museum of Art, New York)*

the heavens after death. The pyramid provided the dead king with everything that he would need in the afterlife. His body had to be preserved from decay if his *ka,* an invisible counterpart of the body, was to live on. So the Egyptians developed an elaborate process of embalming the dead pharaoh and wrapping his corpse in cloth. As an added precaution, they carved a statue of the pharaoh out of hard stone; if anything happened to the fragile mummy, the pharaoh's statue would help keep his ka alive. The need for an authentic likeness accounts for the naturalism of Egyptian portraiture. Artistic renderings of the pharaohs combine accuracy and the abstract in the effort to capture the essence of the living person. This approach produced that haunting quality of Egyptian sculpture – portraits of lifelike people imbued with a solemn, ageless, and serene spirit.

To survive in the spirit world the ka needed

everything that the pharaoh needed in life: food and drink, servants and armed retainers, costly ornaments, and herds of animals. In Egypt's prehistoric period, the king's servants and herdsmen and their flocks were slaughtered at the tomb to provide for the ka. By the time of the Old Kingdom, artists had substituted statues of scribes, officials, soldiers, and servants for their living counterparts. To remind the ka of daily life, artists covered the walls of the tomb with scenes of ordinary life, ranging from agricultural routines to banquets and religious festivities, from hunting parties to gardens and ponds. Designed to give joy to the ka, these paintings, models of furniture, and statuettes today provide an intimate glimpse of Egyptian life 4,500 years ago.

The humor and vivacity of Egyptian tomb paintings are striking, especially when they depict everyday scenes. The scene above, which dates only to about 1300 B.C. is remarkable chiefly because it is typical. This tomb painting shows an Egyptian couple at work in the fields. In the top band the couple reap wheat, while in the second band they harvest flax. To the right in the second band the couple is seen ploughing for the next year's crop. In the bottom two bands are an orchard of date palms and a garden filled with flowers and herbs. The wavy bands represent irrigation canals. The simple agricultural implements include a metal sickle and a light plough drawn by two oxen. Unfortunately, however, research published in 1982 suggests that many Egyptian farmers suffered from various parasites that thrived in the warm, stagnant water of the irrigation canals. Nonetheless, tomb scenes like this one preferred warmth to harsh realities. Other sources of information give a gloomier view of daily life.

THE PHARAOH'S PEOPLE

Because the common folk stood at the bottom of the social and economic scale, they were always at the mercy of grasping officials. The arrival of the tax collector was never a happy occasion. One Egyptian scribe described the worst that could happen:

And now the scribe lands on the river-bank and is about to register the harvest-tax. The janitors carry staves and the Nubians rods of palm, and they say, Hand over the corn, though there is none. The cultivator is beaten all over, he is bound and thrown into a well, soused and dipped head downwards. His wife has been bound in his presence and his children are in fetters.[17]

That was an extreme situation. Nonetheless, taxes might amount to 20 percent of the harvest, and the collection of taxes could often be brutal.

On the other hand, everyone, no matter how lowly, had the right of appeal, and the account of one such appeal, "The Tale of the Eloquent Peasant," was a favorite Egyptian story. The hero of the tale, Khunanup, was robbed by the servant of the high steward, and Khunanup had to bring his case before the steward himself. When the steward delayed his decision, Khunanup openly accused him of neglecting his duty, saying, "The arbitrator is a spoiler; the peace-maker is a creator of sorrow; the smoother over of differences is a creator of soreness."[18] The pharaoh himself ordered the steward to give Khunanup justice, and the case was decided in the peasant's favor.

Egyptian society seems to have been a curious mixture of freedom and constraint. Slavery did not become widespread until the New Kingdom. There was neither a caste system nor a color bar, and humble people could rise to the highest positions if they possessed talent. The most famous example of social mobility (which, however, dates to the New Kingdom) is the biblical story of Joseph, who came to Egypt as a slave and rose to be second only to the pharaoh. On the other hand, most ordinary folk were probably little more than serfs, who could not easily leave the land of their own free will. Peasants were also subject to forced labor, just as they were in early modern France, and this labor included work on the pyramids and canals. Young men were drafted into the pharaoh's army, which served both as a fighting force and as a labor corps.

The vision of thousands of people straining to build the pyramids and countless artists adorning the pharaoh's tomb brings to the modern mind a distasteful picture of oriental despotism. Yet H. Frankfort, one of the most perceptive historians of ancient Egypt, has treated the matter in a purely Egyptian context:

Nothing would be more misleading than to picture the Egyptians in abject submission to their absolute ruler. . . . Their polity was not imposed but evolved from immemorial predilections and was adhered to, without protest, for almost three thousand years. . . . If a god had consented to guide the nation, society held a pledge that the unaccountable forces of nature would be well disposed and bring prosperity and peace. . . . Truth, justice, were "that by which the gods live," an essential element in the established order. Hence, Pharaoh's rule was not tyranny, or his service slavery.[19]

The Egyptian view of life and society is alien to those raised on the Western concepts of individual freedom and human rights. To the ancient Egyptians the pharaoh embodied justice and order – harmony among men and women, nature, and the divine. If the pharaoh was weak, or if he allowed anyone to challenge his unique position, he opened the way to chaos. Twice in Egyptian history the pharaoh failed to maintain rigid centralization. During those two eras, known as the First and Second Intermediate periods, Egypt was exposed to civil war and invasion. Yet even in the darkest times the monarchy survived, and in each period a strong pharaoh arose to crush the rebels or expel the invaders and restore order.

THE HYKSOS IN EGYPT (1640–1570 B.C.)

While Egyptian civilization flourished behind its bulwark of sand and sea, momentous changes were taking place in the ancient Near East, changes that would leave their mark even on rich and insular Egypt. These changes involved enormous and remarkable movements of peoples, especially peoples who spoke Semitic languages.

The original home of the Semites was probably the Arabian peninsula. Some tribes

moved into northern Mesopotamia, others into Syria and Palestine, and still others into Egypt. Shortly after 1800 B.C., people whom the Egyptians called Hyksos, which means "Rulers of the Uplands," began to settle in the Delta. Egyptian tradition, as later recorded by the priest Manetho in the third century B.C., depicted the coming of the Hyksos as a brutal invasion:

In the reign of Toutimaios – I do not know why – the wind of god blew against us. Unexpectedly from the regions of the east men of obscure race, looking forward confidently to victory, invaded our land, and without a battle easily seized it all by sheer force. Having subdued those in authority in the land, they then barbarously burned our cities and razed to the ground the temples of the gods. They fell upon all the natives in an entirely hateful fashion, slaughtering them and leading both their children and wives into slavery. At last they made one of their people king, whose name was Salitis. This man resided at Memphis, leaving in Upper and Lower Egypt tax collectors and garrisons in strategic places.[20]

Although the Egyptians portrayed the Hyksos as a conquering horde, they were probably no more than nomads looking for good land. Their entry into the delta was probably gradual and generally peaceful, much like that of the Hebrews, who did not arrive until around 1500 B.C. Indeed, the Hebrews are typical of the Semitic movement. They were a pastoral people, organized in large tribes whose chiefs and patriarchs directed the life of the community.

The Hyksos "invasion" was one of the fertilizing periods of Egyptian history; it introduced new ideas and techniques into Egyptian life. The Hyksos brought with them the method of making bronze and casting it into tools and weapons. They thereby brought Egypt fully into the Bronze Age culture of the

Mediterranean world, a culture in which the production and use of bronze implements became basic to society. Bronze tools made farming more efficient than ever before because they were sharper and more durable than the copper tools they replaced. The Hyksos' use of bronze armor and weapons as well as horse-drawn chariots and the composite bow, made of laminated wood and horn and far more powerful than the simple wooden bow, revolutionized Egyptian warfare. However much the Egyptians learned from the Hyksos, Egyptian culture eventually absorbed the newcomers. The Hyksos came to worship Egyptian gods and modelled their monarchy on the pharaoh's.

THE NEW KINGDOM: REVIVAL AND EMPIRE (1570–1200 B.C.)

Politically, Egypt was only in eclipse. The Egyptian sun shone again when a remarkable line of kings, the pharaohs of the Eighteenth Dynasty, arose to challenge the Hyksos. The pharaoh Ahmose (1558–1533 B.C.) pushed the Hyksos out of the Delta. Thutmose I (1512–1500 B.C.) subdued Nubia in the south, and Thutmose III (1490–1436 B.C.) conquered Palestine and Syria and fought inconclusively with the Hurrians' new kingdom of Mitanni on the upper Euphrates. These warrior-pharaohs inaugurated the New Kingdom – a period in Egyptian history characterized by enormous wealth and conscious imperialism. During this period, probably for the first time, widespread slavery became a feature of Egyptian life. The pharaoh's armies returned home leading hordes of slaves, who constituted a new labor force for imperial building projects. The Jews, who according to the Old Testament migrated into Egypt during this period to escape a drought, were soon en-slaved and put to work on imperial construction projects.

The kings of the Eighteenth Dynasty created the first Egyptian empire. They ruled Palestine and Syria through their officers, and they incorporated the African region of Nubia. Egyptian religion and customs flourished in Nubia, making a huge impact on African culture there and in neighboring areas. These warrior-kings celebrated their success with monuments on a scale unparalleled since the pharaohs of the Old Kingdom had built the pyramids. Even today the colossal granite statues of these pharaohs and the rich tomb objects of Tutankhamen ("King Tut") testify to the might, wealth, and splendor of the New Kingdom.

AKHENATEN AND MONOTHEISM

One of the most extraordinary of this unusual line of kings was Akhenaten (1367–1350 B.C.), a pharaoh more concerned with religion than conquest. Nefertiti, his wife and queen, encouraged his religious bent. Akhenaten and Nefertiti were monotheists: that is, they believed that the sun-god Aton, whom they worshiped, was universal, the only god. They considered all other Egyptian gods and goddesses frauds, and forbade their worship.

The religious notions and actions of Akhenaten and Nefertiti were in direct opposition to traditional Egyptian beliefs. The Egyptians had long worshiped a host of gods, chief among whom was Amon-Re. Originally Amon and Re had been two distinct sun-gods, but the Egyptians merged them and worshiped Amon-Re as the king of the gods. Besides Amon-Re, the Egyptians honored such other deities as Osiris, Osiris's wife Isis, and his son Horus. Indeed, Egyptian religion had room for many gods and an easy tolerance for new gods.

THE TOMB OF "KING TUT" *The pharaoh Tu-tankhamun was buried in three coffins, one inside the other. Shown here is the removal of the second coffin from the other coffin. The innermost coffin was made of gold. (The Metropolitan Museum of Art. Photograph by Harry Burton)*

THE PHARAOH'S COFFIN *This magnificent coffin from the tomb of "King Tut" depicts the pharaoh in all of his glory. Crossed over his chest are a crook and a flail, which were the emblems of the god Osiris. Richly engraved on the coffin are figures representing both Lower and Upper Egypt. (Metropolitan Museum of Art, New York)*

Herodotus once remarked that the Egyptians "are excessively religious, more so than other men." Akhenaten's attack on the old gods threatened all Egyptians, for the old gods were crucial to the afterlife. Naturally, then, many Egyptians viewed Akhenaten's attack on Osiris, Isis, Anubis, and other gods as a threat to their own chances for immortality. Others were sincerely devoted to the old gods for different reasons. After all, had not Amon-Re driven out the Hyksos and brought Egypt a new era of happiness? To these genuine religious sentiments were added the motives of the traditional priesthood. Although many priests were genuinely scandalized by Akhenaten's monotheism, many others were more concerned about their own welfare. What were the priests of the outlawed gods to do? Akhenaten had destroyed their livelihood and their reason for existence. On grounds of pure self-interest, the established priesthood opposed Akhenaten. Opposition in turn drove the pharaoh to intolerance and persecution. With a vengeance he tried to root out the old gods and their rituals.

Akhenaten celebrated his break with the past by building a new capital, Akhetaten, the modern El-Amarna. There Aton was honored with an immense temple and proper worship. Worship of Aton focused on "truth" (as Akhenaten defined it) and a desire for the natural. The pharaoh and his queen demanded that the "truth" be carried over into art. Unlike Old Kingdom painting and sculpture, which blended the actual and the abstract, the art of this period became relentlessly realistic. Sculptors molded exact likenesses of Akhenaten, despite his ugly features and misshapen body. Artists portrayed the pharaoh in intimate family scenes, playing with his infant daughter or expressing affection to members of his family. On one relief Akhenaten appears gnawing a cutlet of meat, while on another he lolls in a chair. Akhenaten was being portrayed as a mortal man, not as the dignified pharaoh of Egypt.

Akhenaten's monotheism was imposed from above, and failed to find a place among the people. The prime reason for Akhenaten's failure is that his god had no connection with the past of the Egyptian people, who trusted the old gods and felt comfortable praying to them. Average Egyptians were no doubt distressed and disheartened when their familiar gods were outlawed, for they were the heavenly powers that had made Egypt powerful and unique. The fanaticism and persecution that accompanied the new monotheism were in complete defiance of the Egyptian tradition of tolerant polytheism, or worship of several gods. Thus, when Akhenaten died, his religion died with him.

THE HITTITE EMPIRE

At about the time of the Hyksos entry into the Nile Delta, other parts of the Near East were also troubled by the arrival of newcomers. Two new groups of peoples, the Hurrians and Kassites, carved out kingdoms for themselves. Meanwhile the Hittites, who had long been settled in Anatolia (modern Turkey), became a major power in that region and began to expand eastward. Around 1595 B.C., a century and a half after Hammurabi's death, the Hittites and the Kassites brought down the Babylonian kingdom and established Kassite rule there. The Hurrians created the kingdom of Mitanni on the upper reaches of the Euphrates and Tigris.

The Hittites were an Indo-European people. The term *Indo-European* refers to a large family of languages that includes English, most of the languages of modern Europe,

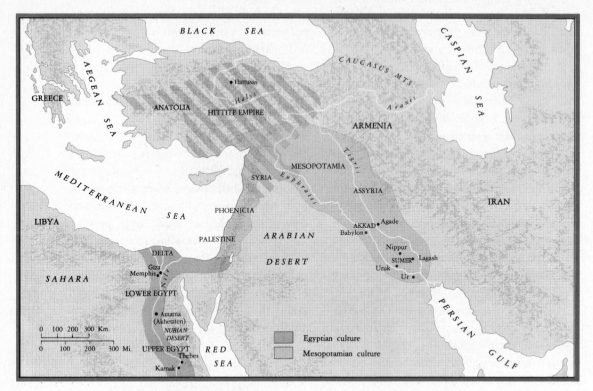

MAP 1.2 BALANCE OF POWER IN THE NEAR
EAST *This map shows the areas controlled by the
Hittites and Egyptians at the height of their power.*

Greek, Latin, Persian, and Sanskrit, the sacred
tongue of ancient India. During the eighteenth and nineteenth centuries, European
scholars learned that peoples who spoke related languages had spread as far west as Ireland and as far east as central Asia. In the
twentieth century, linguists deciphered the
language of the Hittites, and the Linear B
script of Mycenaean Greece. When both languages proved to be Indo-European, scholars
were able to form a clearer picture of these
vast movements. Archaeologists were able to
date them roughly and put them into their
historical context.

The original home of the Indo-Europeans
remains to be identified. Judging primarily
from the spread of the languages, linguists

have suggested that the migrations started
from central Europe. Although two great
waves began around 2000 B.C. and 1200 B.C.,
these migrations were typically sporadic and
gradual. For instance, the Celtic-speaking
Gauls did not move into modern France, Belgium, and Germany until the seventh century
B.C., long after most Indo-Europeans had
found new homes.

Around 2000 B.C., however, Indo-Europeans were on the move on a massive scale.
Peoples speaking the ancestor of Latin pushed
into Italy, and Greek-speaking Mycenaeans
settled in Greece. The Hittites came into
prominence in Anatolia, and other folk thrust
into Iran, India, and central Asia. At first the
waves of Indo-Europeans and others disrupted

existing states, but in time the newcomers settled down.

THE RISE OF THE HITTITES

Until recently, scholars thought that as part of these vast movements the Hittites entered Anatolia only around 1800 B.C. Current archaeological work and new documents, however, prove that Hittites had settled there at least as early as 2700 B.C. Nor did they overrun the country in a sweeping invasion, burning, looting, and destroying as they advanced. Their arrival and diffusion seems in fact to have been rather peaceful, accompanied by intermarriage and alliance with the native population. So well did the Hittites integrate themselves into the local culture of central Anatolia that they even adopted the worship of several native deities.

Although much uncertainty still surrounds the earliest history of the Hittites, their rise to prominence in Anatolia is quite well documented. During the nineteenth century B.C. the native kingdoms in the area engaged in suicidal warfare that left most of Anatolia's once-flourishing towns in ashes and rubble. In this climate of exhaustion the Hittite king Hattusilis I built a hill citadel at Hattusas, the modern Boghazköy, from which he led his Hittites against neighboring kingdoms. Hittite tradition recorded Hattusilis' achievements:

And on whatever campaign he went, he also by his strength kept the hostile country in subjection. And he kept devastating countries, and he made the countries tremble; and he made them boundaries of the sea.[21]

Hattusilis' grandson and successor Mursilis I extended the Hittite arms as far as Babylon. With help from the Kassites, Mursilis captured the city and snuffed out the dynasty of Hammurabi. While the Hittites carried off Babylonian loot, the Kassites took control of the territory. Upon his return home, the victorious Mursilis was assassinated by members of his own family, plunging the kingdom into confusion and opening the door to foreign invasion. The Hittites quickly lost substantial tracts of land in the east and south, and Hattusas itself prepared for attack. Mursilis' career is representative of the success and weakness of the Hittites. They were extremely vulnerable to attack by vigilant and tenacious enemies. Yet once united behind a strong king, they were a power to be reckoned with.

HITTITE SOCIETY

The geography of central Anatolia encouraged the rise of self-contained agricultural communities. Each was probably originally ruled by a petty king, but under the Hittites a group of local officials known as the Elders handled community affairs. Besides the farming population, a well-defined group of artisans fashioned the pottery, cloth, leather goods, and metal tools needed by society. Documents also report that traveling merchants peddled goods and gossip, reminding individual communities that they were part of a larger world. Like many other societies, ancient and modern, the Hittites held slaves, who nonetheless enjoyed certain rights under the law.

At the top of Hittite society was the aristocracy, among whom the relatives of the king constituted a privileged group. The king's relations were a mighty and often unruly group who served as the chief royal administrators. The royal family was often a threat to the king, for some of them, like the assassin of Mursilis I, readily resorted to murder as a method of seizing power. Sons of the king traditionally served as governors of conquered provinces.

THE HITTITE GOD ATARLUHAS   This statue of the god Atarluhas, with two lions at his feet, was set up near the gateway of the Hittite city of Carchemish. A bird-headed demon holds the lions. In 1920 this statue was destroyed in a war between Turkey and Syria. (The British Museum)

Just as the aristocracy stood at the head of society, so the king and queen stood above the aristocracy. The king was supreme commander of the army, chief judge, and supreme priest. He carried on all diplomatic dealings with foreign powers, and in times of war personally led the Hittite army into the field. The queen, who was highly regarded, held a strong, independent position. She had important religious duties to perform, and some queens even engaged in diplomatic correspondence with foreign queens.

The Hittites are typical of many newcomers to the ancient Near East in that they readily assimilated the cultures that they found. On arriving in Anatolia, they adopted much of the local culture. Soon they fell under the far more powerful spell of the superior Mesopotamian culture. The Hittites adopted the cuneiform script for their own language. Hittite kings published law codes, just as Hammurabi had done. Royal correspondence followed Mesopotamian forms. The Hittites delighted in Mesopotamian myths, legends, and epics. Of Hittite art, one scholar has observed that "there is hardly a single Hittite monument which somewhere does not show traces of Mesopotamian influence."[22] To the credit of the Hittites, one must add that they used these Mesopotamian borrowings to create something of their own. Nonetheless, the huge debt of the Hittites and other invaders brilliantly illustrates the great attraction and strength of Mesopotamian culture.

THE ERA OF HITTITE GREATNESS
(CA 1475–CA 1200 B.C.)

The Hittites, like the Egyptians of the New Kingdom, eventually produced an energetic and capable line of kings who restored order and rebuilt Hittite power. Once Telepinus (1525–1500 B.C.) had brought the aristocracy under control, Suppiluliumas I (1380–1346 B.C.) secured central Anatolia and Mursilis II (1345–1315 B.C.) regained Syria. Around 1300 B.C. Mursilis' son stopped the Egyptian army of Rameses II at the battle of Kadesh in Syria. Having fought each other to a standstill, the Hittites and Egyptians first made peace, then an alliance. Alliance was followed by friendship, and friendship by active cooperation. The two greatest powers of the early Near East tried to make war between them impossible.

The Hittites exercised remarkable political

wisdom and flexibility in the organization and administration of their empire. Some states they turned into vassal-kingdoms, ruled by the sons of the Hittite king; the king and his sons promised each other mutual support in times of crisis. Still other kingdoms were turned into protectorates, whose native kings were allowed to rule their populations with considerable freedom. The native kings swore obedience to the Hittite king, and had to contribute military contingents to the Hittite army. Although they also sent tribute to the Hittites, the financial burden was moderate. The common people of these lands probably felt Hittite overlordship little if at all.

While the Hittites were often at war, owing to the sheer number of enemies surrounding them, they often sought diplomatic and political solutions to their problems. They were realistic enough to recognize the limits of their power and far-sighted enough to appreciate the value of peace and alliance with Egypt. Together the two kingdoms provided much of the ancient Near East with a precious interlude of peace.

THE FALL OF EMPIRES (1200 B.C.)

This stable and generally peaceful situation endured until the cataclysm of the thirteenth century B.C., when both the Hittite and Egyptian empires were destroyed by invaders. The most famous of these marauders, called the "Sea Peoples" by the Egyptians, remain one of the puzzles of ancient history. Despite much new work, modern archaeology is still unable to identify the Sea Peoples satisfactorily. It is known, however, that they were part of a larger movement of peoples. Although there is serious doubt about whether the Sea Peoples alone overthrew the Hittites, they did

deal both the Hittites and the Egyptians a hard blow, making the Hittites vulnerable to overland invasion from the north and driving the Egyptians back to the Nile Delta. The Hittites fell under the external blows, but the Egyptians, shaken and battered, retreated to the Delta and held on.

In 1200 B.C., as earlier, both Indo-European and Semitic-speaking peoples were on the move. They brought down the old centers of power and won new homes for themselves. In Mesopotamia the Assyrians destroyed the kingdom of Mitanni and struggled with the Kassites; the Hebrews moved into Palestine; and another wave of Indo-Europeans penetrated Anatolia. But once again these victories were political and military, not cultural. The old cultures — especially that of Mesopotamia — impressed their ideas, values, and ideals on the newcomers. Although the chaos of the thirteenth century B.C. caused a serious material decline throughout the ancient Near East, the old cultures lived on through a dark age.

———◆———

In the long span of years covered by this chapter, human beings made astonishing strides, advancing from primitive hunters to builders of complex and sophisticated civilizations. By harnessing the plant and animal worlds for their welfare, human beings prospered dramatically. With their basic bodily needs more than satisfied, they realized even greater achievements, including more complex social groupings, metal technology, and long-distance trade. The intellectual achievements of these centuries were equally impressive. Ancient Near Eastern peoples created advanced mathematics, monumental architecture, and engaging literature. Although the societies of the Near East suffered stunning blows in the thirteenth century B.C., more persisted than perished. The great achievements of Mesopotamia and Egypt survived to improve and sustain the lives of those who came after.

NOTES

1. L. Eiseley, *The Unexpected Universe,* Harcourt Brace Jovanovich, New York, 1969, p. 102.

2. J. R. Harlan, "The Plants and Animals That Nourish Man," *Scientific American* 235 (September 1976): 89.

3. Xenophon *Anabasis* 1.5.1.

4. W. K. Loftus, *Travels and Researches in Chaldaea and Susiana,* R. Carter & Brothers, New York, 1857, p. 163.

5. J. B. Pritchard, ed., *Ancient Near Eastern Texts,* 3rd ed., Princeton University Press, Princeton, 1969, p. 44. Hereafter called *ANET.*

6. Ibid., p. 104.

7. *ANET,* p. 590.

8. Quoted in S. N. Kramer, *The Sumerians,* University of Chicago Press, Chicago, 1964, p. 238.

9. *ANET,* p. 175.

10. H.L. Mencken, *A Mencken Chrestomathy,* Knopf, New York, 1949, p. 67.

11. *ANET,* p. 67.

12. Kramer, p. 150.

13. *ANET,* p. 171.

14. Kramer, p. 251.

15. *ANET,* p. 372.

16. Herodotus *The Histories* 2.14.

17. Quoted in A. H. Gardiner, "Ramesside Texts Relating to the Taxation and Transport of Corn," *Journal of Egyptian Archaeology* 27 (1941): 19-20.

18. A. H. Gardiner, "The Eloquent Peasant," *Journal of Egyptian Archaeology* 9 (1923): 17.

19. H. Frankfort, *The Birth of Civilization in the Near East,* Doubleday, New York, 1956, pp. 119-120.

20. Manetho *History of Egypt* fr. 42.75-77.

21. E. H. Sturtevant and G. Bechtel, *A Hittite Chrestomathy,* Linguistic Society of America, Philadelphia, 1935, p. 183.

22. M. Vieyra, *Hittite Art* 2300-750 B.C., Alec Tiranti, London, 1955, p. 12.

SUGGESTED READING

The continuing research on the evolution of mankind makes any book quickly outdated, but a commendable exception is R. Leakey and R. Lewin, *Origins* (1977). G. Clark, *Archaeology and Society: Reconstructing the Prehistoric Past,* 3rd ed. (1957), is a study in methodology, and his *The Stone Age Hunters* (1967) describes life and society in the Paleolithic Age. A convenient general treatment is G. Clark and S. Piggott, *Prehistoric Societies* (1965). F. Dahlberg, *Woman the Gatherer* (1981), demonstrates the importance to primitive society of women's role in gathering.

As the text suggests, the origins of agriculture and the Neolithic period have recently received a great deal of attention. Professor Harlan's conclusions, besides the article cited in note 2, are set out in a series of works including "Agricultural Origins: Centers and Noncenters," *Science* 174 (1971): 468-474, and *Crops and Man* (1975). The 1981 Egyptian expedition mentioned in the text is described by F. Wendorf and R. Schild, "The Earliest Food Producers," *Archaeology* 34 (September/October 1981): 30-36. A broad survey of the problem is M. N. Cohen, *The Food Crisis in Prehistory* (1977).

For the societies of Mesopotamia, see A. Leo Oppenheim, *Ancient Mesopotamia,* rev. ed. (1977); M. E. L. Mallowan, *Early Mesopotamia and Iran* (1965); and H. W. F. Saggs, *The Greatness That Was Babylon* (1962). E. Chiera, *They Wrote on Clay* (1938), offers a delightful glimpse of Mesopotamian life, as does H. W. F. Saggs, *Everyday Life in Babylonia and Assyria* (1965).

C. Aldred, *The Egyptians* (1961), provides a good, readable survey of Egyptian developments. More detailed is A. Gardiner, *Egypt of the Pharaohs*

(1961). A. Nibbi, *Ancient Egypt and Some Eastern Neighbors* (1981) looks at Egyptian history in a broad context. See also J. M. White, *Everyday Life in Ancient Egypt* (1963).

Recent general introductions to problems and developments shared by several Near Eastern societies come from D. H. Trump, *The Prehistory of the Mediterranean* (1980), and a series of studies edited by T. A. Wertime and J. D. Muhly, *The Coming of the Age of Iron* (1980). J. B. Pritchard, *The Ancient Near East*, 2 vols. (1958, 1976) is a fine synthesis by one of the world's leading Near Eastern specialists. A sweeping survey is C. Burney, *The Ancient Near East* (1977). Pioneering new work on the origins of writing appears in a series of pieces by D. Schmandt-Besserat, notably "An Archaic Recording System and the Origin of Writing," *Syro-Mesopotamian Studies* 1/2 (1977): 1–32, and "Reckoning before Writing," *Archaeology* 32 (May/June, 1979): 23–31.

O. R. Gurney, *The Hittites*, 2nd ed. (1954) is still a fine introduction by an eminent scholar. Good also is J. G. MacQueen, *The Hittites and Their Contemporaries in Asia Minor* (1975). The 1960s were prolific years for archaeology in Turkey. A brief survey by one of the masters of the field is J. Mellaart, *The Archaeology of Modern Turkey* (1978), which also tests a great number of widely-held historical interpretations. The Sea Peoples have been the subject of two recent studies: A. Nibbi, *The Sea Peoples and Egypt* (1975), and N. K. Sandars, *The Sea Peoples* (1978).

For Near Eastern religion and mythology, good introductions are S. N. Kramer, ed., *Mythologies of the Ancient World* (1961); E. O. James, *The Ancient Gods: The History and Diffusion of Religion in the Ancient Near East and the Eastern Mediterranean* (1960); and J. Gray, *Near Eastern Mythology* (1969). A survey of Mesopotamian religion by one of the foremost scholars in the field is T. Jacobsen, *The Treasures of Darkness: A History of Mesopotamian Religion* (1976).

Surveys of Near Eastern art include H. Frankfort, *The Art and Architecture of the Ancient Orient* (1954), old but still very useful; R. D. Barnett and D. J. Wiseman, *Fifty Masterpieces of Ancient Near Eastern Art* (1969); and J. B. Pritchard's delightful *The Ancient Near East in Pictures*, 2nd ed. (1969). For literature, see S. Fiore, *Voices from the Clay: The Development of Assyro-Babylonian Literature* (1965); W. K. Simpson, ed., *The Literature of Ancient Egypt* (1973); and, above all, J. B. Pritchard, ed., *Ancient Near Eastern Texts* cited frequently in the Notes.

Chapter 2

Small Kingdoms and Mighty Empires in the Near East

THE MIGRATORY INVASIONS that brought down the Hittites and stunned the Egyptians in the thirteenth century B.C. ushered in an era of confusion and weakness. Although much was lost in the chaos, the old cultures of the ancient Near East survived to nurture new societies. In the absence of powerful empires, the Phoenicians, Syrians, Hebrews, and many other peoples carved out small independent kingdoms, until the Near East was a patchwork of them. During this period Hebrew culture and religion evolved under the influence of urbanism, kings, and prophets.

In the ninth century B.C. this jumble of small states gave way to an empire that for the first time embraced the entire Near East. Yet the very ferocity of the Assyrian Empire led to its downfall only two hundred years later. In 550 B.C. the Persians and Medes, who had migrated into Iran, created a "world empire" stretching from Anatolia in the west to the Indus valley in the east. For over two hundred years the Persians gave the ancient Near East peace and stability.

How did Egypt, its political greatness behind it, pass on its cultural heritage to its African neighbors? How did the Jewish state evolve, and what was daily life like in Jewish society? What forces helped to shape Jewish religious thought, still powerfully influential in today's world? What enabled the Assyrians to overrun their neighbors, and how did their cruelty finally cause their undoing? Lastly, how did Iranian nomads create the Persian Empire? This chapter will seek answers to these questions.

EGYPT, A SHATTERED KINGDOM

The invasions of the Sea Peoples ended the great days of Egyptian power. One scribe left behind a somber portrait of Egypt stunned and leaderless:

The land of Egypt was abandoned and every man was a law to himself. During many years there was no leader who could speak for others. Central government lapsed, small officials and headmen took over the whole land. Any man, great or small, might kill his neighbor. In the distress and vacuum that followed . . . men banded together to plunder one another. They treated the gods no better than men, and cut off the temple revenues.[1]

No longer able to dream of foreign conquests, Egypt looked to its own security from foreign invasion. Egyptians suffered a four-hundred-year period of political fragmentation, a new dark age known to Egyptian specialists as the Third Intermediate Period (eleventh–seventh centuries B.C.).

The decline of Egypt was especially sharp in foreign affairs. Whereas the pharaohs of the Eighteenth Dynasty had held sway as far abroad as Syria, their weak successors found it unsafe to venture far from home. In the wake of the Sea Peoples, numerous small kingdoms sprang up in the Near East, each fiercely protective of its own independence. To them Egypt was a memory, and foreign princes often greeted Egyptian officials with suspicion or downright contempt. One Egyptian official, Wen-Amon, left a lively report of his reception in Phoenicia, on an official mission to buy wood. Instead of the respect and deference Wen-Amon expected, he was greeted by the thundering of the king of Byblos:

If the ruler of Egypt were the lord of mine, and I were his servant also, he would not have to send silver and gold, saying: "Carry out the commission of Amon!" There would be no carrying of a royal-gift, such as they used to do for my father. As for me — me also — I am not your servant! I am not the servant of him who sent you either![2]

In the days of Egypt's greatness, no mere king of Byblos would have dared to speak so insolently to an Egyptian official.

Disrupted at home and powerless abroad, Egypt fell prey to invasion by its African neighbors. Libyans from North Africa filtered into the Nile Delta, where they established independent dynasties. Indeed, from 950 to 730 B.C. northern Egypt was ruled by Libyan pharaohs. The Libyans built cities, and for the first time a sturdy urban life grew up in the Delta. Although the coming of the Libyans changed the face of the Delta, the Libyans genuinely admired Egyptian culture, and eagerly adopted Egypt's religion and way of life.

In southern Egypt, meanwhile, the pharaoh's decline opened the way to the energetic Africans of Nubia, who extended their authority northward throughout the Nile valley. Nubian influence in these years, though pervasive, was not destructive. Since the imperial days of the Eighteenth Dynasty (see pages 29–31), the Nubians too had adopted many features of Egyptian culture. Now Nubian kings and aristocrats embraced Egyptian culture wholesale. The thought of destroying the heritage of the pharaohs would have struck them as stupid and barbaric. Thus the Nubians and the Libyans repeated an old Near Eastern phenomenon: new peoples conquered old centers of political and military power, but were themselves assimilated into the older culture.

The reunification of Egypt occurred late and unexpectedly. With Egypt distracted and disorganized by foreign invasions, an independent African state, the Kingdom of Kush, grew up in modern Sudan with its capital at Nepata. These Africans too worshiped Egyptian gods and used Egyptian hieroglyphs to write their language. In the eighth century B.C. their king Piankhy swept through the entire Nile valley from Nepata in the south to the Delta in the north. United once again, Egypt enjoyed a brief period of peace during which Egyptians continued to assimilate their African conquerors. In the Kingdom of Kush, Egyptian methods of administration and bookkeeping, Egyptian arts and crafts, and Egyptian economic practices became common, especially among the aristocracy. Nonetheless, reunification of the realm did not lead to a new Egyptian empire. In the centuries between the fall of the New Kingdom and the recovery of Egypt, several small but vigorous kingdoms had taken root and grown to maturity in the ancient Near East. By 700 B.C. Egypt was once again a strong kingdom, but no longer a mighty empire.

Yet Egypt's legacy to its African neighbors remained vibrant and rich. By trading and exploring southward along the coast of the Red Sea, the Egyptians introduced their goods and ideas as far south as the land of Punt, probably a region on the Somali coast. As early as the New Kingdom Egyptian pharaohs had exchanged gifts with the monarchs of Punt, and contact between the two areas persisted. Egypt was the primary civilizing force in Nubia, which became an African version of the pharaoh's realm, complete with royal pyramids and Egyptian deities, governmental procedures, and language. Egyptian religious beliefs penetrated as far south as Ethiopia. Just as Mesopotamian culture enjoyed wide appeal throughout the Near East, so Egyptian culture had a massive impact on northeastern Africa.

THE CHILDREN OF ISRAEL

The fall of the Hittite Empire and Egypt's collapse created a vacuum of power in the western Near East that allowed for the rise of

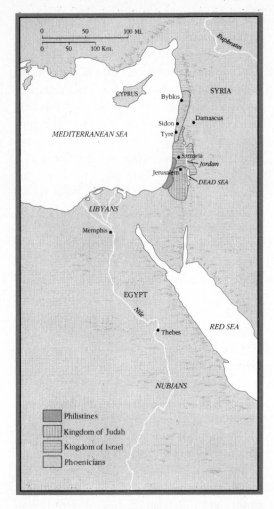

MAP 2.1   SMALL KINGDOMS IN THE NEAR
EAST   This map illustrates the political fragmentation of the Near East after the great wave of thirteenth-century invasions.

numerous small states. No longer crushed between the Hittites in the north and the Egyptians in the south, various peoples – some of
them newcomers – created homes and petty
kingdoms in Syria, Phoenicia, and Palestine.
After the Sea Peoples had raided Egypt, a
branch of them, known in the Bible as Philis-

tines, settled along the coast of modern Israel
(see Map 2.1). Establishing themselves in five
cities somewhat inland from the sea, the Philistines set about farming and raising flocks.

Another sturdy new culture was that of the
Phoenicians, a Semitic-speaking people who
had long inhabited several cities along the
coast of modern Lebanon. They had lived
under the shadow of the Hittites and Egyptians, but in this period the Phoenicians enjoyed full independence. (It was one of their
princes, the king of Byblos, who had given
Wen-Amon an unpleasant taste of the Phoenicians' newly found sense of freedom.) Unlike the Philistine newcomers, who turned
from seafaring to farming, the Phoenicians
took to the sea. They became outstanding
merchants and explorers. In their trading
ventures they sailed as far west as modern
Tunisia, where in 813 B.C. they founded the
city of Carthage, which would one day struggle with Rome for domination of the western
Mediterranean. Phoenician culture was urban,
based on the prosperous commercial centers
of Tyre, Sidon, and Byblos. The Phoenicians'
overwhelming cultural achievement was the
development of an alphabet, which they
handed on to the Greeks sometime in the late
eighth century B.C.

South of Phoenicia arose another small
kingdom, that of the Hebrews or ancient
Jews. Although smaller, poorer, less important, and less powerful than neighboring
kingdoms, the realm of the Hebrews was to
nourish religious ideas that underlie all of
Western civilization. Who were the Jewish
people, and what brought them to this new
land? Earlier Mesopotamian and Egyptian
sources refer to people called Habiru or Ha-
piru, which seems to mean a class of homeless, independent nomads. One such group of
Habiru were the biblical Hebrews. The original homeland of the Hebrews was probably

PHOENICIAN CARGO VESSELS *An Assyrian artist has captured all of the energy and vivacity of the seafaring Phoenicians. The sea is filled with Phoenician cargo ships, which ranged the entire Mediterranean.* *These ships are transporting cedar from Lebanon, some of it stowed on board, while other logs float in their wake. (Giraudon/Louvre)*

northern Mesopotamia, and the most crucial event in their historical development was their enslavement in Egypt. According to the Old Testament, the Hebrews had followed their patriarch Abraham out of Mesopotamia into Canaan, and from there had migrated into the Nile Delta to escape a drought. Arriving during the imperial days of the Eighteenth Dynasty, the Hebrews were soon enslaved and forced to labor on building projects. The passing of Egypt's greatness was the Hebrews' opportunity.

The agent of the Hebrews' deliverance from slavery was Moses, a figure so towering in legendary stature that his actual existence has been doubted. According to the Old Testament, Yahweh – called Jehovah in the Bible – appeared in a burning bush and commanded Moses to lead the Hebrews out of Egypt into Canaan. Thus Moses, in obedience

to the injunctions of Yahweh, directed his people to undertake a political act in the name of their god. The biblical book of Exodus depicts Moses leading the liberated Hebrews from Egypt into Canaan, which was to be their new homeland.

Today archaeologists are trying to ascertain precisely what happened around the time of the Hebrew exodus, and in the process to assess the accuracy of the biblical account. The archaeological record indicates that the thirteenth century B.C. was a time of warfare, disruption, and destruction, and seems to confirm the biblical portrayal of the exodus as a long period of conflict and turmoil. Apparently, nomadic Hebrew tribes filtered into Palestine from Egypt. According to Exodus, the Hebrews at this time consisted of a loose political confederation of twelve disunited tribes, which they believed to be descended from the twelve great-grandsons of Abraham.

In a series of vicious wars and savage slaughters they slowly won a place for themselves in Palestine (see Map 2.1). Success was not automatic, and the Hebrews suffered defeats and setbacks, but gradually they spread their power northward. In some cases they assimilated themselves to the culture of the natives, even going so far as to worship Baal, an ancient Semitic fertility god. In other instances, they carved out little strongholds and enslaved the natives. Even after the conquest, nearly constant fighting was required to consolidate the Hebrews' position.

The greatest danger to the Hebrews came from the Philistines, whose superior technology and military organization at first made them invincible. In Saul (ca 1000 B.C.), a farmer of the tribe of Benjamin, the Hebrews found a champion and a spirited leader. Saul carried the war to the Philistines, often without success. Yet in the meantime he established a monarchy over the twelve Hebrew tribes. Thus, under the peril of the Philistines, the Hebrew tribes evolved from scattered independent units into a centralized political organization in which the king directed the energies of the people.

Saul's work was carried on by David of Bethlehem, who in his youth had followed Saul into battle against the Philistines. Through courage and cunning David became king of Judah, hurled back the Philistines, and waged war against his other neighbors. To give his kingdom a capital he captured the city of Jerusalem, which he enlarged, fortified, and made the religious and political center of his realm. David's military successes won the Hebrews unprecedented security, and his forty-year reign was a period of vitality and political consolidation. David spent his last days dawdling in his harem, and letting the reins of power slip from his hands. Yet his ruin was not Israel's ruin. His work in consolidating the monarchy and enlarging the kingdom paved the way for his son Solomon.

Solomon (ca 965–925 B.C.) applied his energies to creating a nation out of a collection of tribes ruled by a king. He divided the kingdom, for purposes of effective administration, into twelve territorial districts cutting across the old tribal borders. To Solomon the twelve tribes of Israel were far less important than the Hebrew nation. He also yearned to bring his kingdom up to the level of its more sophisticated neighbors, and set about a building program to make Israel a respectable Near Eastern state. Work was begun on a magnificent temple in Jerusalem, on cities, palaces, fortresses, and roads. Solomon worked to bring Israel into the commercial mainstream of the world around it, and kept up good relations with Phoenician cities to the north. To pay for all this activity he imposed taxes far greater than any levied before, much to the displeasure of his subjects.

Solomon dedicated the temple in grand style, and made it the home of the Ark of the Covenant, the cherished chest that contained the holiest of Hebrew religious articles. As is recorded in the Old Testament:

And they [the priests] brought up the ark of the lord, and the tabernacle of the congregation, and all the holy vessels that were in the tabernacle, even these did the priests and the Levites bring up. And king Solomon, and all the congregation of Israel, that were assembled unto him, were with him before the ark, sacrificing sheep and oxen, that could not be told nor numbered for multitude. And the priests brought in the ark of the lord unto his place, into the oracle of the house, to the most holy place.[3]

The temple in Jerusalem was to be the religious heart of the kingdom and the symbol of

Hebrew unity. It also became the stronghold of the priesthood, for a legion of priests was needed to conduct religious sacrifices, ceremonies, and prayers. Yet Solomon's efforts were crowned with strife. He was too liberal in his ways, especially when it came to religion, to please some people, and the financial demands of his building program drained the resources of his people. His use of forced labor for his building projects further fanned popular resentment. However, Solomon had turned a rude kingdom into a state with broad commercial horizons and greater knowledge of the outside world. At his death, the Hebrews broke into two political halves (see Map 2.1). The northern part of the kingdom of David and Solomon became Israel, with its capital at Samaria. The southern half was Judah, and Solomon's city of Jerusalem remained its center. With political division went a religious rift: Israel, the northern kingdom, established rival sanctuaries to gods other than Yahweh. The Hebrew nation was divided, but at least it was divided into two far more sophisticated political units than before the time of Solomon. The Hebrews had taken their place in the increasingly cosmopolitan world of the Near East.

THE EVOLUTION OF JEWISH RELIGION

Hand in hand with their political evolution from fierce nomads to urban dwellers, the Hebrews were evolving spiritual ideas that still permeate Western society. Their chief literary product, the Old Testament, has fundamentally influenced both Christianity and Islam and still exerts a compelling force on the modern world.

It was Moses, the man who led the Hebrews to the promised land, who declared to the Hebrews Yahweh's covenant with them. According to the Old Testament, Yahweh ap-peared to Moses during the Exodus from Egypt, and ordered Moses to tell the Hebrews that he would watch over them, his chosen people. In return the Jews were to obey the Ten Commandments, which enjoined them to worship Yahweh and no other god.

Yahweh was unique because he was a lone god. Unlike the gods of Mesopotamia and Egypt, Yahweh was not the son of another god, nor did he have a divine wife or family. Initially an anthropomorphic god, Yahweh gradually lost his human form and became totally spiritual. Although Yahweh could assume human form, he was not to be depicted in any form. Consequently, the Jews considered graven images — statues and other representations — idolatrous.

At first Yahweh was probably conceived of as no more than the god of the Jews, a god who sometimes faced competition from Baal and other gods in Palestine. Enlil, Marduk, Amon-Re, and the others sufficed for foreigners. In time, however, the Jews came to regard Yahweh as the only god who existed. This was the beginning of true monotheism.

Yahweh was considered the creator of all things; his name means "he causes to be." He governed the cosmic forces of nature, including the movements of the sun, moon, and stars. His presence filled the universe. At the same time Yahweh was a personal god. Despite his awesome power, he was not too mighty or aloof to care for the individual. The Jews even believed that he intervened in human affairs.

Unlike Akhenaten's monotheism, Jewish monotheism was not an unpopular religion imposed from above. It was the religion of a whole people, deeply felt and cherished. Yet the Jews did not consider it their duty to spread the belief in the one god. The Jews rarely proselytized, as later the Christians did. As the chosen people, the chief duty of the

Jews was to maintain the worship of Yahweh as he demanded.

The original form of Yahweh's covenant with the Jews, the Ten Commandments, embodied an ethical code of conduct. It forbade the Jews to steal, murder, lie, and commit adultery. The covenant was a constant force in Jewish life, and the Old Testament records one occasion when the entire nation formally reaffirmed it:

And the king [of the Jews] stood by a pillar, and made a covenant before the lord, to walk after the lord, and to keep his commandments and his testimonies and his statutes with all their heart and all their soul, to perform the words of this covenant that were written in this book [Deuteronomy]. And all the people stood to the covenant.[4]

From the Ten Commandments evolved Jewish law, a code of law and custom originating with Moses and built upon by priests and prophets. The earliest part of this code, the Torah or Mosaic law, was often as harsh as Hammurabi's code, which had a powerful impact upon it. Later tradition, largely the work of prophets who lived from the eleventh to the fifth centuries B.C., was more humanitarian. The work of the prophet Jeremiah (ca 626 B.C.) exemplifies this gentler spirit. According to Jeremiah, Yahweh demanded righteousness from his people and protection for the weak and helpless:

For if ye thoroughly amend your ways and your doings; if ye thoroughly execute judgment between a man and his neighbor; if ye oppress not the stranger, the fatherless, and the widow, and shed not innocent blood in this place, neither walk after other gods to your hurt: then I will cause you to dwell in this place, in the land that I gave your fathers, for ever and ever.[5]

Here the emphasis is on mercy and justice, on avoiding wrongdoing to others because it is displeasing to Yahweh. These precepts replaced the old law's demand for "an eye for an eye." Thus this passage is representative of a subtle and positive shift in Jewish thinking. Jeremiah proclaimed that the god of anger was also the god of forgiveness: "Return, thou backsliding Israel, saith the lord; and I will not cause mine anger to fall upon you; for I am merciful, saith the lord, and I will not keep anger forever."[6] Although Yahweh would punish wrongdoing, he would not destroy those who repented. One generation might be punished for its misdeeds, but Yahweh's mercy was a promise of hope for future generations.

The uniqueness of this phenomenon can be seen by comparing the essence of Hebrew monotheism with the religious outlook of the Mesopotamians. Whereas the Mesopotamians considered their gods capricious, the Jews knew what Yahweh expected of them. The Jews believed that their god would protect them and make them prosper if they obeyed his commandments. The Mesopotamians thought human beings insignificant as compared to the gods, so insignificant that the gods might even be indifferent to them. The Jews too considered themselves puny in comparison to Yahweh. Yet they were Yahweh's chosen people, and he had promised never to abandon them. Finally, though the Mesopotamians believed that the gods generally preferred good to evil, their religion did not demand ethical conduct. The Jews could please their god only by living up to high moral standards in addition to worshiping him.

The evolution of Hebrew monotheism resulted in one of the world's greatest religions, which deeply influenced the development of two others. Many parts of the Old Testament show obvious debts to Mesopotamian culture. Nonetheless, to the Jews goes the credit for developing a religion so emotionally satisfying and ethically grand that it has not only flourished but also profoundly influenced Christianity and Islam. Without Moses there could not have been Jesus or Mohammed. The religious standards of the modern West are deeply rooted in Judaism.

DAILY LIFE IN ISRAEL

Historians generally know far more about the daily life of the aristocracy and the wealthy in ancient societies than about the conditions of the common people. Jewish society is an exception, simply because the Old Testament, which lays down laws for all Jews, has much to say about peasants and princes alike. Comparisons with the social conditions of Israel's ancient neighbors and modern anthropological work among Palestinian Arabs shed additional light on biblical practices. Thus the life of the common people in ancient Israel is better known than, for instance, the lives of ordinary Romans or ancient Chinese.

The nomadic Hebrews first entered Palestine as tribes, consisting of numerous families who thought of themselves as all related to one another. As the Jews consolidated their hold on Palestine, and as the concept of one Jewish nation gained a hold, the importance of the tribes declined.

At first good farm land, pasture land, and watering-spots were held in common by the tribe. Common use of land was – and still is – characteristic of nomadic peoples. Typically each family or group of families in the tribe drew lots every year to determine who worked what fields. But as formerly nomadic peoples turned increasingly to settled agriculture, communal use of land gave way to family ownership. In this respect the experience of the ancient Hebrews seems typical of many early peoples. Slowly but inevitably the shift

from nomad to farmer affected far more than just how people fed themselves. Family relationships reflected evolving circumstances. The extended family, organized in tribes, is even today typical of nomads. With the transition to settled agriculture, the tribe gradually becomes less important than the extended family. With the advent of village life, and finally full-blown urban life, the extended family in turn gives way to the nuclear family.

The family – people related to one another, all living in the same place – was the primary social institution among the Jews. At its head stood the father, who like the Mesopotamian father held great powers. The father was the master of his wife and children, with power of life and death over his family. By the eighth century B.C., the advent of full-blown urban life began to change the shape of family life again. The father's power and the overall strength of family ties relaxed. Much of the father's power passed to the elders of the town, especially the power of life and death over his children. One result of this general development was the liberation of the individual person from the tight control of the family.

Marriage was one of the most important and joyous events in the life of the Hebrew family. When the Jews were still nomads, a man could have only one lawful wife but any number of concubines. Settled life changed marriage customs and later Jewish law allowed men to be polygamous. Not only did kings David and Solomon have harems, but rich men might also have several wives. The chief reason for this custom, as in Mesopotamia, was the desire for children. Given the absence of medical knowledge and the rough conditions of life, women faced barrenness, high infant mortality, and rapid aging. Several women in the family led to some quarrelsome households; and the legal wife, if she were barren, could be scorned and ridiculed by her husband's concubines.

The common man was too poor to afford the luxury of several women in the home. The typical marriage in ancient Israel was monogamous, and a virtuous wife was revered and honored. Perhaps the finest and most fervent song of praise to the good wife comes from the book of Proverbs in the Old Testament:

Who can find a virtuous woman? for her price is far above rubies ... Strength and honour are her clothing; and she shall rejoice in time to come. She openeth her mouth with wisdom; and in her tongue is the law of kindness. She looketh well to the ways of her household, and eateth not the bread of idleness. Her children arise up, and call her blessed; her husband also, and he praiseth her ... Favour is deceitful, and beauty is vain: but a woman that feareth the lord, she shall be praised.[7]

The commandment "honor thy father and thy mother" was fundamental to the Mosaic law. The wife was a pillar of the family, and her work and wisdom were respected and treasured.

Betrothal and marriage were serious matters in ancient Israel. As in Mesopotamia, they were left largely in the hands of the parents. Boys and girls were often married when they were little more than children, and their parents naturally made the marriage arrangements. Rarely were the prospective bride and groom consulted. Marriages were often contracted within the extended family, and commonly among first cousins – a custom still found among Palestinian Arabs today. Although early Jewish custom permitted marriage with foreigners, the fear of alien religions soon led to restrictions against mixed marriages.

The father of the groom offered a bridal gift to the bride's father. This custom, the marriage price, also existed among the Mesopotamians and still survives among modern Palestinian Arabs. The gift was ordinarily money, the amount depending on the social status and wealth of the two families. In other instances, the groom could work off the marriage price by performing manual labor, as Jacob did for Leah and Rachel. At the time of the wedding the man gave his bride and her family wedding presents; unlike Mesopotamian custom, the bride's father did not provide her with a dowry.

As in Mesopotamia, marriage was a legal contract, not a religious ceremony. At marriage a woman left her family and joined the family and clan of her husband. The occasion when the bride joined her husband's household was festive. The groom wore a crown and his best clothes. Accompanied by his friends, also dressed in their finest and carrying musical instruments, the bridegroom walked to the bride's house, where she awaited him in her richest clothes, jewels, and a veil which she removed only later when the couple was alone. The bride's friends joined the group, and together they all marched in procession to the groom's house, their way marked by music and songs honoring the newlyweds. Though the wedding feast might last for days, the couple consummated their marriage on the first night; the next day the bloody linen was displayed to prove the bride's virginity.

Divorce was available only to the husband. He could normally end the marriage very simply and for any of a number of reasons:

When a man hath taken a wife, and married her, and it come to pass that she find no favour in his eyes, because he hath found some uncleanness in her: then let him write her a bill of divorcement, and give it in her hand, and send her out of his house. And when she is departed out of his house, she may go and be another man's wife.[8]

The right to initiate a divorce was denied the wife. Even adultery by the husband was not necessarily grounds for divorce. Jewish law, like the Code of Hammurabi, generally punished adultery with death. Generally speaking, Jewish custom frowned on divorce, and the typical couple entered into marriage fully expecting to spend the rest of their lives together.

The newly married couple was expected to begin a family at once. Children, according to the book of Psalms, "are an heritage of the lord: and the fruit of the womb is his reward."[9] The desire for children to perpetuate the family was so strong that if a man died before he could sire a son, his brother was legally obliged to marry the widow. The son born of the brother was thereafter considered the offspring and heir of the dead man. If the brother refused, the widow had her revenge by denouncing him to the elders in public:

Then shall his brother's wife come unto him in the presence of the elders, and loose his shoe from off his foot, and spit in his face, and shall answer and say, So shall it be done unto that man that will not build up his brother's house.[10]

Sons were especially desired because they maintained the family bloodline and kept the ancestral property within the family. The first-born son had special rights, honor, and responsibilities. At his father's death he became the head of the household, and received a larger inheritance than his younger brothers. Daughters were less highly valued because they would eventually marry and leave the family. Yet in Jewish society, unlike other cultures, infanticide was illegal; Yahweh had forbidden it.

The Old Testament often speaks of the pain of childbirth. Professional midwives frequently assisted at deliveries. The newborn infant was washed, rubbed with salt, and wrapped in swaddling-clothes – bands of cloth that were wrapped around the baby. Normally the mother nursed the baby herself,

and weaned the infant at about the age of three. The mother customarily named the baby immediately after birth, but children were free to change names after they grew up. Eight days after the birth of a son, the ceremony of circumcision – removal of the foreskin of the penis – took place. Circumcision signified that the boy belonged to the Jewish community, and according to Genesis was the symbol of Yahweh's covenant with Abraham.

As in most other societies, so in ancient Israel the early education of children was in the hands of the mother. It was she who taught her children right from wrong and gave them their first instruction in the moral values of their society. As boys grew older, they received more of their education from their fathers. Fathers instructed their sons in religion and the history of their people. Many children were taught to read and write, and the head of each family was probably able to write. Fathers also taught their sons the family craft or trade. Boys soon learned that inattention could be painful, for Jewish custom advised fathers to be strict: "He that spareth his rod hateth his son: but he that loveth him chasteneth him betimes."[11]

Once children grew to adulthood, they entered fully into economic and social life. For most that meant a life on the farm, whose demands and rhythm changed very little over time. Young people began with the lighter tasks. Girls traditionally tended flocks of sheep and drew water from the well for household use. The well was a popular meeting spot, where girls could meet other young people and even travelers passing through the country with camel caravans. After the harvest, young girls followed behind the reapers to glean the fields. Even this work was governed by law and custom: once the girls had gone through the fields, they were not to return, for Yahweh had declared that anything left behind belonged to the needy:

THE SEASONS OF THE YEAR *The Hebrew agricultural year, like that of other peoples, was tied to the sun, seasons, and stars. The center of this mosaic floor shows the sun in its chariot, pulled by four horses. In the outer circle are the signs of the zodiac, while the four seasons of the year peer at the viewer from the corners of the panel. (Consulate General of Israel)*

When thou cuttest down thine harvest in thy field, and hast forgot a sheaf in the field, thou shalt not go again to fetch it: it shall be for the stranger, for the fatherless, and for the widow: that the lord thy God may bless thee in all the work of thine hands.[12]

Boys also tended flocks, especially in wild areas. Like the young David, they practiced their marksmanship with slings and entertained themselves with music. They shared the lighter work, such as harvesting grapes and beating the limbs of olive trees to shake the fruit loose. Only when they grew to full strength did they perform the hard work of harrowing, ploughing, and harvesting.

The land was precious to the family, not simply because it provided a living, but also because it was a link to the past. It was the land of the family's forebears, and held their tombs. The family's feeling for its land was so strong that in times of hardship when land had to be sold, the nearest kin had first right to buy it. Thus the land might at least remain within the extended family.

Ironically, the success of the first Hebrew kings endangered the future of many family farms. With peace, more settled conditions, and increasing prosperity, some Jews began to amass larger holdings by buying out poor and struggling farmers. Far from discouraging this development, the kings created their own huge estates. In many cases slaves, both Jewish and foreign, worked these large farms and estates shoulder-to-shoulder with paid free men. Although the Old Testament called upon the royal and the rich to treat the slave and the laborer with justice and charity, there is no reason to think that Hebrew slavery was different from any other slavery. The prophet Jeremiah thundered against the exploiters:

Woe unto him that buildeth his house by unrighteousness, and his chambers by wrong; that useth his neighbor's service without wages, and giveth him not for his work.[13]

In still later times, rich landowners rented plots of land to poor, free families; the landowners provided the renters with seed and livestock, and normally took half the yield as rent. Although many Old Testament prophets denounced the destruction of the family farm, as the Gracchi were later to condemn the destruction of small Roman farms (Chapter 5), the trend continued toward large estates worked by slaves and hired free men.

The development of urban life among the Jews created new economic opportunities, especially in crafts and trades. People specialized in particular occupations, like milling flour, baking bread, making pottery, weaving cloth, and carpentry. All these crafts were family trades. Sons worked with their father; if the business prospered, they might be assisted by a few paid workers or slaves. The practitioners of a particular craft usually lived in a particular street or section of the town, a custom that is still prevalent in the Middle East today. By the sixth century B.C. craftsmen had formed guilds, intended like European guilds in the Middle Ages (Chapter 11) to protect their interests and aid their members. By banding together, craftsmen gained a corporate status within the community.

Commerce and trade developed later than crafts. In the time of Solomon, foreign trade was in the king's domain. Aided by the Phoenicians, who ranked among the leading merchants of the Near East, Solomon built a fleet to trade with ports on the Red Sea. Solomon also participated in the overland caravan trade. Otherwise, trade with neighboring countries was handled by foreigners, usually Phoenicians. Jews dealt mainly in local trade, and in most instances craftsmen and farmers sold directly to their customers. Only much later, after the great Exile — the period in the sixth century B.C., known as the Babylonian Captivity, when the Babylonians resettled the Jews in Mesopotamia — did Jews become merchants in large numbers. Many of Israel's wise men disapproved of commerce, and like the ancient Chinese, they considered it unseemly to profit from others' work.

Between the eclipse of the Hittites and Egyptians and the rise of the Assyrians, the Hebrews moved from nomadism to urban life and full participation in the mainstream of ancient Near Eastern culture. Retaining their unique religion and customs, they drew from the practices of other peoples and contributed to the lives of their neighbors.

ASSYRIA, THE MILITARY MONARCHY

Small kingdoms like those of the Phoenicians and the Hebrews could exist only in the absence of a major power. The beginning of the ninth century B.C. saw the rise of such a power: the Assyrians of northern Mesopotamia, whose chief capital was at Nineveh on the Tigris river. The Assyrians were a Semitic-speaking people heavily influenced, like so many other peoples of the Near East, by the Mesopotamian culture of Babylon to the south. They were also one of the most warlike peoples in history, largely because throughout their history they were threatened by neighboring folk. Living in an open and exposed land, the Assyrians experienced frequent and devastating attacks by the wild war-loving tribes to their north and east and by the Babylonians to the south. The constant threat to the Assyrians' survival promoted political cohesion and military might.

For over two hundred years the Assyrians labored to dominate the Near East. In 859 B.C. the new Assyrian king Shalmaneser unleashed the first of a long series of attacks on the peoples of Syria and Palestine. Year after relentless year, Assyrian armies hammered at the peoples of the west. These ominous events inaugurated two turbulent centuries marked by Assyrian military campaigns, constant efforts by Syria and the two Jewish kingdoms to maintain or recover their independence, eventual Assyrian conquest of Babylonia and northern Egypt, and periodic political instability in Assyria itself, which prompted stirrings of freedom throughout the Near East.

Under the Assyrian kings Tiglath-pileser III (744-727 B.C.) and Sargon II (721-705 B.C.), both mighty warriors, the Near East trembled as never before under the blows of

ASHURBANIPAL FEASTING *Assyrian art had its gentler side, as in this festive scene, which glorifies the splendor of the king. King Ashurbanipal, reclining on a couch, and his queen, seated opposite him, banquet in an arbor. The harper at the far left provides music, while attendants fan the royal couple. (Reproduced by Courtesy of the Trustees of the British Museum)*

Assyrian armies. The Assyrians stepped up their attacks in Anatolia, Syria, and Palestine. The kingdom of Israel and many other states fell; others, like the kingdom of Judah, became subservient to the warriors from the Tigris. In 717–716 B.C. Sargon led his army in a sweeping attack along the Philistine coast into Egypt. He defeated the pharaoh, who suffered the further ignominy of paying tribute to the foreign conquerors. Sargon also lashed out at Assyria's traditional enemies to the north, and then turned south against a renewed threat in Babylonia. By means of almost constant warfare, Tiglath-pileser III and Sargon carved out an Assyrian empire that stretched from east and north of the Tigris river to central Egypt (see Map 2.2).

An empire forged with so much blood and effort was vulnerable to revolt, and revolt provoked brutal retaliation. The Assyrian king Ashurbanipal (668–633 B.C.) left a grisly account of how he dealt with the Babylonians, who had conspired against him and perhaps earlier against his grandfather, King Sennacherib:

I tore out the tongues of these whose slanderous mouths had uttered blasphemies against my god Ashur and had plotted against me, his god-fearing prince; I defeated them completely. The others, I smashed alive with the very same statues of protective deities with which they had smashed my own grandfather Sennacherib — now finally as a belated burial sacrifice for his soul. I fed their corpses, cut into small pieces, to dogs, pigs, zibu-birds, vultures, the birds of the sky and also to the fish of the ocean. After I had performed this and thus made quiet again the hearts of the great gods, my lords, I removed the corpses of those whom the pestilence had felled, whose leftovers after the dogs and pigs had fed on them were obstructing the streets, filling the places of Babylon, and of those who had lost their lives through the horrible famine.[14]

Revolt against the Assyrians inevitably promised the rebels bloody battles, prolonged sieges accompanied by starvation, plague, and sometimes even cannibalism, and finally surrender followed by systematic torture and slaughter.

Though atrocity and terrorism struck unspeakable fear into Assyria's subjects, Assyria's success was actually due to sophisti-

THE KING OF ASSYRIA ON THE MARCH *The might of the Assyrian king and his retinue shines clearly in this relief. With almost photographic precision the artist has captured the details of the chariot's construction, the harness of the horses, and the weapons and equipment of the accompanying infantrymen. (Metropolitan Museum of Art, New York)*

cated, far-sighted, and effective military organization. By Sargon's time the Assyrians had invented the mightiest military machine the ancient Near East had ever seen. The mainstay of the Assyrian army, the soldier who ordinarily decided the outcome of battles, was the infantryman, armed with a spear and sword and protected by helmet and armor. The Assyrian army also featured archers, some on foot, others on horseback, still others in chariots – the latter ready to wield lances once they had expended their supply of arrows. Some infantry archers wore heavy armor, strikingly similar to the armor worn much later by William the Conqueror's Normans. These soldiers served as a primitive field artillery, whose job was to sweep the enemy's walls of defenders so that others could storm the defenses. Slingers also served as artillery in pitched battles. For mobility on the battlefield, the Assyrians organized a corps of chariots.

Assyrian military genius was remarkable for the development of a wide variety of siege machinery and techniques, including excavation to undermine city walls and battering-rams to knock down walls and gates. Never before in the Near East had anyone applied such technical knowledge to warfare. The Assyrians even invented the concept of a corps of engineers, who bridged rivers with pontoons or provided soldiers with inflatable skins for swimming. Furthermore, the Assyrians knew how to coordinate their efforts, both in open battle and in siege warfare. Sennacherib's account of his siege of Jerusalem in 701 B.C. is a vivid portrait of the Assyrian war machine in action:

As to Hezekiah, the Jew, he did not submit to my yoke, I laid siege to 46 of his strong cities, walled forts and to the countless small villages in their vicinity, and conquered them by means of well-stamped earth-ramps, and battering rams brought thus near to the walls combined with the attack by foot soldiers, using mines, breaches as well as sapper work ... Himself I made prisoner in Jerusalem, his royal residence, like a bird in a cage. I surrounded him with earthwork in order to molest those who were leaving his city's gate ... Hezekiah himself, whom the terror-inspiring splendor of my lordship had overwhelmed and whose irregular and elite troops which he had brought into Jerusalem, his royal residence, in order to strengthen it, had deserted him, did send me, later, to Nineveh,

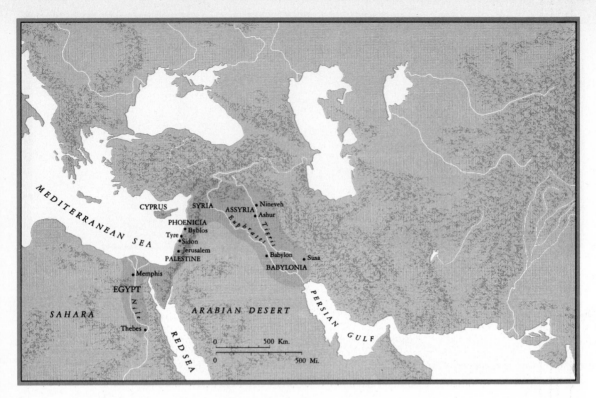

MAP 2.2 THE ASSYRIAN EMPIRE *The Assyrian Empire at its height included almost all of the old centers of power in the ancient Near East.*

my lordly city, together with 30 talents of gold, 800 talents of silver . . . and all kinds of valuable treasures.[15]

Hezekiah and Jerusalem shared the fate of many a rebellious king and capital, and were indeed lucky to escape severe reprisals. The Assyrians were too powerful and well organized and far too tenacious to be turned back by isolated strongholds, no matter how well situated or defended.

ASSYRIAN RULE

Not only did the Assyrians know how to win battles; they also knew how to use their victories. As early as the reign of Tiglath-pileser III, the Assyrian kings began to organize their conquered territories into an empire. The lands closest to Assyria became provinces governed by Assyrian officials. Kingdoms beyond the provinces were not annexed, but became dependent states that followed Assyria's lead. The Assyrian king chose their rulers, either by regulating the succession of native kings or by supporting native kings who appealed to him. The Old Testament recounts how Ahaz, king of Judah, called for help from Tiglath-pileser, and in return for Assyrian support became his vassal:

So Ahaz sent messengers to Tiglath-pileser king of Assyria, saying, I am thy servant and thy son: come up, and save me out of the hand of the king of Syria, and out of the hand of the king of Israel, which rise up against me. And Ahaz took the

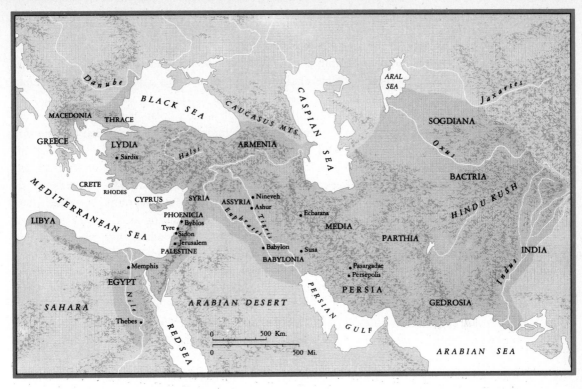

MAP 2.3 THE PERSIAN EMPIRE *The Persian Empire not only included more of the ancient Near East than had the Assyrian Empire, but it also extended as far east as western India.*

silver and gold that was found in the house of the lord, and in the treasures of the king's house, and sent it for a present to the king of Assyria.[16]

Against still more distant states the kings waged frequent war in order to conquer them outright or to make their dependent states secure.

Royal roads and swift mounted messengers linked the Assyrian empire, and Assyrian records describe how these royal messengers brought the king immediate word of unrest or rebellion within the empire. Because of good communications, Assyrian kings could generally move against rebels at a moment's notice. Thus, though rebellion was common in the Assyrian empire, it rarely got off the ground before the king struck back hard.

In the seventh century B.C. Assyrian power seemed secure. From their capitals at Nineveh, Kalah, and Ashur on the Tigris river, the Assyrians ruled a vast empire. Good communications, an efficient army, and calculated terrorism easily kept down the conquered population. With grim efficiency they sacked rebellious cities, leaving forests of impaled prisoners or piles of severed heads to signal their victory. Their ferocity horrified their subjects and bred a vast hatred among them.

Yet the downfall of Assyria was swift and complete. Babylon finally won its independence in 626 B.C. and joined forces with a new people, the Medes, an Indo-European-speaking folk from Iran. Together the Babylonians and the Medes destroyed the Assyrian empire in 612 B.C., paving the way for the rise of the

Persians. The Hebrew prophet Nahum spoke for many when he proclaimed: "Nineveh is laid waste: who will bemoan her?".[17] Their cities destroyed and their power shattered, the Assyrians disappeared from history, remembered only as a cruel people of the Old Testament who oppressed the Hebrews. Two hundred years later, when the Greek adventurer and historian Xenophon passed by the ruins of Nineveh, he marvelled at their extent but knew nothing of the Assyrians. The glory of their empire was forgotten.

Yet modern archaeology has brought the Assyrians out of obscurity. In 1839 the intrepid English archaeologist and traveler A. H. Layard began to excavate Nineveh, then a mound of debris beside the Tigris. His findings electrified the world. In the course of a few years Layard's discoveries shed remarkable new light on Assyrian history. His excavations had an equally stunning impact on the history of art. Layard's workers unearthed masterpieces, including monumental sculpted figures – huge winged bulls, human-headed lions, and sphinxes – as well as brilliantly sculpted friezes. Equally valuable were the numerous Assyrian cuneiform documents, which ranged from royal accounts of mighty military campaigns to simple letters by common people.

Among the most renowned of Layard's finds were the Assyrian palace reliefs, whose number has been increased by the discoveries of twentieth-century archaeologists. Assyrian kings delighted in scenes of war, which their artists depicted in graphic detail. By the time of Ashurbanipal, Assyrian artists had hit upon the idea of portraying a series of episodes – in fact, a visual narrative – of events that had actually taken place. Scene followed scene in a continuous frieze, so the viewer could follow the progress of a military campaign from the time that the army marched out until the

enemy was conquered. So too with another theme of the palace reliefs – the lion hunt. Hunting lions was probably a royal sport, although some scholars have suggested a magical significance. They argue that the hunting scenes depict the king as the protector of his people, the one who wards off evil. In any case, here too the viewer proceeds in sequence, from preparations for the chase through the hunting itself to the killing of the lions. These reliefs, like those depicting warfare, tell a story in pictures, an artistic technique novel in the ancient Near East.

Assyrian art, like much of Egyptian art, was realistic, but the warmth and humor of the Egyptian scenes are absent from the Assyrian reliefs. Assyrian art is stark and often brutal in subject matter, yet marked by an undeniable strength and sophistication of composition. Assyrian realism is well represented by the illustration on page 57, a scene which portrays the climax of the royal lion hunt. The scene is like a photograph, snapped at the height of the action. The king, mounted on horseback, has already fired his arrows into two lions, who nonetheless are still full of fight. The wounded lion on the left has just pounced on a riderless horse, which in a moment will fall mortally wounded. Meanwhile, the king thrusts his spear into another lion, which has begun its spring. The artistic rendering of the figures is exciting and technically flawless. The figures are anatomically correct and in proper proportion and perspective. The whole composition conveys both action and tension. Assyrian art fared better than Assyrian military power. The techniques of Assyrian artists influenced the Persians, who adapted them to gentler scenes.

In fact, many Assyrian innovations, military and political as well as artistic, were taken over wholesale by the Persians. Although the memory of Assyria was hateful throughout

the Near East, the fruits of Assyrian organizational genius helped enable the Persians to bring peace and stability to the same regions where Assyrian armies had spread terror.

THE EMPIRE OF THE PERSIAN KINGS

Like the Hittites before them, the Iranians were Indo-Europeans from central Europe and southern Russia who migrated into a land inhabited by more primitive peoples. Once settled in the area between the Caspian Sea and the Persian Gulf, the Iranians, like the Hittites, fell under the spell of the more sophisticated cultures of their Mesopotamian neighbors. Yet the Iranians went on to create one of the greatest empires of antiquity, one that encompassed hundreds of peoples and cultures. The Persians, the most important of the Iranian peoples, had a far-sighted conception of empire. They respected their subjects

and allowed them to practice their native customs and religions. Thus, the Persians gave the Near East political unity coupled with cultural diversity. Never before had any Near Eastern people viewed empire in such intelligent and humane terms.

THE LAND OF MOUNTAINS AND PLATEAU

Persia – the modern country of Iran – is a stark land of towering mountains and flaming deserts, with a broad central plateau in the heart of the country (see Map 2.3). Iran stretches from the Caspian Sea in the north to the Persian Gulf in the south. Between the Tigris-Euphrates valley in the west and the Indus valley in the east rises an immense plateau, surrounded on all sides by lofty mountains that cut off the interior from the sea.

The central plateau is very high, a landscape of broad plains, scattered oases, and two vast deserts. The high mountains, which catch the moisture coming from the sea, generate ample rainfall for the plain. This semi-tropical area is very fertile, in marked contrast to the aridity of most of Iran. The mountains surrounding the central plateau are dotted with numerous oases, often very fertile, which have from time immemorial served as havens for small groups of people.

At the center of the plateau lies an enormous depression – a forbidding region devoid of water and vegetation, so glowing hot in summer that it is virtually impossible to cross. This depression forms two distinct grim and burning salt deserts, perhaps the most desolate spots on earth. These two deserts form a barrier between east and west.

Iran's geographical position and topography explain its traditional role as the highway between East and West. Throughout history wild, nomadic people migrating from the broad steppes of Russia and Central Asia have streamed into Iran. Confronting the uncrossable salt deserts, most have turned either eastward or westward, moving on until they reached the advanced and wealthy urban centers of Mesopotamia and India. When cities emerged along the natural lines of east-west communication, Iran became the area where nomads met urban dwellers, a meeting-ground of unique significance for the civilizations of both East and West.

THE COMING OF THE MEDES AND THE PERSIANS

The history of human habitation in Iran is long and rich: traces of prehistoric peoples date back as far as 15,000–10,000 B.C. About the prehistoric period, historians and archaeologists still have much to learn. Perhaps the best recent account of prehistoric developments comes from one of the world's foremost experts on ancient Iran, the French scholar Roman Ghirshman:

The arrival of the Iranians in the plateau was preceded by a long period of several millennia, during which there slowly developed the civilization of prehistoric man, who, coming down from his caves, established himself in the plains and valleys. Over the course of more than thirty centuries man acquired the knowledge of and developed agriculture, domesticated animals, took the first steps in metallurgy. His art of painted pottery, doubtless born in the plateau, underwent a rapid rise and extensive diffusion. Man organized his social life by creating villages, and, never remaining isolated, he established and enlarged his contacts with other human groups.[18]

The Iranians entered this land around 1000 B.C. The most historically important of them were the Medes and the Persians, related peoples who settled in different areas. Both groups were part of the vast movement of Indo-European-speaking peoples whose wanderings led them into Europe, the Near East, and India in many successive waves (page 31). These Iranians were nomads, who migrated with their flocks and herds. Like their kinsmen the Aryans, who moved into India, they were also horse-breeders, and the horse gave them a decisive military advantage over the prehistoric peoples of Iran. The Iranians rode into battle in horse-drawn chariots or on horseback, and easily swept the natives before them. Yet because the influx of Iranians went on for centuries, there continued to be constant cultural interchange between conquering newcomers and conquered natives.

Excavations at Siyalk, some 125 miles south of present-day Tehran, provide a valuable glimpse of the encounter of Iranian and native. The village of Siyalk had been inhabited since prehistoric times before falling to the Iranians. The new lords fought all comers: natives, rival Iranians, and even the Assyrians, who often raided far east of the

Tigris. Under the newly-arrived Iranians, Siyalk became a fortified town with a palace and perhaps a temple, all enclosed by a circuit wall strengthened by towers and ramparts. The town was surrounded by fields and farms, for agriculture was the basis of this evolving society.

The Iranians initially created a patchwork of tiny kingdoms, of which Siyalk was one. The chieftain or petty king was basically a warlord who depended on his fellow warriors for aid and support. This band of noble warriors, like the Greek heroes of the *Iliad,* formed the fighting strength of the army. The king owned estates that supported him and his nobles; for additional income the king levied taxes, which were paid in kind and not in cash. He also demanded labor services from the peasants. Below the king and his warrior nobles were free people who held land and others who owned nothing. Artisans produced the various goods needed to keep society running. At the bottom of the social scale were slaves – probably both natives and newcomers – to whom fell the drudgery of hard labor and household service to the king and his nobles.

This early period saw some significant economic developments. The use of iron increased. By the seventh century B.C. iron farm implements had become widespread, leading to increased productivity, greater overall prosperity, and higher standards of living. At the same time Iranian agriculture saw the development of the small estate. Farmers worked small plots of land, and the general prosperity of the period bred a sturdy and free peasantry, who enjoyed greater freedom than their contemporaries in Egypt and Mesopotamia.

Kings exploited Iran's considerable mineral wealth, and Iranian iron, copper, and lapis lazuli attracted Assyrian raiding parties. Even more important, mineral wealth and Iranian horse-breeding stimulated brisk trade with the outside world. Kings found that merchants, who were not usually Iranians, produced large profits to help fill the kings' coffers. Overland trade also put the Iranians in direct contact with their Near Eastern neighbors.

Gradually two groups of Iranians began coalescing into larger units. The Persians had settled in Persis, the modern region of Fars, in southern Iran. Their kinsmen the Medes occupied Media, the modern area of Hamadan in the north, with their capital at Ecbatana. The Medes were exposed to attack by nomads from the north, but their greatest threat was the frequent raids of the Assyrian army. Even though distracted by grave pressures from their neighbors, the Medes united under one king around 710 B.C., and extended their control over the Persians in the south. In 612 B.C. the Medes were strong enough to join the Babylonians in overthrowing the Assyrian Empire. With the rise of the Medes, the balance of power in the Near East shifted for the first time east of Mesopotamia.

THE CREATION OF THE PERSIAN EMPIRE

In 550 B.C. Cyrus the Great (559-530 B.C.), king of the Persians and one of the most remarkable statesmen of antiquity, threw off the yoke of the Medes by conquering them and turning their country into his first satrapy, or province. In the short space of a single lifetime, Cyrus created one of the greatest empires of antiquity. Two characteristics lift Cyrus above the common level of warrior-kings. First, he thought of Iran, not just Persia and Media, as a state. His concept has survived a long, complex, and often turbulent history to play its part in the contemporary world.

Second, Cyrus held an enlightened view of

TOMB OF CYRUS *For all of his greatness Cyrus retained a sense of perspective. His tomb, though monumental in size, is rather simple and unostentatious. Greek writers reported that it bore the following epitaph: "O man, I am Cyrus the son of Cambyses. I established the Persian Empire and was king of Asia. Do not begrudge me my memorial." (Oriental Institute, University of Chicago)*

ancient Near East over two hundred years of peace, prosperity, and security.

Cyrus showed his magnanimity at the outset of his career. Once the Medes had fallen to him, Cyrus united them with his Persians. Ecbatana, the Median capital, became a Persian seat of power. Medes were honored with important military and political posts, and thenceforth helped the Persians to rule the expanding empire. Cyrus' conquest of the Medes resulted not in slavery and slaughter, but in the union of Iranian peoples.

With Iran united, Cyrus looked at the broader world. He set out to achieve two goals: first, to win control of the west, and thus of the terminal ports of the great trade routes that crossed Iran and Anatolia. Secondly, Cyrus strove to secure eastern Iran from the pressure of nomadic invaders. In 550 B.C. neither goal was easy. To the northwest was the young kingdom of Lydia in Anatolia, whose king Croesus was proverbial for his wealth. To the west was Babylonia, enjoying a new period of power now that the Assyrian Empire had been crushed. To the southwest was Egypt, still weak but sheltered behind its bulwark of sand and sea. To the east ranged tough, mobile nomads, capable of massive and destructive incursions deep into Iranian territory.

Cyrus turned first to Croesus' Lydian kingdom, which fell to him around 546 B.C. He established a garrison at Sardis, the capital of Lydia, and ordered his generals to subdue the Greek cities along the coast of Anatolia. Cyrus had thus gained the important ports that looked out to the Mediterranean world. And for the first time the Persians came into direct contact with the Greeks, a people with whom their later history was to be intimately connected.

From Lydia, Cyrus next marched to the far eastern corners of Iran. In a brilliant cam-

empire. Many of the civilizations and cultures that fell to his armies were, he realized, far older, more advanced, and more sophisticated than his. Free of the narrow-minded snobbery of the Egyptians, the religious exclusiveness of the Hebrews, and the calculated cruelty of the Assyrians, Cyrus gave Near Eastern peoples and their cultures his respect, toleration, and protection. Conquered peoples continued to enjoy their institutions, religion, language, and way of life under the Persians. The Persian Empire, which Cyrus created, became a political organization sheltering many different civilizations. To rule such a vast area and so many diverse peoples demanded talent, intelligence, sensitivity, and a cosmopolitan view of the world. These qualities Cyrus and many of his successors possessed in abundance. Consequently, the Persians gave the

paign he conquered the regions of Parthia, Bactria, and even the most westerly part of India. All of Iran was now Persian, from Mesopotamia in the west to the western slopes of the Hindu Kush in the east.

In 540 B.C. Cyrus moved against Babylonia, now isolated from outside help. When Persian soldiers marched quietly into Babylon the next year, the Babylonians welcomed Cyrus as a liberator. Cyrus described the event himself thus:

When I made my gracious entry into Babylon, with rejoicing and pleasure I took up my lordly residence in the royal palace. Marduk, the great lord, turned the noble race of the Babylonians toward me, and I gave daily care to his worship. My numerous troops marched peacefully into Babylon. In all Sumer and Akkad I permitted no unfriendly treatment. The dishonoring yoke was removed from them. Their fallen dwellings I restored; I cleared out the ruins. [19]

Cyrus won the hearts of the Babylonians with toleration of and adherence to Babylonian religion, humane treatment, and support of their efforts to refurbish their capital.

Cyrus was equally generous toward the Jews. He allowed them to return to Palestine, from which they had been deported by the Babylonians. He protected them, gave them back the sacred items they used in worship, and rebuilt the temple of Yahweh in Jerusalem. The Old Testament sings the praises of Cyrus, whom the Jews considered the shepherd of Yahweh, the lord's anointed:

[Yahweh] that saith of Cyrus, he is my shepherd, and shall perform all my pleasure: even saying to Jerusalem, thou shalt be built; and to the temple, thy foundation shall be laid. Thus saith the lord to his anointed, to Cyrus, whose right hand I have holden, to subdue nations before him. [20]

Rarely have conquered people shown such gratitude to their conquerors. Cyrus's benev-

olent policy created a Persian Empire in which the cultures and religions of its members were respected and honored. Seldom have conquerors been as wise, sensitive, and far-sighted as Cyrus and his Persians.

THUS SPAKE ZARATHUSTRA

Iranian religion was originally simple and primitive. Ahuramazda, the chief god, was the creator and benefactor of all living creatures. Yet unlike Yahweh, he was not a lone god. The Iranians were polytheistic. Mithra the sun god, whose cult would later spread throughout the Roman Empire (page 251), saw to justice and redemption. Other Iranian deities personified the natural elements: moon, earth, water, and wind. As in ancient India, fire was a particularly important god. The sacred fire consumed the blood sacrifices that the early Iranians offered to all of their deities.

Early Iranian religion was close to nature and unencumbered by ponderous theological beliefs. A priestly class, the Magi, developed among the Medes to officiate at sacrifices, chant prayers to the gods, and tend the sacred flame. A fine, concise description of this early worship comes from the great German historian Eduard Meyer:

Iranian religion knew neither divine images nor temples. On a hilltop one called upon god and his manifestations — sun and moon, earth and fire, water and wind — and erected altars with their eternal fire. But in other appropriate places one could, without further preparation, pray to the deity and bring him his offerings, with the assistance of the Magi, who in addition chanted the holy formulas. [21]

In time the Iranians built fire temples for these sacrifices. As late as the nineteenth century, fire was still worshiped in Baku, a major city on the Russian-Iranian border.

Around 600 B.C. the prophet Zarathustra — or Zoroaster, as he is more generally known — breathed new meaning into Iranian religion. Of Zoroaster the man, as little is known as of Moses; like his Jewish counterpart, Zoroaster is remembered for his work, which long outlived him. Like Moses, Zoroaster preached a novel concept of divinity and human life. Life, he taught, is a constant battleground between two opposing forces, good and evil. Ahuramazda embodied good and truth but was opposed by Ahriman, a hateful spirit who stood for evil and falsehood. Ahuramazda and Ahriman were locked together in a cosmic battle for the human race, a battle that stretched over thousands of years. But, according to Zoroaster, people were not mere pawns in this struggle. Each person had to choose which side to join — whether to lead a life characterized by good behavior and truthful dealings with others or by wickedness and lies.

Zoroaster emphasized the responsibility of the individual in this decision. He taught that people possessed the free will to decide between Ahuramazda and Ahriman, and that people must rely on their own consciences to guide them through life. Their decisions were crucial, Zoroaster warned, for there would be a time of reckoning. He promised that Ahuramazda would eventually triumph over evil and lies, and that at death each person would stand before the tribunal of good. Ahuramazda, like the Egyptian god Osiris, would judge whether the dead had lived righteously and on that basis would weigh their lives in the balance. Then good and truth would conquer evil and lies. In short, Zoroaster taught the concept of a Last Judgment at which Ahuramazda would decide each person's eternal fate on the basis of that person's deeds in life.

In Zoroaster's thought the Last Judgment was linked to the notion of a divine kingdom after death for those who had lived according to good and truth. They would accompany Ahuramazda to a life of eternal truth in what Zoroaster called "the House of Song" and "the Abode of Good Thought." There they would dwell with Ahuramazda forever. Liars and the wicked, denied this blessed immortality, would be condemned to eternal pain, darkness, and punishment. Thus, Zoroaster preached a Last Judgment that led to a heaven or a hell.

Although tradition has it that Zoroaster met with opposition and coldness, his thought converted Darius (521–486 B.C.), one of the most energetic men ever to sit on the Persian throne. The Persian royal family adopted Zoroastrianism, though without trying to impose it on others. Under the protection of the Persian kings, Zoroastrianism swept through Iran, winning converts and sinking roots that sustained healthy growth for centuries. Zoroastrianism survived the fall of the Persian Empire to influence religious thought in the age of Jesus and to make a vital contribution to Manicheanism, a theology that was to spread through the Byzantine Empire and pose a significant challenge to Christianity. A handful of the faithful still follow the teachings of Zoroaster, whose vision of divinity and human life has transcended the centuries.

PERSIA'S WORLD EMPIRE

Cyrus' successors rounded out the Persian conquest of the ancient Near East. In 525 B.C. Cyrus's son Cambyses (530–522 B.C.) subdued Egypt. Darius (521–486 B.C.) and his son Xerxes (486–464 B.C.) invaded Greece, but were fought to a standstill and forced to retreat (Chapter 3); the Persians never won a permanent foothold in Europe. Yet Darius

DARIUS AND XERXES This relief from the Persian capital of Persepolis shows King Darius and Crown Prince Xerxes in state. Behind them the royal bodyguard stands at attention, as the royal pair receives the guard's commander. (Oriental Institute, University of Chicago)

carried Persian arms into India. Around 513 B.C. western India became the Persian satrapy, or province, of Hindush, which included the valley of the Indus river. Thus, within thirty-seven years the Persians transformed themselves from a subject people to the rulers of an empire that included Anatolia, Egypt, Mesopotamia, Iran, and western India. They had created a "world empire" encompassing all of the oldest and most honored kingdoms and peoples of the ancient Near East. Never before had the Near East been united in one such vast political organization (see Map 2.3).

The Persians knew how to use the peace that they had won on the battlefield. Unlike the Assyrians, they did not resort to royal terrorism to keep order. Like the Assyrians, however, they employed a number of bureaucratic techniques to bind the empire together. The sheer size of the empire made it impossible for one man to rule it effectively. Consequently the Persians divided the empire into some twenty huge satrapies – provinces measuring hundreds of square miles, many of them kingdoms in themselves. Each satrapy had a governor, drawn from the Median and Persian nobility and often a relative of the king; the governor or satrap was directly responsible to the king. An army officer, also responsible to the king, commanded the military forces stationed in the satrapy. Still another official collected the royal taxes. Moreover, the king sent out royal inspectors to watch the satraps and other officials, a method of royal surveillance later used by the medieval king Charlemagne (Chapter 10).

Effective rule of the empire demanded good communications. To meet this need the Persians established a network of roads. The main highway, known as the Royal Road, spanned some 1677 miles from the Greek city of Ephesus on the coast of Asia Minor to Susa in western Iran. The distance was broken into 111 post-stations, each equipped with fresh horses for the king's messengers. Other roads branched out to link all parts of the empire, from the coast of Asia Minor to the valley of the Indus river. Along these roads royal

THE ROYAL PALACE AT PERSEPOLIS *King Darius began and King Xerxes finished building a grand palace worthy of the glory of the Persian Empire. Pictured here is the monumental audience hall,* *where the king dealt with ministers of state and foreign envoys. (Oriental Institute, University of Chicago)*

couriers sped so quickly that the Greek historian and traveler Herodotus marvelled at them:

There is nothing which is mortal that arrives faster than these couriers ... For they say that as many days as the whole journey takes that many horses and men stand at intervals, a horse and man stationed at each daily segment of road. These neither snow nor rain nor heat nor night prevents from traversing their appointed run as fast as possible. The first courier hands over the dispatch to the second, the second to the third. Thereafter from one to another the dispatch passes on.[22]

This system of communications enabled the Persian king to keep in intimate touch with his subjects and officials. He was able to rule efficiently, keep his ministers in line, and protect the rights of the peoples under his control. How effective Persian rule could be, even in small matters, is apparent in a letter from King Darius to the satrap of Ionia, the Greek region of Anatolia. The satrap had transplanted Syrian fruit trees in his province, an experiment Darius praised. Yet the king also learned that his governor had infringed on the rights granted to the sanctuary of the Greek god Apollo, an act that provoked the king to anger:

The King of Kings, Darius the son of Hystaspes says this to Gadatas, his slave [satrap]. I learn that you are not obeying my command in every particular. Because you are tilling my land, transplanting fruit trees from across the Euphrates [Syria] to Asia Minor, I praise your project, and there will be laid up for you great favor in the king's house. But because you mar my dispositions towards the gods, I shall give you, unless you change your ways, proof of my anger when wronged. For you exacted payment from the sacred gardeners of the temple of Apollo, and you ordered them to dig up secular land, failing to understand the attitude of my forefathers towards the god, who told the Persians the truth.[23]

Fruit trees and foreign gods — even such small matters as these were important to the man whom the world called "The King of Kings, the King of Persia, the King of the Provinces."[24] This document alone suggests the efficiency of Persian rule and the compassion of Persian kings. Conquered peoples, left free to enjoy their traditional ways of life, found in the Persian king a capable protector. No wonder that many Near Eastern peoples were, like the Jews, grateful for the long period of peace they enjoyed as the subjects of the Persian Empire.

—◆—

Between around 1200 and 500 B.C. the Near East passed from fragmentation to political unification under the Persian Empire. On the road from chaos to order, from widespread warfare to general peace, peoples in many areas wrought vast and enduring achievements. The Egyptians survived invasion to share their heritage with their African neighbors and later with the Greeks. The homeless Hebrews laboriously built a state and entered the broader world of their neighbors. Simultaneously, they evolved religious and ethical beliefs that permeate the modern West.

Although the Assyrians made the Near East tremble in terror of their armies, they too contributed to the heritage of these long years. Their military and, particularly, political abilities gave the Persians the tools they needed to govern a host of different peoples. Those tools were to be well used. For over two hundred years Persian kings offered their subjects enlightened rule. The Persians gave the ancient Near East a period of peace and stability in which peoples enjoyed their native traditions and lived in concord with their neighbors.

Meanwhile to the west, another people — the Greeks — were slowly shaping cultural and political ideals that were to have an even greater impact on the future. Although Greece and the Near East would eventually become locked in a mighty conflict, the heritage of the East would blend with that of Greece to influence Western civilization in a fundamental way.

NOTES

1. James H. Breasted, *Ancient Records of Egypt,* University of Chicago Press, Chicago, 1907, IV, paragraph 398.

2. J. B. Pritchard, ed., *Ancient Near Eastern Texts,* Princeton University Press, Princeton, 1950, p. 27.

3. 1 Kings 8:4–6.

4. 2 Kings 23:3.

5. Jeremiah 7:5–7.

6. Ibid. 3:12.

7. Proverbs 31:10, 25–30.

8. Deuteronomy 24:1–2.

9. Psalms 128:3.

10. Deuteronomy 25:9.

11. Proverbs 13:24.

12. Deuteronomy 24:19.

13. Jeremiah 23:13.

14. Pritchard, *op. cit.*, p. 288.

15. Ibid.

16. 2 Kings 16:7-8.

17. Nahum 3:7.

18. R. Ghirshman, *L'Iran des origines à l'Islam,* Albin Michel, Paris, 1976, p. 343.

19. Quoted from A. T. Olmstead, *A History of the Persian Empire,* University of Chicago Press, Chicago, 1963, p. 53.

20. Isaiah 44:28-45:1.

21. E. Meyer, *Geschichte des Altertums,* 7th ed., Vol. IV, Part I, Wissenschaftliche Buchgesellschaft, Darmstadt, 1975, pp. 114-115.

22. Herodotus 8.98.

23. R. Meiggs and D. M. Lewis, *A Selection of Greek Historical Inscriptions,* Clarendon Press, Oxford, 1969, no. 12.

24. Behistun Inscription col. 1.1.

SUGGESTED READING

Although late Egyptian history is still largely a specialist's field, K. A. Kitchen, *The Third Intermediate Period in Egypt (1100-650 B.C.)* (1973) is a good synthesis of the period. Valuable too is M. L. Bierbrier's monograph, *Late New Kingdom in Egypt, c. 1300-664 B.C.* (1975). More general is R. David, *The Egyptian Kingdoms* (1975). H. S. Smith, *A Visit to Ancient Egypt: Life at Memphis and Saqqara (c. 500-30 B.C.* (1974) gives a picture of life during the period, and P. L. Shinnie, *Meroe: A Civilization of the Sudan* (1967), does the same for one of Egypt's most important southern neighbors. Those interested in the whole story of Wen-Amon's adventures should read H. Goedicke, *The Report of Wenamun* (1975). Sir A. H. Gardiner, ed., *Late Egyptian Stories* (1973) contains other pieces of late Egyptian literature.

D. Harden, *The Phoenicians,* 2nd ed. (1971) gives a good account of Phoenician history and life. More recently, G. Herm, *The Phoenicians: The Purple Empire of the Ancient World* (1975), treats Phoe-nician seafaring and commercial enterprises. A more general treatment of the entire area is R. Fedden, *Syria and Lebanon,* 3rd ed. (1965). Those interested in individual Phoenician cities should see N. Jidejian, *Byblos through the Ages,* 2nd ed. (1971), *Tyre through the Ages* (1969), and *Sidon through the Ages* (1971). For a history of Phoenicia written at the time of the Roman Empire, see A. I. Baumgarten, *The Phoenician History of Philo of Byblos* (1981).

The Jews have been one of the best studied people in the ancient world, and the reader can easily find many good treatments of Jewish history and society. A readable and balanced book is J. Bright, *A History of Israel,* 2nd ed. (1972). Somewhat older is A. S. Kapelrud, *Israel from Earliest Times to the Birth of Christ* (1966). Other useful general books include G. W. Anderson, *The History and Religion of Israel* (1966), which is a solid scholarly treatment of the subject. The archaeological exploration of ancient Israel is so fast-paced that nearly any book is quickly outdated. Nonetheless, A. Negev, *Archaeological Encyclopedia of the Holy Land* (1973), which is illustrated, is still a good place to start.

S. Yeivin, *The Israelite Conquest of Canaan* (1971), though a bit dated, is a good survey of the Jewish entry into Palestine. M. Pearlman, *In the Footsteps of Moses* (1974), a more popular account, also treats the period. R. de Vaux, *Ancient Israel, Its Life and Institutions,* 2nd ed. (1965), ranges across all eras of Jewish history, and is especially recommended because of its solid base in the ancient sources. The period of Jewish kingship has elicited a good deal of attention. Most recent is B. Halpern, *The Constitution of the Monarchy in Israel* (1981), which makes the significant point that the Jews are the only ancient Near Eastern people to have recorded the decision to adopt monarchy as a form of government. Also valuable in this connection is A. R. Johnson, *Sacral Kingship in Ancient Israel,* 2nd ed. (1967). Solomon's importance as a strong king and an innovator is underlined by a series of studies, especially T. N. Mettinger, *Solomonic State Officials: A Study of the Civil Service Officials of the Israelite Monarchy* (1971); E. W. Heaton, *Solomon's New Men: The*

Emergence of Ancient Israel as a National State (1974); and lastly J. Gutmann, *The Temple of Solomon* (1975).

More specific than de Vaux' splendid general work on Hebrew society is P. A. H. de Boer, *Fatherhood and Motherhood in Israelite and Judean Piety* (1974), which treats a fundamental aspect of Jewish religion and society. A fascinating and ambitious new study of myth and religion is J. O'Brien and W. Major, *In the Beginning: Creation Myths from Ancient Mesopotamia, Israel and Greece* (1981). Lastly, P. R. Ackroyd, *Israel under Babylon and Persia* (1970), gives an informative account of Jewish inability to resist expansion of the great monarchies.

The Assyrians, despite their achievements, have not attracted the scholarly attention that the ancient Jews and other Near Eastern peoples have. Even though outdated, A. T. Olmstead, *History of Assyria* (1928), still possesses the merit of being soundly based in the original sources. Olmstead was a rare scholar who attempted to understand the entire development of the ancient Near East. More recent and more difficult is J. A. Brinkman, *A Political History of Post-Kassite Babylonia, 1158-722 B.C.* (1968), which treats the Babylonian response to the rise of Assyria. M. Cogan, *Imperialism and Religion: Assyria, Judah and Israel in the Eighth and Seventh Centuries B.C.E.* (1973), traces the various effects of Assyrian expansion on the two Jewish kingdoms.

An informative look at the Assyrians themselves comes from J. Laessoe, *People of Ancient Assyria: Their Inscriptions and Correspondence* (1963). Those who appreciate the vitality of Assyrian art should start with the masterful work of R. D. Barnett and W. Forman, *Assyrian Palace Reliefs,* 2nd ed. (1970), an exemplary combination of fine photographs and learned, though not difficult, discussion.

In addition to the works on Iran cited in the Notes, G. C. Cameron, *History of Early Iran* (1969); W. Culican, *The Medes and the Persians* (1965); and J. A. deGobineau, *The World of the Persians* (1971), which is illustrated with color plates, all provide introductions to Persian history. Vastly informative but difficult is E. Herzfeld, *The Persian Empire: Studies in the Geography and Ethnology of the Ancient Near East* (1968), a posthumous work by one of the world's leading authorities on the Persians. Very useful is J. D. Pearson, ed., *A Bibliography of Pre-Islamic Persia* (1975). S. A. Matheson, *Persia: An Archaeological Guide* (1972), is a good guide to Persian monuments. A good brief account of Cyrus the Great's career can be found in M. E. L. Mallowan, "Cyrus the Great (558-529 B.C.)," *Iran* 10 (1972), 1-17.

J. H. Moulton, *Early Zoroastrianism: The Origins, the Prophet, and the Magi* (1972), is a sound treatment of the beginnings and early spread of Zoroastrianism. R. C. Zaehner, *The Dawn and Twilight of Zoroastrianism* (1961) discusses the whole course of Zoroastrianism's history. Zaehner also provides a good introduction to the basic teachings of Zoroastrianism in his *Teachings of the Magi: A Compendium of Zoroastrian Beliefs* (1975).

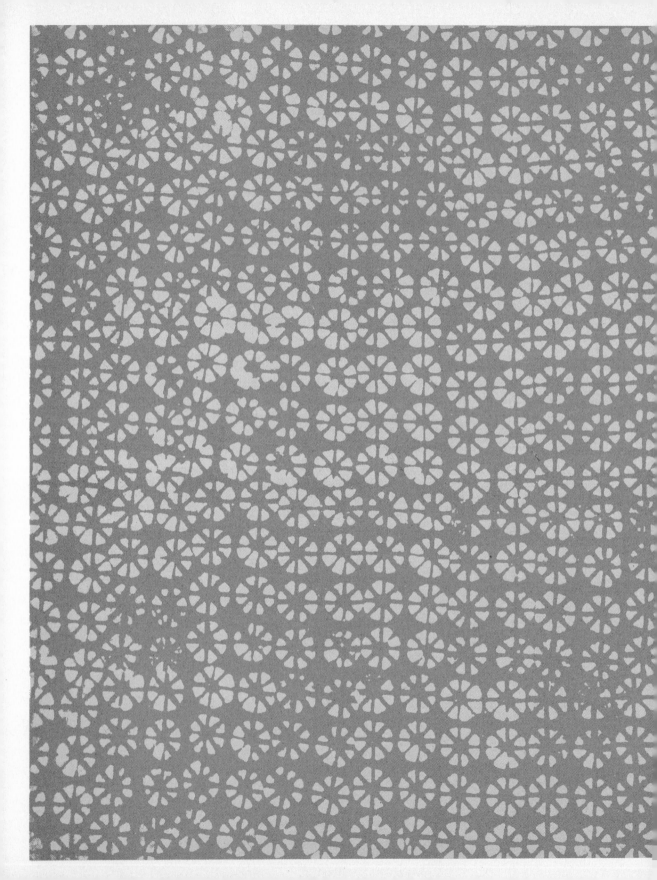

CHAPTER 3

THE LEGACY OF GREECE

THE ANCIENT NEAR EAST was the seat of old cultures and rich empires, but the rocky peninsula of Greece was the home of the civilization that fundamentally shaped Western civilization. The Greeks were the first to explore most of the questions that continue to concern Western thinkers to this day. Going beyond mythmaking and religion, the Greeks strove to understand, in logical, rational terms, the universe and the position of men and women in it. The result was the birth of philosophy and science, which were far more important to most Greek thinkers than religion. The Greeks speculated on human beings and society and created the very concept of politics.

While the scribes of the ancient Near East produced king lists, the Greeks invented history to record, analyze, and understand how people and states functioned in time and space. In poetry, the Greeks spoke as individuals. In drama, they dealt with the grandeur and weakness of humanity and with the demands of society on the individual. The greatest monuments of the Greeks were not temples, statues, or tombs, but profound thoughts set down in terms as fresh and immediate today as they were some 2,400 years ago.

The history of the Greeks is divided into two broad periods: the Hellenic (the subject of this chapter), roughly the time between the arrival of the Greeks and the triumph of Philip of Macedon, and the Hellenistic, the age beginning with Alexander the Great and ending with the Roman conquest (the subject of Chapter 4).

What geographical factors helped to mold the evolution of the city-state and to shape the course of the Greek experience? How did the Greeks develop basic political forms – forms as different as democracy and tyranny – that have influenced all of later Western history?

MAP 3.1 ANCIENT GREECE *In antiquity the home of the Greeks included the islands of the Aegean and the western shore of Turkey as well as the Greek peninsula itself.*

What did the Greek intellectual triumph entail? And, lastly, how and why did the Greek genius eventually fail? These profound questions, which can never be fully answered, are the themes of this chapter.

THE LAND AND THE POLIS

Hellas, as the ancient Greeks called their land, encompassed the Aegean Sea and its islands as well as the Greek peninsula (see Map 3.1). The Greek peninsula itself is an extension of the Balkan system of mountains, stretching in the direction of Egypt and the Near East. Greece is mountainous; its rivers are never more than creeks, and most of them go dry in the summer. It is, however, a land blessed with good harbors, the most important of which look to the east. The islands of the Aegean continue to sweep to the east, and serve as steppingstones between the peninsula and Anatolia. As early as 1000 B.C., Greeks from the peninsula had settled along the coastline of Anatolia (Asia Minor); the heartland of these eastern Greeks was in Ionia. Thus, geography alone encouraged the Greeks to turn their attention to the old civilizations of Asia Minor and Egypt.

Despite the poverty of its soil, Greece is strikingly beautiful, as the eminent German historian K. J. Beloch has written:

Greece is an alpine land, which rises from the waters of the Mediterranean sea, scenically probably the most beautiful region in southern Europe. The noble contours of the mountains, the bare,

BYZANTIUM

ASIA MINOR

LYDIA

Hermus

Maeander

Colophon

IONIA

Erythrae

Miletus

Halicarnassus

RHODES

SAMOS

Hellespont

Troy

LESBOS

CHIOS

AEGEAN SEA

DELOS ⛪

PAROS ⛪

CRETE

Knossos

THASOS

CHALCIDICE

Cape Artemisium

EUBOEA

Chalcis

Oropus

Coronea ✕ BOEOTIA Eretria

MACEDONIA

MT. OLYMPUS ▲

THESSALY

ACHAEA
PHTHIOTIS

MALIS

Thermopylae

DORIS

LOCRIS

PHOCIS ⛪ Delphi
Asea Thebes
MT. HELICON ✕ Plataea

Marathon

ATTICA

Thoricus

Eleusis ⛪
Megara Athens

AEGINA

SALAMIS

Saronic Gulf

MELOS

CYTHERA

Cape Sounion

AETOLIA

ACARNANIA

ITHACA

CORCYRA

Corinthian Gulf

Sicyon

Corinth

ACHAEA

ELIS

Elis

Olympia

ARCADIA

Mantinea
Tegea

MESSENIA

MT. ITHOME ▲

Pylos

Mycenae
Tiryns

Argos

ARGOLIS

P E L O P O N N E S U S

Sparta

LACONIA

Dodona ⛪
EPIRUS

IONIAN SEA

M E D I T E R R A N E A N   S E A

Plains

Sanctuaries ⛪

Major battle ✕

100 Mi.

100 Km.

50

50

0

0

rocky slopes, the dusty green of the conifer forests, the white cover of snow which envelops the higher summits for the greatest part of the year, added to which is the profound blue surface of the sea below, and above everything the diffused brightness of the southern sun; this gives a total picture, the charm of which impresses itself unforgettably on the soul of the observer.[1]

The Greeks gloried in their land, and its beauty was one of the factors that elicited their loyalty to the soil of this hard peninsula. The climate of Greece is mild; though hot in summer, the air is dry and stirred by breezes. In winter snow may blanket the mountain slopes, but rarely covers the lowlands.

Simultaneously, geography acted as an enormously divisive force in Greek life. The mountains of Greece dominate the landscape. They cut the land into many small pockets, and isolate areas of inhabitation from one another. Innumerable peninsulas open to the sea, which is dotted with islands, most of them small and many uninhabitable. The geographical fragmentation of Greece encouraged political fragmentation. Furthermore, communications were extraordinarily poor. Rocky tracks were far more common than roads, and the few roads were unpaved. Usually they were nothing more than a pair of ruts cut into the rock to accommodate the wheels of vehicles. The small physical units of Greece discouraged the growth of great empires.

As in Sumer, the typical Greek political unit was the city-state, which the Greeks called the polis. Rarely did there occur the combination of extensive territory and political unity that allowed one polis to rise above others. Only three city-states were able to muster the resources of an entire region behind them (see Map 3.2): Sparta, which dominated the regions of Laconia and Messenia;

Athens, which united the large peninsula of Attica under its rule; and Thebes, which in several periods marshaled the resources of the fertile region of Boeotia. Otherwise, the political pattern of ancient Greece was one of many small city-states, few of which were much stronger or richer than their neighbors.

Physically, the term *polis* designated a city or town and its surrounding countryside. The typical polis consisted of people living in a compact group of houses within the city. The city's water supply came from public fountains and cisterns. By the fifth century B.C., the city was generally surrounded by a wall. The city contained a point, usually elevated, called the acropolis, and a public square or marketplace (agora). On the acropolis, which in the early period was a place of refuge, stood the temples, altars, public monuments, and various dedications to the gods of the polis. The agora was originally the place where the warrior assembly met, but it became the political center of the polis. In the agora were porticoes, shops, and public buildings, such as council and administrative buildings and courts.

The unsettled territory of the polis was typically the source of its wealth. This territory consisted of arable land, pastureland, and wasteland. Farmers left the city each morning to work their fields or tend their flocks of sheep and goats, and they returned to the city at night. On the wasteland men often quarried stone, mined for precious metals, or at certain times of the year obtained small amounts of fodder. Thus, the polis encompassed a combination of urban and agrarian life.

Regardless of its size or wealth, the polis was fundamental to Greek life. Aristotle, perhaps Greece's greatest thinker, could not envisage civilized life apart from the polis. "The

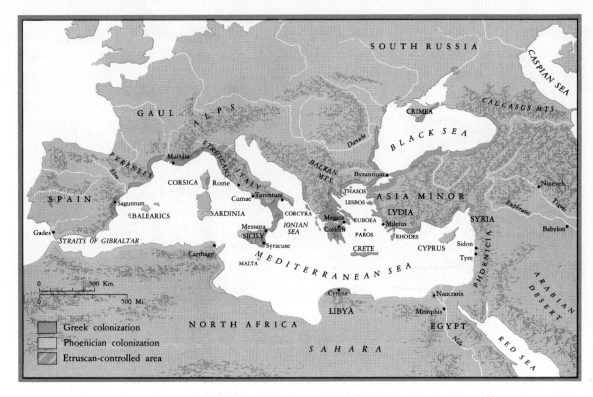

MAP 3.2 COLONIZATION OF THE MEDITER-
RANEAN *Although both the Greeks and Phoenicians colonized the Mediterranean basin at roughly
the same time, the Greeks spread over far greater
areas.*

polis," he wrote, "exists by nature, and man is by nature a being of the polis."[2] Aristotle was summing up the Greek view that the life of men and women in the polis was the only way to live according to nature.

The polis was far more than a political in-stitution. Above all, it was a community of citizens, and the affairs of the community were the concern of all citizens. The intimacy of the polis was an important factor, and one hard for modern city dwellers to imagine. The philosopher Plato thought that five thousand citizens constituted the right population for an ideal polis. Though utopian, Plato was not in this case being unrealistic. Although popu-lation figures for Greece are mostly guess-work, because most city-states were small enough not to need a census, the polis of Thebes in Boeotia is a useful illustration of how small a Greek state was. When Alex-ander the Great destroyed Thebes in 335 B.C., he sold thirty thousand people into slavery. Some six thousand people had died in the fighting, and many others he spared. Thus the free population of Thebes had numbered be-tween thirty and forty thousand at most, and Thebes was a large polis, a major power. Most city-states were far smaller.

The mild climate of Greece meant that much of Greek life was spent outdoors. In a polis, as in a modern Greek village, a person might easily see most other citizens in the course of the day. Nearly everything that happened within the polis was known immediately and discussed at length. Any stranger who arrived with news from abroad found a large and talkative audience at once. Similarly, the citizen would normally see the public buildings and the temples of the polis daily. The monuments of past victories, the tombs of dead warriors, all these would be personal and familiar. In short, life in the polis was very public. The smallness of the polis enabled Greeks to see how the individual fitted into the overall system — how the human parts made up the social whole.

The customs of the community were at the same time the laws of the polis. Rome later created a single magnificent body of law, but the Greeks had as many law codes as they had city-states. Though the laws of one polis might be roughly similar to those of another polis, the law of any given polis was unique simply because the customs and the experience of each polis had been unique.

The polis also had a religious aspect. Although all Greeks customarily worshiped the great deities — Zeus, Hera, Apollo, Athena, and others, who supposedly lived on Mount Olympus — the citizens of each polis had their own particular cults for these gods. Besides the Olympian gods, each polis had its own minor deities, each with his or her own local cult. Participation in the cults and rituals was a civic duty. By honoring the gods and goddesses of the polis, the citizens honored the polis itself. But this civic religion, unlike the religion of the Hebrews, did not entail religious belief. What individuals believed was their own business. Citizens could be total atheists, but they were still expected to participate in the religion of the polis. Their participation did not brand them as hypocrites, but rather as loyal citizens.

The polis could be governed in any of several ways. First, it could be a monarchy, a term derived from the Greek for "the rule of one man." A king could represent the community, reigning according to law and respecting the rights of the citizens. Second, the aristocracy – those who owed their position to birth – could govern the state. Third, the running of the polis could be the duty and prerogative of an oligarchy, which literally means "the rule of a few" – a small group of wealthy citizens, regardless of their status at birth. Or the polis could be governed by a democracy, the rule of the people, which in Greece meant that all the citizens, without respect to birth or wealth, administered the workings of government. How a polis was governed depended on who had the upper hand. When the wealthy held power, they usually instituted oligarchies; when the people could break the hold of the rich, they established democracies. In any case, no polis ever had an iron-clad and unchangeable constitution.

Still another form of Greek government was tyranny. Under tyranny the polis was ruled by a tyrant, a man who had seized power by unconstitutional means. The Greeks did not in theory consider tyranny a legitimate form of government, but in practice it flourished from the seventh century B.C. to the end of the Classical Period. Although the earliest tyrants may have been popular figures, abuses of tyranny soon gave this type of government a bad name. One lasting effect of

tyranny, nevertheless, was to break the exclusive hold of the aristocracy on Greek government. Even so, the Greeks always considered tyranny a political perversion.

Ironically, the very integration of the polis proved to be one of its weaknesses. Because the bonds that held the polis together were so intimate, Greeks were extremely reluctant to allow foreigners to share fully in its life. An alien, even someone Greek by birth, could almost never expect to be made a citizen. Nor could women play a political role in the polis. Women participated in the civic cults, and they served as priestesses, but the polis had no room for them in state affairs. Thus, the exclusiveness of the polis doomed it to a limited horizon.

The individualism of the polis proved to be another serious weakness. The citizens of each polis were determined to remain free and autonomous. Rarely were the Greeks willing to unite in larger political bodies. When they did, they preferred leagues or confederations in which each polis insisted on its autonomy. The political result in Greece, as in Sumer, was almost constant warfare. The polis could dominate, but unlike Rome it could not incorporate.

THE BRONZE AGE
(2000 – 1100 B.C.)

Greek-speaking peoples did not enter the peninsula of Greece until the Bronze Age. Of these early years the ancient Greeks themselves remembered almost nothing. One of the sterling achievements of modern archaeology is the discovery of this lost past. In the nineteenth century, Heinrich Schliemann, a German businessman turned archaeologist, excavated the site of Mycenae in Greece and

PERIODS OF GREEK HISTORY

PERIOD	SIGNIFICANT EVENTS	MAJOR WRITERS
Bronze Age 2000–1100 B.C.	Arrival of the Greeks in Greece Rise and fall of the Mycenaean kingdoms	
Dark Age 1100–800 B.C.	Greek migrations within the Aegean basin Social and political recovery Evolution of the polis Rebirth of literacy	Homer Hesiod
Lyric Age 800–500 B.C.	Rise of Sparta and Athens Colonization of the Mediterranean basin Flowering of lyric poetry Development of philosophy and science in Ionia	Archilochus Sappho Tyrtaeus Solon Anaximander Heraclitus
Classical Age 500–338 B.C.	Persian wars Growth of the Athenian empire Peloponnesian War Rise of drama and historical writing Flowering of Greek philosophy Spartan and Theban hegemonies Conquest of Greece by Philip of Macedon	Herodotus Thucydides Aeschylus Sophocles Euripides Aristophanes Plato Aristotle

the site of Troy in Asia Minor. He discovered the lost past of the Greek people, and to this past he gave the name Mycenaean.

The Mycenaeans entered Greece around 2000 B.C. and settled in central Greece and the Peloponnesus, the peninsula that forms the southernmost part of Greece (see Map 3.1). Mycenaean civilization was utterly unlike anything the later Greeks evolved. The political unit of the Mycenaeans was the kingdom, not the polis. The king and his warrior-aristocracy stood at the top of society. The symbol of the king's power and wealth was the palace, which was also the economic center of the kingdom. Within its walls royal craftsmen fashioned jewelry and rich ornaments, made and decorated fine pottery, forged weapons,

prepared hides and wool for clothing, and manufactured the goods needed by the king and his retainers. Palace scribes kept account of taxes and drew up inventories of the king's possessions. From the palace the king directed the lives of his subjects, and he tightly controlled society. About the king's subjects, almost nothing is known.

The Mycenaean kingdoms were in touch with each other and with the Bronze Age culture of the Minoans in Crete, but these contacts were often violent. The Minoans had established a vibrant and artistically gifted civilization, from which the Mycenaeans derived much of their art. The wealth of the Minoans tempted Mycenaean greed and ambition, and in about 1450 B.C. a band of Mycenaean raiders conquered Cnossus, the most important and the richest Minoan site. This attack was typical of the Mycenaeans, who were consistently a warlike and restless people.

Indeed, the entire history of Mycenaean Greece is a dreary tale of warfare. During the years 1300–1100 B.C., kingdom after kingdom suffered attack and destruction. But not one alien artifact has been found on any of these sites. There are no traces of invading peoples, nothing to suggest that these kingdoms fell to foreign invaders. Instead, the legends preserved by later Greeks told of grim wars between Mycenaean kingdoms and of the fall of great royal families. Apparently Mycenaean Greece destroyed itself in a long series of internecine wars, a pattern that would be repeated by Greeks of later ages.

The fall of the Mycenaean kingdoms ushered in a period of such poverty, disruption, and backwardness that historians usually call it the Dark Age of Greece (1100–800 B.C.). Even literacy was a casualty of the chaos. Yet even this period was important to the development of Greek civilization. It was a time of widespread movements of Greek-speaking peoples. Some Greeks sailed to Crete, where they established new communities. A great wave of Greeks spread eastward through the Aegean to the coast of Asia Minor. These immigrations turned the Aegean into a Greek lake. The people who stayed behind gradually rebuilt Greek society. They thus provided an element of continuity, a link between the Mycenaean period and the Greek culture that emerged from the Dark Age.

The movement of Greek-speaking peoples was not confined to the descendants of the Mycenaeans. During the Dark Age the last peoples who would help create Greek civilization of the historical period moved into Greece. The Boeotians entered Greece from

MINOAN SNAKE GODDESS *This elegant statuette in many ways represents all of the difficulty of interpreting Minoan civilization. Although the Minoans left behind many brilliant pieces of art, they left no history or literature as guides for the understanding of them. Consequently, it is impossible to know what this goddess meant to the Minoans. (Museum of Fine Arts, Boston. Gift of Mrs. W. Scott Fitz)*

THE RETURN OF ODYSSEUS *This fine fifth-century relief portrays one of the most popular episodes from the* Odyssey: *the return of Odysseus from the Trojan War. Although his faithful wife, Penelope,* *and some poor retainers welcomed him eagerly (as this scene suggests), he had singlehandedly to defeat neighboring lords who coveted his kingdom. (Metropolitan Museum of Art, Fletcher Fund, 1930)*

Thessaly and settled in Boeotia. The Dorians, who were nomads, followed the Boeotians and settled in the Peloponnesus. Although the Dorians have traditionally been accused of overthrowing the Mycenaean kingdoms, recent archaeological work has proved that they entered Greece long afterwards. The common language of all these peoples, newcomers and survivors alike, was a bond between them.

HOMER, HESIOD, AND THE HEROIC PAST (1100 – 800 B.C.)

The Greeks, unlike the Hebrews, had no sacred book that chronicled their past. Instead, they had the *Iliad* and the *Odyssey,* the epic poems created by Homer (eighth century B.C.) to describe a time when gods still walked the earth. And they learned the origin and the descent of the gods from the *Theogony,* an epic poem by Hesiod (ca 700 B.C.). For all their importance to Greek thought and literature, Homer and Hesiod were shadowy figures. Later Greeks knew little about them and were not even certain when they had lived. Although some later Greeks thought they had flourished in the tenth century B.C., the historian Herodotus (484-425 B.C.) gave a more accurate date:

It seems to me that the age of Hesiod and Homer was no more than 400 years earlier than my time.

They are the poets who gave the Greeks the gene-alogy of the gods, and they distributed to the gods their honors and acts, and they declared their forms.[3]

This uncertainty over the poets' dates is sig-nificant. It indicates that the Greeks remem-bered very little of their own past, especially the time before they entered Greece. They had also forgotten a great deal about the Bronze and Dark Ages.

Instead of authentic history the poems of Homer and Hesiod offered the Greeks an ideal past, a largely legendary Heroic Age. In terms of pure history these poems contain scraps of information about the Bronze Age, much about the early Dark Age, and some about the poets' own era. Chronologically, then, the Heroic Age falls mainly in the period between the collapse of the Mycenaean world and the rebirth of literacy. Yet it is a mistake to treat the *Iliad* and the *Odyssey* as history; they are magnificent blendings of legends, myth, and a little authentic tradition.

The *Iliad* recounts an expedition of Myce-naeans, whom Homer called Achaeans, to be-siege the city of Troy in Asia Minor. The heart of the *Iliad*, however, is the quarrel be-tween Agamemnon, the king of Mycenae, and Achilles, the tragic hero of the poem, and how their quarrel brought suffering to the Achaeans. Only when Achilles put away his anger and pride did he consent to come for-ward, face, and kill the Trojan hero Hector. The *Odyssey* narrates the adventures of Odys-seus, one of the Achaean heroes who fought at Troy, during his voyage home from the fighting.

The splendor of these poems does not lie in their plots, though the *Odyssey* is a marvelous adventure story. Rather, both poems portray engaging but often flawed characters who are larger than life and yet typically human.

Achilles, the hero of the *Iliad*, is capable of mastering Trojan warriors but can barely con-trol his own anger. Agamemnon commands kings, yet is a man beset by worries. Hector, the hero of the Trojans, is a formidable, noble, and likable foe. Odysseus, the hero of the *Od-yssey*, trusts more to his wisdom and good sense than to his strength. Odysseus' wife Penelope faithfully endures the long years of war and separation, patiently waiting for her beloved husband to return from Troy.

Homer was strikingly successful in depict-ing the deeds of the great gods, who sit on Mount Olympus and watch the fighting at Troy as though they were spectators at a modern baseball game. Sometimes they even participate in the action. Homer's deities are reminiscent of the Mesopotamian gods and goddesses. Hardly a decorous lot, the Olym-pians are raucous, petty, deceitful, and splen-did. In short, they are human. Zeus, the king of the gods, favors the Trojans, but Hera, his wife and queen of the gods, supports the Achaeans. To distract Zeus so that she can aid her favorites, Hera seduces him with wine and sex. Athena, the gray-eyed goddess of wis-dom, squabbles with human beings as though she were a fishwife. In the *Odyssey*, He-phaestus, the god of fire, uses an invisible net to catch his wife, Aphrodite, the goddess of love, sleeping with Ares, the god of war. When Hephaestus summons the other gods to witness the scene, they laugh and joke about his catch. One god even wishes that someday he could be as unlucky as Ares.

Homer at times portrayed the gods in a serious vein, but he never treated them in a systematic fashion, as did Hesiod. Hesiod's epic poem, the *Theogony*, traces the descent of Zeus. Hesiod was influenced by Mesopota-mian myths, which the Hittites had adopted and spread to the Aegean. Hesiod's poem claims that in the beginning there was chaos, the "yawning deep." From chaos came Gaea (Earth), who gave birth to Uranus (Heaven). Gaea and Uranus then gave birth to Cronus and Ocean (the deep-swelling waters). Cronus, the son of Earth and Heaven, like the Mesopotamian Enlil, separated the two and became king of the gods.

Like the Hebrews, Hesiod envisaged his cosmogony – that is, his account of the way the universe developed – in moral terms. Zeus, the son of Cronus, defeated his evil father and took his place as the king of the gods. He then sired Lawfulness, Right, Peace, and other powers of light and beauty. Thus, in Hesiod's conception, Zeus was the god of righteousness, a god who loved justice and hated wrongdoing.

In another epic poem, *Works and Days,* Hesiod wrote of his own time. He lived in the village of Ascra in Boeotia, a scenic place set between beautiful mountains and fertile plains, but Hesiod was a grim pessimist and did not think highly of his village: "Ascra, bad in winter, uncomfortable in summer, never good." Although sometimes portrayed as a common man, Hesiod was a wealthy farmer. He may not, however, have been an aristocrat. The matter of his social standing sets him apart, for all the other great writers of Greece – and, later, Rome – were members of the aristocracy, for only they had the wealth, leisure, and education to create literature. Naturally, then, ancient Greek and Roman literature always reflected the values, cares, and ambitions of the aristocracy. For this reason alone, the common people in Greco-Roman culture are largely unknown to the modern world. Hesiod opens a window to the other side of life.

Hesiod was the victim of injustice. In his will, Hesiod's father had divided his lands between Hesiod and his brother Perses. Perses bribed the aristocratic authorities to give him the larger part of the inheritance and then squandered his wealth. Undaunted by the injustice of the powerful, Hesiod thundered back in a voice reminiscent of Khunanup, the "Eloquent Peasant" (see page 27):

Bribe-devouring lords, make straight
    your decisions,
Forget entirely crooked judgments.
He who causes evil to another harms himself.
Evil designs are most evil to the plotter.[4]

The similarities are striking between the fictional Khunanup and Hesiod, both of whom were oppressed by the rich and powerful. Yet the differences are even more significant. Hesiod, unlike Khunanup, did not receive justice from the political authorities of the day, but he fully expected divine vindication. Hesiod's call for justice has gone ringing through the centuries, its appeal as fresh today as when he first uttered it more than two millennia ago. Hesiod spoke of Zeus as Jeremiah had spoken of Yahweh, warning that Zeus would see that justice was done and injustice punished. He cautioned his readers that Zeus was angered by those who committed adultery and those who harmed orphans and offended the aged. Hesiod's ethical concepts and his faith in divine justice were the product of his belief that the world was governed by the power of good.

Hesiod went on to advise Perses how to become a prosperous farmer. Hesiod's agricultural year was determined by the stars and the seasons. He advised Perses to plow when the constellation Pleiades set and to harvest when it rose. Wood was best cut in autumn, and the farmer should then begin building his plows and wagons and fashioning his tools. When the star Arcturus rose at dusk, it was time to prune the vines. Hesiod warned against doing field work during the time of biting cold, when

all the immense wood roars;
Wild animals shiver and put their tails
*   between their legs,*
Even those whose hide is covered with fur.
For now the cold wind blows through animals
*   even though they be shaggy-breasted.*[5]

In the heat of the summer, however, when the crops were stored in the barn, the farmer rested, sitting in the shade and sipping wine.

In *Works and Days* Hesiod also offered some hardheaded advice on how to live. Although his pessimism was pervasive, his advice was very practical. Hesiod was not theorizing; he was giving his readers tips on how to survive in a hard world. He recommended that a man get a house, an ox, and a slave woman to help with the field work. A man should not take a wife until he was around thirty years old. Then he should be very careful about his prospective bride: "He who trusts women trusts deceivers." Beware of the flirt because "she wants your barn." Marry, he advised, a fine maiden, "for a man gains nothing better than a good wife." Hesiod warned that a couple should have only one son; but if they have a second, they should do so late in life. He insisted upon the importance of good neighbors, because neighbors will help each other in times of trouble. The constant theme of Hesiod's philosophy is to live justly and uprightly, but never trust anyone.

THE LYRIC AGE *(800–500 B.C.)*

Hesiod stood on the threshold of one of the most vibrant periods of Greek history, an era of extraordinary expansion geographically, ar-

tistically, and politically. Greeks ventured as far east as the Black Sea and as far west as Spain (see Map 3.2). With the rebirth of literacy, this period also witnessed a tremendous literary flowering as poets broke away from the heroic tradition and wrote about their own lives. The individualism of the poets typifies this age of adventure and exploration, and the term "Lyric Age" strikingly conveys the spirit of these years. Politically, these were the years when Sparta and Athens – the two poles of the Greek experience – rose to prominence.

OVERSEAS EXPANSION

During the years 1100–800 B.C., the Greeks not only recovered from the breakdown of the Mycenaean world, but also grew in wealth and numbers. This new prosperity brought with it new problems. Greece is a small and not especially fertile country. The increase in population meant that many men and their families had very little land or none at all. Land hunger drove many Greeks to seek new homes outside of Greece. Other factors, largely intangible, played their part as well: the desire for a new start, a love of excitement and adventure, and natural curiosity about what lay beyond the horizon.

The Mediterranean offered the Greeks an escape valve, for they were always a seafaring people. To them the sea was a highway, not a barrier. Through their commercial ventures they had long been familiar with the rich areas of the western Mediterranean. Moreover, the geography of the Mediterranean basin favored colonization. The land and the climate of the Mediterranean region are remarkably uniform. Greeks could travel to new areas, whether to Cyprus in the east or to Malta in the west, and establish the kind of settlement they had had in Greece. They could also raise the same crops that they had raised in Greece. The move to a new home was not a move into totally unknown conditions. Once the colonists had established themselves in their new homes, they continued life essentially as they had lived it in Greece.

From about 750 to 550 B.C., Greeks from the mainland and from Asia Minor poured onto the coasts of the northern Aegean, the Ionian Sea, and the Black Sea, and into North Africa, Sicily, southern Italy, southern France, and Spain (see Map 3.2). Just as the migrations of the Dark Age had turned the Aegean into a Greek lake, this later wave of colonization spread the Greeks and their culture throughout the Mediterranean. Colonization on this scale had a profound impact on the course of Western civilization. It meant that the prevailing culture of the Mediterranean basin would be Greek, and to this heritage Rome would later fall heir.

One man can in many ways stand as the symbol of the vital and robust era of colonization. Archilochus was born on the island of Paros, the bastard son of an aristocrat. He knew that because of his illegitimacy he would never inherit his father's land, and this knowledge seems to have made him self-reliant. He was also a poet of genius, the first of the lyric poets who left an indelible mark on this age. Unlike the epic poets, who portrayed the deeds of heroes, Archilochus sang of himself. He knew the sea, the dangers of sailing, and the price that the sea often exacted. He spoke of one shipwreck in grim terms and even treated the god of the sea with irony: "Of fifty men gentle Poseidon left one, Koiranos, to be saved from shipwreck."

Together with others from Paros he took part in the colonization of Thasos in the northern Aegean. He described the island in less than glowing terms: "Like the spine of an ass it stands, crowned to the brim with a wild forest." His opinion of his fellow colonists was hardly kinder; about them he commented: "So the misery of all Greece came together in Thasos." Yet at Thasos he fell in love with a woman named Neoboule. They did not marry because her father opposed the match. In revenge, Archilochus seduced Neoboule's younger sister, railed at the entire family, and left Thasos to live the life of a mercenary.

His hired lance took him to Euboea, and he left a striking picture of the fighting there:

Not many bows will be strung, nor slings be slung
When Ares begins battle in the plain.
There will be the mournful work of the sword:
For in this kind of battle are the spear-famed
Lords of Euboea experienced.[6]

Through it all, however, Archilochus kept his sardonic humor. Commenting on the death of a relative, for example, he remarked, "I won't cure anything by weeping or make it worse by pursuing pleasures and festivities." For Archilochus the adventure of colonization had a happy, if unusual, ending. The people of Paros, overlooking his waywardness because of his poetic genius, welcomed him back. Later he was killed defending his homeland.

Archilochus exemplifies the energy, restlessness, self-reliance, and sense of adventure that characterizes this epoch. People like him broke old ties, faced homelessness and danger, and built new homes for themselves. They made the Mediterranean Greek.

LYRIC POETS

Archilochus the colonist and adventurer is not nearly as important as Archilochus the lyric poet, whose individualism set a new tone in Greek literature. For the first time in Western civilization, men and women began to write of their own experiences. Their poetry reflected their belief that they had something precious to say about themselves. To them poetry did not belong only to the gods or to the great heroes on the plain of Troy. Some lyric poets used their literary talents for the good of their city-states. They stood forth as individuals and in their poetry urged their countrymen to be patriotic and just.

One of the most unforgettable of these writers is the poet Sappho. Unlike Archilochus, she neither braved the wilds nor pushed into the unknown, yet she was no less individual than he. Sappho was born in the seventh century B.C. on the island of Lesbos, a place of sun, sea, and rustic beauty. Her marriage produced a daughter, to whom she wrote some of her poems. Sappho's poetry is personal and intense. She delighted in her surroundings, which were those of aristocratic women, and she celebrated the little things around her. Hers was a world of natural beauty, of sacred groves, religious festivals, wedding celebrations, and noble companions. Sappho fondly remembered walks with a girlfriend:

There was neither a hill nor a sanctuary
Nor a stream of running water
Which we failed to visit;
Nor when spring began any grove
Filled with the noise of nightingales.[7]

The rising of Hesperus, the evening star, prompted her to welcome it:

Hesperus, bringing back all things
*   Which light-giving dawn disperses,*
You bring back the sheep, you bring back the goat,
*   You bring the child back to its mother.*[8]

Sappho is best known for erotic poetry, for she expressed her love frankly and without shame. She was bisexual, and much of her poetry dealt with her homosexual love affairs.

MOSAIC PORTRAIT OF SAPPHO   *The Greek letters in the upper left corner identify this idealized portrait as that of Sappho. The mosaic, which was found at Sparta, dates to the late Roman Empire and testifies to Sappho's popularity in antiquity. (Photo: Caroline Buckler)*

In one of her poems she remembered the words of her lover:

Sappho, if you don't come out,
Surely I will no longer love you.
O come to us and free your lovely
Strength from your bed.
Lifting off your Chian robe,
Bathe in the waters like a
Pure lily beside a spring.[9]

In another poem Sappho described Aphrodite appearing to her in answer to her prayers. The goddess advised her to be patient: the girl she loved would return her love soon enough.

In antiquity Sappho's name became linked with female homosexual love. Today, the English word *lesbian* is derived from Sappho's island home. Yet to see Sappho as licentious is to misunderstand her and her world completely. The Greeks accepted bisexuality — that men and women could enjoy both ho-

STATUE OF "LEONIDAS" Found at Sparta, this statue is thought by some to represent Leonidas, the Spartan king who was killed at Thermopylae. The statue, with its careful rendering of the muscles and the face, reflects the Spartan ideal of the strong, intelligent, and brave warrior. (Photo: Caroline Buckler)

mosexual and heterosexual lovemaking. Homosexual relationships normally carried no social stigma. In her mature years Sappho was courted by a younger man who wanted to marry her. By then she had already proclaimed her love for several girls, yet the young man was not troubled by these affairs. As it turned out, Sappho refused to marry because she was past child-bearing age.

In their poetry Archilochus and Sappho reveal two sides of Greek life in this period.

Archilochus exemplifies the energy and adventure of the age, while Sappho expresses the intensely personal side of life. The common link is their individualism, their faith in themselves, and their desire to reach out to other men and women in order to share their experiences, thoughts, and wisdom.

THE GROWTH OF SPARTA

During the Lyric Age the Spartans expanded the boundaries of their polis and made it the leading power in Greece. Like other Greeks, the Spartans faced the problems of overpopulation and land hunger. Unlike other Greeks, the Spartans solved these problems by conquest, not by colonization. To gain more land the Spartans set out in about 735 B.C. to conquer Messenia, a rich and fertile region in the southwestern Peloponnesus. This conflict, known as the First Messenian War, lasted for twenty years and ended in a Spartan triumph. The Spartans appropriated Messenian land and turned the Messenians into helots, or state serfs.

In about 650 B.C., Spartan exploitation and oppression of the Messenian helots led to a helot revolt so massive and stubborn that it became known as the Second Messenian War. The Spartan poet Tyrtaeus, a contemporary of these events, vividly portrayed the ferocity of the fighting:

For it is a shameful thing indeed
*   When with the foremost fighters*
An elder falling in front of the young men
*   Lies outstretched,*
Having white hair and grey beard,
Breathing forth his stout soul in the dust,
Holding in his hands his genitals
*   stained with blood.*[10]

Confronted with horrors such as this, Spartan enthusiasm for the war waned. To rally his countrymen Tyrtaeus urged the warriors to face the Messenians:

And let each man coming near
   with his great spear or sword,
Wounding his man cut him down and take him;
And putting foot against foot and leaning shield
   against shield,
Crest upon crest and helmet upon helmet,
And chest to chest, drawing near,
   let him fight his man,
Taking him with the hilt of his sword
   or with his great spear.[11]

Finally, after some thirty years of fighting, the Spartans put down the revolt. Nevertheless, the political and social strain caused by this war led to a transformation of the Spartan polis.

It took the full might of the Spartan people, aristocrat and commoner alike, to win the Second Messenian War. After the victory the nonnobles, who had done much of the fighting, demanded rights equal to those of the nobility. Their agitation disrupted society, until the aristocrats agreed to remodel the state. Although the Spartans later claimed that the changes brought about by this compromise were the work of Lycurgus, a legendary, semidivine lawgiver, they were really the work of the entire Spartan people.

The Lycurgan regimen, as these reforms were called, was a new political, economic, and social system. Political distinctions among the Spartans were eliminated, and all citizens became equal to one another. In effect, the Lycurgan regimen abolished the aristocracy and made the government an oligarchy. Actual governance of the polis was in the hands of two kings, who were primarily military leaders. The kings and twenty-eight elders made up a council that deliberated on foreign and domestic matters and prepared legislation for the assembly, which consisted of all Spartan citizens. The real executive power of the polis was in the hands of five *ephors,* or overseers. The ephors were elected from and by all the people.

To provide for their economic needs the Spartans divided the land of Messenia among all citizens. Helots worked the land, raised the crops, provided the Spartans with their living, and occasionally served in the army. The Spartans kept the helots in line by means of systematic terrorism, hoping to to beat them down and keep them quiet. Spartan citizens were supposed to devote their time exclusively to military training.

In the Lycurgan system every citizen owed primary allegiance to Sparta. Suppression of the individual, together with emphasis on military prowess, led to a barracks state. Family life itself was sacrificed to the polis. If an infant was deformed or handicapped at birth, the polis could demand that the parents put it out to die. In this respect the Spartans were no better or worse than other Greeks. Infanticide was common in ancient Greece and Rome, and many people resorted to it as a way of keeping population down. The difference is that in other Greek states the decision to kill a child belonged to the parents, not to the polis.

Once a Spartan boy reached the age of seven, he lived in barracks with other boys his age. Spartan youth all underwent rugged physical and military training until they reached twenty-four, when they became front-line soldiers. For the rest of their lives, Spartan men kept themselves prepared for combat. Their military training never ceased, and the older men were expected to be models of endurance, frugality, and sturdiness to the younger men. In battle Spartans were supposed to stand and die rather than retreat. An anecdote about one Spartan mother sums up Spartan military values. As her son was setting off to battle, the mother handed him his shield and advised him to come back either victorious carrying the shield or dead being carried upon it. In short, in the Lycurgan regimen Spartans were expected to train vigorously, disdain luxury and wealth, do with little and like it.

THE EVOLUTION OF ATHENS

Like Sparta, Athens too faced pressing social and economic problems during the Lyric Age, but the Athenian response to them was far different from that of the Spartans. Instead of creating an oligarchy, the Athenians extended to all citizens the right and duty of governing the polis. Indeed, the Athenian democracy was one of the most thoroughgoing in Greece.

In the seventh century B.C., however, the aristocracy still governed Athens, as oppressively as the "bribe-devouring lords" against whom Hesiod had railed. The aristocrats owned the best land, met in an assembly to govern the polis, and interpreted the law. Noble landowners were forcing small farmers into economic dependence. Many families were being sold into slavery; others were exiled and their land pledged to the rich. Poor farmers who borrowed from their wealthy neighbors put up their land as collateral. If a farmer was unable to repay the loan, his creditor put a stone on the borrower's field to signify his indebtedness and thereafter took one-sixth of the annual yield until the debt was paid. If the farmer had to borrow again, he pledged himself and at times his family. If he was again unable to repay the loan, he became the slave of his creditor. Because the harvests of the poor farmer were generally small, he normally raised enough to live on but not enough to repay his loan.

The peasants, however, were strong in numbers, and they demanded reforms. They wanted the law to be published so that everyone would know its contents. Under pressure, the aristocrats relented and turned to Draco, a fellow aristocrat, to codify the law. In 621 B.C., Draco published the first law code of the Athenian polis. His code was thought harsh, but it nonetheless embodied the ideal that the law belonged to all citizens. The aristocrats hoped in vain that Draco's law code would satisfy the peasants. Many of the poor began demanding redistribution of the land, and it was obvious that broader reform was needed. Unrest among the peasants continued.

In many other city-states conditions such as those in Athens led to the rise of tyrants. The word *tyrant* brings to mind a cruel and bloody dictator, but the Greeks seem at first to have used the word to denote a leader who seized power without legal right. Many of the first tyrants, though personally ambitious, were men who kept the welfare of the polis in mind. They usually enjoyed the support of the peasants because they reduced the power of the aristocrats. Later tyrants were often harsh and arbitrary – hence the Greeks began to use the word in the modern sense – and when they were, peasants and aristocrats alike suffered.

Only one person in Athens had the respect of both aristocrats and peasants: Solon, himself an aristocrat and poet, but a man opposed to tyrants. Like Hesiod, Solon used his poetry to condemn the aristocrats for their greed and dishonesty. He stormed against

those citizens who are persuaded
to destroy this great city
because they desire reckless wealth.[12]

Solon recited his poems in the Athenian agora, where everyone could hear his relentless call for justice and fairness. The aristocrats realized that Solon was no crazed revolutionary, and the common people trusted him. Around 594 B.C., the aristocrats elected him *archon,* chief magistrate of the Athenian polis, and gave him extraordinary power to reform the state.

Solon immediately freed all people enslaved for debt, recalled all exiles, canceled all debts on land, and made enslavement for debt illegal. He also divided society into four legal groups on the basis of wealth. In the most influential group were the wealthiest citizens, but even the poorest and least powerful group enjoyed certain rights. Solon allowed them into the old aristocratic assembly, where they could take part in the election of magistrates.

In all his work, Solon gave thought to the rights of the poor as well as the rich. He gave the commoners a place in government and a voice in the political affairs of Athens. His work done, Solon insisted that all swear to uphold his reforms. Then, since many were clamoring for him to become tyrant, he left Athens to travel.

Although Solon's reforms solved some immediate problems, they did not bring peace to Athens. Some aristocrats attempted to make themselves tyrants, while others banded together to oppose them. In 546 B.C., Pisistratus, an exiled aristocrat, returned to Athens, defeated his opponents, and became tyrant. Pisistratus reduced the power of the aristocracy while supporting the common people. Under his rule Athens prospered, and his building program began to transform it into one of the splendors of Greece. His reign as tyrant promoted the growth of democratic ideas by arousing in the Athenians rudimentary feelings of equality.

Athenian acceptance of tyranny did not long outlive Pisistratus, for his son Hippias ruled harshly, and his excesses led to his overthrow. After a brief period of turmoil between factions of the nobility, Cleisthenes, a wealthy and prominent aristocrat, emerged triumphant in 508 B.C., largely because he won the support of the people. Cleisthenes created the Athenian democracy, and he did so with the full knowledge and approval of the Athenian people. He reorganized the state completely, but he presented every innovation to the assembly for discussion and ratification. All Athenian citizens had a voice in Cleisthenes' work.

Cleisthenes created a new local unit, the deme, to serve as the basis of his political system. Citizenship was tightly linked to the deme, for each deme kept the roll of those within its jurisdiction who were admitted to citizenship. Cleisthenes also created ten new tribes as administrative units. All the demes were grouped in tribes, which thus formed the link between the demes and the central government. The central government included an assembly of all citizens and a new council of five hundred members. The council prepared legislation for the assembly to consider, and it handled diplomatic affairs. The result of Cleisthenes' work was to make Athens a democracy with a government efficient enough to permit effective popular rule.

Athenian democracy was to prove an inspiring ideal in Western civilization. It demonstrated that a large group of people, not just a few, could efficiently run the affairs of state. By heeding the opinions, suggestions, and wisdom of all its citizens, the state enjoyed the maximum amount of good counsel. Since all citizens could speak their minds, they did not have to resort to rebellion or conspiracy to express their desires.

Athenian democracy must not, however, be thought of in modern terms. In Athens democracy meant a form of government in which poor men as well as rich enjoyed political power and responsibility. In practice, though, most important offices were held by aristocrats. Furthermore, Athenian democracy denied political rights to many people, including women and slaves. Foreigners were seldom admitted to citizenship. Unlike modern democracies, Athenian democracy did not mean that the citizen would merely vote for others who would then run the state. Instead, every citizen was expected to be able to perform the duties of most magistrates. In Athens citizens voted and served. The people were the government. It is this union of the individual and the state — the view that the state exists for the good of the citizen and that the duty of the citizen is to serve it well — that has made Athenian democracy so compelling an ideal.

THE CLASSICAL PERIOD
(500–338 B.C.)

In the years 500–338 B.C., Greek civilization reached its highest peak in politics, thought, and art. In this period the Greeks beat back the armies of the Persian Empire. Then, turning their spears against one another, they destroyed their own civilization in a century of warfare. Some thoughtful Greeks felt prompted to record and analyze these momentous events; the result was the creation of history. This era saw the flowering of philosophy, as thinkers in Ionia and on the Greek mainland began to ponder the nature and meaning of the universe and human experience. Not content to ask "why," they used their intellects to explain the world around them and to determine humanity's place in it.

The Greeks invented drama, and the Athenian tragedians Aeschylus, Sophocles, and Euripides explored themes that still inspire audiences today. Greek architects reached the zenith of their art and created buildings whose very ruins still inspire awe. Because Greek intellectual and artistic efforts attained their fullest and finest expression in these years, this age is called the Classical Period. Few periods in the history of Western society can match it in sheer dynamism and achievement.

THE DEADLY CONFLICTS (499–404 B.C.)

One of the hallmarks of the Classical Period was warfare. In 499 B.C. the Ionian Greeks, with the feeble help of Athens, rebelled against the Persian Empire. In 490 B.C., the Persians struck back at Athens but were beaten off at the Battle of Marathon, a small plain in Attica. This failure only prompted the Persians to try again. In 480 B.C., the Persian king Xerxes led a mighty invasion force into Greece. In the face of this emergency the Greeks united and pooled their resources to resist the invaders. The Spartans provided the overall leadership and commanded the Greek armies. The Athenians, led by the wily Themistocles, provided the heart of the naval forces.

The first confrontation between the Persians and the Greeks occurred at the pass of Thermopylae and in the waters off Artemisium in northern Greece. At Thermopylae the Greek hoplites — the heavily armed troops — showed their mettle. Before the fighting began, a report came in that when the Persian archers shot their bows the arrows darkened the sky. One gruff Spartan merely replied, "Fine, then we'll fight in the shade." The Greeks at Thermopylae fought to the last man, but the Persians took the position. In their next two battles, the Greeks fared better. In 480 B.C., the Greek fleet smashed the Persian navy at Salamis, an island south of Athens. The following year, the Greek army destroyed the Persian forces at Plataea, a small polis at Boeotia.

The significance of these Greek victories is nearly incalculable. By defeating the Persians, the Greeks ensured that oriental monarchy would not stifle the Greek achievement. The Greeks were thus able to develop their particular genius in freedom. These decisive victories meant that Greek political forms and intellectual concepts would be the heritage of the West.

After turning back the invasion, the Greeks took the fight to the Persian Empire. In 478 B.C., the Greeks decided to continue hostilities until they had liberated the Ionians from Persian rule. To achieve that goal a strong navy was essential. The Greeks turned to Athens, the leading naval power in the Aegean, for leadership. Athens and other states, especially those in the Aegean, responded by establishing the Delian League. Athens controlled the Delian League, providing most of the warships for operations and determining how much money each member should contribute to the league's treasury.

Over the next twenty years Athens drove the Persians out of the Aegean and turned the Delian League into an Athenian empire. Athenian rule became severe, and the Athenian polis became openly imperialistic. Although all members of the Delian League were supposed to be free and independent states, Athens reduced them to the status of subjects. A sense of the harshness of Athenian rule can be gained from the regulations the Athenians imposed on their subject allies. After the Athenians had suppressed a revolt in Euboea, they imposed an oath on the people:

I will not revolt from the people of Athens either by any means or devices whatsoever or by word or deed, nor will I be persuaded by anyone who does revolt. And I will pay the tribute to the Athenians that I can persuade the Athenians [to levy]. I will be to them the best and truest ally possible. I will help and defend the people of Athens if anyone wrongs them, and I will obey the people of Athens.[13]

The Athenians dictated to the people of Erythrae, a polis on the coast of Asia Minor, their form of government:

There will be a council of 120 men chosen by lot. . . . The [Athenian] overseers and garrison commander will choose the current council by lot and establish it in office. Henceforth the council and the [Athenian] garrison commander will do these things thirty days before the council goes out of office.[14]

The Athenians also interfered with the economic affairs of the allies and decreed that they use Athenian coins, weights, and measures. The lengths to which the Athenians could go are exemplified in the oath they forced on the people of Colophon, another polis in Asia Minor: "And I will love the Athenian people, and will not desert them . . ." The Athenians were willing to enforce their demands by armed might, and they were ready both to punish violations and to suppress discontent.

The expansion of Athenian power and the aggressiveness of Athenian rule alarmed Sparta and its allies. While relations between Athens and Sparta cooled, Pericles (ca 494–429 B.C.) became the leading statesman in Athens. An aristocrat of solid intellectual ability, he turned Athens into the wonder of Greece. But like the democracy he led, Pericles was aggressive and imperialistic. He made

MAP 3.3   THE PELOPONNESIAN WAR   *This map, which shows the alignment of states during the Peloponnesian War, vividly illustrates the large scale of the war and its divisive impact.*

no effort to allay Spartan fear and instead continued Athenian expansion. At last, in 459 B.C., Sparta and Athens went to war over conflicts between Athens and some of Sparta's allies. The war ended fourteen years later with no serious damage to either side and nothing settled. But this war had divided the Greek world between two great powers.

During the 440s and 430s, Athens continued its severe policies toward its subject allies and came into conflict with Corinth, one of Sparta's leading allies (see Map 3.3). Once

again Athens and Sparta were drifting toward war. In 432 B.C., the Spartans convened a meeting of their allies, who complained of Athenian aggression and demanded that Athens be stopped. With a show of reluctance, the Spartans agreed to declare war. The real reason for war, according to the Athenian historian Thucydides, was very simple:

The truest explanation, though the one least mentioned, was the great growth of Athenian power and the fear it caused the Lakedaimonians [Spartans], which drove them to war.[15]

At the outbreak of this, the Peloponnesian War, a Spartan ambassador warned the Athenians: "This day will be the beginning of great evils for the Greeks." Few men have ever spoken more prophetically. The Peloponnesian War lasted a generation (431-404 B.C.) and brought in its wake fearful plagues, famine, civil wars, widespread destruction, and huge loss of life. Thucydides, the historian who also fought as a general in the war, described its cataclysmic effects:

For never had so many cities been captured and destroyed, whether by the barbarians or by the Greeks who were fighting each other. . . . Never had so many men been exiled or slaughtered, whether in the war or because of civil conflicts.[16]

As the war dragged on, old leaders like Pericles died and were replaced by men of the war generation. In Athens the most prominent of this new breed of politicians was Alcibiades (ca 450-404 B.C.), an aristocrat, a kinsman of Pericles, and a student of the philosopher Socrates. Alcibiades was brilliant, handsome, charming, and popular with the people. He was also self-seeking and egotistical; a shameless opportunist, his first thoughts were always for himself.

Alcibiades' schemes helped bring Athens down to defeat. Having planned an invasion of Sicily that ended in disaster, he deserted to the Spartans and plotted with the Persians, who had sided with Sparta, against his homeland. When his treachery had brought the Athenians to the brink of defeat, he struck a bargain with them. He promised to persuade Persia to throw its support to Athens, if the Athenians would allow him to return home. When they agreed, Alcibiades cheerfully double-crossed the Spartans and led the Athenians against Sparta's forces.

In the end, all of Alcibiades' intrigues failed. The Spartans defeated the Athenian

MOSAIC PORTRAIT OF ALCIBIADES The artist has caught all the craftiness, intelligence, and quickness of Alcibiades, who became a romantic figure in antiquity. Besides the artistic merit of the portrait, the mosaic is interesting because Alcibiades' name in the upper right corner is misspelled. (Photo: Caroline Buckler)

fleet in the Aegean and blockaded Athens by land and sea. Finally, in 404 B.C., the Athenians surrendered and watched helplessly while the Spartans and their allies destroyed the walls of Athens to the music of flute girls. The Peloponnesian War lasted twenty-seven years, and it dealt Greek civilization a serious blow.

THE BIRTH OF HISTORICAL AWARENESS

One positive development grew out of the Persian and Peloponnesian wars: the beginnings of historical writing. Herodotus (ca 485-425 B.C.), known as "the Father of History," was born at Halicarnassus in Asia Minor. As a young man he traveled widely, visiting Egypt, Phoenicia, and probably Babylon. Later he migrated to Athens, which became his intellectual home. In the first lines of his book, *The Histories,* Herodotus explained his reasons for writing history:

This is the publication of the researches of Herodotus of Halicarnassus – so that past deeds will not be forgotten by men through lapse of time – which points out the great and admirable achievements, both those of the Greeks and those of the barbarians, lest they be uncelebrated, and which points out why they waged war against each other.[17]

This introduction bears some resemblance to that of the *Iliad,* and indeed *The Histories* has been called a prose epic. The basic difference is that Herodotus dealt with the real and factual, not with legend. He even gave history its name; his word *historia* originally meant "investigation." Only after his book appeared did the word *historia* gain its modern meaning.

Herodotus chronicled the rise of the Persian Empire, sketched the background of Athens and Sparta, and described the land and customs of the Egyptians and the Scythians, who lived in the region of the modern Crimea. The sheer scope of this work is awesome. Lacking newspapers, sophisticated communications, and easy means of travel, Herodotus nevertheless wrote a history that covered the major events of the Near East and Greece.

Perhaps Herodotus' most striking characteristic is his curiosity. He loved to travel, and like most travelers he accumulated a stock of fine stories. He was an excellent storyteller, and the customs of non-Greek peoples fascinated him. But tales and digressions never obscure the central theme of his work. Herodotus diligently questioned everyone who could tell him anything about the Persian wars. The confrontation between East and West unfolds relentlessly in *The Histories,*

reaching its climax in the great battles of Salamis and Plataea.

In Herodotus' opinion the victory of the Greeks was due to their ability to live life simply, without luxury or wealth. He emphasized this point in describing a meeting between the Persian king Xerxes and a Greek deserter. Xerxes was about to invade Greece, so he questioned the deserter about the Greeks and their land. The deserter told him that

in Greece poverty is ever-present, but excellence is acquired, attained from wisdom and hard law. By making use of them Greece wards off both poverty and despotism.[18]

Herodotus turned to this thought again when he concluded his history with a moral: "Those accustomed to soft lands are themselves soft."

The outbreak of the Peloponnesian War prompted Thucydides (ca 460–ca 400 B.C.) to write a history of its course in the belief that

it would be great and more noteworthy than previous wars, considering that both states were in the prime of all their preparations and seeing that the other Greeks were taking sides with one or the other, some immediately, others intending to do so. For this was the greatest movement among the Greeks and some of the barbarians, and so to speak among most of mankind.[19]

A politician and a general, Thucydides saw action in the war until he was exiled for a defeat. Exile gave him the time and opportunity to question eyewitnesses about the details of events and to visit battlefields. Since he was an aristocrat and a prominent man, he had access to the inner circles of men who made the decisions.

Thucydides was intensely interested in human nature and how it manifested itself during the war. In 430 B.C., a terrible plague struck Athens. Thucydides described both the symptoms of the plague and the reactions of the Athenians in the same clinical terms. He portrayed the virtual breakdown of a society beset by war, disease, desperation, and despair. Similarly, he chronicled the bloody civil war on the island of Corcyra. Instead of condemning the injustice and inhumanity of the fighting, in which citizen turned on citizen and people ruthlessly betrayed their friends, he coolly observed that such things are normal as long as human nature is what it is.

Thucydides saw the Peloponnesian War as highly destructive to Greek character. He noted — with a visible touch of regret — that the old, the noble, and the simple fell before ambition and lust for power. Thucydides interpreted the war and its effects in purely human terms. He firmly rejected any notion that the gods intervened in human affairs. In his view the fate of men and women was, for good or ill, entirely in their own hands.

ATHENIAN ARTS IN THE AGE OF PERICLES

In the last half of the fifth century B.C., Pericles turned Athens into the showplace of Greece. He appropriated Delian League funds to pay for a huge building program, planning temples and other buildings to honor Athena, the patron goddess of the city, and to display to all Greeks the glory of the Athenian polis. Pericles also pointed out that his program would employ a great many Athenians and bring economic prosperity to the city.

Thus began the undertaking that turned the Acropolis into a monument for all time. Construction of the Parthenon began in 447 B.C., followed by the Propylaea, the temple of Athena Nike (Athena the Victorious), and the Erechtheion. Even today in their ruined state they still evoke awe. Plutarch, a Greek writer who lived in the first century A.D., observed:

In beauty each of them was from the outset antique, and even now in its prime fresh and newly made. Thus each of them is always in bloom, maintaining its appearance as though untouched by time, as though an ever-green breath and undecaying spirit had been mixed in its construction.[20]

Even the pollution of modern Athens, although it is destroying the ancient buildings, cannot rob them of their splendor and charm.

The planning of the architects and the skill of the workmen who erected these buildings were both very sophisticated. Visitors approaching the Acropolis first saw the Propylaea, the ceremonial gateway, a building of complicated layout and grand design whose Doric columns seem to hold up the sky.

On the right was the small temple of Athena Nike, whose dimensions harmonize with those of the Propylaea. The temple was built to commemorate the victory over the Persians, and the Ionic frieze above its columns depicted the battle of the Greeks and the Persians. Here for all the world to see was a tribute to Athenian and Greek valor — and a reminder of Athens' part in the victory.

Ahead of the visitors as they stood in the Propylaea was the huge statue of Athena Promachus (the Front-Line Fighter), so gigantic that the crest of Athena's helmet and the point of her spear could be seen by sailors entering the harbor of Athens. This statue celebrated the Athenian victory at the battle of Marathon, and was paid for by the spoils taken from the Persians. To the left stood the Erechtheion, an Ionic temple that housed several ancient shrines. On its southern side is the famous Portico of the Caryatids, a porch whose roof is supported by statues of Athenian maidens. The graceful Ionic columns of the Erechtheion provide a delicate relief from

THE PARTHENON *Stately and graceful, the Parthenon symbolizes the logic, order, and sense of beauty of Greek architecture. The Parthenon was also the centerpiece of Pericles' plan to make Athens the artistic showcase of the Greek world. (Photo: Caroline Buckler)*

the prevailing Doric order of the massive Propylaea and Parthenon.

As visitors walked on they obtained a full view of the Parthenon, thought by many to be the perfect Doric temple. The Parthenon was the chief monument to Athena and her city. The sculptures that adorned the temple portrayed the greatness of Athens and its goddess. The figures on the eastern pediment depicted Athena's birth, those on the west the victory of Athena over the god Poseidon for the possession of Attica. Inside the Parthenon stood a huge statue of Athena, the masterpiece of Phidias, one of the greatest sculptors of all time.

The Parthenon appears to be all rectangle and triangle, yet it is a structure of curves. Both the pavement that supports the columns and the beam above the columns are curved to avoid the illusion of flatness. The columns themselves are gently curved from bottom to top. The Parthenon also appears rigorously regular, but it is actually a collection of irregularities, all designed to compensate for the effects of optical illusion. For instance, the columns are not regularly spaced, and they incline inward; those at the rear are stockier than those at the front end. In all these refinements the Athenian architect showed his knowledge of mathematics, optics, and design. The impression the Parthenon creates is one of perfection. Well might all Athenians, no matter how humble, feel a great burst of pride in themselves, their goddess, and their polis when they gazed on the Parthenon.

In many ways the Athenian Acropolis is

the epitome of Greek art and its spirit. Although the buildings were dedicated to the gods and most of the sculptures portrayed gods, these works nonetheless express the Greek fascination with the human and rational. Greek deities were anthropomorphic, and Greek artists portrayed them as human beings. While honoring the gods, Greek artists were thus celebrating human beings. In the Parthenon sculptures it is visually impossible to distinguish the men and women from the gods and goddesses. This aspect of Greek art made a powerful impression on the American novelist Mark Twain, who visited the Acropolis at night:

As we wandered thoughtfully down the marble-paved length of this stately temple [the Parthenon] the scene about us was strangely impressive. Here and there in lavish profusion were gleaming white statues of men and women, propped against blocks of marble, some of them armless, some without legs, others headless — but all looking mournful in the moonlight and startlingly human![21]

The Acropolis also exhibits the rational side of Greek art. There is no violent emotion in this art, but instead a quiet intensity. Likewise, there is nothing excessive, for "nothing too much" was the canon of artist and philosopher alike. Greek artists portrayed action in a balanced, restrained, and sometimes even serene fashion, capturing the noblest aspects of human beings: their reason, dignity, and promise.

Other aspects of Athenian cultural life were as rooted in the life of the polis as were the architecture and sculpture of the Acropolis. The development of drama was tied to the religious festivals of the city. The polis sponsored the production of plays and required that wealthy citizens pay the expenses of their production. At the beginning of the year dramatists submitted their plays to the archon. He chose those he considered best and assigned a theatrical troupe to each playwright. Although most Athenian drama has perished, enough has survived to prove that the archons had superb taste. Many plays were highly controversial, but the archons neither suppressed nor censored them.

The Athenian dramatists were the first artists in Western society to examine such basic questions as the rights of the individual, the demands of society on the individual, and the nature of good and evil. Conflict is a constant element in Athenian drama. The dramatists used their art to portray, understand, and resolve life's basic conflicts.

Aeschylus (525–456 B.C.), the first of the great Athenian dramatists, was also the first to express the agony of the individual caught in conflict. In his trilogy of plays, *The Oresteia,* Aeschylus deals with the themes of betrayal, murder, and reconciliation. *The Agamemnon,* the first play of the trilogy, depicts Agamemnon's return from the Trojan War and his murder by his wife Clytemnestra and her lover Aegisthus. In the second play, *The Libation Bearers,* Orestes, the son of Agamemnon and Clytemnestra, avenges his father's death by killing his mother and her lover. His act of vengeance is the work of a dutiful son, but the murder of his mother is a sin against his own blood.

The last play of the trilogy, *The Eumenides,* works out the atonement and absolution of Orestes. The Furies, goddesses who avenged murder and unfilial conduct, demand Orestes' death. Orestes stands trial at Athens, with Athena as judge and Apollo as counsel for the defense. When the jury casts six votes to condemn Orestes and six to acquit him, Athena casts the deciding vote in favor of mercy and compassion. Aeschylus used *The Eumenides* to urge reason and justice to reconcile fundamental conflicts. The play concludes with a prayer that civil dissension never be allowed to destroy the city and that the life of the city be one of harmony and grace.

Sophocles (496–406 B.C.) too dealt with matters personal and political. In *Antigone* he examined the relationship between the individual and the state by exploring a conflict between the ties of kinship and the demands of the polis. In the play Polynices has attacked his own state, Thebes, and has fallen in battle. Creon, the Theban king, refuses to allow Polynices' body to be buried. Polynices' sister Antigone is appalled by Creon's action because custom demands that she bury her brother's corpse. Creon is right in refusing to allow Polynices' body to be buried in the polis, but wrong to refuse any burial at all. He continues in his misguided and willful error. As the play progresses, Antigone comes to stand for the precedence of divine law over human defects. Sophocles touches upon the need for recognition of the law and adherence to it as a prerequisite for a tranquil state.

Sophocles' masterpieces have become classics of Western literature, and his themes have inspired generations of playwrights. Perhaps his most famous plays are *Oedipus the King* and its sequel, *Oedipus at Colonus*. *Oedipus the King* is the ironic story of a man doomed by the gods to kill his father and marry his mother. Try as he might to avoid his fate, Oedipus' every action brings him closer to its fulfillment. When at last he realizes that he has carried out the decree of the gods, Oedipus blinds himself and flees into exile. In *Oedipus at Colonus* Sophocles dramatizes the last days of the broken king, whose patient suffering and uncomplaining piety win him an exalted position. In the end the gods honor him for his virtue. The interpretation of these two plays has been hotly debated, but Sophocles seems to be saying that human beings should do the will of the gods, even without fully understanding it, for the gods stand for justice and order.

Euripides (ca 480–406 B.C.), the last of the three great Greek dramatists, also explored the theme of personal conflict within the polis and sounded the depths of the individual. With Euripides drama entered a new, and in many ways more personal, phase. To him the gods were far less important than human beings. Euripides viewed the human soul as a place where opposing forces struggle with each other, where strong passions such as hatred and jealousy come into conflict with reason. The essence of Euripides' tragedy is the flawed character – the men and women who bring disaster on themselves and their loved ones because their passions overwhelm reason. Although Euripides' plays were less popular in his own lifetime than those of Aeschylus and Sophocles, Euripides was a dramatist of genius, and his work later had a significant impact on Roman drama.

Writers of comedy treated the affairs of the polis bawdily and often coarsely. Even so, their plays too were performed at religious festivals. The comic playwrights dealt primarily with the political affairs of the polis and the conduct of its leading politicians. Best known are the comedies of Aristophanes (ca 445–386 B.C.), an ardent lover of his city and a merciless critic of cranks and quacks. He lampooned eminent generals, at times depicting them as morons. He commented snidely on Pericles, poked fun at Socrates and hooted at Euripides. He saved some of his strongest venom for Cleon, a prominent politician. It is a tribute to the Athenians that such devastating attacks could openly and freely be made on the city's leaders and foreign policy. Even at the height of the Peloponnesian War, Aristophanes proclaimed that peace was preferable to the ravages of war. Like Aeschylus, Sophocles, and Euripides, Aristophanes used his art to dramatize his ideas on the right conduct of the citizen and the value of the polis.

Perhaps never were art and political life so intimately and congenially bound together as at Athens. Athenian art was the product of deep and genuine love of the polis. It aimed at bettering the lives of the citizens and the quality of life in the state.

DAILY LIFE IN PERICLEAN ATHENS

In sharp contrast with the rich intellectual and cultural life of Periclean Athens is the simplicity of its material life. The Athenians – and in this respect they were typical of Greeks in general – lived very happily with comparatively few material possessions. In the first place, there were very few material goods to own. The thousands of machines, tools, and gadgets considered essential for modern life had no counterpart in Athenian life. The inventory of Alcibiades' goods, which the Athenians confiscated after his desertion, is enlightening. His household possessions consisted of chests, beds, couches, tables, screens, stools, baskets, and mats. Other necessities of the Greek home included pottery, metal utensils for cooking, tools, luxury goods such as jewelry, and a few other things. These items they had to buy from craftsmen. Whatever else they needed, such as clothes and blankets, they produced at home.

The Athenian house was rather simple. Whether large or small, the typical house consisted of a series of rooms built around a central courtyard, with doors opening onto the courtyard. Many houses had bedrooms on an upper floor. Artisans and craftsmen often set aside a room to use as a shop or work area. The two principal rooms were the men's dining room and the room where the women worked wool. Other rooms included the kitchen and bathroom. By modern standards

there was not much furniture. In the men's dining room were couches, a sideboard, and small tables. Cups and other pottery were often hung on the wall from pegs. Other household furnishings included items such as those confiscated from Alcibiades.

In the courtyard were the well, a small altar, and a washbasin. If the family lived in the country, the stalls of the animals faced the courtyard. The countryman kept oxen for plowing, pigs for slaughtering, sheep for wool, goats for cheese, and mules and donkeys for transportation. Even in the city, chickens and perhaps a goat or two roamed the courtyard together with dogs and cats.

Cooking, done over a hearth in the house, provided welcome warmth in the winter. Baking and roasting were done in ovens. Food consisted of various grains, especially wheat and barley, as well as lentils, olives, figs, and grapes. Garlic and onion were popular garnishes, and wine was always on hand. These foods were stored at home in large jars, and with them the Greek family ate fish, chicken, and vegetables. Women ground wheat into flour at home, baked it into bread, and on special occasions made honey or sesame cakes. The Greeks used olive oil for cooking, as families still do in modern Greece; they also used it as an unguent and as fuel for lamps.

By American standards the Greeks did not eat much meat. On special occasions, such as important religious festivals, the family ate the animal sacrificed to the god and gave the god the exquisite delicacy of the thighbone wrapped in fat. The only Greeks who consistently ate meat were the Spartan warriors. They received a small portion of meat each day, together with the infamous Spartan black broth, a ghastly concoction of pork cooked in blood, vinegar, and salt. One Greek, after tasting the broth, commented that he could easily understand why the Spartans were so willing to die.

In the city a man might support himself as a craftsman — a potter, bronzesmith, sailmaker, or tanner — or he could contract with the polis to work on public buildings, such as the Parthenon and Erechtheion. Men without skills worked as paid laborers but competed with slaves for work. Slaves — usually foreigners, both barbarian and Greek — were paid as much for their labor as were free men.

Slavery was commonplace in Greece, as it was throughout the ancient world. In its essentials Greek slavery resembled Mesopotamian slavery. Slaves received some protection under the law and could buy their freedom. On the other hand, masters could mistreat or neglect their slaves short of killing them, which was illegal. The worst-treated slaves were those of the silver mines at Laurium, who lived, worked, and died in wretchedness. Yet slavery elsewhere was not generally brutal. One crusty aristocrat complained that in Athens one could not tell the slaves from the free. Most slaves in Athens served as domestics and performed light labor around the house. Nurses for children, teachers of reading and writing, and guardians for young men were often slaves. The lives of these slaves were much like those of their owners. Other slaves were skilled workers, who could be found working on public buildings or in small workshops.

The importance of slavery in Athens must not be exaggerated. Apart from the owners of the Laurium mines, Athenians did not own huge gangs of slaves as did Roman owners of large estates. Slave labor competed with free labor and kept wages down, but it never replaced the free labor that was the mainstay of the Athenian economy.

Most Athenians supported themselves by agriculture, but unless the family was fortunate enough to possess holdings in a plain more fertile than most of the land, they found it difficult to reap a good crop from the soil. Wealthy landowners sold their excess produce in the urban marketplace, but many people must have consumed nearly everything they raised. The plow, though wooden, sometimes had an iron share, and was pulled by oxen. Attic farmers were free men. Though hardly prosperous, they were by no means destitute. Greek farmers could usually expect yields of five bushels of wheat and ten of barley per acre for every bushel of grain sown. A bad harvest meant a lean year. In many places farmers grew more barley than wheat because of the nature of the soil. Wherever possible farmers also cultivated vines and olive trees.

For sport both the countryman and the city dweller often hunted for rabbits, deer, or wild boar. A successful hunt supplemented the family's regular diet. Wealthy men hunted on horseback; most others hunted on foot with their dogs. Hunting also allowed a man to display to his fellows his bravery and prowess in the chase. If wild boar were the prey, the sport could be dangerous, as Odysseus discovered when a charging boar slashed open his foot.

The social condition of Athenian women has been the subject of much debate and little agreement. One thing is certain: the status of a free woman of the citizen class was strictly protected by law. Only her children, not those of foreigners or slaves, could be citizens. Only she was in charge of the household and the family's possessions. Yet the law protected her primarily to protect her husband's interests. Raping a free woman was a lesser crime than seducing her because seduction involved the winning of her affections. This law was not concerned with the husband's feelings but with ensuring that he need not doubt the legitimacy of his children.

Ideally, respectable women lived a secluded life in which the only men they saw were relatives. How far this ideal was actually put into practice is impossible to say. At least Athenian women seem to have enjoyed a social circle of other women of their own class. They also attended public festivals, sacrifices, and funerals. Nonetheless, prosperous and respectable women probably spent much of their time in the house. A white complexion – a sign that a woman did not have to work in the fields – was valued highly.

Courtesans lived the freest lives of all Athenian women. Although some courtesans were simply prostitutes, others added intellectual accomplishments to physical beauty. In constant demand, cultured courtesans moved freely in male society. Their artistic talents and intellectual abilities appealed to men who wanted more than sex. The most famous of all courtesans was Aspasia, mistress of Pericles and supposedly friend of Socrates. Under Pericles' roof, she participated in intellectual discussions equally with some of the most stimulating thinkers of the day. Yet her position, like that of most other courtesans, was precarious. After Pericles' death, Aspasia fended for herself, ending her days as the madam of a house of prostitution.

A woman's main functions were to raise the children, oversee the domestic slaves and hired labor, and together with her maids work wool into cloth. The women washed the wool in the courtyard and then brought it into the women's room, where the loom stood. They spun the wool into thread and wove the thread into cloth. They also dyed wool at home and decorated the cloth by weaving in colors and designs. The woman of the household either did the cooking herself or directed her maids. In a sense, poor women lived freer lives than did wealthier women. They performed manual labor in the fields or sold goods in the agora, going about their affairs much as men did.

A distinctive feature of Athenian life, and Greek life in general, was acceptance of homosexuality. The distinguished English scholar K.J. Dover has succinctly described the difference between Greek and modern outlooks on human sexuality:

Greek culture differed from ours in its readiness to recognize the alternation of homosexual and heterosexual preferences in the same individual, its implicit denial that such alternation or coexistence created peculiar problems for the individual or for society, its sympathetic response to the open expression of homosexual desire in words and behavior, and its taste for the uninhibited treatment of homosexual subjects in literature and the visual arts.[22]

No one has satisfactorily explained how the Greek attitude toward homosexual love developed, or determined how common homosexual behavior was. Homosexuality was probably far more common among the aristocracy than among the lower classes. It is impossible to be sure, simply because most of what the modern world knows of ancient Greece and Rome comes from the writings of aristocrats. Since aristocratic boys and girls were often brought up separately, the likelihood of homosexual relationships was very great. This style of life was impossible for the common folk because every member of the family – husband and wife, son and daughter – got out and worked. Among the poorer classes the sexes mingled freely.

Even among the aristocracy attitudes toward homosexuality were complex and sometimes conflicting. Most people saw homosexual love affairs among the young as a stage in the development of a mature heterosexual life. Yet some Athenian aristocrats ridiculed homosexual practices. Comic writers habitually made fun of "boy-crazy men" and "effeminate youths." Others, such as the Spartans and the philosopher Plato, saw in homosexual relationships the opportunity for older men to train their juniors in practical wisdom. For them, the sexual element was supposed to give way to the benefits of education. In Sparta, as in Sappho's Lesbos, noble women loved girls for the same reasons. Warrior-aristocracies generally emphasized the physical side of the relationship in the belief that warriors who were also lovers would fight all the harder to impress each other. They would also be less likely to desert their lovers in battle. Whatever their intellectual and educational content, homosexual love affairs were also overtly sexual.

What effect did homosexual love have on the Greeks? An American psychologist has concluded that the "Greek adolescent... ended up as a non-neurotic, completely (or predominantly) heterosexual adult."[23] Most of Sappho's young lovers went on to marry and raise families. They never regretted the homosexual loves of their past or thought them unusual. Their previous relationships did not prevent them from devoting their primary affection to their new mates. For many Greeks, homosexuality was a normal practice, and they treated it as straightforwardly and honestly as they did heterosexual love and other aspects of life.

Despite some modern speculation to the contrary, relations between Athenian husbands and wives were probably close. The presence of female slaves in the home could be a source of trouble; men were always free to resort to prostitutes; and some men and women engaged in homosexual love affairs. But basically husbands and wives depended on each other for mutual love and support. The wife's position and status in the household were guaranteed by her dowry, which

came from her father and remained her property throughout her married life. If the wife felt that her marriage was intolerable, she could divorce her husband far more easily than could a Mesopotamian wife.

To judge by the evidence of funerary reliefs, there seems to have been nothing radically odd about the relationships of Athenian wives and husbands. One scholar has noted that funerary reliefs express the sorrow of the entire household — husband, children, and slaves — at the death of a wife. An epitaph of the fourth or third century B.C. reads:

Chaerestrate lies in this tomb. When she was alive her husband loved her. When she died he lamented.[24]

THE FLOWERING OF PHILOSOPHY

The myths and epics of the Mesopotamians are ample testimony that speculation about the origin of the universe and of mankind did not begin with the Greeks. The signal achievement of the Greeks was their willingness to treat these questions in rational rather than mythological terms. Although Greek philosophy did not fully flower until the Classical Period, Ionian thinkers had already begun in the Lyric Age to ask what the universe was made of. These men are called the Pre-Socratics, for their work preceded the philosophical revolution begun by the Athenian Socrates. Though they were born observers, the Pre-Socratics rarely undertook deliberate experimentation. Instead they took individual facts and wove them into general theories. Despite appearances, they believed, the universe was actually simple and subject to natural laws. Drawing upon their observations, they speculated about the basic building blocks of the universe.

The first of the Pre-Socratics, Thales (ca

600 B.C.), learned mathematics and astronomy from the Babylonians and geometry from the Egyptians. Yet there was an immense and fundamental difference between Near Eastern thought and the philosophy of Thales. The Near Eastern peoples considered such events as eclipses as evil omens. Thales viewed them as natural phenomena that could be explained in natural terms. In short, he asked *why* things happened. He believed the basic element of the universe to be water. Although he was wrong, the way in which he had asked the question was momentous: it was the beginning of the scientific method.

Thales' follower Anaximander continued his work. Anaximander was the first of the Pre-Socratics to use general concepts, which are essential to abstract thought. One of the most brilliant of the Pre-Socratics, a man of striking originality, Anaximander theorized that the basic element of the universe is "the boundless" or "endless" — something infinite and indestructible. In his view, the earth floats in a void, held in balance by its distance from everything else in the universe.

Anaximander even concluded that mankind had evolved naturally from lower organisms: "In water the first animal arose covered with spiny skin, and with the lapse of time some crawled onto dry land and breaking off their skins in a short time they survived."[25] This remarkable speculation corresponds crudely to Darwin's theory of evolution of species, which it predated by two-and-a-half millennia.

Another Ionian, Heraclitus (ca 500 B.C.) declared the primal element to be fire. He also declared that the world had neither beginning nor end: "This world, the world of all things, neither any god nor man made, but it always was and it is and it will be: an everlasting fire, measures kindling and measures going out."[26] Although the universe was eternal, according to Heraclitus, it changed constantly. An out-growth of this line of speculation was the theory of Democritus that the universe is made of invisible, indestructible atoms. The culmination of Pre-Socratic thought was the theory that four simple substances make up the universe: fire, air, earth, and water.

With this impressive heritage behind them, the philosophers of the Classical Period ventured into new areas of speculation. This development was partly due to the work of Hippocrates (second half of the fifth century B.C.), the father of medicine.

Like Thales, Hippocrates sought natural explanations for natural phenomena. Basing his opinions on empirical knowledge, not on religion or magic, he taught that natural means could be employed to fight disease. In his treatise *On Airs, Waters, and Places,* he noted the influence of climate and environment on health. Hippocrates and his followers put forth a theory that was to prevail in medical circles until the eighteenth century. The human body, they declared, contains four humors, or fluids: blood, phlegm, black bile, and yellow bile. In a healthy body the four humors are in perfect balance; too much or too little of any particular humor causes illness. Hippocrates and his pupils shared the Ionian belief that they were dealing with phenomena that could be explained purely in natural terms. But Hippocrates broke away from the mainstream of Ionian speculation by declaring that medicine was a separate craft — just as ironworking was a craft — and that it had its own principles.

The distinction between natural science and philosophy, upon which Hippocrates insisted, was also promoted by the sophists, who traveled the Greek world teaching young men. Despite differences of opinion on philosophical matters, the sophists all agreed that human beings were the proper subject of study. They also believed that excellence could be taught, and used philosophy and rhetoric to prepare young men for life in the polis. The sophists laid great emphasis on logic and the meanings of words. They criticized traditional beliefs, religion, rituals, and myth, and even questioned the laws of the polis. In essence they argued that nothing is absolute, that everything – even the customs and constitution of the state – is relative. Hence, many Greeks of more traditional inclination considered them wanton and harmful, men who were interested in "making the worse seem the better cause."

One of those whose contemporaries thought him a sophist was Socrates (ca 470–399 B.C.), who sprang from the class of small artisans. Socrates spent his life in investigation and definition. Not strictly speaking a sophist, because he never formally taught or collected fees from anyone, Socrates shared the sophists' belief that human beings and their environment are the essential subjects of philosophical inquiry. Like the sophists, Socrates thought that excellence could be learned and passed on to others. His approach when posing ethical questions and defining concepts was to start with a general topic or problem and to narrow the matter to its essentials. He did so by continuous questioning, a running dialogue. Never did he lecture. Socrates thought that by constantly pursuing excellence, an essential part of which was knowledge, human beings could approach the supreme good and thus find true happiness. Yet, in 399 B.C., Socrates was brought to trial, convicted, and executed on charges of corrupting the youth of the city and introducing new gods.

Socrates' student Plato (427–347 B.C.) carried on his master's search for truth. Unlike Socrates, Plato wrote down his thoughts and theories and founded a philosophical school, the Academy. Plato developed the theory that all visible, tangible things are unreal and temporary, copies of "forms" or "ideas" that are constant and indestructible. Only the mind – not the senses – can perceive the eternal forms. In Plato's view the highest form is the idea of good.

In *The Republic* Plato applied his theory of forms to politics in an effort to describe the ideal polis. His perfect polis is utopian; it aims at providing the greatest good and happiness to all its members. Plato thought that the ideal polis could exist only if its rulers were philosophers. He divided society into rulers, guardians of the polis, and workers. The role of people in each category is decided by the education, wisdom, and ability of the individual. In Plato's republic men and women are equal to one another, and women can become rulers. The utopian polis is a balance, with each individual doing what he or she can to support the state and with each receiving from the state his or her just due.

In a later work, *The Laws,* Plato discarded the ideal polis of *The Republic* in favor of a second-best state. The polis of *The Laws* is grimly reminiscent of the modern dictatorship. At its head is a young tyrant, who is just and good. He meets with a council that sits only at night, and together they maintain the spirit of the laws. Nearly everything about this state is coercive; the free will of the citizens counts for little. The laws speak to every aspect of life; their sole purpose is to make people happy.

Aristotle (384–322 B.C.) carried on the philosophical tradition of Socrates and Plato. A student of Plato, Aristotle went far beyond his teacher in his efforts to understand the universe. The very range of Aristotle's thought is staggering. Everything within human experience was fit subject for his inquiry. In his *Politics* Aristotle followed Plato's lead by writing about the ideal polis. Yet

Aristotle approached the question more realistically than Plato had, and he criticized *The Republic* and *The Laws* on many points. In the *Politics* and elsewhere, Aristotle stressed moderation and concluded that the balance of his ideal state depended on people of talent and education who could avoid extremes.

Not content to examine old questions, Aristotle opened up whole new fields of inquiry. He tried to understand the changes of nature – what caused them and where they led. In the *Physics* and *Metaphysics* he evolved a theory of nature in which he developed the notions of matter, form, and motion. He attempted to bridge the gap between abstract truth and concrete perception that Plato had created.

In *On the Heaven,* Aristotle took up the thread of Ionian speculation. His theory of cosmology added ether to air, fire, water, and earth as building-blocks of the universe. He concluded that the universe revolves and that it is spherical and eternal. He wrongly thought that the earth is the center of the universe, with the stars and other planets revolving around it. The Hellenistic scientist Aristarchus of Samos later realized that the earth revolves around the sun, but Aristotle's view was accepted until the time of the fifteenth-century astronomer Nicolaus Copernicus.

Aristotle's scientific interests also included zoology. In several works he describes various animals and makes observations on animal habits, animal anatomy, and how animals move. He also explored the process of reproduction. Intending to examine the entire animal kingdom, he assigned the world of plants to his follower Theophrastus (see Chapter 4).

Aristotle possessed one of the keenest and most curious philosophical minds of Western civilization. While rethinking the old topics

DEPARTING WARRIOR *Scenes like this were all too common from 431 to 338* B.C., *as young men donned their armor and left for battle. This warrior and a young woman, probably his sister, pour a libation to the gods before he leaves for the war. (Museum of Fine Arts, Boston)*

explored by the Pre-Socratics, he also created whole new areas of study. In short, he tried to learn everything possible about the universe and everything in it. He did so in the belief that all knowledge could be synthesized to produce a simple explanation of the universe and of humanity.

THE FINAL ACT (403–338 B.C.)

The end of the Peloponnesian War only punctuated a century of nearly constant war-

THE LION OF CHAERONEA *Alone on his base, this stylized lion marks the mass grave of nearly 300 elite Theban soldiers who valiantly died fighting the Macedonians at the battle of Chaeronea. After the battle, when Philip viewed the bodies of these brave troops, he said to those around him: "May those who suppose that these men did or suffered anything dishonorable perish wretchedly." (Photo: Caroline Buckler)*

fare that lasted from 431 to 338 B.C. The events of the fourth century demonstrated that no single Greek state possessed enough power and resources to dominate the others. There nevertheless ensued an exhausting struggle for hegemony among the great powers, especially Sparta, Athens, and Thebes. Immediately after the Peloponnesian War, with Athens humbled, Sparta began striving for empire over the Greeks. The arrogance and imperialism of the Spartans turned their former allies against them. Even with Persian help Sparta could not maintain its hold on Greece. In 371 B.C. the Spartans met their match on the plain of Leuctra in Boeotia. A Theban army under the command of Epaminondas, one of Greece's most brilliant generals, destroyed the flower of the Spartan army on a single summer day. The victory at Leuctra left Thebes the most powerful state in Greece. Under Epaminondas the Thebans destroyed Sparta as a first-rank power and checked the ambitions of Athens, but they were unable to bring peace to Greece. In 362 B.C. Epaminondas was killed in battle, and a period of stalemate set in. The Greek states were virtually exhausted.

The man who turned the situation to his own advantage was Philip II, king of Macedonia (359–336 B.C.). Throughout most of Greek history Macedonia, which bordered Greece in the north, in modern Greece and Yugoslavia, had been a backward and disunited kingdom, but Philip's genius, courage, and drive turned it into a major power. One of the ablest statesmen of antiquity, Philip united his powerful kingdom behind him, built a redoubtable army, and pursued his ambition with drive and determination. His horizon was not limited to Macedonia, for he realized that he could turn the rivalry and exhaustion of the Greek states to his own purposes. By clever use of his wealth and superb army Philip won control of the northern Aegean and awakened fear in Athens, which had vital interests there. Demosthenes, an Athenian patriot and a fine orator, warned his fellow citizens against Philip:

Most of all there is this to fear. This cunning and terrible man makes use of his accomplishments, yielding on points when he must, threatening (and he certainly appears to mean it) on others. He slanders us and our inactivity. He fosters and takes for himself anything of value.[27]

Others too saw Philip as a threat. A comic playwright depicted one of Philip's ambassadors warning the Athenians:

*Do you know that your battle will be with men
Who dine on sharpened swords,
And gulp burning firebrands for wine?
Then immediately after dinner the slave
Brings us dessert – Cretan arrows
Or pieces of broken spears.
We have shields and breastplates for
Cushions and at our feet slings and arrows,
And we are crowned with catapults.*[28]

Finally the Athenians joined forces with Thebes, which also appreciated the Macedonian threat, to stop Philip. In 338 B.C. the combined Theban-Athenian army met Philip's veterans at the Boeotian city of Chaeronea. Philip's army won a hard-fought victory: he had conquered Greece and put an end to Greek freedom. Because the Greeks could not put aside their quarrels, they fell to an invader.

———◆———

In a comparatively brief span of time the Greeks progressed from a primitive folk, backward and rude compared to their Near Eastern neighbors, to one of the most influential peoples of history. The originators of science and philosophy asked penetrating questions about the nature of life and society, and came up with deathless responses to many of their own questions. Greek achievements range from the development of sophisticated political institutions to the creation of a stunningly rich literature. Brilliant but quarrelsome, they were their own worst enemies. As the Roman historian Pompeius Trogus later said of their fall:

The states of Greece, while each one wished to rule alone, all squandered sovereignty. Indeed, hastening without moderation to destroy one another in mutual ruin, they did not realize, until they were all crushed, that every one of them lost in the end.[29]

Nonetheless, their achievement outlived their political squabbles to become the cornerstone of all later Western development.

NOTES

1. K. J. Beloch, *Griechische Geschichte,* vol. I, pt. I, K. J. Trübner, Strassburg, 1912, p. 49.

2. Aristotle *Politics* 1253a3-4.

3. Herodotus *The Histories* 2.53.

4. Hesiod *Works and Days* 263–266.

5. Ibid., 511–514.

6. F. Lasserre, *Archiloque,* Société d'Edition "Les Belles Lettres," Paris, 1958, frag. 9, p. 4.

7. W. Barnstable, *Sappho,* Doubleday, Garden City, N.Y., 1965, frag. 24, p. 22.

8. Ibid., frag. 132, p. 106.

9. Ibid., frag. 23, p. 20.

10. J. M. Edmonds, *Greek Elegy and Iambus,* Harvard University Press, Cambridge, Mass., 1931, I.70, frag. 10.

11. Ibid., frag. 11, p. 72.

12. Edmonds, *Greek Elegy and Iambus,* frag. 4, p. 118.

13. R. Meiggs and D. Lewis, *A Selection of Greek Historical Inscriptions,* Clarendon Press, Oxford, 1969, no. 52, lines 21–32.

14. Ibid., no. 40, lines 9–11.

15. Thucydides *History of the Peloponnesian War* 1.23.

16. Ibid.

17. Herodotus *The Histories* 1.1.

18. Ibid., 7.102.

19. Thucydides *The Peloponnesian War* 1.1.

20. Plutarch *Life of Pericles* 13.5.

21. Mark Twain, *The Innocents Abroad,* Signet Classics, New York, 1966, p. 249.

22. K. J. Dover, *Greek Homosexuality,* Random House, New York, 1980, p.1.

23. G. Devereux, "Greek Pseudo-Homosexuality and the 'Greek Miracle'," *Symbolae Osloenses* (1968): 70.

24. S. B. Pomeroy, *Goddesses, Whores, Wives and Slaves,* Schocken, New York, 1975, p. 92.

25. E. Diels and W. Krantz, *Fragmente der Vorsokratiker,* 8th ed. Weidmannsche Verlagsbuchhandlung, Berlin, 1960, Anaximander frag. A30.

26. Ibid., Heraclitus frag. B30.

27. Demosthenes *First Olynthiac* 3.

28. J. M. Edmonds, *The Fragments of Attic Comedy,* E. J. Brill, Leiden, 2.366–369, Mnesimachos frag. 7.

29. Justin 8.1.1–2.

SUGGESTED READING

Translations of the most important writings of the Greeks and Romans can be found in the volumes of the Loeb Classical Library, published by Harvard University Press. Paperback editions of the major Greek and Latin authors are available in the Penguin Classics. Recent translations of documents include those by N. Lewis, *Greek Historical Documents: The Fifth Century* B.C. (1971); J. Wickersham and G. Verbrugghe, *Greek Historical Documents: The Fourth Century* B.C. (1973); and C. Fornara, *Translated Documents of Greece and Rome,* vol. 1: *Archaic Times to the End of the Peloponnesian War* (1977).

Among the many general treatments of Greek history, H. D. F. Kitto, *The Greeks* (1951), is a delightful introduction. V. Ehrenberg in two works, *From Solon to Socrates,* 2nd. ed. (1973) and *The Greek State* (1960), covers major areas of Greek history.

For early Greece the most recent treatments include R. J. Hopper, *The Early Greeks* (1976), and L. H. Jeffery, *Archaic Greece* (1976). No finer introduction to the Lyric Age can be found than A. R. Burn's *The Lyric Age* (1960) and its sequel, *Persia and the Greeks* (1962). A good recent survey of work on Sparta is P. Oliva, *Sparta and Her Social Problems* (1971). Sound discussions of Athenian democracy are available in A. H. M. Jones, *Athenian Democracy* (1957), and C. Hignett, *History of the Athenian Constitution* (1952).

A. J. Graham, *Colony and Mother City in Ancient Greece* (1964), gives a good account of Greek colonization. Athens in the fifth century and the outbreak of the Peloponnesian War are covered in G. E. M. de Ste Croix, *The Origins of the Peloponnesian War* (1972), and R. Meiggs, *The Athenian Empire* (1972).

Several books on fourth-century history have recently appeared. D. M. Lewis' *Sparta and Persia* (1977) is rich in information on the administration of the Persian Empire, Spartan diplomacy, and much else. J. Buckler, *The Theban Hegemony, 371–362 B.C.* (1980) treats the period of Theban ascendancy. J. Cargill, *The Second Athenian League* (1981), a significant new study, traces Athenian policy during the century. J. R. Ellis, *Philip II and Macedonian Imperialism* (1976), and G. Cawkwell, *Philip of Macedon* (1978), analyze the career of the great conqueror.

Daily life, the family, women, and homosexuality receive treatment in Pomeroy's book cited in the Notes; T. B. L. Webster, *Life in Classical Greece* (1969); M. and C. H. B. Quennell, *Everyday Things in Ancient Greece* (1954); and a special issue of the Journal *Arethusa* 6 (1973).

For Greek literature, culture, and science, see A. Lesky, *A History of Greek Literature* (English trans., 1963); W. Jaeger, *Paideia,* 3 vols., (English trans., 1944–1945); H. C. Baldry, *The Greek Tragic Theater* (1971); J. Burnet, *Early Greek Philosophy,* 4th ed.

(1930), and *Greek Philosophy, Thales to Plato* (1914); M. Clagett, *Greek Science in Antiquity* (1971); and E. R. Dodds, *The Greeks and the Irrational* (1951).

The classic treatment of Greek architecture is W. B. Dinsmoor, *The Architecture of the Ancient Greeks,* 3rd ed. (1950). More recent (and perhaps more readable) is A. W. Lawrence, *Greek Architecture,* 3rd ed. (1973). J. Boardman, *Greek Art,* rev. ed. (1973), is both perceptive and sound, as is J. J. Pollitt, *Art and Experience in Classical Greece* (1972).

D. Haynes, *Greek Art and the Idea of Freedom* (1981), traces the evolving freedom of the human personality in Greek art.

J. Pinsent, *Greek Mythology* (1969), is a handy introduction. M. P. Nilsson, *Cults, Myths, Oracles and Politics in Ancient Greece* (1951), examines Greek religion and myth in the contemporary context. See also G. S. Kirk, *The Nature of Greek Myths* (1974).

CHAPTER 4

HELLENISTIC DIFFUSION

TWO YEARS AFTER his conquest of Greece, Philip of Macedon fell victim to an assassin's dagger. Philip's twenty-year-old son, known to history as Alexander the Great (336-323 B.C.) assumed the Macedonian throne. This young man, one of the most remarkable personalities of Western civilization, was to have a profound impact on history. "For in twelve years having conquered not a small part of Europe and nearly all of Asia, he was justly famous and his glory was equal to that of the heroes of old and of the demigods."[1]

By overthrowing the Persian Empire and by spreading Hellenism – Greek culture, language, thought and the Greek way of life – as far as India, Alexander was instrumental in creating a new era, traditionally called Hellenistic to distinguish it from the Hellenic. As a result of Alexander's exploits, the individualistic and energetic culture of the Greeks came into intimate contact with the venerable older cultures of the Near East.

What did the spread of Hellenism mean to the Greeks and the peoples of the Near East? What did the meeting of West and East hold for the development of philosophy, religion, science, medicine, and economics? These are the questions this chapter will explore.

ALEXANDER AND THE GREAT CRUSADE

In 336 B.C., Alexander inherited not only Philip's crown but also his policies. After his victory at Chaeronea, Philip had organized the states of Greece into a huge league under his leadership, and announced to the Greeks his plan to lead them and his Macedonians against the Persian Empire. Fully intending to carry out Philip's designs, Alexander proclaimed to the Greek world that the invasion of Persia was to be a great crusade, a mighty act of revenge for the Persian invasion of Greece in 480 B.C.

Despite his youth, Alexander was well prepared to lead the attack. Philip had groomed his son to become king, and had given him the best education possible. In 343 B.C., Philip invited the philosopher Aristotle to tutor his son. From Aristotle Alexander learned to appreciate Greek culture and literature, and the teachings of the great philosopher left a lasting mark on him. Alexander must also have profited from Aristotle's practical knowledge, but he never accepted Aristotle's political theories. At the age of sixteen Alexander became regent of Macedonia, and two years later at the battle of Chaeronea he helped defeat the Greeks. By 336 B.C., Alexander had acquired both the theoretical and the practical knowledge to rule peoples and lead armies.

In 334 B.C., Alexander led an army of Macedonians and Greeks into Asia Minor. With him went a staff of philosophers and poets, scientists whose job was to map the country and to study strange animals and plants, and the historian Callisthenes, who was to write an account of the campaign. Alexander planned not only to conquer the Persians but to lead an expedition of discovery to open up the East to Greek knowledge.

In the next three years Alexander won three major battles at the Granicus River, Issus, and Gaugamela. As Map 4.1 shows, these battle sites stand almost as road signs marking his march to the East. After his victory at Gaugamela, Alexander captured the principal Persian capital of Persepolis, where he performed a symbolic act of retribution by burning the buildings of Xerxes, the invader of Greece. In 330 B.C., he took Ecbatana, the last Persian capital, and pursued the Persian king to his death.

The Persian Empire had fallen and the war of revenge was over, but Alexander had no intention of stopping. He dismissed his Greek troops, but permitted many of them to serve on as mercenaries. Alexander then began his personal odyssey. With his Macedonian soldiers and Greek mercenaries he set out to conquer the rest of Asia. He plunged deeper into the East, into lands completely unknown to the Greek world. Alexander's way was marked by bitter fighting and bloodshed. It took four more years to conquer Bactria and the easternmost parts of the now-defunct Persian Empire, but still Alexander was determined to march on.

In 326 B.C., Alexander crossed the Indus River and entered India. There too he saw hard fighting, and finally at the Hyphasis River his troops refused to go farther. Alexander was enraged by the mutiny, for he believed that he was near the end of the world. Nonetheless, the army stood firm, and Alexander had to relent. Still eager to explore the limits of the world, Alexander returned south to the Indian Ocean. Even though the tribes in the area did not oppose him, he waged a bloody, ruthless, and unnecessary war against them. After reaching the Indian Ocean and turning west, he led his army through the grim Gedrosian Desert, apparently to punish his troops for their mutiny at the Hyphasis. The army suffered fearfully, and many men died along the way, but in 324 B.C. Alexander reached his camp at Susa. The great crusade was over, and Alexander himself died the next year in Babylon.

COIN OF ALEXANDER *The head on this coin is that of the demigod Heracles, whom Alexander admired and imitated. Alexander claimed that he was descended from Heracles, and on several occasions he even dressed like Heracles. (Courtesy, World Heritage Museum. Photo: Caroline Buckler)*

ALEXANDER'S LEGACY

Of Alexander the man history knows little: he too quickly became a figure of legend, a figure larger than life. Of Alexander's plans and intentions history likewise knows little. Although some scholars have seen him as a high-minded philosopher, his bloody and savage campaigns in the East seem the work of a ruthless and callous conqueror. Yet for the Hellenistic period and for Western civilization in general, what Alexander intended was less important than what he actually did (see Map 4.1).

Alexander was instrumental in changing the face of politics in the eastern Mediterranean. His campaign swept away the Persian Empire, which had ruled the East for over two hundred years. In its place he established a Macedonian monarchy. More important in the long run was his foundation of new cities and military colonies, which scattered Greeks and Macedonians throughout the East. Thus the practical result of Alexander's campaign was to open the East to the tide of Hellenism.

THE POLITICAL LEGACY

In 323 B.C., Alexander the Great died at the age of thirty-two. The main question at his death was whether his vast empire could be

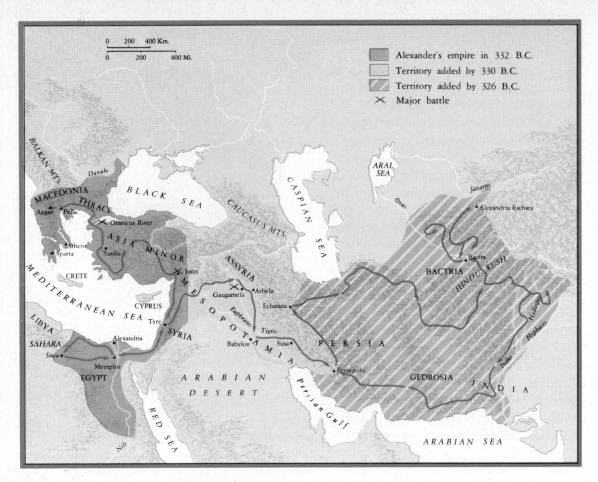

MAP 4.1 ALEXANDER'S CONQUESTS *This
map shows the course of Alexander's invasion of the
Persian Empire and the speed of his progress.*

held together. The answer became obvious
immediately. Within a week of Alexander's
death began a round of fighting that was to
continue for forty years. No single Macedonian general was able to replace Alexander as
emperor of his entire domain. By 275 B.C., as
Map 4.2 shows, three of Alexander's officers
had divided it into large monarchies. Antig-
onus Gonatas became king of Macedonia and
established the Antigonid dynasty, which
ruled until the Roman conquest in 168 B.C.
Ptolemy Lagus made himself king of Egypt,
and his descendants, the Ptolemies, assumed
the powers and position of pharaohs. Se-

leucus, founder of the Seleucid dynasty, carved
out a kingdom that stretched from the coast
of Asia Minor to India. In 263 B.C., Eumenes,
the Greek ruler of Pergamum, a city in western Asia Minor, won his independence from
the Seleucids and created the Pergamene
monarchy. Though the Seleucid kings soon
lost control of their easternmost provinces,
Greek influence in this area did not wane. In
modern Turkestan and Afghanistan another
line of Greek kings established the kingdom
of Bactria, and even managed to spread their
power and culture into northern India.

The political face of Greece itself changed

ALEXANDER AT THE BATTLE OF ISSOS   At the left, Alexander the Great, bareheaded and wearing a breastplate, charges King Darius, who is standing in a chariot. This moment marks the turning point of the battle, as Darius turns to flee from the attack. (Museo Nazionale, Naples. Alinari/Scala)

during the Hellenistic period. The day of the polis was over, and in its place arose leagues of city-states. The two most powerful and most extensive were the Aetolian League in western and central Greece, and the Achaean League in the Peloponnesus. Once-powerful city-states like Athens and Sparta sank to the level of third-rate powers.

The political history of the Hellenistic period was dominated by the great monarchies and the Greek leagues. The political fragmentation and incessant warfare that marked the Hellenic period continued on an even wider and larger scale during the Hel-

lenistic period. Never did the Hellenistic world achieve political stability or lasting peace. Hellenistic kings never forgot the vision of Alexander's empire, spanning Europe and Asia, secure under the rule of one man. Try as they did, they were never able to re-create it. In this respect, Alexander's legacy fell not to his generals but to the Romans of a later era.

THE CULTURAL LEGACY

As Alexander waded ever deeper into the East, distance alone presented him with a serious problem: how was he to retain contact with the Greek world behind him? Communications were vital, for he drew supplies and reinforcements from Greece and Macedonia. Alexander had to be sure that he was never cut off and stranded far from the Mediterranean world. His solution was to plant cities and military colonies in strategic places. In these settlements Alexander left Greek mercenaries and Macedonian veterans no longer up to active campaigning. Besides keeping the road open to the West, these settlements dominated the countryside around them.

Their military significance apart, Alexander's cities and colonies became powerful instruments in the spread of Hellenism throughout the East. Plutarch described Alexander's achievement in glowing terms: "Having founded over 70 cities among barbarian peoples and having planted Greek magistracies in Asia, Alexander overcame its wild and savage way of life."[2] Alexander had indeed opened the East to an enormous wave of immigration, and his successors continued his policy by inviting Greek colonists to settle in their realms. For seventy-five years after Alexander's death, Greek immigrants poured into the East. At least 250 new Hellenistic colonies were established. The Mediterranean world had seen no comparable movement of peoples since the days of Archilochus (see page 82), when wave after wave of Greeks had turned the Mediterranean basin into a Greek-speaking region.

The overall result of Alexander's settlements and those of his successors was the spread of Hellenism as far east as India. Throughout the Hellenistic period Greeks and Easterners became familiar with and adapted themselves to each other's customs, religions, and ways of life. Although Greek culture did not completely conquer the East, it gave the East a vehicle of expression that linked it to the West. Hellenism became a common bond among the East, peninsular Greece, and the western Mediterranean. This pre-existing cultural bond was later to prove supremely valuable to Rome — itself heavily influenced by Hellenism — in its efforts to impose a comparable political unity on the known world.

THE SPREAD OF HELLENISM

When the Greeks and Macedonians entered Asia Minor, Egypt, and the more remote East, they encountered civilizations older than their own. In some ways the Eastern cultures were more advanced than the Greek, in others less so. Thus this third great tide of Greek migration differed from preceding waves, which had spread over land that was uninhabited or inhabited by less-developed peoples.

What did the Hellenistic monarchies offer Greek immigrants, both politically and materially? More broadly, how did Hellenism and the cultures of the East affect one another? What did the meeting of East and West entail for the history of the world?

CITIES AND KINGDOMS

Although Alexander's generals created huge kingdoms, the concept of monarchy never replaced the ideal of the polis. Consequently, the monarchies never won the deep emotional loyalty that Greeks had once felt for the polis. Hellenistic kings needed large numbers of Greeks to run their kingdoms. Otherwise, royal business would grind to a halt, and the conquerors would soon be swallowed up by the far more numerous conquered population. Obviously, then, the kings had to encourage Greeks to immigrate and build new homes.

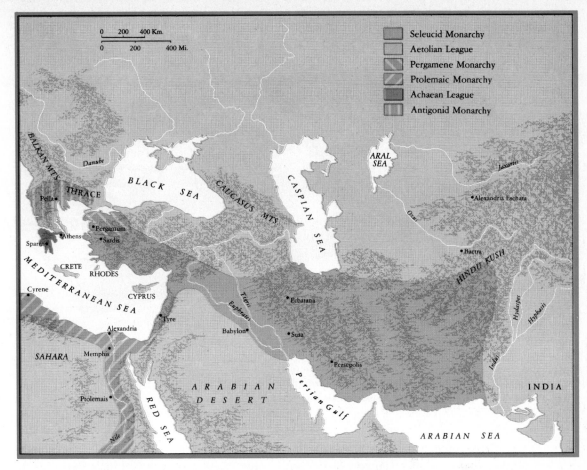

Legend:
- Seleucid Monarchy
- Aetolian League
- Pergamene Monarchy
- Ptolemaic Monarchy
- Achaean League
- Antigonid Monarchy

MAP 4.2 THE HELLENISTIC WORLD After Alexander's death, no single commander could hold his vast conquests together, resulting in the empire's break-up into several kingdoms and leagues.

To these Greeks monarchy was something out of the heroic past, something found in Homer's *Iliad* but not in daily life. The Hellenistic kings thus confronted the problem of making life in the new monarchies resemble the traditional Greek way of life. Since Greek civilization was urban, the kings continued Alexander's policy of establishing cities throughout their kingdoms in order to entice Greeks to immigrate. Yet the creation of these cities posed a serious problem, which the Hellenistic kings failed to solve.

To the Greeks civilized life was unthinkable without the polis, which was far more than a mere city. The Greek polis was by definition sovereign – an independent, autonomous state run by its citizens free from any outside power or restraint. Hellenistic kings, however, refused to grant sovereignty to their cities. In effect, these kings willingly built cities, but refused to build a polis. Instead they attempted a compromise that ultimately failed.

Hellenistic monarchs gave to their cities all the external trappings of a polis. Each had an assembly of citizens, a council to prepare legislation, and a board of magistrates to conduct the political business of the city. Yet however similar to the Greek city-state they appeared,

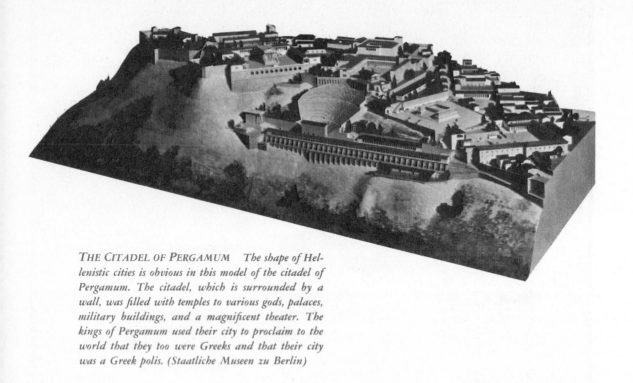

THE CITADEL OF PERGAMUM   *The shape of Hellenistic cities is obvious in this model of the citadel of Pergamum. The citadel, which is surrounded by a wall, was filled with temples to various gods, palaces, military buildings, and a magnificent theater. The kings of Pergamum used their city to proclaim to the world that they too were Greeks and that their city was a Greek polis. (Staatliche Museen zu Berlin)*

these cities could not engage in diplomatic dealings, make treaties, pursue their own foreign policy, or wage their own wars. None could govern its own affairs without interference from the king, who, even if he stood in the background, was the real sovereign. In the eyes of the king the cities were important parts of the kingdom, but the welfare of the kingdom as a whole came first. The cities had to follow royal orders, and the king often placed his own officials in the cities to see that his decrees were carried out.

A new Hellenistic city differed from a Greek polis in other ways as well. The Greek polis had enjoyed political and social unity even though it was normally composed of citizens, slaves, and resident aliens. The polis had one body of law and one set of customs. In the Hellenistic city the Greeks represented an elite citizen class. Natives and non-Greek foreigners who lived in Hellenistic cities usually possessed lesser rights than those of the Greeks and often had their own laws. In some instances this disparity spurred natives to assimilate Greek culture in order to rise both politically and socially. Other peoples, such as the Jews, firmly resisted the essence of Hellenism. The Hellenistic city was not homogeneous, and it could not spark the intensity of feeling that marked the polis.

In many respects, the Hellenistic city resembled a modern city. It was a cultural center with theaters, temples, and libraries. It was a seat of learning, the home of poets, writers, scholars, teachers, and artists. It was the place where people could find amusement. The Hellenistic city was also an economic center that provided a ready market for the grain and produce raised in the surrounding countryside. The city was an emporium, the scene of trade and manufacturing. In short, the Hellenistic city offered cultural and economic opportunities, but did not foster a sense of united, integrated enterprise.

There were no constitutional links between the city and the king. The city was simply his possession. It and its citizens had no voice in how the kingdom was run. The city had no rights except for those the king granted, and even those he could summarily take away. Ambassadors from the city could entreat the king for favors and petition him on such matters as taxes, boundary disputes, and legal cases. But the city had no right to advise the king on royal policy, and it enjoyed no political function within the kingdom.

Hellenistic kings tried to make the kingdom the political focus of citizens' allegiance. If the king could secure the frontiers of his kingdom, he could give it a geographical identity. He could then hope that his subjects would direct their primary loyalty to the kingdom rather than a particular city. However, the kings' efforts to fix their borders led only to sustained warfare. Boundaries were determined by military power, and rule by force became the chief political principle of the Hellenistic world.

Border wars were frequent and exhausting. The Seleucids and the Ptolemies, for instance, waged five wars for the possession of southern Syria. Other kings refused to acknowledge any boundaries at all. These men followed the example of Alexander and waged wars to reunify his empire under their own authority. By the third century B.C., a weary balance of power was reached, but only as the result of stalemate. It was not maintained by any political principle.

The Hellenistic kings failed to create in their kingdoms a political unit to replace the polis. Even the Hellenistic city, despite its beauty and Hellenic trappings, failed to win the devotion and love that the Greeks had readily and enthusiastically given the polis.

Nor did the Hellenistic kings ever give the Greeks anything else to which to attach their political loyalty.

THE GREEKS AND THE OPENING OF THE EAST

If the Hellenistic kings failed to satisfy the Greeks' political yearnings, they nonetheless succeeded in giving them unequaled economic and social opportunities. The ruling dynasties of the Hellenistic world were Macedonian, and Greeks filled all important political, military, and diplomatic positions. These people constituted an upper class that sustained Hellenism in the barbarian East. Besides building Greek cities, Hellenistic kings offered Greeks land and money as a lure to further immigration.

The more splendid, prestigious, and famous the kingdom, the easier it was to attract settlers. Each kingdom strove to be more philhellenic – more Greek-like and more appreciative of Greek culture – than the others. Each claimed the ability to provide Greeks with the necessities of Greek life. The burden of these policies fell upon the native population of the various kingdoms. Easterners paid for these enticements through heavy taxation.

The opening of the East offered ambitious Greeks opportunities for well-paying jobs and economic success. The Hellenistic monarchy, unlike the Greek polis, did not depend solely on its citizens to fulfill its political needs. Talented Greeks could expect to rise quickly within the governmental bureaucracy. Appointed by the king, these administrators did not have to stand for election each year, as had many of the officials of a Greek polis. Since they held their jobs year after year, they had ample time to evolve new administrative techniques. Naturally, they became more efficient than the amateur officials common in the Greek city-states of the Hellenic period. The needs of the Hellenistic monarchy and the opportunities it offered thus gave rise to a professional corps of Greek administrators.

Greeks and Macedonians also found ready employment in the armies and navies of the Hellenistic monarchies. Alexander had proved the Greco-Macedonian style of warfare to be far superior to that of the Easterners, and Alexander's successors, themselves experienced officers, realized the importance of trained Greek and Macedonian soldiers. Moreover, Hellenistic kings were extremely reluctant to arm the native population or to allow them to serve in the army, fearing military rebellions among their conquered subjects. The result of this situation was the emergence of professional armies and navies consisting entirely of Greeks and Macedonians.

Greeks were able to dominate other professions as well. In order to be really philhellenic, the kingdoms and their cities needed Greek writers and artists to create Greek literature, art, and culture on Asian soil. Architects, engineers, and skilled craftsmen found their services in great demand because of the building policies of the Hellenistic monarchs. If Hellenistic kingdoms were to have Greek cities, those cities needed Greek buildings — temples, porticoes, gymnasia, theaters, fountains, and houses. Architects and engineers were sometimes commissioned to design and build whole cities, which they laid out in checkerboard fashion and filled with typical Greek buildings. A truly enormous wave of construction took place during the Hellenistic period.

Despite the opportunities they offered, the Hellenistic monarchies were hampered by their artificial origins. Their failure to win the political loyalty of their Greek subjects and their policy of wooing Greeks with lucrative positions encouraged a feeling of uprootedness and self-serving individualism among Greek immigrants. Once a Greek had left home to take service with, for instance, the army or the bureaucracy of the Ptolemies, he had no incentive beyond his pay and the comforts of life in Egypt to keep him there. If the Seleucid king offered him more money or a promotion, he might well accept it and take his talents to Asia Minor. Why not? In the realm of the Seleucids he, a Greek, would find the same sort of life and environment that the kingdom of the Ptolemies had provided him. Thus professional Greek soldiers and administrators were highly mobile and prone to look to their own interests, not those of the kingdom they joined.

As long as Greeks continued to replenish their professional ranks, the kingdoms remained strong. In the process they drew an immense amount of talent from the Greek peninsula, draining the vitality of the Greek homeland. However, the Hellenistic monarchies could not keep recruiting Greeks forever, in spite of their wealth and willingness to spend lavishly to attract and keep the Greeks coming. In time, the huge surge of immigration slowed greatly. Even then the Hellenistic monarchs were reluctant to recruit Easterners to fill posts normally held by Greeks. The result was at first the stagnation of the Hellenistic world and finally, after 202 B.C., collapse in the face of the young and vigorous Roman Republic.

GREEKS AND EASTERNERS

The Greeks in the East were a minority, and Hellenistic cities were islands of Greek culture in an Eastern sea. But Hellenistic monarchies were remarkably successful in at least partially hellenizing Easterners and spreading a uniform culture throughout the East, a culture to which Rome eventually fell heir. The prevailing institutions, laws, and language of the East became Greek. Indeed, the Near East had seen nothing comparable since the days when Mesopotamian culture had spread throughout the area.

Yet the spread of Greek culture was wider than it was deep. At best it was a veneer, thicker in some places than in others. Hellenistic kingdoms were never entirely unified in language, customs, and thought. Greek culture took firmest hold along the shores of the Mediterranean, but in the Far East, in Persia and Bactria, it eventually gave way to Eastern cultures.

The Ptolemies in Egypt made no effort to spread Greek culture, and unlike other Hellenistic kings they were not city builders. Indeed, they founded only the city of Ptolemais near Thebes. At first the native Egyptian population, the descendants of the pharaoh's people, retained their traditional language, outlook, religion, and way of life. Initially untouched by Hellenism, the natives continued to be the foundation of the state: they fed it by their labor in the fields, and they financed its operations by their taxes.

Under the pharaohs, talented Egyptians had been able to rise to high office, but during the third century B.C. the Ptolemies cut off this avenue of advancement. They tied the natives to the land ever more tightly, making it nearly impossible for them to leave their villages. The bureaucracy of the Ptolemies was ruthlessly efficient, and the native population was viciously and cruelly exploited. Even in times of hardship the king's taxes came first, though payment might mean starvation for the natives. The desperation of the native population was summed up by one Egyptian, who scrawled the warning: "We are worn out; we will run away."[3] To many Egyptians revolt or a life of brigandage was certainly preferable

to working the land under the harsh Ptolemies.

Throughout the third century B.C., the Greek upper class had little to do with the native population. Many Greek bureaucrats established homes in Alexandria and Ptolemais, where they managed finances, served as magistrates, and administered the law. Other Greeks settled in military colonies and supplied the monarchy with fighting men.

In the second century B.C., Greeks and native Egyptians began to intermarry and mingle their cultures. The language of the native population influenced Greek, and many Greeks adopted Egyptian religion and ways of life. Simultaneously, natives adopted Greek customs and language, and began to play a role in the administration of the kingdom and even to serve in the army. While many Greeks and Egyptians remained aloof from each other, the overall result was the evolution of a widespread Greco-Egyptian culture.

Meanwhile the Seleucid kings established many cities and military colonies in western Asia Minor and along the banks of the Tigris and Euphrates rivers in order to nurture a vigorous and numerous Greek population. Especially important to the Seleucids were the military colonies, for they depended on Greeks to defend the kingdom. The Seleucids had no elaborate plan for hellenizing the native population, but the arrival of so many Greeks was bound to have an impact. Seleucid military colonies were generally founded near native villages, thus exposing Easterners to all aspects of Greek life. Many Easterners found Greek political and cultural forms attractive, and imitated them. In Asia Minor and Syria, for instance, numerous native villages and towns developed along Greek lines, and some of them became hellenized cities. Farther East the Greek kings who replaced the Seleucids in the third century B.C. spread Greek culture to their neighbors and even into the Indian subcontinent.

For Easterners the prime advantage of Greek culture was its very pervasiveness. The Greek language became the common speech of the East. Indeed, a common dialect, called *koine*, even influenced the speech of peninsular Greece itself. Greek became the speech of the royal court, the bureaucracy, and the military. It was also the speech of commerce: any Easterner who wanted to compete in business had to learn Greek. As early as the third century B.C., some Greek cities were giving citizenship to hellenized natives.

The vast majority of hellenized Easterners, however, took only the externals of Greek culture while retaining the essentials of their own way of life. Though Greeks and Easterners adapted themselves to each others' ways, there was never a true fusion of cultures. Nonetheless, each found useful things in the civilization of the other, and the two fertilized each other. This fertilization, this mingling of Greek and Eastern elements, is what makes Hellenistic culture unique and distinctive.

HELLENISM AND THE JEWS A prime illustration of how the East took what it wanted from Hellenism while remaining true to itself is the impact of Greek culture on the Jews. At first Jews in Hellenistic cities were treated as resident aliens. As they grew more numerous, they received permission to form a political corporation, a *politeuma,* which gave them a great deal of autonomy. The *politeuma* allowed Jews to attend to their religious and internal affairs without interference from the Greek municipal government. The Jewish politeuma had its own officials, the leaders of the synagogue. In time the Jewish politeuma gained the special right to be judged by its own law and its own officials, thus becoming in effect a Jewish city within a Hellenistic city.

The Jewish politeuma, like the Hellenistic city, obeyed the commands of the king, but there was virtually no royal interference with the Jewish religion. Indeed, the Greeks were always very reluctant to tamper with anyone's religion. Only the Seleucid king Antiochus Epiphanes (175–ca 164 B.C.) tried to suppress the Jewish religion in Judaea. He did so not because he hated the Jews (who were a small part of his kingdom), but because he was trying to unify his realm culturally to meet the threat of Rome. To the Jews he extended the same policy that he applied to all of his subjects. Apart from this instance, Hellenistic Jews suffered no official religious persecution. Some Jews were given the right to become full citizens of Hellenistic cities, but few exercised that right. Citizenship would have allowed them to vote in the assembly and serve as magistrates, but it would also have obliged them to worship the gods of the city – a practice few Jews chose to follow.

Jews living in Hellenistic cities often embraced a good deal of Hellenism. So many Jews learned Greek, especially in Alexandria, that the Old Testament was translated into Greek, and services in the synagogue came to be conducted in Greek. Jews often took Greek names, used Greek political forms, adopted Greek practice by forming their own trade associations, put inscriptions on graves as the Greeks did, and much else. Yet no matter how much of Greek culture or its externals Jews borrowed, they normally remained true to their religion. Their ideas and those of the Greeks were different. The exceptions were some Jews in Asia Minor and Syria who incorporated Greek or local Eastern cults into their worship. To some degree this development was due not only to the strength and attraction of these cults but also to the growing belief among Greeks and Easterners that all peoples, despite differences in cult and ritual, actually worshiped the same gods.

Thus, in spite of their Hellenistic trappings, hellenized Jews remained Jews at heart. The value of Hellenism both to Jews and to other Easterners was its gift of a common cultural background and means of expression.

THE ECONOMIC SCOPE OF THE HELLENISTIC WORLD

Alexander's conquest of the Persian Empire not only changed the political face of the ancient world, it also brought the East fully into the sphere of Greek economics. Yet the Hellenistic period did not see a revolution in the way people lived and worked. The material demands of Hellenistic society remained as simple as those of Athenian society in the fifth century B.C. Clothes and furniture were essentially unchanged, as were household goods, tools, and jewelry. The real achievement of Alexander and his successors was linking East and West in a broad commercial network. The spread of Greeks throughout the East created new markets and stimulated trade. The economic unity of the Hellenistic world, like its cultural bonds, would later prove valuable to the Romans.

COMMERCE

Alexander's conquest of the Persian Empire had immediate effects on trade. In the Persian capitals Alexander had found vast sums of gold, silver, and other treasure. This wealth financed the creation of new cities, the building of roads, and the development of harbors.

Most of the great monarchies coined their money on the Attic standard, which meant that much of the money used in the Hellenistic kingdoms had the same value. Traders were less in need of moneychangers than in the days when each major power coined money on a different standard. As a result of Alexander's conquests, geographical knowledge of the East increased dramatically, making the East far better known to the Greeks than previously. The Greeks spread their law and methods of transacting business throughout the East. Whole new fields lay open to Greek merchants, and they eagerly took advantage of the new opportunities. Commerce itself was a leading area where Greeks and Easterners met on grounds of common interest. In bazaars, ports, and trading centers Greeks learned of Eastern customs and traditions, while spreading knowledge of their own culture.

The Seleucid and Ptolemaic dynasties traded as far afield as India, Arabia, and Africa. Overland trade with India and Arabia was conducted by caravan and was largely in the hands of Easterners. The caravan trade never dealt in bulk items or essential commodities, for only luxury goods could be transported in this very expensive fashion. Once the goods reached the Hellenistic monarchies, Greek merchants took a hand in the trade.

In the early Hellenistic period the Seleucids and Ptolemies ensured that the caravan trade proceeded efficiently. Later in the period – a time of increased war and confusion – they left the caravans unprotected. Taking advantage of this situation, Palmyra in the Syrian desert and Nabataean Petra in Arabia arose as caravan states. Such states protected the caravans from bandits and marauders, and served as dispersal areas of caravan goods.

The Ptolemies discovered how to use monsoon winds to establish direct contact with India. One hardy merchant has left a firsthand account of sailing this important maritime link:

Hippalos, the pilot, observing the position of the ports and the conditions of the sea, first discovered how to sail across the ocean. Concerning the winds of the ocean in this region, when with us the Etesian winds begin, in India a wind between southwest and south, named for Hippalos, sets in from the open sea. From then until now some mariners set forth from Kanes and some from the Cape of Spices. Those sailing to Dimurikes [in southern India] throw the bow of the ship farther out to sea. Those bound for Barygaza and the realm of the Sakas [in northern India] hold to the land no more than three days; and if the wind remains favorable, they hold the same course through the outer sea, and they sail along past the previously mentioned gulfs.[4]

Although this sea route never replaced overland caravan traffic, it kept alive direct relations with the East, stimulating the exchange of ideas as well as goods.

More economically important than this exotic trade were commercial dealings in essential commodities like raw materials, grain, and industrial products. The Hellenistic monarchies usually raised enough grain for their own needs as well as a surplus for export. For the cities of Greece and the Aegean this trade in grain was essential, because many of them could not grow enough of their own. Fortunately for them, abundant supplies of wheat were available nearby in Egypt and in the Crimea in southern Russia.

The large-scale wars of the Hellenistic period often interrupted both the production and distribution of grain. This was especially true when the successors of Alexander were trying to carve out their kingdoms. In addi-

tion, natural calamities, such as excessive rain or drought, frequently damaged harvests. Throughout the Hellenistic period famine or severe food shortage remained a grim possibility.

Most trade in bulk commodities was seaborne, and the Hellenistic merchant ship was the workhorse of the day. The merchant ship had a broad beam and relied on sails for propulsion. It was far more seaworthy than the contemporary warship, which was long, narrow, and built for speed. A small crew of experienced sailors could handle it easily. Maritime trade gave rise to other industries and trades: sailors and shipbuilders, dock workers, merchants, accountants, teamsters, and pirates. Piracy was always a factor in the Hellenistic world and remained so until Rome extended its power throughout the East.

The Greek cities paid for their grain by exporting olive oil and wine. When agriculture and oil production developed in Syria, Greek products began to encounter competition from the Seleucid monarchy. Later in the Hellenistic period Greek oil and wine found a lucrative market in Italy. Another significant commodity was fish, which for export was either salted, pickled, or dried. This trade was doubly important because fish provided poor people with an essential element of their diet. Salt too was often imported, and there was some very slight trade in salted meat, which was a luxury item. Far more important was the trade in honey, dried fruit, nuts, and vegetables. Among raw materials wood ranked high in demand, but there was little trade in manufactured goods.

Slaves were a staple of Hellenistic trade. The wars provided prisoners for the slave market, and to a lesser extent so did kidnapping and capture by pirates. The number of slaves involved cannot be estimated, but there

HARBOR AND WAREHOUSES AT DELOS   During the Hellenistic period Delos became a thriving trading center. Shown here is the row of warehouses at water's edge. From Delos cargoes were shipped to virtually every part of the Mediterranean. (Photo: Caroline Buckler)

is no doubt that slavery flourished. Both the old Greek states and the new Hellenistic kingdoms were ready markets for slaves, as was Rome when it emerged triumphant from the Second Punic War (Chapter 7). The war took a huge toll of Italian manpower, and Rome bought slaves in vast numbers to replace them in the fields.

Throughout the Mediterranean world, slaves were almost always in demand. Only the Ptolemies discouraged both the trade and slavery itself, and they did so only for economic reasons. Their system had no room for slaves, who would only have competed with free labor. Otherwise, slave labor was to be found in the cities and temples of the Hellenistic world, in the factories and fields, and in the homes of wealthier people. In Italy and some parts of the East, slaves performed the manual labor for large estates and worked the mines. They were vitally important to the Hellenistic economy.

SCENE FROM DAILY LIFE   Art in the Hellenistic period often pursued two themes: increased realism and scenes from daily life. This statuette illustrates both themes. Either a peasant or a slave, the man carries a wine jar over his left shoulder and in his right hand a bag, perhaps his lunch. On his back is a basket. He is so heavily loaded that he is walking with difficulty. (Reproduced by Courtesy of the Trustees of the British Museum)

Although demand for goods increased during the Hellenistic period, no new techniques of production appear to have developed. The discoveries of Hellenistic mathematicians and thinkers failed to produce any significant corresponding technological development. Manual labor, not machinery, continued to turn out the raw materials and few manufactured goods the Hellenistic world used. Human labor was so cheap and so abundant that kings had no incentive to encourage the invention and manufacture of laborsaving machinery.

Perhaps only one noteworthy technological innovation dates to the Hellenistic period — the introduction of the Archimedean screw for pumping water out of mines. At Thoricus in Attica miners dug ore by hand and hauled it from the mines for processing. This was grueling work, and invariably miners were slaves, criminals, or forced laborers. The conditions under which they worked were frightful. At Laurium, which provided silver ore for the processing plant at Thoricus, one can still crawl into the labyrinthine shafts. They are narrow and have very low ceilings. The miners dug out the ore on their hands and knees; never did they have a chance to stand upright. Once a miner passed the entrance of the mine and crawled inside, his only light came from the oil lamp that he carried. Ventilation was poor, and the air must have been foul and stifling.

The Ptolemies ran their gold mines along the same harsh lines. One historian gave a grim picture of the miners' lives:

The kings of Egypt condemn [to the mines] those found guilty of wrong-doing and those taken prisoner in war, those who were victims of false accusations and were put into jail because of royal anger. . . . The condemned — and they are very many – all of them are put in chains, and they work persistently and continually, both by day and throughout the night, getting no rest, and carefully cut off from escape.[5]

The Ptolemies even condemned women and children to work in the mines. The strongest men lived and died swinging iron sledgehammers to break up the gold-bearing quartz rock. Others worked underground following the seams of quartz, men who labored with lamps bound to their foreheads and who were whipped by overseers if they slacked off. Once the diggers had cut out blocks of quartz, young boys gathered up the blocks and carried them outside. All of them – men, women, and boys – worked until they died.

Apart from gold and silver, which were used primarily for coins and jewelry, iron was the most important metal, and saw the most varied use. Even so, the method of its production never became very sophisticated. The Hellenistic Greeks did manage to produce a low-grade steel by adding carbon to iron.

Pottery remained an important commodity, and most of it was made locally. The pottery used in the kitchen, the coarse ware, did not change at all. Indeed, it is impossible to tell whether specimens of this type of pottery are Hellenic or Hellenistic. Fancier pots and bowls, decorated with a shiny black glaze, came into use during the Hellenistic period. This ware originated in Athens, but potters in other places began to imitate its style, heavily cutting into the Athenian market. In the second century B.C., a red-glazed ware, often called Samian, burst upon the market and soon dominated it. Athens still held its own, however, in the production of fine pottery. Despite the change in pottery styles, the method of production of all pottery, whether plain or fine, remained essentially unchanged.

Although new techniques of production and wider use of machinery in industry did not occur, the volume of goods produced increased in the Hellenistic period. Such goods were mostly made locally. Small manufacturing establishments existed in nearly all parts of the Hellenistic world.

AGRICULTURE

Hellenistic kings paid special attention to agriculture. Much of their revenue was derived from it: from the produce of royal lands, rents paid by the tenants of royal land, and taxation of agricultural land. Some Hellenistic kings even sought out and supported agricultural experts. The Ptolemies, for instance, sponsored experiments on seed grain, selecting seeds that seemed hardy and productive and trying to improve their characteristics. Hellenistic authors wrote handbooks that discussed how farms and large estates could be most profitably run. These handbooks described soil types, covered the proper times for planting and reaping, and discussed care of farm animals. Whether these efforts had any impact on the average farmer is difficult to determine.

The Ptolemies made the greatest strides in agriculture, but their success was largely political. Egypt had a strong tradition of central authority dating back to the pharaohs, which the Ptolemies inherited and tightened. They could decree what crops Egyptian farmers would plant and what animals would be raised, and they had the power to carry out their commands. The Ptolemies recognized the need for well-planned and constant irrigation, and much native labor went into the digging and maintenance of canals and ditches. The Ptolemies also reclaimed a great deal of land from the desert, including the Fayum, a dried lake bed.

The centralized authority of the Ptolemies

explains how agricultural advances occurred at the local level in Egypt. But such progress was not possible in any other Hellenistic monarchy. Despite royal interest in agriculture and a more studied approach to it in the Hellenistic period, there is no evidence that agricultural productivity increased. Whether Hellenistic agricultural methods had any influence on Eastern practices is unknown.

RELIGION IN THE HELLENISTIC WORLD

In religion Hellenism gave Easterners far less than the East gave the Greeks. At first the Hellenistic period saw the spread of Greek religious cults throughout the East. When Hellenistic kings founded cities, they also built temples and established new cults and priesthoods for the old Olympian gods. The new cults enjoyed the prestige of being the religion of the conquerors, and they were supported by public money.

The most attractive aspects of the Greek cults were their rituals and festivities. Greek cults sponsored literary, musical, and athletic contests, which were staged in beautiful surroundings among impressive Greek buildings. In short, the cults offered bright and lively entertainment, both intellectual and physical. They fostered Greek culture and traditional sports, and thus were a splendid means of displaying Greek civilization in the East.

Despite various advantages, Greek cults suffered from some severe shortcomings. They were primarily concerned with ritual. Participation in the civic cults did not even involve belief. Greeks and others could observe the rituals without believing in the existence of the deities being worshiped. Nor did civic cults impose an ethical code of conduct. Greeks did not have to follow any particular

rule of life, practice certain virtues, or even live decent lives in order to participate in the cults. On the whole, the civic cults neither appealed to religious emotions nor embraced matters such as sin and redemption. Greek mystery religions helped fill this gap, but the centers of these religions were in old Greece. Although the new civic cults were lavish in pomp and display, they could not satisfy deep religious feelings or spiritual yearnings.

Even though the Greeks participated in the new cults for cultural reasons, they felt little genuine religious attachment to them. In comparison to the emotional and sometimes passionate religions of the East, the Greek cults seemed sterile. Greeks increasingly sought solace from other sources. Educated and thoughtful people turned to philosophy as a guide to life, while others turned to superstition, magic, or astrology. Still others might shrug and speak of *Tyche,* which meant Fate or Chance.

In view of the spiritual decline of Greek religion, it is surprising that Eastern religions did not make more immediate headway among the Greeks, but at first they did not. Although Hellenistic Greeks clung to their own cults as expressions of their Greekness rather than for any ethical principles, they did not rush to embrace native religions. Only in the second century B.C., after a century of exposure to Eastern religions, did Greeks begin to adopt them.

Nor did Hellenistic kings make any effort to spread Greek religion among their Eastern subjects. The Greeks always considered religion a matter best left to the individual. Greek cults were attractive only to those socially aspiring Easterners who adopted Greek culture for personal advancement. Otherwise, Easterners were little affected by Greek religion. Nor did native religions suffer from the arrival of the Greeks. Some Hellenistic kings limited the power of native priesthoods, but

RELIGIOUS SYNCRETISM *This relief was found at the Greek outpost of Dura-Europus, located on the Euphrates. In the center sits Zeus Olympius-Baalshamin, a combination of a Greek and a Semitic god. The eastern priest at the left is burning incense on* *an altar, while the figure on the right in Macedonian dress crowns the god. Both the religious sentiments and the style of art show the meeting of East and West. (Yale University Art Gallery, Dura-Europos Collection)*

they also subsidized some Eastern cults with public money. Alexander the Great actually reinstated several Eastern cults that the Persians had suppressed.

The only significant junction of Greek and Eastern religious traditions was the growth and spread of new mystery religions, so called because they featured a body of ritual not to be divulged to anyone not initiated into the cult. The new mystery cults incorporated aspects of both Greek and Eastern religions, and had broad appeal for both Greeks and Easterners who yearned for personal immortality. Since the Greeks were already familiar with old mystery cults, such as the Eleusinian mys-

teries in Attica, the new cults did not strike them as alien or barbarian. Familiar too was the concept of preparation for an initiation. Devotees of the Eleusinian mysteries and other such cults had to prepare themselves mentally and physically before entering the presence of the gods. Thus the new mystery cults fit well with traditional Greek usage.

The new religions enjoyed one tremendous advantage over the old Greek mystery cults. Whereas old Greek mysteries were tied to particular places, such as Eleusis, the new religions spread throughout the Hellenistic world. People did not have to undertake long and expensive pilgrimages just to become

STATUE OF ISIS *Though originally Egyptian, Isis became a Greek goddess during the Hellenistic period. Her cult spread throughout the Hellenistic world, and she became identified with many purely Greek goddesses. Still popular in the Roman period, her cult profoundly influenced the Christian cult of Mary, the mother of Jesus. (Museo Nazionale, Naples)*

members of the religion. In that sense, the new mystery religions came to the people, for temples of the new deities sprang up wherever Greeks lived.

The mystery religions all claimed to save their adherents from the worst that Tyche could do, and they promised life for the soul after death. They all had a single concept in common: the belief that by the rites of initiation the devotees became united with the god, who had himself died and risen from the dead. The sacrifice of the god and his victory over death saved the devotee from eternal death. Similarly, all mystery religions demanded a period of preparation in which the convert strove to become holy – that is, to live by the precepts taught by the religion. Once aspirants had prepared themselves, they went through an initiation in which they learned the secrets of the religion. The initiation was usually a ritual of great emotional intensity, a baptism into a new life.

The Eastern mystery religions that took the Hellenistic world by storm were the Egyptian cults of Serapis and Isis. Serapis, who was invented by King Ptolemy, combined elements of the Egyptian god Osiris with aspects of the Greek gods Zeus, Pluto the prince of the underworld, and Asclepius. Serapis was believed to be the judge of souls, who rewarded virtuous and righteous people with eternal life. Like Asclepius he was a god of healing. Serapis became an international god, and many Hellenistic Greeks thought of him as Zeus. Associated with Isis and Serapis was Anubis, the old Egyptian god who, like Charon in the Greek pantheon, guided the souls of initiates to the realm of eternal life.

The cult of Isis enjoyed even wider appeal than that of Serapis. Isis, the wife of Osiris, claimed to have conquered Tyche, and promised to save any mortal who came to her. She became the most important goddess of the

Hellenistic world, and her worship was very popular among women. Her priests claimed that she bestowed upon humanity the gift of civilization and that she founded law and literature. She was the goddess of marriage, conception, and childbirth, and like Serapis a deity who promised to save the souls of her believers.

There was neither conflict between Greek and Eastern religions nor wholesale acceptance of one or the other. Nonetheless, the Hellenistic world was slowly moving toward belief in a single god who ruled over all people. Greeks and Easterners noticed similarities among one another's deities and assumed that they were worshiping the same gods in different garb. These tendencies toward religious universalism and the desire for personal immortality would prove significant when the Hellenistic world came under the sway of Rome, for Hellenistic developments paved the way for the spread of Christianity.

PHILOSOPHY AND THE COMMON MAN

Philosophy during the Hellenic period was the exclusive province of the wealthy, for only they had leisure enough to pursue philosophical studies. During the Hellenistic period, however, philosophy reached out to touch the lives of more men and women than ever before. The reasons for this development were several. Since the ideal of the polis had declined, politics no longer offered people an intellectual outlet. Moreover, much of Hellenistic life, especially in the new cities of the East, seemed unstable and without venerable traditions. Greeks were far more mobile than they had ever been before, but their very mobility left them feeling uprooted. Many people

in search of something permanent, something unchanging in a changing world, turned to philosophy. Another reason for the increased influence of philosophy was the decline of traditional religion and a growing belief in Tyche. Tyche was more than Fate – it was Chance and Doom, capricious and sometimes malevolent. To protect against the worst that Tyche could do, many Greeks looked to philosophy.

Philosophers themselves became much more numerous, and several new schools of philosophical thought emerged. The Cynics preached the joy of a simple life. The Epicureans taught that pleasure is the chief good. The Stoics emphasized the importance of deeds well done. There was a good deal of rivalry as philosophers tried to demonstrate the superiority of their views, but in spite of their differences the major branches of philosophy agreed on the necessity of making people self-sufficient. They all recognized the need to equip men and women to deal successfully with Tyche. The major schools of Hellenistic philosophy all taught that people could be truly happy only when they had turned their backs on the world around them and focused full attention on one enduring thing. They differed chiefly on what that enduring thing was.

CYNICS

Undoubtedly the most unusual of the new philosophers were the Cynics, who urged a return to nature. They advised men and women to discard traditional customs and conventions (which were in decline anyway) and to live simply. The Cynics believed that by rejecting material things people become free, and that nature will provide all necessities.

The founder of the Cynics was Antisthenes

(b. ca 440 B.C.), but it was Diogenes of Sinope (ca 412–323 B.C.), one of the most colorful men of the period, who spread the philosophy. Diogenes came to Athens to study philosophy and soon evolved his own ideas on the ideal life. He hit upon the solution that happiness was possible only by living according to nature and forgoing luxuries. He attacked social conventions because he considered them contrary to nature. Throughout Greece he gained fame for the rigorous way in which he put his beliefs into practice.

Diogenes' disdain for luxury and social pretense also became legendary. Once when he was living at Corinth, he was supposedly visited by Alexander the Great: "While Diogenes was sunning himself . . . Alexander stood over him and said: 'Ask me whatever gift you like.' In answer Diogenes said to him: 'Get out of my sunlight.' "[6] The story underlines the essence of Diogenes' teachings: even a great, powerful, and wealthy conqueror like Alexander could give people nothing of any real value. Nature had already provided people with everything essential.

Diogenes did not establish a philosophical school in the manner of Plato and Aristotle. Instead, he and his followers took their teaching to the streets and marketplaces. They more than any other philosophical group tried to reach the common man. As part of their return to nature they often did without warm clothing, sufficient food, or adequate housing, which they considered unnecessary. The Cynics also tried to break down political barriers by declaring that people owed no allegiance to any city or monarchy. Rather, they said, all people are cosmopolitan – that is, citizens of the world. The Cynics reached across political boundaries to create a community of people, all sharing their humanity and living as close to nature as humanly possible. The Cynics set a striking example of

how people could turn away from materialism. Although comparatively few men and women could follow such rigorous precepts, the Cynics influenced all the other major schools of philosophy.

EPICUREANS

Epicurus (340–270 B.C.), who founded his own school of philosophy at Athens, based his view of life on scientific theories. Accepting Democritus' theory that the universe is composed of indestructible particles, Epicurus put forth a naturalistic theory of the universe. Although he did not deny the existence of the gods, he taught that they had no effect on human life. The essence of Epicurus' belief was that the principal good of human life is pleasure, which he defined as the absence of pain. He was not advocating drunken revels or sensual dissipation, which he thought actually caused pain. Instead, Epicurus concluded that any violent emotion is undesirable. Drawing on the teachings of the Cynics, he advocated mild self-discipline. Even poverty he considered good, as long as people have enough food, clothing, and shelter. Epicurus also taught that individuals can most easily attain peace and serenity by ignoring the outside world and looking into their personal feelings and reactions. Thus Epicureanism led to quietism.

Epicureanism taught its followers to ignore politics and the issues of the day, for politics led to tumult, which would disturb the soul. Although the Epicureans thought that the state originated through a social contract among individuals, they did not care about the political structure of the state. They were content to live in a democracy, oligarchy, monarchy, or whatever, and they never speculated about the ideal state. Their very ideals stood outside all political forms.

Opposed to the passivity of the Epicureans, Zeno (335–262 B.C.), a Hellenized Phoenician, put forth a different concept of human beings and the universe. When Zeno first came to Athens, he listened avidly to the Cynics. Concluding, however, that the Cynics were extreme, he stayed in Athens to form his own school, the Stoa, named after the building where he preferred to teach.

Stoicism became the most popular philosophy of the Hellenistic world, and the one that later captured the mind of Rome. Zeno and his followers considered nature an expression of divine will, and in their view people could be happy only when they lived in accordance with nature. They stressed the unity of man and the universe, stating that all men were brothers and obliged to help one another. Stoicism's science was derived from Heraclitus, but its broad and warm humanity was the work of Zeno and his followers.

Unlike the Epicureans, the Stoics taught that people should participate in politics and worldly affairs. Yet this idea never led to the belief that individuals ought to try to change the order of things. Time and again the Stoics used the image of an actor in a play: the Stoic plays an assigned part and never tries to change the play. To the Stoics the important question was not whether they achieved anything, but whether they lived virtuous lives. In that way they could triumph over Tyche: for Tyche could destroy achievements but not the goodness and nobility of their lives.

Even though the Stoics evolved the concept of a world order, they thought of it strictly in terms of the individual. Like the Epicureans, they were indifferent to specific political forms. They believed that people should do their duty to the state in which they found themselves. The universal state they preached about was ethical, not political. The most significant practical achievement of the Stoics was the creation of the concept of natural law. The Stoics concluded that since all men were brothers, since all men partook of divine reason, and since all good men were in harmony with the universe, one law – a part of the natural order of life – governed them all.

The Stoic concept of a universal state governed by natural law is one of the finest heirlooms the Hellenistic world passed on to Rome. The Stoic concept of natural law, of one law for all people, became a valuable tool when the Romans began to deal with many different peoples with different laws. The ideal of the universal state gave the Romans a rationale for extending their empire to the farthest reaches of the world. The duty of individuals to their fellows served the citizens of the Roman Empire as the philosophical justification for doing their duty. In this respect, too, the real fruit of Hellenism was to ripen only under the cultivation of Rome.

HELLENISTIC WOMEN

With the growth of monarchy in the Hellenistic period came a major new development: the importance of royal women, many of whom played an active part in political and diplomatic life. In the Hellenic period the polis had replaced kingship, except at Sparta, and queens were virtually unknown, apart from myth and legend. Even in Sparta queens did not participate in politics. Hellenistic queens, however, did exercise political power, either in their own right or by manipulating their husbands. Many Hellenistic queens were depicted as willful or ruthless, especially in power struggles over the throne, and in some cases those charges are accurate. Other Hel-

lenistic royal women, however, set an example of courage and nobility. This is especially true of Cratesiclea, mother of the king Cleomenes.

In 224 B.C., Cleomenes was trying to rebuild Sparta as a major power, but he needed money. King Ptolemy of Egypt promised to help the Spartans because doing so would further his own diplomatic ends. In return for his support Ptolemy demanded that Cleomenes give him his mother, Cratesiclea, as a hostage. Ptolemy's demand was an insult and a grave dishonor to the Spartan lady, yet Cleomenes' plans could not succeed without Ptolemy's money. Reluctant to agree to Ptolemy's terms, Cleomenes was also reluctant to mention the matter to his mother. Plutarch related her reaction:

Finally, when Cleomenes worked up his courage to speak about the matter, Cratesiclea laughed aloud and said: "Is this what you often started to say but flinched from? Rather put me aboard a ship and send me away, wherever you think this body of mine will be most useful to Sparta, before sitting here it is destroyed by old age."[7]

Cratesiclea's selflessness and love of her state became legendary. Other Hellenistic queens and women of royal blood demonstrated the same qualities of self-sacrifice and devotion to duty.

The example of the queens had a profound effect on Hellenistic attitudes toward women in general. In fact, the Hellenistic period saw a great expansion in social and economic opportunities for women. More women than ever before received educations that enabled them to enter the professions and medicine. As the American scholar Sarah Pomeroy has observed: "The serious pursuit of intellectual, artistic, or scientific goals, as an addition, or as a prelude, or even as an alternative to marriage, was a new phenomenon for Greek women."[8] Literacy among women increased dramatically, and their options expanded accordingly. Some won fame as poets, while others studied with philosophers and contributed to the intellectual life of the age. As a rule, however, these developments touched only wealthier women. Poor women, and probably the majority of women, were barely literate, if literate at all.

Women began to participate in politics on at least a limited basis. Often they served as priestesses, as they had in the Hellenic period, but they also began to serve in civil capacities. For their services to the state they received public acknowledgment. Women sometimes received honorary citizenship from foreign cities because of aid given in times of crisis. Few women achieved these honors, however, and those who did were from the upper classes.

This major development was not due to male enlightenment. Although Hellenistic philosophy addressed itself to many new questions, the position of women was not one of them. The Stoics, in spite of their theory of the brotherhood of man, thought of women as men's inferiors. Only the Cynics, who waged war on all accepted customs, treated women as men's equals. The Cynics were interested in women as individuals, not as members of a family or as citizens of the state. Their view did not make much headway. Like other aspects of Cynic philosophy, this attitude was more admired than followed.

The new prominence of women was largely due instead to their increased participation in economic affairs. During the Hellenistic period some women took part in commercial transactions. Nonetheless, they still lived under legal handicaps. In Egypt, for example, a Greek woman needed a male guardian to buy, sell, or lease land, to borrow money, and to represent her in other transactions. Yet often such a guardian was present only to fulfill the letter of the law. The woman was the real agent, and she handled the business being transacted. In Hellenistic Sparta women accumulated large fortunes and vast amounts of land. As early as the beginning of the Hellenistic period women owned two-fifths of the land of Laconia. Spartan women, however, were exceptional. In most other areas, even women who were very wealthy in their own right were at least formally under the protection of a male relative.

These changes do not amount to a social revolution. Women had begun to participate in business, politics, and legal activities. Yet such women were rare, and they labored under handicaps that men did not have. Even so, it was a start.

HELLENISTIC SCIENCE

The area in which Hellenistic culture achieved its greatest triumphs was science. Here too the ancient Near East made contributions to Greek thought. The patient observations of the Babylonians, who for generations had scanned the skies, had provided the raw materials for Thales' speculations, which were the foundation of Hellenistic astronomy. The most notable of the Hellenistic astronomers was Aristarchus of Samos (ca. 310–230 B.C.), who was educated in Aristotle's school. Aristarchus concluded that the sun is far larger than the earth and that the stars are enormously distant from the earth. He argued against Aristotle's view that the earth is the center of the universe. Instead, Aristarchus propounded the heliocentric theory – that is, that the earth and the planets revolve around the sun. His work is all the more impressive because he lacked even a rudimentary telescope. Aristarchus had only the human eye and the human brain, but they were more than enough.

Unfortunately, Aristarchus' theories did not persuade the ancient world. In the second century A.D., Claudius Ptolemy, a mathematician and astronomer in Alexandria, accepted Aristotle's theory of the earth as the center of the universe, and their view prevailed for 1400 years. Aristarchus' heliocentric theory lay dormant until resurrected by the brilliant Polish astronomer Nicolaus Copernicus (1473–1543).

In geometry Hellenistic thinkers discovered little that was new, but Euclid (ca 300 B.C.), a mathematician who lived in Alexandria, compiled a valuable textbook of existing knowledge. His book, *The Elements of Geometry,* has exerted immense influence on Western civilization, for it rapidly became the standard introduction to geometry. Generations of students, from the Hellenistic period to the present day, have learned the essentials of geometry from it.

The greatest thinker of the Hellenistic period was Archimedes (ca 287–212 B.C.), who was a clever inventor as well. He lived in Syracuse in Sicily and watched Rome emerge as a power in the Mediterranean. When the Romans laid siege to Syracuse in the Second Punic War (see Chapter 7), Archimedes invented a number of machines to thwart the Roman army. His catapults threw rocks large enough to sink ships and disrupt battle lines. His grappling devices lifted warships out of the water. The Romans developed a healthy respect for Archimedes, as Plutarch reports: "At last the Romans were so terrified . . . that if a small piece of rope or a small timber was seen protruding from the walls, they bellowed

'There's the thing; Archimedes is unleashing some machine against us,' and turned around and fled."[9]

In the Hellenistic period the practical applications of the principles of mechanics were primarily military, for the building of artillery and siege engines. Archimedes built such machines out of necessity, but they were of little real interest to him. In a more peaceful vein, he invented the Archimedean screw, a device used to pump water into irrigation ditches and out of mines. He also invented the compound pulley. Plutarch described Archimedes' dramatic demonstration of how easily it could move huge weights with little effort:

A three-masted merchant ship of the royal fleet had been hauled on land by hard work and many hands. Archimedes put aboard her many men and the usual freight. He sat far away from her; without haste, but gently working a compound pulley with his hand, he drew her towards him smoothly and without faltering, just as though she were running on the surface of the sea.[10]

Archimedes was far more interested in pure mathematics than in practical inventions. His mathematical research, which covered many fields, was his greatest contribution to Western thought. In his book *On Plane Equilibriums* Archimedes dealt for the first time with the basic principles of mechanics, including the principle of the lever. He once said that if he were given a lever and a suitable place to stand, he could move the world. In his treatise *Sand-Counter* Archimedes devised a system to express large numbers, a difficult matter considering the deficiencies of Greek numerical notation. *Sand-Counter* also discussed the heliocentric theory of Aristarchus. With his treatise *On Floating Bodies* Archimedes founded the science of hydrostatics. He concluded that whenever a solid floats in a liquid, the weight of the solid is equal to the volume of liquid displaced. The way in which he made his discovery has become famous:

When he was devoting his attention to this problem, he happened to go to a public bath. When he climbed down into the bathtub there, he noticed that water in the tub equal to the bulk of his body flowed out. Thus, when he observed this method of solving the problem, he did not wait. Instead, moved with joy, he sprang out of the tub, and rushing home naked he kept indicating in a loud voice that he had indeed discovered what he was seeking. For while running he was shouting repeatedly in Greek, "eureka, eureka" ("I have found it, I have found it").[11]

Archimedes' other works include *On the Measurement of a Circle, On the Sphere and Cylinder, On Conoids and Spheroids,* and *On Spirals.*

Archimedes was willing to share his work, and one of those with whom he communicated was Eratosthenes (285–ca 204 B.C.), a man of almost universal interests. From his native Cyrene in North Africa, Eratosthenes traveled to Athens, where he studied philosophy and learned mathematics. He refused to join any of the philosophical schools, for he was interested in too many things to follow any particular dogma. Hence, his thought was eclectic: he took his doctrines from many schools of thought. For instance, in philosophy Eratosthenes was influenced by Zeno, but Stoicism could not satisfy his mathematical and geographical interests. Besides his scientific work, he devoted time to poetry, in which he showed genuine talent, and he wrote a book on Attic comedy.

Around 245 B.C., King Ptolemy invited Eratosthenes to Alexandria. The Ptolemies had done much to make Alexandria an intellectual, cultural, and scientific center. They had established a lavish library and museum,

undoubtedly the greatest seat of learning in the Hellenistic world. At the crown's expense, the Ptolemies maintained a number of distinguished scholars and poets. Eratosthenes came to Alexandria to become the librarian of the royal library, a position of great prestige. While there he continued his mathematical work and by letter struck up a friendship with Archimedes. Eratosthenes solved the problem of how to double a cube, built a machine to illustrate his proof, and in a short poem dedicated his work to King Ptolemy.

Unlike his friend Archimedes, Eratosthenes did not devote his life entirely to mathematics, although he never lost interest in it. He used his mathematics to further the geographical studies for which he is most famous. He calculated the circumference of the earth geometrically, estimating it as about 24,675 miles. He was not wrong by much: the earth is actually 24,860 miles in circumference. Of this achievement Carl Sagan, the noted contemporary astronomer, has said:

Eratosthenes' only tools were sticks, eyes, feet, and brains, plus a taste for experiment. With them he deduced the circumference of the earth with an error of only a few percent, a remarkable achievement for 2,200 years ago. He was the first person accurately to measure the size of a planet.[12]

Eratosthenes also concluded that the earth is a spherical globe, that the landmass is roughly foursided, and that the land is surrounded by ocean. He discussed the shapes and sizes of land and ocean and the irregularities of the earth's surface. He drew a map of the earth and used his own system of explaining the divisions of the earth's landmass.

Using geographical information gained by Alexander the Great's scientists, Eratosthenes tried to fit the East into Greek geographical knowledge. Although for some reason he ignored the western Mediterranean and Europe, he declared that a ship could sail from Spain either around Africa to India or directly westward to India. Not until the great days of Western exploration did sailors such as Vasco da Gama and Magellan actually prove Eratosthenes' theories. Greek geographers like Eratosthenes also turned their attention southward to Africa. During this period the people of the Mediterranean learned of the climate and customs of Ethiopia, and gleaned some scant information about equatorial Africa.

In his life and work Eratosthenes exemplifies the range and vitality of Hellenistic science. His interests were varied and included the cultural and humanistic as well as the purely scientific. Although his chief interest was in the realm of speculative thought, he did not ignore the practical. He was quite willing to deal with old problems and to break new ground.

In the Hellenistic period the scientific study of botany had its origin. Aristotle's pupil Theophrastus (ca 372–288 B.C.), who became head of the Lyceum, the school established by Aristotle, studied the botanical information made available by Alexander's penetration of the East. Aristotle had devoted a good deal of his attention to zoology, and Theophrastus extended his work to plants. He wrote two books on the subject, *History of Plants* and *Causes of Plants*. He carefully observed phenomena and based his conclusions on what he had actually seen. Theophrastus classified plants and accurately described their parts. He detected the process of germination and realized the importance of climate and soil to plants. Some of Theophrastus' work found its way into agricultural handbooks, but for the most part Hellenistic science did not carry the study of botany any further.

HELLENISTIC MEDICINE

The study of medicine flourished during the Hellenistic period, and Hellenistic physicians carried the work of Hippocrates into new areas. Herophilus, who lived in the first half of the third century B.C., worked at Alexandria and studied the writings of Hippocrates. He accepted Hippocrates' theory of the four humors, and approached the study of medicine in a systematic, scientific fashion. He dissected dead bodies and measured what he observed. He discovered the nervous system and concluded that two types of nerves, motor and sensory, exist. Herophilus also studied the brain, which he considered the center of intelligence, and discerned the cerebrum and cerebellum. His other work dealt with the liver, lungs, and uterus. His younger contemporary, Erasistratus, also conducted research on the brain and the nervous system, and he improved on Herophilus' work. He too followed in the tradition of Hippocrates and preferred to let the body heal itself by means of diet and air.

Both Herophilus and Erasistratus were members of the Dogmatic school of medicine at Alexandria. In this school speculation played an important part in research. So too did the study of anatomy. To learn more about human anatomy Herophilus and Erasistratus dissected corpses and even vivisected criminals whom King Ptolemy contributed for the purpose. Vivisection – cutting into the body of a living animal or person – was seen as a necessary cruelty: the Dogmatists argued that the knowledge gained from the suffering of a few evil men benefited many others. Nonetheless, the practice of vivisection seems to have been short-lived, although dissection continued. Better knowledge of anatomy led to improvements in surgery. These advances enabled the Dogmatists to invent new surgical instruments and new techniques.

In about 280 B.C., Philinus and Serapion, two pupils of Herophilus, led a reaction to the Dogmatists. Believing that the Dogmatists had become too speculative, they founded the Empiric school of medicine at Alexandria. Claiming that the Dogmatists' emphasis on anatomy and physiology was misplaced, they concentrated instead on the observation and cure of illnesses. They also laid heavier stress on the use of drugs and medicine to treat illnesses. Heraclides of Tarentum (perhaps first century B.C.) carried on the Empirical tradition and dedicated himself to observation and use of medicines. He discovered the benefits of opium and worked with other drugs that relieved pain. He also steadfastly rejected magic and sorcery as pertinent to the application of drugs and medicines.

Hellenistic medicine had its dark side, for many physicians were moneygrubbers, fools, and quacks. One of the angriest complaints comes from the days of the Roman Empire:

Of all men only a physician can kill a man with total impunity. Oh no, on the contrary, censure goes to him who dies and he is guilty of excess, and furthermore he is blamed. . . . Let me not accuse their [physicians'] avarice, their greedy deals with those whose fate hangs in the balance, their setting a price on pain, and their demands for down payment in case of death, and their secret doctrines.[13]

Abuses such as these existed already in the Hellenistic period. As is true today, many Hellenistic physicians did not take the Hippocratic oath very seriously.

Besides incompetent and greedy physicians, the Hellenistic world was plagued by people who claimed to cure illnesses through incantations and magic. Their potions included such concoctions as blood from the ear of an ass mixed with water to cure fever, or the liver of a cat, killed when the moon was waning, and preserved in salt. Broken bones could be cured by applying the ashes of a pig's jawbone to the break. The dung of a goat mixed with old wine was good for healing broken ribs. One charlatan claimed that he could cure epilepsy by making the patient drink, from the skull of a man who had been killed but not cremated, water drawn from a spring at night. These quacks even claimed that they could cure mental illness with their remedies. The treatment for a person suffering from melancholy was calf dung boiled in wine. No doubt the patient became too sick to be depressed.

Quacks who prescribed such treatments were very popular, but they did untold harm to the sick and injured. They and the greedy physicians also damaged the reputation of dedicated doctors who honestly and intelligently tried to heal and alleviate pain. The medical abuses that arose in the Hellenistic period were so flagrant that the Romans who later entered the Hellenistic world developed an intense dislike and distrust of physicians. The Romans considered the study of Hellenistic medicine beneath the dignity of a Roman, and even as late as the Roman Empire few Romans undertook the study of Greek medicine. Nonetheless, the work of men like Herophilus and Serapion made valuable contributions to the knowledge of medicine, and the fruits of their work were preserved and handed on to the West.

———◆———

The Hellenistic period fostered the spread of Hellenism throughout the East, disseminating the knowledge, customs, and laws of the Greeks and bringing East and West into intimate contact. Though often called degenerate and stagnant, the Hellenistic period could boast of numerous advances, especially in the sciences and medicine. Hellenistic thinkers created a golden age of scientific discovery and speculation, while Hellenistic philosophy reached out to touch the lives of rich and poor, princes and peasants.

The Hellenistic period also prepared the way for Rome. Although the Hellenistic monarchies, like the Greek city-states, fought to a standstill and seriously weakened each other, they made something new of the East. Greek and Easterner alike changed the East, and into this world Rome moved. Rome brought political stability and Roman law, but in doing so it built upon the society and culture created by Hellenistic men and women.

Notes

1. Diodorus 17.1.4.

2. Plutarch *Moralia* 328E.

3. Quoted in W. W. Tarn and G. T. Griffith, *Hellenistic Civilisation,* Meridian Books, Cleveland and New York, 1961, p. 199.

4. *Periplous of the Erythraian Sea* 57.

5. Diodorus 3.12.2–3.

6. Diogenes Laertius 6.38.

7. Plutarch *Lives of Agis and Cleomenes* 22.5.

8. S. B. Pomeroy, "Technikai kai Mousikai," *American Journal of Ancient History* 2 (1977): 51.

9. Plutarch *Life of Marcellus* 17.4.

10. Ibid., 14.13.

11. Vitruvius *On Architecture* 9 Preface, 10.

12. Carl Sagan, "The Measure of Eratosthenes," *Harvard Magazine* 83 (1980): 10.

13. Pliny the Elder *Natural History* 29.8.18, 21.

Suggested Reading

General treatments of Hellenistic political, social, and economic history can be found in S. A. Cook, et al., *The Cambridge Ancient History,* vol. 7 (1928), and in the shorter and handier works of M. Cary, *A History of the Greek World 323–146 B.C.,* 2nd ed. (1951), and W. W. Tarn and G. T. Griffith, *Hellenistic Civilisation,* 3rd ed. (1951, 1961). M. M. Austin, *The Hellenistic World from Alexander to the Roman Conquest* (1981) is an excellent selection of primary sources in an accurate and readable translation. F. W. Walbank, *The Hellenistic World* (1981) is a fresh new appraisal by one of the foremost scholars of the period. The undisputed classic in this field is M. Rostovtzeff, *The Social and Economic History of the Hellenistic World,* 3 vols. (1941).

Each year brings a new crop of biographies of Alexander the Great. Still the best, however, is J. R. Hamilton, *Alexander the Great* (1973). Old but still useful is U. Wilcken, *Alexander the Great* (English translation, 1967), which has had a considerable impact on scholars and students alike. On the topic of Alexander's place in history, see A. R. Burn, *Alexander the Great and the Hellenistic World* (1947), a lively and sane treatment. Newer is C. B. Welles, *Alexander and the Hellenistic World* (1970). Recent political studies of the Hellenistic period include G. J. D. Aalders, *Political Theory in Hellenistic Times* (1975), and E. V. Hansen, *The Attalids of Pergamon,* 2nd ed. (1971).

On the spread of Hellenism throughout the Near East, see F. E. Peters, *The Harvest of Hellenism* (1970), and most recently, A. Momigliano, *Alien Wisdom: The Limits of Hellenization* (1975).

A. H. M. Jones, *The Greek City from Alexander to Justinian* (1940), deals with urban life during the Hellenistic, Roman, and early Byzantine periods. P. M. Fraser, *Ptolemaic Alexandria,* 3 vols. (1972), covers the life, history, and culture of the most flourishing and prominent of the Hellenistic cities. G. Downey, *A History of Antioch in Syria from Seleucus to the Arab Conquest* (1961), gives a good account of a major city in Asia Minor. Hellenistic Athens is described by C. Mossé, *Athens in Decline, 404–86 B.C.* (1973). G. M. Cohen, *The Seleucid Colo-*

nies (1978), treats all aspects of the Seleucid colonizing effort.

Two general studies of religion within the Hellenistic world are F. Grant, *Hellenistic Religion: The Age of Syncretism* (1953), and H. J. Rose, *Religion in Greece and Rome* (1959). For the effects of Hellenistic religious developments on Christianity, see A. D. Nock, *Early Gentile Christianity and Its Hellenistic Background* (1964). V. Tscherikover, *Hellenistic Civilization and the Jews* (1959) treats the impact of Hellenism on Judaism, and R. E. Witt, *Isis in the Graeco-Roman World* (1971), which is illustrated, studies the origins and growth of the Isis cult. The cult of her consort Osiris is the subject of J. G. Griffiths, *The Origins of Osiris and His Cult* (1980).

Hellenistic philosophy and science have attracted the attention of a number of scholars, and the various philosophical schools are especially well covered. A convenient survey of Hellenistic philosophy is A. A. Long, *Hellenistic Philosophy* (1974). F. Sayre, *The Greek Cynics* (1948), focuses on Diogenes' thought and manners, while C. Bailey, *Epicureans* (1926), although dated, is still a useful study of the origins and nature of Epicureanism. Two recent treatments of Stoicism are J. Rist, *Stoic Philosophy* (1969), and F. H. Sandbach, *The Stoics* (1975). A good survey of Hellenistic science is G. E. R. Lloyd, *Greek Science after Aristotle* (1963), and specific studies of major figures can be found in T. L. Heath's solid work, *Aristarchus of Samos* (1920), still unsurpassed, and E. J. Dijksterhuis, *Archimedes* (1956).

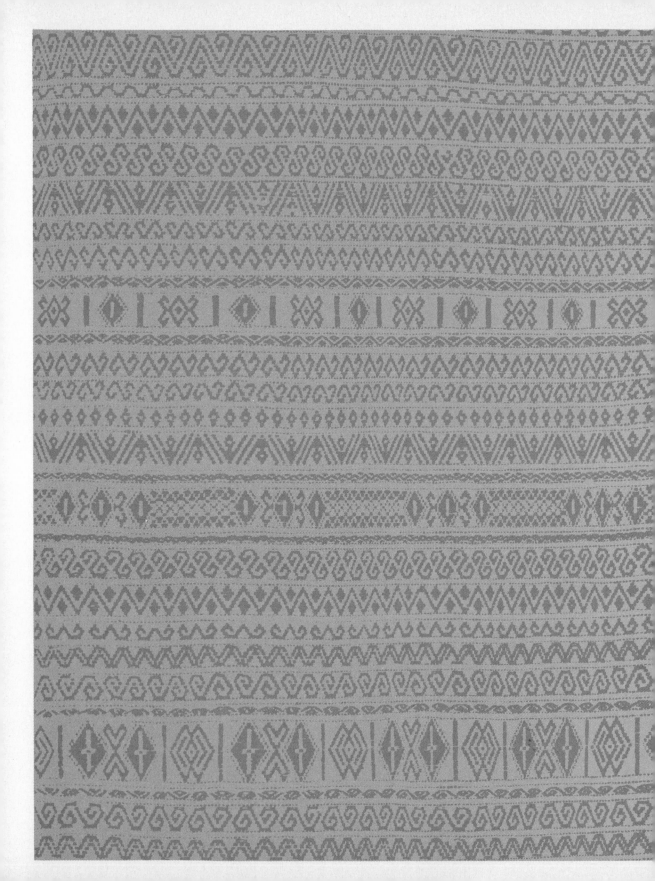

CHAPTER 5

INDIA AND CHINA TO

CA 250 B.C.

WHILE THE GREEKS were spreading their culture and political system throughout the Mediterranean basin, people in India and China were wrestling with similar problems – taming the land, improving agricultural techniques, building cities and urban cultures, and asking basic questions about social organization and the nature of human life.

No single explanation can account for these simultaneous developments, but some similarities are striking. At first glance, the three regions appear far from similar geographically. The Mediterranean basin is a region of mountains and small valleys linked by the sea. Far different are India and China, where large undeveloped and underpopulated tracts of land lay open to Neolithic pioneers. Yet these areas shared certain geographical features that permitted the spread of a common culture. Within each, regional differences in religion, language, and customs flourished, but in all three areas these differences were variations of a pervasive and shared civilization. Agricultural exploitation of the land promoted population increase, and the demands of metal technology encouraged wider contacts within each region.

How did the ancient Indians and Chinese respond to many of the same problems that the people of the Mediterranean were confronting? How did they meet the challenge of the land itself? What kinds of social organization developed in India and China, and what intellectual and religious values did these civilizations generate? These questions will be the central concern of this chapter.

INDIA, THE LAND AND ITS FIRST TAMERS

Ancient India – which encompassed modern Pakistan, Nepal, and part of Afghanistan as well as the modern state of India – was a geographically protected and relatively self-contained land, though regionally highly variable. The subcontinent of India, a land mass as large as western Europe, juts southward into the warm waters of the Indian Ocean. India is a land of contrasts. Some regions are among the wettest on earth; others are dry and even arid desert and scrub land. High mountain ranges in the north drop off to the low river valleys of the Indus and Ganges. These geographical variations greatly influenced the pattern of human development within India.

Three regions of India are of overriding geographical significance: the ring of mountains in the north that separates India from its neighbors, the great river valleys of the Indus and Ganges and their tributaries, and the southern peninsula, especially the narrow coastal plains and the larger Deccan Plateau. The lower reaches of the Himalaya Mountains – the northern geographical boundary of the subcontinent – are covered by some of India's densest forests, sustained by heavy rainfall. Immediately to the south the land drops away to the fertile river valleys of the Indus and Ganges. These lowland plains, which stretch all the way across the subcontinent, are the most fertile parts of India. Here Indian agriculture has traditionally flourished. South of these valleys rise the Vindhya Mountains and the dry, hilly plateau of the Deccan. Only along the coasts do the hills give way to narrow plains. In short, geography set India off from its neighbors, and simultaneously divided the country into many subregions, some of them huge, fertile, and capable of sustaining large and vigorous populations.

The Himalayas, which in many places exceed 25,000 feet in height, protected ancient India from wandering peoples in search of new lands to settle. The Indian Ocean, later a busy avenue to the outside world, served throughout much of antiquity as an immense moat, keeping out invaders while fostering maritime trade with both the Near East and China. Only in the northwest – the area between modern Afghanistan and Pakistan – was India accessible to outsiders. This region, penetrated by the famous Khyber Pass, has traditionally been the highway of invaders – a highway whose other terminus was the flourishing cultures of the ancient Near East. Thus geography segregated India, but it also made possible contact with the ideas, practices, and technology of mankind's earliest civilizations.

The Himalayas shield the subcontinent from the northern cold. They also hold in the monsoon rains that sweep northward from the Indian Ocean each summer. The monsoons in the south and the melting snows of the Himalayas in the north provide India with most of its water. In some areas the resulting moistness and humidity created vast tracts of jungle and swamp; the Ganges was a particularly forbidding region, and only gradually did settlers move there from the tamer west. Much of India, however, is not blessed with abundant water: instead of jungle, the environment is subtropical and dry. In general, the monsoon area of southeastern India experiences the heaviest rainfall, while the driest region is the northwest. Geography and climate, and especially good water resources, combined to make the Punjab and the valley of the Indus River – now in Pakistan – the most attractive regions for India's first settlers, who created the earliest Indian civilization.

THE INDUS CIVILIZATION
(CA 2500–1500 B.C.)

The story of the first civilization in India, known as the Indus civilization, is one of the most dramatic in the entire ancient world. In 1921 archaeologists discovered completely unexpected and astonishing evidence of a thriving and sophisticated urban culture dating to about 2500 B.C. Until that time India had been the home of primitive tribes of hunters and food gatherers; then some newcomers began to develop a truly revolutionary way of life. About the tantalizing problem of the origin of the Indus civilization, the eminent English archaeologist Sir Mortimer Wheeler has commented:

By the middle of the 3rd millennium, something very important was happening in the Indus valley, and happening probably at great speed. Then or rather earlier, certain of the little communities in the Baluch foothills [of modern Pakistan] were emboldened to experiment. Who the first leaders were who led their people, however hesitantly, down to the wide and jungle-ridden plain we shall never know, nor why they ventured; but they were bold men, pioneers in the fullest sense, no mere ejects from the highland zone. Some, perhaps many of them, led forlorn hopes and perished. . . . Seemingly the attempted colonization of the valley continued intermittently, failure succeeding failure, until at last a leader, more determined and far-sighted and fortunate than the rest, won through.[1]

These hardy adventurers created an urban culture based on large-scale agriculture. Like the Mesopotamian city, the Indian city was surrounded by the extensive farmland that fed its inhabitants. These pioneers also developed a script, which is still undeciphered. Contact was early and frequent between the Indus civilization and the great cultures of Mesopotamia. As early as the reign of Sargon of Akkad in the third millennium B.C. (pages 14–15), trade between India and Mesopotamia carried goods and ideas between the two cultures, probably by way of the Persian Gulf.

The Indus civilization extended over fully 1.25 million square kilometers in the Indus valley, an area that exceeded the boundaries of modern Pakistan. Its two best-known cities were Mohenjo-daro in southern Pakistan and

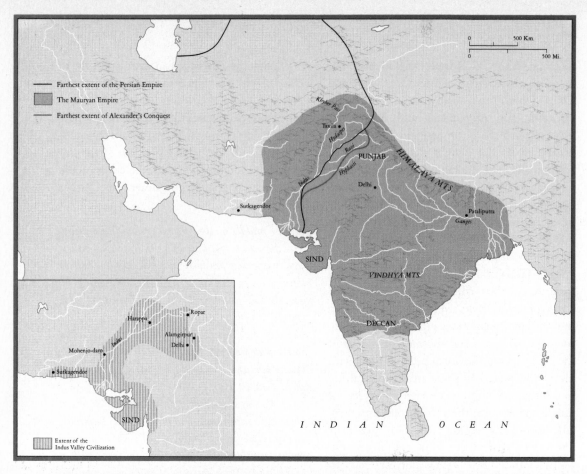

Legend:
- Farthest extent of the Persian Empire
- The Mauryan Empire
- Farthest extent of Alexander's Conquest

Map labels: Khyber Pass, Taxila, Hydaspes, Ravi, PUNJAB, HIMALAYA MTS., Indus, Hyphasis, Delhi, Pataliputra, Ganges, Sutkagendor, SIND, VINDHYA MTS., DECCAN, INDIAN OCEAN

Inset labels: Harappa, Ropar, Alamgirpur, Delhi, Indus, Mohenjo-daro, Sutkagendor, SIND

- Extent of the Indus Valley Civilization

MAP 5.1 THE DEVELOPMENT OF INDIA, CA 2500–CA 250 B.C. *This map shows the development of India from the days of the Indus Valley civilization to the reign of Ashoka. Although northwestern* *India might fall to foreign conquerors like the Persians or Alexander the Great, most of India was unscathed by these incursions. Ashoka created the first real Indian empire.*

Harappa some four hundred miles to the north in the Punjab. Other sites have since been found in southern Pakistan, at Sutkagendor in the west, as far east as Alamgirpur near modern Delhi, and as far north as Ropar (see Map 5.1). Numerous sites are still being excavated, and a full portrait of this vast civilization will have to await their findings. It is already clear, however, that the Indus civilization was marked by a striking uniformity of culture, and simultaneously by marked regional variation.

Some important new linguistic work has suggested that other peoples were also filtering into India from western Asia while the Indus civilization was flourishing. The ancestors of the Dravidians, who are usually considered natives of central and southern India, probably moved through the Indus valley at about this time. In short, the movement of ancient peoples into India was a far more complex process than anyone imagined even a few years ago. Only future work in a variety of fields can clarify this immense phenomenon.

Whatever the future holds, Mohenjo-daro and Harappa are currently the best-understood keys to the Indus civilization. Both cities were huge, over three miles in circumference, and housed large populations. Built of fired mudbrick, Mohenjo-daro and Harappa were largely unfortified, although both were defended by great citadels that towered forty or fifty feet above the surrounding plain. Both cities were logically planned from the outset, not merely villages that grew and sprawled haphazardly. In both, blocks of houses were laid out on a grid plan, centuries before the Greeks used this method of urban design. Streets were straight and wide, varying from 9 to 34 feet. The houses of both cities were substantial, many two stories tall, some perhaps three. As in Greek houses, the focal point of the Indus houses was the central open courtyard, onto which the rooms opened. The houses' brick exteriors were bland and blank, and the city streets must have presented a monotonous face to pedestrians.

Perhaps the most surprising aspect of the elaborate planning of these cities is their complex system of drainage, well preserved at Mohenjo-daro. Each house had a bathroom with a drain connected to the municipal drains located under the major streets. These brick-built channels, which carried off refuse, had openings to allow the clearing of blockages. This system not only demonstrates a sophisticated appreciation of hygiene, but also attests to the existence of a strong central authority capable of urban planning.

Centralized government authority is also apparent in both cities' numerous large structures, which excavators think were public buildings. One of the most important is the state granary, a large storehouse for the community's grain. Moreover, a set of tenement buildings next to a series of round working-floors near the granary at Harappa suggests that the central government dominated the

FIGURINE FROM MOHENJO-DARO *Part of the heritage of the Indus civilization was its artistic creations, such as this figurine of a bearded man. The composition is at once bold and sophisticated. Yet even such glimpses as this give little clue to the origins of the creators of the Indus civilization. (The Bettmann Archive)*

storage and processing of the city's cereal crops. The citadel at Mohenjo-daro further testifies to the power of the city's ruler: here stood monumental buildings, including a marketplace or place of assembly, a palace, and

MOHENJO-DARO The architectural vision and engineering expertise of the Indus civilization are obvious in this view of Mohenjo-daro. The central planning and the huge scale of the city reflect a flourishing community. (Anthro Photo/Horr)

a huge bath featuring a pool some 39 feet by 23 feet and 8 feet deep. The Great Bath, like later Roman baths, was an intricate structure with spacious dressing rooms for the bathers. Because the Great Bath at Mohenjo-daro resembles the ritual purification pools of later Indian society, some scholars have speculated that power was in the hands of a priest-king. They also suggest that the Great Bath played a role in the religious rituals of the city; if so, the dressing rooms may have served the priests who performed the rituals. But little is yet known about the religious life of Mohenjo-daro and Harappa, or about the nature of their government. In the absence of readable written records, archaeology alone

cannot answer these questions. Nonetheless, the power and authority of the government, whether secular or religious, is apparent in the intelligent central planning of these cities.

The prosperity of this civilization depended on constant and intensive cultivation of the rich river valley. The Indus, like the Nile, provided farmers with fertile alluvial soil enriched by annual floods. Farmers built earth embankments to hold the flood waters. The results of this labor were abundant crops of wheat, barley, vegetables, and cotton. The Indus people also domesticated cattle, buffalo, fowl, and possibly pigs and asses. Their efforts led to a high standard of living and to the surpluses that they traded with Mesopotamia.

They were also in contact with neighbors closer to home, trading with the peoples of southern India for gold and the ancient Afghans for silver.

Despite tantalizing glimpses of a serene and stable society, the intellectual and religious life of the Indus people is largely unknown. Fertility was a major concern to them, as it has been to most agricultural people: they apparently worshipped a mother-goddess who looked after the welfare of the community. Some later Indian religious beliefs may have originated in this period. One of the most engaging of the early Indian deities – who is depicted at Mohenjo-daro with his customary three faces, surrounded by wild animals – closely resembles Shiva, a major Hindu god. The Indus peoples' great fondness for animals is apparent in the popularity of terra-cotta animal figurines. Their attitude prefigures the deep respect for the animal world that Indians have traditionally felt. Indeed, they give the impression of having been a people in tune with the world around them, a world they understood and enjoyed. The Indus people maintained their equilibrium with nature for hundreds of years, spreading their culture throughout the valley and enjoying a tranquil development.

Yet this civilization, which appeared in history so suddenly, perished just as mysteriously. After years of prosperity, Mohenjo-daro and Harappa suffered a long decline, perhaps as a result of deforestation, a change in climate, and their huge demands on the land. The first excavators of Mohenjo-daro concluded that the city met a violent end: they found some skeletons of men, women, and children, many with axe or sword wounds, scattered across the ground. Contemporary archaeologists, however, have reinterpreted these findings. Some point out that too few skeletons at Mohenjo-daro showed

INDUS CIVILIZATION *This broken vase presents a light and gay side of the Indus civilization. The people of this civilization were particularly fond of animals, as witnessed by this delicate ibex, with its long, graceful horns. (Art Resource/Scala)*

signs of violence to indicate wholesale slaughter. Others suggest that the population may have fallen prey to diseases such as malaria. Thus the reasons for the disappearance of this intriguing civilization are obscure and disputed. It is known, however, that many of the Indus people lived on, though disrupted and scattered. With them they carried the accomplishments and values of their culture, which became an important element in the development of later Indian civilization.

THE ASCENDANCY OF THE ARYANS (CA 1500–500 B.C.)

Many scholars think that the Indus civilization fell at the hands of the Aryans, an Indo-European people who entered India gradually, relentlessly, and violently from the northwest.

But no one has yet been able to prove the connection. The Aryans — as these newcomers called themselves — may have entered India after the fall of the Indus civilization, much as the Dorians entered Greece after the fall of the Mycenaean kingdoms (page 78). In any case, the arrival of the Aryans was a turning-point in Indian history, an event that forever changed the face of India. The Aryans were part of the enormous movement of Indo-Europeans described in Chapter 1 (pages 31–32). Nomadic wanderers, they came in search of land; the Indus Valley, with its rich plains and predictable climate, lured them on.

Most knowledge of the early Aryans comes from the *Rigveda*, the oldest and most sacred of the Hindu "scriptures." The *Rigveda* is not a history but a collection of hymns in praise of the Aryan gods. Even so, the hymns contain some historical information that sheds light on the Aryans and native Indians. The *Rigveda* and the other *Vedas* are crucial to understanding the social evolution of India during this period, sometimes called the Dark Ages of India.

The *Rigveda* portrays the Aryans as a group of battle-loving pastoral tribes, at war with one another and with the native population of India. Their use of horses and bronze weapons in warfare gave them superiority over the natives. At the head of the Aryan tribe was its chief or *raja*, who led his folk in battle and ruled them in peacetime. Next to the chief was the priest, entrusted with sacrifices to the gods and the knowledge of sacred rituals. In time, as Aryan society laid increasing emphasis on proper performance of the religious rituals, priests evolved into a distinct class possessing precise knowledge of the complex rituals and of the invocations and formulas that accompanied them. The warrior nobility rode to battle in chariots and perhaps on horseback, and expressed their will in assem-

blies. The commoners supported society by tending herds and, increasingly as conditions settled, working the land. To the non-Aryan slaves fell the drudgery of menial tasks. Women held a more favorable position in this period than in later times: they were not yet given in child-marriage, and widows had the right to remarry. In brief, the *Rigveda* portrays the early Aryans, with their pride of conquest and delight in battle, as Indian counterparts of the *Iliad*'s heroes.

Gradually the Aryans pushed farther eastward into the valley of the Ganges River, a land of thick jungle filled with brave and savage tribes. The jungle was as stubborn an enemy as its inhabitants, and clearing it presented a tremendous challenge. The *Mahabharata*, India's greatest epic poem, recounts how the Aryans met that challenge. Agni, the Aryan god of fire, agrees with the god Krishna and the human hero Arjuna to burn the jungle of Khandava and everything in it:

The lord [Agni] took on his fiery form and began to burn the forest. Surrounding it on all sides with his Seven Flames, the Fire angrily burned the Khandava, as though to exhibit the end of the Eon . . . Standing on their chariots at both ends of the forest, the two tigerlike men [Krishna and Arjuna] started a vast massacre of the creatures on every side. Indeed, whenever the heroes saw live creatures escaping, such as lived in the Khandava, they chased them down. They saw no hole to escape, because of the vigorous speed of the chariots — both the grand chariots and their warriors seemed to be strung together. As the Khandava was burning, the creatures in their thousands leaped up in all directions, screeching their terrifying screams. Many were burning in one spot, others were scorched — they were shattered mindlessly, their eyes abursting. Some embraced their sons, others their fathers and mothers, unable to abandon them, and thus went to their perdition. Still others jumped up by the thousands, faces distorted, and darting hither and thither fell into the Fire . . . When they jumped out, the Partha cut them to pieces with his arrows and, laughing, threw them back into the blazing Fire. Their bodies covered with arrows and screeching fiercely, they leaped upward nimbly and fell back into the Fire. The noise of the forest animals, as they were hit by the arrows and left to burn, was like the ocean's when it was being churned.[2]

The Aryans cleared the dense jungle by setting great fires and butchering the natives – portrayed in the poem as forest animals – and by slaughtering the survivors who fled from the conflagration. Once again, the Aryans' ferocity and superior military technology enabled them to wrest control of new territory.

THE SHAPING OF INDIAN SOCIETY

Because the push into the jungle demanded a larger and more tightly organized political entity than before, tribes merged under strong rulers whose power grew increasingly absolute. As rulers claimed sovereignty over specific territory, the nature of political rule shifted from tribal chieftainship to kingship. The priests, or *brahmins,* supported the growth of royal power in return for royal confirmation of their own religious rights, power, and status; the brahmins also served a political function as advisors to the kings. In the face of this royal–priestly alliance, the old tribal assemblies of warriors withered away. The shape of Aryan society was changing under the demands of mastering the new environment and the native population that clung to it so desperately.

Development of the newly won territory led to further changes in Aryan society and its political structure. Once conquered and cleared, the land was ready for cultivation.

FERTILITY IDOL *Found at Harappa, this terra cotta figurine, with elaborate head-dress and prominent physical features, represents a fertility goddess. Fertility goddesses were common not only in the Indus civilization, but in most other ancient agricultural societies as well. (Art Resource/Scala)*

However, constant work was needed to keep the land from reverting to jungle. The typical response to this challenge was the village. It was at this time that India evolved into the land of villages it still is today. Even the later growth of cities did not eclipse the village as the hallmark of Indian society. Yet villages did not conform to a single social pattern throughout India. In the south the typical village consisted of groups of families who considered themselves related to one another. Each such family was a large patriarchal joint or extended family composed of several nuclear families who lived and worked together. In the north, by contrast, marriage outside the village was common, and families' kinship ties extended over wider areas than in the south. What all Indian villages had in common was a tradition of mutual cooperation born of common interests and obligations. The close-knit society of the village has consistently been a stabilizing element in Indian history.

Sustained agriculture and settled conditions promoted prosperity and population growth, which in turn gave rise to the growth of towns and eventually cities. Thus the Aryans gradually transformed themselves from a tribal organization into an urban, as well as a village, society. Prosperity also further enhanced royal power. Another feature of this process was frequent warfare among territorial states, the smaller and weaker of which were conquered and absorbed, giving rise to a number of large kingdoms. By about 500 B.C. the Aryans had created a new political map of India characterized by larger kingdoms, village life, and islands of urban culture.

As the Aryans struggled to dominate the land of India, they increasingly had to contend with its people. Social contact between Aryans and natives led to the development of the complicated system of social organization known as the caste system. A *caste* is a heredi-

tary class of social equals who share the same religion, pursue a specific trade or occupation, and avoid extensive social intercourse with members of other castes. At first this system had two goals: to distinguish Aryans from non-Aryans and to mark birth or descent. Even so, the caste system was fluid at first, and allowed for a surprising amount of social mobility. Even in the early days of conquest the Aryans had mixed with the conquered population, and that slow mingling eventually resulted in the Indian society that emerged into the full light of history. As in Mesopotamia, the process of blending was intellectual and religious as well as social; Aryans and native Indians gradually formed a common and complex culture. Only as conditions stabilized over the years did this system become strict and the number of castes grow.

By about 500 B.C. four main groups of Indian society were steadily evolving: the priest (brahmin), the warrior (kshatriya), the peasant (vaishya), and the serf (shudra). Indians themselves ascribed this development to the gods, as the *Rigveda* testifies:

When they divided the [primeval] Man
  into how many parts did they divide him?
What was his mouth, what were his arms,
  what were his thighs and his feet called?
The brahmin was his mouth, of his
  arms was made the warrior.
His thighs became the vaishya, of
  his feet the shudra was born.[3]

According to this division of duties, the priests conducted religious sacrifices and treasured the religious lore. The warriors defended society on the battlefield, while the peasants grew the food and paid the taxes. The serfs, who were originally the property of the tribe, served the others by performing hard labor. Those without places in this tidy social division — that is, those who entered it later than the others — were the outcastes, who probably earned their livings by performing such undesirable jobs as animal slaughtering and dressing skins. Although their work was economically valuable, it was considered unworthy and socially polluting. These socially impure people were the untouchables. Also among the outcastes were people who had lost their caste status through violations of ritual.

EARLY INDIAN RELIGION

In religion and intellectual life, too, a momentous revolution was occurring in Indian society. The Aryan gods represented natural phenomena. Some of them were great brawling figures, like Agni, the god of fire, Indra, wielder of the thunderbolt and god of war, and Rudra, the divine archer who spread disaster and disease by firing his arrows at mankind. Others were shadowy figures, like Dyaus, the father of the gods, who appears in Greek as Zeus and in Latin as Jupiter. Varuna, the god of order in the universe, was a hard god, quick to punish those who sinned and thus upset the balance of nature. Ushas, the goddess of dawn, was a refreshingly gentle deity who welcomed the birds, gave delight to human beings, and kept off evil spirits. Although the Aryan gods had their duties, they differed from the Greek deities in that they rarely had distinctive personalities or extensive mythologies. All the Aryan gods enjoyed sacrifices, however, and ritual was an essential ingredient in early Aryan religion. Gradually, under the priestly monopoly of the brahmins, correct sacrifice and proper ritual became so important that most brahmins believed a properly performed ritual would force the god to grant the worshipper's wish. Religion became sterile and unsatisfying to many, even among the priestly class.

In search of a faith richer and more mystical, some brahmins retreated to the forests to seek a personal road to the gods. Through asceticism — severe self-discipline and self-denial — and meditation on the traditional teachings of the *Vedas*, these pioneers breathed new life into the old rituals. For one thing, they concluded that disciplined meditation on the ritual sacrifice could produce the same results as the physical ritual itself. Thus they reinterpreted the ritual sacrifices as symbolic gestures with mystical meanings. Slowly Indian religion was changing from primitive worship to a way of thought that nourished human needs and eased human fears. Two cardinal doctrines prevailed: *samsara*, the transmigration of souls by a continual process of rebirth, and *karma*, the tally of good and bad deeds that determined the status of an individual's next life. Gradually the concept arose of a wheel of life, which eventually included the animal and plant worlds and even the gods.

To most people, and especially those on the lower end of the economic and social scale, these concepts were enormously attractive. All existence, no matter how harsh and bitter, could be a climb to better things. By living righteously and doing good deeds, people could improve their lot in the next life. Yet there was another side to these ideas: the wheel of life could be seen as a ruthless treadmill, giving rise to a yearning for release from the wheel's relentless cycle of birth and death. Hence these new concepts created tension in religious thought, as mystics grappled with the problem of the wheel of life.

The solution to this baffling problem appears in the *Upanishads*, a collection of sacred texts created by ascetics who opened up new vistas in religious speculation. The authors of the *Upanishads* fostered the concept of *moksha*, or release from the wheel of life. All people, they taught, have in themselves an eternal

INDIA TO CA 250 B.C.

ca 2500–1500 B.C.	Indus Valley civilization
ca 1500–500 B.C.	Arrival of the Aryans and development of Vedic society
6th–5th centuries B.C.	Development of Hinduism, Jainism, and Buddhism
ca 513 B.C.	Persian conquest of northwestern India and the Indus Valley
326 B.C.	Alexander the Great conquers northwestern India and the Indus Valley
322–298 B.C.	Reign of Chandragupta

truth and reality called *atman*, which corresponds to a greater all-encompassing reality called *Brahman*. The truth in each person and the universal truth are eternal and identical. These mystics and ascetics claimed that life in the world is actually an illusion, and the only way to escape it and the wheel of life is to realize that reality is unchanging. By studying the *Vedas*, by penance, and by meditation, one could join one's individual self with the universal reality. This profound and subtle teaching they summed up in one sentence: "Thou art That." What does this sentence mean? The *Chandogya Upanishad* tells the story of a father explaining it to his son:

'Believe me, my son, an invisible and subtle essence is the Spirit of the whole universe. That is Reality. That is Atman THOU ART THAT.'
'Explain more to me, father', said Svetaketu.
'So be it, my son.
'Place this salt in water and come to me tomorrow morning.'
Svetaketu did as he was commanded, and in the morning his father said to him: 'Bring me the salt you put into the water last night.'

Svetaketu looked into the water, but could not find it, for it had dissolved.
His father then said: 'Taste the water from this side. How is it?'
'It is salt.'
'Taste it from the middle. How is it?'
'It is salt.'
'Taste it from that side. How is it?'
'It is salt.'
'Look for the salt again and come again to me.'
The son did so, saying: 'I cannot see the salt. I only see water.'
His father then said: 'In the same way, O my son, you cannot see the Spirit. But in truth he is here.
'An invisible and subtle essence is the Spirit of the whole universe. That is Reality. That is Truth. THOU ART THAT.'[4]

These great religious thinkers gave society a transcendent means to escape the problems presented by the wheel of life. These revolutionary ideas appealed to those who were dissatisfied with the old brahmin religion of sacrifice, and even won the support of the brahmins and kings. The thought of the

Upanishads gave brahmins a high status to which the poor and lowly could aspire in future life; consequently, the brahmins greeted these concepts, and those who taught them, with tolerance and understanding. They even made a place for them in traditional religious practice. The rulers of Indian society had excellent practical reasons to encourage the new trends. The doctrine of transmigration, and that of righteous living leading to a better future life, encouraged even the poor and oppressed to labor peacefully and dutifully. The revolutionary new doctrines actually promoted stability in social and political life.

By about 500 B.C., all these trends — political, social, and religious — had led to a society, shaped by conqueror and conquered, in which all had a place. Urban life flourished alongside a vigorous village life, both sustained by agriculture. Gone were the warrior chieftains, their place taken by hereditary kings who ruled large territorial states with the support of a hereditary priestly class. Many of India's basic values had already taken shape at this early date.

INDIA'S SPIRITUAL FLOWERING

India's spiritual growth came into full bloom in the sixth and fifth centuries B.C., a period of stunning moral and philosophical thought that gave rise to three of the world's greatest religions, Jainism, Buddhism, and Hinduism. The evolution of these sects is complex and still somewhat obscure. Hinduism is the most direct descendant of the old Vedic religion. Jainism and Buddhism shared that heritage, but reacted against it and Hinduism. Buddhism and Jainism originated as schools of moral philosophy, preoccupied with the nature of ultimate reality and with ethical conduct. Both were originally atheistic, as Jainism remains today: that is, neither denied the existence of gods, but like Epicureanism (page 130) they denied that gods play any important part in the cosmic scheme of things. Although the teachings of the Jains have remained fundamentally unchanged over the years, the sect had become a religious faith, in the sense that it attributed causation to gods, by about 250 B.C. Buddhism too had become a religion within two hundred years of its founding. Hinduism, though influenced by both Buddhism and Jainism, was a religion from the outset. Buddhism reached its full growth much later, and will be considered in more depth in Chapter 6.

JAINISM

The founder and most influential thinker of Jainism, Vardhamana Mahavira (ca 540-468 B.C.), the son of an aristocrat, accepted the doctrines of karma and rebirth but developed the animistic philosophy that human beings, animals, plants, and even inanimate objects and natural phenomena all have living souls. Mahavira taught that the universe and everything in it is composed of souls, usually mixed with matter. These souls are infinite in number and finite in nature, having definite limits. Souls float or sink, according to Mahavira, depending on the amount of matter with which they are mixed; the only way for any soul to reach eternal happiness is to rid itself of all matter so that it can float to the top of the universe.

Mahavira's followers, known as Jains, believed that people could achieve eternal bliss only by living lives of asceticism and avoiding evil thoughts and actions. The Jains considered all life too sacred to be destroyed. Yet if everything in the world possesses a soul, how can one live without destroying other life? The rigorously logical answer is that one cannot. Strictly speaking, the Jains could adhere to their beliefs only by starving to death. Instead of going to this extreme, the Jains created a hierarchy of life, with human beings at the apex, followed by animals, plants, and inanimate objects. The Jain who wished to do the least possible violence to life became a vegetarian. Nonviolence became a cardinal principle of Jainism and soon took root throughout Indian society. Although Jainism never took hold as widely as Hinduism and Buddhism, it has been a profoundly influential strand in Indian thought, and numbers several million adherents in India today.

HINDUISM

Hinduism may be the world's oldest flourishing religion. It is certainly one of the world's largest faiths, with millions of adherents in India and other Asian countries, the West Indies and South Africa; it is also a complex of social customs, doctrines, and beliefs.

Although influenced by Jainism and Buddhism, Hinduism was most firmly rooted in traditional Indian religion. The bedrock of Hinduism is the belief that the *Vedas* are sacred revelations, and that a specific caste system is implicitly prescribed in the *Vedas*. Thus, Hinduism is both a collection of religious beliefs and a sacred division of society complete with its own moral law. Religiously and philosophically, Hinduism is diverse. One of the most tolerant of the world's religions, Hinduism assumes that there are innumerable legitimate ways of worshipping the supreme principle of life. Consequently, it readily incorporates new sects, doctrines, beliefs, rites, and deities. The numerous Hindu gods are all considered aspects of Brahman, the supreme

and undefinable principle of life. According to Hinduism, Brahman suffuses all things, and at the same time transcends all things. The various deities are considered specific manifestations of Brahman, each of whom helps people to reach Brahman by means of rituals.

Hinduism is a guide to life, whose goal is to reach Brahman. There are four steps in this search, progressing from study of the *Vedas* in youth to complete asceticism in old age. In their quest for Brahman, people are to observe *dharma,* a moral law nearly as complex as Hinduism itself. Dharma stipulates the legitimate pursuits of Hindus: material gain, so long as it is honestly and honorably achieved; pleasure and love, for the perpetuation of the family; and finally *moksha,* release from the wheel of life and unity with Brahman. The society that a scrupulous observance of dharma could create is depicted in the *Mahabharata,* a long epic poem in which the law is personified as King Dharma, the bull of the Bharatas:

All the people, relying on King Dharma, lived happily like souls that rely on their own bodies that are favored with auspicious marks and deeds. The bull of the Bharatas cultivated Law, Profit, and Pleasure alike, like a family man honoring three kinsmen alike to himself. To Law, Profit and Pleasure, now incarnated on earth in equal proportions, the king himself appeared as the fourth. In this overlord of men the Vedas *found a superb student, the great sacrifices a performer, the four classes a pure guardian. Luck had found her place, wisdom its apex, all Law its kinsman with this lord of the earth.*[5]

In short, Hinduism spells out the goals of life and how to attain them.

After the third century B.C., Hinduism began to emphasize the roles and personalities of powerful gods, especially Shiva, the cosmic dancer who both creates and destroys, and

Vishnu, the preserver and sustainer of creation. Since these gods are personal manifestations of Brahman, it can be known through them. Thus people could reach Brahman by devotion to personal gods.

India's best-loved sacred hymn, the *Bhagavad Gita,* is a spiritual guide to the most serious problem facing a Hindu – how to live in the world and yet honor dharma, and thus achieve release. The heart of the *Bhagavad Gita* is the spiritual conflict confronting Arjuna, a human hero about to ride into battle against his own kinsmen. As he surveys the battlefield, struggling with the grim notion of killing his relatives, Arjuna voices his doubts to his charioteer, none other than the god Krishna himself. When at last Arjuna refuses to spill his family's blood, Krishna – who is a manifestation of the great god Vishnu – instructs him, as he has instructed generations of Hindus, on the true meaning of Hinduism:

Interwoven in his creation, the Spirit [Brahman] is beyond destruction. No one can bring to an end the Spirit which is everlasting. For beyond time he dwells in these bodies, though these bodies have an end in their time; but he remains immeasurable, immortal. Therefore, great warrior, carry on thy fight. If any man thinks he slays, and if another thinks he is slain, neither knows the ways of truth. The Eternal in man cannot kill; the Eternal in man cannot die. He is never born, and he never dies. He is in Eternity: he is for evermore. Never-born and eternal, beyond times gone or to come, he does not die when the body dies. When a man knows him as never-born, everlasting, never-changing, beyond all destruction, how can that man kill a man, or cause another to kill?[26]

Krishna then clarifies the relation between human reality and the eternal spirit. He explains compassionately to Arjuna the duty to act – to live in the world and carry out his duties as a warrior. Indeed, the *Bhagavad Gita*

urges the necessity of action, which is essential for the welfare of the world.

Early in India's history Hinduism provided it a complex and sophisticated philosophy of life and a religion of enormous emotional appeal. Hinduism also inspired and preserved the vast literature, in Sanskrit and the major regional languages of India, that is India's priceless literary heritage.

INDIA AND THE WEST (CA 513-298 B.C.)

Between the arrival of the Aryans and the evolution of Hinduism, India enjoyed freedom from outside interference. In the late sixth century B.C., however, western India was swept up in events that were changing the face of the ancient Near East. During this period the Persians were creating the first "world empire," which stretched from the western coast of Anatolia to the Indus River (pages 62–65). India became involved in these events when the Persian emperor Darius I conquered the Indus Valley about 513 B.C.

Persian control did not reach far beyond the banks of the Indus, and never extended east of the river. Even so, as part of the Persian empire western India enjoyed immediate contact not only with the old cultures of Egypt and Mesopotamia but also with the young and vital culture of the Greeks. The story of India as the Persian satrapy of Hindush has been told in Chapter 2 (page 63). What effects did contact with Persia and the lands farther west have on India?

Culturally the Persian conquest resembled the Hyksos period in Egypt (pages 28–29) in that it was a fertilizing event, introducing new ideas, techniques, and materials into India. In fact, the period of Persian rule was one of thoroughgoing innovation. As members of the vast Persian Empire, Indians learned the administrative techniques of ruling large tracts of land and huge numbers of people. The adoption of coined money for economic transactions was a far-reaching innovation. From the Persians the Indians learned the technique of minting silver coins; they adopted the Persian standard to facilitate trade with other parts of the empire. Even states in the Ganges Valley, which were never part of the empire, adopted the use of coinage. Another innovation was the introduction of the Aramaic language and script, the official language of the Persian empire. Indians adapted the Aramaic script to their needs and their languages—enabling them to keep records and publish proclamations just as the Persians did.

Likewise, India participated in the larger economic world created by the Persians. Trade increased dramatically with other regions under Persian rule. Once again hardy merchants took the sea route to the West, as had their predecessors of the Indus civilization. Caravan cities grew in number and wealth, as overland trade thrived in the peace brought about by Persian rule. New prosperity and new techniques also gave rise to rough stone architecture, notably at the important city of Taxila in the northern Indus valley. In short, the arrival of the Persians drew India into the mainstream of sophisticated urban, commercial, and political life in the ancient world.

Into this world stormed Alexander the Great, who led his Macedonian and Greek troops through the Khyber Pass into the Indus Valley (page 111) in 326 B.C. What he found in India is most readily apparent in Taxila, a major center of trade in the Punjab. The Greeks described Taxila as "a city great and prosperous, the biggest of those between the Indus River and the Hydaspes [the modern Jhelum] – a region not inferior to Egypt in size, with especially good pastures and rich in fine fruits."[7] Modern archaeology has shed light on Indian urban life in this period, and in the process has proved their praise excessive: despite its prosperity and importance as a seat of Hindu learning, Taxila was an unassuming town, mean and rather poor when compared to the cities of Greece and the Near East. Houses and buildings were constructed of rough, loose masonry, the walls plastered with mud. The streets were narrow and winding, and lacked the extensive drainage system of Mohenjo-daro. The city possessed one large pillared hall that may have been a temple, perhaps the earliest Hindu shrine yet uncovered. The wealth of Indian culture was not reflected in gleaming cities and monumental architecture.

From Taxila, Alexander marched to the mouth of the Indus River before turning west and leaving India forever. The high tide of his penetration was the Hyphasis River (the modern Beas) in the Punjab, from which he fell back to the Hydaspes, a major tributary of the Indus. What is the significance of this turbulent episode in the history of India? The eminent Indian scholar B. G. Gokhale has compared Alexander's passage through India to

a storm that pulls down trees and leaves rubble behind . . . . But its indirect results were many. The invasion left behind many Greek settlements in north-western India which encouraged Greco-Indian cultural contacts and exchange. Alexander's invasion destroyed the kingdoms and petty principalities of the Punjab, and thus was created a political vacuum which was later to be filled by the power of Chandragupta Maurya.[8]

In itself a riot of bloodshed and destruction, Alexander's invasion facilitated the rise of the first kingdom to embrace all of India.

THE KINGDOM OF CHANDRAGUPTA

Alexander had disrupted the political map of western India and died without organizing his conquests, leaving the area in confusion. Chandragupta, the ruler of a small state in the Ganges valley, took advantage of this situation by defeating his enemies piecemeal until by 322 B.C. he had made himself sole master of India. He justified his position as king of India in 304 B.C. by defeating the forces of Seleucus, the general of Alexander the Great who founded the Seleucid monarchy (page 112). In the wake of this battle, Seleucus surrendered the easternmost provinces of his monarchy and concluded a treaty of alliance with Chandragupta. Hence Chandragupta not only defeated one of the mightiest of the Hellenistic kings, but also entered into the world of Hellenistic politics and diplomacy.

The real heir to Alexander's conquest, Chandragupta created the great Maurya Empire, which stretched from the Punjab and Himalayas in the north almost to the tip of the subcontinent, from modern Afghanistan in the west to Bengal in the east. In the administration of his empire, Chandragupta adopted the Persian practice of dividing up the area into provinces. Each province was assigned a governor, most of whom were drawn from Chandragupta's own family. The smallest unit in this system was typically the village, the mainstay of Indian life. From his capital at Pataliputra, in the valley of the Ganges, the king sent agents to the provinces to oversee the workings of government and to keep him informed of conditions in his realm. Chandragupta also enjoyed the able assistance of his great minister Kautilya, who, like Machiavelli later, wrote a practical and sensible treatise on statecraft. For the first time in In-

dian history, one man governed most of the subcontinent, exercising control through delegated power.

Chandragupta applied the lessons learned from Persian rule with stunning effectiveness. A complex bureaucracy was established to see to the operation of the state. A bureaucratic taxation system financed public services. Chandragupta also built a regular army, complete with departments for everything from naval matters to the collection of supplies. In most respects Chandragupta's kingdom resembled the Hellenistic kingdoms, which had also adopted Persian methods of rule.

Megasthenes, a Greek ambassador of King Seleucus, has left a lively description of life at Chandragupta's court. Like many other monarchs, Chandragupta feared treachery and especially assassination, but nonetheless refused to leave government to others. Therefore he took elaborate precautions against intrigue. According to Megasthenes,

Attendance on the king's person is the duty of women, who indeed are bought from their fathers. Outside the gates [of the palace] stand the bodyguards and the rest of the soldiers . . . Nor does the king sleep during the day, and at night he is forced at various hours to change his bed because of those plotting against him. Of his non-military departures [from the palace] one is to the courts, in which he passes the day hearing cases to the end, even if the hour arrives for attendance on his person . . . [When he leaves to hunt,] he is thickly surrounded by a circle of women, and on the outside by spear-carrying bodyguards. The road is fenced off with ropes, and to anyone who passes within the ropes as far as the women death is the penalty.[9]

These measures worked: after resigning the kingship, Chandragupta died the peaceful death of a Jain ascetic in 298 B.C.

Chandragupta left behind a kingdom organized to maintain order and to defend India from invasion. India enjoyed economic prosperity and communications with its neighbors. At a time when many of the major cultures of the world were in direct touch with one another, the Indians, who had created much from their own experience and had learned much from others, could proudly make their own contributions in both the cultural and material spheres. Moreover, Chandragupta's grandson, the great Ashoka, would extend the Mauryan Empire to its greatest scope and would nurture Buddhism within it.

CHINA, THE LAND AND ITS CHALLENGE

While geography had left India an opening to the northwest and thus to the civilizations of the ancient Near East, terrain and distance made China's links to the broader world much more tenuous. Between India and China tower the ice-clad and forbidding peaks of the Himalayas and the Pamirs, and beyond them the vast expanses of Tibet and Chinese Turkestan. Geography isolated China in other directions as well. To the north stretched the Gobi Desert, some 500,000 square miles of desolate waste, and the Mongolian Plateau. To the south rose mountains covered with forests and tracts of jungle. Beyond the shores of China lay Japan, inhabited at this period by primitive peoples, the islands of the South China Sea, and the huge and then-uncharted expanse of the Pacific Ocean. China's main avenue to the major civilizations of the outside world was a thread-like corridor to the northwest, through the vastness of Central Asia, past India, and ultimately to Mesopotamia. Hence, though isolated, China was not sealed

off completely. Like India, it enjoyed a link to other seats of civilization.

China encompasses two immense river basins, those of the Yellow River in the north and the Yangtze in the south. Both rivers rise in the mountains of Tibet and flow eastward across China (see map 5.2). The Yellow River carries tons of loess, a very fine light-colored dust whose color gives the river its name. Loess is exceptionally fertile and easy to cultivate, and this basin was the site of China's earliest agricultural civilization in the Neolithic Period (page 8). Yet like the Tigris in Mesopotamia, the Yellow River can be a rampaging torrent, bringing disastrous floods and changing course unpredictably. Frequently called "China's Sorrow," the Yellow River had to be tamed with dikes. The taming of the river allowed for China's great northern plain to be farmed, eventually nurturing a huge population.

The basins of the Yellow and Yangtze rivers are separated in the west by mountains, which give way to hills, and finally disappear altogether in the flat country near the coast. The two basins are quite distinct, however, when it comes to farming. Dry farming of wheat and millet characterizes the Yellow river basin in the north; irrigated rice agriculture predominates in the warmer and wetter basin of the Yangtze. In the extreme south is the valley of the Hsi, or West, River, an area of mild climate and fertile soil, which would later form the southern boundary of China. Within this enormous expanse of land the climate varies greatly from north to south and from east to west, with milder and wetter conditions prevailing in the south. Except for the river valleys, China is largely mountainous or semi-desert land, too poor to sustain large numbers of people. Geography helped to ensure that human development in China clung to the mighty river systems.

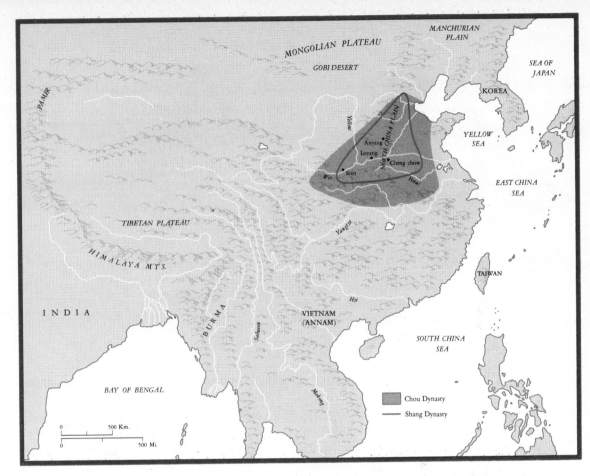

MAP 5.2 CHINA UNDER THE SHANG AND CHOU DYNASTIES, 1523–221 B.C. *The heartland of Chinese development is vividly illustrated by this map, which clearly shows the importance of the Yellow River in early Chinese life. Under the Chou, Chinese authority reached the Yangtze.*

THE SHANG DYNASTY
(CA 1523-1027 B.C.)

At about the time the Aryans were transforming Indian life, the kings of the Shang Dynasty rose to power in northern China. Unlike the Aryans, however, the Shang were natives, very closely linked to indigenous Neolithic peoples. Chinese Neolithic farmers had long since settled into a life of sustained agriculture and animal domestication (page 8).

Asian scholars dispute the nature and degree of outside influence on early Chinese developments, but most agree that ancient Chinese culture was largely a native growth. China did not suffer massive foreign invasion. To this relatively self-contained society, the Shang gave a long period of political rule. Once considered legendary rather than historical, the Shang Dynasty has now been verified from its own written records and the work of modern archaeologists.

The excavations at the modern cities of

SHANG HOUSE *The ordinary farming family of Shang lived in a house very much like its Neolithic ancestors. The house was dark, close, and cramped, but the central hearth provided warmth and light. (From John Hay* Ancient China, *London: The Bodley Head, 1973, p. 41)*

Anyang, the Shang capital, and Chengchow, perhaps the oldest city in China, have shed surprisingly bright light on the Shang kings and the society they ruled. Social divisions among the Shang were apparently simple but sharp: a ruling class of aristocrats, headed by a king and an incipient bureaucracy, directed the work and lives of everyone else. Warfare was a constant feature of Shang life, and the nobles were the warriors of Shang, the men who enforced Shang rule. The Shang kings ruled northern China as a kind of family patrimony. The kings and the aristocracy owned slaves, many of whom had been captured in war. They also controlled the peasantry, who labored as semi-free serfs.

The common people — serf and slave — performed all the economic functions of society. Most were farmers, whose way of life was basically Neolithic. Even in this remote period, however, Shang farmers knew how to cultivate the silkworm; silken threads were woven into fine cloth, and under later emperors silk became China's prime export. Nonetheless, Shang farmers worked their fields with Neolithic tools and methods.

Their homes too were Neolithic in construction: like their ancestors, each family dug a pit in the ground, which served as the living area. Often they dug an entrance passage with a small platform inside the pit to keep water from running down the passage into the house. The central feature of the house was the hearth, which was dug out of the floor of the pit. Beside the hearth were wooden roof-supports, against which the roof-timbers sloped. Lastly the family thatched the roof with reeds and clay, thus making a conical hut-like house. Although they helped create the wealth of Shang, peasant farmers enjoyed little of it themselves.

Other commoners were artisans, dependent upon the nobles, who manufactured the weapons, ritual vessels, jewelry, and other items demanded by the aristocracy. Shang craftsmen worked in stone, bone, and bronze, but are best known for their bronze work; these early Chinese artists created some of the world's most splendid bronze pieces. Among the Shang, bronze was considered a noble metal, fit for weapons and ceremonial vessels but much too precious to be made into tools.

At the top of Shang society lived the king and his nobles, mighty figures elevated far above the common people. They lived in palatial houses, built on huge platforms of pounded earth. The architecture of these houses set a pattern for house-building that has flourished into modern times. They enjoyed the magnificent bronze work of the artisans, and carried bronze weapons into battle. Even after death, the king and his relatives had crucial social roles to play: the living worshipped and entreated them to intercede with the great gods, especially Shang-ti the supreme god, to protect the lives and future hopes of their descendants. At first only the king and his family were worthy of such honors, but this custom is the forerunner of Chinese ancestor worship, an abiding element in Chinese religious belief.

ORIGINS OF WRITING

The origins of Chinese writing appear to be deeply rooted in Shang religion. The kings of Shang were also high priests, and frequently wanted to ask questions of the gods. Their medium was the famous oracle bones of the Shang, generally shoulder bones of oxen or the bottom shells of tortoises. On one side the king or priest wrote his message; on the other side he drilled a small hole, to which he applied a heated point. When the bone or shell split, the priest interpreted the cracks in relation to the writing. Writing developed considerably later in China than in Sumer or India, but the Shang system of writing was already highly developed and sophisticated. Originally pictographic, the signs used by the Shang contained phonetic values. Even so, the Shang and their successors created thousands of signs, resulting in a very complex and cumbersome system. Yet while the Chinese script was laborious, like Sumerian cuneiform and Mycenaean Linear B, mastery of even

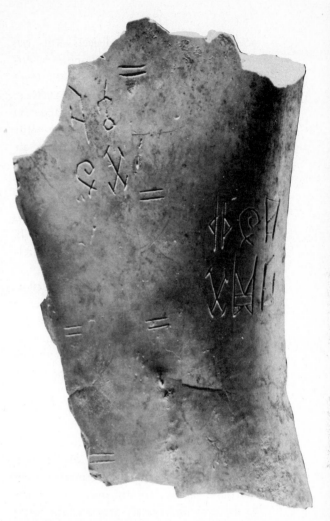

SHANG ORACLE BONE *On one side of the bone the Shang diviner wrote his questions to the gods, and on the other side he applied a hot point. When the cracks in the bone led to the writing, the interpreter read the gods' message. Most questions dealt with the harvest, the weather, travel, and hunting. (The Peabody Museum, Harvard University)*

a few signs enabled people to keep records. Fluent literacy, however, demanded dedication, time, leisure, and thus wealth.

This system of writing, despite its drawbacks, eventually proved very popular and enduring. Later, when the script was simplified and standardized (see Chapter 6), it could be readily written and understood by literate Chinese who spoke different dialects. This was very important, since many Chinese dialects were mutually unintelligible. The script spread throughout China and eventually to Korea and Japan, where it was adapted to local needs. The Koreans adopted the entire Chinese written language, including an approximation of the Chinese pronunciation of the signs. The Japanese went even further than the Koreans, evolving a system in which the Chinese characters served as ideographs that had wholly Japanese pronunciations. In addition, they fashioned two other purely phonetic systems.

Literary mastery required such an effort that those who achieved it represented a learned elite. Literacy was so politically important and socially valuable that education and scholarship were revered; the literate elite was essential to kings and deeply respected by the peasants. Literacy also made possible the growth of a bureaucracy capable of keeping records and conducting correspondence with commanders and governors far from the palace. Hence literacy became the ally of royal rule, furnishing kings quicker communication and more effective control over their realm. At the same time literacy preserved the learning, lore, and experience of early Chinese society, a precious historical heritage for future ages.

THE TRIUMPH OF THE CHOU
(CA 1027-221 B.C.)

Some oracle bones of Shang mention the king of Chou, a small realm in the basin of the Wei River, a tributary of the Yellow River on the western frontier of the Shang domains. The Chou were an agricultural people who had emigrated into the region, perhaps from the northwest. They were also culturally sophisticated masters of bronze and of horse-drawn chariots. In the eleventh century B.C. the Chou king, a dependent of the Shang, became increasingly rebellious and ultimately overturned the Shang Dynasty. Because their contact with the Shang had resulted in their adoption of much of Shang culture, the political victory of the Chou caused no cultural break.

To justify their conquest ideologically, the Chou founders declared that the last Shang king had forfeited his right to rule because of his excesses and incompetence. They asserted that Heaven itself had transferred its mandate to rule China from the Shang house to their worthier rivals, the Chou. This political concept, the Mandate of Heaven, has remained the traditional Chinese legitimization of changes of dynasties.

The victorious Chou confronted the formidable challenge of governing enormous areas of land. Communication within the realm was poor, and it was humanly impossible for one king to administer it all effectively. Moreover, the original Chou capital was near Sian in western China (see map 5.2), too remote for efficient rule of the new domain. The Chou solved these problems by building a second capital at Loyang in the North China plain (see map), and by creating something resembling a feudal state.

Like many medieval European kings, the king of the Chou gave huge tracts of land to members of the royal family and others who had demonstrated their talent and loyalty. At the outset, the newly appointed lords received their authority from the king. In a formal ceremony the king handed the new lord a lump of earth, symbolizing the king's gift of the land to the lord. The lord in turn pledged his loyalty to the king, and usually promised to send the king military forces if he requested.

SHANG BRONZE   *Shang craftsmen turned out some of the most splendid bronze vessels in history. Shang bronzes are marked by technical excellence and artistic grace. (Robert Harding Associates)*

A written record was made of the grant and the new lord's obligations and rights — an unprecedented secular use of writing. In effect, the Chou king was the political overlord of the land. He was also the supreme religious leader, who interceded with the gods for the welfare of Chinese society.

At first the Chou kings exercised strong control over their feudal dependencies. Gradually, however, the lords tried to strengthen their own positions, even at the expense of the king. Furthermore, the power of the lords grew with the prosperity of their holdings. The feudal dependencies of the Chou were actually small islands of settlement scattered all over northern China, separated by wide tracts of undeveloped land. Over several centuries the growing populations of these settlements cleared new land, and eventually permanent cities arose. Once small and vulnerable, these settlements began to coalesce into compact regional states and then to fight among themselves over borders and territories. In this conflict the states in the interior of China

CHOU BRONZE-WORKING   *This bronze vessel testifies that Chou craftsmen had carried on the fine tradition of the Shang. In the shape of a duck with a long neck, this vessel was probably a wine container used primarily on ceremonial occasions. (The Brooklyn Museum, Gift of Mr. and Mrs. Alastair Bradley Martin)*

were eclipsed by those on the borders, which took advantage of their geographical position to expand into new territory. This expansion spread Chinese culture ever wider. While conquering new territory, the lords of the border states were also wringing the most they could from their traditional seats of power. They became absolute rulers in their own right. Around them developed a hereditary class of aristocratic ministers of state, warriors, administrators, and tax collectors. China was gradually becoming a land of numerous independent kingdoms.

Hand in hand with the growing independence of the lords went a decline in the power and stature of the Chou kings. The lords used their troops to realize their own ambitions, and stopped sending forces to the kings in disregard of their feudal obligations. In 771 B.C. a Chou king was defeated and killed by rebel lords, after which the Chou abandoned their western capital and made Loyang, the eastern capital, their permanent seat.

During the period known as the Era of the Warring States (402–221 B.C.), the entire feudal system of the Chou Dynasty disintegrated.

The Chou kings were little more than figure-heads. The dreary cycle of warfare finally ended in 221 B.C., when the ruler of Ch'in, who had forced the abdication of the last Chou king in 256 B.C., conquered all the other states.

SOCIAL CHANGE AND CULTURAL ADVANCEMENT IN THE CHOU PERIOD

The political events of the Chou period had social outcomes that were to have a lasting impact on Chinese society. As the older interior states declined in stature, the aristocracies of these states lost their wealth. Educated, literate, and talented people were forced to seek their fortunes far from home. And the border states, dependent as they were on military and administrative efficiency, needed capable people to keep the wheels of government turning. The upshot was that impoverished aristocrats gravitated to the border states, where their much-needed talents opened the door to careers as ministers and officials. Here merit, not birth, made the difference. This period saw the origins of a trained and able civil service, a group who saw to the daily workings of government and, later, gave a warm reception to the great philosophies of the Chou period.

Despite the long years of warfare and slaughter, the Chou period could boast of some remarkable cultural achievements. Cities grew up around the walled garrisons that the Chou established to hold down the Shang people. Like Roman forts in northern Europe, they evolved from army camps into genuine cities, some with huge populations. The roads and canals built to import food and goods to the city-dwellers stimulated trade and agriculture. Trade was also stimulated and made vastly easier by the invention of coined money.

A dramatic surge in technology during the Chou period permanently altered warfare, agriculture, and ultimately urban life. Under the Chou, craftsmen and artisans discovered the use of iron and rapidly developed its uses. Chou metalsmiths produced both wrought and cast iron – a remarkable achievement, not matched in Europe until the fourteenth century. Chou craftsmen turned out an imposing number of weapons, especially dagger-axes and swords, a mute commentary on life in the period. Use of the chariot in warfare led to improved harnesses for horses. Under the Shang, horses had been harnessed with bands around their girths and throats; this primitive harness actually choked the horse when pulled hard. Although the Chinese did not perfect the harness until a later era (see Chapter 6), they did so centuries before the medieval Europeans.

In agriculture the Chinese under the Chou Dynasty progressed from essentially Neolithic methods of farming to a metal technology. In place of the stone and bone tools of the Shang, Chou farmers used iron. Ploughs with iron shares broke the ground very easily. Iron sickles, knives, and spades made the raising and harvesting of crops easier and far more efficient than ever before. By increasing productivity, metal technology gave Chou farmers the tools to support the thriving urban culture.

THE BIRTH OF CHINESE PHILOSOPHY

The Chou period was an era of outstanding intellectual creativity. Many thoughtful and literate people turned their minds to the basic question of how people could live the happiest and most productive lives in the most efficiently run society. Chinese thinkers were more secular than religious in their outlook.

While Indian mystics were creating a complex socio-religious system, the Chinese were exploring philosophies of political development. Fascinated by political, social, and economic problems, they sought universal rules for human conduct. This period gave rise to three branches of thought – Confucianism, Taoism, and Legalism – that left an indelible stamp on the history of China.

CONFUCIANISM

Of these three schools of thought, Confucianism has had the most profound impact on China. The historical K'ung Fu-tzu (551–479 B.C.) – better known in the West as Confucius – is in many ways as unknown as Socrates. Like Socrates, he was primarily a teacher and did not put his thoughts into writing. His fame comes largely from his students, who collected his sayings in a book called the *Analects.*

Confucius' family was aristocratic but poor, and he had few immediate prospects of success. His family had him educated so that he could take his place in the civil service. Yet he achieved fame as a teacher, not as a minister of state, an irony that failed to satisfy him. Confucius taught the sons of nobles, but yearned to advise lords. Setting out with a small band of students, he sought employment from the lords of the emerging regional states in northeastern China. He served intermittently as a minor official, and continued to spread his ideas. At last Confucius returned home to die among his students, considering himself a failure because he had never held high office.

Confucius' thought centered on the duties and proper behavior of the individual within society. He was far more interested in orderly and stable human relationships than in theology or religious matters. For all his fame,

Confucius was not so much an original thinker as a brilliant synthesizer of old ideas. He taught that there is a universal law that even the sun, moon, and stars follow, and that human beings too should live according to this law. Confucius considered the family the basic unit of society. Within the family, male was superior to female, age to youth: thus husband was obeyed by wife, father by son, elder brother by younger. The eldest male, like the Roman *pater familias,* was the head of the family. This order was to be respected even when those in authority were wrong, according to Confucius:

The Master said, In serving his father and mother a man may gently remonstrate with them. But if he sees that he has failed to change their opinion, he should resume an attitude of deference and not thwart them; he may feel discouraged, but not resentful.[10]

Order in the family was the essential building-block of order in society at large.

Confucius, a man of moderation, was an earnest advocate of gentlemanly conduct. Only such conduct, which involved a virtuous and ethical life, could bring about peaceful social relations and well-run government. The Confucian gentleman was a man of integrity, education, and culture, a man schooled in proper etiquette. Asked to evaluate Tzu-ch'an, a minister of the Cheng state, Confucius discussed the virtues of a gentleman:

in him were to be found four of the virtues that belong to the Way of the true gentleman. In his private conduct he was courteous, in serving his master he was punctilious, in providing for the needs of the people he gave them even more than their due; in exacting service from the people, he was just.[11]

The way in which a gentleman disciplined himself is apparent in the conduct of Master

Tseng, the most important of Confucius' followers:

Master Tseng said, Every day I examine myself on these three points: in acting on behalf of others, have I always been loyal to their interests? In intercourse with my friends, have I always been true to my word? Have I failed to repeat the precepts that have been handed down to me?[12]

Confucius pointed out that aristocratic birth did not automatically make a man a gentleman. Even men of humble birth could reach this exalted level through education and self-discipline. Confucius did not advocate social equality, but his teachings minimized the importance of class distinctions and opened the way for intelligent and talented people to rise in the social scale. The Confucian gentleman was made, not born.

This gentleman found his calling as a civil servant: he advised the ruler wisely, administered the kingdom intelligently, and dealt with the people humanely. Confucianism urged good government, emphasizing the duty of a good ruler to rule his people wisely and with compassion. Confucius commented on the qualities of a good ruler:

A country of a thousand war-chariots cannot be administered unless the ruler attends strictly to business, punctually observes his promises, is economical in expenditure, shows affection towards his subjects in general, and uses the labour of the peasantry only at the proper times of year.[13]

Confucianism was a vital ingredient in the evolution of an effective civil service. As a social movement, Confucianism was a distinct and specially recruited community, whose membership was ideally restricted to learned and talented people who embraced high standards of ethical awareness and conduct. Confucianism offered those in authority a body of expertise on the creation and consolidation of

CONFUCIUS *In this scene Confucius sits sedately under a plum tree playing the lute for some of his followers. The Confucian gentleman was expected to be more than an able administrator. He was to possess social and artistic graces as well. (Library of Congress)*

a well-ordered, sound, and powerful state. That expertise, like medical knowledge, demanded to be taken on its own innate merits, and was thus offered in the form of advice and persuasion; it could not legitimately be applied by violence. Neither revolutionaries nor toadies, Confucian scholar-bureaucrats opposed bad government by upholding in non-violent ways the best ideals of statecraft. The Confucian ideal proved so powerful that it has continued to shape Chinese society nearly to the present day.

ca 1523–ca 1027 B.C.	Shang Dynasty and invention of writing
ca 1027–221 B.C.	Chou Dynasty
551–479 B.C.	Confucius and rise of Confucianism
4th century B.C.	Lao-tzu and development of Taoism
ca 250–208 B.C.	Han Fei-tzu and Li Ssu and development of Legalism

TAOISM

The later Chou period was a time of philosophical ferment. Many others besides Confucius were grappling with the problems of mankind, society, and the universal. Especially significant were the Taoists, followers of a school of thought traditionally ascribed to Lao-tzu. Little is known about Lao-tzu's life; he is supposed to have lived in the sixth century B.C., but his very existence has been questioned. The book attributed to him, *Tao Te Ching (Book of the Way and Its Power),* is probably the work of several people and dates only from the fourth century B.C.

Where Confucian political thought was practical and humanist, Taoism argued that political authority cannot bestow peace and order if it restricts itself to the rules and customs of society. The only effective social control stems, according to Lao-tzu, from adherence to the ultimate nature of reality. The Taoist sage points the way to that nature, and without his mystic vision of nature effective rule is impossible. The only way to achieve this end, Lao-tzu taught, is to follow Tao, or the Way of Nature. *Tao Te Ching* portrays the Way as the creative force of nature, as in this passage:

There is a thing confusedly formed,
Born before heaven and earth.
Silent and void
It stands alone and does not change,
Goes round and does not weary.
It is capable of being the mother of the world.
I know not its name
So I style it 'the way'.[14]

According to Taoists, people could be happy only if they abandoned the world and reverted to nature, living simply and alone. Those who followed the Way had no further need of human society. If the philosophy of Taoism had ever been carried to its logical extreme, Taoism would have created a world of hermits.

Taoism treated the problems of government in a dramatically different way from Confucianism. In essence, the Taoists were convinced that government could do most for people by doing as little as possible. *Tao Te Ching* boldly declares that people are better off left to themselves:

Exterminate the sage, discard the wise,
And the people will benefit a hundredfold;
Exterminate benevolence, discard rectitude,
and the people will again be filial;

Exterminate ingenuity, discard profit,
And there will be no more thieves and bandits.[15]

Lao-tzu argued that public works and services, from roadbuilding to law courts, led to higher taxes, which in turn led to unhappiness and even popular resistance. The fewer laws and rules, the better, Taoists urged. The Taoists also spelled out how, if there had to be a government at all, the people should be ruled:

Therefore in governing the people, the sage empties their minds but fills their bellies, weakens their wills but strengthens their bones. He always keeps them innocent of knowledge and free from desire, and ensures that the clever never dare to act.[16]

The people are to be well treated, according to the Taoists, but they will be happiest if they remain uneducated and materially satisfied.

Taoism was most popular among the rulers and ministers who actually governed Chinese society. It gave them a safety valve in a rough-and-tumble world, a way of coping with the extreme pressures they faced. If a ruler suffered defeat or a minister fell out of favor, he could always resign himself to the chaos of the world. In this respect Taoism became a philosophy of consolation – but only for a chosen few. The elite often adopted Taoism for consolation and Confucianism for serious everyday affairs.

LEGALISM

More pragmatic than Confucianism was Legalism, the collective name later given to a number of distinct but related schools of practical political theory that flourished during the Chou period. Among the founders of Legalism were Han Fei-tzu (d. 233 B.C.) and Li Ssu (d. 208 B.C.), both former Confucians who had been heavily influenced by Taoism.

Both were above all pragmatic realists who thought that the state should possess as much power as possible and extend it relentlessly. Their ideal state was authoritarian: the sensible ruler, in their view, should root out all intellectual dissent or resistance and all competing political ideas. Since human nature is evil, according to the Legalists, the ruler must keep the people disciplined, and even suppressed if they are rebellious. The people should be well treated, but need not be educated. The ruler should appropriate their labor to feed his armies and their wealth to fill his coffers. No frivolity is to be tolerated: people are to work and produce; they should not waste their time on the study of history, philosophy, and other such unproductive pursuits. Legalism was ruthless in its approach to the problems of government. Rather than refute Confucian political ideas, it repressed or dismissed them. In that respect, Legalism is similar to many twentieth-century ideologies. Nonetheless, Legalism was realistic and offered Chinese rulers practical solutions to the problem of governing large populations over great distances.

Legalism was at first very influential in practical affairs. Both Han Fei-tzu and Li Ssu were themselves high officials, in a position to put Legalist theories into practice. Though Legalism offered an effective, if harsh, solution to the problems confronting Chou society, it was ultimately too narrow to compete successfully as an independent school with Confucianism and Taoism.

By roughly 250 B.C. India and China had developed highly accomplished urban civilizations sustained by systematic agriculture. Many of the fundamental ideals, beliefs, customs, and religious practices that would leave their mark on succeeding generations in both cultures had already taken shape. Yet whereas

Indian society was permeated by religion, Chinese thought was largely secular in orientation. During these years scholars, poets, and mystics in both lands created literary and philosophical classics that still profoundly influence life in India and China and in other lands. The intellectual flowering of India and China, like that of Greece and Rome, was to be a proud heritage for centuries to come.

NOTES

1. Sir Mortimer Wheeler, *Early India and Pakistan to Ashoka,* Thames and Hudson, London, 1959, pp. 106–107.

2. J. A. B. van Buitenen, trans., *The Mahabharata,* I. *The Book of the Beginning* University of Chicago Press, Chicago and London, 1973, 216.30–217.15.

3. *Rigveda* 10.90, translated by A. L. Basham, *The Wonder That Was India* Grove Press, New York, 1959, p. 241.

4. Juan Mascaro, trans., *The Upanishads,* Penguin Books, London, 1965, pp. 117–118.

5. van Buitenen, *Mahabharata* I. 214.1–7.

6. Juan Mascaro, trans., *The Bhagavad Gita,* Penguin Books, London, 1962, 2.17–21.

7. Arrian *Anabasis* 5.8.2; Plutarch *Alexander* 59.1.

8. B. G. Gokhale, *Ancient India,* 4th ed., Asia Publishing House, Bombay and London, 1959, 32–33.

9. Strabo 15.1.55.

10. Arthur Waley, trans., *The Analects of Confucius* George Allen and Unwin Ltd., London, 1938, 4.18.

11. Ibid. 5.15.

12. Ibid. 1.4.

13. Ibid. 1.5.

14. D. C. Lau, trans., *Lao Tzu, Tao Te Ching* Penguin Books, London, 1963, 1.25.56.

15. Ibid. 1.19.43.

16. Ibid. 1.3.9.

SUGGESTED READING

Much splendid work has been done on the geographical background of ancient Indian society. Two fine works are O. H. K. Spate and A. T. A. Learmouth, *India and Pakistan: A General and Regional Geography,* 3rd ed. (1967), and B. L. C. Johnson, *South Asia: Selective Studies of the Essential Geography of India, Pakistan, and Ceylon* (1969). A masterpiece in its own right is J. Schwartzberg, ed., *An Historical Atlas of South Asia* (1978), the epitome of what a historical atlas should be. Its contents range well into contemporary times.

General histories of India are too numerous to list, with the exception of A. L. Basham, *The Wonder That Was India* (1959), one of the monuments of the field and a good introduction to nearly every aspect of ancient Indian history. Solid too are R. Thapar's two books, *History of India,* vol. 1 (1966), and *Ancient Indian Social History* (1978). Both are highly recommended.

Work on the Indus civilization continues at a rapid pace. A good recent survey is D. P. Agrawal, *The Archaeology of India* (1982), which is marked by good sense and sound judgment. Equally recent is G. L. Possehl, ed., *Harappan Civilization: A Contemporary Perspective* (1982), which combines excavation reports and analysis of material. His *Ancient Cities of the Indus* (1979) reprints articles by a number of scholars, thus providing a variety of perspectives on early Indus developments. Trade between the Indus and Mesopotamia is treated in E. C. L. During Caspers, "Sumer, Coastal Arabia and the Indus Valley in Protoliterate and Early Dynastic Eras," *Journal of Economic and Social History of the Orient* 22 (1979): 121–135.

For the arrival of the Aryans and subsequent developments N. R. Banerjee, *The Iron Age in India* (1965), and C. Chakraborty, *Common Life in the Rigveda and Atharvaveda* (1977), treat the period from different points of view. More difficult but rewarding is F. Southworth, "Lexical Evidence for Early Contacts between Indo-Aryan and Dravidian," in M. M. Deshpande and P. E. Hook, eds. *Aryan and Non-Aryan in India* (1979): 191–234; the book contains a number of stimulating articles on the period.

Early Indian religion is a complex subject, but a series of books provides a good introduction to the topic. Old but still a classic is A. B. Keith, *Religion and Philosophy of the Vedas and Upanishads,* 2 vols. (1925). T. Hopkins, *Hindu Religious Tradition* (1971), and P. S. Jaini, *The Jaina Path of Purification* (1979), cover two of the major religions. A stimulating and far-reaching discussion of intellectual developments is R. Thapar, "Ethics, Religion, and Social Protest in the First Millennium B.C. in North India," *Daedalus* 104 (Spring 1975):119–132. Good translations of Indian literature discussed in the chapter are listed in the Notes.

Among the numerous works describing India's relations with the Persian Empire and Alexander the Great are several titles cited in the Suggested Readings of Chapters 2 and 4. P. H. L. Eggermont, *Alexander's Campaigns in Sind and Baluchistan* (1975), focuses solely on Alexander's activities in India. Chandragupta's reign is treated in R. K. Mookerji, *Chandragupta Maurya and His Times,* rev. ed. (1966); and J. C. Heesterman, "Kautalya and the Ancient Indian State," *Wiener Zeitschrift* 15 (1971):5–22, analyzes the work and thought of Chandragupta's great minister of state.

The Shang Dynasty, once considered legendary, is now the subject of considerable attention. The best place to start is K. C. Chang, *Shang Civilization* (1981). D. Keightley, "The Religious Commitment: Shang Theology and the Genesis of Chinese Political Culture," *History of Religions* 17 (1978):211–223, studies the development of Shang royal bureaucracy. Early Chinese agriculture is a hotly debated topic. Scholars like Ho Ping-ti, "Loess and the Origins of Chinese Agriculture," *American Historical Review* 75 (1969):1–36, argue that Chinese technological and agricultural methods occurred without any significant outside influence; others, like W. Watson, *Cultural Frontiers in Ancient East Asia* (1971), maintain that the Chinese imported techniques from the West.

For the development of the Chinese language, B. Karlgren, *The Chinese Language* (1949), is a clear discussion, although it ignores the Shang. Newer and more comprehensive in its discussion of earlier writing is Ho Ping-ti, *The Cradle of the East* (1975). A lively and readable account of early life and the origins of writing, told primarily from an archaeological standpoint, is J. Hay, *Ancient China* (1973). More technical are K. C. Chang, *The Archaeology of Ancient China,* 3rd ed. (1977), and *Food in Chinese Culture* (1977), an edited volume containing historical and anthropological material. A somewhat dated but still useful survey of these early periods is provided by T. Cheng, *Archaeology in China,* 3 vols. (1957–1963), which treats the prehistoric, Shang, and Chou periods. H. G. Creel, *The Origins of Statecraft in China* (1970), argues forcefully that early Chou emperors maintained firm control over their feudal dependencies in the first centuries of their dynasty.

A fascinating starting point for the study of early Chinese thought is B. I. Schwartz, "Transcendence in Ancient China," *Daedalus* 104 (Spring 1975):57–68, in which he argues that the emphasis in ancient China was on social and political rather than religious themes. So much has been written on Confucius and the Confucian tradition that only a few works can be singled out for mention. A. Waley's translation of the *Analects of Confucius* (1938) is an eminently readable version of the work attributed to Confucius. H. G. Creel, *Confucius and the Chinese Way* (1960), deals with both the historical and mythological Confucius.

The complexities of Taoism are lucidly set out by H. G. Creel, *What Is Taoism?* (1970), which discusses the differences between purposive and contemplative Taoism. One of the most significant of the contemplative Taoists is Chuang-tzu, whose career is studied by A. C. Graham, *Chuangtzu: The Seven Inner Chapters* (1981). H. G. Creel, one of the foremost scholars of early Chinese thought, also provides a sound introduction to Legalism in *Shen Pu-hai* (1974), which demonstrates that, far from being monolithic, Legalism consisted of a number of schools of practical political theory. D. C. Lau's *Lao Tzu, Tao Te Ching* (1963) is a vigorous translation of Lao-tzu's classic. On the careers of Han Fei-tzu and Li Ssu, see D. Bodde, *China's First Unifier* (1938).

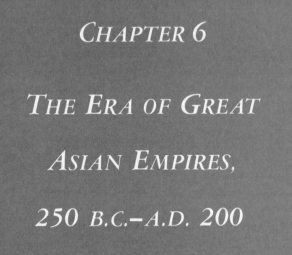

CHAPTER 6

THE ERA OF GREAT

ASIAN EMPIRES,

250 B.C.–A.D. 200

BY ABOUT 250 B.C. the entire vast East was on the threshold of change. Alexander's generals were struggling to hold Iran and the Near East. In India the kingdom created by Chandragupta was coping with the disruption caused by Alexander's whirlwind invasion and other Greek incursions. In China the feudal state of Chou finally disintegrated in civil war. In all three areas, people's responses to these challenging problems led to a new era in their historical development.

The Parthians, originally nomads from Central Asia, first overcame the Greeks and Macedonians in Iran and the Near East and then held off the Roman legions. Ashoka, one of the giants of Indian history, ruled an empire that embraced nearly all of the Indian subcontinent. In China, the emperors of the Ch'in Dynasty put an end to political fragmentation and paved the way for the centuries of prosperity that marked the rule of the Han Dynasty.

How did the Parthians meet the challenge posed by the Western world, and how did they come to serve as a link between China and the Greco-Roman world? How did Ashoka bring security to India, and why did he foster one of the most influential religious developments in the history of the world? How did the Ch'in Dynasty bring political stability to China, and how did the Han perpetuate that stability? What was life like in Han China? These are the questions this chapter will attempt to answer.

THE PARTHIANS, HEIRS OF THE PERSIANS

The Parthians, who now possess the rule of the East – as if a division of the world had been made with the Romans – were once exiles of the Scythians. They were the humblest people in the East in the time of both the Assyrians and the Medes. Afterwards also when the rule of the East passed from the Medes to the Persians, they were a rabble without a name, as though they were the victors' spoils of war. At last, when the Macedonians conquered the East, the Parthians became their slaves, so that it would seem astonishing to everyone that the Parthians, having advanced to such great fortune through their valor, ruled peoples under whose rule they were previously an enslaved mob. Furthermore, provoked by the Romans in three wars . . . , they alone of all people were not equalled, but indeed they proved victorious.[1]

This tribute to the Parthian Empire was written by a Roman, not a Parthian. It is a significant irony that although the Parthians ruled the regions of modern Iran, Iraq, and parts of India for four centuries, virtually everything known about them comes from the observations of foreigners.

The Parthians, despite their power, created little of their own; these nomads-turned-mighty-kings preserved the cultures fashioned under the Persian Empire. After battling the Macedonian successors of Alexander the Great, the Parthians adopted much of Hellenism. The result was a hybrid culture, which they fostered in parts of their empire.

The Parthians stopped the march of Roman armies in the East, but encouraged contact between Greco-Roman culture and the ancient cultures of the Orient. They came into contact with peoples moving westward from the borders of China, and kept open the Silk Road, the great overland caravan route from Han China to the Mediterranean. In India, meanwhile, the Parthians extended their power and administrative methods into the Punjab. Hence, the Parthian Empire spanned the distance between East and West, preserving old cultures and influencing new ones. Above all, the Parthians won their place in history as the heirs of the Persian Empire. They gave Iran centuries of political stability and preserved the heritage of the Persian kings, a heritage that they helped to pass on to posterity.

PARTHIA AND THE SHADOW OF ROME

Although best known for their struggles with Rome, the Parthians' first contacts with the West were their wars with the generals of Alexander the Great. Alexander's successors soon learned that destroying the Persian Empire was far easier than replacing it with a Macedonian empire. There were far too few Greeks and Macedonians to hold down such vast areas, and too many wars ensued among Alexander's successors to permit permanent control of Iran. Into this vacuum moved the Parthians, a band of people who had entered the Iranian plateau from central Asia and had fought with Darius against Alexander. To them ultimately fell the heritage of the Persian Empire and of Alexander's conquests.

Colliding with the Seleucid monarchy, the Parthians under their first king Arsaces (ca 250–248 B.C.) began their conquest of the conquerors of Iran. Further warfare overwhelmed neighboring peoples to the east, including minor Greek strongholds. The Greek kingdom of Bactria in modern Afghanistan (see Map 2.3 on page 55) held out against the Parthians and even extended its sway to northern India. But the Parthians eventually wrested control of part of Greek Bactria, and under their great king Mithridates (ca 171–137 B.C.) they extended their control from Armenia and Babylonia eastward all the way to Bactria. They established a western capital at Ctesiphon in Mesopotamia, near the Seleucid city of Seleucia; in Iran they re-established the old Median capital of Ecbatana, and

PARTHIAN MAILED CAVALRYMAN *This contemporary drawing of a Parthian warrior portrays the type of soldier who overwhelmed Crassus' army and kept the Roman legions at bay. Both rider and horse wear iron armor, and the cavalryman carries a lance and sword. (Yale University Art Gallery, Dura Europas Collection)*

farther east they centered their activities at Hecatompylos in modern Russian Turkestan. Their success was so impressive and undeniable that even the Greeks and Romans marvelled at their achievements, as the testimony of the Greek geographer Strabo (ca 63 B.C.–A.D. 19) attests:

Now at first he [the Parthian king Arsaces] was weak, carrying the war to those whose land he had taken, both he and his successors. In this way the Parthians subsequently became mighty, taking neighboring territory through success in wars, so that accomplishing these feats, they established themselves as lords within the entire area east of the Euphrates. They also took part of Bactria . . . and now they rule so much territory and so many people that they have become in a way rivals of the Romans in the greatness of their empire.[2]

The Parthians had long held firm control of Iran and Mesopotamia when in 92 B.C. the march of empire brought the Romans into the Near East. Although the Hellenistic kings had fallen rather easily to Rome, the Parthians met the Roman advance with iron and courage. The first real test of strength came in 54 B.C. when the Roman general Crassus, friend of Julius Caesar and member of the First Triumvirate (page 171), arrived at the Euphrates with a mighty Roman army. Without provocation, Crassus ordered his army to cross the river into Parthian territory. The Parthians responded by sending an embassy to ask Crassus why he had attacked them without warning or justification:

In response . . . , Crassus boasted that he would give his answer in Seleucia. The oldest of the ambassadors, Vagises, laughing and presenting the palm of his upturned hand, said: "Crassus, hair will grow here before you will see Seleucia."[3]

Near the city of Carrhae in northern Mesopotamia, the Roman legions clashed with the Parthian army under Suren, a military genius. After a long and hard-fought battle, Suren's arrow-firing cavalrymen destroyed Crassus' army in 53 B.C. Parthia had stopped Rome's advance at the Euphrates.

The Romans continued to struggle with Parthia for Mesopotamia, sometimes with fleeting success, but the ancient cultures of Mesopotamia and Iran remained in the Parthian orbit. Crassus' aggressiveness set the pattern for Roman-Parthian relations, but not even Marc Antony and Augustus could overthrow the Parthians. The suffering caused by these wars is apparent in a grim description of the effects of Trajan's two-pronged attack in

114 on a defenseless Parthian subject people, the Mardoi of southern Asia Minor:

A numerous people inhabiting a rugged land, and with such difficulty from it do they, horseless and poor, raise their crops that at present they do not believe in good fortune. The Mardoi were attacked on both sides, being struck by the troops facing them and attacked by those from behind, being pushed back they were perishing.[4]

The Romans made a battleground of Mesopotamia, Armenia, and western Iran, but they never ruled for long. The Parthian bulwark held firm.

PARTHIA AND THE EAST

Parthia played an important and generally far more peaceful role in the East, especially in India. Though usually portrayed as a warrior-folk because of their struggle with Rome, the Parthians actually preferred diplomacy to warfare. Rather than fighting an enemy to the death, they often concluded treaties that benefited both sides. A good example is the Parthians' response to a series of invasions from the East that were nearly as serious as the Roman challenge.

A huge movement of peoples began in the East about 174 B.C. as a result of Chinese efforts to expand their empire. The displaced Huns drove several other folk westward before them. Among these groups were the Shakas, who occupied the area of Tashkent in modern Russia, and the Kushans, who originally dwelt in northwest China. The Shakas, with the Kushans at their heels, overran Bactria and collided with the Parthians, perhaps as early as 130 B.C. The Parthians stubbornly turned back most of the Shakas, who then moved southward into India. The Kushans soon reached Bactria and took control of the area. A complex new distribution of peoples was occurring in the areas of modern Iran, Afghanistan, and Pakistan.

The Parthians simultaneously resisted the invaders and sought peaceful relations with them. They were largely successful. The Shakas adopted Parthian culture wholesale and went on to establish an Indo-Parthian realm in northwestern India. The Shakas paid nominal allegiance to the Parthian kings, but were in fact politically independent; their principal links were cultural rather than political. The Kushans, meanwhile, overthrew the last Greek strongholds in Bactria and created the Kushan Empire in modern Turkestan and Afghanistan. The Kushans made peace with Parthia, and the two powers agreed to a frontier that corresponded closely to that of modern Iran and Afghanistan. By about 60 A.D. the two new empires that had arisen in the East were generally at peace with Parthia and open to Parthian culture. Thus Parthian influence reached beyond the empire's boundaries

and even left its mark on India. In general, the Parthians enjoyed far more peace on their eastern borders than to the west.

THE PARTHIANS BETWEEN EAST AND WEST

The Parthians, though not originators, were culturally cosmopolitan, and this openness helped them to administer their empire. A flexible political organization was a necessity to govern many different peoples across a large area. Like the Seleucids and Persians before them, the Parthians divided their realm into large provinces or satrapies. The central administration of the empire was simple; unlike China, Parthia never had a sophisticated bureaucracy. Nonetheless, the royal secretaries, who were often eunuchs, had important responsibilities. The Parthians spoke Persian among themselves, and Greek and Aramaic were the common tongues of the West. But because they did not impose a common speech on their subjects, Parthian officials had to understand a host of languages. Nor did the Parthians attempt to establish a common culture. They respected the local customs and practices of their subjects, and usually preferred to leave local affairs to local officials. Thanks largely to this policy, the Macedonian conquest of the Persian Empire was more of an interruption than a catastrophe.

The Parthians occupied a position that enabled them to facilitate contact between the Roman and Chinese empires, the two wealthiest and most commercially active realms in the ancient world. Never before in antiquity had the major seats of civilization been in such close contact with one another. The overland lines of communication stretched from China across the vast lands under Parthian control to the eastern provinces of the Roman Empire. Maritime routes linked the Romans to India and even to China. As the middlemen in this trade, the Parthians cleverly tried to keep the Chinese and Romans from making direct contact – and thus from learning how large a cut the Parthians took in commercial transactions.

An elaborate network of roads linked Parthia to China in the east, India in the south, and the Roman Empire in the west. The many branch roads even included routes to southern Russia. The most important of the overland routes was the famous "Silk Road," named for the shipments of silk that passed from China through Parthia to the Roman Empire. Many other luxury items also passed along this route: the Parthians exported exotic fruits, rare birds, ostrich eggs, and other dainties to China in return for iron and delicacies like apricots. Other easily portable luxury goods included gems, gold, silver, spices, and perfumes. From the Roman Empire came glassware, statuettes, and slaves trained as jugglers and acrobats.

Rarely did a merchant travel the entire distance from China to Mesopotamia. Chinese merchants typically sold their wares to Parthians at the Stone Tower, located at modern Tashkurghan in Afghanistan (see Map 6.1). From there Parthian traders carried goods across the Iranian plateau to Mesopotamia or Egypt. This overland trade fostered urban life in Parthia, as cities arose and prospered along the caravan routes. In the process, the Parthians themselves became important consumers of goods, contributing to the volume of trade and reinforcing the commercial ties between East and West.

More than goods passed along these windswept roads. Ideas, religious lore, and artistic inspirations also traveled the entire route. A fine example of how ideas and artistic influences spread across long distances is a Parthian coin that caught the fancy of an artist in China: the coin bore an inscription – a practice the Parthians had adopted from the Greeks – and though the artist could not read it he used the lettering as a motif on a bronze vessel. Similarly, thoughts, ideas, and literary works found ready audiences; Greek plays were performed at the court of the Parthian king. At a time when communication was difficult and often dangerous, trade routes were important avenues for the spread of knowledge about other societies.

This was also an era of exciting maritime exploration. Roman ships sailed from Egyptian ports to the mouth of the Indus River, where they traded local merchandise and wares imported by the Parthians. Merchants who made the voyage had to contend with wind, shoal waters, and pirates, as the Roman writer Pliny the Elder recounts:

For those bound for India the most advantageous sailing is from Ocelis [a city in Arabia]. From there with the wind Hippalos blowing the voyage is forty days to Muziris, the first port in India. It is

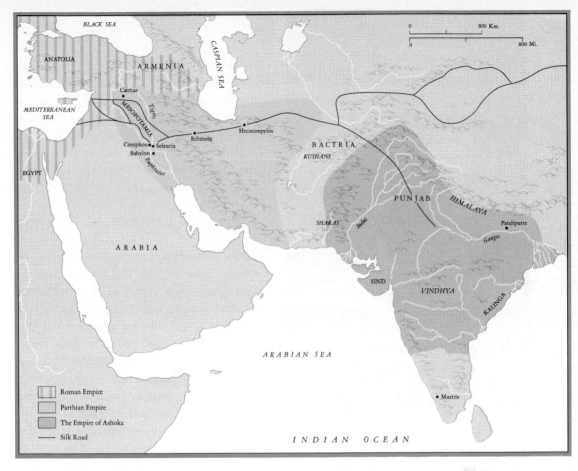

MAP 6.1 THE MAJOR EMPIRES OF CENTRAL
AND SOUTHERN ASIA, CA 250 B.C. From Ana-
tolia in the west to the Himalayas in the east three
great empires ruled western, central, and southern
Asia. During these years, frontiers fluctuated, but the
Silk Road served as a thread connecting them all.

*not a desirable spot because of neighboring pirates,
who occupy a place by the name of Nitrias. Nor is
there an abundance of merchandise there. Besides,
the anchorage for ships is a far distance from
land. Cargoes are brought in and carried out by
lighters [barges].*[5]

Despite such dangers and discomforts, hardy
mariners pushed into the Indian Ocean and
beyond, reaching Malaya, Sumatra, and Java.
Direct maritime trade between China and the
West began in the second century A.D.

For over four hundred years the Parthians
withstood severe pressure on their borders,
preserving the old culture of Iran and fostering Hellenism. During that time they kept
the East and West in constant contact. Eventually, however, the relentless pressure of
Roman attacks weakened Parthian rule in the
Near East. The Roman emperors Septimius
Severus and Caracalla invaded Mesopotamia,
sacking Ctesiphon and Seleucia and dealing
the Parthians their death blow. Yet the Parthians had the last laugh: the Romans crip-

THE ASCETIC BUDDHA *Although often portrayed as a fat and jovial character, the Buddha was sometimes shown as a man on the verge of starvation. Such representations recall the period when the Buddha practiced extreme asceticism in his search for enlightenment. (Giraudon)*

pled the Parthian Empire, but they could not capitalize on their victory. The Parthians had held the line long enough for another Iranian people, the Sassanids, to fill the void left by their fall. The Parthians had upheld the Iranian heritage, and successfully passed it on.

THE MAURYAN EMPIRE IN INDIA

In India the years after Chandragupta's death in 298 B.C. were an epoch of political greatness. Ashoka, one of India's most eminent statesmen, extended the Mauryan Empire to

its farthest limits. The era of Ashoka was enormously important in the religious and intellectual history of the world. A man in search of spiritual solace, Ashoka embraced Buddhism and helped to establish it as an important religion. Buddhism would take deep and lasting root throughout much of the East, but ironically not in India itself.

SIDDHARTHA GAUTAMA AND BUDDHISM

Siddhartha Gautama (ca 536–483 B.C.), better known to the world as the Buddha, meaning the "Enlightened One," was born in northeastern India. As noted in Chapter 5, the Buddha lived at the time when Jainism and Hinduism arose, several hundred years before Ashoka's reign. The Buddha, like Mahavira, the founder of Jainism, was a kshatriya, from a class likely to resent brahmin privilege. They both became dissatisfied with settled life, and abandoned it for a wandering ascetic existence. The Buddha was so distressed by human suffering that he abandoned his family's Hindu beliefs in a quest for a more universal, ultimate enlightenment. He tried techniques of extreme asceticism, including fasting, but came to see that it led nowhere. Only through meditation did he achieve the universal enlightenment in which he comprehended everything, including how the world of *samsara* actually worked. His followers later believed that the Buddha taught them only what was necessary, but that he had seen much more. In this view, what he considered necessary were the "Four Noble Truths" contained in his first sermon. The message of the "Four Noble Truths" is that pain and suffering, frustration and anxiety are ugly but inescapable parts of human life; that suffering and anxiety are caused by the human weaknesses of greed, selfishness, and egoism; that people can understand these weaknesses and triumph over them; and that this triumph is made possible by following a simple code of conduct, what he called "the Eightfold Path."

First, Buddha explained, people have to understand the evils they are suffering. Ultimate release can be achieved only if one has a clear-eyed view of the pain and misery of one's life. Next, one has to decide firmly to free oneself from suffering. This one can do by means of what Buddha called right conduct and right speech, a way of living in which one practices the virtues of love and compassion, joy, and serenity in daily life. The fifth step on the Eightfold Path is to choose "right livelihood," a means of earning a living that does not interfere with the attainment of ultimate enlightenment; the sixth is "right endeavor," the conscious effort to eliminate distracting and harmful desires. People can most readily see the worthlessness of desires, according to Buddha, by recognizing that everything and everyone in the world will pass away. Nothing is permanent. The seventh step is "right awareness," constant contemplation of one's deeds and words, giving full thought to their importance and whether or not they lead to enlightenment. "Right contemplation" is the last step expected of travelers on the Eightfold Path: this step entails deep meditation on the impermanence of everything in the world. With the attainment of the eighth step, the traveler achieves *nirvana,* a state of happiness gained by extinction of self and desires, and release from the effects of *karma.* Thus Buddha propounded his own version of karma and how it worked. Though rooted in Hinduism, Buddhism set off on a road of its own, a road that eventually led out of India altogether, into Ceylon and parts of southeast Asia, through the Kushan Empire and Central Asia into China, Korea, Japan, and Vietnam.

Buddha also taught that if people understand that everything changes with time, they will neither cling to their egos nor worry about what they believe to be their eternal souls. To Buddhists a human being is a collection of parts, physical and mental; as long as these parts remain combined, that combination can be called "I." When that combination changes, as at death, the various parts remain in existence, ready to become the building blocks of different combinations. Buddhism rejected the Hindu doctrine of transmigration of souls but retained the idea of rebirth, casting it in different terms: according to Buddhist teaching, life is passed from person to person as a flame is passed from candle to candle.

Buddhism placed far less emphasis on gods than did Hinduism. The gods might help people out of difficulties like illness, but they could never help people achieve enlightenment. The gods are not, in Buddhist teachings, judges who monitor human life and reign beyond the grave. And, like human beings, the gods too are subject to the laws of change. Nevertheless, Buddha was not strictly an atheist. He conceived of a divine power that was infinite and immortal. As he told his followers, "There is an unborn, an unoriginated, an unmade, an uncompounded; were there not . . . there would be no escape from the world of the born, the originated, the made and the compounded."[6] This unborn and unmade power had nothing to do with the journey to nirvana. That was entirely up to the individual.

The success of Buddhism largely resulted from Buddha's teaching that everyone, noble and peasant, educated and ignorant, could follow the Eightfold Path. Moreover, Buddha was extraordinarily undogmatic. Convinced that each person must achieve enlightenment alone, he emphasized that the Path was important only in that it led the traveler to enlightenment and not for its own sake. He compared it to a raft, essential to cross a river but useless once on the far shore. Buddha warned his followers not to let dogma stand in the way of the journey itself.

Buddha welcomed everyone, regardless of social status or sex, to join him in his exalted journey. He also formed a circle of disciples, the Sangha – in effect, an order of Buddhist monks. Buddha continually reminded his followers that each must reach ultimate fulfillment by individual effort, but he also recognized the value of a group of people striving for the same goal.

After Buddha's death, the Sangha met to decide exactly what Buddhist doctrine was, and to smooth out differences of interpretation that had already sprung up. The result was the early split of Buddhism into two great branches, the Theravada or School of the Elders, and Mahayana or Larger Vehicle. Theravada Buddhism, which claimed to be the purer and stricter form of Buddhist teachings, found its greatest popularity in southeastern Asia from Ceylon to Cambodia.

Far more numerous were the adherents of Mahayana Buddhism, which emphasized the compassionate side of Buddha's teachings. Mahayana Buddhism stressed the possibility of other buddhas yet to come, and taught that all buddhas follow a path open to everyone in the world. Mahayana held that in his previous lives Siddhartha had been a *bodhisattva* – a wise being, a buddha-in-becoming. Bodhisattvas move toward enlightenment, but hold back from it to help others. Later Mahayana Buddhism created a huge pantheon of heavenly buddhas and bodhisattvas to whom people could pray for help toward enlightenment. Mahayana Buddhism eventually won the hearts and minds of the Chinese, Japanese, Koreans, and Vietnamese. Yet it was not until the dramatic conversion of the Indian king Ashoka, some two centuries after the death of

the original Buddha, that Buddhist teachings spread much beyond India.

THE REIGN OF ASHOKA (CA 269–232 B.C.)

Ashoka, the grandson of Chandragupta, was one of India's most remarkable figures. As a young prince, Ashoka served as governor of two important provinces, both seats of Buddhism – still solely an Indian religion – and both commercially wealthy. While governor, Ashoka met and married Devi, a lady of the merchant class who would later end her life spreading Buddhism to Ceylon. The young prince spent his leisure hours hunting and horseback riding, punctuated by lavish feasts. Yet he was also a sensitive and perceptive young man, known for his fondness for and study of birds. In religion Ashoka was deeply influenced by Brahminism and Jainism, which pointed him toward a broader religious outlook.

At the death of his father about 274 B.C., Ashoka rebelled against his older brother, the rightful king, and after four years of fighting succeeded in his bloody bid for the throne. Crowned king of India, he extended Mauryan conquests, initiated or renewed friendly relations with neighboring powers, and reorganized his empire. Ashoka ruled intelligently and energetically. He was equally serious about his pleasures, especially those of the banquet hall and harem. In short, Ashoka in the early years of his reign was an efficient and contented king whose days were divided between business and pleasure.

The change that occurred in the ninth year of his reign affected not just Ashoka and his subjects but the subsequent history of India and the world. That year Ashoka conquered Kalinga, the modern state of Orissa on the east coast of India; in a grim and savage campaign, Ashoka reduced Kalinga by wholesale

ca 269–232 B.C.	Reign of Ashoka
ca 261 B.C.	Kalinga war, leading to spread of Buddhism in India
ca 183–145 B.C.	Greek invasion of India
ca 140 B.C.	First Chinese ambassadors to India
1st century A.D.	Shaka and Kushan invasions of India
A.D. 25–3rd century	Kushan rule in northwestern India
ca A.D. 78	Kushan emperor Kanishka promotes Buddhism

slaughter. As Ashoka himself admitted, "In that (conquest) one hundred and fifty thousand were killed (or maimed) and many times that number died."[7]

Yet instead of exulting like a conqueror, Ashoka was consumed with remorse and revulsion at the horror of war. On the battlefield of Kalinga, the conquering hero looked for a new meaning in life; the carnage of Kalinga gave birth to a new Ashoka. Ashoka embraced Buddhism and used the machinery of his empire to spread Buddhist teachings throughout India.

Ashoka emphasized compassion, nonviolence, and adherence to *dharma*. He may have perceived dharma as a kind of civic virtue, a universal ethical model capable of uniting the diverse people of his extensive empire. Like Constantine, Ashoka erected inscriptions to inform the people of his policy. In one edict, he spoke to his people like a father:

Whatever good I have done has indeed been accomplished for the progress and welfare of the world. By these shall grow virtues namely: proper support of mother and father, regard for preceptors and elders, proper treatment of Brahmins and as-cetics, of the poor and the destitute, slaves and servants.[8]

Ashoka's new outlook can be seen as a form of paternalism, well-meaning government that provides for the people's welfare without granting them much responsibility or freedom. He appointed new officials to oversee the moral welfare of the realm, and made sure that local officials administered humanely.

Ashoka felt the need to protect his new religion and keep it pure. Warning Buddhist monks that he would not tolerate schism – divisions based on differences of opinion about doctrine or ritual – he threw his support to religious orthodoxy. At the same time, Ashoka honored India's other religions: Hinduism and Jainism were revered and respected, and the emperor even built shrines for their worshippers. Buddhism, though royally favored, was just one of India's religions, and it competed peacefully with Hinduism and Jainism for the hearts and minds of the Indian people.

Ashoka felt the need, however, to spread Buddhism beyond India. He sent ambassadors to the larger Hellenistic monarchies to teach

MEMORIAL GATEWAY *This gateway was probably erected by Ashoka in the third century* B.C. *Standing eighteen feet high, the gateway is richly carved and decorated with Buddhist motifs. (The Bettmann Archive)*

the Greeks the message of Buddha. Thus Buddhism and Hellenism came into direct and dramatic contact. The Hellenistic kings were open to new philosophic and religious ideas, but Buddhism never took root in the West; the appeal of Hellenism was too firmly entrenched. Buddhism's great triumph – fully equal to that of Hellenism in the West – was to be in the eastern world.

Ashoka never neglected his duties as emperor. He tightened the central government of the empire and kept a close check on local officials. He also built roads and rest spots to improve communications within the realm. As Ashoka himself described this work:

On the highways Banyan trees have been planted so that they may afford shade to men and animals; mango-groves have been planted; wells have been dug at an interval of every half a kos [approximately every two miles]; resting places have been set up; watering-places have been established for the benefit of animals and men.[9]

These measures also facilitated the march of armies and the armed enforcement of Ashoka's authority. Ashoka's efforts were eminently successful: never before his reign and not again until the modern period did so much of India enjoy peace, prosperity, and humane rule.

INDIA AND ITS INVADERS
(250 B.C.–A.D. 200)

Ashoka's reign was the high point of ancient Indian political history. Although his successors remained on the throne until about 180 B.C., India was thereafter subject to repeated foreign invasions. Like the Aryans, these invaders entered through India's northwestern door. First the Greeks, then the Shakas and Kushans pushed into the Indus Valley, sometimes raiding as far east as the valley of the Ganges. Each wave of invaders overwhelmed its predecessor, but each left its mark on the cultural heritage of India.

The Kushans, whose authority in India lasted until the third century A.D., were particularly significant because their empire encompassed much of central Asia as well as northwestern India. The Kushans put India in closer contact with its eastern neighbors. The Kushan invaders were assimilated into Indian society as *kshatriyas,* of higher status than native Vaisya, Shudra, outcastes, and untouchables, and once again a backward nomadic people fell under the spell of a more sophisticated civilization.

The political map of India after Ashoka was fragmented: the Kushans and earlier invaders held northwestern India, and petty Indian kings ruled small realms in the rest of India. For many years the political history of India was a tale of relentless war among local Indian kings. The energy these wars consumed did nothing for India's capacity to resist the foreign invaders.

Although the Kushans were the final nail in the coffin of Ashoka's political efforts to unite India, they played a valuable role by giving northwest India a long period in which to absorb the newcomers and adapt the cultural innovations introduced by the various invaders. The Kushans were very receptive to external influence, and were themselves subject to many of the influences that acted on the Indians. Kushans and Indians alike absorbed Greek ideas. Greek culture made its greatest impression on Indian art: Greek artists and sculptors working in India adorned Buddhist shrines, modelling the earliest representation of Buddha on Hellenistic statues of Apollo, and were the leading force behind the Gandhara school of art in India. Only the form, however, was Greek; the content was purely Buddhist. In short, India owes a mod-

GANDHARA SCHOOL   This relief shows the impact of Greek art on India. The composition, decoration, and rendering of figures are all typically Greek, but the scene depicts Indians drinking and dancing. (The Cleveland Museum of Art, Dudley P. Allen Fund)

est cultural debt to Hellenism. Just as Ashoka's Buddhist missionaries made no impression on the Greek world, so Hellenism gave India some fresh ideas but had no lasting impact on the essence of Indian life. Only Buddhism, which addressed itself to all human beings rather than any particular culture, was at all significant as a meeting-ground for the Greeks, Indians, and Kushans. Otherwise, the outlooks and values of Greek and Indian cultures were too different and too tenacious for one to assimilate the essence of the other.

The Kushans had even less of a cultural impact on India than did the Greeks, but they proved to be important cultural middlemen. The Kushans stood between the Parthian Empire and China, and they also made direct contact with the early Roman Empire by sea. To India they passed on goods and ideas just as the Parthians had. Having originated on China's western frontier, the Kushans maintained their ties with China and stimulated

Chinese trade with India. This trade awakened interest in India among the Chinese, who as early as about 140 B.C. sent envoys to learn more about their Indian neighbors. One ambassador sent back the following description of India to the Chinese emperor:

The people cultivate the land and live much like the people of Ta-hsia [Bactria]. The region is said to be hot and damp. The inhabitants ride elephants when they go into battle. The kingdom is situated on a great river.[10]

The ambassador's report represents a first groping for contact. The link, once made, held and grew in importance. Knowledge and intellectual curiosity accompanied merchandise along the trade routes, drawing the entire civilized world closer together.

The most important thing the Kushans passed from India to China was Buddhism. According to Buddhist tradition, the Kushan emperor Kanishka – who flourished about 78 A.D. – became a second Ashoka in his devotion to Buddhism, a ruler who wanted to spread Buddha's gentle teachings to the larger world. Kanishka protected the welfare of the Buddhist order. To keep Buddhism pure, he convened a council of Buddhist monks and scholars who reviewed, collected, and edited all Buddhist teachings and philosophy. Kanishka's preference for the Mahayana sect of Buddhism, more compassionate and flexible than its rival Theravada branch, was instrumental in its widespread success. Kanishka and the Kushans carried Mahayana Buddhism to China, transforming it from an Indian sect into an international religion. As champions of Buddhism, the Kushans were instrumental in preserving a priceless heirloom of India's heritage and in changing the course of Chinese history.

Between about 250 B.C. and A.D. 200 India's mightiest empire gave way to foreign invaders in the northwest and political fragmentation elsewhere. The same period saw the flowering and dissemination of Mahayana Buddhism. Culturally India imbibed external influences but gave far more than it received. Indian culture spread to the Kushans, and Buddhism was India's splendid gift to China. India also remained in touch with the leading commercial centers of antiquity. Only in the political sphere, in fact, did India's star fade after Ashoka's reign. Indian culture flourished and enriched the lives of India's neighbors.

CHINA, THE AGE OF EMPIRE

The leader of the state of Ch'in deposed the last Chou king in 256 B.C. Within thirty-five years he had made himself sole ruler of China, taking the title Ch'in Shih Huang Ti or First Emperor. Thus began the Ch'in Dynasty. Although the Ch'in Dynasty lasted only some fifteen years, the work of its emperors endured for centuries. Indeed, the Western name for China is derived from the Ch'in. The First Emperor unified China under a central government as never before, and the Han Dynasty, which replaced the Ch'in, maintained this unity for centuries. Under the emperors of the Ch'in and Han, China flourished economically, culturally, and socially.

THE CH'IN AND UNIFICATION OF CHINA

The ancient Chinese historian Ssu-ma Ch'ien left this vivid description of the victory of the First Emperor:

With its superior strength Ch'in pressed the crumbling forces of its rivals, pursued those who had fled in defeat, and overwhelmed and slaughtered the army of a million until their shields floated upon a river of blood. Following up the advantages of its victory, Ch'in gained mastery over the empire and divided up its mountains and rivers. The powerful states begged to submit to its sovereignty and the weaker ones paid homage at its court.[11]

The Ch'in extended their sway as far south as modern Hong Kong and the South China Sea, introducing Chinese influence into vast new areas. Ch'in armies even penetrated as far as northern Vietnam. With this hard-won victory came political unity, which the First Emperor was determined to maintain.

The First Emperor considered a highly centralized state necessary to ensure a united China. He and his prime minister, Li Ssu, an ardent follower of Legalism, embarked on an imaginative, sweeping, and rigorous program of centralization that touched the lives of nearly everyone in China. At the head of the state stood the emperor, an autocrat possessing absolute power. His first act was to cripple the feudal nobility. As Louis XIV of France was to do many centuries later, the emperor ordered the nobility to leave their lands and appear at his court. Aristocratic families all across China were torn from their estates and transported to Hsienyang, the capital of Ch'in, where they built new homes around the court. The emperor took over their feudal estates and organized China into a system of large provinces, which were further subdivided into smaller units.

The emperor controlled the provinces by appointing governors and lesser administrators, as well as other officials to keep watch on them. These officers were not drawn from the old aristocracy, and owed their power and position entirely to the favor of the emperor. Unlike the old aristocracy, they could not claim hereditary rights to their positions. The governors kept order in the provinces, enforcing laws and collecting taxes. It was one of their most important and least popular duties to draft men for the army and to work on huge building projects.

In the interest of harnessing the enormous human resources of his people, the First Emperor ordered a census of the entire population. This information helped the imperial bureaucracy to plan its activities, estimating the costs of public works and the tax revenues needed to pay for them. The census also enabled the emperor to calculate the labor force available for military service and building projects.

A highly centralized empire needs good communications. Yet communication over an area as vast as China presented a huge challenge, which the emperor met in several ways. First there was the problem of language itself. During the Chou period, the various feudal states often spoke their own distinct dialects of Chinese, which frequently borrowed words from other dialects. Written language also varied from dialect to dialect, some people using signs that were unintelligible to others.

These variations in language made central administration complicated and difficult. However literate, a governor might find himself transferred to a province whose dialect and script were unfamiliar to him; in such a case, he would be handicapped at the outset in carrying out his duties. The First Emperor and his ministers solved this problem by standardizing the written script.

Next the First Emperor standardized the weights, measures, and coinage of the realm. The old coinage was abolished in favor of new round coins with square holes in the center. The new coinage and system of weights and measures made it much easier for the central government to collect taxes. The emperor also standardized the axle-lengths of carts: most Chinese roads at the time were nothing more than deep tracks cut by the wheels of carts; uniform axle-lengths meant that all carts could use the same ruts, improving communications and making travel quicker and more convenient.

The First Emperor initiated land reforms that gave peasant farmers greater rights. He furthered irrigation projects and encouraged land reclamation to bring more soil under cultivation. These efforts, together with the widespread use of iron tools, increased agricultural production and fostered prosperity. The emperor also promoted the weaving of textiles, especially silk, which remained the aristocrat of Chinese fabrics. Thanks to the new road system, goods moved more easily than ever before and trade increased. Although merchants became important figures, their social status remained low; the First Emperor looked down on them as distinctly less than gentlemen. The growth of trade stimulated further growth of towns. Ch'in reforms and centralization helped create a broader and healthier economy, which in turn provided a solid tax base for the government.

THE GREAT WALL OF CHINA   The size and sheer awesomeness of the Great Wall comes through strikingly in this print. Over hill and through valley the Great Wall spanned some 3000 miles of northern China. (From D. Mennie and P. Weale, The Pageant of Peking, *1922)*

FOREIGN DANGER AND INTERNAL UNREST

While the First Emperor was working to bring China unity and prosperity, he faced constant peril on the northern border. For years the Chinese had pushed northward, driving out the nomads and taking over their grassy pasture lands. These nomads were the Huns, who in later centuries would carry death, destruction, and terror to the decaying Roman Empire. Chinese encroachment on their land endangered the very survival of the Huns, scattered tribes each led by its own chieftain. In retaliation the Huns, on horseback and armed with swords and bows, struck back at the Chinese time and again. Sweeping down in quick raids, they plundered prosperous towns and farms and disappeared back into the vastness of the north.

Since Chinese expansion in the north had all along met stiff opposition, the northern states had built long walls for self-protection as early as the fourth century B.C. (page 163). The First Emperor ordered these various stretches of wall to be linked together in one Great Wall, extending from the sea some 3,000 miles to the west. The number of laborers who worked on the wall and the sheer amount of construction material needed are stunning tribute to the First Emperor's power. The Great Wall of China is probably humanity's most immense creation. The Great Wall and the huge numbers of troops guarding the frontier gave the north a period of peace.

Despite their innovations and achievements and the peace they brought to the north, the Ch'in were unpopular rulers. The First Emperor was no altruist. Primarily interested in his own wealth and power, he was determined to reap the profits of his work. Nor was he a man to tolerate opposition: as a Legalist, he distrusted Confucian scholars, some 460 of whom he reportedly had buried alive. He tried to destroy Confucian literature and China's ancient literary heritage by a massive campaign of book-burning. He enforced the tenets of Legalism vigorously and ruthlessly in an effort to wipe out any system of thought that might challenge his autocratic position. The Ch'in demanded obedience, not intelligence.

The common people fared no better than the Confucian scholars. The Ch'in took advantage of the new prosperity to levy heavy taxes, especially on the peasants. Taxation and forced labor on the Great Wall and other projects mercilessly ground down the peasantry. Forced labor and military service disrupted many peasant households; while the men were away, their families worked long, dreary hours to feed themselves and meet the staggering burden of taxes.

The oppressiveness of the Ch'in bred fierce hatred among the people, one of whom described the First Emperor as a monster who "had the heart of a tiger and a wolf. He killed men as though he thought he could never finish, he punished men as though he were afraid he would never get around to them all."[12] The death of the First Emperor in 210 B.C. sparked massive revolts. Huge bands of peasants took up arms against the new emperor. In the ensuing struggle for power, Liu Pang, a peasant and petty official of the Ch'in, defeated his opponents and in 202 B.C. established the Han Dynasty.

THE GLORY OF THE HAN DYNASTY
(202 B.C.–A.D. 220)

The Han Dynasty marked the beginning of China's early imperial age. The dynasty also gave the Chinese their name: they have traditionally called themselves "the men of Han." Liu Pang, the victorious rebel, was no revolutionary. Because he retained the main features of Ch'in administration and made no social reforms, there was no serious break in culture or politics between the two dynasties. The extreme political centralization of the Ch'in was relaxed, but the Han did not revive the feudalism of the Chou emperors. At least in theory, the Han Empire had an autocratic emperor aided by an educated but nonaristocratic bureaucracy. The basis of the empire, as always, was China's vigorous and hard-working peasants.

Under capable emperors like Liu Pang (206–195 B.C.), and his immediate successors, China recovered from the oppression and turmoil of the Ch'in period. Unable to conquer the Huns, who were renewing their threats on the northern border, the Chinese first tried to buy them off with lavish presents and stirred up internal trouble among Hunnish chiefs. In 133 B.C., however, Emperor Han Wu Ti changed this policy and went on the attack. In fourteen years of fighting the Han drove the Huns still farther north. Chinese armies advanced into western Turkestan, where they opened up direct relations with the Kushan Empire and came into closer contact with the Parthian Empire. Equally impressive were the Han emperors' gains in the south. Chinese armies conquered western Korea, where they took over the trade with Japan. The Han also

extended their rule to modern-day Canton and the southeastern coast of China. By III B.C. when the emperor Han Wu Ti conquered northern Vietnam, Chinese rule had spread far beyond the natural boundaries of China.

Han military conquests brought the Chinese into closer contact with distant peoples, which resulted in a dramatic increase in trade with the outside world. It was the Han emperor Wu Ti who took the momentous step of opening the Silk Road to the Parthian and Roman Empires. In exchange for silk and other luxury items, China imported grapes, clover, luxury pieces, and even acrobats and jugglers. By this route the Kushans introduced Buddhism to China.

When Wu Ti conquered northern Vietnam in III B.C., Chinese and foreign merchants moved in and set up trading stations under the supervision of Chinese officials. Southern China and northern Vietnam became meeting-grounds for different cultures. The people of northern Vietnam embraced Chinese culture enthusiastically, while regions not far to the south were falling under the influence of Indian culture carried there by Indian merchants. Indeed, an independent state, called Funan by the Chinese, arose in modern southern Vietnam and Cambodia among Ma-layan people who adopted many aspects of Indian culture.

Chinese rule in the south stimulated trade, and under the Han emperors Chinese merchants opened a new route from southwestern China via the rivers of Vietnam and Burma to ports on the Bay of Bengal. At first the Chinese were content to leave maritime trade in the hands of Indians, Arabs, and other middlemen, but a later Han emperor sent an ambassador direct to the Roman Empire by sea. The ambassador, Kan Ying, sailed to the Roman province of Syria, where during the reign of the Roman emperor Nerva (page 254) he became the first Chinese official to have a firsthand look at the Greco-Roman world. Kan Ying enjoyed himself thoroughly, and in A.D. 97 delivered a fascinating report of his travels to his emperor:

The inhabitants of that country are tall and well-proportioned, somewhat like the Chinese, whence they are called Ta-ts'in. The country contains much gold, silver, and rare precious stones . . . corals, amber, glass . . . gold embroidered rugs and thin silk-cloth and asbestos cloth. All the rare gems of other foreign countries come from there. They make coins of gold and silver. Ten units of silver are worth one of gold. They traffic by sea

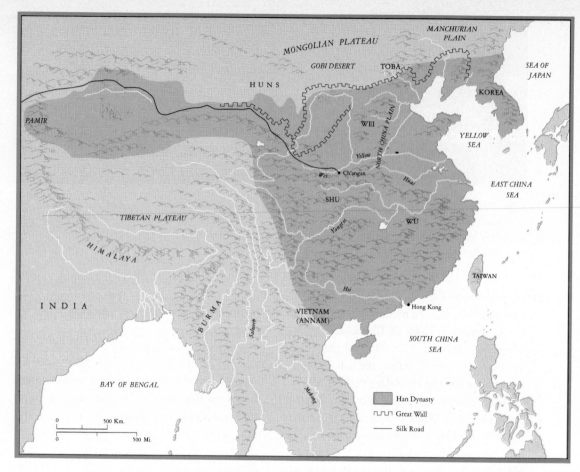

MAP 6.2 CHINA UNDER THE HAN DYNASTY,
206 B.C.–A.D. 220 *The glory of the Han Dynasty
is evident from this map. Unlike China under the
Chou, frontiers have been pushed far into central and
southeastern Asia. The Han ruled over far more territory than any previous dynasty.*

with An-hsi *(Parthia) and T'ien-chu (India),
the profit of which trade is ten-fold. They are
honest in their transactions and there are no double prices. Cereals are always cheap . . . . Their
kings always desired to send embassies to China,
but the An-hsi (Parthians) wished to carry on
trade with them in Chinese silks, and it is for
this reason that they were cut off from communication.*[13]

Trade between China and the Roman Empire
flourished during the Han Dynasty, bringing

the two greatest empires of the ancient world
into largely indirect but constant contact.

Han rule was so successful that China enjoyed unparalleled peace and prosperity. The
Han historian Ssu-ma Ch'ien left a glowing
report of Han administration as it existed
around the year 136 B.C.:

*The nation had met with no major disturbances so
that, except in times of flood or drought, every person was well supplied and every family had enough
to get along on. The granaries in the cities and the*

countryside were full and the government treasuries were running over with wealth. In the capital the strings of cash had stacked up by the hundreds of millions until the cords that bound them had rotted away and they could no longer be counted. In the central granary of the government, new grain was heaped on top of the old until the building was full and the grain overflowed and piled up outside, where it spoiled and became unfit to eat .... Even the keepers of the community gates ate fine grain and meat.[14]

The Han emperors clearly rivalled the Roman emperors not only in the extent of territory under their control but also in the quality of life their subjects enjoyed.

HAN CONFUCIANISM AND INTELLECTUAL REVOLT

Confucianism made a comeback during the Han Dynasty, but it was a changed Confucianism. Confucian texts had fed the First Emperor's bonfires, never to be recovered. Some dedicated scholars had hidden their books, and others had memorized whole books: one ninety-year-old man was able to recite two books virtually in their entirety. These heroic efforts saved much of China's ancient literature and Confucian thought from the Ch'in holocaust.

While trying to reconstruct the past, the new Confucianism was being influenced by other schools of thought, even the hated Legalism. Strengthened by these influences, Confucianism once again took firm hold – a hold so strong that Confucianism has endured as the intellectual and cultural basis in China until the twentieth century. During this period, Confucian scholars pondering China's past elaborated on the theory that dynasties last only as long as they retain the Mandate of Heaven (page 162). Heaven, the chief Chinese deity, gives the ruler the right to govern society. To account for the fall of dynasties, they developed a cyclical theory that dynasties fall when they lose the Mandate of Heaven, which passes on to others.

According to Han Confucianism, the emperor was the intermediary between society and heaven. He served this function by performing all the sacred rites to the deities correctly and scrupulously, and by watching for signs that heaven was displeased. He was also responsible for protecting the empire from outside threats and invasions, and for maintaining order in the empire with as little interference as possible in the lives of the people. If the emperor failed in these tasks, he lost the Mandate of Heaven and risked losing his throne to a worthier claimant. Confucianism explained history by looking to the virtues and vices of individuals, especially emperors and dynasties; Confucian historians saw history not as progressive but as cyclical, consisting of repetitions of the same kinds of events.

In this climate of thought, the study of history flourished. Generations of Chinese scholars devoted their efforts to studying particular dynasties and events, and individual rulers, ministers, and generals. The Chinese, like the Greeks earlier, conceived of history as broader and more complex than the mere chronicling of events. Indeed, during the Han Dynasty China produced one of its finest historians, Ssu-ma Ch'ien (ca 145–86 B.C.). Ssu-ma could be seen as the Chinese equivalent of the Greek Thucydides. Like Thucydides, he believed fervently in visiting the sites where history was made, examining artifacts, and questioning people about events. Ssu-ma was also interested in China's geographical variations, local customs, and local history. As an official of the emperor, he had access to important people and documents and to the imperial library. Having decided to write a history of China down to his own time, Ssu-ma set about interviewing eyewitnesses and those who had shaped events. He also reviewed official documents and written records. The result, ten years in the making, was his classic *Records of the Grand Historian,* a massive work of literary and historical genius.

Nor did Ssu-ma's work die with him. The Pan, a remarkably creative family, took up his study of the Han. Among the most eminent of the Pan was Pan Chao, China's first woman historian and scholar. Pan Chao also wrote poems and essays, notably *Lessons for Women* on the education of women. Taking up Ssu-ma Ch'ien's history, the Pan family wrote the first history of a Chinese dynasty. Thereafter, official court historians wrote the history of every dynasty. Like their Greco-Roman counterparts, Chinese historians considered recent and current history important in their investigations.

Han intellectual pursuits were not limited to history. In medicine, the Han period produced its own Hippocrates, Ching Chi, a practicing physician whose *Treatise on Fevers* became a standard work in Chinese medicine. Chinese surgeons grappled with the problem of reducing the pain of surgery, and the Han physician Hua To developed a drug that, mixed with wine, would render the patient unconscious.

The career of the great mathematician Chang Heng (A.D. 78–139) was strikingly similar to that of the Hellenistic philosopher Eratosthenes (pages 135–136). Both delved deeply into astronomy, and both independently concluded that the world is round, not flat as many contemporaries assumed. Like Eratosthenes, Chang Heng was not content to speculate; he also built models to test his theories. Chang Heng even designed a seismograph capable of discerning the direction

in which an earthquake was taking place, though not its severity. The brilliance of intellectual achievements during the Han period fully matched the breadth of Han intellectual activity.

DAILY LIFE DURING THE HAN DYNASTY

Because the people who chronicled events in Han China were elites writing for other elites, more is known about the upper levels of society than the lower. The lives of the common people were taken for granted or considered too vulgar to write about. Yet though a complete and detailed portrayal is beyond reach, it is possible to sketch the outlines of life in Han China.

The peasant farmer was the backbone of Han society. As in Roman society, agriculture was considered an important and honorable human activity, which distinguished the civilized Chinese from their barbaric and nomadic neighbors. Small households of peasants worked the land, which generated most of the revenue of the empire. The Chinese peasant family was probably small, four or five people, frequently including a grandparent. Both husband and wife performed hard manual labor in the fields, and women were significant economic assets to poor farmers. Men were typically required to spend time each year in the service of the emperor; and while they were away, their wives ran the farm. Farmers' existence was tenuous, for floods, drought, and unduly harsh taxes could wipe them out completely. Especially injurious was harsh and inefficient government. When severely oppressed, peasants revolted, turned to a life of begging or banditry, or, like many common people in the later Roman Empire, put themselves under the protection of powerful landlords. Thus it is easy to understand why the Han emperors were so proud of the peace and security of their reigns, which spared Chinese farmers the worst evils.

The staple grain under cultivation varied depending on soil and climate. In the warmer and wetter south, rice was the traditional crop; in the north, farmers raised millet and wheat wherever possible. In northwestern China peasants raised barley, which thrived on land too poor for wheat. Farmers also grew hemp, which was woven into coarse clothing for common people. Some fortunate farmers had groves of timber or bamboo to supplement their crops. Most fortunate of all were those who grew mulberry trees, the leaves of which nourish silkworms, or groves of lac trees, which produced decorative lacquer. Wherever possible, farmers grew fruit and nut trees; farmers near cities found ready profit growing vegetables and spices, like ginger, for the city folk. Tea and sugar cane were raised in southern China but were still luxury items during the Han period.

Land use became systematic and effective under the Han, probably as a result of experience and of innovations recommended by Chao Kuo, a Han minister. Chao Kuo introduced a regularized ridge-and-furrow system of planting, with seeds planted in lines along the furrows. This method yielded fairly regular harvests, and facilitated land rotation in that the position of the ridges and furrows could change annually. To maintain the fertility of the soil farmers treated their land with manure and crushed bones. The intensive character of Chinese agriculture meant that very little land was available for pasturage. Unlike his Indian counterpart, the Chinese farmer seldom raised cattle, horses, or donkeys. Dogs, pigs, and chickens were the typical domestic farm animals. The lack of draft animals meant that most farm work was done by hand and foot.

Farmers used a variety of tools in their

A HAN FARMSTEAD A pottery model of a wealthy farmstead shows the buildings grouped around a central courtyard. The outer walls of the buildings form a barricade to protect the family and its possessions. (Robert Harding Associates)

work, but the most important was the plough. The earliest wooden plough had been a simple tool, more often pulled by humans than by animals. The new and more effective plough that was introduced during the Han period was fitted with two ploughshares and guided by a pair of handles. This plough too could be pulled by manpower, but was typically pulled by a pair of oxen. The Chinese also developed an elaborate system of long hammers for milling grain and pounding earth. At first these hammers were driven by people working pedals; later they were operated by animals and waterpower. Farmers used fans to blow the chaff from the kernels of grain, and either mortar and pestle or hand mills to grind the grain into flour. Irrigation water was pumped into the fields with devices ranging from a simple pole with attached bucket and counterweight to sophisticated machines worked by foot.

VILLAGE LIFE   These tomb figures depict an ordinary scene of village life in Han China. The two mounted figures represent wealthy men, for most villagers were too poor to keep horses. (The St. Louis Art Museum, Gift of the heirs of Berenice Ballard)

The agricultural year began in mid-February with the breaking up of heavy soil and manuring of the fields. This was the time to sow gourds, onions, melons, and garlic and to transplant oak, pine, and bamboo trees. February was also the beginning of the New Year, a time of celebration and an important religious festival. Besides grain, farmers sowed beans and hemp and a variety of herbs. During the second and third months of the year, farmers practiced their archery to defend themselves against the bandits who infested the countryside; as a further precaution, they repaired the gates and locks of their houses.

The fifth month was the time to cut the hay, and the sixth to hoe the fields. Meanwhile the women of the family were hard at work nurturing silkworms and making silk cloth, which they would later dye. Women also worked the hemp into coarse cloth. With the harvest, processing, and storage of the crop, farmers were ready for winter and the coming year.

City life was varied and hectic compared to the regularity of farming. The wealthiest urbanites lived in splendid houses of two or more stories, surrounded by walls and containing at least one courtyard. These palatial homes shared with ancient Greek houses such features as storage rooms and rooms for animals in the courtyard. The rooms or outhouses used for grain storage were built on stilts to protect against rats and moisture, which could cause rot or mildew.

The house itself was usually four-sided, with the door in one wall. The floors of the poor were covered with animal skins and mats of woven grass, those of the rich with finely embroidered cushions and wool rugs. The bedrooms of wealthy homes were furnished with wooden beds, embroidered draperies, and beautiful screens for privacy. Fine furniture of expensive wood and beautifully lacquered bowls graced the houses of the wealthy.

Wealthy urban dwellers loved costly clothes, and everyone who could afford to bought fine and brightly colored silks. The wealthy also spent money on furs, usually fox and squirrel and sometimes badger. Expensive shoes lined with silk and decorated with leather became extremely popular. Wealthy women wore jewelry of jade and other precious and semiprecious stones, as well as gold earrings and finger rings. The urban poor probably had easier and somewhat cheaper access to silk garments than their rural neighbors, but their clothing was primarily made of coarse hemp cloth.

The diet of city folk, like their clothing, could be rich and varied. Owing to general prosperity, people during the Han period began to eat meat more frequently. Demand increased dramatically for wild game and young animals and fish, which were seasoned with leeks, ginger, and herbs. No longer was rice wine, like meat, a luxury for festival days. It began to be consumed avidly, and very wealthy Chinese began to age vintages for twenty to thirty years. The Chinese, like the Romans, were especially fond of pork, and roast pig was one of the most popular gourmet dishes. Other favorites were minced fish prepared in herbs and spices, and fowl served in orange sauce, together with pickles and a variety of relishes. The Chinese also enjoyed liver and dog meat. Wood and pottery utensils were standard features of common households, but rich people relegated wood and pottery to the kitchen, and dined on dishes decorated with gold and silver.

People with money and taste patronized music, and the very rich often maintained private musical troupes consisting of small choirs, bells, drums, pipes. Flutes and stringed instruments were also popular. People of more common taste flocked to puppet shows and performances of jugglers and acrobats. Magic shows dazzled the impressionable, and cockfighting appealed to bloody tastes. Gambling was popular but considered decidedly vulgar, and archaeologists have found several board games.

As gangs of bandits infested the countryside, so crime plagued the cities. Officials were open to corruption, and sometimes connived with criminals and gangs of thugs who had the support of wealthy and powerful families. Sometimes the situation got so far out of hand that private armies roamed the streets, wearing armor and carrying knives and preying on the weak and helpless. In such situations, poor people who lacked influence often suffered outrages and violence with no hope of justice or retribution.

Silk was in great demand all over the known world during the Han period, and strings of caravans transported bales of it westward. Another distinctive Chinese product was lacquered ware. Parts of China nourish the lac tree, which secretes a resinous fluid refinable to a hard and durable varnish. Han craftsmen developed lacquerwork to a fine art. Because lacquer creates a hard surface that easily withstands wear, it was the ideal preservative for articles of daily use such as cups, dishes, toilet articles, and even parts of carriages. Lacquered boxes and other articles were often decorated with ornamental writing or inlaid with precious metals. Such works of art were of course only for the rich; poor people contented themselves with plain lacquered ware at best. Some of the most splendid examples of lacquerwork are elaborately carved; Chinese craftsmen loved geometric designs, and some of their work is so accurate that it suggests they probably used mechanical tools.

Perhaps the most momentous product of Han imagination was the invention of paper, which the Chinese traditionally date to A.D. 105. Scribes had previously written on strips of bamboo and wood. Fine books like those in the royal library were written on silk rolls, but only the wealthiest could afford such luxury. Ts'ai Lun, to whom the Chinese attribute the invention of paper, worked the fibers of rags, hemp, bark, and other scraps into sheets of paper. Though far less durable than wood, paper was far cheaper than silk. As knowledge of papermaking spread, paper became a cheap and convenient means of conveying the written word. By the fifth century paper had come into common use, paving the way for the later invention of printing.

Han craftsmen continued the Chinese tradition of excellent metallurgy. By the beginning of the first century A.D., China had about fifty state-run ironworking factories. These factories smelted crude iron ore, processed it with chemicals, and fashioned the metal into ingots before turning it over to the craftsmen who worked it into tools and other articles. The products of these factories demonstrate a sophisticated knowledge of metals and refinement. Han workmen turned out iron ploughshares, agricultural tools with wooden handles, and such weapons as swords, spears, armor, and arrowheads. Han metalsmiths were mass-producing superb crossbows long before the crossbow had been dreamed of in Europe.

Iron was replacing bronze in tools, but bronzeworkers still turned out a host of goods. Bronze was prized for jewelry, dishes, and spoons. It was the preferred metal for crossbow triggers and ornate mirrors. Bronze was also used for minting coins and for precision tools like carpenters' rules and adjustable wrenches. Bronze and wood were used for wagon and carriage wheels; Han wheels were made either convex or concave to give a smoother ride. Surviving bronze gear and cog wheels bear eloquent testimony to the sophistication of Han machinery.

Distribution of the products of Han craftsmen was in the hands of merchants, whom Chinese aristocrats, like ancient Hebrew wise men, considered necessary but lowly. In the Chinese scale of values, agriculture was honorable because farmers worked to win the gifts that nature bestowed. Merchants, however, thrived on the toil of others, and the art of winning profits was considered ungentlemanly and not quite legitimate. The first Han emperor took action to put merchants in their place, as the great historian Ssu-ma relates:

After peace had been restored to the empire, Kao-tsu [Liu Pan's posthumous name as emperor] issued an order forbidding merchants to wear silk or ride in carriages, and increased the taxes that they were obliged to pay in order to hamper and humiliate them.[15]

Yet the emperors and ministers of Han China realized fully that merchants had become indispensable. One outcome of this ambiguity was the conclusion that merchants ought to be regulated. Another was an early form of limited socialism — state monopolies on es-

221–210 B.C.	Establishment of the Ch'in Dynasty and unification of China
	Construction of the Great Wall
	Destruction of Confucian literature
202 B.C.–A.D. 220	Establishment of the Han Dynasty
III B.C.	Chinese expansion to the South China Sea and Vietnam
ca 104 B.C.	Opening of the Silk Road to the Parthian and Roman Empires; spread of Buddhism into China begins
A.D. 97	Direct maritime contact begins with the Roman Empire
221–280	Three Kingdoms Era
4th–5th centuries A.D.	Barbarian invasions

sential commodities like iron and salt, which made for price stability.

Retail merchants set up shop in stalls in the markets, grouped together according to their wares. All the butchers, for example, congregated in one part of the market, each trying to outsell the others. Nearly everything could be found in the markets, from food to horses and cattle, from oxcarts and metal hardware to fine silks. The markets were also the haunts of entertainers and fortunetellers. The imperial government stationed officials in the markets to police the selling of goods and to levy taxes on the merchants. The imperial government also chose markets for the public execution of criminals: the rolling of heads served as an example and a warning to would-be criminals and political agitators in the crowd.

The transportation of goods in bulk was still difficult and expensive. Roads were still primitive, but the Han developed several sturdy and effective types of carts and wagons, and a new harness for horses came into widespread use. Where earlier harnesses had fitted around the horse's neck, choking the animal when it pulled a load, the new harness fitted around the horse's chest and over its back, enabling it to pull heavier loads with less effort. This efficient horse collar finally reached medieval Europe in the eighth century A.D., a product of Asian technology that vastly influenced the history of the West.

Because of the difficulty of overland travel, the Chinese relied heavily on water transport. Since the major rivers of China run east-west, canals were cut between the rivers to make north-south traffic possible. Bulk foodstuffs and goods could be transported fairly cheaply and swiftly on river boats, which also provided reasonably comfortable living quarters for crew and passengers. Maintenance of canals and dikes was expensive and made huge demands on the labor force, but these waterways gave China a flexible and effective network of communications.

HAN WATCHTOWER *This sumptuous watchtower not only provided safety, but it was also furnished with comfortable rooms and broad balconies, from which richly dressed figures enjoy the view. (Royal Ontario Museum, George Crofts Collection)*

THE FALL OF HAN CHINA

The Han Empire was an imposing political edifice. Eventually, however, wars on the frontiers and the emperors' enormous building projects put an intolerable strain on society. The emperors drew so heavily on the peasants as soldiers and workers that agricultural production declined severely. Great landlords saw their chance to expand their holdings and to shift the burden of taxation onto the already hard-pressed peasantry. Ground down by ambitious emperors and unscrupulous landowners, many peasants lost their land and sold their children, farm animals, and tools to the landowners, ending as tenants, hired laborers – or outlaws.

The emperor Wang Mang (A.D. 9-23), who was a usurper, attempted to reverse these trends. He tried to re-establish a state monopoly on grain so that private speculators could not exploit famines and shortages to make huge profits. He set about redistributing land to the peasants, and wanted to abolish slavery. Unfortunately, Wang Mang's commendable efforts did little to improve conditions, and he was killed in a peasant uprising. Han Kuang Wu in turn defeated the rebels and established the later Han Empire in A.D. 25.

After a century of peace, the later Han emperors found themselves facing the same problems that Wang Mang had tried to solve. Once again, excessive demands were made on the peasants. Great landlords took over peasants' land and burdened them with heavy taxes. Disorder, intrigue, and assassination at court distracted the government, making intelligent leadership nearly impossible. A murderous rivalry developed between the old scholar-officials, who had traditionally administered political affairs, and the palace eunuchs, men usually of lowly origin who wielded huge influence from their lair among the women of the imperial harem. Turmoil and palace revolt meant that the great landlords were left unhindered. Once again, the peasants staged massive uprisings. When the imperial armies were dispatched to put down the unrest, the victorious generals used their forces to carve out petty kingdoms for themselves. The palace eunuchs revolted against the emperor and his scholar-officials, and the Han Empire collapsed in general turmoil.

In the years that followed, known as the Three Kingdoms Era (A.D. 221-280), China experienced further disorder and barbarian troubles. At precisely the same time, the Roman Empire was facing many of the same problems. The three new kingdoms conformed to the natural geographic divisions of the land: the kingdom of Wei held the north, Shu the upper Yangtze river valley, and Wu the lower Yangtze valley.

China, like Rome, later faced catastrophic barbarian invasions from the north. Most significant were the conquests by the nomadic Toba from Mongolia, who created their own northern dynasty. Early in the fifth century the Toba assumed control of northern China, making the Great Wall their northern boundary. They extended their sway into central Asia and stopped further barbarian invasions of China. Southern China, which remained under Chinese rule, actually benefited from these invasions: thousands of Chinese, among them many scholar-officials, fled to the south, where they devoted their energies and talents to developing southern China economically and culturally.

Barbarian invasions caused China less damage and disruption than did the barbarian invasions of western Europe. The Toba and other nomads quickly came under the spell of Chinese culture linguistically, politically, and economically. The Toba emperor ordered the Toba nobility to speak Chinese at his court,

and to dress and act like Chinese elites. The Toba adopted Chinese agricultural techniques and the bureaucratic method of administering the empire. Chinese culture withstood the impact of invasion so well that it remained vital and essentially unshaken. China's political system was so excellently suited to the land and its people that no barbarian invader could have done without it. That system encompassed not just a bureaucracy fully dependent on the Chinese language, but the culture, religion, and outlook of Chinese society.

———◆———

The regions between Mesopotamia and China all experienced similar developments during the years 250 B.C.–A.D. 200. After a period of warfare the Parthian Empire fell heir to the legacy of the Persian kings, and united Iran and the Near East in a broad and loose political structure. India enjoyed the glories of the Mauryan Empire before being beset by invasion and reduced to numerous petty kingdoms, some ruled by foreign lords. China emerged from feudalism and chaos into an empire that rivalled Rome in extent, wealth, and accomplishment. Yet in China, too, empire was swept away by internal disorder and later by barbarian invasion.

These empires had nurtured the cultural life of the peoples under their sway. The Parthian Empire held back the legions of Rome, enabling the Near East and Iran to develop peacefully along lines of their own making. The Mauryan Empire in India and the Han Empire in China so strengthened their societies that they could survive invasion and political turmoil. Particularly in India and China, the cultures handed on from earlier periods grew strong enough to assimilate newcomers instead of falling before alien cultures.

NOTES

1. Justin 41.1.1–7.

2. Strabo 11.9.2.

3. Plutarch *Crassus* 18.2.

4. Arrian *Parthika* fr. 86–87.

5. Pliny *Natural History* 6.26.

6. Quoted in N. W. Ross, *Three Ways of Asian Wisdom,* Simon and Schuster, New York, 1966, p. 94.

7. Quoted in B. G. Gokhale, *Asoka Maurya,* Twayne Publishers, New York, 1966, p. 157.

8. Pillar Edict 7, quoted by Gokhale, *Asoka,* p. 169.

9. Ibid., pp. 168–169.

10. Burton Watson, trans., *Records of the Grand Historian of China translated from the Shih chi of Ssu-ma Ch'ien,* Columbia University Press, New York and London, 1961, II.269.

11. Ibid., I.31.

12. Ibid., I.53.

13. Quoted in W. H. Schoff, *The Periplus of the Erythraean Sea,* Longmans, Green, London, 1912, p. 276.

14. Watson, *Ssu-ma Ch'ien,* II.81.

15. Ibid., II.79.

SUGGESTED READING

The Parthians remain an enigmatic people, and there is ample room for new work on them. Excellent general introductions are R. Ghirshman, *Iran* (English translation, 1954), ch. 6, and R. N. Frye, *Persia,* 2nd ed. (1969), by two of the foremost scholars in Persian studies. Older and flawed is N. C. Debevoise, *A Political History of Parthia* (1938). Newer and far more comprehensive is M. A. R. Colledge, *The Parthians* (1967), which is illustrated, and his *Parthian Art* (1977), which treats both art and architecture.

The kingdom of Ashoka has attracted much attention, and is consequently far better known than the Parthian Empire. In addition to Gokhale's book cited in the Notes, R. Thapar's excellent *Asoka and the Decline of the Mauryas* (1961) is still an indispensable work on the subject. For the Greek invasions, see W. W. Tarn, *The Greeks in Bactria and India* (1951), a difficult book but still valuable. A. K. Narain's more recent treatment, *The Indo-Greeks* (1967), is equally valuable and a bit more readable. For contact between the Hellenistic world and India, see J. W. Sedlar, *India and the Greek World* (1980), which approaches the problem of cultural transmission between the two civilizations. C. Drekmeier, *Kingship and Community in Early India* (1968), takes a broader approach to early developments.

India's response to the invasions of the Shakas and Kushans is poorly documented, but B. N. Puri, *India Under the Kushanas* (1965), is an admirable effort to unravel a difficult historical period. More recent is F. Ayubi, ed., *Kushan Culture and History* (1971). R. Thapar, "The Image of the Barbarian in Early India," *Comparative Studies in Society and History* 13 (1971):408–436, makes the significant point that Indian society during this period assimilated the invaders even though it considered them barbarians.

Buddhism is such a popular topic that the bibliography is virtually endless. A very valuable introduction by a leading scholar in the field is E. Zürcher, *Buddhism: Its Origins and Spread in Words, Maps, and Pictures* (1962). A shorter and more spiritual approach is E. Conze, *A Short History of Buddhism* (1980). Also enlightening is W. Rahula, *What the Buddha Taught* (1971), which sheds light on the Theravada tradition, and R. Robinson and W. Johnson, *The Buddhist Religion,* 3rd ed. (1982), which is more comprehensive. Still unsurpassed for its discussion of the relations between Buddhism and Hinduism is the grand work of C. N. Eliot, *Hinduism and Buddhism,* 3 vols. (reprinted 1954), which traces the evolution of theistic ideas in both religions. C. Humphreys has written extensively about Buddhism. The student may wish to consult *Buddhism* (1962), *Exploring*

Buddhism (1975) or *The Wisdom of Buddhism* (new ed., 1979).

The political and military success of the Ch'in is the subject of D. Bodde, *China's First Unifier: A Study of the Ch'in Dynasty as Seen in the Life of Li Ssu (280?–208 B.C.)* (1958). P. Nancarrow, *Early China and the Wall* (1978) discusses the importance of the Great Wall of China to early Chinese society. A good account of Ch'in road-building is J. Needham, *Science and Civilization in China,* vol. 4, part 3 (1970). The Han Dynasty has been amply treated by a master scholar, H. H. Dubs, whose *History of the Former Han Dynasty,* 3 vols. (1938–1955) is comprehensive. B. Watson has provided two good studies of Ssu-ma Ch'ien and his historical work: *Records of the Grand Historian of China* (1961) and *Ssu-ma Ch'ien: Grand Historian of China* (1958). China's most important woman scholar is the subject of N. L. Swann, *Pan Chao: Foremost Woman Scholar of China* (1950).

The turmoil of Confucianism in this period is ably treated in a series of studies, especially E. Balazs, *Chinese Civilization and Bureaucracy* (1964); H. Welch and A. Seidel, eds., *Facets of Taoism* (1979), which ranges more broadly than its title might suggest; and especially C. Chang, *The Development of Neo-Confucian Thought* (1957), a very solid discussion of Neo-Confucianism.

M. Loewe, *Everyday Life in Early Imperial China* (1968), paints a vibrant picture of ordinary life during the Han period, a portrayal that attempts to include all segments of Han society. Lastly, W. Zhongshu, *Han Civilization* (1982) excellently treats many aspects of material life under the Han, including architecture, agriculture, manufactures, and burials.

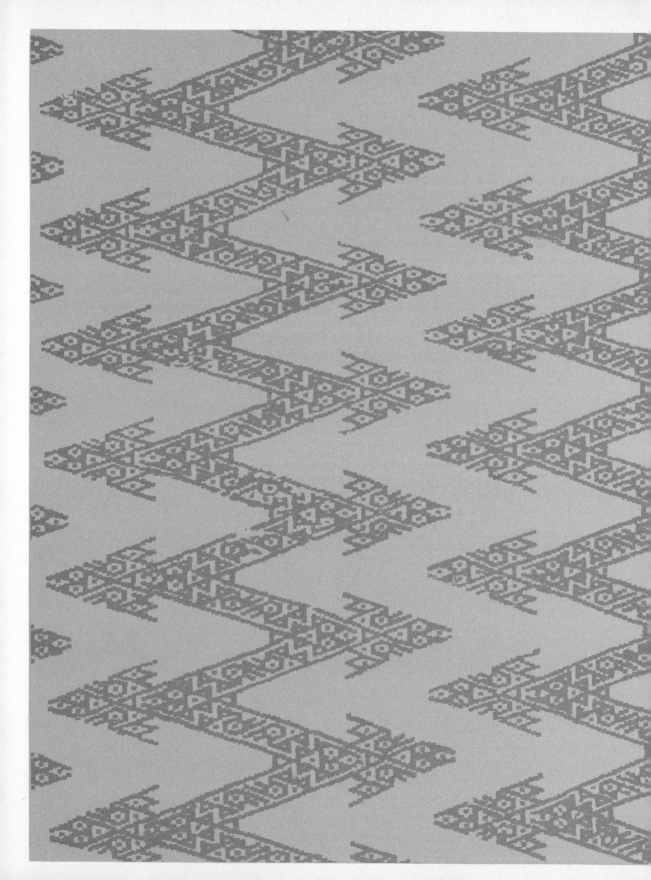

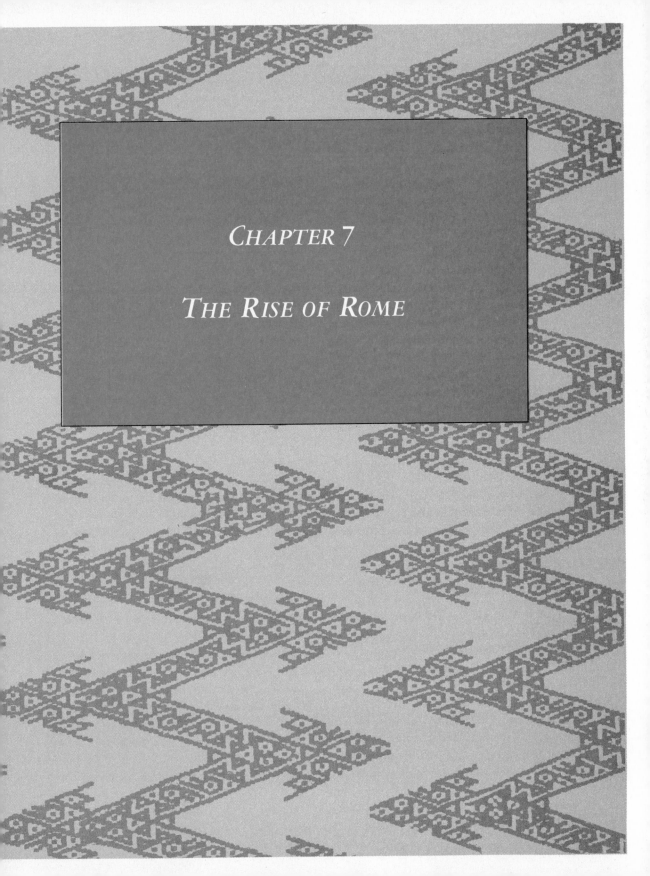

CHAPTER 7

THE RISE OF ROME

"**WHO IS SO THOUGHTLESS** and lazy that he does not want to know in what way and with what kind of government the Romans in less than 53 years conquered nearly the entire inhabited world and brought it under their rule – an achievement previously unheard of?"[1] This question was first asked by Polybius, a Greek historian who lived in the second century B.C. With keen awareness Polybius realized that the Romans were achieving something unique in world history.

What was that achievement? Was it simply the creation of a huge empire? Hardly. The Persians had done the same thing. For that matter, Alexander the Great had conquered vast territories in a shorter time. Was it the creation of a superior culture? Even the Romans admitted that in matters of art, literature, philosophy, and culture they learned from the Greeks. Rome's achievement lay in the ability of the Romans not only to conquer peoples but to incorporate them into the Roman system. Rome succeeded where the Greek polis had failed. Unlike the Greeks, who refused to share citizenship, the Romans extended their citizenship first to the Italians and later to the peoples of the provinces. With that citizenship went Roman government and Roman law. Rome created a world state that embraced the entire Mediterranean area.

Nor was Rome's achievement limited to the ancient world. Rome's law, language, and administrative practices were a precious heritage to medieval and modern Europe. London, Paris, Vienna, and many other modern European cities began as Roman colonies or military camps. When the Founding Fathers created the American Republic they looked to Rome as a model. On the darker side, Napoleon and Mussolini paid their own tribute to Rome by aping its forms. Whether Founding Father or modern autocrat, they were all ac-

knowledging their admiration for the Roman achievement.

Roman history is usually divided into two periods: the Republic, the age in which Rome grew from a small city-state to ruler of an empire, and the Empire, the period when the republican constitution gave way to constitutional monarchy. How did Rome rise to greatness? What effects did the conquest of the Mediterranean have on the Romans themselves? Finally, why did the republic collapse? These are the questions this chapter will attempt to answer.

THE LAND AND THE SEA

To the west of Greece the boot-shaped peninsula of Italy, with Sicily at its toe, occupies the center of the Mediterranean basin. As Map 7.1 shows, Italy and Sicily thrust southward toward Africa: the distance between southwestern Sicily and the northern African coast is at one point only about a hundred miles. Italy and Sicily literally divide the Mediterranean into two basins and form the focal point between the halves.

Like Greece and other Mediterranean lands, Italy enjoys a genial, almost subtropical climate. The winters are rainy, but the summer months are dry. Because of the climate the rivers of Italy usually carry little water during the summer, and some go entirely dry. The low water level of the Arno, one of the principal rivers of Italy, once led Mark Twain to describe it as "a great historical creek with four feet in the channel and some scows

ALPS

Po

Trebia River ✕

Trebia

A
P
P
E
N
N
I
N
E
S

Arno

UMBRIA

ETRURIA ✕
L. Trasimene

PICENUM

Tiber

CORSICA

Veii •

Rome •

LATIUM

SAMNIUM

APULIA

CAMPANIA

Cannae ✕

Tarentum •

CALABRIA

SARDINIA

LUCANIA

T Y R R H E N I A N   S E A

BRUTTIUM

A
D
R
I
A
T
I
C

S
E
A

Messana •

SICILY

Syracuse
✕ •

Carthage •

Cape Bon

Zama ✕

- - - - - Roman boundary before the Punic wars

———— Roman boundary before Augustus

✕ Major battle

———— Major road

0   50   100   150 Km.

0   50   100   150 Mi.

ROME

0   500   1000 m.

0   1500   3000 Ft.

Field of Mars

Tiber

JANICULUM

QUIRINAL

VIMINAL

CAPITOLINE

Senate House

Temple of
Jupiter

Forum

Regia

ESQUILINE

PALATINE

CAELIAN

Circus Maximus

AVENTINE

floating around. It would be a very plausible river if they would pump some water into it."[2] The Arno at least is navigable. Most of Italy's other rivers are not. Clearly, these small rivers were unsuitable for regular, large-scale shipping. Italian rivers, unlike Twain's beloved Mississippi, never became major thoroughfares for commerce and communications.

Geography discouraged maritime trade as well. Italy lacks the numerous good harbors that are such a prominent feature of the Greek landscape. Only in the south are there good harbors, and Greek colonists had early claimed those ports for themselves. Yet geography gave rise to – and the rivers nourished – a bountiful agriculture that sustained a large population. The strength of Italy lay in the land and its produce.

Geography encouraged Italy to look to the Mediterranean. In the north Italy is protected by the Apennine Mountains, which break off from the Alps and form a natural barrier. The Apennines retarded but did not prevent peoples from penetrating Italy from the north. Throughout history, in modern times as well as ancient, various invaders have entered Italy by this route. From the north the Apennines run southward the entire length of the Italian boot; they virtually cut off access to the Adriatic Sea, which further induced Italy to look west to Spain and Carthage rather than east to Greece. Even though most of the land is mountainous, the hill country is not as inhospitable as are the Greek highlands. In antiquity the general fertility of the soil provided the basis for a large population. Nor did the mountains of Italy so carve up the land as to prevent the development of political unity. Geography proved kinder to Italy than to Greece.

In their southward course the Apennines leave two broad and fertile plains, those of

Latium and Campania. These plains attracted settlers and invaders from the time when peoples began to move into Italy. Among these peoples were the Romans, who established their city on the Tiber River in Latium.

This site enjoyed several advantages. The Tiber provided Rome with a constant source of water. Located at an easy crossing-point on the Tiber, Rome thus stood astride the main avenue of communications between northern and southern Italy. The famous seven hills of Rome were defensible and safe from the floods of the Tiber. Rome was in an excellent position to develop the resources of Latium and maintain contact with the rest of Italy.

THE ETRUSCANS AND ROME
(750–509 B.C.)

In recent years archaeologists have found traces of numerous early peoples in Italy. The origins of these cultures and their precise relations with one another are not yet well understood. In fact, no clear account of the prehistory of Italy is yet possible. Of the period before the appearance of the Etruscans (1200–750 B.C.) one fundamental fact is indisputable: peoples speaking Indo-European languages were moving into Italy from the north, probably in small groups. They were part of the awesome but imperfectly understood movement of peoples that spread the Indo-European family of languages from Spain to India.

Only with the coming of the Greeks does Italy enter the light of history. A great wave of Greek immigration swept into southern Italy and Sicily during the eighth century B.C., as was described on pages 81–82. The Greeks brought urban life to these regions, spreading cultural influence far beyond the walls of their city-states.

In the north the Greeks encountered the Etruscans, one of the truly mysterious peoples of antiquity. Who the Etruscans were, where they came from, and what language they spoke are unknown. Nonetheless, this fascinating people was to leave an indelible mark on the Romans. Skillful metal workers, the Etruscans amassed extensive wealth by trading their manufactured goods in Italy and beyond. The strength of their political and military institutions enabled them to form a loosely organized league of cities whose dominion extended as far north as the Po valley and as far south as Latium and Campania (see Map 7.1). In Latium they founded cities and took over control of Rome. Like the Greeks, the Etruscans promoted urban life, and one of the places that benefited from Etruscan influence was Rome.

The Etruscans found the Romans settled on three of Rome's seven hills. The site of the future Forum Romanum, the famous public square and center of political life, was originally the cemetery of the small community. According to Roman legend, Romulus and Remus founded Rome in 753 B.C. Romulus built his settlement on the Palatine Hill, while Remus chose the Aventine (see inset, Map 7.1). Jealous of his brother's work, Remus ridiculed it by jumping over Romulus's unfinished wall. In a rage, Romulus killed his brother and vowed, "So will die whoever else shall leap over my walls." In this instance legend preserves some facts. Archaeological investigation has confirmed that the earliest settlement at Rome was situated on the Palatine and that it dates to the first half of the eighth century B.C. The legend also shows traces of Etruscan influence on Roman customs. The inviolability of Romulus's walls

STATUETTE OF AN ETRUSCAN WARRIOR *The warrior shows the Etruscan military debt to Greece. He wears Greek armor and carries the spear of the Greek heavy infantryman. The artistic rendering of the warrior, however, shows that Italic artists were moving away from Greek models and were creating a style of their own. (Collection of the University Museum, The University of Pennsylvania)*

recalls the Etruscan concept of the *pomerium,* a sacred boundary intended to keep out anything evil or unclean.

During the years 753–509 B.C., the Romans picked up many Etruscan customs. They adopted the Etruscan alphabet, which the Etruscans themselves had adopted from the Greeks. The Romans later handed on this alphabet to medieval Europe and thence to the modern Western world. The Romans also adopted symbols of political authority from the Etruscans. The symbol of the Etruscan king's right to execute or scourge his subjects was a bundle of rods and an ax, called in Latin the *fasces,* which the king's retainer carried before him on official occasions. When the Romans expelled the Etruscan kings, they created special attendants called lictors to carry the fasces before their new magistrates, the consuls. Even the toga, the white woolen robe worn by citizens, came from the Etruscans. In engineering and architecture the Romans adopted from the Etruscans the vault and the arch. Above all, it was thanks to the Etruscans that the Romans truly became urban dwellers.

Etruscan power and influence at Rome were so strong that Roman traditions preserved the memory of Etruscan kings who ruled the city. Under the Etruscans, Rome enjoyed contacts with the larger Mediterranean world, and the city began to grow. In the years 575–550 B.C., temples and public buildings began to grace the city. The Capitoline Hill became the religious center of the city when the temple of Jupiter Optimus Maximus (Jupiter the Best and Greatest) was built there. The forum ceased to be a cemetery and began its history as a public meeting place, much like the agora of a Greek city. Metalwork became common, and the wealthier classes began to import large numbers of

fine Greek vases. The Etruscans had found Rome a collection of villages and made of it a city.

THE ROMAN CONQUEST OF ITALY
(509–290 B.C.)

Early Roman history is an uneven mixture of fact and legend. Roman traditions often contain an important kernel of truth, but that does not make them history. In many cases they are significant because they illustrate the ethics, morals, and ideals that Roman society considered valuable. Rome's early history also presents the historian with another problem. Historical writing did not begin among the Romans until the third century B.C., hundreds of years after the founding of Rome. Much later still, around the time of Jesus, the historian Livy (59 B.C.–A.D. 17) gave final form to these legends.

How much genuine information about the early years did Romans like Livy have? Or did they simply take what they knew and try to make of it an intelligible story? Livy gave his own answer to these questions: "Events before Rome was born or thought of have come down to us in old tales with more of the charm of poetry than of sound historical record, and such traditions I propose neither to affirm nor refute."[3] Livy also admitted that these legends and tales depicted men and women not necessarily as they were, but as Romans should be. For him, the story of early Rome was an impressive moral tale. Today, historians would say that Livy took these legends and made of them a sweeping epic. But they would also admit that the epic preserved the broad outlines of the Roman conquest of Italy and the development of Rome's internal

THE ROMAN FORUM   *The forum was the center of Roman political life. From simple beginnings it developed into the very symbol of Rome's imperial majesty. (Italian Government Travel Office)*

affairs. Both parts of the epic – legend and fact – are worth examining for what they say about the Romans.

According to Roman tradition, the Romans expelled the Etruscan king Tarquin the Proud from Rome in 509 B.C. and founded the republic. In the years that followed, the Romans fought numerous wars with their neighbors on the Italian peninsula. They became soldiers, and the grim fighting bred tenacity, a prominent Roman trait. War also involved diplomacy, at which the Romans became masters. At an early date they learned the value of alliances and how to provide leadership for their allies. Alliances with the Latin towns around them provided them with a large reservoir of manpower. Their alliances also involved the Romans in still other wars and took them farther and farther afield in the Italian peninsula.

One of the earliest wars was with two nearby peoples, the Aequi and the Volsci, and from this contest arose the legend of Cincinnatus. At one point, when the Aequi had launched a serious invasion, the Romans called upon Cincinnatus to assume the office of dictator. In this period the Roman dictator, unlike modern dictators, was a legitimate magistrate given ultimate powers for a specified period of time. The Roman officials found Cincinnatus working his three-acre farm. Wiping the sweat from himself, he listened to the appeal of his countrymen and accepted the office. Fifteen days later, after he had defeated the Aequi, he returned to his farm. Cincinnatus personified the ideal of the Roman citizen – a man of simplicity, a man who put his duty to Rome before any consideration of personal interest or wealth.

Roman tradition tells of grand campaigns

and continuous Roman success in these wars. In reality, most campaigns were neither grand nor always victorious. A good idea of what the fighting was like comes from the legend of the Fabii, one of Rome's noblest families. On one occasion 306 members of the Fabii set out toward Etruscan territory on what was nothing more than a cattle raid. What could be more patriotic than to reduce the enemy's wealth while increasing your own? The Etruscans, however, ambushed the Fabii and surrounded them. One boy escaped from the fighting, but the rest of the Fabii died to the last man, as good Romans were supposed to do. The excessive losses belong to the realm of legend, but the Fabii's type of combat was no doubt typical of the hard-fought border skirmishes and raids, in which the Romans at times took a beating. Gradually, Roman tenacity and numbers exhausted the strength of the enemy. The conflicts also taught the Romans to bounce back from defeat and to modify their institutions to deal effectively with changing problems and situations.

The growth of Roman power was slow but steady. Not until roughly a century after the founding of the republic did the Romans try to drive the Etruscans entirely out of Latium. In 405 B.C. they laid siege to Veii, the last neighboring Etruscan city. Ten years later they captured it. The story of the siege of Veii is in some ways the Roman equivalent of the Greek siege of Troy. But once again tradition preserves a kernel of truth, confirmed now by archaeological exploration of Veii. This was an important Roman victory, for the land of Veii went to the Romans and provided additional resources for Rome's growing population. Rome's concentrated landholdings formed a strong, unified core in central Italy. After the destruction of Veii, Rome overshadowed its Latin allies and its enemies alike.

Although the Romans slowly but steadily advanced their power in central Italy, they suffered a major setback about 390 B.C. A new people, the Celts — or Gauls, as the Romans called them — had been spreading their culture throughout the regions of modern France, Belgium, and southern Germany. By about 550 B.C. the Gauls were trading with the Greek colony of Massilia (modern Marseilles) and with Etruscan cities in the Po valley. Lured by the wealth of northern Italy, bands of Gauls began to push into the Po valley. Around 390 B.C. one band struck as far south as Latium. The great German historian Eduard Meyer has vividly recaptured the terror of the event:

With gloomy fear the sons of the Mediterranean looked upon these giants [the Gauls], with their long red hair and huge moustaches. They were a wild warrior folk who trampled down whatever stood in their way. With the severed heads of their enemies they bedecked their horses and their huts with skulls. Half naked they went into battle, their necks and arms adorned with thick gold rings and chains. Their many-colored mantles they threw aside; only shields covered their bodies. Their weapons were spears and mighty, but slender and wickedly-shaped, swords.[4]

The Gauls swept aside a Roman army and sacked Rome. More intent on loot than land, they agreed to abandon Rome in return for a thousand pounds of gold. The decision to buy off the Gauls made a lasting impression on the Romans. According to Roman tradition, when the Gauls produced their own scale, the Romans howled with indignation. The Gallic chieftain then threw his sword on the scale, exclaiming "Vae victis" — "woe to the conquered." These words, though legendary, became a challenge to the Romans. Thereafter they made it their policy never to accept peace, much less to surrender, as long as the enemy were still in the field.

Although the Gauls left Rome in rubble — another fact confirmed by modern archaeology — they also inadvertently helped the Romans: on their way to central Italy they broke forever the power of the Etruscans. When the Gauls took their gold and returned to the Alps, they left the north open to Roman expansion.

During the century from 390 to 290 B.C., Romans rebuilt their city and recouped their losses. They also reorganized their army to create the mobile legion, a flexible unit capable of fighting on either broken or open terrain. The Romans finally brought Latium and their Latin allies fully under their control, and they conquered Etruria. In 343 B.C., they grappled with the Samnites in a series of bitter wars for the possession of Campania and southern Italy. The Samnites were a formidable enemy, and they inflicted some serious losses on the Romans. But the superior organization, institutions, and manpower of the Romans won out in the end. Although Rome had yet to subdue the whole peninsula, for the first time in history the city stood unchallenged in Italy.

Rome's success in diplomacy and politics was as important as its military victories. Unlike the Greeks, the Romans did not simply conquer and then dominate. Instead, they shared with other Italians both political power and degrees of Roman citizenship. The Romans did not start out to build a system. They were always a practical people — that was one of their greatest strengths. When they found a treaty or a political arrangement that worked, they used it wherever possible. When it did not, they turned to something else. Consequently, Rome had a network of alliances and treaties with other peoples and states.

With many of their oldest allies, such as the Italian cities, they shared full Roman citizenship. In other instances they granted citizenship without the franchise (*civitas sine suffragio*). Allies who held this status enjoyed all the rights of Roman citizenship except that they could not vote or hold Roman offices. They were subject to Roman taxes and calls for military service, but they ran their own local affairs. The Latin allies were able to acquire full Roman citizenship by moving to Rome.

By their willingness to extend their citizenship the Romans took Italy into partnership. Here the political genius of Rome triumphed where Greece had failed: Rome proved itself superior to the Greek polis because it both conquered and shared the fruits of conquest with the conquered. Rome could consolidate where Greece could only dominate. The unwillingness of the Greek polis to share its citizenship condemned it to a limited horizon. Not so with Rome. The extension of Roman citizenship strengthened the state, gave it additional manpower and wealth, and laid the foundations of the Roman Empire itself.

THE ROMAN STATE

The Romans summed up their political existence in a single phrase: *senatus populusque Romanus,* the Roman senate and the people. The real genius of the Romans lay in the fields of politics and law. Unlike the Greeks, they did not often speculate on the ideal state or on political forms; instead, they realistically met actual challenges and created institutions, magistracies, and legal concepts to deal with practical problems. Change was consequently a commonplace feature of Roman political life, and the constitution of 509 B.C. was far simpler than that of 27 B.C. Nonetheless, the principal magistracies and political organs of the state can be briefly sketched.

In the early republic, social divisions determined the shape of politics. Political power was in the hands of the aristocracy – the patricians, who were wealthy landowners. Patrician families formed clans, as did aristocrats in early Greece. They dominated the affairs of state, provided military leadership in time of war, and monopolized knowledge of law and legal procedure. The common people of Rome, the plebeians, had few of the advantages of the patricians. Some plebeians formed clans of their own, and rivaled the patricians in wealth. Many plebeian merchants increased their wealth in the course of Roman expansion, but most plebeians were poor. They were the artisans, the small farmers, and the landless urban dwellers. The plebeians, rich and poor alike, were free citizens and had a voice in politics. Nonetheless, they were overshadowed by the patricians.

Perhaps the greatest institution of the republic was the senate, which had originated under the Etruscans as a council of noble elders who advised the king. During the republic the senate advised the consuls and the other magistrates. Because the senate sat year after year, while magistrates changed annually, it provided stability and continuity. It also served as a reservoir of experience and knowledge. Technically, the senate could not pass legislation; it could only offer its advice. But increasingly because of the senate's prestige its advice came to have the force of law.

The Romans created several assemblies through which the people elected magistrates and passed legislation. The earliest was the *comitia curiata,* which had religious, political, and military functions. According to Roman tradition, king Servius Tullius (578–535 B.C.), who reorganized the state into 193 centuries

(military and political units) for military purposes, created the *comitia centuriata.* Since the patricians shouldered most of the burden of defense, they dominated the *comitia centuriata,* and could easily outvote the plebeians. In 471 B.C., the plebeians won the right to meet in an assembly of their own, the *concilium plebis,* and to pass ordinances. In 287 B.C., the bills passed in the concilium plebis were recognized as binding on the entire population, patrician and plebeian alike.

The chief magistrates of the republic were the two consuls, elected for one-year terms. At first the consulship was open only to the patricians. The consuls commanded the army in battle, administered state business, convened the comitia centuriata, and supervised financial affairs. In effect, they and the senate ran the state. The consuls appointed quaestors to assist them in their duties, and in 421 B.C. the quaestorship became an elective office open to the plebeians. The quaestors took charge of the public treasury and prosecuted criminals in the popular courts.

In 366 B.C., the Romans created a new office, that of praetor, and in 227 B.C. the number of praetors was increased to four. When the consuls were away from Rome, the praetor could act in their place. The praetor dealt primarily with the administration of justice. When he took office, the praetor issued a proclamation declaring the principles along which he would interpret the law. These proclamations became very important because they usually covered areas where the law was vague. Thus, they helped clarify the law.

The lowest officials were the aediles, four in number, who supervised streets and markets and presided over public festivals.

After the age of overseas conquest (pages 219–221), the Romans divided the Mediterranean area into provinces, which were governed by ex-consuls and ex-praetors. Because of their experience in Roman politics, they were well suited to administer the affairs of the provincials and to fit Roman law and custom into new contexts that they might encounter.

One of the most splendid achievements of the Romans was their development of law. Roman law began as a set of rules that regulated the lives and relations of citizens. This civil law, or *ius civile,* consisted of statutes, customs, and forms of procedure. Roman assemblies added to the body of law, and praetors interpreted it. The spirit of the law aimed at protecting the property, lives, and reputations of citizens, redressing wrongs, and giving satisfaction to the victims of injustice.

As the Romans came into more frequent contact with foreigners, they had to devise laws to deal with disputes between Romans and foreigners and between foreigners under Roman jurisdiction. In these instances, where there was no precedent to guide the Romans, the legal decisions of the praetors proved to be of immense importance. The praetors adopted aspects of other legal systems, and they resorted to the law of equity – what they thought was right and just to all parties. Thus, the praetors were in effect free to determine law, and they enjoyed a great deal of flexibility. This situation illustrates the practicality and the genius of the Romans. By addressing specific, actual circumstances the praetors developed a body of law, the *ius gentium,* that applied to Romans and foreigners and that laid the foundation for a universal conception of law. By the time of the late republic Roman jurists were reaching decisions on the basis of the Stoic concept of *ius naturale,* natural law, a universal law that could be applied to all societies.

SOCIAL CONFLICT IN ROME

War was not the only aspect of Rome's early history. In Rome itself a great social conflict, usually known as the Struggle of the Orders, developed between the patricians and the plebeians. What the plebeians wanted was real political representation and safeguards against patrician domination. The efforts of the plebeians to obtain recognition of their rights is the crux of the Struggle of the Orders.

Rome's early wars gave the plebeians the leverage they needed: Rome's survival depended on the army, and the army needed the plebeians. The first showdown between the plebeians and the patricians came, according to tradition, in 494 B.C. To force the patricians to grant concessions, the plebeians seceded from the state; they literally walked out of Rome and refused to serve in the army. Livy tells how Menenius Agrippa, acting as spokesman for the senate, persuaded them to return by relating the story of the belly and the limbs.

Agrippa said that the limbs of the body once went on strike against the stomach because it did nothing but enjoy all the good things it received from the limbs. Yet the limbs found that by starving the stomach they also starved themselves. (In the same vein Benjamin Franklin once told the Founding Fathers that unless they all hung together they would all hang separately.) Livy's story is legend, but once again the legend preserves truth. The Struggle of the Orders was marked by hard bargaining, but also by compromise and concession. Throughout the conflict plebeian and patrician alike were sincerely concerned for the welfare of Rome. Only this true patriotism prevented the conflict from becoming civil war.

The general strike of the plebeians worked. Because of it the patricians made important concessions. They recognized the right of the plebeians to elect their own officials, the tribunes. The tribunes in turn had the right to protect the plebeians from the arbitrary conduct of patrician magistrates. The tribunes brought plebeian complaints and grievances to the senate for resolution. In 471 B.C., when the plebeians won the right to hold their own assembly, the concilium plebis, and to enact ordinances that concerned only themselves, the plebeians became a state within a state. This situation could have led to chaos, but Rome was not a house divided against itself. The plebeians were not bent on undermining the state. Rather, they used their gains only to win full equality under the law.

The law itself was the next target of the plebeians. Only the patricians knew what the law was, and only they could argue cases in court. All too often they had used the law for their own benefit. The plebeians wanted the law codified and published. The result of their agitation was the Law of the Twelve Tables, so called because the laws, which covered civil and criminal matters, were inscribed on large bronze plaques. Like Draco's law code, the Law of the Twelve Tables seems stiff and even harsh. For instance, Table IV commands, "A seriously deformed child should be quickly killed." Table VIII deals handily with slander: "If anyone has sung or composed a song which caused dishonor or disgrace to another, he should be beaten to death with clubs." But at least all Romans could learn their rights and guard against arbitrary judgments. Later still, the plebeians forced the patricians to publish legal procedures as well. They had broken the patricians' legal monopoly. Henceforth, they enjoyed full protection under the law.

The decisive plebeian victory came with the passage of the Licinian-Sextian rogations (or laws) in 367 B.C. Licinius and Sextus were two plebeian tribunes who led a ten-year fight for further reform. Rich plebeians, like Licinius and Sextus themselves, joined the poor to mount a sweeping assault on patrician privilege. Wealthy plebeians wanted the opportunity to provide political leadership for the state. They demanded that the patricians allow them access to all the magistracies of the state. If they could hold the consulship, they could also sit in the senate and advise the senate on policy. The two tribunes won approval from the senate for a law that stipulated that one of the two annual consuls had to be a plebeian.

Licinius and Sextus also protected the interests of the plebeian poor, those who owned little or no land and whose poverty had driven them into debt. These plebeians wanted access to public land so that they could make a new start. The two tribunes sponsored legislation that limited the amount of public land an individual could hold. This restriction struck hard at the patricians, many of whom had used large tracts of public land for their own profit. The new law allowed magistrates to parcel out land in small lots, which plebeians could claim and work for themselves.

The Struggle of the Orders resulted in a Rome stronger and better united than before. It could have led to anarchy, but again the Roman political genius triumphed. Resistance and confrontation never exploded into class warfare. Instead, both sides resorted to compromises to hammer out a realistic solution. Important too were Roman patience and tenacity – and a healthy sense of the practical. These qualities enabled both sides to keep working until they had resolved the crisis. The Struggle of the Orders ended in 367 B.C. with a new concept of Roman citizenship. All citizens shared equally under the law. Theoretically, all could aspire to the highest

THE ROMAN REPUBLIC

509 B.C.	Expulsion of the Etruscan king and founding of the Roman republic
471 B.C.	Plebians win official recognition of their assembly, the *concilium plebis*
ca 450 B.C.	Law of the Twelve Tables
390 B.C.	The Gauls sack Rome
390–290 B.C.	Rebuilding of Rome; reorganization of the army; Roman expansion in Italy
367 B.C.	Licinian-Sextian rogations
287 B.C.	Legislation of the *concilium plebis* made binding on entire population
282–146 B.C.	The era of overseas conquest
264–241 B.C.	First Punic War: Rome builds a navy, defeats Carthage, acquires Sicily
218–202 B.C.	Second Punic War: Scipio defeats Hannibal; Rome dominates the western Mediterranean
200–148 B.C.	Rome conquers the Hellenistic east
149–146 B.C.	Third Punic War: savage destruction of Carthage
133–121 B.C.	The Gracchi introduce land reform; murder of the Gracchi by some senators.
107 B.C.	Marius becomes consul and begins the professionalization of the army.
91–88 B.C.	War with Rome's Italian allies
88 B.C.	Sulla marches on Rome and seizes dictatorship
79 B.C.	Sulla abdicates
78–27 B.C.	Era of civil war
60–49 B.C.	First Triumvirate: Pompey, Crassus, Julius Caesar
45 B.C.	Julius Caesar defeats Pompey's forces and becomes dictator
44 B.C.	Assassination of Julius Caesar
43–36 B.C.	Second Triumvirate: Marc Antony, Lepidus, Octavian
31 B.C.	Octavian defeats Antony and Cleopatra at Actium

political offices. Patrician or plebeian, rich or poor, Roman citizenship was equal for all.

THE AGE OF OVERSEAS CONQUEST (282–146 B.C.)

In 282 B.C., Rome embarked on a series of wars that left it the ruler of the Mediterranean world. There was nothing ideological about these wars. Unlike Napoleon or Hitler, the Romans did not map out grandiose strategies for world conquest. In 282 B.C., they had no idea of what lay in store for them. If they could have looked into the future, they would have stood amazed. In many instances the Romans did not even initiate action; they simply responded to situations as they arose. Nineteenth-century Englishmen were fond of saying, "We got our empire in a fit of absence of mind." The Romans could not go quite that far. Even though they sometimes declared war reluctantly, they nonetheless felt the need to dominate, to eliminate any state that could threaten them.

Rome was imperialistic, and its imperialism took two forms. In the barbarian West, the home of fierce tribes, Rome resorted to bald aggression to conquer new territory. In areas like Spain, and later in Gaul, the fighting was fierce and savage, and gains came slowly. In the civilized East, the world of Hellenistic states, Rome tried to avoid annexing territory. The East was already heavily populated, and those people would have become Rome's responsibility. New responsibilities meant new problems, and such headaches the Romans shunned. In the East the Romans preferred to be patrons rather than masters. Only when that policy failed did they directly annex land. But in 282 B.C., all this lay in the future.

The Samnite wars had drawn the Romans into the political world of southern Italy. In 282 B.C., alarmed by the powerful newcomer, the Greek city of Tarentum in southern Italy called for help from Pyrrhus, king of Epirus in western Greece. A relative of Alexander the Great and an excellent general, Pyrrhus won two furious battles but suffered heavy casualties – thus the phrase "Pyrrhic victory" for a victory involving severe losses. Roman bravery and tenacity led him to comment: "If we win one more battle with the Romans, we'll be completely washed up." Against Pyrrhus's army the Romans threw new legions, and in the end Roman manpower proved decisive. In 275 B.C., the Romans drove Pyrrhus from Italy and extended their sway over southern Italy. Once they did, the island of Sicily became important to them.

Pyrrhus once described Sicily as a future "wrestling ground for the Carthaginians and Romans." The Phoenician city of Carthage, in North Africa (see Map 7.2), had for centuries dominated the western Mediterranean. Sicily had long been a Carthaginian target. Since Sicily is the steppingstone to Italy, the Romans could not let it fall to an enemy. In 264 B.C., Carthage and Rome came to blows over the city of Messina, which commanded the straits between Sicily and Italy. This conflict, the First Punic War, lasted for twenty-three years. The Romans quickly learned that they could not conquer Sicily unless they controlled the sea. Yet they lacked a fleet and hated the sea as fervently as cats hate water. Nevertheless, with grim resolution the Romans built a navy and challenged the Carthaginians at sea. The Romans fought seven major naval battles with the Carthaginians and won six. Twice their fleet went down in gales. But finally the Romans wore down the Carthaginians. In 241 B.C., the Romans de-

MODEL OF A ROMAN WARSHIP *This rare ancient model was found off the southern coast of the Peloponnesus near Sparta. The bow of the warship is capped by a ram, behind which run the seats for the rowers. At the stern is the poop, the station of the officers and steersmen. (Photo: Caroline Buckler)*

feated them and took possession of Sicily, which became their first real province. Once again Rome's resources, manpower, and determination proved decisive.

The First Punic War was a beginning, not an end. Carthage was still a formidable enemy. After the First Punic War the Carthaginians expanded their power to Spain and turned the Iberian Peninsula into a rich field of operations. By 219 B.C., Carthage had found its avenger – Hannibal. In Spain, Hannibal learned how to lead armies and to wage war on a large scale. A brilliant general, he realized the advantages of swift mobile forces, and he was an innovator in tactics.

In 219 B.C., Hannibal defied the Romans by laying siege to the small city of Saguntum in Spain. When the Romans declared war the following year, he gathered his forces and led them on one of the most spectacular marches in ancient history. Hannibal carried the Second Punic War to the very gates of Rome. Starting in Spain, he led his troops – infantry,

cavalry, and elephants – over the Alps and into Italy on a march of more than a thousand miles. Once in Italy, he defeated one Roman army at the battle of Trebia and later another at the battle of Lake Trasimene in 217 B.C. At the battle of Cannae in 216 B.C. Hannibal inflicted some forty thousand casualties on the Romans. He spread devastation throughout Italy, but failed to crush Rome's iron circle of Latium, Etruria, and Samnium. The wisdom of Rome's political policy of extending rights and citizenship to its allies showed itself in these dark hours. Italy stood solidly with Rome against the invader. And Rome fought back.

The Roman general Scipio Africanus copied Hannibal's methods of mobile warfare. He streamlined the legions by making their components capable of independent action and by introducing new weapons. Scipio gave his new army combat experience in Spain, which he wrested from the Carthaginians. Meanwhile the Roman fleet dominated the western

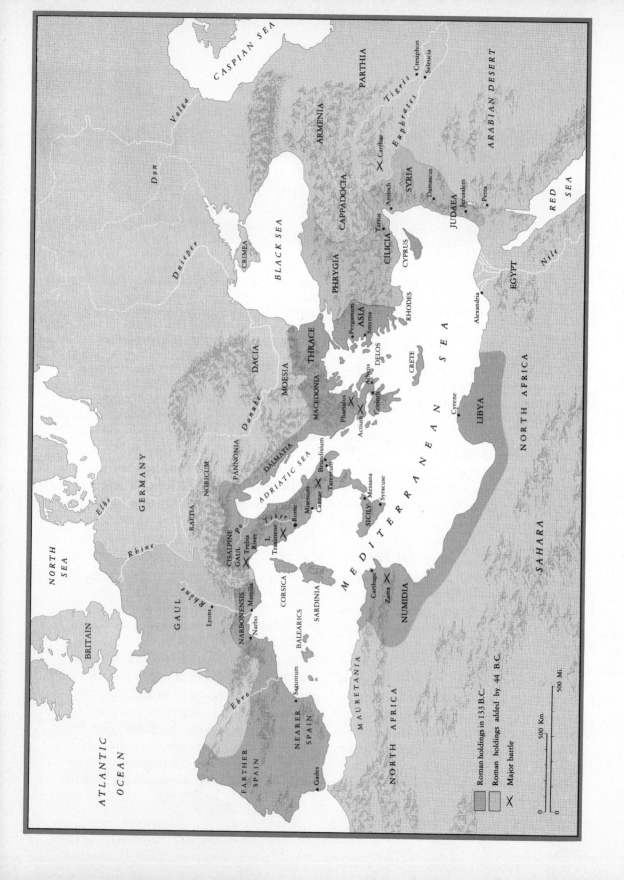

CASPIAN SEA

Volga

Don

Dnieper

CRIMEA

BLACK SEA

PARTHIA

ARMENIA

Tigris

Euphrates

Ctesiphon
Seleucia
Carrhae ✕

ARABIAN DESERT

CAPPADOCIA

SYRIA
Damascus
Antioch

JUDAEA
Jerusalem
Petra

RED SEA

PHRYGIA

CILICIA
Tarsus

CYPRUS

EGYPT

Nile

THRACE

Pergamum
ASIA
Smyrna

DELOS
RHODES

Alexandria

MACEDONIA

Athens

CRETE

MEDITERRANEAN SEA

Pharsalus ✕
Actium ✕
Corinth

Cyrene

LIBYA

NORTH AFRICA

DACIA

MOESIA

Danube

DALMATIA

PANNONIA

NORICUM

RAETIA

ADRIATIC SEA

Brundisium
Tarentum

Misenum
Cannae ✕
SICILY Messana
Syracuse

GERMANY

Elbe

Rhine

Po
CISALPINE GAUL ✕
Trebia
Rome
Tiber
Trasimene ✕

Carthage
Zama ✕
NUMIDIA

NORTH SEA

GAUL

Rhône

Lyons

NARBONENSIS
Narbo
Massilia

CORSICA

SARDINIA

BALEARICS

MAURETANIA

NORTH AFRICA

SAHARA

BRITAIN

ATLANTIC OCEAN

Ebro

Saguntum

NEARER SPAIN

FARTHER SPAIN

Gades

Roman holdings in 133 B.C.

Roman holdings added by 44 B.C.

✕ Major battle

500 Km.

500 Mi.

0
0

Mediterranean and interfered with Carthaginian attempts to reinforce Hannibal. In 204 B.C., the Roman fleet landed Scipio in Africa, which prompted the Carthaginians to recall Hannibal from Italy to defend the homeland.

In 202 B.C., near the town of Zama (see Map 7.2), Scipio Africanus defeated Hannibal in one of the world's truly decisive battles. Scipio's victory meant that the world of the western Mediterranean would henceforth be Roman. Roman language, law, and culture, fertilized by Greek influences, would in time permeate this entire region. The victory at Zama meant that Rome's heritage — not Carthage's — would be passed on to the Western world.

The Second Punic War contained the seeds of still other wars. Unabated fear of Carthage led to the Third Punic War, a needless, unjust, and savage conflict that ended in 146 B.C., when Scipio Aemilianus, grandson of Scipio Africanus, destroyed the old hated rival. As the Roman conqueror watched the death pangs of that great city, he turned to his friend Polybius with the words: "I fear and foresee that someday someone will give the same order about my fatherland." It would, however, be centuries before an invader would stand before the gates of Rome.

During the war with Hannibal the Romans had invaded Spain, a peninsula rich in material resources and the home of fierce warriors. When the Roman legions tried to reduce Spanish tribesmen, they met with bloody and determined resistance. Not until 133 B.C., after years of brutal and ruthless warfare, did Scipio Aemilianus finally conquer Spain.

When the Romans intervened in the Hellenistic East, they went from triumph to triumph. The Romans dealt with the Greeks in a civilized fashion. There were hard-fought battles in the East, but the bloodletting and carnage that marked the battles in the West were not repeated in the cultured East. Even so, the results were essentially the same. The kingdom of Macedonia fell to the Roman legions, as did Greece and the Seleucid monarchy. By 146 B.C., the Romans stood unchallenged in the eastern Mediterranean, and they had turned many states and kingdoms into provinces. In 133 B.C., the king of Pergamum in Asia Minor left his kingdom to the Romans in his will. The Ptolemies of Egypt meekly obeyed Roman wishes. The following years would bring the Romans new victories, and they would establish their system of provincial administration. But by 146 B.C., the work of conquest was largely done. The Romans had turned the entire Mediterranean basin into *mare nostrum* — "our sea."

OLD VALUES AND GREEK CULTURE

Rome had conquered the Mediterranean world, but some Romans considered that victory a misfortune. The historian Sallust (86–34 B.C.), writing from hindsight, complained that the acquisition of an empire was the beginning of Rome's troubles:

But when through labor and justice our Republic grew powerful, great kings defeated in war, fierce nations and mighty peoples subdued by force, when Carthage the rival of the Roman people was wiped out root and branch, all the seas and lands lay open, then fortune began to be harsh and to throw everything into confusion. The Romans had easily

BATTLE BETWEEN THE ROMANS AND THE
GAULS   *All the brutality and fury of Rome's wars
with the barbarians of western Europe come to life in
this Roman sarcophagus of 225 B.C. Even the bravery*
*and strength of the Gauls were no match for the stead-
iness and discipline of the Roman legions. (Alinari/
Scala)*

*borne labor, danger, uncertainty, and hardship. To
them leisure, riches — otherwise desirable — proved
to be burdens and torments. So at first money, then
desire for power grew great. These things were a
sort of cause of all evils.[5]*

Sallust was not alone in his feelings. At the
time, some senators had opposed the destruction of Carthage on the grounds that fear of
their old rival would keep the Romans in
check. Did Rome gain the whole world only
to lose its soul? Sallust obviously thought so,
and he could have made a good case. It is true
that the new empire provided many Romans
with golden opportunities to amass fortunes
wrung from the conquered. It is true that numerous generals, provincial governors, and
other magistrates oppressed the vanquished
for their personal gain. But it is also true that
Rome continued to produce patriotic, noble,
and hard-working men and women, just as it
had in the past. Rome did not suddenly become weak and evil, but Roman society was

undergoing a fundamental change. In the
process, Rome's early period became senti-
mentalized as the "good old days," a golden
age of virtue the early Romans themselves
would never have recognized.

In the second century B.C., Romans learned
that they could not return to what they fondly
considered a simple life. They were world
rulers. The responsibilities they faced were
complex and awesome. They had to change
their institutions, their social patterns, and
their way of thinking to meet the new era.
They were in fact building the foundations of
a great imperial system. It was an awesome
challenge, and there were failures along the
way. Roman generals and politicians would
destroy each other. Even the republican constitution would eventually be discarded. But
in the end Rome triumphed here just as it had
on the battlefield, for out of the turmoil
would come the pax Romana — the Roman
peace.

How did the Romans of the day meet these

challenges? How did they lead their lives and cope with these momentous changes? Obviously, there are as many answers to these questions as there were Romans. Yet two men can be taken to represent the major trends of the second century B.C. Cato the Elder shared the mentality of those who longed for the good old days and idealized the traditional agrarian way of life. Scipio Aemilianus led those who embraced the new urban life with its eager acceptance of Greek culture. Fortynine years older than Scipio, Cato was a product of an earlier generation, one that confronted a rapidly changing world. Cato and Scipio were both aristocrats and neither of them was typical, even of the aristocracy. But they do exemplify opposing sets of attitudes that marked Roman society and politics in the age of conquest.

CATO AND THE TRADITIONAL IDEAL

Marcus Cato was born a plebeian, but his talent and energy carried him to Rome's highest offices. He cherished the old virtues and consistently imitated the old ways. Cato had inherited an estate north of Rome and began his career as a man of moderate means. Near his estate were the fields and cottage of Manius Curius, the general who had driven Pyrrhus from Italy forty years before Cato was born. Curius had been another Cincinnatus; although Curius had held the consulship and commanded armies, he worked his small farm alone. He once refused a large bribe, saying that a man of his simple tastes did not need gold. It was the example of Curius that Cato constantly held before his eyes.

In Roman society ties within the family were very strong. In this sense Cato and his family were typical. Cato was *paterfamilias,* a term that meant far more than merely "father." The paterfamilias was the oldest

dominant male of the family. He held nearly absolute power over the lives of his wife and children so long as he lived. He could legally kill his wife for adultery or divorce her at will. He could kill his children or sell them into slavery. He could force them to marry against their will. Until the paterfamilias died, his sons could not legally own property. At his death, his wife and children inherited his property.

Despite his immense power, the paterfamilias did not necessarily act alone or arbitrarily. To deal with important family matters he usually called a council of the adult males. In this way the leading members of the family aired their views. They had the opportunity to give their support to the paterfamilias or to dissuade him from harsh decisions. In these councils the women of the family had no formal part, but it can safely be assumed that they played an important behind-the-scenes role. Although the possibility of serious conflicts between a paterfamilias and his grown sons is obvious, no one in ancient Rome ever complained about the institution. Perhaps in practice the paterfamilias preferred to be lenient rather than absolute.

Cato's wife (whose name is unknown) was the matron of the family, a position of authority and respect. The virtues expected of a Roman matron were those of Lucretia, a legendary figure from the early republic. According to Livy's account, the son of the last Etruscan king wanted to sleep with Lucretia. One night while her husband was away, the king's son slipped into her room and tried to seduce her. When she refused him, he threatened to kill her and then he raped her. When he had gone, Lucretia sent for her father and husband and told them the whole story. They tried to console her, telling her that she had been helpless and was free from any shame. Her answer was short: "Never shall Lucretia

provide a precedent for unchaste women to escape what they deserve." She demanded vengeance, the death of the king's son. Then, innocent though she was, she drew a knife and killed herself. Clearly, Lucretia was the ideal, but numerous funerary inscriptions testify that the virtues of chastity and modesty were highly valued. The tribute of one husband to his wife is typical of many:

Here is laid a woman dutiful, temperate, pure, chaste, Sempronia Moschis, to whom thanks are returned by her husband for her merits.[6]

Like most Romans, Cato and his family began the day early in the morning. The Romans divided the period of daylight into twelve hours and the darkness into another twelve. The day might begin as early as half past four in summer, as late as half past seven in winter. Because Mediterranean summers are invariably hot, the farmer and his wife liked to take every advantage of the cool mornings. Cato and his family, like modern Italians, ordinarily started the morning with a light breakfast, usually nothing more than some bread and cheese. After breakfast the family went about its work.

Because of his political aspirations Cato often used the mornings to plead law cases. He walked to the marketplace of the nearby town and defended anyone who wished his help. He received no fees for these services, but did put his neighbors in his debt. In matters of law and politics Roman custom was very strong. It demanded that Cato's clients give him their political support or their votes in repayment whenever he asked for them. These clients knew and accepted their obligations to Cato for his help.

Cato's wife shared her husband's love for the old ways. While he was in town, she ran the household. She spent the morning spinning and weaving wool for the clothes they wore. She supervised the domestic slaves, planned the meals, and devoted a good deal of attention to her son. In wealthy homes during this period the matron had begun to employ a slave as a wet nurse. Cato's wife refused to delegate her maternal duties. Like most ordinary Roman women, she nursed her son herself. She also bathed and swaddled him daily. Later, the boy was allowed to play with toys and terra-cotta dolls. Roman children, like children everywhere, kept pets. Dogs were especially popular, and they were valuable as house guards. Children played all sorts of games, and games of chance were very popular. Until the age of seven the child was under the matron's care. During this time the mother began to educate her daughter in the management of the household. After the age of seven, the son — and in many wealthy households the daughter too — began formal education.

In the country, Romans like Cato continued to take their main meal at midday. This meal included either coarse bread made from the entire husk of wheat or porridge made with milk or water; it also included turnips, cabbage, olives, and beans. When Romans ate meat, they preferred pork. Unless they lived by the sea, the average farm family did not eat fish, which was an expensive delicacy. Cato once complained that Rome was a place where a fish could cost more than a cow. With the midday meal the family drank an ordinary wine mixed with water. Afterward any Roman who could took a nap. This was especially true in the summer, when the Mediterranean heat can be fierce. Slaves, artisans, and hired laborers, however, went about their work. In the evening the Romans ate a light meal and went to bed about nightfall.

The agricultural year followed the sun and the stars; they were the farmer's calendar. Like Hesiod in Boeotia, the Roman farmer looked to the sky to determine when to plant, weed, shear sheep, and perform other chores. Varro (116–27 B.C.), one of the most famous writers on agriculture, did everything by the sun and stars. He advised farmers in Italy to harvest their grain crops between the summer solstice and the rising of the Dog Star. He suggested that they sow at the setting of the Pleiades. Varro's book on agriculture owed much to Hellenistic Greek manuals, but it also reflected actual Roman practice. Besides, the farmer could not depend on the civil calendar. The lunar year is 354 days long, and the solar year is 365¼ days long. So the civil calendar had to be adjusted to both lunar and solar years. To make matters worse, politicans often tampered with the calendar. In 46 B.C., when Julius Caesar reformed the civil calendar, it was some 2½ months out of step with the solar year. Obviously, farmers had to depend on something more reliable than this. Their solution was the sun, moon, and stars.

Spring was the season for plowing. Roman farmers plowed their land at least twice and preferably three times. The third plowing was to cover the sown seed in ridges and to use the furrows to drain off excess water. The Romans used a variety of plows. Some had detachable shares. Some were heavy for thick soil, others light for thin, crumbly soil. Farmers used oxen and donkeys to pull the plow. They collected the dung of their animals for fertilizer. Besides spreading manure, some farmers fertilized their fields by planting lupines and beans; when they began to pod, farmers plowed them under. The main money crops, at least for rich soils, were wheat and flax. Forage crops included clover, vetch, and alfalfa. Prosperous farmers like Cato raised olive trees chiefly for the oil. They also raised grapevines for the production of wine. Cato and his neighbors harvested their cereal crops in summer and their grapes in autumn. Harvests varied depending on the soil, but farmers could usually expect yields of 5½ bushels of wheat or 10½ bushels of barley per acre.

MANUMISSION OF SLAVES   During the Republic some Roman masters began to free slaves in public ceremonies. Here two slaves come before their master or a magistrate, who is in the process of freeing the kneeling slave by touching him with a manumission-rod. The other slave shows his gratitude and his good faith with a handshake. (Collection Waroque, Mariemont, Belgium. © A. C. L. Brussels)

In the early republic the master of the household worked the farm himself. By the second century B.C., however, Cato was noticeably old-fashioned because he stripped to the waist in summer and sweated alongside his slaves and day laborers.

An influx of slaves resulted from Rome's wars and conquests. Prisoners from Spain, Africa, and the Hellenistic East, and even some blacks from Hannibal's army, came to Rome as the spoils of war. The Roman attitude toward slaves and slavery had little in common with modern views. To the Romans slavery was a misfortune that befell some people. But slavery did not entail any racial theories. Races were not enslaved because the Romans thought them inferior. The black African slave was treated no worse — and no better — than the Spaniard. Indeed, some slaves were valued because of their physical distinctiveness: black Africans and blond Germans were particular favorites. For the talented slave, the Romans always held out the hope of eventual freedom. Manumission — the freeing of individual slaves by their masters — became so common that it had to be limited by law. Not even Christians questioned the institution of slavery. It was just a fact of life.

Slaves were entirely the property of their master, and they might be treated with great cruelty. Many Romans were practical enough to realize that they got more out of their slaves by kindness than by severity. Yet in Sicily slave owners treated their slaves viciously. They bought slaves in huge numbers, branded them for identification, put them in irons, and often made them go without food and clothing. In 135 B.C., these conditions gave rise to a major slave revolt, during which many of the most brutal masters died at the hands of their slaves. Italy too had trouble with slave unrest, but conditions there were generally better than in Sicily.

Cato urged his countrymen to treat slaves humanely. Varro suggested that masters should control slaves with knowledge and not with whips. Yet even Cato could be hardhearted. Although he worked and ate with his slaves, he never forgot their money value. When they grew too old to work, he sold them to save the expense of feeding them.

Not all Romans were Catos, though. Between many slaves and masters there developed genuine bonds of affection. On numerous occasions slaves risked or gave their lives to protect kind masters.

Part of the reason for such good relations probably stems from the fact that many slaves came from the Hellenistic East. They were certainly not barbarians. Many of them were more cultured than their owners. Greek male slaves frequently became the tutors of the master's children. These men especially were likely to receive their freedom. Slaves who gained their freedom also became Roman citizens. Freedmen and freedwomen often continued to live with their previous owners. And it was not unusual for Romans to permit their ex-slaves to be buried with them.

For Cato and most other Romans, religion played an important part in life. Originally, the Romans thought of the gods as invisible and shapeless natural forces. Only through Etruscan and Greek influence did Roman deities take on human form. Jupiter, the sky god, and his wife Juno became equivalent to the Greek Zeus and Hera. Mars was the god of war, but he was also the god who guaranteed the fertility of the farm and protected it from danger. Cato habitually sacrificed a pig, a ram, and a bull to Mars to obtain his help and protection. Cato or one of his farmhands led the animals around the boundaries of the farm and then called upon Mars the Father

that you hold back, repel, and turn away disease seen and unseen, blight and devastation; that you allow my crops, grain, vines, and thickets to increase and flourish; that you keep my shepherd and flocks safe; that you watch over and give good health and strength to me, my house, and household.[7]

Cato then sacrificed the animals to Mars and

offered the god small cakes. The Romans used a similar ritual, the Robigalia, to protect the grain crops from mildew. The Robigalia later gave rise to the Christian practice of purifying farms on Rogation Days, when the priest and his congregation marched in procession around the farms while calling upon Jesus and the saints for protection. Cato would have approved.

These two religious practices are illustrative of Roman religion in general. The gods of the Romans were not loving and personal. They were stern, powerful, and aloof. But as long as the Romans honored the cults of their gods, they could expect divine favor.

Along with the great gods the Romans believed in spirits who haunted fields, forests, crossroads, and even the home itself. Some of these deities were hostile, and only magic could ward them off. The spirits of the dead, like ghosts in modern horror films, frequented the places where they had lived. They too had to be placated, but they were ordinarily benign. As the poet Ovid (43 B.C.–A.D. 17) put it:

The spirits of the dead ask for little.
They are more grateful for piety than for an expensive gift —
Not greedy are the gods who haunt the Styx below.
A rooftile covered with a sacrificial crown,
Scattered kernels, a few grains of salt,
Bread dipped in wine, and loose violets —
These are enough.
Put them in a potsherd and leave them in the middle of the road.[8]

A good deal of Roman religion consisted of such rituals as those Ovid describes. These practices lived on long after the Romans had lost interest in the great gods. Even Christianity could not entirely wipe them out. Instead, Christianity was to incorporate many of these rituals into its own style of worship.

SCIPIO: GREEK CULTURE AND
URBAN LIFE

The old-fashioned ideals that Cato represented came into conflict with a new spirit of wealth and leisure. The conquest of the Mediterranean world and the spoils of war made Rome a great city. Some, like the historian Velleius Paterculus (first century A.D.), viewed these developments with distaste:

Scipio Africanus opened the way for Roman power. Scipio Aemilianus opened the way for luxury. Indeed, when Rome was free of the fear of Carthage, and its rival in empire was removed, Rome fell, not gradually but in headlong course, from virtue towards vice. The old discipline was deserted and the new introduced. The state turned from vigilance to sleep, from military affairs to pleasures, from work to leisure.[9]

Roman life, especially in the cities, *was* changing and becoming less austere. The spoils of war went to the building of baths, theaters, and other places of amusement. Romans and Italian townsmen began to spend more of their time in leisure pursuits. But simultaneously the new responsibilities of governing the world produced in Rome a sophisticated society. Romans developed new tastes and a liking for Greek culture and literature. They began to learn the Greek language. It became common for an educated Roman to speak both Latin and Greek. Hellenism dominated the cultural life of Rome. Even diehards like Cato found a knowledge of Greek essential for political and diplomatic affairs. The poet Horace (64–8 B.C.) summed it up well: "Captive Greece captured her rough conqueror and introduced the arts into rustic Latium."

One of the most avid devotees of Hellenism and the new was Scipio Aemilianus, the destroyer of Carthage. Scipio was also the man whom Velleius had accused of introducing luxury into Rome. Scipio realized that broad and worldly views had to replace the old Roman narrowness. The new situation called for new ways. Rome was no longer a small city on the Tiber; it was the capital of the world, and Romans had to adapt themselves to that fact. Scipio was ready to become an innovator both in politics and culture. He broke with the past in the conduct of his political career. He embraced Hellenism wholeheartedly. Perhaps more than anyone else of his day, Scipio represented the new Roman – imperial, cultured, and independent.

Scipio even dared to be independent in his political career, which differed from that of traditional politicians. He set out on a course of personal politics, determined to carve out a career for himself on the strength of his own merits. In doing so he set an example for future politicians. One of the most successful of Scipio's imitators would be Julius Caesar.

In his education and interests, too, Scipio broke with the past. As a boy, he had received the traditional Roman training, learning to read and write Latin and becoming acquainted with the law. He mastered the fundamentals of rhetoric and learned how to throw the javelin, fight in armor, and ride a horse. But later Scipio also learned Greek and became a fervent Hellenist. As a young man he formed a lasting friendship with the historian Polybius, who actively encouraged him in his study of Greek culture and in his intellectual pursuits. In later life Scipio's love of Greek learning, rhetoric, and philosophy became legendary. Scipio also promoted the spread of Hellenism in Roman society. He became the center of the Scipionic Circle, a small group of Greek and Roman artists, philosophers, historians, and poets. Conservatives like Cato tried to stem the rising tide of Hellenism, but men like Scipio carried the day and helped make the heritage of Greece an abiding factor in Roman life.

The new Hellenism profoundly stimulated the growth and development of Roman art and literature. The Roman conquest of the Hellenistic East resulted in wholesale confiscation of Greek paintings and sculpture to grace Roman temples, public buildings, and private homes. Roman artists copied many aspects of Greek art, but their emphasis on realistic portraiture carried on a native tradition.

Fabius Pictor (second half of the third century B.C.), a senator, wrote the first *History of Rome* in Greek. Other Romans translated Greek classics into Latin. Still others, like the poet Ennius (239–169 B.C.), the father of Latin poetry, studied Greek philosophy, wrote comedies in Latin, and adapted many of Euripides' tragedies for the Roman stage. Ennius also wrote a history of Rome in Latin verse. Plautus (ca 254–184 B.C.) specialized in rough humor. He too decked out Greek plays in Roman dress, but was no mere imitator. Indeed, his play *Amphitruo* was itself copied eighteen hundred years later by the French playwright Molière and the English poet John Dryden. The Roman dramatist Terence (ca 195–159 B.C.), a member of the Scipionic Circle, wrote comedies of refinement and grace that owed their essentials to Greek models. His plays lacked the energy and the slapstick of Plautus's rowdy plays. All of early Roman literature was derived from the Greeks, but it managed in time to speak in its own voice and to flourish because it had something of its own to say.

The conquest of the Mediterranean world brought the Romans leisure, and Hellenism influenced how they spent their free time. During the second century B.C., the Greek custom of bathing became a Roman passion and an important part of the day. In the early republic Romans had bathed infrequently, especially in the winter. Now large buildings containing pools and exercise rooms went up in great numbers, and the baths became an essential part of the Roman city. Architects built intricate systems of aqueducts to supply the bathing establishments with water. Conservatives railed at this Greek custom too, calling it a waste of time and an encouragement to idleness. The conservatives were correct in that bathing establishments were more than just places to take a bath. They included gymnasia, where men exercised and played ball. Women had places of their own to bathe, generally sections of the same baths used by men; for some reason, women's facilities lacked gymnasia. The baths contained hot-air rooms to induce a good sweat and pools of hot and cold water to finish the actual bathing. They also contained snack bars and halls where people chatted and read. The baths were socially important places where men and women went to see and be seen: social climbers tried to talk to "the right people" and wangle invitations to dinner; politicians took advantage of the occasion to discuss the affairs of the day. Despite the protests of conservatives and moralists, the baths at least provided people – rich and poor – with places for clean and healthy relaxation.

This period also saw a change in the eating habits of urban dwellers. The main meal of the day shifted from midday to evening. Dinner became a more elaborate meal and dinner parties became fashionable. Although Scipio Aemilianus detested fat people, more and more Romans began to eat excessively. Rich men and women displayed their wealth by serving exotic dishes and gourmet foods. After a course of vegetables and olives came the main course of meat, fish, or fowl. Pig was a favorite dish, and a whole suckling pig might be stuffed with sausage. A lucky guest might even dine on peacock and ostrich, each

BATHS OF CARACALLA   Once introduced into the Roman world, social bathing became a passion. These baths, which date to the Roman Empire, are the ultimate development of sophistication and size. (Italian Government Travel Office)

served with rich sauces. Dessert, as in Italy today, usually consisted of fruit. With the meal the Romans served wine, and during this period vintage wines became very popular. Household slaves sometimes read poetry or performed music during the meal. People of more vulgar tastes hired jesters. Dwarves were in great demand, and the evening's entertainment consisted of buffoonery and coarse jokes. After dinner the party drank wine and talked, often late into the night.

Although the wealthy gorged themselves whenever they could, poor artisans and workers could rarely afford rich meals. Their dinners resembled Cato's. Yet they too occasionally spent generously on food, especially during the major festivals. The Roman calendar was crowded with religious festivals, occasions not of dreary piety but of cheerful celebration. One such was the festival of Anna Perenna, a festival of fertility, longevity, and prosperity. It was an occasion for fun and exuberant but harmless excess. The poet Ovid caught all the joy and charm of the event in these lines:

> *The ordinary people come [to the banks of the Tiber];*
> *   And scattering themselves over the green grass,*
> *They drink and lie down, each man with his woman.*
> *Some remain under the open sky, a few put up tents,*
> *   Others build leafy huts of twigs.*
> *Some set up reeds instead of unbending columns,*
> *   Over which they spread their togas.*
> *Yet they grow warm with sun and wine, and pray*
> *   For as many years as cups of wine they take, and they drink that many.*

. . . .

There also they sing the songs they have heard in
  the theaters,
  And they beat time to the words with lively
  hands.
Putting down the bowl, they join in rough ring
  dances,
  And the trim girlfriend dances with her hair
  flying.
As they return home, they stagger and are a spectacle to the vulgar.
  When meeting them, the crowd calls them
  blessed.
The procession came my way recently (a worthy
  sight in my opinion):
  A drunk woman dragged along a drunk old
  man.[10]

Robust religious festivals and a decided love
of good food and drink were characteristics of
the average Roman, whether rich or poor.

Did Hellenism and the new social customs
corrupt the Romans? Perhaps the best answer
is simply this: the Roman state and the empire it ruled continued to exist for six more
centuries. Rome did not collapse; the state
continued to prosper. The golden age of literature was still before it. The high tide of its
prosperity still lay in the future. The Romans
did not like change, but they took it in stride.
That was part of their practical turn of mind
and part of their genius.

THE LATE REPUBLIC (133–27 B.C)

The wars of conquest created serious problems for the Romans, some of the most
pressing of which were political. The republican constitution had suited the needs of a
simple city-state, but it was inadequate to
meet the requirements of Rome's new position in international affairs (see Map 7.2).

Sweeping changes and reforms were necessary
to make it serve the demands of empire. A
whole system of provincial administration
had to be established. Officials had to be
appointed to govern the provinces and to
administer the law. These officials and
administrative organs had to find places
within the constitution. Armies had to be
provided to defend the provinces, and a system of tax collection had to be created.

Other political problems were equally serious. During the wars Roman generals commanded huge numbers of troops for long
periods of time. Men such as Scipio Aemilianus were on the point of becoming too
mighty for the state to control. Although
Rome's Italian allies had borne much of the
burden of the fighting, they received fewer
rewards than did Roman officers and soldiers.
Italians began to agitate for full Roman citizenship and a voice in politics.

There were serious economic problems too.
Hannibal's operations and the warfare in Italy
had left the countryside a shambles. The
movements of numerous armies had disrupted
agriculture. The prolonged fighting had also
drawn untold numbers of Roman and Italian
men away from their farms for long periods.
The families of these soldiers could not keep
the land under full cultivation. The people
who defended Rome and conquered the world
for Rome became impoverished for having
done their duty.

These problems, complex and explosive,
largely account for the turmoil of the closing
years of the republic. The late republic was
one of the most dramatic eras in Roman history. It produced some of Rome's most
famous figures: Marius, Sulla, Cicero, Pompey, and Julius Caesar, among others. In one
way or another each of these men attempted
to solve Rome's problems.

When the legionaries returned to their

farms in Italy, they encountered an appalling situation. All too often their farms looked like the farms of people they had conquered. Two courses of action were open to them. They could rebuild as their forefathers had done. Or they could take advantage of an alternative not open to their ancestors: they could sell their holdings. The wars of conquest had made some men astoundingly rich. These men wanted to invest their wealth in land. They bought up small farms to create huge estates, which the Romans called latifundia.

The purchase offers of the rich landowners appealed to the veterans for a variety of reasons. Many veterans had seen service in the East, where they had tasted the rich city life of the Hellenistic states. They were reluctant to return home and settle down to a dull life on the farm. Often their farms were so badly damaged that rebuilding hardly seemed worth the effort. Besides, it was hard to make big profits from small farms. Nor could the veterans supplement their income by working on the latifundia. Although the owners of the latifundia occasionally hired free men as day laborers, they preferred to use slaves to work their land. Slaves could not strike, and they could not be drafted into the army. Confronted by these conditions, veterans and their families opted to sell their land. They took what they could get for their broken farms and tried their luck elsewhere.

Most veterans migrated to the cities, especially to Rome. Although some found work, most did not. Industry and small manufacturing were generally in the hands of slaves. Even when there was work, slave labor kept the wages of free men low. Instead of a new start, veterans and their families encountered slum conditions that matched those of modern American cities. Sanitation was virtually non-existent. Housing was frequently shabby and

structurally unsound, but expensive nonetheless. Fire and police protection were unknown. These conditions were especially prevalent in Rome and some larger cities. Within a brief period of time Rome became the home of a large body of urban poor.

This trend held ominous consequences for the strength of Rome's armies. The Romans had always believed that only landowners should serve in the army, for only they had something to fight for. Landless men, even if they were Romans and lived in Rome, could not be conscripted into the army. These landless men may have been veterans of major battles and numerous campaigns; they may have won distinction on the battlefield. But once they sold their land they became ineligible for further military service. A large pool of experienced manpower was going to waste. The landless ex-legionaries wanted a new start, and they were willing to support any leader who would provide it.

One man who recognized the plight of Rome's peasant farmers and urban poor was an aristocrat, Tiberius Gracchus (163–133 B.C.). Appalled by what he saw, Tiberius warned his countrymen that the legionaries were losing their land even while fighting Rome's wars:

The wild beasts that roam over Italy have every one of them a cave or lair to lurk in. But the men who fight and die for Italy enjoy the common air and light, indeed, but nothing else. Houseless and homeless they wander about with their wives and children. And it is with lying lips that their generals exhort the soldiers in their battles to defend sepulchres and shrines from the enemy, for not a man of them has an hereditary altar, not one of all these many Romans an ancestral tomb, but they fight and die to support others in luxury, and though they are styled masters of the world, they have not a single clod of earth that is their own.[11]

Until his death, Tiberius Gracchus sought a solution to the problems of the veterans and the urban poor.

After his election as tribune of the people, Tiberius in 133 B.C. proposed that public land be given to the poor in small lots. His was an easy and sensible plan, but it angered many wealthy and noble people who had usurped large tracts of public land for their own use. They had no desire to give any of it back, and they bitterly resisted Tiberius's efforts. Violence broke out in Rome when a large body of senators killed Tiberius in cold blood. It was a black day in Roman history. The very people who directed the affairs of state and administered the law had taken the law into their own hands. The death of Tiberius was the beginning of an era of political violence. In the end that violence would bring down the republic.

Although Tiberius was dead, his land bill became law. Furthermore, Tiberius's brother Gaius (153–121 B.C.) took up the cause of reform. Gaius was a veteran soldier with an enviable record, but this fiery orator made his mark in the political arena. Gaius also became tribune, and demanded even more extensive reform than had his brother. To help the urban poor Gaius pushed legislation to provide them with cheap grain for bread. He defended his brother's land law and suggested other measures for helping the landless. He proposed that Rome send many of its poor and propertyless people out to form colonies in southern Italy. The poor would have a new start and could lead productive lives. The city of Rome would immediately benefit because excess and nonproductive families would leave for new opportunities abroad. Rome would be less crowded, sordid, and dangerous.

Gaius went a step further and urged that all Italians be granted full rights of Roman citizenship. This measure provoked a storm of opposition, and it was not passed in Gaius's

UNUSUAL ROMAN HELMET *Not standard issue, this metal helmet is a craftsman's masterpiece. The helmet itself is decorated with battle scenes and originally probably bore a crest. The molded face is actually a hinged visor. (Reproduced by Courtesy of the Trustees of the British Museum)*

lifetime. Yet in the long run he proved wiser than his opponents. In 91 B.C., many Italians revolted against Rome over the issue of full citizenship. After a brief but hard-fought war the senate gave Roman citizenship to all Italians. Had the senate listened to Gaius earlier, it could have prevented a great deal of bloodshed. Instead, reactionary senators rose against Gaius and murdered him and three thousand of his supporters. Once again the cause of reform had met with violence. Once again it was Rome's leading citizens who flouted the law.

More trouble for Rome came from an unexpected source. In 112 B.C., war broke out in North Africa, when a Numidian king named Jugurtha rebelled against Rome. The Roman legions made little headway against him until 107 B.C., when Gaius Marius, an Italian "new man" (a politician not from the traditional Roman aristocracy), became consul. Marius's values were those of the military camp. A man of fierce vigor and courage, Marius saw the army as the tool of his ambition. To prepare for the war with Jugurtha, Marius reformed the Roman army. He was the first Roman officer to recruit an army by permitting landless men to serve in the legions. Marius thus tapped Rome's vast reservoir of idle manpower. His volunteer army was a professional force, not a body of draftees. Marius also reorganized the Roman legion into smaller units, called cohorts, which made the legion more mobile and flexible. He rearmed the legion by making the sword and javelin the standard weapons of the legionaries.

There was, however, a disturbing side to Marius's reforms, one that would henceforth haunt the republic. To encourage enlistments, Marius promised land to his volunteers after the war. Poor and landless veterans flocked to him, and together they handily defeated Jugurtha. When Marius proposed a bill to grant land to his veterans, the senate refused to act, in effect turning its back on the soldiers of Rome. This was a disastrous mistake. Henceforth, the legionaries expected their commanders — not the senate or the state — to protect their interests. Through Marius's reforms the Roman army became a professional force, but it owed little allegiance to the state. By failing to reward the loyalty of Rome's troops, the senate set the stage for military rebellion and political anarchy.

Nor was trouble long in coming. The senate's refusal to honor Marius's promises to his soldiers, and the brief but bitter war between the Romans and their Italian allies (91–88 B.C.), set off serious political disturbances in Rome. In 88 B.C., the Roman general and conqueror Sulla marched on Rome with his army to put an end to the turmoil. Sulla made himself dictator — a far cry from Cincinnatus's dictatorship. He put his enemies to death and confiscated their land. The constitution thus disrupted was never effectively put back together.

In 79 B.C. Sulla voluntarily abdicated as dictator and permitted the republican constitution to function normally once again. Yet his dictatorship cast a long shadow over the late republic. Sulla the political reformer proved far less influential than Sulla the successful general and dictator. Civil war was to be the constant lot of Rome for the next fifty years, until the republican constitution gave way to the empire of Augustus in 27 B.C. The history of the late republic is the story of the power struggles of some of Rome's most famous figures: Julius Caesar and Pompey, Augustus and Marc Antony. One figure who stands apart is Cicero (106–43 B.C.), a practical politician whose greatest legacy to the Roman world and to Western civilization is his mass of political and oratorical writings.

Pompous, vain, and sometimes silly, Cicero was nonetheless one of the few men of the period to urge peace and public order. As consul in 63 B.C. he put down a conspiracy against the republic, but he refused to use force to win political power. Instead, he developed the idea of "concord of the orders," an idealistic and probably unattainable balance among the elements that constituted the Roman state. A truly brilliant master of Latin prose and undoubtedly Rome's finest orator, Cicero used his vast literary ability to promote political and social reforms and to explore the underlying principles of statecraft. Yet Cicero commanded no legions, and only legions commanded respect.

In the late republic the Romans were grappling with the simple and inescapable fact that their old city-state constitution was unequal to the demands of overseas possessions and the problems of governing provinces. Thus even Sulla's efforts to put the constitution back together again proved hollow. Once the senate and the other institutions of the Roman state had failed to come to grips with the needs of empire, once the authorities had lost control of their own generals and soldiers, and once the armies put their faith in their commanders instead of in Rome, the republic was doomed.

Sulla's real political heirs were Pompey and Julius Caesar, who realized that the days of the old republican constitution were numbered. Pompey, a man of boundless ambition, began his career as one of Sulla's lieutenants. After his army put down a rebellion in Spain, he himself threatened to rebel unless the senate allowed him to run for consul. He and another ambitious politician, Crassus, pooled their political resources and both won the consulship. They dominated Roman politics until the rise of Julius Caesar, who became consul in 59 B.C. Together the three concluded a political alliance, the First Triumvirate, in which they agreed to advance each other's interests.

The man who cast the longest shadow over these troubled years was Julius Caesar (100–44 B.C.). More than a mere soldier, Caesar was a cultivated man. Born of a noble family, he received an excellent education, which he furthered by studying in Greece with some of the most eminent teachers of the day. He had serious intellectual interests, and his literary ability was immense. Caesar was a superb orator, though second to Cicero, and his affable personality and wit made him popular. He was also a shrewd politician of unbridled ambition. Since military service was an effective stepping-stone to politics, Caesar launched his military career in Spain, where his courage won the respect and affection of his troops. Personally brave and tireless, Caesar was a military genius who knew how to win battles and how to turn victories into permanent gains.

In 58 B.C., Caesar became governor of Gaul, the region of modern France, a huge area he had conquered in the name of Rome. Caesar's account of his operations, his *Commentaries* on the Gallic wars, became a classic in Western literature and most schoolchildren's introduction to Latin. By 49 B.C., the First Triumvirate had fallen apart. Crassus had died in battle, and Caesar and Pompey, each suspecting the other of treachery, came to blows. The result was a long and bloody civil war, which raged from Spain across northern Africa to Egypt. Although Pompey enjoyed the official support of the government, Caesar finally defeated Pompey's forces in 45 B.C. He had overthrown the republic and made himself dictator.

Julius Caesar was not merely another victorious general. Politically brilliant, he was determined to make basic reforms, even at the expense of the old constitution. He took the first long step to break down the barriers between Italy and the provinces, extending citizenship to many of the provincials who had supported him. Caesar also took measures to cope with Rome's burgeoning population. By Caesar's day perhaps 750,000 people lived in Rome. Caesar drew up plans to send his veterans and some 80,000 of the poor and unemployed to colonies throughout the Mediterranean. He founded at least twenty colonies, most of which were located in Gaul,

Spain, and North Africa. These colonies were important agents in spreading Roman culture in the western Mediterranean. Caesar's work would eventually lead to a Roman empire composed of citizens, not subjects.

In 44 B.C., a group of conspirators assassinated Caesar and set off another round of civil war. Caesar had named his eighteen-year-old grandnephew, Octavian – or Augustus, as he is better known to history – as his heir. Augustus joined forces with two of Caesar's lieutenants, Marc Antony and Lepidus, in a pact known as the Second Triumvirate, and together they hunted down and defeated Caesar's murderers. In the process, however, Augustus and Antony came into conflict. Antony, "boastful, arrogant, and full of empty exultation and capricious ambition," proved to be the major threat to Augustus's designs.[12] In 33 B.C., Augustus branded Antony a traitor and a rebel. Augustus painted lurid pictures of Antony lingering in the eastern Mediterranean, a romantic and foolish captive of the seductive Cleopatra, queen of Egypt and bitter enemy of Rome. In 31 B.C., with the might of Rome at his back, Augustus met and defeated the army and navy of Antony and Cleopatra at the battle of Actium in Greece. Augustus's victory put an end to an age of civil war that had lasted since the days of Sulla.

———◆———

The final days of the republic, even though filled with war and chaos, should not obscure the fact that much of the Roman achievement survived the march of armies. The Romans had conquered the Mediterranean world only to find that conquest required them to change their way of life. Socially, they imbibed Greek culture and adjusted themselves to the superior civilization of the Hellenistic East. Politically, their city-state constitution broke down

and expired in the wars of the late republic. Even so, men like Caesar and later Augustus sought new solutions to the problems confronting Rome. The result, as Chapter 8 will describe, was a system of government capable of administering an empire with justice and fairness. Out of the failure of the republic arose the pax Romana of the empire.

NOTES

1. Polybius *The Histories* 1.1.5.

2. Mark Twain, *The Innocents Abroad,* Signet Classics, New York, 1966, p. 176.

3. Livy *History of Rome* Preface 6.

4. E. Meyer, *Geschichte des Altertums,* 6th ed., vol 5, Wissenschaftliche Buchgesellschaft, Darmstadt, 1975, pp. 144–145.

5. Sallust *War with Catiline* 10.1–3.

6. *Corpus Inscriptionum Latinarum,* vol. 6, G. Reimer, Berlin, 1882, no. 26192.

7. Cato *On Agriculture* 141.2–3.

8. Ovid *Fasti* 2.535–539.

9. Velleius Paterculus *History of Rome* 2.1.1.

10. Ovid *Fasti* 3.525–542.

11. Plutarch *Life of Tiberius Gracchus* 9.5–6.

12. Plutarch *Life of Antony* 2.8.

SUGGESTED READING

H. H. Scullard covers much of Roman history in a series of books: *The Etruscan Cities and Rome* (1967), *A History of the Roman World, 753–146 B.C.,* 3rd ed. (1961), and *From the Gracchi to Nero,* 4th ed. (1976). The Etruscans have inspired much new work, most notably L. Banti, *The Etruscan Cities and Their Culture* (English translation, 1973), M. Pallottino, *The Etruscans,* rev. ed. (1975), and R. M. Ogilvie, *Early Rome and the Etruscans* (1976), an excellent account of Rome's early relations with them.

Roman expansion is the subject of J. Heurgon, *The Rise of Rome to 264 B.C.* (English translation, 1973), R. M. Errington, *The Dawn of Empire* (1971), and W. V. Harris, *War and Imperialism in Republican Rome 327–70 B.C.* (1979). J. F. Lazenby, *Hannibal's War: A Military History of the Second Punic War* (1978), is a recent and detailed treatment of one of Rome's greatest struggles. More general and encompassing is E. Gabba, *Republican Rome, the Army, and the Allies* (English translation, 1976). One of the best studies of Rome's political evolution is the classic, A. N. Sherwin-White, *The Roman Citizenship,* 2nd ed. (1973), a work of enduring value.

The great figures and events of the late republic have been the object of much new work. E. S. Gruen, *The Last Generation of the Roman Republic* (1974), treats the period as a whole. Very important are the studies of E. Badian, *Roman Imperialism in the Late Republic* (1968) and *Publicans and Sinners* (1972). R. Syme, *The Roman Revolution,* revised ed. (1952) is a classic. Valuable also are P. A. Brunt, *Social Conflicts in the Roman Republic* (1971); A. J. Toynbee, *Hannibal's Legacy,* 2 vols. (1965); and A. W. Lintott, *Violence in the Roman Republic* (1968).

Many new works deal with individual Romans who left their mark on this period. H. C. Boren, *The Gracchi* (1968), treats the work of the two brothers, and B. Levick, *Tiberius the Politician* (1976), offers closer scrutiny of the elder of the brothers, as does A. Bernstein, *Tiberius Sempronius Gracchus, Tradition and Apostacy* (1978). A. E. Astin has produced two works that are far more extensive than their titles indicate: *Scipio Aemilianus* (1967) and *Cato the Censor* (1978). J. Leach, *Pompey the Great* (1978), surveys the career of this politician, and B. Rawson, *The Politics of Friendship, Pompey and Cicero* (1978), treats both figures in their political environment. M. Gelzer, *Caesar, Politician and Statesman* (English translation, 1968) is easily the best study of one of history's most significant figures. Those interested in learning more about Caesar and the importance of his writings in the late Republic should see the fine article by L. Raditsa, "Julius Caesar and His Writings," in *Aufstieg und Niedergang der römischen Welt,* vol. I, part 3 (1973), pp. 417–456. His one-time colleague Marcus Crassus is treated in B. A. Marshall, *Crassus: A Political Biography* (1976), and A. Ward, *Marcus Crassus and the Late Roman Republic* (1977).

K. D. White, *Roman Farming* (1970), deals with agriculture, and J. P. V. D. Balsdon covers social life in the republic and the empire in two works: *Life and Leisure in Ancient Rome* (1969) and *Roman Women,* revised ed. (1974). Greek cultural influence on Roman life is the subject of A. Wardman, *Rome's Debt to Greece* (1976). F. Schulz, *Classical Roman Law* (1951) is a useful introduction to an important topic. Lastly, H. H. Scullard, *Festivals and Ceremonies of the Roman Republic* (1981), gives a fresh look at religious practices.

CHAPTER 8

THE PAX ROMANA

HAD THE ROMANS conquered the entire Mediterranean world only to turn it into their battlefield? Would they, like the Greeks before them, become their own worst enemies, destroying each other and wasting their strength until they perished? At Julius Caesar's death in 44 B.C. it must have seemed so to many. Yet finally, in 31 B.C., Augustus restored peace to a tortured world, and with peace came prosperity, new hope, and a new vision of Rome and Rome's destiny. The Roman poet Virgil expressed this vision most nobly:

You, Roman, remember — these are your arts:
To rule nations, and to impose the ways of peace,
To spare the humble and to war down the proud.[1]

In place of the republic, Augustus established a constitutional monarchy. He attempted to achieve a lasting cooperation in government and a balance among the people, the magistrates, the senate, and the army. His efforts were not always successful. His settlement of Roman affairs did not permanently end civil war. Yet he carried on Caesar's work. It was Augustus who created the structure that the modern world calls the Roman Empire. He did his work so well, and his successors so capably added to it, that Rome realized Virgil's hope. For the first and second centuries A.D. the lot of the Mediterranean world was peace — the *pax Romana,* a period of security, order, and harmony, of flourishing culture and expanding economy. It was a period that saw the wilds of Gaul, Spain, Germany, and eastern Europe introduced to Greco-Roman culture. By the third century A.D., when the empire gave way to the medieval world, the greatness of Rome and the blessings of Roman culture had left an indelible mark on the yet-unseen ages to come.

How did the Roman emperors govern the empire, and how did they spread Roman influence into northern Europe? What were the fruits of the pax Romana? Why did Christianity, originally a minor and local religion, sweep across the Roman world to change it fundamentally? Finally, how did the empire meet the grim challenge of barbarian invasion and economic decline? These are the main questions this chapter will consider.

AUGUSTUS'S SETTLEMENT (31 B.C.–A.D. 14)

When Augustus put an end to the civil wars that had raged since 83 B.C., he faced monumental problems of reconstruction. Rome and the entire Mediterranean world were in his power, and the legions were obedient to his word. Sole ruler as no Roman had ever been, he had a rare opportunity to shape the future. But how was that to be accomplished?

Augustus could easily have declared himself dictator as Caesar had, but the thought was repugnant to him. Augustus was neither an autocrat nor a revolutionary. His solution was to restore the republic. But was that possible? Some eighteen years of anarchy and civil war had shattered the republican constitution. It could not be rebuilt in a day. Augustus recognized these problems, but did not let them stop him. From 29 to 23 B.C., he toiled to heal Rome's wounds. The first problem facing him was to rebuild the constitution and the organs of government. Next he had to demobilize the army and care for the welfare of the provinces. Then he had to meet the danger of barbarians at Rome's European frontiers. Augustus was highly successful in meeting these challenges; his gift of peace to a war-torn world sowed the seeds of a literary flowering that produced some of the finest fruits of the Roman mind.

The Principate and the Restored Republic

Restoring the republic and creating a place for himself in it proved to be the biggest challenges to Augustus. Typically Roman, he preferred not to create anything new; he intended instead to modify republican forms and offices to meet new circumstances. Augustus planned for the senate to take upon itself a serious burden of duty and responsibility. He expected it to administer some of the provinces, to continue to be the chief deliberative body of the state, and to act as a court of law. Yet he did not give the senate enough power to become his partner in government. As a result, the senate failed to live up to its responsibilities, and increasingly its prerogatives shifted to Augustus by default.

Augustus's own position within the restored republic was something of an anomaly. He could not simply surrender the reins of power, for someone else would only have seized them. But how was he to fit into a republican constitution? Again Augustus had his own answer. He became *princeps civitatis,* "the First Citizen of the State." This prestigious title carried no power; it indicated only that Augustus was the most distinguished of all Roman citizens. In effect, it designated Augustus as the first among equals and a little more equal than anyone else in the state. His real power resided in the magistracies he held, the powers granted him by the senate, and his control of the army. Clearly, much of the principate, as the position of First Citizen is known, was a legal fiction. Yet that need not imply that Augustus, like a modern dictator, tried to clothe himself with constitutional legitimacy. In an inscription known as *Res Gestae (The Deeds of Augustus),* Augustus described his constitutional position in these terms:

COIN OF AUGUSTUS   *This portrait shows Augustus as a mature* princeps. *Like many of his coins, this one too has a propaganda value. On the reverse is his grandson Gaius. Augustus may have minted this coin to publicize Gaius's participation in Tiberius's campaign against the Germans. (Courtesy, World Heritage Museum. Photo: Caroline Buckler)*

In my sixth and seventh consulships [28–27 B.C.], I had ended the civil war, having obtained through universal consent total control of affairs. I transferred the Republic from my power to the authority of the Roman people and the senate. . . . After that time I stood before all in rank, but I had power no greater than those who were my colleagues in any magistracy.[2]

Augustus was not being a hypocrite. As consul he had no more constitutional and legal power than his fellow consul. Yet in addition to the consulship Augustus held many other magistracies, which his fellow consul did not. Constitutionally, his ascendancy within the state stemmed from the number of magistracies he held and the power granted him by the senate. At first he held the consulship annually, and then the senate voted him permanent proconsular power. The senate also voted him *tribunicia potestas* – the full power of the tribunes. Tribunician power gave Augustus the right to call the senate into session, present legislation to the people, and defend their rights. He held either high office or the powers of the chief magistrate year in and year out. No other magistrate could do the same. In 12 B.C., he became *pontifex maximus,* chief priest of the state. By assuming this position of great honor, Augustus became the chief religious official within the state.

The main source of Augustus's power was his position as commander of the Roman army. His title *imperator,* with which Rome customarily honored a general after a major victory, came to mean "emperor" in the modern sense of the term. Augustus governed the provinces where troops were needed for defense. The frontiers were his special concern. There Roman legionaries held the German barbarians at arm's length. The frontiers were also the areas where fighting could be expected to break out. Augustus made sure that Rome went to war only at his command. He controlled the deployment of the Roman army and paid its wages. He granted it bonuses and gave veterans retirement benefits. Thus, he avoided the problems with the army that the old senate had created for itself. Augustus never shared control of the army, and no Roman found it easy to defy him militarily.

The very size of the army was a special problem for Augustus. Rome's legions numbered thousands of men, far more than were necessary to maintain peace. What was Augustus to do with so many soldiers? This sort of problem had constantly plagued the late republic, whose leaders never found a solution to it. Augustus gave his own answer in the *Res Gestae:* "I founded colonies of soldiers in Africa, Sicily, Macedonia, Spain, Achaea, Gaul, and Pisidia. Moreover, Italy has 28 colonies under my auspices."[3] At least forty new colonies arose, most of them in the western Mediterranean. Augustus's veterans took abroad with them their Roman language and culture. His colonies, like those of Julius Caesar, were a significant tool in the further spread of Roman culture throughout the West.

Roman colonies were very different from the Greek colonies of Archilochus's time (pages 81–82). Greek colonies were independent. Once founded, they went their own way. Roman colonies were part of a system – the Roman Empire – that linked East with West in a mighty political, social, and economic network. The glory of the Roman Empire was its great success in uniting the Mediterranean world and spreading Greco-Roman culture throughout it. Roman colonies played a crucial part in that process, and deservedly did Augustus boast of his foundations.

What is to be made of Augustus's constitutional settlement? Despite his claims to the contrary, Augustus had not restored the republic. In fact, he would probably have agreed with the words of John Stuart Mill, the nineteenth-century English philosopher: "When society requires to be rebuilt, there is no use in attempting to rebuild it on the old plan." Augustus had created a constitutional monarchy, something completely new in Roman history. The title *princeps,* "First Citizen," came to mean in Rome, as it does today, "prince" in the sense of a sovereign ruler.

Augustus also failed to solve a momentous problem. He never found a way to institutionalize his position with the army. The ties between the princeps and the army were always personal. The army was loyal to the princeps but not necessarily to the state. The

Augustan Principate worked well at first, but by the third century A.D. the army would make and break emperors at will. Nonetheless, it is a measure of Augustus's success that his settlement survived as long and as well as it did.

AUGUSTUS'S ADMINISTRATION OF THE PROVINCES

To gain an accurate idea of the total population of the empire, Augustus ordered a census to be taken in 28 B.C. In Augustus's day the population of the Roman empire was between 70 and 100 million people, fully 75 percent of whom lived in the provinces. In the areas under his immediate jurisdiction Augustus put provincial administration on an ordered basis. He improved its functioning as well. Believing that the cities of the empire should look after their own affairs, he encouraged and fostered local self-government and urbanism. Augustus respected local customs and ordered his governors to do the same. The lengths he was willing to go to can be seen in Judaea.

Augustus wished to avoid antagonizing the Jews. As early as 40 B.C., long before he had put an end to the civil war, he and Antony had prevailed upon the senate to give the Jews their own king, Herod the Great, as a gesture of goodwill. Also, when the Roman legionaries stationed outside of Jerusalem entered the city, they left their standards behind in deference to the Jewish belief that the standards showed graven images. This was a magnanimous gesture, the equivalent of a modern army leaving its national flags behind. Augustus saw no reason to interfere with the customs, institutions, and traditions of cities as long as they functioned peacefully and effectively.

As a spiritual bond between the provinces and Rome, Augustus encouraged the cult of Roma, the goddess and guardian of the state. In the Hellenistic East, where king-worship was an established custom, the cult of Roma et Augustus grew up and spread rapidly. Augustus then introduced it in the West. By the time of his death in A.D. 14, nearly every province in the Empire could boast an altar or shrine to Roma et Augustus. In the West it was not the person of the emperor who was worshiped but his *genius* – his guardian spirit. In praying for the good health and welfare of the emperor Romans and provincials were praying for the empire itself. The cult became a symbol of Roman unity.

ROMAN EXPANSION INTO NORTHERN AND WESTERN EUROPE

For the history of Western civilization one of the most momentous aspects of Augustus's reign was Roman expansion into the wilderness of northern and western Europe (see Map 8.1). In this Augustus was following in Julius Caesar's footsteps. Between 58 and 51 B.C., Caesar had subdued Gaul and unsuccessfully attacked Britain. Carrying on his work, Augustus pushed Rome's frontier into the region of modern Germany. The Germanic tribes were tough opponents, and the Roman legions saw much bitter fighting against them in the north.

For the common soldier this fighting must have been exceptionally grim. Forests were believed to be the haunts of evil spirits, places of dim light and unidentifiable sounds. As early as the third century B.C. Roman armies habitually skirted the forests of Etruria. The vast forests of central Germany, with their thick, impenetrable gloom, must have oppressed even veteran legionaries. The thought of coming suddenly onto a war party of tall bearded Germans was not particularly pleasing either. Even so, the Roman legionary was

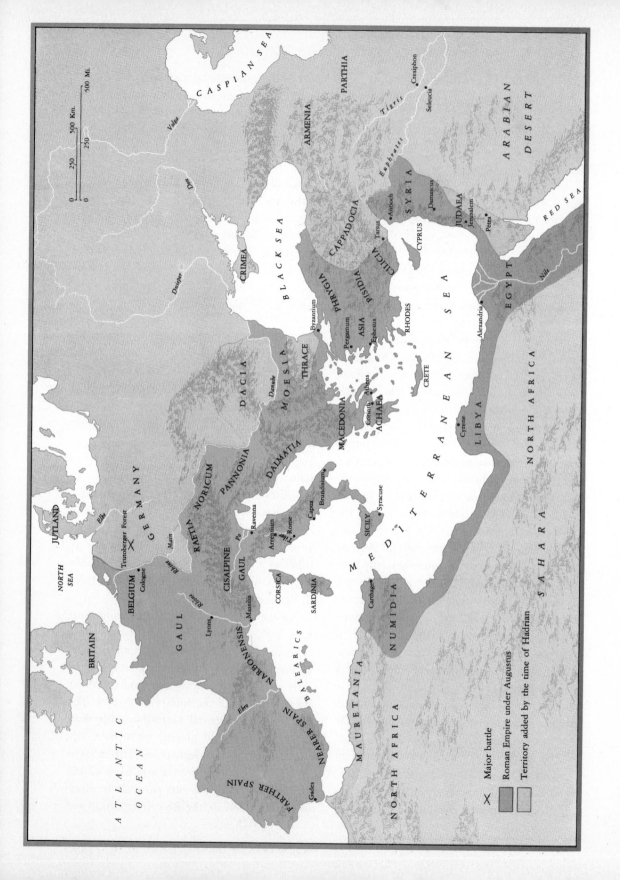

CASPIAN SEA

PARTHIA

ARMENIA

Tigris

Ctesiphon •
Seleucia •

ARABIAN

DESERT

Euphrates

SYRIA

Antioch •   • Damascus

JUDAEA

RED SEA

CAPPADOCIA

CILICIA

Tarsus •

CYPRUS

Jerusalem •
Petra •

PHRYGIA

PISIDIA

500 Mi.

500 Km.

250

250

0

0

CRIMEA

BLACK SEA

Byzantium •

Pergamum •

ASIA

Ephesus •

RHODES

MEDITERRANEAN SEA

EGYPT

Nile

Alexandria •

Volga

Dnieper

Don

Dniester

DACIA

Danube

MOESIA

THRACE

MACEDONIA

Athens •

Corinth •

ACHAEA

CRETE

LIBYA

Cyrene •

NORTH AFRICA

SAHARA

NORICUM

PANNONIA

DALMATIA

Main

RAETIA

Rhine

GERMANY

Teutoberger Forest ✕

BELGIUM

Cologne •

CISALPINE
GAUL

Po

Ravenna •

Arretium •
Rome •
Ostia •

Capua •

Brundisium •

SICILY

Syracuse •

JUTLAND

Elbe

NORTH
SEA

BRITAIN

ATLANTIC

OCEAN

GAUL

Lyons •

NARBONENSIS

Massilia •

CORSICA

SARDINIA

BALEARICS

NEARER SPAIN

Ebro

FARTHER SPAIN

Gades •

Carthage •

NUMIDIA

MAURETANIA

NORTH AFRICA

✕   Major battle

Roman Empire under Augustus

Territory added by the time of Hadrian

stouthearted, and these obstacles did not stop Roman expansion.

Augustus began his work in the north by completing the conquest of Spain. In Gaul, apart from minor campaigns, most of his work was peaceful. He founded twelve new towns. The Roman road system linked new settlements with one another and with Italy. But the German frontier, along the Rhine River, was the scene of hard fighting. In 12 B.C., Augustus ordered a major invasion of Germany beyond the Rhine. Roman legions advanced to the Elbe River, and a Roman fleet explored the North Sea and Jutland. The area north of the Main River and west of the Elbe was on the point of becoming Roman. But in 9 B.C., Augustus's general Varus lost some twenty thousand troops at the battle of the Teutoburger Forest. Thereafter the Rhine remained the Roman frontier.

Meanwhile, more successful generals extended the Roman standards as far as the Danube. Roman legions penetrated the area of modern Austria and western Hungary. The regions of modern Serbia, Bulgaria, and Rumania fell to Roman troops. Within this area the legionaries built fortified camps. Roads linked these camps with one another, and settlements grew up around the camps. Traders began to frequent the frontier and to traffic with the barbarians. Thus Roman culture — the rough-and-ready kind found in military camps — gradually spread into the northern wilderness.

Augustus's achievements in the north were monumental. For the first time in history, Greco-Roman culture spread beyond the sunny Mediterranean into the heart of Europe.

Amid the vast expanse of forests, Roman towns, trade, language, and law began to exert a civilizing influence on the barbarians. The Roman way of life attracted the barbarians, who soon recognized the benefits of assimilating Roman culture. Military camps often became towns; many modern European cities owe their origins to the forts of the Roman army. For the first time, the barbarian north came into direct, immediate, and continuous contact with Mediterranean culture.

LITERARY FLOWERING

The Augustan settlement's gift of peace inspired a literary flowering unparalleled in Roman history. With good reason this period is known as the golden age of Latin literature. Augustus and many of his friends actively encouraged poets and writers. As Virgil, Rome's greatest poet, summed up Augustus and his era:

Here is the man, here is he whom you often hear promised to you,
Augustus Caesar, offspring of the deified [Julius Caesar], who will establish
Once more a golden age in Latium.[4]

Virgil was not alone in this sentiment. The poet Horace felt the same:

With Caesar [Augustus] the guardian of the state
Not civil rage nor violence shall drive out peace,
Nor wrath which forges swords
And turns unhappy cities against each other.[5]

These lines are not empty flattery, despite Augustus's support of many contemporary Latin writers. To a generation that had known only vicious civil war, Augustus's settlement was an unbelievable blessing.

The tone and ideal of Roman literature, like that of the Greeks, was humanistic and

ARA PACIS   This scene from the Ara Pacis, the Altar of Peace, celebrates Augustus's restoration of peace and the fruits of peace. Here Mother Earth is depicted with her children. The cow and the sheep under the goddess represent the prosperity brought by peace, especially the agricultural prosperity so highly cherished by Virgil. (Alinari/Scala)

worldly. Roman poets and prose writers celebrated the dignity of humanity and the range of its accomplishments. They stressed the physical and emotional joys of a comfortable, peaceful life. Their works were highly polished, elegant in style, and intellectual in conception. Roman poets referred to the gods frequently and treated mythological themes, but always the core of their work was human, not divine.

Virgil (70-19 B.C.) celebrated the new age in the *Georgics,* four books of poems on agriculture. Virgil delighted in his own farm, and his poems sing of the pleasures of peaceful farm life. The *Georgics* are also a manual of agriculture written in meter. The poet tells how to keep bees, grow grapes and olives, plow, and manage a farm. Throughout the

Georgics Virgil wrote about things he himself had seen, rather than drawing his theme from the writings of others. For instance, he describes the worker bees returning to the hive at nightfall:

The weary young bees come back late at night,
Their legs full of thyme. Far and wide they feed
         on arbutus and grey-green willows and red
         crocus
And rich linden and rust-colored hyacinth.[6]

Virgil could be vivid and graphic as well as pastoral. Even a small event could be a drama for him. The death of a bull while plowing is hardly epic material; yet Virgil captures the sadness of the event in the image of the farmer unyoking the remaining animal:

Look, the bull, shining under the rough plough,
falls to the ground
and vomits from his mouth blood mixed with
foam,
and releases his dying groan.
Sadly moves the ploughman, unharnessing the
young steer grieving for the death of his brother
and leaves in the middle of the job
the plough stuck fast.[7]

Virgil's poetry is robust yet graceful. A sensitive man who delighted in simple things, Virgil left in his *Georgics* a charming picture of life in the Italian countryside in a period of peace.

Virgil's masterpiece is the *Aeneid,* an epic poem that is the Latin equivalent of the Greek *Iliad* and *Odyssey.* In the *Aeneid* Virgil expressed his admiration for Augustus's work by celebrating the shining ideal of a world blessed by the pax Romana. Virgil's account of the founding of Rome and the early years of the city gave final form to the legend of Aeneas, the Trojan hero who escaped to Italy at the fall of Troy. The principal Roman tradition held that Romulus was the founder of Rome, but the legend of Aeneas was also very old; it was known by the Etruscans as early as the fifth century B.C. Although Rome could not have had two founders, Virgil linked the legends of Aeneas and Romulus and kept them both. In so doing he also connected Rome with Greece's heroic past. Recounting the story of Aeneas and Dido, the queen of Carthage, Virgil made their ill-fated love affair the cause of the Punic wars. But above all, the *Aeneid* is the expression of Virgil's passionate belief in Rome's greatness. It is a vision of Rome as the protector of the good and noble against the forces of darkness and disruption.

In its own way Livy's history of Rome, entitled simply *Ab Urbe Condita* (*From the Founding of the City*), is the prose counterpart

of the *Aeneid.* Livy (59 B.C.–A.D. 17) received training in Greek and Latin literature, rhetoric, and philosophy. He even urged the future emperor Claudius to write history. Livy loved and admired the heroes and the great deeds of the republic, but he was also a friend of Augustus and a supporter of the principate. He especially approved of Augustus's efforts to restore the old republican virtues and morality.

Livy's history began with the legend of Aeneas and ended with the reign of Augustus. His theme of the greatness of the republic fitted admirably with Augustus's program of restoring the republic. Livy's history was colossal, consisting of 142 books of which only 25 percent still exists. Livy was a sensitive writer, and something of a moralist. Like Thucydides, he felt that history should be applied to the present. His history later became one of Rome's legacies to the modern world. During the Renaissance *Ab Urbe Condita* found a warm admirer in the poet Petrarch and left its mark on Machiavelli, who read it avidly.

The poet Horace (65–8 B.C.) rose from humble beginnings to friendship with Augustus. The son of an ex-slave and tax collector, Horace nonetheless received an excellent education. He loved Greek literature and finished his education in Athens. After Augustus's victory he returned to Rome and became Virgil's friend. Horace acquired a small farm north of Rome, which delighted him. He was as content as Virgil on his farm, and expressed his joy in a few lines:

Strive to add nothing to the myrtle plant!
The myrtle befits both you, the servant,
And me the master, as I drink under the
Thick-leaved vine.[8]

Horace happily turned his pen to celebrating Rome's newly won peace and prosperity. One of his finest odes commemorates Augustus's victory over Cleopatra at Actium in 31 B.C. Cleopatra is depicted as a frenzied queen, drunk with desire to destroy Rome. Horace saw in Augustus's victory the triumph of West over East, of simplicity over oriental excess. One of the truly moving aspects of Horace's poetry, like Virgil's, is his deep and abiding gratitude for the pax Romana.

For Rome, Augustus's age was one of hope and new beginnings. Augustus had put the empire on a new foundation. Constitutional monarchy was firmly established, and government was to all appearances a partnership between the princeps and the senate. The Augustan settlement was a delicate structure, and parts of it would in time be discarded. Nevertheless it worked, and by building on it later emperors would carry on Augustus's work.

The solidity of Augustus's work became obvious at his death in A.D. 14. Since the principate was not technically an office, Augustus could not legally hand it to a successor. Augustus had recognized this problem, and long before his death had found a way to solve it. He shared his consular and tribunician powers with his adopted son Tiberius, thus grooming him for the principate. In his will Augustus left most of his vast fortune to Tiberius, and the senate formally requested Tiberius to assume the burdens of the principate. All the formalities apart, Augustus had succeeded in creating a dynasty.

JUDAISM AND THE RISE OF CHRISTIANITY

During the reign of the emperor Tiberius (A.D. 14–37), perhaps in A.D. 29, Pontius Pilate, prefect of Judaea, condemned Jesus of Nazareth to death. At the time a minor event, this has become one of the best-known moments in history. How did these two men come to their historic meeting? The question is not idle, for Rome was as important as Judaea to Christianity. Jesus was born in a troubled time, when Roman rule aroused hatred and unrest among the Jews. This climate of hostility affected the lives of all who lived in Judaea, Roman and Jew alike. It forms the backdrop of Jesus' life, and it had a fundamental impact on his ministry. Without an understanding of this age of anxiety in Judaea, Jesus and early Christianity cannot properly be appreciated.

The entry of Rome into Jewish affairs was anything but peaceful. The civil wars that destroyed the republic wasted the prosperity of Judaea and the entire eastern Mediterranean world. Jewish leaders took sides in the fighting, and Judaea suffered its share of ravages and military confiscations. Peace brought little satisfaction to the Jews. Although Augustus treated Judaea generously, the Romans won no popularity by making Herod king of Judaea. King Herod gave Judaea prosperity and security, but the Jews hated his acceptance of Greek culture. He was also a bloodthirsty prince, who murdered his own wife and sons. Upon his death, the Jews broke out in revolt. For the next ten years Herod's successor waged almost constant war against the rebels. Added to the horrors of civil war were years of crop failure, which caused famine and plague. Men who called themselves prophets proclaimed the approach of the end of the world and the coming of the Messiah, the savior of Israel.

At length the Romans intervened to restore order. Augustus put Judaea under the charge of a prefect answerable directly to the emperor. Religious matters and local affairs became the responsibility of the Sanhedrin, the highest Jewish judicial body. Although many prefects tried to perform their duties scrupulously and conscientiously, many others were rapacious and indifferent to Jewish culture. Often acting from fear rather than cruelty, some prefects fiercely stamped out any signs of popular discontent. Pontius Pilate, prefect in A.D. 26–36, is typical of such incompetent officials. Although eventually relieved of his duties in disgrace, Pilate brutally put down even innocent demonstrations. Especially hated were the Roman tax collectors, called publicans, many of whom pitilessly gouged the Jews. Publicans and sinners – the words became synonymous. Clashes between Roman troops and Jewish guerrillas inflamed the anger of both sides.

In A.D. 40 the emperor Caligula undid part of Augustus's good work by ordering his statue erected in the temple at Jerusalem. The order, though never carried out, further intensified Jewish resentment. Thus, the Jews became embittered by Roman rule because of taxes, sometimes unduly harsh enforcement of the law, and a misguided interference in their religion.

Among the Jews two movements spread. First was the rise of the Zealots, extremists who worked and fought to rid Judaea of the Romans. Resolute in their worship of Yahweh, they refused to pay any but the tax levied by the Jewish temple. Their battles with the Roman legionaries were marked by savagery on both sides. As usual, the innocent caught in the middle suffered grievously. As Roman policy grew tougher, even moderate Jews began to hate the conquerors. Judaea came more and more to resemble a tinderbox, ready to burst into flames at a single spark.

The second movement was the growth of militant apocalyptic sentiment – the belief that the coming of the Messiah was near. This belief was an old one among the Jews. But by the first century A.D. it had become more

widespread and fervent than ever before. Typical was the Apocalypse of Baruch, which foretold the destruction of the Roman Empire. First would come a period of great tribulation, misery, and injustice. At the worst of the suffering, the Messiah would appear. The Messiah would destroy the Roman legions and all the kingdoms that had ruled Israel. Then the Messiah would inaugurate a period of happiness and plenty.

This was no abstract notion among the Jews. As the ravages of war became ever more widespread and conditions worsened, more and more people prophesied the imminent coming of the Messiah. One such was John the Baptist, "the voice of one crying in the wilderness, prepare ye the way of the lord."[9] Many Jews did just that. The sect described in the Dead Sea Scrolls readied itself for the end of the world. Its members were probably Essenes, and their social organization closely resembled that of the early Christians. Members of this group shared their possessions, precisely as John the Baptist urged people to do. Yet this sect, unlike the Christians, also made military preparations for the day of the Messiah.

Into this climate of Roman severity, fanatical Zealotry, and Messianic hope came Jesus of Nazareth (ca 3 B.C.–A.D. 29). He was raised in Galilee, the stronghold of the Zealots. Yet Jesus himself was a man of peace. Jesus urged his listeners to love god as their father and each other as god's children. The kingdom that he proclaimed was no earthly one, but one of eternal happiness in a life after death. Jesus' teachings are strikingly similar to those of Hillel (30 B.C.–A.D. 9), a great rabbi and interpreter of the Scriptures. Hillel taught the Jews to love one another as they loved god. He taught them to treat others as they themselves wished to be treated. Jesus' preaching was in this same serene tradition.

Jesus' teachings were entirely and thoroughly Jewish. He declared that he would change not one jot or tittle of the Jewish law. His orthodoxy enabled him to preach in the synagogue and the temple. His only deviation from orthodoxy was his insistence that he taught in his own name, not in the name of Yahweh. Was he then the Messiah? A small band of followers thought so, and Jesus revealed himself to them as the Messiah. Yet Jesus had his own conception of the Messiah. Unlike the Messiah of the Apocalypse of Baruch, Jesus would not destroy the Roman Empire. He told his disciples flatly that they were to "render unto Caesar the things that are Caesar's." Jesus would establish a spiritual kingdom, not an earthly one. Repeatedly he told his disciples that his kingdom was "not of this world."

Of Jesus' life and teachings the prefect Pontius Pilate knew little and cared even less. All that concerned him was the maintenance of peace and order. The crowds following Jesus at the time of the Passover, a highly emotional time in the Jewish year, alarmed Pilate, who faced a volatile situation. Some Jews believed that Jesus was the long-awaited Messiah. Others were disappointed because he refused to preach rebellion against Rome. Still others who hated and feared Jesus wanted to be rid of him. The last thing that Pilate wanted was a riot on his hands. Christian tradition has made much of Pontius Pilate. In the medieval West he was considered a monster. In the Ethiopian church he is considered a saint. Neither monster nor saint, Pilate was simply a hard-bitten Roman official. He did his duty, at times harshly. In Judaea his duty was to enforce the law and to keep the peace. These were the problems on his mind when Jesus stood before him. Jesus as King of the Jews did not worry him. The popular agitation surrounding Jesus did. To avert a riot

and bloodshed Pilate condemned Jesus to death.

Once Pilate's soldiers had carried out the sentence, the entire matter seemed to be closed. There were rumors that Jesus had risen from the dead or that his disciples had stolen his body, but otherwise the tumult subsided. Jesus' followers lived quietly and peacefully, unmolested by Roman or Jew. Pilate had no quarrel with them, and Judaism already had many minor sects. Peter (d. A.D. 67?), the first of Jesus' followers, became the head of the sect, which continued to observe Jewish law and religious customs. Peter, a man of traditional Jewish beliefs, felt that Jesus' teachings were meant exclusively for the Jews. Only in their practices of baptism and the Lord's Supper did the sect differ from normal Jewish custom. Meanwhile, they awaited the return of Jesus.

Christianity might have remained a purely Jewish sect had it not been for Paul of Tarsus (A.D. 5?–67?). The conversion of Hellenized Jews and of Gentiles (non-Jews) to Christianity caused the sect grave problems. Were the Gentiles subject to the law of Moses? If not, was Christianity to have two sets of laws? The answer to these questions was Paul's momentous contribution to Christianity. Paul was unlike Jesus or Peter. Born in a thriving and busy city filled with Romans, Greeks, Jews, Syrians, and others, he was at home in the world of Greco-Roman culture. After his conversion to Christianity he taught that his native Judaism was the preparation for the Messiah, and that Jesus by his death and resurrection had fulfilled the prophesy of Judaism and initiated a new age. Paul taught that Jesus was the Son of God, the beginning of a new law, and he preached that Jesus' teachings were to be proclaimed to all people, whether Jew or Gentile. Paul thus made a significant break with Judaism, Christianity's parent religion, for Judaism was exclusive and did not seek converts.

Paul's influence was far greater than that of any other early Christian. He traveled the length and breadth of the eastern Roman world, spreading his doctrine and preaching of Jesus. To little assemblies of believers in cities as distant as Rome and Corinth he taught that Jesus had died to save all people. Paul's vision of Christianity won out over Peter's traditionalism. Christianity broke with Judaism and embarked on its own course.

What was Christianity's appeal to the Roman world? What did this obscure sect give people that other religions did not? Christianity possessed many different attractions. One of its appeals was its willingness to embrace both men and women, slaves and nobles. Many of the Eastern mystery religions with which Christianity competed were exclusive in one way or another. Mithraism, a mystery religion descended from Zoroastrianism, spread throughout the entire empire. Mithras the sun god embodied good and warred against evil. Like Christianity, Mithraism offered elaborate and moving rituals including a form of baptism, a code of moral conduct, and the promise of life after death. Unlike Christianity, however, Mithraism permitted only men to become devotees. Much the same was true of the ancient Eleusinian mysteries of Greece, which were open only to Greeks and Romans.

Christianity appealed to common people and to the poor. Its communal celebration of the Lord's Supper gave men and women a sense of belonging. Christianity also offered its adherents the promise of salvation. Christians believed that Jesus on the cross had defeated evil, and that he would reward his followers with eternal life after death. Christianity also offered the possibility of forgiveness. Human nature was weak, and even the best Christians would fall into sin. But Jesus loved sinners and forgave those who repented. In its doctrine of salvation and forgiveness alone Christianity had a powerful ability to give solace and strength to those who believed.

Christianity was attractive to many because it gave the Roman world a cause. Hellenistic philosophy had attempted to make men and women self-sufficient: people who became indifferent to the outside world could no longer be hurt by it. That goal alone ruled out any cause except the attainment of serenity. The Romans, who were never innovators in philosophy, merely elaborated this lonely and austere message. Instead of passivity Christianity stressed the ideal of striving for a goal. Each and every Christian, no matter how poor or humble, worked to realize the triumph of Christianity on earth. This was God's will, a sacred duty for every Christian. By spreading the word of Christ, Christians played their part in God's plan. No matter how small a part each Christian played, that part was important. Since this duty was God's will, Christians believed that sooner or later the goal would be achieved. The Christian was not to be discouraged by temporary setbacks, believing Christianity to be invincible.

Christianity gave its devotees a sense of community. No Christian was alone. All members of the Christian community strived toward the same goal of fulfilling God's plan. Each individual community was in turn a member of a greater community. And that community, the Church General, was indestructible. After all, Jesus himself had promised, "Thou art Peter, and upon this rock I will build my church; and the gates of hell shall not prevail against it."[10]

So Christianity's attractions were many, from forgiveness of sin to an exalted purpose for each individual. Its insistence on the importance of the individual gave solace and encouragement, especially to the poor and meek. Its claim to divine protection fed hope in the eventual success of the Christian community. Christianity made participation in the universal possible for each and every person. The ultimate reward promised by Christianity was eternal bliss after death. Though at first the educated and wealthy scoffed at this message, they too succumbed to its charm. It was unlike anything the average man and woman had ever known.

THE JULIO-CLAUDIANS AND THE FLAVIANS (27 B.C.–A.D. 96)

For fifty years after Augustus's death the dynasty that he established – known as the Julio-Claudians because they were all members of the Julian and Claudian clans – provided the emperors of Rome. Some of the Julio-Claudians, like Tiberius and Claudius, were sound rulers and able administrators. Others, like Caligula and Nero, were weak and frivolous men who exercised their power stupidly and brought misery to the empire. Writers such as the biting and brilliant historian Tacitus (ca A.D. 55–ca 116) and the gossipy Suetonius (ca A.D. 75–150) have left unforgettable – and generally hostile – portraits of these emperors that are literary masterpieces. Yet the venom of Tacitus and Suetonius cannot obscure the fact that Julio-Claudians were responsible for some notable achievements and that during their reigns the empire on the whole prospered.

One of the most momentous achievements of the Julio-Claudians was Claudius's creation of an imperial bureaucracy composed of professional administrators. Even the most energetic emperor could not run the empire alone.

The numerous duties and immense reponsibilities of the emperor prompted Claudius to delegate power. He began by giving the freedmen of his household official duties, especially in the field of finances. It was a simple, workable system. Claudius knew his ex-slaves well and could discipline them at will. The effect of Claudius's innovations was to enable the emperor to rule the empire more easily and efficiently.

One of the worst defects of Augustus's settlement – the army's ability to interfere in politics – became obvious during the Julio-Claudian period. Augustus had created a special standing force, the Praetorian Guard, as an imperial bodyguard. In A.D. 41 one of the praetorians murdered Caligula while others hailed Claudius as the emperor. Under the threat of violence the senate ratified the praetorians' choice. It was a story repeated frequently. During the first three centuries of the empire the Praetorian Guard all too often murdered emperors they were supposed to protect and saluted emperors of their own choosing.

In A.D. 69, Nero's inept rule led to an extensive military uprising that caused widespread disruption. No fewer than four men became emperor that year, known as the Year of the Four Emperors. Roman armies in Gaul, on the Rhine, and in the East marched on Rome to make their commanders emperor. The man who emerged triumphant was Vespasian, commander of the eastern armies, who entered Rome in 70 and restored order. Nonetheless, the Year of the Four Emperors proved that the Augustan settlement had failed to end civil war.

Not a brilliant politician, Vespasian did not institute reforms as had Augustus or tackle the problem of the army in politics. To prevent usurpers from claiming the throne Vespasian designated his sons Titus and Domitian as his successors. By establishing the Flavian (the name of Vespasian's clan) dynasty Vespasian turned the principate into an open and admitted monarchy. He also expanded the power of the emperor by increasing the size of the budding bureaucracy Claudius had created.

One of Vespasian's first tasks was to suppress rebellions that had erupted at the end of Nero's reign. The most famous had taken place in Judaea, which still seethed long after Jesus' crucifixion. Long-standing popular unrest and atrocities committed by Jews and Romans alike sparked a massive revolt in A.D. 66. Four years later a Roman army reconquered Judaea and reduced Jerusalem by siege. The Jewish survivors were enslaved, their state destroyed. The mismanagement of Judaea was one of the few — and worst — failures of Roman imperial administration.

The Flavians carried on Augustus's work on the frontiers. Domitian, the last of the Flavians, won additional territory in Germany and consolidated it in two new provinces. He defeated barbarian tribes on the Danube frontier and strengthened that area as well. Nonetheless, Domitian was one of the most hated of Roman emperors, and he fell victim to an assassin's dagger. Nevertheless, the Flavians had given the Roman world peace and had kept the legions in line. Their work paved the way for the era of the "Five Good Emperors," the golden age of the empire.

THE AGE OF THE FIVE GOOD EMPERORS (A.D. 96–180)

In the second century of the Christian era, the Empire of Rome comprehended the fairest part of the earth, and the most civilised portion of mankind. The frontiers of that extensive monarchy

THE PRAETORIAN GUARD *Instituted by Augustus as the imperial bodyguard, the Praetorian Guard began making and breaking emperors as early as the Julio-Claudian period. For all of their power, they were not crack troops, but their access to the emperor gave them an influence far greater than their numerical strength or fighting ability. (Giraudon)*

were guarded by ancient renown and disciplined valour. The gentle but powerful influence of laws and manners had gradually cemented the union of the provinces. Their peaceful inhabitants enjoyed and abused the advantages of wealth and luxury. The image of a free constitution was preserved with decent reverence: the Roman senate appeared to possess the sovereign authority, and devolved on the emperors all the executive powers of government. During a happy period (A.D. 98–180) of more than fourscore years, the public administration was conducted by the virtue and abilities of Nerva, Trajan, Hadrian, and the two Antonines.[11]

Thus Edward Gibbon (1737–1794) began his monumental *History of the Decline and Fall* of the Roman Empire. Gibbon saw the era of Nerva, Trajan, Hadrian, Antoninus Pius, and Marcus Aurelius – the "five good emperors" – as the happiest period in human history, the last burst of summer before the autumn of failure and barbarism. Gibbon recognized a great truth: the age of the Antonines, as the "five good emperors" are often called, was one of almost unparalleled prosperity. Wars were minor and confined to the frontiers. Even the serenity of Augustus's day seemed to pale in comparison. These emperors were among the noblest, most dedicated, and ablest men in Roman history. Yet fundamental political and military changes had taken place since Augustus's day.

THE ANTONINE MONARCHY

The age of the Antonines was the age of full-blown monarchy. Gibbon wrote:

The obvious definition of a monarchy seems to be that of a state, in which a single person, by what-soever name he may be distinguished, is entrusted with the execution of the laws, the management of the revenue, and the command of the army.[12]

Augustus clearly fits Gibbon's definition of a monarch in all essentials. But there is a significant difference between Augustus's position and that of an emperor like Hadrian.

Augustus claimed that his influence arose from the collection of offices the senate had bestowed upon him. However, there was in law no such office as emperor. Augustus was merely the First Citizen. Under the Flavians the principate became a full-blown monarchy, and by the time of the Antonines the principate was an office with definite rights, powers, and prerogatives. In the years between Augustus and the Antonines the emperor had become an indispensable part of the imperial machinery. In short, without the emperor the

empire would quickly fall to pieces. Augustus had been monarch in fact but not in theory; the Antonines were monarchs in both.

The Antonines were not power-hungry autocrats. The concentration of power was the result of empire, as the American historian M. Hammond has pointed out:

Monarchy was indeed an inescapable result of the existence of the empire; the more efficient the imperial government became, the more it assumed new functions; and the more that increasing pressure made its task heavier, so much the more it became monarchical.[13]

In short, the easiest and most efficient way to run the Roman Empire was to invest the emperor with vast powers. Furthermore, Roman emperors on the whole proved to be effective rulers and administrators. As capable and efficient emperors took on new tasks and functions, the hand of the emperor was felt in more and more areas of life and government. Increasingly, the emperors became the source of all authority and guidance within the empire. The five good emperors were benevolent and exercised their power intelligently, but they were absolute kings all the same. Lesser men would later throw off the façade of constitutionality and use this same power in a despotic fashion.

Typical of the five good emperors is the career of Hadrian, who became emperor in A.D. 117. He was born in Spain, a fact that illustrates the importance of the provinces in Roman politics. Hadrian received his education at Rome and became an ardent admirer of Greek culture. He caught the attention of his elder cousin Trajan – the future emperor – who started him on a military career. At age nineteen Hadrian served on the Danube frontier, where he learned the details of how the Roman army lived and fought and saw for himself the problems of defending the fron-

ROMAN HISTORY AFTER AUGUSTUS

PERIOD	IMPORTANT EMPERORS	SIGNIFICANT EVENTS
Julio-Claudians 27 B.C.–A.D. 68	Augustus, 27 B.C.–A.D. 14 Tiberius, 14–37 Caligula, 37–41 Claudius, 41–54 Nero, 54–68	Augustan settlement Beginning of the principate Birth and death of Jesus Expansion into northern and western Europe Creation of the imperial bureaucracy
Year of the Four Emperors, 68–69	Nero Galba Otho Vitellius	Civil war Major breakdown of the concept of the principate
Flavians 69–96	Vespasian, 69–79 Titus, 79–81 Domitian, 81–96	Growing trend toward the concept of monarchy Defense and further consolidation of the European frontiers
Antonines 96–192	Nerva, 96–98 Trajan, 98–117 Hadrian, 117–138 Antoninus Pius, 138–161 Marcus Aurelius, 161–180 Commodus, 180–192	The "golden age" – the era of the "five good emperors" Economic prosperity Trade and growth of cities in northern Europe Beginning of barbarian menace on the frontiers
Severi 193–235	Septimius Severus, 193–211 Caracalla, 211–217 Elagabalus, 218–222 Severus Alexander, 222–235	Military monarchy All free men within the empire given Roman citizenship
"Barracks Emperors" 235–284	Twenty-two emperors in forty-nine years	Civil war Breakdown of the Empire Barbarian invasions Severe economic decline
Tetrarchy 284–337	Diocletian, 284–305 Constantine, 306–337	Political recovery Autocracy Legalization of Christianity Transition to the Middle Ages in the West Birth of the Byzantine Empire in the East

tiers. When Trajan became emperor in A.D. 98, he began giving Hadrian high military and administrative positions in which he learned how to defend and run the empire. At Trajan's death in 117, Hadrian assumed the reins of power.

Roman government had changed since Augustus's day. One of the most significant changes was the enormous growth of the imperial bureaucracy created by Claudius. Hadrian reformed this system by putting the bureaucracy on an organized, official basis. He established imperial administrative departments to handle the work formerly done by the imperial freedmen. Hadrian also separated civil service from military service. Men with little talent or taste for the army could instead serve the state as administrators. Hadrian's bureaucracy demanded professionalism from its members. Administrators made a career of the civil service. These innovations made for more efficient running of the empire, and increased the authority of the emperor, who was the ruling power of the bureaucracy.

CHANGES IN THE ARMY

The Roman army had also changed since Augustus's time. The Roman legion had once been a mobile unit, but its duties under the empire no longer called for mobility. The successors of Augustus called a halt to further conquests. The army was expected to defend what had already been won. Under the Flavian emperors (A.D. 69–96) the frontiers became firmly fixed. Forts and watch stations guarded the borders. Behind the forts the Romans built a system of roads, which allowed the forts to be quickly supplied and reinforced in times of trouble. The army had evolved into a garrison force, with legions guarding specific areas for long periods.

The personnel of the legions was changing too. Italy could no longer supply all the recruits needed for the army. Increasingly, only the officers came from Italy and from the more Romanized provinces. The legionaries were mostly drawn from the less civilized provinces, especially the ones closest to the frontiers. A major trend was already obvious in Hadrian's day: fewer and fewer Roman soldiers were really Roman. In the third century A.D., the barbarization of the army would result in an army indifferent to Rome and its traditions. In the age of the Antonines, however, the army was still a source of economic stability and a Romanizing agent. Provincials and even barbarians joined the army to learn a trade and to gain Roman citizenship. Even so, the signs were ominous. Julius Caesar's veterans would hardly have recognized Hadrian's troops as Roman legionaries.

LIFE IN THE GOLDEN AGE

If a man were called to fix the period in the history of the world, during which the condition of the human race was most happy and prosperous, he would without hesitation, name that which elapsed from the death of Domitian to the accession of Commodus.[14]

Thus, according to Gibbon, the age of the five good emperors was a golden age in human history. How does Gibbon's picture correspond to the popular image of Rome as a city of bread, brothels, and gladiatorial games? If the Romans were degenerates who spent their time carousing, who kept Rome and the empire running? Can life in Rome be taken as representative of life in other parts of the empire?

Truth and exaggeration are mixed both in Gibbon's view and in the popular image of Rome. Rome and the provinces must be treated separately. Rome no more resembled a provincial city like Cologne than New York resembles Keokuk, Iowa. Rome was unique and must be seen as such. Only then can one turn to the provinces to obtain a full and reasonable picture of the empire under the Antonines.

IMPERIAL ROME

Rome was truly an extraordinary city, especially by ancient standards. It was also an enormous city, with a population somewhere between 500,000 and 750,000. Although Rome could boast of stately palaces, noble buildings, and beautiful residential areas, most people lived in jerrybuilt apartment houses. Fire and crime were perennial problems, even after Augustus created fire and urban police forces. Streets were narrow and drainage inadequate. During the republic sanitation had been a common problem. Numerous inscriptions record prohibitions against the dumping of human refuse and even cadavers within the grounds of sanctuaries and cemeteries. Under the empire this situation improved. By comparison with medieval and early modern European cities, Rome was a healthy enough place to live.

Rome was such a huge city that the surrounding countryside could not feed it. Because of the danger of starvation, the emperor, following republican practice, provided the citizen population with free grain for bread, and later included oil and wine. By feeding the citizenry the emperor prevented bread riots caused by shortages and high prices. For the rest of the urban population who did not enjoy the rights of citizenship,

COIN OF HADRIAN   *The emperor Hadrian not only energetically ruled the Roman Empire, he also helped to set a new fashion in Rome by sporting a full beard. Since Scipio Aemilianus's day, Romans had ordinarily been clean-shaven. (Courtesy, World Heritage Museum. Photo: Caroline Buckler)*

the emperor provided grain at low prices. This measure was designed to prevent speculators from forcing up the price of grain in times of crisis. By maintaining the grain supply the emperor kept the favor of the people and insured that Rome's poor and idle did not starve.

The emperor also entertained the Roman populace, often at vast expense. The most popular forms of public entertainment were gladiatorial contests and chariot racing. Gladiatorial fighting was originally an Etruscan funerary custom, a blood sacrifice for the dead. Even a humane man like Hadrian staged extravagant contests. In A.D. 126 he sponsored six days of such combats, during which 1,835

APARTMENT HOUSES AT OSTIA   At heavily populated places such as Rome and Ostia, which was the port of Rome, apartment buildings housed urban dwellers. The brick construction of this building is a good example of solid Roman work. In Rome some apartment buildings were notoriously shoddy and unsafe. (Italian Government Travel Office)

pairs of gladiators dueled, usually with swords and shields. Many gladiators were criminals, some of whom were sentenced to be slaughtered in the arena. These convicts were given no defensive weapons and stood little real chance of survival. Other criminals were sentenced to fight in the arena as fully armed gladiators. Some gladiators were the slaves of gladiatorial trainers; others were prisoners of war. Still others were free men who volunteered for the arena. Even women at times engaged in gladiatorial combat. What drove these men and women? Some obviously had no other choice. For a criminal condemned to death, the arena was preferable to the imperial mines, where convicts worked digging ore and died under wretched conditions. At least

in the arena the gladiator might fight well enough to win his or her freedom. Others no doubt fought for the love of danger and for fame. Although some Romans protested against gladiatorial fighting, most delighted in it – one of their least attractive sides. Not until the fifth century did Christianity put a stop to it.

The Romans were even more addicted to chariot racing than to gladiatorial shows. Under the empire four permanent teams competed against one another. Each team had its own color – red, white, green, or blue. Some Romans claimed that people cared more about their favorite team than about the race itself. Two-horse and four-horse chariots ran a course of seven laps, about five miles. A successful driver could be the hero of the hour. One charioteer, Gaius Appuleius Diocles, raced for twenty-four years. During that time he drove 4,257 starts and won 1,462 of them. His admirers honored him with an inscription that proclaimed him the champion of all charioteers.

But people like the charioteer Diocles were no more typical of the common Roman than Babe Ruth is of the average American. Ordinary Romans have left their mark in the inscriptions that grace their graves. These inscriptions offer a glimpse of Roman life. Ordinary Romans were proud of their work and accomplishments. They were affectionate toward their families and friends, and eager to be remembered after death. They did not spend their lives in idleness, watching gladiators or chariot races. They had to make a living. They dealt with everyday problems and rejoiced over small pleasures. An impression of them and their cares can be gained from their epitaphs. The funerary inscription of Paprius Vitalis to his wife is particularly engaging:

If there is anything good in the lower regions – I, however, finish a poor life without you – be happy there too, sweetest Thalassia . . . married to me for 40 years.[15]

As moving is the final tribute of a patron to his ex-slave:

To Grania Clara, freedwoman of Aulus, a temperate freedwoman. She lived 23 years. She was never vexatious to me except when she died.[16]

In another epitaph the wife of a merchant honored her husband for his honest dealings. Even the personal philosophies of typical Romans have come down from antiquity. Marcus Antonius Encolpus erected a funerary inscription to his wife that reads in part:

Do not pass by my epitaph, traveler.
But having stopped, listen and learn, then go your way.
There is no boat in Hades, no ferryman Charon,
no caretaker Aiakos, no dog Cerberus.
All we who are dead below
have become bones and ashes, but nothing else.
I have spoken to you honestly, go on, traveler,
lest even while dead I seem loquacious to you.[17]

Others put it more simply: "I was, I am not, I don't care." "To each his own tombstone." These Romans went about their lives much as people have always done. Though fond of brutal spectacles, they also had their loves and their dreams.

THE PROVINCES

In the provinces and even on the frontiers many men and women would have agreed with Gibbon's opinion of the second century. The age of the Antonines was one of extensive prosperity, especially in western Europe. The Roman army had beaten back the barbarians and exposed them to the civilizing effects of Roman traders. The resulting peace and security opened Britain, Gaul, Germany, and the lands of the Danube to immigration. Agriculture flourished as large tracts of land came under cultivation. Most of this land was in the hands of free tenant farmers. From the time of Augustus slavery had declined in the empire, as had the growth of latifundia (see page 232). Augustus and his successors encouraged the rise of free farmers. Under the Antonines this trend continued, and the holders of small parcels of land thrived as never before. The Antonines provided loans on easy terms to farmers. These loans enabled them to rent land previously worked by slaves. It also permitted them to cultivate the

SCENE FROM TRAJAN'S COLUMN From 101 to 107 Trajan fought the barbarian tribes along the Danube. This scene depicts Roman soldiers unloading supplies at a frontier city, which forms the background. Not only did such walled cities serve as Roman strong points, they were also centers of Roman civilization, with their shops, homes, temples, and amphitheaters. (Alinari/Scala)

new lands that were being opened up. Consequently, the small tenant farmer was becoming the backbone of Roman agriculture.

In continental Europe the army was largely responsible for the new burst of expansion. The areas where the legions were stationed readily became Romanized. When legionaries retired from the army, they often settled in the locality where they had served. Since they had usually learned a trade in the army, they brought essential skills to areas that badly needed trained men. These veterans took their retirement pay and used it to set themselves up in business.

Since the time of Augustus towns had gradually grown up around the camps and forts. The roads that linked the frontier with the rearward areas served as commercial lifelines for the new towns and villages. Part Roman, part barbarian, these towns were truly outposts of civilization, much like the raw towns of the American West. In the course of time many of them grew to be Romanized cities. As they did, emperors gave them the status of full Roman municipalities, with charters and constitutions. This development was very pronounced along the Rhine and Danube frontiers. Thus while defending the borders, the army also spread Roman culture. This process would go so far that in A.D. 212 the emperor Caracalla would grant Roman citizenship to every free man within the empire.

The eastern part of the empire also participated in the boom. The Roman navy had swept the sea of pirates, and Eastern merchants traded their wares throughout the Mediterranean. The flow of goods and produce in the East matched that of the West. Venerable cities like Corinth, Antioch, and Ephesus flourished as rarely before. The cities of the East built extensively, bedecking themselves with new amphitheaters, temples, fountains, and public buildings. For the East, the age of the Antonines was the heyday of the city. Urban life there grew ever richer and more comfortable.

Trade among the provinces increased dramatically. Britain and Belgium became prime producers of grain, much of their harvests going to the armies of the Rhine. Britain's famous wool industry probably got its start under the Romans. Italy and southern Gaul produced wine in huge quantities. The wines of Italy went principally to Rome and the Danube, while Gallic wines were shipped to Britain and the Rhineland. Roman colonists had introduced the olive to southern Spain and northern Africa, an experiment so successful that these regions produced most of the oil consumed in the western empire. In the East, Syrian farmers continued to cultivate the olive, and the production of oil reached an all-time high. Egypt was the prime grain producer of the East, and tons of Egyptian wheat went to feed the populace of Rome. The Roman army in Mesopotamia consumed a high percentage of the raw materials and manufactured products of Syria and Asia Minor. The spread of trade meant the end of isolated and self-contained economies. By the time of the Antonines the empire had become an economic reality as well as a political one.

One of the most striking features of this period was the growth of industry in the provinces. Cities in Gaul and Germany eclipsed the old Mediterranean manufacturing centers. Italian cities were particularly hard-hit by this development. Cities like Arrentium and Capua had dominated the production of glass, pottery, and bronze ware. Yet in the second century A.D. Gaul and Germany took over the pottery market. Lyons in Gaul became the new center of the glassmaking industry. The technique of glass blowing spread to Britain and Germany, and later in the second century Cologne replaced Lyons in glass production. The cities of Gaul were nearly unrivaled in the manufacture of bronze and brass. Gallic craftsmen invented a new technique of tin-plating and decorated their work with Celtic designs. Their wares soon drove Italian products out of the northern European market. For the first time in history northern Europe was able to rival the Mediterranean as a producer of manufactured goods. Europe had entered fully into the economic and cultural life of the Mediterranean world.

The age of the Antonines was generally one of peace, progress, and prosperity. The work of the Romans in northern and western Europe was a permanent contribution to the history of Western society. The cities that grew up in Britain, Belgium, Gaul, Germany, Austria, and elsewhere survived the civil wars that racked the empire in the third century A.D. Likewise, they survived the barbarian invasions that destroyed the western empire, and handed on a precious heritage, both cultural and material, to the medieval world. The period of the Antonine monarchy was also one of consolidation. Roads and secure sea-lanes linked the empire in one vast web. The empire had become a commonwealth of cities, and urban life was the hallmark of this civilization.

CIVIL WARS AND INVASION IN THE THIRD CENTURY

The age of the Antonines gave way to a period of chaos and stress. During the third century A.D., the empire was stunned by civil wars and barbarian invasions. By the time peace was restored, the economy was shattered, cities had shrunk in size, and agriculture was becoming manorial (see pages 267–268). In the disruption of the third century and the reconstruction of the fourth, the medieval world had its origins.

After the death of Marcus Aurelius, the last of the five good emperors, his son Commodus came to the throne, a man who was totally unsuited to govern the empire. His misrule led to his murder and a renewal of civil war. After a brief but intense spasm of fighting, the African general Septimius Severus defeated other rival commanders and established the Severan dynasty (A.D. 193–235). Although Septimius Severus was able to stabilize the empire, his successors proved incapable of disciplining the legions. When the last of the Severi was killed by one of his own soldiers, the empire plunged into still another grim, destructive, and this time prolonged round of civil war.

Over twenty different emperors ascended the throne in the forty-nine years between 235

and 284, and many rebels died in the attempt to seize power. At various times, parts of the empire were lost to rebel generals, one of whom, Postumus, set up his own empire in Gaul for about ten years (A.D. 259–269). Yet other men like the iron-willed Aurelian (A.D. 270–275) dedicated their energies to restoring order. So many military commanders seized rule that the middle of the third century has become known as the age of the "barracks emperors." The Augustan Principate had become a military monarchy, and that monarchy was nakedly autocratic.

The disruption caused by civil war opened the way for widespread barbarian invasions. Throughout the empire, barbarian invasions and civil war devastated towns, villages, and farms and caused a catastrophic economic depression. Indeed, the Roman Empire seemed on the point of collapse.

BARBARIANS ON THE FRONTIERS

The first and most disastrous result of the civil wars was trouble on the frontiers. It was Rome's misfortune that this era of anarchy coincided with immense movements of barbarian peoples. Historians still dispute the precise reason for these migrations, though their immediate cause was pressure from tribes moving westward across Asia. In the sixth century A.D., Jordanes, a Christianized Goth, preserved the memory of innumerable wars among the barbarians in his *History of the Goths*. Goths fought Vandals, Huns fought Goths. Steadily, the defeated and displaced tribes moved toward the Roman frontiers. Finally, like "a swarm of bees" – to use Jordanes's image – the Goths burst into Europe in A.D. 258.

When the barbarians reached the Rhine and Danube frontiers, they often found huge gaps in the Roman defenses. Typical is the case of Decius, a general who guarded the Danube frontier in Dacia (modern Rumania). In A.D. 249, he revolted and invaded Italy in an effort to become emperor. Decius left the frontier deserted, and the Goths easily poured in looking for new homes. Through much of the third century A.D., bands of Goths devastated the Balkans as far south as Greece. They even penetrated Asia Minor. The Alamanni, a German people, swept across the Danube. At one point they entered Italy and reached Milan before they were beaten back. Meanwhile the Franks, still another German folk, hit the Rhine frontier. The Franks then invaded eastern and central Gaul and northeastern Spain. Saxons from Scandinavia entered the English Channel in search of loot. In the East the Sassanids, of Persian stock, overran Mesopotamia. If the army had been guarding the borders instead of creating and destroying emperors, none of these invasions would have been possible. The "barracks emperors" should be credited with one accomplishment, however: they fought barbarians when they were not fighting each other. Only that kept the empire from total ruin.

TURMOIL IN FARM AND VILLAGE LIFE

How did the ordinary people cope with this period of iron and blood? What did it mean to the lives of men and women on farms and in villages? How did local officials continue to serve their emperor and their neighbors? Some people became outlaws. Others lived their lives more prosaically. Some voiced their grievances to the emperor, thereby leaving a record of the problems they faced. In a sur-

prising number of cases the barbarians were less of a problem than the lawlessness of soldiers, imperial officials, and local agents. For many ordinary people official corruption was the tangible and immediate result of the breakdown of central authority. In one instance some tenant farmers in Lydia (modern Turkey) complained to the emperor about arbitrary arrest and the killing of prisoners. They claimed that police agents had threatened them and prevented them from cultivating the land. Tenant farmers in Phrygia (modern Turkey) voiced similar complaints. They suffered extortion at the hands of public officials. Military commanders, soldiers, and imperial agents requisitioned their livestock and compelled the farmers to forced labor. The farmers were becoming impoverished, and many people deserted the land to seek safety elsewhere. The inhabitants of an entire village in Thrace (modern Bulgaria) complained that they were being driven from their homes. From imperial and local officials they suffered insolence and violence. Soldiers demanded to be quartered and given supplies. Many villagers had already abandoned their homes to escape. The remaining villagers warned the emperor that unless order was restored, they too would flee.

Local officials were sometimes unsympathetic or violent toward farmers and villagers because of their own plight. They were responsible for the collection of imperial revenues. If their area could not meet its tax quota, they paid the deficit from their own pockets. For instance, Aurelius Hermophilus complained that he could no longer perform public duties because he had gone bankrupt. When Aemilius Stephanus, a wealthy Roman in Egypt, learned that he had been nominated to the local council of his town, he surrendered all his property to the man who had nominated him. In one Egyptian municipality fistfights broke out among the officials. Finally the emperor had to forbid fighting in the council house. Because the local officials were so hard-pressed, they squeezed whatever they could from the villagers and farmers.

RECONSTRUCTION UNDER DIOCLETIAN AND CONSTANTINE (A.D. 284–337)

At the close of the third century A.D., the emperor Diocletian (284–305) put an end to the period of turmoil. Repairing the damage done in the third century was the major work of the emperor Constantine (306–337) in the fourth. But the price was high.

Under Diocletian, Augustus's polite fiction of the emperor as "first among equals" gave way to the emperor as absolute autocrat. The princeps became *dominus* – lord. The emperor claimed that he was "the elect of god" – that he ruled because of god's favor. Constantine even claimed to be the equal of Jesus' first twelve followers. To underline the emperor's exalted position, Diocletian and Constantine adopted the gaudy court ceremonies and trappings of the Persian Empire. People entering the emperor's presence prostrated themselves before him and kissed the hem of his robes. Constantine went so far as to import Persian eunuchs to run the palace. The Roman emperor had become an oriental monarch.

No mere soldier, Diocletian gave serious thought to the ailments of the empire. He recognized that the empire and its difficulties had become too great for one man to handle. He also realized that during the third century provincial governors had frequently used their positions to foment or participate in rebellions. To solve the first of these problems

MAP 8.2 *THE ROMAN WORLD DIVIDED Under Diocletian, the Roman empire was first divided into a western and an eastern half, a development that foreshadowed the medieval division between the Latin West and the Byzantine East.*

Diocletian divided the empire into a western half and an eastern half (see Map 8.2). Diocletian assumed direct control of the eastern part; he gave the rule of the western part to a colleague, along with the title *augustus,* which had become synonymous with emperor. Diocletian and his fellow augustus further delegated power by appointing two men to assist them. Each man was given the title of *caesar* to indicate his exalted rank. Although this system is known as the Tetrarchy because four men ruled the empire, Diocletian was clearly the senior partner and the final source of authority.

Each half of the empire was further split into two prefectures, governed by a prefect responsible to an augustus. Diocletian reduced the power of the old provincial governors by dividing provinces into smaller units: he organized the prefectures into smaller administrative units called dioceses, which were in turn subdivided into small provinces. Provincial governors were also deprived of their military power, leaving them only civil and administrative duties.

Diocletian's division of the empire into two parts was a momentous step, for it became permanent. Constantine and later emperors tried hard to keep the empire together, but without success. Throughout the fourth century A.D., the East and the West drifted apart. In later centuries the western part witnessed the fall of Roman government and the rise of barbarian kingdoms, while the eastern empire evolved into the majestic Byzantine Empire.

The most serious immediate matters con-

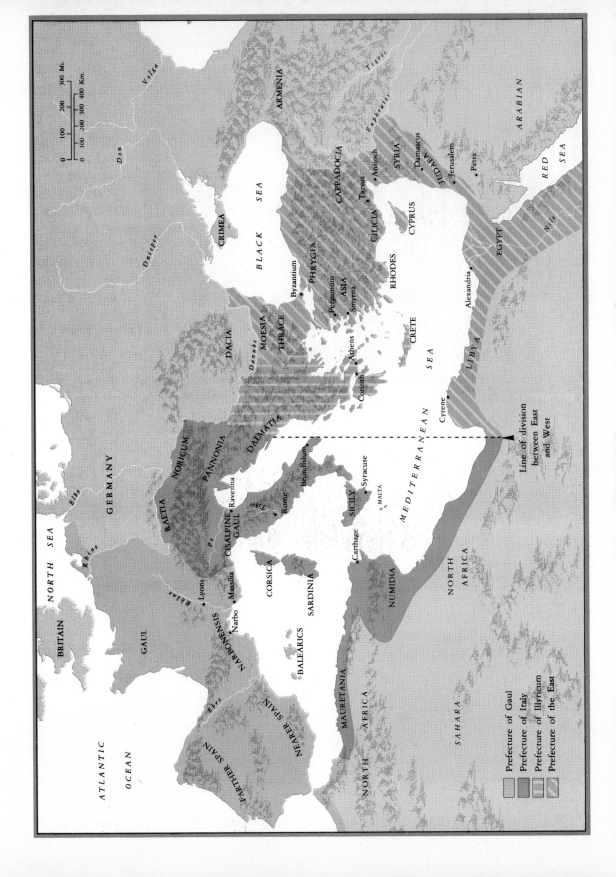

ATLANTIC
OCEAN

NORTH SEA

BRITAIN

GERMANY

GAUL

NARBONENSIS

Lyons
Massilia
Narbo

Ebro

FARTHER SPAIN

NEARER SPAIN

BALEARICS

CORSICA

SARDINIA

MAURETANIA

NORTH AFRICA

SAHARA

Elbe

Rhine

Rhône

Po

RAETIA

NORICUM

PANNONIA

CISALPINE GAUL
Ravenna

Rome

Brundisium

SICILY
Syracuse
MALTA

Carthage

NUMIDIA

NORTH AFRICA

MEDITERRANEAN SEA

DALMATIA

DACIA

Danube

MOESIA

THRACE

Byzantium

CRIMEA

Dnieper

Don

Volga

BLACK SEA

ARMENIA

CAPPADOCIA

Tigris

PHRYGIA

Pergamum
ASIA
Smyrna

Athens
Corinth

CRETE

RHODES

CYPRUS

CILICIA
Tarsus

SYRIA
Antioch
Damascus

JUDAEA
Jerusalem
Petra

EGYPT

Alexandria

Nile

Euphrates

RED SEA

ARABIAN SEA

LIBYA

Cyrene

Line of division
between East
and West

300 Mi.
200
100
0

400 Km.
300
200
100
0

Prefecture of Gaul
Prefecture of Italy
Prefecture of Illyricum
Prefecture of the East

THE ARCH OF CONSTANTINE *To celebrate the victory which made him emperor, Constantine built this triumphal arch at Rome. Rather than decorate the arch with the inferior work of his own day, Constantine plundered other Roman monuments, including those of Trajan and Marcus Aurelius. (Italian Government Travel Office)*

fronting Diocletian and Constantine were economic, social, and religious. They needed additional revenues to support the army and the imperial court. Yet the wars and the barbarian invasions had caused widespread destruction and poverty. The fighting had struck a serious blow to Roman agriculture, which the emperors tried to revive. Christianity had become too strong either to ignore or to crush. How Diocletian, Constantine, and their successors dealt with those problems helped create the economic and social patterns medieval Europe inherited.

INFLATION AND TAXES

The barracks emperors had dealt with economic hardship by depreciating the currency: they cut the silver content of coins until money was virtually worthless. As a result the entire monetary system fell into ruin. In Egypt governors had to order bankers to accept imperial money. The immediate result was a crippling inflation throughout the empire.

The empire was less capable of recovery than in earlier times. Wars and invasions had disrupted normal commerce and the means of production. Mines were exhausted in the attempt to supply much-needed ores, especially gold and silver. War and invasion had hit the cities especially hard. Markets were disrupted, and travel became dangerous. Craftsmen, artisans, and traders rapidly left devastated regions. The prosperous industry and commerce of Gaul and the Rhineland declined markedly. Those who owed their prosperity to commerce and the needs of urban life likewise suffered. Cities were no longer places where trade and industry thrived. The devastation of the countryside increased the difficulty of feeding and supplying the cities. The destruction was so extensive that many wondered whether the ravages could be repaired at all.

The response of Diocletian and Constantine to these problems was marked by compulsion, rigidity, and loss of individual freedom. Diocletian's attempt to curb inflation illustrates the methods of absolute monarchy: in a move unprecedented in Roman history, he issued an edict that fixed maximum prices and wages throughout the empire. The measure failed because it was unrealistic and unenforceable.

The emperors dealt with the tax system just as strictly and inflexibly. As in the past, local officials bore the responsibility of collecting imperial taxes. Constantine made these officials into a hereditary class; son followed father whether he wanted to or not. In this period of severe depression, many localities could not pay their taxes. In such cases these local officials had to make up the difference from their own funds. This system soon wiped out a whole class of moderately wealthy people.

With the monetary system in ruins, most imperial taxes became payable in kind — that is, in goods or produce instead of money. The major drawback of payment in kind is its demands on transportation. Goods have to be moved from where they are grown or manufactured to where they are needed. Accordingly, the emperors locked into their occupations all those involved in the growing, preparation, and transportation of food and essential commodities. A baker or shipper could not go into any other business, and his son took up the trade upon his death. The late Roman Empire had a place for everyone, and everyone had a place.

THE DECLINE OF SMALL FARMS

The late Roman heritage to the medieval world is most obvious in agriculture. Because of worsening conditions, free tenant farmers were reduced to serfdom. During the third century A.D., many were killed or fled the land to escape the barbarians, or abandoned farms ravaged in the fighting. Consequently, large tracts of land lay deserted. Great landlords with ample resources began at once to reclaim as much of this land as they could. The huge estates that resulted were the forerunners of medieval manors. Like manors, villas were self-sufficient. Since they often produced more than they consumed, they successfully competed with the declining cities by selling their surplus in the countryside. They became islands of stability in an unsettled world.

While the villas were growing, the small farmers who remained on the land barely held their own. They were too poor and powerless to stand against the tide of chaos. They were exposed to the raids of barbarians or brigands and to the tyranny of imperial officials. For relief they turned to the great landlords. After all, the landowners were men of considerable resources, lords in their own right. They were wealthy, and they had many people working

A Large Roman Villa   During the third and fourth centuries, as the Roman Empire was breaking up, large villas such as this often became the focus of life. The villa was at once a fortress, as can be seen by the towers at the corner of the building, and the economic and social center of the neighborhood. (Courtesy, German Archeological Institute)

their land. They were independent and capable of defending themselves. If need be, they could – and at times did – field a small force of their own. Already influential, they stood up to imperial officials.

In return for the protection and security that landlords could offer, the small landholders gave over their lands. Free men and their families became clients of the landlords, and lost much of their freedom. To guarantee a steady supply of labor the landlords bound them to the soil. They could no longer decide to move elsewhere. Henceforth, they and their families worked the land of their patrons. Free men and women were in effect becoming serfs.

THE LEGALIZATION OF CHRISTIANITY

In religious affairs Constantine took the decisive step of recognizing Christianity as a legitimate religion. No longer would Christians suffer persecution for their beliefs. Constantine himself died a Christian in 337. Constantine has been depicted both as a devout convert to Christianity and as a realistic opportunist who used the young religion to his own imperial ends. Certainly Constantine was realistic enough to recognize and appreciate Christianity's spread and hold on his subjects. He correctly gauged the strength of the Christian ecclesiastical organization, and realized that the new church could serve as a friend of his empire. Yet there is no solid reason to doubt the sincerity of his conversion to the Christian religion. In short, Constantine was a man personally inclined toward Christianity and an emperor who could bestow on it a legal and legitimate place within the Roman empire.

Why had the pagans – those who believed in the Greco-Roman gods – persecuted Christians in the first place? Polytheism is by nature tolerant of new gods and accommodating in religious matters. Why was Christianity singled out for violence? These questions are still matters of scholarly debate, but some broad answers can be given.

Even an educated and cultured man like the historian Tacitus opposed Christianity. He believed that Christians hated the whole human race. As a rule early Christians, like Jews, kept to themselves. Romans distrusted and feared their exclusiveness, which seemed unsociable and even subversive. Most pagans genuinely misunderstood Christian practices. They thought that the Lord's Supper, at which Christians said they ate and drank the body and blood of Jesus, was an act of cannibalism. Pagans thought that Christians indulged in immoral and indecent rituals. They considered Christianity one of the worst of the oriental mystery cults, for one of the hallmarks of many of those cults was disgusting rituals.

Even these feelings of distrust and revulsion do not entirely account for persecution. The main reason seems to have been sincere religious conviction on the part of the pagans. Time and again they accused Christians of atheism. Indeed, Christians either denied the existence of pagan gods or called them evil spirits. For this same reason many Romans hated the Jews. Tacitus no doubt expressed the common view when he said that Jews despised the gods. Christians went even further than Jews – they said that no one should worship pagan gods.

At first, some pagans were repelled by the fanaticism of these monotheists. No good could come from scorning the gods. The whole community might end up paying for the wickedness and blasphemy of the Christians. Besides – and this is important – pagans did not demand that Christians *believe* in pagan gods. Greek and Roman religion was never a matter of belief or ethics. It was purely a religion of ritual. One of the clearest statements of pagan theological attitudes comes from the Roman senator Symmachus:

We watch the same stars; heaven is the same for us all; the same universe envelops us: what importance is it in what way anyone looks for truth? It is impossible to arrive by one route at such a great secret.[18]

Yet Roman religion was inseparable from the state. An attack on one was an attack on the other. The Romans were being no more fanatical or intolerant than an eighteenth-century English judge who declared the Christian religion part of the law of the land. All the pagans expected was performance of the ritual act, a small token sacrifice. Any Christian who sacrificed went free, no matter what he or she personally believed. The earliest persecutions of the Christians were minor and limited. Even Nero's famous persecution was temporary and limited to Rome. Subsequent persecutions were sporadic and local.

As time went on, pagan hostility decreased.

Pagans gradually realized that Christians were not working to overthrow the state and that Jesus was no rival of Caesar. The emperor Trajan forbade his governors to hunt down Christians. Trajan admitted that he thought Christianity an abomination, but he preferred to leave Christians in peace.

The stress of the third century, however, seemed to some emperors the punishment of the gods. What else could account for such anarchy? With the empire threatened on every side, a few emperors thought that one way to appease the gods was by offering them the proper sacrifices. Such sacrifices would be a sign of loyalty to the empire, a show of Roman solidarity. Consequently, a new wave of persecutions began. Yet even they were never very widespread or long-lived; by the late third century, pagans had become used to Christianity. Although a few emperors, including Diocletian, vigorously persecuted Christians, most pagans left them alone. Nor were they very sympathetic to the new round of persecutions. Pagan and Christian alike must have been relieved when Constantine legalized Christianity.

In time the Christian triumph would be complete. In 380, the emperor Theodosius made Christianity the official religion of the Roman Empire. At that point Christians began to persecute the pagans for their beliefs. History had come full circle.

THE CONSTRUCTION OF CONSTANTINOPLE

The triumph of Christianity was not the only event that made Constantine's reign a turning-point in Roman history. Constantine took the bold step of building a new capital for the empire. Constantinople, the New Rome, was constructed on the site of Byzantium, an old Greek city on the Bosporus. Throughout the third century, emperors had found Rome and

the West hard to defend. The eastern part of the empire was more easily defensible, and escaped the worst of the barbarian devastation. It was wealthy and its urban life still vibrant. Moreover, Christianity was more widespread in the East than in the West, and Constantinople was intended to be a Christian city.

THE AWFUL REVOLUTION

On the evening of October 15, 1764, Edward Gibbon, a young Englishman, sat in Rome among the ruins of the Capitol listening to the chanting of some monks. As the voices of the Christian present echoed against the stones of the pagan past, Gibbon wondered how the Roman Empire had given way to the medieval world. His curiosity aroused, he dedicated himself to the study of what he considered the greatest problem in history.

Twelve years later, in 1776, Gibbon published *The History of the Decline and Fall of the Roman Empire,* one of the monuments of English literature, a brilliant work fashioned with wit, learning, humor, and elegance.

Gibbon's thesis is, as the title of his work indicates, that the Roman Empire, after the first two centuries of existence, declined in strength, vitality, and prosperity and then fell into ruin. His concept of Rome's "decline and fall," a process he called "the awful revolution," has dominated historical thought for two hundred years. Even those who disagree with Gibbon over details have usually accepted his concept of "decline and fall." What explanations did Gibbon give for the fate of the Roman Empire, and how have others responded to his views? Is Gibbon's concept valid, and is it the only way of looking at this problem?

GIBBON'S RATIONALISTIC THEORIES

Gibbon was a true son of the Enlightenment, the eighteenth-century mode of thought that honored reason and despised faith. He regarded Christianity with contempt and as nothing more than vile superstition. In Gibbon's view the glory of the ancient world, with its learning, arts, manners, and philosophy, gleamed in comparison with the "Dark Ages" of the medieval period, when the church held Europe in the thrall of ignorance and sorcery. Christianity emphasized the virtues of humility, patience, and piety — qualities hardly masculine or imperial and totally inadequate for the maintenance of a proud and vigorous empire. Christianity praised chastity and the monastic life, which, in Gibbon's view, drained the empire of vitality and creativity. Nor did he admire the Germans who invaded and infiltrated the empire. Uncivilized and uncouth, they were, in Gibbon's eyes, even incapable of using reason. Although he acknowledged their hardiness and manly vigor, he scorned them as savages who ate horsemeat.

Despite the value of Gibbon's work, Christianity cannot reasonably be made the villain of the piece. True, many very able minds and forceful characters devoted their lives and energies to the Christian church and not to the empire. True, monasticism flourished and led to a passive and politically unproductive existence. Yet the numbers involved in these pursuits were small in proportion to the total population. Furthermore, the Byzantine Empire, which evolved from the eastern part of the Roman Empire, demonstrated that Christians could handle the sword and spear as well as the cross.

Gibbon also argued that the empire had grown so large that it fell of its own weight. In his words, "the decline of Rome was the natural and inevitable effect of immoderate greatness. . . . The story of its ruin is simple and obvious; and instead of inquiring *why* the Roman empire was destroyed, we should rather be surprised that it had subsisted so long."[19] In effect, Gibbon begs his own question, and instead chronicles the later history of the Roman world.

PSEUDOSCIENTIFIC THEORIES: SCIENCE ABUSED

Gibbon is not alone in trying to explain Rome's fate. The question has absorbed the attention of many, some of whom have misused scientific techniques in their search. They have applied bits of scientific fact and method to a vast and imperfectly known historical development, ignoring the simple fact that the end of the Roman Empire, unlike the composition of DNA, cannot be scientifically determined.

A slightly altered form of Gibbon's view of natural decline has recently found supporters who look at historical developments in biological terms. According to them, states and empires develop like living organisms, progressing through periods of birth and growth to maturity and consolidation, followed by decrepitude, decline, and collapse. This argument is simply false analogy, unsupported by any scientific evidence.

Some twentieth-century writers have resorted to pseudoscientific theories blaming the "collapse" of the empire on racial corruption. As the physically strong, morally pure, and creatively intelligent Romans conquered inferior Asian and African peoples, so the explanation goes, they intermingled with them. The physical and intellectual traits of the less fit came to predominate. This "mongrelization" of the empire steadily sapped the physical and moral fibre of the Romans. When faced with a military crisis, Rome was too weak to cope. Even taken on its own terms, this theory is nonsense. The eastern half of the empire, the home of the "inferior" Asiatics, survived a thousand years longer than the "superior" western one.

Not all those who have used science to explain Rome's fate have been cranks. Some writers have tried to use statistical information and demographic arguments to explain Rome's fall. According to this view, a sharp decline in population diminishes a society's ability to defend itself and weakens its economy and ultimately the entire civilization. In 167 A.D., they argue, the bubonic plague swept the empire and apparently killed large numbers of people. Yet it is a serious error to conclude that the ravages of disease in the second century were responsible for later catastrophes. Economic historians have demonstrated that even severe epidemics have only a short-term economic effect, after which conditions quickly normalize themselves. There was ample time for the empire to recover from this plague.

Population did decline in the third and fourth centuries, for which the most likely explanation is losses due to war and devastation. Even so, the population of the Roman Empire outnumbered the invading barbarians, and there were more than enough people to defend the empire.

THE SOCIOECONOMIC THEORIES OF FERDINAND LOT

The twentieth-century French scholar Ferdinand Lot relied on economics to explain "the awful revolution." He acknowledged that the causes of Rome's "decline" were many and interrelated, but maintained that the basic causes were socioeconomic. Lot pointed out that the Roman economy was badly adjusted;

in fact, according to him, it never really developed. Although the Romans had technological skill, Rome never industrialized. An almost limitless supply of slaves provided cheap labor and discouraged the development of labor-saving methods. Roman conquests brought a steady stream of slaves to the West. Slaves worked the land on the latifundia and produced what little was manufactured in the West. The Roman aristocracy lived on the revenues from their estates. The few people involved in trade and commerce served as middlemen, moneylenders, tax collectors, or civil bureaucrats. A commercial and industrial middle class failed to develop.

Western products – primarily, in Lot's view, raw materials – did not begin to equal the value of imports. Increasingly, the balance of trade within the empire worsened: the western part bought much more than it sold and paid for purchases with precious metals. The pressure of the German invasions made social and economic conditions worse. Once the West was cut off from sources of goods and without goods of its own to export, it reverted to an agrarian and isolated economy. The level of learning deteriorated and technical skills were lost. According to Lot, economic collapse accelerated political ruin. Moreover, great cities in the West drastically declined in population, and simultaneously trade and commerce slowed to a trickle. With the tax base gone, cultural movements and intellectual activities could not be maintained.

The force of Lot's argument is weakened by the fact that large-scale emancipation of slaves occurred during the empire. Roman emperors encouraged the growth of a prosperous class of small tenant farmers. Slavery also existed in the East, and did not prevent the West from industrializing. Cities in Gaul and Germany became centers of manufacturing, and even managed to dominate the production of glass, pottery, and bronze ware. Furthermore, these industries were usually manned by free labor, not slaves.

Lot's theories also make too little of political factors. The economic woes of the empire began during the civil wars and invasions of the middle of the third century — wars that left wide tracts of land desolate and manufacturing centers in shambles. Roman failure to create a stable form of government exposed the empire to serious disruption that could not fail to have dire economic effects. Though enlightening in many respects, Lot's theories are incapable of explaining the "decline and fall."

POLITICAL EXPLANATIONS

Over the years political explanations have won the widest acceptance. The Roman imperial government never solved the problem of succession: it never devised a peaceful and regular way to pass on the imperial power when an emperor died. The legions enjoyed too much power, often creating and destroying civil governments at will, and in the process disrupting the state. The assassinations of emperors and frequent changes of government produced chronic instability, weakening the state's ability to solve its problems.

From the late third century onward, successive approaches to Rome's economic difficulties proved disastrous. Emperors depreciated the coinage. The middle classes carried an increasingly heavy burden of taxation, and all the while the imperial bureaucracy grew bigger, though not more efficient. These factors combined to destroy the ordinary citizen's confidence in the state. Consequently, according to the political explanation, with the economy and society undermined, the empire was destroyed by its internal difficulties.

There is no question that the Roman Empire suffered from severe political problems, which were never solved. Energy that could have been spent defending the frontiers or policing the sea-lanes was all too often squandered in bloody and costly civil war. The same fate had overtaken the republic, but at least then there were no land-hungry barbarian tribes ready to turn Roman weakness to their own advantage. Political explanations, too, have their defects, for emperors such as Diocletian showed how the empire could survive even fearful ravages. Nor do political theories adequately explain why the West "fell" while the East survived for another millennium.

CONTINUITY AND CHANGE

Some writers have rejected the whole idea of decline. As early as 1744, before Gibbon had contemplated writing the *Decline and Fall of the Roman Empire,* the Frenchman Abbé Galliani wrote: "The fall of empires? What can that mean? Empires being neither up nor down do not fall. They change their appearance."[20] The concept of change and development, instead of decline, has much to recommend it, inasmuch as many aspects of the Roman world survived to influence the medieval and eventually the modern world. Roman law left its traces on the legal and political systems of most European countries. Roman roads, aqueducts, bridges, and buildings remained in use, standing as constant reminders of the Roman past and its link with the present. The Latin language, with its rich vocabulary and its strict but rational grammatical rules, facilitated communication over a wide area and allowed for precision of expression. For almost two thousand years Latin language and literature remained the core of all education in the West. Those who studied Latin came to some degree under the spell of

Rome, as Roman attitudes and patterns of thought fertilized the intellectual lives of generation after generation of Europeans. Slowly, almost imperceptibly, the Roman Empire gave way to the medieval world.

———◆———

Never before in Western history and not again until modern times did one state govern so many people over so much of the world for so long a span of time. The true heritage of Rome is its long tradition of law and freedom. Under Roman law and government the West enjoyed relative peace and security for extensive periods of time. Under the auspices of Rome northern Europe entered into the civilized world of the Mediterranean. Through Rome the best of ancient thought and culture was preserved to make its contribution to modern life. Perhaps no better epitaph for Rome can be found than the words of Virgil:

While rivers shall run to the sea,
While shadows shall move across the valleys of
  mountains,
While the heavens shall nourish the stars,
Always shall your honor and your name and your
  fame endure.[21]

NOTES

1. Virgil *Aeneid* 6.851–853.
2. Augustus *Res Gestae* 6.34.
3. Ibid., 5.28.
4. Virgil *Aeneid* 6.791–794.
5. Horace *Odes* 4.15.
6. Virgil *Georgics* 4.180–183.
7. Ibid., 3.515–519.
8. Horace *Odes* 1.38.
9. Matthew 3:3.
10. Matthew 16:18.
11. Edward Gibbon, *The History of the Decline and Fall of the Roman Empire,* Modern Library, New York, n.d., 1.1.
12. Ibid., 1.52.
13. M. Hammond, *The Antonine Monarchy,* American Academy in Rome, Rome, 1959, p. x.
14. Gibbon, 1.70.
15. *Corpus Inscriptionum Latinarum,* vol. 6, G. Reimer, Berlin, 1882, no. 9792.
16. Ibid., vol. 10, no. 8192.
17. Ibid., vol. 6, no. 14672.
18. Symmachus *Relations* 3.10.
19. Gibbon, 2.438.
20. Quoted in F. W. Walbank, *The Awful Revolution,* University of Toronto Press, Toronto, 1969, p. 121.
21. Virgil *Aeneid* 1.607–609.

SUGGESTED READING

Of the works cited in the Notes, that by Hammond is a classic in the field, and Gibbon's *Decline and Fall* is of course one of the masterpieces of English literature. Some good general treatments of the empire include B. Cunliffe, *Rome and Her Empire* (1978), which is profusely illustrated, and P. Petit, *Pax Romana* (English translation, 1976). The role of the emperor is superbly treated by F. Millar, *The Emperor in the Roman World* (1977), and the defense of the empire is brilliantly studied by E. N. Luttwak, *The Grand Strategy of the Roman Empire* (1976). The army that carried out that strategy is the subject of G. Webster, *The Roman Imperial Army* (1969).

Favorable to Augustus is M. Hammond, *The Augustan Principate* (1933), and G. W. Bowersock, *Augustus and the Greek World* (1965), is excellent intellectual history. C. M. Wells, *The German Policy of Augustus* (1972), uses archaeological findings to illustrate Roman expansion into northern Europe.

The commercial life of the empire is the subject of M. P. Charlesworth, *Trade Routes and Commerce of* the Roman Empire, 2nd ed. (1926). Newer, if briefer, is the stimulating article by L. Casson, "Rome's Trade with the East: The Sea Voyage to Africa and India," *Transactions of the American Philological Association* 110 (1980): 21-36. R. Duncan-Jones, *The Economy of the Roman Empire: Quantitative Studies,* 2nd ed. (1982), employs new techniques of historical inquiry. J. Percival, *The Roman Villa* (1976), is a lively study of an important institution. The classic treatment, which ranges across the empire, is M. Rostovtzeff, *The Economic and Social History of the Roman Empire* (1957).

Social aspects of the empire are the subject of R. Auguet, *Cruelty and Civilization: The Roman Games* (English translation, 1972); P. Garnsey, *Social Status and Legal Privilege in the Roman Empire* (1970); and A. N. Sherwin-White, *Racial Prejudice in Imperial Rome* (1967). A general treatment is R. MacMullen, *Roman Social Relations, 50 B.C. to A.D. 284* (1981). N. Kampen, *Image and Status: Roman Working Women in Ostia* (1981) is distinctive for its treatment of ordinary Roman women. An important feature of Roman history is treated by R. P. Saller, *Personal Patronage under the Early Empire* (1982).

Christianity, paganism, and Judaism receive treatment in E. M. Smallwood, *The Jews under Roman Rule* (corrected ed., 1981); R. A. Markus, *Christianity in the Roman World* (1975); and A. D. Momigliano, *The Conflict between Paganism and Christianity in the Fourth Century* (1963). Two important topics in the study of early Christianity are treated in W. H. C. Frend, *Martyrdom and Persecution in the Early Church* (1965); and M. Hengel, *Acts and the History of Earliest Christianity* (1979). The significance of the cult of Roma in the empire is well treated by R. Mellor, "The Goddess Roma", in *Aufstieg und Niedergang der römischen Welt,* vol. II, part 17 (1981), pp. 952-1030.

A convenient survey of Roman literature is J. W. Duff, *Literary History of Rome from the Origins to the Close of the Golden Age* (1953) and *Literary History of Rome in the Silver Age,* 3rd ed. (1964).

The fall of Rome continues to be a fertile field of investigation: A. H. M. Jones, *The Decline of the Ancient World* (1966); F. W. Walbank, *The Awful Revolution* (1969); and R. MacMullen's two books: *Soldier and Civilian in the Later Roman Empire* (1963) and *Enemies of the Roman Order: Treason, Unrest, and Alienation in the Empire* (1966).

CHAPTER 9

THE MAKING OF EUROPE

THE CENTURIES BETWEEN approximately 400 and 900 present the student with a paradox. These years witnessed the disintegration of the Roman Empire, which had been one of humanity's great political and cultural achievements. On the other hand, these five centuries were a creative and important period, during which Europeans laid the foundations for the development of medieval and modern Europe. It is not too much to say that this period saw the making of Europe.

The basic ingredients that went into the making of a distinctly European civilization were the cultural legacy of Greece and Rome, the customs and traditions of the Germanic peoples, and the Christian faith. The most important of these was Christianity, because it absorbed and assimilated the other two. It reinterpreted the classics in a Christian sense. It instructed the Germanic peoples and gave them new ideals of living and social behavior. Christianity became the cement that held European society together.

During this period the Byzantine Empire centered at Constantinople served as a protective buffer between Europe and savage peoples to the east. The Greeks preserved the philosophical and scientific texts of the ancient world, which later formed the basis for study in science and medicine; and they produced a great synthesis of Roman law, the Justinian Code. In the urbane and sophisticated life led at Constantinople, the Greeks set a standard far above the primitive existence of the West.

In the seventh and eighth centuries, Arabic culture spread around the southern fringes of Europe – to Spain, Sicily, and North Africa, and to Syria, Palestine, and Egypt. The Arabs translated the works of such Greek thinkers as Euclid, Hippocrates, and Galen, and made important contributions in mathematics, astronomy, and physics. In Arabic translation,

Greek texts trickled to the West, and most later European scientific study rested on the Arabic work.

European civilization resulted from the fusion of Germanic traditions, the Greco-Roman heritage, and the Christian faith. How did these components act upon one another? How did they bring about the making of Europe? What influence did the Byzantine and Islamic cultures have on the making of European civilization? These are the questions discussed in this chapter.

THE MIGRATION OF THE GERMANIC PEOPLES

The migration of peoples from one area to another has been a dominant and continuing feature of European history. Mass movements of Europeans occurred in the fourth through sixth centuries, in the ninth and tenth centuries, and in the twelfth and thirteenth centuries. From the sixteenth century to the present such movements have been almost continuous, and have involved not just the European continent but the entire world. The causes of these migrations varied, and they are not thoroughly understood by scholars. But there is no question that they profoundly affected both the regions to which peoples moved and the ones they left behind.

The *völkerwanderungen*, or migrations of the Germanic peoples, was an important factor in the decline of the Roman Empire. Many twentieth-century historians and sociologists have tried to explain who the Germans were and why they emigrated, but scholars have not had much success at answering these questions. The surviving evidence is primarily archaeological, scanty, and not yet adequately explored. Conclusions are still tentative.

VANDAL LANDOWNER   *The adoption of Roman dress — short tunic, cloak, and sandals — reflects the way the Germanic tribes accepted Roman lifestyles. Likewise both the mosaic art form and the man's stylized appearance show the Germans' assimilation of Roman influences. (Notice that the rider has a saddle but not stirrups.) (The British Museum)*

What answers do exist rest on archaeological evidence found later inside the borders of the Roman Empire: bone fossils, cooking utensils, jewelry, instruments of war, and other surviving artifacts. Like the Vikings, who first terrorized and then settled in many sections of Europe in the ninth and tenth centuries, the Germans came from eastern Germany and the areas of modern Denmark, Sweden, and Norway. Ethnically they were Scandinavians.

Since about 250, Germanic tribes had pressed along the Rhine-Danube frontier of the Roman Empire. Depending upon their closeness to that border, these tribes differed considerably from one another in level of civilization. Some tribes, such as the Visigoths and Ostrogoths, led a settled existence, engaged in agriculture and trade, and accepted an unorthodox form of Christianity called Arianism. Long acquaintance with Roman ways made them very civilized, and some had been welcomed into the empire and served as mercenaries in the imperial army. Tribes such as the Anglo-Saxons and the Huns, who lived far from the Roman frontiers, were not af-

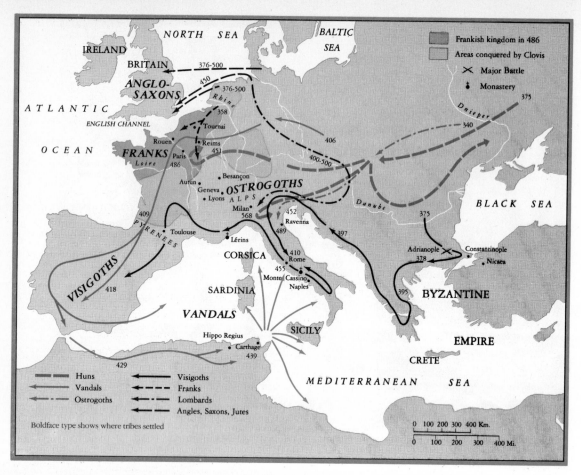

MAP 9.1 THE GERMANIC MIGRATIONS *The
Germanic tribes infiltrated and settled in all parts of
Western Europe. The Huns, who were not German
ethnically, originated in central Asia.*

fected by the civilizing influences of Rome.
They remained primitive, nomadic, even barbaric peoples.

Historians do not know exactly when the
Mongolian tribe called the Huns began to
move westward from China, but about 370
they pressured the Goths living along the
Rhine-Danube frontier. The Huns easily defeated the Ostrogoths, and the frightened Visigoths petitioned the emperor to be allowed
to settle within the empire. Once inside,
however, they revolted. In 378, a Visigothic

army decisively defeated the emperor's army.
This date marks the beginning of massive
Germanic invasions; Germans flooded into
the empire (see Map 9.1).

Why did the Germans emigrate? In the absence of literary evidence one can only speculate. Perhaps overpopulation and food
shortages resulting from polygamy (the practice of having several wives simultaneously)
caused migration. Perhaps victorious tribes
forced the vanquished ones to move south.
Perhaps tales of the luxurious lifestyle of the

cities of the Roman Empire attracted settlers. Perhaps the Germans migrated for a combination of all these reasons.

Some tribes that settled within the borders of the Roman Empire numbered perhaps no more than ten thousand individuals. Others, such as the Ostrogoths and Visigoths, were about twenty or thirty times larger. Because they settled near and quickly intermingled with Romans and Romanized peoples, it is impossible to specify numbers of the original migrators. Dense forests, poor soil, and inadequate equipment probably kept food production low. This meant that the Germans could not increase very rapidly in their new locations.

Except for the Lombards, whose conquests of Italy persisted through the sixth and seventh centuries, the movements of Germanic peoples on the Continent ended about 600. Between 450 and 565, the Germans established a number of kingdoms, but none except the Frankish kingdom lasted very long. Since the German kingdoms were not states with definite geographical boundaries, their locations are approximate. The Visigoths overran much of southwestern Gaul. Establishing their headquarters at Toulouse, they exercised a weak domination over Spain until a great Muslim victory at Guadalete in 711 ended Visigothic rule. The Vandals, whose destructive ways are commemorated in the word *vandal,* settled in North Africa. In northern and western Europe in the sixth century, the Burgundians established rule over lands roughly circumscribed by the old Roman army camps at Lyons, Besançon, Geneva, and Autun.

In northern Italy, the sixth-century Ostrogothic king Theodoric pursued a policy of assimilation between Germans and Romans. He maintained close relations with the Roman emperor at Constantinople and drew Roman scholars and diplomats into the royal civil service. He was a crude German, however, and his reign was disliked by the pagan Roman aristocrats. Moreover, he was an Arian Christian, so Roman Catholics hated him as heretical. His royal administration fell apart during the reconquest of Italy by the Byzantine emperor Justinian in the sixth century. Weakness, war, and plague then made northern Italy ripe for the Lombard conquest in the seventh century.

The most enduring Germanic kingdom was established by the Frankish chieftain Clovis (481-511). Originally only a petty chieftain with headquarters in the region of Tournai in northwestern Gaul (modern Belgium), Clovis began to expand his territories in 486. His defeat of the Gallo-Roman general Syagrius extended his jurisdiction to the Loire. Clovis's conversion to orthodox Christianity in 496 won him the crucial support of the papacy and the bishops of Gaul. As the defender of Roman Catholicism against heretical German tribes, he went on to conquer the Visigoths, extending his domain as far as the Pyrenees and making Paris his headquarters. Because he was descended from the half-legendary chieftain Merovech, the dynasty Clovis founded has been called Merovingian. Clovis's sons subjugated the Burgundians in eastern Gaul and the Ostrogothic tribes living north of the Alps.

GERMANIC SOCIETY

The Germans replaced the Romans as rulers of most of the European continent, and German customs and traditions formed the basis of European society for centuries. What pat-

THE BAPTISM OF CLOVIS In this thirteenth-century representation, Remigius, Bishop of Rheims, blesses Clovis, a noble holds the crown symbolizing royal victory, while the Holy Spirit descends with holy oil. Clovis respected Remigius and supported his work of conversion; Remegius urged obedience to Clovis. (Biblothèque Nationale, Paris)

terns of social and political life characterized the Germans? What kind of economy did they practice?

Scholars are hampered in answering these questions because the Germans could not write, and so kept no written records before their conversion to Christianity. The earliest information about them comes from moralistic accounts by such Romans as the historian Tacitus, who was acquainted only with the tribes living closest to the borders of the empire. Furthermore, Tacitus wrote his *Germania* at the end of the first century A.D., and by the fifth century German practices differed from those of Tacitus's time. Our knowledge of the Germans depends largely on information in

records written in the sixth and seventh centuries and projected backward.

KINSHIP AND CUSTOM

The Germans had no notion of the state as we in the twentieth century use that concept; they thought in social, not political, terms. The basic social unit of the Germans was the tribe, or folk. Members of the folk believed they were all descended from a common ancestor. Blood united them. Kinship protected them. Law was custom — unwritten, preserved in the minds of the elders of the tribe, and handed down by word of mouth from generation to generation. Custom regulated everything. Every tribe had its customs, and every member of the tribe knew what they were. Members were subject to their tribe's customary law wherever they went, and friendly tribes respected one another's laws.

Germanic tribes were led by a king, or tribal chieftain. The chief was that member of the folk recognized as the strongest, the bravest in battle. He was elected from among the male members of the strongest family. He led the tribe in war, settled disputes among tribal members, conducted negotiations with outside powers, and offered sacrifices to the gods. Closely associated with the king was the *gesith,* or war band (known in Latin as the *comitatus*). The members of the war band were usually the bravest young men in the tribe. They swore loyalty to the chief and fought with him in battle. They were not supposed to leave the battlefield without him; to do so implied cowardice and disloyalty and brought terrible disgrace.

LAW

As long as custom determined all behavior, the early Germans had no need for written law. Beginning in the late sixth century, however, German tribal chieftains began to collect, write, and publish lists of their customs. Why then? The Christian missionaries who were slowly converting the Germans to Christianity wanted to know the tribal customs, and they encouraged German rulers to set down their customs in written form. Churchmen wanted to read about German ways in order to assimilate the tribes to Christianity. Moreover, by the sixth century the German kings needed rules and regulations for the Romans living under their jurisdiction as well as for their own people.

Today if a person holds up a bank, American law maintains that the robber attacks both the bank and the state in which it exists. That is a sophisticated notion involving the abstract idea of the state. In early German law, all crimes were regarded as crimes against a person.

According to the code of the Salian Franks, every person had a particular monetary value to the tribe. This value was called the *wergeld,* which literally means man-money or "money to buy off the spear." Men of fighting age had the highest wergeld, then women of childbearing age, then children, and finally the aged. Everyone's value reflected his or her potential military worthiness. If a person accused of a crime agreed to pay the wergeld, and if the victim and his or her family accepted the payment, there was peace (hence the expression "money to buy off the spear"). If the accused refused to pay the wergeld, or if the victim's family refused to accept it, a blood feud ensued. Individuals depended on their kin for protection, and kinship served as a force of social control.

Historians and sociologists have difficulty applying the early law codes, partly because they are patchwork affairs studded with additions made in later centuries. For example, the Salic Law — the law code of the Salian Franks — was issued by Clovis in the late fifth century and amended first in the eighth and again in the ninth century. Thus it cannot be taken as an entirely accurate representation of conditions in the sixth century. Nevertheless, it does offer a general picture of Germanic life and problems in the early Middle Ages, and it is typical of the law codes of other tribes, such as the Visigoths, the Burgundians, the Lombards, and the Anglo-Saxons.

The Salic Law lists the money fines to be paid to the victim or the family for such injuries as theft, rape, assault, arson, and murder:

If any person strike another on the head so that the

brain appears, and the three bones which lie above the brain shall project, he shall be sentenced to 1200 denars, which make 300 shillings.

But if it shall have been between the ribs or in the stomach, so that the wound appears and reaches to the entrails, he shall be sentenced to 1200 denars – which make 300 shillings – besides five shillings for the physician's pay.

If any one have hit a free woman who is pregnant, and she dies, he shall be sentenced to 2800 denars, which make 700 shillings.

If any one have killed a free woman after she has begun bearing children, he shall be sentenced to 2400 denars, which make 600 shillings.

If any one shall have drawn a harrow through another's harvest after it has sprouted, or shall have gone through it with a waggon where there was no road, he shall be sentenced to 120 denars, which make 30 shillings.

If any one shall have killed a free Frank, or a barbarian living under the Salic law, and it have been proved on him, he shall be sentenced to 8000 denars.

But if any one have slain a man who is in the service of the king, he shall be sentenced to 2400 denars, which make 600 shillings.

If any one have slain a Roman who eats in the king's palace, and it have been proved on him, he shall be sentenced to 1200 denars, which make 300 shillings.[1]

This is not really a code of law at all, but a list of tariffs or fines for particular offenses. German law aimed at the prevention or reduction of violence. It was not concerned with justice.

At first Romans had been subject to Roman law, and Germans to Germanic custom. As German kings accepted Christianity, and as Romans and Germans increasingly intermarried, the distinction between the two laws blurred and, in the course of the seventh and eighth centuries, disappeared. The result

of the fusion would be the new feudal law, to which all people were subject.

LIFE IN THE FORESTS

How did the Germans live? The dark, dense forests that dotted the continent of Europe were the most important physical and psychological factor in the lives of the Germanic peoples who were not quickly Romanized. Forests separated one tribe from another. The pagan Germans believed that gods and spirits inhabited the forests. Trees were holy, and to cut them down was an act of grave sacrilege. Thus the Germans cut no trees. They also feared building a mill or a bridge on a river, lest the river spirit be offended. This attitude prevented the clearing of land for farming and tended to keep the Germans isolated.

In the course of the sixth through eighth centuries, the Germans slowly adapted to Greco-Roman and Christian attitudes and patterns of behavior. Acceptance of Christianity and the end of animistic beliefs that spiritual forces live in natural objects had profound consequences. In fact, the decline of animistic beliefs marks a turning-point in the economic and intellectual progress of the West. A more settled and less nomadic way of life developed as people no longer feared to make use of natural resources such as rivers and forests. Once animistic beliefs were dispelled, the forests were opened to use, and all members of the community had common rights in them. Trees provided everyone with wood for building and for fuel; the forests served as the perfect place for grazing animals throughout the Middle Ages. The steady reduction of forest land between the sixth and thirteenth centuries was a major step in the agricultural development of Europe.

Within the forests the Germans clustered in small villages of a few families. Individual families lived in huts made of mud, wood, or wattle (poles intertwined with twigs or reeds) and thatched with straw. Recent archaeological excavations at Thetford in East Anglia in England uncovered a sixth-century village. Evidence from places on the Continent suggests that this English village was typical. It contained a number of one-room huts about twelve feet long, most without a fireplace. Uprights in the center of the gable supported the roof. These dwellings were scattered over a small cleared area, without alignment or evidence of town planning.

Each German family owned its plot of land and passed it on to the next generation. All members of the small community worked together to cultivate the clearing. Apparently, the land farmed was adjacent to the dwellings. Farmers helped one another to plow and harvest, and all had to agree on the uniform rotation of crops. It is difficult to generalize about agricultural methods. The German plow dug deeper than the Roman plow, but it was hard to turn around at the end of the furrow. The difficulty of this operation probably brought about the division of arable land into long narrow strips.

Bread was the basic food, and oats and rye the predominant grains in the fifth and sixth centuries. Later these cereals were held in low esteem, and wheat was raised everywhere it would grow. Peas and beans (a source of protein), turnips, onions, and cabbage supplemented the diet. Beside the field under cultivation, another stood fallow. Cattle grazed on it and fertilized it.

ANGLO-SAXON ENGLAND

The island of Britain, conquered by Rome during the reign of Claudius, shared fully in the life of the Roman Empire during the first four centuries of the Christian era. A military

THE TARA BROOCH   Men and women of the Germanic tribes wore brooches to fasten their cloaks at the shoulder. This elaborately decorated brooch (a reproduction) was worn by a person of the warrior aristocracy. Ordinary people used a thorn. (Courtesy, World Heritage Museum. Photo: Caroline Buckler)

aristocracy governed, and the official religion was the cult of the emperor. Towns were planned in the Roman fashion, with temples, public baths, theaters, and amphitheaters. In the countryside large manors controlled the surrounding lands. Roman merchants brought Eastern luxury goods and Eastern religions – including Christianity – into Britain. The native Britons, a gentle Celtic people, had become thoroughly Romanized. Their language was Latin. Their lifestyle was Roman.

But an event in the distant eastern province of Thrace changed all this. In 378, the Visigoths crossed the Danube and inflicted a severe defeat on the Roman emperor Valens at Adrianople. Even Britain felt the consequences. Rome was forced to retrench, and in 407 Roman troops were withdrawn from the island, leaving it unprotected. The savage Picts from Scotland continued to harass the

MAP 9.2 *ANGLO-SAXON ENGLAND Can you identify the seven kingdoms of the Heptarchy? Where is Bede's monastery Jarrow?*

north. Teutonic tribes from Scandinavia and modern-day Belgium – the Angles, Saxons, and Jutes – stepped up their assaults, attacking in a hit-and-run fashion. Their goal was plunder, and at first their invasions led to no permanent settlements. As more Germans arrived, however, they took over the best lands and humbled the Britons. Increasingly, the natives fled to the west and settled in Wales. These sporadic raids continued for over a century and led to Germanic control of most of Britain. Historians have labeled the period 500 to 1066 Anglo-Saxon.

Except for the Jutes, who probably came from Frisia (modern Belgium), the Teutonic tribes came from the least Romanized and least civilized parts of Europe. They destroyed Roman culture in Britain. Tribal custom superseded Roman law.

The beginnings of the Germanic kingdoms in Britain are very obscure, but scholars suspect they came into being in the seventh and eighth centuries. Writing in the eighth century, the scholar Bede (pages 331–332) described seven kingdoms: the Jutish kingdom of Kent; the Saxon kingdoms of the East Saxons (Essex), South Saxons (Sussex), and West Saxons (Wessex); and the kingdoms of the Angles, Mercians, and Northumbrians (see Map 9.2). The names imply that these peoples thought of themselves in tribal rather than geographical terms. They referred to the kingdom of the West Saxons, for example, rather than simply Wessex. Because of Bede's categorization, scholars refer to the Heptarchy, or seven kingdoms of Anglo-Saxon Britain. The suggestion of total Anglo-Saxon domination, however, is not entirely accurate. Germanic tribes never subdued Scotland, where the Picts remained strong, or Wales, where the Celts and native Britons continued to put up stubborn resistance.

Thus Anglo-Saxon England was divided along racial and political lines. The Teutonic kingdoms in the south, east, and center were opposed by the Britons in the west, who wanted to get rid of the invaders. The Anglo-Saxon kingdoms also fought among themselves, with the result that boundaries shifted constantly. Finally in the ninth century, under pressure of the Danish, or Viking, invasions, the Britons and the Germanic peoples were molded together under the leadership of King Alfred of Wessex (871–899).

THE SURVIVAL AND GROWTH OF THE EARLY CHRISTIAN CHURCH

While many elements of the Roman Empire disintegrated, the Christian church survived and grew. Having gained the support of the fourth-century emperors, the church gradually adopted the Roman system of organization. Christianity had a dynamic missionary policy, and the church slowly succeeded in assimilating – that is, adapting – pagan peoples, both Germans and Romans, to Christian teaching. Moreover, the church possessed able administrators and leaders and highly literate and creative thinkers. These factors help to explain the survival and growth of the early Christian church in the face of repeated Germanic invasions.

THE CHURCH AND THE ROMAN EMPERORS

The early church benefited considerably from the support of the emperors. In return, the emperors expected the support of the Christian church in the maintenance of order and unity. Constantine had legalized the practice of Christianity within the empire in 312. Although he himself was not baptized until he was on his deathbed, Constantine encouraged Christianity throughout his reign. He freed the clergy from imperial taxation. At the churchmen's request, he helped to settle theological disputes and thus to preserve doctrinal unity within the church. Constantine generously endowed the building of Christian churches, and one of his gifts – the Lateran Palace in Rome – remained the official residence of the popes until the fourteenth century. Constantine also declared Sunday a public holiday, a day of rest for the service of God. As the result of its favored position within the empire, Christianity slowly became the leading religion.

At the end of the fourth century, the emperor Theodosius went further than Constantine and made Christianity the official religion of the empire. Theodosius stripped Roman pagan temples of their statues, made the practice of the old Roman state religion a treasonable offense, and persecuted Christians who dissented from orthodox doctrine. Most significant, he allowed the church to establish its own courts. Church courts began to develop their own body of law, called canon law. These courts, not the Roman government, had jurisdiction over the clergy and ecclesiastical disputes. At the death of Theodosius, the Christian church was completely independent of the authority of the Roman state. The foundation for the power of the medieval church had been laid.

What was to be the church's relationship to secular powers? How was the Christian to render unto Caesar the things that were his while returning to God his due? This problem had troubled the earliest disciples of Christ. The toleration of Christianity and the coming to power of Christian emperors in the fourth century did not make it any easier. Striking a balance between responsibility to secular rulers and loyalty to spiritual duties was difficult.

In the fourth century, theological disputes arose within Christianity – primarily disagreements about the nature of Christ. Constantine, to whom religious disagreement meant civil disorder, intervened. In 325, Constantine summoned a council of church leaders to Nicaea in Asia Minor, and presided over it personally.

The council debated whether Christ was of a different substance from God, as Arius, a priest of Alexandria, maintained, or of the same substance, as Bishop Athanasius of Alexandria held. The council decided against the Arians and supported the doctrine that Christ was of the same substance as God. This became the orthodox position. Anxious to preserve the unity of the empire, Constantine insisted on its acceptance by all Christians. The participation of the emperor in a theological dispute within the church paved the way for later rulers to claim they could do the same.

So active was the emperor Theodosius's participation in church matters that he eventually came to loggerheads with Bishop Ambrose of Milan (339–397). Theodosius ordered Ambrose to hand over his cathedral church to the emperor. Ambrose's response had important consequences for the future:

At length came the command, "Deliver up the Basilica"; I reply, "It is not lawful for us to deliver it up, nor for your Majesty to receive it. By no law can you violate the house of a private man, and do you think that the house of God may be taken away? It is asserted that all things are lawful to the Emperor, that all things are his. But do not burden your conscience with the thought that you have any right as Emperor over sacred things. Exalt not yourself, but if you would reign the longer, be subject to God. It is written, God's to God and Caesar's to Caesar. The palace is the Emperor's, the Churches are the Bishop's. To you is committed jurisdiction over public, not over sacred buildings."[2]

Ambrose's statement was to serve as the cornerstone of the ecclesiastical theory of state-church relations throughout the Middle Ages. Ambrose insisted that the church was independent of the state's jurisdiction. The two powers were, he maintained, separate and autonomous. He insisted that in matters relating to the faith or the church, the bishops were to be the judges of emperors, not the other way around. In a Christian society, harmony and peace depended upon agreement between the bishop and the secular ruler. But if disagreement developed, the church was ultimately the superior power because the church was responsible for the salvation of all individuals (including the emperor).

Theodosius accepted Ambrose's argument and bowed to the church. In later centuries theologians, canonists, and propagandists repeatedly cited Ambrose's position as the basis of relations between the two powers. The precedent set by Theodosius was repeatedly recalled by church leaders in the Middle Ages as proof that secular power had to yield to ecclesiastical authority.

INSPIRED LEADERSHIP

The early Christian church benefited from the brilliant administrative abilities of some church leaders and from identification of the authority and dignity of the bishop of Rome with the grand imperial traditions of the city. Some highly able Roman citizens accepted baptism and applied their intellectual powers and administrative skills to the service of the church rather than the empire. With the empire in decay, educated people joined and worked for the church in the belief that it was the one institution able to provide leadership. Bishop Ambrose, for example, was the son of the Roman prefect of Gaul, a trained lawyer and governor of a province. As bishop of Milan, he exercised considerable responsibility and influence in the temporal as well as ecclesiastical affairs of northern Italy.

During the reign of Diocletian (284–305), the Roman Empire had been divided for administrative purposes into geographical units called dioceses. Gradually the church made use of this organizational structure. Christian bishops – the leaders of early Christian communities, popularly elected by the Christian people – established their headquarters, or sees, in the urban centers of the old Roman dioceses. Their jurisdiction extended throughout all parts of the diocese. The center of the bishop's authority was his cathedral (the word derives from the Latin *cathedra*, meaning "chair"). Thus church leaders capitalized on the Roman imperial method of organization and adapted it to ecclesiastical purposes.

After the removal of the capital and the emperor to Constantinople (page 270), the bishop of Rome exercised vast influence in the West because he had no real competitor there. Bishops of Rome – known as popes from the Latin word *papa,* meaning "father" – began to identify their religious offices with the imperial traditions of the city. They stressed that Rome had been the capital of a worldwide empire, and they emphasized the special importance of Rome within the framework of that empire. Successive bishops of Rome reminded Christians in other parts of the world that Rome was the burial-place of Saint Peter and Saint Paul. Moreover, according to tradition Saint Peter, the chief of Christ's first twelve followers, had lived and been executed in Rome. No other city in the world could make such claims.

In the fifth century, the bishops of Rome began to stress their supremacy over other Christian communities and to urge other churches to appeal to Rome for the resolution of complicated doctrinal issues. Thus Pope Innocent I (401–417) wrote to the bishops of Africa:

[*We approve your action in following the principle*] *that nothing which was done even in the most remote and distant provinces should be taken as finally settled unless it came to the notice of this See, that any just pronouncement might be confirmed by all the authority of this See, and that the other churches might from thence gather what they should teach. . . .*[3]

The prestige of Rome and the church as a whole was also enhanced by the courage and leadership of the Roman bishops. According to tradition, Pope Leo I (440–461) met the advancing army of Attila the Hun in 452 and, through his power of persuasion, saved Rome from a terrible sacking. Three years later, Leo repeated this performance and secured concessions from the Vandal leader Gaiseric.

By the time Gregory I (590–604) became pope, there was no civic authority left to handle the problems pressing the city. Flood, famine, plague, and invasion by the Lombards made for an almost disastrous situation. Pope Gregory concluded a peace with the Lombards, organized relief services that provided water and food for the citizens, and established hospitals for the sick and dying. The fact that it was Christian leaders, rather than imperial administrators, who responded to the city's dire needs could not help but increase the prestige and influence of the church.

MISSIONARY ACTIVITY

The word *catholic* derives from a Greek word meaning "general," "universal," or "worldwide." Early Christians believed that Christ's teaching was intended for all peoples, and they sought to make their faith catholic – that is, believed everywhere. This could be accomplished only through missionary activity. As Saint Paul had written to the Christian community at Colossae in Asia Minor:

You have stripped off your old behavior with your old self, and you have put on a new self which will progress towards true knowledge the more it is renewed in the image of its creator; and in that image there is no room for distinction between Greek and Jew, between the circumcised or the uncircumcised, or between barbarian or Scythian, slave and free man. There is only Christ; he is everything and he is in everything.[4]

Paul urged Christians to bring the "good news" of Christ to all peoples. The Mediterranean served as the highway over which Christianity spread to the cities of the empire.

During the Roman occupation, there were

also scattered and isolated Christian communities in Gaul, Britain, and Ireland. However, they had no wide impact on the populations of their countries, and the migration of the German tribes in the fourth and fifth centuries virtually destroyed Christianity in remote and isolated Britain. The Christianization of the Germans really began in 597, when Pope Gregory I sent a delegation of monks under the Roman Augustine to Britain to convert the Britons. Augustine's approach, adopted by all subsequent missionaries, was to concentrate on converting the king. When he succeeded in converting Ethelbert, king of Kent, the baptism of Ethelbert's people took place as a matter of course. Augustine established his headquarters, or cathedral seat, at Canterbury, the capital of Kent.

In the course of the seventh century, two Christian forces competed for the conversion of the pagan Anglo-Saxons: Roman-oriented missionaries traveling north from Canterbury, and Celtic monks from Ireland and northwestern Britain. Monasteries were established at Iona, Lindisfarne, Jarrow, Whitby, and York (see Map 9.2).

The Roman and Celtic traditions differed completely in their forms of church organization, types of monastic life, and methods of arriving at the date of the central feast of the Christian calendar, Easter. At the Synod (ecclesiastical council) of Whitby in 664, the Roman tradition was completely victorious. The conversion of the English, and the close attachment of the English church to Rome, had far-reaching consequences, because Britain later served as a base for the Christianization of the Continent.

Between the fifth and tenth centuries, the great majority of peoples living on the European continent and the nearby islands accepted the Christian religion – that is, they received baptism, though baptism in itself did not automatically transform people into Christians.

Religion influenced all aspects of tribal life. All members of the tribe participated in religious observances, because doing so was a social duty. Religion was not a private or individual matter; the religion of the chieftain or king determined the religion of the people. Thus missionaries concentrated their initial efforts not on the people but on kings or tribal chieftains. According to custom, tribal chiefs negotiated with all foreign powers, including the gods. Because the Christian missionaries represented a "foreign" power (the Christian God), the king dealt with them. If the ruler accepted Christian baptism, his people did so too. The result was mass baptism.

Once a ruler had marched his people to the waters of baptism, however, the work of Christianization had only begun. Baptism meant either sprinkling the head or immersing the body in water. Conversion meant mental and heartfelt acceptance of the beliefs of Christianity. What does it mean to be a Christian? This question has troubled sincere people from the time of Saint Paul to the present. The problem rests in part in the basic teaching of Jesus in the Gospel:

Then fixing his eyes on his disciples he said:
"How happy are you who are poor: yours is the kingdom of God. Happy you who are hungry now: you shall be satisfied. Happy you who weep now: you shall laugh.
"Happy are you when people hate you, drive you out, abuse you, denounce your name as criminal, on account of the Son of man. Rejoice when that day comes and dance for joy, then your reward will be great in heaven. This was the way their ancestors treated the prophets."

THE CURSES
"But alas for you who are rich: you are having

your consolation now. Alas for you who have your fill now: you shall go hungry. Alas for you who laugh now: you shall mourn and weep.

"Alas for you when the world speaks well of you: This was the way their ancestors treated the false prophets."

LOVE OF ENEMIES

"But I say this to you who are listening: Love your enemies, do good to those who hate you, bless those who curse you, pray for those who treat you badly. To the man who slaps you on one cheek, present the other cheek too; to the man who takes your cloak from you, do not refuse your tunic. Give to everyone who asks you, and do not ask of your property back from the man who robs you. Treat others as you would like them to treat you."[5]

These ideas are among the most radical and revolutionary the world has heard, and it has proved very difficult to get people to live by them.

The German peoples were warriors who idealized the military virtues of physical strength, ferocity in battle, and loyalty to the leader. Victors in battle enjoyed the spoils of success and plundered the vanquished. The greater the fighter, the more trophies and material goods he collected. Thus the Germans had trouble accepting the Christian precepts of "love your enemies" and "turn the other cheek." How could a person be poor and happy at the same time, as Christians claimed?

The Germanic tribes found the Christian notions of sin and repentance virtually incomprehensible. Sin in Christian thought meant disobedience to the will of God as revealed in the Ten Commandments and the teachings of Christ. Good or "moral" behavior to the barbarians meant the observance of tribal customs and practices. Dishonorable behavior caused social ostracism. The inculcation of Christian ideals took a very long time.

CONVERSION AND ASSIMILATION

In Christian theology, conversion involves a turning toward God – that is, a conscious effort to live according to the gospel message. How did missionaries and priests get masses of pagan and illiterate peoples to understand and live by Christian ideals and teachings? Through preaching, through assimilation, and through the penitential system. Preaching aimed at instruction and edification. Instruction presented the basic teachings of Christianity. Edification was intended to strengthen the newly baptized in their faith through stories about the lives of Christ and the saints. Deeply ingrained pagan customs and practices could not be stamped out by words alone, or even by imperial edicts. Christian missionaries often pursued a policy of assimilation, easing the conversion of pagan men and women by stressing similarities between their customs and beliefs and those of Christianity. A letter that Pope Gregory I wrote to Augustine of Canterbury beautifully illustrates this policy. The letter, carried to Augustine in Britain by one Mellitus in 601, expresses the pope's intention that pagan buildings and practices be given a Christian significance:

To our well beloved son Abbot Mellitus: Gregory servant of the servants of God.... Therefore, when by God's help you reach our most reverent brother, Bishop Augustine, we wish you to inform him that we have been giving careful thought to the affairs of the English, and have come to the conclusion that the temples of the idols among that people should on no account be destroyed. The idols are to be destroyed, but the temples themselves are to be aspersed with holy water, altars set up in them, and relics deposited there. For if these temples are well-built, they must be purified from the worship of demons and dedicated to the service of the true God. In this way, we hope that the people, seeing

THE PANTHEON (INTERIOR) *Originally a temple for the gods, the Pantheon later served as a Christian church. As such, it symbolizes the adaptation of pagan elements to Christian purposes. (Alinari/Scala)*

that their temples are not destroyed, may abandon their error and, flocking more readily to their accustomed resorts, may come to know and adore the true God. And since they have a custom of sacrificing many oxen to demons, let some other solemnity be substituted in its place, such as a day of Dedication or the Festivals of the holy martyrs whose relics are enshrined there. On such occasions they might well construct shelters of boughs for themselves around the churches that were once temples, and celebrate the solemnity wth devout feasting. . . . For it is certainly impossible to eradicate all errors from obstinate minds at one stroke, and whoever wishes to climb to a mountain top climbs gradually step by step, and not in one leap.[6]

How assimilation works is perhaps best appreciated through the example of a festival familiar to all Americans, Saint Valentine's Day. There were two Romans named Valentine. Both were Christian priests, and both were martyred for their beliefs around the middle of February in the third century. Since about 150 B.C. the Romans had celebrated the festival of Lupercalia, at which they asked the gods for fertility for themselves, their fields, and their flocks. This celebration occurred in mid-February, shortly before the Roman New Year and the arrival of spring. Thus the early church "converted" the old festival of Lupercalia into Saint Valentine's Day. (Nothing in the lives of the two Christian martyrs connects them with lovers or the exchange of messages and gifts. That practice began in the later Middle Ages.) February 14 was still celebrated as a festival, but it had taken on Christian meaning.

Assimilation is a slow process. Probably more immediate in its impact on the unconverted masses was the penitential system. Penitentials were manuals for the examination of conscience. Irish priests wrote the earliest ones, which English missionaries then carried to the Continent. The illiterate penitent knelt beside the priest, who questioned the penitential about sins he or she might have committed. The recommended penance was then imposed. Penance usually meant fasting for three days each week on bread and water, which served as a "medicine" for the soul. Here is a section of the penitential prepared by Archbishop Theodore of Canterbury (668–690), which circulated widely at the time:

If anyone commits fornication with a virgin he shall do penance for one year. If with a married woman, he shall do penance for four years, two of these entire, and in the other two during the three forty-day periods and three days a week.

A male who commits fornication with a male shall do penance for three years.

If a woman practices vice with a woman, she shall do penance for three years.

Whoever has often committed theft, seven years is his penance, or such a sentence as his priest shall determine, that is, according to what can be arranged with those whom he has wronged. And he who used to steal, when he becomes penitent, ought always to be reconciled to him against whom he has offended and to make restitution according to the wrong he has done to him; and [in such case] he shall greatly shorten his penance.

If a layman slays another with malice aforethought, if he will not lay aside his arms, he shall do penance for seven years; without flesh and wine, three years.

If one slays a monk or a cleric, he shall lay aside his arms and serve God, or he shall do penance for seven years.

He who defiles his neighbor's wife, deprived of his own wife, shall fast for three years two days a week and in the three forty-day periods.

If [the woman] is a virgin, he shall do penance for one year without meat and wine and mead.

If he defiles a vowed virgin, he shall do penance for three years, as we said above, whether a child is born of her or not.

Women who commit abortion before [the fetus] has life, shall do penance for one year or for the three forty-day periods or for forty days, according to the nature of the offense; and if later, that is, more than forty days after conception, they shall do penance as murderesses, that is for three years on Wednesdays and Fridays and in the three forty-day periods. This according to the canons is judged [punishable by] ten years.

If a mother slays her child, if she commits homicide, she shall do penance for fifteen years, and never change except on Sunday.

If a poor woman slays her child, she shall do penance for seven years. In the canon it is said that if it is a case of homicide, she shall do penance for ten years.[7]

As this sample suggests, writers of penitentials were preoccupied with sexual transgressions. Penitentials are much more akin to the Jewish law of the Old Testament than to the spirit of the New Testament. They provide an enormous amount of information about the ascetic ideals of early Christianity and about the crime-ridden realities of Celtic and Germanic societies. Penitentials also reveal the ecclesiastical foundations of some modern attitudes toward sex, birth control, and abortion. Most important, the penitential system led to the growth of a different attitude toward religion: formerly public, corporate, and social, religious observances became private, personal, and individual.[8]

Christian Attitudes Toward Classical Culture

Probably the major dilemma the early Christian church faced concerned Greco-Roman culture. The Roman Empire as a social, political, and economic force gradually disintegrated. Its culture, however, survived. In Greek philosophy, art, and architecture, in Roman law, literature, education, and engineering, the legacy of a great civilization continued. The Christian religion had begun and spread within this intellectual and psychological milieu. What was to be the attitude of Christians to the Greco-Roman world of ideas?

Hostility

Christians in the first and second centuries believed that the end of the world was near. Christ had promised to return, and Christians expected to witness that return. Therefore they considered knowledge useless and learning a waste of time. The important duty of the Christian was to prepare for the Second Coming of the Lord.

Early Christians harbored a strong hatred of pagan Roman culture – in fact, of all Roman civilization. Had not the Romans crucified Christ? Had not the Romans persecuted Christians and subjected them to the most horrible tortures? Did not the Book of Revelation in the New Testament call Rome the great whore of the world, filled with corruption, sin, and every kind of evil? Roman culture was sexual, sensual, and materialistic. The sensual poetry of Ovid, the pornographic descriptions of the satirist Petronius, the political poetry of Virgil, even the rhetorical brilliance of Cicero represented a threat, in the eyes of serious Christians, to the spiritual aims and ideals of Christianity. Good Christians who sought the Kingdom of Heaven through the imitation of Christ believed they had to disassociate themselves from the filth that Roman culture embodied.

As Saint Paul wrote, "The wisdom of the world is foolishness, we preach Christ crucified." Tertullian (ca 160–220), an influential African Christian writer, condemned all secular literature as foolishness in the eyes of God. He called the Greek philosophers, such as Aristotle, "hucksters of eloquence" and compared them to "animals of self-glorification." "What has Athens to do with Jerusalem," he demanded, "the Academy with the Church? We have no need for curiosity since Jesus Christ, nor for inquiry since the gospel." Tertullian insisted that Christians would find in the Bible all the wisdom they needed.

Compromise and Adjustment

At the same time, Christianity encouraged adjustment to the ideas and institutions of the Roman world. Some Biblical texts clearly urged Christians to accept the existing social, economic, and political establishment. In a letter specifically addressed to Christians living among non-Christians in the hostile environment of Rome, Saint Peter had written about the obligations of Christians:

TOWARDS PAGANS
Always behave honourably among pagans, so that they can see your good works for themselves and, when the day of reckoning comes, give thanks to God for the things which now make them denounce you as criminals.

TOWARDS CIVIL AUTHORITY
For the sake of the Lord, accept the authority of every social institution: the emperor, as the supreme authority, and the governors as commissioned by

*him to punish criminals and praise good citizen-
ship. God wants you to be good citizens. . . . Have
respect for everyone and love for your community;
fear God and honour the emperor.*[9]

Christians really had little choice. Greco-Roman culture was the only culture they knew. Only men received a formal education, and they went through the traditional curriculum of grammar and rhetoric. They learned to be effective speakers in the forum or law courts. No other system of education existed. Many early Christians had grown up as pagans, been educated as pagans, and were converted only as adults. Toward homosexuality, for example, Christians of the first three or four centuries simply imbibed the attitude of the world in which they lived. Many Romans indulged in homosexual activity, and contemporaries did not consider such behavior (or inclinations to it) immoral, bizarre, or harmful. Several emperors were openly homosexual, and homosexuals participated freely in all aspects of Roman life and culture. Early Christians too considered homosexuality a conventional expression of physical desire, and they were no more susceptible to anti-homosexual prejudices than pagans were. Some prominent Christians experienced loving same-gender relationships that probably had a sexual element. What eventually led to a change in public and Christian attitudes toward sexual behavior was the shift from the sophisticated urban culture of the Greco-Roman world to the rural culture of medieval Europe.[10]

Even had early Christians wanted to give up their classical ideas and patterns of thought, they would have had great difficulty doing so. Therefore, they had to adapt or adjust their Roman education to their Christian beliefs. Saint Paul himself believed there was a good deal of truth in pagan thought, as long

THE ANTIOCH CHALICE *This earliest surviving Christian chalice, which dates from the fourth century A.D., combines the typical Roman shape with Christian motifs. The chalice is decorated with figures of Christ and the apostles, leaves, and grapes, which represent the sacrament of the Eucharist. (The Metropolitan Museum of Art; the Cloisters Collection; purchase, 1950)*

as it was correctly interpreted and properly understood.

The result was a compromise. Christians gradually came to terms with Greco-Roman culture. Saint Jerome (340–419), a distinguished theologian and linguist, remains famous for his translation of the Old and New Testaments from the Hebrew and Greek into vernacular Latin. Called the Vulgate, his edition of the Bible served as the official translation until the sixteenth century, and even today scholars rely on it. Saint Jerome was also familiar with the writings of such classical authors as Cicero, Virgil, and Terence. He believed that Christians should study the best of ancient thought, because it would direct their minds to God. Jerome maintained that the best ancient literature should be interpreted in light of the Christian faith.

SYNTHESIS: SAINT AUGUSTINE

The finest representative of the blending of classical and Christian ideas, and indeed one of the most brilliant thinkers in the history of the Western world, was Saint Augustine of Hippo (354–430). Aside from the scriptural writers, no one else has had a greater impact on Christian thought in succeeding centuries. Saint Augustine was born into an urban family in what is now Algeria in North Africa. His father was a pagan, his mother a devout Christian. Because his family was poor – his father was a minor civil servant – the only avenue to success in a highly competitive world was a classical education.

Augustine's mother believed that a good classical education, though pagan, would make her son a better Christian, so Augustine's father scraped together the money to educate him. The child received his basic education in the local school. By modern and even medieval standards, that education was extremely narrow: textual study of the writings of the poet Virgil, the orator-politician Cicero, the historian Sallust, and the playwright Terence. At that time, learning meant memorization. Education in the late Roman world aimed at appreciation of words, par-

ticularly those of renowned and eloquent orators.

At the age of seventeen, Augustine went to nearby Carthage to continue his education. There he took a mistress with whom he lived for fifteen years. At Carthage, Augustine entered a difficult psychological phase and began an intellectual and spiritual pilgrimage that led him through experiments with several philosophies and heretical Christian sects. In 383, he traveled to Rome, where he endured illness and disappointment in his teaching: his students fled when their bills were due.

Finally, in Milan in 387, through his friendship with Ambrose and the insights he gained from reading Saint Paul's Letter to the Romans, Augustine was converted and received Christian baptism. He later became bishop of the seacoast city of Hippo Regius in his native North Africa. He was a renowned preacher to Christians there, a vigorous defender of orthodox Christianity, and the author of over ninety-three books and treatises.

Augustine's autobiography, *The Confessions,* is a literary masterpiece and one of the most influential books in the history of Europe. Written in the form of a prayer to God, its language is often incredibly beautiful:

Great are thou, O Lord, and exceedingly to be praised: great is thy power and of thy wisdom there is no reckoning. And man, indeed, one part of thy creation, has the will to praise thee: yea, man, though he bears his mortality about with him . . . even man, a small portion of thy creation, has the will to praise thee. Thou dost stir him up, that it may delight him to praise thee, for thou hast made us for thyself, and our hearts are restless till they find repose in thee.[11]

Too late have I loved thee, O beauty ever ancient and ever new, too late have I loved thee! And be-

hold! Thou wert within and I without, and it was without that I sought thee. Thou wert with me, and I was not with thee. Those creatures held me far from thee which, were they not in thee, were not at all. Thou didst call, thou didst cry, thou didst break in upon my deafness; thou didst gleam forth, thou didst shine out, thou didst banish my blindness; thou didst send forth thy fragrance, and I drew breath and yearned for thee; I tasted and still hunger and thirst; thou didst touch me, and I was on flame to find thy peace.[12]

The Confessions describes Augustine's moral struggle, the conflict between his spiritual and intellectual aspirations and his sensual and material self. It tells the eternally human story of a man constantly tempted by sin but aware also of the providence of God. *The Confessions* reveals the change and development of a human mind and personality steeped in the philosophy and culture of the ancient world.

Greek and Roman philosophers had taught that knowledge and virtue are the same thing: a person who really knows what is right will do what is right. Augustine rejected this idea. He believed that a person may know what is right but fail to act righteously because of the innate weakness of the human will. People do not always act on the basis of rational knowledge. Here Augustine made a profound contribution to the understanding of human nature: he demonstrated that a very learned person can also be corrupt and evil. *The Confessions,* written in the rhetorical style and language of late Roman antiquity, marks the synthesis of Greco-Roman forms and Christian thought.

When the Visigothic chieftain Alaric conquered Rome in 410, horrified pagans blamed the disaster on the Christians. In response, Augustine wrote *City of God.* This profoundly original work contrasts Christianity with the secular society in which it existed. *City of God* presents a moral interpretation of the Roman government, and in fact of all history. Written in Latin and filled with references to ancient history and mythology, it is the best statement of the Christian philosophy of history.

According to Augustine, history is the account of God acting in time. Human history reveals that there are two kinds of people: those who live according to the flesh in the city of Babylon and those who live according to the spirit in the City of God. In other words, humanity is composed of individuals who live entirely according to their selfish inclinations and individuals who live according to the Word of God. The former will endure eternal hellfire, the latter eternal bliss.

Augustine maintained that states came into existence as the result of Adam's fall and people's inclination to sin. The state is a necessary evil, responsible only for providing the peace and order Christians need in order to pursue their pilgrimage to the City of God. The particular form of government — whether monarchy, aristocracy, or democracy — is basically irrelevant. Any civil government that fails to provide order, law, and justice is no more than a band of gangsters.

Since the state results from moral lapse, from sin, it follows that the church, which is concerned with salvation, is responsible for everyone, including Christian rulers. Churchmen in the Middle Ages used Augustine's theory to defend their belief in the ultimate superiority of the spiritual power over the temporal. This remained the dominant political theory until the late thirteenth century.

Augustine had no objection to drawing on pagan knowledge to support Christian thought. Augustine used Roman history as evidence to defend Christian theology. In doing so he assimilated Roman history, and indeed all of classical culture, into Christian teaching.

MONASTICISM AND THE RULE OF SAINT BENEDICT

Christianity began and spread as a city religion. Since the first century, however, some especially pious Christians had felt that the only alternative to the decadence of urban life was complete separation from the world. All-consuming pursuit of material things, gross sexual promiscuity, and general political corruption disgusted them. They believed that the Christian life as set forth in the Gospel could not be lived in the midst of such immorality. They rejected the established values of Roman society and were the first real nonconformists in the church.

At first individuals and small groups left the cities and went to live in caves or rude shelters in the desert or the mountains. These people were called hermits, from the Greek word *eremos,* meaning "desert." There is no way of knowing how many hermits there were in the fourth and fifth centuries, partly because their conscious aim was a secret and hidden life known only to God.

Several factors worked against the eremitical variety of monasticism in western Europe. First was the climate. The cold, snow, ice, and fog that covered much of Europe for many months of the year discouraged isolated living. Dense forests filled with wild animals and wandering barbaric German tribes presented obvious dangers. Furthermore, church leaders did not really approve of the eremitical life. Hermits sometimes claimed to have mystical experiences, direct communications with God. No one could verify these experiences.

But if hermits could communicate directly with the Lord, what need had they for the priest and the institutional church? The church hierarchy, or leaders, encouraged coenobitic monasticism – that is, communal living in monasteries.

In the fifth and sixth centuries, many experiments in communal monasticism were made in Gaul, Italy, Spain, Anglo-Saxon England, and Ireland. John Cassian, after studying both eremitical and coenobitic mysticism in Egypt and Syria, established two monasteries near Marseilles in Gaul around 415. One of Cassian's books, *Conferences,* based on conversations he had had with holy men in the East, discussed the dangers of the isolated hermit's life. The abbey or monastery of Lérins on the Mediterranean Sea near Cannes (ca 410) also had significant contacts with monastic centers in the Middle East and North Africa. Lérins encouraged the severely penitential and extremely ascetic behavior common in the East, such as long hours of prayer, fasting, and self-flagellation. It was this tradition of harsh self-mortification that the Roman-British monk Saint Patrick carried from Lérins to Ireland in the fifth century. Church organization in Ireland became closely associated with the monasteries, and Irish monastic life followed the ascetic Eastern form.

Around 540, the Roman senator Cassiodorus retired from public service and established a monastery, the Vivarium, on his estate in Italy. Cassiodorus wanted the Vivarium to become an educational and cultural center, and enlisted highly educated and sophisticated men for it. He set the monks to copying both sacred and secular manuscripts, intending this to be their sole occupation. Cassiodorus started the association of monasticism with scholarship and learning. This developed into a great tradition in the medieval and modern worlds. But Cassiodorus's experiment did not become the most influential form of monasticism in European society. The fifth and sixth centuries witnessed the appearance of many other monastic lifestyles.

In 529 Benedict of Nursia (480–543), who had experimented with both the eremitical and the communal forms of monastic life, wrote a brief set of regulations, or rules, for the monks who had gathered around him at Monte Cassino between Rome and Naples. This guide for monastic life slowly replaced all others. *The Rule of Saint Benedict* has influenced all forms of organized religious life in the Roman church.

THE RULE OF SAINT BENEDICT

Saint Benedict conceived of his *Rule* as a simple code for ordinary men. It outlined a monastic life of regularity, discipline, and moderation. Each monk had ample food and adequate sleep. Self-destructive acts of mortification were forbidden. In an atmosphere of silence, the monk spent part of the day in formal prayer, which Benedict called the Work of God. This consisted of chanting psalms and other prayers from the Bible in that part of the monastery church called the choir. The rest of the day was passed in study and manual labor. After a year of probation, the monk made three vows.

First, the monk vowed stability: he promised to live his entire life in the monastery of his profession. The vow of stability was Saint Benedict's major contribution to Western monasticism; his object was to prevent the wandering so common in his day. Second, the monk vowed conversion of manners — that is, to strive to improve himself and to come closer to God. Third, he promised obedience, the most difficult vow because it meant the complete surrender of his will to the abbot, or head of the monastery. The first sentence of

ST. BENEDICT *from Agnolo Gaddi,* Madonna Enthroned with Saints, *ca 1385. The first word of his Rule, which Benedict holds in his left hand, is "Listen." Listening was the posture of students, and St. Benedict called his monastery a "School of the Lord's Service," where the monks listened not only to their abbot but through the abbot to Christ himself. In his right hand, Benedict carries the rods of correction. (National Gallery of Art, Washington, Andrew W. Mellon Collection)*

the *Rule* urged the monk, by the labor of obedience, to return to God, from whom he had departed "by the sloth of disobedience."

The Rule of Saint Benedict expresses the assimilation of the Roman spirit into Western monasticism. It reveals the logical mind of its creator and the Roman concern for order, organization, and respect for law. Its spirit of moderation and flexibility is reflected in the patience, wisdom, and understanding with which the abbot is to govern, and, indeed, the entire life is to be led. The *Rule* could be used in vastly different physical and geographical circumstances, in damp and cold Germany as well as in warm and sunny Italy. The *Rule* was quickly adapted for women, and many convents of nuns were established in the early Middle Ages.

Saint Benedict's *Rule* implies that a person who wants to become a monk or nun need have no previous ascetic experience or even a particularly strong bent toward the religious life. Thus, it allowed for the admission of newcomers with different backgrounds and personalities. This flexibility helps to explain the attractiveness of Benedictine monasticism throughout the centuries. *The Rule of Saint Benedict* is a superior example of the way in which the Greco-Roman heritage and Roman patterns of thought were preserved.

At the same time, the *Rule* no more provides a picture of actual life within a Benedictine abbey of the seventh or eighth (or twentieth) century than the American Constitution of 1789 describes living conditions in the United States today. A code of laws cannot do that. Monasteries were composed of individuals, and human beings defy strict classification according to rules, laws, or statistics. *The Rule of Saint Benedict* had one fundamental purpose. The exercises of the monastic life were designed to draw the individual, slowly but steadily, away from attachment to the world and love of self and toward the love of God.

THE SUCCESS OF BENEDICTINE MONASTICISM

Why was the Benedictine form of monasticism so successful? Why did it eventually replace other forms of Western monasticism? The answer lies partly in its spirit of flexibility and moderation and partly in the balanced life it provided. Early Benedictine monks and nuns spent part of the day in prayer, part in

study or some other form of intellectual activity, and part in manual labor. The monastic life as conceived by Saint Benedict did not lean too heavily in any one direction; it struck a balance between asceticism and idleness. It thus provided opportunities for persons of entirely different abilities and talents – from mechanics to gardeners to literary scholars. Benedict's *Rule* contrasts sharply with Cassiodorus's narrow concept of the monastery as a place for aristocratic scholars and bibliophiles.

Benedictine monasticism also suited the social circumstances of early medieval society. The German invasions had fragmented European life: the self-sufficient rural estate replaced the city as the basic unit of civilization. A monastery too had to be economically self-sufficient. It was supposed to produce from its lands and properties all that was needed for food, clothing, buildings, and liturgical service of the altar. The monastery fitted in – indeed, represented – the trend toward localism.

Benedictine monasticism also succeeded partly because it was so materially successful. In the seventh and eighth centuries, monasteries pushed back forest and wasteland, drained swamps, and experimented with crop rotation. For example, the abbey of Saint Wandrille, founded in 645 near Rouen in northwestern Gaul, sent squads of monks to clear the forests that surrounded it. Within seventy-five years the abbey was immensely wealthy. The abbey of Jumièges, also in the diocese of Rouen, followed much the same pattern. Such Benedictine houses made a significant contribution to the agricultural development of Europe. The socialistic nature of their organization, whereby property was held in common and profits pooled and reinvested, made this contribution possible.

Finally, monasteries conducted schools for the education of the young people of the neighborhood. Some learned about prescriptions and herbal remedies for disease, and

JUSTINIAN AND HIS COURT The Emperor Justinian (center) with ecclesiastical and court officials personifies the unity of the Byzantine state and the orthodox church in the person of the emperor. Just as the emperor was both king and priest, so all his Greek subjects belonged to the orthodox church. (Alinari/Scala)

went on to provide medical treatment for their localities. A few copied manuscripts and wrote books. This training did not go unappreciated in a society desperately in need of it. Local and royal governments drew upon the services of the literate men, the able administrators whom the monasteries produced. This was not what Saint Benedict had intended, but the effectiveness of the institution he designed made it perhaps inevitable.

THE BYZANTINE EAST
(CA 400–788)

Constantine (306–337) had tried to maintain the unity of the Roman Empire, but during the fifth and sixth centuries the western and eastern halves drifted apart. Later emperors worked to hold the empire together. Justinian (527–565) waged long and hard-fought wars against the Ostrogoths and temporarily regained Italy and North Africa. But his conquests had disastrous consequences. Justinian's wars exhausted the resources of the Byzantine state, destroyed Italy's economy, and killed a large part of its population. The wars paved the way for the easy conquest of Italy by another Germanic tribe, the Lombards, shortly after Justinian's death. In the late sixth century, the territory of the western Roman Empire came under Germanic sway, while in the East the Byzantine Empire continued the traditions and institutions of the caesars.

Latin Christian culture was only one legacy the Roman Empire bequeathed to the Western world. The Byzantine culture centered at Constantinople – Constantine's New Rome – was another. The Byzantine Empire maintained a high standard of living, and for centuries the Greeks were the most civilized people in the Western world. The Byzantine Empire held at bay, or at least hindered, barbarian peoples who could otherwise have wreaked additional devastation on western Europe, retarding its development. Most important, however, is the role of Byzantium as preserver of the wisdom of the ancient world. Throughout the long years when barbarians in western Europe trampled down the old and then painfully built something new, Byzantium protected and then handed on to the West the intellectual heritage of Greco-Roman civilization.

BYZANTINE EAST AND GERMANIC WEST

As imperial authority disintegrated in the West during the fifth century, civic functions were performed first by church leaders and then by German chieftains. As we have seen, Pope Leo I negotiated with Attila the Hun and persuaded him to withdraw from Rome. There was no other authority in Rome to do so. The death of the Roman emperor Romulus Augustus in 476 signaled the end of the empire in the West. Thereafter, German chieftains held power.

Meanwhile in the East, the Byzantines preserved the forms and traditions of the old Roman Empire, and even called themselves Romans. Byzantine emperors traced their lines back past Constantine to Augustus. The senate that sat in Constantinople carried on the traditions and preserved the glory of the old Roman senate. The army that defended the empire was the direct descendant of the

old Roman legions. Even the chariot factions of the Roman Empire lived on under the Byzantines, who cheered their favorites as enthusiastically as had the Romans of Hadrian's day.

The position of the church differed considerably in the Byzantine East and the Germanic West. The fourth-century emperors Constantine and Theodosius had wanted the church to act as a unifying force within the empire, but the Germanic invasions made that impossible. The bishops of Rome repeatedly called upon the emperors at Constantinople for military support against the invaders, but rarely could the emperors send it. The church in the West steadily grew away from the empire and became involved in the social and political affairs of Italy and the West. Nevertheless, until the eighth century, the popes, who were selected by the clergy of Rome, continued to send announcements of their elections to the emperors at Constantinople – a sign that the Roman popes long thought of themselves as bishops of the Roman Empire.

The popes were preoccupied with conversion of the Germans, the Christian attitude toward classical culture, and relations with the German rulers. The church in the West concentrated on its missionary function. It took time for the clergy to be organized and for the papacy to get in touch with all clerics. Most of the theology of the church in the West came from the East, and the overwhelming majority of popes were themselves of Eastern origin.

Tensions occasionally developed between church officials and secular authorities in the West. The dispute between Bishop Ambrose of Milan and the emperor Theodosius is a good example. A century later, Pope Gelasius I (492–496) insisted that bishops, not civil authorities, were responsible for the administration of the church. Gelasius maintained that two powers governed the world, the sacred authority of the popes and the royal power of kings. Because priests have to answer to God even for kings, the sacred power was the greater.

Such an assertion was virtually unheard of in the East, where the emperor's jurisdiction over the church was fully acknowledged. The emperor in Constantinople nominated the patriarch, as the highest prelate of the church in the East was called. The emperor looked upon religion as a branch of the state. Religion was such a vital aspect of the social life of the people that the emperor devoted considerable attention to it. He considered it his duty to protect the faith, not only against heathen enemies but also against heretics within the empire. In case of doctrinal disputes, the emperor, following Constantine's example at Nicaea, summoned councils of bishops and theologians to settle problems.

In the East, Christianity was the established religion. All citizens of the Byzantine Empire were Christians; to be Byzantine meant to be Christian. The Greek church was an imperial state church subject to and guided by the emperor. The clergy were well organized. The level of theological debate was high. Fine points of Christian theology held the attention of the leaders of the Greek church.

The expansion of the Arabs in the Mediterranean in the seventh and eighth centuries furthered the separation of the churches by dividing the two parts of Christendom. Separation bred isolation. Isolation, combined with prejudice on both sides, bred hostility. Finally, in 1054, a theological disagreement led the bishop of Rome and the patriarch of Constantinople to excommunicate each other. The outcome was a permanent schism, or split, between the Roman Catholic and the Greek Orthodox churches.

In spite of religious differences, the Byzantine Empire served as a bulwark for the West, protecting it against invasions from the east. The Greeks stopped the Persians in the seventh century. They blunted – though they could not stop – Arab attacks in the seventh and eighth centuries, and they fought courageously against Turkish invaders until the fifteenth century, when they were finally overwhelmed. Byzantine Greeks slowed the impetus of the Slavic incursions in the Balkans and held the Russians at arm's length.

Turning from war to the arts of peace, the Byzantines set about civilizing the Slavs, both in the Balkans and in Russia. Byzantine missionaries spread the word of Christ, and one of their triumphs was the conversion of the Russians. The Byzantine missionary Cyril adapted the Greek alphabet to the Russian language, and this script (called the Cyrillic alphabet) is still in use today. Cyrillic script made possible the birth of Russian literature. Similarly, Byzantine art and architecture became the basis and inspiration of Russian forms. The Byzantines were so successful that the Russians claimed to be the successors of the Byzantine Empire. For a time Moscow was even known as "the Third Rome" (the second Rome being Constantinople).

THE LAW CODE OF JUSTINIAN

One of the most splendid achievements of the Byzantine emperors was the preservation of Roman law for the medieval and modern worlds. Roman law had developed from many sources – decisions by judges, edicts of the emperors, legislation passed by the senate, and the opinions of jurists expert in the theory and practice of law. By the fourth century, Roman law had become a huge bewildering mass. Its sheer bulk made it almost unusable. Some laws had become outdated, some repeated others, and some contradicted others. Faced with this vast, complex, and confusing hodgepodge, the emperor Theodosius decided to clarify and codify the law. He explained the need to do so:

When we consider the enormous multitude of books, the diverse modes of process and the difficulty of legal cases, and further the huge mass of imperial constitutions, which hidden as it were under a rampart of gross mist and darkness precludes men's intellects from gaining a knowledge of them, we feel that we have met a real need of our age, and dispelling the darkness have given light to the laws by a short compendium. . . . Thus having swept away the clouds of volumes, on which many wasted their lives and explained nothing in the end, we established a compendious knowledge of the Imperial constitutions since the time of the divine Constantine. [13]

Theodosius's work was only a beginning. He left centuries of Roman law untouched.

A far more sweeping and systematic codification took place under the emperor Justinian. Justinian intended to simplify the law and to make it known to everyone. He appointed a committee of eminent jurists to sort through and organize the laws. In 529, Justinian published the *Code*, which distilled the legal genius of the Romans into a coherent whole, eliminated outmoded laws, eliminated contradictions, and clarified the law itself. Not content with the *Code*, Justinian set about bringing order to the equally huge body of Roman jurisprudence, the science or philosophy of law.

During the second and third centuries the foremost Roman jurists, at the request of the emperors, had expressed learned opinions on complex legal problems, but often these opinions differed from one another. To harmonize this body of knowledge, Justinian directed his jurists to clear up disputed points and to issue definitive rulings. Accordingly, in 533 his lawyers published the *Digest,* which codified Roman legal thought. Finally, Justinian's lawyers compiled a handbook of civil law, the *Institutes.*

These three works — the *Code, Digest,* and *Institutes* — are the backbone of the *corpus juris civilis,* the body of civil law, which is the foundation of law for nearly every modern European nation. Even England, which developed its own common law, has been influenced by it. The work of Justinian and his dedicated band of jurists still affects the life of the modern world nearly fifteen hundred years later.

BYZANTINE INTELLECTUAL LIFE

Among the Byzantines education was highly prized, and because of them many masterpieces of ancient Greek literature survived to fertilize the intellectual life of the modern world. The literature of the Byzantine Empire was predominantly Greek, although Latin was long spoken among top politicians, scholars, and lawyers. Indeed, Justinian's *Code* was first written in Latin. Among the reading public, which was quite large, history was a favorite subject. Generations of Byzantines read the historical works of Herodotus, Thucydides, and others. Some Byzantine historians abbreviated long histories, such as those of Polybius, while others wrote detailed narratives of their own days.

The most remarkable Byzantine historian was Procopius (ca 500–ca 562), who left a rousing account of Justinian's reconquest of North Africa and Italy. Proof that the wit and venom of ancient writers like Archilochus and Aristophanes lived on in the Byzantine era can be found in Procopius's *Secret History,* a vicious and uproarious attack on Justinian and his wife, the empress Theodora. Although the

Byzantines are often depicted as dull and life-less, such opinions are hard to defend in the face of Procopius's descriptions of Justinian's character:

For he was at once villainous and amenable; as people say colloquially, a moron. He was never truthful with anyone, but always guileful in what he said and did, yet easily hoodwinked by any who wanted to deceive him. His nature was an unnat-ural mixture of folly and wickedness.[14]

Procopius even accused Justinian of being a demon who possessed strange powers:

And some of those who have been with Justinian at the palace late at night, men who were pure of spirit, have thought they saw a strange demonaic form taking his throne and walked about, and indeed he was never wont to remain sitting for long, and immediately Justinian's head vanished, while the rest of his body seemed to ebb and flow; whereat the beholder stood aghast and fearful, wondering if his eyes were deceiving him. But presently he perceived the vanished head filling out and joining the body again as strangely as it had left it.[15]

The *Secret History* may not be great history, but it is robust literature.

Later Byzantine historians chronicled the victories of their emperors and the progress of their barbarian foes. Like Herodotus before them, they were curious about foreigners. They have left striking descriptions of the Turks, who eventually overwhelmed Byzantium. They painted unflattering pictures of the uncouth and grasping princes of France and England, who saw in the Crusades the perfect combination of faith and piety, blood-shed and profit.

In mathematics and geometry the Byzantines discovered nothing new. Yet they were exceptionally important as catalysts, for they passed Greco-Roman learning on to the

LID–BYZANTINE BOX *Probably made in Alexandria, Egypt in the fifth century, this medicine box (15.2 cm. high and 8.9 cm. wide) was divided into six compartments intended to hold various medicines. The female figure on the lid carries a rudder in one hand, symbolizing Alexandria's maritime activities, and a cornucopia suggesting material prosperity or good health in the other. Alexandria was a great medical center until about 700 A.D., after which leadership in medical practice passed to Constantinople. (Dumbarton Oaks Center for Byzantine Studies, Trustees of Harvard University)*

Arabs, who assimilated it and made remarkable advances upon it. The Byzantines were equally uncreative in astronomy and natural science, but they at least faithfully learned what the ancients had to teach.

Only when science could be put to military use did the Byzantines make advances. The best-known Byzantine scientific discovery was chemical – "Greek fire," a combustible liquid that was the medieval equivalent of the flame thrower. In mechanics the Byzantines continued the work of Hellenistic and Roman inventors of artillery and seige machinery. Just as Archimedes had devised machines to stop the Romans, so Byzantine scientists improved and modified devices for defending their empire.

The Byzantines devoted a great deal of attention to medicine, and the general level of medical competence was far higher in the Byzantine Empire than it was in the medieval West. The Byzantines assimilated the discoveries of Hellenic and Hellenistic medicine but added very few of their own. The basis of their medical theory was Hippocrates' concept of the four humors of the body (page 101). Byzantine physicians emphasized the importance of diet and rest, and relied heavily on drugs made from herbs. Perhaps their chief weakness was their excessive use of bleeding and burning, which often succeeded only in further weakening an already feeble patient. Hospitals were a prominent feature of Byzantine life, and the army too had a medical corps.

THE ARABS AND ISLAM

Around 610, in the obscure town of Mecca in what is now Saudi Arabia, a moderately successful merchant called Mohammed began to

have religious visions. By the time he died in 632, all Arabia had accepted his creed. A century later his followers controlled Syria, Palestine, Egypt, all of North Africa, Spain, and part of France. This Arabic expansion profoundly affected the development of European culture. Through centers at Salerno in southern Italy and Toledo in central Spain, Arabic and Greek learning reached the West. Arabic mathematicians not only preserved ancient learning but also made original contributions. Western knowledge, especially in medicine, mathematics, and engineering, rests heavily on Arabic achievements.

THE ARABS

In Mohammed's time, Arabia was inhabited by Semitic tribes, most of whom were Bedouins. These primitive and warlike peoples grazed their goats and sheep on the sparse patches of grass that dotted the vast semi-arid peninsula. Other Arabs, called Hejaz, lived in the southern valleys and coastal towns along the Red Sea – in Yemen, Mecca, and Medina. The Hejaz led a more sophisticated life and supported themselves by agriculture and trade. Their caravan routes crisscrossed Arabia and carried goods to Byzantium, Persia, and Syria. The Hejaz had wide commercial dealings, but avoided cultural contacts with their Jewish, Christian, and Persian neighbors. The wealth produced by their business transactions led to luxurious and extravagant living in the towns.

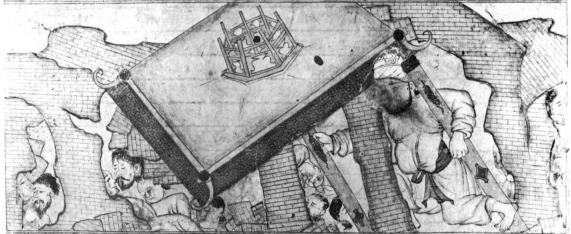

Although the nomadic Bedouins condemned the urbanized lifestyle of the Hejaz as immoral and corrupt, Arabs of both types deeply respected each other's local tribal customs. They had no political unity beyond their tribal bonds. Tribal custom regulated their lives. Custom demanded the rigid observance of family obligations and the performance of religious rituals. Custom insisted that an Arab be proud, generous, and swift to take revenge. Custom required manly courage in public and avoidance of shameful behavior that could bring social disgrace.

Although the various tribes differed markedly, they did have certain religious rules in common. For example, all Arabs kept three months of the year as sacred, and during that time fighting stopped so that everyone could attend the holy ceremonies in peace. The city of Mecca was the religious center of the Arab world, and fighting was never tolerated there. All Arabs prayed at the Kaaba, the sanctuary in Mecca. Within the Kaaba was a sacred black stone that Arabs revered because they believed it had fallen from heaven.

What eventually molded the diverse Arab tribes into a powerful political and social unity was the religion founded by Mohammed.

MOHAMMED AND THE FAITH OF ISLAM

Except for a few vague autobiographical remarks in the Koran, the sacred book of Islam, Mohammed (ca 571–632) left no account of his life. Arab tradition accepts as historically true some of the sacred legends that developed about him, but those legends were not written down until about a century after his death. Orphaned at the age of six, Mohammed was brought up by his grandfather. As a young man he became a merchant in the caravan trade. Later he entered the service of a wealthy widow, and their subsequent marriage brought him financial independence. The Koran reveals him as an extremely devout man, ascetic, self-disciplined, literate but not educated.

Since childhood Mohammed had had strange seizures, or fits, during which he completely lost consciousness and had visions. After 610, these attacks and the accompanying visions apparently became more frequent. Unsure for a time what he should do, Mohammed discovered his mission after a vision in which the angel Gabriel instructed him to preach. Mohammed described his visions in verse form and used these verses as his Qur'an (Koran) or prayer recitation. During his lifetime Mohammed's secretary, Zaid ibn Thabit, jotted down these revelations haphazardly. After Mohammed's death, scribes organized the revelations into chapters, and in 651 Mohammed's second successor as religious leader, Othman, published an official version of them known as the Koran.

The religion Mohammed founded is called Islam; a believer in that faith is called a Muslim. Mohammed's religion eventually attracted great numbers of people, partly because of the simplicity of its doctrines. The subtle and complex reasoning Christianity had acquired by the seventh century was absent from Islam. Nor did Islam emphasize study and learning, as did Judaism.

The strictly monotheistic theology outlined in the Koran has only a few tenets. Allah, the Muslim god, is all-powerful and all-knowing. Mohammed, Allah's prophet, preached his word and carried his message. Mohammed described himself as the successor both of the Jewish patriarch Abraham and of Christ, and claimed that his teachings replaced theirs. Mohammed invited and won converts from Judaism and Christianity.

Because Allah is all-powerful, believers

must submit themselves to him. ("Islam" literally means "submission to the word of God.") This Islamic belief is closely related to the central feature of Muslim doctrine, the coming Day of Judgment. Muslims need not be concerned about *when* judgment will occur, but they must believe with absolute and total conviction that the Day of Judgment *will* come. Consequently, all of a Muslim's thoughts and actions at every hour of every day should be oriented toward the Last Judgment.

The Islamic Day of Judgment will be very similar to the Christian one: on that day God will separate the saved and the damned. Mohammed described in lengthy detail the frightful tortures with which Allah will punish the damned: scourgings, beatings with iron clubs, burnings, and forced drinking of boiling water. The prophet's depiction of the heavenly rewards of the saved and the blessed are just as graphic but different in kind from those of Christian theology. The Muslim vision of heaven features lush green gardens surrounded by refreshing streams. There the saved, clothed in rich silks, lounge about on soft cushions and couches, nibbling ripe fruits, sipping delicious beverages served by handsome youths, and enjoying the companionship of plump black-eyed maidens. It is not difficult to understand how these particular sensual delights would appeal to a people living in or near the hot, dry desert.

In order to merit the rewards of heaven, Mohammed prescribed a strict code of morality and behavior. The Muslim must recite a profession of faith in Allah and in Mohammed as God's prophet: "There is no god but Allah and Mohammed is his prophet." The believer must pray five times a day, fast and pray during the sacred month of Ramadan, make a pilgrimage to the holy city of Mecca once during his or her lifetime, and give alms to the poor. The Koran forbids alcoholic beverages and gambling. It condemns usury in business — that is, lending money at high interest rates or taking advantage of market demands for products by charging high prices for them. Some foods, such as pork, are forbidden, a dietary regulation adopted directly from the Mosaic law of the Jews.

By earlier Arab standards, the Koran sets forth an austere sexual morality. Muslim jurisprudence condemned licentious behavior on the part of men as well as women, and the status of women in Muslim society gradually improved. About marriage, illicit intercourse, and inheritance, the Koran states:

(Of) . . . women who seem good in your eyes, marry but two, three, or four; and if ye still fear that ye shall not act equitably, then only one; or the slaves whom ye have acquired: this will make justice on your part easier.
The whore and the fornicator: whip each of them a hundred times. . . .
The fornicator shall not marry other than a whore; and the whore shall not marry other than a fornicator. . . .
They who defame virtuous women, and fail to bring four witnesses (to swear that they did not), are to be whipped eighty times. . . .
Men who die and leave wives behind shall bequeath to them a year's maintenance. . . .
And your wives shall have a fourth part of what you leave, if you have no issue; but if you have issue, then they shall have an eighth part. . . .
With regard to your children, God commands you to give the male the portion of two females; and if there be more than two females, then they shall have two-thirds of what their father leaves; but if there be one daughter only, she shall have the half. (The man who is shamed at the birth of a daughter) hides himself from the people because of the ill tidings: shall he keep it with disgrace or

bury it in the dust? Are not his judgments wrong? ... Kill not your children for fear of want: for them and for you will we provide. Verily, the killing of them is a great wickedness.

By contrast, Western law has tended to punish prostitutes but not their clients. Westerners tend to think polygamy degrading to women, but in a military society where there are apt to be many widows, polygamy provided women a measure of security. The prohibition against killing unwanted female infants by burial obviously represents a more humane attitude. With respect to matters of property, Muslim women were more emancipated than Western women. For example, a Muslim woman retained complete jurisdiction over one-third of her property when she married, and she could dispose of it in any way she wished. A Western woman had no such power.[16]

The Muslim who faithfully observed the laws of the Koran could hope for salvation. The believer who suffered and died for his faith in battle was assured the sensual rewards of the Muslim heaven immediately. According to the Koran, salvation is by Allah's grace and choice alone. A Muslim will not "win" salvation as a reward for good behavior. Because Allah is all-knowing and all-powerful, he knows from the moment of a person's conception whether or not that person will be saved. Nevertheless, Mohammed maintained, predestination gave the believer the will and the courage to try to achieve the impossible. Devout Muslims came to believe that mechanical performance of the basic rules of the faith would automatically gain them salvation.

Historians and ecumenically minded theologians have pointed out many similarities among Islam, Christianity, and Judaism. All three religions are monotheistic. Like Jews, Muslims are forbidden to eat pork. Like Christians, Muslims are urged to practice charity and to be generous to the poor and the weak. And like Christians, Muslims believe in the Last Judgment. Mohammed probably had a general familiarity with the Old and New Testaments, and he must have learned something about Jewish and Christian cultures on his commercial travels.

In the Koran, Mohammed gave his believers a holy book of revelation, moral principles, and history on a par with the Old and New Testaments. Like Jews and Christians, Muslims became people with a sacred book. But the Koran was not only a sacred book. It was written with great eloquence and poetic charm, qualities the Arabs of Mohammed's day especially valued.

MUSLIM EXPANSION IN THE WEST

Mohammed's preaching at first did not appeal to many people. Legend has it that for the first three years he attracted only fourteen believers. One explanation for the slow acceptance of Islam is that Mohammed urged the destruction of the idols in the sanctuary at Mecca. This site drew thousands of devout Arabs annually and thus brought important revenue to the city. The townspeople turned against Mohammed, and he and his followers were forced to flee to Medina. This Hegira, or flight, occurred in 622, and Muslims subsequently dated the beginning of their era from that event. At Medina, Mohammed attracted increasing numbers of believers, and his teachings began to have an impact.

The social and political effects of Islam were massive. Mohammed destroyed the communal and tribal quality of Arab life. Individuals could perform the religious rituals, such as the five daily prayers, alone. Although

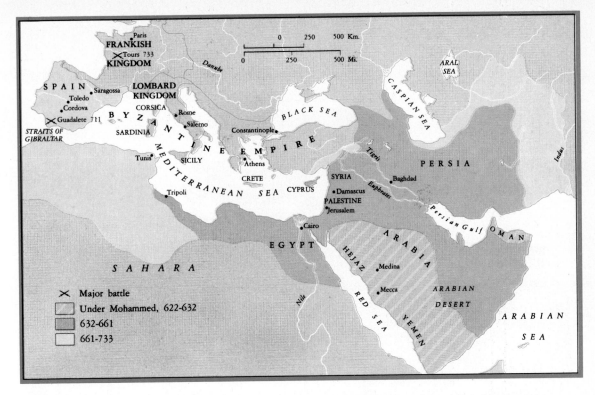

Muslims customarily worshiped together at sundown on Fridays, no assembly or organized church was essential. Islam lacked the public and corporate aspects of tribal religion. Every Muslim hoped that by following the simple requirements of Islam he or she could achieve salvation. For the believer, the significance of the petty disputes and conflicts of tribal society paled before the simple teachings of Allah. On this basis Mohammed united the nomads of the desert and the merchants of the cities. The doctrines of Islam, instead of the ties of local custom, bound all Arabs.

The faith of Allah, having united the Arabs, redirected their warlike energies. Hostilities were launched outward. By the time Mohammed died in 632, he had welded together all the Bedouin tribes. The crescent of Islam, the Muslim symbol, controlled the entire Arabian peninsula. In the following century, between 632 and 733, one rich province of the old Roman Empire after another came under Muslim domination – first Syria, then Egypt and Persia, and then all of North Africa (see Map 9.3). The governmental headquarters of this vast new empire was established at Damascus in Syria by the ruling Omayyad family. A contemporary proverb speaks of the Mediterranean as a Muslim lake.

In 711, a Muslim force crossed the Straits of Gibraltar and at Gaudalete easily defeated the weak Visigothic kingdom in Spain. The Muslims swept across Spain in seven years

DOME OF THE ROCK *Built in 691 by Mohammed's second successor, the Caliph Abd al-Malik, this domed mosque was the first Islamic religious building in Jerusalem after the Arab conquest of Palestine. Because the* Koran *forbade representations of the human figure, geometrical designs decorate the walls. (Israel Government Tourist Administration)*

and, as one scholar has written, "What was lost in seven years, it took seven hundred to regain."[17] A few Christian princes supported by the Frankish rulers held out in northern mountain fortresses, but the Muslims controlled most of Spain until the twelfth century. The political history of Spain in the Middle Ages is the history of the *reconquista,* or Christian reconquest of that country.

In 719, the Arabs pushed beyond the Pyrenees into the kingdom of the Franks. At the battle of Tours in 733, the Frankish ruler Charles Martel defeated the Arabs and halted their further expansion. Ultimately Charlemagne expelled them from France.

Nor was Muslim expansion confined to northern Africa and southern Europe. From the Arabian peninsula, Muslims also carried their faith deep into Africa and across Asia all the way to India. In the West, however, Arab political influence was felt almost exclusively in Spain. A member of the Omayyad dynasty, Abdurrahman (756–788), established the Moorish kingdom of Spain with its capital at

Cordova. (The Spanish kingdom and Spanish culture were called Moorish after the dark-skinned Moors of North Africa, also known as Berber-Arabs, who had conquered the Iberian Peninsula.) Jewish people were generally well treated in Moorish Spain, and Christians were tolerated as long as they paid a small tax.

Toledo became an important center of learning through which Arab intellectual achievements entered and influenced western Europe. Arabic knowledge of science and mathematics, derived from the Chinese, Greeks, and Hindus, was highly sophisticated. The Muslim mathematician Al-Khwarizmi (d.830) wrote the important treatise *Algebra*, the first work in which the word *algebra* is used mathematically, to mean the transposing of negative terms in an equation to the opposite side. Al-Khwarizmi used Arabic numerals in *Algebra*, and applied mathematics to problems of physics and astronomy. Muslims also instructed Westerners in the use of the zero, which permitted the execution of complicated problems of multiplication and long division. Use of the zero represented an enormous advance over the clumsy Roman numerals.

Muslim medical knowledge was also far superior to that of Westerners. By the ninth century, Arab physicians had translated most of the treatises of Hippocrates and Galen. Unfortunately, these Greek treatises came to the West as translations from Greek to Arabic to Latin, and inevitably lost a great deal in translation. Nevertheless, in the ninth and tenth centuries, Arabic knowledge and experience in anatomy and pharmaceutical prescriptions much enriched Western knowledge. Later, Greek philosophical thought passed to the West by way of Arabic translation.

There is no question that Islam was a significant ingredient in the making of Europe.

Muslim expansion meant that Mediterranean civilization would be divided into three spheres of influence, the Byzantine, the Arabic, and the Western. Beginning in the ninth century, Arabic mathematics, medicine, philosophy, and science played a decisive role in the formation of European culture. A few of the words that came into English from Arabic suggest the extent of Arabic influence: alcohol, admiral, algebra, almanac, candy, cipher, coffee, damask, lemon, orange, sherbet, zero.[18]

———◆———

Saint Augustine died in 430 as the Vandals approached the coastal city of Hippo. Scholars have sometimes described Augustine as standing with one foot in the ancient world and one in the Middle Ages. Indeed, Augustine does represent the end of ancient culture and the birth of what has been called the Middle Ages. A new and different kind of society was gestating in the mid-fifth century.

The world of the Middle Ages combined Germanic practices and institutions, classical ideas and patterns of thought, Christianity, and a significant dash of Islam. Christianity, because it creatively and energetically fashioned the Germanic and the classical legacies, was the most powerful agent in the making of Europe. Saint Augustine of Hippo, dogmatic thinker and Christian bishop, embodies the coming world-view.

Notes

1. E. F. Henderson, ed., *Select Historical Documents of the Middle Ages*, G. Bell & Sons, London, 1912, pp. 176–189.

2. R. C. Petry, ed., *A History of Christianity: Read-*

ings in the History of Early and Medieval Christianity, Prentice-Hall, Englewood Cliffs, N.J., 1962, p. 70.

3. H. Bettenson, ed., *Documents of the Christian Church,* Oxford University Press, Oxford, 1947, p. 113.

4. Colossians 3:9-11 (*Jerusalem Bible*).

5. Luke 6:20-32 (*Jerusalem Bible*).

6. L. Sherley-Price, trans., *Bede: A History of the English Church and People,* Penguin Books, Baltimore, 1962, pp. 86-87.

7. J. T. McNeill and H. Gamer, trans., *Medieval Handbooks of Penance,* Octagon Books, New York, 1965, pp. 184-197.

8. L. White, "The Life of the Silent Majority," in *Life and Thought in the Early Middle Ages,* ed. R. S. Hoyt, University of Minnesota Press, Minneapolis, 1967, p. 100.

9. I Peter 2:11-20 (*Jerusalem Bible*).

10. See John Boswell, *Christianity, Social Tolerance, and Homosexuality: Gay People in Western Europe from the Beginning of the Christian Era to the Fourteenth Century,* University of Chicago Press, Chicago, 1980, chs. 3 and 5, esp. pp. 87, 127-131.

11. F. J. Sheed, trans., *The Confessions of St. Augustine,* Sheed & Ward, New York, 1953, book I, pt. 3.

12. Ibid., book 10, pt. 27, p. 236.

13. Quoted by J. B. Bury, *History of the Later Roman Empire,* vol. I, Dover Publications, New York, 1958, pp. 233-234.

14. R. Atwater, trans., *Procopius: The Secret History,* University of Michigan Press, Ann Arbor, 1963, book 8.

15. Ibid., book 12.

16. Julia O'Faolain and Lauro Martines, eds., *Not in God's Image: Women in History from the Greeks to the Victorians,* Harper & Row, New York, 1973, pp. 108-115.

17. J. H. Elliott, *Imperial Spain, 1496-1716,* St. Martin's Press, London, 1966, p. 26.

18. F. B. Artz, *The Mind of the Middle Ages,* Alfred A. Knopf, New York, 1967, p. 178.

SUGGESTED READING

In addition to the studies listed in the Notes, this chapter leans on the following works, which students may consult for a broader treatment of the characteristics of the early Middle Ages.

P. Brown, *The World of Late Antiquity, A.D. 150-750* (1971), is a well-illustrated and lucidly written introduction to the entire period, with an emphasis on social and cultural change. B. Lyon, *The Origins of the Middle Ages: Pirenne's Challenge to Gibbon* (1972), is an excellent bibliographical essay with extensive references. For the Germans, see J. M. Wallace-Hadrill, *The Barbarian West, The Early Middle Ages A.D. 400-1000* (1962), and A. Lewis, *Emerging Europe, A.D. 400-1000* (1967), both of which describe German customs and society and the Germanic impact on the Roman Empire. F. Lot, *The End of the Ancient World* (1965), emphasizes the economic and social causes of Rome's decline.

There is a rich literature on the Christian church and its role in the transition between ancient and medieval civilizations. F. Oakley, *The Medieval Experience: Foundations of Western Cultural Singularity* (1974), stresses the Christian roots of Western cultural uniqueness. J. Danielou and H. Marrou, *The Christian Centuries,* vol. 1: *The First Six Hundred Years* (1964), is a clearly written and comprehensive history. G. Le Bras, "The Sociology of the Church in the Early Middle Ages," in S. L. Thrupp, ed., *Early Medieval Society* (1967), discusses the Christianization of the barbarians. Students interested in the synthesis of classical and Christian cultures should see C. N. Cochrane, *Christianity and Classical Culture* (1957), a deeply learned monograph. T. E. Mommsen, "Saint Augustine and the Christian Idea of Progress: The Background of the City of God," *Journal of the History of Ideas* 12 (1951):346-374, and G. B. Ladner, *The Idea of Reform* (1959), examine ideas of history and progress among the early fathers of the Christian church. The best biography of St. Augustine is

P. Brown, *Augustine of Hippo* (1967), which treats him as a symbol of change.

Monasticism has attracted the interest of Westerners from sixth-century Germans to twentieth-century hippies. L. Doyle, trans., *St. Benedict's Rule for Monasteries* (1957), presents the monastic guide in an accessible pocket-size form; a more scholarly edition is J. McCann, ed. and trans., *The Rule of Saint Benedict* (1952). Two beautifully illustrated syntheses by distinguished authorities are D. Knowles, *Christian Monasticism* (1969), which sketches monastic history through the middle of the twentieth century, and G. Zarnecki, *The Monastic Achievement* (1972), which focuses on the medieval centuries. L. J. Daly, *Benedictine Monasticism* (1965), stresses the day-to-day living of the monks, and H. B. Workman, *The Evolution of the Monastic Ideal* (1962), concentrates on monasticism as a spiritual and intellectual ideal.

For Byzantium and the Arabs, see J. Hussey, *The Byzantine World* (1961); A. A. Vasiliev, *History of the Byzantine Empire* (1968); S. Runciman, *Byzantine Civilization* (1956); B. Lewis, *The Arabs in History* (1966); T. Andrae, *Mohammed: The Man and His Faith* (1970); M. Rodinson, *Mohammed* (1974); and G. E. von Grunebaum, *Medieval Islam* (1961), which are all excellent treatments of the subject.

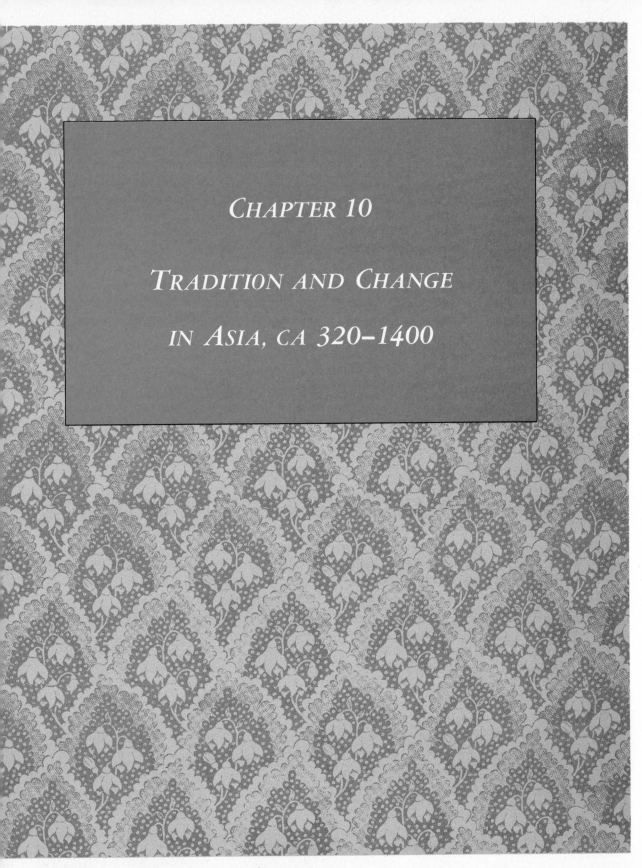

CHAPTER 10

TRADITION AND CHANGE

IN ASIA, CA 320–1400

BETWEEN ABOUT 320 AND 1400 the various societies of Asia continued to evolve their own distinct social, political, and religious institutions. These same years saw momentous changes sweep across Asia. The tide of change surged back and forth between East and West. In the first half of the period Arab conquerors and their new Muslim faith reached the Indian subcontinent and Afghanistan. In Central Asia they met the Turks moving westward from the borders of China. The result of this contact was wholesale conversion of the Turks to Islam. Muslim Turks then spread their new religion to northern India, which they conquered. Others continued westward, settling in Anatolia and sinking the ethnic and cultural roots of modern Turkey. Meanwhile, Japan emerged into the light of history. Although affected by Chinese culture, philosophy, and religion, the Japanese adapted these influences to their way of life.

In the second half of the period the Mongols swept from their homeland north of China westward as far as the plains of Hungary and eastward all the way to the Pacific Ocean. Their catastrophic intrusion into the Islamic world of the Middle East was marked by their destruction of Baghdad. The Mongols conquered China and unsuccessfully hurled two vast fleets at Japan. At the very end of the period, the travels of the Venetian merchant Marco Polo to Peking gave promise of a new era when the peoples of Europe and Asia would meet face to face.

This chapter will explore three main questions. What effect did these enormous movements of peoples have on the traditional societies of Asia? How were new religious and cultural ideas received by the long-established cultures of the East? And what political and economic effects did these events have on newcomer and native alike?

INDIA, FROM TRIUMPH TO INVASION (CA 320–1400)

Under the Gupta kings, India enjoyed one of the most magnificent cultural flowerings in its long history. By about 800 the caste system had fully evolved, dividing Indian society into thousands of self-contained subcastes. The incursion of the Muslim Turks — the second permanent foreign influence on India — introduced a new religion and spelled the decline of Buddhism in India. Ultimately the presence of Islam in the subcontinent would lead to the creation of the modern states of Pakistan and Bangladesh.

THE GUPTA EMPIRE (CA 320–480)

For years after the fall of Mauryan power India suffered fragmentation and foreign domination, but even political turmoil did not interrupt the evolution of Indian culture. Not until about 320 did another line of Indian kings, the Guptas, extend their authority over much of the subcontinent. Founded by Chandragupta — unrelated to the founder of the Mauryan Empire by the same name — the Guptas' original home was in the area of modern Bihar in the Ganges valley. Although the Guptas failed to restore Ashoka's empire, they united northern India under their rule and received tribute from states in Nepal and the Indus valley. They also gave large parts of India a long period of peace and political unity.

The real creator of the Gupta Empire was Chandragupta's son Samudragupta (ca 335–375), who defeated many of the rulers of southern India and then restored them to their thrones as his subjects. With frontier states he made alliances and extended his pro-

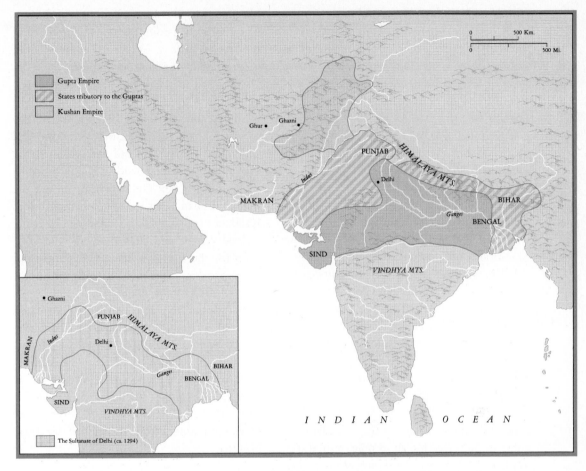

MAP 10.1 POLITICAL MAP OF INDIA, CA
400–CA 1294 *This map and its insert show the political face of India from the time of the imperial
Guptas to the arrival of Muslim invaders. It also demonstrates the importance of the Indus and Ganges
river valleys, perhaps the most coveted area in India.*

tection. By means of military conquest and
political shrewdness, Samudragupta brought
much of India from the Himalayas in the
north to the Vindhya Mountains in the south
under his government (see Map 10.1).

Once firmly in power, Samudragupta preferred leniency and diplomacy to force of
arms. Like Ashoka, he adhered to the ideal of

a just king who ruled according to *dharma*.
Following Ashoka's example, he erected inscriptions proclaiming the glories of his reign.
In one of his most important pronouncements, inscribed on a stone pillar erected by
Ashoka some six hundred years earlier, Samudragupta extolled his own fame, power, and
personal qualities:

His far-reaching fame, deep-rooted in peace, ema-
nated from the restoration of the sovereignty of
many fallen royal families. . . . He, who had no
equal in power in the world, eclipsed the fame of
the other kings by the radiance of his versatile vir-
tues, adorned by innumerable good actions. He,
who was enigmatic, was the real force that gener-
ated good and destroyed the evil. Having a com-
passionate heart, he could easily be won over by
faithfulness, loyalty, and homage.[1]

Samudragupta had reason to boast of his accomplishments. By putting an end to weakness and fragmentation, he laid the foundations of India's golden age.

Samudragupta's many achievements were matched by those of his son Chandragupta II (ca 375-415), under whom the glory of the Guptas reached its height. Perhaps Chandragupta's most significant exploit was the overthrow of the Shakas in western India. As a result of that victory, the busy maritime trade conducted by the rich seaports of western India with the Middle East and China came under the protection of the Guptas. Chandragupta II put the Indian people into direct touch with the wider world once again, and as in the past this contact involved ideas as well as goods.

The great crisis of the Gupta Empire was the invasion of the Huns, the nomads whose migration from Central Asia shook the known world. As seen in Chapter 9, the Huns hammered at the Roman Empire. By at least 450 a group of them known as the White Huns thundered into India. Mustering his full might, Skandagupta (ca 455-467) threw back the invaders; only a few Huns settled in northern India, where they were in time absorbed by the native population. Although the Huns failed to uproot the Gupta Empire, they dealt the dynasty a fatal blow. By 500 the glory of the Gupta kings was past. Later kings

like the great Harsha (ca 606-647) made valiant efforts to reunite the Gupta Empire, but the country once again reverted to a pattern of local kingdoms in constant conflict.

Although they failed to unite India permanently, the Guptas set the stage for one of the most splendid epochs in Indian cultural history. Sanskrit masterpieces were preserved, and traditional epic poems and verses on mythological themes were reworked and polished to a higher sheen. The Gupta period also saw the rise of Indian drama; India's greatest poet Kalidasa (ca 380-450), like Shakespeare, melded poetry and drama. Poets composed epics for the courts of the Gupta kings, and other writers experimented with prose romances and popular tales.

In science too the Gupta period could boast of some impressive intellectual achievements. Science never appealed to the Indians as much as religion, but Indian mathematicians arrived at the concept of zero, which is necessary for higher mathematics. Other scientific thinkers wrestled with the concept of gravitation long before the day of Sir Isaac Newton.

The greatness of the Guptas is neither limited to their political achievements nor diminished by their ultimate failure. They saved India for a long period from political fragmentation, foreign domination, and confusion. The peace they established released cultural and intellectual energies that shaped one of the sunniest epochs in India's long history.

DAILY LIFE IN INDIA

The first reliable and abundant information about the daily life of the Indian people dates from the period of the Gupta Empire and its long aftermath. One of the most instructive and, to modern minds, amazing characteristics of Indian society is its remarkable stability

VILLAGE SCENE *This relief portrays the community life of the Indian village. Seated at the door of their houses, couples converse and watch the comings and goings of their neighbors. In the background rich* *and abundant foliage suggests fertility, and the whole air of the relief is one of quiet prosperity. (André Martin, Paris)*

and veneration for its age-old customs and traditions. Indians did not oppose progress and innovation, but they preferred the old familiar ways. Since Indian society changed slowly and gradually, it is possible to take a good long look at daily life and social customs in the millennium between the fourth and the fourteenth centuries.

Although Indian agriculture ranged from subsistence farming to the working of huge estates, agricultural life ordinarily meant village life. The average farmer worked a small plot of land outside the village, aided by the efforts of the extended family (page 150). The entire family pooled their resources – human, animal, and material – under the direction of the head of the family. Shared work, shared sacrifice, and joint confrontation of hazards strengthened family ties. The Indian farming family usually lived close to the bone, bad weather and heavy taxes frequently condemning them to a lean year of poverty and discomfort.

To all Indian farmers, rich and poor, water supply was crucial. India's great scourge is its merciless droughts, which cause plants to wither, the earth to crack, and famine to stalk the countryside. Indian farmers quickly learned to drill deep into the ground to tap permanent sources of water. They also irrigated their fields by diverting rivers and digging reservoirs and canals. As in Hammurabi's Mesopotamia, maintenance of waterworks demanded constant effort, and disputes over water rights often led to local quarrels.

The agricultural year began with spring ploughing. The ancient plough, drawn by two oxen, wearing yokes and collars, had an iron-tipped share and a handle with which the farmer guided it. Similar ploughs are still used in parts of India. Once ploughed and sown, the land yielded a rich variety of crops. Rice, the most important and popular grain, was sown at the beginning of the long rainy season. Beans, lentils, and peas were the farmer's friends, since they grew during the cold season and were harvested in the spring when fresh food was scarce. Cereal crops like wheat, barley, and millet provided carbohydrates and other nutrients, and large estates grew sugar cane. Some families cultivated vegetables, spices, and flowers in their gardens. Village orchards kept people supplied with fruit, and the inhabitants of well-situated villages could eat their fill of fresh and dried fruit, and sell the surplus at a nearby town.

Indian farmers raised and bred livestock, the most highly valued of which were cattle. Cattle were used for ploughing and esteemed for their milk. Their hides and horns were precious raw materials, as were the fleeces of rams and sheep. All the animals of the community were in the hands of the village cowherd or shepherd, who led them to and from pasture and protected them from wild animals and thieves.

Farmers fortunate enough to raise surpluses found ready markets in towns and cities. There they came into contact with merchants and traders, some of whom dealt in local commodities and others in East-West trade. Unlike their ancient Jewish and Chinese counterparts, Indian merchants enjoyed a respectable place in society. Given India's central geographical position between China and the West, there were huge profits to be made in foreign commerce. Daring Indian sailors founded new trading centers along the coasts of southeast Asia, and in the process spread Indian culture. Other Indian merchants specialized in the caravan trade that continued to link China, Iran, India, and the West. These hardy merchants conducted cargoes from Indian seaports northward to the overland routes across Central Asia.

Local craftsmen and tradesmen lived and worked in specific parts of the town or village. Their shops were open to the street, with the family living on the floor above. The busiest tradesmen dealt in milk and cheese, oil, spices, and perfumes. Equally prominent but disreputable were tavern keepers. Like the taverns of ancient Mesopotamia, Indian taverns were haunts of criminals and con men, and in the worst of them fighting was as common as drinking. In addition to these tradesmen and merchants a host of peddlers shuffled through towns and villages selling everything from bath salts to fresh-cut flowers.

Although leather-workers were economically important, their calling was considered beneath the dignity of anyone but outcastes; Indian religious and social customs condemned those who made a living handling the skins of dead animals. Masons, carpenters, and brickmakers were more highly respected. As in all agricultural societies, blacksmiths were essential. Pottery was used in all households, but Indian potters, unlike their counterparts in the ancient Near East and the Greco-Roman world, neither baked their wares in kilns nor decorated them. Indian potters restricted themselves to the functional. The economic life of the village, then, consisted of a harmonious balance of agriculture and small business.

What of the village itself – its people and its daily sights? Encircled by walls, the typical village was divided into quarters by two main streets that intersected at the center of the village. The streets were unpaved, and the rainy season turned them into a muddy soup. Cattle and sheep roamed as freely as people.

The villagers shared their simple houses with such household pets as cats, parrots, and geese. Half-wild mongooses served as effective protection against snakes. The pond outside the village that served as its main source of water also bred fish, birds, and mosquitoes. Women drawing water frequently encountered water buffaloes wallowing in the shallows. When the farmers returned from the fields in the evening, the village gates were closed until morning.

Towns and cities were also typically laid out in a square or rectangular pattern, always situated near a lake or river. They too were fortified by walls and towers and entered through gates. A city was usually surrounded by a moat, into which the gutters flowed; the moat often served as a source of drinking water. The streets of cities and towns were paved and flanked by gutters. Every sizable city or town had a marketplace where villagers could sell their surpluses to townspeople and peddlers hawked their wares. Nearby were temples, houses, and the usual shops and craftsmen's stalls. Part of every major city was devoted to parks, fountains, and gardens. The populations of particularly prosperous cities often spilled over outside the walls into crowded and squalid slums. Here worked some of the most despised elements of the population: butchers, public executioners, and undertakers. Sometimes the slums evolved into cities that ringed the original city.

The period following the fall of the Guptas saw the slow proliferation and hardening of the caste system. Early Indian society was divided into four major groups, the brahmins, warriors, peasants, and serfs (page 150). Further subdivisions arose, reflecting differences in trade or profession, tribal or racial affiliation, religious beliefs, and place of residence. By about 800 these distinctions had solidified

into an approximation of the caste system as it is known today. Eventually Indian society consisted of more than three thousand castes. The caste sustained its members, giving them a sense of belonging and helping to define their relations to members of other castes. Yet the caste system further fragmented society. Each caste had its own governing body, which enforced the rules of the caste among its members. Those incapable of living up to the rules were expelled, becoming outcastes. These unfortunates lived despised and miserable lives, performing tasks that others considered unclean or lowly.

For all members of Indian society, regardless of caste, marriage and the family were the very focus of life. Once again, far more is known about the upper levels of society than the lower. As in earlier eras, the Indian family of this period was an extended family, in which grandparents, uncles and aunts, cousins, nieces and nephews lived together in the same house or compound. The joint family was under the authority of the eldest male, who might take several wives. The family affirmed its solidarity by the religious ritual of honoring its dead ancestors, which linked the living and the dead.

Special attention was devoted to the raising of sons, but all children were pampered. The great poet Kalidasa depicts children as the greatest joy of their father's life:

With their teeth half-shown in causeless laughter,
and their efforts at talking so sweetly uncertain,
when children ask to sit on his lap
a man is blessed, even by the dirt on their bodies.[2]

In poor households children worked as soon as they were able. In wealthier homes children faced the age-old irritations of reading, writing, and arithmetic. Less attention was paid to daughters, though in more prosperous families they were usually literate.

The three upper castes welcomed boys fully into the life of the caste and society with a religious initiation symbolizing a second birth. Ideally, a boy then entered into a period of asceticism and religious training, during which he mastered at least part of one *Veda*. Such education was at the hands of *gurus*, brahmin teachers with whom the boys boarded. In reality, relatively few went through this expensive education.

Having completed their education, young men were ready to lead adult lives, the first and foremost step in which was marriage. Child-marriage, unknown in the ancient and medieval periods, later became customary. Indians considered child-marriage desirable, in part, because of their attitudes toward women. Girls were thought to be unusually fascinated by sex. Lawgivers feared that, left to their own whims, young girls would take lovers as soon as they reached puberty and become pregnant before they were married. Girls who had lost their virginity could seldom hope to find good husbands, and would become financial burdens and social disgraces to their families. Indian law even warned fathers that they sinned grievously unless they betrothed a daughter before her first menstrual period. Indian custom also held that in the best marriages the husband was at least three times as old as his wife. Thus daughters were customarily betrothed before they reached puberty, often to men they had never seen. The wedding and consummation of the marriage did not take place, however, until after the girl had reached puberty and could start a family.

After an elaborate wedding ceremony, a newly married couple set up quarters in the house or compound of the bridegroom's father. In contrast to ancient Jewish practice, newlyweds were not expected to consummate their marriage on the first night. Indian custom delicately acknowledged that two strangers, though married, might need some time to adjust to their new mode of life. Hindu ritual advised couples to forgo sex for the first three nights so that they could become acquainted.

An Indian wife had two main duties – to manage the house and to produce children, preferably sons. Her husband was her master, to whom she owed obedience; Indian women spent their entire lives, from childhood to decrepitude, under the authority of men. Indian law was blunt:

A woman is not independent, the males are her masters. . . . Their fathers protect them in childhood, their husbands protect them in youth, and their sons protect them in age; a woman is never fit for independence.[3]

Denied a significant role in life outside the home, wives made the household their domain. All domestic affairs were under their control. As a rule, women rarely left the house, and then only with a chaperone. They did accompany their husbands to weddings, great festivals, and quiet outings with the family. Among one stratum of high-caste Hindus, the kshatriyas, wives' bonds with their husbands were so strong that a widow was expected to perform the act of *sati*, throwing herself on his funeral pyre. During the medieval period it was strongly felt that a true and faithful wife – a sati, for whom the practice was named – should have no life apart from her husband's.

Within the home, the position of a wife often depended chiefly on her own intelligence and strength of character. In the best of cases a wife was considered a part of her husband, his friend and comforter as well as his wife. Wives were traditionally supposed to be humble, cheerful, and diligent even toward worthless husbands. In reality, some women took matters into their own hands. Far from being docile, they ruled the roost. An Indian verse paints a vivid picture of what a henpecked husband could expect:

But when she has him in her clutches
it's all housework and errands!
'Fetch a knife to cut this gourd!'
  'Get me some fresh fruit!'

'We want wood to boil the greens,
  and for a fire in the evening!'
'Now paint my feet!'
  'Come and massage my back!'

So ... resist the wiles of women,
  avoid their friendship and company
The little pleasure you get from them
will only lead you into trouble![4]

Most women, however, led lives frankly and unashamedly subservient to their husbands. Despite the severe limitations of her society, the typical wife lived her days honored, cherished, and loved by her husband and family.

In Indian life the most eagerly desired event was the birth of children. Marriage had no other purpose. Before consummating their marriage, the newlyweds repeated the traditional prayers that the wife would immediately become pregnant. While pregnant, the wife was treated like a queen, nearly suffocated with affection and attention, and rigorously circumscribed by religious ritual. Members of the family carefully watched her diet and exercise, and women of her caste prayed that she would bear sons. Labor and birth were occasions of religious ritual. While the women of the household prepared for the birth, the husband performed rituals intended to guarantee an easy delivery and a healthy child. After the child's birth, the parents performed rituals intended to bring the baby happiness, prosperity, and desirable intellectual, physical, and moral qualities. Infants

were pampered until they reached the age of schooling and preparation for the adult world.

INDIA AND SOUTHEAST ASIA

During this period, and particularly between about 650 and 1250, Indian merchants and missionaries disseminated Indian culture throughout Southeast Asia. Its impact was so pervasive that scholars generally refer to this phenomenon as "the Indianization of Southeast Asia." In this region Indians encountered both indigenous peoples and newcomers moving southward from the frontiers of China. Their relations with these peoples varied greatly: contact with the vigorous tribes moving into the southern areas of the mainland was generally peaceful; but with the native states in the Malay Peninsula and the islands of the Indian Ocean, commercial rivalry sometimes led to active warfare. Although many of the events of these years are imperfectly known, a fairly clear picture has emerged of the Indianization of the Vietnamese, Thais, Burmans, and Cambodians and the native peoples of the islands (see Map 10.2).

On the mainland three major groups of newcomers pushed southward toward the Indian Ocean from the southern borders of China. Their movements entailed prolonged fighting, as each people strove to win a homeland. As in other such extensive migrations, the newcomers fought each other as often as the native populations. The Vietnamese established themselves on the eastern coast of the mainland. In 939 they became independent of China and extended their power southward along the coast of present-day Vietnam. Of all these peoples, they were the least influenced by Indian culture. The Thais lived to their west in what is today southwestern China and northern Burma. In the eighth century the Thai tribes united in a confederacy, and even

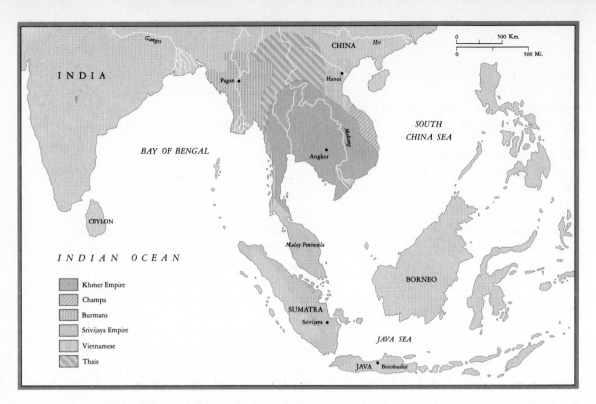

MAP 10.2 THE STATES OF SOUTHEAST ASIA *This map illustrates the greatest extent of several major Southeast Asian states between ca 650 and ca 1250. The boundaries are somewhat approximate, for states gained and lost territory several times during this long period.*

expanded northward against T'ang China; like the Chinese themselves, however, the Thai confederacy fell to the Mongols in 1253. Still farther west another tribal people, the Burmans, migrated in the eighth century to the area of modern Burma. They too established a state, Pagan, and came into direct contact with India and Ceylon.

The most important mainland state was the Khmer Empire of Cambodia, which controlled the heart of the region. The Khmers were indigenous to the area, and around 400 they had created an independent state. Their empire, founded in 802, eventually extended its southern borders to the sea and the northeastern Malay Peninsula. Generally successful in a long series of wars with the Vietnamese,

Khmer power reached its peak and then declined in ca 1218.

Far different from these land-based states was the maritime empire of Srivijaya, which originated as a city-state on the island of Sumatra. Like the Khmers, the people of Srivijaya were indigenous. Their wealth was based on sea-borne trade and tolls on ships passing through their waters. To protect their commercial interests they created a navy strong enough to rule the waters around Sumatra, Java, and Borneo. At its height the Srivijaya Empire controlled the coast of Sumatra, the southern half of the Malay Peninsula, and the western tip of Java. Though long predominant in the area, Srivijaya suffered a stunning blow in 1025: a commercial rival in southern

India launched a large naval raid that succeeded in capturing the king and capital of Srivijaya. Unable to hold their gains, the Indians retreated, but the Srivijaya Empire never recovered its former vigor. By the mid-thirteenth century it was further weakened by the arrival of Chinese traders, and eventually fell to local rivals.

Although the political histories of all these peoples varied, their responses to Indian culture were generally similar. The coastal states were the first to adopt Indian ways, which originally appealed most keenly to the elites of Southeast Asia. Indeed, the very concept of kingship reached them from India. Local rulers and their elites, like good Indian kings, began to observe *dharma*, the sacred law, and adopted the Sanskrit language and script. Indian mythology took hold, as did Indian architecture and sculpture. Some of the world's greatest edifices were erected in central Java and Cambodia, inspired by Indian building principles, techniques, and cultural ideals. Kings and their courts, the first to embrace Indian culture, consciously spread it to their subjects.

Indian religion was also instrumental in this process. Hinduism proved popular, but Buddhism took Southeast Asia by storm. Buddhism emphasized the value of popular education, and its temples, monasteries, and missionaries helped bring education to the common people. Especially influential was the Buddhist concept of the *bodhisattva*, a buddha-in-becoming. Inspired by this ideal, many kings and local rulers strove to give their subjects good and humane government. Buddhist missionaries from India played a prominent role in these developments. Local converts continued the process by making pilgrimages to India and Ceylon to worship and observe Indian life for themselves.

By the twelfth century Indian culture, secular and religious, had found a permanent new home in Southeast Asia. Although Chinese influence flourished more strongly among the Vietnamese, and Islam would later rival Buddhism, Indian culture persisted, especially in the southern part of the region. Even today the West pays tribute to this phenomenon by calling the Southeast Asian islands "Indonesia," meaning the islands of India. Seldom has the world seen such a protracted and pervasive cultural diffusion. It stands as a monument to the vitality and magnetism of Indian civilization.

INDIA UNDER SIEGE

Between roughly 650 and 1400 India experienced turmoil and invasion, as wave after wave of foreign armies moved into the subcontinent. Arabs, Turks, and Mongols all swept into weak and disorganized India. Particularly for the six centuries from 636 to 1296, invaders beat against India and its neighbors. This complex and imperfectly understood phenomenon had four distinct phases. The Muslim Arabs' attack on the Sind (636–713) was followed by the battle for Afghanistan (643–870). Muslims next pushed into the Punjab (870–1030), and finally conquered the valley of the Ganges (1175–1206). Between onslaughts, conflict persisted between newcomer and native.

Arabs under the leadership of Muhammad ibn Qasim reached the coast of modern West Pakistan in 636, and pushed on into Sind and the Indus valley. But the Islamic conquest of northern India came at the hands of Turkish converts to Islam, not these first Arab invaders. While huge numbers of Turks advanced on the Byzantine Empire and won control of Asia Minor, others remained in the East. One group established a small kingdom in northeastern Iran and Afghanistan, with

ANGKOR WAT *The great artistic achievement of the Khymers was the planning and building of Angkor Wat, an enormous and lavishly decorated temple. The temple also reflects Indian influence, for the god chiefly honored here is Vishnu. (Art Resource)*

their capital at Ghazni. In 986 Sabuktigin, a Turkish chieftain and devout Muslim, launched an initial raid into the Punjab. Once again, India suffered its age-old fate: invasion by a strong and confident power through the northwestern corridor. Sabuktigin's son Mahmud stepped up the frequency and intensity of the raids until he had won the Punjab. Then, like other invaders before him, he began pushing toward the Ganges. Mahmud systematically looted secular palaces and Hindu shrines, and destroyed Indian statues as infidel idols. Even the Arab conquerors of Sind fell to him. The Indus valley, the Punjab, and the rest of northwestern India were in the grip of the invader.

Mahmud's death gave India roughly a century and a half of fitful peace, marred by local conflicts. Then a new line of Turkish rulers that had arisen in Afghanistan, with their capital at Ghur southwest of modern Kabul, renewed Muslim attacks on India. Muhammed of Ghur planned to annex the land he attacked, rather than merely plundering it. After conquering Mahmud's Indian holdings, he struck eastward toward the Ganges in 1192. Muhammed's generals captured Delhi, and by the end of the twelfth century had extended their control nearly throughout northern India. Like Mahmud, Muhammed and his generals considered Hindu and Buddhist religious statues nothing more than idols; Muslim troops destroyed them in vast numbers. Buddhist centers of worship and learning suffered grievously. The great Buddhist university at Nalanda in Bihar was utterly destroyed by a Turkish raiding party in 1193. Most Buddhists took refuge from this dual military and religious assault in Tibet and places farther east. Buddhism, which had thrived so long in peaceful and friendly competition with Hinduism, was pushed out of its native soil by the invaders.

When Muhammed fell to an assassin in 1206, one of his generals, the ex-slave Qutb-ud-din, seized the reins of power and made his capital at Delhi. Qutb-ud-din established the Sultanate of Delhi, a Muslim kingdom that ruled northern India from the Indus to Bengal from 1206 to 1526. As early as 1327 the Muslim sultans of Delhi had brought most of India under their control. The Muslims, like the Aryans, were a conquering minority. To prevent assimilation by the far more numerous Indians, they recruited Turks and Iranians from outside India; they also provided a haven for elite Muslim refugees fleeing the widespread Mongol devastation of Iran and the Middle East. Both groups of newcomers reinforced the Islamic impact on India. Under the Sultanate of Delhi, Iranian influences deeply affected Hindu art and architecture. Iranians introduced the minaret – an essential architectural feature of the mosque – as well as the arch and the dome. So great was the impact of Iranian Muslims that Urdu, the official language of modern Pakistan, evolved as a mixture of Persian with Arabic and Hindi.

The most lasting impact of the invader was religious. Islam replaced Hinduism and Buddhism in the Indus Valley (modern Pakistan) and in Bengal at the mouth of the Ganges (modern Bangladesh). Elsewhere in India, where Muslim influence was far less powerful, Hinduism resisted the newcomers and their religion. Most Indians looked on the successful invaders simply as a new ruling caste, capable of governing and taxing them but otherwise peripheral to their lives. Hinduism was bolstered in this attitude by the caste system: the myriad castes largely governed themselves, isolating the newcomers. Hinduism also enjoyed profound devotion on the part of the Indian people. The years of war and invasion had not hindered the development of a pious, devotional Hinduism called *bhakti*. Bhakti

INDIA, CA 350–CA 1400

ca 320–480	Gupta Empire
ca 380–450	Kalidasa, India's greatest poet
636–1206	Muslim invasions of India
1192	Destruction of Buddhism in India
1290–1320	Delhi Sultanate
1398	Timur conquers the Punjab and Delhi

emphasized personal reverence for and worship of a Hindu deity such as Krishna, Shiva, or Rama. Bhakti nourished impassioned love of the Hindu gods among ordinary folk. In some instances the bhakti tradition sought synthesis with Islam; in others, converts to Islam retained much of Hindu tradition. In all cases there was a certain amount of mutual borrowing. In general, Hinduism's beliefs and social organization had a strong hold over the people of India; roughly 75 percent remained Hindu.

Muslim control over most of the subcontinent was short-lived. By 1336 a native Indian kingdom in the south effectively resisted the Muslims. In the north, the Muslims retained political dominance longer, but still suffered the traditional fate of foreign conquerors of the north. In 1398 the Turkish chieftain Timur, lord of central Asia, Iran, and Mesopotamia, pushed into the Punjab and captured Delhi. To Timur, India was merely a source of loot. When his troops were sated with destruction and slaughter, Timur retired from India, leaving the Muslims and Hindus to pick up the pieces.

By about 1400 India was again as politically divided as before the Gupta Empire. Yet the events of the preceding millennium had had more than political and military significance. The march of armies had brought Islam into India and driven Buddhism out. Meanwhile Hinduism had flourished. These developments were to be critically important for the future of the entire region, for in them lie the origins of modern India, Pakistan, and Bangladesh.

CHINA'S GOLDEN AGE
(580–CA 1400)

The years between the fall of the Han Dynasty in the third century and the rise of the Ming in the fourteenth brought some of China's brightest days and some of its darkest. During this period the Chinese absorbed foreign influences, notably Buddhism, that fundamentally shaped their society. Chinese cultural traditions, especially Confucianism, drew new strength and vitality from abroad. This was a golden era of enormous intellectual and artistic creativity in Chinese history.

Sui, T'ang, and Sung emperors and statesmen reunited the empire, repaired the foundations of national strength, and once again made China one of the world's unrivalled states. Even later political disruption, particularly the invasion of the Mongols, could not undo the achievements of those who shaped the history of these years. Nor were invasions and internal chaos enough to break the spirit of the Chinese people. The Mongols were the first foreigners ever to rule all of China, but their domination lasted only ninety-seven years, until the Ming emperors once again united the land under a native dynasty.

BUDDHISM REACHES CHINA

Between the fall of the Han Dynasty in 220 and the rise of the Sui in 589, Buddhism reached China from the west. Merchants and travelers from India and the Kushan Empire spread word of the new religion in the north, while Indian sailors were introducing it into China's southern ports. Buddhism reached China at a time when many thinkers were doubting the value of traditional Confucian thought and many ordinary people wanted a message of hope. Buddhism initially won a place for itself in China because it offered a refreshing and novel solution to social disruption and political chaos (pages 180–182). Buddhism was ultimately successful in China because it had powerful appeal for many different segments of society. To Chinese scholars, the Buddhist concepts of transmigration of souls, *karma,* and *nirvana* posed a stimulating intellectual challenge. For rulers the Buddhist church was a source of magical power and a political tool: since it was neither barbarian nor Chinese, this foreign faith could embrace both groups equally. To the middle and lower classes, Buddhism's egalitarianism – the teaching that enlightenment was available to all – came as a breath of fresh air. Buddhism spoke to all, regardless of their so-cial class. Thus the lower orders of society believed that they had as much chance as the elites to live according to Buddha's precepts. For them especially, simple faith and devotion alone could win salvation. For many, regardless of social status, Buddhism's promise of eternal bliss as the reward for a just and upright life was deeply comforting. In a rough and tumultuous age, moreover, Buddhism's emphasis on kindness and the value of human life offered hope of a better future on earth. Similarly, Buddhist teachings on the value of charity and good works had a profound impact on Chinese morality. Besides holding out a path to salvation in the next world, Buddhism offered a practical program for improving life in this world.

If Buddhism changed Chinese life, China likewise changed Buddhism. Mahayana Buddhism, the more flexible and widespread of Buddhism's two schools (page 182), gave rise to several new sects responsive to specific Chinese needs. The T'ien-t'ai sect, which later gave rise to the Tendai in Japan, was favored by Chinese scholars, who attempted to resolve the numerous intellectual problems in Buddhism and to organize its doctrines in keeping with traditional Chinese thought. The most popular and numerically largest new growth was the Pure Land sect, which retained many of the most appealing aspects of Mahayana Buddhism. It too would later have a vast impact on Japanese society. Like its Indian counterpart, this sect was very lenient. Instead of following Buddha's Eightfold Path, people had only to declare their sincere faith in Buddha to reach paradise, the "pure land." Many simple and uneducated people found in the Pure Land sect a comforting route to joy scarcely attainable on earth. Meanwhile the True Word sect, which won more popularity in Japan than in China, promised its adherents immortality through magic, rituals, and

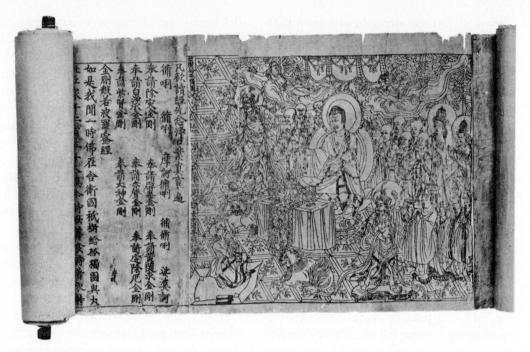

BUDDHISM REACHES CHINA This scene brilliantly illustrates the spread of Buddhism from India to China. The writing at the left, printed in Chinese characters, is a translation of a Buddhist text origi- *nally written in Sansrit. This scene of Buddha addressing a follower is also the earliest dated example of blockprinting. (The British Library)*

chants. Lastly, the Ch'an sect, the forerunner of Zen in Japan, combined elements of Buddhism and Taoism. Like Taoism itself, Ch'an dreamed of a return to nature and simplicity, and preached that individuals were responsible for their own ultimate enlightenment. In this respect Ch'an was quite similar to the teaching of Buddha himself that each person must tread the path of enlightenment alone. Ch'an emphasized meditation and the individual search for enlightenment instead of the learning and scholarship of the T'ien-t'ai sect. One of the prime reasons for Buddhism's success in China was its extraordinary ability to accommodate itself to local thought, beliefs, and conditions. Rarely has a religion fared so well in a foreign land.

Buddhist monks from abroad introduced

monasticism to China, and the resulting monasteries became more than merely centers for religious practice and study. Like their counterparts in medieval Europe, monasteries played an active role in social, economic, and political life. The missionary monks traveled the trade routes with Buddhist merchants, who gave the newly formed monasteries a secular function: increasingly, they entrusted their money and wares to the monasteries for safekeeping, in effect transforming the monasteries into banks and warehouses. Buddhist merchants often endowed monks with money or land to support temples and monasteries. The monks, who thus became powerful landlords, hired peasants to work the monastic and temple lands, and the tenants in turn became ready converts to Buddhism. Formidable in wealth and numbers, monasteries became influential participants in politics, rivalling the traditional Chinese landlords in power. The monasteries' prosperity and political power further protected converts from local Chinese lords and reinforced the spread of Buddhism.

Buddhism also had a profound impact on the artistic life of China. Buddhist art, like its religious message, first reached China along the Silk Road. At Tun-huang in northwest China, thousands of artists worked for centuries to transform a mile-long stretch of hillside into a monumental shrine. It was at Tun-huang that the Chinese first encountered the Greek-inspired Gandhara school of Indian sculpture (page 185), which led Chinese artists toward a new realism. The life of Buddha also offered Chinese painters and sculptors a wealth of new themes. From the fourth century on, Buddha and his life became inseparable from Chinese art.

Thus Buddhism's appeal to the Chinese was religious, social, and artistic. Its message struck a sympathetic chord among nobles and peasants alike. It endowed China with a new view of human dignity, the promise of personal salvation, and a compelling vision of peace.

THE T'ANG DYNASTY (618–907)

The T'ang emperors rose to greatness on the shoulders of their predecessors, the Sui Dynasty (580–618). The Sui resembled the Ch'in of the third century B.C. (pages 187–190) in that both were short-lived dynasties that restored political order to a storm-tossed land and set the stage for splendid successors. Sui land reforms helped to restore economic prosperity, and their waterworks strengthened ties between northern and southern China. Their crowning achievement was the Grand Canal,

connecting the western reaches of the Yellow River to the eastern waters of the Huai and Yangtze rivers (see Map 10.3). The canal facilitated the shipping of tax grain from the recently developed Yangtze delta to the centers of political and military power in north China. Henceforth the rice-growing Yangtze valley and southern China generally played an ever more influential role in economic and political life, strengthening China's internal cohesion.

Though successful as reformers, the Sui emperors fell prey to a grim combination of military defeat and massive peasant uprisings. From these unlikely conditions rose the T'ang Dynasty, probably the greatest dynasty in Chinese history. Its founder, who took the imperial name T'ai Tsung, was far more than a mere upstart who eliminated the last Sui emperor. In addition to being an able general and astute politician, T'ai Tsung was also an educated and far-sighted administrator who followed conscientiously the lessons of Chinese history. Having seen the results of oppression, T'ai Tsung avoided extravagance and continued Sui reforms.

T'ai Tsung tried first to alleviate the poverty of the peasants. Building on the Sui system, he ordered that land be divided among the peasants as equally as possible, and that imperial officials safeguard the peasants' holdings. A prosperous peasantry, in T'ai Tsung's view, would provide a secure and steady base of income for the empire. In practice, the attempt to equalize landholdings quickly broke down, and by 780 the law was revoked. Even so, T'ai Tsung's efforts were not entirely in vain: he had done enough to give agriculture a much-needed boost, and productivity increased in both grain and livestock. Not since the Han Dynasty had the peasants been so well off.

In the civil sphere, T'ang accomplishments

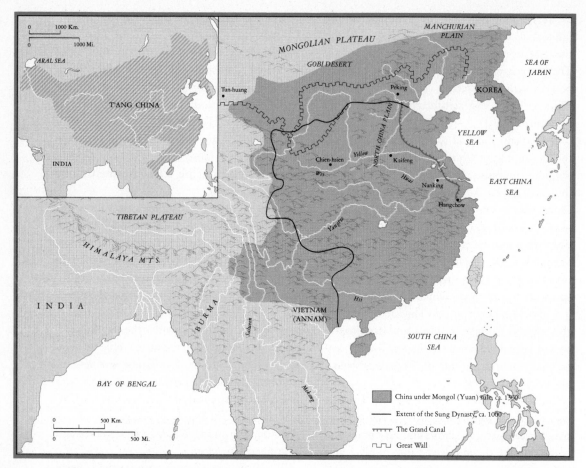

MAP 10.3 THE POLITICAL DIVISIONS OF CHINA FROM THE T'ANG TO YUAN DYNASTIES, 618–1368 This map and its insert illustrate how the T'ang Dynasty and its successors were able to sustain the expanded frontiers of the Han Dynasty, although their hold in the west was always somewhat tenuous.

far outstripped anything known in Europe until the growth of national states in the seventeenth century (Chapter 20). T'ang emperors subdivided the administration of the empire into departments, much like the numerous agencies of modern governments. T'ang departments oversaw military organization, maintenance and supply of the armies, foreign affairs, administration of justice, finance, building and transportation, education, and much else. During this period no other state on earth was as politically sophisticated as the T'ang empire.

A bureaucracy of this scope demanded huge numbers of educated and trained personnel; as in earlier eras of strong central government, the imperial administration offered a lucrative career to talented Chinese. T'ang emperors revived the Han method of hiring and promoting government officials on the basis of education, ability, and merit. This process reinforced Confucian values, ethics, and emphasis on scholarship. Candidates for official positions were expected to learn the Confucian classics, to master the rules of poetry, and to discuss practical administrative and political matters. Universities were founded to train able and dedicated young men. Graduates passed a demanding battery of oral and written examinations to prove their ability. Training was hard and long; though they did not endure the physical discipline of Mesopotamian scribes, they sacrificed much to achieve success.

Students who passed the official examinations had unlimited futures ahead of them. Talent, education, and a bureaucracy theoretically based on merit promised them high office, wealth, and prestige. Although the rich and powerful often sidestepped the system of formal examinations, the T'ang created an effective civil service long before anything comparable developed in Europe. The T'ang emperors deserve full credit for the mandarin system of professional public service. Despite weaknesses and loopholes for the influential, the effectiveness of the T'ang administrative system was such that it lasted even into the twentieth century.

Mandarin scholar-officials also played an important cultural role. Since much of the official's training involved the study of literature, history, and politics, China's literary heritage became integral to contemporary life. Because nearly any literate man in the empire could take the examinations, centers for study sprouted throughout China. Knowledge of the classics spread throughout the empire, encouraging cultural unity. The weakness of the mandarin system was its narrow outlook and inflexibility, which stifled originality and independence of thought. Nonetheless, the mandarin system was an institution in which people from every part of China could meet on a common ground.

In foreign affairs the T'ang turned their attention first to the Turks, who had spread their power from the northern borders of China to the Byzantine Empire in Asia Minor. By T'ai Tsung's death in 649 Chinese armies had conquered all of Turkestan in the west. The T'ang also turned to Korea, but they had much less success there than the Han had had seven centuries earlier. Chinese influence in Tibet came somewhat more peacefully, despite some Sino-Tibetan rivalries and wars. For years the Tibetans had lived a partly nomadic and partly agricultural life on China's western border. Then in the early seventh century one of their chieftains unified the Tibetan tribes and sought a marriage alliance with T'ai Tsung. The emperor sent his daughter to Tibet with musicians, craftsmen, and technicians to introduce new tools and techniques, along with books on Chinese agricultural methods. The Tibetans modelled their culture partially on the T'ang; the Koreans and Japanese adopted Chinese culture more enthusiastically. China's script and literature, Buddhism, crafts, political ideas and techniques spread widely, making Chinese culture dominant throughout East Asia.

THE SUNG DYNASTY (960-1279)

In the middle of the eighth century T'ang foreign policy collapsed in rout and rebellion. The defeat of Chinese armies in central Asia and on the southwestern border undercut the emperor's authority. The sources of this crisis varied from the changing demands of frontier defense to stupid imperial decisions. At last in 755 a powerful general, An Lu-shan, revolted in response to imperial maltreatment. An Lu-shan was defeated, but other generals followed his example. The T'ang Dynasty ended in a devastating conflagration of military rebellions, peasant uprisings, and barbarian invasions. The period from 907 to 960, known as the Era of the Five Dynasties, resembled the age of the "barracks emperors" of the Roman Empire (page 262). In northern China rival generals struggled against barbarians and one another to establish permanent dynasties. Southern China fragmented into ten independent states. Weak and distracted, China presented an easy target to the barbarians, and one group of nomads known as the Khitan captured Peking and most of northeastern China and Manchuria.

The founder of the Sung Dynasty, the northern general Chao K'uang-yin, made his bid for empire in 960. Unsuccessful against the Khitans in the northeast and the Tanguts, a now-extinct ethnic group, in the northwest, Chao K'uang-yin recognized that he lacked the resources to engage all his enemies simultaneously, and sought peace with the Khitan and Tanguts by paying them both annual tribute. He then mapped out a broad strategy to annex the economically prosperous southern states, most of which fell to him easily. Gradually Chao K'uang-yin – known as emperor as Sung T'ai Tsu – unified southern China and extended his influence as far as Indonesia.

Despite sporadic warfare, the early Sung period enjoyed broad-based economic prosperity for a variety of demographic and economic reasons. The population had increased to an unprecedented 100 million. Rapidly increasing urbanization went hand in hand with greatly expanded agricultural productivity. Advances in the technology and production of coal and iron also played quite a significant part, as did improvements in communications. Efficient water transport fostered the development of a national market for domestic products. The tea trade boomed: in the Han period tea had been a luxury item, but under the T'ang tea had become immensely popular throughout China. Trade was brisk in other commodities

as well. Porcelain continued to be a prime export and domestic product. Salt continued to be a state monopoly. By bringing political stability to southern China, the Sung fostered commercial expansion.

The political success of the Sung permitted the cultural and technological innovations of the T'ang period to reach full growth. Foremost among them was the invention of printing, which changed the history of China and the entire world. T'ang craftsmen developed the art of carving words and pictures onto wooden blocks, inking them, and then pressing the block onto paper. Each block consisted of an entire page of text and illustrations. Such whole-page blocks were being printed as early as the middle of the ninth century, and in the eleventh century moveable type was invented. Moveable type was never widely used in China, but when this Chinese invention reached Europe in the thirteenth century (pages 595–597), it revolutionized the communication of ideas. In China as in Europe, the invention and spread of printing dramatically increased the availability of books and lowered their price. Scholarship flourished, and literacy spread rapidly among the general population.

The T'ang and Sung periods were rich in technological innovation. The T'ang invented gunpowder, originally for use in fireworks. By the early Sung period people were using gunpowder to propel arrows – in effect, the first rockets. Later, projectiles were given a gunpowder charge so that they exploded on impact. Although the cannon still lay in the future, the Chinese began to develop artillery long before it was known in western Europe.

Other inventions included the abacus, which, like the modern computer, allowed quick computation of complicated sums. The combination of the water wheel and the bellows enabled smelters to increase the output

220–589	Buddhism reaches China
580–618	Sui Dynasty and restoration of public order
618–907	T'ang Dynasty: economic, political, and artistic flowering
907–960	Era of the Five Dynasties: warfare and revolt
960–1279	Sung Dynasty and Neo-Confucian thought
1021–1086	Wang An-shih, author and political reformer
1215–1368	Mongol conquest of China
ca 1300	Marco Polo travels in China

of pig iron. Under the Sung, government-operated spinning and weaving mills produced cheap, durable, and comfortable cotton clothing.

Economic vitality and the consolidation of Sung rule gave a great impetus to urbanization. In fact, city dwellers were becoming economically more important than the landed gentry during the years of Sung rule. Rich urbanites indulged in increasingly costly dress and food. Women suffered a severe decline in social standing, the cruellest expression of which was the custom of footbinding. So long as women's labor was needed to help keep starvation from the door, they possessed a certain status, albeit lowly. In prosperous urban households, however, women no longer fulfilled an economic function, and became ornaments of status. To show the world that they need not work mothers bound the feet of their infant daughters until the arches broke and the foot healed to half its normal growth. Not until the twentieth century was this custom abandoned.

The Sung, although they unified central and southern China and created the climate for new prosperity, never fully solved the problem of political relations with the Khitan and Tangut states in the north. Whenever possible, the Sung used diplomacy to avoid war and play off one state against the other. In 1114, however, the political situation became more complex. The Jurchen, a people from the northeastern frontier, threw off the yoke of the Khitan state, and in 1125 toppled their former overlords. Flushed with success, the Jurchen marched against the Sung, and in 1126 they sacked the Sung capital and drove the remnants of the imperial court to the southern city of Hangchow.

The Sung emperors who governed from Hangchow, commonly known as the Southern Sung Dynasty, held on to the area below the Yangtze River from 1127 to 1279. The Southern Sung resisted the northerners, but established a stable border with them. Although there never was genuine peace between the two, fighting was usually limited to border areas. For 152 years the Southern Sung flourished, despite the annual tribute they paid to the northerners.

The Southern Sung period is especially notable for a great increase in the volume of maritime trade, both oceanic and coastal. Chinese shipwrights built large, stable junks with huge cargo capacity. These ships enabled Chinese merchants to sail direct to Korea and Japan, which became eager importers of Chinese goods. Ocean voyages were rendered considerably easier and safer by the invention of the magnetic compass, which was widely used in China at least two centuries earlier than in western Europe. The shipping of Chinese goods to the West was mostly in the hands of Arabs, who like their Roman and Indian predecessors, used the annual monsoons to sail to ports in India and east Africa. Thus, southern China under the Sung entered fully and prosperously into a commercial network that stretched from the Mediterranean all the way to Japan.

The increased volume of trade and the invention of printing led to two momentous innovations, the use of paper money and the development of banking. The standardized currency introduced under the First Emperor had been bulky copper coinage (page 188). Paper money originated under the Sung as notes of deposit – documents certifying that a person had deposited a specific amount of copper coinage with the government. Notes of deposit rapidly gave way to true paper money, which anyone could cash in for copper coins. The Venetian merchant and adventurer Marco Polo (1254-1342) wrote one of the earliest descriptions of how Chinese paper money was issued:

The coinage of this paper money is authenticated with as much form and ceremony as if it were actually of pure gold or silver; for to each note a number of officers, specially appointed, not only subscribe their names, but affix their signets also; and when this has been regularly done by the whole of them, the principal officer ... having dipped

into vermillion the royal seal committed to his custody, stamps with it the piece of paper, so that the form of the seal tinged with the vermillion remains impressed upon it.[5]

To this day American paper money carries the signatures of federal officials, the seals of the Federal Reserve Bank, and the Great Seal of the United States; only the vermillion is absent.

Merchants increasingly used the convenient and portable paper money as a medium of exchange. The popularity of paper money also gave rise to the new profession of counterfeiting; Chinese counterfeiters risked their heads, since those inept or unlucky enough to be caught were decapitated. Paper money in turn gave rise to a system of credit and banking that enabled merchants to deposit money, take out loans, and invest in commercial ventures. Facilitated by the new monetary and banking systems, trade burgeoned so much that the Sung government derived more revenue from taxes on trade than from the traditional land tax.

Yet despite their political and economic success, the Southern Sung emperors were living in the twilight of a great era: in the north a new and unforeseen danger, the Mongols, were on the verge of shaking the world from China to Hungary.

CULTURAL BLOSSOMING OF THE T'ANG AND SUNG

The economic reforms, political stability, and military successes of the T'ang and Sung nourished a splendid era in the history of Chinese culture. Although the T'ang period is best known for its poetry, many forms of art flourished during these years. Chinese potters produced porcelain of extraordinarily high quality and delicate balance. The finest porcelain was produced in state factories for use at court or as royal gifts to foreign dignitaries. Later, porcelain of uniformly high quality became a major item of export to the West.

Within the past ten years the excavations of T'ang imperial tombs at modern Chien-hsien in Shensi province have shed welcome new light on the sculpture and painting of this vibrant period. T'ang emperors were customarily accompanied to their graves by a crowd of monumental stone figures and ceramic statuettes. At Chien-hsien scores of life-sized statues of horses and warriors guard the tombs, while rows of statues of dignitaries, lions, and sheep stand in silent audience. Inside the tombs, ceramic statuettes of ceremonial troops serve as guardians.

The royal tombs display T'ang painting at its best. The walls are graced with the painted figures of respectful mandarins, court ladies, and warrior guards. Scenes of hunting and polo lend an air of energy and vivacity. Mythological creatures ward off evil spirits. Realistic and graceful in form, the paintings exhibit a sophisticated sense of perspective. The total effect is joyous, even gay. T'ang painters captured life accurately and with a deft touch.

Poetry in the T'ang period enjoyed a luxuriant growth, and new developments widened the horizons of prose writing. The translation of Buddhist texts originally written in Indian and Central Asian languages introduced new concepts, styles of writing, and literary devices to Chinese. In turn, translators had to adapt Chinese to these foreign languages. Mandarins too needed a flexible literary medium in which to write their official reports. Writers consciously aimed at greater clarity and easier means of expression. Some writers used this new flexibility to create the prose essay as a literary form. Prose in the T'ang period became a more useful tool for the bureaucracy and a distinctive literary genre.

The glory of T'ang literature was its poetry, which achieved unmatched elegance and brilliance. T'ang poetry was sophisticated, urbane, and learned. Thoroughly familiar with earlier poetry and with history, T'ang poets were also influenced by Chinese and foreign folk songs. They were consummate masters of meter and rhythm, their poems often gem-like. Though formal and rigorous in composition, T'ang poetry expresses genuine emotion, frequently with humor and sensitivity. Some poets strung songs together to accompany drama, in effect creating Chinese opera. T'ang poets created new vehicles for verse, and themselves became the models for their Sung successors and all later Chinese poets.

One of the most delightful of the T'ang poets was Li Po (701–762), whose poetry is polished, learned, and good-natured. Unlike most T'ang poets, Li Po was never a mandarin official, although he was familiar with the cultivated life of the imperial court. He was a member in good standing of the literary circle known as the "Eight Immortals of the Wine Cup," and his poems allude often to his love of wine. Even banishment from the court did not dampen his spirits, for Li Po loved his wine, his art, and all of nature too much ever to become morose. One of his most famous poems describes an evening of drinking with only the moon and his shadow for company:

A cup of wine, under the flowering trees;
I drink alone, for no friend is near.
Raising my cup I beckon the bright moon,
For he, with my shadow, will make three men.
The moon, alas, is no drinker of wine;
Listless, my shadow creeps about at my side.

. . . .

Now we are drunk, each goes his way.
May we long share our odd, inanimate feast,
And we meet at last on the cloudy River of the sky.[6]

CHINESE RIVER FESTIVAL   All of the beauty and delicacy of Chinese painting is obvious in this lively scene of people enjoying a river festival. Like the great poets, Chinese painters delighted in scenes from daily life. (The Metropolitan Museum of Art, Rogers Fund, 1911)

Another poem captures a moment of joy while walking in the mountains on a summer day:

Gently I stir a white feather fan,
With open shirt sitting in a green wood.
I take off my cap and hang it on a jutting stone;
A wind from the pine-trees trickles on my bare head.[7]

Li Po is said to have died one night in the company of his old friend the moon.

Less cheerful but no less talented was Po Chü-i (772-846), whose poems often reflect the concerns of a scholar-official. He felt the weight of his responsibilities as governor of several small provinces and sympathized with the people whom he governed. At times Po Chü-i worries whether he is doing his job justly and well:

From my high castle I look at the town below
Where the natives of Pa cluster like a swarm of flies.
How can I govern these people and lead them aright?
I cannot even understand what they say.
But at least I am glad, now that the taxes are in,
To learn that in my province there is no discontent.[8]

Watching the reapers in the fields, he describes their work and wonders about their fate and his:

Tillers of the soil have few idle months;

. . . .

Suddenly the hill is covered with yellow corn.
Wives and daughters shoulder baskets of rice;
Youths and boys carry the flasks of wine.
Following after they bring a wage of meat
To the strong reapers toiling on the southern hill,
Whose feet are burned by the hot earth they tread,
Whose backs are scorched by flames of the shining
  sky.

. . . .

And I to-day . . . by virtue of what right
Have I never once tended field or tree?

. . . .

Thinking of this, secretly I grew ashamed;
And all day the thought lingered in my head.[9]

Like most other T'ang poets, Po Chü-i keenly appreciated nature. Though a high official, he enjoyed such simple things as the pine trees growing around his house and a river babbling over its stony bed. Forced to retire from official life owing to persistent ill health, he took discomfort and retirement in graceful stride. Finally, at age seventy-four he succumbed to a stroke, comforted by his wine and poetry. He had lived a long life with few regrets.

The artists and thinkers of the Sung period brought to fulfillment what the T'ang had so brilliantly begun. Buoyed by political stability and economic prosperity, the Sung explosion of learning and thought was a direct result of the invention of printing. The availability of books enabled scholars to amass their own libraries, and thus to pursue their studies more easily and deeply. Sung scholars formed circles to discuss their interests and ideas and to share their work with others. Sung publishers printed the classics of Chinese literature in huge editions to satisfy scholarly appetites. Works on philosophy, science, and medicine were also consumed avidly. Han and T'ang poetry and historical works became the models for Sung writers' own work. One very popular literary innovation was the encyclopedia, which first appeared in the Sung period, at least five centuries before the philosophe Diderot began publishing his great encyclopedia in France.

One of the most influential Sung schools of thought was that of Wang An-shih (1021–1086), whose interests embraced economics, politics, literary style, and the classics of Chinese literature. As a Sung minister of state, Wang An-shih launched a series of political and economic innovations with his "New Laws." The "Young Shoots" law extended low-interest loans to poor farmers, as some governments do today. Another law substituted a graduated tax for forced labor on state work projects. Like the Roman emperor Diocletian (page 264), Wang An-shih introduced official price controls and limitations on profits; he went further than Diocletian by coupling this measure with a plan to equalize the land tax. Though marked by realism and good sense, Wang An-shih's innovations ultimately failed. When his imperial patron died, he was left powerless and defenseless. Ideological warfare and heavy bureaucratic infighting among officials stifled action. The "New Laws" also met with serious opposition from wealthy merchants and great landowners.

Other schools of Neo-Confucian thought confronted purely intellectual problems, and left a more enduring imprint. The Ch'eng-Chu school achieved one of the greatest intellectual feats of a great age by adding a metaphysical dimension to traditional Confucianism's secular approach to human life and the universe. Metaphysics — the theoretical philosophy of being — gave Confucianism an intellectual depth and sophistication that equipped it to challenge what had long been a Buddhist monopoly of ultimate truth.

Neo-Confucians mined Confucian, Buddhist, and Taoist thought to create this new metaphysics. Meanwhile one of the finest minds of the age, Chu Hsi (1120–1200), addressed himself to the metaphysical problem of evil, evolving ideas that correspond roughly to Plato's theory of forms (page 102). Like Plato, Chu Hsi concluded that everything that exists has a specific form, or *li*. *Ch'i*, or matter, combines with *li* to make up the material world. When the two are out of balance, the result is evil. People can correct this imbalance, Chu Hsi taught, through Confucian study and Buddhist meditation. In effect, Chu Hsi explained not only how evil develops in the world but how it can be corrected.

Chu Hsi's talents extended to the classics of Chinese literature, on which he wrote learned commentaries. He was also the premier historian of his day. In striving for a unified view of life and the universe, he interpreted history and literature in support of his philosophical ideas. Unparalleled among Neo-Confucians, Chu Hsi himself became a classic, whose works have been read, revered, and imitated for centuries. He and other intellectuals breathed new life into Confucianism to meet the challenge of Buddhism.

Sung poets and painters matched the greatness of their T'ang predecessors. The Sung particularly excelled at painting. Two dramatically dissimilar approaches to art arose: some painters, like Li Lung-mien (ca 1040–1106), stressed exact realism; others, like Mi Fei (ca 1051–1107), pursued a mystical romanticism in which space and natural elements were suggested with a few brush strokes.

The culture of the T'ang and Sung periods is remarkable for its breadth and variety, as well as its brilliance. From painting to poetry, from philosophy to history, these years gave rise to exquisite masterpieces.

THE MONGOL CONQUEST (1215–1368)

In 1215 the Southern Sung and their northern neighbors felt the first tremor of what was to be among the most remarkable movements of people in all history. Genghis Khan (1167–1227), a leader of the Mongols – a people who gave their name to modern-day Mongolia – united the Mongol tribes with neighboring Tatars and Turks. Once united, this mighty swell of humanity burst upon northern China. Marco Polo has left a vivid description of their endurance and military skill:

They are brave in battle, almost to desperation, setting little value upon their lives, and exposing themselves without hesitation to all manner of danger. Their disposition is cruel. They are capable of supporting every kind of privation, and when there is a necessity for it, can live for a month on the milk of their mares, and upon such wild animals as they may chance to catch. Their horses are fed upon grass alone, and do not require barley or other grain. The men are habituated to remain on horseback during two days and two nights, without dismounting; sleeping in that situation whilst their horses graze. No people on earth can surpass them in fortitude under difficulties, nor show greater patience under wants of every kind.[10]

In 1215 Genghis Khan and his Mongol scourge overwhelmed the Jurchens in the north and captured Peking. All of northern China fell in 1234. From this base Genghis Khan's successors launched a stunning move on the West. Some detachments of Mongols struck as far into Europe as Hungary. The main force, known as the Golden Horde, overwhelmed southern Russia. Another detachment carved out a kingdom in Iran. By 1241 Mongol rule stretched from Hungary eastward all the way to the Pacific.

The Southern Sung held out tenaciously against these world shakers, but Genghis

MARBLE GATE NEAR THE GREAT WALL   *This majestic arch, which was erected in 1345, marks the site where the Mongol leader Genghis Khan fought and won a major battle against the Chinese. Although it is the monument of a foreign ruler, the arch is typically Chinese in its design and decoration. (D. Mennie and P. Weale,* The Pageant of Peking, *1922)*

Khan's grandson Kublai Khan (1216–1294) extinguished the dynasty and annexed all of southern China by 1279. For the first time in history, all of China was ruled by foreigners. By 1271 Kublai Khan proclaimed himself emperor of China and founder of the Yuan Dynasty (1271–1368). The Mongols distrusted the traditional mandarin class, yet needed their bureaucratic system. They compromised by assigning foreigners – Turks, Muslims from Central Asia, and even a handful of European adventurers – to the highest administrative posts but allowed Chinese to hold lower offices. The Mongol conquest did not hinder China's trade, which continued the expansion begun under the Sung. By establishing his capital at Peking, Kublai Khan helped reunite northern and southern China commercially in that the wealth of the south flowed north to sustain the capital.

As a conquering minority, the Mongols proclaimed repressive laws against the far more numerous Chinese. They divided society into four classes with varying rights, privileges, and legal protection. The Mongols themselves enjoyed full protection under the law; below them were their foreign administrators. The northern Chinese, who had been conquered first, had broader political and legal rights than the southerners, but bore a far heavier burden of taxes and services; the southern Chinese shouldered a very light tax load but suffered heavy legal and political discrimination. The Mongols disarmed the Chinese population and forbade them to assemble in large numbers and even to travel by night. The Chinese were captives in their own country.

Into this world wandered the remarkable Marco Polo (ca 1254–1324) with his father and uncle. The three Polos had journeyed by land across Asia to the court of Kublai Khan, who received them with warmth and curiosity. Adept in four Asian languages, Marco Polo was uniquely equipped to collect accurate information about China. He probably never traveled far from Peking, but drew heavily on Chinese accounts. He trained his insatiable curiosity on the land of China, its people and their customs, and everything likely to stimulate commerce. After seventeen years in China, the Polos returned to Italy, where Marco wrote a vivid account of their farflung travels. At first considered sheer fantasy, his book was widely read and contributed enormously to familiarizing Europeans with the East.

Mongol repression bred bitter resentment throughout China. By the middle of the fourteenth century, moreover, the Mongol hold on the East was weakening. Struggles among claimants to the Yuan throne seriously compromised the Great Khan's power and prestige, and Kublai Khan's successors proved weak and incompetent. In this atmosphere of crisis, some Chinese formed secret societies – underground resistance groups dedicated to overthrowing the oppressor. The most effective secret society, known as the Red Turbans, consisted of peasants and artisans, who had suffered the most from Mongol rule. In 1351 the rebels were ready to strike. Their rebellion caught the Mongols totally off guard. One of these rebels, a poor peasant and ex-monk best known to history as Hung Wu, later became the first Ming emperor. In 1356 Hung Wu and his followers stormed the important city of Nanking. Securing control over southern and central China, they pushed the Mongols northward, and by 1368 the Chinese had driven the Mongols completely out of China. Hung Wu established the Ming Dynasty (1368–1644). Once again China was united under one of its sons.

JAPAN, DAWN OF THE RISING SUN

Japan entered the light of history late, and Japanese historical writing originated even later. The earliest reliable information on Japan comes from sporadic notices in Chinese histories, the first of which dates only from A.D. 57. Little is known about the origins and formative years of the Japanese people. By the time of their first appearance in history, they had already had extensive exposure to Chinese culture. Yet though the Japanese derived much from the Chinese, they molded their borrowings to suit their special needs. Early Japan saw the growth of an indigenous culture influenced, but never overwhelmed, by the Chinese.

THE JAPANESE ISLANDS

The heart of Japan is its four major islands, the largest and most important of which is Honshu. The three southern islands surround the Inland Sea, a narrow stretch of water dotted with smaller islands (see Map 10.4). All four islands are mountainous, with craggy interiors and some active volcanoes. Rugged terrain divides the land into numerous small valleys watered by streams. There is little flat land, and only 16 percent of the total area is arable. Japan's climate ranges from subtropical in the south, which the Pacific bathes in warm currents, to a region of cold winters in the north. Rainfall is abundant, favoring rice production. Yet nature can be harsh: Japan is a land buffeted by earthquakes, typhoons, and tidal waves.

Despite its occasional rages, the sea provides a rich harvest, and the Japanese have traditionally been fishermen and mariners.

CREATION OF JAPAN *This Japanese painting portrays two deities standing in the clouds above the Pacific Ocean. The god, sword at his side, stirs the waters with a lance and thereby creates the home islands of Japan. (Courtesy, Museum of Fine Arts, Boston, Bigelow Collection)*

can and Allied troops stepped ashore after the Japanese surrender in 1945. Consequently, the Japanese have for long periods been free to develop their way of life without external interference. Continuity has been a consistent hallmark of Japanese history.

EARLY JAPAN AND THE YAMATO STATE

The beginnings of Japanese history are lost in the mists of legend. The Chinese historian Wei Chih wrote one of the earliest reliable descriptions of Japanese life in A.D. 297:

The land of Wa [Japan] is warm and mild. In winter as in summer the people live on raw vegetables and go barefooted. They live in houses; father and mother, elder and younger, sleep separately. They smear their bodies with pink and scarlet, just as the Chinese use powder. They serve food on bamboo and wooden trays, helping themselves with their fingers.[11]

The society that Wei Chih and other Chinese sources portray was based on agriculture and dominated by a warrior aristocracy. Clad in helmet and armor, these warriors wielded swords and battleaxes, and often the bow. Some of them rode into battle on horseback. Social stratification was rigid, peasants serving at the command of nobles. At the bottom of the social scale were the slaves, who were usually house servants. Slaves may have accounted for approximately 5 percent of the total population.

Early Japan was divided into numerous political units, although by about 513 their number had been greatly reduced. Each pocket of local authority was under the rule of a particular clan — a large group of families who all claimed descent from a common ancestor and worshipped a common deity. Each clan had its own chieftain, who marshalled its forces for battle and served as its chief priest.

Since the land is rugged and lacking in navigable waterways, political unification by land has been difficult until the modern period. The Inland Sea, like the Aegean in Greece, was the readiest avenue of communications. Hence the land bordering the Inland Sea developed as the political and cultural center of early Japan. Geography also blessed Japan with a moat. Great powers like the Han and T'ang Dynasties and the Mongols might overrun the continent, but their grasp never reached to the Japanese islands. Japan did not suffer a single successful invasion until Ameri-

In Japan as in many other ancient societies, political power was a function of family strength, organization, and cohesion.

By the third century A.D. the Yamato clan had seized the fertile area south of modern Kyoto, near Osaka Bay (see Map 10.4). At the center of the Yamato holdings was a rich plain, which constituted the chief economic resource of the clan. Gradually the Yamato clan, who traced their descent from the sun-goddess, subordinated a huge number of other clans to create the Yamato state. The chieftain of the Yamato clan proclaimed himself emperor and ruler over the other chieftains. The Yamato harnessed the loyalty of their subordinates by giving them specific duties, functions, and gifts, and by including them in a religious hierarchy. Clans that recognized Yamato dominion continued to exercise local authority, and some clans were given specific military or religious functions to fulfill. In an effort to centralize further the administration of the state, the emperor created a council of chieftains, who were treated as though they were appointed officials.

The Yamato also used their religion to subordinate the gods of their supporters, much as Hammurabi had used Marduk (page 18). Creating a hierarchy of gods under the authority of their sun-goddess, they established her chief shrine in eastern Honshu, where the sun-goddess could catch the first rays of the rising sun. Around the shrine there grew up local clan cults, giving rise to a native religion that the Japanese called *Shinto,* the Way of the Gods. Shinto was a unifying force: the chief deity of Shinto, the sun-goddess, became the protectress of the nation. Shinto also stressed the worship of ancestors, thus strengthening the link between the present and the past. Much of its appeal arose from the simple fact that it was a happy religion. Its cheerful rituals celebrated the beauty of nature instead of invoking the hazards of fate or divine wrath. Shinto emphasized ritual cleanliness, and its annual festival was marked by wine, song, and good cheer.

By the sixth century the powerful Yamato state was struggling to dominate Korea. From the dawn of their history the Japanese had held parts of Korea, but by 562 the Koreans had driven them out. Yet Japanese-Korean contact was neither entirely hostile nor limited to warfare. Early Japanese society easily absorbed migrating Koreans, and its holdings in Korea enriched the Japanese economically.

Much more important, however, was Korea's role as the avenue through which Chinese influence reached Japan. Chinese impact on the Japanese was profound and wide-ranging. The Japanese adapted the Chinese system of writing and record keeping, which allowed for bureaucratic administration along Chinese lines, and set the stage for literature, philosophy, and written history.

Another influence was of lasting importance to the Japanese – Buddhism. In 538 a Korean king sent the Yamato court Buddhist images and scriptures. The new religion immediately became a political football, one faction of the ruling clan favoring its official adoption and others opposing it. The resulting turmoil, both religious and political, ended only in 587, when the pro-Buddhists defeated their opponents on the battlefield. Buddhism proved important to Japanese life for three broad reasons. First, it was a new and sophisticated but appealing religion that met needs not envisaged by Shinto. Second, it served as an influential carrier of Chinese culture. Finally, its influence with Japan's rulers enabled it to play an influential role in politics.

The victorious pro-Buddhists undertook a sweeping reform of the state, partly to strengthen Yamato rule and partly to intro-

PRINCE SHOTOKU *Prince Shotoku, the author of the "Seventeen Article Constitution," is shown here with many of the attributes of a Chinese mandarin official. His sword shows that he was more than a mere administrator, and was ready to resist those who opposed his reforms. (The Bettmann Archive)*

duce Chinese political and bureaucratic concepts. The architect of this effort was Prince Shotoku (574–622), the author of the "Seventeen Article Constitution," a triumph of Buddhist ethical and Confucian political thought. Issued in 604, the constitution was not a blueprint for government but a list of moral and ethical Buddhist precepts stressing righteous political conduct. It upheld the rights of the ruler and commanded his subjects to obey him. The constitution recommended an intricate bureaucracy like China's, and admonished the nobility to avoid strife and opposition. Although the Seventeen Article Constitution

never became the law of the entire land, it spelled out what Shotoku considered the proper goals of government and pointed the way to future reform.

Shotoku realized that Japan lacked the trained personnel to put his reforms into effect. To build a corps of professional administrators he sent a large embassy of talented Japanese to T'ang China in 607, to learn Chinese methods and arts at the source. Other students studied at Buddhist monasteries in China, and then carried the message of Buddha accurately and fully to Japan. At first their numbers were small, but over the course of years thousands of young men studied in China and returned home to share what they had learned.

The death of Shotoku in 622 set off twenty years of political chaos. Finally in 654 supporters of his policies, aided by students trained in China, overthrew the government. The following year they proclaimed the Taika Reforms, a bold effort to create a complete imperial and bureaucratic system like that of the T'ang empire. For all their hopes, the Taika Reforms failed to make Japan a small-scale copy of T'ang China. Nonetheless the reformers created a nation, with all the political trappings of its neighbors. The symbol of this new political awareness was the establishment in 710 of Japan's first capital and first city, modelled on the T'ang capital, at Nara, just north of modern Osaka. Nara gave its name to an era that lasted until 784, an era characterized by the continued importation of Chinese ideas and methods. Buddhism triumphed both religiously and politically. The Buddhist monasteries that ringed the capital were both religious centers and wealthy landlords, and the monks were active in the political life of the capital. In the Nara Era, Buddhism and the imperial court went hand in hand.

THE HEIAN ERA (794–1185)

Buddhist influence at Nara showed its dark side when in 770 a Buddhist priest tried to usurp the throne. The results were twofold. The imperial family removed the capital to Heian – modern Kyoto – where it remained until 1867. And a strong reaction against Buddhism and Chinese culture soon set in, strikingly symbolized by the severance of relations with China after 838. Thereafter the Japanese assimilated and adapted what they had imported. In a sense their intellectual and cultural childhood had come to an end, and they were ready to go their own way.

Though under a cloud, Buddhism not only survived the reaction but actually made gains. Before closing the door on China, the Japanese admitted two new Buddhist cults that gradually became integral parts of Japanese life. In 805 a Japanese monk introduced the Tendai sect (Chinese T'ien-t'ai, page 331). Though a complex product of China's high culture, Tendai proved popular because it held out the possibility of salvation to all. In addition to its religious message, Tendai preached the Confucian ideal of service to the state. The Shingon (True Word) sect arrived in 806 on the heels of Tendai. Like its Chinese precursor, this Japanese sect promised salvation through ritual, magical incantations, and masses for the dead.

Patronized initially by the nobility, both sects held the seeds of popular appeal. The common people cared nothing for Tendai and Shingon as metaphysical and intellectual systems, but were strongly attracted by their magic and the prospect of personal salvation. As Tendai and Shingon spread Buddhism throughout Japan, they were gradually transformed into distinctively Japanese religions.

Only later, during the Kamakura Shogunate (1185–1333), did Buddhism begin a vigorous proselytizing campaign. The emphasis on equality and salvation that was the hallmark of both Tendai and Shingon prepared the way for two sects that promised their followers sure and immediate salvation. The Pure Land sect (page 331) preached that Buddha's paradise of eternal bliss, the Pure Land, could be reached through simple faith in Buddha. Neither philosophical understanding of Buddhist scriptures nor devotion to rituals was necessary. People had only to repeat Buddha's name to be saved. The second sect, an offshoot of the first, was the Lotus sect of Nichiren (1222–1281), a fiery and intolerant preacher who reduced Buddhism to a single moment of faith. To be saved, according to Nichiren, people had only to call sincerely upon Buddha. Nothing else was necessary. Stripped of its intellectual topweight, Buddhism made greater headway in the countryside than ever before.

The eclipse of Chinese influence liberated Japanese artistic and cultural impulses. The Japanese continued to draw on Chinese models, but forged new paths of their own. Japanese architects evolved a light, simple, and graceful style of building beautifully in keeping with the country's natural surroundings. The Heian Era fostered a unique development in painting, the "Yamato pictures," paintings of everyday scenes in which figures and objects are outlined and then painted in with bright colors. Equally great strides were made in writing itself. In order to express themselves more easily and clearly, Japanese scholars modified the Chinese script they had adopted during the Yamato period. The Japanese produced two syllabaries in which phonetic signs stand for syllables instead of whole words. This development made it possible for the first time to write the Japanese language in the native syntax.

The reform of their written language un-

FIVE-STORIED PAGODA   This splendid pagoda is a good example of Japanese architecture of the Heian period. Buildings were intended to complement their natural surroundings.. (Art Resource, Orian Press)

shackled Japanese writers. No longer bound in the straitjacket of Chinese, they created their own literary style and modes of expression. The writing of history, which had begun in the Nara Era, received a huge boost, as did poetry. Completely original was the birth of the novel, one of the finest of which is *The Tale of Genji*. This ageless novel by the court lady Murasaki Shikibu (978–ca 1016) treats court life, paying minute attention to dialogue and exploring personalities. Not merely a novelist, she also wrote about the mission of the novelist and the purpose of the novel. The novel was taken up by other writers; Sei Shonagon's *Pillow Book* is yet another masterpiece. These works bore no resemblance to any works in Chinese literature. The Japanese were launched on their own independent and fertile literary tradition.

Politically, the Heian Era gave rise to two opposing tendencies: while the emperors were trying to extend their power and centralize their authority, aristocrats were striving to free themselves from imperial control. The aristocrats quickly won out over the emperors. The biggest winners were the Fujiwara family, who in the ninth century had regularly served as regents for the emperor. As other families too rose to prominence, setting the stage for intrigue and infighting at court, the effectiveness of the imperial government was further diminished.

The emperors contributed to their own eclipse by decreeing disastrous land laws. The imperial government's efforts to appropriate land and redistribute it to peasants wrecked its own economic base. The government was too weak to overcome widespread resistance and evasion of the laws, and the emperors themselves permitted too many loopholes to make them effective. The result was precisely the opposite of what the central government intended: vast tracts of land were made exempt from taxation and imperial control, and land became consolidated in fewer hands. Those who profited most were local lords and high government officials, members of the imperial court and Buddhist monasteries, all of whom became great landlords at the emperor's expense. Instead of a peasantry of small landholders paying taxes to the imperial treasury, the emperors and even the Fujiwara regents had to contend with strong aristocratic families who were increasingly difficult to control.

In 1156 open rebellion and civil war erupted, fed by declining central power, feuds among the great families, and the ambitions of local lords. The two most powerful contenders in the struggle were the Taira and Minamoto clans, who quickly outstripped both the emperor and the Fujiwara. The Taira drew their political strength from their vast landholdings, while the Minamoto dominated the Kanto plain, a rich agricultural area near modern Tokyo. Both clans relied on *samurai,* skilled warriors who were rapidly consolidating as a new social class. By 1192 the Minamoto had vanquished all opposition, and their leader Yoritomo (1147–1199) became *shogun* or general-in-chief. With him began the Kamakura Shogunate, which lasted until 1333.

FEUDALISM AND THE SAMURAI

The twelfth-century events that culminated in the Kamakura Shogunate involved the evolution of Japanese feudalism. Some experts see no value in comparing Japanese feudalism with that of medieval Europe. Large-scale human developments like feudalism are not easy to interpret, and the rich variety of cultures around the world rarely provide exact parallels. Even so, a comparison of Japanese and European feudalism is potentially en-

lightening, particularly since the two developments occurred totally independently and under different circumstances. Whereas feudalism in Europe was a response to foreign invasions, in Japan it evolved out of the gradual breakdown of central authority. No external factors were involved.

The distinguished American scholar John W. Hall offers a balanced definition of feudalism:

Perhaps the most useful way to conceive of feudalism is the simplest, namely that it is a condition of society in which there is at all levels a fusion of the civil, military, and judicial elements of government into a single authority. This fusion of public and private functions being achieved in the person of the locally powerful military figure, it is also natural that military practices and values become predominant in the total society.[12]

Hall sees the military element as the linchpin that held feudal society together. But since a warrior class cannot exist without economic support, it is only part of a larger system. The Japanese warrior aristocracy, the samurai, depended economically on the *shoen,* a private domain outside imperial control that somewhat resembled the medieval European manor (pages 425–426). The shoen typically consisted of a village and its farmland, normally land capable of growing rice. In both Japan and Europe, land was a fundamental component in feudalism.

Samurai and shoen were basic elements of Japanese feudalism. But what conditions gave rise to them, and how did they fuse? Both owed their origins directly to the gradual breakdown of central authority in the Heian Era. The shoen had its roots in the ninth century, when local lords began escaping imperial taxes and control by formally giving their land to a Buddhist monastery, which was exempt from taxes, or to a court official who

JAPAN, CA 350–CA 1400

3rd century A.D.	Creation of the Yamato state
538	Introduction of Buddhism
604	Shotoku's "Seventeen Article Constitution"
655	Taika reforms
710–784	Nara era, creation of Japan's first capital and first city
794–1185	Heian era and literary flowering
1185–1333	Kamakura Shogunate and Japanese feudalism
1274 and 1281	Unsuccessful Mongol invasion of Japan

could get special privileges from the emperor. The local lord then received his land back as a tenant who paid his protector a nominal rent. The monastery or official received a steady income from the land, while the tenant was thereafter free of imperial taxes and jurisdiction. The local lord continued to exercise actual authority over the land – all the more so, in fact, since imperial officials could no longer touch him. In spite of his legal status as a tenant, he was the real boss of his estate.

The many other people who were economically, politically, and legally dependent upon the shoen, and who had various and often overlapping rights and functions within it, were known as *shiki*. The lord often entrusted the actual running of the estate to a manager, who received a share of its produce in payment. The shoen was cultivated either by independent farmers (*myoshu*) who owned specific fields, or dependent farmers, or, typically, a combination of both. Unlike peasants in medieval Europe, dependent farmers never became serfs.

To keep order on the shoen and to protect it

from harm lords organized private armies. As the central government weakened, local lords and their armies – the only source of law and order in the countryside – grew stronger. Thus the inability of central authority to defend its subjects sparked the rise of local armies of professional soldiers – the samurai.

The samurai and his lord, like the European knight and lord, had a twofold bond. In both societies the lord extended his authority over the vassal in return for the latter's loyalty and service. In both the vassal received from his lord a fief to support him. In both Japan and Europe the vassal entered into his lord's service in a formal ceremony, whose religious element was far more central in Europe than in Japan. Another difference is that Japanese vassals originally received only shiki rights – a certain portion of the estate's produce – and not a grant of land. Only later did the true landed fief appear in Japan. Another striking difference between Japanese and European feudalism is that initially the lord-samurai relationship, far from being the only government, existed alongside the anemic imperial system.

Not until the Ashikaga Shogunate, which lasted from 1338 to 1573 (page 355), did the military aristocracy take over from imperial officers.

Like the European knight, the samurai had his own military and social code of conduct, later called *Bushido* or The Way of the Warrior. The bedrock of the samurai's code was loyalty to his lord, to which everything else was secondary. Yoritomo founded the Kamakura Shogunate upon the samurai and his code, and attitudes that blossomed in his lifetime long outlasted the political system he built. Perhaps the eminent scholar George Sansom has best caught the flavor of the samurai's devotion to lord and duty:

The warrior does not question the commands of his lord, but obeys them regardless of his own life, his family, and all his private interests. In defeat he must bear in mind what he owes for past favors and must be ready to die in the cause of his lord, or in the cause of the family or clan of which he is a member. It follows that a warrior's life belongs to his lord, and he may not dispose of it to suit his own ends, or merely to preserve his own reputation.[13]

Preferring death to dishonor, the samurai showed his complete dedication in the act of *seppuku* (sometimes called *harakiri*), ritual suicide by disemboweling oneself.

By the end of the twelfth century the samurai had left their mark on cultural life as well as military affairs. They constituted the ruling class at the local level, aristocrats who were close to the land and those who worked it. While samurai values were not those of the court aristocracy, their code of conduct was by no means rude or vulgar. Like the chivalric code of the medieval knight, the principles of the samurai embraced religion, personal conduct, and practical affairs. As articulated in the later code of Bushido, samurai were expected to respect the gods, keep honorable company, be fair and even generous to others, and be sympathetic to the weak and helpless.

The symbols of the samurai were their swords, with which they were expected to be expert, and the cherry blossom, which falls with the spring wind, signifying the way in which samurai gave their lives for their lords. Like knights, samurai went into battle in armor and often on horseback. Like the ancient Spartans, samurai were expected to make do with little and like it. Physical hardship became routine, and soft living was despised as weak and unworthy. Although the full-blown samurai code did not take final shape until the later Ashikaga Shogunate, samurai were making an irresistible impact on Japanese life by the end of the twelfth century.

THE KAMAKURA SHOGUNATE (1185–1333)

The Kamakura Shogunate derives its name from Kamakura, the seat of the Minamoto clan and of Yoritomo's shogunate. Yoritomo's victory meant that the emperor continued to be an ornament, honored and esteemed but largely powerless. Yoritomo's victory also inaugurated an era of feudalism that lasted until around 1600.

Based on the loyalty of his followers, Yoritomo's rule was an extension of the way in which he ran his own estate. Having established his *Bakufu* (Tent Government) at Kamakura, Yoritomo created three bodies, staffed by his retainers, to handle political and legal matters. His adminstrative board drafted government policy, another board regulated lords and samurai, and a board of inquiry served as the court of the land. For administration at the local level, Yoritomo created two groups of officials. The military land stewards were responsible for the collection of taxes. Charged with governing most estates, they saw to their proper operation and maintained law and order in return for a share of the produce. The second body of officials were the military governors, who oversaw the military and police protection of the provinces. They supervised the conduct of the military land stewards in peacetime, and commanded the provincial samurai in war. Yet Yoritomo's system suffered from a weakness: before the end of the twelfth century, the military governors and military land stewards had become hereditary officials – local rulers in their own right – whose allegiance to the Kamakura Shogunate was waning.

Yoritomo's successors did not inherit his ability, and in 1219 the Hojo family, a powerful vassal, reduced the shogun to a figurehead. Thenceforth until 1333, the Hojo family held the reins of power by serving as regents of the shogun. The shogun had joined the emperor as a political figurehead.

Internal affairs continued unchanged during the Hojo Regency, but a formidable challenge appeared from abroad. Japan's self-imposed isolation was rudely interrupted in the thirteenth century by a massive seaborne invasion whose lingering effects weakened the Hojo Regency and eventually led to the downfall of the Kamakura Shogunate. The Mongol leader Kublai Khan, having overrun China and Korea, turned his eyes toward Japan. In 1274 and again in 1281 he sent huge numbers of ships and men to storm the islands. On both occasions the Mongols managed to land but were beaten back by samurai. What proved ultimately decisive, however, were two fierce storms that destroyed the Mongol fleets. Marco Polo recounts what he heard about one invasion force:

The expedition sailed from the ports of Zai-tun and Kin-sai, and crossing the intermediate sea, reached the island in safety. . . . It happened, after

some time, that a north wind began to blow with great force, and the ships of the Tartars, which lay near the shore of the island, were driven foul of each other. . . . The gale, however, increased to so violent a degree that a number of vessels foundered. The people belonging to them, by floating upon the pieces of the wreck, saved themselves upon an island lying about four miles from the coast of Zipangu [Japan].[14]

The Japanese claimed that they were saved by the *kamikaze*, the Divine Wind – which lent its name to the thousands of Japanese aviators who tried to become a second divine wind in World War Two by crashing their airplanes on American warships.

Although the Hojo regents had successfully defended Japan, they could not reward their vassals satisfactorily because little booty was found among the wreckage. Discontent grew among the samurai, and by the fourteenth century the entire political system was breaking down. Both the imperial and shogunate families were divided among themselves, and discontent increased among the samurai, who were rapidly growing in number. Since the land could not adequately support more samurai, many samurai families became increasingly impoverished. This phenomenon had two results. First, poverty created a pool of warriors ready for plunder. Second, samurai shifted their loyalty from the Kamakura Shogunate to local officials who could offer them adequate maintenance.

The explosive combination of factional disputes among Japan's leading families and samurai unrest blew up in 1331, when the emperor Go-Daigo tried to recapture real power. His attempt sparked an uprising by the great families, local lords, samurai, and even Buddhist monasteries, which commanded the allegiance of thousands of samurai. Go-Daigo destroyed the Kamakura Shogunate but lost

REPULSE OF THE MONGOLS   Although this scene shows the Japanese samurai heroically resisting the Mongol fleet, Kublai Khan's invasion plans were actually ruined by fierce storms, which the Japanese called the kamikaze, or Divine Wind. (The Bettmann Archive)

the loyalty of his followers. One of his most important military leaders, Ashikaga Takauji, made his own bid for power. By 1338 the rebel had defeated the emperor and established the Ashikaga Shogunate, which lasted until 1573. Takauji's victory was also a victory for the samurai, who took over civil authority throughout Japan. The day of the samurai had fully dawned.

By about 1400 traditional religious, social, and intellectual values had been challenged and fertilized by new peoples and new ideas throughout Asia. Most of India clung to Hinduism, while Islam took root in modern Pakistan and Bangladesh. China incorporated and distilled Buddhism, which won a place next to Confucianism in Chinese life. Japan imported much of Chinese culture only to mold it into something distinctly Japanese. Finally, firm economic and cultural links made it virtually impossible for any Asian people to continue to develop in total isolation.

NOTES

1. Translated by O. P. Singh Bhatia, *The Imperial Guptas,* New India Press, New Delhi, 1962, p. 79.

2. Translated by A. L. Basham, *The Wonder That Was India,* Grove Press, New York, 1954, p. 161.

3. Vasishtha 4.5.1–2, translated by G. Bühler, *The Sacred Laws of the Aryas,* Part II: *Vasishtha and Baudhayana,* Clarendon Press, Oxford, 1882, p. 31.

4. *Sutrakritanga* 1.4.2, quoted in Basham, *The Wonder That Was India,* pp. 459–460.

5. *The Travels of Marco Polo, the Venetian,* J. M. Dent and Sons, London and Toronto, 1908, p. 203.

6. Translated by A. Waley, *More Translations from the Chinese,* Alfred A. Knopf, New York, 1919, p. 27.

7. Ibid., p. 29.

8. Ibid., p. 71.

9. Ibid., p. 41.

10. *The Travels of Marco Polo,* p. 128.

11. R. Tsunoda et al., *Sources of the Japanese Tradition,* Columbia University Press, New York, 1958, p. 6

12. John W. Hall, *Japan, From Prehistory to Modern Times,* Delacorte Press, New York, 1970, p. 77.

13. *A History of Japan to 1334,* Stanford University Press, Stanford, 1958, p. 360.

14. *The Travels of Marco Polo,* pp. 325–326.

SUGGESTED READING

The reign of the Guptas is especially well documented. O. P. Singh Bhatia, *The Imperial Guptas* (1962), treats the entire dynasty. In a series of works S. K. Maity covers many facets of the period: *Gupta Civilization: A Study* (1974), *The Imperial Guptas and Their Times* (1975), and *Economic Life in North India in the Gupta Period* (1975). D. H. H. Ingalls, "Kalidasa and the Attitudes of the Golden Age," *Journal of the American Oriental Society* 96 (1976):15–26, studies the writings of India's greatest poet and dramatist in their historical context.

Good treatments of Indian society and daily life can be found in A. L. Basham, *The Wonder That Was India* (1959), ch. 6, and J. Auboyer, *Daily Life in Ancient India from 200 B.C. to A.D. 700* (1965).

An extensive survey of the Islamic invasions of India is J. F. Richards, "The Islamic Frontier in the East: Expansion into South Asia," *South Asia* 4 (1974):90–109, in which Richards makes the point that many Indian princes put up stiff resistance to the invaders. Much broader studies of the impact of Islam on the subcontinent are A. Embree, ed., *Muslim Civilization in India* (1964), and I. H. Qureshi, *History of the Muslim Community of the Indo-Pakistan Subcontinent* (1961), which is very pro-Pakistan. A good treatment of early Islam in India is K. A. Nizami, *Some Aspects of Religion and Politics in India during the Thirteenth Century* (reprinted 1970). In two books, *Islam in the Indian Subcontinent* (1980) and *Islam in India and Pakistan* (1982), A. Schimmel surveys many aspects of Islam, including architecture, life, art, and traditions in the subcontinent. G. S. Pomerantz, "The Decline of Buddhism in India," *Diogenes* 96 (1976):38–66, treats the demise of Buddhism on its native soil.

Two works concentrate on the Delhi Sultanate, M. Habib and K. A. Nizami, eds., *Comprehensive History of India,* vol. 5, *Delhi Sultanate* (1970), and P. Hardy, "The Growth of Authority over a Conquered Political Elite: the Early Delhi Sultanate as a Possible Case Study," in J. F. Richards, ed., *Kingship and Authority in South Asia* (1978).

O. W. Wolters, *Early Indonesian Commerce: A Study of the Origins of Srivijaya* (1967), is perhaps the most comprehensive treatment of that kingdom. Much broader in scope are H. G. Q. Wales, *The Making of Greater India,* 2nd ed. (1961), and *The Indianization of China and of South-East Asia* (1967).

The standard work on the arrival of Buddhism in China is E. Zürcher, *The Buddhist Conquest of China,* 2 vols. (1959). Also good on the intellectual climate of the time are E. Balazs, *Chinese Civilization and Bureaucracy* (1964), and H. Welch and A. Seidel, eds., *Facets of Taoism* (1979). Shorter and more popular is A. Wright, Buddhism in Chinese History (1959). Finally, K. Ch'en, *Buddhism in China* (1964) and *The Chinese Transformation of Buddhism* (1973), cover the early evolution of Buddhism in China. B. Gray, *Buddhist Cave Paintings at Tunhuang* (1959), is the place to begin study of the artistic impact of Buddhism on China.

Political events from the time of the Sui to Sung Dynasties are particularly well covered. Though old, W. Bingham, *The Founding of the T'ang Dynasty: The Fall of Sui and Rise of T'ang* (1941), is still useful. C. P. Fitzgerald, *Son of Heaven: A Biography of Li Shih-min, Founder of the T'ang Dynasty* (1933), is likewise an old treatment of the first T'ang emperor. Newer and broader is J. Perry and B. Smith, eds., *Essays on T'ang Society* (1976). The career of An Lu-shan is admirably discussed by E. G. Pullyblank, *The Background of the Rebellion of An Lu-shan* (1955). The difficult period of the Five Dynasties is well covered by G. Wang, *The Structure of Power in North China during the Five Dynasties* (1963). Various aspects of Sung developments receive attention in J. T. C. Liu and P. Golas, eds., *Changes in Sung China* (1969), and E. A. Kracke, Jr., *Civil Service in Early Sung China (960–1067)* (1953). Wang An-shih still generates controversy, and a variety of views can be found in J. T. C. Liu, *Reform in Sung China: Wang An-shih (1021–1086) and His New Policies* (1959), and J. Meskill, ed., *Wang An-shih – Practical Reformer?* (1963). Lastly, A. F. Wright, *The Sui Dynasty* (1978) has become the standard work on this important dynasty.

Those interested in further discussion of the great poets of the period can find no better place to start than the work of A. Waley, a gifted translator: *The Life and Times of Po Chü-i* (1949) and *The Poetry and Career of Li Po, 701–762* (1950). A brief treatment of the T'ang tombs at Chien-hsien, well illustrated with color plates, is N. H. Dupree, "T'ang Tombs in Chien County, China," *Archaeology* 32, no. 4 (1979):34–44.

For the Mongols in their native setting, see L. Kwanten, *Imperial Nomads: A History of Central Asia, 500–1500 A.D.* (1979), a comprehensive picture of Central Asian developments. H. D. Martin, *The Rise of Chinghis Khan and His Conquest of North China* (1950), studies the rise of the Mongols to greatness. J. Dardess, "From Mongol Empire to Yuan Dynasty: Changing Forms of Imperial Rule in Mongolia and Central Asia," *Monumenta Serica* 30 (1972–1973):117–165, traces the evolution of Mongol government. His *Conquerors and Confucians: Aspects of Political Change in Late Yuan China* (1973) continues the study for a somewhat later period. Lastly, Dardess' "The Transformations of Messianic Revolt and the Founding of the Ming Dynasty," *Journal of Asian Studies* 29 (1970):539–558, treats some of the factors behind the overthrow of the Yuan Dynasty.

Among the many fine general works on Japan, the following are especially recommended in addition to those cited in the Notes: G. Sansom, *Japan: A Short Cultural History,* rev. ed. (1943), and *A History of Japan to 1334* (1958); G. Trewartha, *Japan: A Geography* (1965); and E. O. Reischauer and J. K. Fairbank, *East Asia: The Great Tradition* (1960).

For early Japanese history, G. J. Groot, *The Prehistory of Japan* (1951), is still useful, though rapidly becoming dated. The same is true of J. E. Kidder, *Japan Before Buddhism* (1959). Newer and quite readable is Kidder's *Early Buddhist Japan* (1972), which is well illustrated. J. M. Kitagawa, *Religion in Japanese History* (1966), discusses both Shinto and Buddhism.

Early Japanese literary flowering has attracted much attention. I. Morris, *The World of the Shining Prince: Court Life in Ancient Japan* (1964), provides a general treatment of the climate in which early Japanese artists lived. Shikibu Murasaki's *The Tale of Genji* has been translated by A. Waley (1933), and I. Morris has translated *The Pillow Book of Sei Shonagon,* 2 vols. (1967).

Japanese feudalism, like its medieval European counterpart, continues to excite discussion and disagreement. Some provocative works include K. Asakawa, *Land and Society in Medieval Japan* (1965); P. Duus, *Feudalism in Japan* (1969); J. W. Hall's penetrating *Government and Local Power in Japan: 500–1700: A Study Based on Bizen Province* (1966); and E. O. Reischauer, "Japanese Feudalism," in R. Coulborn, ed., *Feudalism in History* (1956):26–48.

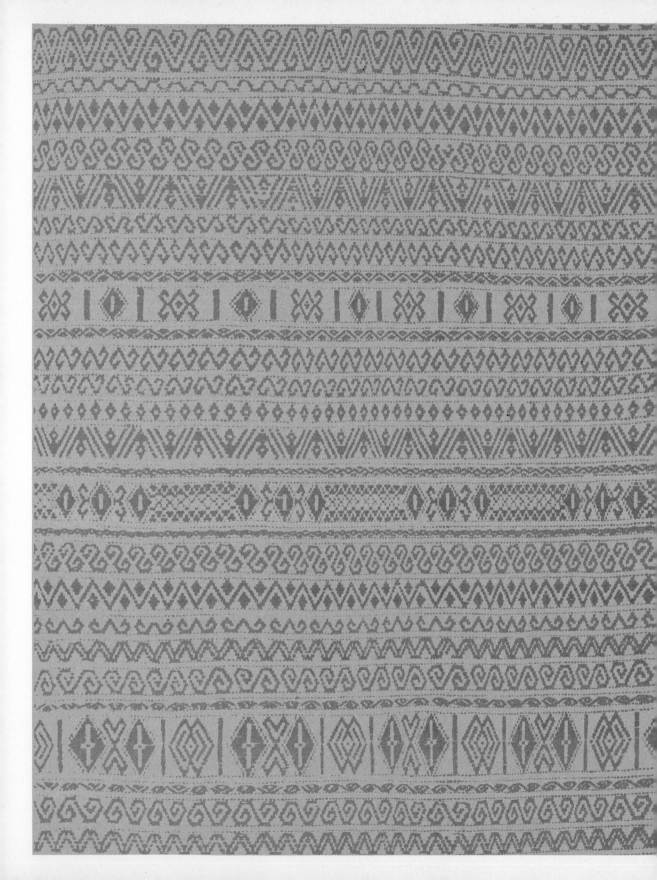

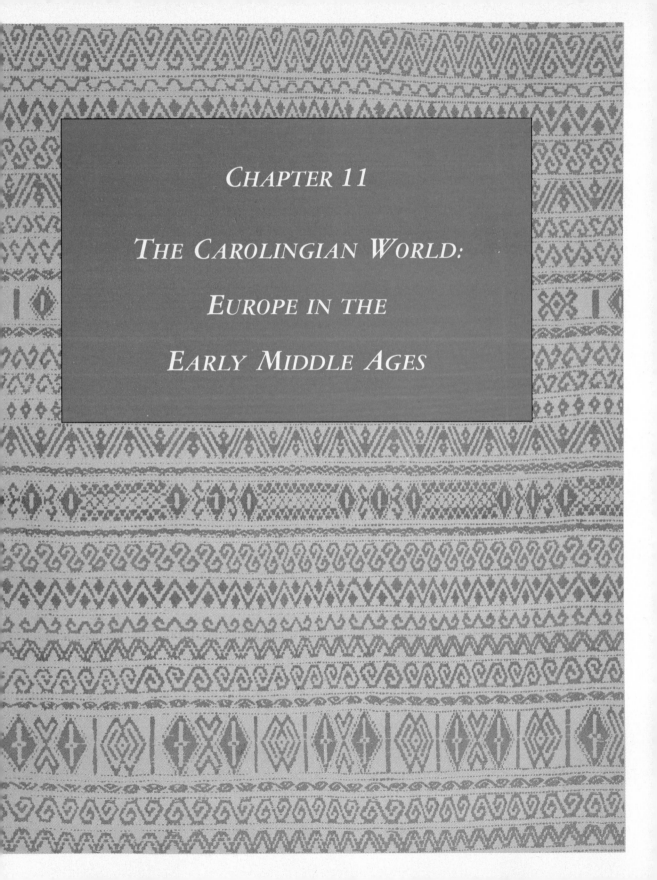

CHAPTER 11

THE CAROLINGIAN WORLD:

EUROPE IN THE

EARLY MIDDLE AGES

IN 733, the Frankish chieftain Charles Martel defeated the Muslim invaders at the battle of Tours in central France. At the time it was only another skirmish in the struggle between Christians and Muslims, but in retrospect it looms as one of the great battles of history: this Frankish victory halted Arab expansion in Europe. A century later, in 843, Charles Martel's three great-great-grandsons, after a bitter war, concluded the Treaty of Verdun, which divided the European continent among themselves.

Between 733 and 843, a society emerged that was distinctly European. A new kind of social and political organization, later called feudalism, appeared. And for the first time since the collapse of the Roman Empire, most of western Europe was united under one government. That government reached the peak of its development under Charles Martel's grandson, Charlemagne. Christian missionary activity among the Germanic peoples continued, and strong ties were forged with the Roman papacy. A revival of study and learning, sometimes styled the Carolingian Renaissance, occurred under Charlemagne.

This chapter will explore the following questions. What was feudalism? How did it come about? How did Charlemagne acquire and govern his vast empire? What was the significance of the relations between Carolingian rulers and the church? What was the Carolingian Renaissance? The culture of the Carolingian Empire has been described as "the first European civilization." What does this mean?

THE EIGHTH CENTURY: END OF THE ANCIENT WORLD?

Scholars have traditionally designated the fifth century as the end of the ancient world. But an influential twentieth-century historian, the Belgian Henri Pirenne, has argued that the eighth century was the real turning-point in Western civilization.

Pirenne's thesis focuses on the Mediterranean Sea. The Roman Empire had controlled the Mediterranean from the Bosporus in the east to the Straits of Gibraltar in the west. Roman trade, Roman armies, and Greco-Roman ideas had travelled on the Mediterranean; it was the highway that united the empire. Although the German tribes had conquered the western provinces in the fifth and sixth centuries, they had perpetuated many Roman ways. The Germans gradually converted to Christianity, and with Christianization came Romanization. German rulers in the West continued trade and economic relations with the East, and the Germans shared in the economic and cultural unity the Mediterranean provided.

But the Muslim conquests of the seventh and eighth centuries ended all this. The Mediterranean, long the thoroughfare of the Greco-Roman world, became a Muslim lake. By the time of Charlemagne in the late eighth century, the Muslims controlled the Mediterranean and the land bordering three sides of it. According to Pirenne, their control meant the real end of the ancient world, which had centered on the Mediterranean. In the eighth century, western Europe, which had been relying on Eastern imports, was cut off from its sources of supply. An isolated and agrarian economy developed as a result. Charlemagne's capital at Aix-la-Chapelle was a sign of the shift of political and military power to the north, away from the Mediterranean. For the next five hundred years, northern Europe, rather than Rome and Italy, was to be the center of culture and civilization. Thus the imperial coronation of Charlemagne by Pope Leo III on Christmas Day in the year 800 can be seen as the symbolic end of the ancient world and the start of the medieval.

Pirenne's argument rests heavily on Mohammed; indeed, as Pirenne put it, "It is therefore strictly correct to say that without Mohammed, Charlemagne would have been inconceivable."[1] By this he meant that the entire empire of Charlemagne was centered in northern Europe and oriented to the West as the direct consequence of Muslim expansion. Pirenne's interpretation has provoked vigorous debate. Historians have questioned his facts and disputed his conclusions. For one thing, considerable evidence suggests that trade between the East and the West continued through the eighth and ninth centuries and was not shut off by Muslim control of the Mediterranean. As this debate vividly illustrates, the division of time spans into distinct periods is always subject to interpretation. Whatever the merits of Pirenne's thesis, the eighth century deserves attention as a great turning point.

EQUESTRIAN STATUE OF CHARLEMAGNE *A medieval king was expected to be fierce (and successful) in battle, to defend the church and the poor, and to give justice to all. This majestic and idealized figure of Charlemagne conveys these qualities. The horse is both the symbol and the means of his constant travels. (French Embassy Press and Information Division)*

TOWARD A FEUDAL SOCIETY

In the period of the Germanic invasions the Roman imperial government had been compelled to retrench. Roman troops and Roman administrators were withdrawn from the provinces. Gallo-Romans in Gaul and Romanized natives in Britain were forced to cope as best they could. No authority was strong enough to provide peace over a wide area.

Men who could fight, or who owned horses, or who were wealthy and had the time to learn how to fight and ride could join a local band of warriors. But the vast defenseless majority, compelled to work the land for their livelihood, had little choice but to seek out some local strongman and ask that "lord" for protection. Local lords replaced Roman administrators. Western Europe was governed by the simple law that he should take who has the power, and he should keep who can.

FEUDALISM

Between the sixth and eighth centuries, European society evolved toward a condition that scholars later termed feudalism. Feudalism may be defined as a kind of social organization in which public political power resided in the private hands of a small military elite. The fundamental strength of the feudal elite rested on its military might. The ethos, the values – indeed, the entire culture of feudal society –

was military. Almost everything was determined by war or the preparation for war. Thus, loyalty was the highest virtue. It was the cement that held a warring society together.

In order to ensure the support of his fighters, a lord gave them land in exchange for their loyalty. Charles Martel got land to distribute to his men by confiscating church property. Lesser lords, as they defeated weaker neighbors and seized their property, divided it among their followers. Early feudalism resulted from a fusion of the Germanic custom of swearing allegiance to a warrior leader with the Roman practice of granting an estate or the booty of war to fighters or important servants. The mounted warrior became a vassal (from the Celtic word for "a well-born young man") of the lord. Though he was obliged to perform services in return for holding the land – his feud, or fief – the vassal lost nothing in social status.

The political power of the ruling class rested upon the ability to raise a contingent of fighting men, to hold courts, to coin money, and to conduct relations and make agreements with outside powers. These powers were held by many lords, both lay and ecclesiastical, and not just by monarchs. Many men became the vassals of several lords in order to acquire more land or money and thus improve their economic position. Feudal lords everywhere were out for themselves, and everywhere they tended to resist the centralizing ambitions of kings.

The ceremony by which a man became the vassal of another involved the use of religious objects, such as the Bible or relics of the saints, and the presence of a priest. The vassal knelt, placed his folded hands between those of the lord, and declared his intention to become the lord's man. By this he meant that he would fight for the lord or perform some

other kind of military service, such as castle-guard. The vassal then rose and swore his faith (or fidelity) on the Bible or the relics. Lord and vassal exchanged a kiss on the mouth, symbolizing peace between two social equals. The conclusion of the ceremony was marked by the lord's investing his new vassal with a symbol of his fief, such as a clump of earth.

Because feudal society was a military society, men held the dominant positions in it. A high premium was put on physical strength, fighting skill, and bravery. The legal and social position of women was not as insignificant as might be expected, however. Charters recording gifts to the church indicate that women held land in many areas. Women frequently endowed monasteries, churches, and other religious establishments. The possession of land obviously meant economic power. Moreover, women inherited fiefs. In southern France and Catalonia in Spain, women inherited feudal property as early as the tenth century. Other kinds of evidence attest to the status of women. In parts of northern France, children sometimes identified themselves in legal documents by their mother's name rather than their father's name, indicating that the mother's social position in the community was higher than the father's.

In a treatise he wrote in 822 on the organization of the royal household, Archbishop Hincmar of Reims placed the queen directly above the treasurer. She was responsible for giving the knights their annual salaries. She supervised the manorial accounts. Thus, in the management of large households, with many knights to oversee and complicated manorial records to supervise, the lady of the manor had highly important responsibilities. With such responsibility went power and influence.[2]

Feudalism concerned the rights, powers, and lifestyle of the military elite; manorialism involved the services and obligations of the peasant classes. The *economic* power of the warring class rested upon landed estates, which were worked by peasants. Hence feudalism and manorialism were inextricably linked. Peasants needed protection, and lords demanded something in return for that protection. Free peasants surrendered themselves and their lands to the lord's jurisdiction. The land was given back, but the peasants became tied to the land by various kinds of payments and services. In France, England, Germany, and Italy, local custom determined precisely what those services were, but certain practices became common everywhere. The serf was obliged to turn over to the lord a percentage of the annual harvest, usually in produce, sometimes in cash. The peasant paid a fee to marry someone from outside the lord's estate. He paid a fine, often his best beast, to inherit property. Above all, the peasant became part of the lord's permanent labor force. With vast stretches of uncultivated virgin land and a tiny labor population, lords encouraged population growth and immigration. The most profitable form of capital was not land but laborers. The small feudal class led lives devoted to war and leisure; toil was the usual fate of those who were not warriors or clerics.

In entering into a relationship with a feudal lord, the free farmer lost status. His position became servile, and he became a serf. That is, he was bound to the land and could not leave it without the lord's permission. He was also subject to the jurisdiction of the lord's court in any dispute over property or suspicion of criminal behavior.

The transition from freedom to serfdom was slow; its speed was closely related to the degree of political order in a given geographical region. Even in the late eighth century there were still many free men. And within the legal category of serfdom there were many economic levels, ranging from the highly prosperous to the desperately poor. Nevertheless, a social and legal revolution was taking place. Around the year 800, perhaps 60 percent of the population of Western Europe – completely free a century before – had been reduced to serfdom. The ninth-century Viking assaults on Europe created extremely unstable conditions and individual insecurity, leading to additional loss of personal freedom. Chapter 10 will look in detail at the lives of the peasants. As we shall see, although the later Middle Ages witnessed considerable upward social mobility, serfdom remained the condition of most Europeans, in fact if not in law, for almost a thousand years.

THE RISE OF THE CAROLINGIAN DYNASTY

In the seventh century, the kingdom of the Franks steadily deteriorated. Weak and incompetent rulers lost power to local strongmen. Central authority collapsed in the face of brute force. The administrative agencies of the Merovingian kings slipped into the hands of local powers.

The rise of the Carolingian family – whose name derives from the Latin *Carolus,* for "Charles" – began with the efforts of Pippin I in the mid-seventh century. Pippin made himself mayor of the palace of Austrasia, which meant that he was head of the Frankish administration. His grandson Pippin II (d. 714) also gained the title of mayor of the palace, and from that position worked to reduce the power of the Frankish aristocracy.

It was Pippin's son Charles Martel (714–741) who defeated the Muslims at Tours and thus checked Arab expansion into Europe. Charles's wars against the Saxons, the Burgundians, and the Frisians broke those weakening forces. His victory over the infidels and his successful campaigns within the Frankish kingdom added to the prestige of his family the reputation of great military strength. Charles Martel held the real power in the Frankish kingdom; the Merovingians were king in name only.

The rise of the Carolingian dynasty rested partly on papal support. In the early eighth century, while Charles Martel and his son Pippin III were attempting to bring the various Germanic tribes under their jurisdiction, they gained the support of two Anglo-Saxon missionaries, Willibrord and Wynfrith. The Northumbrian monk Willibrord crossed the English Channel and preached to the pagans on the Frisian Islands and in the area of the modern Netherlands, Belgium, and Luxembourg. With enormous zeal Willibrord organized the church of Friesland, established the see of Utrecht, and acted as the first archbishop. He also founded the abbey of Echternach (in what is now Luxembourg), which subsequently became an important missionary center.

Even more spectacular were the achievements of Wynfrith, or Boniface (680–754), as he was later called. A native of Devonshire in England, Boniface preached in Bavaria and Hesse in southern Germany. There, assisted by other monks from Britain, his many conversions attracted the attention of both Charles Martel and Pope Gregory II. Boniface traveled to Rome several times and was made a bishop. He became an enthusiastic champion of ecclesiastical principles and of papal authority in the Frankish kingdom.

Given the semibarbarous peoples with whom he was dealing, Boniface's achievements were remarkable. He founded the see of Mainz, the chief see of Germany, and the abbey of Fulda, which became one of the great centers of Christian culture in the ninth century. He built churches. He established the *Rule of Saint Benedict* in all the monasteries he founded or reformed. With the full support of Pippin III, Boniface held several councils that reformed the Frankish church. He even succeeded in cutting down the famous Oak of Thor, the center of a pagan cult.

Saint Boniface preached throughout Germany against divorce, polygamous unions, and incest. On these matters German custom and ecclesiastical law completely disagreed. The Germans allowed divorce simply by the mutual consent of both parties. The Germanic peoples also practiced polygamy and incest – sexual relations between brothers and sisters or between parents and children – on a wide scale. (Incest, in fact, is a major theme of a seventh-century German legend about the twins Sigmund and Siglinda, whose tragic love and the life of their son Siegfried were immortalized in three operas by the nineteenth-century composer Richard Wagner.) Church councils in the sixth and seventh centuries repeatedly condemned incest, indicating that it was common. And theologians since Saint Augustine had stressed that marriage, validly entered into, could not be ended.

Boniface's preaching was not without impact, for in 802 Charlemagne prohibited incest, and decreed that a husband might separate from an adulterous wife. The woman could be punished, and the man could not remarry in her lifetime. Charlemagne also encouraged severe punishment for adulterous men. In so doing, he contributed to the dignity of marriage, the family, and women.

Saint Boniface, known as the Apostle of Germany, is one of the most important fig-

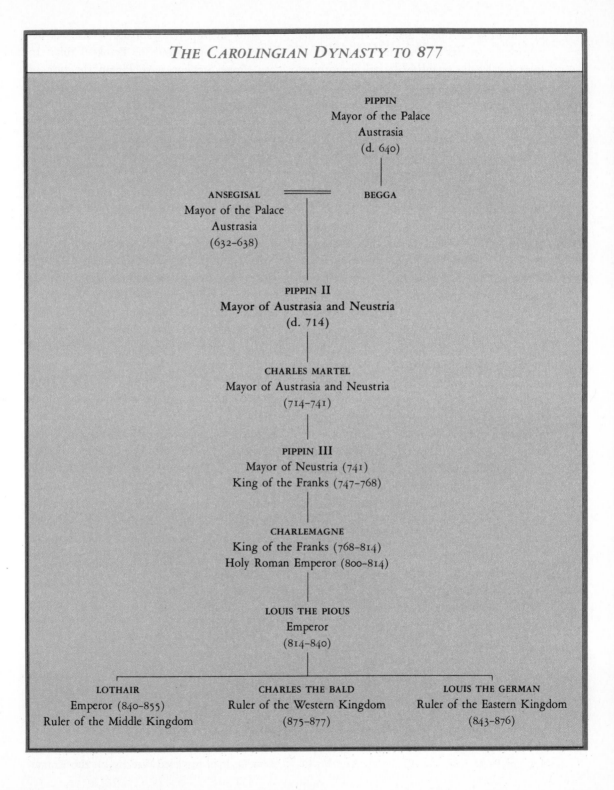

THE CAROLINGIAN DYNASTY TO 877

PIPPIN
Mayor of the Palace
Austrasia
(d. 640)

ANSEGISAL ═══ **BEGGA**
Mayor of the Palace
Austrasia
(632–638)

PIPPIN II
Mayor of Austrasia and Neustria
(d. 714)

CHARLES MARTEL
Mayor of Austrasia and Neustria
(714–741)

PIPPIN III
Mayor of Neustria (741)
King of the Franks (747–768)

CHARLEMAGNE
King of the Franks (768–814)
Holy Roman Emperor (800–814)

LOUIS THE PIOUS
Emperor
(814–840)

LOTHAIR
Emperor (840–855)
Ruler of the Middle Kingdom

CHARLES THE BALD
Ruler of the Western Kingdom
(875–877)

LOUIS THE GERMAN
Ruler of the Eastern Kingdom
(843–876)

ures in early European history. In all of his missionary activity he promoted peace and respect for legally established civil authorities. Charles Martel and Pippin III protected Boniface, and he preached Christian obedience to rulers. Because of his staunch adherence to Roman ideas, Roman traditions, and the Roman pope, the Romanization of Europe accompanied Christianization.

Charles Martel had been king of the Franks in fact but not in title. His son Pippin III (747–768) made himself king in title as well as in fact. In Germanic custom — and custom was law — the kingship had to pass to someone with royal blood. Pippin did not want to do away with the ineffectual Merovingian king, but he did want the kingship. Because the missionary activity of Boniface had spread Christian ideals and enhanced papal influence in the Frankish kingdom, Pippin decided to consult the pope about the kingship. Accordingly, Pippin sent Boniface to Rome to ask the pope whether the man who has the power is entitled to be king. Pope Zacharias, guided by the Augustinian principle that the real test of kingship is whether it provides for order and justice, responded in 751 that he who has the power should also have the title. This answer constituted recognition of the Carolingians.

Just as the emperors Constantine and Theodosius in the fourth century had taken actions that would later be cited as precedents in the relations between church and state (pages 287 and 288), so Pippin III in the eighth century took papal confirmation as official approval of his title. In 752, Pippin III was formally elected king of the Franks by the great lords, or magnates, of the Frankish territory. Two years later the pope — who needed Pippin's protection from the Lombards — came to Gaul and personally anointed Pippin king at Paris.

Thus an important alliance was struck between the papacy and the Frankish ruler. In 754, Pope Stephen gave Pippin the title of protector of the Roman church. Pippin in turn agreed to restore to the papacy territories in northern Italy recently seized by the Lombards; he promptly marched into Italy and defeated the Lombards. The Carolingian family had received official recognition and anointment from the leading spiritual power in Europe. The papacy had gained a military protector.

On a second successful campaign in Italy in 756, Pippin made a large donation to the papacy. The gift was estates in central Italy that technically belonged to the Byzantine emperor at Constantinople. Known as the Papal States, they existed over a thousand years, until the newly formed kingdom of Italy abolished them in 1870.

Because of his anointment, Pippin's kingship took on a special spiritual and moral character. Before Pippin, only priests and bishops had received anointment: Pippin became the first lay person to be anointed with the sacred oils. His person was considered sacred. He was acknowledged as *rex et sacerdos* (king and priest). Pippin also cleverly eliminated possible threats to the Frankish throne, and the pope promised him support in the future. When Pippin died, his son Charlemagne succeeded him.

THE EMPIRE OF CHARLEMAGNE

Charles the Great (768–814) built on the military and diplomatic foundations of his ancestors. Charles's secretary and biographer, the Saxon Einhard, wrote a lengthy description of this warrior-ruler. It has serious flaws, partly because it is modeled directly on the Roman author Suetonius's *Life of the Emperor Augustus*. Still, it is the earliest medieval biography of a layman, and historians consider it generally accurate:

Charles was large and strong, and of lofty stature, though not disproportionately tall . . . the upper part of his head was round, his eyes very large and animated, nose a little long, hair fair, and face laughing and merry. Thus his appearance was always stately and dignified . . . although his neck was thick and somewhat short, and his belly rather prominent; but the symmetry of the rest of his body concealed these defects. His gait was firm, his whole carriage manly, and his voice clear, but not so strong as his size led one to expect. His health was excellent, except during the four years preceding his death. . . . Even in those years he consulted rather his own inclinations than the advice of physicians, who were almost hateful to him, because they wanted him to give up roasts, to which he was accustomed, and to eat boiled meat instead. In accordance with the national custom, he took frequent exercise on horseback and in the chase, accomplishments in which scarcely any people in the world can equal the Franks. He enjoyed the exhalations from natural warm springs, and often practiced swimming, in which he was such an adept that none could surpass him; and hence it was that he built his palace at Aix-la-Chapelle, and lived there constantly during his latter years until his death. He used not only to invite his sons to his bath, but his nobles and friends, and now and then a troop of his retinue or bodyguard. . . .

He used to wear the national, that is to say, the Frank, dress — next his skin a linen shirt and linen breeches, and above these a tunic fringed with silk; while hose fastened by bands covered his lower limbs, and shoes his feet, and he protected his shoulder and chest in winter by a close-fitting coat of otter or marten skins. Over all he flung a blue cloak, and he always had a sword girt about him, usually one with a gold or silver hilt and belt; he
sometimes carried a jeweled sword, but only on great feastdays or at the reception of ambassadors from foreign nations.[3]

Though crude and brutal, Charlemagne was a man of enormous intelligence. He appreciated good literature, such as Saint Augustine's *City of God*, and Einhard considered him an unusually effective speaker. On the other hand, he could not even write his own name.

For all Charles's concern for moderation in food and wine, he had three wives, one after the other, and after they died, three concubines simultaneously. The austere code of sexual morality he published for the empire reflects the attitude of the clerics who wrote it far more than the behavior of the warriorking. The most striking feature of Charlemagne's character was his phenomenal energy, which helps to account for his great military achievements.

TERRITORIAL EXPANSION

Continuing the expansionist policies of his ancestors, Charlemagne fought more than fifty campaigns and became the greatest warrior of the early Middle Ages. In what is now France, he subdued all of the north. In the south, the lords of the mountainous ranges of Aquitaine — what is now called Basque country — fought off his efforts at total conquest. The Muslims in northeastern Spain were checked by the establishment of strongly fortified areas known as marches.

Charlemagne's greatest successes were in what is today called Germany. There, his concerns were basically defensive. In the course of a thirty-year war against the semibarbaric Saxons, he added most of the northwestern German tribes to the Frankish kingdom. The story goes that because of their repeated rebellions, Charlemagne ordered more than four thousand Saxons slaughtered on one day.

To the south, he achieved spectacular results. In 773–774, the Lombards in northern Italy once again threatened the papacy. Charlemagne marched south, overran fortresses at Pavia and Spoleto, and incorporated Lombardy – including Venetia, Istria, and Dalmatia – into the Frankish kingdom. To his title as king of the Franks, he added king of the Lombards. This victory ended all serious attempts at the unification of Italy until the nineteenth century.

By around 805, the Frankish kingdom included all of continental Europe except Spain, Scandinavia, southern Italy, and the Slavic fringes of the east (see Map 11.1). Not since the third century A.D. had any ruler controlled so much of the Western world. Not until Napoleon Bonaparte in the early nineteenth century was the feat to be repeated.

THE GOVERNMENT OF THE CAROLINGIAN EMPIRE

Charlemagne ruled a vast rural world dotted with isolated estates and characterized by constant petty violence. His empire was definitely not a state as people today understand that term; it was a collection of primitive peoples and semibarbarian tribes. Apart from a small class of warrior-aristocrats and clergy, almost everyone engaged in agriculture. Trade and commerce played only a small part in the economy. Cities served as the headquarters of bishops and as ecclesiastical centers.

By constant travel, personal appearances, and the sheer force of his personality, Charlemagne sought to awe his conquered peoples with his fierce presence and his terrible justice. By confiscating the estates of the great territorial magnates, he acquired land with which to gain the support of lesser lords.

Charles divided his kingdom into counties, which served as administrative units. Two or three hundred counts were appointed as the king's representatives. They had full military and judicial powers to maintain law and order and to dispense justice at the local level. They held their offices for life. As a link between local authorities and the central government of the emperor, Charles appointed officials called *missi dominici,* agents of the lord king. The empire was divided into visitorial districts. Each year, beginning in 802, two missi, usually a count and a bishop or abbot, visited assigned districts. They held courts and investigated the judicial, financial, and clerical activities of the district. They held commissions to regulate crime, moral conduct, the clergy, education, the poor, and many other matters. The missi checked up on the counts and worked to prevent the counts' positions from becoming hereditary: strong counts with hereditary estates would have weakened the power of the emperor.

In especially barbarous areas, such as the Spanish and Danish borders, Charles set up areas called marks. There, royal officials called margraves had extensive powers to govern their dangerous localities.

A modern state has institutions of government, such as a civil service, courts of law, financial agencies for the collection and apportionment of taxes, and police and military powers with which to maintain order internally and defend against foreign attack. These simply did not exist in Charlemagne's empire. What held society together were relationships of dependence cemented by oaths promising faith and loyalty.

Although the empire lacked viable institutions, some of the Carolingians involved in governing did have vigorous political ideas. The abbots and bishops who served as Charlemagne's advisers worked out what was for

IRELAND

NORTHUMBRIA
Jarrow
York

DANISH
MARCH

MERCIA
EAST
ANGLIA
NORTH WALES
WESSEX KENT
WEST WALES ESSEX
SUSSEX

SAXONY
804
Fulda

Aix-la-Chapelle
AUSTRASIA
Mainz
Echternach

TRIBUTARY SLAVIC PEOPLES

BRITTANY
811
NEUSTRIA
Rouen
Paris
Tours

ALEMANNIA
BAVARIA
788

BURGUNDY
Lyons

VENETIA
Milan
Pavia
ISTRIA

DALMATIA

AQUITAINE
Bordeaux

Marseilles

OMMAYAD KINGDOM OF SPAIN

Roncevalles

SPANISH MARCH
811
Barcelona

CORSICA

PAPAL
STATES
Spoleto
Rome
Monte Cassino
DUCHY
OF
BENEVENTO
Salerno

Toledo

Cordova

SARDINIA

BYZANTINE EMPIRE

SICILY

Monasteries
Tributary peoples
Byzantine Empire

Frankish Kingdom, 768
Areas conquered by Charlemagne

0   100   200 Km.
0   100   200 Mi.

MAP 11.1   THE CAROLINGIAN WORLD   The
extent of Charlemagne's nominal jurisdiction was extraordinary; it was not equalled until the nineteenth
century.

THE IMPERIAL CORONATION OF CHARLE-
MAGNE *Contemporary evidence for Charlemagne's
coronation by Pope Leo III is literary and contradictory. This fifteenth-century illustration supports the
ecclesiastical view that Charlemagne (kneeling) hum-*
*bly accepted the crown, which the papacy could grant
or withhold. The presence of two cardinals (in
broad-brimmed hats) and the dress of all show this is
a late medieval interpretation of the event. (Musée
Condé, Chantilly/Giraudon)*

their time a sophisticated political ideology.
In letters and treatises they set before the emperor high ideals of behavior and of government. They wrote that a ruler may hold
power from God, but he is responsible to the
law. Just as all subjects of the empire were
required to obey him, so he too was obliged
to respect the law. They envisioned a unified
Christian society presided over by a king who
was responsible for the maintenance of peace,
which would enable Christians to pursue their
pilgrimage to the City of God. They encouraged the emperor to maintain law and
order and to do justice, without which neither
the ruler nor the "state" has any justification.
These views derived largely from Saint Augustine's theories of kingship. Inevitably, they
could not be realized in an illiterate, half-

Christianized, and preindustrial society. But
they were the seeds from which medieval and
even modern ideas of government were to
develop.

THE IMPERIAL CORONATION OF CHARLEMAGNE (800)

In the autumn of the year 800, Charlemagne
paid a momentous visit to Rome. Here are
two accounts of what happened.

According to the Frankish *Royal Annals*, a
year-by-year description of events:

*On the very day of the most holy nativity of the
Lord [Christmas], when the king at Mass had
risen from prayer before the tomb of Blessed Peter
the Apostle, Pope Leo placed the crown on his
head, and by all the people of Rome he was ac-*

claimed: Long Life and Victory to the August Charles, the Great and Peace-Giving Emperor, crowned by God. And after the ovations, the pope did obeisance to him according to the custom observed before the ancient emperors, and the title of Patricius [Protector] being dropped, he was called Emperor and Augustus.[4]

Charlemagne's secretary Einhard wrote:

His last journey there [to Rome] was due to another factor, namely that the Romans, having inflicted many injuries on Pope Leo – plucking out his eyes and tearing out his tongue, he had been compelled to beg the assistance of the king. Accordingly, coming to Rome in order that he might set in order those things which had exceedingly disturbed the condition of the Church, he remained there the whole winter. It was at the time that he accepted the name of Emperor and Augustus. At first he was so much opposed to this that he insisted that although that day was a great [Christian] feast, he would not have entered the Church if he had known beforehand the pope's intention. But he bore very patiently the jealousy of the Roman Emperors [that is, the Byzantine rulers] who were indignant when he received these titles. He overcame their arrogant haughtiness with magnanimity, a virtue in which he was considerably superior to them, by sending frequent ambassadors to them and in his letters addressing them as brothers.[5]

Charlemagne became *Holy* Roman emperor, adding the sacred authority of the Christian church to the universal authority of the Roman emperor. Einhard says that Charlemagne seldom used the imperial title. But the fact that he sometimes used it illustrates a significant point. Charlemagne governed most of continental Europe. He considered himself a Christian king ruling a Christian people. The title expressed his connection with the Rome of the caesars and the Rome of the popes. By using it, Charlemagne was consciously perpetuating the old Roman imperial

notions, while at the same time identifying with the new Rome of the Christian church. Charlemagne and his government represent a combination of German feudal practices and Christian ideals. These two elements were basic constituents of Europe in the early Middle Ages.

For centuries scholars have debated the significance of the imperial coronation of Charlemagne. Did Charles plan the coronation in St. Peter's on Christmas Day? What did he have to gain from the imperial title? Did Pope Leo III arrange the coronation in order to identify the Frankish monarchy with the papacy and papal policy? Did a coronation actually happen, or are accounts of it later inventions?

Although final answers will probably never be found, two things are certain. First, later German rulers were anxious to gain the imperial title and to associate themselves with the legend of Charlemagne and with ancient Rome. They wanted to use the ideology of imperial Rome to strengthen their own positions. Second, ecclesiastical authorities continually cited the event as proof that the dignity of the imperial crown could be granted only by the pope. The imperial coronation of Charlemagne, whether event or nonevent, was to have a profound effect on the course of German history and on the later history of Europe.

THE CAROLINGIAN INTELLECTUAL REVIVAL

It is ironic that Charlemagne's most enduring legacy was the stimulus he gave to scholarship and learning. Barely literate himself, preoccupied with the control of vast territories, much more of a warrior than a thinker, he nevertheless set in motion a cultural revival that had "international" and long-lasting consequences. The revival of learning associated with Charlemagne and his court at Aix-la-Chapelle drew its greatest inspiration from seventh- and eighth-century intellectual developments in the Anglo-Saxon kingdom of Northumbria, situated on the northernmost tip of the old Roman world.

NORTHUMBRIAN CULTURE

The victory of the Roman forms of Christian liturgy and monastic life at the Synod of Whitby in 664 marked the official end of the Celtic church in Britain (page 290). But Whitby did not end the Celtic influence on Christianity in Northumbria. Irish-Celtic culture – through such monasteries as Lindisfarne and York – permeated the Roman church in Britain and resulted in a flowering of artistic and scholarly activity.

Northumbrian creativity owes a great deal to the intellectual curiosity and collecting zeal of Saint Benet Biscop (ca 628–689). Descended from a noble Northumbrian family, Benet Biscop became a monk at Lérins, an island monastery in the Mediterranean that enjoyed valuable contacts with the Eastern monastic tradition of Syria and Egypt. He returned to Britain in the company of the Syrian archbishop of Canterbury, Theodore of Tarsus. Between 674 and 682, Benet Biscop founded the monasteries of Wearmouth and Jarrow. A strong supporter of Benedictine monasticism, he introduced the Roman form of ceremonial into the new religious houses and encouraged it in older ones. Benet Biscop made five dangerous trips to Italy, raided the libraries, and brought back to Northumbria manuscripts, relics, paintings, and other treasures. These books and manuscripts formed the libraries on which much later study was based.

Northumbrian monasteries produced scores of books: missals (used for the celebration of the mass), psalters (which contained the 150 psalms and other prayers used by the monks in their devotions), commentaries on the Scriptures, illuminated manuscripts, law codes, and collections of letters and sermons. The finest product of Northumbrian art is probably the Gospel book produced at Lindisfarne around 700. The incredible expense involved in the publication of such a book – for vellum, coloring, gold leaf – represents in part an aristocratic display of wealth. The script, called uncial, is a Celtic version of contemporary Greek and Roman handwriting. The illustrations have a strong Eastern quality. They combine the abstract style of the Christian Middle East and the narrative approach of classical Roman art. Likewise, the use of geometrical decorative designs shows the influence of Syrian art. Many scribes, artists, and illuminators must have participated in its preparation.

The finest representative of Northumbrian and indeed all Anglo-Saxon scholarship is the Venerable Bede (ca 673–735). The simplicity of Bede's life illustrates his greatness. Given by his parents when he was seven years old as an oblate or "offering" to Benet Biscop's monastery at Wearmouth, he was later sent to the new monastery at Jarrow five miles away. There, surrounded by the books Benet Biscop had brought from Italy, Bede spent the rest of his life.

Bede's scrupulous observance of the *Rule of Saint Benedict* expressed his deep piety. His days were punctuated only by the bells for choir and other religious duties. As a scholar, his patience and diligence reflected his deep love for learning. Contemporaries revered Bede for his learned commentaries on the Scriptures and for the special holiness of his life, which earned him the title "Venerable." He was the most widely read author in the entire Middle Ages.

Modern scholars praise Bede for his *Ecclesiastical History of the English Nation.* Broader in scope than the title suggests, it is the chief source of information about early Britain. Bede searched far and wide for his information, discussed the validity of his evidence, compared various sources, and exercised a rare critical judgment. For these reasons, he has been called "the first scientific intellect among the Germanic peoples of Europe."[6]

Bede was probably the greatest master of chronology of the Middle Ages. He began the system of dating events from the birth of Christ, rather than from the foundation of the city of Rome, as the Romans had done, or from the regnal years of kings, as the Germans did. Bede introduced the term *anno Domini,* "in the year of the Lord," abbreviated A.D. He fit the entire history of the world into this new dating method. (The reverse, or diminishing, dating system of B.C., before Christ, does not seem to have been widely used before 1700.) The Anglo-Saxon missionary Saint Boniface introduced this system of reckoning time throughout the Frankish empire of Charlemagne.

At the very time that monks at Lindisfarne were producing their Gospel book, and Bede at Jarrow was writing his *History,* another Northumbrian monk was at work on a nonreligious epic poem that provides considerable information about the society that produced it. The poem *Beowulf* is perhaps the finest expression of the secular literature of the eighth century. Though the tale is almost childish in its simplicity, scholars have hailed it as a masterpiece of Western heroic literature.

The great hall of the Danish king Hrothgar has been ravaged for twelve years by a half-human monster called Grendel. Hrothgar and his men cannot stop Grendel's attacks. Finally Beowulf, a relative of the Swedish royal house, hears of Grendel's murderous destruc-

THE SCRIBE EZRA   Monks at Bede's monastery at Jarrow made this copy of an early Christian manuscript showing the Jewish scribe Ezra writing his chronicle. The backless bench on which he works appears very uncomfortable. Books were stored against theft and climate in heavy chests or cabinets. (Scala/ Editorial Photocolor Archives)

tion. With a bodyguard of fourteen trusted warriors, Beowulf sails to Denmark and in a brutal battle destroys Grendel. Hrothgar and his queen, Wealhtheow, give a great banquet for Beowulf and his followers. Afterward, Grendel's mother enters the hall and carries off one of Hrothgar's closest advisers to revenge her son's death. Beowulf ultimately catches and destroys her. This victory is followed by more feasting, and Beowulf returns home to Sweden laden with rich gifts.

Beowulf later becomes king of a Swedish tribe and rules them for fifty years. When his country is ravaged by a terrible dragon, the aged Beowulf challenges him. In the ensuing battle, Beowulf is overwhelmed by the dragon's fiery breath, and all but one of his followers flee. Beowulf defeats the dragon, but is mortally wounded and dies.[7]

The story resembles ordinary Norse legends, but it is actually permeated with classical, Germanic, and Christian elements. Though the poem was written in England, all the action takes place in Scandinavia. This reflects the "international" quality of the culture of the age, or at least the close ties between England and the Continent in the eighth century. (Britain exported wool to the settlements in Frisia that later became the flourishing commercial centers at Ypres and Bruges, which produced cloth.)

Beowulf's entire life was devoted to fighting and war. His values are military and aristocratic: the central institution in the poem is the *gesith,* or Germanic band of warriors united to fight with Beowulf. The highest virtue is loyalty to him, and loyalty is maintained by the giving of gifts. Yet the author was a Christian monk, and the basic theme of the poem is the conflict between good and evil. Beowulf, however, does not exhibit any Christian humility. Never one to hide his light under a bushel, he boasts of his exploits unashamedly. In this, he embodies the classical idea of fame, the notion that fame is the greatest achievement because it is all that a person leaves behind.

Pagan and Germanic symbols and practices suffuse Beowulf. Fighting, feasting, and drinking preoccupy its warrior heroes. There is no glimpse of those who raised and prepared the food they consume. The author did not think peasants deserved mention. In a famous scene Hrothgar's beautiful queen Wealhtheow enters the great hall, dispensing grace and gifts. The scene suggests that women of the upper class served a decorative function in aristocratic society. But Wealhtheow may have been handing out presents to the warriors because she had custody of and responsibility for her husband's treasure.

In another scene the body of a dead king, along with considerable treasure, is put on a ship and floated out to sea. That this was a typical method of burial for Scandinavian kings is known from the ship burial uncovered at Sutton Hoo in England in 1939. Such customs are a far cry from traditional Christian burial. A monk may have composed *Beowulf,* but the persistence of this practice indicates that conversion was still imperfect in much of Europe.

Reading *Beowulf,* one enters a world of darkness, cold, gloom, and pessimism, pierced by a weak ray of Christian hope. It is the foremost expression of the psychological complexities and spiritual contradictions of what has been called the heroic age of Scandinavia — the eighth and ninth centuries.

A less serious literary genre than the epic poem, highly popular in Anglo-Saxon England and Carolingian Europe, was the riddle. Riddles were more than a guessing game for children; in the riddle a poet took on the characteristics or personality of someone or something. Riddles were intended to instruct and to entertain:

Swings by his thigh a thing most magical!
Below the belt, beneath the folds
of his clothes it hangs, a hole in its front end,
stiff-set & stout, but swivels about.

Levelling the head of this hanging instrument,
its wielder hoists his hem above the knee:
it is his will to fill a well-known hole
that it fits fully when at full length.

He has often filled it before. Now he fills it again.[8]

The answer is a key. Riddling was a popular

game in monasteries, and the subjects were not always pious.

The physical circumstances of life in the seventh and eighth centuries make Northumbrian cultural achievements all the more remarkable. Learning was pursued under terribly primitive conditions. Monasteries such as Jarrow and Lindisfarne stood on the very fringes of the European world. The barbarian Picts, just an afternoon's walk from Jarrow, were likely to attack at any time.

Food was not the greatest problem. The North Sea and the nearby rivers, the Tweed and the Tyne, yielded abundant salmon and other fish, which could be salted or smoked for winter, a nutritious if monotonous diet. Climate was another matter. Winter could be extremely harsh. In 664, for example, deep snow was hardened by frost from early winter until mid-spring. When it melted away, many animals, trees, and plants were found dead. To make matters worse, disease and sickness could take terrible tolls. Bede described events in the year 664:

In the same year of our Lord 664 there was an eclipse of the sun on the third day of May at about four o'clock in the afternoon. Also in that year a sudden pestilence first depopulated the southern parts of Britain and then attacked the kingdom of the Northumbrians as well. Raging far and wide for a long time with cruel devastation it struck down a great multitude of men. . . . This same plague oppressed the island of Ireland with equal destruction.[9]

Damp cold with bitter winds blowing across the North Sea must have pierced everyone and everything, even the stone monasteries. Inside, only one room, the calefactory or warming room, had a fire. Scribes in the scriptorium, or writing room, had to stop frequently to rub the circulation back into their numb hands. These monk-artists and

BINDING OF THE LINDAU GOSPELS This splendid example of the Carolingian revival combines the geometric forms of Anglo-Irish art with the Roman portrait tradition. The strong face of Christ shows no suffering. The semiprecious stones around the border are raised to catch the light. (The Pierpont Morgan Library)

monk-writers paid a very high physical price for what they gave to posterity.

Had they remained entirely insular, Northumbrian cultural achievements would have been of slight significance. As it happened, an Englishman from Northumbria played a decisive role in the transmission of English learning to the Carolingian Empire and continental Europe.

THE CAROLINGIAN RENAISSANCE

Charlemagne's empire disintegrated shortly after his death in 814. But the support he gave to education and learning preserved the writings of the ancients and laid the foundations for all subsequent medieval culture. Charlemagne promoted a revival that scholars have named the Carolingian Renaissance.

At his court at Aix-la-Chapelle, Charlemagne assembled learned men from all over Europe. From Visigothic Spain came Theodulf, the best writer of Latin verse of the day. From Pavia in Lombardy came the monk-historian Paul the Deacon, who later wrote the invaluable *History of the Lombards,* still the chief source for the history of the sixth and seventh centuries. From the abbey of Fulda came Einhard, who served as a royal administrator and Charlemagne's closest adviser and biographer.

The most important scholar and the leader of the palace school was the Northumbrian Alcuin. He was born about a year after Bede's death (ca 735) and educated at the cathedral school at York. On a visit to Italy in 781, Alcuin met Charlemagne, who invited him to his court. From then until his death in 804, Alcuin remained the emperor's major adviser on religious and educational matters.

Alcuin was an unusually prolific scholar. He prepared some of the emperor's official documents, and wrote many moral *exempla,* or models, which set high standards for royal behavior and constitute a treatise on kingship. Alcuin's letters to Charlemagne set forth political theories on the authority, power, and responsibilities of a Christian ruler.

What did the scholars at Charlemagne's court do? They copied books and manuscripts and built up libraries. They devised the beautifully clear handwriting known as Carolingian minuscule, from which modern Roman type is derived. (This script is called minuscule because it has lower-case letters; the Romans had only capitals.) They established schools all across Europe, attaching them to

monasteries and cathedrals. They placed great emphasis on the education of priests, trying to make all of them at least able to read, write, and do simple arithmetical calculations. The greatest contribution of the scholars at Aix-la-Chapelle was not so much the originality of their ideas as their hard work of salvaging and preserving the thought and writings of the ancients. Thus the Carolingian Renaissance was a rebirth of interest in, and the study and preservation of, the ideas and achievements of classical Greece and Rome.

Language has been called "the nourishing mother of history." It is the core, the center, of all culture and civilization. Without the ability to communicate ideas, grammatically and effectively, orally and in writing, an individual or a society is barbaric. The revival of learning inspired by Charlemagne and directed by the Northumbrian Alcuin halted the dangers of barbaric illiteracy on the European continent. Although hardly widespread by later standards, basic literacy was established among the clergy and even among some of the nobility. The small group of scholars at Aix-la-Chapelle preserved Greek and Latin culture from total extinction in the West.

Meanwhile, the common people spoke their local or vernacular languages. The Bretons, for example, retained their local dialect, and the Saxons and Bavarians could not understand each other (see Map 11.1). Communication among the diverse peoples of the Carolingian Empire was possible only through the medium of Latin.

Once basic literacy was established, monastic and other scholars went on to more difficult work. By the middle years of the ninth century there was a great outpouring of more sophisticated books. Collections of canon law, illustrated manuscripts, codes of Frankish law, commentaries on the Bible and on the church

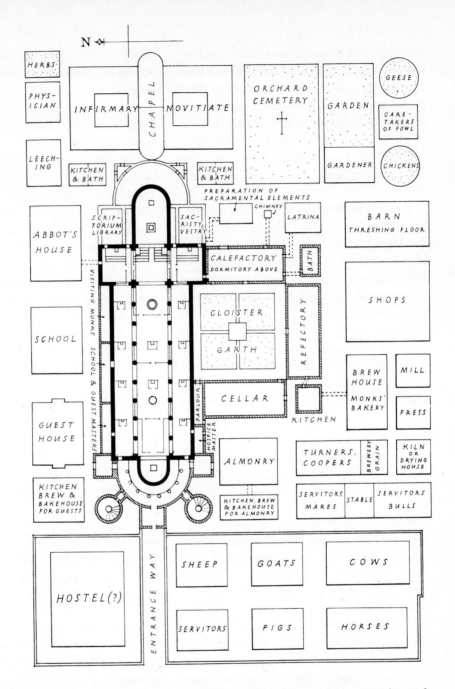

N

HERBS

PHYS-
ICIAN

LEECH-
ING

KITCHEN
& BATH

ABBOT'S

HOUSE

SCHOOL

GUEST

HOUSE

KITCHEN
BREW &
BAKEHOUSE
FOR GUESTS

HOSTEL(?)

INFIRMARY

CHAPEL

NOVITIATE

KITCHEN
& BATH

ORCHARD
CEMETERY

GARDEN

GARDENER

GEESE

CARE-
TAKERS
OF FOWL

CHICKENS

SCRIP-
TORIUM
LIBRARY

SAC-
RISTY
VESTRY

PREPARATION OF
SACRAMENTAL ELEMENTS

CHIMNEY

LATRINA

BARN
THRESHING FLOOR

CALEFACTORY
DORMITORY ABOVE

BATH

VISITING MONKS SCHOOL & GUEST MASTERS

CLOISTER

GARTH

REFECTORY

SHOPS

CELLAR

PARLOUR

KITCHEN

BREW
HOUSE

MONKS'
BAKERY

MILL

PRESS

HOSPICE MASTER

ALMONRY

KITCHEN, BREW
& BAKEHOUSE
FOR ALMONRY

TURNERS,
COOPERS

BREWERY GRAIN

KILN
OR
DRYING
HOUSE

SERVITORS
MARES

STABLE

SERVITORS
BULLS

ENTRANCE WAY

SHEEP

SERVITORS

GOATS

PIGS

COWS

HORSES

PLAN FOR AN IDEAL MONASTERY *This is a ninth-century architectural design for a self-supporting monastic community of 270 members. The monks' lives centered around the church and the cloister (center). Note the herb garden close to the physician's quarters. The western entrance for visitors was sur-* *rounded by the hostel for poor guests and pens for farm animals — with all the inevitable smells. (Kenneth John Conant,* Carolingian and Romanesque Architecture, 800–1200. Pelican History of Art, 2nd rev. ed. New York. 1978. p. 57)*

fathers flowed from monastic and cathedral scriptoria. Ecclesiastical writers, imbued with the legal ideas of ancient Rome and the theocratic ideals of Saint Augustine, instructed the semibarbarian rulers of the West. And it is no accident that medical study in the West began, at Salerno in southern Italy, in the late ninth century, *after* the Carolingian Renaissance.

Alcuin completed the work of his countryman Boniface – the Christianization of northern Europe. Latin Christian attitudes penetrated deeply into the consciousness of European peoples. By the tenth century, the patterns of thought and lifestyles of educated western Europeans were those of Rome and Latin Christianity. Even the violence and destruction of the great invasions of the late ninth and tenth centuries could not destroy the strong foundations laid by the Northumbrian Alcuin and his colleagues.

HEALTH AND MEDICAL CARE IN THE EARLY MIDDLE AGES

Scholars' careful examination of medical treatises, prescription (or herbal) books, manuscript illustrations, and archaeological evidence has recently revealed a surprising amount of information about medical treatment in the early Middle Ages. In a society devoted to fighting, warriors and civilians alike stood a strong chance of wounds from sword, spear, battle-axe, or some blunt instrument. Trying to eke a living from poor soil with poor tools, perpetually involved in pushing back forest and wasteland, the farmer and his family daily ran the risk of accidents. Poor diet weakened everyone's resistance to disease. People bathed rarely. Low standards of personal hygiene increased the danger of

infection. This being the case, what medical or surgical attention was available to medieval people?

The Germanic peoples had no rational understanding of the causes of and cures for disease. They believed that sickness was due to one of three factors: elf-shot, in which elves hurled darts that produced disease and pain; wormlike creatures in the body; and the number 9. Treatment involved the use of charms, amulets, priestly incantations, and potions. Drinks prepared from mistletoe, for example, were thought to serve as an antidote to poison and to make women fertile.

Medical practice consisted primarily of drug and prescription therapy. Through the monks' efforts and through the recovery of Greek and Arabic manuscripts, a large body of the ancients' prescriptions was preserved and passed on. For almost any ailment, several recipes were likely to exist in the prescription lists. Balsam was recommended for coughs. For asthma an ointment combining chicken, wormwood, laurel berries, and oil of roses was to be rubbed on the chest. The scores of prescriptions to rid the body of lice, fleas, and other filth reflect the frightful standards of personal hygiene. The large number of prescriptions for eye troubles suggests that they too must have been very common. This is understandable, given the widespread practice of locating the fireplace in the center of the room. A lot of smoke and soot filtered into the room, rather than going up the chimney. One remedy calls for bathing the eyes in a solution of herbs mixed with honey, balsam, rainwater, saltwater, or wine.

Poor diet caused frequent stomach disorders and related ailments such as dysentery, constipation, and diarrhea. The value of dieting and avoiding greasy foods was recognized. For poor circulation, a potion of meadow wort, oak rind, and lustmock was recommended. Pregnant women were advised to abstain from eating the flesh of almost all male animals, because their meat might deform the child. Men with unusually strong sexual appetites were advised to fast and to drink at night the juice from agrimony (an herb of the rose family) boiled in ale. If a man suffered from a lack of drive, the same plant boiled in milk gave him "courage."

Physicians were not concerned with the treatment of specific diseases or illnesses. They did not examine patients. The physician, or leech, as he was known in Anglo-Saxon England, treated only what he could see or deduce from the patient's obvious symptoms. Treatment consisted of the application of herbal, animal, or superstitious remedies to these symptoms. The physician knew little about the pathology of disease or physiological functions. He knew little of internal medicine. He had no accurate standards of weights and measures. Prescriptions called for "a pinch of" or "a handful" or "an eggshell full."

Warfare and the dangers inherent in working the land made broken bones, wounds, and burns common. All wounds and open injuries invited infection, and infection invited gangrene. Several remedies were known for wounds. Physicians appreciated the antiseptic properties of honey, and prescriptions recommended that wounds be cleaned with it. When an area or limb had become gangrenous, a good technique of amputation existed. The physician was instructed to cut above the diseased flesh, that is, to cut away some healthy tissue and bone, in order to hasten cure. The juice of white poppy plants — the source of heroin — could be added to wine and drunk as an anesthetic. White poppies, however, grew only in southern Europe and North Africa. If a heavy slug of wine was not enough to dull the patient, he or she had to be held down forcibly while the physician

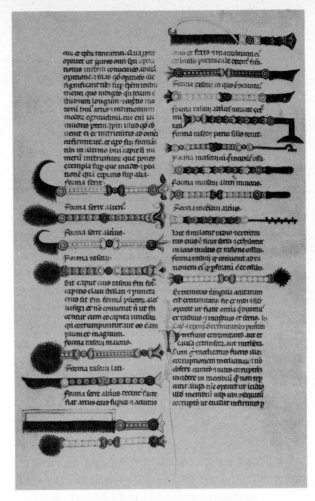

MEDICAL INSTRUMENTS *Medieval physicians invented hundreds of instruments for surgical operations. This page shows a number of knives and saws. The accompanying text explains which instrument to use for various operations. (Yale Medical Library)*

cut. Butter and egg whites, which have a soothing effect, were prescribed for burns.

Teeth survive long periods of burial and give reasonably good information about disease. Evidence from early medieval England shows that the incidence of tooth decay was very low. In the adult population, the rate of cavities was only one-sixth that of the present day. Cavities below the gum line, however, were very common, due to the prevalence of carbohydrates and starch in the diet. The result was abscesses of the gums. These and other forms of periodontal disease were widespread after the age of thirty.[10]

The spread of Christianity in the Carolingian era had a beneficial effect on medical knowledge and treatment. Several of the church fathers expressed serious interest in medicine. Some of them even knew something about it. The church was deeply concerned about human suffering, whether physical or mental. Christian teaching vigorously supported concern for the poor, sick, downtrodden, and miserable. Churchmen taught that while all knowledge came from God, he had supplied it so that people could use it for their own benefit.

In the period of the bloodiest violence, the sixth and seventh centuries, medical treatment was provided by the monasteries. No other places offered the calm and quiet atmosphere necessary for treatment and recuperation. Monks took care of the sick. They collected and translated the ancient medical treatises. They cultivated herb gardens from which medicines were prepared. Monks practiced medicine throughout the Middle Ages, as did lay people.

The foundation of a school at Salerno in southern Italy sometime in the ninth century gave a tremendous impetus to medical study by lay people. Its location attracted Arabic, Greek, and Jewish physicians from all over the Mediterranean region. Students flocked there from northern Europe. The Jewish physician Shabbathai Ben Abraham (931–982) left behind pharmacological notes that were widely studied in later centuries.

By the eleventh century, the medical school at Salerno enjoyed international fame. Its most distinguished professor then was Constantine the African. A native of Carthage, he had studied medicine throughout the Middle East and, because of his thorough knowledge of oriental languages, served as an important transmitter of Arabic culture to the West. Constantine taught and practiced medicine at Salerno for some years before becoming a monk at Monte Cassino.

Several women physicians also contributed to the celebrity of the school. Trotula, an authority on gynecological problems, wrote a book called *On Female Disorders.* Though not connected with the Salerno medical school, the abbess Hildegard (1098–1179) of Rupertsberg in Hesse, Germany, reputedly treated the emperor Frederick Barbarossa. Hildegard's treatise *On the Physical Elements* shows a remarkable degree of careful scientific observation.

How available was medical treatment? Most people lived on isolated rural estates, and had to take such advice and help as was available locally. Physicians were very few. They charged a fee, which only the rich could afford. Most illnesses, apparently, simply took their course. People had to develop a stoical attitude. Death came early. A person of forty was considered old. People's vulnerability to ailments for which there was no probable cure contributed to a fatalistic acceptance of death at an early age. Early medical literature shows that attempts to relieve pain and suffering were primitive and crude. Still, it is significant that serious attempts *were* made.

DIVISION AND DISINTEGRATION OF THE CAROLINGIAN EMPIRE (814–887)

Charlemagne left his vast empire to his only surviving son, Louis the Pious (814–840), who had actually been crowned emperor in his father's lifetime. Deeply religious he was, and well educated, but Louis was no soldier. Thus he could not retain the respect and loyalty of the warrior-aristocracy on whom he depended for troops and for administration of his territories. Disintegration began almost at once.

The basic reason for the collapse of the Carolingian Empire is simply that it was too big. In Charlemagne's lifetime it was held together by the sheer force of his personality and driving energy. After his death, it began to fall apart. The empire lacked a bureaucracy like that of the Roman Empire – the administrative machinery necessary for strong and enduring government. It was a collection of tribes held together at the pleasure of warrior-aristocrats, men most interested in strengthening their own local positions and insuring that they could pass on to their sons the offices and estates they had amassed. Counts, abbots, bishops – both lay and ecclesiastical magnates needed estates to support themselves and reward their followers. In their localities, they simply assumed judicial, military, and financial functions. Why should they obey an unimpressive distant ruler who represented a centralizing power, a power that threatened their localistic interests? What counted was strength in one's own region and the preservation of family holdings.

Bad roads filled with thugs and rivers swarming with pirates made communication within the empire very difficult. Add to this the Frankish custom of dividing estates among all male heirs. Between 817 and his death in 840, Louis the Pious made several divisions of the empire. Dissatisfied with their portions and anxious to gain the imperial title, Louis's sons, Lothair, Louis the German, and Charles the Bald fought bitterly among themselves. Finally, in the Treaty of Verdun of 843, the brothers agreed to partition the empire (see Map 11.2).

MAP 11.2   THE DIVISION OF THE CAROLINGIAN EMPIRES, 843   *The treaty of Verdun (843), which divided the empire among Charlemagne's grandsons, is frequently taken as the start of the separate development of Germany, France, and Italy. The "Middle Kingdom" of Lothair, however, lacking defensive borders and any political or linguistic unity, soon broke up into several territories.*

Lothair, the eldest, received the now-empty title of emperor and the "middle kingdom," which included Italy and the territories bordered by the Meuse, Saône, and Rhône rivers in the west and the Rhine in the east. Almost immediately this kingdom broke up into many petty principalities extending diagonally across Europe from Flanders to Lombardy. When the French and German monarchs were trying to build strong central governments in the twelfth and thirteenth centuries, this area was constantly contested between them. Even in modern times, the "middle kingdom" of Lothair has been blood-soaked.

The eastern and most Germanic part of the Carolingian Empire passed to Louis the German. The western kingdom went to Charles the Bald; it included the provinces of Aquitaine and Gascony and formed the basis of medieval and modern France. The descendants of Charles the Bald held on in the west until 987, when the leading magnates elected Hugh Capet as king. The heirs of Louis the German ruled the eastern kingdom until 911, but real power was in the hands of local chieftains. Everywhere in the tenth century, fratricidal warfare among the descendants of Charlemagne accelerated the spread of feudalism.

GREAT INVASIONS OF THE NINTH CENTURY

After the Treaty of Verdun and the division of Charlemagne's empire among his grandsons, continental Europe presented an easy target for foreign invaders. All three kingdoms were torn by domestic dissension and disorder. No European political power was strong enough to put up effective resistance to external attacks. The frontier and coastal defenses erected by Charlemagne and maintained by Louis the Pious were completely neglected.

From the moors of Scotland to the mountains of Sicily there arose in the ninth century the Christian prayer "Save us, O God, from the violence of the Northmen." The Northmen, also known as Normans or Vikings, were Germanic peoples from Norway, Sweden, and Denmark who had remained beyond the sway of the Christianizing and civilizing influences of the Carolingian Empire. Some scholars believe that the name "Viking" derives from the Old Norse word *vik,* meaning creek. A Viking, then, was a pirate who waited in a creek or bay to attack passing vessels.

Charlemagne had established marches, fortresses, and watchtowers along his northern coasts to defend his territory against Viking raids. Their assaults began around 787, and by the mid-tenth century they had brought large chunks of continental Europe and Britain under their sway. In the east they pierced the rivers of Russia as far as the Black Sea. In the west they sailed as far as Greenland and even to the coast of North America, perhaps as far south as Boston.

The Vikings were superb seamen. Their advanced methods of boatbuilding gave them great speed and maneuverability. Propelled either by oars or sails, deckless, about sixty-five feet long, a Viking ship could carry between forty and sixty men — quite enough to harass an isolated monastery or village effectively. These boats, navigated by thoroughly experienced and utterly fearless sailors, moved through the most complicated rivers, estuaries, and waterways in Europe. They could move swiftly, attack, and get away before help could arrive.

Scholars disagree about the reasons for these migrations. Some maintain that because the Vikings practiced polygamy, their countries were vastly overpopulated. Since the property of a family passed to the oldest son, other sons had to emigrate. Others argue that climatic conditions and crop failures forced migration. Still others insist that the Northmen were looking for trade and new commercial contacts. What better targets of plunder, for example, than the mercantile centers of northern France and Frisia?

Plunder they did. Viking attacks were bitterly savage. At first they attacked and sailed off laden with booty. Later, they returned, settled down, and colonized the areas they had conquered. For example, the Vikings overran a large part of northwestern France and called

VIKING SHIP MODEL *The Norwegian original was built entirely of oak, weighed over twenty tons, and could carry a sizable contingent of men and horses. With fleets of these ships, the Vikings conducted piratical raids, territorial conquests, and colonizing ventures. (Courtesy, World Heritage Museum. Photo: Caroline Buckler)*

the territory Norsemanland, from which the word "Normandy" is derived.

Scarcely had the savagery of the Viking assaults begun to subside when Europe was hit from the east and south (see Map 11.3). Beginning around 862, Magyar, or Hungarian, tribes crossed the Danube and pushed steadily westward. They subdued northern Italy, compelled Bavaria and Saxony to pay tribute, and penetrated even into the Rhineland and Burgundy. These roving bandits attacked isolated villages and monasteries, taking prisoners and selling them in the Eastern slave markets. The Magyars were not colonizers; their sole object was booty and plunder.

The Magyars and Vikings depended upon fear. In their initial attacks on isolated settlements, every man, woman, and child was put to the sword. A few attractive women might be spared to satisfy the lusts of the conquerors or to be sold into slavery. The Hungarians and Scandinavians struck such terror in rural and defenseless peoples that they often gave up without a struggle. Many communities bought peace by paying tribute.

From the south the Muslims began new encroachments, concentrating on the two southern peninsulas, Italy and Spain. Their goal too was plunder. In Italy the monks of Monte Cassino were forced to flee. The Muslims drove northward and sacked Rome in 846. Most of Spain had remained under their

TO GREENLAND AND
NORTH AMERICA

ICELAND
874

FAEROES
800

SHETLANDS
700

VIKINGS

Novgorod 820

Volga

IRELAND
839

866-878

841-884

BRITAIN

Vistula

Elbe

Oder

882

Dnieper

Rouen

Aix-la-Chapelle

895

NORMANDY

Seine

Loire

896-911

Rhine

Rhine

900

MAGYARS

883

843-882

Bordeaux

917

Rhône

899

907 911

866

Santiago

Garonne

Marseilles

895

Danube

Lisbon
844

Tagus

Barcelona

CORSICA

Rome

Monte
Cassino

Constantinople

BALEARICS

859-861

846

0   200   400 Km.

844

SARDINIA

0   200   400 Mi.

842

827

SICILY

MUSLIMS

840-896

♱ Monastery

───── Vikings

▄ ▄ ▄ Magyars

───── Muslims

MAP 11.3 THE GREAT INVASIONS OF THE
NINTH CENTURY *Note the Viking penetration of
eastern Europe and their probable expeditions to
North America. What impact did their various invasions have on European society?*

domination since the sixth century (page 311). Expert seamen, they sailed around the Iberian peninsula, braved the notoriously dangerous shoals and winds of the Atlantic coast, and attacked the settlements along the coast of Provence. Muslim attacks on the European continent in the ninth and tenth centuries were less destructive, primarily because in comparison to the rich and sophisticated culture of the Arab capitals, northern Europe was primitive, backward, and offered little.

What was the effect of these invasions on the structure of European society? Viking, Magyar, and Muslim attacks accelerated the development of feudalism. Lords capable of rallying fighting men, supporting them, and putting up resistance to the invaders did so. They also assumed political power in their territories. Weak and defenseless people sought the protection of local strongmen. Free men sank to the level of serfs. Consequently, European society became further fragmented. Public power became increasingly decentralized.

FEUDALISM AND HISTORY

The adjective *feudal* is often used disparagingly to describe something antiquated and barbaric. It is similarly commonplace to think of medieval feudalism as a system that let a small group of lazy military leaders exploit the producing class, the tillers of the soil. This is not a very useful approach. Preindustrial societies from ancient Greece to the American South before the Civil War to some twentieth-century Latin American countries have been characterized by sharp divisions between the "exploiters" and the "exploited." To call all such societies feudal strips the term

of significant meaning and distorts our understanding of medieval feudalism. As many twentieth-century scholars have demonstrated, when feudalism developed it served the needs of medieval society.

The term *feudalism* was first coined in the late seventeenth century. The men who used it meant a type of government in which political power was treated as a private possession and divided among a large number of lords. Later, abolition of feudalism was among the main rallying-cries of the French Revolution and other eighteenth-century democratic revolutions. (What the revolutionaries really meant was manorialism and aristocratic privilege; by that time, feudalism had not existed in France for several hundred years.)

Scholars agree that feudalism was a persistent feature of medieval European culture. It was, however, far from uniform. The feudalism developing in Charlemagne's ninth-century Frankish kingdom was vastly different from the feudalism of thirteenth-century France under Louis IX. The feudalism of eleventh-century Normandy was considerably different from that of eleventh-century Anglo-Saxon England just twenty-six miles away. The word itself inaccurately implies the constancy of the feud, the land a lord gave to a vassal in return for his promise to fight or perform some other service. In fact, the giving of land was largely a tenth-century development. Eighth-century lords maintained their vassals in their own households, and even in the tenth century most vassals in France held no land. Some lords gave their vassals cash instead of land.

Feudalism is often characterized as a pyramid with weak men at the bottom, ever more important lords in the middle, and the king at the top. But lords and kings never arranged themselves so neatly. Many men became vassals of several lords in order to acquire more land or money. Medieval European feudalism frequently lacked organization, regularity, and rational connections. Feudal lords everywhere were out for themselves, and everywhere they tended to oppose the centralizing ambitions of kings.

The central point about medieval society is that economic and political power were in the hands of military leaders. Successful lords provided protection for the peasants who worked the land. They also exercised political and judicial authority over the dependent serfs. When the lord was a bishop or abbot, he had ecclesiastical as well as civil jurisdiction over his peasants. Because almost all communities were rural, isolated, and vulnerable to attack, the basic need of society was physical security. Consequently, the military virtues and values of the feudal nobility infused all aspects of the culture.

———◆———

The culture that emerged in Europe between 733 and 843 has justifiably been called the first European civilization. That civilization had definite characteristics: it was feudal, Christian, and infused with Latin ideas and models. A military elite controlled most forms of economic and political power. Almost all peoples were baptized Christians. Latin was the common language of educated people everywhere; what was written was written in Latin. In spite of the disasters of the ninth and tenth centuries, these features remained basic aspects of European culture for centuries to come.

The century and a half after the death of Charlemagne in 814 witnessed a degree of disintegration, destruction, and disorder un-

paralleled in Europe until the twentieth century. The Viking, Magyar, and Muslim invasions made a frightful situation absolutely disastrous. The Carolingian Empire was split into several parts, each tending to go its own way. No civil or religious authority could maintain stable government over a very wide area. Local strongmen provided what little security existed. Commerce and long-distance trade were drastically reduced. Leadership of the church became the political football of Roman aristocratic families. The rich became warriors; the poor sought protection. The result was that society underwent feudalization.

NOTES

1. H. Pirenne, *Mohammed and Charlemagne,* Barnes & Noble, New York, 1955, pp. 234–235.

2. See D. Herlihy, "Land, Family, and Women in Continental Europe, 701–1200," in *Women in Medieval Society,* ed. S. M. Stuart, University of Pennsylvania Press, Philadelphia, 1976, pp. 13–45.

3. Einhard, *The Life of Charlemagne,* with a foreword by S. Painter, University of Michigan Press, Ann Arbor, 1960, pp. 50–51.

4. B. D. Hill, ed., *Church and State in the Middle Ages,* John Wiley & Sons, New York, 1970, p. 45.

5. Ibid., pp. 46–47.

6. R. W. Southern, *Medieval Humanism and Other Studies,* Basil Blackwell, Oxford, 1970, p. 3.

7. D. Wright, trans., *Beowulf,* Penguin Books, Baltimore, 1957, pp. 9–19.

8. M. Alexander, trans., *The Earliest English Poems,* Penguin Books, Baltimore, 1972, p. 99.

9. L. Sherley-Price, trans., *Bede: A History of the English Church and Peoples,* Penguin Books, Baltimore, 1962, book 3, chap. 27, p. 191.

10. See S. Rubin, *English Medieval Medicine,* Barnes & Noble, New York, 1974.

SUGGESTED READING

In spite of centuries of war, violence, and destruction, a sizable literature survives from the period once inaccurately described as the Dark Ages. Scholars have devoted considerable attention to that literature because it was produced in such a crucial period, and the enterprising student who seeks further information about it may find the following works useful.

Chapters 4, 5, and 6 of J. B. Russell, *A History of Medieval Christianity: Prophecy and Order* (1968), describe the mind of the Christian church and show how it gradually made an impact on pagan Germanic peoples. C. Dawson, *Religion and the Rise of Western Culture* (1958), emphasizes the religious origins of Western culture. C. H. Talbot, ed., *The Anglo-Saxon Missionaries in Germany* (1954), gives a good picture, through biographies and correspondence, of eighth-century religious life.

Einhard's *Life of Charlemagne* is probably the best starting point for study of the great chieftain. There is no easily accessible and thorough treatment of the man and his government, but the advanced student with a knowledge of French should see L. Halphen, *Charlemagne et L'Empire Carolingien* (1949), the standard scholarly treatment. Recent research has been incorporated in E. Perroy, "Carolingian Administration," in S. Thrupp, ed., *Early Medieval Society* (1967). J. Brondsted, *The Vikings* (1960), is an excellently illustrated study of many facets of the culture of the Northmen.

In addition to the references to Bede, Beowulf, and Anglo-Saxon poetry in the Notes, D. L. Sayers, trans., *The Song of Roland* (1957), provides an excellent key, in epic form, to the values and lifestyles of the feudal classes. For the eighth-century revival of learning, see W. Levison, *England and the Continent in the Eighth Century* (1946); M. L. W. Laistner, *Thought and Letters in Western Europe, 500–900* (1931); and the beautifully written evocation by P. H. Blair, *Northumbria in the Days of Bede* (1976). E. S. Duckett, *Alcuin, Friend of Charlemagne* (1951),

makes light and enjoyable reading. L. Wallach, *Alcuin and Charlemagne*, rev. ed. (1968), is a technical study of Alcuin's treatises for the advanced student. The best treatment of the theological and political ideas of the period is probably K. F. Morrison, *The Two Kingdoms: Ecclesiology in Carolingian Political Thought* (1964), a difficult book.

Those interested in the role of women and children in early medieval society should see two articles: D. Herlihy, "Land, Family, and Women in Continental Europe, 701–1200," and E. Coleman, "Infanticide in the Early Middle Ages," both in S. M. Stuart, ed., *Women in Medieval Society* (1976).

For health and medical treatment, the curious student should consult S. Rubin, *Medieval English Medicine, A.D. 500–1300* (1974), especially pp. 97–149; W. H. McNeill, *Plagues and Peoples* (1976); A. Castiglioni, *A History of Medicine,* trans. E. B. Krumbhaar (1941); and the important article by J. M. Riddle, "Theory and Practice in Medieval Medicine," *Viator* 5 (1974): 157–184.

The literature on feudalism and manorialism is very rich. F. L. Ganshof, *Feudalism* (1961), and J. R. Strayer, "Feudalism in Western Europe," in *Feudalism in History,* ed. R. Coulborn (1956), are probably the best introductions. M. Bloch, *Feudal Society,* trans. L. A. Manyon (1961) remains the standard scholarly study. The more recent treatments of Perry Anderson, *Passages from Antiquity to Feudalism* (1978), and Georges Duby, *The Early Growth of the European Economy: Warriors and Peasants from the Seventh to the Twelfth Century* (1978), stress the evolution of social structures and mental attitudes. For the significance of the ceremony of vassalage, see Jacques Le Goff, "The Symbolic Ritual of Vassalage," in his *Time, Work, & Culture in the Middle Ages,* trans. Arthur Goldhammer (1982), a collection of provocative but difficult essays that includes his "The Peasants and the Rural World in the Literature of the Early Middle Ages." The best broad treatment of peasant life and conditions is Georges Duby, *Rural Economy and Country Life in the Medieval West,* trans. C. Postan (1968).

CHAPTER 12

REVIVAL, RECOVERY,

AND REFORM

BY THE LAST QUARTER of the tenth century, after a long and bitter winter of discontent, the first signs of European spring were appearing. The European springtime lasted from the early eleventh century to the end of the thirteenth century. This period from about 1050 to 1300 has often been called the High Middle Ages. The term designates a time of crucial growth and remarkable cultural achievement between two eras of economic, political, and social crisis.

What were the ingredients of revival? How did they come about? What was the social and economic impact of the recovery of Europe? How did reform of the Christian church affect relations between the church and civil authorities? These are the questions discussed in this chapter.

POLITICAL REVIVAL

The eleventh century witnessed the beginnings of political stability in western Europe. Foreign invasions gradually declined, and domestic disorder subsided. This development gave people security in their persons and property. Security and political stability, supported by the peace movements of the church, contributed to a slow increase in population. Political order and stability paved the way for economic recovery.

THE DECLINE OF INVASION AND CIVIL DISORDER

The most important factor in the revival of Europe after the disasters of the ninth century was the gradual decline in foreign invasions and the reduction of domestic violence. In 911 the Norwegian leader Rollo subdued large parts of what was later called Normandy. The West Frankish ruler Charles the Simple, unable to oust the Northmen, went along with that territorial conquest. He recognized Rollo as duke of Normandy on the condition that Rollo swear allegiance to him and hold the territory as a sort of barrier against future Viking assaults. This agreement, embodied in the treaty of Saint-Clair-sur-Epte, marks the beginning of the rise of Normandy.

Rollo kept his word. He exerted strong authority over Normandy and in troubled times supported the weak Frankish king. Rollo and his men were baptized as Christians. Although additional Viking settlers arrived, they were easily pacified. The tenth and eleventh centuries saw the steady assimilation of Normans and French. Major attacks on France had ended.

Rollo's descendant, Duke William I (1035–1087), made feudalism work as a system of government in Normandy. William attached specific quotas of military or knight service to the lands he distributed. Vassals who defaulted on their military obligations or refused attendance at the duke's court were ruthlessly executed. William forbade the construction of private castles, always the symbol of feudal independence. He limited private warfare and vigorously supported a peace movement sponsored by the church. He kept strict control over the coinage and maintained strong supervision over the church, actively participating in church councils and in the selection of abbots and bishops. By 1066 – the year William and the Normans invaded England – the duchy of Normandy was the strongest and the most peaceful territory in Western Europe.

Recovery followed a somewhat different pattern in England. Between 960 and 1040,

England was part of a vast Scandinavian empire that stretched from Normandy to Iceland and even to the eastern coast of North America. The Danish ruler Canute, king of England (1016–1035) and after 1030 king of Norway as well, made England the center of his empire. Canute promoted a policy of assimilation and reconciliation between Anglo-Saxons and Vikings.

Canute governed with the help of a *witan* – literally, a council of wise men – composed of Anglo-Saxons and Danes. He republished the laws of tenth-century Anglo-Saxon kings to show the continuity of his government with theirs. Canute and his followers accepted Christianity and Christian ideas about the responsibilities of a good and just king. Slowly the two peoples were molded together. The assimilation of Viking and Anglo-Saxon was personified by King Edward the Confessor (1042–1066), the son of an Anglo-Saxon father and a Norman mother who had taken Canute as her second husband.

In the East the German king Otto I (936–973) inflicted a crushing defeat on the Hungarians on the banks of the Lech River in 955. This battle halted the Magyars' westward expansion and threat to Germany, and made Otto a great hero to the Germans. It also signified the revival of the German monarchy and demonstrated that Otto was a worthy successor to Charlemagne.

When he was chosen king, Otto had selected Aix-la-Chapelle as the site of his coronation to symbolize his intention to continue the work and tradition of Charlemagne. The basis of his power was to be an alliance with, and control of, the church. Otto asserted the right to invest bishops and abbots with the symbols of their office – the ring, which symbolized the bishop's union with his dioceses, and the staff, which was the symbol of his pastoral authority. This assertion gave Otto effective control over ecclesiastical appointments. Before receiving religious consecration, bishops and abbots had to perform feudal homage for the lands that accompanied the church office. (This practice, later known as lay investiture, was to create a grave crisis in the eleventh century.)

Otto realized that he had to use the financial and military resources of the church to halt feudal anarchy. He used the higher clergy extensively in his administration, and the bulk of his army came from monastic and other church lands. Between 936 and 955, Otto succeeded in breaking the territorial power of the great German dukes.

In 962 Otto was crowned Holy Roman emperor by the pope. The imperial coronation had important results. It revived the Holy Roman Empire and its traditions, and it showed that Otto had the full support of the church in Germany and Italy. The uniting of the kingship with the imperial crown advanced German interests. Otto filled a power vacuum in northern Italy and brought about peace among the great aristocratic families. He established stable government there for the first time in over a century. Peace and political stability in turn promoted the revival of northern Italian cities, such as Venice.

By the start of the eleventh century, the Italian maritime cities were seeking a place in the rich Mediterranean trade. Pisa and Genoa fought to break Muslim control of the trade and shipping with the Byzantine Empire and the Orient. Once the Muslim fleets had been destroyed, the Italian cities of Venice, Genoa, and Pisa embarked on the road to prosperity. The eleventh century witnessed their steadily rising strength and wealth. Freedom from invasion and domestic security made economic growth possible all over western Europe.

The Peace Movements of the Church

Meanwhile the church was working to end arson, rape, homicide, and wanton destruction. The knights were developing a consciousness of themselves as a class, and the social gap between knight and serf was widening. Local lords ignored all laws and restraints, and attacks on churches were common. Physical assaults on the peasants and the devastation of their fields caused terrible suffering.

In the last quarter of the tenth century, councils of bishops met in Burgundy. The place is significant, for Burgundy was the part of the Carolingian Empire where anarchy was worst and where the clergy and the poor had no defenders whatsoever. The bishops accordingly proclaimed the Peace of God. It placed certain persons – monks who lived in monasteries, clergy who lived in villages and cathedral cities, and the poor – and certain places – church buildings and peasant fields – under ecclesiastical protection. Those who attacked such persons and places were anathematized, which meant that they were to be totally excluded from contact with all Christians. The bishops convinced their relatives among the aristocracy to participate in trying to enforce the peace.

In 1027, a council published the Truce of God, which attempted to regulate the times of fighting. An agreement was sworn that "in order to enable every man to show respect for the Lord's Day," no one was to attack an enemy between Saturday evening and Monday morning. Before 1050, the number of restricted days was increased. Thursday, Friday, and Saturday were added as reminders of the Last Supper, the Crucifixion, and the Entombment. Gradually, some saints' days were added and then the seasons of Advent (the four weeks before Christmas) and Lent (the six weeks before Easter). Lords and knights were urged to form groups to preserve the peace. How effective they were is not known, but without strong and determined lay support they would not have been very successful.

The chief importance of the peace movements lies in their influence on secular rulers. Around 1050, Duke William of Normandy compelled his vassals to join the movement. His backing, and eventually that of other leaders, was an important element in the promotion of peace.

Increasing Population and Mild Climate

A steady growth of population also contributed to the general recovery of Europe. The decline of foreign invasions and of internal civil disorder reduced the number of people killed and maimed. Feudal armies in the eleventh through thirteenth centuries continued their destruction, but they were very small by modern standards and fought few pitched battles. Most medieval warfare consisted of the besieging of castles or fortifications. As few as twelve men could defend a castle. With sufficient food and an adequate water supply, they could hold out for a long time. Monastic chroniclers, frequently bored and almost always writing from hearsay evidence, tended to romanticize medieval warfare (as long as it was not in their own neighborhoods). Most conflicts were petty skirmishes with slight loss of life. The survival of more young people, those most often involved in warring activities, and those usually the most sexually active meant a population rise.

Nor was there any "natural," or biological, hindrance to population expansion. Between the tenth and fourteenth centuries, Europe was not hit by any major plague or other medical scourge, though leprosy and malaria did strike down some people. Leprosy had entered Europe in the early Middle Ages. Although caused by a virus, the disease was not very contagious and, if contracted, worked slowly. Lepers presented a frightful appearance: the victim's arms and legs rotted away, and gangrenous sores emitted a horrible smell. Physicians had no cure. For these reasons, and because of the command in the thirteenth chapter of Leviticus that lepers be isolated, medieval lepers were segregated in hospitals called leprosaria.

Malaria, spread by protozoa-carrying mosquitoes that infested swampy areas, also caused problems. Malaria is characterized by alternate chills and fevers, and leaves the afflicted person extremely weak. Peter the Venerable, the ninth abbot of the monastery of Cluny (1122–1156), suffered for many of his later years from recurring bouts of malaria contracted on a youthful trip to Rome. Still, relatively few people caught malaria or leprosy. Crop failure and the ever-present danger of starvation were much more pressing threats.

The weather cooperated with the revival. Meteorologists believe that a slow but steady retreat of polar ice occurred between the ninth and the eleventh centuries. A significant warming trend occurred and continued until about 1200. The century between 1080 and 1180 witnessed exceptionally clement weather in England, France, and Germany, with mild winters and dry summers.

Good weather helps to explain advances in population growth, land reclamation, and agricultural yield. Increased agricultural output had a profound impact on society: it affected Europeans' health, commerce, trade, industry, and general lifestyle.

The greatest manifestation of the recovery of Europe was the rise of towns and the development of a new business and commercial class. This development was to lay the foundations for Europe's transformation, centuries later, from a rural and agricultural society into an industrial and urban society. This change, which had global implications, had its beginnings in the Middle Ages.

Why did these developments occur when they did? What sorts of people first populated the towns and where did they come from? What is known of town life in the High Middle Ages? What relevance did towns have for medieval culture? Part of the answer to at least one of these questions has already been given. Without increased agricultural output, there would not have been an adequate food supply for new town dwellers. Without a rise in population, there would have been no one to people the towns. Without a minimum of peace and political stability, merchants could not have transported and sold goods. (Merchants dislike nothing more than domestic disorder.)

THE RISE OF TOWNS

Medieval society was traditional, agricultural, and rural. The emergence of a new class that was none of these constituted a social revolution. The new class — artisans and merchants — came from the peasantry. They were landless younger sons of large families, driven away by land shortage. Or they were forced by war and famine to seek new possibilities. Or they were unusually enterprising and adventurous, curious and willing to take a chance.

One of the most exciting aspects of the

THE CITY WALLS OF MANTUA *Town walls protected citizens from theft and physical attack. Upkeep of the walls was usually the town's heaviest expense. (The Granger Collection)*

study of history is that facts and evidence may be explained in a variety of ways. There is no final or definitive interpretation. Serious investigation of the origin of European towns began only in the twentieth century. Historians have proposed three basic theories. Some scholars believe towns began as boroughs — that is, as forts or fortifications erected during the ninth-century Viking invasions. According to this view, towns were at first places of

defense or security into which farmers from the surrounding countryside moved when their area was attacked. Later, merchants were attracted to the fortifications because they had something to sell and wanted to be where the potential customers were. But most residents of the early towns made their livings by farming outside the town.

The Belgian historian Henri Pirenne maintained that towns sprang up when merchants who engaged in long-distance trade gravitated toward attractive or favorable spots, such as near a fort. Usually traders settled just outside the walls, in the *faubourgs* or *suburbs* – both of which mean "outside," or "in the shelter of the walls." As their markets prospered and as their number outside the walls grew, the merchants built a new wall around themselves. Such construction might be necessary every century or so. According to Pirenne, a medieval town consisted architecturally of a number of concentric walls, and the chief economic pursuit of its residents was trade and commerce.

A third explanation focuses on the great cathedrals and monasteries. The large numbers of clergy attached to a cathedral or monastery represented a demand for goods and services. Cathedrals such as Notre Dame in Paris conducted schools, which drew students from far and wide. Consequently, traders and merchants settled near the religious establishments to cater to the residents' economic needs. Concentrations of people accumulated, and towns came into being.

All three theories have validity, though none of them explains the origins of *all* medieval towns. Few towns of the tenth and eleventh centuries were "new" in the sense that American towns and cities were new in the seventeenth and eighteenth centuries. They were not carved out of forest and wilderness. Some medieval towns that had become flourishing centers of trade by the mid-twelfth century had originally been Roman army camps: York in northern England, Bordeaux in west central France, and Cologne in west central Germany are good examples of ancient towns that underwent revitalization in the eleventh century. Some Italian seaport cities, such as Pisa and Genoa, had been centers of shipping and commerce in earlier times. Muslim attacks and domestic squabbles had cut their populations and drastically reduced the volume of their trade in the early Middle Ages, but trade with Constantinople and the Orient had never stopped entirely. The restoration of order and political stability promoted rebirth and new development. Pirenne's interpretation accurately describes the Flemish towns of Bruges and Ypres. It does not fit the course of development in the Italian cities or in such centers as London.

Whether evolving from a newly fortified place or an old Roman army camp, from a cathedral site or a river junction or a place where several overland routes met, all medieval towns had a few common characteristics. Walls enclosed the town. (The terms "burgher" and "bourgeois" derive from the Old English and Old German words *burg, burgh, borg,* and *borough* for a walled or fortified place. Thus, a burgher or bourgeois was originally a person who lived or worked inside the walls.) The town had a marketplace. It often had a mint for the coining of money and a court to settle disputes.

In each town many people inhabited a small, cramped area. Census records do not exist for most of Europe before the early eighteenth century, but tax returns reveal the populations of many English towns in 1377. The largest city, London, had 23,314 people. The second largest city, Bristol, had only 6,345 citizens. Some continental cities, such as Paris, were probably much bigger. Size was not important; the real strength of the medieval towns rested in their people (Map 12.1).

By the late eleventh century many towns in Western Europe had small Jewish populations. Jews had emigrated in post-Roman times from the large cities of the Mediterranean region to France, the Rhineland, and Britain. During the Carolingian period Jews had the reputation of being richer and more

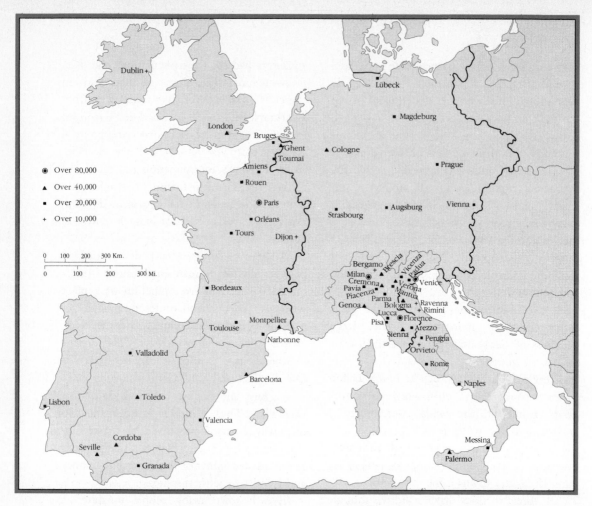

MAP 12.1   POPULATION OF EUROPEAN URBAN
AREAS, CA LATE THIRTEENTH CENTURY
Although there were scores of urban centers in the
thirteenth century, the Italian and Flemish towns had
the largest concentrations of people. By modern stan-
dards, Paris was Europe's only real city.

learned than the semibarbarian peoples among
whom they lived. They typically earned their
livelihoods in the lesser trades or by lending
money at interest, and Jews engaged in trade
had to be literate to keep records. The laws of
most countries forbade Jews to own land,
though they could hold land pledged to them
for debts. As townspeople they often possessed cultural eminence over their neighbors.
By the twelfth century many Jews were
usurers: they lent to consumers but primarily

to new or growing business enterprises. New
towns and underdeveloped areas where cash
was scarce welcomed Jewish settlers. Like
other businesspeople, the Jews preferred to
live near their work; they also settled close to
their synagogue or school. Thus originated
the Jews' street or quarter or ghetto. Such
neighborhoods gradually became legally defined sections where Jews were required to
live.

In their backgrounds and abilities, townspeople represented diversity and change. They constituted an entirely new element in medieval society. They fit into none of the traditional categories. Their occupations, their preoccupations, their very lives were different from those of the feudal nobility and the laboring peasantry. They were the "middle" class.

The aristocratic nobility glanced down with contempt and derision at the money-grubbing townspeople, but were not above borrowing from them. The rural peasantry peered up with suspicion and fear at the town dwellers. What was the point, the farmers wondered, of making money? Only land had real permanence.

Nor did the new commercial classes make much sense initially to churchmen. The immediate goal of the middle class was obviously not salvation. It was to be a good while before churchmen developed a theological justification for the new classes.

TOWN LIBERTIES

In the words of the Greek poet Alcaeus, "Not houses finely roofed or well built walls, nor canals or dockyards make a city, but men able to use their opportunity."[1] Men and opportunity. That is fundamentally what medieval towns meant – concentrations of people and varieties of chances. No matter where groups of traders congregated, they settled on someone's land and had to secure from king or count, abbot or bishop, permission to live and trade. Aristocratic nobles and churchmen were suspicious of and hostile to the middle class. They soon realized, however, that profits and benefits flowed to them and their territories from the markets set up on their land.

The history of towns in the eleventh through thirteenth centuries consists largely of the efforts of merchants to acquire "liberties." In the Middle Ages, liberties meant special privileges. For the town dweller, liberties included the privilege of living and trading on the lord's land. The most important privilege a medieval townsperson could gain was freedom. It gradually developed that an individual who lived in a town for a year and a day was free of servile obligations and status. More than anything else, perhaps, the liberty of personal freedom that came with residence in a town contributed to the emancipation of the serfs in the High Middle Ages. Liberty meant citizenship, and citizenship in a town implied the right to buy and sell goods there. Unlike foreigners and outsiders of any kind, the full citizen did not have to pay taxes and tolls in the market. Obviously, this increased profits.

In the twelfth and thirteenth centuries towns fought for, and slowly gained, legal and political rights. Since the tenth century, some English boroughs had held courts with jurisdiction over members of the town in civil and criminal matters. In the twelfth century, such English towns as London and Norwich developed courts that applied a special kind of law, called law merchant. It dealt with commercial transactions, debt, bankruptcy, proof of sales, and contracts. Law merchant was especially suitable to the needs of the new bourgeoisie. Around 1116, the count of Flanders granted to the burgesses of Ypres the right to hold a municipal court that alone could judge members of the town. Gradually, other towns across Europe acquired the same right. In effect it gave them judicial independence.[2]

In the acquisition of full rights of self-government, the merchant guilds played a large role. Medieval men were long accustomed to communal enterprises. In the late tenth and early eleventh centuries, men who were engaged in foreign trade joined together in merchant guilds; united enterprise provided them greater security and less risk of losses than did individual action. At about the same time, the artisans and craftsmen of particular trades formed guilds of their own. These were the butchers, the bakers, and the candlestick makers. Members of the craft guilds determined the quality, quantity, and price of the goods produced and the number of apprentices and journeymen affiliated with the guild. Terrible conflicts were to arise between the craft guilds and the merchant guilds in the thirteenth and fourteenth centuries, but that is a later story.

Women engaged in every kind of urban commercial activity, both as helpmates to their husbands and independently. In many manufacturing trades women predominated, and in some places women were a large percentage of the labor force. In fourteenth-century Frankfurt, for example, about 33 percent of the crafts and trades were entirely female, about 40 percent wholly male, and the remaining crafts roughly divided between the sexes. Craft guilds provided greater opportunity for women than did merchant guilds. In late twelfth-century Cologne, women and men had equal rights in the turners' guild (those who made wooden objects on a lathe). Most members of the Paris silk and woolen trades were women, and some achieved the mastership. Widows frequently followed their late husbands' professions, but if they remarried outside the craft they lost the mastership. Between 1254 and 1271 the chief magistrate of Paris drew up the following regulations for the silk industry:

Any woman who wishes to be a silk spinster (woman who spins) on large spindles in the city of Paris – i.e. reeling, spinning, doubling and re-

twisting – may freely do so, provided she observe the following customs and usages of the craft:

No spinster on large spindles may have more than three apprentices, unless they be her own or her husband's children born in true wedlock; nor may she contract with them for an apprenticeship of less than seven years or for a fee of less than 20 Parisian sols to be paid to her, their mistress. . . . If a working woman comes from outside Paris and wishes to practice the said craft in the city, she must swear before the guardians of the craft that she will practice it well and loyally and conform to its customs and usages. . . . No man of this craft who is without a wife may have more than one apprentice; . . if, however, both husband and wife practice the craft, they may have two apprentices and as many journeymen as they wish.[3]

Guild records show that women received lower wages than men for the same work, on the grounds that they needed less income.

By the late eleventh century, especially in the towns of the Low Countries (present-day Belgium and Holland) and northern Italy, the leading men in the merchant guilds were quite rich and powerful. They constituted an oligarchy in their towns, controlling economic life and bargaining with kings and lords for political independence. Full rights of self-government included the right to hold a town court, the right to select the mayor and other municipal officials, and the right to tax and collect taxes. Kings often levied on their serfs and unfree townspeople arbitrary taxes called tallage, or the taille. Such taxes (also known as customs) called attention to the fact that men were not free. Citizens of a town much preferred to levy and collect their own taxes.

A charter that King Henry II of England granted to the merchants of Lincoln around

1157 nicely illustrates the town's rights. The emphasized passages clearly suggest that the merchant guild had been the governing body in the city for almost a century and that anyone who lived in Lincoln for a year and a day was considered free:

Henry, by the grace of God, etc., to the bishop of Lincoln, and to the justices, sheriffs, barons, servants and all his liegemen, both French and English, of Lincoln, greeting. Know that I have granted to my citizens of Lincoln all their liberties and customs and laws which they had in the time of Edward [King Edward the Confessor] *and William and Henry, kings of England.* And I have granted them their gild-merchant, comprising men of the city and other merchants of the shire, as well and freely as they had it in the time of our aforesaid predecessors, kings of England. *And all the men who live within the four divisions of the city and attend the market, shall stand in relation to gelds* [taxes] *and customs and the assizes* [ordinances or laws] *of the city as well as ever they stood in the time of Edward, William and Henry, kings of England. I also confirm to them that if* anyone has lived in Lincoln for a year and a day without dispute from any claimant, *and has paid the customs, and if the citizens can show by the laws and customs of the city that the claimant has remained in England during that period and has made no claim,* then let the defendant remain in peace in my city of Lincoln as my citizen, *without* [having to defend his] *right.*[4]

Kings and lords were reluctant to grant towns self-government, fearing loss of authority and revenue if they gave the merchant guilds full independence. But the lords discovered that towns attracted increasing numbers of people to an area — people whom the lords could tax. Moreover, when burghers bargained for a town's political independence, they offered sizable amounts of ready cash. Consequently, feudal lords ultimately agreed to self-government.

TOWN LIFE

Protective walls surrounded almost all medieval towns and cities. The valuable goods inside a town were too much of a temptation to marauding bands for the town to be without the security of bricks and mortar. The walls were pierced by gates, and visitors waited at the gates to gain entrance to the town. When the gates were opened early in the morning, guards inspected the quantity and quality of the goods brought in and collected the customary taxes. Part of the taxes went to the king or lord on whose land the town stood, part to the town council for civic purposes. Constant repair of the walls was usually the town's greatest expense.

Peasants coming from the countryside and merchants traveling from afar set up their carts as stalls just inside the gates. The result was that the road nearest the gate was the widest thoroughfare. It was the ideal place for a market, because everyone coming in or going out used it. Most streets in a medieval town were marketplaces as much as passages for transit. They were narrow, just wide enough to transport goods through.

Medieval cities served, above all else, as markets. In some respects the entire city was a marketplace. The place where a product was made and sold was also typically the merchant's residence. Usually the ground floor was the scene of production. A window or door opened from the main workroom directly onto the street. The window displayed the finished product, and passersby could look in and see the goods being produced. The

MEDIEVAL STREET SCENE *Merchants displayed their goods from shop windows on the ground floor: tailors, furriers, a barber, and a grocer. Merchants with shops on the street that linked the two main town gates naturally profited more than did those on side streets which were blocked by the town wall. (Bibliothèque Nationale, Paris)*

merchant and his family lived above the business on the second or third floor. As his business and his family expanded, he built additional stories on top of his house.

Because space within the walls of the town was limited, expansion occurred upward. Second and third stories were built jutting out over the ground floor and thus over the street. Neighbors on the opposite side of the road did the same. Since the streets were narrow to begin with, houses thus lacked fresh air and light. Initially, houses were made of wood and thatched with straw. Fire represented a con-

stant danger, and because houses were built so close together, fires spread rapidly. Municipal governments consequently urged construction in stone or brick.

Most medieval cities developed haphazardly. There was little town planning. As the population increased, space became more and more limited. Air and water pollution presented serious problems. Many families raised pigs for household consumption in sties next to the house. Horses and oxen, the chief means of transportation and power, dropped tons of dung on the streets every year. It was universal practice in the early towns to dump household waste, both animal and human, into the road in front of one's house. The stench must have been abominable. In 1298, the burgesses of the town of Boutham in Yorkshire, England, received the following order (one long, vivid sentence):

To the bailiffs of the abbot of St. Mary's York, at Boutham. Whereas it is sufficiently evident that the pavement of the said town of Boutham is so very greatly broken up and that all the singular passing and going through that town sustain immoderate damages and grievances, and in addition the air is so corrupted and infected by the pigsties situated in the king's highways and in the lanes of that town and by the swine feeding and frequently wandering about in the streets and lanes and by dung and dunghills and many other foul things placed in the streets and lanes, that great repugnance overtakes the king's ministers staying in that town and also others there dwelling and passing through, the advantage of more wholesome air is impeded, the state of men is grievously injured, and other unbearable inconveniences and many other injuries are known to proceed from such corruption, to the nuisance of the king's ministers aforesaid and of others there dwelling and passing through, and to the peril of their lives, and to the manifest shame and reproach of the bailiffs and other the inhabitants of that town: the king, being unwilling longer to tolerate such great and unbearable defects there, orders the bailiffs to cause the pavement to be suitably repaired within their liberty before All Saints next, and to cause the pigsties, aforesaid streets and lanes to be cleansed from all dung and dunghills, and to cause them to be kept thus cleansed hereafter, and to cause proclamation to be made throughout their bailiwick forbidding any one, under pain of grievous forfeiture, to cause or permit their swine to feed or wander outside his house in the king's streets or the lanes aforesaid.[5]

A great deal of traffic passed through Boutham in 1298 because of the movement of the English troops to battlefronts in Scotland. Conditions there were probably not typical. Still, this document suggests that problems of space, air pollution, and sanitation bedeviled urban people in medieval times just as they do today.

The church took a great interest in townspeople as Christians. Parish clergy catered to their spiritual needs. As the bourgeoisie gained in wealth, they expressed their continuing Christian faith by refurbishing old churches, constructing new ones, and giving stained-glass windows, statues, and carvings. The twelfth-century chronicler William of Newburgh, writing about 1170, could proudly boast that the city of London had 126 parish churches, in addition to 13 monastic churches and the great cathedral of St. Paul's.

Some literary descriptions of medieval cities survive, but they do not tell all that we would like to know. Most illustrations of walls, streets, and houses date only from the fifteenth century. Medieval cities, like modern ones, changed a great deal in the course of decades and, of course, centuries. A fifteenth-century picture is not a very accurate representation of twelfth-century conditions. William of Newburgh, however, left a detailed description of the city of London around 1175:

Among the noble and celebrated cities of the world that of London, the capital of the kingdom of the English, is one which extends its glory farther than all the others and sends its wealth and merchandise more widely into distant lands. Higher than all the rest does it lift its head. . . .

It has on the east the Palatine castle [the Tower of London], very great and strong: the keep and walls rise from very deep foundations and are fixed with a mortar tempered by the blood of an-

A FIFTEENTH-CENTURY HOUSE *Medieval merchants conducted their business on the ground floor and lived with their families on the floors above. As additional stories were added on, they jutted out one over the other. Since this form of building was done on both sides of the street, streets received little light during the day and were dangerously dark at night. (Royal Commission on Historical Monuments, England)*

imals. On the west there are two castles very strongly fortified, and from these there runs a high and massive wall with seven double gates and with towers along the north at regular intervals. London was once also walled and turreted on the south, but the mighty Thames, so full of fish, has with the sea's ebb and flow washed against, loosened, and thrown down those walls in the course of time. Upstream to the west there is the royal palace [*the Palace of Westminster*]. . . .

Everywhere outside the houses of those living in the suburbs, and adjacent to them, are the spacious and beautiful gardens of the citizens, and these are planted with trees. Also there are on the north side pastures and pleasant meadow lands through which flow streams wherein the turning of mill-wheels makes a cheerful sound. Very near lies a great forest with woodland pastures in which there are the lairs of wild animals: stags, fallow deer, wild boars and bulls. . . .

Those engaged in business of various kinds, sellers of merchandise, hirers of labour, are distributed every morning into their several localities according to their trade. Besides, there is in London on the river bank among the wines for sale in ships and in the cellars of the vintners a public cook-shop. There daily you may find food according to the season, dishes of meat, roast, fried and boiled, large and small fish, coarser meats for the poor and more delicate for the rich, such as venison and big and small birds. If any of the citizens should unexpectedly receive visitors, weary from their journey, who would fain not wait until fresh food is bought and cooked, or until the servants have brought bread or water for washing, they hasten to the river bank and there find all they need. . . .

Immediately outside one of the gates there is a field [*Smithfield*] which is smooth both in fact and in name. On every sixth day of the week, unless it be a major feast-day, there takes place there a famous exhibition of fine horses for sale. Earls, barons and knights, who are in the town, and many citizens come out to see or to buy. It is pleasant to see the high-stepping palfreys with their gleaming coats, as they go through their paces, putting down their feet alternately on one side together. . . .

By themselves in another part of the field stand the goods of the countryfolk: implements of husbandry, swine with long flanks, cows with full udders, oxen of immense size, and woolly sheep. There also stand the mares fit for plough, some big with foal, and others with brisk young colts closely following them.

To this city from every nation under heaven merchants delight to bring their trade by sea. The Arabian sends gold; the Sabaean spice and incense. The Scythian brings arms, and from the rich, fat lands of Babylon comes oil of palms. The Nile sends precious stones; the men of Norway and Russia, furs and sables; nor is China absent with purple silk. The Gauls come with their wines. . . .

We now come to speak of the sports of the city, for it is not fitting that a city should be merely useful and serious-minded, unless it be also pleasant and cheerful. . . .

Furthermore, every year on the day called Carnival — to begin with the sports of boys (for we were all boys once) — scholars from the different schools bring fighting-cocks to their masters, and the whole morning is set apart to watch their cocks do battle in the schools, for the boys are given a holiday that day. After dinner all the young men of the town go out into the fields in the suburbs to play ball. The scholars of the various schools have their own ball, and almost all the followers of each occupation have theirs also. The seniors and the fathers and the wealthy magnates of the city come on horseback to watch the contests of the younger generation, and in their turn recover their lost youth: the motions of their natural heat seem to be stirred in them at the mere sight of such strenuous activity and by their participation in the joys of unbridled youth.

Every Sunday in Lent after dinner a fresh swarm of young men goes forth into the fields on war-horses, steeds foremost in the contest, each of which is skilled and schooled to run in circles. From the gates there sallies forth a host of laymen, sons of the citizens, equipped with lances and

shields, the younger ones with spears forked at the top, but with the steel point removed. They make a pretence at war, carry out field-exercises and indulge in mimic combats. Thither too come many courtiers, when the king is in town, and from the households of bishops, earls and barons come youths and adolescents, not yet girt with the belt of knighthood, for the pleasure of engaging in combat with one another. Each is inflamed with the hope of victory. . . .

On feast-days throughout the summer the young men indulge in the sports of archery, running, jumping, wrestling, slinging the stone, hurling the javelin beyond a mark and fighting with sword and buckler. . . .

Others, more skilled at winter sports, put on their feet the shin-bones of animals, binding them firmly around their ankles, and, holding poles shod with iron in their hands, which they strike from time to time against the ice, they are propelled swift as a bird in flight or a bolt shot from an engine of war. . . .[6]

People wanted to get into medieval cities because they represented a means of economic advancement, social mobility, and improvement in legal status. For the adventurous, the ambitious, and the shrewd, cities offered tremendous opportunities.

THE REVIVAL OF LONG-DISTANCE TRADE

The eleventh century witnessed a remarkable revival of trade as artisans and craftsmen manufactured goods for local and foreign consumption (see Map 12.2). Most trade centered in towns and was controlled by professional traders. Because long-distance trade was risky and required large investments of capital, it could be practiced only by professionals. The transportation of goods involved serious risks. Shipwrecks were common. Pirates infested the sea-lanes, and robbers and thieves roamed virtually all of the land routes. Since the risks were so great, merchants preferred to share them. A group of men would thus pool some of their capital to finance an expedition to a distant place. When the ship or caravan returned and the goods brought back were sold, the investors would share the profits. If disaster struck the caravan, an investor's loss was limited to the amount of his investment.

What goods were exchanged? What towns took the lead in medieval "international" trade? In the late eleventh century, the Italian cities, especially Venice, led the West in trade in general and completely dominated the oriental market. Ships carried salt from the Venetian lagoon, pepper and other spices from North Africa, and silks and purple textiles from the Orient to northern and western Europe. Venetian caravans brought slaves from the Crimea and Chinese silks from Mongolia to the town markets and regional fairs of France, Flanders, and England. (Fairs were periodic gatherings that attracted buyers, sellers, and goods from all over Europe.) Flanders controlled the cloth industry. The towns of Bruges, Ghent, and Ypres built up a vast industry in the manufacture of cloth. Italian merchants exchanged their products for Flemish tapestries, fine broadcloths, and various other textiles.

Two circumstances help to explain the lead Venice and the Flemish towns gained in long-distance trade. Both enjoyed a high degree of peace and political stability. Geographical factors were equally if not more important. Venice was ideally located at the northwestern end of the Adriatic Sea, with easy access to both the transalpine land routes and the Adriatic and Mediterranean sea-lanes. The markets of North Africa, Byzantium, and Russia and the great fairs of Ghent in Flanders and Champagne in France provided commercial opportunities that Venice quickly seized. The

geographical situation of Flanders also offered unusual possibilities. Just across the Channel from England, Flanders had easy access to English wool. Indeed, Flanders and England developed a very close economic relationship.

Sheep had been raised for their wool in England since Roman times. The rocky soil and damp climate of Yorkshire and Lincolnshire, though poorly suited for agriculture, were excellent for sheep farming. Beginning in the early twelfth century, but especially after the arrival of Cistercian monks around 1130, the size of the English flocks doubled and then tripled. Scholars have estimated that by the end of the twelfth century roughly 6 million sheep grazed on the English moors and downs. They produced fifty thousand sacks of wool a year.[7] Originally, a "sack" of wool was the burden one packhorse could carry, an amount eventually fixed at 364 pounds; fifty thousand sacks, then, represented huge production.

Wool was the cornerstone of the English medieval economy. Population growth in the twelfth century and the success of the Flemish and Italian textile industries created foreign demand for English wool. The production of English wool stimulated Flemish manufacturing, and the expansion of the Flemish cloth industry in turn spurred the production of English wool. The availability of raw wool also encouraged the development of domestic cloth manufacture within England. The towns of Lincoln and York in the north, Leicester and Northampton in the central counties, Winchester in the south, and Exeter in the west became important cloth-producing

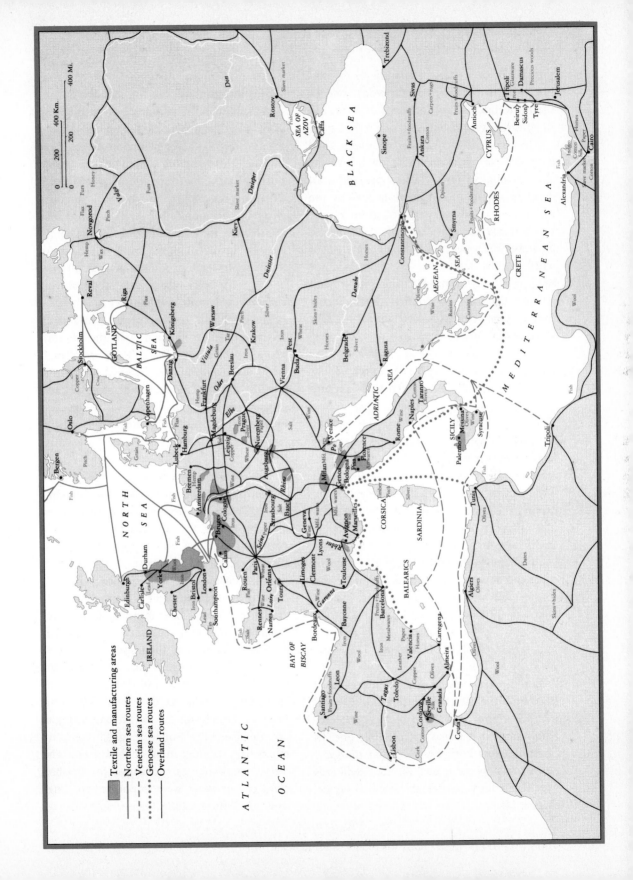

Textile and manufacturing areas

Northern sea routes

Venetian sea routes

Genoese sea routes

Overland routes

400 Mi.

400 Km.

200

200

0

0

ATLANTIC OCEAN

NORTH SEA

BALTIC SEA

MEDITERRANEAN SEA

BLACK SEA

SEA OF AZOV

ADRIATIC SEA

AEGEAN SEA

BAY OF BISCAY

IRELAND

GOTLAND

CRETE

CYPRUS

RHODES

SICILY

SARDINIA

CORSICA

BALEARICS

Don
Volga
Dnieper
Dniester
Danube
Vistula
Oder
Elbe
Rhine
Rhône
Loire
Garonne
Tagus
Po

Edinburgh
Durham
Carlisle
York
Chester
Bristol
London
Southampton
Calais
Bruges
Rennes
Nantes
Paris
Rouen
Orléans
Tours
Limoges
Clermont
Lyons
Toulouse
Bayonne
Bordeaux
Leon
Santiago
Lisbon
Toledo
Córdova
Seville
Granada
Almeira
Valencia
Cartegena
Barcelona
Ceuta
Algiers
Tunis
Marseilles
Avignon
Geneva
Basel
Strasbourg
Troyes
Cologne
Bremen
Amsterdam
Hamburg
Lübeck
Magdeburg
Frankfurt
Nuremberg
Augsburg
Prague
Leipzig
Breslau
Kraków
Warsaw
Königsberg
Danzig
Riga
Reval
Stockholm
Copenhagen
Oslo
Bergen
Novgorod
Kiev
Rostov
Caffa
Sinope
Trebizond
Sivas
Ankara
Smyrna
Constantinople
Belgrade
Ragusa
Vienna
Buda
Pest
Milan
Genoa
Bologna
Pisa
Florence
Venice
Rome
Naples
Taranto
Palermo
Messina
Syracuse
Tripoli
Antioch
Beirut
Sidon
Tyre
Tripoli
Damascus
Jerusalem
Cairo
Alexandria

Fish
Furs
Furs
Furs
Honey
Wax
Pitch
Flax
Hemp
Wax
Slave market
Grain
Silver
Iron
Wheat
Wheat
Skins + hides
Horses
Horses
Horses
Silver
Wine
Wine
Raisins
Currants
Olives
Olive oil
Wool
Fish
Olives
Olives
Skins + hides
Dates
Wool
Fish
Fish
Cotton
Opium
Fruits + foodstuffs
Carpets + rugs
Fruits + foodstuffs
Fruits + foodstuffs
Cotton
Indigo
Cotton
Silk
Paper
Slave market
Cotton
Precious woods
Glassware
Iron
Olives
Wine
Timber
Silver
Olives
Olives
Wool
Iron
Wool
Wine
Cork
Cotton
Salt
Leather
Copper
Olives
Horses
Metalwares
Paper
Iron
Fruits + foodstuffs
Horses
Fish
Salt
Wine
Flax
Lead
Iron
Lead
Tin
Lead
Iron
Wool
Fish
Wine
Wine
Mid. wares
Mid. wares
Wine
Salt
Paper
Copper
Wheat
Wine
Wine
Iron
Salt
Glass
Silk
Iron
Fustian
Copper
Copper
Iron
Hemp
Grain + flax
Fish
Pitch
Fish
Copper
Flax
Flax
Iron
Pitch
Wine
Pitch
Tar

towns. The port cities of London, Hull, Boston, and Bristol thrived on the wool trade. In the thirteenth century commercial families in these towns grew fabulously rich.

The wool and cloth trades serve as a good barometer of the economic growth and decline of English towns. The supply of wool depended upon such natural factors as the amount of land devoted to grazing, the weather, and the prevalence of sheep disease or scab. The price of wool, unlike that of wheat or other foodstuffs, was determined not by supply but by demand. Changes in demand – often the result of political developments over which merchants had no control – could severely damage the wool trade. In the 1320s, for example, violent disorder exploded in the Flemish towns, causing a sharp drop in demand for English wool. When wool exports fell, the economies of London, Hull, and Southampton slumped. Then, during the Hundred Years' War (pages 508–509), the English Crown laid increasingly high export taxes on raw wool, and again the wool trade hurt. On the other hand, the decline of wool exports encouraged the growth of cloth manufacturing in older centers such as Lincoln and in new ones such as Tiverton and Lavenham. In the fourteenth century these towns experienced some population growth and considerable prosperity – a prosperity directly linked to the cloth industry.

THE COMMERCIAL REVOLUTION

A steadily expanding volume of international trade from the late eleventh through the thirteenth centuries was a sign of the great economic surge, but it was not the only one. In cities all across Europe trading and transportation firms opened branch offices. Credit was widely extended, considerably facilitating exchange. Merchants devised the letter of credit,

which made unnecessary the slow and dangerous shipment of coin for payment.

A new capitalistic spirit developed. Professional merchants were always on the lookout for new markets and new opportunities. They invested their surplus capital in new enterprises to make more money. They diversified their interests and got involved in a wide variety of operations. The typical prosperous merchant in the later thirteenth century might well be involved in buying and selling, in shipping, in lending some capital at interest, and in other types of banking. Medieval merchants were fiercely competitive.

Some scholars consider capitalism a modern phenomenon, beginning in the fifteenth or sixteenth century. But in their use of capital to make more money, in their speculative pursuits and willingness to gamble, in their competitive spirit, and in the variety of their interests and operations, medieval businessmen displayed the essential traits of capitalists.

The ventures of the English cloth industry in the fourteenth century illustrate these impulses. Profits had steadily accumulated in the cloth-producing towns, where manufacturers often had close ties with wool dealers. With the Flemish cloth industry in trouble, English merchant-manufacturers invaded Flemish markets on the continent and invested their capital in a variety of enterprises. Cloth merchants began to deal in French wines, Flemish tapestries, Baltic fish, furs, and naval stores, and Italian silks. English businessmen established trading centers called factories with long-term residents at Antwerp, Bergen in Norway, Danzig on the Baltic, and Cologne on the Rhine; a single English company might have factories in all of these cities. The foreign commodities exchanged for finished cloth or raw wool were imported into England for domestic sale. These activities re-

A FLEMISH DOCK SCENE *Flemish towns early developed commercial ties with neighboring countries. The Flemish purchased wool from England and manufactured excellent textiles, which they sold to* *merchants from all over Europe. This print shows bales of cloth being loaded at dockside for transport abroad. (Bodleian Library)*

quired capital, willingness to take risks, and the aggressive pursuit of opportunities – the essential ingredients of capitalism. They also yielded fat profits.

These developments added up to what one modern scholar who knows the period well has called "a commercial revolution, . . probably the greatest turning point in the history of our civilization."[8] This is not a wildly extravagant statement. In the long run the commercial revolution of the High Middle Ages brought about radical change in European society and culture. One remarkable aspect of this change is that the commercial classes did not constitute a large part of the total population – never more than 10 percent. They exercised an influence far in excess of their actual numbers.

The commercial revolution created a great deal of new wealth. Wealth meant a higher standard of living. The new availability of something as simple as spices, for example, allowed for variety in food. Dietary habits gradually changed. Taste became more sophisticated. Contact with Eastern civilizations introduced Europeans to eating utensils such as forks. Table manners improved. People learned to eat with forks and knives, instead of tearing the meat from the roast with their hands. They began to use napkins, instead of wiping their greasy fingers on the dogs lying under the table.

The existence of wealth did not escape the attention of kings and other rulers. Wealth could be taxed, and through taxation kings could create strong and centralized states. In the years to come, alliances with the middle classes were to enable kings to defeat feudal powers and aristocratic interests and to build the states that came to be called modern.

The commercial revolution also provided the opportunity for thousands of serfs to improve their social position. The slow but steady transformation of European society from almost completely rural and isolated to relatively more sophisticated constituted the greatest effect of the commercial revolution that began in the eleventh century.

Even so, merchants and businesspeople did not run medieval communities, except in central and northern Italy and in the county of Flanders. Towns remained small: as late as the 1320s a town of 5000 people was considered sizable, and Paris with about 80,000 souls was Europe's greatest city. The castle, the manorial village, and the monastery dominated the landscape. The feudal nobility and churchmen determined the preponderant social attitudes, values, and patterns of thought and behavior. The commercial changes of the eleventh and twelfth centuries did, however, lay the economic foundations for the development of urban life and culture that occurred during the Renaissance.

REVIVAL AND REFORM IN THE CHRISTIAN CHURCH

The eleventh century also witnessed the beginnings of a remarkable religious revival. Monasteries, always the leaders in ecclesiastical reform, remodeled themselves under the leadership of the Burgundian abbey of Cluny. Subsequently, new religious orders, such as the Cistercians, were founded and became a broad spiritual movement.

The papacy itself, after a century of corruption and decadence, was cleaned up. The popes worked to clarify church doctrine and to codify church law. They and their officials sought to communicate with all the clergy and peoples of Europe through a clearly defined and obedient hierarchy of bishops. The popes wanted the basic loyalty of all members of the clergy. Pope Gregory VII (1073-1085) tried to enforce an entirely new theory of Christian kingship, and his assertion of papal power caused profound changes and serious conflicts with secular authorities. The revival of the Christian church was manifested in the twelfth and thirteenth centuries by a flowering of popular piety, reflected in the building of magnificent cathedrals.

MONASTIC REVIVAL

In the early Middle Ages the best Benedictine monasteries had been citadels of good Christian living and centers of education and learning. Between the seventh and ninth centuries,

MONT ST.-MICHEL   *At the summit of a 250-foot cone of rock rising out of the sea and accessible only at low tide, Mont St.-Michel combined fortified castle and monastery. Thirteenth century monarchs considered it crucial to their power in northwestern France,* *and it played a decisive role in French defenses against the English during the Hundred Years War. The abbots so planned the architecture that monastic life went on undisturbed by military activity. (Mark Sheridan OSB)*

religious houses like Bobbio in northern Italy, Luxeuil in France, and Jarrow in England copied and preserved manuscripts, maintained schools, and set high standards of monastic observance. Charlemagne had encouraged and supported these monastic activities, and the collapse of the Carolingian Empire had disastrous effects.

The Viking and Muslim invaders attacked and ransacked many monasteries across Europe. Some communities fled and dispersed. In the period of political disorder that followed the disintegration of the Carolingian Empire, many religious houses fell under the control and domination of local feudal lords. Powerful laymen appointed themselves or their relatives as abbots, while keeping their wives or mistresses. They took for themselves the lands and goods of monasteries. They spent monastic revenues and sold monastic offices. Temporal powers all over Europe dominated the monasteries. The level of spiritual observance and intellectual activity declined.

In 909 William the Pious, duke of Aquitaine, established the abbey of Cluny near Mâcon in Burgundy. This was to be a very important event. In his charter of endowment Duke William declared that Cluny was to enjoy complete independence from all feudal or secular lordship. The new monastery was to be subordinate only to the authority of Saints Peter and Paul as represented by the pope. The duke then renounced his own possession of and influence over Cluny.

This monastery and its foundation charter came to exert vast religious influence. The first two abbots of Cluny, Berno (910–927) and Odo (927–942), set very high standards of religious behavior. They stressed strict observance of the *Rule of Saint Benedict,* the development of a personal spiritual life by the individual monk, and the importance of the liturgy. In the church as a whole, Cluny gradually came to stand for clerical celibacy and the suppression of simony (the sale of church offices). Within a generation neighboring monasteries sought Cluny's help and were reformed along Cluniac lines.

In the course of the eleventh century, Cluny was fortunate in having a series of extremely able abbots, who all ruled for a long time. They paid careful attention to sound economic management and to the principle of independence from lay influence. In the Holy Roman Empire, Cluniac reform had the strong and significant support of the emperor Henry III (1039–1056). He aided the religious houses in their struggle for independence from the lay aristocracy. Hundreds of monasteries across Europe, in France, Germany, Italy, Spain, and England, placed themselves under Cluny's jurisdiction. By the time of the

sixty-year reign of Abbot Hugh (1049–1109), the Cluniac reforming spirit was felt everywhere.

Success for an institution, as for an individual, is measured by the degree to which it lives up to the goals it sets for itself. In religion nothing leads to failure like material success. By the last quarter of the eleventh century, some monasteries enjoyed wide reputations for the beauty and richness of their chant and the piety of the monks' lives. Deeply impressed laymen showered gifts upon them. Jewelry, rich vestments and elaborately carved sacred vessels, lands and properties poured into some houses. With this wealth came the influence of laymen. As the monasteries became richer, the lifestyle of the monks became luxurious. Monastic observance and spiritual fervor declined.

Once again the ideals of the pristine Benedictine life were threatened. Fresh demands for reform were heard, and the result was the founding of new religious orders in the late eleventh and early twelfth centuries. The best representatives of the new reforming spirit and monastic piety of the twelfth century were the Cistercians.

In 1098 a group of monks left the rich abbey of Molesmes in Burgundy and founded a new house in the swampy forest of Cîteaux. They had specific goals and high ideals. They planned to avoid all involvement with secular feudal society. They decided to accept only uncultivated lands far from regular habitation. They intended to refuse all gifts of mills, serfs, tithes, ovens – the traditional manorial sources of income. The early Cistercians determined to avoid elaborate liturgy and ceremony and to keep their chant simple. Finally, they refused to allow the presence of high and powerful laymen in their monasteries, because they knew that such influence was usually harmful to careful observance.

To the Cistercian reformers the older Benedictine monasteries represented power, wealth, and luxurious living, which violated the spirit of the *Rule of Saint Benedict*. The Cistercian life was to be a new kind of commune. It was to be simple, isolated, austere, and purified of all the economic and religious complexities found in the Benedictine houses.

These Cistercian goals coincided perfectly with the needs of twelfth-century society. The late eleventh and early twelfth centuries witnessed energetic agricultural expansion and land reclamation all across Europe. The early Cistercians wanted to farm only land that had previously been uncultivated, or swampland, or fenland, and that was exactly what needed to be done. They thus became the great pioneers of the twelfth century. Their churches had to be plain, and they wanted their daily lives to be simple. A pioneer existence in a commune where all had to work hard and all resources were pooled obviously had enormous economic and social possibilities. Unavoidably the success of the Cistercians' efforts brought wealth, and wealth brought power and influence.

The first monks at Cîteaux experienced sickness, a dearth of recruits, and terrible privations. Their obvious sincerity and high idealism eventually attracted attention. In 1112, a twenty-three-year-old nobleman called Bernard joined the community at Cîteaux, together with thirty of his aristocratic friends and companions. Thereafter, this reforming movement gained wide impetus. Cîteaux founded hundreds of new monasteries in the course of the twelfth century, and its influence on European society was profound.

REFORM OF THE PAPACY

Some scholars believe that the monastic revival spreading from Cluny influenced reform of the Roman papacy and eventually of the entire Christian church. Certainly, Abbot Odilo of Cluny (994-1048) was a close friend of the German emperor Henry III, who promoted reform throughout the empire. Pope Gregory VII, who carried the ideals of reform to extreme lengths, had spent some time at Cluny. And the man who consolidated the reform movement and strengthened the medieval papal monarchy, Pope Urban II (1088-1099), had been a monk and prior at Cluny. The precise degree of Cluny's impact on the reform movement cannot be measured. But the broad goals of the Cluniac movement and those of the Roman papacy were the same.

The papacy provided little leadership to the Christian peoples of western Europe in the tenth century. Factions in Rome sought to control the papacy for their own material gain. Popes were appointed to advance the political ambitions of their families – the great aristocratic families of the city – and not because of special spiritual qualifications. The office of pope, including its spiritual powers and influence, was frequently bought and sold, though this grave crime, called simony, had been condemned by Saint Peter. The licentiousness and debauchery of the papal court scandalized people. According to a contemporary chronicler, for example, Pope John XII (955-963), who had secured the papal office at the age of eighteen, wore himself out from sexual excesses before he was twenty-eight. Such conditions weakened the religious prestige and moral authority of the pope.

At the local parish level there were many married priests. Taking Christ as the model for the priestly life, the Roman church had always encouraged clerical celibacy, and it had been an obligation for ordination since the fourth century. But in the tenth and eleventh

centuries, probably a majority of the priests of Europe were married or living with a woman. Such priests were called Nicolaites from a reference in the Book of Revelation to early Christians who advocated a return to pagan sexual practices.

Several factors may account for the uncelibate state of the clergy. The explanation may lie in the basic need for warmth and human companionship. Perhaps village priests could not survive economically on their small sala-

ries and needed the help of a mate. Perhaps the tradition of a married clergy was so deeprooted by the tenth century that each generation simply followed the example of its predecessor. In any case, the disparity between the law and the reality shocked people in the lay community and bred disrespect for the clergy.

Serious efforts at reform began under Pope Leo IX (1049-1054). Not only was Leo related to Emperor Henry III but, as bishop of Toul and a German, he was also an outsider who owed nothing to any Roman faction. Leo traveled widely and held councils at Pavia, Reims, and Mainz that issued decrees against simony, Nicolaism, and violence. Leo's representatives held church councils across Europe, pressing for moral reform. They urged individuals who could not secure justice at home to appeal to the pope, the ultimate source of justice.

Leo himself was a man of deep humility and great pastoral zeal. By his character and his actions, he set high moral standards for the West. The reform of the papacy had legal as well as moral aspects. During Leo's pontificate a new collection of ecclesiastical law was prepared – the Collection of 74 Titles. Based on letters of popes and the decrees of councils, the Collection of 74 Titles laid great emphasis on papal authority. The substance of the Collection was to stress the rights, the legal position, and the supreme spiritual prerogatives of the bishop of Rome as the successor of Saint Peter.

Papal reform continued after Leo IX. In the short reign of Nicholas II (1058-1061), a council held in the ancient church of St. John Lateran in 1059 reached a momentous decision. A new method was devised for electing the pope. Since the eighth century the priests of the major churches in and around Rome had constituted a special group, called a college, that advised the pope when he summoned them to meetings. These chief priests were called cardinals from the Latin word *cardo,* meaning "hinge." The cardinals were the hinges on which the church turned. The Lateran Synod of 1059 decreed that the authority and power to elect the pope rested solely in this college of cardinals. The college retains that power today.

The object of the decree was to remove this crucial decision from the secular squabbling of Roman aristocratic factions. When the office of pope was vacant, the cardinals were responsible for the government of the church. (In the Middle Ages the college of cardinals numbered around twenty-five or thirty, most of them from Italy. In 1586, the figure was set at seventy. In the 1960s, Pope Paul VI virtually doubled that number, appointing men from the remotest parts of the globe to reflect the international character of the church.) By 1073, the progress of reform in the Christian church was well advanced. The election of Cardinal Hildebrand as Pope Gregory VII changed the direction of reform from a moral to a political one.

THE GREGORIAN REVOLUTION

The papal reform movement of the eleventh century is frequently called the Gregorian reform movement, after Pope Gregory VII. The label is not accurate, in that reform began long before Gregory's pontificate and continued after it. Gregory's reign did, however, inaugurate a radical or revolutionary phase that had important political and social consequences.

In contrast to his predecessors and successors in the eleventh century, Cardinal Hildebrand – who took the name Gregory when he was elected pope – was not of aristocratic descent but the son of poor Tuscan peasants. Some historians have argued that his bitter clash with the German emperor Henry IV was the result of a lowborn upstart's desire to humble the chief secular power in Europe. This idea is intriguing, if not thoroughly convincing. Gregory's education probably had more influence on his mature attitudes than his social origins did. He received a good education at Rome and spent some time at Cluny, where his strict views of clerical life were strengthened. Hildebrand had served in the papal secretariat under Leo IX, and after 1065 was probably the chief influence there.

Hildebrand was dogmatic, inflexible, and unalterably convinced of the truth of his own views. He believed that the pope, as the successor of Saint Peter, was the Vicar of God on earth and that papal orders were the orders of God. His ideas of kingship were even more notorious – and threatening – to his contemporaries. In a Christian society, he believed, the king was responsible for providing peace and order so that Christians could pursue their pilgrimage to the City of God.

The king was obliged to act righteously. If he did not, he was a tyrant, to whom *no one* owed allegiance. Who was to decide if a ruler was a tyrant? The pope, as the Vicar of God, would make that decision and, Hildebrand maintained, could release subjects from their duty of obedience. This had been the Christian view of kingship since the time of Saint Augustine. But Hildebrand wanted to put the theory into practice, and in that respect he was very much a radical.

Once Hildebrand became pope, the reform of the papacy took on a new dimension. Its goal was not just the moral regeneration of the clergy and centralization of the church under papal authority. Gregory and his assistants began to insist upon "the freedom of the church." By this they meant the freedom of all churchmen to obey the newly codified canon law, and freedom from control and interference by laymen.

"Freedom of the church" pointed to the end of lay investiture – the selection and appointment of church officials by secular authority. Ecclesiastical opposition to lay investiture was not new in the eleventh century. It too had been part of church theory for centuries. But Gregory's attempt to put theory into practice was a radical departure from tradition. Since feudal monarchs depended upon churchmen for the operation of their governments, Gregory's program seemed to spell disaster for stable royal administration. It provoked a terrible crisis.

The Controversy Over Lay Investiture

In February 1075, Pope Gregory held a council at Rome. It published decrees not only against Nicolaism and simony but also, for the first time, against lay investiture:

If anyone henceforth shall receive a bishopric or abbey from the hands of a lay person, he shall not be considered as among the number of bishops and abbots. . . . Likewise if any emperor, king . . . or any one at all of the secular powers, shall presume to perform investiture with bishoprics or with any other ecclesiastical dignity . . . he shall feel the divine displeasure as well with regard to his body as to his other belongings.[9]

In short, clerics who accepted investiture

from laymen were to be deposed, and laymen who invested clerics were to be excommunicated (cut off from contact with other Christians).

The church's penalty of excommunication relied for its effectiveness on public opinion. Since most Europeans favored Gregory's moral reforms, he believed that excommunication would compel rulers to abide by his changes. Immediately, however, Henry IV in the German Empire, William the Conqueror in England, and Philip I in France protested.

The strongest reaction came from Germany. Henry IV had strongly supported the moral aspects of church reform within the empire. In fact, they would not have achieved much success without his support. But of all the countries of Europe, the Holy Roman Empire most depended upon the services of churchmen. Governing a vast territory of half Christianized and half pagan peoples, the emperor relied heavily upon the assistance of churchmen. His fledgling bureaucracy could not survive without the literacy and administrative knowhow of bishops and abbots. Naturally, then, he had selected and invested most of them.

Over and beyond the subject of lay investiture, however, a more fundamental issue was at stake. Gregory's decree raised the question of the proper role of the monarch in a Christian society. Did a king have ultimate jurisdiction over all his subjects, including the clergy? For centuries tradition had answered this question in favor of the ruler; so it is no wonder that Henry vigorously protested the papal assertions about lay investiture. By implication they undermined imperial power and sought to make papal authority supreme.

An increasingly bitter exchange of letters ensued. Gregory accused Henry of lack of respect for the papacy and insisted that disobedience to the pope was disobedience to God. Henry protested in a now-famous letter beginning, "Henry King not by usurpation, but by the pious ordination of God, to Hildebrand, now not Pope, but false monk."

Within the empire, those who had most to gain from the dispute quickly took advantage of it. In January 1076, in the southwestern German city of Worms on the Rhine, the German bishops who had been invested by Henry withdrew their allegiance from the pope. Gregory replied by excommunicating them and the emperor. The lay nobility delighted in the bind the emperor had been placed in: with Henry IV excommunicated and cast outside the fold of the Christian faithful, they did not have to obey him and could advance their own interests. Gregory hastened to support them. The Christmas season of 1075 witnessed an ironic situation within Germany: the greater clergy supported the emperor, while the great nobility favored the pope.

Henry outwitted Gregory. Crossing the Alps in January, he approached the pope's residence at Canossa in northern Italy. According to legend, Henry stood for three days in the snow seeking forgiveness. As a priest, Pope Gregory was obliged to grant absolution and to readmit the emperor to the Christian community. Henry's going to Canossa is often described as the most dramatic incident in the High Middle Ages. Some historians claim that it marked the peak of papal power because the most powerful ruler in Europe, the Holy Roman emperor, had bowed before the pope. Actually, Henry scored a temporary victory. When the sentence of excommunication was lifted, Henry regained the kingship and his authority over his rebellious subjects. But in the long run, in Germany and elsewhere, secular rulers were reluctant to pose a

TWELFTH-CENTURY ROMANESQUE CROZIER This ivory crozier or staff (a reproduction) shows Saint John baptizing Christ in the Jordan River, while the Holy Spirit in the form of a dove descends and God the Father blesses the event. Old Testament prophets with scrolls surround the head of the crozier. (Courtesy, World Heritage Museum. Photo: Caroline Buckler)

serious challenge to the papacy for the next two hundred years.

For the German empire the incident at Canossa settled nothing. The controversy over lay investiture and the position of the king in Christian society continued. In 1080 Gregory VII again excommunicated and deposed the emperor, but this time it appeared to public opinion that Henry was being persecuted. The papal edicts had little effect. Moreover, Henry invaded Italy, captured Rome, and controlled the city when Gregory died in exile in 1085. But Henry won no lasting victory. Gregory's successors encouraged Henry's sons to revolt against their father. With lay investiture the ostensible issue, the conflict between the papacy and the successors of Henry IV continued into the twelfth century.

The kings of England and France were just as guilty of lay investiture as the German emperor. William the Conqueror (1066-1087) ignored papal decrees against the practice. He selected bishops and counted them among his most important tenants-in-chief. He presided over church councils and refused to allow papal letters or legates into England without his permission. He did, though, work to achieve in England the moral goals of reform. Under the Conqueror's sons William Rufus and Henry I, however, disagreement with the popes over lay investiture was long and violent.

Philip I (1060-1108) of France also quarreled with Gregory, but the subject of their dispute was more Philip's adulterous marriage than lay investiture. Philip enjoyed the profits he received from the sale of church offices. And he probably thought that a church independent of royal control would be a real threat to the French monarchy. Rome's conflict with the western rulers never reached the proportions of the dispute with the German emperor. Gregory VII and his successors had the diplomatic sense to avoid creating three enemies at once.

A long and exhausting propaganda campaign followed the confrontation at Canossa. Finally, in 1122, at a conference held at Worms, the issue was settled by compromise. The terms, as it happened, were the same as those agreed on by the papacy and the English king Henry I in 1107. Bishops were to be chosen according to canon law – that is, by the clergy – in the presence of the emperor or his delegate. The emperor surrendered the right of investing bishops with the ring and staff. But, since lay rulers were permitted to be present at ecclesiastical elections and to accept or refuse feudal homage from the new prelates, they still possessed an effective veto over ecclesiastical appointments. At the same time, the papacy achieved technical success, because rulers could no longer invest. Papal power was enhanced. Thus neither side won a clear victory. The real winners in Germany were the great princes and the lay aristocracy.

The long controversy had tremendous social and political consequences in Germany. For half a century, between 1075 and 1125, civil war was chronic within the empire. Preoccupied with Italy and the quarrel with the papacy, emperors could do little about it. To control their lands, great lords built castles, symbolizing their increased power and growing independence. (In no European country do more castles survive today.) The castles were both military strongholds and centers of administration for the surrounding territories. The German aristocracy subordinated the knights and reinforced their dependency with strong feudal ties. They reduced freemen and serfs to an extremely humble and servile position. Henry IV and Henry V were compelled to surrender rights and privileges to the nobility. Particularism, localism, and feudal independence characterized the Holy Roman Empire in the High Middle Ages. The investiture controversy had a catastrophic effect there, severely retarding the development of a strong centralized monarchy.

THE PAPACY IN THE HIGH MIDDLE AGES

In the late eleventh century and throughout the twelfth, the papacy pressed Gregory's campaign for reform of the church. Pope

Urban II laid the real foundations for the papal monarchy by reorganizing the central government of the Roman church, the papal writing office (the chancery) and papal finances. He recognized the college of cardinals as a definite consultative body. These agencies, together with the papal chapel, constituted the papal court, or curia – the papacy's administrative bureaucracy and its court of law. The papal curia, although not fully developed until the mid-twelfth century, was the first well-organized institution of monarchial authority in medieval Europe.

The Roman curia had its greatest impact as a court of law. As the highest ecclesiastical tribunal, it formulated canon law for all of Christendom. It was the instrument with which the popes pressed the goals of reform and centralized the church. The curia sent legates to hold councils in various parts of Europe. Councils published decrees and sought to enforce the law. When individuals in any part of Christian Europe felt they were being denied justice in their local church courts, they could appeal to Rome. Slowly but surely, in the High Middle Ages the papal curia developed into the court of final appeal for all of Christian Europe.

In the course of the twelfth century, appeals to the curia steadily increased. The majority of cases related to disputes over church property or ecclesiastical elections and above all to questions of marriage and annulment. Significantly, most of the popes in the twelfth and thirteenth centuries were themselves canon lawyers. The most famous of them, the man whose pontificate represented the height of medieval papal power, was Innocent III (1198-1216).

Innocent judged a vast number of cases. He compelled King Philip Augustus of France to take back his wife, Ingeborg of Denmark. He arbitrated the rival claims of two disputants to the imperial crown of Germany. He forced King John of England to accept as archbishop of Canterbury a man whom John did not really want. Innocent exerted papal authority in the Iberian Peninsula, in Norway and Sweden, in the Balkans, and even in distant Cyprus and Armenia.

By the early thirteenth century, papal efforts at reform begun more than a century before had attained phenomenal success. The popes themselves were men of high principles and strict moral behavior. The frequency of clerical marriage had declined considerably. The level of violence had dropped sharply. Simony was much more the exception than the rule. The church enjoyed a huge success in most places and provided leadership for Christian Europe.

Yet the seeds of future difficulties were being planted. As the volume of appeals to Rome multiplied, so did the size of papal bureaucracy. As the number of lawyers increased, so did concern for legal niceties and technicalities, fees, and church offices. As early as the mid-twelfth century, John of Salisbury, an Englishman working in the papal curia, had written a blistering critique of the expanding curial bureaucracy. The people, he wrote, condemned the curia for its greed and indifference to human suffering. Nevertheless, the trend continued.

Thirteenth-century popes, a long series of canon lawyers, devoted their attention to the bureaucracy and to their conflicts with the German emperor Frederick II. Some, like Gregory IX (1227-1241), abused their prerogatives to such an extent that their moral impact was seriously weakened. Even worse, Innocent IV (1243-1254) used secular weapons, including military force, to maintain his leadership. These popes badly damaged papal prestige and influence. By the early fourteenth century, the seeds of disorder would grow into a vast and sprawling tree, and once again cries for reform would be heard.

———◆———

The end of the great invasions signaled the beginning of profound changes in European society – economic, social, political, and ecclesiastical. In the year 1000, having enough to eat was the rare privilege of a few noblemen, priests, and monks. In the course of the eleventh century, however, manorial communities slowly improved their agricultural equipment; this advance, aided by warmer weather, meant more food and increasing population. Surplus population on the land led to the growth of old towns and the foundation of new ones. Towns and cities represented an entirely new social class, new opportunities, and a more sophisticated way of life.

In the eleventh century, also, rulers and local authorities gradually imposed some degree of order within their territories. Peace and domestic security, vigorously pushed by the church, meant larger crops for the peasants and improved trading conditions for the townspeople. The church overthrew the domination of lay influences, and the spread of the Cluniac and the Cistercian orders marked the ascendancy of monasticism. Having put its own house in order, the Roman papacy in the twelfth and thirteenth centuries built the first strong governmental bureaucracy. In the High Middle Ages the church exercised general leadership of European society.

NOTES

1. Quoted by R. S. Lopez, "Of Towns and Trade," in *Life and Thought in the Early Middle Ages,* ed. R.

S. Hoyt, University of Minnesota Press, Minneapolis, 1967, p. 33.

2. H. Pirenne, *Economic and Social History of Medieval Europe,* Harcourt Brace, New York, 1956, p. 53.

3. Quoted by Julia O'Faolain and Lauro Martines, eds., *Not In God's Image: Women in History from the Greeks to the Victorians,* Harper & Row, New York, 1973, pp. 155-156.

4. D. Douglas and G. W. Greenaway, eds., *English Historical Documents,* Eyre & Spottiswoode, London, 1961, 2.969.

5. H. Rothwell, ed., *English Historical Documents,* Eyre & Spottiswoode, London, 1975, 3.854.

6. Douglas and Greenaway, 2.956-961.

7. M. M. Postan, *The Medieval Economy and Society: An Economic History of Britain in the Middle Ages,* Penguin Books, Baltimore, 1975, pp. 213-214.

8. R. S. Lopez, "The Trade of Medieval Europe: The South," in *The Cambridge Economic History of Europe,* ed. M. M. Postan and E. E. Rich, Cambridge University Press, Cambridge, 1952, 2.289.

9. B. D. Hill, ed., *Church and State in the Middle Ages,* John Wiley & Sons, New York, 1970, p. 68.

SUGGESTED READING

In addition to the references in the Notes, the curious student will find a fuller treatment of many of the topics raised in this chapter in the following works.

Both C. D. Burns, *The First Europe* (1948), and G. Barraclough, *The Crucible of Europe: The Ninth and Tenth Centuries in European History* (1976), survey the entire period and emphasize the transformation from a time of anarchy to one of great creativity; Barraclough also stresses the importance of stable government. His *The Origins of Modern Germany* (1963) is essential for central and eastern Europe. For the social significance of the peace movements, see H. E. J. Cowdray, "The Peace and the Truce of God in the Eleventh Century," *Past and Present* 46 (1970): 42-67.

For economic and social history, see Gerald A. J.

Hodgett, *A Social and Economic History of Medieval Europe* (1974), a broad survey, and Carlo M. Cipolla, *Before the Industrial Revolution: European Society and Economy, 1000–1700* (1980), which draws on a wealth of recent research to treat demographic shifts, technological change, and business practices. The effect of climate on population and economic growth is discussed in the remarkable work of E. L. Ladurie, *Times of Feast, Times of Famine: A History of Climate since the Year 1000,* trans. B. Bray (1971). A masterful account of agricultural changes and their sociological implications is to be found in G. Duby, *The Early Growth of the European Economy: Warriors and Peasants from the Seventh to the Twelfth Centuries* (1978).

Students interested in the origins of medieval towns and cities will learn how historians use the evidence of coins, archeology, tax records, geography, and laws in J. F. Benton, ed., *Town Origins: The Evidence of Medieval England* (1968). H. Pirenne, *Medieval Cities* (1956), is an important and standard work, which concentrates on the Low Countries. H. Saalman, *Medieval Cities* (1968), gives a fresh description of the layouts of medieval cities, with an emphasis on Germany, and shows how they were places of production and exchange. Colin Platt's well-illustrated *The English Medieval Town* (1979) makes excellent use of archeological evidence and contains detailed information on the wool and cloth trades. Richard Muir, *The English Village* (1980), offers a broad survey of many aspects of the daily lives of ordinary people. For readability, few works surpass J. and F. Gies, *Life in a Medieval City* (1973).

For the Christian church, the papacy, and ecclesiastical developments, G. Barraclough's richly illustrated *The Medieval Papacy* (1968) is a good general survey that emphasizes the development of administrative bureaucracy. The advanced student may tackle W. Ullmann, *A Short History of the Papacy in the Middle Ages* (1972). S. Williams, ed., *The Gregorian Epoch: Reformation, Revolution, Reaction?* (1964), contains significant interpretations of the eleventh-century reform movements. Ullmann's *The Growth of Papal Government in the Middle Ages,* rev. ed. (1970) traces the evolution of papal law and government. G. Tellenbach, *Church, State, and Christian Society at the Time of the Investiture Contest* (1959), emphasizes the revolutionary aspects of the Gregorian reform program. The relationship of the monks to the ecclesiastical crisis of the late eleventh century is discussed by N. F. Cantor, "The Crisis of Western Monasticism," *American Historical Review* 66 (1960), and by H. E. J. Cowdray, *The Cluniacs and the Gregorian Reform* (1970), an impressive but difficult study. J. B. Russell, *A History of Medieval Christianity: Prophecy and Order* (1968), is an important and sensitively written work.

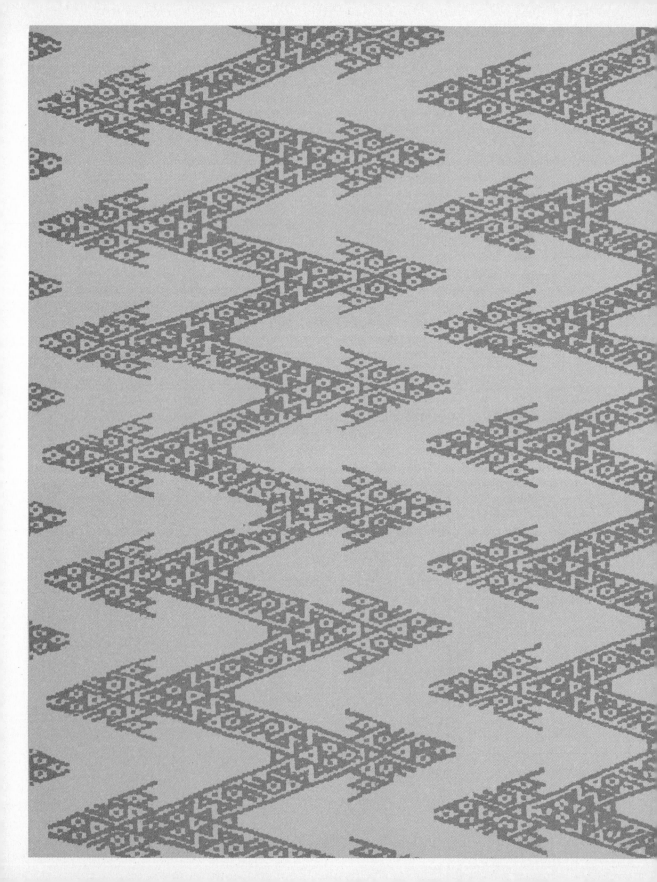

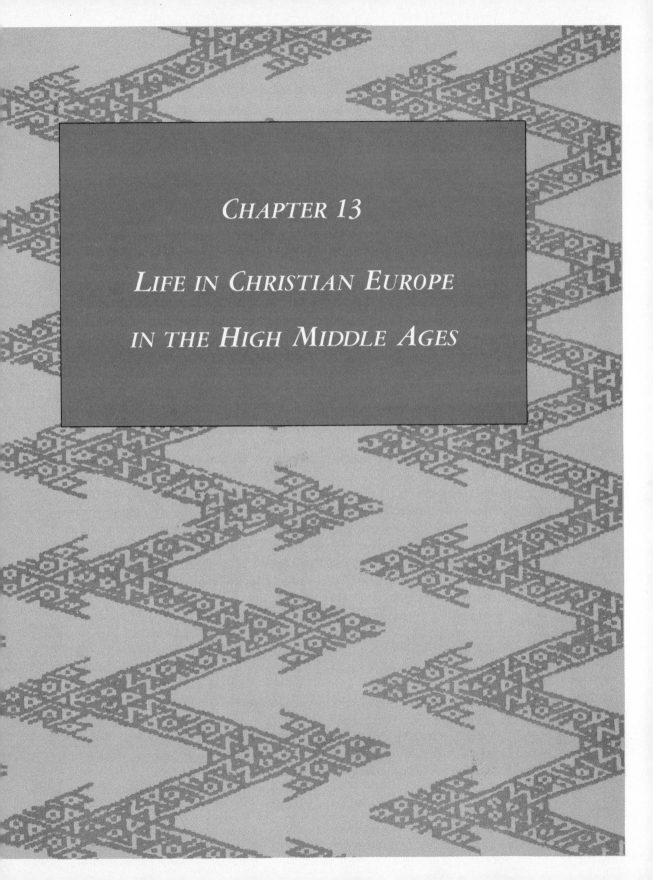

CHAPTER 13

LIFE IN CHRISTIAN EUROPE IN THE HIGH MIDDLE AGES

THE REVIVAL OF TRADE and commerce in the eleventh century brought into being a new class of merchants and businessmen. However, traders and other city dwellers were not typical of medieval society. They may have represented the wave of the future, but in the twelfth century that future was far in the distance. Some historians, trying to show the links between medieval and modern urban society, have concentrated their attention on the medieval commercial classes. In doing so, they have presented a distorted and anachronistic picture of medieval society. Other scholars have painted medieval society as static and unchanging. This picture also is inaccurate, because there was a good deal of movement, change, and migration.

In his biography of the Anglo-Saxon king Alfred, the tenth-century monk Asser described Christian society as composed of those who pray (the monks), those who fight (the nobles), and those who work (the peasants). This description, which was widely accepted and frequently repeated by other writers in the High Middle Ages, set forth the basic social composition of the medieval world. It does not take into consideration the emerging commercial classes. But medieval people were usually contemptuous (at least officially) of profit-making activities, and long after the appearance of commercial and urban groups, the general medieval view of Christian society remained the one formulated by Asser in the tenth century.

The most representative figures of Christian society in the High Middle Ages were peasants, monks, and nobles. How did these people actually live? What were their preoccupations and lifestyles? To what extent was social mobility possible for them? These are some of the questions this chapter seeks to answer.

THOSE WHO WORK

The largest and economically most productive group in medieval European society was the peasants. The men and women who worked the land in the twelfth and thirteenth centuries made up the overwhelming majority of the population, probably more than 90 percent. Yet it is difficult to form a coherent picture of them. The records that serve as historical sources were written by and for the aristocratic classes. Since farmers did not perform what were considered "noble" deeds, the aristocratic monks and clerics did not waste time or precious paper and ink on them. When peasants were mentioned, it was usually with contempt or in terms of the services and obligations they owed.

Usually – but not always. In the early twelfth century, Honorius, a monk and teacher at Autun who composed a popular handbook of sermons, wrote: "What do you say about the agricultural classes? Most of them will be saved because they live simply and feed God's people by means of their sweat."[1] This sentiment circulated widely. Honorius's comment suggests that peasant workers may have been appreciated and in a sense respected more than is generally believed.

In the last twenty-five years, historians have made remarkable advances in their knowledge of the medieval European peasantry. They have been able to do so by bringing fresh and different questions to old documents, by paying greater attention to such natural factors as geography and climate, and by studying demographic changes. Nevertheless, this new information raises additional questions, and a good deal remains unknown.

In 1932, a distinguished economic historian

wrote, "The student of medieval social and economic history who commits himself to a generalization is digging a pit into which he will later assuredly fall and nowhere does the pit yawn deeper than in the realm of rural history."[2] This remark is virtually as true today as when it was written. It is, therefore, important to remember that peasants' conditions varied widely across Europe, that geographical and climatic features as much as human initiative and local custom determined the peculiar quality of rural life. The problems that faced the farmer in Yorkshire, England, where the soil was rocky and the climate rainy, were very different from those of the Italian peasant in the sun-drenched Po valley.

Another difficulty has been historians' tendency to group all peasants into one social class. That is a serious mistake. It is true that medieval theologians simply lumped everyone who worked the land into the category of "those who work." In actual fact, however, there were many gradations, classes, and levels of peasants, ranging all the way from complete slaves to free and very rich farmers. The period from 1050 to 1250 was one of considerable fluidity with no little social mobility. The status of the peasantry varied widely all across Europe.

SLAVERY, SERFDOM, AND UPWARD MOBILITY

Slaves were found in western Europe in the High Middle Ages, but in steadily declining numbers. That the word *slave* derives from "Slav" attests to the widespread trade in men and women from the Slavic areas in the early Middle Ages. Around the year 1200, there were in aristocratic and upper-middle-class households in Provence, Catalonia, Italy, and Germany a few slaves — blond Slavs from the Baltic, olive-skinned Syrians, and blacks from Africa.

Since ancient times, it had been a universally accepted practice to reduce conquered peoples to slavery. The church had long taught that all baptized Christians were brothers in Christ and that all Christians belonged to one "international" community. Although the church never issued a blanket condemnation of slavery, it did vigorously oppose the enslaving of Christians. In attacking the enslavement of Christians and in criticizing the reduction of pagans and infidels to slavery, the church made a contribution to the development of human liberty.

In western Europe during the Middle Ages legal language differed considerably from place to place, and the distinction between slave and serf was not always clear. Both lacked freedom — the power to do as one wished — and were subject to the arbitrary will of one man, the lord. A serf, however, could not be bought and sold like an animal or an inanimate object, as the slave could.

The serf was required to perform labor services on the lord's land. The number of workdays varied but it was usually three days a week, except in the planting or harvest seasons, when it would be more. Serfs frequently had to pay arbitrary taxes. When a man married, he had to pay his lord a fee. When he died, his son or heir had to pay an inheritance tax to inherit his parcels of land. The precise amounts of tax paid to the lord on these important occasions depended upon local custom and tradition. Every manor had its particular obligations. A free person had to do none of these things. For his or her landholding, rent had to be paid to the lord, and that was often the sole obligation. A free person could move and live as he or she wished.

Serfs were tied to the land, and serfdom was a hereditary condition. A person born a serf was likely to die a serf, though many did secure their freedom. About 1187, Glanvill, an official of King Henry II and an expert on English law, described how villeins (literally, inhabitants of small villages) — as English serfs were called — could be made free:

A person of villein status can be made free in several ways. For example, his lord, wishing him to achieve freedom from the villeinage by which he is subject to him, may quit-claim him from himself and his heirs; or he may give or sell him to another with intent to free him. It should be noted, however, that no person of villein status can seek his freedom with his own money, for in such a case he could, according to the law and custom of the realm, be recalled to villeinage by his lord, because all the chattels of a villein are deemed to such an extent the property of his lord that he cannot redeem himself from villeinage with his own money, as against his lord. If, however, a third party pro-

vides the money and buys the villein in order to free him, then he can maintain himself for ever in a state of freedom as against his lord who sold him. . . . If any villein stays peaceably for a year and a day in a privileged town and is admitted as a citizen into their commune, that is to say, their gild, he is thereby freed from villeinage.[3]

Many energetic and hardworking serfs acquired their freedom in the High Middle Ages. More than anything else, the economic revival that began in the eleventh century advanced the cause of individual liberty. The revival saw the rise of towns, increased land productivity, the growth of long-distance trade, and the development of a money economy. With the advent of a money economy, serfs could save money and buy their freedom.

Another opportunity for increased personal freedom, or at least for a reduction in traditional manorial obligations and dues, was provided by the reclamation of waste and forest land in the eleventh and twelfth centuries. Resettlement on newly cleared land offered unusual possibilities for younger sons and for those living in areas of acute land shortage or on overworked, exhausted soil. Historians still do not know very much about this movement: how the new frontier territory was advertised, how men were recruited, how they and their households were transported, and how the new lands were distributed. It is certain, however, that there was significant migration and that only a lord with considerable authority over a wide territory could sponsor such a movement. Great lords supported the fight against the marshes of northern and eastern Germany and against the sea in the Low Countries.

As land long considered poor was brought under cultivation, there was a steady nibbling away at the wasteland on the edges of old villages. Clearings were made in forests. Marshes and fens were drained and slowly made arable. This type of agricultural advancement frequently improved the peasants' social and legal condition. A serf could clear a patch of fen or forest land, make it productive, and, through prudent saving, buy more land and eventually purchase his freedom. There were in the thirteenth century many free tenants on the lands of the bishop of Ely in eastern England, tenants who had moved into the area in the twelfth century and drained the fens. Likewise, settlers on the low lands of the abbey of Bourbourg in Flanders, who had erected dikes and extended the arable lands, possessed hereditary tenures by 1159. They secured personal liberty and owed their overlord only small payments.

Peasants who remained in the villages of their birth often benefited because landlords, threatened with the loss of serfs, relaxed ancient obligations and duties. While it would be unwise to exaggerate the social impact of the settling of new territories, frontier lands in the Middle Ages did provide opportunities for upward mobility.

THE MANOR

In the High Middle Ages, most European peasants, free and unfree, lived on estates called manors. The word *manor* derives from a Latin term meaning "dwelling," "residence," or "homestead." In the twelfth century it meant the estate of a lord and his dependent tenants.

The manor was the basic unit of medieval rural organization and the center of rural life. All other generalizations about manors and manorial life have to be limited by variations in the quality of the soil, local climatic conditions, and methods of cultivation. Some

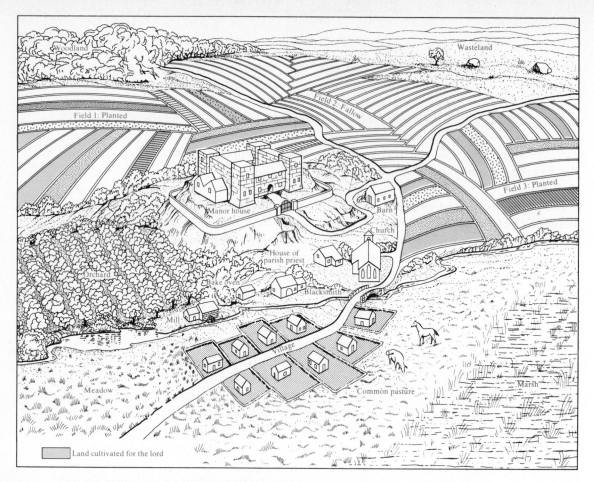

Woodland

Wasteland

Field 1: Planted

Field 2: Fallow

Field 3: Planted

Manor house

Barn

Church

House of parish priest

Orchard

Bake oven

Blacksmith

Mill

Village

Meadow

Common pasture

Marsh

Land cultivated for the lord

FIGURE 13.1   A MEDIEVAL MANOR *The basic unit of rural organization and the center of life for most people, the manor constituted the medieval peasants' world. Since manors had to be economically self-sufficient, life meant endless toil.*

manors were vast, covering several thousand acres of farmland; others were no larger than 120 acres. A manor might include several villages or none at all, but usually it contained a single village and was subject to one lord (see Figure 13.1).

The arable land of the manor was divided into two sections. The demesne, or home farm, was cultivated for the lord. The other part was held by the peasantry. Usually, the peasants' portion was larger, held on condition that they cultivate the lord's demesne. All the arable, both the lord's and the peasants',

was divided into strips, and the strips belonging to any given individual were scattered throughout the manor. All peasants cooperated in the cultivation of the land, working it as a group. This meant that all shared in any disaster as well as any large harvest.

A manor usually held pasture or meadowland for the grazing of cattle, sheep, and sometimes goats. Often the manor had some forest land as well. Forests had enormous economic importance: they were the source of wood for building and resin for lighting; ash for candles, and ash and lime for fertilizers and all sorts of sterilizing products; wood for fuel and bark for the manufacture of rope. From the forests came wood for the construction of barrels, vats, and all sorts of storage containers. Last but hardly least, the forests were used for the feeding of pigs, cattle, and domestic animals on nuts, roots, and wild berries. If the manor was intersected by a river, it had a welcome source of fish and eels.

AGRICULTURAL METHODS

The fundamental objective of all medieval agriculture was the production of an adequate food supply. According to the method historians have called the open-field system, at any one time half the manorial land was under cultivation and the other half lay fallow; the length of the fallow period was usually one year. Every peasant farmer had strips scattered in both halves. One part of the land under cultivation was sown with winter cereals, such as wheat and rye, the other with spring crops, such as peas, beans, and barley. What was planted in a particular field varied each year when the crops were rotated.

Local needs, the fertility of the soil, and dietary customs determined what was planted and the method of crop rotation. Where one or several manors belonged to a great aristocratic establishment, such as the abbey of Cluny, which needed large quantities of oats for horses, more of the arable land would be planted in oats than in other cereals. Where the land was extremely fertile, such as the Alsace region of France, a biennial cycle was used: one crop of wheat was sown and harvested every other year, and in alternate years all the land lay fallow. The author of an English agricultural treatise advised his readers to stick to a two-field method of cultivation and insisted that a rich harvest every second year was preferable to two mediocre ones

every three years. Farmers everywhere obviously sought to use the land in the most productive way and to get the greatest output.

Nor were they ignorant of the value of animal fertilizers. Chicken manure, because of its high nitrogen content, was the richest but limited in quantity. Sheep manure was also valuable. Gifts to English Cistercian monasteries were frequently given on condition that the monks' sheep be allowed to graze at certain periods on the benefactor's demesne. Because cattle were fed on the common pasture and were rarely stabled, gathering their manure was laborious and time-consuming. Nevertheless, whenever possible, animal manure was gathered and thinly spread. So also was house garbage – eggshells, fruit cores, onion skins – that had disintegrated on a compost heap.

Tools and farm implements are often shown in medieval manuscripts. But accepting such representations at face value is misleading. Rather than going out into a field to look at a tool, medieval artists simply copied drawings from classical and other treatises. Thus a plow or harrow pictured in a book written in the Ile-de-France may actually have been used in England or Italy a half century before.

In the early twelfth century the production of iron increased greatly. There is considerable evidence for the manufacture of iron plowshares (the part of the plow that cuts the furrow into and grinds up the earth). In the thirteenth century the wooden plow continued to be the basic instrument of agricultural production, but its edge was strengthened with iron. Only after the start of the fourteenth century, when lists of manorial equipment began to be kept, is there evidence for pitchforks, spades, axes, and harrows. Harrows were used to smooth out the soil after it had been broken up. A crude harrow appears

LATE MEDIEVAL WHEELLESS PLOW *This plow has a sharp-pointed colter, which cut the earth while the attached mold-board lifted, turned, and pulverized the soil. As the man steers the plow, his wife prods the oxen. The caption reads, "God speed the plow, and send us corn (wheat) now." (Trinity College Library, Cambridge)*

in the illustration for the month of October in the *Très riches heures du duc de Berry,* completed in the mid-fifteenth century. The harrow is made of wood and weighted down with a large stone to force it to cut more deeply into the earth.

The harrow was drawn by horses. The use of horses rather than oxen in the agricultural economy increased in the later thirteenth century. Horses were a large investment, perhaps comparable to a modern tractor. They had to be shod (another indication of increased iron production) and the oats they ate were costly. But horses represented an important element in the improvement of the medieval agricul-tural economy. Because of their greater strength, horses brought far greater efficiency to farming than oxen. Indeed, some scholars believe that the use of the horse in agriculture is one of the decisive ways in which western Europe advanced over the rest of the world. But horses were not universally adopted. The Mediterranean countries, for example, did not use horsepower. And, at the same time, tools remained pitifully primitive.

Agricultural yields varied widely from place to place and from year to year. Even with good iron tools, horsepower, and careful use of seed and fertilizer, medieval peasants were at the mercy of the weather. Even today, lack of rain or too much rain can cause terrible financial loss and extreme hardship. How much more vulnerable was the medieval peasant with his primitive tools! By twentieth-century standards medieval agricultural yields were very low. The inadequate preparation of the soil, the poor selection of seed, the lack of sufficient manure – all made this virtually inevitable.

Yet there was striking improvement over time. Between the ninth and early thirteenth centuries, it appears that yields of cereals approximately doubled, and that on the best-managed estates, for every bushel of seed planted, the farmer harvested five bushels of grain. This is a very tentative conclusion. Because of the great scarcity of manorial inventories before the thirteenth century, the student of medieval agriculture has great difficulty determining how much the land produced. The author of a treatise on land husbandry, Walter of Henley, who lived in the mid-thirteenth century, wrote that the land should yield three times its seed; that amount was necessary for sheer survival. The surplus would be sold to grain merchants in the nearest town. Townspeople were wholly dependent on the surrounding countryside for food, which could not be shipped a long distance. A poor harvest meant that both town and rural people suffered.

Grain yields were probably greatest on the large manorial estates, where there was more professional management. For example, the estates of Battle Abbey in Sussex, England, enjoyed a very high yield of wheat, rye, and oats in the century and a half between 1350 and 1499. This was due to heavy seeding, good crop rotation, and the use of manure from the monastery's sheep flocks. Battle Abbey's yields seem to have been double those of smaller, less efficiently run farms. A modern Illinois farmer expects to get 40 bushels

of soybeans, 150 bushels of corn, and 50 bushels of wheat for every bushel of seeds planted. Of course, modern costs of production in labor, seed, and fertilizer are quite high, but this yield is at least ten times that of the farmer's medieval ancestor. The average manor probably got a yield of 5:1 in the thirteenth century.[4] As low as that may seem by current standards, it marked a rise in the level of productivity equal to that of the years just before the great agricultural revolution of the eighteenth century.

LIFE ON THE MANOR

Life for most people in medieval Europe meant country life. A person's horizons were largely restricted to the manor on which he or she was born. People rarely traveled more than twenty-five miles beyond their villages. Everyone's world was small, narrow, and provincial in the original sense of the word: limited by the boundaries of the province. This way of life did not have entirely unfortunate results. A farmer had a strong sense of family and the certainty of its support and help in time of trouble. People knew what their life's work would be – the same as their mother's or father's. They had a sense of place, and pride in that place was reflected in adornment of the village church. Religion and the village gave people a sure sense of identity and with it psychological peace. Modern people – urban, isolated, industrialized, rootless, and thoroughly secular – have lost many of these reinforcements.

On the other hand, even aside from the unending physical labor, life on the manor was dull. Medieval men and women must have had a crushing sense of frustration. They lived lives of quiet desperation. Often they sought escape in heavy drinking. English judicial records of the thirteenth century reveal

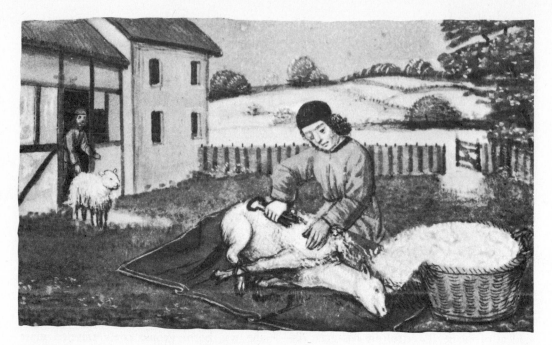

SHEEPSHEARING   After the sheep was tied up, the farmer clipped the wool and bagged it. English wool was internationally famous for its fine quality, and the English and the Flemish economies depended upon the wool trade. (The British Museum)

a surprisingly large number of "accidental" deaths. Strong, robust, and commonsensical farmers do not ordinarily fall down on their knives and stab themselves, or slip out of a boat and drown, or get lost in the woods on a winter's night, or fall from their horses and get trampled. They were probably drunk. Many of these accidents occurred, as the court records say, "coming from an ale." Brawls and violent fights were frequent at taverns. They reflect in part the drudgery of life and simple human frustration.

Women played a significant role in the agricultural life of medieval Europe. This obvious fact is often overlooked by historians. Women shared with their fathers and husbands the backbreaking labor in the fields, work that was probably all the more difficult for them because of weaker muscular development and frequent pregnancies. The adage from the Book of Proverbs – "Houses and riches are the inheritances of fathers: but a prudent wife is from the Lord" – was seldom more true than in an age when the wife's prudent management was often all that separated a household from starvation in a year of crisis. And starvation was a very real danger to the peasantry until the eighteenth century.

Women managed the house. The size and quality of peasants' houses varied according to their relative prosperity, and that prosperity usually depended upon the amount of land held. Poorer peasants lived in windowless cottages built of wood and clay or wattle and thatched with straw. These cottages consisted of one large room that served as the kitchen and living quarters for all. Everyone slept there. The house had an earthen floor and a fireplace. The lack of windows meant that the room was very sooty. A trestle table, several stools, one or two beds, and a chest for storing clothes constituted the furniture. A shed attached to the house provided storage for tools and shelter for animals. Prosperous peasants added rooms and furniture as they could be afforded, and some wealthy peasants in the early fourteenth century had two-story houses with separate bedrooms for parents and children.

Every house had a small garden and an outbuilding. Onions, garlic, turnips, and carrots were grown and stored through the winter in the main room of the dwelling or in the shed attached to it. Cabbage was raised almost everywhere and, after being shredded, salted, and packed in vats in hot water, was turned into kraut. Peasants ate vegetables not because they appreciated their importance for good health but because there was usually little else. Some manors had fruit trees – apple, cherry, and pear in northern Europe; lemon, lime, and olive in the south. But because of the high price of sugar, when it was available, fruit could not be preserved. Preserving and storing other foods were the basic responsibility of the women and children.

Women also had to know the correct proportions of barley, water, yeast, and hops to make beer – the universal drink of the common people in northern Europe. By modern American standards the rate of beer consumption was heroic. Each monk of Abingdon Abbey in England in the twelfth century was allotted three gallons a day, and a man working in the fields for ten or twelve hours a day probably drank much more.

The mainstay of the diet for peasants everywhere – and for all other classes – was bread. It was a hard, black substance made of barley, millet, and oats, rarely of expensive wheat flour. The housewife usually baked the supply for the household once a week. Where sheep, cows, or goats were raised, she also made cheese. In places like the Bavarian Alps region of southern Germany, where hundreds of sheep grazed on the mountainsides, or at Cheddar in southwestern England, cheese was a staple of the diet.

The diet of those living in an area with access to a river, lake, or stream would be supplemented with fish, which could be preserved by salting. In many places there were severe laws against hunting and trapping in the forests. Deer, wild boars, and other game were strictly reserved for the king and nobility. These laws were flagrantly violated, however, and stolen rabbits and wild game often found their way to the peasants' tables. Woods and forests also provided nuts, which housewives and small children would gather in the fall.

Lists of peasant obligations and services to the lord, such as the following from a manor in Battle Abbey in England, commonly included the payment of chickens and eggs:

John of Coyworth holds a house and thirty acres of land, and owes yearly 2 p at Easter and Michaelmas; and he owes a cock and two hens at Christmas, of the value of 4 d.[5]

Chickens and eggs must have been highly valued in the prudently managed household. Except for the rare chicken or the illegally caught wild game, meat appeared on the table only on the great feast days of the Christian year: Christmas, Easter, and Pentecost. Then, the meat was likely to be pork from the pig that had been slaughtered in the fall and salted for the rest of the year. Some scholars believe that by the mid-thirteenth century there was a great increase in the consumption of meat generally. If so, this improvement in

WORKING IN THE FIELDS Women shared with men all the difficult agricultural work. These farm scenes show women hoeing, sowing seed, cutting and tying the grain, and carrying it to the mill. Although the sickles and the spade appear to have an iron tip, the hoe is entirely wooden. (Rheinisches Landesmuseum, Bonn)

the diet is further evidence of a better standard of living.

Breakfast, eaten at dawn before the farmer departed for his work, might well consist of bread, an onion (easily stored through the winter months), and a piece of cheese, washed down with milk or beer. Farmers then as now ate their main meal around noon. This was often soup – a thick *potage* of boiled cabbage, onions, turnips, and peas, seasoned with a bone or perhaps a sliver of meat. The evening meal, taken at sunset, consisted of leftovers from the noon meal, perhaps with bread, cheese, milk, or beer.

Once children were able to walk, they helped their parents in the hundreds of chores that had to be done. Small children were set to collecting eggs, if the family possessed chickens, or gathering twigs and sticks for firewood. As they grew older, children had more responsible tasks, such as weeding the family vegetable garden, milking the cows, shearing the sheep, cutting wood for fires, helping with the planting or harvesting, and assisting their mothers in the endless tasks of baking, cooking, and preserving. Because of poor diet, terrible sanitation, and lack of medical care, the death rate among children was phenomenally high.

POPULAR RELIGION

Apart from the land and the weather and the peculiar conditions that existed on each manor, the Christian religion had the greatest impact on the daily lives of ordinary people in the High Middle Ages. Religious practices varied widely from country to country and even from province to province. But nowhere was religion a one-hour-on-Sunday or High Holy Days affair. Christian practices and attitudes shaded and permeated virtually all aspects of everyday life.

In the ancient world participation in religious rituals was a public and social duty. As the Germanic and Celtic peoples were Christianized, their new religion became a fusion of Jewish, pagan, Roman, and Christian practices. By the High Middle Ages, religious rituals and practices represented a synthesis of many elements, and all people shared as a natural and public duty in the religious life of the community.

The village church was the center of manorial life — social, political, and economic as well as religious. Most of the important events in a person's life took place in or around the church. A person was baptized there, within hours of birth. Men and women confessed their sins to the village priest there and received, usually at Easter and Christmas, the sacrament of the Eucharist. In front of the church, the bishop reached down from his horse and confirmed a person as a Christian by placing his hands over the candidate's head and making the sign of the cross on the forehead. (Bishops Thomas Becket of Canterbury and Hugh of Lincoln were considered especially holy men because they got down from their horses to confirm.) Young people courted in the churchyard and, so the sermons of the priests complained, made love in the church cemetery. They were married before the altar in the church.

The stone in the church altar contained relics of the saints, often a local saint to whom the church itself had been dedicated. In the church women and men could pray to the Virgin and the local saints. The saints had once lived on earth and thus could well understand human problems. They could be helpful intercessors with Christ or God the Father. According to official church doctrine, the center of the Christian religious life was the mass, the re-enactment of Christ's sacrifice on the cross. Every Sunday and on holy days, the villager stood at mass or squatted on the floor (there were no chairs), breaking the painful routine of work. Finally, people wanted to be buried in the church cemetery, close to the holy place and the saints believed to reside there.

The church was the center of village social life. The feasts that accompanied baptisms, weddings, funerals, and other celebrations were commonly held in the churchyard. Medieval drama originated within the church. Mystery plays, based on biblical episodes, were performed first in the sanctuary, then on the church porch, and finally in the village square, which was often in front of the west door.

From the church porch the priest read to his parishioners orders and messages from royal and ecclesiastical authorities. Royal judges traveling on circuit opened their courts on the church porch. The west front of the

church, with its scenes of the Last Judgment, was the background against which the justices disposed of civil and criminal cases. Farmers from outlying districts pushed their carts to the marketplace in the village square near the west front. In busy mercantile centers such as London, business agreements and commercial exchanges were made in the aisles of the church itself, as at St. Paul's.

Popular religion consisted largely of rituals heavy with symbolism. Before slicing a loaf of bread, the good wife tapped the sign of the cross on it with her knife. Before the planting, the village priest customarily went out and sprinkled the fields with water, symbolizing refreshment and life. Shortly after a woman had successfully delivered a child, she was "churched." This was a ceremony of thanksgiving, based on the Jewish rite of purification. When a child was baptized, a few grains of salt were dropped on its tongue. Salt had been the symbol of purity, strength, and incorruptibility for the ancient Hebrews, and the Romans had used it in their sacrifices. It was used in Christian baptism both to drive away demons and to strengthen the infant in its new faith.

The entire calendar was designed with reference to the great festivals of the Christian year — Easter, Christmas, and Pentecost. Saints' days were legion. Everyone participated in village processions. The colored vestments the priests wore at mass gave the villagers a sense of the changing seasons of the church's liturgical year. The signs and symbols of Christianity were visible everywhere.

Was popular religion entirely a matter of ritualistic formulas and ceremonies? What did the peasants actually *believe*? They accepted what family, customs, and the clergy ingrained in them. They learned the fundamental teachings of the church from the homilies of the village priests. The mass was in Latin, but the priest delivered homilies on the gospel in the vernacular. People grasped the meaning of biblical stories and church doctrines from the paintings on the village church wall. If their parish was wealthy, the scenes depicted in the church's stained-glass windows instructed them. Illiterate and uneducated, they certainly could not reason out the increasingly sophisticated propositions of clever theologians. Still, scriptural references and proverbs dotted everyone's language. Christianity was a basic element in the common people's culture; indeed, it was their culture.

Christians had long had special reverence and affection for the Virgin Mary, as the Mother of Christ. In the eleventh century theologians began to emphasize the depiction of Mary at the crucifixion in the Gospel of John:

But standing by the cross of Jesus were his mother, and his mother's sister, Mary the wife of Clopas, and Mary Magdalene. When Jesus saw his mother and the disciple whom he loved standing near, he said to his mother, "Woman, behold, your son!" Then he said to the disciple, "Behold, your mother!"[6]

Medieval scholars interpreted this passage as expressing Christ's compassionate concern for all humanity and Mary's spiritual motherhood of all Christians. The huge outpouring of popular devotions to Mary concentrated on her role as Queen of Heaven and, because of her special relationship to Christ, as all-powerful intercessor with Him. Masses on Saturdays specially commemorated her, sermons focused on her unique influence with Christ, and hymns and prayers to her multiplied. The most famous prayer, *Salve Regina*, perfectly expresses medieval people's attitude toward Mary:

Hail, holy Queen, Mother of Mercy! Our life, our sweetness, and our hope. To thee we cry, poor banished children of Eve; to thee we send up our sighs, mourning and weeping in this valley of tears. Turn, then, most gracious advocate, thy merciful eyes upon us; and after this our exile show us the blessed fruit of thy womb, Jesus. O merciful, O loving, O sweet Virgin Mary!

The prayer vividly and lovingly declares medieval people's confidence in Mary, to whom they recommend themselves as the exiled sons

BURIAL OF THE VIRGIN *Carved in a piece of ivory 5" × 2½", this detailed scene of Mary's burial reflects both the profound faith of the age and the incredible skill of medieval artists. (Courtesy, World Heritage Museum. Photo: Caroline Buckler)*

of Eve in this world, and in her power as advocate with Christ.

Peasants had a strong sense of the universal presence of God. They believed that God intervened directly in human affairs and could reward the virtuous and bring peace, health, and material prosperity. They believed, too, that God punished men and women for their sins with disease, poor harvests, and the destructions of war. Sin was caused by the Devil, who lurked everywhere. The Devil constantly incited people to evil deeds and sin, especially sins of the flesh. Sin frequently took place in the dark. Thus, evil and the Devil were connected in the peasant's mind with darkness or blackness. In medieval literature the Devil is often portrayed as a Negro, an identification that has had a profound and sorry impact on Western racial attitudes.

For peasants, life was not only hard but short. Few lived much beyond the age of forty. They had a great fear of nature: storms, thunder, and lightning terrified them. They had a terror of hell, whose geography and awful tortures they knew from sermons. And they certainly saw that the virtuous were not always rewarded but sometimes suffered considerably on earth. These things, which they could not explain, bred in them a deep pessimism.

No wonder, then, that pilgrimages to shrines of the saints were so popular. They offered hope in a world of gloom. They satisfied a strong emotional need. They meant change, adventure, excitement. The church granted indulgences to those who visited the shrines of great saints. Though indulgences only reduced the priest-imposed penalties for sin, people equated them with salvation. They generally believed that the indulgence received from a pilgrimage cut down the amount of time one would spend in hell. Thus pilgrimages "promised" salvation. Vast numbers embarked on pilgrimages to the shrines of St. James at Santiago de Compostella in Spain, Thomas Becket at Canterbury, St.-Gilles de Provence, and Saints Peter and Paul at Rome.

THOSE WHO FIGHT

In the High Middle Ages members of the nobility were those who fought. Also from the nobility came the great majority of monks and clerics, as well as the opinions, attitudes, and behavior that, to a considerable extent, shaped the lives of other classes. How did the lifestyle and social status of the nobility in the twelfth and thirteenth centuries differ from what they had been in the tenth century? What political and economic role did the nobility play?

Nobility was a legal status that a person acquired automatically at birth or received from a king or ruler as a reward for outstanding fighting skill or unusual services. Nobles considered themselves aristocrats — the word *aristocrat* derives from a Greek term meaning "the best" — but only toward the end of the twelfth century did the European nobility begin to develop a definite class consciousness. Nobles had a way of life based on a chivalric code and the observance — at least among those they considered social equals — of ideals of courtesy, generosity, graciousness, and hospitality. Most monks came from noble families, and the opinions they expressed were aristocratic.

The aristocratic nobility, though a small fraction of the total population, strongly influenced all aspects of culture — political, economic, religious, educational, and artistic. For that reason European society in the twelfth and thirteenth centuries may be termed aristocratic. In spite of scientific, industrial, and political revolutions, the nobility continued to hold the real political and social power in Europe down to the nineteenth century. In order to account for this continuing influence in later centuries, it is important to understand its development in the High Middle Ages.

The noble was almost always a military man, and he frequently used the Latin title *miles,* or knight, to indicate his nobility. He possessed a horse and a sword. These, and the leisure time in which to learn how to use them in combat, were the visible signs of his nobility.

Members of the nobility enjoyed a special legal status. The noble was free personally and in his possessions. He had immunity from almost all outside authorities. He was limited only by his military obligation to king, duke, or prince. As the result of his liberty, he had certain rights and responsibilities. He raised troops and commanded them in the field. He held courts that dispensed a sort of justice. Sometimes he coined money for use within his territories. He conducted relations with outside powers. He was the political, military, and judicial lord of the people who settled on his lands. He made political decisions affecting them, he resolved disputes among them, and he protected them in time of attack. The liberty of the noble and the privileges that went with his liberty were inheritable; they were perpetuated by blood and not by wealth alone.

Women whose fathers or husbands were noble were considered noble too, but not in their own right. Noble ladies often performed the political and military obligations of the men of their class, but there is no evidence of a woman being raised to the nobility. The values of a society are largely determined by its needs, and in the High Middle Ages those needs were military. Fighting was usually done by men, and so men were given noble status.

In the course of the twelfth century, the aristocratic knights slowly evolved into a distinct and closely knit class with feelings of superiority and an attitude of exclusivity. They had a common culture based on consciousness of family, the veneration of ancestors, and a sense of their own worth. Those who were or aspired to be aristocrats wanted

CHAIN MAIL *This long shirt of interlinked metal rings, though heavy and uncomfortable, was flexible and allowed movement. Knights wore it because before the manufacture of plate armor, chain mail provided a fair degree of protection. (Courtesy, World Heritage Museum. Photo: Caroline Buckler)*

to possess a castle, the symbol of feudal independence and of a military lifestyle. Nobles almost always married within their class.

INFANCY AND CHILDHOOD

Some very exciting research has been done on childbirth in the Middle Ages. Most information comes from manuscript illuminations, which depict the birth process from the moment of coitus through pregnancy to delivery. An interesting thirteenth-century German miniature from Vienna shows a woman in labor. She is sitting on a chair or stool surrounded by four other women, who are pres-

MIDWIVES HASTENING DELIVERY   Relatives or midwives assist the woman in childbirth by shaking her up and down. Significantly, no physician is present. With such treatment, the death-rate for both mothers and infants was high. (Bildarchiv der Österreichischen Nationalbibliothek)

ent to help her in the delivery. They could be relatives or neighbors. If they are midwives, the woman in labor is probably noble or rich, since midwives charged a fee. Two midwives seem to be shaking the mother up and down to hasten delivery. One of the women is holding a coriander seed near the mother's vagina. Coriander is an herb of the carrot family, and its seeds were used for cleaning purposes. They were thought to be helpful for expelling gas from the alimentary canal — hence their value for speeding up delivery.

The rate of infant mortality in the High Middle Ages must have been staggering. Such practices as jolting the pregnant woman up and down and inserting a seed into her surely contributed to the death rate of both the newborn and the mother. Natural causes — disease and poor or insufficient food — also resulted in many deaths. Infanticide, however, which was common in the ancient world, seems to have declined in the High Middle Ages. Ecclesiastical pressure worked steadily against it. High mortality due to foreign invasions and the generally violent and unstable conditions of the ninth and tenth centuries also made unnecessary the deliberate killing of one's own children. On the other hand, English court records from the counties of Warwickshire, Staffordshire, and Gloucestershire for 1221 reveal a suspiciously large number of children dying from "accidental deaths" — drowning, falling from carts, disappearing into the woods, falling into the fire. Still, accidental deaths in rural conditions are more common than is usually thought. Until more research is done, we cannot be certain about the prevalence of infanticide in the High Middle Ages.

Noble women did not nurse their own children. They sent newborns out to wet nurses — women who had recently given birth and therefore had milk. When Richard Plantagenet was born to Henry II and Eleanor on September 8, 1157, his mother immediately gave him to a woman of St. Alban's to nurse. The wet nurse had also had a son on September 8. How long the infant Richard and other medieval children were nursed is not known.

Swaddling appears to have been common in the Middle Ages. Strips of cloth were wrapped tightly around the child's arms, legs, and entire body until it was immobile. The infant was often strapped to a board, which could be set down in a corner or hung up in an out-of-the-way spot. Swaddling depressed the bodily functions: the heartbeat slowed, the child slept more and cried less. Theoretically, this practice arose from adult fears that the child would harm itself if its limbs were free. Probably, too, swaddling was a convenience to the nurse or parent. A swaddled child could be ignored for hours.[7] Any number of unfortunate things could happen to the inert infant, not the least of which was lying for a long time in its own filth. Swaddling surely led to body rashes, disease, and death.

For children of aristocratic birth, the years from infancy to around the age of seven or eight were primarily years of play. Infants had their rattles, as the twelfth-century monk Guibert of Nogent reports, and young children their special toys. Of course, then as now, children would play with anything handy — balls, rings, pretty stones, horns, any small household object. Gerald of Wales, who later became a courtier of King Henry II, describes how as a child he built monasteries and churches in the sand while his brothers were making castles and palaces. Vincent of Beauvais, who composed a great encyclopedia around 1250, recommended that children be bathed twice a day, fed well, and given ample playtime.

Guibert of Nogent speaks in several places in his autobiography of "the tender years of childhood" — the years from six to twelve. Describing the severity of the tutor whom his mother assigned to him, Guibert wrote:

Placed under him, I was taught with such purity and checked with such honesty from the vices which commonly spring up in youth that I was kept from ordinary games and never allowed to leave my master's company, or to eat anywhere else than at home, or to accept gifts from anyone without his leave; in everything I had to show self-control in word, look, and deed, so that he seemed to require of me the conduct of a monk rather than a clerk. While others of my age wandered everywhere at will and were unchecked in the indulgence of such inclinations as were natural at their age, I, hedged in with constant restraints and dressed in my clerical garb, would sit and look at the troops of players like a beast awaiting sacrifice. Even on Sundays and saints' days I had to submit to the severity of school exercises. At hardly any time, and never for a whole day, was I allowed to take a holiday; in fact, in every way and at all times I was driven to study. Moreover, he devoted himself exclusively to my education, since he was allowed to have no other pupil.[8]

Guibert's mother had intended him for the church. Other boys and girls had more playtime and more freedom.

Aristocrats deliberately had large families in order to insure the continuation of the family. Although many women died in childbirth and many children died before the age of seven, the survival of four or five children was not uncommon. Parents decided upon the futures of their children as soon as they were born or when they were still toddlers. Sons were prepared for one of the two positions considered suitable to their birth and position. Careers for the youngest sons might well be found in the church; for the rest, a suitable position meant a military career. Likewise, parents determined early which daughters would be married – and to whom – and which would become nuns.

At about the age of seven a boy of the noble class who was not intended for the church was placed in the household of one of his father's friends or relatives. There he became a servant to the lord and received his formal training in arms. He was expected to serve the lord at the table, to assist him as a private valet when called upon to do so, and, as he gained experience, to care for the lord's

horses and equipment. The boy might have a great deal of work to do, depending upon the size of the household and the personality of the lord. The work children did, medieval people believed, gave them experience and preparation for later life.

Training was in the arts of war. The boy learned to ride and to manage a horse. He had to acquire skill in wielding a sword, which sometimes weighed as much as twenty-five pounds. He had to be able to hurl a lance, shoot with a bow and arrow, and care for armor and other equipment. In the eleventh and twelfth centuries, noble youths were rarely taught to read and write. On thousands of charters from that period nobles signed with a cross (+) or some other mark. Literacy for the nobility became a little more common in the thirteenth century. Formal training was concluded around the age of eighteen with the ceremony of knighthood.

By the twelfth century, all men who were legally and socially noble had been formally knighted and could use the titles *dominus* and *messire,* which mean "lord." The ceremony of knighthood was one of the most important in a man's life. Once knighted, a young man was supposed to be courteous, generous, and if possible handsome and rich. Above all, he was to be loyal to his lord and brave in battle. Loyalty was the greatest and most important virtue. In a society lacking strong institutions of government, loyalty was the cement that held aristocratic society together. That is why the greatest crime was called a felony, which meant treachery to one's lord.

YOUTH

Knighthood, however, did not mean adulthood, power, and responsibility. Sons were completely dependent upon their fathers for support. Unless a young man's father was dead, he was still considered a youth. He remained a youth until he was in a financial position to marry — that is, until his father died. That might not happen until he was in his late thirties, and marriage at forty was not uncommon. A famous English soldier of fortune, William Marshal, had to wait until he was forty-five to take a wife. One factor — the inheritance of land and the division of properties — determined the lifestyle of the aristocratic nobility. The result was tension, frustration, and sometimes violence.

Once he had been knighted, the young man traveled. His father selected a group of friends to accompany, guide, and protect him. The band's chief pursuit was fighting. They meddled in local conflicts. Sometimes they departed on crusades. They did the tournament circuit. The tournament, in which a number of men competed from horseback (in contrast to the joust, which involved only two competitors), gave the bachelor knight experience in pitched battle. Since the horses and equipment of the vanquished were forfeited to the victors, the knight could also gain a reputation and a profit. The group hunted. They took great delight in spending money on horses, armor, gambling, drinking, and women. Everywhere these bands of youths went they stirred up trouble. It is no wonder that kings supported the Crusades. Those foreign excursions rid their countries of considerable violence caused by bands of footloose young knights.

The period of traveling lasted two or three years. Although some young men met violent death and others were maimed or injured, many returned home, still totally dependent upon their fathers for support. Serious trouble frequently developed at this stage, for the father was determined to preserve intact the properties of the lordship and to maintain his power and position within the family. Young men could not marry and set up a household on their own without the father's approval.

When fathers survived until advanced years, marriage and independence had to be long postponed.

Parents often wanted to settle their daughters' futures as soon as possible. Men, even older men, tended to prefer young brides. A woman in her late twenties or thirties would have fewer years of married fertility, limiting the number of children she could produce and thus threatening the survival of the family. Therefore, aristocratic girls in the High Middle Ages were married at around the age of sixteen.

The future of many young women was not enviable. For a girl of sixteen, marriage to a man in his thirties was not the most attractive prospect, and marriage to a widower in his forties and fifties would be even less so. If there were a large number of marriageable young girls in a particular locality, their market value was reduced. In the early Middle Ages it had been the custom for the groom to present a dowry to the bride and her family, but by the late twelfth century the process was reversed. Thereafter, the size of the marriage portions offered by brides and their families rose higher and higher.

Many girls of aristocratic families did not marry at all, although there were few professions a well-born lady could honorably enter. She certainly could not be apprenticed to a trader or artisan. Even less did her blood and dignity allow her to perform any manual labor. The sole alternative was the religious life. Benedictine abbeys for women provided "career opportunities" for some unmarriageable girls. Parents commonly decided upon this option, especially if there were several daughters in the family, when the child was under ten. If a girl felt no particular inclination toward becoming a nun, her mother changed her mind quickly enough. The girl of eleven or twelve years was taken to the childbed of a relative or neighbor to observe the pain and blood that was the lot of married women. It was an event she would not quickly forget. This traumatic experience made her willing to go along with her parent's wishes.

In England in the later Middle Ages there were 138 nunneries, whose residents were overwhelmingly women from the nobility and the upper middle classes. Most convents were small, however, and did not have places for everyone desiring entrance. The new religious orders of the thirteenth century, the Franciscan and the Dominican, provided some relief by establishing many convents for girls and women of the upper class.

Within noble families and within medieval society as a whole, paternal control of the family property and wealth led to serious difficulties. Because marriage was long delayed for men, a considerable age difference existed between husbands and wives and between fathers and their sons. Because of this generation gap, as one scholar has written, "the father became an older, distant, but still powerful figure. He could do favors for his sons, but his very presence, once his sons had reached maturity, blocked them in the attainment and enjoyment of property and in the possession of a wife."[9] Consequently, disputes between the generations were common in the twelfth and thirteenth centuries. Older men held on to property and power. Younger sons wanted a "piece of the action." This helps explain the conflicts and rebellions that occurred in the years 1173-1189 between Henry II of England and his sons Henry, Geoffrey, and John. Their case was quite typical.

The relationship between the mother and her sons was also affected. Closer in years to her children than her husband, she was perhaps better able to understand their needs and frustrations. She often served as a mediator between conflicting male generations. One

authority, discussing the role of the mother in French epic poetry, has written, "In extreme need, the heroes betake themselves to their mother, with whom they always find love, counsel and help. She takes them under her protection, even against their father."[10]

When society included so many married young women and unmarried young men, sexual tensions also arose. The young male noble, unable to marry for a long time, could satisfy his lust with peasant girls or prostitutes. But what was a young woman unhappily married to a much older man to do? The literature of courtly love is filled with stories of young bachelors in love with young married women. How hopeless their love was is not known. The cuckolded husband is a stock figure in such masterpieces as *The Romance of Tristan and Isolde,* Chaucer's *The Merchant's Tale,* and Boccaccio's *Fiammetta's Tale.*

In the High Middle Ages, for economic reasons, a man might remain a bachelor knight – a "youth" – for a very long time. The identification of bachelorhood with youth has survived into modern times, and the social attitude persists that marriage makes a man mature – an adult. Marriage, however, is no guarantee of that.

POWER AND RESPONSIBILITY

A member of the nobility became an adult when he came into the possession of his property. He then acquired vast authority over lands and people. With it went responsibility. The first obligation of the noble was to fight. He was supposed to be the protector and the defender of Christian society against its enemies. In the words of Honorius of Autun:

Soldiers: You are the arm of the Church, because you should defend it against its enemies. Your duty

FRENCH CASTLE UNDER SIEGE *Most medieval warfare consisted of small skirmishes and the besieging of castles. If surrounded by a moat and supplied with food and water, a few knights could hold a castle against large armies for a long time. Notice the use of engines to hurl missiles. (The British Museum)*

is to aid the oppressed, to restrain yourself from rapine and fornication, to repress those who impugn the Church with evil acts, and to resist those who are rebels against priests. Performing such a service, you will obtain the most splendid of benefices from the greatest of Kings.[11]

Nobles rarely lived up to this ideal, and there are countless examples of nobles attacking the church. In the early thirteenth century, Peter of Dreux, count of Brittany, spent so much of his time attacking the church that he was known as "the Scourge of the Clergy."

The nobles' conception of rewards and gratification did not involve the kind of postponement envisioned by the clergy. They wanted rewards immediately. Since by definition a military class is devoted to war, those rewards came through the pursuit of arms. When nobles were not involved in local squabbles with neighbors – usually disputes over property or over real or imagined slights – they participated in tournaments.

Complete jurisdiction over his properties allowed the noble, at long last, to gratify his desire for display and lavish living. Since his status in medieval society depended upon the size of his household, he would be anxious to increase the number of his household retainers. The elegance of his clothes, the variety and richness of his table, the number of his horses and followers, the freedom with which he spent money — all these things were public indications of his social standing. The aristocratic lifestyle was luxurious and extravagant. To maintain it, nobles often had to borrow from Jewish financiers or wealthy monasteries.

At the same time nobles had a great deal of work to do. The responsibilities of a noble in the High Middle Ages depended upon the size and extent of his estates, the number of his dependents, and his position in his territory relative to others of his class and to the king. As a vassal he was required to fight for his lord or for the king when called upon to do so. By the mid-twelfth century this service was limited in most parts of western Europe to forty days a year. He might have to perform guard duty at his lord's castle for a certain number of days a year. He was obliged to attend his lord's court on important occasions when the lord wanted to put on great displays, such as at Easter, Pentecost, and Christmas. When the lord knighted his eldest son or married off his eldest daughter, he called his vassals to his court. They were expected to attend and to present a contribution known as a gracious aid.

Throughout the year a noble had to look after his own estates. He had to appoint prudent and honest overseers and to make sure that they paid him the customary revenues and services. Since the estates of a great lord were usually widely scattered, he had to travel frequently.

Until the late thirteenth century, when royal authority intervened, a noble in France or England had great power over the knights and peasants on his estates. He maintained order among them and dispensed justice to them. Holding the manorial court, which

punished criminal acts and settled disputes, was one of his gravest obligations. The quality of justice varied widely: some lords were vicious tyrants who exploited and persecuted their peasants; others were reasonable and evenhanded. In any case, the quality of life on the manor and its productivity were related in no small way to the temperament and decency of the lord — and his lady.

Women played a large and important role in the functioning of the estate. They were responsible for the practical management of the household's "inner economy" — cooking, brewing, spinning, weaving, overseeing servants, caring for yard animals. The lifestyle of the medieval warrior nobles required constant travel, both for purposes of war and for the supervision of distant properties. When the lord was away for long periods, the women frequently managed the herds, barns, granaries, and outlying fields as well.

Frequent pregnancies and the reluctance to expose women to hostile conditions kept the lady at home and therefore able to assume supervision over the family's fixed properties. When a husband went away on crusade — and his absence could last anywhere from two to five years, if he returned at all — his wife was often the sole manager of the family properties. When her husband went to the Holy Land between 1060 and 1080, the lady Hersendis was the sole manager of the family properties in the Vendomois region in northern France.

Nor were the activities of women confined to managing family households and estates in the absence of their husbands. Medieval warfare was largely a matter of brief skirmishes, and few men were killed in any single encounter. But altogether the number slain ran high, and there were many widows. Aristocratic widows frequently controlled family properties and fortunes and exercised great authority. Although the evidence is scattered and sketchy, there are indications that women performed many of the functions of men. In Spain, France and Germany they bought, sold, and otherwise transferred property. Gertrude, labeled "Saxony's almighty widow" by the chronicler Ekkehard of Aaura, took a leading role in the conspiracies against the emperor Henry V. Sophia, wife of Berthold of Zohringer, assisted her brother Henry the Proud with eight hundred knights at the siege of Falkenstein in 1129. And Eilika Billung, the widow of Count Otto of Ballenstedt, built a castle at Burgwerben on the Saale River and, as advocate of the monastery of Goseck, removed one abbot and selected his successor. From her castle at Bernburg, the countess Eilika was also reputed to ravage the countryside.

Throughout the High Middle Ages fighting remained the dominant feature of the noble lifestyle. The church's preachings and condemnations reduced but did not stop violence. Lateness of inheritance, depriving the nobility of constructive outlets for their energy, together with the military ethos of their culture, encouraged petty warfare and disorder. The nobility thus represented a constant source of trouble for monarchy. In the thirteenth century kings drew on the financial support of the middle classes to build the administrative machinery that gradually laid the foundations for strong royal government. The Crusades relieved the rulers of France, England, and the German Empire of some of their most dangerous elements. Complete royal control of the nobility, however, came only in modern times.

THOSE WHO PRAY

According to Asser, monks performed the most important service to society. In the

MONKS IN CHOIR *Seven times during the day and once during the night monks went to the church to chant the psalms and other prayers, performing what everyone believed to be a valuable service for the rest of society. (The British Museum)*

Middle Ages prayer was looked upon as a vital social service, one that was just as crucial as the agricultural labor of the farmers and the military might of the nobles. Just as the knights protected and defended society with the sword, and the peasants provided food and sustenance through their toil, so the monks with their prayers and chants worked to secure God's blessing for society.

Monasticism represented some of the finest aspirations of medieval civilization. The monasteries were devoted to prayer, and their standards of Christian behavior influenced the entire church. The monasteries produced the educated elite that was continually drawn into the administrative services of kings and great lords. Monks kept alive the remains of classical culture and experimented with new styles of architecture and art. They introduced new techniques of estate management and land reclamation. Although relatively few in number in the High Middle Ages, the monks played a significant role in medieval society.

RECRUITMENT

Toward the end of his *Ecclesiastical History of England and Normandy,* when he was a man well into his sixties, Orderic Vitalis, a monk of the Norman abbey of St. Evroul, interrupted his narrative to explain movingly how he happened to become a monk:

It was not thy will, O God, that I should serve thee longer in that place, for fear that I might be less attentive to thee among kinsfolk, who are often a burden and an impediment to thy servants, or might in any way be distracted from obeying the law through human affection for my family. And so, O glorious God, you didst inspire my father Odeleric to renounce me utterly and submit me in all things to thy goverance. So, weeping, he gave me, a weeping child, into the care of the monk Reginald, and sent me away into exile for love of thee, and never saw me again. And I, a mere boy, did not presume to oppose my father's wishes, but obeyed him in all things, for he promised me for his part that if I became a monk I should taste of the joys of Heaven with the Innocents after my death. . . . And so, a boy of ten, I crossed the English channel and came into Normandy as an exile, unknown to all, knowing no one. Like Joseph in Egypt I heard a language which I could not understand. But thou didst suffer me through thy grace to find nothing but kindness among strangers. I was received as an oblate in the abbey of St.

Evroul by the venerable abbot Mainier in the eleventh year of my life. . . . The name of Vitalis was given me in place of my English name, which sounded harsh to the Normans.[12]

Orderic Vitalis (ca 1075– ca 1140) was one of the leading scholars of his times. As such, he is not a representative figure or even a typical monk. Intellectuals, those who earn their living or spend most of their time working with ideas, are never typical figures of their times. In one respect, however, Orderic was quite representative of the monks of the High Middle Ages: although he had no doubt that God wanted him to be a monk, the decision was actually made by his parents who gave him to a monastery as a child-oblate. Orderic was the third son of Odeleric, a knight who fought for William the Conqueror at the battle of Hastings (1066). For his participation in the Norman conquest of England, Odeleric was rewarded with lands in western England. Concern for the provision of his two older sons probably led him to give his youngest to the monastery.

Medieval monasteries were religious institutions whose organization and structure fulfilled the social needs of the feudal nobility. Between the tenth and thirteenth centuries, economic necessities compelled great families, or aspiring ones, to seek a life in the church for some members. There simply were not sufficient resources or career opportunities to provide suitable, honorable positions in life for all the children in aristocratic families. The monasteries provided these children an honorable and aristocratic life and opportunities for ecclesiastical careers.[13]

Until well into modern times, and certainly in the Middle Ages, almost everyone believed in and accepted the thorough subjection of children to their parents. This belief was the logical consequence of the fact that young noblemen were not expected to work and were therefore totally dependent on their fathers. Some men did become monks as adults, and apparently for a wide variety of reasons: belief in a direct call from God, disgust with the materialism and violence of the secular world, the encouragement and inspiration of others, economic failure or lack of opportunity, poverty, sickness, the fear of hell. However, most men who became monks, until about the early thirteenth century, seem to have been given as child-oblates by their parents.

In the thirteenth century, the older Benedictine and Cistercian orders had to compete with the new orders of friars – the Franciscans and the Dominicans. More and more monks had to be recruited from the middle class, that is, from small landholders or traders in the district near the abbey. As medieval society changed economically, and as European society ever so slowly developed middle-class traits, the monasteries almost inevitably drew their manpower, when they were able, from the middle classes. Until that time, they were preserves of the aristocratic nobility.

MONK HARVESTING GRAIN *Saint Benedict wrote, "they are truly monks when they live by the labor of their hands" (Rule, chapter 48). The isolated and localized nature of life in the early Middle Ages required that monasteries be entirely self-supporting. (Bibliothèque Publique de Dijon)*

PRAYER AND OTHER WORK

The pattern of life within individual monasteries varied widely from house to house and from region to region. Each monastic community was shaped by the circumstances of its foundation and endowment, by tradition, by the interests of its abbots and members, and by local conditions. It would therefore be a mistake to think that Christian monasticism in the High Middle Ages was everywhere the same. One central activity, however – the work of God – was performed everywhere. Daily life centered around the liturgy.

Seven times a day and once during the night, the monks went to choir to chant the psalms and other prayers prescribed by Saint Benedict. Prayers were offered for peace, rain, good harvests, the civil authorities, the monks' families, and their benefactors. Monastic patrons in turn lavished gifts upon the monasteries, which often became very wealthy. Through their prayers the monks performed a valuable service for the rest of society.

Prayer justified the monks spending a large percentage of their income on splendid objects to enhance the liturgy; monks praised God, they believed, not only in prayer but in everything connected with prayer. They sought to accumulate priestly vestments of the finest silks, velvets, and embroideries; and sacred vessels – chalices, patens, and thuribles – of embossed silver and gold. Thuribles

MONK INSTRUCTING ILLUMINATOR All monks had to learn to read in order to perform the religious services. A few of the intellectually and artistically gifted were often taught to copy and to illuminate manuscripts. (The Pierpont Morgan Library)

containing sweet-smelling incense brought at great expense from the Orient were used for the incensation of the altars, following ancient Jewish ritual. The pages of gospel books were richly decorated with gold leaf and the books' bindings were ornamented and bejewelled. Every monastery tried to acquire the relics of its patron saint, which necessitated the production of a beautiful reliquary to house the relics. The liturgy, then, inspired a great deal of art, and the monasteries became the crucibles of art in Western Christendom.

The monks fulfilled their social responsibility by praying. It was generally agreed that they could best carry out this duty if they were not distracted by worldly matters. Thus, great and lesser lords gave the monasteries lands that would supply the community with

necessities. Each manorial unit was responsible for provisioning the abbey for a definite period of time, and the expenses of each manor were supposed to equal its income.

The administration of the abbey's estates and properties consumed considerable time. The operation of a large establishment, such as Cluny in Burgundy or Bury St. Edmunds in England, which by 1150 had several hundred monks, involved planning, prudence and wise management. Although the abbot or prior had absolute authority in making assignments, common sense advised that tasks be allotted according to the ability and talents of individual monks.

The usual method of economic organization was the manor. Many monastic manors were small enough and close enough to the abbey to be supervised directly by the abbot. But if a monastery held and farmed vast estates, the properties were divided into administrative units under the supervision of one of the monks of the house. The lands of the German abbey of St. Emmeran at Regensburg, for example, were divided into thirty-three manorial centers.

Because the choir monks were aristocrats, they did not till the land themselves. In each house one monk, the cellarer or general financial manager, was responsible for supervising the peasants or lay brothers who did the actual agricultural labor. Lay brothers were vowed religious drawn from the servile classes, with simpler religious and intellectual obligations than those of the choir monks. The cellarer had to see to it that the estates of the monastery produced enough income to cover its expenses. Another monk, the almoner, was responsible for feeding and caring for the poor of the neighborhood. At the French abbey of St.-Requier in the eleventh century, 110 persons were fed every day. At Corbie, fifty loaves of bread were distributed daily to the poor.

The precentor, or cantor, was responsible for the library and the careful preservation of books. The sacristan of the abbey had in his charge all the materials and objects connected with the liturgy — vestments, candles, incense, sacred vessels, altar cloths, and hangings. The novice master was responsible for the training of recruits, instructing them in the *Rule*, the chant, the Scriptures, and the history and traditions of the house. For a few of the monks, work was some form of intellectual activity, such as the copying of books and manuscripts, the preparation of manuals, and the writing of letters.

Although the church forbade monks to study law and medicine, that rule was often ignored. In the twelfth and thirteenth cen-

turies, many monks gained considerable reputations for their knowledge and experience in the practice of both the canon law of the church and the civil law of their countries. For example, the Norman monk Lanfranc, because of his legal knowledge and administrative ability, became the chief adviser of William the Conqueror.

Although knowledge of medicine was primitive by twentieth-century standards, monastic practitioners were less ignorant than one would suspect. Long before 1066, a rich medical literature had been produced in England. The most important of these treatises was *The Leech Book of Bald* ("leech" means medical). This work exhibits a wide knowledge of herbal prescriptions, familiarity with ancient authorities, and evidence based on empirical practice. Bald discusses diseases of the lungs and stomach together with their remedies and demonstrates his acquaintance with surgery. *The Leech Book of Bald* was copied and circulated widely in the eleventh through thirteenth centuries, and many monastic libraries in England and on the Continent had a copy of it. Medical knowledge was sometimes rewarded. King Henry II of England made his medical adviser, the monk Robert de Veneys, abbot of Malmesbury.

The religious houses of medieval Europe usually took full advantage of whatever resources and opportunities their location offered. For example, the raising of horses could produce income in a world that depended on horses for travel and for warfare. Some monasteries, such as the Cistercian abbey of Jervaulx in Yorkshire, became famous for and quite wealthy from their production of prime breeds. In the eleventh and twelfth centuries, a period of considerable monastic expansion, large tracts of swamp, fen, forest, and wasteland were brought under cultivation — principally by the Cistercians.

The Cistercians, whose constitution insisted that they accept lands far from human habitation and forbade them to be involved in the traditional feudal-manorial structure, were ideally suited to the agricultural needs and trends of their times. In the Low Countries they built dikes to hold back the sea, and the reclaimed land was put to the production of cereals. In the eastern parts of the Holy Roman Empire – in Silesia, Mecklenburg, and Pomerania – they took the lead in draining swamps and cultivating wasteland. Because of a labor shortage, they advertised widely all across Europe for monks and brothers. Because of their efforts, the rich, rolling land of French Burgundy was turned into lush vineyards. In northern and central England, the rocky soil and damp downs of Lincolnshire, poorly suited to agriculture, were turned into sheep runs; by the third quarter of the twelfth century, the Cistercians were raising sheep and playing a very large role in the production of England's staple crop, wool.

Some monasteries got involved in iron and lead mining. In 1291, the Cistercian abbey of Furness operated at least forty forges. The German abbeys of Königsbronn, Waldsassen, and Saarbegen also mined iron in the thirteenth century. The monks entered this industry first to fill their own needs, but in an expanding economy they soon discovered a large market. Iron had hundreds of uses. Nails, hammers, plows, armor, spears, axes, stirrups, horseshoes, and many weapons of war were all made from this basic metal. When King Richard of England was preparing to depart on crusade in 1189, he wanted to take fifty thousand horseshoes with him. Lead also had a great variety of uses. It could be used for the roofing of buildings, and as alloy for strengthening the silver coinage, for framing pane-glass windows in parish, mon-astery, and cathedral churches, and even for lavatory drainpipes.

Whatever work particular monks did and whatever economic activities individual monasteries were involved in, monks also performed social services and exerted an influence for the good. Monasteries often ran schools that gave primary education to young boys. Abbeys like St. Albans, situated north of London on a busy thoroughfare, served as hotels and resting-places for travelers. Monasteries frequently operated "hospitals" and leprosaria, which provided care and attention to the sick, the aged, and the afflicted – primitive care, it is true, but often all that was available. In short, they performed a variety of social services in an age when there was no "state" and no conception of social welfare as a public responsibility.

ECONOMIC DIFFICULTIES

In the twelfth century, expenses in the older Benedictine monastic houses increased more rapidly than did income, leading to a steadily worsening economic situation. Cluny is a good example. Life at Cluny was lavish and extravagant. There were large quantities of rich food. The monks' habits were made of the best cloth available. Cluny's abbots and priors traveled with sizable retinues, as great lords were required to do. The abbots worked to make the liturgy ever more magnificent, and large sums were spent on elaborate vestments and jeweled vessels. Abbot Hugh embarked on an extraordinarily expensive building program. He entirely rebuilt the abbey church, and when Pope Urban II consecrated it in 1095 it was the largest church in Christendom. The monks lived like lords, which in a sense they were.

Revenue came from the hundreds of monasteries scattered across France, Italy, Spain,

CLUNY, CA 1157   Begun in 1085 and supported by the generosity of kings and peasants, the church (right center) and monastery of Cluny was the administrative center of a vast monastic and feudal empire. Note the apse around the east end of the church and the large foreground complex, which served as monastic infirmary and guest hostel. (The Mediaeval Academy of America)

and England that Cluny had reformed in the eleventh century; each year they paid Cluny a cash sum. Novices were expected to make a gift of land or cash when they entered. For reasons of security, knights departing on crusade often placed their estates under Cluny's authority. Still, this income was not enough. The management of Cluny's manors all across Europe was entrusted to bailiffs or wardens who were not monks and who were given lifetime contracts. Frequently these bailiffs were poor managers and produced no profits. But they could not be removed and replaced. In order to meet expenses, Cluny had to rely on cash reserves. For example, Cluny's estates produced only a small percentage of needed

food supplies; the rest had to be bought and paid for from cash reserves.

Cluny had two basic alternatives – improve management to cut costs or borrow money. The abbey could have placed the monastic manors under the jurisdiction of monks, rather than hiring bailiffs who would grow rich as middlemen. It could have awarded annual rather than lifetime contracts, supervised all revenues, and tried to cut costs within the monastery. Cluny chose the second alternative – borrowing. Consequently, the abbey spent hoarded reserves of cash and fell into debt.

In contrast to the abbot of Cluny, Suger (1122–1151), the superior of the royal abbey of St.-Denis near Paris, was a shrewd manager. Although he too spared no expense to enhance the beauty of his monastery and church, Suger kept an eye on costs and made sure that his properties were soundly managed. But the management of St.-Denis was unusual. Far more typical was the economic mismanagement at Cluny. By the later twelfth century, small and great monasteries were facing comparable financial difficulties.

———◆———

During the eleventh century the term *chevaliers,* meaning "horsemen" or "knights," gained widespread currency in France. Non-French peoples gradually adopted it to refer to the nobility, "who sat up high on their warhorses, looking down on the poor masses and terrorizing the monks."[14] By 1100 the knightly class was united in its ability to fight on horseback, its insistence that each member was descended from a valorous ancestor, its privileges, and its position at the top of the social hierarchy. The interests and activities of the nobility centered around warfare, but its economic power rested upon its ability to extract labor services and rents from the peasants. Generalizations about peasant life in the High Middle Ages must always be qualified by manorial customs, by the weather in a given year, and by the personalities of local lords. Everywhere, however, the performance of agricultural services and the payment of rents preoccupied peasants. Although they led hard lives, social mobility was possible through exceedingly hard work, luck, or flight to a town.

The monks exercised a profound influence on matters of the spirit. In their prayers the monks battled for the Lord, just as the chivalrous knights did on the battlefield. In their chant and rich ceremonial, in the Romanesque architecture of their buildings, and in the ex-

ample of many monks' lives, the monasteries inspired Christian peoples to an incalculable degree. As the crucibles of sacred art, the monasteries became the cultural centers of Christian Europe.

NOTES

1. Honorius of Autun, "Elucidarium sive Dialogus de Summa Totius Christianae Theologiae," in *Patrologia Latina,* ed. J. P. Migne, Garnier Bros., Paris, 1854, vol. 172, col. 1149.

2. E. Power, "Peasant Life and Rural Conditions," in J. R. Tanner et al., *The Cambridge Medieval History,* Cambridge University Press, Cambridge, 1958, 7.716.

3. Glanvill, "De Legibus Angliae," book 5, chap. 5, in *Social Life in Britain from the Conquest to the Reformation,* ed. G. G. Coulton, Cambridge University Press, London, 1956, pp. 338–339.

4. G. Duby, *Early Growth of the European Economy,* Cornell University Press, Ithaca, N.Y., 1977, pp. 213–219.

5. S. R. Scargill-Bird, ed., *Custumals of Battle Abbey in the Reign of Edward I and Edward II,* Camden Society, London, 1887, p. 19.

6. John 19: 25–27.

7. L. Demause, "The Evolution of Childhood," in *The History of Childhood,* ed. L. Demause, Psychohistory Press, New York, 1974, pp. 32–37.

8. J. F. Benton, ed. and trans., *Self and Society in Medieval France: The Memoirs of Abbot Guibert of Nogent,* Harper & Row, New York, 1970, p. 46.

9. D. Herlihy, "The Generation Gap in Medieval History," *Viator* 5 (1974): 360.

10. Cited in ibid., p. 361.

11. Honorius of Autun in *Patrologia Latina,* vol. 172, col. 1148.

12. M. Chibnall, ed. and trans., *The Ecclesiastical History of Orderic Vitalis,* Oxford University Press, Oxford, 1972, 2.xiii.

13. R. W. Southern, *Western Society and the Church in the Middle Ages,* Penguin Books, Baltimore, 1970, pp. 224–230, esp. p. 228.

14. G. Duby, *The Age of the Cathedrals: Art and Society, 980–1420,* trans. Eleanor Levieux and Barbara Thompson, University of Chicago Press, Chicago, 1981, p. 38.

SUGGESTED READING

The best short introduction to the material of this chapter is C. Brooke, *The Structure of Medieval Society* (1971), a beautifully illustrated book. The student interested in aspects of medieval slavery, serfdom, or the peasantry should begin with M. Bloch, "How Ancient Slavery Came to an End" and "Personal Liberty and Servitude in the Middle Ages, Particularly in France," in *Slavery and Serfdom in the Middle Ages: Selected Essays,* trans. W. R. Beer (1975). There is an excellent discussion of these problems in the magisterial work of G. Duby, *Rural Economy and Country Life in the Medieval West,* trans. C. Postan (1968). G. C. Homans, *English Villagers of the Thirteenth Century* (1975), is a fine combination of sociological and historical scholarship, while the older study of H. S. Bennett, *Life on the English Manor: A Study of Peasant Conditions* (1960), contains much useful information presented in a highly readable fashion. Emmanuel LeRoy Ladurie, *Montaillou: Cathars and Catholics in a French Village, 1294–1324,* trans. Barbara Bray (1978), is a fascinating glimpse of village life. G. Duby, *The Early Growth of the European Economy: Warriors and Peasants from the Seventh to the Twelfth Century* (1977), is a superb synthesis by a leading authority. Advanced students should see the same author's *The Three Orders: Feudal Society Imagined* (1980), a brilliant but difficult book.

For the nobility, see L. Genicot, "The Nobility in Medieval Francia: Continuity, Break, or Evolution?"; A. Borst, "Knighthood in the High Middle Ages: Ideal and Reality"; and two studies by G. Duby, "The Nobility in Eleventh and Twelfth Century Maconnais" and "Northwestern France: The 'Youth' in Twelfth Century Aristocratic Society": all these articles appear in F. L. Cheyette, ed., *Lordship and Community in Medieval Europe: Selected Readings* (1968). Social mobility among both aristocracy and peasantry are discussed in T. Evergates, *Feudal Society in the Bailliage of Troyes under the Counts of Champagne, 1152–1284* (1976). M. Bloch, *Feudal Society* (1966), remains the standard.

E. Power, *Medieval Women* (1976), is a nicely illustrated sketch of the several classes of women. For women, marriage, and the family in the High Middle Ages, J. McNamara and S. F. Wemple, "Sanctity and Power: The Dual Pursuit of Medieval Women," in *Becoming Visible: Women in European History* (1977), ed. R. Bridenthal and C. Koonz; and E. R. Coleman, "Medieval Marriage Characteristics: A Neglected Factor in the History of Medieval Serfdom," in *The Family in History: Interdisciplinary Essays* (1973), ed. T. K. Rabb and R. I. Rotberg, make interesting reading.

There is no dearth of good material on the monks in medieval society. The titles listed in the Suggested Reading for Chapter 7 represent a useful starting point for study. Anne Boyd, *The Monks of Durham* (1975), is an excellently illustrated sketch of many facets of monastic culture in the High Middle Ages. L. J. Lekai, *The Cistercians: Ideals and Reality* (1977), is a broad scholarly survey of the White Monks. Georges Duby, *The Age of the Cathedrals,* cited in the Notes to this chapter, is especially strong on the monastic origins of medieval art. Both W. Braunfels, *Monasteries of Western Europe: the Architecture of the Orders* (1972), and C. Brooke, *The Monastic World* (1974), have splendidly illustrated texts and good bibliographies.

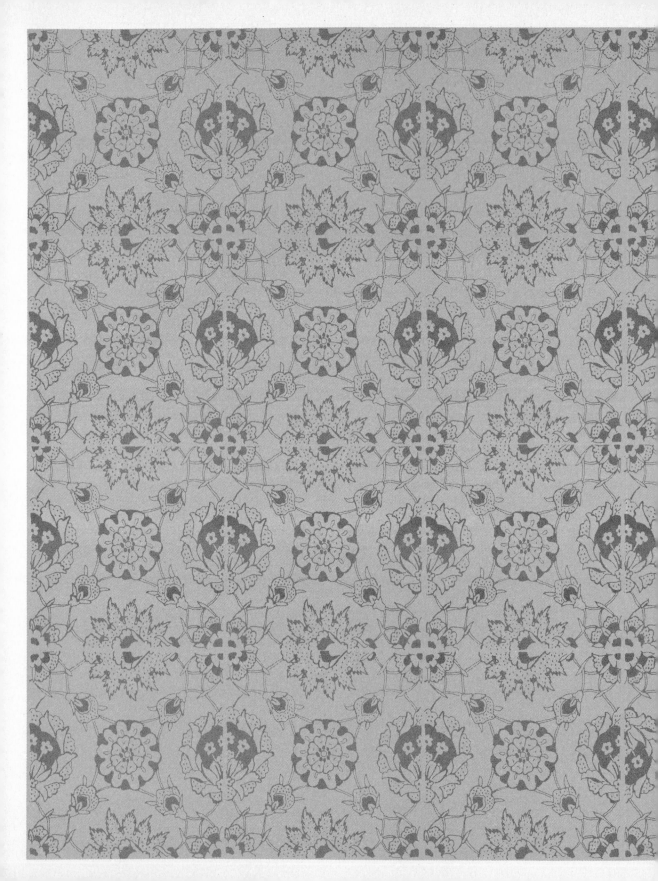

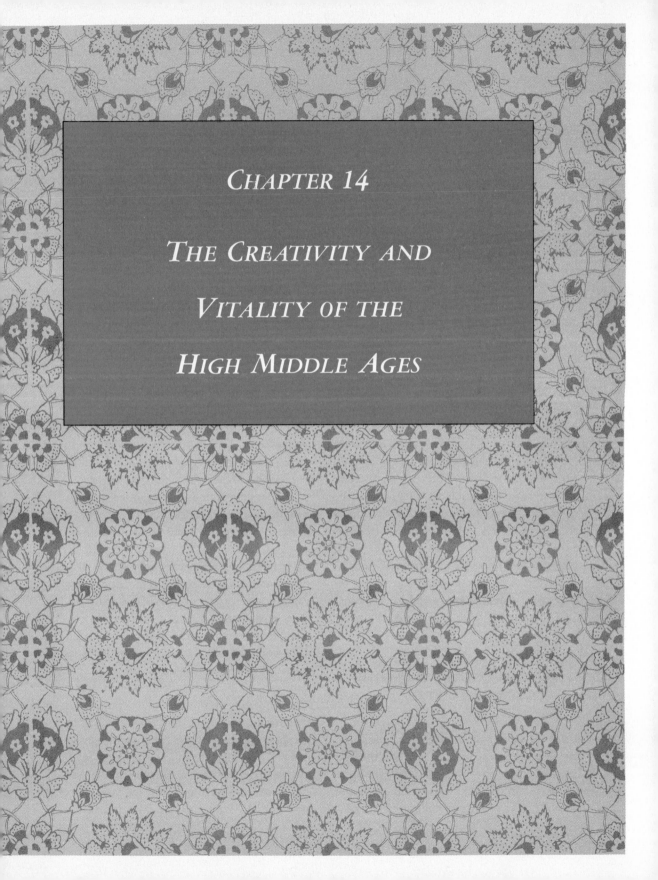

CHAPTER 14

THE CREATIVITY AND

VITALITY OF THE

HIGH MIDDLE AGES

THE HIGH MIDDLE AGES witnessed some of the most remarkable achievements in the entire history of Western society. Europeans displayed tremendous creativity and vitality in many realms of culture. Rulers tried to establish contact with all of their peoples, developed new legal and financial institutions, and slowly consolidated power in the hands of the monarchy. The kings of England and France succeeded in laying the foundations of the modern national state. The university, a uniquely Western contribution to civilization and a superb expression of medieval creativity, came into being at the same time. The Gothic cathedral manifested medieval peoples' deep Christian faith and their appreciation for the worlds of nature, man, and God. The Crusades, a series of holy wars to recover the Holy Land from the Muslims, also expressed European Christians' strong, even fanatical, religious faith.

This chapter will discuss the following questions. How did medieval rulers in England, France, and the Holy Roman Empire work to solve their problems of government? How did universities develop, and what needs of medieval society did they serve? What does the Gothic cathedral reveal about the ideals, attitudes, and interests of medieval people? What functions did the cathedral serve? Finally, what combination of motives inspired the Crusades, and what results did they have?

MEDIEVAL ORIGINS OF THE MODERN STATE

Rome's great legacy to Western civilization had been the concepts of the state and the law, but for almost five hundred years after the disintegration of the Roman Empire in the West the state as a reality did not exist. Political authority was completely decentralized. Power was spread among many feudal lords, who gave their localities such protection and security as their strength allowed. The fiefdoms, kingdoms, and territories that covered the continent of Europe did not have the qualities or provide the services of a modern state. They did not have jurisdiction over many people, and their laws affected a relative few. In the mid-eleventh century, there existed many layers of authority – earls, counts, barons, knights – between a king and the ordinary people.

In these circumstances, medieval kings had common goals. The rulers of England, France, and the Holy Roman Empire wanted to strengthen and extend royal authority within their territories. They wanted to establish an effective means of communication with all peoples in order to increase public order. They wanted more revenue and efficient state bureaucracies. The solutions they found to these problems laid the foundations for modern national states.

The modern state is an organized territory with definite geographical boundaries that are recognized by other states. It has a body of law and institutions of government. If the state claims to govern according to law, it is guided in its actions by the law. The modern national state counts on the loyalty of its citizens, or at least a majority of them. It provides order so that citizens can go about their daily work and other activities. It protects its citizens in their persons and property. The state tries to prevent violence and to apprehend and punish those who commit it. It supplies a currency or medium of exchange that permits financial and commercial transactions. The state conducts relations with foreign governments. In order to accomplish even these minimal functions, the state must have officials, bureaucracies, laws and courts

THE BAYEUX TAPESTRY *Measuring 231' by 19½", the Bayeux Tapestry gives a narrative description of the events surrounding the Norman Conquest of England. The tapestry provides an important historical source for the clothing, armor, and lifestyles of the Norman and Anglo-Saxon warrior class. (Tapisserie de la Reine Mathilde, Ville de Bayeux)*

of law, soldiers, information, and money. States with these attributes are relatively recent developments.

UNIFICATION AND COMMUNICATION

ENGLAND   Under the pressure of the Danish (or Viking) invasions of the ninth and tenth centuries, the seven kingdoms of Anglo-Saxon England united under one king. At the same period, for reasons historians still cannot fully explain, England was divided into local units called shires, or counties, each under the jurisdiction of a sheriff appointed by the king. The Danish king Canute (1016–1035) and his successor Edward the Confessor (1042–1066) exercised broader authority than any contemporary ruler on the Continent. All the English thegns, or local chieftains, recognized the central authority of the kingship.

The kingdom of England, therefore, had a political head start on the rest of Europe.

When Edward the Confessor died, his cousin Duke William of Normandy claimed the English throne and in 1066 defeated the Anglo-Saxon claimant on the battlefield of Hastings. As William subdued the rest of the country, he distributed lands to his Norman followers and assigned specific military quotas to each estate. He also required all feudal lords to swear an oath of allegiance to him as king.

William the Conqueror (1066–1087) preserved the Anglo-Saxon institution of sheriffs representing the king at the local level, but replaced Anglo-Saxon sheriffs with Normans. A sheriff, who always lived in the county where he worked, had heavy duties. He maintained order in the shire. He caught criminals and punished them in the shire court, over which he presided. He collected taxes and, when the king ordered him to do so, raised an army of foot soldiers. The sheriff also organized adult males in groups of ten, with each member liable for the good behavior of the others. The Conqueror thus made local people responsible for order in their communities. For all his efforts, the sheriff received no pay. This system, whereby unpaid officials governed the county, served as the basic pattern of English local government for many centuries. It cost the Crown nothing, but restricted opportunities for public service to the well-to-do.

William also retained another Anglo-Saxon device, the writ. This brief administrative order written in the vernacular (Anglo-Saxon) by a government clerk was the means by which the central government communicated with people at the local level. Sheriffs were empowered to issue writs relating to matters in their counties.

In 1086 the Conqueror introduced into England a major innovation, the Norman inquest. At his Christmas court in 1085, William discussed the state of the kingdom with his vassals and decided to conduct a systematic investigation of the entire country. The survey was to be made by means of inquests, or general inquiries, held throughout England. William wanted to determine how much wealth there was in his new kingdom, who held what land, and what lands had been disputed among his vassals since the conquest of 1066. In 1086 groups of royal officials or judges were sent to every part of the country. In every village and farm, the priest and six ordinary people were put under oath to answer the questions asked of them by the king's commissioners. Everybody and everything was counted and listed. In the words of a contemporary chronicler:

He sent his men over all England into every shire and had them find out how many hundred hides

there were in the shire, or what land and cattle the king himself had, or what dues he ought to have in twelve months from the shire. Also ... what or how much everybody had who was occupying land in England, in land or cattle, and how much money it was worth. So very narrowly did he have it investigated, that there was no single hide nor yard of land, nor indeed ... one ox nor one cow nor one pig was there left out, and not put down in his record: and all these records were brought to him afterwards.[1]

The resulting record, called *Domesday Book* from the Anglo-Saxon word *doom* meaning "judgment," still survives. It is an invaluable source of social and economic information about medieval England.

The Conqueror's scribes compiled *Domesday Book* in less than a year, using the evidence given by local people. *Domesday Book* provided William and his descendants with information vital for the exploitation and government of the country. Knowing the amount of wealth every area possessed, the king could tax accordingly. Knowing the amount of land his vassals had, he could allot knight service fairly. *Domesday Book* was a unique document. Its inclusion of material about all of England helped enable English kings to think of their country as a single unit and to work to bind it together. Across the English Channel, state building took a different course.

FRANCE In the early twelfth century, France consisted of a number of virtually independent provinces. Each was governed by its local ruler; each had its own laws and customs; each had its own coinage; each had its own dialect. Unlike the king of England, the king of France had jurisdiction over a very small area. Chroniclers called King Louis VI (1108–1137) *roi de St.-Denis,* king of St.-Denis, because the territory he controlled was limited to Paris and the St.-Denis area surrounding the city. This region, called the Ile-de-France or royal domain, became the nucleus of the French state. The clear goal of the medieval French monarchy was to increase the royal domain and extend the power and authority of the king (see Map 14.1).

The work of unifying France began under Louis VI's grandson Philip II (1180–1223). Rigord, Philip's biographer, gave him the title "Augustus" (from a Latin word meaning "to increase") because he vastly enlarged the territory of the kingdom of France. By defeating a baronial plot against the Crown, Philip Augustus acquired the northern counties of Artois and Vermandois. When King John of England, who was Philip's vassal for the rich province of Normandy, defaulted on his feudal obligation to come to the French court, Philip declared Normandy forfeit to the French crown. He enforced this declaration militarily, and in 1204 Normandy fell to the French. Within two years Philip also gained the prosperous farmlands of Maine, Touraine, and Anjou. By the end of his reign Philip was effectively master of northern France.

In the thirteenth century Philip Augustus's descendants made important acquisitions in the south. Louis VIII (1223–1226) added the county of Poitou to the kingdom of France by war. Louis IX (1226–1270) gained Toulouse and a vital interest in the Mediterranean province of Provence through his marriage to Margaret of Provence. Louis' son Philip III (1270–1285) secured Languedoc through inheritance. By the end of the thirteenth century, most of the provinces of modern France had been added to the royal domain through diplomacy, marriage, war, and inheritance. The king of France was stronger than any group of antagonistic French nobles who might try to challenge his authority.

Philip Augustus devised a method of governing the provinces and providing for communication between the central government in Paris and local communities. Philip decided that each province would retain its own institutions and laws. But royal agents, called baillis in the north and seneschals in the south, were sent from Paris into the provinces as the king's official representatives with authority to act for him. Often middle-class lawyers, these men possessed full judicial, financial, and military jurisdiction in their districts. The baillis and seneschals were appointed by, paid by, and responsible to the king. Unlike the English sheriffs, they were never natives of the provinces to which they were assigned, and they could not own land there. This policy reflected the fundamental principle of French administration that royal interests superseded local interests.

While English governmental administration was based on the services of unpaid local officials, France was administered by a professional royal bureaucracy. Bureaucracy was the cornerstone of French royal government. As new territories came under royal control, the bureaucracy expanded. So great was the variety of customs, laws, and provincial institutions that any attempt to impose uniformity would have touched off a rebellion. The French system was characterized by diversity at the local level and centralization at the top. Although it sometimes fell into disrepair, the basic system that Philip Augustus created worked so well that it survived until the Revolution of 1789.

THE HOLY ROMAN EMPIRE   The political problems of the Holy Roman Empire differed considerably from those of France and England. The eleventh-century investiture controversy between the German emperor and the Roman papacy had left the empire shattered and divided (pages 414–416). In the twelfth and thirteenth centuries, the Holy Roman Empire was split into hundreds of indepen-

Map 14.1 *The Growth of the Kingdom of France* *Some scholars believe that Philip II received the title "Augustus" (from a Latin word meaning "to increase"), because he vastly expanded the territories of the kingdom of France. In spite of differences, what similarities among peoples made expansion from Paris likely?*

Within the map:

ENGLAND

ENGLISH CHANNEL

BAY OF BISCAY

SPAIN

MEDITERRANEAN SEA

HOLY ROMAN EMPIRE

• Bruges
Ghent
• Ypres
Calais •
FLANDERS
Bouvines 1214
ARTOIS
Arras •
VERMANDOIS
• Amiens
• Rouen
Soissons •
Reims •
NORMANDY
CHAMPAGNE
Paris •
• Troyes
Seine
Chartres •
ILE-DE-FRANCE
(ROYAL DOMAIN)
MAINE
BLOIS
Orléans •
BRITTANY
Loire
BURGUNDY
ANJOU
Tours
Nantes •
TOURAINE
Bourges •
POITOU
BOURBON
Cluny •
• Poitiers
Clermont •
Lyons •
AQUITAINE
Rhône
Bordeaux •
Garonne
TOULOUSE
Avignon •
GASCONY
PROVENCE
• Toulouse
Montpellier •
Marseilles •
LANGUEDOC
Meuse

Legend:

Crown lands in 1180
Added by Philip Augustus, 1180-1223
Added 1223-1270
Added 1270-1314
Royal fiefs
✕ Major battle

0   50   100 Km.
0   50   100 Mi.

dent provinces, principalities, bishoprics, duchies, and free cities. Princes, dukes, and local rulers held power over small areas.

There were several barriers to the development of a strong central government. The German rulers lacked a strong royal domain, like that of the French kings, to use as a source of revenue and a base from which to expand royal power. No accepted principle of succession to the throne existed, and as a result the death of the emperor was often followed by disputes, civil war, and anarchy. Moreover, German rulers were continually attracted south by the wealth of the northern Italian cities or by dreams of restoring the imperial glory of Charlemagne. Time after time the German emperors got involved in Italian affairs, and in turn the papacy, fearful of a strong German power in northern Italy, interfered in German affairs. German princes took bribes from whichever authority — the emperor or the pope — best supported their own particular ambitions. Consequently, the centralization of authority in Germany, in contrast to that in France and England, occurred very slowly. In medieval Germany, power remained in the hands of numerous princes instead of the emperor.

Through most of the first half of the twelfth century, civil war wracked the Holy Roman Empire as the emperors tried to strengthen their position by playing off baronial factions against one another. When the emperor Conrad III died in 1152, the resulting anarchy was so terrible that the electors — the seven princes responsible for choosing the emperor — decided that the only alternative to continued chaos was the selection of a strong ruler. They chose Frederick Barbarossa of the house of Hohenstaufen.

Frederick Barbarossa (1152–1190) tried valiantly to unify the empire. Just as the French rulers branched out from their compact do-main in the Ile-de-France, Frederick tried to use his family duchy of Swabia in southwestern Germany as a power base (see Map 14.2). Just as William the Conqueror had done, Frederick required all vassals in Swabia to take an oath of allegiance to him as emperor, no matter who their immediate lord might be. He appointed officials called ministeriales, men of low social origin, to exercise the full imperial authority over administrative districts of Swabia. Ministeriales linked the emperor and local communities.

Outside of Swabia, Frederick tried to make feudalism work as a system of government. The princes throughout the empire exercised tremendous power, and Frederick tried to subordinate them to the authority of the royal government. He made alliances with the great lay princes in which they acknowledged that their lands were fiefs of the emperor, and he in turn recognized their military and political jurisdiction over their territories. Frederick also compelled the great churchmen to become his vassals, so that when they died he could control their estates. Frederick solved the problem of chronic violence by making the princes responsible for the establishment of peace within their territories. At a great assembly held at Roncaglia in 1158, private warfare was forbidden and severe penalties were laid down for violations of the peace.

Unfortunately Frederick Barbarossa did not concentrate his efforts and resources in one area. He too became embroiled in the affairs of Italy. He too wanted to restore the Holy Roman Empire, joining Germany and Italy. In the eleventh and twelfth centuries, the northern Italian cities had grown rich on trade, and Frederick believed that if he could gain the imperial crown, he could cash in on Italian wealth. Frederick saw that although the Italian cities were populous and militarily strong, they lacked stable governments and

Scale bar:
0   100   200 Km.
0   100   200 Mi.

Lübeck
HOLSTEIN
POMERANIA
Bremen
BRANDENBURG
FRISIA
SAXONY
Brandenburg
LUSATIA
Goslar
POLAND
Cologne
Aix-la-Chapelle
THURINGIA
MEISSEN
LOWER LORRAINE
FRANCONIA
Mainz
Prague
Trier
Worms
BOHEMIA
UPPER LORRAINE
MORAVIA
Verdun
Toul
BAVARIA
AUSTRIA
FRANCE
Augsburg
SWABIA
Salzburg
STYRIA
Besançon
CARINTHIA
BURGUNDY–ARLES
HUNGARY
CARNIOLA
VERONA
LOMBARDY
✕ Legnano 1176
Milan
Venice
Pavia
Roncaglia
REPUBLIC OF VENICE
Avignon
Arles   PROVENCE
Florence
Marseilles
TUSCANY
PAPAL STATES
Rome
APULIA
KINGDOM OF SICILY
Naples
Salerno
Messina
✕ Major battle
Holy Roman Empire, ca 1200
Kingdom of Sicily
Republic of Venice
Palermo
SICILY

were often involved in struggles with one another. The German emperor mistakenly believed that moneygrubbing infantrymen could not stand up against his tough aristocratic knights. He did not realize that the merchant oligarchs who ran the city governments of Milan, Venice, and Florence considered themselves just as noble as he; they prized their independence and were determined to fight for it. Frederick's desire to control the papacy and to end papal claims to suzerainty over the empire also attracted him southward. He did not know that the popes feared a strong German state in northern Italy even more than they feared the rich and (the popes suspected) slightly heretical Italian cities.

Between 1154 and 1188, Frederick made six expeditions into Italy. His scorched-earth policy was successful at first, making for significant conquests in the north. The brutality of his methods, however, provoked revolts, and the Italian cities formed an alliance with the papacy. In 1176, Frederick suffered a catastrophic defeat at Legnano (see Map 14.2). This battle marked the first time a feudal cavalry of armed knights was decisively defeated by bourgeois infantrymen. Frederick was forced to recognize the independence of the northern Italian cities. Germany and Italy remained separate countries and followed separate courses of development.

Frederick Barbarossa's Italian ventures contributed nothing to the unification of the German states. Because the empire lacked a stable bureaucratic system of government, his presence was essential for the maintenance of peace. In Frederick's absences, the fires of independence and disorder spread. The princes

and magnates consolidated their power, and the unsupervised royal ministeriales gained considerable independence. By 1187, Frederick had to accept again the reality of private warfare. The power of the princes grew at the expense of a centralized monarchy.

FINANCE

As medieval rulers expanded their territories and extended their authority, they required more officials, larger armies, and more and more money. Officials and armies had to be paid, and kings had to find ways to raise revenue.

In England, William the Conqueror's son Henry I (1100–1135) established a bureau of finance called the Exchequer (for the checkered cloth at which his officials collected and audited royal accounts). Henry's income came from a variety of sources: from taxes paid by peasants living on the king's estates; from the Danegeld, an old tax originally levied to pay tribute to the Danes; from the *dona,* an annual gift from the church; from money paid to the Crown for settling disputes; and from fines paid by people found guilty of crimes. Henry also received income because of his position as feudal lord. If, for example, one of his vassals died and the son wished to inherit the father's properties, the heir had to pay Henry a relief tax. The sheriff in each county was responsible for collecting all these sums and for paying them twice a year to the king's Exchequer. Henry, like other medieval kings, made no distinction between his private income and state revenues.

An accurate record of expenditures and income is needed to insure a state's solvency. Henry assigned a few of the barons and bishops at his court to keep careful records of the monies paid into and out of the royal treasury. These financial officials, called barons of the Exchequer, gradually developed into a professional organization with its own rules, procedures, and esprit de corps. The Exchequer, which always sat in London, became the first institution of the governmental bureaucracy of England. Because of its work, an almost complete series of financial records for England dating back to 1130 survives; after 1154 the series is complete.

The development of royal financial agencies in most continental countries lagged behind the English Exchequer. Twelfth-century French rulers derived their income from their royal estates in the Ile-de-France. As Philip Augustus and his successors added provinces to the royal domain, the need for money became increasingly acute. Philip made the baillis and seneschals responsible for collecting taxes in their districts. This income came primarily from fines and confiscations imposed by the courts. Three times a year the baillis and seneschals reported to the king's court with the monies they had collected.

In the thirteenth century, French rulers found additional sources of revenue. They acquired some income from the church and some from people living in the towns. Townspeople paid tallage — a tax arbitrarily laid by the king. In all parts of the country feudal vassals owed military service to the king when he called for it. Louis IX converted this military obligation into a cash payment, called host tallage, and thus increased his revenues. Philip Augustus, Louis VIII, and Louis IX all taxed the Jews mercilessly.

Medieval people believed that a good king lived on the income of his own land and taxed only in time of a grave emergency — that is, a just war. Because the church, and not the state, performed what twentieth-century people call social services, such as education and care of the sick, the aged, and orphaned children, there was no ordinary need for the government to tax. Taxation meant war

financing. The French monarchy could not continually justify taxing the people on the grounds of the needs of war. Thus the French kings were slow to develop an efficient bureau of finance. French localism — in contrast to England's early unification — also retarded the growth of a central financial agency. Not until the fourteenth century, as a result of the demands of the Hundred Years' War, did a state financial bureau emerge — the Chamber of Accounts.

The one European government other than England that developed an efficient financial bureaucracy in the High Middle Ages was the kingdom of Sicily. Sicily is a good example of how strong government could be built on a feudal base by determined rulers.

Like England, Sicily had come under Norman domination. Between 1061 and 1091, a bold Norman knight, Roger de Hauteville, with a small band of mercenaries had defeated the Muslims and Greeks who controlled the island. Like William the Conqueror in England, Roger introduced Norman feudalism in Sicily and made it work as a system of government. Roger distributed scattered fiefs to his followers, so that no vassal had a centralized power base. He took an inquest of royal properties and rights, and he forbade private warfare. Roger adapted his Norman experience to Arabic and Greek governmental practices. Thus he retained the Muslims' main financial agency, the *diwan*, a sophisticated bureau for recordkeeping.

His son and heir, Count Roger II (1130–1154), continued the process of state building. He subdued the province of Apulia in southern Italy, united it with his Sicilian lands, and had himself crowned king of Sicily (1130–1154). Roger II organized the economy in the interests of the state; for example, the Crown secured a monopoly on the sale of salt and lumber. With the revenues thus acquired, Roger hired mercenary troops. His judiciary welcomed appeals from local communities. The army, the judiciary, and the *diwan* were staffed by Greeks and Muslims as well as Normans.

Under Frederick II Hohenstaufen (1212–1250), grandson of Roger II, Sicily underwent remarkable development. Frederick, also the grandson and heir of Frederick Barbarossa, was a brilliant legislator and administrator, and he constructed the most advanced bureaucratic state in medieval Europe. The institutions of the kingdom of Sicily were harnessed in the service of the state as represented by the king.

Frederick banned private warfare, and he placed all castles and towers under royal administration. Frederick also replaced town officials with royal governors. In 1231, he published the Constitutions of Melfi, a collection of laws that vastly enhanced royal authority. Both feudal and ecclesiastical courts were subordinated to the king's courts. Each year royal judges visited all parts of the kingdom, and the supreme court at Capua heard appeals from all lesser courts. Thus churchmen accused of crimes were tried in the royal courts. Royal control of the nobility, of the towns, and of the judicial system added up to great centralization, which required a professional bureaucracy and sound state financing.

In 1224, Frederick founded the University of Naples to train clerks and officials for his bureaucracy. University-educated administrators and lawyers emphasized the stiff principles of Roman law, such as the Justinian maxim that "what pleases the prince has the force of law." Frederick's financial experts regulated agriculture, public works, and even business. His customs service carefully supervised all imports and exports, collecting taxes for the Crown on all products. Royal revenues increased tremendously. Moreover, Frederick strictly regulated the currency and forbade the export of gold and silver bullion.

GERMAN BRONZE DRAGON *Dating from the thirteenth century, this dragon swallowing a man curves its tail over its winged body to form the handle of an aquamanile. Aquamanilia were made in imaginative, often playful forms. They held water for the washing of priests' hands during the celebration of mass, and they were also used in households for the washing of hands at meals. The water comes out of a hole beneath the man's head. (Metropolitan Museum of Art, The Cloisters Collection, 1947)*

Finally, Frederick secured the tacit consent of his people to regular taxation. This was an incredible achievement in the Middle Ages, when most people believed that taxes should be levied only in time of grave emergency, the just war. Frederick defined emergency broadly. For much of his reign he was involved in a bitter dispute with the papacy. Churchmen hardly considered the emperor's wars with the popes as just, but Frederick's position was so strong that he could ignore criticism and levy taxes.

Frederick's contemporaries called him "The Transformer of the World." He certainly transformed the kingdom of Sicily, creating a state that was in many ways modern. But Frederick was highly ambitious: he wanted to control the entire peninsula of Italy. The popes, fearful of being encircled, waged a long conflict to prevent that. The kingdom of Sicily required constant attention, and Frederick's absences took their toll. Shortly after he died, the unsupervised bureaucracy he had built fell to pieces. The pope, claiming feudal suzerainty over Sicily, called in a French prince to rule.

Frederick showed little interest in Germany. He concentrated his attention on Sicily rather than the historic Hohenstaufen stronghold in Swabia, and the focus of imperial concerns shifted southward. When he visited the empire, in the expectation of securing German support for his Italian policy, he made sweeping concessions to the princes, bishops, duchies, and free cities. In 1220, for example, he exempted German churchmen from taxation and from the jurisdiction of imperial authorities. In 1231, he gave lay princes the same exemptions and even threw in the right to coin money. Frederick gave away so much that imperial authority was seriously weakened. In the later Middle Ages, lay and ecclesiastical princes held sway in the Holy Roman Empire. The centralizing efforts of Frederick Barbarossa were destroyed by his grandson Frederick II.

LAW AND JUSTICE

Throughout Europe, the form and application of laws depended upon local and provincial custom and practice. In the twelfth and thirteenth centuries the law was a hodgepodge of Germanic customs, feudal rights, and provincial practices. Kings wanted to blend these elements into a uniform system of rules acceptable and applicable to all their peoples. In France and England kings successfully contributed to the development of national states through the administration of their laws. Legal developments in continental countries like France were strongly influenced by Roman law, while England slowly built up a unique unwritten common law.

The French king Louis IX was famous in his time for his concern for justice. Each French province, even after being made part of the kingdom of France, retained its unique laws and procedures, but Louis IX created a royal judicial system. He established the Parlement of Paris, a kind of supreme court that welcomed appeals from local administrators and from the courts of feudal lords throughout France. By the very act of appealing the decisions of feudal courts to the Parlement of Paris, French people in far-flung provinces were recognizing the superiority of royal justice. By reviewing the decisions of baronial courts, the Parlement of Paris dispensed the king's justice to all French people.

Louis sent royal judges to all parts of the country to check up on the work of the baillis and seneschals and to hear complaints of injustice. He was the first French monarch to publish laws for the entire kingdom. The Parlement of Paris registered (or announced) these laws, which forbade private warfare, judicial duels, gambling, blaspheming, and prostitution. Louis sought to identify justice with the kingship, and gradually royal justice touched all parts of the kingdom.

Under Henry II (1154-1189), England developed and extended a common law, a law common to and accepted by the entire country. No other country in medieval Europe did so. Henry I had occasionally sent out circuit judges (royal officials who traveled a given circuit or district) to hear civil and criminal cases. Henry II made this way of extending royal justice an annual practice. Every year royal judges left London and set up court in the counties. Wherever the king's judges sat, there sat the king's court. Slowly, the king's court gained jurisdiction over all property disputes and criminal actions.

Henry made an important innovation in civil or property law. Disputes over land and movable property had caused a great deal of violence. Henry established a procedure whereby a person who felt unjustly deprived of possessions could seek a remedy in the royal court. The aggrieved person applied to the sheriff for help. The sheriff summoned a jury of local people before the king's judges, and there in the royal court the jury answered questions about rightful possession. On the basis of the jury's verdict, the disputed property was awarded. Thus, rather than attempting to get property back by force, English people had recourse to the king's court.

Henry also improved procedure in criminal justice. In 1166, he instructed the sheriffs to summon local juries to conduct inquests and draw up lists of known or suspected criminals. These lists, sworn to by the juries, were to be presented to the royal judges when they arrived in the community. This accusing jury is the ancestor of the modern grand jury.

An accused person formally charged with a crime did *not* undergo trial by jury. He or she was tried by ordeal. The accused was tied hand and foot and dropped in a lake or river. People believed that water was a pure substance and would reject anything foul or unclean. Thus a person who sank was considered innocent, and a person who floated was considered guilty. Trial by ordeal was a ritual that appealed to the supernatural for judgment. God determined innocence or guilt, and thus a priest had to be present to bless the water. Henry II and others considered this ancient

Germanic method irrational and a poor way of determining results, but they knew no alternative. In 1215, the Fourth Lateran Council of the church forbade the presence of priests at trials by ordeal and thus effectively abolished them. Gradually, in the course of the thirteenth century, the king's judges adopted the practice of calling upon twelve people (other than the accusing jury) to consider the question of innocence or guilt. This became the jury of trial, but it was very slowly accepted because medieval people had more confidence in the judgment of God than in that of twelve ordinary people.

Henry's innovations in civil procedure, the use of the accusing jury, and regular visits by circuit judges marked a decisive step forward. As the judges advanced the notion that any serious crime belonged under the king's jurisdiction, crime was no longer considered a violent act against an individual to be avenged by the victim and his or her family. Criminal acts became deeds against the state, or against the king as the embodiment of the state.

One aspect of Henry's judicial reforms encountered stiff resistance from an unexpected source: a friend and former chief adviser whom Henry had made archbishop of Canterbury – Thomas Becket. Henry selected Becket as archbishop in 1162 because he believed he could depend on Becket's support. But when Henry wanted to bring all persons in the kingdom under the jurisdiction of the royal courts, Thomas Becket's opposition led to another dramatic conflict between temporal and spiritual powers.

In the 1160s, many literate people accused of crimes claimed "benefit of clergy," even though they were not clerics and often had no intention of being ordained. "Benefit of clergy" gave the accused the right to be tried in church courts, which meted out mild punishments. A person found guilty in the king's court might suffer mutilation – loss of a hand

THE MARTYRDOM OF THOMAS BECKET
Becket's murder evoked many illustrations in the thirteenth century. This illumination faithfully follows the manuscript sources: while one knight held off the archbishop's defenders, the other three attacked. With a powerful stroke, the crown of his head was slashed off and his brains scattered on the cathedral floor. (Walters Art Gallery)

or foot, or castration — or even death. Ecclesiastical punishments tended to be an obligation to say certain prayers or to make a pilgrimage. In 1164 Henry II insisted that everyone, including clerics, be subject to the royal courts.

Becket vigorously protested that church law required clerics to be subject to church courts. When he proceeded to excommunicate one of the king's vassals, the issue became more complicated. Because no one was sup-

posed to have any contact with an excommunicated person, it appeared that the church could arbitrarily deprive the king of necessary military forces. The disagreement between Henry II and Becket dragged on for years. Becket maintained that as archbishop he had to defend the rights of the church. Henry insisted that the Crown should have full jurisdiction over all its subjects. The king grew increasingly bitter that his appointment of Becket had proved to be such a mistake. Late in December 1170, in a fit of rage, Henry expressed the wish that Becket be destroyed. Four knights took the king at his word, went to Canterbury, and killed the archbishop in his cathedral as he was leaving evening services.

What Thomas Becket could not achieve in life, he gained in death. The assassination of an archbishop in his own church during the Christmas season turned public opinion in England and throughout western Europe against the king. Within months miracles were recorded at Becket's tomb, and in a short time Canterbury Cathedral became a major pilgrimage and tourist site. Henry had to back down. He did public penance for the murder and gave up his attempts to bring clerics under the authority of the royal court.

Henry II's sons Richard I ("the Lion-Hearted") (1189-1199) and John (1199-1216) lacked their father's interest in the work of government. Handsome, athletic, and with an international reputation for military prowess, Richard looked upon England as a source of revenue for his military enterprises. Soon after his accession, he departed on crusade to the Holy Land. During his reign he spent only six months in England, and the government was run by ministers trained under Henry II.

Unlike Richard, King John was incompetent as a soldier and unnecessarily suspicious that the barons were plotting against him. His basic problems, however, were financial. King John inherited a heavy debt from his father and brother. The country had paid dearly for Richard's crusading zeal. Returning from the Holy Land, Richard had been captured, and England had paid an enormous ransom to secure his release. In 1204, John lost the rich province of Normandy to Philip Augustus of France and then spent the rest of his reign trying to get it back. To finance that war, he got in deeper and deeper trouble with his barons. John squeezed as much money as possible from his position as feudal lord. He took scutage, a tax paid by his vassals in lieu of performing knight service. Each time John collected it, he increased the amount due. He forced widows to pay exorbitant fines to avoid unwanted marriages. He sold young girls who were his feudal wards to the highest bidder. These actions antagonized the nobility.

John also alienated the church and the English townspeople. He rejected Pope Innocent III's nominee to the see of Canterbury. And he infuriated the burghers of the towns by extorting money from them and threatening to revoke their charters of self-government.

All the money John raised did not bring him success. In July 1214, John's coalition of Flemish, German, and English cavalry suffered a severe defeat at the hands of Philip Augustus of France at Bouvines in Flanders. This battle ended English hopes for the recovery of territories from France. The battle of Bouvines also strengthened the barons' opposition to John. On top of his heavy taxation, his ineptitude as a soldier in a society that idealized military glory was the final straw. Rebellion begun by a few hotheaded northern barons eventually grew to involve a large number of the English nobility, including the archbishop of Canterbury and the earl of Pembroke, the leading ecclesiastical and lay

peers. After lengthy negotiations in the spring of 1215, John met the barons at Runnymede, a meadow along the Thames River. There he was forced to sign the treaty called Magna Carta, which became the cornerstone of English justice and law.

Magna Carta signifies the principle that the king and the government shall be under the law, that everyone including the king must obey the law. It contains clauses to protect the rights and property of all English people. It defends the interests of widows, orphans, townspeople, and freemen. Some clauses contain the germ of the idea of due process of law and of the right to a fair and speedy trial. Every English king in the Middle Ages reissued Magna Carta as evidence of his promise to observe the law. Because it was reissued frequently, and because later generations appealed to Magna Carta as a written statement of English liberties, it acquired an almost sacred importance as a guarantee of law and justice.

In the thirteenth century, the judicial precedents set under Henry II slowly evolved into permanent institutions. The king's judges asserted the royal authority and applied the same principles everywhere in the country. English people found the king's justice more rational and more evenhanded than the justice meted out in the baronial courts. The royal courts gained popularity, and the baronial courts lost rights and business. Respect for the king's law and the king's courts promoted loyalty to the Crown. By the time of Henry's great-grandson, Edward I (1272-1307), one law, the common law, operated all over England.

In the later Middle Ages, the English common law developed features that differed strikingly from the system of Roman law operative in continental Europe. The common law relied on precedents: a decision in an important case served as an authority for deciding similar cases. By contrast, continental judges, trained in Roman law, used the fixed legal maxims of the Justinian Code (pages 303–304) to decide their cases. Thus the common-law system evolved according to the changing experience of the people, while the Roman-law tradition tended toward an absolutist approach. In countries influenced by the common law, such as Canada and the United States, the court is open to the public; in countries with Roman-law traditions, such as France and the Latin American nations, courts need not be public. Under the common law, the accused in criminal cases has a right to access to the evidence against him; under the other system, he need not. The common law requires that judges be strictly impartial; in the Roman-law system judges interfere freely in many activities in their court rooms. Finally, whereas torture is foreign to the common-law tradition, it was once widely used in the Roman legal system.

The extension of royal law and justice led to a phenomenal amount of legal codification all over Europe. Governments wanted the law written down in an orderly and systematic fashion. The English judge Henry of Bracton (d. 1268) wrote a *Treatise on the Laws and Customs of England,* the French jurist Philippe de Beaumanoir (1250–1296) produced the *Customs of Beauvais,* and an anonymous German scholar compiled the *Sachsenspiegel* (1253). Legal texts and encyclopedias exalted royal authority, consolidated royal power, and emphasized political and social uniformity. The pressure for social conformity in turn contributed to a rising hostility toward minorities, Jews, and homosexuals.

Early Christians, as we have seen (page 295), displayed no special prejudice against homosexuals. While some of the Church Fathers, such as St. John Chrysostom (347–407), preached against them, a general in-

difference to homosexual activity prevailed throughout the early Middle Ages. In the early twelfth century a large homosexual literature circulated. Publicly known homosexuals such as Ralph, archbishop of Tours (1087–1118), and King Richard the Lion-Hearted of England held high ecclesiastical and political positions.

Beginning in the late twelfth century, however, a profound change occurred in public attitudes toward homosexual behavior. Why, if prejudice against homosexuals cannot be traced to early Christianity? Scholars have only begun to investigate this question, and the root cause of intolerance rarely yields to easy analysis. In the thirteenth century a fear of foreigners, especially Muslims, became associated with the crusading movement. Heretics were the most despised minority in an age that stressed religious and social uniformity. The notion spread that both Muslims and heretics, the great foreign and domestic menaces to the security of Christian Europe, were inclined to homosexual relations. Finally, the systematization of law and the rising strength of the state made any religious or sexual distinctiveness increasingly unacceptable. Whatever the precise cause, "between 1250 and 1300 homosexual activity passed from being completely legal in most of Europe to incurring the death penalty in all but a few legal compilations."[2] Spain, France, England, Norway, and several Italian city-states adopted laws condemning homosexual acts. Most of these laws remained on statute books until the twentieth century.

MEDIEVAL UNIVERSITIES

Just as the first strong secular states emerged in the thirteenth century, so did the first universities. This was no coincidence. The new bureaucratic states needed educated administrators, and universities were a response to this need. The word *university* derives from the Latin *universitas,* meaning "corporation" or "guild." Medieval universities were educational guilds that produced educated and trained individuals. They were also an expression of the tremendous vitality and creativity of the High Middle Ages. Their organization, methods of instruction, and goals continue to influence institutionalized learning in the Western world.

In the early Middle Ages, anyone who received any education got it from a priest. Priests instructed the clever boys on the manor in the Latin words of the mass, and taught them the rudiments of reading and writing. Few boys acquired elementary literacy, however, and girls did not even obtain that. The peasant who wished to send his son to school had to secure the permission of his lord, because the result of formal schooling tended to be a career in the church or some trade. If a young man were to pursue either profession, he had to leave the manor and gain free status. Because the lord stood to lose the services of educated peasants, he carefully limited the number of serfs who were sent to school.

Few schools were available anyway. Society was organized for war and defense and gave slight support to education. By the late eleventh century, however, social conditions had markedly improved. There was greater political stability, and favorable economic conditions had advanced many people beyond the level of bare subsistence. The curious and able felt the lack of schools and teachers.

Since the time of the Carolingian Empire, monasteries and cathedral schools had offered the only formal instruction available. The monasteries were geared to religious concerns, and the monastic curriculum consisted of studying the Scriptures and the writings of the church fathers. Monasteries wished to maintain an atmosphere of seclusion and silence and were unwilling to accept large numbers of noisy lay students. In contrast, schools attached to cathedrals and run by the bishop and his clergy were frequently situated in bustling cities, and in Italian cities like Bologna wealthy businessmen had established municipal schools. Cities inhabited by peoples of many backgrounds and "nationalities" stimulated the growth and exchange of ideas. In the course of the twelfth century, cathedral schools in France and municipal schools in Italy developed into universities (see Map 14.3).

The school at Chartres Cathedral in France became famous for its studies of the Latin classics and for the broad literary interests it fostered in its students. The most famous graduate of Chartres was the Englishman John of Salisbury (d. 1180), who wrote *The Statesman's Book,* an important treatise on the corrupting effects of political power. But Chartres, situated in the center of rich farmland remote from the currents of commercial traffic and intellectual ideas, did not develop into a university. The first European universities appeared in Italy, at Bologna in the north and Salerno in the south.

The growth of the University of Bologna coincided with a revival of interest in Roman law. The study of Roman law as embodied in the Justinian Code had never completely died out in the West, but this sudden burst of interest seems to have been inspired by Irnerius (d. 1125), a great teacher at Bologna. His fame attracted students from all over Europe. Irnerius not only explained the Roman law of the Justinian Code, he applied it to difficult practical situations. An important school of civil law was founded at Montpellier in

BALTIC
SEA

SCOTLAND

NORTH
SEA

DENMARK

■ St. Andrews

■ Glasgow

Copenhagen ■

✝✝ Jarrow
Durham
Rivaulx ✝
York ⛫

IRELAND

ENGLAND

HOLY

Magdeburg ⛫

Peterborough ■
Cambridge ■   ■ Bury
■   St. Edmunds
■ Oxford

Leipzig ■

Louvain ■   ■ Cologne
Fulda ✝

Prague ■

Salisbury ■ ⛫ Winchester ⛫ Canterbury

Mainz ⛫   ⛫ Bamberg

ROMAN

Mont St.
Michel

ATLANTIC

OCEAN

✝ Jumièges
Bec ✝
Notre Dame ■ St.-Denis ✝
Paris ✝
Savigny ✝   ⛫ Chartres

Orléans ■
✝ Tours

Laon ⛫
⛫ Reims

Heidelberg ■

Regensburg ✝
Hirsau ■   ✝ Lorch

Vienna ■

Clairvaux ✝

Fleury ✝

Citeaux ■   Basel ■   ■ St.-Gall

Bourges ■

■ Poitiers

Cluny ■

EMPIRE

FRANCE

Bordeaux ■

Cahors ■

Grenoble ■

Pavia ■   ■ Padua
Piacenza ■
Bologna ■

Montpellier ■ ■ Avignon

Florence ■ ■ Vallombrosa
Perugia ■

Toulouse ■

CORSICA

SPAIN

Valladolid ■

Salamanca ■

Coimbra ■

⛫ Toledo

SARDINIA

Rome ■
Monte Cassino ■
Naples ■
■ Salerno

Seville ■

MEDITERRANEAN   SEA

Palermo ■
SICILY

■   University

✝   Monastery school

⛫   Cathedral school

0   100   200   300 Km.

0   100   200   300 Mi.

MAP 14.3   INTELLECTUAL CENTERS OF MEDIE-
VAL EUROPE   *Universities obviously provided more
sophisticated instruction than did monastic and cathedral schools. What other factors distinguish the
three kinds of intellectual centers?*

southern France, but Bologna remained the greatest law school throughout the Middle Ages.

At Salerno, interest in medicine had persisted for centuries. Greek and Muslim physicians there had studied the use of herbs as cures for disease, and they had experimented with surgery. The twelfth century ushered in a new interest in Greek medical texts and in the work of Arab and Greek doctors. Students of medicine poured into Salerno, and their study soon attracted royal attention. In 1140, when King Roger II of Sicily took the practice of medicine under royal control, his ordinance stated:

Who, from now on, wishes to practice medicine, has to present himself before our officials and examiners, in order to pass their judgment. Should he be bold enough to disregard this, he will be punished by imprisonment and confiscation of his entire property. In this way we are taking care that our subjects are not endangered by the inexperience of the physicians.

Nobody dare practice medicine unless he has been found fit by the convention of the Salernitan masters.[3]

King Roger sought to protect the people of the kingdom of Sicily from incompetent doctors.

In the first decades of the twelfth century, students converged upon Paris. They crowded into the cathedral school of Notre Dame and spilled over into the area later called the Latin Quarter – whose name probably reflects the Italian origin of many of the students attracted to Paris by the surge of interest in the classics, logic, and theology. The cathedral

school's international reputation had already drawn to Paris scholars from all over Europe, one of the most famous of whom was Peter Abélard.

The son of a minor Breton knight, Peter Abélard (1079–1142) studied in Paris, quickly absorbed a large amount of material, and set himself up as a teacher. Abélard was fascinated by logic, which he believed could be used to solve most problems. He had a brilliant mind and, although orthodox in his philosophical teaching, appeared to challenge ecclesiastical authorities. His book *Sic et Non (Yes and No)* was a list of apparently contradictory propositions drawn from the Bible and the writings of the church fathers. One such proposition, for example, stated that sin is pleasing to God and is not pleasing to God. Abélard used a method of systematic doubting in his writing and teaching. As he put it in the preface to *Sic et Non,* "By doubting we come to questioning, and by questioning we perceive the truth." While other scholars merely asserted theological principles, Abélard discussed and analyzed them. Through reasoning he even tried to describe the attributes of the three persons of the Trinity, the central mystery of the Christian faith. Abélard was severely censured by a church council, but his cleverness, boldness, and imagination made him highly popular with students.

The influx of students eager for learning, together with dedicated and imaginative teachers, created the atmosphere in which universities grew. In northern Europe – at Paris and later at Oxford and Cambridge in England – associations or guilds of professors organized universities. They established the curriculum, set the length of time for study, and determined the form and content of examinations. In 1200, King Philip Augustus officially recognized the University of Paris, and in 1208 Pope Innocent III, who had studied there, designated the community of students and scholars a *universitas*.

INSTRUCTION AND CURRICULUM

University faculties grouped themselves according to academic disciplines, called schools – law, medicine, philosophy, and theology. The professors, known as schoolmen or scholastics, developed a method of thinking, reasoning, and writing in which questions were raised and authorities cited on both sides of the question. The goal of the scholastic method was to arrive at definitive answers and to provide a rational explanation for what was believed on faith. Schoolmen held that reason and faith constitute two harmonious realms in which the truths of faith and reason complement each other. The scholastic approach rested upon the recovery of classical philosophical texts.

Ancient Greek and Arabic texts had entered Europe in the early twelfth century, primarily through Toledo in Muslim Spain. Thirteenth-century philosophers relied on Latin translations of these texts, especially those of Aristotle. Aristotle had stressed direct observation of nature, as well as the principles that theory must follow fact and that knowledge of a thing requires an explanation of its causes. The schoolmen reinterpreted Aristotelian texts in a Christian sense.

In exploration of the natural world, Aristotle's axioms were not precisely followed. Medieval scientists argued from authority, such as the Bible, the Justinian Code, or an ancient scientific treatise, rather than from direct observation and experimentation, as modern scientists do. Thus, the conclusions of medieval scientists were often wrong. Nevertheless, natural science gradually emerged as a discipline distinct from philosophy. Scholastics made important contributions to the advancement of knowledge. They preserved the Greek and Arabic texts that contained the body of ancient scientific knowledge, which would otherwise have been lost. And, in asking questions about nature and the universe, scholastics laid the foundations for later scientific work.

Many of the problems that scholastic philosophers raised dealt with theological issues. They addressed, for example, the question that interested all Christians, educated and uneducated: how is a person saved? St. Augustine's thesis – that, as the result of Adam's fall, human beings have a propensity to sin – had become a central feature of medieval church doctrine. The church taught that it possessed the means to forgive the sinful: through grace conveyed through the sacraments. However, although grace provided a predisposition to salvation, the scholastics held that one must also *decide* to use the grace received. In other words, a person must use his or her reason to advance to God.

Thirteenth-century scholastics devoted an enormous amount of time to collecting and organizing knowledge on all topics. These collections were published as *summa,* or reference books. There were summa on law, philosophy, vegetation, animal life, theology. Saint Thomas Aquinas (1225–1274), a professor of theology at Paris, produced the most famous collection, the *Summa Theologica,* which deals with a vast number of theological questions.

Aquinas drew an important distinction between faith and reason. He maintained that, although reason can demonstrate many basic Christian principles such as the existence of God, other fundamental teachings such as the Trinity and original sin cannot be proven by logic. That reason cannot establish them does not, however, mean they are contrary to reason. People can gain an understanding of such doctrines through revelation embodied in Scripture. Scripture cannot contradict reason, nor reason Scripture:

The light of faith that is freely infused into us does not destroy the light of natural knowledge [reason] implanted in us naturally. For although the natural light of the human mind is insufficient to show us these things made manifest by faith, it is nevertheless impossible that these things which the divine principle gives us by faith are contrary to those implanted in us by nature [reason]. Indeed, were that the case, one or the other would have to be false, and, since both are given to us by God, God would have to be the author of untruth, which is impossible. . . . it is impossible that those things which are of philosophy can be contrary to those things which are of faith.[4]

Aquinas also investigated the branch of philosophy called epistemology, which is concerned with how a person knows something. Aquinas stated that one knows, first, through sensory perception of the physical world – seeing, hearing, touching, and so on. He maintained that there can be nothing in the mind that is not first in the senses. Secondly, knowledge comes through reason, the mind exercising its natural abilities. Aquinas stressed the power of human reason to know, even to know God. Proofs of the existence of God exemplify the scholastic method of knowing.

Aquinas begins with the things of the natural world – earth, air, trees, water, birds. From these things, he inquires back to their original source or cause, the mover, creator, planner who started it all. Everything, Aquinas maintained, has an ultimate and essential explanation, a reason for existing. Here he was following Aristotle. Aquinas went further and identified the reason for existing, or first mover, with God. Thomas Aquinas and all medieval intellectuals held that the end

of both faith and reason was the knowledge of, and union with, God. His work later became the fundamental text of Roman Catholic doctrine.

At all universities, the standard method of teaching was the lecture – that is, a reading. The professor read a passage from the Bible, the Justinian Code, or one of Aristotle's treatises. He then explained and interpreted the passage; his interpretation was called a gloss. Students wrote down everything. Texts and glosses were sometimes collected and reproduced as textbooks. For example, the Italian Peter Lombard (d. 1160), a professor at Paris, wrote what became the standard textbook in theology, *Sententiae (The Sentences),* which was a compilation of basic theological principles.

Because books had to be copied by hand, they were extremely expensive and few students could afford them. Students therefore depended for study on their own or friends' notes accumulated over a period of years. The choice of subjects was narrow. The syllabus at all universities consisted of a core of ancient texts that everyone studied and, if they wanted to get ahead, mastered.

There were no examinations at the end of a series of lectures. Examinations were given after three, four, or five years of study, when the student applied for a degree. The professors determined the amount of material students had to know for each degree, and students frequently insisted that the professors specify precisely what that material was. When the candidate for a degree believed himself prepared, he presented himself to a committee of professors for examination.

Examinations were oral and very difficult. (Not only did paper and ink cost a great deal, the examination was designed to test the student's ability to think quickly on his feet and to express his thoughts effectively.) If the candidate passed, he was awarded the first, or

A UNIVERSITY LECTURE Some students doze, some chat, and some are attentive to the lecturer. All students appear much older than undergraduates today. (Bildarchiv Preussischer Kulturbesitz)

bachelor's, degree. Further study, about as long, arduous, and expensive as it is today, enabled the graduate to try for the master's and doctor's degrees. All degrees certified competence in a given subject, and degrees were technically licenses to teach. Most students, however, did not become teachers.

STUDENT LIFE

The students and faculties of medieval universities were from the middling rungs of society, very much like many of the students and teachers at American state universities today. Most students (all of whom were male) came from families of lesser knights, burgesses of the towns, merchants, and artisans — the group that today would be called middle-class. Undergraduates were usually in their twenties and thirties, poor, ambitious, and aggressively upwardly mobile. They wanted and received an education that was practical, utilitarian, and vocational.

Students wanted to acquire as quickly as

possible the knowledge necessary for a secure, well-paying job in the service of the church or secular government. Consequently, once the first degree had been attained, law was the subject most often pursued for an advanced degree. Students studied law because governments needed the expertise of lawyers. Philip Augustus of France employed law graduates as baillis and seneschals. Frederick II, when he established the University of Naples, had clearly stated in the university's charter that the school's purpose was to train men who would dispense the law throughout his kingdom.

Medieval students exercised more power in their universities than do students today. In the Middle Ages students often traveled long distances to work with great scholars. They arrived as foreigners in the countries where they studied, and, fearful of the natives, formed associations for mutual security. Some guilds were set up for sheer physical protection; others sought to defend students from the high rates charged by local boarding-houses and innkeepers. Student guilds, especially in southern Italy, hired the professors, paid their fees, and demanded that teachers cover the syllabus within an agreed-upon time. If they became dissatisfied with incompetent professors or the financial gouging of townspeople, students did not hesitate to boycott lectures or to leave the town entirely. Cambridge University, for example, began when students at Oxford got fed up with conditions there.

Municipal court records of towns like Paris, Oxford, and Cambridge reveal that in the thirteenth and fourteenth centuries student riots and rebellions were common. Townspeople resented what they considered the wasteful lives of students. Students protested the high costs of living in university towns or what they felt were the unfair deci-sions of professors or university officials. Friction between students and townspeople or between students and university authorities was common. But the aim of medieval student movements was never to reform society as a whole. Medieval students had no interest in changing the basic social system. They wanted, instead, to get into the system; they wanted a piece of the action.

Medieval universities did not have luxurious dormitories, semiprofessional athletic teams, vast administrations, or even class-rooms. The first professors lectured in rented halls. In the later thirteenth century, first at Paris and then at Oxford, noblemen and wealthy businessmen established colleges, or residence halls, and endowed scholarships for poor students. Most students lived in abject poverty, and before the sixteenth century they led a cold, uncomfortable, and hand-to-mouth existence. Nevertheless, in establishing the system of lectures, textbooks, faculties, examinations, and degrees, medieval universities laid the foundations for modern institutional learning.

GOTHIC ART

Medieval churches stand as the most spectacular manifestations of the vitality and creativity of the High Middle Ages. It is difficult for twentieth-century people to appreciate the extraordinary amounts of energy, imagination, and money involved in building them. Between 1180 and 1270 in France alone, eighty cathedrals, about five hundred abbey churches, and tens of thousands of parish churches were constructed. This construction represents a remarkable investment for a country of scarcely 18 million people. More stone was quarried for churches in medieval France than

ROMANESQUE AND GOTHIC ARCHES The round barrel vault characterizes the Romanesque style. Cross vaults built on arches and supported by buttresses typify the Gothic.

had been mined in ancient Egypt, where the Great Pyramid alone consumed 40.5 million cubic feet of stone. All these churches displayed a new architectural style. Fourteenth-century critics called the new style "Gothic" because they mistakenly believed the Goths of the fifth century had invented it. The Gothic style actually developed partly in reaction to an earlier style named Romanesque, which supposedly resembled ancient Roman architecture.

Gothic cathedrals were built in towns, and they reflect both bourgeois wealth and enormous civic pride. The manner in which a society spends its wealth expresses its values. Cathedrals, abbeys, and village churches testify to the deep religious faith and piety of medieval people. If the dominant aspect of medieval culture had not been the Christian faith, the builder's imagination and the merchant's money would have been used in other ways.

FROM ROMANESQUE GLOOM TO "UNINTERRUPTED LIGHT"

The relative political stability and increase of ecclesiastical wealth in the eleventh century encouraged the arts of peace. In the ninth and tenth centuries, the Vikings and Magyars had burned hundreds of wooden churches. In the eleventh century, abbots wanted to rebuild in a more permanent fashion, and after the year 1000 church building increased on a wide scale. Because fireproofing was essential, the ceiling had to be made of stone. Therefore, builders replaced wooden roofs with arched stone ceilings called vaults. The stone ceilings were heavy; only thick walls would support them. Because the walls were so thick, the windows were small, allowing little light into the interior of the church. The basic features of Romanesque architecture, as this style is called, are stone vaults in the ceiling, a rounded arch over the nave (the central part of the church), and thick, heavy walls. In northern Europe, twin bell towers often crowned the Romanesque churches, giving them a powerful, fortresslike appearance. Built primarily by the monasteries, Romanesque churches reflect the quasi-military, aristocratic, and pre-urban society that built them.

The inspiration for the Gothic style originated in the brain of one monk, Suger, abbot of St.-Denis (1122–1151), whose life is a remarkable medieval success story. Born of very poor parents, he was given as a child-oblate to the abbey of St.-Denis. St.-Denis was a royal abbey, closely associated with the French monarchy, the custodian of the royal insignia, and the burial place of the French kings. Suger became chief adviser to Louis VI and

Louis VII; and when Louis VII was away on crusade, he served as the regent of France. When Suger became abbot, he decided to reconstruct the old Carolingian abbey church at St.-Denis. Work began in 1137. On June 11, 1144, King Louis VII and a large crowd of bishops, dignitaries, and common people witnessed the solemn consecration of the first Gothic church in France.

The basic features of Gothic architecture — the pointed arch, the ribbed vault, and the flying buttress — were not unknown before 1137. What was without precedent was the interior lightness they made possible. Since the ceiling of a Gothic church weighed less, the walls could be thinner. Windows were cut into the stone, allowing the church to be flooded with light. Stained-glass windows crowned the Gothic style. The bright interior was astounding. Suger, describing his achievement, exulted:

Moreover, it was cunningly provided that ... the central nave of the old nave should be equalized, by means of geometrical and arithmetical instruments, with the central nave of the new addition; and, likewise, that the dimensions of the old side-aisles should be equalized with the dimensions of the new side-aisles, except for that elegant and praiseworthy extension, in [the form of] a circular string of chapels, by virtue of which the whole [church] would shine with the wonderful and uninterrupted light of most sacred windows, pervading the interior beauty.[5]

Thirteenth-century people referred to Gothic architecture as "the new style," or "the Frankish work." Begun in the Ile-de-France, Gothic architecture spread throughout France with the expansion of royal power. French architects were soon invited to design and supervise the construction of churches in other parts of Europe. For example, William of Sens, an experienced architect, was commis-

FOURTEENTH-CENTURY FRENCH STAINED GLASS *Stained glass illuminated both the church and, in the stories told, the minds of the viewers. In the left lancet the prophet Isaiah holds a scroll predicting that a Virgin will bear a son; in the right Mary Magdalene weeps because she cannot find Christ. (Metropolitan Museum of Art, The Cloisters, New York)*

WEST FRONT OF NOTRE DAME CATHEDRAL
In this powerful vision of the Last Judgment, Christ sits
in judgment surrounded by angels, the Virgin, and
Saint John. Scenes of paradise fill the arches on
Christ's right, scenes of hell on the left. In the lower

lintel, the dead arise incorruptible, and in the upper
lintel (below Christ's feet), the saved move off to
heaven, while devils push the damned to hell. Below,
the twelve apostles line the doorway. (Alinari/Scala)

sioned to rebuild Canterbury Cathedral after a disastrous fire in 1174. The distinguished scholar John of Salisbury was then in Canterbury and observed William's work. After John became bishop of Chartres, he wanted William of Sens to assist in the renovation of Chartres Cathedral. Through such contacts "the new style" traveled rapidly over Europe.

THE CREATIVE OUTBURST

The construction of a Gothic cathedral represented a gigantic investment of time, money, and corporate effort. It was the bishop and the clergy of the cathedral who made the decision to build, but they depended on the support of all the social classes. Bishops raised revenue from contributions by people in their dioceses, and the clergy appealed to the king and the nobility. The French rulers were generous benefactors of many cathedrals. Louis IX endowed so many churches in the Ile-de-France – most notably Sainte Chapelle, a small chapel he built to house the crown of thorns – that scholars speak of a "court style" of Gothic. Noble families often gave in order to have their crests in the stained-glass windows. Above all, the church relied on the financial help of those with the greatest amount of ready cash, the commercial classes.

Money was not the only need. A great number of craftsmen had to be assembled: quarrymen, sculptors, stonecutters, masons, mortar makers, carpenters, blacksmiths, glassmakers, roofers. Each master craftsman had his own apprentices, and unskilled laborers had to be recruited for the heavy work. The construction of a large cathedral was rarely completed in one lifetime; many were never finished at all. Because generation after generation of craftsmen added to the building, many Gothic churches show the architectural influences of two or even three centuries.

The surge of church building in the twelfth and thirteenth centuries is intimately associated with the growth of towns and the increase of commercial wealth. The medieval cathedrals are monuments to the interest and support of the business classes. Townspeople had secured their independence from feudal authorities, and they celebrated that freedom by building splendid cathedrals. A large and magnificent church also reflected the wealth and prosperity of the townspeople – and the cleverness and industry needed to acquire that wealth. What better way to display that wealth than in the house of God?

Since cathedrals were symbols of bourgeois civic pride, towns competed to build the largest and most splendid church. In northern France in the late twelfth and early thirteenth centuries, cathedrals grew progressively taller. In 1163, the citizens of Paris began Notre Dame cathedral, intending it to reach a height of 114 feet. Reconstruction on Chartres Cathedral was begun in 1194: it was to be 119 feet. The people of Beauvais exceeded everyone: their church, started in 1247, reached 157 feet; unfortunately, the weight imposed on the vaults was too great, and the building collapsed in 1284. Medieval people built cathedrals to glorify God – and if mortals were impressed, so much the better.[6]

Cathedrals served secular as well as religious purposes. The sanctuary containing the altar and the bishop's chair belonged to the clergy, but the rest of the church belonged to the people. In addition to marriages, baptisms, and funerals, there were scores of feast days on which the entire town gathered in the cathedral for festivities. Amiens Cathedral could hold the entire town of ten thousand people. Local guilds, which fulfilled the economic, fraternal, and charitable functions of

CROUCHING BLACK MAN *From the north transept of Chartres Cathedral, ca 1230. The thousands of representations of blacks in medieval art show that Europeans were familiar with them — from commercial contacts with Muslim parts of Spain and Italy, the crusades, and the slave trade. Europeans' attitudes reflected a curious fascination with the social feeling, as here implied, that black people should occupy menial positions. The black man supports the Queen of Sheba, who symbolizes the pagan world in need of conversion. (Mark Sheridan OSB)*

modern labor unions, met in the cathedrals to arrange business deals and plan recreational events and the support of disabled members. Magistrates and municipal officials held political meetings there. Some towns never built town halls, because all civic functions took place in the cathedral. Pilgrims slept there, lovers courted there, traveling actors staged plays there. The cathedral belonged to all.

The structure of the Gothic cathedral mirrored the interests of all classes of medieval society. The clergy planned the design of the building along orderly theological principles, putting into practice the axiom of the fifth-century mystical writer Dennis the Areopagite, "Through the senses man may rise to the contemplation of the divine." The cathedral was intended to teach the people the doctrines of the Christian faith through visual images.

Architecture became the servant of theology. The main altar was at the east end, pointing toward Jerusalem, the city of peace. The west front of the cathedral faced the setting sun, and its wall was usually devoted to scenes of the Last Judgment. The north side, which received the least sunlight, displayed events from the Old Testament. The south side, washed in warm sunshine for much of the day, depicted scenes from the New Testament. This symbolism implied that the Jewish people of the Old Testament lived in darkness and that the gospel brought by Christ illuminated the world. Every piece of sculpture, furniture, and stained glass had some religious or social significance.

Stained glass beautifully reflects the creative energy of the High Middle Ages. It is both an integral part of Gothic architecture and a distinct form of painting. The glassmaker "painted" his picture with small fragments of glass held together with strips of lead. As Gothic churches became more skeletal and had more windows, stained glass replaced manuscript illumination as the leading kind of painting.

Contributors to the cathedral and the workmen left their imprint upon it. The stonecutter cut his mark on every block of stone, partly so that he would be paid, partly

too so that his work would be remembered. At Chartres Cathedral the craft and merchant guilds – drapers, furriers, haberdashers, tanners, butchers, bakers, fishmongers, and wine merchants – donated money and are memorialized in the stained-glass windows. The incredibly beautiful window of the wine merchants depicts their business in three central medallions: a wine merchant and his cart; a man pouring wine from a cask; and the wine being used at the mass. Thousands of scenes in the cathedral celebrate nature,

country life, and the activities of ordinary people. All members of medieval society had a place in the City of God, which the Gothic cathedral represented. No one, from kings to milkmaids, was excluded.

Tapestry making also came into its own in the fourteenth century. Heavy woolen tapestries were first made in monasteries and convents as wall hangings for churches. Because they could be moved and lent an atmosphere of warmth, they subsequently replaced mural paintings. Early tapestries depicted religious scenes, but later hangings produced for the knightly class bore secular designs, especially romantic forests and hunting spectacles.

The drama, derived from the church's liturgy, emerged as a distinct art form during the same period. For centuries skits based on Christ's Resurrection and Nativity had been performed in monasteries and cathedrals. Beginning in the thirteenth century, plays based on these and other biblical themes and on the lives of the saints were performed in the towns. Guilds financed these "mystery plays," so called because they were based on the mysteries of the Christian faith; in a long production, each of a town's guilds was responsible for a different scene. Actors used very simple costumes and props, and comical or vulgar farces from the lives of ordinary people were interspersed with serious religious scenes. Performed first at the cathedral altar, then in the church square, and later in the town marketplace, mystery plays enjoyed great popularity. They allowed the common people to understand and identify with religious figures and the mysteries of their faith. While provoking the individual conscience to reform, mystery plays were also an artistic manifestation of local civic pride.

THE CRUSADES

Crusades in the late eleventh and early twelfth centuries were holy wars sponsored by the papacy for the recovery of the Holy Land from the Muslim Arabs or the Turks. In the later twelfth and through the thirteenth century, crusades were also directed against Europe's domestic enemies, heretics. Between 1096 and 1270 there were at least eight campaigns to wrest the Holy Land from the in-fidels. Throughout this period Christians alone and in groups left Europe in a steady trickle for the Middle East. Although people of all ages and classes participated in the Crusades, so many knights did so that crusading became a distinctive feature of the upper-class lifestyle. In an aristocratic military society men coveted a reputation as a Crusader; the Christian knight who had been to the Holy Land enjoyed great prestige. The Crusades manifested the religious and chivalric ideals – as well as the tremendous vitality – of medieval society.

The Crusades of the High Middle Ages grew out of earlier conflict between Christians and Muslims in Spain. The concept of a holy war originated in the Spanish peninsula and gradually influenced all parts of western Europe. In the eighth century, the Arabs had overrun the peninsula, and Christian lords had fled into the mountains in the north. In the tenth century, Christians started the *reconquista,* or holy war of reconquest. Christian warriors made slow progress – not until 1492 did Isabella and Ferdinand finally succeed in expelling the Arabs – but by about 1100 Christian kings had regained about a fourth of the peninsula. The *reconquista* dominates the history of medieval Spain.

The Roman papacy supported the holy war in Spain, and by the late eleventh century had strong reasons for wanting to launch an expedition against Muslim infidels in the Middle East as well. The papacy had been involved in a bitter struggle over investiture with the German emperors. If the pope could muster a large army against the enemies of Christianity, his claim to be the leader of Christian society in the West would be strengthened.

Moreover, in 1054 a serious theological disagreement had split the Greek church of Byzantium and the Roman church of the

West. The pope believed that a crusade would lead to strong Roman influence in Greek territories and eventually the reunion of the two churches. Then, in 1071 at Manzikert in eastern Anatolia, Turkish soldiers in the pay of the Arabs defeated a Greek army and occupied much of Asia Minor. The emperor at Constantinople appealed to the West for support. Shortly afterward, the holy city of Jerusalem, the scene of Christ's preaching and burial, fell to the Turks. Pilgrimages to holy places in the Middle East became very dangerous, and the papacy was outraged that the holy city was in the hands of infidels.

In 1095, Pope Urban II journeyed to Clermont in France and called for a great Christian holy war against the infidels. He stressed the sufferings and persecution of Christians in Jerusalem. He urged Christian knights who had been fighting one another to direct their energies against the true enemies of God, the Muslims. Urban proclaimed an indulgence, or remission of sin, to those who would fight for and regain the holy city of Jerusalem. Few speeches in history have had such a dramatic effect as Urban's call at Clermont for the First Crusade.

The response was fantastic. Godfrey of Bouillon, Geoffrey of Lorraine, and many other great lords from northern France immediately had the cross of the Crusader sewn on their tunics. Encouraged by popular preachers like Peter the Hermit, and by papal legates in Germany, Italy, and England, thousands of people of all classes joined the crusade. Although most of the Crusaders were French, pilgrims from all countries streamed southward from the Rhineland, through Germany and the Balkans. No development in the High Middle Ages better reveals Europeans' religious zeal and emotional fervor, and the influence of the reformed papacy, than the incredible outpouring of support for the First Crusade.

Religious convictions inspired many, but mundane motives were also involved. Except for wives, who had to remain at home to manage estates, many people expected to benefit from the crusade. For the curious and the adventurous, it offered foreign travel and excitement; it promised escape from the dullness of everyday life. The crusade provided kings, who were trying to establish order and to build states, the perfect opportunity to get rid of troublemaking knights. It gave land-hungry younger sons a chance to acquire fiefs in the Middle East. Even some members of the middle class who stayed at home profited from the crusade. Nobles often had to borrow money from the middle class to pay for their expeditions, and they put up part of their land as security. If a noble did not return home or could not pay the interest on the loan, the middle-class creditor took over the land.

The First Crusade was successful mostly because of the dynamic enthusiasm of the participants. The Crusaders had little more than religious zeal. They knew nothing about the geography or climate of the Middle East. Although among the host there were several counts with military experience, the Crusaders could never agree on a leader, and the entire expedition was marked by disputes among the great lords. Lines of supply were never set up. Starvation and disease wracked the army, and the Turks slaughtered hundreds of noncombatants. Nevertheless, convinced that "God wills it" – the war cry of the Crusaders – the army pressed on and in 1099 captured Jerusalem. Although the Crusaders fought bravely, Arab disunity was a chief reason for their victory. At Jerusalem, Edessa, Tripoli, and Antioch, Crusader kingdoms were founded on the Western feudal model (see Map 14.4).

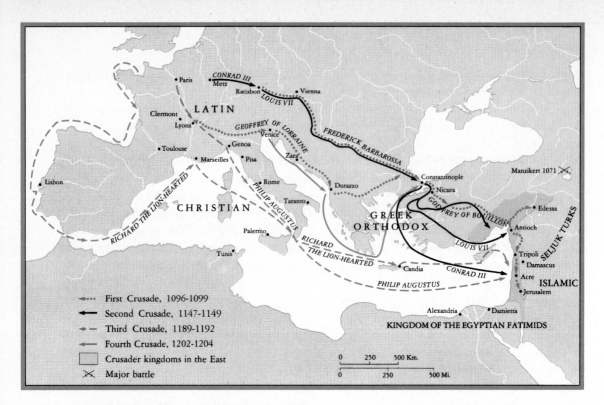

MAP 14.4 *THE ROUTES OF THE CRUSADES*
The crusades led to a major cultural encounter be-
tween Muslim and Christian values. What significant
intellectual and economic effects resulted?

Between 1096 and 1270, the crusading ideal was expressed in eight papally approved expeditions to the East. In addition to those eight, the papacy in 1208 proclaimed a crusade against heretics in southern France. In the same year, two expeditions of children set out on a crusade to the Holy Land. One contingent turned back; the other was captured and sold into slavery. And, in 1227 and 1239, the pope launched a crusade against the emperor Frederick II. None of the crusades against the Muslims achieved very much. The third one (1189–1192) was precipitated by the recapture of Jerusalem by the sultan Saladin in 1187. Frederick Barbarossa of the Holy Roman Empire, Richard the Lion-Hearted of England, and Philip Augustus of France participated, and the Third Crusade was better financed

than previous ones. But disputes among the leaders and strategic problems prevented any lasting results.

During the Fourth Crusade (1198–1204), careless preparation and inadequate financing had disastrous consequences for Byzantine-Latin relations. Hoping to receive material support from the Greeks, the leaders of the crusade took the expedition to Constantinople before advancing to Jerusalem. But once there, they sacked the city and established the Latin Empire of Constantinople. This assault by one Christian people on another, when one of the goals of the crusade was the reunion of the Greek and Latin churches, helped to discredit the entire crusading movement. Two later crusades undertaken by King Louis IX of France added to his prestige as a pious ruler. Apart from that, the last of the official crusades accomplished nothing at all.

Crusades were also mounted against groups perceived as Christian Europe's social enemies. In 1208 Pope Innocent III proclaimed a crusade against the Albigensians, a heretical sect. The Albigensians, whose name derived from the southern French town of Albi where they were concentrated, rejected orthodox doctrine on the relationship of God and man, the sacraments, and the hierarchy. Believing the Albigensians a political threat, the French monarchy joined the crusade. Under Count Simon de Montfort the French inflicted a savage defeat on the Albigensians at Muret in 1213; the county of Toulouse passed to the authority of the French Crown. The popes in the mid-thirteenth century, fearful of encirclement by imperial territories, promoted crusades against Emperor Frederick II. This use of force against a Christian ruler backfired, damaging papal credibility as the sponsor of peace.

The Crusades brought few cultural changes to western Europe. By the late eleventh century, strong economic and intellectual ties with the East had already been made. The Crusades testify to the religious enthusiasm of the High Middle Ages. But, as Steven Runciman, a distinguished scholar of the Crusades, concluded in his three-volume history:

The triumphs of the Crusade were the triumphs of faith. But faith without wisdom is a dangerous thing. . . . In the long sequence of interaction and fusion between Orient and Occident out of which our civilization has grown, the Crusades were a tragic and destructive episode. . . . There was so much courage and so little honour, so much devotion and so little understanding. High ideals were besmirched by cruelty and greed, enterprise and endurance by a blind and narrow self-righteousness; and the Holy War itself was nothing more than a *long act of intolerance in the name of God, which is the sin against the Holy Ghost.*[7]

Societies, like individuals, cannot maintain a high level of energy indefinitely. In the later years of the thirteenth century, Europeans seemed to run out of steam. The crusading movement gradually fizzled out. No new cathedrals were constructed, and if a cathedral had not been completed by 1300, the chances were that it never would be. The strong rulers of France and England, building on the foundations of their predecessors, increased their authority and gained the loyalty of all their subjects. The vigor of those kings, however, did not pass to their immediate descendants. The church, which for two centuries had guided Christian society, began to face grave difficulties. A violent dispute between the papacy and the kings of France and England badly damaged papal prestige.

In 1296, Kind Edward I of England and Philip the Fair of France declared war upon each other. To finance this war both kings laid taxes on the clergy. Kings had been taxing the church for decades. Pope Boniface VIII (1294–1303), a staunch defender of papal supremacy, forbade churchmen to pay the taxes. But Edward and Philip refused to accept this decree, partly because it hurt royal finances, and partly because the papal order threatened royal authority within their countries. Edward immediately denied the clergy the protection of the law, which meant that they could be attacked with impunity. Philip halted the shipment of all ecclesiastical revenue to Rome. Boniface had to back down.

Philip the Fair and his ministers continued their attack on all powers in France outside royal authority. Philip arrested a French bishop who was also the papal legate. When

THE CAPTURE OF JERUSALEM IN 1099 *As engines hurl stones to breach the walls, crusaders enter
on scaling ladders. Scenes from Christ's passion
(above) identify the city as Jerusalem. (Bibliothèque
Nationale, Paris)*

Boniface defended the ecclesiastical status and
diplomatic immunity of the bishop, Philip replied with the trumped-up charge that the
pope was a heretic. The papacy and the French
monarchy waged a bitter war of propaganda.
Finally in 1302, in a letter entitled *Unam
Sanctam* (because its opening sentence spoke
of one holy Catholic church), Boniface insisted that Philip, like everyone else, submit
to papal authority. Philip's university-trained
advisers responded with an argument drawn
from Roman law: they maintained that the
king of France was completely sovereign in
his kingdom and responsible to God alone.
French mercenary troops went to Italy and
arrested the aged pope at Anagni. Although
Boniface was soon freed, he died shortly afterward. The incident at Anagni marked a decisive turning point.

The French attack on the leadership of the
church signaled the weakening of religious
authority. The Christian church had been the

ART: A MIRROR OF SOCIETIES

Art reveals the interests and values of societies and frequently gives unique and intimate glimpses of how people actually lived. In portraits and statues, whether of gods, ghanas, saints, samurai, maharanas, or merchants, it preserves the memory and fame of people who shaped societies. In paintings, carvings, and drawings, art also shows how people worked, played, prayed, suffered, and triumphed. Art, therefore, is useful to the historian, especially for distant periods and remote cultures where written records are scarce or hard to understand.

The art of early societies, apart from public buildings such as temples, cathedrals, and mosques, was created for an aristocratic elite and reflected their tastes and values. Only a wealthy Greek could afford a richly painted vase or wine cup. Only a rich Aztec chief could build an extensive palace, faced with adobe or stone and surrounded by patios. The royal standard of Ur, below, shows aspects of Sumerian society in peacetime. In its

upper band, a triangular box on a pole used on ceremonial occasions, depicts a royal banquet, with the king and his nobles drinking and listening to music. In the lower band herdsmen lead animals. (By courtesy of the British Museum.) Art was created to represent the power of kings and the social distinction of nobles. Upper class people commissioned mosaics, illuminated manuscripts, jewelry and carved objects, miniatures and paintings. African obas ordered bronze plaques to symbolize their power and authority. Japanese samurai displayed their wealth with elegant silk screens with genre and erotic scenes. Art also instructed. In Christian Europe, Shiite Persia, and Mughal India books were considered especially valuable objects, because of the skill, time, and precious materials needed to produce them. Copies of monastic psalters, Persian poetry, and the Muslim Koran taught the reader the tenets of his or her faith and represented the wealth of the possessor. Artists ev-

erywhere illuminated manuscripts with religious, court, and battle scenes. While Western monks decorated the borders of pages with floral designs and animal scenes, Muslim artists used geometrical or calligraphic motifs.

Art shows the changes and continuity of life and the impact of societies and cultures upon one another. Scenes of agriculture and commerce have been popular from classical to modern times. As values changed, so did major artistic themes. Religious art of the early Middle Ages replaced the sensuous pagan subjects of antiquity. In turn, the art of the later Middle Ages and of the Renaissance displayed secular interests. As trade carried the techniques and media of cultures around the world, individual societies learned and adapted them to convey their own particular messages. In the remarkable Persian garden scene, Chinese building tiles were used to depict a European merchant showing cloth to a lady; the tableau combines Chinese, European, and Persian qualities.

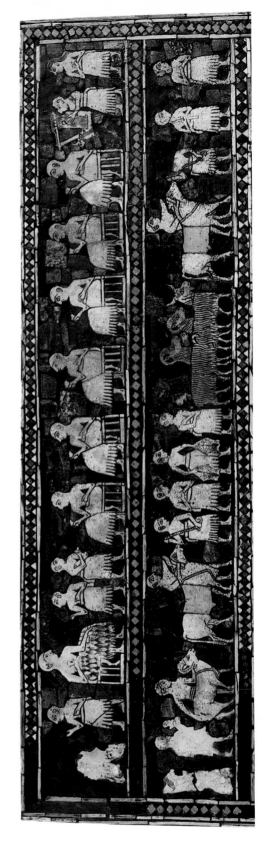

INCAN EAR PLUGS (above) In the Moche period (ca A.D. 200–600) Peruvian goldsmiths achieved a remarkable degree of artistry. These heavy gold ear plugs with stone and shell inlays were probably designed for a relative of the Inca himself: They immediately identified the wearer as a great lord. (The Metropolitan Museum of Art, Gift of Mrs. Harold Bache, 1966)

PALESTRINA MOSAIC (below) Fish and birds abound as boatsmen steer among rocks and try their hand at spearing fish. The Nile was legendary for its fertility and the exotic animals that could be encountered along its course. Mosaics such as this were common in the ancient world and could be found in temples and the homes of the wealthy. (Scala/EPA)

CHINESE POLO PLAYER (above left) Han sculptors, like their ancient Greek counterparts, developed a distinctive realistic style of art. Here the sculptor has portrayed a polo player astride a powerful horse. The sport of polo was naturally popular among a people who relied heavily on cavalry in their warfare. (Art Resource)

LES TRÈS RICHES HEURES DU JEAN, DUC DE BERRY (above, right) This illustrates March in a book of calendar miniatures produced for the duke of Berry, brother of the king of France. With exquisite detail the artists capture four scenes of agricultural life in the early fifteenth century. A shepherd with a dog guards a flock of sheep. Three peasants prune vines while another works in a different field. And an aged farmer guides a wheeled plow and oxen. Symbolically, the vast castle of Lusignan dominates the landscape. (Chantilly, Musée Condé/Giraudon)

THE CAMPIN ALTARPIECE (ca 1425–1428), by Robert Campin (d. 1444). This 4-by 2-ft. painting in oil on wood was intended to hang behind the altar, facing the people. The Annunciation scene in the center panel occurs in the house of a Flemish burgher. Every detail has significance. For example, the serious, modestly dressed middle-class donors in the left panel are memorialized observing the mystery, the lilies on the table in the center panel represent the Virgin's chastity, and Joseph in the right panel carves a delicately painted view of a fifteenth-century city in the right panel carves a mousetrap, symbolizing Christ, the bait set to catch the devil. (The Metropolitan Museum of Art, The Cloisters Collection.)

FEAST OF THE GODS (above) Giovanni Bellini (1430?–1516). In this pastoral scene based on a story of the Roman poet Ovid, Olympian gods picnic in a wooded grove as satyrs and nymphs serve them. The peacock in the tree symbolizes the gods' immortality. The pagan theme, the appreciation for perspective and nature, and the sensual atmosphere make this painting a fine example of Italian Renaissance classicism. (National Gallery of Art, Washington, D.C.)

BUILDING TILES: IN A PERSIAN GARDEN (below) Isfahan under Shah Abbas I held great fame for beautiful palaces, mosques, and gardens, and attracted thousands of European merchants. In this brilliant scene the reclining lady buys cloth from a European merchant, as the kneeling gentleman advises her, and servants bring refreshments to conclude the deal. In Safavid Persia the garden symbolized paradise. (Metropolitan Museum of Art, Rogers Fund, 1903. [03.9c])

SUNG TAPESTRY (overleaf) Attributed to the Emperor Hui-Tsung (1082–1135). This vignette depicts women pounding silk. A talented painter, Hui-Tsung may have copied this scene from an eighth century T'ang work or his court artists may have done so. The hair styles and garments are archaizing and inaccurate. The work is still one of the earliest and finest examples of anachronism in Chinese art. (Courtesy, Museum of Fine Arts, Boston. Chinese and Japanese Special Fund)

strongest influence in medieval society, but now a new power, the national secular state, was emerging in western Europe. Boniface's successors not only retracted *Unam Sanctam* but apologized for it. The centralized power of the French monarchy, which had been growing for over a century, scored a victory over the papacy. The presence of King Philip the Fair at the coronation of Pope Clement V at Lyons in 1305 was symbolic: Clement was French, and he established the papal court at Avignon, within the borders of the Holy Roman Empire but very much a French city. For the next sixty years, the Roman papacy was strongly influenced by France. Anagni foreshadowed serious difficulties within the Christian church, but additional difficulties awaited Western society in the fourteenth century.

NOTES

1. D. C. Douglas and G. E. Greenaway, eds., *English Historical Documents,* II, Eyre & Spottiswoode, London, 1961, p. 853.

2. This section leans heavily on John Boswell, *Christianity, Social Tolerance, and Homosexuality: Gay People in Western Europe from the Beginning of the Christian Era to the Fourteenth Century,* University of Chicago Press, Chicago, 1980, pp. 270–293; the quotation is from p. 293.

3. Quoted by H. E. Sigerist, *Civilization and Disease,* University of Chicago Press, Chicago, 1943, p. 102.

4. Quoted by John H. Mundy, *Europe in the High Middle Ages, 1150–1309,* Basic Books, New York, 1973, pp. 474–475.

5. E. Panofsky, trans., *Abbot Suger on the Abbey Church of St.-Denis and Its Art Treasures,* Princeton University Press, Princeton, 1946, p. 101.

6. See J. Gimpel, *The Cathedral Builders,* Grove Press, New York, 1961, pp. 42–49.

7. S. Runciman, *A History of the Crusades,* vol. 3, *The Kingdom of Acre,* Cambridge University Press, Cambridge, 1955, p. 480.

SUGGESTED READING

The achievements of the High Middle Ages have attracted considerable scholarly attention, and the curious student will have no difficulty finding exciting material on the points raised in this chapter. Three general surveys of the period 1050–1300 are especially recommended: J. R. Strayer, *Western Europe in the Middle Ages* (1955), a masterful synthesis; J. W. Baldwin, *The Scholastic Culture of the Middle Ages* (1971), which stresses the intellectual features of medieval civilization; and F. Heer, *The Medieval World* (1963).

G. O. Sayles, *The Medieval Foundations of England* (1961), traces English conditions to the end of the thirteenth century, while R. Fawtier, *The Capetian Kings of France* (1962), shows how the French monarchy built a nation. G. Barraclough, *Origins of Modern Germany* (1963), provides the best explanation of the problems and peculiarities of the Holy Roman Empire; this is a fine example of a Marxist interpretation of medieval history. Tom Corfe, *Archbishop Thomas Becket and King Henry II* (1980), treats many aspects of the political and religious life of twelfth century England, as well as the conflict between those two persons, in a cleverly illustrated little study: this book is in the Cambridge History of Mankind series. J. R. Strayer, *On the Medieval Origins of the Modern State* (1972), is an excellent treatment of the political and bureaucratic development of European states, also with emphasis on France and England. The advanced student of French medieval administrative history should consult Joseph R. Strayer, *The Reign of Philip the Fair* (1980). Students interested in approaching the High Middle Ages through biographies of leading political figures will find D. C. Douglas, *William the Conqueror* (1964); W. L. Warren, *Henry II* (1974); and E. Kantorowicz, *Frederick II* (1931), interesting and thorough.

For the new currents of thought in the High Middle Ages, see C. Brooke, *The Twelfth Century Renaissance* (1970), a splendidly illustrated book with copious quotations from the sources; E. Gilson, *Héloise and Abélard* (1960) which treats the medieval origins of modern humanism against the background of Abélard the teacher; D. W. Robertson, Jr., *Abélard and Héloise* (1972), which is highly readable, commonsensical, and probably the best recent study of Abélard and the love affair he supposedly had; and C. W. Hollister, ed., *The Twelfth Century Renaissance* (1969), a well-constructed anthology with source materials on many aspects of twelfth-century culture. N. Orme, *English Schools in the Middle Ages* (1973), focuses on the significance of schools and literacy in English Medieval society, while J. Leclercq, *The Love of Learning and the Desire of God* (1974), discusses monastic literary culture.

On the medieval universities, C. H. Haskins, *The Rise of the Universities* (1959), is a good introduction, while H. Rashdall, *The Universities of Europe in the Middle Ages* (1936), is the standard scholarly work. G. Leff, *Paris and Oxford Universities in the Thirteenth and Fourteenth Centuries* (1968), gives a fascinating sketch and includes a useful bibliography.

Students will find a good general introduction to Romanesque and Gothic architecture in N. Pevsner, *An Outline of European Architecture* (1963), a standard work. D. Grivot and G. Zarnecki, *Gislebertus, Sculptor of Autun* (1961), is the finest appreciation of Romanesque architecture written in English. For the actual work of building, see D. Macaulay, *Cathedral: The Story of Its Construction* (1973), a prizewinning, simply written, and cleverly illustrated re-creation of the problems and duration of cathedral building. J. Gimpel, *The Cathedral Builders* (1961), explores the engineering problems involved in cathedral building and places the subject within its social context. Advanced students will enjoy E. Mâle, *The Gothic Image: Religious Art in France in the Thirteenth Century* (1958), which contains a wealth of fascinating and useful detail. For the most important cathedrals in France, architecturally and politically, see A. Temko, *Notre Dame of Paris, the Biography of a Cathedral* (1968); G. Henderson, *Chartres* (1968); and A. Katzenellenbogen, *The Sculptural Programs of Chartres Cathedral* (1959), by a distinguished art historian. E. Panofsky, *Abbot Suger on the Abbey Church of St.-Denis and Its Art Treasures* (1946), provides a contemporary background account of the first Gothic building. E. G. Holt, ed., *A Documentary History of Art* (1957), contains source materials useful for writing papers. J. Gimpel, *The Medieval Machine: The Industrial Revolution of the Middle Ages* (1977), discusses the mechanical and scientific problems involved in the earlier industrial revolution and shows how construction affected the medieval environment; this is an extremely useful book.

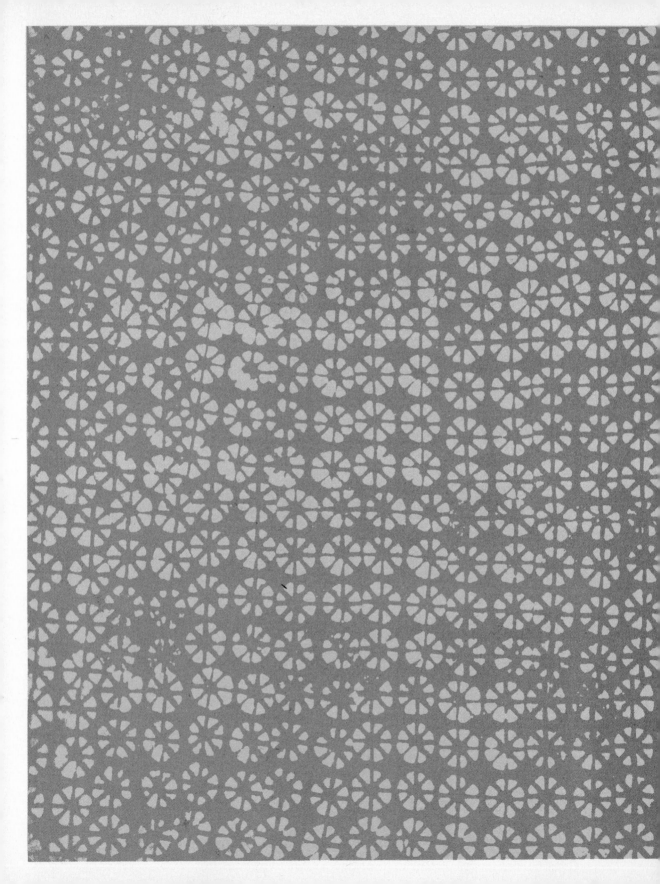

CHAPTER 15

THE CRISIS OF THE

LATER MIDDLE AGES

IN THE LATER MIDDLE AGES, the last book of the New Testament, the Book of Revelation, inspired thousands of sermons and hundreds of religious tracts. The Book of Revelation deals with visions of the end of the world, with disease, war, famine, and death. It is no wonder this part of the Bible was so popular. Between 1300 and 1450, Europeans experienced a frightful series of shocks: economic dislocation, plague, war, social upheaval, and increased crime and violence. Death and preoccupation with death make the fourteenth century one of the gloomiest periods in Western civilization.

The miseries and disasters of the later Middle Ages bring to mind a number of questions. What were the social and psychological effects of repeated attacks of plague and disease? Some scholars maintain that war is often the catalyst for political, economic, and social change. Does this theory have validity for the fourteenth century? Finally, what provoked the division of the church in the fourteenth century? What other ecclesiastical difficulties was the schism a sign of, and what impact did it have on the faith of the common people? This chapter seeks to answer these questions.

PRELUDE TO DISASTER

The fourteenth century began with serious economic problems. In the first decade, the countries of northern Europe experienced a considerable price inflation. The costs of grain, livestock, and dairy products rose sharply. Bad weather made a serious situation worse. An unusual number of storms brought torrential rains. Almost everywhere, heavy rains ruined the wheat, oats, and hay crops on which people and animals depended. Since long-distance transportation of food was ex-

pensive and difficult, most urban areas depended for bread and meat on areas no more than a day's journey away. Poor harvests – and one in four was likely to be poor – led to scarcity and starvation. Almost all of northern Europe suffered a terrible famine in the years 1315–1317.

Hardly had western Europe begun to recover from this disaster when another struck. An epidemic of typhoid fever carried away thousands. In 1316, 10 percent of the population of the city of Ypres in Belgium may have died between May and October alone. Then in 1318 disease hit cattle and sheep, drastically reducing the herds and flocks. Another bad harvest in 1321 brought famine, starvation, and death.

The large province of Languedoc in southern France presents a classic example of agrarian crisis. For over 150 years, Languedoc had enjoyed continual land reclamation, steady agricultural expansion, and enormous population growth. Then the fourteenth century opened with four years of bad harvests, 1302 through 1305. Torrential rains in 1310 ruined the harvest and brought on terrible famine. Harvests failed again in 1322 and 1329. In 1332, desperate peasants survived the winter on raw herbs. In the half-century from 1302 to 1348, poor harvests occurred twenty times. The undernourished population was ripe for the Grim Reaper, who appeared in 1348 in the form of the Black Death.

These catastrophes had inevitable social consequences. Poor harvests meant that marriages had to be postponed. Later marriages and the deaths caused by famine and disease meant a further reduction in population. Thus, after the steady population growth of the twelfth and thirteenth centuries, western Europe suffered a gradual decline in the first third of the fourteenth century. Meanwhile, the international character of trade and commerce meant that a disaster in one country had serious implications elsewhere. For example, the infection that attacked English sheep in 1318 caused a sharp decline in wool exports in the following years. Without wool, Flemish weavers could not work, and thousands were laid off. Without woolen cloth, the businesses of Flemish, French, and English merchants suffered. Unemployment encouraged many men to turn to crime.

To none of these problems did governments have any solutions. In fact, they even lacked policies. After the death of Edward I in 1307, England was governed by the incompetent and weak Edward II (1307–1327), whose reign was dominated by a series of baronial conflicts. In France the three sons of Philip the Fair who followed their father to the French throne between 1314 and 1328 took no interest in the increasing economic difficulties. In the Holy Roman Empire power drifted into the hands of local rulers. The only actions the governments took tended to be in response to the demands of the upper classes. Economic and social problems were aggravated by the appearance in western Europe of a frightful disease.

THE BLACK DEATH

Around 1331, the bubonic plague broke out in China. In the course of the next fifteen years, merchants, traders, and soldiers carried the disease across the Asian caravan routes until, in 1346, it reached the Crimea in southern Russia. From there the plague had easy access to the Mediterranean lands and western Europe.

In 1291, Genoese sailors had opened the Straits of Gibraltar to Italian shipping by defeating the Moroccans. Then, shortly after 1300, important advances were made in the design of Italian merchant ships. A square rig was added to the mainmast, and ships began to carry three masts instead of just one. Additional sails better utilized wind power to propel the ship. The improved design permitted year-round shipping for the first time, and Venetian and Genoese merchant ships could sail the dangerous Atlantic coast even in the winter months. With ships continually at sea, the rats that bore the disease spread rapidly beyond the Mediterranean to Atlantic and North Sea ports.

In October 1347, Genoese ships brought the plague to Messina, from which it spread to Sicily. Venice and Genoa were hit in January 1348, and from the port of Pisa the disease spread south to Rome and north to Florence and all Tuscany. By late spring southern Germany was attacked. Frightened French authorities chased a galley bearing the disease from the port of Marseilles, but not before plague had infected the city, from which it spread to Languedoc and Spain. In June 1348, two ships entered the Bristol Channel and introduced it into England. All Europe felt the scourge of this horrible disease (see Map 15.1).

PATHOLOGY

Modern understanding of the bubonic plague rests on the research of two bacteriologists, one French and one Japanese, who in 1894 independently identified *Pasteurella pestis,* the bacillus that causes the plague (so labeled after the French scientist's teacher, Louis Pasteur). The bacillus liked to live in the bloodstream of an animal or, ideally, in the stomach of a flea. The flea in turn resided in the hair of a rodent, sometimes a squirrel but preferably the hardy, nimble, and vagabond black rat. Why the host black rat moved so much, sci-

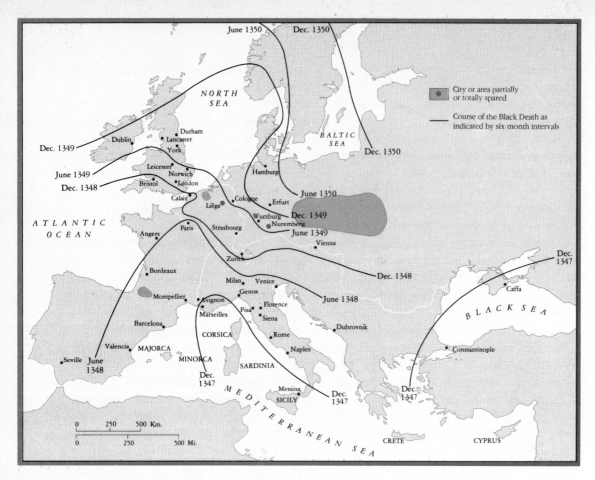

**MAP 15.1   THE COURSE OF THE BLACK DEATH
IN FOURTEENTH-CENTURY EUROPE** *Note the
routes that the bubonic plague took across Europe.
How do you account for the fact that several regions
were spared the "dreadful death"?*

entists still do not know, but it often traveled
by ship. There the black rat could feast for
months on a cargo of grain or live snugly
among bales of cloth. Fleas bearing the bacillus also had no trouble nesting in saddlebags.[1]
Comfortable, well fed, and often having
greatly multiplied, the black rats ended their
ocean voyage and descended upon the great
cities of Europe.

Although by the fourteenth century urban
authorities from London to Paris to Rome
had begun to try to achieve a primitive level
of sanitation, urban conditions remained ideal
for the spread of disease. Narrow streets filled

with mud, refuse, and human excrement were
as much cesspools as thoroughfares. Dead animals and sore-covered beggars greeted the
traveler. Houses whose upper stories projected over the lower ones eliminated light
and air. And extreme overcrowding was commonplace. When all members of an aristocratic family lived and slept in one room, it
should not be surprising that six or eight
persons in a middle-class or poor household
slept in one bed — if they had one. Closeness,
after all, provided warmth. Houses were beginning to be constructed of brick, but many
remained of wood, clay, and mud. A deter-

mined rat had little trouble entering such a house.

Standards of personal hygiene remained frightfully low. Since water was considered dangerous, partly for good reasons, people rarely bathed. Skin infections, consequently, were common. Lack of personal cleanliness, combined with any number of temporary ailments such as diarrhea and the common cold, naturally weakened the body's resistance to serious disease. Fleas and body lice were universal afflictions: everyone from peasants to archbishops had them. One more bite did not cause much alarm. But if that nibble came from a bacillus-bearing flea, an entire household or area was doomed.

The symptoms of the bubonic plague started with a growth the size of a nut or an apple in the armpit, the groin, or on the neck. This was the boil, or *buba,* that gave the disease its name and caused agonizing pain. If the *buba* was lanced and the pus thoroughly drained, the victim had a chance of recovery. The secondary stage was the appearance of black spots or blotches caused by bleeding under the skin. (This syndrome did not give the disease its common name; contemporaries did not call the plague the Black Death. Sometime in the fifteenth century the Latin phrase *atra mors,* meaning "dreadful death" was translated "black death," and the phrase stuck.) Finally, the victim began to cough violently and spit blood. This stage, indicating the presence of thousands of bacilli in the bloodstream, signaled the end, and death followed in two or three days. Rather than evoking compassion for the victim, a French scientist has written, everything about the bubonic plague provoked horror and disgust: "All the matter which exuded from their bodies let off an unbearable stench; sweat, excrement, spittle, breath, so fetid as to be overpowering; urine turbid, thick, black or red."[2]

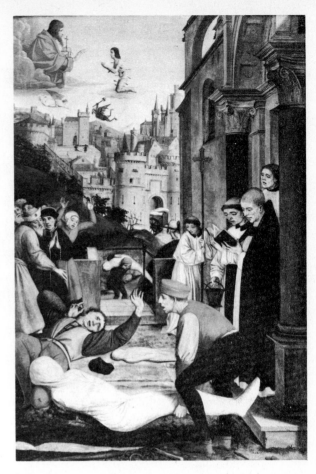

THE PLAGUE-STRICKEN   *Even as the dead were wrapped in shrouds and collected in carts for mass burial, the disease struck others. The man collapsing has the symptomatic buba on his neck. As Saint Sebastian pleads for mercy (above), a winged devil, bearer of the plague, attacks an angel. (Walters Art Gallery)*

Medieval people had no rational explanation for the disease nor any effective medical treatment for it. Fourteenth-century medical literature indicates that physicians could sometimes ease the pain, but they had no cure. Most people — lay, scholarly, and medical — believed that the Black Death was caused by some "vicious property in the air" that carried the disease from place to place. All authorities assumed that some corruption of the atmosphere caused the disease.

PROCESSION OF FLAGELLANTS *The horrors of the Black Death provoked terrible excesses. People believed that the disease was God's punishment for humanity's sins, which could be atoned for only through severe penances. In this procession of robed and hooded flagellants, two of the men flog those ahead of them. (Bibliothèque Royale Albert I, Brussels)*

The Italian writer Giovanni Boccaccio (1313–1375), describing the course of the disease in Florence in the preface to his book of tales, *The Decameron*, pinpointed the cause of the spread:

Moreover, the virulence of the pest was the greater by reason that intercourse was apt to convey it from the sick to the whole, just as fire devours things dry or greasy when they are brought close to it. Nay, the evil went yet further, for not merely by speech or association with the sick was the malady communicated to the healthy with consequent peril of common death, but any that touched the clothes of the sick or aught else that had been touched or used by them, seemed thereby to contract the disease.[3]

The highly infectious nature of the plague was recognized by a few sophisticated Arabs.

When the disease struck the town of Salé in Morocco, Ibu Abu Madyan shut in his household with sufficient food and water and allowed no one to enter or leave until the plague had passed. Madyan was entirely successful. In European cities, those who could afford it fled to the countryside, which generally suffered less. Few were so wise or lucky, however, and the plague took a staggering toll.

The mortality rate cannot be specified, because population figures for the period before the arrival of the plague do not exist for most countries and cities. The largest amount of material survives for England, but it is difficult to use and, after enormous scholarly controversy, only educated guesses can be made. Of a total population of perhaps 4.2 million, probably 1.4 million died of the Black Death in its several visits.[4] Densely populated Italian cities endured incredible losses. Florence lost between half and two-thirds of its 1347 population of 85,000 when the plague visited in 1348. In general, rural areas suffered much less than urban ones. The disease recurred intermittently in the 1360s and 1370s and reappeared several times down to 1700. There have been twentieth-century outbreaks in such places as Hong Kong, Bombay, and Uganda.

SOCIAL AND PSYCHOLOGICAL CONSEQUENCES

Predictably, the poor died more rapidly than the rich, because the rich enjoyed better health to begin with; but the powerful were not unaffected. In England two archbishops of Canterbury fell victim to the plague in 1349, King Edward III's daughter Joan died, and many leading members of the London guilds followed her to the grave.

It is noteworthy that in an age of mounting criticism of clerical wealth and luxury, the behavior of the clergy during the plague was often exemplary. Priests, monks, and nuns cared for the sick and buried the dead. In places like Venice, where even physicians ran away, priests remained to give what ministrations they could. Consequently, their mortality rate was phenomenally high. The German clergy, especially, suffered a severe decline in personnel in the years after 1350. With the ablest killed off, the wealth of the German church fell into the hands of the incompetent and weak. The situation was already ripe for reform.

The plague accelerated the economic decline that had begun in the early part of the fourteenth century. In many parts of Europe there had not been enough work for the people to do. The Black Death was a grim remedy to this problem. Population decline, however, led to an increased demand for labor and to considerable mobility among the peasant and working classes. Wages rose sharply. The shortage of labor and steady requests for higher wages put landlords on the defensive. They retaliated with such measures as the English Statute of Laborers (1351), which attempted to freeze salaries and wages at pre-1347 levels. The statute could not be enforced and therefore the move was largely unsuccessful.

Even more frightening than the social effects were the psychological consequences. The knowledge that the disease meant almost certain death provoked the most profound pessimism. Imagine an entire society in the grip of the belief that it was at the mercy of a frightful affliction about which nothing could be done, a disgusting disease from which family and friends would flee, leaving one to die alone and in agony. It is not surprising that some sought release in orgies and gross sensuality while others turned to the severest forms of asceticism and frenzied religious fervor. Some extremists joined groups of flagellants, who collectively whipped and scourged themselves as penance for their and society's sins in the belief that the Black Death was God's punishment for humanity's wickedness.

The literature and art of the fourteenth century reveal a terribly morbid concern with death. One highly popular artistic motif, the Dance of Death, depicted a dancing skeleton leading away a living person. No wonder survivors experienced a sort of shell shock and a terrible crisis of faith. Lack of confidence in the leaders of society, lack of hope for the future, defeatism, and malaise wreaked enormous anguish and contributed to the decline of the Middle Ages. A long international war added further misery to the frightful disasters of the plague.

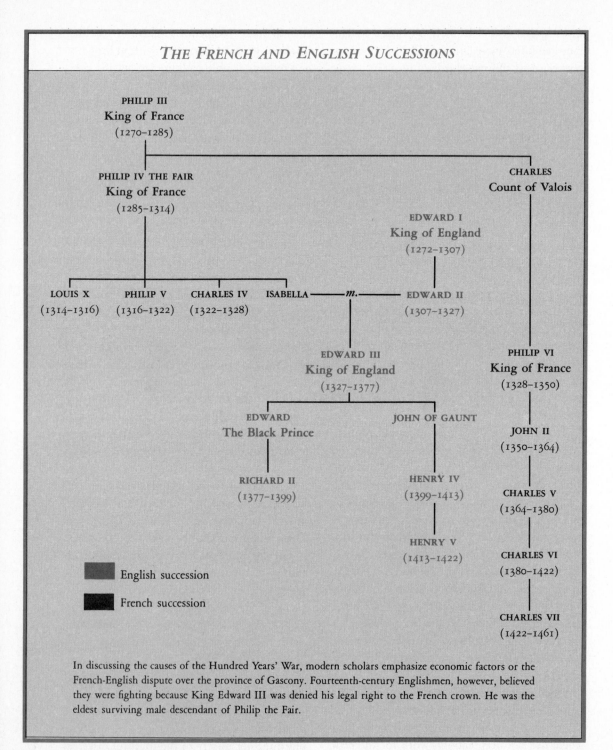

THE FRENCH AND ENGLISH SUCCESSIONS

PHILIP III
King of France
(1270–1285)

PHILIP IV THE FAIR
King of France
(1285–1314)

CHARLES
Count of Valois

EDWARD I
King of England
(1272–1307)

LOUIS X
(1314–1316)

PHILIP V
(1316–1322)

CHARLES IV
(1322–1328)

ISABELLA —— *m.* —— **EDWARD II**
(1307–1327)

EDWARD III
King of England
(1327–1377)

PHILIP VI
King of France
(1328–1350)

EDWARD
The Black Prince

JOHN OF GAUNT

JOHN II
(1350–1364)

RICHARD II
(1377–1399)

HENRY IV
(1399–1413)

CHARLES V
(1364–1380)

HENRY V
(1413–1422)

CHARLES VI
(1380–1422)

English succession

French succession

CHARLES VII
(1422–1461)

In discussing the causes of the Hundred Years' War, modern scholars emphasize economic factors or the French-English dispute over the province of Gascony. Fourteenth-century Englishmen, however, believed they were fighting because King Edward III was denied his legal right to the French crown. He was the eldest surviving male descendant of Philip the Fair.

THE HUNDRED YEARS' WAR
(CA 1337–1453)

In January 1327, Queen Isabella of England, her lover Mortimer, and a group of barons, having deposed and murdered Isabella's incompetent husband King Edward II, proclaimed his fifteen-year-old son king as Edward III. A year later Charles IV of France, the last surviving son of the French king Philip the Fair, died childless. With him ended the Capetian dynasty. An assembly of French barons, intending to exclude Isabella – who was Charles's sister and daughter of Philip the Fair – and her son Edward III from the French throne, proclaimed that "no woman nor her son could succeed to the [French] monarchy." The barons passed the crown to Philip VI of Valois (1328–1350), a nephew of Philip the Fair. In these actions lie the origins of another phase of the centuries-old struggle between the English and the French monarchies, one that was fought intermittently from 1337 to 1453.

CAUSES

Edward III of England, as the eldest surviving direct male descendant of Philip the Fair of France, believed he was entitled to the French throne. God had given him the French kingdom, he maintained, and it was his special duty to claim it. Edward was also duke of Aquitaine, in France (see Map 15.2), and in 1329 he did homage to Philip VI for the duchy. Thus Edward was a vassal of the French ruler, though their interests were diametrically opposed. Moreover, the dynastic argument had feudal implications: in order to increase their independent power, French vassals of Philip VI used the excuse that they had to transfer their loyalty to a more legitimate overlord, Edward III. This position resulted in widespread conflicts.

Economic factors involving the wool trade, the ancient dispute over Aquitaine, control of the Flemish towns – for centuries these had served as justifications for war between France and England. The causes of the conflicts known as the Hundred Years' War were dynastic, feudal, political, and economic. Recent historians have stressed the economic factors. The wool trade between England and Flanders served as the cornerstone of the economies of both countries; they were closely interdependent. Flanders was a fief of the French crown, and the Flemish aristocracy was highly sympathetic to the monarchy in Paris. But the wealth of the Flemish merchants and cloth manufacturers depended on English wool, and the Flemish burghers strongly supported the claims of Edward III. The disruption of their commerce with England threatened their prosperity.

It is impossible to measure the precise influence of the Flemings on the cause and course of the war. Certainly, Edward could not ignore their influence, because it represented money he needed to carry on the war. Although the war's impact on commerce fluctuated, over the long run it badly hurt the wool trade and the cloth industry.

Why did the struggle last so long? One historian has written in jest that if Edward III had been locked away in a castle with a pile of toy knights and archers to play with, he would have done far less damage.[5] The same might be said of Philip VI. Both rulers glorified war and saw it as the perfect arena for the realization of their chivalric ideals. Neither king possessed any sort of policy for dealing with his kingdom's social, economic, or political ills. Both sought military adventure as a means of diverting attention from domestic problems.

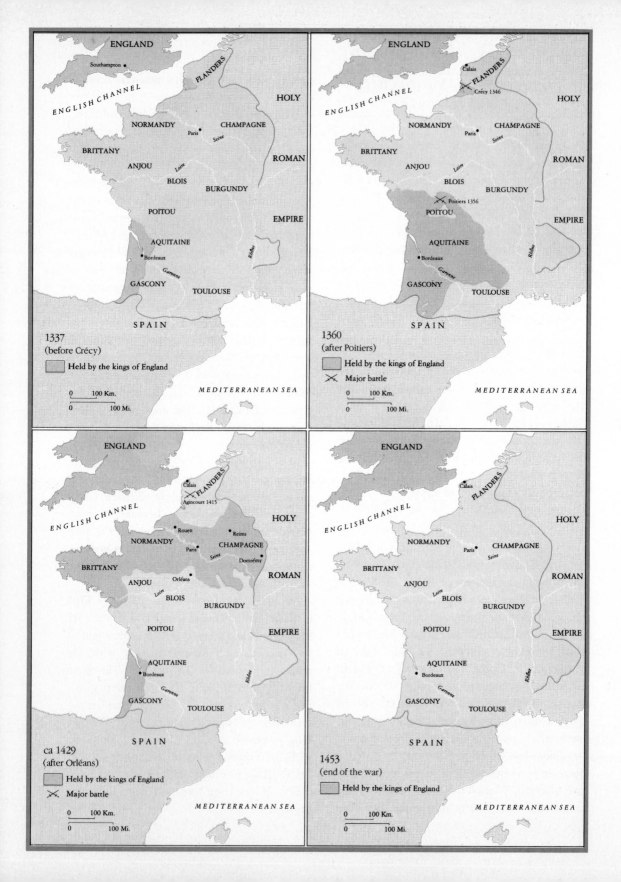

1337
(before Crécy)

▨ Held by the kings of England

0   100 Km.
0   100 Mi.

ENGLAND
Southampton
ENGLISH CHANNEL
NORMANDY
BRITTANY
ANJOU
Paris
Seine
CHAMPAGNE
FLANDERS
HOLY
ROMAN
BLOIS
BURGUNDY
Loire
POITOU
EMPIRE
AQUITAINE
Bordeaux
Garonne
Rhône
GASCONY
TOULOUSE
SPAIN
MEDITERRANEAN SEA

1360
(after Poitiers)

▨ Held by the kings of England
✕ Major battle

0   100 Km.
0   100 Mi.

ENGLAND
Calais
ENGLISH CHANNEL
Crécy 1346
FLANDERS
HOLY
ROMAN
NORMANDY
BRITTANY
ANJOU
Paris
Seine
CHAMPAGNE
BLOIS
BURGUNDY
Loire
Poitiers 1356
POITOU
EMPIRE
AQUITAINE
Bordeaux
Garonne
Rhône
GASCONY
TOULOUSE
SPAIN
MEDITERRANEAN SEA

ca 1429
(after Orléans)

▨ Held by the kings of England
✕ Major battle

0   100 Km.
0   100 Mi.

ENGLAND
ENGLISH CHANNEL
Calais
Agincourt 1415
FLANDERS
HOLY
ROMAN
Rouen
Reims
NORMANDY
Paris
Seine
Domrémy
CHAMPAGNE
BRITTANY
Orléans
ANJOU
Loire
BLOIS
BURGUNDY
POITOU
EMPIRE
AQUITAINE
Bordeaux
Garonne
Rhône
GASCONY
TOULOUSE
SPAIN
MEDITERRANEAN SEA

1453
(end of the war)

▨ Held by the kings of England

0   100 Km.
0   100 Mi.

ENGLAND
ENGLISH CHANNEL
Calais
FLANDERS
HOLY
ROMAN
NORMANDY
Paris
Seine
CHAMPAGNE
BRITTANY
ANJOU
Loire
BLOIS
BURGUNDY
POITOU
EMPIRE
AQUITAINE
Bordeaux
Garonne
Rhône
GASCONY
TOULOUSE
SPAIN
MEDITERRANEAN SEA

THE POPULAR RESPONSE

The governments of both England and France manipulated public opinion to support the war. Whatever significance modern students ascribe to the economic factor, public opinion in fourteenth-century England held that the war was waged for one reason: to secure for King Edward the French crown he had been denied.[6] Edward III issued letters to the sheriffs describing in graphic terms the evil deeds of the French and listing the royal needs. Royal letters instructed the clergy to deliver sermons filled with patriotic sentiment. Frequent assemblies of Parliament — which theoretically represented the entire nation — spread royal propaganda for the war. The royal courts sensationalized the wickedness of the other side and stressed the great fortunes to be made from the war. Philip VI sent agents to warn communities about the dangers of invasion and to stress the French Crown's revenue needs to meet the attack.

The royal campaign to rally public opinion was highly successful, at least in the early stage of the war. Edward III gained widespread support in the 1340s and 1350s. The English developed a deep hatred of the French and feared that King Philip intended "to have seized and slaughtered the entire realm of England." As England was successful in the field, pride in the country's military proficiency increased.

Most important of all, the war was popular because it presented unusual opportunities for wealth and advancement. Poor and unemployed knights were promised regular wages.

Criminals who enlisted were granted pardons. The great nobles expected to be rewarded with estates. Royal exhortations to the troops before battles repeatedly stressed that, if victorious, the men might keep whatever they seized. The French chronicler Jean Froissart wrote that at the time of Edward III's expedition of 1359, men of all ranks flocked to the king's banner. Some came to acquire honor, but many came in order "to loot and pillage the fair and plenteous land of France."[7]

THE INDIAN SUMMER OF MEDIEVAL CHIVALRY

The period of the Hundred Years' War witnessed the final flowering of the aristocratic code of medieval chivalry. Indeed, the enthusiastic participation of the nobility in both France and England was in response primarily to the opportunity the war provided to display chivalric behavior. Chivalry was a code of conduct originally devised by the clergy to improve the crude and brutal behavior of the knightly class. A knight was supposed to be brave, anxious to win praise, courteous, loyal to his commander, gracious, and generous. What better place to display these qualities than on the field of battle?

War was considered an ennobling experience; there was something elevating, manly, fine, and beautiful about it. When Shakespeare in the sixteenth century wrote of "the pomp and circumstance of glorious war," he was echoing the fourteenth- and fifteenth-century chroniclers who had glorified the trappings of war. Describing the French army before the battle of Poitiers (1356), a contemporary said, "Then you might see banners and pennons unfurled to the wind, whereon fine gold and azure shone, purple, gules and ermine. Trumpets, horns and clarions — you might hear sounding through the camp; the Dauphin's great battle made the earth ring."[8]

The chronicler Froissart repeatedly speaks of the beauty of an army assembled for battle. Writing of the French army before the battle of Bergues in 1383, Froissart reflected the attitudes of the aristocratic classes: it was "a great beauty to see the banners, pennons, and basinets glittering against the sun, and such a great multitude of men-at-arms that the eye of man could not take them in, and it seemed that they bore a veritable forest of lances." At Poitiers, it was marvelous and terrifying to hear the thundering of the horses' hooves, the cries of the wounded, the sound of the trumpets and clarions, and the shouting of war cries. The tumult was heard at a distance of more than three leagues. And it was a great grief to see and behold the flower of all the nobility and chivalry of the world go thus to destruction, to death, and to martyrdom on both sides.

This romantic and "marvelous" view of war holds little appeal for modern men and women, who are more conscious of the slaughter, brutality, dirt, and blood that war inevitably involves. Also, modern thinkers are usually conscious of the broad mass of people, while the chivalric code applied only to the aristocratic military elite. Chivalry had no reference to those outside the knightly class.

The knight was supposed to show courtesy, graciousness, and generosity to his social equals, but certainly not to his social inferiors. When English knights fought French ones, they were social equals fighting according to a mutually accepted code of behavior. The infantry troops were looked upon as inferior beings. When a peasant force at Longueil destroyed a contingent of English knights, their comrades mourned them because "it was too much that so many good fighters had been killed by mere peasants."[9]

Armies in the field were commanded by rulers themselves, by princes of the blood such as Edward III's son Edward, the Black Prince — so-called because of the color of his armor — or by great aristocrats. Knights formed the cavalry; the despised peasantry served as infantrymen, pikemen, and archers. Edward III set up recruiting boards in the counties to enlist the strongest peasants. Perhaps 10 percent of the adult population of England was involved in the actual fighting or in supplying and supporting the troops. The French contingents were even larger. By medieval standards, the force was astronomically large, especially considering the difficulty of transporting men, weapons, and horses across the English Channel. The costs of these armies stretched French and English resources to the breaking point.

The war was fought almost entirely in France and the Low Countries. It consisted mainly of a series of random sieges and cavalry raids. In 1335 the French began supporting Scottish incursions into northern England, ravaging the countryside in Aquitaine, and sacking and burning English coastal towns, such as Southampton. Naturally, such tactics lent weight to Edward III's propaganda campaign. In fact, royal propaganda on both sides fostered a kind of early nationalism.

In the early stages of the war, England was highly successful. At Crécy in northern France in 1346, English longbowmen scored a great victory over French knights and crossbowmen. Although the fire of the longbow was not very accurate, it allowed for rapid reloading, and the English archers could send off three arrows to the French crossbowmen's one. The result was a blinding shower of arrows that unhorsed the French knights and caused mass confusion. The firing of cannon —

THE BATTLE OF CRÉCY, 1346 *Pitched battles were unusual in the Hundred Years' War. At Crécy, however, the English (on the right with lions on their royal standard) scored a spectacular victory. The longbow proved a more effective weapon than the French crossbow, and the low-born English archers withstood a charge of the aristocratic French knights. (Photo: Larousse)*

probably the first use of artillery in the West — created further panic. Thereupon the English horsemen charged and butchered the French.

This was not war according to the chivalric rules that Edward III would have preferred. The English victory at Crécy rests on the skill and swiftness of the despised peasant archers, who had nothing at all to do with the chi-

valric ideals for which the war was being fought. Ten years later Edward the Black Prince, using the same tactics as at Crécy, smashed the French at Poitiers, captured the French king, and held him for ransom. Again at Agincourt near Arras in 1415, the chivalric English soldier-king Henry V (1413–1422) gained the field over vastly superior numbers. Henry followed up his triumph at Agincourt

FIFTEENTH-CENTURY ARMOR *This kind of expensive plate armor was worn by the aristocratic nobility in the fifteenth and sixteenth centuries. The use of gunpowder gradually made armor outmoded. (Courtesy, World Heritage Museum. Photo: Caroline Buckler)*

with the reconquest of Normandy. By 1419, the English had advanced to the walls of Paris (see Map 15.2).

But the French cause was not lost. Though England had won the initial victories, France won the war.

JOAN OF ARC AND FRANCE'S VICTORY

The ultimate French success rests heavily on the actions of an obscure French peasant girl, Joan of Arc, whose vision and work revived French fortunes and led to victory. A great deal of pious and popular legend surrounds Joan the Maid, because of her peculiar appearance on the scene, her astonishing success, her martyrdom, and her canonization by the Catholic church. The historical fact is that she saved the French monarchy, which was the embodiment of France.

Born in 1412 in the village of Domrémy in Champagne to well-to-do peasants, Joan of Arc grew up in a religious household. During adolescence she began to hear voices, which she later said belonged to Saint Michael, Saint Catherine, and Saint Margaret. In 1428, these voices spoke to her with great urgency, telling her that the dauphin (the uncrowned King Charles VII) had to be crowned and the English expelled from France. Joan went to the French court, persuaded the king to reject the rumor that he was illegitimate, and secured his support for her relief of the besieged city of Orléans.

The astonishing thing is not that Joan the Maid overcame serious obstacles to see the dauphin, not even that Charles and his advisers listened to her. What is amazing is the swiftness with which they were convinced. French fortunes had been so low for so long that the court believed only a miracle could save the country. Because Joan cut her hair short and dressed like a man, she scandalized the court. But hoping she would provide the necessary miracle, Charles allowed her to accompany the army that was preparing to raise the English siege of Orléans.

In the meantime Joan, herself illiterate, dictated the following letter calling upon the English to withdraw:

JHESUS MARIA

King of England, and you Duke of Bedford, calling yourself regent of France, you William Pole, Count of Suffolk John Talbot, and you Thomas Lord Scales, calling yourselves Lieutenants of the said Duke of Bedford, do right in the King of Heaven's sight. Surrender to The Maid *sent hither by God the King of Heaven, the keys of all the good towns you have taken and laid waste in France. She comes in God's name to establish the Blood Royal, ready to make peace if you agree to abandon France and repay what you have taken. And you, archers, comrades in arms, gentles and others, who are before the town of Orléans, retire in God's name to your own country. If you do not, expect to hear tidings from* The Maid *who will shortly come upon you to your very great hurt. And to you, King of England, if you do not thus, I am a chieftain of war, and whenever I meet your followers in France, I will drive them out; if they will not obey, I will put them all to death. I am sent here in God's name, the King of Heaven, to drive you body for body out of all France.*[10]

Joan apparently thought of herself as an agent of God.

Joan arrived before Orléans on April 28, 1429. Seventeen years old, she knew little of warfare and believed that if she could keep the French troops from swearing and frequenting whorehouses, victory would be theirs. On May 8, the English, weakened by disease and lack of supplies, withdrew from Orléans. Ten days later, Charles VII was crowned king at Reims. These two events marked the turning point in the war.

JOAN OF ARC   *Later considered the symbol of the French state in its struggle against the English, Joan of Arc here carries a sword in one hand and a banner with the royal symbol of fleur-de-lis in the other. Her face, which scholars believe to be a good resemblance, shows inner strength and calm determination. (Archives Nationales, Paris/Giraudon)*

In 1430 England's allies, the Burgundians, captured Joan and sold her to the English. When the English handed her over to the ecclesiastical authorities for trial, the French court did not intervene. While the English wanted Joan eliminated for obvious political reasons, sorcery (witchcraft) was the ostensible charge at her trial. Witch persecution was increasing in the fifteenth century and Joan's wearing of men's clothes appeared not only aberrant but indicative of contact with the devil. Asked why she did so, Joan replied, "It is a little thing and of small importance. I did not don it by the advice of men of this world. I donned it only by the command of God and the angels."[11]

Joan of Arc's political impact on the course of the Hundred Years' War and on the development of the kingdom of France has led scholars to examine her character and behavior very closely. Besides being an excellent athlete and a superb rider, she usually dressed like a rich and elegant young nobleman. Some students maintain that Joan's manner of dress suggests uncertainty about her own sexual identity. She did not menstruate — very rare in a healthy girl of eighteen — though she was female in every external respect: many men, including several dukes, admired her beautiful breasts. Perhaps, as Joan said, wearing men's clothes meant nothing at all. On the other hand, as some writers believe, she may have wanted to assume a completely new identity. Joan always insisted that God had specially chosen her for her mission. The richness and masculinity of her clothes, therefore, emphasized her uniqueness and made her highly conspicuous.[12] In 1431 the court condemned her as a heretic — her claim of direct inspiration from God, thereby denying the authority of church officials, constituted heresy — and burned her at the stake in the marketplace in Rouen. A fresh trial in 1456 rehabilitated her name. In 1902 she was canonized and declared a holy maiden, and today she is revered as the second patron saint of France. The nineteenth-century French historian Jules Michelet extolled Joan of Arc as a symbol of the vitality and strength of the French peasant classes.

The relief of Orléans stimulated French pride and rallied French resources. In England, as the war dragged on, loss of life mounted, and money appeared to be flowing into a bottomless pit, demands for an end increased. The clergy and the intellectuals pressed for peace. Parliamentary opposition to additional war grants stiffened. Slowly the French reconquered Normandy and, finally, ejected the English from Aquitaine. At the end of the war, in 1453, only the town of Calais remained in English hands.

COSTS AND CONSEQUENCES

For both France and England, the war proved a disaster. In France, the English had slaughtered thousands of soldiers and civilians. In the years after the sweep of the Black Death, this additional killing meant a grave loss of population. The English had laid waste to hundreds of thousands of acres of rich farmland, leaving the rural economy of many parts of France in a shambles. The war had disrupted trade and the great fairs, resulting in the drastic reduction of French participation in international commerce. Defeat in battle and heavy taxation contributed to widespread dissatisfaction and aggravated peasant grievances.

In England, only the southern coastal ports experienced much destruction; yet England fared little better than France. The costs of war were tremendous: England spent over £5 million in the war effort, a huge sum in the fourteenth and fifteenth centuries. The worst loss was in manpower. Between 10 and 15 percent of the adult male population between the ages of fifteen and forty-five fought in the army or navy. In the decades after the plague, when the country was already suffering a severe manpower shortage, war losses made a bad situation frightful. Peasants serving in France as archers and pikemen were desperately needed to till the fields. The knights who ordinarily handled the work of local government as sheriffs, coroners, jurymen, and justices of the peace were abroad, and their absence contributed to the breakdown of order at the local level. The English government attempted to finance the war effort by raising taxes on the wool crop. Because of steadily increasing costs, the Flemish and Italian buyers could not afford English wool. Consequently, wool exports slumped drastically between 1350 and 1450.

Many men of all social classes had volunteered for service in France in the hope of acquiring booty and becoming rich. The chronicler Walsingham, describing the period of Crécy, tells of the tremendous prosperity and abundance resulting from the spoils of war: "For the woman was of no account who did not possess something from the spoils of ... cities overseas in clothing, furs, quilts, and utensils ... tablecloths and jewels, bowls of murra [semiprecious stone] and silver, linen and linen cloths."[13] Walsingham is referring to 1348, in the first generation of war. As time went on, most fortunes seem to have been squandered as fast as they were made.

If English troops returned with cash, they did not invest it in land. In the fifteenth century, returning soldiers were commonly described as beggars and vagabonds, roaming about making mischief. Even the large sums of money received from the ransom of the great – such as the £250,000 paid to Edward III for the freedom of King John of France – and the monies paid as indemnities by captured towns and castles did not begin to equal the £5 million-plus spent. England suffered a serious net loss.[14]

The long war also had a profound impact on the political and cultural lives of the two countries. Most notably, it stimulated the development of the English Parliament. Edward III's constant need for money to pay for the war compelled him to summon not only the great barons and bishops but knights of the shires and burgesses from the towns as well. Between the outbreak of the war in 1337 and the king's death in 1377, parliamentary assemblies met twenty-seven times. Parliament met in thirty-seven of the fifty years of Edward's reign.

The frequency of the meetings is significant. Representative assemblies were becoming a habit, a tradition. Knights and burgesses – or the Commons, as they came to be called – recognized their mutual interests and began to meet apart from the great lords. The Commons gradually realized that they held the country's purse strings, and a parliamentary statute of 1341 required that all nonfeudal levies have parliamentary approval. When Edward III signed the law, he acknowledged that the king of England could not tax without Parliament's consent. Increasingly, during the course of the war, money grants were tied to royal redress of grievances: if the government was to raise money, it had to correct the wrongs its subjects protested.

As the Commons met in a separate chamber – the House of Commons – it also developed its own organization. The speaker came to preside over debates in the House of Commons and to represent the Commons before the House of Lords and the king. Clerks kept a record of what transpired during discussions in the Commons.

In England theoretical consent to taxation and legislation was given in one assembly for the entire country. France had no such single assembly; instead, there were many regional or provincial assemblies. Why did a national representative assembly fail to develop in France? The initiative for convening assemblies rested with the king, who needed revenue almost as much as the English ruler. But the French monarchy found the idea of representative assemblies thoroughly distasteful. The advice of a counselor to King Charles VI (1380–1422), "above all things be sure that no great assemblies of nobles or of *communes* take place in your kingdom,"[15] was accepted. Charles VII (1422–1461) even threatened to punish those proposing a national assembly.

The English Parliament was above all else a court of law, a place where justice was done and grievances remedied. No French assembly (except that of Brittany) had such competence. The national assembly in England met frequently. In France general assemblies were so rare that they never got the opportunity to develop precise procedures or to exercise judicial functions.

No one in France wanted a national assembly. Linguistic, geographic, economic, legal, and political differences were very strong. People tended to think of themselves as Breton, Norman, Burgundian, or whatever, rather than as French. Through much of the fourteenth and early fifteenth centuries, weak monarchs lacked the power to call a national assembly. Provincial assemblies, highly jealous of their independence, did not want a national assembly. The costs of sending delegates to it would be high, and the result was likely to be increased taxation. Finally, the Hundred Year's War itself hindered the growth of a representative body. Violence on dangerous roads discouraged travel. As the fifteenth-century English jurist Sir John Fortescue wrote, "Englishmen made such war in France that the three Estates dared not come together."[16]

In both countries, however, the war did promote the growth of nationalism – the feeling of unity and identity that binds together a people who speak the same language, have a common ancestry and customs, and live in the same area. In the fourteenth century, nationalism largely took the form of hostility to foreigners. Both Philip VI and Edward III drummed up support for the war by portraying the enemy as an alien, evil people. Edward III linked his personal dynastic quarrel with England's national interests. As the Parliament Roll of 1348 states:

The Knights of the shires and the others of the Commons were told that they should withdraw together and take good counsel as to how, for with-standing the malice of the said enemy and for the salvation of our said lord the King and his Kingdom of England ... the King could be aided.[17]

After victories, each country experienced a surge of pride in its military strength. Just as English patriotism ran strong after Crécy and Poitiers, so French national confidence rose after Orléans. French national feeling demanded the expulsion of the enemy not merely from Normandy and Aquitaine but from French soil. Perhaps no one expressed this national consciousness better than Joan of Arc, when she exulted that the enemy had been "driven out of *France.*"

VERNACULAR LITERATURE

Few developments expressed the emergence of national consciousness more vividly than the emergence of national literatures. Across Europe people spoke the language and dialect of their particular locality and class. In England, for example, the common people spoke regional English dialects, while the upper classes conversed in French. Official documents and works of literature were written in Latin or French. Beginning in the fourteenth century, however, national languages – the vernacular – came into use not only in verbal communication but in literature as well. Three masterpieces of European culture, Dante's *Divine Comedy* (1321), Chaucer's *Canterbury Tales* (1387-1400), and Villon's *Grand Testament* (1461) brilliantly manifest this new national pride.

Dante Aligheri (1265-1321) descended from an aristocratic family in Florence, where he held several positions in the city government. Dante called his work a comedy because

he wrote it in Italian and in a different style from the "tragic" Latin; a later generation added the adjective "divine," referring both to its sacred subject and to Dante's artistry. The *Divine Comedy* is an allegorical trilogy of one hundred cantos (verses) whose three equal parts (1+33+33+33) each describe one of the realms of the next world, Hell, Purgatory, and Paradise. Dante recounts his imaginary journey through these regions toward God. The Roman poet Virgil, representing reason, leads Dante through Hell where he observes the torments of the damned and denounces the disorders of his own time, especially ec-clesiastical ambition and corruption. Passing up into Purgatory, Virgil shows the poet how souls are purified of their disordered inclinations. In Paradise, home of the angels and saints, St. Bernard — representing mystic contemplation — leads Dante to the Virgin Mary. Through her intercession he at last attains a vision of God.

The *Divine Comedy* portrays contemporary and historical figures, comments on secular and ecclesiastical affairs, and draws on scholastic philosophy. Within the framework of a symbolic pilgrimage to the City of God, the *Divine Comedy* embodies the psychological tensions of the age. A profoundly Christian poem, it also contains bitter criticism of some church authorities. In its symmetrical structure and use of figures from the ancient world, such as Virgil, the poem perpetuates the classical tradition, but as the first major work of literature in the Italian vernacular it is distinctly modern.

Geoffrey Chaucer (1340–1400), the son of a London wine merchant, was an official in the administrations of the English kings Edward III and Richard II who wrote poetry as an avocation. Chaucer's *Canterbury Tales* is a collection of stories in a lengthy rhymed narrative. On a pilgrimage to the shrine of St. Thomas Becket at Canterbury (see page 468), thirty people of various social backgrounds each tell a tale. The Prologue sets the scene and describes the pilgrims, whose characters are further revealed in the story each person tells. For example, the gentle Christian Knight relates a chivalric romance; the gross Miller tells a vulgar story about a deceived husband; the earthy Wife of Bath, who earns her living as a weaver and has buried five husbands, sketches a fable about the selection of a spouse; and the elegant Prioress, who violates her vows by wearing jewelry, delivers a homily on the Virgin. In depicting the interests and behavior of all types of people, Chaucer presents a rich panorama of English social life in the fourteenth century. Like the *Divine Comedy,* the *Canterbury Tales* reflects the cultural tensions of the times. Ostensibly Christian, many of the pilgrims are also materialistic, sensual, and worldly, suggesting the ambivalence of the broader society's concern for the next world and frank enjoyment of this one.

Our knowledge of François Villon (1413–1463), probably the greatest poet of late medieval France, derives from Paris police records and his own poetry. Born to desper-ately poor parents in the year of Joan of Arc's execution, Villon was sent by his guardian to the University of Paris where he earned the Master of Arts degree. A rowdy and free-spirited student, he disliked the stuffiness of academic life. In 1455 Villon killed a man in a street brawl; banished from Paris, he joined one of the bands of wandering thieves that harassed the countryside after the Hundred Years' War. For his fellow bandits he composed ballads in thieves' jargon.

Villon's *Lais* (1456), a pun on the word *legs* (meaning "legacy"), is a series of farcical bequests to his friends and enemies. *Ballade des Pendus* (Ballad of the Hanged) was written while contemplating that fate in prison. (His execution was commuted.) Villon's greatest and most self-revealing work, the *Grand Testament,* contains another string of bequests, including a legacy to a prostitute, and describes his unshakeable faith in the beauty of life here on earth. The *Grand Testament* possesses elements of social rebellion, bawdy humor, and rare emotional depth. While the themes of Dante's and Chaucer's poetry are distinctly medieval, Villon's celebration of the human condition here on earth brands him as definitely modern. While he used medieval forms of versification, Villon's language was the despised vernacular of the poor and the criminal.

THE DECLINE OF THE CHURCH'S PRESTIGE

In times of crisis or disaster, people of all faiths have sought the consolation of religion. In the fourteenth century, however, the official Christian church offered very little solace. In fact, the leaders of the church added to the sorrow and misery of the times.

THE BABYLONIAN CAPTIVITY

From 1309 to 1372, the popes lived in the city of Avignon in southeastern France. In order to control the church and its policies, Philip the Fair of France pressured Pope Clement V to settle in Avignon (page 489). Clement, critically ill with cancer, lacked the will to resist Philip. This period in church history is often called the Babylonian Captivity (referring to the seventy years the ancient Hebrews were held captive in Mesopotamian Babylon).

The Babylonian Captivity badly damaged papal prestige. The Avignon papacy reformed its financial administration and centralized its government. But the seven popes at Avignon concentrated on bureaucratic matters to the exclusion of spiritual objectives. Although some of the popes led austere lives at Avignon, the general atmosphere was one of luxury, splendor, and extravagance. The leadership of the church was cut off from its historic roots and the source of its ancient authority, the city of Rome. In the absence of the papacy, the Papal States in Italy lacked stability and good government. The economy of Rome had long been based on the presence of the papal court and the rich tourist trade the papacy attracted. The Babylonian Captivity left Rome poverty-stricken. As long as the French crown dominated papal policy, papal influence in England (with whom France was intermittently at war) and in Germany declined.

Many devout Christians urged the popes to return to Rome. The Dominican mystic Catherine of Siena, for example, made a special trip to Avignon to plead with the pope to return. In 1377, Pope Gregory XI brought the papal court back to Rome. Unfortunately, he died shortly after the return. At Gregory's death, Roman citizens demanded an Italian pope who would remain in Rome. Deter-

mined to influence the papal conclave (the assembly of cardinals who choose the new pope) to elect an Italian, a Roman mob surrounded St. Peter's Basilica, blocked the roads leading out of the city, and seized all boats on the Tiber River. Between the time of Gregory's death and the opening of the conclave, great pressure was put on the cardinals to elect an Italian. At the time, none of them protested this pressure.

Sixteen cardinals — eleven Frenchmen, four Italians, and one Spaniard — entered the conclave on April 7, 1378. After two ballots they unanimously chose a distinguished administrator, the archbishop of Bari, Bartolomeo Prignano, who took the name Urban VI. Each of the cardinals swore that Urban had been elected "sincerely, freely, genuinely, and canonically."

Urban VI (1378–1389) had excellent intentions for church reform: he wanted to abolish simony, pluralism (holding several church offices at the same time), absenteeism, clerical extravagance, and ostentation. These were the very abuses being increasingly criticized by Christian peoples across Europe. Unfortunately, Pope Urban went about the work of reform in a tactless, arrogant, and bullheaded manner. The day after his coronation he delivered a blistering attack on cardinals who lived in Rome while drawing their income from benefices elsewhere. His criticism was well-founded but ill-timed, and provoked opposition among the hierarchy before Urban had consolidated his authority.

In the weeks that followed Urban stepped up attacks on clerical luxury, denouncing individual cardinals by name. He threatened to strike the cardinal archbishop of Amiens. Urban even threatened to excommunicate certain cardinals, and when he was advised that such excommunications would not be lawful unless the guilty had been warned three times, he shouted, "I can do anything, if it be my will and judgment."[18] Urban's quick temper and irrational behavior have led scholars to question his sanity. Whether he was medically insane or just drunk with power is a moot point. In any case, Urban's actions brought on disaster.

In groups of two and three, the cardinals slipped away from Rome and met at Anagni. They declared Urban's election invalid because it had come about under threats from the Roman mob, and they asserted that Urban himself was excommunicated. The cardinals then proceeded to the city of Fondi between Rome and Naples and elected Cardinal Robert of Geneva, the brother of King Charles V of France, as pope. Cardinal Robert took the name Clement VII. There were thus two popes – Urban at Rome and the anti-pope Clement VII (1378–1394), who set himself up at Avignon in opposition to the legally elected Urban. So began the Great Schism, which divided Western Christendom until 1417.

THE GREAT SCHISM

The powers of Europe aligned themselves with Urban or Clement along strictly political lines. France naturally recognized the French anti-pope, Clement. England, France's historic enemy, recognized Pope Urban. Scotland, whose attacks on England were subsidized by France, followed the French and supported Clement. Aragon, Castile, and Portugal hesitated before deciding for Clement at Avignon. The German emperor, who enjoyed the title of king of the Romans and bore ancient hostility to France, recognized Urban VI. At first the Italian city-states recognized Urban; when he alienated them, they opted for Clement.

John of Spoleto, a professor at the law school at Bologna, eloquently summed up intellectual opinion of the schism:

The longer this schism lasts, the more it appears to be costing, and the more harm it does: scandal, massacres, ruination, agitations, troubles and disturbances . . . this dissention is the root of everything: divers tumults, quarrels between kings, seditions, extortions, assassinations, acts of violence, wars, rising tyranny, decreasing freedom, the impunity of villains, grudges, error, disgrace, the madness of steel and of fire given license.[19]

The scandal of competing popes "rent the seamless garment of Christ," as the church was called, and provoked horror and vigorous cries for reform. The common people, wracked by inflation, wars, and plague, were thoroughly confused about which pope was legitimate. The schism weakened the religious faith of many Christians and gave rise to instability and religious excesses. It brought the leadership of the church into serious disrepute. At a time when ordinary Christians needed the consolation of religion and confidence in their religious leaders, church officials were fighting among themselves for power.

THE CONCILIAR MOVEMENT

Calls for reform of the church were not new. A half-century before the Great Schism, in 1324, Marsiglio of Padua, then rector of the University of Paris, had published *Defensor Pacis* (*The Defender of the Peace*). Dealing as it did with the authority of the state and the church, *Defensor Pacis* proved to be one of the most controversial works written in the Middle Ages.

Marsiglio argued that the state was the great unifying power in society and that the church was subordinate to the state. He put forth the revolutionary ideas that the church had no inherent jurisdiction and should own no property. Authority in the Christian church, according to Marsiglio, should rest in a general council, made up of laymen as well as priests and superior to the pope. These ideas directly contradicted the medieval notion of a society governed by the church and the state, with the church ultimately supreme.

Defensor Pacis was condemned by the pope and Marsiglio was excommunicated. But the idea that a general council representing all of the church had a higher authority than the pope was repeated by John Gerson (1363-1429), a later chancellor of the University of Paris and influential theologian.

Even more earthshaking than the theories of Marsiglio of Padua were the ideas of the English scholar and theologian John Wyclif (1329-1384). Wyclif wrote that papal claims of temporal power had no foundation in the Scriptures, and that the Scriptures alone should be the standard of Christian belief and practice. He urged the abolition of such practices as the veneration of saints, pilgrimages, pluralism, and absenteeism. Every sincere Christian, according to Wyclif, should read the Bible for himself. Wyclif's views had broad social and economic significance. He urged that the church be stripped of its property. His idea that every Christian free of mortal sin possessed lordship was seized upon by peasants in England during a revolt in 1381 and used to justify their goals.

In advancing these views, Wyclif struck at the roots of medieval church structure and religious practices. Consequently, he has been hailed as the precursor of the Reformation of the sixteenth century. Although Wyclif's ideas were vigorously condemned by ecclesiastical authorities, they were widely disseminated by humble clerics and enjoyed great popularity in the early fifteenth century. Wyclif's followers were called Lollards. The term, meaning mumblers of prayers and psalms, refers to what they criticized. After the Czech king Wenceslaus's sister Anne married Richard II of England, members of Queen Anne's household carried Lollard principles back to Bohemia, where they were spread by John Hus, rector of the University of Prague.

While John Wyclif's ideas were being spread, two German scholars at the University of Paris, Henry of Langenstein and Conrad of Gelnhausen, produced treatises urging the summoning of a general council. Conrad wrote that the church, as the congregation of all the faithful, was superior to the pope. Although canon law held that only a pope might call a council, a higher law existed, the common good. The common good of Christendom required the convocation of a council.

In response to continued Europe-wide calls for a council, the two colleges of cardinals — one at Rome, the other at Avignon — summoned a council at Pisa in Italy in 1409. A distinguished gathering of prelates and theologians deposed both popes and selected another. Neither the Avignon pope nor the Roman pope would resign, however, and the appalling result was a threefold schism.

Finally, due to the pressure of the German emperor Sigismund, a great council met at Constance in Switzerland (1414-1418). It had three objectives: to end the schism, to reform the church "in head and members" (from top to bottom), and to wipe out heresy. The council condemned the Lollard ideas of John Hus, and he was burned at the stake. The council eventually deposed both the Roman pope and the successor of the pope chosen at Pisa, and it isolated the Avignonese anti-pope. A conclave elected a new leader, the Roman Cardinal Colonna, who took the name Martin V (1417-1431).

Martin proceeded to dissolve the council. Nothing was done about reform. The schism was over, and the conciliar movement in effect ended. For a time thereafter, the papacy concentrated on Italian problems to the exclusion of universal Christian interests. But the schism and the conciliar movement had exposed the crying need for ecclesiastical reform, thus laying the foundations for the great reform efforts of the sixteenth century.

THE LIFE OF THE PEOPLE

In the fourteenth century, economic and political difficulties, disease, and war profoundly affected the lives of European peoples. Decades of slaughter and destruction, punctuated by the decimating visits of the Black Death, made a grave economic situation virtually disastrous. In many parts of France and the Low Countries fields lay in ruin or untilled for lack of manpower. In England, as taxes increased, criticism of government policy and mismanagement multiplied. Crime, always a factor in social history, aggravated economic troubles, and throughout Europe the frustrations of the common people erupted into widespread revolts. For most people, marriage and the local parish church continued to be the center of their lives.

FUR-COLLAR CRIME

The Hundred Years' War had provided employment and opportunity for thousands of idle and fortune-seeking knights. But during periods of truce and after the war finally ended, many nobles once again had little to do. Inflation also hurt them. Although many were living on fixed incomes, their chivalric code demanded lavish generosity and an aristocratic lifestyle. Many nobles turned to crime as a way of raising money. The fourteenth and fifteenth centuries witnessed a great deal of "fur-collar crime," so-called for the miniver fur the nobility alone were allowed to wear on their collars. England provides a good case study of upper-class crime.

Fur-collar crime rarely involved such felonies as homicide, robbery, rape, and arson. Instead, nobles used their superior social status to rob and extort from the weak and then to corrupt the judicial process. Groups of noble brigands roamed the English countryside stealing from both rich and poor. Sir John de Colseby and Sir William Bussy led a gang of thirty-eight knights who stole goods worth £3,000 in various robberies. Operating exactly like modern urban racketeers, knightly gangs demanded that peasants pay "protection money" or else have their hovels burned and their fields destroyed. Members of the household of a certain Lord Robert of Payn beat up a victim and then demanded money for protection from future attack.

Attacks on the rich often took the form of kidnaping and extortion. Individuals were grabbed in their homes, and wealthy travelers were seized on the highways and held for ransom. In northern England a gang of gentry led by Sir Gilbert de Middleton abducted Sir Henry Beaumont and his brother, the bishop-elect of Durham, and two Roman cardinals in England on a peacemaking visit. Only after a ransom was paid were the victims released.[20]

Fur-collar criminals were terrorists, but like some twentieth-century white-collar criminals who commit nonviolent crimes, medieval aristocratic criminals got away with their outrages. When accused of wrongdoing, fur-collar criminals intimidated witnesses. They threatened jurors. They used "pull" or influence or cash to bribe judges. As a fourteenth-century English judge wrote to a young nobleman, "For the love of your father I have hindered charges being brought against you and have prevented execution of indictment actually made."[21]

The ballads of Robin Hood, a collection of folk legends from late medieval England, describe the adventures of the outlaw hero and his band of followers, who lived in Sherwood Forest and attacked and punished those who violated the social system and the law. Most of the villains in these simple tales are fur-collar criminals – grasping landlords, wicked sheriffs such as the famous sheriff of Nottingham, and mercenary churchmen. Robin and his merry men performed a sort of retributive justice. Robin Hood was a popular figure, because he symbolized the deep resentment of aristocratic corruption and abuse; he represented the struggle against tyranny and oppression.

Criminal activity by nobles continued decade after decade because governments were not strong enough to stop it. Then, too, much of the crime was directed against a lord's own serfs, and the line between a noble's legal jurisdiction over his peasants and criminal behavior was a very fine one indeed. Persecution by lords, coming on top of war, disease, and natural disasters, eventually drove long-suffering peasants all across Europe to revolt.

PEASANT REVOLTS

Peasant revolts occurred often in the Middle Ages. Early in the thirteenth century, the French preacher Jacques de Vitry asked rhetorically, "How many serfs have killed their lords or burnt their castles?"[22] Social and economic conditions in the fourteenth and fifteenth centuries caused a great increase in peasant uprisings.

In 1358, when French taxation for the Hundred Years' War fell heavily on the poor, the frustrations of the French peasantry exploded in a massive uprising called the *Jacquerie,* after the nickname of a supposedly happy agricultural laborer, Jacques Bonhomme (Good Fellow). Peasants in Picardy and Champagne went on the rampage.

Crowds swept through the countryside slashing the throats of nobles, burning their castles, raping their wives and daughters, killing or maiming their horses and cattle. Peasants blamed the nobility for oppressive taxes, for the criminal brigandage of the countryside, for defeat in war, and for the general misery. Artisans, small merchants, and parish priests joined the peasants. Urban and rural groups committed terrible destruction, and for several weeks the nobles were on the defensive. Then the upper class united to repress the revolt with savage and merciless ferocity. Thousands of the "Jacques," innocent as well as guilty, were cut down.

This forcible supppression of social rebellion, without some effort to alleviate its underlying causes, could only serve as a stopgap measure and drive protest underground. Between 1363 and 1484, serious peasant revolts swept the Auvergne; in 1380, uprisings occurred in the Midi; and in 1420, they erupted in the Lyonnais region of France.

The Peasants' Revolt in England in 1381, involving perhaps a hundred thousand people, was probably the largest single uprising of the entire Middle Ages. The causes were complex and varied from place to place. In general, though, the thirteenth century had witnessed the steady commutation of labor services for cash rents, and the Black Death had drastically cut the labor supply. As a result, peasants demanded higher wages and fewer manorial obligations. The parliamentary Statute of Laborers of 1351 (see page 499) declared:

Whereas to curb the malice of servants who after the pestilence were idle and unwilling to serve without securing excessive wages, it was recently ordained . . . that such servants, both men and women, shall be bound to serve in return for salaries and wages that were customary . . . five or six years earlier.[23]

THE JACQUERIE *Because social revolt on the part of war-weary, frustrated poor seemed to threaten the natural order of Christian society, the upper classes everywhere exacted terrible vengeance on peasants and* artisans. *In this scene some* jacques *are cut down, some beheaded, and others drowned. (Bibliothèque Nationale, Paris)*

This statute was an attempt by landlords to freeze wages and social mobility.

The statute could not be enforced. As a matter of fact, the condition of the English peasantry steadily improved in the course of the fourteenth century. Some scholars believe that the peasantry in most places was better off in the period 1350–1450 than it had been for centuries before or was to be for four centuries after.

Why then was the outburst in 1381 so serious? It was provoked by a crisis of rising expectations. The relative prosperity of the la-boring classes led to demands that the upper classes were unwilling to grant. Unable to climb higher, the peasants' frustration found release in revolt. Economic grievances combined with other factors. Decades of aristocratic violence, much of it perpetrated against the weak peasantry, had bred hostility and bitterness. In France frustration over the lack of permanent victory increased. In England the social and religious agitation of the popular preacher John Ball fanned the embers of discontent. Such sayings as Ball's famous couplet

When Adam delved and Eve span
Who was then the gentleman?

reflect real revolutionary sentiment. But the lords of England believed that God had permanently fixed the hierarchical order of society and that nothing man could do would change that order. Moreover, the south of England, where the revolt broke out, had been subjected to frequent and destructive French raids. The English government did little to protect the south, and villages grew increasingly scared and insecure. Fear erupted into violence.

The straw that broke the camel's back in England was a head tax on all adult males. Although it met widespread opposition in 1380, the royal council ordered the sheriffs to collect it again in 1381 on penalty of a huge fine. Beginning with assaults on the tax collectors, the uprising in England followed much the same course as had the Jacquerie in France. Castles and manors were sacked; manorial records were destroyed. Many nobles, including the archbishop of Canterbury, who had ordered the collection of the tax, were murdered.

Although the center of the revolt was the highly populated and economically advanced south and east, sections of the north and the Midlands also witnessed rebellions. Violence took different forms in different places. The townspeople of Cambridge expressed their hostility to the university by sacking one of the colleges and building a bonfire of academic property. In towns containing skilled Flemish craftsmen, fear of competition led to their attack and murder. Urban discontent merged with rural violence. Apprentices and journeymen, frustrated because the highest positions in the guilds were closed to them, rioted.

The boy-king Richard II (1377-1399) met the leaders of the revolt, agreed to charters insuring peasants' freedom, tricked them with false promises, and then proceeded to crush the uprising with terrible ferocity. Although the nobility tried to restore ancient duties of serfdom, virtually a century of freedom had elapsed, and the commutation of manorial services continued. Rural serfdom had disappeared in England by 1550.

Conditions in England and France were not unique. In Florence in 1378, the *ciompi,* the poorest workmen, revolted. Serious social trouble occurred in Lübeck, Brunswick, and other cities of the Holy Roman Empire. In Spain in 1391, aristocratic attempts to impose new forms of serfdom combined with demands for tax relief led to massive working-class and peasant uprisings in Seville and Barcelona. These took the form of vicious attacks on Jewish communities. Rebellions and uprisings everywhere reveal deep peasant and working-class frustration and the general socioeconomic crisis of the times.

MARRIAGE

Marriage and the family provided such peace and satisfaction as most people attained. In fact, life for those who were not clerics or nuns meant marriage. Apart from sexual and emotional urgency, the community expected people to marry. For a girl, childhood was a preparation for marriage. In addition to the thousands of chores involved in running a household, girls learned obedience, or at least subordination. Adulthood meant living as a wife or widow. However, sweeping statements about marriage in the Middle Ages have limited validity. Most peasants were illiterate and left slight record of their feelings toward their spouses or about marriage as an institution. The gentry, however, often could write, and the letters exchanged between

Margaret and John Paston, upper-middle-class people who lived in Norfolk, England, in the fifteenth century, provide important evidence of the experience of one couple.

John and Margaret Paston were married about 1439, after an arrangement concluded entirely by their parents. John spent most of his time in London fighting through the law courts to increase his family properties and business interests; Margaret remained in Norfolk to supervise the family lands. Her enormous responsibilities involved managing the Paston estates, hiring workers, collecting rents, ordering supplies for the large household, hearing complaints and settling disputes among tenants, and marketing her crops. In these duties she proved herself a remarkably shrewd businessperson. Moreover, when an army of over a thousand men led by the aristocratic thug Lord Moleyns attacked her house, she successfully withstood the siege. When the Black Death entered her area, Margaret moved her family to safety.

Margaret Paston did all this on top of raising eight children (there were probably other children who did not survive childhood). Her husband died before she was forty-three, and she later conducted the negotiations for the children's marriages. Her children's futures, like her estate management, were planned with an eye toward economic and social advancement. When one daughter secretly married the estate bailiff, an alliance considered beneath her, the girl was cut off from the family as if she were dead.[24]

The many letters surviving between Margaret and John reveal slight tenderness toward their children. They seem to have reserved their love for each other, and during many of his frequent absences they wrote to express mutual affection and devotion. How typical the Paston relationship was, modern historians cannot say, but the marriage of John and Margaret, although completely arranged by their parents, was based on respect, responsibility, and love.[25]

In the later Middle Ages, as earlier – indeed, until the late nineteenth century – economic factors, rather than romantic love or physical attraction, determined whom and when a person married. The young agricultural laborer on the manor had to wait until he had sufficient land. Thus most men had to wait until their fathers died or yielded the holding. The age of marriage was late, which in turn affected the number of children a couple had. The journeyman craftsman in the urban guild faced the same material difficulties. Prudent young men selected (or their parents selected for them) girls who would bring the most land or money to the union. Once a couple married, the union ended only with the death of one partner.

Divorce – the complete dissolution of the contract between a woman and man lawfully married – did not exist in the Middle Ages. The church held that a marriage validly entered into could not be dissolved. A valid marriage consisted of the oral consent or promise of the two parties made to each other. Church theologians of the day urged that the marriage be publicized by banns, or announcements made in the parish church, and that the couple's union be celebrated and witnessed in a church ceremony and blessed by a priest.

A great number of couples did not observe the church's regulations. Some treated marriage as a private act – they made the promise and spoke the words of marriage to each other without witnesses and then proceeded to enjoy the sexual pleasures of marriage. This practice led to a great number of disputes, because one or the other of the two parties could later deny having made a marriage agreement. The records of the ecclesiastical courts reveal many cases arising from privately made contracts. Here is a typical case heard by the ecclesiastical court at York in England in 1372:

[The witness says that] one year ago on the feast day of the apostles Philip and James just past, he was present in the house of William Burton, tanner of York. . . . when and where John Beke, saddler . . . called the said Marjory to him and said to her, "Sit with me." Acquiescing in this, she sat down. John said to her, "Marjory, do you wish to be my wife?" And she replied, "I will if you wish." And taking at once the said Marjory's right hand, John said, "Marjory, here I take you as my wife, for better or worse, to have and to hold until the end of my life; and of this I give you my faith." The said Marjory replied to him, "Here I take you John as my husband, to have and to hold until the end of my life, and of this I give you my faith." And then the said John kissed the said Marjory. . . .[26]

This was a private arrangement, made in secret and without the presence of the clergy. Evidence survives of marriages contracted in a garden, in a blacksmith's shop, at a tavern, and, predictably, in a bed. Church courts heard a great number of similar cases. The records of those courts that relate to marriage reveal that rather than suits for divorce, the great majority of petitions asked the court to enforce the marriage contract that one of the parties believed she or he had validly made. Annulments were granted in extraordinary circumstances, such as male impotence, on the grounds that a lawful marriage had never existed.

LIFE IN THE PARISH

In the later Middle Ages, the land and the parish remained the focus of life for the European peasantry. Work on the land continued to be performed collectively. All men, for example, cooperated in the annual tasks of planting and harvesting. The close association

of the cycle of agriculture and the liturgy of the Christian calendar endured. The parish priest blessed the fields before the annual planting, offering prayers on behalf of the people for a good crop. If the harvest was a rich one, the priest led the processions and celebrations of thanksgiving.

How did the common people feel about their work? Since the vast majority were illiterate and inarticulate, it is difficult to say. It is known that the peasants hated the ancient services and obligations on the lords' lands and tried to get them commuted for money rents. When lords attempted to reimpose service duties, the peasants revolted.

In the thirteenth century, the craft guilds provided the small minority of men living in towns and cities with the psychological satisfaction of involvement in the manufacture of a superior product. The guild member also had economic security. The craft guilds set high standards for their merchandise. The guilds looked after the sick, the poor, the widowed, and the orphaned. Masters and journeymen worked side by side.

In the fourteenth century, those ideal conditions began to change. The fundamental objective of the craft guild was to maintain a monopoly on its product, and to do so recruitment and promotion were carefully restricted. Some guilds required a high entrance fee for apprentices; others admitted only the sons or relatives of members. Apprenticeship increasingly lasted a long time, seven years. Even after a young man had satisfied all the tests for full membership in the guild and had attained the rank of master, other hurdles had to be crossed, such as finding the funds to open his own business or special connections just to get in a guild. Restrictions limited the number of apprentices and journeymen to the anticipated openings for masters. The larger a particular business was, the greater was the likelihood that the master did not know his

MASKED MUMMERS *People of all ages and classes enjoyed mummers' shows, which were performed by groups of masked actors who burlesqued some well-known event or person. Sometimes mummers accom-* *panied their shows with primitive musical instruments, such as drums or tambourines. (Bibliothèque Nationale, Paris)*

employees. The separation of master and journeyman and the decreasing number of openings for master craftsmen created serious frustrations. Strikes and riots occurred in the Flemish towns, in France, and in England.

The recreation of all classes reflected the fact that late medieval society was organized for war and that violence was common. The aristocracy engaged in tournaments or jousts; archery and wrestling had great popularity among ordinary people. Everyone enjoyed the cruel sports of bullbaiting and bearbaiting. As the great French scholar Marc Bloch wrote, "Violence was an element in manners. Medieval men had little control over their immediate impulses; they were emotionally insensitive to the spectacle of pain, and they had small regard for human life . . ."[27] Thus, the

hangings and mutilations of criminals were exciting and well-attended events, with all the festivity of a university town before a Saturday football game. Chronicles exulted in describing executions, murders, and massacres. Here a monk gleefully describes the gory execution of William Wallace in 1305:

Wilielmus Waleis, a robber given to sacrilege, arson and homicide . . . was condemned to most cruel but justly deserved death. He was drawn through the streets of London at the tails of horses, until he reached a gallows of unusual height, there he was suspended by a halter; but taken down while yet alive, he was mutilated, his bowels torn out and burned in a fire, his head then cut off, his body divided into four, and his quarters transmitted to four principal parts of Scotland.

Behold the end of the merciless man, who himself perished without mercy.[28]

Violence was as English as roast beef and plum pudding, as French as bread, cheese, and *potage.*

Alcohol, primarily beer or ale, provided solace to the poor, and the frequency of drunkenness reflects their terrible frustrations.

In the fourteenth and fifteenth centuries, the laity began to exercise increasing influence and control over the affairs of the parish. Churchmen were criticized. The constant quarrels of the mendicant orders (the Franciscans and Dominicans), the mercenary and grasping attitude of the parish clergy, the scandal of the Great Schism and a divided Christendom — all these did much to weaken the spiritual mystique of the clergy in the popular mind. The laity steadily took responsibility for the management of parish lands. Laymen and laywomen organized associations to vote on and purchase furnishings for the church. And ordinary lay people secured jurisdiction over the structure of the church building, its vestments, books, and furnishings. These new responsibilities of the laity reflect the increased dignity of the parishioners in the late Middle Ages.[29]

Late medieval preachers likened the crises of their times to the Four Horsemen of the Apocalypse in the Book of Revelation, who brought famine, war, disease, and death. The crises of the fourteenth and fifteenth centuries were acids that burned deeply into the fabric of traditional medieval European society. Bad weather brought poor harvests, which contributed to the international economic depression. Disease, over which people also had little control, fostered widespread psychological depression and dissatisfaction. Population losses caused by the Black Death and the Hundred Years' War encouraged the working classes to try to profit from the labor shortage by selling their services higher: they wanted to move up the economic ladder. The socialistic ideas of thinkers like John Wyclif, John Hus, and John Ball fanned the flames of social discontent. When peasant frustrations exploded in uprisings, the frightened nobility and upper middle class crushed the revolts and condemned heretical preachers as agitators of social rebellion. But the war had heightened social consciousness among the poor.

The Hundred Years' War served as a catalyst for the development of representative government in England. The royal policy of financing the war through Parliament-approved taxation gave the middle classes an increased sense of their economic power. They would pay taxes in return for some influence in shaping royal policies.

In France, on the other hand, the war stiffened opposition to national assemblies. The disasters that wracked France decade after decade led the French people to believe that the best solutions to complicated problems lay not in an assembly but in the hands of a strong monarch. France became the model for continental countries in the evolution toward royal absolutism.

The war also stimulated technological experimentation, especially with artillery. After about 1350, the cannon, although highly inaccurate, was commonly used all over Europe.

Religion remained the cement that held society together. European culture was a Christian culture. But the Great Schism weakened the prestige of the church and people's faith in papal authority. The conciliar movement, by denying the church's universal sovereignty, strengthened the claims of secular governments to jurisdiction over all their peoples. The later Middle Ages witnessed a steady shift of basic loyalty from the Christian church to the emerging national states.

ALBRECHT DÜRER: THE FOUR HORSEMEN OF
THE APOCALYPSE   From right to left, representa-
tives of war, strife, famine, and death gallop across
Christian society leaving thousands dead or in misery.
The horrors of the age made this subject extremely
popular in art, literature, and sermons. (Courtesy,
Museum of Fine Arts, Boston)

NOTES

1. W. H. McNeill, *Plagues and Peoples,* Doubleday, New York, 1976, pp. 151–168.

2. Quoted by P. Ziegler, *The Black Death,* Pelican Books, Harmondsworth, England, 1969, p. 20.

3. J. M. Rigg, trans., *The Decameron of Giovanni Boccaccio,* J. M. Dent & Sons, London, 1903, p. 6.

4. Ziegler, pp. 232–239.

5. N. F. Cantor, *The English: A History of Politics and Society to 1760,* Simon & Schuster, New York, 1967, p. 260.

6. J. Barnie, *War in Medieval English Society: Social*
Values and the Hundred Years' War, Cornell University Press, Ithaca, N.Y., 1974, p. 6.

7. Quoted by Barnie, p. 34.

8. Ibid., p. 73.

9. Ibid., pp. 72–73.

10. W. P. Barrett, trans., *The Trial of Jeanne d'Arc,* George Routledge, London, 1931, pp. 165–166.

11. Quoted by Edward A. Lucie-Smith, *Joan of Arc,* W. W. Norton, New York, 1977, p. 32.

12. Ibid., pp. 32–35.

13. Quoted by Barnie, pp. 36–37.

14. M. M. Postan, "The Costs of the Hundred Years' War," *Past and Present* 27 (April 1964):34–53.

15. Quoted by P. S. Lewis, "The Failure of the Medieval French Estates," *Past and Present* 23 (November 1962):6.

16. Ibid., p. 10.

17. C. Stephenson and G. F. Marcham, eds., *Sources of English Constitutional History,* rev. ed., Harper & Row, New York, 1972, p. 217.

18. Quoted by J. H. Smith, *The Great Schism 1378: The Disintegration of the Papacy,* Weybright & Talley, New York, 1970, p. 141.

19. Ibid., p. 15.

20. B. A. Hanawalt, "Fur Collar Crime: The Pattern of Crime Among the Fourteenth-Century English Nobility," *Journal of Social History* 8 (Spring 1975):1–14.

21. Ibid., p. 7.

22. Quoted by M. Bloch, *French Rural History,* trans. Janet Sondheimer, University of California Press, Berkeley, 1966, p. 169.

23. Stephenson and Marcham, p. 225.

24. A. S. Haskell, "The Paston Women on Marriage in Fifteenth Century England," *Viator* 4 (1973):459–469.

25. Ibid., p. 471.

26. Quoted by R. H. Helmholz, *Marriage Litigation in Medieval England,* Cambridge University Press, Cambridge, 1974, pp. 28–29.

27. M. Bloch, *Feudal Society,* trans. L. A. Manyon, Routledge & Kegan Paul, London, 1961, p. 411.

28. A. F. Scott, ed., *Everyone a Witness: The Plantagenet Age,* Thomas Y. Crowell, New York, 1976, p. 263.

29. See E. Mason, "The Role of the English Parishioner, 1000–1500," *Journal of Ecclesiastical History* 27:1 (January 1976):17–29.

SUGGESTED READING

Students who wish further elaboration of the topics covered in this chapter should consult the following studies, on which the chapter leans extensively. For the Black Death and health generally, see W. H. McNeill, *Plagues and Peoples* (1976), a fresh, challenging, and comprehensive study; F. F. Cartwright, *Disease and History* (1972), which contains an interesting section on the Black Death; P. Ziegler, *The Black Death* (1969), a fascinating and highly readable book; and H. E. Sigerist, *Civilization and Disease* (1970), which presents a worthwhile treatment of the many social implications of disease.

The standard study of the long military conflicts of the fourteenth and fifteenth centuries remains that of E. Perroy, *The Hundred Years' War* (1959). J. Henneman, *Royal Taxation in Fourteenth Century France: The Development of War Financing, 1322–1356* (1971), is an important technical work by a distinguished historian. J. Barnie's *War in Medieval English Society: Social Values and the Hundred Years' War* (1974), treats the attitude of patriots, intellectuals, and the general public. Desmond Seward, *The Hundred Years' War: The English in France, 1337–1453* (1981), tells an exciting story, and John Keegan, *The Face of Battle* (1977), Chapter 2, "Agincourt," describes what war meant to the ordinary soldier. Barbara Tuchman, *A Distant Mirror: The Calamitous 14th Century* (1980), gives a vivid picture of many facets of fourteenth-century life, while concentrating on the war. The best treatment of the financial costs of the war is probably M. M. Postan, "The Costs of the Hundred Years' War," *Past and Present* 27 (April 1964):34–53. E. Searle and R. Burghart, "The Defense of England and the Peasants' Revolt," *Viator* 3 (1972), is a fascinating study of the peasants' changing social attitudes.

For political and social conditions in the fourteenth and fifteenth centuries, the following studies are all useful: P. S. Lewis, *Later Medieval France: The Polity* (1968), and "The Failure of the French Medieval Estates," *Past and Present* 23 (November 1962); L. Romier, *A History of France* (1962); G. O. Sayles, *The King's Parliament of England* (1974); M. Bloch, *French Rural History* (1966); I. Kershaw, "The Great Famine and Agrarian Crisis in England, 1315–1322," *Past and Present* 59 (May 1973); B. A. Hanawalt, "Fur Collar Crime: The Pattern of Crime Among the Fourteenth-Century English Nobility," *Journal of Social History* 8 (Spring 1975): 1–17, a fascinating discussion; K. Thomas, "Work and Leisure in Pre-Industrial Society," *Past and Present* 29 (December 1964); M. Keen, *The Outlaws of Medieval Legend* (1961) and "Robin Hood – Peasant or Gentleman?," *Past and Present* 19 (April 1961):7–18; P. Wolff, "The 1391 Pogrom in Spain, Social Crisis or Not?," *Past and Present* 50 (February 1971):4–18; and R. H. Helmholz, *Marriage Litigation in Medieval England* (1974). Students are especially encouraged to consult the brilliant achievement of E. L. Ladurie, *The Peasants of Languedoc,* trans. John Day (1976).

The poetry of Dante, Chaucer, and Villon may be read in the following editions: Dorothy Sayers, trans., *Dante: The Divine Comedy,* 3 vols. (1963); Nevil Coghill, trans., *Chaucer's Canterbury Tales* (1977); Peter Dale, trans., *The Poems of Villon* (1973). The social setting of Chaucer's *Canterbury Tales* is brilliantly evoked in D. W. Robertson, Jr., *Chaucer's London* (1968).

Many of the preceding titles treat the religious history of the period. In addition, the following contain interesting and valuable information: G. Barraclough, *The Medieval Papacy* (1968), which is splendidly illustrated; W. Ullmann, *A Short History of the Papacy in the Middle Ages* (1972); E. Mason, "The Role of the English Parishioner, 1000–1500," *Journal of Ecclesiastical History* 27 (January 1976):17–29; and J. H. Smith, *The Great Schism 1378: The Disintegration of the Medieval Papacy* (1970).

CHAPTER 16

AFRICA AND THE AMERICAS

BEFORE EUROPEAN INTRUSION,

CA 400–1500

DURING THE PERIOD that historians of western Europe call the Middle Ages, Africa and the Americas gave rise to highly sophisticated civilizations alongside a wide spectrum of more simply organized societies. Until fairly recently, Americans and Europeans have known relatively little about Africa or about America before the arrival of Columbus. The more that historians and sociologists have learned about medieval Africa and pre-Columbian America, the more they have appreciated the richness, diversity, and dynamism of their cultures.

As we look at the major civilizations of Africa and America before 1500, this chapter will explore the following questions. What sources of information help us to understand Africa in the period that Westerners call the Middle Ages? What patterns of social and political organization prevailed among the peoples of Africa and South America? What types of agriculture and commerce did African and American peoples engage in? What values do their art, architecture, and religions express? What internal social difficulties among American and African peoples in the early sixteenth century contributed to their conquest by Europeans?

THE LAND AND PEOPLES OF AFRICA

Africa is immense: the world's second largest continent, it covers 20 percent of the earth's land surface. Five distinct geographical zones roughly divide the continent (see Map 16.1 on page 531). Fertile land with good rainfall and dense vegetation borders the Mediterranean coast in the north and the southwestern coast of the Cape of Good Hope in the south. Inland from these areas lies dry steppe country, called the Sahel in the north, with little plant life. These regions in turn gradually give way to Africa's great deserts, the Sahara and Libyan deserts in the north and the Namib and Kalahari in the south. The vast Sahara – 3.5 million square miles – takes its name from an ancient Arabic word resembling the sound of a parched man's gasp for water. The equatorial region takes in most of central Africa, a territory heavily influenced by dense, humid tropical rain forests. Finally, savanna lands extend in a swath across the widest part of Africa, as well as parts of south-central Africa and the eastern coast. The savanna's grassy prairies, open forests, high plateaux, and evergreen-dotted mountains make it one of the richest habitats in the world. Because it invites migration and cultural contacts, the savanna is far and away the most important region of West Africa historically.

The climate of the entire continent is tropical. Temperate climates exist only at high elevations; subtropical climates are limited to the northern and southern coasts and at high elevations. Rainfall is concentrated in the fall and winter seasons in most parts of the continent, and is very sparse in desert and semi-desert areas.

On the basis of archeological and linguistic evidence, anthropologists believe that five distinct peoples inhabited Africa by 8000 B.C. The Berbers of North Africa, a Semitic people, have intermingled with Mediterranean and Middle Eastern peoples since classical times. The great Saint Augustine of Hippo (pages 232-233) was a Berber. The Egyptians, a cultural rather than a racial group, were well known to the ancient Greeks, and their land served as the breadbasket of the Roman Empire. Black Africans inhabited the region south of the Sahara and Libyan deserts, encompassing the savanna from the Atlantic coast to Ethiopia on the east coast, and the rain forests. Short-statured peoples sometimes called Pygmies inhabited the equatorial rain forests. South of these forests, in the southern third of the continent, lived peoples collectively known as the Khoisan, a major language grouping.

THE STUDY OF AFRICAN HISTORY

Until the fifteenth century, non-Africans knew only the coastal fringes of Africa. Until the nineteenth century, in fact, they knew virtually nothing about the interior of the African continent. In discussing the "discoveries" that Europeans and Americans made in Africa, it is important to remember that they were discoveries only for outsiders. Africans had known about them all along.

The Greeks and Romans called North Africa "Libya." Since Libya was part of the Roman Empire, the Romans knew the geography of Africa's Mediterranean coast; but the vast interior south of the coastal fringe was a great mystery to them. Classical geographers speculated that Africa was entirely surrounded by oceans. They also thought that trade routes crisscrossed it, because gold, ivory, and slaves flowed across the Mediterranean from North Africa to the cities of the empire. According to the second-century Alexandrian geographer Claudius Ptolemy, below Libya lay Ethiopia — by which he meant all the territory south of the Sahara Desert. Until the sixteenth century, many European languages still used the term *Ethiopian* to designate all African or black peoples.

In the centuries before Christ, Greeks and Romans explored the northwestern coast of Africa. By the second century A.D. Arab and Indian merchant-sailors were trading along the eastern coast, probably as far south as Zanzibar. In the eighth century Muslim geographers began to write about the African peoples of the Upper Nile region and the south-

ern Saharan and Sudan belt of West Africa. Then, beginning in the late fifteenth century, Portuguese explorers reached the southern end of the continent, proved that Africa was bounded by two oceans, and recorded valuable descriptions of coastal regions and peoples. Even so, as late as the eighteenth century so little was known about the interior of Africa that the English satirist Jonathan Swift could write:

Geographers in Afric maps
with savage pictures fill their Gaps
and o'er inhabitable Downs
Place Elephants for want of Towns.

In the nineteenth century, trade, missionary efforts and imperialistic enterprises prompted the European powers to undertake systematic investigations of the interior plateaux of Africa. The English explorers Richard Burton and John Speke discovered the source of the Nile — the longest river in the world — at Victoria Nyanza, 4,187 miles inland from its mouth. The Scottish missionary-explorer David Livingstone, who had gone to Africa "to open a path for commerce and Christianity," discovered Victoria Falls and Lake Nyasa in 1855. An American reporter for the New York *Herald,* Henry Morton Stanley, originally sent to find the "lost" Livingstone, explored central and eastern Africa and blazed a trail to Lake Tanganyika in southeastern Africa. On a later trip in 1888, he discovered the magnificent Ruwenzori mountains in the central part of the continent. Explorers such as these laid the foundations for our knowledge of Africa's rich, highly diverse terrain.

Only since about 1950 has there been significant archeological activity in Africa. In 1959 the British anthropologists Louis and Mary Leakey discovered at Olduvai Gorge in Tanganyika the fossil skull of a creature either human or directly ancestral to humans. Careful paleontological examination proved that the skull dated from around 1,750,000 B.C.; near it were stone tools and the bones of animals that had been eaten. The discovery in 1974 at the Afar Depression in Ethiopia of a human jawbone and tooth fossils apparently between 1 and 3 million years old not only confirmed the Leakeys' findings but represented earlier evidence of human existence. These discoveries seem to confirm Charles Darwin's theory that man evolved from a simian ancestor in the tropics, and probably in Africa.[1]

Linguistics – study of the origins, structure, and modification of languages – can also yield valuable information for the historian. Language provides insight into the thought processes, interests, customs, ideals, and attitudes of a people: it is the central manifestation of their culture. When an area's present-day speech closely resembles the language spoken in the same region centuries before, we know that the people who speak the language have lived in isolation from outside influences. For example, until the advent of television around 1950, the people of Appalachia in the southeastern United States spoke a version of English strikingly similar to that of the early colonists who arrived around 1650. Scholars have classified more than a thousand distinct languages in Africa, including several dozen in the West African states of Liberia, Guinea, and Sierra Leone alone. One group, the Limba of Sierra Leone, speak a tongue completely different from the languages of their neighbors. The Limba, therefore, have probably lived in the region longer than any other people.

If many languages are spoken in a particular area, the implication is that some of its peoples immigrated into the region. If only a small percentage of a region's people speak a particular language, the likelihood is strong

MAP 16.1 AFRICA BEFORE 1500, SHOWING TRADE ROUTES For centuries trade linked Africa with Mediterranean and Asian societies. Note especially the trans-Saharan trade routes and those along the East African coast.

that their ancestors were at some point overwhelmed by stronger peoples or tribes. When a dominant language contains many words "borrowed" from another language, it is highly likely that speakers of the dominant language were in contact with or conquered by the people whose words they adopted. For example, the Hausa people of Nigeria "borrowed" words of key cultural importance from the Kanuri people, who pressured them from the east.[2] When a language has been severely modified or, in the extreme case, has disappeared entirely, so have other aspects of its speakers' culture.

Africa's traditional oral historians have preserved a record of past events by prodigious feats of historical memory. In the western Sudan, for instance, a professional class of minstrels called *griots* have for centuries preserved and recited the history of their people. Griots narrate family and tribal histories, descent, the succession of village chiefs and local kings, battles and migrations. Some twentieth-century griots have related incidents known to have occurred in the thirteenth century, their accounts passed down by word of mouth over twenty generations. Because facts can be garbled, distorted, and falsified when transmitted orally, scholars cannot take for granted the accuracy of oral history. Moreover, oral history can be recast to justify an existing political situation. Yet some scholars have concluded that there is a kernel of historical truth in the Greek poet Homer's *Iliad*, and he too discussed events that happened seven centuries before his time. The Bible is

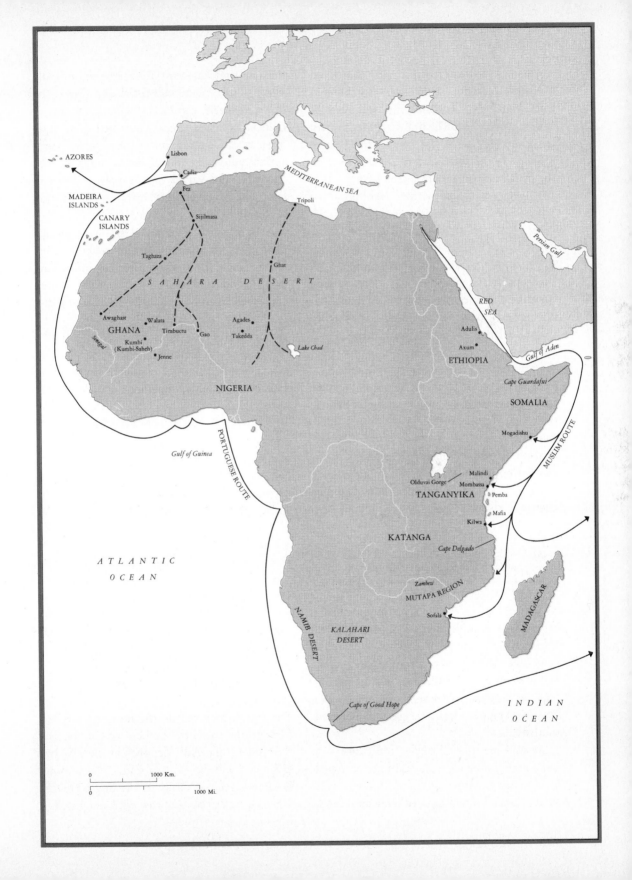

AZORES

Lisbon
Cadiz
MADEIRA
ISLANDS
CANARY
ISLANDS

Fez
Sijilmasa

MEDITERRANEAN SEA

Tripoli

S A H A R A   D E S E R T

Taghaza

Ghat

Persian Gulf

*RED
SEA*

Awaghast
Walata
Agades
Takedda

GHANA
Timbuctu
Gao
Senegal
Kumbi
(Kumbi-Saheh)
Jenne

Lake Chad

Adulis

Axum

Gulf of Aden

ETHIOPIA

NIGERIA

Cape Guardafui

SOMALIA

Mogadishu

MUSLIM ROUTE

Gulf of Guinea

PORTUGUESE ROUTE

Olduvai Gorge
Malindi
Mombassa
Pemba

TANGANYIKA

Mafia
Kilwa

KATANGA

Cape Delgado

*A T L A N T I C
O C E A N*

Zambezi
MUTAPA REGION
Sofala

MADAGASCAR

*NAMIB
DESERT*

*KALAHARI
DESERT*

Cape of Good Hope

*I N D I A N
O C E A N*

0   1000 Km.

0   1000 Mi.

accepted as an inspired document based on historical memory. Moreover, archeologists have found that historical memory can be amazingly accurate. The oral accounts of African griots can, when used with care, help to reconstruct the social and political history of the distant and the more recent past.[3]

A wide variety of written records – the conventional raw materials of the historian's craft – survive from early African history. Those parts of Africa that had commercial, intellectual, military, or religious contacts with Islam possess a body of documents dating from the eighth century. Both Arab and African converts to the faith of Allah kept memorials of events, and many North African and West African records survive, some in Arabic, some written in African languages with Arabic characters. All sorts of materials survive from the sixteenth through early twentieth centuries: travelers' accounts, ships' logs, shipping bills, papal letters, missionaries' letters and diaries, and official government documents from colonial offices. To these records recent scholars have brought new and old questions.

EARLY AFRICAN SOCIETIES

Africa was one of the sites where agriculture began. Several millennia before the birth of Christ, African farmers learned to domesticate plants, including millet, sorghum, and yams. Ironworking was introduced south of the Sahara in the first millennium B.C. From the Egyptian empire, ideas and goods penetrated southward.

Around the time of Christ, the Bantu – a small group of people who had long occupied modern-day eastern Nigeria on Africa's west coast – began to move out of their homeland.

Pushing southeastward, they settled in central Africa south of the equatorial rain forest. In this new locale, significant agricultural development occurred: easily cultivated yams and bananas, introduced into Africa from Asia, and the adoption of livestock raising made for an ample and varied food supply. Adequate food led in turn to a massive population explosion.

Because much of central Africa is a plateau, its topsoil is thin and groundwater scarce. These conditions promote shifting cultivation in preference to settled agriculture. The Bantu continued to move gradually south and east, reaching present-day Rhodesia by the eighth century and the southeastern coast by the sixteenth century. Describing the village life of Bantu people, the nineteenth-century British explorer David Livingstone wrote, "Food abounds, and very little labor is required for its cultivation. . . . When a garden becomes too poor for good crops. . . . the owner removes a little farther into the forest, applies fire round the roots of the larger trees to kill them, cuts down the smaller, and a new, rich garden is ready for the seed." Livingstone's observation captures "the essence of . . . the whole process of migratory agriculture which characterized most indigenous African societies."[4] Knowledge of ironworking gave the Bantu a distinct advantage over the Khoisans and Pygmies they encountered, hunting-and-gathering peoples whom they absorbed and displaced.

THE WESTERN SUDAN

The region bounded on the north by the Sahara, on the south by the Gulf of Guinea, on the west by the Atlantic, and on the east by Lake Chad and the modern state of Cameroon is known geographically as the Sudan. (This region is not to be confused with the modern

AFRICA CA 400–1500

ca 1st century A.D.	Beginning of Bantu migrations
ca A.D. 200	First use of the camel for trans-Saharan transportation
600–1500	Extensive slave trade from sub-Saharan Africa to the Mediterranean
11th century	Islam penetrates sub-Saharan Africa
11th century	Height of the Kingdom of Ghana
13th and 14th centuries	Kingdom of Mali
1312–1337	Mansa Musa, medieval Africa's most famous ruler
14th and 15th centuries	Height of the Swahili (East African) City-States
4th century	Ethiopia accepts Christianity
6th and 7th centuries	Political and commercial ascendancy of Ethiopia
9th century	Decline of Ethiopia

nation of Sudan, south of Egypt.) In the savanna lands of the western Sudan – where the Bantu migrations originated – a series of dynamic kingdoms emerged in the millennium before European intrusion.

Between 1000 B.C. and A.D. 200 the peoples of the western Sudan made the momentous shift from nomadic hunting to settled agriculture. They cultivated crops with iron tools and domesticated animals for food. The rich savanna proved ideally suited to the production of cereals, especially rice, millet, and sorghum, and people situated near the Senegal River and Lake Chad supplemented their diet with fish. As we have seen, food supply tends to have a direct effect on a people's rate of reproduction, and the peoples of the region – known as the Mande and the "Chadic speakers" or "Sao" – increased dramatically in number. By A.D. 400 the entire savanna, par-

ticularly the areas around Lake Chad, the Niger Bend, and present-day central Nigeria (see Map 16.1) had a large population.

Families and clans affiliated by blood kinship lived together in villages or small city-states. Above and beyond the extended family, the basic social unit was the village, governed by a chief in consultation with a council of elders. Some city-states and villages seem to have formed kingdoms: village chiefs were responsible to regional heads, who answered to provincial governors, who were in turn responsible to the king. The various chiefs and their families formed a sort of aristocracy. Kingship in the Sudanese region may have emerged from the priesthood, who made rain and had contact with spirit powers. African kings always had religious sanction, and were often themselves considered divine. (In this respect, early African kingship bears a strong

CASBAH IN MOROCCO   *The medieval sultanate of Morocco traded heavily with the West African kingdoms and, through trade, strongly influenced the architecture of the Sudanic cities. Note the defensive wall and towers (Robert Harding Associates/Sassoon)*

resemblance to the Germanic kingship of the same period: the authority of both rested in part on their ability to negotiate with outside powers, such as the gods.) The most prominent feature of early African society was a strong sense of community, based partly on the blood relationship and partly on religion.

African religions were largely animistic. That is, most people believed that a Supreme Being had created the universe and was the source of all life, but that people could not know or communicate with the Being. The Supreme Being had originally breathed spirit

into all living things, and the *anima* or spirits residing in such things as trees, water, and earth had to be appeased. In the cycle of the agricultural year, for example, all the spirits had to be propitiated from the time of clearing the land through sowing the seed to the final harvesting. (The early Germanic tribes had a similar belief.) Because special ceremonies and rituals were necessary to satisfy these spirits, special priests were needed with the knowledge and power to communicate with them. Thus the practice of African religion consisted primarily of sacred rituals performed by priests who were also the heads of families or villages. The head of each family was also responsible for maintaining the family ritual cults — ceremonies honoring the dead and living members of the family.[5]

In sum, extended families made up the villages that collectively formed small kingdoms. What spurred the expansion of these small kingdoms into formidable powers controlling sizable territory was the development of long-distance trade. And what made long-distance or trans-Saharan trade possible was the introduction of the camel.

THE TRANS-SAHARAN TRADE

The camel had an impact on African trade comparable to that of the horse on European agriculture (page 322). Although scholars dispute exactly when the camel was introduced from central Asia — first into North Africa and then into the Sahara and the Sudan — they agree it was before A.D. 200. Camels can carry about 500 pounds as much as 25 miles a day, and can go for days without drink, living on the water stored in their humps. Although stupid and sometimes vicious, the camel is much more efficient for desert travel than either the horse or the ox. Use of this beast to transport heavy and bulky freight led to profound economic and social changes in West Africa.

Between A.D. 200 and 700 a network of caravan routes developed between the Mediterranean coast and the Sudan (see Map 16.1, page 531). One route, the Morocco-Niger route, ran from Fez to Sijilmasa on the edge of the desert, and then south via Walata and Taghaza and back to Fez; another route originated at Sijilmasa and extended due south to Timbuctu with a stop at Taghaza. A third itinerary ran south from Tripoli in Egypt to Lake Chad and then swung south and west. A fourth ran from Egypt to Gao by way of the Saharan oases of Ghat and Agades, and then on to Takedda. The long expedition across the Sahara testifies to the indomitable spirit of the traders and to their passionate ambition for wealth. The Arab traveler Ibn-Batuta, who made the journey in the fourteenth century when the trans-Saharan traffic was at its height, wrote an account of the experience. Because of the blistering sun and daytime temperatures of 110°, the caravan drivers preferred to travel at night, when the temperature might drop to the low 20s. Nomadic robbers, the Tuareg Berbers, posed a serious threat. The Tuaregs lived in the desert uplands and preyed on the caravans as a way of life. Consequently, merchants made safe-conduct agreements with the Tuaregs and selected guides from among them. Caravans of twelve thousand camels were reported in the fourteenth century, meaning that many merchants crossed the desert together to discourage attack. Blinding sandstorms often isolated part of a line of camels, and on at least one occasion buried alive some camels and drivers. Water was the biggest problem. The Tuaregs sometimes poisoned wells to wipe out caravans and steal their goods. In order to satisfy normal thirst and to compensate for constant sweating, a gallon of water a day per man was required. Desperate thirst sometimes forced the traders to kill camels and drink the foul, brackish water in their stomachs. It took Ibn-Batuta twenty-five days to travel from Sijilmasa to the oasis of Taghaza; from Taghaza to the important market town of Waleta took another sixty days, making the entire trip almost three months long.

The Arabo-Berber merchants from North Africa who controlled the caravan trade carried manufactured goods — silk and cotton cloth, beads, mirrors — as well as dates and the essential salt from the Saharan oases and

TABLE 16.1 ESTIMATED MAGNITUDE OF TRANS-SAHARAN SLAVE TRADE, A.D. 650–1500

Years	Annual Average of Slaves Traded	Total
650–800	1,000	150,000
800–900	3,000	300,000
900–1100	8,700	1,740,000
1100–1400	5,500	1,650,000
1400–1500	4,300	430,000

Source: Austen, "The Trans-Saharan Slave Trade." For full citation see note 6, p. 576.

was black Africa's major industry. The gold trade connected sub-Saharan Africa with the Mediterranean, the Middle East, and Europe.

West Africa's next most valuable export was slaves. Who were these slaves? The lack of strong evidence permits only a speculative answer. As was true among early European and Asian peoples, African slaves were peoples captured in war. In the Muslim cities of North Africa, southern Europe, and southwestern Asia, demand for household slaves was high among the elite classes. Some slaves were needed to work the gold and salt mines. Recent research suggests, moreover, that large numbers of black slaves were recruited through the trans-Saharan trade for Muslim military service. The armed forces of medieval Islamic regimes in Tunisia, Morocco, and Egypt consisted largely of slaves. High death rates from disease, manumission (Muslim law required that slaves be freed on their owners' death, though the law was not usually observed), and the assimilation of some blacks into Muslim society meant that demand for slaves remained high for centuries. Table 16.1 shows one careful scholar's tentative conclusions, based on many kinds of evidence, about the scope of the trans-Saharan slave trade. The total number of blacks enslaved over an 850-year period may be tentatively estimated at over 4 million.[6]

mines to the Sudan. These products were exchanged for the much-coveted commodities of the West African savanna – gold, ivory, gum, kola nuts (eaten as a stimulant), and slaves. The steady growth of this trans-Saharan trade had three important effects on West African society.

First of all, trade stimulated gold mining and the search for slaves. Parts of modern-day Senegal, Nigeria, and Ghana contained rich veins of gold. Both sexes shared in mining it: the men sunk the shafts, hacked out gold-bearing rocks and crushed them, separating the gold from the soil; the women washed the gold in gourds. Where the gold was alluvial (mixed with soil, sand, or gravel), as in Upper Senegal, it was separated from the soil by panning. Scholars estimate that by the eleventh century nine tons were exported to Europe annually – a prodigious amount, since even with modern machinery and sophisticated techniques the total gold exports from the same region in 1937 amounted to only twenty-one tons. Because of the huge demand for African gold in North Africa, Europe, and Asia during the Middle Ages, gold mining

Slavery in Muslim societies as in European and Asian countries before the fifteenth century, was not based strictly on skin color. The slaves that West Africa exported were all black, but Muslims also enslaved Caucasians who had been purchased, seized in war, or kidnapped from Europe. The households of wealthy Muslims in Cordova or Alexandria or Tunis often included slaves of several races, all of whom had been completely cut off from their cultural roots. Likewise, West African

MOSQUE IN MALI *This mosque is in a Malian town that was the terminus of one trans-Saharan trade route. The remains of this thirteenth-century mosque reflect the penetration of Muslim ideas and institutions in the western and central Sudan, the modern states of which are almost entirely Muslim. (Robert Harding Associates/Patrick Matthews)*

kings who sold blacks to traders from the north also bought a few white slaves – Slavic, British, and Turkish – for their domestic needs. Race had very little to do with the phenomenon of slavery.[7]

The trans-Saharan trade also stimulated the development of vigorous urban centers in West Africa. Scholars date the growth of African cities from around the beginning of the ninth century. Families that had profited from the trade in gold, ivory, and slaves tended to congregate in the border zones between the savanna and the Sahara. Thus centrally located, they acted as middlemen between the miners to the south and Muslim merchants from the north. Modest profits aroused ambitions for greater wealth and for control of trading activities and routes. By the early thirteenth century, these families had become powerful black merchant dynasties comparable to the Medici of Florence in the fifteenth century or the Fuggers of Augsburg in the sixteenth. Muslim traders from the Mediterranean settled permanently in these trading depots, from which they organized the trans-Saharan caravans. The concentration of people stimulated agriculture and the handicraft industries. Gradually, cities of sizable population emerged. Jenne, Gao, and Timbuctu, which enjoyed commanding positions on the Niger River bend, became centers of the export-import trade. Sijilmasa, the northern terminus of one of the trans-Saharan trade routes, grew into a thriving market center. Kumbi, with 15,000-20,000 inhabitants, was probably the largest city in the western Sudan in the twelfth century. By European standards this was an enormous metropolis; London and Paris achieved that size only in the late thirteenth century. Between 1100 and 1400 these cities played a dynamic role in the commercial life of West Africa and Europe, and became centers of intellectual creativity.

Perhaps the most influential consequence of the trans-Saharan trade was the impact of Islam on West African society. Muslim expansion began soon after Mohammed's death in 632 (pages 308-310). In the eighth century, Arab armies swept across and easily subdued the North African coast as far west as Morocco. By the tenth century the Muslim Berbers controlled the north-south trade routes to the savanna, and by the eleventh century the African rulers of Gao and Timbuctu had accepted Islam. The king of Ghana was also influenced by Islam. Muslims quickly became integral to West African government and society.

Conversion to Islam introduced West Afri-

cans to a rich and sophisticated culture. By the late eleventh century, Islam encompassed not only theological doctrines and a way of life, but a body of legal traditions and writings, efficient techniques of government and statecraft, advanced scientific knowledge and engineering skills, and collections of lyric poetry and popular romances. At approximately the same time, Muslims were aiding the Norman king Roger of Sicily in the construction of his state bureaucracy (pages 464-465) and guiding the ruler of Ghana in the operation of his administrative machinery. The king of Ghana adopted the Muslim *diwan,* a sophisticated agency for keeping financial records, as his treasury. Because efficient government depends upon the preservation of records, the arrival of Islam in West Africa marked the advent of written African documents.

Arab Muslims also taught the rulers of Ghana how to manufacture bricks, and royal palaces and mosques began to be built of them. African rulers corresponded with Muslim architects, theologians, and other intellectuals who advised them on statecraft and religion. In sum, Islam accelerated the development of the African empires of the fourteenth through sixteenth centuries.

AFRICAN KINGDOMS AND EMPIRES (CA 800–1450)

The period from about 800 to 1450 witnessed the flowering of several powerful African states. So remarkable was the kingdom of Ghana during this great age in African history that writers throughout the medieval world praised it as a model for imitation by other rulers. "The king of Ghana is the richest monarch in the world," reported the tenth-century traveler Ibn-Hawkal. The twelfth-century chronicler al-Idrisi told the Norman king Roger of Sicily that the lords of Ghana often fed tens of thousands of people at lavish banquets. No doubt an exaggeration, al-Idrisi's account certainly contains an element of truth: the rulers of Ghana possessed fabulous wealth. Medieval Ghana also holds a central place in the historical consciousness of the modern state of Ghana. Since this former British colony attained independence in 1957, its political leaders have hailed the medieval period as a glorious heritage. The name of the modern republic of Ghana — which in fact lies far from the site of the old city — was selected specifically to signify the rebirth of an age of gold and glory in black Africa.

THE KINGDOM OF GHANA (CA 900–1100)

The nucleus of the territory that became the kingdom of Ghana was inhabited by Soninke people who called their ruler *ghana,* or war chief. Muslim traders and other foreigners applied the word to the region where the Soninke lived, and by the late eighth century the term *Ghana* was used to designate the black kingdom south of the Sahara. The Soninke themselves called their land Aoukar or Awkar, by which they meant the region north of the Senegal and Niger rivers. Only the southern part of Aoukar received enough rainfall to be agriculturally productive, and it was in this region that the black civilization of Ghana developed. Skillful farming and an efficient system of irrigation led to the production of abundant crops, which eventually supported a population of as many as 200,000 people.

The Soninke name for their king — war chief — aptly describes his major preoccupation in the tenth century. In 992 Ghana captured the Berber town of Awdaghast, strate-gically situated on the trans-Saharan trade route. Thereafter Ghana controlled the southern portion of a major caravan route. Before 1000 the rulers of Ghana had extended their influence almost to the Atlantic coast, as well as capturing a number of small kingdoms in the south and east. By the beginning of the eleventh century, the king exercised sway over a vast territory. No other African power could successfully challenge him.

Throughout this vast area, possibly 250,000 square miles — larger than modern France, approximately the size of Texas — all authority sprang from the king, whose people considered him semi-sacred. His position was hereditary in the matrilineal line — that is, the heir of the ruling king was one of his sister's sons (presumably the eldest or fittest for battle). According to the eleventh-century Spanish Muslim geographer al-Bakri, whom this system obviously puzzled, "This is their custom . . . the kingdom is inherited only by the son of the king's sister. He the king has no doubt that his successor is a son of his sister, while he is not certain that his son is in fact his own, and he does not rely on the genuineness of this relationship."[8] A council of ministers assisted the king in the work of government, and from the ninth century onward most of these ministers were Muslims. Detailed evidence about the early Ghanaian bureaucracy has not survived, but scholars suspect that separate agencies were responsible for taxation, royal property, foreigners, forests, and the army. The royal administration was well served by Muslim ideas, skills, and especially Muslim literacy. The king and his people, however, clung to their ancestral religion, and the basic political institutions of Ghana remained African.

The king of Ghana held his court at the city of Kumbi, which consisted of two sections, one inhabited by Muslim traders and

ROYAL WOMAN FROM BENIN   *The elaborate gold headdress, the gold braided in her hair, and the heavy gold necklace indicate that this woman is from the royal class and attest to the wealth of the region. (Lee Boltin)*

officials. al-Bakri provides a valuable picture of Kumbi in the eleventh century:

The city of Ghana consists of two towns lying on a plain, one of which is inhabited by Muslims and is large, possessing twelve mosques — one of which is a congregational mosque for Friday prayer; each has its imām, its muezzin and paid reciters of the Qurān. The town possesses a large number of juris-consults and learned men.[9]

The town inhabited by the king is six miles from the Muslim one and is called Al Ghana.

The land separating the two towns is filled with dwellings. These houses are built of stone and aca-cia wood. The residence of the king consists of a palace and a number of dome-shaped dwellings, all of them surrounded by a strong enclosure, like a city wall. In the town where the king lives, not far from the royal court of justice, there is a mosque, where Muslims who come on diplomatic missions to the king pray. The town where the king lives is surrounded by domed huts, woods, and copses where priest-magicians live; in these woods also are the religious idols and tombs of the kings. Special guards protect this area and prevent anyone from entering it so that no foreigners know what is in-side. Here also are the king's prisons, and if any-one is imprisoned there, nothing more is heard of him. The king's interpreters, his treasurer, and most of his ministers are selected from among the Muslim community.[10]

This passage reveals a great deal about the Muslim community in Ghana, which must have been large and prosperous to have sup-ported twelve mosques. Either for their own protection or to preserve their special identity, the Muslims lived in their own quarter or ghetto, separate from the African population of artisans and tradespeople. The imām was the religious leader who conducted the ritual worship, especially the main prayer service on Fridays. Since Islamic worship had political connotations as well as religious meaning, the imām was, then as now, both a political and a religious authority in the Muslim community. The muezzin leads the prayer responses after the imām; he must have a strong voice so that those at a distance and the women in the harīm, or enclosure, can hear. Muslim reli-gious leaders exercised civil authority over their co-religionists in much the same way that rabbis had civil jurisdiction over the Jew-ish communities of medieval England. The presence in Ghana of the imām, jurisconsults and other learned men also suggests vigorous intellectual activity.

al-Bakri also describes the royal court:

The king adorns himself, as do the women here, with necklaces and bracelets; on their heads they wear caps decorated with gold, sewn on material of fine cotton stuffing. When he holds court in order to hear the people's complaints and to do justice, he sits in a pavilion around which stand ten horses wearing golden trappings; behind him ten pages stand, holding shields and swords decorated with gold; at his right are the sons of the chiefs of the country, splendidly dressed and with their hair sprinkled with gold. The governor of the city sits on the ground in front of the king with other officials likewise sitting around him. Excellently pedigreed dogs guard the door of the pavilion: they never leave the place where the king is; they wear collars of gold and silver studded with bells of the same material. The noise of a sort-of drum, called a daba, and made from a long hollow log, announces the start of the royal audience. When the king's coreligionists appear before him, they fall on their knees and toss dust on their heads — this is their way of greeting their sovereign. Muslims show respect by clapping their hands. [11]

Religious ceremonies and court rituals emphasized the sacredness of the king and served to strengthen his authority.

What sort of juridical system did Ghana have? How was the guilt or innocence of an accused person determined? Justice derived from the king, who heard cases at court or on travels throughout his kingdom. As al-Bakri recounts:

When a man is accused of denying a debt or of having shed blood or some other crime, a headman (village chief) takes a thin piece of wood, which is sour and bitter to taste, and pours upon it some water which he then gives to the defendant to drink. If the man vomits, his innocence is recognized and he is congratulated. If he does not vomit and the drink remains in his stomach, the accusation is accepted as justified. [12]

This appeal to the supernatural for judgment was very similar to the justice by ordeal that prevailed among the English and Germanic peoples of western Europe at the same time. Complicated cases in Ghana seem to have been appealed to the king, who often relied on the advice of Muslim legal experts.

The king's elaborate court, the administrative machinery he built, and the extensive territories he governed were all costly. The king of Ghana needed a great deal of money, and he apparently had three main sources of support. The royal estates — some hereditary, others conquered in war — produced an annual revenue, mostly in the form of foodstuffs for the royal household. The king also received tribute annually from subordinate chieftains. Lack of evidence prevents us from estimating the value of this tax. The third and probably largest source of income was customs duties on goods entering and leaving the country. Salt — especially necessary to health in tropical climates where the loss from perspiration is great — was the largest import. According to al-Bakri, "for every donkey that enters the country, the king takes a duty of one gold dinar and two [for one] that leaves." [13] Berber merchants paid a tax to the king on the cloth, metalwork, weapons, and other goods they brought into the country from North Africa; in return these traders received royal protection from bandits. African traders bringing gold into Ghana from the south also paid the customs duty, and the royal treasury held a monopoly on the export of gold.

The gold industry was undoubtedly the king's largest source of income. What impressed contemporaries about Ghana was its gold: it was upon gold that the fame of medieval Ghana rested. The eighth-century astronomer al-Fazari characterized Ghana as "the land of gold," and the ninth-century geographer al-Ya-qubi wrote, "Its king is mighty, and in his lands are gold mines. Under his authority are various other kingdoms — and in all this region there is gold."[14] In sum, the strength of Ghana rested upon two valuable minerals, salt from the north and gold from the south.

The governing aristocracy — the king, his court, and Muslim administrative officials — occupied the highest rank on the Ghanian social ladder. The next rung consisted of the merchant class. Considerably below merchants stood the farmers, cattle breeders, supervisors of the gold mines, skilled craftsmen and weavers — what today might be called the middle class. Some merchants and miners must have enjoyed great wealth and a luxurious lifestyle, but, as in all aristocratic societies, money alone did not suffice. High status was based on blood and royal service. At the bottom of the social scale were the slaves, who worked in households, on farms and in the mines. We know very little about them. As in Asian and European societies of the time, slaves accounted for only a small percentage of the population.

Apart from these various social classes stood the army. According to al-Bakri, "the king of Ghana can put 200,000 warriors in the field, more than 40,000 being armed with bow and arrow."[15] Like most medieval estimates, this is probably a gross exaggeration. Even a modern industrialized state with sophisticated means of transportation, communication, and supply lines would have enormous difficulty mobilizing so many men for battle. The king

of Ghana, however, was not called war chief for nothing. He maintained at his palace a crack standing force of a thousand men, comparable to the Roman Praetorian Guard (page 188). These thoroughly disciplined, well-armed, totally loyal troops protected the king and the royal court. They lived in special compounds, enjoyed the favor of the king, and sometimes acted as his personal ambassadors to subordinate rulers. In wartime, this regular army was augmented by levies of soldiers from conquered peoples and by the use of slaves and free reserves. The force that the king could field was sizable, if not as huge as al-Bakri estimated.

THE KINGDOM OF MALI (CA 1200–1450)

During the century after the collapse of Kumbi, a cloud of obscurity hangs over the Western Sudan. As its former subject peoples seized their independence, the kingdom of Ghana split into several small kingdoms that feuded among themselves. One of these peoples, the Mandinke, lived in the kingdom of Kangaba on the Upper Niger River. The Mandinke had long been part of the Ghanaian empire, and the Mandinke and Soninke belonged to the same language group. Kangaba formed the core of the new empire of Mali. Building on Ghanaian foundations, Mali developed into a better-organized and more

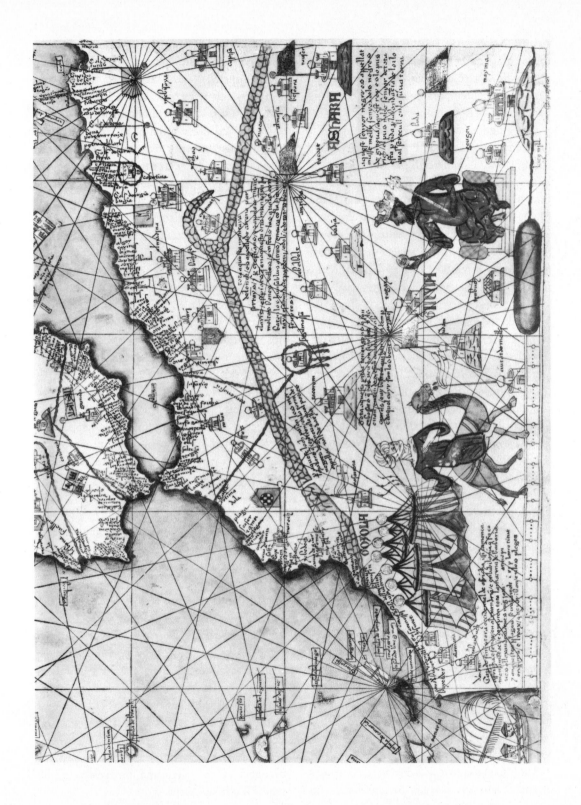

powerful state than Ghana had been. In the fourteenth and fifteenth centuries Mali achieved a degree of wealth and cultural brilliance that contemporary Muslim and Christian writers praised highly.

The kingdom of Mali owed its greatness to two fundamental assets. First, its strong agricultural and commercial base provided for large population and enormous wealth. Second, Mali had two rulers, Sundiata and Mansa Musa, who combined military success with exceptionally creative personalities. Although the structure of Mali's society and government closely resembled that of Ghana, Mali's rulers used Islam more effectively.

The earliest surviving evidence about the Mandinke people, dating from the early eleventh century, indicates that they were extremely successful at agriculture. Consistently large harvests throughout the twelfth and thirteenth centuries meant a plentiful supply of food, which encouraged steady population growth. The geographical location of Kangaba also placed them in an ideal position in the West African trade. Earlier, during the period of Ghanaian hegemony, the Mandinke had acted as middlemen in the gold and salt traffic flowing north and south. In the thirteenth century Mandinke traders formed companies, travelled widely, and gradually became a major force in the entire West African trade.

Sundiata (ca 1230-1255) set up his capital at Niani, and, adopting a scheme that especially favored mercantile interests, transformed the city into an important financial and trading center. He then embarked upon a policy of imperial expansion. Through a series of military victories, Sundiata and his successors absorbed into Mali the territories of the former kingdom of Ghana and established hegemony over the trading cities of Gao, Jenne, and Walata.

These expansionist policies were continued in the fourteenth century by Sundiata's descendant Mansa Musa (ca 1312-1337), medieval Africa's most famous ruler. In the language of the Mandinke, *mansa* means emperor, which attests to Musa's imperial ascendancy. Mansa Musa fought many campaigns and checked every attempt at rebellion. Ultimately, his influence extended northward to several Berber cities in the Sahara, eastward to the cities of Timbuctu and Gao, and in the west as far as the Atlantic Ocean. Throughout his territories he maintained strict royal control over the rich trans-Saharan trade. Consequently this empire, roughly twice the size of the Ghanaian kingdom and containing perhaps 8 million people, brought Mansa Musa fabulous wealth.

Mansa Musa built on the foundations of his predecessors. The stratified aristocratic structure of Malian society perpetuated the pattern set in Ghana, as did the system of provincial administration. The emperor took responsibility himself for the territories that formed the heart of the empire, and appointed governors to rule the outlying provinces or dependent kingdoms. Mansa Musa made a significant innovation: in a practice strikingly similar to the French *appanages* of the time, he chose members of the royal family as provincial governors. He could count on their loyalty, and they received valuable experience in the work of government. As in the Ghanaian period, the subordinate provinces paid him an annual tribute.

In another aspect of administration, Mansa Musa differed from his predecessors. He became a devout Muslim. While most of the Mandinke clung to their ancestral animism, Islamic practices and influences in Mali multiplied. Just as the Christian monks of medieval Europe praised the deeds of kings who favored monasticism, so the Muslim *'ulamas* (learned Islamic writers) lauded and perhaps exaggerated the piety and prosperity of the reign of Mansa Musa.

The most celebrated event of Mansa Musa's reign was his pilgrimage to Mecca in 1324–1325, during which he paid a state visit to the sultan of Egypt. Mansa Musa's entrance into Cairo was magnificent. Preceded by five hundred slaves, each carrying a six-pound staff of gold, he followed with a huge host of retainers including one hundred elephants each bearing one hundred pounds of gold. Several hundred additional camels carrying food, supplies, and weapons brought up the rear. The emperor lavished his wealth on the citizens of the Egyptian capital. Writing twelve years later, al-Omari, one of the sultan's officials, recounts:

This man [Mansa Musa] spread upon Cairo the flood of his generosity: there was no person, officer of the court, or holder of any office of the Sultanate who did not receive a sum of gold from him. The people of Cairo earned incalcuable sums from him, whether by buying and selling or by gifts. So much gold was current in Cairo that it ruined the value of money. . . . Let me add that gold in Egypt had enjoyed a high rate of exchange up to the moment of their arrival. . . . But from that day onward, its value dwindled; the exchange was ruined, and even now it has not recovered. . . . That is how it has been for twelve years from that time, because of the great amounts of gold they brought to Egypt and spent there.[16]

Mansa Musa's gold caused a terrible inflation throughout Egypt. For the first time, however, the Mediterranean world gained concrete knowledge of the wealth and power of the black kingdom of Mali, and it began to be known as one of the great empires of the world. When the Majorcan mapmaker Abraham Cresques drew his atlas of Africa in 1375, he showed Mansa Musa enthroned in Mali as traders from North Africa marched toward his markets. Mali retained this international reputation in the fourteenth and fifteenth centuries.

Musa's pilgrimage also had significant consequences within Mali. He gained some understanding of the Mediterranean countries, and opened diplomatic relations with the Muslim rulers of Morocco and Egypt. His zeal for the Muslim faith and Islamic culture increased. Musa brought back from Arabia the distinguished architect as-Saheli, whom he commissioned to construct new mosques at Timbuctu and other cities. These mosques served as centers for the conversion of Africans. Musa employed Muslim engineers to build in brick where pounded clay had formerly been used. He also encouraged Malian merchants and traders to wear the distinctive flowing robes and turbans of Muslim males.

Timbuctu began as a campsite for desert nomads. Under Mansa Musa it grew into a thriving commercial entrepôt, attracting merchants and traders from North Africa and all parts of the Mediterranean world. Business people brought sophisticated attitudes and cosmopolitan ideas. In the fifteenth century Timbuctu developed into a great center for scholarship and learning. Architects, astronomers, poets, lawyers, mathematicians, and theologians flocked there. One hundred and fifty "schools of divinity" were devoted to the study of the Koran. The school of Islamic law enjoyed an international distinction in Africa comparable to the prestige of the law school at Bologna as a center of civil and canon law in Europe. A vigorous trade in books flourished in Timbuctu; when immigrants introduced Islam into the Hausa state of Kano in the central Sudan, they brought Muslim books on divinity and etymology from Timbuctu. Leo Africanus, the sixteenth-century Muslim traveler and writer who later converted to Christianity, recounts that around 1500 Timbuctu had a "great store of doctors, judges, priests, and other learned men that are bountifully maintained at the king's cost and charges. And hitherto are brought diverse

TIMBUCTU *Begun as a Tuareg seasonal camp in the eleventh century, Timbuctu emerged as a great commercial entrepot in the fourteenth century and as an important Muslim educational center of the* Songhai empire in the sixteenth century. A strong agricultural base, watered by the nearby Niger River, supported a sizable population. (Library of Congress)

manuscripts or written books out of Barbarie [the north African states, from Egypt to the Atlantic Ocean] which are sold for more money than any other merchandise." It is easy to understand why the university of Timbuctu was called by a contemporary writer "the Queen of the Sudan." Timbuctu's tradition and reputation for scholarship lasted until the eighteenth century.

In the fourteenth and fifteenth centuries Muslim intellectuals and Arabic traders frequently married native African women. These unions brought into being a group of racially mixed people. The necessity of living together harmoniously, the intellectual tradition of awareness of diverse cultures, and the cosmopolitan atmosphere of the city all contributed to a rare degree of racial toleration and understanding. After visiting the court of Mansa Musa's successor in 1352–1353, the Arab traveler Ibn-Batuta observed that

the Negroes possess some admirable qualities. They are seldom unjust, and have a greater abhorrence of injustice than any other people. Their sultan shows no mercy to anyone who is guilty of the least act of it. There is complete security in their country. Neither traveler nor inhabitant in it has anything to fear from robbers. ... They do not confiscate the property of any white man who dies in their country, even if it be uncounted wealth. On the contrary, they give it into the charge of some trustworthy person among the whites, until the rightful heir takes possession of it. They are careful to observe the hours of prayer, and assiduous in attending them in congregations, and in bringing up their children to them. On Fridays, if a man does not go early to the mosque, he cannot find a corner to pray in, on account of the crowd.[17]

For a person of Ibn-Batuta's globe-trotting experience and urbanity, this is high praise indeed.

THE EAST AFRICAN CITY-STATES

In the first century A.D., a merchant-seaman from Alexandria in Egypt, possibly acting as an agent of the Roman imperial government, sailed down the Red Sea and out into the Indian Ocean. Along the coasts of East Africa and India he found seaports. He took careful notes on all he observed, and the result, the *Periplus of the Erythraean Sea* (as the Greeks called the Indian Ocean), is the earliest surviving literary evidence of the city-states of the East African coast. Although primarily preoccupied with geography and navigation, the *Periplus* includes accounts of the local peoples and their commercial activities. Even in the days of the Roman emperors, the *Periplus* testifies, the East African coast had strong commercial links with India and the Mediterranean.

Greco-Roman ships travelled from Adulis on the Red Sea around the tip of the Gulf of Aden and down the African coast that the Greeks called Azania, in modern-day Kenya and Tanzania (see Map 16.1 on page 531).

These ships carried manufactured goods – cotton cloth, copper and brass, iron tools, and gold and silver plate. At the African coastal emporia, Mediterranean merchants exchanged these goods for cinnamon, myrrh and frankincense, slaves, and animal by-products such as ivory, rhinoceros horns, and tortoise shells. Somewhere around Cape Delgado on the Horn of Africa, the ships caught the monsoon winds eastward to India, where ivory was in great demand. In the first few centuries of the Christian era, many merchants and seamen from the Mediterranean settled in East African coastal towns. The fifth-century geographer Claudius Ptolemy called the native women they married "Ethiopian," by which he meant black. Since the author of the first-century *Periplus* did not describe the natives as "Ethiopian," and apparently did not find their skin color striking enough to comment on, scholars have deduced that the Bantu migrations reached the eastern coast between the first and fifth centuries.

Succeeding centuries saw the arrival of more traders. The great emigration from Arabia after the death of Mohammed accelerated Muslim penetration of the East African coast, which the Arabs called the Zanj, land of the blacks. Arab Muslims established small trading colonies along the coast, whose local peoples were ruled by kings and practiced various animistic religions. Social historians remain uncertain about the precise relationship between the Arab immigrants and the native black peoples. Some scholars maintain that Arab trading posts gradually achieved political hegemony over the indigenous blacks, who became acculturated to Islam. Other writers argue that the ancient African trading centers grew to serve the commercial needs of local African royal houses, and that through the influence of Arab merchants the Africans slowly converted to Islam. Whatever was the

SIXTEENTH-CENTURY IVORY SALT CELLAR
Mande-speaking people of Bullom (modern Sierra Leone in West Africa) carved this beautiful egg-shaped salt container which is supported by intricately carved African men and women. (Sotheby Parke-Bernet/Art Resource)

case, indigenous African religions remained strong in the interior of the continent.

Beginning in the late twelfth century, fresh waves of Arabs and of Persians from Shiraz poured down the coast, first settling at Mogadishu and then pressing southward to Kilwa (see Map 16.1 on page 531). Everywhere they landed, they introduced Islamic culture to the indigenous black population. Similarly, Indonesians crossed the Indian Ocean and settled on the African coast and the large island of Madagascar, or Malagasy (itself an Indonesian word) from the earliest Christian centuries through the Middle Ages. All these immigrants intermarried with Africans, and the resulting society combined Asian, African, and especially Islamic characteristics.

This East African coastal culture was called Swahili, after a Bantu tribal group of the region. The Swahili language is characterized by poetic forms linked with Arabic, grammar derived from Bantu, and a vocabulary similar to both. The thirteenth-century Muslim mosque at Mogadishu and the fiercely Muslim populations of Mombassa and Kilwa in the fourteenth century attest to strong Muslim influence.

Much of our knowledge about life in these trading societies, such as Mombassa, Pemba, Kilwa, and Mogadishu (see Map 16.1 on page 531), rests on the account of the indomitable Ibn-Batuta. These cities were great commercial empires in the fourteenth and fifteenth centuries, comparable to Venice and Genoa. Like those Italian city-states, Kilwa, Mombassa, and Mafia were situated on offshore islands; the tidal currents that isolated them from the mainland also protected them from landside attack.

When Ibn-Batuta arrived at Mogadishu, the sheikh dressed him in robes of heavy Chinese silk and turbans of Egyptian cloth. Ibn-Batuta was impressed, in the words of a modern historian,

with the size of the town, the lavish hospitality of the sheikh effectively carried out in his richly appointed palace. Traveling on to Kilwa, he found the city large and elegant, its buildings, as was typical along the coast, constructed of stone and coral rag [roofing slate]. Houses were generally single storied, consisting of a number of small rooms separated by thick walls supporting heavy stone roofing slabs laid across mangrove poles. Some of the more formidable structures contained second and third stories, and many were embellished with cut stone decorative borders framing the entranceways. Tapestries and ornamental niches covered the walls and the floors were carpeted. Of course, such appointments were only for the wealthy; the poorer classes occupied the timeless mud and straw huts of Africa, their robes a simple loincloth, their dinner a millet porridge supplemented by wild fruits gathered in the nearby forest.[18]

On the mainland were fields and orchards of rice, millet, oranges, mangoes, and bananas, and pastures and yards for cattle, sheep, and poultry. Yields were apparently high; Ibn-Batuta noted that the rich enjoyed three enormous meals a day and were very fat.

From among the rich mercantile families that controlled the coastal cities, a ruler arose who had by the fourteenth century taken the Arabic title of *sheikh,* or sultan. The sheikh governed both the island city and the nearby mainland. Further inland, tribal chiefs ruled with the advice of councils of elders. By the late thirteenth century Kilwa had become the most powerful city on the coast, exercising political hegemony as far north as Pemba and as far south as Sofala (see Map 16.1 on page 531).

The Portuguese, approaching the East African coastal cities in the early sixteenth century, were astounded at their enormous wealth and prosperity. This wealth rested on monopolistic control of all trade in the area. Some coastal cities manufactured goods for export: Mogadishu produced a cloth for the Egyptian market, Mombassa and Molindi processed iron tools, and Sofala made Cambay cottons for the interior trade. The bulk of the cities' exports, however, were animal products – tortoise shell, ambergris, leopard skins, ivory – and gold. The gold originated in the Mutapa region south of the Zambezi River (see Map 16.1 on page 531), where the Bantus mined it. As in tenth-century Ghana, gold was a royal monopoly in the fourteenth-century coastal city-states: the Mutapa kings received it as annual tribute, prohibited outsiders from entering the mines or participating in the trade, and controlled shipments down the Zambezi River to the coastal markets. The prosperity of Kilwa rested upon its traffic in gold.

African goods satisfied the widespread aristocratic demand for luxury goods. In Arabia, the leopard skins were made into saddles, the shells into combs, and ambergris was used in the manufacture of perfumes. Because the tusks of African elephants were larger and more durable than those of Indian elephants, African ivory was in great demand in India for sword and dagger handles, carved decorative objects, and the ceremonial bangles used in Hindu marriage rituals. In China, the wealthy valued African ivory for use in the construction of sedan chairs.

In exchange for these natural products, the Swahili cities bought pottery, glassware and beads, and many varieties of cloth. Swahili kings imposed enormous duties on imports, perhaps more than 80 percent of the value of the goods themselves. Even so, merchants who came to Africa to trade made fabulous profits.

ETHIOPIAN FOLK ART   In Christian Ethiopia the arts, which were shaped by folk tradition, served the church and the state. These scenes, a free intermingling of scriptural events, royal occasions, and apocryphal gospel episodes, show no European or Byzantine artistic influence; they thus reflect Ethiopia's cultural isolation. (The American Museum of Natural History)

ETHIOPIA: THE CHRISTIAN KINGDOM OF AXUM

The great eighteenth-century historian Edward Gibbon wrote that "Ethiopians slept near a thousand years." Gibbon meant that, for a near-millennium between the seventh and fifteenth centuries, Europeans knew nothing about Ethiopia. In the fourth century Ethiopia had accepted Christianity, and the appointment of a bishop by the Egyptian patriarch of Alexandria led to close ties with the Egyptian Coptic Church. At the time, the capital city of Axum was a powerful cosmopolitan center whose mercantile activities played a major part in international commerce and whose military and political power was the dominant influence in East Africa.

The expansion of Islam in the eighth century severed Axum's commercial contacts with the Byzantine Empire and ended its control of the Red Sea routes. The kingdom declined as a major power. Ethiopia's high Abyssinian mountains encouraged an inward concentration of attention and hindered access from the outside. Twelfth-century crusaders returning from the Middle East told of a powerful Christian ruler, Prester John, whose lands lay behind Muslim lines and who was anxious to help restore the Holy Land to Christian control. Europeans identified that kingdom with Ethiopia. In the later thirteenth century, the dynasty of the Solomonid kings witnessed a literary and artistic renais-

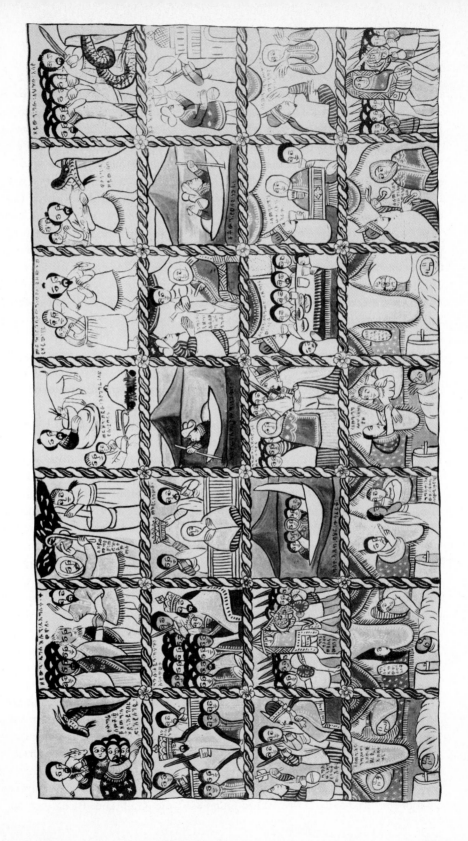

sance particularly notable for works of hagiography, biblical exegesis, and manuscript illumination. The most striking feature of Ethiopian society in the period 500–1500 was the close relationship between the church and the state. Coptic Christianity inspired a fierce devotion and tended to equate doctrinal heresy with political rebellion, thus reinforcing central monarchial power.

Early Africa encompassed a wide variety of political systems, so many that it is difficult to classify them into meaningful categories. Nevertheless, all African societies shared one basic feature: a close relationship between political and social organization. Ethnic or blood ties bound the clan together. What scholars call "stateless societies" were culturally homogeneous ethnic societies, the smaller ones numbering fewer than 100 people, who pursued a nomadic hunting existence; larger stateless societies of perhaps several thousand people lived a settled and often agricultural or herding life. The Pygmies of the tropical rain forest exemplify a type of stateless society. In the western Sudan, large empires with complicated royal bureaucracies developed. In the Christian kingdom of Ethiopia in east central Africa, kings relied on the strong Christian faith of their people to strengthen political authority. The East Coast gave rise to powerful city-states based on sophisticated mercantile activities. Before the intrusion of Europeans, Africa was a rich mosaic of political and social systems.

THE PEOPLES AND GEOGRAPHY OF THE AMERICAS

In 1501–1502 the Florentine explorer Amerigo Vespucci (1451–1512) sailed down the coast of Brazil. Convinced that he had found a new world, Vespucci published an account of his voyage. Shortly thereafter the geographer Martin Waldseemüller proposed that this New World be called America to preserve Vespucci's memory. Initially applied only to South America, by the end of the sixteenth century the term *America* was used for both continents in the Western Hemisphere.

To the people of the Americas, of course, the notion of a discovery meant nothing. The New World was, in a sense, a European invention. And even for Europeans the concept of discovery presented problems. In matters of geography as in other branches of knowledge, medieval Europeans believed that all human knowledge was contained in the Scriptures, the writings of the Church Fathers, and the Greek and Roman authors, none of whom mentioned a new world. The adventurous explorers of the fifteenth and sixteenth centuries sailed west searching for Asia and Africa because, for Europeans, those continents and Europe were the only world that existed. They did not expect to find a new continent. Long before the arrival of Europeans, however, sophisticated civilizations had flourished in Central and South America.

From the Bering Straits to the southern tip of South America is about 11,000 miles, or about the distance from Greenland to Cape Town, South Africa. A mountain range extends all the way from Alaska to the tip of South America, crossing Central America from northwest to southeast, and making for rugged country along virtually the entire west coast of both continents.

Mexico, whose name derives from that of the Aztecs who settled in central Mexico, is dominated by high plateaus bounded by coastal plains. Geographers have labelled the plateau regions "Cold Lands," the valleys between the plateaus "Temperate Lands," and the Gulf and Pacific coastal regions "Hot

Lands." The Caribbean coast of Central America – modern Guatemala, Honduras, Nicaragua, El Salvador, Costa Rica, and Panama – is characterized by thickly jungled lowlands, heavy rainfall, and torrid heat, generally unhealthy for humans. Central America's western uplands, with their more temperate climate and good agricultural land, support the densest population in the region.

The continent of South America, south of the Isthmus of Panama, contains twelve nations: in descending order of size, Brazil, Argentina, Peru, Colombia, Bolivia, Venezuela, Chile, Ecuador, Guyana, Uruguay, Surinam and French Guiana. Brazil – 3 times the size of Argentina and almost 100 times larger than French Guiana – is about the same size as the United States including Alaska. Like Africa, South America is a continent of extremely varied terrain. The entire western coast is edged by the Andes, the highest mountain range in the hemisphere. Mt. Alcanqua in Argentina rises 23,000 feet, or 3,000 feet higher than the tallest mountain in the United States. On the east coast another mountain range, called the Brazilian highlands, accounts for one quarter of the area of Brazil. Yet three quarters of South America – almost the entire periphery of the continent – is plains. The Amazon River, at 4,000 miles the second longest river in the world, bisects the north-central part of the continent. The Amazon drains 2.7 million square miles of land in Brazil, Colombia, and Peru. Tropical lowland rain forests, characterized by dense growth and annual rainfall in excess of eighty inches a year, extend from the Amazon and Orinoco River basins northward all the way to southern Mexico. This jungle, the largest in the world, covers parts of Brazil, Venezuela, and Ecuador.

Most scholars believe that people began crossing the Bering Straits from Russian Si-

beria only about 20,000 years ago, when the straits were narrower. Skeletal finds indicate that these immigrants belonged to several ethnic groups. Anthropologists classify the earliest of them as Amurians, short-statured people with long flat heads and coppery skin – a physical type once common in Asia and Europe. The last to arrive, at about the time of Christ, had strong Mongoloid features, large faces, and yellowish skin. The American Indians, or Amerinds, represent a hybrid of Amurians and Mongoloids.

Nomadic and extremely primitive, Amerinds lived by hunting small animals, fishing, and gathering wild fruits. As soon as an area had been exploited and the group had grown too large for the land to support, some families moved on, usually southward. Food supply and climate forced them to migrate.

Gradually the newcomers spread throughout the Americas, losing contact with one another. At the time the Europeans arrived, most of the peoples of North America and the huge Amazon Basin were Neolithic hunters and farmers, some migratory and some living in villages. Linguistic studies have revealed a mosaic of languages: 250 languages, most of them mutually unintelligible, were spoken between the northern border of Mexico and the southern border of Guatemala alone. Even today, inhabitants of neighboring villages in southern Mexico speak totally different tongues and must communicate in a third language. Like Africa, America exhibits enormous cultural diversity.

Some of the peoples of the Americas became big-game hunters, armed with heavy stone missiles. These hunters, who roamed the plains until the arrival of Europeans, necessarily travelled in small groups. Sizable populations grew, however, among the peoples who learned to cultivate the soil. By necessity or experimentation or accident, they discov-

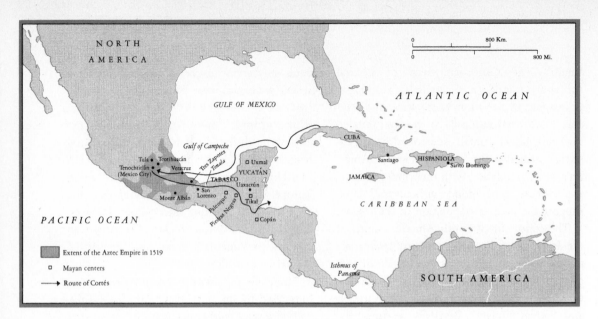

MAP 16.2 THE AZTEC EMPIRE, 1519 *The
Aztecs controlled much of central Mexico, the Maya
the Yucatan peninsula and some of modern Guatemala. Note the number of cities.*

ered how to domesticate plants. Archeological
excavations in Mexico City have unearthed
fossilized corn at depths of around 50 feet,
indicating that corn was grown there around
2500 B.C. Corn requires very little work to
grow, and yields a fantastic harvest. In central
Mexico, the Amerinds built *chinampas* or
floating gardens, constructed by dredging soil
from the bottom of a lake or pond, placing
the soil on mats of woven twigs, and planting
crops in the soil; chinampas were enormously
productive, yielding up to three harvests a
year. So extensive was this method of agriculture that central Mexico became known as the
chinampas region. In Peru, meanwhile, the
Andean mountain slopes were terraced with
stone retaining walls to keep the hillsides
from sliding. Both chinampas and terraced
slopes required large labor forces. Stable settlement, therefore, became essential. Before
2300 B.C. the Amerinds raised corn, beans,
squash, pumpkins, and, in the area of modern
Peru, white potatoes. Careful cultivation of

the land meant a reliable and steady food supply, which contributed to a higher fertility
rate and in turn to a population boom. Because corn and potatoes require much less
labor than grain, Amerindian civilizations
were able to use their large labor forces in the
construction of religious and political buildings and as standing armies.[19] Agricultural advancement thus had definitive social and political consequences.

THE OLMEC, TEOTIHUACAN, AND TOLTEC CIVILIZATIONS OF MEXICO

Population growth led to the development of
the first distinct Mesoamerican civilization,
the Olmec, which scholars estimate to have
thrived from approximately 1500 B.C. to A.D.
300 (Scholars use the term *Mesoamerican* to
designate the area of present-day Mexico and
Central America.) All subsequent Meso-

american cultures have rested on the Olmec. Originating at modern San Lorenzo in the region of southern Veracruz and Tabasco (see Map 16.2 on page 554), Olmec society revolved around groups of large stone buildings where the political elite and the priestly hierarchy resided with their retainers. Peasant farmers inhabited the surrounding countryside. From careful study of the great surviving architectural monuments and their richly carved jade sculptures, scholars have learned more about Olmec culture: a small hereditary elite governed the mass of workers; the clustered buildings served as sites for religious ceremonies and as marketplaces for the exchange of agricultural produce and manufactured goods. The Olmecs also possessed a form of writing. Around 900 B.C. San Lorenzo was destroyed, probably by migrating peoples from the north, and power passed to La Venta in Tabasco.

At La Venta, archeological excavation has uncovered the huge volcano-shaped Great Pyramid. Built 110 feet high at an inaccessible site on an island in the Tonala River, the Great Pyramid was the center of the Olmec religious cult. Like the cathedrals of medieval Europe, the upward thrust of this monument may have represented the human effort to get closer to the gods. Built of huge stone slabs, the Great Pyramid required, scholars have estimated, some 800,000 man-hours of labor. It testifies to the region's bumper harvests, which supported a labor force large enough to build such a monument. Around 300 B.C., however, La Venta fell. Tres Zapotes, 100 miles to the northwest, became the leading Olmec site. Olmec ceremonialism, magnificent sculpture, skillful stone work, social organization, and writing were important cultural advances that paved the way for the developments of the Classic Period.

During the period from about A.D. 300 to A.D. 900, which specialists in Mesoamerican culture call "the Golden Age" or "the Classic Period," the Teotihuacan valley in central Mexico witnessed the flowering of a remarkable civilization. The culture of Teotihuacan seems to have been built by a new people from regions east and south of the Valley of Mexico. The city of Teotihuacan had a population of over 200,000 – larger than any European city at the time. The inhabitants of Teotihuacan were stratified into distinct social classes: the rich and powerful elite resided in a special precinct, in houses of palatial splendor. Ordinary working people, tradespeople, artisans, and obsidian craftsmen lived in apartment compounds on the edge of the city. Around A.D. 600 each of these compounds housed about a hundred people; archeological research is slowly yielding information about their standard of living. The inhabitants of the barrio compounds seem to have been very poor, related by kinship ties, and perhaps shared common ritual interests. Agricultural laborers lived outside the city. Teotihuacan was a great commercial center, the entrepôt for trade and culture for all of Mesoamerica. It was also the ceremonial center of an entire society, a capital filled with artworks, a mecca that attracted thousands of pilgrims a year.

In the center of the city stood the great pyramids of the sun and moon. The former, each of whose sides was 700 feet long and 200 feet high, was built of sun-dried bricks and faced with stone. The smaller pyramid of the moon god was similar in construction. In lesser temples, natives and outlanders worshipped the rain god and the feathered serpent, later called Quetzalcoatl. These gods were all associated with the production of corn, the staple of the people's diet.

Although Teotihuacan dominated Mesoamerican civilization during the Classic Period, other centers also flourished. In the isolated valley of Oaxaca at modern-day Monte Albán (see Map 16.2 on page 554), for example, Zapotecan-speaking peoples established a great religious center whose temples and elaborately decorated tombs testify to the wealth of the nobility. The art – and probably the entire culture – of Monte Albán and other such centers derived from Teotihuacan.

As had happened earlier to San Lorenzo and La Venta, Teotihuacan collapsed before new invaders. Around A.D. 700 semi-barbarian hordes from either the Jalisco region or southern Zacatecas burned Teotihuacan, and Monte Albán fell shortly afterwards. By 900 the Golden Age of Mesoamerica had ended.

There followed an interregnum known as "the Time of Troubles" (ca A.D. 800–1000), characterized by disorders and an extreme militarism. Whereas nature gods and their priests seem to have governed the great cities of the earlier period, militant gods and warriors dominated the petty states that now arose. Among these states, the most powerful heir to Teotihuacan was the Toltec confederation. Like previous invading peoples, the Toltecs admired the culture of their predecessors and sought to absorb and preserve it; through intermarriage, they assimilated with the Teotihuacan. Thus every new Mesoamerican confederation – a weak union of strong states – became the cultural successor of earlier ones.

Under the semi-legendary figure Toliptzin (ca 980–1000), the Toltecs extended their hegemony over most of central Mexico from coast to coast. Apparently Toliptzin adopted the name Quetzalcoatl, signifying his position as high priest of the god worshipped by the Toltecs. He established his capital at Tula, whose splendor and power became legendary during his reign. According to the "Song of Quetzalcoatl," a long Aztec glorification of him:

He [Toliptzin-Quetzalcoatl] was very rich and had everything necessary to eat and drink, and the corn [under his reign] was in abundance, and the squash very fat, an arm's length around, and the ears of corn were so tall that they were carried with both arms.... and they sowed and reaped cotton in all colors, red and incarnate and yellow and brown and whitish, green and blue and blackish and gray and orange and tawny, and these colors of the cotton were natural.... And more than that the said Quetzalcoatl had all the wealth in the world, gold and silver and green stones [jade] and other precious things and a great abundance of cocao trees in different colors, and the said vassals of the said Quetzalcoatl were very rich and lacked nothing.... nor did they lack corn, nor did they eat the small ears but rather they used them like firewood to heat up their baths.[20]

Aztec legends describe a powerful struggle between the Toltecs' original tribal god, Tezcatlipoca, who required human sacrifices, and the newer Toltec-Teotihuacan god, Quetzalcoatl, who gave his people bumper corn crops, fostered learning and the arts, and asked only the sacrifice of animals like butterflies and snakes. Tezcatlipoca won this battle, and the priest-king Toliptzin-Quetzalcoatl was driven into exile. As he departed, he promised to return and regain his kingdom.

Whatever reality lies behind this legend, it became a cornerstone of later Aztec tradition. It also played a profound role in Mexican history: by a remarkable coincidence, the year that Quetzalcoatl had promised to return happened to be the year when the Spanish conquistador Cortés landed in Mexico. Belief in the Quetzalcoatl legend helps explain the Aztec emperor Montezuma's indecisiveness about the Spanish adventurers, and his ultimate fate.

After the departure of Toliptzin-Quetzalcoatl, troubles beset the Toltec state. Drought led to crop failure. Northern barbarian peoples, the Chichimec, attacked the borders in waves. Weak, incompetent rulers could not quell domestic uprisings. When its last king committed suicide in 1174, the Toltec state collapsed. In 1224 the Chichimec captured Tula.

The last of the Chichimec to arrive in central Mexico were the Aztecs. As before, the vanquished strongly influenced the victors: the Aztecs absorbed the cultural achievements of the Toltecs. The Aztecs – building on Olmec, Teotihuacan, and Toltec antecedents— created the last unifying civilization in Mexico before the arrival of the Europeans.

AZTEC SOCIETY: RELIGION AND WAR

When the Aztecs appeared in the valley of Mexico, they spoke the same Nahuatl language as the Toltecs. Otherwise, however, they had nothing in common with their advanced predecessors. Poor, unwelcome, looked upon as foreign barbarians, they had to settle on a few swampy islands in Lake Texoco. There, in 1325, they founded a city consisting of a few huts and an altar for their war-god Huitzilopochtli, who had protected them during 150 years of wandering. From these unpromising beginnings the Aztecs rapidly assimilated the cultural legacy of the Toltecs and in 1428 embarked on a policy of territorial expansion. By the time Hernando Cortés arrived in 1520, less than a century later, the Aztec confederation encompassed all of central Mexico from the Gulf to the Pacific and as far south as Guatemala. The rulers of neighboring Texoco and Tlacopan bowed to the Aztec king, and thirty-eight subordinate provinces paid him tribute.

QUETZALCOATL *Just as the Aztec gods required nourishment from human sacrifice, so Aztec sculpture displays brutal and terrifying aspects. Here Quetzalcoatl is shown as the bringer of civilization and god of flowing water. (The Brooklyn Museum, Henry L. Batlerman and Frank S. Benson Funds)*

The growth of a strong mercantile class led to an influx of tropical wares and luxury goods: cotton, feathers, cocoa, skins, turquoise jewelry, and gold. The upper classes consequently enjoyed an elegant and extravagant life style; the court of the Emperor Montezuma II (1502–1520) was more magnificent than anything in western Europe. How, in less than two hundred years, had the Mexicans (from the Aztec word *mizquitl,* meaning desolate land, or from Mixitli, the Aztec god of war) grown from an insignificant tribe of wandering nomads to a people of vast power and fabulous wealth?

Aztec pictorial records attribute their own success to the power of their god Huitzilopochtli and to the Aztecs' drive and indomitable will power. Will and determination they unquestionably had, but there is another explanation: the Aztec state was geared for war. In the course of the fifteenth century, the primitive tribesmen who had arrived in the Mexican valley in 1325 transformed themselves into professional soldiers. As the territory under Aztec control gradually expanded and military campaigns continued, warriors had to be in perpetual readiness. They were constantly subduing new states and crushing rebellions. A strong standing army was the backbone of the Mexican state, and war had become the central feature of Mexican culture.

WAR AND HUMAN SACRIFICE

In Aztec society, war was the dominant cultural institution. War shaped the social hierarchy, the education people received, and the level of economic prosperity. War was also an article of religious faith.

Chief among the Aztecs' many gods was Huitzilopochtli, who symbolized the sun blazing at high noon. The sun, the source of all life, had to be kept moving in its orbit if darkness was not to overtake the world. To keep it moving, Mexicans believed, the sun had to be frequently fed precious fluid—that is, human blood. Human sacrifice was therefore a sacred duty, essential for the preservation and prosperity of humankind. The bleeding heart ripped from the victim's chest averted the disasters that constantly threatened to destroy the universe. Black-robed priests carried out the sacred ritual in the following manner:

The victim was stretched out on his back on a slightly convex stone with his arms and legs held by four priests, while a fifth ripped him open with a flint knife and tore out his heart. The sacrifice also often took place in a manner which the Spanish described as gladiatorio: *the captive was tied to a huge disk of stone . . . by a rope that left him free to move; he was armed with wooden weapons, and he had to fight several normally-armed Aztec warriors in turn. If, by an extraordinary chance, he did not succumb to their attacks, he was spared; but nearly always the 'gladiator' fell, gravely wounded, and a few moments later he died on the stone, with his body opened by the black-robed, long-haired priests. The warriors who were set apart for this kind of death wore ornaments and clothes of a special nature, and they were crowned with white down, as a symbol of the first light of dawn when the soul of the resuscitated warrior takes its flight in the greyness towards our father the sun.*[21]

The large Aztec armies sometimes took thousands of prisoners in a single battle:

In addition to daily sacrifices of small numbers of prisoners and slaves at major and minor shrines, then, mass sacrifices involving hundreds and thousands of victims could be carried out to commemorate special events. The Spanish chroniclers were told, for example, that at the dedication in 1487, of the great pyramid of Tenochitlán four lines of prisoners stretching for two miles each were sacrificed by a team of executioners who worked night and day for four days. Alloting two minutes for sacrifice, the demographer and historian Sherbourne Cook estimated that the number of victims associated with that single event was 14,100. The scale of these rituals could be dismissed as exaggerations were it not for the encounters of Bernal Diaz and Andres de Tapia (companions of Cortés) with methodically racked and hence easily counted rows of human skulls in the plazas of the Aztec cities. Diaz writes that in the plaza of Xocotlan "there were piles of human skulls so regularly arranged that one could count them, and I estimated them at more than a hundred thousand. I repeat again there were more than one hundred thousand of them."[22]

The Aztecs held that these sacrifices provided sustenance for Huitzilopochtli and appeased the gods of earth, rain, and the other forces of nature. Hence, human sacrifice represented the only means of satisfying the deities and of preventing chaos in a basically unstable world. The bodies of many victims were eaten after their hearts had been torn out. How ought we to understand the practice of human sacrifice and cannibalism?

Anthropologists have recently proposed a variety of explanations, none of them completely satisfactory. Some have suggested that sacrificing people to the gods served to regulate population growth, keeping the population consistent with the food supply that the area could produce. Yet the ritual slaughter of human beings had been practiced by earlier peoples – the Olmecs, the Teotihuacans, and the Toltecs – in all likelihood before population density had reached the point of threatening the available food supply. Moreover, since almost all those sacrificed were men – warriors captured in battle – population growth could still have exceeded the death rate. It would have had more effect on population to execute women of childbearing age.

According to a second hypothesis, the Aztecs lived on a diet of corn, beans, squash, tomatoes, and peppers; dog meat, chicken, turkey, and fish was virtually restricted to the upper classes, since wildlife was scarce. Continual population growth meant that meat was unavailable to ordinary people. A protein deficiency resulted, and the Aztec rulers kept the masses quiet by feeding them the carcasses of human beings.[23] Even if we ignore the testimony of modern nutritionists that beans supply ample protein, other evidence weakens the validity of this gruesome notion: in an area teeming with wild game, the Huron Indians of North America ritually executed captives and feasted on their stewed bodies. Meat shortage could not have been a nutritional problem for the Hurons.

A third theory holds that ritual human sacrifice was an instrument of state terrorism. The Aztecs controlled a large confederation of city-states by sacrificing prisoners seized in battle; by taking hostages from among defeated peoples as ranson against future revolt; and by demanding from subject states an annual tribute of people to be sacrificed to Huitzilopochtli. Thus, the argument goes, Aztec rulers crushed dissent with terror. Unsuccessful generals, corrupt judges and careless public officials, even people who accidentally entered forbidden precincts of the royal palaces, were routinely sacrificed. When the supply of such victims ran out, slaves, plebians, even infants torn from their mothers suffered ritual execution. The emperor Montezuma II (ca 1502-1520), who celebrated his coronation with the sacrifice of 5,100 people, could be said to have ruled by holocaust. Trumpets blasted and drums beat all day long announcing the sacrifice of yet another victim. Blood poured down the steps of the pyramids.

Death stalked everywhere, fear haunted the land. Ordinary people appear to have endured this living nightmare by escaping into intoxicating drink and drugs.[24] The enthusiasm with which subject city-states greeted Cortés on his march to the Mexican capital lends plausibility to the thesis that human sacrifice was an instrument of state terrorism.

THE LIFE OF THE PEOPLE

A wealth of information survives about fifteenth- and sixteenth-century Mexico. The Aztecs were deeply interested in their own past, and in their pictographic script wrote many books recounting their history, geography, and religious practices. They loved making speeches, and every public or social occasion gave rise to lengthy orations, which scribes copied down. The Aztecs also preserved records of their legal disputes, which alone amounted to vast files. The Spanish conquerors subsequently destroyed much of this material. But many documents remain, making it possible to construct a picture of the Mexican people at the time of the Spanish intrusion.

During their early migrations, no sharp social distinctions existed among the Aztecs. All were equally poor. The head of the family was both provider and warrior, and a sort of tribal democracy prevailed in which all adult males participated in important decisionmaking. By the early sixteenth century, however, a stratified social structure had come into being, and the warrior aristocracy exercised great power and authority.

Scholars do not yet understand precisely how this social stratification evolved. According to Aztec legend, the Mexicans admired the Toltecs and chose their first king, Acamapichti, from among them. The many children he fathered with Aztec women formed the nucleus of the noble class. At the time of the Spanish intrusion into Mexico, men who had distinguished themselves in war occupied the highest military and social positions in the state. The highest generals, the leading judges, and the governors of provinces were appointed by the emperor from among his servants who had earned reputations as war heroes. These great lords, or *tecuhtli,* dressed luxuriously and lived in palaces. The provincial governors exercised full political, judicial, and military authority on the emperor's behalf. In their territories they maintained order, settled disputes and judged legal cases, oversaw the cultivation of land, and made sure that tribute – in food or gold – was paid to the emperor. The governors also led contingents of troops in wartime. These functions resembled those of feudal lords in western Europe during the Middle Ages (pages 361–363). Just as only nobles of France and England could wear fur and carry a sword, so in Aztec society, only the *tecuhtli* could wear jewelry and embroidered cloaks.

Beneath the great nobility of soldiers and imperial officials resided the class of warriors. Theoretically, every free man could be a warrior, and parents dedicated their male children to war: the parents buried the child's umbilical cord with some arrows and a shield on the day of his birth. In actuality, the sons of nobles enjoyed advantages deriving from their fathers' position and influence in the state. At the age of six, the boy entered a school that trained him for war. Future warriors were taught to fight with a *macana,* a paddle-shaped wooden club edged with bits of obsidian, a volcanic rock similar to granite but as sharp as glass. This weapon could be brutally effective: during the Spanish invasion, Aztec warriors armed with macanas slashed off the heads of horses at one blow. Youths were also trained in the use of spears, bows and arrows, and lances with obsidian points. They learned to live on little food and sleep, and to accept bodily pain without complaint. At about age eighteen a warrior fought his first campaign; if he captured a prisoner for ritual sacrifice, he acquired the title of *iyac,* or warrior. If in later campaigns he succeeded in killing or capturing four of the enemy, he became a *tequiua–*one of those who shared in the booty, and thus a member of the nobility. The warrior class enjoyed a proud and privileged position in Mexican society because they provided the state with the victims necessary for its survival. If, however, a young man failed in several campaigns to capture the required four prisoners, he joined the *maceualti,* the plebian or working class.

The maceualtin were the ordinary citizens, the backbone of Aztec society and the vast majority of the population. The word *maceualti* means worker, and implied boorish speech and vulgar behavior. Members of this class performed all sorts of agricultural, military, and domestic services and carried heavy public burdens, which noble warriors did not. Government officials assigned the maceualtin work on the temples, roads and bridges. Army officers called them up for military duty, but Mexicans considered this an honor and a religious rite, not a burden. Maceualtin paid taxes, which nobles, priests, orphans, and slaves did not do. On the other hand, the maceualtin in the capital possessed certain rights: they held their plots of land for life, and they received a small share of the tribute paid by the provinces to the emperor. Maceualtin in subject provinces enjoyed none of these rights.

Beneath the maceualtin were the *thalmaitl,* the landless workers or serfs. Some social his-

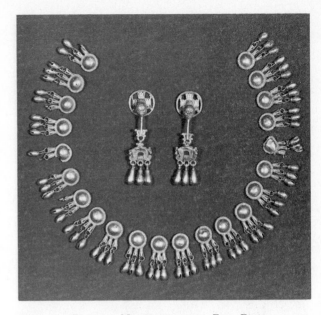

MIXTECA-PUEBLA NECKLACE AND EAR BOBS
Aztec men and women of the warrior class loved elaborate jewelry such as this rich necklace and ear rings of cast gold, one of the few examples of Aztec artistry to escape the Spanish melting pot. (Dumbarton Oaks Research Library and Collections, Washington, D.C.)

torians speculate that this class originated during the period of migrations and upheavals, when weak and defenseless people placed themselves under the protection of strong warriors. The thalmaitl provided agricultural labor at times of planting and harvesting, paid rents in kind, and were bound to the soil – they could not move off the land. The thalmaitl resembled in many ways the serfs of western Europe, but unlike serfs performed military service when called on to do so. They enjoyed some rights as citizens and generally were accorded more respect than slaves.

THE GODDESS TLAZOLTEOTL *The Aztecs believed that Tlazolteotl (sometimes called the "Mother of the Gods"), in her eating refuse, consumed the sins of humankind, thus leaving them pure. As the goddess of childbirth, Tlazolteotl was extensively worshipped. Note the squatting position for childbirth, then common all over the world. (Dumbarton Oaks Research Library and Collections, Washington, D.C.)*

Slaves were the lowest social class. Like European and African slaves, most were prisoners captured in war or kidnapped from enemy tribes but usually not sacrificed. Aztecs who stole from a temple or private house or plotted against the emperor could also be en-

slaved. Also people in serious debt sometimes voluntarily sold themselves into slavery. Female slaves often became their masters' concubines. Mexican slaves, however, differed fundamentally from European ones: "Tlatlocotin (slaves) could possess goods, save money, buy land and houses and even slaves for their own service."[25] Slaves could purchase their freedom; if a slave married a free woman, their offspring were free, and a slave who escaped and managed to enter the emperor's palace was automatically free. Most slaves eventually gained their freedom. Mexican slavery, therefore, had humane qualities, in marked contrast with the methods the Spanish later introduced into South America and those the English imposed in North America.

Alongside these secular social classes stood the temple priests. The sun-god Huitzilopochtli and the many lesser gods each had many priests to oversee the upkeep of the temple, assist at religious ceremonies, and perform the ritual sacrifices. The priests also did a brisk business in divination, foretelling the future on the basis of signs and omens. Aztecs were deeply concerned about coming events, and consulted priests on such matters as the selection of wives and husbands and the future careers of newborn babies; they routinely did so before journeys and when departing for war. Because the emperor and the wealthy showered gifts on the gods, temples possessed enormous wealth in gold and silver ceremonial vessels, statues, buildings and land. For example, fifteen provincial villages had to provide food for the temple at Texoco and wood for its eternal fires. The priests who had custody of all this property did not marry and were expected to live moral and upright lives. From the temple revenues and resources, the priests supported schools, aided the poor, and maintained hospitals. The chief priests had the ear of the emperor, having participated in his election and often exercised great power and influence.

At the peak of the social pyramid stood the emperor. The various Aztec historians contradict each other about the origin of the imperial dynasty, but modern scholars tend to accept the verdict of one sixteenth-century authority that "the custom has always been preserved among the Mexicans (that) the sons of kings have not ruled by right of inheritance, but by election."[26] The monarchy passed from the emperor to the ablest son of one of his legitimate wives (not his many concubines); a small oligarchy of the chief priests, warriors, and state officials made the selection. If none of the sons proved satisfactory, a brother or nephew of the emperor was chosen, but election was always restricted to the royal family. The nineteenth-century historian William Prescott vividly described the imperial coronation:

The new monarch was installed in his regal dignity with much parade of religious ceremony; but not until, by a victorious campaign he had obtained a sufficient number of captives to grace his triumphal entry into the capital, and to furnish victims for the dark and bloody rites which stained the Aztec superstition. Amidst this pomp of human sacrifice, he was crowned. The crown, resembling a mitre in its form, and curiously ornamented with gold, gems, and feathers, was placed on his head by the lord of Tezcuco, the most powerful of his royal allies. The title of King, by which the earlier Aztec princes are distinguished by Spanish writers, is supplanted by that of Emperor in the later reigns, intimating, perhaps, his superiority over the confederated monarchies of Tlacopan and Tezcuco.

The Aztec princes, especially towards the close of the dynasty, lived in a barbaric pomp, truly oriental. Their spacious palaces were provided with halls for the different councils, who aided the monarch in the transaction of business. The chief of these was a sort of privy council, composed in part, probably, of the four electors chosen by the nobles . . . It was the business of this body, so far as can be gathered from the very loose accounts given of it, to advise the king, in respect to the government of the provinces, the administration of the revenues, and, indeed, on all great matters of public interest.

In the royal buildings were accomodations, also, for a numerous body-guard of the sovereign, made up of the chief nobility.[27]

Prescott's account exhibits some of the Anglo-Saxon cultural arrogance typical of nineteenth-century scholars, but is evocative and apparently accurate.

The Aztec emperor was expected to be a great warrior; one of his titles was *tlacatecuhtli*, lord of the men. He led Mexican and allied armies into battle. His other duties all pertained to the welfare of his people. It was up to the emperor to see that justice was done – he was the final court of appeal. He also held ultimate responsibility for insuring an adequate food supply, and for protecting against famine and other disasters. The emperor Montezuma I (1440–1467) distributed 20,000 loads of stockpiled grain when a flood hit the city. The records show that the Aztec emperors took their public duties very seriously.

THE CITIES OF THE AZTECS

When the Spanish entered Mexico City in November, 1519, they could not believe their eyes. According to Bernal Diaz, one of Cortés's companions:

And when we saw all those cities and villages built in the water, and other great towns on dry

land, and that straight and level causeway lead-
ing to Mexico, we were astounded. These great
towns and cues (temples) and buildings rising from
the water, all made of stone, seemed like an en-
chanted vision from the tale of Amadis. Indeed,
some of our soldiers asked whether it was not all a
dream.[28]

The credulous Diaz, the calculating Cortés –
all the Spanish agreed on the astonishing
beauty of the city.

Tenochtitlan – the Aztec name for Mexico
City – had about 60,000 households. The
upper class practiced polygamy and had many
children, and many households included servants and slaves; thus the total population
probably numbered at least 500,000 people.
No European city and few Asian ones could
boast a population even half that size. The
total Aztec empire has been estimated at
around 5 million inhabitants.

Originally built on salt marshes, Tenochtitlan was approached by four great highways
that connected it with the mainland. Wide
straight streets and canals criss-crossed the
city, and the bridges over the canals were so
broad and solidly built that ten horsemen
could ride abreast over them. Boats and
canoes plied the canals. Lining the roads and
canals stood thousands of rectangular one-
story houses of mortar faced with stucco. Although space was limited, many houses had
small gardens, which along with the numerous parks blazed with the colors and scents of
flowers. The Mexicans loved flowers and used
them in ritual ceremonies.

A large aqueduct whose sophisticated engineering astounded Cortés carried pure water
from distant springs and supplied fountains in
the parks. Streets and canals opened onto
public squares. The Spanish marvelled that
the large square containing the main marketplace was "twice as big as that of Salamanaca
(in Spain), with arcades all around, where

more than sixty thousand people came every
day."[29] Tradespeople offered every kind of
merchandise: butchers hawked turkeys, ducks,
chickens, rabbits, and deer, while grocers sold
kidney beans, squash, avocados, corn, and all
kinds of peppers. Artisans sold intricately designed gold, silver, and feathered jewelry.
Seamstresses offered sandals, loincloths and
cloaks for men and blouses and long skirts for
women – the traditional dress of ordinary
people – and embroidered robes and cloaks
for the rich. Slaves for domestic service, wood
for building, herbs for seasoning and medicinal purposes, honey and sweets, knives, jars
and utensils, smoking tobacco, even human
excrement used to cure animal skins – all
these wares made so dazzling a spectacle that
Bernal Diaz exclaimed: "If I describe everything in detail, I shall never be done."[30]

At one side of the central square of Tenochtitlan stood the great temple of Huitzilopochtli. Built as a pyramid and approached
by three flights of 120 steps each, the temple
was about 100 feet high and dominated the
city's skyline. According to Cortés's account,
the temple was

so large that within the precincts, which are sur-
rounded by a very high wall, a town of some five
hundred inhabitants could easily be built. All
round inside this wall there are very elegant
quarters with very large rooms and corridors where
their priests live. There are as many as forty
towers, all of which are so high that in the case of
the largest there are fifty steps leading up to the
main part of it; and the most important of these
towers is higher than that of the cathedral of Se-
ville. They are so well constructed in both their
stone and woodwork that there can be none better
in any place, for all the stonework inside the
chapels where they keep their idols is in high relief
with figures and little houses... All these towers
are burial places of chiefs, and the chapels therein
are each dedicated to the idol which he venerated.[31]

Assessing the Aztec way of life for the emperor Charles V, Cortés concluded:

I will say only that these people live almost like those in Spain, and in such harmony and order as there, and considering that they are barbarous and so far from the knowledge of God and cut off from all civilized nations, it is truly remarkable to see what they have achieved in all things.[32]

While Cortés's views reflect his own culture and outlook, it is undeniable that Aztec civilization was remarkable.

The strange end of the Aztec nation remains one of the most fascinating events in the annals of human societies. The Spanish adventurer Hernando Cortés landed at Vera Cruz in February 1519. In November, he entered Tenochtitlan and soon had the emperor Montezuma in custody. Within less than two years he had destroyed the monarchy, gained complete control of the Mexican capital, and extended his jurisdiction over much of the Aztec empire. Why did a strong people defending its own territory succumb so quickly to a handful of Spaniards fighting in dangerous and completely unfamiliar circumstances? How indeed, since Montezuma's scouts sent him detailed reports of the Spaniard's movements? The answer lies in the Spaniards' boldness and timing, and in Aztec psychology, political structure, attitude toward war, and level of technology.

The Spaniards arrived in late summer, when the Aztecs were preoccupied with harvesting their crops and not thinking of war. From the Spaniards' perspective, their timing was ideal. Then, a series of natural phenomena, signs, and portents seemed to augur coming disaster. A comet was seen in daytime, a column of fire appeared every midnight for a year, and two temples were suddenly destroyed, one by lightning unaccompanied by thunder. These and other apparently inexplicable events raised the specter of the return of Quetzalcoatl, and had a pervasively unnerving emotional effect on the Aztecs. They looked upon the Europeans riding "wild beasts" as extraterrestrial forces coming to establish a new social order. Defeatism then swept the nation and paralyzed its will.

The Aztecs had never developed an effective method of governing subject peoples. The Aztec "empire" was actually a group of subject communities lacking legal or governmental ties to what we call the state. The Aztecs controlled them through terror, requiring from each clan an annual tribute of humans to be sacrificed to the gods. Tributary peoples seethed with revolt. When the Spaniards appeared, the Totonacs greeted them as liberators, and other subject groups joined them against the Aztecs.

Montezuma refrained from attacking the Spaniards as they advanced toward his capital, and welcomed Cortés and his men into Tenochtitlan. Historians have often condemned the Aztec ruler for vacillation and weakness. Is this a fair assessment? Montezuma relied on the advice of his state council, itself divided, and on the dubious loyalty of tributary communities. When Cortés – with incredible boldness – took Montezuma hostage, the emperor's influence over his people crumbled.

But the major explanation for the collapse of the Aztec empire to fewer than 600 Spaniards lies in the Aztec notion of warfare and level of technology. Forced to leave Tenochtitlan to settle a conflict elsewhere, Cortés placed his lieutenant Alvarado in charge. Alvarado's harsh rule drove the Aztecs to revolt, and they almost succeeded in destroying the Spanish garrison. When Cortés returned just in time, the Aztecs allowed his reinforcements to join Alvarado's beseiged force. No threatened European or Oriental state would have conceived of doing such a thing: dividing an enemy's army and destroying the separate parts was basic to European military tactics. But for the Aztecs warfare was a ceremonial act, in which "divide and conquer" had no place.

Having allowed the Spanish forces to reunite, the entire population of Tenochtitlan attacked the invaders. The Aztecs killed many Spaniards, who in retaliation executed Montezuma. The Spaniards escaped from the city, and inflicted a crushing defeat on the Aztec army at Otumba near Lake Texoco on July 7, 1520. The Spaniards won because "the simple Indian methods of mass warfare were of little avail against the manoeuvring of a well-drilled force."[33] Aztec weapons proved no match for the terrifyingly noisy and lethal Spanish cannon, muskets, crossbows, and steel swords. European technology decided the battle. Cortés began the systematic conquest of Mexico.

THE MAYA OF CENTRAL AMERICA

Between about A.D. 300 and 900 another Amerindian people, the Maya of Central America, attained a level of intellectual and artistic achievement equalled by no other Indian people in the Western hemisphere and by few peoples throughout the world. The Maya were the only Indian people to develop an original system of writing. They also invented a calendar considered more accurate than the European Gregorian calendar. And the Maya made advances in mathematics that Europeans did not match for several centuries. Who were the Maya and where did they come from? What was the basis of their culture? What is the significance of their intellectual and artistic achievement?

The word *Maya* seems to derive from *Zamnā*, the early Maya culture god. On the basis of linguistic evidence, scholars believe

ca 20,000 B.C.	Migration across the Bering Sea to the Americas
ca 1500B.C.–A.D. 300	Rise of Olmec culture
A.D. 300–900	Classic period of Teotihuacan civilization
ca A.D. 800–1000	"Time of Troubles" in Mesoamerica
ca 1000–1300	Toltec hegemony
ca 1325	Arrival of the Aztecs in the Valley of Mexica
mid-15th century	Height of Aztec culture
1519	Arrival of the Spanish
1521	Collapse of the Aztecs
ca A.D. 600–900	Peak of Mayan civilization
ca 1000	Beginning of Incan expansion
1438–1493	Great Age of Incan imperialism
1532	Spanish execution of the Incan king and collapse of Incan empire

that the first Maya were a small North American Indian group who emigrated from southern Oregon and northern California to the western highlands of Guatemala. Between the third and second millennia B.C., various groups, including the Cholans and Tzeltalans, broke away from the parent group and settled in northern Guatemala, Tabasco and southern Campeche in Mexico, Belize and Rio Motague in Guatemala, and in a narrow portion of western Honduras. Since the Cholan-speaking Maya occupied the area during the time of great cultural achievement, the Cholan Maya apparently created the culture.

Mayan culture rested on an agricultural basis. Like the Aztecs, the Maya grew maize, beans, squashes, chili peppers, some root crops, and fruit trees. Turkeys were domesti-

cated, but barkless dogs fattened on corn seem to have been the main source of protein. In the Yucatan men trapped fish along the shores and in inland streams. Cotton was widely exported, as the discovery of rich Mayan textiles all over Mesoamerica attests.

Abundant food supported large population centers, and the entire Mayan region could have had as many as 14 million inhabitants. At Uxmal, Uxactum, Copan, Piedras, and Tixal (see Map 16.2 on page 554), archeologists have uncovered the palaces of nobles, elaborate pyramids where nobles were buried, engraved stelae, masonry temples, altars, sophisticated polychrome pottery, and courts for games played with a rubber ball. The largest site, Tikal, may have had 40,000 people. Since these centers lacked commercial and industrial activities, scholars avoid calling them cities. Rather, they were religious and ceremonial centers.

Although the Maya traded with the Aztecs, Mayan sources rarely mention marketplaces in their own population centers, and they had no distinct mercantile class. Yet sharply defined social classes characterized the culture. A hereditary elite nobility possessed private land, defended the society as warriors, carried on business activities as merchants, directed the religious rituals as priests, and held all political power. The rest of the people were free workers, serfs, and slaves. The intellectual class also belonged to the ruling nobility.

A method of measuring and recording time to arrange and commemorate events in the life of a society and to plan the agricultural and ceremonial year is a basic feature of all advanced societies. From careful observation of the earth's movements around the sun, the Maya invented a calendar of eighteen 20-day months and one 5-day month, for a total of 365 days. Using a system of bars ($-$ $=5$) and dots ($\circ=1$), the Maya devised a form of mathematics based on the vigesimal (20) rather than the decimal system. Having developed a system of hieroglyphic writing with 850 characters, the Maya recorded chronology, religion, and astronomy in books of barkpaper and deerskin. In sum, the Central American Maya proved themselves masters of abstract knowledge – notably in astronomy, mathematics, calendric development, and the recording of history.

THE INCAS OF PERU

The Aztec civilization of Mexico had already passed its peak when the Spanish landed in America. So too had a greater culture to the south, that of the Incas of Peru. Like the Aztecs, the Incas were, in the words of a distinguished anthropologist, "a small militaristic group that came to power late, conquered surrounding groups, and established one of the most extraordinary empires in the world."[34] Gradually, Inca culture spread throughout Peru. Modern knowledge of the Incas is concentrated on the last century before Spanish intrusion (1438–1532); contemporary scholars know far less about earlier developments.

Peru consists of three radically different geographical regions: a 2,000-mile-long semi-desert coastland skirting the Pacific Ocean; tropical jungle lowlands bordering modern Bolivia and Brazil; and in the center, the cold highlands of the Andes Mountains. Six valleys of fertile and wooded land at altitudes of 8,000–11,000 feet punctuate highland Peru, the largest of which are Huaylas, Cuzco, and Titicaca. It was in these valleys that Inca civilization developed and flourished.

Inca culture rested on remarkable agricultural progress between A.D. 600 and 1000. Hillside terracing and irrigation, use of the foot plow and bronze hoe, and of guano (the dried excrement of sea birds) as fertilizer produced bumper crops. By the fifteenth century, enough corn, beans, chili peppers, squash, tomatoes, sweet potatoes, peanuts, avocados, and white potatoes (which alone grow at high altitudes) were harvested to feed not only the farmers themselves but also massive armies, administrative bureaucracies, and thousands of industrial workers. Wild animals had become almost extinct and were the exclusive preserve of the nobility; common people rarely ate any meat other than guinea pigs, which most families raised. Chicha, a beer fermented from corn, was the staple drink.

INCAN IMPERIALISM

Who were the Incas? *Inca* was originally the name of the governing family of one Amerindian group that settled in the basin of Cuzco; from that family, the name was gradually extended to all Indians living in the Andes valleys. The Incas themselves used the word to identify their chief or emperor; here the term is used for both the ruler and the people. Around A.D. 1000 the Incas were only one of many small groups fighting among themselves for land and water. As they began to conquer their neighbors, a body of religious lore came into being that ascribed divine origin to their earliest king, Manco Capac (ca 1200), and promised warriors the gods' favor and protection. Strong historical evidence dates only from the reign of Pachacuti Inca (1438-1471), who launched the imperialist phase of Incan civilization. By threats, promises, and brute conquest, Pachacuti and his son Topa Inca (1471–1493) extended Incan domination to the frontier of modern Ecuador and Colombia in the north and to the Maule River in Chile in the south (see Map 16.3 on page 570), an area of about 350,000 square miles. Some authorities rank Pachacuti and Topa Inca with Alexander the Great and Napoleon among the world's greatest conquerors. By the time of the Spanish conquest, about 16 million people owed allegiance to the Inca emperor.

Inca civilization was the culmination of the fusion and assimilation of earlier Amerindian cultures in the Andes valleys. Each group that had entered the region had its own distinct language. These languages were not written, and have become extinct. Scholars will probably never understand the linguistic condition of Peru before the fifteenth century when Pachacuti made Quechua (pronounced *keshwa*) the official language of his people. Quechua became the language of administration; Quechua-speaking peoples were sent as colonists to subject regions, and conquered peoples were forced to adopt it. Quechua thus superseded native dialects, and spread the Inca way of life throughout the Andes. Although not written until the Spanish in Peru adopted it as a second official language, Quechua had replaced local languages by the seventeenth and eighteenth centuries and is still spoken by most Peruvians today.

Whereas the Aztecs controlled their subject peoples through a prolonged reign of terror, the Incas governed by means of imperial unification. They imposed not only their Quechua language but their entire panoply of gods: the sun god, divine ancestor of the royal family, his wife the moon god, and the thunder god, who brought life-giving rain. Magnificent temples scattered throughout the expanding empire housed idols of these gods, whom state-appointed priests attended. Priests led prayers and elaborate rituals, and on such occasions as a terrible natural disaster or a great military victory, they sacrificed human beings to the gods. Subject peoples were required to worship the state gods. Imperial unification was also achieved through the forced participation of local chieftains in the central bureaucracy, and through a policy of colonization called *mitima*. To prevent rebellion in newly conquered territories, Pachacuti transferred all their inhabitants to other parts of the empire, replacing them with workers who had lived longer under Incan rule and whose independent spirit had been broken.[35] Finally, an excellent system of roads — averaging three feet in width, some paved and others not — provided for the transportation of armies and the rapid communication of royal orders by runners. Incan roads followed

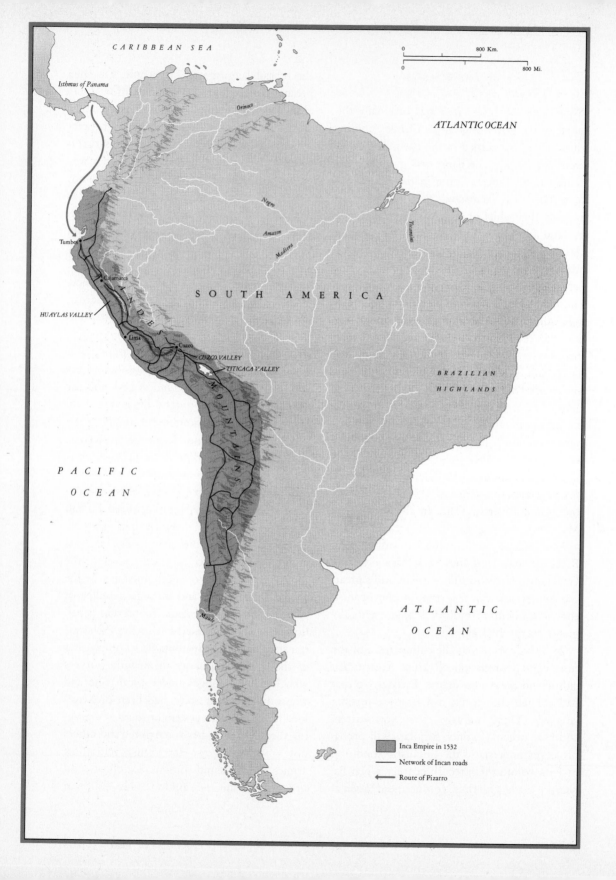

CARIBBEAN SEA

Isthmus of Panama

ATLANTIC OCEAN

Orinoco

Negro

Amazon

Madeira

Tocantins

SOUTH AMERICA

Tumbes

Cajamarca

HUAYLAS VALLEY

ANDES

Lima

Cuzco

CUZCO VALLEY

TITICACA VALLEY

BRAZILIAN
HIGHLANDS

PACIFIC
OCEAN

MOUNTAINS

ATLANTIC
OCEAN

Maule

0   800 Km.

0   800 Mi.

Inca Empire in 1532

Network of Incan roads

Route of Pizarro

straight lines wherever possible; but they also crossed marshes and causeways, rivers and streams, on pontoon bridges and tunnelled through hills. This great feat of engineering bears striking comparison with ancient Roman roads, which also linked an empire.

INCAN SOCIETY

The fundamental unit of early Incan society had been the clan, or *ayllu*. Kinship was its basis: an ayllu consisted of all those who claimed a common male ancestor. A village typically consisted of several ayllus: each had its own farmland and woodland, which all members cooperated in farming. The chief, or *curacas,* of the ayllu, to whom all members owed allegiance, conducted relations with outsiders.

In the fifteenth century, Pachacuti and Topa Inca superimposed imperial institutions on those of kinship. The Incas ordered allegiance to be paid to the ruler at Cuzco, rather than to the local curacas. They drafted local men for distant wars, and changed the entire populations of certain regions through the system of mitimas. Entirely new ayllus were formed. Residence rather than kinship became the basis of social organization. Emperors sometimes gave newly acquired lands to victorious generals, distinguished civil servants, and favorite nobles; these lords subsequently exercised authority previously held by the native curacas. Whether longtime residents or new colonists, all had the status of peasant farmers, which entailed heavy agricultural or other obligations. Just as in medieval Europe peasants worked several days each week on their lord's lands, so in Incan Peru people had to work on state lands (that is, the Inca's lands), or on lands assigned to the temple. Peasant workers also performed forced labor on roads and bridges; they terraced and irrigated new arable land; served on construction crews for royal palaces, temples, and public buildings such as fortresses; acted as runners on the post roads; and excavated in the imperial gold, silver, and copper mines. The imperial government annually determined the number of laborers needed for these various undertakings and each district had to supply an assigned quota. The government also made the ayllu responsible for the state-owned granaries and for the production of cloth for army uniforms.

The state required everyone to marry, and even decided when and sometimes whom a person should marry. As in medieval Europe, a person was not considered an adult until he or she married, started a household, and became liable to public responsibilities. Men married around the age of twenty, women a little younger. A young man who wanted a certain girl "hung around" her father's house and shared in the work. The Incas did not especially prize virginity, and premarital sexual relations were common. The marriage ceremony consisted of the joining of hands and the exchange of a pair of sandals. This ritual was followed by a large wedding feast, at which the state presented the bride and groom with two complete sets of clothing, one for everyday wear and one for festive occasions. If a man or woman did not find a satisfactory mate, the provincial governor selected one for him or her. Travel was forbidden, so couples necessarily came from the same region. Like most warring societies (such as the medieval Muslims) with high male death rates, the Incas practiced polygamy, though the cost of supporting many wives restricted it largely to the upper classes. Polygamy provided social security ·for the many widows.

In many aspects of daily life, the common people were regimented and denied both choice and initiative. On the other hand, the Inca took care of the poor and aged who could not look after themselves, distributed grain in time of shortage and famine, and supplied assistance in natural disasters. Scholars have debated whether Incan society was socialistic, totalitarian, or a forerunner of the welfare state; it may be merely a matter of definition. Although the Incan economy was strictly regulated, there certainly was not an equal distribution of wealth. Everything above and beyond the masses' basic needs went to the emperor and the nobility. The back-breaking labor of ordinary people in the fields and mines made possible the luxurious lifestyle of the nobility. The great Incan nobility – called big ears, or *orejones* by the Spanish, because they pierced their ears and distended the lobes with heavy jewelry – consisted of the Inca's kinsmen. Lesser nobles included the curacas, royal household servants, public officials, and entertainers. As the empire expanded in the fifteenth century, there arose a noble class of warriors, governors, and local officials, whose support the Inca secured with gifts of land, precious metals, llamas and alpacas. (Llamas were used as beasts of burden, alpacas raised for their long fine wool.) The nobility was exempt from agricultural work and other kinds of public service.

THE FALL OF THE INCAS

In 1527 the Inca emperor ruled as a benevolent despot. His power was limited only by custom. His millions of subjects looked upon him as a god, firm but just to his people, merciless to his enemies. ("Looked upon" is figurative: only a few of the Inca's closest relatives dared look at his divine face, the nobility approached him on their knees, and the masses kissed the dirt as he rode by in his litter.) The borders of his vast empire were well fortified, threatened by no foreign invaders. No sedition or civil disobedience disturbed the domestic tranquillity. Grain was plentiful, and apart from an outbreak of smallpox in a distant province – introduced by the Spaniards – no natural disaster upset the general peace. An army of 50,000 loyal troops stood at the Inca's instant disposal. Why, then, did this powerful empire fall so easily to Francisco Pizarro (page 734) and his band of 175 men armed with one small ineffective cannon? This question has troubled students for centuries. There can be no definitive answers, but several explanations have been offered.

First, the Incas were totally isolated. They had no contact with other Amerindian cultures, and knew nothing at all of Aztec civilization nor its collapse to the Spaniards in 1521. Since about 1500 Inca scouts had reported "floating houses" on the seas, manned by white men with beards. Tradesmen told of strange large animals with feet of silver (as horseshoes appeared in the brilliant sunshine). Having observed a border skirmish between Indians and white men, intelligence sources advised the Inca that the Europeans' swords were as harmless as women's weaving battens. A coastal chieftain had poured chicha down the barrel of a gun to appease the god of thunder. These incidents suggest that Inca culture provided no basis for interpreting such phenomena – that the Incas lacked the faintest understanding of the Spaniards and the significance of their arrival. Moreover, if the strange pale men planned war, there were

MACHU PICCHU *The citadel of Machu Picchu, surrounded by mountains in the clouds, clings to a spectacular crag in upland Peru. It was discovered only in 1911, by the young American explorer Hiram* *Bingham. Both its origin and the reason for its abandonment remain unknown. (Ira Kirschenbaum, Stock, Boston)*

very few of them, and the Incas believed that they could not be reinforced from the sea.[36]

At first the Incas did not think that the strangers intended trouble. They believed the old Inca legend that the creator-god Virocha — who had brought civilization to them, become displeased, and sailed away promising to return someday — had indeed returned. Like a similar Aztec superstition, belief in this legend prevented the Incas from taking prompt action.

A political situation may also have lain at the root of their difficulty. The Incas apparently had no definite principle for the succes-

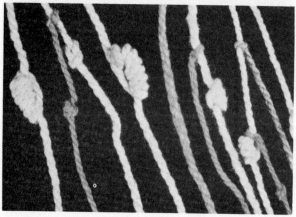

QUIPUS *A Quipu (pronounced kee-poo) consisted of a main cord (ranging from one to several feet in length) with small colored strings which had knots (quipus) at intervals. Quipus were systems of recording information, such as royal dynasties, census counts, wealth in llamas, among other things. (Loren McIntyre)*

sion of the emperor. The reigning emperor, with the advice of his council, chose his successor – usually the most capable son of his chief wife. In 1527, however, the Inca Huayna Capac died without naming his heir. The council chose Huascar, son of his chief wife, who was accordingly crowned at Cuzco with the imperial *borla,* the fringed headband symbolizing the imperial office. The people and the generals, however, supported Atahualpa, son of a secondary wife and clearly Huayna's favorite son. A bitter civil war ensued. Atahualpa emerged victorious, but the five-year struggle may have exhausted him and damaged his judgment.

Soon after Francisco Pizarro landed at Tumbes on May 13, 1532 – the very day Atahualpa won the decisive battle against his brother – he learned of all these events. As Pizarro advanced across the steep Andes toward the capital at Cuzco, Atahualpa – simultaneously proceeding to the capital for his coronation – stopped at the provincial town of Cajamarca. He, too, was kept fully informed. The Inca's strategy was to lure the Spanish into a trap, seize their horses and ablest men for his army, and execute the rest. What had the Inca, surrounded by his thousands of troops, to fear? Atahualpa thus accepted Pizarro's invitation to come with his bodyguards "unarmed so as not to give offense" into the central plaza of Cajamarca. He rode right into the Spaniard's trap. Pizarro knew that if he could capture the person of the Inca, from whom all power devolved, he would have the "Kingdom of Gold" for which he had come to the New World. The Inca's litter arrived in the ominously quiet town square. One cannon blast terrified the Indians. The Spaniards rushed out from hiding and ruthlessly slaughtered the Indians. Atahualpa's headband was instantly torn from his head. He offered to purchase his freedom with a roomful of gold. Pizarro agreed to this ransom, and an appropriate document was drawn up and signed. After the gold had been gathered from all parts of the empire to fill the room — 17 feet by 22 feet by 9 feet — the Spaniards trumped up charges against the Inca and strangled him. The Inca empire lay at Pizarro's feet.

———◆———

In the late fifteenth century the African continent contained a variety of very different societies and civilizations. While the Christian kingdom of Ethiopia led an isolated, inward-looking existence, the city-states of the East African coast conducted complicated mercantile activities with the Muslim Middle East, India, and China. The sizable Muslim populations of East Africa's bustling port cities were in touch with the cultures of the Mediterranean and the Indian Ocean. Some West African kingdoms, such as Mali, had for centuries carried on a brisk trade in salt, gold, and slaves. The faith of Islam had accompanied this trade, leading to the conversion of African rulers, the growth of intellectual centers such as Timbuctu, and sometimes to the strong influence of Muslim *ulamas* (religious specialists or teachers, especially of the *Sharia,* or law) in the affairs of West African states. Islam was the dominant foreign influence on traditional African societies.

Across the Atlantic, the great Amerindian cultures of the Aztec, the Maya, and the Inca had passed their intellectual peaks by 1500. The Aztec built a unified civilization based heavily on their Toltec heritage, distinguished by sophisticated achievements in engineering, sculpture, and architecture. The Inca revealed a genius for organization; the imperial Incan state was virtually unique for the time in assuming responsibility for the social welfare of

all its people. The Maya are justly renowned for their accomplishments in abstract thought. Why did these cultures fall? Some scholars have attributed their collapse before the Spanish invaders to their shared status as highly centralized theocracies with unclear royal successions. (The Maya differed from the Inca and the Aztec in that they had no single governmental authority whose overthrow could bring down an empire. The Maya, moreover, used ambushes and jungle guerrilla warfare to oppose the Spanish advance, and continued to fight the Spaniards throughout most of the sixteenth century.) But the lack of an unclear royal succession is not a fully convincing explanation. Neither the English nor the Russians had fully solved the constitutional problem of the royal succession by the sixteenth or even the seventeenth centuries. The governments of Spain, France, and England also relied heavily on theocratic legitimacy.

The Spaniards triumphed over the Amerindian nations of the New World largely for the same reason that the English defeated the Spanish Armada at the end of the same century: because of superior technology and fighting skills. Cannon, horses, and well-disciplined troops gave the Spaniards enormous advantages over Aztec and Incan methods of mass attack. Modern weapons and tactics destroyed the pre-Columbian civilizations, but they live on today in the Mexican, Central American, and Peruvian peoples.

NOTES

1. See J. Desmond Clark, *The Prehistory of Africa,* Thames and Hudson, London, 1970, pp. 23, 46–59.
2. See Joseph H. Greenberg, "Linguistic Evidence for the Influence of the Kanuri on the Hausa," *Journal of African History* I, (1960): 205 ff.

3. See Daniel F. McCall, *Africa in Time Perspective: A Discussion of Historical Reconstruction from Unwritten Sources,* Oxford University Press, New York, 1969, pp. 52–56.

4. Cited in Robert W. July, *Precolonial Africa: An Economic and Social History,* Charles Scribner's Sons, New York, 1975, p. 135.

5. J. Spencer Trimingham, *Islam in West Africa,* Oxford University Press, Oxford, 1959, pp. 6–9.

6. Ralph A. Austen, "The Trans-Saharan Slave Trade: A Tentative Census," in *The Uncommon Market: Essays in the Economic History of the Atlantic Slave Trade,* ed. Henry A. Gemery and Jan S. Hogendorn, Academic Press, New York, 1979, pp. 1–71, esp. p. 66.

7. July, pp. 124–129.

8. Cited in J. O. Hunwick, "Islam in West Africa, A.D. 1000–1800," in *A Thousand Years of West African History,* ed. J. F. Ade Ajayi and Ian Espie, Humanities Press, New York, 1972, pp. 244–245.

9. Cited in A. Adu Boahen, "Kingdoms of West Africa, c. A.D. 500–1600," in *The Horizon History of Africa,* American Heritage, New York, 1971, p. 183.

10. Al Bakri, *Kitāb al-mughrib fī dhikr bilād Ifrīqīya wa'l-Maghrib.* French edition, *Description de l'Afrique Septentrionale,* by De Shane. Paris, Adrien-Maisonneuve, 1965, pp. 328–329.

11. Cited in Roland Oliver and Caroline Oliver, eds., *Africa in the Days of Exploration,* Prentice-Hall, Englewood Cliffs, N.J., 1965, p. 10.

12. Cited in Boahen, p. 184.

13. Ibid.

14. Cited in E. Jefferson Murphy, *History of African Civilization,* Delta Publishing Company, New York, 1972, p. 109.

15. Cited in Murphy, p. 111.

16. Cited in Murphy, p. 120.

17. Cited in Oliver and Oliver, p. 18.

18. July, p. 209.

19. See Fernand Braudel, *The Structures of Everyday Life: Civilization and Capitalism 15th-18th Century,* vol. I, trans. Sian Reynolds, Harper & Row, New York, 1981, pp. 160–161.

20. Cited in Ignacio Bernal, *Mexico Before Cortez: Art, History, and Legend,* rev. ed., trans. Willis Barnstone, Anchor Books, New York, 1975, p. 68.

21. Jacques Soustelle, *Daily Life of the Aztecs on the Eve of the Spanish Conquest,* trans. Patrick O'Brian, Stanford University Press, Stanford, 1970, p. 97.

22. See Marvin Harris, *Cannibals and Kings,* Random House, New York, 1977, pp. 99–110, esp. p. 106.

23. Ibid., pp. 109–110.

24. See Richard Padden, *The Hummingbird and the Hawk,* Ohio State University Press, Columbus, 1967, pp. 76–99.

25. Soustelle, p. 74.

26. Cited in Soustelle, p. 89.

27. William H. Prescott, *The Conquest of Mexico and the Conquest of Peru,* New York, 1847, p. 20–21.

28. Bernal Diaz, *The Conquest of New Spain,* trans. J. M. Cohen, Penguin Books, New York, 1978, p. 214.

29. Cited in J. H. Parry, *The Discovery of South America,* Taplinger, New York, 1979, p. 159.

30. Diaz, p. 233.

31. Cited in Parry, pp. 161–163.

32. Cited in Parry, p. 163.

33. G. C. Vaillant, *Aztecs of Mexico,* Penguin Books, New York, 1979, p. 241. Chapter 15, on which this section leans, is fascinating.

34. J. Alden Mason, *The Ancient Civilizations of Peru,* Penguin Books, New York, 1978, p. 108.

35. Ibid., p. 123.

36. Victor W. Von Hagen, *Realm of the Incas,* New American Library, New York, 1961, pp. 204–207.

SUGGESTED READING

For good introductions to the problems involved in the study of early African history, see Creighton Gobel and Norman R. Bennett, eds., *Reconstructing African Cultural History* (1967); J. D. Fage, *Africa Discovers Her Past* (1970); Colin M. Turnbull, *Man in Africa* (1976); and Richard E. Leakey and Roger Lewin, *Origins: What New Discoveries Reveal about the Emergence of Our Species and Its Possible Future* (1977). Roland Oliver and J. D. Fage, *A Short History of Africa* (1975), and Richard Olaniyan, *African History and Culture* (1982), are useful general surveys.

For specific topics raised in early African history, see, in addition to the titles listed in the Notes, Roland Oliver and Gervase Mathew, eds., *History of East Africa* (1963), the standard work on the eastern part of the continent, with a valuable chapter on the coastal city-states; G. S. P. Freeman-Grenville, *The East African Coast: Select Documents from the First to the Earlier Nineteenth Century* (1962), which contains excellent material from Arabic, Chinese, and Portuguese perspectives; David Conrad and Humphrey Fisher, "The Conquest that Never Was: Ghana and the Almoravids," in *History of Africa* 9 (1982): 21–59; Martin Klein and Paul E. Lovejoy, "Slavery in West Africa," in *The Uncommon Market: Essays in the Economic History of the Atlantic Slave Trade,* ed. Henry A. Gemery and Jan S. Hogendorn, (1979); and R. S. Smith, *Warfare and Diplomacy in Pre-Colonial West Africa* (1976). On the important topic of Islam, see John Spencer Trimingham, *A History of Islam in West Africa* (1970) and the same scholar's *Islam in East Africa* (1974), which are standard works. J. Kritzeck and W. H. Lewis, eds., *Islam in Africa* (1969), and Maurice Lombard, *The Golden Age of Islam* (1975), are also helpful.

Students interested in exploring aspects of pre-Columbian South America will have no trouble finding a rich literature. G. C. Vaillant, *Aztecs of Mexico* (1979); J. Alden Mason, *The Ancient Civilizations of Peru;* and Michael D. Coe, *The Maya,* rev. ed. (1980), are all sound and well-illustrated surveys. Coe's *Mexico* (1977) is probably the most comprehensive treatment of Mexican civilizations, with excellent illustrations and a good bibliography. The clever sketches of Victor W. Von Hagen, *Realm of the Incas* (1961), and *The Aztec: Man and Tribe* (1961), are popular archeological accounts. Ignacio Bernal, *Mexico before Cortez: Art, History, Legend* (1975), brings out the social significance of Mexican art. Paul Westheim, *The Sculpture of Ancient Mexico,* trans. Ursula Bernard (1963), also focuses on the importance of art and sculpture for an understanding of the civilization.

More specialized recent studies include Muriel Porter Weaver, *The Aztec, Maya and Their Predecessors* (1981), which is highly readable and splendidly illustrated; Karl W. Luckert, *Olmec Religion: A Key to Middle America and Beyond* (1976), an iconographical study of Olmec and Aztec religious symbolism; B. C. Brundage, *A Rain of Darts: The Mexican Aztecs* (1973); and Nigel Davies, *The Aztecs until the Fall of Tula* (1977), a highly detailed but fascinating book; Eric R. Wolf, ed., *The Valley of Mexico: Studies in Pre-Hispanic Ecology and Society* (1976), an important collection of significant articles; and Louis Baudin, *A Socialist Empire: The Incas of Peru* (1961).

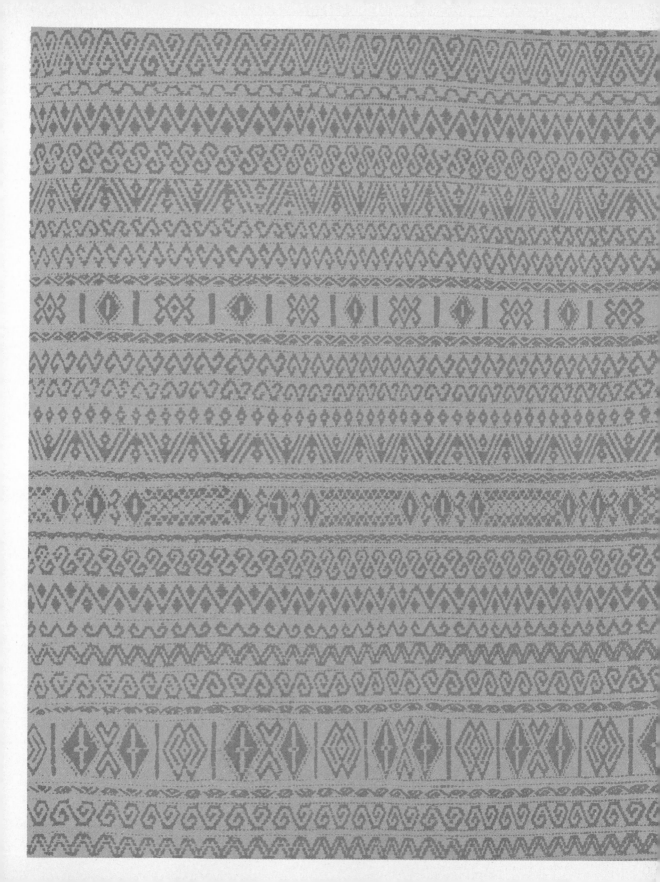

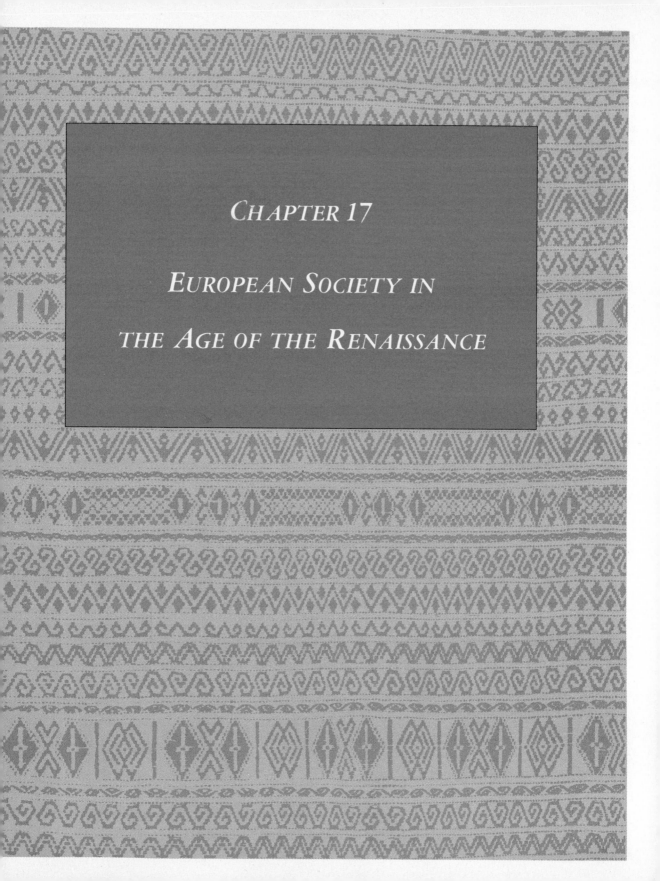

CHAPTER 17

EUROPEAN SOCIETY IN
THE AGE OF THE RENAISSANCE

WHILE THE FOUR HORSEMEN of the Apocalypse carried war, plague, famine, and death across the Continent, a new culture was emerging in southern Europe. The fourteenth century witnessed the beginnings of remarkable changes in many aspects of Italian society. In the fifteenth century, these phenomena spread beyond Italy and gradually influenced society in northern Europe. These cultural changes have been collectively labeled the Renaissance. What does the term *Renaissance* mean? How did the Renaissance manifest itself in politics, government, and social organization? What developments occurred in the evolution of the nation state? Did the Renaissance involve shifts in religious attitudes? This chapter explores these questions.

THE IDEA OF THE RENAISSANCE

The Renaissance was an intellectual movement that began in Italy in the fourteenth century. It was characterized by hostility to the culture of the Middle Ages and fascination with the ancient world. Writers and artists of the Renaissance displayed great concern for individualism, a serious interest in human nature based on the study of the Greek and Latin classics, and a new excitement about life in this world. The cultural movement scholars have called the Renaissance was limited to a small, self-conscious, educated elite; it never directly involved the masses of people.

The realization that something new and unique was happening first came to men of letters of the fourteenth century, especially to the poet and humanist Francesco Petrarch (1304-1374). Petrarch thought that he was living at the start of a new age, a period of light following a long night of Gothic gloom. He believed that the first and second centuries of the Roman Empire represented the peak in the development of human civilization. The Germanic invasions had caused a sharp cultural break with the glories of Rome and inaugurated what Petrarch called "the Dark Ages." Medieval people had believed that they were continuing the glories that had been ancient Rome, and had recognized no cultural division between the world of the emperors and their own times. But for Petrarch and many of his contemporaries, the thousand-year period between the fourth and the fourteenth centuries constituted a barbarian, or Gothic, or middle age. The sculptors, painters, and writers of the Renaissance spoke contemptuously of their medieval predecessors and identified themselves with the thinkers and artists of Greco-Roman civilization. Petrarch believed he was witnessing a new golden age of intellectual achievement – a rebirth or, to use the French word that came into English, a renaissance. The division of historical time into periods is often arbitrary and done for the convenience of historians. In terms of the way most people lived and thought, no sharp division exists between the Middle Ages and the Renaissance. Nevertheless, Petrarch's categorization of time periods has had great influence. Most scholars use the word *Renaissance* to mean the artistic and cultural developments in western Europe that began in the fourteenth century and lasted into the seventeenth.

ITALIAN ORIGINS OF THE RENAISSANCE

The Renaissance began in Italy. Why did a brilliant flowering of artistic and intellectual creativity occur in Italy in the fourteenth through sixteenth centuries? This question has troubled scholars for a long time, and they still have not arrived at a definite answer. Some have offered economic explanations for Italy's cultural flowering, emphasizing the material prosperity without which the arts cannot flourish.

By the middle of the fourteenth century, the commercial classes of Florence and other Italian cities had acquired enough money that they could finance non-moneymaking activities. The cornerstone of northern Italian economic activity was international trade, commerce, and banking. The northern Italian cities had led the way in the commercial revival of the eleventh century. By the middle of the twelfth century, Venice, Genoa, Florence, and Milan were enjoying a great volume of trade with the Middle East and with northern Europe. These Italian cities fully exploited their geographical position as natural crossroads for exchange between the East and the West. Venice had profited tremendously from the Fourth Crusade. In the early fourteenth century, furthermore, Genoa and Venice made important strides in shipbuilding, allowing their ships for the first time to sail all year long. Improvements in the construction of cargo ships enabled the Venetians and Genoese to carry more bulk and to navigate the dangerous Atlantic Ocean. Most goods were purchased directly from the producers and sold a good distance away. For example, Italian merchants bought fine English wool directly from the Cistercian abbeys of Yorkshire in northern England. The wool was transported to the bazaars of North Africa either overland or by ship through the Straits of Gibraltar. The risks in such an operation were great, but the profits were enormous. These profits were continually reinvested to earn more.

It is generally agreed that the first manifestations of the Italian Renaissance – in art, ar-

BUSINESS ACTIVITIES IN A FLORENTINE BANK The Florentines early developed new banking devices. One man (left) presents a letter of credit or a bill of exchange, forerunners of the modern check, which allowed credit in distant places. A foreign merchant (right) exchanges one kind of currency for another. The bank profited from the fees it charged for these services. (Prints Division; New York Public Library; Astor, Lenox and Tilden Foundation)

chitecture, and literary creativity – appeared in Florence, and Florence possessed enormous wealth. Geography had not helped Florence; it was an inland city without easy access to water transportation. But toward the end of the thirteenth century, Florentine merchants and bankers acquired control of papal banking. From their position as tax collectors for the papacy, Florentine mercantile families began to dominate European banking on both sides of the Alps. These families had offices in Paris and London, Barcelona and Marseilles, Tunis and the North African ports, and, of course, Naples and Rome. The profits from loans, investments, and money exchanges that poured back to Florence were pumped into urban industries. Such profits contributed to the city's economic vitality.

The Florentine wool industry, however, was the major factor in the city's financial expansion and population increase. Florence purchased the best-quality wool from England and Spain, developed remarkable techniques for its manufacture, and employed thousands of workers to turn it into cloth. Florentine weavers produced immense quantities of superb woolen cloth, which brought the highest prices in the fairs, markets, and bazaars of Europe, Asia, and Africa.

By the first quarter of the fourteenth century, the economic foundations of Florence were so strong that even two severe crises could not destroy the city. In 1344, King Edward III of England repudiated his huge debts to Florentine bankers and forced some of them into bankruptcy. Florence also suffered frightfully from the Black Death, losing perhaps half its population. Still, the basic Florentine economic structure remained stable. Driving enterprise, technical know-how, and competitive spirit saw Florence through the difficult economic period of the late fourteenth century.[1]

One inconsistency in this economic explanation of the origins of the Renaissance lies in the fact that in the middle of the fourteenth century the Florentine wool and banking industries experienced a serious depression. Trade declined, affected by the Black Death and the international business slump. Moreover, such cities as Genoa, which had at one time enjoyed considerable prosperity, made no profound contribution to the Renaissance. It may be, however, that Florentine businessmen who found foreign markets closed invested instead in art, expecting a financial return from art works that increased in value.

A leading interpretation of the Italian Renaissance traces its origins to the development of civic humanism, or public pride, in Florence. In the 1380s, Florence was severely threatened by the conquests of Gian Galeazzo Visconti, duke of Milan. The Florentines put up a heroic and successful resistance, and in so doing came to appreciate the special virtues of their republican form of government – in contrast to the tyranny represented by Visconti. Awareness of their unique political heritage, which they traced back to the time of the Roman Empire, led the Florentines to take great pride in their city. Civic humanism took the form of public respect for Florence's achievements, whether in trade or architecture, education or the arts. They embarked upon a policy of beautification. This civic self-consciousness eventually spread to the other city-states of Italy.

Unlike the countries of northern Europe, Italy had never been heavily feudalized. Italian feudal lords rarely exercised the vast independent powers held by the barons of France, England, and the Holy Roman Empire. Although the volume of urban trade and the size of urban populations severely declined in the early Middle Ages, cities survived as commercial centers. In the twelfth and thirteenth centuries, northern Italian cities like Venice and Milan gained control of their surrounding territories. The wealth they steadily gained was used to acquire and solidify their independence; the Holy Roman emperors never fully exploited the wealth of the cities.

Italian society in the fourteenth century meant urban society, and this fundamental fact helps to account for the Italian origin of the Renaissance. The cities of Milan, Venice, Florence, Genoa, and Pisa were visited by traders and businessmen from all parts of the Western world. Foreigners brought with them their own customs, traditions, and values, and considerable social interchange inevitably took place. The merchant Francesco Datini, for example, was involved in commercial transactions with two hundred cities,

THE WEDDING FEAST *This picture was one of a series Botticelli produced illustrating a story in Boccaccio's* Decameron. *The classical architecture with its vision of nature beyond, the pomp with which the* meal *is served, and the philosophical discussion at the tables — all represent the tastes and ideals of the Florentine aristocracy under the Medici. (Courtesy of Christie's)*

from Alexandria and Beirut in the south to Stockholm in the north. Italians gained an awareness of different parts of the world. They grew more refined, more sophisticated in their tastes and lifestyles, more worldly and urbane. Although Italians remained devoted sons and daughters of the church, they grew more secular in their outlook and behavior. Class distinctions remained strong in Renaissance Italy, but those distinctions were based on wealth rather than birth. And enterprise, imagination, and hard work could lead to wealth in the urban environment.

Moreover, the wealthy burghers of the cities began to strike military and marital contracts with the rural nobility of northern Italy. These alliances enabled the nobles to maintain a high standard of living in a rising money economy and gave the cities military support and protection. When the rich merchants united with the rural nobility, two significant developments occurred: the possession of land gradually came into the hands of bankers and merchants, and as a result the cities obtained political as well as economic jurisdiction over the surrounding countryside. In no other part of Europe did cities acquire such political power, primarily because the aristocratic ethos forbade feudal barons to unite with the moneygrubbing bourgeoisie. Nor did cities elsewhere have the commercial and financial strength of the Italian towns.

A foreign element also played a significant role. Beginning in the late fourteenth century, a steady stream of educated Greek refugees came from Byzantium to Italy to escape Turkish domination. Greek scholars like Manuel

Chrysoloras, John Bessarion, and Jonus Lascaris taught the Greek language and translated important Greek literary classics into Latin. Venice became the center of Greek scholarship, but Florence and Rome also gained an international reputation for Greek learning. Greek emigration to Italy broadened the intellectual horizon and enriched Italian Renaissance culture.

Finally, the Renaissance started in Italy because Italian poets, sculptors, painters, and philosophers of the fifteenth and sixteenth centuries considered themselves the natural heirs of the ancient Romans. Italy still possessed the literary manuscripts, the architectural monuments, the roads that constituted the heritage of Roman civilization. The national past of Italy was visible everywhere. Above all, Italians retained the historical memory of Roman power and imperial grandeur, and looked back on Roman antiquity as the golden age, as an ideal to be restored and reborn.

Increased wealth afforded more leisure time. Wealth in itself is usually not sufficient to satisfy the human psyche. When the physical and material needs of life are fulfilled and there is a surplus, then the spirit can be enriched by esthetic and intellectual interests.

The Renaissance, then, was an artistic and intellectual movement that began in the Italian cities and was supported and sustained by urban wealth.

HALLMARKS OF THE RENAISSANCE

The Renaissance was characterized, as we have seen, by the self-conscious awareness among fourteenth- and fifteenth-century Italians that they were living in a new era. The Renaissance also manifested itself in a new attitude toward men and women and the world – an attitude that may be described as individualism. A humanism characterized by a deep interest in the Latin classics and the deliberate attempt to revive antique lifestyles emerged, as did a bold new secular spirit.

INDIVIDUALISM

In the Middle Ages individuals thought of themselves as part of a group – as a member of a guild, as a resident of a particular area. The very few people who considered themselves so unusual that they indulged in autobiography – Saint Augustine in the fifth century and Guibert of Nogent in the twelfth, for example – were unique for that very reason. Christian humility and the concept of Western society as an organic entity encouraged people to define themselves in terms of a larger religious, economic, or social group.

This organic view of society eroded during the fourteenth and fifteenth centuries in Italy. The Renaissance witnessed the emergence of many distinctive personalities who gloried in their uniqueness. Italians of unusual abilities were self-consciously aware of their singularity, and unafraid to be unlike their neighbors; they had enormous confidence in their ability to achieve great things. Leon Battista Alberti (1404–1474), a writer, architect, and mathematician, remarked, "Men can do all things if they will."[2] Completely lacking in modesty, real or false, talented people of the Renaissance were proud of their abilities and eager for everyone to know about them. The Florentine goldsmith and sculptor Benvenuto Cellini (1500–1574) prefaced his *Autobiography* with a sonnet that declares:

My cruel fate hath warr'd with me in vain:
Life, glory, worth, and all unmeasur'd skill,
Beauty and grace, themselves in me fulfill
That many I surpass, and to the best attain.[3]

Cellini, certain of his genius, wrote so that the whole world might appreciate it.

Individualism stressed personality, genius, uniqueness, and the fullest development of capabilities and talents. Artist, athlete, painter, scholar, sculptor, whatever – a person's potential should be stretched until fully realized. Thirst for fame, a driving ambition, a burning desire for success drove such people to the complete achievement of their potential. The quest for glory was central to Renaissance individualism.

THE REVIVAL OF ANTIQUITY

In the cities of Italy, and especially in Rome, civic leaders and the wealthy populace showed phenomenal archaeological zeal for the recovery of manuscripts, statues, and monuments. Pope Nicholas V (1447-1455), a distinguished scholar, planned the Vatican Library for the nine thousand manuscripts he had collected. Pope Sixtus IV (1471-1484) built that library, which remains one of the richest repositories of ancient and medieval documents.

Patrician Italians consciously copied the lifestyle of the ancients and even searched out pedigrees dating back to ancient Rome. Aeneas Silvius Piccolomini, a native of Siena who became Pope Pius II (1458-1464), once pretentiously declared, "Rome is as much my home as Siena, for my House, the Piccolomini, came in early times from the capital to Siena, as is proved by the constant use of the names Aeneas and Silvius in my family."[4]

The revival of antiquity also took the form of profound interest in and study of the Latin classics. This feature of the Renaissance became known as the "new learning," or simply "humanism," the term of the Florentine rhetorician and historian Leonardo Bruni (1370-1444). The words *humanism* and *humanist* derive ultimately from the Latin *humanitas,* which Cicero used to mean the literary culture needed by anyone who would be considered educated and civilized. Humanists studied the Latin classics to learn what they reveal about human nature. Humanism emphasized human beings, their achievements, interests, and capabilities. Although churchmen supported the new learning, Italian humanism was a preponderantly lay phenomenon.

Appreciation for the literary culture of the Romans had never died completely in the West. Bede, Alcuin, and Einhard in the eighth century, and Ailred of Rievaulx, Bernard of Clairvaux, and John of Salisbury in the twelfth century had all studied and imitated the writings of the ancients. Medieval writers, however, had studied the ancients in order to come to know God. Medieval thinkers held that human beings are the noblest of god's creatures, and that though they have fallen, they are still capable of regeneration and thus deserving of respect. Medieval scholars interpreted the classics in a Christian sense and invested the ancients' poems and histories with Christian meaning.

Renaissance philosophers and poets also emphasized human dignity, but usually not in a Christian context. In a remarkable essay, "On the Dignity of Man," the Florentine writer Pico della Mirandola maintained that man's place in the universe may be somewhere between the beasts and the angels but that there are no limits to what he can accomplish.

Humanists tried to approach the classical texts with an open mind, to learn what the ancients had thought. They rejected the religious interpretations and systematic and formal scholastic works of the Middle Ages. They hated scholasticism because they believed it denied humanity and destroyed style.

The fourteenth- and fifteenth-century humanists loved the language of the classics and considered it superior to the corrupt Latin of the medieval schoolmen. Renaissance writers were very excited by the purity of ancient Latin. They eventually became concerned more about form than content, more about the way an idea was expressed than about the significance and validity of the idea. Literary humanists of the fourteenth century wrote each other highly stylized letters imitating ancient authors, and they held witty philosophical dialogues in conscious imitation of the Platonic Academy of the fifth century B.C. Wherever they could, Renaissance humanists heaped scorn on the "barbaric" Latin style of the medievalists. The leading humanists of the early Renaissance were rhetoricians, seeking effective and eloquent communication, both oral and written.

SECULAR SPIRIT

Secularism involves a basic concern with the material world instead of eternal and spiritual interests. A secular way of thinking tends to find the ultimate explanation of everything and the final end of human beings within the limits of what the senses can discover. In a religious society, such as the medieval, the focus is on the other-worldly, on life after death. In a secular society, attention is concentrated on the here and now, often on the acquisition of material things. The fourteenth and fifteenth centuries witnessed the slow but steady growth of secularism in Italy.

The economic changes and rising prosperity of the Italian cities in the thirteenth century worked a fundamental change in social and intellectual attitudes and values. In the Middle Ages the feudal nobility and the higher clergy had determined the dominant patterns of culture. The medieval aristocracy expressed disdain for moneymaking. Christian ideas and values infused literature, art, politics, and all other aspects of culture. In the Renaissance, by contrast, the business concerns of the urban bourgeoisie required constant and rational attention.

Worries about shifting rates of interest, shipping routes, personnel costs, and employee relations did not leave much time for thoughts about penance and purgatory. The busy bankers and merchants of the Italian cities calculated ways of making and increasing their money. Money allowed greater material pleasures, a more comfortable life, the leisure time to appreciate and patronize the arts. Money could buy many sensual gratifications, and the rich, social-climbing patricians of Venice, Florence, Genoa, and Rome came to see life more as an opportunity to be enjoyed than as a painful pilgrimage to the City of God.

In *On Pleasure,* the humanist Lorenzo Valla (1406–1457) defended the pleasures of the senses as the highest good. Scholars praise Valla as the father of modern historical criticism. His study *On the False Donation of Constantine* (1444) demonstrated by careful textual examination that an anonymous eighth-century document supposedly giving the papacy jurisdiction over vast territories in western Europe was a forgery. Medieval people had accepted the Donation of Constantine as a reality, and the proof that it was an invention seriously weakened the foundations of papal claims to temporal authority. Lorenzo Valla's work exemplifies the application of critical scholarship to old and almost sacred writings, as well as the new secular spirit of the Renaissance. The tales in the *Decameron* by the Florentine Boccaccio (1313-1375), which describe ambitious merchants, lecherous friars, and cuckolded husbands, portray a frankly acquisitive, sensual, and secular society. The "contempt of the world" theme, so pervasive in medieval literature, had disappeared. Renaissance writers justified the accumulation and enjoyment of wealth with references to ancient authors.

Nor did church leaders do much to combat the new secular spirit or set high moral standards. In the fifteenth and early sixteenth centuries, the papal court and the households of the cardinals were just as worldly as those of great urban patricians. Of course, most of the popes and higher church officials had come from the bourgeois aristocracy. The Medici pope Leo X (1513-1521), for example, supported artists and men of letters because patronage was an activity he had learned in the household of his father, Lorenzo the Magnificent. Renaissance popes beautified the city of Rome and patronized the arts. They expended enormous enthusiasm and huge sums of money on the re-embellishment of the city. A new papal chancellery, begun in 1483 and finished in 1511, stands as one of the architectural masterpieces of the High Renaissance (roughly the period 1500-1530). Pope Julius II (1503-1513) tore down the old St. Peter's Basilica and began work on the present structure in 1506. Michelangelo's dome for St. Peter's is still considered his greatest work. Papal interests, far removed from spiritual concerns, fostered rather than discouraged the new worldly attitude.

But the broad mass of the people and even the intellectuals and leaders of society remained faithful to the Christian church. Few people questioned the basic tenets of the Christian religion. Italian humanists and their aristocratic patrons were antiascetic, antischolastic, and anticlerical, but they were not agnostics or skeptics. The thousands of pious paintings, sculptures, processions, and pilgrimages of the Renaissance period prove that strong religious feeling persisted.

ART AND THE ARTIST

No feature of the Renaissance evokes greater admiration than its artistic masterpieces. The 1400s (quattrocento) and 1500s (cinquecento) witnessed a dazzling creativity in painting, architecture, and sculpture. In all the arts, the city of Florence consistently led the way. According to the Renaissance art historian Giorgio Vasari (1511-1574), the painter Perugino once asked why it was in Florence and not elsewhere that men achieved perfection in the arts. The first answer he received was, "There were so many good critics there, for the air of the city makes men quick and perceptive and impatient of mediocrity."[5]

Some historians and art critics have maintained that the Renaissance "rediscovered" the world of nature and of human beings. This is nonsense, as a quick glance at a Gothic cathedral reveals. The enormous detail applied to the depiction of animals' bodies, the careful carving of leaves, flowers, and all kinds of vegetation, the fine sensitivity frequently shown in human faces – these clearly show medieval and ancient people's appreciation for nature in all its manifestations. Saint Francis of Assisi (1181-1226) encouraged throughout his entire life an awareness of nature. No historical period has a monopoly on the appreciation of nature or beauty.

ART AND SOCIETY

Significant changes in the realm of art did occur in the fourteenth century. Art served

BOTTICELLI: ADORATION OF THE MAGI *The Florentine artist, biographer, and Medici courtier Giorgio Vasari (1511-1574) says that this painting contains the most faithful likenesses of Cosimo (kneel-* *ing before the Christ child) and Lorenzo (far left). Although the subject is Christian, the painting has a secular spirit, introduces individual portraits, and serves to glorify the Medici family. (Alinari/Scala)*

the newly rich middle class as well as the institutional church. The patrons of Renaissance art were more frequently laypeople than ecclesiastics. Patrician merchants and bankers supported the arts as a means of self-glorification and self-perpetuation. Art may also have been a form of financial investment. Great families, such as the Medicis in Florence, used works of art as a means of gaining and maintaining public support for their rule. A magnificent style of living, enriched by works of art, seemed to prove the greatness of the rulers.

As the fifteenth century advanced, the subject matter of art became steadily more secular. The study of classical texts and manuscripts brought deeper understanding of ancient ideas. Classical themes and motifs, such as the lives and loves of pagan gods and goddesses, figured increasingly in painting and sculpture. Religious topics, such as the Annunciation of the Virgin and the Nativity, remained popular among both patrons and artists, but frequently the patron had himself and his family portrayed in the picture. In Botticelli's *Adoration of the Magi,* for example,

Cosimo de' Medici appears as one of the Magi kneeling before the Christ child. People were conscious of their physical uniqueness, and they wanted their individuality immortalized. Paintings cost money and thus were also means of displaying wealth. Although many Renaissance paintings have classical or Christian themes, the appearance of the patron reflects the new spirit of individualism and secularism.

The style of Renaissance art was decidedly different from that of the Middle Ages. The individual portrait emerged as a distinct artistic genre. In the fifteenth century members of the newly-rich middle class often had themselves painted in a scene of romantic chivalry or in courtly society. Rather than reflecting a spiritual ideal, as medieval painting and sculpture tended to do, Renaissance portraits mirrored reality. The Florentine painter Giotto (1276-1337) led the way in the depiction of realism; his treatment of the human body and face replaced the formal stiffness and artificiality that had for so long characterized the representation of the human body. The sculptor Donatello (1386-1466) probably exerted the greatest influence of any Florentine artist before Michelangelo. His many statues express an appreciation of the incredible variety of human nature. While medieval artists had depicted the nude human body only in a spiritualized and moralizing context, Donatello revived the classical figure with its balance and self-awareness. The short-lived Florentine Masaccio (1401-1428), sometimes called the father of modern painting, inspired a new style characterized by great realism, narrative power, and remarkably effective use of light and dark.

Narrative artists depicted the body in a more scientific and natural manner. The female figure is voluptuous and sensual. The male body, as in Michelangelo's *David* and *The Last Judgment,* is strong and heroic. Renaissance glorification of the human body reveals the secular spirit of the age. Filippo Brunelleschi (1377-1446), together with Piero della Francesca (1420-1492), seems to have pioneered perspective in painting, the linear representation of distance and space on a flat surface. *The Last Supper* of Leonardo da Vinci (1452-1519), with its stress on the tension between Christ and the disciples, is an incredibly subtle psychological interpretation.

THE STATUS OF THE ARTIST

In the Renaissance the social status of the artist improved. The lower-middle-class medieval master mason had been viewed in the same light as a mechanic. The artist in the Renaissance was considered an independent intellectual worker. Some artists and architects achieved not only economic security but very great wealth. All aspiring artists received a practical (not theoretical) education in a recognized master's workshop. For example, Michelangelo (1475-1564) was apprenticed at age thirteen to the artist Ghirlandaio (1449-1494), although he later denied the fact to make it appear he never had any formal training. The more famous the artist, the more he attracted assistants or apprentices. Lorenzo Ghiberti (1378-1455) had twenty assistants during the period he was working on the bronze doors of the Baptistery in Florence, his most famous achievement.

Ghiberti's salary of two hundred florins a year compared very favorably with that of the head of the city government, who earned five hundred florins. Moreover, at a time when a man could live in a princely fashion on three hundred ducats a year, Leonardo da Vinci was making two thousand annually. Michelangelo was paid three thousand ducats for painting

HANS MEMLING: MARIA AND TOMMASO POR-TINARI A Florentine citizen, Tommaso Portinari *earned a fortune as representative of the Medici bank-ing interests in Bruges, Flanders. Husband and wife are dressed in a rich but durable black broadcloth;*

Maria's necklace displays their wealth. Although both faces show a sharp intelligence, there is a melancholy sadness about them, suggestive of the pessimism of northern religious piety. (The Metropolitan Museum of Art: Bequest of Benjamin Altman, 1913)

the ceiling of the Sistine Chapel. When he agreed to work on St. Peter's Basilica, he re-fused a salary; he was already a wealthy man.[6]

Renaissance society respected and rewarded the distinguished artist. In 1537, the prolific letter writer, humanist, and satirizer of princes Pietro Aretino (1492–1556), wrote to Michelangelo while he was painting the Sis-tine Chapel:

TO THE DIVINE MICHELANGELO:
Sir, just as it is disgraceful and sinful to be un-mindful of God so it is reprehensible and dishon-ourable for any man of discerning judgement not to honour you as a brilliant and venerable artist whom the very stars use as a target at which to shoot the rival arrows of their favour. You are so accomplished, therefore, that hidden in your hands

lives the idea of a new king of creation, whereby the most challenging and subtle problem of all in the art of painting, namely that of outlines, has been so mastered by you that in the contours of the human body you express and contain the purpose of art.... And it is surely my duty to honour you with this salutation, since the world has many kings but only one Michelangelo.[7]

When the Holy Roman emperor Charles V (1519–1556) visited the workshop of the great Titian (1477–1576) and stooped to pick up the artist's dropped paintbrush, the em-peror was demonstrating that the patron himself was honored in the act of honoring the artist. The social status of the artist of genius was immortally secured.

Renaissance artists were not only aware of

their creative power; they boasted about it. The architect Brunelleschi had his life written, and Ghiberti and Cellini wrote their autobiographies. Many medieval sculptors and painters had signed their own works; Renaissance artists almost universally did so, and many of them incorporated self-portraits, usually as bystanders, in their paintings. These actions reflect an acute consciousness of creative genius.

The Renaissance, in fact, witnessed the birth of the concept of the artist as genius. In the Middle Ages people believed that only God created, albeit through individuals; the medieval conception recognized no particular value in artistic originality. Renaissance artists and humanists came to think that a work of art was the deliberate creation of a unique personality, of an individual who goes beyond traditions, rules, and theories. A genius has a peculiar gift, which ordinary laws should not inhibit. Cosimo de'Medici described a painter, because of his genius, as "divine," implying that the artist shared in the powers of God. The word *divine* was widely applied to Michelangelo. The Renaissance thus bequeathed the idea of genius to the modern world.

The student must guard against interpreting Italian Renaissance culture in twentieth-century democratic terms. The culture of the Renaissance was that of a small mercantile elite, a business patriciate with aristocratic pretensions. Renaissance culture did not directly affect the broad middle classes, let alone the vast urban proletariat. The typical small tradesman or craftsman could not read the sophisticated Latin essays of the humanists, even if he had the time to do so. He could not afford to buy the art works of the great masters. A small, highly educated minority of literary humanists and artists created the culture of and for an exclusive elite. They cared little

for ordinary people. Castiglione, Machiavelli, and Vergerio, for example, thoroughly despised the masses. Renaissance humanists were a smaller and narrower group than the medieval clergy had ever been. High churchmen had commissioned the construction of the Gothic cathedrals, but, once finished, the buildings were for all to enjoy. The modern visitor can still see the deep ruts in the stone floors of Chartres and Canterbury where the poor pilgrims slept at night. Nothing comparable was built in the Renaissance. Insecure, social-climbing merchant princes were hardly egalitarian.[8] The Renaissance ushered in a gulf between the learned minority and the uneducated multitude that has survived for many centuries.

SOCIAL CHANGE

The Renaissance changed many aspects of Italian, and subsequently European, society. The new developments brought about real breaks with the medieval past. What impact did the Renaissance have on educational theory and practice, on political thought? How did printing, the era's most stunning technological discovery, affect fifteenth- and sixteenth-century society? Did women have a Renaissance?

EDUCATION AND POLITICAL THOUGHT

One of the central preoccupations of the humanists was education and moral behavior. Humanists poured out treatises, often in the form of letters, on the structure and goals of education and the training of rulers. In one of the earliest systematic programs for the young, Peter Paul Vergerio (1370–1444) wrote Ubertinus, the ruler of Carrara:

*SCHOOL OF LUCA DELLA ROBBIA: VIRGIN AND
CHILD   In the late fifteenth century, della Robbia's
invention of the process of making polychrome-glazed
terracottas led contemporaries to consider him a great
artistic innovator. The warm humanity of this roundel (circular panel) is characteristic of della Robbia's
art. (Marion Gray. By permission of St. Anselm's
Abbey, Washington, D.C.)*

The lives of men of position are passed, as it were, in public view; and are fairly expected to serve as witness to personal merit and capacity on the part of those who occupy such exceptional place amongst their fellow men. You therefore, Ubertinus, ... the representative of a house for many generations sovereign in our ancient and most learned city of Padua, are peculiarly concerned in attaining this excellence in learning of which we speak.... Progress in learning ... as in character, depends largely on ourselves.

For the education of children is a matter of more than private interest; it concerns the State, which indeed regards the right training of the young as, in certain aspects, within its proper sphere.... In order to maintain a high standard of purity all enticements of dancing, or suggestive spectacles, should be kept at a distance: and the society of women as a rule carefully avoided. A bad companion may wreck the character. Idleness, of mind and body, is a common source of temptation to indulgence, and unsociable, solitary temper must be disciplined, and on no account encouraged. Tutors and comrades alike should be chosen from amongst those likely to bring out the best qualities, to attract by good example, and to repress the first signs of evil.... Above all, respect for Divine ordinances is of the deepest importance; it should be inculcated from the earliest years. Reverence towards elders and parents is an obligation closely akin. In this, antiquity offers us a beautiful illustration. For the youth of Rome used to escort the Senators, the Fathers of the City, to the Senate House: and awaiting them at the entrance, accompany them at the close of their deliberations on their return to their homes. In this the Romans saw an admirable training in endurance and in patience. This same quality of reverence will imply courtesy towards guests, suitable greeting to elders, to friends and to inferiors....

We call those studies liberal *which are worthy of a free man; those studies by which we attain and practise virtue and wisdom; that education*
which calls forth, trains and develops those highest gifts of body and of mind which ennoble men, and which are rightly judged to rank next in dignity to virtue only....[9]

Part of Vergerio's treatise specifies subjects for the instruction of young men in public life: history teaches virtue by examples from the past; ethics focuses on virtue itself; and rhetoric or public speaking trains for eloquence.

No book on education achieved wider fame or broader influence than Baldassare Castiglione's *The Courtier* (1528). This treatise sought to train, discipline, and fashion the young man into the courtly ideal, the gentleman. According to Castiglione, the educated man of the upper class should have a broad background in many academic subjects, and his spiritual and physical, as well as intellectual, capabilities should be trained. The courtier should have easy familiarity with dance, music, and the arts. Castiglione envisioned a man who could compose a sonnet, wrestle, sing a song and accompany himself on an instrument, ride expertly, solve difficult mathematical problems, and, above all, speak and write eloquently. With these accomplishments, he would be the perfect Renaissance man. Whereas the medieval chivalric ideal stressed the military virtues of bravery and loyalty, the Renaissance man had to develop his artistic and intellectual potential as well as his fighting skills.

In contrast to the pattern of medieval education, the Renaissance courtier had the aristocrat's hostility to specialization and professionalism. Medieval higher education, as offered by the universities, had aimed at providing a practical grounding in preparation for a career. After exposure to the rudiments of grammar and rhetoric, which the medieval student learned mainly through memorization, he was trained for a profession

– usually law – in the government of the state or the church. Education was very functional and, by later standards, middle class.

In manner and behavior, the Renaissance courtier had traits his medieval predecessor probably had not had time to acquire. The gentleman was supposed to be relaxed, controlled, always composed and cool, elegant but not ostentatious, doing everything with a casual and seemingly effortless grace. In the sixteenth and seventeenth centuries, *The Courtier* was widely read. It influenced the social mores and patterns of conduct of elite groups in Renaissance and early modern Europe. The courtier became the model of the European gentleman.

No Renaissance book on any topic, however, has been more widely read and studied in all the centuries since its publication than the short political treatise *The Prince,* by Niccolò Machiavelli (1469–1527). Some political scientists maintain that Machiavelli was describing the actual competitive framework of the Italian states with which he was familiar. Other thinkers praise *The Prince* because it revolutionized political theory and destroyed medieval views of the nature of the state. Still other scholars consider this work a classic because it deals with eternal problems of government and society.

Born to a modestly wealthy Tuscan family, Machiavelli received a good education in the Latin classics. He entered the civil service of the Florentine government and served on thirty diplomatic missions. When the exiled Medicis returned to power in the city in 1512, they expelled Machiavelli from his position as officer of the city government. In exile he wrote *The Prince.*

The subject of *The Prince* is political power: how the ruler should gain, maintain, and increase his power. In this, Machiavelli implicitly addresses the question of the citizen's

relationship to the state. As a good humanist, he explores the problems of human nature and concludes that human beings are selfish, corrupt, and out to advance their own interests. This pessimistic view leads him to maintain that the prince should manipulate the people in any way he finds necessary:

The manner in which men live is so different from the way in which they ought to live, that he who leaves the common course for that which he ought to follow will find that it leads him to ruin rather than to safety. For a man who, in all respects, will carry out only his professions of good, will be apt to be ruined amongst so many who are evil. A prince therefore who desires to maintain himself must learn to be not always good, but to be so or not as necessity may require.[10]

The prince should combine the cunning of a fox with the ferocity of a lion to achieve his goals. Asking rhetorically whether it is better for a ruler to be loved or feared, Machiavelli wrote:

A prince, therefore, should not mind the ill repute of cruelty, when he can thereby keep his subjects united and loyal; for a few displays of severity will really be more merciful than to allow, by an excess of clemency, disorders to occur, which are apt to result in rapine and murder; for these injure a whole community, whilst the executions ordered by the prince fall only upon a few individuals. And, above all others, the new prince will find it almost impossible to avoid the reputation of cruelty, because new states are generally exposed to many dangers. . . .

. . . This, then, gives rise to the question "whether it be better to be loved than feared, or to be feared than be loved." It will naturally be answered that it would be desirable to be both the one and the other; but as it is difficult to be both at the same time, it is much more safe to be feared than to be loved, when you have to choose between the

two. For it may be said of men in general that they are ungrateful and fickle, dissemblers, avoiders of danger, and greedy of gain. So long as you shower benefits upon them, they are all yours. . . . And the prince who relies upon their words, without having otherwise provided for his security, is ruined; for friendships that are won by rewards, and not by greatness and nobility of soul, although deserved, yet are not real, and cannot be depended upon in time of adversity.[11]

Medieval political theory derived ultimately from Saint Augustine's view that the state arose as a consequence of Adam's fall and people's propensity to sin. The test of good government was whether it provided justice, law and order. Political theorists and theologians from Alcuin to Marsiglio of Padua had stressed the way government ought to be; they set high moral and Christian standards for the ruler's conduct.

Machiavelli divorced government from moral and ethical considerations. He was concerned not with the way things ought to be but with the way they actually are. Consequently, the sole test of a "good" government was whether it was effective, whether the ruler increased his power. The state Machiavelli envisioned was a dynamic, amoral force.

Scholars have debated whether Machiavelli was writing a satire, trying to ingratiate himself with the Medicis, objectively describing contemporary Italian events, or advocating a fierce Italian nationalism that would achieve the unification of the peninsula. In any case, the word *Machiavellian* entered English as a synonym for devious, crafty, and corrupt politics in which the end justifies any means.

THE PRINTED WORD

Sometime in the thirteenth century, paper money and playing cards from China reached the West. They were block printed – that is, Chinese characters or pictures were carved into a wooden block, inked, and the words or illustrations put on paper. Since each word, phrase, or picture was on a separate block, this method of reproduction was extraordinarily expensive and time-consuming.

Around 1455, probably through the combined efforts of three men – Johan Gutenberg, Johan Fust, and Peter Schoffer, all experimenting at Mainz – movable type came into being. The mirror image of each letter (rather than entire words or phrases) was carved in relief on a small block. Individual letters, easily movable, were put together to form words; words separated by blank spaces formed lines of type; and lines of type were brought together to make up a page. Once the printer had placed wooden pegs around the type for a border, and locked the whole in a frame, the page was ready for printing. Since letters could be arranged into any format, an infinite variety of texts could be printed by reusing and rearranging pieces of type.

By the middle of the fifteenth century, paper was no problem. The technologically advanced but extremely isolated Chinese knew how to manufacture paper as early as the first century A.D. This knowledge reached the West in the twelfth century, when the Arabs introduced the process into Spain. Europeans quickly learned that old rags could be shredded, mixed with water, placed in a mold, squeezed, and dried to make a durable paper, far less expensive than the vellum (calfskin) and parchment (sheepskin) on which medieval scribes had relied for centuries.

The effects of the invention of movable-type printing were not felt overnight. Nevertheless, within a half-century of the publication of Gutenberg's Bible in 1456, movable type brought about radical changes. The costs of reproducing books were drasti-

THE PRINT SHOP *Sixteenth-century printing in-*
volved a division of labor. Two persons (left) at sepa-
rate benches set the pieces of type. Another (center,
rear) inks the chase (or locked plate containing the set
type). Another (right) operates the press which prints
the sheets. The boy removes the printed pages and sets
them to dry. Meanwhile, a man carries in fresh paper
on his head. (BBC Hulton Picture Library)

cally reduced. It took less time and money to print a book by machine than to make copies by hand. The press also reduced the chances of error. If the type had been accurately set, all the copies would be correct no matter how many were reproduced. The greater the number of pages a scribe copied, the greater the chances for human error.

Printing stimulated the literacy of the laity. Although most of the earliest books dealt with religious subjects, students, business-men, and upper- and middle-class people sought books on all kinds of subjects. Thus, intellectual interests were considerably broad-ened. International communication was enor-mously facilitated. The invention of printing permitted writers and scholars of different countries to learn about one another's ideas and discoveries quickly. Intellectuals working in related fields got in touch with each other and cooperated in the advancement of knowl-edge.

Within the past twenty-five years, two in-ventions have revolutionized life for most Americans, television and the computer. By the late 1960s, the tired business executive or mechanic could return home in the evening, flip on "the tube," and while eating dinner watch battles in Vietnam or Israel that had occurred only a few hours before. The Ameri-can tourist in Copenhagen or Florence or Tokyo who suddenly needs to draw on a bank account in New Orleans or Portland can have the account checked by computer in a matter of minutes. The impact of these relatively recent developments has been absolutely phenomenal. The invention of movable type likewise transformed European society in the fifteenth century.

The process of learning was made much easier by printing. In the past, students had had to memorize everything because only the cathedral, monastery, or professor possessed the book. The greater availability of books meant that students could begin to buy their own. If information was not at the tip of the tongue, it was at the tip of the fingers. The number of students all across Europe multiplied. It is not entirely accidental that between 1450 and 1517 seven new universities were established in Spain, three in France, nine in Germany, and six new colleges were set up at Oxford in England.

Printing also meant that ideas critical of the established order in state or church could be more rapidly disseminated. In the early sixteenth century, for example, the publication of Erasmus's *The Praise of Folly* helped pave the way for the Reformation. After 1517, the printing press played no small role in the spread of Martin Luther's political and social views. Cartoons and satirical engravings of all kinds proliferated. They also provoked state censorship, which had been very rare in the Middle Ages. The printed word eventually influenced every aspect of European culture: educational, economic, religious, political, and social.

WOMEN

The status of upper-class women declined during the Renaissance. If women in the High Middle Ages are compared with those of fifteenth- and sixteenth-century Italy with respect to the education they received, the kind of work they performed, their access to property and political power, and the role they played in shaping the outlook of their society, it is clear that ladies in the Renaissance ruling classes generally had less power than comparable ladies of the feudal age.

In the cities of Renaissance Italy, girls received the same education as boys. Young ladies learned their letters and studied the classics. Many read Greek as well as Latin, knew the poetry of Ovid and Virgil, and could speak one or two "modern" languages, such as French or Spanish. In this respect, Renaissance humanism represented a real educational advance for women. Girls also received some training in painting, music, and dance. What were they to do with this training? They were to be gracious, affable, charming – in short, decorative. Renaissance women were better educated than their medieval counterparts. But whereas education trained a young man to rule and to participate in the public affairs of the city, it prepared a woman for the social functions of the home. An educated lady was supposed to know how to attract artists and literati to her husband's court; she was to grace her husband's household.

A striking difference also exists between the medieval literature of courtly love, the etiquette books and romances, and the widely studied Renaissance manual on courtesy and good behavior, Castiglione's *The Courtier*. In the medieval books manners shaped the man to please the lady; in *The Courtier* the lady was to make herself pleasing to the man. With respect to love and sex, the Renaissance witnessed a downward shift in women's status. In contrast to the medieval tradition of relative sexual equality, Renaissance humanists laid the foundations for the bourgeois double standard. Men, and men alone, operated in the public sphere; women belonged in the home. Castiglione, the foremost spokesman of Renaissance love and manners, completely separated love from sexuality. For women, sex was restricted entirely to marriage. Ladies were bound to chastity, to the roles of wife and mother in a politically arranged marriage. Men, however, could pursue sensual indulgence outside marriage. The Italian Renaissance courts accepted a dual sexual standard, as the medieval courts had not. Although some noble ladies were highly educated and some exercised considerable political power, Renaissance culture did little to advance the dignity of women. They usually served as decorative objects in a male society.[12]

Popular attitudes toward rape provide another index of the status of women in the Renaissance. A careful study of the legal evidence from Venice in the years 1338–1358 is informative. The Venetian shipping and merchant elite held economic and political power and made the laws. Those laws reveal that rape was not considered a particularly serious crime against either the victim or society. Noble youths committed a higher percentage of rapes than their small numbers in Venetian society would imply, despite government-regulated prostitution. The rape of a young girl of marriageable age or a child under twelve was considered a graver crime than the rape of a married woman. Still, the punishment for rape of a noble marriageable girl was only a fine or about six months' imprisonment. In an age when theft and robbery were punished by mutilation, and forgery and sodomy by burning, this penalty was very mild indeed. When a youth of the upper class was convicted of the rape of a nonnoble girl, his punishment was even lighter.

By contrast, the sexual assault on a noble-woman by a man of working-class origin, which was extraordinarily rare, resulted in se-vere penalization because the crime had social and political overtones.

In the eleventh century, William the Conqueror had decreed that rapists should be castrated, thus implicitly according women protection and a modicum of respect. But in the early Renaissance, rape was treated as a minor offense. Venetian laws and their enforcement show that the populace believed that rape damaged, but only slightly, men's property – women.[13]

Evidence from Florence in the fifteenth century also sheds light on infanticide, which historians are only now beginning to study in the Middle Ages and the Renaissance. Early medieval penitentials and church councils had legislated against abortion and infanticide, though it is known that Pope Innocent III (1198–1216) was moved to establish an orphanage "because so many women were throwing their children into the Tiber."[14] In the fourteenth and early fifteenth centuries, a considerable number of children died in Florence under suspicious circumstances. Some were simply abandoned outdoors. Some were said to have been crushed to death while sleeping in the same bed with their parents. Some died from "crib death" or suffocation. These deaths occurred too frequently to have all been accidental. And far more girls than boys died thus, reflecting societal discrimination against girl children as inferior and less useful than boys. The dire poverty of parents led them to do away with unwanted children.

The gravity of the problem of infanticide, which violated both the canon law of the church and the civil law of the state, forced the Florentine government to build the Foundling Hospital. Supporters of the institution maintained that without public responsibility, "many children would soon be found dead in the rivers, sewers, and ditches, unbaptized."[15] The city fathers commissioned

TITIAN: THE RAPE OF EUROPA *According to Greek myth, the Phoenician princess Europa was carried off to Crete by the god Zeus disguised as a white bull. The story was highly popular in the Renaissance with its interests in the classics. In this masterpiece, the erotic and voluptuous female figure reveals the new interest in the human form and the secular element in Renaissance art. (Isabella Stewart Gardner Museum)*

Filippo Brunelleschi, who had recently completed the dome over the Cathedral of Florence, to design the building. (Interestingly enough, the Foundling Hospital – completed in 1445 – is the very first building to use the revitalized Roman classic design that characterizes Renaissance architecture.) The unusually large size of the hospital suggests that great numbers of children were abandoned.

BLACKS IN RENAISSANCE SOCIETY

Ever since the time of the Roman republic, a few black people had lived in Western Europe. They had come, along with white slaves, as the spoils of war. Even after the collapse of the Roman Empire, Muslim and Christian merchants continued to import them. The evidence of medieval art attests to the presence of Africans in the West and Eu-

Baldung: Adoration of the Magi Early
sixteenth-century German artists produced thousands
of adoration scenes depicting a black man as one of the
three kings: these paintings were based on direct observation, reflecting the increased presence of blacks in
Europe. The elaborate costumes, jewelry, and landscape expressed royal dignity, Christian devotion, and
oriental luxury. (Gemälde galerie. Staatliche Museen
Preussischer Kulturbesitz, Berlin [West])

ropeans' awareness of them. In the twelfth and thirteenth centuries a large cult surrounded St. Maurice, martyred in the fourth century for refusing to renounce his Christian faith, who was portrayed as a black knight. St. Maurice received the special veneration of the nobility. The numbers of blacks, though, had always been small.

Beginning in the fifteenth century, however, hordes of black slaves entered Europe. Portuguese explorers imported perhaps a thousand a year and sold them at the markets of Seville, Barcelona, Marseilles, and Genoa. The Venetians specialized in the import of white slaves, but blacks were so greatly in demand at the Renaissance courts of northern Italy that the Venetians defied papal threats of excommunication to secure them. What roles did blacks play in Renaissance society? What image did Europeans have of Africans?

The medieval interest in curiosities, the exotic, and the marvelous continued into the Renaissance. Because of their rarity, black servants were highly prized and much sought after. In the late fifteenth century Isabella, the wife of Gian Galeazzo Sforza, took pride in the fact that she had ten blacks, seven of them females; a black lady's maid was both a curiosity and a symbol of wealth. In 1491 Isabella of Este, Duchess of Mantua, instructed her agent to secure a black girl between four and eight years old, "shapely and as black as possible." The duchess saw the child as a source of entertainment: "we shall make her very happy and shall have great fun with her." She hoped that the little girl would become "the best buffoon in the world."[16] The cruel ancient tradition of a noble household retaining a professional "fool" for the family's amusement persisted through the Renaissance — and even down to the twentieth century.

Adult black slaves filled a variety of positions. Many served as maids, valets, domestic servants; Italian aristocrats such as the Marchesa Elena Grimaldi had their portraits painted with their black page boys to indicate their wealth. The Venetians employed blacks – slave and free – as gondoliers and stevedores on the docks. Tradition, stretching back at least as far as the thirteenth century, connected blacks with music and dance. In Renaissance Spain and Italy blacks performed as dancers, as actors and actresses in courtly dramas, and as musicians, sometimes composing full orchestras.[17]

Before the sixteenth-century "discoveries" of the non-European world, Europeans had little interest in Africans and African culture. Consequently, Europeans knew little about them beyond biblical accounts. The European attitude toward Africans was ambivalent. On the one hand, Europeans perceived Africa as a remote place, the home of strange people isolated by heresy and Islam from superior European civilization. Africans' contact even as slaves with Christian Europeans could only "improve" the blacks. Most Europeans' knowledge of the black as a racial type was based entirely on theological speculation. Theologians taught that God is light. Blackness, the opposite of light, therefore represented the hostile forces of the underworld: evil, sin, and the devil. Thus the devil was commonly represented as a black man in medieval and early Renaissance art. Blackness, however, also possessed certain positive qualities. It symbolized the emptiness of worldly goods, the humility of the monastic way of life. Black clothes permitted a conservative and discreet display of wealth. Black vestments and funeral trappings indicated grief, and Christ had said that those who mourn are blessed. Until the exploration and observation of the sixteenth, seventeenth, and nineteenth centuries allowed, ever so slowly, for the development of more scientific knowledge, the Western conception of Africa and black people remained bound up with religious notions.[18]

THE ENVIRONMENT

Historians and natural scientists are only today beginning to study the attitude of peoples in earlier centuries toward their natural environment. An enormous amount of exciting research, which could improve ecological knowledge and aid in the solution of present-day problems, waits to be done. The measures the city of Florence took against water pollution in the fifteenth century provide some interesting information.

In 1450, the Florentine governing body expressed concern that fishermen and others several miles southeast of the city were using toxic substances to harvest more fish from the Arno River, which flowed through the city and was the source of much of Florence's fish. Fewer fresh fish reached the city markets. Ecclesiastical law required Christians to abstain from meat during the Fridays of the year and during the seasons of Advent and Lent. Fish was an obvious substitute, and the fishing industry was large and influential. The law of 1450 states:

Whereas it often happens, especially in parts of the Casentino and areas near there, that poisons and toxic substances are put and inserted into the neighboring rivers and waters to capture and angle fish more easily and in greater number . . .

This is done where those fish are procreated and made which are called Trout, and truly noble and impressive fish they are. The result is that the said fish are destroyed and wasted.

And certainly if this were not so, our city and also other neighboring areas would continually and far more abound in the said fish. So that, therefore, the said genus of fish is preserved, and

our city and the other said areas have a copious and abundant supply of such fish, the magnificent . . . lords priors . . . ordain . . .[19]

The citizens of Florence apparently did not understand the ecological problem and were not concerned about conservation. While they appreciated the beauty of the "noble trout," their concern was only that if upstream waters were polluted and the fish there killed, there would be fewer fish caught and brought to market in Florence. Government officials did not object to the damage to the river as a source of beauty, pleasure, and drinking water. Variations of the law of 1450 were put on the statute books in 1455, 1460, 1471, and 1477,[20] suggesting that these early conservation measures could not be enforced.

THE RENAISSANCE IN THE NORTH

In the last quarter of the fifteenth century, Renaissance thought and ideals penetrated northern Europe. Students from the Low Countries, France, Germany, and England flocked to Italy, imbibed the "new learning," and carried it back to their countries. Northern humanists interpreted Italian ideas about and attitudes toward classical antiquity, individualism, and humanism in terms of their own traditions. The cultural traditions of northern Europe tended to remain more distinctly Christian, or at least pietistic, than those of Italy. Thus while the Renaissance in Italy was characterized by a secular and pagan spirit and focused on Greco-Roman motifs and scholarship, north of the Alps the Renaissance had a religious character and emphasized biblical and early Christian themes. Scholars have termed the northern Renaissance "Christian humanism."

Christian humanists were interested in the development of an ethical way of life. To achieve it they believed that the best elements of classical and Christian cultures should be combined. For example, the classical ideals of calmness, stoical patience, and broad-mindedness should be joined in human conduct with the Christian virtues of love, faith, and hope. Northern humanists also stressed the use of reason, rather than acceptance of dogma, as the foundation for an ethical way of life. Like the Italians, they were extremely impatient with scholastic philosophy. Christian humanists had a profound faith in the power of the human intellect to bring about moral and institutional reform. They believed that although human nature had been corrupted by sin it was fundamentally good and capable of improvement through education, which would lead to piety and an ethical way of life.

This optimistic viewpoint found expression in scores of lectures, treatises, and collections of precepts. Treatises such as Erasmus's *The Education of a Christian Prince* express the naive notion that peace, harmony among nations, and a truly ethical society will result from a new system of education. This hope has been advanced repeatedly in Western history – by the ancient Greeks, by the sixteenth-century Christian humanists, by the eighteenth-century philosophers of the Enlightenment, and by nineteenth-century advocates of progress. The proposition remains highly debatable, but each time the theory has reappeared education has been further democratized.

The work of the French priest Jacques Lefèvre d'Etaples (ca 1455–1536) is one of the early attempts to apply humanistic learning to religious problems. A brilliant thinker and able scholar, he believed that more accurate texts of the Bible would lead people to live better lives. According to Lefèvre, a solid ed-ucation in the Scriptures would increase piety and raise the level of behavior in Christian society. Lefèvre produced an edition of the Psalms and a commentary on Saint Paul's Epistles. In 1516, when Martin Luther lectured to his students at Wittenberg on Paul's Letter to the Romans, he relied on Lefèvre's texts.

Lefèvre's English contemporary John Colet (1466–1519) also published lectures on Saint Paul's Epistles, approaching them in the new critical spirit. Unlike the medieval theologians, who studied the Bible for allegorical meanings, Colet, who was a priest, interpreted the Pauline letters historically – that is, within the social and political context of the times when they were written. Both Colet and Lefèvre d'Etaples were later suspected of heresy, as humanistic scholarship got entangled with the issues of the Reformation.

Colet's friend and countryman Thomas More (1472–1535) towers above other figures in sixteenth-century English social and intellectual history. More's political stance at the time of the Reformation (page 650), a position that in part flowed from his humanist beliefs, got him into serious trouble with King Henry VIII and has tended to obscure his contribution to Christian humanism.

The early career of Thomas More presents a number of paradoxes that reveal the marvelous complexity of the man. Trained as a lawyer, More lived as a student in the London Charterhouse, a Carthusian monastery. He subsequently married and practiced law, but became deeply interested in the classics, and his household served as a model of warm Christian family life and a mecca for foreign and English humanists. Following the career pattern of such Italian humanists as Petrarch, he entered government service under Henry VIII and was sent as ambassador to Flanders. There More found the time to write *Utopia*

THE LATER MIDDLE AGES, RENAISSANCE, AND PROTESTANT AND CATHOLIC REFORMATIONS, 1300–1600

As is evident in this chronology, early manifestations of the Renaissance and Protestant Reformation coincided in time with major events of the Later Middle Ages.

1300–1321	Dante, *The Divine Comedy*
1304–1374	Petrarch
1309–1372	Babylonian Captivity of the papacy
1337–1453	Hundred Years' War
1347–1351	The Black Death
ca 1350	Boccaccio, *The Decameron*
1356	Golden Bull: transforms the Holy Roman Empire into an aristocratic federation
1358	The Jacquerie
ca 1376	John Wyclif publishes *Civil Dominion* attacking the church's temporal power and asserting the supremacy of Scripture
1377–1417	The Great Schism
1378	Laborers' revolt in Florence
1381	Peasants' Revolt
1385–1400	Chaucer, *Canterbury Tales*
1414–1418	Council of Constance: ends the schism, postpones reform, executes John Hus
1431	Joan of Arc is burned at the stake
1434	Medici domination of Florence begins
1438	Pragmatic Sanction of Bourges: declares autonomy of the French church from papal jurisdiction
1453	Capture of Constantinople by the Ottoman Turks, ending the Byzantine Empire
1453–1471	Wars of the Roses in England
1456	Gutenberg Bible
1492	Columbus reaches the Americas
	Unification of Spain under Ferdinand and Isabella; expulsion of Jews from Spain
1494	France invades Italy, inaugurating sixty years of war on Italian soil
	Florence expels the Medici and restores republican government

1509	Erasmus, *The Praise of Folly*
1512	Restoration of the Medici in Florence
1512–1517	Lateran Council undertakes reform of clerical abuses
1513	Balboa discovers the Pacific
	Macchiavelli, *The Prince*
1516	Concordat of Bologna between France and the papacy: rescinds the Pragmatic Sanction of 1438, strengthens French monarchy, establishes Catholicism as the national religion
	Thomas More, *Utopia*
1517	Martin Luther proclaims the 95 Theses
1519–1522	Magellan's crew circumnavigates the earth
1523	Luther's translation of the New Testament into German
1524	Peasants' Revolt in Germany
1527	Sack of Rome by mercenaries of Holy Roman Emperor Charles
1528	Castiglione, *The Courtier*
1530	Confession of Augsburg, official formulation of Lutheran theology
1534	Act of Supremacy inaugurates the English Reformation
1534–1541	Michelangelo, *The Last Judgment*
1535	Execution of Thomas More for treason
1536	John Calvin, *Institutes of the Christian Religion*
1540	Loyola founds the Society of Jesus (Jesuits)
1541	Calvin establishes a theocracy in Geneva
1543	Copernicus, *On the Revolutions of the Heavenly Spheres*
1545–1563	Council of Trent
1555	Peace of Augsburg: German princes determine the religion of their territories; no privileges for Calvinism
1572	St. Bartholemew's Day Massacre
1588	Spanish Armada
1598	Edict of Nantes grants French Protestants freedom of worship in certain towns
1603	Shakespeare, *Hamlet*
1605	Sir Francis Bacon, *The Advancement of Learning*

(1516), which presented a revolutionary view of society.

Utopia, which literally means "nowhere," describes an ideal socialistic community on a South Sea island. All its children receive a good education, primarily in the Greco-Roman classics, and learning does not cease with maturity, for the goal of all education is to develop rational faculties. Adults divide their days equally between manual labor or business pursuits (the Utopians were thoroughly familiar with advanced Flemish business practices) and various intellectual activities.

Because the profits from business and property are held strictly in common, there is absolute social equality. The Utopians use gold and silver to make chamber pots or to prevent wars by buying off their enemies. By this casual use of precious metals, More meant to suggest that the basic problems in society were caused by greed. Utopian law exalts mercy above justice. Citizens of Utopia lead an ideal and nearly perfect existence because they live by reason; their institutions are perfect.

More's ideas were profoundly original in the sixteenth century. Contrary to the long-prevailing view that vice and violence exist because women and men are basically corrupt, More maintained that *society's* flawed institutions are responsible for corruption and war. Today most people take this view so much for granted that it is difficult to appreciate how radical it was in the sixteenth century. According to More, the key to improvement and reform of the individual was reform of the social institutions that mold the individual.

Better known by his contemporaries than Thomas More was the Dutch humanist Desiderius Erasmus of Rotterdam (1469?–1536). Orphaned as a small boy, Erasmus was forced to enter a monastery. Although he intensely disliked the religious life, he developed there an excellent knowledge of the Latin language and a deep appreciation for the Latin classics. During a visit to England in 1499, Erasmus met John Colet, who decisively influenced his life's work: the application of the best humanistic learning to the study and explanation of the Bible. As a mature scholar with an international reputation stretching from Krakow to London, Erasmus could boast with truth, "I brought it about that humanism, which among the Italians...savored of nothing but pure paganism, began nobly to celebrate Christ."[21]

Erasmus's long list of publications includes *The Adages* (1500), a list of Greek and Latin precepts on ethical behavior; *The Education of a Christian Prince* (1504), which combines idealistic and practical suggestions for the formation of a ruler's character through the careful study of Plutarch, Aristotle, Cicero, and Plato; *The Praise of Folly* (1509), a satire on monasticism and a plea for the simple and spontaneous Christian faith of children; and, most important of all, a critical edition of the Greek New Testament (1516). In the preface to the New Testament Erasmus explained the purpose of his great work:

Only bring a pious and open heart, imbued above all things with a pure and simple faith.... For I utterly dissent from those who are unwilling that the sacred Scriptures should be read by the unlearned translated into their vulgar tongue, as though Christ had taught such subtleties that they can scarcely be understood even by a few theologians.... Christ wished his mysteries to be published as openly as possible. I wish that even the weakest woman should read the Gospel — should read the epistles of Paul. And I wish these were translated into all languages, so that they might be read and understood, not only by Scots and Irishmen, but also by Turks and Saracens. To make them understood is surely the first step. It may be that they might be ridiculed by many, but some would take them to heart. I long that the husbandman should sing portions of them to himself as he follows the plough, that the weaver should hum them to the tune of his shuttle, that the traveller should beguile with their stories the tedium of his journey. . . .

Why do we prefer to study the wisdom of Christ in men's writings rather than in the writing of Christ himself?[22]

Two fundamental themes run through all of Erasmus's scholarly work. First, education was the means to reform, the key to moral and intellectual improvement. The core of education ought to be study of the Bible and the classics. Second, the essence of Erasmus's thought is, in his own phrase, "the philosophy of Christ." By this Erasmus meant that Christianity is an inner attitude of the heart or spirit. Christianity is not formalism, special ceremonies, law; Christianity is Christ – his life and what he said and did, not what theologians and commentators have written about him. The Sermon on the Mount, for Erasmus, expressed the heart of the Christian message.

While the writings of Colet, Erasmus, and More have strong Christian themes and have drawn the attention primarily of scholars, the stories of the French humanist François Rabelais (1490?–1553) possess a distinctly secular flavor and have attracted broad readership among the literate public. Rabelais' *Gargantua* and *Pantagruel* (serialized between 1532 and 1552) belong among the great comic masterpieces of world literature. These stories' gross and robust humor introduced the adjective *Rabelaisian* into the language.

Gargantua and *Pantagruel* can be read on several levels: as comic romances about the adventures of the giant Gargantua and his son Pantagruel; as a spoof on contemporary French society; as a program for educational reform; or as illustrations of Rabelais' prodigious learning. The reader enters a world of Renaissance vitality, ribald joviality, and intellectual curiosity. On his travels Gargantua meets various absurd characters, and within their hilarious exchanges there occur serious discussions on religion, politics, philosophy, and education. Rabelais had received an excellent humanistic education in a monastery, and Gargantua discusses the disorders of contemporary religious and secular life. Like More and Erasmus, Rabelais did not denounce institutions directly. Like Erasmus, Rabelais satirized hypocritical monks, pedantic academics, and pompous lawyers. But where Erasmus employed intellectual cleverness and sophisticated wit, Rabelais applied wild and gross humor. Like Thomas More, Rabelais believed that institutions molded individuals and that education was the key to a moral and healthy life. While the middle-class inhabitants of More's *Utopia* lived lives of restrained moderation, the aristocratic residents of Rabelais' Thélème lived for the full gratification of their physical instincts and rational curiosity.

Thélème, the abbey Gargantua establishes, parodies traditional religion and other social institutions. Thélème, whose motto is "Do as Thou Wilt," admits women *and* men, allows all to eat, drink, sleep, and work when they choose, provides excellent facilities for swimming, tennis, and football, and encourages sexual experimentation and marriage. Rabelais believed profoundly in the basic goodness of human beings and the rightness of instinct.

The most roguishly entertaining Renaissance writer, Rabelais was convinced that "laughter is the essence of manhood." A convinced believer in the Roman Catholic faith, he included in Gargantua's education an appreciation for simple and reasonable prayer.

JEROME BOSCH: DEATH AND THE MISER   Netherlandish painters frequently used symbolism, and Bosch (ca 1450–1516) is considered the master-artist of symbolism and fantasy. Here, rats, which because of their destructiveness symbolize evil, control the miser's gold. Bosch's imagery appealed strongly to twentieth-century surrealist painters. (National Gallery of Art, Washington, D.C., Samual H. Kress Collection)

Rabelais combined the Renaissance zest for life and enjoyment of pleasure with a classical insistence on the cultivation of the body and the mind.

The distinctly religious orientation of the literary works of the Renaissance in the north also characterized northern art and architecture. Some Flemish painters, notably Jan van Eyck (1366–1441), were the equals of Italian painters. One of the earliest artists successfully to use oil on wood panels, van Eyck, in paintings such as the *Ghent Altarpiece* and the portrait of *Giovanni Arnolfini and His Bride,* shows the Flemish love for detail; the effect is great realism. Van Eyck's paintings also demonstrate remarkable attention to human personality, as do those of Hans Memling (d. 1494) in his studies of *Tommaso Portinari and His Wife.* Typical of northern piety, the Portinari are depicted in an attitude of prayer (see page 590).

Another Flemish painter, Jerome Bosch (c. 1450–1516) frequently used religious themes, but in combination with grotesque fantasies, colorful imagery, and peasant folk legends. Many of Bosch's paintings reflect the confusion and anguish often associated with the end of the Middle Ages. In *Death and the Miser,* Bosch's dramatic treatment of the Dance of Death theme, the miser's gold, increased by usury, is ultimately controlled by diabolical rats and toads, while his guardian angel urges him to choose the crucifix.

A quasi-spiritual aura likewise infuses architectural monuments in the north. The city halls of wealthy Flemish towns like Bruges, Brussels, Louvain, and Ghent strike the viewer more as shrines to house the bones of saints than as settings for the mundane decisions of politicians and businessmen. Northern architecture was little influenced by the classical revival so obvious in Renaissance Rome and Florence.

POLITICS AND THE STATE IN THE RENAISSANCE (CA 1450–1521)

The High Middle Ages had witnessed the origins of many of the basic institutions of the modern national state. Sheriffs, inquests, juries, circuit judges, bureaucracies, and representative assemblies all trace their origins to the twelfth and thirteenth centuries (pages (457–470). The linchpin for the development of states, however, was strong monarchy, and during the period of the Hundred Years' War no ruler in western Europe was able to provide effective leadership. The resurgent power of feudal nobilities weakened the centralizing work begun earlier.

Beginning in the fifteenth century, rulers utilized the aggressive methods implied by Renaissance political ideas to rebuild their governments. First in Italy, then in France, England, and Spain, rulers began the work of reducing violence, curbing unruly nobles and troublesome elements, and establishing domestic order. Within the Holy Roman Empire of Germany, the lack of centralization helps to account for the later German distrust of the Roman papacy. Divided into scores of independent principalities, Germany could not deal with the Roman church as an equal.

The dictators and oligarchs of the Italian city-states, however, together with Louis XI of France, Henry VII of England, and Ferdinand of Spain, were tough, cynical, and calculating rulers. In their ruthless push for power and strong governments, they subordinated morality and considerations of right and wrong to the achievement of hard results. They preferred to be secure, if feared, rather than loved. Whether or not they actually read Machiavelli's *The Prince,* they acted as if they had.

Some historians have called Louis XI (1461–1483), Henry VII (1485–1509), and Ferdinand and Isabella of Spain (1474–1516) "new monarchs." The term is only partly appropriate. These monarchs were new in that they invested kingship with a strong sense of royal authority and national purpose. They stressed that monarchy was the one institution that linked all classes and peoples within definite territorial boundaries. Rulers emphasized the "royal majesty" and royal sovereignty and insisted that all must respect and be loyal to them. They ruthlessly suppressed opposition and rebellion, especially from the nobility. They loved the business of kingship and worked hard at it.

In other respects, however, the methods of these rulers, which varied from country to country, were not so new. They reasserted long-standing ideas and practices of strong monarchs in the Middle Ages. The Holy Roman emperor Frederick Barbarossa, the English Edward I, and the French King Philip the Fair had all applied ideas drawn from Roman law in the High Middle Ages. Renaissance princes also did so. They seized upon the maxim of the Justinian Code, "What pleases the prince has the force of law," to advance their authority. Some medieval rulers, such as Henry I of England, had depended heavily upon middle-class officials. Renaissance rulers too tended to rely on civil servants of middle-class background. With tax revenues, medieval rulers had built armies to crush feudal anarchy. Renaissance townspeople with commercial and business interests naturally wanted a reduction of violence and usually were willing to be taxed in order to achieve domestic order.

Scholars have often described the fifteenth-century "new monarchs" as crafty, devious, and thoroughly Machiavellian in their methods. Yet contemporaries of the Capetian Philip the Fair considered him every bit as devious and crafty as his Valois descendants, Louis XI and Francis I, were considered in the fifteenth and sixteenth centuries. Machiavellian politics were not new in the age of the Renaissance. What was new was a marked acceleration of politics, whose sole rationalization was the acquisition and expansion of power. Renaissance rulers spent precious little time seeking a religious justification for their actions. With these qualifications of the term "new monarchs" in mind, let us consider the development of national states in Italy, France, England, and Spain in the period 1450 to 1521.

THE ITALIAN CITY-STATES

In the fourteenth century, the Holy Roman emperors had made several efforts to impose imperial authority in Italy and continue the tradition begun by Charlemagne. But the German emperors, economically and militarily weak, could not defeat the powerful, though separate, city-states. The Italian city-states were thus entirely independent of the Holy Roman Empire.

In the fifteenth century, five powers dominated the Italian peninsula – Venice, Milan, Florence, the Papal States, and the kingdom of Naples (see Map 17.1). The rulers of the city-states – whether despots in Milan, patrician elitists in Florence, or oligarchs in Venice – governed as monarchs. They crushed proletarian revolts, levied taxes, killed their enemies, and used massive building programs to employ, and the arts to overawe, the masses.

Venice, with enormous trade and a vast colonial empire, ranked as an international power. Although Venice had a sophisticated constitution and was a republic in name, an oligarchy of merchant-aristocrats actually ran

the city. Milan was also called a republic, but despots of the Sforza family ruled harshly and dominated the smaller cities of the north. Likewise in Florence the form of government was republican, with authority vested in several councils of state. In reality, between 1434 and 1494, power in Florence was held by the great Medici banking family. Although they did not hold public office, Cosimo (1434–1464) and Lorenzo (1469–1492) ruled from behind the scenes.

A republic is a state in which political power resides in the people and is exercised by them or their chosen representatives. The Renaissance nostalgia for the Roman form of republican government, combined with a calculating shrewdness, prompted leaders of Venice, Milan, and Florence to preserve the old forms: the people could be deceived into thinking they still possessed the decisive voice.

Central Italy consisted mainly of the Papal States, which during the Babylonian Captivity had come under the sway of important Roman families. Pope Alexander VI (1492–1503), aided militarily and politically by his son Cesare Borgia, reasserted papal authority in the papal lands. Cesare Borgia became the hero of Machiavelli's *The Prince* because he began the work of uniting the peninsula by ruthlessly conquering and exacting total obedience from the principalities making up the Papal States.

South of the Papal States was the kingdom of Naples, consisting of virtually all of southern Italy and, at times, Sicily. The kingdom of Naples had long been disputed by the Aragonese and by the French. In 1435, it passed to Aragon.

The major Italian city-states controlled the smaller ones, such as Siena, Mantua, Ferrara, and Modena, and competed furiously among themselves for territory. The large cities used

HOLY ROMAN EMPIRE

DUCHY OF SAVOY

Turin

SALUZZO

DUCHY OF MILAN

Milan
Lodi
Pavia

REP. OF GENOA

Genoa

M. OF MANTUA

D. OF MODENA

D. OF FERRARA

Padua

Venice

REPUBLIC OF VENICE

DALMATIA

OTTOMAN EMPIRE

Bologna

Ravenna

REP. OF LUCCA

REP. OF FLORENCE

Arno
Pisa

Florence

Siena

REP. OF SIENA

Urbino

PAPAL STATES

Assisi

ADRIATIC SEA

Tiber

Rome

CORSICA (to Genoa)

SARDINIA

KINGDOM OF NAPLES

Naples
Salerno

Bari

MEDITERRANEAN SEA

Palermo

KINGDOM OF SICILY

| 0 | 50 | 100 Km. |
| 0 | 50 | 100 Mi. |

MAP 17.1 THE ITALIAN CITY-STATES, CA 1494 *In the fifteenth century the Italian city-states represented great wealth and cultural sophistication. The political divisions of the peninsula invited foreign intervention.*

diplomacy, spies, paid informers, and any other means to get information that could be used to advance their ambitions. While the states of northern Europe were moving toward centralization and consolidation, the world of Italian politics resembled a jungle where the powerful dominated the weak.

In one significant respect, however, the Italian city-states anticipated future relations among competing European states after 1500. Whenever one Italian state appeared to gain a predominant position within the peninsula, other states combined to establish a balance of power against the major threat. In 1450, for example, Venice went to war against Milan in protest against Francesco Sforza's acquisition of the title of duke of Milan. Cosimo de' Medici of Florence, a long-time supporter of a Florentine-Venetian alliance, switched his po-

sition and aided Milan. Florence and Naples combined with Milan against powerful Venice and the papacy. In the peace treaty signed at Lodi in 1454, Venice received territories in return for recognizing Sforza's right to the duchy. This pattern of shifting alliances continued until 1494.

At the end of the fifteenth century, Venice, Florence, Milan, and the papacy possessed great wealth and represented high cultural achievement. Their imperialistic ambitions at each other's expense, however, and their inability to form a common alliance against potential foreign enemies, made Italy an inviting target for invasion. When Florence and Naples entered into an agreement to acquire Milanese territories, Milan called upon France for support.

At Florence the French invasion had been

predicted by the Dominican friar Girolamo Savonarola (1452–1498). In a number of fiery sermons between 1481 and 1494, Savonarola attacked what he considered the paganism and moral vice of the city, the undemocratic government of Lorenzo de' Medici, and the corruption of Pope Alexander VI. For a time Savonarola enjoyed wide popular support among the ordinary people; he became the religious leader of Florence and as such contributed to the fall of the Medici. Eventually, however, people wearied of his moral denunciations, and he was excommunicated and executed. As an enemy of secularism, Savonarola stands as proof that the common people did not share the worldly outlook of the commercial and intellectual elite. His career also illustrates the internal instability of Italian cities such as Florence, an instability that invited foreign invasion.

The invasion of Italy in 1494 by the French king Charles VIII (1483–1498) inaugurated a new period in Italian and European power politics. Italy became the focus of international ambitions and the battleground of foreign armies. Charles swept down the peninsula with little opposition, and Florence, Rome, and Naples soon bowed before him. When Piero de' Medici, Lorenzo's son, went to the French camp seeking peace, the Florentines exiled the Medicis and restored republican government.

Charles's success simply whetted French appetites. In 1508, his successor, Louis XII, formed the League of Cambrai with the pope and the German emperor Maximilian for the purpose of stripping rich Venice of its mainland possessions. Pope Leo X soon found the French a dangerous friend, and in a new alliance called upon the Spanish and Germans to expel the French from Italy. This anti-French combination was temporarily successful. But the French returned in 1522, and after Charles V succeeded his grandfather Maximilian as Holy Roman emperor, there began the series of conflicts called the Habsburg-Valois wars (named for the German and French dynasties), whose battlefield was Italy.

In the sixteenth century, the political and social life of Italy was upset by the relentless competition for dominance between France and the empire. The Italian cities suffered severely from the continual warfare, especially in the frightful sack of Rome in 1527 by imperial forces under Charles V. Thus the failure of the city-states to form some federal system, or to consolidate, or at least to establish a common foreign policy, led to the continuation of the centuries-old subjection of the peninsula by outside invaders. Italy was not to achieve unification until 1870.

FRANCE

The Hundred Years' War left France badly divided, drastically depopulated, commercially ruined, and agriculturally weak. Nonetheless, the ruler whom Joan of Arc had seen crowned at Reims, Charles VII (1422–1461), revived the monarchy and France. He seemed an unlikely person to do so. Frail, ugly, feeble, hypochondriacal, mistrustful, called "the son of a madman and a loose woman," Charles VII began France's long recovery.

Charles reconciled the Burgundians and Armagnacs, who had been waging civil war for thirty years. By 1453, French armies had expelled the English from French soil except in Calais. Charles reorganized the royal council, giving increased influence to the middle-class men, and he strengthened royal finances through such taxes as the gabelle (on salt) and the taille (a land tax). These taxes remained the Crown's chief sources of state income until the Revolution of 1789.

Charles also reformed the justice system

FRENCH TRADESMEN *A bootmaker, a cloth merchant (with bolts of material on shelves), and a dealer in gold plate and silver share a stall. Through sales taxes, the French crown received a share of the profits. (Bibliothèque Municipale, Rouen/Giraudon)*

and remodeled the army. By establishing regular companies of cavalry and archers — recruited, paid, and inspected by the state — Charles created the first permanent royal army. In 1438, Charles published the Pragmatic Sanction of Bourges, asserting the superiority of a general council over the papacy, giving the French crown control over the appointment of bishops, and depriving the pope of French ecclesiastical revenues. The Pragmatic Sanction established the Gallican (or French) liberties, because it affirmed the autonomy of the French church from the Roman papacy. Greater control over the church, the army, and justice helped to consolidate the authority of the French crown.

Charles's son Louis XI, called "the Spider King" by his subjects because of his treacherous and cruel character, was very much a Renaissance prince. Facing the perpetual French problems of unification of the realm and reduction of feudal disorder, he saw money as the answer. Louis promoted new industries, such as silk weaving at Lyons and Tours. He welcomed tradesmen and foreign craftsmen, and he entered into commercial treaties with England, Portugal, and the towns of the Hanseatic League, a group of cities that played an important role in the development of towns and commercial life in northern Germany. The revenues raised through these economic activities and severe taxation were used to improve the army. With the army Louis stopped aristocratic brigandage and slowly cut into urban independence.

Luck favored his goal of expanding royal authority and unifying the kingdom. On the timely death of Charles the Bold, duke of Burgundy, in 1477 Louis invaded Burgundy and gained some territories. Three years later, the extinction of the house of Anjou brought Louis the counties of Anjou, Bar, Maine, and Provence.

Some scholars have credited Louis XI with laying the foundations for later French royal absolutism. Louis summoned only one meeting of the Estates General, and the delegates requested that they not be summoned in the future. Thereafter the king would decide. Building on the system begun by his father, Louis XI worked tirelessly to remodel the government following the debacle of the fourteenth and fifteenth centuries. In his reliance on finances supplied by the middle classes to fight the feudal nobility, Louis is typical of the new monarchs.

Two further developments strengthened the French monarchy. The marriage of Louis XII and Anne of Brittany retained the large western duchy of Brittany for the French state. Then, the French king Francis I and Pope Leo X reached a mutually satisfactory agreement in 1516. The new treaty, the Concordat of Bologna, rescinded the Pragmatic Sanction's assertion of the superiority of a general council over the papacy and approved the pope's right to receive the first year's income of new bishops and abbots. In return, Leo X recognized the French ruler's right to select French bishops and abbots. French kings thereafter effectively controlled the appointment and thus the policies of church officials within the kingdom.

ENGLAND

English society suffered severely from the disorders of the fifteenth century. The aristocracy dominated the government of Henry IV (1399–1413) and indulged in mischievous violence at the local level. Population, decimated by the Black Death, continued to decline. While Henry V (1413–1422) gained chivalric prestige for his military exploits in France, he was totally dependent upon the feudal magnates who controlled the royal council and Parliament. Henry V's death, leaving a nine-month-old son, the future Henry VI (1422–1461), gave the barons a perfect opportunity to entrench their power. Between 1455 and 1471, adherents of the ducal houses of York and Lancaster waged civil war, commonly called the Wars of the Roses because the symbol of the Yorkists was a white rose and that of the Lancastrians a red one. Although only a small minority of the nobility participated, the chronic disorder hurt trade, agriculture, and domestic industry. Under the pious but spineless Henry VI, the authority of the monarchy sank lower than it had been in centuries.

Edward IV (1461-1483) began establishing domestic tranquility. He succeeded in defeating the Lancastrian forces and after 1471 began to reconstruct the monarchy and consolidate royal power. Edward, his brother Richard III (1483-1485), and Henry VII of the Welsh house of Tudor worked to restore royal prestige, to crush the power of the nobility, and to establish order and law at the local level. All three rulers used methods Machiavelli would have praised – ruthlessness, efficiency, and secrecy.

The Hundred Years' War had cost the nation dearly, and the money to finance it had been raised by Parliament. Dominated by various baronial factions, Parliament had been the arena where the nobility exerted its power. As long as the monarchy was dependent on the lords and the commons for revenue, the king had to call Parliament. Thus Edward IV revived the medieval ideal that he would "live of his own," meaning on his own financial resources. He reluctantly established a policy the monarchy was to follow with rare exceptions down to 1603. Edward, and subsequently the Tudors, conducted foreign policy on the basis of diplomacy, avoiding expensive wars. Thus the English monarchy did not depend on Parliament for money, and the Crown undercut that source of aristocratic influence.

Henry VII did, however, summon several meetings of Parliament in the early years of his reign. He used these assemblies primarily to confirm laws. Parliament remained the highest court in the land, and a statute registered (approved) there by the lords, bishops, and commons gave the appearance of broad national support plus thorough judicial authority.

The center of royal authority was the royal council, which governed at the national level. There too Henry VII revealed his distrust of the nobility: although they were not completely excluded, very few great lords were among the king's closest advisers. Regular representatives on the council numbered between twelve and fifteen men, and while many gained high ecclesiastical rank (the means, as it happened, by which the Crown paid them), their origins were the lesser landowning class and their education was in law. They were in a sense middle class.

The royal council handled any business the king put before it – executive, legislative, judicial. For example, the council conducted negotiations with foreign governments and secured international recognition of the Tudor dynasty through the marriage in 1501 of Henry VII's eldest son Arthur to Catherine of Aragon, the daughter of Ferdinand and Isabella of Spain. The council prepared laws for parliamentary ratification. The council dealt with real or potential aristocratic threats through a judicial offshoot, the court of Star Chamber, so-called because of the stars painted on the ceiling of the room.

The court of Star Chamber applied principles of Roman law, and its methods were terrifying: the accused was not entitled to see evidence against him; sessions were secret; torture could be applied to extract confessions; and juries were not called. These procedures ran directly counter to English common-law precedents, but they effectively reduced aristocratic troublemaking.

Unlike the continental countries of Spain and France, England had no standing army or professional civil-service bureaucracy. The Tudors relied upon the support of unpaid local officials, the justices of the peace. These influential landowners in the shires handled all the work of local government. They apprehended and punished criminals, enforced parliamentary statutes, supervised conditions of service, fixed wages and prices, maintained proper standards of weights and measures, and even checked up on moral behavior. Justices of the peace were appointed and supervised by the council. From the royal point of view, they were an inexpensive method of government.

The Tudors won the support of the influential upper middle class because the Crown linked government policy with their interests. A commercial or agricultural upper class fears and dislikes few things more than disorder and violence. If the Wars of the Roses served any useful purpose, it was killing off dangerous nobles and thus making the Tudors' work easier. The Tudors promoted peace and social order, and the gentry did not object to arbitrary methods like the court of Star Chamber, because the government had halted the long period of anarchy.

Grave, secretive, cautious, and always thrifty, Henry VII rebuilt the monarchy. He encouraged the cloth industry and built up the English merchant marine. Both English exports of wool and the royal export tax on that wool steadily increased. Henry crushed an invasion from Ireland and secured peace with Scotland through the marriage of his daughter Margaret to the Scottish king. When Henry VII died in 1509, he left a country at peace both domestically and internationally, a fat treasury, and the dignity of the royal majesty much enhanced.

SPAIN

Political development in Spain followed a pattern different from that of France and England. The central theme in the history of medieval Spain – or, more accurately, of the separate kingdoms Spain comprised – was disunity and plurality. The various peoples who lived in the Iberian Peninsula lacked a common cultural tradition. Different languages, different laws, and different religious communities made for a rich diversity. Complementing the legacy of Hispanic, Roman, and Visigothic peoples, Muslims and Jews had made significant contributions to Spanish society.

The centuries-long *reconquista* – the attempts of the northern Christian kingdoms to control the entire peninsula – had both military and religious objectives: expulsion or conversion of the Arabs and Jews and political control of the south. By the middle of the fifteenth century, the kingdoms of Castile and Aragon dominated the weaker Navarre, Granada, and Portugal, and, with the exception of Granada, the Iberian Peninsula had been won for Christianity. The wedding in 1469 of the dynamic and aggressive Isabella, heiress of Castile, and the crafty and persistent Ferdinand, heir of Aragon, was the final major step in the unification and Christianization of Spain. This marriage, however, constituted a dynastic union of two royal houses, not the political union of two peoples. Although Ferdinand and Isabella pursued a common foreign policy, Spain under their rule remained a loose confederation of separate states. Each kingdom continued to maintain its own cortes (parliament), laws, courts, bureaucracies, and systems of coinage and taxation.

Isabella and Ferdinand determined to strengthen royal authority. In order to curb the rebellious and warring aristocracy, they revived an old medieval institution. Popular groups in the towns called *hermandades,* or brotherhoods, were given the authority to act both as local police forces and as judicial tribunals. Local communities were made responsible for raising troops and apprehending and punishing criminals. The *hermandades* repressed violence with such savage punishments that by 1498 they could be disbanded.

The second step Ferdinand and Isabella

took to curb aristocratic power was the restructuring of the royal council. Aristocrats and great territorial magnates were rigorously excluded; thus the influence of the nobility on state policy was greatly reduced. Ferdinand and Isabella intended the council to be the cornerstone of their governmental system, with full executive, judicial, and legislative power under the monarchy. The council was also to be responsible for the supervision of local authorities. The king and queen, therefore, appointed to the council only people of middle-class background. The council and various government boards recruited men trained in Roman law, a system that exalted the power of the Crown as the embodiment of the state.

In the extension of royal authority and the consolidation of the territories of Spain, the church was the linchpin. The church possessed vast power and wealth, and churchmen enjoyed exemption from taxation. Most of the higher clergy were descended from great aristocratic families, controlled armies and strategic fortresses, and fully shared the military ethos of their families.

The major issue confronting Isabella and Ferdinand was the appointment of bishops. If the Spanish crown could select the higher clergy, then the monarchy could influence ecclesiastical policy, wealth, and military resources. Through a diplomatic alliance with the papacy, especially with the Spanish pope Alexander VI, the Spanish monarchs secured the right to appoint bishops in Spain and in the Hispanic territories in America. This power enabled the "Catholic Kings of Spain," a title granted Ferdinand and Isabella by the papacy, to establish, in effect, a national church.[23]

The Spanish rulers used their power to reform the church, and they used some of its wealth for national purposes. For example,

they appointed a learned and zealous churchman, Cardinal Jiménez (1436–1517), to reform the monastic and secular clergy. Jiménez proved effective in this task, and established the University of Alcalá in 1499 for the education of the clergy, although instruction did not actually begin until 1508. A highly astute statesman, Jiménez twice served as regent of Castile.

Revenues from ecclesiastical estates provided the means to raise an army to continue the *reconquista*. The victorious entry of Ferdinand and Isabella into Granada on January 6, 1492, signaled the culmination of eight centuries of Spanish struggle against the Arabs in southern Spain and the conclusion of the *reconquista* (see Map 17.2). Granada in the south was incorporated into the Spanish kingdom, and in 1512 Ferdinand conquered Navarre in the north.

Although the Arabs had been defeated, there still remained a sizable and, in the view of the Catholic sovereigns, potentially dangerous minority, the Jews. Since ancient times, governments had never tolerated religious pluralism; religious faiths that differed from the official state religion were considered politically dangerous. Medieval writers quoted the fourth-century Byzantine theologian Saint John Chrysostom, who had asked rhetorically, "Why are the Jews degenerate? Because of their odious assassination of Christ." John Chrysostom and his admirers in the Middle Ages chose to ignore two facts: that it was the Romans who had killed Christ (because they considered him a *political* troublemaker), and that Christ had forgiven his executioners from the cross. France and England had expelled their Jewish populations in the Middle Ages, but in Spain Jews had been tolerated. In fact, Jews had played a decisive role in the economic and intellectual life of the several Spanish kingdoms.

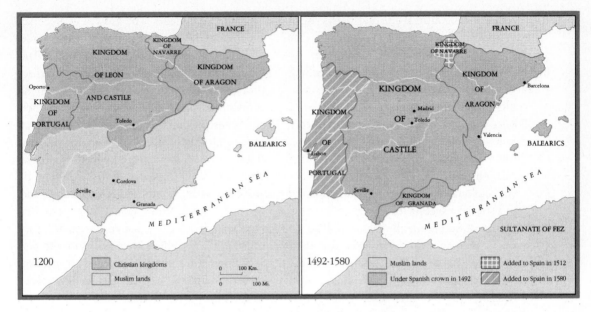

MAP 17.2 THE CHRISTIANIZATION AND UNI-
FICATION OF SPAIN *The political unification of
Spain was inextricably tied up with conversion or ex-
pulsion of the Muslims and the Jews. Why?*

Anti-Semitic riots and pogroms in the late fourteenth century had led many Jews to convert; they were called *conversos*. By the middle of the fifteenth century, many conversos held high positions in Spanish society as financiers, physicians, merchants, tax collectors, and even officials of the church hierarchy. Numbering perhaps 200,000 in a total population of about 7.5 million, Jews exercised an influence quite disproportionate to their numbers. Aristocratic grandees who borrowed heavily from Jews resented their financial dependence, and churchmen questioned the sincerity of Jewish conversions. At first, Isabella and Ferdinand continued the policy of royal toleration – Ferdinand himself had inherited Jewish blood from his mother. But many conversos apparently reverted to the faith of their ancestors, prompting Ferdinand and Isabella to secure Rome's permission to revive the In-

quisition, a medieval judicial procedure for the punishment of heretics.

Although the Inquisition was a religious institution established to insure the Catholic faith, it was controlled only by the Crown and served primarily as a politically unifying force in Spain. Because the Spanish Inquisition commonly applied torture to extract confessions, first from lapsed conversos, then from Muslims, and later from Protestants, it gained a notorious reputation. Thus, the word *inquisition,* meaning "any judicial inquiry conducted with ruthless severity," came into the English language. The methods of the Spanish Inquisition were cruel, though not as cruel as the investigative methods of some twentieth-century governments. In 1478 the deeply pious Ferdinand and Isabella introduced the Inquisition into their kingdoms to handle the problem of backsliding conversos. They solved the problem in a dire and drastic manner. Shortly after the reduction of the Moorish stronghold at Granada in 1492, Isabella and Ferdinand issued an edict expelling all practicing Jews from Spain. Of the community of perhaps 200,000 Jews, 150,000 fled. (Efforts were made through last-minute conversions to retain good Jewish physicians.) Absolute religious orthodoxy served as the foundation of the Spanish national state.

The diplomacy of the Catholic rulers of Spain achieved a success they never anticipated. Partly out of hatred for the French and partly to gain international recognition for their new dynasty, Ferdinand and Isabella in 1496 married their second daughter, Joanna, heiress to Castile, to the archduke Philip, heir through his mother to the Burgundian Netherlands and through his father to the Holy Roman Empire. Philip and Joanna's son, Charles V (1519–1556), thus succeeded to a vast patrimony on two continents. When Charles's son Philip II united Portugal to the Spanish crown in 1580, the Iberian Peninsula was at last politically united.

———◆———

Fourteenth-century Italy witnessed the rebirth of a strong interest in the ancient world, a Renaissance whose classicizing influences affected law and literature, government, education, religion, and art. Expanding outside Italy, this movement affected the entire culture of Europe. The chief features of the Renaissance were a secular attitude toward life, a belief in individual potential, and a serious interest in the Latin classics. The printing press revolutionized communication. Meanwhile the status of women in society declined, and black people entered Europe in sizable numbers for the first time since the collapse of the Roman Empire.

These changes rested upon important economic developments. The growth of Venetian and Genoese shipping and long-distance trade, Florentine banking and manufactures, Milanese and Pisan manufactures – these activities brought into being wealthy urban classes. As commercial oligarchies, they governed their city-states. In northern Europe city merchants and rural gentry allied with rising monarchies. With taxes provided by businesspeople, kings provided a greater degree of domestic peace and order, conditions essential for trade. In Spain, France, and England, rulers also emphasized royal dignity and authority, and they utilized Machiavellian ideas to insure the preservation and continuation of their governments. Feudal monarchies gradually evolved in the direction of nation states.

NOTES

1. A. Brucker, *Renaissance Florence,* John Wiley & Sons, New York, 1969, chap. 2.

2. Quoted by J. Burckhardt, *The Civilization of the Renaissance in Italy,* Phaidon Books, London, 1951, p. 89.

3. *Memoirs of Benvenuto Cellini; A Florentine Artist; Written by Himself,* Everyman's Library, J. M. Dent & Sons, London, 1927, p. 2.

4. Quoted by Burckhardt, p. 111.

5. B. Burroughs, ed., *Vasari's Lives of the Artists,* Simon & Schuster, New York, 1946, pp. 164–165.

6. See chap. 3, "The Social Status of the Artist," in A. Hauser, *The Social History of Art,* vol. 2, Vintage Books, New York, 1959, esp. pp. 60, 68.

7. G. Bull, trans., *Aretino: Selected Letters,* Penguin Books, New York, 1976, p. 109.

8. Hauser, pp. 48–49.

9. Quoted by W. H. Woodward, *Vittorino da Feltre and Other Humanist Educators,* Cambridge University Press, Cambridge, 1897, pp. 96–97.

10. C. E. Detmold, trans., *The Historical, Political*

and *Diplomatic Writings of Niccolò Machiavelli*, J. R. Osgood & Co., Boston, 1882, pp. 51–52.

11. Ibid., pp. 54–55.

12. This account rests on the excellent study of J. Kelly-Gadol, "Did Women Have a Renaissance?" in R. Bridenthal and C. Koonz, eds., *Becoming Visible: Women in European History,* Houghton Mifflin, Boston, 1977, pp. 137–161, esp. p. 161.

13. G. Ruggiero, "Sexual Criminality in the Early Renaissance: Venice 1338–1358," *Journal of Social History* 8 (Spring 1975):18–31.

14. Quoted by R. C. Trexler, "Infanticide in Florence: New Sources and First Results," *History of Childhood Quarterly* 1:1 (Summer 1973): 99.

15. Ibid., p. 100.

16. See Jean Devisse and Michel Mollat, *The Image of the Black in Western Art,* vol. II, part 2, trans. William Granger Ryan, William Morrow and Company, New York, 1979, pp. 187–188.

17. Ibid., pp. 190–194.

18. Ibid., pp. 255–258.

19. Quoted by R. C. Trexler, "Measures against Water Pollution in Fifteenth-Century Florence," *Viator* 5 (1974):463.

20. Ibid., pp. 464–467.

21. Quoted by E. H. Harbison, *The Christian Scholar and His Calling in the Age of the Reformation,* Charles Scribner's Sons, New York, 1956, p. 109.

22. Quoted by F. Seebohm, *The Oxford Reformers,* Everyman's Library, J. M. Dent & Sons, London, 1867, p. 256.

23. See J. H. Elliott, *Imperial Spain 1469–1716,* Mentor Books, New York, 1963, esp. pp. 97–108 and p. 75.

SUGGESTED READING

There are scores of exciting studies available on virtually all aspects of the Renaissance. In addition to the titles given in the Notes, the curious student interested in a broad synthesis should see J. H. Plumb, *The Italian Renaissance* (1965), a superbly written book based on deep knowledge and understanding; this book is probably the best starting point. J. R. Hale, *Renaissance Europe: The Individual and Society, 1480–1520* (1978), is an excellent treatment of individualism by a distinguished authority. F. H. New, *The Renaissance and Reformation: A Short History* (1977), gives a concise, balanced, and up-to-date account. M. P. Gilmore, *The World of Humanism* (1962), is an older but sound study that recent scholarship has not superseded on many subjects. Students interested in the problems the Renaissance has raised for historians should see K. H. Dannenfeld, ed., *The Renaissance: Medieval or Modern* (1959), an anthology with a variety of interpretations, and W. K. Ferguson, *The Renaissance in Historical Thought* (1948), a valuable but difficult book. For the city where much of it originated, G. A. Brucker, *Renaissance Florence* (1969), gives a good description of Florentine economic, political, social, and cultural history.

J. R. Hale, *Machiavelli and Renaissance Italy* (1966), is the best short biography of Machiavelli and broader in scope than the title would imply. G. Bull, trans., *Machiavelli: The Prince* (1959), is a readable and easily accessible edition of the political thinker's major work. C. Singleton, trans., *The Courtier* (1959), presents an excellent picture of Renaissance court life.

The best introduction to the Renaissance in northern Europe and a book that has greatly influenced twentieth-century scholarship is J. Huizinga, *The Waning of the Middle Ages: A Study of the Forms of Life, Thought, and Art in France and the Netherlands in the Dawn of the Renaissance* (1954). The leading northern humanist is sensitively treated in M. M. Philips, *Erasmus and the Northern Renaissance* (1965), and in J. Huizinga, *Erasmus of Rotterdam* (1952), probably the best biography. The standard biography of *Thomas More* remains that of R. W. Chambers (1935), but see also E. E. Reynolds, *Thomas More* (1962). Jacques LeClercq, trans., *The Complete Works of Rabelais* (1963), is easily available.

Renaissance art has understandably inspired vast researches. In addition to Vasari's volume of biographical sketches on the great masters referred to in the Notes, A. Martindale, *The Rise of the Artist in the Middle Ages and Early Renaissance* (1972), is a splendidly illustrated introduction. B. Berenson, *Italian Painters of the Renaissance* (1957), the work of an American expatriate who was an internationally famous art historian, has become a classic. W. Sypher, *Four Stages of Renaissance Style* (1956), relates drama and poetry to the visual arts of painting and sculpture. One of the finest appreciations of Renaissance art, written by one of the greatest art historians of this century, is E. Panofsky, *Meaning in the Visual Arts* (1955). Both Italian and northern painting are treated in the brilliant study of M. Meiss, *The Painter's Choice: Problems in the Interpretation of Renaissance Art* (1976), a collection of essays dealing with Renaissance style, form, and meaning. The splendidly illustrated work of Mary McCarthy, *The Stones of Florence* (1959), celebrates the energy and creativity of the greatest Renaissance city.

The student who wishes to study blacks in medieval and early modern European society should see the rich and original achievement of Jean Devisse and Michel Mollat, *The Image of the Black in Western Art,* vol. II: Part 1, *From the Demonic Threat to the Incarnation of Sainthood,* and Part 2, *Africans in the Christian Ordinance of the World: Fourteenth to Sixteenth Century,* trans. William Granger Ryan, William Morrow & Co., New York, 1979.

The following works are not only useful for the political and economic history of the age of the Renaissance but also contain valuable bibliographical information: A. J. Slavin, ed., *The "New Monarchies" and Representative Assemblies* (1965), a collection of interpretations; R. Lockyer, *Henry VII* (1972), a biography with documents illustrative of the king's reign; J. H. Elliott, *Imperial Spain: 1469–1716* (1966), with a balanced treatment of Isabella and Ferdinand; and I. Origo, *The Merchant of Prato* (1957), a perceptive and detailed account of one busy Florentine businessman.

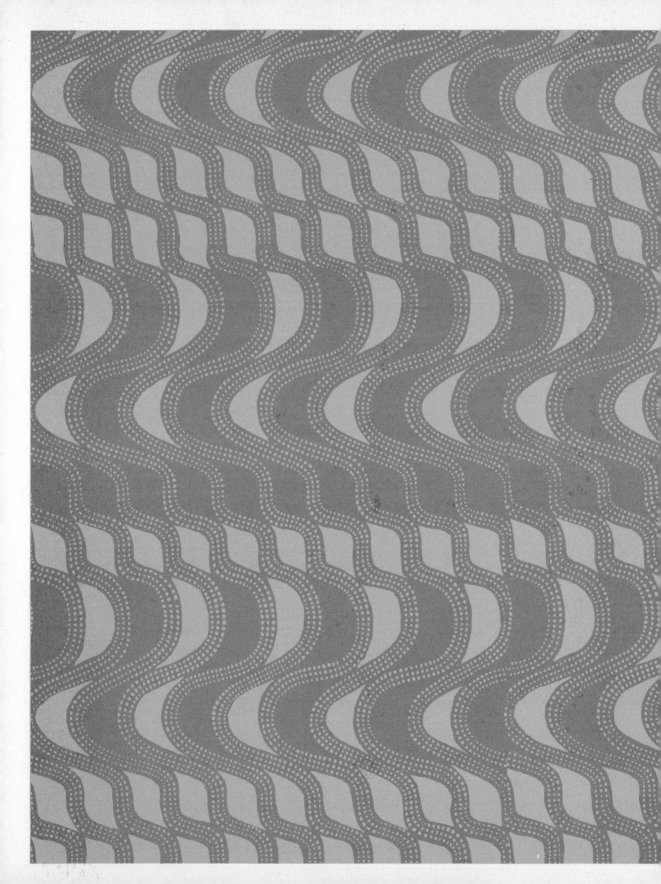

CHAPTER 18

REFORM AND RENEWAL

IN THE CHRISTIAN CHURCH

THE IDEA OF REFORM is as old as Christianity itself. In his letter to the Christians of Rome, Saint Paul exhorted: "Do not model yourselves on the behavior of the world around you, but let your behavior change, reformed by your new mind. That is the only way to discover the will of God and know what is good, what it is that God wants, what is the perfect thing to do."[1] In the early fifth century, Saint Augustine of Hippo, describing the final stage of world history, wrote, "In the sixth age of the world our reformation becomes manifest, in newness of mind, according to the image of Him who created us." In the middle of the twelfth century, Saint Bernard of Clairvaux complained about the church of his day: "There is as much difference between us and the men of the primitive Church as there is between muck and gold."

The need for reform of the individual Christian and of the institutional church is central to the Christian faith. The Christian humanists of the late fifteenth and early sixteenth centuries – More, Erasmus, Lefèvre d'Etaples, and Jiménez – urged reform of the church on the pattern of the early church primarily through educational and social change. Men and women of every period believed the early Christian church represented a golden age, and critics in every period called for reform.

Sixteenth-century cries, therefore, were hardly new. Why then did sixteenth-century demands for reform lead to revolution in the Christian church and to lasting divisions in Christian society? What role did social and political factors play in the several reformations? What were the consequences of religious division? To resolve these questions, the related issue of the condition of the church within European society must first be explored.

THE CONDITION OF THE CHURCH (CA 1400–1517)

The papal conflict with the German emperor Frederick II in the thirteenth century, followed by the Babylonian Captivity and then by the Great Schism, badly damaged the prestige of church leaders. In the fourteenth and fifteenth centuries, conciliarists reflected educated public opinion when they called for the reform of the church "in head and members." The secular humanists of Italy and the Christian humanists of the north denounced corruption in the church. As Machiavelli put it, "We Italians are irreligious and corrupt above others, because the Church and her representatives set us the worst example."[2] In *The Praise of Folly,* Erasmus condemned the absurd superstitions of the parish clergy and the excessive rituals of the monks. The records of episcopal visitations of parishes, civil court records, and even such literary masterpieces as Chaucer's *Canterbury Tales* and Boccaccio's *Decameron* tend to confirm the sarcasms of the humanists.

Concrete evidence of disorder is spotty and scattered. Since a great deal of corruption may have gone unreported, the moral situation may have been worse than the evidence suggests. On the other hand, bishops' registers and public court records mention the exceptional, not the typical. The thousands of priests who quietly and conscientiously went about their duties and did not warrant correction received no mention in the documents.

The religious life of most people in early sixteenth-century Europe took place at the village or local level. Any assessment of the moral condition of the parish clergy must take into account one fundamental fact: parish priests were peasants, and they were poor. All too frequently the spiritual quality of their lives was not much better than that of the people to whom they ministered. The clergy identified religion with life; that is, they injected religious symbols and practices into everyday living. Some historians, therefore, have accused the clergy of vulgarizing religion. But if the level of belief and practice was vulgarized, still the lives of rural, isolated, and semipagan people were spiritualized.

SIGNS OF DISORDER

In the early sixteenth century, critics of the church concentrated their attacks on three disorders: clerical immorality, clerical ignorance, and clerical pluralism with the related problem of absenteeism. There was little pressure for doctrinal change; the emphasis was on moral and administrative reform.

Since the fourth century, church law had required that candidates for the priesthood accept absolute celibacy. It had always been difficult to enforce. Many priests, especially those ministering to country people, had concubines, and reports of neglect of the rule of celibacy were common. Immorality, of course, included more than sexual transgressions. Clerical drunkenness, gambling, and indulgence in fancy dress were frequent charges. There is no way of knowing how many priests were guilty of such behavior. But because such conduct was so much at odds with the church's rules and moral standards, it scandalized the educated faithful.

The bishops enforced regulations regarding the education of priests very casually. As a result, standards for ordination were shockingly low. Many priests could barely read and write, and critics laughed at the illiterate priest mumbling the Latin words of the mass, which he could not understand. Predictably, this was

the disorder the Christian humanists, with their concern for learning, particularly condemned.

Absenteeism and pluralism constituted the third major abuse. Many clerics, especially higher ecclesiastics, held several benefices (or offices) simultaneously but seldom visited their benefices, let alone performed the spiritual responsibilities those offices entailed. Instead, they collected revenues from all of them and paid a poor priest a fraction of the income to fulfill the spiritual duties of a particular local church.

Many Italian officials in the papal curia held benefices in England, Spain, and Germany. Revenues from those countries paid the Italian priests' salaries, provoking not only charges of absenteeism but nationalistic resentment. King Henry VIII's chancellor Thomas Wolsey was archbishop of York for fifteen years before he set foot in his diocese. The French king Louis XII's famous diplomat Antoine du Prat is perhaps the most notorious example of absenteeism: as archbishop of Sens, the first time he entered his cathedral was in his own funeral procession. Critics condemned pluralism, absenteeism, and the way money seemed to change hands when a bishop entered into his office.

Although royal governments strengthened their positions and consolidated their territories in the fifteenth and sixteenth centuries, rulers lacked sufficient revenues to pay and reward able civil servants. The Christian church, with its dioceses and abbeys, possessed a large proportion of the wealth of the countries of Europe. What better way to reward government officials than with high church offices? After all, the practice was sanctioned by centuries of tradition. Thus in Spain, France, England, and the Holy Roman Empire – in fact, all over Europe – because

THE CHURCH CONTRASTED *Satirical woodcuts as well as the printed word attacked conditions in the church. Here the mercenary spirit of the sixteenth-century papacy is contrasted with the attitude of Christ toward money changers: Christ drove them from the temple, but the pope kept careful records of revenues owed to the church. (Photos: Caroline Buckler)*

church officials served their monarchs, those officials were allowed to govern the church.

The broad mass of the people, in supporting the church, supported everything that churchmen did. Bishops and abbots did a lot of work for secular governments. Churchmen served as royal councilors, diplomats, treasury

officials, chancellors, viceroys, and judges. These positions had nothing whatsoever to do with spiritual matters. Bishops worked for their respective states as well as for the church, and they were paid by the church for their services to the state. It is astonishing that so many conscientiously tried to carry out their religious duties on top of their public burdens.

The prodigious wealth of the church inevitably stimulated criticism. For centuries devout laymen and laywomen had bequeathed land, money, rights, and privileges to religious institutions. By the sixteenth century, these gifts and shrewd investments had resulted in vast treasure. Some was spent in the service of civil governments. Much of it was used to alleviate the wretched condition of the poor. But some also provided a luxurious lifestyle for the church hierarchy.

In most countries except England, members of nobility occupied the highest positions in the church. The sixteenth century was definitely not a democratic age. The spectacle of proud, aristocratic prelates living in magnificent splendor contrasted very unfavorably with the simple fishermen who were Christ's first disciples. Nor did the popes of the period 1450–1550 set much of an example. They lived like secular Renaissance princes. Pius II (1458–1464), although deeply learned and a tireless worker, enjoyed a reputation as a clever writer of love stories and witty Latin poetry. Sixtus IV (1471–1484) beautified the city of Rome, built the famous Sistine Chapel, and generously supported several artists. Innocent VIII (1484–1492) made the papal court a model of luxury and scandal. All three popes used papal power and papal wealth to advance the material interests of their own families.

The court of the Spanish pope Rodrigo Borgia, Alexander VI (1492–1503), who publicly acknowledged his mistress and children, reached new heights of impropriety. Because of the prevalence of intrigue, sexual promiscuity, and supposed poisonings, the name Borgia became a synonym for moral corruption. Julius II (1503–1513), the nephew of Sixtus IV, donned military armor and personally led papal troops against the French invaders of Italy in 1506. After him, Giovanni de' Medici, the son of Lorenzo the Magnificent, carried on as Pope Leo X (1513–1521) the Medicean tradition of being a great patron of the arts.

Through the centuries, papal prestige and influence had rested heavily on the moral quality of the popes' lives – that is, on their strong fidelity to Christian teaching as revealed in the Gospel. The lives of Renaissance popes revealed little of this Gospel message.

SIGNS OF VITALITY

Calls for reform testify to the spiritual vitality of the church as well as to its problems. Before a patient can be cured of sickness, he or she must acknowledge that a problem exists. In the late fifteenth and early sixteenth centuries, both individuals and groups within the church were working actively for reform. In Spain, Cardinal Francisco Jiménez visited religious houses, encouraged the monks and friars to keep their rules and constitutions, and set high standards for the training of the diocesan clergy. Jiménez founded the University of Alcalá (1499) partly for the education of priests.

Lefèvre d'Etaples in France and John Colet in England called for a return to the austere Christianity of the early church. Both men stressed the importance of sound preaching of the Scriptures.

In Holland, beginning in the late fourteenth century, a group of pious laymen and laywomen called the Brethren of the Common Life lived in stark simplicity while daily carrying out the Gospel teaching of feeding the hungry, clothing the naked, and visiting the sick. The Brethren also established schools for the education of the young, their most famous pupil being Erasmus of Rotterdam. The spirituality of the Brethren of the Common Life found its finest expression in the classic *The Imitation of Christ* by Thomas à Kempis. As its title suggests, *The Imitation of Christ* urges ordinary Christians to take Christ as their model and to seek perfection in a simple way of life. The movement, which spread to Germany, France, and Italy, was a real religious revival.

So too were the activities of the Oratories of Divine Love in Italy. The oratories were groups of priests living in communities who worked to revive the church through prayer and preaching. They did not withdraw from the world as medieval monks had done, but devoted themselves to pastoral and charitable activities such as founding hospitals and orphanages. Oratorians served God in an active ministry.

If external religious observances are a measure of depth of heartfelt conviction, Europeans in the early sixteenth century remained deeply pious and loyal to the Roman Catholic church. Villagers participated in processions honoring the local saints. Middle-class people made pilgrimages to the great national shrines, as the enormous wealth of Saint Thomas Becket's tomb at Canterbury in England and the shrine of Saint James de Compostella in Spain testify. The upper classes continued to remember the church in their wills. In England, for example, between 1480 and 1490 almost £30,000, a prodigious sum in those days, was bequeathed to religious foundations. People of all social classes devoted an enormous amount of their time and

GRUNEWALD: CRUCIFIXION *The bloodless hands, tortured face, and lacerated body reveal profound sorrow for Christ's physical agony and suggest the intense piety of northern Europe. Grunewald, court* *painter to Albert of Brandenburg, shows in this painting (ca 1510) his strong attraction to Luther's ideas. (National Gallery of Art, Washington, D.C. Samual H. Kress Collection)*

income to religious causes and foundations. Sixteenth-century society remained deeply religious; all across Europe people sincerely yearned for salvation.

The papacy also expressed concern for reform. Pope Julius II summoned an ecumenical (universal) council, which met in the church of St. John Lateran in Rome from 1512 to 1517. Since most of the bishops were Italian and did not represent a broad cross-section of international opinion, the term *ecumenical* is not appropriate. Nevertheless, the bishops and theologians present strove earnestly to reform the church. They criticized the ignorance of priests, lamenting that only 2 percent of the clergy could understand the Latin of the liturgical books. The Lateran Council also condemned superstitions believed by many of the laity. The council recommended higher standards for education of the clergy and instruction of the common people. The bishops placed the responsibility for eliminating bureaucratic corruption squarely on the papacy and suggested significant doctrinal reforms. But many obstacles stood in the way of ecclesiastical change. Nor did the actions of an obscure German friar immediately force the issue.

MARTIN LUTHER AND THE BIRTH OF PROTESTANTISM

As the result of a personal religious struggle, a German Augustinian friar, Martin Luther (1483-1546), launched the Protestant Reformation of the sixteenth century. Luther was not a typical person of his time; miners' sons who become professors of theology are never typical. But Luther is representative of his time in the sense that he articulated the widespread desire for reform of the Christian church and the deep yearning for salvation. In the sense that concern for salvation motivated Luther and other reformers, the sixteenth-century Reformation was in part a continuation of the medieval religious search.

LUTHER'S EARLY YEARS

Martin Luther was born at Eisleben in Saxony, the second son of a hardworking and ambitious copper miner. At considerable sacrifice, his father sent him to school and then to the University of Erfurt, where Martin earned a master's degree with distinction at the young age of twenty-one. Hans Luther intended his son to proceed to the study of law and a legal career, which had since Roman times been the steppingstone to public office and material success. Badly frightened during a thunderstorm, however, Martin Luther vowed to become a friar. Without consulting his father, he entered the monastery of the Augustinian friars at Erfurt in 1505. Luther was ordained a priest in 1507, and after additional study earned the doctorate of theology. From 1511 until his death in 1546, he served as professor of Scripture at the new University of Wittenberg.

Martin Luther was exceedingly scrupulous in his monastic observances and devoted to prayer, penances, and fasting; nevertheless, the young friar's conscience troubled him constantly. The doubts and conflicts felt by any sensitive young person who has just taken a grave step were especially intense in young Luther. He had terrible anxieties about sin and worried continually about his salvation. Luther intensified his monastic observances but still found no peace of mind.

A recent psychological interpretation of Luther's early life suggests that he underwent a severe inner crisis in the years 1505-1515. Luther had disobeyed his father, thus viola-

salvation comes not through external observances and penances but through a simple faith in Christ. Faith is the means by which God sends humanity his grace, and faith is a free gift that cannot be earned. Thus Martin Luther discovered himself, God's work for him, and the centrality of faith in the Christian life.

THE NINETY-FIVE THESES

An incident illustrative of the condition of the church in the early sixteenth century propelled Martin Luther onto the stage of history and brought about the Reformation in Germany. The University of Wittenberg lay within the ecclesiastical jurisdiction of the archdiocese of Magdeburg. The twenty-seven-year-old archbishop of Magdeburg, Albert, was also administrator of the see of Halberstadt and had been appointed archbishop of Mainz. To hold all three offices simultaneously – blatant pluralism – required papal dispensation. At that moment Pope Leo X was anxious to continue the construction of St. Peter's Basilica, but was hard pressed for funds. Archbishop Albert borrowed money from the Fuggers, a wealthy banking family of Augsburg, to pay for the papal dispensation allowing him to hold the several episcopal benefices. Only a few powerful financiers and churchmen knew the details of the arrangement, but Leo X authorized Archbishop Albert to sell indulgences, or pardons, in Germany. With the proceeds the archbishop could repay the Fuggers.

Wittenberg was in the political jurisdiction of Frederick of Saxony, one of the seven electors of the Holy Roman Empire. When Frederick forbade the sale of indulgences within his duchy, people of Wittenberg, including some of Professor Luther's students, streamed

YOUNG LUTHER *Lucas Cranach, court painter to Elector Frederick of Saxony and a friend of Luther's, captured the piety, the strength, and the intense struggle of the young friar. (Photo: Caroline Buckler)*

ting one of the Ten Commandments, and serious conflict persisted between them. The religious life seemed to provide no answers to his mental and spiritual difficulties. Three fits that he suffered in the monastic choir during those years may have been outward signs of his struggle.[3] Luther was grappling, as had thousands of medieval people before him, with the problem of salvation and thus the meaning of life. He was also searching for his life's work.

Luther's wise and kindly confessor, Staupitz, directed him to the study of Saint Paul's letters. Gradually, Luther arrived at a new understanding of the Pauline letters and of all Christian doctrine. He came to believe that

across the border from Saxony into Jüteborg in Thuringia to buy indulgences.

What was an indulgence? According to Catholic theology, individuals who sin alienate themselves from God and his love. In order to be reconciled to God, the sinner must confess his or her sins to a priest and do the penance assigned. For example, the man who steals must first return the stolen goods and then perform the penance given by the priest, usually certain prayers or good works. This is known as the temporal (or earthly) penance, since no one knows what penance God will ultimately require.

The doctrine of indulgence rested on three principles. First, God is merciful, but he is also just. Second, Christ and the saints, through their infinite virtue, established a "treasury of merits," which the church, through its special relationship with Christ and the saints, can draw upon. Third, the church has the authority to grant to sinners the spiritual benefits of those merits. Originally, an indulgence was a remission of the temporal (priest-imposed) penalties for sin. Beginning in the twelfth century, the papacy and bishops had given Crusaders such indulgences. By the later Middle Ages people widely believed that an indulgence secured total remission of penalties for sin – on earth or in purgatory – and assured swift entry into heaven.

Archbishop Albert hired the Dominican friar John Tetzel to sell the indulgences. Tetzel mounted a blitz advertising campaign. One of his slogans – "As soon as coin in coffer rings, the soul from purgatory springs" – brought phenomenal success. Men and women could buy indulgences not only for themselves but for deceased parents, relatives, or friends. Tetzel even drew up a chart with specific prices for the forgiveness of particular sins. The

massive amounts of junk that "sophisticated" Americans buy today should make one cautious in condemning the gullibility of sixteenth-century German peasants. Who wouldn't want a spiritual insurance policy?

Luther was severely troubled that ignorant people believed that they had no further need for repentance once they had purchased an indulgence. Accordingly, in the academic tradition of the times, on the eve of All Saints' Day (October 31) 1517, he attached to the door of the church at Wittenberg castle a list of ninety-five theses (or propositions) on indulgences. By this act Luther intended only to start a theological discussion of the subject and to defend the theses publicly.

Some of the theses challenged the pope's power to grant indulgences, and others criticized papal wealth: "Why does not the Pope, whose riches are at this day more ample than those of the wealthiest of the wealthy, build the one Basilica of St. Peter's with his own money, rather than with that of poor believers . . . ?"[4] Luther at first insisted that the pope had not known about the traffic in indulgences, for if he had known, he would have put a stop to it.

The theses were soon printed and read by Germans all over the empire. Immediately, broad theological issues were raised. When questioned, Luther insisted that Scripture persuaded him of the invalidity of indulgences. He rested his fundamental argument on the principle that there was no biblical basis for indulgences. But, replied Luther's opponents, to deny the legality of indulgences was to deny the authority of the pope who had authorized them. The issue was drawn: where did authority lie in the Christian church?

Through 1518 and 1519, Luther studied the history of the papacy. Gradually, he gained the conviction, like Marsiglio and Hus before him (pages 514–515), that ultimate authority in the church belonged not to the papacy but to a general council. Then, in 1519, in a large public disputation with the Catholic debater John Eck at Leipzig, Luther denied both the authority of the pope and the infallibility of a general council. The Council of Constance, he said, had erred when it condemned John Hus in 1415.

The papacy responded with a letter condemning some of Luther's propositions, ordering that his books be burned, and giving him two months to recant or be excommunicated. Luther retaliated by publicly burning the letter. Shortly afterward – January 3, 1521 – his excommunication became final. By this time the controversy involved more than theological issues. The papal legate wrote, "All Germany is in revolution. Nine-tenths shout 'Luther' as their war-cry; and the other tenth cares nothing about Luther, and cries 'Death to the court of Rome.' "[5]

In this highly charged atmosphere the twenty-one-year-old emperor Charles V held his first diet (assembly of the Estates of the empire) at Worms and summoned Luther to appear before it. When ordered to recant, Luther replied in language that rang all over Europe:

Unless I am convinced by the evidence of Scripture or by plain reason – for I do not accept the authority of the Pope or the councils alone, since it is established that they have often erred and contradicted themselves – I am bound by the Scriptures I have cited and my conscience is captive to the Word of God. I cannot and will not recant anything, for it is neither safe nor right to go against conscience. God help me. Amen.[6]

Luther was declared an outlaw of the empire, which meant that he was denied legal protection.

Between 1520 and 1530, Luther worked out the basic theological tenets that became the articles of faith for his new church and subsequently for all Protestant groups. The word *Protestant* derives from the protest drawn up by a small group of reforming German princes at the Diet of Speyer in 1529. The princes "protested" the decisions of the Catholic majority. At first Protestant meant Lutheran, but with the appearance of many protesting sects it became a general term applied to all non-Catholic Christians. Lutheran Protestant thought was officially formulated in the Confession of Augsburg in 1530.

Ernst Troeltsch, a German student of the sociology of religion, has defined Protestantism as a "modification of Catholicism, in which the Catholic formulation of questions was retained, while a different answer was given to them." Luther provided new answers to four old, basic theological issues.

First, how is a person to be saved? Traditional Catholic teaching held that salvation was achieved by both faith *and* good works. Luther held that salvation comes by *faith alone*. Women and men are saved, said Luther, by the arbitrary decision of God, irrespective of good works or the sacraments.

Second, where does religious authority reside? Christian doctrine had long maintained that authority rests both in the Bible and in the traditional teaching of the church. Luther maintained that authority rests in the Word of God as revealed in the Bible alone and as interpreted by an individual's conscience. He urged that each person read and reflect upon the Scriptures.

Third, what is the church? Luther reemphasized the Catholic teaching that the church consists of the entire community of

Christian believers. The medieval church had tended to identify the church with the clergy. Luther insisted upon the priesthood of all believers.

Finally, what is the highest form of Christian life? The medieval church had stressed the superiority of the monastic and religious life over the secular. Luther argued that all vocations have equal merit, whether ecclesiastical or secular, and that every person should serve God in his or her individual calling.[7] Protestantism, in sum, represented a reformulation of the Christian heritage.

THE SOCIAL IMPACT OF LUTHER'S BELIEFS

In the sixteenth century, religion infused many aspects of life, and theological issues had broad social implications. The Lutheran movement started a religious revolution, which soon led to social revolt. As early as 1521, Luther had a vast following. Every encounter with ecclesiastical or political authorities attracted attention to him. Pulpits and printing presses spread his message all over Germany. By the time of his death, people of all social classes had become "Lutheran."

What was the immense appeal of Luther's religious ideas? Historians have puzzled over this question for centuries. It is always difficult to distinguish between spiritual and altruistic motives and materialistic, self-serving ones. The attraction of the German peasants to Lutheran beliefs was logical and almost predictable. Luther himself came from a peasant background, and he knew their ceaseless toil. The peasants must have admired Luther's defiance of the authority of the church. Moreover, they thrilled to the words Luther used in his treatise *On Christian Liberty* (1520): "A Christian man is the most free lord of all and

subject to none." Taken by themselves, these words easily contributed to social unrest.

In the early sixteenth century, the economic condition of the peasantry varied from place to place, but was generally worse than it had been in the fifteenth century and was continuing to deteriorate. Although the lords did not attempt to reimpose or increase servile obligations that had been set aside after the Black Death, nevertheless rising prices hurt people living on fixed incomes. A huge number of beggars swelled the populations of the towns. At Hamburg, for example, perhaps 20 percent of the people were paupers.

The upper classes viewed the peasants and their wretched conditions with contempt. Nobles looked upon peasants as little more than animals, "the ox without horns." Luther's fellow professor and colleague in reform at Wittenberg, Philip Melanchthon, enjoyed a great reputation as a Christian humanist, yet dismissed the peasants with Luther's words "the ass *will* have blows and the people *will* be ruled by force."

In June 1524, a massive revolt broke out near the Swiss frontier and swept into the Rhineland, Swabia, Franconia, and Saxony. As many townspeople as farm laborers participated. Urban proletariat and agricultural laborers poured their grievances into the *Twelve Articles,* published in 1525. The peasants wanted complete abolition of serfdom, an end to oppressive taxes and tithes, reform of the clergy, confiscation of church property, and such basic privileges as the right to cut wood in the lords' forests. The slogans of the crowds that swept across Germany came directly from Luther's writings. "God's righteousness" and "the Word of God" were invoked in the effort to secure social and economic justice.[8]

The poor who expected Luther's support

THE PEASANTS' REVOLT *The peasants were attracted to Luther's faith because it seemed to give religious support to their economic grievances. Carrying the banner of the Peasants' League and armed with pitchforks and axes, a group of peasants surround a knight. (Photo: Caroline Buckler)*

were soon disillusioned. Background, education, and monastic observance all inclined him toward obedience to political authority and respect for social superiors. Luther had written of the "freedom" of the Christian, but he had meant the freedom to obey the Word of God, for in sin men and women lose their freedom and break their relationship with God. Freedom for Luther meant independence from the authority of the Roman church; it did *not* mean opposition to legally established secular powers. Accordingly he tossed off a tract, *Against the Murderous, Thieving Hordes of the Peasants,* calling upon the nobility to

put down the unlawful revolt. The German nobility crushed it with ferocity. Historians have estimated that as many as a hundred thousand peasants were slaughtered.

Luther took literally these words of Saint Paul's letter to the Romans: "Let every soul be subject to the higher powers. For there is no power but of God: the powers that be are established by God. Whosoever resists the power, resists the ordinance of God: and they that resist shall receive to themselves damnation."[9] As it developed, Lutheran theology exalted the state, subordinated the church to the state, and everywhere championed "the powers that be." The consequences for German society were profound and have redounded into the twentieth century. After the revolt, the condition of the working classes worsened, and their religion taught complete obedience to divinely appointed authority, the state.

Scholars in many disciplines have attributed Luther's fame and success to the new invention of the printing press, which rapidly reproduced and made known his ideas. Equally important is Luther's incredible skill with language. Some thinkers have lavished praise on the Wittenberg reformer; others have bitterly condemned him. But, in the words of psychologist Erik Erikson:

The one matter on which professor and priest, psychiatrist and sociologist, agree is Luther's immense gift for language: his receptivity for the written word; his memory for the significant phrase; and his range of verbal expression (lyrical, biblical, satirical, and vulgar) which in English is paralleled only by Shakespeare.[10]

Language proved to be the weapon with which this peasant's son changed the world.

Educated people and humanists, like the peasants, were much attracted by Luther's words. He advocated a simpler, personalized religion based on faith, a return to the spirit of the early church, the centrality of the Scriptures in the liturgy and in the Christian life, the abolition of elaborate ceremonial — precisely the reforms the nothern Christian humanists had been calling for. Ulrich Zwingli (1483–1531), for example, a humanist of Zurich, was strongly influenced by Luther's writings; they stimulated Zwingli's reforms in that Swiss city. The nobleman Ulrich von Hutton (1488–1523), who had published several humanistic tracts, in 1519 dedicated his life to the advancement of Luther's reformation. And as we shall see, the

Frenchman John Calvin (1509–1564), often called the organizer of Protestantism, owed a great deal to Luther's thought.

The publication of Luther's German translation of the New Testament in 1523 democratized religion. His insistence that everyone should read and reflect upon the Scriptures attracted the literate and thoughtful middle classes partly because Luther appealed to their intelligence. Moreover, the business classes, preoccupied with making money, envied the church's wealth, disapproved of the luxurious lifestyle of some churchmen, and resented tithes and ecclesiastical taxation. Luther's doctrines of salvation by faith and the priesthood of all believers not only raised the religious status of the commercial classes but protected their pocketbooks as well.

Martin Luther's attitude toward women became the standard for German and Protestant women for centuries. Luther believed that marriage was a woman's career. A student recorded Luther as saying, early in his public ministry, "Let them bear children until they are dead of it; that is what they are for." A happy marriage to the ex-nun Katharine von Bora mellowed him, and another student later quoted him as saying, "Next to God's Word there is no more precious treasure than holy matrimony. God's highest gift on earth is a pious, cheerful, God-fearing, home-keeping wife, with whom you may live peacefully, to whom you may entrust your goods, and body and life."[11] Although Luther deeply loved his "dear Katie," he believed that women's concerns revolved exclusively around the children, the kitchen, and the church. A happy woman was a patient wife, an efficient manager, and a good mother.

Luther's viewpoint reflected contemporary values: German women were no more oppressed than Italian, Spanish, or even French ones. But few men considered women intelligent enough to handle a profession outside the home.

GERMANY AND THE PROTESTANT REFORMATION

The history of the Holy Roman Empire in the later Middle Ages is a story of dissension, disintegration, and debility. Unlike Spain, France, and England, the empire lacked a strong central power. The Golden Bull of 1356 created government by an aristocratic federation. Each of seven electors – the archbishops of Mainz, Trier, and Cologne, the margrave of Brandenburg, the duke of Saxony, the count palatine of the Rhine, and the king of Bohemia – gained virtual sovereignty in his own territory. The agreement ended disputed elections in the empire; it also reduced the central authority of the emperor. Thereafter, Germany was characterized by weak borders, localism, and chronic disorder. The nobility strengthened their territories, while imperial power declined.

Against this background of decentralization and strong local power, Martin Luther had launched a movement to reform the church. Two years after Luther posted the Ninety-Five Theses, the electors chose as emperor a nineteen-year-old Habsburg prince, who ruled as Charles V. How did the goals and interests of the emperor influence the course of the Reformation in Germany? What impact did the upheaval in the Christian church have on the political condition in Germany?

THE RISE OF THE HABSBURG DYNASTY

The marriage in 1477 of Maximilian I of the house of Habsburg and Mary of Burgundy was a decisive event in early modern European history. Through this union with the rich and powerful duchy of Burgundy, the Austrian house of Habsburg became the strongest ruling family within the empire. Its fortunes became permanently linked to those of the empire.

In the fifteenth and sixteenth centuries, as in the Middle Ages, relations among states continued to be greatly affected by the connections of royal families. Marriage often determined the diplomatic status of states. The Habsburg-Burgundian marriage angered the French, who considered Burgundy part of French territory. Louis XI of France repeatedly ravaged parts of the Burgundian Netherlands until he was able to force Maximilian to accept French terms: the Treaty of Arras (1482) emphatically declared Burgundy a part of the kingdom of France. The Habsburgs, however, never really renounced their claim to Burgundy, and intermittent warfare over it continued between France and Maximilian. Within the empire, German principalities that resented Austria's pre-eminence began to see that they shared interests with France. The marriage of Maximilian and Mary was to inaugurate two centuries of conflict between the Austrian house of Habsburg and the Valois kings of France. And Germany was to be the chief arena of the struggle.

"Other nations wage war; you, Austria, marry." Historians dispute the origins of the adage, but no one questions its accuracy. The heir of Mary and Maximilian, Philip of Burgundy, married Joanna of Castile, daughter of Ferdinand and Isabella of Spain. Philip and Joanna's son Charles V (1500–1558) fell heir to a vast conglomeration of territories. Through a series of accidents and unexpected deaths, Charles inherited Spain from his mother, together with her possessions in the New World and the Spanish dominions in

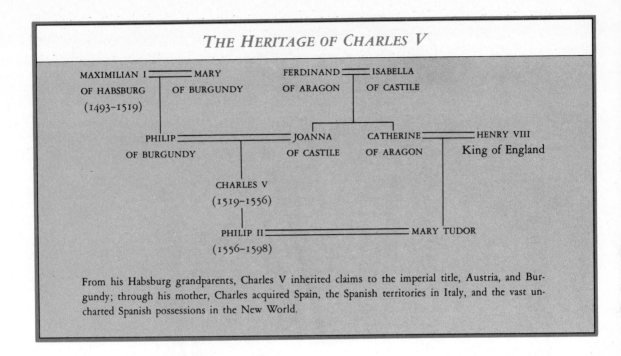

THE HERITAGE OF CHARLES V

```
MAXIMILIAN I ═══════ MARY          FERDINAND ═══════ ISABELLA
OF HABSBURG          OF BURGUNDY    OF ARAGON          OF CASTILE
(1493–1519)

        PHILIP ═══════════════════ JOANNA      CATHERINE ═══════ HENRY VIII
        OF BURGUNDY                 OF CASTILE  OF ARAGON         King of England

              CHARLES V
              (1519–1556)

              PHILIP II ════════════════════════════════ MARY TUDOR
              (1556–1598)
```

From his Habsburg grandparents, Charles V inherited claims to the imperial title, Austria, and Burgundy; through his mother, Charles acquired Spain, the Spanish territories in Italy, and the vast uncharted Spanish possessions in the New World.

Italy, Sicily, Sardinia, and Naples. From his father he inherited the Habsburg lands in Austria, southern Germany, the Low Countries, and Franche-Comté in east central France.

Charles's inheritance was an incredibly diverse collection of states and peoples, each governed in a different manner and held together only by the person of the emperor. Charles's Italian adviser, the grand chancellor Gattinara, told the young ruler: "God has set you on the path towards world monarchy." Charles not only believed this; he was convinced that it was his duty to maintain the political and religious unity of Western Christendom. In this respect Charles V was the last medieval emperor.

Charles needed and in 1519 secured the imperial title. Forward-thinking Germans proposed governmental reforms. They urged placing the administration in the hands of an imperial council whose president, the emperor's appointee, would have ultimate executive power. Reforms of the imperial finances, the army, and the judiciary were also recommended. Such ideas did not interest the young emperor at all. When he finally arrived in Germany from Spain and opened his first diet at Worms in January 1521, he naively announced that "the empire from of old has had not many masters, but one, and it is our intention to be that one." Charles went on to say that he was to be treated as of greater account than his predecessors because he was more powerful than they had been. In view of the long history of aristocratic power, Charles's notions were pure fantasy.

Charles continued the Burgundian policy of his grandfather Maximilian. That is, German revenues and German troops were subordinated to the needs of other parts of the empire, first Burgundy and then Spain. Habs-

EMPEROR CHARLES V   Sometimes called a second Charlemagne, Charles V unsuccessfully tried to unite millions of people divided by geography, custom, language, and centuries of historical development under his family rule. The full beard partially conceals the long jutting jaw, a Habsburg family trait. (Photo: Caroline Buckler)

burg international interests came before the need for reform in Germany.

THE POLITICAL IMPACT OF LUTHER'S BELIEFS

In the sixteenth century, the practice of religion remained a public matter. Everyone participated in the religious life of the community, just as almost everyone shared in the local agricultural work. Whatever spiritual convictions individuals held in the privacy of their consciences, the emperor, king, prince, magistrate, or other civil authority determined the official form of religious practice within his jurisdiction. Religion had too many social implications to be left to individual judgment. Almost everyone believed that the presence of a faith different from that of the majority represented a political threat to the security of the state. Only a tiny minority, and certainly none of the princes, believed in religious liberty.

Against this background, the religious storm launched by Martin Luther swept across northern and central Germany. Several elements in his religious reformation stirred patriotic feelings. Anti-Roman sentiment ran high. Humanists lent eloquent intellectual support. And Luther's translation of the New Testament into German evoked national pride. Lutheranism contributed to the development of German nationalism.

For decades devout laymen and churchmen had called on the German princes to reform the church. In 1520, Luther took up the cry in his *Appeal to the Christian Nobility of the German Nation.* Unless the princes destroyed papal power in Germany, Luther argued, reform was impossible. He urged the princes to confiscate ecclesiastical wealth and to abolish indulgences, dispensations, pardons, and clerical celibacy. He told them that it was their public duty to bring about the moral reform of the church. Luther based his argument in part on the papacy's financial exploitation of Germany:

Now that Italy is sucked dry, they come into Germany, and begin, oh so gently. But let us beware, or Germany will soon become like Italy. Already we have some cardinals; what the Romans seek by that the "drunken Germans" are not to understand until we have not a bishopric, a monastery, a living, a benefice, a mite or a penny left. . . . They skim the cream off the bishoprics, monasteries, and benefices, and because they do not yet venture to turn them all to shameful use, as they have done in Italy, they only practice for the present the sa-

cred trickery of coupling together ten or twenty prelacies and taking a yearly portion from each of them so as to make a tidy sum after all. The priory of Würzburg yields a thousand gulden; that of Bamberg, something; Mainz, Trier, and the others, something more; and so . . . that a cardinal might live at Rome like a rich king.

How comes it that we Germans must put up with such robbery and such extortion of our property at the hands of the pope? If the Kingdom of France has prevented it, why do we Germans let them make such fools and apes of us? It would all be more bearable if in this way they only stole our property; but they lay waste the churches and rob Christ's sheep of their pious shepherds, and destroy the worship and the Word of God. Even if there were not a single cardinal, the Church would not go under. As it is they do nothing for the good of Christendom; they only wrangle about the incomes of bishoprics and prelacies, and that any robber could do. . . .

Since we here come to the heart of the matter, we will pause a little, and let it be seen that the Germans are not quite such gross fools as not to note or understand the sharp practices of the Romans. I do not now complain that at Rome God's command and Christian law are despised; for such is the state of Christendom, and particularly of Rome, that we may not now complain of such high matters. Nor do I complain that natural or temporal law and reason count for nothing. The case is worse even than that. I complain that they do not keep their own self-devised canon law, though it is, to be sure, mere tyranny, avarice, and temporal splendor, rather than law. . . .[12]

These words fell on welcome ears and itchy fingers. Luther's appeal to German patriotism gained him strong support, and national feeling influenced many princes otherwise confused by or indifferent to the complexities of the religious issues.

The church in Germany possessed great

wealth. And, unlike other countries, Germany had no strong central government to check the flow of gold to Rome. Rejection of Roman Catholicism and adoption of Protestantism would mean the legal confiscation of lush farmlands, rich monasteries, and wealthy shrines. Some German princes, such as the prince-archbishop of Cologne, Hermann von Wied, were sincerely attracted to Lutheranism, but many civil authorities realized that they had a great deal to gain by embracing the new faith. A steady stream of duchies, margraviates, free cities, and bishoprics secularized church property, accepted Lutheran theological doctrines, and adopted simpler services conducted in German. The decision reached at Worms in 1521 to condemn Luther and his teaching was not enforced because the German princes did not want to enforce it.

Charles V was a vigorous defender of Catholicism, and contemporary social and political theory denied the possibility of two religions coexisting peacefully in one territory. Thus, many princes used the religious issue to extend their financial and political independence. When doctrinal differences became linked to political ambitions and financial receipts, the results proved unfortunate for the improvement of German government. The Protestant movement ultimately proved a political disaster for Germany.

Charles V must share blame with the German princes for the disintegration of imperial authority in the empire. He neither understood nor took an interest in the constitutional problems of Germany, and he lacked the material resources to oppose Protestantism effectively there. Throughout his reign he was preoccupied with his Flemish, Spanish, Italian, and American territories.

Five times between 1521 and 1555, Charles V went to war with the Valois kings of France. The issue each time was the Habsburg lands acquired by the marriage of Maximilian and Mary of Burgundy. Much of the fighting occurred in Germany. The cornerstone of French foreign policy in the sixteenth and seventeenth centuries was the desire to keep the German states divided. Thus Europe witnessed the paradox of the Catholic king of France supporting the Lutheran princes in their challenge to his fellow Catholic, Charles V. French policy was successful. The long dynastic struggle commonly called the Habsburg-Valois wars advanced the cause of Protestantism and promoted the political fragmentation of the German empire.

Charles's efforts to crush the Lutheran states were unsuccessful. Finally in 1555 he agreed to the Peace of Augsburg, which, in accepting the status quo, officially recognized Protestantism. Each prince was permitted to determine the religion of his territory. Most of northern and central Germany became Lutheran, while the south remained Roman Catholic. There was no freedom of religion, however. Princes or town councils established state churches to which all subjects of the area had to belong. Dissidents, whether Lutheran or Catholic, had to convert or leave. The political difficulties Germany inherited from the Middle Ages had been compounded by the religious crisis of the sixteenth century.

THE GROWTH OF THE PROTESTANT REFORMATION

The printing press publicized Luther's defiance of the Roman church and spread his theological ideas all over Europe. Working people discovered in Luther's ideas the economic theories they wanted to find. Christian humanists believed initially that Luther supported their own educational and intellectual goals. Princes steadily read in Luther's theories an expansion of state power and authority. What began as one man's religious search in a small corner of Germany soon became associated with many groups' interests and aspirations.

By 1555, much of northern Europe had broken with the Roman Catholic church. All of Scandinavia, England, Scotland, and such self-governing cities as Geneva and Zurich in Switzerland and Strasbourg in eastern France had rejected the religious authority of Rome and adopted new faiths. In that a common religious faith had been the one element uniting all of Europe for almost a thousand years, the fragmentation of belief led to profound changes in European life and society. The most significant new form of Protestantism was Calvinism, of which the Peace of Augsburg had made no mention at all.

CALVINISM

In 1509, while Luther was studying for the doctorate at Wittenberg, John Calvin (1509–1564) was born in Noyon in northwestern France. Luther inadvertently launched the Protestant Reformation. Calvin, however, had the greater impact on future generations. His theological writings profoundly influenced the social thought and attitudes of Europeans and English-speaking peoples all over the world, especially in Canada and the United States. Although he had originally intended to have an ecclesiastical career, Calvin studied law, which had a decisive impact on his mind and later thought. In 1533, he experienced a religious crisis, as a result of which he converted to Protestantism.

JOHN CALVIN *The lean, ascetic face with the strong jaw reflects the iron will and determination of the organizer of Protestantism. The fur collar represents his training in law. (Photo: Caroline Buckler)*

Calvin believed that God had delegated him to reform the church. Accordingly, he accepted an invitation to assist in the reformation of the Swiss city of Geneva. There, beginning in 1541, Calvin established a theocracy, which was, according to contemporary theory, a society ruled by God through reformed ministers and civil magistrates. Geneva, "a city that was a Church," became the model of a Christian community for sixteenth-century Protestant reformers.

To understand Calvin's Geneva, it is necessary to understand Calvin's ideas. These he embodied in *The Institutes of the Christian Re-*

ligion, first published in 1536 and definitively issued in 1559. The cornerstone of Calvin's theology was his belief in the absolute sovereignty and omnipotence of God and the total weakness of humanity. Before the infinite power of God, he asserted, men and women are as insignificant as grains of sand:

Our souls are but faint flickerings over against the infinite brilliance which is God. We are created, he is without beginning. We are subject to ignorance and shame. God in his infinite majesty is the summation of all virtues. Whenever we think of him we should be ravished with adoration and astonishment. . . . The chief end of man is to enjoy the fellowship of God and the chief duty of man is to glorify God. . . .[13]

Calvin did not grant free will to human beings, because that would detract from the sovereignty of God. Men and women cannot actively work to achieve salvation; rather, God in his infinite wisdom decided at the beginning of time who would be saved and who damned. This viewpoint constitutes the theological principle called predestination:

Predestination we call the eternal decree of God, by which he has determined in himself, what he would have become of every individual of mankind. For they are not all created with a similar destiny; but eternal life is foreordained for some, and eternal damnation for others. . . .

In conformity, therefore, to the clear doctrine of the Scripture, we assert, that by an eternal and immutable counsel, God has once for all determined, both whom he would admit to salvation, and whom he would condemn to destruction. We affirm that this counsel, as far as concerns the elect, is founded on his gratuitous mercy, totally irrespective of human merit; but that to those whom he devotes to condemnation, the gate of life

is closed by a just and irreprehensible, but incomprehensible, judgment.

How exceedingly presumptuous it is only to inquire into the causes of the Divine will; which is in fact, and is justly entitled to be, the cause of everything that exists. . . . For the will of God is the highest justice; so that what he wills must be considered just, for this very reason, because he wills it.[14]

Many people have found this a pessimistic view of the nature of God, who revealed himself in the Old and New Testaments as merciful as well as just. Calvin's response was that although individuals cannot know whether they will be saved – and the probability is that they will be damned – still, good works are a "sign" of election. In any case, people should concentrate on worshiping God and doing his work and not waste time worrying about salvation.

While Luther subordinated the church to the state, Calvin made the state subordinate to the church, and he succeeded in arousing Genevans to a high standard of public and private behavior. For Calvin, God was perpetually active, vigilant, and busy, and he selected certain individuals to do his work. Calvin, convinced that he was one of those individuals, worked tirelessly to transform Geneva into the perfect Christian community. Those who denied predestination were banished.

Austere living, religious instruction for all, public fasting, and evening curfew became the order of the day. Dancing, card playing, fashionable clothes, and heavy drinking were absolutely prohibited. The ministers investigated the private morals of citizens but were unwilling to punish the town prostitutes as severely as Calvin would have preferred.

Calvin reserved his harshest condemnation for religious dissenters. He declared:

If anybody slanders a mortal man he is punished and shall we permit a blasphemer of the living God to go unscathed? If a prince is injured, death appears to be insufficient for vengeance. And now when God, the sovereign Emperor, is reviled by a word, is nothing to be done? God's glory and our salvation are so conjoined that a traitor to God is also an enemy to the human race and worse than a murderer because he brings souls to perdition. Some object that since the offense consists only in words, there is no need for severity. But we muzzle dogs, and shall we leave men free to open their mouths as they please? Those who object are dogs and swine. They murmur that they will go to America where nobody will bother them.

God makes plain that the false prophet is to be stoned without mercy. We are to crush beneath our heel all affections of nature when His honor is concerned. The father should not spare his child, nor brother his brother, nor husband his own wife or the friend who is dearer to him than life. No human relationship is more than animal unless it be grounded in God[15]

Calvin translated his words into action. In the 1550s, the Spanish humanist Michael Servetus had gained international notoriety for his publications denying the Christian dogma of the Trinity, which holds that God is three divine persons, Father, Son, and Holy Spirit. Servetus had been arrested by the Spanish Inquisition, but escaped to Geneva, where he hoped for support. He was promptly re-arrested. At his trial he not only held to his belief that there is no scriptural basis for the Trinity but rejected child baptism and insisted that a person under twenty cannot commit a mortal sin. The city fathers considered this last idea dangerous to public morality, "especially in these days when the young are so corrupted." Although Servetus begged that he be punished by banishment, Calvin and the

town council maintained that the denial of child baptism and the Trinity amounted to a threat to all society. Whispering "Jesus, Son of the eternal God, have pity on me," Servetus was burned at the stake.

To many sixteenth-century Europeans, Calvin's Geneva seemed "the most perfect school of Christ since the days of the Apostles." Religious refugees from France, England, Spain, Scotland, and Italy poured into the city. Subsequently, Calvin's church served as the model for the Presbyterian church in Scotland, the Huguenot church in France, and Puritan churches in England and New England.

Calvinism became the compelling force in international Protestantism. The Calvinist ethic of the "calling" dignified all work with a religious aspect. Hard work, well done, was pleasing to God. This doctrine encouraged an aggressive, vigorous social activism. In the *Institutes* Calvin provided a systematic theology for Protestantism. The reformed church of Calvin had a strong and well-organized machinery of government. These factors, together with the social and economic applications of Calvin's theology, made Calvinism the most dynamic force in sixteenth- and seventeenth-century Protestantism.

THE ANABAPTISTS

The name *Anabaptist* derives from a Greek word meaning "to baptize again." The Anabaptists, sometimes described as "the left wing of the Reformation," believed that only adults could make a free choice about religious faith, baptism, and entry into the Christian community. Thus they considered the practice of baptizing infants and children preposterous and claimed there was no scriptural basis for it. They wanted to rebaptize believers who had been baptized as children.

Anabaptists took the Gospel and, at first, Luther's teachings absolutely literally and favored a return to the kind of church that had existed among the earliest Christians – a voluntary association of believers who had experienced an inner light.

Anabaptists maintained that only a few people would receive the inner light. This position meant that the Christian community and the Christian state were not identical. In other words, Anabaptists believed in the separation of church and state and in religious tolerance. They almost never tried to force their values on others. In an age that believed in the necessity of state-established churches, Anabaptist views on religious liberty were far ahead of their time.

Each Anabaptist community or church was entirely independent; it selected its own ministers and ran its own affairs. In 1534 the community at Münster in Germany, for example, established a legal code that decreed the death penalty for insubordinate wives. Moreover, the Münster community also practiced polygamy and forced all women under a certain age to marry or face expulsion or execution.

Anabaptist attitudes toward women were sexist and discriminatory, although Anabaptists admitted women to the priesthood. They shared goods as the early Christians had done, refused all public offices, and would not serve in the armed forces. In fact, they laid great stress on pacifism. A favorite Anabaptist scriptural quotation was "By their fruits you shall know them," meaning that if Christianity was a religion of peace, the Christian should not fight. Good deeds were the sign of Christian faith, and to be a Christian meant to imitate the meekness and mercy of Christ. With such beliefs Anabaptists were inevitably a minority. Anabaptism attracted the poor,

the unemployed, the uneducated. Geographically, Anabaptists drew their members from depressed urban areas – from among the followers of Zwingli in Zurich, and from Basel, Augsburg, and Nuremberg.

Ideas such as absolute pacifism and the distinction between the Christian community and the state brought down upon these unfortunate people fanatical hatred and bitter persecution. Zwingli, Luther, Calvin, and Catholics all saw – quite correctly – the separation of church and state as leading ultimately to the complete secularization of society. The powerful rulers of Swiss and German society immediately saw the connection between religious heresy and economic dislocation. Civil authorities feared that the combination of religious differences and economic grievances would lead to civil disturbances. In Saxony, in Strasbourg, and in the Swiss cities, Anabaptists were either banished or cruelly executed ,by burning, beating, or drowning. Their ideas, however, survived.

Later, the Quakers with their gentle pacifism; the Baptists with their emphasis on an inner spiritual light, the Congregationalists with their democratic church organization; and, in 1789, the authors of the United States Constitution with their concern for the separation of church and state – all these trace their origins in part to the Anabaptists of the sixteenth century.

THE ENGLISH REFORMATION

As on the Continent, the Reformation in England had social and economic causes as well as religious ones. As elsewhere, too, Christian humanists had for decades been calling for the purification of the church. When the political matter of the divorce of King Henry VIII (1509-1547) became enmeshed with other issues, a complete break with Rome resulted.

Demands for ecclesiastical reform dated back to the fourteenth century. The Lollards (pages 515-516) had been driven underground in the fifteenth century, but survived in parts of London, East Anglia, west Kent, and southern England. Working-class people, especially cloth workers, were attracted to their ideas. The Lollards stressed the individual's reading and interpretation of the Bible, which they considered the only standard of Christian faith and holiness. Consequently, they put no stock in the value of the sacraments and were vigorously anticlerical. Lollards opposed ecclesiastical wealth, the veneration of the saints, prayers for the dead, and all war. Although they had no notion of justification by faith, like Luther they insisted upon the individual soul's direct responsibility to God.

The work of the English humanist William Tyndale (ca 1494-1536) stimulated cries for reform. Tyndale visited Luther at Wittenberg in 1524, and a year later at Antwerp he began printing an English translation of the New Testament. From Antwerp merchants carried the New Testament into England, where it was distributed by Lollards. Fortified with copies of Tyndale's English Bible and some of Luther's ideas, the Lollards represented the ideal of "a personal, scriptural, non-sacramental, and lay-dominated religion."[16] Thus, in this manner, doctrines that would later be called Protestant flourished underground in England before any official or state-approved changes.

In the early sixteenth century the ignorance of much of the parish clergy, and the sexual misbehavior of some, compared unfavorably with the education and piety of lay people. In 1510 Dr. William Melton, an official of York Cathedral, exhorted the newly ordained priests of the diocese:

...from this darkness of ignorance ... arises that great and deplorable evil throughout the whole Church of God, that everywhere throughout town and countryside there exists a crop of oafish and boorish priests, some of whom are engaged in ignoble and servile tasks, while others abandon themselves to tavern haunting, swilling and drunkenness. Some cannot get along without their wenches; others pursue their amusement in dice and gambling and other such trifling all day long. ... This is inevitable, for since they are completely ignorant of good literature, how can they obtain improvement or enjoyment in reading and study. Nay rather, they throw aside their books in contempt and everywhere they return to the wretched and unlovely life I have mentioned. ... We must avoid and keep far from ourselves that grasping, deadly plague of avarice for which practically every priest is accused and held in disrepute before the people, when it is said that we are greedy for rich promotions, or harsh and grasping in retaining and amassing money. ...[17]

Even more than the ignorance and lechery of the lower clergy, the wealth of the English church fostered resentment and anticlericalism. The church controlled perhaps 20 percent of the land, and also received an annual tithe of the produce of lay people's estates. Since the church had jurisdiction over wills, the clergy also received mortuary fees, revenues paid by the deceased's relatives. Mortuary fees led to frequent lawsuits, since the common lawyers nursed a deep jealousy of the ecclesiastical courts.

The career of Thomas Wolsey (1474?-1530) provides an extreme example of pluralism in the English church in the early sixteenth century. The son of a butcher, Wolsey became a priest and in 1507 secured an

HENRY VIII's "VICTORY" *This cartoon shows Henry VIII, assisted by Cromwell and Cranmer, triumphing over Pope Clement VII. Although completely removed from the historical facts, such illustrations were effectively used to promote antipapal feeling in late sixteenth-century England. (Photo: Caroline Buckler)*

appointment as chaplain to Henry VII. In 1509 Henry VIII made Wolsey a privy councillor, where his remarkable ability and energy won him rapid advancement. In 1515 he became a cardinal and lord chancellor, and in 1518 papal legate. As chancellor, Wolsey dominated domestic and foreign policy, prosecuted the rich in the royal courts, and attacked the nobility in Parliament. As papal legate he ruled the English church, with final authority in all matters relating to marriage, wills, the clergy, and ecclesiastical appointments. Wolsey had more power than any previous royal minister, and he used that power to amass a large number of church offices, including the archbishopric of York, the rich bishoprics of Winchester and Lincoln, and the abbacy of St. Albans. He displayed the vast wealth these positions brought him with ostentation and arrogance, which in turn fanned the embers of anticlericalism. The divorce of Henry VIII ignited all these glowing coals.

Having fallen in love with Anne Boleyn, sister of his cast-off mistress Mary Boleyn, Henry wanted to divorce his wife Catherine of Aragon. Legal, diplomatic, and theological problems stood in his way, however. Catherine had first been married to Henry's brother Arthur. Contemporaries doubted that Arthur's union with Catherine had been consumated during the short time Arthur lived, and theologians therefore believed that no true marriage existed between them. When Henry married Catherine in 1509, he boasted that she was a virgin. According to custom, and in order to eliminate all doubts and legal technicalities about Catherine's marriage to Arthur, Henry secured a dispensation from Pope Julius II. For eighteen years Catherine and Henry lived together in what contemporaries thought a happy marriage. Catherine produced six children, but only the princess Mary survived childhood.

Precisely when Henry lost interest in his wife as a woman is unknown, but around 1527 he began to quote from a passage in the Old Testament Book of Leviticus: "You must not uncover the nakedness of your brother's wife; for it is your brother's nakedness. . . . The man who takes to wife the wife of his brother: that is impurity; he has uncovered his brother's nakedness, and they shall be childless."[18] Henry insisted that God was denying him a male heir to punish him for marrying his brother's widow. Henry claimed that he wanted to spare England the dangers of a disputed succession. The anarchy and disorders of the Wars of the Roses would surely be repeated if a woman, the princess Mary, inherited the throne. Although Henry contended that the succession was the paramount issue in his mind, his behavior suggests otherwise.

Henry went about the business of insuring a peaceful succession in a most extraordinary manner. He petitioned Pope Clement VII for an annulment of his marriage to Catherine. Henry wanted the pope to declare that a legal marriage with Catherine had never existed, in which case Princess Mary was illegitimate and thus ineligible to succeed to the throne. The pope was an indecisive man whose attention at the time was focused on the Lutheran revolt in Germany and the Habsburg-Valois struggle for control of Italy. Clement delayed acting on Henry's request. The capture and sack of Rome in 1527 by the emperor Charles V, Queen Catherine's nephew, thoroughly tied the pope's hands. Charles could hardly allow the pope to grant the annulment, thereby acknowledging that Charles's aunt, the queen of England, was a loose woman who had lived in sin with Henry VIII.

Accordingly, Henry determined to get his divorce in England. The convenient death of the archbishop of Canterbury allowed Henry to appoint a new archbishop, Thomas Cranmer (1489-1556). Cranmer heard the case in his archiepiscopal court, granted the annulment, and thereby paved the way for Henry's marriage to Anne Boleyn. English public opinion was against this marriage and strongly favored Queen Catherine as a woman much wronged. By rejecting Catherine, Henry ran serious political risks, and all for a woman whom contemporaries found neither very intelligent nor very attractive. The only distinguishing feature they noticed was a sixth finger on her right hand. The marriage between Henry and Anne was publicly announced on May 28, 1533. In September the princess Elizabeth was born.

Since Rome had refused to support Henry's matrimonial plans, he decided to remove the English church from papal jurisdiction. Henry used Parliament to legalize the Reformation in England. The Act in Restraint of Appeals (1533) declared that:

Where, by divers sundry old authentic histories and chronicles, it is manifestly declared and expressed that this realm of England is an empire, and so hath been accepted in the world, governed by one supreme head and king having the dignity and royal estate of the imperial crown of the same (he being also institute and furnished by the goodness and sufferance of Almighty God with plenary, whole, and entire power, pre-eminence, authority, prerogative, and jurisdiction to render and yield justice and final determination to all manner of folk residents or subjects within this his realm, in all causes, matters, debates, and contentions happening to occur, insurge, or begin within the limits thereof, without restraint or provocation to any foreign princes or potentates of the world. . . .).[19]

The act went on to forbid all judicial appeals to the papacy, thus establishing the Crown as the highest legal authority in the land. In effect, the Act in Restraint of Appeals placed sovereign power in the king. The Act for the Submission of the Clergy (1534) required churchmen to submit to the king and forbade the publication of all ecclesiastical laws without royal permission. The Supremacy Act of 1534 declared the king the supreme head of the Church of England.

Englishmen had long criticized ecclesiastical abuses. Sentiment for reform was strong, and a minority of people held distinctly Protestant doctrinal views. Still, it is difficult to gauge the degree of popular support for Henry's break with Rome. Scholars have pointed out that the king had to bribe, threaten, and intimidate the House of Commons to get his legislation passed. Some op-

posed the king. John Fisher, the bishop of Rochester, a distinguished scholar and humanist who had preached the oration at the funeral of Henry VII, lashed the clergy with scorn for their cowardice. Another humanist, Thomas More, resigned the chancellorship to protest the passage of the Act for the Submission of the Clergy and would not take an oath recognizing Anne's heir. Fisher, More, and other dissenters were beheaded.

When Anne Boleyn failed in her second attempt to produce a male child, Henry VIII charged her with adulterous incest and in 1536 had her beheaded. Parliament promptly proclaimed the princess Elizabeth illegitimate and, with the royal succession thoroughly confused, left the throne to whomever Henry chose. His third wife, Jane Seymour, gave Henry the desired son, Edward, and then died in childbirth. Henry went on to three more wives. Before he passed to his reward in 1547, he got Parliament to reverse the decision of 1536, relegitimating Mary and Elizabeth and fixing the succession first in his son and then in his daughters.

Between 1535 and 1539, under the influence of his chief minister, Thomas Cromwell, Henry decided to dissolve the English monasteries because, he charged, they were economically mismanaged and morally corrupt. Actually, he wanted their wealth. Justices of the peace and other local officials who visited religious houses throughout the land found the contrary. Ignoring their reports, the king ended nine hundred years of English monastic life, dispersed the monks and nuns, and confiscated their lands. Hundreds of properties were later sold to the middle and upper classes and the proceeds spent on war. The dissolution of the monasteries did not achieve a more equitable distribution of land and wealth or advance the cause of social justice. Rather, the "bare ruined choirs where late the

HOLBEIN: SIR THOMAS MORE *This powerful portrait (1527), revealing More's strong character and humane sensitivity, shows Holbein's complete mastery of detail—down to the stubble on More's chin. The chain was an emblem of More's service to Henry VIII. (© The Frick Collection, New York)*

sweet birds sang" – as Shakespeare described the desolate religious houses – testified to the loss of a valuable esthetic and cultural force in English life.

The English Reformation under Henry VIII was primarily a matter of political, social, and economic issues, rather than religious ones. In fact, the Henrician Reformation retained such traditional Catholic practices and doctrines as confession to a priest, clerical celibacy, and transubstantiation (the doctrine of the real presence of Christ in the bread and wine of the Eucharist). On the other hand, Protestant literature circulated, Protestant doctrines captured increasing numbers of people, and Henry approved the selection of men with known Protestant sympathies as tutors for his son. Until late in the century the religious situation remained fluid.

The nationalization of the church and the dissolution of the monasteries led to important changes in governmental administration. Vast tracts of land came temporarily under the Crown's jurisdiction, and new bureaucratic machinery had to be developed to manage those properties. New departments had to be coordinated with old ones. Medieval government had been household government: all branches of the state were associated with the person and personality of the monarch. In finances, for example, no distinction was made between the king's personal income and state revenues. Each branch of government was supported with funds from a specific source; if the source had a bad year, that agency suffered while other branches of government were well in the black. Massive confusion and overlapping of responsibilities existed.

Thomas Cromwell reformed and centralized the king's household, the council, the secretariats, and the Exchequer. New departments of state were set up. Surplus funds from all departments went into a liquid fund to be applied to areas where there were deficits. This balancing resulted in greater efficiency and economy. In Henry VIII's reign can be seen the growth of the modern centralized bureaucratic state.

For several decades after Henry's death in 1547, the English church shifted left and right. In the short reign of Henry's sickly son Edward VI (1547–1553), the strongly Protestant ideas of Archbishop Thomas Cranmer exerted a significant influence on the religious life of the country. Cranmer drastically simplified the liturgy, invited Protestant theologians to England, and prepared the first *Book of Common Prayer* (1549). In stately and dignified English, the *Book of Common Prayer* included, together with the Psalter, the order for all services of the Church of England.

The equally brief reign of Mary Tudor (1553–1558) witnessed a sharp move back to Catholicism. The devoutly Catholic daughter of Catherine of Aragon, Mary rescinded the Reformation legislation of her father's reign and fully restored Roman Catholicism. Mary's marriage to her cousin Philip of Spain, son of the emperor Charles V, proved highly unpopular in England, and her persecution and execution of several hundred Protestants further alienated her subjects. During her reign many Protestants fled to the Continent. Mary's death raised to the throne her sister Elizabeth (1558–1603) and inaugurated the beginnings of religious stability.

For a long time, Elizabeth's position as queen was insecure. Although the populace cheered her accession, many questioned her legitimacy. On the one hand, Catholics wanted a Roman Catholic ruler. On the other hand, a vocal number of returned English exiles wanted all Catholic elements in the Church of England destroyed. The latter, because they wanted to "purify" the church, were called Puritans.

Elizabeth had been raised a Protestant, but if she had genuine religious convictions she kept them to herself. Probably one of the shrewdest politicians in English history, Elizabeth chose a middle course between Catholic and Puritan extremes. She insisted upon dignity in church services and political order in the land. She did not care what people believed as long as they kept quiet about it. Avoiding precise doctrinal definitions, Elizabeth had herself styled "Supreme Governor of the Church of England, Etc.," and left it to her subjects to decide what the "Etc." meant.

The parliamentary legislation of the early years of Elizabeth's reign – laws sometimes labeled the "Elizabethan Settlement" – required outward conformity to the Church of England and uniformity in all ceremonies. Everyone had to attend Church of England services; those who refused were fined. In 1563, a convocation of bishops approved the Thirty-Nine Articles, a summary in thirty-nine short statements of the basic tenets of the Church of England. During Elizabeth's reign, the Anglican church (for the Latin *Ecclesia Anglicana*), as the Church of England was called, moved in a moderately Protestant direction. Services were conducted in English, monasteries were not re-established, and the clergy were allowed to marry. But the bishops remained as church officials, and apart from language, the services were quite traditional.

THE ESTABLISHMENT OF THE CHURCH OF SCOTLAND

Reform of the church in Scotland did not follow the English model. In the early sixteenth century, the church in Scotland presented an extreme case of clerical abuse and corruption, and Lutheranism initially attracted sympathetic support. In Scotland as elsewhere, political authority was the decisive influence in

reform. The monarchy was very weak, and factions of virtually independent nobles competed for power. King James V and his daughter Mary, Queen of Scots (1560–1567), staunch Catholics and close allies of Catholic France, opposed reform. The Scottish nobles supported it. One man, John Knox (1505?–1572) dominated the movement for reform in Scotland.

In 1559, Knox, a dour, narrow-minded, and fearless man with a reputation as a passionate preacher, set to work reforming the church. He had studied and worked with Calvin in Geneva, and was determined to structure the Scottish church after the model of Calvin's Geneva. In 1560, Knox persuaded the Scottish parliament, which was dominated by reform-minded barons, to enact legislation ending papal authority. The mass was abolished and attendance at it forbidden under penalty of death. Knox then established the Presbyterian Church of Scotland, so named because presbyters, or ministers – not bishops – governed it. The Church of Scotland was strictly Calvinist in doctrine, adopted a simple and dignified service of worship, and laid great emphasis on preaching. Knox's *Book of Common Order* (1564) became the liturgical directory for the church. The Presbyterian Church of Scotland was a national, or state, church, and many of its members maintained close relations with English Puritans.

PROTESTANTISM IN IRELAND

To the ancient Irish hatred of English political and commercial exploitation, the Reformation added the bitter antagonism of religion. Henry VIII wanted to "reduce that realm to the knowledge of God and obedience to us." English rulers in the sixteenth century regarded the Irish as barbarians, and a policy of complete extermination was rejected only because "to enterprise [attempt] the whole extirpation and total destruction of all the Irishmen in the land would be a marvelous sumptious charge and great difficulty."[20] In other words, it would have cost too much.

In 1536, on orders from London, the Irish parliament, which represented only the English landlords and the people of the Pale (the area around Dublin), approved the English laws severing the church from Rome and making the English king sovereign over ecclesiastical organization and practice. The Church of Ireland was established on the English pattern, and the (English) ruling class adopted the new reformed faith. Most of the Irish, probably for political reasons, defiantly remained Roman Catholic. Monasteries were secularized. Catholic property was confiscated and sold, and the profits shipped to England. With the Roman church driven underground, the Catholic clergy acted as national as well as religious leaders.

LUTHERANISM IN SWEDEN, NORWAY, AND DENMARK

In Sweden, Norway, and Denmark the monarchy took the initiative in the religious reformation. The resulting institutions were Lutheran state churches. Since the late fourteenth century, the Danish kings had ruled Sweden and Norway as well as Denmark. In 1520, the Swedish nobleman Gustavus Vasa led a successful revolt against Denmark, and Sweden became independent. As king, Gustavus Vasa seized church lands and required the bishops' loyalty to the Swedish crown. The Wittenberg-educated Swedish reformer Olaus Petri (1493–1552) translated the New Testament into Swedish and, with the full support of Gustavus Vasa, organized the church along strict Lutheran lines. This consolidation of the Swedish monarchy in the

sixteenth century was to have a profound effect on Germany in the seventeenth century.

In Denmark, King Christian III (1534–1559) secularized church property and set up a Lutheran church. Norway, which was governed by Denmark until 1814, became Lutheran under Danish influence.

THE CATHOLIC AND THE COUNTER REFORMATIONS

Between 1517 and 1547, the reformed versions of Christianity known as Protestantism made remarkable advances. All of England, Scotland, Scandinavia, half of Germany, and sizable parts of France and Switzerland adopted the creeds of Luther, Calvin, and other reformers. Still, the Roman Catholic church made a significant comeback. After about 1540, no new large areas of Europe, except for the Netherlands, accepted Protestant beliefs (see Map 18.1).

Historians distinguish between two types of reform within the Catholic church in the sixteenth and seventeenth centuries. The Catholic Reformation began before 1517 and sought renewal basically through the stimulation of a new spiritual fervor. The Counter Reformation started in the 1530s as a reaction to the rise and spread of Protestantism. The Counter Reformation involved Catholic efforts to convince dissidents or heretics to return to the church lest they corrupt the entire community of Catholic believers. Fear of the "infection" of all Christian society by the religious dissident was a standard sixteenth-

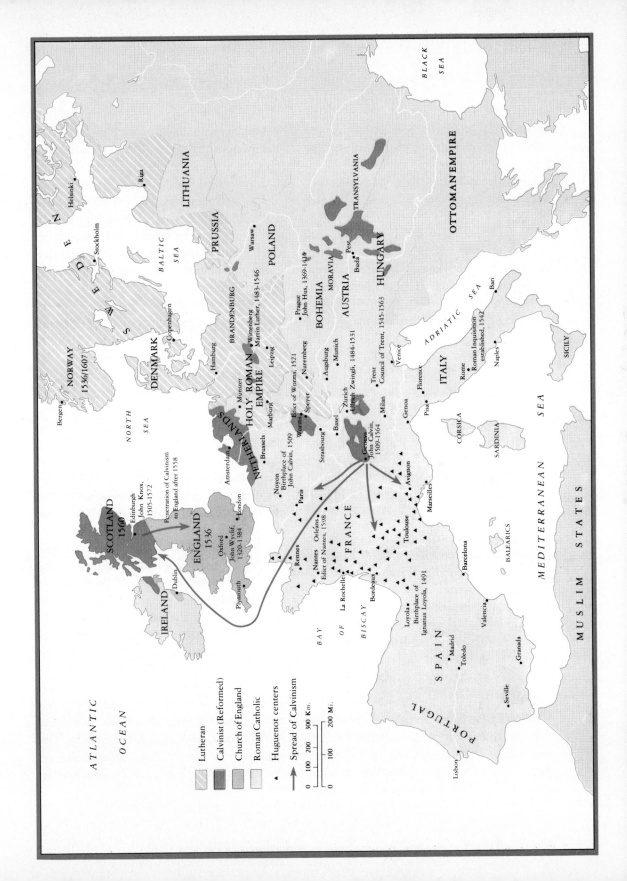

ATLANTIC

OCEAN

NORWAY
1536/1607

Bergen

NORTH

SEA

SWEDEN

Helsinki
Riga

Stockholm

BALTIC
SEA

LITHUANIA

PRUSSIA

POLAND

BLACK
SEA

OTTOMAN EMPIRE

TRANSYLVANIA

Warsaw

BRANDENBURG

DENMARK

Copenhagen

Hamburg

Leipzig

HOLY ROMAN
EMPIRE

Wittenberg
Martin Luther, 1483–1546

Edict of Worms, 1521

Nuremberg

Augsburg

Munich

Prague
John Hus, 1369–1415

BOHEMIA

MORAVIA

Budi

Pest

HUNGARY

AUSTRIA

Trent
Council of Trent, 1545–1563

Venice

ADRIATIC
SEA

Bari

NETHERLANDS

Münster

Marburg

Worms

Speyer

Strasbourg

Basel

Zürich
Ulrich Zwingli, 1484–1531

Milan

Genoa

Florence

ITALY

Rome

Roman Inquisition
established, 1542

Naples

SICILY

Amsterdam

Brussels

Noyon
Birthplace of
John Calvin, 1509

Paris

Geneva
John Calvin,
1509–1564

Pisa

CORSICA

SARDINIA

MEDITERRANEAN

SEA

SCOTLAND
1560

Edinburgh
John Knox,
1505–1572

Penetration of Calvinism
to England after 1558

ENGLAND
1536

Oxford
John Wyclif,
1320–1384

London

IRELAND

Dublin

Plymouth

Rennes

Nantes
Edict of Nantes, 1598

Orléans

FRANCE

Toulouse

Avignon

Marseilles

BAY

OF

BISCAY

La Rochelle

Bordeaux

Loyola
Birthplace of
Ignatius Loyola, 1491

SPAIN

Madrid

Toledo

Barcelona

BALEARICS

Valencia

Granada

Seville

PORTUGAL

Lisbon

MUSLIM STATES

Lutheran

Calvinist (Reformed)

Church of England

Roman Catholic

▲ Huguenot centers

Spread of Calvinism

0   100   200   300 Km.

0   100   200 Mi.

century attitude. If the heretic could not be persuaded to reconvert, counter-reformers believed it necessary to call upon temporal authorities to defend Christian society by expelling or eliminating the dissident. The Catholic Reformation and the Counter Reformation were not mutually exclusive; in fact, after about 1540 they progressed simultaneously.

What factors influenced the attitudes and policies of the papacy? Why did church leaders wait so long before dealing with the issues of schism and reform? How did the Catholic church succeed in reforming itself and in stemming the tide of Protestantism?

THE SLOWNESS OF INSTITUTIONAL REFORM

The Renaissance princes who sat on the throne of Saint Peter were not blind to the evils that existed. Modest reform efforts had begun with the Lateran Council called in 1512 by Pope Julius II. The Dutch pope Adrian VI (1522–1523) had instructed his legate in Germany to

say that we frankly confess that God permits this [Lutheran] persecution of his church on account of the sins of men, especially those of the priests and prelates. . . . We know that in this Holy See now for some years there have been many abominations, abuses in spiritual things, excesses in things commanded, in short that all has become perverted. . . . We have all turned aside in our ways, nor was there, for a long time, any who did right – no, not one.[21]

Why did the popes, spiritual leaders of the Western church, move so slowly? The answers lie in the personalities of the popes themselves, their preoccupation with political affairs in Italy, and the awesome difficulty of reforming so complicated a bureaucracy as the Roman curia.

Pope Leo X (1513–1521), who opened his pontificate with the words "Now that God has given us the papacy, let us enjoy it," typified the attitude of the Renaissance papacy. Leo concerned himself with artistic beauty and sensual pleasures. He first dismissed the Lutheran revolution as "a monkish quarrel," and by the time he finally acted with a letter condemning Luther, much of northern Germany had already rallied around the sincere Augustinian.

Adrian VI tried desperately to reform the church and to check the spread of Protestantism. His reign lasted only thirteen months, however, and the austerity of his life and his Dutch nationality provoked the hostility of pleasure-loving Italian curial bureaucrats.

Clement VII, a true Medicean, was far more interested in elegant tapestries and Michelangelo's painting of the Last Judgment than in theological disputes in barbaric Germany. Indecisive and vacillating, Pope Clement must bear much of the responsibility for the great spread of Protestantism. While Emperor Charles V and the French king Francis I competed for the domination of divided Italy, the papacy worried about the security of the Papal States. Clement tried to follow a middle course, backing first the emperor and then the French ruler. At the battle of Pavia in 1525, Francis I suffered a severe defeat and was captured. In a reshuffling of diplomatic alliances, the pope switched from Charles and the Spaniards to Francis I. The emperor was victorious once again, however, and in 1527 his Spanish and German mercenaries sacked and looted Rome and captured the pope. Obviously, papal concern about Italian affairs and the Papal States diverted attention from reform.

The idea of reform was closely linked to the idea of a general council representing the entire church. Early in the sixteenth century, Ferdinand of Spain appointed a committee of Spanish bishops to draft materials for conciliar reform of the church. In France, the University of Paris also pressed for a council. (French monarchs subsequently used this academic demand to support their military intervention in Italy.) The emperor Charles V, increasingly disturbed by the Lutheran threat, called for "a free Christian council in German lands." German Catholic bishops drew up lists of "oppressive disorders" that needed reform. A strong contingent of countries from beyond the Alps – from Spain, Germany, and France – wanted to reform the vast bureaucracy of Latin officials, reducing offices, men, and revenues.

Popes from Julius II to Clement VII, remembering fifteenth-century conciliar attempts to limit papal authority, resisted calls for a council. The papal bureaucrats who were the popes' intimates warned the popes against a council, fearing loss of power and prestige. Five centuries before, Saint Bernard of Clairvaux had anticipated the situation: "The most grievous danger of any Pope lies in the fact that, encompassed as he is by flatterers, he never hears the truth about his own person and ends by not wishing to hear it."[22]

THE COUNCIL OF TRENT

In the papal conclave that followed the death of Clement VII, Cardinal Alexander Farnese promised two German cardinals that if he were elected pope he would summon a council. He won the election and ruled as Pope Paul III (1534-1549). This Roman aristocrat, humanist, and astrologer, who immediately made his teenage grandsons cardinals, seemed an unlikely person to undertake serious reform. Yet Paul III appointed as cardinals several learned churchmen, such as Caraffa (later Pope Paul IV), established the Inquisition in the Papal States and – true to his word – called a council, which finally met at Trent in northern Italy.

The Council of Trent met intermittently from 1545 to 1563. It was called not only to reform the church but to secure reconciliation with the Protestants. Lutherans and Calvinists were invited to participate, but their insistence that the Scriptures be the sole basis for discussion made reconciliation impossible. Other problems bedeviled all the sessions of the council. International politics repeatedly cast a shadow over the theological debates. Charles V opposed discussions on any matter that might further alienate his Lutheran subjects, fearing the loss of additional imperial territory to Lutheran princes. Meanwhile, the French kings worked against the reconciliation of Roman Catholicism and Lutheranism: as long as religious issues divided the German states, the empire would be weakened, and a weak and divided empire meant a stronger France.

Trent had been selected as the site for the council because of its proximity to Germany. The city's climate, small size, and poor accommodations, the advanced age of many bishops, the difficulties of travel in the sixteenth century, and the refusal of Charles V and Henry II of France to allow their national bishops to attend certain sessions – these factors drastically reduced attendance. Portugal, Poland, Hungary, and Ireland sent representatives, but very few German bishops attended.

Another problem was the persistence of the conciliar theory of church government. Some bishops wanted a concrete statement asserting the supremacy of a church council over the

The text within the engraving reads:

THE
COUNCIL
of
TRENT

The Representation of the Fathers assembled in the
Council of Trent: begun about the end of the year 1545.
Concluded towards the end of 1563. under y Pontificate
of Paul III. Iulius III. Marcel II. Paul IV. and Pius IV.
There were XXV. Sessions, in which were present
VII. Cardinals Whereof were the Popes Legates,
XVI. Ambassadours from Kings, Princes & Repub-
licks, CCL. Patriarchs, Archbishops, Bishops,—
Abbots and Generals of Orders, All Divines
and Doctours of the Civil and Canon Law.

THE COUNCIL OF TRENT *This seventeenth-
century engraving depicts one of the early and sparsely
attended sessions of the Council of Trent. The tridentine sessions of 1562–63 drew many more bishops and
laymen, but there were never many representatives
from northern Europe. (Photo: Caroline Buckler)*

papacy. The adoption of the conciliar principle could have led to a divided church. The bishops had a provincial and national outlook; only the papacy possessed an international perspective. Fortunately, the centralizing tenet was established that all acts of the council required papal approval.

In spite of the obstacles, the achievements of the Council of Trent are impressive. It dealt with both doctrinal and disciplinary matters. The council gave equal validity to the Scriptures and to tradition as sources of religious truth and authority in the church. It reaffirmed the seven sacraments and the traditional Catholic teaching on transubstantiation — the belief in the conversion of the bread and wine used in the Mass into the actual body and blood of Christ. Thus, Lutheran and Calvinist positions were rejected.

The council tackled the problems arising from ancient abuses by strengthening ecclesiastical discipline. Tridentine (from *Tridentum,* the Latin word for Trent) decrees required bishops to reside in their own dioceses, suppressed pluralism and simony, and forbade the sale of indulgences. Clerics who kept concubines were to be warned to give them up and, if they refused, stripped of all ecclesiastical income. The jurisdiction of bishops over all the clergy of their dioceses was made almost absolute, and bishops were ordered to visit every religious house within the diocese at least once every two years. In a highly original canon, the council required every diocese to establish a seminary for the education and training of the clergy; the council even prescribed the curriculum and insisted that preference for admission be given to sons of the poor. Finally, great emphasis was laid on preaching and instructing the laity, especially the uneducated.

The Council of Trent did not meet everyone's expectations. Reconciliation with Prot-

estantism was not achieved, nor was reform brought about immediately. Nevertheless, the Tridentine decrees laid a solid basis for the spiritual renewal of the church and for the enforcement of correction. For four centuries the doctrinal and disciplinary legislation of Trent served as the basis for Roman Catholic faith, organization, and practice.

NEW RELIGIOUS ORDERS

The establishment of new religious orders within the church reveals a central feature of the Catholic Reformation. These new orders developed in response to one crying need: to raise the moral and intellectual level of the clergy. Education was a major goal of them all.

The Ursuline order of nuns founded by Angela Merici (1474–1540) attained enormous prestige for the education of women. The daughter of a country gentleman, Angela Merici worked for many years among the poor, sick, and uneducated around her native Brescia in northern Italy. In 1535 she established the Ursuline order to combat heresy through Christian education. The first religious order concentrating exclusively on teaching young girls, the Ursulines sought to re-Christianize society by training future wives and mothers. Approved as a religious community by Paul III in 1544, the Ursulines rapidly grew and spread to France and the New World. Their schools in North America, stretching from Quebec to New Orleans, provided superior education for young women and inculcated the spiritual ideals of the Catholic Reformation.

The Society of Jesus, founded by Ignatius Loyola (1491–1556), a former Spanish soldier, played a powerful international role in resisting the spread of Protestantism, converting Asians and Latin American Indians to Catholicism, and spreading Christian education all over Europe. While recuperating from a severe battle wound in his legs, Loyola studied a life of Christ and other religious books and decided to give up his military career and become a soldier of Christ. During a year spent in seclusion, prayer, and personal mortification, he gained the religious insights that went into his great classic, *Spiritual Exercises.* This work, intended for study during a four-week period of retreat, directed the individual imagination and will to the reform of life and a new spiritual piety.

Loyola was apparently a man of considerable personal magnetism. After study at the universities in Salamanca and Paris, he gathered a group of six companions and in 1540 secured papal approval of the new Society of Jesus, whose members were called Jesuits. Their goals were the reform of the church primarily through education, preaching the Gospel to pagan peoples, and fighting Protestant heresy. Within a short time, the Jesuits had attracted many recruits.

The Society of Jesus was a highly centralized, tightly knit organization. Candidates underwent a two-year novitiate, in contrast to the usual one-year probation. Although new members took the traditional vows of poverty, chastity, and obedience, the emphasis was on obedience. Carefully selected members made a fourth vow of obedience to the pope and the governing members of the society. As faith was the cornerstone of Luther's life, so obedience became the bedrock of the Jesuit tradition.

The Jesuits had a modern, quasi-military quality; a sort of ecclesiastical Green Berets, they achieved phenomenal success for the papacy and the reformed church. Jesuit schools adopted modern teaching methods, and while they first concentrated on the children of the poor, they were soon educating the sons of the nobility. As confessors and spiritual directors to kings, Jesuits exerted great political influence. Operating on the principle that the end sometimes justifies the means, they were not above spying. Indifferent to physical comfort and personal safety, they carried Christianity to the Moluccan Islands, Ceylon, and Japan before 1550, to Brazil and the Congo in the seventeenth century. Within Europe, the Jesuits brought southern Germany and much of eastern Europe back to Catholicism.

THE SACRED CONGREGATION OF THE HOLY OFFICE

In 1542, Pope Paul III established the Sacred Congregation of the Holy Office with jurisdiction over the Roman Inquisition, which became a powerful instrument of the Counter Reformation. The Inquisition was a committee of six cardinals with judicial authority over all Catholics and with the power to arrest, imprison, and execute. Under the direction of the fanatical Cardinal Caraffa, it vigorously attacked heresy.

The Roman Inquisition operated under the principles of Roman law. It accepted hearsay evidence, was not obliged to inform accused people of the charges against them, and sometimes applied torture. Echoing one of Calvin's remarks about heresy, Cardinal Caraffa wrote, "No man is to lower himself by showing toleration towards any sort of heretic, least of all a Calvinist."[23] The Holy Office published the *Index of Prohibited Books,* a catalog of forbidden reading that included the publications of many printers.

Within the Papal States in central Italy, the Inquisition effectively destroyed heresy (and many heretics). Outside the papal territories, however, its influence was slight. Governments had their own judicial systems for the suppression of treasonable activities, as religious heresy was then considered. The republic of Venice is a good case in point.

In the sixteenth century, Venice was one of the great publishing centers of Europe. The Inquisition and the Index could have badly damaged the Venetian book trade. Authorities there cooperated with the Holy Office only when heresy became a great threat to the security of the republic. The Index had no influence on scholarly research in nonreligious areas, such as law, classical literature, and mathematics. Venetians and Italians, as a result of the Inquisition, were not cut off from the main currents of European learning.[24]

———◆———

The age of the Reformation presents very real paradoxes. The break with Rome and the rise of Lutheran, Anglican, Calvinist, and other faiths destroyed the unity of Europe as an organic Christian society. Saint Paul's exhortation, "There should be no schism in the body [of the church]. . . . You are all one in Christ,"[25] was gradually ignored. On the other hand, religious belief remained tremendously strong. In fact, the strength of religious convictions caused political fragmentation. In the later sixteenth century and through most of the seventeenth, religion and religious issues continued to play a major role in the lives of individuals and in the policies and actions of governments. Religion, whether Protestant or Catholic, decisively influenced the growth of national states.

For almost a thousand years, the church had taught Europeans "to believe in order that you may know." In the seventh through ninth centuries, European peoples had been led in massive numbers to the waters of Christian baptism. The Christian faith and Christian practices, however, meant little to the pagan barbarians of the early Middle Ages.

Many centuries passed before the church had a significantly Christianizing impact on those peoples. Therein lies another paradox. At the moment when literature, sermons, and especially art were expressing the widespread desire for individual and emotional experience within a common spiritual framework, the schism brought confusion, divisiveness, and destruction. The Reformation was, ironically, a tribute to the successful educational work of the medieval church.

Finally, scholars have maintained that the sixteenth century witnessed the beginnings of the modern world. They are both right and wrong. The sixteenth-century revolt from the church paved the way for the eighteenth-century revolt from the Christian God, one of the strongest supports of life in Western culture. In this respect, the Reformation marked the beginning of the modern world, with its secularism and rootlessness. At the same time, it can equally be argued that the sixteenth century represented the culmination of the Middle Ages. Martin Luther's anxieties about salvation show him to be very much a medieval man. His concerns had deeply troubled serious individuals since the time of Saint Augustine. Modern people tend to be less troubled by this issue. The sixteenth century was a definite watershed.

NOTES

1. Romans 12:2-3.

2. Quoted by J. Burckhardt, *The Civilization of the Renaissance in Italy,* Phaidon Books, London, 1951, p. 262.

3. See E. Erickson, *Young Man Luther: A Study in Psychoanalysis and History,* W. W. Norton, New York, 1962, passim.

4. T. C. Mendenhall et al., eds., *Ideas and Institu-*

tions in European History: 800–1715, Henry Holt, New York, 1948, p. 220.

5. Quoted by O. Chadwick, *The Reformation*, Penguin Books, Baltimore, 1976, p. 55.

6. Quoted by E. H. Harbison, *The Age of Reformation*, Cornell University Press, Ithaca, N.Y., 1963, p. 52.

7. I have leaned heavily here on Harbison, pp. 52–55.

8. H. Hillerbrand, *Men and Ideas in the Sixteenth Century*, Rand McNally, Chicago, 1969, p. 28.

9. Romans 13:1–2.

10. Erickson, p. 47.

11. Quoted by J. Atkinson, *Martin Luther and the Birth of Protestantism*, Penguin Books, Baltimore, 1968, pp. 247–248.

12. *Martin Luther: Three Treatises*, Muhlenberg Press, Philadelphia, 1947, pp. 28–31.

13. Quoted by R. Bainton, *The Travail of Religious Liberty*, Harper & Brothers, New York, 1958, p. 65.

14. J. Allen, trans., *John Calvin: The Institutes of the Christian Religion*, Westminster Press, Philadelphia, 1930, book 3, chap. 21, paras. 5, 7.

15. Quoted by Bainton, pp. 69–70.

16. A. G. Dickens, *The English Reformation*, Schocken Books, New York, 1964, p. 36.

17. A. G. Dickens and Dorothy Carr, eds., *The Reformation in England to the Accession of Elizabeth I*, Edward Arnold, London, 1969, pp. 15–16.

18. Leviticus 18:16, 20, 21.

19. C. Stephenson and G. F. Marcham, *Sources of English Constitutional History*, Harper & Row, New York, 1937, p. 304.

20. Quoted by P. Smith, *The Age of the Reformation*, rev. ed., Henry Holt, New York, 1951, p. 346.

21. Ibid., p. 84.

22. Quoted by H. Jedin, *A History of the Council of Trent*, Nelson & Sons, London, 1957, 1.126.

23. Quoted by Chadwick, p. 270.

24. See P. Grendler, *The Roman Inquisition and the Venetian Press, 1540–1605*, Princeton University Press, Princeton, N.J., 1977.

25. I Corinthians 1:25, 27.

SUGGESTED READING

There are many lucidly written and easily accessible studies of the religious reformations of the sixteenth century. O. Chadwick, *The Reformation* (1976); E. H. Harbison, *The Age of Reformation* (1963); R. Bainton, *The Reformation of the Sixteenth Century* (1961); and H. Hillerbrand, *Men and Ideas in the Sixteenth Century* (1969), are all good general introductions. P. Smith's *The Age of the Reformation*, rev. ed. (1951) is an older but comprehensive and often amusing treatment. The recent work of Steven Ozment, *The Age of Reform, 1250–1550: An Intellectual and Religious History of Late Medieval and Reformation Europe* (1980), provides a sophisticated survey of the ideas of the period.

Students who wish to explore aspects of Luther's life and work in greater detail should see, in addition to the titles in the Notes, R. Bainton, *Here I Stand* (1960); J. Atkinson, *Martin Luther and the Birth of Protestantism* (1968); and the sensitively scholarly work of H. Boehmer, *Martin Luther: Road to Reformation* (1960), a well-balanced book by a distinguished Protestant theologian. The perceptive study of H. G. Haile, *Luther: An Experiment in Biography* (1980), focuses on the character of the mature and aging reformer. The pioneering work of Gerald Strauss, *Luther's House of Learning: The Indoctrination of the Young in the German Reformation* (1978), describes how plain people were imbued with Reformation ideas and behavior. The best biography of the central political figure in the period of the German Reformation remains K. Brandi, *Charles V* (1954), while G. Barraclough, *The Origins of Modern Germany* (1952), gives a closet Marxist treatment.

The best introduction to Calvin as a man and theologian is probably the balanced account of F. Wendel, *Calvin: The Origins and Development of His Thought*, trans. P. Mairet (1963). J. T. McNeill, *History and Character of Calvinism* (1954), presents useful and previously inaccessible information. W. E. Monter, *Calvin's Geneva* (1967), is an excellent account of the impact of Calvinism on the social and economic life of that Swiss city. R. T. Kendall,

Calvinism and English Calvinism to 1649 (1981), treats English conditions, while Robert M. Mitchell, *Calvin and the Puritan View of the Protestant Ethic* (1979), offers a good interpretation of the socioeconomic implications of Calvin's thought. Students interested in the left wing of the reformation should see the profound study of G. H. Williams, *The Radical Reformers* (1962), a highly detailed and difficult book.

For England, in addition to the fundamental works by Dickens cited in the Notes, see S. T. Bindoff, *Tudor England* (1959), a good short synthesis. The following works contain excellent background material on the social and religious history of England in the pre-reformation period: Louis Brewer Hall, *The Perilous Vision of John Wyclif* (1983), a highly readable biography of the great fourteenth century reformer; Geoffrey Hindley, *England in the Age of Caxton* (1979), which shows how the London cloth dealer and book publisher symbolized the social and intellectual themes of his times; and John Gillingham, *The Wars of the Roses. Peace and Conflict in Fifteenth Century England* (1983), which denies that the Wars of the Roses brought widespread civil disorder and violence and thus provides a significant revisionist interpretation of the period.

The complex character of Henry VIII has naturally attracted the attention of many scholars. The best biography, with an exhaustive analysis of the legal and canonical implications of Henry's divorce from Catherine of Aragon, is that of J. J. Scarisbrick, *Henry VIII* (1968), while Catherine herself receives sympathetic treatment from G. Mattingly, *Catherine of Aragon* (1949). H. A. Kelly, *The Matrimonial Trials of Henry VIII* (1975) treats the legal aspects of all of Henry's marriages and divorces. L. B. Smith, *Henry Eighth. The Mask of Royalty* (1980) is a splendidly written account of Henry's old age. A provocative treatment of Henry's possible syphilis and its effects on his children is given in F. S. Cartwright, *Disease and History* (1972).

For two central figures of the Henrician reformation, Thomas More and Cardinal Wolsey, Jasper Ridley, *Statesman and Saint. Cardinal Wolsey, Sir Thomas More and the Politics of Henry VIII* (1983) gives an interesting revisionist interpretation. Karl Kautsky, *Thomas More and His Utopia* (1927) presents More as the great forerunner of modern socialism, while E. E. Reynolds, *The Field is Won. The Life and Death of Thomas More* (1968) emphasizes the spiritual and intellectual character of the man. In addition to Ridley's book, Wolsey receives sympathetic treatment in N. Williams, *The Cardinal and the Secretary* (1975).

Muriel St. Clare Byrne, ed., *The Lisle Letters*, selected by Bridget Boland (1983) contains a superb record of English social history in the crucial years of Reformation (1536-1540), based on the records of a family close to the court and important events; this is a very significant new work. On the dissolution of the English monasteries, see D. Knowles, *The Religious Orders in England*, vol. 3 (1959), one of the finest examples of historical prose written in the twentieth century. Knowles's *Bare Ruined Choirs* (1976) is an attractively illustrated abridgement of Religious Orders. G. R. Elton, *The Tudor Revolution in Government* (1959), discusses the modernization of English government under Thomas Cromwell. The standard Roman Catholic interpretation of the English Reformation remains Philip Hughes, *The Reformation in England*, 3 vols. (1952-54).

The recent study of John Julius Norwich, *A History of Venice* (1982) contains a good account of the vicissitudes of a major Italian city-state during the Reformation, while William H. McNeill, *The Pursuit of Power. Technology, Armed Force, and Society since 1000 A.D.* (1982) includes a masterful discussion of the changes in the nature of warfare in the sixteenth century.

For examples of the exciting work that has recently been done on women, the family, and sexuality in early modern times, see, for women, Sherrin Marshall Wyntjes, "Women in the Reformation Era," in Renate Bridenthal and Claudia Koonz eds., *Becoming Visible. Women in European History* (1977), which treats the importance of women's support for the advancement of the Protestant cause; for France, Jean Louis Flandrin, *Families in Former Times – Kinship, Household and Sexuality in Early Modern France* (1977) and Edward Shorter, *The Making of the Modern Family* (1977); for England, see Lawrence Stone, "The Rise of the Nuclear Family in Early Modern England," in Charles E. Rosenberg ed., *The Family in History* (1978) and Stone's monumental *The Family, Sex and Marriage in England, 1500–1800* (1977), and Jack Goody, Joan Thirsk, and E. P. Thompson eds., *Family and Inheritance. Rural Society in Western Europe 1200–1800* (1978), which contains articles on Germany and France, as well as on England.

The best comprehensive treatment of the Catholic reformation from a Catholic point of view is Erwin Iserloh, Joseph Glazik, and Hubert Jedin, *Reformation and Counter Reformation,* trans. Anselm Biggs and Peter W. Becker (1980), while the older and briefer study of P. Janelle, *The Catholic Reformation* (1951) is still reliable. A. G. Dickens, *The Counter Reformation* (1969) gives the Protestant standpoint in a beautifully illustrated book. For a virtually definitive study of the Council of Trent, one should consult H. Jedin, *A History of the Council of Trent,* 3 vols., (1957–1961).

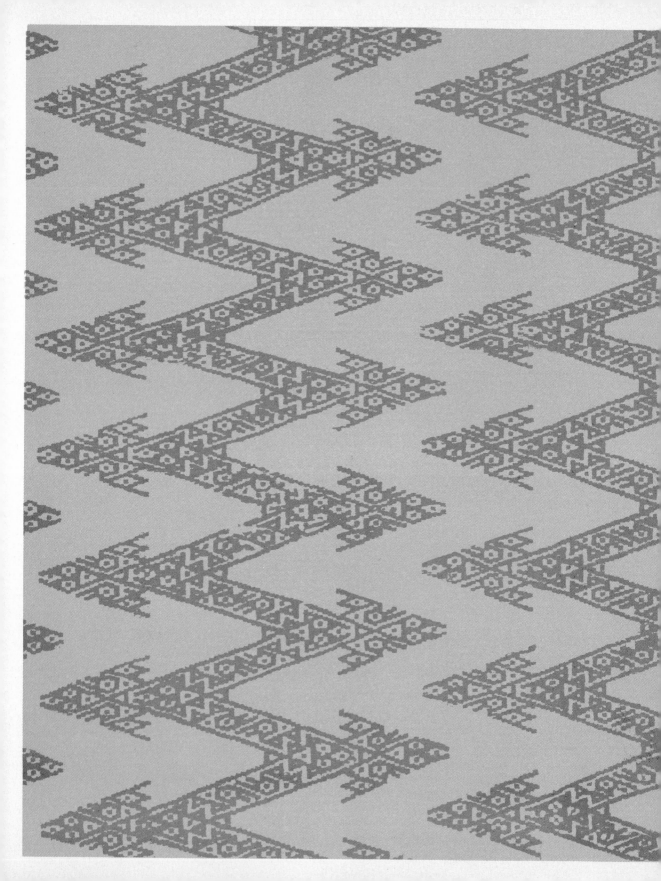

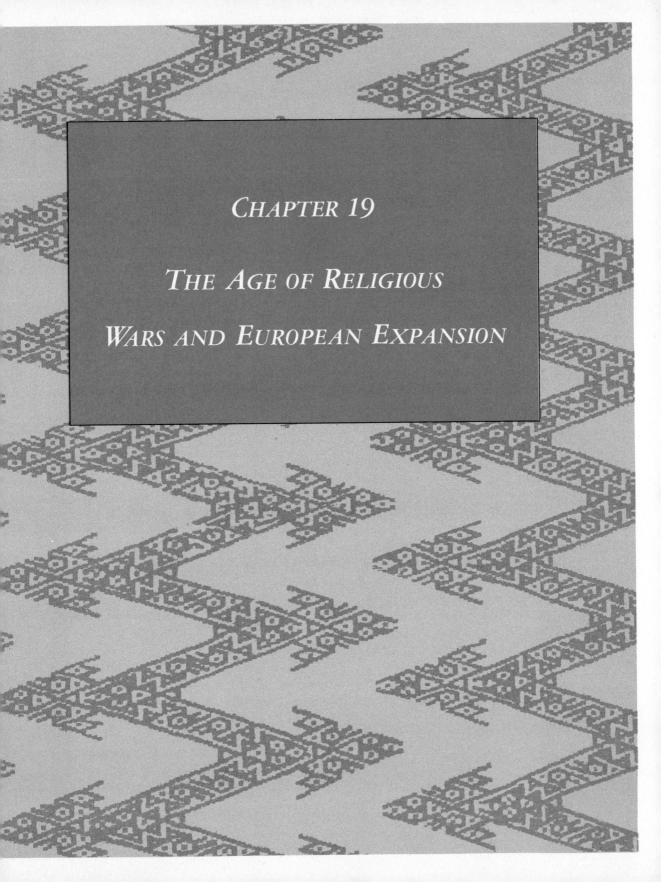

CHAPTER 19

THE AGE OF RELIGIOUS

WARS AND EUROPEAN EXPANSION

THE RENAISSANCE and the reformations of the fifteenth and sixteenth centuries drastically altered intellectual, political, religious, and social life in Europe. But even before Martin Luther initiated the movement to reform the church, European peoples had been involved in overseas activities that had profound consequences for the domestic life of Europe and for the rest of the world. In the middle of the fifteenth century, Europeans began to confront ancient civilizations in Africa, Asia, and the Americas. These confrontations led first to conquest, then to exploitation, and finally to significant changes in both Europe and the conquered territories. European expansion took place amidst domestic and international conflict.

For much of the period 1560–1648, war and religious issues dominated the politics of European states. Wars were fought for power and territorial expansion, although religion was commonly used to rationalize those wars. Meanwhile Europeans carried their political, religious, and social attitudes to the new continents they subdued. This chapter seeks to explore the following questions. Why, in the sixteenth and seventeenth centuries, did European peoples expand overseas? How were a relatively small number of people living on the edge of the Eurasian landmass able to gain control of the major sea-lanes of the world and establish economic and political hegemony on distant continents far from home? What effect did overseas expansion have on Europe and on conquered societies?

DISCOVERY, RECONNAISSANCE, AND EXPANSION

Historians have variously called the period 1450–1650 "The Age of Discovery," "The

Age of Reconnaissance," and "The Age of Expansion." All three labels are appropriate. "The Age of Discovery" refers to the era's phenomenal advances in geographical knowledge and in technology, often achieved through trial and error. In 1350, it took as long to sail from the eastern end of the Mediterranean to the western end as it had taken a thousand years earlier, in 350. Even in the fifteenth century, Europeans knew little more about the earth's surface than the Romans had known. By 1650, however, Europeans had made an extensive reconnaissance – or preliminary exploration – and had sketched fairly accurately the physical outline of the whole earth. Much of the geographical information they had gathered was tentative and not fully understood – hence the appropriateness of the term "The Age of Reconaissance."

The designation of the era as "The Age of Expansion" refers to the migration of Europeans to other parts of the world. This colonization resulted in political control of much of South America and North America, coastal regions of Africa, India, China, Japan, and many Pacific islands. Political hegemony was accompanied by economic exploitation, religious domination, and the introduction of European patterns of social and intellectual life. The sixteenth-century expansion of European society launched a new age in world history.

The outward expansion of Europe began with the Viking voyages across the Atlantic in the tenth and eleventh centuries. Under Eric the Red and Leif Ericson, the Vikings discovered Greenland and the eastern coast of North America. They may even have traveled down the New England coast as far south as Boston. The Crusades of the eleventh through thirteenth centuries were another phase in Europe's attempt to explore, Christianize, and exploit territories and peoples on the periphery of the Continent. But these early thrusts outward resulted in no permanent settlements. The Vikings made only quick raids in search of booty. Lacking stable political institutions in Scandinavia, they had no workable forms of government to impose on distant continents. In the twelfth and thirteenth centuries, the lack of a strong territorial base, weak support from the West, and sheer misrule combined to make the medieval Crusader kingdoms short-lived. Even in the mid-fifteenth century, Europe seemed ill-prepared for international ventures. By 1450, a grave new threat had appeared in the East – the Ottoman Turks.

Combining excellent military strategy with efficient administration of their conquered territories, the Turks had subdued most of Asia Minor and begun to settle on the Western side of the Bosporus. The Ottoman Turks under Sultan Mohammed II (1451–1481) captured Constantinople in 1453, pressed southwest into the Balkans, and by the early sixteenth century controlled the eastern Mediterranean. The Turkish menace badly frightened Europeans. In France in the fifteenth and sixteenth centuries, twice as many books were printed about the Turkish threat as about the American discoveries. The Turks imposed a military blockade on eastern Europe, thus forcing Europeans' attention westward. Yet the fifteenth and sixteenth centuries witnessed a fantastic continuation, on a global scale, of European expansion: great discoveries led to overseas empires.

Political centralization in Spain, France, and England helps to explain those countries' outward push. In the fifteenth century, Isabella and Ferdinand had consolidated their several kingdoms to achieve a united Spain. The Catholic rulers slashed the powers of the nobility, revamped the Spanish bureaucracy, and humbled dissident elements, notably the Muslims and the Jews. The Spanish monarchy was stronger than ever before, and in a position to support foreign ventures; it could bear the costs and dangers of exploration. But Portugal, situated on the extreme southwestern edge of the European continent, got the start on the rest of Europe.

Portugal's taking of Ceuta, an Arab city in northern Morocco, in 1415 marked the beginning of European exploration and control of overseas territory. The objectives of Portuguese policy included the historic Iberian crusade to Christianize Muslims, and the search for gold, for an overseas route to the spice markets of India, and for the mythical Christian ruler of Ethiopia, Prester John.

In the early phases of Portuguese exploration, Prince Henry (1394–1460), called "the Navigator" because of the annual expeditions he sent down the western coast of Africa, played the leading role. In the fifteenth century, most of the gold that reached Europe came from the Sudan in West Africa and from Ashanti blacks living near the gold coast. Muslim caravans brought the gold from the African cities of Niani and Timbuktu and carried it north across the Sahara to Mediterranean ports. Then the Portuguese muscled in on this commerce in gold. Prince Henry's carefully planned expeditions succeeded in reaching Guinea, and under King John II (1481-1495), the Portuguese established trading posts and forts on the Guinea coast and penetrated into the continent all the way to Timbuktu (see Map 19.1). Portuguese ships transported gold to Lisbon, and by 1500 Portugal controlled the flow of gold to Europe. The golden century of Portuguese prosperity had begun.

Still the Portuguese pushed farther south down the west coast of Africa. In 1487, Bartholomew Diaz rounded the Cape of Good Hope at the southern tip, but storms and a threatened mutiny forced him to turn back. On a second expedition (1497-1499), the Portuguese mariner Vasco da Gama reached India and returned to Lisbon loaded with samples of Indian wares (see Map 19.1). King Manuel (1495-1521) promptly dispatched thirteen ships under the command of Pedro Alvares Cabral, assisted by Diaz, to set up trading posts in India. On April 22, 1500, the coast of Brazil in South America was sighted and claimed for the crown of Portugal. Cabral then proceeded south and east around the Cape of Good Hope and reached India. Half the fleet was lost on the return voyage, but the six spice-laden vessels that dropped anchor in Lisbon harbor in July 1501 more than paid for the entire expedition. Thereafter, convoys were sent out every March. Lisbon became the entrance port for Asian goods into Europe — but not without a fight.

For centuries the Muslims had controlled the rich spice trade of the Indian Ocean, and they did not surrender it willingly. Portuguese commercial activities were accompanied by the destruction or seizure of strategic Muslim coastal forts, which later served Portugal as both trading posts and military bases.

Alfonso de Albuquerque, whom the Portuguese crown appointed as governor of India (1509-1515), decided that these bases and not inland territories should control the Indian Ocean. Accordingly, his cannon blasted open the ports of Calicut, Ormuz, Goa, and Malacca, the vital centers of Arab domination of south Asian trade. This bombardment laid the foundation for Portuguese imperialism in the sixteenth and seventeenth centuries: a strange way to bring Christianity to "those who were in darkness." As one scholar wrote about the opening of China to the West, "while Buddha came to China on white elephants, Christ was borne on cannon balls."[1]

In March 1493, between the first and second voyages of Vasco da Gama, Spanish ships entered Lisbon harbor bearing a triumphant Italian explorer in the service of the Spanish monarchy. Christopher Columbus (1451-1506), a Genose mariner, had secured Spanish support for an expedition to the East. He sailed from Palos, Spain, to the Canary Islands and crossed the Atlantic to the Bahamas, landing in October 1492 on an island that he named San Salvador and believed to be the coast of India.

Columbus explained the motives for his expedition in the journal of his voyage, entitled *Book of the First Navigation and Discovery of the Indies:*

And Your Highnesses, as Catholic Christians and Princes devoted to the Holy Christian Faith and the propagators thereof, and enemies of the sect of Mahomet and of all idolatries and heresies, resolved to send me Christopher Columbus to the said regions of India, to see the said princes and peoples and lands and [to observe] the disposition of them and of all, and the manner in which may be undertaken their conversion to our Holy Faith, and ordained that I should not go by land (the usual

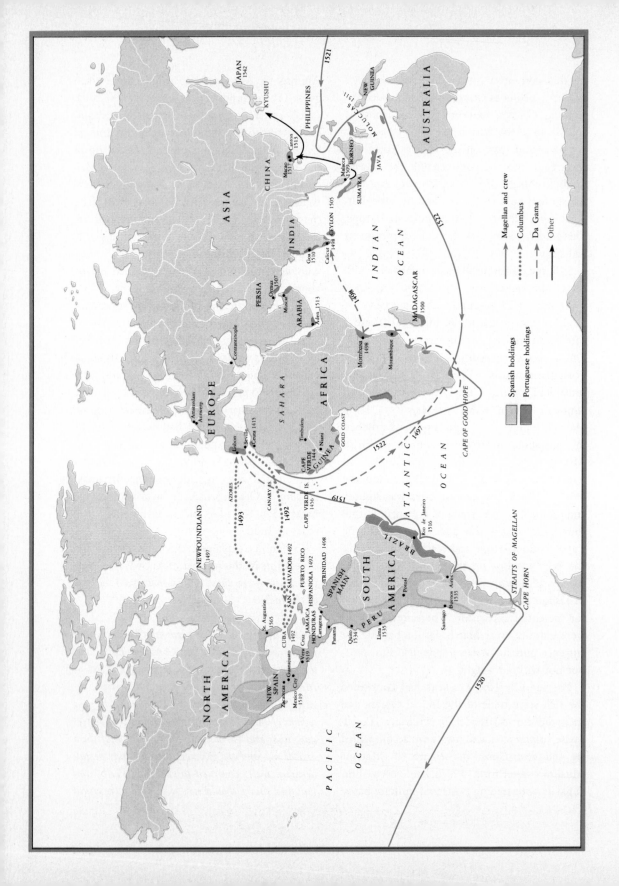

MAP 19.1 *OVERSEAS EXPLORATION AND CON-QUEST, FIFTEENTH AND SIXTEENTH CEN-TURIES The voyages of discovery marked another phase in the centuries-old migrations of European peoples. Consider the major contemporary significance of each of the three voyages depicted on the map.*

way) to the Orient, but by the route of the Occident, by which no one to this day knows for sure that anyone has gone.[2]

Like most people of his day, Christopher Columbus was a deeply religious man. The crew of his flagship, *Santa Maria,* recited vespers every night and sang a hymn to the Virgin, the "Salve Regina," before going to bed. Nevertheless, the Spanish fleet, sailing westward to find the East, sought wealth as well as souls to convert to Christianity.

Between 1492 and 1502, Columbus made four voyages to America, discovering all the major islands of the Caribbean – Haiti (which he called Dominica and the Spanish named Hispaniola), San Salvador, Puerto Rico, Jamaica, Cuba, Trinidad – and Honduras in Central America. Columbus believed until he died that the islands he found were off the coast of India. In fact, he had opened up for the rulers of Spain a whole new world. The Caribbean islands – the West Indies – represented to Spanish missionary zeal millions of Indian natives for conversion to Christianity. Hispaniola, Cuba, and Puerto Rico also offered gold.

Forced labor, disease, and starvation in the Spaniards' gold mines rapidly killed off the Indians of Hispaniola. When Columbus arrived in 1493, the population had been approximately 100,000; in 1570, 300 people survived. Indian slaves from the Bahamas and black Africans from Guinea were then imported to do the mining.

The search for precious metals determined the direction of Spanish exploration and expansion into South America. When it became apparent that placer mining in the Caribbean islands was slow and the rewards slim, new routes to the East and new sources of gold and silver were sought.

In 1519, the Spanish ruler Charles V commissioned Ferdinand Magellan (1480–1521) to find a direct route to the Moluccan Islands off the southeast coast of Asia. Magellan sailed southwest across the Atlantic to Brazil, and proceeded south around Cape Horn into the Pacific Ocean (see Map 19.1). He crossed the Pacific, sailing west, to the Malay Archipelago, which he called the Western Isles. (These islands were conquered in the 1560s and named the Philippines for Philip II of Spain.)

Although Magellan was killed, the expedition continued, returning to Spain in 1522 from the east by way of the Indian Ocean, the Cape of Good Hope, and the Atlantic. Terrible storms, mutiny, starvation, and disease haunted this voyage. Nevertheless, it verified Columbus's theory that the earth was round and brought information about the vastness of the Pacific. Magellan also proved that the earth was much larger than Columbus and others had believed.

In the West Indies, the slow recovery of gold, the shortage of a healthy labor force, and sheer restlessness speeded up Spain's search for wealth. In 1519, the year Magellan departed on his worldwide expedition, a brash and determined Spanish adventurer Hernando Cortez (1485–1547), crossed from Hispaniola to mainland Mexico with six hundred men, seventeen horses, and ten canon. Within three years, Cortez had conquered the fabulously rich Aztec empire, taken captive the Aztec emperor Montezuma, and founded Mexico City as the capital of New Spain. The subjugation of northern Mexico took longer, but between 1531 and 1550 the Spanish gained

COLUMBUS LANDS ON SAN SALVADOR The printed page and illustrations, such as this German woodcut, spread reports of Columbus's voyage all over Europe. According to Columbus, a group of naked Indians greeted the Spaniards' arrival. Pictures of the Indians as "primitive" and "uncivilized" instilled prejudices which centuries have not erased. (Photo: Caroline Buckler)

control of Zacatecas and Guanajuato, where rich silver veins were soon tapped.

Another Spanish conquistador, Francisco Pizzaro (1470–1541), repeated Cortez's feat in Peru. Between 1531 and 1536, with even fewer resources, Pizzaro crushed the Inca empire in northern South America and established the Spanish viceroyalty of Peru with its center at Lima. In 1545, Pizzaro opened at Potosí in the Peruvian highlands what became the richest silver mines in the New World.

Between 1525 and 1575, the riches of the Americas poured into the Spanish port of Seville and the Portuguese capital of Lisbon. For all their new wealth, however, Lisbon and Seville did not become important trading centers. It was the Flemish city of Antwerp, although controlled by the Spanish Habsburgs, that developed into the great entrepôt for overseas bullion and Portuguese spices and served as the commercial and financial capital of the entire European world.

Since the time of the great medieval fairs, cities of the Low Countries – so called because much of the land lies below sea level – had been important sites for the exchange of products from the Baltic and Italy. Antwerp, ideally situated on the Scheldt River at the intersection of many trading routes, steadily expanded as the chief intermediary for international commerce and finance. English woolens, Baltic wheat, fur, and timber, Portuguese spices, German iron and copper, Spanish fruit, French wines and dyestuffs, Italian silks, marbles, and mirrors, together with vast amounts of cash, were exchanged at Antwerp. The city's harbor could dock 2,500 vessels at once, and 5,000 merchants from many nations gathered daily in the bourse (or exchange). Spanish silver was drained to the Netherlands to pay for food and luxury goods. Even so, the desire for complete economic independence from Spain was to play a major role in the Netherlands' revolt in the late sixteenth century.

By the end of the century, Amsterdam had overtaken Antwerp as the financial capital of Europe. The Dutch had also embarked on foreign exploration and conquest. The Dutch East India Company, founded in 1602, became the major organ of Dutch imperialism and within a few decades expelled the Portuguese from Ceylon and other East Indian islands. By 1650, the Dutch West India Company had successfully horned in on the Spanish possessions in America and gained control of much of the African and American trade.

English and French explorations lacked the immediate and sensational results of the Spanish and Portuguese. In 1497 John Cabot, a Genoese merchant living in London, sailed for Brazil but discovered Newfoundland. The next year he returned and explored the New England coast and perhaps as far south as Delaware. Since these expeditions found no spices or gold, the English king Henry VII lost interest in exploration. Between 1534 and 1541, the Frenchman Jacques Cartier made several voyages and explored the St. Lawrence region of Canada, but the first permanent French settlement, at Quebec, was not founded until 1608.

COLONIAL ADMINISTRATION

Columbus, Cortez, and Pizzaro claimed the lands they had "discovered" for the crown of Spain. How were they to be governed? According to the Spanish theory of absolutism, the Crown was entitled to exercise full authority over all imperial lands. In the sixteenth century the Crown divided its New World territories into four viceroyalties or administrative divisions: New Spain, which consisted of Mexico, Central America, and present-day California, Arizona, New Mexico, and Texas, with the capital at Mexico City; Peru, originally all the lands in continental South America, later reduced to the territory of modern Peru, Chile, Bolivia, and Equador, with the viceregal seat at Lima; New Granada, including present-day Venezuela, Colombia, Panama, and after 1739 Ecuador, with Bogata as its administrative center; and La Plata, consisting of Argentina, Uruguay, and Paraguay,

with Buenos Aires as the capital. Within each territory, the viceroy or imperial governor exercised broad military and civil authority as the direct representative of the sovereign in Madrid. The viceroy presided over the *audiencia,* a board of twelve to fifteen judges, which served as his advisory council and the highest judicial body. The enlightened Spanish king Charles III (1716–1788) introduced the system of intendants. These royal officials possessed broad military, administrative, and financial authority within their intendancy, and were responsible not to the viceroy but to the Crown in Madrid.

From the early sixteenth century to the beginning of the nineteenth, the Spanish monarchy acted on the mercantilist principle that the colonies existed for the financial benefit of the mother country. The mining of gold and silver was always the most important industry in the colonies. The Crown claimed the *quinto,* one-fifth of all precious metals mined in South America. Gold and silver yielded the Spanish monarchy 25 percent of its total income. In return, it shipped manufactured goods to America and discouraged the development of native industries.

The Portuguese governed their colony of Brazil in a similar manner. After the union of the crowns of Portugal and Spain in 1580, Spanish administrative forms were introduced. Local officials called *corregidores* held judicial and military powers. Mercantilist policies placed severe restrictions on Brazilian industries that might compete with those of Portugal. In the seventeenth century the use of black slave labor made possible the cultivation of coffee and cotton, and in the eighteenth century Brazil led the world in the production of sugar. The unique feature of colonial Brazil's culture and society was its thoroughgoing intermixture of Indians, whites, and blacks.

THE ECONOMIC EFFECTS OF SPAIN'S DISCOVERIES IN THE NEW WORLD

The sixteenth century has often been called the golden century of Spain. The influence of Spanish armies, Spanish Catholicism, and Spanish wealth was felt all over Europe. This greatness rested largely upon the influx of precious metals from the New World.

The mines at Zacatecas and Guanajuato in Mexico and Potosí in Peru poured out huge quantities of precious metals. To protect this treasure from French and English pirates, armed convoys transported it each year to Spain. Between 1503 and 1650, 16 million kilograms of silver and 185,000 kilograms of gold entered the port of Seville. Scholars have long debated the impact of all this bullion on the economies of Spain and Europe as a whole. Spanish predominance, however, proved temporary.

In the sixteenth century, Spain experienced a steady population increase, creating a sharp rise in the demand for food and goods. Spanish colonies in the Americas also represented a demand for products – olive oil, wine, wool, steel cutlery, and a variety of luxury goods. Since Spain had expelled some of the best farmers and businessmen, the Muslims and the conversos, in the fifteenth century, the Spanish economy was already suffering and could not meet the new demands. Prices rose. Because the costs of manufacturing cloth and other goods increased, Spanish products could not compete in the international market with cheaper products made elsewhere. The textile industry was badly hurt. Prices spiraled upward, faster than the government could levy taxes to dampen the economy. (Higher taxes would have cut the public's buying power; with fewer goods sold, prices would have come down.)

Several times between 1557 and 1647, Philip II and his successors were forced to repudiate the state debt, which in turn undermined confidence in the government. The enormous flow of silver and gold from the Americas thus contributed to the destruction of Spanish agriculture and industry. When the flow declined in the seventeenth century, the economy was in a shambles.

As Philip II paid his armies and foreign debts with silver bullion, the Spanish inflation was transmitted to the rest of Europe. Between 1560 and 1600, much of Europe experienced large price increases. Prices doubled and in some cases quadrupled. Spain suffered most severely, but all European countries were affected. People who lived on fixed incomes, such as the continental nobles, were badly hurt because their money bought less. Those who owed fixed sums of money, such as the middle class, prospered: in a time of rising prices, debts had less value each year. Food costs rose most sharply, and the poor fared worst of all.

TECHNOLOGICAL STIMULI TO EXPLORATION

Technological developments were the key to Europe's remarkable outreach. By 1350, cannon – iron or bronze guns that fired iron or stone balls – had been fully developed in western Europe. These pieces of artillery emitted frightening noises and great flashes of fire and could batter down fortresses and even city walls. Sultan Mohammed II's siege of Constantinople in 1453 provides a classic illustration of the effectiveness of cannon fire.

Constantinople had the strongest walled fortifications in the West. The sultan secured the services of a Western technician who built fifty-six small cannon and a gigantic gun that could hurl stone balls weighing about eight hundred pounds. The gun could be moved only by several hundred oxen, and loaded and fired only by about a hundred men working together. Reloading took two hours. This awkward but powerful weapon breached the walls of Constantinople before it cracked on the second day of the bombardment. Lesser cannon finished the job.

Early cannon posed serious technical difficulties. Iron cannon were cheaper than bronze to construct, but they were difficult to cast effectively and were liable to crack and injure the artillerymen. Bronze guns, made of copper and tin, were less subject than iron to corrosion, but they were very expensive. All cannon were extraordinarily difficult to move, required considerable time for reloading, and were highly inaccurate. They thus proved inefficient for land warfare. However, they could be used at sea.

The mounting of cannon on ships and improved techniques of shipbuilding gave impetus to European expansion.[3] Since ancient times, most seagoing vessels had been narrow open boats called galleys, propelled by manpower. Slaves or convicts who had been sentenced to the galleys manned the oars of the ships that sailed the Mediterranean, and both cargo and warships carried soldiers for defense. Although well suited to the placid and thoroughly explored waters of the Mediterranean, galleys could not withstand the rough winds and uncharted shoals of the Atlantic. The need for sturdier craft, as well as population losses caused by the Black Death, forced the development of a new style of ship that would not require soldiers for defense.

In the course of the fifteenth century, the Portuguese developed the caravel, a small, light, three-masted sailing ship. Although somewhat slower than the galley, the caravel held more cargo and was highly maneuverable. When fitted with cannon, it could dominate larger vessels, such as the round ships commonly used as merchantmen. The substitution of windpower for manpower, and artillery fire for soldiers, signaled a great technological advance and gave Europeans navigational and fighting ascendancy over the rest of the world.[4]

Other fifteenth-century developments in navigation helped make possible the conquest of the Atlantic. The magnetic compass enabled sailors to determine their direction and position at sea. The astrolabe, an instrument used to determine the altitude of the sun and other celestial bodies, permitted mariners to plot their latitude, or position north or south of the equator. Steadily improved maps and sea charts provided information about distance, sea depths, and general geography.

THE EXPLORERS' MOTIVES

The expansion of Europe was not motivated by demographic pressures. The Black Death had caused serious population losses from which Europe had not recovered in 1500. Few Europeans emigrated to North or South America in the sixteenth century. Half of those who did sail to begin a new life in America died en route; half of those who reached the New World eventually returned to their homeland. Why, then, did explorers brave the Atlantic and Pacific oceans, risking their lives to discover new continents and spread European culture?

The reasons are varied and complex. People of the sixteenth century were still basically medieval, in the sense that their attitudes and values were shaped by religion and expressed in religious terms. In the late fifteenth century, crusading fervor remained a basic part of the Portuguese and Spanish national ideal. The desire to Christianize Muslims and pagan peoples played a central role in European expansion. Queen Isabella of Spain, for example, showed a fanatical zeal for converting the Muslims to Christianity, but she concentrated her efforts on the Arabs in Granada. After the abortive crusading attempts of the thirteenth century, Isabella and other rulers realized full well that they lacked the material resources to mount the full-scale assault on Islam necessary for victory. Crusading impulses thus shifted from the Muslims to the pagan peoples of Africa and the Americas.

Government sponsorship and encouragement of exploration also help to account for the results of the various voyages. Mariners and explorers could not afford, as private individuals, the massive sums needed to explore mysterious oceans and to control remote continents. The strong financial support of Prince Henry the Navigator led to Portugal's phenomenal success in the spice trade. Even the grudging and modest assistance of Isabella and Ferdinand eventually brought untold riches – and complicated problems – to Spain. The Dutch in the seventeenth century, through such government-sponsored trading companies as the Dutch East India Company, reaped enormous wealth, and although the Netherlands was a small country in size, it dominated the European economy in 1650. In England, by contrast, Henry VII's lack of interest in exploration delayed English expansion for a century.

Scholars have frequently described the European discoveries as a manifestation of Renaissance curiosity about the physical universe, the desire to know more about the geography and peoples of the world. There is truth to this explanation. Cosmography, natural history, and geography aroused enormous interest among educated people in the fifteenth and sixteenth centuries. Just as science fiction and speculation about life on other planets excite readers today, quasi-scientific literature about Africa, Asia, and the Americas captured the imaginations of literate Europeans. Oviedo's *General History of the Indies*, a detailed eyewitness account of plants, animals, and peoples, was widely read.

Spices were another important incentive to undertake voyages of discovery. Introduced into western Europe by the Crusaders in the twelfth century, nutmeg, mace, ginger, cinnamon, and pepper added flavor and variety to the monotonous diet of Europeans. Spices were also used in the preparation of medicinal drugs and in the manufacture of incense for religious ceremonies. In the late thirteenth century, the Venetian Marco Polo (1254?–1324?), the greatest of the medieval travelers, had visited the court of the Chinese emperor. The widely publicized account of his travels in the *Book of Various Experiences* stimulated a rich trade in spices between Asia and Italy. The Venetians came to hold a monopoly of the spice trade in western Europe.

Spices were grown in India and China, shipped across the Indian Ocean to ports on the Persian Gulf, and then transported by Arabs across the Arabian Desert to Mediterranean ports. But the rise of the Ming dynasty in China in the late fourteenth century resulted in the expulsion of foreigners. And the steady penetration of the Ottoman Turks into the eastern Mediterranean and of hostile Muslims across North Africa forced Europeans to seek a new route to the Asian spice markets.

The basic reason for European exploration and expansion, however, was the quest for material profit. Mariners and explorers frankly admitted this. As Bartholomew Diaz put it, his motives were "to serve God and His Majesty, to give light to those who were in darkness and to grow rich as all men desire to do." When Vasco da Gama reached the port of Calicut, India, in 1498, a native asked what the Portuguese wanted. Da Gama replied, "Christians and spices."[5] The bluntest of the Spanish conquistadors, Hernando Cortez, announced as he prepared to conquer Mexico, "I have come to win gold, not to plow the fields like a peasant."[6]

Spanish and Portuguese explorers carried the fervent Catholicism and missionary zeal of the Iberian Peninsula to the New World, and once in America they urged home governments to send clerics "to bring light to those who were in darkness." At bottom, however, wealth was the driving motivation. A sixteenth-century diplomat, Ogier Gheselin de Busbecq, summed up this paradoxical attitude well: in expeditions to the Indies and the Antipodes, he said, "religion supplies the pretext and gold the motive."[7] The mariners, explorers, and conquistadors were religious and "medieval" in justifying their actions, materialistic and "modern" in their behavior.

POLITICS, RELIGION, AND WAR

In 1559, France and Spain signed the Treaty of Cateau-Cambrésis, which ended the long conflict known as the Habsburg-Valois wars. This event marks a decisive watershed in early modern European history. Spain was the victor. France, exhausted by the struggle, had to acknowledge Spanish dominance in Italy, where much of the war had been fought. Spanish governors ruled in Sicily, Naples, and Milan, and Spanish influence was strong in the Papal States and Tuscany.

The emperor Charles V had divided his attention between the Holy Roman Empire and Spain. Under his son Philip II (1556–1598), however, the center of the Habsburg empire and the political center of gravity for all of Europe shifted westward to Spain. Before 1559, Spain and France had fought bitterly for control of Italy; after 1559, the two Catholic powers aimed their guns at Protestantism. The Treaty of Cateau-Cambrésis ended an era of dynastic wars and initiated a period of conflicts in which religion played a dominant role.

Because a variety of issues were stewing, it is not easy to generalize about the wars of the late sixteenth century. Some were continuations of struggles between the centralizing goals of monarchies and the feudal reactions of nobilities. Some were crusading battles between Catholics and Protestants. Some were struggles for national independence or for international expansion.

These wars differed considerably from earlier wars. Sixteenth- and seventeenth-century armies were bigger than medieval ones; some forces numbered as many as fifty thousand men. Because large armies were expensive, governments had to reorganize their administrations to finance them. The use of gunpowder altered both the nature of war and popular attitudes toward it. Guns and cannon killed and wounded from a distance, indiscriminately. Writers scorned gunpowder as a coward's weapon that allowed a common soldier to kill a gentleman. The Italian poet Ariosto lamented:

Through thee is martial glory lost, through
Thee the trade of arms becomes a worthless art:
And at such ebb are worth and chivalry that
The base often plays the better part.[8]

Gunpowder destroyed the notion, common during the Hundred Years' War, that warfare was an ennobling experience. Governments had to utilize propaganda, pulpits, and the printing press to arouse public opinion to support war.[9]

Late-sixteenth-century conflicts fundamentally tested the medieval ideal of a unified Christian society governed by one political ruler, the emperor, to whom all rulers were theoretically subordinate, and one church, to which all people belonged. The Protestant Reformation had killed this ideal, but few people recognized it as dead. Catholics continued to believe that Calvinists and Lutherans could be reconverted; Protestants persisted in thinking that the Roman church should be destroyed. Catholics and Protestants alike feared people of the other faith living in their midst. The settlement finally achieved in 1648, known as the Peace of Westphalia, signaled the end of the medieval ideal.

THE ORIGINS OF DIFFICULTIES IN FRANCE (1515–1559)

In the first half of the sixteenth century, France continued the recovery begun under Louis XI (page 615). The population losses caused by the plague and the disorders accompanying the Hundred Years' War had created such a labor shortage that serfdom virtually disappeared. Cash rents replaced feudal rents and servile obligations. This development clearly benefited the peasantry. Meanwhile, the declining buying power of money hurt the nobility. The steadily increasing French population brought new lands under cultivation, but the division of property among sons meant that most peasant holdings were very small. Domestic and foreign trade picked up; mercantile centers such as Rouen and Lyons expanded; and in 1517 a new port city was founded at Le Havre.

ROSSO AND PRIMATICCIO: THE GALLERY OF FRANCES I Flat paintings alternating with rich sculpture provide a rhythm that directs the eye down the long gallery at Fontainebleau, the construction of which occupied much of Francis I's attention from 1530 to 1540. He sought to re-create in France the elegant Renaissance lifestyle he had discovered in Italy. (Giraudon)

The charming and cultivated Francis I (1515–1547) and his athletic, emotional son Henry II (1547–1559) governed through a small, efficient council. Great nobles held titular authority in the provinces as governors, but Paris-appointed officials, the baillis and seneschals, continued to exercise actual fiscal and judicial responsibility (pages 459–460). In 1539, Francis issued an ordinance that placed all France under the jurisdiction of the royal law courts and made French the language of those courts. This act had a powerful centralizing impact. The taille, a tax on land, provided such strength as the monarchy had and supported a strong standing army. Unfortunately, the tax base was too narrow for France's extravagant promotion of the arts and ambitious foreign policy.

Deliberately imitating the Italian Renaissance princes, the Valois monarchs lavished money on a magnificent court and vast building program, and on Italian artists. Francis I commissioned the Paris architect Pierre Lescot to rebuild the palace of the Louvre. Francis secured the services of Michelangelo's star pupil, Il Rosso, who decorated the wing of the Fontainebleau chateau, subsequently called the Gallery Francis I, with rich scenes of classical and mythological literature. After acquiring Leonardo da Vinci's Mona Lisa, Francis brought Leonardo himself to France, where he soon died. Henry II built a castle at Dreux for his mistress, Diana de Poitiers, and a palace in Paris, the Tuileries, for his wife, Catherine de' Medici. Art historians credit

Francis I and Henry II with importing Italian Renaissance art and architecture to France. Whatever praise these monarchs deserve for their cultural achievement, they spent far more than they could afford.

The Habsburg-Valois wars, waged intermittently through the first half of the sixteenth century, also cost more than the government could afford. Financing the war posed problems. In addition to the time-honored practices of increasing taxes and heavy borrowing, Francis I tried two new devices to raise revenue: the sale of public offices and a treaty with the papacy. The former proved to be only a temporary source of money. The offices sold tended to become hereditary within a family, and once a man bought an office he and his heirs were tax-exempt. The sale of public offices thus created a tax-exempt class called the nobility of the robe, which held positions beyond the jurisdiction of the Crown.

The treaty with the papacy was the Concordat of Bologna (page 615), in which Francis agreed to recognize the supremacy of the papacy over a universal council. In return, the French crown gained the right to appoint all French bishops and abbots. This understanding gave the monarchy a rich supplement of money and offices and a power over the church that lasted until the Revolution of 1789. The Concordat of Bologna helps to explain why France did not later become Protestant: it in effect established Catholicism as the national religion. Because they possessed control over appointments and had a vested financial interest in Catholicism, French rulers had no need to revolt from Rome.

However, the Concordat of Bologna perpetuated disorders within the French church. Ecclesiastical offices were used primarily to pay and reward civil servants. Churchmen in France, as elsewhere, were promoted to the hierarchy not for any special spiritual qualifications but because of their services to the state. Such bishops were unlikely to work to elevate the intellectual and moral standards of the parish clergy. Few of the many priests in France devoted scrupulous attention to the needs of their parishioners. The teachings of Luther and Calvin, as the presses disseminated them, found a receptive audience.

Luther's tracts first appeared in France in 1518, and his ideas attracted some attention. After the publication of Calvin's *Institutes* in 1536, sizable numbers of French people were attracted to the "reformed religion," as Calvinism was called. Because Calvin wrote in French, rather than Latin, his ideas gained wide circulation. Initially, Calvinism drew converts from among reform-minded members of the Catholic clergy, the industrious middle classes, and from artisan groups. Most Calvinists lived in major cities, such as Paris, Lyons, Meaux, and Grenoble.

In spite of condemnation by the universities, government bans, and massive burnings at the stake, the numbers of Protestants grew steadily. When Henry II died in 1559, there were 40 well-organized and 2,150 mission churches in France. Perhaps one-sixth of the population had become Calvinist.

RELIGIOUS RIOTS AND CIVIL WAR IN FRANCE (1559–1589)

For thirty years, from 1559 to 1589, violence and civil war divided and shattered France. The feebleness of the monarchy was the seed from which the weeds of civil violence germinated. The three weak sons of Henry II who occupied the throne could not provide the necessary leadership. Francis II (1559–1560) died after seventeen months. Charles IX (1560–1574) succeeded at the age of ten and was thoroughly dominated by his opportunis-

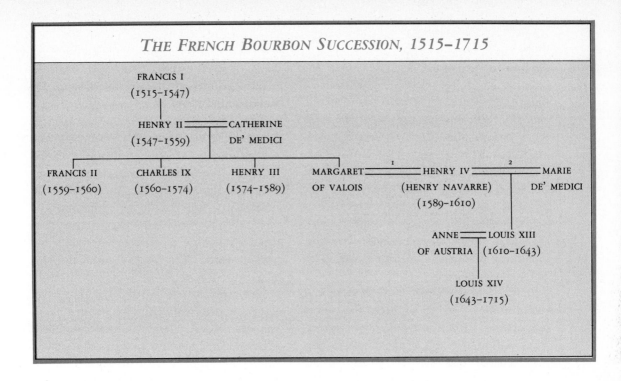

THE FRENCH BOURBON SUCCESSION, 1515–1715

FRANCIS I
(1515–1547)

HENRY II ——— CATHERINE
(1547–1559)   DE' MEDICI

FRANCIS II   CHARLES IX   HENRY III   MARGARET ——1—— HENRY IV ——2—— MARIE
(1559–1560)   (1560–1574)   (1574–1589)   OF VALOIS   (HENRY NAVARRE)   DE' MEDICI
                                                                    (1589–1610)

                                                   ANNE ——— LOUIS XIII
                                                   OF AUSTRIA (1610–1643)

                                                   LOUIS XIV
                                                   (1643–1715)

tic mother, Catherine de' Medici, who would support any party or position to maintain her influence. The intelligent and cultivated Henry III (1574–1589) divided his attention between debaucheries with his male lovers and frantic acts of repentance.

The French nobility took advantage of this monarchial weakness. In the second half of the sixteenth century, between two-fifths and half of the nobility at one time or another became Calvinist. Just as German princes in the Holy Roman Empire had adopted Lutheranism as a means of opposition to the emperor Charles V, so French nobles frequently adopted the "reformed religion" as a religious cloak for their independence. No one believed that peoples of different faiths could coexist peacefully within the same territory. The Reformation thus led to a resurgence of feudal disorder. Armed clashes between Catholic royalist lords and Calvinist antimonarchial lords occurred in many parts of France.

Among the upper classes the Catholic-Calvinist conflict was the surface issue, but the fundamental object of the struggle was power. Working-class crowds composed of skilled craftsmen and the poor wreaked terrible violence on people and property. Both Calvinists and Catholics believed that the others' books, services, and ministers polluted the community. Preachers incited violence, and ceremonies like baptisms, marriages, and funerals triggered it. Protestant pastors encouraged their followers to destroy statues and liturgical objects in Catholic churches. Catholic priests urged their flocks to shed the blood of the Calvinist heretics.

In 1561 in the Paris church of St.-Médard, a Protestant crowd cornered a baker guarding a box containing the consecrated Eucharistic bread. Taunting "Does your God of paste protect you now from the pains of death?"[10] the mob proceeded to kill the poor man. Calvinists believed that the Catholic emphasis on symbols in their ritual desecrated what was truly sacred and promoted the worship of images. In scores of attacks on Catholic churches religious statues were knocked down, stained-glass windows smashed, and sacred vestments, vessels, and Eucharistic elements defiled. In 1561, a Catholic crowd charged a group of just-released Protestant prisoners, killed them, and burned their bodies in the street. Hundreds of Huguenots, as French Calvinists were called, were tortured, had their tongues or throats slit, were maimed or murdered.

In the fourteenth and fifteenth centuries, crowd action – attacks on great nobles and rich prelates – had expressed economic grievances. Religious rioters of the sixteenth century believed that they could assume the power of public magistrates and rid the community of corruption. Municipal officials criticized the crowds' actions, but the participation of pastors and priests in these demonstrations lent riots a sort of legitimacy.[11]

A savage Catholic attack on Calvinists in Paris on August 24, 1572 (Saint Bartholomew's Day) followed the usual pattern. The occasion was a religious ceremony, the marriage of the king's sister Margaret of Valois to the Protestant Henry of Navarre. Among the many Calvinists present for the wedding festivies was the admiral de Coligny, head of one of the great noble families of France and leader of the Huguenot party. Coligny had recently replaced Catherine in influence over the young king Charles IX. When, the night before the wedding, the leader of the Catholic aristocracy, Henry of Guise, had Coligny murdered, rioting and slaughter followed. The Huguenot gentry in Paris were massacred, and religious violence spread to the provinces. Between August 25 and October 3, perhaps twelve thousand Huguenots perished at

Meaux, Lyons, Orléans, and Paris. The contradictory orders of the unstable Charles IX worsened the situation.

The Saint Bartholomew's Day massacre launched the War of the Three Henrys, a civil conflict among factions led by the Catholic Henry of Guise, the Protestant Henry of Navarre, and King Henry III, who succeeded the tubercular Charles IX in 1574. Although he remained Catholic, King Henry realized that the Catholic Guise group represented his greatest danger. The Guises wanted, through an alliance of Catholic nobles called the Holy League, not only to destroy Calvinism but also to replace Henry III as king with a member of the Guise family. Violence continued. France suffered fifteen more years of religious rioting and domestic anarchy. Agriculture in many areas was destroyed; commercial life declined severely; starvation and death haunted the land.

What ultimately saved France was a small group of Catholic moderates called *politiques* who believed that only the restoration of strong monarchy could reverse the trend toward collapse. No religious creed was worth the incessant disorder and destruction. Therefore the *politiques* supported religious toleration. The death of Catherine de' Medici, followed by the assassinations of Henry of Guise and King Henry III, paved the way for the accession of Henry of Navarre, who became Henry IV (1589–1610).

This glamorous prince, "who knew how to fight, to make love and to drink," as a contemporary remarked, wanted above all a strong and united France. He knew too that the majority of the French were Roman Catholics. Declaring "Paris is worth a mass," Henry knelt before the archbishop of Bourges and was received into the Roman Catholic church. Henry's willingness to sacrifice religious principles to political necessity saved France. The Edict of Nantes, which Henry published in 1598, granted to Huguenots liberty of conscience and liberty of worship in certain specified towns, such as La Rochelle. The reign of Henry IV and the Edict of Nantes prepared the way for French absolutism in the seventeenth century by helping to restore internal peace in France.

THE NETHERLANDS UNDER CHARLES V

In the last quarter of the sixteenth century, the political stability of England, the international prestige of Spain, and the moral influence of the Roman papacy all became mixed up with the religious crisis in the Low Countries. The Netherlands was the pivot around which European money, diplomacy, and war revolved. What began as a movement for the reformation of the church developed into a struggle for Dutch independence.

The emperor Charles V (1519-1556) had inherited the seventeen provinces that compose present-day Belgium and Holland (pages 638-639). Ideally situated for commerce between the Rhine and Scheldt rivers, the great towns of Bruges, Ghent, Brussels, Arras, and Amsterdam made their living by trade and industry. The French-speaking southern towns produced fine linens and woolens, while the wealth of the Dutch-speaking northern cities rested on fishing, shipping, and international banking. The city of Antwerp was the largest port and the greatest money market in Europe. In the cities of the Low Countries trade and commerce had produced a vibrant cosmopolitan atmosphere, which was well personified by the urbane Erasmus of Rotterdam.

Each of the seventeen provinces of the Netherlands possessed historic liberties: each was self-governing and enjoyed the right to make its own laws and collect its own taxes. Only the recognition of a common ruler in the person of the emperor Charles V united the provinces. Delegates from each province met together in the Estates General, but important decisions had to be referred back to each province for approval. In the middle of the sixteenth century, the seventeen provinces had a limited sense of federation.

In the Low Countries as elsewhere, corruption in the Roman church and the critical spirit of the Renaissance provoked pressure for reform. Lutheran tracts and Dutch translations of the Bible flooded the seventeen provinces in the 1520s and 1530s, attracting many people to Protestantism. Charles V's government responded with condemnation and mild repression. This policy was not particularly effective, however, because ideas circulated freely in the cosmopolitan atmosphere of the commercial centers. But Charles's personality checked the spread of Lutheranism. Charles had been born in Ghent and raised in the Netherlands; he was Flemish in language and culture. He identified with the Flemish and they with him.

In 1556, however, Charles V abdicated, dividing his territories between his brother Ferdinand, who received Austria and the Holy Roman Empire, and his son Philip, who inherited Spain, the Low Countries, and the Spanish possessions in America. Charles delivered his abdication speech before the Estates General at Brussels. The emperor was then fifty-five years old, white-haired, and so crippled in the legs that he had to lean for support on the young Prince William of Orange. According to one account:

His under lip, a Burgundian inheritance, as faithfully transmitted as the duchy and county, was heavy and hanging, the lower jaw protruding so far beyond the upper that it was impossible for him to bring together the few fragments of teeth which still remained, or to speak a whole sentence in an intelligible voice.[12]

Charles spoke in Flemish. His small, shy, and sepulchral son Philip responded in Spanish; he could speak neither French nor Flemish. The Netherlanders had always felt Charles one of themselves. They were never to forget that Philip was a Spaniard.

THE REVOLT OF THE NETHERLANDS (1566–1587)

By the 1560s, there was a strong, militant minority of Calvinists in most of the cities of the Netherlands. The seventeen provinces possessed a large middle-class population, and the "reformed religion," as a contemporary remarked, had a powerful appeal "to those who had grown rich by trade and were therefore ready for revolution."[13] Calvinism appealed to the middle classes because of its intellectual seriousness, moral gravity, and emphasis on any form of labor well done. It took deep root among the merchants and financiers in Amsterdam and the northern provinces. Working-class people were also converted, partly because their employers would hire only fellow Calvinists. Well-organized and with the backing of rich merchants, Calvinists quickly gained a wide following. Lutherans taught respect for the powers that be; the "reformed religion," however, tended to encourage opposition to "illegal" civil authorities.

In 1559, Philip II appointed his half-sister Margaret as regent of the Netherlands (1559–1567). A proud, energetic, and strong-willed woman who once had Ignatius Loyola as her confessor, Margaret pushed Philip's orders to wipe out Protestantism. She introduced the Inquisition. Her more immediate problem, however, was revenue to finance the government of the provinces. Charles V had steadily increased taxes in the Low Countries. When Margaret appealed to the Estates General, they claimed that the Low Countries were more heavily taxed than Spain. Nevertheless, Margaret raised taxes. In so doing, she quickly succeeded in uniting the opposition to the government's fiscal policy with the opposition to official repression of Calvinism.

In August 1566, fanatical Calvinists, primarily of the poorest classes, embarked upon a rampage of frightful destruction. As in France, Calvinist destruction in the Low Countries was incited by popular preaching, and attacks were aimed at religious images as symbols of false doctrines, not at people. The Cathedral of Notre Dame at Antwerp was the first target. Begun in 1124 and finished only in 1518, this church stood as a monument to the commercial prosperity of Flanders, the piety of the business classes, and the artistic genius of centuries. On six successive summer evenings, crowds swept through the nave. While the town harlots held tapers to the greatest concentration of art works in northern Europe, people armed with axes and sledgehammers smashed altars, statues, paintings, books, tombs, ecclesiastical vestments, missals, manuscripts, ornaments, stained-glass windows, and sculptures. Before the havoc was over, thirty more churches had been sacked and irreplaceable libraries burned. From Antwerp the destruction spread to Brussels and Ghent and north to the provinces of Holland and Zeeland.

From Madrid, Philip II sent twenty thousand Spanish troops under the duke of Alva to pacify the Low Countries. Alva interpreted

"pacification" to mean the ruthless extermination of religious and political dissidents. On top of the Inquisition he opened his own tribunal, soon called the Council of Blood. On March 3, 1568, fifteen hundred men were executed. Even Margaret was sickened and resigned her regency. Alva resolved the financial crisis by levying a 10 percent sales tax on every transaction, which in a commercial society caused widespread hardship and confusion.

For ten years, between 1568 and 1578, civil war raged in the Netherlands between Catholics and Protestants and between the seventeen provinces and Spain. A series of Spanish generals could not halt the fighting. In 1576, the seventeen provinces united under the leadership of Prince William of Orange, called "the Silent" because of his remarkable discretion. In 1578, Philip II sent his nephew Alexander Farnese, duke of Parma, to crush the revolt once and for all. A general with a superb sense of timing, an excellent knowledge of the geography of the Low Countries, and a perfect plan, Farnese arrived with an army of German mercenaries. Avoiding pitched battles, he fought by patient sieges. One by one the cities of the south fell — Maastricht, Tournai, Bruges, Ghent, and finally the financial capital of northern Europe, Antwerp. Calvinism was forbidden in these territories, and Protestants were compelled to convert or leave. The collapse of Antwerp marked the farthest extent of Spanish jurisdiction and the political division of the Netherlands.

The ten southern provinces, the Spanish Netherlands (the future Belgium), remained under the control of the Spanish Habsburgs. The seven northern provinces, led by Holland, formed the Union of Utrecht, and in 1581 declared their independence from Spain. Thus was born the United Provinces of the Netherlands (see Map 19.2).

Geography, language and sociopolitical structure differentiated the two countries. The northern provinces were ribboned with sluices and canals and therefore were highly defensible. Several times the Dutch had broken the dikes and flooded the countryside to halt the advancing Farnese. In the southern provinces the Ardennes mountains interrupt the otherwise flat terrain. The Dutch spoken in the north was akin to German, while the Flemish spoken in the south was close to French. In the north the commercial aristocracy possessed the predominant power; in the south the landed nobility had the greater influence. The north was Protestant; the south remained Catholic.

Philip II and Alexander Farnese did not accept this geographical division, and the struggle continued after 1581. The United Provinces repeatedly begged the Protestant Queen Elizabeth of England for assistance.

The crown on the head of Elizabeth I (pages 652–653) did not rest easily. She had steered a moderately Protestant course between the Puritans, who sought the total elimination of Roman Catholic elements in the English church, and the Roman Catholics, who wanted full restoration of the old religion. Elizabeth survived a massive uprising by the Catholic north in 1569–1570. She survived two serious plots against her life. In the 1570s, the presence in England of Mary, Queen of Scots, a Roman Catholic and the legal heir to the English throne, produced a very embarrassing situation. Mary was the rallying point of all opposition to Elizabeth, yet the English sovereign hesitated to set the terrible example of regicide by ordering Mary executed.

Elizabeth faced a grave dilemma. If she responded favorably to Dutch pleas for military support against the Spanish, she would antagonize Philip II. The Spanish king had the steady flow of silver from the Americas at his disposal, and Elizabeth, lacking such treasure, wanted to avoid war. But if she did not help the Protestant Netherlands and they were crushed by Farnese, the likelihood was that the Spanish would invade England.

Three developments forced Elizabeth's hand. First, the wars in the Low Countries — the chief market for English woolens — badly hurt the English economy. When wool was not exported, the Crown lost valuable customs revenues. Second, the murder of William the Silent in July 1584 eliminated not only a great Protestant leader but the chief military check on the Farnese advance. Third, the collapse of Antwerp appeared to signal a

Catholic sweep throughout the Netherlands. The next step, the English feared, would be a Spanish invasion of their island. For these reasons, Elizabeth pumped £250,000 and two thousand troops into the Protestant cause in the Low Countries between 1585 and 1587. Increasingly fearful of the plots of Mary, Queen of Scots, Elizabeth finally signed her death warrant. Mary was beheaded on February 18, 1587. Sometime between March 24 and 30, the news of Mary's death reached Philip II.

PHILIP II AND THE SPANISH ARMADA

Philip pondered the Dutch and English developments at the Escorial northwest of Madrid. Begun in 1563 and completed under the king's personal supervision in 1584, the Monastery of Saint Lawrence of the Escorial served as a monastery for Jeromite monks, a tomb for the king's Habsburg ancestors, and a royal palace for Philip and his family. The vast buildings resemble a gridiron, the instrument on which Saint Lawrence (d. 258) had supposedly been roasted alive. The royal apartments were in the center of the Italian Renaissance building complex. King Philip's tiny bedchamber possessed a concealed sliding window that opened directly onto the high altar of the monastery church so he could watch the services and pray along with the monks. In this somber atmosphere, surrounded by a community of monks and close to the bones of his ancestors, the Catholic ruler of Spain and of much of the globe passed his days.

Philip of Spain considered himself the international defender of Catholicism and the heir to the medieval imperial power. Hoping to keep England within the Catholic church when his wife Mary Tudor died, Philip had asked Elizabeth to marry him; she had em-

MAP 19.2 THE NETHERLANDS, 1578-1609
Although small in geographical size, the Netherlands held a strategic position in the religious struggles of the sixteenth century. Why?

phatically refused. Several popes had urged him to move against England. When Pope Sixtus V (1585–1590) heard of the death of the queen of Scots, he promised to pay Philip 1 million gold ducats the moment Spanish troops landed in England. Alexander Farnese had repeatedly warned that to subdue the Dutch, he would have to conquer England and cut off the source of Dutch support. Philip worried that the vast amounts of South American silver he was pouring into the conquest of the Netherlands seemed to be going down a bottomless pit. Two plans for an expedition were considered. Philip's naval adviser recommended that a fleet of 150 ships sail from Lisbon, attack the English navy in the Channel, and invade England. In Antwerp, Farnese urged Philip to assemble a collection of barges and troops in Flanders to stage a cross-Channel assault. With the "inevitable" support of English Catholics, Spain would achieve a great victory.

Philip compromised. He prepared a vast armada to sail from Lisbon to Flanders, fight off Elizabeth's navy *if* it attacked, rendezvous with Farnese, and escort his barges across the English Channel. The expedition's purpose was to transport the Flemish army.

On May 9, 1588, *la felicissima armada* – "the most fortunate fleet," as it was ironically called in official documents – sailed from Lisbon harbor on the last medieval crusade. The Spanish fleet of 130 vessels carried 123,790 cannon balls and perhaps 30,000 men, every one of whom had confessed his sins and received the Eucharist. An English fleet of about 150 ships met the Spanish in the Channel. It was composed of smaller, faster, more maneuverable ships, many of which had greater firing power. A combination of storms and squalls, spoiled food and rank water, inadequate Spanish ammunition, and, to a lesser extent, English fire ships that caused the Spanish to panic and scatter, gave England the victory. Many Spanish ships went to the bottom of the ocean; perhaps 65 managed to crawl home by way of the North Sea.

The battle in the Channel has frequently been described as one of the decisive battles in the history of the world. In fact, it had mixed consequences. Spain soon rebuilt its navy, and after 1588 the quality of the Spanish fleet improved. The destruction of the Armada did not halt the flow of silver from the New World. More silver reached Spain between 1588 and 1603 than in any other fifteen-year period. The war between England and Spain dragged on for years.

The defeat of the Spanish Armada was decisive, however, in the sense that it prevented Philip II from reimposing unity on western Europe by force. He did not conquer England, and Elizabeth continued her financial and military support of the Dutch. In the Netherlands, however, neither side gained significant territory. The borders of 1581 tended to become permanent. In 1609, Philip III of Spain (1598–1621) agreed to a truce, in effect recognizing the independence of the United Provinces.

THE THIRTY YEARS' WAR (1618–1648)

While Philip II dreamed of building a second armada and Henry IV began the reconstruction of France, the political-religious situation in central Europe deteriorated. An uneasy truce had prevailed in the Holy Roman Empire since the Peace of Augsburg of 1555 (page 642). The Augsburg settlement, in recognizing the independent power of the German princes, had destroyed the authority of the central government. The Habsburg ruler in Vienna enjoyed the title of emperor but had no power.

According to the Augsburg settlement, the faith of the prince determined the religion of his subjects. Later in the century, though, Catholics grew alarmed because Lutherans, in violation of the Peace of Augsburg, were steadily acquiring north German bishoprics. The spread of Calvinism further confused the issue. The Augsburg settlement had pertained only to Lutheranism and Catholicism, but Calvinists ignored it and converted several princes. Lutherans feared that the Augsburg principles would be totally undermined by

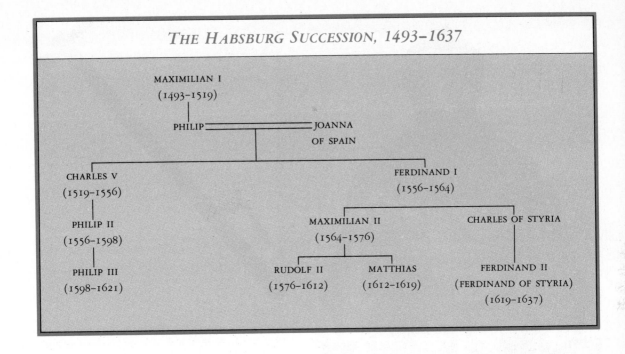

THE HABSBURG SUCCESSION, 1493–1637

MAXIMILIAN I
(1493–1519)

PHILIP ══════════ JOANNA
OF SPAIN

CHARLES V
(1519–1556)

FERDINAND I
(1556–1564)

PHILIP II
(1556–1598)

MAXIMILIAN II
(1564–1576)

CHARLES OF STYRIA

PHILIP III
(1598–1621)

RUDOLF II
(1576–1612)

MATTHIAS
(1612–1619)

FERDINAND II
(FERDINAND OF STYRIA)
(1619–1637)

Catholic and Calvinist gains. Also, the militantly active Jesuits had reconverted several Lutheran princes to Catholicism. In an increasingly tense situation, Lutheran princes formed the Protestant Union (1608) and Catholics retaliated with the Catholic League (1609). Each alliance was determined that the other should make no religious (that is, territorial) advance. The empire was composed of two armed camps.

Dynastic interests were also involved in the German situation. When Charles V abdicated in 1556, he had divided his possessions between his son Philip II and his brother Ferdinand I. This partition began the Austrian and Spanish branches of the Habsburg family. Ferdinand inherited the imperial title and the Habsburg lands in central Europe, including Austria, Bohemia, and Hungary. Ferdinand's

grandson, Matthias, had no direct heirs and promoted the candidacy of his fanatically Catholic cousin, Ferdinand of Styria. The Spanish Habsburgs strongly supported the goals of their Austrian relatives: the unity of the empire and the preservation of Catholicism within it.

In 1617, Ferdinand of Styria secured election as king of Bohemia, a title that gave him jurisdiction over Silesia and Moravia as well as Bohemia. The Bohemians were Czech and German in nationality, and Lutheran, Calvinist, Catholic, and Hussite in religion; all these faiths enjoyed a fair degree of religious freedom. When Ferdinand proceeded to close some Protestant churches, the heavily Protestant Estates of Bohemia protested. On May 23, 1618, Protestants hurled two of Ferdinand's officials from a castle window in

SIXTEENTH-CENTURY GERMAN BATTLE HAM-
MER   *Held in the hand with the leather thong se-*
cured around the wrist, a powerful blow from this
battle hammer could instantly crush a skull or smash
a rib cage. (Photo: Caroline Buckler)

SEVENTEENTH-CENTURY BATTLE ARMOR   *Ar-*
mor remained a symbol of the noble's high social status
and military profession, although armor gave much
less protection after the invention of gun powder. The
maker had a sense of humor. (Photo: Caroline
Buckler)

Prague. They fell seventy feet but survived: Catholics claimed that angels had caught them; Protestants said the officials fell on a heap of soft horse manure. Called "the defenestration of Prague," this event marked the beginning of the Thirty Years' War.

Historians traditionally divide the war into four phases. The first or Bohemian phase (1618–1625) was characterized by civil war in Bohemia between the Catholic League, led by Ferdinand, and the Protestant Union, headed by Prince Frederick of the Palatinate. The Bohemians fought for religious liberty and independence from Habsburg rule. In 1618, the Bohemian Estates deposed Ferdinand and gave the crown of Bohemia to Frederick, thus uniting the interests of German Protestants with those of the international enemies of the Habsburgs. Frederick wore his crown only a few months. In 1620, he was totally defeated by Catholic forces at the battle of the White Mountain. Ferdinand, who had recently been elected Holy Roman emperor as Ferdinand II, followed up his victories by wiping out Protestantism in Bohemia through forcible conversions and the activities of militant Jesuit missionaries. Within ten years, Bohemia was completely Catholic.

The second or Danish phase of the war (1625–1629) — so called because of the participation of King Christian IV of Denmark (1588–1648), the ineffective leader of the Protestant cause — witnessed additional Catholic victories. The Catholic imperial army led by Albert of Wallenstein scored smashing victories. It swept through Silesia, north through Schleswig and Jutland to the Baltic, and east into Pomerania. Wallenstein had made himself indispensable to the emperor Ferdinand, but he was an unscrupulous opportunist who used his vast riches to build an army loyal only to himself. The general

seemed interested more in carving out an empire for himself than in aiding the Catholic cause. He quarreled with the Catholic League, and soon the Catholic forces were badly divided. Religion was eclipsed as a basic issue of the war.

The year 1629 marked the peak of Habsburg power. The Jesuits persuaded the emperor to issue the Edict of Restitution, whereby all Catholic properties lost to Protestantism since 1552 were to be restored and only Catholics and Lutherans (*not* Calvinists, Hussites, or other sects) were to be allowed to practice their faiths. Ferdinand appeared to be embarked on a policy to unify the empire. When Wallenstein began ruthless enforcement of the edict, Protestants throughout Europe feared a complete collapse of the balance of power in north central Europe.

The third or Swedish phase of the war (1630–1635) began with the arrival in Germany of the Swedish king Gustavus Adolphus (1594–1632). The ablest administrator of his day and a devout Lutheran, Gustavus Adolphus intervened to support the oppressed Protestants within the empire and to assist his relatives, the exiled dukes of Mecklenburg. Cardinal Richelieu, the chief minister of King Louis XIII of France (1610–1643) subsidized the Swedes, hoping to weaken Habsburg power in Europe. In 1631, with a small but well-disciplined army equipped with superior muskets and warm uniforms, Gustavus Adolphus won a brilliant victory at Breitenfeld. Again in 1632, he was victorious at Lützen, although he was fatally wounded in the battle.

The participation of the Swedes in the Thirty Years' War proved decisive for the future of Protestantism and of later German history. When Gustavus Adolphus landed on German soil, he had already brought Denmark, Poland, Finland, and the smaller Baltic states under Swedish influence. The Swedish victories ended the Habsburg ambition of uniting all the German states under imperial authority.

The death of Gustavus Adolphus, followed by the defeat of the Swedes at the battle of Nördlingen in 1634, prompted the French to enter the war on the side of the Protestants. Thus began the French, or international, phase of the Thirty Years' War (1635-1648). For almost a century French foreign policy had been based on opposition to the Habsburgs, because a weak empire divided into scores of independent principalities enhanced France's international stature. In 1622, when the Dutch had resumed the war against Spain, the French had supported Holland. Now, in 1635, Cardinal Richelieu declared war on Spain and again sent financial and military assistance to the Swedes and the German Protestant princes. The war dragged on. French, Dutch, and Swedes, supported by Scots, Finns, and German mercenaries, burned, looted, and destroyed German agriculture and commerce. The Thirty Years' War lasted so long because neither side had the resources to win a quick, decisive victory. Finally, in October 1648, peace was achieved.

The treaties signed at Münster and Osnabrück, commonly called the Peace of Westphalia, mark a turning point in European political, religious, and social history. The treaties recognized the sovereign independent authority of the German princes. Each ruler could govern his particular territory and make war and peace as well. With power in the hands of more than three hundred princes, with no central government, courts, or means of controlling unruly rulers, the Holy Roman Empire as a real state was effectively destroyed (see Map 19.3).

The independence of the United Provinces of the Netherlands was acknowledged. The

MAP 19.3 EUROPE IN 1648 *Which country emerged from the Thirty Years War as the strongest European power? What dynastic house was that country's major rival in the early modern period?*

international stature of France and Sweden was also greatly improved by the Peace of Westphalia. The political divisions within the empire, the weak German frontiers, and the acquisition of the province of Alsace increased France's size and prestige. The treaties allowed France to intervene at will in German affairs. Sweden received a large cash indemnity and jurisdiction over German territories along the Baltic Sea. The powerful Swedish presence in northeastern Germany subsequently posed a major threat to the future kingdom of Brandenburg-Prussia. The treaties also denied the papacy the right to participate in German religious affairs – a restriction symbolizing the reduced role of the Roman Catholic church in European politics.

In religion the Westphalian treaties stipulated that the Augsburg agreement of 1555 should stand permanently. The sole modification was that Calvinism, along with Catholicism and Lutheranism, would become a legally permissible creed. In practice the north German states remained Protestant, the south German states Catholic. The war settled little. Both sides had wanted peace, and with remarkable illogic they fought for thirty years to get it.

GERMANY AFTER THE THIRTY YEARS' WAR

The Thirty Years' War was a disaster for the German economy and society, probably the most destructive event in German history before the twentieth century. Population losses were frightful. Perhaps one-third of the urban residents and two-fifths of the inhabitants of

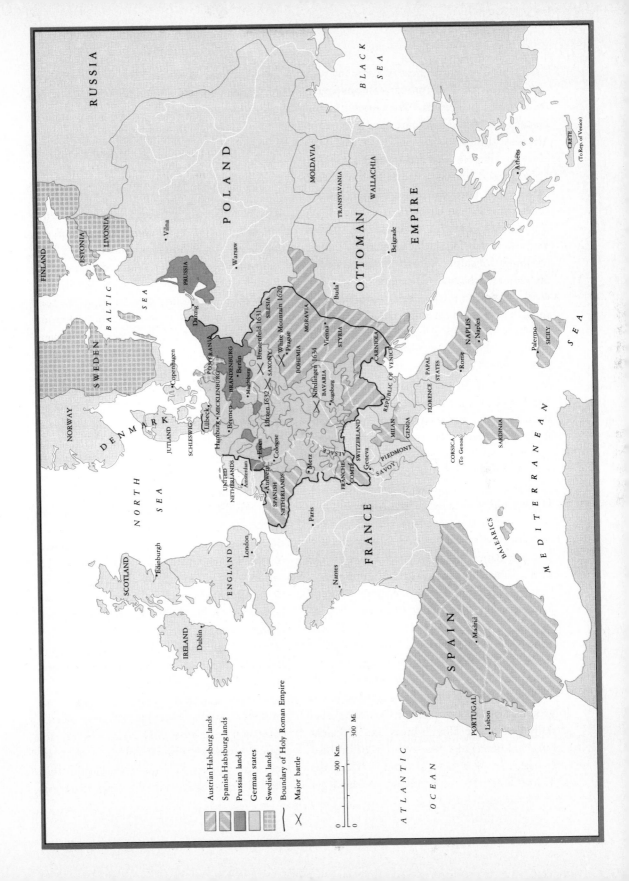

RUSSIA

BLACK SEA

POLAND

FINLAND

ESTONIA

LIVONIA

•Vilna

MOLDAVIA

WALLACHIA

TRANSYLVANIA

•Warsaw

•Belgrade

OTTOMAN EMPIRE

SWEDEN

BALTIC SEA

PRUSSIA

•Danzig

SILESIA

White Mountain 1620

MORAVIA

•Buda

Breitenfeld 1631

•Copenhagen

POMERANIA

MECKLENBURG

BRANDENBURG

•Berlin

SAXONY

Magdeburg

Prague•

BOHEMIA

Vienna•

STYRIA

CARNIOLA

Palermo

SICILY

CRETE
(To Rep. of Venice)

•Athens

NORWAY

DENMARK

Lübeck•

Hamburg•

JUTLAND

SCHLESWIG

Lützen 1632

Nördlingen 1634

BAVARIA

•Augsburg

REPUBLIC OF VENICE

NAPLES

•Naples

•Rome

PAPAL STATES

FLORENCE

MEDITERRANEAN SEA

NORTH SEA

Bremen•

Essen•

Cologne•

MILAN

GENOA

Geneva•

SAVOY

PIEDMONT

SARDINIA

CORSICA
(To Genoa)

SCOTLAND

•Edinburgh

UNITED NETHERLANDS

Amsterdam•

Antwerp•

SPANISH NETHERLANDS

ALSACE

FRANCHE COMTÉ

SWITZERLAND

•Metz

ENGLAND

London•

IRELAND

•Dublin

•Paris

FRANCE

Nantes•

BALEARICS

SPAIN

•Madrid

PORTUGAL

Lisbon•

ATLANTIC OCEAN

Austrian Habsburg lands

Spanish Habsburg lands

Prussian lands

German states

Swedish lands

Boundary of Holy Roman Empire

Major battle

300 Mi.

300 Km.

rural areas died. Entire areas of Germany were depopulated, partly by military actions, partly by disease – typhus, dysentery, bubonic plague, and syphilis accompanied the movements of armies – and partly by the thousands of refugees who fled to safer areas.

In the late sixteenth and early seventeenth centuries, all Europe experienced an economic crisis primarily caused by the influx of silver from South America. Because the Thirty Years' War was fought on German soil, these economic difficulties were badly aggravated in the empire. Scholars still cannot estimate the value of losses in agricultural land and livestock, in trade and commerce. The trade of southern cities like Augsburg, already hard hit by the shift in transportation routes from the Mediterranean to the Atlantic, was virtually destroyed by the fighting in the south. Meanwhile, towns like Lübeck, Hamburg, and Bremen in the north and Essen in the Ruhr actually prospered because of the many refugees they attracted. The destruction of land and foodstuffs, compounded by the flood of Spanish silver, brought on a severe price rise. During and after the war, inflation was worse in Germany than anywhere else in Europe.

Agricultural areas suffered catastrophically. The population decline caused a rise in the value of the labor, and owners of great estates had to pay more for agricultural workers. Farmers who needed only small amounts of capital to restore their lands started over again. Many small farmers, however, lacked the revenue to rework their holdings and had to become day laborers. Nobles and landlords bought up many small holdings and acquired great estates. In some parts of Germany, especially east of the Elbe in areas like Mecklenburg and Pomerania, peasants' loss of land led to the rise of a new serfdom.[14] Thus the Thirty Years' War contributed to the legal and economic decline of the largest segment of German society.

THE GREAT EUROPEAN WITCH-HUNT

The period of the religious wars witnessed a startling increase in the phenomenon of witch-hunting, whose prior history was long but sporadic. "A witch," according to Chief Justice Coke of England, "was a person who hath conference with the Devil to consult with him or to do some act." This definition by the highest legal authority in England demonstrates that educated people, as well as the ignorant, believed in witches. Belief in witches – individuals who could mysteriously injure other people, for instance by causing them to become blind or impotent, and who could harm animals, for example by preventing cows from giving milk – dates back to the dawn of time. For centuries tales had circulated about old women who made nocturnal travels on greased broomsticks to "sabbats," or assemblies of witches, where they participated in sexual orgies and feasted on the flesh of infants. In the popular imagination witches had definite characteristics: the vast majority were married women or widows between fifty and seventy years old, crippled or bent with age, with pockmarked skin; they often practiced midwifery or folk medicine, and most had sharp tongues and were quick to scold.

In the sixteenth century religious reformers' extreme notions of the devil's powers, and the insecurity created by the religious wars, contributed to the growth of belief in witches. The idea developed that witches made pacts with the devil in return

for the power to work mischief on their enemies. Since pacts with the devil meant the renunciation of God, witchcraft was considered heresy, and all religions persecuted it.

Fear of witches took a terrible toll of innocent lives in parts of Europe. In southwestern Germany 3,229 witches were executed between 1561 and 1670, most by burning. The communities of the Swiss Confederation tried 8,888 persons between 1470 and 1700 and executed 5,417 of them as witches. In all the centuries before 1500 witches in England had been suspected of causing perhaps "three deaths, a broken leg, several destructive storms and some bewitched genitals." Yet between 1559 and 1736 witches were thought to have caused thousands of deaths, and in that period almost 1,000 witches were executed in England.[15]

Historians and anthropologists have offered a variety of explanations for the great European witch-hunt. Some scholars maintain that charges of witchcraft were a means of accounting for inexplicable misfortunes. Just as the English in the fifteenth century had blamed their military failures in France on Joan of Arc's sorcery, so in the seventeenth century the English Royal College of Physicians attributed undiagnosable illnesses to witchcraft. Some scholars hold that in small communities, which typically insisted on strict social conformity, charges of witchcraft were a means of attacking and eliminating the nonconformist; witches, in other words, served the collective need for scapegoats. The evidence of witches' trials, some writers suggest, shows that women were not accused because they harmed or threatened their neighbors; rather, their communities believed such women worshiped the devil, engaged in wild sexual activities with him, and ate infants. Other scholars argue the exact opposite:

that people were tried and executed as witches because their neighbors feared their evil powers. Finally, there is the theory that the unbridled sexuality of which witches were accused was a psychological projection on the part of their accusers, resulting from Christianity's repression of sexuality. The reasons for the persecution of witches probably varied from place to place. Perhaps witches, symbolizing unacceptable ideas or practices, were "victims of society's constant pressure towards intellectual conformity."[16]

SEXISM, RACISM, AND SKEPTICISM

The age of religious wars revealed extreme and violent contrasts. It was a deeply religious period in which men fought passionately for their beliefs; seventy percent of the books printed dealt with religious subjects. Yet the times saw the beginnings of religious skepticism. Europeans explored new continents, partly with the missionary aim of Christianizing the peoples they encountered. Yet the Spanish, Portuguese, Dutch, and English proceeded to enslave the Indians and blacks they encountered. While Europeans indulged in gross sensuality, the social status of women declined. Sexism, racism, and skepticism had all originated in ancient times. But late in the sixteenth century they began to take on their familiar modern forms.

THE STATUS OF WOMEN

The decades between 1560 and 1648 witnessed another decline in the status of women in European society. The Reformation did not help women. The early reformers had urged study of the Bible as the means of improving human conduct. Scriptural study, however, tended to revive Saint Paul's notion that women are the source of sin and vice in the world. Also, the violence and upheaval of the religious wars was followed by a period of reaction and retrenchment. While early humanists such as Erasmus and Zwingli had allowed divorce on grounds of insanity and extreme cruelty, by 1600 all faiths firmly opposed divorce on any grounds. In England, for example, only an act of Parliament could dissolve a marriage.

Although private opinions and public laws relating to the social position of women varied widely, the weight of evidence from the sixteenth and seventeenth centuries indicates that women were considered to be decidedly inferior beings. Their social value rested on their ability to produce heirs. A few women, of course, had power and influence. Margaret of Austria, Charles V's aunt, and Louise of Savoy, Francis I's mother – they cannot be identified apart from their male relatives – conducted the diplomatic negotiations that in 1529 led to the Peace of Cambrai and the end of the second phase of the Habsburg-Valois wars. Jeanne d'Albret, the mother of Henry of Navarre (later Henry IV of France), legalized Calvinism in her domain and aided its spread through France; she was known as "the Saint of the Reform." Likewise, Mary Tudor reestablished Catholicism in England. All these women, however, were of royal blood.

The great majority of women were treated either as grown-up children to be teasingly indulged or as hopelessly irrational. The attitude of John Knox, the Calvinist reformer of the Scottish church, was not atypical: "Nature doth paint them forth to be weak, frail, impatient, feeble and foolish, and experience hath declared them to be unconstant, variable, cruel, and void of the spirit of council and regiment." (Knox had in mind the Catholic

VERONESE: MARS AND VENUS UNITED BY LOVE Taking a theme from classical mythology, the Venetian painter Veronese celebrates in clothing, architecture, and landscape the luxurious wealth of the aristocracy (painted ca 1580). The lush and curvaceous Venus and the muscular and powerfully built Mars suggest the anticipated pleasures of sexual activity and the frank sensuality of the age. (Metropolitan Museum of Art, New York, Kennedy Fund, 1910)

Mary, Queen of Scots, whom he had good political reasons for fearing.) In 1595, the professors at Wittenberg University solemnly debated whether or not women are human beings. Humanists repeated the ancient story of woman the temptress and cause of sin in the world.

Artists' drawings of plump, voluptuous women and massive, muscular men reveal the contemporary standards of physical beauty. It was a sensual age that gloried in the delights of the flesh. Some people, such as the humanist-poet Aretino, found sexual satisfaction with both sexes. Reformers and public officials simultaneously condemned and condoned sexual "sins." The oldest profession had many practitioners, and when in 1566 Pope Pius IV expelled all the prostitutes from Rome, so many people left and the city suffered such a loss of revenue that in less than a month the pope was forced to rescind the order. Scholars debated Saint Augustine's notion that whores serve a useful social function by preventing worse sins. Prostitution was common, because desperate poverty forced women and young men into it. The general public took it for granted. Consequently, civil authorities in both Catholic and Protestant countries licensed houses of public prostitution. These establishments were intended for the convenience of single men, and some Protestant cities, such as Geneva and Zurich, installed officials in the brothels with the ex-

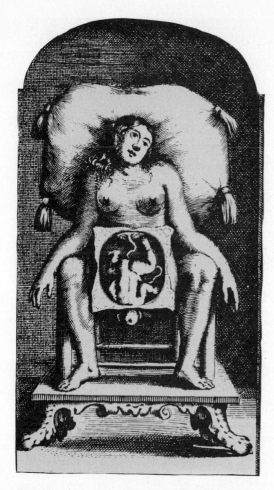

WOMAN IN LABOR *The production of male heirs was women's major social responsibility. Long into modern times a sitting or squatting position for the delivery of babies was common, because it allowed the mother to push. The calm and wistful look on the mother's face suggests a remarkably easy delivery; it is the artist's misconception of the process. (Photo: Caroline Buckler)*

press purpose of preventing married men from patronizing them.

Marriage for all social classes remained a serious business, entered into primarily to advance the economic interests of the parties. There are some remarkable success stories. Elizabeth Hardwick, the orphaned daughter of an obscure English country squire, made four careful marriages, each of which brought her more property and carried her higher up the social ladder. She managed her estates, amounting to more than a hundred thousand acres, with a degree of business sense rare in any age. The two great mansions she built, Chatsworth and Hardwick, stand today as monuments to her acumen. As countess of Shrewsbury, "Bess of Hardwick" so thoroughly enjoyed the trust of Queen Elizabeth that Elizabeth appointed her jailer of Mary, Queen of Scots. Having established several aristocratic dynasties, the countess of Shrewsbury died in 1608, past her eightieth year, one of the richest people in England.[17]

While the Catholic church held up the ideal of celibacy and the religious life as the highest form of Christian life, Protestantism exalted the dignity of marriage. Luther insisted that absolute celibacy was impossible. In the Middle Ages, and later in Catholic countries, the religious life provided a career option for women who did not choose or could not afford to marry. For Protestant women, marriage became the only professional possibility. Protestant marriages took on the form of a contract, whereby each partner promised the other support, understanding, and sharing of material goods. Within marriage many women certainly controlled their own destinies, but there was no question of social or legal equality: wives were subordinate to their husbands.

If some nuns in the later Middle Ages

lacked a religious vocation, and if some religious houses witnessed moral laxness and financial mismanagement, nevertheless convents provided the only scope for the literary, artistic, and administrative talents of unmarried women. In abolishing the religious houses, Protestantism threw out the baby with the bathwater. Marriage became virtually the only occupation for Protestant women, which helps to explain why Anglicans, Calvinists, and Lutherans established communities of religious women in the eighteenth and nineteenth centuries.

Many sixteenth-century reformers, including Luther, Erasmus, and several popes, believed polygamy less of an evil than divorce. (By polygamy they meant a man having several wives at the same time, not a woman having more than one husband.) Theologians found scriptural justification for their position on polygamy. Except among the Anabaptists, however, polygamy was rarely practiced.

If the partners to a monogamous marriage found themselves unsuited, there was virtually no socially acceptable way out. In Catholic countries as well as Protestant ones, a woman could not secure a divorce on grounds of extreme cruelty, desertion, adultery, or complete incompatibility. Women's social and legal position became steadily more confined, and, apart from the upper classes, that position would not change much before the nineteenth century. Death alone dissolved a legitimate marriage. When a spouse died, the great majority of survivors remarried.[18]

ORIGINS OF NORTH AMERICAN RACISM: THE AFRICAN SLAVE TRADE

The Age of Discovery opened up vast new continents for European exploration and exploitation. Once across the Atlantic, the major problem European settlers faced was a shortage of labor. As early as 1495, the Spanish solved the problem by enslaving the native Indians. In the sixteenth and seventeenth centuries, the Portuguese, the Dutch, and the English followed suit.

Unaccustomed to any form of manual labor, and certainly to panning gold for more than twelve hours a day in the broiling sun, the Indians died "like fish in a bucket," as one Spanish settler reported.[19] In 1515, a Spanish missionary, Bartholomé de Las Casas (1474-1566), who had seen the evils of Indian slavery, urged Emperor Charles V to end Indian slavery in his American dominions. Las Casas recommended the importation of blacks from Africa, both because church law did not strictly forbid black slavery and because blacks could better survive under South American conditions. The emperor agreed, and in 1518 the African slave trade began.

Several European nations participated in the African slave trade. Spain brought the first slaves to Brazil; by 1600, 44,000 were being imported annually. Between 1619 and 1623, the Dutch West India Company, with the full support of the government of the United Provinces, transported 15,430 Africans to Brazil. Only in the late seventeenth century, with the chartering of the Royal African Company, did the English get involved. Thereafter, large numbers of African blacks poured into the North American colonies. In 1790, there were 757,181 Negroes in a total United States population of 3,929,625. When the first census was taken in Brazil in 1798, Negroes numbered about 2 million in a total population of 3.25 million.

Almost all peoples in the world have engaged in slavery at some time in their histories. Since ancient times, victors in battle had enslaved conquered peoples. European slavers found slavery widespread in Africa when they arrived in the sixteenth and seventeenth centuries, and they had no difficulty finding Africans willing to sell their captured tribal enemies for cloth, jewelry, guns and whiskey. In seeking slaves in Africa, Europeans encouraged more slave hunting.

Almost as soon as the institution of black slavery was introduced into the New World, controversy arose about it. Las Casas and others soon became disgusted with the Spanish treatment of blacks, and criticized black slavery on the same grounds as Indian slavery: it was inhumane. By the late seventeenth century, abolitionist movements existed in both South and North America.

European settlers brought to the New World the racial attitudes they had absorbed in Europe. North American attitudes derive basically from England. On the eve of the Age of Discovery, the English were overwhelmingly a rural people. Tough, sober, accustomed to unending hard work relieved by few physical comforts, a quarrelsome but rarely violent people, they accepted life with stoical patience. The age was cruel, and the English were not compassionate. The public execution of criminals and the stoning of wretches tied up in the village stocks were major occasions for public entertainment. When a good workman fell from a ladder and was permanently disabled, his community was more concerned that he would become a public charge than about his misfortune.[20]

Early Christian writers in the fourth and fifth centuries had identified blackness with sin and corruption. This notion had become deep-rooted over the centuries. Thus in 1550, when the first black Africans appeared on the streets of London, the concept of blackness was already loaded with emotional meaning. Black meant "deeply stained with dirt, soiled,

THE SPANISH IN AMERICA   The Spanish used barbaric methods to frighten and subdue the Indians. Based on the eyewitness accounts of the Spanish missionary Bartholomew de las Casas, illustrations of Spanish cruelties satisfied Europeans' curiosity about the New World, gratified appetites for bizarre tortures, and promoted anti-Spanish and anti-Catholic feelings. (Photo: Caroline Buckler)

dirty, foul … malignant, having dark or deadly purposes."[21] White, on the other hand, connoted purity and virginity, goodness and cleanliness. Physical beauty to the English meant an almost alabaster white skin tinged with pink. The Negro's black skin, "disfigured" facial features, and curled hair seemed the exact opposite of the physical ideal.

Art and literature had already given English people some acquaintance with "Ethiopians," as black Africans had been called since Roman times. In the sixteenth and seventeenth centuries, the English were still extremely curious about Africans' lives and customs, and slavers' accounts were extraordinarily popular. Travel literature depicted Africans as savages because of their eating habits, morals, clothing, and social customs; as barbarians because of their language and methods of war; and as heathens because they were not Christian. English people saw similarities between apes and Africans; thus, the terms "bestial" and "beastly" were frequently applied to Africans. Africans were believed to possess a potent sexuality and to be extremely lustful. One seventeenth-century observer considered Africans "very lustful and impudent, .. (for a Negroes hiding his members, their extraordinary greatness) is a token of their lust." African women were considered sexually aggressive and "possessed of a temper hot and lascivious."[22]

The English used the heathenism of the Africans as a justification for enslaving them.

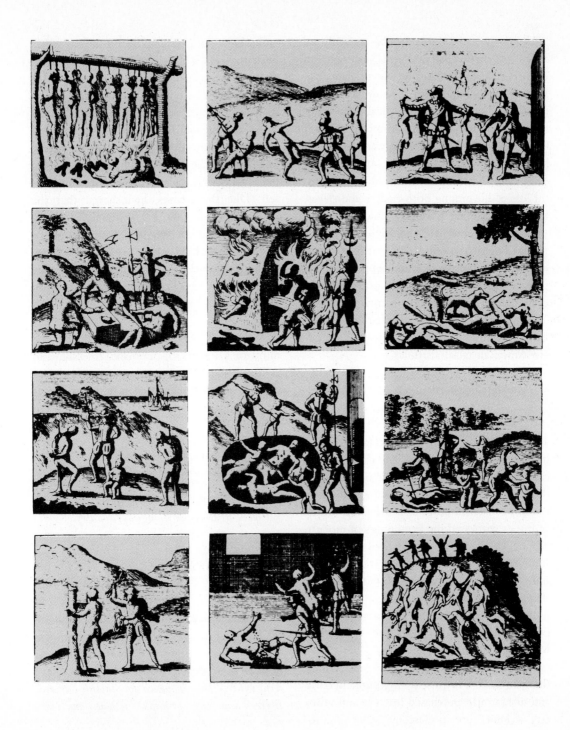

Africans appeared to suit the agricultural needs of the underpopulated continent of North America. Unlike the North American Indians, who were armed, however primitively, and had the psychological support of their tribes, the Africans, stripped of their languages and tribal cultures, were powerless in the New World. Moreover, in spite of the dangers of the trade in Africa and the frightful loss of life among both traders and slaves, the profits in slavery were enormous.

In the seventeenth and eighteenth centuries, English colonists in North America continued to believe in these supposed social characteristics of Africans. Gradually they became part of the American mental furniture. The myths of black savagery, barbarism, and lechery became the classic stereotypes of modern American racial attitudes.

THE ORIGIN OF MODERN SKEPTICISM: MICHEL DE MONTAIGNE

The decades of religious fanaticism, bringing in their wake death, famine, and civil anarchy, caused both Catholics and Protestants to doubt that any one faith contained absolute truth. The late sixteenth and early seventeenth centuries witnessed the beginnings of modern skepticism. Skepticism is a school of thought founded on doubt that total certainty or definitive knowledge is ever attainable. The skeptic is cautious and critical, and suspends judgment. Perhaps the finest representative of early modern skepticism is the Frenchman Michel de Montaigne (1533–1592).

Montaigne came from a bourgeois family that had made a fortune selling salted herring and in 1477 had purchased the title and property of Montaigne in Gascony. Montaigne received a classical education before studying law and securing a judicial appointment in 1554. Although a member of the nobility, in

embarking on a judicial career he identified with the new nobility of the robe. He condemned the ancient nobility of the sword for being more concerned with war and sports than with the cultivation of the mind.

At the age of thirty-eight, Montaigne resigned his judicial post, retired to his estate, and devoted the rest of his life to study, contemplation, and the effort to understand himself. Like the Greeks, he believed that the object of life was to "know thyself," for self-knowledge teaches men and women how to live in accordance with nature and God. Montaigne developed a new literary genre, the essay – from the French *essayer,* meaning to test or try – to express his thoughts and ideas.

Montaigne's *Essays* provide insight into the mind of a remarkably humane, tolerant, and civilized man. He was a humanist; he loved the Greek and Roman writers and was always eager to learn from them. In his essay "On Solitude," he quoted the Roman poet Horace:

Reason and sense remove anxiety,
Not villas that look out upon the sea

Ambition, avarice, irresolution, fear, and lust do not leave us when we change our country.

Some said to Socrates that a certain man had grown no better by his travels. "I should think not," he said; "he took himself along with him. . . ."
We should have wife, children, goods, and above all health, if we can; but we must not bind ourselves to them so strongly that our happiness depends on them. We must reserve a back shop all our own, entirely free, in which to establish our real liberty and our principal retreat and solitude. . . .[23]

From the ancient authors, especially the Roman stoic Seneca, Montaigne acquired a sense of calm, inner peace, and patience. The ancient authors also inculcated in him a tolerance and broad-mindedness. Montaigne had grown up during the French civil wars, perhaps the worst kind of war. Religious ideology had set family against family, even brother against brother. He wrote:

In this controversy . . . France is at present agitated by civil wars, the best and soundest side is undoubtedly that which maintains both the old religion and the old government of the country. However, among the good men who follow that side (for I speak not of those who use it as a pretext either to wreak their private vengeances, or to supply their avarice, or to pursue the favor of princes; but of those who follow it out of true zeal toward their religion and a holy concern for maintaining the peace and the status of their fatherland) — of these, I say, we see many whom passion drives outside the bounds of reason, and makes them sometimes adopt unjust, violent, and even reckless courses. . . .[24]

Although he remained a Catholic, Montaigne possessed a detachment, an independence, an openness of mind, and a willingness to look at all sides of a question. As he wrote, "I listen with attention to the judgment of all men; but so far as I can remember, I have followed none but my own. Though I set little value upon my own opinion, I set no more on the opinions of others."

In a violent and cruel age, Montaigne was a gentle and sensitive man. In his famous essay "On Cruelty," he said:

Among other vices, I cruelly hate cruelty, both by nature and by judgment, as the extreme of all vices. . . .

I live in a time when we abound in incredible examples of this vice, through the license of our civil wars; and we see in the ancient histories nothing more extreme than what we experience of this every day. But that has not reconciled me to it at all.[25]

In the book-lined tower where Montaigne passed his days, he became a deeply learned man. Yet he was not ignorant of the world of affairs, and he criticized scholars and bookworms who ignored the life around them. Montaigne's essay "On Cannibals" reflects the impact of overseas discoveries on Europeans' consciousness. His tolerant mind rejected the notion that one culture is superior to another:

I long had a man in my house that lived ten or twelve years in the New World, discovered in these latter days, and in that part of it where Villegaignon landed [Brazil]. . . .

I find that there is nothing barbarous and savage in [that] nation, by anything that I can gather, excepting, that every one gives the title of barbarism to everything that is not in use in his own country. As, indeed, we have no other level of truth and reason, than the example and idea of the opinions and customs of the place wherein we live: there is always the perfect religion, there is perfect government, there the most exact and accomplished usage of all things. . . .[26]

In his belief in the nobility of human beings in the state of nature, uncorrupted by organized society, and in his cosmopolitan attitude toward different civilizations, Montaigne anticipated many eighteenth-century thinkers.

The thought of Michel de Montaigne marks a sharp break with the past. Faith and religious certainty had characterized the intellectual attitudes of Western society for a millennium. Montaigne's rejection of any kind of dogmatism, his secularism, and his skepticism thus represent a basic change. In his own time, and throughout the seventeenth century, few would have agreed with him. The publication of his ideas, however, anticipated a basic shift in attitudes. Montaigne inaugurated an era of doubt. "Wonder," he said, "is the foundation of all philosophy, research is the means of all learning, and ignorance is the end."[27]

ELIZABETHAN AND JACOBEAN LITERATURE

The age of the religious wars and European expansion also experienced an extraordinary degree of intellectual ferment. In addition to the development of the essay as a distinct literary genre, the late sixteenth and early seventeenth centuries fostered remarkable creativity in other branches of literature. England, especially, in the latter part of Elizabeth's reign and the first years of her successor James I (1603–1625), witnessed unparalleled brilliance. The terms *Elizabethan* and *Jacobean* (referring to the reign of James) are used to designate the English music, poetry, prose, and drama of this period. The poetry of Sir Philip Sidney (1554–1586), such as *Astrophel and Stella*, strongly influenced later poetic writing. *The Faerie Queene* of Edmund Spenser (1552–1599) endures as one of the greatest moral epics in any language. The rare poetic beauty of the plays of Christopher Marlowe (1564–1593), such as *Tamburlaine* and *The Jew of Malta*, paved the way for the work of Shakespeare. Above all, the immortal dramas of Shakespeare and the stately prose of the Authorized or King James Bible mark the Elizabethan and Jacobean periods as the golden age of English literature.

William Shakespeare (1564–1616), the son of a successful glove manufacturer who rose to the highest municipal office in the Warwickshire town of Stratford-on-Avon, chose a career on the London stage. By 1592 he had gained recognition as an actor and playwright.

Between 1599 and 1603 Shakespeare performed in the Lord Chamberlain's Company and became co-owner of the Globe Theater, which after 1603 presented his plays.

Shakespeare's genius lies in the originality of his characterizations, the diversity of his plots, his understanding of human psychology, and his unexcelled gift for language. Shakespeare was a Renaissance man in his deep appreciation for classical culture, individualism, and humanism. Such plays as *Julius Caesar, Pericles,* and *Antony and Cleopatra* deal with classical subjects and figures. Several of his comedies have Italian Renaissance settings. The nine history plays, including *Richard II, Richard III,* and *Henry IV,* enjoyed the greatest popularity among Shakespeare's contemporaries. Written during the decade after the defeat of the Spanish Armada, the history plays express English national consciousness; lines such as these from *Richard II* reflect this sense of national greatness with unparalleled eloquence:

This royal Throne of Kings, this scepter'd Isle,
This earth of Majesty, this seat of Mars,
This other Eden, demi-paradise,
This fortress built by Nature for herself,
Against infection and the hand of war:
This happy breed of men, this little world,
This precious stone, set in the silver sea,
Which serves it in the office of a wall,
Or as a moat defensive to a house,
Against the envy of less happier Lands,
This blessed plot, this earth, this Realm, this
     England...

Shakespeare's later plays, above all the tragedies *Hamlet, Othello,* and *Macbeth,* explore an enormous range of human problems and are capable of an almost infinite variety of interpretations. *Othello,* which the nineteenth-century historian Thomas Macaulay called "perhaps the greatest work in the world,"

A ROYAL PICNIC   *The English court imitated the Italian Renaissance devotion to nature. (See Bellini's* Feast of the Gods — *in first color section.) In this pastoral atmosphere suggestive of classical mythology, Queen Elizabeth interrupts the day's hunt for a picnic in the forest. The meal seems to consist of fowl, bread, wine, and perhaps pastries. (The Huntington Library, San Marino, California)*

portrays an honorable man destroyed by a flaw in his own character and the satanic evil of his supposed friend Iago. *Macbeth's* central theme is exorbitant ambition. Shakespeare analyzes the psychology of sin in the figures of Macbeth and Lady Macbeth whose mutual love under the pressure of ambition leads to their destruction. The central figure in *Hamlet,* a play suffused with individuality, wrestles with moral problems connected with revenge and with man's relationship to life and death. The soliloquy in which Hamlet debates suicide is perhaps the most widely quoted passage in English literature:

To be, or not to be: that is the question:
Whether 'tis nobler in the mind to suffer
The slings and arrows of outrageous fortune,
Or to take arms against a sea of troubles,
And by opposing end them? To die: to sleep;
No more; and by a sleep to say we end
The heart-ache and the thousand natural shocks
That flesh is heir to, 'tis a consummation
Devoutly to be wish'd.

Hamlet's sad cry, "There is nothing either good or bad but thinking makes it so," expresses the anguish and uncertainty of modern man. *Hamlet* has always enjoyed great popularity, because in his many-faceted personality people have seen an aspect of themselves.

Shakespeare's dynamic language bespeaks his extreme sensitivity to the sounds and

meanings of words. Perhaps no phrase better summarizes the reason for his immortality than this line, slightly modified, from *Antony and Cleopatra:* "Age cannot wither [him], nor custom stale/[his] infinite variety."

The other great masterpiece of the Jacobean period was the *Authorized Bible.* At a theological conference in 1604, a group of Puritans urged James I to support a new translation of the Bible. The king in turn assigned the task to a committee of scholars, who published their efforts in 1611. Based on the best scriptural research of the time and divided into chapters and verses, the Authorized Version is actually a revision of earlier Bibles more than an original work. Yet it provides a superb expression of the mature English vernacular in the early seventeenth century. Thus, Psalm 37:

Fret not thy selfe because of evill doers, neither bee thou envious against the workers of iniquitie.
For they shall soone be cut downe like the grasse; and wither as the greene herbe.
Trust in the Lord, and do good, so shalt thou dwell in the land, and verely thou shalt be fed.
Delight thy selfe also in the Lord; and he shall give thee the desires of thine heart.
Commit thy way unto the Lord: trust also in him, and he shall bring it to passe.
And he shall bring forth thy righteousness as the light, and thy judgement as the noone day.

The Authorized Version, so-called because it was produced under royal sponsorship – it had no official ecclesiastical endorsement – represented the Anglican and Puritan desire to encourage lay people to read the Scriptures. It quickly achieved great popularity and displaced all earlier versions. British settlers carried this Bible to the North American colonies, where it became known as the *King*

James Bible. For centuries the *King James Bible* has had a profound influence on the language and lives of English-speaking peoples.

———◆———

In the sixteenth and seventeenth centuries, Europeans explored and for the first time gained access to large parts of the globe. European peoples had the intellectual curiosity, the driving ambition, and the scientific technology to attempt feats that were as difficult and expensive then as is going to the moon in our own time. Exploration and exploitation contributed to a more sophisticated standard of living, in the form of spices and Asian luxury goods, and to a terrible international inflation resulting from the influx of South American silver and gold. Governments, the upper classes, and the peasantry were badly hurt by the inflation. Meanwhile the middle class of bankers, shippers, financiers, and manufacturers prospered for much of the seventeenth century.

European expansion and colonization took place against a background of religious conflict and budding national consciousness. The seventeenth century was by no means a secular period. Although the medieval religious framework had broken down, people still thought largely in religious terms. Europeans explained what they did politically and economically in terms of religious doctrine. Religious ideology served as a justification for a variety of goals: the French nobles' opposition to the Crown, the Dutch struggle for political and economic independence from Spain. In Germany religious pluralism and foreign ambitions added to political difficulties. After 1648, the divisions between Protestant and Catholic tended to become permanent. Religious skepticism and racial attitudes were harbingers of developments to come.

NOTES

1. Quoted by C. M. Cipolla, *Guns, Sails, and Empires: Technological Innovation and the Early Phases of European Expansion, 1400–1700,* Minerva Press, New York, 1965, pp. 115–116.

2. Quoted by S. E. Morison, *Admiral of the Ocean Sea: A Life of Christopher Columbus,* Little, Brown, Boston, 1946, p. 154.

3. Cipolla, pp. 90–131.

4. J. H. Parry, *The Age of Reconnaissance,* Mentor Books, New York, 1963, chaps. 3 and 5.

5. Quoted by Cipolla, p. 132.

6. Quoted by F. H. Littell, *The Macmillan Atlas History of Christianity,* Macmillan, New York, 1976, p. 75.

7. Quoted by Cipolla, p. 133.

8. Quoted by J. Hale, "War and Public Opinion in the Fifteenth and Sixteenth Centuries," *Past and Present* 22 (July 1962):29.

9. See ibid., pp. 18–32.

10. Quoted by N. Z. Davis, "The Rites of Violence: Religious Riot in Sixteenth Century France," *Past and Present* 59 (May 1973):59.

11. See ibid., pp. 51–91.

12. Quoted by J. L. Motley, *The Rise of the Dutch Republic,* David McKay, Philadelphia, 1898, 1.109.

13. Quoted by P. Smith, *The Age of the Reformation,* Henry Holt, New York, 1951, p. 248.

14. H. Kamen, "The Economic and Social Consequences of the Thirty Years' War," *Past and Present* 39 (April 1968):44–61.

15. Norman Cohn, *Europe's Inner Demons: An Enquiry Inspired by the Great Witch-Hunt,* Basic Books, New York, 1975, pp. 253–254; Keith Thomas, *Religion and the Decline of Magic,* Charles Scribner's Sons, New York, 1971, pp. 450–455.

16. See Keith Thomas, op. cit., pp. 435–446; Cohn, op. cit., pp. 258–263.

17. See D. Durant, *Bess of Hardwick: Portrait of an Elizabethan Dynast,* Weidenfeld & Nicolson, London, 1977.

18. S. M. Wyntjes, "Women in the Reformation Era," in *Becoming Visible: Women in European History,* ed. R. Bridenthal and C. Koonz, Houghton Mifflin, Boston, 1977, p. 187.

19. Quoted by D. P. Mannix, *Black Cargoes: A History of the Atlantic Slave Trade,* Viking, New York, 1968, p. 5.

20. W. Notestein, *The English People on the Eve of Colonization,* Harper & Brothers, New York, 1954, p. 14.

21. Quoted by W. D. Jordan, *The White Man's Burden: Historical Origins of Racism in the United States,* Oxford University Press, New York, 1974, p. 6.

22. Ibid., p. 19.

23. Quoted by D. M. Frame, trans., *The Complete Works of Montaigne,* Stanford University Press, Stanford, Calif., 1958, pp. 175–176.

24. Ibid., p. 177.

25. Ibid., p. 306.

26. Quoted by C. Cotton, trans., *The Essays of Michel de Montaigne,* A. L. Burt, New York, 1893, pp. 207, 210.

27. Ibid., p. 523.

SUGGESTED READING

Perhaps the best starting point for the study of European society in the age of exploration is J. H. Parry, *The Age of Reconnaissance* (1963), which treats the causes and consequences of the voyages of discovery. Parry's splendidly illustrated *The Discovery of South America* (1979) examines Europeans' reactions to the maritime discoveries and treats the entire concept of new *discoveries.* The urbane studies of C. M. Cipolla present fascinating material on technological and sociological developments written in a lucid style: *Guns, Sails, and Empires: Technological Innovation and the Early Phases of European Expansion, 1400–1700* (1965); *Clocks and Culture, 1300–1700* (1967); *Cristofano and the Plague: A Study in the History of Public Health in the Age of*

Galileo (1973); and *Public Health and the Medical Profession in the Renaissance* (1976). S. E. Morison, *Admiral of the Ocean Sea: A Life of Christopher Columbus* (1946), is the standard biography of the great discoverer.

For the religious wars, in addition to the references in the Suggested Reading for Chapter 14 and in the Notes to this chapter, see J. H. M. Salmon, *Society in Crisis: France in the Sixteenth Century* (1975), which traces the fate of French institutions during the civil wars. A. N. Galpern, *The Religions of the People in Sixteenth-Century Champagne* (1976), is a useful case study in religious anthropology, and William A. Christian, Jr., *Local Religion in Sixteenth Century Spain* (1981) traces the attitudes and practices of ordinary people.

A beautifully illustrated introduction to Holland is K. H. D. Kaley, *The Dutch in the Seventeenth Century* (1972). The best comprehensive treatment of the religious strife and civil wars in the Low Countries remains that of J. L. Motley, *The Rise of the Dutch Republic,* 3 vols. (1898). The student who reads French will find a wealth of material in H. Hauser, *La prépondérance espagnole, 1559–1660* (1948).

Of the many biographies of Elizabeth of England, Wallace T. MacCaffrey, *Queen Elizabeth and the Making of Policy, 1572–1588* (1981), examines the problems posed by the Reformation and how Elizabeth solved them. J. E. Neale, *Queen Elizabeth I* (1957), remains valuable, and L. B. Smith, *The Elizabethan Epic* (1966), is a splendid evocation of the age of Shakespeare with Elizabeth at the center.

Nineteenth- and early twentieth-century historians described the defeat of the Spanish Armada as a great victory for Protestantism, democracy, and capitalism, which those scholars tended to link together. Recent historians have treated the event in terms of its contemporary significance. G. Mattingly, *The Armada* (1959), combines superb readability with the highest scholarly standards: this is history at its best. M. Lewis, *The Spanish Armada* (1972), tells a good story from the English perspective; David Howarth, *The Voyage of the Armada: the Spanish Story* (1981), presents the other side in an exciting narrative. C. V. Wedgwood, *The*

Thirty Years' War (1961), must be qualified in light of recent research on the social and economic effects of the war, but it is still a good (if detailed) starting point on a difficult period. A variety of opinions on the causes and results of the war are given in T. K. Rabb's anthology, *The Thirty Years' War* (1981). The following articles, all of which appear in the scholarly journal *Past and Present,* provide some of the latest important findings: H. Kamen, "The Economic and Social Consequences of the Thirty Years' War," no. 39 (1968); J. Hale, "War and Public Opinion in the Fifteenth and Sixteenth Centuries," no. 22 (1962); J. V. Polišenský, "The Thirty Years' War and the Crises and Revolutions of Sixteenth Century Europe," no. 39 (1968); and for the overall significance of Sweden, M. Roberts, "Queen Christina and the General Crisis of the Seventeenth Century," no. 22 (1962).

As background to the intellectual changes instigated by the Reformation, D. C. Wilcox, ed., *In Search of God and Self: Renaissance and Reformation Thought* (1975), contains perceptive articles, and T. Ashton, ed., *Crisis in Europe, 1560–1660* (1967), is fundamental. On witches and witchcraft, see, in addition to the titles by Norman Cohn and Keith Thomas in the Notes, Jeffrey B. Russell, *Witchcraft in the Middle Ages* (1976); Montague Summers, *The History of Witchcraft and Demonology* (1973); and H. R. Trevor-Roper, *The European Witch-Craze of the Sixteenth and Seventeenth Centuries* (1967), a brilliant collection of essays. Among the fascinating studies on North American racism, the interested student should consult W. D. Jordan, *The White Man's Burden: Historical Origins of Racism in the United States* (1974), and D. P. Mannix in collaboration with M. Cowley, *Black Cargoes: A History of the Atlantic Slave Trade* (1968), a hideously fascinating account. South American conditions may be contrasted in C. R. Boxer, *Four Centuries of Portuguese Expansion* (1969). The leading authority on Montaigne is D. M. Frame. See his *Montaigne's Discovery of Man* (1955), and his translation, *The Complete Works of Montaigne* (1958).

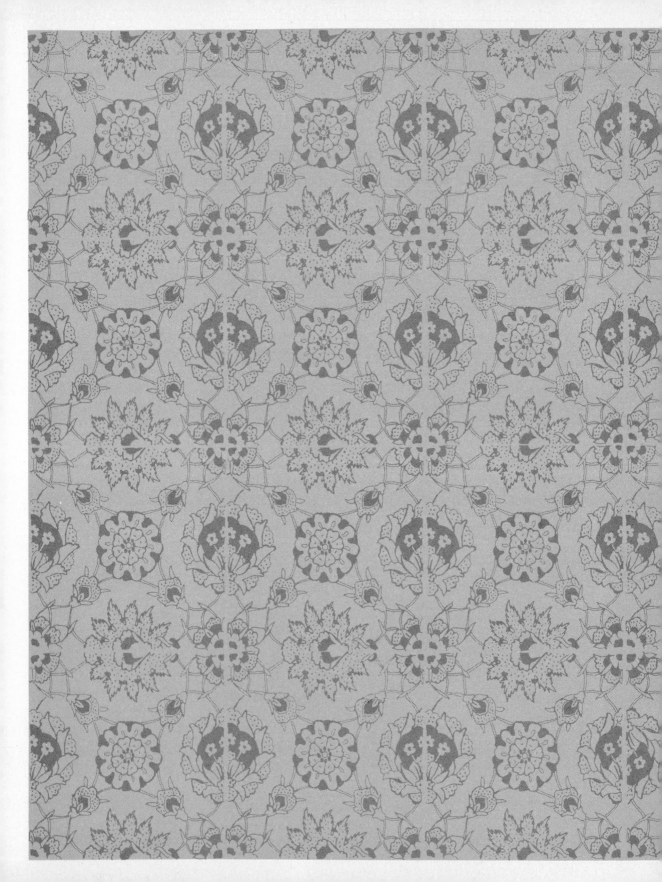

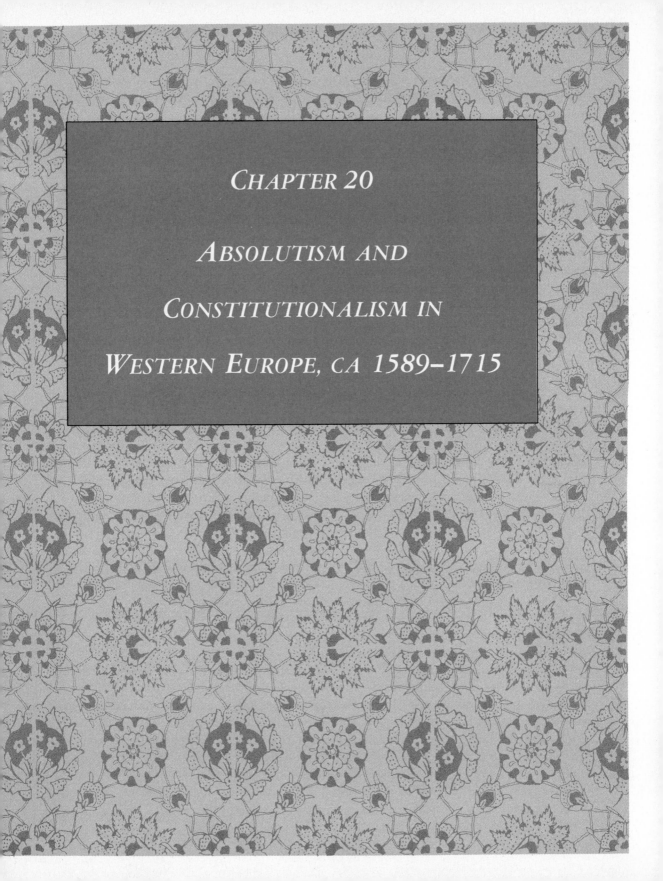

CHAPTER 20

ABSOLUTISM AND

CONSTITUTIONALISM IN

WESTERN EUROPE, CA 1589–1715

THE SEVENTEENTH CENTURY was a period of revolutionary transformation. Some of its most profound developments were political: the seventeenth century has been called the century when government became modern. The sixteenth century had witnessed the emergence of the nation-state. The long series of wars fought in the name of religion – but actually contests between royal authority and aristocratic power – brought social dislocation and agricultural and commercial disaster. Increasingly, strong national monarchy seemed the only solution. Spanish and French monarchs gained control of the major competing institution in their domains, the Roman Catholic church. In England and some of the German principalities, where rulers could not completely regulate the church, they set up national churches. In the German Empire the Treaty of Westphalia placed territorial sovereignty in the hands of the princes. The kings of France, England, and Spain claimed the basic loyalty of their subjects. Monarchs made laws, to which everyone within their borders was subject. These powers added up to something close to sovereignty.

A nation may be termed sovereign when it possesses a monopoly over the instruments of justice and the use of force within clearly defined boundaries. In a sovereign state no system of courts, such as ecclesiastical tribunals, competes with state courts in the dispensation of justice; and private armies, such as those of feudal lords, present no threat to royal authority because the national army is stronger. Royal law touches all persons within the country. Sovereignty had been evolving in the late sixteenth century. Seventeenth-century governments now faced the problem of *which* authority within the state would possess sovereignty – the Crown or the nobility.

In the period between roughly 1589 and 1715, two basic patterns of government emerged in Europe: absolute monarchy and the constitutional state. Almost all subsequent governments have been modeled on one or the other of these patterns. How were these forms of government "modern"? How did they differ from the feudal and dynastic monarchies of earlier centuries? Which countries best represent the new patterns of political organization? This chapter will be concerned with these political questions.

ABSOLUTISM

In the absolutist state, sovereignty is embodied in the person of the ruler. The ruler is not restrained by any legal authority. Absolute kings claimed to rule by divine right, meaning that they were responsible to God alone. (Medieval kings had governed "by the grace of God," but invariably they acknowledged that they had to respect and obey the law.) Absolute monarchs in the seventeenth and eighteenth centuries were not checked by national assemblies. Estates general and parliaments met at the wish and in response to the needs of kings. Because these meetings provided opportunities for opposition to the Crown to coalesce, absolute monarchs eventually stopped summoning them.

Absolute rulers effectively controlled all competing jurisdictions, all institutions or interest groups within their territories. They regulated religious sects. They abolished the liberties (privileges) long held by certain areas, groups, or provinces. Absolute kings also secured mastery over the one class that historically had posed the greatest threat to monarchy, the nobility. Medieval governments had been able to do none of these things. They had been restrained by the church, by the feudal nobility, and by their own financial limitations.

In some respects the key to the power and success of absolute monarchs lay in how they solved their financial problems. The solution was the creation of new state bureaucracies, which directed the economic life of the country in the interests of the king, raising ever higher taxes or devising other methods of raising revenue.

Bureaucracies were composed of career officials, appointed by and solely accountable to the king. The backgrounds of these civil servants varied. Absolute monarchs sometimes drew on the middle class, as in France, or utilized members of the nobility, as in Spain and eastern Europe. Where there was no middle class or an insignificant one, as in Austria, Prussia, Spain, and Russia, the government of the absolutist state consisted of an interlocking elite of monarchy, aristocracy, and bureaucracy.

Royal agents in medieval kingdoms had used their public offices and positions to benefit themselves and their families. In England, for example, Crown servants from Thomas Becket to Thomas Wolsey had treated their high offices as their personal private property, and reaped considerable profit from the positions they held. The most striking difference between seventeenth-century bureaucracies and their medieval predecessors was that seventeenth-century civil servants served the state as represented by the king. Bureaucrats recognized that the offices they held were public, or state, positions. The state paid them salaries to handle revenues that belonged to the Crown, and they were not supposed to use their official positions for private gain. Bureaucrats gradually came to distinguish between public duties and private property.

Absolute monarchs also maintained permanent standing armies. Medieval armies had been raised by feudal lords for particular wars or campaigns, after which the troops were disbanded. In the seventeenth century, mon-archs alone recruited and maintained armies – in peacetime as well as during war. Kings deployed their troops both inside and outside the country in the interests of the monarchy. Armies became basic features of absolutist, and modern, states. Absolute rulers also invented new methods of compulsion. They concerned themselves with the private lives of potentially troublesome subjects, often through the use of secret police.

Thus rule of absolute monarchs was not all-embracing because they lacked the financial and military resources and the technology to make it so. Thus the absolutist state was not the same as a totalitarian state. Totalitarianism is a twentieth-century phenomenon; it seeks to direct all facets of a state's culture – art, education, religion, the economy, and politics – in the interests of the state. By definition totalitarian rule is *total* regulation. By twentieth-century standards, the ambitions of an absolute monarch were quite limited: he sought the exaltation of himself as the embodiment of the state. When King Louis XIV of France declared, "L'état, c'est moi!" ("I am the state!"), he meant that he personally was the incarnation of France. Yet the absolutist state did foreshadow recent totalitarian regimes in two fundamental respects: in the glorification of the state over all other aspects of the national culture, and in the use of war and an expansionist foreign policy to divert attention from domestic ills.

All of this is best illustrated by the experience of France, aptly known as the model of absolute monarchy.

THE FOUNDATIONS OF ABSOLUTISM IN FRANCE: HENRY IV AND SULLY

The ingenious Huguenot-turned-Catholic, Henry IV (pages 684–685), ended the French religious wars with the Edict of Nantes. The first of the Bourbon dynasty, and probably the first French ruler since Louis IX in the thirteenth century genuinely to care about the French people, Henry IV and his great minister Sully (1560–1641) laid the foundations of later French absolutism. Henry denied influence on the royal council to the nobility, which had harassed the countryside for half a century. Maintaining that "if we are without compassion for the people, they must succumb and we all perish with them," Henry also lowered the severe taxes on the overburdened peasantry.

Sully proved himself a financial genius. He not only reduced the crushing royal debt but began to build up the treasury. He levied an annual tax, the *paulette,* on people who had purchased financial and judicial offices and had consequently been exempt from royal taxation. One of the first French officials to appreciate the significance of overseas trade, Sully subsidized the Company for Trade with the Indies. He started a countrywide highway system and even dreamed of an international organization for the maintenance of peace.

In twelve short years Henry IV and Sully restored public order in France and laid the foundations for economic prosperity. By late-sixteenth-century standards, Henry IV's government was both progressive and promising. His murder in 1610 by a crazed fanatic plunged the country into civil war and threatened to undo his work.

THE CORNERSTONE OF FRENCH ABSOLUTISM: LOUIS XIII AND RICHELIEU

After the death of Henry IV, the queen-regent Marie de' Medici led the government for the child-king Louis XIII (1610–1643), but in fact feudal nobles and princes of the blood dominated the political scene. In 1624, Marie de' Medici secured the appointment of Armand Jean du Plessis – Cardinal Richelieu (1585–

1642) – to the council of ministers. It was a remarkable appointment. The next year Richelieu became president of the council, and after 1628 he was first minister of the French crown and the actual ruler of France. Richelieu used his strong influence over King Louis XIII to exalt the French monarchy as the embodiment of the French state. One of the greatest servants of the French state, Richelieu set in place the cornerstone of French absolutism, and his work served as the basis for France's cultural domination of Europe in the later seventeenth century.

Richelieu's policy was the total subordination of all groups and institutions to the French monarchy. The French nobility, with its selfish and independent interests, had long constituted the foremost threat to the centralizing goals of the Crown and to a strong national state. Therefore, Richelieu broke the power of the nobility. He leveled castles, long the symbol of feudal independence. He crushed aristocratic conspiracies with quick executions. For example, when the duke de Montmorency, the first peer of France and the godson of Henry IV, became involved in a revolt in 1632, he was summarily put to death. Richelieu abolished the great medieval military dignities that had exalted the prestige and local power of some great nobles. He banned dueling. He prevented the great lords from sitting in the king's council.

The constructive genius of Cardinal Richelieu is best reflected in the administrative system he established. He extended the use of royal commissioners called intendants. France was divided into thirty-two *généralités* (districts), in each of which a royal intendant had complete responsibility for justice, police, and finances. The intendants were authorized "to decide, order and execute all that they see good to do." Usually members of the upper middle class or minor nobility, the intendants were appointed directly by the monarch, to whom they were solely responsible. They had complete power in their districts and were to use that power for two related purposes: to enforce royal orders in the *généralités* of their jurisdiction and to weaken the power and influence of the regional nobility. The system of government by intendants derived from Philip Augustus's baillis and seneschals, and ultimately from Charlemagne's *missi dominici*. As the intendants' power grew during Richelieu's administration, so did the power of the centralized state.

Although Richelieu succeeded in building a rational and centralized political machine in the intendant system, he was not the effective financial administrator Sully had been. France lacked a sound system of taxation, a method of raising sufficient revenue to meet the needs of the state. Richelieu reverted to the old device of selling offices. He increased the number of sinecures, tax exemptions, and benefices that were purchasable and inheritable. In 1624, this device brought in almost 40 percent of royal revenues.

The rising cost of foreign and domestic policies led to the auctioning of tax farms, the system whereby a man bought the right to collect taxes. Tax farmers kept a very large part of the receipts they collected. The sale of offices and this antiquated system of tax collection were improvisations that promoted confusion and corruption. Even worse, state offices, once purchased, were passed on to heirs, which meant that a family that held a state office was eternally exempt from taxation. Richelieu's inadequate and temporary solutions created grave financial problems for the future.

The cardinal perceived that Protestantism all too often served as a cloak for the political intrigues of ambitious lords. When the Huguenots revolted in 1625, under the duke de

Rohan, Richelieu personally supervised the siege of their walled city, La Rochelle, and forced it to surrender. Thereafter, fortified places of security were abolished. Huguenots were allowed to practice their faith, but they no longer possessed armed strongholds or the means to be an independent party in the state. Another aristocratic prop was knocked down.

French foreign policy under Richelieu was aimed at the destruction of the fence of Habsburg territories that surrounded France. Consequently, Richelieu supported the Habsburgs' enemies. In 1631, he signed a treaty with the Lutheran king Gustavus Adolphus promising French support against the Catholic Habsburgs in what has been called the Swedish phase of the Thirty Years' War (page 693). French influence became an important factor in the political future of the German empire. Richelieu added Alsace in the east (1639) and Arras in the north (1640) to French territory.

Richelieu's efforts at centralization extended even to literature. In 1635 he gave official recognition to a group of philologists who were interested in grammar and rhetoric. Thus was born the French Academy. With Richelieu's encouragement, the Academy began the preparation of a *dictionary* to standardize the French language; it was completed in 1694. The French Academy survives as a prestigious learned society, whose membership has been broadened to include people outside the field of literature.

Richelieu personified the increasingly secular spirit of the seventeenth century. Although a bishop of the Roman Catholic church, he gave his first loyalty to the French state. Although a Roman Catholic cardinal, he gave strong support to the Protestant Lutherans of Germany. The portrait of Richelieu by Philippe de Champaigne – with its penetrating eyes, expression of haughty and imperturbable cynicism, and dramatic sweep of rich red robes – reveals the authority, grandeur, and power the cardinal wanted to convey as first minister of France. Just before Richelieu died in 1642, worn out with work and ulcers, the curé of St.-Eustache asked him to forgive his enemies. Richelieu replied, characteristically, that he had no enemies save those of the king and the state.

Richelieu had persuaded Louis XIII to appoint his protegé Jules Mazarin (1602-1661) as his successor. An Italian diplomat of great charm, Mazarin served on the Council of State under Richelieu, acquiring considerable political experience. He became a cardinal in 1641 and a French citizen in 1643. When Louis XIII followed Richelieu to the grave in 1643 and a regency headed by Queen Anne of Austria governed for the child-king Louis XIV, Mazarin became the dominant power in the government. He continued the antifeudal and centralizing policies of Richelieu, but his attempts to increase royal revenues led to the civil wars known as the Fronde.

The word *fronde* means slingshot or catapult, and a *frondeur* was originally a street urchin who threw mud at the passing carriages of the rich. The term came to be used for anyone who opposed the policies of the government. Richelieu had stirred up the bitter resentment of the aristocracy, who felt its constitutional status and ancient privileges threatened. He also bequeathed to the Crown a staggering debt, and when Mazarin tried to impose financial reforms the monarchy incurred the enmity of the middle classes. Both groups plotted against Anne and Mazarin. Most historians see the Fronde as the last serious effort by the French nobility to oppose the monarchy by force. When in 1648 Mazarin proposed new methods for raising income, bitter civil war ensued between the monarchy on the one side and the frondeurs

(the nobility and the upper-middle classes) on the other. Riots and public turmoil wracked Paris and the nation. The violence continued intermittently for almost twelve years. Factional disputes among the nobles led to their ultimate defeat.

The conflicts of the Fronde had two significant results for the future: a badly disruptive effect on the French economy and a traumatic impact on the young Louis XIV. The king and his mother were frequently threatened and sometimes treated as prisoners by aristocratic factions. On one occasion a mob broke into the royal bedchamber to make sure the king was actually there; it succeeded in giving him a bad fright. Louis never forgot such humiliations. The period of the Fronde formed the cornerstone of his political education and of his unalterable conviction that the sole alternative to anarchy was absolute monarchy.

THE ABSOLUTE MONARCHY OF LOUIS XIV

According to the court theologian Bossuet, the clergy at the coronation of Louis XIV in Reims Cathedral asked God to cause the splendors of the French court to fill all who beheld it with awe. God subsequently granted that prayer. In the reign of Louis XIV (1643-1715), the longest in European history, the French monarchy reached the peak of absolutist development. In the magnificence of his court, in his absolute power, in the brilliance of the culture over which he presided and which permeated all of Europe, and in his remarkably long life, Louis XIV dominated his age. No wonder scholars have characterized the second half of the seventeenth century as "The Grand Century," "The Age of Magnificence," and, echoing the eighteenth-century philosopher Voltaire, "The Age of Louis XIV."

Who was this phenomenon of whom it was said that when Louis sneezed, all Europe caught cold? Born in 1638, king at the age of five, he entered into personal, or independent, rule in 1661. One of his first recorded remarks reveals the astonishing sense of self that was to awe French people and foreigners alike. Taken as a child to his father's deathbed, he identified himself as "Louis Quatorze" ("Louis the fourteenth").

In old age Louis claimed that he had grown up learning very little, and many historians have agreed. He knew little Latin and only the rudiments of arithmetic, and was thus by Renaissance standards not well educated. On the other hand, he learned to speak Italian and Spanish fluently; he knew some French history, and more European geography than the ambassadors accredited to his court. He imbibed the devout Catholicism of his mother Anne of Austria, and throughout his long life scrupulously performed his religious duties. Religion, Anne, and Mazarin all taught Louis that God had established kings as His rulers on earth. The royal coronation consecrated him to God's service, and he was certain – to use Shakespeare's phrase – that there was a divinity that doth hedge a king. Although kings were a race apart, they could not do as they pleased: they must obey God's laws and rule for the good of the people.

Louis's education was more practical than formal. Under Mazarin's instruction he studied state papers as they arrived, and he attended council meetings and sessions at which French ambassadors were dispatched abroad and foreign ambassadors received. He learned by direct experience and gained professional training in the work of government. Above all, the misery he suffered during the Fronde gave Louis an eternal distrust of the nobility and a profound sense of his own isolation. Accordingly, silence, caution, and secrecy be-

came political tools for the achievement of his goals. His characteristic answer to requests of all kinds became the enigmatic "Je verrai" ("I shall see").

Louis grew up with an absolute sense of his royal dignity. Tall and distinguished in appearance, he was inclined to fatness because of the gargantuan meals in which he indulged. Seduced by one of his mother's maids when he was sixteen, the king matured into a highly sensual man easily aroused by an attractive female face and figure. It is to his credit, however, that neither his wife, Queen Maria Theresa, whom he married as the result of a diplomatic agreement with Spain, nor his mistresses ever possessed any political influence. Extraordinarily selfish, Louis doted on flattery, which he interpreted as glory.

Whatever his negative qualities, Louis XIV worked extremely hard and succeeded in being "every moment and every inch a king." Because he so thoroughly relished the role of king, historians have had difficulty distinguishing the man from the monarch. Louis XIV was a consummate actor, and his "terrifying majesty" awed all who saw him.

The reign of Louis XIV witnessed great innovations in style but few in substance; Louis extended and intensified earlier practices and trends. The most significant development was his acquisition of absolute control over the French nobility. Indeed, it is often said that Louis achieved the complete "domestication" of the nobility.

Louis XIV turned the royal court into a fixed institution. In the past the king of France and the royal court had traveled constantly, visiting the king's properties, the great noblemen, and his *bonnes villes* or good towns. Since the time of Louis IX, or even Charlemagne, rulers had traveled to maintain order in distant parts of the realm, to impress humbler subjects with the royal dignity and

AERIAL VIEW OF VERSAILLES *Awe-inspiring, monumental, and over a quarter of a mile long, Versailles is the supreme example of classical baroque architecture in the service of absolute monarchy. The vast formal gardens with their geometric regularity pro-* *vided the outdoor setting for Louis XIV's festivities, while the three avenues radiating from the palace symbolize the king as source of all power. (French Government Tourist Office)*

magnificence, and in so doing to bind the country together through loyalty to the king. Since the early Middle Ages, the king's court had consisted of his family, trusted advisers and councilors, a few favorites, and servants. Except for the very highest officials of the state, members of the council had changed constantly.

Louis XIV installed the court at Versailles, a small town ten miles from Paris. He required all the great nobility of France, at the peril of social, political, and sometimes economic disaster, to come live at Versailles for at least part of the year. Today, Versailles stands as the best surviving museum of a vanished society on earth. In the seventeenth century, it became a model of rational order, the center of France and thus the center of Western civilization, the perfect symbol of the king's absolute power.

Louis XIII had begun Versailles as a hunting lodge, a retreat from a queen he did not

HALL OF MIRRORS AT VERSAILLES *This long and magnificently impressive room takes up much of the central block of Versailles. The hundreds of mirrors, which give the illusion of width, reflected the court spectacles and the king's glory. The splendor of* *this hall and many other adjacent palace rooms was a far cry, however, from the cramped conditions that many nobles were forced to live with at the royal court. (French Government Tourist Office)*

like. His son's architects, Le Nôtre and Le Vau, turned what Saint-Simon called "the most dismal and thankless of sights" into a veritable paradise. Wings were added to the original building to make the palace U-shaped. Everywhere at Versailles the viewer has a sense of grandeur, vastness, and incredible elegance. Enormous state rooms became display galleries for inlaid tables, Italian marble statuary, Gobelin tapestries woven at the state factory in Paris, silver ewers, and beauti-

ful (if uncomfortable) furniture. If genius means attention to detail, Louis XIV and his designers had it: the décor was perfected down to the last doorknob and keyhole. In the gigantic Hall of Mirrors, which was later to reflect so much of German as well as French history, hundreds of candles illuminated the domed ceiling, where allegorical paintings celebrated the king's victories.

The Ambassador's Staircase is of brilliantly colored marble, with part of the railing gold-plated. The staircase is dominated by a great bust of the king, which when completed so overwhelmed a courtier that he exclaimed to the sculptor Bernini, "Don't do anything more to it, it's so good I'm afraid you might spoil it." The statue, like the staircase – and the entire palace – succeeded from the start in its purpose: it awed.

The formal, carefully ordered, and perfectly landscaped gardens at Versailles express at a glance the spirit of the age of Louis XIV. Every tree, every bush, every foot of grass, every fountain, pool, and piece of statuary within three miles is perfectly laid out. The vista is of the world made rational and absolutely controlled. Nature itself was subdued to enhance the greatness of the king.

Under the vast terrace stands one of the great architectural splendors of France, the Orangerie. Designed to house the king's twelve hundred potted palms and orange trees, the Orangerie is a huge vaulted space, so large that when it was completed in 1686 several operas could be performed there simultaneously without inconvenience. The Siamese ambassador is reputed to have said that the magnificence of Louis XIV must indeed be great, since he had raised so superb a palace simply for his orange trees.

Against this background of magnificent splendor, as the great aristocrat Saint-Simon describes, Louis XIV

reduced everyone to subjection, and brought to his court those very persons he cared least about. Whoever was old enough to serve did not dare demur. It was still another device to ruin the nobles by accustoming them to equality and forcing them to mingle with everyone indiscriminately....

... To keep everyone assiduous and attentive, the King personally named the guests for each festivity, each stroll through Versailles, and each trip. These were his rewards and punishments. He

knew there was little else he could distribute to keep everyone in line. He substituted idle rewards for real ones and these operated through jealousy, the petty preferences he showed many times a day, and his artfulness in showing them. No one was more ingenious than him in nourishing the hopes and satisfactions to which these petty preferences and distinctions gave birth....

... Upon rising, at bedtime, during meals, in his apartments, in the gardens of Versailles, everywhere the courtiers had a right to follow, he would glance right and left to see who was there; he saw and noted everyone; he missed no one, even those who were hoping they would not be seen.... For the most distinguished persons, it was a demerit not to put in a regular appearance at court. It was just as bad for those of lesser rank to come but rarely, and certain disgrace for those who never, or almost never, came....

... Louis XIV took great pains to inform himself on what was happening everywhere, in public places, private homes, and even on the international scene.... Spies and informers of all kinds were numberless....

... But the King's most vicious method of securing information was opening letters....[1]

Through ritual and ceremony the king turned the proud and ancient nobility into a pack of trained seals. He destroyed their ancient right to advise and counsel the monarch. Operas, fetes, and balls occupied the nobles' time and attention. They become solely instruments of the king's pleasure. Louis XIV may have had limited native intelligence, but through painstaking attention to detail and precisely calculated showmanship, he emasculated the major threat to his absolute power. He separated power from grandeur: the nobility enjoyed the grandeur in which they lived; the king alone enjoyed the power.

The art and architecture of Versailles served as fundamental tools of state policy under

Louis XIV. Architecture was the device the king used to overawe his subjects and foreign visitors. Versailles was seen as a reflection of French genius. Thus the Russian czar Peter the Great imitated Versailles in the construction of his palace, Peterhof, as did the Prussian emperor Frederick the Great in his palace at Potsdam outside Berlin.

As in architecture, so too in language. Beginning in the reign of Louis XIV, French became the language of polite society and the vehicle of diplomatic exchange. French also gradually replaced Latin as the language of international scholarship and learning. The wish of other kings to ape the courtly style of Louis XIV and the imitation of French intellectuals and artists spread the French language all over Europe. The royal courts of Sweden, Russia, Poland, and Germany all spoke French. In the eighteenth century, the great Russian aristocrats were more fluent in French than in Russian. In England the First Hanoverian king, George I, spoke French but no English. France inspired a cosmopolitan European culture in the late seventeenth century, and that culture was inspired by the king. That is what Voltaire meant when he called the period "The Age of Louis XIV."

Louis dominated the court, and the court was the center of France. In the king's scheme of things, the court was more significant than the government. Louix XIV made no innovations in the government of France. He continued the system of the intendants, appointing them entirely from the middle class. By curbing the power of the local aristocracy and gentry, the intendants advanced royal sovereignty in the provinces. Members of the royal councils – such as the Council of State, which dealt with diplomacy, war, and peace – were drawn from the class Saint-Simon called "the bookkeepers," the middle class.

Louis feared and distrusted the nobility, and so he eliminated them from government. Throughout his long reign, and in spite of increasing financial problems, he never called the French nobility together in a meeting of the Estates General. The nobility, therefore, had no means of united expression or action. Nor did Louis have a first minister, freeing him from worry about the inordinate power of a Richelieu. Louis's use of terror – a secret police force, a system of informers, and the practice of opening private letters – foreshadowed some of the devices of the modern state. French government remained highly structured, bureaucratic, centered in Paris, and responsible to Louis XIV.

ECONOMIC MANAGEMENT UNDER LOUIS XIV: COLBERT AND MERCANTILISM

As controller-general of finances, the king named Jean Baptiste Colbert. The son of a draper of Reims, Colbert (1619–1683) came to manage the entire royal administration and proved himself a financial genius. Colbert's central principle was that the economy and the wealth of France should serve the state. He did not invent the economic system or program called mercantilism, but he rigorously applied it to France.

Mercantilism is a system for the regulation of economic activities, especially commercial activities, by and for the state. In seventeenth- and eighteenth-century economic theory, a nation's international power was thought to be based on its wealth, specifically its gold supply. To accumulate gold, a country should always sell abroad more than it bought. Colbert believed that a successful economic policy meant more than a favorable balance of trade. He insisted that the French sell abroad and buy *nothing* back. France should be self-sufficient, able to produce within its borders everything the subjects of the French king needed. Consequently, the outflow of gold would be halted and the power and prestige of the state enhanced.

Colbert attempted to accomplish self-sufficiency through state support for both old industries and newly created ones. He subsidized the established cloth industries at Abbeville, St.-Quentin, and Carcassonne. He granted special royal privileges to the rug and tapestry industries at Paris, Gobelin, and Beauvais. New factories at St.-Antoine in Paris manufactured mirrors to replace Venetian imports. Looms at Chantilly and Alençon competed with English lacemaking, and foundries at St.-Etienne made steel and firearms that cut Swedish imports. To insure a high-quality finished product, Colbert set up a system of state inspection and regulation. To insure order within every industry he compelled all craftsmen to organize into guilds, and within every guild he gave the masters absolute power over their workers. Colbert encouraged skilled foreign craftsmen and manufacturers to immigrate to France, and he gave them special privileges. To protect French products, Colbert enacted high tariffs, which prevented foreign goods from competing with French ones.

Colbert's most important work was the creation of a powerful merchant marine to transport French goods. He gave bonuses to French shipowners and builders, and established a method of maritime conscription, arsenals, and academies for the training of sailors. In 1661, France possessed 18 unseaworthy vessels; by 1681, France had 276 frigates, galleys, and ships of the line. Colbert tried to organize and regulate the entire French economy for the glory of the French state as embodied in the king.

Colbert hoped to make Canada – rich in untapped minerals and some of the best agricultural land in the world – part of a vast French empire. He gathered four thousand peasants from western France and shipped them to Canada, where they peopled the province of Quebec. (In 1608, one year after the English arrived at Jamestown, Virginia, Sully had established the city of Quebec, which became the capital of French Canada.) Subsequently, the Jesuit Marquette and the merchant Joliet sailed down the Mississippi River and took possession of the land on both sides as far south as present-day Arkansas. In 1684, the French explorer La Salle continued down the Mississippi to its mouth and claimed vast territories and the rich delta for Louis XIV. The area was called, naturally, Louisiana.

Nothing did more to destroy Colbert's system of commercial and colonial regulation than the revocation of the Edict of Nantes – an event that, on the surface at least, had little to do with economic life. For almost a century the edict had granted equal political and some religious rights to the Huguenots of France. Scholars have debated at length the reasons for Louis XIV's revocation of it in 1685. Was the revocation due to the powerful influence of the king's Catholic wife, Madame de Maintenon? Was it the result of pressure from Catholic business interests who resented the competition of the clever Huguenots? Did Louis abolish freedom of religion because of his pride and religious intolerance, which could not countenance the existence in France of a sizable group with a faith different from his own? Or was it sheer ignorance of the large numbers of his Calvinist subjects and their social and economic importance to the state, an ignorance attributable to the isolation of the court? Whatever the exact causes of the revocation, its consequences proved disastrous.

Perhaps 300,000 French citizens chose to emigrate rather than convert. Some of the best craftsmen, businessmen, soldiers, and sailors fled to England, Holland, and Prussia. They left their goods behind but carried their skills and hatred of Louis XIV with them. The loss of so many experts and the taxes they represented – on top of Louis's chronic need for money – severely aggravated the national financial situation. After 1685, the French government had to resort again to the expediency of creating offices and selling them on a broad scale. This stopgap measure paid for the present by mortgaging the future, since officeholders and their descendants paid no taxes.

Most catastrophic of all, the revocation of the Edict of Nantes provoked domestic turmoil within France and fear and hatred abroad. Calvinist peasants in Languedoc revolted, for example, and Louis was ultimately forced to back down. The Protestant states of northern Europe – Holland, Brandenburg, and Sweden – united against Louis XIV, and from 1688 until his death France was almost continually at war. With some justification, historians have called the revocation of the Edict of Nantes the greatest error the Bourbon dynasty committed.

FRENCH CLASSICISM

Scholars characterize the art and literature of the age of Louis XIV as French Classicism. By this they mean that the artists and writers of the late seventeenth century deliberately imitated the subject matter and style of classical antiquity; that their work resembles that of Renaissance Italy; and that French art possessed the classical qualities of discipline, balance, and restraint. Classicism was the official style of Louis's court. In painting, however, French classicism had already reached its peak before 1661, the beginning of the king's personal government.

Nicholas Poussin (1593–1665) is generally considered the finest example of French classicist painting. Poussin spent all but eighteen months of his creative life in Rome because he found the atmosphere in Paris uncongenial. Deeply attached to classical antiquity, he believed that the highest aim of painting was to represent noble actions in a logical and orderly, but not realistic, way. His masterpiece, "The Rape of the Sabine Women," exhibits these qualities. Its subject is an incident in Roman history; the figures of people and horses are ideal representations, and the emotions expressed are studied, not spontaneous. Even the buildings are exact architectural models of ancient Roman structures.

While Poussin selected grand and "noble" themes, Louis Le Nain (1593–1648) painted genre scenes of peasant life. At a time when artists favored Biblical and classical allegories, Le Nain's paintings are unique for their depiction of peasants. The highly realistic group assembled in "The Peasant Family" have great human dignity. The painting itself is reminiscent of portrayals of peasants by seventeenth-century Dutch painters.

Le Nain and Poussin, whose paintings still had individualistic features, did their work before 1661. After Louis's accession to power, the principles of absolutism molded the ideals of French classicism. Individualism was not allowed, and artists' efforts were directed to the glorification of the state as personified by the king. Precise rules governed all aspects of culture, with the goal of formal and restrained perfection.

Contemporaries said that Louis XIV never

ceased playing the role of grand monarch on the stage of his court. If the king never fully relaxed from the pressures and intrigues of government, he did enjoy music and theater and used them as a backdrop for court ceremonial. Louis favored Jean-Baptiste Lully (1632–1687), whose orchestral works combine lively animation with the restrained austerity typical of French classicism. Lully also composed court ballets, and his operatic productions achieved a powerful influence throughout Europe. Louis supported Francois Couperin (1668–1733), whose harpsicord and organ works possess the regal grandeur the king loved, and Marc-Antoine Charpentier (1634–1704), whose solemn religious music entertained him at meals. Charpentier received a pension for the *Te Deums,* hymns of thanksgiving he composed to celebrate French military victories.

Louis XIV loved the stage, and in the plays of Molière and Racine his court witnessed the finest achievements in the history of the French theater. When Jean-Baptiste Poquelin (1622–1673), the son of a prosperous tapestry maker, refused to join his father's business and entered the theater, he took the stage name Molière. As playwright, stage manager, director, and actor, Molière produced comedies that exposed the hypocrisies and follies of society though brilliant caricature. *Tartuffe* satirized the religious hypocrite, *Le Bourgeois Gentilhomme (The Would-Be Gentleman)* attacked the social parvenu, and *Les Femmes savantes (The Learned Women)* mocked the fashionable pseudo-intellectuals of the day. In structure Molière's plays followed classical models, but they were based on careful social observation. Molière made the bourgeoisie the butt of his ridicule; he stopped short of criticizing the nobility, thus reflecting the policy of his royal patron.

While Molière dissected social mores, his

contemporary Jean Racine (1639–1699) analyzed the power of love. Racine based his tragic dramas on Greek and Roman legends, and his persistent theme is the conflict of good and evil. Several plays – *Andromache, Berenice, Iphigenie,* and *Phedre* – bear the names of women and deal with the power of passion in women. Louis preferred *Mithridates* and *Brittanicus* because of the "grandeur" of their themes. For simplicity of language, symmetrical structure, and calm restraint, the plays of Racine represent the finest examples of French classicism. His tragedies and Molière's comedies are still produced today.

LOUIS XIV'S WARS

Just as the architecture and court life at Versailles served to reflect the king's glory, and as the economy of the state under Colbert was managed to advance the king's prestige, so did Louis XIV use war to exalt himself above the other rulers and nations of Europe. He visualized himself as a great military hero. "The character of a conqueror," he remarked, "is regarded as the noblest and highest of titles." Military glory was his aim. In 1666, Louis appointed François le Tellier (later Marquis de Louvois) as secretary of war. Louvois created a professional army, which was modern in the sense that the French state, rather than private nobles, employed the soldiers.

Because of the justifiable fear that an army of native French soldiers would turn on their oppressors, the army of Louis XIV was re-

cruited heavily from Swiss, German, and Irish mercenaries. Officers were French, the ranks largely foreign. A foreign mercenary army could more easily be employed against rebellious peasants whose language they did not speak. It is one of the ironies of Louis' wars that a French army of Protestant Swiss and German troops was sent against the Protestant Dutch.

A commissariat was established to feed the troops, in place of the ancient practice of living off the countryside. An ambulance corps was designed to look after the wounded. Uniforms and weapons were standardized. Finally, a rational system of recruitment, training, discipline, and promotion was imposed. With this new military machine, for the first time in Europe's history one national state, France, was able to dominate the politics of Europe.

Louis continued on a broader scale the expansionist policy begun by Cardinal Richelieu. In 1667, using a dynastic excuse, he invaded Flanders, part of the Spanish Netherlands, and Franche-Comté in the east. In consequence he acquired twelve towns, including the important commercial centers of Lille and Tournai (see Map 20.1). Five years later, Louis personally led an army of over a hundred thousand men into Holland, and the Dutch ultimately saved themselves only by opening the dikes and flooding the countryside. This war, which lasted six years and eventually involved the German empire and Spain, was concluded by the Treaty of Nijmegen (1678). Louis gained additional Flemish towns and the whole of Franche-Comté.

Encouraged by his successes, by the weakness of the German empire, and by divisions among the other European powers, Louis continued his aggression. In 1684 he seized the city of Trier, and the province of Lorraine was permanently occupied by France. At that moment, the king seemed invincible.

In fact, Louis had reached the limit of his expansion at Nijmegen. The wars of the 1680s and 1690s brought him no additional territories. In 1689, the Dutch prince William of Orange, a bitter foe of Louis XIV, became king of England. William joined the League of Augsburg – which included the German emperor, the kings of Spain and Sweden, and the electors of Bavaria, Saxony, and the Palatinate – adding British resources and men to the alliance. Neither the French nor the league won any decisive victories. The alliance served instead as preparation for the long-expected conflict known as the War of the Spanish Succession.

This struggle (1701–1713), provoked by the territorial disputes of the past century, also involved the dynastic question of the succession to the Spanish throne. It was an open secret in Europe that the king of Spain, Charles II (1665–1700), was mentally defective and sexually impotent. In his will Charles left his territories to his grandnephew, Philip of Anjou, who was also Louis XIV's grandson. When Charles died on November 1, 1700, the line of the Spanish Habsburgs ended. Immediately, Louis claimed the Spanish throne on behalf of his grandson.

The union of the French and Spanish crowns would have totally upset the European balance of power, and Louis's declaration that "the Pyrenees no longer exist" provoked the long-anticipated crisis. In May 1702 England, Holland, and the Holy Roman Empire declared war on France. They claimed that they were fighting to prevent France from becoming too strong in Europe, but during the previous half-century overseas maritime rivalry among France, Holland, and England had created serious international tension. The secondary motive of the Allied Powers was to check France's expanding commercial power in North America, Asia, and Africa. In the

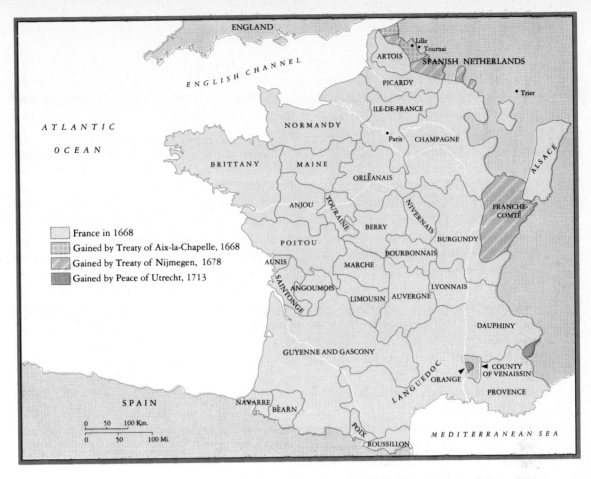

ENGLAND

ENGLISH CHANNEL

Lille
Tournai

ARTOIS

SPANISH NETHERLANDS

PICARDY

Trier

ILE-DE-FRANCE

ATLANTIC

OCEAN

NORMANDY

Paris   CHAMPAGNE

ALSACE

BRITTANY

MAINE

ORLÉANAIS

ANJOU

TOURAINE

NIVERNAIS

FRANCHE-
COMTÉ

BERRY

BURGUNDY

POITOU

BOURBONNAIS

AUNIS

MARCHE

SAINTONGE

ANGOUMOIS

LIMOUSIN   AUVERGNE

LYONNAIS

DAUPHINY

GUYENNE AND GASCONY

LANGUEDOC   ORANGE

COUNTY
OF VENAISSIN

PROVENCE

SPAIN

NAVARRE

BÉARN

FOIX

ROUSSILLON

MEDITERRANEAN SEA

France in 1668

Gained by Treaty of Aix-la-Chapelle, 1668

Gained by Treaty of Nijmegen, 1678

Gained by Peace of Utrecht, 1713

0   50   100 Km.

0   50   100 Mi.

*MAP 20.1   THE ACQUISITIONS OF LOUIS XIV,
1668–1713   The desire for glory and the weakness
of his German neighbors encouraged Louis' expansionist policy. But he paid a high price for his acquisitions.*

ensuing series of conflicts, two great soldiers dominated the alliance against France: Eugene, prince of Savoy, representing the Holy Roman Empire, and the Englishman John Churchill, subsequently duke of Marlborough. Eugene and Churchill inflicted a crushing defeat on Louis in 1704 at Blenheim in Bavaria. Marlborough followed with another victory at Ramillies near Namur in Brabant.

The war was finally concluded at Utrecht in 1713, where the principle of partition was applied. Louis's grandson Philip became the first Bourbon king of Spain on the understanding that the French and Spanish crowns would never be united. France surrendered Newfoundland, Nova Scotia, and the Hudson Bay territory to England, which also acquired Gibraltar, Minorca, and the *asiento,* or control of the African slave trade from Spain. The Dutch received little because the former Spanish Netherlands was given to Austria.

The Peace of Utrecht had important international consequences. It represented the balance-of-power principle in operation, setting limits on the extent to which any one power, in this case France, could expand. The treaty completed the decline of Spain as a great power. It vastly expanded the British Empire. Finally, Utrecht gave European powers experience in international cooperation and thus prepared them for the great alliances against France at the end of the eighteenth century.

For Louis XIV, Utrecht was a severe defeat. He had waged his wars in the quest for glory. He had gained little (see Map 20.1). Utrecht marked the end of French expansion. To raise revenue for the wars, forty thousand additional offices had been sold, thus increasing the number of families exempt from future taxation. Constant war had disrupted trade, which meant the state could not tax the profits of trade. Widespread starvation in the provinces provoked peasant revolts, especially in Brittany. In 1714, France hovered on the brink of financial bankruptcy. Louis had exhausted the country without much compensation. It is no wonder that when he died on September 1, 1715, Saint-Simon wrote, "Those . . . wearied by the heavy and oppressive rule of the King and his ministers, felt a delighted freedom. . . . Paris . . . found relief in the hope of liberation. . . . The provinces . . . quivered with delight . . . [and] the people, ruined, abused, despairing, now thanked God for a deliverance which answered their most ardent desires."[2]

THE DECLINE OF ABSOLUTIST SPAIN IN THE SEVENTEENTH CENTURY

Spanish absolutism and greatness had preceded that of the French. In the sixteenth century, Spain had developed the standard features of absolute monarchy: a permanent bureaucracy staffed by professionals employed in the various councils of state, a standing army, and national taxes, the *servicios,* which fell most heavily on the poor.

France depended upon financial and admin-

VELAZQUEZ: THE MAIDS OF HONOR The Infanta Margarita painted in 1656 with her maids and playmates has invaded the artist's studio, while her parents' image is reflected in the mirror on the back wall. Velazquez (extreme left), who powerfully influenced nineteenth-century impressionist painters, imbued all of his subjects, including the pathetic dwarf (right, in black) with a sense of dignity. (Giraudon)

istrative unification within its national borders; Spain had developed an international absolutism on the basis of silver bullion from Peru. Spanish gold and silver, Spanish armies, and Spanish glory had dominated the continent of Europe for most of the sixteenth century, but by the 1590s the seeds of disaster were sprouting. While France in the seventeenth century represented the classic model of the modern absolute state, Spain was experiencing steady decline and decay. Fiscal disorder, political incompetence, population decline, intellectual isolation, and psychological malaise — all combined to reduce Spain, by 1715, to the rank of a second-rate power.

The fabulous and seemingly inexhaustible flow of silver from Mexico and Peru had led Philip II (page 689) to assume the role of defender of Roman Catholicism in Europe. In order to humble the Protestant Dutch and to control the Spanish Netherlands, Philip believed that England, the Netherlands' greatest supporter, had to be crushed. He poured millions of Spanish ducats and all of Spanish hopes into the vast fleet that sailed in 1588. When the "Invincible Armada" went down in the North Sea, a century of Spanish pride and power went with it. After 1590, a spirit of defeatism and disillusionment crippled almost all efforts at reform.

Philip II's Catholic crusade had been financed by the revenues of the Spanish-Atlantic economy. These included, in addition to silver and gold bullion, the sale of cloth,

grain, oil, and wine to the colonies. In the early seventeenth century, the Dutch and English began to trade with the Spanish colonies, cutting into the revenues that had gone to Spain. Mexico and Peru themselves developed local industries, further lessening their need to buy from Spain. Between 1610 and 1650, Spanish trade with the colonies fell 60 percent.

At the same time the native Indians and African slaves, who worked the South American silver mines under conditions that would have disgraced the ancient Egyptian pharaohs, suffered frightful epidemics of disease. Moreover, the lodes started to run dry. Consequently, the quantity of metal produced for Spain steadily declined. Nevertheless, in Madrid royal expenditures constantly exceeded income. The remedies applied in the face of a mountainous state debt and declining revenues were devaluation of the coinage and declarations of bankruptcy. In 1596, 1607, 1627, 1647, and 1680 Spanish kings found no solution to the problem of an empty treasury other than cancellation of the national debt. Naturally, public confidence in the state deteriorated.

Spain, in contrast to the other countries of western Europe, had only a tiny middle class. Disdain for money, in a century of increasing commercialism and bourgeois attitudes, reveals a significant facet of the Spanish national character. Public opinion, taking its cue from the aristocracy, condemned moneymaking as vulgar and undignified. Those with influence or connections sought titles of nobility and social prestige. Thousands entered economically unproductive professions and became priests, monks, and nuns: there were said to be nine thousand monasteries in the province of Castile alone. The flood of gold and silver had produced severe inflation, pushing the

costs of production in the textile industry higher and higher, to the point that Castilian cloth could not compete in colonial and international markets. Many manufacturers and businessmen found so many obstacles in the way of profitable enterprise that they simply gave up.[3]

Spanish aristocrats, attempting to maintain an extravagant lifestyle they could no longer afford, increased the rents on their estates. High rents and heavy taxes in turn drove the peasants from the land. Agricultural production suffered and the peasants departed for the large cities, where they swelled the ranks of unemployed beggars.

Their most Catholic majesties, the kings of Spain, had no solutions to these dire problems. The portraits of Philip III (1598-1622), Philip IV (1622-1665), and Charles II hanging in the Prado, the Spanish national museum in Madrid, reflect the increasing weakness of the dynasty. Their faces – the small beady eyes, the long noses, the jutting Habsburg jaws, the constipated and pathetically stupid expressions – tell a story of excessive inbreeding and decaying monarchy. These Spanish kings all lacked force of character. Philip III, a pallid, melancholy, and deeply pious man "whose only virtue appeared to reside in a total absence of vice," handed the government over to the lazy duke of Lerma, who used it to advance his personal and familial wealth. Philip IV left the management of his several kingdoms to Count Olivares.

Olivares was an able administrator. He did not lack energy and ideas; he devised new sources of revenue. But he clung to the grandiose belief that the solution to Spain's difficulties rested in a return to the imperial tradition. Unfortunately, the imperial tradition demanded the revival of war with the Dutch at the expiration of a twelve-year truce in 1622 and a long war with France over Mantua (1628–1659). These conflicts on top of an empty treasury brought disaster.

In 1640, Spain faced serious revolts in Naples and Portugal, and in 1643 the French inflicted a crushing defeat on a Spanish army in Belgium. By the Treaty of the Pyrenees of 1659, which ended the French-Spanish wars, Spain was compelled to surrender extensive territories to France. This treaty marked the end of Spain as a great power.

Seventeenth-century Spain was the victim of its past. It could not forget the grandeur of the sixteenth century and look to the future. The bureaucratic councils of state continued to function as symbols of the absolute Spanish monarchy. But because those councils were staffed by aristocrats, it was the aristocracy that held the real power. Spanish absolutism had been built largely on slave-produced gold and silver. When the supply of bullion decreased, the power and standing of the Spanish state declined.

The most cherished Spanish ideals were military glory and strong Roman Catholic faith. In the seventeenth century, Spain lacked the finances and the manpower to fight the expensive wars in which it foolishly got involved. Spain also ignored the new mercantile ideas and scientific methods, because they came from heretical nations, Holland and England. The incredible wealth of South America destroyed the tiny Spanish middle class and created contempt for business and manual labor.

The decadence of the Habsburg dynasty and the lack of effective royal councilors also contributed to Spanish failure. Spanish leaders seemed to lack the will to reform. Pessimism and fatalism permeated national life. In the reign of Philip IV, a royal council was appointed to plan the construction of a canal linking the Tagus and Manzanares rivers in Spain. After interminable debate, the committee decided that "if God had intended the rivers to be navigable, He would have made them so."

In the novel *Don Quixote*, the Spanish writer Cervantes (1547–1616) produced one of the great masterpieces of world literature. The main character, Don Quixote, lives in a world of dreams, traveling about the countryside seeking military glory. From the title of this book English has borrowed the word *quixotic*. Meaning idealistic but impractical, it characterizes seventeenth-century Spain.

CONSTITUTIONALISM

The seventeenth century, which witnessed the development of absolute monarchy, also saw the appearance of the constitutional state. While France and later Prussia, Russia, and Austria solved the question of sovereignty with the absolutist state, England and Holland evolved toward the constitutional state. What is constitutionalism? Is it the same as democracy?

Constitutionalism is the limitation of government by law. Constitutionalism also implies a balance between the authority and power of the government on the one hand, and the rights and liberties of the subjects on the other. The balance is often very delicate.

A nation's constitution may be written or unwritten. In may be embodied in one basic document, occasionally revised by amendment or judicial decision, like the Constitution of the United States. Or a constitution may be partly written and partly unwritten and include parliamentary statutes, judicial decisions, and a body of traditional procedures and practices, like the English and Canadian constitutions. Whether written or unwritten, a constitution gets its binding force from the government's acknowledgment that it must respect that constitution — that is, that the state must govern according to the laws. Likewise, in a constitutional state, the people look upon the law and the constitution as the protectors of their rights, liberties, and property.

Modern constitutional governments may take either a republican or a monarchial form. In a constitutional republic, the sovereign power resides in the electorate and is exercised by the electorate's representatives. In a constitutional monarchy, a king or queen serves as the head of state and possesses some residual political authority, but again the ultimate or sovereign power rests in the electorate.

A constitutional government is not, however, quite the same as a democratic government. In a complete democracy, *all* the people have the right to participate either directly, or indirectly through their elected representatives, in the government of the state. Democratic government, therefore, is intimately tied up with the franchise (the vote). Most men could not vote until the late nineteenth century. Even then, women — probably the majority in Western societies — lacked the franchise; they gained the right to vote only in the twentieth century. Consequently, although constitutionalism developed in the seventeenth century, full democracy was achieved only in very recent times.

THE DECLINE OF ROYAL ABSOLUTISM IN ENGLAND (1603-1649)

In the late sixteenth century the French monarchy was powerless; a century later the king's power was absolute. In 1588, Queen Elizabeth I of England exercised very great personal power; by 1689, the English monarchy was severely circumscribed and limited. Change in England was anything but orderly: England in the seventeenth century displayed as much political stability as some African states in the twentieth. They executed one king, experienced a bloody civil war, experimented with military dictatorship, then restored the son of the murdered king, and finally, after a bloodless revolution, established a constitutional monarchy. Political stability came only in the 1690s. How do we account for the fact that after such a violent and tumultuous century, England laid the foundations for a constitutional monarchy? What combination of political, socioeconomic, and religious factors brought on first a civil war in 1642-1649 and then the constitutional settlement of 1688-1689?

The extraordinary success of Elizabeth I had rested on her political shrewdness and flexibility, her careful management of finances, her wise selection of ministers, her clever manipulation of Parliament, and her sense of royal dignity and devotion to hard work. The aging queen had always refused to discuss the succession. After her Scottish cousin James Stuart succeeded her as James I (1603-1625), Elizabeth's strengths seemed even greater than they actually had been. The Stuarts lacked every quality Elizabeth had possessed.

King James was well educated and learned but lacking in common sense — he was once called "the wisest fool in Christendom." He also lacked the common touch. Urged to wave at the crowds who waited to greet their new ruler, James complained that he was tired, and threatened to drop his breeches "so they can cheer at my arse." Having left barbarous and violent Scotland for rich and prosperous England, James believed he had entered "the Promised Land." As soon as he got to London, the new English king went to see the Crown jewels.

Abysmally ignorant of English law and of the English Parliament, but sublimely arrogant, James was devoted to the theory of the divine right of kings. He expressed his ideas about divine right in his essay "The Trew Law of Free Monarchy." According to James I, a monarch has a divine (or God-given) right to his authority, and is responsible only to God. Rebellion is the worst of political crimes. If a king orders something evil, the subject should respond with passive disobedience but should be prepared to accept any penalty for non-compliance.

James substituted political theorizing and talk for real work. He lectured the House of Commons: "There are no privileges and immunities which can stand against a divinely appointed King." This notion, implying total royal jurisdiction over the liberties, persons, and properties of English men and women, formed the basis of the Stuart concept of absolutism. Such a view ran directly counter to the long-standing English idea that a person's property could not be taken away without due process of law. James's expression of such views before the English House of Commons constituted a grave political mistake.

The House of Commons guarded the pocketbook of the nation, and James and later Stuart kings badly needed to open that pocketbook. Elizabeth had bequeathed to James a sizable royal debt. Through prudent management the debt could have been gradually reduced, but James I looked upon all revenues as a happy windfall to be squandered on a lavish court and favorite courtiers. In fact, the extravagance and licentiousness of James' court, and the public flaunting of his male lovers, weakened respect for the monarchy.

Elizabeth had also left to her Stuart successors a House of Commons that appreciated its

THE LAMENTABLE COMPLAINTS OF NICK FROTH the Tapster, and RVLEROST the Cooke. Concerning the restraint lately set forth, against drinking, potting, and piping on the Sabbath day, and against selling meate.

Printed in the yeare, 1641.

PURITAN IDEALS OPPOSED The Puritans preached sober living and abstention from alcoholic drink, rich food, and dancing. This pamphlet reflects the common man's hostility to such restraints. "Potting" refers to tankards of beer; "piping" means making music. (The British Museum)

own financial strength and intended to use that strength to acquire a greater say in the government of the state. The knights and burgesses who sat at Westminster in the early seventeenth century wanted to discuss royal expenditures, religious reform, and foreign affairs. In short, the Commons wanted what amounted to sovereignty.

Profound social changes had occurred since the sixteenth century. The English House of Commons during the reigns of James I and his son Charles I (1625-1649) was very different from the assembly Henry VIII had terrorized into passing his Reformation legislation. A social revolution had brought about the change. The dissolution of the monasteries and the sale of monastic land had enriched many people. Agricultural techniques like the draining of wasteland and the application of fertilizers improved the land and its yield. Old manorial common land had been enclosed and turned into sheep runs; breeding was carefully supervised, and the size of the flocks increased. In these activities, as well as in renting and leasing parcels of land, precise accounts were kept.

Many men invested in commercial ventures at home, such as the expanding cloth industry, and in partnerships and joint stock companies engaged in foreign enterprises. They made prudent marriages. All these developments led to a great deal of social mobility. Both in commerce and in agriculture, the English in the late sixteenth and early seventeenth centuries were capitalists, investing their profits to make more money. Although the international inflation of the period hit everywhere, in England commercial and agricultural income rose faster than prices. Wealthy country gentry, rich city merchants, and financiers invested abroad.

The typical pattern was for the commercially successfully to set themselves up as country gentry, thus creating an elite group that possessed a far greater proportion of land and of the national wealth in 1640 than had been the case in 1540. Small wonder that in 1640 someone could declare in the House of Commons, probably accurately, "We could buy the House of Lords three times over." Increased wealth had also produced a better-educated and more articulate House of Commons. Many members had acquired at least a

smattering of legal knowledge, and they used that knowledge to search for medieval precedents from which to argue against the king. The class that dominated the Commons wanted political power corresponding to its economic strength.

In England, unlike France, there was no social stigma attached to paying taxes. Members of the House of Commons were willing to tax themselves provided they had some say in the expenditure of those taxes and in the formulation of state policies. The Stuart kings, however, considered such ambitions intolerable presumption and a threat to their divine-right prerogative. Consequently, at every Parliament between 1603 and 1640 bitter squabbles erupted between the Crown and the wealthy, articulate, and legal-minded Commons. Charles I's attempt to govern without Parliament (1629-1640), and to finance his government by arbitrary nonparliamentary levies, brought the country to a crisis.

An issue graver than royal extravagance and Parliament's desire to make the law also disturbed the English and embittered relations between the king and the House of Commons. That problem was religion. In the early seventeenth century, increasing numbers of English men and women felt dissatisfied with the Church of England established by Henry VIII and reformed by Elizabeth. Many believed the Reformation had not gone far enough. They wanted to "purify" the Anglican church of Roman Catholic elements — elaborate vestments and ceremonial, the position of the altar at the east end of the church, even the giving and wearing of wedding rings. These people were called Puritans.

It is very difficult to establish what proportion of the English population was Puritan. It is clear, however, that many English men and women were attracted by the socioeconomic implications of John Calvin's theology. Calvinism emphasized hard work, sobriety, thrift, competition, and postponement of pleasure, and tended to link sin and poverty with weakness and moral corruption. These attitudes fit in precisely with the economic approaches and practices of many (successful) businessmen and farmers. These values have frequently been called the Protestant, or middle-class, or capitalist, ethic. While it is hazardous to identify capitalism and progress with Protestantism – there were many successful Catholic capitalists – the "Protestant virtues" represented the prevailing values of the great majority of members of the House of Commons.

James I and Charles I both gave the impression of being highly sympathetic to Roman Catholicism. Charles supported the policies of William Laud, archbishop of Canterbury (1573-1645), who tried to impose elaborate ritual and rich ceremonial on all churches. Laud insisted on complete uniformity of church services, and enforced that uniformity through an ecclesiastical court called High Commission. People believed the country was being led back to Roman Catholicism. When in 1639 Laud attempted to impose a new prayer book, modeled on the Anglican Book of Common Prayer, on the Presbyterian Scots, the Scots revolted. In order to finance an army to put down the Scots, King Charles was compelled to summon Parliament in November 1640.

For eleven years Charles I had ruled without Parliament, financing his government through extraordinary stopgap levies, considered illegal by most English people. For example, the king revived a medieval law requiring coastal districts to help pay the cost of ships for defense, but levied the tax, called ship money, on inland as well as coastal counties. When the issue was tested in the courts, the judges, having been suborned, decided in the king's favor.

Most members of Parliament believed that such taxation without consent amounted to arbitrary and absolute despotism. Consequently, they were not willing to trust the king with an army. Accordingly, this Parliament, commonly called the Long Parliament because it existed from 1640 to 1660, proceeded to enact legislation that limited the power of the monarch and made arbitrary government impossible.

In 1641, the Commons passed the Triennial Act, which compelled the king to summon Parliament every three years. The Commons impeached Archbishop Laud and abolished the House of Lords and the Court of High Commission. It went further and threatened to abolish the institution of episcopacy. King Charles, fearful of a Scottish invasion – the original reason for summoning Parliament – accepted these measures. Understanding and peace were not achieved, however, partly because radical members of the Commons pushed increasingly revolutionary propositions, partly because Charles maneuvered to rescind those he had already approved. An uprising in Ireland precipitated civil war.

Ever since Henry II had conquered Ireland in 1171, English governors had mercilessly ruled the Irish, and English landlords had ruthlessly exploited them. The English Reformation had made a bad situation worse: because the Irish remained Catholic, religious differences became united with economic and political oppression. Without an army, Charles I could neither come to terms with the Scots nor put down the Irish rebellion, and the Long Parliament remained unwilling to place an army under a king it did not trust.

Charles thus instigated military action against parliamentary forces. He recruited an army drawn from the nobility and their cavalry staff, the rural gentry, and mercenaries. The Parliamentary army was composed of the militia of the City of London, country squires with business connections, and men with a firm belief in the spiritual duty of serving.

The English Civil War (1642–1646) tested whether sovereignty in England was to reside in the king or in Parliament. The Civil War did not resolve that problem, although it ended in 1649 with the execution of King Charles on the charge of high treason – a severe blow to royal power. The period between 1649 and 1660, called the Interregnum because it separated two monarchial periods, saw England's one experience of military dictatorship.

PURITANICAL ABSOLUTISM IN ENGLAND: CROMWELL AND THE PROTECTORATE

The problem of sovereignty was vigorously debated in the middle years of the seventeenth century. In *Leviathan,* the English philosopher and political theorist Thomas Hobbes (1588–1679) maintained that sovereignty is ultimately derived from the people, who transfer it to the monarchy by implicit contract. The power of the ruler is absolute, but kings do not hold their power by divine right. This view pleased no one in the seventeenth century.

When Charles I was beheaded on January 30, 1649, the kingship was abolished. A commonwealth, or republican form of government, was proclaimed. Theoretically, legislative power rested in the surviving members of Parliament and executive power in a council of state. In fact, the army that had defeated the royal forces controlled the government, and Oliver Cromwell controlled the army.

Although called the Protectorate, the rule of Cromwell (1653–1658) constituted military dictatorship.

Oliver Cromwell (1599–1658) came from the country gentry, the class that dominated the House of Commons in the early seventeenth century. He himself had sat in the Long Parliament. Cromwell rose in the parliamentary army, and achieved nationwide fame by infusing the army with his Puritan convictions and molding it into the highly effective military machine, called the New Model Army, that defeated the royalist forces.

Parliament had written a constitution, the Instrument of Government (1653), that invested executive power in a lord protector (Cromwell) and a council of state. The Instrument provided for triennial parliaments and gave Parliament the sole power to raise taxes. But after repeated disputes Cromwell tore the document up. He continued the standing army and proclaimed quasi-martial law. He divided England into twelve military districts, each governed by a major general. On the issue of religion Cromwell favored broad toleration, and the Instrument of Government gave all Christians, except Roman Catholics, the right to practice their faith. Toleration meant state protection of many different Protestant sects, and most English people had no enthusiasm for such a notion; the idea was far ahead of its time. Cromwell identified Irish Catholicism with sedition. In 1649 he crushed rebellion there with merciless savagery, leaving a legacy of Irish hatred for England that has not yet subsided. The state rigorously censored the press, forbade sports, and kept the theaters closed.

Cromwell's regulation of the nation's economy had features typical of seventeenth-century absolutism. The lord protector's policies were mercantilist, similar to those Colbert established in France. Cromwell enforced a navigation act requiring that English goods be transported on English ships. The navigation act was a great boost to the development of an English merchant marine, and brought about a short but successful war with the commercially threatened Dutch. Cromwell also welcomed the immigration of Jews, because of their skills, and they began to return to England in larger numbers after four centuries of absence.

Absolute government collapsed when Cromwell died in 1658. Absolutism failed because the English got fed up with military rule. They longed for a return to civilian government, restoration of the common law, and social stability. Moreover, the strain of creating a community of puritanical saints proved too psychologically exhausting. Government by military dictatorship was an unfortunate experiment that English men and women never forgot and never repeated. By 1660, they were ready to restore the monarchy.

THE RESTORATION OF THE ENGLISH MONARCHY

The Restoration of 1660 re-established the monarchy in the person of Charles II (1660–1685), eldest son of Charles I. At the same time both houses of Parliament were restored, together with the established Anglican church, the courts of law, and the system of local government through justices of the peace. The Restoration failed to resolve two serious problems. What was to be the attitude of the state toward Puritans, Catholics, and dissenters from the established church? And what was to be the constitutional position of the king – that is, what was to be relationship between the king and Parliament?

About the first of these issues, Charles II, a relaxed, easygoing, and sensual man, was basically indifferent. He was not interested in

THE HOUSE OF COMMONS   *This seal of the Commonwealth shows the small House of Commons in session with the speaker presiding; the legend "in the third year of freedom" refers to 1651, three years after the abolition of the monarchy. In 1653, however, Cromwell abolished this "Rump Parliament" — so-called because it consisted of the few surviving members elected before the Civil War — and he and the army governed the land. (The British Museum)*

doctrinal issues. Parliamentarians were, and they proceeded to enact a body of laws that sought to compel religious uniformity. Those who refused to receive the sacrament of the Church of England could not vote, hold public office, preach, teach, attend the universities, or even assemble for meetings, according to the Test Act of 1673. These restrictions could not be enforced. When the Quaker William Penn held a meeting of his friends and was arrested, the jury refused to convict him.

In politics, Charles II was determined "not to set out in his travels again," which meant that he intended to get along with Parliament. Charles II's solution to the problem of the relationship between the king and the House of Commons had profound importance for later constitutional development. Generally good rapport existed between the king and the strongly royalist Parliament that had restored him. This rapport was due largely to the king's appointment of a council of five men who served both as his major advisers and as members of Parliament, thus acting as liaison agents between the executive and the legislature. This body – known as the Cabal from the names of its five members (Clifford, Arlington, Buckingham, Ashley-Cooper and Lauderdale) – was an ancestor of the later cabinet system. It gradually came to be accepted that the Cabal was answerable in Parliament for the decisions of the king. This development gave rise to the concept of ministerial responsibility: royal ministers must answer to the Commons.

Harmony between the Crown and Parliament rested on the understanding that Charles would summon frequent parliaments and that Parliament would vote him sufficient revenues. However, although Parliament believed Charles had a virtual divine right to govern, it did not grant him an adequate income. Accordingly, Charles entered into a secret agreement with Louis XIV. The French king would give Charles £200,000 annually, and in return Charles would relax the laws against Catholics, gradually re-Catholicize England, and support French policy against the Dutch.

When the details of this secret treaty leaked out, a great wave of anti-Catholic fear swept England. This fear was compounded by a crucial fact: although Charles had produced several bastards, he had no legitimate children. It therefore appeared that his brother and heir, James, Duke of York, who had publicly acknowledged his Catholicism, would inaugu-

rate a Catholic dynasty. The combination of hatred for the French absolutism embodied in Louis XIV, hostility to Roman Catholicism, and fear of a permanent Catholic dynasty produced virtual hysteria. The Commons passed an exclusion bill denying the succession to a Roman Catholic, but Charles quickly dissolved Parliament and the bill never became law.

James II (1685–1688) did succeed his brother, and almost at once the worst English anti-Catholic fears were realized. In direct violation of the Test Act, James appointed Roman Catholics to positions in the army, the universities, and local government. When these actions were tested in the courts, the judges, whom James had appointed, decided for the king. The king was suspending the law at will, and appeared to be reviving the absolutism of his father and grandfather. He went further. Attempting to broaden his base of support with Protestant dissenters and nonconformists, James issued a declaration of indulgence granting religious freedom to all.

Two events gave the signals for revolution. First, seven bishops of the Church of England petitioned the king that they not be forced to read the declaration of indulgence because of their belief it was an illegal act. They were imprisoned in the Tower of London but subsequently acquitted amid great public enthusiasm. Second, in June 1688, James's queen produced a male heir. A Catholic dynasty seemed assured. The fear of a Roman Catholic monarchy, supported by France and ruling outside the law, prompted a group of eminent persons to offer the English throne to James's Protestant daughter Mary and her Dutch husband, Prince William of Orange. In November 1688, James II, his queen, and infant son fled to France and became pensioners of Louis XIV.

The English call the events of 1688 the Glorious Revolution. The revolution was indeed glorious in the sense that it replaced one king with another with a minimum of bloodshed. It also represented the destruction, once and for all, of the idea of divine-right monarchy. William and Mary accepted the English throne from Parliament, and in so doing explicitly recognized the supremacy of Parliament. The revolution of 1688 established the principle that sovereignty, the ultimate power in the state, rested in Parliament, and that the king ruled with the consent of the governed.

The men who had brought about the revolution quickly framed their intentions in the Bill of Rights, which is the cornerstone of the modern British constitution. The basic principles of the Bill of Rights were formulated in direct response to Stuart absolutism. Law was to be made in Parliament; once made, the law could not be suspended by the Crown. Parliament had to be called at least every three years. Both elections to and debate in Parliament were to be free in the sense that the Crown was not to interfere in them; this aspect of the Bill was widely disregarded in the eighteenth century. Judges would hold their offices "during good behavior," which assured the independence of the judiciary. No longer could the Crown get the judicial decisions it wanted by threats of removal. There was to be no standing army in peacetime – a limitation designed to prevent the repetition of either Stuart or Cromwellian military government. The Bill of Rights granted "that the subjects which are Protestants may have arms for their defense suitable to their conditions and as al-

lowed by law,"[4] meaning that Catholics could not possess firearms because the Protestant majority feared them. Additional parliamentary legislation granted freedom of worship to Protestant dissenters and nonconformists and required that the English monarch always be Protestant in faith.

The Glorious Revolution found its best defense in the political philosopher John Locke's "Second Treatise on Civil Government" (1690). A spokesman for the great land-owning class that had brought about the revolution, Locke (1632–1704) maintained that men set up civil governments in order to defend property. Thus the purpose of government is to protect life, liberty, and property. Locke's ideas, though not profound, had great influence throughout the eighteenth century.

However glorious, the events of 1688–1690 did not constitute a *democratic* revolution. The revolution placed sovereignty in Parliament, and Parliament represented the upper classes. The great majority of English people acquired no say in their government. The English revolution established a constitutional monarchy; it also inaugurated an age of aristocratic government, which lasted at least until 1832 and probably until 1914.

In the course of the eighteenth century, the cabinet system of government evolved. The term *cabinet* refers to the small private room in which English rulers consulted their chief ministers. In a cabinet system the leading ministers, who must have seats in and the support of a majority of the House of Commons, formulate common policy and conduct the business of the country. During the administration of one royal minister, Sir Robert Walpole (1721–1742), the idea developed that the cabinet was responsible to the House of Commons. The king normally presided at cabinet meetings, but because the Hanoverian king George I (1714–1727) did not understand enough English to follow the discussions, he stopped attending cabinet sessions. George II (1727–1760) followed that precedent. The influence of the Crown in decision making accordingly declined. Walpole enjoyed the favor of the monarchy and of the House of Commons, and came to be called the king's first, or prime, minister. In the English cabinet system both legislative and executive power are held by the leading ministers, who form the government.

THE DUTCH REPUBLIC IN THE SEVENTEENTH CENTURY

The seventeenth century witnessed an unparalleled flowering of Dutch scientific, artistic, and literary achievement. In this period, often called "the golden age of the Netherlands," Dutch ideas and attitudes played a profound role in shaping a new and modern worldview. At the same time the Republic of the United Provinces of the Netherlands represents another model of the development of the modern state.

In the late sixteenth century, the seven northern provinces of the Netherlands, of which Holland and Zeeland were the most prosperous, succeeded in throwing off Spanish domination. This success was based on their geographical lines of defense, the wealth of the cities, the brilliant military strategy of William the Silent, the preoccupation of Philip II of Spain with so many other concerns, and the northern provinces' vigorous Calvinism. In 1581 the seven provinces of the Union of Utrecht had formed the United Provinces (page 688). Philip II continued to try to crush the Dutch with the Armada but in 1609 his son Philip III agreed to a truce that implicitly recognized the independence of the United Provinces. At the time neither side

expected the peace to be permanent. The Peace of Westphalia in 1648, however, confirmed the Dutch republic's independence.

Within each province an oligarchy of wealthy merchants called regents handled domestic affairs in the local Estates. The provincial Estates held virtually all the power. A federal assembly, or States General, handled matters of foreign affairs, such as war. But the States General did not possess sovereign authority, since all issues had to be referred back to the local Estates for approval. The States General appointed a representative, the stadholder, in each province. As the highest executive there, the stadholder carried out ceremonial functions and was responsible for defense and good order. The sons of William the Silent, Maurice and William Louis, held the office of stadholder in all seven provinces. The regents in each province jealously guarded local independence and resisted efforts at centralization. Nevertheless, Holland, which had the largest navy and the most wealth, dominated the republic and the States General. Significantly, the Estates assembled at Holland's capital, The Hague.

The government of the United Provinces fits none of the standard categories of seventeenth-century political organization. The Dutch were not monarchial, but fiercely republican. The government was controlled by wealthy merchants and financiers. Although rich, their values were not aristocratic but strongly middle-class, emphasizing thrift, hard work, and simplicity in living. The Dutch republic was not a strong federation but a confederation – that is, a weak union of strong provinces. The provinces were a temptation to powerful neighbors, yet the Dutch resisted the long Spanish effort at reconquest and withstood both French and English attacks in the second half of the century. Louis XIV's hatred of the Dutch was proverbial. They

MODEL OF A SEVENTEENTH-CENTURY FLUYT
The Dutch surpassed all nations in the design of fast-sailing ships. The fluyt or fluteship was cheap to construct, carried a large cargo, and required only a *small crew. It gave the Dutch a great advantage, resulting in their notable commercial success. (Photo: Caroline Buckler)*

represented all that he despised — middle-class values, religious toleration, and political independence.

The political success of the Dutch rested on the phenomenal commercial prosperity of the Netherlands. The moral and ethical bases of that commercial wealth were thrift, frugality, and religious toleration. John Calvin had written, "From where do the merchant's profits come except from his own diligence and industry"; this attitude undoubtedly encouraged a sturdy people who had waged a centuries-old struggle against the sea.

Alone of all European peoples in the seventeenth century, the Dutch practiced religious toleration. Peoples of all faiths were welcome within their borders. It is a striking testimony to the urbanity of Dutch society that in a century when patriotism was closely identified with religious uniformity, the Calvinist province of Holland allowed its highest official, Jan van Oldenbarneveldt, to continue to practice his Roman Catholic faith. As long as a businessman conducted his religion in private, the government did not interfere with him.

Toleration also paid off: it attracted a great deal of foreign capital and investment. Deposits at the Bank of Amsterdam were guaranteed by the city council, and in the middle years of the century the bank became Europe's best source of cheap credit and commercial intelligence, and the main clearinghouse for bills of exchange. Men of all races and creeds traded in Amsterdam, at whose docks on the Amstel River five thousand ships, half the merchant marine of the United Provinces, were berthed. Joost van den Vondel, the poet of Dutch imperialism, exulted:

God, God, the Lord of Amstel cried, hold every
  conscience free;
And Liberty ride, on Holland's tide, with billow-
  ing sails to sea,
And run our Amstel out and in; let freedom gird
  the bold,
And merchant in his counting house stand elbow
  deep in gold.[5]

The fishing industry was the cornerstone of the Dutch economy. For half the year, from June to December, fishing fleets combed the dangerous English coast and the North Sea, raking in tiny herring. Profits from herring stimulated shipbuilding, and even before 1600 the Dutch were offering the lowest shipping rates in Europe. Although Dutch cities became famous for their exports – diamonds, linen from Haarlem, pottery from Delft – Dutch wealth depended less on exports than on transport. The merchant marine was the largest in Europe.

In 1602, a group of the regents of Holland formed the Dutch East India Company, a joint stock company. Each investor received a percentage of the profits proportional to the amount of money he had put in. Within half a century, the Dutch East India Company had cut heavily into Portuguese trading in the Far East. The Dutch seized the Cape of Good

VERMEER: WOMEN WEIGHING GOLD Vermeer painted pictures of middle-class women involved in ordinary activities in the quiet interiors of their homes. Unrivaled among Dutch masters for his superb control of light, in this painting (ca 1657) Vermeer illuminates the pregnant woman weighing gold on her scales, as Christ in the painting on the wall weighs the saved and the damned. (National Gallery of Art, Washington, D.C. Widener Collection)

Hope, Ceylon, and Malacca, and established trading posts in each place. In the 1630s, the Dutch East India Company was paying its investors about 35 percent return annually on their investments. The Dutch West India Company, founded in 1621, traded extensively with Latin America and Africa.

Although the initial purpose of both companies was commercial – the import of spices and silks to Europe – the Dutch found themselves involved in the imperialistic exploitation of large parts of the Pacific and Latin America. Amsterdam, the center of a worldwide Dutch empire, became the commercial and financial capital of Europe. During the seventeenth century the Dutch translated their commercial acumen and flexibility into political and imperialist terms with striking success. But war with France and England in the 1670s hurt the United Provinces. The long War of the Spanish Succession, in which the Dutch supported England against France, was a costly drain on Dutch manpower and financial resources. The peace signed in 1715 to end the war marked the beginning of Dutch economic decline.

———◆———

According to Thomas Hobbes, the central drive in every man is "a perpetual and restless desire of Power, after Power, that ceaseth only in Death." The seventeenth century solved the problem of *sovereign power* in two fundamental

ways, absolutism and constitutionalism. The France of Louis XIV witnessed the emergence of the fully absolutist state. The king commanded all the powers of the state: judicial, military, political, and to a great extent ecclesiastical. France developed a centralized bureaucracy, a professional army, a state-directed economy, all of which Louis personally supervised. For the first time in history all the institutions and powers of the national state were effectively controlled by a single person. The king saw himself as the representative of God on earth, and it has been said that "to the seventeenth century imagination God was a sort of image of Louis XIV."[6]

As Louis XIV personifies absolutism, so Stuart England exemplifies the evolution of the first modern constitutional state. The conflicts between Parliament and the first two Stuart rulers, James I and Charles I, tested where sovereign power would rest in the state. The resulting Civil War did not solve the problem. The Instrument of Government, the document produced in 1653 by the victorious parliamentary army, provided for a balance of governmental authority and recognition of popular rights; as such, the Instrument has been called the first modern constitution. Unfortunately, it lacked public support. James II's absolutist tendencies brought on the Revolution of 1688, and the people who made that revolution settled three basic issues. Sovereign power was divided between king and parliament, with parliament enjoying the greater share. Government was to be based on the rule of law. And the liberties of English people were made explicit in written form, in the Bill of Rights. The framers of the English constitution left to later generations the task of making constitutional government work.

The models of governmental power established by seventeenth-century England and France strongly influenced other states then and ever since. As the Mississippi novelist William Faulkner wrote, "The past isn't dead; it's not even past."

NOTES

1. S. de Gramont, ed., *The Age of Magnificence: Memoirs of the Court of Louis XIV by the Duc de Saint-Simon,* Capricorn Books, New York, 1964, pp. 141–145.
2. Ibid., p. 183.
3. S. H. Elliott, *Imperial Spain, 1469–1716,* Mentor Books, New York, 1963, pp. 306–308.
4. C. Stephenson and G. F. Marcham, *Sources of English Constitutional History,* Harper & Row, New York, 1937, p. 601.
5. Quoted by D. Maland, *Europe in the Seventeenth Century,* Macmillan, New York, 1967, pp. 198–199.
6. Quoted by Carl J. Friedrich and Charles Blitzer, *The Age of Power,* Cornell University Press, Ithaca, New York, 1957, p. 112.

SUGGESTED READING

Students who wish to explore the problems presented in this chapter in greater depth will easily find a rich and exciting literature with many titles available in paperback editions. Geoffrey Parker, *Europe in Crisis, 1598–1618* (1980), provides a readable introduction to the religious, social, and economic tensions of the period. C. Friedrich, *The Age of the Baroque, 1610–1660* (1962), is a good survey. Perhaps the best recent study of absolutism is P. Anderson, *Lineages of the Absolutist State* (1974), a Marxist interpretation of absolutism in western and eastern Europe. The short study of M. Beloff, *The Age of Absolutism* (1967), concentrates on the social forces that underlay administrative change. H. Rosenberg, "Absolute Monarchy and Its Legacy," in *Early Modern Europe, 1450–1650* (1967), ed. N. F. Cantor and S. Werthman, is a seminal study. T. Aston, ed., *Crisis in Europe, 1560–1660* (1967), contains stimulating essays by leading authorities. The classic treatment of constitutionalism remains that of C. H. McIlwain, *Constitutionalism: Ancient and Modern* (1940), written by a great scholar during the rise of German fascism. S. B. Crimes, *English Constitutional History* (1967), is an excellent survey with valuable chapters on the sixteenth through eighteenth centuries.

Louis XIV and his age have seduced the attention of many scholars. The best contemporary biography is J. Wolf, *Louis XIV* (1968), which stresses Louis' contribution to the development of the modern bureaucratic state. For a variety of opinions about Louis, see William F. Church, ed., *Louis XIV in Historical Thought* (1978). Two works of W. H. Lewis, *The Splendid Century* (1957) and *The Sunset of the Splendid Century* (1963), make delightful reading and contain useful material on social history. R. Hatton, *Europe in the Age of Louis XIV* (1979), is a splendidly illustrated survey of many aspects of European culture in the seventeenth century. O. Ranum, *Paris in the Age of Absolutism* (1968), describes the geographical, political, economic, and architectural significance of the cultural capital of Europe. R. Mousnier, *Peasant Uprisings in Seventeenth-Century France, Russia, and China* (1970), an important study in comparative history, treats agrarian relationships and social stratification. V. L. Tapie, *The Age of Grandeur: Baroque Art and Architecture* (1960), is a magnificently illustrated book that emphasizes the relationship between art and politics. Part 4 of L. Romier, *A History of France*, trans. A. L. Rowse (1962), offers an intelligible and nationalistic narrative. For Spain, J. H. Elliott, *Imperial Spain, 1469–1716*, rev. ed. (1977), is a sensitively written and authoritative study.

G. M. Trevelyan, *England Under the Stuarts* (1960), is a good starting point for English social and political history. Brief accounts of many facets of English culture are contained in M. Ashley, *England in the Seventeenth Century* (1961), and J. H. Plumb, *England in the Eighteenth Century* (1961). M. Weber, *The Protestant Ethic and the Spirit of Capitalism* (1958), traces the relationship between Protestantism and socioeconomic developments. W. Haller, *The Rise of Puritanism* (1957), is the best treatment of English Puritanism, but it is for the advanced student. For the background to the Civil War and the war itself, see C. V. Wedgwood, *The King's Peace* (1969) and *The King's War* (1959), both highly readable; the old but scholarly biography of Cromwell by C. Firth, *Oliver Cromwell* (1956); and the recent popular study by A. Fraser, *Cromwell* (1975). C. Brinton, *The Anatomy of Revolution* (1952), contains an interesting analysis of the English Civil War and contrasts it with the French and Russian revolutions. L. Stone, *The Crisis of the Aristocracy, 1558–1641* (1967), is broader in scope than the title implies and in fact treats many aspects of English social history. Stone is a leading authority on English family history.

On Holland, the best introduction to the relationship between commercial development and the growth of democratic ideas and institutions remains Henri Pirenne, *Early Democracies in the Low Countries* (1963), especially chapters X and XI. C. R. Boxer, *The Dutch Seaborne Empire* (1980), and the appropriate chapters of D. Maland, *Europe in the Seventeenth Century* (1967), are useful for Dutch overseas expansion and the reasons for Dutch prosperity. K. H. D. Haley, *The Dutch in the Seventeenth Century* (1972), is a splendidly illustrated appreciation of Dutch commercial and artistic achievements. No recent work has replaced the well-written, thorough narrative of J. L. Motley, *The Rise of the Dutch Republic*, 3 vols., (1898).

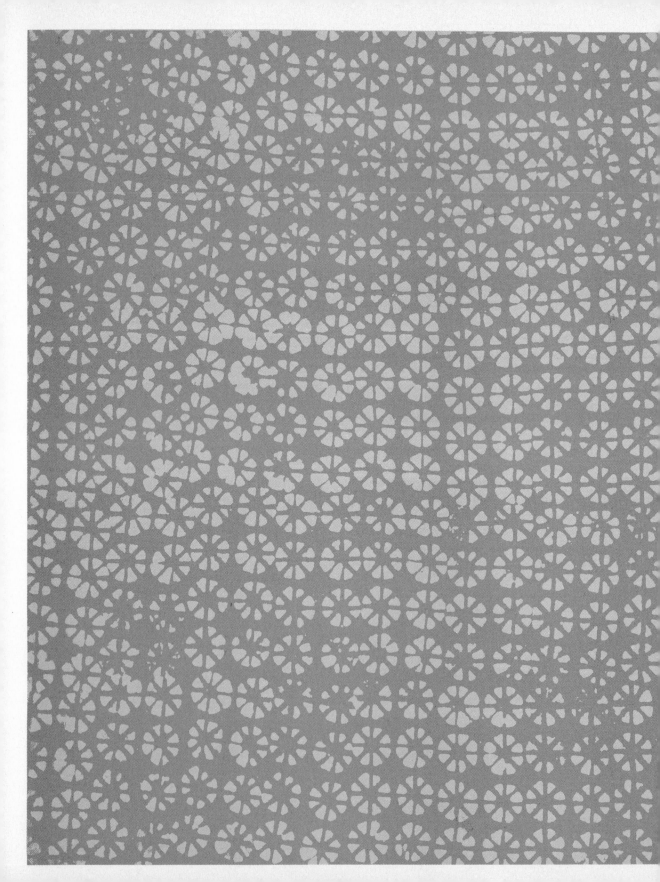

CHAPTER 21

ABSOLUTISM IN EASTERN EUROPE

THE SEVENTEENTH CENTURY witnessed a struggle between constitutionalism and absolutism in eastern Europe. With the notable exception of the kingdom of Poland, monarchial absolutism was everywhere triumphant in eastern Europe; constitutionalism was decisively defeated. Absolute monarchies emerged in Austria, Prussia, and Russia. This was a development of great significance: these three monarchies exercised enormous influence until 1918, and they created a strong authoritarian tradition that is still dominant in eastern Europe.

Although the monarchs of eastern Europe were greatly impressed by Louis XIV and his model of royal absolutism, their states differed in several important ways from their French counterpart. Louis XIV built French absolutism on the heritage of a well-developed medieval monarchy and a strong royal bureaucracy. And when Louis XIV came to the throne the powers of the nobility were already somewhat limited, the French middle class was relatively strong, and the peasants were generally free from serfdom. Eastern absolutism rested upon a very different social reality: a powerful nobility, a weak middle class, and an oppressed peasantry condemned to serfdom.

These differences in social conditions raise three major questions. First, why did the basic structure of society in eastern Europe move away from that of western Europe in the early modern period? Second, how and why, in their different social environments, did the rulers of Austria, Prussia, and Russia manage to build powerful absolute monarchies, which proved more durable than that of Louis XIV? Finally, how did the absolute monarchs' interaction with artists and architects contribute to the splendid achievements of baroque culture? These are the questions this chapter seeks to answer.

LORDS AND PEASANTS IN EASTERN EUROPE

When absolute monarchy took shape in eastern Europe in the seventeenth century, it built on social and economic foundations laid between roughly 1400 and 1650. In those years the princes and the landed nobility of eastern Europe rolled back the gains made by the peasantry during the High Middle Ages and reimposed a harsh serfdom on the rural masses. The nobility also reduced the importance of the towns and the middle classes. This process differed profoundly from developments in western Europe at the same time. In the west peasants won greater freedom and the urban capitalistic middle class continued its rise. Thus, the east that emerged contrasted sharply with the west – another aspect of the shattered unity of medieval Latin Christendom.

THE MEDIEVAL BACKGROUND

Between roughly 1400 and 1650, nobles and rulers re-established serfdom in the eastern lands of Bohemia, Silesia, Hungary, eastern Germany, Poland, Lithuania, and Russia. The east – the land east of the Elbe River in Germany, which historians often call "East Elbia" – gained a certain social and economic unity in the process. But eastern peasants lost their rights and freedoms. They became bound first to the land they worked and then, by degrading obligations, to the lords they served.

This development was a tragic reversal of trends in the High Middle Ages. The period from roughly 1050 to 1300 had been a time of general economic expansion characterized by the growth of trade, towns, and population. Expansion also meant clearing the forests and colonizing the frontier beyond the Elbe River. Anxious to attract German settlers to their sparsely populated lands, the rulers and nobles of eastern Europe had offered potential newcomers attractive economic and legal incentives. Large numbers of incoming settlers obtained land on excellent terms and gained much greater personal freedom. These benefits were also gradually extended to the local Slavic populations, even those of central Russia. Thus by 1300 there had occurred a very general improvement in peasant conditions in eastern Europe. Serfdom all but disappeared. Peasants bargained freely with their landlords and moved about as they pleased. Opportunities and improvements east of the Elbe had a positive impact on western Europe, where the weight of serfdom was also reduced between 1100 and 1300.

After about 1300, however, as Europe's population and economy both declined grievously, mainly because of the Black Death, the east and the west went in different directions. In both east and west there occurred a many-sided landlord reaction, as lords sought to solve their tough economic problems by more heavily exploiting the peasantry. Yet this reaction generally failed in the west. In many western areas by 1500 almost all of the peasants were completely free, and in the rest of western Europe serf obligations had declined greatly. East of the Elbe, however, the landlords won. By 1500, eastern peasants were well on their way to becoming serfs again.

Throughout eastern Europe, as in western Europe, the drop in population and prices in the fourteenth and fifteenth centuries caused severe labor shortages and hard times for the nobles. Yet rather than offer better economic and legal terms to keep old peasants and attract new ones, eastern landlords used their political and police power to turn the tables on the peasants. They did this in two ways.

First, the lords made their kings and princes issue laws that restricted or eliminated the peasants' precious, time-honored right of free movement. Thus, a peasant could no longer leave to take advantage of better opportunities elsewhere without the lord's permission, and the lord had no reason to make such concessions. In Prussian territories by 1500, the law required that runaway peasants be hunted down and returned to their lords; a runaway servant was to be nailed to a post by one ear and given a knife to cut himself loose. Until the middle of the fifteenth century, medieval Russian peasants had been free to move wherever they wished and seek the best landlord. Thereafter this freedom was gradually curtailed, so that by 1497 a Russian peasant had the right to move only during a two-week period after the fall harvest. Eastern peasants were losing their status as free and independent men and women.

Second, lords steadily took more and more of their peasants' land and imposed heavier and heavier labor obligations. Instead of being independent farmers paying reasonable, freely negotiated rents, peasants tended to become forced laborers on the lords' estates. By the early 1500s, lords in many territories could command their peasants to work for them without pay as many as six days a week. A German writer of the mid-sixteenth century described peasants in eastern Prussia who "do not possess the heritage of their holdings and have to serve their master whenever he wants them."[1]

The gradual erosion of the peasantry's economic position was bound up with manipulation of the oppressive legal system. The local lord was also the local prosecutor, judge, and jailer. As a matter of course, he ruled in his own favor in disputes with his peasants. There were no independent royal officials to provide justice or uphold the common law.

Between 1500 and 1650, the social, legal, and economic conditions of peasants in eastern Europe continued to decline. Free peasants lost their freedom and became serfs. In Poland, for example, nobles gained complete control over their peasants in 1574, after which they could legally inflict the death penalty on their serfs whenever they wished. In Prussia a long series of oppressive measures reached their culmination in 1653. Not only were all the old privileges of the lords reaffirmed, but peasants were assumed to be in "hereditary subjugation" to their lords unless they could prove the contrary in the lords' courts, which was practically impossible. Prussian peasants were serfs tied to their lords as well as to the land.

In Russia the right of peasants to move from a given estate was "temporarily" suspended in the 1590s and permanently abolished in 1603. In 1649, a new law code completed the process. At the insistence of the lower nobility, the Russian tsar lifted the nine-year time limit on the recovery of runaways. Henceforth, runaway peasants were to be returned to their lords whenever they were caught, as long as they lived. The last small hope of escaping serfdom was gone. Control of serfs was strictly the lords' own business, for the new law code set no limits on the lords' authority over their peasants. Although the political development of the various eastern states differed, the legal re-establishment of permanent hereditary serfdom was the common fate of peasants in the east by the middle of the seventeenth century.

The consolidation of serfdom between 1500 and 1650 was accompanied by the growth of estate agriculture, particularly in Poland and eastern Germany. In the sixteenth century European economic expansion and population growth resumed after the great declines of the late Middle Ages. Prices for agricultural commodities also rose sharply as gold and silver flowed in from the New World. Thus, Polish and German lords had powerful economic incentives to increase the production of their estates. And they did.

Lords seized more and more peasant land for their own estates and then demanded and received ever more unpaid serf labor on those enlarged estates. Even when the estates were inefficient and technically backward, as they generally were, the great Polish nobles and middle-rank German lords squeezed sizable, cheap, and thus very profitable surpluses out of their impoverished peasants. These surpluses in wheat and timber were easily sold to big foreign merchants, who exported them to the growing cities of the west. The poor east helped feed the much wealthier west.

The re-emergence of serfdom in eastern Europe in the early modern period was clearly a momentous human development, and historians have advanced a variety of explanations for it. As always, some scholars have stressed the economic interpretation. Agricultural depression and population decline in the fourteenth and fifteenth centuries led to a severe labor shortage, they have argued, and thus eastern landlords naturally tied their precious peasants to the land. With the return of prosperity and the development of export markets in the sixteenth century, the landlords finished the job, grabbing the peasants' land and making them work as unpaid serfs on the enlarged estates. This argument by itself is not very convincing, for almost identical economic developments "caused" the opposite result in the west. Indeed, some historians have maintained that labor shortage and subsequent renewed expansion were key factors in the virtual disappearance of serfdom in western Europe.

PUNISHING SERFS *This seventeenth-century illustration from Olearius's famous* Travels to Moscovy *suggests what eastern serfdom really meant. The scene* *is eastern Poland. There, according to Olearius, a common command of the lord was, "Beat him till the skin falls from the flesh." (Photo: Caroline Buckler)*

It seems fairly clear, therefore, that political rather than economic factors were crucial in the simultaneous rise of serfdom in the east and decline of serfdom in the west. Specifically, eastern lords enjoyed much greater political power than their western counterparts. In the late Middle Ages, when much of eastern Europe experienced innumerable wars and general political chaos, the noble landlord class greatly increased its political power at the expense of the ruling monarchs. There were, for example, many disputed royal successions, so that weak kings were forced to grant political favors to win the support of the nobility. Thus while strong "new monarchs" were rising in Spain, France, and England and providing effective central government, kings were generally losing power in the east. Such weak kings could not resist the demands of the lords regarding their peasants.

Moreover, most eastern monarchs did not want to resist even if they could. The typical king was only "first among equals" in the noble class. He too thought mainly in "private" rather than "public" terms. He too wanted to squeeze as much as he could out of *his* peasants and enlarge *his* estates. The western concept and reality of sovereignty, as embodied in a king who protected the interests of all his people, was not well developed in eastern Europe before 1650.

The political power of the peasants was also weaker in eastern Europe, and declined steadily after about 1400. Although there were occasional bloody peasant uprisings against the oppression of the landlords, they never succeeded. Nor did eastern peasants effectively resist day-by-day infringements on their liberties by their landlords. Part of the reason was that the lords, rather than the kings, ran the courts – one of the important concessions nobles extorted from weak monarchs. It has also been suggested that peasant solidarity was weaker in the east, possibly reflecting the lack of long-established village communities on the eastern frontier.

Finally, with the approval of weak kings, the landlords systematically undermined the medieval privileges of the towns and the power of the urban classes. Instead of selling their products to local merchants in the towns, as required in the Middle Ages, the landlords sold directly to big foreign capitalists. For example, Dutch ships sailed up the rivers of Poland and eastern Germany to the loading docks of the great estates, completely short-circuiting the local towns. Moreover, "town air" no longer "made people free," for the eastern towns lost their medieval right of refuge and were compelled to return runaways to their lords. The population of the towns and the importance of the urban middle classes declined greatly. This development both reflected and promoted the supremacy of noble landlords in most of eastern Europe in the sixteenth century.

THE RISE OF AUSTRIA AND PRUSSIA

In spite of the strength of the nobility and the weakness of many monarchs before 1600,

strong kings did begin to emerge in many lands in the course of the seventeenth century. War and the threat of war aided rulers greatly in their attempts to build absolute monarchies. There was an endless struggle for power, as eastern rulers not only fought each other but also battled with hordes of Asiatic invaders. In this atmosphere of continuous wartime emergency, monarchs reduced the political power of the landlord nobility. Cautiously leaving the nobles the unchallenged masters of their peasants, the absolutist monarchs of eastern Europe gradually gained and monopolized political power in three key areas. They imposed and collected permanent taxes without consent. They maintained permanent standing armies, which policed their subjects in addition to fighting abroad. And they conducted relations with other states as they pleased.

As with all general historical developments, there were important variations on the absolutist theme in eastern Europe. The royal absolutism created in Prussia was stronger and more effective than that established in Austria. This advantage gave Prussia a thin edge over Austria in the struggle for power in east-central Europe in the eighteenth century. That edge had enormous long-term political significance, for it was a rising Prussia that unified the German people in the nineteenth century and imposed upon them a fateful Prussian stamp.

AUSTRIA AND THE OTTOMAN TURKS

Like all the peoples and rulers of central Europe, the Habsburgs of Austria emerged from the Thirty Years' War (pages 690–696) impoverished and exhausted. The effort to root out Protestantism in the German lands had failed utterly, and the authority of the Holy Roman Empire and its Habsburg em-

THE OTTOMAN SLAVE TAX *This contemporary drawing shows Ottoman officials rounding up male Christian children in the Balkans. The children became part of a special slave corps, which served the* sultan for life as soldiers and administrators. The slave tax and the slave corps were of great importance to the Ottoman Turks in the struggle with Austria. (The British Museum)

perors had declined almost to the vanishing point. Yet defeat in central Europe also opened new vistas. The Habsburg monarchs were forced to turn inward and eastward in the attempt to fuse their diverse holdings into a strong unified state.

An important step in this direction had actually been taken in Bohemia during the Thirty Years' War. Protestantism had been strong among the Czechs of Bohemia, and in 1618 the Czech nobles who controlled the Bohemian Estates — the semiparliamentary body of Bohemia — had risen up against their Habsburg king. Not only was this revolt crushed, but the old Czech nobility was wiped out as well. Those Czech nobles who did not die in 1620 at the battle of the White Mountain (page 693), a momentous turning point in Czech history, had their estates confiscated. The Habsburg king, Ferdinand II (1619–1637), then redistributed the Czech lands to a motley band of aristocratic soldiers of fortune from all over Europe.

In fact, after 1650, 80 to 90 percent of the Bohemian nobility was of recent foreign origin and owed everything to the Habsburgs.

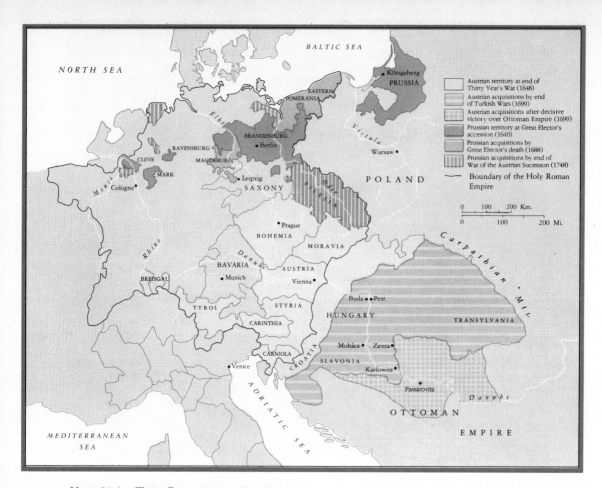

MAP 21.1 THE GROWTH OF AUSTRIA AND BRANDENBURG-PRUSSIA TO 1748 *Austria expanded to the southwest into Hungary and Transylvania at the expense of the Ottoman Empire. But it was unable to hold the rich German province of Silesia, which was conquered by Brandenburg-Prussia.*

With the help of this new nobility, the Habsburgs established strong direct rule over reconquered Bohemia. The condition of the enserfed peasantry worsened: three days per week of unpaid labor – the *robot* – became the norm, and a quarter of the serfs worked for their lords every day but Sundays and religious holidays. Serfs also paid the taxes, which further strengthened the alliance between the Habsburg monarch and the Bohemian nobility. Protestantism was also stamped out, in the course of which a growing unity of religion was brought about. The reorgani-

zation of Bohemia was a giant step toward absolutism.

After the Thirty Years' War, Ferdinand III centralized the government in the old hereditary provinces of Austria proper, the second part of the Habsburg holdings (see Map 21.1). For the first time he created a permanent standing army, which stood ready to put down any internal opposition. The Habsburg monarchy was then ready to turn toward the vast plains of Hungary, which it claimed as the third and largest part of its dominion, in opposition to the Ottoman Turks.

The Ottomans came out of the Anatolia, in present-day Turkey, and they created one of history's greatest military empires. At their peak in the middle of the sixteenth century under Suleiman the Magnificent (1520–1566), they ruled the most powerful empire in the world, bar none. Their possessions stretched from western Persia across North Africa and up into the heart of central Europe. Apostles of Islam, the Ottoman Turks were old and determined foes of the Catholic Habsburgs. Their armies had almost captured Vienna in 1529, and for more than 150 years thereafter they ruled all of the Balkans, almost all of Hungary, and part of southern Russia.

The Ottoman Empire was originally built on a fascinating and very non-European conception of state and society. There was an almost complete absence of private landed property. All the agricultural land of the empire was the personal hereditary property of the sultan, who exploited the land as he saw fit according to Ottoman political theory. There was, therefore, no security of landholding and no hereditary nobility. Everyone was dependent upon the sultan and virtually his slave.

Indeed, the top ranks of the bureaucracy were staffed by the sultan's slave corps. Every year the sultan levied a "tax" of one to three thousand male children upon the conquered Christian populations in the Balkans. These and other slaves were raised in Turkey as Muslims, and trained to fight and to administer. The most talented slaves rose to the top of the bureaucracy; the less fortunate formed the brave and skillful core of the sultan's army, the so-called janissary corps.

As long as the Ottoman Empire expanded, the system worked well. As the sultan won more territory, he could impose his slave tax on larger populations. Moreover, he could amply reward loyal and effective servants by letting them draw a carefully defined income from conquered Christian peasants on a strictly temporary basis. For a long time Christian peasants in eastern Europe were economically exploited less by the Muslim Turks than by Christian nobles, and they were not forced to convert to Islam. After about 1570, however, the powerful, centralized Ottoman system slowly began to disintegrate as the Turks' western advance was stopped. Temporary landholders became hard-to-control permanent oppressors. Weak sultans left the glory of the battlefield for the delights of the harem, and the army lost its dedication and failed to keep up with European military advances.

Yet in the late seventeenth century, under vigorous reforming leadership, the Ottoman Empire succeeded in marshaling its forces for one last mighty blow at Christian Europe. After wresting territory from Poland, fighting a long inconclusive war with Russia, and establishing an alliance with Louis XIV of France, the Turks turned again on Austria. A huge Turkish army surrounded Vienna and laid siege to it in 1683. But after holding out against great odds for two months, the city was relieved by a mixed force of Habsburg, Saxon, Bavarian, and Polish troops, and the Ottomans were forced to retreat. Soon the retreat became a rout. As their Russian and Venetian allies attacked on other fronts, the Habsburgs conquered all of Hungary and Transylvania (part of present-day Rumania) by 1699.

The Turkish wars and this great expansion strengthened the Habsburg army and promoted some sense of unity in the Habsburg lands. The Habsburgs moved to centralize their power and make it as absolute as possible. These efforts to create a fully developed, highly centralized, absolutist state were only partly successful.

The Habsburg state was composed of three separate and distinct territories – the old "hereditary provinces" of Austria, the kingdom of Bohemia, and the kingdom of Hungary. These three parts were tied together primarily by their common ruler – the Habsburg monarch. Each part had its own laws and political life, for the three noble-dominated Estates continued to exist, though with reduced powers. The Habsburgs themselves were well aware of the fragility of the union they had forged. In 1713, Charles VI (1711–1740) proclaimed the so-called Pragmatic Sanction, which stated that the Habsburg possessions were never to be divided and were always to be passed intact to a single heir, who might be female since Charles had no sons. Charles spent much of his reign trying to get this principle accepted by the various branches of the Habsburg family, by the three different Estates of the realm, and by the states of Europe. His fears turned out to be well founded.

The Hungarian nobility, despite its reduced strength, effectively thwarted the full development of Habsburg absolutism. Time and again throughout the seventeenth century, Hungarian nobles – the most numerous in Europe, making up from 5 to 7 percent of the Hungarian population – rose in revolt against the attempts of Vienna to impose absolute rule. They never triumphed decisively, but neither were they ever crushed and replaced as the Czech nobility had been in 1620.

Hungarians resisted because many of them were Protestants, especially in the area long ruled by the more tolerant Turks, and they hated the heavy-handed attempts of the conquering Habsburgs to re-Catholicize everyone. Moreover, the lords of Hungary often found a powerful military ally in Turkey. Finally, the Hungarian nobility, and even part of the peasantry, had become attached to a national ideal long before most of the peoples of Europe. They were determined to maintain as much independence and local control as possible. Thus when the Habsburgs were bogged down in the War of the Spanish Succession (page 730), the Hungarians rose in one last patriotic rebellion under Prince Francis Rakoczy in 1703. Rakoczy and his forces were eventually defeated, but this time the Habsburgs had to accept a definitive compromise. Charles VI restored many of the traditional privileges of the Hungarian aristocracy in return for Hungarian acceptance of hereditary Habsburg rule. Thus Hungary, unlike Austria or Bohemia, never came close to being fully integrated into a centralized, absolute Habsburg state.

PRUSSIA IN THE SEVENTEENTH CENTURY

After 1400, the status of east German peasants declined steadily; their serfdom was formally spelled out in the early seventeenth century. While the local princes lost political power and influence, a revitalized landed nobility became the undisputed ruling class. The Hohenzollern family, which ruled through its senior and junior branches as the electors of Brandenburg and the dukes of Prussia, had little real princely power. The Hohenzollern rulers were nothing more than the "first among equals," the largest landowners in a landlord society.

Nothing suggested that the Hohenzollerns and their territories would ever play an important role in European or even German affairs. The elector of Brandenburg's right to help choose the Holy Roman emperor with six other electors was of little practical value, and the elector had no military strength whatsoever. The territory of his cousin, the duke of Prussia, was actually part of the kingdom of Poland. Moreover, geography conspired against the Hohenzollerns. Brandenburg, their power base, was completely cut off from the sea (see Map 21.1). A tiny part of the vast north European plain that stretches from France to Russia, Brandenburg lacked natural frontiers and lay open to attack from all directions. The land was poor, a combination of sand and swamp. Contemporaries contemptuously called Brandenburg "the sand-box of the Holy Roman Empire."[2]

Brandenburg was a helpless spectator in the Thirty Years' War, its territory alternately ravaged by Swedish and by Habsburg armies. Population fell drastically, and many villages disappeared. The power of the Hohenzollerns reached its lowest point. Yet the devastation of the country prepared the way for Hohenzollern absolutism, because foreign armies dramatically weakened the political power of the Estates — the representative assemblies of the realm. This weakening of the Estates helped the very talented young elector Frederick William (1640–1688), later known as the Great Elector, to ride roughshod over traditional parliamentary liberties and to take a giant step toward royal absolutism. This constitutional struggle, often unjustly neglected by historians, was the most crucial in Prussian history for hundreds of years, until that of the 1860s.

When he came to power in 1640, the twenty-year-old Great Elector was determined to unify his three quite separate provinces and to add to them by diplomacy and war. These provinces were historic Brandenburg, the area around Berlin; Prussia, inherited in 1618 when the junior branch of the Hohenzollern family died out; and completely separate, scattered holdings along the Rhine in western Germany, inherited in 1614 (see Map 21.1). Each of the three provinces was inhabited by Germans; but each had its own Estates, whose power had increased until about 1600 as the power of the rulers declined. Although the Estates had not met regularly during the chaotic Thirty Years' War, they still had the power of the purse in their respective provinces. Taxes could not be levied without their consent. The Estates of Brandenburg and Prussia were dominated by the nobility and the landowning classes, known as the Junkers. But it must be remembered that this was also true of the English Parliament before and after the Civil War. Had the Estates successfully resisted the absolutist demands of the Great Elector, they too might have evolved toward more broadly based constitutionalism.

The struggle between the Great Elector and the provincial Estates was long, complicated, and intense. After the Thirty Years' War, the representatives of the nobility zealously reasserted the right of the Estates to vote taxes, a right the Swedish armies of occupation had simply ignored. Yet first in Brandenburg in 1653, and then in Prussia between 1661 and 1663, the Great Elector eventually had his way.

To pay for the permanent standing army he first established in 1660, Frederick William forced the Estates to accept the introduction of permanent taxation without consent. Moreover, the soldiers doubled as tax collectors and policemen, becoming the core of the rapidly expanding state bureaucracy. The power of the Estates declined rapidly thereafter, for the Great Elector had both financial independence and superior force. He turned the screws of taxation: the state's total revenue tripled during his reign. The size of the army leaped about tenfold. In 1688, a population of one million was supporting a peacetime standing army of thirty thousand. Many of the soldiers were French Huguenot immigrants, whom the Great Elector welcomed as the talented, hardworking citizens they were.

In accounting for the Great Elector's fateful triumph, two factors appear central. As in the formation of every absolutist state, war was a decisive factor. The ongoing struggle between Sweden and Poland for control of the

Baltic after 1648 and the wars of Louis XIV in western Europe created an atmosphere of permanent crisis. The wild Tartars of southern Russia swept through Prussia in the winter of 1656–1657, killing and carrying off as slaves more than fifty thousand people, according to an old estimate. This invasion softened up the Estates and strengthened the urgency of the elector's demands for more money for more soldiers. It was no accident that, except for commercially minded Holland, constitutionalism won out only in England, the only major country to escape devastating foreign invasions in the seventeenth century.

Second, the nobility had long dominated the government through the Estates, but only for its own narrow self-interest. When the crunch came, the Prussian nobles proved unwilling to join the representatives of the towns in a consistent common front against royal pretensions. The nobility was all too concerned with its own rights and privileges, especially its freedom from taxation and its unlimited control over the peasants. When, therefore, the Great Elector reconfirmed these privileges in 1653 and after, even while reducing the political power of the Estates, the nobility growled but did not bite. It accepted a compromise whereby the bulk of the new taxes fell upon towns, and royal authority stopped at the landlords' gates. The elector could and did use naked force to break the liberties of the towns. The main leader of the urban opposition in the key city of Königsberg, for example, was simply arrested and imprisoned for life without trial.

THE CONSOLIDATION OF PRUSSIAN ABSOLUTISM

By the time of his death in 1688, the Great Elector had created a single state out of scattered principalities. But his new creation was still small and fragile. All the leading states of Europe had many more people – France with 20 million was fully twenty times as populous – and strong monarchy was still a novelty. Moreover, the Great Elector's successor, Elector Frederick III, "the Ostentatious" (1688–1713), was weak of body and mind.

Like so many of the small princes of Germany and Italy at the time, Frederick III imitated Louis XIV in every possible way. He built his own very expensive version of Versailles. He surrounded himself with cultivated artists and musicians and basked in the praise of toadies and sycophants. His only real political accomplishment was to gain the title of king from the Holy Roman emperor, a Habsburg, in return for military aid in the War of the Spanish Succession, and in 1701 he was crowned King Frederick I.

This tendency toward luxury-loving, happy, and harmless petty tyranny was completely reversed by Frederick William I (1713–1740), "the Soldiers' King." A crude, dangerous psychoneurotic, Frederick William I was nevertheless the most talented reformer ever produced by the Hohenzollern family. It was he who truly established Prussian absolutism and gave it its unique character. It was he who created the best army in Europe, for its size, and who infused military values into a whole society. In the words of a leading historian of Prussia:

For a whole generation, the Hohenzollern subjects were victimized by a royal bully, imbued with an obsessive bent for military organization and military scales of value. This left a deep mark upon the institutions of Prussiandom and upon the molding of the "Prussian spirit."[3]

Frederick William's passion for the army and military life was intensely emotional. He had, for example, a bizarre, almost pathological love for tall soldiers, whom he credited

THE "TOBACCO PARLIAMENT" In absolutist Prussia the informal discussion of politics by the king and his friends over a pipe after dinner was the only parliament. (Historical Picture Service, Chicago)

with superior strength and endurance. Austere and always faithful to his wife, he confided to the French ambassador: "The most beautiful girl or woman in the world would be a matter of indifference to me, but tall soldiers – they are my weakness." Like some fanatical modern-day basketball coach in search of a championship team, he sent his agents throughout both Prussia and all of Europe, tricking, buying, and kidnapping top recruits. Neighboring princes sent him their giants as gifts to win his gratitude. Prussian mothers told their sons: "Stop growing or the recruiting agents will get you."[4]

Profoundly military in temperament, Frederick William always wore an army uniform, and he lived the highly disciplined life of the professional soldier. He began his work by five or six in the morning; at ten he almost always went to the parade ground to drill or inspect his troops. A man of violent temper, Frederick William personally punished the

MOLDING THE PRUSSIAN SPIRIT *Discipline was strict and punishment brutal in the Prussian army. This scene, intended to instruct school children, shows one soldier being flogged while another is being beaten with canes as he walks between rows of troops. (Photo: Caroline Buckler)*

most minor infractions on the spot: a missing button off a soldier's coat quickly provoked a savage beating with his heavy walking stick.

Frederick William's love of the army was also based on a hardheaded conception of the struggle for power and a dog-eat-dog view of international politics. Even before ascending the throne he bitterly criticized his father's ministers: "They say that they will obtain land and power for the king with the pen; but I say it can be done only with the sword." Years later he summed up his life's philoso-phy in his instructions to his son: "A formidable army and a war chest large enough to make this army mobile in times of need can create great respect for you in the world, so that you can speak a word like the other powers."[5] This unshakable belief that the welfare of king and state depended upon the army above all else reinforced Frederick William's personal passion for playing soldier.

The cult of military power provided the rationale for a great expansion of royal absolutism. As the king himself put it with his characteristic ruthlessness: "I must be served with life and limb, with house and wealth, with honour and conscience, everything must be committed except eternal salvation – that belongs to God, but all else is mine."[6] To make good these extraordinary demands, Frederick William created a strong centralized bureaucracy. More commoners probably rose to top positions in the civil government than at any other time in Prussia's history. The last traces of the parliamentary Estates and local self-government vanished.

The king's grab for power brought him into considerable conflict with the noble landowners, the Junkers. In his early years, he even threatened to destroy them; yet, in the end, the Prussian nobility was not destroyed but enlisted – into the army. Responding to a combination of threats and opportunities, the Junkers became the officer caste. By 1739, all but 5 of 245 officers with the rank of major or above were aristocrats, and most of them were native Prussians. A new compromise had been worked out, whereby the proud nobility imperiously commanded the peasantry in the army as well as on its estates.

Coarse and crude, penny-pinching and hardworking, Frederick William achieved results. Above all, he built a first-rate army on the basis of third-rate resources. The standing army increased from 38,000 to 83,000 during his reign. Prussia, twelfth in Europe in population, had the fourth largest army by 1740. Only the much more populous states of France, Russia, and Austria had larger forces, and even France's army was only twice as large as Prussia's. Moreover, soldier for soldier, the Prussian army became the best in Europe, astonishing foreign observers with its precision, skill, and discipline. For the next two hundred years, Prussia and then Prussianized Germany would almost always win the crucial military battles.

Frederick William and his ministers also built an exceptionally honest and conscientious bureaucracy, which not only administered the country but tried with some success to develop it economically. Finally, like the miser he was, living very frugally off the income of his own landholdings, the king loved his "blue boys" so much that he hated to "spend" them. This most militaristic of kings was, paradoxically, almost always at peace.

Nevertheless, the Prussian people paid a heavy and lasting price for the obsessions of the royal drillmaster. Civil society became rigid and highly disciplined. Prussia became "the Sparta of the North"; unquestioning obedience was the highest virtue. As a Prussian minister later summed it up, "To keep quiet is the first civic duty."[7] Thus, the policies of Frederick William I combined with harsh peasant bondage and Junker tyranny to lay the foundations for what later evolved into probably the most militaristic country of modern times.

Frederick II (1740–1786), also known as Frederick the Great, built masterfully upon his father's work. This was somewhat surprising, for like many children with tyrannical (or kindly) parents, he rebelled against his parents' wishes in his early years. Rejecting the crude life of the barracks, Frederick embraced culture and literature, even writing poetry and fine prose in French, a language his father detested. He threw off his father's dour Calvinism and dabbled with atheism. After trying, unsuccessfully, to run away at age eighteen in 1730, he was virtually imprisoned and even compelled to watch his companion in flight beheaded at his father's command. Yet, like many other rebellious youths, Frederick eventually reached a reconciliation with his father, and by the time he came to the throne ten years later he was determined to follow in his father's footsteps.

When, therefore, the emperor of Austria, Charles VI, also died in 1740 and his young and beautiful daughter, Maria Theresa, became queen of the Habsburg dominions, Frederick suddenly and without warning invaded her rich all-German province of Silesia. This action defied solemn Prussian promises to respect the Pragmatic Sanction, which guaranteed Maria Theresa's succession, but no matter. For Frederick, it was the opportunity of a lifetime to expand the size and power of Prussia. Although Maria Theresa succeeded in dramatically rallying the normally quarrelsome Hungarian nobility, her multinational army was no match for Prussian precision. In 1742, as other greedy powers were falling upon her lands in the general European War of the Austrian Succession (1740-1748), she was forced to cede all of Silesia to Prussia. In one stroke Prussia doubled its population to 6 million people. Now Prussia unquestionably towered above all the other German states and stood as a European Great Power.

Frederick had to spend much of his reign fighting against great odds not only to hold onto his initial gains but to save Prussia from total destruction. In the end he succeeded, worthy heir of "the Soldiers' King" he sought to please. In 1760, at the very height of his struggle against invading armies on all sides, Frederick recounted a dream in which he met his father with his favorite general at the palace. "Have I done well?" he asked. "Very well," Frederick William replied. "That pleases me greatly," said Frederick. "Your approval means more to me than that of the whole world."[8]

THE DEVELOPMENT OF RUSSIA

One of the favorite parlor games of nineteenth-century Russian (and non-Russian) in-

tellectuals was debating whether Russia was a part of western European civilization or was a "nonwestern," "Asiatic" civilization. This question was particularly fascinating because it was unanswerable. A good case could be made for either position. To this day Russia differs fundamentally from the West in some basic ways, though Russian history has paralleled that of the West in other ways. Thus the hypnotic attraction of Russian history.

The differences between Russia and the West were particularly striking before 1700, when Russia's overall development began to draw progressively closer to that of its western neighbors. These early differences and Russia's long isolation from Europe explain why little has so far been said here about Russia. Yet it is impossible to understand how Russia has increasingly influenced and been influenced by western European civilization since roughly the late seventeenth century without looking at the course of early Russian history. Such a brief survey will also help explain how, when absolute monarchy finally and decisively triumphed under the rough guidance of Peter the Great in the early eighteenth century, it was a quite different type of absolute monarchy from that of France or even Prussia.

THE VIKINGS AND THE KIEVAN PRINCIPALITY

In antiquity the Slavs lived as a single people in central Europe. With the start of the mass migrations of the late Roman Empire, the Slavs moved in different directions and split into three groups. Between the fifth and ninth centuries the eastern Slavs, from whom the Ukrainians, the Russians, and the White Russians descend, moved into the vast and practically uninhabited area of present-day European Russia (see Map 21.2).

This enormous area consisted of an immense virgin forest to the north, where most of the eastern Slavs settled, and an endless prairie grassland to the south. Probably organized as tribal communities, the eastern Slavs, like many North American pioneers much later, lived off the great abundance of wild game and a crude "slash and burn" agriculture. After clearing a piece of the forest to build log cabins, they burned the stumps and brush. The ashes left a rich deposit of potash and lime, and the land gave several good crops before it was exhausted. The people then moved on to another untouched area and repeated the process.

In the ninth century the Vikings, those fearless warriors from Scandinavia, appeared in the lands of the eastern Slavs. Called Varangians in the old Russian chronicles, the Vikings were interested primarily in international trade, and the opportunities were good, since the Muslim conquests of the eighth century had greatly reduced Christian trade in the Mediterranean. Moving up and down the rivers, the Vikings soon linked Scandinavia and northern Europe with the Black Sea and the Byzantine Empire with its capital at Constantinople. They built a few strategic forts along the rivers, from which they raided the neighboring Slavic tribes and collected tribute. Slaves were the most important article of tribute, and the word *Slav* even became the word for slave in several European languages.

In order to increase and protect their international commerce, the Vikings declared themselves the rulers of the eastern Slavs. According to tradition, the semilegendary chieftain Ruirik founded the princely dynasty about 860. In any event, the Varangian ruler Oleg (878–912) established his residence at Kiev. He and his successors ruled over a loosely united confederation of Slavic territories – the Kievan state – until 1054. The Viking prince and his clansmen quickly became assimilated into the Slavic population, taking local wives and emerging as the noble class.

Assimilation and loss of Scandinavian ethnic identity was speeded up by the conversion of the Vikings to Eastern Orthodox Christianity by missionaries from the Byzantine Empire. The written language of these missionaries, Slavic – Church Slavonic – was subsequently used in all religious and nonreligious documents in the Kievan principality. Thus the rapidly Slavified Vikings left two important legacies for the future. They created a loose unification of Slavic territories under a single ruling prince and a single ruling dynasty. And they imposed a basic religious unity by accepting Orthodox Christianity, as opposed to Roman Catholicism, for themselves and the eastern Slavs.

Even at its height under Great Prince Iaroslav the Wise (1019–1054), the unity of the Kievan principality was extremely tenuous. Trade, rather than government, was the main concern of the rulers. Moreover, the Slavified Vikings failed to find a way of peacefully transferring power from one generation to the next. In medieval western Europe this fundamental problem of government was increasingly resolved by resort to the principle of primogeniture: the king's eldest son received the crown as his rightful inheritance when his father died. Civil war was thus averted; order was preserved. In early Kiev, however, there were apparently no fixed rules and much strife accompanied each succession.

Possibly to avoid such chaos, before his death in 1054 Great Prince Iaroslav divided the Kievan principality among his five sons, who in turn divided their properties when they died. Between 1054 and 1237, Kiev disintegrated into more and more competing units, each ruled by a prince claiming to be a descendant of Ruirik. Even when only one prince was claiming to be the great prince, the whole situation was very unsettled.

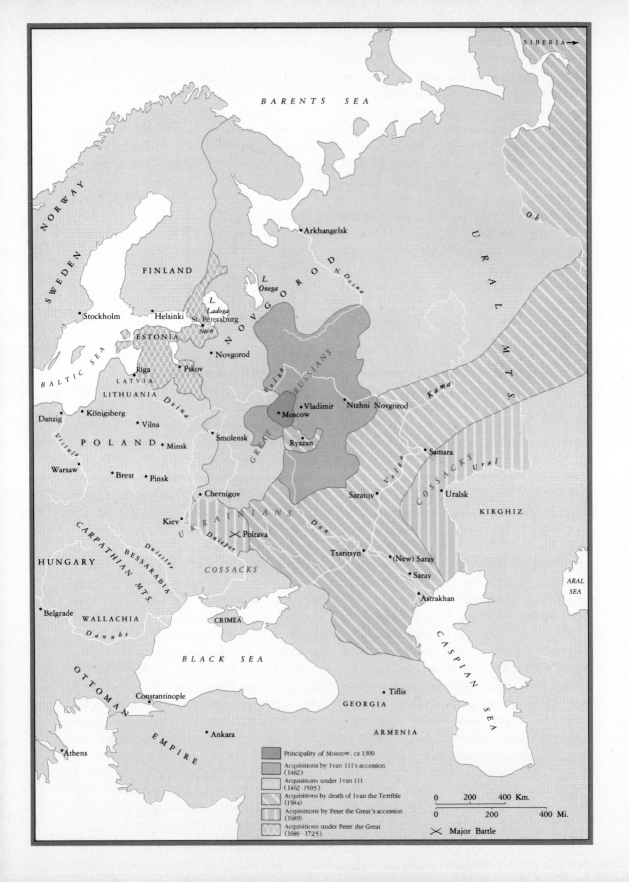

BARENTS SEA

SIBERIA →

NORWAY

SWEDEN

FINLAND

Stockholm
Helsinki
St. Petersburg
ESTONIA
Riga
LATVIA
LITHUANIA

BALTIC SEA

Danzig
Königsberg
Vilna

POLAND
Minsk

Warsaw
Brest
Pinsk

HUNGARY

CARPATHIAN MTS.
BESSARABIA

Belgrade
WALLACHIA
Danube

OTTOMAN

Constantinople

EMPIRE

Athens

Ankara

• Arkhangelsk

L. Onega

N. Dvina

L. Ladoga
Neva

NOVGOROD

Novgorod
Pskov

Dvina

GREAT

Smolensk

• Chernigov

Kiev
UKRAINIANS
Dnieper

Dniester

COSSACKS

CRIMEA

BLACK SEA

Volga

RUSSIANS

Moscow
Vladimir
Nizhni Novgorod

Ryazan

Kama

URAL MTS.

Ob

Samara

Saratov

Don

Volga

Ural

COSSACKS

Uralsk

KIRGHIZ

Tsaritsyn

(New) Saray

Saray

Astrakhan

ARAL
SEA

GEORGIA

Tiflis

ARMENIA

CASPIAN SEA

Poltava

☐ Principality of Moscow, ca 1300

☐ Acquisitions by Ivan III's accession (1462)

☐ Acquisitions under Ivan III (1462–1505)

☐ Acquisitions by death of Ivan the Terrible (1584)

☐ Acquisitions by Peter the Great's accession (1689)

☐ Acquisitions under Peter the Great (1689–1725)

0   200   400 Km.

0   200   400 Mi.

✕ Major Battle

MAP 21.2 THE EXPANSION OF RUSSIA TO
1725 *After the disintegration of the Kievan state
and the Mongol conquest, the princes of Moscow and
their descendants gradually extended their rule over
an enormous territory.*

The princes divided their land like private
property because they thought of it as private
property. A given prince owned a certain
number of farms or landed estates, and had
them worked directly by his people, mainly
slaves, called *kholops* in Russian. Outside of
these estates, which constituted the princely
domain, the prince exercised only very limited
authority in his principality. Excluding the
clergy, two kinds of people lived there: the
noble boyars and the commoner peasants.

The boyars were the descendants of the
original Viking warriors, and they also held
their lands as free and clear private property.
And although the boyars normally fought in
princely armies, the customary law declared
they could serve any prince they wished. The
ordinary peasants were also truly free. The
peasants could move at will wherever opportunities were greatest. In the touching phrase
of the times, theirs was "a clean road, without
boundaries."[9] In short, fragmented princely
power, private property, and personal freedom
all went together.

THE MONGOL YOKE AND THE RISE OF
MOSCOW

The eastern Slavs, like the Germans and the
Italians, might have emerged from the Middle
Ages weak and politically divided, had it not
been for a development of extraordinary importance – the Mongol conquest of the Kievan state. Wild nomadic tribes from present-
day Mongolia, the Mongols were temporarily
unified in the thirteenth century by Jenghiz
Khan (1162–1227), one of history's greatest

conquerors. In five years his armies subdued
all of China. His successors then wheeled
westward, smashing everything in their path
and reaching the plains of Hungary vic-
toriously before they pulled back in 1242. The
Mongol army – the Golden Horde – was savage in the extreme, often slaughtering the entire population of cities before burning them
to the ground. On route to Mongolia, Archbishop John of Plano Carpini, the famous
papal ambassador to Mongolia, passed through
Kiev in southern Russia in 1245–1246 and
wrote an unforgettable eyewitness account:

*The Mongols went against Russia and enacted a
great massacre in the Russian land. They destroyed towns and fortresses and killed people. They
besieged Kiev which had been the capital of Russia,
and after a long siege they took it and killed the
inhabitants of the city. For this reason, when we
passed through that land, we found lying in the
field countless heads and bones of dead people; for
this city had been extremely large and very populous, whereas now it has been reduced to nothing:
barely two hundred houses stand there, and those
people are held in the harshest slavery.*[10]

Having devastated and conquered, the
Mongols ruled the eastern Slavs for more than
two hundred years. They built their capital of
Saray on the lower Volga (see Map 21.2).
They forced all the bickering Slavic princes to
submit to their rule and to give them tribute
and slaves. If the conquered peoples rebelled,
the Mongols were quick to punish with death
and destruction. Thus, the Mongols unified
the eastern Slavs, for the Mongol khan was
acknowledged by all as the supreme ruler.

The Mongol unification completely
changed the internal political situation. Although the Mongols conquered, they were
quite willing to use local princes as their obedient servants and tax collectors. Therefore
they did not abolish the title of great prince,

bestowing it instead upon the prince who served them best and paid them most handsomely.

Beginning with Alexander Nevsky in 1252, the previously insignificant princes of Moscow became particularly adept at serving the Mongols. They loyally put down popular uprisings and collected the khan's harsh taxes. By way of reward the princes of Moscow emerged as hereditary great princes. Eventually the Muscovite princes were able to destroy their princely rivals and even to replace the khan as supreme ruler. In this complex process, two princes of Moscow after Alexander Nevsky – Ivan I and Ivan III – were especially noteworthy.

Ivan I (1328–1341) was popularly known as Ivan the Moneybag. A bit like Frederick William of Prussia, he was extremely stingy and built up a large personal fortune. This enabled him to buy more property and to increase his influence by loaning money to less frugal princes to pay their Mongol taxes. Ivan's most serious rival was the prince of Tver, whom the Mongols at one point appointed as great prince.

In 1327, the popultion of Tver revolted against Mongol oppression, and the prince of Tver joined his people. Ivan immediately went to the Mongol capital of Saray, where he was appointed commander of a large Russian-Mongol army, which then laid waste to Tver and its lands. For this proof of devotion, the Mongols made Ivan the general tax collector for all the Slavic lands they had subjugated and named him great prince. Ivan also convinced the metropolitan of Kiev, the leading churchman of all eastern Slavs, to settle in Moscow; Ivan I thus gained greater prestige, while the church gained a powerful advocate before the khan.

In the next hundred-odd years, in the course of innumerable wars and intrigues, the great princes of Moscow significantly in-

creased their holdings. Then, in the reign of Ivan III (1462–1505), the long process was largely completed. After purchasing Rostov, Ivan conquered and annexed other principalities, of which Novgorod with its lands extending as far as the Baltic Sea was most crucial (see Map 21.2). Thus, more than four hundred years after Iaroslav the Wise had divided the embryonic Kievan state, the princes of Moscow defeated all the rival branches of the house of Ruirik and became the unique holder of princely power.

Another dimension to princely power developed. Not only were the princes of Moscow the *unique* rulers, they were the *absolute* rulers, the autocrat, the *tsar* – the Slavic contraction for caesar, with all its connotations. This imperious conception of absolute power is expressed in a famous letter from the aging Ivan III to the Holy Roman emperor Frederick III (1440–1493). Frederick had offered Ivan the title of king in conjunction with the marriage of his daughter to Ivan's nephew. Ivan proudly refused:

We by the grace of God have been sovereigns over our domains from the beginning, from our first forebears, and our right we hold from God, as did our forebears.... As in the past we have never needed appointment from anyone, so now do we not desire it.[11]

The Muscovite idea of absolute authority was powerfully reinforced by two developments. First, about 1480 Ivan III stopped acknowledging the khan as his supreme ruler. There is good evidence to suggest that Ivan and his successors saw themselves as khans. Certainly they assimilated the Mongol concept of kingship as the exercise of unrestrained and unpredictable power.

Second, after the fall of Constantinople to the Turks in 1453, the tsars saw themselves as the heirs of both the caesars and Orthodox Christianity, the one true faith. All the other kings of Europe were heretics: only the tsars were rightful and holy rulers. This idea was promoted by Orthodox churchmen, who spoke of "holy Russia" and "the Third Rome." As the metropolitan Zosima stated in 1492: "Two Romes have fallen, the third Rome will be Moscow and a fourth is not to be."[12] Ivan's marriage to Sofia, the daughter of the last Byzantine emperor, further enhanced the aura of an eastern imperial inheritance for Moscow. Worthy successor to the mighty khan and the true Christian emperor, the Muscovite tsar was a king above all others.

TSAR AND PEOPLE TO 1689

By 1505, the great prince of Moscow – the tsar – had emerged as the single hereditary ruler of "all the Russias" – of all the lands of the eastern Slavs – and he was claiming unrestricted power as his God-given right. In effect, the tsar was demanding the same kind of total authority over all his subjects that the princely descendants of Ruirik had long exercised over their slaves on their own landed estates. This was an extremely radical demand.

While peasants had begun losing their freedom of movement in the fifteenth century, so had the noble boyars begun to lose power and influence. Ivan III pioneered in this regard, as in so many others. When Ivan conquered the principality of Novgorod in the 1480s, he confiscated fully 80 percent of the land, executing the previous owners or resettling them nearer Moscow. He then kept more than half of the confiscated land for himself, and distributed the remainder to members of a new emerging service nobility. The boyars had previously held their land as hereditary private property and been free to serve the prince of their choosing. The new service nobility held the tsar's land on the explicit condition that they serve in the tsar's

ST. BASIL'S CATHEDRAL in Moscow, with its steeply sloping roofs and proliferation of multicolored onion-shaped domes, was a striking example of powerful Byzantine influences on Russian culture. According to tradition, an enchanted Ivan the Terrible blinded the cathedral's architects, to insure they would never duplicate their fantastic achievement. (The New York Public Library)

army. Moreover, Ivan III began to require boyars outside of Novgorod to serve him if they wished to retain their lands. Since there were no competing princes left to turn to, the boyars had to yield.

The rise of the new service nobility accelerated under Ivan IV (1533-1584), the famous Ivan the Terrible. Having ascended the throne at age three, Ivan had suffered insults and neglect at the hands of the haughty boyars after his mother mysteriously died, possibly poisoned, when he was just eight. At age sixteen he suddenly pushed aside his hated boyar advisers. In an awe-inspiring ceremony complete with gold coins pouring down upon his head, he majestically crowned himself and officially took the august title of tsar for the first time.

Selecting the beautiful and kind Anastasia of the popular Romanov family for his wife and queen, the young tsar soon declared war on the remnants of Mongol power. He defeated the faltering khanates of Kazan and Astrakhan between 1552 and 1556, adding vast new territories to Russia. In the course of these wars Ivan virtually abolished the old distinction between hereditary boyar private property and land granted temporarily for service. All nobles, old and new, had to serve the tsar in order to hold any land.

The process of transforming the entire nobility into a service nobility was completed in the second part of Ivan the Terrible's reign. In 1557, Ivan turned westward, and for the next twenty-five years Muscovy waged an exhausting, unsuccessful war primarily with the large Polish-Lithuanian state, which controlled not only Poland but much of the Ukraine in the sixteenth century. Quarreling with the boyars over the war and blaming them for the sudden death of his beloved Anastasia in 1560, the increasingly cruel and demented Ivan turned to strike down all who stood in his way.

Above all, he struck down the ancient Muscovite boyars with a reign of terror. Leading boyars, their relatives, and even their peasants and servants were executed en masse by a special corps of unquestioning servants. Dressed in black and riding black horses, they were the forerunners of the modern dictator's secret police. Large estates were confiscated, broken up, and reapportioned to the lower service nobility. The great boyar families were

severely reduced. The newer, poorer, more nearly equal service nobility, which was still less than .5 percent of the total population, was totally dependent upon the autocrat.

Ivan also took giant strides toward making all commoners servants of the tsar. His endless wars and demonic purges left much of central Russia depopulated. It grew increasingly difficult for the lower service nobility to squeeze a living for themselves out of the peasants left on their landholdings. As the service nobles demanded more from the remaining peasants, more and more peasants fled toward the wild, recently conquered territories to the east and south. There they formed free groups and outlaw armies known as Cossacks. The Cossacks maintained a precarious independence beyond the reach of the oppressive landholders and the tsar's hated officials. The solution to this problem was to complete the tying of the peasants to the land, to make them serfs perpetually bound to serve the noble landholders, who were bound in turn to serve the tsar.

In the time of Ivan the Terrible urban traders and artisans were also bound to their towns and jobs, so that the tsar could tax them more heavily. Ivan assumed that the tsar owned Russia's trade and industry, just as he owned all the land. In the course of the sixteenth and seventeenth centuries, the tsars therefore took over the mines and industries and monopolized the country's important commercial activities. The urban classes had no security in their work or property, and even the wealthiest merchants were basically dependent agents of the tsar. If a new commercial activity became profitable, it was often taken over by the tsar and made a royal monopoly. This royal monopolization was in sharp contrast to developments in western Europe, where the capitalist middle classes were gaining strength and security in their private property. The tsar's service obligations checked the growth of the Russian middle classes, just as they led to the decline of the boyars, the rise of the lower nobility, and the final enserfment of the peasants.

Ivan the Terrible's system of autocracy and compulsory service struck foreign observers forcibly. Sigismund Herberstein, a German traveler to Russia, wrote in 1571: "All the people consider themselves to be *kholops,* that is slaves of their Prince." At the same time Jean Bodin, the French thinker who did so much to develop the modern concept of sovereignty, concluded that Russia's political system was fundamentally different from those of all other European monarchies and comparable only to that of the Turkish empire. In both Turkey and Russia, as in other parts of Asia and Africa, "the prince is become lord of the goods and persons of his subjects . . . governing them as a master of a family does his slaves."[13] The Mongol inheritance weighed heavily upon Russia.

As has so often been the case in Russian history, the death of an iron-fisted tyrant – in this case Ivan the Terrible in 1584 – ushered in an era of confusion and violent struggles for power. Events were particularly chaotic after Ivan's son Theodore died in 1598 without an heir. The years from 1598 to 1613 are aptly called the Time of Troubles.

The close relatives of the deceased tsar intrigued against and murdered each other, alternately fighting and welcoming the invading Swedes and Poles, who even occupied Moscow. Most serious for the cause of autocracy, there was a great social upheaval as Cossack bands marched northward, rallying peasants and slaughtering nobles and officials. The mass of Cossacks and peasants called for the "true tsar," who would restore their freedom of movement and allow them to farm for whomever they pleased, who would reduce their heavy taxes and lighten the yoke imposed by the landlords.

This social explosion from below, which combined with a belated surge of patriotic opposition to Polish invaders, brought the nobles, big and small, to their senses. In 1613, they elected Ivan's sixteen-year-old grand-nephew, Michael Romanov, the new hereditary tsar. Then they rallied around him in the face of common internal and external threats. Michael's election was a real restoration, and his reign saw the gradual re-establishment of tsarist autocracy. Michael was understandably more kindly disposed toward the supportive nobility than toward the sullen peasants. Thus while peasants were completely enserfed in 1649, Ivan's heavy military obligations upon the nobility were relaxed considerably. In the long reign of Michael's successor, the pious Alexis (1645-1676), this asymmetry of obligations was accentuated. The nobility gained more exemptions from military service, while the peasants were further ground down.

The result was a second round of mass upheaval and protest. In the later seventeenth century the unity of the Russian Orthodox church was torn apart by a great split. The surface question was the religious reforms introduced in 1652 by the patriarch Nikon, a dogmatic purist who wished to bring "corrupted" Russian practices of worship into line with the Greek Orthodox model. The self-serving church hierarchy quickly went along, but the intensely religious common people resisted. They saw Nikon as the anti-Christ, who was stripping them of the only thing they had – the true religion of "holy Russia."

Great numbers left the church and formed illegal communities of Old Believers, who were hunted down and persecuted. As many as twenty thousand people burned themselves alive, singing the "halleluyah" in their chants three times rather than twice as Nikon had demanded and crossing themselves in the old style, with two rather than three fingers, as they went down in flames. After the great split the Russian masses were alienated from the established church, which became totally dependent upon the state for its authority.

Again the Cossacks revolted against the state, which was doggedly trying to catch up with them on the frontiers and reduce them to serfdom. Under Stenka Razin they moved up the Volga River in 1670–1671, attracting a great undisciplined army of peasants, murdering landlords and high church officials, and proclaiming freedom from oppression. This rebellion to overthrow the established order was finally defeated by the government. In response the thoroughly scared upper classes tightened the screws of serfdom even further. Holding down the peasants, and thereby maintaining the tsar, became almost the principal obligation of the nobility until 1689.

THE REFORMS OF PETER THE GREAT

It is now possible to understand the reforms of Peter the Great (1689–1725) and his kind of monarchial absolutism. Contrary to some historians' assertions, Peter was interested primarily in military power and not in some grandiose westernization plan. A gigantic, seven-foot-tall man of enormous energy and will power, Peter was determined to redress the defeats the tsar's armies had occasionally suffered in their wars with Poland and Sweden since the time of Ivan the Terrible.

To be sure, these western foes had never seriously threatened the existence of the tsar's vast kingdom, except perhaps when they had added to the confusion of civil war and domestic social upheaval in the Time of Troubles. Russia had even gained a large mass of the Ukraine from the kingdom of Poland in 1667 (see Map 21.2). And tsarist forces had completed the conquest of the primitive tribes of all Siberia in the seventeenth century. Muscovy, which had been as large as all the rest

of Europe combined in 1600, was three times as large as the rest of Europe in 1689 and by far the largest kingdom on earth. But territorial expansion was the soul of tsardom, and it was natural that Peter would seek further gains. The thirty-six years of his reign knew only one year of peace.

When Peter came to the throne, the heart of his army still consisted of cavalry made up of boyars and service nobility. Foot soldiers played a secondary role, and the whole army served on a part-time basis. The Russian army was lagging behind the professional standing armies being formed in Europe in the seventeenth century. The core of such armies was a highly disciplined infantry – an infantry that fired and refired rifles as it fearlessly advanced, until it charged with bayonets fixed. Such a large permanent army was enormously expensive and could be created only at the cost of great sacrifice. Given the desire to conquer more territory, Peter's military problem was serious.

Peter's solution was, in essence, to tighten up Muscovy's old service system and really make it work. He put the nobility back in harness, with a vengeance. Every nobleman, great or small, was once again required to serve in the army or in the civil administration – for life. Since a more modern army and government required skilled technicians and experts, Peter created schools and even universities. One of his most hated reforms required five years of compulsory education away from home for every young nobleman. Peter established an interlocking military-civilian bureaucracy with fourteen ranks, and he decreed that all must start at the bottom and work toward the top. More people of non-noble origins rose to high positions in the embryonic meritocracy. Peter searched out talented foreigners – twice in his reign he went abroad to study and observe – and placed them in his service. These measures combined to make the army and government more powerful and more efficient.

Peter also greatly increased the service requirements of the commoners. He established a regular standing army of more than 200,000 soldiers, made up mainly of peasants commanded by officers from the nobility. In addition, special forces of Cossacks and foreigners numbered more than 100,000. The departure of a drafted peasant boy was celebrated by his family and village almost like a funeral, as indeed it was, since the recruit was drafted for life. The peasantry also served with its taxes, which increased threefold during Peter's reign, as people – "souls" – replaced land as the primary unit of taxation. Serfs were also arbitrarily assigned to work in the growing number of factories and mines. Most of these industrial enterprises were directly or indirectly owned by the state, and they were worked almost exclusively for the military. In general, Russian serfdom became more oppressive under the reforming tsar.

The constant warfare of Peter's reign consumed 80 or 85 percent of all revenues but brought only modest territorial expansion. Yet the Great Northern War with Sweden, which lasted from 1700 to 1721, was crowned in the end by Russian victory. After initial losses, Peter's new war machine crushed the smaller army of Sweden's Charles XII in southern Russia at Poltava in 1709, one of the most significant battles in Russian history. Sweden never really regained the offensive, and Russia eventually annexed Estonia and much of present-day Latvia (see Map 21.2), lands that had never before been under Russian rule. Russia became the dominant power on the Baltic Sea and very much a European Great Power. If victory or defeat is the ultimate criterion for historical judgment, Peter's reforms were a success.

REFORMING THE NOBILITY   After a military revolt in 1698 Peter took revenge by decreeing that all nobles adopt Western manners and dress. This contemporary cartoon shows a gigantic Peter personally cutting off the long beard of a noble, thereby humiliating him and symbolically imposing more modern values. (The New York Public Library)

There were other important consequences of Peter's reign. Because of his feverish desire to use modern technology to strengthen the army, many westerners and western ideas flowed into Russia for the first time. A new class of educated Russians began to emerge. At the same time vast numbers of Russians, especially among the poor and weak, hated Peter's massive changes. The split between the enserfed peasantry and the educated nobility thus widened, even though all were caught up in the endless demands of the sovereign.

A new idea of state interest, as distinct from the tsar's personal interests, began to take hold. Peter himself fostered this conception of the public interest by claiming time and again to be serving the common good. For the first time a Russian tsar attached explanations to his decrees in an attempt to gain the confidence and more enthusiastic support of the populace. Yet, as before, the tsar alone decided what the common good was. Here was a source of future tension between tsar and people.

In sum, Peter built on the service obligations of old Muscovy. His monarchial absolutism was truly the culmination of the long development of a unique Russian civilization. Yet the creation of a more modern army and state introduced much that was new and western to that civilization. This development paved the way for Russia to move much closer to the European mainstream in its thought and institutions during the Enlightenment, especially under that famous administrative and sexual lioness, Catherine the Great.

ABSOLUTISM AND THE BAROQUE

The rise of royal absolutism in eastern Europe had many consequences. Nobles served their powerful rulers in new ways while the great inferiority of the urban middle classes and the peasants was reconfirmed. Armies became larger and more professional, while taxes rose and authoritarian traditions were strengthened. Nor was this all. Royal absolutism also interacted with baroque culture and art, baroque music and literature. Inspired in part by Louis XIV of France, the great and not-so-great rulers called upon the artistic talent of the age to glorify their power and magnifi-

cence. This exaltation of despotic rule was particularly striking in architecture, whose lavish masterpieces reflected and reinforced the spirit of absolutism.

BAROQUE ART AND MUSIC

Throughout European history, the cultural tastes of one age have often seemed quite unsatisfactory to the next. So it was with the baroque. The term *baroque* itself may have come from the Portuguese word for an "odd-shaped, imperfect pearl," and was commonly used by late-eighteenth-century art critics as an expression of scorn for what they considered an overblown, unbalanced style. The hostility of these critics, who also scorned the Gothic style of medieval cathedrals in favor of a classicism inspired by antiquity and the Renaissance, has long since passed. Specialists agree that the triumphs of the baroque marked one of the high points in the entire history of Western culture.

The early development of the baroque is complex, but most scholars stress the influence of Rome and the revitalized Catholic church of the later sixteenth century. The papacy and the Jesuits encouraged the growth of an intensely emotional, exuberant art. These patrons wanted artists to go beyond the Renaissance focus on pleasing a small, wealthy cultural elite. They wanted artists to appeal to the senses, and thereby touch the souls and kindle the faith of ordinary churchgoers, while proclaiming the power and confidence of the reformed Catholic church. In addition to this underlying religious emotionalism, the baroque drew its sense of drama, motion, and ceaseless striving from the Catholic Reformation. The interior of the famous Jesuit Church of Jesus in Rome – the Gesù – combined all these characteristics in its lavish, shimmering, wildly active decorations and frescoes.

Taking definite shape in Italy after 1600, the baroque style in the visual arts developed with exceptional vigor in Catholic countries – in Spain and Latin America, Austria, southern Germany, and Poland. Yet baroque art was more than just "Catholic art" in the seventeenth century and the first half of the eighteenth. True, neither Protestant England nor the Netherlands ever came fully under the spell of the baroque, but neither did Catholic France. And Protestants accounted for some of the finest examples of baroque style, especially in music. The baroque style spread partly because its tension and bombast spoke to an agitated age, which was experiencing great violence and controversy in politics and religion.

In painting, the baroque reached maturity early with Peter Paul Rubens (1577–1640), the most outstanding and representative of baroque painters. Studying in his native Flanders and in Italy, where he was influenced by the masters of the High Renaissance such as Michelangelo, Rubens developed his own rich, sensuous, colorful style, which was characterized by animated figures, melodramatic contrasts, and monumental size. Although Rubens excelled in glorifying monarchs, like queen mother Marie de' Medici of France, he was also a devout Catholic. Nearly half of his pictures treat Christian subjects. Yet one of Rubens' trademarks was fleshy, sensual nudes, who populate his canvasses as Roman goddesses, water nymphs, and remarkably voluptuous saints and angels.

Rubens was enormously successful. To meet the demand for his work, he established a large studio and hired many assistants to execute his rough sketches and gigantic murals. Sometimes the master artist added only the finishing touches. Rubens' wealth and position – on occasion he was given special diplomatic assignments by the Habs-burgs – attest that distinguished artists continued to enjoy the high social status they had won in the Renaissance.

In music the baroque style reached its culminating point almost a century later in the dynamic, searching, soaring lines of the endlessly inventive Johann Sebastian Bach (1685–1750), one of the greatest composers the Western world has ever produced. Organist and choirmaster of several Lutheran churches across Germany, Bach was equally at home writing secular concertos and sublime religious cantatas. Bach's organ music, the greatest ever written, combined with unsurpassed mastery the baroque spirit of invention, tension, and emotion in an unforgettable striving toward the infinite. Unlike Rubens, Bach was not fully appreciated in his lifetime, but since the early nineteenth century his reputation has grown steadily.

PALACES AND POWER

As soaring Gothic cathedrals expressed the idealized spirit of the High Middle Ages, so dramatic baroque palaces symbolized the age of absolutist power. By 1700, palace building had become a veritable obsession with the rulers of central and eastern Europe. These baroque palaces were clearly intended to overawe the people with the monarch's strength. The great palaces were also visual declarations of equality with Louis XIV, Europe's most awesome ruler, and were therefore modeled after Versailles to a greater or lesser extent. One such palace was Schönbrunn, an enormous Viennese Versailles, begun in 1695 by Emperor Leopold to celebrate Austrian military victories and Habsburg might. Charles XI of Sweden, having reduced the power of the aristocracy, ordered the construction in 1693 of his Royal Palace, which dominates the center of Stockholm to this day. Frederick I of Prussia began his imposing new royal residence in Berlin in 1701, a year after he attained the title of king.

Petty princes also contributed mightily to the palace-building mania. Frederick the Great of Prussia noted that every descendant of a princely family "imagines himself to be something like Louis XIV. He builds his Versailles, has his mistresses, and maintains his army."[14] The not very important elector-archbishop of Mainz, the ruling prince of that city, confessed apologetically that "building is a craze which costs much, but every fool likes his own hat."[15] The archbishop of Mainz's own "hat" was an architectural gem, like that of another churchly ruler, the prince-bishop of Würzburg. So too was the Zwinger palace of Dresden, built by Augustus the Strong of Saxony, who managed to get himself elected king of Poland and unsuccessfully challenged Prussia for leadership among the German states.

In central and eastern Europe the favorite noble servants of royalty became extremely rich and powerful, and they too built grandiose palaces in the capital cities. These palaces were in part an extension of the monarch, for they surpassed the buildings of less favored nobles and showed all with eyes to see the high road to fame and fortune. Take, for example, the palaces of Prince Eugene of Savoy. A French nobleman by birth and education, Prince Eugene entered the service of Leopold I with the relief of besieged Vienna in 1683, and he became Austria's most outstanding military hero. It was he who reorganized the Austrian army, smashed the Turks, fought Louis XIV to a standstill, and generally guided the triumph of absolutism in Austria. Rewarded with great wealth by his grateful royal employer, Eugene called upon the leading architects of the day, J. B. Fischer von Erlach and Johann Lukas von Hildebrandt, to consecrate his glory in stone and fresco. Fischer built Eugene's Winter (or Town) Palace in Vienna, and he and Hildebrandt collaborated on the prince's Summer Palace on the city's outskirts.

The Summer Palace was actually two enormous buildings, the Lower Belvedere and the Upper Belvedere, completed in 1713 and 1722 respectively, and joined by one of the most exquisite gardens in Europe. The Upper Belvedere, Hildebrandt's masterpiece, stood gracefully, even playfully, behind a great sheet of water. One entered through magnificent iron gates into a fantastic hall where sculptured giants crouched as pillars, and then moved on to a great staircase of dazzling whiteness and luscious ornamentation. Even today the emotional impact of this building is great: here, indeed, art and beauty create a sense of immense power and wealth.

Palaces like the Upper Belvedere were magnificent examples of the baroque style. They expressed the baroque delight in bold, sweeping statements, which were intended to provide a dramatic emotional experience. To create this experience baroque masters dissolved the traditional artistic frontiers: the architect permitted the painter and the artisan to cover his undulating surfaces with wildly colorful paintings, graceful sculptures, and fanciful carvings. Space was used in a highly original way, to blend everything together in a total environment. These techniques shone in all their glory in the churches of southern Germany and in the colossal entrance halls of palaces like that of the prince-bishop of Würzburg. Artistic achievement and political statement reinforced each other.

ROYAL CITIES

Absolute monarchs and baroque architects were not content with fashioning ostentatious

THE WÜRZBURG RESIDENCE *This palace was a masterpiece of German baroque architecture. Here, in the Hall of the Kaiser, painter, sculptor, and architect have combined to create a dramatic visual experience. (AMA/Adelmann/EPA)*

palaces. They remodeled existing capital cities, or even built new ones, to reflect royal magnificence and the centralization of political power. Karlsruhe, founded in 1715 as the capital city of a small German principality, is only an extreme example. There, broad, straight avenues radiated out from the palace, so that all roads – like all power – were fo-

cused upon the ruler. More typically, the monarch's architects added new urban areas alongside the old city; these areas then became the real heart of the expanding capital.

The distinctive features of these new additions were their broad avenues, their imposing government buildings, and their rigorous mathematical layout. Along these major thoroughfares the nobles built elaborate baroque townhouses; stables and servants' quarters were built on the alleys behind. Wide avenues also facilitated the rapid movement of soldiers through the city to quell any disturbance (the king's planners had the needs of the military constantly in mind). Under the arcades along the avenues appeared smart and very expensive shops, the first department stores, with plateglass windows and fancy displays.

The new avenues brought reckless speed to the European city. Whereas everyone had walked through the narrow, twisting streets of the medieval town, the high and mighty raced down the broad boulevards in their elegant carriages. A social gap opened up between the wealthy riders and the ordinary, gaping, dodging pedestrians. "Mind the carriages!" wrote one eighteenth-century observer in Paris:

Here comes the black-coated physician in his chariot, the dancing master in his coach, the fencing master in his surrey – and the Prince behind six horses at the gallop as if he were in the open country.... The threatening wheels of the overbearing rich drive as rapidly as ever over stones stained with the blood of their unhappy victims.[16]

Speeding carriages on broad avenues, an endless parade of power and position: here was the symbol and substance of the baroque city.

THE GROWTH OF ST. PETERSBURG

No city illustrated better than St. Petersburg the close ties among politics, architecture, and urban development in this period. In 1700, when the Great Northern War between Russia and Sweden began, the city did not exist. There was only a small Swedish fortress on one of the water-logged islands at the mouth of the Neva River, where it flows into the Baltic Sea. In 1702, Peter the Great's armies seized this desolate outpost. Within a year the reforming tsar had decided to build a new city there and to make it, rather than ancient Moscow, his capital.

Since the first step was to secure the Baltic coast, military construction was the main concern for the next eight years. A mighty fortress was built on Peter Island, and a port and shipyards were built across the river on the mainland, as a Russian navy came into being. The land was swampy and uninhabited, the climate damp and unpleasant. But Peter cared not at all: for him, the inhospitable northern marshland was a future metropolis, gloriously bearing his name.

After the decisive Russian victory at Poltava in 1709 greatly reduced the threat of Swedish armies, Peter moved into high gear. In one imperious decree after another, he ordered his people to build a city that would equal any in the world. Such a city had to be western and baroque, just as Peter's army had to be western and permanent. From such a new city, his "window on Europe," Peter also believed it would be easier to reform the country militarily and administratively. The hand of tradition would rest lightly on the banks of the Neva.

These general political goals matched Peter's architectural ideas, which had been influenced by his travels in western Europe. First, Peter wanted a comfortable, "modern" city. Modernity meant broad, straight, stone-paved avenues, houses built in a uniform line and not haphazardly set back from the street, large parks, canals for drainage, stone bridges, and street lighting. Second, all building had to conform strictly to detailed architectural regulations set down by the government. Finally, each social group – the nobility, the merchants, the artisans, and so on – was to live in a certain section of town. In short, the city and its population were to conform to a

carefully defined urban plan of the baroque type.

Peter used the traditional but reinforced methods of Russian autocracy to build his modern capital. The creation of St. Petersburg was just one of the heavy obligations he dictatorially imposed on all social groups in Russia. The peasants bore the heaviest burdens. Just as the government drafted peasants for the army, it also drafted twenty-five to forty thousand men each summer to labor in St. Petersburg for three months, without pay. Every ten to fifteen peasant households had to furnish one such worker each summer, and then pay a special tax in order to feed that worker in St. Petersburg.

Peasants hated this forced labor in the capital, and each year a fourth to a third of those sent risked brutal punishments and ran away. Many peasant construction workers died each summer from hunger, sickness, and accidents. Many also died because peasant villages tended to elect old men or young boys to labor in St. Petersburg, since strong and able-bodied men were desperately needed on the farm in the busy summer months. Thus beautiful St. Petersburg was built on the shoveling, carting, and paving of a mass of conscripted serfs.

Peter also drafted more privileged groups to his city, but on a permanent basis. Nobles were summarily ordered to build costly stone houses and palaces in St. Petersburg and to live in them most of the year. The more serfs a noble possessed, the bigger his dwelling had to be. Merchants and artisans were also commanded to settle and build in St. Petersburg. These nobles and merchants were then required to pay for the city's avenues, parks, canals, embankments, pilings, and bridges, all of which were very costly in terms of both money and lives because they were built upon a swamp. The building of St. Petersburg was, in truth, an enormous direct tax levied on the wealthy, who in turn forced the peasantry to do most of the work. The only real beneficiaries were the indispensable foreign architects and urban planners, whose often-princely salaries added to the tax burden. No wonder so many Russians hated Peter's new city.

Yet the tsar had his way. By the time of his death in 1725 there were at least six thousand houses and numerous impressive government buildings in St. Petersburg. Under the remarkable women who ruled Russia throughout most of the eighteenth century, St. Petersburg blossomed fully as a majestic and well-organized city, at least in its wealthy showpiece sections. Peter's youngest daughter, the quick-witted, sensual beauty Elizabeth (1741–1762), named as her chief architect Bartolomeo Rastrelli, who had come to Russia from Italy as a boy of fifteen in 1715. Combining Italian and Russian traditions into a unique, wildly colorful St. Petersburg style, Rastrelli built many palaces for the nobility and all the larger government buildings erected during Elizabeth's reign. He also rebuilt the Winter Palace as an enormous,

aqua-colored royal residence, now the Hermitage Museum. There Elizabeth established a flashy, luxury-loving, and slightly crude court, which Catherine in turn made truly imperial. All the while St. Petersburg grew rapidly, and its almost 300,000 inhabitants in 1782 made it one of the world's largest cities. Peter and his successors had created out of nothing a magnificent and harmonious royal city, which unmistakably proclaimed the power and grandeur of Russia's rulers.

From about 1400 to 1650 social and economic developments in eastern Europe increasingly diverged from those in western Europe. In the east peasants and townspeople lost precious freedoms, while the nobility increased its power and prestige. It was within this framework of resurgent serfdom and entrenched nobility that Austrian and Prussian monarchs fashioned absolutist states in the seventeenth and early eighteenth centuries. Thus monarchs won absolutist control over standing armies, permanent taxes, and legislative bodies. But they did not question the underlying social and economic relationships. Indeed, they enhanced the privileges of the nobility, which furnished the leading servitors for enlarged armies and growing state bureaucracies.

In Russia the social and economic trends were similar but the timing of political absolutism was different. Mongol conquest and rule was a crucial experience, and a harsh indigenous tsarist autocracy was firmly in place by the reign of Ivan the Terrible in the sixteenth century. More than a century later Peter the Great succeeded in tightening up Russia's traditional absolutism and modernizing it by reforming the army, the bureaucracy, and the defense industry. In Russia and throughout eastern Europe, war and the needs of war weighed heavily in the triumph of absolutism.

Triumphant absolutism interacted spectacularly with the arts. Baroque art, which had grown out of the Catholic Reformation's desire to move the faithful and exalt the true faith, admirably suited the secular aspirations of eastern rulers. They built grandiose baroque palaces, monumental public squares, and even whole cities to glorify their power and majesty. Thus baroque art attained magnificent heights in eastern Europe, symbolizing the ideal and harmonizing with the reality of imperious royal absolutism.

NOTES

1. Quoted by F. L. Carsten, *The Origins of Prussia*, Clarendon Press, Oxford, 1954, p. 152.

2. Ibid., p. 175.

3. H. Rosenberg, *Bureaucracy, Aristocracy, and Autocracy: The Prussian Experience, 1660–1815*, Beacon Press, Boston, 1966, p. 38.

4. Quoted by R. Ergang, *The Potsdam Führer: Frederick William I, Father of Prussian Militarism*, Octagon Books, New York, 1972, pp. 85, 87.

5. Ibid. pp. 6–7, 43.

6. Quoted by R. A. Dorwart, *The Administrative Reforms of Frederick William I of Prussia*, Harvard University Press, Cambridge, Mass., 1953, p. 226.

7. Quoted by Rosenberg, p. 40.

8. Quoted by Ergang, p. 253.

9. Quoted by R. Pipes, *Russia Under the Old Regime*, Charles Scribner's Sons, New York, 1974, p. 48.

10. Quoted by N. V. Riasanovsky, *A History of Russia*, Oxford University Press, New York, 1963, p. 79.

11. Quoted by I. Grey, *Ivan III and the Unification of Russia*, Collier Books, New York, 1967, p. 39.

12. Quoted by R. Mousnier, *Peasant Uprisings in*

Seventeenth-Century France, Russia, and China, Harper & Row, New York, 1970, p. 154.

13. Both quoted by Pipes, pp. 65, 85.

14. Quoted by Ergang, p. 13.

15. Quoted by J. Summerson, in *The Eighteenth Century: Europe in the Age of Enlightenment,* ed. A. Cobban, McGraw-Hill, New York, 1969, p. 80.

16. Quoted by L. Mumford, *The Culture of Cities,* Harcourt Brace Jovanovich, New York, 1938, p. 97.

SUGGESTED READING

All of the books cited in the Notes are highly recommended. F. L. Carsten's *The Origins of Prussia* (1954) is the best study on early Prussian history, and H. Rosenberg, *Bureaucracy, Aristocracy, and Autocracy: The Prussian Experience, 1660–1815* (1966), is a masterful analysis of the social context of Prussian absolutism. In addition to R. Ergang's exciting and critical biography of ramrod Frederick William I, *The Potsdam Führer* (1972), there is G. Ritter, *Frederick the Great* (1968), a more sympathetic study of the talented son by one of Germany's leading conservative historians. G. Craig, *The Politics of the Prussian Army, 1640–1945* (1964), expertly traces the great influence of the military on the Prussian state over three hundred years. R. J. Evans, *The Making of the Habsburg Empire, 1550–1770* (1979), and R. A. Kahn, *A History of the Habsburg Empire, 1526–1918* (1974), analyze the development of absolutism in Austria, as does A. Wandruszka, *The House of Habsburg* (1964). J. Stoye, *The Siege of Vienna* (1964), is a fascinating account of the last great Ottoman offensive, which is also treated in the interesting study by P. Coles, *The Ottoman Impact on Europe, 1350–1699* (1968). The Austro-Ottoman conflict is also a theme of L. S. Stavrianos, *The Balkans Since 1453* (1958), and D. McKay's fine biography, *Prince Eugene of Savoy* (1978).

On eastern peasants and serfdom, J. Blum, "The Rise of Serfdom in Eastern Europe," *American His-*

torical *Review* 62 (July 1957):807–836, is a good point of departure, while R. Mousnier, *Peasant Uprisings in Seventeenth-Century France, Russia, and China* (1970), is an engrossing comparative study. J. Blum, *Lord and Peasant in Russia from the Ninth to the Nineteenth Century* (1961), provides a good look at conditions in rural Russia, and P. Avrich, *Russian Rebels, 1600–1800* (1972), treats some of the violent peasant upheavals those conditions produced. R. Hellie, *Enserfment and Military Change in Muscovy,* (1971), is outstanding, as is Alexander Yanov's provocative *Origins of Autocracy: Ivan the Terrible in Russian History* (1981). In addition to the fine surveys by Pipes and Riasanovsky cited in the Notes, J. Billington, *The Icon and the Axe* (1970), is a stimulating history of early Russian intellectual and cultural developments, such as the great split in the church. M. Raeff, *Origins of the Russian Intelligentsia* (1966), skillfully probes the mind of the Russian nobility in the eighteenth century. B. H. Sumner, *Peter the Great and the Emergence of Russia* (1962), is a fine brief introduction, which may be compared with the brilliant biography by Russia's greatest prerevolutionary historian, Vasili Klyuchevsky, *Peter the Great* (trans. 1958), and with R. Massie, *Peter the Great* (1980). G. Vernadsky and R. Fisher, eds., *A Source Book for Russian History from Early Times to 1917,* 3 vols. (1972), is an invaluable, highly recommended collection of documents and contemporary writings.

Three good books on art and architecture are E. Hempel, *Baroque Art and Architecture in Central Europe* (1965); G. Hamilton, *The Art and Architecture of Russia* (1954); and N. Pevsner, *An Outline of European Architecture,* 6th ed. (1960). Bach, Handel, and other composers are discussed intelligently by M. Bufkozer, *Music in the Baroque Era* (1947).

CHAPTER 22

TOWARD A NEW WORLD-VIEW

MOST PEOPLE are not philosophers, but nevertheless they have certain ideas and assumptions about the world in which they live. These ideas and assumptions add up to a basic outlook on life, a more or less coherent world-view. At the risk of oversimplification, one may say that the world-view of medieval and early modern Europe was primarily religious and theological. Not only did Christian or Jewish teachings form the core of people's spiritual and philosophical beliefs, but religious teachings also permeated all the rest of human thought and activity. Political theory relied on the divine right of kings, for example, and activities ranging from marriage and divorce to eating habits and hours of business were regulated by churches and religious doctrines.

In the course of the eighteenth century, this religious and theological world-view of the educated classes of western Europe underwent a fundamental transformation. Many educated people came to see the world primarily in secular and scientific terms. And while few abandoned religious beliefs altogether, many became openly hostile to established Christianity. The role of churches and religious thinking in earthly affairs and in the pursuit of knowledge was substantially reduced. Among many in the upper and middle classes a new critical, scientific, and very "modern" world-view took shape. Why did this momentous change occur? How did this new outlook on life affect society and politics? This chapter seeks to answer these questions.

THE SCIENTIFIC REVOLUTION

The foremost cause of the change in world-view was the scientific revolution. Modern science – precise knowledge of the physical world based upon the union of experimental observations with sophisticated mathematics – crystallized in the seventeenth century. Whereas science had been secondary and subordinate in medieval intellectual life, it became independent and even primary for many educated people.

The emergence of modern science was a development of tremendous long-term significance. A noted historian has even said that the scientific revolution of the late sixteenth and seventeenth centuries "outshines everything since the rise of Christianity and reduces the Renaissance and Reformation to the rank of mere episodes, mere internal displacements, within the system of medieval Christendom." The scientific revolution was "the real origin both of the modern world and the modern mentality."[1] This statement is an exaggeration, but not much of one. Of all the great civilizations, only that of the West developed modern science. It was with the scientific revolution that Western society began to acquire its most distinctive traits.

Although historians agree that the scientific revolution was enormously important, they approach it in quite different ways. Some scholars believe that the history of scientific achievement in this period had its own basic "internal" logic and that "nonscientific" factors had quite limited significance. These scholars write brilliant, often highly technical, intellectual studies, but they neglect the broader historical context. Other historians stress "external" economic, social, and religious factors, brushing over the scientific developments themselves. Historians of science now realize that these two approaches need to be brought together, but they are only beginning to do so. It is best, therefore, to examine the milestones on the fateful march toward modern science first and then to search for nonscientific influences along the route.

ARISTOTLE'S UNIVERSE In this late medieval woodcut the great Greek mathematician Archimedes stands on the motionless earth, surrounded by the other three elements — water, air, and fire. Beyond fire is the perfect celestial world of the sun, the planets, and the stars. (Royal Astronomical Society/Ann Ronan Picture Library)

SCIENTIFIC THOUGHT IN 1500

Since developments in astronomy and physics were at the heart of the scientific revolution, one must begin with the traditional European conception of the universe and movement in it. In the early 1500s, traditional European ideas about the universe were still based primarily upon the ideas of Aristotle, the great Greek philosopher of the fourth century B.C. These ideas had gradually been recovered during the Middle Ages and then brought into harmony with Christian doctrines by medieval theologians. According to this revised Aristotelian view, a motionless earth was fixed at the center of the universe. Around it moved ten separate, transparent, crystal spheres. In the first eight spheres were embedded, in turn, the moon, the sun, the five known planets, and the fixed stars. Then followed two spheres added during the Middle Ages to account for slight changes in the positions of the stars over the centuries. Beyond the tenth sphere was heaven, with the throne of God and the souls of the saved. Angels kept the spheres moving in perfect circles.

Aristotle's views, suitably revised by medieval philosophers, also dominated thinking about physics and motion on earth. Aristotle had distinguished sharply between the world of the celestial spheres and that of the earth — the sublunar world. The spheres consisted of a perfect, incorruptible "quintescence," or fifth essence. The sublunar world, however, was made up of four imperfect, changeable elements. The "light" elements — air and fire — naturally moved upward, while the "heavy" elements — water and earth — naturally moved downward. The natural directions of motion did not always prevail, however, for elements were often mixed together, and could be affected by an outside force such as a human being. Aristotle and his followers also believed that a uniform force moved an object at a constant speed and that the object would stop as soon as that force was removed.

Aristotle's ideas about astronomy and physics were accepted with minor revisions for two thousand years, and with good reason. First, they offered an understandable common-sense explanation for what the eye actually saw. Second, Aristotle's science, as interpreted by Christian theologians, fit neatly with Christian doctrines. It established a home for God and a place for Christian souls. It put human beings at the center of the universe, and made them the critical link in a "great chain of being" that stretched from the throne of God to the most lowly insect on earth. Thus science was primarily a branch of theology, and it reinforced religious thought. At the same time, medieval "scientists" were already providing closely reasoned explanations of the universe, explanations they felt were worthy of God's perfect creation.

THE COPERNICAN HYPOTHESIS

The desire to explain and thereby glorify God's handiwork led to the first great departure from the medieval system. This departure was the work of the Polish clergyman and as-

tronomer Nicolaus Copernicus (1473–1543). As a young man Copernicus studied church law and astronomy in various European universities. He saw how professional astronomers were still dependent for their most accurate calculations on the work of Ptolemy, the last great ancient astronomer, who had lived in Alexandria in the second century A.D. Ptolemy's achievement had been to work out complicated rules to explain the minor irregularities in the movement of the planets. These rules enabled stargazers and astrologers to track the planets with greater precision. Many people then (and now) believed that the changing relationships between planets and stars influenced and even determined an individual's future.

The young Copernicus was uninterested in astrology, and felt that Ptolemy's cumbersome and occasionally inaccurate rules detracted from the majesty of a perfect Creator. He hit upon an old Greek idea being discussed in Renaissance Italy: the idea that the sun rather than the earth was at the center of the universe. Finishing his university studies and returning to a church position in east Prussia, Copernicus worked on his hypothesis from 1506 to 1530. Never questioning the Aristotelian belief in crystal spheres or the idea that circular motion was most perfect and divine, Copernicus theorized that the stars and planets, including the earth, revolve around a fixed sun. Yet Copernicus was a cautious man. Fearing the ridicule of other astronomers, he did not publish his *On the Revolutions of the Heavenly Spheres* until 1543, the year of his death.

Copernicus's theory had enormous scientific and religious implications, many of which the conservative Copernicus was unaware of. First, it put the stars at rest, their apparent nightly movement simply a result of the earth's rotation. Thus it destroyed the main reason for believing in crystal spheres capable of moving the stars around the earth. Second, Copernicus's theory suggested a universe of staggering size. If in the course of a year the earth moved around the sun and yet the stars appeared to remain in the same place, then the universe was unthinkably large or even infinite. Finally, by characterizing the earth as just another planet, Copernicus destroyed the basic idea of Aristotelian physics – the idea that the earthly world was quite different from the heavenly one. Where, then, was the realm of perfection? Where was heaven and the throne of God?

The Copernican theory quickly brought sharp attacks from religious leaders, especially Protestant leaders. Hearing of Copernicus's work even before it was published, Martin Luther spoke of Copernicus as "the new astrologer who wants to prove that the earth moves and goes round. . . . The fool wants to turn the whole art of astronomy upside down." Luther did, however, note that "as the Holy Scripture tells us, so did Joshua bid the sun stand still and not the earth." Calvin also condemned Copernicus, citing as evidence the first verse of Psalm 93: "The world also is established that it cannot be moved." "Who," asked Calvin, "will venture to place the authority of Copernicus above that of the Holy Spirit?"[2] Catholic reaction was milder at first. The Catholic church had never been hypnotized by literal interpretations of the Bible, and not until 1616 did it officially declare the Copernican theory false.

This slow reaction also reflected the slow progress of Copernicus's theory for many years. Other events were almost as influential in creating doubts about traditional astronomical ideas. In 1572, a new star appeared and shone very brightly for almost two years. The new star, which was actually a distant exploding star, made an enormous impression upon people. It seemed to contradict the idea that the heavenly spheres were unchanging and therefore perfect. In 1577, a new comet suddenly moved through the sky, cutting a straight path across the supposedly impenetrable crystal spheres. It was time, as a typical scientific writer put it, for "the radical renovation of astronomy."[3]

FROM TYCHO BRAHE TO GALILEO

One astronomer who agreed was Tycho Brahe (1546–1601). Born into a leading Danish noble family and earmarked for a career in government, Brahe was at an early age tremendously impressed by a partial eclipse of the sun. It seemed to him "something divine that men could know the motions of the stars so accurately that they were able a long time beforehand to predict their places and relative positions."[4] Completing his studies abroad and returning to Denmark, Brahe established himself as Europe's leading astronomer with his detailed observations of the new star of 1572. Aided by generous grants from the king of Denmark, which made him one of the richest men in the country, Brahe built the most sophisticated observatory of his day. For twenty years he meticulously observed the stars and planets with the naked eye. An imposing man who had lost a piece of his nose in a duel and replaced it with a special bridge of gold and silver alloy, a noble who exploited his peasants arrogantly and approached the heavens humbly, Brahe's great contribution was his mass of data. His limited understanding of mathematics prevented him, however, from making much sense out of his data. Part Ptolemaic, part Copernican, he believed that all the planets revolved around the sun and that the entire group of sun and planets revolved in turn around the earth-moon system.

TYCHO BRAHE'S MAIN OBSERVATORY Lavishly financed by the king of Denmark, Brahe built his magnificent observatory at Uraniborg between 1576 and 1580. For twenty years he studied the heavens and accumulated a mass of precise but undigested data. (The British Library)

It was left to Brahe's brilliant young assistant, Johannes Kepler (1571–1630), to go much farther. Kepler was a medieval figure in many ways. Coming from a minor German noble family and trained for the Lutheran ministry, he long believed that the universe was built on mystical mathematical relationships and a musical harmony of the heavenly bodies. Working and reworking Brahe's

mountain of observations in a staggering sustained effort after the Dane's death, this brilliant mathematician eventually went beyond mystical intuitions.

Kepler formulated three famous laws of planetary motion. First, building upon Copernican theory, he demonstrated in 1609 that the orbits of the planets around the sun are elliptical rather than circular. Second, he demonstrated that the planets do not move at a uniform speed in their orbits. Third, in 1619 he showed that the time a planet takes to make its complete orbit is precisely related to its distance from the sun. Kepler's contribution was monumental. Whereas Copernicus had speculated, Kepler proved mathematically the precise relations of a sun-centered (solar) system. His work demolished the old system of Aristotle and Ptolemy, and in his third law he came close to formulating the idea of universal gravitation.

While Kepler was unraveling planetary motion, a young Florentine name Galileo Galilei (1564–1642) was challenging all the old ideas about motion. Like so many early scientists, Galileo was a poor nobleman first marked for a religious career. However, he soon became fascinated by mathematics. A brilliant student, Galileo became a professor of mathematics in 1589 at age twenty-five. He proceeded to examine motion and mechanics in a new way. Indeed, his great achievement was the elaboration and consolidation of the modern experimental method. Rather than speculate about what might or should happen, Galileo conducted controlled experiments to find out what actually *did* happen.

In his famous "acceleration experiment," he showed that a uniform force – in this case gravity – produced a uniform acceleration. Here is how Galileo described his pathbreaking method and conclusion in his *Two New Sciences:*

A piece of wooden moulding . . . was taken; on its edge was cut a channel a little more than one finger in breadth. Having made this groove very straight, smooth and polished, and having lined it with parchment, also as smooth and polished as possible, we rolled along it a hard, smooth and very round bronze ball. . . . Noting . . . the time required to make the descent . . . we now rolled the ball only one-quarter the length of the channel; and having measured the time of its descent, we found it precisely one-half of the former. . . . In such experiments [over many distances], repeated a full hundred times, we always found that the spaces traversed were to each other as the squares of the times, and that this was true for all inclinations of the plane.[5]

With this and other experiments, Galileo also formulated the law of inertia. That is, rather than "rest" being the natural state of objects, an object continues in motion forever unless stopped by some external force. Aristotelian physics was in a shambles.

In the tradition of Brahe, Galileo also applied the experimental method to astronomy. His astronomical discoveries had a very great impact on scientific development. On hearing that the telescope had just been invented in Holland, Galileo made one for himself and trained it on the heavens. He quickly discovered the first four moons of Jupiter, which clearly suggested that Jupiter could not possibly be embedded in any impenetrable crystal sphere. This discovery provided new evidence for the Copernican theory, in which Galileo already believed.

Galileo then pointed his telescope at the moon. He wrote in 1610 in *Siderus Nuncius:*

I feel sure that the moon is not perfectly smooth, free from inequalities, and exactly spherical, as a large school of philosophers considers with regard to the moon and the other heavenly bodies. On the

contrary, it is full of inequalities, uneven, full of hollows and protuberances, just like the surface of the earth itself, which is varied everywhere by lofty mountains and deep valleys. . . . The next object which I have observed is the essence or substance of the Milky Way. By the aid of a telescope anyone may behold this in a manner which so distinctly appeals to the senses that all the disputes which have tormented philosophers through so many ages are exploded by the irrefutable evidence of our eyes, and we are freed from wordy disputes upon the subject. For the galaxy is nothing else but a mass of innumerable stars planted together in clusters. Upon whatever part of it you direct the telescope straightway a vast crowd of stars presents itself to view; many of them are tolerably large and extremely bright, but the number of small ones is quite beyond determination.[6]

Reading these famous lines, one feels that a crucial corner in Western civilization is being turned. The traditional religious and theological world-view, which rested on determining and then accepting the proper established authority, is beginning to give way in certain fields to a critical, "scientific" method. This new method of learning and investigating was the greatest accomplishment of the entire scientific revolution, for it has proved capable of enormous extension. A historian critically investigating the documents of the past, for example, is not much different from a Galileo investigating stars and rolling balls.

Galileo was employed in Florence by the Medici grand dukes of Tuscany, and his work eventually aroused the ire of some theologians. The issue was presented in 1624 to Pope Urban VII, who permitted Galileo to write about different possible systems of the world, as long as he did not presume to judge which one actually existed. After the publication in Italian of his widely read *Dialogue on the Two Chief Systems of the World* in 1632, which too openly lampooned the traditional views of Aristotle and Ptolemy and defended those of Copernicus, Galileo was tried for heresy by the papal Inquisition. Imprisoned and threatened with torture, the aging Galileo recanted, "renouncing and cursing" his Copernican errors. Of minor importance in the development of science, Galileo's trial later became for some writers the perfect symbol of the inevitable conflict between religious belief and scientific knowledge.

NEWTON'S SYNTHESIS

The accomplishments of Kepler, Galileo, and other scientists had had their effect by about 1640. The old astronomy and physics were in ruins, and several fundamental breakthroughs had been made. The new findings had not, however, been fused together in a new synthesis, a synthesis that would provide a single set of explanations for motion both on earth and in the skies. That synthesis, which prevailed until the twentieth century, was the work of Isaac Newton (1642–1727).

Newton was born into the lower English gentry, and attended Cambridge University. He was a very complex individual. A great genius who spectacularly united the experimental and theoretical-mathematical sides of modern science, Newton was also fascinated by alchemy. He sought the elixir of life and a way to change base metals into gold and silver. Not without reason did the twentieth-century economist John Maynard Keynes call Newton "the last of the magicians." Newton was intensely religious. He had a highly suspicious nature, lacked all interest in women and sex, and in 1693 had a nervous breakdown from which he later recovered. He was far from being the perfect rationalist so endlessly eulogized by writers in the eighteenth and nineteenth centuries.

Of his intellectual genius and incredible powers of concentration there can be no doubt, however. Arriving at some of his most basic ideas about physics in 1666 at age twenty-four, but unable to prove these theories mathematically, he attained a professorship and studied optics for many years. In 1684, Newton returned to physics for eighteen extraordinarily intensive months. For weeks on end he seldom left his room except to read his lectures. His meals were sent up but he usually forgot to eat them, his mind fastened like a vise on the laws of the universe. Thus did Newton open the third book of his immortal *Mathematical Principles of Natural Philosophy,* published in Latin in 1687 and generally known as the *Principia,* with these lines:

In the preceding books I have laid down the principles of philosophy [that is, science]. . . . These principles are the laws of certain motions, and powers or forces, which chiefly have respect to philosophy. . . . It remains that from the same principles I now demonstrate the frame of the System of the World.

Newton made good his grandiose claim. His towering accomplishment was to integrate in a single explanatory system the astronomy of Copernicus, as corrected by Kepler's laws, with the physics of Galileo and his predecessors. Newton did this by means of a set of mathematical laws that explain motion and mechanics. These laws of dynamics are complex, and it took scientists and engineers two hundred years to work out all their implications. Nevertheless, the key feature of the Newtonian synthesis was the law of universal gravitation. According to this law, every body in the universe attracts every other body in the universe in a precise mathematical relationship, whereby the force of attraction is proportional to the quantity of matter of the objects and inversely proportional to the square of the distance between them. The whole universe – from Kepler's elliptical orbits to Galileo's rolling balls – was unified in one majestic system.

CAUSES OF THE SCIENTIFIC REVOLUTION

With a charming combination of modesty and self-congratulation, Newton once wrote: "If I have seen further [than others], it is by standing on the shoulders of Giants."[7] Surely the path from Copernicus to Newton confirms the "internal" view of the scientific revolution as, first of all, a product of towering individual genius. The problems of science were inherently exciting, and solution of those problems was its own reward for inquisitive, high-powered minds. Yet there were certainly broader causes as well.

The long-term contribution of medieval intellectual life and medieval universities to the scientific revolution was much more considerable than historians unsympathetic to the Middle Ages once believed. By the thirteenth century, permanent universities with professors and large student bodies – six thousand in Paris in 1300, for example – had been established in western Europe. The universities were supported by society because they trained the lawyers, doctors, and church leaders society required. By 1300, philosophy had taken its place alongside law, medicine, and theology. Medieval philosophers developed a limited but real independence from theologians and a sense of free inquiry. They nobly pursued a body of knowledge and tried to arrange it meaningfully by means of abstract theories.

Within this framework, science was able to emerge as a minor but distinct branch of philosophy. In the fourteenth and fifteenth centuries, first in Italy and then elsewhere in Europe, leading universities established new professorships of mathematics, astronomy, and physics (natural philosophy) within their faculties of philosophy. The prestige of the new fields was still low among both professors and students. Nevertheless, this pattern of academic science, which grew out of the medieval commitment to philosophy and did not change substantially until the late eighteenth century, undoubtedly promoted scientific development. Rational, critical thinking was applied to scientific problems by a permanent community of scholars. And an outlet existed for the talents of a Galileo or a Newton: all of the great pathbreakers just considered either studied or taught at universities.

The Renaissance also stimulated scientific progress. One of the great deficiencies of medieval science was its rather rudimentary mathematics. The recovery of the finest works of Greek mathematics – a by-product of Renaissance humanism's ceaseless search for the knowledge of antiquity – greatly improved European mathematics well into the early seventeenth century. The recovery of more texts also showed that classical mathematicians had had their differences, and Europeans were forced to try to resolve these ancient controversies by means of their own efforts. Finally, the Renaissance pattern of patronage, especially in Italy, was often scientific as well as artistic and humanistic. Various rulers and wealthy businessmen supported scientific investigations, just as the Medicis of Florence supported those of Galileo.

The navigational problems of long sea voyages in the age of overseas expansion were a third factor in the scientific revolution. Ship captains on distant shores needed to be able to chart their positions as accurately as possible, so that reliable maps could be drawn and the risks of international trade reduced. As early as 1484, the king of Portugal appointed a commission of mathematicians to perfect tables to help seamen find their latitude. This resulted in the first European navigation manual.

The problem of fixing longitude was much more difficult. In England, the government and the great capitalistic trading companies turned to science and scientific education in an attempt to solve this pressing practical problem. When the famous Elizabethan financier Sir Thomas Gresham left a large amount of money to establish Gresham College in London, he stipulated that three of the college's seven professors had to concern themselves exclusively with scientific subjects. The professor of astronomy was directed to teach courses on the science of navigation. A seventeenth-century popular ballad took note of the new college's calling:

This college will the whole world measure
Which most impossible conclude,
And navigation make a pleasure
By finding out the longitude.[8]

At Gresham College scientists had, for the first time in history, an important, honored role in society. They enjoyed close ties with the top officials of the Royal Navy and with the leading merchants and shipbuilders. Gresham College became the main center of scientific activity in England in the first half of the seventeenth century. The close tie between practical men and scientists also led to the establishment in 1662 of the Royal Society of London, which published scientific papers and sponsored scientific meetings.

Navigational problems were also critical in the development of many new scientific instruments, such as the telescope, the barometer, the thermometer, the pendulum clock, the microscope, and the air pump. Better instruments, which permitted more accurate observations, often led to very important new

knowledge almost automatically. Galileo with his telescope was by no means unique.

Better instruments were part of the fourth factor, the development of better ways of obtaining knowledge about the world. Two important thinkers, Francis Bacon (1561-1626) and René Descartes (1596-1650), represented key aspects of this improvement in scientific methodology.

The English politician and writer Francis Bacon was the greatest early propagandist for the new experimental method, as Galileo was its greatest early practitioner. Rejecting the Aristotelian and medieval method of using speculative reasoning to build general theories, Bacon argued that new knowledge had to be pursued through empirical, experimental research. That is, the researcher who wants to learn more about leaves or rocks should not speculate about the subject, but rather collect a multitude of specimens and then compare and analyze them. Thus freed from sterile "medieval" speculation, the facts will speak for themselves and knowledge will increase. Bacon's contribution was to formalize the empirical method, which had already been used by scientists like Brahe and Galileo, into a general theory of deductive reasoning, which we call empiricism.

Bacon claimed that the empirical method would result not only in more knowledge, but in highly practical, extremely useful knowledge. According to Bacon, scientific discoveries, like those so avidly sought at Gresham College, would bring about much greater control over the physical environment and make people rich and nations powerful. Thus Bacon helped provide a radically new, highly effective justification for private and public support of scientists and scientific inquiry.

The French philosopher René Descartes was a true genius who made his first great discovery in mathematics. As a young, twenty-three-year-old soldier serving in the Thirty Years' War, he experienced on a single night in 1619 a life-changing intellectual vision. What Descartes saw was that there was a perfect correspondence between geometry and algebra, and that geometrical, spatial figures could be expressed as algebraic equations and vice-versa. A great step forward in the history of mathematics, Descartes' discovery of analytic geometry provided scientists with an important new tool. Descartes also made contributions to the science of optics, but his greatest achievement was to develop his initial vision into a whole philosophy of knowledge and science.

Like Bacon, Descartes scorned traditional science and had great faith in the powers of the human mind. Yet Descartes was much more systematic and mathematical than Bacon. He decided it was necessary to doubt everything that could reasonably be doubted and then, as in geometry, to use deductive reasoning from self-evident principles to ascertain scientific laws. Descartes' reasoning ultimately reduced all substances to *matter* and *mind* – that is, to the physical and the spiritual. His view of the world as consisting of two fundamental entities is known as Cartesian dualism. Descartes was a profoundly original and extremely influential thinker.

It is important to realize that the modern scientific method, which began to crystallize in the late seventeenth century, has combined Bacon's inductive experimentalism and Descartes' deductive, mathematical rationalism. Neither of these extreme approaches was sufficient by itself. Bacon's inability to appreciate the importance of mathematics and his obsession with practical results clearly showed the limitations of antitheoretical empiricism. Likewise, some of Descartes' positions – he believed, for example, that it was possible to deduce the whole science of medicine from

STATE SUPPORT *Governments supported scientific research because they thought it might be useful. Here Louis XIV visits the French Royal Academy of Sciences in 1671 and examines a plan for better military fortifications. The great interest in astronomy, anatomy, and geography is evident. (Bibliothèque Nationale, Paris)*

first principles – aptly demonstrated the inadequacy of rigid, dogmatic rationalism. Significantly, Bacon faulted Galileo for his use of abstract formulas, while Descartes criticized the great Italian for being too experimental and insufficiently theoretical. Thus the modern scientific method has typically combined Bacon and Descartes. It has joined precise observations and experimentalism with the search for general laws that may be expressed in rigorously logical, mathematical language.

Finally, there is the question of science and religion. Just as some historians have argued that Protestantism led to the rise of capitalism, others have concluded that Protestantism was a fundamental factor in the rise of modern science. Protestantism, particularly in its Calvinist varieties, supposedly made scientific inquiry a question of individual conscience and not religious doctrine. The Catholic church, on the other hand, supposedly suppressed scientific theories that conflicted with its teachings and thus discouraged scientific progress.

The truth of the matter is more complicated. *All* religious authorities – Catholic, Protestant, and Jewish – opposed the Copernican system to a greater or lesser extent until about 1630, by which time the scientific revolution was definitely in progress. The Catholic church was initially less hostile than Protestant and Jewish religious leaders. This early Catholic toleration and the scientific interests of Renaissance Italy help account for the undeniable fact that Italian scientists played a crucial role in scientific progress right up to the trial of Galileo in 1633. Thereafter the Counter Reformation church became more hostile to science, which helps account for the decline of science in Italy (but not in Catholic France) after 1640. At the same time some Protestant countries became quite "pro-science," especially if the country lacked a strong religious authority capable of imposing religious orthodoxy on scientific questions.

This was the case with England after 1630. English religious conflicts became so intense that it was impossible for the authorities to impose religious unity on anything, including science. It is significant that the forerunners of the Royal Society agreed to discuss only "neutral" scientific questions, so as not to come to blows over closely related religious and political disputes. The work of Bacon and his many followers during Cromwell's Commonwealth helped solidify the neutrality and independence of science. Bacon advocated the experimental approach precisely because it was open-minded and independent of any preconceived religious or philosophical ideas. Neutral and useful, science became an accepted part of life and developed rapidly in England after about 1640.

SOME CONSEQUENCES OF THE SCIENTIFIC REVOLUTION

The rise of modern science had many consequences, some of which are still unfolding. First, it went hand in hand with the rise of a new and expanding social group – the scientific community. Members of this community were linked together by learned societies, common interests, and shared values. Expansion of knowledge was the primary goal of this community, and scientists' material and psychological rewards depended on their success in this endeavor. Thus science became quite competitive, and ever more scientific advance was inevitable.

Second, the scientific revolution introduced not only new knowledge about nature but also a new and revolutionary way of obtaining such knowledge – the modern scientific method. In addition to being both theoretical and experimental, this method was highly critical, and it differed profoundly from the old way of getting knowledge about nature. It refused to base its conclusions on tradition and established sources, on ancient authorities and sacred texts.

The scientific revolution had few consequences for economic life and the living standards of the masses until the late eighteenth century at the very earliest. True, improvements in the techniques of navigation facilitated overseas trade and helped enrich leading merchants. But science had relatively few practical economic applications, and the hopes of the early Baconians were frustrated. The close link between theoretical, or pure, science and applied technology, which we take for granted today, simply did not exist before the nineteenth century. Thus, the scientific revolution of the seventeenth century was first and foremost an intellectual revolution. It is not surprising that for more than a hundred years its greatest impact was on how people thought and believed.

THE ENLIGHTENMENT

The scientific revolution was the single most important factor in the creation of the new world-view of the eighteenth-century Enlightenment. This world-view, which has played a very large role in shaping the modern mind, was made up of a rich mix of ideas, sometimes conflicting, for intellectuals delight in playing with ideas as athletes delight in playing games. In this rich diversity, three central concepts stand out.

The most important and original idea of the Enlightenment was that the methods of natural science could and should be used to examine and understand all aspects of life. This was what intellectuals meant by *reason,* a favorite word of Enlightenment thinkers. Nothing was to be accepted on faith. Everything was to be submitted to the rational, critical, "scientific" way of thinking. This approach brought the Enlightenment into a head-on conflict with the established churches, which rested their beliefs on the special authority of the Bible and Christian theology. A second important Enlightenment concept was that the scientific method was capable of discovering the laws of human society as well as those of nature. Thus was "social science" born. Its birth led to the third key idea, the idea of progress. Armed with the proper method of discovering the laws of human existence, Enlightenment thinkers be-

lieved it was at least possible to create better societies and better people. Their belief was strengthened by some genuine improvements in economic and social life during the eighteenth century, as we shall see in the next two chapters.

The Enlightenment was, therefore, profoundly secular. It revived and expanded the Renaissance concentration on worldly explanations. In the course of the eighteenth century, the Enlightenment had a profound impact on the thought and culture of the urban middle and upper classes. It did not have much appeal for the poor and the peasants.

THE EMERGENCE OF THE ENLIGHTENMENT

The Enlightenment reached its maturity about 1750, when a brilliant band of French thinkers known as the philosophes effectively propagandized the new world-view across Europe. Yet it was the generation that came of age between the publication of Newton's masterpiece in 1687 and the death of Louis XIV in 1715 that tied the crucial knot between the scientific revolution and a new outlook on life.

Talented writers of that generation popularized the hard-to-understand scientific achievements for the educated elite. The most famous and influential popularizer was a very versatile French man of letters, Bernard de Fontenelle (1657–1757). Fontenelle practically invented the technique of making highly complicated scientific findings understandable to a broad nonscientific audience. He set out to make science witty and entertaining, as easy to read as a novel. This was a tall order, but Fontenelle largely succeeded.

His most famous work, *Conversations on the Plurality of Worlds* of 1686, begins with two elegant figures walking in the gathering shadows of a large park. One is a woman, a so-

POPULARIZING SCIENCE *The frontpiece illustration of Fontenelle's* Conversations on the Plurality of Worlds *invites the reader to share the pleasures of astronomy with an elegant lady and an entertaining teacher. (Photo: Caroline Buckler)*

phisticated aristocrat, and the other is her friend, perhaps even her lover. They gaze at the stars, and their talk turns to a passionate discussion of . . . astronomy! He confides that "each star may well be a different world." She is intrigued by his novel idea: "Teach me about these stars of yours." And he does, gently but persistently stressing how error is giving way to truth. At one point he explains:

There came on the scene a certain German, one Copernicus, who made short work of all those various circles, all those solid skies, which the ancients had pictured to themselves. The former he abolished; the latter he broke in pieces. Fired with the noble zeal of a true astronomer, he took the earth and spun it very far away from the center of the universe, where it had been installed, and in that center he put the sun, which had a far better title to the honor.[9]

Rather than tremble in despair in the face of these revelations, Fontenelle's lady rejoices in the advance of knowledge. Fontenelle thus went beyond entertainment to instruction, suggesting that the human mind was capable of making great progress.

This idea of progress was essentially a new idea of the later seventeenth century. Medieval and Reformation thinkers had been concerned primarily with sin and salvation. The humanists of the Renaissance had emphasized worldly matters, but they had been backward-looking. They had believed it might be possible to equal the magnificent accomplishments of the ancients, but they did not ask for more. Fontenelle and like-minded writers had come to believe that, at least in science and mathematics, their era had gone far *beyond* antiquity. Progress, at least intellectual progress, was clearly possible. During the eighteenth century, this idea would sink deeply into the consciousness of the European elite.

Fontenelle and other literary figures of his generation were also instrumental in bringing science into conflict with religion. Contrary to what is often assumed, many seventeenth-century scientists, both Catholic and Protestant, believed that their work exalted God. They did not draw antireligious implications from their scientific findings. The greatest scientist of them all, Isaac Newton, was a devout if unorthodox Christian who saw all of his studies as directed toward explaining God's message. Newton devoted far more of his time to angels and biblical prophecies than to universal gravitation, and he was convinced that all of his inquiries were equally "scientific."

Fontenelle, on the other hand, was skeptical about absolute truth and cynical about the claims of organized religion. Since such views could not be stated openly in Louis XIV's France, Fontenelle made his point through subtle editorializing about science. His depiction of the cautious Copernicus as a self-conscious revolutionary was typical. In his *Eulogies of Scientists* Fontenelle exploited with endless variations the basic theme of rational, progressive scientists versus prejudiced, reactionary priests. Time and time again Fontenelle's fledgling scientists attended church and studied theology; then, at some crucial moment, each was converted from the obscurity of religion to the clarity of science.

The progressive and antireligious implications that writers like Fontenelle drew from the scientific revolution reflected a very real crisis in European thought at the end of the seventeenth century. This crisis had its roots in several intellectual uncertainties and dissatisfactions, of which the demolition of Aristotelian-medieval science was only one.

A second uncertainty involved the whole question of religious truth. The destructive wars of religion had been fought, in part, because religious freedom was an intolerable idea in the early seventeenth century. Both Catholics and Protestants had believed that religious truth was absolute and therefore worth fighting and dying for. It was also generally believed that a strong state required unity in religious faith. Yet the disastrous results of the many attempts to impose such religious unity, such as Louis XIV's expulsion of the French Protestants in 1685, led some people to ask if ideological conformity in re-

ligious matters was really necessary. Others skeptically asked if religious truth could ever be known with absolute certainty, and concluded that it could not.

The most famous of these skeptics was Pierre Bayle (1647–1706), a French Huguenot who took refuge in Holland. A teacher by profession and a crusading journalist by inclination, Bayle critically examined the religious beliefs and persecutions of the past in his *Historical and Critical Dictionary,* published in 1697. Demonstrating that human beliefs had been extremely varied and very often mistaken, Bayle concluded that nothing can ever be known beyond all doubt. In religion as in philosophy, humanity's best hope was open-minded toleration. Bayle's skeptical views were very influential. Many eighteenth-century writers mined his inexhaustible vein of critical skepticism for ammunition for their attacks on superstition and Christian theology. Bayle's four-volume *Dictionary* was more frequently found in the private libraries of eighteenth-century France than any other book.

The rapidly growing travel literature on non-European lands and cultures was a third cause of uncertainty. In the wake of the great discoveries, Europeans were learning that the peoples of China, India, Africa and the Americas all had their own very different beliefs and customs. Europeans shaved their faces and let their hair grow. The Turks shaved their heads and let their beards grow. In Europe a man bowed before a woman to show respect. In Siam a man turned his back on a woman when he met her, because it was disrespectful to look directly at her. Countless similar examples discussed in the travel accounts helped change the perspective of educated Europeans. They began to look at truth and morality in relative rather than absolute terms. Anything was possible, and who could say what was right or wrong? As one Frenchman wrote: "There is nothing that opinion, prejudice, custom, hope, and a sense of honor cannot do." Another wrote disapprovingly of religious skeptics who were corrupted "by extensive travel and lose whatever shreds of religion that remained with them. Every day they see a new religion, new customs, new rites."[10]

A fourth cause and manifestation of European intellectual turmoil was John Locke's epoch-making *Essay Concerning Human Understanding.* Published in 1690 – the same year Locke published his famous *Second Treatise on Civil Government* – Locke's essay brilliantly set forth a new theory about how human beings learn and form their ideas. In doing so he rejected the prevailing view of Descartes, who had held that all people are born with certain basic ideas and ways of thinking. Locke insisted that all ideas are derived from experience. The human mind is like a blank tablet at birth, a tablet on which environment writes the individual's understanding and beliefs. Human development is, therefore, determined by education and social institutions, for good or for evil. Locke's *Essay Concerning Human Understanding* passed through many editions and translations. It was, along with Newton's *Principia,* one of the dominant intellectual inspirations of the Enlightenment.

THE PHILOSOPHES AND THEIR IDEAS

By the death of Louis XIV in 1715, many of the ideas that would soon coalesce into the new world-view had been assembled. Yet Christian Europe was still strongly attached to its traditional beliefs, as witnessed by the powerful revival of religious orthodoxy in the first half of the eighteenth century. By the outbreak of the American Revolution in 1775, however, a large portion of western Europe's educated elite had embraced many of the new ideas. This acceptance was the work of one of history's most influential groups of intellectuals, the philosophes. It was the philosophes who proudly and effectively proclaimed that they, at long last, were bringing the light of knowledge to their ignorant fellow creatures in a great Age of Enlightenment.

Philosophe is the French word for philosopher, and it was in France that the Enlightenment reached its highest development. The French philosophes were indeed philosophers. They asked fundamental philosophical questions about the meaning of life, about God, human nature, good and evil, and cause and effect. But, in the tradition of Bayle and Fontenelle, they were not content with abstract arguments or ivory-tower speculations among a tiny minority of scholars and professors. They wanted to influence and convince a broad audience.

The philosophes were intensely committed to reforming society and humanity, yet they were not free to write as they wished, since it was illegal in France to criticize openly either church or state. Their most radical works had to circulate in France in manuscript form, very much as critical works are passed from hand to hand in unpublished form in dictatorships today. Knowing that direct attacks would probably be banned or burned, the philosophes wrote novels and plays, histories and philosophies, dictionaries and encyclopedias, all filled with satire and double meanings to spread the message.

One of the greatest philosophes, the baron de Montesquieu (1689–1755), brilliantly pioneered this approach in *The Persian Letters,* an extremely influential social satire published in 1721. Montesquieu's work consisted of amusing letters supposedly written by Persian travelers, who see European customs in "strange ways" and thereby cleverly criticize existing practices and beliefs. Having shown wit to be a powerful weapon against the cruelty and superstition he despised, Montesquieu turned to political theory and as we shall see in Chapter 26, contributed greatly to the development of liberalism.

The most famous and in many ways most representative philosophe was François Marie Arouet, who was known by the pen name of Voltaire (1694–1778). In his long career this son of a comfortable middle-class family wrote over seventy witty volumes, hobnobbed with kings and queens, and died a millionaire because of shrewd business speculations. His early career, however, was turbulent. In 1717, Voltaire was imprisoned for eleven months in the Bastille in Paris for insulting the regent of France. In 1726, a barb from his sharp tongue led a great French nobleman to have him beaten and arrested. This experience made a deep impression upon Voltaire. All his life he struggled against legal injustice and class inequalities before the law.

Released from prison after promising to leave the country, Voltaire lived in England for three years. He then wrote various works praising English institutions and popularizing English scientific progress. Newton, he wrote, was history's greatest man, for he had used his genius for the benefit of humanity. "It is," wrote Voltaire, "the man who sways our minds by the prevalence of reason and the native force of truth, not they who reduce mankind to a state of slavery by force and downright violence . . . that claims our reverence and admiration."[11] In the true style of the Enlightenment, Voltaire mixed the glorification of science and reason with an appeal for better people and institutions.

Yet, like almost all of the philosophes, Voltaire was a reformer and not a revolutionary in social and political matters. Returning to France, he was eventually appointed royal historian in 1743, and his *Age of Louis XIV* portrayed Louis as the dignified leader of his age. Voltaire also began a long correspon-

VOLTAIRE was a prodigious worker. This painting shows him dictating from the very moment he hops out of bed. (Bulloz)

dence with Frederick the Great, and he accepted Frederick's flattering invitation to come brighten up the Prussian court in Berlin. The two men later quarreled, but Voltaire always admired Frederick as a freethinker and an enlightened monarch.

Voltaire pessimistically concluded that the best one could hope for in the way of government was an enlightened monarch, since human beings "are very rarely worthy to govern themselves." Nor did he believe in social equality in human affairs. The idea of making servants equal to their masters was "absurd and impossible." The only realizable equality Voltaire thought was that "by which the citizen only depends on the laws which protect the freedom of the feeble against the ambitions of the strong."[12]

Voltaire's philosophical and religious positions were much more radical. In the tradition of Bayle, his voluminous writings challenged – often indirectly – the Catholic church and Christian theology at almost every point. Although he was considered by many devout Christians to be a shallow blasphemer, Voltaire's religious views were influential and quite typical of the mature Enlightenment. The essay on religion from his widely read *Philosophical Dictionary* sums up many of his criticisms and beliefs:

I meditated last night; I was absorbed in the contemplation of nature; I admired the immensity, the course, the harmony of these infinite globes which the vulgar do not know how to admire.

I admired still more the intelligence which directs these vast forces. I said to myself: "One must be blind not to be dazzled by this spectacle; one must be stupid not to recognize its author; one must be mad not to worship the Supreme Being."

I was deep in these ideas when one of those genii who fill the intermundane spaces came down to me . . . and transported me into a desert all covered with piles of bones. . . . He began with the first pile. "These," he said, "are the twenty-three thousand Jews who danced before a calf, with the twenty-four thousand who were killed while lying with Midianitish women. The number of those massacred for such errors and offences amounts to nearly three hundred thousand.

"In the other piles are the bones of the Christians slaughtered by each other because of metaphysical disputes. . . ."

"What!" I cried, "brothers have treated their brothers like this, and I have the misfortune to be of this brotherhood! . . . Why assemble here all these abominable monuments to barbarism and fanaticism?"

"To instruct you. . . . Follow me now." . . .

I saw a man with a gentle, simple face, who seemed to me to be about thirty-five years old. From afar he looked with compassion upon those piles of whitened bones, through which I had been led to reach the sage's dwelling place. I was astonished to find his feet swollen and bleeding, his hands likewise, his side pierced, and his ribs laid bare by the cut of the lash. "Good God!" I said to him, "is it possible for a just man, a sage, to be in this state? . . . Was it . . . by priests and judges that you were so cruelly assassinated?"

With great courtesy he answered, "Yes."

"And who were these monsters?"

"They were hypocrites."

"Ah! that says everything; I understand by that one word that they would have condemned you to the cruelest punishment. Had you then proved to them, as Socrates did, that the Moon was not a goddess, and that Mercury was not a god?"

"No, it was not a question of planets. My countrymen did not even know what a planet was; they were all arrant ignoramuses. Their superstitions were quite different from those of the Greeks."

"Then you wanted to teach them a new religion?"

"Not at all; I told them simply: 'Love God with all your heart and your neighbor as yourself, for that is the whole of mankind's duty.' Judge yourself if this precept is not as old as the universe; judge yourself if I brought them a new religion." . . .

"Did you not say once that you were come not to bring peace, but a sword?"

"It was a scribe's error; I told them that I brought peace and not a sword. I never wrote anything; what I said can have been changed without evil intention."

"You did not then contribute in any way by your teaching, either badly reported or badly interpreted, to those frightful piles of bones which I saw on my way to consult with you?"

"I have only looked with horror upon those who have made themselves guilty of all these murders."

. . . [Finally] I asked him to tell me in what true religion consisted.

"Have I not already told you? Love God and your neighbor as yourself."

"What! Can we love God and still eat meat on Friday?"

"I always ate what was given me; for I was too poor to give dinner to anyone."

"Must I take sides for either the Greek or the Latin church?"

"When I was in the world I never made any distinction between the Jew and the Samaritan."

"Well, if that is so, I take you for my only master." Then he made me a sign with his head which filled me with consolation. The vision disappeared, and a clear conscience stayed with me.[13]

This passage requires careful study, for it suggests many Enlightenment themes of religion and philosophy. As the opening paragraphs show, Voltaire clearly believed in a God. But the God of Voltaire and most philosophes was a distant, deistic God, a great Clockmaker who built an orderly universe and then stepped aside and let it run. Finally, the philosophes hated all forms of religious intolerance. They believed that people had to be wary of dogmatic certainty and religious disputes, which often led to fanaticism and savage, inhuman action. Simple piety and human kindness – the love of God and the golden rule – were religion enough, even Christianity enough, as Voltaire's interpretation of Christ suggests.

The ultimate strength of the philosophes lay, however, in their numbers, dedication, and organization. The philosophes felt keenly that they were engaged in a common undertaking that transcended individuals. Their greatest and most representative intellectual achievement was, quite fittingly, a group effort – the seventeen-volume *Encyclopedia: The Rational Dictionary of the Sciences, the Arts, and the Crafts,* edited by Denis Diderot (1713–1774) and Jean le Rond d'Alembert (1717–1783). Diderot and d'Alembert made a curious pair. Diderot began his career as a hack writer, first attracting attention with a skeptical tract on religion that was quickly burned by the judges of Paris. D'Alembert was one of Europe's leading scientists and mathematicians, the orphaned and illegitimate son of celebrated aristocrats. Moving in different circles and with different interests, the two men set out to find coauthors who would examine the whole of rapidly expanding human knowledge. Even more fundamentally, they set out to teach people how to think critically and objectively about all matters. As Diderot said, he wanted the *Encyclopedia* to "change the general way of thinking."[14]

The editors of the *Encyclopedia* had to conquer innumerable obstacles. After the appearance in 1751 of the first volume, which dealt with such controversial subjects as atheism, the soul, and blind people – all words beginning with *a* in French – the government temporarily banned publication. The pope later placed it on the Index and pronounced excommunication on all who read or bought it. The timid publisher mutilated some of the articles in the last ten volumes without the editors' consent in an attempt to appease the authorities. Yet Diderot's unwavering belief in the importance of his mission held the encyclopedists together for fifteen years, and the enormous work was completed in 1765. Hundreds of thousands of articles by leading scientists and famous writers, skilled workers and progressive priests, treated every aspect of life and knowledge.

Not every article was daring or original, but the overall effect was little short of revolutionary. Science and the industrial arts were exalted, religion and immortality questioned. Intolerance, legal injustice, and out-of-date social institutions were openly criticized. More generally, the writers of the *Encyclopedia* showed that human beings could use the proc-

CANAL WITH LOCKS   The articles on science and the industrial arts in the Encyclopedia *carried lavish explanatory illustrations. This typical engraving from the section on water and its uses shows advances in canal building and reflects the encyclopedists' faith in technical progress. (Photo: Caroline Buckler)*

ess of reasoning to expand human knowledge. Encyclopedists were convinced that greater knowledge would result in greater human happiness, for knowledge was useful and made possible economic, social, and political progress. The *Encyclopedia* was extremely influential in France and throughout western Europe as well. It summed up the new world-view of the Enlightenment.

THE LATER ENLIGHTENMENT

After about 1770, the harmonious unity of the philosophes and their thought began to break down. As the new world-view became increasingly accepted by the educated public, some thinkers sought originality by exaggerating certain ideas of the Enlightenment to the exclusion of others. These latter-day philosophes built rigid, dogmatic systems.

In his *System of Nature* (1770) and other works, the aristocratic Baron Paul d'Holbach (1723–1789) argued that human beings were machines completely determined by outside forces. Free will, God, and immortality of the soul were foolish myths. D'Holbach's rabid atheism and determinism, which were coupled with extreme hostility toward Christianity and all other religions, dealt the Enlightenment movement a severe blow. Deists like Voltaire, who believed in God but not in established churches, found d'Holbach's inflexible atheism repulsive. They saw in him the same dogmatic intolerance they had been fighting all their lives.

Another aristocrat, the marquis Marie-Jean

de Condorcet (1743-1794), transformed the Enlightenment belief in gradual, hard-won progress into fanciful utopianism. In his *Progress of the Human Mind,* written in 1793 during the French Revolution, Condorcet traced the nine stages of human progress that had already occurred and predicted that the tenth would bring perfection. Ironically, Condorcet wrote this work while fleeing for his life. Caught and condemned by revolutionary extremists, he preferred death by his own hand to the blade of the guillotine.

Other thinkers and writers after about 1770 began to attack the Enlightenment's faith in reason, progress, and moderation. The most famous of these was the Swiss Jean-Jacques Rousseau (1712-1778), a brilliant but difficult thinker, an appealing but neurotic individual. Born into a poor family of watchmakers in Geneva, Rousseau went to Paris and was greatly influenced by Diderot and Voltaire. Always extraordinarily sensitive and suspicious, Rousseau came to believe his philosophe friends were plotting against him. In the mid-1750s he broke with them personally and intellectually, living thereafter as a lonely outsider with his uneducated common-law wife and going in his own highly original direction.

Like other Enlightenment thinkers, Rousseau was passionately committed to individual freedom. Unlike them, however, he attacked rationalism and civilization as destroying rather than liberating the individual. Warm, spontaneous feeling had to complement and correct the cold intellect. Moreover, the individual's basic goodness had to be protected from the cruel refinements of civilization. As we shall see in Chapter 28, these ideas greatly influenced the early romantic movement, which rebelled against the culture of the Enlightenment in the late eighteenth century. Applying his heartfelt ideas to children,

Rousseau had a powerful impact upon the development of modern education. In his famous novel *Emile* (1762) he argued that education must shield the naturally unspoiled child from the corrupting influences of civilization and too many books. According to Rousseau, children must develop naturally and spontaneously, at their own speed and in their own way. It is eloquent testimony to Rousseau's troubled life and complicated personality that he placed all five of his own children in orphanages.

Rousseau also made an important contribution to political theory in the *Social Contract* (1762). His fundamental ideas were the general will and popular sovereignty. According to Rousseau, the general will is sacred and absolute, reflecting the common interests of the people, who have displaced the monarch as the holder of the sovereign power. The general will is not necessarily the will of the majority, however, although minorities have to subordinate themselves to it without question. Little noticed before the French Revolution, Rousseau's dogmatic concept of the general will appealed greatly to democrats and nationalists after 1789. The concept has also been used since 1789 by many dictators, who have claimed that they, rather than some momentary majority of the voters, represent the general will and thus the true interests of the sovereign masses.

THE SOCIAL SETTING OF THE ENLIGHTENMENT

The philosophes were splendid talkers as well as effective writers. Indeed, sparkling conversation in private homes spread Enlightenment ideas to Europe's upper middle class and aristocracy. Paris set the example, and other French cities and European capitals followed. In Paris a number of talented and often rich women presided over regular social gatherings of the great and near-great in their elegant drawing rooms, or salons. There, a d'Alembert and a Fontenelle could exchange witty, uncensored observations on literature, science, and philosophy with great aristocrats, wealthy middle-class financiers, high-ranking officials, and noteworthy foreigners. These intellectual salons practiced the equality the philosophes preached. They were open to all men and women with good manners, provided only that they were famous or talented, rich or important. More generally, the philosophes championed greater rights and expanded education for women, arguing that the subordination of females was an unreasonable prejudice and the sign of a barbaric society.

One of the most famous salons was that of Madame Geoffrin, the unofficial godmother of the *Encyclopedia*. Having lost her parents at an early age, the future Madame Geoffrin was married at fifteen by her well-meaning grandmother to a rich and boring businessman of forty-eight. It was the classic marriage of convenience – the poor young girl and the rich old man – and neither side ever pretended that love was a consideration. After dutifully raising her children, Madame Geoffrin sought to break out of her gilded cage as she entered middle age. The very proper businessman's wife became friendly with a neighbor, the marquise de Tencin. In her youth the marquise had been rather infamous as the mistress of the regent of France, but she had settled down to run a salon that counted Fontenelle and the philosopher Montesquieu among its regular guests.

When the marquise died in 1749, Madame Geoffrin tactfully transferred these luminaries to her spacious mansion for regular dinners. At first Madame Geoffrin's husband loudly protested the arrival of this horde of "para-

sites." But his wife's will was much stronger than his, and he soon opened his purse and even appeared at the twice-weekly dinners. "Who was that old man at the end of the table who never said anything?" an innocent newcomer asked one evening. "That," replied Madame Geoffrin without the slightest emotion, "was my husband. He's dead."[15]

When M. Geoffrin's death became official, Madame Geoffrin put the large fortune and spacious mansion she inherited to good use. She welcomed the encyclopedists – Diderot, d'Alembert, Fontenelle, and a host of others. She gave them generous financial aid and helped to save their enterprise from collapse, especially after the first eight volumes were burned by the authorities in 1759. She also corresponded with the king of Sweden and Catherine the Great of Russia. Madame Geoffrin was, however, her own woman. She remained a practicing Christian, and would not tolerate attacks on the church in her house. It was said that distinguished foreigners felt they had not seen Paris unless they had been invited to one of her dinners. The plain and long-neglected Madame Geoffrin managed to become the most renowned hostess of the eighteenth century.

There were many other hostesses, but Madame Geoffrin's greatest rival, Madame du Deffand, was one of the most interesting. While Madame Geoffrin was middle-class, pious, and chaste, Madame du Deffand was a skeptic from the nobility who lived fast and easy, at least in her early years. Another difference was that women – mostly highly intelligent, worldly members of the nobility – were fully the equal of men in Madame du Deffand's intellectual salon. Forever pursuing fulfillment in love and life, Madame du Deffand was an accomplished and liberated woman. An exceptionally fine letter writer, she carried on a vast correspondence with

leading men and women all across Europe. Voltaire was her most enduring friend.

Madame du Deffand's closest female friend was Julie de Lespinasse, a beautiful, talented young woman whom she befriended and made her protégée. The never-acknowledged illegitimate daughter of noble parents, Julie de Lespinasse had a hard youth, but she flowered in Madame du Deffand's drawing room — so much so that she was eventually dismissed by her jealous patroness.

Once again Julie de Lespinasse triumphed.

Her friends gave her money so that she could form her own salon. Her highly informal gatherings — she was not rich enough to supply more than tea and cake — attracted the keenest minds in France and Europe. As one philosophe marveled, "Nowhere was the conversation more brilliant nor better supervised.... She could toss out an idea for debate, make her contribution with clarity and sometimes with eloquence, and direct the conversation with the skill of a fairy." Another philosophe wrote:

She could unite the different types, even the most antagonistic, sustaining the conversation by a well-aimed phrase, animating and guiding it at will. . . . Politics, religion, philosophy, news: nothing was excluded. Her circle met daily from five to nine. There one found men of all ranks in the State, the Church, and the Court, soldiers and foreigners, and the leading writers of the day.[16]

Thus in France the ideas of the Enlightenment thrived in a social setting that graciously united members of the intellectual, economic, and social elites. Never before and never again would social and intellectual life be so closely and so pleasantly joined. In such an atmosphere the philosophes and the French nobility and upper middle class increasingly influenced one another. Critical thinking became fashionable, and flourished alongside hopes for human progress through greater knowledge.

ENLIGHTENED ABSOLUTISM

How did the Enlightenment influence political developments? To this important question there is no easy answer. On the one hand, the philosophes were primarily interested in converting people to critical "scientific" thinking and were not particularly concerned with politics. On the other hand, such thinking naturally led to political criticism and interest in political reform. Educated people, who belonged mainly to the nobility and middle class, came to regard political change as both possible and desirable.

Until the American Revolution, however, most Enlightenment thinkers believed that political change should come from above – from the ruler – rather than from below, especially in central and eastern Europe. There were several reasons for this essentially moderate belief. First, royal absolutism was a fact

of life, and the kings and queens of Europe's leading states clearly had no intention of giving up their great powers. Second, the philosophes generally believed that a benevolent absolutism offered the best opportunities for improving society. Critical thinking was turning the art of good government into an exact science. Therefore, it was necessary only to educate and "enlighten" the monarch, who could then swiftly and successfully make good laws and promote human happiness. Third, the philosophes turned toward the rulers because the rulers seemed to be listening. Just as the philosophes and the increasingly receptive upper middle class and nobility influenced one another, so did the philosophes and the "enlightened monarchs" come to form a mutual admiration society. Finally, although the philosophes did not dwell on this fact, they distrusted the masses. Known simply as "the people" in the eighteenth century, the peasant masses and the urban poor were, according to the philosophes, still enchained by the superstitions of the priests. Moreover, violent passions rather than logical thinking guided the people's actions. No doubt the people were maturing, but they were still children in need of firm parental guidance.

Encouraged and instructed by the philosophes, several absolutist rulers of the later eighteenth century tried, to the best of their abilities, to govern in an enlightened manner. The actual programs of these rulers varied greatly. Let us, therefore, examine these monarchs at close range before trying to form any overall judgment regarding the success or failure of enlightened absolutism.

THE "GREATS": FREDERICK OF PRUSSIA AND CATHERINE OF RUSSIA

Just as the French absolutism of Louis XIV had been the model for European rulers in the late seventeenth century, the enlightened absolutism of the French philosophes inspired European monarchs in the second half of the eighteenth century. French was the international language of the educated classes, and the education of future kings and queens across Europe lay in the hands of French tutors espousing Enlightenment ideas. France's cultural leadership was reinforced by the fact that it was still the wealthiest and most populous country in Europe. Thus, absolutist monarchs in several west German and Italian states, as well as in Spain and Portugal, proclaimed themselves more enlightened. By far the most influential of the new-style monarchs were Frederick II of Prussia and Catherine II of Russia, both styled "the Great."

FREDERICK THE GREAT   Frederick II, as we have seen (pages 765–766), carried on most of the stern military traditions he inherited from his father. His unprovoked attack on Maria Theresa's Austria in 1740 in order to seize Silesia helped contribute to a generation of warfare and almost resulted in the destruction of Prussia in the Seven Years' War (1756–1763). Yet in spite of his aggression and the philosophes' hatred of war, Frederick II was universally acknowledged as an "enlightened" absolute monarch, for two basic reasons.

First of all, Frederick adopted the cultural outlook of the Enlightenment. He wrote verse in French, delighted in witty conversation, and openly made fun of Christian doctrines. Yet he tolerantly allowed his subjects to believe as they wished in religious and philosophical matters. He also promoted the advancement of knowledge, improving his country's schools and universities.

Second, Frederick tried to improve the lives of his subjects. As he wrote his friend Voltaire: "I must enlighten my people, cultivate their manners and morals, and make them as happy as human beings can be, or as happy as the means at my disposal permit." The legal system and the bureaucracy were Frederick's primary tools. Prussia's laws were simplified, and judges decided cases quickly and impartially. Prussian officials became famous for their hard work and honesty. After the Seven Years' War ended in 1763, Frederick's government also energetically promoted the reconstruction of agriculture and industry in his war-torn country. In all this Frederick set a good example. He worked hard and lived modestly, claiming that he was "only the first servant of the state." Thus, Frederick justified monarchy in terms of practical results and said nothing of the divine right of kings.

Frederick's dedication to high-minded principles went only so far, however. He never tried to change Prussia's existing social structure. True, he condemned serfdom in the abstract, but he accepted it in practice and did not even free the serfs on his own estates. He accepted the old privileges of the nobility and extended new ones as well. It became practically impossible for a middle-class person to gain a top position in the government. The Junker nobility remained the backbone of the army and the entire Prussian state.

CATHERINE THE GREAT   Catherine the Great of Russia (1762–1796) was one of the most remarkable rulers who ever lived, and the philosophes adored her. Catherine was a German princess from Anhalt-Zerbst, a totally insignificant principality sandwiched between Prussia and Saxony. Her father commanded a regiment of the Prussian army, but her mother was related to the Romanovs of Russia, and that proved to be her chance.

Peter the Great had abolished the hereditary succession of tsars so that he could name his successor and thus preserve his policies. This move opened a period of palace intrigue and a rapid turnover of rulers until Peter's youngest daughter Elizabeth came to the Russian throne in 1741. A crude, shrewd woman noted for her hard drinking and hard loving – one of her official lovers was an illiterate shepherd boy – Elizabeth named her nephew Peter heir to the throne and chose Catherine to be his wife in 1744. It was a mismatch from the beginning. The fifteen-year-old Catherine was intelligent and attractive; her husband was stupid and ugly, his face badly scarred by smallpox. Ignored by her childish husband, Catherine carefully studied Russian, endlessly read writers like Bayle and Voltaire, and made friends at court. Soon she knew what she wanted. "I did not care about Peter," she wrote in her *Memoirs,* "but I did care about the crown."[17]

As the old empress Elizabeth approached death, Catherine plotted against her unpopular husband. A dynamic, sensuous woman, Catherine used her powerful sexual desire to good political advantage. She selected as her new lover a tall, dashing young officer named Gregory Orlov, who with his four officer brothers commanded considerable support among the soldiers stationed in St. Petersburg. When Peter came to the throne in 1762, his first act was to withdraw Russian troops from the coalition against the hard-pressed Frederick of Prussia, whom he greatly admired. This decision saved Prussia from certain destruction, but it further alienated the army. Nor did Peter III's attempt to gain support from the Russian nobility by freeing it from compulsory state service succeed. At the end of six months Catherine and the military conspirators deposed Peter III in a palace revolution. Then the Orlov brothers murdered him. The German princess became empress of Russia.

Catherine had drunk deeply at the Enlightenment well. Never questioning the common assumption that absolute monarchy was the best form of government, she set out to rule in an enlightened manner. One of her most enduring goals was to bring the sophisticated culture of western Europe to backward Russia. To do so, she imported Western architects, sculptors, musicians, and intellectuals. She bought masterpieces of Western art in wholesale lots and created one of the best collections in all Europe. Throughout her reign Catherine patronized the philosophes. An enthusiastic letter writer, she corresponded extensively with Voltaire and praised him as "the champion of the human race." When the French government banned the *Encyclopedia,* she offered to publish it in St. Petersburg. She discussed reform with Diderot in St. Petersburg; and when Diderot needed money, she purchased his library for a small fortune but allowed him to keep it during his lifetime. With these and countless similar actions, Catherine skillfully won a good press for herself and for her country in the West. Moreover, this intellectual ruler, who wrote plays and articles and loved good talk, set the tone for the entire Russian nobility. Peter the Great westernized Russian armies, but it was Cahterine who westernized the thinking of the Russian nobility.

Catherine's second goal was domestic reform, and she began her reign with sincere and ambitious projects. Better laws were a major concern. In 1767, she drew up enlightened instructions for the special legislative commission she appointed to prepare a new law code. No new unified code was ever produced, but Catherine did restrict the practice of torture and allowed limited religious toleration. She also tried to improve education and strengthen local government. The philosophes applauded these measures and hoped more would follow.

Such was not the case. In 1773, a simple Cossack soldier named Emelian Pugachev sparked a gigantic uprising of serfs, very much as Stenka Razin had done a century earlier (page 774). Proclaiming himself the true tsar, Pugachev issued "decrees" abolishing serfdom, taxes, and army service. Thousands joined his cause, slaughtering landlords and officials over a vast area of southwestern Russia. Pugachev's hordes eventually proved no match for Catherine's noble-led regular army. Betrayed by his own men, Pugachev was captured and savagely executed.

Pugachev's rebellion was a decisive turning point in Catherine's domestic policy. On coming to the throne she had condemned serfdom in theory, but she was smart enough to realize that any changes would have to be very gradual or else she would quickly follow her departed husband. Pugachev's rebellion put an end to any illusions she might have had about reforming serfdom. The peasants were clearly dangerous, and her empire rested on the support of the nobility. After 1775, Catherine gave the nobles absolute control of their serfs. She extended serfdom into new areas, such as the Ukraine. In 1785, she formalized the nobility's privileged position, freeing them forever from taxes and state service. She also confiscated the lands of the Russian Orthodox church and gave them to favorite officials. Under Catherine the Russian nobility attained its most exalted position, and serfdom entered its most oppressive phase.

Catherine's third goal was territorial expansion, and in this respect she was extremely successful. Her armies subjugated the last descendants of the Mongols, the Crimean Tartars, and began the conquest of the Caucasus.

Her greatest coup by far was the partitioning of Poland. Poland had failed to build a strong absolutist state. For decades all important decisions had required the unanimous agreement of every Polish noble, which meant that nothing could ever be done. When be-

CATHERINE THE GREAT Intelligent, pleasure-loving, and vain, Catherine succeeded in bringing Russia closer to western Europe than ever before. (John R. Freeman)

tween 1768 and 1772 Catherine's armies scored unprecedented victories against the Turks and thereby threatened to disturb the balance of power between Russia and Austria in eastern Europe, Frederick of Prussia obligingly came forward with a deal. He proposed that Turkey be let off easily, and that Prussia, Austria, and Russia each "compensate" itself by taking a gigantic slice of Polish territory. Catherine jumped at the chance. The first partition of Poland took place in 1772. Two more partitions, in 1793 and 1795, gave all three powers more Polish territory, and the kingdom of Poland simply vanished from the map (see Map 22.1).

Expansion helped Catherine keep the nobility happy, for it provided her vast new lands to give to her faithful servants. Expansion also helped Catherine reward her lovers, of whom twenty-one have been definitely identified. Upon all these royal favorites she lavished large estates with many serfs, as if to make sure there were no hard feelings when her interest cooled. Until the end this remarkably talented woman – who always believed that, in spite of her domestic setbacks, she was slowly civilizing Russia – kept her zest for life. Fascinated by a new twenty-two-year-old flame when she was a roly-poly grandmother in her sixties, she happily reported her good fortune to a favorite former lover: "I have come back to life like a frozen fly; I am gay and well."[18]

ABSOLUTISM IN FRANCE AND AUSTRIA

LOUIS XV OF FRANCE   In building French absolutism, Louis XIV successfully drew on the middle class to curb the powers of the nobility. As long as the Grand Monarch lived, the nobility could only grumble and, like the duke of Saint-Simon in his *Memoirs,* scornfully lament the rise of "the vile bourgeoisie." But

when Louis XIV finally died in 1715, to be succeeded by his five-year-old great-grandson Louis XV (1715-1774), the nobility staged a rapid comeback. The duke of Orléans, who governed as regent until 1723, favored the high nobility.

The duke restored to the high court of Paris – the Parlement – the right to "register" and thereby approve the king's decrees. This was a fateful step. By the eighteenth century, the judges of the Parlement of Paris were mostly nobles. Moreover, they actually owned their seats on the bench and passed them as private property from father to son. They could not be replaced by the king. By establishing the right of this intensely aristocratic group to register the king's laws, the duke of Orléans practically destroyed French absolutism.

This result became clear when the heavy expenses of the War of the Austrian Succession (page 766) plunged France into a financial crisis. In 1748, Louis XV appointed a finance minister who decreed a 5 percent income tax on every individual regardless of social status. Exemption from taxation had been one of the most hallowed privileges of the nobility. The nobility immediately exploded in angry indignation, and the Parlement of Paris refused to ratify the new tax. All the other groups that had over time bought or extracted special privileges in taxation – the clergy, the large towns, certain wealthy bourgeoisie – added their voices to the protest. The monarchy retreated; the new tax was dropped. Following the disastrously expensive Seven Years' War the same drama was re-enacted. The government tried to maintain emergency taxes after the war ended. The nobility, effectively led by the Parlement of Paris, protested violently. The government caved in and withdrew the wartime measures in 1764.

Indolent and sensual by nature, more inter-

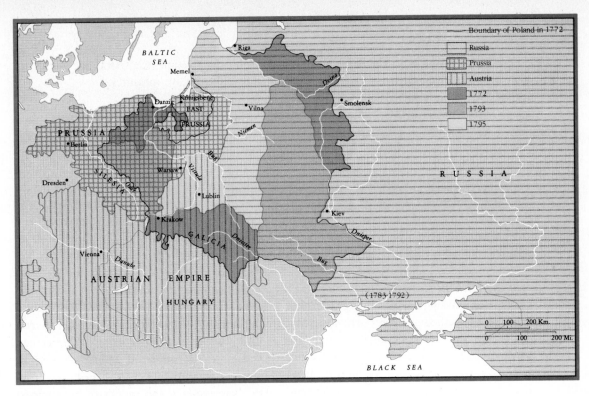

MAP 22.1 THE PARTITION OF POLAND AND
RUSSIA'S EXPANSION, 1772–1795 Although all
three of the great eastern absolutist states profited from
the division of large but weak Poland, Catherine's
Russia gained the most.

ested in his many mistresses than in affairs of state, Louis XV finally roused himself for a determined attempt to salvage his absolutist inheritance. "The magistrates," he angrily told the Parlement of Paris in a famous face-to-face confrontation, "are my officers. . . . In my person only does the sovereign power rest."[19] In 1768, Louis appointed a tough career official named René de Maupeou as chancellor and ordered him to end the usurpations of the Paris judges.

Maupeou abolished the Parlement of Paris and exiled its members. He created a new and docile parlement of royal officials and began once again to tax the privileged groups. Most of the philosophes applauded these measures: the sovereign was using his power to introduce badly needed reforms for the common

good. And in spite of the predictable cries from the nobility and their privileged allies, Louis XV might have prevailed – if he had lived to a very ripe old age.

But Louis XV died in 1774. The new king, Louis XVI (1774–1792), was a shy twenty-year-old with good intentions. Taking the throne, he is reported to have said: "What I should like most is to be loved."[20] The eager-to-please monarch immediately collapsed before the noble-led opposition, dismissing Maupeou and repudiating the great minister's work. The old Parlement of Paris was reinstated and the old ways were once again embraced. Royal absolutism, enlightened or otherwise, no longer existed in France. The country was drifting toward renewed financial crisis and political upheaval.

JOSEPH II OF AUSTRIA In some ways Joseph II (1780–1790) of Austria was the most spectacular enlightened absolutist of all. Named co-regent with his mother, the empress Maria Theresa, in 1765 but able to exercise little influence on her policies of gradual reform, Joseph sought to make up for lost time after her death. Determined to improve the life of the people, he saw the nobility and the clergy as the chief obstacles to this goal.

In a series of revolutionary decrees Joseph attacked the privileged groups head-on. He abolished serfdom and gave the peasants secure tenure of their land. He taxed all groups equally. Establishing complete religious toleration even for atheists, Joseph took education out of the hands of the Catholic church. He granted equal civil rights to Protestants and Jews. To accomplish this revolution from above, Joseph strengthened the central state and tried to erase the old provincial differences. Although guided to a considerable extent by very personal beliefs, Joseph demonstrated that Enlightenment ideas had revolutionary social and political implications if pushed to their logical extreme.

Joseph II was a heroic but colossal failure. He encountered opposition from all the privileged groups. His top officials and local bureaucrats, who were of necessity drawn largely from the nobility since the middle class was small and weak, subverted his program at every turn. Hungary and other parts of the empire rose up in open revolt. Joseph died prematurely at forty-nine, a broken and disillusioned man. His brother Leopold (1790–1792) came to the throne and was forced to cancel almost all of Joseph's revolutionary edicts in order to re-establish order. The nobles won back most of their traditional privileges, and the peasants lost most of their gains. Once again peasants were required to do forced labor for their lords. After Leopold's death in 1792, the reaction born of the French Revolution swept away the rest of Joseph's progressive measures.

AN OVERALL EVALUATION

In spite of their differences, the leading monarchs of the later eighteenth century all clearly believed that they were acting on the principles of the Enlightenment. The philosophes generally agreed with this assessment and cheered them onward. It is now possible to evaluate the enlightened absolutists and understand what they did and did not do.

The enlightened monarchs, especially Catherine and Frederick, encouraged and spread the cultural values of the Enlightenment. Perhaps this was their greatest achievement. Skeptical in religion and intensely secular in basic orientation, they unabashedly accepted the here-and-now and sought their happiness in the enjoyment of it. At the same time they were proud of their intellectual accomplishments and good taste, and they supported knowledge, education, and the arts. No wonder the philosophes felt the monarchs were kindred spirits.

The enlightened absolutists also tried to make life better for their subjects by enacting needed reforms. They had some successes, notably in Prussia and in the general area of the law and religious toleration. Yet cautious Frederick, ambitious Catherine, lazy Louis XV, and radical Joseph II all ended up with modest results. The life of the masses remained very hard in the eighteenth century. Everywhere the gap between the privileged nobility and the heavily burdened people remained as great as ever.

Some historians have concluded that the enlightened absolutists were not really sincere in their reform efforts. This interpretation, however, fits only in some instances. It probably applies to Catherine after Pugachev's rebellion, but it does not explain the failure of the fanatically committed Joseph II. It ignores Frederick's genuine concern for his subjects. It overlooks Louis XV's all-out effort to curb the Parlement of Paris and tax the nobility during Maupeou's administration. For a better explanation of the limited accomplishments of enlightened absolutism, one must look beyond motives to the structure of political and social power.

Chapters 20 and 21 have described how European monarchs dramatically strengthened their authority in the later seventeenth and early eighteenth centuries. With the striking exceptions of England, Holland, and Poland, European rulers created absolutist states. Arbitrarily and without consent, they raised standing armies, waged war, and imposed new taxes. In doing so, absolutist monarchs like Louis XIV and the Great Elector of Prussia reduced some of the power of the nobility, the only group besides themselves that really mattered politically.

Yet royal absolutism went only so far. It never touched the social and economic privileges of the nobility in any fundamental way. Indeed, nobles in eastern Europe often succeeded in working out very advantageous compromises: in return for accepting the monarch's greater control over the state, they won greater control over their peasants and the towns. The power of even the most absolute monarch was still balanced and restrained by the social and economic power of the nobles. Thus, the social and economic reforms of enlightened absolutists were of necessity limited and superficial: powerful nobilities simply would not permit radical measures to succeed.

More fundamentally, monarchs as a group were partners with the nobility and could not seriously support antinoble reforms for very long. Monarchy and nobility were like the husband and wife in an old-fashioned marriage. They loved and quarreled, cooperated

ENLIGHTENMENT CULTURE *was elegant, intellectual, and international. This painting shows the seven-year-old Austrian child prodigy, Wolfgang Amadeus Mozart (1756–1791), playing his own composition while his older sister sings and his father plays the violin. The elder Mozart displayed his children in the houses of leading aristocrats all across Europe. (Musée Condé de Chantilly/Giraudon)*

and changed; but they always knew they were joined together forever for better or worse. European monarchs and nobles were privileged groups in a society that used hierarchy and inequality as its basic organizing principles. Both appealed primarily to tradition to justify their inherited position, and the great privileges of one could hardly be secure without those of the other. No wonder that when monarchs built their absolutist states they normally turned to nobles to lead their armies and expanded bureaucracies. And if Louis XIV quite exceptionally preferred middle-class officials, Louis XV and Louis XVI did not: between 1714 and 1789, all but three of France's ministers were titled nobles.

The great eighteenth-century philosophe and aristocrat Montesquieu summed it all up in one famous line: "No monarchy, no nobility; no nobility, no monarchy."[21] Montesquieu was right: for centuries monarchy and nobility flourished together in Europe, and together they later declined and have almost disappeared.

———◆———

This chapter has focused on the complex development of a new world-view in Western civilization. This new view of the world was essentially critical and secular, drawing its inspiration from the Scientific Revolution and crystallizing in the Enlightenment.

The decisive breakthroughs in astronomy and physics in the seventeenth century, which demolished the imposing medieval synthesis of Aristotelian philosophy and Christian theology, had only limited practical consequences despite the expectations of scientific enthusiasts like Bacon. Yet the impact of new scientific knowledge on intellectual life became great. Interpreting scientific findings and Newtonian laws in an antitraditional, antireligious manner, the French philosophes of the Enlightenment extolled the superiority of rational, critical thinking. This new method, they believed, promised not just increased knowledge but even the discovery of the fundamental laws of human society, which could then be implemented by enlightened rulers for the general good. Although social and political realities frustrated these fond hopes, the philosophes succeeded in spreading their radically new world-view. That was a momentous accomplishment.

NOTES

1. H. Butterfield, *The Origins of Modern Science,* Macmillan, New York, 1951, p. viii.

2. Quoted by A. G. R. Smith, *Science and Society in the Sixteenth and Seventeenth Centuries,* Harcourt Brace Jovanovich, New York, 1972, p. 97.

3. Quoted by Butterfield, p. 47.

4. Quoted by Smith, p. 100.

5. Ibid. pp. 115–116.

6. Ibid. p. 120.

7. A. R. Hall, *From Galileo to Newton, 1630–1720,* Harper & Row, New York, 1963, p. 290.

8. Quoted by R. K. Merton, *Science, Technology and Society in Seventeenth-Century England,* rev. ed., Harper & Row, New York, 1970, p. 164.

9. Quoted by P. Hazard, *The European Mind, 1680–1715,* Meridian Books, Cleveland, 1963, pp. 304–305.

10. Ibid., pp. 11–12.

11. Quoted by L. M. Marsak, ed., *The Enlightenment,* John Wiley & Sons, New York, 1972, p. 56.

12. Quoted by G. L. Mosse et al., eds., *Europe in Review,* Rand McNally, Chicago, 1964, p. 156.

13. M. F. Arouet de Voltaire, *Oeuvres complètes,* Firmin-Didot Frères, Fils et Cie, Paris, 1875, VIII, 188-90.

14. Quoted by P. Gay, "The Unity of the Enlightenment," *History* 3 (1960):25.

15. Quoted by G. P. Gooch, *Catherine the Great and Other Studies,* Archon Books, Hamden, Conn., 1966, p. 112.

16. Ibid., p. 149.

17. Ibid., p. 15.

18. Ibid., p. 53.

19. Quoted by R. R. Palmer, *The Age of Democratic Revolution,* Princeton University Press, Princeton, 1959, 1.95-96.

20. Quoted by G. Wright, *France in Modern Times,* Rand McNally, Chicago, 1960, p. 42.

21. Quoted by P. Anderson, *Lineages of the Absolutist State,* LLB, London, 1974, p. 298.

SUGGESTED READING

The first three authors cited in the Notes – H. Butterfield (rev. ed. 1966), A. G. R. Smith, and A. R. Hall – have written excellent general interpretations of the scientific revolution. Another good study is M. Boas, *The Scientific Renaissance, 1450–1630* (1966), which is especially insightful on the influence of magic on science and on Galileo's trial. T. Kuhn, *The Copernican Revolution* (1957), is the best treatment of the subject; his *The Structure of Scientific Revolutions* (1962) is a challenging, much-discussed attempt to understand major breakthroughs in scientific thought over time. Two stimulating books on the ties between science and society in history are B. Merton, *Science, Technology and Society in Seventeenth-Century England,* rev. ed. (1970), and J. Ben-David, *The Scientist's Role in Society* (1971). E. Andrade, *Sir Isaac Newton* (1958), is a good, short biography, which may be compared with F. Manuel, *The Religion of Isaac Newton* (1974).

P. Hazard, *The European Mind, 1680–1715* (1963), is a classic study of the formative years of Enlightenment thought, and his *European Thought in the Eighteenth Century* (1954) is also recommended. A famous, controversial interpretation of the Enlightenment is that of C. Becker, *The Heavenly City of the Eighteenth Century Philosophes* (1932), which maintains that the world-view of medieval Christianity continued to influence the philosophes greatly. Becker's ideas are discussed interestingly in R. O. Rockwood, ed., *Carl Becker's Heavenly City Revisited* (1958). P. Gay has written several major studies on the Enlightenment: *Voltaire's Politics* (1959) and *The Party of Humanity* (1971) are two of the best. I. Wade, *The Structure and Form of the French Enlightenment* (1977), is a recent major synthesis. F. Baumer's *Religion and the Rise of Skepticism* (1969), H. Payne's *The Philosophes and the People* (1976), K. Rogers's *Feminism in Eighteenth-Century England* (1982), and J. B. Bury's old but still ex-

citing *The Idea of Progress* (1932) are stimulating studies of important aspects of Enlightenment thought. Above all, one should read some of the philosophes and let them speak for themselves. Two good anthologies are C. Brinton, ed., *The Portable Age of Reason* (1956), and F. Manuel, ed., *The Enlightenment* (1951). Voltaire's most famous and very amusing novel, *Candide,* is highly recommended, as are S. Gendzier, ed., *Denis Diderot: The Encyclopedia: Selections* (1967) and A. Wilson's biography, *Diderot* (1972).

In addition to the works mentioned in the Suggested Reading for Chapters 16 and 17, the monarchies of Europe are carefully analyzed in Charles Tilly, ed., *The Formation of National States in Western Europe* (1975), and ably discussed in J. Gagliardo, *Enlightened Despotism* (1967), both of which have useful bibliographies. Other recommended studies on the struggle for power and reform in different countries are: F. Ford, *Robe and Sword* (1953), which traces the resurgence of the French nobility after the death of Louis XIV; R. Herr, *The Eighteenth-Century Revolution in Spain* (1958), on the impact of Enlightenment thought in Spain; and P. Bernard, *Joseph II* (1968). In addition to I. de Madariaga's masterful *Russia in the Age of Catherine the Great* (1981) and D. Ransel's solid *Politics of Catherinean Russia* (1975), the ambitious reader should look at A. N. Radishchev, *A Journey From St. Petersburg to Moscow* (trans. 1958), a famous 1790 attack on Russian serfdom and an appeal to Catherine the Great to free the serfs, for which Radishchev was exiled to Siberia.

The culture of the time may be approached through A. Cobban, ed., *The Eighteenth Century,* (1969), a richly illustrated work with excellent essays, and C. B. Behrens, *The Ancien Régime* (1967). C. Rosen, *The Classical Style: Haydn, Mozart, Beethoven* (1972), brilliantly synthesizes music and society, as did Mozart himself in his great opera *The Marriage of Figaro,* where the count is the buffoon and his servant the hero.

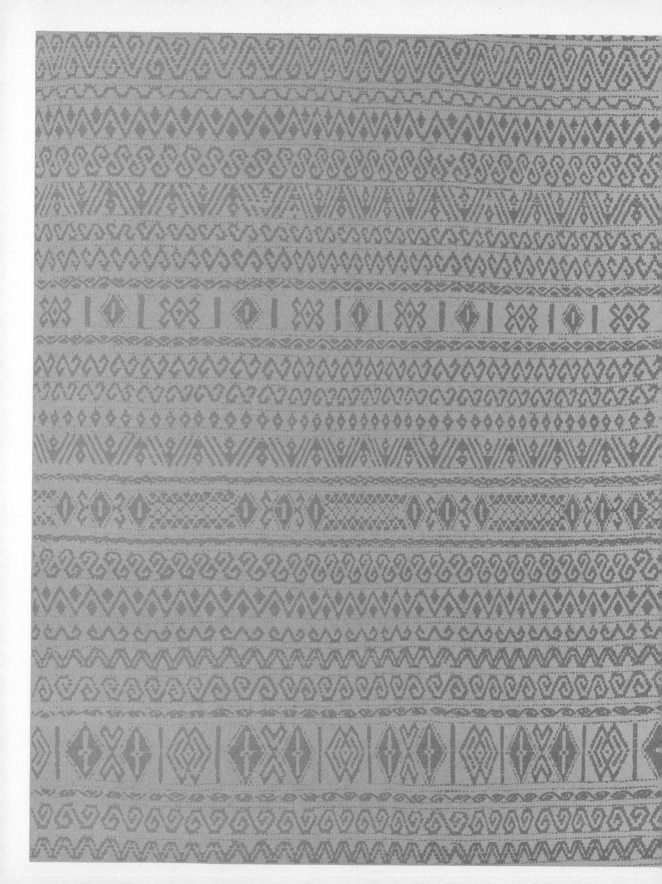

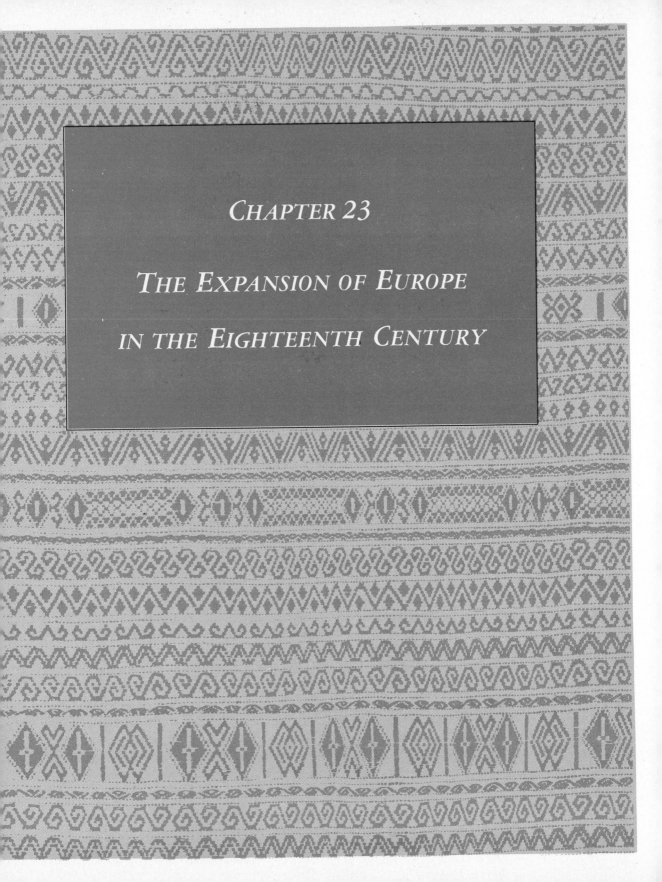

CHAPTER 23

THE EXPANSION OF EUROPE

IN THE EIGHTEENTH CENTURY

THE WORLD OF ABSOLUTISM and aristocracy, a combination of raw power and elegant refinement, was a world apart from that of ordinary men and women. For the overwhelming majority of the population in the eighteenth century, life remained a struggle with poverty and uncertainty, with the landlord and the tax collector. In 1700, peasants on the land and artisans in their shops lived little better than had their ancestors in the Middle Ages. Only in science and thought, and there only among a few intellectual leaders, had Western society succeeded in going beyond the great achievements of the High Middle Ages, achievements that in turn owed so much to Greece and Rome.

Everyday life was a struggle because the men and women of European societies, despite their best efforts, still could not produce very much by modern standards. Ordinary people might work like their beasts in the fields, and they often did, but there was seldom enough good food, warm clothing, and decent housing. Life went on; history went on. The wars of religion ravaged Germany in the seventeenth century; Russia rose to become a Great Power; the kingdom of Poland simply disappeared; monarchs and nobles continuously jockeyed for power and wealth. In 1700 or even 1750, the idea of progress – the idea that the lives of great numbers of people could improve substantially here on earth – was still only the dream of a small elite in their fashionable salons.

Yet the economic basis of European life was beginning to change. In the course of the eighteenth century, the European economy emerged from the long crisis of the seventeenth century, responded to challenges, and began to expand once again. Some areas were more fortunate than others. The rising Atlantic powers – Holland, France, and above all England – and their colonies led the way.

Agriculture and industry, trade and population, began a surge comparable to that of the eleventh- and twelfth-century springtime of European civilization. Only this time development was not cut short. This time the response to new challenges led toward one of the most influential developments in human history, the Industrial Revolution, which we shall consider in Chapter 27. What were the causes of this renewed surge? Why were the fundamental economic underpinnings of European society beginning to change, and what were the dimensions of those changes? How did these changes affect people and their work? These are the questions this chapter will try to answer.

AGRICULTURE AND THE LAND

At the end of the seventeenth century the economy of Europe was agrarian, as it had been for several hundred years. With the possible exception of Holland, at least 80 percent of the people of all western European countries drew their livelihoods from agriculture. In eastern Europe the percentage was considerably higher.

Men and women lavished their attention on the land, plowing fields and sowing seed, reaping harvests and storing grain. The land repaid these efforts, year after year yielding up the food and most of the raw materials for industry that made life possible. Yet the land was stingy. Even in a rich agricultural region like the Po valley in northern Italy, every bushel of wheat sown yielded on average only five or six bushels of grain at harvest during the seventeenth century. The average French yield in the same period was somewhat less. Such yields were barely more than those attained in fertile, well-watered areas in the

FARMING THE LAND *Agricultural methods in Europe changed very slowly from the Middle Ages to the early eighteenth century. This realistic picture from Diderot's* Encyclopedia *has striking similarities with agricultural scenes found in medieval manuscripts. (Photo: Caroline Buckler)*

thirteenth century or in ancient Greece. By modern standards output was distressingly low. (For each bushel of wheat seed sown today on fertile land with good rainfall, an American or French farmer can expect roughly forty bushels of produce.) In 1700, European agriculture was much more ancient and medieval than modern.

If the land was stingy, it was also capricious. In most regions of Europe in the six-

teenth and seventeenth centuries, harvests were poor, or even failed completely, every eight or nine years. The vast majority of the population who lived off the land might survive a single bad harvest by eating less and drawing on their reserves of grain. But when the land combined with persistent bad weather – too much rain rotting the seed, or drought withering the young stalks – the result was catastrophic. Meager grain reserves were soon exhausted, and the price of grain soared. Provisions from other areas with better harvests were hard to obtain.

In such crisis years, which periodically stalked Europe in the seventeenth and even into the eighteenth century, a terrible tightening knot in the belly forced people to tragic substitutes – the "famine foods" of a desperate population. People gathered chestnuts and stripped bark in the forests; they cut dandelions and grass; and they ate these substitutes to escape starvation. In one community in Norway in the early 1740s people were forced to wash dung from the straw in old manure piles in order to bake a pathetic substitute for bread. Even cannibalism occurred in the seventeenth century.

Such unbalanced and inadequate food in famine years made people weak and extremely susceptible to illness and epidemics. The eating of rough material like bark or grass – really unfit for human consumption – resulted in dysentery and intestinal ailments of every kind. Influenza and smallpox preyed with particular savagery upon populations weakened by famine. In famine years the number of deaths soared far above normal. A third of a village's population might disappear in a year or two. The 1690s were as dismal as many of the worst periods of earlier times. One county in Finland, which was probably typical of the entire country, lost fully 28 percent of its inhabitants in 1696 and 1697. Certain well-studied villages in the Beauvais region of northern France suffered a similar fate. In preindustrial Europe the harvest was the real king, and the king was seldom generous and often cruel.

To understand why Europeans produced barely enough food in good years and occasionally agonized through years of famine throughout the later seventeenth century, one must follow the plowman, his wife, and his children into the fields to observe their battle for food and life. There the ingenious pattern of farming that Europe had developed in the Middle Ages, a pattern that allowed fairly large numbers of people to survive but could never produce material abundance, was still dominant.

THE OPEN-FIELD SYSTEM

The greatest accomplishment of medieval agriculture was the open-field system of village agriculture developed by European peasants (page 427). That system divided the land to be cultivated by the peasants into a few large fields, which were in turn cut up into long narrow strips. The fields were open and the strips were not enclosed into small plots by fences or hedges. An individual peasant family – if it were fortunate – held a number of strips scattered throughout the various large fields. The land of those who owned but did not till, primarily the nobility, the clergy, and wealthy townsmen, was also in scattered strips. The peasant community farmed each large field as a community, with each family following the same pattern of plowing, sowing, and harvesting in accordance with tradition and the village leaders.

The ever-present problem was exhaustion of soil. If the community planted wheat year after year in a field, the nitrogen in the soil was soon depleted and crop failure was certain. Since the supply of manure for fertilizer was limited, the only way for the land to recover its life-giving fertility was for a field to lie fallow for a period of time. In the early Middle Ages a year of fallow was alternated with a year of cropping, so that half the land stood idle in a given year. With time three-year rotations were introduced, especially on more fertile lands. This system permitted a year of wheat or rye to be followed by a year

MILLET: THE GLEANERS *Poor French peasant women search for grains and stalks the harvesters (in the background) have missed. The open-field system seen here could still be found in parts of Europe in 1857, when this picture was painted. Millet is known for his great paintings expressing social themes. (Cliché des Musées Nationaux, Paris)*

of oats or beans, and only then by a year of fallow. Even so, only awareness of the tragic consequences of continuous cropping forced undernourished populations to let a third (or a half) of their land lie constantly idle, especially when the fallow had to be plowed two or three times a year to keep down the weeds.

Traditional rights reinforced the traditional pattern of farming. In addition to rotating the field crops in a uniform way, villages maintained open meadows for hay and natural pasture. These lands were "common" lands, set aside primarily for the draft horses and oxen so necessary in the fields, but open to the cows and pigs of the village community as well. After the harvest, the people of the village also pastured their animals on the wheat or rye stubble. In many places such pasturing followed a brief period, also established by tradition, for the gleaning of grain. Poor women would go through the fields picking up the few single grains that had fallen to the ground in the course of the harvest. The subject of a great nineteenth-century painting, *The Gleaners* by Jean François Millet, this backbreaking work by hardworking but impoverished women meant quite literally the slender margin of survival for some people in the winter months.

In the age of absolutism and nobility, state and landlord continued to levy heavy taxes and high rents as a matter of course. In so doing they stripped the peasants of much of their meager earnings. The level of exploitation varied. Conditions for the rural population were very different in different areas.

Generally speaking, the peasants of eastern Europe were worst off. As we have seen in Chapter 21, they were still serfs, bound to their lords in hereditary service. Though serfdom in eastern Europe in the eighteenth century had much in common with medieval serfdom in central and western Europe, it was, if anything, harsher and more oppressive. In much of eastern Europe there were no real limitations on the amount of forced labor the lord could require, and five or six days of unpaid work per week on the lord's land was not uncommon. Well into the nineteenth century individual Russian serfs and serf families were regularly sold with and without land. Serfdom was often very close to slavery. The only compensating factor in much of eastern Europe was that, as with slavery, differences in well-being among serfs were slight. In Russia, for example, the land available to the serfs for their own crops was divided among them almost equally.

Social conditions were considerably better in western Europe. Peasants were generally free from serfdom. In France and western Germany they owned land and could pass it on to their children. Yet life in the village was unquestionably hard, and poverty was the great reality for most people. For the Beauvais region of France at the beginning of the eighteenth century, it has been carefully estimated that in good years and bad only a tenth of the peasants could live satisfactorily off the fruits of their landholdings. Owning less than half of the land, the peasants had to pay heavy royal taxes, the church's tithe, and dues to the lord, as well as set aside seed for the next season. Left with only half of their crop for their own use, they had to toil and till for others and seek work far afield in a constant scramble for a meager living. And this was in a country where peasants were comparatively well off. The privileges of the ruling elites weighed heavily upon the people of the land.

AGRICULTURAL REVOLUTION

The social conditions of the countryside were well entrenched. The great need was for new farming methods that would enable Europeans to produce more and eat more. The idle fields were the heart of the matter. If peasants could replace the fallow with crops, they could increase the land under cultivation by 50 percent. So remarkable were the possibilities and the results that historians have often spoken of the progressive elimination of the fallow, which occurred slowly throughout Europe from the late seventeenth century onward, as an Agricultural Revolution.

This agricultural revolution, which took longer than historians used to believe, was a great milestone in human development. The famous French scholar Marc Bloch, who gave his life in the resistance to the Nazis in World War Two, summed it up well: "The history of the conquest of the fallow by new crops, a fresh triumph of man over the earth that is just as moving as the great land clearing of the Middle Ages, [is] one of the noblest stories that can be told."[1]

Because grain crops exhaust the soil and make fallowing necessary, the secret to eliminating the fallow lies in alternating grain with certain nitrogen-storing crops. Such crops not only rejuvenate the soil even better than fallowing, but give more produce as well. The most important of these land-reviving crops are peas and beans, root crops such as turnips and potatoes, and clovers and grasses. In the eighteenth century, peas and beans were old standbys; turnips, potatoes, and clover were newcomers to the fields. As time went on, the number of crops that were systematically rotated grew, and farmers developed increasingly sophisticated patterns of rotation to suit different kinds of soils. For example, farmers in French Flanders near Lille in the late eighteenth century used a ten-year rotation, alternating a number of grain, root, and hay crops on a ten-year schedule. Continuous experimentation resulted in more scientific farming.

Improvements in farming had multiple effects. The new crops made ideal feed for animals. Because peasants and larger farmers had more fodder — hay and root crops — for the winter months, they could build up their small herds of cattle and sheep. More animals meant more meat and better diets for the people. More animals also meant more manure for fertilizer, and therefore more grain for bread and porridge. The vicious cycle in which few animals meant inadequate manure, which meant little grain and less fodder, which led to fewer animals, and so on, could be broken. The cycle became positive: more animals meant more manure, which meant more grain and more fodder, which meant more animals.

Technical progress had its price, though. The new rotations were scarcely possible within the traditional framework of open fields and common rights. A farmer who wanted to experiment with new methods would have to control the village's pattern of rotation. To wait for the entire village to

agree might mean waiting forever. The improving, innovating agriculturalist needed to enclose and consolidate his scattered holdings into a compact fenced-in field. In doing so, he would also seek to enclose his share of the natural pasture, the "common." Yet the common rights were precious to many rural people. Thus when the small landholders and the poor could effectively oppose the enclosure of the open fields, they did so. Only powerful social and political pressures could overcome the traditionalism of rural communities.

The old system of unenclosed open fields and the new system of continuous rotation coexisted in Europe for a very long time. In large parts of central Russia, for example, the old system did not disappear until after the Communist Revolution in 1917. It could also be found in much of France and Germany in the early years of the nineteenth century. Indeed, until the end of the eighteenth century the promise of the new system was extensively realized only in the Low Countries — present-day Holland, Belgium, and French Flanders — and in England.

THE LEADERSHIP OF THE LOW COUNTRIES AND ENGLAND

The new methods of the agricultural revolution originated in the Low Countries. The vibrant, dynamic middle-class society of seventeenth-century republican Holland was the most advanced in Europe in many areas of human endeavor. In shipbuilding and navigation, in commerce and banking, in drainage and agriculture, the people of the Low Countries, especially the Dutch, provided models the jealous English and French sought to copy or to cripple.

By the middle of the seventeenth century, intensive farming was well established throughout much of the Low Countries. Enclosed fields, continuous rotation, heavy manuring, and a wide variety of crops: all these innovations were present. Agriculture was highly specialized and commercialized. The same skills that grew turnips produced flax to be spun into linen for clothes and tulip bulbs to lighten the heart with their beauty. The fat cattle of Holland, so beloved by Dutch painters, gave the most milk in Europe. Dutch cheeses were already world-renowned.

The reasons for early Dutch leadership in farming were basically threefold. In the first place, since the end of the Middle Ages the Low Countries had been one of the most densely populated areas in Europe. Thus, in order to feed themselves and provide employment, the Dutch were forced at an early date to seek maximum yields from their land, and to increase it through the steady draining of marshes and swamps. Even so, they had to import wheat from Poland and eastern Germany.

The pressure of population was connected with the second cause, the growth of towns and cities in the Low Countries. Stimulated by commerce and overseas trade, Amsterdam grew from 30,000 to 200,000 in its golden seventeenth century. The growth of urban population provided Dutch peasants with good markets for all they could produce and allowed each region to specialize efficiently in what it did best.

Finally, there was the quality of the people. Oppressed neither by grasping nobles nor warminded monarchs, the Dutch could develop their potential in a free and capitalistic society. The Low Countries became "the Mecca of foreign agricultural experts who came . . . to see Flemish agriculture with their own eyes, to write about it and to propagate its methods in their home lands."[2]

The English were the best students. Indeed, they were such good students that it is often forgotten that they had teachers at all. Drainage and water control was one subject in which they received instruction. Large parts of seventeenth-century Holland had once been sea and sea marsh, and the efforts of centuries had made the Dutch the world's leaders in the skills of drainage. In the first half of the seventeenth century, Dutch experts made a great contribution to draining the extensive marshes, or fens, of wet and rainy England.

The most famous of these Dutch engineers, Cornelius Vermuyden, directed one large drainage project in Yorkshire and another in Cambridgeshire. The project in Yorkshire was supported by Charles I and financed by a group of Dutch capitalists, who were to receive one-third of all land reclaimed in return for their investment. Despite local opposition, Vermuyden drained the land by means of a large canal – his so-called Dutch river – and settlers cultivated the new fields in the Dutch fashion. In the Cambridge fens, Vermuyden and his Dutch workers eventually reclaimed forty thousand acres, which were then farmed intensively in the Dutch manner. Although all these efforts were disrupted in the turbulent 1640s by the English Civil War, Vermuyden and his countrymen largely succeeded. A swampy wilderness was converted into thousands of acres of some of the best land in England. On such new land, where traditions and common rights were not established, farmers introduced new crops and new rotations fairly easily.

Dutch experience was also important to Viscount Charles Townsend (1674–1738), one of the pioneers of English agricultural improvement. This lord from the upper reaches of the English aristocracy learned about turnips and clover while serving as English ambassador to Holland. In the 1710s, he was using these crops in the sandy soil of his large

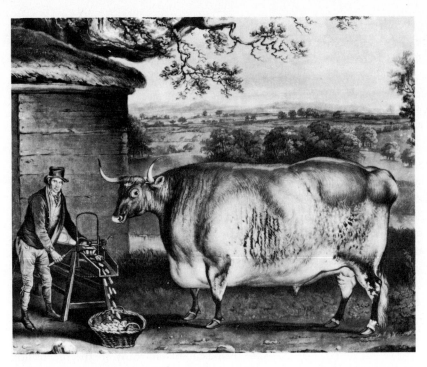

SELECTIVE BREEDING meant bigger livestock and more meat on English tables. This gigantic champion, one of the new improved shorthorn breed, was known as the Newbus Ox. Such great fat beasts were pictured in the press and praised by poets. (Institute of Agricultural History and Museum of English Rural Life, University of Reading)

estates in Norfolk in eastern England, already one of the most innovative agricultural areas in the country. When Lord Charles retired from politics in 1730 and returned to Norfolk, it was said that he spoke of turnips, turnips, and nothing but turnips. This led some wit to nickname his lordship "Turnip" Townsend. But Townsend had the last laugh. Draining extensively, manuring heavily, and sowing crops in regular rotation without fallowing, the farmers who leased Townsend's lands produced larger crops. They and he earned higher incomes. Those who had scoffed reconsidered. By 1740, agricultural improvement in various forms had become something of a craze among the English aristocracy.

Jethro Tull (1674–1741), part crank and part genius, was another important English innovator. A true son of the early Enlightenment, Tull constantly tested accepted ideas about farming in an effort to develop better methods through empirical research. He was especially enthusiastic about horses, in preference to slower-moving oxen. He also advocated sowing seed with drilling equipment, rather than scattering it by hand. Drilling distributed seed evenly and at the proper depth. There were also improvements in livestock, inspired in part by the earlier successes of English country gentlemen in breeding ever-faster horses for the races and fox hunts that were their passions. Selective breeding of ordinary livestock was a marked improvement over the old pattern, which has been graphically described as little more than "the haphazard union of nobody's son with everybody's daughter."

By the mid-eighteenth century, English agriculture was in the process of a radical and desirable transformation. The eventual result was that by 1870 English farmers produced 300 percent more food than they had produced in 1700, although the number of people working the land had increased by only 14 percent. This great surge of agricultural production provided food for England's rapidly growing urban population. It was a tremendous achievement.

THE DEBATE OVER ENCLOSURE

To what extent was technical progress a product of social injustice? There are sharp differences of opinion among historians. The oldest and still widely accepted view is that the powerful ruling class, the English landowning aristocracy, enclosed the open fields and divided up the common pasture in such a way that poor people lost their small landholdings and were pushed off the land. The large landowners controlled Parliament, which made the laws. They had Parliament pass hundreds of "enclosure acts," each of which authorized the fencing of open fields in a given district and abolished common rights there. Small farmers who had little land and cottagers who had only common rights could no longer make a living. They lost position and security and had to work for a large landowner for wages or else move to town in search of work. This view, popularized by Karl Marx in

the nineteenth century, has remained dear to many historians to this day.

There is some validity to this idea, but more recent studies have shown that the harmful consequences of enclosure in the eighteenth century have often been exaggerated. In the first place, as much as half of English farmland was already enclosed by 1750. A great wave of enclosure of English open fields into sheep pastures had already occurred in the sixteenth and early seventeenth centuries, in order to produce wool for the thriving textile industry. In the later seventeenth and early eighteenth centuries, many open fields were enclosed fairly harmoniously by mutual agreement among all classes of landowners in English villages. Thus, parliamentary enclosure, the great bulk of which occurred after 1760 and particularly during the Napoleonic wars early in the nineteenth century, only completed a process that was in full swing. Nor did an army of landless farm laborers appear only in the last years of the eighteenth century. Much earlier, and certainly by 1700, there were perhaps two landless agricultural workers in England for every self-sufficient farmer. In 1830, after the enclosures were complete, the proportion of landless laborers on the land was not much greater.

Indeed, by 1700 a highly distinctive pattern of landownership existed in England. At one extreme were a few large landowners, at the other a large mass of laborers who held little land and worked for wages. In between stood two other groups: small self-sufficient farmers who owned their own land, and substantial tenant farmers who rented land from the big landowners and hired wage laborers. Yet the small independent English farmers were already declining in number by 1700, and they continued to do so in the eighteenth century.

They could not compete with the profit-minded, market-oriented tenant farmers.

The tenant farmers, many of whom had formerly been independent owners, were the key to mastering the new methods of farming. Well financed by the large landowners, the tenant farmers fenced fields, built drains, and improved the soil with fertilizers. Such improvements actually increased employment opportunities for wage workers in the countryside. So did new methods of farming, for land was farmed more intensively without the fallow, and new crops like turnips required more care and effort. Thus, enclosure did not force people off the land by eliminating jobs. By the early nineteenth century, rural poverty was often greatest in those areas of England where the new farming techniques had not been adopted.

THE BEGINNING OF THE POPULATION EXPLOSION

There was another factor that affected the existing order of life and forced economic changes in the eighteenth century. This was the remarkable growth of European population, the beginning of the "population explosion." This population explosion continued in Europe until the twentieth century, by which time it was affecting non-Western areas of the globe. What caused the growth of population, and what did the challenge of more mouths to feed and more hands to employ do to the European economy?

LIMITATIONS ON POPULATION GROWTH

Many commonly held ideas about population in the past are wrong. One such mistaken idea

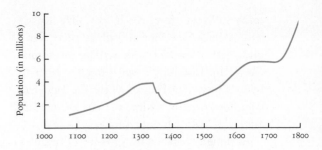

FIGURE 23.1 THE GROWTH OF POPULATION IN ENGLAND 1000–1800. *England is a good example of both the uneven increase of European population before 1700 and the third great surge of growth, which began in the eighteenth century. (Source: E. A. Wrigley,* Population and History, *McGraw-Hill, New York, 1969)*

is that people always married young and had large families. A related error is the belief that past societies were so ignorant that they could do nothing to control their numbers and that population was always growing too fast. On the contrary, until 1700 the total population of Europe grew slowly much of the time, and by no means constantly (see Figure 23.1). There were very few occurrences of the frightening increases so common in many poor countries today.

In seventeenth-century Europe, births and deaths, fertility and mortality, were in a crude but effective balance. The birthrate – annual births as a proportion of the population – was fairly high, but far lower than it would have been if all women between ages fifteen and forty-five had been having as many children as biologically possible. The death rate in normal years was also high, though somewhat lower than the birthrate. As a result, the population grew modestly in normal years at a rate of perhaps .5 to 1 percent, or enough to double the population in 70 to 140 years. This is, of course, a generalization encompassing many different patterns. In areas like Russia and colonial New England, where there was a great deal of frontier to be settled, the annual rate of increase might well exceed 1 percent. In a country like France, where the land had long been densely settled, the rate of increase might be less than .5 percent.

Although population growth of even 1 percent per year is fairly modest by the standards of many African and Latin American countries today – some of which are growing at about 3 percent annually – it will produce a very large increase over a long period. An annual increase of even 1 percent will result in sixteen times as many people in three hundred years. Such gigantic increases simply did not occur in agrarian Europe before the eighteenth century. In certain abnormal years and tragic periods, many more people died than were born. Total population fell sharply, even catastrophically. A number of years of modest growth would then be necessary to make up for those who had died in such an abnormal year. Such savage increases in deaths helped check total numbers and kept the population from growing rapidly for long periods.

The grim reapers of demographic crisis were famine, epidemic disease, and war. Famine, the inevitable result of poor farming methods and periodic crop failures, was particularly murderous because it was accompanied by disease. With a brutal one-two punch, famine stunned and weakened a population and disease finished it off. Disease could also ravage independently, even in years of adequate harvests. Bubonic plague returned again and again to Europe for more than three hundred years after the ravages of the Black Death in the fourteenth century. Not until the late 1500s did most countries have as many people as in the early 1300s. Epidemics of dysentery and smallpox also operated independently of famine.

War was another scourge. The indirect effects were more harmful than the organized killing. War spread disease. Soldiers and camp followers passed venereal disease through the countryside to scar and kill. Armies requisitioned scarce food supplies for their own use and disrupted the agricultural cycle. The Thirty Years' War (pages 689–695) witnessed all possible combinations of distress. In the German states, the number of inhabitants declined by more than *two-thirds* in some large areas and by at least one-third almost everywhere. The Thirty Years' War reduced total German population by no less than 40 percent. But numbers inadequately convey the dimensions of such human tragedy. One needs the vision of the artist. The great sixteenth-century artist, Albrecht Dürer, captured the horror of demographic crisis in his chilling woodcut *The Four Horsemen of the Apocalypse*. Death, accompanied by his trusty companions War, Famine, and Disease, takes his merciless ride of destruction. The narrow victory of life over death that prevails in normal times is being undone.

THE NEW PATTERN OF THE EIGHTEENTH CENTURY

In the eighteenth century, the population of Europe began to grow markedly. This increase in numbers occurred in all areas of Europe – western and eastern, northern and southern, dynamic and stagnant. Growth was especially dramatic after about 1750, as Figure 23.2 shows.

Although it is certain that Europe's population grew greatly, it is less clear why. Recent painstaking and innovative research in population history has shown that, because population grew everywhere, it is best to look for general factors and not those limited to individual countries or areas. What, then, caused fewer people to die or, possibly, more babies to be born? In some kinds of families women may have had more babies than before. Yet the basic cause was a decline in mortality – fewer deaths.

The bubonic plague mysteriously disappeared. Following the Black Death in the fourteenth century, plagues remained a part of the European experience, striking again and again with savage force, particularly in towns. As a German writer of the early sixteenth century noted, "It is remarkable and astonishing that the plague should never wholly cease, but it should appear every year here and there, making its way from one place to another. Having subsided at one time, it returns within a few years by a circuitous route."[3]

As late as 1720, a ship from Syria and the Levant, where plague was ever-present, brought the monstrous disease to Marseilles. In a few weeks, forty thousand of the city's ninety thousand inhabitants died. The epidemic swept southern France, killing a third, a half, even three-fourths of those in the larger towns. Once again an awful fear swept across Europe. But the epidemic passed, and that was the last time plague fell upon western and central Europe. The final disappearance of plague was due in part to stricter measures of quarantine in Mediterranean ports and along the Austrian border with Turkey. Human carriers of plague were carefully isolated. Chance and plain good luck were more important, however.

It is now understood that bubonic plague is, above all, a disease of rats. The epidemic spreads among humans only after they are bitten by fleas that have fed on diseased rats. More precisely, it is the black rat that spreads major epidemics, for the black rat's flea is the principal carrier of the plague bacillus. After 1600, for reasons unknown, a new rat of Asiatic origin – the brown, or wander, rat –

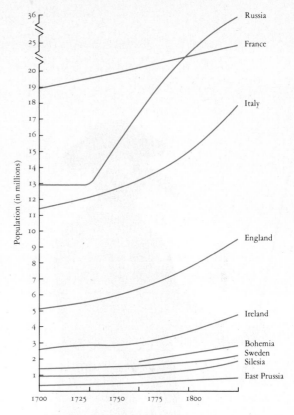

FIGURE 23.2   THE INCREASE OF POPULATION IN EUROPE IN THE EIGHTEENTH CENTURY   The number of people grew substantially all across Europe. France's large population continued to support French political and intellectual leadership, but Russia emerged as Europe's most populous state.

began to drive out and eventually eliminate its black competitor. In the words of a noted authority, "This revolution in the animal kingdom must have gone far to break the lethal link between rat and man."[4] Although the brown rat also contracts the plague, another kind of flea is its main parasite. That flea carries the plague poorly and, for good measure, has little taste for human blood.

DOCTOR IN PROTECTIVE CLOTHING Most doctors believed, incorrectly, that poisonous smells carried the plague. This doctor has placed strong-smelling salts in his "beak" to protect himself against deadly plague vapors. (Germanisches Nationalmuseum, Nuremberg)

Advances in medical knowledge did not contribute much to reducing the death rate in the eighteenth century. The most important advance in preventive medicine in this period was inoculation against smallpox. Yet this great improvement was long confined mainly to England and probably did little to reduce deaths throughout Europe until the later part of the century. Improvements in the water supply and sewerage promoted somewhat better public health and helped reduce such diseases as typhoid and typhus in some urban areas of western Europe. Yet those early public-health measures had only limited general significance. In fact, changes in the rat population helped millions of human beings in their struggle against untimely death much more than did doctors and medical science in the eighteenth century.

Human beings were more successful in their efforts to safeguard the supply of food and protect against famine. The eighteenth century was a time of considerable canal and road building in western Europe. These advances in transportation, which were among the more positive aspects of enlightened absolutism, lessened the impact of local crop failure and famine. Emergency supplies could be brought in. The age-old spectacle of localized starvation became less frequent. Wars became more gentlemanly and less destructive than in the seventeenth century and spread fewer epidemics. New foods, particularly the potato, were introduced. Potatoes served as an important alternative source of vitamins A and C for the poor, especially when the grain crops were skimpy or failed. In short, population grew in the eighteenth century primarily because years of abnormal death rates were less catastrophic. Famines, epidemics, and wars continued to occur, but their severity moderated.

The growth of population in the eighteenth century cannot be interpreted as a sign of human progress. Plague faded from memory, transport improved, people learned to eat potatoes; yet for the common people life was still a great struggle. Indeed, for many it was more of a struggle than ever, for in many areas increasing numbers led to overpopulation. A serious imbalance between the number of people and the economic opportunities available to them developed. There was only so much land available, and tradition slowed the adoption of better farming methods. Therefore, agriculture could not provide enough work for the rapidly growing labor force. Everyone might work steadily during planting and harvesting, when many hands were needed, but at other times rural people were often unemployed or underemployed.

Growing numbers increased the challenge of poverty, especially the severe poverty of the rural poor. People in the countryside had to look for new ways to make a living. Even if work outside of farming paid poorly, small wages were better than none. Thus, in the eighteenth century growing numbers of people and acute poverty were even more influential than new farming methods as forces for profound changes in agrarian Europe.

THE GROWTH OF COTTAGE INDUSTRY

The growth of population contributed to the development of industry in rural areas. The poor in the countryside were eager to supplement their earnings from agriculture with other types of work, and capitalists from the city were eager to employ them, often at lower wages than urban workers commanded.

Manufacturing with hand tools in peasant cottages grew markedly in the eighteenth century. Rural industry became a crucial feature of the European economy.

To be sure, peasant communities had always made some clothing, processed some food, and constructed some housing for their own use. But in the High Middle Ages peasants did not produce manufactured goods on a large scale for sale in a market; they were not handicraft workers as well as farmers and field laborers. Industry in the Middle Ages was dominated and organized by urban craft guilds and urban merchants, who jealously regulated handicraft production and sought to maintain it as an urban monopoly. By the eighteenth century, however, the pressures of rural poverty and the need for employment in the countryside had proved too great, and a new system was expanding lustily. The new system had many names. Sometimes referred to as cottage industry or domestic industry, it has often been called "the putting-out system."

THE PUTTING-OUT SYSTEM

The two main participants in the putting-out system were the merchant-capitalist and the rural worker. The merchant lent or put out raw materials — raw wool, for example — to several cottage workers. Those workers processed the raw material in their own homes, spinning and weaving the wool into cloth in this case, and returned the cloth to the merchant. The merchant paid the outworkers for their work by the piece and proceeded to sell the finished product. There were endless variations on this basic relationship. Sometimes rural workers would buy their own materials and work as independent producers before they sold to the merchant. The relative im-

RURAL INDUSTRY IN ACTION *This French engraving suggests just how many things could be made
in the countryside with simple hand tools. These men
are making inexpensive but long-lasting wooden shoes,
which were widely worn by the poor. (Photo: Caroline
Buckler)*

portance of earnings from the land and from
industry varied greatly for handicraft workers.
In all cases, however, the putting-out system
was a kind of capitalism. Merchants needed
large amounts of capital, which they held in
the form of goods being worked up and sold
in distant markets. They sought to make
profits and increase their capital in their businesses.

The putting-out system was not perfect,
but it had definite advantages. It increased
employment in the countryside and provided
the poor with additional income. Since pro-

duction in the countryside was unregulated,
workers and merchants could change procedures and experiment as they saw fit. Because
they did not need to meet rigid guild standards, which maintained quality but discouraged the development of new methods,
cottage industry became capable of producing
many kinds of goods. Textiles, all manner of
knives, forks, and housewares, buttons and
gloves, clocks and musical instruments could
be produced quite satisfactorily in the countryside. Luxury goods for the rich, such as
exquisite tapestries and fine porcelain, de-

WOMEN WORKING   This mother and her daughters may well be knitting, lace-making, and spinning for some merchant capitalist. The close ties between cottage industry and agriculture are well illustrated in this summer scene. (Photo: Caroline Buckler)

manded special training, close supervision, and centralized workshops. Yet such goods were as exceptional as those who used them. The skills of rural industry were sufficient for everyday articles.

Rural manufacturing did not spread across Europe at an even rate. It appeared first in England and developed most successfully there, particularly for the spinning and weaving of woolen cloth. By 1500, half of England's textiles were being produced in the countryside. By 1700, English industry was generally more rural than urban and heavily reliant on the putting-out system. Continental countries developed rural industry more slowly.

In France at the time of Louis XIV, Colbert had revived the urban guilds and used them as a means to control the cities and collect taxes (page 725). But the pressure of rural poverty proved too great. In 1762 the special privileges of urban manufacturing were abolished in France, and the already-developing rural industries were given free rein from then on. The royal government in France had come to believe that the best way to help the poor

THE WOOLEN INDUSTRY *Many steps went into the production of woolen cloth. This illustration suggests schematically how cottage workers combed out the fleece of the sheep and made raw wool ready for spinning.*

peasants was to encourage the growth of cottage manufacturing. Thus in France, as in Germany and other areas, the later part of the eighteenth century witnessed a remarkable expansion of rural industry in certain densely populated regions. The pattern established in England was spreading to the Continent.

THE TEXTILE INDUSTRY

Throughout most of history, until at least the nineteenth century, the industry that has always employed the most people has been textiles. The making of linen, woolen, and eventually cotton cloth was the typical activity of cottage workers engaged in the putting-out system. A look inside the cottage of the English rural textile worker illustrates a way of life as well as an economic system.

The rural worker lived in a small cottage, with tiny windows and little space. Indeed, the worker's cottage was often a single room that served as workshop, kitchen, and bedroom. There were only a few pieces of furni-

ture, of which the weaver's loom was by far the largest and most important. That loom had changed somewhat in the early eighteenth century, when John Kay's invention of the flying shuttle enabled the weaver to throw the shuttle back and forth between the threads with one hand. Aside from that improvement, however, the loom was as it had been for much of history. In the cottage there were also spinning wheels, tubs for dyeing cloth and washing raw wool, and carding pieces to comb and prepare the raw material.

These different pieces of equipment were necessary because cottage industry was first and foremost a family enterprise. All the members of the family helped in the work, so that "every person from seven to eighty (who retained their sight and who could move their hands) could earn their bread," as one eighteenth-century English observer put it.[5] While the women and children prepared the raw material and spun the thread, the man of the house wove the cloth. There was work for everyone, even the youngest. After the dirt was beaten out of the raw cotton, it had to be thoroughly cleaned with strong soap in a tub, where tiny feet took the place of the agitator in a washing machine. George Crompton, the son of Samuel Crompton, who in 1784 invented the mule for cotton spinning, recalled that "soon after I was able to walk I was employed in the cotton manufacture. . . . My mother tucked up my petticoats about my waist, and put me into the tub to tread upon the cotton at the bottom."[6] Slightly older children and aged relatives carded and combed the cotton or wool, so the woman and the older daughter she had taught could spin it into thread. Each member had a task. The very young and very old worked in the family unit as a matter of course.

There was always a serious imbalance in this family enterprise: the work of four or five spinners was needed to keep one weaver steadily employed. Therefore, the wife and the husband had constantly to try to find more thread and more spinners. Widows and unmarried women – those "spinsters" who spun for their living – were recruited by the wife. Or perhaps the weaver's son went off on horseback to seek thread. The need for more thread might even lead the weaver and his wife to become small capitalist employers. At the end of the week, when they received the raw wool or cotton from the merchant-manufacturer, they would put out some of this raw material to other cottages. The following week they would return to pick up the thread and pay for the spinning – spinning that would help keep the weaver busy for a week until the merchant came for the finished cloth.

Relations between workers and employers were not always harmonious. In fact, there was continuous conflict. An English popular song written about 1700, called "The Cloth-ier's Delight, or the Rich Men's Joy and The Poor Men's Sorrow," has the merchant boasting of his countless tricks used to "beat down wages":

We heapeth up riches and treasure great store
Which we get by griping and grinding the poor.
*   And this is a way for to fill up our purse*
*   Although we do get it with many a curse.*[7]

There were constant disputes over weights of materials and the quality of the cloth. Merchants accused workers of stealing raw materials, and weavers complained that merchants delivered underweight bales. Both were right; each tried to cheat the other, even if only in self-defense.

There was another problem, at least from the merchant-capitalist's point of view. Rural labor was cheap, scattered, and poorly organized. For these reasons it was hard to control. Cottage workers tended to work in spurts. After they got paid on Saturday afternoon, the men in particular tended to drink and carouse for two or three days. Indeed, Monday was called "holy Monday" because inactivity was so religiously observed. By the end of the week the weaver was probably working feverishly to make his quota. But if he did not succeed, there was little the merchant could do. When times were good and the merchant could easily sell everything produced, the weaver and his family did fairly well and were particularly inclined to loaf, to the dismay of the capitalist. Thus, in spite of its virtues, the putting-out system in the textile industry had definite shortcomings. There was an imbalance between spinning and weaving. Labor relations were often poor, and the merchant was unable to control the quality of the cloth or the schedule of the workers. The merchant-capitalist's search for new methods of production became intense.

BUILDING THE ATLANTIC ECONOMY

In addition to agricultural improvement, population pressure, and expanding cottage industry, the expansion of Europe in the eighteenth century was characterized by the growth of world trade. Spain and Portugal revitalized their empires and began drawing more wealth from renewed development. Yet, once again, the countries of northwestern Europe – the Netherlands, France, and above all Great Britain – benefited most. Great Britain (formed in 1707 by the union of England and Scotland in a single kingdom), became the leading maritime power. In the eighteenth century, British ships and merchants succeeded in dominating long-distance trade, particularly the fast-growing intercontinental trade across the Atlantic Ocean. The British played the critical role in building a fairly unified Atlantic economy, which offered remarkable opportunities for them and their colonists.

MERCANTILISM AND COLONIAL WARS

Britain's commercial leadership in the eighteenth century had its origins in the mercantilism of the seventeenth century (page 725). European mercantilism was a system of economic regulations aimed at increasing the power of the state. As practiced by a leading advocate like Colbert under Louis XIV, mercantilism aimed particularly at creating a favorable balance of foreign trade in order to increase a country's stock of gold. A country's gold holdings served as an all-important treasure chest, to be opened periodically to pay for war in a violent age.

Early English mercantilists shared these views. As Thomas Mun, a leading merchant and early mercantilist, wrote in *England's Treasure by Foreign Trade* (1630, published 1664): "The ordinary means therefore to increase our wealth and treasure is by foreign trade wherein we must observe this rule; to sell more to strangers yearly than we consume of theirs in value." What distinguished English mercantilism was the unusual idea that governmental economic regulations could and should serve the private interests of individuals and groups as well as the public needs of the state. As Josiah Child, a very wealthy brewer and director of the East India Company, put it, in the ideal economy "Profit and Power ought jointly to be considered."[8]

In France and other continental countries, by contrast, seventeenth-century mercantilists generally put the needs of the state far above those of businessmen and workers. And they seldom saw a possible harmony of public and private interests for a common good.

The result of the English desire to increase both its military power and private wealth was the mercantile system of the Navigation Acts. Oliver Cromwell established the first of these laws in 1651, and the restored monarchy of Charles II extended them further in 1660 and 1663; the Navigation Acts of the seventeenth century were not seriously modified until 1786. The acts required that most goods imported from Europe into England and Scotland be carried on British-owned ships with British crews, or on ships of the country producing the article. Moreover, these laws gave British merchants and shipowners a virtual monopoly on trade with the colonies. The colonists were required to ship their products – sugar, tobacco, and cotton – on British ships, and to buy almost all of their European goods from the mother country. It was believed that these economic regulations would provide British merchants and workers with profits and employment, and colonial

THE PORT OF DIEPPE IN 1754 *This painting by Joseph Vernet (1714–1789) was one of fourteen in a famous series of port scenes commissioned by Louis XV. Vernet's work admirably captures the spirit and excitement of French maritime expansion. (Louvre/ Giraudon)*

plantation owners and farmers with a guaranteed market for their products. And the state would develop a shipping industry with a large number of tough, experienced deepwater seamen, who could be drafted when necessary into the Royal Navy to protect the island nation.

The Navigation Acts were a form of economic warfare. Their initial target was the Dutch, who were far ahead of the English in shipping and foreign trade in the mid-seventeenth century. The Navigation Acts, in conjunction with three Anglo-Dutch wars between 1652 and 1674, did seriously damage Dutch shipping and commerce. The thriving Dutch colony of New Amsterdam was seized

in 1664 and rechristened New York. By the later seventeenth century, when the Dutch and the English became allies to stop the expansion of France's Louis XIV, the Netherlands was falling behind England in shipping, trade, and colonies.

As the Netherlands followed Spain into relative decline, France emerged as a far more serious rival. Rich in natural resources and endowed with a population three or four times that of England, France too was intent upon building a powerful fleet and a worldwide system of rigidly monopolized colonial trade. And France, aware that Great Britain coveted large parts of Spain's American empire, was determined to revitalize its Spanish ally. Thus, from 1701 to 1763, Britain and France were locked in a series of wars to decide, in part, which nation would become the leading maritime power and claim a lion's share of the profits of Europe's overseas expansion (see Map 23.1).

The first round was the War of the Spanish Succession (page 730), which started when Louis XIV declared his willingness to accept the Spanish crown willed to his grandson. Besides upsetting the continental balance of power, a union of France and Spain threatened to destroy the British colonies in North America. The thin ribbon of British settlements along the Atlantic seaboard from Massachusetts to the Carolinas would be surrounded by a great arc of Franco-Spanish power stretching south and west from French Canada to Florida and the Gulf of Mexico (see Map 23.1). Defeated by a great coalition of states after twelve years of fighting, Louis XIV was forced in the Peace of Utrecht (1713) to cede Newfoundland and Nova Scotia to Britain. Spain was compelled to give Britain control of the lucrative West African slave trade – the so-called *asiento* – and to let Britain send one ship of merchandise into the Spanish colonies annually, through Porto Bello on the Isthmus of Panama.

France was still a mighty competitor. The War of the Austrian Succession (1740-1748), which started when Frederick the Great of Prussia seized Silesia from Austria's Maria Theresa, became a world war, including Anglo-French conflicts in India and North America. Indeed, it was the seizure of French territory in Canada by New England colonists that forced France to sue for peace in 1748, and to accept gladly a return to the territorial situation existing in North America at the beginning of the war. France's Bourbon ally, Spain, defended itself surprisingly well and Spain's empire remained intact.

MAP 23.1 THE ECONOMY OF THE ATLANTIC BASIN IN 1701 *The growth of trade encouraged both economic development and military conflict in the Atlantic Basin.*

This inclusive stand-off helped set the stage for the Seven Years' War (1756-1763). In central Europe, Austria's Maria Theresa sought to win back Silesia and crush Prussia, thereby re-establishing the Habsburgs' traditional leadership in German affairs. She almost succeeded, skillfully winning France – the Habsburgs' long-standing enemy – and Russia to her cause. Yet the Prussian state survived, saved by its army and the sudden decision of the newly crowned Peter III of Russia to withdraw from the war in 1762.

Outside of Europe, the Seven Years' War was the decisive round in the Franco-British competition for colonial empire. Led by William Pitt (1708-1788), whose grandfather had made a fortune as a trader in India, the British concentrated on using superior sea power to destroy the French fleet and choke off French commerce around the world. Capturing Quebec in 1759 and winning a great naval victory at Quiberon Bay, the British also strangled France's valuable sugar trade with its Caribbean islands and smashed French forts in India. After Spain entered the war on France's side in 1761, the surging British temporarily occupied Havana in Cuba, and Manila in the Philippines. With the Treaty of Paris (1763), France lost all its possessions on the mainland of North America. French Canada as well as French territory east of the Mississippi River passed to Britain, and France ceded Louisiana to Spain as compensation for Spain's loss of Florida to Britain. France also gave up most of its holdings in India, opening the way to British dominance on the subcontinent. By 1763, British naval power, built in large part upon the rapid growth of the British shipping

Great Britain
France
Portugal
Spain

HUDSON'S BAY

LOUISIANA

MEXICO

NEW FRANCE
QUEBEC

Mississippi

Ohio

NEWFOUNDLAND
(To Gr. Br., 1713)

GREAT BRITAIN

ACADIA
(NOVA SCOTIA)
(To Gr. Br., 1713)

Furs

NETH.

FLORIDA

Tobacco

Colonial products

Manufactured goods

FRANCE

Silver

AUSTRIA

CUBA

Sugar

PORTUGAL   SPAIN

JAMAICA
(ENGLAND, 1670)

SANTO DOMINGO
(FRANCE, 1697)

Porto Bello

Asiento
(Spain; to Gr. Br.,
1713)

CANARY IS.
(SPAIN)

LESSER
ANTILLES
(English and
French since
about 1630)

A T L A N T I C   O C E A N

NEW GRANADA

Sugar

GUIANA

(DUTCH)

(FRENCH)

A F R I C A

PERU

CAPE VERDE IS.
(PORT.)

European forts and trading stations

BRAZIL

Slaves

ANGOLA

industry after the passage of the Navigation Acts, had triumphed decisively. Britain had realized its goal of monopolizing a vast trading and colonial empire for its exclusive benefit.

LAND AND WEALTH IN
NORTH AMERICA

Of all Britain's colonies, those on the North American mainland proved most valuable in the long run. The settlements along the Atlantic coast provided an important outlet for surplus population, so that migration abroad limited poverty in England, Scotland, and northern Ireland. The settlers also benefited. In the mainland colonies, they had privileged access to virtually free and unlimited land. The availability of farms was a precious asset in preindustrial Europe, where agriculture was the main source of income and prestige.

The possibility of having one's own farm was particularly attractive to ordinary men and women from the British Isles. Land in England was already highly concentrated in the hands of the nobility and gentry in 1700, and became more so with agricultural improvement in the eighteenth century. White settlers who came to the colonies as free men and women, or as indentured servants pledged to work seven years for their passage, or as prisoners and convicts, could obtain their own farms on easy terms as soon as they had their personal freedom. Many poor white farmers also came to the mainland from the British West Indies, crowded out of those islands by the growth of big sugar plantations using black slave labor. To be sure, life in the mainland colonies was hard and rough, especially on the frontier. Yet the settlers succeeded in paying little or no rent to grasping landlords, and taxes were very low. Unlike the great majority of European peasants, who had

to accept high rents and taxes as part of the order of things, American farmers could keep most of what they managed to produce.

The availability of land made labor expensive in the colonies. This basic fact, rather than any repressive aspects of the Navigation Acts, limited the growth of industry in the colonies. As the Governor of New York put it in 1767:

The price of labor is so great in this part of the world that it will always prove the greatest obstacle to any manufacturers attempting to set up here, and the genius of the people in a country where everyone can have land to work upon leads them so naturally into agriculture that it prevails over every other occupation.[9]

The advantage for colonists was in farming, and farm they did.

Cheap land and scarce labor were also critical factors in the growth of slavery in the southern colonies. By 1700 British indentured servants were carefully avoiding the Virginia lowlands, where black slavery was spreading, and by 1730 the large plantations there had gone over completely to black slaves. Slave labor permitted an astonishing tenfold increase in tobacco production between 1700 and 1774, and created a wealthy aristocratic planter class in Maryland and Virginia.

In the course of the eighteenth century, the farmers of New England and, particularly, the middle colonies of Pennsylvania and New Jersey began to produce more food than they needed. They exported ever more food stuffs, primarily to the West Indies. There the owners of the sugar plantations came to depend on the mainland colonies for grain and dried fish to feed their slaves. The plantation owners, whether they grew tobacco in Virginia and Maryland or sugar in the West Indies, had the exclusive privilege of supplying the British Isles with their products. Eng-

COLONIAL COMPETITION AND WAR, 1651–1763

1651–1663	British Navigation Acts create the mercantile system, which is not seriously modified until 1786
1652–1674	Three Anglo-Dutch wars damage Dutch shipping and commerce
1664	New Amsterdam is seized and renamed New York
1701–1714	War of the Spanish Succession
1713	Peace of Utrecht: Britain wins parts of Canada from France and control of the west African slave trade from Spain
1740–1748	War of the Austrian Succession, resulting in no change in territorial holdings in North America
1756–1763	Seven Years' War (known in North America as the French and Indian War), a decisive victory for Britain
1763	Treaty of Paris: Britain receives all French territory on the North American mainland and achieves dominance in India

lishmen could not buy cheaper sugar from Brazil, nor were they allowed to grow tobacco in the home islands. Thus the colonists too had their place in the protective mercantile system of the Navigation Acts. The American shipping industry grew rapidly in the eighteenth century, for example, because colonial shippers enjoyed the same advantages as their fellow British citizens in the mother country.

The abundance of almost free land resulted in a rapid increase in the colonial population in the eighteenth century. In a mere three-quarters of a century after 1700, the white population of the mainland colonies multiplied a staggering ten times as immigrants arrived and colonial couples raised large families. In 1774, 2.2 million whites and 330,000 blacks inhabited what would soon become the independent United States.

Rapid population growth did not reduce the settlers to poverty. On the contrary, agricultural development resulted in fairly high standards of living for mainland colonists, in eighteenth-century terms. There was also an unusual degree of economic equality, by the standards of Europe. Few people were extremely rich and few were extremely poor. Most remarkable of all, on the eve of the American Revolution, the *average* white man or woman in the mainland British colonies probably had the highest income and standard of living in the world. It has been estimated that between 1715 and 1775 the real income of the average American was increasing about 1 percent per year per person, almost two-thirds as fast as it increased with massive industrialization between 1840 and 1959. When one considers that between 1775 and 1840 Americans experienced no improvement in their standard of living, it is clear just how

BUILDING THE ATLANTIC ECONOMY

TOBACCO was a key commodity in the Atlantic trade. This engraving from 1775 shows a merchant and his slaves preparing a cargo for sail. (The British Museum)

much the colonists benefited from hard work and the mercantile system created by the Navigation Acts.[10]

THE GROWTH OF FOREIGN TRADE

England also profited greatly from the mercantile system. Above all, the rapidly growing and increasingly wealthy agricultural populations of the mainland colonies provided an expanding market for English manufactured goods. This situation was extremely fortunate, for England in the eighteenth century was gradually losing, or only slowly expanding, its sales to many of its traditional European markets. However, rising demand for manufactured goods from North America, as well as from the West Indies, Africa, and Latin America, allowed English cottage industry to continue to grow and diversify. Merchant-capitalists and manufacturers found

new and exciting opportunities for profit and wealth.

Since the late Middle Ages, England had relied very heavily on the sale of woolen cloth in foreign markets. Indeed, as late as 1700 woolen cloth was the only important manufactured good exported from England, and fully 90 percent of it was sold to Europeans. In the course of the eighteenth century, the states of continental Europe were trying to develop their own cottage textile industries in an effort to deal with rural poverty and overpopulation. Like England earlier, these states adopted protectionist, mercantilist policies. They tried by means of tariffs and other measures to exclude competing goods from abroad, whether English woolens or the cheap but beautiful cotton calicos the English East India Company brought from India and sold in Europe.

France had already closed its markets to the

English in the seventeenth century. In the eighteenth century, German states purchased much less woolen cloth from England and encouraged cottage production of coarse, cheap linens, which became a feared competitor in all of central and southern Europe. By 1773, England was selling only about two-thirds as much woolen cloth to northern and western Europe as it had in 1700. The decline of sales to the Continent meant that the English economy badly needed new markets and new products in order to develop and prosper.

Protected colonial markets came to the rescue. More than offsetting stagnating trade with Europe, they provided a great stimulus for many branches of English manufacturing. The markets of the Atlantic economy led the way, as may be seen in Figure 23.3. English exports of manufactured goods to continental Europe increased very modestly, from roughly £2.9 million in 1700 to only £3.3 million in 1773. Meanwhile, sales of manufactured products to the Atlantic economy – primarily the mainland colonies of North America and the West Indian sugar islands, with an important assist from West Africa and Latin America – soared from £500,000 to £3.9 million. Sales to other "colonies" – Ireland and India – also rose substantially in the eighteenth century.

English exports became much more balanced and diversified. To America and Africa went large quantities of metal items – axes to frontiersmen, firearms, chains for slaveowners. There were also clocks and coaches, buttons and saddles, china and furniture, musical instruments and scientific equipment, and a host of other things. By 1750, half the nails made in England were going to the colonies. Foreign trade became the bread-and-butter of some industries.

Thus, the mercantile system formed in the seventeenth century to attack the Dutch and

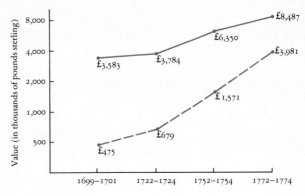

Note: Data exclude English re-exports.

FIGURE 23.3 EXPORTS OF ENGLISH MANU-FACTURED GOODS 1700–1774 *While trade with Europe stagnated after 1700, English exports to Africa and the Americas boomed and greatly stimulated English economic development. (Source: R. Davis, "English Foreign Trade, 1700–1774," Economic History Review, 2d series, 15 (1962); 302–303)*

win power and profit for England continued to shape trade in the eighteenth century. The English concentrated in their hands much of the demand for manufactured goods from the growing Atlantic economy. The pressure of demand from three continents upon the cottage industry of one medium-sized country heightened the efforts of English merchant-capitalists to find new and improved ways to produce more goods. By the 1770s, England stood on the threshold of radical industrial change, as we shall see in Chapter 27.

REVIVAL IN COLONIAL LATIN AMERICA

When the last Spanish Habsburg, the feeble-minded Charles II, died in 1700 (page 730), Spain was "little less cadaverous than its defunct master."[11] Its vast empire lay before

Europe awaiting dismemberment. Yet, in one of those striking reversals with which history is replete, Spain revived. The empire held together and even prospered, while a European-oriented landowning aristocracy enhanced its position in colonial society.

Spain recovered in part because of better leadership. Louis XIV's grandson, who took the throne as Philip V (1700–1746), brought new men and fresh ideas with him from France, and rallied the Spanish people to his Bourbon dynasty in the long War of the Spanish Succession. When peace was restored, a series of reforming ministers reasserted royal authority, overhauling state finances and strengthening defense. To protect the colonies, they restored Spain's navy to a respectable third place in Europe behind Great Britain and France. Philip's ministers also promoted the economy with vigorous measures that included a gradual relaxation of the state monopoly on colonial trade. The able Charles III (1759–1788), a truly enlightened monarch, further extended economic and administrative reform.

Revitalization in Madrid had positive results in the colonies. The colonies succeeded in defending themselves from numerous British attacks and even increased in size. Spain received Louisiana from France in 1763, and missionaries and ranchers extended Spanish influence all the way to northern California.

Political success was matched by economic improvement. After declining markedly in the seventeenth century, silver mining recovered in Mexico and Peru. Output quadrupled between 1700 and 1800, when Spanish America accounted for half of world silver production. Ever a risky long shot at sudden riches, silver mining encouraged a gambler's attitude toward wealth and work. The big profits of the lucky usually went into land. Silver min-

ing also encouraged food production for large mining camps and gave the creoles – people of Spanish blood born in the Americas – the means to purchase more and more European luxuries and manufactured goods. A class of wealthy merchants arose to handle this flourishing trade, which often relied on smuggled goods from Great Britain. As in British North America, industry remained weak, although workshops employing forced Indian labor made Mexican and Peruvian wool into coarse fabrics for the Latin American masses. Spain's colonies were an important part of the Atlantic economy.

Economic development strengthened the creole elite, which came to rival the top government officials dispatched from Spain. As in most preindustrial societies, land was the main source of wealth. In contrast to British America but like Spain and eastern Europe, creole estate owners controlled much of the land. Small independent farmers were rare.

The Spanish crown had given large holdings to the conquering pioneers and their followers, and beginning in the late sixteenth century many big tracts of state land were sold to favored settlers. Thus, although the Crown decreed that Indian communities were to retain the use of their tribal lands, a class of big landholders grew up in sparsely settled regions and in the midst of the defeated Indian populations.

The Spanish settlers strove to become a genuine European aristocracy, and they largely succeeded. As good aristocrats, they believed that work in the fields was the proper occupation of a depressed, impoverished peasantry. The defenseless Indians suited their needs. As the Indian population recovered in numbers, slavery and periodic forced labor gave way to widespread debt peonage from 1600 onward. Under this system, a planter or rancher would keep his Christianized, increasingly Hispanicized Indians in perpetual debt bondage by periodically advancing food, shelter, and a little money. Debt peonage subjugated the Indians and was a form of agricultural serfdom.

The landowning class practiced primogeniture, passing everything from eldest son to eldest son to prevent fragmentation of land and influence. Also like European nobles, wealthy creoles built ornate townhouses, contributing to the development of a lavish colonial baroque style that may still be seen in Lima, Peru, and Mexico City. The creole elite followed European cultural and intellectual trends. Enlightenment ideas spread to colonial salons and universities, encouraging a questioning attitude and preparing the way for the creoles' rise to political power with the independence movements of the early nineteenth century.

There were also creoles of modest means, especially in the cities, since estate agriculture discouraged small white farmers. (Chile was an exception: since it had few docile Indians to exploit, white settlers had to work their small farms to survive.) The large middle group in Spanish colonies consisted of racially mixed *mestizos,* the offspring of Spanish men and Indian women. The most talented mestizos realistically aspired to join the creoles, for enough wealth and power could make one white. This ambition siphoned off the most energetic mestizos and lessened the build-up of any lower-class discontent. Thus, by the end of the colonial era roughly 20 percent of the population was classified as white and about 30 percent as mestizo. Pure-blooded Indians accounted for most of the remainder, for only on the sugar plantations of Cuba and Puerto Rico did black slavery ever take firm root in Spanish America.

The situation was quite the opposite in Portuguese Brazil. As in the West Indies, enormous numbers of blacks were brought in chains to work the sugar plantations. About half the population of Brazil was of African origin in the early nineteenth century. Even more than in the Spanish territories, the people of Brazil intermingled sexually and culturally. In contrast to North America, where racial lines were hard and fast, at least in theory, colonial Brazil made a virtue of miscegenation and the population grew to include every color in the racial rainbow.

———◆———

While some European intellectual elites were developing a new view of the world in the eighteenth century, Europe as a whole was experiencing a gradual but far-reaching expansion. As agriculture showed signs of modest improvement across the continent, first the Low Countries and then England succeeded in launching the epoch-making Agricultural Revolution. Plague disappeared and the populations of all countries grew significantly, encouraging the progress of cottage industry and merchant capitalism.

Europeans also continued their overseas expansion, fighting for empire and profit and consolidating their hold on the Americas in particular. A revived Spain and its Latin American colonies participated fully in this expansion. As in agriculture and cottage industry, however, England and its empire proved most successful. The English concentrated much of the growing Atlantic trade in their hands, which challenged and enriched English industry and intensified the search for new methods of production. Thus, by the 1770s, England was on the verge of an economic breakthrough fully as significant as the great political upheaval destined to develop shortly in neighboring France.

NOTES

1. M. Bloch, *Les caractères originaux de l'histoire rurale française,* Librarie Armand Colin, Paris 1960, 1.244-245.

2. B. H. Slicher van Bath, *The Agrarian History of Western Europe,* A.D. *500-1850,* St. Martin's Press, New York, 1963, p. 240.

3. Quoted in E. E. Rich and C. H. Wilson, eds., *Cambridge Economic History of Europe,* Cambridge University Press, Cambridge, England, 4.74.

4. Ibid., p. 85.

5. Quoted by I. Pinchbeck, *Women Workers and the Industrial Revolution, 1750-1850,* F. S. Crofts, New York, 1930, p. 113.

6. Quoted by S. Chapman, *The Lancashire Cotton Industry,* Manchester University Press, Manchester, 1903, p. 13.

7. Quoted by P. Mantoux, *The Industrial Revolution in the Eighteenth Century,* Harper & Row, New York, 1961, p. 75.

8. Quoted by C. Wilson, *England's Apprenticeship, 1603-1763,* Longmans, Green, London, 1965, p. 169.

9. Quoted by D. Dillard, *Economic Development of the North Atlantic Community,* Prentice-Hall, Englewood Cliffs, N.J., 1967, p. 192.

10. G. Taylor, "America's Growth Before 1840," *Journal of Economic History* 24 (December 1970):427-444.

11. J. Rippy, *Latin America: A Modern History,* rev. ed., University of Michigan Press, Ann Arbor, 1968, p. 97.

SUGGESTED READING

B. H. Slicher van Bath, *The Agrarian History of Western Europe,* A.D. *500-1850* (1963), is a wide-ranging general introduction to the gradual transformation of European agriculture, as is M. Bloch's great classic, cited in the Notes, which has been translated as *French Rural History* (1966). J. Blum, *The End of the Old Order in Rural Europe* (1978), is an impressive comparative study. J. de Vries, *The Dutch Rural Economy in the Golden Age, 1500-1700* (1974), skillfully examines the causes of early Dutch leadership in farming, and E. L. Jones, *Agriculture and Economic Growth in England, 1650-1815* (1967), shows the importance of the agricultural revolution for England. Two recommended and complementary studies on landowning nobilities are R. Forster, *The Nobility of Toulouse in the Eighteenth Century* (1960), and G. E. Mingay, *English Landed Society in the Eighteenth Century* (1963). A. Goodwin, ed., *The European Nobility in the Eighteenth Century* (1967), is an exciting group of essays on aristocrats in different countries. R. and E. Forster, eds., *European Society in the Eighteenth Century* (1969), assembles a rich collection of contemporary writing on a variety of economic and social topics. Le Roy Ladurie, *The Peasants of Languedoc* (1976), a brilliant and challenging study of rural life in southern France for several centuries, complements J. Goody et al., eds., *Family and Inheritance: Rural Society in Western Europe, 1200-1800* (1976). Life in small-town preindustrial France comes alive in P. Higonnet, *Pont-de-Montvert: Social Structure and Politics in a French Village, 1700-1914* (1971), while O. Hufton deals vividly and sympathetically with rural migration, work, women, and much more in *The Poor in Eighteenth-Century France* (1974). P. Mantoux, *The Industrial Revolution in the Eighteenth Century* (1928), and D. Landes, *The Unbound Prometheus* (1969), provide excellent discussions of the development of cottage industry.

Two excellent multivolume series, *The Cambridge Economic History of Europe,* and C. Cipolla, ed., *The Fontana Economic History of Europe,* cover the sweep of economic developments from the Middle Ages to the present and have extensive bibliographies. In the area of trade and colonial competition, V. Barbour, *Capitalism in Amsterdam* (1963), and C. R. Boxer, *The Dutch Seaborne Empire* (1970), are very interesting on Holland. C. Wilson, *Profit and Power: A Study of England and the Dutch Wars* (1957), is exciting scholarship, as are W. Dorn, *The*

Competition for Empire, 1740–1763 (1963), D. K. Fieldhouse, *The Colonial Empires* (1971), and R. Davies, *The Rise of Atlantic Economies* (1973). R. Pares, *Yankees and Creoles* (1956), is a short, lively work on trade between the mainland colonies and the West Indies. E. Williams, *Capitalism and Slavery* (1966), provocatively argues that slavery provided the wealth necessary for England's industrial development. Another exciting work is J. Nef, *War and Human Progress* (1968), which examines the impact of war on economic and industrial development in European history between about 1500 and 1800 and may be compared with M. Gutmann, *War and Rural Life in the Early Modern Low Countries* (1980). J. Fagg's *Latin America* (1969) provides a good introduction to the colonial period and has a useful bibliography, while C. Haring, *The Spanish in America* (1947), is a fundamental modern study.

Three very fine books on the growth of population are C. Cipolla's short and lively *The Economic History of World Population* (1962); E. A. Wrigley's more demanding *Population and History* (1969); and T. McKeown's scholarly *The Modern Rise of Population* (1977). In addition to works on England cited in the Suggested Reading for Chapter 22, D. George, *England in Transition* (1953), and C. Wilson, *England's Apprenticeship, 1603–1763* (1965), are highly recommended. The greatest novel of eighteenth-century English society is Henry Fielding's unforgettable *Tom Jones,* although Jane Austen's novels about country society, *Emma* and *Pride and Prejudice* are not far behind.

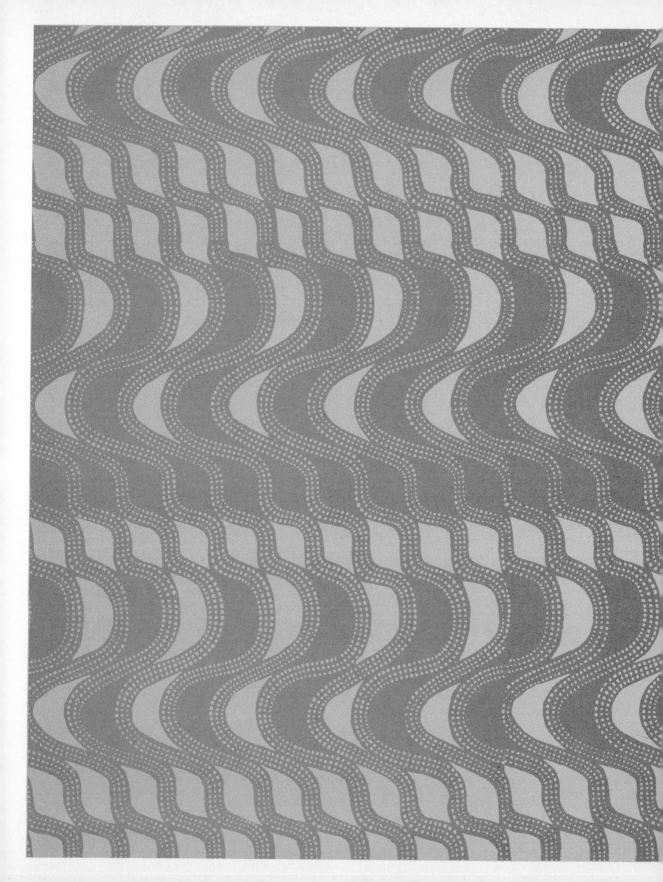

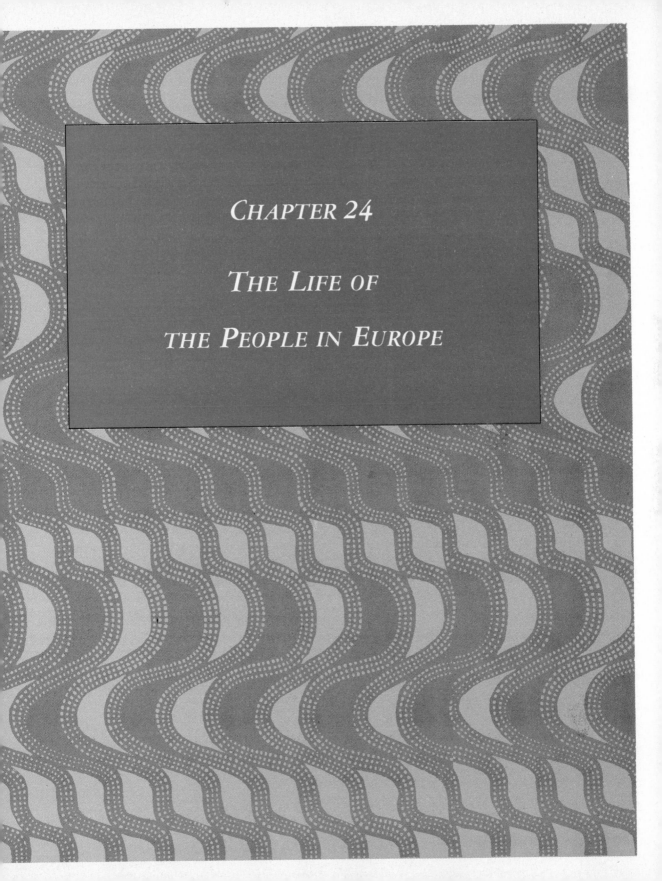

CHAPTER 24

THE LIFE OF
THE PEOPLE IN EUROPE

THE DISCUSSION OF AGRICULTURE and industry in the last chapter showed the ordinary man and woman at work, straining to make ends meet and earn a living. Yet work is only part of human experience. What about the rest? What about such basic things as marriage and childhood, food and drink, diet and medicine? How, in short, did "the people" — the peasant masses and the urban poor — really live in western Europe before the age of revolution began at the end of the eighteenth century? This is the simple but profound question that the economic and social developments naturally raise.

MARRIAGE AND THE FAMILY

The basic unit of social organization is the family. It is within the structure of the family that human beings love, mate, and reproduce themselves. It is primarily the family that teaches the child, imparting values and customs that condition an individual's behavior for a lifetime. The family is also an institution woven into the web of history. It evolves and changes, and it has taken different forms in different times and places.

EXTENDED AND NUCLEAR FAMILIES

In many traditional Asian and African societies, the typical family has often been an extended family. A newly married couple, instead of establishing their own home, will go to live with either the bride's or the groom's family. The couple raises their children while living under the same roof with their own brothers and sisters, who may also be married. The family is a big three- or four-generation clan, headed by a patriarch or perhaps a matriarch, and encompassing everyone from the youngest infant to the oldest grandparent.

Extended families, it is often said, provide security for adults and children in traditional agrarian peasant economies. Everyone has a place within the extended family, from cradle to grave. Sociologists frequently assume that the extended family gives way to the conjugal, or "nuclear," family with the advent of industrialization and urbanization. Couples establish their own households and their own family identities when they marry. They live with the children they raise, apart from their parents. Something like this is indeed happening in much of Asia and Africa today. And since Europe was once agrarian and preindustrial, it has often been believed that the extended family must also have prevailed in Europe before it was destroyed by the Industrial Revolution.

In fact, the situation was quite different in western and central European societies. By 1700, the extended three-generational family was a great rarity in western and central Europe. Indeed, the extended family may never have been common in Europe, although it is hard to know about the Middle Ages because there are fewer records for the historian to study. When young European couples married, they normally established their own households and lived apart from their parents. When a three-generation household came into existence, it was usually a parent who moved in with a married child, rather than a newly married couple moving in with either set of parents. The married couple, and the children that were sure to follow, were on their own from the beginning.

Perhaps because European couples set up separate households when they married, people did not marry young in the seventeenth and early eighteenth centuries. By the standards of today the average person, who was neither rich nor aristocratic, married suprisingly late, many years after reaching adulthood and many more after beginning to work. In one well-studied typical English village, both men and women married for the first time at an average age of twenty-seven or older in the seventeenth and eighteenth centuries. For one long period, the average age for women at first marriage was thirty years. In early eighteenth-century France the average man and woman marrying for the first time were in their late twenties. Moreover, a substantial portion of men and women never married at all.

Between two-fifths and three-fifths of European women capable of bearing children — that is, women between fifteen and forty-four — were unmarried at any given time. The contrast with traditional non-Western societies is once again striking. In those societies the pattern has very often been almost universal and very early marriage. The union of a teenage bride and her teenage groom has been the general rule.

The custom of late marriage and nuclear family was a distinctive characteristic of European society. The consequences have been tremendous, though still only partially explored. It seems likely that the dynamism and creativity that have characterized European society were due in large part to the pattern of marriage and family. This pattern fostered and required self-reliance and independence. In preindustrial western Europe in the sixteenth through eighteenth centuries, marriage normally joined a mature man and a mature woman — two adults who had already experienced a great deal of life and could transmit self-reliance and real skills to the next generation.

Why was marriage delayed? The main reason was that couples normally could not marry until they could support themselves economically. The land was the main source of income. The peasant son often needed to wait until his father's death to inherit the family farm and marry his sweetheart. Similarly, the peasant daughter and her family needed to accumulate a small dowry to help her boy friend buy land or build a house.

There were also laws and regulations to temper impetuous love and physical attraction. In some areas couples needed the legal permission or tacit approval of the local lord or landowner in order to marry. In Austria and Germany there were legal restrictions on marriage, and well into the nineteenth century poor couples had particular difficulty securing the approval of local officials. These officials believed that freedom to marry for the lower classes would mean more paupers, more abandoned children, and more money for welfare. Thus prudence, custom, and law combined to postpone the march to the altar. This pattern helped society maintain some kind of balance between the number of people and the available economic resources.

WORK AWAY FROM HOME

Many young people worked within their families until they could start their own households. Boys plowed and wove; girls spun and tended the cows. Many others left home to work elsewhere. In the towns a lad might be apprenticed to a craftsman for seven or fourteen years to learn a trade. During that time he would not be permitted to marry. In most trades he earned little and worked hard, but if he were lucky he might eventually be admitted to a guild and establish his economic independence. More often, the young man would drift from one tough job to another: hired hand for a small farmer, laborer on a new road, carrier of water in a nearby town. He was always subject to economic fluctua-

THE CHIMNEY SWEEP *Some boys and girls found work as chimney sweeps, especially if they were small. Climbing up into chimneys was dirty, dangerous work. Hot stones could set the sweep's clothing on fire. (Photo: Caroline Buckler)*

tions, and unemployment was a constant threat.

Girls also left their families to work, at an early age and in large numbers. The range of opportunities open to them was more limited, however. Service in another family's household was by far the most common job. Even middle-class families often sent their daughters into service (as they sent their sons to workshops and counting houses) and hired others as servants in return. Thus, a few years

away from home as a servant was a normal part of growing up. If all went well, the girl (or boy) would work hard and save some money for parents and marriage. At the least, there would be one less mouth to feed at home.

The legions of young servant girls worked hard but had little real independence. Sometimes the employer paid the girl's wages directly to her parents. Constantly under the eye of her mistress, her tasks were many – cleaning, shopping, cooking, caring for the baby – and often endless, for there were no laws to limit her exploitation. Few girls were so brutalized that they snapped under the strain, like the Russian servant girl Varka in Chekhov's chilling story, "Sleepy," who, driven beyond exhaustion, finally quieted her mistress's screaming child by strangling it in its cradle. But court records are full of complaints by servant girls of physical mistreatment by their mistresses. There were many others like the fifteen-year-old English girl in the early eighteenth century who told the judge that her mistress had not only called her "very opprobrious names, as Bitch, Whore and the like," but also "beat her without provocation and beyond measure."[1]

There was also the pressure of seducers and sexual attack. In theory, domestic service offered protection and security for a young girl leaving home. The girl had food, lodging, and a new family. She did not drift in a strange and often dangerous environment. But in practice, she was often the easy prey of a lecherous master, or his sons, or his friends. Indeed, "the evidence suggests that in all European countries, from Britain to Russia, the upper classes felt perfectly free to exploit sexually girls who were at their mercy."[2] If the girl became pregnant, she was quickly fired and thrown out in disgrace to make her own way. Prostitution and petty thievery were often the harsh alternatives that lay ahead. "What are we?" exclaimed a bitter Paris prostitute during the French Revolution. "Most of us are unfortunate women, without origins, without education, servants and maids for the most part."[3]

PREMARITAL SEX AND BIRTH-CONTROL PRACTICES

Did the plight of some ex-servant girls mean that late marriage in preindustrial Europe went hand in hand with premarital sex and many illegitimate children? For most of western and central Europe, until at least 1750, the answer seems to be no. English parish registers, in which the clergy recorded the births and deaths of the population, seldom list more than one bastard out of every twenty children baptized. Some French parishes in the seventeenth century had extraordinarily low rates of illegitimacy, with less than one percent of the babies born out of wedlock. Illegitimate babies were apparently a rarity, at least as far as the official church records are concerned.

At the same time premarital sex was clearly commonplace. In one well-studied English village one-third of all first children were conceived before the couple was married, and many were born within three months of the marriage ceremony. No doubt many of these couples were already betrothed, or at least "going steady," before they entered into an intimate relationship. But the very low rates of illegitimate birth also reflect the powerful social controls of the traditional village, particularly the open-field village with its pattern of cooperation and common action. Irate parents and village elders, indignant priests and authoritative landlords, all combined to

pressure any young people who wavered about marriage in the face of unexpected pregnancy. These controls meant that premarital sex was not entered into lightly. In the countryside it was generally limited to those contemplating marriage.

Once a woman was married, she generally had several children. This does not mean that birth control within marriage was unknown in western and central Europe before the nineteenth century. But it was primitive and quite undependable. The most common method was coitus interruptus – withdrawal by the male before ejaculation. The French, who were apparently early leaders in contraception, were using this method extensively to limit family size by the end of the eighteenth century. The same technique was apparently used in some English communities and no doubt elsewhere, since awareness of this way to prevent conception was widespread. Withdrawal as a method of birth control was in keeping with the European pattern of nuclear family, in which the father bore the direct responsibility of supporting his children. Withdrawal – a male technique – was one way to meet that responsibility.

Mechanical and other means of contraception were not unknown in the eighteenth century, but they appear to have been used mainly by certain sectors of the urban population. The "fast set" of London used the "sheath" regularly, although primarily to protect against venereal disease, not pregnancy. Prostitutes used various contraceptive techniques to prevent pregnancy, and such information was probably available to anyone who really sought it. The second part of an indictment for adultery against a late-sixteenth-century English vicar charged that the wayward minister was "also an instructor of young folks [in] how to commit the sin of adultery or fornication and not to beget or bring forth children."[4]

NEW PATTERNS OF MARRIAGE AND ILLEGITIMACY

In the second half of the eighteenth century, the pattern of late marriage and few illegitimate children began to break down. It is hard to say why. Certainly, changes in the economy had a gradual but profound impact. The growth of cottage industry created new opportunities for earning a living, opportunities not tied to limited and hard-to-get land. Because a scrap of ground for a garden and a cottage for the loom and spinning wheel could be quite enough for a modest living, young people had greater independence and did not need to wait for a good-sized farm. A contemporary observer of an area of rapidly growing cottage industry in Switzerland at the end of the eighteenth century described these changes: "The increased and sure income offered by the combination of cottage manufacture with farming hastened and multiplied marriages and encouraged the division of landholdings, while enhancing their value; it also promoted the expansion and embellishment of houses and villages."[5]

As a result cottage workers not only married earlier, but for different reasons. Nothing could be so businesslike, so calculating, as a peasant marriage, which was often dictated by the needs of the couple's families. After 1750, however, courtship became more extensive and freer as cottage industry grew. It was easier to yield to the attraction of the opposite sex and fall in love. The older generation was often shocked by the lack of responsibility they saw in the early marriages of the poor, the union of "people with only two spinning wheels and not even a bed." But the laws and regulations they imposed, especially in Germany, were often disregarded. Unions based on love rather than economic considerations were increasingly the pattern for cottage workers. Factory workers, numbers of whom first began to appear in England after about 1780, followed the path blazed by cottage workers.

Changes in the timing and motivation of marriage went hand in hand with a rapid increase in illegitimate births between about 1750 and 1850. Some historians even speak of an "illegitimacy explosion," a phrase that is no exaggeration in many instances. In Frankfurt, Germany, for example, only about 2 percent of all births were illegitimate in the early 1700s. This figure rose to 5 percent in about 1760, to about 10 percent in 1800, and peaked at about 25 percent around 1850. In Bordeaux, France, illegitimate births rose steadily until by 1840 fully one out of every three babies was born out of wedlock. Small towns and villages less frequently experienced such startlingly high illegitimacy rates, but increases from a range of 1 to 3 percent initially to 10 to 20 percent between 1750 and 1850 were commonplace. A profound sexual and cultural transformation was taking place. Fewer girls were abstaining from premarital intercourse, and fewer boys were marrying the girls they got pregnant.

It is hard to know exactly why this change occurred and what it meant. The old idea of a safe, late, economically secure marriage did not reflect economic and social realities. The growing freedom of thought in the turbulent years beginning with the French Revolution in 1789 influenced sexual and marital behavior. And illegitimate births, particularly in Germany, were also the result of open rebellion against class laws limiting the right of the poor to marry. Unable to show a solid financial position and thereby obtain a marriage license, couples asserted their independence and lived together anyway. Children were the natural and desired result of "true love" and greater freedom. Eventually, when the stuffy old-fashioned propertied classes gave in and repealed their laws against "imprudent marriage," poor couples once again went to the altar, often accompanied by their children, and the number of illegitimate children declined.

More fundamentally, the need to seek work outside farming and the village made young people more mobile. Mobility in turn encouraged new sexual and marital relationships, which were less subject to parental pressure and village tradition. As in the case of young servant girls who became pregnant and were then forced to fend for themselves, some of these relationships promoted loose living or prostitution. This resulted in more illegitimate births and strengthened an urban subculture of habitual illegitimacy.

EARLY SEXUAL EMANCIPATION?

It has been suggested that the increase in illegitimate births represented a stage in the emancipation of women. According to this view, new economic opportunities outside the home, in the city and later in the factory, revolutionized women's attitudes about themselves. Young working women became individualistic and rebelled against old restrictions like late marriage. They sought fulfillment in the pleasure of sexuality. Since there was little birth control, freer sex for single women meant more illegitimate babies.

No doubt single working women in towns and cities were of necessity more independent and self-reliant. Yet, until at least the late nineteenth century, it seems unlikely that such young women were motivated primarily by visions of emancipation and sexual liberation. Most women were servants or textile workers. These jobs paid poorly, and the possibility of a truly independent "liberated" life was correspondingly limited. Most women in the city probably looked to marriage and family life as an escape from hard, poorly paid work and as the foundation of a satisfying life.

Hopes and promises of marriage from men of the working girl's own class led naturally enough to sex.[6] In one medium-sized French city in 1787–1788 the great majority of unwed mothers stated that sexual intimacy had followed promises of marriage. Many soldiers, day laborers, and male servants were no doubt sincere in their proposals. But their lives were insecure, and many hesitated to take on the heavy economic burdens of wife and child. Nor were their backbones any longer stiffened by the traditional pressures of the village.

In a growing number of cases, therefore, the intended marriage did not take place. The romantic yet practical dreams and aspirations of many young working women and men were frustrated by low wages, inequality, and changing economic and social conditions. Old patterns of marriage and family were breaking down among the common people. Only in the late nineteenth century would more stable patterns reappear.

WOMEN AND CHILDREN

In the traditional framework of preindustrial Europe women married late, but then began bearing children rapidly. If a woman married before she was thirty, and if both she and her husband lived to forty-five, the chances were roughly one in two that she would give birth to six or more children. The newborn child entered a dangerous world. Infant mortality – the number of babies who would die

THE FACE OF POVERTY   *A poor Italian peasant woman nurses her infant and stoically begs for her children in this realistic painting by Ceruti. Begging was quite common in the eighteenth century. (Collection G. Testori, Novate)*

creases the likelihood of pregnancy for the average woman by delaying the resumption of ovulation. Although women may have been only vaguely aware of the link between nursing and not getting pregnant, they were spacing their children – from two and a half to three or more years apart in many communities – and limiting their fertility by nursing their babies. If a newborn baby died, nursing stopped and a new life could be created. Nursing also saved lives: the breast-fed infant was more likely to survive on its mother's milk than on any artificial foods. In many areas of Russia, where common practice was to give a new child a sweetened (and germ-ladened) rag to suck on for its subsistence, half the babies did not survive for the first year.

In contrast to the laboring poor, the women of the aristocracy and upper middle class seldom nursed their own children. The upper-class woman felt that breast-feeding was crude and common, and well beneath her dignity. Instead she hired a wet nurse – a nursing mother from the poor – to suckle her child. The mother of more modest means – the wife of a shopkeeper or artisan – also commonly used a wet nurse, sending her baby to some poor woman in the country as soon as possible.

Wet-nursing was a very widespread and flourishing business in the eighteenth century, a dismal business within the framework of the putting-out system. The traffic was in babies rather than in wool and cloth, and two or three years often passed before the wet-nurse worker finished her task. The great French historian Jules Michelet described with compassion the plight of the wet nurse, who was still going to the homes of the rich in the early nineteenth century in France:

People do not know how much these poor women are exploited and abused, first by the vehicles

before their first birthday – was high. One in five was sure to die, and one in three was quite likely to in the poorer areas. Newborn children are very likely to catch infectious diseases of the stomach and chest. Not until the late nineteenth century were these diseases and their treatment understood. Thus little could be done for an ailing child, even in rich families. Childhood itself was dangerous. Parents in preindustrial Europe could count themselves fortunate if half their children lived to adulthood.

CHILD CARE AND NURSING

Women of the lower classes generally breast-fed their infants, and for much longer periods than is customary today. Breast-feeding de-

which transport them (often barely out of their confinement), and afterward by the employment offices which place them. Taken as nurses on the spot, they must send their own child away, and consequently it often dies. They have no contact with the family that hires them, and they may be dismissed at the first caprice of the mother or doctor. If the change of air and place should dry up their milk, they are discharged without any compensation. If they stay there [in the city] they pick up the habits of the easy life, and they suffer enormously when they are forced to return to their life of [rural] poverty. A good number become servants in order to stay in the town. They never rejoin their husbands, and the family is broken.[7]

Other observers noted the flaws of wet nurses. It was a common belief that a nurse passed her bad traits to the baby with her milk. When a child turned out poorly, it was assumed that "the nurse changed it." Many observers charged that nurses were often negligent and greedy. They claimed that there were large numbers of "killing nurses" with whom no child ever survived. The nurse let the child die quickly, so that she could take another child and another fee. No matter how the adults fared in the wet-nurse business, the child was a certain loser.

FOUNDLINGS AND INFANTICIDE

In the ancient world and in Asian societies it was not uncommon to allow or force newborn babies, particularly girl babies, to die when there were too many mouths to feed. To its great and eternal credit the early medieval church, strongly influenced by Jewish law, denounced infanticide as a pagan practice and insisted that every human life was sacred. The willful destruction of newborn children became a crime punishable by death. And yet, as the reference to "killing nurses" suggests, direct and indirect methods of eliminating

unwanted babies did not disappear. There were, for example, many cases of "overlaying" – parents rolling over and suffocating the child placed between them in their bed. Such parents claimed they were drunk and had acted unintentionally. In Austria in 1784, suspicious authorities made it illegal for parents to take children under five into bed with them. Severe poverty on the one hand, and increasing illegitimacy on the other, conspired to force the very poor to thin their own ranks.

The young girl – very likely a servant – who could not provide for her child had few choices. If she would not stoop to abortion or the services of a killing nurse, she could bundle up her baby and leave it on the doorstep of a church. In the late seventeenth century Saint Vincent de Paul was so distressed by the number of babies brought to the steps of Notre Dame in Paris that he established a home for foundlings. Others followed his example. In England the government acted on a petition calling for a foundling hospital "to prevent the frequent murders of poor, miserable infants at birth" and "to suppress the inhuman custom of exposing newborn children to perish in the streets."

In much of Europe in the eighteenth century, foundling homes became a favorite charity of the rich and powerful. Great sums were spent on them. The foundling home in St. Petersburg, perhaps the most elaborate and lavish of its kind, occupied the former palaces of two members of the high nobility. In the early nineteenth century it had 25,000 children in its care and was receiving 5,000 new babies a year. At their best, the foundling homes of the eighteenth century were a good example of Christian charity and social concern in an age of great poverty and inequality.

Yet the foundling home was no panacea. By the 1770s, one-third of all babies born in

ABANDONED CHILDREN *At this Italian found-lings' home a frightened, secretive mother could dis-creetly deposit her baby. (Bettmann Archive)*

Paris were immediately abandoned to the foundling home by their mothers. Fully a third of all those foundlings were abandoned by married couples, a powerful commentary on the standard of living among the working poor, for whom an additional mouth to feed often meant tragedy. In London competition for space in the foundling home soon became so great that it led "to the disgraceful scene of women scrambling and fighting to get to the door, that they might be of the fortunate few to reap the benefit of the Asylum."[8]

Furthermore, great numbers of babies entered, but few left. Even in the best of these homes half the babies normally died within a year. In the worst, fully 90 percent did not survive! They succumbed to long journeys over rough roads, the intentional and unintentional neglect of their wet nurses, and the customary childhood illnesses. So great was the carnage that some contemporaries called the foundling hospitals "legalized infanticide."

Certainly, some parents and officials looked upon the hospitals as a dump for unwanted babies. In the early 1760s, when the London Foundling Hospital was obliged to accept all babies offered, it was deluged with babies from the countryside. Many parish officers placed with the foundling home the abandoned children in their care, just as others apprenticed five-year-old children to work in factories. Both practices reduced the cost of welfare at the local level. Throughout the eighteenth century, millions of children of the poor continued to exit after the briefest of appearances upon the earthly stage. True, they died after being properly baptized, an important consideration in still-Christian Europe. Yet those people who would dream of an idyllic past should do well to ponder the foundling's fate.

What were the more typical circumstances of children's lives? Did the treatment of foundlings reflect the attitudes of normal parents? Harsh as it may sound, the young child was very often of little concern to its parents and to society in the eighteenth century. This indifference toward children was found in all classes; rich children were by no means exempt. The practice of using wet nurses, who were casually selected and often negligent, is one example of how even the rich and the prosperous put the child out of sight and out of mind. One French moralist, writing in 1756 about how to improve humanity, observed that "one blushes to think of loving one's children." It has been said that the English gentleman of the period "had more interest in the diseases of his horses than of his children."[9]

Parents believed that the world of the child was an uninteresting one. When parents did stop to notice their offspring, they often treated them as dolls or playthings – little puppies to fondle and cuddle in a moment of relaxation. The psychological distance between parent and child remained vast.

Much of the indifference was due to the terrible frequency, the terrible banality, of death among children of all classes. Parents simply could not afford to become too emotionally involved with their children, who were so unlikely to survive. The great eighteenth-century English historian Edward Gibbon (1737-1794) wrote that "the death of a new born child before that of its parents may seem unnatural but it is a strictly probable event, since of any given number the greater part are extinguished before the ninth year, before they possess the faculties of the mind and the body." Gibbon's father named all his boys Edward, hoping that at least one of them would survive to carry his name. His prudence was not misplaced. Edward the future historian and eldest survived. Five brothers and sisters who followed him all died in infancy.

Doctors were seldom interested in the care of children. One contemporary observer quoted a famous doctor as saying that "he never wished to be called to a young child because he was really at a loss to know what to offer for it." There were "physicians of note who make no scruple to assert that there is nothing to be done for children when they are ill." Children were caught in a vicious circle: they were neglected because they were very likely to die, and they were likely to die because they were neglected.

Indifference toward children often shaded off into brutality. When parents and other adults did turn toward children, it was normally to discipline and control them. The novelist Daniel Defoe (1660?-1731), always delighted when he saw very young children working hard in cottage industry, coined the axiom "Spare the rod and spoil the child." He meant it. So did Susannah Wesley, mother of John Wesley (1703-1791), the founder of Methodism. According to her, the first task of a parent toward her children was "to conquer the will, and bring them to an obedient temper." She reported that her babies were "taught to fear the rod, and to cry softly; by which means they escaped the abundance of correction they might otherwise have had, and that most odious noise of the crying of children was rarely heard in the house, but the family lived in as much quietness as if there had not been a child among them."[10]

It was hardly surprising – indeed, it was quite predictable – that when English parish officials dumped their paupers into the first

THE FIVE SENSES *Published in 1774, J. B. Base-*
dow's Elementary Reader *helped spread new atti-*
tudes toward child development and education.
Drawing heavily upon the theories of Locke and
Rousseau, the German educator advocated nature
study and contact with everyday life. In this illustra-
tion for Basedow's reader, gentle teachers allow un-
corrupted children to learn about the five senses
through direct experience. (Photo: Caroline Buckler)

factories late in the eighteenth century, the
children were beaten and brutalized, as we
shall see. That was part of the childrearing
pattern – widespread indifference on the one
hand and strict physical discipline on the
other – that prevailed through most of the
eighteenth century.

Late in the century this pattern came under
attack. Critics like Jean-Jacques Rousseau
called for greater love, tenderness, and understanding toward children. In addition to supporting foundling homes to discourage
infanticide and urging wealthy women to

nurse their own babies, these new voices ridiculed the practice of swaddling. Wrapping
youngsters in tight-fitting clothes and blankets
was generally believed to form babies properly
by "straightening them out." By the end of
the century small children were often dressed
in simpler, more comfortable clothing, allowing much greater freedom of movement.
More parents expressed a delight in the love
and intimacy of the child and found real pleasure in raising their offspring. These changes
were part of the general growth of humani-
tarianism and optimism about human poten-

tial that characterized the eighteenth-century Enlightenment.

SCHOOLS AND EDUCATION

The role of formal education outside the home, in those special institutions called schools, was growing more important. The aristocracy and the rich had led the way in the sixteenth century with special colleges, often run by the Jesuits. But "little schools," charged with elementary education of the children of the masses, did not appear until the seventeenth century. Unlike medieval schools, which mingled all age groups, the little schools specialized in boys and girls from seven to twelve, who were instructed in basic literacy and religion.

Although large numbers of common people got no education at all in the eighteenth century, the beginnings of popular education were recognizable. France made a start in 1682 with the establishment of Christian schools, which taught the catechism and prayers as well as reading and writing. The Church of England and the dissenting congregations established "charity schools" to instruct the children of the poor. As early as 1717, Prussia made attendance at elementary schools compulsory. Inspired by the old Protestant idea that every believer should be able to read and study the Bible in the quest for personal salvation, and by the new idea of a population capable of effectively serving the state, Prussia led the way in the development of universal education. Religious motives were also extremely important elsewhere. From the middle of the seventeenth century, Presbyterian Scotland was convinced that the path to salvation lay in careful study of the Scriptures, and this belief led to an effective network of parish schools for rich and poor alike. The Enlightenment commitment to greater

knowledge through critical thinking reinforced interest in education in the eighteenth century.

The result of these efforts was a remarkable growth of basic literacy between 1600 and 1800, especially after 1700. Whereas in 1600 only one male in six was barely literate in France and Scotland, and one in four in England, by 1800 almost 90 percent of the Scottish male population was literate. At the same time two out of three males were literate in France, and in advanced areas such as Normandy literacy approached 90 percent. More than half of English males were literate by 1800. In all three countries the bulk of the jump occurred in the eighteenth century. Women were also increasingly literate, although they probably lagged behind men somewhat in most countries. (For example, in England in 1840 – the first date for which there is complete census evidence – two-thirds of newly married men and half of newly married women were literate.) Some elementary education was becoming a reality for European peoples, and schools were of growing significance in everyday life.

THE EUROPEAN'S FOOD

Plague, starvation, and economic crisis, which recurred often in the seventeenth century, gradually disappeared in the eighteenth century. This phenomenon probably accounts in large part for the rapid growth in the total number of Europeans and for their longer lives. The increase in the average life span, allowing for regional variations, was remarkable. In 1700, the average European could expect at birth to live only twenty-five years. A century later, a newborn European could expect to live fully ten years longer, to age thirty-five. The doubling of the adult life span meant that there was more time to produce and create, and more reason for parents to stress learning and preparation for adulthood.

People also lived longer because ordinary years were progressively less deadly. People ate better and somewhat more wisely. Doctors and hospitals probably saved a few more lives than they had in the past. How and why did health and life expectancy improve, and how much did they improve? And what were the differences between rich and poor? To answer these questions, it is necessary first to follow the eighteenth-century family to the table, and then to see what contribution doctors made.

DIETS AND NUTRITION

Although the accomplishments of doctors and hospitals are constantly in the limelight today, the greater if less spectacular part of medicine is preventive medicine. The great breakthrough of the second half of the nineteenth century was the development of public health techniques – proper sanitation and mass vaccinations – to prevent outbreaks of communicable diseases. Even before the nineteenth century, when medical knowledge was slight and doctors were of limited value, prevention was the key to longer life. Good clothing, warm dry housing, and plentiful food make for healthier populations, much more capable of battling off disease. Clothing and housing for the masses probably improved only modestly in the eighteenth century, but the new agricultural methods and increased agricultural output had a beneficial effect. The average European ate more and better food and was healthier as a result in 1800 than in 1700. This pattern is apparent if we look at the fare of the laboring poor.

At the beginning of the eighteenth century,

ordinary men and women depended on grain as fully as they had in the past. Bread was quite literally the staff of life. Peasants in the Beauvais region of France ate two pounds of bread a day, washing it down with water, green wine, beer, or (if they were lucky) a little skimmed milk. Their dark bread was made from a mixture of rough-ground wheat and rye – the standard flour of the poor. The poor also ate grains in soup and gruel. In rocky northern Scotland, for example, people depended on oatmeal, which they often ate half-cooked so it would swell in their stomachs and make them feel full. No wonder, then, that the supply of grain and the price of bread were always critical questions for most of the population.

The poor, rural and urban, also ate a fair quantity of vegetables. Indeed, vegetables were considered "poor people's food." Peas and beans were probably the most common; grown as field crops in much of Europe since the Middle Ages, they were eaten fresh in late spring and summer. Dried, they became the basic ingredients in the soups and stews of the long winter months. In most regions other vegetables appeared on the tables of the poor in season, primarily cabbages, carrots, and wild greens. Fruit was uncommon and limited to the summer months.

The European poor loved meat and eggs, but even in England – the wealthiest country in Europe in 1700 – they seldom ate their fill. Meat was too expensive. When the poor did eat meat – on a religious holiday or at a wedding or other special occasion – it was most likely lamb or mutton. Sheep could survive on rocky soils and did not compete directly with humans for the slender resources of grain.

Milk was rarely drunk. It was widely believed that milk caused sore eyes, headaches, and a variety of ills, except among the very young and very old. Milk was used primarily to make cheese and butter, which the poor liked but could afford only occasionally. Medical and popular opinion considered whey, the watery liquid left after milk was churned, "an excellent temperate drink."

The diet of the rich – aristocrats, officials, and the comfortable bourgeoisie – was traditionally quite different from that of the poor. The men and women of the upper classes were rapacious carnivores, gorging on meat, meat, and more meat. To a large extent a person's standard of living and economic well-being was judged by the amount of meat eaten. A truly elegant dinner among the great and the powerful consisted of one rich meat after another – a chicken pie, a leg of lamb, a grilled steak, for example. Three separate meat courses might be followed by three fish courses, laced with piquant sauces and complemented with sweets, cheeses, and nuts of all kinds. Fruits and vegetables were not often found on the tables of the rich. The long-standing dominance of meat and fish in the diet of the upper classes continued throughout the eighteenth century. There was extravagant living, and undoubtedly great overeating and gluttony, not only among the aristocracy but among the prosperous business and professional classes as well.

There was also an enormous amount of drunkenness and overdrinking among the rich. The English squire, for example, who loved to ride with his hounds, loved drink with a similar passion. He became famous as the "four-bottle man." With his dinner he drank red wine from France or white wine from the Rhineland, and with his dessert he took sweet but strong port or Madeira from Portugal. Sometimes he ended the evening under the table in a drunken stupor, but very often he did not. The wine and the meat were consumed together in long hours of sustained excess, permitting the "gentleman" and his guests to drink enormous quantities.

The diet of small traders, master craftsmen, minor bureaucrats – the people of the towns and cities – was probably less monotonous than that of the peasantry. The markets, stocked by market gardens in the outskirts, provided a substantial variety of meats, vegetables, and fruits, although bread and beans still formed the bulk of the poor family's diet.

There were also regional dietary differences in 1700. Generally speaking, northern, Atlantic Europe ate better than southern Mediterranean Europe. The poor of England probably ate best of all. Contemporaries on both sides of the Channel often contrasted the Englishman's consumption of meat with the French peasant's greater dependence on bread and vegetables. The Dutch were also considerably better fed than the average European, in large part because of their advanced agriculture and diversified gardens.

THE IMPACT OF DIET ON HEALTH

How were the poor and the rich served by their quite different diets? Good nutrition depends on a balanced supply of food, as well as on an adequate number of calories. Modern research has shown that the chief determinant of nutritional balance is the relationship between carbohydrates (sugar and starch) and proteins. A diet consisting primarily of carbohydrates is seriously incomplete.

At first glance the diet of the laboring poor, relying as it did on carbohydrates, seems unsatisfactory. Even when a peasant got his daily two or three pounds of bread, his supply of protein and essential vitamins would seem too low. A closer look reveals a brighter picture. Most bread was "brown" or "black," made from wheat or rye. Flour was quite different from that used in the mushy white bread of an American supermarket. The flour of the eighteenth century was a whole-meal flour, produced by stone grinding. It contained most of the bran – the ground-up husk – and the all-important wheat germ. The bran and germ contain higher proportions of some minerals, vitamins, and good-quality proteins than does the rest of the grain. Only when they are removed does bread become a foodstuff providing relatively more starch and less of the essential nutrients.

In addition, the field peas and beans eaten by poor people since Carolingian days contained protein that complemented the proteins in whole-meal bread. The proteins in whey, cheese, and eggs, which the poor ate at least occasionally, also supplemented the value of the protein in the bread and vegetables. Indeed, a leading authority concludes that if a pint of milk and some cheese and whey were eaten each day, the balance of the poor people's diet "was excellent, far better indeed than in many of our modern diets."[11]

The basic bread-and-vegetables diet of the poor *in normal times* was satisfactory. It protected effectively against most of the disorders associated with a deficiency of the vitamin-B complex, for example. The lack of sugar meant that teeth were not so plagued by cavities. Constipation was almost unknown to peasants and laborers living on coarse cereal breads, which provided the roughage modern diets lack. The common diet of the poor also generally warded off anemia, although anemia among infants was not uncommon.

The key dietary problem was probably getting enough green vegetables (or milk), particularly in the late winter and early spring, to insure adequate supplies of vitamins A and C. A severe deficiency of vitamin C produces scurvy, an awful disease that leads to loose

teeth and rotting, stinking gums, swelling of the limbs, and great weakness. Before the season's first vegetables, many people had used up their bodily reserves of vitamin C and were suffering from mild cases of scurvy. Sailors on long voyages suffered most. By the end of the sixteenth century the exceptional antiscurvy properties of lemons and limes led to the practice of supplying some crews with a daily ration of lemon juice, which had highly beneficial effects. English sailors came to be known as "limeys" because of their habit of sucking on limes. "Scurvy grass" – a kind of watercress – also guarded against scurvy, and this disease was increasingly controlled on even the longest voyages.

The practice of gorging on meat, sweets, and spirits caused the rich their own nutritional problems. They too were very often deficient in vitamins A and C, because of their great disdain for fresh vegetables. Gout was a common affliction of the overfed and underexercised rich. No wonder they were often caricatured dragging their flabby limbs and bulging bellies to the table, to stuff their swollen cheeks and poison their livers. People of moderate means, who could afford some meat and dairy products with fair regularity but who had not abandoned the bread and vegetables of the poor, were probably best off from a nutritional standpoint.

New Foods and New Knowledge

In nutrition and food consumption, Europe in the early eighteenth century had not gone

beyond its medieval accomplishments. This situation began to change markedly as the century progressed. Although the introduction of new methods of farming was confined largely to the Low Countries and England, a new food – the potato – came to the aid of the poor everywhere.

Introduced into Europe from the Americas, along with corn, squash, tomatoes, chocolate, and many other useful plants, the humble potato is an excellent food. It contains a good supply of carbohydrates and calories. More important, it is rich in vitamins A and C, especially if the skin is eaten and it is not overcooked. The lack of green vegetables that could lead to scurvy was one of the biggest deficiencies in the poor person's winter and early spring diet. The potato, which gave a much higher caloric yield than grain for a given piece of land, provided the needed vitamins and supplemented the bread-based diet. Doctors, increasingly aware of the dietary benefits of potatoes, prescribed them for the general public and in institutions such as schools and prisons.

For some poor people, especially desperately poor peasants who needed to get every possible calorie from a tiny plot of land, the potato replaced grain as the primary food in the eighteenth century. This happened first in Ireland, where in the seventeenth century Irish rebellion had led to English repression and the perfection of a system of exploitation worthy of the most savage Eastern tyrant. The foreign (and Protestant) English landlords took the best land, forcing large numbers of poor (and Catholic) peasants to live off tiny scraps of rented ground. By 1700, the poor in Ireland lived almost exclusively on the bountiful fruits of the potato plot. And since intensive cultivation gave so much good food from so little land, ever more people were able to eke out a meager existence.

Elsewhere in Europe the potato took hold more slowly. Potatoes were first fed to pigs and livestock, and there was considerable debate over whether they were fit for humans. In Germany the severe famines caused by the Seven Years' War (page 811) settled the matter: potatoes were edible and no "famine food." By the end of the century the potato was an important dietary supplement in much of Europe.

There was also a general growth of market gardening and a greater variety of vegetables in towns and cities. Potatoes, cabbages, peas, beans, radishes, spinach, asparagus, lettuce, parsnips, carrots, and other vegetables were much more common. They were sold in central markets and streets, from "moveable shops that run upon wheels, attended by ill looking fellows," according to one London observer. In the course of the eighteenth century the large towns and cities of maritime Europe began to receive semitropical fruit, such as oranges, lemons, and limes, from Portugal and the West Indies, although they were not cheap.

The growing variety of food was matched by some improvement in knowledge about diet and nutrition. For the poor, such improvement was limited primarily to the insight that the potato and other root crops improved health in the winter and helped to prevent scurvy. The rich began to be aware of the harmful effects of their meat-ladened, wine-drowned meals.

The waning influence of Galen's medical teachings was another aspect of progress. Galen's Roman synthesis of ancient medical doctrines held that the four basic elements – air, fire, water, and earth – combine to produce in each person a complexion and a corresponding temperament. Foods were grouped into four categories appropriate for each complexion. Galen's notions dominated the dietary thinking of the seventeenth-century medical profession: "Galen said that the flesh of a hare preventeth fatness, causeth sleep and cleanseth the blood," and so on for a thousand things.

Conventional wisdom had also held, quite erroneously, that vegetables and fruits caused poor health. Vegetables were seen as "windy" and tending to cause fevers, and fruits were considered dangerous except in very small amounts. Similarly, butter, an excellent food rich in vitamin A, which the poor used on bread whenever they could, was regarded with great suspicion by the rich and the medical profession. It was believed bad for children because, according to typical opinion, it choked the "glands and capillaries" and made children "weakly, corpulent, big-belly'd, very subject to breakings-out, and to breed lice."

The growth of scientific experimentation in the seventeenth century led to a generally beneficial questioning of the old views. Haphazardly, by trial and error, and influenced by advances in chemistry, saner ideas developed. Experiments with salts led to the belief that foods were by nature either acid (all fruits and most vegetables) or alkaline (all meats). Doctors and early nutritionists came to believe that one key to good health was a *balance* of the two types.

An English doctor writing at the end of the century as the "Soldier's Friend" on "the means of preserving the health of military men" stated categorically that "ripe fruits, in moderate quantity, are wholesome; and, contrary to the vulgar prejudice, tend rather to prevent than to induce bowel complaints."[12] Excessive consumption of meat was identified by some medical men as a dangerous practice. Gout, the class hazard of the rich, was linked with overeating and lack of exercise. Thus, the eighteenth century saw increased understanding of the importance of a balanced diet

for proper health. Such awareness – and the potato – were no doubt important factors in the rise in life expectancy and the growth of Europe's population.

Not all changes in the eighteenth century were for the better. Bread began to change, most noticeably in England. Rising incomes and new tastes led to a shift from whole-meal black or brown bread to white bread made from finely ground and sifted flour. On the Continent such white bread was generally limited to the well-to-do. To the extent that the preferred wheaten flour was stone-ground and sifted for coarse particles only, white bread remained satisfactory. But the desire for "bread as white as snow" was already leading to a decline in nutritional value.

The coarser bran, which is necessary for roughage, and at least some of the germ, which darkened the bread but contained the grain's nutrients, were already being sifted out to some extent. Bakers in English cities added the chemical alum to their white loaves to make them smoother, whiter, and larger. In the nineteenth century, "improvements" in milling were to lead to the removal of almost all the bran and germ from the flour, leaving it perfectly white and perfectly reduced in nutritional value. The only saving grace in the sad deterioration of bread was that people began to eat less of it and therefore depended on it less.

Another sign of nutritional decline was the growing consumption of sweets in general and sugar in particular. Initially a luxury, sugar dropped rapidly in price, as slave-based production increased in the Americas, and it was much more widely used in the eighteenth century. This development probably led to an increase in cavities and to other ailments as well. Overconsumption of refined sugar can produce, paradoxically, low blood sugar (hypoglycemia) and, for some individuals at least, a variety of physical and mental ailments. Of course the greater or lesser poverty of the laboring poor saved most of them from the problems of the rich and well-to-do.

MEDICAL SCIENCE AND THE SICK

Advances in medical science played a very small part in improving the health and lengthening the lives of people in the eighteenth century. Such seventeenth-century advances as William Harvey's discovery of the circulation of blood were not soon translated into better treatment. The sick had to await the medical revolution of the later nineteenth century for much help from doctors.

Yet developments in medicine reflected the general thrust of the Enlightenment. The prevailing focus on discovering the laws of nature and on human problems, rather than on God and the heavens, gave rise to a great deal of research and experimentation. The century saw a remarkable rise in the number of doctors, and a high value was placed on their services. Thus when the great breakthroughs in knowledge came in the nineteenth century, they could be rapidly diffused and applied. Eighteenth-century medicine, in short, gave promise of a better human existence, but most of the realization lay far in the future.

THE MEDICAL PROFESSIONALS

Care of the sick was the domain of several competing groups – faith healers, apothecaries, surgeons, and physicians. Since the great majority of common ailments have a tendency to cure themselves, each group could point to successes and win adherents. When the doctor's treatment made the patient worse, as it often did, the original medical problem could always be blamed.

Faith healers, who had been one of the most important kinds of physicians in medieval Europe, remained active. They and their patients believed that demons and evil spirits caused disease by lodging in people and that the proper treatment was to exorcise or drive out the offending devil. Good Christians became exorcists: had not Jesus himself cured by casting out devils? The men and women who cast out devils had to be careful to keep their mouths closed, for the devil could jump from the patient's mouth into their own. By the eighteenth century, this demonic view of disease was still common among the poor, especially in the countryside, as was faith in the healing power of religious relics, prayer, and the laying on of hands. Faith healing was particularly effective in the treatment of mental disorders like hysteria and depression, where the link between attitude and illness is most direct.

Apothecaries, or pharmacists, sold a vast number of herbs, drugs, and patent medicines for every conceivable "temperament and distemper." Early pharmacists were seldom regulated, and they frequently diagnosed as freely as the doctors whose prescriptions they filled. Their prescriptions were incredibly complex – a hundred or more drugs might be included in a single prescription – and often very expensive. Some of the drugs undoubtedly worked: strong laxatives were given to the rich for their constipated bowels. The apothecary regularly and profitably administered enemas for the same purpose. Indeed, the medical profession continued to believe that regular "purging" of the bowels was essential for good health and the treatment of illness. Much purging was harmful, however, and only bloodletting for the treatment of disease was more effective in speeding patients to their graves.

Drugs were prescribed and concocted in a helter-skelter way. With so many different drugs being combined, it was impossible to isolate cause and effect. Nor was there any standardization. A complicated prescription filled by ten different pharmacists would result in ten different preparations with different medical properties.

Surgeons competed vigorously with barbers and "bone benders," the forerunners of chiropractors. The eighteenth-century surgeon (and patient) labored in the face of incredible difficulties. Almost all operations were performed without any pain killer, for anesthesia was believed too dangerous. The terrible screams of people whose limbs were being sawed off shattered hospitals and battlefields. Such operations were common, because a surgeon faced with an extensive wound sought to obtain a plain surface that he could cauterize with fire. Thus, if a person broke an arm or a leg and the bone stuck out, off came the limb. Many patients died from the agony and shock of such operations.

Surgery was also performed in the midst of filth and dirt. There simply was no knowledge of bacteriology and the nature of infection. The simplest wound treated by a surgeon festered, often fatally. In fact, surgeons encouraged wounds to fester in the belief — a remnant of Galen's theory — that the pus was beneficially removing the base portions of the body.

Physicians, the fourth major group, were trained like surgeons. They were apprenticed in their teens to a practicing physician for several years of on-the-job training. This training was then rounded out with hospital work or some university courses. To their credit, physicians in the eighteenth century

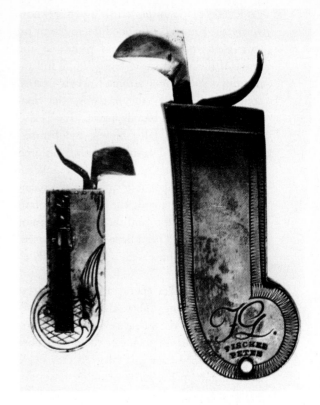

KNIVES FOR BLOODLETTING *In the eighteenth century doctors continued to use these diabolical instruments to treat almost every illness, with disastrous results. (Courtesy, World Heritage Museum. Photo: Caroline Buckler)*

were increasingly willing to experiment with new methods, but the hand of Galen lay heavily upon them. Bloodletting was still considered a medical cure-all. It was the way "bad blood," the cause of illness, was removed and the balance of humors necessary for good health restored.

According to a physician practicing medicine in Philadelphia in 1799, "No operation of surgery is so frequently necessary as bleeding.... But though practiced by midwives, gardeners, blacksmiths, etc., very few know when it is proper." The good doctor went on to explain that bleeding was proper at the onset of all inflammatory fevers, in all inflammations, and for "asthma, sciatic pains, coughs, head-aches, rheumatisms, the apoplexy, epilepsy, and bloody fluxes." It was also necessary after all falls, blows, and bruises. The doctor warned against bleeding children with leeches, the common practice. With leeches, it was impossible to know the quantity of blood taken, and "the bleeding is often very difficult to stop, and the wounds are not easily healed."[13] With a little care, he advised, a child could be bled with a knife as easily as an adult.

Physicians, like apothecaries, laid great stress on purging. They also generally believed that disease was caused by bad odors, and for this reason they carried canes whose heads contained ammonia salts. As they made their rounds in the filthy, stinking hospitals, physicians held their canes to their noses to protect themselves from illness.

While ordinary physicians were bleeding, apothecaries purging, surgeons sawing, and faith healters praying, the leading medical thinkers were attempting to pull together and assimilate all the information and misinformation they had been accumulating. The attempt was ambitious: to systematize medicine around simple, basic principles, as Newton had done in physics. But the schools of thought resulting from such speculation and theorizing did little to improve medical care. Proponents of animism explained life and disease in terms of *anima,* the "sensitive soul," which they believed was present throughout the body and prevented its decay and self-destruction. Another school, vitalism, stressed "the vital principle," which inhabited all parts of the body. Vitalists tried to classify diseases systematically.

More interesting was the homeopathic system of Samuel Hahnemann of Leipzig. Hahnemann believed that very small doses of drugs that produce certain symptoms in a healthy person will cure a sick person with those symptoms. This theory was probably preferable to most eighteenth-century treatments, in that it was a harmless alternative to the extravagant and often fatal practices of bleeding, purging, drug taking, and induced vomiting. The patient gained confidence, and the body had at least a fighting chance of recovering. Hahnemann engaged in bitter debate with the apothecaries, whom he accused of incompetence and greed with their expensive treatments.

HOSPITALS

Hospitals were terrible throughout most of the eighteenth century. There was no isolation of patients. Operations were performed in the patient's bed. The nurses were old, ignorant, greedy, and often drunk women. Fresh air was considered harmful, and infections of every kind were rampant. Diderot's article in the *Encyclopedia* on the Hôtel-Dieu in Paris, the "richest and most terrifying of all French hospitals," vividly describes normal conditions of the 1770s:

Imagine a long series of communicating wards filled with sufferers of every kind of disease who are sometimes packed three, four, five or even six into a bed, the living alongside the dead and dying, the air polluted by this mass of unhealthy bodies, passing pestilential germs of their afflictions from one to the other, and the spectacle of suffering and agony on every hand. That is the Hôtel-Dieu.

The result is that many of these poor wretches come out with diseases they did not have when they went in, and often pass them on to the people they go back to live with. Others are half-cured and

HOSPITAL LIFE *Patients crowded into hospitals like this one in Hamburg in 1746 had little chance of recovery. A priest by the window administers last rites, while in the center a surgeon coolly saws off the leg of a man who has received no anesthesia. (Germanisches Nationalmuseum, Nuremberg)*

spend the rest of their days in an invalidism as hard to bear as the illness itself; and the rest perish, except for the fortunate few whose strong constitutions enable them to survive.[14]

No wonder the poor of Paris hated hospitals and often saw confinement there as a plot to kill paupers.

In the last years of the century, the humanitarian concern already reflected in Diderot's description of the Hôtel-Dieu led to a movement for hospital reform through western Europe. Efforts were made to improve ventilation and eliminate filth, on the grounds that bad air caused disease. The theory was wrong, but the results were beneficial, since the spread of infection was somewhat reduced.

MENTAL ILLNESS

Mental hospitals too were incredibly savage institutions. The customary treatment for mental illness was bleeding and cold water, administered more to maintain discipline than to effect a cure. Violent persons were chained to the wall and forgotten. A breakthrough of sorts occurred in the 1790s, when William Tuke founded the first humane sanatorium in

England. In Paris an innovative warden, Philippe Pinel, took the chains off the mentally disturbed in 1793 and tried to treat them as patients rather than prisoners.

In the eighteenth century, there were all sorts of wildly erroneous ideas about mental illness. One was that moonlight caused madness, a belief reflected in the word *lunatic* – someone harmed by lunar light. Another mid-eighteenth-century theory, which lasted until at least 1914, was that masturbation caused madness, not to mention acne, epilepsy, and premature ejaculation.

The initial form of this theory was the work of a Swiss doctor, Samuel Tissot. In 1758, Tissot argued that semen was

the Essential Oil of the animal liquors . . . the dissipation whereof leaves the other humors weak. . . . The seminal liquor has so great an influence upon the corporeal powers that . . . the physicians of all ages have been unanimously of the opinion that the loss of an ounce of this humor would weaken more than that of forty ounces of blood.[15]

This being the case, parents, religious institutions, and schools waged relentless war on masturbation by males, although they were curiously uninterested in female masturbation. In the nineteenth century this misguided idea was to reach its greatest height, resulting in increasingly drastic medical treatment. Doctors ordered their "patients" to wear mittens, fitted them with wooden braces between the knees, or simply tied them up in straitjackets.

Medical Experiments and Research

In the second half of the eighteenth century, medicine in general turned in a more practical and experimental direction. Some of the experimentation was creative quackery involving the recently discovered phenomenon of electricity. One magnificent quack, James Graham of London, opened a great hall filled with the walking sticks, crutches, eyeglasses, and ear trumpets of supposedly cured patients, which he kept as symbols of his victory over disease. Great glass globes, mysterious sphinxes, and the rich perfumes of burning incense awaited all who entered. Graham's principal treatment involved his Celestial Bed, which stood on forty pillars of rich glass and was decorated with magnets and electrical devices. Graham claimed that by sleeping in it youths would keep their good looks, their elders would be rejuvenated, and couples would have beautiful, healthy children. The fee for a single night in the Medico-Magnetico-Musico-Electrical Bed was £100 – a great sum of money.

The rich could buy expensive treatments, but the prevalence of quacks and the general lack of knowledge meant they often got little for their money. Because so many treatments were harmful, the poor were probably much less deprived by their almost total lack of access to medical care than one might think.

Renewed experimentation and the intensified search for solutions to human problems also led to some real advances in medicine after 1750, although most were still modest compared to the advances of the nineteenth and twentieth centuries. The eighteenth century's greatest medical triumph was the conquest of smallpox.

With the progressive decline of bubonic plague, smallpox became the most terrible of the infectious diseases. In the words of the historian Thomas Macaulay, "smallpox was always present, filling the churchyard with corpses, tormenting with constant fears all whom it had not stricken." In the seventeenth century, one in every four deaths in the British Isles was due to smallpox, and it is estimated that 60 million Europeans died of it in

THE FIGHT AGAINST SMALLPOX *This Russian illustration dramatically urges parents to inoculate their children against smallpox. The good father's healthy youngsters flee from their ugly and infected playmates, who hold their callous father responsible for their shameful fate. (Yale Medical Library)*

the eighteenth century. Fully 80 percent of the population was stricken at some point in life, and 25 percent of the total population was left permanently scarred. If ever a human problem cried out for a humane solution, it was smallpox.

The first step in the conquest of this killer came in the early eighteenth century. An English aristocrat whose great beauty had been marred by the pox, Lady Mary Wortley Montague, learned about the practice of inoculation in the Ottoman Empire while her husband was serving as British ambassador

there. She had her own son successfully inoculated in Constantinople, and was instrumental in spreading the practice in England after her return in 1722.

Inoculation against smallpox had long been practiced in the Middle East. The skin was deliberately broken, and a small amount of matter taken from the pustule of a smallpox victim was applied. The person thus contracted a mild case of smallpox that gave lasting protection against further attack. Inoculation was risky. Some of the very first to undergo it in England were felons sentenced to death, who were granted a pardon in return for inoculation. All these unsung heroes recovered and escaped hanging. Generally, about one person in fifty died from inoculation. Soon it was discovered that people who had been inoculated were just as infectious as those who had caught the disease by chance. Inoculated people thus spread the disease, and the practice of inoculation against smallpox was widely condemned in the 1730s.

Success in overcoming this problem in British colonies led the British College of Physicians in 1754 to strongly advocate inoculation. The procedure became complicated, however, involving elaborate and expensive preparatory treatment with bleeding, purging, blisters, and so on. Doctors reaped fine fees and large fortunes, and only people of substantial means could afford inoculation.

A successful search for cheaper methods led to something approaching mass inoculation in England in the 1760s. One specialist treated seventeen thousand patients and only five died. Both the danger and the cost had been reduced, and deadly smallpox struck all classes less frequently. On the Continent, the well-to-do were also inoculated, beginning with royal families like those of Maria Theresa and Catherine the Great. The practice then spread to the middle classes. Smallpox inoculation played some part in the decline of the death rate at the end of the century and the increase in population.

The final breakthrough against smallpox came at the end of the century. Edward Jenner (1749–1823), a talented country doctor, noted that in the English countryside there was a longstanding belief that dairy maids who had contracted cowpox did not get smallpox. Cowpox produces sores on the cow's udder and on the hands of the milker. The sores resemble those of smallpox, but the disease is mild and not contagious.

For eighteen years Jenner practiced a kind of Baconian science, carefully collecting data on protection against smallpox by cowpox. Finally, in 1796, he performed his first vaccination on a young boy, using matter taken from a milkmaid with cowpox. Two months later he inoculated the boy with smallpox pus, but the disease did not take. In the next two years twenty-three successful vaccinations were performed, and in 1798 Jenner published his findings. There was some skepticism and hostility, but after Austrian medical authorities replicated Jenner's results, the new method of treatment spread rapidly. Smallpox soon declined to the point of disappearance in Europe and then throughout the world. Jenner eventually received prizes of £30,000 from the British government for his great discovery, a fitting recompense for a man who gave an enormous gift to humanity and helped lay the foundation for the rise of the science of immunology in the nineteenth century. The struggle against fate and death, against the unknown but not unknowable, had won a great victory.

In recent years imaginative research has greatly increased the specialist's understanding of ordinary life and social patterns in the past. The human experience, as recounted by historians, has become richer and more meaningful, and many mistaken ideas have fallen. This has been particularly true of eighteenth-century, preindustrial Europe. The intimacies of family life, the contours of women's history and of childhood, and vital problems of medicine and nutrition are emerging from obscurity. Nor is this all. A deeper, truer understanding of the life of Europe's common people can shed light on the great economic and political developments of longstanding concern, as we shall see in Chapters 26 and 27.

1. Quoted by J. M. Beattie, "The Criminality of Women in Eighteenth-Century England," *Journal of Social History* 8 (Summer 1975):86.

2. W. L. Langer, "Infanticide: A Historical Survey," *History of Childhood Quarterly* 1 (Winter 1974):357.

3. Quoted by R. Cobb, *The Police and the People: French Popular Protest, 1789–1820,* Clarendon Press, Oxford, 1970, p. 238.

4. Quoted by E. A. Wrigley, *Population and History,* McGraw-Hill, New York, 1969, p. 127.

5. Quoted in D. S. Landes, ed., *The Rise of Capitalism,* Macmillan, New York, 1966, pp. 56–57.

6. See L. A. Tilly, J. W. Scott, and M. Cohen, "Women's Work and European Fertility Patterns," *Journal of Interdisciplinary History* 6 (Winter 1976):447–476.

7. J. Michelet, *The People,* trans. with an introduction by J. P. McKay, University of Illinois Press, Urbana, 1973 (original publication, 1846), pp. 38–39.

8. J. Brownlow, *The History and Design of the Foundling Hospital,* London, 1868, p. 7.

9. Quoted by B. W. Lorence, "Parents and Children in Eighteenth-Century Europe," *History of Childhood Quarterly* 2 (Summer 1974):1–2.

10. Ibid., pp. 13, 16.

11. J. C. Drummond and A. Wilbraham, *The Englishman's Food: A History of Five Centuries of English Diet,* 2nd ed., Jonathan Cape, London, 1958, p. 75.

12. Ibid., p. 235.

13. Quoted by L. S. King, *The Medical World of the Eighteenth Century,* University of Chicago Press, Chicago, 1958, p. 320.

14. Quoted by R. Sand, *The Advance to Social Medicine,* Staples Press, London, 1952, pp. 86–87.

15. Quoted by R. P. Neuman, "Masturbation, Madness, and the Modern Concepts of Childhood and Adolescence," *Journal of Social History* 8 (Spring 1975):2.

Although often ignored in many general histories of the Western world, social topics of the kind considered in this chapter flourish in specialized journals today. The articles cited in the Notes are typical of the exciting work being done, and the reader is strongly advised to take time to look through recent volumes of some leading journals: *Journal of Social History, Past and Present, History of Childhood Quarterly,* and *Journal of Interdisciplinary History.* In addition, the number of book-length studies has begun to expand rapidly.

Among general introductions to the history of the family, women, and children, E. A. Wrigley, *Population and History* (1969), is excellent. P. Laslett, *The World We Have Lost* (1965), is an exciting pioneering investigation of England before the Industrial Revolution, though some of his conclusions have been weakened by further research. Lawrence Stone, *The Family, Sex and Marriage in England, 1500–1800* (1977), is a brilliant general interpretation, and L. Tilly and J. Scott, *Women, Work and Family* (1978), is excellent. P. Ariès, *Centuries of Childhood: A Social History of Family Life* (1962), is another stimulating study. E. Shorter, *The Making of the Modern Family* (1975), is an all-too-lively and rather controversial interpretation. All four works are highly recommended. T. Rabb and R. I. Rothberg, eds., *The Family in History* (1973), is a good collection of articles dealing with both Europe and the United States. A. MacFarlane, *The Family Life of Ralph Josselin* (1970), is a brilliant re-creation of the intimate family circle of a seventeenth-century English clergyman who kept a detailed diary; MacFarlane's *Origins of English Individualism: The Family, Property and Social Transition* (1978) is a major work. I. Pinchbeck and M. Hewitt, *Children in English Society* (1973), is a good introduction. E. Flexner has written a fine biography on the early feminist Mary Wollstonecraft (1972). Various aspects of sexual relationships are treated imaginatively by M. Foucault, *The History of Sexuality* (1981), and R. Wheaton and T. Hareven, eds., *Family and Sexuality in French History* (1980).

J. Burnett, *A History of the Cost of Living* (1969), has a great deal of interesting information about what people spent their money on in the past and complements the fascinating work of J. C. Drummond and A. Wilbraham, *The Englishman's Food: A History of Five Centuries of English Diet* (1958). J. Knyveton, *Diary of a Surgeon in the Year 1751–1752* (1937), gives a contemporary's unforgettable picture of both eighteenth-century medicine and social customs. Good introductions to the evolution of medical practices are B. Ingles, *History of Medicine* (1965); O. Bettmann, *A Pictorial History of Medicine* (1956); and H. Haggard's old but interesting *Devils, Drugs, and Doctors* (1929). W. Boyd, *History of Western Education* (1966), is a standard survey, which may be usefully supplemented by an important article by L. Stone, "Literacy and Education in England, 1640–1900," *Past and Present* 42 (February 1969):69–139. M. D. George, *London Life in the Eighteenth Century* (1965), is a delightfully written book, while L. Chevalier, *Labouring Classes and Dangerous Classes* (1973), is a keen analysis of the poor people of Paris in a slightly later period. G. Rudé, *The Crowd in History, 1730–1848* (1964), is an innovative effort to see politics and popular protest from below. An important series edited by Robert Forster and Orest Ranuum considers neglected social questions such as diet, abandoned children, and deviants, as does Peter Burke's excellent study, *Popular Culture in Early Modern Europe* (1978). Finally, J. Howard, *State of the Prisons,* first published in 1777 and reissued in 1929, takes one on an exhaustive tour of European jails in the eighteenth century and shows the beginning of concern for humanitarian reform of unbelievably harsh penal conditions.

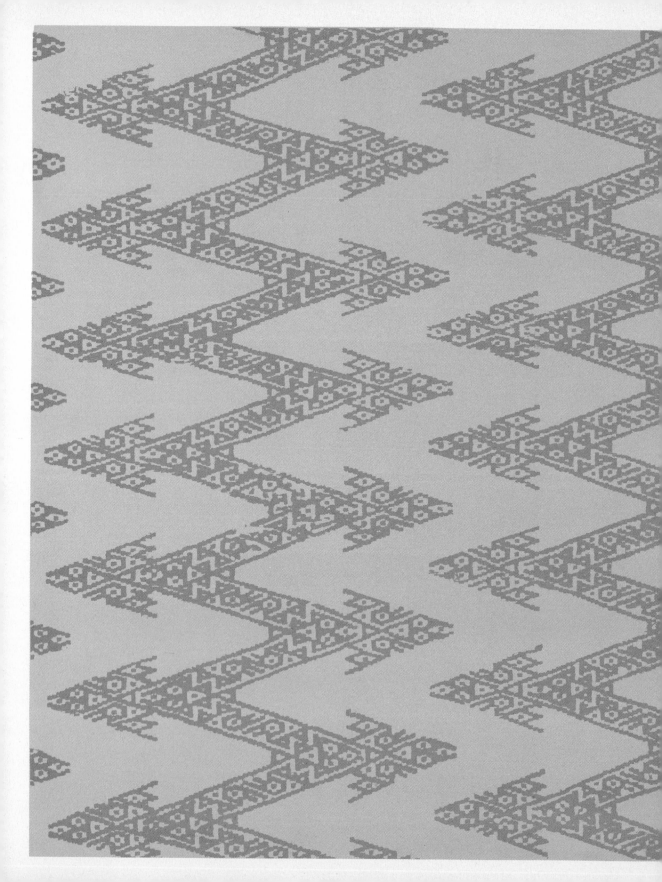

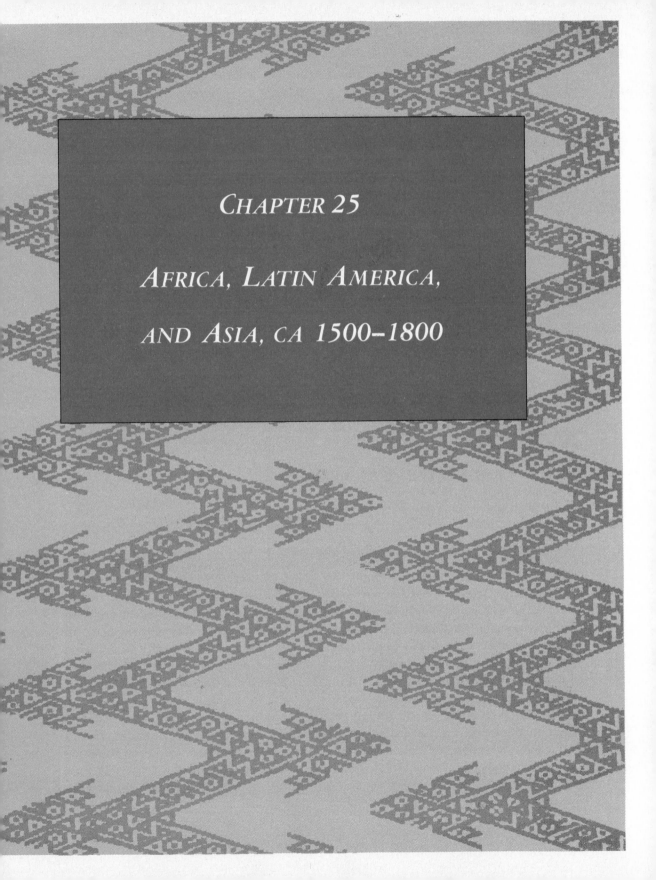

CHAPTER 25

AFRICA, LATIN AMERICA, AND ASIA, CA 1500–1800

WHEN THE PORTUGUESE admiral Alfonso de Albuquerque attacked Malacca in present-day Indonesia in 1511, he justified the assault on the grounds of "the great service we shall perform to our Lord in casting Moors [Muslims] out of the country and quenching the fire of the sect of Mohamet . . . and the service we shall render to King Don Manuel in taking this city because it is the source of all the spiceries and drugs." Religion provided the pretext for European overseas expansion; wealth was the actual motive, and European seapower offered the means of reaching all parts of the globe. Seapower brought Europeans into contact for the first time with societies in sub-Saharan Africa, India, China, and Japan. Between 1500 and 1800, the business of discovery coincided with the discovery of business possibilities.

African states and societies represented a wide variety of languages, cultures, and kinds of economic and political development. European intrusion in Africa led to the transatlantic slave trade, one of the great forced migrations in world history. Meanwhile the Mughal leader Babur and his successors conquered the Indian subcontinent, and Mughal rule inaugurated a period of radical administrative reorganization and the flowering of intellectual and architectural creativity. Indian spices and cloth attracted European businessmen, and economic penetration eventually gave way to political dominion. In China, the Ming dynasty replaced the Yüan dynasty of the Mongols and was in turn replaced by the Ch'ing, beginning a long period of peace, relative prosperity, and population expansion. Under the Ch'ing, the Chinese empire reached its greatest territorial extent. Vast public monuments rose, and literary and artistic creativity reached an unparalleled apogee. The Japanese islands, united by the Tokugawa shogunate, experienced further evolution of the feudal military aristocracy; although Japan developed in near-total isolation from outside influences, its sociopolitical system bore some striking similarities to medieval European feudalism.

These changes suggest a number of questions. What economic, political, and demographic effects did foreign trade, and especially the slave trade, have on African kingdoms and societies? How did Muslim governmental reform and artistic inspiration affect the dominant Hindu population in India? What political and social conditions in India enabled the British to gain power there? What features characterized the governments of the Ming and Ch'ing in China and the Tokugawa shogunate in Japan? How were Chinese and Japanese societies affected by agricultural and commercial developments? What ethical and religious values influenced Asian societies' subsequent attitudes and behavior toward Westerners? This chapter will attempt to answer these questions.

THE SOUTH AMERICAN HOLOCAUST

About 200,000 Spaniards emigrated to the New World in the sixteenth century. Soldiers demobilized from the Spanish and Italian campaigns, adventurers and drifters unable to find work in Spain, they did not intend to work in the New World either. After having assisted in the conquest of the Aztecs of central Mexico and the subjugation of the Incas in Peru, these drifters wanted to settle down and become a ruling class. In the temperate grazing areas they carved out vast estates and imported Spanish sheep, cattle, and horses for the kinds of ranching with which they were familiar. In the coastal tropics, unsuited for grazing animals, the Spanish erected huge sugar plantations. Columbus had introduced sugar into the West Indies; Cortez into Mexico. Sugar was a great luxury in Europe, and demand for it was high. Around 1550 the discovery of silver at Zacatecas and Guanajuato in Mexico and Potosi in present-day Bolivia stimulated silver rushes. How were the cattle ranches, sugar plantations, and silver mines to be worked? Obviously, by the Indians.

The Spanish quickly established the *encomiendas* system, whereby the Crown granted the conquerors the right to employ groups of Indians in a town or area as agricultural or mining laborers or as tribute-payers. Theoretically, the Spanish were forbidden to enslave the Indian natives; in actuality, the encomiendas were a legalized form of slavery. The European demand for sugar, tobacco, and silver prompted the colonists to expoit the Indians mercilessly. Unaccustomed to forced labor, especially in the blistering heat of tropical cane fields or the dark, dank, and dangerous mines, Indians died like flies. Recently scholars have tried to reckon the death rate of the Amerindians in the sixteenth century. Some historians maintain that when Columbus landed at Hispaniola (modern Haiti and the Dominican Republic) in 1492, the island's population stood at 100,000; in 1570, 300 people survived. The Indian population of Peru is estimated to have fallen from 1.3 million in 1570 to 600,000 in 1620; central Mexico had 25.3 million Indians in 1519 and 1 million in 1605.[1] Some demographers dispute these figures, but all scholars agree that the decline of the native Indian population in all of Spanish-occupied America amounted to a catastrophe greater in scale than any that has occurred even in the twentieth century.

What were the causes of this devastating slump in population?

Students of the history of medicine have suggested the best explanation: disease. The major cause of widespread epidemics is migration, and those peoples isolated longest from other societies suffer most. Contact with disease builds up bodily resistance. At the beginning of the sixteenth century, American Indians probably had the unfortunate distinction of longer isolation from the rest of humankind that any other people on earth. With little or no resistance to diseases brought from the Old World, the inhabitants of the highlands of Mexico and Peru, especially, fell victim to smallpox. According to one expert, smallpox caused "in all likelihood the most severe single loss of aboriginal population that ever occurred."[2]

Disease was the prime cause of the Indian holocaust, but the Spaniards contributed heavily to the Indians' death rate.[3] According to the Franciscan missionary Bartolomé de Las Casas, the Spanish maliciously murdered thousands:

This infinite multitude of people [the Indians] was so created by God, as that they were without fraud, without subtilty or malice, to their natural Governours most faithful and obedient. Toward the Spaniards whom they serve, patient, meek and peaceful, and who laying all contentious and tumultuous thoughts aside, live without any hatred or desire of revenge; the people are most delicate and tender, enjoying such a feeble constitution of body as does not permit them to endure labour, so that the Children of Princes and great persons here, are not more nice and delicate then the Children of the meanest Country-man in that place. The Nation is very poor and indigent, possessing little, and by reason that they gape not after temporal goods, neither proud nor ambitious.

To these quiet Lambs, endued with such blessed qualities, came the Spaniards like most c(r)uel Tygres, Wolves and Lions, enrag'd with a sharp and tedious hunger; for these forty years past, minding nothing else but the slaughter of these un-

fortunate wretches, whom with divers kinds of torments neither seen nor heard of before, they have so cruelly and inhumanely butchered, that of three millions of people which Hispaniola *it self did contain, there are left remaining alive scarce three hundred persons. And for the Island of* Cuba, *which contains as much ground in length, as from* Valladolid *to* Rome; *it lies wholly desert, until'd and ruin'd. The Islands of St. John and Jamaica lie waste and desolate. The Lucayan Islands neighbouring toward the North upon Cuba and Hispaniola, being above Sixty or thereabouts with those Islands that are vulgarly called the islands of the Gyants, of which that which is least fertile is more fruitful than the King of Spains Garden of Sevil [Seville], being situated in a pure and temperate air, are now totally unpeopled and destroyed; the inhabitants thereof amounting to above 5,000,000 souls, partly killed, and partly forced away to work in other places.*[4]

Las Casas's remarks concentrate on the tropical lowlands, but the death rate in the highlands was also staggering.

The Christian missionaries who accompanied the conquistadors and settlers – Franciscans, Dominicans, and Jesuits – played an important role in converting the Indians to Christianity, teaching them European methods of agriculture, and inculcating loyalty to the Spanish Crown. In terms of numbers of people baptized, missionaries enjoyed phenomenal success, though the depth of the Indians' understanding of Christianity remains debatable. Missionaries, especially Las Casas, asserted that the Indians had human rights, and through Las Casas's persistent pressure the emperor Charles V abolished the worst abuses of the encomiendas system.

Some scholars offer a psychological explanation for the colossal death rate of the Indians: they simply lost the will to survive. Their gods appeared to have abandoned them

to a world over which they had no control. Hopelessness, combined with frightfully abusive treatment and excessive overwork, pushed many men to suicide, many women to abortion or infanticide. Whatever its precise causes, the astronomically high death rate created a severe labor shortage in Spanish America. As early as 1511, king Ferdinand of Spain observed that the Indians seemed to be "very frail" and that "one black could do the work of four Indians."[5] Thus was born an absurd myth and the massive importation of black slaves from Africa.

AFRICAN KINGDOMS AND SOCIETIES (CA 1500-1800)

It is said that the darkest thing about Africa has always been our ignorance of it. Although Africa's relationship with the Western world stretches back a very long time, only recently have historians, economists, and anthropologists begun to ask critical questions about African societies in early modern times. Without Africa, European and North and Latin American societies would not have developed as they did socially, economically, politically, or culturally. Thus the study of early African societies is essential both for its own sake and for an understanding of Europe and the Western Hemisphere. What kinds of states and societies existed in Africa during the period that Western historians call early modern times? How did the slave trade operate? What were the geographical and societal origins of the slaves shipped to the Americas and to Asia?

SENEGAMBIA AND BENIN

In the mid-fifteenth century, Africa consisted of a wide variety of kingdoms and states –

political entities ruled by princes who governed defined areas through bureaucratic hierarchies — and of societies that lacked political structure but were held together by family or kinship ties.

A number of kingdoms flourished along the two-thousand-mile West coast between Senegambia and modern Cameroun. Because much of the coastal region is covered by tropical rain forest, in contrast to the Western Sudan (see Map 25.1 on page 889), it is called the West African Forest region. The Senegambian states in the north possessed a homogeneous culture and a common history. For centuries Senegambia — named for its two rivers — had served as an important entrepôt for desert caravan contact with the Islamic civilization of North Africa and the Middle East. Through the slave trade, Senegambia contributed more than any other African region to the repopulation of the New World between 1450 and about 1650. From the late seventeenth century, when the Atlantic slave trade became a significant feature of African commerce, Senegambia had important maritime contacts with Europe and the Americas. Thus Senegambia felt the impact of Islamic culture from the north and of European influences from the maritime West.

The medieval kingdoms of Ghana and Mali (pages 539–547) had incorporated parts of Senegambia, but by 1450 several northern states, such as Ñomi, Ñaani, Wuuli, Badibu, and Wolof, were completely independent; southern states like Kaabu and Kantora remained under Mali's hegemony. Mali's influence disintegrated after 1450, giving rise to a number of successor kingdoms that were independent but connected to one another through family ties. Stronger states rose and temporarily exercised power over weaker ones.

Scholars are still exploring the social and political structures of the various Senegambian states. The peoples of Senegambia spoke Wolof, Seerer, and Pulaar, which are all members of the West African language group. Both the Wolof and Seerer had clearly defined classes: royalty, nobility, warriors, peasants, low-caste artisans such as blacksmiths and leather workers, and slaves. Slaves consisted of those pawned for debt, house servants who could not be sold, and those acquired through war or purchase. Senegambian slavery, though it varied from society to society, bore little resemblance to Western slavery. Neither plantation nor chattel slavery, it was instead a basic part of complex African social structures. Many slaves were not considered property that could be bought and sold, and some slaves served as royal advisors and enjoyed great power and prestige.[6]

Among the Wolof the nobility elected the king, who immediately acquired authority and a special religious charisma. He commanded contingents of soldier-slaves and appointed the village chiefs. Kings gained their revenues from the chiefs, from merchants, and from taxes on defeated peoples.[7] The Wolof had a well-defined governmental hierarchy. Among the stateless societies of Senegambia, where kinship and lineage groups tended to fragment communities, age-grade systems evolved. Age-grades were groups of men and women whom the society initiated into adulthood at the same time. Age-grades cut across family ties, created community-wide loyalties, and provided a means of local law enforcement, since the group was mutually responsible for the behavior of all its members.

The typical Senegambian community was a small self-supporting agricultural village of closely related families. Custom assigned a high value to cultivation of the land, the shared objective of the group; work was understood more in terms of social relationships than as labor in the abstract. Fields were cut from the surrounding forest, and the average farm of six or eight acres supported a moderate-sized family. Often the family worked the land for a common harvest; sometimes individuals had their own private fields. Millet and sorghum were the staple grains in northern Senegambia; further south, forest dwellers cultivated yams, often as big as a man's arm, as a staple. Senegambians supplemented their diet with plantain, beans, and bananas. Fish, oysters, small game such as rabbits and monkeys provided protein. Along the Guinea coast rice was the basic cereal, and okra, onions, melons, and pepper spiced the regular diet. Frequent fairs in neighboring villages served as markets for the exchange of produce and opportunities for outside news and social diversion. As a distinguished scholar has put it, "Life was simple, government largely limited to the settlement of disputes by family heads or elders, the basic economy scarcely more than the production and consumption of food, social life centered on the ceremony accompanying birth, death, and family alliance, recreation preoccupied with the eternal round of visit and gossip which were the main pursuits of leisure time."[8]

The fifteenth and sixteenth centuries saw the emergence of the great forest kingdom of Benin in what is now southern Nigeria. Although scholars still know little about Benin's origins, its history seems to have been characterized by a power struggle between the king and the nobility that neither side ever completely won. An elaborate court ceremonial emerged exalting the position of the *oba*, or king, and lending stability to the state. In the later fifteenth century, the *oba* Ewuare played off his palace chiefs against the village chiefs and thereby maintained a balance of power. A great warrior, Ewuare strengthened his army and pushed Benin's borders as far as

MAP 25.1   WEST AFRICAN KINGDOMS AND SLAVE TRADE, CA 1500–1800   Consider the role that rivers and other geographical factors played in the development of the West African slave trade. Why would Luanda and Benguela be the logical Portuguese source for slaves?

the Niger river on the east, westward into Yoruba country, and south to the Atlantic (see Map 25.1). During the late sixteenth and early seventeenth centuries the office of *oba* evolved from a warrior kingship to a position of spiritual leadership.

At its height in the late sixteenth century, Benin controlled a vast territory, and European visitors described a strong and sophisticated society. The capital, Benin City,

was a stronghold twenty-five miles in circumference, protected by walls and natural defenses, containing an elaborate royal palace and neatly laid-out houses with verandas and balustrades, and divided by broad avenues and smaller intersecting streets. The power of the oba was apparent in his wealth, his divinity, his domination over commercial transactions, and his large and lavish court. In this prosperous society, the wealthier classes dressed and lived very well. Beef, mutton, chicken, and yams were staples, while the less well-to-do made do with yams, dried fish, beans and bananas.[9]

Visitors also noted that Benin City was kept scrupulously clean and had no beggars, and that public security was so effective that theft was unknown.

Beginning in 1485 the Portuguese and other Europeans appeared in Benin in pursuit of trade. A small exchange in pepper and slaves developed, but never acquired importance in the Benin economy. Nor did the Portuguese have much success in converting the staunchly animistic people to Christianity. Europe's impact on Benin was minimal. In the late seventeenth century, Benin's tributary

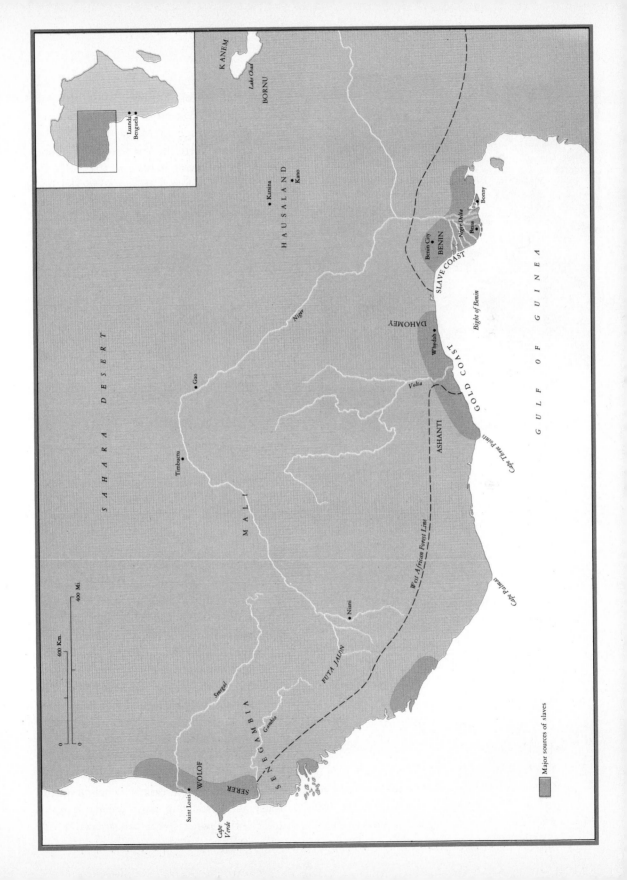

KANEM

Lake Chad

BORNU

Luanda
Benguela

SAHARA DESERT

HAUSALAND

Katsina
Kano

Niger

Benin City
BENIN

Benin City

Niger Delta
Brass
Bonny

SLAVE COAST

Bight of Benin

GULF OF GUINEA

DAHOMEY

Whydah

Gao

Volta

GOLD COAST

Cape Three Points

Timbuctu

ASHANTI

MALI

West African Forest Line

Niani

Cape Palmas

400 Mi.

400 Km.

FUTA JALON

Senegal

SENEGAMBIA

Gambia

WOLOF

SERER

Saint Louis

Cape Verde

Major sources of slaves

THE OBA OF BENIN *The walls of the Oba's palace were decorated with bronze plaques that may date to the 16th-18th centuries. This plaque vividly conveys the Oba's power, majesty, and authority. The necklace (or choker) is his symbol of royalty. Attendants hold up his hands, while warriors raise shields over his head as sunshades. (Courtesy of Museum of Primitive Art, New York)*

states seceded and stronger neighbors nibbled at its frontiers. The exact reasons for Benin's decline in the eighteenth and nineteenth centuries remain uncertain.

THE SUDAN: SONGHAY, KANEM-BORNU, AND HAUSALAND

The kingdom of Songhay, a successor state of Ghana and Mali, dominated the whole Niger region of the western and central Sudan (see Map 25.1 on page 889). Muhammad Toure (1492–1528) completed the expansionist and administrative consolidation begun by his predecessors. A convert to Islam, Muhammad made a pilgrimage to Mecca; impressed by what he saw there, he tried to bring about greater centralization in his own territories. In addition to building a strong army and improving taxation procedures, he replaced local Songhay officials with more efficient Arab ones in an effort to substitute royal institutions for ancient kinship ties. Islamic institutions failed to take root in the countryside, however, and Muslim officials alienated the king from his people. His reforms were a failure. Nor was Muhammad able to ensure a peaceful succession. His death inaugurated a period of political instability that led to the slow disintegration of the Songhay kingdom. Beginning in 1582 the sultanate of Morocco pressed southward in search of a greater share of the trans-Saharan trade. The people of Songhay, lacking effective leadership and believing the desert to be a sure protection against invasion, took no defensive precautions. In 1591 a Moroccan army of three thousand soldiers equipped with European muskets – many of whom were slaves of European origin – crossed the Sahara and inflicted a crushing defeat on the Songhay at Tondibi. This battle spelled the end of the Songhay empire; a moderate-sized kingdom lingered on in the south for a century or so. Weak political units arose, but not until the eighteenth century did kingdoms able to exercise wide authority emerge again.

To the east of Songhay lay the kingdoms of Kanem-Bornu and Hausaland (see Map 25.1 on page 889). Under the dynamic military leader Idris Alooma (1571–1603), Kanem-Bornu subdued weaker peoples and gained jurisdiction over an extensive area. Well-drilled and equipped with firearms, camel-mounted cavalry and a standing army decimated warriors fighting with spears and arrows. Idris

Alooma perpetuated the feudal pattern of government in which lands were granted to able fighters in return for loyalty and the promise of future military assistance. Meanwhile agriculture occupied most people, peasants and slaves alike. Kanem-Bornu shared in the trans-Saharan trade, shipping eunuchs and young girls to North Africa in return for horses. A devout Muslim, Idris Alooma elicited high praise from Ibn Fartua, who wrote a history of his reign called *The Kanem Wars:*

So he made the pilgrimage and visited Taba [Medina] with delight . . . He was enriched by visiting the tomb of the pious Sahaba [the Companions of the Prophet], the chosen, the perfect ones . . .

Then he prepared to return to the kingdom of Bornu. When he reached the land called Barak [Wadi Barak, east of Lake Chad] he killed all the inhabitants who were warriors. They were strong but after this they became weak; they became conquered, where formerly they had been con- *querors. Among the benefits which God, the Most High, of His bounty conferred upon the Sultan [Idris Alooma] was the acquisition of Turkish musketeers and numerous household slaves who became skilled in firing muskets.*

Hence the Sultan was able to kill the people of Amsaka with muskets, and there was no need for other weapons, so that God gave him great victory by reason of his superiority in arms.

Among the most surprising of his acts was the stand he took against obscenity and adultery, so that no such thing took place openly in his time. Formerly the people had been indifferent to such offences, committed openly or secretly by day or night. In fact he was a power among his people and from him came their strength.

The Sultan was intent on the clear path laid down by the Qur'an . . . in all his affairs and actions.[10]

Idris Alooma built mosques at his capital city of N'gazargamu, and substituted Muslim courts and Islamic law for African tribunals and ancient customary law. His eighteenth-century successors lacked his vitality and military skills, however, and the empire declined.

Between Songhay and Kanem-Bornu were the lands of the Hausa. An agricultural people living in small villages, the Hausa grew millet, sorghum, barley, rice, cotton, livestock, and citrus fruit. Some Hausa merchants carried on a heavy trade in slaves and kola nuts with North African communities across the Sahara. Obscure trading posts evolved into important Hausa city-states like Katsina and Kano, through which Islamic influences entered the region. Kano and Katsina became Muslim intellectual centers, and in the fifteenth century attracted scholars from distant Timbuctu. The Muslim chronicler of the reign of king Muhammad Rimfa of Kano (1463-1499) records that Muhammad introduced the Muslim practices of purdah or wife-seclusion, of the *idal-fitr* or festival after the fast of Ramadan, and of assigning eunuchs to the high offices of state.[11] As in Songhay and Kanem-Bornu, however, Islam made no strong imprint on the mass of the Hausa people, however, until the nineteenth century.

ETHIOPIA

At the beginning of the sixteenth century, the powerful East African Christian kingdom of Ethiopia extended from Massawa in the north to the tributary states of Fatajar, Doaro, and Bali in the south (see Map 25.1 on page 889). The ruling Solomonid dynasty, however, faced serious troubles. Adal, a Muslim state along the southern base of the Red Sea, began incursions into Ethiopia, and in 1529 the Adal general Ahman ibn Ghazi inflicted a disastrous defeat on the Ethiopian emperor Lebna Dengel (1508-1540). Ahmad followed up his victory with systematic devastation of the land, destruction of many Ethiopian artistic and literary works, and the forced conversion of thousands to Islam. Lebna Dengel fled to the mountains and appealed to Portugal for assistance. The Portuguese, eager for a share in the wealth of the East African coast and interested in the conversion of Ethiopia to Roman Catholicism, responded with a force of musketeers. In 1541 they decisively defeated the Muslims near Lake Tana.

No sooner had the Muslim threat ended than Ethiopia encountered three more dangers. The Galla, Cushitic-speaking peoples, moved northward in great numbers, occupying portions of Harar, Shoa, and Amhara. The Ethiopians could not defeat them militarily, and the Galla were not interested in assimilation. For the next two centuries the two peoples lived together in an uneasy truce. Simultaneous with the Galla migrations, the Ottoman Turks seized Massawa and other coastal cities; the Ethiopian emperor could not dislodge them. Then the Jesuits arrived, anxious to capitalize on earlier Portuguese support, and attempted to force Roman Catholicism on a proud people whose form of Christianity long antedated the European version. The overzealous Jesuit missionary Alphonse Mendez tried to revamp the Ethiopian liturgy, rebaptize the people, and replace ancient Ethiopian customs and practices with Roman ones. Since Ethiopian national sentiment was closely tied up with Coptic Christianity, violent rebellion and anarchy ensued. In 1633 the Jesuit missionaries were expelled. For the next two centuries hostility to foreigners, weak political leadership, and regionalism characterized Ethiopia. Civil conflicts between Galla and Ethiopians erupted continually. The Coptic Church, though lacking strong authority, survived as the cornerstone of Ethiopian national identity.

THE SWAHILI CITY-STATES

The Swahili city-states on the east coast of Africa enjoyed a worldwide reputation for commercial prosperity in the late fifteenth century. Mogadishu, Mombasa, Kilwa, and Sofala continued their ancient trade with the Arabian and Persian Gulf ports, and also exchanged goods with Indonesia, India, and China. The Swahili cities traded ivory, gold, and slaves for Indian beads, Chinese silks, textiles, and porcelains. Kilwa dominated the lesser states, including Sofala through which poured gold from the inland mines. The cities' culture was cosmopolitan and their standard of living, based on inland agriculture, was very high.

The arrival of the Portuguese explorer Vasco da Gama (page 671) in 1498 spelled the end of the Swahili cities' independence. Da Gama wanted to build a Portuguese maritime empire in the Indian Ocean, and between 1502 and 1507 the southern ports of Kilwa, Zanzibar, and Sofala fell before Portuguese guns and became Portuguese tributary states. The better-fortified northern cities, such as Mogadishu, survived as important entrepôts for goods to India. But the Portuguese victory in the south proved hollow: rather than accept Portuguese commercial restrictions, the residents deserted the towns and their economies crumbled. Large numbers of Kilwa's people, for example, emigrated to northern cities. The flow of gold from inland mines to Sofala slowed to a trickle. Swahili passive resistance successfully prevented the Portuguese from gaining control of the local coastal trade.

Initially lured to the Indian Ocean by the spice trade, the Portuguese wanted a station on the East African coast. After the intermittent bombardment of several cities, Portugal finally won an administrative stronghold near

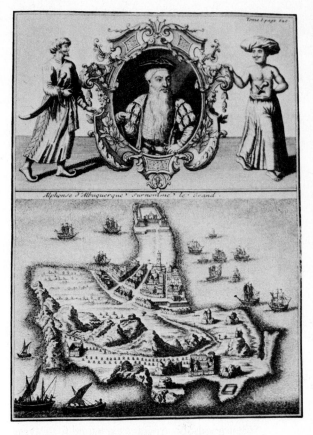

ALFONSO DE ALBUQUERQUE On his voyages to the Indies, the Portuguese admiral Alfonso de Albuquerque (1453–1515) seized Goa, making it the center of Portuguese power in India; took Malacca, extending Portuguese influence in southeast Asia; and captured Hormuz, ending Muslim control of the spice trade in the Arabian Sea. Two muscular Indians, symbolizing power and wealth, pay him homage. (Courtesy The Oliveira Lima Library, The Catholic University of America. Photo: Paul McKane, OSB)

Mombassa in 1589. Called Fort Jesus, it remained a Portuguese base for over a century. In the late seventeenth century, pressures from the northern European maritime powers – the Dutch, French, and English – aided greatly by the Arabs of Oman, combined with local African rebellions to bring about the collapse of Portuguese influence. Portuguese presence remained only at Mozambique in the far south.

AFRICA AND THE TRANSATLANTIC SLAVE TRADE

Until recently scholars advanced two basic theories about the Atlantic slave trade. One school of thought maintained that slavery had long existed in Africa, and that by transporting slaves to the New World Europeans rescued them from conditions of primitive barbarism; the slave trade and later Western colonialism started the process whereby Africa entered the modern world of the nineteenth and twentieth centuries. Other scholars held that African kingdoms had had well-developed civilizations since the time of the Egyptian pharoahs, civilizations that the slave trade destroyed; moreover, the slave trade was itself a form of barbarism. New research has shifted the focus of scholarly interest, and different questions have recently been raised. What regions of Africa were the sources of slaves? What goods did Africans exchange for slaves? What business procedures were involved in the transactions? What were the economic, social, political, and demographic effects of the slave trade on African societies?

As we have seen, the search for a sea route to India led the Portuguese in the fifteenth century to explore the West African coast. The transatlantic slave trade actually began when Christopher Columbus returned to Spain from the West Indies in 1493 with five hundred Indian slaves. The westward exchange of slaves began under the Portuguese flag and lasted almost four centuries, until about 1870. Portugal essentially monopolized the slave trade until 1600 and continued to play a large role in the seventeenth century, though increasingly threatened by rivals such as the Dutch, French, and English. From 1690 until the House of Commons abolished the slave trade in 1807, England was the leading carrier of African slaves.

Sources of slaves generally followed the route of European exploration down the West African coast. In the sixteenth and early seventeenth centuries the Senegambian coast and the area near the mouth of the Congo River yielded the greatest numbers. By the late seventeenth century the British found the Ivory Coast the most profitable territory; a century later the Bight of Benin and the Gold Coast had become the largest suppliers. The Portuguese acquired the bulk of their slaves from Angola. Transatlantic wind patterns partly determined the routes of exchange. Shippers naturally preferred the swiftest crossing – that is, from the African port nearest the latitude of the intended American destination. Thus Portuguese shippers carried their cargoes from Angola to Brazil, and British merchants sailed from the Bight of Benin to the Caribbean. The great bulk of slaves were intended for the sugar and coffee plantations extending from the Caribbean islands to Brazil.[12]

The African region south of the Congo River, which the Portuguese named Angola, produced 26 percent of all African slaves and 70 percent of all Portuguese slaves. Trading networks extending deep into the interior culminated at two major ports on the Angolan coast, Luanda and Beneguela. Between the 1730s and 1770s Luanda shipped between 8,000 and 10,000 slaves each year; at the end of the eighteenth century Benguela's numbers equalled those of Luanda. In 1820, the peak year, 18,957 blacks left Luanda. Although a few slaves were acquired through warfare, the Portuguese secured the vast majority through trade with African dealers; no whites participated in the inland markets. Almost all Portuguese shipments went to satisfy the virtually insatiable Brazilian demand for slaves.[13]

CITY OF LUANDA, ANGOLA Founded by the Portuguese in 1575, Luanda was a center of the huge slave trade to Brazil. In this 18th century print, offices and warehouses line the streets, while in right foreground slaves are dragged to the ships for transportation to America. (Courtesy of The New York Public Library, Astor, Lenox, and Tilden Foundations)

Unlike Great Britain, France, and the Netherlands, Portugal did not have a strong mercantile class involved in slaving in the eighteenth century. Instead of the mother country, the Portuguese colony of Brazil provided the ships, capital, and goods for the slave trade. Credit played a major role in the trade: Brazilian-controlled firms in Luanda extended credit to African operators, who had to make payments in slaves six or eight months later. Portuguese ironwares and wine, Brazilian tobacco and brandies, European and Asian textiles, firearms, and beads were the main goods exchanged for slaves. All commodities entered Angola from Brazil. Since the Luandan (or Beneguelan) merchant determined the value of the goods in relation to a

prime young slave, since the dealer under-valued the worth of the slave and overpriced what he sold, and since sharp dealing was commonplace, the African dealer frequently ended up in debt to the merchant. In order to keep the price of slaves high in Brazil, Portuguese merchants in Angola and Brazil sought to maintain a steady trickle from the African interior of Luanda and across the ocean to Rio de Janeiro: a flood of slaves would have depressed the market. Rio, the port-capital through which most slaves passed, commanded the Brazilian trade. Planters and mine operators from the provinces travelled to Rio to buy slaves. Between 1795 and 1808, approximately 10,000 Angolans per year stood in the Rio slave market. In 1810 the figure rose to 18,000, and in 1828 it reached 32,000.[14]

The English port cities of London, Bristol, and particularly Liverpool dominated the British slave trade. In the eighteenth century Liverpool was the world's greatest slave-trading port. In all three cities, small and cohesive merchant classes exercised great public influence. The cities also had huge stores of industrial products for export, growing shipping industries, and large amounts of ready cash for investment abroad. Merchants generally formed partnerships to raise capital and to share risks; each voyage was a separate business enterprise.

Slaving ships from Bristol searched the Gold Coast, the Bight of Benin, Bonny, and Calabar, while the ships of Liverpool drew slaves from Gambia, the Windward Coast, and the Gold Coast. To Africa, British ships carried textiles, gunpowder and flint, beer and spirits, British and Irish linens, and woolen cloth. African dealers wanted to trade their slaves for an equivalent value in desirable consumer goods, while European traders wanted to sell their goods at a profit calculated in their own national currency. Thus a system based on both barter and monetary exchange developed. A collection of goods was grouped together into what was called "the sorting." An English or Portuguese sorting might include bolts of cloth, firearms, alcohol, tobacco, and hardware; this batch of goods would be traded for an individual slave or a quantity of gold, ivory, or dyewood. When Europeans added a markup for profit, Africans followed suit. Currency was not exchanged; instead it served as a standard of value and a method of keeping accounts.[15]

European traders had two systems for exchange. First, especially on the Gold Coast, they established fort-factories, which were expensive to maintain but proved useful for fending off rival Europeans. In the second or shore method of trading, European ships sent boats into shore or invited African dealers to bring traders and slaves out to the ships. The English captain John Adams, who made ten voyages to Africa between 1786 and 1800, described the shore method of trading at Bonny:

This place is the wholesale market for slaves, as not fewer than 20,000 are annually sold here; 16,000 of whom are natives of one nation called Ibo, so that this single nation has not exported a less number of its people, during the last twenty years, than 320,000; and those of the same nation sold at New and Old Calabar, probably amounted in the same period of time to 50,000 more, making an aggregate amount of 370,000 Ibos.... Fairs where the slaves of the Ibo nation are obtained are held every five or six weeks at several villages, which are situated on the banks of the rivers and creeks in the interior, and to which the [African] traders of Bonny resort to purchase them.

The preparation necessary for going to these fairs generally occupies the Bonny people some days. Large canoes, capable of carrying 120 persons, are launched and stored for the voyage. The traders augment the quantity of their merchandise, by obtaining from their friends, the captains of the slave ships, a considerable quantity of goods on credit, according to the extent of business they are in the habit of transacting. Evening is the period chosen for the time of departure, when they proceed in a body, accompanied by the noise of drums, horns, and gongs. At the expiration of the sixth day, they generally return bringing with them 1,500 or 2,000 slaves, who are sold to Europeans the evening after their arrival, and taken on board the ships....

It is expected that every vessel, on her arrival [at Bonny], will fire a salute the instant the anchor is let go, as a compliment to the black mon-

arch who soon afterwards makes his appearance in a large canoe, at which time, all those natives who happen to be alongside the vessel are compelled to proceed in their canoes to a respectful distance, and make way for his Majesty's barge. After a few compliments to the captain, he usually enquires after brother George [meaning the King of England, George III], and hopes he and his family are well. He is not pleased unless he is regaled with the best the ship affords. . . . His power is absolute; and the surrounding country, to a considerable distance, is subject to his dominion. . . .

Some of the [African] traders have become extremely opulent in consequence of the great extent to which the trade in slaves has been carried on by them, and are in possession of European articles to a considerable amount, especially wrought iron and copper. . . .

A trader here, named Africa John, and who has been [on] several voyages to England, is endowed with an extraordinary memory. I have known him to have open running accounts with fourteen or fifteen vessels at the same time, wherein the debit sides exhibited long lists of various articles received by him at periods on credit; yet he could tell to a bunch of beads the exact state of each account when he came to settle it, although he could neither read nor write.[16]

The shore method of buying slaves allowed the ship to move easily from market to market. The final prices of slaves depended upon their ethnic origin, their availability when the shipper arrived, and their physical health when offered for sale in the West Indies or the North or South American colonies.

What economic impact did European trade have on African societies? Lacking a developed technology, African agricultural communities naturally desired European manufactured goods. Africans exchanged slaves, ivory, pepper, animal skins, and gold to bullion-hungry Europe for cloth, jewelry, tobacco, alcoholic spirits, and iron bars and tools. Africans thus spent their profits on luxury and consumer goods, just as Europeans did on American sugar, coffee, and oriental silks and porcelains. Their earnings were not retained within Africa. African states eager for expansion or controlling commerce bought European firearms, which may have encouraged warfare. The difficulty of maintaining guns, however, gave their owners only marginal superiority over effective bowmen.[17] In sum, international trade did not lead to the economic development of Africa. Neither technological growth nor the gradual spread of economic benefits occurred in early modern times.

The arrival of Europeans did cause basic social changes in some West African societies. In Senegambia, for example, chattel slavery seems to have been unknown before the growth of the transatlantic trade. By the late eighteenth century, however, chiefs were using the slave labor of craftsmen, sailors, and farm workers; if the price was right, they were sold off. Moreover, those who committed crimes had traditionally paid fines; with the urgent demands for slaves, many misdemeanors became punishable by sale to slave dealers. Europeans introduced corn, pineapple, cassava, and sweet potatoes to West Africa, which had important consequences for population growth. Finally, the intermarriage of French traders and Wolof women in Senegambia created a *métis* or mulatto class. In the emerging urban centers at St. Louis and Gorée, this small class adopted the French language, Roman Catholic faith, and a French manner of life. The *métis* exercised considerable political and economic power. When granted French citizenship in the late eighteenth century, they sent Senegalese grievances to the Estates General of 1789.[18] How-

TABLE 25.1 ESTIMATED SLAVE IMPORTS BY DESTINATION, 1451–1870

Destination	Estimated Total Slave Imports (Curtin)	(Rawley)
British North America	399,000	523,000
Spanish America	1,552,100	1,687,000
British Caribbean	1,665,000	2,443,000
French Caribbean	1,600,200	1,655,000
Dutch Caribbean	500,000	500,000
Danish Caribbean	28,000	50,000
Brazil	3,646,800	4,190,000
Old World	175,000	297,000
	9,556,100	11,345,000

Source: Philip D. Curtin, *Economic Change in Precolonial Africa: Senegambia in the Era of the Slave Trade,* University of Wisconsin Press, Madison, 1975; James A. Rawley, *The Transatlantic Slave Trade: A History,* W. W. Norton, New York, 1981, p. 428.

ever, European cultural influences did not penetrate to West African society beyond the sea coast.

The political consequences of the slave trade varied from place to place. In the kingdom of the Kongo the perpetual Portuguese search for slaves undermined the monarchy, destroyed political unity, and led to constant disorder and warfare; power passed to the village chiefs. Likewise in Angola, which became a Portuguese proprietary colony, the slave trade decimated and scattered the population and destroyed the local economy. On the other hand, the military kingdom of Dahomey, which entered into the slave trade in the eighteenth century and made it a royal monopoly, prospered enormously from trading in slaves; the economic strength of the state rested upon it. The royal army raided deep into the interior, and in the late eighteenth century Dahomey had become one of the major West African sources of slaves. When slaving expeditions failed to produce sizable catches, and when European demands declined, the resulting depression in the Dahomeyian economy caused serious political unrest. Iboland inland from the Niger Delta, from whose great port cities of Bonny and Brass the British drained tens of thousands of slaves, experienced minimal political effects and suffered no permanent population loss. A high birthrate kept pace with the incursions of the slave trade, and Ibo societies remained demographically and economically strong.

Finally, what of the overall demographic impact? Table 25.1 reports the somewhat divergent recent findings of two careful scholars.

The total number of slaves who left Africa over a four-hundred-year period seems to lie somewhere between 9 and 12 million. These numbers represent only the transatlantic slave trade; they do not include slaves exported from East Africa or across the Sahara. Furthermore, these are export figures; they do not include the approximately 10–15 percent who died during procurement or in transit. The demographic impact varied with time and place: the effect was obviously less severe in places where fewer blacks were enslaved, and African societies that raided the interior for slaves suffered less than did those that sold their own members. West Africa, the main supplier of slaves, lost an enormous labor supply, primarily of strong young men. Many other African societies, particularly those organized in strong kingdoms, remained strong and suffered no significant population loss. The Atlantic slave trade was one of the great forced migrations of world history. Although it caused terrible human misery and individual degradation, the present scholarly consensus seems to be that its overall impact on Africa was slight.

THE OTTOMAN AND SAFAVID EMPIRES

The spiritual descendants of Mohammed controlled three vast and powerful empires around 1500: the Ottoman empire of Turkey, the Safavid empire of Persia, and the Mughal empire of India. From West Africa to central Asia, from the Balkans to southeast Asia, Muslim arms pursued the religious ideal of the Holy War. The greatest of these empires, that of the Ottoman Turks, so severely threatened Italy and southeastern Europe that the aged Pope Pius II himself shouldered the cross of the crusader in 1464. The Turks inspired such fear that even in distant Iceland the Lutheran *Book of Common Prayer* begged God for protection from "the cunning of the Pope and the terror of the Turk."

Who were the Ottomans and the Safavids, and what political and religious factors gave rise to their empires? What were their sources of power and how did they govern? What intellectual developments characterized the Ottoman and Safavid cultures? We will consider the Mughals of India in the next section.

THE OTTOMAN MILITARY STATE

The Ottomans took their name from Osman (1299–1326), the ruler of a Turkish-speaking people in western Anatolia who began expansionist moves in the fourteenth century. The Ottomans gradually absorbed other peoples in the peninsula, and the Ottoman state emerged as one of many small Turkish states during the breakup of the empire of the Seljuk Turks. The first Ottoman state thus occupied the border between Islam and Byzantine Christendom. The Ottoman ruler called himself "border chief" or leader of the Gazis, frontier fighters in the holy war. The earliest Ottoman

historical source, a fourteenth-century saga, defines the Gazis as "the instrument of God's religion.... God's scourge who cleanses the earth from the filth of polytheism ... God's pure sword."[19] The principle of *jihad*, or Muslim holy war, was the cornerstone of Ottoman political theory and then of the Ottoman state. Europe was the frontier of the Muslim crusading mission. In 1389 in southern Yugoslavia the Ottomans defeated a combined force of Serbs and Bosnians, and in 1396 they crushed King Sigismund of Hungary supported by French, German, and English knights on the Danube in modern Bulgaria. The reign of Sultan Mehmed II (1451–1481) saw the end of all Turkish dynasties in Anatolia, and the Ottoman conquest of Constantinople, capital of the Byzantine empire (see Map 25.2).

The six-week seige of Constantinople remains one of the dramatic events in world history, because Constantinople had symbolized the continuation of imperial Rome. The Byzantine emperor Constantine IX Palaeologus with only about 10,000 men relied on the magnificent system of circular walls and stone fortifications that had protected the city for a thousand years. Mehmed II had over 100,000 men and a large fleet, but iron chains spanning the harbor kept him out of the Golden Horn. Western technology eventually decided the battle: a renegade Hungarian working for the Ottomans cast huge bronze cannon on the spot, since it was easier to bring raw materials to the scene of military action than to move guns long distances.[20] When the thirty-inch bombard shattered a city gate, the Turks forced an entry. For three days the city suffered looting and rape. The historian Oruç describes the Muslim conquest of the city:

The ruler of Istanbul was brave and asked for no quarter. The priests said that according to what

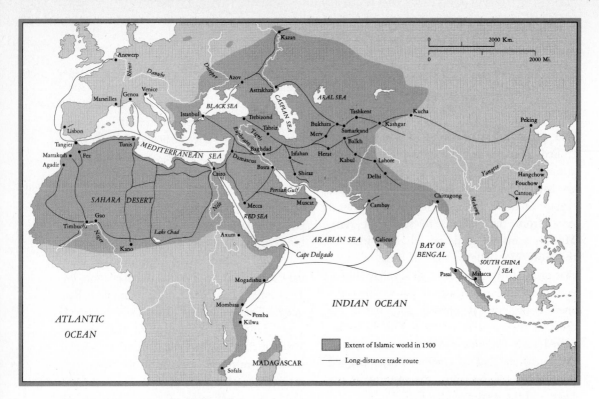

MAP 25.2 ISLAMIC EXPANSION TO CA 1500
Islam spread along the commercial arteries that extended from the eastern Mediterranean all the way to China, southeast Asia, and Malaysia.

was written in the gospels the city could not be captured. Believing in their words, he set up guns and muskets on every side to defend the towers. While his men went into the body of the tower, they talked all kinds of nonsense. God forfend, they blasphemed against the reverence of the Prophet and spoke nonsensical words. Because of their pride, almighty God visited this disaster upon them. Sultan Mehmed, the son of Sultan Murad, inspired by zeal, said "in the cause of God" and commanded plunder. The gazis, entering by force on every side, found a way in through the breaches in the fortress made by the guns and put the infidels in the fortress to the sword. The way was opened to the rest of the soldiers. They came through the trenches and set up ladders. They threw these against the walls of the towers and climbed up them. Mounting on the tower they de-

stroyed the infidels who were inside and entered the city. They looted and plundered. They seized their money and possessions and made their sons and daughters slaves. Sultan Mehmed also gave orders to plunder the houses. In this way what could be taken was taken. The Muslims took so much booty that the wealth gathered in Istanbul since it was built 2400 years before became the portion of the gazis. They plundered for three days, and after three days plunder was forbidden.[21]

The Gazis were frontier fighters who believed they were waging a holy war against infidels.

The conquest of Constantinople inaugurated the imperial phase of the Ottoman military state. The Ottoman emperors considered themselves successors of the Byzantine emperor – as their title Sultan-i-Rum (Sultan of Rome) attests. From Constantinople, their new capital, the Ottomans pushed down the Aegean and up the Adriatic. In 1480 a fleet took the Italian port of Otranto; serious plans were laid for the conquest of all Italy. Only a disputed succession following the death of Mehmed II in 1481 caused the postponement – and, later, cancellation – of those plans. (The political vacuum in Italy in the late fifteenth century, and the ease with which the French conquered several Italian states after 1494, suggest that the history of Renaissance Italy and of all Europe would have been vastly different if the Turks had persisted.)

The Ottomans conquered Syria and Palestine (1516) and Egypt (1517), and drove across North Africa to Algiers in Morocco. The Mediterranean became virtually an Ottoman lake. With Greece and the Balkans already under Ottoman domination, Suleiman II's army crushed the Hungarians in 1526, killing the king and thousands of his nobles. Three years later the Turks besieged the Hapsburg capital at Vienna. Once again, only an accident – the army's insistence on returning home before winter – prevented Muslim control of all central Europe. In virtually every area, the Ottomans' success was due to the weakness and political disunity of their enemies and to superior Turkish military organization and artillery. Gunpowder, invented by the Chinese and adapted to artillery use by Europeans, played an influential role in the development of the Ottoman state.

Military organization also dominated the Ottoman social and administrative systems, which reached classic form under Suleiman the Magnificent (1494–1566). The seventeenth-century Ottoman historian Mustafa Naima divided Muslim society into producers of wealth, Muslim and non-Muslim, and the military. Naima held that there could be no

state without the military; wealth was needed to support the military; the state's subjects raised the wealth; subjects could prosper only through justice; and that without the state there could be no justice.[22]

The ruling class consisted exclusively of Muslims, totally loyal to the sultan and fully immersed in the complex Islamic culture. Under Suleiman the Magnificent, the Ottoman ruling class consisted in part of descendants of Turkish families that had formerly ruled parts of Anatolia. In return for bureaucratic service to the sultan, they held *timars* (landed estates) on *sipahinek* (property) only for the duration of their lifetimes. Since all property belonged to the sultan and reverted to him on the holder's death, Turkish nobles – unlike their European counterparts – could not put down roots. Thus the Ottoman empire did not develop a feudal structure before 1600.

Secondly, slaves purchased from Spain, North Africa, and Venice, captured in battle, and acquired through the system known as *devshirme* – by which the sultan's agents swept the provinces for Christian youths – were recruited for the imperial civil service and the army. Islamic law forbade the enslavement of Muslims. Southern Europeans did not shrink from selling people into slavery, and as the Ottoman *jihad* advanced in the fifteenth and sixteenth centuries, Albanian, Bosnian, Wallachian, and Hungarian slave-boys filled Ottoman imperial needs. All were converted to Islam. The brightest 10 percent entered the palace school, where they learned to read and write Arabic, Ottoman Turkish, and Persian, received special religious instruction, and were trained for the civil service. Other boys were sent to Turkish farms where they acquired physical toughness in preparation for military service. Known as *janissaries* (Turkish for recruit), these men formed the elite army corps. Thoroughly indoctrinated and absolutely loyal to the sultan, the janissary slave corps eliminated the influence of old Turkish families and played the central role in Ottoman military affairs in the sixteenth century. Some formerly Christian boys of Slavic origin rose to high positions in the Ottoman state as theologians, poets, jurists, and generals.

All authority theoretically emanated from the sultan and flowed from him to his state servants: police officers, provincial governors, heads of the treasury, generals. These men were frequently designated *pashas,* a title of distinction granted by the sultan.

The reign of Suleiman II (1520–1566), who extended Ottoman jurisdiction to its widest geographical extent, and presided over an extraordinary artistic flowering, represents the peak of Ottoman influence and culture. Muslims called Suleiman 'the Lawgiver' because of his educational and legal reforms, which remained in effect until the nineteenth century. Europeans described Suleiman as 'the Magnificent' because of the grandeur of his court. With annual state revenues of about $80 million, at a time when Elizabeth of England could expect $150,000 and Francis I of France perhaps $1 million, with thousands of servants to cater to his every whim, and a lifestyle no European monarch could begin to rival, Suleiman was indeed 'Magnificent.' Suleiman used his fabulous wealth and power to adorn Constantinople with palaces and mosques. Some of his undertakings, such as his reconstruction of the water systems of the great pilgrimage sites at Mecca and Jerusalem, also benefited his subjects. The Ottomans under Suleiman demonstrated splendid creativity in carpetweaving, textiles, ceramics, and, above all, in architecture. In the buildings of Pasha Sinan (1491–1588), the Christian slave who rose to become imperial architect, the Ottoman spirit is powerfully expressed. A contemporary of Michelangelo, Sinan designed 312 public buildings – mosques, schools, hospitals, public baths, palaces, and burial chapels. His masterpieces, the Shehzade and Suleimaniye mosques at Constantinople, represented solutions to spatial problems unique to domed buildings. As Sinan wrote in his memoirs:

Christians say that they have defeated the Muslims because no dome has been built in the Islamic world which can rival the dome of St. Sophia. It greatly grieved my heart that they should say that to build so large a dome was so difficult a task. I determined to erect such a mosque, and with the help of God, in the reign of Sultan Selim Khan, I made the dome of this mosque six cubits wider and four cubits deeper than the dome of St. Sophia.[23]

Sinan's mosque expresses the discipline, power, the devotion to Islam that characterized the Ottoman empire under Suleiman the Magnificent. With pardonable exaggeration, Suleiman began a letter to the king of France, with whom he was allied against the Hapsburgs after 1536, "I who am the sultan of sultans, the sovereign of sovereigns, the dispenser of crowns to the monarchs on the face of the earth . . . to thee who art Francis, King of the land of France. . . ."[24]

Following Suleiman's reign, repeated crises occurred over the succession. The sultan's oldest son was designated his heir, but to prevent threats of usurpation he was denied a role in governing and isolated in circumstances of lavish sensuality. When the prince succeeded his father, years of dissipation had often rendered him alcoholic or insane or exhausted from excessive sexual activity. An imperial councillor, the grand vizier, exercised the actual power.

In the seventeenth century a series of weak and incompetent rulers enabled the janissaries to destroy the influence of the old Turkish families. Members of the elite army corps secured permanent military and administrative offices for their sons through bribery, and thus made their positions hereditary. The janissaries thus became the powerful feudal class in Ottoman Turkey.

THE PERSIAN THEOCRATIC STATE

Persia, after a long period of Arab and Mongol domination, emerged as a powerful Muslim state under the Safavid dynasty in the early sixteenth century. Between 1501 and 1510, Ismail (1502–1524), the founder of the dynasty, defeated petty Turkish leaders, united all of Persia under his sovereign rule, and proclaimed himself shah. Shah Ismail declared the Shiite form of Islam the state religion. The Shiites claimed ultimate descent from Ali, Mohammed's son-in-law, and believed that leadership among Muslims rightfully belonged to the Prophet's descendants. (The Safavid dynasty takes its name from Ismail's ancestor Safi-al-Din (d. 1334), who asserted his descent from Ali.) The Shiites also believed that they possessed a secret interpretation of the Koran, transmitted from Mohammed to Ali, from whom it passed to his heirs. The guardians of this knowledge, the *ulama,* claimed infallible religious and political authority. The Safavids ruled a theocratic state. With its puritanical emphasis on the holy law and on self-flagellation in penance for any disloyalty to Ali, the Safavid state represented theocracy triumphant throughout the first half-century of its existence.

Safavid power reached its height under Shah Abbas (1587–1629), whose military achievements, support for trade and commerce, and endowment of the arts earned him the epithet 'the Great.' The Persian army had hitherto consisted of tribal units under tribal leadership. Shah Abbas built a national army

DANCING MEN Persian, 1523. Sufism, the Islamic form of mysticism, sought to cultivate the inner attitude with which the believer performed his ritual duties. Based on a poem of the poet Hafiz (d. 1389), the Sufis believed that through such collective rituals as dancing, one could have an ecstatic experience and come closer to God. (Courtesy, Freer Gallery of Art, Smithsonian Institution, Washington, D.C.)

on the Ottoman model, composed of Armenian and Georgian recruits paid by and loyal to himself. Utilizing the engineering skills of the English adventurer Sir Anthony Sherley, who supplied the Persian artillery with cannon, Shah Abbas campaigned against the Turks and captured Baghdad, Mosul, and Diarbakr in Mesopotamia.

Military victories explain only part of Shah Abbas's claim to greatness. Determined to improve his country's export trade, he built the small cottage business of carpetweaving into a national industry. In the capital city of Isfahan alone, factories employed over 25,000 weavers who produced woolen carpets, brocades, and silks of brilliant color, design, and quality. Three hundred Chinese potters were imported to make glazed building tiles, which adorned the great Safavid buildings and captured much of the European tile market.

The jewel of Safavid greatness was Isfahan, whose prosperity and beauty rested upon trade and industry. Shah Abbas himself supervised the reconstruction of the city. A seventeenth-century English visitor described Isfahan's bazaar as "the surprisingest piece of Greatness in Honour of commerce the world can boast of." Besides splendid rugs, stalls displayed pottery and fine china, metalwork of exceptionally high quality, silks and velvets of stunning weave and design. A city of perhaps 750,000 people, Isfahan boasted 162 mosques, 48 *madrasas* or seminaries where future ulamas learned the sacred Muslim sciences, 273 public baths, and the vast imperial palace. Private houses had their own garden courts, and public gardens, pools, and parks adorned the wide streets. Tales of the beauty of Isfahan circulated worldwide, attracting thousands of tourists annually in the seventeenth and eighteenth centuries.

Shah Abbas was succeeded by inept rulers whose heavy indulgence in wine and the plea-

sures of the harem weakened the monarchy and fed the slow disintegration of the state. The harem dominated the court. Shiite theologians seized power. Internal weakness encouraged foreign aggression. In the eighteenth century the Turks, Afghans, and Russians invaded and divided Persia among themselves. Political anarchy and social chaos characterized Persian life.

INDIA: FROM MUGHAL DOMINATION TO BRITISH DOMINION (CA 1498–1805)

While African societies were experiencing their first large-scale contacts with Europeans, the Asian subcontinent of India achieved a remarkable culture under the domination of the Mughals. In 1504 Babur (1483–1530), ruler of the small Mughal territory in central Asia, captured Kabul and established a kingdom in Afghanistan. From Kabul he was driven southward into India. In 1525 Babur launched a serious invasion; a year later, with a force of only twelve thousand men, he defeated the decrepit sultan of Delhi at the battle of Panipat. Babur's capture of the cities of Agra and Delhi paved the way for further conquests in northern India (see Map 25.3). Thus began the Mughal rule that lasted until the eighteenth century, when domestic disorder and incompetent government opened the door to lengthy European intervention.

THE RULE OF THE MUGHALS

Babur's conquests laid the foundation for the Mughal conquest of India. Babur's son Humayun (r. 1530–1540 and 1555–1556), however, lost most of the territories his father had acquired when the Afghans of northern India

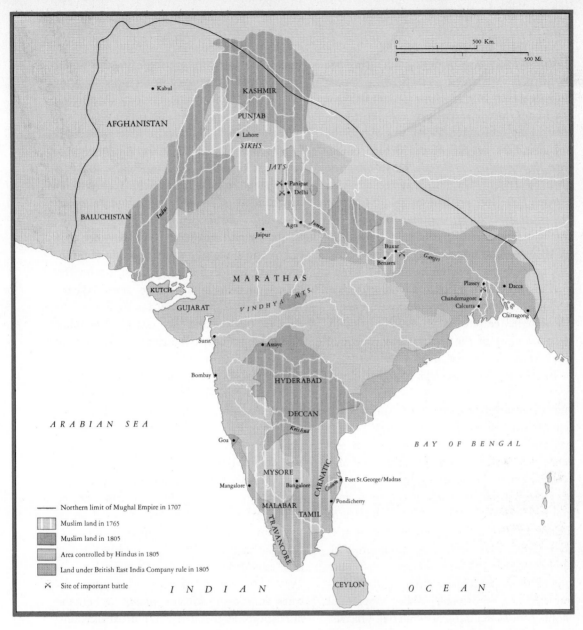

MAP 25.3 INDIA, 1707–1805 *In the eighteenth century Mughal power gradually yielded to the Hindu Marathas, the Sikhs, and the British East India Company.*

rebelled. Humayun went into temporary exile in Persia, where he developed a deep appreciation for Persian art and literature. This interest was to lead to a remarkable efflorescence of Mughal art under his son Akbar.

The reign of Akbar (1556–1605) may well have been the greatest in the history of India. Under his dynamic leadership the Mughal state took definite form. A boy of thirteen when he became *badshah*, or imperial ruler,

Akbar was ably assisted during his early years by his father's friend Bairam Khan, a superb military leader. In 1555 Bairam Khan defeated the Hindu forces at Panipat, and shortly afterward he recaptured Delhi and Agra, the key fortresses of the north. Before falling from power in 1560, Bairam Khan took the great fortress of Gwalior, annexed the rich province of Jaunpur, and prepared for war against Malwa. Akbar continued this expansionist policy, gradually adding the territories of Malwa, Gondwana, and Gujarat (see Map 25.3 on page 905). Because the Afghan tribesmen in Bengal put up tremendous resistance, it took Akbar several years to acquire Bengal. The Mughal empire under Akbar eventually included most of the subcontinent north of the Godavari river (see Map 25.3).

To govern this vast region Akbar developed an efficient bureaucracy staffed by able and well-trained officials, both Muslim and non-Muslim. As in the early modern nations of Europe (pages 463–464), Mughal state solvency depended upon the establishment of a careful system for recording income and expenditures. Under Akbar's *diwan*, or finance minister Raja Todar Mal, a Hindu, a bureau of finance and royal mint came into existence. Raja Todar Mal devised methods for the assessment and collection of taxes that were applied throughout the entire empire. To administer the provinces, Akbar appointed about 800 *mansabdars* or imperial officials, who performed a wide variety of financial, military, and judicial functions at the local level. The central government, however, rarely interfered in the life of village communities. Akbar's policies laid the basis for all later Mughal administration in India.

The cornerstone of Akbar's policies was religious toleration: he sought the peaceful mutual assimilation of Hindus and Muslims, especially in his government. Although this was not a radical innovation – a few Hindus had long been employed in the imperial army and in the administration – very deep prejudices divided the two peoples. When the refusal of many Hindus to serve under a Muslim ruler, or to learn Persian, the court language, thwarted Akbar's goal, he took decisive steps to heal the breach. According to his principle of *sulahkul*, or universal tolerance, the *badshah* assumed responsibility for all the people, regardless of religion. In 1564 Akbar ended the pilgrim tax, which won him the gratitude of the many Hindus who travelled to various pilgrimage sites. Akbar's most widely acclaimed act was to abolish the *jizya*, a tax imposed on non-Muslim adult males. He immediately earned the support of the Hindu warrior class and the goodwill of the general Hindu population. Twice Akbar married Hindu princesses, one of whom became the mother of his heir Jahangir. Hindus eventually accounted for 30 percent of the imperial bureaucracy.

Scholars have heatedly debated Akbar's own religious beliefs. Although he considered himself an orthodox Muslim and demonstrated great devotion to the shrine of an Islamic mystic at Ajmer, he supported an eclectic assortment of theological ideas, a policy that caused serious domestic difficulties. In 1575 Akbar sponsored public theological debates among the Muslim *ulama*. When the discussions degenerated into mutual recriminations, Akbar declared himself the final interpreter of Islamic law. Orthodox Muslims became alarmed. After 1579 Akbar encouraged further debate, inviting Zoroastrians, Jains, Hindus, and Jesuits, as well as the Muslim ulama, to participate. From these discussions Akbar and his courtiers created the *Din-i-Illah* (literally, "divine faith"), which some advisors called a syncretic religion. The Din-i-Illah borrowed the concept of great respect for animal life from the Jains and reverence for the sun from Zoroastrianism, but it was primarily based on the rationalistic elements in the Islamic tradition and stressed the emperor as a Perfect Man. Some scholars interpret it as a reflection of Akbar's "cult of personality," intended to serve as a common bond for the court nobility. In any case, the Din-i-Illah antagonized all sects and provoked serious Muslim rebellions. Although misinterpreted by contemporaries and misunderstood later, the Din-i-Illah established Akbar's reputation as a philosopher-king.

The birth of his son Jahangir, which Akbar saw as fulfillment of a prophecy by a holy man, Shaikh Salim Chisti, inspired Akbar to build a new city, Fatehpur-Sikri. Akbar personally supervised the construction of the new city, named in part for the site of his great military victory over Gujarat, and in part for the home of Salim Chisti. It combined the Muslim tradition of domes, arches, and spacious courts with the Hindu tradition of flat stone beams, ornate decoration, and solidity. According to Abu-l-Fazl, the historian of Akbar's reign, "His majesty plans splendid edifices, and dresses the work of his mind and heart in the garment of stone and clay."[25] Completed in 1578, the city included an imperial palace, a mosque, lavish gardens, and a Hall of Worship, as well as thousands of houses for ordinary people. Along with the ancient cities of Delhi and Agra, Fatehpur-Sikri served as an imperial capital and the center of Akbar's lavish court. Its construction reflects Akbar's desire to assimilate Hindus and Muslims and the vaunting power of his empire.

Although illiterate, Akbar was gifted with a creative intellect and imagination. He enthusiastically supported artists who produced magnificent paintings and books in the Indo-Persian style. In Mughal India as throughout the Muslim world, books were regarded as precious objects. Time, talent, and expensive materials went into their production, and they were highly coveted because they reflected wealth, learning, and power. Akbar reportedly possessed 24,000 books when he died. Abu-l-Fazl described the library in this way:

His Majesty's library is divided into several parts; some of the books are kept within, and some without, the Harem. Each part of the library is subdivided, according to the value of the books and the estimation in which the sciences are held of which the books treat. Prose works, poetical works, Hindi, Persian, Greek, Kashmirian, Arabic, are all separately placed. In this order they are also inspected. Experienced people bring them daily and read them before His Majesty, who hears every book from beginning to end. At whatever page the reader stops, His Majesty makes with his own pen a sign, according to the number of pages; and rewards the readers with presents of cash either in gold or silver, according to the number of leaves read out by them. Among books of renown there are few that are not read in His Majesty's assembly hall; and there are no historical facts of past ages, or curiosities of science, or interesting points of philosophy, with which His Majesty, a leader of impartial sages, is unacquainted.[26]

Official court biographers almost always exaggerate the achievements of their subjects, but Akbar's library attests to his sincere appreciation for learning. Akbar's son Jahangir (1605–1628) lacked his father's military abilities and administrative genius but did succeed in consolidating Mughal rule in Bengal. His patronage of the arts and lavish court have led scholars to characterize his reign as 'the age of splendor.'

Jahangir's son Shah Jahan (1628–1658) launched fresh territorial expansion. Faced with dangerous revolts by the Muslims in Ahmadnagar and the resistance of the newly arrived Portuguese in Bengal, Shah Jahan not only crushed them but strengthened his northwestern frontier. He reasserted Mughal authority in the Deccan and Golkunda.

The new capital that Shah Jahan founded at Delhi superseded Agra, Akbar's main capital. Situated on the rich land linking the Indus and Ganges valleys, Delhi or Shahjahanabad eventually became one of the great cities of the Muslim world. The city boasted one of the finest mosques in Islam, the Juma Masjid, and magnificent boulevards. The Red Fort, named for its red sandstone walls, housed the imperial palace, the headquarters of the imperial administration, the imperial treasury, an arsenal, and a garrison. Subsequent Mughal rulers held their *durbar,* or court, at Delhi until the city fell to the British in 1857.

Shah Jahan also ordered the construction of the Peacock Throne. This famous device, actually a cot-bedstead resting on golden legs, was encrusted with emeralds, diamonds, pearls, and rubies, took seven years to fashion, and cost the equivalent of $5 million. It served as the imperial throne of India until 1739, when the Persian warrior Nadir Shah seized it as plunder and carried it to Persia.

Shah Jahan's most enduring monument is the Taj Mahal, the supreme example of the garden tomb. The English word *paradise* derives from the old Persian *pairidaeza,* a walled garden. The Mughals sought to bring their vision of paradise alive in the walled garden tombs in which they buried their dead. Twenty thousand workers toiled eighteen years to build this memorial to Shah Jahan's favorite wife, Mumtaz Mahal, who died giving birth to their fifteenth child. One of the most beautiful structures in the world, the Taj Mahal is both an expression of love and a superb architectural blending of Islamic and Indian culture. It also asserted the power of the Mughal dynasty.

The Mughal state never developed a formal procedure for the imperial succession, and a crisis occurred toward the end of Shah Jahan's reign. Competition among his sons ended with the victory of Aurangzeb, who executed his elder brother and locked his father away until his death in 1666. A puritanically devout and strictly orthodox Muslim, a skillful general and a clever diplomat, Aurangzeb ruled more of India than did any previous badshah. His reign witnessed the culmination of Mughal power and the beginning of its decline.

The combination of religious zeal and financial necessity seems to have prompted Aurangzeb to introduce a number of reforms. He appointed censors of public morals in important cities to enforce Islamic laws against gambling, prostitution, drinking, and the use of narcotics. He forbade the *sati* – the self-immolation of widows on their husbands' funeral pyres – and the castration of boys to sell them as eunuchs. He also abolished all taxes not authorized by Islamic law. This measure led to a serious loss of state revenues; to replace them, Aurangzeb in 1679 reimposed the *jizya,* the tax on non-Muslims. It fell most heavily on the Hindu majority.

Regulating Indian society according to Islamic law meant modifying the religious toleration and cultural cosmopolitanism instituted by Akbar. Aurangzeb ordered the destruction of some Hindu temples. He required Hindus to pay higher customs duties than Muslims. Out of fidelity to Islamic law, he even criticized his mother's tomb, the Taj Mahal: "The lawfulness of a solid construction over a grave is doubtful, and there can be no doubt about the extravagance involved."[27] On the other hand, Aurangzeb employed more Hindus in the imperial administration than any previous Mughal ruler. But his religious policy proved highly unpopular with

TAJ MAHAL AT AGRA   The finest example of Muslim architecture in India. The white marble exterior is inlaid with semi-precious stones in Arabic inscriptions and floral designs. The oblong pool reflects the building, which asserts the power of the Mughal dynasty. (Stock, Boston/Ira Kirschenbaum)

the majority of his subjects. Although his indomitable military strength and persistent activity staved off difficulties and maintained the unity of the empire, Aurangzeb created problems weaker successors could not handle.

Aurangzeb's military ventures also had mixed results. A tireless general, he pushed the conquest of the south and succeeded in annexing the Golkunda and Bijapur sultanates. The stiffest opposition came from the Marathas, a militant Hindu group centered in the western Deccan. From 1681 until his death in 1707 at the age of ninety, Aurangzeb led repeated sorties through the Deccan. He took many forts and won several battles. Total destruction of the Maratha guerrilla bands eluded him, however, and after his death they played an important role in the collapse of the Mughal empire.

Aurangzeb's eighteenth-century successors

faced formidable problems. Repeated disputes over the succession contributed to the instability of the monarchy. Court intrigues replaced the battlefield as the testing ground for the nobility. Mughal provincial governors began to rule independently, giving only minimal allegiance to the *badshahs* at Delhi. The Marathas, who revolted and pressed steadily northward, constituted the gravest threat to Mughal authority. No ruler could defeat them.

In 1739 the Persian adventurer Nadir Shah invaded India, defeated the Mughal army, looted Delhi, and after a savage massacre carried off a huge amount of treasure, including the Peacock Throne. When Nadir Shah withdrew to Afghanistan, he took with him the prestige of the Mughal government. Constant skirmishes between the Afghans and the Marathas for control of the Punjab and northern India ended in 1761 at the battle of Panipat, where the Marathas were crushingly defeated. India no longer had any power capable of imposing order on the subcontinent or of checking the rapacious penetration of the Europeans.

EUROPEAN RIVALRY FOR THE INDIAN TRADE

Shortly before Babur's invasion of India, the Portuguese under the navigator Pedro Cabral had opened the subcontinent to Portuguese trade. In 1510 they established the port of Goa on the Arabian Sea as their headquarters, and through a policy of piracy and terrorism the Portuguese swept the Muslims off the Indian and Arabian Oceans (page 893). Attempting to justify Portuguese seizure of commercial traffic that the Muslims had long dominated, the Portuguese historian Barroes wrote:

It is true that there does exist a common right to all to navigate the seas and in Europe we recognize the rights which others hold against us; but the right does not extend beyond Europe and therefore the Portuguese as Lords of the Sea are justified in confiscating the goods of all those who navigate the seas without their permission.[28]

For Europeans, in short, Western principles of international law did not apply in Asia. For almost a century the Portuguese controlled the spice trade over the Indian Ocean.

In 1602 the Dutch formed the United Dutch East India Company with the stated goal of wresting the enormously lucrative spice trade from the Portuguese. The first dividends the Company declared were 132 percent. The scent of fabulous profits also attracted the English. With a charter signed by Queen Elizabeth, eighty London merchants organized the British East India Company: their object was to crack the Dutch monopoly of the Indian spice and cotton trade. Although the English initially had no luck, in 1619 Emperor Jahangir granted a British mission led by Sir Thomas Roe important commercial concessions at the port of Surat on the Gulf of Cambay. Gifts, medical services, and bribes to Indian rulers soon enabled the British to set up twenty-seven other forts along the coasts. The Fort of St. George on the eastern coast became the modern city of Madras. In 1669 the island of Bombay, given to England when the Portuguese princess Catherine of Braganza married King Charles II, was leased to the Company. This event marks the virtually total British absorption of Portuguese power in India. Meanwhile the Dutch concentrated their efforts in Indonesia. In 1690 Job Charnock, a Company official, established a fort that eventually became the city of Calcutta. Thus the three places that subsequently became centers of British economic

VIEW OF GOA *The Portuguese admiral Albuquerque seized Goa (on the Arabian Sea) in 1510, attracted by the wealth of the Mughal Empire. Notice the elegant dress and jewels of the veiled Muslim lady whose slave boy, imported from East Africa, holds a parasol as a sunshade. (Courtesy The Oliveira Lima Library, The Catholic University of America. Photo: Paul McKane, OSB)*

and political imperialism – Bombay, Calcutta, and Madras – had already come into existence before 1700.

FACTORY-FORT SOCIETIES

The British called their trading post at Surat a *factory,* and the word was later used for all European settlements in India. The term did not signify manufacturing; it designated the walled compound containing the residences, gardens, and offices of Company officials and the warehouses where goods were stored before shipping to Europe. The Company president exercised political authority over all residents.

In exchange for English minerals – silver, copper, zinc, and lead – and fabrics, the Company bought Indian cotton goods, silks, pepper and other spices, sugar, and opium. By the late seventeenth century the Company was earning substantial profits; profitability increased even more after 1700 when it began to trade with China. Because the directors of the British East India Company in London discouraged all unnecessary expenses and financial risks, they opposed any interference in local Indian politics and even missionary activities. Indian conditions, however, brought about a fundamental change in the nature of the Company's factories.

The violent disorders and political instabil-

ity that wracked India during Aurangzeb's reign and in the early eighteenth century led to the evolution of the factories into forts and then into territorial settlements. In order to protect their trading interests, Company officials transformed the factories into defensive installations manned by small garrisons of native troops. When warlords appeared or an uprising occurred, people from the surrounding countryside flocked into the fort. Because of the lack of a strong central government and because local princes were unable to provide security, the Company factory-forts gradually came to exercise political authority over the territories around them.

Factory-forts existed to make profits for the Asian-European trade, and the factory port towns evolved into flourishing centers of Indian economic profit. Some Indian merchants in Calcutta and Bombay made gigantic fortunes from the country trade — that is, trade within Asia. In the European economies, however, Asian goods created serious problems. Indian and Chinese wares enjoyed great popularity in England and on the European continent in the late seventeenth and early eighteenth centuries. The middle classes wanted Indian textiles, which were colorful, durable, cheap, and washable. The upper classes desired Chinese wallpaper and porcelains, Indian silks and brocades. The import of these products into England threatened domestic goods, and as early as 1695 English manufacturers called for an embargo on Indian cloth, while silk weavers picketed the House of Commons. Moreover, trade with Asia was one-way: Asians had little interest in European manufactured articles. The United Dutch East India Company found the Siamese so oblivious to traditional Dutch goods that the company tried to interest them in collections of pornography. Europeans had to pay for everything they bought from Asia with precious metals. This circumstance gave rise to insistent pressure within England, France, and the Netherlands against the East India Companies' import of Asian goods. As one authority explains it:

The root of the argument from which grew a tree of many branches was the old fear of the drain of gold. When the English pamphleteers professed to be shocked by the transparency of Indian fabrics, their care for the modesty of English females was a disguise, not less transparent than muslin, for the objections of those who on general grounds deplored sending gold and silver abroad or on particular grounds were anxious to protect domestic industries.[29]

THE RISE OF THE BRITISH EAST INDIA COMPANY

The French were the last to arrive in India. Louis XIV's financial wizard Colbert (page 725) planned the French East India Company for trade in the Eastern Hemisphere, and in the 1670s the Company established factories at Chandernagore in Bengal, Pondicherry, and elsewhere. Joseph Dupleix (1697-1764), who was appointed governor general at Pondicherry in 1742, was the first European to appreciate fully the political as well as economic potential of India. He understood the instability of the Mughal empire and realized that one European power would eventually govern India. Dupleix also knew that, since the French East India Company could expect no support from the government in Paris, it would have to be economically self-sufficient and acquire territory. He made allies with Indian princes and built an army of native troops, called *sepoys,* who were trained as infantrymen. The British likewise built an army with Indian surrogates trained in Western military drill and tactics. War broke out at midcentury.

From 1740 to 1763 Britain and France were almost continually engaged in a great global struggle (see the timeline on page 845). India, like North America, became a battleground and a prize. The French and the English both bid for the support of the rulers of the Deccan. In 1746 Dupleix captured Madras, and in 1751 the French gained control of the huge Deccan and Carnatic regions. But while the French won land battles, English seapower decided the first phase of the war. Then in 1757, the English commander Robert Clive, having bought up most of the officers of the French-supported *nawab* (Muslim governor) of Bengal, defeated him at Plassey. In a series of brilliant victories Clive went on to destroy

French power in southern India. By preventing French reinforcements, British seapower again proved to be the determining factor, and Clive soon extended British jurisdiction over the important northern province of Bengal. The Treaty of Paris of 1763 recognized British control of much of India, and scholars acknowledge it as the beginning of the British Empire in India.

How was the vast subcontinent to be governed? The British Parliament believed that the British East India Company had too much power and considered the Company largely responsible for the political disorders there, which were bad for business. Parliament attempted to solve Indian problems with special legislation. The Regulating Act of 1773 deprived the Company of some of its political power. The newly created office of governor general would, with an advisory council, exercise political authority over the territory controlled by the Company. The India Act of 1784 required that the governor general be chosen from outside the Company, and made its directors subject to parliamentary supervision.

Implementation of these reforms fell to Warren Hastings, the governor of Bengal and first governor general (1774-1784) with jurisdiction over Bombay and Madras. Hastings tried to build an effective administrative system and to turn the British East India Company into a government. He laid the foundations for the first Indian civil service, abolished tolls to facilitate internal trade, placed the salt and opium trades under government control, and planned a codification of Muslim and Hindu laws. He sought allies among Indian princes and, in imitation of Dupleix's plan, built an army of sepoy troops trained as infantrymen to support the British artillery. The biggest problem facing Hastings's administration was a coalition of the rulers of Mysore and the Marathas aimed at the expulsion of the British. Hastings's skillful diplomacy offset this alliance temporarily. In 1785, however, Hastings resigned his office and returned to England. Charges that he had interfered in provincial administrations, extorted money from Indian princes, and ordered the murder of an Indian merchant led to his impeachment; he was finally acquitted in 1795.

Hastings's successor Lord Charles Cornwallis (whom George Washington defeated at Yorktown) served as Governor General of India from 1786 to 1794. Cornwallis continued the work of building a civil service and the war against the Mysore. His introduction of the British style of property relations in effect converted a motley collection of ex-Mughal officers, tax collectors, and others into English-style landlords. A new land revenue system resulted. The third governor general, the Marquess Richard Wellesley (1797–1805) defeated the Mysore in 1799, and four years later crushed the Marathas at the Battle of Assaye. Building upon the work of his predecessors, he vastly extended British influence in India. Like most nineteenth-century British governors of India, Wellesley believed that British rule strongly benefited the Indians. With supreme condescension, he wrote that British power should be established over the Indian princes in order "to deprive them of the means of prosecuting any measure or of forming any confederacy hazardous to the security of the British empire, and to enable us to preserve the tranquility of India by exercising a general control over the restless spirit of ambition and violence which is characteristic of every Asiatic government."[30]

At the beginning of the nineteenth century, the authority and power of the British East India Company had yielded to the government in London. Subsequent British rule rested upon three foundations: the support of puppet Indian princes, who exercised the trappings but not the reality of power; a large army of sepoys of dubious loyalty; and an increasingly effective civil service, manned largely by Englishmen with Hindus and Muslims in minor positions.

CHINA: FROM THE MING DYNASTY TO THE MID-MANCHU (CA 1368-1795)

The combination of Mongol repression, rapid inflation of the currency, disputes over the succession among the Khans, and the growth of peasant secret societies led to the decay of Mongol government in China (pages 342–344). By 1368, Hung Wu, the leader of a secret society called the Red Turbans, had pushed the Mongols out of China. Hung Wu (1368–1398), the founder of the Ming dynasty, stands out in Chinese history along with Liu Pang, founder of the Han dynasty, as the only peasants who founded major dynasties. The Ming regime (1368–1644) is the only dynasty that originated south of the Yangtze River.

Under the Ming, China experienced remarkable change. Agricultural development and commercial reconstruction followed a long period of chaos and stagnation. Hung Wu introduced far-reaching social and political institutions, intended to be hereditary, but by the middle of the fifteenth century his administrative framework had begun to decay. Ming government tended to be harshly autocratic. Externally, the Ming emperors strove to push back the Mongol borders in the north. Chinese defeats in Mongolia in the later fifteenth century led to a long period of steady Chinese withdrawal.

CHINESE PEASANTS AT WORK   *The Western artist who sketched this picture in the 17th century seems to be telling us that the use of human power in agriculture was as common in China as animal power.*   *Coco palm trees (left) have many important uses, though they are not usually found as far north as China. The pigtailed men date the picture from the Manchu period. (Photo: Caroline Buckler)*

THE MING AGRICULTURAL AND COMMERCIAL REVOLUTIONS

Mongol exploitation and the civil disorders that accompanied the breakdown of Yüan rule had left China in economic chaos. Vast stretches of farmland were laid waste, some entirely abandoned. Damaged dikes and canals proved unusable, causing trade to decline.

A profound economic reconstruction occurred between 1370 and 1398. The agricultural revolution that China underwent in the Ming period was in part a gigantic effort at recovery after the disaster of Mongol rule, and in part a continuation of developments begun under the Sung. This revolution involved radical improvement in methods of rice produc-

tion. More than bread in Europe, rice supplied almost the total nourishment of the population. Terracing and irrigation of mountain slopes, introduced in the eleventh century, had led to larger rice harvests. The introduction of Indo-Chinese, or Champa, rice proved an even greater boon. Champa was drought-resistant, yielded larger harvests, and could be sown earlier in the year. Although Champa rice was of lower nutritional quality than traditional Chinese rice, it considerably increased the total output of food. Ming farmers experimented with Champa rice that required only sixty days from planting to harvesting, instead of the usual hundred days. Peasants soon reaped two harvests a year, an enormous increase in production.

Other innovations also had good results. Because the roots of rice plants require a rich supply of oxygen, the water in which rice grows must be kept in motion so that oxygenation can occur. Ming-era peasants introduced irrigation pumps worked by pedals. Farmers also began to stock the rice paddies with fish, which continuously fertilized the rice fields, destroyed malaria-bearing mosquitoes, and enriched the diet. Fish farming in the paddies eventually enabled large parts of southern China, previously uninhabitable, to be brought under cultivation. Farmers also discovered the possibilities of commercial cropping in cotton, sugar cane, and indigo. Finally, new methods of crop rotation allowed for continuous cultivation and more than one harvest per year from a single field.

The Ming rulers promoted the repopulation and colonization of devastated regions through massive transfers of people; immigrants received large plots and exemption from taxation for many years. Table 25.2, based on fourteenth-century records of newly-tilled land, helps tell the story.[31]

Reforestation of the land was a dramatic aspect of the agricultural revolution. In 1391 the Ming government ordered 50 million trees planted in the Nanking area; the trees were intended for the construction of a maritime fleet. In 1392 each family holding colonized land in Anhwei province had to plant 200 mulberry trees, 200 jujube trees, and 200 persimmon trees. In 1396 peasants in the present-day provinces of Hunan and Hupei planted 84 million fruit trees. Historians have estimated that 1 billion trees were planted in the Hung Wu period.[32]

What were the social consequences of this agricultural growth? Increased food production led to steady population growth. Demographers date the start of the Chinese population boom at about 1550, as a direct result of improved methods of rice produc-

TABLE 25.2   LAND RECLAMATION IN EARLY MING CHINA

Year	Reclaimed Land (in hectares: 1 hectare = 2.5 acres)
1371	576,000
1373	1,912,000
1374	4,974,000
1379	1,486,000

tion. Increases in total yields differed fundamentally, however, from comparable agricultural growth in Europe: Chinese grain harvests were improved through intensification of peasant labor. This meant lower income per capita.

Another outcome of population increase seems to have been the multiplication of towns and small cities. Urbanization in the Ming (and, later, Ch'ing) eras involved the proliferation of market centers and small towns, rather than the growth of large cities that characterized Europe and China in the Sung period. Most people lived in tiny hamlets or villages, without markets. What distinguished a village from a town was that a town had a market. Towns held markets twice a week; in southern China, where a week was ten days long, markets were held three times a week. Town markets consisted of little open-air shops that sold essential goods — pins, matches, oil for lamps, candles, paper, incense, tobacco — to the country people who came in from surrounding hamlets. The market usually included a tea room or tavern where tea and rice wine was sold, entertainers performed, and moneylenders and pawnshops sometimes did business. Because itinerant salesmen depended on the city market for their wares, town markets were not held on days when the nearest city had its market.

Tradesmen, who carried their wares on their backs, and small craftsmen — carpenters, barbers, joiners, locksmiths — moved constantly from market to market. Large towns and cities became the focus for foodstuffs from the countryside and for rare and precious goods from distant places. Cities gradually became islands of sophistication in the highly localized Chinese economy. Nanking, for example, because of the residence of the imperial court and bureaucracy, spread out enormously. The concentration of people in turn created demand for goods and services. Industrial development was stimulated. Small businesses manufactured textiles and paper, and luxury goods such as silks and porcelains. Nanking and Shanghai became centers for the production of cotton and silks, while Hsin-an specialized in the grain and salt trade and in silver. While small towns remained embedded in peasant culture, large towns and cities pursued contacts with the wider world.

THE GOVERNMENT OF HUNG WU

Hung Wu's governmental reforms rested upon a few strong centralizing principles. He established China's capital at Nanking (literally, southern capital), his old base on the Yangtze river. He stripped many nobles of their estates and divided them among the peasantry. Although Hung Wu had been a monk, he confiscated many of the temples' tax-exempt lands, thereby increasing the proceeds of the state treasury. Unlike the Sung period, when commercial taxes fed the treasury, imperial revenues in the Ming (and, later, Ch'ing) periods came mainly from agriculture. Farmers produced the state's resources.

Hung Wu ordered a general survey of all China's land and several censuses of the population; the information gathered was recorded in official registers. These registers provided valuable information about the taxes that landlords, temples, and peasants owed. According to the registers, the capital was owed 8 million shih, or 160,000 tons, of rice per year. Such thorough fiscal information contributed to the efficient operation of the state.

To secure soldiers for the army and personnel for his administration and to generate revenue, Hung Wu adopted the Yüan practice of requiring service to the state. He made all occupations hereditary. The entire Chinese population was classified into three hereditary categories: peasants, artisans, and soldiers. The state ministry with jurisdiction over a particular category designated the individual's obligations to the state. The Ministry of Finance oversaw the peasants, who provided the bulk of the taxes and performed public labor services. The Ministry of Public Works supervised artisans and all people with special skills and crafts. The Ministry of the Army controlled the standing army of 2 million men. Every person entered a state category at birth, on the basis of his father's occupation; one's descendants belonged to the same category. When a soldier died or proved unable to fight, his family had to provide a replacement. Finally, each social category prevailed in a particular geographical region. Army families lived along the coasts and lengthy frontiers that they defended, craftsmen lived mainly in the neighborhoods of the cities for which they produced goods, and the peasants lived in the countryside.

The Ming emperor wielded absolute and despotic power. Access to his personal favor was the only means of acquiring privilege or some limited derivative power. The complex ceremonial and court ritual surrounding any public appearance by the emperor, the vast imperial palace staffed only by servile women and eunuchs, and the precise procedures of

IMPERIAL PALACE AT PEKING *Within the Imperial City stood the Forbidden City, filled with blocks of glazed tiled buildings at the heart of which was the Emperor's Palace. Later Ming emperors lived in great magnificence and oppressive, bureaucrat-ordered monotony. (Photo: Caroline Buckler)*

the imperial bureaucracy – which blamed all difficulties on the emperor's advisors – all lent the throne a rarified aura and exalted the emperor's authority. Hung Wu also forced the military nobles (his old rebel comrades-in-arms) to live at his court in Nanking, where he could keep an eye on them. He raised many generals to the nobility, which carried honor and financial benefits but no political power whatsoever.

Late in his reign Hung Wu executed many nobles and divided China into principalities, putting one of his sons in charge of each. Suspicious even of his sons' loyalty, he carefully circumscribed their power. Positions in the imperial administration were filled in part by civil service examinations, whose re-establish-

ment proved to be Hung Wu's most enduring reform. The examination system later became the exclusive channel for official recruitment, lasting until the twentieth century. In the Ming period these examinations took on three inflexible characteristics: they required minute knowledge of the ancient Chinese classics, a formal and precise literary style, and they discouraged all originality. These features promoted conservatism and opposition to innovation in the bureaucracy.

After 1426 the eunuch-dominated secret police controlled the palace guards and the imperial workshops, infiltrated the civil service, and headed all foreign missions. Through blackmail, spies, and corruption, the secret police exercised enormous domestic power.

How did eunuchs acquire such power? Without heirs, they had no immediate family concerns. Drawn from the lowest classes of society, looked upon with distaste by respectable people, eunuchs had no hope of gaining status except by satisfying every whim of the emperor. They were indifferent to public opinion. Because their submission to the emperor seemed total, the emperors believed them absolutely trustworthy. Several eunuchs – Wang Chih in the 1470s, Liu Chin in the 1500s, and Wei Chung-hsien in the 1620s – gained dictatorial power when their emperors lost interest in affairs of state.

Foreign affairs occupied much of Hung Wu's attention. He sought to control all Chinese contacts with the outside world and repeatedly invaded Mongolia, but the strengthening and extension of the Great Wall stands as Hung Wu's and his Ming successors' most enduring achievement. According to one record of his reign, the *Book on Military Affairs, History of the Ming Dynasty,* the defense system of the Great Wall throughout the Ming period "stretched 10,000 *li* [a *li* is about one-third of a mile] in an unbroken chain from the Yalu River in the east to Jiayuguan [in modern Gansu province] in the west...."[33] The wall served as a protective girdle around the northern parts of the empire, sheltering towns, cities, and the inner countryside. The forts, beacon towers, and garrisons that pierced the wall at militarily strategic spots kept in close contact with the central government of the emperor. Because of the steady pressure of Mongol attacks in the fifteenth century, Hung Wu's successors continued the work of reinforcing the Great Wall.

Hung Wu forbade free commercial contacts along the coasts between Chinese and foreign merchants. He insisted that foreign states eager to trade with China acknowledge his suzerainty by offering tribute. The early Ming emperors displayed greater military and diplomatic efficiency than had any Chinese ruler for centuries. By the mid-fifteenth century, however, the emperors could not restrict the commercial demands of Chinese and foreign traders within tight commercial channels. Mongol raids by land and Japanese piracy at sea, often with the hidden cooperation of the local Chinese, were commonplace. Along the coasts of Kiangsu, Chekiang, and Fukien provinces, Japanese entered China disguised as merchants. If they were dissatisfied with the official rates of exchange, they robbed and destroyed. Neither fortresses and the transfer of coastal settlements inland, nor precautionary attacks on Japanese merchant raiders and their Chinese allies suppressed the problem. The imperial court came to regard foreigners arriving by ship as barbarians. When Europeans arrived in the sixteenth century, they too were commonly called barbarians.

DECLINE OF THE MING DYNASTY

A bitter struggle for the throne ensued when Hung Wu died. Eventually his fourth son prevailed, taking the regnal name Yung Lo (1403–1424). The bloody wars that brought Yung Lo to the throne devastated the territory between the Yellow River and the Yangtze, and he promoted a policy of resettlement there. Yung Lo continued his father's policies of civil-service examinations, controlling the nobility, and trying to restrain the Japanese pirates. His most significant act, however, proved to be the transfer of the capital back to Peking. Yung Lo had served as governor *(wang)* of the north during his father's reign, and he felt greater support there than in the south. Peking was also closer to the northern frontier, and thus a better place for strategic defense against China's ancient enemies, the

Mongols. This move pleased the military faction, but hurt the new gentry and mercantile groups whose economic interests centered around Nanking.

The extravagance of the imperial court also caused economic difficulties. Hung Wu had exercised fiscal restraint, but Yung Lo and his successors tried to outdo the splendor and magnificence of the Mongols. Yung Lo rebuilt his palaces and temples in a monumental style, whose grandeur surpassed that of Louis XIV's Versailles. The emperor and the court lived in the Forbidden City, a quarter-mile compound filled with palatial buildings, ceremonial halls, marbled terraces, and lengthy galleries. The Forbidden City was surrounded

by the Imperial City, an area of no less than three square miles, also closed to the public. Within the enclosure were numerous avenues and artificial lakes. In addition to imperial villas, temples, and residences of eunuch officials inside the compound, there were also supply depots and material-processing plants. Among them was the court of Imperial Entertainments, which had the capacity to serve banquets for up to 15,000 men on short notice. Next to the bakery, distillery, and confectionery were the emperor's stable, armory, printing-office, and book depository. In sum, the palace was completely self-sufficient.[34]

A century and a half later, in the reign of the emperor Wan-li (1573–1620), everything required for the maintenance of the Imperial City was manufactured or deposited there. Approximately 20,000 eunuchs, some of whom held top positions in the imperial entourage, worked there. Some 3,000 female domestics performed household tasks. The emperor's immediate court – councillors, bodyguards, relatives, concubines, and official wives – numbered several thousand people. Supporting so many people on so lavish a scale placed a terrible burden on the treasury,

and financial difficulties played a major role in the decline of the Ming.

Yung Lo's successors lacked his drive and ability. The Mongols continued to press on the northern borders, and the Chinese had to yield some territory. In 1449 an ill-prepared and thoroughly inexperienced expedition launched by the eunuch Wang Zhen, with the participation of the young emperor Ying-tsung (1436–1450 and 1457–1464), met total disaster. The emperor himself was captured and remained a prisoner of the Mongols for seven years. He regained his throne only with great difficulty. In the south, a Chinese army of 200,000 had pressed into northern Vietnam in 1406. This imperialistic move led to temporary Chinese domination of the Red river basin and of much of central Vietnam. A Vietnamese liberation movement retaliated, and by 1427 had driven the occupiers out. In 1471 the Chinese also had to withdraw from the province of Annam in present-day North Vietnam, which had been annexed in Yung Lo's reign. In the sixteenth century the Japanese accelerated their coastal raids and even sacked the cities of Ningpo and Yangchow. Difficulties in collecting taxes hindered the government's ability to strengthen the army. It was commonplace in the eleven hundred counties of Ming China for people to delay or simply refuse to pay their taxes, aware that no magistrate could prosecute thousands of delinquents. Their taxes were eventually written off. Without adequate revenues, the empire could not maintain a strong army to defend itself.

In spite of these foreign pressures, the empire did not fall apart. In fact, southern China enjoyed considerable prosperity in the late sixteenth and early seventeenth centuries. Why? Japanese, Portuguese, and Dutch merchants paid in silver for the Chinese silks and ceramics they bought. The steady flow of silver into China from the illicit trade with Japan – and, later, from the mines of Mexico and Peru via Spain – had momentous consequences. The value of Chinese paper currency, which had been in circulation since the eleventh century, drastically declined. Unable to control either the state economy or local commercial activity, the imperial government had to adopt a more liberal attitude and simply acquiesce in foreign trade. The emperor also had to recognize the triumph of silver as a medium of exchange.

Also, merchants in the southern maritime provinces, where trade flourished with Japan, the Philippines, and Indonesia, invested surplus capital in new ventures in the towns. Peasants migrated to the towns seeking employment, and agriculture declined. Some businesses employed several hundred workers, many of them women. According to a French scholar, "Peasant women took jobs at Sungchiang, southwest of Shanghai in the cotton mills. According to contemporary descriptions, in the big workshops the employees were already the anonymous labor force that we regard as characteristic of the industrial age."[35] Sungchiang developed into a large cotton-weaving center, Soochow became famous for its luxury silks, and by the end of the sixteenth century paper factories at Kiangsi employed 50,000 workers.

By the late sixteenth century China was participating in the emerging global economy. Portuguese ships carried Chinese silks and ceramics to Nagaski and returned with Japanese silver. The huge Ming merchant marine, built from the trees planted by Hung Wu and more technically proficient for long sea voyages than the Spanish and Portuguese fleets, transported textiles, porcelains, silk, and paper to Manila in the Philippines and brought back sweet potatoes, tobacco, firearms, and silver. From Manila the Spanish fleet carried Chinese

goods to the markets of Barcelona, Antwerp, and Venice. The Dutch transported tea by the boatload from Fukien and Chekiang for the castles and drawing rooms of Europe.[36] Europeans paid for most of their imports with silver. Recent scholars argue that between one-third and one-half of *all* the silver mined in the Americas between 1527 and 1821 wound up in China. Spanish galleons carried it from Acapulco to Manila and thence to Chinese ports.[37]

In 1600 the Ming dynasty faced grave political and economic problems. The Manchus threatened from the north. Wars against the Japanese and Koreans had depleted the imperial treasury. As rich landowners bought up the lands assigned to farm families, the social structures set up by Hung Wu had broken down. The government had to hire mercenaries; the military, considered a disreputable profession, drew the dregs of society. According to the Jesuit missionary Matteo Ricci (1552–1610), "All those under arms lead a despicable life, for they have not embraced this profession out of love of their country or devotion to their king or love of honour and glory, but as men in the service of a provider of employment."[38]

Maintenance of the army placed a heavy burden on the state. The imperial court continued to squander vast sums on an ostentatious lifestyle and the allowances of the extended imperial family. Under the Emperor Wan-li (1517–1619), forty-five princes of the first rank received annual incomes of 10,000 *shih* (the money equivalent of 10,000 tons of grain), while 21,000 lesser nobles also received large allowances. The emperors increased domestic sales taxes, established customs posts for export-import duties, and laid ever-more-crushing taxes on the peasants. New taxes provoked violent riots in the large commercial centers of Soochow, Hangchow,

CHINESE SCHOLARS *The civil service examina-*
tions, the chief means of access to governmental posi-
tions and social status, inculcated total submission to
the autocratic state. The largest number of candidates
took the examinations in general knowledge and liter-
ary ability. Here candidates stand at writing desks,
composing essays. (Bibliothèque Nationale, Paris)

and Peking. Between 1619 and 1627 greedy
court eunuchs helped precipitate the crisis.
The eunuch Wei Chung-hsien (1563–1627)
exercised a two-year reign of terror and sent
hundreds of honest civil servants to their
deaths as 'conspirators.' The bureaucracy that
the eunuchs controlled was so torn by factions that it could not function.

Finally, the emperors became victims of
their training, and servants rather than masters of the bureaucracy. A Ming emperor was
taught that his primary duties were to vener-

ate heaven and to follow the precedents set by his ancestors. So long as the emperor performed certain time-honored rituals, he retained the Mandate of Heaven. In a society lacking a strong army and effective bureaucratic institutions, it was imperial ritual that connected the ordinary person to the state by imbuing awe, respect, and loyalty. Thus the emperors spent a large part of each day in the performance of imperial ceremonies, which they came to resent.

The reign of the Emperor Wan-li (1573-1620), who ruled longer than any other member of the dynasty, illustrates what happened when the emperor was at odds with the system. An intelligent man with some good ideas, Wan-li felt that the bureaucrats opposed everything he wanted to do. When he tried to increase the size of the army and to improve its effectiveness through drills and maneuvers, civil-service officials sent him lengthy memorials calling for an end to such exercises. When he wanted to take personal command of the army at a time of foreign invasion, bureaucrats told him that precedent forbade him to leave the Imperial City. Wan-li gradually reached the conclusion that the monarchy had become no more than a set of stylized performances. Stymied in whatever he wanted to do, he simply refused to make state decisions. He devoted his time to his horses and, while still a young man, to the construction of his tomb. Imperial decisions were postponed. Factional strife among the court eunuchs and bureaucrats increased. The wheels of government ground to a halt.[39]

Meanwhile, the Manchus, a Tungusic people from Manchuria, pressed against China's northwestern border. Under their leader Nurhachi (1559-1626), they built a powerful military and administrative organization and gained the allegiance of the Mongols and other tribes. As the Ming government in Peking floundered, public anger at bureaucratic

corruption mounted. Ming troops, their pay in arrears, turned outlaw. Droughts led to crop failures, which in turn caused widespread famines. Starving peasants turned to banditry, and entire provinces revolted. The general decay paved the way for Manchu conquest.

MANCHU RULE

The Manchus declared a new dynasty, the Ch'ing, in 1644, and went on to capture Peking and slowly gain control of all China. Their initial success was due more to the internal weaknesses of the Ming than to special strengths of their own. Other developments help explain their ultimate victory and rule. The gentry and business classes, centered in the south around Nanking, were alienated by the Ming court's fiscal mismanagement and demands for more taxes. Although various Ming princelings and local bandit groups rose against the Manchus, the Ming army lacked good equipment and staying power and gradually collapsed. The entry of the Manchus' imperial armies into Yunnan in 1681 marked their complete military triumph.

There remained the influential academic and intellectual classes. By purging the civil service of the old court eunuchs and troublesome factions, and by offering Chinese intellectuals positions in the bureaucracy, the Manchus gained the support of the intellectuals. Chinese scholars flocked to Peking. The Manchu government, staffed by able and honest Chinese, became much more efficient than the Ming.

The Ch'ing dynasty – the name adopted by the Manchus means "pure" or "unsullied" – ruled until 1912. In its heydey in the eighteenth century, the Ch'ing empire covered much of Asia: China proper, Manchuria, Mongolia, Tibet, Sinkiang; and enjoyed tribute from Burma, Nepal, Laos, Siam, Annam, and Korea (see Map 25.4). China had the

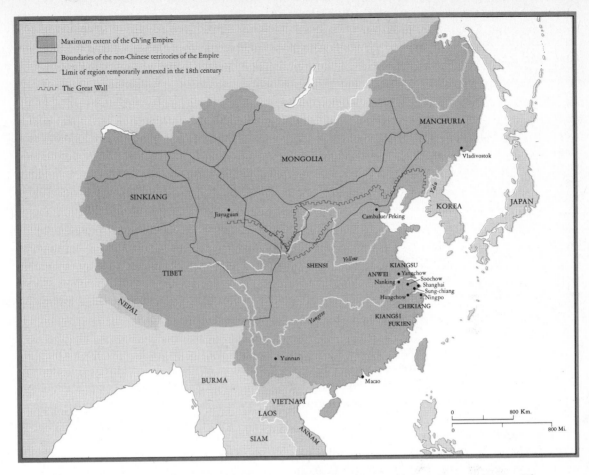

MAP 25.4 *CHINA: CH'ING EMPIRE, 1759 The sheer size of the Chinese empire almost inevitably led to its profound cultural influence on the rest of Asia. What geographical and political factors limited the extent of the Ch'ing empire?*

largest population on earth, and it achieved an unprecedented degree of prosperity.

How did 1 million Manchus govern 350 million Chinese? The Ch'ing dynasty retained the basic structures of Ming and Confucian government. The emperor governed as supreme and autocratic ruler with the Mandate of Heaven. The bureaucracies continued as they had in Ming and earlier times: while the imperial household bureaucracy managed the emperor's palaces and households, the central bureaucracy administered his vast empire. Positions in the latter were mostly assigned on the basis of candidates' performances in the

civil-service examinations in the Confucian classics. The highest positions in Peking and in the provinces of China were open to Chinese as well as Manchus. These measures pacified the Chinese economic and intellectual elites. The Manchus, however, maintained a distinct and privileged status in society. They wore distinctive clothes, did not practice footbinding, retained their own language and alphabetic script, and maintained ethnic separatism by forbidding intermarriage with the Chinese. The Manchus required male Chinese to wear their hair in a pigtail as a sign of subjection to the Ch'ing.

TABLE 25.3   POPULATION OF CHINA, 1578-1974

Year	Government	Population Families	Individuals
1578	Ming Dynasty	10.6 million	60.7 million
1662	Ch'ing Dynasty	19.2 million	100 million
1710		23.3 million	116 million
1729		25.5 million	127 million
1741			143.4 million
1754			184.5 million
1778			243 million
1796			275.7 million
1814			374.6 million
1850			414.5 million
1953	People's Republic		601.9 million
1974			800 million

The agricultural improvements begun in the Ming period had profound social effects in the eighteenth century. China experienced a population explosion, as Table 25.3 statistics illustrate.

Internal peace and relative prosperity, and engineering methods that prevented flooding of the countryside, contributed to the steady growth of population. Continued population increases without increased agricultural output led, in the late eighteenth century, to rebellions, uprisings, and general weakness of the Manchu dynasty.

The Manchu dynasty reached its zenith under the Emperor K'ang-hsi (1662-1722). K'ang-hsi, an exact contemporary of the Indian ruler Aurangzeb, France's Louis XIV, and the Russian Czar Peter the Great, demonstrated exceptional intelligence, energy, and concern for the welfare of his people. He also enjoyed much greater freedom of action than had the Ming emperor Wan-li a century earlier. Where Wan-li had been a captive of precedent, incapable of making changes, K'ang-hsi cut both court expenses and taxes, and travelled extensively throughout his domains. On these trips he investigated the conduct of local bureaucrats in an effort to prevent them from

oppressing the people. Where Wan-li had vacillated in the face of domestic revolt and foreign invasion, the K'ang-hsi emperor squarely faced a massive rebellion in south China in 1678 and thoroughly crushed it. He personally led an army into Mongolia and smashed the forces of the Mongol leader Galdan. This victory permanently eliminated the danger of a reinvigorated Mongolian empire on China's borders.

The K'ang-hsi emperor also cultivated the arts of peace. He invited scholars to his court and subsidized the compilation of a huge encyclopedia and two monumental dictionaries. *The Complete Library of the Four Treasuries*, a collection of all of Chinese literature that required the work of 15,000 calligraphers and 361 editors, preserved the Chinese literary tradition. K'ang-hsi's contributions to literature hold a distinguished place in the long history of Chinese culture. Europe and America, however, appreciate the period primarily for its excellent porcelain. The word *china* entered the English language and became synonymous with fine pottery and tableware. An imperial factory at Kiangsi, directly controlled by the K'ang-hsi court, produced porcelain masterpieces: monochrome vases, bowls, and dishes in oxblood, pale green and dark blue, and polychromes in blue and white enjoyed enormous popularity in Paris, London, and New York in the eighteenth century and ever since.

The family is the fundamental unit of every society. In Ming and Ch'ing China, however, the family exercised greater social influence than it did anywhere else, and far more than in Western societies. The family directed the moral education of the child, the economic advancement and marriage of the young, and religious life through ceremonial rites honoring the family's ancestors. The Chinese family discharged many of the roles that the Christian Church performed in the European Middle Ages, and that the state carries out today. It assumed total responsibility for the sick, the indigent, and the aged. The family expected and almost invariably received the full devotion and loyalty of its members. A person without a family had no material or psychological support.

Poor families tended to be "nuclear" – that is, couples established their own households and raised their own children. The educated, middle-class, and wealthy frequently resided in extended families – several generations of patrilineal relatives and their wives lived together in one large house or compound, individual families occupying different sections. In both kinds of families, the paternal head of the family held autocratic power over all members of the household. On his death, his authority passed to his eldest son. The father led the family in the ancient Confucian rites honoring its ancestors. If these ceremonies were not continued into the next generation, the family suffered social disgrace and the dead were believed to endure great misery. Thus marriage was extremely important. Almost everyone married. Reverence for one's parents, maintenance of the family, and perpetuation of the line required that sons marry shortly after reaching puberty. The father and family elders discussed the possibilities and employed a local go-between to negotiate with the prospective bride's family. The go-between drew up a marriage contract specifying the property, furniture, clothing, and gifts the two young people would bring to the union. As elsewhere, parents wanted to make the most economically and socially advantageous union for their children. The couple had no part in these arrangements; many never even saw each other until the groom lifted the bride's veil on their wedding day. But they had been brought up to accept this.

A Chinese bride became part of her husband's family, and became subject to him and to her in-laws. Her first duty was to bear sons. If she did not, she might adopt one. Failure to give her husband heirs gave him grounds for divorce, which brought great disgrace upon her family. A woman, however, could not divorce her husband for any reason. Divorce was extremely rare in Chinese society, but a wealthy man with a "nonproductive" wife might take concubines who lived in the house with his wife. Because males performed the all-important ceremonies in honor of the family ancestors, they held a much higher position in society than did women. The desperately poor often practiced infanticide of girl babies or sold their daughters as concubines. Young brides came under the direct control of their mothers-in-law, whose severity and cruelty is a common theme in Chinese literature. A strong-willed woman, once she had sons, gained increasing respect as the years went by. The Chinese deeply respected age. Women of the wealthy classes, with servants to do the household chores, spent their days in semi-seclusion nibbling dainties, smoking opium, and gambling. Poor women worked in the fields beside their husbands, in addition to bearing children and managing the household.

The educational system during the Ming and Ch'ing periods had both virtues and weaknesses. Most villages and all towns and cities operated schools that prepared boys for the all-important civil-service examinations. Boys learned to write with a brush the approximately 3,000 commonly used characters of literary Chinese; they learned from memory the standard texts of Confucian philosophy, ethics, and history. The curriculum was very limited, and the instructional method stressed memorization and discouraged imagination. The successful civil-service candidate received no practical training in the work of government. On the other hand, the system yielded a high percentage of literate men (relative to Europe at the same time); it preserved the ethical values of Chinese culture, and it gave Chinese society cohesion and stability. All educated Chinese shared the same basic literary culture, much as medieval Europeans were formed by Latin Christian culture. As in medieval Europe too, educational opportunities for girls were severely limited. Rich men occasionally hired tutors for their daughters, and a few women achieved exceptional knowledge. Most women of all classes received training that prepared them for roles as wives and mothers: courteous behavior, submission to their husbands, and the administration of a household.

In sharp contrast to the social structure of Europe, Chinese society had few hard-and-fast lines. The emperors fought the development of a hereditary aristocracy, which would have worked against the interest of absolute monarchy. Few titles of nobility were granted in perpetuity. Meanwhile the state bureaucracy provided opportunities and motivation for upward mobility. The entire family supported and encouraged intelligent sons to prepare for the civil-service examinations, and the work and self-sacrifice of the parents bore fruit in the sons. Positions in the bureaucracy brought salaries and gifts, which the family invariably invested in land. The competitive examinations – open, with few exceptions, to all classes – prevented the formation of a ruling caste. Since everyone accepted the Confucian principle that the nation should be led by the learned and civilized, scholars held the highest rank in the social order. They, along with Heaven, Earth, the emperor, and parents, deserved special veneration. With the possible exception of the Jewish people, no other nation has respected learning as much as the Chinese, who gave special deference to the teacher-scholar. Farmers merited esteem because they produced food; merchants less so because they supposedly lived off the profits of others' toil. Merchants tried to marry into the scholar class in order to rise on the social ladder, but China did not develop an articulate bourgeoisie. At the bottom of society were actors, prostitutes, and the many beggars.

The Chinese found recreation and relaxation in many ways. All classes gambled at cards and simple numbers games. The teahouse served as the local meeting-place to exchange news and gossip, and to listen to the tales of professional storytellers, who enjoyed great popularity. The affluent indulged in an alcoholic drink made from fermented and distilled rice, and both men and women liked pipes and tobacco. Everyone who could afford to went to theaters, which were a central part of Chinese culture. The actors wore happy and sad masks like their ancient Greek counterparts, and their gestures were formal and heavily stylized; the plays typically dramatized episodes from Chinese history and literature. The Chinese associated athletics, riding, and horse racing with soldiers, at best a necessary evil, and regarded the active life as the direct antithesis of the scholarly contemplation they most valued. Thus sports found little favor.

The first Christian missionaries in China had little impact on the bulk of the population, but among the intellectual classes their work was significant. In 1582 the Italian Jesuit Matteo Ricci (1552-1610), the most famous Christian missionary to Asia, settled at Macao on the mouth of the Canton River. Like the Christian monks who had converted the Germanic tribes of early medieval Europe, Ricci sought first to convert the emperor and elite groups and then, through gradual assimilation as in Europe (pages 289-291), to win the throngs of Chinese. Ricci tried to present Christianity to the Chinese in Chinese terms. He understood the Chinese respect for learning and worked to win converts among the scholarly class. When Ricci was admitted to the Imperial City at Peking, he addressed the Emperor Wan-li:

Li Ma-tou [Ricci's name transliterated into Chinese], your Majesty's servant, comes from the Far West, addressed himself to Your Majesty with respect, in order to offer gifts from his country. Your Majesty's servant comes from a far distant land which has never exchanged presents with the Middle Kingdom [the Chinese name for China, based on the belief that the Chinese empire occupied the middle of the earth and was surrounded by barbarians]. Despite the distance, fame told me of the remarkable teaching and fine institutions with which the imperial court has endowed all its peoples. I desired to share these advantages and live out my life as one of Your Majesty's subjects, hoping in return to be of some small use.[40]

Ricci presented the emperor with two clocks, one of them decorated with dragons and eagles in the Chinese style. The emperor's growing fascination with clocks gave Ricci the opportunity to display other examples of Western technology. He instructed court scholars about astronomical equipment and the manufacture of cannons, and drew for them a map of the world — with China at its center. These inventions greatly impressed the Chinese intelligentsia, and in the 1730s a Jesuit wrote, "The Imperial Palace is stuffed with clocks, ... watches, carillons, repeaters, organs, spheres, and astronomical clocks of all kinds — there are more than four thousand pieces from the best masters of Paris and London."[41] Nevertheless the Jesuits made only a few converts to Christianity, most of them from the small but crucially important scholar class.

Christian missionary efforts miscarried over the "Rites Controversy," a dispute over ritual between the Jesuits and other Roman Catholic religious orders. The Jesuits supported the celebration of the Mass in Chinese and the performance of other ceremonies in terms understandable by the Chinese. Other missionaries, such as the Franciscans, felt that the Jesuits had sold out the essentials of the Christian faith in order to win converts. One burning issue was whether the Chinese reverence for ancestors was homage to the good the dead had done during their lives, or an act of worship. The Franciscans secured the support of the Roman authorities, who considered themselves authorities on Chinese culture and decided against the Jesuits. In 1704 and again in 1742 Rome decreed that Roman ceremonial practice (that is, in Latin) was to be the law for Chinese missions. This decision continued to govern Roman Catholic missionary activity until the Second Vatican Council in 1962.

JAPAN (CA 1400-1800)

Between the late fourteenth and the late sixteenth centuries, Japanese society experienced almost continual violence and civil war. The weak central governments could not maintain order. Throughout the islands, local strongmen destroyed weak ones: around 1450, 250 *daimyōs*, or lords, held power; by 1600, there were only 12 daimyōs. Successful military leaders carved out large territories and governed them as independent rulers. Political and social conditions in fifteenth- and sixteenth-century Japan strongly resembled those of western Europe in the tenth and eleventh centuries. Political power was in the hands of a small group of military leaders. Historians often use the same term – feudalism – to describe the Japanese and the European experience. As in medieval Europe, feudalism paved the way for the rise of a strong centralized state in seventeenth-century Japan.

FEUDALISM IN JAPAN

Feudalism played a powerful role in Japanese culture until the nineteenth century. The similarities between feudalism in Japan and in medieval Europe have fascinated scholars, as have their very significant differences. Feudalism in Europe emerged out of the fusion of Germanic and Roman social institutions, and flowered under the impact of Muslim and Viking invasions. In Japan, on the other hand, feudalism evolved in complete isolation from outside cultural forces. Japan was more secluded from alien influences than any other country of comparable cultural development. When foreign pressures finally opened up Japan in the nineteenth century, Japanese feudalism collapsed.

The two constituent elements of Japanese feudalism appeared between the eighth and the twelfth centuries: the *shō* or land with its *shiki* or rights, and the military warrior clique. Some scholars have equated the shō with the European manor, but the comparison needs careful qualification. A manor corresponded to one composite village, while a particular family's shō were widely scattered. Those who held shō possessed the shiki there – that is,

the right to the income or rice produced by the land. On the other hand, just as several persons might hold rights – military, judicial, grazing – on a medieval manor, and all these rights yielding income, so several persons frequently held shiki on a Japanese estate. The Japanese samurai warrior resembled the knight of twelfth-century France. Both were armed with expensive weapons, and both fought on horseback. Just as the knight was supposed to live according to the chivalric code (pages 503–504), so Japanese samurai were expected to live according to *Bushido*, a code that stressed military honor, courage, stoical acceptance of hardship, and, above all, loyalty. Samurai and knights were both highly conscious of themselves as aristocrats; but while knights fought as groups, samurai fought as individuals.

By the middle of the sixteenth century Japanese feudalism had taken on other distinctive features. As the number of shō decreased and the powerful daimyōs consolidated their territories, the practice of primogeniture became common. Instead of dividing an estate among all the lord's children, the shō were kept intact and assigned to the eldest or ablest son. Also, only a small proportion of samurai attained the rank of daimyō and possessed shō; most warriors received support in rice, not in land. In this respect they resembled European knights supported by cash or money fiefs. They were salaried fighters with no connection to land. Third, the nature of warfare changed in two basic ways. Daimyōs employed large numbers of foot soldiers equipped with spears, along with armed cavalrymen. The countryside also saw the construction of new castles. As in medieval Europe, the typical method of warfare was to besiege a castle and wait for it to surrender. Around 1540 the introduction of the musket from Europe made infantrymen effective against mounted samurai; the use of Western cannon

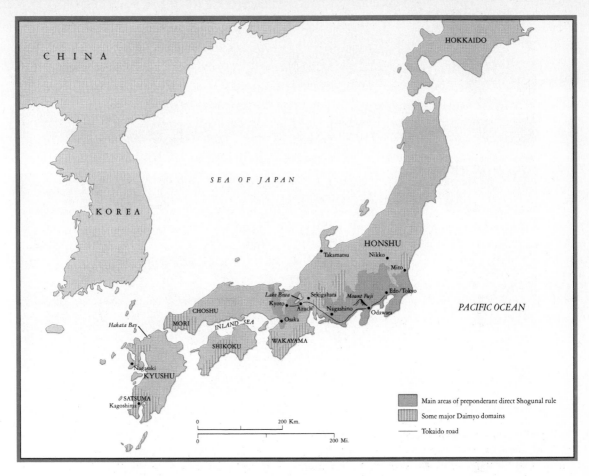

MAP 25.5 TOKUGAWA JAPAN *Consider the cultural and political significance of the fact that Japan is an island. How did the concentration of Shogunate lands affect its government of Japan?*

required more elaborately fortified castles. These military and social developments occurred during a century of turbulence and chronic disorder, out of which emerged a leader who ended the chaos and began the process of Japanese unification. Oda Nobunaga (1534-1582) laid the foundations of the modern Japanese national state.

NOBUNAGA AND NATIONAL UNIFICATION

A samurai of the lesser daimyō class, Nobunaga won control of his native province of Owari in 1559. He began immediately to ex-

tend his power and made himself lord of the eastern province of Mikawa. Nobunaga defeated a powerful daimyō in 1560, and eight years later seized Kyoto, the capital city. As a result, Nobunaga became the virtual ruler of central Japan.

Scholars have called the years 1568-1600 "the period of National Unification." During it the country underwent aggressive and dynamic change. Adopting the motto, "Rule the Empire by Force," Nobunaga set out to subdue all real and potential enemies of unification. With the support of a brilliant but low-born general, Toyotomi Hideyoshi, he

HANABUSA ITCHŌ: MARKETPLACE Perhaps the greatest cartoon artist in Japanese history. Itchō (1652–1724) worked with ink and color on paper. This elegantly simple representation of a vegetable market shows Itchō's appreciation for the activities of everyday life and helps explain his enormous contemporary popularity. (Courtesy, Freer Gallery of Art, Smithsonian Institution, Washington, D.C.)

subdued most of western Japan. In 1575 Nobunaga's use of firearms at the battle of Nagashino led to a decisive victory that added the province of Totomi to his domains. When Hideyoshi smashed the great fortress of Odawara, eastern and northern Japan came under Nobunaga's control as well.

The great Buddhist temple-fortresses proved to be Nobunaga's biggest problem. Some of these monasteries possessed vast wealth and armed retainers, and they actively intervened in secular affairs. During the civil wars the Buddhists had supported various daimyōs in their private wars, but Nobunaga would tolerate no such interference. The strategically located monastery on Mt. Hiei near Kyoto had long provided sanctuary for political factions, but previous daimyōs had refused to attack it because it was sacred. Nobunaga

had his troops surround Mt. Hiei and set fire to the thickets on the lower slopes of the mountain. As the monks and lay people fled the fire, Nobunaga's men slaughtered them by the thousands. The destruction of Japan's most powerful monastery ended Buddhist influence as a political force.

Although Nobunaga won control of most of Japan by the sword, he backed up his conquests with governmental machinery and a policy of conciliation. He gave lands and subordinate positions in the army to his defeated enemies. Trusted daimyōs received complete civil jurisdiction over entire provinces. At strategic points, such as Nijo near Kyoto and Azuchi on the shore of Lake Biwa, Nobunaga built castles to serve as key administrative and defensive centers for the surrounding territories. He opened the little fishing village of

Nagasaki to foreign commerce; it soon grew into the nation's largest port. He standardized the currency, eliminated customs barriers, and encouraged the development of trade and industry. When Nobunaga was murdered by one of his vassals, his general and staunchest adherent Hideyoshi carried on his work.

The son of a peasant, Hideyoshi had risen to power by his military bootstraps: he was an exceptionally able field commander. Hideyoshi made two significant contributions to the unification and centralization of Japan. In 1582 he attacked the great fortress of Takamatsu; when direct assault failed, he had his troops flood the surrounding moat until the castle was forced into submission. When Takamatsu fell, so did the large province of Mori. Successful seige of the town of Kagoshima then brought the southern island of Kyushu under his domination. Hideyoshi conciliated the vanquished daimyōs as Nobunaga had done – with lands and military positions – but he also required them to swear allegiance and to obey him "down to the smallest particular."[42]

Having reduced his most dangerous adversaries and taken steps to control the daimyōs, Hideyoshi ordered a survey of the entire country. The military power of the unified Japanese state depended upon a strong agricultural basis, and Hideyoshi wanted to exploit the peasantry fully. His agents collected detailed information about the daimyōs' lands, and about towns, villages, agricultural produce, and industrial output all over Japan. A sort of Japanese equivalent of the *Domesday Book* (page 458), this material enabled him to assess military quotas and taxable property. Hideyoshi's surveys tied the peasant population to the land and tightened the collection of the land tax. When Hideyoshi died in 1598, he left a strong centralized state. Brute force had created a unified Japan.

On his deathbed the old soldier had set up a council of regents to govern during the minority of his infant son. The strongest regent was Hideyoshi's long-time supporter, Tokugawa Ieyasu, who ruled vast territories around Edo, modern-day Tokyo. Ieyasu quickly eliminated the young ruler, and in 1600 at Sekigahara he smashed a coalition of daimyō defenders of the heir. This battle marked the beginning of the Tokugawa regime.

THE TOKUGAWA REGIME

Japanese children are taught that "Ieyasu ate the pie Nobunaga made and Hideyoshi baked." As the aphorism suggests, Ieyasu took over and completed the work begun by his able predecessors. He took decisive steps to solidify his dynasty and control the feudal nobility, and to maintain peace and prosperity in Japan. The Tokugawa regime that Ieyasu fashioned worked remarkably well, lasting until 1867.

Ieyasu obtained from the emperor the title of shōgun, which meant that he and his heirs had the right to command everyone. Constitutionally, the emperor exercised sovereign authority; in practice, authority and power – both the legal right and the physical means – were held by the Tokugawa shōgun. Ieyasu declared the emperor and his court at Kyoto "very precious and decorative, like gold and silver," and surrounded the imperial court with all the ceremonial trappings and none of the realities of power.

In a scheme reminiscent of Louis XIV of France (page 720) and Peter the Great of Russia (page 782), Ieyasu forced the feudal lords to establish "alternate residence" at his capital city of Edo, to spend every other year there, and to leave their wives and sons there – essentially as hostages. This device had obvious advantages: the shōgun could keep close tabs on the daimyōs, control them through their children, and weaken them financially with the burden of maintaining two residences. Ieyasu justified this institution by invoking the Bushido code, with its emphasis on loyalty. Using strategems like those practiced by the English William the Conqueror, Ieyasu forbade members of the nobility to marry without his consent, thus preventing the formation of dangerous alliances. The Tokugawa shōguns also severely restricted the construction of castles – symbols, in Japan as in medieval Europe, of feudal independence. The aristocratic samurai class, however, alone possessed the right to wear two swords, and they exercised full administrative powers within their own domains. In effect, the country was governed by martial law in peacetime. Only warriors could hold official positions in the state bureaucracy. Finally, again like the system of Louis XIV, a network of spies kept close watch on the nobility.

As in medieval Europe and early modern China, the agricultural class held a respected position in Japanese society because they provided it with sustenance. Even so, farmers had to mind their betters, and they bore a disproportionate share of the tax load. According to the survey made by Hideyoshi, taxes were imposed on villages, not individuals; the tax varied between 30 and 40 percent of the rice crop.

As in Europe and China, the commercial classes occupied the lowest rungs on the social ladder because they profited from the toils of others. The peace that the Tokugawa imposed in the seventeenth century brought a steady rise in population and prosperity. As demand for goods grew, so did the numbers of merchants. To maintain stability, the early Tokugawa shōguns froze the four social categories – imperial court nobility, samurai, peasants, and merchants. Laws rigidly prescribed what each class could and could not do. Nobles, for example, were "strictly forbidden whether by day or by night, to go saunter through the streets or lanes in places where they have no business to be." Daimyōs were prohibited from moving troops outside their frontiers, making alliances, and coining money. Designated dress and stiff rules of etiquette distinguished one class from another.[43] This kind of stratification succeeded in its purpose: it protected the Tokugawa from daimyō attack and inaugurated a long era of peace.

To maintain dynastic stability and internal peace, Ieyasu's descendants imposed measures called *sakoku*, or "the closed country policy," which sealed Japan's borders around 1636. Japanese were forbidden to leave the country; foreigners were excluded. Shortly after the Jesuit missionary Francis Xavier landed at Kagoshima in 1549, he had made many converts among the poor and even some among the daimyōs. By 1600 there were 300,000 baptized Christians, most of them on the southernmost island of Kyushu where the shōgun's power was weakest and the loyalty of the daimyōs most doubtful. In 1615 bands of Christian samurai had supported Ieyasu's enemies at the fierce battle of Osaka. In 1637 30,000 peasants in the heavily Catholic area of northern Kyusu revolted. The shōguns therefore associated Christianity with domestic disorder and feudal rebellion. Accordingly, what had earlier been mild persecution became ruthless repression after 1639. Foreign priests were expelled or tortured and thousands of Japanese Christians suffered crucifixion. The policy of sakoku remained in force for almost two centuries as a means of controlling religious organizations and securing political order. The shōgunate kept Japan isolated.

THE LIFE OF THE PEOPLE

Two hundred years of peace is no mean achievement in the history of world societies. Moreover, profound social and economic development occurred in spite of Japan's near-total isolation. The lives of the Japanese people changed profoundly in the seventeenth and eighteenth centuries.

The Tokugawa shōgunate subdued the nobility by emasculating it politically. Stripped of power and required to spend every other year at Edo, the daimyōs and samurai passed their lives pursuing pleasure. They spent frantically on fine silks, paintings, concubines, boys, the theater, and the redecoration of their castles. Around 1700 one scholar observed that the entire military class was living "as in an inn, that is consuming now and paying later."[44] Eighteenth-century Japanese novels, plays, and histories portray the samurai as engrossed in tavern brawls and sexual orgies. These frivolities, plus the heavy costs of maintaining an alternate residence at Edo, travelling with their retinues, and the sophisticated pleasures of the capital gradually ruined the warrior class.

They spent heavily on the *kabuki* theater, which enjoyed enormous popularity. An art form created by townspeople, kabuki drama consisted of crude and bawdy skits dealing with love and romance or aspects of prostitution, an occupation in which the actors and actresses had usually had professional experience. Performances featured elaborate costumes, singing, dancing, and recitation of poetry. Because female actresses were thought to be corrupting the public morals, the Tokugawa government banned them from the stage in 1629. When women were excluded from the stage, men played all the parts. Male actors in female dress and makeup performed as seductively as possible in order to entice the burly samurai who thronged the theaters. Homosexuality, long accepted in Japan, was widely practiced among the samurai, who pursued the actors and spent profligately on them. According to one seventeenth-century Edo writer,

"Youth's kabuki" began with beautiful youths being made to sing and dance, whereupon droll fools...had their hearts captivated and their souls stolen. As they rapturously gave themselves up to visiting the youths in high spirits, the early depletion of even substantial fortunes was like light snow exposed to the spring sun. How much worse it was for those whose fortunes were slight to begin with. There were many of these men who soon had run through their fortunes...I have heard that men of the capital have also done this.... Even though the lineage of every one of the youths was extremely base, these beautiful youths were respected by the stupid; they flapped about like kites and owls and, going into the presence of the exalted [distinguished persons], befouled the presence; and these were scoundrels who, saying insolent things as it pleased them, ruined men and held them in contempt.[45]

Some moralists and bureaucrats periodically complained, but the Tokugawa government accepted kabuki and prostitution as necessary evils. They provided employment, gratified the tastes of samurai and townspeople, and diverted former warriors from potential criminal and political mischief.[46] How did the samurai pay for their pleasures? In the same way their European counterparts did — by fleecing the peasants and borrowing from the merchants.

According to Japanese theory, farmers deserved respect. In practice, peasants were sometimes severely oppressed and led miserable lives. It was government policy to tax them to the level of bare subsistence, and official legislation repeatedly defined their duties. In 1649 every village in Japan received these regulations:

• *Peasants must rise early and cut grass before cultivating the fields. In the evening they are to make straw rope or straw bags, all such work to be done with great care.*

- *They must not buy tea or sake [a fermented liquor made from rice] to drink nor must their wives.*
- *Men must plant bamboo or trees round the farmhouse and must use the fallen leaves for fuel so as to save expense.*
- *Peasants are people without sense or forethought. Therefore they must not give rice to their wives and children at harvest time, but must save food for the future. They should eat millet, vegetables, and other coarse food instead of rice. Even the fallen leaves of plants should be saved as food against famine.... During the seasons of planting and harvesting, however, when the labor is arduous, the food taken may be a little better...*
- *The husband must work in the fields, the wife must work at the loom. Both must do night work. However good-looking a wife may be, if she neglects her household duties by drinking tea or sightseeing or rambling on the hillsides, she must be divorced.*
- *Peasants must wear only cotton or hemp — no silk. They may not smoke tobacco. It is harmful to health, it takes up time, and costs money. It also creates a risk of fire.*[47]

The state demanded that peasants work continually and live frugally. The conspicuous consumption of the upper classes led them in the course of the seventeenth and eighteenth centuries to increase taxes from 30 percent to 50 percent of the rice crop. Mountains cover much of Japan, and only 20 percent of its land is arable. Although the amount of cultivated land rose from about 5 million acres in 1600 to roughly 11.5 million in 1860, the long period of peace brought a great increase in population. The merchants who bought farm produce fixed the price of rice so low that it seemed to farmers that the more they produced, the less they earned. They found release from their frustrations either in flight from the village or in revolt. After 1704, peasant rebellions became chronic. Oppressive taxation provoked 84,000 farmers in the prov-

ince of Iwaki to revolt in 1739. Following widespread burning and destruction, their demands were met. In other instances the shōguns ordered savage repression, and natural disasters added to the peasants' misery. In the 1770s fires, floods, and volcanic eruptions hit all parts of Japan. Drought and torrential rain led to terrible famines in 1783–1788 and again in 1832–1836. Oppressive taxation, bad weather, and the contempt of lords and the central government often combined to make the lot of peasants virtually unrelieved wretchedness.

This picture of the Japanese peasantry tells only part of the story. The Japanese peasantry in the Tokugawa period was not a single homogeneous class. Recent scholarship has demonstrated that peasant society was more "a pyramid of wealth and power.... that rose from the tenant farmer at the bottom through small landholders to wealthy peasants at the top."[48] Agricultural productivity increased substantially during the Tokugawa period, and, although assessed taxes remained high, they were fixed. Therefore, peasants who improved their lands and increased their yields continued to pay the same assessed tax, but they paid proportionately less and pocketed the surplus as profit. Their social situation accordingly rose. By the early nineteenth century there existed a large class of relatively wealthy, educated, and ambitious peasant families. This upper stratum of village peasants resembled the middle ranks of the warrior class more than it did most peasants.

The Tokugawa witnessed a major transformation of agriculture, a great leap in productivity and specialization. The rural population increased, but surplus labor was drawn to other employment and to the cities; the agricultural population did not increase. In fact, Japan suffered an acute shortage of farm labor from 1720 to 1868. In some villages, industry became almost as important as agriculture. At

PLEASURE QUARTER OF KYOTO *These scenes give superb information about the dress and customs of the Japanese upper class in the mid-seventeenth century. In the foreground people pace in front of elegant bordellos. In the interior garden, beautifully dressed courtesans entertain wealthy patrons. The expensive materials used — ink, colors, and gold on paper — suggest that the folding screens were made for a rich merchant. (Museum of Fine Arts, Boston, Gift of Denman Waldo Ross)*

Hirano near Osaka, for example, 61.7 percent of all arable land was sown in cotton. Since the peasants ginned the cotton locally before transporting it to wholesalers in Osaka, they had a thriving industry. In many rural places, as many peasants worked in the manufacture of silk, or cotton, or vegetable oil as in the production of rice.[49]

The urban commercial classes, scorned for benefitting from the misery of the peasants and the appetites of the samurai, theoretically occupied the bottom rung of the social ladder. Merchants had no political power but they accumulated wealth, sometimes great wealth. They also proved the possibility of social mo-

bility, and thus the inherent weakness of the regime's system of strict social stratification. The commercial class grew in response to the phenomenal development of urban life. The seventeenth-century surplus rural population, together with underemployed samurai, desperately poor peasants, and the ambitious and adventurous, thronged to the cities. All wanted a better way of life than could be found in the dull farming villages. Japan's cities grew tremendously: Kyoto, the imperial capital of the emperor and his pleasure-loving court; Edo, the political capital, with its multitudes of government bureaucrats, daimyōs in alternate residence, intellectuals, and police;

and Osaka, by this time the greatest commercial city in Japan with its huge grain exchange and commercial banks. In the eighteenth century, Edo's population of almost 1 million represented the largest demand for goods and services in the world. The Tokugawa shōguns provided order and political stability, and turned the samurai into urban consumers by denying them military opportunities. Merchants stood ready to serve them. Towns offered all kinds of luxury goods and catered to every extravagant and exotic taste. By marketing the daimyōs' grain, they gave the aristocrats the cash they needed to support their rich establishments. Merchants formed guilds and banks and lent money to the samurai. Those who defaulted on their debts found themselves cut off from further credit.[50]

The despised merchant class grew steadily wealthier, and by contemporary standards anywhere in the world the Japanese "middle" class lived very well. The ruling samurai with their fixed stipends became increasingly poorer. In 1705 the shōgunate confiscated the wealth of the merchant house of Yodoya in Osaka "for conduct unbecoming a member of the commercial class." The government seized fifty pairs of gold screens, 360 carpets, several mansions, 48 granaries and warehouses scattered around the country, and hundreds of thousands of gold pieces. Yodoya possessed fabulous wealth, but other merchants too enjoyed a rich lifestyle. The actual reason for the confiscation was that influential daimyōs and samurai who owed the Yodoya gigantic debts and resented their wealth had pressured the shōgun to cut Yodoya down.[51]

———◆———

At the beginning of the nineteenth century, African societies were developing autonomously. Europeans exported upwards of 12 million slaves from Africa to meet the labor needs of Latin America, but the overall impact of the slave trade was slight. Although French culture influenced the coastal fringes of Senegal, the English maintained factories along the Gold Coast, and the Portuguese held Angola as a colony and maintained an insecure hold on Mozambique in East Africa, European influence hardly penetrated the African interior at all. It appeared around 1810 that Africa's development would be entirely autonomous.

The Indian subcontinent, for centuries the economic prize of European commercial interests, began to experience British political domination. Bitter hostility between Hindu and Muslim persisted as a dominant theme of Indian life.

China had undergone a rapid increase in both prosperity and population in the eighteenth century. On the basis of highly developed agriculture, the Ch'ing empire supported a population of 200 million in 1762 and 380 million in 1812, compared to only 193 million in all of Europe in 1800. Ch'ing China was also geographically larger than the present People's Republic of China, encompassing some of present-day Russia. But China's political and economic systems began to deteriorate in the late eighteenth and early nineteenth centuries. The country suffered from excessive centralization, in that all local questions had to be referred to Peking. The extravagant court placed an intolerable drain on the state treasury. Graft and corruption pervaded the imperial bureaucracy, provincial administration, and the army. The population explosion led to a severe land shortage, causing tension and frequent revolts in the countryside. The massive opium trade also had a disastrous effect on Chinese society: The volume of opium smuggled by the British East India Company into China increased tenfold between 1790 and 1820. So vast was the amount of opium imported, relative to Chinese exports of tea and silk, that China suffered a highly unfavorable balance of trade. The outflow of silver severely damaged the Chinese economy and thus the Manchu dynasty.

In 1800 Tokugawa Japan was reaping the rewards of two centuries of peace and social order. Steady economic growth and improved agricultural technology had swelled the population. The samurai class had been transformed into peaceful city dwellers and civil bureaucrats. The wealth of the business classes grew, and the samurai, dependent upon fixed agricultural rents in a time of rising standards of living, fell into debt. Although the shōgunate maintained a policy of national isolation, and no foreign power influenced Japan's political or social life, Japan was not really cut off from outside cultural contacts. Through the port of Nagasaki, Western scientific ideas and some Western technology entered the country through the persistent interest of Japanese scholars. The Japanese readily absorbed foreign technological ideas.

NOTES

1. Nicolas Sanchez-Albornoz, *The Population of Latin America: A History.* trans. W. A. R. Richardson, University of California Press, Berkeley, 1974, p. 41.

2. Cited in Alfred W. Crosby, *The Columbian Exchange: Biological and Cultural Consequences of 1492,* Greenwood Publishing Company, Westport, Conn., 1972, p. 39.

3. Crosby, Chapter 2, "Conquistador y Pestilencia," pp. 35–59.

4. Cited in Charles Gibson, ed., *The Black Legend: Anti-Spanish Attitudes in the Old World and the New,* Alfred Knopf, New York, 1971, pp. 74–75.

5. Cited in Leslie B. Rout, Jr., *The African Experience in Spanish America,* Cambridge University Press, New York, 1976, p. 23.

6. Philip D. Curtin, *Economic Change in Precolonial Africa: Senegambia in the Era of the Slave Trade,* University of Wisconsin Press, Madison, 1975, pp. 34–35; James A. Rawley, *The Transatlantic Slave Trade: A History,* W. W. Norton, New York, 1981, p. 12.

7. Robert W. July, *A History of the African People,* 3rd ed., Charles Scribner's Sons, New York, 1980, pp. 128–129.

8. Robert W. July, *Precolonial Africa: An Economic and Social History,* Charles Scribner's Sons, New York, 1975, p. 99.

9. July, *History of the African People,* p. 141.

10. Ahmad ibn Fartura, "The Kanem Wars," in *Nigerian Perspectives,* ed. Thomas Hodgkin, Oxford University Press, London, 1966, pp. 114–115.

11. "The Kano Chronicle" cited in Hodgkin, *Nigerian Perspectives,* pp. 89–90.

12. Rawley, p. 45.

13. Ibid., pp. 28–29.

14. Ibid., pp. 45–47.

15. July, *History of the African People,* p. 208.

16. John Adams, "Remarks on the Country Extending from Cape Palmas to the River Congo," in Hodgkin, *Nigerian Perspectives,* pp. 178–180.

17. Rawley, p. 426.

18. July, *History of the African People,* pp. 201–202.

19. Cited in Bernard Lewis, *The Muslim Discovery of Europe,* W. W. Norton, New York, 1982, p. 29.

20. William H. McNeill, *The Pursuit of Power: Technology, Armed Force, and Society since A.D. 1000,* University of Chicago Press, Chicago, 1982, p. 87.

21. Cited in Lewis, p. 30.

22. Francis Robinson, *Atlas of the Islamic World since 1500,* Facts on File, New York, 1982, p. 72.

23. Cited in Robinson, p. 79.

24. Cited in Philip K. Hitti, *The Near East in History,* D. Van Nostrand Company, Princeton, 1961, p. 336.

25. Cited in Vincent A. Smith, *The Oxford History*

of India, Oxford University Press, Oxford, 1967, p. 398.

26. Cited in Milo Cleveland Beach, *The Imperial Image: Painting for the Mughal Court,* Freer Gallery of Art, Smithsonian Institution, Washington, D.C., 1981, pp. 9–10.

27. Cited in S. M. Ikram, *Muslim Civilization in India,* Columbia University Press, New York, 1964, p. 202.

28. Cited in K. M. Panikkar, *Asia and Western Dominance,* George Allen & Unwin, London, 1965, p. 35.

29. Cited in Panikkar, p. 53.

30. Cited in Woolbridge Bingham, Hilary Conroy, and Frank W. Ikle, *A History of Asia,* vol. II, Allyn & Bacon, Boston, 1967, p. 74.

31. Jacques Gernet, *A History of Chinese Civilization,* Cambridge University Press, New York, 1982, p. 391.

32. Ibid.

33. Luo Zewen et al., *The Great Wall,* McGraw-Hill, New York, 1981, p. 140.

34. Ray Huang, *1587: A Year of No Significance. The Ming Dynasty in Decline,* Yale University Press, New Haven, 1981, p. 13.

35. Gernet, pp. 425–426.

36. John E. Wills, Jr., "Maritime China from Wang Chih to Shih Long," *From Ming to Ching: Conquest, Region, and Continuity in Seventeenth-Century China,* ed. Jonathan D. Spence and John E. Wills, Jr., Yale University Press, New Haven, 1979, pp. 203–216.

37. Fernand Braudel, *The Wheels of Commerce: Civilization and Capitalism, 15th–18th Century,* vol. 2, trans. Sian Reynolds, Harper & Row, New York, 1982, pp. 198–199.

38. Gernet, p. 431.

39. See Huang, pp. 120–129.

40. Cited in Stephen Neill, *A History of Christian Missions,* Penguin Books, New York, 1977, p. 163.

41. Cited in Carlo M. Cipolla, *Clocks and Culture,* W. W. Norton, New York, 1978, p. 86.

42. See George B. Sansom, *A History of Japan,* *1334–1615,* vol. II, Stanford University Press, Stanford, California, 1961, chs. XX–XXI.

43. Ibid., ch. XXV.

44. Cited in Donald H. Shively, "Bakufu versus Kabuki," in *Studies in the Institutional History of Early Modern Japan,* ed. John W. Hall, Princeton University Press, Princeton, 1970, p. 236.

45. Ibid., pp. 241–242.

46. Ibid.

47. Cited in George Sansom, *A History of Japan, 1615–1867,* Stanford University Press, Stanford, California, 1978, p. 99.

48. See Thomas C. Smith, "The Japanese Village in the Seventeenth Century," in Hall, p. 280.

49. Thomas C. Smith, *The Agrarian Origins of Modern Japan,* Stanford University Press, Stanford, California, 1959, pp. 78–79.

50. See Bingham et al., pp. 140–142.

51. George B. Sansom, *Japan: A Short Cultural History,* rev. ed., Appleton-Century-Crofts, New York, 1943, p. 472.

SUGGESTED READING

Students should have little difficulty finding interesting and sound material on the topics raised in this chapter. For Africa in the era of the slave trade, in addition to the titles given in the Notes, see A. F. C. Ryder, *Benin and the Europeans, 1485–1897* (1969); R. E. Bradbury, *Benin Studies* (1973), which contains useful articles on government, art, and society; Elizabeth Isichei, *The Ibo People and the Europeans* (1973), which treats internal migrations and the impact of the slave trade on society; and David Gamble, *The Wolof of Senegambia* (1967), which discusses Wolof economy, political structure, and social organization. Lawrence W. Henderson, *Angola: Five Centuries of Conflict* (1979), provides a good survey of the Portuguese in Angola, while Gerald J. Bender, *Angola under the Portuguese: The Myth and the Reality* (1978), focuses on the nineteenth and twentieth centuries with some background sections. For the Swahili city-states, C.

S. Nicholls, *The Swahili Coast* (1971), is an important work. William Bascom and Melville J. Herskovits, eds., *Continuity and Change in African Cultures* (1959), treats many facets of African cultures with emphasis on linguistics and ethnohistory. The standard reference works on African history are R. Oliver, ed., *The Cambridge History of Africa,* vol. III: *ca 1050–1600* (1977), and R. Gray, ed., *The Cambridge History of Africa,* vol. IV: *ca 1600–ca 1870* (1975).

The best up-to-date accounts of Ottoman history are Halil Inalcik, *The Ottoman Empire: The Classical Age, 1300–1600* (1973), and Norman Itzkowitz, *Ottoman Empire and Islamic Tradition* (1972). Ogier Ghiselin de Busbecq, *Turkish Letters,* trans. E. S. Foster (1967), is a first-hand report of the court of Suleiman the Magnificent. Geoffrey Goodwin, *A History of Ottoman Architecture* (1971), is probably the best available general study, and the famous architect Sinan has found his biographer in Arthur Stratton, *Sinan* (1972). Ivo Andric, *The Bridge on the Drina,* trans. L. F. Edwards (1959), is a brilliant novel evoking Balkan life under Turkish rule; it earned its author the Nobel Prize for Literature. Islam's understanding of the West is studied in the excellent work of Bernard Lewis, *The Muslim Discovery of Europe* (1982), and R. W. Southern, *Western Views of Islam* (1962), is a fine summary of the Western viewpoint.

There is no up-to-date treatment of Mughal India, but the curious student might start with P. M. Holt et al., eds., *The Cambridge History of Islam,* 2 vols. (1970). M. Mujeeb, *The Indian Muslims* (1967), and I. Habib, *The Agrarian System of Mughal India 1556–1707* (1963), are both useful. Bamber Gascoigne, *The Great Moghuls* (1971), and Gavin Hambly, *The Cities of Mughal India: Delhi, Agra, and Fatehpur Sikri* (1968), are well illustrated and highly readable.

The best starting-point for the weaknesses of Yüan rule and the early development of the Ming dynasty in China is Charles O. Hucker, *The Ming Dynasty: Its Origins and Evolving Institutions* (1978), but see also Edward L. Dreyer, *Early Ming China: A Political History, 1355–1435* (1982), which contains a valuable up-to-date bibliography. Charles O. Hucker, *The Traditional Chinese State in Ming Times, 1368–1644* (1962), is a standard study written in simple, untechnical language. Jonathan D. Spence, *Ts'ao Yin and the K'ang-hsi Emperor, Bondservant and Master* (1966) uses the life of an official in the Chinese bureaucracy to describe the era and institutional framework in which he operated. Jonathan D. Spence and John E. Wills, Jr., eds., *From Ming to Ch'ing: Conquest, Region, and Continuity in Seventeenth-Century China* (1979) focuses on the transition from Ming to Ch'ing in a collection of wide-ranging essays by leading scholars.

The best one-volume survey of Japanese history and culture is Edwin O. Reischauer, *Japan: The Story of a Nation,* 3rd ed. (1981), which combines expert knowledge with superb readability. G. B. Sanson, *Japan: A Short Cultural History* (1962), is an older but still useful account. More detailed treatments of Japanese history are Albert M. Craig and Edwin O. Reischauer, *Japan: Tradition and Transformation* (1978), and Sir George Sansom, *A History of Japan,* 3 vols. (1958–1963). For Japanese feudalism, see Peter Duus, *Feudalism in Japan* (1976), and John W. Hall and Jeffrey P. Maas, eds., *Medieval Japan: Essays in Institutional History* (1974). The following studies are valuable for specific topics: Martin Colcutt, *Five Mountains: the Zen Monastic Institution in Medieval Japan* (1980); C. R. Boxer, *The Christian Century in Japan, 1549–1650* (1967); R. P. Dore, *Education in Tokugawa Japan* (1965); Thomas C. Smith, *The Agrarian Origins of Modern Japan* (1965); C. D. Sheldon, *The Rise of the Merchant Class in Tokugawa Japan, 1600–1868* (1958). Japan's greatest literary classic, *The Tale of Genji,* by Lady Murasaki, has been translated by Arthur Waley (1955).

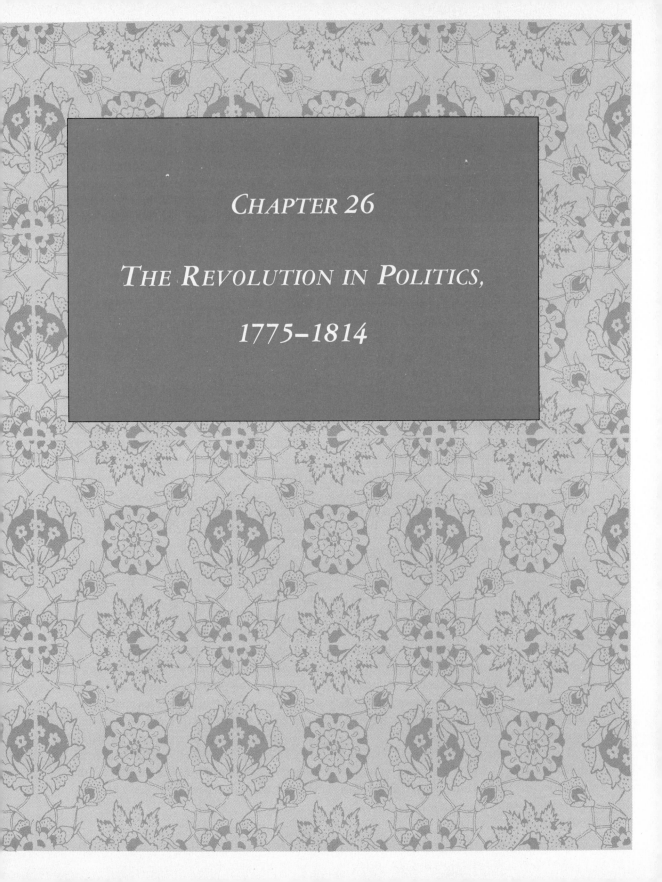

CHAPTER 26

THE REVOLUTION IN POLITICS,

1775–1814

THE LAST YEARS of the eighteenth century were a time of great upheaval. A series of revolutions and revolutionary wars challenged the old order of kings and aristocrats. The ideas of freedom and equality, ideas that have not stopped shaping the world since that era, flourished and spread. The revolution began in North America in 1775. Then in 1789 France, the largest and most influential country in Europe, became the leading revolutionary nation. It established first a constitutional monarchy, then a radical republic, and finally a new empire under Napoleon. The armies of France also joined forces with patriots and radicals abroad in an effort to establish new governments based on new principles throughout much of Europe. The world of modern domestic and international politics was born.

What caused this era of revolution? What were the ideas and objectives of the men and women who rose up violently to undo the established system? What were the gains and losses for privileged groups and for ordinary people in a generation of war and upheaval? These are the questions this chapter will seek to answer in an examination of the French and American revolutions.

LIBERTY AND EQUALITY

Two ideas fueled the revolutionary period in both America and Europe: liberty and equality. What did eighteenth-century politicians and other people mean by liberty and equality, and why were those ideas so radical and revolutionary in their day?

The call for liberty was first of all a call for individual human rights. Even the most enlightened monarchs customarily claimed that it was their duty to regulate what people wrote and believed. Liberals of the revolutionary era protested such controls from on high. They demanded freedom to worship according to the dictates of their consciences instead of according to the politics of their prince. They demanded the end of censorship and the right to express their beliefs freely in print and at public meetings. They demanded freedom from arbitrary laws and from judges who simply obeyed orders from the government.

These demands for basic personal freedoms, which were incorporated into the American Bill of Rights and other liberal constitutions, were very far-reaching. Indeed, eighteenth-century revolutionaries demanded more freedom than most governments today believe it is desirable to grant. The Declaration of the Rights of Man, issued at the beginning of the French Revolution, proclaimed, "Liberty consists in being able to do anything that does not harm another person." A citizen's rights had, therefore, "no limits except those which assure to the other members of society the enjoyment of these same rights." Liberals called for the freedom of the individual to develop and to create to the fullest possible extent. In the context of aristocratic and monarchial forms of government that then dominated Europe, this was a truly radical idea.

The call for liberty was also a call for a new kind of government. The revolutionary liberals believed that the people were sovereign — that is, that the people alone had the authority to make laws limiting the individual's freedom of action. In practice, this system of government meant choosing legislators who represented the people and who were accountable to them. Moreover, liberals of the revolutionary era believed that every people —

every ethnic group – had this right of self-determination, and thus the right to form a free nation.

By equality, eighteenth-century liberals meant that all citizens were to have identical rights and civil liberties. Above all, the nobility had no right to special privileges based on the accident of birth.

Liberals did not define equality as meaning that everyone should be equal economically. Quite the contrary. As Thomas Jefferson wrote in an early draft of the American Declaration of Independence, before changing "property" to the more noble-sounding "happiness," everyone was equal in "the pursuit of property." Jefferson and other liberals certainly did not expect equal success in that pursuit. Great differences in wealth and income between rich and poor were perfectly acceptable to liberals. The essential point was that everyone should legally have an equal chance. French liberals and revolutionaries said they wanted "careers opened to talent." They wanted employment in government, in business, and in the professions to be based on ability, not on family background or legal status.

Equality of opportunity was a very revolutionary idea in eighteenth-century Europe. Legal inequality between classes and groups was the rule, not the exception. Society was still legally divided into groups with special privileges, such as the nobility and the clergy, and groups with special burdens, like the peasantry. In many countries, various middle-class groups – professionals, businessmen, townspeople, and craftsmen – enjoyed privileges that allowed them to monopolize all sorts of economic activity. It was this kind of economic inequality, an inequality based on artificial legal distinctions, against which liberals protested.

The ideas of liberty and equality – the central ideas of classical liberalism – have deep roots in Western history. The ancient Greeks and the Judeo-Christian tradition had affirmed for hundreds of years the sanctity and value of the individual human being. The Judeo-Christian tradition, reinforced by the Reformation, had long stressed personal responsibility on the part of both common folk and exalted rulers, thereby promoting the self-discipline without which liberty becomes anarchy. The hounded and persecuted Protestant radicals of the later sixteenth century had died for the revolutionary idea that individuals were entitled to their own religious beliefs.

Although the liberal creed had roots deep in the Western tradition, classical liberalism first crystallized at the end of the seventeenth century and during the Enlightenment of the eighteenth century.

Liberal ideas reflected the Enlightenment's stress on human dignity and human happiness on earth. They shared the Enlightenment's general faith in science, rationality, and progress: the adoption of liberal principles meant better government and a better society for all. Almost all the writers of the Enlightenment were passionately committed to greater personal liberty. They preached religious toleration, freedom of press and speech, and fair and equal treatment before the law. Yet many of the French philosophers – Voltaire was typical – believed that these liberties could be realized through the enlightened absolutism of a wise king or queen. A minority of eighteenth-century thinkers thought otherwise. It was these thinkers who were mainly responsible for wedding the liberal concept of self-government to the Enlightenment's concern with personal freedom and legal equality.

Almost all the great proponents of the liberal theory of self-government came from England and France. Two of them were particularly influential. John Locke, who was so influential in giving the Enlightenment new ideas about how human beings learn (page 801), turned to English history as a basis for his political theory. England's long political tradition rested, according to Locke, on "the rights of Englishmen" and on representative government through Parliament. Thus in the controversy over excluding the strong-minded James, Duke of York, from the English throne, Locke argued for strict limitations on monarchy in order to preserve liberty. An admirer of the great Whig noblemen who subsequently made the bloodless revolution of 1688 (pages 742–743), Locke maintained that a government that oversteps its proper function – protecting the natural rights of life, liberty, and private property – becomes a tyranny. In such extreme cases the people have the natural right of rebellion. Locke thought such drastic action could usually be avoided, if the government respected the rights of its citizens and the people were zealous in the defense of their liberty. Thus Locke helped to revive the powerful idea, inherited from ancient Greece and Rome (page 131), that there are natural or universal rights that are equally valid for all peoples and societies.

It is important to note that Locke's strong defense of economic liberty and private property was linked to his love of political freedom. Locke prophetically saw that there was a close relationship between economic freedom and political freedom. If a significant number of citizens, such as the large English landowners, were not economically independent, there would be no basis for independent political opposition. Locke's ideas, as well as those of other English thinkers who lauded liberty and denounced the danger of tyranny, were particularly popular in colonial America.

Few of the French philosophes were particularly interested in political theorizing, but the baron de Montesquieu (1689–1755) was a towering exception. Having made his name as a social satirist, he turned to liberal political philosophy in the course of the eighteenth century. Montesquieu was a great noble, and he was dismayed by the triumph of absolute government in France under Louis XIV. Inspired by the example of the physical sciences, Montesquieu set out to apply the critical method to the problem of government in *The Spirit of Laws* (1748). The result was a comparative study of republics, monarchies, and despotisms – a great pioneering inquiry in the emerging social sciences.

Fearful of the tyrannical possibility of an unrestrained state, as was Locke, Montesquieu developed the idea that despotism would be avoided if political power were divided – among legislative, executive, and judicial branches of government. Each branch would check the tendency of the other to usurp power and curtail liberty. Montesquieu especially admired England and the English balance of power among the king, the Parliament, and the independent courts. Montesquieu's theory of separation of powers had great impact: the constitutions of the young United States in 1789 and of France in 1791 were based in large part on this theory.

THE ATTRACTION OF LIBERALISM

Locke and Montesquieu were spokesmen for liberal ideals. Were they also, as is often said, spokesmen for "a rising middle class," a class impatient with the pretensions of monarchy and the privileges of aristocracy? To some extent, they were. Equality before the law and equality of opportunity were ideals particularly dear to ambitious and educated bourgeois. Yet liberal ideas about individual rights and political freedom also appealed to much of the aristocracy, at least in western Europe and as formulated by Montesquieu. Representative government did not mean democracy, which liberal thinkers tended to equate with mob rule. Rather, they envisioned voting for representatives as being restricted to those who owned property, those with "a stake in society." England had shown the way. After 1688, it had combined a parliamentary system and considerable individual liberty with a restricted franchise and unquestionable aristocratic pre-eminence.

Eighteenth-century liberalism, then, appealed not only to the middle class, but also to some aristocrats. It found broad support among the educated elite and the substantial classes in western Europe. What it lacked from the beginning was strong mass support. For comfortable liberals, the really important questions were theoretical and political. They had no need to worry about their stomachs and the price of bread. For the much more numerous laboring poor, the great questions were immediate and economic. Getting enough to eat was the crucial challenge. These differences in outlook and well-being were to lead to many misunderstandings and disappointments for both groups in the revolutionary era.

THE AMERICAN REVOLUTION, 1775–1789

The era of liberal revolution began in the New World. The thirteen mainland colonies of British North America revolted against their mother country and then succeeded in establishing a new unified government.

Americans have long debated the meaning of their revolution. Some have even questioned whether or not it was a real revolution, as opposed to a war for independence. According to some scholars, the revolution was conservative and defensive in that its demands were for the traditional liberties of Englishmen; Americans were united against the British, but otherwise they were a satisfied people and not torn by internal conflict. Other scholars have argued that, on the contrary, the American Revolution was quite radical. It split families between patriots and Loyalists and divided the country. It achieved goals that were fully as advanced as those obtained by the French in their great revolution a few years later.

How does one reconcile these positions? Both contain large elements of truth. The American revolutionaries did believe they were demanding only the traditional rights of English men and women. But those traditional rights were liberal rights, and in the American context they had very strong democratic and popular overtones. Thus, the American Revolution was fought in the name of established ideals that were still quite radical in the context of the times. And in founding a government firmly based on liberal principles, the Americans set an example that had a forceful impact on Europe and speeded up political development there.

THE ORIGINS OF THE REVOLUTION

The American Revolution had its immediate origins in a squabble over increased taxes. The British government had fought and decisively won the Seven Years' War (page 842) on the strength of its professional army and navy.

THE BOSTON TEA PARTY   In this 1789 engraving men disguised as Indians dump East India Company tea into the harbor. The large crowd on shore indicates widespread support. (Library of Congress)

The American colonists had furnished little real aid. The high cost of the war to the British, however, had led to a doubling of the British national debt. Anticipating further expense defending its recently conquered western lands from Indian uprisings like that of Pontiac, the British government in London set about reorganizing the empire with a series of bold, largely unprecedented measures. Breaking with tradition, the British decided to maintain a large army in North America after peace was restored in 1763. Moreover, they sought to exercise strict control over their newly conquered western lands and to tax the colonies directly. In 1765, the government pushed through Parliament the

Stamp Act, which levied taxes on a long list of commercial and legal documents, diplomas, pamphlets, newspapers, almanacs, dice, and playing cards. A stamp glued to each article indicated the tax had been paid.

The effort to increase taxes as part of tightening up the empire seemed perfectly reasonable to the British. Heavier stamp taxes had been collected in Great Britain for two generations, and Americans were being asked only to pay a share of their own defense. Moreover, Americans had been paying only very low local taxes. The Stamp Act would have doubled taxes to about two shillings per person. No other people in the world (except the Poles) paid so little. The British, meanwhile, paid the world's highest taxes in about 1765 – twenty-six shillings per person. It is not surprising that taxes per person in the newly independent American nation were much higher in 1785 than in 1765, when the British no longer subsidized American defense. The colonists protested the Stamp Act vigorously and violently, however, and after rioting and boycotts against British goods, Parliament reluctantly repealed the new tax.

As the fury of the Stamp Act controversy revealed, much more was involved than taxes. The key question was political. To what extent could the home government refashion the empire and reassert its power while limiting the authority of colonial legislatures and their elected representatives? Accordingly, who should represent the colonies, and who had the right to make laws for Americans? While a troubled majority of Americans searched hard for a compromise, some radicals began to proclaim that "taxation without representation is tyranny." The British government replied that Americans were represented in Parliament, albeit indirectly (like most Englishmen themselves), and that the absolute supremacy of Parliament throughout the empire could not be questioned. Many Americans felt otherwise. As John Adams put it, "A Parliament of Great Britain can have no more rights to tax the colonies than a Parliament of Paris." Thus imperial reorganization and Parliamentary supremacy came to appear as grave threats to Americans' existing liberties and time-honored institutions.

Americans had long exercised a great deal of independence and gone their own way. In British North America, unlike England and Europe, there was no powerful established church, and personal freedom in questions of religion was taken for granted. The colonial assemblies made the important laws, which were seldom overturned by the home govern-

ment. The right to vote was much more widespread than in England. In many parts of colonial Massachusetts, for example, as many as 95 percent of the adult males could vote.

Moreover, greater political equality was matched by greater social and economic equality. Neither a hereditary nobility nor a hereditary serf population existed, although the slavery of the Americas consigned blacks to a legally oppressed caste. Independent farmers were the largest group in the country and set much of its tone. In short, the colonial experience had slowly formed a people who felt themselves separate and distinct from the home country. The controversies over taxation intensified those feelings of distinctiveness and separation and brought them to the fore.

In 1773, the dispute over taxes and representation flared up again. The British government had permitted the financially hard-pressed East India Company to ship its tea from China directly to its agents in the colonies, rather than through London middlemen who then sold to independent merchants in the colonies. Thus, the company secured a virtual monopoly on the tea trade, and colonial merchants were suddenly excluded from a highly profitable business. The colonists were quick to protest.

In Boston, men disguised as Indians had a rowdy "tea party," and threw the company's tea into the harbor. This led to extreme measures. The so-called Coercive Acts closed the port of Boston, curtailed local elections and town meetings, and greatly expanded the royal governor's power. County conventions in Massachusetts protested vehemently and urged that the acts be "rejected as the attempts of a wicked administration to enslave America." Other colonial assemblies joined in the denunciations. In September 1774, the First Continental Congress met in Philadelphia, where the more radical members argued successfully against concessions to the Crown. Compromise was also rejected by the British Parliament and in April 1775 fighting began at Lexington and Concord.

INDEPENDENCE

The fighting spread, and the colonists moved slowly but inevitably toward open rebellion and a declaration of independence. The uncompromising attitude of the British government and its use of German mercenaries went a long way toward dissolving long-standing loyalties to the home country and rivalries among the separate colonies. *Common Sense* (1775), a brilliant attack by the recently arrived English radical Thomas Paine, also mobilized public opinion in favor of independence. A runaway best seller with sales of 120,000 copies in a few months, Paine's tract ridiculed the idea of a small island ruling a great continent. In his call for freedom and republican government, Paine expressed Americans' growing sense of separateness and moral superiority.

On July 4, 1776, the Second Continental Congress adopted the Declaration of Independence. Written by Thomas Jefferson, the Declaration of Independence boldly listed the tyrannical acts committed by George III (1760–1820) and confidently proclaimed the natural rights of man and the sovereignty of the American states. Sometimes called the world's greatest political editorial, the Declaration of Independence in effect universalized the traditional rights of Englishmen and made them the rights of all mankind. It stated that "all men are created equal . . . they are endowed by their Creator with certain unalienable rights . . . among these are life, liberty, and the pursuit of happiness." No other American political document has ever caused

such excitement, both at home and abroad.

Many American families remained loyal to Britain; many others divided bitterly. After the Declaration of Independence, the conflict often took the form of a civil war pitting patriot against Loyalist. The Loyalists tended to be wealthy and politically moderate. Many patriots too were wealthy – individuals such as John Hancock and George Washington – but willingly allied themselves with farmers and artisans in a broad coalition. This coalition harassed the Loyalists and confiscated their property to help pay for the American war effort. The broad social base of the revolutionaries tended to make the liberal revolution democratic. State governments extended the right to vote to many more people in the course of the war and re-established themselves as republics.

On the international scene, the French were sympathetic to the rebels from the beginning. They wanted revenge for the humiliating defeats of the Seven Years' War. Officially neutral until 1776, they supplied the great bulk of guns and gunpowder used by the American revolutionaries, very much as neutral Great Powers supply weapons for "wars of national liberation" today. In 1778, the French offered the Americans a formal alliance, and in 1779 and 1780 the Spanish and Dutch declared war on Britain. Catherine the Great of Russia helped organize a League of Armed Neutrality in order to protect neutral shipping rights, which Britain refused to recognize.

Thus by 1780, Great Britain was engaged in an imperial war against most of Europe as well as the thirteen colonies. In these circum-

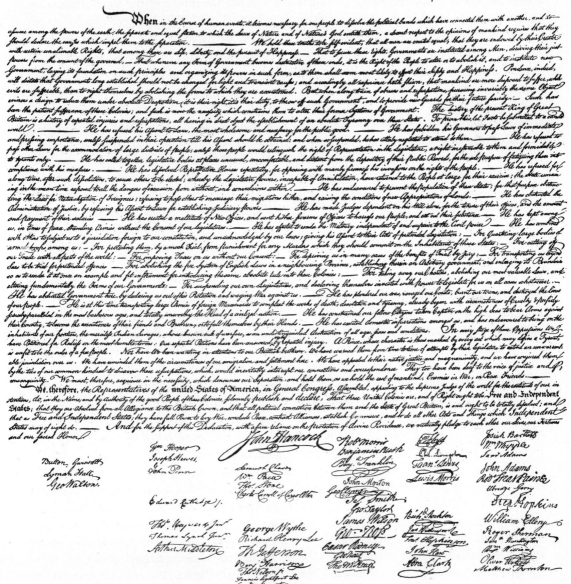

In CONGRESS. July 4, 1776.

The unanimous Declaration of the thirteen united States of America,

stances, and in the face of severe reverses in India, the West Indies, and at Yorktown in Virginia, a new British government decided to cut its losses. American negotiators in Paris were receptive. They feared that France wanted a treaty that would bottle up the new United States east of the Alleghenies and give British holdings west of the Alleghenies to France's ally, Spain. Thus the American negotiators ditched the French and accepted the extraordinarily favorable terms Britain offered.

By the Treaty of Paris of 1783, Britain ceded all its territory between the Appalachians and the Mississippi River to the Americans and recognized the independence of the thirteen colonies. Out of the no-win rivalries of the Old World, the Americans snatched dominion over half a continent.

FRAMING THE CONSTITUTION

The liberal program of the American Revolution was consolidated by the federal Constitution, the Bill of Rights and the creation of a national republic. Assembling in Philadelphia in the summer of 1787, the delegates to the Constitutional Convention were determined to end the period of economic depression, social uncertainty, and very weak central government that had followed independence. The delegates decided, therefore, to grant the federal, or central, government important powers: regulation of domestic and foreign trade, the right to levy taxes, and the means to enforce its laws.

Strong rule was placed squarely in the context of representative self-government. Senators and congressmen would be the lawmaking delegates of the voters, and the president of the republic would be an elected official. The central government was to operate in a Lockean framework of checks and balances. The executive, legislative, and judicial branches would systematically balance each other. The power of the federal government would in turn be checked by the powers of the individual states.

When the results of the secret deliberation of the Constitutional Convention were presented to the states for ratification, a great public debate began. The opponents of the proposed constitution – the Anti-Federalists – charged that the framers of the new document had taken too much power from the individual states and made the federal government too strong. Moreover, many Anti-Federalists feared for the personal liberties and individual freedoms for which they had just fought. In order to overcome these objections, the Federalists solemnly promised to spell out these basic freedoms as soon as the new constitution was adopted. The result was the first ten amendments to the Constitution, which the first Congress passed shortly after it met in New York in March 1789. These amendments formed an effective bill of rights to safeguard the individual. Most of them – trial by jury, due process of law, right to assembly, freedom from unreasonable search – had their origins in English law and the English Bill of Rights of 1689. Others – the freedoms of speech, the press, and religion – reflected natural-law theory and the American experience.

The American Constitution and the Bill of Rights exemplified the great strengths and the limits of what came to be called classical liberalism. Liberty meant individual freedoms and political safeguards. Liberty also meant representative government, but did not necessarily mean democracy with its principle of the one man, one vote.

Equality – slaves excepted – meant equality

before the law, not equality of political participation or economic well-being. Indeed, economic inequality was resolutely defended by the elite who framed the Constitution. The right to own property was guaranteed by the Fifth Amendment, and if the government took private property the owner was to receive "just compensation." The radicalism of liberal revolution in America was primarily legal and political, not economic or social.

THE REVOLUTION'S IMPACT ON EUROPE

Hundreds of books, pamphlets, and articles analyzed and romanticized the American upheaval. Thoughtful Europeans noted, first of all, its enormous long-term implications for international politics. A secret report by the Venetian ambassador to Paris in 1783 stated what many felt: "If only the union of the Provinces is preserved, it is reasonable to expect that, with the favorable effects of time, and of European arts and sciences, it will become the most formidable power in the world."[1] More generally, American independence fired the imaginations of those few aristocrats who were uneasy with their privileges and of those commoners who yearned for greater equality. Many Europeans believed that the world was moving now and that America was leading the way. As one French writer put it in 1789: "This vast continent which the seas surround will soon change Europe and the universe."

Europeans who dreamed of a new era were fascinated by the political lessons of the American Revolution. The Americans had begun with a revolutionary defense against tyrannical oppression, and they had been victorious. They had then shown how rational beings could assemble together to consolidate their gains in a permanent written constitu-

tion – a new social contract. All this gave greater reality to the concepts of individual liberty and representative government. It reinforced one of the primary ideas of the Enlightenment, the idea that a better world here on earth was possible.

THE FRENCH REVOLUTION, 1789–1791

No country felt the consequences of the American Revolution more directly than France. Hundreds of French officers served in America and were inspired by the experience. The most famous of these, the young and impressionable Marquis de Lafayette (1757–1834), left home wanting only to fight France's traditional foe, England. He returned with a love of liberty and firm republican convictions. French intellectuals and publicists engaged in passionate analysis of the federal Constitution, as well as the constitutions of the various states of the new United States. The American Revolution undeniably hastened upheaval in France.

Yet the French Revolution did not mirror the American example. It was more violent and more complex, more influential and more controversial, more loved and more hated. For Europeans and most of the rest of the world, it was *the* great revolution of the eighteenth century, the revolution that opened the modern era in politics.

THE CRISIS OF THE OLD ORDER

Like the American Revolution, the French Revolution had its immediate origins in the financial difficulties of the government. War with England had greatly increased France's

LOUIS XVI *Louis was a handsome, well-meaning youth when he came to the throne in 1774. This stunning portrait by Duplessis idealizes him as a majestic, self-confident ruler, worthy heir of Louis XIV and French absolutism. Actually, Louis XVI was shy, indecisive, and somewhat stupid. (Chateau de Versailles / Giraudon)*

national debt; bankruptcy or a sharp rise in taxes became inevitable. The government's yearly income from taxation and other sources was, quite simply, less than it spent. For a long time the government had been living with the problem by means of haphazard deficit financing, borrowing ever more money from bankers and the well-to-do. By 1788, fully half of France's annual budget went for ever-increasing interest payments on the ever-increasing debt. Another quarter went to maintain the military, while 6 percent was absorbed by the costly and extravagant king and his court at Versailles. Less than one-fifth of the entire national budget was available for the productive functions of the state, such as transportation and general administration. It was an impossible financial situation.

One way out would have been for the government to declare partial bankruptcy, forcing its creditors to accept greatly reduced payments on the debt. Following widespread medieval practice, the powerful Spanish monarchy had regularly repudiated large portions of its debt in the late sixteenth and seventeenth centuries. France had done likewise in the early eighteenth century, after an attempt by John Law, a Scottish adventurer, to establish a French national bank ended in financial disaster in 1720. Yet by the 1780s the French debt was held by an army of aristocratic and bourgeois creditors, and the French monarchy, though absolute in theory, had become far too weak for such a drastic and unpopular action.

Nor could the king and his ministers, unlike modern governments, print money and create inflation to cover their deficits. Unlike England and Holland, which had far larger national debts relative to their populations, France after John Law's unsuccessful experiment had no central bank, no paper currency, and no means of creating credit. French money was good gold coin. Even in times of severe economic crisis the government could not create credit and paper money. It could only beg, unsuccessfully, for new gold loans from its frightened and hard-pressed population. Bound up in the straitjacket of a primitive banking system, the monarchy had no alternative but to try to increase taxes.

TAXES AND PRIVILEGES

France's system of taxation was unfair and out of date. Increased taxes were possible only in conjunction with developing new sources of revenue, and such tax reform opened a Pandora's box of social and political demands. Taxes were based on the inequality of a society still legally divided into the medieval orders or "estates" – the clergy, the nobility, and everyone else – and were apportioned among the estates very unequally.

Constituting only about 100,000 of France's 24 million inhabitants, the clergy had important privileges. It owned about 10 percent of the land in France and was lightly taxed. Moreover, it levied on the crops of the peasantry an oppressive tax (the tithe) that averaged somewhat less than 10 percent. The clergy's top jobs, soft and overpaid, were jealously monopolized by nobles, to the intense dissatisfaction of the poor parish priests of lower-class origin.

The second estate consisted of some 400,000 noblemen and noblewomen, whose privileges were not only great but growing. Fully in keeping with the general European compromise of bureaucratic absolutism, the French nobility in the late eighteenth century had come to hold almost all the top positions in the government. The nobles also owned fully 25 percent of all the land in the country and were very lightly taxed by the government. Like the clergy, they taxed the peasantry for their own profit. This was done by means of exclusive rights to hunt and fish, village monopolies on baking bread and pressing grapes for wine, fees for justice, and a host of other privileges. Thus in France, as in most of Europe, the wealthiest group in the country – the nobility – systematically exploited the poorest – the peasantry. Long accustomed to a sumptuous banquet of privilege, the appetite of the French nobility had only increased with eating. Ironically, in view of all that followed, it was the pretensions of the nobility that turned a financial crisis into a revolution.

Everyone else was a commoner, a member of the third estate. A few commoners were extremely rich businessmen or highly successful doctors and lawyers. Many more were urban artisans and unskilled day laborers. The vast majority of the third estate consisted of the peasants and agricultural workers in the countryside. Thus, the third estate was a conglomeration of vastly different social groups, united only by their shared legal status as distinct from the privileged nobility and clergy.

FORMATION OF THE NATIONAL ASSEMBLY

The Revolution was under way by 1787, though no one could have realized what was to follow. That year Louis XVI's minister of finance dusted off old proposals to impose a general tax on all landed property, and he convinced the king to call an Assembly of Notables to gain support for the idea. The assembled notables, who were mainly important noblemen and high-ranking clergy of noble birth, were not in favor of it. In return for their support they demanded control over all government spending and decision making through provincial assemblies, which they expected to control. Denouncing arbitrary taxation by the king, the nobility sought in the name of liberty to assure its own domination of the state. The king tried to reassert his authority. A great wave of protest swept the country. Finlly, in July 1788, a beaten Louis XVI called for a spring session of the Estates General, the old representative body of all three estates that had not met since 1614. Absolute monarchy was falling.

What would replace it? Throughout the winter of 1788-1789, that question excited France. The Estates General of 1614 had sat as three separate houses – clergy, nobility, and commoners. Any action had required the agreement of all three branches, a requirement that had guaranteed control by the privileged orders. The nobility expected that history would repeat itself. The noble judges of the Parlement of Paris – a kind of supreme court in the eighteenth century – did their part. Accustomed to thundering against the rule of despotism, they ruled that the Estates should sit separately.

This ruling infuriated middle-class intellectuals. They wanted the three estates to meet as a single house, so that commoners from the third estate would have the dominant voice and be able to prevent aristocratic control. This issue and many others were thoroughly discussed in pamphlets and in the drafting of grievance petitions at the local level. There was great popular participation. Almost all male commoners twenty-five years or older had the right to vote for their representatives to the Estates General. However, the voting for the representatives required two, three, or even four stages, which meant that most of the representatives finally selected by the third estate were well-educated and prosperous members of the middle class. Most of them were not businessmen, but lawyers and government officials. Social status and prestige were matters of great concern to this economic elite. There were hardly any representatives from the great mass of laboring poor – the peasants, the artisans, and the day laborers.

In May 1789, the twelve hundred delegates of the three estates paraded in medieval pageantry through the streets of Versailles to an opening session clothed in feudal magnificence. The estates were almost immediately deadlocked. Delegates of the third estate refused to transact any business until the king ordered the privileged orders to sit with them in a single body. Finally, after a six-week war of nerves, a few parish priests began to go over to the third estate, which on June 17 voted to call itself the National Assembly. On June 20, excluded from their hall because of "repairs," they moved to a large indoor tennis court. There they swore the famous Oath of the Tennis Court, pledging never to disband until they had written a new constitution.

The king's actions were then somewhat contradictory. On June 23 he made a conciliatory speech to a joint session, urging reforms, and then ordered the three estates to meet together. At the same time he apparently followed the advice of the nobles, who saw things working out quite differently than they had expected and urged the king to dissolve the Estates General. The king called an army of eighteen thousand troops toward Versailles, and on July 11 he dismissed his finance minister and his more liberal ministers. Faced first with aristocratic and then with bourgeois revolt, Louis XVI had resigned himself to bankruptcy. Now he sought again to reassert his divine and historic right to rule. The middle-class delegates had done their best, but they were resigned to being disbanded at the point of bayonets. One third-estate delegate reassured a worried colleague: "You won't hang – you'll only have to go back home."[2]

THE REVOLT OF THE POOR AND THE OPPRESSED

While the third estate struggled at Versailles for symbolic equality with the nobility and clergy in a single legislative body, economic hardship gripped the masses of France in a tightening vise. Grain was the basis of the diet of ordinary people, and in 1788 the harvest had been extremely poor. The price of bread, which had been rising gradually since 1785, began to soar. By July 1789, the price of bread in the provinces climbed as high as eight sous per pound. In Paris, where bread was subsidized by the government in an attempt to prevent popular unrest, the price rose to four sous. The poor could scarcely afford to pay two sous per pound, for even at that price a laborer with a wife and three children had to spend half of his wages to buy the family's bread.

Harvest failure and high bread prices unleashed a classic economic depression of the preindustrial age. With food so expensive and with so much uncertainty, the demand for manufactured goods collapsed. Thousands of artisans and small traders were thrown out of work. By the end of 1789, almost half of the French people would be in need of relief. One person in eight was a pauper, living in extreme want. In Paris, the situation was desperate in July 1789: perhaps 150,000 of the city's 600,000 people were without work.

Against this background of dire poverty and desperation, the people of Paris entered decisively onto the revolutionary stage. They believed in a general though ill-defined way that their economic distress had human causes. They believed that they should have steady work and enough bread to survive. Specifically, they feared that the dismissal of the king's moderate finance minister would throw them at the mercy of aristocratic landowners and grain speculators. Stories, like that quoting the wealthy financier Joseph François Foulon as saying that the poor "should eat grass, like my horses," and rumors that the king's troops would sack the city, began to fill the air. Angry crowds formed and passionate voices urged action. On July 13, the people began to seize arms for the defense of the city, and on July 14, several

STORMING THE BASTILLE *This contemporary drawing conveys the fury and determination of the revolutionary crowd on July 14, 1789. This successful popular action had enormous symbolic significance, and July 14 has long been France's most important national holiday. (Photo: Flammarion)*

hundred of the most determined people marched to the Bastille to search for gunpowder.

An old medieval fortress with walls ten feet thick and eight great towers each a hundred feet high, the Bastille had long been used as a prison. It was guarded by eighty retired soldiers and thirty Swiss guards. The governor of the fortress-prison refused to hand over the powder, panicked, and ordered his men to fire, killing ninety-eight people attempting to enter. Cannon were brought to batter the main gate, and fighting continued until the governor of the prison surrendered. While he was being taken under guard to city hall, a band of men broke through and hacked him to death. His head and that of the mayor of Paris, who had been slow to give the crowd arms, were stuck on pikes and paraded through the streets. The next day a committee of citizens appointed Lafayette commander of the city's armed forces. Paris was lost to the king, who was forced to recall the finance minister and to disperse his troops. The uprising of the masses of Paris had saved the National Assembly.

As the delegates resumed their long-winded and inconclusive debates at Versailles, the people in the countryside sent them a radical and unmistakable message. All across France peasants began to rise in spontaneous, violent, and effective insurrection against their lords. Neither middle-class landowners, who often owned manors and village monopolies, nor the larger, more prosperous farmers, were spared. In some areas the nobles and bourgeoisie combined forces and organized patrols to protect their property. Yet the peasant insurrection went on. Recent enclosures were undone; old common lands were reoccupied; and the forests were seized. Taxes went unpaid. Fear of vagabonds and outlaws – the so-called Great Fear – seized the countryside and fanned the flames of rebellion. The long-suffering peasants were doing their best to free themselves from aristocratic privilege and exploitation.

Faced with chaos and fearful of calling on the king to restore order, the more liberal aristocrats and bourgeois at Versailles responded to peasant demands with a surprise maneuver on the night of August 4, 1789. The duke of Aiguillon, one of the greatest landowners in France, declared that

in several provinces the whole people forms a kind of league for the destruction of the manor houses, the ravaging of the lands, and especially for the seizure of the archives where the title deeds to feudal properties are kept. It seeks to throw off at last a yoke that has for many centuries weighted it down.[3]

He urged equality in taxation and the elimination of feudal dues. In the end, all the old exactions were abolished, generally without compensation: serfdom where it still existed, exclusive hunting rights for nobles, fees for justice, village monopolies, the right to make peasants work on the roads, and a host of others. The church's tithe was also abolished. Thus the French peasantry, which already owned about 30 percent of all the land, quickly achieved a great and unprecedented victory. Henceforth, the French peasants would seek mainly to consolidate their triumph. As the Great Fear subsided, they became a force for order and stability.

A LIMITED MONARCHY

The National Assembly moved forward. On August 27, 1789, it issued the Declaration of the Rights of Man. This great liberal document had a very American flavor, and Lafayette even discussed his draft in detail with the American ambassador in Paris, Thomas Jefferson, the author of the American Declaration of Independence. According to the French declaration, "men are born and remain free and equal in rights." Mankind's natural rights are "liberty, property, security, and resistance to oppression." Also, "every man is presumed innocent until he is proven guilty." As for law, "it is an expression of the general will; all citizens have the right to concur personally or through their representatives in its formation.... Free expression of thoughts and opinions is one of the most precious rights of mankind: every citizen may therefore speak, write, and publish freely." In short, this clarion call of the liberal revolutionary ideal guaranteed equality before the law, representative government for a sovereign people, and individual freedom. This revolutionary credo, only two pages long, was propagandized throughout France and Europe and around the world.

Moving beyond general principles to draft a constitution proved difficult. The questions of how much power the king should retain

À Versailles À Versailles du 5 Octobre 1789.

"TO VERSAILLES" *This print is one of many commemorating the women's march on Versailles. Notice on the left that the fashionable lady from the well-to-do is a most reluctant revolutionary. (Photo: Flammarion)*

and whether he could permanently veto legislation led to another deadlock. Once again the decisive answer came from the poor, in this instance the poor women of Paris.

To understand what happened one must remember that the work and wages of women and children were essential in the family economy of the laboring poor. In Paris great numbers of women worked, particularly within the putting-out system in the garment industry – making lace, fancy dresses, embroidery, ribbons, bonnets, corsets, and so on. Most of these goods were beautiful luxury items, destined for an aristocratic and international clientele.[4] Immediately after the fall of the Bastille, many of France's greatest nobles

began to leave for foreign courts, so that demand for luxuries began to plummet. International markets also declined, and the church was no longer able to give its traditional grants of food and money to the poor. Unemployment and hunger increased further, and the result was another popular explosion.

On October 5, some seven thousand desperate women marched the twelve miles from Paris to Versailles to demand action. A middle-class deputy looking out from the assembly saw "multitudes arriving from Paris including fishwives and bullies from the market, and these people wanted nothing but bread." This great crowd invaded the assembly, "armed with scythes, sticks and pikes."

One coarse, tough old woman directing a large group of younger women defiantly shouted into the debate: "Who's that talking down there? Make the chatterbox shut up. That's not the point: the point is that we want bread."[5] Hers was the genuine voice of the people, without which any understanding of the French Revolution is hopelessly incomplete.

The women invaded the royal apartments, slaughtered some of the royal bodyguards, and furiously searched for the despised queen, Marie Antoinette. "We are going to cut off her head, tear out her heart, fry her liver, and that won't be the end of it," they shouted, surging through the palace in a frenzy. It seems likely that only the intervention of Lafayette and the National Guard saved the royal family. But the only way to calm the disorder was for the king to go and live in Paris, as the crowd demanded.

The next day the king, the queen, and their son left for Paris in the midst of a strange procession. The heads of two aristocrats, stuck on pikes, led the way. They were followed by the remaining members of the royal bodyguard, unarmed and surrounded and mocked by fierce men holding sabers and pikes. A mixed and victorious multitude surrounded the king's carriage, hurling crude insults at the queen. There was drinking and eating among the women. "We are bringing the baker, Mrs. Baker, and the baker's wife," they joyfully sang. The National Assembly followed the king to Paris. Reflecting the more radical environment, it adopted a constitution that gave the virtually imprisoned "baker" only a temporary veto in the law-making process. And, for a time, he and the government made sure that the masses of Paris did not lack bread.

The next two years until September 1791 saw the consolidation of the constructive phase of the Revolution. The National Assembly established a constitutional monarchy, which Louis XVI reluctantly accepted in July 1790. The king remained the head of state, but all lawmaking power was placed in the hands of the National Assembly, elected by the economic upper half of French males. Counties or departments of approximately equal size replaced the complicated old patchwork of provinces with their many historic differences. The jumble of weights and measures that varied from province to province was abolished and replaced by the simple, rational metric system. The National Assembly promoted economic freedom. Monopolies and guilds were prohibited, and barriers to trade within France were abolished in the name of economic liberty. Thus, the National Assembly applied the critical spirit of the Enlightenment to reform France's laws and institutions completely.

The assembly also seized the property of nobles who had left France, and it nationalized the property of the church. The government used former church property as collateral to guarantee a new paper currency, the so-called assignats, and then sold these properties in an attempt to put the state's finances on a solid footing. Although the church's land was sold in large blocks, a procedure that favored nimble speculators and the rich, peasants eventually purchased much of it as it was subdivided. These purchases strengthened their attachment to the revolutionary state.

The most unfortunate aspect of the reorganization of France was that it brought the new government into conflict with the Catholic church. Many middle-class delegates to the National Assembly, imbued with the rationalism and skepticism of the eighteenth-century philosophes, harbored a deep distrust of "superstitious religion." They were interested in the church only to the extent they could seize its land and use the church to strengthen the new state. In the Civil Constitution of the Clergy of 1790 they established a national church. In the face of resistance, the National Assembly required the clergy to take a loyalty oath to the new government. The clergy became just so many more employees of the state. The pope formally condemned this attempt to subjugate the church. Against such a backdrop, it is not surprising that only half the priests of France took the oath of allegiance. The result was a deep division within the country on the religious question, and confusion and hostility among French Catholics were pervasive. The attempted reorganization and subjugation of the Catholic church was the revolutionary government's first great failure.

WORLD WAR AND REPUBLICAN FRANCE, 1791–1799

When Louis XVI accepted the final version of the completed constitution in September 1791, a young and still obscure provincial lawyer and member of the National Assembly named Maximilien Robespierre (1758–1794) evaluated the work of two years and concluded "The Revolution is over." Robespierre was both right and wrong. He was right in the sense that most of the constructive and lasting reforms were in place. Nothing substantial in the way of liberty and equality would be added in the next generation, though much would be lost. He was wrong in the sense that the most tormented and most radical stages lay ahead. New heroes and new myths were to emerge in revolutionary wars and international conflict.

The outbreak and progress of revolution in France produced great excitement and a sharp division of opinion in Europe and the United States. Liberals and radicals such as the English scientist Joseph Priestley (1733–1804) and the American patriot Tom Paine (1739–1809) saw a mighty triumph of liberty over despotism. Conservative spirits like Edmund Burke (1729–1797) were deeply troubled. In 1790, Burke published *Reflections on the Revolution in France,* one of the great intellectual defenses of European conservatism. He defended inherited privileges in general and those of the English monarchy and aristocracy in particular. He predicted that unlimited reform would lead only to chaos and renewed tyranny. By 1791, fear was growing outside France that the great hopes raised by the revolution might be tragically dashed. The moderate German writer Friederich von Gentz was apprehensive that if moderate and intelligent revolution failed in France, all the old evils would be ten times worse: "It would be felt that men could be happy only as slaves, and every tyrant, great or small, would use this confession to seek revenge for the fright that the awakening of the French nation had given him."[6]

The kings and nobles of Europe, who had at first welcomed the revolution in France as weakening a competing power, began to feel threatened themselves. At their courts they listened to the French aristocrats who had fled France and were urging intervention in France's affairs. When Louis XVI and Marie Antoinette were arrested and returned to Paris after trying unsuccessfully to slip out of France in June 1791, the kings of Austria and Prussia issued the Declaration of Pillnitz. This carefully worded statement declared their willingness to intervene in France, but only with the unanimous agreement of all the Great Powers, which they did not expect to receive. Austria and Prussia expected their threat to have a sobering effect on revolutionary France without causing war.

The crowned heads of Europe misjudged the revolutionary spirit in France. When the National Assembly had disbanded, it had sought popular support by decreeing that none of its members would be eligible for election to the new Legislative Assembly. This meant that when the new representative body was duly elected and convened in October 1791, it had a different character. The great majority were still prosperous, well-educated, and middle class, but they were younger and more reckless than their predecessors. Loosely allied as Jacobins, so named after their political club, the new representatives were passionately committed to liberal revolution.

The Jacobins were full of hatred toward aristocrats and despotic monarchs, and easily whipped themselves into a patriotic fury with bombastic oratory. So the courts of Europe were attempting to incite a war of kings against France; well then, "we will incite a war of people against kings. . . . Ten million Frenchmen, kindled by the fire of liberty, armed with the sword, with reason, with eloquence would be able to change the face of the world and make the tyrants tremble on their thrones."[7] Only Robespierre and a very few others argued that people do not welcome liberation at the point of a gun. Such warnings were brushed aside. France would "rise to the full height of her mission," as one deputy urged. In April 1792, France declared war on the king of Austria.

France's crusade against tyranny went poorly at first. Prussia joined Austria in the Austrian Netherlands (present-day Belgium), and French forces broke and fled at their first encounter with armies of this First Coalition. The road to Paris lay open, and it is possible that only conflict between the eastern monarchs over the division of Poland saved France from defeat.

Military reversals and Austro-Prussian threats caused a wave of patriotic fervor to sweep France. The Legislative Assembly declared the country in danger. Volunteer armies from the provinces streamed through Paris, fraternizing with the people and singing patriotic songs like the stirring *Marseillaise,* later the French national anthem.

In this supercharged wartime atmosphere, rumors of treason by the king and queen spread in Paris. Once again, as in the storming of the Bastille, the common people of Paris acted decisively. On August 10, 1792, a revolutionary mob attacked the royal palace at the Tuileries, capturing it after heavy fighting with the Swiss Guards. The king and his family fled for their lives to the nearby Legislative Assembly, which suspended the king from all his functions, imprisoned him, and called for a new National Convention to be elected by universal male suffrage. Monarchy in France was on its deathbed, mortally wounded by war and popular revolt.

THE SECOND REVOLUTION

The fall of the monarchy marked a rapid radicalization of the Revolution, which historians often call "the second revolution." Louis's imprisonment was followed by the September Massacres, which disgraced the Revolution in the eyes of most of its remaining foreign supporters. Wild stories seized the city that imprisoned counter-revolutionary aristocrats and priests were plotting with the allied invaders. As a result, frenzied crowds invaded the pris-

THE END OF LOUIS XVI   *Some cheered and others wept at the sight of Louis's severed head. The execution of the king was a victory for the radicals, but it horrified Europe's monarchs and conservatives. (Photo: Flammarion)*

ons of Paris and summarily slaughtered half the men and women they found. In late September 1792, the new, popularly elected National Convention proclaimed France a republic. The republic adopted a new revolutionary calendar, and citizens were expected to address each other with the friendly "thou" of the people, rather than with the formal "you" of the rich and powerful.

All of the members of the National Convention were Jacobins and republicans, and the great majority continued to come from the well-educated middle class. But the convention was increasingly divided into two well-defined, bitterly competitive groups —

the Girondists and the Mountain, so called because its members, led by Danton and Robespierre, sat on the uppermost left-hand rows of the assembly hall. Many indecisive members seated in "the Plain" below floated back and forth between the rival factions.

The division was clearly apparent after the National Convention overwhelmingly convicted Louis XVI of treason. By a single vote, 361 of the 720 members of the convention then unconditionally sentenced him to death in January 1793. Louis died with tranquil dignity on the newly invented guillotine. One of his last sentences was, "I am innocent and shall die without fear. I would that my death might bring happiness to the French, and ward off the dangers which I foresee."[8]

Both the Girondists and the Mountain were determined to continue the "war against tyranny." The Prussians had been stopped at the indecisive battle of Valmy on September 20, 1792, one day before the republic was proclaimed. Republican armies then successfully invaded Savoy and captured Nice. A second army corps invaded the German Rhineland and took the city of Frankfurt. To the north the revolutionary armies won their first major battle at Jemappes and occupied the entire Austrian Netherlands by November 1792. Everywhere they went, French armies of occupation chased the princes, "abolished feudalism," and found support among some peasants and middle-class people.

But the French armies also lived off the land, requisitioning food and supplies and plundering local treasures. The liberators looked increasingly like foreign invaders. International tensions mounted. In February 1793 the National Convention, at war with Austria and Prussia, declared war on Britain, Holland, and Spain as well. Republican France was now at war with almost all of Europe, a great war that would last almost without interruption until 1815.

As the forces of the First Coalition drove the French from the Austrian Netherlands, peasants in western France revolted against being drafted into the army. They were supported and encouraged by devout Catholics, royalists, and foreign agents.

In Paris, the quarrelsome convention found itself locked in a life-and-death political struggle between the Girondists and the Mountain. The two groups were in general agreement on questions of policy. Sincere republicans, they hated privilege and wanted to temper economic liberalism with social concern. Yet personal hatreds ran deep. The Girondists feared a bloody dictatorship by the Mountain, and the Mountain was no less convinced that the more moderate Girondists would turn to conservatives and even royalists in order to retain power. With the middle-class delegates so bitterly divided, the laboring poor of Paris emerged as the decisive political factor.

The great mass of the Parisian laboring poor always constituted – along with the peasantry in the summer of 1789 – the elemental force that drove the Revolution forward. It was the artisans, shopkeepers, and day laborers who had stormed the Bastille, marched on Versailles, driven the king from the Tuileries, and carried out the September Massacres. The laboring poor were often known as the *sans-culottes,* "without breeches," because they wore trousers instead of the knee breeches of the aristocracy and the solid middle class. The immediate interests of the sans-culottes were mainly economic, and in the spring of 1793 the economic situation was as bad as the military situation. Rapid inflation, unemployment, and food shortages were again weighing heavily on the poor.

Moreover, by the spring of 1793 the sans-culottes were keenly interested in politics. Encouraged by the so-called "angry men," such as the passionate young ex-priest and journalist Jacques Roux, the sans-culottes were demanding radical political action to guarantee them their daily bread. At first the Mountain joined the Girondists in violently rejecting these demands. But in the face of military defeat, peasant revolt, and hatred of the Girondists, the Mountain and especially Robespierre became more sympathetic. The Mountain joined with sans-culottes activists in the city government to engineer a popular uprising, which forced the convention to arrest thirty-one Girondist deputies for treason on June 2. All power passed to the Mountain.

THE FRENCH REVOLUTION

May 5, 1789	Estates General convene at Versailles
June 17, 1789	Third Estate declares itself the National Assembly
June 20, 1789	Oath of the Tennis Court
July 14, 1789	Storming of the Bastille
July–August 1789	The Great Fear in the countryside
August 4, 1789	National Assembly abolishes feudal privileges
August 27, 1789	National Assembly issues Declaration of the Rights of Man
October 5, 1789	Parisian women march on Versailles and force royal family to return to Paris
November 1789	National Assembly confiscates church lands
July 1790	Civil Constitution of the Clergy establishes a national church
	Louis XVI reluctantly agrees to accept a constitutional monarchy
June 1791	Arrest of the royal family while attempting to flee France
August 1791	Declaration of Pillnitz by Austria and Prussia
April 1792	France declares war on Austria
August 1792	Parisian mob attacks palace and takes Louis XVI prisoner
September 1792	September Massacres
	National Convention declares France a republic and abolishes monarchy

Robespierre and others from the Mountain joined the recently formed Committee of Public Safety, to which the Convention had given dictatorial power to deal with the national emergency. These developments in Paris triggered revolt in leading provincial cities, such as Lyons and Marseilles, where moderates denounced Paris and demanded a decentralized government. The peasant revolt spread and the republic's armies were driven back on all fronts. By July 1793, only the areas around Paris and on the eastern frontier were firmly controlled by the central government. Defeat appeared imminent.

TOTAL WAR AND THE TERROR

A year later, in July 1794, the Austrian Netherlands and the Rhineland were once again in the hands of conquering French armies, and the First Coalition was falling apart. This remarkable change of fortune was due to the revolutionary government's success in harnessing, for perhaps the first time in history, the explosive forces of a planned economy, revolutionary terror, and modern nationalism in a total war effort.

Robespierre and the Committee of Public Safety advanced with implacable resolution on

	The French Revolution (continued)	
January 1793	Execution of Louis XVI	
February 1793	France declares war on Britain, Holland, and Spain	
	Revolts in provincial cities	
March 1793	Bitter struggle in the National Convention between Girondists and the Mountain	
April–June 1793	Robespierre and the Mountain organize the Committee of Public Safety and arrest Girondist leaders	
September 1793	Price controls to aid the sans-culottes and mobilize war effort	
1793–1794	Reign of Terror in Paris and the provinces	
Spring 1794	French armies victorious on all fronts	
July 1794	Execution of Robespierre	
	Thermidorean Reaction begins	
1795–1799	The Directory	
1795	End of economic controls and suppresion of the sans-culottes	
1797	Napoleon defeats Austrian armies in Italy and returns triumphant to Paris	
1798	Austria, Great Britain, and Russia form the Second Coalition against France	
1799	Napoleon overthrows the Directory and seizes power	

several fronts in 1793–1794. In an effort to save revolutionary France, they collaborated with the fiercely patriotic and democratic sans-culottes. They established, as best they could, a planned economy with egalitarian social overtones. Rather than let prices be determined by supply and demand, the government decreed the maximum allowable prices, fixed in paper assignats, for a host of key products. Although the state was too weak to enforce all its price regulations, it did fix the price of bread in Paris at levels the poor could afford. Rationing and ration cards were introduced to make sure that the limited supplies of bread were shared fairly. Quality was also controlled. Bakers were permitted to make only the "bread of equality" – a brown bread made of a mixture of all available flours. White bread and pastries were outlawed as frivolous luxuries. The poor of Paris may not have eaten well, but they ate.

They also worked, mainly to produce arms and munitions for the war effort. Craftsmen and small manufacturers were told what to produce and when to deliver. The government nationalized many small workshops and requisitioned raw materials and grain from the peasants. Sometimes planning and control did

THE REIGN OF TERROR *A man, woman, and child accused of political crimes are brought before a special revolutionary committee for trial. The Terror's iron dictatorship crushed individual rights as well as treason and opposition. (Photo: Flammarion)*

not go beyond orders to meet the latest emergency: "Ten thousand soldiers lack shoes. You will take the shoes of all the aristocrats in Strasbourg and deliver them ready for transport to headquarters at 10 A.M. tomorrow." Failures to control and coordinate were failures of means and not of desire: seldom if ever before had a government attempted to manage an economy so thoroughly. The second revolution and the ascendancy of the sans-culottes had produced an embryonic emergency socialism, which was to have great influence on the subsequent development of socialist ideology.

While radical economic measures supplied the poor with bread and the armies with weapons, a Reign of Terror (1793–1794) was solidifying the home front. Special revolutionary courts, responsible only to Robespierre's Committee of Public Safety, tried rebels and "enemies of the nation" for political crimes. Drawing on popular, sans-culottes support centered in the local Jacobin clubs, these local courts ignored normal legal procedures and judged severely. Forty thousand French men and women were executed. Another 300,000 suspects crowded the prisons and often brushed close to death in a revolutionary court.

Robespierre's Reign of Terror was one of the most controversial phases of the French Revolution. Most historians now believe that the Terror was not directed against any single class. Rather, it was a political weapon directed impartially against all who might oppose the revolutionary government. For many Europeans of the time, however, the Reign of Terror represented a terrible perversion of the generous ideals of 1789. It strengthened the belief that France had foolishly replaced a weak king with a bloody dictatorship.

The third and perhaps decisive element in the French republic's victory over the First Coalition was its ability to continue drawing on the explosive power of patriotic dedication to a national state and a national mission. This is the essence of modern nationalism. With a common language and a common tradition, newly reinforced by the idea of popular sovereignty, the French people were stirred by a common loyalty. The shared danger of foreign foes and internal rebels unified all classes in a heroic defense of the nation.

In such circumstances war was no longer the gentlemanly game of the eighteenth century, but a life-and-death struggle between good and evil. Everyone had to participate in the national effort. According to a famous decree of August 1793:

The young men shall go to battle and the married men shall forge arms. The women shall make tents and clothes, and shall serve in the hospitals; children shall tear rags into lint. The old men will be guided to the public places of the cities to kindle the courage of the young warriors and to preach the unity of the Republic and the hatred of kings.

Like the wars of religion, war in 1793 was a crusade; this war, though, was fought for a secular rather than a religious ideology.

As all unmarried young men were subject to the draft, the French armed forces swelled to 1 million men in fourteen armies. A force of this size was unprecedented in the history of European warfare. The soldiers were led by young, impetuous generals, who had often risen rapidly from the ranks and personified

the opportunities the Revolution seemed to offer gifted sons of the people. These generals used mass attacks at bayonet point by their highly motivated forces to overwhelm the enemy. By the spring of 1794, French armies were victorious on all fronts. The republic was saved.

THE THERMIDORIAN REACTION AND THE DIRECTORY, 1794–1799

The success of the French armies led Robespierre and the Committee of Public Safety to relax the emergency economic controls, but they extended the political Reign of Terror. Their lofty goal was increasingly an ideal democratic republic, where justice would reign and there would be neither rich nor poor. Their lowly means were unrestrained despotism and the guillotine, which struck down any who might seriously question the new order. In March 1794, to the horror of many sans-culottes, Robespierre's Terror wiped out many of the "angry men," led by the radical social democrat Jacques Hébert. Two weeks later, several of Robespierre's long-standing collaborators, led by the famous orator Danton, marched up the steps to the guillotine. Knowing that they might be next, a strange assortment of radicals and moderates in the convention organized a conspiracy. They howled down Robespierre when he tried to speak to the convention on 9 Thermidor (July 27, 1794). On the following day it was Robespierre's turn to be shaved by the revolutionary razor.

As Robespierre's closest supporters followed their leader, France unexpectedly experienced a thorough reaction to the despotism of the Reign of Terror. In a general way this "Thermidorian reaction" recalled the early days of the Revolution. The respectable middle-class lawyers and professionals who had led the liberal Revolution of 1789 reasserted their authority. Drawing support from their own class, the provincial cities, and the better-off peasants, the convention abolished many economic controls, printed more paper currency, and let prices rise sharply. It severely restricted the local political organizations where the sans-culottes had their strength. And all the while, the wealthy bankers and new-rich speculators celebrated the sudden end of the Terror with an orgy of self-indulgence and ostentatious luxury.

The collapse of economic controls coupled with runaway inflation hit the working poor very hard. The gaudy extravagance of the rich wounded their pride. The sans-culottes accepted private property, but they believed passionately in small business and the right of all to earn a decent living. Increasingly disorganized after Robespierre purged their radical spokesmen, the common people of Paris finally revolted against the emerging new order in early 1795. The Convention quickly used the army to suppress these insurrections. For the first time since the fall of the Bastille, bread riots and uprisings by Parisians living on the edge of starvation were effectively put down by a government that made no concessions to the poor.

In the face of all these catastrophes the revolutionary fervor of the laboring poor finally subsided. As far as politics was concerned, their interest and influence would remain very limited until 1830. There arose, especially from the women, a great cry for peace and a turning toward religion. As the government looked the other way, the women brought back the Catholic church and the worship of God. In one French town women fought with each other over which of their children should be baptized first. After six tumultuous years the women of the poor concluded that the Revolution was a failure.

As for the middle-class members of the convention, they wrote yet another constitution, which they believed would guarantee their political supremacy. The mass of the population could vote only for "electors," who would be men of means. The electors then elected the members of a reorganized assembly, as well as important officials throughout France. The assembly also chose the five-man executive – the Directory.

The men of the Directory continued to support French military expansion abroad. War was no longer so much a crusade as a means to meet the ever-present, ever-unsolved economic problem. Large, victorious French armies reduced unemployment at home, and they were able to live off the territories they conquered and plundered.

The unprincipled action of the Directory reinforced widespread disgust with war and starvation. This general dissatisfaction revealed itself clearly in the national elections of 1797, which returned a large number of conservative and even monarchial deputies who favored peace at almost any price. Fearing for their skins, the members of the Directory used the army to nullify the elections and began to govern dictatorially. Two years later, Napoleon Bonaparte ended the Directory in a coup d'état and substituted a strong dictatorship for a weak one. The Revolution was over.

THE NAPOLEONIC ERA, 1799–1814

For almost fifteen years, from 1799 to 1814, France was in the hands of a keen-minded military dictator masquerading first as a Roman consul and then as an emperor. Napoleon Bonaparte was clever enough to end the civil strife in France, in order to consolidate his rule. Had he stopped there, his achievement would have been considerable. But he did not, for the military dictator was also a military adventurer. Peace was boring; the dream of universal empire was irresistible. Napoleon pushed onward with wars of aggression, steadfastly rejecting compromises with his foes until, at last, he destroyed himself.

NAPOLEON'S RULE OF FRANCE

In 1799, when he seized power, young General Napoleon was a national hero. Born in Corsica into an impoverished noble family in 1769, Napoleon left home to become a lieutenant in the French artillery in 1785. Ever the opportunist, he went back to Corsica to fight for the island's independence in 1789. When that adventure failed miserably after about four years, he returned to France as a French patriot and a dedicated revolutionary. Rising rapidly in the new army, Napoleon was placed in command of French forces in Italy and won brilliant victories there in 1796 and 1797. His next campaign, in Egypt, was a failure, but Napoleon succeeded in abandoning his army and returning to France before the fiasco was generally known.

Napoleon soon learned that some prominent members of the assembly were plotting against the Directory. The dissatisfaction of these plotters stemmed not so much from the fact that the Directory was a dictatorship, but that it was a weak dictatorship. Ten years of upheaval and gore had made firm rule much more appealing than liberty and popular politics to these disillusioned revolutionaries. The abbé Sieyès personified this evolution in thinking. In 1789 he had written in his famous pamphlet *What Is the Third Estate?* that the nobility was useless and that the entire people should rule the French nation.

"EMPEROR NAPOLEON" *Napoleon soon minted new gold coins like this one. In doing so, he ended a decade of financial upheaval and gained support from the middle class. (Courtesy of the American Numismatic Society, New York)*

Now Sieyès' motto was "confidence from below, authority from above."

Like the other members of his group, Sieyès wanted a strong military ruler. The flamboyant thirty-year-old Napoleon was ideal. Thus the conspirators and Napoleon organized a takeover. On November 9, 1799, soldiers disbanded the assembly at bayonet point. Napoleon was named first consul of the republic, and a new constitution consolidating his position was overwhelmingly approved in a plebiscite in December 1799. Republican appearances were maintained for the moment, but Napoleon was the virtual dictator of France.

The essence of Napoleon's domestic policy was to use dictatorial powers to maintain order and put an end to civil strife. He did so by working out unwritten agreements with powerful groups in France, whereby these groups received favors in return for obedient service. Napoleon's bargain with the solid middle class was codified in the famous civil code of 1804, which reasserted two of the fundamental principles of this class and of their moderate revolution of 1789: equality of all citizens before the law, and absolute security of wealth and private property. Napoleon and the leading bankers of Paris established a privately owned Bank of France, which loyally served the interests of both the state and the financial oligarchy. Napoleon's devotion to the economic status quo also appealed to the peasants, who had bought some of the lands confiscated from the church and nobility. Thus, Napoleon accepted the gains of the peasantry and reassured the middle class, which had lost its revolutionary illusions in the face of social upheaval.

At the same time Napoleon accepted and strengthened the position of the French bureaucracy. France became a thoroughly centralized state. A network of prefects, subprefects, and centrally appointed mayors depended on Napoleon and served him well. Nor were members of the old nobility slighted. In 1800 and again in 1802 Napoleon granted amnesty to a hundred thousand émigrés on the condition that they return to France and take a loyalty oath. Members of this returning elite soon ably occupied many high posts in the expanding centralized state. Only a thousand diehard monarchists were exempted and remained abroad. Napoleon also created a new, ostentatious imperial nobility in order to reward his most talented generals and officials.

Napoleon's policy of buying off important groups in return for their support is illustrated by his treatment of the Catholic church in France. In 1800, the French clergy was still divided into two groups: those who had taken an oath of allegiance to the revolutionary government, and those in exile or hiding who had refused to do so. Personally uninterested in religion, Napoleon wanted to heal the religious division so that a united Catholic church in France could serve as one of the pillars of his regime. After long and arduous negotiations, Napoleon and Pope Pius VII (1800–1823) signed the Concordat of 1801. The pope gained for French Catholics the precious right to practice their religion freely, but Napoleon gained the most politically. His government now nominated bishops, paid the clergy, and exerted great influence over the church in France. Thus was Napoleon successful in using religion to strengthen his rule.

Napoleon's autocratic and supposedly efficient reorganization of France's church, bureaucracy, laws, and finances has led some historians to call him "the last of the enlightened despots." This discription is flattering, for it neglects Napoleon's endless foreign aggression and insatiable power drive, which might better earn him the epithet "the first of the modern madmen." Be that as it may, the characterization of Napoleon as an enlightened despot is at least half accurate: he was thoroughly despotic. Free speech and freedom of the press – fundamental rights of the liberal revolution, enshrined in the Declaration of the Rights of Man – were constantly and cynically violated. Shortly after seizing power, Napoleon reduced the number of newspapers in Paris from seventy-three to thirteen. By 1811, only four were left, and they were rigorously censored – little more than organs of government propaganda.

In 1802, Napoleon tried and failed to restore the black slavery the Revolution had abolished in France's former colony of Haiti; on the French islands of Martinique and Gua-

THE NAPOLEONIC ERA

November 1799	Napoleon overthrows the Directory
December 1799	French voters overwhelmingly approve Napoleon's new constitution
1800	Napoleon founds the Bank of France
1801	France defeats Austria and acquires Italian and German territories in the Treaty of Lunéville
	Napoleon signs a concordat with the pope
1802	Treaty of Amiens with Britain
March 1804	Execution of the Duke of Engheim
December 1804	Napoleon crowns himself emperor
October 1805	Battle of Trafalgar: Britain defeats the French and Spanish fleets
December 1805	Battle of Austerlitz: Napoleon defeats Austria and Prussia
1807	Treaties of Tilsit: Napoleon redraws the map of Europe
1810	Height of the Grand Empire
June 1812	Napoleon invades Russia with 600,000 men
Winter 1812	Disastrous retreat from Russia
March 1814	Russia, Prussia, Austria, and Britain form the Quadruple Alliance to defeat France
April 1814	Napoleon abdicates and is exiled to Elba

deloupe, he succeeded. Here as elsewhere, the military dictator betrayed the revolutionary ideals of freedom and liberty.

Napoleon could honestly boast that his government was based on three forces: "My policemen, my officials, and my priests." The occasional elections were a farce. Later laws prescribed harsh penalties for political offenses. Whereas the Revolution had established that a person was presumed innocent until proven guilty, Napoleon's penal code placed the burden of proving one's innocence upon the defendant.

These changes in the law were part of the creation of a police state in France. Since Napoleon was usually busy making war, this task was largely left to Joseph Fouché, an unscrupulous opportunist who had earned a reputation for brutality during the Reign of Terror. As minister of police – a kind of super police chief at the national level – Fouché organized a ruthlessly efficient spy system, which kept thousands of citizens under continuous police surveillance. People even suspected of subversive thoughts were arbitrarily detained, placed under house arrest, or – shades of modern totalitarian states – consigned to insane asylums. After 1810 political suspects were held in state prisons, as they had been during the Terror. There were about 2,500 such political prisoners in 1814.

NAPOLEON'S WARS AND FOREIGN POLICY

Napoleon was above all a military man, and a great one. After coming to power in 1799, he sent peace feelers to Austria and Great Britain, the two remaining members of the Second Coalition, which had been formed against France in 1798. When these overtures were rejected, French armies led by Napoleon decisively defeated the Austrians. In the Treaty of Lunéville (1801) Austria accepted the loss of its Italian possessions, and German territory on the west bank of the Rhine was incorporated into France. Once more, as in 1797, the British were alone, and war-weary, like the French.

Still seeking to consolidate his regime domestically, Napoleon concluded the Treaty of Amiens with Great Britain in 1802. Britain agreed to return Trinidad and the Caribbean islands, which it had seized from France since 1792. The treaty said very little about Europe, though. France remained in control of Holland, the Austrian Netherlands, the west bank of the Rhine, and most of the Italian peninsula. Napoleon was free to reshape the German states as he wished. To the dismay of British businessmen, the Treaty of Amiens did not provide for expansion of the commerce between Britain and the Continent. It was clearly a diplomatic triumph for Napoleon, and peace with honor and profit increased his popularity at home.

In 1802, Napoleon was secure but unsatisfied. Always more of a romantic gambler than an enlightened administrator, he could not contain his power drive. Aggressively redraw-

ing the map of Germany so as to weaken Austria and attract the secondary states of southwestern Germany toward France, Napoleon was also almost entirely responsible for renewed war with Great Britain. Regarding war with Britain as inevitable, he threatened British interests in the eastern Mediterranean and tried to restrict British trade with all of Europe. Britain had technically violated the Treaty of Amiens by failing to evacuate the island of Malta, but it was Napoleon's decision to renew war. Like Hitler in 1940, he concentrated his armies in the French ports on the Channel in the fall of 1803 and began making preparations to invade England. Yet Great Britain remained mistress of the seas. When Napoleon tried to bring his Mediterranean fleet around Gibraltar to northern France, a combined French and Spanish fleet was, after a series of mishaps, virtually annihilated by Lord Nelson at the battle of Trafalgar on October 21, 1805. Invasion of England was henceforth impossible.

Renewed fighting had its advantages, however, for the cunning first consul used the wartime atmosphere to have himself proclaimed emperor. He secretly supplied money to French royalists in England, who were organizing a conspiracy to restore the Bourbons, and then fell upon the émigrés caught in his trap when they got to France in early 1804. Unable to find any clear tie between the captured émigrés and any of the Bourbons, Napoleon nonetheless seized a Bourbon prince, the duke of Enghien, in the neutral German state of Baden in March 1804. Subsequently, aware that his widely publicized charges against the duke of Enghien were in fact false, Napoleon nevertheless had the duke executed immediately after his arrival in Paris. On the basis of these plots and lies, Napoleon then asked the people to make him emperor. He needed more power to save the nation

from the Bourbons! It worked, and France accepted a restored monarchy.

Austria, Russia, and Sweden joined with Britain to form the Third Coalition against France shortly before the battle of Trafalgar. Actions like the execution of the duke of Enghein and Napoleon's decision to make himself king of Italy had convinced both Alexander I of Russia and Francis II of Austria that Napoleon had to be checked. Yet the Austrians and the Russians were no match for Napoleon, who scored a brilliant victory over

them at the battle of Austerlitz in December 1805. Alexander I decided to pull back, and Austria accepted large territorial losses in return for peace as the Third Coalition collapsed.

Victorious at Austerlitz, Napoleon proceeded to reorganize the German states to his liking. In 1806, he abolished many of the tiny German states as well as the ancient Holy Roman Empire, whose emperor had traditionally been the king of Austria. Napoleon established by decree a German Confederation of the Rhine, a union of fifteen German states minus Austria, Prussia, and Saxony. Naming himself "protector" of the confederation, Napoleon controlled western Germany with an iron hand. In 1806, for example, a Nuremberg bookseller named Johann Philipp Palm distributed a short work entitled *Germany in Her Deepest Humiliation*. Palm's pamphlet appealed to the kings of Saxony and Prussia to free the German people from Napoleon's destruction. Napoleon ordered Palm executed for this relatively minor offense.

Napoleon's actions in Germany alarmed the Prussians, who had been at peace with France for more than a decade. Expecting help from his ally Russia, Frederick William III of Prussia mobilized his armies. Napoleon attacked and won two more brilliant victories in October 1806 at Jena and Auerstadt, where the Prussians were outnumbered two to one. The war with Prussia and Russia continued into the following spring, and after Napoleon's larger armies won another victory Alexander decided to seek peace.

For several days in June 1807, the young tsar and the French emperor negotiated face-to-face on a raft anchored in the middle of the Niemen River. All the while, the helpless Frederick William rode back and forth on the shore, anxiously awaiting the results. As the German poet Heinrich Heine said later, Napoleon had but to whistle and Prussia would have ceased to exist. In the subsequent treaties of Tilsit, Prussia lost half of its population, while Russia accepted Napoleon's reorganization of western and central Europe, and Napoleon promised Alexander help against the Turks. A secret clause called upon Alexander I to declare war on Britain if Napoleon could not make peace on favorable terms with his island enemy.

After the victory of Austerlitz and even

MAP 26.1   NAPOLEONIC EUROPE IN 1810

more after the treaties of Tilsit, Napoleon saw himself as the emperor of Europe and not just of France. The so-called Grand Empire he built had three parts. The core was an ever-expanding France, which by 1810 included Belgium, Holland, parts of northern Italy, and much German territory on the east bank of the Rhine. Beyond French borders Napoleon established a number of dependent satellite kingdoms, upon the thrones of which he placed (and replaced) the members of his large family. Third, there were the independent but allied states of Austria, Prussia, and Russia. Both satellites and allies were expected after 1806 to support Napoleon's continental system, and thus to cease all trade with Britain.

The impact of the Grand Empire on the peoples of Europe was considerable. In the areas incorporated into France and in the satellites (see Map 26.1) Napoleon introduced many French laws, abolishing feudal dues and serfdom where French revolutionary armies had not already done so. Some of the peasants and middle-class benefited from these reforms. These benefits were purchased, however, at the price of heavy taxes in money and men for Napoleon's armies. Napoleon came to be regarded much more as a conquering tyrant than an enlightened liberator.

The first great revolt occurred in Spain. In 1808 a coalition of Catholics, monarchists, and patriots rebelled against Napoleon's attempts to make Spain a French satellite with a Bonaparte as its king. French armies occupied Madrid, but the foes of Napoleon fled to the hills and waged uncompromising guerrilla warfare. Spain was a clear warning. It was time to stop.

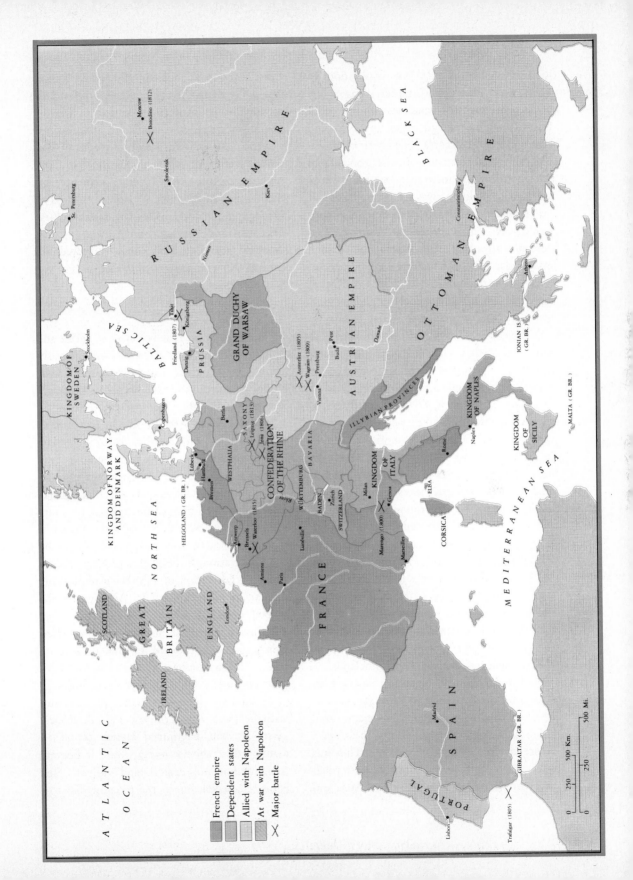

ATLANTIC OCEAN

SCOTLAND

IRELAND

GREAT BRITAIN

ENGLAND

London

NORTH SEA

KINGDOM OF SWEDEN

Stockholm

BALTIC SEA

St. Petersburg

RUSSIAN EMPIRE

Moscow

Borodino (1812)

Smolensk

Kiev

Niemen

KINGDOM OF NORWAY AND DENMARK

Copenhagen

HELGOLAND (GR. BR.)

Hamburg

Lübeck

Bremen

Berlin

WESTPHALIA

Tilsit

Friedland (1807)

Königsberg

Danzig

PRUSSIA

GRAND DUCHY OF WARSAW

AUSTRIAN EMPIRE

Austerlitz (1805)

Wagram (1809)

Pest

Buda

Danube

Pressburg

Vienna

SAXONY

Leipzig (1813)

Jena (1806)

CONFEDERATION OF THE RHINE

BAVARIA

WÜRTEMBURG

BADEN

Zurich

SWITZERLAND

Rhine

Lunéville

KINGDOM OF ITALY

Milan

Marengo (1800)

Genoa

ILLYRIAN PROVINCES

OTTOMAN EMPIRE

BLACK SEA

Constantinople

IONIAN IS. (GR. BR.)

Athens

Antwerp

Brussels

Waterloo (1815)

Amiens

Paris

FRANCE

Marseilles

ELBA

Rome

CORSICA

KINGDOM OF NAPLES

Naples

KINGDOM OF SICILY

MALTA (GR. BR.)

MEDITERRANEAN SEA

SPAIN

Madrid

PORTUGAL

Lisbon

GIBRALTAR (GR. BR.)

Trafalgar (1805)

French empire
Dependent states
Allied with Napoleon
At war with Napoleon
✕ Major battle

500 Mi.

500 Km.

250

250

0

Yet Napoleon would not, could not. In 1810, when the Grand Empire was at its height, Britain still remained at war with France, helping the guerrillas in Spain and Portugal (see Map 26.1). The continental system, organized to exclude British goods from the Continent and force that "nation of shopkeepers" to its knees, was a failure. Instead, it was France that suffered from Britain's counterblockade, which created hard times for Napoleon's strongest supporters – the French middle class. Perhaps looking for a scapegoat, Napoleon turned upon Alexander I of Russia, who had been fully supporting Napoleon's war of prohibitions against British goods.

Napoleon's invasion of Russia began in June 1812 with a force that eventually numbered 600,000, probably the largest force yet assembled in a single army. Only one-third of this force was French, however; nationals of all the satellites and allies were drafted into the operation. Originally planning to winter in the Russian city of Smolensk if Alexander did not sue for peace, Napoleon reached Smolensk and recklessly pressed on. The great battle of Borodino that followed was a draw, and the Russians retreated in good order. Alexander ordered the evacuation of Moscow, which then burned, and he refused to negotiate. Finally, after five weeks in the burned-out city, Napoleon ordered a retreat. That retreat was one of the great military disasters in history. The Russian army and the Russian winter cut Napoleon's army to pieces. Only 100,000 men returned to their homelands.

As before in Egypt, Napoleon deserted his troops and fled to Paris to raise yet another army. He might still have had peace and saved his throne if he had been willing to accept a France reduced to its historic size. This was what Austria's foreign minister Metternich proposed. But Napoleon refused. Austria and

Prussia deserted Napoleon and joined Russia and Great Britain in the Fourth Coalition. All across Europe patriots called for a "war of liberation" against Napoleon's oppression, and the well-disciplined regular armies of Napoleon's enemies closed in for the kill. This time the coalition held together, cemented by the Treaty of Chaumont, which created a Quadruple Alliance to last for twenty years. Less than a month later, on April 4, 1814, a defeated, abandoned Napoleon abdicated his throne. An era had ended. Peace in Europe was possible.

◆

The revolution that began in America and spread to France was a liberal revolution. Inspired by English history, especially the Glorious Revolution, and some of the teachings of the Enlightenment, revolutionaries on both sides of the Atlantic sought to establish civil liberties and equality before the law within the framework of representative government. Success in America was subsequently matched by success in France, thanks to the decisive action of the poor and the oppressed – the sans-culottes and the peasants. The government and society established by the Declaration of the Rights of Man and the French constitution of 1791 were remarkably similar to those created in America by the federal Constitution and the Bill of Rights. All classes except the nobility benefited from this great step forward in human history, though the prosperous middle class may have profited most.

Yet the revolution in France did not end with the liberal victory of 1789-1791. As Robespierre led the determined French people in a total effort against foreign foes, it became more democratic, radical, and violent. This effort succeeded, but at the price of dictatorship, first by Robespierre himself and then by the Directory and Napoleon. Some historians blame the excesses of the French revolutionaries for the emergence of dictatorship, while others hold the conservative monarchs of Europe responsible. In any case, historians have often concluded that the French Revolution ended in failure.

This conclusion is highly debatable, though. After the fall of Robespierre the solid middle class with its liberal philosophy and Enlightenment world-view reasserted itself. Under the Directory it salvaged a good portion of the social and political gains that it and the peasantry had made between 1789 and 1791. In so doing, the middle-class leaders repudiated the radical social and economic measures associated with Robespierre, but they never reestablished the old order of privileged nobility and absolute monarchs. And although Napoleon drastically curtailed thought and speech, his dictatorship used rather than weakened the middle class and the peasantry. Careers were open to talent, and private wealth remained secure. In spite of a generation of war and upheaval, a very substantial part of the liberal triumph of 1789–1791 survived in France in 1814. Old Europe would never be the same.

NOTES

1. Quoted by R. R. Palmer, *The Age of Democratic Revolution,* Princeton University Press, Princeton, N.J., 1959, 1.239.

2. G. Lefebvre, *The Coming of the French Revolution,* Vintage Books, New York, 1947, p. 81.

3. P. H. Beik, ed., *The French Revolution,* Walker, New York, 1970, p. 89.

4. O. Hufton, "Women in Revolution," *Past and Present* 53 (November 1971): 91–95.

5. G. Pernoud and S. Flaisser, eds., *The French Revolution,* Fawcett Publications, Greenwich, Conn., 1960, p. 61.

6. L. Gershoy, *The Era of the French Revolution, 1789–1799,* Van Nostrand, New York, 1957, p. 135.

7. Ibid., p. 150.

8. Pernoud and Flaisser, pp. 193–194.

SUGGESTED READING

In addition to the fascinating eyewitness reports on the French Revolution in P. Beck, *The French Revolution,* and G. Pernoud and S. Flaisser, eds., *The French Revolution* (1960), A. Young's *Travels in France During the Years 1787, 1788 and 1789* (1969) offers an engrossing contemporary description of France and Paris on the eve of revolution. Edmund Burke, *Reflections on the Revolution in France,* first published in 1790, is the classic conservative indictment. The intense passions the French Revolution has generated may be seen in the nineteenth-century French historians, notably the enthusiastic Jules Michelet, *History of the French Revolution;* the hostile Hippolyte Taine; and the judicious Alexis de Tocqueville, whose masterpiece, *The Old Regime and the French Revolution,* was first published in 1856. Important recent general studies on the entire period are R. R. Palmer, *The Age of Democratic Revolution* (1959, 1964), which paints a comparative international picture; E. J. Hobsbawm, *The Age of Revolution, 1789–1848* (1962); C. Breunig, *The Age of Revolution and Reaction, 1789–1850* (1970); O. Connelly, *French Revolution – Napoleonic Era* (1979); and L. Dehio, *The Precarious Balance: Four Centuries of the European Power Struggle* (1962). C. Brinton's older but delightfully written *A Decade of Revolution, 1789–1799* (1934) complements his stimulating *Anatomy of Revolution* (1952), an ambitious comparative approach to revolution in England, America, France, and Russia. A. Cobban, *The Social Interpretation of the French Revolution* (1964), is an exciting reassessment of many well-worn ideas, to be compared with W. Doyle, *Origins of the French Revolution* (1981); G. Lefebvre, *The Coming of the French Revolution* (1947); and N. Hampson, *A Social History of the French Revolution* (1963). G. Rudé makes the men and women of the great days of upheaval come alive in his *The Crowd in the French Revolution* (1959). R. R. Palmer studies sympathetically the leaders of the Terror in *Twelve Who Ruled* (1941). Two other particularly interesting detailed works are C. L. R. James, *The Black Jacobins* (1938), on black slave revolt in Haiti, and J. C. Herold, *Mistress to an Age* (1955), on the remarkable Madame de Staël. On revolution in America, E. Morgan, *The Birth of the Republic, 1763–89,* and B. Bailyn, *The Ideological Origins of the American Revolution* (1967), are noteworthy. Three important recent studies on aspects of revolutionary France are D. Jordan's vivid *The King's Trial: Louis XVI vs. the French Revolution* (1979); W. Sewell, Jr.'s imaginative *Work and Revolution in France: The Language of Labor from the Old Regime to 1848* (1980); and R. Phillips' *Family Breakdown in Late Eighteenth-Century France: Divorces in Rouen, 1792–1803* (1980).

P. Geyl, *Napoleon, For and Against* (1949), is a delightful discussion of changing historical interpretations of Napoleon. Good biographies are J. M. Thompson, *Napoleon Bonaparte: His Rise and Fall* (1952); F. H. M. Markham, *Napoleon* (1964); and E. Ludwig's popular novel *Napoleon* (1915). Other wonderful novels inspired by this period are Raphael Sabatini, *Scaramouche,* a swashbuckler of revolutionary intrigue with accurate historical details; Charles Dickens's classic *Tale of Two Cities;* and Leo Tolstoy's monumental saga of Napoleon's invasion of Russia (and much more), *War and Peace.*

CHAPTER 27

THE REVOLUTION IN

ENERGY AND INDUSTRY

AT ABOUT THE TIME the French Revolution was opening a new political era, another revolution was transforming economic and social life. This was the Industrial Revolution, which began in England in the 1780s and spread after 1815 to continental Europe and then around the world. Because the Industrial Revolution was less dramatic than the French Revolution, some historians see industrial development as basically moderate and evolutionary. In the long perspective, however, it was rapid and brought about radical changes. Perhaps only the development of agriculture in Neolithic times had a similar impact and significance.

The Industrial Revolution profoundly modified much of human experience. It changed patterns of work, transformed the social class structure, and eventually even altered the international balance of political power. It may quite possibly have saved Europe from the poverty of severe overpopulation and even from famine. How did this happen? How and why did drastic changes occur in industry, and how did these changes affect people and society? These are the questions this chapter will seek to answer. Chapter 30 will examine in detail the emergence of accompanying changes in urban civilization.

THE INDUSTRIAL REVOLUTION IN ENGLAND

The Industrial Revolution began in England. It was something new in history, and it was quite unplanned. With no models to copy and no idea of what to expect, England had to pioneer not only in industrial technology but also in social relations and urban living. Between 1793 and 1815, these formidable tasks were complicated by almost constant war with

France. As the trailblazer in economic development, as France was in political changes, England must command special attention.

EIGHTEENTH-CENTURY ORIGINS

The Industrial Revolution grew out of the expanding Atlantic economy of the eighteenth century, which served mercantilist England remarkably well. England's colonial empire, augmented by a strong position in Latin America and in the African slave trade, provided a growing market for English manufactured goods. So did England itself. In an age when it was much cheaper to ship goods by water than by land, no part of England was more than twenty miles from navigable water. Beginning in the 1770s, a canal-building boom greatly enhanced this natural advantage (see Map 27.1). Nor were there any tariffs within the country to hinder trade, as there were in France before 1789 and in politically fragmented Germany.

Agriculture played a central role in bringing about the Industrial Revolution in England. English farmers were second only to the Dutch in productivity in 1700, and they were continuously adopting new methods of farming as the century went on. The result, especially before 1760, was a period of bountiful crops and low food prices. The ordinary English family did not have to spend almost everything it earned just to buy bread. It could spend more on other items, on manufactured goods — leather shoes or a razor for the man, a bonnet or a shawl for the woman, toy soldiers for the son, and a doll for the daughter. Thus, demand for goods within the country complemented the demand from the colonies.

England had other assets that helped give rise to the Industrial Revolution. Unlike eighteenth-century France, England had an effective central bank and well-developed credit markets. The monarchy and the aristocratic oligarchy, which had jointly ruled the country since 1688, provided stable and predictable government. At the same time the government let the domestic economy operate fairly freely and with few controls, encouraging personal initiative, technical change, and a free market. Finally, England had long had a large class of hired agricultural laborers, whose numbers were further increased by the enclosure movement of the late eighteenth century. These rural wage earners were relatively mobile – compared to village-bound peasants in France and western Germany, for example – and along with cottage workers they formed a potential industrial labor force for capitalist entrepreneurs.

All these factors combined to initiate the Industrial Revolution, which began in the 1780s – after the American war for independence and just before the French Revolution. Thus the great economic and political revolutions that have shaped the modern world occurred almost simultaneously, though they began in different countries. The Industrial Revolution was, however, a longer process. It was not complete in England until 1830 at the earliest, and it had no real impact on continental countries until after the Congress of Vienna ended the era of revolutionary wars in 1815.

THE FIRST FACTORIES

The pressure to produce more goods for a growing market was directly related to the first decisive breakthrough of the Industrial Revolution – the creation of the world's first large factories in the English cotton textile industry. Technological innovations in the manufacture of cloth led to a whole new system of production and social relationships. Since no other industry experienced such a

MAP 27.1 COTTAGE INDUSTRY AND TRANSPORTATION IN EIGHTEENTH-CENTURY ENGLAND *England had an unusually good system of navigable waterways even before river-linking canals made it better.*

rapid or complete transformation before 1830, these trail-blazing developments deserve special consideration.

Although the putting-out system of merchant capitalism (page 835) was expanding all across Europe in the eighteenth century, this pattern of rural industry was most fully developed in England. Thus it was in England, under the pressure of growing demand, that the system's shortcomings first began to outweigh its advantages. This was especially true in the textile industry after about 1760.

The constant shortage of thread in the textile industry focused attention on ways of improving spinning. Many a tinkering worker knew that a better spinning wheel promised rich rewards. Spinning of the traditional raw materials – wool and flax – proved hard to change, but cotton was different. Cotton textiles had first been imported into England from India by the East India Company, and by 1760 there was a tiny domestic industry in northern England. After many experiments over a generation, a gifted carpenter and jack-of-all trades, James Hargreaves, invented his cotton spinning jenny about 1765. At almost the same moment a barber-turned-manufacturer named Richard Arkwright invented (or possibly pirated) another kind of spinning machine, the water frame. These breakthroughs produced an explosion in the infant industry. By 1790, the new machines produced ten times as much cotton yarn as had been made in 1770. By 1800, the production of cotton thread was England's most important industry.

Hargreaves' jenny was simple and inexpensive. It was also hand-operated. In early models, from six to twenty-four spindles were mounted on a sliding carriage, and each spindle spun a fine slender thread. The woman moved the carriage back and forth with one hand and turned a wheel to supply power with the other. Now it was the weaver who could not keep up with his vastly more efficient wife.

Arkwright's water frame employed a different principle. It quickly acquired a capacity of several hundred spindles, and required much more power – water power. The water frame thus required large specialized mills, factories that employed as many as a thousand workers from the very beginning. The water frame could spin only coarse strong thread, which was then put out for respinning on innumerable hand-powered cottage jennies. Around 1790 Samuel Crompton's innovation, the "mule," began to require more power than the human arm could supply. (Crompton's invention was called the mule because it united the best aspects of the jenny and the water frame, as a mule combines the traits of its mother the horse and its father the donkey.) After that time, all cotton spinning was gradually concentrated in factories.

The first consequences of these revolutionary developments were much more beneficial than is usually believed. Cotton goods became much cheaper, and they were bought and treasured by all classes. In the past only the wealthy could afford the comfort and cleanliness of underwear, which was called body linen because it was made from expensive linen cloth. Now millions of poor people could afford to wear cotton slips and underpants, who had earlier worn nothing underneath their coarse, filthy outer garments.

The family was freed from its constant search for adequate yarn from scattered, part-time spinners, since all the thread needed could be spun in the cottage on the jenny or obtained from a nearby factory. The wages of weavers, now hard pressed to keep up with the spinners, rose markedly until about 1792. Weavers were among the best-paid workers in England. They were known to walk proudly through the streets with £5 notes stuck in their hatbands, and they dressed like the middle class.

One result of this unprecedented prosperity was that large numbers of agricultural laborers became weavers. Meanwhile, however, mechanics and capitalists were seeking to invent a power loom to save on labor costs. This Edmund Cartwright achieved in 1785. But the power looms of the factories worked poorly at first, and handloom weavers continued to receive good wages until at least 1800.

HARGREAVES SPINNING JENNY This early model was rapidly improved. By 1783 one woman could easily spin by hand a hundred threads of cotton at a time. (Photo: Caroline Buckler)

Working conditions in the early factories were less satisfactory than those of cottage weavers and spinners. But until the late 1780s most English factories were in rural areas, where they had access to water power. These factories employed a relatively small percentage of all cotton textile workers. People were reluctant to work in them, partly because they resembled the poorhouses where destitute inmates had to labor for very little pay. Therefore, factory owners turned to young children as a source of labor. More precisely, they turned to children who had been abandoned by their parents and put in the care of local parishes. The parish officers often "apprenticed" such unfortunate orphans to factory owners. The parish thus saved money and the factory owners gained workers over whom they exercised almost the authority of slaveowners. The hours were terrible, the conditions appalling. But only the nakedness of this exploitation was new. These children, and the women who came to work beside them in the next generation, were simply doing in the factory, under different conditions, the same kind of work they had long done in their cottages. It is some consolation that such exploitation of small children was at this point more nearly ending than beginning.

The creation of the world's first modern factories in the English cotton textile industry in the 1770s and 1780s, which grew out of the putting-out system of cottage production, was a momentous development. Both symbolically and in substance, the big new cotton mills marked the beginning of the Industrial Revo-

MAKING CHARCOAL *After wood was carefully cut and stacked, iron masters slowly burned it to produce charcoal. Before the Industrial Revolution, a* *country's iron industry depended in large part on the size of its forests. (Photo: Caroline Buckler)*

lution in England in the 1780s and the acceleration of English industrial development.

THE PROBLEM OF ENERGY

The growth of the cotton textile industry might have been stunted or cut short, however, if water from rivers and streams had re- mained the primary source of power for the new factories. But this did not occur. Instead, an epoch-making solution was found to the age-old problem of energy and power. It was this solution to the energy problem – a problem once again very much before us today – that permitted continued rapid development in cotton textiles, the gradual generalization of the factory system, and the triumph of the Industrial Revolution.

Human beings, like all living organisms, require energy. Adult men and women need from 2,000 to 4,000 calories (calories are units of energy) daily simply to fuel their bodies, work, and survive. Energy comes from a variety of sources; energy also takes different forms and one form may be converted into another. Plants have been converting solar energy into caloric matter for eons. And human beings have used their toolmaking abilities to construct machines that convert one form of energy into another for their own benefit.

Prehistoric people relied on plants and plant-eating animals as their sources of energy. With the development of agriculture, the early civilizations were able to increase the number of "useful" plants and thus the supply of energy. Some plants could be fed to domesticated animals, like the horse. Stronger than human beings, these animals converted the energy in the plants into useful work. In the medieval period people began to develop water mills to grind their grain and windmills to pump water and drain swamps. More efficient use of water and wind in the sixteenth and seventeenth centuries enabled human beings to accomplish more; intercontinental sailing ships are a prime example. Nevertheless, even into the eighteenth century society continued to rely for energy mainly on plants, and human beings and animals continued to perform most useful work. This dependence meant that Western civilization remained poor in energy and power.

Lack of power lay at the heart of the poverty that afflicted the large majority of people. The man behind the plow and the woman at the spinning wheel could employ only horsepower and human muscle in their labor. No matter how hard they worked, they could not produce very much. What people needed were new sources of energy and more power at their disposal. Then they would be able to work more efficiently, produce more, and live better.

Where was more energy to be found? Almost all energy came directly or indirectly from plants, and therefore from the land: grain for people, hay for animals, and wood for heat. The land was also the principal source of raw materials needed for industrial production: wool and flax for clothing, leather for shoes, wood for housing, tools, and ironmaking. And although swamps could be drained and marshes reclaimed from the sea, it was difficult to expand greatly the amount of land available. True, its yield could be increased, such as by the elimination of fallow; yet there were definite limits to such improvements.

The shortage of energy was becoming particularly severe in England by the eighteenth century. Because of the growth of population, most of the great forests of medieval England had long ago been replaced by fields of grain and hay. Wood was in ever shorter supply; yet it remained tremendously important. It was the primary source of heat for all homes and industries. It was also the key to transportation, since ships and wagons were made of wood. Moreover, wood was, along with iron ore, the basic raw material of the iron industry. Processed wood (charcoal) was the fuel mixed with iron ore in the blast furnace to produce pig iron. The iron industry's appetite for wood was enormous, and even very modest and constant levels of iron production had gone far toward laying bare the forests of England, as well as parts of Europe. By 1740, the English iron industry was stagnating. Vast forests enabled Russia in the eighteenth century to become the world's leading producer of iron, much of which was exported to England. But Russia's potential for growth was limited too, and in a few decades Russia would reach the barrier of inadequate energy that was already holding England back.

"STEAM IS AN ENGLISHMAN"

As this early energy crisis grew worse, England looked toward its abundant and widely scattered reserves of coal as an alternative to its vanishing wood. Coal was first used in England in the late Middle Ages as a source of heat. By 1640, most homes in London were heated with it, and it also provided heat for making beer, glass, soap, and other products. Coal was not used, however, to produce mechanical energy or to power machinery. It was there that coal's potential was enormous, as a simple example shows.

One pound of good bituminous coal contains about 3,500 calories of heat energy. A miner who eats 3,500 calories of food can dig out 500 pounds of coal a day, using hand tools. Even an extremely inefficient converter, which transforms only 1 percent of the heat energy in coal into mechanical energy, will produce 27 horsepower-hours of work from the 500 pounds of coal the miner cut out of the earth. (The miner, by contrast, produces only about 1 horsepower-hour in the course of a day.) Much more energy is consumed by the converter, but much more work can be done.

Early steam engines were just such inefficient converters. As more coal was produced, mines were dug deeper and deeper and were constantly filling with water. Mechanical pumps, usually powered by animals walking in circles at the surface, had to be installed. At one mine, fully 500 horses were used in pumping. Such power was expensive and bothersome. In an attempt to overcome these disadvantages, Thomas Savery in 1698 and

Thomas Newcomen in 1705 invented the first primitive steam engines.

Both of these engines were extremely inefficient. Both burned coal to produce steam, which was then injected into a cylinder or reservoir. In Newcomen's engine the steam in the cylinder was cooled, creating a partial vacuum in the cylinder. This vacuum allowed the pressure of the earth's atmosphere to push the piston in the cylinder down and operate a pump. By the 1770s, many Savery engines and hundreds of Newcomen engines were working successfully, though inefficiently, in English mines.

In the early 1760s, a gifted young Scot named James Watt (1736–1819) was drawn to a critical study of the steam engine. Watt was employed at the time by the University of Glasgow as a skilled craftsman making scientific instruments. The Scottish universities were pioneers in practical technical education, and in 1763 Watt was called on to repair a Newcomen engine being used in a physics course. After a series of observations, Watt saw why the Newcomen engine wasted so much energy: the cylinder was being heated and cooled for every single stroke of the piston. To remedy this problem Watt added a separate condenser, where the steam could be condensed without cooling the cylinder. This splendid invention greatly increased the efficiency of the steam engine.

To invent something in a laboratory is one thing; to make it a practical success is quite another. Watt needed skilled workers, precision parts, and capital, and the relatively advanced nature of the English economy proved crucial. A partnership with a wealthy, progressive toymaker, Matthew Boulton of Birmingham, provided risk capital and a manufacturing plant. In the craft tradition of locksmiths, tinsmiths, and millwrights Watt found skilled mechanics who could install,

The ENGINE for Raising Water (with a power made) by Fire

THE NEWCOMEN ENGINE *The enormous steam-filled cylinder (C) was cooled by injecting cold water from the tank above (G) by means of a pipe (M). Atmospheric pressure then pushed the piston down, raised the beam, and pumped water from the mine. (Science Museum, London)*

regulate, and repair his sophisticated engines. From ingenious manufacturers like the cannonmaker John Wilkinson, who learned to bore cylinders with a fair degree of accuracy, Watt was gradually able to purchase precision parts. This support allowed him to create an effective vacuum and regulate a complex engine. In more than twenty years of constant effort Watt made many further improvements. By the late 1780s, the steam engine was a practical and commercial success in England.

As a nineteenth-century saying put it, "Steam is an Englishman."

The steam engine of Watt and his followers was the Industrial Revolution's most fundamental advance in technology. For the first time in history humanity had, at least for a few generations, almost unlimited power at its disposal. For the first time inventors and engineers could devise and implement all kinds of power equipment to aid people in their work. For the first time abundance was at least a possibility for ordinary men and women.

The steam engine was quickly put to use in many industries in England. It made possible the production of ever more coal, to feed steam engines elsewhere. The steam-power plant began to replace water power in the cotton spinning mills during the 1780s, contributing greatly to that industry's phenomenal ascension. Steam also took the place of water power in flour mills, in the malt mills used in breweries, in the flint mills supplying the china industry, and in the mills exported to the West Indies to crush sugar cane.

Steam power promoted important breakthroughs in other industries. The English iron industry was radically transformed. The use of powerful steam-driven bellows in the blast furnaces helped ironmakers switch over rapidly from limited charcoal to unlimited coke (which is made from coal) in the smelting of pig iron after 1770. In the 1780s, Henry Cort developed the puddling furnace, which allowed pig iron to be refined in turn with coke. Strong, skilled ironworkers – the puddlers – "cooked" molten pig iron in a great vat, raking off globs of refined iron for further processing. Cort also developed heavy-duty steam-powered rolling mills, which were capable of spewing out finished iron in every shape and form.

The economic consequence of these technical innovations was a great boom in the English iron industry. In 1740, annual British iron production was only 17,000 tons. With the spread of coke smelting and the first impact of Cort's inventions, production reached 68,000 tons in 1788, 125,000 tons in 1796, and 260,000 tons in 1806. In 1844, Britain produced 3 million tons of iron. This was truly phenomenal expansion. Once scarce and expensive, iron became the cheap, basic building-block of the economy.

Sailing ships had improved noticeably since the age of discoveries, and the second half of the eighteenth century saw extensive construction of hard and relatively smooth roads, particularly in France before the Revolution. Yet it was passenger traffic that benefited most from this construction. Overland shipment of freight, relying as it did solely on horsepower, was still quite limited and frightfully expensive; shippers relied on rivers and canals for heavy freight whenever possible. It was logical therefore that inventors would try to use steam power to improve inland transportation.

As early as 1800, an American ran a "steamer on wheels" through city streets. Other experiments followed. In the 1820s, English engineers perfected steam cars capable of carrying fourteen passengers at ten miles an hour – as fast as the mail coach. But the noisy, heavy steam automobiles frightened passing horses and damaged themselves as well as the roads with their vibrations. For the rest of the century horses continued to reign on highways and city streets.

The coal industry had long been using plank roads and rails to move coal wagons within mines and at the surface. Rails reduced friction and allowed a horse or a human being to pull a heavier load. Thus once a rail capable of supporting a heavy locomotive was developed in 1816, all sorts of experiments with steam engines on rails went forward. In 1825, after ten years of work, George Stephenson built an effective locomotive. In 1830, his *Rocket* sped down the track of the just-completed Liverpool and Manchester Railway at sixteen miles per hour. This was the world's first important railroad, fittingly steaming in the heart of industrial England.

The line from Liverpool to Manchester was

THE THIRD-CLASS CARRIAGE *The French comic artist Honoré Daumier (1808–1879) was fascinated by the railroad and its human significance. This great painting focuses on the peasant grandmother, old and weary, absorbed in memories. The nursing mother is* *love and creativity, while the sleeping boy represents childhood innocence. (The Metropolitan Museum of Art. Bequest of Mrs. H. O. Havemeyer, 1929. The H. O. Havemeyer Collection)*

a financial as well as a technical success, and many private companies were quickly organized to build more rail lines. These companies had to get permission for their projects from Parliament and pay for the rights of way they needed; otherwise, their freedom was great. Within twenty years they had completed the main trunk lines of Great Britain. Other countries followed quickly with their own railway construction.

The significance of the railroad was tremendous. The railroad dramatically reduced the cost and uncertainty of shipping freight overland. This advance had many economic consequences. Previously, markets had tended to be small and local; as the barrier of high transportation costs was lowered, they became larger and even nationwide. Larger markets encouraged larger factories with more sophisticated machinery. Such factories could make goods cheaper, enabling people to pay less for them. They also tended to drive most cottage workers, many urban artisans, and some other manufacturers out of business.

In all countries the construction of railroads contributed to the growth of a class of urban workers. Cottage workers, farm laborers, and small peasants did not generally leave their jobs and homes to go directly to work in factories. However, the building of railroads created a strong demand for labor, especially unskilled labor, throughout a country. Like farm work, hard work on construction gangs was done in the open air with animals and hand tools. Many farm laborers and poor peasants, long accustomed to leaving their villages for temporary employment, went to build railroads. By the time the work was finished, life back home in the village often seemed dull and unappealing, and many men drifted to towns in search of work – with the railroad companies, in construction, in factories. By the time they sent for their wives and sweethearts to join them, they had become urban workers.

The railroad changed the outlook and values of the entire society. The last and culminating invention of the Industrial Revolution, the railroad dramatically revealed the power and increased the speed of the new age. Racing down a track at sixteen miles per hour or, by 1850, at a phenomenal fifty miles per hour was a new and awesome experience. As the noted French economist Michel Chevalier put it after a ride on the Liverpool and Manchester in 1833, "There are certain impressions that one cannot put into words!"

Some great painters like J. M. W. Turner (1775–1851) and Claude Monet (1840–1926) succeeded in expressing this sense of power and awe. So did the massive new train stations, the cathedrals of the industrial age. The leading railway engineers, like Isambard Kingdom Brunel and Thomas Brassey, whose tunnels pierced mountains and whose bridges spanned valleys, became the idols of the public – the astronauts of their day. Everyday speech absorbed the images of railroading.

After you got up a "full head of steam," you "highballed" along. And if you didn't "go off the track," you might "toot your own whistle." The railroad fired the imagination.

BRITAIN AT MIDCENTURY

In 1851, London was the site of a famous industrial fair. This exposition was held in the newly built Crystal Palace, an architectural masterpiece made entirely of glass and iron, both of which were now cheap and abundant. For the hundreds of thousands who visited, one fact stood out. The little island of Britain – England, Wales, and Scotland – was "the workshop of the world." It alone produced two-thirds of the world's coal and more than half of its iron and cotton cloth. Britain was the first industrial nation (see Map 27.2).

Britain had unlocked and developed a new source of energy. With practically unlimited power, the British economy had enormously increased its production of manufactured goods. Between 1780 and 1800, Britain doubled its production of industrial goods. Between 1801 and 1851, the gross national product – the GNP that present-day newspapers and politicians are always talking about – rose three and a half times at constant prices. In other words, the British increased enormously their wealth and their national income. At the same time the population of Great Britain boomed, growing from about 9 million in 1780 to almost 21 million in 1851.

Since the economy grew much faster than the number of people, average real income per person grew markedly. (Real income is what people's money wages really buy after adjusting for the effects of inflation or deflation.) In fact, average real income per person in Britain just about *doubled* between 1801 and 1851, from £13 per person to £24 per person. Put very simply, and all other things being equal, the woman or man of 1851 could buy twice as much as the woman or man of 1801. Considering the poverty of the eighteenth century, poverty that all the drama and excitement of the French Revolution did little or nothing to reduce, this would appear to be a monumental achievement.

But perhaps all other things were not equal. Perhaps workers, farmers, and ordinary people did not share in the new wealth. Perhaps only the rich got richer, while the poor got poorer or made no progress. We shall turn to this great issue after looking at the spread of the Industrial Revolution to continental countries.

THE SPREAD OF THE INDUSTRIAL REVOLUTION

The new methods of the Industrial Revolution spread rather slowly at first. Whereas Britain's economy began to speed up about 1780 and had created an industrial urban society by 1850, the economies of continental Europe began to follow only after 1815 and particularly after about 1830. First Belgium took up the challenge; then between about 1840 and 1860, France and the various states of Germany began developing rapidly, as did the United States. After 1870 Sweden, Russia, and Japan joined in and during the twentieth century many more countries have done so.

THE CHALLENGE OF INDUSTRIALIZATION

If poverty was so widespread in Europe and if industrial development created so much more wealth per person in Great Britain, why did

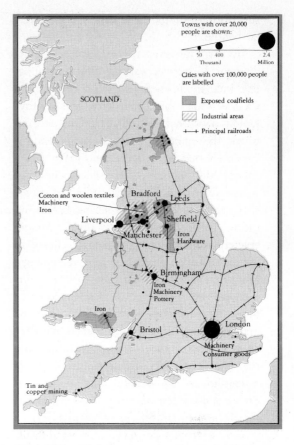

MAP 27.2 THE INDUSTRIAL REVOLUTION IN ENGLAND, CA 1850 *Industry concentrated in the rapidly growing cities of the north and the midlands, where rich coal and iron deposits were in close proximity.*

continental countries wait years and even decades before they followed the British example? The eighteenth century was certainly an era of agricultural improvement, population increase, expanding foreign trade, and growing cottage industry. England led in these developments, but other countries participated in the general trend. Thus, when the pace of English industry began to accelerate in the 1780s, countries like France began to copy the new methods. English industry enjoyed clear superiority, but the Continent was not very far behind.

By 1815, however, the situation was quite different. In spite of wartime difficulties, English industry maintained the momentum of the 1780s and continued to grow and improve rapidly between 1789 and 1815. On the Continent the unending political and economic upheavals that began with the French Revolution had another effect. They disrupted trade, created runaway inflation, and fostered social anxiety. War severed normal communications between England and the Continent, severely handicapping continental efforts to use new British machinery and technology. Moreover, the years from 1789 to 1815 were, even for the privileged French economy, a time of "national catastrophe" – in the graphic words of a recent French scholar.[1] Thus, whatever the French Revolution and the Napoleonic era meant politically, economically and industrially they meant that France and the rest of Europe were much farther behind Britain in 1815 than in 1789.

This widening gap made it more difficult for other countries to follow the British example in energy and industry after 1815. British goods were being produced very economically, and they had come to dominate world markets completely while the continental states were absorbed in war between 1792 and 1815. In addition, British technology had become so advanced and complicated that very few engineers or skilled technicians outside England understood it. Moreover, the technology of steam power had grown much more expensive. It involved large investments in the iron and coal industries and, after 1830, required the existence of railroads, which were very costly. Continental businessmen had great difficulty finding the large sums of money the new methods demanded, and there was a shortage of laborers accustomed to

working in factories. Landowners and government officials were often so suspicious of the new form of industry and the changes it brought that they did little at first to encourage it. All these disadvantages slowed the spread of modern industry (see Map 27.3).

After 1815, however, when continental countries began to industrialize seriously, they had at least two important advantages. First, they did not need to develop, ever so slowly and expensively, their own advanced technology. Instead, they could simply "borrow" the new methods developed in Great Britain, as well as engineers and some of the financial resources they lacked. European countries like France and Russia had a second asset that many non-Western areas lacked in the nineteenth century. They had strong independent governments, which did not fall under foreign political control. These governments could fashion economic policies to serve their own interests, and they did. They could, eventually, use the power of the state to promote the growth of industry.

AGENTS OF INDUSTRIALIZATION

To understand better the spread of modern industry, let us look at the fascinating careers of a few of the businessmen, workers, and apostles of industrialization who were involved. For economic life is as much the product of particular human efforts as of vast impersonal forces.

The British realized the great value of their technical discoveries and tried to keep knowledge of them to themselves. Until 1825 it was illegal for artisans and skilled mechanics to leave Britain; until 1843 the export of textile machinery and other equipment was forbidden. Many talented, ambitious workers, however, slipped out of the country illegally and introduced the new methods abroad.

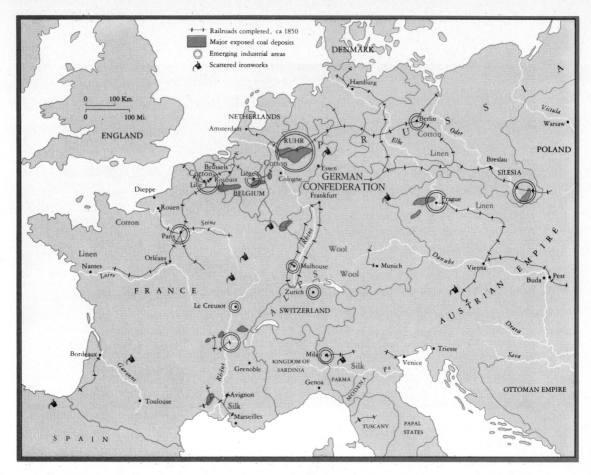

Map legend:
- Railroads completed, ca 1850
- Major exposed coal deposits
- Emerging industrial areas
- Scattered ironworks

MAP 27.3 CONTINENTAL INDUSTRIALIZATION, CA 1850 Although continental countries were beginning to make progress by 1850, they still lagged far behind England. For example, continental railroad building was still in an early stage, whereas the English rail system was essentially complete (see page 995).

One such man was William Cockerill, a Lancashire carpenter. He and his sons began building cotton-spinning equipment in French-occupied Belgium in 1799. In 1817, the most famous son, John Cockerill, purchased the old summer palace of the deposed bishops of Liège in southern Belgium. Cockerill converted the palace into a large industrial enterprise, which produced machinery, steam engines, and then railway locomotives. He also established modern ironworks and coal mines at Liège, as well as other operations throughout western Europe.

Cockerill's plant at Seraing became an industrial nerve center, continually gathering new information and transmitting it across Europe. Many skilled British workmen came, illegally, to work for Cockerill, and some went on to found their own companies throughout Europe. Newcomers brought the latest plans and secrets, so that Cockerill could boast that ten days after an industrial advance occurred in Britain he knew all about it in Belgium. Thus, British technicians and skilled workers were a powerful force in the spread of early industrialization.

Another instructive career is that of Fritz Harkort, a pioneer in the German machinery

COCKERILL'S WORKS *light up the night and display the awesome power of the new industrial technology in this lithograph of 1852. (The British Museum)*

industry. Harkort came from an old commercial family in Westphalia. He studied engineering developments in England while serving there as a Prussian army officer during the Napoleonic wars. Impressed and enchanted with what he saw, Harkort concluded that Germany had to match all these English achievements as quickly as possible. Setting up shop in an abandoned castle in the still-tranquil Ruhr Valley, Harkort felt an almost religious calling to build steam engines and become "the Watt of Germany."

Harkort's basic idea was simple, but it was enormously difficult to carry out. Steam engines had been greatly improved in the course of thirty years, and the new models Harkort was trying to copy required much accuracy and know-how. Lacking skilled laborers to do the job, Harkort turned to England for experienced, though expensive, mechanics. He could not be choosy. As he later reminisced, "I had to cut several of my English workers down from the gallows, so to speak, if only in order to get some of them."[2] He longed for the day he could replace the haughty foreigners with his own countrymen.

Getting materials posed a great problem as well. German ironsmiths could not supply the thick iron boilers Harkort needed, and he had to import them from England at great cost and with frequent damage. There was a modest market for Harkort's engines, for the German coal industry was beginning to expand. But German roads were so bad – Harkort denounced them as death traps for man and beast – that steam engines had to be built at the works, completely dismantled and shipped piece by piece to the buyer, and then reassembled by Harkort's technicians. No wonder Harkort was a very early promoter of railroads, which, he predicted in 1829, "will bring countless revolutions to the world."

In spite of all these problems, Harkort built engines, sold them throughout Germany and the rest of Europe, and won fame and praise. His ambitious efforts also resulted in large financial losses for himself and his partners. These proved fatal, for Harkort's enterprise, like almost all the others of the day, was a private, capitalistic undertaking. It could not lose money indefinitely. In 1832, after sixteen years of activity and accomplishment, Harkort was forced out of his company by his financial backers, who cut back operations to reduce losses. In one sense, then, his career was a failure; yet Harkort was a pioneering visionary, the most creative German businessman of his era. His career illustrates both the great efforts of a few key business leaders to copy the British achievement and the extreme difficulty of the task.

Support from the government often helped businessmen in continental countries overcome some of their difficulties. Tariff protection was one such support. For example, after Napoleon's wars ended in 1815, France was suddenly flooded with cheaper and better English goods. The French government responded by laying high tariffs on many English imports, in order to protect the French economy. After 1815, continental governments bore the cost of building roads and canals to improve transportation, and they also bore much of the cost of building railroads.

The career of the German journalist and thinker Friedrich List (1789-1846) reflects government's greater role in the Industrial Revolution on the Continent than in England. List considered the growth of modern industry of the utmost importance because manufacturing was a primary means of increasing people's well-being and relieving their poverty. Moreover, List was a dedicated nationalist. He wrote that "the wider the gap between the backward and advanced nations becomes, the more dangerous it is to remain behind," for an agricultural nation was not only poor but weak, increasingly unable to defend itself and maintain its political independence. To promote industry was to defend the nation.

The practical policy List focused on in articles and in his *National System of Political Economy* (1841) was the tariff. He supported the formation of a customs union, or Zollverein, among the separate German states. Such a tariff union came into being in 1834. It allowed goods to move between the German member states without tariffs, and a single uniform tariff was erected against all other nations. List wanted a high protective tariff, which would encourage "infant industries," allowing them to develop and eventually to hold their own against their more advanced British counterparts. List denounced the English doctrine of free trade as little more than England's attempt "to make the rest of the world, like the Hindus, its serfs in all industrial and commercial relations." By the 1840s, List's ideas were increasingly popular in Germany and elsewhere.

Banks, like governments, also played a larger and more creative role on the Continent than in England. Previously, almost all banks in Europe had been private, organized as secretive partnerships. Such banks were content to deal with a few rich clients and a few big merchants. They avoided industry. In the 1830s, two Belgian banks pioneered in a new direction. The General Society of Belgium and the Bank of Belgium were big corporations with many stockholders, large and small. Thus their financial resources were large. The banks were able to use that money to develop industrial companies. They became in short, industrial banks.

Similar banks became important in France and Germany in the 1850s. They established and developed many railroads and many companies working in heavy industry. The most famous such bank was the Crédit Mobilier of Paris, founded by Isaac and Emile Pereire, two young Jewish journalists from Bordeaux. The Crédit Mobilier advertised extensively. It used the savings of thousands of small investors, as well as the resources of big ones. The activities of the bank were far-reaching; it built railroads all over France and Europe. As Emile Pereire had said in 1835, "It is not enough to outline gigantic programs on paper. I must write my ideas on the earth."

Industrial banks like the Crédit Mobilier mobilized the savings of thousands of small investors and invested those savings in industry and transportation, particularly in the 1850s. In doing so, the directors of these banks helped their countries find the capital needed for industrialization. They also often made themselves very wealthy.

CAPITAL AND LABOR

Industrial development brought new social relations and problems between capital and labor. A new group of factory owners and big industrial capitalists arose. These men strengthened the wealth and size of the middle class, which had previously been made up mainly of merchants and professional people. The nineteenth century became the golden age of the middle class. Modern industry also created a much larger group – the factory workers. For the first time large numbers of men and women came together under one roof to work with complicated machinery for big capitalists and big companies. What was the nature of relations between these two new groups – between capital and labor? Did the new industrial middle class ruthlessly exploit the workers, as Karl Marx and others have charged?

THE NEW CLASS OF FACTORY OWNERS

Early industrialists operated in a highly competitive economic system. As the careers of Watt and Harkort illustrate, there were countless problems of production, and success and large profits were by no means certain. Manufacturers, therefore, waged a constant battle to cut their costs of production and stay afloat. Most profit had to go back into the business for new and better machinery. "Dragged on by the frenzy of this terrible life," according to one of his dismayed critics, the struggling manufacturer had "no time for niceties. He must conquer or die, make a fortune or drown himself."[3]

The early industrialists came from a variety of backgrounds. Many, like Harkort, were from well-established merchant families, which provided capital and contacts. Others, like Watt and Cockerill, were of very modest means, especially in the early days. Artisans and skilled workmen of exceptional ability had unparalleled opportunities. The ethnic and religious groups that had been discrimin-

LARGE-SCALE INDUSTRY This fascinating drawing shows the main composing room of the central railroad printing shop in Paris in the 1870s. Most appropriately, the millions of tickets, timetables, and notices are being printed in a building of iron and glass, while France's cultural heroes look down approvingly. (Photo: Caroline Buckler)

ated against in the traditional occupations controlled by the landed aristocracy jumped at the new chances. Quakers and Scots were tremendously important in England; Protestants and Jews dominated banking in Catholic France. Many of the industrialists were newly rich, and they were very proud and self-satisfied.

As factories grew larger, opportunities declined, at least in well-developed industries. It became considerably harder for a gifted but poor young mechanic to end up as a wealthy manufacturer. Formal education became more important as a means of advancement, and formal education at the advanced level was expensive. In England by 1830 and in France and Germany by 1860, leading industrialists were more likely to have inherited their well-established enterprises, and they were financially much more secure than their fathers and grandfathers. They were also aware of a greater gap between themselves and their workers.

THE NEW FACTORY WORKERS

The social consequences of the Industrial Revolution have long been hotly debated. Since any honest observer will see that some conditions got better and others got worse, vigorous debate is likely to continue. (Also, industry promoted rapid urbanization with its own great problems, as we shall see in Chapter 30.) Nevertheless, for workers and ordinary families, the Industrial Revolution brought a great transformation, which was, on balance, desirable. It marked a great step forward from the pattern of preindustrial life for the poor and the oppressed.

The condition of English workers in the Industrial Revolution has always generated the most controversy among historians, because England was the first country to industrialize and because the social consequences seem harshest there. Before 1850, other countries had not proceeded very far with industrialization, and almost everyone agrees that the economic conditions of European workers improved after 1850. The countries that followed England were able to benefit from English experience in social as well as technical matters. Thus, the early English Industrial Revolution provides the strongest case for the harmful social consequences of modern industrial development, at least prior to 1914, and it is fitting to focus on it.

From the beginning the Industrial Revolution in England had its critics. Among the first were the romantic poets. William Blake (1757–1827) called the early factories "satanic mills" and protested against the hard life of the London poor. William Wordsworth (1770–1850) lamented the destruction of the rural way of life and the pollution of the land and water. Doctors and reformers wrote eloquently of problems in the factories and new towns. Some handicraft workers, notably the Luddites who attacked whole factories in northern England in 1812 and after, smashed the new machines, which they believed were putting them out of work.

Another early critic was Friedrich Engels (1820–1895), the future revolutionary and colleague of Karl Marx. After studying conditions in northern England, this young middle-class German published *The Condition of the Working Class in England* in 1844. Engels

cast the problem of industrial life in class terms. "At the bar of world opinion," he wrote, "I charge the English middle classes with mass murder, wholesale robbery, and all the other crimes in the calendar."[4] Engels's charge of middle-class exploitation and increasing worker poverty was embellished by Marx and later socialists. It was extremely influential.

Meanwhile other observers believed that conditions were improving for the working class. Andrew Ure wrote in 1835 in his study of the cotton industry that conditions in most factories were not harsh and were even quite good. Edwin Chadwick, a great and conscientious government official well acquainted with the problems of the working class, concluded that "the whole mass of the laboring community" was increasingly able "to buy more of the necessities and minor luxuries of life."[5] Other observers were equally optimistic.

If all the contemporary indictments of observers like Engels and all the defenses of those like Ure were counted up, those who thought conditions were getting worse for working people would probably be the majority. Yet it is clear that opinions differed greatly. In an attempt to go deeper into the problem, historians must look at different kinds of sources.

Statistical evidence is one such source. It should help resolve the conflicting opinions of contemporary and often biased observers. If working people suffered a great decline, as Engels and later socialists asserted, then they must have bought less and less food, clothing, and other necessities as time went on. The purchasing power of the working person's wages must have declined drastically.

At the end of the nineteenth century, dispassionate British statisticians tried to pull together all the evidence on wages and prices and thereby measure what working-class peo-

ple could or could not have bought. Such an approach was only partially successful. England was not in a prestatistical age during its Industrial Revolution, but there were many gaps and shortcomings in the available numbers. Nevertheless, this approach does offer important insights.

During the period from about 1750 to 1790, when cottage industry was still dominant, the purchasing power of the average British laborer's wages seems to have risen somewhat. The workers – primarily cottage workers, artisans, and farm hands – could buy more goods, like food and clothing, over the years. Wages in industry were substantially higher than in agriculture, and all kinds of

wages rose faster in the industrializing areas of the north than in the purely agricultural counties of the south. The cautious conclusion must be that from 1750 to 1790 the growth of industry made for a more abundant life for working people, in terms of material goods.

The years from 1792 to 1815, a period of constant war against revolutionary and Napoleonic France, brought very different circumstances. Wages rose, but they did not keep up with inflation. Food prices rose most, as the price of wheat approximately doubled from 1790 to 1810. The condition of the working poor declined.

Between 1815 and 1850, the purchasing

power of workers' wages increased again. Money wages remained steady or fell somewhat, but prices fell more. The fullest studies show that the real wages of the average worker – agricultural and industrial – increased 25 percent between 1800 and 1825 and another 40 percent between 1825 and 1850.[6] The trend was definitely upward but the course was erratic. Between 1820 and 1840, real wages increased by only 5 to 10 percent. However, the wages of unskilled workers in British industry were again, as before 1790, about twice as high as those of unskilled workers in British agriculture. In short, throughout the Industrial Revolution, with the exception of the wartime period, there was apparently substantial economic improvement for British workers.

This important conclusion must be qualified, though. Increased purchasing power meant more goods, but it did not necessarily mean greater happiness. People do not live by bread alone. Also, these figures do not say anything about how the level of unemployment may have risen, for the simple reason that there are no good unemployment statistics from this period. Furthermore, the hours in the average workweek increased; to an unknown extent, workers earned more simply because they worked more. Finally, the wartime decline was of great importance. The war years were formative years for the new factory labor force. They were also some of the hardest. They colored the early experience of modern industrial life in somber tones.

Another way to consider the workers' standard of living is to look at the goods they purchased. Again, the evidence is somewhat contradictory. Speaking generally, workers ate somewhat more and better as the Industrial Revolution progressed, except in wartime. Diets became more varied; people ate more potatoes and dairy products and more fruits and vegetables.

Clothing improved, but housing for working people did not. In short, per capita use of specific goods supports the position that the standard of living of the working classes rose, at least moderately, during the Industrial Revolution. The rich did get richer. So did the poor to some extent, especially if they worked in industry.

CONDITIONS OF WORK

What about working conditions? Did workers earn more only at the cost of working longer and harder? Were workers exploited harshly by the new factory owners?

The first factories were cotton mills, which began functioning along rivers and streams in the 1770s. Cottage workers, accustomed to the putting-out system, were reluctant to work in factories even when they received relatively good wages, because factory work was different from what they were used to and unappealing. In the factory, workers had to keep up with the machine and follow its tempo. They had to show up every day and work long, monotonous hours. Factory workers had to adjust their daily lives to the shrill call of the factory whistle.

Cottage workers were not used to that kind of life and discipline. All members of the family worked hard and long but in spurts, setting their own pace. They could interrupt their work when they wanted to. Women and children could break up their long hours of spinning with other tasks. On Saturday afternoon the head of the family delivered the week's work to the merchant-manufacturer and got paid. Saturday night was a time of relaxation and drinking, especially for the

COTTON MILL NEAR MANCHESTER *The simple rural scene in the foreground of this 1834 engraving contrasts vividly with the massive brick factory building dominating the landscape. (Photo: Caroline Buckler)*

men. Recovering from his hangover on Tuesday, the weaver bent to his task on Wednesday and then worked like crazy to meet his deadline on Saturday. Like some students today, he might "pull an all-nighter" on Thursday or Friday, in order to get his work in.

Also, early factories resembled English poorhouses, where totally destitute people went to live on welfare. Some poorhouses were industrial prisons, where the inmates had to work in order to receive their food and lodging. The similarity between large brick factories and large stone poor-houses increased the cottage workers' fear of factories and their hatred of factory discipline.

It was cottage workers' reluctance to work in factories that prompted the early cotton-mill owners to turn to abandoned and pauper children for their labor. As we have seen, they contracted with local officials to employ large numbers of these children, who had no say in the matter. Pauper children were often badly treated and terribly overworked in the mills, as they were when they were apprenticed as chimney sweeps, market girls, shoemakers, and so forth. In the eighteenth century, semi-forced child labor seemed necessary and was socially accepted. From our modern point of view, it was cruel exploitation and a blot on the record of the new industrial system.

GIRL DRAGGING COAL TUBS *Published by reformers in Parliament in 1842, this picture shocked public opinion and contributed to the Mines Act of 1842. Such work for children was not new, but with rapid industrialization it touched more people. (The British Museum)*

By 1790, the early pattern was rapidly changing. The use of pauper apprentices was in decline, and in 1802 it was forbidden by Parliament. Many more factories were being built, mainly in urban areas, where they could use steam rather than water power and attract a work force more easily than in the countryside. The need for workers was great. And, indeed, people came from near and far to work in the cities, both as factory workers and as laborers, builders, and domestic servants. Yet as they took these new jobs, working people did not simply give in to a system of labor that had formerly repelled them. Rather, they helped modify the system by carrying over old, familiar working traditions.

For one thing, they came to the mills and the mines as family units. This was how they had worked on farms and in the putting-out system. The mill or mine owner bargained with the head of the family and paid him or her for the work of the whole family. In the cotton mills children worked for their mothers or fathers, collecting wastes and "piecing" broken threads together. In the mines children sorted coal and worked the ventilation equipment. Their mothers hauled coal in the narrow tunnels below the surface, while their fathers hewed with pick and shovel at the face of the seam.

The preservation of the family as an economic unit in the factories from the 1790s on made the new surroundings more tolerable, both in Great Britain and in other countries during the early stages of industrialization. Parents disciplined their children, making firm measures socially acceptable, and directed their upbringing. The presence of the whole family meant that children and adults worked the same long hours (twelve-hour shifts were normal in cotton mills in 1800). In the early years, some very young children were em-

ployed solely to keep the family together. Je-
dediah Strutt, for example, believed children
should be at least ten years old to work in his
mills, but he reluctantly employed seven-year-
olds to satisfy their parents. Adult workers
were not particularly interested in limiting the
minimum working age or hours of their children, as long as they worked side by side.
Only when technical changes threatened to
place control and discipline in the hands of
impersonal managers and foremen did they
protest against inhuman conditions in the
name of their children.

But some enlightened employers and social
reformers in Parliament definitely felt otherwise. "In an age of rising standards of hu-
manitarianism the few were determined to
impose higher standards on the many; and
were able to exploit developing means of mass
communication to do it."[7] These reformers
had important successes.

Their first major accomplishment was the
Factory Act of 1833. It limited the work day
for children between nine and thirteen to
eight hours and that of adolescents between
fourteen and eighteen to twelve hours. The
law also prohibited the employment of children under nine; they were to be enrolled in
the elementary schools factory owners were
required to establish. Since efficiency required
standardized shifts for all workers, the Factory
Act shattered the pattern of whole families
working together in the factory. The employment of children declined rapidly. Similarly,
the Mines Act of 1842 prohibited women and
boys under ten from working underground.

Ties of blood and kinship remained important in other ways in England in the formative
years between about 1790 and 1840. Many
manufacturers and builders hired workers not
directly but through subcontractors. They
paid the subcontractors on the basis of what
the subcontractors and their crews pro-

duced – for smelting so many tons of pig
iron or moving so much dirt or gravel for a
canal or roadbed. Subcontractors in turn hired
and fired their own workers, many of whom
were friends and relations. The subcontractor
might be as harsh as the greediest capitalist,
but the relationship between subcontractor
and work crew was close and personal. This
kind of traditional relationship was more acceptable to workers than impersonal factory
discipline. This system also provided people
an easy way to find a job. Even today, a friend
or cousin who is a foreman is often worth a
hundred formal application forms.

Ties of kinship were particularly important
for newcomers, who often travelled considerable distances to find work. Many urban
workers in Great Britain were from Ireland.
Forced out of rural Ireland by population
growth and deteriorating economic conditions from 1817 on, Irish in search of jobs
could not be choosy; they took what they
could get. As early as 1824 most of the workers in the Glasgow cotton mills were Irish; in
1851 one-sixth of the population of the great
port of Liverpool was Irish. Even when Irish
workers were not related directly by blood,
they were held together by ethnic and religious ties. Like other immigrant groups elsewhere, they worked together, formed their
own neighborhoods, and not only survived
but thrived.

A MATURE WORKING CLASS

By about 1850, the working people of urban
Britain had, like British industry, gone a long
way toward attaining maturity. Family employment in the factory had given way to the
employment of adults, for whom the discipline of the clock and the regularity of the
machine were familiar taskmasters. Gone were
violent demonstrations against industrializa-

tion. In their place were increasing acceptance of the emerging industrial system and an ongoing effort to make that system serve workers better.

In Great Britain, and in other countries later on, workers slowly created a labor movement to serve their needs. In 1799, partly in panicked reaction to the French Revolution, Parliament had passed the Combination Acts outlawing unions and strikes. These acts were widely disregarded by workers. Societies of skilled factory workers organized unions, as printers, papermakers, carpenters, and other such craftsmen had long since done. The unions sought to control the number of skilled workers, limit apprenticeship to members' own children, and bargain with owners over wages. They were not afraid to strike; there was, for example, a general strike of adult cotton spinners in Manchester in 1810. In the face of widespread union activity, Parliament repealed the Combination Acts in 1824, and unions were tolerated though not fully accepted after 1825.

The next stage in the development of the British trade-union movement was the attempt to create a single large national union. This effort was led not so much by working people as by social reformers like Robert Owen (1771–1858). Owen, a self-made cotton manufacturer, had pioneered in industrial relations by combining firm discipline with concern for the health, safety, and hours of his workers. After 1815, he experimented with cooperative and socialist communities, including one at New Harmony, Indiana. Then, in 1834, Owen organized one of the largest and most visionary of the early national unions, the Grand National Consolidated Trades Union. When this and other grandiose schemes collapsed, the British labor movement moved once again after 1851 in the direction of bread-and-butter craft unions. The

most famous of these "new model" unions was the Amalgamated Society of Engineers. These craft unions won real benefits for their members by fairly conservative means and thus helped make unions an accepted part of the industrial scene.

The maturity of British workers was also expressed in direct political activity in defense of their own interests. After the collapse of Owen's national trade union, a great deal of the energy of working people went into the Chartist movement, whose goal was political democracy. The key Chartist demand – that all men be given the right to vote – became the great hope of millions of aroused people. Workers were also active in campaigns to limit the workday in the factories to ten hours and to permit duty-free importation of wheat into Great Britain to secure cheap bread. Thus working people played an active role in shaping the new industrial system. Clearly, they were neither helpless victims nor passive beneficiaries.

THE ALTERNATIVE TO INDUSTRIALIZATION

What was the alternative to the Industrial Revolution and the new urban society? What would have been the likely course of events – the likely alternative for Europe – if industrialization had not occurred? It is impossible to know exactly, yet a look at general developments and at the case of Ireland, which did not industrialize, may shed some light on this question.

THE GROWTH OF POPULATION

The drama of industrialization must be viewed alongside the drama of rapid population growth. As we have seen, Europe's population began growing after 1720 (pages 832–835), leading to severe pressures on available resources and overpopulation in many areas. Large numbers of people had serious difficulty growing or buying the food they needed. There was widespread underemployment, acute poverty, and constant migration in search of work.

All these forces operated during and after the era of the French Revolution. Europe had roughly 140 million people in 1750, 188 million in 1800, and 266 million in 1850 – an increase of almost 40 percent in each half-century. Overpopulation worsened between 1800 and 1850 on much of the Continent, most noticeably in Flanders, parts of Scandinavia, and southwestern Germany. One result was migration from the countryside to nearby cities and towns, where unskilled laborers were already irregularly employed and poorly paid. Another result was that growing numbers of peasants liquidated their small and inadequate landholdings and went abroad. Thus in the early nineteenth century, particularly in the hungry 1840s, many German and Swedish settlers tried their luck and skill on prairie lands of the American Midwest.

The pressure of increasing numbers and rural poverty was most severe in Ireland. Although Ireland supplied many workers for factories in Britain, Ireland itself did not industrialize in the nineteenth century. Therefore, although Ireland was a particularly oppressed and exploited nation, its fate could have been that of much of Europe if not for the Industrial Revolution.

THE POTATO FAMINE IN IRELAND

Late-eighteenth-century Ireland was a conquered country. The great mass of the population (outside the northern counties of Ulster which were partly Presbyterian) were Irish Catholic peasants, who rented their land from a tiny minority of Church of England Protestants, many of whom lived in England (page 870). These Protestant landlords lacked the improving zeal of their English counterparts. They knew they were perched on top of a volcano that erupted periodically, but they were quite content to use their powers to grab as much as possible, as quickly as possible.

The result was that the condition of the Irish peasantry around 1800 was abominable. The typical peasant family lived in a wretched cottage made of mud and could afford neither shoes nor stockings. Hundreds of shocking accounts describe hopeless poverty. Sir Walter Scott wrote:

The poverty of the Irish peasantry is on the extreme verge of human misery; their cottages would scarce serve for pig styes even in Scotland; and their rags seem the very refuse of a sheep, and are spread over their bodies with such an ingenious variety of wretchedness that you would think nothing but some sort of perverted taste could have assembled so many shreds together.

For a French traveler, Ireland was "pure misery, naked and hungry.... I saw the American Indian in his forests and the black slave in his chains, and I believed that I was seeing in their pitiful condition the most extreme form of human misery; but that was before I knew the lot of poor Ireland."[8] Yet in spite of these terrible conditions, population growth sped onward. The 3 million of 1725 reached 4 million in 1780, and doubled to 8 million in 1840. Between 1780 and 1840, 1.75 million men and women left Ireland for Britain and America.

The population of Ireland grew so quickly for three reasons: extensive cultivation of the potato, early marriage, and hideous exploitation of peasants by landlords. The potato, first

IRISH EMIGRANTS   The potato famine forced hundreds of thousands of desperate Irish peasants, like these waiting to sail from Cork in 1850, to leave their native land. (Bettmann Archive)

introduced into Ireland in the late sixteenth century, was the principal food of the Irish peasantry by the last years of the eighteenth century. The reason for dependence on the potato was originally the pressure of numbers, which forced the peasants to wring as many calories as they could out of a given piece of land. But once peasants began to live almost exclusively on potatoes, many more people could exist. A single acre of land spaded and planted with potatoes could feed a family of six for a year, whereas it would take at least two and probably four acres of grain and pasture to feed the same number. Moreover, the potato was not choosy and could thrive on boggy wastelands.

Needing only a potato patch of an acre or two for survival, Irish boys and girls married much earlier than did their counterparts in rural England and France by the end of the eighteenth century. Setting up housekeeping was easy, for a cabin of mud and stone could be slapped together in a few days with the willing assistance of the young couple's neighbors and relatives. A mat for a bed, a chair or two, a table, and an iron pot to boil potatoes were easily acquired. To be sure, the young couple was accepting the life of extreme poverty that travelers and people of good conscience lamented. They would literally live on potatoes – ten pounds a day every day all year long for the average male – moistened with a cup of milk if they were lucky.

Nonetheless, the decision to marry early and have large families was quite reasonable, given Irish conditions. The landlords, not the peasants, owned and controlled the land. Because land was leased only for short periods on uncertain terms, peasants had no incentive to make permanent improvements. Any increase in profits went to the landlord, and anything beyond what preserved the peasants from absolute starvation was extorted from them. Poverty thus being inescapable in rural Ireland, it was better shared with a wife or husband. Children were a precious asset, as in many poor countries today, for there was no welfare or social security system, and an infirm or aged person's best hope of escaping starvation was a dutiful son or a loving daughter.

As the population continued to grow, conditions became increasingly precarious. The peasantry depended on a single crop, the size of which varied substantially from year to year. Potato failures cannot be detected in time to plant other crops, nor can potatoes be stored for more than a year. Furthermore, a potato economy is a subsistence economy. It lacks a well-developed network of roads and trade capable of distributing other foods in time of disaster. From 1820 onward, deficiencies in the potato crop became increasingly serious. Disease in the potato crop was becoming more common, and the accompanying fever epidemics that struck the population were growing more frequent. Some great catastrophe in the near future was almost completely inevitable.

In 1845 and 1846, and again in 1848 and 1851, the potato crop failed in Ireland and throughout much of Europe. The general result was high food prices, widespread suffering, and social unrest. In Ireland, which was farthest down the road to rural overpopulation and dependence on a disease-prone plant, the result was unmitigated disaster – the Great Famine. Blight attacked the young plants, the leaves withered, and the tubes rotted. Widespread starvation and mass fever epidemics followed. Cannibalism occurred, although starving people generally lived on the carcasses of diseased cattle, dogs, and horses, and on herbs of the field. In some places dead people were found with grass in their mouths.

Total losses were staggering. The population of Ireland was roughly 8 million in 1845, and without the famine it would have reached 9 million in 1851. But that year Ireland's population was only 6.5 million. Fully a million emigrants fled the famine between 1845 and 1851 (2 million left between 1840 and 1855), going primarily to the United States and Great Britain. Thus at least 1.5 million people died or went unborn because of the disaster. The British government's efforts at famine relief were too little and too late. Moreover, the government continued to collect its taxes and the landlords continued to demand their rents. Tenants who could not pay were evicted and their homes broken up or burned. Famine or no, Ireland was still the conquered jewel of foreign landowners.

The Great Famine shattered and reversed the pattern of Irish population growth. Alone among the nations of Europe, Ireland's numbers declined in the nineteenth century, to 4.4 million in 1911. Ireland remained a land of continuous out-migration. It also became a land of late marriage and widespread celibacy, as the landowning classes discouraged potato farming and converted much of the country into pasture for cattle and sheep. After great population decline and untold suffering, Ireland found a new demographic equilibrium within the framework of a poor pastoral economy.

———◆———

The fate of Ireland has real relevance for an understanding of the Industrial Revolution. The rapid population growth without industrialization that occurred in Ireland between 1780 and 1845 occurred elsewhere too – in central Russia, in western Germany, and in southern Italy, to name only three crucial regions. In these areas there were indications of acute poverty and overpopulation, and the potato played a crucial role as it had done in Ireland. In Prussia, for example, annual potato production grew from 1 to 11 million tons from 1815 to 1860. By 1850 in some parts of Europe bread was a luxury; workers and peasants were subsisting almost entirely on potatoes. In 1500 the average German had eaten about 200 pounds of meat a year; in 1850 his counterpart ate about 40 pounds.[9] The standard of living was declining. Other Irelands were in the making.

Population growth threatened to produce a morass of rural poverty, a demographic catastrophe, or both. In this connection, the historian T. S. Ashton once argued that the Industrial Revolution was the salvation rather than the curse of England and of the parts of Europe fortunate enough to follow England's lead. He may have overstated the case, but Ashton was surely closer to the truth than those who persist in arguing the contrary. The alternative to the revolution in energy and industry would probably have been, sooner or later, disaster.

NOTES

1. M. Lévy-Leboyer, *Les banques européennes et l'industrialisation dans la première moitié du XIXe siècle,* Presses Universitaires de France, Paris, 1964, p. 29.

2. Quoted by D. S. Landes, *The Unbound Prometheus: Technological Change and Industrial Development in Western Europe from 1750 to the Present,* Cambridge University Press, Cambridge, 1969, p. 150.

3. J. Michelet, *The People,* University of Illinois Press, Urbana, 1973 (originally published, 1846), p. 64.

4. F. Engels, *The Condition of the Working Class in England,* trans. and ed. W. O. Henderson and W. H. Chaloner, Stanford University Press, Stanford, 1968, p. xxiii.

5. Quoted in W. A. Hayek, ed., *Capitalism and the Historians,* University of Chicago Press, Chicago, 1954, p. 126.

6. P. Deane and W. A. Cole, *British Economic Growth, 1688–1959,* Cambridge University Press, Cambridge, 1964, p. 25.

7. P. Mathias, *The First Industrial Nation: An Economic History of Britain, 1700–1914,* Charles Scribner's Sons, New York, 1969, p. 205.

8. Quoted by G. O'Brien, *The Economic History of Ireland from the Union to the Famine,* Longmans, Green, London, 1921, pp. 21–24.

9. W. L. Langer, *Political and Social Upheaval, 1832–1852,* Harper & Row, New York, 1969, p. 188.

SUGGESTED READING

There is a vast and exciting literature on the Industrial Revolution. D. Landes's *The Unbound Prometheus* (1969), cited in the Notes, and S. Pollard, *Peaceful Conquest: The Industrialization of Europe* (1981), are the best general treatments of European industrial growth since 1750. P. Mathias, *The First Industrial Nation: An Economic History of Britain, 1700–1914* (1969); P. Deane, *The First Industrial Revolution* (1966); and P. Mantoux, *The Industrial Revolution in the Eighteenth Century* (1961), admirably discuss the various aspects of the English breakthrough and offer good bibliographies. (See also the Suggested Reading for Chapter 23.) W. Rostow, *The Stages of Economic Growth: A Non-Communist Manifesto* (1960), is a popular, provocative study. R. Cameron brilliantly traces the spread of railroads and industry across Europe in *France and the Economic Development of Europe, 1800–1914* (1961). The recent works of A. S. Milward and S. B. Saul, *The Economic Development of Continental Europe, 1780–1870* (1973), and *The Development of the Economies of Continental Europe, 1850–1914* (1977), may be compared with J. Clapham's old-fashioned classic, *Economic Development of France and Germany* (1963). C. Kindleberger, *Economic Growth in France and Britain, 1851–1950* (1964), is a stimulating study, especially for those with some background in economics. Other important works in recent years on industrial developments are C. Tilly and E. Shorter, *Strikes in France, 1830–1848* (1974); D. Ringrose, *Transportation and Economic Stagnation in Spain, 1750–1850* (1970); L. Schofer, *The Formation of a Modern Labor Force* (1975), which focuses on the Silesian part of Germany; and W. Blackwell, *The Industrialization of Russia,* 2nd ed. (1982).

The debate between "optimists" and "pessimists" about the consequences of industrialization in England goes on. P. Taylor, ed., *The Industrial Revolution: Triumph or Disaster?* (1970), is a useful introduction to different viewpoints, while W. A. Hayek, ed., *Capitalism and the Historians* (1954), is a good collection of essays stressing positive aspects. It is also fascinating to compare Friedrich Engels's classic condemnation, *The Condition of the Working Class in England,* with Andrew Ure's optimistic defense, *The Philosophy of Manufactures,* first published in 1835 and reprinted recently. E. P. Thompson continues and enriches the Engels tradition in *The Making of the English Working Class* (1963), an exciting book rich in detail and early working-class lore. An unorthodox but moving account of a doomed group is D. Bythell, *The Handloom Weavers* (1969). F. Klingender, *Art and the Industrial Revolution,* rev. ed. (1968), is justly famous, and M. Ignatieff, *A Just Measure of Pain* (1980), is an engrossing study of prisons during English industrialization.

Among general studies, many of which are cited in the Suggested Reading for Chapter 23, G. S. R. Kitson Clark, *The Making of Victorian England* (1967), is particularly imaginative. A. Briggs, *Victorian People* (1955), provides an engrossing series of brief biographies. H. Ausubel discusses a major reformer in his work, *John Bright* (1966), and B. Harrison skillfully illuminates the problem of heavy drinking in *Drink and the Victorians* (1971). On poverty and politics in Ireland, K. H. Connell, *The Population of Ireland, 1750–1850* (1950), and S. Cronin, *Irish Nationalism: A History of Its Roots and Ideology* (1981), are excellent points of departure. The most famous contemporary novel dealing with the new industrial society is Charles Dickens's *Hard Times,* an entertaining but exaggerated story. *Mary Barton* and *North and South* by Elizabeth Gaskill are more realistic portrayals and both are highly recommended, as is Emile Zola's *Germinal,* a grim, powerful story of love and hate during a violent strike by French coal miners.

CHAPTER 28

IDEOLOGIES AND UPHEAVALS,

1815–1850

THE MOMENTOUS ECONOMIC and political transformation of modern times began in the late eighteenth century with the Industrial Revolution in England and then the French Revolution. Until about 1815, these revolutions were separate, involving different countries and activities and proceeding at very different paces. The Industrial Revolution created the factory system and new groups of capitalists and industrial workers in northern England, but almost continuous warfare with France checked its spread to continental Europe. Meanwhile, England's ruling aristocracy suppressed all forms of political radicalism at home and joined with crowned heads abroad to oppose and eventually defeat revolutionary and Napoleonic France. The economic and political revolutions worked at cross-purposes and even neutralized each other.

After peace returned in 1815, the situation changed. Economic and political changes tended to fuse, reinforcing each other and bringing about what the historian Eric Hobsbawm has incisively called "the dual revolution." For instance, the growth of the industrial middle class encouraged the drive for representative government, while the demands of the French sans-culottes in 1793–1794 inspired many socialist thinkers. Gathering strength and threatening almost every aspect of the existing political and social framework, the dual revolution rushed on to alter completely first Europe and then the world. Much of world history in the last two centuries can be seen as the progressive unfolding of the dual revolution.

Yet three qualifications must be kept firmly in mind. In Europe in the nineteenth century, as in Asia and Africa in more recent times, the dual revolution was not some inexorable mechanical monster grinding peoples and cultures into a homogenized mass. The economic and political transformation it wrought was built on complicated histories, strong traditions, and highly diverse cultures. Radical change was eventually a constant, but the particular results varied enormously.

Nor should the strength of the old forces be underestimated. In Europe especially, the traditional elites – the monarchs, noble landowners, and bureaucrats – long proved capable of defending their privileges and even of rerouting the dual revolution to serve their interests.

Finally, the dual revolution posed a tremendous intellectual challenge. The meanings of the economic, political, and social changes that were occurring, as well as the ways they could be shaped by human action, were anything but clear. These questions fascinated observers and stimulated new ideas and ideologies.

How then did the political revolution, derailed by class antagonisms in France and resisted by European monarchs, break out again in the era of early industrialization? And what ideas did thinkers develop to describe and shape the transformation going on before their eyes?

THE PEACE SETTLEMENT

The eventual triumph of revolutionary economic and political forces was by no means certain in 1814. Quite the contrary. The conservative, aristocratic monarchies with their preindustrial armies and economies (Great Britain excepted) appeared firmly in the driver's seat once again. France had been decisively defeated by the off-again, on-again alliance of Russia, Prussia, Austria, and Great Britain. That alliance had been strengthened and reaffirmed in March 1814, when the allies pledged not only to defeat France but to hold it in line for twenty years thereafter. This goal was the basis of the Quadruple Alliance. Allied armies had then entered Paris, and Napoleon had abdicated his throne.

Most people felt an intense and profound longing for peace. The great challenge for statesmen in 1814 was to construct a peace settlement that would last and not sow the seeds of another war. Their efforts were largely successful and contributed to a century unmarred by destructive, generalized war (see Map 28.1).

GOALS AND PRINCIPLES

The allied powers were concerned first and foremost with the defeated enemy, France. Uncertain and somewhat divided about the future government of France, they agreed to the restoration of the Bourbon dynasty, in part because demonstrations led by a few dedicated French monarchists indicated some support among the French people for that course of action. This support was temporarily consolidated when the new monarch, Louis XVIII (1814-1824), issued the Constitutional Charter which accepted many of France's revolutionary changes and established a fairly liberal regime. The allies signed the first Peace of Paris with the restored Bourbon monarchy on May 30, 1814.

The allies were quite lenient toward France. France was given the boundaries it possessed in 1792, which were larger than those of 1789. France lost only the territories it had conquered in Italy, Germany, and the Low Countries, in addition to a few colonial possessions. Although there was some sentiment for levying a fine on France to pay for the war, the allies did not press the matter when Louis XVIII stated firmly that his government would not pay any reparations. France was even allowed to keep the art treasures Napoleon's agents had looted from the museums of Europe. Thus, the victorious powers did not punish harshly, and they did not foment a spirit of injustice and revenge in the defeated country.

At the same time a number of barriers were raised against renewed French aggression. The Low Countries – Belgium and Holland – were united under an enlarged Dutch monarchy capable of opposing France more effectively. Moreover, Prussia received considerably more territory on France's eastern border, so as to stand as the "sentinel on the Rhine" against France. In these ways the Quadruple Alliance combined leniency toward France with strong defensive measures. They held out a carrot with one hand and picked up a bigger stick with the other.

THE BALANCE OF POWER

In their moderation toward France the allies were motivated by self-interest and traditional ideas about the balance of power. To Metternich and Castlereagh, the foreign ministers of Austria and Great Britain, as well as their French counterpart Talleyrand, the balance of power meant an international equilibrium of political and military forces, which would preserve the freedom and independence of each of the Great Powers. Such a balance would discourage aggression by any combination of states or, worse, the domination of Europe by any single state. As they saw it, the task of the powers was thus twofold. They had to make sure that France would not dominate Europe again, and they also had to arrange international relations so that none of the victors would be tempted to strive for domination in its turn. Such a balance involved many considerations and all of Europe. The Great Powers, assisted in a minor way by

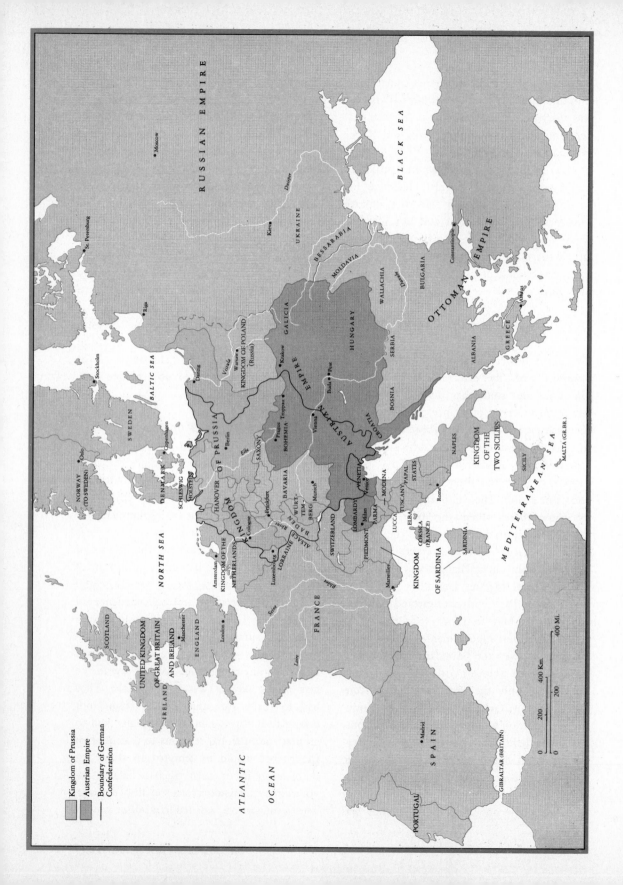

RUSSIAN EMPIRE

BLACK SEA

OTTOMAN EMPIRE

• Moscow

• St. Petersburg

• Riga

Dnieper

• Kiev

UKRAINE

BESSARABIA

MOLDAVIA

WALLACHIA

Danube

BULGARIA

• Constantinople

SWEDEN

BALTIC SEA

• Stockholm

Danzig

KINGDOM OF POLAND
(Russia)

Vistula

• Warsaw

GALICIA

• Kraków

• Buda • Pest

HUNGARY

SERBIA

BOSNIA

CROATIA

ALBANIA

GREECE

• Athens

NORWAY
(TO SWEDEN)

• Oslo

DENMARK

• Copenhagen

SCHLESWIG

(HOLSTEIN)

HANOVER

KINGDOM OF PRUSSIA

• Berlin

SAXONY

Elbe

BOHEMIA

• Prague • Troppau

AUSTRIAN EMPIRE

• Vienna

VENETIA

• Venice

MODENA

PARMA

TUSCANY

PAPAL
STATES

LUCCA

• Rome

NAPLES

KINGDOM
OF THE
TWO SICILIES

SICILY

MALTA (GR. BR.)

MEDITERRANEAN SEA

UNITED KINGDOM
OF GREAT BRITAIN
AND IRELAND

SCOTLAND

IRELAND

ENGLAND

• Manchester

• London

NORTH SEA

KINGDOM OF THE
NETHERLANDS

• Amsterdam

• Luxembourg

BADEN

WÜRT-
TEM-
BERG

BAVARIA

• Munich

BERG

• Cologne

• Frankfurt

Rhine

ALSACE

LORRAINE

SWITZERLAND

LOMBARDY

• Milan

PIEDMONT

• Marseilles

KINGDOM
OF SARDINIA

ELBA

CORSICA
(FRANCE)

SARDINIA

FRANCE

Rhone

Seine

Loire

ATLANTIC

OCEAN

SPAIN

• Madrid

PORTUGAL

GIBRALTAR (BRITAIN)

Kingdom of Prussia

Austrian Empire

Boundary of German
Confederation

400 Km.

400 Mi.

200

200

0

0

the smaller European states, began a series of negotiations in Vienna in October 1814 to resolve these challenges.

The balance of power was the mechanism used by the Great Powers – Austria, Britain, Prussia, Russia, and France – to settle their own disputes, which became quite dangerous. There was general agreement among the victors that each of them should receive compensation in the form of territory for their successful struggle against the French. Great Britain had already won colonies and strategic outposts during the long wars, and these it retained. Metternich's Austria gave up territories in Belgium and southern Germany but expanded greatly elsewhere, taking the rich provinces of Venetia and Lombardy in northern Italy as well as its former Polish possessions and new lands on the eastern coast of the Adriatic (see Map 28.1). There was also agreement that Prussia and Russia should be compensated. But where, and to what extent? That was the ticklish question that almost led to renewed war in January 1815.

The vaguely progressive, impetuous Alexander I of Russia had already taken Finland and Bessarabia on his northern and southern borders. Yet he burned with ambition to restore the ancient kingdom of Poland, on which he expected to bestow the benefits of his autocratic rule. The Prussians were willing to go along and give up their Polish territories, provided they could swallow up the large and wealthy kingdom of Saxony, their German neighbor to the south.

These demands were too much for Castlereagh and Metternich, who feared an unbalancing of forces in central Europe. In an as-

tonishing about-face, they turned for diplomatic support to the wily Talleyrand and the defeated France he represented. On January 3, 1815, Great Britain, Austria, and France signed a secret alliance directed against Russia and Prussia. As Castlereagh concluded somberly, it appeared that "the peace we have so dearly purchased will be of short duration."[1]

The outcome, however, was compromise rather than war. When rumors of the alliance were intentionally leaked, the threat of war caused the rulers of Russia and Prussia to moderate their demands. They accepted Metternich's proposal: Russia established a small Polish kingdom, and Prussia received two-fifths rather than all of Saxony (see Map 28.1). This compromise was very much within the framework of balance-of-power ideology and eighteenth-century diplomacy: Great Powers became greater, but not too much greater. In addition, France had been able to intervene and tip the scales in favor of the side seeking to prevent undue expansion of Russia and Prussia. In so doing France regained its Great Power status and was no longer isolated, as Talleyrand gleefully reported to Louis XVIII.

As the final touches were being put on the peace settlement, Napoleon suddenly reappeared on the scene. After his unconditional abdication, the victorious allies had granted Napoleon the island of Elba off the coast of Italy as his own tiny state. Napoleon was allowed to keep his imperial title, and France was required to pay him a large yearly income of 2 million francs. But Napoleon was Napoleon, and he soon tired of his "comic kingdom." Hearing of diplomatic tensions in Vienna and political unrest in France, he escaped from Elba in February 1815. Landing in France, Napoleon issued appeals for support and marched on Paris with a small band. French officers and soldiers who had fought

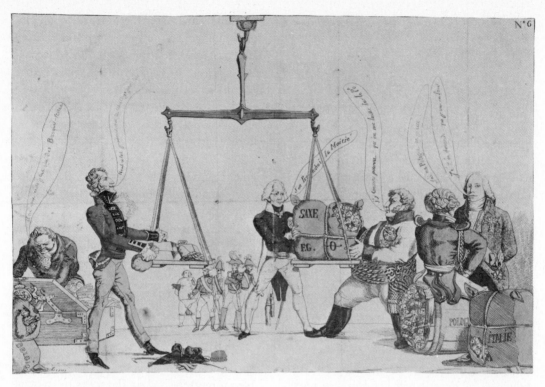

ADJUSTING THE BALANCE   The Englishman on the left uses his money to counterbalance the people that the Prussian and the fat Metternich are gaining in Saxony and Italy. Alexander I sits happily on his prize, Poland. The cartoon captures the essence of balance-of-power diplomacy in 1814. (Bibliothèque Nationale, Paris)

so long with Napoleon joined with him. Louis XVIII fled, and once more Napoleon took command. But his wild gamble was doomed, for the allies were united against him. At the end of a frantic hundred days they crushed his forces at Waterloo and imprisoned him on the rocky island of St. Helena, far off the western coast of Africa.

Once again, Napoleon had done much harm and little good. Even so, the resulting peace – the second Peace of Paris – was still relatively moderate toward France. Fat old Louis XVIII was restored to his throne. France lost some territory, had to pay an indemnity of 700 million francs, and had to support a large army of occupation for five years. The rest of the settlement already concluded at Vienna was left intact. The allies did, however, agree to meet periodically to discuss their "common interests" and to consider appropriate measures for the "maintenance of peace in Europe." This agreement marked the beginning of the European "congress system," which lasted long into the nineteenth century and settled international crises by means of diplomatic conferences.

INTERVENTION AND REPRESSION

There was also a domestic political side to the re-establishment of peace. Within their own countries the leaders of the victorious states were much less flexible. In 1815, under Metternich's leadership, Austria, Prussia, and Russia embarked on a crusade against the ideas and politics of the dual revolution. The crusade lasted until 1848.

The first step was the Holy Alliance, formed by Austria, Prussia, and Russia in September 1815. First proposed by Russia's Alexander I, the alliance proclaimed the intention of the three eastern monarchs to rule exclusively on the basis of Christian principles and to work together to maintain peace and justice on all occasions. Castlereagh refused to sign, characterizing the vague statement of principle as "a piece of sublime mysticism and nonsense." Yet it soon became a practical instrument for the repression of liberal and revolutionary movements all over Europe.

In 1820, revolutionaries succeeded in forcing the monarchs of Spain and the southern Italian kingdom of the Two Sicilies to grant liberal constitutions against their wills. Metternich was horrified: revolution was rising once again. Calling a conference at Troppau in Austria, he and Alexander I proclaimed the principle of active intervention to maintain all autocratic regimes, whenever they were threatened. Austrian forces then marched into Naples and restored Ferdinand I to the throne of the Two Sicilies. The French armies of Louis XVIII likewise restored the Spanish regime – after the Congress of Troppau had rejected Alexander's offer to send his Cossacks riding across Europe to teach the Spanish an unforgettable lesson.

Great Britain remained aloof, arguing that intervention in the domestic politics of foreign states was not an object of British diplomacy. In particular, Great Britain opposed any attempts by the restored Spanish monarchy to reconquer its former Latin American possessions, which had gained their independence during and after the Napoleonic wars. Encouraged by the British position, the young United States proclaimed its celebrated Monroe Doctrine in 1823. This bold document declared that European powers were to keep their hands off the New World and in no way attempt to re-establish their political system there. In the United States constitutional liberalism, an ongoing challenge to the conservatism of continental Europe, retained its cutting edge.

In the years following the crushing of liberal revolution in southern Italy in 1821 and in Spain in 1823, Metternich continued to battle against liberal political change. Sometimes he could do little, as in the case of the new Latin American republics. Nor could he undo the dynastic changes of 1830 in western Europe. Yet until 1848 his system was quite effective in central Europe, where his power was greatest.

Metternich's policies dominated not only Austria and the Italian peninsula but the entire German Confederation, which the peace settlement of Vienna had called into being. The confederation was composed of thirty-eight independent German states, including Prussia and Austria. (The Hungarian half of the Austrian Empire was not a member.) These states met in complicated assemblies dominated by Austria, with Prussia a willing junior partner in the planning and execution of repressive measures.

It was through the German Confederation that Metternich had the infamous Carlsbad Decrees issued in 1819. The decrees required the thirty-eight German member states to root out subversive ideas in their universities and newspapers. They also established a permanent committee with spies and informers to investigate and punish any liberal or radical organizations. Metternich's ruthless imposition of repressive internal policies on the governments of central Europe contrasted with the intelligent moderation he had displayed in the general peace settlement in 1815.

METTERNICH AND CONSERVATISM

Metternich's determined defense of the status quo made him a villain in the eyes of most progressive, optimistic historians of the nineteenth century. Yet rather than denounce the man, it is more useful to try to understand him and the general conservatism he represented.

Born into the middle ranks of the landed nobility of the Rhineland, Prince Klemens von Metternich (1773–1859) was an internationally oriented aristocrat. In 1795 his splendid marriage to Eleonora von Kaunitz, granddaughter of Austria's famous statesman and heiress to vast estates, opened the door to the highest court circles and a brilliant diplomatic career. Austrian ambassador to Napoleon's court in 1806 and Austrian foreign minister from 1809 to 1848, the cosmopolitan Metternich always remained loyal to his class and jealously defended its rights and privileges to the day he died. Like most other conservatives of his time, he did so with a clear conscience. The nobility was one of Europe's most ancient institutions, and conservatives regarded tradition as the basic source of human institutions. In their view, the proper state and society remained that of pre-1789 Europe, which rested on a judicious blend of monarchy, bureaucracy, and aristocracy.

Metternich's commitment to conservatism was coupled with a passionate hatred of liberalism. He firmly believed that liberalism, as embodied in revolutionary America and France, had been responsible for a generation of war with untold bloodshed and suffering. Liberal demands for representative government and civil liberties had unfortunately captured the imaginations of some middle-class lawyers, businessmen, and intellectuals. Metternich thought that these groups had been and still were engaged in a vast conspiracy to impose their beliefs on society and destroy the existing order. Like many conservatives then and since, Metternich blamed liberal revolutionaries for stirring up the lower classes, whom he believed to be indifferent or hostile to liberal ideals, desiring nothing more than peace and quiet.

The threat of liberalism appeared doubly dangerous to Metternich because it generally went with national aspirations. Liberals, especially liberals in central Europe, believed that each people, each national group, had a right to establish its own independent government and seek to fulfill its own destiny. The idea of national self-determination was repellent to Metternich. It not only threatened the existence of the aristocracy, it also threatened to destroy the Austrian Empire and revolutionize central Europe.

The vast Austrian Empire of the Habsburgs was a great dynastic state. Formed over centuries by war, marriage, and luck, it was made up of many peoples speaking many languages (see Map 28.2). The Germans, long the dominant element, had supported and profited by the long-term territorial expansion of Austria; yet they accounted for only a quarter of the population. The Magyars (Hungarians), a substantially smaller group, dominated the kingdom of Hungary – which was part of the Austrian Empire – though they did not account for a majority of the population even there.

The Czechs, the third major group, were concentrated in Bohemia and Moravia. There were also large numbers of Italians, Poles, and Ukrainians, as well as smaller groups of Slovenes, Croats, Serbs, Ruthenians, and Rumanians. The various Slavic peoples represented a widely scattered and completely divided ma-

METTERNICH *This portrait by Sir Thomas Lawrence reveals much of Metternich the man. Handsome, refined, and intelligent, Metternich was a great aristocrat passionately devoted to the defense of his class and its interests. (Bettmann Archive)*

jority in an empire dominated by Germans and Hungarians. Different ethnic groups often lived in the same provinces and even the same villages. Thus, the different parts and provinces of the empire differed in languages, customs, and institutions. They were held to-

gether primarily by their ties to the Habsburg emperor.

The multinational state Metternich served was both strong and weak. It was strong because of its large population and vast territories; it was weak because of its many and

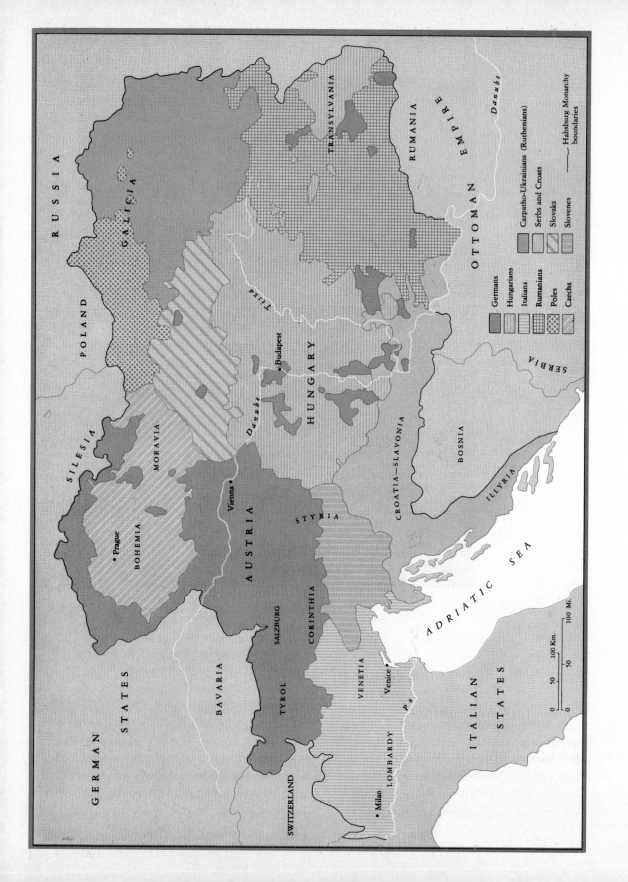

RUSSIA

POLAND

GALICIA

SILESIA

GERMAN

STATES

MORAVIA

BOHEMIA

• Prague

Vienna •

AUSTRIA

SALZBURG

BAVARIA

TYROL

CORINTHIA

STYRIA

SWITZERLAND

• Milan

LOMBARDY

VENETIA

Venice •

Po

HUNGARY

• Budapest

Tisza

Danube

TRANSYLVANIA

RUMANIA

OTTOMAN EMPIRE

Danube

SERBIA

CROATIA–SLAVONIA

BOSNIA

ILLYRIA

ADRIATIC SEA

ITALIAN

STATES

Germans

Hungarians

Italians

Rumanians

Poles

Czechs

Carpatho-Ukrainians (Ruthenians)

Serbs and Croats

Slovaks

Slovenes

Habsburg Monarchy boundaries

100 Km.

100 Mi.

50

50

0

0

MAP 28.2 *PEOPLES OF THE HABSBURG MON-*
ARCHY, 1815   The old dynastic state was a patch-
work of nationalities. Note the widely scattered pockets
of Germans and Hungarians.

potentially dissatisfied nationalities. In these circumstances Metternich virtually had to oppose liberalism and nationalism, for Austria was simply unable to accommodate those ideologies of the dual revolution. Other conservatives supported Austria because they could imagine no better fate for the jumble of small nationalities wedged precariously between masses of Germans and hordes of Russians in east central Europe. Castlereagh even went so far as to say that Austria was "the great hinge upon which the fate of Europe must ultimately depend." Metternich's repressive conservatism may not appeal to many people today, but it had understandable roots in the dilemma of a multinational state in an age of rising nationalism.

RADICAL IDEAS AND EARLY SOCIALISM

The years following the peace settlement of 1815 were years of profound intellectual activity. Intellectuals and social observers were seeking to understand the revolutionary changes that had occurred and were still taking place. These efforts led to ideas that still motivate the world.

Almost all of these basic ideas were radical. In one way or another they opposed the old deeply felt conservatism that Metternich exemplified so well. That revived conservatism, with its stress on tradition, a hereditary monarchy, a strong and privileged landowning aristocracy, and an official church, was rejected by radicals. Instead, radicals developed and re-

fined alternative visions – alternative ideologies – and tried to convince society to act on them. With time, they were very successful.

LIBERALISM

The ideas of liberalism – liberty and equality – were by no means defeated in 1815. First realized successfully in the American Revolution and then achieved in part in the French Revolution, this political and social philosophy continued to pose a radical challenge to revived conservatism. Liberalism demanded representative government as opposed to autocratic monarchy, equality before the law as opposed to legally separate classes. Liberty also continued to mean specific individual freedoms: freedom of the press, freedom of speech, freedom of assembly, and freedom from arbitrary arrest. In Europe, only France with Louis XVIII's Constitutional Charter and Great Britain with its Parliament and historic rights of English men and women had realized much but by no means all of the liberal program in 1815. Elsewhere, liberal demands were still a call for revolutionary change.

Yet although "classical" liberalism still had its cutting edge, it was not as sharp a tool as it had been. This was especially true of liberal economic principles, which called for unrestricted private enterprise and no government interference in the economy. This philosophy was popularly known as the doctrine of laissez-faire.

The idea of a free economy had first been persuasively formulated by a Scottish professor of philosophy, Adam Smith (1723–1790). Smith, whose *Inquiry into the Nature and Causes of the Wealth of Nations* (1776) founded modern economics, was highly critical of eighteenth-century mercantilism. Mercantilism, he said, meant stifling government regulations as well as unjust privileges for private monopolies and government favorites. Far preferable was free competition, which would give all citizens a fair and equal opportunity to do what they did best. Smith argued effectively that freely competitive private enterprise would result in greater income for everyone, not just the rich.

Unlike some of his contemporaries, Smith applauded the modest rise in real wages of British workers in the eighteenth century and went so far as to say, "No society can surely be flourishing and happy, of which the far greater part of the members are poor and miserable." Smith also believed that greater competition meant higher wages for workers, since manufacturers and "masters are always and everywhere in a sort of tacit, but constant and uniform, combination, not to raise the wages of laborers above their actual rate." In short, Adam Smith was a spokesman for general economic development, not narrow business interests.

In the early nineteenth century, the British economy was progressively liberalized, as old restrictions on trade and industry were relaxed or eliminated. This liberalization promoted continued rapid economic growth in the Industrial Revolution. At the same time, however, economic liberalism and laissez-faire economic thought were tending to become a doctrine serving business interests. Businessmen used the doctrine to defend their right to do exactly as they wished in their factories. Labor unions were outlawed because they supposedly restricted free competition and the individual's "right to work."

The teachings of a kindly parson, Thomas Malthus (1766–1834), helped make economic liberalism an ideology of business interests in many people's minds. In his *Essay on the Principle of Population* (1798) Malthus argued that population would always tend to grow faster than the supply of food. In Malthus's opinion, the only hope of warding off such "positive checks" to population growth as war, famine, and disease was "prudential restraint." That is, young men and women had to limit the growth of population by the old tried-and-true means of marrying late in life. But Malthus was not optimistic about this possibility. The powerful attraction of the sexes would cause most people to marry early and have many children.

The wealthy English stockbroker and economist David Ricardo (1772–1823) was even less optimistic. His depressing "iron law of wages" posited that, because of the pressure of population growth, wages would always sink to the subsistence level. That is, wages would be just high enough to keep the workers from starving. Malthus and Ricardo thought of themselves as objective social scientists. Yet their teachings were often used by industrial and middle-class interests in England, the Continent, and the United States to justify opposing any kind of government intervention to protect workers and improve the lot of common people: if workers were poor, it was their own fault, the result of their breeding like rabbits.

In the early nineteenth century, liberal political ideals also became more closely associated with narrow class interests. Early nineteenth-century liberals favored representative government, but they generally wanted property qualifications attached to the right to vote. In practice, this meant limiting the vote to well-to-do aristocratic landowners, substantial businessmen, and successful members of the professions. Workers and peasants as well as the lower middle class of shopkeepers, clerks, and artisans did not own the necessary property and thus could not vote.

As liberalism became increasingly middle-class after 1815, some intellectuals and foes of conservatism felt that it did not go nearly far enough. Inspired by memories of the French Revolution and the contemporary example of exuberant Jacksonian democracy in the young American republic, they called for universal voting rights, at least for males. Giving all men the vote, they believed, would allow the masses to participate in government and would lead to democracy.

Many people who believed in democracy also believed in the republican form of government. They detested the power of the monarchy, the privileges of the aristocracy, and the great wealth of the upper middle class. These democrats and republicans were more radical than the liberals. Taking for granted much of the liberal program, they sought to go beyond it. Democrats and republicans were also more willing than most liberals to endorse violent upheaval to achieve goals. All of which meant that liberals and radical, democratic republicans could join forces against conservatives only up to a point.

NATIONALISM

Between 1815 and 1850, most people who believed in either liberalism or radical, democratic republicanism also believed in nationalism. Conversely, many early nineteenth-century nationalists, like the Italian patriot Giuseppe Mazzini and the French historian Jules Michelet, were just as committed to liberty as they were to nationalism. Many governments, however, have been very nationalistic without favoring liberty and democracy. Why then was love of liberty almost synonymous with love of nation in the early nineteenth century?

GIUSEPPE MAZZINI *First imprisoned for revolutionary agitation in 1830 and spending much of his life in exile, Mazzini ceaselessly preached the doctrine of Italian rebirth in a free, democratic, and united Italy. (The Mansell Collection)*

A common faith in the creativity and nobility of the people was perhaps the single most important reason for people's linking these two concepts. Liberals and especially democrats saw the people as the ultimate source of all government. The people (or some of them) elected their officials and governed themselves within a framework of personal liberty. Yet such self-government would be possible only if the people were united by common traditions and common loyalties. In practice, common loyalties rested, first of all, on a common language. A shared language forged the basic unity of a people, a unity that transcended local or provincial interests and was not weakened by close contact with other ethnic groups.

Early nationalists usually believed that every nation, like every citizen, has the right to exist in freedom and to develop its character and spirit. They were confident that the independence and freedom of other nations, as in the case of other citizens within a nation, would not lessen the freedom of their own country. Rather, the symphony of nations would promote the harmony and ultimate unity of all peoples. As the historian Jules Michelet put it in *The People* in 1846, each citizen "learns to recognize his country . . . as a note in the grand concert; through it he himself participates and loves the world." Similarly, Mazzini believed that "in laboring according to the true principles of our country we are laboring for Humanity." Thus, the liberty of the individual and the love of a free nation overlapped greatly in the early nineteenth century.

Nationalism also had a negative side. Even as they talked of serving the cause of humanity, early nationalists stressed the differences between peoples. The German pastor and philosopher Johann Herder (1744–1803) had argued that every people has its own particular spirit and genius, which it expresses through its culture and language. Yet Herder (and others after him) could not define the uniqueness of the French, German, and Slavic peoples without comparing and contrasting one people with another. Thus, even early nationalism developed a strong sense of "we" and "they."

"They" were often the enemy. The leader of the Czech cultural revival, the passionate democrat and nationalist historian Francis Palacký, is a good example of this tendency. In his histories he lauded the achievements of the Czech people, which he characterized as a long struggle against brutal German domina-

tion. To this "we-they" outlook, it was all too easy for nationalists to add two other highly volatile ingredients: a sense of national mission and a sense of national superiority. As Mazzini characteristically wrote, "Peoples never stop before they have achieved the ultimate aim of their existence, before having fulfilled their mission." Even Michelet, so alive to the aspirations of other peoples, could not help speaking in 1846 of the "superiority of France"; the principles espoused in the French Revolution had made France the "salvation of mankind."

German and Spanish nationalists had a very different opinion of France. To them the French often seemed as oppressive as the Germans seemed to the Czechs, as hateful as the Russians seemed to the Poles. The despised enemy's mission might seem as oppressive as the American national mission – as the American journalist and strident nationalist John Louis O'Sullivan sketched it in 1845 after the annexation of Texas – seemed to the Mexicans. O'Sullivan wrote that taking land from an "imbecile and distracted Mexico" was a laudable step in the "fulfillment of our manifest destiny to overspread the continent allotted by Providence for the free development of our yearly multiplying millions."[2]

Early nationalism was thus ambiguous. Its main thrust was liberal and democratic. But below the surface lurked ideas of national superiority and national mission, which could lead to aggressive crusades and countercrusades, as had happened in the French Revolution and in the "wars of liberation" against Napoleon.

FRENCH UTOPIAN SOCIALISM

To understand the rise of socialism, one must begin with France. Despite the fact that France lagged far behind Great Britain in developing modern industry, almost all the early socialists were French. Although they differed on many specific points, these French thinkers were acutely aware that the political revolution in France and the rise of modern industry in England had begun a transformation of society. Yet they were disturbed by what they saw. Liberal practices in politics and economics appeared to be fomenting selfish individualism and splitting the community into isolated fragments. There was, they believed, an urgent need for a further reorganization of society to establish cooperation and a new sense of community. Starting from this shared outlook, individual French thinkers went in many different directions. They searched the past, analyzed existing conditions, and fashioned luxurious utopias. Yet certain ideas tied their critiques and visions together.

Early French socialists believed in economic planning. Inspired by the emergency measures of 1793 and 1794 in France, they argued that the government should rationally organize the economy and not depend on destructive competition to do the job. Early socialists also shared an intense desire to help the poor and to protect them from the rich. With passionate moral fervor they preached that the rich and the poor should be more nearly equal economically. Finally, socialists believed that private property should be abolished and replaced by state or community ownership. Planning, greater economic equality, and state ownership of property: these were the key ideas of early French socialism and of all socialism since.

One of the most influential of these thinkers was a nobleman, Count Henri de Saint-Simon (1760-1825). A curious combination of radical thinker and successful land speculator, Saint-Simon optimistically proclaimed the tremendous possibilities of industrial development: "The age of gold is before

us!" The key to progress was proper social organization. Such an arrangement of society required the "parasites" – the court, the aristocracy, lawyers, churchmen – to give way, once and for all, to the "doers" – the leading scientists, engineers, and industrialists. The doers would carefully plan the economy and guide it forward by undertaking vast public-works projects and investment banks. Saint-Simon also stressed in highly moralistic terms that every social institution ought to have as its main goal improved conditions for the poor. Saint-Simon's stress on industry and science inspired middle-class industrialists and bankers, like the Pereire brothers, founders of the Crédit Mobilier.

After 1830, the socialist critique of capitalism became sharper. Charles Fourier (1772-1837), a lonely, saintly man with a tenuous hold on reality, described a socialist utopia in lavish mathematical detail. Hating the urban wage system, Fourier envisaged self-sufficient communities of 1,620 people living communally on 5,000 acres devoted to a combination of agriculture and industry. Fourier was also an early proponent of the total emancipation of women, abolition of marriage, and complete sexual freedom. Although Fourier waited in vain each day at noon in his apartment for a wealthy philanthrophist to endow his visionary schemes, he was very influential. Several utopian communities were founded along the lines he prescribed, mainly in the United States.

Louis Blanc (1811-1882), a sharp-eyed, intelligent journalist, was much more practical. In his *Organization of Work* (1839) he urged workers to agitate for universal voting rights and to take control of the state peacefully. Blanc believed that the full power of the state should be directed at setting up government-backed workshops and factories to guarantee full employment. The "right to work" had to become as sacred as any other right. Finally, there was Pierre Joseph Proudhon (1809–1865), a self-educated printer, who wrote a pamphlet in 1840 entitled *What Is Property?* His answer was that it was nothing but theft. Property was profit that was stolen from the worker, who was the source of all wealth. Unlike most socialists, Proudhon feared the power of the state and thus was often considered an anarchist.

Thus, a variety of French thinkers blazed the way with utopian socialism in the 1830s and 1840s. Their ideas were very influential, particularly in Paris, where poverty-stricken workers with a revolutionary tradition were attentive students. Yet the economic arguments of the French utopians were weak, and their specific programs usually seemed too fanciful to be taken seriously. To Karl Marx was left the task of establishing firm foundations for modern socialism.

MARXIAN SOCIALISM

In 1848, the thirty-year-old Karl Marx and the twenty-eight-year-old Friedrich Engels published the *Communist Manifesto,* the Bible of socialism. The son of a Jewish lawyer who had converted to Christianity, the atheistic young Marx had studied philosophy at the University of Berlin before turning to journalism and economics. He read widely in French socialist thought and was developing his own socialist ideas by the time he was twenty-five.

Early French socialists often appealed to the middle class and the state to help the poor. Marx argued that the interests of the middle class and those of the industrial working class are inevitably opposed to each other. Indeed, according to the *Manifesto,* "the history of all previously existing society is the history of class struggles." In Marx's view, one class had

always exploited the other, and with the advent of modern industry, society was split more clearly than ever before: split between the middle class – the bourgeoisie – and the modern working class – the proletariat. Moreover, the bourgeoisie had reduced everything to a matter of money and "naked self-interest." "In a word, for exploitation, veiled by religious and political illusions, the bourgeoisie had substituted naked, shameless, direct brutal exploitation."

Just as the bourgeoisie had triumphed over the feudal aristocracy, Marx predicted, the proletariat was destined to conquer the bourgeoisie in a violent revolution. While a tiny minority owned the means of production and grew richer, the ever-poorer proletariat was constantly growing in size and in class consciousness. In this process the proletariat was aided, according to Marx, by a portion of the bourgeoisie who had gone over to the proletariat and who (like Marx and Engels) "had raised themselves to the level of comprehending theoretically the historical moment." And the critical moment was very near. "Let the ruling classes tremble at a Communist revolution. The proletarians have nothing to lose but their chains. They have a world to win. WORKING MEN OF ALL COUNTRIES, UNITE!" So ends the *Communist Manifesto.*

In brief outline, Marx's ideas may seem to differ only slightly from the wild and improbable ideas of the utopians of his day. Yet whatever one may think of the validity of Marx's analysis, he must be taken seriously. He united sociology, economics, and all human history in a vast and imposing edifice. He synthesized in his socialism not only French utopian schemes but English classical economics and German philosophy – the major intellectual currents of his day.

Marx's debt to England was great. He was

the last of the classical economists. Following David Ricardo, who had taught that labor was the source of all value, Marx went on to argue that profits were really wages stolen from the workers. Moreover, Marx incorporated Engels's charges of terrible oppression of the new class of factory workers in England; thus his doctrines seemed to be based on hard facts.

Marx's theory of historical evolution was built on the philosophy of the German Georg Hegel (1770–1831). Hegel believed that history is "ideas in motion": each age is characterized by a dominant set of ideas, which produces opposing ideas and eventually a new synthesis. The idea of being had been dominant initially, for example, and it had produced its antithesis, the idea of nonbeing. This idea in turn had resulted in the synthesis of becoming. History has, therefore, pattern and purpose.

Marx retained Hegel's view of history as a dialectic process of change, but made economic relationships between classes the driving force. This dialectic explained the decline of agrarian feudalism and the rise of industrial capitalism. And Marx stressed again and again that "the bourgeoisie, historically, has played a most revolutionary part. . . . During its rule of scarcely one hundred years the bourgeoisie has created more massive and more colossal productive forces than have all preceding generations together." Here was a convincing explanation for people trying to make sense of the dual revolution. Marx's next idea, that it was now the bourgeoisie's turn to give way to the socialism of revolutionary workers, appeared to many the irrefutable capstone of a brilliant interpretation of humanity's long development. Thus, Marx pulled together powerful ideas and insights to create one of the great secular religions out of the intellectual ferment of the early nineteenth century.

KARL MARX   In 1849 the exiled Marx settled in London. There he laboriously wrote Capital, *the weighty exposition of his socialist theories, and played a leading role in the successful organization of the First International of socialists in 1864. (The Mansell Collection)*

THE ROMANTIC MOVEMENT

Developing radical concepts of politics and society were accompanied by comparable changes in literature and other arts during the dual revolution. The early nineteenth century marked the acme of the romantic movement, which profoundly influenced the arts and enriched European culture immeasurably.

The romantic movement was in part a revolt against classicism and the Enlightenment. Classicism was essentially a set of artistic rules and standards that went hand in glove with the Enlightenment's belief in rationality, order, and restraint. The classicists believed that the ancient Greeks and Romans had discovered eternally valid esthetic rules long ago and that playwrights and painters should continue to follow them. Classicists could enforce these rules in the eighteenth century because they dominated the courts and academies for which artists worked.

Forerunners of the romantic movement appeared from about 1750 on. Of these, Rousseau (pages 807–808) – the passionate advocate of feeling, freedom, and natural goodness – was most influential. Romanticism then crystallized fully in the 1790s, primarily in England and Germany. The French Revolution kindled the belief that radical reconstruction was also possible in cultural and artistic life (even though many early English and German romantics became disillusioned with events in France and turned from liberalism to conservatism in politics). Romanticism gained strength until the 1840s, when realism began to challenge it seriously.

ROMANTICISM

Romanticism was characterized by a belief in emotional exuberance, unrestrained imagination, and spontaneity in both art and personal life. In Germany early romantics of the 1770s and 1780s called themselves the Storm and Stress *(Sturm und Drang)* group, and many romantic artists of the early nineteenth century lived lives of tremendous emotional intensity. Suicide, duels to the death, madness, and strange illnesses were not uncommon among leading romantics. Romantic artists typically led bohemian lives, wearing their

DELACROIX: LIBERTY LEADING THE PEOPLE *This great romantic painting idealistically glorifies the July Revolution in Paris in 1830. Raising the revolutionary tricolor on high, pure and beautiful Liberty unites the worker, the bourgeois, and the street child in a righteous crusade against privilege and oppression. (Louvre, Paris / Giraudon)*

hair long and uncombed in preference to powdered wigs, and living in cold garrets rather than frequenting stiff drawing rooms. They rejected materialism and sought to escape to lofty spiritual heights through their art. Great individualists, the romantics believed the full development of one's unique human potential to be the supreme purpose in life. The romantics were driven by a sense of an unlimited universe and by a yearning for the unattained, the unknown, the unknowable.

Nowhere was the break with classicism more apparent than in romanticism's general conception of nature. Classicism was not particularly interested in nature. In the words of the eighteenth-century English author Samuel Johnson, "A blade of grass is always a blade of grass; men and women are my subjects of inquiry." Nature was portrayed by classicists as beautiful and chaste, like an eighteenth-century formal garden. The romantics, on the other hand, were enchanted by nature. Sometimes they found it awesome and tempestuous, as in Théodore Géricault's painting *The Raft of the Medusa,* which shows the survivors of a shipwreck adrift in a turbulent sea. Others saw nature as a source of spiritual inspiration. As the great English landscape artist John Constable (1776–1837) declared, "Nature is Spirit visible."

Most romantics saw the growth of modern industry as an ugly, brutal attack on their beloved nature and on the human personality. They sought escape – in the unspoiled "Lake

District" of northern England, in exotic North Africa, in an idealized Middle Ages. Yet some romantics found a vast, awesome, terribly moving power in the new industrial landscape. In ironworks and cotton mills they saw the flames of Hell and the evil genius of Satan himself. One of John Martin's last and greatest paintings, *The Great Day of His Wrath* (1850), vividly depicts the last judgment foretold in Revelations VI, "when the sun became black as sackcloth of hair, and the moon became as blood; and the stars of heaven fell unto the earth. . . ." Martin's romantic masterpiece was inspired directly by a journey through the Black country of the industrial Midlands in the dead of night. According to Martin's son:

The glow of the furnaces, the red blaze of light, together with the liquid fire, seemed to him truly sublime and awful. He could not imagine anything more terrible even in the regions of everlasting punishment. All he had done or attempted in ideal painting fell far short, very far short, of the fearful sublimity.[3]

Fascinated by color and diversity, the romantic imagination turned toward the study and writing of history with a passion. For romantics, history was not a minor branch of philosophy from which philosophers picked suitable examples to illustrate their teachings. History was beautiful, exciting, and important in its own right. It was the art of change over time – the key to a universe that was now perceived to be organic and dynamic, no longer mechanical and static as it had appeared to the philosophes of the eighteenth-century Enlightenment.

Historical studies supported the development of national aspirations and encouraged entire peoples to seek in the past their special destinies. This trend was especially strong in Germany and eastern Europe. As the famous English historian Lord Acton put it, the growth of historical thinking associated with the romantic movement was a most fateful step in the story of European thought.

LITERATURE

Britain was the first country where romanticism flowered fully in poetry and prose, and the British romantic writers were among the most prominent in Europe. Wordsworth, Coleridge, and Scott were all active by 1800, to be followed shortly by Byron, Shelley, and Keats. All were poets: romanticism found its distinctive voice in poetry as the Enlightenment had in prose.

A towering leader of English romanticism, William Wordsworth (1770-1850) traveled in France after his graduation from Cambridge. There he fell passionately in love with a French woman named Annette Vallon, who bore him a daughter. He was deeply influenced by the philosophy of Rousseau and the spirit of the early French Revolution. Back in England, prevented by war and the Terror from returning to France, Wordsworth settled in the countryside with his sister Dorothy and Samuel Taylor Coleridge (1772-1834).

In 1798, the two poets published their *Lyrical Ballads,* one of the most influential literary works in the history of the English language. In defiance of classical rules, Wordsworth and Coleridge abandoned flowery poetic conventions for the language of ordinary speech, while simultaneously endowing simple subjects with the loftiest majesty. This twofold rejection of classical practice was at first ignored and then harshly criticized, but by 1830 Wordsworth had triumphed.

One of the best examples of Wordsworth's romantic credo and genius is "Daffodils":

I wandered lonely as a cloud
That floats on high o'er vales and hills,
When all at once I saw a crowd,
A host, of golden daffodils;
Beside the lake, beneath the trees,
Fluttering and dancing in the breeze.

Continuous as the stars that shine
And twinkle on the Milky Way,
They stretched in never-ending line
Along the margin of a bay:
Ten thousand saw I at a glance,
Tossing their heads in sprightly dance.

The waves beside them danced, but they
Out-did the sparkling waves in glee:
A poet could not but be gay,
In such a jocund company:
I gazed – and gazed – but little thought
What wealth the show to me had brought:

For oft, when on my couch I lie
In vacant or in pensive mood,
They flash upon that inward eye
Which is the bliss of solitude;
And then my heart with pleasure fills,
And dances with the daffodils.

Here indeed is simplicity and love of nature in commonplace forms. Here too is Wordsworth's romantic conviction that nature has the power to elevate and instruct, especially when interpreted by a high-minded poetic genius. Wordsworth's conception of poetry as "the spontaneous overflow of powerful feeling recollected in tranquillity" is well illustrated by the last stanza.

Born in Edinburgh, Walter Scott (1771–1832) personified the romantic movement's fascination with history. Raised on his grandfather's farm, Scott fell under the spell of the old ballads and tales of the Scottish border. He was also deeply influenced by German romanticism, and particularly by the immortal poet and dramatist Johann Wolfgang von Goethe (1749–1832). Scott translated Goethe's famous play about a sixteenth-century knight who revolted against centralized authority and championed individual freedom – at least in Goethe's romantic drama. A natural storyteller, Scott then composed long narrative poems and a series of historical novels. Scott excelled in faithfully recreating the spirit of bygone ages and great historical events, especially those of Scotland.

At first the strength of classicism in France inhibited the growth of romanticism there. Then, between 1820 and 1850, the romantic impulse broke through in the poetry and prose of Lamartine, Alfred de Vigny, Victor Hugo, Alexander Dumas, and George Sand. Of these, Victor Hugo (1802–1885) was the greatest in both poetry and prose.

Son of a Napoleonic general, Hugo achieved an amazing range of rhythm, language, and image in his lyric poetry. His powerful novels exemplified the romantic fascination with fantastic characters, strange settings, and human emotions. The hero of Hugo's famous *Hunchback of Notre Dame* (1831) is the great cathedral's deformed bellringer, a "human gargoyle" overlooking the teeming life of fifteenth-century Paris. A great admirer of Shakespeare, whom classical critics had derided as undisciplined and excessive, Hugo also championed romanticism in drama. His play *Hernani* (1830) consciously broke all the old rules, as Hugo renounced his early conservatism and equated freedom in literature with liberty in politics and society. Hugo's political evolution was thus exactly the opposite of Wordsworth's, in whom youthful radicalism gave way to middle-aged caution. As the contrast between the two artists suggests, romanticism was a cultural movement compatible with many political beliefs.

George Sand (1804–1876), a strong-willed and gifted woman, defied the narrow conventions of her time in an unending search for self-fulfillment. After eight years of unhappy marriage in the provinces, she abandoned her dullard of a husband and took her two children to Paris to pursue a career as a writer. There she soon achieved fame and wealth, eventually writing over eighty novels on a variety of romantic and social themes. All were shot through with a typically romantic love of nature and moral idealism. George Sand's striking originality and individualism went far beyond her flamboyant preference for men's clothing and taste for cigars and her notorious affairs with the poet Alfred Musset and the composer Frédéric Chopin, among others. Her semi-autobiographical novel *Lélia* was shockingly modern, delving deeply into her tortuous quest for sexual and personal freedom.

In central and eastern Europe literary romanticism and early nationalism often reinforced each other. Seeking a unique greatness in every people, well-educated romantics plumbed their own histories and cultures. Like modern anthropologists, they turned their attention to peasant life and transcribed the folk songs, tales, and proverbs that the cosmopolitan Enlightenment had disdained. The brothers Jacob and Wilhelm Grimm were particularly successful at rescuing German fairy tales from oblivion. In the Slavic lands, romantics played a decisive role in converting spoken peasant languages into modern written languages. The greatest of all Russian poets, Alexander Pushkin (1799–1837), rejecting eighteenth-century attempts to force Russian poetry into a classical strait-

jacket, used his lyric genius to mold the modern literary language.

ART AND MUSIC

The greatest and most moving romantic painter in France was Eugène Delacroix (1798–1863), probably the illegitimate son of the French foreign minister Talleyrand. Delacroix was a master of dramatic, colorful scenes that stir the emotions. He was fascinated with remote and exotic subjects, whether lion hunts in Morocco or the languishing, sensuous women of a sultan's harem. Yet he was also a passionate spokesman for freedom. His masterpiece, *Liberty Leading the People,* celebrated the nobility of popular revolution in general and revolution in France in particular.

In England the most outstanding romantic painters were J. M. W. Turner (1775–1851) and John Constable (1776–1837). Both were fascinated by nature but their interpretations of it contrasted sharply, aptly symbolizing the tremendous emotional range of the romantic movement. Turner depicted nature's power and terror; wild storms and sinking ships were favorite subjects. Constable painted gentle Wordsworthian landscapes in which human beings are at one with their environment, the comforting countryside of unspoiled rural England.

It was in music that romanticism realized most fully and permanently its goals of free expression and emotional intensity. Whereas the composers of the eighteenth century had remained true to well-defined structures, like the classical symphony, the great romantics used a great range of forms to paint a thousand landscapes and evoke a host of powerful emotions. Romantic composers also transformed the small classical orchestra, tripling its size by adding wind instruments, percus-

HEROES OF ROMANTICISM   Liszt plays for a gathering of friends. From left to right sit Alexander Dumas, George Sand (characteristically wearing men's clothing), and Marie d'Agoult, Liszt's mistress.

Standing from left to right are Victor Hugo, Paganini, and Rossini. A portrait of Byron and a bust of Beethoven look down. (Bildarchiv Preussischer Kulturbisitz)

sion, and more brass and strings. The crashing chords evoking the surge of the masses in Chopin's "Revolutionary" etude, the bottomless despair of the funeral march in Beethoven's Third Symphony, the solemn majesty of a great religious event in Schumann's Rhenish Symphony: such were the modern orchestra's musical paintings that plumbed the depth of human feeling.

This range and intensity gave music and musicians much greater prestige and importance than in the past. Music no longer simply complemented a church service or helped a nobleman digest his dinner. Music became a

sublime end in itself. It became for many the greatest of the arts, precisely because it achieved the most ecstatic effect and most perfectly realized the endless yearning of the soul. It was worthy of great concert halls and the most dedicated sacrifice. The unbelievable one-in-a-million performer – the great virtuoso who could transport the listener to ecstasy and hysteria – became a cultural hero. The composer Franz Liszt (1811–1886) vowed to do for the piano what Paganini had done for the violin, and he was lionized as the greatest pianist of his age. People swooned for Liszt as they scream for rock idols today.

Though romanticism dominated music until late in the nineteenth century, no composer ever surpassed its first great master, Ludwig van Beethoven (1770–1827). Extending and breaking open classical forms, Beethoven used contrasting themes and tones to produce dramatic conflict and inspiring resolutions. As the contemporary German novelist Ernst Hoffmann (1776–1822) wrote, "Beethoven's music sets in motion the lever of fear, of awe, of horror, of suffering, and awakens just that infinite longing which is the essence of Romanticism." Beethoven's range was tremendous; his output included symphonies, chamber music, sonatas for violin and piano, masses, an opera, and a great many songs.

At the peak of his fame, in constant demand as a composer and recognized as the leading concert pianist of his day, Beethoven began to lose his hearing. He considered suicide, but eventually overcame despair: "I will take fate by the throat; it will not bend me completely to its will."[4] Beethoven continued to pour out immortal music. Among other achievements, he fully exploited for the first time the richness and beauty of the piano. Beethoven never heard much of his later work, including the unforgettable choral finale to the Ninth Symphony, for his last years were silent, spent in total deafness.

REFORMS AND REVOLUTIONS

While the romantic movement was developing, liberal, national, and socialist forces battered against the conservatism of 1815. In some countries change occurred gradually and peacefully. Elsewhere pressure built up like steam in a pressure cooker without a safety valve, and eventually caused an explosion in 1848. Three important countries – Greece, Great Britain, and France – experienced variations on this basic theme.

NATIONAL LIBERATION IN GREECE

National, liberal revolution, frustrated in Italy and Spain by conservative statesmen, succeeded first after 1815 in Greece. Since the fifteenth century, the Greeks had been living under the domination of the Ottoman Turks. In spite of centuries of foreign rule the Greeks had survived as a people, united by their language and the Greek Orthodox religion. It was perfectly natural that the general growth of national aspirations and a desire for independence would inspire some Greeks in the early nineteenth century. This rising national movement led to the formation of secret societies and then to revolt in 1821, led by Alexander Ypsilanti, a Greek patriot and a general in the Russian army.

The Great Powers, and particularly Metternich, were opposed to all revolution, even revolution against the Islamic Turks. They refused to back Ypsilanti and supported the Ottoman Empire. Yet for many Europeans the Greek cause became a holy cause. Educated Americans and Europeans were in love with the culture of classical Greece; Russians were stirred by the piety of their Orthodox brethren. Writers and artists, moved by the romantic impulse, responded enthusiastically to the Greek struggle. The flamboyant, radical poet Lord Byron went to Greece and died there in the struggle "that Greece might still be free." Turkish atrocities toward the rebels fanned the fires of European outrage and Greek determination. One of Delacroix's romantic masterpieces memorialized the massa-

March 1814	Russia, Prussia, Austria, and Britain form the Quadruple Alliance to defeat France
April 1814	Napoleon abdicates
May–June 1814	Restoration of the Bourbon monarchy; Louis XVIII issues Constitutional Charter accepting civil liberties and representative government
1814	First Peace of Paris: allies combine leniency with defensive posture toward France
October 1814–June 1815	Congress of Vienna peace settlement: establishes balance-of-power principle and creates the German Confederation
February 1815	Napoleon escapes from Elba and marches on Paris
June 1815	Battle of Waterloo
September 1815	Austria, Prussia, and Russia form the Holy Alliance to repress liberal and revolutionary movements
November 1815	Second Peace of Paris and renewal of Quadruple Alliance: punishes France and establishes the European "congress system"
1819	Carlsbad Decrees: Metternich imposes repressive measures throughout the German Confederation
1820	Revolution in Spain and the Kingdom of the Two Sicilies
	Congress of Troppau: Metternich and Alexander I of Russia proclaim principle of intervention to maintain autocratic regimes
1821	Austria crushes liberal revolution in Naples and restores the Sicilian autocracy
	Greek revolt against the Ottoman Turks
1823	French armies restore the Spanish regime
	United States proclaims the Monroe Doctrine
1824	Reactionary Charles X succeeds Louis XVIII in France
1830	Charles X repudiates the Constitutional Charter; insurrection and government collapse; Louis Philippe succeeds to the throne and maintains a narrowly liberal regime to 1848
	Greece wins independence from the Ottoman Empire
1832	Reform Bill expands British electorate and encourages the middle class
1839	Louis Blanc, *Organization of Work*
1840	Pierre Joseph Proudhon, *What Is Property?*
1846	Jules Michelet, *The People*
1848	Karl Marx and Friedrich Engels, *The Communist Manifesto*

cre at Chios, where the Turks slaughtered nearly 100,000 Greeks.

The Greeks, though often quarreling among themselves, battled on against the Turks and hoped for the eventual support of European governments. In 1827 Great Britain, France, and Russia responded to popular demands at home and directed Turkey to accept an armistice. When the Turks refused, the navies of these three powers trapped the Turkish fleet at Navarino and destroyed it. Russia then declared another of its periodic wars of expansion against the Turks. This led to the establishment of a Russian protectorate over much of present-day Rumania, which had also been under Turkish rule. Great Britain, France, and Russia finally declared Greece independent in 1830 and installed a German prince as king of the new country in 1832. In the end the Greeks had won: a small nation had gained its independence in a heroic war against a foreign empire.

LIBERAL REFORM IN GREAT BRITAIN

Eighteenth-century British society had been both flexible and remarkably stable. It was dominated by the landowning aristocracy, but that class was neither closed nor rigidly defined. Successful business and professional people could buy land and become gentlemen, while the common people had more than the usual opportunities of the preindustrial world. Basic civil rights for all were balanced by a tradition of deference to one's social superiors. Parliament was manipulated by the king and was thoroughly undemocratic. Only about 6 percent of the population could vote for representatives to Parliament, and by the 1780s there was growing interest in some kind of political reform.

But the French Revolution threw the aristocracy into a panic for a generation, making it extremely hostile to any attempts to change the status quo. The Tory party, completely controlled by the landed aristocracy, was particularly fearful of radical movements at home and abroad. Castlereagh initially worked closely with Metternich to restrain France and restore a conservative balance in central Europe. This same intense conservatism motivated the Tory government at home. After 1815 the aristocracy defended its ruling position by repressing every kind of popular protest.

The first step in this direction was the Corn Law of 1815. During a generation of war with France the British had been unable to import food. As shortages occurred and agricultural prices skyrocketed, a great deal of marginal land had been brought under cultivation. This development had been a bonanza for the landed aristocracy, whose fat rent rolls became even fatter. Peace meant that grain could be imported again and that the price of wheat and bread would go down. To almost everyone except the aristocracy, lower prices seemed highly desirable. The aristocracy, however, rammed the Corn Law through Parliament. This law prohibited the importation of foreign grain unless the price at home rose above eighty shillings per quarter-ton – a level reached only in time of harvest disaster before 1790. Seldom has a class legislated more selfishly for its own narrow economic advantage.

The Corn Law, coming at a time of widespread unemployment and postwar adjustment, led to protests and demonstrations by urban laborers. They were supported by radical intellectuals, who campaigned for a reformed House of Commons that would serve the nation and not just the aristocracy. In 1817, the Tory government responded by temporarily suspending the traditional rights of peaceable assembly and habeas corpus. Two years later Parliament passed the infamous Six Acts, which among other things controlled a heavily taxed press and practically eliminated all mass meetings. These acts followed an enormous but orderly protest at St. Peter's Fields in Manchester, which had been savagely broken up by armed cavalry. Nicknamed the battle of Peterloo, in scornful reference to the British victory at Waterloo, this incident expressed the government's determination to repress and stand fast.

Ongoing industrial development was not only creating urban and social problems but also strengthening the upper middle classes. The new manufacturing and commercial groups insisted on a place for their new wealth alongside the landed wealth of the aristocracy in the framework of political power and social prestige. They called for certain kinds of liberal reform: reform of town government, organization of a new police force, and more rights for Catholics and dissenters. In the 1820s, a less frightened Tory government led by Robert Peel moved in the direction of better urban administration, greater economic liberalism, and civil equality for Catholics. The prohibition on imports of foreign grain was replaced by a heavy tariff. These actions encouraged the middle classes to press on for reform of Parliament, so they could have a larger say in government and perhaps repeal the revised Corn Law – that symbol of aristocratic domination.

The Whig party, though led like the Tories by great aristocrats, had by tradition been more responsive to commercial and manufacturing interests. In 1830, a Whig ministry introduced "an act to amend the representation of the people of England and Wales." Defeated, then passed by the House of Commons, this reform bill was rejected by the House of Lords. But when in 1832 the Whigs got the king to promise to create enough new peers to pass the law, the House of Lords reluctantly gave in rather than see its snug little club ruined by upstart manufacturers and plutocrats. A mighty surge of popular protest had helped the king and lords make up their minds.

The Reform Bill of 1832 had profound significance. The House of Commons had emerged as the all-important legislative body. In the future an obstructionist House of Lords could always be brought into line by the threat of creating new peers. The new industrial areas of the country gained representation in the Commons, and many old "rotten boroughs" – electoral districts with very few voters that the landed aristocracy had bought and sold – were eliminated.

The redistribution of seats reflected the shift in population to the northern manufacturing counties and the gradual emergence of an urban society. As a result of the Reform Bill of 1832, the number of voters increased about 50 percent. Comfortable members of the urban population, as well as some substantial farmers who leased their land, received the vote. Thus the pressures building up in Great Britain were successfully – though only temporarily – released. A major reform had been achieved peacefully, without revolution or civil war. More radical reforms within the system appeared difficult but not impossible.

The principal radical program was embodied in the "People's Charter" of 1838 and the Chartist movement (page 1008). Partly inspired by the economic distress of the working class, the Chartists' core demand was universal male (not female) suffrage. They saw complete political democracy and rule by

THE BRITISH LION IN 1850;

OR, THE EFFECTS OF FREE TRADE.

FREE TRADE OPTIMISM *Appearing in* Punch *in 1846 as the Corn Law was being repealed, this cartoon looked to the future and reflected British self-confidence. Socially and economically advanced Great Britain had no need for protective tariffs. The British economy actually did boom after 1850. (The British Library)*

the common people as the means to a good and just society. Hundreds of thousands of people signed gigantic petitions calling on Parliament to grant all men the right to vote, first and most seriously in 1839, again in 1842, and yet again in 1848. Parliament rejected all three petitions. In the short run the working poor failed with their Chartist demands, but they learned a valuable lesson in mass politics.

While calling for universal suffrage, many working-class people joined with middle-class manufacturers in the Anti-Corn Law League, founded in Manchester in 1839. Mass participation made possible a popular crusade against the tariff on imported grain and against the landed aristocracy. People were fired up by dramatic popular orators such as John Bright and Richard Cobden. These fighting liberals argued that lower food prices and more jobs in industry depended on repeal of the Corn Law. Much of the working class agreed. The climax of the movement came in 1845, when Ireland's potato crop failed and famine seemed likely in England. In 1846, the Tory prime minister Robert Peel joined with the Whigs and a minority of his own party to repeal the Corn Law. Thereafter, free trade became almost sacred doctrine in Great Britain.

The following year the Tories passed a bill designed to help the working classes, but in a different way. This was the Ten Hours Act of 1847, which limited the workday for women and young people in factories to ten hours. Tory aristocrats continued to champion legislation regulating factory conditions. They were competing vigorously with the middle class for the support of the working class. This healthy competition between a still-vigorous aristocracy and a strong middle class was a crucial factor in Great Britain's peaceful

evolution. The working classes could make temporary alliances with either competitor to better their own conditions.

THE REVOLUTION OF 1830 IN FRANCE

Louis XVIII's Constitutional Charter of 1814 – theoretically a gift from the king but actually a response to political pressures – was basically a liberal constitution (page 1017). The economic gains of the middle class and the prosperous peasantry were fully protected; great intellectual and artistic freedom was permitted; and a real parliament with upper and lower houses was created. Immediately after Napoleon's abortive Hundred Days, the moderate, worldly-wise king refused to bow to the wishes of diehard aristocrats like his brother Charles, who wished to sweep away all the revolutionary changes and return to a bygone age of royal absolutism and aristocratic pretension. Instead, Louis appointed as his ministers moderate royalists, who sought and obtained the support of a majority of the representatives elected to the lower Chamber of Deputies between 1816 and Louis' death in 1824.

Louis XVIII's charter was anything but democratic. Only about 100,000 of the wealthiest people out of a total population of 30 million had the right to vote for the deputies, who, with the king and his ministers, made the laws of the nation. Nonetheless, the "notable people" who did vote came from very different backgrounds. There were wealthy businessmen, war profiteers, successful professionals, ex-revolutionaries, large landowners from the middle class, Bourbons, and Bonapartists.

The old aristocracy with its pre-1789 mentality was a minority within the voting population. It was this situation that Louis' successor, Charles X (1824–1830), could not abide. Crowned in a lavish, utterly medieval, five-hour ceremony in the cathedral of Reims in 1824, Charles was a true reactionary. He wanted to re-establish the old order in France. Increasingly blocked by the opposition of the deputies, Charles finally repudiated the Constitutional Charter in an attempted coup in July 1830. He issued decrees stripping much of the wealthy middle class of its voting rights, and he censored the press. The reaction was an immediate insurrection. In "three glorious days" the government collapsed. Paris boiled with revolutionary excitement, and Charles fled. Then the upper middle class, which had fomented the revolt, skillfully seated Charles's cousin, Louis Philippe, duke of Orléans, on the vacant throne.

Louis Philippe (1830–1848) accepted the Constitutional Charter of 1814, adopted the red, white, and blue flag of the French Revolution, and admitted that he was merely the "king of the French people." In spite of such symbolic actions, the situation in France remained fundamentally unchanged. As Casimir Périer, a wealthy banker and Louis Philippe's new chief minister, bluntly told a deputy who complained when the vote was extended only from 100,000 to 170,000 citizens: "The trouble with this country is that there are too many people like you who imagine that there has been a revolution in France."[5] The wealthy "notable" elite actually tightened its control as the old aristocracy retreated to the provinces to sulk harmlessly. For the upper middle class there had been a change in dynasty, in order to protect the status quo and the narrowly liberal institutions of 1815. Republicans, democrats, social reformers, and the poor of Paris were bitterly disappointed. They had made a revolution, but it seemed for naught.

THE REVOLUTIONS OF 1848

In 1848, revolutionary political and social ideologies combined with economic crisis and the romantic impulse to produce a vast upheaval. Only the most advanced and the most backward major countries – reforming Great Britain and immobile Russia – escaped untouched. Governments toppled; monarchs and ministers bowed or fled. National independence, liberal-democratic constitutions, and social reform: the lofty aspirations of a generation seemed at hand. Yet, in the end, the revolutions failed. Why was this so?

A DEMOCRATIC REPUBLIC IN FRANCE

The late 1840s in Europe were hard economically and tense politically. The potato famine in Ireland in 1845 had echoes on the Continent. Bad harvests jacked up food prices and caused misery and unemployment in the cities. "Prerevolutionary" outbreaks occurred all across Europe: an abortive Polish revolution in the northern part of Austria in 1846, a civil war between radicals and conservatives in Switzerland in 1847, and an armed uprising in Naples, Italy, in January 1848. Revolution was almost universally expected, but it took revolution in Paris – once again! – to turn expectations into realities.

From its beginning in 1830, Louis Philippe's "bourgeois monarchy" was characterized by stubborn inaction. There was a glaring lack of social legislation, and politics was dominated by corruption and selfish special interests. The king's chief minister in the 1840s, François Guizot, was complacency personified. Guizot was especially satisfied with the electoral system. Only the rich could vote for deputies, and many of the deputies were

DAUMIER: THE LEGISLATIVE BELLY   Protected by freedom of the press after 1830, French republicans and radicals bitterly attacked the do-nothing government of Louis Philippe. Here Daumier, the master of caricature, savagely ridicules the corruption of the Chamber of Deputies and the bloated bellies of its greedy members. (Charles Deering Collection. Courtesy of the Art Institute of Chicago)

docile government bureaucrats. It was the government's stubborn refusal to consider electoral reform that touched off popular revolt in Paris. Barricades went up on the night of February 22, 1848, and by February 24 Louis Philippe had abdicated in favor of his grandson. But the common people in arms would tolerate no more monarchy. This refusal led to the proclamation of a provisional republic, headed by a ten-man executive committee and certified by cries of approval from the revolutionary crowd.

In the flush of victory, there was much about which Paris revolutionaries could agree. A generation of historians and journalists had praised the First French Republic, and their work had born fruit: the revolutionaries were firmly committed to a republic as opposed to any form of constitutional monarchy, and they immediately set about drafting a constitution for France's Second Republic. Moreover, they wanted a truly popular and democratic republic, so that the healthy, lifegiving forces of the common people – the peasants and the workers – could reform society with wise legislation. In practice, building such a republic meant giving the right to vote to every adult male, and this was quickly done. Revolutionary compassion and sympathy for freedom were expressed in the freeing of all slaves in French colonies, abolition of the death penalty, and the establishment of a ten-hour workday for Paris.

Yet there were profound differences within the revolutionary coalition in Paris. On the one hand there were the moderate, liberal republicans of the middle class. They viewed universal manhood suffrage as the ultimate concession to be made to popular forces, and strongly opposed any further radical social measures. On the other hand were the radical republicans. Influenced by the critique of capitalism and unbridled individualism elaborated by a generation of utopian socialists, and appalled by the poverty and misery of the urban poor, the radical republicans were committed to socialism. To be sure, socialism came in many utopian shapes and sizes for the Parisian working poor and their leaders, but that did not make their commitment to it any less real. Finally, wedged in between were individuals like the poet Lamartine and the democrat Ledru-Rollin, who were neither doctrinaire socialists nor stand-pat liberals and who sought to escape an impending tragedy.

Worsening depression and rising unemployment brought these conflicting goals to the fore. Louis Blanc (page 1029), who along with the worker Albert represented the republican socialists in the provisional government, pressed for recognition of a socialist "right to work." Blanc asserted that permanent government-sponsored cooperative workshops should be established for workers. Such workshops would be an alternative to capitalist employment and a decisive step toward a new social order.

The moderate republicans wanted no such thing. They were willing to provide only temporary relief. The resulting compromise set up national workshops – soon to become a vast program of pick-and-shovel public works – and established a special commission under Louis Blanc to "study the question." This satisfied no one. As bad as the national workshops were, though, they were better than nothing. An army of desperate poor from the French provinces and even from foreign countries streamed into Paris to sign up. The number enrolled in the workshops soared from 10,000 in March to 120,000 by June, and another 80,000 were trying unsuccessfully to join.

While the workshops in Paris grew, the French masses went to the polls in late April. Voting in most cases for the first time, the people elected to the new Constituent Assembly about five hundred moderate republicans, three hundred monarchists, and one hundred radicals who professed various brands of socialism. One of the moderate republicans was the author of *Democracy in America,* Alexis de Tocqueville (1805–1859), who had predicted the overthrow of Louis Philippe's government. To this brilliant observer, socialism was the most characteristic aspect of the revolution in Paris.

This socialist revolution had evoked a violent reaction not only among the frightened middle and upper classes but also among the bulk of the population – the peasants. The French peasants owned land, and, according to Tocqueville, "private property had become with all those who owned it a sort of bond of fraternity."[6] The countryside, Tocqueville wrote, had been seized with a universal hatred of radical Paris. Returning from Normandy to take his seat in the new Constituent Assembly, Tocqueville saw that a majority of the members were firmly committed to the republic and strongly opposed to the socialists, and he shared their sentiments.

The clash of ideologies – of liberal capitalism and socialism – became a clash of classes and arms after the elections. The new government's executive committee dropped Louis Blanc and thereafter included no representative of the Parisian working class. Fearing that their socialist hopes were about to be dashed, the workers invaded the assembly on May 15 and tried to proclaim a new revolutionary state. But the government was ready and used the middle-class National Guard to squelch this uprising. As the workshops continued to fill and grow more radical, the fearful but powerful propertied classes in the assembly took the offensive. On June 22 the government dissolved the national workshops in Paris, giving the workers the choice of joining the army or going to workshops in the provinces.

The result was a spontaneous and violent uprising. Frustrated in their attempts to create a socialist society, masses of desperate men and women were now losing even their life-sustaining relief. As a voice from the crowd cried out when the famous astronomer François Arago counseled patience: "Ah, Monsieur Arago, you have never been hungry!"[7] Barricades sprang up in the narrow streets of Paris, and a terrible class war began. Working men and women fought with the courage of utter desperation, but the government had the army and the support of peasant France. After three terrible "June Days" and the death or injury of more than ten thousand people, the republican army under General Louis Cavaignac stood triumphant in a sea of working-class blood and hatred.

The revolution in France thus ended in spectacular failure. The February coalition of the middle and working classes had in four short months become locked in mortal combat. In place of a generous democratic republic, the Constituent Assembly completed a constitution featuring a strong executive. This allowed Louis Napoleon, nephew of Napoleon Bonaparte, to win a landslide victory in the election of December 1848. The appeal of his great name, as well as the desire of the propertied classes for order at any cost, had produced a semi-authoritarian regime.

THE AUSTRIAN EMPIRE IN 1848

Throughout central Europe news of the upheaval in France evoked feverish excitement and eventually revolution. Liberals demanded written constitutions, representative government, and greater civil liberties. When governments hesitated, popular revolts followed. Urban workers and students served as the shock troops, but they were allied with middle-class liberals and peasants. In the face of this united front, monarchs collapsed and granted almost everything. The popular revolutionary coalition, having secured great and easy victories, then broke down as it had in France. The traditional forces – the monarchy, the aristocracy, and the regular army – recovered their nerve, reasserted their authority, and took back many though not all of the concessions. Reaction was everywhere victorious.

The revolution in the Austrian Empire began in Hungary. Nationalism had been growing among Hungarians since about 1790, and in 1848 under the leadership of Louis Kossuth the Hungarians demanded national autonomy, full civil liberties, and universal suffrage. When the monarchy in Vienna hesi-

THE REVOLUTIONS OF 1848

February	Revolt in Paris against Louis Philippe's "bourgeois monarchy"; Louis Philippe abdicates; proclamation of a provisional republic
February–June	Establishment and rapid growth of government-sponsored workshops in France
March 3	Hungarians under Kossuth demand autonomy from Austrian Empire
March 13	Uprising of students and workers in Vienna; Metternich flees to London
March 19–21	Frederick William IV of Prussia is forced to salute the bodies of slain revolutionaries in Berlin and agrees to a liberal constitution and merger into a new German state
March 20	Ferdinand I of Austria abolishes serfdom and promises reforms
March 26	Workers in Berlin issue a series of socialist demands
April 22	French voters favor moderate republicans over radicals 5–1
May 15	Parisian socialist workers invade the Constitutional Assembly and unsuccessfully proclaim a new revolutionary state
May 18	Frankfurt Assembly begins writing a new German constitution
June 17	Austrian army crushes working-class revolt in Prague
June 22–26	French government abolishes the national workshops, provoking an uprising
	June Days: republican army defeats rebellious Parisian working class
October	Austrian army besieges and retakes Vienna from students and working-class radicals
December	Conservatives force Ferdinand I of Austria to abdicate in favor of young Francis Joseph
	Frederick William IV disbands Prussian Constituent Assembly and grants Prussia a conservative constitution
	Louis Napoleon wins a landslide victory in French presidential elections
March 1849	Frankfurt Assembly elects Frederick William IV of Prussia emperor of the new German state; Frederick William refuses and reasserts royal authority in Prussia
June–August 1849	Habsburg and Russian forces defeat the Hungarian independence movement

tated, Viennese students and workers took to the streets on March 13 and added their own demands. Peasant disorders broke out in parts of the empire. The Habsburg emperor Ferdinand I (1835–1848) capitulated and promised reforms and a liberal constitution. Metternich fled in disguise toward London. The old order seemed to be collapsing with unbelievable rapidity.

The coalition of revolutionaries was not completely stable, though. The Austrian Empire was overwhelmingly agricultural, and serfdom still existed. On March 20, as part of its capitulation before upheaval, the monarchy abolished serfdom with its degrading forced labor and feudal services. Peasants throughout the empire felt they had won a victory reminiscent of France in 1789. Newly free, men and women of the land lost interest in the political and social questions agitating the cities. The government had in the peasants a potential ally of great importance, especially since in central Europe as in France the bulk of the army was made up of peasants.

The coalition of March was also weakened – and ultimately destroyed – by conflicting national aspirations. In March the Hungarian revolutionary leaders pushed through an extremely liberal, almost democratic, constitution granting widespread voting rights and civil liberties, and ending feudal obligations. So far, well and good. Yet the Hungarian revolutionaries were also nationalists with a mission. They wanted the ancient Crown of Saint Stephen, with its mosaic of provinces and nationalities, transformed into a unified centralized Hungarian nation. To the minority groups that formed half the population of the kingdom of Hungary – the Croats, the Serbs, and the Rumanians – such unification was completely unacceptable. Each felt entitled to political

autonomy and cultural independence. The Habsburg monarchy in Vienna exploited the fears of the minority groups, and they were soon locked in armed combat with the new Hungarian government.

In a somewhat different fashion, Czech nationalists in Bohemia and the city of Prague, led by the Czech historian Palacký, came into conflict with German nationalists. Like the minorities in Hungary, the Czechs saw their struggle for autonomy as a struggle against a dominant group – the Germans. Thus the national aspirations of different peoples in the Austrian Empire came into sharp conflict, and the monarchy was able to play off one group against the other.

Nor was this all. The urban working classes of poor artisans and day laborers were not as radical in the Austrian Empire as they were in France, but then neither were the middle class and lower middle class. Throughout Austria and the German states, where Metternich's brand of absolutism had so recently ruled supreme, the middle class wanted liberal reform, complete with constitutional monarchy, limited voting rights, and modest social measures. They wanted a central European equivalent of the English Reform Bill of 1832 and the Corn Law repeal of 1846. When the urban poor rose in arms, as they did in the Austrian cities of Vienna, Prague, and Milan and throughout the German Confederation as well, and presented their own demands for universal voting rights and socialist workshops, the prosperous middle classes recoiled in alarm. As in Paris, the union of the urban poor and the middle class was soon a mere memory, and a bad memory at that.

Finally, the conservative aristocratic forces gathered around Emperor Ferdinand I regained their nerve and reasserted their great strength. The archduchess Sophia, a conservative but intelligent and courageous Bavarian princess married to the emperor's brother, provided a rallying-point. Deeply ashamed of the emperor's collapse before "a mess of students,"[8] she insisted that Ferdinand, who had no heir, abdicate in favor of her eighteen-year-old son, Francis Joseph. Powerful nobles who held high positions in the government, the army, and the church agreed completely. They organized around Sophia in a secret conspiracy to reverse and crush the revolution.

Their first breakthrough came when one of the most dedicated members of the group, Prince Alfred Windischgrätz, bombarded Prague and savagely crushed a working-class revolt there on June 17. Other Austrian officials and nobles began to lead the minority nationalities of Hungary against the revolutionary government proclaimed by the Hungarian patriots. Another Austrian army under General Josef Radetzky reconquered Austria's possessions in northern Italy in late July 1848. Revolution failed as miserably in Italy as everywhere else. At the end of October the well-equipped, predominantly peasant troops of the regular Austrian army attacked the student and working-class radicals in Vienna, and retook the city at the cost of more than four thousand casualties. Thus, the determination of the Austrian aristocracy and the loyalty of its army were the final ingredients in the triumph of reaction and the defeat of revolution.

Only in Hungary were the forces represented by Sophia's son Francis Joseph (1848–1916), crowned emperor of Austria immediately after his eighteenth birthday in December 1848, at first unsuccessful. Yet another determined conservative, Nicholas I of Russia (1825–1855), obligingly lent his iron hand. On June 6, 1849, 130,000 Russian troops poured into Hungary. After bitter fighting – in which the Hungarian army supported the revolutionary Hungarian government – they subdued the country. For a number of years the Habsburgs ruled Hungary as a conquered territory.

PRUSSIA AND THE FRANKFURT ASSEMBLY

The rest of the states in the German Confederation generally recapitulated the ebb and flow of developments in France and Austria. The key difference was the additional goal of unifying the thirty-eight states of the German Confederation, with the possible exception of Austria, into a single sovereign nation. Therefore events in Germany were extraordinarily complex, since they were occurring not only in the individual principalities but at the all-German level as well.

After Austria, Prussia was the largest and most influential German kingdom. Prior to 1848, the goal of middle-class Prussian liberals had been to transform absolutist Prussia into a liberal constitutional monarchy. Such a monarchy would then take the lead in merging itself and all the other German states into a liberal unified nation. The agitation following the fall of Louis Philippe encouraged Prussian liberals to press their demands. When they were not granted, the artisans and factory workers in Berlin exploded. The autocratic yet paternalistic Frederick William IV (1840–1861), already displaying the instability that later became insanity, vacillated. Humiliated by the revolutionary crowd, which forced him to salute from his balcony the blood-spattered corpses of workers who had fallen in an uprising on March 18, the nearly hysterical king finally caved in. On March 21, he promised to grant Prussia a liberal constitution and to merge it into a new national German state that was to be created. He appointed two wealthy businessmen from the Rhineland – perfect representatives of moderate liberalism – to form a new government.

The situation might have stabilized at this point, if the workers had not wanted much more and the Prussian aristocracy much less. On March 26, the workers issued a series of radical and vaguely socialist demands: universal voting rights, a ministry of labor, a minimum wage, and a ten-hour day. At the same time a wild-tempered Prussian landowner and aristocrat, Otto von Bismarck, joined the conservative clique gathered around the king to urge counterrevolution. While these tensions in Prussia were growing, an elected assembly arrived in Berlin to write a constitution for the Prussian state.

To add to the complexity of the situation, a self-appointed committee of liberals from various German states successfully called for the formation of a national constituent assembly to begin writing a federal constitution for a unified German state. That body met for the first time on May 18 in St. Paul's Church in Frankfurt. The Frankfurt National Assembly was a most curious revolutionary body. It was really a serious middle-class body whose 820 members included some 200 lawyers, 100 professors, many doctors, judges, and officials, and 140 businessmen for good measure.

Called together to write a constitution, the learned body was soon absorbed in a battle with Denmark over the provinces of Schleswig and Holstein. Jurisdiction over them was a hopelessly complicated issue from a legal point of view. Britain's Foreign Minister Lord Palmerston once said that only three people had ever understood the Schleswig-Holstein question, and of those one had died, another had gone mad, and he himself had forgotten the answer. The provinces were inhabited primarily by Germans but were ruled by the king of Denmark, although Holstein was a member of the German Confederation. When Frederick VII, the new nationalistic king of Denmark, tried to integrate both provinces into the rest of his state, the Germans there revolted.

Hypnotized by this conflict, the National Assembly at Frankfurt debated ponderously and finally called on the Prussian army to oppose Denmark in the name of the German nation. Prussia responded and began war with Denmark. As the Schleswig-Holstein issue demonstrated, the national ideal was a crucial factor motivating the German middle classes in 1848.

Almost obsessed with the fate of Germans under Danish rule, many members of the Frankfurt assembly also wanted to bring the German-speaking provinces of Austria into the new German state. Yet resurgent Austria resolutely opposed any division of its territory. Once this Austrian action made a "big German" state impossible, the Frankfurt assembly completed drafting a liberal constitution. Finally, in March 1849, the assembly elected King Frederick William of Prussia emperor of the new German national state (minus Austria and Schleswig-Holstein).

By early 1849, however, reaction had been successful almost everywhere. Frederick William reasserted his royal authority, disbanded the Prussian Constituent Assembly, and granted his subjects a limited, essentially conservative, constitution. Reasserting that he ruled by divine right, Frederick William contemptuously refused to accept the "crown from the gutter." The reluctant revolutionaries in Frankfurt had waited too long and acted too timidly.

When Frederick William, who really wanted to be emperor but only on his own authoritarian terms, tried to get the small monarchs of Germany to elect him emperor, Austria balked. Supported by Russia, Austria forced Prussia to renounce all its schemes of unification in late 1850. The German Confederation was re-established. After two turbulent years the political map of the German states remained unchanged. Attempts to unite the Germans – first in a liberal national state and then in a conservative Prussian empire – had failed completely.

———◆———

The liberal and nationalistic revolutions of 1848 were abortive. Political, economic, and social pressures that had been building since 1815 exploded dramatically, but very few revolutionary goals were realized. The moderate, nationalistic middle classes were unable to consolidate their initial victories in France or elsewhere in Europe. Instead, they drew back when artisans, factory workers, and radical socialists rose up to present their own much more revolutionary demands. This retreat facilitated the efforts of dedicated aristocrats in central Europe, and made possible the crushing of Parisian workers by a coalition of solid bourgeoisie and landowning peasantry in France. A host of fears, a sea of blood, and a torrent of disillusion had drowned the lofty ideals and utopian visions of a generation. The age of romantic revolution was over.

Notes

1. A. J. May, *The Age of Metternich, 1814–1848,* rev. ed., Holt, Rinehart & Winston, New York, 1963, p. 11.

2. H. Kohn, *Nationalism,* Van Nostrand, New York, 1955, pp. 141–142.

3. Quoted by F. D. Klingender, *Art and the Industrial Revolution,* Paladin, St. Albans, England, 1972, p. 117.

4. Quoted by F. B. Artz, *From the Renaissance to Romanticism: Trends in Style in Art, Literature, and Music, 1300–1830,* University of Chicago Press, Chicago, 1962, pp. 276, 278.

5. Quoted by G. Wright, *France in Modern Times,* Rand McNally, Chicago, 1960, p. 145.

6. A. de Tocqueville, *Recollections,* Columbia University Press, New York, 1949, p. 94.

7. M. Agulhon, *1848,* Editions du Seuil, Paris, 1973, pp. 68–69.

8. Quoted by W. L. Langer, *Political and Social Upheaval, 1832–1852,* Harper & Row, New York, 1969, p. 361.

Suggested Reading

All of the works cited in the Notes are highly recommended. May's is a good brief survey, while Kohn has written perceptively on nationalism in many books. Wright's *France in Modern Times* is a lively introduction to French history with stimulating biographical discussions; Langer is a balanced synthesis with an excellent bibliography. Among general studies C. Morazé, *The Triumph of the Middle Classes* (1968), a wide-ranging procapitalist interpretation, may be compared with E. J. Hobsbawm's flexible Maxism in *The Age of Revolution, 1789–1848* (1962). For English history, A. Briggs's socially oriented *The Making of Modern England, 1784–1867* (1967), and D. Thomson's *England in the Nineteenth Century, 1815–1914* (1951), are excellent. Restoration France is sympathetically portrayed by Guillaume de Bertier de Sauvigny in *The Bourbon Restoration* (1967). T. Hamerow studies the social implications of the dual revolution in Germany in *Restoration, Revolution, Reaction 1815–1871* (1966), which may be compared to H.

Treitschke's bombastic, pro-Prussian *History of Germany in the Nineteenth Century* (1915–1919), a classic of nationalistic history, and L. Snyder, *Roots of German Nationalism* (1978). H. Kissinger, *A World Restored* (1957), offers not only a provocative interpretation of the Congress of Vienna but also insights into the mind of Richard Nixon's famous Secretary of State. Compare with H. Nicolson's entertaining *The Congress of Vienna* (1946). On 1848, L. B. Namier's highly critical *1848: The Revolution of the Intellectuals* (1964), and P. Robertson's *Revolutions of 1848: A Social History* (1960), are outstanding. I. Deak, *The Lawful Revolution: Louis Kossuth and the Hungarians, 1848–49* (1979), is a noteworthy study of an interesting figure.

On early socialism and Marxism, there are W. Sewell, Jr.'s *Work and Revolution in France* (1980), and E. Wilson's engrossing survey of nineteenth-century developments, *To the Finland Station* (1953), as well as G. Lichtheim's high-powered *Marxism* (1961) and his *Short History of Socialism* (1970). J. Schumpeter, *Capitalism, Socialism and Democracy* (1947), is magnificent but difficult, a real mind-stretcher. On liberalism, there is R. Heilbroner's entertaining *The Worldly Philosophers* (1967), and G. de Ruggiero's classic *History of European Liberalism* (1959). J. Barzun, *Classic, Romantic and Modern* (1961), skillfully discusses the emergence of romanticism, while R. Stromberg, *An Intellectual History of Modern Europe* (1966), is a readable general survey. The important place of religion in nineteenth-century thought is considered from different perspectives in H. McLeod, *Religion and the People of Western Europe* (1981), and O. Chadwick, *The Secularization of the European Mind in the Nineteenth Century* (1976).

The thoughtful reader is strongly advised to delve into the incredibly rich writing of contemporaries. J. Bowditch and C. Ramsland, eds., *Voices of the Industrial Revolution* (1961), is an excellent starting point, with well-chosen selections from leading economic thinkers and early socialists. H. Hugo, ed., *The Romantic Reader,* is another fine anthology. Jules Michelet's compassionate masterpiece *The People,* a famous historian's anguished examination of French social divisions on the eve of 1848, draws one into the heart of the period and is highly recommended. Alexis de Tocqueville covers some of the same ground less romantically in his *Recollections,* which may be compared with Karl Marx's white-hot "instant history," *Class Struggles in France, 1848–1850* (1850). Great novels that accurately portray aspects of the times are Victor Hugo, *Les Misérables,* an exciting story of crime and passion among France's poor; Honoré de Balzac, *Cousin Bette* and *Père Goriot;* and Thomas Mann, *Buddenbrooks,* a wonderful historical novel that traces the rise and fall of a prosperous German family over three generations during the nineteenth century.

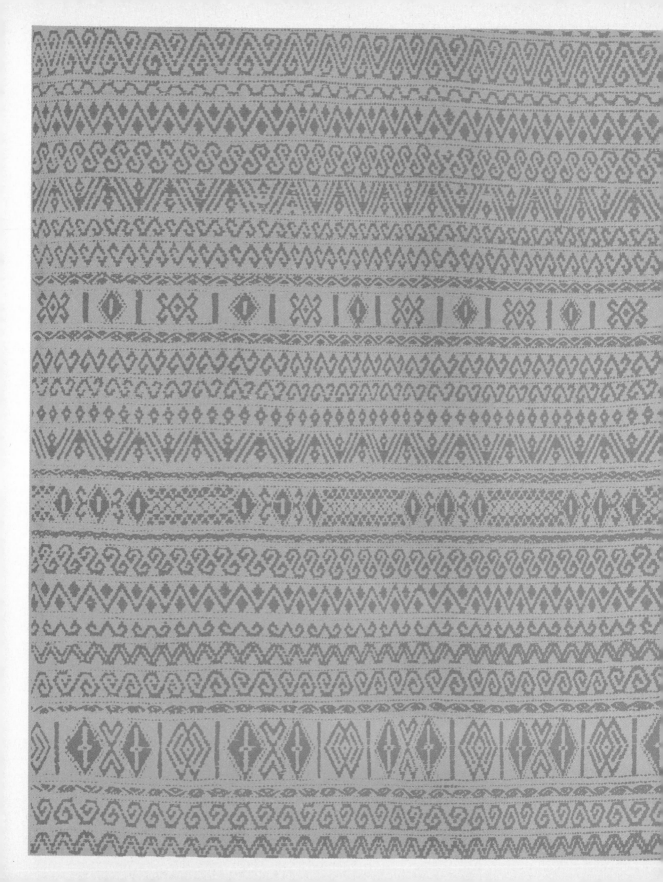

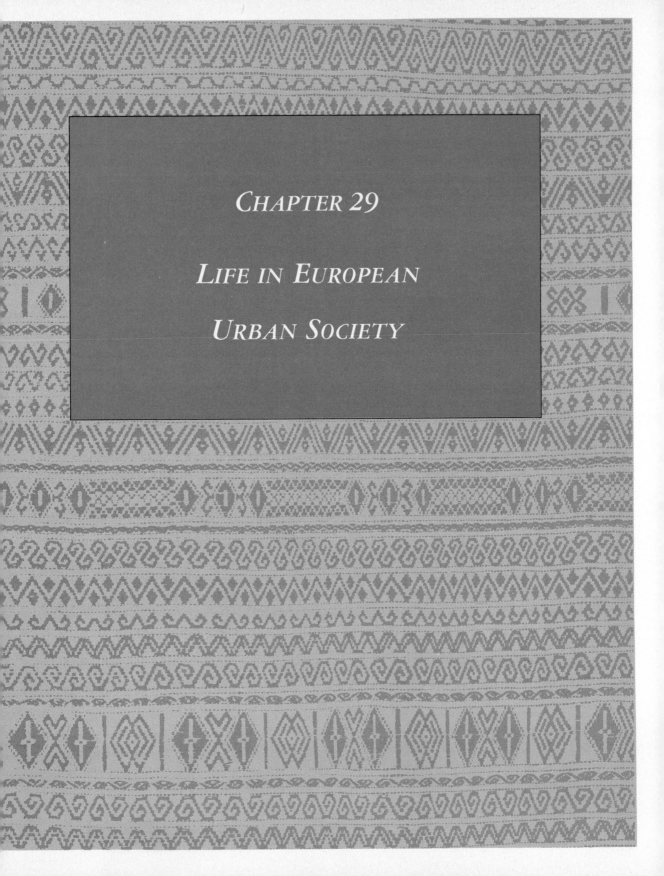

CHAPTER 29

LIFE IN EUROPEAN

URBAN SOCIETY

THE ERA OF INTELLECTUAL and political upheaval that culminated in the revolutions of 1848 was also an era of rapid urbanization. After 1848 Western political development veered off in a novel and uncharted direction, but the growth of towns and cities rushed forward with undiminished force. Thus Western society was urban and industrial in 1900, as surely as it had been rural and agrarian in 1800. The urbanization of society was both a result of the Industrial Revolution and a reflection of its enormous impact. What was life like in the cities, and how did it change? What did the emergence of urban industrial society mean for rich and poor and in between? How did families cope with the challenges and respond to the opportunities of the developing urban civilization? Finally, what changes in thought and culture inspired and gave expression to this new civilization? These are the questions this chapter will investigate.

TAMING THE CITY

The consequences of economic transformation were, from the beginning, more positive than historians have often recognized. Indeed, given the poverty and uncertainty of preindustrial life, the history of industrialization is probably better written in terms of increasing opportunities than of greater hardships. But does not this relatively optimistic view of the consequences of industrialization neglect the quality of life in urban areas? Were not the new industrial towns and cities awful places where people, and especially the poor, suffered from bad housing, lack of sanitation, and a sense of hopelessness? Did not these drawbacks more than cancel out higher wages and greater opportunity?

INDUSTRY AND THE GROWTH OF CITIES

Since the Middle Ages European cities had been centers of government, culture, and large-scale commerce. They had also been congested, dirty, and unhealthy. People were packed together almost as tightly as possible within the city limits. The typical city was a "walking city": for all but the wealthiest classes, walking was the only available form of transportation.

Infectious disease spread with deadly speed in cities, and people were always more likely to die in the city than in the countryside. In the larger towns more people died each year than were born, on the average, and urban populations were able to maintain their numbers only because newcomers were continuously arriving from rural areas. Little could be done to improve these conditions. Given the pervasive poverty, absence of urban transportation, and lack of medical knowledge, the deadly and overcrowded conditions could only be accepted fatalistically. They were the urban equivalents of bad weather and poor crops, the price of urban excitement and opportunity.

Clearly, deplorable urban conditions did not originate with the Industrial Revolution. What the Industrial Revolution did was to reveal those conditions more nakedly than ever before. The steam engine freed industrialists from dependence on the energy of fast-flowing streams and rivers, which meant that by 1800 there was every incentive to build new factories in urban areas. Cities had better shipping facilities, and thus better supplies of coal and raw materials. There were also many hands wanting work in the cities, for cities drew people like a magnet. And it was a great advantage for a manufacturer to have other factories nearby to supply his needs and buy his products. Therefore, as industry grew,

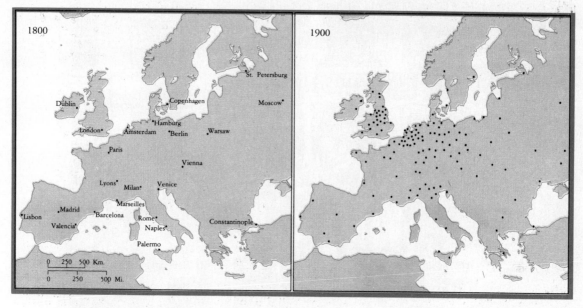

MAP 29.1 EUROPEAN CITIES OF 100,000 OR
MORE, 1800 AND 1900 *There were more large
cities in Great Britain in 1900 than in all Europe in
1800.*

there was also a rapid expansion of already overcrowded and unhealthy cities.

The challenge of the urban environment was felt first and most acutely in Great Britain. The number of people living in cities of 20,000 or more in England and Wales jumped from 1.5 million in 1801 to 6.3 million in 1851, and reached 15.6 million by 1891. Such cities accounted for 17 percent of the total English population in 1801, 35 percent as early as 1851, and fully 54 percent in 1891. Other countries duplicated the English pattern as they industrialized. An American observer was hardly exaggerating when he wrote in 1899 that "the most remarkable social phenomenon of the present century is the concentration of population in cities"[1] (see Map 29.1).

In the 1820s and 1830s, people in Britain and France began to worry about the condi-

tion of their cities. In those years the populations of a number of British cities were increasing by 40 to 70 percent each decade. Manchester, the cotton city, grew by 40 percent between 1811 and 1821, and by 47 percent between 1821 and 1831. The population of the principal Scottish manufacturing city, Glasgow, grew by 30 percent or more each decade between 1801 and 1841. With urban areas expanding at such previously undreamed-of rates, people's traditional fatalistic indifference to overcrowded, unsanitary urban living conditions began to give way to active concern. Something had to be done.

On one point everyone could agree: except on the outskirts, each town and city was using every scrap of land to the fullest extent. Parks and open areas were almost nonexistent. A British parliamentary committee reported in 1833 that "with a rapidly increasing popula-

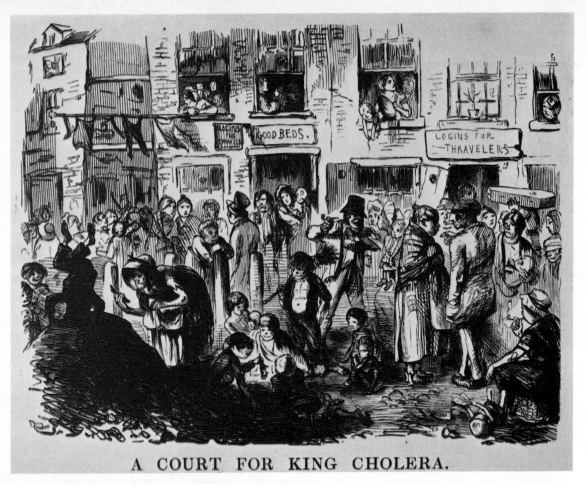

A COURT FOR KING CHOLERA.

FILTH AND DISEASE   This drawing from Punch *in 1852 tells volumes about the unhealthy living conditions of the urban poor. In the foreground children play with a dead rat and a woman scavenges a dungheap. Cheap rooming houses provide shelter for the frightfully overcrowded population. (The British Museum)*

tion, lodged for the most part in narrow courts and confined streets, the means of occasional exercise and recreation in fresh air are every day lessened, as inclosures [of vacant areas] take place and buildings spread themselves on every side."[2] Buildings were erected on the smallest possible lots, in order to pack the maximum number of people into a given space. Narrow houses were built wall-to-wall, in long rows. These row houses had neither front nor back yards, and only a narrow alley in back separated one row from the next. Or buildings were built around tiny courtyards completely enclosed on all four sides. Many people lived in cellars and attics. The tiny rooms within such buildings were often overcrowded. "Six, eight, and even ten occupying one room is anything but uncommon," wrote a doctor from Aberdeen in Scotland for a government investigation in 1842.

These highly concentrated urban populations lived in extremely unsanitary and unhealthy conditions. Open drains and sewers flowed alongside or down the middle of unpaved streets. Due to poor construction and an absence of running water, the sewers often filled with garbage and excrement. Toilet facilities were primitive in the extreme. In parts of Manchester as many as two hundred people shared a single outhouse. Such privies filled up rapidly, and since they were infrequently emptied, sewage often overflowed and seeped into cellar dwellings.

The extent to which filth lay underfoot and the smell of excrement filled the air is hard to believe; yet it was abundantly documented between 1830 and 1850. One London construction engineer found, for example, that the cellars of two large houses on a major road were "full of night-soil [human excrement], to the depth of three feet, which had been permitted for years to accumulate from the overflow of the cesspools." Moreover, courtyards in poorer neighborhoods sometimes became dunghills, collecting excrement that was sometimes sold as fertilizer. By the 1840s there was among the better-off classes a growing, shocking "realization that, to put it as mildly as possible, millions of English men, women, and children were living in shit."[3]

Who or what was responsible for these awful conditions? The crucial factors were the tremendous pressure of ever more people coupled with the *total* absence of public transportation. People simply had to jam themselves together if they were to be able to walk to shops and factories. Another factor was that government in Great Britain, both local and national, was slow to provide sanitary facilities and establish adequate building codes. This slow pace was probably attributable more to a need to explore and identify what precisely should be done than to rigid middle-class opposition to government action. Certainly Great Britain had no monopoly on overcrowded and unhealthy urban conditions; many continental cities were every bit as bad.

Most responsible of all was the sad legacy of rural housing conditions in preindustrial society, combined with appalling ignorance. As the author of a recent study concludes, there "were rural slums of a horror not surpassed by the rookeries of London.... The evidence shows that the decent cottage was the exception, the hovel the rule."[4] Thus housing was far down the newcomer's list of priorities, and it is not surprising that many carried the filth of the mud floor and the dung of the barnyard with them to the city.

Indeed, ordinary people generally took dirt and filth for granted, and some even prized it. As one English miner told an investigator, "I do not think it usual for the lasses [in the coal mines] to wash their bodies; my sisters never wash themselves." As for the men, "their legs and bodies are as black as your hat." When poor people were admitted to English workhouses, they often resisted the required bath. One man protested that it was "equal to robbing him of a great coat which he had had for some years."[5]

THE PUBLIC HEALTH MOVEMENT

Although cleanliness was not next to godliness in most people's eyes, it was becoming so for some reformers. The most famous of these was Edwin Chadwick, one of the commissioners charged with the administration of relief to paupers under the revised Poor Law of 1834. Chadwick was a good Benthamite — that is, a follower of the radical philosopher Jeremy Bentham (1748–1832). Bentham had taught that public problems ought to be dealt with on a rational, scientific basis and according to the "greatest good for the greatest number." Applying these principles, Chadwick soon saw that much more than economics was involved in the problems of poverty and the welfare budget. Indeed, he soon became convinced that sickness and disease actually caused poverty, simply because a sick worker was an unemployed worker, and orphaned children were poor children. Most important, Chadwick believed that disease could be prevented by quite literally cleaning up the urban environment. That was his "sanitary idea."

Building on a growing number of medical and sociological studies, Chadwick collected detailed reports from local Poor Law officials on the "sanitary conditions of the laboring population." After three years of investigation these reports and Chadwick's hard-hitting commentary were published in 1842 to wide publicity. This mass of evidence proved that disease was related to filthy environmental conditions, which were in turn caused largely by lack of drainage, sewers, and garbage collection. Putrefying, smelly excrement was no longer simply disgusting. For reformers like Chadwick, it was a threat to the entire community. It polluted the atmosphere and caused disease.

The key to the energetic action Chadwick proposed was an adequate supply of clean piped water. Such water was essential for personal hygiene, public bathhouses, street cleaning, firefighting, and industry. Chadwick correctly believed that the stinking excrement of communal outhouses could be dependably carried off by water through sewers at less than one-twentieth the cost of removing it by hand. The cheap iron pipes and tile drains of the industrial age would provide running water and sewerage for all sections of town, not just the wealthy ones. In 1848, spurred on by the cholera epidemic of 1846, Chadwick's report became the basis of Great Britain's first public health law, which created a national

health board and gave cities broad authority to build modern sanitary systems.

The public health movement won dedicated supporters in the United States, France, and Germany from the 1840s on. As in Great Britain, governments accepted at least limited responsibility for the health of all citizens. Moreover, they adopted increasingly concrete programs of action, programs that broke decisively with the age-old fatalism of urban populations in the face of shockingly high mortality. Thus, despite many people's skepticism about sanitation, European cities were making real progress toward adequate water supplies and sewage systems by the 1860s and 1870s. And city dwellers were beginning to reap the reward of better health.

THE BACTERIAL REVOLUTION

Effective control of communicable disease required more than a clean water supply and good sewers. Victory over disease also required a great leap forward in medical knowledge and biological theory. Reformers like Chadwick were seriously handicapped by the prevailing miasmatic theory of disease – the belief that people contract disease when they breathe the bad odors of decay and putrefying excrement; in short, the theory that smells cause disease. The miasmatic theory was a reasonable deduction from empirical observations: cleaning up filth did produce laudable results. Yet the theory was very incomplete.

Keen observation by doctors and public health officials in the 1840s and 1850s pinpointed the role of bad drinking water in the transmission of disease and suggested that contagion was spread *through* filth and not caused by it. Examples of particularly horrid stenches, such as that of the sewage-glutted Thames River at London in 1858, that did not lead to widely feared epidemics also weakened the miasmatic idea. Another factor was the successful merging of anatomical and clinical approaches to medicine between 1800 and 1850, particularly at the Paris school of medicine. Doctors there recognized a definite connection between the symptoms of certain illnesses observed at the bedside and the diseased organs seen when the body was dissected at autopsy. Medical research began zeroing in on specific diseases in an attempt to find specific treatments. When an improved theory was developed, progress could be rapid.

The breakthrough was the development of the germ theory of disease by Louis Pasteur (1822–1895). Pasteur was a French chemist by profession, not a physician. After important discoveries about the structure of crystals, he turned in 1854 to the study of fermentation. For ages people had used fermentation to make bread and wine, beer and cheese, but without really understanding what was going on. And from time to time beer and wine would mysteriously spoil for no apparent reason. As rapidly growing cities provided a vast, concentrated demand, big brewers and winemakers were seeking ways to prevent spoilage and financial loss. Responding to their calls for help, Pasteur used his microscope to develop a simple test brewers could use to monitor the fermentation process and avoid spoilage. He then investigated various kinds of fermentation.

Pasteur found that fermentation depended on the growth of living organisms. Moreover, he demonstrated that the activity of these organisms could be suppressed by heating the wine or milk – by *pasteurizing* it. The breathtaking implication was that specific diseases were caused by specific living organisms – germs – and that those organisms could be

controlled in people as well as in milk and wine. This theory was confirmed in 1868. After three years of intensive research, Pasteur isolated and controlled parasitic micro-organisms that were killing off the silkworms used in France's large silk industry. Once again, scientific research had been stimulated by and had responded to the needs of the emerging industrial society.

By 1870, the work of Pasteur and others had demonstrated the general connection between germs and disease. When in the middle of the 1870s the German country doctor Robert Koch and his coworkers developed pure cultures of harmful bacteria and described their life cycles, the dam broke. Over the next twenty years researchers – mainly Germans – identified the organisms responsible for disease after disease, often identifying several in a single year. At the same time Pasteur and his colleagues concentrated on modifying and controlling the virulence of disease-producing germs. Building on the example of Edward Jenner's pioneering conquest of smallpox, Pasteur and his team developed a number of effective vaccines. The most famous was his vaccination for rabies in 1885, a crucial step in the development of modern immunology.

Acceptance of the germ theory brought about dramatic improvements in the deadly environment of hospitals and in surgery. The English surgeon Joseph Lister (1827–1912) had noticed that patients with simple fractures were much less likely to die than those with compound fractures, in which the skin was broken and internal tissues were exposed to the air. In 1865, when Pasteur showed that air was full of bacteria, Lister immediately grasped the connection between aerial bacteria and the problem of wound infection. He reasoned that a chemical disinfectant applied to a

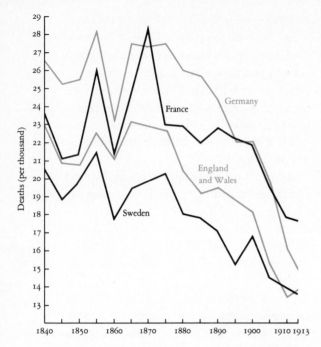

FIGURE 29.1 THE DECLINE OF DEATH RATES IN ENGLAND AND WALES, GERMANY, FRANCE, AND SWEDEN, 1840–1913 *A rising standard of living, improvements in public health, and better medical knowledge all contributed to the dramatic decline of death rates in the nineteenth century.*

wound dressing would "destroy the life of the floating particles." Lister's "antiseptic principle" worked wonders. In the 1880s, German surgeons developed the more sophisticated practice of sterilizing not only the wound but everything – hands, instruments, clothing – that entered the operating room.

The achievements of the bacterial revolution coupled with the ever-more-sophisticated public health movement saved millions of lives, particularly after about 1890. Mortality rates began to decline dramatically in European countries (see Figure 29.1) as the awful death sentences of the past – diphtheria, typhoid and typhus, cholera, yellow fever – became vanishing diseases. City dwellers benefited especially from these developments. By 1910, the likelihood of death for people of all ages in urban areas was generally no greater than in rural areas, and sometimes it was less. Particularly striking was the decline in infant mortality in the cities after 1890. In many countries, an urban mother was less likely than a rural mother to see her child die before its first birthday by 1910. A great silent revolution had occurred: the terrible ferocity of death from disease-carrying bacteria in the cities had almost been tamed.

URBAN PLANNING AND PUBLIC TRANSPORTATION

Public health was only part of the urban challenge. Overcrowding, bad housing, and lack of transportation could not be solved by sewers and better medicine; yet in these areas too important transformations improved the quality of urban life after midcentury.

More effective urban planning was one of the keys to improvement. Earlier urban planning had declined by the early nineteenth century; after 1850 it was revived and extended. France took the lead during the rule of Napoleon III (1848–1870), who sought to stand above class conflict and promote the welfare of all his subjects through government action. He believed that rebuilding much of Paris would provide employment, improve living conditions, and testify to the power and glory of his empire. In the baron Georges Haussmann, an aggressive, impatient Alsatian whom he placed in charge of Paris, Napoleon III found an authoritarian planner capable of bulldozing over both buildings and opposition. In twenty years Paris was quite literally transformed.

The Paris of 1850 was a labyrinth of narrow, dark streets, the results of desperate overcrowding. In an area of the central city

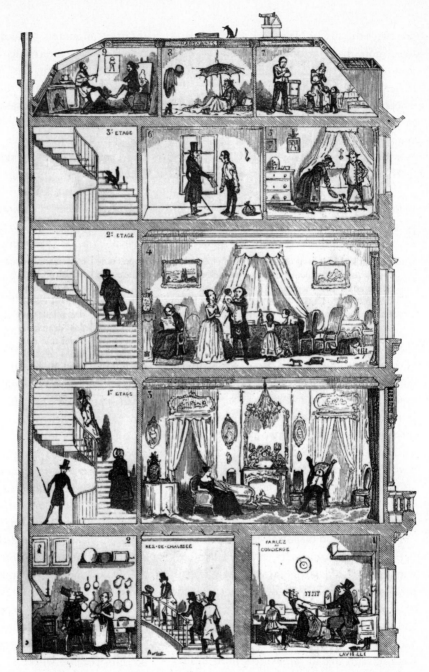

APARTMENT LIVING IN PARIS *This realistic contemporary drawing shows how different social classes lived close together in European cities about 1850. Passing the middle-class family on the first floor (American second floor), the economic condition of the tenants declined until one reached abject poverty in the garret. (Bibliothèque Nationale, Paris)*

not twice the size of New York's Central Park lived more than one-third of the city's 1 million inhabitants. Terrible slum conditions and extremely high death rates were facts of life. There were few open spaces and only two public parks for the entire metropolis. Public transportation played a very small role in this enormous walking city.

Haussmann and his fellow planners proceeded on many interrelated fronts. With a bold energy that often shocked their contemporaries, they razed old buildings in order to cut broad, straight, tree-lined boulevards through the center of the city as well as in new quarters on the outskirts. These boulevards, designed in part to prevent the easy construction and defense of barricades by revolutionary crowds, also permitted traffic to flow freely. Their construction also demolished some of the worst slums. New streets stimulated the construction of better housing, especially for the middle classes. Small neighborhood parks and open spaces were created throughout the city, and two very large parks suitable for all kinds of holiday activities were developed on either side of the city. The city also improved its sewers, and a system of aqueducts more than doubled the city's supply of good fresh water.

Haussmann and Napoleon III tried to make Paris a more beautiful city, and to a large extent they succeeded. The broad, straight boulevards, such as those radiating out like the spokes of a wheel from the Arch of Triumph and those centering on the new Opera House, afforded impressive vistas. If for most people Paris remains one of the world's most beautiful and enchanting cities, it is in part because of the transformations of the Second Empire.

The rebuilding of Paris provided a new model for urban planning and stimulated modern urbanism throughout Europe, particularly after 1870. In city after city public authorities mounted a coordinated attack on many of the interrelated problems of the urban environment. As in Paris, improvements in public health through better water supply and waste disposal often went hand in hand with new boulevard construction. Cities like Vienna and Cologne followed the Parisian example of tearing down old walled fortifications and replacing them with broad circular boulevards on which office buildings, town halls, theaters, opera houses, and museums were erected. These ring roads and the new boulevards that radiated out from them toward the outskirts eased movement and encouraged urban expansion. "Zoning expropriation" laws, which allowed a majority of the owners of land in a given quarter of the city to impose major street or sanitation improvements on a reluctant minority, were an important mechanism of the new urbanism.

The development of mass public transportation was also of great importance in the improvement of urban living conditions. Such transportation came late, but in a powerful rush. In the 1870s many European cities authorized private companies to operate horse-drawn streetcars, which had been developed in the United States, to carry riders along the growing number of major thoroughfares. Then, in the 1890s, came the real revolution: European countries adopted another American transit innovation, the electric streetcar.

Electric streetcars were wonderfully cheaper, faster, more dependable, and more comfortable than their horse-drawn counterparts. Service improved dramatically. Millions of Europeans – workers, shoppers, schoolchildren – hopped on board during the workweek. And on weekends and holidays streetcars carried millions on happy outings to parks and countryside, racetracks and music halls. In 1886, the horse-drawn streetcars of Austria-Hungary, France, Germany,

and Great Britain were carrying about 900 million riders. By 1910, electric streetcar systems in the four countries were carrying 6.7 billion riders.[6] Each man, woman, and child was using public transportation four times as often in 1910 as in 1886.

Good mass transit helped greatly in the struggle for decent housing. Just as the new boulevards and horse-drawn streetcars had facilitated the middle-class move to better housing in the 1860s and 1870s, so electric streetcars gave people of modest means access to new, improved housing after 1890. The still-crowded city was able to expand and be-

come less congested. In England in 1901, only 9 percent of the urban population was "overcrowded," in terms of the official definition of more than two persons per room. On the Continent many city governments in the early twentieth century were building electric streetcar systems that provided transportation to new public and private housing developments in outlying areas of the city for the working classes. Poor, overcrowded housing, long one of the blackest blots on the urban landscape, was in retreat – another graphic example of the gradual taming of the urban environment.

RICH AND POOR AND IN BETWEEN

General improvements in health and in the urban environment had beneficial consequences for all kinds of people. Yet differences in living conditions between social classes remained gigantic.

SOCIAL STRUCTURE

How much had the almost-completed journey to an urban, industrialized world changed the social framework of rich and poor? The first great change was a substantial and undeniable increase in the standard of living for the average person. The real wages of British workers, for example, which had already risen substantially by 1850, almost doubled between 1850 and 1906. Similar unmistakable increases occurred in continental countries as industrial development quickened after 1850. Ordinary people took a great step forward in the centuries-old battle against poverty, reinforcing efforts to improve many aspects of human existence.

There is another side to the income coin, however, and it must be stressed as well. Greater economic rewards for the average person did *not* eliminate poverty, *nor* did they make the wealth and income of the rich and the poor significantly more equal. In almost every advanced country around 1900, the richest 5 percent of all households in the population received fully one-third of all national income. The richest one-fifth of households received anywhere from 50 to 60 percent of all national income, while the entire bottom four-fifths received only 40 to 50 percent. Moreover, the bottom 30 percent of households received 10 percent or less of all

income. These enormous differences are illustrated in Figure 29.2.

The middle classes were smaller than they are today and accounted for only about 20 percent of the population; thus, statistics show that the upper and middle classes alone received less altogether than the two richest The poorest four-fifths – the working classes, including peasants and agricultural laborers – received less altogether than the two richest classes. And since many wives and teenagers in poor families worked, these figures actually understate the enduring gap between rich and poor. Moreover, income taxes on the wealthy were light or nonexistent. Thus the gap between rich and poor remained enormous at the beginning of the twentieth century. It was probably almost as great as it had been in the age of agriculture and aristocracy, before the Industial Revolution.

The great gap between rich and poor endured, in part, because industrial and urban development made society more diverse and less unified. By no means did society split into two sharply defined opposing classes, as Marx had predicted. Instead, economic specialization enabled society to produce more effectively, and in the process created more new social groups than it destroyed. There developed an almost unlimited range of jobs, skills, and earnings; one group or subclass shaded off into another in a complex, confusing hierarchy. Thus, the tiny elite of very rich and the sizable mass of dreadfully poor were separated from each other by many subclasses, each filled with individuals struggling to rise, or at least to hold their own in the social order. In this atmosphere of competition and hierarchy, neither the middle classes nor the working classes acted as a unified force. The age-old pattern of great economic inequality remained firmly intact.

THE MIDDLE CLASSES

By the beginning of the twentieth century, the diversity and range within the urban middle class was striking. Indeed, it is more meaningful to think of a confederation of middle classes, loosely united by occupations requiring mental rather than physical skill. At the top stood the upper middle class, composed mainly of the most successful business families from banking, industry, and large-scale commerce. These families were the prime beneficiaries of modern industry and scientific progress. As the incomes of people in the upper middle class rose, and as they progressively lost all traces of radicalism after the trauma of 1848, they were almost irresistibly drawn toward the aristocratic lifestyle.

As the aristocracy had long divided the year between palatial country estates and lavish town houses during "the season," so the upper middle class purchased country places or built beach houses for weekend and summer use. (Little wonder that a favorite scenario in late-nineteenth-century middle-class novels was a mother and children summering gloriously in the country home, with only sporadic weekend intrusions by a distant, shadowy father.) The number of servants was an important indicator of wealth and standing for the middle class, as it had always been for the aristocracy. The first sign of real wealth in a middle-class household was a male servant; two or three were a mark of opulence. (In England well-paid butlers had to be tall; footmen were six inches shorter on the average than butlers and earned only half as much.) Private coaches and carriages, ever an expensive item in the city, were also signs of rising social status. More generally, the rich businessman and certainly his son devoted less time to business and more to "culture" and

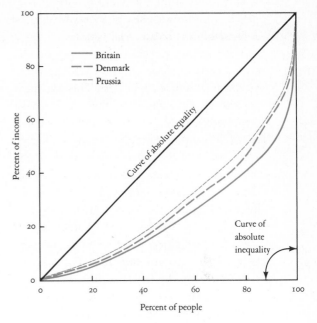

DISTRIBUTION OF INCOME

Country	Richest 5%	Richest 10%	Richest 20%	Poorest 60%
Britain	43%		59%	
Denmark	30	39%	55	31%
Prussia	30		50	33

FIGURE 29.2 *THE DISTRIBUTION OF INCOME IN BRITAIN, DENMARK, AND PRUSSIA IN 1913* The so-called Lorenz curve is useful for showing the degree of economic inequality in a given society. The closer the actual distribution of income lies to the (theoretical) curve of absolute equality, where each 20 percent of the population receives 20 percent of all income, the more nearly equal incomes are. European society was very far from any such equality before World War I. Notice that incomes in Prussia were somewhat more equal than in Britain. (Source: S. Kuznets, Modern Economic Growth, Yale University Press, New Haven, 1966, pp. 208–209)

easy living than was the case in less wealthy or well-established commercial families.

The topmost reaches of the upper middle class tended to shade off into the old aristocracy to form a new upper class. This was the 5 percent of the population that, as we have seen, received roughly one-third of the national income in European countries before 1914. Much of the aristocracy welcomed this development. Having experienced a sharp decline in its relative income in the course of industrialization, the landed aristocracy had met big business coming up the staircase and was often delighted to trade titles, country homes, and snobbish elegance for good hard cash. Some of the best bargains were made through marriages to American heiresses. Correspondingly, wealthy aristocrats tended increasingly to exploit their agricultural and mineral resources like businessmen. Bismarck was not the only proud noble to make a fortune distilling brandy on his estates.

Below the wealthy upper middle class were much larger, much less wealthy, and increasingly diversified middle-class groups. Here one found the moderately successful industrialists and merchants, as well as professionals in law and medicine. This was the middle middle class, solid and quite comfortable but lacking great wealth. Below them were independent shopkeepers, small traders, and tiny manufacturers – the lower middle class. Both of these traditional elements of the middle class expanded modestly in size with economic development.

Meanwhile the traditional middle class was gaining two particularly important additions. The expansion of industry and technology created an ever-growing demand for experts with specialized knowledge. The most valuable of the specialties became solid middle-class professions. Engineering, for example, emerged from the world of skilled labor as a full-fledged profession of great importance, considerable prestige, and many branches. Architects, chemists, accountants, and surveyors – to name only a few – first achieved professional standing in this period. They established criteria for advanced training and certification and banded together in organizations to promote and defend their interests.

Management of large public and private institutions also emerged as a kind of profession, as governments provided more services and as very large corporations like railroads came into being. Government officials and many private executives were not capitalists in the sense that they owned business enterprises. But public and private managers did have specialized knowledge and the capacity to earn a good living. And they shared most of the values of the business-owning entrepreneurs and the older professionals.

Industrialization also expanded and diversified the lower middle class. The number of independent, property-owning shopkeepers and small businessmen grew and so did the number of white-collar employees – a mixed group of traveling salesmen, bookkeepers, store managers, and clerks who staffed the offices and branch stores of large corporations. White-collar employees were propertyless and often earned no more than the better-paid skilled or even semi-skilled workers did. Yet white-collar workers were fiercely committed to the middle class and to the ideal of "moving up" in society. In the Balkans, for example, clerks let their fingernails grow very long to distinguish themselves sharply from people who worked with their hands. The tie, the suit, and soft clean hands were no-less-subtle marks of class distinction than wages.

Relatively well educated but without complex technical skills, many white-collar groups aimed at achieving professional standing and the accompanying middle-class status. Ele-

"A CORNER OF THE TABLE" With photographic precision this 1904 oil painting by the French academic artist Paul-Emile Chabas (1867–1937) skillfully idealizes the elegance and intimacy of a sumptuous dinner party. (Granger Collection)

mentary-school teachers largely succeeded in this effort. From being miserably paid part-time workers in the early nineteenth century, teachers rode the wave of mass education to respectable middle-class status and income. Nurses also rose from the lower ranks of un-skilled labor to precarious middle-class stand-ing. Dentistry was taken out of the hands of working-class barbers and placed in the hands of highly trained (and middle-class) profes-sionals.

In spite of their growing occupational di-versity and conflicting interests, the middle classes were loosely united by a certain style of life. Food was the largest item in the house-hold budget, for middle-class people liked to eat very well. In France and Italy, the middle classes' love of good eating meant that, even in large cities, activity ground almost to a halt between half past twelve and half past two on weekdays, as husbands and schoolchildren re-turned home for the midday meal. Around eight in the evening the serious business of eating was taken up once again.

The English were equally attached to big substantial meals, which they ate three times a day if income allowed. The typical English breakfast of bacon and eggs, toast and mar-malade, and stewed fruits – not to mention sardines, kidneys, or fresh fish – always astonished French and German travelers, though large-breakfast enthusiasts like the Dutch and Scandinavians were less awed. The European middle classes consumed meat in abundance, and a well-off family might spend fully 10 percent of its substantial earnings on meat alone. In the 1890s even a very prosperous English family – with an income of, say, $10,000 a year when the average working-class family earned perhaps $400 a year – spent fully one-quarter of its income on food and drink.

Spending on food was also great because the dinner party was this class's favored social occasion. A wealthy family might give a lavish party for eight to twelve almost every week, while more modest households would settle for once a month. Throughout middle-class Europe such dinners were served in the "French manner" (which the French had borrowed from the Russian aristocracy): eight or nine separate courses, from appetizers at the beginning to coffee and liqueurs at the end. In summer, a "picnic" was in order. But what a picnic! For a party of ten, one English cookbook suggested five pounds of cold salmon, a quarter of lamb, eight pounds of pickled brisket, a beef tongue, a chicken pie, salads, cakes, and six pounds of strawberries. An ordinary family meal normally consisted of only four courses – soup, fish, meat, and dessert.

The middle-class wife could cope with this endless procession of meals, courses, and dishes because she had both servants and money at her disposal. The middle classes were solid members of what some contemporary observers called the "servant-keeping classes." Indeed, the presence of at least one enormously helpful full-time maid to cook and clean was the best single sign that a family had crossed the vague line separating the working classes from the middle classes. The

greater its income, the greater the number of servants a family employed. The all-purpose servant gave way to a cook and a maid, then to a cook, a maid, and a boy, and so on. A prosperous English family far up the line with $10,000 a year in 1900 spent fully one-fourth of its income on a hierarchy of ten servants: a manservant, a cook, a kitchen maid, two housemaids, a serving maid, a governess, a gardener, a coachman, and a stable boy. Domestic servants were the second largest item in the budget of the middle classes. Thus, food and servants absorbed about one-half of income at all levels of the middle classes.

Well-fed and well-served, the middle classes were also well-housed by 1900. Many quite prosperous families rented rather than owned their homes. Apartment living, complete with tiny rooms for servants under the eaves of the top floor, was commonplace (outside Great Britain), and wealthy investors and speculative builders found good profits in middle-class housing. By 1900 the middle classes were also quite clothes-conscious. The factory, the sewing machine, and the department store had all helped to reduce the cost and expand the variety of clothing. Middle-class women were particularly attentive to the fickle dictates of fashion.

Education was another growing expense, as middle-class parents tried to provide their children with ever-more-crucial advanced education. The keystones of culture and leisure were books, music, and travel. The long realistic novel, the heroics of Wagner and Verdi, the diligent striving of the dutiful daughter on an "isn't-it-beautiful" piano, and the "we-wanted-a-change-from-the-seashore" packaged tour to a foreign country were all sources of middle-class pleasure.

Finally, the middle classes were loosely united by a shared code of expected behavior and morality. This code was strict and demanding. It laid great stress on hard work and personal achievement. Men and women who fell into crime or poverty were generally assumed to be responsible for their own circumstances. Traditional Christian morality was reaffirmed by this code and preached tirelessly by middle-class people who took pride in their own good conduct. Drinking and gambling were denounced as vices, sexual purity and fidelity celebrated as virtues. In short, the middle-class person was supposed to know right from wrong and was expected to act accordingly.

THE WORKING CLASSES

About four out of five people belonged to the working classes at the turn of the century. Many members of the working classes – that is, people whose livelihoods depended on physical labor and who did not employ domestic servants – were still small landowning peasants and hired farm hands. This was especially true in eastern Europe. In western and central Europe, however, the typical worker had left the land. In Great Britain less than 8 percent of the people worked in agriculture, while in rapidly industrializing Germany only one person in four was employed in agriculture and forestry. Even in less-industrialized France less than half of the people depended on the land in 1900.

The urban working classes were even less unified and homogeneous than the middle classes. In the first place, economic development and increased specialization expanded the traditional range of working-class skills, earnings, and experiences. Meanwhile the old sharp distinction between highly skilled artisans and unskilled manual workers was gradually breaking down. To be sure, highly

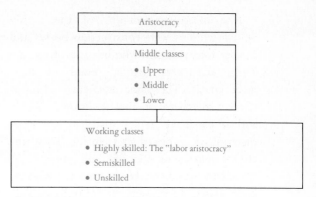

FIGURE 29.3   THE URBAN SOCIAL HIERARCHY

skilled printers and masons, as well as unskilled dock workers and common laborers, continued to exist. But between these extremes there were ever more semiskilled groups, many of which were composed of factory workers and machine tenders (see Figure 29.3).

In the second place, skilled, semiskilled, and unskilled workers had widely divergent lifestyles and cultural values, and their differences contributed to a keen sense of social status and hierarchy within the working classes. The result was great variety and limited class unity.

Highly skilled workers, who comprised about 15 percent of the working classes, were a real "labor aristocracy." By 1900 they were earning about £2 a week in Great Britain, or roughly $10 a week and $500 per year. This was only about two-thirds the income of the bottom ranks of the "servant-keeping" classes. But it was fully twice as much as the earnings of unskilled workers, who averaged about $5 per week, and substantially more than the earnings of semiskilled workers, who averaged perhaps $7 per week. Other European countries had a similar range of earnings.

The most "aristocratic" of the highly skilled workers were construction bosses and factory foremen, men who had risen from the ranks and were fiercely proud of their achievement. The labor aristocracy also included members of the traditional highly skilled handicraft trades that had not been mechanized or placed in factories. These included makers of scientific and musical instruments, cabinetmakers, potters, jewelers, bookbinders, engravers, and printers. This group as a whole was under constant long-term pressure. Irregularly but inexorably, factory methods were being extended to ever more crafts, and many skilled artisans were being replaced by lower-paid, semiskilled factory workers. Traditional woodcarvers and watchmakers virtually disappeared, for example, as the making of furniture and timepieces was taken out of the shop and put into the factory.

At the same time a contrary movement was occurring. The labor aristocracy was consistently being enlarged by the growing need for highly skilled workers, such as shipbuilders, machine-tool makers, railway locomotive engineers, fine cotton textile spinners, and some metalworkers. Thus, the labor elite was in a state of flux as individuals and whole crafts moved in and out of it.

To maintain their precarious standing, the upper working class adopted distinctive values and strait-laced, almost puritanical, behavior. Like the middle classes, the labor aristocracy was strongly committed to the family and to economic improvement. Families in the upper working class saved money regularly, worried about their children's education, and valued good housing. Despite these similarities, which superficial observers were quick to exaggerate, skilled workers viewed themselves not as aspirants to the middle class but as the pacesetters and natural leaders of all the working classes. Well aware of the poverty and degradation not so far below them, they practiced self-discipline and stern morality.

The upper working class in general frowned on heavy drinking and sexual permissiveness. The organized temperance movement was strong in the countries of northern Europe, such as Great Britain, where a generation advocated tea as "the cup that cheers but does not inebriate." As one German labor aristocrat somberly warned, "the path to the brothel leads through the tavern" and from there quite possibly to drastic decline or total ruin for person and family.[7]

Men and women of the labor aristocracy were quick to find fault with those below them who failed to meet their standards. In 1868, William Lovett, an English labor aristocrat if ever there was one, denounced "this ignorant recklessness and improvidence that produce the swarms of half-starved, neglected, and ignorant children we see in all directions; who mostly grow up to become the burdens and often the pests of society, which the industrious and frugal have to support."[8] Finally, many members of the labor aristocracy had definite political and philosophical beliefs, whether Christian or socialist, or both. Such beliefs further strengthened the stern moral code of the upper working class.

Below the labor aristocracy stood semiskilled and unskilled urban workers. The enormous complexity of this sector of the world of labor is not easily summarized. Workers in the established crafts – carpenters, bricklayers, pipefitters – stood near the top of the semiskilled hierarchy, often flirting with (or having backslid from) the labor elite. A large number of the semiskilled were factory workers, who earned highly variable but relatively good wages and whose relative importance in the labor force was increasing.

The unskilled was the larger group, made

THE LONDON COFFEE STALL   *The cities of the nineteenth century teemed with street-sellers. The battered top hat and baggy overcoat of this coffee vendor show how such petty capitalists struggled to reach the lower middle class. (Photo: Caroline Buckler)*

up of day laborers such as longshoremen, wagon-driving teamsters, teenagers, and every kind of "helper." Many of these people had real skills and performed valuable services, but they were unorganized and divided, united only by the common fate of meager earnings. The same lack of unity characterized street vendors and market people – self-employed workers who competed savagely with each other and with the established shopkeepers of the lower middle classes.

One of the largest components of the unskilled group was domestic servants, whose numbers grew steadily in the nineteenth century. In advanced Great Britain, for example, one out of every seven employed persons was

SERVANTS SEEKING WORK *in Moscow bargained with prospective employers (or their agents) in this special hiring yard just outside the ancient city walls. Moscow's bustling "market for servants" was open* *every day of the year and was busiest on Sundays. The shed in the center provided some protection from the weather. (Photo: Caroline Buckler)*

a domestic servant in 1911. The majority were women; indeed, one out of every three girls in Britain between the ages of fifteen and twenty was a domestic servant. Throughout Europe and America, a great many female domestics in the cities were recent migrants from rural areas. As in earlier times, domestic service was still hard work at low pay with limited personal independence. For the full-time general maid in a lower-middle-class family, there was an unending routine of babysitting, shopping, cooking, and cleaning. In the great households the girl was at the bottom of a rigid hierarchy; status-conscious butlers and housekeepers were determined to stand almost as far above her as the wealthy master and mistress.

Nonetheless, domestic service had real attractions for "rough, country girls" with strong hands and few specialized skills. Marriage prospects were better, or at least more varied, in the city. And though wages were low, they were higher and more regular than in hard agricultural work. Finally, as one London observer noted, young girls and other migrants were drawn to the city by "the contagion of numbers, the sense of something going on, the theaters and the music halls, the brightly lighted streets and busy crowds – all, in short, that makes the difference between the Mile End fair on a Saturday night, and a dark and muddy country lane, with no glimmer of gas and with nothing to do."[9]

Many young domestics from the countryside made the successful transition to working-class wife and mother. Yet with an unskilled or unemployed husband and a growing family, such a woman often had to join the broad ranks of working-women in the "sweated industries." These industries resembled the old putting-out and cottage industries of the eighteenth and early nineteenth centuries. The women normally worked at home, though sometimes together in some loft or garret, for tiny merchant-manufacturers. Paid by the piece and not by the hour, these women (and their young daughters), for whom organization was impossible earned pitiful wages and lacked any job security.

Some women did hand-decorating of every conceivable kind of object; the majority, however, made clothing, especially after the advent of the sewing machine. Foot-powered sewing machines allowed the poorest wife or widow in the foulest dwelling to rival and eventually supplant the most highly skilled male tailor. By 1900 only a few such tailors lingered on in high-priced "tailor-made" shops. An army of poor women accounted for the bulk of the inexpensive "ready-made" clothes displayed on department store racks and in tiny shops. All of these considerations graphically illustrates the rise and fall of groups and individuals within the working classes.

The urban working classes sought fun and recreation, and they found it. Across the face of Europe drinking was unquestionably the favorite leisure-time activity of working people. For many middle-class moralists, as well as moralizing historians since, love of drink has been a curse of the modern age — a sign of social dislocation and popular suffering. Certainly, drinking was deadly serious business. One English slum dweller recalled that "drunkenness was by far the commonest cause of dispute and misery in working class homes. On account of it one saw many a decent family drift down through poverty into total want."[10] As in Soviet Russia today, where a worker may earn $200 a month and some of the world's best bread costs only twenty-five cents a loaf but foul vodka costs five dollars a bottle, heavy drinking by only one family member could make the difference between modest dignity and dire, violent poverty for many a working-class family.

Generally, however, heavy "problem" drinking declined by the late nineteenth century, as it became less and less socially acceptable. This decline reflected in part the firm moral leadership of the upper working class. At the same time drinking became more public and social, especially as on-the-job drinking, an ancient custom of field laborers and urban artisans, declined. Cafés and pubs became increasingly bright, friendly places. Working-class political activities, both moderate and radical, were also concentrated in taverns and pubs. Moreover, social drinking by married couples and sweethearts became accepted and widespread for the first time. Greater participation by women undoubtedly helped to civilize the world of drink and hard liquor.

The two other leisure-time passions of the working classes were sports and music halls. By the late nineteenth century there had been a great decline in "cruel sports," such as bull-baiting and cockfighting, throughout Europe. Their place was filled by modern spectator sports, of which racing and soccer were the most popular. There was a great deal of gambling on sports events, and for many a workingman the desire to decipher the racing forms was a powerful incentive toward literacy. Music halls and vaudeville theaters, the working-class counterparts of middle-class opera and classic theater, were enormously

SWEATED INDUSTRY   This photo captures the essence of sweated industry. Women and young boys labor for low wages in a necktie workshop in New York about 1890. (Jacob A. Riis Collection, Museum of the City of New York)

popular throughout Europe. In the words of one English printer, "It is to the music halls that the vast body of working people look for recreation and entertainment."[11] In 1900 there were more than fifty in London alone. Music-hall audiences were thoroughly mixed, which may account for the fact that drunkenness, pregnancy before marriage, marital difficulties, and mothers-in-law were favorite themes of broad jokes and bittersweet songs.

THE FAMILY

Urban life wrought many fundamental changes in the family. Although much is still unknown, it seems clear that by the late nineteenth century the family had stabilized considerably after the disruption of the late eighteenth and early nineteenth centuries. The home became more important for both men and women. The role of women and attitudes toward children underwent substantial change, and adolescence emerged as a distinct stage of life. These are but a few of the transformations that affected all social classes in varying degrees.

PREMARITAL SEX AND MARRIAGE

By 1850, the preindustrial pattern of lengthy courtship and mercenary marriage was pretty well dead among the working classes. In its place the ideal of romantic love had triumphed. As one French observer in a small seaport remarked about 1850: "The young men are constantly letting partners with handsome dowries go begging. When they marry, it's ordinarily for inclination and not for advantage."[12] Couples were ever more likely to come from different, even distant, towns and to be more nearly the same age, further indicating that romantic sentiment was replacing tradition and financial considerations. The calculating practice whereby wealthy old craftsmen took pretty young brides, who as comfortable middle-aged widows later married poor apprentices, was increasingly heard of only in old tales and folk songs.

Sexual experimentation before marriage had also triumphed as had illegitimacy. As we have seen, there was an "illegitimacy explosion" between about 1750 and 1850 (page 858). By the 1840s, as many as one birth in three was occurring outside of wedlock in many large cities. Although poverty and economic uncertainty undoubtedly prevented many lovers from marrying, there were also many among the poor and propertyless who saw little wrong with having illegitimate offspring. As one young Bavarian woman answered happily when asked why she kept having illegitimate children: "It's O.K. to make babies. . . . The king has o.k.'d it!"[13]

Thus, the pattern of romantic ideals, premarital sexual activity, and widespread illegitimacy was firmly established by midcentury among the urban working classes.

It is hard to know how European couples managed sex, pregnancy, and marriage in the second half of the nineteenth century, because such questions were considered improper both in polite conversation and in public opinion polls. Yet there are many telltale clues. The rising rate of illegitimacy was reversed: more babies were born to married mothers. Some observers have argued that this shift reflected the growth of puritanism and a lessening of sexual permissiveness among the unmarried. This explanation, however, is unconvincing.

The percentage of brides who were pregnant continued to be high, and showed little or no tendency to decline. In many parts of urban Europe around 1900 as many as one woman in three was going to the altar an expectant mother. Moreover, unmarried people almost certainly used the cheap rubbers and diaphragms the industrial age had made available to prevent pregnancy, at least in predominantly Protestant countries.

Unmarried young people were probably engaging in just as much sexual activity as their parents and grandparents who had created the illegitimacy explosion of 1750–1850. But toward the end of the nineteenth century, pregnancy usually meant marriage and the establishment of a two-parent household. This important development reflected the growing respectability of the working classes, as well as their gradual economic improvement. Skipping out was less acceptable, and marriage was less of an economic disaster. Thus, the urban working-class couple became more stable, and their stability strengthened the family as an institution.

Economic considerations in marriage long

remained much more important to the middle classes than to the working classes. In France, dowries and elaborate legal marriage contracts were standard practice, and marriage was for many families life's most crucial financial transaction. A popular author advised young Frenchmen that "marriage is in general a means of increasing one's credit and one's fortune and of insuring one's success in the world."[14] This preoccupation with money led many middle-class men, in France and elsewhere, to marry late and to choose women considerably younger and less sexually experienced than themselves. These differences between husband and wife became a source of tension in many middle-class marriages.

A young woman of the middle class found her romantic life carefully supervised by her well-meaning mother, who schemed for a proper marriage and guarded her daughter's virginity like the family's credit. After marriage, middle-class morality sternly demanded fidelity.

Middle-class boys were watched too, but not as vigilantly. By the time they reached late adolescence they had usually attained considerable sexual experience with maids or prostitutes. With marriage a distant, uncertain possibility, it was all too easy for the young man of the middle classes to turn to the urban underworld of whoredom and sexual exploitation to satisfy his desires.

PROSTITUTION

In Paris alone 155,000 women were registered as prostitutes between 1871 and 1903, and 750,000 others were suspected of prostitution in the same years. Men of all classes visited prostitutes, but the middle and upper classes supplied much of the motivating cash. Thus, though many middle-class men abided by the publicly professed code of stern puritanical morality, many others indulged their appetites for prostitutes and sexual promiscuity.

My Secret Life, the anonymous eleven-volume autobiography of an English sexual adventurer from the servant-keeping classes, provides a remarkable picture of such a man. Beginning at an early age with a maid, the author becomes progressively obsessed with sex and devotes his life to living his sexual fantasies. In almost every one of his innumerable encounters all across Europe, this man of wealth simply buys his pleasure. The underlying theme of the rake's progress is the clink of copper, silver, and gold. Usually meetings are arranged in a businesslike manner: regular and part-time prostitutes quote their prices; working-class girls are corrupted by hot meals and warm baths.

At one point, however, he offers a young girl a sixpence for a kiss and gets it. Learning that the pretty, unskilled working girl earns nine pence a day – she fills seed packets at a nursery – he offers her the equivalent of a week's salary for a few moments of fondling. When she finally agrees, he savagely exults that "*her* want was my opportunity."[15] Later he offers more money for more gratification, and when she refuses he tries unsuccessfully to rape her in a hackney cab. On another occasion he takes a farm worker by force: "Her tears ran down. If I had not committed a rape, it looked uncommonly like one." He then forces his victim to take money to prevent a threatened lawsuit, while the foreman advises the girl to keep quiet and realize that "you be in luck if he likes you."

Obviously atypical in its excesses, the encyclopedic thoroughness of *My Secret Life* does mirror accurately the dark side of sex and class in urban society. Thinking of their wives largely in terms of money and social position, the men of the comfortable classes often purchased sex and even affection from poor girls both before and after marriage. Moreover, the great continuing differences between rich and poor made for every kind of debauchery and sexual exploitation, including the brisk trade in poor virgins the author of *My Secret Life* particularly relished. Brutal sexist behavior was part of life – a part the sternly moral women (and men) of the upper working class detested and tried to shield their daughters against. For many poor young women, prostitution, like domestic service, was a stage of life. Having passed through it, they went on to marry men of their own class and establish homes and families.

KINSHIP TIES

Within working-class homes, ties to relatives after marriage – kinship ties – were normally much stronger than superficial social observers have recognized. Most newlyweds tried to live near their parents, though not in the same house. Indeed, for many married couples in the cities, ties to mothers and fathers, uncles and aunts became more important, and ties to nonrelated acquaintances became weaker.

People turned to their families for help in coping with sickness, unemployment, death, and old age. Although governments were generally providing more welfare services by 1900, the average couple and their children inevitably faced crises. Funerals, for example, were an economic catastrophe, requiring a sudden large outlay for special clothes, carriages, and burial services. Unexpected death or desertion could leave widows and orphans in need of financial aid or perhaps a foster home. Relatives responded to such cries, knowing full well that their time of need and repayment would undoubtedly come.

Relatives were also valuable at less tragic moments. If a couple was very poor, an aged

THE GREAT SOCIAL EVIL.

TIME :—Midnight. A Sketch not a Hundred Miles from the Haymarket.

Bella. " AH ! FANNY ! HOW LONG HAVE YOU BEEN *GAY ?*"

PROSTITUTION was commonly known as "the great social evil" because it was so widespread. This Punch *cartoon of 1857 shows two weary streetwalkers and involves a play on words. (In the nineteenth century "gays" were prostitutes, not homosexuals.) (The British Museum)*

relation often moved in to cook and mind the children so the wife could earn badly needed income outside the home. Sunday dinners and holiday visits were often shared, as was outgrown clothing and useful information. Often the members of a large family group all lived in the same neighborhood.

WOMEN AND FAMILY LIFE

Industrialization and the growth of modern cities brought great changes to the lives of European women. These changes were particularly consequential for married women, and most women did marry in the nineteenth century.

The work of most wives became quite distinct and separate from that of their husbands. Husbands became wage earners in factories and offices, while wives tended to stay home and manage the household and care for the children. The preindustrial pattern among both peasants and cottage workers, in which husbands and wives worked together and divided up household duties and childrearing, declined. Only in a few occupations, such as retail trade, did married couples live where they worked and struggle together to make their Mom and Pop operations a success. Factory employment for married women also declined as the early practice of hiring entire families in the factory disappeared.

As economic conditions improved late in the nineteenth century, women generally worked outside the home after marriage only in poor families. One old English worker recalled that "the boy wanted to get into a position that would enable him to keep a wife and family, as it was considered a thoroughly unsatisfactory state of affairs if the wife had to work to help maintain the home."[16] The ideal was a strict division of labor by sex: the wife

as mother and homemaker, the husband as wage earner.

This rigid division of labor meant that married women faced great injustice if they tried to move into the man's world, the world of employment outside the home. Husbands were unsympathetic or hostile. Well-paying jobs were off-limits to women, and a woman's wage was almost always less than a man's even for the same work. No wonder some women rebelled by the second half of the nineteenth century and began the long-continuing fight for equality of the sexes and the rights of women. More generally, rigidly separate roles narrowed women's horizons and fenced in their world.

There was a brighter side to the same coin. As home and children became the wife's main concerns, her control and influence there apparently became increasingly absolute throughout Europe. Among the English working classes it was the wife who generally determined how the family's money was spent. In many families the husband gave all his earnings to his wife to tend. She returned to him only a small allowance for carfare, beer, tobacco, and union dues. All the major domestic decisions, from the children's schooling and religious instruction to the selection of new furniture or a new apartment, were hers. In France women had even greater power in their assigned domain. One English feminist noted in 1908 that "though legally women occupy a much inferior status than men [in France], in practice they constitute the superior sex. They are the power behind the throne." Another Englishwoman believed that "in most French households, women reign with unchallenged sway."[17]

Women ruled at home partly because running the urban household was a complicated and extremely demanding task. Twice-a-day food shopping, penny-pinching, economizing, and the growing crusade against dirt – not to mention child raising – were a full-time occupation. Nor were there any laborsaving appliances to help. The wife also ruled at home because a good deal of her effort was directed toward pampering her husband as he expected. In countless humble households she saw that he had meat while she ate bread, that he relaxed by the fire while she did the dishes.

The woman's guidance of the household went hand in hand with the increased emotional importance of home and family. The home she ran was idealized as a warm shelter in a hard and impersonal urban world. By the 1820s one observer of the comfortable middle classes in Marseilles had noted, for example, that "the family father, obliged to occupy himself with difficult business problems during the day, can relax only when he goes home.... Family evenings together are for him a time of the purest and most complete happiness."[18]

In time the central place of the family spread down the social scale. For a child of the English slums in the early 1900s

home, however poor, was the focus of all love and interests, a sure fortress against a hostile world. Songs about its beauties were ever on people's lips. "Home, sweet home," first heard in the 1870s, had become "almost a second national anthem." Few walls in lower-working-class houses lacked "mottoes" – colored strips of paper, about nine inches wide and eighteen inches in length, attesting to domestic joys: EAST, WEST, HOME'S BEST; BLESS OUR HOME; GOD IS MASTER OF THIS HOUSE; HOME IS THE NEST WHERE ALL IS BEST.[9]

By 1900 home and family were what life was all about for millions of people of all classes.

One of the most striking signs of deepening emotional ties within the family was the mother's love and concern for her tiny infants. This was a sharp break with the past. It may seem scarcely believable today that the typical mother in preindustrial Western society was very often indifferent toward her baby. This indifference – unwillingness to make real sacrifices for the welfare of the infant – was giving way among the comfortable classes by the later part of the eighteenth century, but the ordinary mother adopted new attitudes only as the nineteenth century progressed. The baby became more important, and women became better mothers.

Women also developed stronger emotional ties to their husbands. Even in the comfortable classes, marriages were increasingly founded on sentiment and sexual attraction rather than money and calculation. Affection and eroticism became more central to the couple after marriage. Gustave Droz, whose book *Mr., Mrs., and Baby* went through 121 editions between 1866 and 1884, saw love within marriage as the key to human happiness. He condemned men who made marriage sound dull and practical, men who were exhausted by prostitutes and rheumatism and who wanted their young wives to be little angels. He urged women to follow their hearts and marry a man more nearly their own age:

A husband who is stately and a little bald is all right, but a young husband who loves you and who drinks out of your glass without ceremony, is better. Let him, if he ruffles your dress a little and places a kiss on your neck as he passes. Let him, if he undresses you after the ball, laughing like a fool. You have fine spiritual qualities, it is true, but your little body is not bad either and when one loves, one loves completely. Behind these follies lies happiness.[20]

A WORKING-CLASS HOME, 1875   *Emotional ties within ordinary families grew stronger in the nineteenth century. (Illustrated London News, LXVI, 1875. Photo courtesy of Boston Public Library)*

Many French marriage manuals of the late 1800s stressed that women had legitimate sexual needs, such as "the right to orgasm." Perhaps the French were a bit more enlightened in these matters than other nationalities. But the rise of public socializing by couples in cafés and music halls, as well as franker affection within the family, suggest a more erotic, more pleasurable intimate life for women throughout Western society. This too helped make the woman's role as mother and homemaker acceptable and even satisfying.

CHILD RAISING

Children benefited from the freer expression of affection within the family circle. Mothers increasingly breast-fed their own infants, for example, rather than paying wet nurses to do so. Breast-feeding involved sacrifice – a temporary loss of freedom, if nothing else. Yet in an age when there was no good alternative to mother's milk, it saved lives. The surge of maternal feeling also gave rise to a wave of specialized books on childrearing and infant hygiene, such as Droz's phenomenally successful best-seller *Mr., Mrs., and Baby.* Droz urged fathers to get into the act, and pitied those "who do not know how to roll around on the carpet, play at being a horse and a great wolf, and undress their baby."[21] Another sign, from France, of increased affection is that fewer illegitimate babies were abandoned as foundlings, especially after about 1850. Moreover, the practice of swaddling – wrapping a baby like a tiny mummy – disappeared completely. Instead, ordinary mothers allowed their babies freedom of movement and delighted in their spontaneity.

The loving care lavished on infants was matched by greater concern for older children and adolescents. They too were wrapped in the strong emotional ties of a more intimate and more protective family. For one thing, European women began to limit the number of children they bore in order to care adequately for those they had. It was evident by the end of the century that the birthrate was declining across Europe, as Figure 29.4 shows, and it continued to do so until after World War Two. The Englishwoman who married in the 1860s, for example, had an average of about six children; her daughter marrying in the 1890s had only four; and her granddaughter marrying in the 1920s had only two or possibly three.

The most important reason for this revolutionary reduction in family size, in which the comfortable and well-educated classes took the lead, was parents' desire to improve their economic and social position and that of their children. Children were no longer an economic asset. By having fewer youngsters, parents could give those they had valuable advantages, from music lessons and summer vacations to long expensive university educations and suitable dowries. A young German skilled worker with only one child

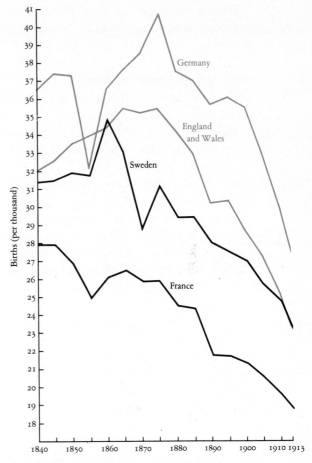

FIGURE 29.4   *THE DECLINE OF BIRTHRATES IN ENGLAND AND WALES, FRANCE, GERMANY, AND SWEDEN, 1840–1913 Women had fewer babies for a variety of reasons, including the fact that their children were increasingly less likely to die before they reached adulthood. Compare with Figure 29.2 on page 1067.*

spoke for many in his class when he said, "We want to get ahead, and our daughter should have things better than my wife and sisters did."[22] Thus, the growing tendency of couples in the late nineteenth century to use a variety of contraceptive methods – rhythm, withdrawal, and mechanical devices – certainly reflected increased concern for children.

Indeed, many parents were probably *too* concerned about their children, unwittingly subjecting them to an emotional pressure cooker of almost unbearable intensity. The result was that many children and especially adolescents came to feel trapped and in desperate need of greater independence.

Biological and medical theories led parents to believe that their own emotional characteristics were passed on to their offspring, and that they were thus directly responsible for any abnormality in a child. The moment the child was conceived was thought to be of enormous importance. "Never run the risk of conception when you are sick or over-tired or unhappy," wrote one influential American woman. "For the bodily condition of the child, its vigor and magnetic qualities, are much affected by conditions ruling this great moment."[23] So might the youthful "sexual excesses" of the father curse future generations. Although this was true in the case of syphilis, which could be transmitted to unborn children, the rigid determinism of such views left little scope for the child's individual development.

Another aspect of excessive parental concern was the sexual behavior of the child. Masturbation was viewed with horror, for it represented an act of independence and even defiance. Diets, clothing, games, and sleeping were carefully regulated. Girls were discouraged from riding horses and bicycling because rhythmic friction simulated masturbation. Boys were dressed in trousers with shallow and widely separated pockets. Between 1850 and 1880, there were surgical operations for children who persisted in masturbating. Thereafter until about 1905, various restraining apparatuses were more often used.

These and less blatant attempts to repress the child's sexuality were a source of unhealthy tension, often made worse by the rigid division of sexual roles within the family. It was widely believed that mother and child love each other easily, but that relations between the father and the child are necessarily difficult and often tragic. The father was a stranger; his world of business was far removed from the maternal world of spontaneous affection. Moreover, the father was demanding, often expecting the child to succeed where he himself had failed and making his love conditional on achievement. Little wonder that the imaginative literature of the late nineteenth century came to deal with the emotional and destructive elements of father-son relationships. In the Russian Feodor Dostoevsky's great novel *The Brothers Karamazov* (1880–1881), for example, four sons work knowingly or unknowingly to destroy their father. Later, at the murder trial, one of the brothers claims to speak for all mankind and screams out: "Who doesn't wish his father dead?"

Sigmund Freud (1856–1939), the Viennese founder of psychoanalysis, formulated the most striking analysis of the explosive dynamics of the family, particularly the middle-class family in the late nineteenth century. A physician by training, Freud began his career treating mental illness. He noted that the hysteria of his patients appeared to originate in bitter early childhood experiences, wherein the child had been obliged to repress strong feelings. When these painful experiences were recalled and reproduced under hypnosis or through the patient's free association of ideas, the patient could be brought to understand his or her unhappiness and eventually to deal with it.

One of Freud's most influential ideas concerned the Oedipal tensions, resulting from the son's instinctive competition with the father for the mother's love and affection. More generally, Freud postulated that much of human behavior is motivated by unconscious emotional needs, whose nature and origins are kept from conscious awareness by various mental devices he called defense mechanisms. Freud concluded that much unconscious psychological energy is sexual energy, which is in turn repressed and precariously controlled by rational thinking and moral rules. If Freud exaggerated the sexual and familial roots of adult behavior, that exaggeration was itself a reflection of the tremendous emotional intensity of family life in the late nineteenth century.

The working classes probably had more avenues of escape from such tensions than did the middle classes. Unlike their middle-class counterparts, who remained economically dependent on their families until a long education was finished or a proper marriage secured, working-class boys and girls went to work when they reached adolescence. Earning wages on their own, they could bargain with their parents for greater independence within the household by the time they were sixteen or seventeen. If they were unsuccessful, they could and did leave home, to live cheaply as paying lodgers in other working-class homes. Thus, the young person from the working classes broke away from the family more easily when emotional ties became oppressive. In the twentieth century middle-class youth would follow this lead.

Science and Thought

Major changes in Western thought accompanied the emergence of urban society. Two aspects of these complex intellectual developments stand out as especially significant. Scientific knowledge expanded rapidly and came to influence the Western world-view even more profoundly than it had since the Scientific Revolution and the early Enlightenment. And, between about the 1840s and the 1890s, European literature underwent a shift from soaring romanticism to tough-minded realism.

The Triumph of Science

As the pace of scientific advance quickened, and as theoretical advances resulted in great practical benefits, science exercised growing influence on human thought. The intellectual achievements of the Scientific Revolution had resulted in few such benefits, and theoretical knowledge had also played a relatively small role in the Industrial Revolution in England. But breakthroughs in industrial technology enormously stimulated basic scientific inquiry, as researchers sought to explain theoretically how such things as steam engines and blast furnaces actually worked. The result was an explosive growth of fundamental scientific discoveries from the 1830s onward. And unlike earlier periods, these theoretical discoveries were increasingly transformed into material improvements for the general population.

A perfect example of the translation of better scientific knowledge into practical human benefits was the work of Pasteur and his followers in biology and the medical sciences. Another was the development of the branch of physics known as thermodynamics. Building on Newton's laws of mechanics and on studies of steam engines, thermodynamics investigated the relationship between heat and mechanical energy. By midcentury, physicists had formulated the fundamental laws of thermodynamics, which were then applied to mechanical engineering, chemical processes, and many other fields. The law of conservation of energy held that different forms of energy – such as heat, electricity, and magnetism – could be converted but neither created nor destroyed. Nineteenth-century thermodynamics demonstrated that the physical world is governed by firm unchanging laws.

Chemistry and electricity were two other fields characterized by extremely rapid progress. Chemists devised ways of measuring the atomic weight of different elements, and in 1869 the Russian chemist Dmitri Mendeleev (1834–1907) codified the rules of chemistry in the periodic law and the periodic table. Chemistry subdivided into many specialized branches, such as organic chemistry – the study of the compounds of carbon. Applying theoretical insights gleaned from this new field, researchers in large German chemical companies discovered ways of transforming the dirty, useless coal-tar that accumulated in coke ovens into beautiful, expensive synthetic dyes for the world of fashion. The basic discoveries of Michael Faraday (1791–1867) on electromagnetism in the 1830s and 1840s resulted in the first dynamo (generator) and opened the way for the subsequent development of electric motors, electric lights, and electric streetcars.

The triumph of science and technology had at least three significant consequences. First, though ordinary citizens continued to lack detailed scientific knowledge, everyday experience and innumerable popularizers impressed the importance of science on the popular mind.

As science became more prominent in popular thinking, the philosophical implications of science formulated in the Enlightenment spread to broad sections of the population. Natural processes appeared to be determined by rigid laws, leaving little room for either divine intervention or human will. Yet scientific and technical advance had also fed the Enlightenment's optimistic faith in human progress, which now appeared endless and automatic to many middle-class minds.

Finally, the methods of science acquired unrivaled prestige after 1850. For many, the union of careful experiment and abstract theory seemed the only reliable route to truth and objective reality. The "unscientific" intuitions of poets and the revelations of saints were hopelessly inferior.

SOCIAL SCIENCE AND EVOLUTION

From the 1830s onward, many thinkers tried to apply the objective methods of science to the study of society. In some ways these efforts simply perpetuated the critical thinking of the philosophes. Yet there were important differences. The new "social scientists" had access to the massive sets of numerical data that governments had begun to collect, on everything from children to crime, from population to prostitution. In response, they developed new statistical methods to analyze these facts "scientifically" and supposedly to test their theories. And the systems of the leading nineteenth-century social scientists were more unified, all-encompassing, and dogmatic than those of the philosophes. Marx was a prime example (see pages 1030–1031).

Another extremely influential system builder was the French philosopher Auguste Comte (1798–1857). Initially a disciple of the utopian socialist Saint-Simon, Comte wrote a six-volume *System of Positive Philosophy* (1830–1842) that was largely overlooked during the romantic era. But when the political failures of 1848 completed the swing to realism, Comte's philosophy came into its own. Its influence has remained great to this day.

Comte postulated that all intellectual activity progresses through predictable stages:

The great fundamental law . . . is this: – that each of our leading conceptions – each branch of our knowledge – passes successively through three different theoretical conditions: the Theological, or fictitious; the Metaphysical, or abstract; and the Scientific, or positive. . . . The first is the necessary point of departure of human understanding, and the third is the fixed and definitive state. The second is merely a transition.[24]

By way of example, Comte noted that the prevailing explanation of cosmic patterns had shifted, as knowledge of astronomy developed, from the will of God (the theological) to the will of an orderly Nature (the metaphysical) to the rule of its own unchanging laws (the scientific). Later, this same intellectual progression took place in increasingly complex fields – physics, chemistry, and, finally, the study of society. By applying the scientific, positivist method, Comte believed, his new discipline of sociology would soon discover the eternal laws of human relations. This colossal achievement would in turn enable expert social scientists to impose a disciplined harmony and well-being on less-enlightened citizens. Dismissing the "fictions" of traditional religions, Comte became the chief priest of the religion of science and rule by experts.

Comte's stages of knowledge exemplify the nineteenth-century fascination with the idea of evolution and dynamic development. Thinkers in many fields, like the romantic historians and "scientific" Marxists, shared and applied this basic concept. In geology, Charles Lyell (1797–1875) effectively discredited the longstanding view that the earth's surface had been formed by short-lived cataclysms, such as biblical floods and earthquakes. Instead, according to Lyell's principle of uniformitarianism, the same geological processes that are at work today slowly formed the earth's surface over an immensely long time. The evolutionary view of biological development, first proposed by the Greek Anaximander in the sixth century B.C., re-emerged in a more modern form in the work of Jean Baptiste Lamarck (1744–1829). Lamarck asserted that all forms of life had arisen through a long process of continuous adjustment to the demands of the environment.

Lamarck's work was flawed – he believed that characteristics parents acquired in the course of their lives could be inherited by their children – and was not accepted, but it helped prepare the way for Charles Darwin (1809–1882), the most influential of all nineteenth-century evolutionary thinkers. As the official naturalist on a five-year scientific cruise to Latin America and the South Pacific in 1831, Darwin carefully collected specimens of the different animal species he encountered on the voyage. Back in England and convinced by fossil evidence and by his friend Lyell that the earth and life upon it were immensely ancient, Darwin came to doubt the general belief in a special divine creation of each species of animals. Instead, he concluded, all life had gradually evolved from a common ancestral origin in an unending "struggle for survival." After long hesitation, Darwin published his research, which immediately attracted wide attention.

Darwin's great originality lay in suggesting precisely *how* biological evolution might have occurred. His theory is summarized in his title – *On the Origin of Species by the Means of Natural Selection* (1859). Decisively influenced by Malthus's gloomy theory that populations naturally grow faster than their food supplies, Darwin argued that chance differences among the members of a given species help some to survive while others died. Thus, the variations that prove useful in the struggle for survival are selected naturally and gradually spread to the entire species through reproduction. Darwin did not explain why such variations occurred in the first place, and not until the early twentieth century did the study of genetics and the concept of mutation provide some answers.

As the capstone of already-widespread evolutionary thinking, Darwin's theory had a powerful and many-sided influence on European thought. Darwin was hailed as the great scientist par excellence, "the Newton of biology," who had revealed once again the fantastic powers of objective science. Darwin's findings also reinforced the teachings of secularists like Comte and Marx, who scornfully dismissed religious belief in favor of agnostic materialism. In the great cities especially, religion was on the defensive. Finally, many writers applied the theory of biological evolution to human affairs. Herbert Spencer (1820–1903), an English disciple of Auguste Comte, saw the human race as driven forward to ever-greater specialization and progress by the brutal economic struggle that efficiently determined "the survival of the fittest." The poor were the ill-fated weak, the prosperous the chosen strong. Understandably, Spencer and other Social Darwinists were especially popular with the upper middle class.

REALISM IN LITERATURE

In 1868 Emile Zola (1840–1902), the giant of the realist movement in literature, defended his violently criticized first novel against charges of pornography and corruption of morals. Such accusations were meaningless, Zola claimed: he was only a purely objective scientist using "the modern method, the universal instrument of inquiry of which this age makes such ardent use to open up the future."

I chose characters completely dominated by their nerves and their blood, deprived of free-will, pushed to each action of their lives by the fatality of their flesh. . . . I have simply done on living bodies the work of analysis which surgeons perform on corpses.[25]

Zola's literary manifesto articulated the key themes of realism, which had emerged in the 1840s and continued to dominate Western culture and style until the 1890s. Realist writers believed that literature should depict life exactly as it was. Forsaking poetry for prose and the personal, emotional viewpoint of the romantics for strict, scientific objectivity, the realists simply observed and recorded – content to let the facts speak for themselves.

The major realist writers focused their extraordinary powers of observation on contemporary everyday life. Emphatically rejecting the romantic search for the exotic and the sublime, they energetically pursued the typical and commonplace. Beginning with a dissection of the middle classes, from which most of them sprang, many realists eventually focused on the working classes, especially the urban working classes, who had been neglected in imaginative literature before this time. They put a microscope to many unexplored and taboo subjects – raw sex, strikes, violence, alcoholism – and hastened to report that slums and factories teemed with savage behavior. Many shocked middle-class critics denounced realism as ugly sensationalism, wrapped provocatively in pseudo-scientific declarations and crude language.

The realists' claims of objectivity did not prevent the elaboration of a definite world-view. Unlike the romantics, who had gloried in individual freedom and an unlimited universe, realists such as Zola were strict determinists. Human beings, like atoms, were components of the physical world, and all human actions were caused by unalterable natural laws. Heredity and environment determined human behavior; good and evil were merely social conventions.

The realist movement began in France, where romanticism had never been completely dominant, and three of its greatest practitioners – Balzac, Flaubert, and Zola – were French. Honoré de Balzac (1799-1850) spent thirty years writing a vastly ambitious panorama of postrevolutionary French life. Known collectively as *The Human Comedy,* this series of nearly one hundred books vividly portrays more than two thousand characters from virtually all sectors of French society. Balzac pictures urban society as grasping, amoral, and brutal, characterized by a Darwinian struggle for wealth and power. In *Père Goriot* (1835), the hero, a poor student from the provinces, eventually surrenders his idealistic integrity to feverish ambition and society's all-pervasive greed.

Madame Bovary (1857), the masterpiece of Gustave Flaubert (1821-1880), is far narrower in scope than Balzac's work but unparalleled in its depth and accuracy of psychological insight. Unsuccessfully prosecuted as an outrage against public morality and religion, Flaubert's carefully crafted novel tells the ordinary, even banal, story of a frustrated middle-class housewife who has an adulterous love affair and is betrayed by her lover. Without moralizing, Flaubert portrays the provincial middle class as petty, smug, and hypocritical.

Zola was most famous for his seamy, an-imalistic view of working-class life. But he also wrote gripping, carefully researched stories featuring the stock exchange, the big department store, and the army, as well as urban slums and bloody coal strikes. Like many later realists, Zola sympathized with socialism, a sympathy evident in his overpowering *Germinal* (1885).

Realism quickly spread beyond France. In England, Mary Ann Evans (1819-1880), who wrote under the pen name George Eliot, brilliantly achieved a more deeply felt, less sensational kind of realism. "It is the habit of my imagination," George Eliot wrote, "to strive after as full a vision of the medium in which a character moves as of the character itself." Her great novel *Middlemarch: A Study of Provincial Life* examines masterfully the ways in which people are shaped by their social medium as well as their own inner strivings, conflicts, and moral choices. Thomas Hardy (1840-1928) was more in the Zola tradition. His novels, like *Tess of the D'Urbervilles* (1891), depicted men and women frustrated and crushed by fate and bad luck.

The greatest Russian realist, Count Leo Tolstoy (1828-1910), combined realism in description and character development with an atypical moralizing, which came to dominate his later work. Tolstoy's greatest work was *War and Peace,* a monumental novel set against the historical background of Napoleon's invasion of Russia in 1812. Tolstoy probes deeply into the lives of a multitude of unforgettable characters, such as the ill-fated Prince Andrei, the shy, fumbling Pierre, and the enchanting, level-headed Natasha. Tolstoy goes to great pains to develop his fatalistic theory of history, which regards free will as an illusion and the achievements of even the greatest leaders as only the channeling of historical necessity. Yet Tolstoy's central message

GEORGE ELIOT *Reared in a strict religious atmosphere against which she later rebelled, Mary Ann Evans accepted scientific attitudes but never lost a strong moral sense of personal responsibility. Her first novels appeared when she was in her early forties. (Historical Pictures Service)*

is one that most of the people discussed in this chapter would readily accept: human love, trust, and everyday family ties are life's enduring values.

Thoroughgoing realism (or naturalism, as it was often called) arrived late in the United States, most arrestingly in the work of Theodore Dreiser (1871–1945). Dreiser's first novel, *Sister Carrie* (1900), the story of an ordinary farm girl who does well going wrong in Chicago, so outraged conventional morality that the publisher withdrew the book. The

United States subsequently became a bastion of literary realism in the twentieth century, after the movement had faded away in Europe.

———◆———

The Industrial Revolution had a decisive influence on the urban environment. The populations of towns and cities grew rapidly because it was economically advantageous to locate factories and offices in urban areas. This rapid growth worsened longstanding overcrowding and unhealthy living conditions, and posed a frightening challenge for society. Eventually government leaders, city planners, reformers, scientists, and ordinary citizens responded. They took effective action in public health and provided themselves with other badly needed urban services. Gradually they tamed the ferocious savagery of the traditional city.

As urban civilization came to prevail, there were major changes in family life. Especially among the lower classes, family life became more stable, more loving, and less mercenary. These improvements had a price, though. Sex roles for men and women became sharply defined and rigidly separate. Women especially tended to be locked into a subordinate and stereotypic role. Nonetheless, on balance, the quality of family life improved for all family members. Better, more stable family relations reinforced the benefits for the masses of higher real wages, expanding social security systems, greater political participation, and more education.

While the quality of urban and family life improved, the class structure became more complex and diversified than before. Urban society featured many distinct social groups, which existed in a state of constant flux and competition. Thus, the gap between rich and poor remained enormous and really quite traditional in mature urban society, although

there were countless gradations between the extremes. Large numbers of poor women in particular continued to labor as workers in sweated industries, as domestic servants, and as prostitutes in order to satisfy the demands of their masters in the servant-keeping classes. Urban society in the late nineteenth century represented a great step forward for humanity, but it remained very unequal.

Inequality was a favorite theme of realist novelists like Balzac and Zola. More generally, literary realism reflected Western society's growing faith in science, progress, and evolutionary thinking. The emergence of urban, industrial civilization accelerated the secularization of Western thought and the Western world-view.

NOTES

1. A. Weber, *The Growth of Cities in the Nineteenth Century,* Columbia University Press, New York, 1899, p. 1.

2. Quoted by W. Ashworth, *The Genesis of Modern British Town Planning,* Routledge & Kegan Paul, London, 1954, p. 17.

3. S. Marcus, "Reading the Illegible," in *The Victorian City: Images and Realities,* ed. H. J. Dyos and Michael Wolff, Routledge & Kegan Paul, London, 1973, 1.266.

4. E. Gauldie, *Cruel Habitations: A History of Working-Class Housing, 1780–1918,* George Allen & Unwin, London, 1974, p. 21.

5. Quoted in E. Chadwick, *Report on the Sanitary Condition of the Labouring Population of Great Britain,* ed. M. W. Flinn, University Press, Edinburgh, 1965 (originally published, 1842), pp. 315–316.

6. J. P. McKay, *Tramways and Trolleys: The Rise of Urban Mass Transport in Europe,* Princeton University Press, Princeton, N.J., 1976, p. 81.

7. Quoted by R. P. Neuman, "The Sexual Ques-

tion and Social Democracy in Imperial Germany," *Journal of Social History* 7 (Winter 1974):276.

8. Quoted by B. Harrison, "Underneath the Victorians," *Victorian Studies* 10 (March 1967):260.

9. Quoted by J. A. Banks, "The Contagion of Numbers," in Dyos and Wolff, 1.112.

10. R. Roberts, *The Classic Slum: Salford Life in the First Quarter of the Century,* University Press, Manchester, 1971, p. 95.

11. Quoted by B. Harrison, "Pubs," in Dyos and Wolff, 1.175.

12. Quoted by E. Shorter, *The Making of the Modern Family,* Basic Books, New York, 1975, p. 150.

13. Quoted by J. M. Phayer, "Lower-Class Morality: The Case of Bavaria," *Journal of Social History* 8 (Fall 1974):89.

14. Quoted by T. Zeldin, *France, 1848–1945,* Clarendon Press, Oxford, 1973, 1.288.

15. Quoted by S. Marcus, *The Other Victorians: A Study of Sexuality and Pornography in Mid-Nineteenth-Century England,* Basic Books, New York, 1966, p. 142.

16. Quoted by G. S. Jones, "Working-Class Culture and Working-Class Politics in London, 1870–1900: Notes on the Remaking of a Working Class," *Journal of Social History* 7 (Summer 1974): 486.

17. Quoted by Zeldin, 1.346.

18. Quoted by Shorter, pp. 230–231.

19. R. Roberts, p. 35.

20. Quoted by Zeldin, 1.295.

21. Ibid., 1.328.

22. Quoted by Neuman, p. 281.

23. Quoted by S. Kern, "Explosive Intimacy: Psychodynamics of the Victorian Family," *History of Childhood Quarterly* 1 (Winter 1974):439.

24. A. Comte, *The Positive Philosophy of Auguste Comte,* trans. H. Martineau, J. Chapman, London, 1853, 1. 1–2.

25. Quoted by G. J. Becker, ed., *Documents of Modern Literary Realism,* Princeton University Press, Princeton, N.J., 1963, p. 159.

SUGGESTED READING

All of the books and articles cited in the Notes are highly recommended; each in its own way is an important contribution to social history and life in the urban society. Note that the *Journal of Social History,* which has a strong European orientation, is excellent both for its articles and for its reviews of new books. T. Zeldin, *France, 1848–1945,* 2 vols. (1973, 1977), is a pioneering social history that opens many doors.

On the European city, D. Pinkney, *Napoleon III and the Rebuilding of Paris* (1972), is fascinating, as are G. Masur, *Imperial Berlin* (1970), and M. Hamm, ed., *The City in Russian History* (1976). So also are N. Evenson's beautifully illustrated *Paris: A Century of Change, 1878–1978* (1979), D. Grew's authoritative *Town in the Ruhr: A Social History of Bochum, 1860–1914* (1979), and the essays in J. Merriman, ed., *French Cities in the 19th Century: Class, Power, and Urbanization* (1982). D. Olsen's scholarly *Growth of Victorian London* (1978) complements H. Mayhew's wonderful contemporary study, *London Labour and the Labouring Poor* (1861), reprinted recently. M. Crichton's realistic historical novel on organized crime, *The Great Train Robbery* (1976), is excellent. J. J. Tobias, *Urban Crime in Victorian England* (1972), is a lively, scholarly approach to declining criminal activity in the nineteenth century, with a wealth of detail. G. Rosen, *History of Public Health* (1958), is an excellent introduction to medical developments. For society as a whole, J. Burnett, *History of the Cost of Living* (1969), cleverly shows how different classes spent their money, and B. Tuchman, *The Proud Tower* (1966), draws an unforgettable portrait of people and classes before 1914. J. Laver's handsomely illustrated *Manners and Morals in the Age of Optimism, 1848–1914* (1966), investigates the urban underworld and relations between the sexes. Sexual attitudes are also examined by E. Trudgill, *Madonnas and Magdalenas: The Origin and Development of Victorian Sexual Attitudes* (1976), A. McLaren, *Sexuality and Social Order: Birth Control in Nine-*

teenth-Century France (1982), and J. Phayer, *Sexual Liberation and Religion in Nineteenth Century Europe* (1977).

Women are coming into their own in historical studies. In addition to the general works by Shorter, Wrigley, Stone, and Tilly and Scott cited in Chapter 20, there are a growing number of eye-opening, specialized investigations. These include L. Davidoff, *The Best Circles* (1973), on upper-class society types; O. Banks, *Feminism and Family Planning in Victorian England* (1964); and Patricia Branca, *Women in Europe Since 1750* (1978). L. Holcombe, *Victorian Ladies at Work* (1973), pioneers in examining middle-class women at work. M. Vicinus, ed., *Suffer and Be Still* (1972), and *A Widening Sphere* (1981), are far-ranging collections of essays on women's history, as is R. Bridenthal and C. Koonz, eds., *Becoming Visible: Women in European History* (1976). Feminism is treated perceptively in R. Evans, *The Feminists: Women's Emancipation in Europe, America, and Australia* (1979), and K. Blair, *The Clubwoman as Feminist: True Womanhood Redefined, 1868–1914* (1980). J. Gillis, *Youth and History* (1974), is a good introduction. D. Ransel, ed., *The Family in Imperial Russia* (1978), is an important work on the subject, as is J. Donzelot, *The Policing of Families* (1979), which stresses the loss of family control of all aspects of life to government agencies.

Among studies of special groups, J. Scott, *The Glass-Workers of Carmaux* (1974), is outstanding on skilled French craftsmen, and D. Lockwood, *The Blackcoated Worker* (1958), carefully examines class consciousness in the English lower middle class. Two fine studies on universities and their professors are S. Rothblatt, *Revolution of the Dons: Cambridge and Society in Victorian England* (1968), and F. Ringer, *The Decline of the German Mandarins* (1969). Servants and their employers receive excellent treatment in T. McBride, *The Domestic Revolution: The Modernization of Household Service in England and France, 1820–1920* (1976), and B. Smith, *Ladies of the Leisure Class: The Bourgeoises of Northern France in the Nineteenth Century* (1981), which may be compared with the innovative study by M. Miller, *The Bon Marché: Bourgeois Culture and the Department Store, 1869–1920* (1981).

On Darwin, M. Ruse, *The Darwinian Revolution* (1979), is a good starting point. The masterpieces of the great realist social novelists remain one of the best and most memorable introductions to nineteenth-century culture and thought. In addition to the novels discussed in this chapter, and those cited in the Suggested Reading for Chapters 22 and 23, Ivan Turgenev's *Fathers and Sons* and Zola's *The Dram-Shop (L'Assommoir)* are especially recommended.

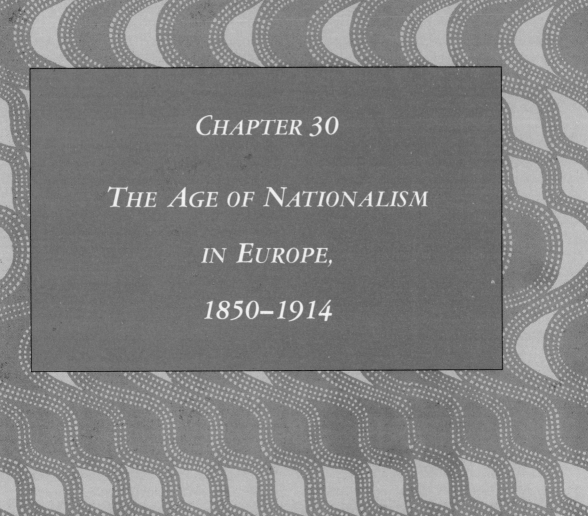

CHAPTER 30

THE AGE OF NATIONALISM

IN EUROPE,

1850–1914

THE REVOLUTIONS OF 1848 closed one era and opened another. Urban industrial society began to take strong hold on the Continent, as it already had in Great Britain. Internationally, the repressive peace and diplomatic stability of Metternich's time was replaced by a period of war and rapid change. In thought and culture soaring romanticism gave way to tough-minded realism. In the European economy the hard years of the 1840s were followed by good times and prosperity throughout most of the 1850s and 1860s. Perhaps most important of all, European society progressively found, for better or worse, a new and effective organizing principle, capable of coping with the many-sided challenge of the dual revolution and the emerging urban civilization. That principle was nationalism – dedication to and identification with the nation-state.

The triumph of nationalism in Europe after 1850 is a development of enormous historical significance. It was by no means completely predictable. After all, nationalism had been a powerful force since at least 1789. Yet it had repeatedly failed to realize its goals, most spectacularly so in 1848. Why, then, did nationalism become in one way or another an almost universal faith in Europe between 1850 and 1914? More specifically, how did nationalism evolve so that it appealed not only to predominantly middle-class liberals but to the broad masses of society as well? These are the weighty questions this chapter seeks to answer.

NAPOLEON III IN FRANCE

Early nationalism was at least liberal and idealistic and often democratic and radical as well. The ideas of nationhood and popular sovereignty posed an awesome revolutionary threat to conservatives like Metternich. Yet, from the vantage point of the twentieth century, it is clear that nationalism wears many masks: it may be democratic and radical, as it was for Mazzini and Michelet; but it can also flourish in dictatorial states, which may be conservative, fascist, or communist. Napoleon I's France had already combined national devotion with authoritarian rule. Significantly, it was Napoleon's nephew, Louis Napoleon, who revived and extended this merger. It was he who showed how governments could reconcile popular and conservative forces in an authoritarian nationalism. In doing so, he provided a model for political leaders elsewhere.

THE SECOND REPUBLIC AND LOUIS NAPOLEON

The overwhelming victory of Louis Napoleon Bonaparte in the French presidential elections of December 1848 has long puzzled historians. The nephew of Napoleon I, Louis Napoleon had lived most of his life outside of France and played no part in French politics before 1848. Why did universal manhood suffrage give such an unproven nobody 5.5 million votes, while the runner-up, General Cavaignac of June Days fame, polled only 1.5 million and the other three candidates (including the poet Lamartine) received insignificant support?

The usual explanation is that, though Louis Napoleon had only his great name in common with his uncle, that was enough. According to some historians, the Napoleonic legend – a monument to the power of romanticism between 1820 and 1848 – had transformed a dictator into a demigod in the minds of the unsophisticated French masses.

Another explanation, popularized by Karl Marx, has stressed the fears of middle-class and peasant property owners in the face of the socialist challenge of urban workers. These classes wanted protection. They wanted a tough cop with a big stick on the beat. They found him in Louis Napoleon, who had indeed served briefly as a special constable in London at the height of the Chartist agitation.

These explanations are not wrong, but there was more to Louis Napoleon's popularity than stupidity and fear. In late 1848, Louis Napoleon had a positive "program" for France, which was to guide him throughout most of his long reign. This program had been elaborated earlier in two pamphlets, *Napoleonic Ideas* and *The Elimination of Poverty,* which Louis Napoleon had written while imprisoned for a farcical attempt to overthrow Louis Philippe's government. The pamphlets had been widely circulated prior to the presidential election.

Louis Napoleon believed that the government should represent the people and that it should also try hard to help them economically. How was this to be done? Parliaments and political parties were not the answer, according to Louis Napoleon. Politicians represented special interest groups, particularly middle-class ones. When they ran a parliamentary government, they stirred up class hatreds because they were not interested in helping the poor. This had occurred under Louis Philippe, and it was occurring again under the Second Republic. The answer was a strong, even authoritarian, national leader, like the first Napoleon, who would serve all the people, rich and poor. This leader would be linked to the people by direct democracy and universal male suffrage. Sovereignty would flow from the entire population to the leader, and would not be diluted or corrupted by politicians and legislative bodies.

These political ideas went hand in hand with Louis Napoleon's vision of national unity and social progress. Unlike his uncle, who had reduced unemployment and social tensions by means of foreign wars, Louis Napoleon favored peaceful measures to relieve the awful poverty of the poor. Rather than doing nothing or providing only temporary relief, the state and its leader had a sacred duty to provide jobs and stimulate the economy. All classes would benefit by such action.

Louis Napoleon's political and social ideas were at least vaguely understood by large numbers of French peasants and workers in December 1848. To many common people he appeared to be both a strong man *and* a forward-looking champion of their interests, and that is why they voted for him.

Elected to a four-year term, President Louis Napoleon had to share power with a conservative National Assembly. With some misgivings he signed a bill to increase greatly the role of the Catholic church in primary and secondary education. In France as elsewhere in Europe after 1848, anxious "haves" saw religion as a bulwark against radicalism. As one leader of the church in France put it, "There is only one recipe for making those who own nothing believe in property-rights: that is to make them believe in God, who dictated the Ten Commandments and who promises eternal punishment to those who steal."[1] Very reluctantly, Louis Napoleon also signed another conservative law depriving many poor people of the right to vote. He took these conservative measures for two main reasons: he wanted the assembly to vote funds to pay his personal debts, and he wanted it to change the constitution so he could run for a second term.

The assembly did neither. Thus, in 1851 Louis Napoleon began to organize a conspiracy with key army officers. On December 2, 1851, he illegally dismissed the assembly and seized power in a coup d'état. There was some armed resistance in Paris and other cities, but the actions of the assembly had left the Second Republic with few defenders. Like his uncle, Louis Napoleon called on the French people to legalize his actions. They did. Ninety-two percent voted to make him a strong president for ten years. A year later, 97 percent agreed in a national plebiscite to make him hereditary emperor. For the third time, and by the greatest margin yet, the authoritarian Louis Napoleon was overwhelmingly elected by universal male suffrage to lead the French nation.

NAPOLEON III'S SECOND EMPIRE

Louis Napoleon – now Emperor Napoleon III – experienced both success and failure between 1852 and 1870. His greatest success was with the economy, particularly in the 1850s. His government encouraged the new investment banks and massive railroad construction that were at the heart of the industrial revolution on the Continent. General economic expansion was also fostered by the government's ambitious program of public works, which included the rebuilding of Paris to improve the urban environment. The profits of businessmen soared with prosperity, and the working classes did not fare poorly either. Their wages more than kept up with inflation, and jobs were much easier to find. France's economy benefited from a worldwide economic boom and other external events, such as gold discoveries in California and Australia. Yet the contribution of Napoleon III's economic policies was real all the same.

Louis Napoleon always hoped that economic progress would reduce social and political tensions. This hope was at least partially realized. Until the mid-1860s there was little active opposition and even considerable support for his government from France's most dissatisfied group, the urban workers. Napoleon III's regulation of pawnshops and his support of credit unions and better housing for the working class were evidence of positive concern in the 1850s. In the 1860s, he granted workers the right to form unions and the right to strike – important economic rights denied by earlier governments.

At first, political power remained in the hands of the emperor. He alone chose his ministers, and they had great freedom of action. At the same time Napoleon III restricted but did not abolish the assembly. To be sure, the French parliament in the 1850s had little power. It could not initiate legislation, and it did not control the budget. Parliamentary sessions were not open to the public, and the government permitted only a dry summary of its debates to be published. Yet the members of the assembly were elected by universal male suffrage every six years. In each district the government put up its candidate and permitted opposition candidates, although it restricted speeches and discussions during the electoral campaigns.

Louis Napoleon and his government took the parliamentary elections very seriously. They tried to entice notable people, even those who had opposed the regime, to stand as government candidates in order to expand its base of support. Moreover, the government rewarded districts that elected government candidates. It used its officials and appointed mayors to spread the word that the election of the government's candidate was the key to roads, schools, tax rebates, and a thousand other local concerns.

In 1857 and again in 1863, Louis Napo-

REBUILDING PARIS Cutting new boulevards through Paris was like smashing superhighways through cities today. Expensive and time-consuming, it brought massive demolitions, considerable slum clearance, and protests that the old city was being ruined.

In addition to expecting economic benefits, Napoleon III rightly believed that broad boulevards would be harder for revolutionaries to barricade than narrow twisting streets. (The Mansell Collection)

leon's system worked well and produced overwhelming electoral victories. The poet-politician Alphonse de Lamartine was convinced that Louis Napoleon was France's greatest politician since Talleyrand, and possibly even greater than he. Yet in the course of the 1860s Napoleon III's electoral system gradually disintegrated, for several reasons. France's problems in Italy and the rising power of Prussia led to increasing criticism at home from his Catholic and nationalist sup-

porters. With increasing effectiveness, the middle-class liberals who had always detested his dictatorship continued to denounce his rule as a disgrace to France's republican tradition.

Napoleon was always sensitive to the public mood. Public opinion, he once said, always wins the last victory. Thus in the 1860s he progressively "liberalized" his empire. He gave the assembly greater powers and the opposition candidates greater freedom, which they used to good advantage. In 1869 the opposition, consisting of republicans, monarchists, and liberals, polled almost 45 percent of the vote.

The following year a sick and weary Louis Napoleon once again granted France a new constitution, which combined a basically parliamentary regime with a hereditary emperor as chief of state. In a final great plebiscite on the eve of a disastrous war with Prussia, 7.5 million Frenchmen voted in favor of the new constitution, and only 1.5 million opposed it. Napoleon III's attempt to reconcile a strong national state with universal manhood suffrage was still evolving, in a democratic direction.

NATION BUILDING IN ITALY AND GERMANY

Louis Napoleon's triumph in 1848 and his authoritarian rule in the 1850s provided the old ruling classes of Europe with a new model in politics. As the great Swiss historian Jacob Burckhardt later noted, "Louis Napoleon had risked universal suffrage for the elections, and others followed his lead. The conservative streak in the rural populations had been recognized, though no attempt had been made to assess precisely how far it might be extended from the elections to everything and everybody."[2] To what extent was it possible that the expanding urban middle classes and even the growing working classes might, like people in rural areas, rally to a strong and essentially conservative national state? This was one of the great political questions in the 1850s and 1860s. In central Europe a resounding and definitive answer came with the national unification of Italy and Germany.

Italy had never been a united nation prior to 1860. Part of Rome's great empire in ancient times, the Italian peninsula was divided in the Middle Ages into competing city-states, which led the commercial and cultural revival of the West with amazing creativity. A battleground for great powers after 1494, Italy had been reorganized in 1815 at the Congress of Vienna. The rich northern provinces of Lombardy and Venetia were taken by Metternich's Austria. Sardinia and Piedmont were under the rule of an Italian monarch, and Tuscany with its famous capital of Florence shared north central Italy with several smaller states. Central Italy and Rome were ruled by the papacy, which had always considered an independent political existence necessary to fulfill its spiritual mission. Naples and Sicily were ruled, as they had been for almost a hundred years, by a branch of the Bourbons. Metternich was not wrong in dismissing Italy as "a geographical expression" (see Map 30.1).

Between 1815 and 1848, the goal of a unified Italian nation captured the imaginations of increasing numbers of Italians. There were three basic approaches. The first was the radical program of the idealistic patriot Mazzini, who preached a centralized democratic republic based on universal suffrage and the will of the people. The second was that of Gioberti, a Catholic priest, who called for a federation of existing states under the presidency of a progressive pope. Finally, there were those who looked for leadership toward the autocratic kingdom of Sardinia-Piedmont, much as many Germans looked toward Prussia.

The third alternative was strengthened by the failures of 1848, when Austria smashed and discredited Mazzini's republicanism. Almost by accident, Sardinia's monarch Victor

AUSTRIAN EMPIRE

SWITZERLAND

FRANCE

Legend:
- Kingdom of Sardinia before 1859
- To Kingdom of Sardinia, 1859
- To Kingdom of Sardinia, 1860
- To Kingdom of Italy, 1866, 1870
- ✕ Major battle

SAVOY
To France 1860

LOMBARDY
From Austria

VENETIA
From Austria, 1866

Trieste

Magenta ✕ • Milan
Turin

Villafranca
Solferino ✕

Venice

Po

PARMA

PIEDMONT

MODENA

Genoa

ROMAGNA

Bologna

To France 1860 ➔

NICE

THE MARCHES

ADRIATIC SEA

OTTOMAN EMPIRE

Nice

Pisa

Florence

Marseilles

TUSCANY

Tiber

KINGDOM

CORSICA
(FRANCE)

OF

SARDINIA

PAPAL STATES
(1870)

Rome

Naples

Bari

Taranto

SARDINIA

TYRRHENIAN SEA

KINGDOM OF
THE TWO SICILIES

MEDITERRANEAN SEA

Palermo

Straits of Messina

SICILY

0   50   100 Km.
0   50   100 Mi.

MAP 30.1 THE UNIFICATION OF ITALY, 1859–1870 The leadership of Sardinia-Piedmont and nationalist fervor were decisive factors in the dramatic political unification of the Italian peninsula.

Emmanuel retained the liberal constitution granted under duress in March 1848. This constitution provided for a fair degree of civil liberties and real parliamentary government, complete with elections and parliamentary control of taxes. To the Italian middle classes, Sardinia appeared to be a liberal, progressive state, ideally suited to achieve the goal of national unification. By contrast, Mazzini's brand of democratic republicanism seemed quixotic and too radical. As for the papacy, Pius IX's cautious support for unification had given way to fear and hostility during the upheavals of 1848. For a long generation, the papacy would stand resolutely opposed not only to national unification but to almost all modern trends.

CAVOUR AND GARIBALDI

Sardinia had the good fortune of being led by a brilliant statesman, Count Camillo Benso di Cavour, the dominant figure in the Sardinian government from 1850 until his death in 1861. Cavour's development was an early sign of the coming tacit alliance between the aristocracy and the solid middle class throughout much of Europe. Beginning as a successful manager of his father's large landed estates in Piedmont, Cavour was also an economic liberal. He turned toward industry and made a substantial fortune in sugar mills, steamships, banks, and railroads. Economically secure, he then entered the world of politics and became chief minister in the liberalized Sardinian monarchy. Cavour's national goals were limited and realistic. Until 1859, he sought unity only for the states of northern and perhaps central Italy in a greatly expanded kingdom of Sardinia. It was not one of his goals to incorporate the papal states or the kingdom of the Two Sicilies, with their very different cultures

and governments, into an Italy of all the Italians. Cavour was a moderate nationalist.

In the 1850s, Cavour worked to consolidate Sardinia as a liberal state capable of leading northern Italy. His program of highways and railroads, of civil liberties and opposition to clerical privilege, increased support for Sardinia throughout nothern Italy. Yet Cavour realized that Sardinia could not drive Austria out of Lombardy and Venetia and unify northern Italy under Victor Emmanuel without the help of a powerful ally. He sought that ally in the person of Napoleon III, who sincerely believed in the general principle of nationality, as well as modest expansion for France.

In a complicated series of diplomatic maneuvers, Cavour in 1854 entered the Crimean War against Russia on the side of Great Britain and France, and tenaciously worked for a diplomatic alliance with Napoleon III against Austria. Finally, he succeeded. In July 1858, Cavour and Napoleon III agreed orally in the utmost secrecy that if Cavour could goad Austria into attacking Sardinia, France would come to Sardinia's "defense."

For a time Cavour feared that an international congress and a diplomatic compromise would thwart his plans. But in the end Austria obligingly issued an ultimatum and declared war. Napoleon III came to Sardinia's defense. Then, after the victory of the combined Franco-Sardinian forces, he did a complete about-face. Nauseated by the gore of war and criticized by French Catholics for supporting the pope's declared enemy, Napoleon III abandoned Cavour. He made a compromise peace with the Austrians at Villafranca in July 1859. Sardinia would receive only Lombardy, the area around Milan. The rest of the map of Italy would remain essentially unchanged. Cavour resigned in a rage.

Yet Cavour's plans were salvaged by popular revolts and Italian nationalism. While the war against Austria had raged in the north, dedicated nationalists in central Italy had risen and driven out their rulers. Nationalist fervor seized the urban masses. Large crowds demonstrated, chanting "Italy and Victor Emmanuel," and singing passionately, "Foreigners, get out of Italy!" Buoyed up by this enthusiasm, the leaders of the nationalist movement in central Italy ignored the compromise peace of Villafranca and called for fusion with Sardinia. This was not at all what France and the other Great Powers wanted, but the nationalists held firm and eventually had their way. Cavour returned to power in early 1860 and worked out a diplomatic deal with Napoleon III. The people of central Italy voted overwhelmingly to join a greatly enlarged kingdom of Sardinia. Cavour had achieved his original goal of a north Italian state (see Map 30.1).

For superpatriots like Giuseppe Garibaldi (1801–1882), the job of unification was still only half done. The son of a poor sailor, Garibaldi personified the romantic, revolutionary nationalism of Mazzini and 1848. As a lad of seventeen he had traveled to Rome and been converted to "the New Italy, the Italy of all the Italians." As he later wrote in his *Autobiography,* "The Rome that I beheld with the eyes of youthful imagination was the Rome of the future – the dominant thought of my whole life." Sentenced to death in 1834 for his part in an uprising in Genoa, Garibaldi escaped to South America. For twelve years he led a guerrilla band in Uruguay's struggle for independence. "Shipwrecked, ambushed, shot through the neck," he found in a tough young woman, Anna da Silva, a mate and companion in arms. Their first children nearly starved in the jungle while Garibaldi, clad in his long red shirt, fashioned a legend not unlike that of the Cuban Ché Guevara in recent times. He returned to Italy to fight in 1848, and led a corps of volunteers against Austria in 1859. By the spring of 1860, Garibaldi had emerged as a powerful independent force in Italian politics.

Partly to use him and partly to get rid of him, Cavour secretly supported Garibaldi's bold plan to "liberate" Sicily. Landing in Sicily in May 1860, Garibaldi's guerrilla band of a thousand "Red Shirts" captured the imagination of the Sicilian peasantry. Outwitting the twenty-thousand-man royal army, the guerrilla leader took Palermo. Then he and his men crossed to the mainland, marched triumphantly toward Naples, and prepared to attack Rome and the pope. But the wily Cavour quickly sent Sardinian forces to occupy most of the Papal States (but not Rome) and to intercept Garibaldi.

Cavour realized that an attack on Rome would bring about war with France, and he also feared Garibaldi's popular appeal. Therefore, he immediately organized a plebiscite in the conquered territories. Despite the urging of some of his more radical supporters, the patriotic Garibaldi did not oppose Cavour, and the people of the south voted to join Sardinia. When Garibaldi and Victor Emmanuel rode through Naples to cheering crowds, they symbolically sealed the union of north and south, of monarch and people.

Cavour had succeeded. He had controlled Garibaldi and had turned popular nationalism in a conservative direction. The new kingdom of Italy, which did not include Venice until 1866 or Rome until 1870, was neither radical nor democratic. Italy was a parliamentary monarchy under Victor Emmanuel, but in accordance with the Sardinian constitution only a small minority of Italians had the right to

GARIBALDI LANDING IN SICILY *With a thousand volunteers the flamboyant Garibaldi conquered
the kingdom of the Two Sicilies in 1860 and paved the
way for Italian unification. (Historical Pictures Service, Chicago)*

vote. There was a definite division between the propertied classes and the common people. There was also a great social and cultural gap between the progressive, industrializing north and the stagnant, agrarian south. This gap would increase, since peasant industries in the south would not be able to survive. Italy was united politically. Other divisions remained.

GERMANY BEFORE BISMARCK

In the aftermath of 1848, while Louis Napoleon consolidated his rule and Cavour schemed, the German states were locked in a political stalemate. With Russian diplomatic support, Austria had blocked the halfhearted attempt of Frederick William IV of Prussia (1840-1861) to unify Germany "from above." This action contributed to a growing tension between Austria and Prussia, as each power sought to block the other within the reorganized German Confederation (pages 1021 and 1050). Stalemate also prevailed in the domestic politics of the individual states, as Austria, Prussia, and the smaller German kingdoms entered a period of reaction and immobility.

At the same time powerful economic forces were undermining the political status quo. As we have seen, modern industry grew rapidly in Europe throughout the 1850s. Nowhere was this growth more rapid than within the German customs union (Zollverein). Developing gradually under Prussian leadership after 1818 and founded officially in 1834 to stimulate trade and increase the revenues of member states, the customs union had not included Austria. After 1848, it became a crucial factor in the Austro-Prussian rivalry.

Tariff duties were substantially reduced so that Austria's highly protected industry could not bear to join. In retaliation, Austria tried to destroy the Zollverein by inducing the south German states to leave it, but without success. Indeed, by the end of 1853 all the German states except Austria had joined the customs union. A new Germany excluding Austria was becoming an economic reality, and the middle class and business groups were finding solid economic reasons to bolster their idealistic support of national unification. Thus, economic developments helped Prussia greatly in its struggle against Austria's traditional supremacy in German affairs.

The national uprising in Italy in 1859 made a profound impression in the German states. In Prussia, great political change and war — perhaps with Austria, perhaps with France — seemed quite possible. The tough-minded William I of Prussia (1858-1888), who had replaced the unstable Frederick William IV as regent in 1858 and became king in 1861, and his top military advisers were convinced of the need for major army reforms. William I wanted to double the size of the regular army. He also wanted to reduce the importance of the reserve militia, a semipopular force created during the Napoleonic wars. William had contempt for the "dirty reservists," those "civilians in uniform," who lacked efficiency and complete obedience. By drafting every young man into the army for three years, the king and his conservative supporters hoped to promote military attitudes in daily life. Of course, reform of the army meant a bigger defense budget and higher taxes.

Prussia had emerged from 1848 with a parliament of sorts, and by 1859 the Prussian parliament was in the hands of the liberal middle class. The middle class, like the landed aristocracy, was overrepresented by the Prussian electoral system, and it wanted society to be less, not more, militaristic. Above all, middle-class representatives wanted to establish

OTTO VON BISMARCK This photo accurately portrays Bismarck's ferocity and determination as a political fighter. Helmets and uniforms were worn by civilian officials as well as soldiers in Prussia. (Bettmann Archive)

coach." King William considered abdicating in favor of his more liberal son. In the end, he called on Count Otto von Bismarck to head a ministry and defy the parliament. It was a momentous choice.

BISMARCK TAKES COMMAND

The most important figure in German history between Luther and Hitler, Otto von Bismarck (1815–1898) has been the object of enormous interest and debate. Like his contemporary Abraham Lincoln, Bismarck stood at the very center of a nation's development in a critical era.

A great hero to some, a great villain to others, Bismarck was above all a master of politics. Born into the Prussian landowning aristocracy, the young Bismarck was a wild and tempestuous student, given to duels and drinking. Proud of his Junker heritage – "my fathers have been born and have lived and died in the same rooms for centuries" – and always devoted to his Prussian sovereign, Bismarck had a strong personality and an unbounded desire for power.

Bismarck entered the civil service, which was the only socially acceptable career except the army for a Prussian aristocrat. But he soon found bureaucratic life unbearable and fled to his ancestral estate. The civil servant was like a musician in an orchestra, he said, and "I want to play the tune the way it sounds to me or not at all. . . . My pride bids me command rather than obey."[3] Yet in his drive for power, power for himself and for Prussia, Bismarck was extraordinarily flexible and pragmatic. "One must always have two irons in the fire," he once said. He kept his options open, pursuing one policy and then another as he moved with skill and cunning toward his goal.

Bismarck first honed his political skills as a

once and for all that parliament, not the king, had the ultimate political power. They also wanted to insure that the army was responsible to the people and not "a state within a state." These demands were popular. The parliament rejected the military budget in 1862, and the liberals triumphed so completely in new elections that the conservatives "could ride to the parliament building in a single

diplomat. Acquiring a reputation as an ultra-conservative in the Prussian assembly in 1848, he fought against Austria as the Prussian ambassador to the German Confederation from 1851 to 1859. Transferred next to St. Petersburg and then to Paris, Bismarck had an excellent opportunity to evaluate Alexander II and Napoleon III at close range. A blunt, expansive talker, especially after a few drinks, Bismarck's basic goal was well known in 1862 – to build up Prussia's strength and consolidate Prussia's precarious Great Power status.

To achieve this goal, Bismarck was convinced that Prussia had to control completely the northern, predominantly Protestant part of the German Confederation. He saw three possible paths open before him. He might work with Austria to divide up the smaller German states lying between them. Or he might combine with foreign powers – France and Italy, or even Russia – against Austria. Or he might ally with the forces of German nationalism to defeat and expel Austria from German affairs. Each possibility was explored in many complicated diplomatic maneuvers, but in the end the last path was the one Bismarck took.

That Bismarck would join with the forces of German nationalism to increase Prussia's power seemed unlikely when he took office in 1862. Bismarck's appointment made a strong but unfavorable impression. One of the liberal middle-class members of the Prussian parliament expressed enlightened public opinion throughout Prussia and the other German states: "Bismarck, that is to say: government without budget, rule by the sword in home affairs, and war in foreign affairs. I consider him the most dangerous Minister for Prussia's liberty and happiness."[4]

Bismarck's speeches were a sensation and a scandal. Declaring that the government would rule without parliamentary consent, Bismarck lashed out at the middle-class opposition: "The great questions of the day will not be decided by speeches and resolutions – that was the blunder of 1848 and 1849 – but by blood and iron." In 1863 he told the Prussian Parliament, "If a compromise cannot be arrived at and a conflict arises, then the conflict becomes a question of power. Whoever has the power then acts according to his opinion." Denounced for this view that "might makes right," Bismarck and the bureaucracy nevertheless collected taxes and reorganized the army. And for four years, from 1862 to 1866, the voters of Prussia continued to express their opposition by sending large liberal majorities to the parliament.

THE AUSTRO-PRUSSIAN WAR OF 1866

Opposition at home spurred the search for success abroad. The ever-knotty question of Schleswig-Holstein provided a welcome opportunity. When the Danish king tried again, as in 1848, to bring the provinces into a centralized Danish state against the will of the German Confederation, Prussia joined Austria in a short and successful war against Denmark in 1864. Then, rather than following nationalist sentiment and allowing the conquered provinces to become another medium-sized independent state within the German Confederation, Bismarck maneuvered Austria into a tricky position. Prussia and Austria agreed to joint administration of the conquered provinces, thereby giving Bismarck a weapon he could use either to force Austria into peacefully accepting Prussian domination in northern Germany or to start a war against Austria.

Bismarck knew that a war with Austria would have to be a localized war. He had to be certain that Prussian expansion did not provoke a mighty armed coalition, such as the coalition that had almost crushed Frederick the Great in the eighteenth century. Russia, the great bear to the east, was no problem. Bismarck had already gained Alexander II's gratitude by supporting Russia's repression of a Polish uprising in 1863. Napoleon III – the "sphinx without a riddle," according to Bismarck – was another matter. But Bismarck charmed him into neutrality with vague promises of more territory along the Rhine. Thus, when Austria proved unwilling to give up its historic role in German affairs, Bismarck was in a position to engage in a war of his own making.

The Austro-Prussian War of 1866 lasted only seven weeks. Utilizing railroads to mass troops and the new breechloading needle gun for maximum firepower, the reorganized Prussian army overran northern Germany and defeated Austria decisively at the battle of Königgrätz in Bohemia. Anticipating Prussia's future needs, Bismarck offered Austria realistic, even generous, peace terms. Austria paid no reparations and lost no territory to Prussia, although Venice was ceded to Italy. But the German Confederation was dissolved, and Austria agreed to withdraw from German affairs. The states north of the Main River were grouped in a new North German Confederation led by an expanded Prussia. The mainly Catholic states of the south were permitted to remain independent, while forming military alliances with Prussia. Bismarck's fundamental goal of Prussian expansion was being realized (see Map 30.2).

THE TAMING OF PARLIAMENT

Bismarck had long been convinced that the old order he so ardently defended should make peace – on its own terms – with the liberal middle class and the nationalist movement. Inspired somewhat by Louis Napoleon, he realized that nationalism was not necessarily hostile to conservative, authoritarian government. Moreover, Bismarck believed that because of the events of 1848 the German middle class could be led to prefer the reality of national unity to a long uncertain battle for truly liberal institutions. During the constitutional struggle over army reform and parliamentary authority, he had delayed but not abandoned this goal. Thus, during the attack on Austria in 1866 he increasingly identified Prussia's fate with the "national development of Germany."

In the aftermath of victory Bismarck fashioned a federal constitution for the new North German Confederation. Each state retained its own local government, but the king of Prussia was to be president of the confederation and the chancellor – Bismarck – was to be responsible only to the president. The federal government – William I and Bismarck – controlled the army and foreign affairs. There was also a legislature, consisting of an upper house whose delegates were appointed by the different states and a lower house. Both houses shared equally in the making of laws. Members of the lower house were elected by universal, equal manhood suffrage. With this radical innovation, Bismarck opened the door to popular participation and went over the head of the middle class directly to the people. All the while, however, ultimate power rested as securely as ever in the hands of Prussia and its king and army.

Events within Prussia itself were even more significant than those at the federal level. In the flush of victory the ultraconservatives expected Bismarck to suspend the Prussian constitution or perhaps abolish the Prussian parliament altogether. Yet he did nothing of

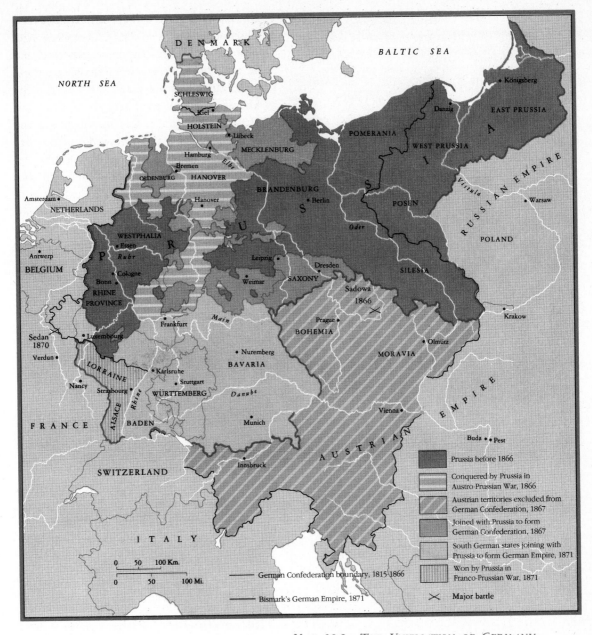

NORTH SEA

DENMARK

BALTIC SEA

SCHLESWIG

Kiel

HOLSTEIN

Lübeck

Hamburg

Bremen

MECKLENBURG

POMERANIA

WEST PRUSSIA

Königsberg

EAST PRUSSIA

Danzig

S

I

A

RUSSIAN EMPIRE

Amsterdam

NETHERLANDS

OLDENBURG

HANOVER

Hanover

Berlin

BRANDENBURG

S

U

R

Oder

POSEN

Vistula

Warsaw

POLAND

Antwerp

BELGIUM

P

WESTPHALIA

Essen

Ruhr

Cologne

Bonn

RHINE
PROVINCE

Leipzig

Weimar

SAXONY

Dresden

Sadowa
1866

SILESIA

Krakow

Frankfurt

Main

Prague

BOHEMIA

Olmütz

MORAVIA

Sedan
1870

Luxembourg

Verdun

Nuremberg

BAVARIA

LORRAINE

Nancy

Karlsruhe

Strasbourg

Stuttgart

ALSACE

Rhine

WÜRTTEMBERG

Danube

Munich

Vienna

AUSTRIAN EMPIRE

FRANCE

BADEN

Innsbruck

SWITZERLAND

Buda

Pest

Prussia before 1866

Conquered by Prussia in
Austro-Prussian War, 1866

Austrian territories excluded from
German Confederation, 1867

ITALY

Joined with Prussia to form
German Confederation, 1867

South German states joining with
Prussia to form German Empire, 1871

Won by Prussia in
Franco-Prussian War, 1871

0   50   100 Km.

0   50   100 Mi.

German Confederation boundary, 1815–1866

Bismark's German Empire, 1871

× Major battle

MAP 30.2   THE UNIFICATION OF GERMANY,
1866–1871   *This map deserves careful study. Note
how Prussian expansion, Austrian expulsion from the
old German Confederation, and the creation of a new
German Empire went hand in hand. Austria lost no
territory but Prussia's neighbors in the north suffered
grievously or simply disappeared.*

Sein erster Gedanke von Th. Th. Heine

Ueberschreiten der Geleise verboten!

Fatal! Jetzt kann ich nicht mehr Reserveoffizier sein.

"HIS FIRST THOUGHT"   This 1896 cartoon provides a brilliant commentary on German middle-class
attitudes. Suddenly crippled, the man's first thought is
"Disaster! Now I can no longer be an army reserve
officer." Being a part-time junior officer, below the
dominant aristocratic career officers, became a great
middle-class status symbol. (Photo: Caroline Buckler)

the sort. Instead, he held out an olive branch
to the parliamentary opposition. Marshalling
all his diplomatic skill, Bismarck asked the
parliament to pass a special indemnity bill to
approve after the fact all of the government's
spending between 1862 and 1866. Most of the
liberals snatched at the chance to cooperate.

For four long years they had opposed and
criticized Bismarck's "illegal" measures. And
what had happened? Bismarck, the king, and
the army had persevered, and in the end these
conservative forces had succeeded beyond the
wildest dreams of the liberal middle class. In
1866, German unity was in sight, and the
people were going to be allowed to participate
actively in the new state. Many liberals repented their "sins" and were overjoyed that
Bismarck would forgive them.

None repented more ardently or more
typically than Hermann Baumgarten, a
mild-mannered, thoroughly decent history
professor and member of the liberal opposition. In an essay entitled "A Self Criticism of
German Liberalism," he confessed in 1866:

We thought by agitation we could transform Germany. But . . . almost all the elements of our political system have been shown erroneous by the
facts themselves. . . . Yet we have experienced a
miracle almost without parallel. The victory of our
principles would have brought us misery, whereas
the defeat of our principles has brought boundless
salvation.[5]

The constitutional struggle was over. The
German middle class was bowing respectfully
before Bismarck and the monarchial authority
and aristocratic superiority he represented.
They did not stand upright again in the years
before 1914.

THE FRANCO-PRUSSIAN WAR OF 1870–1871

The rest of the story of German unification is
anticlimactic. In 1867, Bismarck brought the
four south German states into the customs
union and established a customs parliament.
But the south Germans were reluctant to go
further because of their different religious and
political traditions. Bismarck realized that a
patriotic war with France would drive the

south German states into his arms. The French obligingly played their part. The apparent issue – whether a distant relative of Prussia's William I (and France's Napoleon III) might become king of Spain – was only a diplomatic pretext. By 1870 the French leaders of the Second Empire, alarmed by their powerful new neighbor on the Rhine, had decided on a war to teach Prussia a lesson.

As soon as war against France began in 1870, Bismarck had the wholehearted support of the south German states. With other governments standing still – Bismarck's generosity to Austria in 1866 was paying big dividends – German forces under Prussian leadership decisively defeated Louis Napoleon's armies at Sedan on September 1, 1870. Three days later French patriots in Paris proclaimed yet another French republic and vowed to continue fighting. But after five months, in January 1871, a starving Paris surrendered, and France went on to accept Bismarck's harsh peace terms. By this time the south German states had agreed to join a new German Empire. The victorious William I was proclaimed emperor of Germany in the Hall of Mirrors in the palace of Versailles, outside of Paris. Europe had a nineteenth-century German "sun king." As in the 1866 constitution, the king of Prussia and his ministers had ultimate power in the new empire, and the lower house of the legislature was elected popularly by universal male suffrage.

The Franco-Prussian War of 1870–1871, which Europeans generally saw as a test of nations in a pitiless Darwinian struggle for existence, released an enormous surge of patriotic feeling in Germany. Bismarck's genius, the invincible Prussian army, the solidarity of king and people in a unified nation – these and similar themes were trumpeted endlessly during and after the war. The weakest of the

Great Powers in 1862 – after Austria, Britain, France, and Russia – Prussia fortified by the other German states had become the most powerful state in Europe in less than a decade. Most Germans were enormously proud, enormously relieved. And they were somewhat drunk with success, blissfully imagining themselves the fittest and best of the European species. Semi-authoritarian nationalism had triumphed. Only a few critics remained dedicated to the liberal ideal of truly responsible parliamentary government.

THE MODERNIZATION OF RUSSIA

In Russia, unlike Italy and Germany, there was no need to build a single state out of a jumble of principalities. The vast Russian Empire was a great multinational state. In the early nineteenth century, nationalism there was a subversive ideology identified with revolution. After 1853, however, old autocratic Russia was in serious trouble. It became clear to Russia's leaders that the country had to embrace the process of "modernization."

A vague and often overworked term, *modernization* is a great umbrella under which some writers place most of the major developments of the last two hundred or even five hundred years. Yet defined narrowly – as changes that enable a country to compete effectively with the leading countries at a given time – modernization can be a useful concept. It fits Russia after the Crimean War particularly well.

THE "GREAT REFORMS"

In the 1850s, Russia was a poor agrarian society. Industry was little developed, and almost 90 percent of the population lived on

"FAREWELL,"   says the triumphant German soldier on the left in this French cartoon. "No, till we meet again," replies the French soldier. "Visits must be returned." German victory and Bismarck's seizure of French territory poisoned Franco-German relations after 1871. (Photo: Caroline Buckler)

the land. Agricultural techniques were backward: the ancient open-field system reigned supreme. Serfdom was still the basic social institution. Bound to the lord on a hereditary basis, the peasant serf was little more than a slave. Individual serfs and serf families were regularly sold, with and without land, in the early nineteenth century. Serfs were obliged to furnish labor services or money payments as the lord saw fit. Moreover, the lord could choose freely among them for army recruits, who had to serve for twenty-five years, and he could punish a serf with deportation to Si-

beria whenever he wished. Sexual exploitation of female serfs by their lords was common.

Serfdom had become the great moral and political question for the government by the 1840s, but it might still have lasted many more years had it not been for the Crimean War of 1853–1856. The war began as a dispute with France over who should protect certain Christian shrines in the Ottoman Empire. Because the fighting was concentrated in the Crimean peninsula in the Black Sea, Russia's transportation network of rivers and wagons failed to supply the distant Russian armies adequately. France and Great Britain, aided by Sardinia, inflicted a humiliating defeat on Russia.

The military defeat marked a turning point in Russian history. The Russian state had been built on the military, and Russia had not lost a major war for a century and a half. This defeat demonstrated that Russia had fallen behind the rapidly industrializing nations of western Europe in many areas. At the very least Russia needed railroads, better armaments, and reorganization of the army if it were to maintain its international position. Moreover, the disastrous war had caused hardship and raised the specter of massive peasant rebellion. Reform of serfdom was imperative. And, as the new tsar, Alexander II (1855–1881), told the serf owners, it would be better if reform came from above rather than below. Military disaster thus forced Alexander II and his ministers along the path of rapid social change and general modernization.

The first and greatest of the reforms was the freeing of the serfs in 1861. Human bondage was abolished forever, and the emancipated peasants received, on the average, about half of the land. Yet they had to pay fairly high prices for their land, and because the land was owned collectively each peasant village was jointly responsible for the payments of all the families in the village. The government hoped that collective responsibility would strengthen the peasant village as a social unit and prevent the development of a class of landless peasants. In practice, collective ownership and responsibility made it very difficult for individual peasants to improve agricultural methods or leave their villages. Thus the effects of the reform were limited, for it did not encourage peasants to change their old habits and attitudes.

Most of the later reforms were also halfway measures. In 1864, the government established a new institution of local government, the *zemstvo*. Members of this local assembly were elected by a three-class system of towns, peasant villages, and noble landowners. A zemstvo executive council dealt with local problems. The establishment of the zemstvos marked a significant step toward popular participation, and Russian liberals hoped it would lead to a national parliament. They were soon disappointed. The local zemstvo remained subordinate to the traditional bureaucracy and the local nobility, who were heavily favored by the property-based voting system. More successful was reform of the legal system, which established independent courts and equality before the law. "Almost overnight it transformed the Russian judiciary from one of the worst to one of the best in the civilized world."[6] Education was also liberalized somewhat, and censorship was relaxed but not removed.

THE INDUSTRIALIZATION OF RUSSIA

Until the twentieth century, Russia's greatest strides toward modernization were economic rather than political. Industry and transport, both so vital to the military, were transformed in two industrial surges. The first of these came after 1860. The government encouraged and subsidized private railway companies, and construction boomed. In 1860, the empire had only about 1,250 miles of railroads; by 1880, it had about 15,500 miles. The railroads enabled agricultural Russia to export grain and thus earn money for further industrialization. Domestic manufacturing was stimulated, and by the end of the 1870s Russia had a sophisticated and well-developed railway-equipment industry. Industrial suburbs grew up around Moscow and St. Petersburg, and a class of modern factory workers began to take shape.

Industrial development strengthened Russia's military forces and gave rise to territorial expansion to the south and east. Imperial expansion greatly excited many ardent Russian nationalists and superpatriots, who became some of the government's most enthusiastic supporters. Industrial development also contributed mightily to the spread of Marxian thought and the transformation of the Russian revolutionary movement after 1890.

In 1881, Alexander II was assassinated by a small group of terrorists. The era of reform came to an abrupt end, for the new tsar, Alexander III (1881–1894), was a determined reactionary. Russia, and indeed all of Europe, experienced hard times economically in the 1880s. Political modernization remained frozen until 1905, but economic modernization sped forward in the massive industrial surge of the 1890s. As it had after the Crimean War, nationalism played a decisive role. The key leader was Sergei Witte, the tough, competent minister of finance from 1892 to 1903. Early in his career Witte found in the writings of Friedrich List (page 999) an analysis and a program for action. List had stressed the peril for Germany of remaining behind England in the 1830s and 1840s. Witte saw the same threat of industrial backwardness threatening Russia's power and greatness.

NOVGOROD MERCHANTS DRINKING TEA *This photograph from the late nineteenth century suggests how Russian businessmen were slow to abandon old-fashioned dress and traditional attitudes in the face of change. Stern authoritarians in the family circle and staunchly devoted to church and tsar, Russian businessmen were often suspicious of foreigners as well as of the lawyers and journalists who claimed to speak for the nation's middle class. (BBC Hulton Picture Library)*

Witte moved forward on several fronts. A railroad manager by training, he believed that railroads were "a very powerful weapon . . . for the direction of the economic development of the country."[7] Therefore the government built railroads rapidly, doubling the network to 35,000 miles by the end of the century. The gigantic trans-Siberian line connecting Moscow with Vladivostok on the Pacific Ocean 5,000 miles away was Witte's pride, and it was largely completed during his term of office. Following List's advice, Witte raised high protective tariffs to build Russian industry, and he put the country on the gold standard of the "civilized world" in order to strengthen Russian finances.

Witte's greatest innovation, however, was to use the West to catch up with the West. He aggressively encouraged foreigners to use their abundant capital and advanced technology to build great factories in backward Russia. As he told the tsar, "The inflow of foreign capital is . . . the only way by which our industry will be able to supply our country quickly with abundant and cheap products."[8] This policy was brilliantly successful, especially in southern Russia. There, in the eastern Ukraine, foreign capitalists and their engineers built an enormous and very modern steel and coal industry almost from scratch in little more than a decade. By 1900, only the United States, Germany, and Great Britain were producing more steel than Russia. The Russian petroleum industry had even pulled up alongside that of the United States and was producing and refining half the world's output of oil.

Witte knew how to keep foreigners in line.

Once a leading foreign businessman came to him and angrily demanded that the Russian government fulfill a contract it had signed and pay certain debts immediately. Witte asked to see the contract. He read it and then carefully tore it to pieces and threw it in the waste-paper basket without a word of explanation. It was just such a fiercely independent Russia that was catching up with the advanced nations of the West.

THE REVOLUTION OF 1905

Catching up partly meant vigorous territorial expansion, for this was the age of Western imperialism. By 1903, Russia had established a sphere of influence in Chinese Manchuria and was casting greedy eyes on northern Korea. When the protests of equally imperialistic Japan went unanswered, the Japanese launched a surprise attack in February 1904. To the world's amazement, Russia suffered repeated losses and was forced to accept a humiliating defeat in August 1905.

As is often the case, military disaster abroad brought political upheaval at home. The business and professional classes had long wanted to match economic modernization with political modernization. Their minimal goal was to turn the last of Europe's absolutist monarchies into a liberal, representative regime. Factory workers, strategically concentrated in the large cities, had all the grievances of early industrialization and were organized in a radical labor movement. Peasants had gained little from the era of reforms and were suffering from poverty and overpopulation. Finally, nationalist sentiment was emerging among the empire's minorities. The politically and culturally dominant ethnic Russians were only about 45 percent of the population, and by 1900 some intellectuals among the subject nationalities were calling for self-rule and au-

tonomy. Separatist nationalism was strongest among the Polish and Ukrainians. With the army pinned down in Manchuria, all these currents of discontent came together in the revolution of 1905.

The beginning of the revolution pointed up the incompetence of the government. On a Sunday in January 1905, a massive demonstration of workers and their families converged peacefully on the Winter Palace in St. Petersburg to present a petition to the tsar. The workers were led by a trade unionist priest named Father Gapon, who had been secretly supported by the police as a preferable alternative to more radical unions. Carrying icons and respectfully singing "God Save the Tsar," the workers did not know Nicholas II had fled the city. Suddenly troops opened fire, killing and wounding hundreds. The "Bloody Sunday" massacre turned ordinary workers against the tsar and produced a wave of general indignation.

Outlawed political parties came out into the open, and by the summer of 1905 strikes, peasant uprisings, revolts among minority nationalities, and troop mutinies were sweeping the country. The revolutionary surge culminated in October 1905 in a great paralyzing general strike, which forced the government to capitulate. The tsar issued the October Manifesto, which granted full civil rights and promised a popularly elected Duma (parliament) with real legislative power. The Manifesto split the opposition. It satisfied most moderate and liberal demands, but the Social Democrats rejected it and led a bloody workers' uprising in Moscow in December 1905. Frightened middle-class moderates helped the government repress the uprising and survive as a constitutional monarchy.

On the eve of the opening of the first Duma in May 1906, the government issued the new constitution, the Fundamental Laws.

The tsar retained great powers. The Duma, elected indirectly by universal male suffrage, and a largely appointive upper house could debate and pass laws, but the tsar had an absolute veto. As in Bismarck's Germany, the emperor appointed his ministers, who did not need to command a majority in the Duma.

The disappointed, predominantly middle-class liberals, the largest group in the newly elected Duma, saw the Fundamental Laws as a great step backwards. Efforts to cooperate with the tsar's ministers soon broke down. The government then dismissed the Duma, only to find that a more hostile and radical opposition was elected in 1907. After three months of deadlock, the second Duma was also dismissed. Thereupon the tsar and his reactionary advisors unilaterally rewrote the electoral law so as to increase greatly the weight of the propertied classes at the expense of workers, peasants, and national minorities.

The new law had the intended effect. With landowners assured half the seats in the Duma, the government finally secured a loyal majority in 1907 and again in 1912. Thus armed, the tough, energetic chief minister, Peter Stolypin, pushed through important agrarian reforms designed to break down collective village ownership of land and to encourage the more enterprising peasants – the so-called "wager on the strong." On the eve of the First World War, Russia was partially modernized, a conservative constitutional monarchy with a peasant-based but industrializing economy.

THE RESPONSIVE NATIONAL STATE, 1871–1914

For central and western Europe, the unification of Italy and Germany by "blood and iron" marked the end of a dramatic period of nation building. After 1871, the heartland of Europe was organized in strong national states. Only on the borders of Europe – in Ireland and Russia, in Austria-Hungary and the Balkans – did subject peoples still strive for political unity and independence. Despite national differences, European domestic politics after 1871 had a common framework – the firmly established national state. The common themes within that framework were the emergence of mass politics and growing mass loyalty toward the national state.

For good reason, ordinary people – the masses of an industrializing, urbanizing society – felt increasing loyalty to their governments. More and more people could vote. By 1914, universal manhood suffrage was the rule rather than the exception. This development had as much psychological as political significance. Ordinary men were no longer denied the right to vote because they lacked wealth or education. They counted; they could influence the government to some extent. They could feel that they were becoming "part of the system."

Women began to demand the right to vote. The women's suffrage movement achieved its first success in the western United States, and by 1913 women could vote in twelve states. Europe too moved slowly in this direction. In 1914, Norway gave the vote to most women. Elsewhere, women like the English Emmeline Pankhurst were very militant in their demands. They heckled politicians and held public demonstrations. These efforts generally failed before 1914, but they prepared the way for the triumph of the women's suffrage movement immediately after World War One.

As the right to vote spread, politicians and parties in national parliaments represented the people more responsively. Most countries soon had many political parties. The multi-

THE GERMAN REICHSTAG IN 1871 *Bismarck (second from left on the floor) presents the government's program to the new Reichstag. The creation of a national parliament, duly elected by universal manhood suffrage, convinced many that Germany was making healthy progress. (Bildarchiv Preussischer Kulturbisitz)*

party system meant that parliamentary majorities were built on shifting coalitions, which were unstable but did give parties leverage. They could obtain benefits for their supporters. Governments increasingly passed laws to alleviate general problems and to help specific groups. Governments seemed to care, and they seemed more worthy of support.

THE GERMAN EMPIRE

Politics in Germany after 1871 reflected many of these developments. The new German Em- pire was a federal union of Prussia and twenty-four smaller states. Much of the everyday business of government was conducted by the separate states, but there was a strong national government with a chancellor – Bismarck until 1890 – and a popularly elected parliament, called the Reichstag. Although Bismarck refused to be bound by a parliamentary majority, he tried nonetheless to maintain such a majority. This situation gave the political parties opportunities. Until 1878, Bismarck relied mainly on the National Liberals, who had rallied to him after 1866. They supported legislation useful for further economic and legal unification of the country.

Less wisely, they backed Bismarck's attack on the Catholic church, the so-called *Kulturkampf,* or "struggle for civilization." Like Bismarck, the middle-class National Liberals were alarmed by Pius IX's declaration of papal infallibility in 1870. That dogma seemed to put loyalty to the church above loyalty to the nation. Only in Protestant Prussia did the *Kulturkampf* have even limited success. Catholics throughout the country generally voted for the Catholic Center party, which blocked passage of national laws hostile to the church. Finally, in 1878, Bismarck abandoned his attack. Indeed, he and the Catholic Center party entered into an uneasy but mutually advantageous alliance. The reasons were largely economic.

After a worldwide financial bust in 1873, European agriculture was in an increasingly difficult position. Wheat prices plummeted as cheap grain poured in from the United States, Canada, and Russia. New lands were opening up in North America and Russia, and the combination of railroads and technical improvements in shipping cut freight rates drastically for grain. European peasants with their smaller, less efficient farms could not compete in cereal production, especially in western and southern Germany. The peasantry there was largely Catholic, and the Catholic Center party was thus converted to the cause of higher tariffs to protect the economic interests of its supporters.

The same competitive pressures caused the Protestant Junkers who owned large estates in eastern Germany to embrace the cause of higher tariffs. They were joined by some of the iron and steel magnates of the Prussian Rhineland, who had previously been for free trade. With three such influential groups lob-

bying energetically, Bismarck was happy to go along with a new protective tariff in 1879. In doing so he won new supporters in parliament – the Center party of the Catholics and the Conservative party of the Prussian landowners – and he held on to most of the National Liberals.

Bismarck had been looking for a way to increase taxes and raise more money for the government. The solution was higher tariffs. Many other governments acted similarly. The 1880s and 1890s saw a widespread return to protectionism. France in particular established very high tariffs to protect agriculture and industry, peasants and manufacturers. Thus, the German government and other governments responded to a major economic problem and simultaneously won greater loyalty.

At the same time, Bismarck tried to stop the growth of German socialism because he genuinely feared its revolutionary language and allegiance to a movement transcending the nation state. In 1878, after two attempts on the life of William I by radicals (though not socialists), Bismarck succeeded in ramming through the Reichstag a law repressing socialists. Socialist meetings and publications were strictly forbidden. The Social Democratic party was outlawed and driven underground. However, German socialists displayed a discipline and organization worthy of the Prussian army itself. Bismarck had to try another tack.

Thus Bismarck's state pioneered with social measures designed to win the support of working-class people. In 1883, he pushed through the parliament the first of several modern social security laws to help wage earners. The laws of 1883 and 1884 established national sickness and accident insurance; the law of 1889 established old-age pensions and retirement benefits. Henceforth, sick, injured, and retired workers could look forward to regular weekly benefits from the state. This national social security system, paid for through compulsory contributions by wage earners and employers as well as grants from the state, was the first of its kind anywhere. It was to be fifty years before similar measures would be taken in the United States. Bismarck's social security system did not wean workers from socialism, but it did protect them from some of the uncertainties of the complex urban industrial world. This enormously significant development was a product of political competition and governmental efforts to win popular support.

Increasingly, the great issues in German domestic politics were socialism and the Marxian Social Democratic party. In 1890 the new emperor, the young, idealistic, and unstable William II (1888–1918), opposed Bismarck's attempt to renew the law outlawing the Social Democratic party. Eager to rule in his own right, as well as to earn the support of the workers, William II forced Bismarck to resign. After the "dropping of the pilot," German foreign policy changed profoundly and mostly for the worse, but the government did pass new laws to aid workers and to legalize socialist political activity.

Yet William II was no more successful than Bismarck in getting workers to renounce socialism. Indeed, socialist ideas spread rapidly, and more and more Social Democrats were elected to the parliament in the 1890s. After opposing a colonial war in German Southwest Africa in 1906 and thus suffering important losses in the general elections of 1907, the German Social Democratic party broadened its base in the years before World War One. In the elections of 1912 the party scored a great victory, becoming the largest single party in the Reichstag. The "revolu-

tionary" socialists were, however, becoming less and less revolutionary in Germany. In the years before World War One, the strength of socialist opposition to greater military spending and imperialist expansion declined greatly. German socialists marched under the national banner.

REPUBLICAN FRANCE

In 1871, France seemed hopelessly divided once again. The patriotic republicans who proclaimed the Third Republic in Paris after the military disaster at Sedan refused to admit defeat. They defended Paris with great heroism for weeks, living off rats and zoo animals, until they were quite literally starved into submission by German armies in January 1871. When national elections then sent a large majority of conservatives and monarchists to the National Assembly, the traumatized Parisians exploded and proclaimed the Paris Commune in March 1871. Vaguely radical, the leaders of the Commune wanted to govern Paris without interference by the conservative French countryside. The National Assembly, led by the aging politician Adolphe Thiers, would hear none of it. The Assembly ordered the French army into Paris and brutally crushed the Commune. Twenty thousand people died in the fighting. As in June 1848, it was Paris against the provinces, French against French.

Out of this tragedy France slowly formed a new national unity, achieving considerable stability before 1914. How is one to account for this? Luck played a part. Until 1875, the monarchists in the "republican" National Assembly had a majority but could not agree who should be king. The compromise Bourbon candidate refused to rule except under the white flag of his ancestors – a completely un-

THE FACE OF CIVIL WAR *Enraged radicals and anarchists set countless fires as the French army smashed the troops of the Paris Commune, which are pictured here. Most fire bombers were women. Terrible atrocities were committed on both sides. (Photo: Caroline Buckler)*

acceptable condition. In the meantime Thiers' slaying of the radical Commune and his other firm measures showed the fearful provinces and the middle class that the Third Republic might be moderate and socially conservative. France therefore retained the republic, though reluctantly and unenthusiastically. As President Thiers cautiously said, it was "the government which divides us least."

Another stabilizing factor was the skill and determination of the moderate republican leaders in the early years. The most famous of these was Léon Gambetta, the son of an Italian grocer, a warm, easygoing, unsuccessful lawyer turned professional politician. A master of emerging mass politics, Gambetta combined eloquence with the personal touch as he preached a republic of truly equal opportunity. Gambetta was also instrumental in establishing absolute parliamentary supremacy between 1877 and 1879, when the somewhat autocratic President Marie Edmé MacMahon was forced to resign. By 1879, the great majority of members of both the upper and lower houses of parliament were republicans. Although these republicans were split among many parliamentary groups and later several parties – a situation that led to constant coalition politics and the rapid turnover of ministers – the Third Republic had firm foundations after almost a decade.

The moderate republicans sought to preserve their creation by winning the hearts and minds of the next generation. Trade unions were fully legalized, and France acquired a colonial empire. More importantly, under the leadership of Jules Ferry, the moderate republicans of small towns and villages passed a series of laws between 1879 and 1886 establishing free compulsory elementary education for both girls and boys. At the same time, they greatly expanded the state system of public tax-supported schools.

This was a fundamental change. Most elementary and much secondary education had traditionally been in the parochial schools of the Catholic church, which had long been hostile to republics and to much of secular life. Free compulsory elementary education in France became secular republican education. The pledge of allegiance and the national anthem replaced the catechism and the *Ave Maria*. Militant young elementary teachers carried the ideology of patriotic republicanism into every corner of France. In their classes they sought to win the loyalty of the young citizens to the republic, so that France would never again vote en masse for dictators like the two Napoleons.

Although these educational reforms disturbed French Catholics, many of them rallied to the republic in the 1890s. The limited acceptance of the modern world by the more liberal Pope Leo XIII (1878-1903) eased tensions between church and state. Unfortunately, the Dreyfus affair changed all that.

Alfred Dreyfus, a Jewish captain in the French army, was falsely accused and convicted of treason. His family never doubted his innocence and fought unceasingly to reopen the case, enlisting the support of prominent republicans and intellectuals such as the novelist Emile Zola. In 1898 and 1899, the case split France apart. On one side was the army, which had manufactured evidence against Dreyfus, joined by anti-Semites and most of the Catholic establishment. On the other side stood the civil libertarians and most of the more radical republicans.

This battle, which eventually led to Dreyfus's being declared innocent, revived republican feeling against the church. Between 1901 and 1905, the government severed all ties between the state and the Catholic church. The salaries of priests and bishops were no longer paid by the government, and all churches were given to local committees of lay Catholics. Catholic schools were put completely on their own financially, and in a short time they lost a third of their students. The state school system's power of indoctrination was greatly strengthened. In France only the growing socialist movement, with its very different and thoroughly secular ideology, stood in opposition to patriotic, republican nationalism.

GREAT BRITAIN AND IRELAND

Britain in the late nineteenth century has often been seen as a shining example of peaceful and successful political evolution. Germany had gotten stuck with a manipulated parliament that gave an irresponsible emperor too much power; France had a quarrelsome parliament that gave its presidents too little power. Great Britain, in contrast, seemed to enjoy an effective two-party parliament that skillfully guided the country from classical liberalism to full-fledged democracy with hardly a misstep.

This view of Great Britain is not so much wrong as incomplete. The right to vote, granted to males of the solid middle class in 1832, was further extended to all middle-class men and the best-paid workers by Prime Minister Benjamin Disraeli and the Conservatives via the Second Reform Bill of 1867. The son of a Jewish stockbroker, himself a novelist and urban dandy, the ever-fascinating Disraeli (1804–1881) was willing to risk this "leap in the dark" in order to gain new supporters. The Conservative party, he believed, needed to broaden its traditional base of aristocratic and landed support if it was to survive. After 1867 English political parties and electoral campaigns became more modern, and the "lower orders" appeared to vote as responsibly as their "betters." Hence the

Third Reform Bill of 1884 gave the vote to almost every adult male.

While the House of Commons was drifting toward democracy, the House of Lords was content to slumber nobly. Between 1901 and 1910, however, that bastion of aristocratic conservatism tried to reassert itself. Acting as supreme court of the land, it ruled against labor unions in two important decisions. And, after the Liberal party came to power in 1906, the Lords vetoed several measures passed by the Commons, including the so-called People's Budget. The Lords finally capitulated, as they had done in 1832, when the king threatened to create enough new peers to pass the bill.

Aristocratic conservatism yielded to popular democracy, once and for all. The result was that extensive social welfare measures, slow to come to Great Britain, were passed in a spectacular rush between 1906 and 1914. During those years the Liberal party, inspired by the fiery Welshman David Lloyd George (1863–1945), substantially raised taxes on the rich as part of the People's Budget. This income helped the government pay for national health insurance, unemployment benefits, old-age pensions, and a host of other social measures. The state was integrating the urban masses socially as well as politically.

This record of accomplishment was only part of the story, though. On the eve of World War One the ever-emotional, ever-unanswered question of Ireland brought Great Britain to the brink of civil war. In the 1840s Ireland had been decimated by famine, which fueled an Irish revolutionary movement. Thereafter, the English slowly granted concessions, such as the abolition of the privileges of the Anglican church and rights for Irish peasants. The Liberal prime minister William Gladstone (1809–1898), who had proclaimed twenty years earlier that "my mission is to pacify Ireland," introduced bills to give Ireland self-government in 1886 and in 1893. They failed to pass. After two decades of relative quiet, Irish nationalists in the British Parliament saw their chance. They supported the Liberals in their battle for the People's Budget and received passage of a home-rule bill for Ireland in return.

Thus Ireland, the emerald isle, achieved self-government – but not quite, for Ireland is composed of two peoples. As much as the Irish Catholic majority in the southern counties wanted home rule, precisely that much did the Irish Protestants of the northern counties of Ulster come to oppose it. Motivated by the accumulated fears and hostilities of generations, the Protestants of Ulster refused to submerge themselves in a Catholic Ireland, just as Irish Catholics had refused to submerge themselves in a Protestant Britain.

The Ulsterites vowed to resist home rule in northern Ireland. By December 1913 they had raised 100,000 armed volunteers, and they were supported by much of English public opinion. Thus in 1914 the Liberals in the House of Lords introduced a compromise home-rule law that did not apply to the northern counties. This bill, which openly betrayed promises made to Irish nationalists, was rejected and in September the original home-rule plan was passed but simultaneously suspended for the duration of hostilities. The momentous Irish question had been overtaken by earth-shattering world war in August 1914.

Irish developments illustrated once again the power of national feeling and national movements in the nineteenth century. Moreover, they were proof that governments could not elicit greater loyalties unless they could capture and control that elemental current of national feeling. Though Great Britain had much going for it – power, Parliament, pros-

perity – none of these availed in the face of Irish nationalism in its Catholic and Protestant versions. Similarly, progressive Sweden was powerless to stop the growth of the Norwegian national movement, which culminated in Norway's breaking away from Sweden and becoming a fully independent nation in 1905. In this light, one can also see how hopeless was the case of the Ottoman Empire in Europe in the later nineteenth century. It was only a matter of time before the Serbs, the Bulgarians, and the Rumanians would break away, and they did.

THE AUSTRO-HUNGARIAN EMPIRE

The dilemma of conflicting nationalisms in Ireland also helps one appreciate how desperate the situation in the Austro-Hungarian Empire had become by the early twentieth century. In 1849 Magyar nationalism had driven Hungarian patriots to declare an independent Hungarian republic, which was savagely crushed by Russian and Austrian armies (pages 1049–1050). Throughout the 1850s Hungary was ruled as a conquered territory, and Emperor Francis Joseph and his bureaucracy tried hard to centralize the state and "Germanize" the language and culture of the different nationalities.

Then, in the wake of defeat by Prussia in 1866, a weakened Austria was forced to strike a compromise and establish the so-called dual monarchy. The empire was divided in two and the nationalistic Magyars gained virtual independence for Hungary. Henceforth each half of the empire agreed to deal with its own "barbarians" – its own minorities – as it saw fit. The two states were joined only by a shared monarch and common ministries for finance, defense, and foreign affairs. After 1867, the disintegrating force of competing nationalisms continued unabated, for both

Austria and Hungary had several "Irelands" within their borders.

In Austria, ethnic Germans were only one-third of the population, and by the late 1890s many Germans saw their traditional dominance threatened by Czechs, Poles, and other Slavs. A particularly emotional and divisive issue in the Austrian parliament was the language used in government and elementary education at the local level. From 1900 to 1914, the parliament was so divided that ministries generally could not obtain a majority and ruled instead by decree. Efforts by both conservatives and socialists to defuse national antagonisms by stressing economic issues cutting across ethnic lines – which led to the introduction of universal male suffrage in 1907 – proved largely unsuccessful.

One aspect of such national antagonisms was anti-Semitism, which was particularly virulent in Austria. The Jewish populations of Austrian cities grew very rapidly after Jews obtained full legal equality in 1867, reaching 10 percent of the population of Vienna by 1900. Many Jewish businessmen were quite successful in banking and retail trade, while Jewish artists, intellectuals, and scientists, like the world-famous Sigmund Freud, played a major role in making Vienna a leading center of European culture and modern thought. When extremists charged the Jews with controlling the economy and corrupting German culture with alien ideas and ultra-modern art, anxious Germans of all classes tended to listen. The popular mayor of Vienna from 1897 to 1910, Dr. Karl Lueger, combined anti-Semitic rhetoric with calls for "Christian socialism" and municipal ownership of basic services. Lueger appealed especially to the German lower middle class – and to an unsuccessful young artist named Adolf Hitler.

In Hungary, the Magyar nobility in 1867 restored the constitution of 1848 and used it to dominate both the Magyar peasantry and the minority populations until 1914. Only the wealthiest fourth of adult males had the right to vote, making the parliament the creature of the Magyar elite. Laws promoting use of the Magyar (Hungarian) language in schools and government were rammed through and bitterly resented, especially by the Croatians and Rumanians. While Magyar extremists campaigned loudly for total separation from Austria, the radical leaders of the subject nationalities dreamed in turn of independence from Hungary. Unlike most major countries, which were able to harness nationalism to strengthen the state after 1871, the Austro-Hungarian Empire was progressively weakened and eventually destroyed by it.

THE SOCIALIST MOVEMENT

Nationalism served, for better or worse, as a new unifying principle. But what about socialism? Did the rapid growth of socialist parties, which were generally Marxian parties, dedicated to an international proletarian revolution, mean that national states had failed to gain the support of workers? Certainly, many prosperous and conservative citizens were greatly troubled by the socialist movement. And many historians have portrayed the years before 1914 as a time of ever-increasing conflict between revolutionary socialism on the one hand and a nationalist alliance between conservative aristocracy and the prosperous middle class on the other. This question requires close examination.

THE SOCIALIST INTERNATIONAL

The growth of socialist parties after 1871 was phenomenal. Neither Bismarck's antisocialist laws nor his extensive social security system checked the growth of the German Social Democratic party, which espoused the Marxian ideology. By 1912, it had attracted millions of followers and was the largest party in the parliament. Socialist parties also grew in other countries, though nowhere else with quite such success. In 1883, Russian exiles in Switzerland founded the Russian Social Democratic party, which grew rapidly in the 1890s and thereafter despite internal disputes. In France various socialist parties re-emerged in the 1880s after the carnage of the Commune. Most of them were finally unified in a single, increasingly powerful Marxian party, called the French Section of the Workers International in 1905. Belgium and Austria-Hungary also had strong socialist parties of the Marxian persuasion.

As the name of the French party suggests, Marxian socialist parties were eventually linked together in an international organization. As early as 1848, Marx had declared in the *Communist Manifesto* that "the working men have no country," and he had urged proletarians of all nations to unite against their governments. Joining the flood of radicals and republicans who fled continental Europe for England and America after the revolutions of 1848, Marx settled in London. Poor and depressed, he lived on his meager earnings as a journalist and the gifts of his friend Engels. Marx never stopped thinking of revolution. Digging deeply into economics and history, he concluded that revolution follows economic crisis, and tried to prove it in *Critique of Political Economy* (1859) and his greatest theoretical work *Capital* (1867).

The bookish Marx also excelled as a practical organizer. In 1864, Marx played an important role in founding the First International of socialists – the International Working Men's Association. In the following years he

SOCIALIST PROPAGANDA, RUSSIAN STYLE "We work for you; we feed you," groan the masses. "We eat for you," boast the wealthy. Above, the army ("We shoot you"), the church ("We deceive you"), the bureaucracy ("We govern you"), and the monarchy ("We rule over you") all exploit the workers and the peasants. (Courtesy, Thames and Hudson Ltd., from The Nineteenth Century, *edited by Asa Briggs, 1970)*

battled successfully to control the organization and used its annual meetings as a means of spreading his realistic, "scientific" doctrines of inevitable socialist revolution. Then Marx enthusiastically embraced the passionate, vaguely radical patriotism of the Paris Commune and its terrible conflict with the French National Assembly as a giant step toward socialist revolution. This impetuous action frightened many of his early supporters, especially the more moderate British labor leaders. The First International collapsed.

Yet international proletarian solidarity remained an important objective for Marxists. In 1889, as the individual parties in different countries grew stronger, socialist leaders came together to form the Second International, which lasted until 1914. Although the International was only a federation of various national socialist parties, it had great psychological impact. Every three years delegates from the different parties met to interpret Marxian doctrines and plan coordinated action. May 1 – May Day – was declared an annual international one-day strike, a day of marches and demonstrations. A permanent executive for the International was established. Many feared and many others rejoiced in the growing power of socialism and the Second International.

UNIONS AND REVISIONISM

Was socialism really radical and revolutionary in these years? On the whole, it was not. Indeed, as socialist parties grew and attracted large numbers of members, they looked more and more toward gradual change and steady improvement for the working class, less and less toward revolution. The mainstream of European socialism became militantly moderate; that is, they increasingly combined radical rhetoric with sober action.

Workers themselves were progressively less inclined to follow radical programs. There were several reasons for this. As workers gained the right to vote and to participate politically in the nation state, their attention focused more on elections than on revolutions. And as workers won real, tangible benefits, this furthered the process. Workers were not immune to patriotic education and indoctrination during military service, however ar-

dently socialist intellectuals might wish the contrary. Nor were workers a unified social group, as we have seen in Chapter 29.

Perhaps most important of all, workers' standard of living rose substantially after 1850 as the promise of the Industrial Revolution was at least partially realized. In Great Britain, for example, workers could buy almost twice as much with their wages in 1906 as in 1850, and most of the increase came after 1870. Workers experienced similar increases in most continental countries after 1850, though much less strikingly in late-developing Russia. Improvement in the standard of living was much more than merely a matter of higher wages. The quality of life improved dramatically in urban areas. For all these reasons, workers tended more and more to become militantly moderate: they demanded gains, but they were less likely to take to the barricades in pursuit of them.

The growth of labor unions reinforced this trend toward moderation. In the early stages of industrialization, modern unions were generally prohibited by law. A famous law of the French Revolution had declared all guilds and unions illegal in the name of "liberty" in 1791. In Great Britain, attempts by workers to unite were considered criminal conspiracies after 1799. Other countries had similar laws, and these obviously hampered union development. In France, for example, about two hundred workers were imprisoned each year between 1825 and 1847 for taking part in illegal combinations. Unions were considered subversive bodies, only to be hounded and crushed.

From this sad position workers struggled to escape. Great Britain led the way in 1824–1825, when unions won the right to exist but (generally) not the right to strike. After the collapse of Robert Owen's attempt to form one big union in the 1830s (page 1008), new and more practical kinds of unions appeared. Limited primarily to highly skilled workers such as machinists and carpenters, the "new unions" avoided both radical politics and costly strikes. Instead, their sober, respectable leaders concentrated on winning better wages and hours for their members through collective bargaining and compromise. This approach helped pave the way to full acceptance in Britain in the 1870s, when unions won the right to strike without being held legally liable for the financial damage inflicted on employers. After 1890 unions for unskilled workers developed, and between 1901 and 1906 the legal position of British unions was further strengthened.

Germany was the most industrialized, socialized, and unionized continental country by 1914. German unions were not granted important rights until 1869, and until the antisocialist law was repealed in 1890 they were frequently harassed by the government as socialist fronts. Nor were socialist leaders particularly interested in union activity, believing as they did in the iron law of low wages and the need for political revolution. The result was that as late as 1895 there were only about 270,000 union members in a male industrial work force of nearly 8 million. Then, with German industrialization still storming ahead and almost all legal harrassment eliminated, union membership skyrocketed to roughly 3 million in 1912.

This great expansion both reflected and influenced the changing character of German unions. Increasingly, unions in Germany focused on concrete bread-and-butter issues — wages, hours, working conditions — and not on instilling pure socialist doctrine. Genuine collective bargaining, long opposed by socialist intellectuals as a "sellout," was officially recognized as desirable by the German Trade Union Congress in 1899. When employers proved unwilling to bargain, a series of strikes forced them to change their minds.

Between 1906 and 1913, successful collective bargaining was gaining a prominent place in German industrial relations. In 1913 alone, over 10,000 collective bargaining agreements affecting 1.25 million workers were signed. Further gradual improvement, not revolution, was becoming the primary objective of the German trade union movement.

The German trade unions and their leaders were in fact, if not in name, thoroughgoing revisionists. "Revisionism" – that most awful of sins in the eyes of militant Marxists in the twentieth century – was an effort by various socialists to update Marxian doctrines to reflect the realities of the time. Thus, the socialist Edward Bernstein argued in 1899 in his *Evolutionary Socialism* that Marx's predictions of ever-greater poverty for workers and ever-greater concentration of wealth in ever-fewer hands had been proven false. Therefore, Bernstein suggested, socialists should reform their doctrines and tactics. They should combine with other progressive forces to win gradual evolutionary gains for workers through legislation, unions, and further economic development. These views were formally denounced as heresy by the German Social Democratic party and later by the entire Second International. Nevertheless, the revisionist, gradualist approach continued to gain the tacit acceptance of many German socialists, particularly in the trade unions.

Moderation found followers elsewhere. In France the great humanist and socialist leader Jean Jaurès formally repudiated revisionist doctrines in order to establish a unified socialist party, but he remained at heart a gradualist. Questions of revolutionary versus gradualist policies split Russian Marxists.

Socialist parties before 1914 had clear-cut national characteristics. Russians and socialists in the Austro-Hungarian Empire tended to be the most radical. The German party talked revolution and practiced reformism, greatly influenced by its enormous trade union movement. The French party talked revolution and tried to practice it, unrestrained by a trade union movement that was both very weak and very radical. In England, the socialist but non-Marxian Labour party, reflecting the well-established union movement, was formally committed to gradual reform. In Spain and Italy, Marxian socialism was very weak. There anarchism, seeking to smash the state rather than the bourgeoisie, dominated radical thought and action.

In short, socialist policies and doctrines varied from country to country. Socialism itself was to a large extent "nationalized" behind the imposing façade of international unity. This helps explain why, when war came in 1914, socialist leaders almost without exception supported their governments.

From the mid-nineteenth century onward, Western society became nationalistic as well as urban and industrial. Nation states and strong-minded national leaders gradually enlisted widespread support and gave men and women a sense of belonging. Even socialism became increasingly national in orientation, gathering strength as a champion of working-class interests in domestic politics. Yet, while nationalism served to unite peoples, it also drove them apart. Though most obvious in Austria-Hungary and Ireland, this was in a real sense true for all of Western civilization. For the universal national faith, which reduced social tensions within states, promoted a bitter, almost Darwinian competition between states and thus ominously threatened the progress and unity it had helped to build.

NOTES

1. Quoted by G. Wright, *France in Modern Times,* Rand McNally, Chicago, 1960, p. 179.

2. J. Burckhardt, *Reflections on History,* G. Allen & Unwin, London, 1943, p. 165.

3. Quoted by O. Pflanze, *Bismarck and the Development of Germany: The Period of Unification, 1815–1871,* Princeton University Press, Princeton, N.J., 1963, p. 60.

4. Quoted by E. Eyck, *Bismarck and the German Empire,* W. W. Norton, New York, 1964, p. 59.

5. Quoted by H. Kohn, *The Mind of Germany: The Education of a Nation,* Charles Scribner's Sons & Macmillan, New York, 1960, pp. 156–161.

6. N. Riasanovsky, *A History of Russia,* Oxford University Press, New York, 1963, p. 418.

7. Quoted by T. von Laue, *Sergei Witte and the Industrialization of Russia,* Columbia University Press, New York, 1963, p. 78.

8. Quoted by J. P. McKay, *Pioneers for Profit: Foreign Entrepreneurship and Russian Industrialization, 1885–1913,* Chicago University Press, Chicago, 1970, p. 11.

SUGGESTED READING

In addition to the general works mentioned in the Suggested Reading for Chapter 23, which treat the entire nineteenth century, G. Craig, *Germany, 1866–1945* (1980), and B. Moore, *Social Origins of Dictatorship and Democracy* (1966), are outstanding.

Among specialized works of high quality, R. Williams, *Gaslight and Shadows* (1957), brings the world of Napoleon III vibrantly alive, while another engaging collective biography by R. Shattuck, *The Banquet Years* (1968), captures the spirit of artistic and intellectual Paris at the end of the century. E. Weber, *Peasants into Frenchmen* (1976), stresses the role of education and modern communications in the transformation of rural France after 1870. E. Thomas, *The Women Incendiaries*

ART AND THE HUMAN EXPERIENCE

Art offers rich insights into human history. It reveals the interests and values of different societies, and suggests how they change over time. It captures the life of the people, presenting a striking visual record to complement the written sources that historians usually rely upon.

Art also has its own dynamic and its own integrity, growing out of a universal need for beauty and artistic expression. This need for beauty and expression has taken many forms throughout history. It shows itself in the ceremonial artifacts of unknown masters as well as in the stunning canvases of great painters like the French impressionists, who introduced new techniques to capture reality as they saw it while simultaneously delighting in pure color and abstract design. Enriching our understanding of the past, art stands proud in its own right – a magnificent triumph of the human spirit.

LE MOULIN DE LA GALETTE À MONTMARTRE (1876) Renoir (1841–1919). Auguste Renoir was a joyous painter whose whole work optimistically affirmed the beauty and value of modern life. In this masterpiece, painted for the third exhibition of French impressionists in 1877, Renoir has transformed a popular outdoor dance hall of the urban masses into a happy fairyland, where beautiful women and gallant men share the enchantment of music and romance. (Cliché des Musées Nationaux, Paris.)

RED BOATS AT ARGENTEUIL (above) Monet (1840–1926). The impressionists were city dwellers who often found the light and open air they admired in the suburbs of Paris. Monet rented a houseboat at the little holiday village of Argenteuil. There he and his friends painted the happy world of sailboats and weekend relaxation, of radiant sunshine and shimmering water shot through with reflections and many shades of blue. (Courtesy of the Fogg Art Museum, Harvard University. Bequest – Collection of Maurice Wertheim, Class of 1906.)

THE WOODCUTTER (left) Katsushika Hokusai (1760–1849). Considered the most original nineteenth-century Japanese *ukiyo-e* artist, one who had a profound influence on the French impressionists Manet and Degas, and one of the great artists of the world, Hokusai produced masterpieces in many genres. This simple woodcutter with a pipe in his mouth and humorous face reflects the imagination and wit for which Hokusai was famous. (Courtesy, Freer Gallery)

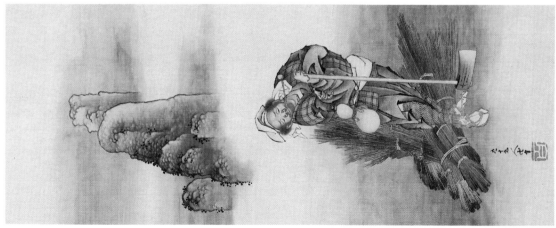

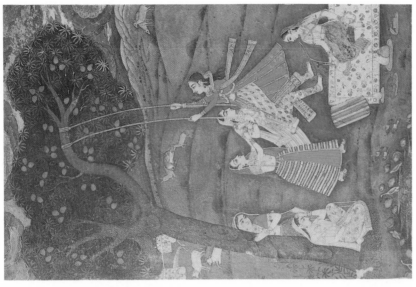

INDIAN HUNTING SCENE (above left) The aristocratic sport of hunting wild boar was especially popular in the heavily wooded province of Udaipur in northwestern India. The great detail given to plants and animals reveals the strong interest of Indian Rajput art in landscapes, zoology, and botany. (EPA)

INDIAN LADIES IN THE COUNTRY (above right) Rich color and a delicacy and sinuous grace in the depiction of the human form characterized the painting at the Hindu Rajput courts of northwestern India. As one lady in a diaphanous sari sits on an elegant Persian carpet, some companions play in the swing while others gaze off dreamily. Note the soft facial features, the heavy jewelry, and the small feet, all typical of their aristocratic social class. (Scala New York/Florence)

THE CARD PLAYERS (below) Cezanne (1839–1906). An immensely important artist, Paul Cezanne rejected his early impressionistic style as too light and delicate. In *The Card Players* (1892) Cezanne shows the dignity of ordinary people in everyday life, as well as the devotion to form and solidity which made him the father of modern abstract art. (The Metropolitan Museum of Art: Bequest of Stephen C. Clark, 1960.)

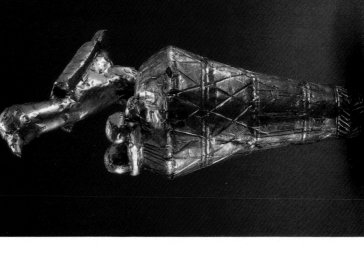

HAITIAN LANDSCAPE (detail) (above) Jean-Gilles (b. 1943). The folk art of Latin America has achieved wide popularity in recent times. The oil paintings of the young Haitian Joseph Jean-Gilles convey a special joy with their fresh, unaffected view of the world. In this outstanding example hundreds of multicolored trees dot the green landscape as farmers cultivate the fields below. (Museum of Modern Art of Latin America, Washington, D.C. Photo by Angel Hurtado.)

ASHANTI STAFF TOP (right) In the early eighteenth century, the Ashanti of central Ghana expanded northward, subdued various peoples, and established a powerful successor state to the medieval African kingdoms of Ghana and Mali. The gold trade was the linchpin of its economic and political power. A splendid example of the Ashanti's superb skill in goldworking, this staff top reflects the region's proverbial wealth. (Lee Boltin)

HELMET MASK OF KUBA TRIBE (far right) The Kuba, a Bantu-speaking people who settled in the Congo region, believed their king ruled by divine appointment. Symbolic of his authority is this ferocious mask made of cloth, shells, beads and hemp. (Lee Boltin)

THE STARRY NIGHT (overleaf) Van Gogh (1853–1890). The tragic Dutchman Vincent van Gogh absorbed impressionism in Paris, but under the burning sun of southern France he went beyond portraying the world of external reality. In works like *The Starry Night* he feverishly painted his own inner world of intense emotion and wild imagination, thereby contributing greatly to the rise of expressionism in modern art. (Collection, the Museum of Modern Art, New York. Acquired through the Lillie P. Bliss Bequest.)

(1966), examines radical women in the Paris Commune. D. Johnson, *France and the Dreyfus Affair* (1967), is a careful examination of the famous case. In *Jean Barois,* Nobel Prize winner R. M. Du Gard accurately recreates in novel form the Dreyfus affair, and Emile Zola's novel *The Debacle* treats the Franco-Prussian War realistically. D. M. Smith has written widely on Italy, and his *Garibaldi* (1956) and *Italy: A Modern History,* rev. ed. (1969), are recommended. P. Schroeder, *Austria, Great Britain and the Crimean War* (1972), is an outstanding and highly original diplomatic study. In addition to the important studies on Bismarck and Germany by Pflanze, Eyck, and Kohn cited in the Notes, F. Stern, *Gold and Iron* (1977), is a fascinating examination of relations between Bismarck and his financial adviser, the Jewish banker Bleichröder. G. Iggers, *The German Conception of History* (1968), and K. D. Barkin, *The Controversy Over German Industrialization, 1890–1902* (1970), are valuable in-depth investigations. H. Glasser, ed., *The German Mind in the Nineteenth Century,* is an outstanding anthology, as is P. Mendes-Flohr, *The Jew in the Modern World: A Documentary History* (1980). P. Gay, *Freud, Jews, and Other Germans* (1978), is brilliant on the development of modern culture. R. Kann, *The Multinational Empire,* 2 vols. (1950, 1964), probes the intricacies of the nationality problem in Austria-Hungary, while S. Stavrianos has written extensively on southeastern Europe, including *The Balkans, 1815–1914* (1963).

In addition to the studies on Russian industrial development by von Laue and McKay cited in the Notes, W. Blackwell, *The Industrialization of Russia,* 2nd. ed. (1982), is recommended. Among fine studies on Russian social development and modernization, T. Emmons, *The Russian Landed Gentry and the Peasant Emancipation of 1861* (1968); R. Zelnik, *Labor and Society in Tsarist Russia, 1855–1870* (1971); R. Johnson, *Peasant and Proletarian: The Working Class of Moscow at the End of the Nineteenth Century* (1979); and H. Troyat, *Daily Life in Russia Under the Last Tsar* (1962), are particularly noteworthy. W. E. Mosse, *Alexander II and the Modernization of Russia* (1958), provides a good discussion of midcentury reforms, while C. Black, ed., *The Transformation of Russian Society* (1960), offers a collection of essays on Russian modernization. Ivan Turgenev's great novel *Fathers and Sons* probes the age-old conflict of generations as well as nineteenth-century Russian revolutionary thought. G. Dangerfield, *The Strange Death of Liberal England* (1961), brilliantly examines social tensions in Ireland as well as Englishwomen's struggle for the vote before 1914. W. Arnstein convincingly shows how the Victorian aristocracy survived and even flourished in nineteenth-century Britain in F. Jaher, ed., *The Rich, the Well-Born, and the Powerful* (1973), an interesting collection of essays on social elites in history. The theme of aristocratic strength and survival is expanded in A. Mayer's provocative *Persistence of the Old Regime: Europe to the Great War* (1981). On late-nineteenth-century socialism, C. Schorske, *German Social Democracy, 1905–1917* (1955), is a modern classic; V. Lidtke, *The Outlawed Party* (1966), ably treats the German socialists between 1878 and 1890. H. Goldberg, *The Life of Jean Jaurès* (1962), is a sympathetic account of the great French socialist leader. P. Stearns, who has written several books on European labor history, considers radical labor leaders in *Revolutionary Syndicalism and French Labor* (1971). M. Hanagan, *The Logic of Solidarity* (1980), examines the working class in three French towns between 1870 and 1914.

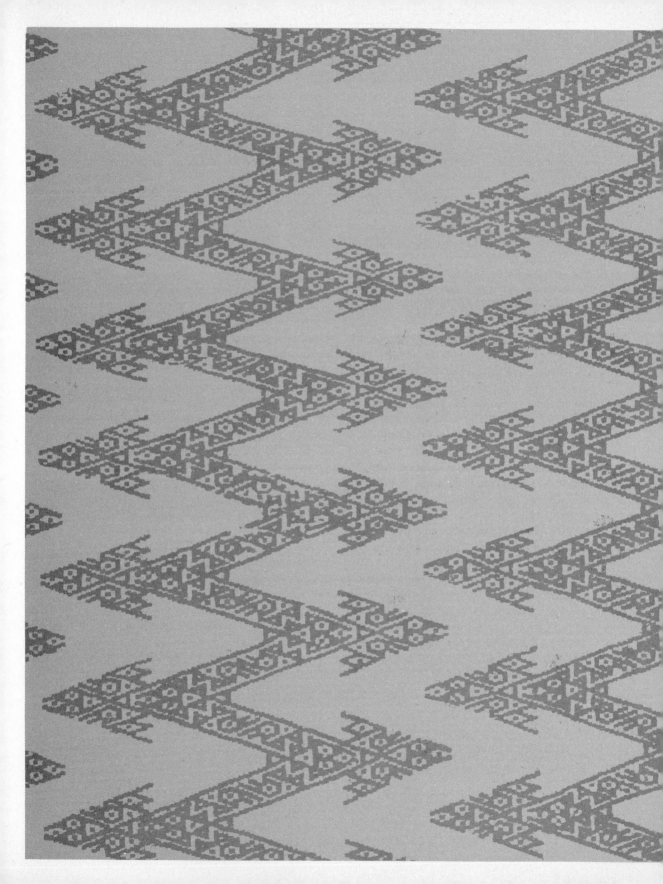

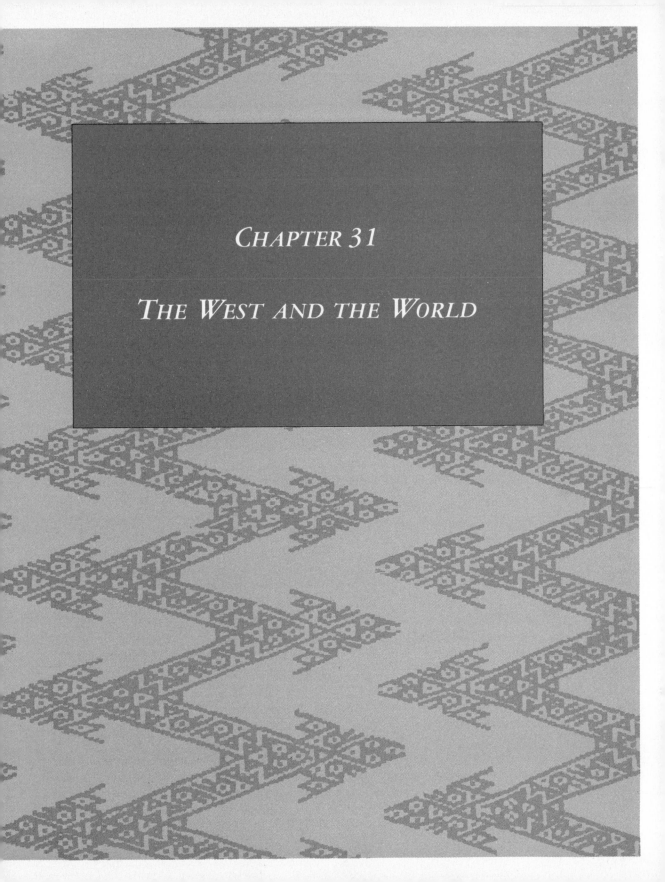

CHAPTER 31

THE WEST AND THE WORLD

WHILE NATIONALISM and urban life were transforming Western society, Western society itself was reshaping the world. At the peak of its power and pride, the West entered the third and most dynamic phase of the aggressive expansion that began with the Crusades and continued with the great discoveries and the rise of seaborne colonial empires. An ever-growing stream of products, people, and ideas flowed out from Europe in the nineteenth century. Hardly any corner of the globe was left untouched. The most spectacular manifestations of Western expansion came in the late nineteenth century, when the leading European nations established or enlarged their far-flung political empires. The political annexation of territory in the 1880s – the "new imperialism," as it is often called by historians – was the capstone of a profound underlying economic and technological process. How and why did this many-sided, epochmaking expansion occur, and what were some of its consequences for the West and the rest of the world? These are the questions this chapter seeks to answer.

BUILDING A WORLD ECONOMY

The Industrial Revolution created, first in Great Britain and then in Europe and North America, a growing and tremendously dynamic economic system. In the course of the nineteenth century that system was extended across the face of the earth. Much of this extension into non-Western areas was peaceful and beneficial for all concerned, for the West had many products and techniques the rest of the world desired. If peaceful methods failed, however, Europeans did not stand on ceremony. They used their superior military power to force non-Western nations to open their doors to trade and investment.

TRADE AND COMMUNICATIONS

Commerce between nations has always been a powerful stimulus to economic development. Never was this more true than in the nineteenth century, when world trade grew prodigiously. As Figure 31.1 shows, world trade grew modestly until about 1840, and then it took off. After a slowdown in the last years of the century, another surge lasted until World War One. The value of world trade in 1913 was roughly *twenty-five* times what it had been in 1800. This figure actually understates growth, since average prices of both manufactured goods and raw materials were substantially *lower* in 1913 than in 1800. In a general way, the enormous increase in international commerce summed up the growth of an interlocking world economy, centered in and directed by Europe.

Great Britain played a key role in using trade to tie all corners of the world together economically. In 1815, Britain already had a colonial empire, for India, Canada, Australia, and other scattered areas remained British possessions after American independence. The technological breakthroughs of the Industrial Revolution allowed Britain to manufacture cotton textiles, iron, and other goods ever more cheaply and to far outstrip domestic demand for such products. By 1820 Britain was exporting half of its cotton textiles, for example. As European nations and the United States erected protective tariff barriers and began to industrialize, British cotton-textile manufacturers aggressively sought and found other foreign markets. In 1820, Europe bought half of Britain's cotton-textile exports and India bought only 6 percent. By 1850, India bought 25 percent and Europe only 16 percent of a much larger total.

Moreover, after the repeal of the Corn Laws in 1846, Britain's commitment to free trade was unswerving. The decisive argument in the battle against tariffs on imported grain had been, "We must give, if we mean honestly to receive, and buy as well as sell." Until 1914, Britain thus remained the world's emporium, where not only agricultural products and raw materials but also manufactured goods entered freely. Free access to the enormous market of Britain and its empire stimulated business activities around the world.

The growth of trade was facilitated by the conquest of distance. The earliest railroad construction occurred in Europe (including Russia) and in America north of the Rio Grande; other parts of the globe saw the building of rail lines after 1860. By 1920, more than one-quarter of the world's railroads were in Latin America, Asia, Africa, and Australia. Wherever railroads were built, they drastically reduced transportation costs, opened new economic opportunities, and called forth new skills and attitudes. Moreover, in the areas of massive European settlement – North America and Australia – they were built in advance of the population and provided a means of settling the land.

The power of steam revolutionized transportation by sea as well as by land. In 1807, inhabitants of the Hudson Valley in New York saw "the Devil on the way to Albany in a saw-mill," as Robert Fulton's steamship *Clermont* traveled 150 miles upstream in thirty-two hours. Steam power, long used to drive paddle-wheelers on rivers, particularly in Russia and North America, finally began to supplant sails on the oceans of the world in the late 1860s. Lighter, stronger, cheap steel replaced iron, which had replaced wood. Screw propellers superseded paddle wheels, while mighty compound steam engines cut fuel consumption by half. Passenger and freight rates tumbled, and the intercontinental shipment of low-priced raw materials became feasible. In addition to the large passenger liners and freighters of the great shipping

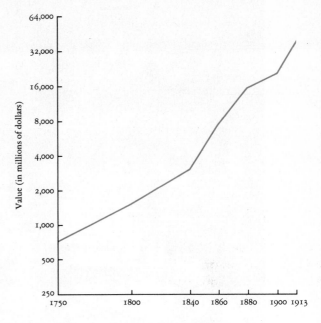

Note: Data show total world exports and total world imports.

FIGURE 31.1 THE GROWTH OF WORLD TRADE, 1750–1913 IN 1913 DOLLARS The expansion of international commerce encouraged and reflected Western economic development in the nineteenth century. (Source: W. Woodruff, Impact of Western Man: A Study of Europe's Role in the World Economy. *St. Martin's Press, New York, 1967, p. 313 and references cited there.)*

companies, there were innumerable independent tramp steamers searching endlessly for cargo around the world.

An account of an actual voyage by a typical tramp freighter will highlight developments in global trade in the nineteenth century. The ship left England in 1910, carrying rails and general freight to western Australia. From there it carried lumber to Melbourne in southeastern Australia, where it took on harvester combines for Argentina. In Buenos Aires it loaded wheat for Calcutta, and in Calcutta took on jute for New York. From New York it carried a variety of industrial products to Australia, before returning to England with lead, wool, and wheat after a

CHEAP LAND in distant North America was an irresistible magnet for millions of Europeans. This picture shows the special, low-cost sleeping cars for immigrants on the Canadian Pacific Railroad. (Historical Picture Service, Chicago)

voyage of 72,000 miles to six continents in seventeen months.

The revolution in land and sea transportation helped European pioneers to open up vast new territories and to produce agricultural products and raw materials there for sale in Europe. Moreover, the development of refrigerated railway cars and, from the 1880s, refrigerator ships enabled first the United States and then Argentina, Australia, and New Zealand to ship mountains of chilled or frozen beef and mutton to European (mainly British) consumers. From Asia, Africa, and Latin America came not only the traditional tropical products – spices, tea, sugar, coffee – but new raw materials for industry, such as jute, rubber, cotton, and coconut oil.

Intercontinental trade was enormously facilitated by the Suez and Panama canals. Of great importance too was large and continuous investment in modern port facilities, which made loading and unloading cheaper, faster, and more dependable. Finally, transoceanic telegraph cables inaugurated rapid communications among the financial centers of the world. While a British tramp freighter steamed from Calcutta to New York, a broker in London was arranging, by telegram, for it to carry an American cargo to Australia. World commodity prices were also instantaneously conveyed by the same network of communications.

In surveying these dramatic and impressive developments one must remember that, in terms of value, most *trade* (as opposed to most *shipping*) was among European nations, the United States, and Canada. It was not between Europe and the colonial-tropical lands of Africa, Asia, and Latin America. For example, Britain and Germany, both great world traders, carried on a very large and profitable trade with each other before World War One. Between 1900 and 1913, Britain's second-best customer in the entire world was Germany (after India), and Britain was Germany's largest single customer. Germany sold twice as much to Britain alone as to all of Africa and Asia combined. Before 1914, world trade was centered in the prosperous, tightly integrated European economy.

FOREIGN INVESTMENT

The growth of trade and the conquest of distance encouraged the expanding European economy to make massive foreign investments. Beginning about 1840, European capitalists started to invest large sums in foreign lands. They did not stop until the outbreak of World War One in 1914. By that year Europeans had invested more than $40 billion abroad. Great Britain, France, and Germany were the principal investing countries, although by 1913 the United States was emerging as a substantial foreign investor. The sums involved were enormous (see Map 31.1). In the decade before 1914, Great Britain was investing 7 percent of its annual national income abroad, or slightly more than it was investing in its entire domestic economy. The great gap between rich and poor meant

that the wealthy and moderately well-to-do could and did send great sums abroad in search of interest and dividends.

Contrary to what many people assume, most of the capital exported did *not* go to European colonies or protectorates in Asia and Africa. About three-quarters of total European investment went to other European countries, the United States and Canada, Australia and New Zealand, and Latin America. The reason was simple: Europe found its most profitable opportunities for investment in construction of the railroads, ports, and utilities that were necessary to settle and develop those almost-vacant lands. By loaning money for a railroad in Argentina or in Canada's prairie provinces, for example, Europeans not only collected interest but also enabled white settlers to buy European rails and locomotives, developed sources of cheap wheat, and opened still more territory for European settlement. Much of this investment – such as in American railroads, fully a third of whose capital in 1890 was European, or in Russian railroads, which drew heavily on loans from France – was peaceful and mutually beneficial. The victims were native American Indians and Australian aborigines, who were decimated by the diseases, liquor, and guns of an aggressively expanding Western civilization.

THE OPENING OF CHINA AND JAPAN

Europe's relatively peaceful development of robust "offshoots" in sparsely populated North America, Australia, and much of Latin America absorbed huge quantities of goods, investments, and migrants. From a Western point of view, that was the most important aspect of Europe's global thrust. Yet Europe's economic and cultural penetration of old, densely populated civilizations was also pro-

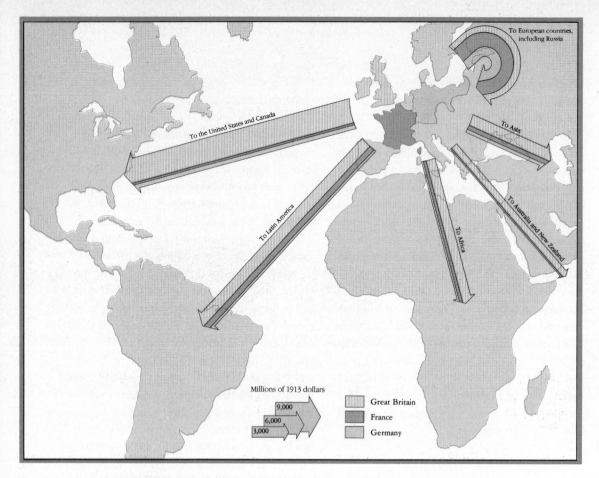

To European countries, including Russia

To the United States and Canada

To Asia

To Latin America

To Africa

To Australia and New Zealand

Millions of 1913 dollars

9,000

6,000

3,000

Great Britain
France
Germany

MAP 31.1 EUROPEAN INVESTMENT TO 1914
Foreign investment grew rapidly after 1850, and
Britain, France, and Germany were the major investing nations. As the map shows, most European investment did not go to the area seized by the "new
imperialism."

foundly significant, especially for the non-European peoples affected by it. With such
civilizations Europeans also increased their
trade and profit. Moreover, as had been the
case ever since Vasco da Gama and Christopher Columbus, expanding Western society
was prepared to use force to attain its desires,
if necessary. This was what happened in China
and Japan, two crucial examples of the general
pattern of intrusion into non-Western lands.

Traditional Chinese civilization was self-
sufficient. For centuries China had sent more
to Europe in the way of goods and inventions

than it received, and this was still the case in
the eighteenth century. Europeans and the
English in particular had developed a taste for
Chinese tea, but they had to pay for it with
hard silver since China was supremely uninterested in European wares. Trade with
Europe was carefully regulated by the Chinese
imperial government – the Manchu dynasty – which was more interested in isolating and controlling the strange "sea
barbarians" than in pursuing commercial exchange. The imperial government refused to
establish diplomatic relations with the "infe-

rior" European states, and it required all foreign merchants to live in the southern city of Canton, and to buy and sell only from the local merchant monopoly. Practices considered harmful to Chinese interests, such as the sale of opium and the export of silver from China, were strictly forbidden.

For years the little community of foreign merchants in Canton had to accept the Chinese system. By the 1820s, however, the dominant group, the British, was flexing its muscles. Moreover, in the smoking of opium – that "destructive and ensnaring vice" denounced by Chinese decrees – they had found something the Chinese really wanted. Grown legally in British-occupied India, opium was smuggled into China by means of fast ships and bribed officials. The more this rich trade developed, the greedier British merchants became and the more they resented the patriotic attempts of the Chinese government to stem the tide of drug addiction. By 1836, the aggressive goal of the British merchants in Canton was an independent British colony in China and "safe and unrestricted liberty" in trade. They pressured the British government to take decisive action, and enlisted the support of British manufacturers with visions of vast Chinese markets to be opened.

At the same time the Manchu government decided that the opium trade had to be stamped out for it was ruining the people and stripping the empire of its silver, which was going to British merchants to pay for the opium. The government began to prosecute Chinese drug dealers vigorously and in 1839 sent special envoy Lin Tse-hsü to Canton. Lin Tse-hsü ordered the foreign merchants to obey China's laws, "for our great unified Manchu Empire regards itself as responsible for the habits and morals of its subjects and cannot rest content to see any of them become victims of a deadly poison."[1] The British merchants refused and were expelled, whereupon war soon broke out.

Using troops from India and in control of the seas, the British occupied several coastal cities and forced China to surrender. In the Treaty of Nanking in 1842, the imperial government was forced to cede the island of Hong Kong to Britain forever, pay an indemnity of $100 million, and open up four large cities to foreign trade with low tariffs.

Thereafter the opium trade flourished, and Hong Kong developed rapidly as an Anglo-Chinese enclave. China continued to nurture illusions of superiority and isolation, however, and refused to accept foreign diplomats to Peking, the imperial capital. Finally, there was a second round of foreign attack between 1856 and 1860, culminating in the occupation of Peking by seventeen thousand British and French troops and the intentional burning of the emperor's summer palace. Another round of harsh treaties gave European merchants and missionaries greater privileges and protection. Thus did Europeans use military aggression to blow a hole in the wall of Chinese seclusion and open the country to foreign trade and foreign ideas.

China's neighbor, Japan, had its own highly distinctive civilization and even less use for westerners. European traders and missionaries first arrived in Japan in the sixteenth century. By 1640, Japan had reacted quite negatively to their presence. The government decided to seal off the country from all European influences, in order to preserve its traditional culture and society. It ruthlessly persecuted Japanese Christians and expelled all but a few Dutch merchants, who were virtually imprisoned in a single port and rigidly controlled. When American and British whaling ships began to appear off Japanese coasts almost two hundred years later, the policy of exclusion was still in effect. An order of 1825 commanded Japanese officials to "drive away foreign vessels without second thought."[2]

Japan's unbending isolation seemed hostile and barbaric to the West, particularly to the United States. It complicated the practical problems of shipwrecked American sailors and provisioning of whaling ships and China traders sailing in the eastern Pacific. It also thwarted the hope of trade and profit. Also, Americans shared the self-confidence and dynamism of expanding Western society. They had taken California from Mexico in 1848, and Americans felt destined to play a great role in the Pacific. It seemed, therefore, the United States' duty to force the Japanese to share their ports and behave like a "civilized" nation.

After several unsuccessful American attempts to establish commercial relations with Japan, Commodore Matthew Perry steamed into Edo (now Tokyo) Bay in 1853 and demanded diplomatic negotiations with the emperor. Japan entered a grave crisis. Some Japanese warriors urged resistance, but senior officials realized how defenseless their cities were against naval bombardment. Shocked and humiliated, they reluctantly signed a treaty with the United States that opened two ports and permitted trade. Over the next five years more treaties spelled out the rights and privileges of the Western nations and their merchants in Japan. Japan was "opened." What the British had done in China with war, the Americans had done in Japan with the threat of war.

WESTERN PENETRATION OF EGYPT

Egypt's experience illustrates not only the explosive power of the expanding European economy and society but also their seductive appeal in non-Western lands. Of great importance in African and Middle Eastern history, the ancient land of the pharaohs had since 525 B.C. been ruled by a succession of foreigners – Persians, Macedonian Greeks, Romans, Byzantine Greeks, Arabs, Mameluks, and Ottoman Turks. In 1798, French armies under young General Napoleon Bonaparte invaded the Egyptian part of the Ottoman Empire and occupied the territory for three years. Into the power vacuum left by the French withdrawal stepped an extraordinary Albanian-born Turkish general, Mohammed Ali.

First appointed governor of Egypt by the Turkish sultan, Mohammed Ali soon disposed of his political rivals and set out to build his own state on the strength of a large, powerful army. He conquered the Sudan to the south of Egypt in order to seize black warriors for a slave army. When this traditional practice did not give the desired results, he decided to build military might on the European model. Mohammed Ali drafted for the first time the illiterate, despised peasant masses of Egypt, and he hired French and Italian army officers to train these raw recruits and their Turkish officers. The government was also reformed, new lands were cultivated, and communications improved. By the time of his death in 1848, Mohammed Ali had established a strong and virtually independent Egyptian state, to be ruled by his family on an hereditary basis, even though Egypt was still officially part of the Turkish empire.

Mohammed Ali's policies of modernization attracted large numbers of Europeans to the banks of the Nile. As one Arab sheikh of the Ottoman Empire remarked in the 1830s, "Englishmen are like ants; if one finds a bit of meat, hundreds follow."[3] The port city of Alexandria, which had fewer than a hundred European residents in 1798, had more than fifty thousand by 1864, most of them Italians,

THE OPENING OF THE SUEZ CANAL in 1869 revolutionized communications between Europe and Asia. (BBC Hulton Picture Library)

Greeks, French, and English. Europeans served not only as army officers but also as engineers, doctors, high government officials, and policemen. Others found their "meat" in trade, finance, and shipping. This was particularly true after 1863, when Mohammed Ali's grandson Ismail began his sixteen-year rule as Egypt's khedive, or prince.

Educated at France's leading military academy and as fluent in French as a Parisian, Ismail was a westernizing autocrat. He dreamed of using European technology and capital to modernize Egypt quickly, and he conquered territory and tried to build a vast empire in northwest Africa. The large irrigation net-

works he promoted caused cotton production and exports to Europe to boom. Ismail also borrowed large sums to install modern communications, and with his support the Suez Canal was completed by a French company in 1869. The Arabic of the masses rather than the Turkish of the conquerors became the official language, and young Egyptians educated in Europe helped spread new skills and new ideas in the bureaucracy. Cairo acquired modern boulevards, Western hotels, and an opera house. As Ismail proudly declared: "My country is no longer in Africa, we now form part of Europe."[4]

Yet Ismail was too impatient and too reckless. His projects were enormously expensive, and the sale of his stock in the Suez Canal to the British government for $20 million did not relieve the situation. By 1876, Egypt owed foreign bondholders a colossal $450 million (up from $16 million when Ismail took power), and the country could not pay the interest on its debt. Rather than let Egypt go bankrupt and repudiate its loans, as had some Latin American countries and U.S. state governments in the early nineteenth century, the governments of France and Great Britain intervened politically in support of the European bankers who held the Egyptian bonds. They forced Ismail to appoint French and British commissioners to oversee Egyptian finances, in order that the Egyptian debt would be paid in full. This was a momentous decision. It implied direct European political control and a loss of Egyptian autonomy. Such direct political control was a sharp break with the previous pattern of trade, investment, and relatively peaceful economic and cultural penetration. Some English critics denounced this action as naked aggression, cloaked in hypocrisy about guarding the Suez Canal, the "life line to India."

Foreign financial control evoked a violent nationalistic reaction among Egyptian religious leaders, young intellectuals, and army officers. In 1879, under the leadership of Colonel Ahmed Arabi, they formed the Egyptian Nationalist Party. Continuing diplomatic pressure, which forced Ismail to abdicate in favor of his weak son Tawfiq (1879–1892), resulted in bloody anti-European riots in Alexandria in 1882. A number of Europeans were killed, and Tawfiq and his court had to flee to British ships for safety. When the British fleet bombarded Alexandria, more riots swept the country, and Colonel Arabi declared that "an irreconcilable war existed between the Egyptians and the English." Britain had superior

military power, and a British expeditionary force decimated Arabi's forces and occupied all of Egypt.

The British said their occupation was temporary, but British armies remained in Egypt until 1956. They maintained the façade of the khedive's government as an autonomous province of the Ottoman Empire, but the khedive was a mere puppet. The able British consul general Evelyn Baring, later Lord Cromer, ruled the country after 1883. Once a vocal opponent of involvement in Egypt, Baring was a paternalistic reformer who had come to believe that "without European interference and initiative reform is impossible here." Baring's rule did result in better conditions for peasants and tax reforms, while foreign bondholders tranquilly clipped their coupons and Egyptian nationalists nursed their injured pride.

In Egypt, Baring and the British reluctantly but spectacularly provided a new model for European expansion in densely populated lands. Such expansion was based on military force, absolute political domination, and a self-justifying ideology of beneficial reform. As we shall see, this model of expansion was to predominate until 1914.

THE GREAT MIGRATION

A poignant human drama was interwoven with economic expansion: literally millions of people picked up stakes and left their ancestral lands in the course of history's greatest migration. To millions of ordinary people, for whom the opening of China and the interest on the Egyptian debt had not the slightest significance, this great movement was the central experience in the saga of Western expansion. It was, in part, because of this great migration that the West's impact on the world in the nineteenth century was so many-sided, going far beyond economic matters.

THE PRESSURE OF POPULATION

We have seen that in the early eighteenth century the growth of European population entered its third and decisive stage, which continued unabated until the twentieth century (page 831). Birthrates eventually declined in the nineteenth century, but so did death rates, mainly because of the rising standard of living and secondarily because of the medical revolution. Thus the population of Europe (including Asiatic Russia) more than doubled, from approximately 188 million in 1800 to roughly 432 million in 1900.

These figures actually understate Europe's population explosion, for between 1815 and 1932 more than 60 million people left Europe. These migrants went primarily to the "areas of European settlement" – North and South America, Australia, New Zealand, and Siberia – where they contributed to a rapid growth of numbers. The population of North America (the United States and Canada) alone grew from 6 million to 81 million between 1800 and 1900 because of continuous immigration and the high fertility rates of North American women. Since population grew more slowly in Africa and Asia than in Europe, as Figure 31.2 shows, Europeans and people of European origin jumped from about 22 percent of the world's total to about 38 percent on the eve of World War One.

The growing number of Europeans provided further impetus for Western expansion. It was a driving force behind emigration. As in the eighteenth century, the rapid increase in numbers put pressure on the land and led to land hunger and relative overpopulation in area after area. In most countries migration

ELLIS ISLAND in New York harbor was the main entry point into the United States after 1892. For millions of migrants the first frightening experience in the new land was being inspected and processed through its crowded "pens." (Culver Pictures)

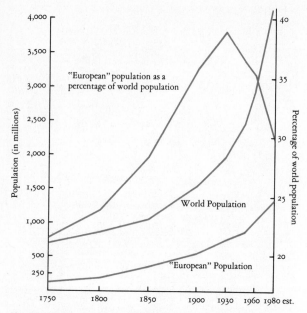

Population (in millions)

4,000
3,500
3,000
2,500
2,000
1,500
1,000
500
250

"European" population as a
percentage of world population

World Population

"European" Population

1750   1800   1850   1900   1930   1960 1980 est.

Percentage of world population

40
35
30
25
20

Note: "European" population includes Europe and also areas of predominantly European settlement – Asiatic Russia, North America, South America, and Australia/New Zealand.

FIGURE 31.2   THE INCREASE OF EUROPEAN AND WORLD POPULATIONS, 1750–1975 (Source: W. Woodruff, Impact of Western Man: A Study of Europe's Role in the World Economy. St. Martin's Press, New York, 1967, p. 103 and references cited there.)

increased twenty years after a rapid growth in population, as many children of the baby boom grew up, saw little available land and few opportunities, and migrated. This pattern was especially prevalent when rapid population increase predated extensive industrial development, which offered the best long-term hope of creating jobs within the country and reducing poverty. Thus millions of country folk went abroad, as well as to nearby cities, in search of work and economic opportunity. The case of the Irish, who left en masse for Britain during the Industrial Revolution and for the United States after the potato famine, was extreme but not unique.

Before looking at the people who migrated, let us consider three facts. First, the number of men and women who left Europe increased steadily until World War One. As Figure 31.3 shows, more than 11 million left in the first decade of the twentieth century, over five times the number departing in the 1850s. Although figures on migration are notoriously poor, the outflow of migrants was clearly an enduring characteristic of European society for the entire period.

Second, different countries had very different patterns of movement. As Figure 31.3 also shows, people left Britain and Ireland (which are not distinguished in the British figures) in large numbers from the 1840s on. This emigration reflected not only rural poverty but also the movement of skilled, industrial technicians and the preferences shown to British migrants in the British Empire. Ultimately, about one-third of all European migrants between 1840 and 1920 came from the British Isles. German migration was quite different. It grew irregularly after about 1830, reaching a first peak in the early 1850s and another in the early 1880s. Thereafter it declined rapidly, for Germany's rapid industrialization was providing adequate jobs at home. This pattern contrasted sharply with that of Italy. More and more Italians left the country right up to 1914, reflecting severe problems in Italian villages and relatively slow industrial growth. In sum, migration patterns mirrored social and economic conditions in the various European countries and provinces.

Third, although the United States absorbed the largest number of European migrants, it may surprise Americans to learn that only slightly more than half went to the United States. Asiatic Russia, Canada, Argentina, Brazil, and Australia also attracted large numbers, as Figure 31.4 shows. Moreover, migrants accounted for a larger proportion of the total population in Argentina, Brazil, and Canada than in the United States. Between 1900 and 1910, for example, new arrivals represented 3 percent of Argentina's population each year, as opposed to only 1 percent for the United States. The American assumption that European migration meant migration to the United States is quite inaccurate.

EUROPEAN MIGRANTS

What kind of people left Europe, and what were their reasons for doing so? Most were poor people from rural areas, though seldom from the poorest classes. Indeed, the European migrant was most often a small peasant landowner or a village craftsman, whose traditional way of life was threatened by too little land, estate agriculture, and cheap factory-made goods. German peasants who left the Rhineland and southwestern Germany between 1830 and 1854, for example, felt trapped by what Friedrich List called the "dwarf economy," with its tiny landholdings and declining craft industries. Selling out and moving to buy much cheaper land in the American Midwest became a common response. Contrary to what is often said, the European migrant was generally not a desperately impoverished landless peasant or urban proletarian, but an energetic small farmer or skilled artisan trying hard to stay ahead of poverty.

Determined to maintain or improve their status, migrants were a great asset to the countries that received them. This was doubly so because the vast majority were young and very often unmarried. Fully two-thirds of those admitted to the United States were under thirty-one years of age, and 90 percent were under forty. They came in the prime of life and were ready to work hard in the new land, at least for a time.

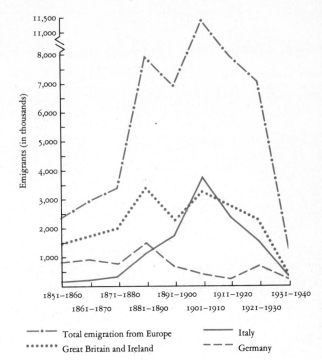

FIGURE 31.3 EMIGRATION FROM EUROPE BY DECADES, 1851–1940 (Source: W. Woodruff, Impact of Western Man: A Study of Europe's Role in the World Economy. *St. Martin's Press, New York, 1967, pp. 106–107 and references cited there.*)

Many Europeans, especially by the end of the nineteenth century, were truly migrants as opposed to immigrants – that is, they returned home after some time abroad. One in two migrants to Argentina, and probably one in three to the United States, eventually returned to their native land. The likelihood of repatriation varied greatly by nationality. Seven out of eight people who migrated from the Balkans to the United States in the late nineteenth century returned to their countries. At the other extreme, only one person in ten from Ireland and only one in twenty among east European Jews returned to the country of origin.

Once again the possibility of buying land in the old country was of central importance.

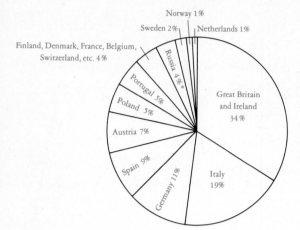

* Not including migrants to Asiatic Russia.

FIGURE 31.4 ORIGIN AND DESTINATION OF EUROPEAN EMIGRANTS, 1851–1960 (Source: W. Woodruff, Impact of Western Man: A Study of Europe's Role in the World Economy. *St. Martin's Press, New York, 1967, pp. 108–109 and references cited there.)*

Land in Ireland (as well as in England and Scotland) was tightly held by large, often-absentee landowners, and little land was available for purchase. In Russia, Jews were left in relative peace until the assassination of Alexander II by non-Jewish terrorists in 1881 brought a new tsar and an official policy of pogroms and savage discrimination. Russia's 5 million Jews were already confined to the market towns and small cities of the so-called "Pale of [Jewish] Settlement," where they worked as artisans and petty traders. Most land was held by non-Jews. When, therefore, Russian Jewish artisans began in the 1880s to escape both factory competition and oppression by migrating – a migration that eventually totaled 2 million people – it was basically a once-and-for-all departure. Non-Jewish migrants from Russia, who constituted a majority of those leaving the tsar's empire after 1905, had access to land, and thus returned much more frequently to their peasant villages in central Russia, Poland, and the Ukraine.

The mass movement of Italians illustrates many of the characteristics of European migration. As late as the 1880s, which was for Italians as for Russian Jews the first decade of substantial exodus, three in every four Italians depended on agriculture. With the influx of cheap North American wheat, the longstanding problems of the Italian village became more acute. And since industry was not advancing fast enough to provide jobs for the rapidly growing population, many Italians began to leave their country for economic reasons. Most Italian migrants were not landless laborers from areas dominated by large estates; such people tended to stay in Italy and turned increasingly toward radical politics. Instead, most were small landowning peasants, whose standard of living was falling because of rural overpopulation and agricultural depression. Migration provided them both an escape valve and a possible source of income to buy more land.

Many Italians went to the United States, but before 1900 more went to Argentina and Brazil. Indeed, two out of three migrants to those two developing countries came from Italy. In Brazil the big coffee planters, faced with the collapse of black slavery, attracted Italians to their plantations with subsidized travel and promises of high wages. In fact, Italian agricultural workers in Brazil were harshly exploited, although many sons and daughters of the first generation eventually did become independent farmers after World War One.

Many Italians had no intention of settling abroad permanently. Some called themselves "swallows": after harvesting their own wheat and flax in Italy, they "flew" to Argentina to harvest wheat between December and April. Returning to Italy for the spring planting, they repeated the exhausting process. This was a very hard life, but a frugal worker could save $250 to $300 in the course of a season. A one-way passage from Latin America to Italy usually cost only $25 to $30, and sometimes as little as $8. Italian migrants also dominated the building trades and the architectural profession in Latin America, and succeeded in giving a thoroughly Italian character to many Latin American cities.

Other Italians migrated to other European countries. France was a favorite destination. In 1911, the Italian-born population of France was roughly a third as large as that in the United States. Like other European nationalities, Italian migrants fanned out in many directions.

Ties of family and friendship played a crucial role in the movement of peoples. There are many examples of people from a given province or village settling together in rural enclaves or tight-knit urban neighborhoods

thousands of miles away. Very often a strong individual – a businessman, a religious leader – would blaze the way and others would follow.

Many landless young European men and women were spurred to leave by a spirit of revolt and independence. In Sweden and in Norway, in Jewish Russia and in Italy, these young people felt frustrated by the small privileged classes, who often controlled both church and government and resisted demands for change and greater opportunity. Many a young Norwegian seconded the passionate cry of their national poet, Bjørnson: "Forth will I! Forth! I will be crushed and consumed if I stay."[5]

Many young Jews wholeheartedly agreed with a spokesman of Kiev's Jewish community in 1882, who declared, "Our human dignity is being trampled upon, our wives and daughters are being dishonored, we are looted and pillaged; either we get decent human rights or else let us go wherever our eyes may lead us."[6] Thus, for many, migration was a radical way to "get out from under." Migration slowed down when the people won fundamental political and social reforms, such as the right to vote and social security.

ASIAN MIGRANTS

Not all migration was from Europe. A substantial number of Chinese, Japanese, Indians, and Filipinos – to name only four key groups – responded to rural hardship with temporary or permanent migration. At least 3 million Asians (as opposed to more than 60 million Europeans) moved abroad before 1920. Most went as indentured laborers to work under incredibly difficult conditions on the plantations or in the goldfields of Latin America, southern Asia, Africa, California, Hawaii, and Australia. White estate owners

THE CHINESE EXCLUSION ACT *This vicious cartoon from a San Francisco newspaper celebrates American laws shutting off Chinese migration. Americans and Europeans generally shared the same attitudes regarding the non-Western world. (Photo: Caroline Buckler)*

very often used Asians to replace or supplement blacks after the suppression of the slave trade.

In the 1840s, for example, there was a strong demand for field hands in Cuba, and the Spanish government actively recruited Chinese laborers. They came under eight-year contracts, were paid about twenty-five cents a day, and were fed potatoes and salted beef. Between 1853 and 1873, when such migration was stopped, more than 130,000 Chinese laborers went to Cuba. The majority spent their lives there as virtual slaves. The great landlords of Peru also brought in more than 100,000 workers from China in the nineteenth century, and there were similar movements of Asians elsewhere.

Such migration from Asia would undoubtedly have grown to much greater proportions if planters and mineowners in search of cheap

labor had had their way. But they did not. Asians fled the plantations and goldfields as soon as possible, seeking greater opportunities in trade and towns. There they came into conflict with other brown-skinned peoples – such as in Malaya and East Africa – and with white settlers in areas of European settlement.

These settlers demanded a halt to Asian migration. One Australian brutally summed up the typical view: "The Chinaman knows nothing about Caucasian civilization.... In fact, a Chinaman is a mere dumb animal... and could never be anything else. It would be less objectionable to drive a flock of sheep to the poll than to allow Chinamen to vote. The sheep at all events would be harmless."[7] By the 1880s, Americans and Australians were building "great white walls" – discriminatory laws designed to keep Asians out. Thus, a final crucial factor in the migrations before

1914 was the general policy of "whites only" in the open lands of possible permanent settlement. Racism meant that Asian migration was always of secondary importance in the world of expanding European society.

WESTERN IMPERIALISM

The expansion of Western society reached its apex between about 1880 and 1914. In those years the leading European nations not only continued to send massive streams of migrants, money, and manufactured goods around the world, but also rushed to create or enlarge vast *political* empires abroad. This political empire building contrasted sharply with the economic penetration of non-Western territories between 1816 and 1880, which had left a China or a Japan "opened" but politically independent. By contrast, the empires of the late nineteenth century recalled the old European colonial empires of the seventeenth and eighteenth centuries and led contemporaries to speak of the "new imperialism."

Characterized by a frantic rush to plant the flag over as many people and as much territory as possible, the new imperialism had momentous consequences. It resulted in new tensions between competing European states, and it led to wars and rumors of war with non-European powers. The new imperialism was aimed primarily at Africa and Asia. It put millions of black, brown, and tan peoples directly under the rule of whites. How and why did whites come to rule these peoples?

THE SCRAMBLE FOR AFRICA

The most spectacular manifestation of the new imperialism was the seizure of Africa, which broke sharply with previous patterns and fascinated contemporary Europeans and Americans.

As late as 1880, European nations controlled only 10 percent of the African continent, and their possessions were hardly increasing. The French had begun conquering Algeria in 1830, and by 1880 substantial numbers of French, Italian, and Spanish settlers lived among the overwhelming Arab majority.

At the other end of the continent, in South Africa, the British had taken possession of the Dutch settlements at Capetown during the wars with Napoleon I. This takeover had led disgruntled Dutch cattlemen and farmers in 1835 to make their so-called Great Trek into the interior, where they fought the Zulu and Xhosa peoples for land. After 1853, while British colonies like Canada and Australia were beginning to evolve toward self-government, the Boers (as the Dutch in south Africa were called) proclaimed their political independence and defended it against British armies. By 1880 Dutch and British settlers, who detested each other, had wrested control of much of South Africa from the Zulu and the Xhosa.

European trading posts and forts dating back to the age of discoveries and the slave trade dotted the coast of West Africa. The Portuguese proudly but ineffectively held their old possessions in Angola and Mozambique. Elsewhere, over the great mass of the continent, Europeans did not rule.

Between 1880 and 1900, the situation changed completely. Britain, France, Germany, and Italy scrambled for African possessions as if their lives depended on it. By 1900, nearly the whole continent had been carved up and placed under European rule: only Ethiopia in northeast Africa and Liberia on the west African coast remained independent. Even the Dutch settler republics of southern

Africa were conquered by the British in the bloody Boer War (1899–1902). In the years before 1914, the European powers tightened their control and established colonial governments to rule their gigantic empires (see Map 31.2).

In the complexity of the European seizure of Africa, certain events and individuals stand out. Of enormous importance was the British occupation of Egypt, which established the new model of formal political control. There was also the role of Leopold II of Belgium (1865–1909), an energetic, strong-willed monarch with a savage lust for distant territory. "The sea bathes our coast, the world lies before us," he had exclaimed in 1861. "Steam and electricity have annihilated distance, and all the non-appropriated lands on the surface of the globe can become the field of our operations and of our success."[8] By 1876 Leopold was focusing on Africa, and he organized in Brussels the International Association for the Exploration and Civilization of Central Africa. Subsequently, Leopold formed a financial syndicate under his personal control to send H. M. Stanley, a sensation-seeking journalist and part-time explorer, to the Congo basin. Stanley established trading stations, signed "treaties" with African chiefs, and planted the flag of Leopold's International Association. Leopold's actions alarmed the French, who quickly sent out an expedition under Pierre de Brazza. In 1880 de Brazza signed a treaty of protection with the chief of the large Teke tribe and began to establish a French protectorate on the north bank of the Congo River.

Leopold's buccaneering intrusion into the Congo area raised the question of the political fate of black Africa – Africa south of the Sahara. By the time the British successfully invaded and occupied Egypt, the richest and most developed land in Africa in 1882,

MAP 31.2 THE PARTITION OF AFRICA *European nations carved up Africa after 1880 and built vast political empires.*

Europe had caught "African fever." There was a gold-rush mentality, and the race for territory was on.

To lay down some basic rules for this new and dangerous game of imperialist competition, Jules Ferry of France and Bismarck of Germany arranged an international conference on Africa in Berlin in 1884 and 1885. The conference established the principle that European claims to African territory had to rest on "effective occupation" in order to be recognized by other states. This principle was very important. It meant that Europeans would push relentlessly into interior regions from all sides, and that no single European power would be able to claim the entire continent. The conference recognized Leopold's personal rule over a neutral Congo Free State and declared all of the Congo basin a free-trade zone. The conference also agreed to work to stop slavery and the slave trade in Africa.

The Berlin conference coincided with Germany's sudden emergence as an imperial power. Prior to about 1880 Bismarck, like many European leaders at the time, had seen little value in colonies. Colonies reminded him, he said, of a poor but proud nobleman who wore a fur coat when he could not afford a shirt underneath. Then, in 1884 and 1885, as political agitation for expansion increased, Bismarck did an abrupt about-face, and Germany established protectorates over a number of small African kingdoms and tribes in Togo, Cameroon, South West Africa, and later in East Africa.

In acquiring colonies Bismarck cooperated against the British with France's Jules Ferry, who was as ardent for empire as he was for

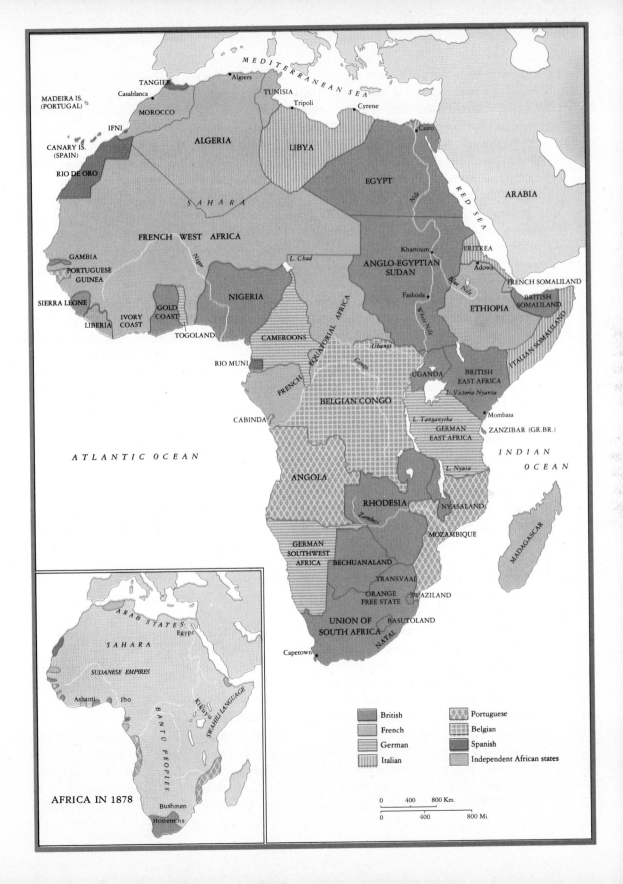

MEDITERRANEAN SEA

MADEIRA IS.
(PORTUGAL)

TANGIER
• Algiers
Casablanca
MOROCCO
• Tripoli
TUNISIA
• Cyrene

IFNI

CANARY IS.
(SPAIN)

RIO DE ORO

ALGERIA

LIBYA

EGYPT
• Cairo

Nile

RED SEA

ARABIA

SAHARA

FRENCH WEST AFRICA

L. Chad

Khartoum •

ANGLO-EGYPTIAN
SUDAN

ERITREA
• Adowa
FRENCH SOMALILAND
BRITISH
SOMALILAND

GAMBIA
PORTUGUESE
GUINEA

Niger

Blue Nile

SIERRA LEONE

NIGERIA

IVORY
COAST

GOLD
COAST

Fashoda •

White Nile

ETHIOPIA

LIBERIA

TOGOLAND

CAMEROONS

FRENCH EQUATORIAL AFRICA

Ubangi

UGANDA

BRITISH
EAST
AFRICA

ITALIAN SOMALILAND

RIO MUNI

Congo

L. Victoria Nyanza

BELGIAN CONGO

• Mombasa

CABINDA

L. Tanganyika

GERMAN
EAST AFRICA

ZANZIBAR (GR.BR.)

ATLANTIC OCEAN

INDIAN
OCEAN

L. Nyasa

ANGOLA

RHODESIA

NYASALAND

Zambesi

MOZAMBIQUE

MADAGASCAR

GERMAN
SOUTHWEST
AFRICA

BECHUANALAND

TRANSVAAL

ORANGE
FREE STATE

SWAZILAND

BASUTOLAND

UNION OF
SOUTH AFRICA

NATAL

Capetown •

ARAB STATES
Egypt

SAHARA

SUDANESE EMPIRES

Ashanti   Ibo

Kikuyu

SWAHILI LANGUAGE

BANTU PEOPLES

AFRICA IN 1878

Bushmen

Hottentots

	British		Portuguese
	French		Belgian
	German		Spanish
	Italian		Independent African states

0   400   800 Km.

0   400   800 Mi.

education. With Bismarck's tacit approval the French pressed vigorously southward from Algeria, eastward from their old forts on the Senegal coast, and northward from de Brazza's newly formed protectorate on the Congo River. The object of these three thrusts was Lake Chad, a malaria-infested swamp on the edge of the Sahara Desert.

Meanwhile, the British began enlarging their west African enclaves and impatiently pushing northward from the Cape Colony and westward from Zanzibar. Their thrust southward from Egypt was blocked in the Sudan by fiercely independent Muslims, who massacred a British force under General Charles "Chinese" Gordon at Khartoum in 1885.

A decade later another British force under General Horatio H. Kitchener moved cautiously and more successfully up the Nile River, building a railroad to supply arms and reinforcements as it went. Finally, in 1898, these British troops met their foe at Omdurman, where Muslim tribesmen charged time and time again only to be cut down by the recently invented machine gun. For one smug participant, the young British officer Winston Churchill, it was "like a pantomime scene" in a play. "These extraordinary foreign figures . . . march up one by one from the darkness of Barbarism to the footlights of civilization . . . and their conquerors, taking their possessions, forget even their names. Nor will history record such trash." For another more somber English observer, "It was not a battle but an execution. The bodies were not in heaps . . . but they spread evenly over acres and acres."[9] In the end eleven thousand fanatical Muslim tribesmen lay dead, while only twenty-eight Britons had been killed.

Continuing up the Nile after the battle of Omdurman, Kitchener's armies found that a small French force under Major Jean-Baptiste Marchand had already occupied the village at Fashoda. Locked in imperial competition ever since Britain had occupied Egypt, France had tried to beat the British to one of Africa's last unclaimed areas – the upper reaches of the Nile. The result was a serious diplomatic crisis, and even the threat of war. Eventually, wracked by the Dreyfus affair (page 1121) and unwilling to fight, France backed down and ordered Marchand to withdraw.

The reconquest of the Sudan exemplifies the general process of empire building in Africa. The fate of the Muslim force at Omdurman was eventually inflicted on all native peoples who resisted European rule: they were blown away by vastly superior military force. But however much the European powers squabbled for territory and privilege around the world, they always had the sense to stop short of actually fighting each other for it. Imperial ambitions were not worth a great European war.

IMPERIALISM IN ASIA

Although the sudden division of Africa was more spectacular, Europeans also extended their political control in Asia. In 1815, the Dutch ruled little more than the island of Java in the East Indies. Thereafter they gradually brought almost all of the three-thousand-mile archipelago under their political authority, though – in good imperialist fashion – they had to share some of the spoils with Britain and Germany. In the critical decade of the 1880s, the French under the leadership of Jules Ferry took Indochina. India, Japan, and China also experienced a profound imperialist impact (see Map 31.3).

Two other great imperialist powers, Russia and the United States, also acquired rich territories in Asia. Russia, whose history since the later Middle Ages has been marked by almost continuous expansion, moved steadily

OMDURMAN, 1898   The Sudan was conquered and a million square miles was added to the British Empire. (The Mansell Collection)

forward on two fronts throughout the nine-teenth century. Russians conquered Muslim areas to the south in the Caucasus and in central Asia, and also nibbled greedily on China's outlying provinces in the Far East, especially in the 1890s.

The United States' great conquest was the Philippines, taken from Spain in 1898 after the Spanish-American War. When it quickly became clear that the United States had no intention of granting independence, Philippine patriots under Emile Aguinaldo rose in revolt and were suppressed only after long, bitter fighting. (Not until 1933 was a timetable for independence established.) Some Americans protested the taking of the Philippines, but to no avail. Thus another great

Western power joined the imperialist ranks in Asia.

CAUSES OF THE NEW IMPERIALISM

Many factors contributed to the late-nineteenth-century rush for territory and empire, which was in turn one aspect of Western society's generalized expansion in the age of industry and nationalism. Little wonder that heated controversies have raged over interpretation of the new imperialism, especially since authors of every persuasion have often exaggerated particular aspects in an attempt to prove their own theories. Yet in spite of complexity and controversy, basic causes are clearly identifiable.

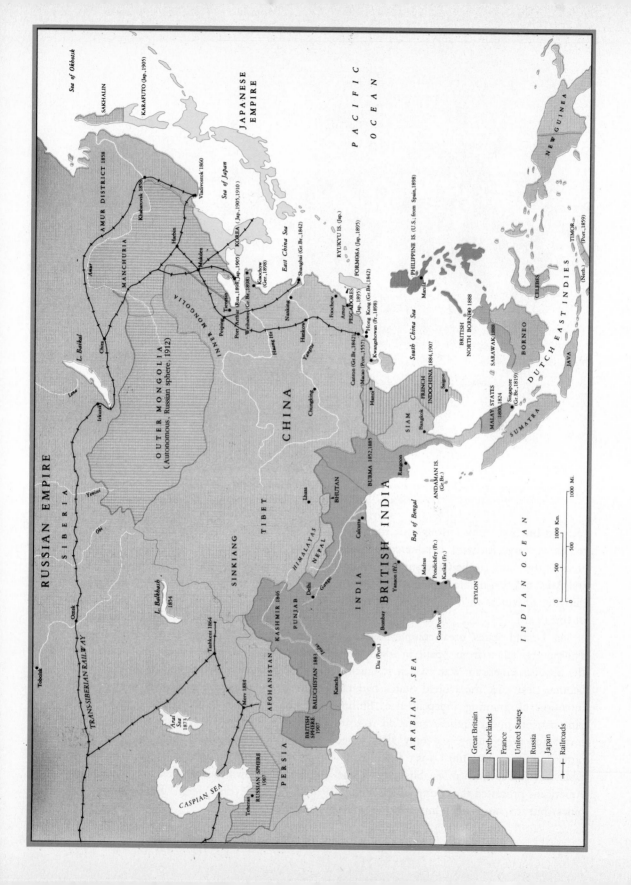

Sea of Okhotsk

SAKHALIN

KARAFUTO (Jap., 1905)

RUSSIAN EMPIRE

SIBERIA

AMUR DISTRICT 1858

MANCHURIA

Amur

Khabarovsk 1850

Vladivostok 1860

JAPANESE EMPIRE

Sea of Japan

KOREA (Jap., 1905, 1910)

Harbin

Mukden

Peiping

Tientsin

Port Arthur (Rus., 1898, 1905)

Weihaiwei (Gr. Br., 1898)

Kiaochow (Ger., 1898)

Shanghai (Gr. Br., 1842)

East China Sea

RYUKYU IS. (Jap.)

FORMOSA (Jap., 1895)

PESCADORES (Jap., 1895)

PHILIPPINE IS. (U.S. from Spain, 1898)

Manila

PACIFIC OCEAN

NEW GUINEA

TIMOR (Port., 1859)

L. Baikal

Irkutsk

China

Lena

INNER MONGOLIA

OUTER MONGOLIA (Autonomous, Russian sphere, 1912)

Yenisei

Ob

CHINA

Nanking

Hankow

Yangtze

Hwang Hô

Foochow

Amoy

Canton (Gr. Br., 1842)

Macao (Port., 1557)

Hong Kong (Gr. Br., 1842)

Kwangchowan (Fr., 1898)

South China Sea

BRITISH NORTH BORNEO 1888

SARAWAK 1888

BORNEO

CELEBES

DUTCH EAST INDIES

JAVA

(Neth.)

L. Balkhash

1854

SINKIANG

TIBET

Chungking

Lhasa

HIMALAYAS

NEPAL

BHUTAN

BURMA 1852, 1885

Rangoon

FRENCH INDOCHINA 1884, 1907

Hanoi

Saigon

SIAM

Bangkok

MALAY STATES 1800, 1824

Singapore (Gr. Br., 1819)

SUMATRA

Tashkent 1864

AFGHANISTAN

KASHMIR 1846

PUNJAB

Delhi

Ganges

Indus

BALUCHISTAN 1883

Karachi

BRITISH SPHERE 1907

Bombay

Diu (Port.)

INDIA

BRITISH INDIA

Calcutta

Bay of Bengal

ANDAMAN IS. (Gr. Br.)

Madras

Pondichéry (Fr.)

Karikal (Fr.)

Yanaon (Fr.)

Goa (Port.)

CEYLON

INDIAN OCEAN

Merv 1884

Aral Sea 1873

RUSSIAN SPHERE 1907

PERSIA

Teheran

CASPIAN SEA

ARABIAN SEA

TRANS-SIBERIAN RAILWAY

Tobolsk

Omsk

1000 Km.

1000 Mi.

500

500

Great Britain

Netherlands

France

United States

Russia

Japan

Railroads

MAP 31.3 ASIA IN 1914 *India remained under British rule while China precariously preserved its political independence.*

Economic motives played an important role in the extension of political empires, especially the British Empire. By the late 1870s, France, Germany, and the United States were industrializing rapidly behind rising tariff barriers. Great Britain was losing its early lead and facing increasingly tough competition in foreign markets. In this new economic situation Britain came to value old possessions, such as India and Canada, more highly. The days when a leading free-trader like Richard Cobden could denounce "the bloodstained fetish of Empire" and statesman Benjamin Disraeli could call colonies "a millstone round our necks" came to an abrupt end. When continental powers began to grab any and all unclaimed territory in the 1880s, the British followed suit immediately. They feared that France and Germany would seal off their empires with high tariffs and restrictions, and that future economic opportunities would be lost forever.

Actually, the overall economic gains of the new imperialism proved quite limited before 1914. The new colonies were simply too poor to buy much, and they offered few immediately profitable investments. Nonetheless, even the poorest, most barren desert was jealously prized, and no territory was ever abandoned. Colonies became important for political and diplomatic reasons. Each leading country saw colonies as crucial to national security, military power, and international prestige. For instance, safeguarding the Suez Canal played a key role in the British occupation of Egypt, and protecting Egypt in turn led to the bloody reconquest of the Sudan. National security was a major factor in the United States'

decision to take the Panama Canal Zone in 1903.

The widespread belief that great states needed great navies in turn necessitated a string of naval bases and coaling stations around the world.

Many people were convinced that colonies were essential to great nations. "There has never been a great power without great colonies," wrote one French publicist in 1877. "Every virile people has established colonial power," echoed the famous nationalist historian of Germany, Heinrich von Treitschke. "All great nations in the fullness of their strength have desired to set their mark upon barbarian lands and those who fail to participate in this great rivalry will play a pitiable role in time to come."[10]

Treitschke's harsh statement reflects not only the increasing aggressiveness of European nationalism after Bismarck's wars of German unification but also social Darwinian theories of brutal competition between races. As the English economist Walter Bagehot argued, "the strongest nation has always been conquering the weaker . . . and the strongest tend to be best." Thus, European nations, which were seen as racially distinct parts of the dominant white race, had to seize colonies to show they were strong and virile. Moreover, since racial struggle was nature's inescapable law, the conquest of inferior peoples was just. "The path of progress is strewn with the wreck . . . of inferior races," wrote one professor in 1900. "Yet these dead peoples are, in very truth, the stepping stones on which mankind has risen to the higher intellectual and deeper emotional life of to-day."[11] Social Darwinism and racial doctrines fostered imperial expansion.

Finally, certain special-interest groups in each country were powerful agents of expansion. Shipping companies wanted lucrative subsidies. White settlers on dangerous, turbulent frontiers constantly demanded more land and greater protection. Missionaries and humanitarians wanted to spread religion and stop the slave trade. Explorers and adventurers sought knowledge and excitement. Military men and colonial officials, whose role has often been overlooked by writers on imperialism, foresaw rapid advancement and high-paid positions in growing empires. The actions of such groups and the determined individuals who led them thrust the course of empire forward.

Western society did not rest the case for empire solely on naked conquest and a Darwinian racial struggle, or on power politics and the need for naval bases on every ocean. In order to satisfy their consciences and answer their critics, imperialists developed additional arguments.

A favorite idea was that Europeans could and should "civilize" more primitive nonwhites. According to this view, nonwhites would eventually receive the benefits of modern economies, cities, advanced medicine, and higher standards of living. In time, they might be ready for self-government and Western democracy. Thus, French people spoke of their sacred "civilizing mission." Rudyard Kipling (1865–1936), who wrote masterfully of Anglo-Indian life and was perhaps the most influential writer of the 1890s, exhorted Europeans to unselfish service in distant lands:

Take up the White Man's Burden –
  Send forth the best ye breed –
Go bind your sons to exile
  To serve your captives' need,
To wait in heavy harness,
  On fluttered folk and wild –
Your new-caught, sullen peoples
  Half-devil and half-child.[12]

Many Americans accepted the ideology of the white man's burden. It was an important factor in the decision to rule rather than liberate the Philippines after the Spanish-American War. Like their European counterparts, these Americans sincerely believed that their civilization had reached unprecedented heights, and that they had unique benefits to bestow on all "less-advanced" peoples. Another argument was that imperial government protected natives from tribal warfare as well as cruder forms of exploitation by white settlers and businessmen.

Peace and stability under European control also permitted the spread of Christianity – the "true" religion. In Africa, Catholic and Protestant missionaries competed with Islam south of the Sahara, seeking converts and building schools to spread the gospel of Jesus Christ. Many Africans' first real contact with whites was in mission schools. As late as 1942, for example, 97 percent of Nigeria's student population was in mission schools. Some peoples, like the Ibos in Nigeria, became highly Christianized.

Such occasional successes in black Africa contrasted with the general failure of missionary efforts in India, China, and the Islamic world. There, Christians often preached in vain to peoples with ancient, complex religious beliefs. Yet the number of Christian believers around the world did increase substantially in the nineteenth century, and missionary groups kept trying. Unfortunately, "many missionaries had drunk at the well of European racism," and this probably prevented them from doing better.[13]

CRITICS OF IMPERIALISM

The expansion of empire aroused sharp, even bitter, critics. A forceful attack was delivered in 1902, after the unpopular Boer War, by the radical English economist J. A. Hobson (1858–1940) in his *Imperialism,* a work that influenced Lenin and others. Hobson contended that the rush to acquire colonies was due to the economic needs of unregulated capitalism, particularly the need of the rich to find outlets for their surplus capital. Yet, Hobson argued, imperial possessions do not pay off economically for the country as a whole. Only unscrupulous special-interest groups profit from them, at the expense of both the European taxpayer and the natives. Moreover, the quest for empire diverts attention from domestic reform and closing the gap between rich and poor. These and similar arguments were not very persuasive. Most people then (and now) believed that imperialism was economically profitable for the homeland, and a broad and genuine enthusiasm for empire developed among the masses.

Hobson and many other critics struck home, however, with their moral condemnation of whites imperiously ruling nonwhites. They rebelled against crude Darwinian thought. "O Evolution, what crimes are committed in thy name!" cried one foe. Another sardonically coined a new beatitude: "Blessed are the strong, for they shall prey on the weak."[14] Kipling and his kind were lampooned as racist bullies, whose rule rested on brutality, racial contempt, and the Maxim machine gun. Henry Labouchère, a member of Parliament and prominent spokesman for this position, mocked Kipling's famous poem:

Pile on the Brown Man's burden!
And if ye rouse his hate,
Meet his old-fashioned reasons
With Maxims up to date,
With shells and Dum-Dum bullets
A hundred times plain
The Brown Man's loss must never
Imply the White Man's gain.[15]

In *Heart of Darkness,* the Polish-born novelist Joseph Conrad (1857–1924) castigated the "pure selfishness" of Europeans in "civilizing" Africa; the main character, once a liberal scholar, turns into a savage racist.

Critics charged Europeans with applying a degrading double standard and failing to live up to their own noble ideals. At home, Europeans had won or were winning representative government, individual liberties, and a certain equality of opportunity. In their empires, Europeans imposed military dictatorships on Africans and Asians, forced them to work involuntarily almost like slaves, and discriminated against them shamelessly. Only by renouncing imperialism, its critics insisted, and giving captive peoples the freedoms Western society had struggled for since the French Revolution, would Europeans be worthy of their traditions. Europeans who denounced the imperialist tide provided colonial peoples with a Western ideology of liberation.

RESPONSES TO WESTERN IMPERIALISM

To consider the great surge of European expansion from the Western point of view is to see half the story. It is time to try to examine what foreign domination and imperialism meant to those who were ruled.

To peoples in Africa and Asia, Western expansion represented a profoundly disruptive assault. Everywhere it threatened traditional ruling classes, traditional economies, and traditional ways of life. Christian missionaries and European secular ideologies challenged established beliefs and values. Non-Western peoples experienced a crisis of identity, a crisis made all the more painful by the power and arrogance of the white intruders.

SENEGALESE SCOUTS, 1913 *Europeans recruited large numbers of native soldiers to expand and enforce their rule in Africa and Asia. Senegalese scouts were the pride of the French army in black Africa. (Roger-Viollet)*

The initial response of African and Asian rulers was to try to drive the unwelcome foreigners away. This was the case in China, Japan, and the upper Sudan, as we have seen. Violent antiforeign reactions exploded elsewhere, again and again, but the superior military technology of the industrialized West almost invariably prevailed. Beaten in battle, many Africans and Asians concentrated on preserving their cultural traditions at all cost. Others found themselves forced to reconsider their initial hostility. Some (like Ismail of Egypt) concluded that the West was indeed superior in some ways and that it was therefore necessary to reform their societies and copy European achievements. Thus, it is possible to think of responses to the Western impact as a spectrum, with "traditionalists" at one end, "westernizers" or "modernizers" at the other, and many shades of opinion in between. Both before and after European domination, the struggle among these groups was often intense. With time, however, the modernizers tended to gain the upper hand.

When the power of both the traditionalists and the modernizers was thoroughly shattered by superior force, the great majority of Asians and Africans accepted imperial rule. Political participation in non-Western lands was historically limited to small elites, and the masses were used to doing what their rulers told them. In these circumstances Europeans, clothed in power and convinced of their righteousness, governed smoothly and effectively. They received considerable support from both traditionalists – local chiefs, landowners, religious leaders – and modernizers – the Western-educated professional classes and civil servants.

Nevertheless, imperial rule was in many ways a hollow shell built on sand. Support for European rule among the conforming and accepting millions was shallow and weak. Thus, the conforming masses followed with greater or lesser enthusiasm a few determined personalities who came to oppose the Europeans. Such leaders always arose, both when Europeans ruled directly and when they manipulated native governments, for at least two basic reasons.

First, the nonconformists – the eventual anti-imperial leaders – developed a burning desire for human dignity. They came to feel that such dignity was incompatible with foreign rule with its smirks and smiles, its paternalism and condescension. Second, potential leaders found in the Western world the ideologies and justification for their protest. They discovered liberalism with its credo of civil liberty and political self-determination. They echoed the demands of anti-imperialists in Europe and America that the West live up to its own ideals.

More important, they found themselves attracted to modern nationalism, which asserted that every people had the right to control its own destiny. After 1917, anti-imperialist revolt would find another weapon in Lenin's version of Marxian socialism. Thus, the anti-imperialist search for dignity drew strength from Western culture, as is apparent in the development of three major Asian countries, India, Japan, and China.

EMPIRE IN INDIA

India was the jewel of the British Empire, and no colonial area experienced a more profound British impact. Unlike Japan and China, which maintained a real or precarious independence, and unlike African territories, which were annexed by Europeans only at the end of the nineteenth century, India was ruled more or less absolutely by Britain for a very long time.

Arriving in India on the heels of the Portuguese in the seventeenth century, the British East India Company had conquered the last independent native state by 1848. The last "traditional" response to European rule – the attempt by the established ruling classes to drive the white man out by military force – was broken in India in 1857 and 1858. Those were the years of the Great Rebellion (which the British called a mutiny), when an insurrection by Muslim and Hindu mercenaries in the British army spread throughout northern and central India before it was finally crushed, primarily by loyal native troops from southern India. Thereafter Britain ruled India directly. India illustrates, therefore, for better and for worse, what generations of European domination might produce.

After 1858, India was ruled by the British Parliament in London and administered by a tiny all-white civil service in India. In 1900 this elite consisted of fewer than 3,500 top officials, for a population of 300 million. The white elite, backed by white officers and native troops, was competent and generally well-disposed toward the welfare of the Indian peasant masses. Yet it practiced strict job discrimination and social segregation, and most of its members quite frankly considered the jumble of Indian peoples and castes to be racially inferior. As Lord Kitchener, one of the

THE BRITISH IN INDIA *This photo suggests not only the incredible power and luxury of the British ruling class in India but its confidence and self-satisfaction as well. As one British viceroy said: "We are all British gentlemen engaged in the magnificent work of governing an inferior race." (BBC Hulton Picture Library)*

most distinguished top military commanders of India, stated:

It is this consciousness of the inherent superiority of the European which has won for us India. However well educated and clever a native may be, and however brave he may prove himself, I believe that no rank we can bestow on him would cause him to be considered an equal of the British officer.[16]

When, for example, the British Parliament in 1883 was considering a major bill to allow Indian judges to try white Europeans in India, the British community rose in protest and defeated the measure. The idea that they might be judged by Indians was inconceivable to Europeans, for it was clear to the Europeans that the empire in India rested squarely on racial inequality.

In spite of (perhaps even because of) their strong feelings of racial and cultural superiority, the British acted energetically and introduced many desirable changes to India. Realizing that they needed well-educated Indians to serve as skilled subordinates in the government and army, the British established a modern system of progressive secondary education in which all instruction was in English. Thus, through education and government service the British offered some Indians excellent opportunities for economic and social advancement. High-caste Hindus were particularly quick to respond, and emerged as skillful intermediaries between the British rulers and the Indian people – a new elite profoundly influenced by Western thought and culture.

This new bureaucratic elite played a crucial role in modern economic development, which was a second result of British rule. Irrigation projects for agriculture, the world's third largest railroad network for good communications, and large tea and jute plantations geared to the world economy were all developed. Unfortunately, the lot of the Indian masses improved little, for the increase in production was quite literally eaten up by population increase.

Finally, with a well-educated, English-speaking Indian bureaucracy and modern communications, the British created a unified, powerful state. They placed under the same general system of law and administration the different Hindu and Muslim peoples and the vanquished kingdoms of the entire subcontinent – groups that had fought each other for centuries during the Middle Ages and had been repeatedly conquered by Muslim and Mongol invaders. It was as if Europe, with its many states and varieties of Christianity, had been conquered and united in a single great empire.

In spite of these achievements, the decisive reaction to European rule was the rise of nationalism among the Indian elite. No matter how Anglicized and necessary a member of the educated classes became, he or she could never become the white ruler's equal. The top jobs, the best clubs, the modern-style hotels, and even certain railroad compartments were sealed off to brown-skinned men and women. The peasant masses might accept such inequality as the latest version of age-old oppression, but the well-educated, English-speaking elite eventually could not. For the elite, racial discrimination meant not only injured pride but bitter injustice. It flagrantly contradicted those cherished Western concepts of human rights and equality. Moreover, it was based on dictatorship, no matter how benign.

By 1885, when educated Indians came together to found the predominantly Hindu Indian National Congress, demands were increasing for the equality and self-government Britain enjoyed and had already granted white-settler colonies, such as Canada and Australia. By 1907, emboldened in part by Japan's success (see the next section), the radicals in the Indian National Congress were calling for complete independence. Even the moderates were demanding home rule for India through an elected parliament. Although there were sharp divisions between Hindus and Muslims, Indians were finding an answer to the foreign challenge. The common heritage of British rule and Western ideals, along with the reform and revitalization of the Hindu religion, had created a genuine movement for national independence.

THE EXAMPLE OF JAPAN

When Commodore Perry arrived in Japan in 1853 with his crude but effective gunboat diplomacy, Japan was a complex feudal society. At the top stood a figurehead emperor, but for more than two hundred years real power had been in the hands of a hereditary military governor, the shogun. With the help of a warrior nobility known as samurai, the shogun governed a country of hardworking, productive peasants and city dwellers. Often poor and restless, the intensely proud samurai were deeply humiliated by the sudden American intrusion and the unequal treaties with Western countries.

When foreign diplomats and merchants began to settle in Yokohama, radical samurai reacted with a wave of antiforeign terrorism and antigovernment assassinations between 1858 and 1863. The imperialist response was swift and unambiguous. An allied fleet of American, British, Dutch, and French warships demolished key forts, which further weakened the power and prestige of the shogun's government. Then, in 1867, a coalition led by patriotic samurai seized control of the government with hardly any bloodshed and restored the political power of the emperor. This was the Meiji Restoration, a great turning point in Japanese development.

The immediate, all-important goal of the new government was to meet the foreign threat. The battle cry of the Meiji reformers was "enrich the state and strengthen the armed forces." Yet how was this to be done? In an about-face that was one of history's most remarkable chapters, the young but well-trained, idealistic but flexible leaders of Meiji Japan dropped their antiforeign attacks. Convinced that Western civilization was indeed superior in its military and industrial aspects, they initiated from above a series of measures to reform Japan along modern lines. They were convinced that "Japan must be reborn with America its mother and France its father."[17] In the broadest sense, the Meiji

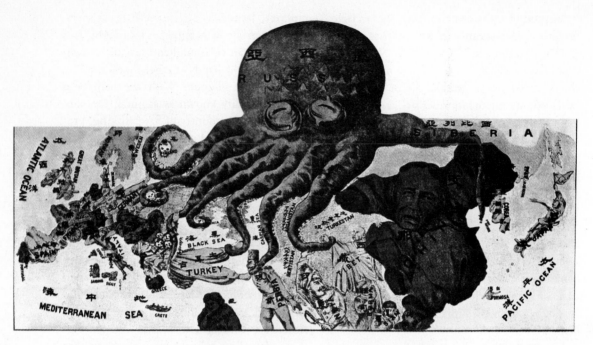

"THE RUSSIAN OCTOPUS" *This Japanese cartoon gives an Asian view of Russian imperialism and celebrates Japanese victories in 1904. "The ugly black octopus stretches out its eight arms in all directions," says* the cartoon's sly caption, "but sometimes it happens that it gets seriously wounded by a little fish because of its excessive greed." By 1904, Japan was definitely a "big fish" in Asian waters. (The Mansell Collection)

leaders tried to harness the power inherent in Europe's dual revolution, in order to protect their country and catch up with the West.

In 1871, the new leaders abolished the old feudal structure of aristocratic, decentralized government and formed a strong unified state. Following the example of the French Revolution, they dismantled the four-class legal system and declared social equality. They decreed freedom of movement in a country where traveling abroad had been a most serious crime. They created a free, competitive, government-stimulated economy. Japan began to build railroads and modern factories. Thus, the new generation adopted many principles of a free, liberal society; and, as in Europe, such freedom resulted in a tremendously creative release of human energy.

Yet the overriding concern of Japan's political leadership was always a powerful state, and to achieve this more than liberalism was borrowed from the West. The army was completely reorganized along French and German lines, with three-year military service for all males and a professional officer corps. This army of draftees effectively put down disturbances in the countryside, and in 1877 it was used to crush a major rebellion by feudal elements protesting the loss of their privileges. Japan also borrowed rapidly and adopted skillfully the West's science and modern technology, particularly in industry, medicine, and education. Many Japanese were encouraged to study abroad, and the government paid large salaries to attract highly qualified foreign experts. These experts were always carefully controlled, though, and they were replaced by well-trained Japanese as soon as possible.

By 1890, when the new state was firmly established, the wholesale borrowing of the early restoration had given way to more selective emphasis on those things foreign that were in keeping with Japanese tradition. Following the model of the German Empire, Japan established an authoritarian constitution and rejected democracy. The power of the emperor and his ministers was vast, that of the legislature limited.

Japan successfully copied the imperialism of Western society. Expansion not only proved that Japan was strong; it also cemented the nation together in a great mission. Having "opened" Korea with the gunboat diplomacy of imperialism in 1876, Japan decisively defeated China in a war over Korea in 1894 and took Formosa. In the next years Japan competed aggressively with the leading European powers for influence and territory in China, particularly in Manchuria. There Japanese and Russian imperialism met and collided. In 1904, Japan attacked Russia without warning, and after a bloody war Japan emerged with a valuable foothold in China, Russia's former protectorate over Port Arthur (see Map 31.3). By 1910, when it annexed Korea, Japan was a major imperial power, continuously expanding its influence in China in spite of sharp protests from its distant Pacific neighbor, the United States.

Japan became the first non-Western country to use an ancient love of country to transform itself and thereby meet the many-sided challenge of Western expansion. Moreover, Japan demonstrated convincingly that a modern Asian nation could defeat and humble a great Western power. Many Chinese nationalists were fascinated by Japan's achievement. A group of patriots in French-ruled southern Vietnam sent Vietnamese students to Japan to learn the island empire's secret of success. Japan provided patriots in Asia and Africa with an inspiring example of national recovery and national liberation.

TOWARD REVOLUTION IN CHINA

In 1860, the two-hundred-year-old Manchu dynasty in China appeared on the verge of collapse. Efforts to repel the foreigner had failed, and rebellion and chaos wracked the country. Yet the government drew on its traditional strengths and made a surprising comeback that lasted more than thirty years.

Two factors were crucial in this reversal. First, the traditional ruling groups temporarily produced new and effective leadership. Loyal scholar-statesmen and generals quelled disturbances like the great Tai Ping rebellion. A truly remarkable woman, the empress dowager Tzu Hsi, governed in the name of her young son and combined shrewd insight with vigorous action to revitalize the bureaucracy.

Second, destructive foreign aggression lessened, for the Europeans had obtained their primary goal of commercial and diplomatic relations. Indeed, some Europeans contributed to the dynasty's recovery. A talented Irishman named Robert Hart honestly and effectively reorganized China's customs office and increased the government tax receipts, while a sympathetic American diplomat, Anson Burlingame, represented China in foreign lands and helped strengthen the central government. Such efforts dovetailed with the dynasty's efforts to adopt some aspects of Western government and technology while maintaining traditional Chinese values and beliefs.

The parallel movement toward domestic reform and limited cooperation with the West collapsed under the blows of Japanese imperi-

CRUSHING THE BOXER REBELLION   *A captured Boxer is about to lose his head in a public execution before European troops. (BBC Hulton Picture Library)*

alism. The Sino-Japanese war of 1894–1895 and the subsequent harsh peace treaty revealed China's helplessness in the face of aggression, triggering a rush for foreign concessions and protectorates in China. At its high point in 1898, it appeared that the European powers might actually divide China among themselves, as they had recently divided Africa. Probably only the jealousy each nation felt toward its imperial competitors saved China from partition, although the United States' "Open Door" policy, which opposed formal

annexation of Chinese territory, may have helped tip the balance. In any event, the tempo and impact of foreign penetration accelerated dramatically after 1894.

So too did the intensity and radicalism of the Chinese reaction. Like the men of the Meiji Restoration, some modernizers saw salvation in Western institutions. In 1898, the government launched a desperate "hundred days of reform" in an attempt to meet the foreign challenge. More radical reformers like the revolutionary Sun Yat-sen (1866–1925), who came from the peasantry and was educated in Hawaii by Christian missionaries, sought to overthrow the dynasty altogether and establish a republic.

On the other side, some traditionalists turned back toward ancient practices, political conservatism, and fanatical hatred of the "foreign devils." "Protect the country, destroy the foreigner" was their simple motto. Such conservative, antiforeign patriots had often clashed with foreign missionaries, whom they charged with undermining reverence for ancestors and thereby threatening the Chinese family and the entire society. In the agony of defeat and unwanted reforms, secret societies like the Boxers rebelled. In northeastern China, more than two hundred foreign missionaries and several thousand Chinese Christians were killed. Once again the imperialist response was swift and harsh. Peking was occupied and plundered by foreign armies. A heavy indemnity was imposed.

The years after the Boxer Rebellion (1900–1903) were ever more troubled. Anarchy and foreign influence spread, as the power and prestige of the Manchu dynasty declined still further. Antiforeign, antigovernment revolutionary groups agitated and plotted. Finally, in 1912, a spontaneous uprising toppled the Manchu dynasty. After thousands of years of emperors and empires, a loose coalition of revolutionaries proclaimed a Western-style republic and called for an elected parliament. The transformation of China under the impact of expanding Western society entered a new phase, and the end was not in sight.

———

In the nineteenth century the West entered the third and most dynamic phase of its centuries-old expansion into non-Western lands. In so doing Western nations forged an integrated world economy, sent forth millions of emigrants, and established political influence in Asia and vast political empires in Africa. The reasons for this culminating surge were many, but the economic thrust of robust industrial capitalism, an ever-growing lead in technology, and the competitive pressures of European nationalism were particularly important.

Western expansion had far-reaching consequences. For the first time in human history the world became, in many ways, a single unit. Moreover, European expansion diffused the ideas and techniques of a highly developed civilization. Yet the West relied on force to conquer and rule, and it treated non-Western peoples as racial inferiors. Thus non-Western elites, often armed with Western doctrines, gradually responded to the Western challenge. They launched a national, anti-imperialist struggle for dignity, genuine independence, and modernization. This struggle would emerge as a central drama of world history after the great European civil war of 1914–1918, which reduced the West's technological advantage and shattered its self-confidence and complacent moral superiority.

NOTES

1. Quoted by A. Waley, *The Opium War Through Chinese Eyes,* Macmillan, New York, 1958, p. 29.

2. Quoted by J. W. Hall, *Japan, from Prehistory to Modern Times,* Delacorte Press, New York, 1970, p. 250.

3. Quoted by R. Hallett, *Africa to 1875,* University of Michigan Press, Ann Arbor, 1970, p. 109.

4. Quoted by Earl of Cromer, *Modern Egypt,* London, 1911, p. 48.

5. Quoted by T. Blegen, *Norwegian Migration to America,* Norwegian-American Historical Association, Northfield, Minn., 1940, 2.468.

6. Quoted by I. Howe, *World of Our Fathers*, Harcourt Brace Jovanovich, New York, 1976, p. 25.

7. Quoted by C. A. Price, *The Great White Walls Are Built: Restrictive Immigration to North America and Australia, 1836–1888*, Australian National University Press, Canberra, 1974, p. 175.

8. Quoted by W. L. Langer, *European Alliances and Alignments, 1871–1890*, Vintage Books, New York, 1931, p. 290.

9. Quoted by J. Ellis, *The Social History of the Machine Gun*, Pantheon Books, New York, 1975, pp. 86, 101.

10. Quoted by G. H. Nadel and P. Curtis, eds., *Imperialism and Colonialism*, Macmillan, New York, 1964, p. 94.

11. Quoted by W. L. Langer, *The Diplomacy of Imperialism*, 2nd ed., Knopf, New York, 1951, pp. 86, 88.

12. Rudyard Kipling, *The Five Nations*, London, 1903, quoted by the permission of Mrs. George Bambridge, Methuen & Company, and Doubleday & Company, Inc.

13. E. H. Berman, "African Responses to Christian Mission Education," *African Studies Review* 17:3 (1974):530.

14. Quoted in Langer, *Diplomacy of Imperialism*, p. 88.

15. Quoted by Ellis, pp. 99–100.

16. Quoted by K. M. Panikkar, *Asia and Western Dominance*, George Allen & Unwin, London, 1959, p. 116.

17. Quoted by Hall, p. 289.

SUGGESTED READING

Hall and Hallett, cited in the Notes, are excellent introductions to the histories of Japan and Africa. A. Waley, also cited in the Notes, has written extensively and well on China. K. Latourette, *The Chinese: Their History and Culture*, rev. ed. (1964), is a fine survey with many suggestions for further reading. Howe and Blegen, cited in the Notes, provide dramatic accounts of Jewish and Norwegian migration to the United States. Most other migrant groups have also found their historians: M. Walker, *Germany and the Emigration, 1816–1885* (1964), and W. Adams, *Ireland and Irish Emigration to the New World* (reissued 1967), are outstanding. Langer's volumes consider the diplomatic aspects of imperialism in exhaustive detail. Ellis's well-illustrated study of the machine gun is fascinating, as is Price on the restriction of Asian migration to Australia. All these works are cited in the Notes.

General surveys of European expansion in a broad perspective include R. Betts, *Europe Overseas* (1968); A. Thornton, *Imperialism in the 20th Century* (1977); T. Smith, *The Patterns of Imperialism* (1981); and W. Woodruff, *Impact of Western Man* (1967), which has an extensive bibliography. D. K. Fieldhouse has also written two fine surveys, *Economics and Empire, 1830–1914* (1970), and *Colonialism, 1870–1945* (1981). G. Barraclough, *An Introduction to Contemporary History* (1964), argues powerfully that Western imperialism and the non-Western reaction to it have been crucial in world history since about 1890. J. A. Hobson's classic *Imperialism* (1902) is readily available, and the Marxist-Leninist case is effectively presented in V. G. Kieran, *Marxism and Imperialism* (1975). Two excellent anthologies on the problem of European expansion are G. Nadel and P. Curtis, eds., *Imperialism and Colonialism* (1964), and H. Wright, ed., *The "New Imperialism,"* rev. ed. (1975).

Britain's leading position in European imperialism is examined in a lively way by B. Porter, *The Lion's Share* (1976); J. Morris, *Pax Britannica* (1968); and D. Judd, *The Victorian Empire* (1970), a stunning pictorial history. B. Semmel has written widely on the intellectual foundations of English expansion, as in *The Rise of Free Trade Imperialism* (1970). G. Himmelfarb, *Darwin and the Darwinian Revolution* (1968), shrewdly considers the philosophy so often used to justify the race for territory. H. Brunschwig, *French Colonialism, 1871–1914* (1966), and W. Baumgart, *Imperialism: The Idea and Reality of British and French Colonial Expansion* (1982), are well-balanced studies. A. Moorehead, *The White Nile* (1971), tells the fascinating story of the European exploration of the mysterious upper Nile. Volumes 5 and 6 of K. Latourette, *History of the Expansion of Christianity,* 7 vols. (1937–1945), examines the powerful impulse for missionary work in non-European areas. D. Headrick stresses Western technological superiority in *Tools of Empire* (1981).

Two unusual and provocative studies on personal relations between European rulers and non-European subjects are D. Mannoni, *Prospero and Caliban: The Psychology of Colonialization* (1964), and F. Fanon, *Wretched of the Earth* (1965), a bitter attack on white racism by a black psychologist active in the Algerian revolution. Novels also bring the psychological and human dimensions of imperialism alive. H. Rider Haggard, *King Solomon's Mines,* portrays the powerful appeal of adventure in exotic lands, while Rudyard Kipling, the greatest writer of European expansion, is at his stirring best in *Kim* and *Soldiers Three.* Joseph Conrad unforgettably probes European motives in *Heart of Darkness,* while André Gide, *The Immoralist,* closely examines European moral corruption in North Africa.

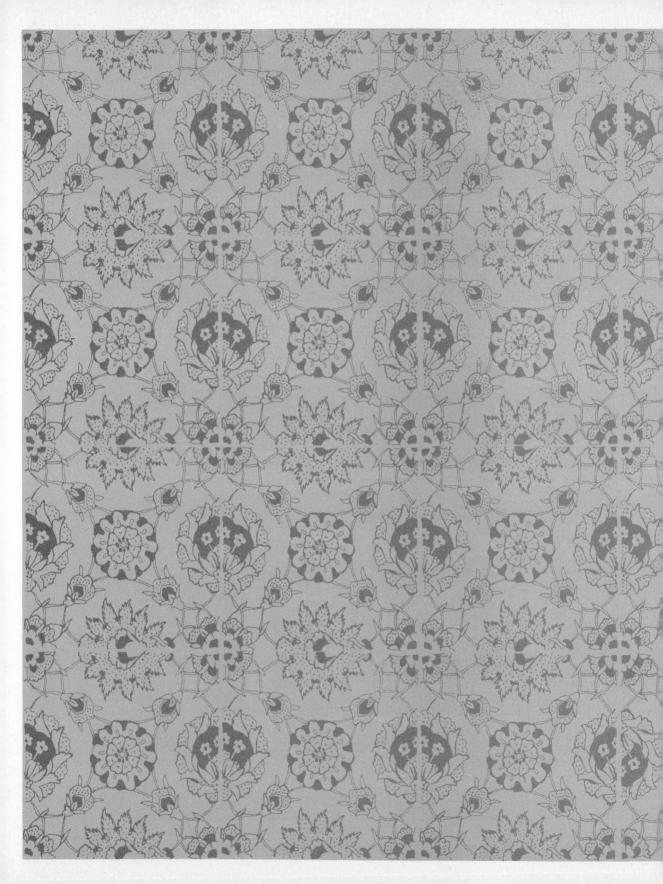

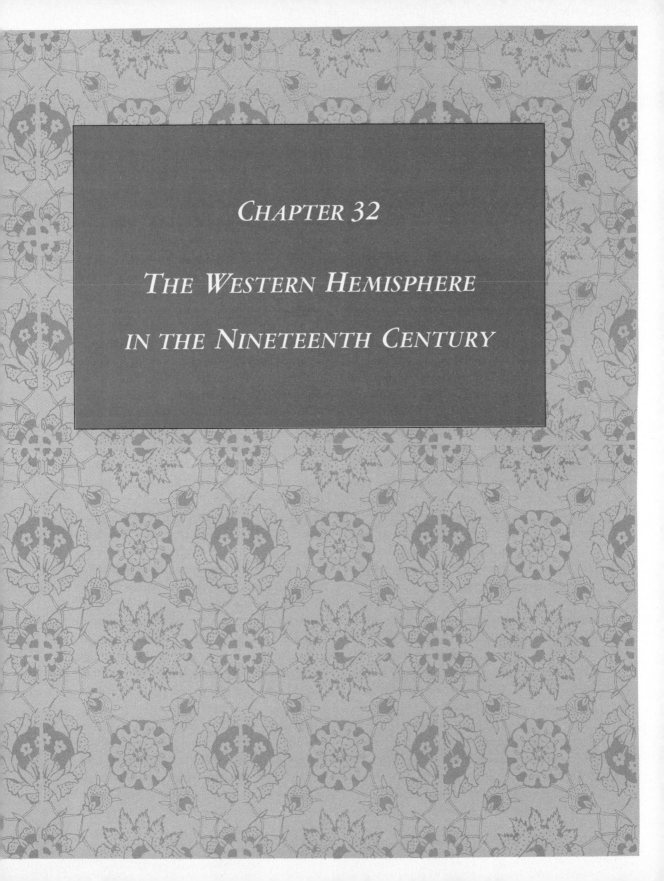

CHAPTER 32

THE WESTERN HEMISPHERE
IN THE NINETEENTH CENTURY

IN THE WESTERN HEMISPHERE as in Europe, the nineteenth century was a period of nation-building. It was also an era of geographic expansion and dynamic industrial and commercial growth. The century witnessed unparalleled waves of migration from Europe and Asia to the Americas. The millions of immigrants who braved the oceans populated and built the new nations; they also linked the Western Hemisphere with the rest of the globe. The countries of North and South America became highly diverse ethnically and culturally. One aspect of this pluralism was racial differences, and the issue of race created serious tensions throughout the hemisphere. In the United States it helped to bring on the Civil War, which jeopardized the existence of the Union itself. In the late nineteenth and early twentieth century European immigration directly affected the ways with which the United States and the Latin American nations coped with racial situations.

At the end of the eighteenth century, the several countries of South America and Canada remained colonies, whose European mother countries looked upon the democratic experiment of the infant United States with suspicion and scorn. By 1914 the Latin American states and Canada were enjoying political independence and playing a crucial role in the world economy. The United States had achieved the stature of a colossus, upon which the Old World depended in the First World War. How had this transformation come about? Why and how did the Spanish colonies of Latin America shake off European domination and develop into national states? What role did the concept of manifest destiny play in the evolution of the United States? How did the Americas absorb new peoples and what was their social impact? How did slavery affect the black family in the United States? This chapter seeks to answer these questions.

LATIN AMERICA (CA 1800–1929)

In 1800 the Spanish empire in the Western Hemisphere stretched from the headwaters of the Mississippi river in present-day Minnesota to the tip of Cape Horn in the Antarctic. The Spanish Crown claimed 7 million square miles, roughly one-third of the entire hemisphere. According to the Kentucky statesman Henry Clay, "Within this vast region, we behold the most sublime and interesting objects of creation: the loftiest mountains, the most majestic rivers in the world; the richest mines of precious metals, the choicest productions of the earth."[1] Spain believed that this great wealth existed for its benefit, and Spanish policies fostered bitterness and the desire for independence in the colonies.

Between 1806 and 1825 the Spanish colonies in Latin America were convulsed by upheavals that ultimately resulted in their separation from Spain. Some scholars regard these insurrections as wars of revolution; others call them wars of independence; still others consider them civil wars. All three characterizations contain elements of truth. The Latin American wars were revolutions in the sense that the colonists revolted against the domination of Spain and fought for direct self-government. They were wars of independence in that the colonies sought economic liberation and management of their own commercial affairs. They were civil wars in the sense that social and racial groups fought one another. The *Creoles* – people of Spanish descent born in America – resented the economic and political dominance of the *peninsulares,* as natives of Spain or Portugal were called. Peninsulares controlled the rich export-import trade, intercolonial trade, and the mining industries. At the same time *mestizos* of mixed Spanish and Indian background, and *mulattoes* of mixed

Spanish and African heritage sought an end to their systematic subordination.

Between 1850 and the worldwide depression of 1929, the countries of Latin America developed into national states. The predominant factors in this evolution were the heritage of colonial exploitation, a "neocolonial" economic structure, massive immigration from Europe and Asia, and the resulting fusion of Amerindian, Caucasian, African, and Asian peoples. The Latin American societies that emerged in the twentieth century can best be understood against this background.

THE ORIGINS OF THE REVOLUTIONS

Because of regional, geographic, and racial diversities, the Latin American movements for independence took different forms in different places. Everywhere, however, they grew out of recent colonial economic grievances. By the late seventeenth century the Spanish colonies had achieved a high degree of economic diversity and independence. The mercantilist imperialism of the days of Cortés and Pizarro, which held that the colonies existed for Spain's financial benefit and should be economically dependent upon Spain, had faded away. The colonies had become agriculturally and commercially self-sufficient producers of foodstuffs, wine, textiles, and consumer goods. What was not produced domestically was secured through trade between colonies. Despite formidable geographic obstacles, a healthy intercolonial trade had developed independent of Spain.

In Peru, for example, domestic agriculture supported the large mining settlements, and the colony did not have to import food. Craft workshops owned by the state or by private individuals produced consumer goods for the working class; what was not manufactured locally was bought from Mexico and transported by the Peruvian merchant marine. By 1700 Mexico and Peru were sending shrinking percentages of their revenues to Spain, and retaining more for public works, defense, and administration. The colonies lived for themselves and not for Spain.

The reforms of the Spanish Bourbons radically reversed this economic independence. Spain's humiliating defeat in the War of the Spanish Succession prompted demands for sweeping reform of all its institutions, including colonial policies and practices (page 675). To improve administrative efficiency, the enlightened monarch Charles III (1759–1788) carved the region of modern Colombia, Venezuela, and Ecuador out of the vast viceroyalty of Peru; it became the new viceroyalty of New Granada with its capital at Bogotá. The Crown also created the viceroyalty of Rio de la Plata (present-day Argentina) with its capital at Buenos Aires (see Map 32.1 on page 1170). Far more momentous was Charles III's radical overhaul of colonial trade policies, to enable Spain to compete with Great Britain and Holland in the great eighteenth-century struggle for empire. The Spanish Crown intended that the colonies serve as sources of raw materials and as markets for Spanish manufactured goods. Charles III's free-trade policies cut duties drastically for Spanish merchants. All Iberian ports, no longer just Cadiz, were allowed to trade with the colonies. In America these actions stimulated production of crops in demand in Europe: coffee in Venezuela; sugar in Cuba and throughout the Caribbean; hides, leather, and salted beef in the Rio de la Plata. In Mexico and Peru, production of silver climbed steadily in the last quarter of the century. The volume of Spain's trade with the colonies soared, possibly as much as 700 percent between 1778 and 1788.[2]

Colonial manufacturing, which had been

Disputed by England,
Spain, and Russia

Effective frontier of
Spanish settlement

ATLANTIC

OCEAN

COAHUILA
VICEROYALTY
OF NEW SPAIN

BAJÍO LEÓN

Mexico City •   • Veracruz

Havana

CUBA   HAITI/SAINT DOMINIQUE

JAMAICA   PUERTO RICO

CARIBBEAN SEA

• Guatemala

Caracas

Bogotá •   VICEROYALTY OF
NEW GRANADA   GUIANA

Amazon

VICEROYALTY
Lima •   OF PERU

VICEROYALTY OF BRAZIL

PACIFIC

OCEAN

Bahia

Río de Janeiro

São Paulo

VICEROYALTY OF
RÍO DE LA PLATA

Santiago •

Montevideo

AUDIENCIA
OF CHILE

Buenos Aires

FALKLAND/MALVINAS ISLANDS

0   1000 Km.

0   1000 Mi.

MAP 32.1 LATIN AMERICA BEFORE INDEPEN-
DENCE Consider the factors that led to the bounda-
ries of the various Spanish and Portuguese colonies in
North and South America.

growing steadily, suffered severely. Better made and cheaper European goods drove colonial goods out of the marketplace. Colonial textiles, chinaware, and wine, for example, could not compete with cheap Spanish products. For one thing, American free laborers were paid more than European workers in the eighteenth century; this helps explain the great numbers of immigrants to the colonies. Also, intercolonial transportation costs were higher than transatlantic costs: in Buenos Aires, for example, Spanish wines were actually cheaper than locally produced Mendoza wine.

In the Rio de la Plata region, heavy export taxes and light import duties shattered the wine industry. When the wine merchants complained of "tyrannical taxes" and asked an end to the import of Spanish wines, the imperial government rejected their appeal. Geographic obstacles also hampered Latin American economic development. Mountains, deserts, jungles, and inadequate natural harbors frustrated colonial efforts to promote economic integration.

Having made the colonies dependent on essential Spanish goods, Spain found that it could not keep the sea routes open. After 1789 the French Revolutionary and Napoleonic Wars isolated Spain from Latin America. Foreign traders, especially from the United States, swarmed into Spanish-American ports. In 1796 the Madrid government lifted the restrictions against neutrals trading with the colonies, thus acknowledging Spain's inability to supply the colonies with needed goods and markets.[3] All these difficulties spelled disaster for colonial trade and industry.

At the end of the eighteenth century colo-

nists also complained bitterly that only peninsulares were appointed to the *audiencias* – the colonies' highest judicial bodies, which also served as councils to the viceroys – and other positions in the colonial governments, to the exclusion of creoles. According to the nineteenth-century Mexican statesman and historian Lucas Alaman,

this preference shown to Spaniards in political offices and ecclesiastical benefices has been the principal cause of the rivalry between the two classes; add to this the fact that Europeans possessed great wealth, which although it may have been the just reward of effort and industry, excited the envy of Americans and was considered as so much usurpation from them; consider that for all these reasons the Spaniards had obtained a decided preponderance over those born in the country; and it will not be difficult to explain the increasing jealousy and rivalry between the two groups which culminated in hatred and enmity.[4]

In the late seventeenth and early eighteenth centuries, large numbers of Creoles had been appointed to government positions, including the audiencias. Then, beginning in 1751, the Crown drastically reduced appointments of Creoles. The upper levels of colonial bureaucracies became overwhelmingly Spanish. Between 1730 and 1750, fully 53 percent of appointees to the audiencias had been Creoles; from 1751 to 1775, only 13 percent were Creoles.[5] This change in imperial policy provoked American outrage. From the perspective of the Creole elite of Spanish America, the world seemed "upside down."[6] Creoles hungered for political office and resented their successful Spanish rivals.

Madrid's tax reforms aggravated discontent. In the 1770s and 1780s the Spanish Crown needed income to finance imperial defense. Colonial ports had to be fortified and standing armies built. Like Great Britain, Spain believed its Latin American colonies

DIAMOND MINING IN BRAZIL *The discovery of gold and diamonds in Brazil in the 17th-century increased the demand for slave labor. The English geologist John Mawe made this dramatic engraving of slaves washing for diamonds in the early 19th-century. (Courtesy, Oliveira Lima Library, The Catholic University of America. Photo: Paul McKane, OSB)*

should bear some of the costs of their own defense. Accordingly, Madrid raised the prices of tobacco and liquor and increased the *alcabala* (a sales tax of Arabic origin) on many items. Improved governmental administration made tax collection more efficient. Creole business and agricultural interests resented the Crown's monopoly of the tobacco industry and opposed new taxes.

Like the thirteen North American colonies a decade earlier, the Latin American protest movements claimed that the colonies were being taxed unconstitutionally. However, where the merchants of Boston and Philadel-

phia had protested taxation without representation, the Spanish colonies had no tradition of legislative approval of taxes. Creole mercantile leaders argued instead that the constitutional system was being violated when taxes were imposed without *consultation*. They asserted that relations between imperial authorities and colonial interests stayed on an even keel through consultation and compromise; when the Crown imposed taxes without consultation, therefore, it violated ancient constitutional practice.

North American ships calling at Spanish American ports had introduced the subversive writings of Thomas Paine and Thomas Jefferson. The imperial government recognized the potential danger of the North American example: although Spain had joined France on the side of the rebel colonies against Great Britain during the American Revolution, the Madrid government refused in 1783 to grant diplomatic recognition to the new United States. For decades the ideas of Voltaire, Rousseau, and Montesquieu also trickled into Latin America. In 1794 the Colombian Antonio Nariño translated and published the French *Declaration of the Rights of Man and the Citizen.* Although Spanish authorities sentenced him to ten years in an African prison, Nariño lived to become the father of Colombian independence. By 1800 the Creole elite throughout Latin America was familiar with liberal enlightenment political thought.[7]

RACE IN THE COLONIAL PERIOD

The Creoles assumed the "rights of man" to be limited to themselves; they had no thought of sharing such rights with the Indian and black masses. The racial complexion of Latin American societies is perhaps the most complicated in the world. Few European women emigrated to the colonies; thus Spanish males took their pleasure with Indian and African women. African men deprived of black women sought Indian women. The result was a population composed of every possible combination of Indian, Spanish, and African blood. Spanish theories of racial purity rejected people of mixed blood, and particularly those of African descent. A person's social status depended upon the degree of European blood he or she possessed or appeared to possess. Peninsulares and Creoles reinforced their privileged status by showing contempt for the non-white. As the great nineteenth-century German scientist Alexander von Humboldt put it, having spent five years travelling throughout South America, "Any white person, although he rides his horse barefoot, imagines himself to be of the nobility of the country." Coupled with the Spaniard's aristocratic disdain for manual labor, a three-hundred-year tradition had instilled in the minds of Latin Americans the notion that dark skin and manual labor went together. Owners of mines, plantations, and factories had a vested interest in keeping blacks and Indians in a servile position. A pervasive racism and discrimination characterized all the Latin American colonies.

In spite of the catastrophes that had befallen them in the sixteenth and seventeenth centuries, Indians still constituted the majority of the population of Latin America at the end of the colonial period. Demographers estimate that Indians accounted for between three-fifths and three-fourths of the total population. The colonies that became Peru and Bolivia had Indian majorities; the regions that became Argentina and Chile had European majorities. As the Indians declined in the seventeenth century, the Spanish grabbed up Indian lands for wheat, corn, cattle, and sheep raising. Indians and black slaves toiled in the silver and gold mines of Mexico, Colombia,

and Peru, the wheat fields of Chile, the humid mosquito-ridden cane brakes of Mexico and the Caribbean, the diamond mines and coffee plantations of Brazil.

Nevertheless, non-whites did experience some social mobility in the colonial period, certainly more than in North America. In Mexico, decreasing reliance on slaves in the economic system led to a great increase in manumissions. Once freed, however, Negroes immediately became subject to the payment of tribute, as were the Indians. Freedmen also incurred the obligation of military service. A few mulattoes rose in the army, some as high as the rank of colonel; the army and the Church seem to have offered the greatest opportunities for social mobility. Many black slaves gained their freedom by fleeing to the jungles or mountains, where they established self-governing communities. Around 1800 Venezuela counted 24,000 fugitive slaves in a total population of 87,000.

Conditions varied, but many Indians were still subject to the *mita* and *repartimiento*. The mita, a system of forced labor requiring that all adult Indian males work for part of each year in the silver mines, was thinly disguised slave labor; the silver mines were deathtraps. The law of repartimiento required Indians to buy goods solely from the local *corregidores*. The new taxes of the 1770s and 1780s fell particularly heavily on the Indians. When Indian opposition to these taxes and to oppressive conditions exploded into violence, Creoles organized the protest movements and assumed leadership of them.

THE COMUNERO REVOLUTION

In Peru in November 1779 the wealthy, well-educated mestizo Tupac Amaru, a descendant of the Inca kings, captured, tried, and executed the local *corregidor,* the official who collected taxes. Tupac Amaru and his mostly Indian followers demanded the abolition of the alcabala and the mita, and replacement of the corregidores with Indian governors. Proclaiming himself liberator of the people, Tupac Amaru waged a war of blood and fire against the Spanish governors. Violence swept the Peruvian highlands. Thousands lost their lives and a vast amount of private property was destroyed. Poor communication among the rebel forces and the superior organization of the imperial armies enabled the Spanish to crush the revolt. Tupac Amaru, his family, and his captains were captured and savagely executed. Frightened colonial administrators did, however, grant some reforms. The Crown repealed the repartimiento, reduced the mita, and replaced the corregidores with a lighter system of intendants. The condition of the Indians temporarily improved.

News of the rebellion of Tupac Amaru trickled northward, where it helped stimulate revolution in New Granada. Disorders occurred first at Socorro in modern Colombia (see Map 32.2 on page 1178). Throughout the eighteenth century Socorro had prospered. Sugar cane, corn, and cattle flourished on its exceptionally fertile soil. Large cotton crops stimulated the production of textiles, mostly in a primitive cottage industry worked by women. Socorro's location on the Suarez river made it an agricultural and manufacturing center and an entrepôt for trade with the hinterland. Hard-working Spanish immigrants had prospered and often intermarried with the Indians, creating a sizable mestizo population. When the viceroy published new taxes on tobacco and liquor and reorganized the alcabala, riots broke out in Socorro in March 1781 and spread to other towns. Representatives of peasants and artisan groups from many towns elected a *comun,* or central committee, to lead the insurrection. Each town elected its local comun and the captain of its militia. Known

as the Comunero Revolution, the insurrection in New Granada enjoyed broad-based support and good organization, and appeared far more threatening to governmental authorities than had the uprising in Peru.

An Indian peasant army commanded by Creole captains marched on Bogotá. Government officials, lacking adequate military resources, sent a commission to play for time by negotiating with the comuneros. On June 4 the commission agreed to the rebels' terms: reduction of the alcabala and of the Indians' forced tribute, abolition of the new taxes on tobacco, and preference for Creoles over peninsulares in governmental positions. The joyful Indian army disbanded and went home. What they did not know was that the commission had already secretly disclaimed the agreement with the rebels on the grounds that it had been taken by force. Having succeeded in dispersing the Indians, the government at Bogotá won over the Creole leaders with promises of pardons and then moved in reserve troops who captured large numbers of rebels. When the last rebel holdout – that of Jose Antonio Galan – had been captured, the kangaroo court that tried him declared

that the punishment of this prisoner and his associates should serve as an exemplary warning, so that no one subsequently can claim ignorance of the horrible crime that a person commits when obstructing the laws and ordinances emanating from legitimate superiors.[9]

He was condemned

to be taken out of jail, dragged and taken to the place of execution where he will be hung until dead, that his head be removed from his dead body, that the rest of his body be quartered, that his torso be committed to flames for which purpose a fire shall be lit in front of the platform. His head shall be sent to. Guaduas, the scene of his scandalous insults, his right arm shall be displayed in the

1764–1780	Charles III of Spain's administrative and economic reforms
1781	Communero revolution in New Granada
1810–1825	Latin American wars of independence against Spain
1822	Proclamation by Portugal of Brazil's independence
1826	Call by Simon Bolivar for Panama Conference on Latin American union
1825–ca 1870	Political instability in most Latin American nations
ca 1870–1919	Latin American neo-colonialism
1876–1911	Porfirio Diaz' control of Mexico
1888	Emancipation of slaves in Brazil; final abolition of slavery in Western Hemisphere
1880–1914	Massive immigration from Europe and Asia to Latin America
1898	Spanish American War; end of Spanish control over Cuba; transfer of Puerto Rico to United States

main square of Socorro, his left arm shall be displayed in the square of San Gil, his right leg shall be displayed in Charala his birthplace, and his left leg in the parish of Mogotes. All his descendants shall be declared infamous, all his property shall be confiscated by the royal treasury, his home shall be burnt, and the ground salted, so that in this fashion his infamous name may be forgotten.[10]

Thus ended the revolt of the comuneros in New Granada. The comuneros failed to win self-rule, but they forced the authorities to act in accordance with the spirit of the "unwritten constitution," whose guiding principle was consultation and compromise. Although the authorities used Galan's execution as a stick to kill social revolution, over the next twenty years they extended the carrot of governmental concern to promote colonial prosperity.

INDEPENDENCE

Napoleon Bonaparte lit the fuse of the Latin American powder keg. In 1808, as part of his effort to rule Europe, Napoleon deposed the Spanish king Ferdinand VII and placed his own brother on the Spanish throne (page 976). In Latin America the Creoles seized the opportunity: since everything in Spanish America was done in the name of the king, the Creoles argued that the removal of the legitimate king shifted sovereignty to the people – that is, themselves. The small, wealthy Creole aristocracy used the removal of the Spanish king as justification for their seizure of political power and their preservation of that power.

Thus began the war for independence. An able scholar has described it as "a prolonged, confused, and in many ways contradictory

SIMON BOLIVAR (1783–1830)   His success in defeating Spanish armies earned him the title 'the Liberator.' President of Greater Colombia, Bolivar organized the government of Peru, created Bolivia, and dreamt of a United Spanish America. He is respected as the greatest Latin American hero. (Courtesy of the Organization of American States)

It had no single recognized leader like Washington. The struggle for independence had no agency to provide the movement with funds or to authorize recruitment of an army. Each part of the continent fought the war, which lasted from 1810 to 1824, in its own way. If there was no central direction, no centrally recognized leadership, likewise there was no formally accepted political doctrine."[11] The Creoles who led the various movements for independence did not intend a radical redistribution of property or reconstruction of society; they merely rejected the authority of the Spanish Crown.

"In the final battle . . . , the soldiers on the field came from Venezuela, Colombia, Ecuador, Peru, Argentina, and Chile, and among the officers there were Frenchmen and Englishmen who had opposed each other in the Napoleonic Wars. It was a continental, if not an international, army. The war stopped but did not officially end. There was no treaty of peace. There was no recognition of the new states. There was no definite agreement as to the form of government or even as to national boundaries. . . . Just as there was no Continental Congress, there was no Constitutional Convention where all of the former colonies united to establish a government. In Latin America each separate area went its own way. Central America broke away from Mexico and then splintered into five separate nations. Uruguay, Paraguay, and Bolivia separated themselves from Argentina, Chile from Peru, and Bolivar's attempt to federate the state of *Gran Colombia* (Venezuela, Colombia, and Ecuador) with Peru and Bolivia under a centralized government broke down."[12]

Simon Bolivar (1783–1830), the great hero of the movement for independence, is considered the Spanish-American George Washington. A very able general, Bolivar's victories over the royalist armies won him the presi-

movement. In Mexico it began as a popular social movement [and] ended many years later as a conservative uprising against a liberal Spanish constitution. In Venezuela it came to be a war unto the death; in other places it was a war between a small [Creole] minority and the Spanish authorities. It was not an organized movement with a central revolutionary directorate. It had no Continental Congress.

dency of Greater Colombia. Bolivar dreamt of a continental union, and in 1826 he summoned a conference of South American republics at Panama. The meeting achieved little. Bolivar organized the government of Bolivia and became the head of the new state of Peru. The territories of Greater Colombia splintered apart, however, and a sadly disillusioned Bolivar went into exile, saying "America is ungovernable. Those who served the revolution plowed the seas." The failure of pan-Americanism isolated individual countries, prevented collective action, and later paved the way for the political and economic intrusion of the United States and other powers.

Portuguese Brazil's quest for independence was unique: Brazil won its independence without violent upheaval. When Napoleon's troops entered Portugal, the king and the royal family fled to Brazil and made Rio de Janeiro the capital of the Portuguese empire. The new government immediately lifted the old mercantilist restrictions and opened Brazilian ports to the ships of all friendly nations. Under popular pressure, Pedro I proclaimed Brazil's independence in 1822 and published a constitution. Pedro's administration was wracked by factional disputes between Portuguese courtiers and Brazilian Creoles, a separatist movement in the Rio Grande do Sul region, and provincial revolts. His successor Pedro II (1840–1889) restored order and laid the foundations of the modern Brazilian state. His reign witnessed the expansion of the coffee industry, the beginnings of the rubber industry, and massive immigration.

THE CONSEQUENCES OF INDEPENDENCE

The wars of independence ended around 1825. What effects did they have on South American societies? How were South American countries governed in the nineteenth century?

What factors worked against the development of modern nations? Because the movements for independence differed in character and course in different regions and countries, generalizations about Mexico, the Caribbean islands, and South America are likely to be misleading. Significant changes did occur, however, throughout South America.

The newly independent nations did not achieve immediate political stability when the wars of independence ended around 1825. The Spanish Crown had served as a unifying symbol, and its disappearance left a power vacuum. Civil disorder typically followed. The Creole leaders of the revolutions had no experience in government, and the wars had left a legacy of military, not civilian, leadership. Throughout the continent, idealistic but impractical leaders proclaimed republics – independent states governed by an assembly of representatives of the electorate. In practice, the generals ruled. In Argentina, for example, Juan Manuel de Rosa assumed power amid widespread public disorder in 1835 and ruled as dictator. In Mexico, liberals declared a federal republic, but incessant civil strife led to the rise of the dictator Antonia Lopez de Santa Anna. Likewise in Venezuela, strongmen, dictators, and petty aristocratic oligarchs governed from 1830 to 1892. Some countries suffered constant revolutions: in the course of the century Bolivia had sixty and Venezuela fifty-two. The rule of force prevailed almost everywhere. Enlightened dictatorship was the typical form of government.

The wars of liberation disrupted the economic life of most Latin American countries. The prosperity many areas had achieved toward the end of the colonial period was destroyed. Mexico and Venezuela in particular lost almost half their populations and suffered great destruction of farmland and animals. Even countries that saw relatively little vio-

UNITED STATES

ATLANTIC

OCEAN

MEXICO

Havana

Mexico City • • Veracruz

CUBA

DOMINICAN REP.

BR. HONDURAS

JAMAICA   HAITI

PUERTO RICO

Guatemala •

GUATEMALA   HONDURAS

CARIBBEAN SEA

NICARAGUA

COSTA RICA

Caracas •

BR. GUIANA

VENEZUELA

DUTCH GUIANA

FR. GUIANA

• Bogota

COLOMBIA

Quito •

ECUADOR

Amazon

PERU

B R A Z I L

Lima •

La Paz •

Bahia •

BOLIVIA

PACIFIC

São Paulo •

OCEAN

PARAGUAY

Rio de Janeiro •

Paraná

Valparaiso •

Santiago •

URUGUAY

CHILE

Buenos Aires •

ARGENTINA

• Montevideo

Bahia Blanca •

Independent nations

FALKLAND/MALVINAS ISLANDS

0   1000 Km.

0   1000 Mi.

lence, such as Chile and New Granada, experienced a weakening of economic life. Armies were frequently recruited by force, and when the men were demobilized many did not return home. The consequent population dislocation hurt agriculture and mining. Guerrilla warfare disrupted trade and communications; forced loans and the seizure of private property for military use ruined many people. In the 1820s Peru's economy staggered under the burden of supporting large armies. Isolated territories such as Paraguay and much of Central America suffered little damage, but most countries gained independence at the price of serious economic problems.

Independence accelerated the abolition of slavery. The destruction of agriculture in countries such as Mexico and Venezuela caused the collapse of the plantation system, and fugitive slaves could not be recaptured. Also, both the royalists and the patriot generals Bolivar and San Martin offered slaves freedom in exchange for military service. The result was that slaves constituted a large part of the military forces, perhaps a third of San Martin's army. Finally, most of the new independent states adopted republican constitutions declaring the legal equality of all men. For Indians and blacks, however, these noble words were meaningless, since the revolution brought about no redistribution of property. Nor could ancient racist attitudes be eliminated by the stroke of a pen.

Although the edifice of racism persisted in the nineteenth century, Latin America experienced much more assimilation and offered Negroes greater economic and social mobility than did the United States. As a direct result of their heroic military service in the wars of

independence, a substantial number of Negroes improved their social status. Some even attained the political heights: the Mexican revolutionary Vincente Guerrero, who served as president of his country in 1829; Juan José Flores, a general under Bolivar, architect of the nation of Ecuador and its first president; Andrés Santa Cruz, president of Bolivia; Antonio Guzman, who governed Venezuela as a benevolent dictator; and Ramon Castilla, whose term as president of Peru witnessed the strengthening of state financing.

What accounts for the relative racial permeability of Latin America in comparison with the system of severe segregation in the United States? As the Dutch scholar Hoetink points out, Latin American countries evolved a three-tiered sociracial structure, in contrast to the two-tiered racial edifice in the United States. Legally and socially, Latin American societies classified people as white, colored, or black, and marriages between whites and light-skinned colored people were commonly accepted. Legislative discrimination against colored people proved unenforceable. Thus light skin allowed for gradual assimilation into the middle and upper social echelons. In the United States, by contrast, anyone who was not "pure" white was classified as black.

Hoetink explains the problem partly in terms of the large population of poor whites in the United States. "Nowhere, but in the North American mainland, did the number of extremely poor whites always exceed the number of slaves. Nowhere, but in the [U.S.] South, were special police forces predominantly manned by poor whites."[13] Also, Latin American elites' perception of "whiteness" and of physical beauty seems to have been broader than that of the white majority in the United States.

The advantages of assimilation did not, and do not, apply to dark-skinned people in Latin

SOCIAL LIFE IN LATIN AMERICA *The easy mingling of blacks and whites in many Latin American cities led to large mulatto populations. Note the elaborate dress of the women reflecting Spanish and African styles. (Courtesy, The Oliveira Lima Library, the Catholic University of America. Photo: Paul McKane, OSB)*

America. While substantial numbers of light-skinned colored people rose economically and socially, the great mass of dark-skinned blacks continued to experience all the consequences of systematic and insistent racism.

NEOCOLONIALISM

The leaders of the Latin American revolutions had hoped that their nations, once independent, would attract European and North American investment. Instead, political instability and the preoccupation of European and North American financiers with industrial expansion in their own countries discouraged investment. The advent of stable dictator-

ships, however, eventually paved the way for real economic growth. After 1870 capital began to flow south and across the Atlantic. In Mexico, North American capital supported the production of hemp (used in the United States for grain harvesting), sugar, bananas, and rubber, frequently on American-owned plantations. British and American interests backed the development of Mexican tin, copper, and gold mining; oil drilling leapt forward, and by 1911 Mexico had taken third place among the world's oil producers. British financiers built Argentina's railroads, meat-packing industry, and utilities. British businessmen in Chile developed the copper and nitrate industries (nitrate is used in the production of pharmaceuticals and fertilizers); by 1890 the British controlled 70 percent of the nitrate industry. Likewise in Brazil, foreign capital – mainly British – flowed into coffee, cotton, and sugar production and manufacturing. In 1889 Brazil produced 56 percent of the world's coffee; by 1904 that figure had risen to 76 percent. When massive overproduction of coffee led to a sharp drop in prices in 1902, a commission of British, American, German, and French bankers rescued the Brazilian government from near-disaster.

The economic development of Latin America at the end of the nineteenth century was purchased at the high price of a new, economic form of domination. Foreign investors had acquired control of the railroads, mineral resources, and banking, and they had made heavy inroads into agriculture, real estate, and manufacturing. British investments led all others, but U.S. interests followed closely. Beginning in 1898 the United States flexed its imperialistic muscles and sent gunboats and troops to defend its dollars in the Caribbean and Central America. By the turn of the century the Latin American nations were active participants in the international economic order, but foreigners controlled most of their industries.

Another distinctive feature of the neo-colonial order was the cultivation of one crop. Each country's economy revolved around only one or two products: sugar in Cuba, nitrates and copper in Chile, meat in Argentina, coffee in Brazil. A sharp drop in the world market demand for a product could destroy the industry and with it the nation's economic structure. The outbreak of the First World War in 1914 drastically reduced exports of Latin American raw materials and imports of European manufactured goods, provoking general economic crisis.[14]

Throughout the eighteenth century the Spanish-owned *haciendas* – large landed estates – had continued to expand to meet the needs of commercial agriculture: wheat for the cities, corn for the Indians' consumption, sugar for export to Europe and North America. By means of purchase, forced removal of Indians, and outright seizure, the Spanish continued to take Indian land, as they had in the seventeenth century. Some land was acquired merely to eliminate Indian competition by depriving them of their fields, which were then left fallow.

The late nineteenth century witnessed ever-greater concentrations of land in ever-fewer hands. In places like the Valley of Mexico, a few large haciendas controlled all the land. Under the dictatorship of General Porfirio Diaz, the Mexican government in 1883 passed a law allowing real-estate companies (controlled by Diaz' political cronies) to survey public and "vacant" lands and to retain one-third of the land they surveyed. An 1894 law provided that land could be declared vacant if legal title to it could not be produced. Since few Indians could come up with deeds to the land their ancestors had worked for centuries, the door swung open to wholesale expropriation of small landowners and entire villages. Shrewd speculators tricked illiterate Indians into selling their lands for trifling sums. Thousands of litigants immobilized the courts. Indians who dared armed resistance were crushed by government troops and carried off to virtual slave labor. Vast stretches of land came into the hands of private individuals – in one case, 12 million acres. According to one authority, "the government had divested itself of an area roughly equal to that of California or equal to the combined totals of Ohio, Indiana, Illinois, and half of Kentucky; ... nearly one-fifth of the total land area of Mexico."[15] The Indians, stripped of their lands, represented a ready labor supply.

MEXICAN STRIKE *Subsistence wages and inhuman working conditions in foreign-owned firms led to massive strikes like this one at the Rio Blanco textile factory in Mexico in 1909. Government troops crushed the strike amid considerable bloodshed. (Brown Brothers)*

They were mercilessly exploited. Debt peonage became standard practice: landowners paid their laborers not in cash but in vouchers, redeemable only at the company store, whose high prices and tricky bookkeeping kept the peons permanently in debt.

Some scholars maintain that the owners of these huge estates hardly exploited their land at all, letting it lie fallow until it rose in value or attracted American investors. The lack of cultivation, they assert, kept the prices of corn and other crops artificially high. Where the land was cultivated, landowners used antiquated machinery and old-fashioned methods of irrigation and fertilization. The owners themselves, supported by rents, passed indo-

lent lives in extravagant luxury in Mexico City and other cities.

Recent scholars deny all this. They argue that the haciendas were in fact efficient capitalistic enterprises whose owners sought to maximize profits on invested capital. The Sanchez Navarros family of northwestern Mexico, for instance, engaged in a wide variety of agricultural and commercial pursuits, exploiting their lands and resources as fully as possible. The Sanchez Navarros controlled 800,000 acres in 1821, and continued to acquire chunks of land; ultimately their *latifundio* — an estate of two or more haciendas — was about the size of West Virginia. Along with vast cattle ranches and sheep runs containing as many as 250,000 sheep, the Sanchez Navarros cultivated maize, wheat, and cotton. They invested heavily and profitably in silver mining and manufacturing, and lent sizable sums at high interest. Although they brutally exploited their peons and practiced debt peonage, the Sanchez Navarros lived very modestly on their own estates rather than luxuriating in the capital. We must await further investigation to determine whether the Sanchez Navarros were unique or representative of a type of magnate prevalent in the agricultural and business communities of nineteenth-century Mexico.[16]

THE IMPACT OF IMMIGRATION

In 1852 the Argentine political philosopher Juan Bautista Alberdi published a book, *Bases and Points of Departure for Argentine Political Organization,* arguing that "to govern is to populate." Alberdi meant that the development of his country – and, by extension, all of Latin America – depended upon immigration. Argentina actually had an adequate labor supply, but it was unevenly distributed throughout the country. Moreover, Alberdi maintained, the Indians and blacks lacked basic skills and it would take too long to train them. Therefore he pressed for massive immigration from the "advanced" countries of northern Europe and the United States. Alberdi's ideas won immediate acceptance and were even incorporated into the Argentine constitution, which declared that "the Federal government will encourage European immigration." Other Latin American countries adopted similar policies promoting immigration.[17]

European needs coincided perfectly with those of Latin America (pages 1143–1145). After 1880, Ireland, Great Britain, Germany, Italy, Spain, and the Central European nations experienced greater population growth than their labor markets could absorb. Meanwhile the growing industries of Europe needed South American raw materials and markets for their finished goods, and South American countries wanted European markets for their minerals, coffee, sugar, beef, and manufactured goods. Italian, Spanish, and Portuguese peoples poured into Latin America, and immigration linked the two hemispheres.

Immigration led to rapid urbanization, which meant Europeanization and industrialization. By 1900, Buenos Aires, Rio de Janeiro, and Sao Paulo had populations of more than 500,000 people; Mexico City, Montevideo, Santiago de Chile, and Havana also experienced spectacular growth. Portuguese, Italian, French, Chinese, and Japanese immigrants gave an international flavor to the cities, and a more vigorous tempo replaced the somnolent Spanish atmosphere.

By 1914 Buenos Aires had emerged as one of the most cosmopolitan cities in the world. In less than half a century, the population of the city and its province had grown from 500,000 to 3.6 million. Argentina's political capital, the city housed all its governmental bureaucracies and agencies. The meat-packing, food processing, flour milling, and wool industries concentrated in Buenos Aires; half of all overseas tonnage passed through the city, which was also the heart of the nation's railroad network. The University of Buenos Aires was the intellectual hub of the nation. The elegant shops near the Plaza de Mayo catered to the expensive tastes of the elite upper classes, who constituted about 5 percent of the population.

Meanwhile the thousands of immigrants who toiled twelve hours a day, six days a week, on the docks and construction sites and in the meat-packing plants crowded into the city's *conventillos,* or tenements:

completed the furnishings. Light came from the open door and one window, from an oil or gas lamp, or occasionally from a bare electric light bulb. On the once-whitewashed walls were tacked pictures of popular heroes, generals, or kings torn from magazines, an image of the Madonna and a couple of saints, perhaps a faded photograph of family members in Europe. The women often eked out miserable incomes by taking in laundry and washing and drying it in the patios. Others ironed or sewed on a piecework basis. Some men worked here: in one corner a shoemaker might ply his trade, in another a man might bend over a small table repairing watches.[18]

DOMESTIC SCENES IN MID-NINETEENTH CEN-TURY RIO The servants, lace table cloth, and fancy dress of the mistress imply that this is a well-to-do household; the bare pine floors and the nude slave children prove that the family is aspiring. The meal, consisting of meat, bread, fruit, and wine, seems to be eaten on imported china. (Courtesy, Oliveira Lima Library, The Catholic University of America. Photo: Paul McKane, OSB)

The one-room dwelling . . . served a family with two to five children or a group of four or five single men. At the door to each room stood a pile of wooden boxes. One generally held a basin for washing; another a charcoal brazier on which to cook the daily watery stew, or puchero; *and garbage accumulated in a third. Two or three iron cots, a pine table, a few wooden chairs, an old trunk, perhaps a sewing machine, and more boxes*

Immigrants dreamed of rapid economic success in the New World, and there was in fact plenty of upward social mobility. The first generation almost always did manual labor, but their sons often advanced to upper blue-collar or white-collar jobs. The rare Genoese or Neapolitan immigrant whose labor and thrift made his son a millionaire quickly learned the meaning of assimilation: the son typically assumed the dress, style, and values of the Spanish elite. Hispanic attitudes toward class, manual labor, and egalitarianism prevailed, and the new immigrant rich imitated the Spanish nobility.[19]

Europeans gave an enormous boost to the development of industry and commerce. Italian and Spanish settlers in Argentina stimulated the expansion of the cattle industry and the development of the wheat and shoe industries. In Brazil, English investments facilitated the growth of the iron industry and the railroads. Swiss immigrants built the cheese business, Italians gained a leading role in the coffee industry, and the Japanese pioneered the development of the cotton industry. In Peru, the British controlled railroad construction, Italians became influential in banking and the restaurant business, while the French dominated jewelry, dressmaking, and pharmaceutical ventures. The arrival of millions of migrants changed the entire commercial structure of South America.

Immigration also promoted further ethnic integration. The vast majority of migrants were unmarried males; seven out of ten people who landed in Argentina between 1857 and 1924 were single males between thirteen and forty years old. Those who stayed often sought out Indian or other lower-class women. This kind of assimilation also occurred in Brazil, Mexico, Peru, and other South American countries. Male settlers from eastern Europe and women of all nationalities preferred to marry within their own ethnic groups. But men greatly outnumbered women, and a man who chose to marry usually had to marry an Indian.[20] Immigration, then, furthered racial mixture of Europeans, Asians, and native South Americans.

For Latin America's sizable black population, immigration proved a calamity. Slavery had been technically abolished in Spanish America after independence and in Portuguese Brazil by 1888, but the economic and social status of the Negro population had scarcely changed. Accustomed to working the rural coffee plantations and the mines, blacks had no preparation for urban living. Lacking skills, they could not compete with white labor for city jobs, and they lacked the time to acquire the necessary skills. In 1893, 71.2 percent of the working population of Sao Paulo was foreign-born. Anxious to adapt to America and to climb the economic ladder, immigrants quickly learned the ancient racial prejudices. Negro women usually found work as domestics, but employers excluded black males from good jobs. As a distinguished scholar of the problem has put it,

Although the competition from the immigrant affected the whole native population, only the negroes and mulattoes suffered its impact as a kind of social cataclysm. Excluded from the labor market or forced to its fringes, the colored men found themselves condemned to chronic unemployment, seasonal work, depressed wages, and adjustment to a type of life in which, inevitably, misery went hand in hand with social disintegration.[21]

Racial prejudice kept the vast bulk of the South American black population in a wretched socioeconomic position until the Second World War.

After independence, the social structure of most Latin American countries remained basically unchanged. Republican constitutions declared all men (but not women) equal under the law, but everywhere – except perhaps in Venezuela – an aristocratic white agrarian class exercised wealth and power. European ideas, such as utopian socialism, entered Latin American ports and stimulated mild intellectual ferment, but made only a slight impact on social change before the twentieth century. In the United States, by contrast, a dynamic commercial and capitalistic elite held economic and political power at the turn of the century. As Great Britain and the United States came to hold neocolonial control over the Latin American economy, the ruling aristocracy gradually became receptive to capitalistic values and ideals. European styles of dress became highly popular because they signified social status. Modernization in industry and commerce, however, came only in the twentieth century.

THE UNITED STATES
(CA 1789–1929)

The victory of the North American colonies and the founding of the United States seemed to validate the Enlightenment idea that a better life on earth was possible (pages 945–946).

Americans carried over into the nineteenth and twentieth centuries an unbounded optimism about the future. The vastness of the land and its untapped resources reinforced that faith. The young nation, confident of its "manifest destiny," pushed relentlessly across the continent. Westward movement, however, threatened to extend black slavery, which generated increasing disagreement between the industrialized North and the agricultural South. The ensuing Civil War cost more lives than any other war the nation was to fight. Union victory did not resolve the racial issue that had caused the war, but it did preserve the federal system and American confidence in the future.

The years between 1865 and 1917 witnessed the building of a new industrialized nation. Massive waves of immigrants pursued the frontier to its end, provided the labor to exploit the country's huge mineral resources, turned small provincial towns into sophisticated centers of ethnic and cultural diversity, and built the railroads that tied the country together. However, the American economy absorbed immigrants faster than American society did. The ideology of manifest destiny lived on after the frontier closed, and considerably affected United States–Latin American relations. In the First World War, American aid and American troops were the deciding factor in the Allied victory. After the war, "normalcy" and the facade of prosperity supported a persistent optimism. Only the Great Depression, beginning in 1929 and bringing enormous unemployment and terrible social problems, shook Americans' confidence in their potential and their future.

MANIFEST DESTINY

In an 1845 issue of the *United States Magazine and Democratic Review,* editor John L. O'Sulli-

MAP 32.3   TERRITORIAL GROWTH OF THE UNITED STATES   *The Cumberland Road between Cumberland, Maryland and — by 1833 — Columbus, Ohio and the Erie Canal, which linked New York City and the Great Lakes region, carried thousands of easterners and immigrants to the Old Northwest and the frontier beyond. Transcontinental railroads subsequently made all the difference.*

van boldly declared that foreign powers were trying to prevent American annexation of Texas in order to impede "the fulfillment of our manifest destiny to overspread the continent allotted by Providence for the free development of our yearly multiplying millions." O'Sullivan was articulating a sentiment prevalent in the United States since early in its history: that God had foreordained the nation to cover the entire continent. After a large-circulation newspaper picked up the phrase "manifest destiny," it was used on the floor of Congress and soon entered the language as a catchword for and justification of expansion. The concept of manifest destiny played an important role in some basic developments in American history: the settlement of peoples of diverse nationalities, the issue of slavery, the conflict over whether the United States was to remain agrarian or become a commercial and industrial society.

When George Washington took the presidential oath of office on Wall Street in 1789, fewer than 4 million people inhabited the thirteen states on the eastern seaboard. By the time Abraham Lincoln became the sixteenth president in 1861, the United States was as large as it is today, excepting Alaska and Hawaii, and had 31 million inhabitants. During the colonial period, pioneers had pushed westward to the Appalachian mountains. After independence, westward movement accelerated. The eastern states claimed all the land from the Atlantic to the Mississippi river, but two

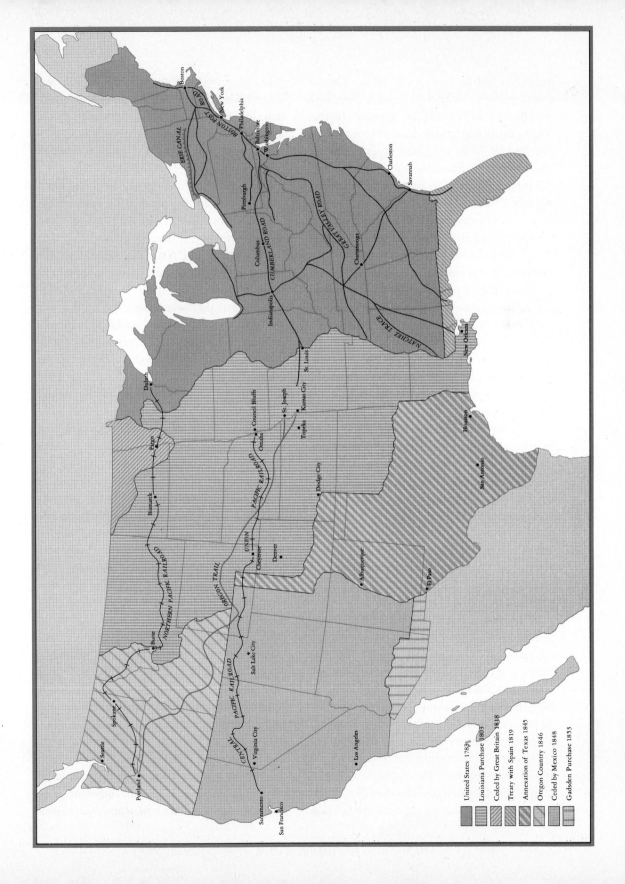

BOSTON POST ROAD

ERIE CANAL

New York

Boston

Philadelphia

Baltimore

Washington

Pittsburgh

Columbus

CUMBERLAND ROAD

GREAT VALLEY ROAD

Charleston

Savannah

Indianapolis

Chattanooga

NATCHEZ TRACE

New Orleans

St. Louis

Duluth

Council Bluffs

St. Joseph

Kansas City

Omaha

Topeka

Houston

Fargo

PACIFIC RAILROAD

Dodge City

San Antonio

Bismarck

NORTHERN PACIFIC RAILROAD

UNION

Cheyenne

Denver

Albuquerque

El Paso

OREGON TRAIL

Butte

CENTRAL PACIFIC RAILROAD

Salt Lake City

Spokane

Seattle

Virginia City

Los Angeles

Portland

Sacramento

San Francisco

United States 1783

Louisiana Purchase 1803

Ceded by Great Britain 1818

Treaty with Spain 1819

Annexation of Texas 1845

Oregon Country 1846

Ceded by Mexico 1848

Gadsden Purchase 1853

forces blocked immediate expansion. The Indians, trying to save their lands, allied with the British in Canada to prevent further American encroachment. Secondly, the federal government, with an almost empty treasury, wanted revenue from land sales. In 1794 special commissioner John Jay concluded a treaty whereby Britain agreed to evacuate border forts in the Northwest Territory, which meant the end of British support for the Indians. A similar treaty with Spain paved the way for southeastern expansion.

Events in Europe and the Caribbean led to a massive increase in American territory. In 1800 Spain ceded the Louisiana Territory – the land between the Mississippi and the Rocky Mountains – to France. Napoleon intended to use the Louisiana Territory to make France an imperial power in America, but a black revolution on the island of Hispaniola (present-day Haiti and Santa Domingo) upset his plans. Under Toussaint L'Ouverture, Haiti's 500,000 slaves revolted against their 40,000 white owners. Napoleon quickly dispatched troops with orders to crush the revolt, seize New Orleans, and take possession of the Louisiana Territory. President Thomas Jefferson, alarmed at the prospect of a French army on U.S. territory, ordered the American minister in Paris, Robert Livingston, to negotiate to buy the Louisiana Territory.

When yellow fever and Haitian bullets carried off most of the French troops, Napoleon relinquished his grandiose plans. He was planning war with Great Britain, and realized that France's weak sea power could not prevent Britain from taking Louisiana. The day Napoleon opened hostilities with England, his foreign minister Talleyrand casually asked Livingston, "What would you give us for the whole of Louisiana?" The astonished American proposed $4 million. "Too low!" said Talleyrand. "Reflect and see me tomorrow." Less

than three weeks later the deed of sale was signed. The United States paid only $12 million for millions of acres of some of the world's richest farmland; the Louisiana Purchase has proved to be the greatest bargain in U.S. history.

Scarcely was the ink dry on the treaty when pressure rose in the western sections of the United States for war with England: western settlers wanted further expansion. Repeated British attacks on American vessels on the high seas and British interference in American trade provided diplomatic justification for war. In fact, the "war hawks" believed a war with Britain would yield Canada, permanently end Indian troubles, and open up vast forest land for additional expansion. The treaty of Ghent (1814) ended the conflict; ultimately the boundary situation prior to 1812 prevailed.

Peace launched the "Great Migration" as settlers poured into the Northwest and the Gulf Plains. Congress sold land in lots of 160 acres at $2 an acre; only $80 was needed as down payment, enabling even the poorest person to buy a farm. Irish and German immigrants rapidly put the black earth of Indiana and Illinois under cultivation; pioneers of American stock planted cotton in the lush delta of the Gulf Plains; Scandinavian and German settlers found the softly rolling hills of the Wisconsin country ideal for cattle herds. As a popular song of the era ran, "Ioway, Ioway, that's where the tall corn grows."

Meanwhile Spain, preoccupied with South American rebellions, sold the Florida territory to the federal government. Beginning in 1821 settlers poured into the Mexican territory of Texas, whose soil proved excellent for the production of cotton and sugar. Contemptuous of the dictatorial and incompetent government of the Mexican President Santa

SIOUX CAMP IN SOUTH DAKOTA The Sioux were a nomadic people, who lived in harmony with the natural environment. Once they moved on from a place, the abandoned landscape looked almost undisturbed. This photograph, taken in 1891, shows a scene characteristic of their camps. (Library of Congress)

Anna, Texans seceded from Mexico and proclaimed an independent republic in 1836. Southern politicians, fearing that Texas would become a refuge for fugitive slaves, pressured President Tyler to admit Texas to the Union. A joint resolution of Congress, hastily signed by Tyler, did so in 1845.

The absorption of Texas's 267,339 square miles (France, by comparison, covers 211,200 square miles) whetted American appetites for the rest of the old Spanish empire in North America. Some expansionists even dreamt of

Cuba and Central America. President Polk tried to buy California from Mexico, but Mexicans harbored a grudge over the annexation of Texas and refused to do business. Exploiting Mexico's political instability, Polk goaded Mexico into war. When a cavalry skirmish in disputed border territory led to several American deaths, Polk announced to Congress, "The cup of forbearance has been exhausted. After reiterated menaces, Mexico has passed the boundary of the United States, has invaded our territory and shed American blood on American soil." Congress obligingly responded that "by act of the Republic of Mexico, a state of war exists between that Government and the United States." Texas and the Mississippi valley states, eager for more slave territory, rushed 49,000 soldiers "to revel in the halls of Montezuma." Mexico suffered total defeat. In the treaty of Guadalupe Hidalgo (1848), Mexico surrendered its claims to Texas, yielded New Mexico and California, and recognized the Rio Grande as the international border. A treaty with Great Britain in 1846 had already recognized the American settlement in the Oregon territory. The continent had been acquired. The nation's "manifest destiny" was fulfilled.

THE FATE OF THE INDIANS

But what of the millions of Indians – the only native Americans – who inhabited this vast territory? As the dean of American historians, Samuel Eliot Morison, recounts, "An American journalist who had spent several years in India, and whose small children had come to love the Indians, came home in 1958. Shortly thereafter he found the boys crying as they watched a TV 'Western' because, as one moaned, 'They're killing Indians!' Papa had to explain that these were not Indians of India but Red Indians, and that to kill them was part of the American Way of Life."[22] And so it was.

While the Indians faithfully observed their treaties with the United States, "white pioneers in the Northwest committed the most wanton and cruel murders of them, for which it was almost impossible to obtain a conviction from a pioneer jury."[23] Government officials frequently manipulated the Indians by gathering a few chiefs, plying them with cheap whiskey, and then inducing them to hand over their tribes' hunting grounds. By

MAP 32.4   INDIAN CESSION OF LANDS TO THE UNITED STATES   *Forced removal of the Creek, Cherokee, and Chickasaw Indians led to the deaths of thousands on the famous Trail of Tears to reservations in Oklahoma, and the destruction of their cultures.*

this method William Henry Harrison, superintendent of the Indians of the Northwest Territory and a future president, got the native Americans to part with 48 million acres. He had the full backing of President Jefferson.

The policy of pushing the Indians westward across the Mississippi, which President Monroe's administration had adopted early in the century, accelerated during Andrew Jackson's presidency (1829–1837). Thousands of Delaware, Shawnee, and Wyandot, tricked into moving from the Northwest Territory to reservations west of Missouri, died of cholera and measles during the journey. The survivors found themselves hopelessly in debt for supplies and farming equipment. The state of Georgia, meanwhile, was nibbling away at Cherokee lands, which were theoretically protected by treaty with the United States government. Then gold was discovered on the Cherokee lands, and a gold rush occurred. A Vermont missionary, the Reverend Samuel C. Worcester, carried the Indians' case to the Supreme Court. When Chief Justice John Marshall ruled that the laws of Georgia had no force within the Cherokee territory – which meant that white settlers and gold rustlers had to leave – President Jackson retorted, "John Marshall has made his decision. Now let him enforce it." The Creek, Cherokee, and other tribes were rounded up, expelled, and sent beyond the western boundaries of Missouri and Arkansas; they were guaranteed complete possession of their new reservations "as long as grass grows and water runs."[24] The shameful price of westward expansion was the dislocation and extermination of millions of native Americans.

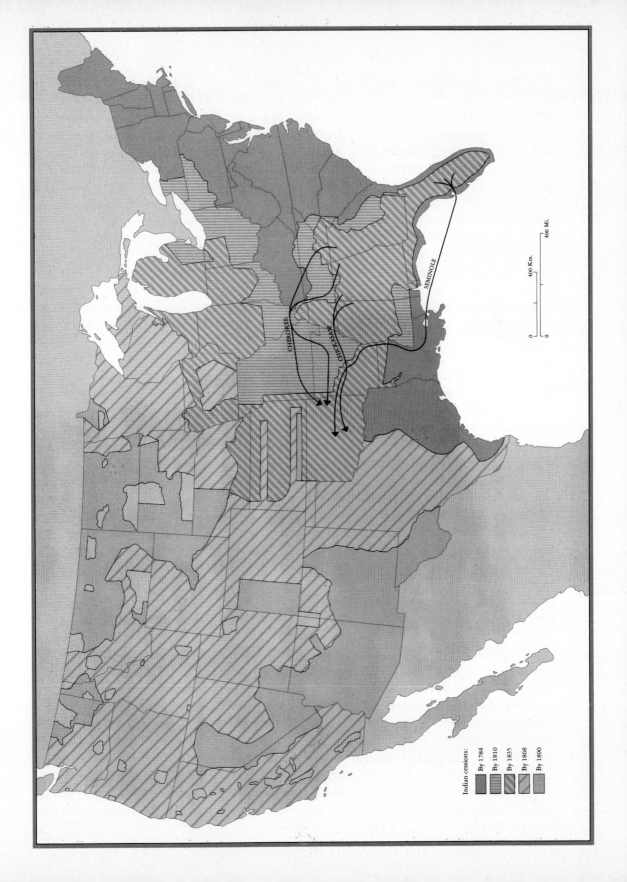

SEMINOLE

CHEROKEE

CHICKASAW

400 Km.

400 Mi.

0

0

Indian cessions:

By 1784
By 1810
By 1835
By 1868
By 1890

BLACK SLAVERY IN THE SOUTH

Since the first black slaves landed in the Virginia colony in 1619, slavery and race relations have posed a serious dilemma for the American majority. A powerful array of moral, legal, political, and sociological arguments have characterized slavery as a great evil, an irrational and peculiar institution, a violation of the central principle of the Declaration of Independence that all men are created equal. Eighteenth- and nineteenth-century Americans, however, could not decide whether the ringing words of the Declaration applied to Negroes. As one scholar recently posed the question,

How did the slave-holding class, which was molded by the same forces that shaped the nation, which fought America's wars and helped inspire its Revolution, a class which boasted of its patriotism, its devotion to freedom, its adherence to the major tenets of liberalism — how did such a class justify its continuing commitment to slavery and remain so steadfast in that commitment that it willingly separated from the Union it had helped to create? In short, how could the slaveholders' ideology prove so malleable as to reinforce simultaneously their devotion to black slavery and to democratic freedom? It is here, in the triumph of the slaveholders' liberalism, that the legacy of slavery becomes a truly American dilemma.[25]

The answer can be summarized in one word: profit. A long line of historians have argued that slavery was not financially productive, and that different social and economic values prevailed in the South than in the North. The North exhibited "bourgeois capitalist" values, the South embraced "aristocratic anti-capitalist" values. As one scholar put it, "Whereas in the North people followed the lure of business and money for their own sake, in the South specific forms of property carried the badges of honor, prestige, and power."[26] In other words, slaveowners cared about profits, but they cared more about the social prestige and political power that the slaveowner enjoyed in the Old South. But this was not so. The economic historians Fogel and Engerman have convincingly demonstrated that southern planters were not indolent aristocrats but "hard, calculating businessmen who priced their slaves, and other assets, with as much shrewdness as could be expected of any northern capitalist."[27] Across the entire South, slaveowners realized an annual net return of 10 percent of the purchase price of their slaves, both male and female. A man with fifty slaves had an annual net income of about $7,500 (roughly the equivalent of $75,000 today), which was more than sixty times the per-capita income in 1860; he was a very rich man. Planters engaged in slave agriculture because they wanted to make a profit, and they usually did so.

They and subsequently all of American society, however, paid a high price in guilt and psychological conflict. Some slaveholders, like President George Washington, found the subject too uncomfortable even to talk about: "I shall frankly declare to you that I do not like even to think, much less talk of it."[28] In the half-century before the Civil War, most slaveowners were deeply religious. On the one hand, they taught their children to get rich by the accumulation of land and slaves; on the other hand, they taught that God would punish the greedy with eternal damnation. Slaveholders justified slavery by dismissing blacks as inferior, but religion preached that in the eyes of God black and white were equal and would ultimately be judged on that basis. This posed a terrible psychological contradiction that few could resolve. Some slaveowners felt completely trapped by the system. As one

DANCING THE JUBA Recreation was a major way that slaves preserved their African culture. This painting executed on a South Carolina plantation in the late eighteenth century shows musical instruments (*stringed* molo *and* gudugudu *drum*), women's headscarves, man's use of cane, and dance steps of Yoruba origin — all revealing continuation of African customs. (*Abby Aldridge Rockefeller Folk Art Center, Williamsburg, Virginia*)

master wrote, "I cannot just take them up and sell them though that would be clearly the best I could do for myself. I cannot free them. I cannot keep them with comfort... What would I not give to be freed from responsibility for these poor creatures." The Alabamian Henry Watson, who in 1835 said "I abominate slavery," wrote to his wife fifteen years later when he had become a prosperous slaveowner, "If we do commit a sin in owning slaves, it is certainly one which is attended with great conveniences."[29] Perhaps even more than men, women of the planter class felt troubled by slavery. The South Carolina aristocrat Mary Boykin Chesnut confided to her diary in 1861,

I wonder if it be a sin to think slavery a curse to any land. Sumner [the Massachusetts senator and abolitionist who bitterly denounced slavery in the U.S. Senate] said not one word of this hated institution which is not true. Men and women are punished when their masters and mistresses are brutes and not when they do wrong.... God forgive us, but ours is a monstrous *system and wrong and iniquity. Perhaps the rest of the world is as bad — this only I see. Like the patriarchs of old our men live all in one house with their wives and their concubines, and the mulattoes one sees in every family exactly resemble the white children — and every lady tells you who is the father of all the mulatto children in everybody's household, but those in her own she seems to think drop from the clouds, or pretends so to think. . . . my disgust sometimes is boiling over. . . . Thank God for my countrywomen — alas for the men! No worse than men everywhere but the lower their mistresses, the more degraded they must be.*[30]

Mary Chesnut believed that most white women of the South were abolitionists in their hearts, and fiery ones too. Though Mary Chesnut enjoyed the attentions and services of her slaves, when Lincoln issued the Emancipation Proclamation she welcomed it with "an unholy joy."[31]

WESTWARD EXPANSION AND CIVIL WAR

Cotton was king in the mid-nineteenth century, and cotton carried slavery westward. It was westward expansion, not moral outrage, that brought the controversy over slavery to a head. As Congress created new territories, the question of whether slavery would be extended arose again and again (see Map 32.5). For years elaborate compromises were worked out, but the North increasingly feared that the South was intent on controlling the nation. The South feared that free territories would harbor fugitive slaves. Issues of sectional political power became more and more heated.

In the 1850s the question of the further expansion of slavery agitated the nation. Perhaps no statesman better summarized the dilemma than Lincoln in a speech in 1854:

When they [southern proponents of expansion] remind us of their constitutional rights, I acknowledge them, not grudgingly, but fully, and fairly;

and I would give them any legislation for the reclaiming of their fugitives, which should not, in its stringency, be more likely to carry a free man into slavery, than our ordinary criminal laws are to hang an innocent one. . . . But all this, to my judgment, furnishes no more excuse for permitting slavery to go into our own free territory, than it would for reviving the African slave trade by law.

Slavery is founded in the selfishness of man's nature — opposition to it, in his love of justice. These principles are in eternal antagonism; and when brought into collision so fiercely, as slavery extension brings them, shocks, and throes, and convulsions must ceaselessly follow.[32]

Accepting the Republican Party nomination for a seat in the U.S. Senate in 1858, Lincoln predicted the tragic events ahead:

A house divided against itself cannot stand.

I believe this government cannot endure, permanently half slave and half free.

I do not expect the Union to be dissolved — I do not expect the house to fall — but I do expect it will cease to be divided.

It will become all one thing, or all the other.

Either the opponents of slavery, will arrest the further spread of it, and place it where the public mind shall rest in the belief that it is in the course of ultimate extinction; or its advocates will push it forward, till it shall become alike lawful in all the States, old as well as new — North as well as South.[33]

In this and every other speech Lincoln made between 1854 and his election to the presidency in 1860, he argued against slavery less on moral or legal grounds than in terms of free labor's self-interest. If slavery continued to expand, Lincoln insisted, it would become a nationwide institution. He appealed to both immigrants and native-born whites when he declared that slavery should be excluded from new territories so that they could be "an out-

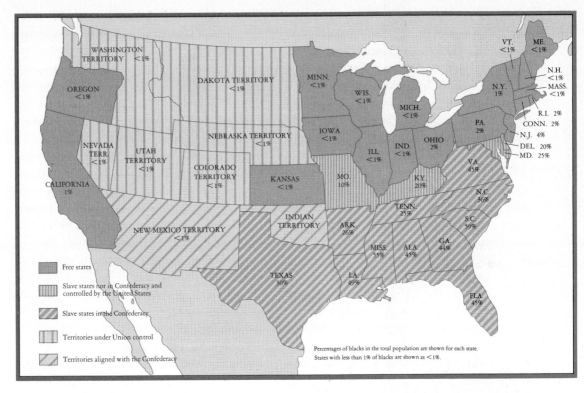

Free states

Slave states not in Confederacy and controlled by the United States

Slave states in the Confederacy

Territories under Union control

Territories aligned with the Confederacy

Percentages of blacks in the total population are shown for each state.
States with less than 1% of blacks are shown as <1%.

MAP 32.5 SLAVERY IN THE UNITED STATES, 1860 *The Confederacy waged an heroic struggle, but the North's industrial might and the waves of immigrants who fought in the Union army decided the war. Note the slave populations of such states as South Carolina and Mississippi and consider how they influenced the later social and economic history of those regions.*

let for free white people everywhere, the world over – in which Hans, and Baptiste, and Patrick, and all other men from all the world, may find new homes and better their condition in life."[34] Free white workers, in other words, could not compete in the labor market against blacks. Therefore the territories should be kept open. To protest Lincoln's victory in the election of 1860, South Carolina seceded from the Union in December 1860. Ten southern states soon followed South Carolina's example and formed

the Confederacy with its capital at Richmond, Virginia.

When the Civil War began in 1861, Lincoln fought it to preserve the Union and to maintain the free labor system; the abolition of slavery was a secondary outcome, which he in fact tried to avoid. When a general in the field declared the slaves of South Carolina and Georgia free, Lincoln overruled the order. He wanted to bring the seceding states back into the Union with their institutions intact. To many people it seemed absurd to fight the

Confederacy, which depended upon slavery to wage the war, without abolishing slavery. As one historian has put it, Lincoln wanted "to conduct the war for the preservation of the *status quo,* which had produced the war."[35] Only when the war dragged on and the slaughter had become frightful on both sides, only when it appeared that Great Britain might recognize the Confederacy, and when it had been proved obvious that the southern war effort benefited considerably from slave labor – only then did Lincoln, reluctantly, resolve on emancipation. The Emancipation Proclamation, which became effective on January 1, 1863, expressed no moral indignation. It freed slaves only in those states and areas in rebellion against the United States – the very places it was least effective; it preserved slavery in states loyal to the United States or under military jurisdiction. As the London *Spectator* sneered, "The principle is not that a human being cannot justly own another, but that he cannot own him unless he is loyal to the United States."[36] The Emancipation Proclamation nevertheless spelled the doom of North American slavery. The Proclamation transformed the war from a political struggle to preserve the Union into a moral crusade for the liberty of all Americans.

European and English liberals greeted the announcement with great joy. A gathering of working people in Manchester, England, wrote President Lincoln:

The erasure of that foul blot upon civilization and Christianity – chattel slavery – during your Presidency will cause the name of Abraham Lincoln to be honoured and revered by posterity. Accept our high admiration of your firmness in upholding the proclamation of freedom.[37]

As Lincoln acknowledged, this statement reflects enormous charity, because the Civil War deeply affected Manchester working people. In fact, it had a worldwide impact socially and economically.

Because the English and continental textile industries relied on raw American cotton, the Confederacy sought European help. In 1861, however, England had a 50 percent oversupply of fiber and cotton cloth; a huge crop, 23 billion pounds, shipped before the Union blockade, filled British warehouses. Cotton brokers in Manchester and Liverpool sold their stock at huge profits. By 1862, however, the English picture had changed. Deprived of cotton, the mills of Lancashire closed. Tens of thousands of workers were thrown out of work and starved. Many emigrated to the United States. Between 1862 and 1864, efforts to alleviate the terrible suffering severely taxed the resources of the British government. The depression forced English manufacturers to search for new markets, and the Civil War stimulated cotton production in Egypt, India, and Brazil. The demands of English industry for Egyptian and Indian cotton played a significant role in the expansion of the English merchant marine fleet, and in decisions about the construction of the Suez canal and the political penetration of Egypt.

The war also had important political consequences in Europe. In 1861 British and European opinion had divided along class lines. The upper classes sympathized with the American South, while the commercial classes and working people sided with the North. The English people interpreted the northern victory as a triumph for the democratic experiment over aristocratic oligarchy. The Union success proved that popular government worked. Thus, the United States gave a powerful stimulus to those in Britain and elsewhere who supported the cause of political democracy. When parliaments debated the extension of suffrage, the American example was frequently cited.

Military historians describe the American Civil War as the first modern war. "It was the first conflict in which the massive productive capacities of the Industrial Revolution were placed at the disposal of the military machine. It witnessed the first prominent use of mass production of goods to sustain mass armies, mass transportation on railroads, and telegraphic communication between different theaters and on the battlefield. It saw also the first use of such devices of the future as armored warships, breech-loading and repeating rifles, rifled artillery, land and sea mines, submarines, balloons, precursors of the machine gun, and trench warfare. . . . in no previous war had so many of the methods and weapons made possible by modern industry been so apparent. In its material manifestations alone, in its application of the resources of technology to the business of killing, the Civil War presaged the later world wars."[38]

In April 1865, the Confederate general Robert E. Lee surrendered his army at Appomattox Court House in Virginia, ending the costliest and bloodiest war Americans had ever fought. Lincoln had called for "malice toward none and charity for all" in his second inaugural address in 1864, and planned a generous policy toward the defeated South. The bullet that killed Lincoln brought on a different kind of reconstruction, the central figure in which was the Negro.

During Reconstruction (1865–1877), the vanquished South adjusted to a new social and economic order without slavery, and the eleven Confederate states rejoined the Union. Congress and the nation debated the political and social status of the Negro in the reconstructed South. For former slaves, Reconstruction represented the opportunity to exer-

cise their new freedom, but southerners detested the very notion of social equality and northerners were ambivalent on the subject. In practical terms, Reconstruction meant the reunion of black families separated before emancipation. Blacks wanted land to farm but, lacking cash, they soon accepted the sharecropping system: farmers paid landowners about half of the year's crops at harvest time in return for a cabin, food, mules, seed, and tools the rest of the year. Believing that education was the key to economic advancement, blacks flocked to country schools and to colleges supported by northern religious groups. Although the 15th Amendment forbade states to deny anyone the vote "on account of race, color, or previous condition of servitude," whites used violence, terror, and, between 1880 and 1920, new Jim Crow laws to prevent blacks from voting and to enforce rigid racial segregation. Lacking strong northern support, blacks did not gain legal equality or suffrage in many parts of the old Confederacy until the 1960s.

THE BLACK FAMILY

What impact did slavery have on the black family? Able scholars, both black and white, have long maintained that the enslavement of Africans in the eighteenth century led to the deterioration of the black family as a social unit in the nineteenth and twentieth centuries. As two authorities put it, "The most rudimentary type of family organization was not permitted to survive, to say nothing of the extensions of the family. The mother-child family, with the father either unknown, absent, or, if present, incapable of wielding influence, was the only type of family that could survive." Other writers, basing their arguments upon received scholarly opinion, maintained that "the experience of slavery left as its most serious heritage a steady weakness in the Negro family."[39] However, Herbert G. Gutman's authoritative *The Black Family in Slavery and Freedom, 1750–1925* has demonstrated that such notions arise more from fantasy than from fact. In spite of the destructive effects of slavery, Afro-Americans established strong family units.

Most slave couples had long marriages. A study of the entire adult slave population of North Carolina in 1860 has shown that 25 percent of slave marriages lasted between ten and nineteen years, 20 percent lasted at least twenty years, and almost 10 percent endured thirty years or more. Most slave women spent their entire adult lives in settled unions with the same husband. In 1864–1865 Union Army officers who recorded slave marriages were deeply impressed by their durability. As one white soldier wrote, "It is not pretended that all marriages that have taken place were well advised, or will be happy, or faithfully observed. When marriages among whites shall all prove so, without exception, it will be time to look for such a happy state among blacks.... Marriage is not treated as a light matter."[40] Planters encouraged slave marriages, because, as one owner put it, "marriage adds to the comfort, happiness, and health of those entering upon it, besides insuring a greater increase." Large slave families advanced owners' economic interests, and planters rewarded slave women who had many children.[41]

Forcible separation due to the sale of one partner proved the greatest threat to the permanence of slave marriages. In spite of illiteracy, separated spouses tried to remain in touch with one another. Once slavery had been abolished, separated couples went to enormous lengths to reunite their families.

Evidence from all parts of the South reveals that this was the common pattern.

Women often had to resist the attentions of the slaveowners themselves. As an ex-Tennessee slave reported, "Old Buford – his darkies had chillun by him, and mammy wouldn't do it; and I've seen him take a paddle with holes in it and beat her." Not infrequently owners supplied slave women with black men who had reputations for sexual prowess. Slave women, however, made choices: they tried to select their own husbands, rejecting – up to the point of risking being sold – mates chosen by their owners. Historians of medicine know little about the birth-control methods used by slave couples. Considerable information survives, however, about abortion. In 1860 a Tennessee physician reported that slave women tried to abort by "medicine," "violent exercise," and other means. Cotton plants were "habitually and effectively resorted to by slaves of the South for producing abortion."[42]

Typically, slave women had their first child around the age of nineteen. The continual labor shortage in the South led slave owners to encourage slaves to produce children rapidly. Owners urged slave women to begin bearing children as teenagers, and to have more children rapidly thereafter. On the Good Hope plantation in South Carolina, for example, 80 percent of slave couples had at least four children. Almost all women had all their children by one husband, and most children grew to teenage in households with both parents present. Although premarital intercourse was common among slaves – though not as common as among young American adults in 1970–1980 – the weight of the evidence shows that women rarely engaged in sexual activity outside of marriage.

Settled slave marriages provided models for growing children, which allowed them to pass

HARLEM HELLFIGHTERS   Returning to New York in 1919 aboard the U.S.S. Stockholm, *these black men of the famed U.S. 369th Division had fought in the bloody battle of the Meuse-Argonne during the* First World War. The French government awarded 150 of them the coveted Croix de Guerre. (Springer/ Bettman Film Archive)

a strong tradition of marital and kin obligations from generation to generation. The pattern of stable black marriages lasted well into the present century. Research on black households in New York City in 1925 shows that 85 percent were headed by two parents.[43] The period since the great depression of 1929 has witnessed a general decline in the stability of American families, both white and black. Shifting values throughout American society, such as changed sexual attitudes and an enormous increase in the divorce rate, have increased the proportion of black families headed by one parent. In recent decades, the 1980 census shows, the difference between black and white wages has narrowed, but total household income has remained highly divergent because many more black households depended on the income of a single parent. The decline in family stability has proved an obstacle to black economic advancement.

INDUSTRIALIZATION AND IMMIGRATION

After the Civil War the United States underwent a gigantic industrial boom based on exploitation of the country's natural resources. The federal government turned over vast amounts of land and mineral resources to industry for development. In particular, the railroads — the foundation of industrial expansion — received 130 million acres. By 1900

THE IRISH VOTE As Irish immigrants arrived in torrential waves in the 1880s and 1890s, American politicians began to recognize the potential of the Irish vote. A British cartoonist viciously caricatured both leading politicians, kowtowing, and "the Irish Vote." (Puck; courtesy of American Heritage Picture Library)

the American railroad system was 193,000 miles long, connected every part of the nation, and represented 40 percent of the railroad mileage of the entire world. Immigrant workers built it.

The late nineteenth and early twentieth centuries witnessed the immigration of unprecedented numbers of Europeans and Asians to the United States (pages 1143–1147). Between 1860 and 1900 14 million immigrants came, and during the peak years between 1900 and 1914 another 14 million passed through the customs inspection at Ellis Island in New York City. All sought a better life and a higher standard of living. The immigrants' ambitions precisely matched the labor needs of the times. Chinese, Scandinavian, and Irish immigrants laid 30,000 miles of railroad tracks between 1867 and 1873, and another 73,000 miles in the 1880s. Poles, Hungarians, Bohemians, and Italians poured into the coal and iron mines of western Pennsylvania and Appalachia. The steel magnate Andrew Carnegie recruited southern and eastern European immigrants for his smoking mills around Pittsburgh, Cleveland, and Gary, Indiana. The Carnegie Steel Corporation (later United States Steel), worked almost entirely by Slavs and Italians, produced one-third of the world's total annual steel supply in 1900. John D. Rockefeller, whose Standard Oil Company earned tens of billions of dollars, employed thousands of Czechs, Poles, and other Slavs in his oil fields around the country. Lithuanians, Poles, Croats, Scandinavians, Irish, and Negroes entered the Chicago stockyards and built the meatpacking industry. Irish immigrants continued to operate the spinning frames and knitting machines of New England's textile mills. Industrial America developed on the sweat and brawn — the cheap labor — of its immigrant millions.

As industrial expansion transformed the eastern half of the United States, settlers conquered the trans-Mississippi West. Thousands of land-hungry farmers moved westward, where land was still only $1.25 an acre. In the final third of the nineteenth century, the last pioneers acquired 430 million acres and put 225 million of them under cultivation.

The West also held precious metals. The discovery of gold and silver in California, Colorado, Arizona, Montana, and on the reservations of the Sioux Indians of South Dakota precipitated huge rushes. Even before 1900, miners had extracted $1.24 billion in gold and $901 million in silver from western mines. Some miners left the West as soon as they had made their piles, but others settled down to farm and help their territories toward statehood. By 1912 the West had been won and the last frontier closed.

In the entire movement westward, women shared with men the long and dangerous journey, and then the dawn-to-dusk backbreaking work of carving a homestead out of the wilderness. It fell to women to "make a home" out of crude log cabins without windows or doors or tarpaper shacks with mud floors, if they were lucky; more frequently, settlers lacked even a roof over their heads. One "gently reared" bride of seventeen took one look at her mud roof and dirt floor and indignantly announced, "My father had a much better house for his hogs!" Lacking cookstoves, they had to prepare food over open fireplaces, using all kinds of substitutes for ingredients easily available "back East." Before they could wash clothes, women had to make soap out of lye and carefully saved household ashes. Considered the carriers of "high culture," women organized such educational, religious, musical, and recreational activities as frontier society possessed. Frontierswomen also had to defend their homes against prairie fires and Indian attacks. These burdens were accompanied by frequent pregnancies, and women often gave birth without medical help or even the support of other women. Frontier women often used such contraceptive devices as spermicides, condoms, and, after 1864, vaginal diaphragms and abortifacients. Even so, frontier women had large families; the death rate for infants and young children ran as high as 30 percent in the mid-nineteenth century. Generally speaking, the frontier blurred sex roles: women commonly did the same agricultural work as men.[44]

As in South America, immigration led to rapid urbanization. In 1790 only 5.1 percent of Americans had lived in centers of 2500 or more people. By 1860 this figure had risen to 19.9 percent, and by 1900 almost 40 percent lived in cities. The overwhelming majority of the southern and eastern Europeans who came to North America at the turn of the century became urban industrial workers, their entire existence framed by the factory and the tenement. Newly uprooted from rural Europe, Italians, Greeks, Croats, Hungarians, Czechs, Poles, Russians, and Jews contrasted sharply with urban surroundings and with each other. Older residents saw only "a sea of strange faces, babbling in alien tongues and framed by freakish clothes. Walking through these mul-

WESTERN WOMEN *Some women who made the long trek west did all the work that men did, not only managing their farms and ranches, but branding their cattle. (Courtesy, Colorado Historical Society)*

titudes now was really like a voyage round the globe."[45]

Between 1880 and 1920 industrial production soared. New inventions such as the steam engine, the dynamo (generator), and the electric light were given industrial and agricultural applications. Transcontinental railroads and technological innovations like the sewing machine and the assembly line made large-scale production more economical. Large factories replaced small ones, because only large factories could buy large machines, operate them at full capacity, and take advantage of railroad discount rates. In the automobile industry, for example, Henry Ford of Detroit set up assembly lines where each worker, instead of assembling an entire car, performed only one task in the flow of automobile construction. In 1910 Ford sold 10,000 cars; in 1914, a year after he inaugurated the first moving assembly line, he sold 248,000 cars.

Such developments changed the face of American society. Sewing machines made cheap, varied, mass-produced clothing available to city people in department stores, and to country people through mail-order catalogues. The automobile increased opportunities for travel, general mobility, and change.

By the 1890s factory managers were stressing industrial efficiency and the importance of time. Management engineers wanted to produce more at lower cost, which meant reducing labor costs by eliminating unnecessary workers. As the quantity rather than the quality of goods produced became the measure of acceptable work, workers' skills were less valued. As assembly-line workers increasingly performed only monotonous and time-determined work, in effect they became interchangeable parts of the machines they operated.

Despite accelerated production, and perhaps because of overproduction, the national economy experienced repeated cycles of boom-and-bust in the late nineteenth century. Serious depressions in 1873, 1884, and 1893 slashed prices and threw many people out of work. Leading industrialists responded by establishing larger corporations and trusts. Trusts granted control of their stock to a board of trustees, which then managed the operation of all the companies the trust owned. The legalization of trusts led to huge conglomerates, such as John D. Rockefeller's Standard Oil Company, which as a result of the merger of several smaller oil companies controlled 84 percent of the nation's oil in 1898. Standard Oil also controlled most American pipelines and was involved in natural-gas production. Standard Oil monopolized the oil industry, J. P. Morgan's United States Steel the iron and steel industries, and Swift & Co. of Chicago the meat-processing industry.

Industrialization led to the creation of a vast class of salaried workers who depended totally on their employers for work. Corporate managers, however, were always preoccupied with cutting labor costs. Thus employers paid workers piecemeal for the number of articles produced, to encourage the use of the new machines; managers hired more women and children and paid them much less than men. Most women worked in the textile industry; some earned as little as $1.56 for seventy hours work, while men received $7 to $9 for the same work. And employers reduced wages, forcing workers to toil longer and harder to maintain the same incomes. Because owners fought in legislatures and courts against the installation of safety devices, working conditions in mines and mills were frightful. In 1913, even after some safety measures had been taken, 25,000 people died in industrial accidents, and between 1900 and 1917, 72,000 railroad worker deaths occurred.

Workers responded with strikes, violence, and, gradually, unionization.

Urbanization brought serious problems. In *How the Other Half Lives* (1890), a newspaper reporter and recent immigrant from Denmark, Jacob Riis, drew national attention to what he called "the foul core of New York's slums." His phrase "the other half" soon became a synonym for the urban poor. Riis estimated that 300,000 people inhabited a single square mile on New York's Lower East Side. Overcrowding, poor sanitation, and lack of health services caused frequent epidemics. The blight of slums increased crime, prostitution, alcoholism, and other drug-related addictions. Riis attacked the vicious economic exploitation of the immigrant poor and the dangers to our political system:

The slum complaint had been chronic in all ages, but the great changes which the nineteenth century saw, the new industry, political freedom, brought on an acute attack which put that very freedom in jeopardy. Too many of us had supposed that, built as our commonwealth was on universal suffrage, it would be proof against the complaints that harassed older states; but in fact it turned out that there was extra hazard in that. Having solemnly resolved that all men are created equal and have certain inalienable rights, among them life, liberty, and the pursuit of happiness, we shut our eyes and waited for the formula to work.... When after a hundred years, we opened our eyes, it was upon sixty cents a day as the living wage of the working-woman in our cities; upon "knee pants" at forty cents a dozen for the making; upon the Potter's Field [a cemetery for paupers] taking tithe of our city life, ten per cent each year for the trench, truly the Lost Tenth of the slum. Our country had grown great and rich; through our ports was poured food for the millions of Europe. But in the back streets multitudes huddled in ignorance and want.... Political freedom we had won; but the problem of helpless poverty, grown vast with the added offscourings of the Old World, mocked us, unsolved. Liberty at sixty cents a day set presently its stamp upon the government of our cities, and it became the scandal and the peril of our political system.[46]

New York City was not unique; slums and the social problems resulting from them existed in all large American cities. Reformers fought for slum clearance, but public apathy and vested economic interests delayed massive urban renewal until after the Second World War.

European and Asian immigrants aroused nativist sentiments – that is, intense hostility to their foreign and "un-American" looks, behavior, and loyalties on the part of native-born Americans. Some of this antagonism sprang from the deep-rooted Anglo-Saxon racism of many Americans. Some grew out of old Protestant suspicion of Roman Catholicism, the faith of most of the new arrivals. A great deal of the dislike of the foreign-born sprang from fear of economic competition. To most Americans, the Chinese with their exotic looks and willingness to work for very little seemed the most dangerous. Increasingly violent agitation against orientals led to race riots in California and finally culminated in the Chinese Exclusion Act of 1882, which denied Chinese laborers entrance to the country.

Immigrants from Europe seized upon white racism as a way of improving themselves in the job market: they could compensate for their immigrant status by claiming superiority to ex-slaves and their descendants. The arrival of thousands of Irish immigrants in the 1850s, followed by millions of Italians and Slavs in the period 1880–1914, aggravated an already bad situation. What the German scientist Alexander von Humbolt wrote about the attitude of peninsulares toward Creoles in

Latin America in the early nineteenth century – "the lowest, least educated, and uncultivated European believes himself superior to the white born in the New World"[47] – precisely applies to the outlook of Irish, Italian, or Slavic immigrants to the United States at the turn of this century if one merely substitutes *black* for *white*. In the eyes of all ethnic groups, the social status of blacks remained the lowest while that of immigrants rose. As the United States underwent expansion and industrialization in the course of the nineteenth century, negroes remained the worst off *because of* immigration.[48]

In the 1890s the nation experienced a severe economic depression. Faced with overproduction, the rich and politically powerful owners of mines, mills, and factories fought the organization of labor unions, laid off thousands, slashed wages, and ruthlessly exploited their workers. Workers in turn feared that immigrant labor would drive salaries lower. The frustrations provoked by pitifully low salaries in "good times," by unemployment during the depression, and by all the unresolved problems of industrial urban society boiled over into savage attacks on the foreign-born. One of the bloodiest incidents occurred in western Pennsylvania in 1897, when about 150 unarmed Polish and Hungarian coal miners tried to persuade others to join their walkout. The coal owners convinced the local sheriff that the strike was illegal. As the strikers approached, the sheriff panicked and ordered his deputies to shoot. Twenty-one immigrants died and forty were wounded. The sheriff subsequently explained that the miners were only "infuriated foreigners ... like wild beasts." Local people agreed that if the strikers had been American-born, no blood would have been shed.[49]

Pressures to restrict immigration varied with economic conditions: it slackened in

New York's Lower East Side For the thousands of East European Jews who fled the shtetls (rural communities) of Russia and Poland, American cities were their first experience of urban life. Besides the frightful squalor of the tenements, the noise, size of buildings, and rush of daily existence were terrifying experiences. Fierce determination backed by centuries of social endurance gave them the moral power to persevere. (Courtesy, Library of Congress)

times of relative prosperity and increased in periods of recession. After the First World War, labor leaders lobbied Congress for restrictions because they feared losing the wage gains achieved during the war. Some intellectuals argued that immigrants from southern and eastern Europe, with their unfamiliar cultural traditions, threatened to destroy American society. Italians were feared because of possible Cosa Nostra connections; eastern Europeans were thought to have Communist connections. In the 1920s Congress responded with laws that set severe quotas – 2 percent of resident nationals as of the 1890 census –

on immigration from southern and eastern Europe. The Japanese were completely excluded. These racist laws remained on the books until 1965.

———◆———

In the later years of the nineteenth century, industrialization, expansion, and the assimilation of foreign peoples preoccupied the nations of the Western Hemisphere. Political instability slowed the development of most Latin American countries. A few reformers sought closer relations between North and

South America, but little of significance was accomplished. In 1889, for example, a Pan-American Conference in Washington rejected a proposal to settle disputes among nations by arbitration.

A revolt in Cuba against incompetent Spanish administration had more far-reaching consequences. The American "yellow press" luridly described the horrors of the concentration camps where the Spanish incarcerated the rebels. When the battleship *Maine* was mysteriously blown up in Havana harbor, inflamed public opinion swept the United States into war. The Spanish-American War of 1898 – the "splendid little war," as Secretary of State John Hay called it – lasted just ten weeks and resulted in the United States acquiring Cuba and the Philippine Islands. Denying any imperialistic ambitions in the Philippines, President William McKinley declared that the United States wanted only "to take them all and educate the Filipinos and uplift and civilize and Christianize them." McKinley, like most Americans, did not know that the Filipinos had an old and sophisticated culture and had been Christians for three centuries.

The notion of manifest destiny had swept the United States into the Caribbean and across the Pacific. Between 1900 and 1929 the United States intervened in Latin American affairs whenever it felt its economic interests were threatened. Americans secured control of the Panama Canal on their own terms, and in 1912 and 1926 U.S. Marines intervened in Nicaragua to bolster conservative governments. The result has been a bitter legacy of anti-American feeling throughout Latin America. Only with the launching of President Franklin D. Roosevelt's Good Neighbor Policy did relations between the two halves of the hemisphere begin to improve.

NOTES

1. Cited in William Spence Robertson, *Rise of the Spanish American Republics,* The Free Press, New York, 1965, p. 19.

2. See Benjamin Keen and Mark Wasserman, *A Short History of Latin America,* Houghton Mifflin, Boston, 1980, pp. 109–115.

3. John Lynch, *The Spanish American Revolutions, 1808–1826,* W.W. Norton, New York, 1973, pp. 13–14; Keen and Wasserman, pp. 145–146.

4. Cited in Lynch, p. 18.

5. Mark Burkholder and D. S. Chandler, *From Impotence to Authority. The Spanish Crown and the American Audiencias, 1687–1808,* University of Missouri Press, Columbia, 1977, p. 145.

6. Ibid., p. 141.

7. Keen and Wasserman, p. 146.

8. Cited in Phelan, p. 62; see also Leslie B. Rout, *The African Experience in Spanish America,* Cambridge University Press, New York, 1977, p. 165.

9. Ibid., p. 209.

10. Ibid., pp. 206–207.

11. Frank Tannenbaum, *Ten Keys to Latin America,* Random House, New York, 1962, pp. 69–71.

12. Ibid.

13. H. Hoetink, *Slavery and Race Relations in the Americas,* Harper & Row, New York, 1973, p. 14.

14. Keen and Wasserman, pp. 201–204.

15. Ibid., p. 207.

16. See Charles H. Harris, *A Mexican Family Empire. The Latifundio of the Sanchez Navarros, 1765–1867,* University of Texas Press, Austin, 1975, *passim.*

17. Nicolas Sanchez-Albornoz, *The Population of Latin America: A History.* trans. W. A. R. Richardson, University of California Press, Berkeley, 1974, pp. 151–152.

18. James R. Scobie, "Buenos Aires as a Commercial-Bureaucratic City, 1880–1910: Characteristics of a City's Orientation," in *American Historical Review* 77, no. 4 (October 1972): 1046.

19. Ibid., p. 1064.

20. See Magnus Morner, ed., *Race and Class in Latin America.* Part II: Immigration, Stratification, and Race Relations, Columbia University Press, New York, 1971, pp. 73–122; Sanchez-Albornoz, pp. 160–167.

21. Florestan Fernandes, "Immigration and Race Relations in Sao Paulo," in Magnus Morner, p. 127.

22. Samuel Eliot Morison, *The Oxford History of the American People,* Oxford University Press, New York, 1965, p. 445.

23. Ibid., pp. 380–381.

24. Ibid., pp. 446–452.

25. James Oakes, *The Ruling Race: A History of American Slaveholders,* Alfred A. Knopf, New York, 1982, pp. x–xi.

26. Cited in Robert William Fogel and Stanley L. Engerman, *Time on the Cross: The Economics of American Negro Slavery,* Little Brown, Boston, 1974, p. 64.

27. Ibid., p. 73.

28. Cited in Oakes, p. 120.

29. Cited in Oakes, pp. 120–121.

30. C. Vann Woodward, ed., *Mary Chesnut's Civil War,* Yale University Press, New Haven, 1981, p. 29.

31. Ibid., pp. xlix–l.

32. Roy P. Basler ed., *The Collected Works of Abraham Lincoln,* vol II, Rutgers University Press, New Brunswick, N.J., 1953, pp. 255–256, 271.

33. Ibid., pp. 461–462.

34. Cited in Richard Hofstadter, *The American Political Tradition,* Random House, New York, 1948, p. 114.

35. T. Harry Williams cited in Hofstadter, pp. 128–129.

36. Cited in Hofstadter, p. 132.

37. Cited in Morison, p. 654.

38. T. Harry Williams, *The History of American Wars: From Colonial Times to World War I,* Alfred A. Knopf, New York, 1981, p. 202.

39. Cited in Herbert G. Gutman, *The Black Family in Slavery and Freedom, 1750–1925,* Random House, New York, 1977, pp. xvii–xix.

40. Ibid., pp. 14–16, 21–22.

41. Cited in Fogel and Engerman, p. 84.

42. Ibid., pp. 81–82.

43. Gutman, p. xix.

44. Sandra L. Myres, *Westering Women and the Frontier Experience, 1800–1915,* University of New Mexico Press, Albuquerque, 1982, chs. 6 and 7.

45. Gunther Barth, *City People: The Rise of Modern City Culture in the Nineteenth Century,* Oxford University Press, New York, 1980, p. 15.

46. Cited in Daniel Boorstin, ed., *An American Primer,* New American Library, New York, 1966, pp. 667–668.

47. Cited in Lynch, p. 18.

48. Hoetink, p. 18.

49. Cited in John Higham, *Strangers in the Land: Patterns of American Nativism, 1860–1925,* Atheneum, New York, 1971, pp. 89–90.

SUGGESTED READING

Perhaps the best introduction to the independence movements in Latin America is John Lynch, *The Spanish-American Revolutions* (1973), which is soundly researched and includes a good bibliography. The most useful biographies of Simon Bolivar are those of Gerhard Masur, *Simon Bolivar,* 2nd ed. (1969), and J. J. Johnson and D. M. Ladd, *Simon Bolivar and Spanish American Independence, 1783–1830* (1968), which contains good selections of Bolivar's writings. J. C. J. Metford, *San Martin the Liberator* (1950), is a good short life of that revolutionary. For Brazil, see K. R. Maxwell, *Conflicts and Conspiracies: Brazil and Portugal, 1750–1808* (1973), and A. J. R. Russell-Wood, ed., *From Colony to Nation: Essays in the Independence of Brazil* (1975). A. P. Whitaker, *The United States and the Independence of Latin America, 1800–1830* (1941), remains the standard study of the role of the United States.

Jan Bazant, *A Concise History of Mexico* (1978), is a good starting-point for the study of Mexican history, but M. C. Meyer and W. L. Sherman, *The Course of Mexican History* (1979), is the most thorough treatment. Tulio Halperin-Donghi, *The Aftermath of Revolution in Latin America* (1973), and C. C. Griffin, "Economic and Social Aspects of the Era of Spanish-American Independence," *Hispanic American Historical Review* 29 (1949), provide important interpretations of the consequences of the revolutions.

The following studies offer good treatments of society and politics in Latin America in the nineteenth century: Richard Graham and P. H. Smith, eds., *New Approaches to Latin American History* (1974); Ralph Roeder, *Juarez and His Mexico*, 2 vols. (1947), perhaps the best available work in English; H. S. Ferns, *Argentina* (1969); Jay Kinsbruner, *Chile: A Historical Interpretation* (1973); A. J. Bauer, *Chilean Rural Society from the Spanish Conquest to 1930* (1975); E. B. Burns, *A History of Brazil* (1970); Robert Conrad, *The Destruction of Brazilian Slavery, 1850–1888* (1973); and R. B. Toplin, *The Abolition of Slavery in Brazil* (1972).

For social and economic developments and the triumph of neocolonialism, the following titles are useful: Robert Cortes Conde, *The First Stages of Modernization in Spanish America* (1967); Jan Bazant, *A Concise History of Mexico from Hidalgo to Cardenas, 1805–1940* (1978); R. Knowlton, *Church Property and the Mexican Reform, 1856–1910* (1976); R. D. Anderson, *Outcasts in Their Own Land: Mexican Industrial Workers, 1906–1911* (1976); James Scobie, *Argentina: A City and A Nation*, 2nd ed. (1971); M. J. Mamalakis, *The Growth and Structure of the Chilean Economy from Independence to Allende* (1976), which provides an excellent economic overview; Andre Gunder Frank, *Capitalism and Underdevelopment in Latin America: Historical Studies of Chile and Brazil* (1969); David Rock, *Politics in Argentina, 1890–1930: The Rise and Fall of Radicalism* (1975); Richard Graham, *Britain and the Onset of Modernization in Brazil, 1850–1914* (1968).

The major themes in United States history have been extensively treated by many able scholars, and

students will have no difficulty finding a wealth of material. James MacGregor Burns, *The Vineyard of Liberty* (1982), traces the origins and development of American society, politics, and culture, emphasizing the growth of liberty, from the 1780s to 1863; this work is a classic achievement. The standard study of manifest destiny remains Frederick Merk, *Manifest Destiny and Mission in American History: A Reinterpretation* (1963), but see also K. Jack Bauer, *The Mexican-American War, 1846–1848* (1976). In *The Only Land They Knew: The Tragic Story of the American Indians in the Old South* (1981), J. Leitch Wright recounts the interaction of Native Americans, Africans, and Europeans in the American South. On slavery, see Stanley M. Elkins, *Slavery: A Problem in American Institutional and Intellectual life*, 3rd rev. ed. (1976), a great achievement, which includes a good comparison of slavery in the United States and Latin America and a fine bibliographical essay. Eugene D. Genovese, *Roll, Jordan, Roll: The World the Slaves Made* (1974), is a comprehensive Marxist treatment of plantation slavery, stressing the paternalism of the planter class. For the origins and development of racial attitudes in both North and South America, see Winthrop D. Jordan, *White Over Black: American Attitudes Toward the Negro, 1550–1812* (1969).

On the black family, see, in addition to Gutman's book cited in the Notes, the following studies: August Meier and Elliott M. Rudwick, *From Plantation to Ghetto: An Interpretive History of American Negroes* (1968); E. Franklin Frazier, *Black Bourgeoisie*, 15th ed. (1975); Benjamin Quarles, *The Negro in the Making of America* (1974); and Gerda Lerner, ed., *Black Women in White America: A Documentary History* (1973).

The literature on the Civil War and Reconstruction is mammoth, and the following titles treat important aspects of it: David Donald, ed., *Why the North Won the Civil War* (1977); John Hope Franklin, *Reconstruction* (1965); Harold M. Hyman, *A More Perfect Union* (1973); and James McPherson, *The Abolitionist Legacy* (1975).

Thomas C. Cochrane, *Business in American Life* (1977); Alfred D. Chandler, *Strategy and Structure: Chapters in the History of American Industrial Enter-*

prise (1966); Harold C. Livesay, *Andrew Carnegie and the Rise of Big Business* (1975); and David F. Hawkes, *John D.: The Founding Father of the Rockefellers* (1980), are fine studies of industrialism and corporate growth in the late nineteenth century.

On the lives of Jews and other immigrants in American cities, see Irving Howe's brilliant achievement, *World of Our Fathers* (1976), which is splendidly illustrated and contains a good bibliography.

CHAPTER 33

THE GREAT BREAK:

WAR AND REVOLUTION

IN THE SUMMER OF 1914 the nations of Europe went willingly to war. They believed they had no other choice. Moreover, both peoples and governments confidently expected a short war leading to a decisive victory. Such a war, they believed, would "clear the air," and European society would go on as before.

These expectations were almost totally mistaken. The First World War was long, indecisive, and tremendously destructive. To the shell-shocked generation of survivors, it was known simply as the Great War: the war of unprecedented scope and intensity. From today's perspective it is clear that the First World War marked a great break in the course of Western historical development since the French and Industrial Revolutions. A noted British political scientist has gone so far as to say that even in victorious and relatively fortunate Great Britain, the First World War was *the* great turning point in government and society, "as in everything else in modern British history.... There's a much greater difference between the Britain of 1914 and, say, 1920, than between the Britain of 1920 and today."[1]

This is a very strong statement, but it contains much truth, for all of Europe as well as for Britain. It suggests three questions this chapter will try to answer. What caused the Great War? How and why did war and revolution have such enormous and destructive consequences? And where in the trauma and bloodshed were formed elements of today's world, many of which people now accept and even cherish?

THE FIRST WORLD WAR

The First World War was so long and destructive because it involved all the Great Powers and because it quickly degenerated into a senseless military stalemate. Like two evenly matched boxers in an old-time hundred-round championship bout, each side tried to wear down its opponent and break its body and spirit. There was no referee to call a draw, only the blind hammering of a life-or-death struggle.

THE BISMARCKIAN SYSTEM OF ALLIANCES

The Franco-Prussian War and the foundation of the German Empire opened a new era in international relations. France was decisively defeated in 1871 and forced to pay a large war indemnity and give up Alsace-Lorraine. In ten short years, from 1862 to 1871, Bismarck had made Prussia-Germany – traditionally the weakest of the Great Powers – the most powerful nation in Europe (pages 1106-1111). Had Bismarck been a Napoleon I or a Hitler, for whom no gain was ever sufficient, continued expansion would no doubt sooner or later have raised a powerful coalition against the new German Empire. Yet he was not. As Bismarck never tired of repeating after 1871, Germany was a "satisfied" power. Germany had no territorial ambitions and only wanted peace in Europe.

But how was peace to be preserved? The most serious threat to peace came from the east, from Austria-Hungary and from Russia. Those two enormous multinational empires had many conflicting interests, particularly in the Balkans, where the Ottoman Empire – "the sick man of Europe" – was ebbing fast. There was a real threat that Germany might be dragged into a great war between the two rival empires. Bismarck's solution was a system of alliances to restrain both Russia and Austria-Hungary, to prevent conflict between them, and to isolate a hostile France.

THE CONGRESS OF BERLIN, 1878   *With the Austrian representative on his right and with other participants looking on, Bismarck the mediator symbolically seals the hard-won agreement by shaking* *hands with the chief Russian negotiator. The Great Powers often relied on such special conferences to settle their international disputes. (Bettmann Archive)*

A first step was the creation in 1873 of the conservative Three Emperors' League, which linked the monarchs of Austria-Hungary, Germany, and Russia in an alliance against radical movements. In 1877–1878, when Russia's victories over Turkey threatened the balance of Austrian and Russian interests in the Balkans and the balance of British and Russian interests in the Middle East, Bismarck played the role of sincere peacemaker. At the Congress of Berlin in 1878, he saw that Austria obtained the right to "occupy and administer" the Ottoman provinces of Bosnia and Herzegovina to counterbalance Russian gains, while independent Balkan states were also carved from the disintegrating Ottoman Empire.

Bismarck's balancing efforts at the Congress of Berlin infuriated Russian nationalists, which led Bismarck to conclude a defensive military alliance with Austria against Russia in 1879. Motivated by tensions with France, Italy joined Germany and Austria in 1882, thereby forming the Triple Alliance.

Bismarck continued to work for peace in eastern Europe, seeking to neutralize tensions between Austria-Hungary and Russia. In 1881, he capitalized on their mutual fears and cajoled them both into a secret alliance with Germany. This Alliance of the Three Emperors lasted until 1887. It established the principle of cooperation among all three powers in any further division of Turkey, while each state pledged friendly neutrality in case one of the three found itself at war with a fourth power (except Turkey).

Bismarck also maintained good relations with Britain and Italy, while cooperating with France in Africa but keeping France isolated in Europe. In 1887, Russia declined to renew the Alliance of the Three Emperors because of new tensions in the Balkans. Bismarck craftily substituted a Russian-German Reinsurance Treaty, by which both states promised neutrality if the other was attacked.

Bismarck's accomplishments in foreign policy after 1871 were great. For almost a generation he maintained German leadership in international affairs, and he worked successfully for peace by managing conflicts and by restraining Austria-Hungary and Russia with defensive alliances.

THE RIVAL BLOCS

In 1890, the young, impetuous emperor William II dismissed Bismarck, in part because of the chancellor's friendly policy toward Russia since the 1870s. William then adamantly refused to renew the Russian-German Reinsurance Treaty, in spite of Russian pleas to do so. This fateful departure in foreign affairs prompted long-isolated republican France to court absolutist Russia, offering loans, arms, and friendship. In both countries there were enthusiastic public demonstrations, and in St. Petersburg the autocratic Nicholas II stood bareheaded on a French battleship while a band played the "Marseillaise," the hymn of the Revolution. A preliminary agreement between the two countries was reached in 1891, and in early 1894 France and Russia became military allies. This alliance was to remain in effect as long as the Triple Alliance of Austria, Germany, and Italy: continental Europe was

FIGURE 33.1 THE ALLIANCE SYSTEM AFTER 1871

dangerously divided into two rival blocks.

The policy of Great Britain became increasingly crucial. Long content with "splendid isolation" and no permanent alliances, Britain after 1891 was the only uncommitted Great Power. Could Britain afford to remain isolated, or would it feel compelled to take sides? Alliance with France or Russia certainly seemed highly unlikely. With its vast and rapidly expanding empire, Britain was often in serious conflict with these countries around the world in the heyday of imperialism.

Britain also squabbled with Germany, for Emperor William II was a master of tactless public statements, and Britain found Germany's pursuit of greater world power after about 1897 vaguely disquieting. Nevertheless, many Germans and some Britons believed that their statesmen would eventually formalize the "natural alliance" they felt already united the advanced, racially related Germanic and Anglo-Saxon peoples. Alas, such an understanding never materialized. Instead, the generally good relations that had prevailed between Prussia and Great Britain ever since the mid-eighteenth century, and certainly under Bismarck, gave way to a bitter Anglo-German rivalry.

There were several reasons for this tragic development. The hard-fought Boer War (1899–1902) between the British and the tiny Dutch republics of South Africa had a major impact on British policy. British statesmen saw that Britain was overextended around the world. The Boer War also brought into the open widespread anti-British feeling, as edi-

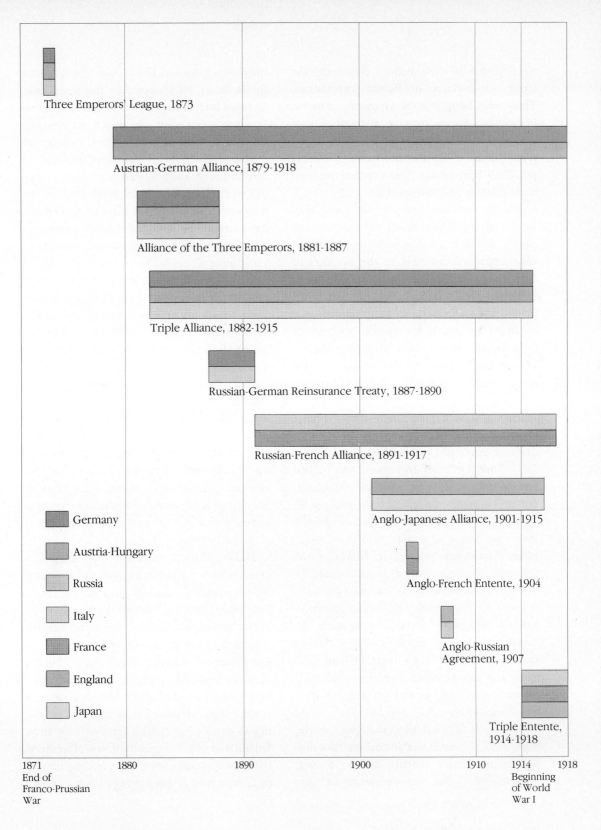

Three Emperors' League, 1873

Austrian-German Alliance, 1879-1918

Alliance of the Three Emperors, 1881-1887

Triple Alliance, 1882-1915

Russian-German Reinsurance Treaty, 1887-1890

Russian-French Alliance, 1891-1917

Anglo-Japanese Alliance, 1901-1915

Germany

Austria-Hungary

Russia

Italy

France

England

Japan

Anglo-French Entente, 1904

Anglo-Russian
Agreement, 1907

Triple Entente,
1914-1918

1871
End of
Franco-Prussian
War

1880

1890

1900

1910

1914
Beginning
of World
War I

1918

torial writers in many nations denounced the latest manifestation of British imperialism. There was even talk of Germany, Austria, France, and Russia forming a grand alliance against the bloated but insatiable British Empire. Therefore British statesmen prudently set about shoring up their exposed position with alliances and agreements.

Britain improved its often-strained relations with the United States and in 1902 concluded a formal alliance with Japan. Britain then responded favorably to the advances of France's skillful foreign minister, Théophile Delcassé, who wanted better relations with Britain and was willing to accept British rule in Egypt in return for British support of French plans to dominate Morocco. The resulting Anglo-French Entente of 1904 settled all outstanding colonial disputes between Britain and France.

Frustrated by Britain's turn toward France in 1904, Germany decided to test the strength of the entente and drive Britain and France apart. First, Germany threatened and bullied France into dismissing Delcassé. However, rather than accept the typical territorial payoff of imperial competition – a slice of French jungle in Africa or a port in Morocco – in return for French primacy in Morocco, the Germans foolishly rattled their swords in 1905. They insisted on an international conference on the whole Moroccan question without presenting precise or reasonable demands. Germany's crude bullying forced France and Britain closer together, and Germany left the Algeciras Conference of 1906 empty-handed and isolated (except for Austria-Hungary).

The result of the Moroccan crisis and the Algeciras Conference was something of a diplomatic revolution. Britain, France, Russia, and even the United States began to see Germany as a potential threat, which might seek to dominate all Europe. At the same time, German leaders began to see sinister plots to "encircle" Germany and block its development as a world power. In 1907, Russia, battered by the disastrous war with Japan and the revolution of 1905, agreed to settle its quarrels with Great Britain in Persia and central Asia with a special Anglo-Russian Agreement. As a result of that agreement, Germany's blustering paranoia increased and so did Britain's thinly disguised hostility.

Germany's decision to add a large, enormously expensive fleet of big-gun battleships to its already expanding navy also heightened tensions after 1907. German nationalists, led by the all-too-persuasive Admiral Tirpitz, saw a large navy as the legitimate mark of a great world power. But British leaders like Lloyd George saw it as a detestable military challenge, which forced them to spend the "People's Budget" on battleships rather than on social welfare. Economic rivalry also contributed to distrust and hostility between the two nations. Unscrupulous journalists and special-interest groups portrayed healthy competition in foreign trade and investment as a form of economic warfare.

Many educated shapers of public opinion and ordinary people in Britain and Germany were increasingly locked in a fateful "love-hate" relationship between the two countries. Proud nationalists in both countries simultaneously admired and feared the power and accomplishments of their nearly equal rival. In 1909, the mass-circulation London *Daily Mail* hysterically informed its readers in a series of reports that "Germany is deliberately preparing to destroy the British Empire."[2] By then, Britain was psychologically if not officially in the Franco-Russian camp. The leading nations of Europe were divided into two hostile blocs, dangerously ill prepared to deal with upheaval on Europe's southeastern frontier.

THE OUTBREAK OF WAR

In the early years of this century, war in the Balkans was as inevitable as anything can be in human history. The reason was simple: nationalism was destroying the Ottoman Empire and threatening to break up the Austro-Hungarian Empire. The only questions were what kind of wars would occur and where they would lead.

Greece had long before led the struggle for national liberation, winning its independence in 1832. In 1875, widespread nationalist rebellion in the Ottoman Empire had resulted in Turkish repression, Russian intervention, and Great Power tensions. Bismarck had helped resolve this crisis at the 1878 Congress of Berlin, which worked out the partial division of Turkish possessions in Europe. Austria-Hungary obtained the right to "occupy and administer" Bosnia and Herzegovina. Serbia and Rumania won independence, and a part of Bulgaria won local autonomy. The Ottoman Empire retained important Balkan holdings, for Austria-Hungary and Russia each feared the other's domination of totally independent states in the area (see Map 33.1).

After 1878, the siren call of imperialism lured European energies, particularly Russian energies, away from the Balkans. This division helped preserve the fragile balance of interests in southeastern Europe. By 1903, however, Balkan nationalism was on the rise once again. Serbia led the way, becoming openly hostile toward both Austria-Hungary and the Ottoman Empire. The Serbs, a Slavic people, looked to Slavic Russia for support of their national aspirations. To block Serbian expansion and to take advantage of Russia's weak-

"IMMODEST ENGLAND" This irreverent 1903 French view of King Edward VII reflected widespread hostility toward Britain before the Anglo-French Entente. French newspapers still delight in spreading scandalous rumors about the English royal family. (L'Impudique Albion from L'Assiette au Beurre, 1903)

ness after the revolution of 1905, Austria in 1908 formally annexed Bosnia and Herzegovina with their predominantly Serbian populations. The kingdom of Serbia erupted in rage, but could do nothing without Russian support.

Then in 1912 in the First Balkan War, Serbia turned southward. With Greece and Bulgaria it took Macedonia from the Ottoman Empire and then quarreled with its ally Bulgaria over the spoils of victory – a dispute

MAP 33.1 *THE BALKANS AFTER THE CON-GRESS OF BERLIN, 1878* *The Ottoman Empire suffered large territorial losses but remained a power in the Balkans.*

June 28, 1914, during a state visit to the Bosnian capital of Sarajevo. The assassins were closely connected to the ultranationalist Serbian society, The Black Hand. This revolutionary group was secretly supported by members of the Serbian government and was dedicated to uniting all Serbians into a single state. Although the leaders of Austria-Hungary did not and could not know all the details of Serbia's involvement in the assassination plot, they concluded after some hesitation that Serbia had to be severely punished once and for all. After a month of maneuvering, Austria-Hungary presented Serbia with an unconditional ultimatum, on July 23.

The Serbian government had just forty-eight hours in which to agree to cease all subversion in Austria and all anti-Austrian propaganda in Serbia as well. Moreover, a thorough investigation of all aspects of the assassination at Sarajevo was to be undertaken in Serbia by a joint commission of Serbian and Austrian officials. These demands amounted to virtual control of the Serbian state. When Serbia replied moderately but evasively, Austria began to mobilize and then declared war on Serbia on July 28. Thus, a desperate multinational Austria-Hungary deliberately chose war in a last-ditch attempt to stem the rising tide of hostile nationalism. The "Third Balkan War" had begun (see Map 33.2).

Of prime importance in Austria-Hungary's fateful decision was Germany's unconditional support. Emperor William II and Chancellor Theobald von Bethmann-Hollweg gave Austria-Hungary a "blank check" and urged aggressive measures in early July, even though they realized that war between Austria and Russia was the most probable result. They knew Russian pan-Slavs saw Russia not only as the protector, but also as the eventual liberator, of southern Slavs. As one pan-Slav had

that led in 1913 to the Second Balkan War. Austria intervened in 1913 and forced Serbia to give up Albania. After centuries, nationalism had finally destroyed the Ottoman Empire in Europe. This sudden yet long-awaited event elated the Balkan nationalists and dismayed the leaders of multinational Austria-Hungary. The former hoped, and the latter feared, that Austria might be next to be broken apart.

Within this tense context, Archduke Francis Ferdinand, heir to the Austrian and Hungarian thrones, and his wife Sophie were assassinated by Bosnian revolutionaries on

said much earlier, "Austria can hold her part of the Slavonian mass as long as Turkey holds hers and vice versa."[3] At the very least a resurgent Russia could not stand by, as in the Bosnian crisis, and simply watch the Serbs be crushed. Yet Bethmann-Hollweg apparently hoped that while Russia (and therefore France) would go to war, Great Britain would remain neutral, unwilling to fight for "Russian aggression" in the distant Balkans. After all, Britain had reached only "friendly understandings" with France and Russia on colonial questions and had no alliance with either power.

In fact, the diplomatic situation was already out of control. Military considerations began to dictate policy. Russia, a vast country, required much longer to mobilize its armies than did Germany and Austria-Hungary. On July 28, as Austrian armies bombarded Belgrade, Russian Foreign Minister Sergei Sazonov ordered a "partial mobilization" against Austria-Hungary. Almost immediately he found that this was impossible. All the complicated mobilization plans of the Russian general staff had assumed a war with both Austria *and* Germany: Russia could not mobilize against one without mobilizing against the other. On July 29, therefore, Russia ordered full mobilization and in effect declared general war. For as the French general Boisdeffre had said to the agreeing Russian tsar when the Franco-Russian military convention was being negotiated in 1892, "mobilization is a declaration of war."[4]

The same tragic subordination of political considerations to military strategy descended on Germany. The German general staff had also thought only in terms of a two-front war. Their plan for war – the Schlieffen plan, the work of Count Alfred von Schlieffen, chief of the German general staff from 1891 to 1906 and a professional military man – called for

MAP 33.2 THE BALKANS IN 1914 *Ethnic boundaries did not follow political boundaries, and Serbian national aspirations threatened Austria-Hungary.*

knocking out France first with a lightning attack through neutral Belgium before turning on Russia.

Thus on August 2, 1914, General Helmuth von Moltke, "acting under a dictate of self-preservation," demanded that Belgium permit German armies to pass through its territory. Belgium, whose neutrality was solemnly guaranteed by all the great states including Prussia, refused. Germany attacked. Thus Germany's terrible, politically disastrous response to a war in the Balkans was an all-out invasion of France by way of the plains of neutral Belgium on August 3. In the face of this act of aggression, Great Britain declared war on Germany the following day. The First World War had begun.

REFLECTIONS ON THE ORIGINS OF THE WAR

Although few events in history have aroused such interest and controversy as the coming of the First World War, the question of immediate causes and responsibilities can be answered with considerable certainty. Austria-Hungary deliberately started the "Third Balkan War." A war for the right to survive was Austria-Hungary's desperate, if understandable, response to the aggressive, yet understandable, revolutionary drive of Serbian nationalists to unify their people in a single state. In spite of Russian intervention in the quarrel, it is clear from the beginning of the crisis that Germany not only pushed and goaded Austria-Hungary onward but was also responsible for instantly turning a little war into the Great War by means of its sledge-hammer attack on Belgium and France.

After Bismarck's resignation in 1890, German leaders lost control of the international system. They felt increasingly that Germany's status as a world power was declining while that of Britain, France, Russia, and the United States was growing. And indeed the powers of what officially became the Triple Entente — Great Britain, France and Russia — in August 1914 were checking Germany's vague but real aspirations, as well as working to strangle Austria-Hungary, Germany's only real ally. Germany's aggression in 1914 reflected the failure of all European statesmen, not just German leaders, to incorporate Bismarck's mighty empire permanently and peacefully into the international system.

There were other underlying causes. The new overseas expansion – imperialism – did not play a direct role, since the European powers always settled their colonial conflicts peacefully. Yet the easy imperialist victories did contribute to a general European over-confidence and reinforced national rivalries. In this respect it was influential.

The triumph of nationalism was a crucial underlying precondition of the Great War. Nationalism was at the heart of the Balkan wars, in the form of Serbian aspirations and the grandiose pan-German versus pan-Slavic racism of some fanatics. Nationalism drove the spiraling arms race. More generally, as we have seen in Chapter 30, the aristocracy and middle classes arrived at nationalistic compromises, while ordinary people looked toward increasingly responsive states for psychological and material well-being.

Broad popular commitment to "my country right or wrong" weakened groups that thought in terms of international communities and consequences. Thus the big international bankers, who were frightened by the prospect of war in July 1914, and the extreme-left socialists, who believed that the enemy was at home and not abroad, were equally out of step with national feeling.

Finally, the wealthy governing classes underestimated the risk of war in 1914. They had forgotten that great wars and great social revolutions very often go together in history. Metternich's alliance of conservative forces in support of international peace and the domestic status quo had become only a distant memory.

THE FIRST BATTLE OF THE MARNE

When the Germans invaded Belgium in August 1914, they and everyone else believed that the war would be short, for urban society rested on the food and raw materials of the world economy: "The boys will be home by Christmas." The Belgian army heroically defended its homeland, however, and fell back in good order to join a rapidly landed British army corps near the Franco-Belgian border. This action complicated the original Schlieffen plan of concentrating German armies on the right wing and boldly capturing Paris in a vast encircling movement. Moreover, the German left wing in Lorraine failed to retreat, thwarting the plan to suck French armies into Germany and then annihilate them. Instead, by the end of August dead-tired German soldiers were advancing along an enormous front in the scorching summer heat. The neatly designed prewar plan to surround Paris from the north and west had been thrown into confusion.

French armies totaling 1 million, reinforced by more than 100,000 British troops, had retreated in orderly fashion before Germany's 1.5 million men in the field. Under the leadership of the steel-nerved General Joseph Joffre, the French attacked a gap in the German line at the battle of the Marne on September 6. For three days France threw everything into the attack. At one point the French government desperately requisitioned all the taxis of Paris to rush reserves to the front. Finally, the Germans fell back. Paris and France had been miraculously saved.

STALEMATE AND SLAUGHTER

The attempts of French and British armies to turn the German retreat into a rout were unsuccessful, and so were moves by both sides to outflank each other in northern France. As a result, both sides began to dig trenches to protect themselves from machine-gun fire. By November 1914, an unbroken line of trenches extended from the Belgian ports through northern France past the fortress of Verdun and on to the Swiss frontier.

In the face of this unexpected stalemate, slaughter on the western front began in earnest. The defenders on both sides dug in behind rows of trenches, mines, and barbed wire. For days and even weeks ceaseless shelling by heavy artillery supposedly "softened up" the enemy in a given area (and also signaled the coming attack). Then young draftees and their junior officers went "over the top" of the trenches in frontal attacks on the enemy's line.

The cost in lives was staggering; the gains in territory minuscule. The massive French and British offensives during 1915 never gained more than three miles of blood-soaked earth from the enemy. In the battle of the Somme in the summer of 1916, the British and French gained an insignificant 125 square miles at the cost of 600,000 dead or wounded, while the Germans lost half a million men. That same year the unsuccessful German campaign against Verdun cost 700,000 lives on both sides. The British poet Siegfried Sassoon (1886–1967) wrote of the Somme offensive: "I am staring at a sunlit picture of Hell."

Terrible 1917 saw General Robert Nivelle's French army almost destroyed in a grand spring attack at Champagne, while at Passchendaele in the fall the British traded 400,000 casualties for fifty square miles of Belgian Flanders. The hero of Erich Remarque's great novel *All Quiet on the Western Front* (1929) describes one such attack:

We see men living with their skulls blown open; we see soldiers run with their two feet cut off. . . . Still the little piece of convulsed earth in which we lie is held. We have yielded no more than a few hundred

PREPARING THE ATTACK *The great offenses of the First World War required the mobilization of men and material on an unprecedented scale. This photo shows American troops moving up. (U.S. Army Signal Corps)*

yards of it as a prize to the enemy. But on every yard there lies a dead man.

Such was war on the western front.

The war of the trenches shattered an entire generation of young men. Millions who could have provided political creativity and leadership after the war were forever missing.

Moreover, those who lived through the holocaust were maimed, shell-shocked, embittered, and profoundly disillusioned. The young soldiers went to war believing in the world of their leaders and elders, the pre-1914 world of order, progress, and patriotism. Then, in Remarque's words, "the first bombardment showed us our mistake, and under it the

world as they had taught it to us broke in pieces." For many the sacrifice and comradeship of the battlefield became life's crucial experience, an experience that "soft" civilians could never understand. A chasm opened up between veterans and civilians, making the difficult postwar reconstruction all the more difficult.

THE WIDENING WAR

On the eastern front slaughter did not degenerate into suicidal trench warfare. With the outbreak of war, the "Russian steamroller" immediately moved into eastern Germany. Very badly damaged by the Germans under Generals Paul von Hindenburg and Erich

Ludendorff at the battles of Tannenberg and the Masurian Lakes in August and September 1914, Russia never threatened Germany again. On the Austrian front enormous armies see-sawed back and forth, suffering enormous losses. Austro-Hungarian armies were repulsed twice by little Serbia in bitter fighting. But with the help of German forces they reversed the Russian advances of 1914 and forced the Russians to retreat deep into their own territory in the eastern campaign of 1915. A staggering 2.5 million Russians were killed, wounded, or taken prisoner that year.

These changing tides of victory and defeat brought neutral countries into the war (see Map 33.3). Italy, a member of the Triple Alliance since 1882, had declared its neutrality in 1914 on the grounds that Austria had launched a war of aggression. Then, in May 1915, Italy joined the Triple Entente of Great Britain, France, and Russia in return for promises of Austrian territory. Bulgaria allied with Austria and Germany, now known as the Central Powers, in September 1915 in order to settle old scores with Serbia. The Austro-Hungarian grand offensive against Italy in June 1916 allowed Russia's most talented commander, General Alexei Brusilov, to reconquer Austria-Hungary's Polish provinces before bogging down once again.

The entry of Italy and Bulgaria in 1915 was part of a general widening of the war. The Balkans, with the exception of Greece, came to be occupied by the Central Powers, and British forces were badly defeated in 1915 trying to take the Dardanelles from Turkey, Germany's ally. More successful was the entente's attempt to incite Arab nationalists against their Turkish overlords. An enigmatic British colonel, soon known to millions as Lawrence of Arabia, aroused the Arab princes to revolt in early 1917. In 1918, British armies from Egypt smashed the Ottoman Empire

once and for all. In their Middle East campaign the British drew on forces from Australia, New Zealand, and India. Contrary to German hopes, the colonial subjects of the British (and French) did not revolt but loyally supported their foreign masters. Instead, the European war extended around the globe as Great Britain, France, and Japan seized Germany's colonies.

A crucial development in the expanding conflict came in April 1917, when the United States declared war on Germany. American intervention grew out of the war at sea, sympathy for the entente, and the increasing desperation of total war. At the beginning of the war, Britain and France had established a naval blockade to strangle the Central Powers. They refused to accept the traditional distinction under international law between military equipment (contraband) and nonmilitary (noncontraband) articles such as food and clothing. No neutral ship was permitted to sail to Germany with any cargo. The blockade annoyed Americans, but effective propaganda over German atrocities in occupied Belgium and lush profits from selling war supplies to Britain and France blunted American indignation.

Moreover, in early 1915 Germany launched a counterblockade using the murderously effective submarine, a new weapon that violated traditional niceties of fair warning under international law. In May 1915, after sinking about ninety ships in the British war zone, a German submarine sank the British passenger liner *Lusitania,* which was also carrying arms and munitions. More than a thousand lives, among them 139 Americans, were lost. Presi-

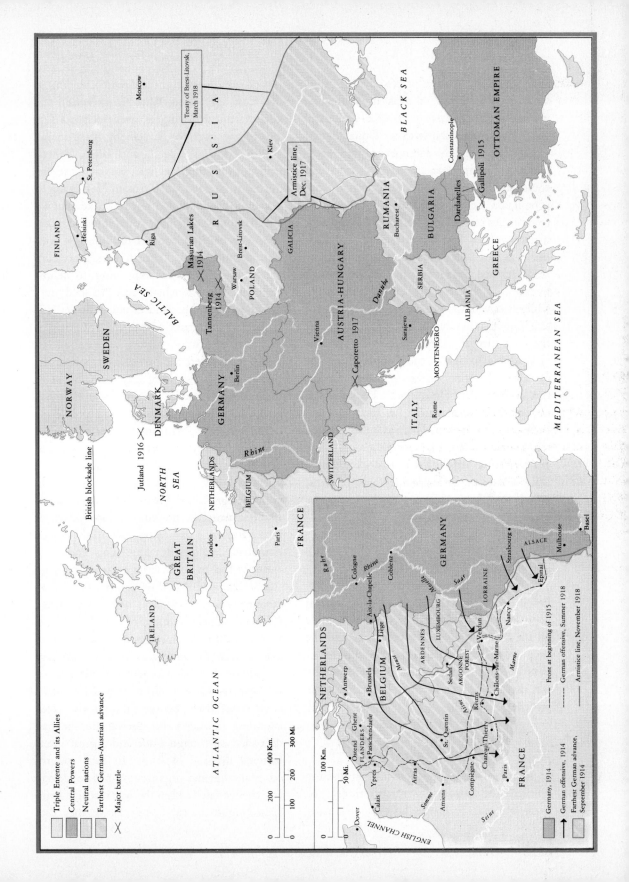

Treaty of Brest Litovsk, March 1918

Armistice line, Dec. 1917

Moscow

St. Petersburg

Helsinki

FINLAND

Riga

Kiev

R U S S I A

BLACK SEA

Constantinople

Gallipoli 1915

OTTOMAN EMPIRE

Dardanelles

RUMANIA

Bucharest

BULGARIA

GALICIA

SERBIA

GREECE

Masurian Lakes 1914

Warsaw

Brest-Litovsk

POLAND

Tannenberg 1914

AUSTRIA-HUNGARY

Danube

Vienna

Caporetto 1917

Sarajevo

MONTENEGRO

ALBANIA

SWEDEN

NORWAY

DENMARK

BALTIC SEA

GERMANY

Berlin

Rhine

SWITZERLAND

ITALY

Rome

MEDITERRANEAN SEA

Jutland 1916

NORTH SEA

British blockade line

NETHERLANDS

BELGIUM

FRANCE

Paris

GREAT BRITAIN

London

IRELAND

ATLANTIC OCEAN

Triple Entente and its Allies

Central Powers

Neutral nations

Farthest German-Austrian advance

Major battle

200   400 Km.

0

300 Mi.

0   100   200

GERMANY

Ruhr

Rhine

Cologne

Coblenz

Aix-la-Chapelle

Liège

Moselle

Saar

LORRAINE

Strasbourg

ALSACE

Mulhouse

Basel

Epinal

Nancy

Verdun

ARGONNE FOREST

Châlons-sur-Marne

Marne

Château-Thierry

Reims

Aisne

St. Quentin

Sedan

LUXEMBOURG

ARDENNES

Meuse

Antwerp

Brussels

BELGIUM

NETHERLANDS

Ghent

Ostend

FLANDERS

Passchendaele

Ypres

Calais

Dover

ENGLISH CHANNEL

Arras

Somme

Amiens

Compiègne

Paris

Seine

FRANCE

Germany, 1914

German offensive, 1914

Farthest German advance, September 1914

Front at beginning of 1915

German offensive, Summer 1918

Armistice line, November 1918

50 Mi.

0

100 Km.

0

dent Woodrow Wilson protested vigorously. Germany was forced to relax its submarine warfare for almost two years; the alternative was almost certain war with the United States.

Early in 1917, the German military command, confident that improved submarines could starve their island enemy Britain into submission before the United States could come to its rescue, resumed unrestricted submarine warfare. Like the invasion of Belgium, this was a reckless gamble. British shipping losses reached staggering proportions, though by late 1917 shippers came up with the inevitable effective response, the convoy system for safe transatlantic shipping. In the meantime the embattled President Wilson had told a sympathetic Congress and people that "the German submarine warfare against commerce is a warfare against mankind." Thus the last uncommitted great nation, as fresh and enthusiastic as Europe had been in 1914, entered the world war in April 1917, almost three years after it began. Eventually, the United States was to tip the balance in favor of Great Britain and France.

THE HOME FRONT

Before looking at the last year of the Great War, let us turn our attention to the people on the "home front." The people behind the lines were tremendously involved in the titanic struggle. War's impact on them was no less massive than on the men crouched in the trenches.

MOBILIZING FOR TOTAL WAR

In August 1914, most people had greeted the outbreak of hostilities enthusiastically. In every country the masses believed that their nation was in the right and was defending itself from aggression. With the exception of a few extreme left-wingers, even socialists supported the war. Tough standby plans to imprison socialist leaders and break general strikes protesting the war proved quite unnecessary in 1914. In Germany, for example, the trade unions voted not to strike, and socialists in the parliament voted money for war credits in order to counter the threat of Russian despotism. A German socialist volunteered for the front, explaining to fellow members of the Reichstag that "to shed one's blood for the fatherland is not difficult: it is enveloped in romantic heroism."[5] William II said that he saw no parties, only good Germans. Everywhere the patriotic support of the masses and the working class contributed to national unity and an energetic war effort.

By mid-October generals and politicians began to realize that more than patriotism would be needed to win the war, whose end was not in sight. Each country experienced a relentless, desperate demand for men and weapons. In France, for example, the generals found themselves needing 100,000 pieces of heavy artillery a day, as opposed to the 12,000 they had anticipated using. This enormous quantity had to come from a French steel industry that had lost three-fourths of its iron resources in the first days of the war, when Germany seized the mines of French Lorraine. In Great Britain shortages of jute for sandbags and flax for tents soon became matters of life and death, while Germany found itself cut off from the Chilean nitrates needed to make explosives. Each belligerent quickly faced countless shortages, for prewar Europe had depended on foreign trade and a great international division of labor. In each country economic life and organization had to change and change fast to keep the war machine from sputtering to a stop. And change they did.

In each country a government of national unity began to plan and control economic and social life in order to wage "total war." Free-market capitalism was abandoned, at least "for the duration." Instead, government planning boards established priorities and decided what was to be produced and consumed. Rationing, price and wage controls, and even restrictions on workers' freedom of movement were imposed by government. Only through such regimentation could a country make the greatest possible military effort. Thus, though there were national variations, the great nations all moved toward planned economies commanded by the established political leadership.

This revolutionary development would burn deeply into the twentieth-century consciousness. The planned economy of "total war" released the tremendous energies first harnessed by the French under Robespierre during the French Revolution. Total war, however, was based on tremendously productive industrial economies not confined to a single nation. The result was an effective – and therefore destructive – war effort on all sides.

Moreover, the economy of total war

blurred the old distinction between soldiers on the battlefield and civilians at home. As President Wilson told Americans shortly after the United States entered the war, there were no armies in the struggle in the traditional sense. Rather, "there are entire nations armed. Thus the men [and women] who remain to till the soil and man the factories are not less a part of the army than the men beneath the battle flags."[6] The war was a war of whole peoples, entire populations, and the loser would be the society that cracked first.

Finally, however awful the war was, the ability of governments to manage and control highly complicated economies strengthened the cause of socialism. With the First World War, socialism became for the first time a realistic economic blueprint as opposed to a utopian program.

Germany illustrates the general trend. It also went farthest in developing a planned economy to wage total war. As soon as war began, Walter Rathenau, the talented, foresighted Jewish industrialist in charge of Germany's largest electrical company, convinced the government to set up a War Raw Materials Board to ration and distribute raw materials. Under Rathenau's direction, every useful material from foreign oil to barnyard manure was inventoried and rationed. Moreover, the board launched successful attempts to produce substitutes, such as synthetic rubber and synthetic nitrates. Without the spectacular double achievement of discovering a way to "fix" nitrogen present in the air and then of producing synthetic nitrates in enormous quantity, the blockaded German war machine would have stalled in a matter of months.

Food was also rationed in accordance with physical need. Men and women doing hard manual work were given extra rations. During the last two years of the war, only children and expectant mothers received milk rations. Sometimes mistakes were made that would have been funny if they had not been tragic. In early 1915, German authorities calculated that greedy pigs were eating food that hungry people needed, and ordered a "hog massacre" only to find that there were too few pigs left to eat an abundant potato crop. Germany also failed to tax the war profits of private firms heavily enough. This contributed to massive deficit financing, inflation, the growth of a black market, and the eventual re-emergence of class conflict.

Following the terrible battles of Verdun and the Somme in 1916, the military leaders Hindenburg and Ludendorff became the real rulers of Germany, and they decreed the ultimate mobilization for total war. Germany, said Hindenburg, could win only "if all the treasures of our soil that agriculture and industry can produce are used exclusively for the conduct of the War. . . . All other considerations must come second."[7] This goal, they believed, required that every German man, woman, and child be drafted into the service of the war. Thus, in December 1916 the military leaders rammed through the parliament the Auxiliary Service Law, which required all males between seventeen and sixty to work only at jobs considered critical to the war effort.

Although women and children were not specifically mentioned, this forced-labor law was also aimed at them. Many women already worked in war factories, mines, and steel mills, where they labored like men at the heaviest and most dangerous jobs. With the passage of the Auxiliary Service Law, many more women followed. Children were organized by their teachers into garbage brigades to collect every scrap of useful material: grease strained from dishwater, coffee grounds, waste paper, tin cans, metal door knockers, bottles, rags, hair, bones, and so forth, as well as acorns, chestnuts, pinecones, and rotting leaves. Potatoes gave way to turnips, and people averaged little more than a thousand calories a day. Thus, in Germany total war led to the establishment of history's first "totalitarian" society, and war production increased while some people literally starved to death.

Great Britain mobilized for total war less rapidly and less completely than Germany, for it could import materials from its empire and from the United States. By 1915, however, a serious shortage of shells led to the establishment of a Ministry of Munitions under David Lloyd George. The ministry organized private industry to produce for the war, controlled profits, allocated labor, fixed wage rates, and settled labor disputes. By December 1916, when Lloyd George became prime minister, the British economy was almost totally planned and regulated. More than two hundred factories and 90 percent of all imports were bought and allocated directly by the state. Food was strictly rationed, and the hours for public drinking drastically reduced, while war production soared. Great Britain had followed very successfully in Germany's footsteps.

THE SOCIAL IMPACT

The social impact of total war on society was no less profound than the economic, though again there were important national variations. The millions of men at the front and the insatiable needs of the military created a tremendous demand for workers. Jobs were available for absolutely everyone. This situation had seldom if ever been seen before 1914, when unemployment and widespread poverty had been facts of urban life. The exceptional

demand for labor brought about great and momentous changes.

One such change was greater power and prestige for labor unions. Having proved their loyalty in August 1914, labor unions became an indispensable partner of government and private industry in the planned war economy. Unions cooperated with war governments on work rules, wages, and production schedules in return for real participation in important decisions. This entry of labor leaders and unions into policy-making councils paralleled the entry of socialist leaders into the war governments. Thus did organized labor gain, for the first time, something like real equality with employers in industrial society.

The role of women changed dramatically. In every country large numbers of women left home and domestic service to work in industry, transportation, and offices. By 1917, women formed fully 43 percent of the labor force in Russia. The number of women driving buses and streetcars increased tenfold in Great Britain. Moreover, women became highly visible – not only as munitions workers but as bank tellers, mail carriers, even policewomen.

At first, the male-dominated unions were hostile to women moving into new occupations, believing that their presence would lower wages and change work rules. But government pressure and the principle of equal pay for equal work (until the end of the war) overcame these objections. Women also served as nurses and doctors at the front. In general, the war greatly expanded the range of women's activities and changed attitudes toward them. As a direct result of their many-sided war effort, Britain, Germany, and Austria granted women the right to vote immediately after the war. Women also showed a growing spirit of independence during the war, as they bobbed their hair, shortened their skirts, and smoked in public.

War also promoted greater social equality, blurring class distinctions and lessening the gap between rich and poor. This blurring was most apparent in Great Britain, where wartime hardship was never extreme. In fact, the bottom third of the population generally lived *better* than ever before, for the poorest gained most from the severe shortage of labor. The English writer Robert Roberts recalled how his parents' tiny grocery store in the slums of Manchester thrived as never before during the war, when people who had scrimped to buy bread and soup bones were able to afford fancy cakes and thick steaks. In 1924, a British government study revealed that the distribution of income had indeed shifted in favor of the poorest: only half as many families lived in severe poverty as in 1911, even though total production of goods had not increased. In continental countries greater equality was reflected in full employment, rationing according to physical needs, and a sharing of hardships. There too society became more uniform and more egalitarian, in spite of some war profiteering.

Finally, death itself had no respect for traditional social distinctions. It savagely decimated the young aristocratic officers who led the charge, and it fell heavily on the mass of drafted peasants and unskilled workers who followed. Yet death often spared the aristocrats of labor. Their lives were too valuable to squander at the front, for they were needed to train and direct the newly recruited women and older unskilled men laboring valiantly in war plants at home.

GROWING POLITICAL TENSIONS

During the first two years of war most soldiers and civilians supported their govern-ments. Even in Austria-Hungary – the most vulnerable of the belligerents, with its competing nationalities – loyalty to the state and monarchy remained astonishingly strong through 1916. Belief in a just cause, patriotic nationalism, the planned economy, and a sharing of burdens united peoples behind their various national leaders. Furthermore, each government did its best to control public opinion to bolster morale. Newspapers, letters, and public addresses were rigorously censored. Good news was overstated; bad news was repressed or distorted.

Each government used both crude and subtle propaganda to maintain popular support. German propaganda hysterically pictured black soldiers from France's African empire raping German women, while German atrocities in Belgium and elsewhere were ceaselessly recounted and exaggerated by the French and British. Patriotic posters and slogans, slanted news and biased editorials inflamed national hatreds and helped sustain superhuman efforts.

By the spring of 1916, however, people were beginning to crack under the strain of total war. In April 1916, Irish nationalists in Dublin tried to take advantage of this situation and rose up against British rule in their great Easter Rebellion. A week of bitter fighting passed before the rebels were crushed and their leaders executed. Strikes and protest marches over inadequate food began to flare up on every home front. Soldiers' morale began to decline. Russian troops mutinied. Numerous French units refused to fight after General Nivelle's disastrous offensive of May 1917. Only tough military justice and a tacit agreement with his troops that there would be no more grand offensives enabled the new general in chief, Henri-Philippe Pétain, to restore order. A rising tide of war-weariness and defeatism also swept France's civilian popula-

Daddy, what did YOU do in the Great War?

On les aura!

2ᴱ EMPRUNT
DE
LA DÉFENSE NATIONALE

Souscrivez

DEVAMBEZ Imp PARIS

WARTIME PROPAGANDA was skillful and effective. Before the draft was introduced to Britain in 1916, the famous poster on the left shamed many able-bodied men into volunteering for military service. The patriotic poster on the right encouraged many French people to buy bonds to finance the war effort. (By courtesy of the Trustees of the Imperial War Museum)

tion before Georges Clemenceau emerged as a ruthless and effective wartime leader in November 1917. Clemenceau established a virtual dictatorship, pouncing on strikers and jailing without trial journalists and politicians who dared to suggest a compromise peace with Germany.

The strains were worse for the Central Powers. In October 1916, the chief minister of Austria was assassinated by a young social-

ist crying, "Down with Absolutism! We want peace!"[8] The following month, when the feeble old Emperor Francis Joseph died sixty-eight years after his mother Sophia had pushed him onto the throne in 1848 (page 1050), a symbol of unity disappeared. In spite of absolute censorship, political dissatisfaction and conflicts among nationalities grew. In April 1917, Austria's chief minister summed up the situation in the gloomiest possible terms. The country and army were exhausted. Another winter of war would bring revolution and disintegration. "If the monarchs of the Central Powers cannot make peace in the coming months," he wrote, "it will be made for them by their peoples."[9] Both Czech and Yugoslav leaders demanded autonomous democratic states for their peoples. The allied blockade kept tightening; people were starving.

The strain of total war and the Auxiliary Service Law was also evident in Germany. In the winter of 1916–1917, Germany's military position appeared increasingly desperate. Stalemates and losses in the west were matched by Russian advances (the Brusilov offense) in the east: hence the military's insistence on the all-or-nothing gamble of unrestricted submarine warfare when the entente refused in December 1916 to consider peace on terms favorable to the Central Powers.

Also, the national political unity of the first two years of war was collapsing as the social conflict of prewar Germany re-emerged. A growing minority of socialists in the parliament began to vote against war credits, calling for a compromise "peace without annexations or reparations." In July 1917 a coalition of socialists and Catholics passed a resolution in the parliament to that effect. Such a peace was unthinkable for conservatives and military leaders. So also was the surge in revolutionary agitation and strikes by war-weary workers that occurred in early 1917. When the bread ration was further reduced in April, more than 200,000 workers struck and demonstrated for a week in Berlin, returning to work only under the threat of prison and military discipline. Thus militaristic Germany, like its ally Austria-Hungary (and its enemy France), was beginning to crack in 1917. Yet it was Russia that collapsed first and saved the Central Powers, for a time.

THE RUSSIAN REVOLUTION

The Russian Revolution of 1917 was one of modern history's most momentous events. Directly related to the growing tensions of World War One, its significance went far beyond the wartime agonies of a single European nation. The Russian Revolution opened a new era. For some, it was Marx's socialist vision come true; for others, it was the triumph of dictatorship. To all, it presented a radically new kind of state and society.

THE FALL OF IMPERIAL RUSSIA

Like its allies and its enemies, Russia embraced war with patriotic enthusiasm in 1914. At the Winter Palace, while throngs of people knelt and sang "God Save the Tsar," Tsar Nicholas II (1894–1917) repeated the oath Alexander I had made in 1812 and vowed never to make peace as long as the enemy stood on Russian soil. Russia's lower house, the Duma, voted war credits. Conservatives anticipated expansion in the Balkans, while liberals and most socialists believed alliance with Britain and France would bring democratic reforms. For a moment, Russia was united.

Soon, however the strains of war began to take their toll. The unprecedented artillery barrages used up Russia's supplies of shells and ammunition, and better-equipped German armies inflicted terrible losses. For a time in 1915 substantial numbers of Russian soldiers were sent to the front without rifles; they were told to find their arms among the dead. There were 2 million Russian casualties in 1915 alone. Morale declined among soldiers and civilians. Yet Russia's battered peasant army did not collapse but continued to fight courageously until early 1917.

Under the shock of defeat, Russia moved

toward full mobilization on the home front. The Duma and the organs of local government took the lead, setting up special committees to coordinate defense, industry, transportation, and agriculture. These efforts improved the military situation. Russian factories produced more than twice as many shells in 1916 as in 1915, for example, and monthly shell production in late 1916 was forty times its prewar level. Yet there were many failures, and Russia mobilized less effectively for total war than the other warring nations.

The great problem was leadership. Under the constitution resulting from the revolution of 1905 (pages 1115–1116), the tsar had retained complete control over the bureaucracy and the army. Legislation proposed by the Duma, which was weighted in favor of the wealthy and conservative classes, was subject to the tsar's veto. Moreover, Nicholas II fervently wished to maintain the sacred inheritance of supreme royal power, which with the Orthodox Church was for him the key to Russia's greatness. A kindly, slightly stupid man, of whom a friend said he "would have been an ideal country gentleman, devoting his life to wife and children, his farms and his sport," Nicholas failed to form a close partnership with his citizens in order to fight the war more effectively. He relied instead on the old bureaucratic apparatus, distrusting the moderate Duma, rejecting popular involvement, and resisting calls to share power.

As a result the Duma, the educated middle classes and the masses became increasingly critical of the tsar's leadership. Following Nicholas's belated dismissal of the incompetent minister of war, demands for more democratic and responsive government exploded in the Duma in the summer of 1915. "From the beginning of the war," declared one young liberal, "public opinion has understood the character and magnitude of the struggle; it has understood that short of organizing the whole country for war, victory is impossible. But the Government has not understood, the Government has rejected every offer of help with disdain."[10] In September parties ranging from conservative to moderate socialist formed the Progressive Bloc, which called for a completely new government responsible to the Duma instead of the tsar. In answer, Nicholas temporarily adjourned the Duma and announced that he was going to the front to lead and rally Russia's armies.

His departure was a fatal turning point. With the tsar in the field commanding the troops, control of the government was taken over by the hysterical empress, Tsarina Alexandra, and a debauched adventurer, the monk Rasputin. A minor German princess and granddaughter of England's Queen Victoria, Nicholas's wife was a devoted mother with a sick child, a strong-willed woman with a hatred of parliaments. Having constantly urged her husband to rule absolutely, Alexandra tried to do so herself in his absence. She seated and unseated the top ministers. Her most trusted adviser was "our Friend Grigori," an uneducated Siberian preacher who was appropriately nicknamed Rasputin – the "Degenerate."

Rasputin began his career with a sect noted for mixing sexual orgies with religious ecstasies, and his influence rested on mysterious healing powers. Alexis, Alexandra's fifth child and heir to the throne, suffered from a rare disease, hemophilia. The tiniest cut meant uncontrollable bleeding, terrible pain, and possible death. Medical science could do nothing. Only Rasputin could miraculously stop the bleeding, perhaps through hypnosis. The empress's faith in Rasputin was limitless. "Believe more in our Friend," she wrote her husband in 1916. "He lives for you and Rus-

FAMILY PORTRAIT *With husband Nicholas II standing behind, the beautiful but tense Alexandra shows one of her daughters, who could not inherit the Russian throne, to her grandmother, Queen Victoria of England, and Victoria's son, the future Edward VII. European monarchs were closely related by blood and breeding before 1914. (Nicholas A. de Basily Collection, Hoover Institution)*

sia." In this atmosphere of unreality, the government slid steadily toward revolution.

In a desperate attempt to right the situation and end unfounded rumors that Rasputin was the empress's lover, three members of the high aristocracy murdered Rasputin in December 1916. The empress went into semipermanent shock, her mind haunted by the dead man's prophecy: "If I die or you desert me, in six months you will lose your son and your throne."[11] Food shortages in the cities worsened, morale declined. On March 8, women in Petrograd (formerly St. Petersburg) calling for bread started riots, which spontaneously spread to the factories and throughout the city. From the front the tsar ordered the troops to restore order, but discipline broke down and the soldiers joined the revolutionary crowd. The Duma responded by declaring a provisional government on March 12, 1917. Three days later Nicholas abdicated without protest.

THE PROVISIONAL GOVERNMENT

The March revolution was the result of an unplanned uprising of hungry, angry people in the capital, but it was joyfully accepted throughout the country. The patriotic upper and middle classes rejoiced at the prospect of a more determined and effective war effort, while workers happily anticipated better wages and more food. All classes and political parties called for liberty and democracy. They were not disappointed. As Lenin said, Russia became the freest country in the world. After generations of arbitrary authoritarianism the provisional government quickly established equality before the law; freedom of religion, speech, and assembly; the right of unions to organize and strike; and the rest of the classic liberal program.

Yet both the liberal and moderate socialist leaders of the provisional government rejected social revolution. The government formed in May 1917 by the fiery agrarian socialist Alexander Kerensky refused to confiscate large landholdings and give them to peasants, fearing that such drastic action in the countryside would only complete the disintegration of Russia's peasant army. For the patriotic Kerensky, as for other moderate socialists, the continuation of war was still the all-important national duty. There would be plenty of time for land reform later, and all Kerensky's efforts were directed toward a last offensive in early July. Human suffering and war-weariness grew, sapping the limited strength of the provisional government.

From its first day the provisional government had to share power with a formidable rival – the Petrograd Soviet (or "council") of Workers' and Soldiers' Deputies. Modeled on the revolutionary soviets of 1905, the Petrograd Soviet was a huge, fluctuating mass meeting of two to three thousand workers, soldiers, and socialist intellectuals. Seeing itself as a true grass-roots revolutionary democracy, this "counter" or "half" government suspiciously watched the provisional government and issued its own radical orders, further weakening Kerensky's government. The most famous of these orders was "Army Order No. 1," issued to all Russian military forces the very day the provisional government was formed.

Order No. 1 stripped officers of their authority and placed power in the hands of elected committees of common soldiers. Designed primarily to protect the revolution from some counterrevolutionary Bonaparte on horseback, Army Order No. 1 instead led to a total collapse of army discipline. Many an officer was hanged for his sins. Meanwhile, following the foolhardy summer offensive, masses of peasant soldiers began "voting with their feet," to use Lenin's graphic phrase. That is, they began returning to their villages to help their families get a share of the land, land that peasants were simply seizing as they settled old scores in a great agrarian upheaval. All across the country liberty was turning into anarchy in the summer of 1917. It was an unparalleled opportunity for the most radical and most talented of Russia's many socialist leaders, Vladimir Ilyich Lenin (1870–1924).

LENIN AND THE BOLSHEVIK REVOLUTION

From his youth Lenin's whole life was dedicated to the cause of revolution. Born into the middle class, the seventeen-year-old Lenin became an implacable enemy of imperial Russia when his older brother was executed for plotting to kill the tsar in 1887. As a law student he began searching for a revolutionary faith. He found it in Marxian socialism, which began to win converts among radical intellectuals as industrialization surged forward in Russia in the 1890s. Exiled to Siberia for three years because of socialist agitation, Lenin studied Marxist doctrines with religious intensity. After his release, the young priest of socialism joined fellow believers in western Europe. There he lived for seventeen years and developed his own revolutionary interpretations of the body of Marxian thought.

Three interrelated ideas were central for Lenin. First, turning to the early fire-breathing Marx of 1848 and the *Communist Manifesto* for inspiration, Lenin stressed that capitalism could be destroyed only by violent revolution. He tirelessly denounced all revisionist theories of a peaceful evolution to socialism as betraying Marx's message of unending class conflict. Lenin's second, more original idea was that,

under certain conditions, a socialist revolution was possible even in a relatively backward country like Russia. Though capitalism was not fully developed there, and the industrial working class was small, the peasants were poor and thus potential revolutionaries.

Lenin believed that at a given moment revolution was determined more by human leadership than by vast historical laws. Thus Lenin's third basic idea: the necessity of a highly disciplined workers' party, strictly controlled by a dedicated elite of intellectuals and full-time revolutionaries like Lenin himself. Unlike ordinary workers and trade union officials, this elite would never be seduced by short-term gains. It would not stop until revolution brought it to power.

Lenin's theories and methods did not go unchallenged by other Russian Marxists. At the meetings of the Russian Social Democratic Labor party in London in 1903, matters came to a head. Lenin demanded a small, disciplined, elitist party, while his opponents wanted a more democratic party with mass membership. The Russian party of Marxian socialism promptly split into two rival factions. Lenin's camp was called "Bolsheviks" or "Majority"; his opponents were "Mensheviks" or "Minority." Lenin's majority did not last, but Lenin did not care. He kept the fine-sounding name "Bolshevik" and developed the party he wanted: tough, disciplined, revolutionary.

Unlike most socialists, Lenin did not rally round the national flag in 1914. Observing events from neutral Switzerland, he saw the war as a product of imperialistic rivalries and a marvelous opportunity for class war and socialist upheaval. The March revolution was, Lenin felt, a step in that direction. Since propaganda and internal subversion were accepted weapons of total war, the German government graciously provided the impatient Lenin, his wife, and about twenty trusted colleagues with safe passage across Germany and back into Russia in April 1917. The Germans hoped that Lenin would undermine the sagging war effort of the world's freest society. They were not disappointed.

Arriving triumphantly at Petrograd's Finland Station on April 3, Lenin attacked at once. To the great astonishment of local Bolsheviks, he rejected all cooperation with the "bourgeois" provisional government of the liberals and moderate socialists. His slogans were radical in the extreme: "All power to the Soviets." "All land to the peasants." "Stop the war now." Never a slave to Marxist determinism, the brilliant but not unduly intellectual Lenin was a superb tactician. The moment was now.

Yet Lenin almost overplayed his hand. An attempt by the Bolsheviks to seize power in July collapsed, and Lenin fled and went into hiding. He was charged with being a "German agent," and indeed he and the Bolsheviks were getting money from Germany.[12] But no matter. Intrigue between Kerensky and his commander-in-chief General Lavr Kornilov, a popular war hero "with the heart of a lion and the brains of a sheep," resulted in Kornilov's leading a feeble attack against the provisional government in September. In the face of this rightist "counterrevolutionary" threat, the Bolsheviks were rearmed and redeemed. Kornilov's forces disintegrated, but Kerensky lost all credit with the army and its officer corps, the only force that might have saved him and liberal government in Russia.

TROTSKY AND THE SEIZURE OF POWER

Throughout the summer the Bolsheviks had appealed very effectively to the workers and soldiers of Petrograd, markedly increasing their popular support. Party membership had soared from 50,000 to 240,000 and in October the Bolsheviks gained a fragile majority in the Petrograd Soviet. Moreover, Lenin had found a strong right arm – Leon Trotsky, the second most important person in the Russian Revolution.

A spellbinding revolutionary orator and independent radical Marxist, Trotsky (1879–1940) supported Lenin wholeheartedly in 1917. It was he who brilliantly executed the Bolshevik seizure of power. Painting a vivid but untruthful picture of German and counterrevolutionary plots, Trotsky first convinced the Petrograd Soviet to form a special Military-Revolutionary Committee in October and make him its leader. Military power in the capital passed into Bolshevik hands. Trotsky's second master stroke was to insist that the Bolsheviks reduce opposition to their coup by taking power in the name not of the Bolsheviks but of the more popular and democratic soviets, which were meeting in Petrograd from all over Russia in early November. On the night of November 6, militants from Trotsky's committee joined with trusty Bolshevik soldiers to seize government buildings and pounce on members of the provisional government. Then on to the Congress of Soviets! There a Bolshevik majority – roughly 390 of 650 turbulent delegates – declared that all power had passed to the soviets and named Lenin head of the new government.

The Bolsheviks came to power for three key reasons. First, by late 1917 democracy had given way to anarchy: power was there for those who would take it. Second, in Lenin and Trotsky the Bolsheviks had utterly determined and truly superior leadership, which both the tsarist government and the provisional government lacked. Third, in 1917 the Bolsheviks

VLADIMIR LENIN   Dramatically displaying both his burning determination and his skill as a revolutionary orator, Lenin addresses the victorious May Day celebration of 1918 in Moscow's Red Square. (Culver Pictures)

succeeded in appealing to many soldiers and urban workers, people who were exhausted by war and eager for socialism. With time many workers would become bitterly disappointed, but for the moment they had good reason to believe they had won what they wanted.

DICTATORSHIP AND CIVIL WAR

History is full of short-lived coups and unsuccessful revolutions. The truly monumental accomplishment of Lenin, Trotsky, and the rest of the Bolsheviks was not taking power but keeping it. In the next four years the Bolsheviks went on to conquer the chaos they had helped to create, and they began to build their kind of dictatorial socialist society. The conspirators became conquerors. How was this done?

Lenin had the genius to profit from developments over which he and the Bolsheviks had no control. Since summer a peasant revolution had been sweeping across Russia, as the tillers of the soil invaded and divided among themselves the great and not-so-great estates of the landlords and the church. Peasant seizure of the land – a Russian 1789 – was not very Marxist, but it was quite unstoppable in 1917. Thus Lenin's first law, which supposedly gave land to the peasants, actually merely approved what peasants were already doing. Urban workers' great demand in November was direct control of individual factories by local workers' committees. This too Lenin ratified with a decree in November.

Unlike many of his colleagues, Lenin acknowledged that Russia had lost the war with Germany, that the Russian army had ceased to exist, and that the only realistic goal was peace at any price. The price was very high indeed. Germany demanded in December 1917 that the Soviet government give up all its western territories. These areas were inhabited by Poles, Finns, Lithuanians, and other non-Russians – all those peoples who had been conquered by the tsars over three centuries and put into the "prisonhouse of nationalities," as Lenin had earlier called the Russian Empire.

At first Lenin's fellow Bolsheviks would not accept such great territorial losses. But when German armies resumed their unopposed march into Russia in February 1918, Lenin had his way in a very close vote in the Central Committee of the party. "Not even his greatest enemy can deny that at this moment Lenin towered like a giant over his Bolshevik colleagues."[13] A third of old Russia's population was sliced away by the German meat ax in the Treaty of Brest-Litovsk in March 1918. With peace Lenin had escaped the certain disaster of continued war and could uncompromisingly pursue his goal of absolute political power for the Bolsheviks – now renamed Communists – within Russia.

In November 1917, the Bolsheviks had cleverly proclaimed their regime only a "provisional workers' and peasants' government," promising that a freely elected Constituent Assembly would draw up a new constitution. But the freest elections in Russia's history – both before and after 1917 – produced a stunning setback for the Bolsheviks, who won less than one-fourth of the elected delegates. The Socialist Revolutionaries – the peasants' party – had a clear majority. The Constituent Assembly met for only one day, on January 18, 1918. It was then permanently disbanded by Bolshevik soldiers acting under Lenin's orders. Thus, even before the peace with Germany, Lenin was clearly establishing a one-party government.

The destruction of the democratically elected Constituent Assembly helped feed the flames of civil war. People who had risen up for self-rule in November saw that once again they were getting dictatorship from the capital. For the next three years, "Long live the [democratic] soviets; down with the Bolsheviks" was to be a popular slogan. The officers of the old army took the lead in organizing the so-called White opposition to the Bolsheviks in southern Russia and the Ukraine, in Siberia, and to the west of Petrograd. The Whites came from many social groups and were united only by their hatred of the Bolsheviks – the Reds.

By the summer of 1918, *eighteen* self-proclaimed regional governments – several of which represented minority nationalities – competed with Lenin's Bolsheviks in Moscow. By the end of the year White armies were on the attack. In October 1919, it appeared they might triumph, as they closed in on Lenin's government from three sides. Yet they did not. By the spring of 1920, the White armies had been almost completely defeated, and the Bolshevik Red Army had

THE RUSSIAN REVOLUTION

1914	Russia enthusiastically enters the First World War
1915	Two million Russian casualties
	Progressive Bloc calls for a new government responsible to the Duma, not the tsar
	Tsar Nicholas adjourns the Duma and departs for the front; control of the government falls to Alexandra and Rasputin
December 1916	Murder of Rasputin
March 8, 1917	Bread riots in Petrograd (St. Petersburg)
March 12, 1917	Duma declares a provisional government
March 15, 1917	Tsar Nicholas abdicates without protest
April 3, 1917	Lenin returns from exile and denounces the provisional government
May 1917	Kerensky forms a moderate socialist government and continues the war
	Petrograd Soviet issues Army Order no. 1, granting military power to committees of common soldiers
Summer 1917	Agrarian upheavals: peasants seize estates, peasant soldiers desert the army to join in
October 1917	Bolsheviks gain a majority in the Petrograd Soviet
November 6, 1917	Bolsheviks seize power; Lenin heads the new "provisional workers' and peasants' government"
November 1917	Lenin ratifies peasant seizure of land and worker control of factories; all banks nationalized
January 1918	Lenin permanently disbands the Constituent Assembly
February 1918	Lenin convinces the Bolshevik Central Committee to accept a humiliating peace with Germany in order to pursue the revolution
March 1918	Treaty of Brest-Litovsk: Russia loses one-third of its population
	Trotsky as war commissar begins to rebuild the Russian army
	Government moves from Petrograd to Moscow
1918–1920	Great Civil War
Summer 1918	Eighteen competing regional governments; White armies oppose the Bolshevik revolution
1919	White armies on the offensive but divided politically; they receive little benefit from Allied intervention
1920	Lenin and Red armies victorious, retaking Belorussia and the Ukraine

retaken Belorussia and the Ukraine. The following year the Communists also reconquered the independent nationalist governments of the Caucasus. The civil war was over; Lenin had won.

Lenin and the Bolsheviks won for several reasons. Strategically, they controlled the center, while the Whites were always on the fringes and disunited. Moreover, the poorly defined political program of the Whites was vaguely conservative, and it did not unite all the foes of the Bolsheviks under a progressive, democratic banner. For example, the most gifted of the White generals, the nationalistic General Anton Denikin, refused to call for a democratic republic and a federation of nationalities, although he knew doing so would help his cause. Most important, the Communists quickly developed a better army, an army for which the divided Whites were no match.

Once again Trotsky's leadership was decisive. The Bolsheviks had preached democracy in the army and had elected officers in 1917. But beginning in March 1918, Trotsky as war commissar re-established the draft and the most drastic discipline for the newly formed Red Army. Soldiers deserting or disobeying an order were summarily shot. Moreover, Trotsky made effective use of former tsarist army officers, who were actively recruited and given unprecedented powers of discipline over their troops. In short, Trotsky formed a highly disciplined and very effective fighting force.

The Bolsheviks also effectively mobilized the home front. Establishing "war communism" – the application of the "total war" concept to a civil conflict – they seized grain from the peasants, introduced rationing, nationalized all banks and industry, and required everyone to work. Although these measures contributed to a breakdown of normal economic activity, they also served to maintain labor discipline and to keep the Red Army supplied.

"Revolutionary terror" also contributed to the Communist victory. The old tsarist secret police was re-established as the Cheka, which hunted down and executed thousands of real or supposed foes, like the tsar's family and other "class enemies." At one point, shortly after the government moved from Petrograd to Moscow in March 1918, a circus clown in Moscow was making fun of the Bolsheviks to an appreciative audience. Chekists in the crowd quickly pulled out their guns and shot several laughing people. Moreover, people were shot or threatened with being shot for minor nonpolitical failures. The terror aroused by the secret police became a tool of the government. The Cheka sowed fear, and fear silenced opposition.

Finally, foreign military intervention in the civil war ended up helping the Communists. After Lenin made peace with Germany, the Allies (the Americans, British, and Japanese) sent troops to Archangel and Vladivostok to prevent war materiel they had sent the provisional government from being captured by the Germans. After the Soviet government nationalized all foreign-owned factories without compensation, and refused to pay all of Russia's foreign debts, Western governments and particularly France began to support White armies. Yet these efforts were small and halfhearted. In 1919, Western peoples were sick of war, and few Western politicians believed in a military crusade against the Bolsheviks. Thus, Allied intervention in the civil war did not aid the Whites effectively, though it did permit the Communists to appeal to the patriotic nationalism of ethnic Russians, which was particularly strong among former tsarist army officers. Allied intervention was both too little and too much.

The Russian Revolution and the Bolshevik triumph was, then, one of the reasons why the First World War was such a great turning point in modern history. A radically new government, based on socialism and one-party dictatorship, came to power in a great European state, maintained power, and eagerly encouraged worldwide revolution. Although halfheartedly constitutional monarchy in Russia was undoubtedly headed for some kind of political crisis before 1914, it is hard to imagine the triumph of the most radical proponents of change and reform except in a situation of total collapse. That was precisely what happened to Russia in the First World War.

THE PEACE SETTLEMENT

In 1918 the guns of world war finally fell silent. After winning great concessions from Lenin in the Treaty of Brest-Litovsk in March 1918, the Germans launched their last major attack against France. Yet this offensive failed like those before it. With breathtaking rapidity the United States, Great Britain, and France decisively defeated Germany militarily. Then, as civil war spread in Russia and as chaos engulfed much of eastern Europe, the victorious Western Allies came together in Paris to establish a lasting peace.

Expectations were high; optimism was almost unlimited. The Allies labored intensively and soon worked out terms for peace with Germany and for the creation of the peacekeeping League of Nations. Nevertheless, the hopes of peoples and politicians were soon disappointed, for the peace settlement of 1919 turned out to be a terrible failure. Rather than

creating conditions for peace, it sowed the seeds of another war. Surely this was the ultimate tragedy of the Great War, a war that directly and indirectly cost $332 billion and left 10 million dead and another 20 million wounded. How did it happen? Why was the peace settlement unsuccessful?

THE END OF THE WAR

In early 1917, the strain of total war was showing everywhere. After the Russian Revolution in March there were major strikes in Germany. In July a coalition of moderates passed a "peace resolution" in the German parliament, calling for peace without territorial annexations. To counter this moderation born of war-weariness, the German military established a virtual dictatorship and aggressively exploited the collapse of Russian armies after the Bolshevik Revolution. Victory in the east having quieted the German moderates, General Ludendorff and company fell on France once more in the great spring offensive of 1918. For a time German armies pushed forward, coming within thirty-five miles of Paris. But Ludendorff's exhausted, overextended forces never broke through. They were decisively stopped in July at the second battle of the Marne, where 140,000 fresh American soldiers saw action. Adding 2 million men in arms to the war effort by August, the late but massive American intervention decisively tipped the scales in favor of Allied victory.

By September, British, French, and American armies were advancing steadily on all fronts, and a panicky General Ludendorff realized that Germany had lost the war. Yet he insolently insisted that moderate politicians shoulder the shame of defeat, and on October 4 the emperor formed a new, more liberal German government to sue for peace. As negotiations over an armistice dragged on, an angry and frustrated German people finally rose up. On November 3, sailors in Kiel mutinied, and throughout northern Germany soldiers and workers began to establish revolutionary councils on the Russian soviet model. The same day Austria-Hungary surrendered to the Allies and began breaking apart. Revolution broke out in Germany, and masses of workers demonstrated for peace in Berlin. With army discipline collapsing, the emperor was forced to abdicate and fled to Holland. Socialist leaders in Berlin proclaimed a German republic on November 9 and simultaneously agreed to tough Allied terms of surrender. The armistice went into effect November 11, 1918. The war was over.

REVOLUTION IN GERMANY

Military defeat brought political revolution to Germany and Austria-Hungary, as it had to Russia. In Austria-Hungary the revolution was primarily nationalistic and republican in character. Having started the war to preserve an antinationalist dynastic state, the Habsburg Empire had perished in the attempt. In its place independent Austrian, Hungarian, and Czechoslovakian republics were proclaimed, while a greatly expanded Serbian monarchy united the south Slavs and took the name of Yugoslavia. The prospect of firmly establishing the new national states overrode class considerations for most people in east central Europe.

The German revolution of November 1918 resembled the Russian Revolution of March 1917. In both cases a genuine popular uprising toppled an authoritarian monarchy and established a liberal provisional republic. In both countries liberals and moderate socialists took control of the central government, while workers' and soldiers' councils formed a "countergovernment." In Germany, however,

THE FALL OF MONARCHY   *Entitled simply "November 1918," this eloquent drawing from a popular German magazine shows the crowns of Europe scattered like driftwood after the final wave of war and revolution. (Photo: Caroline Buckler)*

the moderate socialists won and the Lenin-like radical revolutionaries in the councils lost. In communist terms, the liberal, republican revolution in Germany in 1918 was only "half" a revolution: a "bourgeois" political revolution without a communist second installment. It was Russia without Lenin's Bolshevik triumph.

There were several reasons for the German outcome. The great majority of Marxian socialist leaders in the Social Democratic party were, as before the war, really pink and not red. They wanted to establish real political democracy and civil liberties, and they favored the gradual elimination of capitalism. They were also German nationalists, appalled by the prospect of civil war and revolutionary terror. Moreover, there was much less popular support among workers and soldiers for the extreme radicals than in Russia. Nor did the German peasantry, which already had most of the land, at least in western Germany, provide the elemental force that has driven all great modern revolutions, from the French to the Chinese.

Of crucial importance also was the fact that the moderate German Social Democrats, unlike Kerensky and company, accepted defeat and ended the war the day they took power. This act ended the decline in morale among soldiers and prevented the regular army with its conservative officer corps from disintegrating. When radicals headed by Karl Liebknecht and Rosa Luxemburg and their supporters in the councils tried to seize control of the government in Berlin in January, the moderate socialists called on the army to crush the uprising. Liebknecht and Luxemburg were arrested and then brutally murdered by army leaders. Finally, even if the moderate socialists had taken the Leninist path, it is very unlikely they would have succeeded. Civil war in Germany would certainly have followed, and the Allies, who were already occupying western Germany according to the terms of the armistice, would have marched on to Berlin and ruled Germany directly. Historians have often been unduly hard on Germany's moderate socialists.

THE TREATY OF VERSAILLES

The peace conference opened in Paris in January 1919 with seventy delegates representing twenty-seven victorious nations. There were great expectations. A young British diplomat,

Harold Nicolson, wrote later that the victors "were convinced that they would never commit the blunders and iniquities of the Congress of Vienna [of 1815]." Then "the misguided, reactionary, pathetic aristocrats" had cynically shuffled populations; now "we believed in nationalism, we believed in the self-determination of peoples." Indeed, "we were journeying to Paris . . . to found a new order in Europe. We were preparing not Peace only, but Eternal Peace."[14] The general optimism and idealism had been greatly strengthened by President Wilson's January 1918 peace proposal, the Fourteen Points, which stressed national self-determination and the rights of small countries.

The real powers at the conference were the United States, Great Britain, and France, for Germany was not allowed to participate and Russia was locked in civil war and did not attend. Italy was considered part of the Big Four, but its role was quite secondary. Almost immediately the three great allies began to quarrel. President Wilson, who was wildly cheered by European crowds as the spokesman for a new idealistic and democratic international cooperation, was almost obsessed with creating a League of Nations. Wilson insisted that this question come first, for he passionately believed that only a permanent international organization could protect member states from aggression and avert future wars. Wilson had his way, although Lloyd George of Great Britain and especially Clemenceau of France were unenthusiastic. They were primarily concerned with punishing Germany.

Playing on British nationalism, Lloyd George had already won a smashing electoral victory in December on the popular platform of making Germany pay for the war. "We shall," he promised, "squeeze the orange until the pips squeak." Personally inclined to make

THE TREATY OF VERSAILLES was signed in the magnificent Hall of Mirrors. The Allies did not allow Germany to participate in the negotiation of the peace treaty. (National Archives)

a somewhat moderate peace with Germany, Lloyd George was to a considerable extent a captive of demands for a total victory worthy of the sacrifices of total war against a totally depraved enemy. As Rudyard Kipling summed up the general British feeling at the end of the war, the Germans were "a people with the heart of beasts."[15]

France's Georges Clemenceau, "the Tiger," who had broken wartime defeatism and led his country to victory, wholeheartedly agreed. Like most French people, Clemenceau quite frankly wanted old-fashioned revenge. He also wanted lasting security for France. This, he believed, required the creation of a buffer state between France and Germany, the permanent demilitarization of Germany, and vast German reparations. He feared that sooner or later Germany with its 60 million people would attack France with its 40 million, unless the Germans were permanently weakened. Moreover, France had no English Channel (or Atlantic Ocean) as a reassuring barrier against German aggression. Wilson, supported by Lloyd George, would hear none of it. Clemenceau's demands seemed vindictive, violating morality and the principle of national self-determination. By April the conference was deadlocked on the German question, and Wilson packed his bags to go home.

Clemenceau's obsession with security reflected his anxiety about France's long-term weakness. In the end, convinced that France should not break with its allies because France could not afford to face Germany alone in the future, he agreed to a compromise. He gave up the French demand for a Rhineland buffer state in return for a formal defensive alliance with the United States and Great Britain. Under the terms of this alliance, both Wilson and Lloyd George promised that their countries would come to France's aid in the event of a German attack. Thus, Clemenceau appeared to win his goal of French security, as Wilson had won his of a permanent international organization. The Allies moved quickly to finish the peace settlement, believing that necessary adjustments would later be possible within the dual framework of a strong Western alliance and the League of Nations (see Map 33.4).

The Treaty of Versailles between the Allies and Germany was the key to the settlement, and the terms were not unreasonable as a first step toward re-establishing international order. (Had Germany won, it seems certain that France and Belgium would have been treated with greater severity, as Russia had been at Brest-Litovsk.) Germany's colonies were given to France, Britain, and Japan as League of Nations mandates. Germany's territorial losses within Europe were minor,

thanks to Wilson. Alsace-Lorraine was returned to France. Areas of Germany inhabited primarily by Poles were ceded to the new Polish state, in keeping with the principle of national self-determination. Predominantly German Danzig was also placed within the Polish tariff lines, but as a self-governing city under League of Nations protection. Germany had to limit its army to 100,000 men and agree to build no military fortifications in the Rhineland.

More harshly, the Allies declared that Germany (with Austria) was responsible for the war and had therefore to pay reparations equal to all civilian damages caused by the war. This unfortunate and much-criticized clause expressed inescapable popular demands for German blood, but the actual figure was not set and there was the clear possibility that reparations might be set at a reasonable level in the future, when tempers had cooled.

When presented with the treaty, the German government protested vigorously. But there was no alternative, especially in that Germany was still starving because the Allies had not yet lifted their naval blockade. On June 28, 1919, German representatives of the ruling moderate Social Democrats and the Catholic party signed the treaty in the Sun King's Hall of Mirrors at Versailles, where Bismarck's empire had been joyously proclaimed almost fifty years before.

Separate peace treaties were concluded with the other defeated powers – Austria, Hungary, Bulgaria, and Turkey. For the most part, these treaties merely ratified the existing situation in east central Europe following the breakup of the Austro-Hungarian Empire. Like Austria, Hungary was a particularly big loser, as its "captive" nationalities (and some interspersed Hungarians) were ceded to Rumania, Czechoslovakia, Poland, and Yugo-

Legend:

Boundaries of German, Austrian, and Russian Empires in 1914

Areas lost by Austro-Hungarian Empire

Areas lost by Russian Empire

Areas lost by German Empire

Areas lost by Bulgaria

Demilitarized Zone

Boundaries of 1926

NORWAY
SWEDEN
FINLAND
Helsinki
Stockholm
Tallinn
Leningrad (St. Petersburg)
ESTONIA
DENMARK
NORTH SEA
BALTIC SEA
Riga
LATVIA
Memel
LITHUANIA
NETHERLANDS
Amsterdam
GERMANY
Berlin
Danzig
EAST PRUSSIA
POLISH CORRIDOR
Vistula
Warsaw
POLAND
Kiev
Brussels
BELGIUM
RUHR
Cologne
Frankfurt
Weimar
Elbe
Prague
Paris
Versailles
LUXEMBOURG
CZECHOSLOVAKIA
GALICIA
LORRAINE
Rhine
Dniester
ALSACE
Strasbourg
Ruhr
BESSARABIA
FRANCE
Berne
SWITZERLAND
Vienna
Geneva
Locarno
AUSTRIA
Budapest
HUNGARY
RUMANIA
S. TYROL
Milan
Trieste
Zagreb
Genoa
Rapallo
Venice
CROATIA
YUGOSLAVIA
Belgrade
Bucharest
BLACK SEA
SERBIA
BULGARIA
ITALY
Rome
MONTENEGRO (To Yugoslavia, 1921)
Sofia
Istanbul (Constantinople)
ALBANIA
Naples
MEDITERRANEAN SEA
GREECE
TURKEY
Athens

0   300 Km.
0   150   300 Mi.

MAP 33.4 SHATTERED EMPIRES AND TERRITORIAL CHANGES AFTER WORLD WAR ONE
The Great War brought tremendous changes in eastern Europe. New nations were established, and a dangerous power vacuum was created between Germany and Soviet Russia.

slavia. Italy got some Austrian territory. The Turkish empire was broken up. France received Lebanon and Syria, while Britain took Iraq and Palestine, which was to include a Jewish national homeland first promised by Britain in 1917. Officially League of Nations mandates, these acquisitions of the Western powers were one of the more imperialistic elements of the peace settlement. Another was mandating Germany's holdings in China to Japan. The age of Western imperialism lived on. National self-determination was still only for Europeans and their offspring.

AMERICAN REJECTION OF THE VERSAILLES TREATY

The rapidly concluded peace settlement of early 1919 was not perfect, but within the context of war-shattered Europe it was an acceptable beginning. The principle of national self-determination, which had played such a large role in starting the war, was accepted and served as an organizing framework. Germany had been punished but not dismembered. A new world organization complemented a traditional defensive alliance of satisfied powers. The serious remaining problems could be worked out in the future. Moreover, Allied leaders had seen speed as essential for another reason: they detested Lenin and feared that his Bolshevik Revolution might spread. They realized that their best answer to Lenin's unending calls for worldwide upheaval was peace and tranquillity for war-weary peoples.

There were, however, two great interrelated obstacles to such peace: Germany and the United States. Plagued by communist uprisings, reactionary plots, and popular disillusionment with losing the war at the last

minute, Germany's moderate socialists and their liberal and Catholic supporters faced an enormous challenge. Like French republicans after 1871, they needed time (and luck) if they were to establish firmly a peaceful and democratic republic. Progress in this direction required understanding yet firm treatment of Germany by the victorious Western Allies, and particularly by the United States.

However, the United States Senate and, to a lesser extent, the American people rejected Wilson's handiwork. Republican senators led by Henry Cabot Lodge refused to ratify the Treaty of Versailles without changes in the articles creating the League of Nations. The key issue was the league's power — more apparent than real — to require member states to take collective action against aggression.

Lodge and others believed that this requirement gave away Congress's constitutional right to declare war. No doubt Wilson would have been wise to accept some reservations. But, in failing health, Wilson with narrow-minded self-righteousness rejected all attempts at compromise. He instructed loyal Democratic senators to vote against any reservations whatsoever to the Treaty of Versailles. In doing so, Wilson assured that the treaty was never ratified by the United States in any form and that the United States never joined the League of Nations. Moreover, the Senate refused to ratify Wilson's defensive alliance with France and Great Britain. America turned its back on Europe.

Understandable perhaps in the light of American traditions, the Wilson-Lodge fiasco and the new-found gospel of isolationism represented nevertheless a tragic and cowardly renunciation of America's responsibility. Using America's action as an excuse, Great Britain too refused to ratify its defensive alliance with France. Bitterly betrayed by its allies, France stood alone. Very shortly, France was to take actions against Germany that would feed the fires of German resentment and seriously undermine democratic forces in the new republic. The great hopes of early 1919 were turning to ashes by the end of the year. The Western alliance had collapsed, and a grandiose plan for permanent peace had given way to a fragile truce. For this, and for what came later, the United States must share a large part of the guilt.

———◆———

Why did World War One have such revolutionary consequences? Why was it such a great break with the past? World War One was, first of all, a war of committed peoples. In France, Britain, and Germany in particular, governments drew on genuine popular support. This support reflected not only the diplomatic origins of the war but also the way western European society had been effectively unified under the nationalist banner in the later nineteenth century. The relentlessness of total war helps explain why so many died, why so many were crippled physically and psychologically, and why Western civilization would in so many ways never be the same again. More concretely, the war swept away monarchs and multinational empires. National self-determination apparently triumphed, not only in Austria-Hungary but in much of Russia's western borderlands as well. Except in Ireland and parts of Soviet Russia, the revolutionary dream of national unity, born of the French Revolution, had finally come true.

Two other revolutions were products of the war. In Russia the Bolsheviks established a radical regime, smashed existing capitalist institutions, and stayed in power with a new kind of authoritarian rule. Whether the new Russian regime was truly Marxian or socialist was questionable, but it indisputably posed a powerful, ongoing revolutionary challenge within Europe and in Europe's colonial empires.

More subtle, but quite universal in its impact, was an administrative revolution. This revolution, born of the need to mobilize entire societies and economies for total war, greatly increased the power of government. And after the guns grew still, government planning and wholesale involvement in economic and social life did not disappear in Europe. Liberal market capitalism and a well-integrated world economy were among the many casualties of the administrative revolution, and greater social equality was everywhere one of its results. Thus, even in European countries, such as Britain or France, where a communist takeover never came close to occurring, society still experienced a great revolution.

Tragically, the "war to end war" did not bring peace but only a fragile truce: in the West the Allies failed to maintain their wartime solidarity. Germany remained unrepentant and would soon have more grievances to nurse. Moreover, the victory of national self-determination in eastern Europe created a power vacuum between a still-powerful Germany and a potentially mighty Communist Russia. A vast area lay open to military aggression from two sides.

Finally, and perhaps most importantly from the viewpoint of world history, the bloody struggle in Europe had profound consequences for many African and Asian peoples. They, too, were drawn into the conflict, and their wartime experiences encouraged radically different attitudes toward European states and European power, as we shall see in the next chapter.

NOTES

1. M. Beloff, *U.S. News and World Report,* 8 March 1976, p. 53.

2. Quoted by J. Remak, *The Origins of World War I,* Holt, Rinehart & Winston, New York, 1967, p. 84.

3. Quoted by W. E. Mosse, *Alexander II and the Modernization of Russia,* Collier Books, New York, 1962, pp. 125–126.

4. Quoted by Remak, p. 123.

5. Quoted by J. E. Rodes, *The Quest for Unity: Modern Germany 1848–1970,* Holt, Rinehart & Winston, New York, 1971, p. 178.

6. Quoted by F. P. Chambers, *The War Behind the War, 1914–1918,* Faber & Faber, London, 1939, p. 444.

7. Ibid., p. 168.

8. Quoted by R. O. Paxton, *Europe in the Twentieth Century,* Harcourt Brace Jovanovich, New York, 1975, p. 109.

9. Quoted by Chambers, p. 378.

10. Ibid., p. 110.

11. Ibid., pp. 302, 304.

12. A. B. Ulam, *The Bolsheviks,* Collier Books, New York, 1968, p. 349.

13. Ibid., p. 405.

14. H. Nicolson, *Peacemaking 1919,* Grosset & Dunlap Universal Library, New York, 1965, pp. 8, 31–32.

15. Ibid., p. 24.

SUGGESTED READING

Both J. Remak, *The Origins of World War I* (1967), and L. Lafore, *The Long Fuse* (1971), are highly recommended studies of the causes of the First World War. A. J. P. Taylor, *The Struggle for Mastery in Europe, 1848–1919* (1954), is an outstanding survey of diplomatic developments with an exhaustive bibliography. V. Steiner, *Britain and the Origins of the First World War* (1978), and G. Kennan, *The Decline of Bismarck's European Order: Franco-Russian Relations, 1875–1890* (1979), are also major contributions. K. Jarausch's *The Enigmatic Chancellor* (1973) is an important recent study on Bethmann-Hollweg and German policy in 1914. C. Falls, *The Great War* (1961), is the best brief introduction to military aspects of the war. B. Tuchman, *The Guns of August* (1962), is a marvelous account of the dramatic first month of the war and the beginning of military stalemate. G. Ritter provides an able study in *The Schlieffen Plan* (1958). A. J. P. Taylor, *The First World War* (1963), is a strikingly illustrated history of the war, and A. Horne, *The Price of Glory: Verdun 1916* (1979), is a moving account of the famous siege.

F. L. Carsten, *War Against War* (1982), considers radical movements in Britain and Germany. The best single volume on the home fronts is still F. Chambers, *The War Behind the War, 1914–1918* (1939). Chambers drew heavily on the many fine books on the social and economic impact of the war in different countries published by the Carnegie Endowment for International Peace under the general editorship of J. T. Shotwell. A. Marwick, *The Deluge* (1970), is a lively account of war and society in Britain, while G. Feldman, *Army, Industry, and Labor in Germany, 1914–1918* (1966), shows the impact of total war and military dictatorship on Germany. Two excellent collections of essays, J. Roth, ed., *World War I* (1967), and R. Albrecht-Carrié, ed., *The Meaning of the First World War* (1965), deftly probe the enormous consequences of the war for people and society. The debate over Germany's guilt and aggression, which has been reopened in recent years, may be best approached through G. Feldman, ed., *German Imperialism, 1914–1918* (1972). M. Fainsod, *International Socialism and the World War* (1935), ably discusses the splits between radical and moderate socialists during the conflict. In addition to Erich Maria Remarque's great novel *All Quiet on the Western Front,* Henri Barbusse, *Under Fire* (1917), and Jules Romains, *Verdun* (1939), are highly recommended for their fictional yet realistic recreations of the war.

A. Ulam's *The Bolsheviks* (1968), which focuses

on Lenin, is a masterful introduction to the Russian Revolution, as is B. Wolfe, *Three Who Made a Revolution* (1955), a collective biography of Lenin, Trotsky, and Stalin. Leon Trotsky himself wrote the colorful and exciting *History of the Russian Revolution* (1932), which may be compared with the classic eyewitness account of the young, pro-Bolshevik American John Reed, *Ten Days That Shook the World* (1919). R. Daniels, *Red Ocotober* (1969), provides a clear account of the Bolshevik seizure of power, and R. Pipes, *The Formaton of the Soviet Union* (1968), is recommended for its excellent treatment of the nationality problem during the Revolution. A. Wildman, *The End of the Russian Imperial Army* (1980), is a fine account of the soldiers' revolt, and G. Leggett, *The Cheka: Lenin's Secret Police* (1981), shows revolutionary terror in action. Boris Pasternak's justly celebrated *Doctor Zhivago* is a great historical novel of the revolutionary era. R. Massie, *Nicholas and Alexandra* (1971), is a moving popular biography of Russia's last royal family and the terrible health problem of the heir to the throne. H. Nicolson, *Peacemaking 1919* (1965), captures the spirit of the Versailles settlement. T. Bailey, *Woodrow Wilson and the Lost Peace* (1963), and W. Widenor, *Henry Cabot Lodge and the Search for an American Foreign Policy* (1981), are also highly recommended. A. Mayer provocatively stresses the influence of domestic social tensions and widespread fears of further communist revolution in *The Politics and Diplomacy of Peacemaking* (1969).

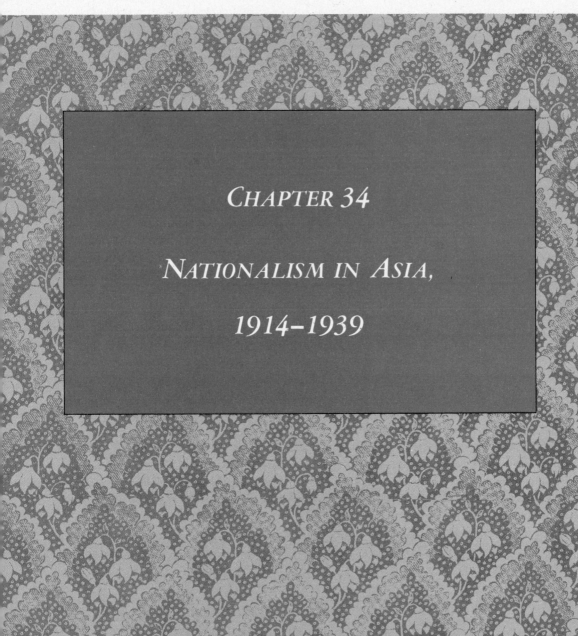

CHAPTER 34

NATIONALISM IN ASIA,

1914–1939

FROM AN ASIAN PERSPECTIVE the First World War was a European civil war. As a result it decisively shattered the united front of Western imperialism and convulsed prewar relationships in Asia. Most crucially, the war speeded up the development of modern nationalism in Asia. As we saw in Chapter 31, the nationalist gospel of anti-imperialist political freedom and racial equality had already won converts among Asia's Westernized-educated elites before 1914. In the 1920s and 1930s it increasingly won the souls of the masses. As in Europe in the nineteenth century, nationalism became a mass movement with potentially awesome power.

There were at least two reasons for the upsurge of nationalism in Asia. For one thing, nationalism in Asia possessed the power to transform ancient agrarian societies, as it had in Europe beginning with the French Revolution. As a faith in a certain kind of unified and bureaucratized state, nationalism challenged old political practices and beliefs. More generally, nationalism was a conduit through which the European secular world view – grounded in the Renaissance, the Scientific Revolution, and the Enlightenment – spread to the non-Western world. Moreover, nationalism promoted the kinds of social and economic change associated with the dual revolution (page 1016), in part because it strengthened the modernizers in their contest for influence and power with the conservative traditionalists (pages 1105–1110). Nationalist ideology gave the modernizers a vision of a glorious future for a rejuvenated people, a vision they could use to mobilize the masses and ennoble the sacrifices that the struggle would require.

Also, it is often overlooked that the growth of nationalism stimulated bitter conflicts and even wars between Asian peoples, as it had in the West. Not only did nationalism undermine and eventually destroy European political empires and challenge successfully even more widespread foreign economic domination; it also served to rally Chinese against Japanese, Indian Muslims against Indian Hindus, Arabs against Jews, and vice versa. Nationalism in Asia brought disasters as well as benefits in its wake.

Although modern nationalism has everywhere exhibited certain shared characteristics, it has never been monolithic. Nowhere was this truer than in Asia, where the new and often narrow ideology of nationalism was grafted onto old, rich, and complex civilizations. Between the world wars each Asian country developed its own distinct national movement, rooted in its unique culture and particular historical experience. Each people created its own national reawakening, which renovated thought and culture as well as politics and economics.

How did modern nationalism – the dominant force in most of the world in the twentieth century – develop in Asia between the First and Second World Wars? How did national movements arise in different countries, and how did some of these parallel movements come into brutal conflict? These are the questions this chapter seeks to answer.

THE FIRST WORLD WAR AND WESTERN IMPERIALISM

Every Asian national movement shared in a burning desire for genuine freedom from foreign imperialism. The First World War had a profound effect on these aspirations by altering relations between Asia and Europe.

As a distinguished Indian historian has written, "the Great War of 1914–1918 was from the Asian point of view a civil war within the European community of nations."[1] For four years Asians watched the haughty bearers of the white man's burden vilifying and destroying each other. Far from standing united and supremely self-confident in an apparently unbeatable imperialistic phalanx, the Western nations were clawing at each other in total disarray. The impact of this spectacle was enormous. Japan's defeat of imperial Russia in 1904 (page 1115) had shown that an Asian power could best a European great power; now for the first time Asians saw the entire West as divided and vulnerable.

Few Asians particularly cared who won the vicious family quarrel in distant Europe. But the Europeans, particularly the British and the French, were driven by the harsh logic of total war to draft their colonial subjects into the conflict. The British and French uprooted hundreds of thousands of Asians and Africans to fight the Germans and Turks. This too had major consequences. An Indian or Vietnamese soldier who fought in France and came in contact there with democratic and republican ideas was likely to be less willing to accept foreign rule when he returned home.

The British and the French also made rash promises to gain the support of colonial peoples during the war. Thus British leaders were promising Jewish nationalists in Europe a homeland in Palestine even as they promised Arab nationalists independence from the Ottoman Empire. To counteract popular unrest in India due to inflation and heavy taxation, the British in 1917 were forced to announce a new policy of self-governing institutions. After the war, afflicted with second thoughts, the colonial powers found that the nationalist genie they had released refused to slip meekly back into the bottle.

The idealistic war aims of President Wilson also raised the hopes of peoples under colonial rule. In January 1918 Wilson proposed to make peace on the basis of his Fourteen Points (page 1244), whose key idea was national self-determination for the peoples of Europe and of the Ottoman Empire. Wilson also proposed that in all colonial questions "the interests of native populations be given equal weight with the desires of European governments." Wilson's program seemed to call for national self-rule, the rights of weak nations, and international justice. This subversive, even revolutionary, message was spread around the world by American propagandists in 1918 and 1919. It had enormous appeal for educated Asians, fuelling their hopes of freedom and dignity.

Military service and Wilsonian self-determination also fired the hopes of some Africans and some visionary American black supporters of African freedom. But World War One had less impact on European imperialism in black Africa – Africa south of the Sahara – than in Asia and the Arab world. Because the European conquest of Africa was not completed until 1900, Africans outside of certain coastal areas had not experienced foreign domination long enough for nationalist movements to develop. For black Africa, as we shall see in Chapter 38, the Great Depression and World War Two were to prove much more influential in the growth of nationalist movements.

Once the Allies had won the war, they tried to shift gears and re-establish or increase their political and economic domination in Asia and Africa. Although fatally weakened, in retrospect, Western imperialism remained very much alive in 1918. First of all, President Wilson was no revolutionary. At the Versailles Peace Conference he proved willing to compromise on colonial questions in order to achieve some of his European goals and the creation of the League of Nations. Also, Allied statesmen and ordinary French and British citizens quite rightly believed that their colonial empires had contributed to their ultimate victory over the Central Powers. They were in no mood to give up such valuable possessions voluntarily. Third, the victors remained convinced of the superiority of their civilization. They believed that their rule was best for colonial peoples. A few "discontented" Asian or African intellectuals might agitate for self-rule; but Europeans in general, and colonial officials in particular, believed that the humble masses were grateful for the law and order brought by the white man's administration. If pressed, Europeans said that such administration was preparing colonial subjects for eventual self-rule, but only in the distant future.

The compromise at Versailles between Wilson's vague, moralistic idealism and the European preoccupation with "good administration" was the establishment of a system of League of Nations mandates over Germany's former colonies and the old Ottoman Empire. Article 22 of the League of Nations Covenant, which was part of the Treaty of Versailles, assigned territories "inhabited by peoples incapable of governing themselves" to various "developed nations." "The well-being and development of such peoples" was declared "a sacred trust of civilization." A Permanent Mandates Commission was created to oversee the developed nations' fulfillment of their international responsibility; most of the members of the Permanent Mandates Commission came from European countries with colonies. Thus the League elaborated a new principle, development toward the eventual goal of self-government, but left its implementation to the colonial powers themselves.

The mandates system clearly demonstrated that Europe was determined to maintain its imperial rule. It is no wonder that Asian patriots were bitterly disappointed after the First

World War. They saw France, Great Britain, and other nations — industrialized Japan was the only Asian state to obtain mandates — grabbing Germany's colonies as spoils of war and creating more colonial protectorates in the old Ottoman Empire. Yet Asian patriots were not about to give up. They preached the nationalist creed and struggled to build mass movements capable of achieving independence.

In this struggle they were encouraged and sometimes inspired by Soviet Communism. Immediately after the October Revolution, Lenin and his fellow Bolsheviks declared that the Asian peoples conquered by the tsars, now inhabitants of the Soviet Union, were complete equals of the Russians with a right to their own development. (In actuality this hardly happened, but the propaganda was effective nonetheless.) The communists also denounced European (and American) imperialism and pledged to support revolutionary movements in all colonial countries, even when they were primarily movements of national independence led by "middle-class" intellectuals. Foreign political and economic exploitation was the immediate enemy, they said, and socialist revolution could wait until after Western imperialism had been defeated.

The example, ideology, and support of Russian communists exerted a powerful influence in the 1920s and 1930s, particularly in China and French Indochina. Middle-class nationalists were strengthened in their battle with foreign rule, and the ranks of communist nationalists also swelled. A nationalistic young Vietnamese, who had pled the cause of Vietnamese independence unsuccessfully at the Versailles Peace Conference, described his feelings when he read Lenin's statement on national self-determination for colonial peoples, adopted by the Communist Third International in 1920:

DELEGATES TO THE PEACE CONFERENCE OF 1919 *Standing in the foreground is Prince Faisal, third son of King Hussein of Hejaz and frustrated spokesman for the Arab cause at Versailles. The Brit-* *ish officer T. E. Lawrence — popularly known as Lawrence of Arabia — is second from the right in the middle row. (Bettmann Archive)*

These resolutions filled me with great emotion, enthusiasm, and faith. They helped me see the problem clearly. My joy was so great I began to cry. Alone in my room I wrote the following words, as if I were addressing a great crowd: "My dear compatriots, so miserable and oppressed, here is what we need. Here is the path to our liberation."[2]

The young nationalist was Ho Chi Minh, who was to fight a lifetime to create an independent, communist Vietnam.

Yet the appeal of nationalism in Asia was not confined to territories under direct European rule, like French Indochina and League of Nations mandates. The extraordinary growth of international trade after 1850 had drawn millions of peasants and shopkeepers throughout Asia into the Western-dominated world economy, disrupting local markets and often creating hostility toward European businessmen. Moreover, Europe and the United States had forced even the most solid Asian states, China and Japan, to accept unequal treaties and humiliating limitations on their sovereignty. Thus the nationalist promise of genuine independence and true equality with the West appealed as powerfully in weak states like China as in colonial territories like British India.

Finally, as in Russia after the Crimean War

or Japan after the Meiji Restoration, the nationalist creed went hand in hand with acceptance of modernization by the educated elites. Modernization promised changes that would enable old societies to compete effectively with the world's leading nations.

THE MIDDLE EAST

The most flagrant attempt to expand the scope of Western imperialism occurred in the Middle East, where the British and the French sought to replace the defunct Ottoman Empire with their own rule. Arab, Turkish, and Iranian nationalists, as well as Jewish nationalists arriving from Europe, reacted violently. Their struggles to win dignity and independence sometimes brought nationalists into sharp conflict with each other, most notably in Palestine.

THE ARAB REVOLT

The Ottoman Empire, which had long been subject to European pressure and had adopted European military and educational reforms in the 1820s and 1830s, became increasingly weak and autocratic in the late nineteenth century. The combination of declining international stature and domestic tyranny eventually led to an upsurge of revolutionary activity among idealistic exiles and nationalistic young army officers, who wanted to seize power and save the Ottoman state. These fervent patriots, the so-called Young Turks, succeeded in the Revolution of 1908, and subsequently they were determined to hold the vast empire together. Defeated by Bulgaria, Serbia, and Greece in the Balkan War of 1912, stripped of practically all territory in Europe, the Young Turks redoubled their ef-

forts in Asia. The most important of their Asian possessions were Syria – consisting of modern-day Lebanon, Syria, Israel and Jordan – and Iraq; the Ottoman Turks claimed the Arabian peninsula but exercised only a loose control there.

For centuries the largely Arabic populations of Syria and Iraq had been tied to their Ottoman rulers by their common faith in Islam (though there were Christian Arabs as well). Yet beneath the surface ethnic and linguistic tensions simmered between Turks and Arabs, who were as different as Chinese and Japanese or French and Germans. As early as 1883, a Frenchman who had traveled widely in the Arab provinces reported:

Everywhere I came upon the same abiding and universal sentiment: hatred of the Turks. The notion of concerted action to throw off the detested yoke is gradually shaping itself.... An Arab movement, newly-risen, is looming in the distance; a race hitherto downtrodden will presently claim its due place in the destinies of Islam.[3]

The actions of the Young Turks after 1908 made the "Arab movement" a reality. Although some Turkish reformers argued for an Ottoman liberalism that would give equal political rights to all ethnic and religious groups within the empire, the majority successfully insisted on a narrow Turkish nationalism. They further centralized the Ottoman Empire, and extended the sway of the Turkish language, culture, and race. In 1909 the Turkish government brutally slaughtered thousands of Armenian Christians. Meanwhile the Arab revolt gathered strength. By 1914 the great majority of Arab leaders believed that armed conflict with their Turkish masters was inevitable.

When the Young Turks made the fatal decision to side with Germany in 1914, Arab leaders suddenly found an unexpected ally in

Great Britain. The foremost Arab leader was Hussein Ibn Ali, a direct descendant of the prophet Mohammed through the house of Quraysh. As the *sharif* or chief magistrate of Mecca, the most holy city in the Muslim world, Hussein governed much of the territory along the Red Sea, known as the Hejaz. Basically anti-Turkish, Hussein refused to second the Turkish sultan's call for a holy war against the Triple Entente. His refusal pleased the British, who feared that such calls would trigger a Muslim revolt in India.

In 1915 Hussein managed to win vague British commitments to Arab independence, and the next year he revolted against the Turks, proclaiming himself king of the Arabs. Hussein joined forces with the British under T. E. Lawrence, who in 1917 led Arab tribesmen and Indian soldiers in a highly successful guerrilla war against the Turks on the Arabian peninsula. In September 1918, British armies and their Arab allies smashed into Syria. This last great offensive culminated in the triumphal entry of Hussein's son Faisal into Damascus. There was wild Arab rejoicing, and many nationalists expected independence to rise from the dust of the Ottoman collapse.

Within two years, however, many Arab nationalists felt bitterly betrayed by Great Britain and its allies. The issues involved are complex, controversial, and highly emotional, but it is undeniable that this bitterness left an enduring legacy of hatred toward the West. When Britain and France set about implementing secret wartime treaties to divide and rule the old Ottoman Empire, Arab nationalists felt betrayed. In the secret Sykes-Picot Agreement of 1916, Britain and France had agreed that France would receive modern-day Lebanon, Syria, and much of southern Turkey, and Britain would receive Palestine, Jordan, and Iraq. These treaties, drawn up to reinforce Allied determination to fight on, contradicted British (and Wilsonian) promises concerning Arab independence after the war.

A related source of Arab bitterness was Britain's wartime commitment to a Jewish homeland in Palestine. The famous Balfour Declaration of November 1917 declared:

His Majesty's Government views with favor the establishment in Palestine of a National Home for the Jewish People, and will use their best endeavors to facilitate the achievement of this object, it being clearly understood that nothing shall be done which may prejudice the civil and religious rights of existing non-Jewish communities in Palestine, or the rights and political status enjoyed by Jews in any other country.

As careful reading reveals, the Balfour Declaration made contradictory promises to European Jews and Middle Eastern Arabs, and it has been a subject of passionate debate ever since. Some British Cabinet members apparently believed such a declaration would appeal to German, Austrian, and American Jews and thus help the British war effort; others sincerely supported the Zionist vision of a Jewish homeland. In any event, Arabs were dismayed. In 1914 Jews accounted for about 11 percent of the predominantly Arab population of the Ottoman province of Palestine. A "Jewish national home" seemed to the Arabs to imply some kind of Jewish state incompatible with majority rule. Also, a state founded on religious and ethnic exclusivity was out of keeping with both Islamic and Ottoman tradition, which had historically been more tolerant of religious diversity and minorities than had the Christian monarchs or nation-states in Europe.

Despite strong French objections, Hussein's son Faisal was allowed to attend the Paris Peace Conference; but the Allies made clear that he represented only the Kingdom of Hejaz, not all Arabs. Faisal invoked Wilson's

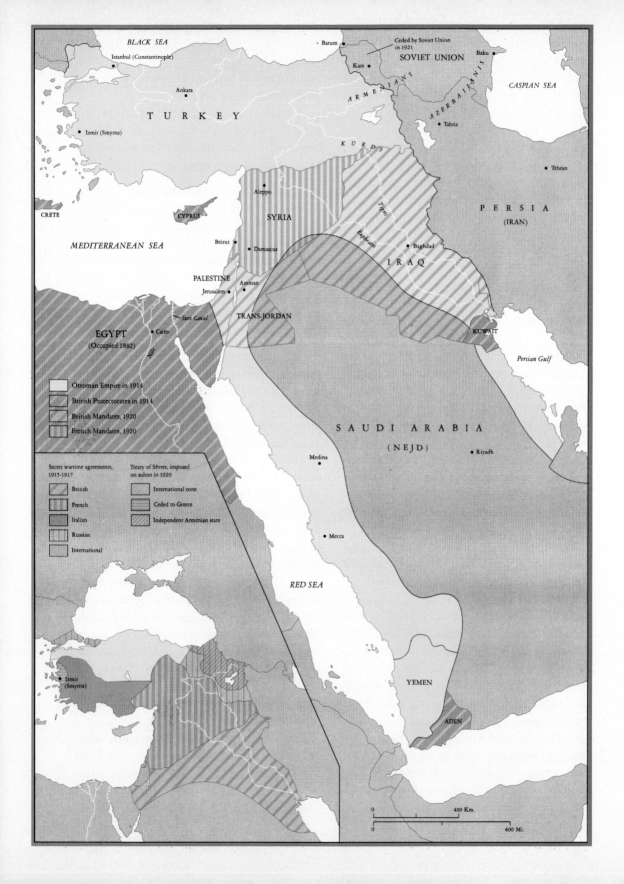

BLACK SEA

Istanbul (Constantinople)

• Batum

Ceded by Soviet Union
in 1921

SOVIET UNION

• Baku

Kars

CASPIAN SEA

Ankara

A R M E N I A N S

A Z E R B A I J A N I S

TURKEY

• Tabriz

Izmir (Smyrna)

K U R D S

• Tehran

PERSIA
(IRAN)

CRETE

CYPRUS

Aleppo

SYRIA

Tigris

Euphrates

• Baghdad

IRAQ

MEDITERRANEAN SEA

Beirut

• Damascus

PALESTINE

Amman

Jerusalem

TRANS-JORDAN

KUWAIT

Suez Canal

Persian Gulf

EGYPT
(Occupied 1882)

• Cairo

Nile

SAUDI ARABIA
(NEJD)

Medina

• Riyadh

	Ottoman Empire in 1914
	British Protectorates in 1914
	British Mandates, 1920
	French Mandates, 1920

Secret wartime agreements,
1915-1917

Treaty of Sèvres, imposed
on sultan in 1920

	British		International zone
	French		Ceded to Greece
	Italian		Independent Armenian state
	Russian
	International

• Mecca

RED SEA

Izmir
(Smyrna)

YEMEN

ADEN

0   400 Km.

0   400 Mi.

idea of self-determination, but despite Wilson's lukewarm support his effort came to nothing. Faisal was forced to accept Franco-British demands regarding the mandate system and the Balfour Declaration. On his return to Syria, Faisal's followers repudiated his compromise. In March 1920 they met as the Syrian National Congress and proclaimed Syrian independence with Faisal as king. A similar congress declared Iraq an independent kingdom.

Western reaction was swift and decisive. France and Britain convened the League of Nations to approve the mandates they wanted. Then a French army stationed in Lebanon attacked Syria, taking Damascus in July 1920. Faisal fled and the French took over. Meanwhile the British put down an uprising in Iraq in bloody fighting and established military rule there. Western imperialism appeared to have replaced Turkish rule in the Middle East.

THE TURKISH REVOLUTION

In November 1918 the Allied fleet entered Constantinople (modern Istanbul), the Ottoman capital. A young English official vividly described the strange and pathetic situation he encountered:

I found the Ottoman Empire utterly smashed, her vast territories stripped into pieces, and her conquered populations blinded and bewildered by their sudden release. The Turks were worn out, dead-tired, and without bitterness awaited their fate. . . . The debris of the old order waited to be constructed into a new system.[4]

The Allies' "new system" was blatant imperialism, and it proved harsher for the Turks than for the Arabs. A treaty forced upon the helpless sultan dismembered Turkey and reduced it to a puppet state. Not only did Great Britain and France occupy parts of Turkey; Italy and Greece claimed their shares as well. There was a sizeable Greek minority in western Turkey, and Greek nationalists cherished the "Great Idea" of incorporating this territory into a modern Greek empire modeled on long-dead Christian Byzantium. In 1919 a Greek army carried by British ships landed on the Turkish coast at Smyrna. The sultan ordered his exhausted troops not to resist, and Greek armies advanced into the interior. Turkey seemed finished.

But Turkey produced a great leader, and revived to become an inspiration to the entire Middle East. Mustafa Kemal (1881–1938), the father of modern Turkey, was a military man. The son of a petty government official and sympathetic to the Young Turk movement, Kemal distinguished himself in World War One by directing the successful defense of the Dardanelles against British attack, the only great Turkish victory of the war. Back in Istanbul after the armistice, Mustafa Kemal watched with anguish the Allies' aggression and the sultan's cowardice. In early 1919 he moved to central Turkey and began working to unify the Turkish resistance.

The sultan, bowing to Allied pressure, initially denounced Kemal, but the cause of national liberation proved more powerful. The

MUSTAFA KEMAL *explains his radical reform of the written language. Impeccably elegant European dress symbolizes Kemal's conception of a modernized Turkey. (The Historical Pictures Service, Inc., Chicago)*

catalyst was the Greek invasion and attempted annexation of much of western Turkey. One young woman who was to play a major role in the Turkish revolution described feelings she shared with countless others:

After I learned about the details of the Smyrna occupation [by Greek armies], I hardly opened my mouth on any subject except when it concerned the sacred struggle. . . . I suddenly ceased to exist as an individual. I worked, wrote and lived as a unit of that magnificent national madness.[5]

Refusing to acknowledge the Allied dismemberment of their country, the Turks battled on through 1920 despite staggering defeats. The next year the Greeks, egged on by the British, advanced almost to Ankara,

the nationalist stronghold in central Anatolia. There Mustafa Kemal's forces took the offensive and won a great victory. The Greeks and their British allies sued for peace. After long negotiations, the resulting Treaty of Lausanne abolished the hated Capitulations, imposed by European powers in the nineteenth century to give their citizens special privileges in the Ottoman Empire, and recognized the territorial integrity of a truly independent Turkey; Turkey lost only its former Arab provinces.

Mustafa Kemal, a nationalist without religious faith, believed that Turkey should modernize and secularize along Western lines. His first moves were political. Drawing on his great prestige as a war hero, Kemal called upon the somewhat reluctant National Assembly to depose the sultan and establish a republic. He had himself elected president and moved the capital from cosmopolitan Istanbul to Ankara in the Turkish heartland. Kemal savagely crushed the demands for autonomy of ethnic minorities like the Armenians and the Kurds, but realistically abandoned all thought of winning back lost Arab territories. He focused instead on internal affairs, creating a one-party system – partly inspired by the Bolshevik example – to work his will.

The most radical of Kemal's changes pertained to religion and culture. For centuries, most of the intellectual and social activities of believers had been sternly regulated by Islamic religious authorities, in keeping with the Sacred Law. Profoundly influenced by the example of western Europe, Mustafa Kemal set out, like the philosophers of the Enlightenment, to restrict the place of religion and religious leaders in daily affairs. Like Russia's Peter the Great, he employed dictatorial measures rather than reason to reach his goal. Kemal and his followers simply decreed a revolutionary separation of church and state. Religious courts were abolished, replaced by a completely new legal system based on European law codes. Religious schools gave way to state schools that taught such secular subjects as science, mathematics, and social sciences.

To dramatize the break with the past, Mustafa Kemal struck down many entrenched patterns of behavior. Women, traditionally secluded and dominated by males in Islamic society, received the right to vote. Marriage was now governed by civil law on a European model, rather than the Islamic code. Women were allowed to seek divorces, and no longer could a wealthy man take a second, third, or fourth wife, as under Islamic law. Men were forbidden to wear the tall red fez as headgear; government employees were ordered to wear business suits and felt hats, erasing the visible differences between Muslims and "infidel" Europeans. The old Arabic script was replaced with a new Turkish alphabet, based on Roman letters, that made the written language closer to the spoken vernacular. This revolutionary change isolated Turks from their historical heritage and literature, as the radical reformers probably hoped. The simpler, more phonetic alphabet also facilitated massive government efforts to spread basic literacy after 1928. Finally, in 1935, family names on the European model were introduced. The National Assembly granted Mustafa Kemal the surname Atatürk, which means "father of the Turks."

By the time of his death in 1938, Atatürk and his supporters had consolidated their pioneering revolution. Government-sponsored industrialization was fostering urban growth and new attitudes. Turks no longer considered business and science beneath their dignity. Poverty persisted in rural areas, as did some religious discontent among devout Muslims, which caused Turkish governments after World War Two to modify some of Atatürk's most radical reforms in a conservative direc-

tion. But like the Japanese after the Meiji Restoration, the Turkish people had rallied around the nationalist banner to repulse European imperialism and were building a modern secular state.

IRAN AND AFGHANISTAN

In Persia, renamed Iran in 1935, brutal efforts to build a unified modern nation ultimately proved less successful than in Turkey.

The late nineteenth century had been a sorry period in Iran's long and sometimes glorious history. Iran was subject to extreme foreign pressure, the Russians pressing relentlessly from the north and the British pushing upward from India and the Persian Gulf. Like China in a similar predicament at the same time, Iran managed to play the Great Powers against each other to maintain a precarious independence. However, the spectacle of the shah granting economic privileges to foreigners alienated native merchants. At the same time an inspired religious leader, Jamal al-Din al-Afghani, preached governmental reform as a means of reviving Islamic civilization. In 1906 a nationalistic coalition of merchants, religious leaders, and intellectuals revolted. The despotic shah was forced to grant a constitution and establish a national assembly, the Majlis. Nationalist hopes ran high.

Yet the Iranian revolution of 1906 was doomed to failure, largely because of European imperialism. Without consulting Iran, Britain and Russia in 1907 simply divided the country into spheres of influence. Britain's sphere ran along the Persian Gulf; the Russian sphere encompassed the whole northern half of Iran. Thereafter Russia intervened constantly. It blocked reforms, occupied cities, and completely dominated the country by 1912. When Russian power temporarily collapsed in the Bolshevik Revolution, British

1914	Ottoman Empire enters First World War on Germany's side
1916	Allies agree secretly to partition Ottoman Empire
1916–1917	Arab revolt against Turkish rule grows
November 1917	Balfour Declaration pledges British support for a Jewish homeland in Palestine
October 1918	Arabs and British triumph as Ottoman Empire collapses
1919	Treaty of Versailles divides old Ottoman Empire into League of Nations mandates
1919	Mustafa Kemal mounts nationalist struggle against foreign occupation
1920	Faisal proclaimed king of Syria but quickly deposed by the French, who establish their mandate in Syria
Early 1920s	Tide of Jewish immigration surges into British mandate of Palestine
1923	Treaty of Lausanne recognizes independent Turkey and Mustafa Kemal begins secularizing Turkish society
1925	Reza Shah takes power in Iran and rules to 1941
1932	Iraq gains political independence in return for long-term military alliance with Great Britain
1936	Syrian nationalists sign treaty of friendship with France in return for promises of independence
late 1930s	Tensions mount between Arabs and Jews in Palestine

armies rushed into the power vacuum. By bribing corrupt Iranians liberally, Great Britain secured a 1919 agreement installing British "advisors" in every department of the government.

This blatant attempt to make Iran a British satellite was a key event in the development of Iranian nationalism. It aroused the national spirit. The Majlis refused to ratify the treaty, which confirmed Iranians' worst suspicions about Britain and the West. More important, in 1921 this reaction against the British brought to power a military dictator, Reza Shah, who proclaimed himself shah in 1925 and ruled until 1941.

Inspired throughout his reign by the example of Turkey's Mustafa Kemal, the patriotic, religiously indifferent Reza Shah had three basic goals: to build a modern nation, to free Iran from foreign domination, and to rule with an iron fist. The challenge was enormous. Iran was a vast, backward country of deserts, mountain barriers, and rudimentary communications. Most of the rural population was poor and illiterate, and there were sizeable ethnic minorities with their own aspirations among the Persian majority. Furthermore, Iran's powerful religious leaders hated Western (Christian) domination, but were no less opposed to a more secular, less Islamic society.

To realize his vision of a strong Iran, the energetic shah created a modern army, built railroads, and encouraged commerce and industry. He won control over the ethnic minorities, like the Kurds in the north and the Arab tribesmen on the border with Iraq. He withdrew many of the privileges granted to foreigners and raised taxes on the powerful Anglo-Persian Oil Company. Yet Reza Shah was ultimately less successful than Atatürk. Because the European-educated elite was smaller than in Turkey, the idea of recreating Persian greatness on the basis of a secularized society attracted fewer determined supporters. Many powerful religious leaders turned against him. Reza Shah became increasingly brutal, greedy, and tyrannical, murdering his enemies and lining his pockets. His support of Hitler's Nazi Germany also exposed Iran's tenuous and fragile independence to international conflicts.

Afghanistan, meanwhile, was nominally independent in the nineteenth century, but the British imposed political restrictions and constantly meddled in the country. In 1919 the new violently anti-British amir Ammanullah declared a holy war on the British government in India and won complete independence for the first time. Ammanullah then decreed revolutionary reforms designed to hurl his primitive country into the twentieth century. The result was tribal and religious revolt, civil war, and retreat from reform. Islam remained both religion and law. A powerful but primitive patriotism had enabled Afghanistan to win political freedom from the West, but modest efforts to build a modern society met little success.

The establishment of French and British mandates at the point of a gun forced Arab nationalists to seek independence by gradual means after 1920. Arab nationalists were indirectly aided by Western taxpayers, who wanted cheap empires – that is, peaceful ones. The result was that Arabs won considerable control over local affairs in the mandated states, except Palestine, though they remained European satellites in international and economic affairs.

The wily British chose Faisal, whom the French had so recently deposed in Syria, as king of Iraq. Faisal obligingly signed an alliance giving British advisors broad behind-the-scenes control. Faisal (1921–1933) proved an excellent ruler, gaining the support of his people and encouraging moderate reforms. In 1932 he secured Iraqi independence at the price of a long-term military alliance with Great Britain.

Egypt, occupied by Great Britain ever since 1882 (page 1140) and a British protectorate since 1914, pursued a similar path. Following intense nationalist agitation after the war, Great Britain in 1922 proclaimed Egypt formally independent but continued to occupy the country militarily. In 1936, the British agreed to a treaty restricting their troops to the Suez Canal Zone.

The French were less compromising in Syria. They practiced a policy of divide-and-rule, carving out a second mandate in Lebanon and generally playing off ethnic and religious minorities against each other. Lebanon eventually became a republic, dominated by the Christian majority and under French protection. Syrian nationalists finally won promises of independence in 1936 in return for a treaty of friendship with France.

In short, the Arab states freed themselves

from Western mandates but not from Western influence. Foreign companies' seizure of control over the newly discovered oil fields also helped to convince radical nationalists that genuine independence had not yet been achieved. The struggle against the West had to continue.

Relations between the Arabs and the West were complicated by the tense situation in the British mandate of Palestine, which deteriorated in the interwar years. Both Arabs and Jews denounced the British, who tried unsuccessfully to compromise with both sides, but the anger of Arab nationalists was aimed primarily at Jewish settlers. The key issue was Jewish migration from Europe to Palestine. A small Jewish community had survived in Palestine ever since the destruction of Jerusalem and the dispersal of the Jews in Roman times. But Jewish nationalism, known as Zionism, was a recent phenomenon of European origin. The Dreyfus affair and anti-Jewish riots in Russia had convinced a cultured Austrian journalist named Theodore Herzl that even nonreligious Jews would never be fully accepted in Europe. Only the re-creation of a Jewish state in Palestine could guarantee Jews dignity and security. Under Herzl's leadership, the Zionist movement encouraged Jews from all over the world to settle in the province of Palestine on lands purchased by Jewish philanthropists, with the approval of the relatively tolerant Ottoman rulers. Some Jewish idealists from Russia and central Europe were attracted to Palestine by the Zionist vision; but until 1921 the great majority of Jewish emigrants preferred the United States (page 1205).

After World War One the situation changed radically. An isolationist United States drastically limited immigration from eastern Europe, where war and revolution had caused chaos and kindled anti-Semitism. Moreover, the British began honoring the Balfour Declaration despite Arab protests.

Thus the number of Jewish immigrants to Palestine from turbulent interwar Europe grew rapidly. The first surge came in the early 1920s, the second in the 1930s when German (and Polish) persecution created a mass of Jewish refugees. By 1939 the Jewish population of Palestine had increased almost fivefold over 1914, and accounted for about 30 percent of all inhabitants.

Jewish settlers in Palestine faced formidable economic and political difficulties. Much of the land purchased by the Jewish National Fund was productive, but most Jewish immigrants came from urban backgrounds and preferred to establish new cities like Tel Aviv or live in existing towns. There economic and cultural friction often hardened Arab protest into Arab hatred, and serious anti-Jewish riots and even massacres ensued. The British gradually responded to Arab pressure and tried to slow down Jewish immigration. This satisfied neither Jews nor Arabs, and by 1938 the two communities were engaged in an undeclared civil war. When, on the eve of World War Two, the frustrated British proposed an independent Palestine whose Jewish population would be permanently limited to one third of the total, the Zionists believed themselves in grave danger.

In the face of adversity, Jewish settlers from many different countries gradually succeeded in forging a cohesive community. Hebrew, which for centuries had been used only in religious worship, was revived as a living language to bind a people together. Despite its slow beginnings, rural development achieved often-spectacular results. The key unit of agricultural organization was the kibbutz, a cooperative farm on which each member shared equally in the work, rewards, and defense of the farm. Men and women labored side by side; a nursery cared for the children and a common dining hall served meals. Some cooperative farms turned arid

ENTERING PALESTINE *This rare photo, showing poor Russian Jews arriving on foot in Palestine, poignantly captures both the hardships and the* *determination of the early Zionists. (the Bettmann Archive/BBC Hulton)*

grazing land into citrus groves and irrigated gardens. An egalitarian socialist ideology also characterized industry, which grew rapidly and was owned largely by the Jewish trade unions. By 1939 a new but old nation was emerging in the Middle East.

TOWARD SELF-RULE IN INDIA

The national movement in British India grew out of two interconnected cultures, Hindu and Muslim, which came to see themselves as fundamentally different in rising to challenge British rule. Nowhere has the power of modern nationalism, both to unify and to divide, been more strikingly demonstrated than in India.

PROMISES AND REPRESSION (1914–1919)

Indian nationalism had emerged in the late nineteenth century (page 1159), and when World War One began the British feared revolt. Instead, somewhat like Europe's equally mistrusted socialist workers, Indians loyally supported the war effort. About 1.2 million Indian soldiers and laborers volunteered for duty and served in Europe, Africa, and the Middle East. The British government in India and the native Indian princes sent large supplies of food, money, and ammunition. In return, the British opened more good government jobs to Indians and made other minor concessions.

As the war in distant Europe ground on, however, inflation, high taxes, food shortages, and a terrible influenza epidemic created widespread suffering and discontent. The prewar

AN INDIAN PRINCE entertained British officers in 1907. India's native princes often lived in fabulous luxury, but the British always held the real power. (The Bettmann Archive/BBC Hulton)

nationalist movement revived, stronger than ever, and the moderate and radical wings of the Indian National Congress joined forces. Moreover, in 1916 the Hindus leading the Congress party hammered out an alliance with India's Muslim League. Founded in 1906 to uphold Muslim interests, the League had grown out of fears that under British rule the once-dominant Muslim minority had fallen behind the Hindu majority, especially in the Western education necessary for good jobs in the government. The important 1916 alliance, known as the Lucknow Pact, forged a powerful united front and called for putting India on equal footing with self-governing white dominions like Canada, Australia, and New Zealand.

The British response was contradictory. On the one hand, the Secretary of State for India made the unprecedented announcement in August 1917 that British policy in India called for "the gradual development of self-governing institutions and the progressive realization of responsible government." The means of achieving this great step forward was spelled out in late 1919 in the Government of India Act, which established a dual administration, part Indian and elected, part British and authoritarian. Such noncontroversial activities as agriculture, health, and education were transferred to Indian officials, accountable to elected provincial assemblies. More sensitive matters like taxes, police, and prisons remained solely in British hands.

The positive impact of this reform, so typical of the British tradition of gradual political change, was seriously undermined by old-fashioned repression. Despite the unanimous opposition of the elected Indian members, the British in 1919 rammed the Rowlatt Acts through India's Imperial Legislative Council. These Acts indefinitely extended wartime "emergency measures" designed to curb unrest and root out "conspiracy." The result was a wave of rioting across India.

In these tense conditions an unsuspecting crowd of some ten thousand gathered to celebrate a Hindu religious festival in an enclosed square in Amritsar, a city in the northern province of Punjab. The local English commander, General Dyer, had, unknown to the crowd, banned all public meetings that very day. Dyer marched his native Gurkha troops onto the field and, without warning, ordered them to fire. The soldiers kept firing into the unarmed mass at point-blank range until the ammunition ran out. A total of 1,650 rounds were fired, killing 379 and wounding 1,137; nine of every ten rounds claimed a victim. The Amritsar Massacre shattered wartime hopes in a frenzy of postwar reaction. India stood on the verge of more violence and repression, and, sooner or later, terrorism and guerrilla war. That India took a different path to national liberation was due largely to Mohandas "Mahatma" Gandhi, the most fascinating and influential Indian since Ashoka.

HINDU SOCIETY AND MAHATMA GANDHI

By the time of Gandhi's birth in 1869, the Indian subcontinent was firmly controlled by the British. Part of the country was directly ruled by British (and subordinate Indian) officials, ultimately answerable to the British Parliament in London. These areas included Bengal and its teeming capital of Calcutta in eastern India, Bombay and its hinterland in western India, the Punjab in the northwest and Madras on the southeast coast. Meanwhile, the so-called protected states were more sheltered from European ideas and the world economy. Many of the old ways remained intact. The native prince — usually known as the maharaja — remained the titular ruler, though he was bound to the British by unequal treaties and had to accept the "advice" of the British resident assigned to his court.

It was in just such a tiny backwater protected state that Gandhi grew up. His father was a member of the merchant caste; *gandhi* means grocer in the Gujarati language. But the Indian caste system has always been more flexible and dynamic than unsympathetic Westerners have wanted to believe. For six generations the heads of Gandhi's family had served as hereditary prime ministers in various minuscule realms on the Kathiawar peninsula, north of Bombay on the Arabian Sea.

The extended (or joint) family, which had for generations been the most important unit of Indian society, powerfully influenced young Gandhi. Gandhi's father was the well-to-do head of the clan, which included five brothers and their wives, children, and children's children. The big three-story ancestral home swarmed with relatives — a whole community crowded into the labyrinth of tiny rooms and spilled out into the open courtyards. There the entire extended family celebrated holidays and Hindu festivals. There the prime minister routinely entertained a score of dinner guests each day. In such a communal atmosphere, patience, kindness, and a good-natured love of people were essential virtues; the aggressive, solitary individualism so prized in Europe and America would have threatened group harmony. So it was for Gandhi.

In the Hindu family the woman is subordinate but respected. She is "worshipped as a mother, venerated as a wife, loved as a sister, but not much regarded as a woman. Woman as woman is the handmaid of man; her duty is to worship her husband, to bear and rear his children."[6] Every Hindu girl married young, often before puberty; her husband was chosen by her parents. The young bride moved into her father-in-law's house, where, according to one famous Indian nationalist, it was "the common rule for intercourse to take place on that very night when she has the first menstruation. . . . This custom has been practiced for at least 2500 years."[7]

Marriage was a sacrament that could not be dissolved by divorce or even by death. Widows were forbidden by custom to remarry and, until the British abolished the practice in 1829, a dutiful wife from a high-ranking caste was expected to throw herself on her husband's funeral fire and join him immediately in the world beyond. More generally, a woman's fate was linked to that of the family, in which she was the trusted guardian of orthodox Hindu values.

Gandhi's mother was the ideal Hindu housewife. Married as a young illiterate girl to a forty-two-year-old man whose first wives had died without male children, Putali Ba bore three boys and a girl. According to Gandhi, his ever-cheerful mother was "the first to rise and the last to go to bed . . . and she never made any distinction between her own children and other children in the family."[8] Very devoted but undogmatic in religious matters, Putali Ba fasted regularly and exercised a strong influence on her precocious son. Gandhi was married at thirteen to a local girl who became his lifelong companion.

After his father's death, Gandhi decided to study law in England. No member of his subcaste had ever done so and the local elders declared Gandhi an outcaste, claiming Hindu practices were impossible in alien England. Gandhi disagreed. To win over his wife and anxious mother, he swore that he would not touch meat, women, or wine in the foreign land. Gandhi kept his word and became a zealous vegetarian, refusing even to eat eggs because they were potential living creatures. After passing the English bar, he returned to India. But his practice in Bombay failed, and in 1893 he decided to try his luck as a lawyer for wealthy Indian merchants in South Africa. It was a momentous decision.

THE ROOTS OF MILITANT NONVIOLENCE

Soon after arriving in South Africa, the elegant young lawyer in Western dress took a business trip by train. A white man entered Gandhi's first-class compartment, took one look, and called the conductor. Gandhi was ordered to ride in the baggage car. When he protested, a policeman threw him off the train. Years later Gandhi recalled this experience as a critical turning-point in his life. He had refused to bow to naked racial injustice.

As Gandhi's law practice flourished, he began to examine the plight of Indians in South Africa. After the British abolished black slavery in the Empire, plantation owners in South Africa and elsewhere had developed a "new system of slavery"[9]: they imported desperately poor Indians as indentured laborers on five-year renewable contracts. When some thrifty, hardworking Indians completed their terms and remained in South Africa as free persons and economic competitors, the Dutch and British settlers passed brutally discriminatory laws. The law books called Indians "semi-barbarous Asiatics," and some towns even prohibited Indians from walking on the sidewalks. Poor Indians had to work on white-owned plantations or return to India; rich Indians lost the vote. Gandhi undertook the legal defense of his countrymen, infuriating the whites, and in 1896 a hysterical mob almost lynched the "coolie lawyer."

Meanwhile Gandhi was searching for a spiritual theory of social action. Identifying with South Africa's black majority as well as his own countrymen, he meditated on the Hindu pursuit of spiritual strength through fasting, sexual abstinence, devotion to duty, and reincarnation. He also studied Christian teachings. Gradually Gandhi developed and articulated a weapon for the weak that he called *Satyagraha*. *Satya* in Hindi means spiritual truth, which equals love; *agraha* is strength or force. Gandhi conceived of Satyagraha, loosely translated as "Soul Force," as a means of striving for truth and social justice through love, suffering, and conversion of the oppressor. Its tactic is courageous nonviolent resistance. Satyagraha owed a good deal to the Christian Gospels, for Christ's call to "love your enemies" touched Gandhi to the core.

As the undisputed leader of South Africa's Indians before the First World War, Gandhi put his philosophy into action. When the white government of South Africa severely restricted Asian immigration and internal freedom of movement, he led a campaign of mass resistance. Thousands of Indian men and women marched across forbidden borders and peacefully withstood beatings, arrest, and imprisonment. Indian coal miners went on strike and many "sisters" became active resisters.

The struggle was hard and the odds long, but Gandhi never wavered. He remarked to a friend at the time, "Men say I am a saint losing myself in politics. The fact is I am a politician trying my hardest to be a saint."[10] In 1914, South Africa's exasperated whites

MOHANDAS "MAHATMA" GANDHI A profoundly original thinker, Gandhi also preserved a common touch that endeared him to millions of ordinary Indians. (Historical Pictures Service, Inc., Chicago)

agreed to many of the Indians' demands. A law was passed abolishing discriminatory taxes on Indian traders, recognizing the legality of non-Christian marriages, and permitting continued immigration of free Indians. Satyagraha — militant nonviolence in pursuit of social justice — had proved itself a powerful force in Gandhi's hands.

GANDHI LEADS THE WAY

In 1915 Gandhi returned to India. His reputation had preceded him: the masses hailed him as a "Mahatma," or "Great Soul" – a Hindu title of veneration for a man of great knowledge and humanity – and the name stuck. Feeling his way into Indian affairs, Gandhi crisscrossed India on third-class trains dressed in peasant garb, listening to common folk and talking to Congress party leaders. Moved by the wretched misery of the very poor, he led some sharecroppers against British landowners and organized a strike of textile workers in his native Gujarat. But it was the aftermath of the Amritsar Massacre that catapulted Gandhi to leadership of the national movement in India.

Drawing on his South African experience, Gandhi in 1920 launched a national campaign of nonviolent resistance to British rule. Denouncing British injustice, he urged his countrymen to boycott British goods, jobs, and honors. He returned medals he had won in South Africa and told peasants not to pay taxes or buy heavily-taxed liquor. Gandhi electrified the people.

The result was nothing less than a revolution in Indian politics. The nationalist movement had previously touched only the tiny prosperous Western-educated elite. Now both the illiterate masses of village India and the educated classes heard a voice that seemed to be in harmony with their profoundest values. Even Gandhi's renunciation of sex – with his wife's consent – accorded with a popular Hindu belief attributing special power to those who do not squander their life force in sexual intercourse. Gandhi's call for militant nonviolence was particularly appealing to the masses of Hindus who were not members of the warrior caste or the so-called "military races," and who were traditionally passive and nonviolent. The British had regarded ordinary Hindus as cowards. Gandhi told them they could be courageous, and even morally superior:

Formerly, when people wanted to fight with one another, they measured between them their bodily strength; now it is possible to take away thousands of lives by one man working behind a gun from a hill.

Our difficulties are of our own creation. God set a limit to man's locomotive ambition in the construction of his body. Man immediately proceeded to discover means of overriding the limit.

What do you think? Wherein is courage required – in blowing others to pieces from behind a cannon, or with a smiling face to approach a cannon and be blown to pieces? Who is the true warrior – he who keeps death always as a bosomfriend, or he who controls the death of others? Believe me that a man devoid of courage and manhood can never be a passive resister.[11]

Gandhi made Congress into a mass political party, welcoming members from every ethnic group and cooperating closely with the Muslim minority.

In 1922, some Indian resisters turned to violence. A mob murdered twenty-two policemen and savage riots broke out. Gandhi abruptly called off his campaign. Arrested for fomenting rebellion, Gandhi told the British judge that he had committed "a Himalayan blunder to believe that India had accepted nonviolence."[12] Released from prison after two years, Gandhi set up a commune, established a national newspaper, and set out to reform Indian society and improve the lot of the poor. He welcomed the outcaste untouchables into his fellowship. He worked to help child widows, promote cottage industry, and end the use of alcohol. For Gandhi, moral improvement, social progress, and the national movement always went hand in hand.

The resistance campaign of 1920–1922 left the British severely shaken. Although moderate Indians had participated effectively in the system of dual government, the commission the British formed in 1927 to consider further steps toward self-rule included no Indian members. Indian resentment was intense. In 1929, the radical nationalists, led by the able and aristocratic Jawaharlal Nehru, pushed through the National Congress a resolution calling for virtual independence within a year. The British predictably stiffened, and Indian radicals talked of a bloody showdown.

In this tense situation Gandhi masterfully reasserted his leadership. He took a hard line toward the British, to satisfy the extremists, but controlled them by insisting on nonviolent methods. He then organized another massive resistance campaign, this time against the hated salt tax, which affected every Indian family. Gandhi himself led 50,000 people in a spectacular march to the sea to make salt without paying a tax, in defiance of the law. A Western journalist described their reception:

Suddenly, at a word of command, scores of native policemen rushed upon the advancing marchers and rained blows on their heads.... No one of the marchers even raised an arm to fend off the blows. They went down like ten-pins. From where I stood I heard the whack of the clubs on unprotected skulls.... Those struck down fell sprawling, unconscious or writhing with fractured skulls or broken shoulders.... The survivors, without breaking ranks, silently and doggedly marched on until struck down.[13]

Over the next few months 60,000 protesters went to jail, but this time there was very little rioting. Finally, in 1931, the frustrated, unnerved British released Gandhi from jail and sat down to negotiate with him, as an equal, over self-rule for India. There were many complications, including the determined opposition of diehard imperialists like Winston Churchill. But in 1935 the negotiations resulted in a new constitution, which greatly strengthened India's parliamentary representative institutions. It was virtually a blueprint for independence.

Gandhi inspired people far beyond India's borders. Martin Luther King was later to be deeply influenced by his tactic and philosophy of nonviolent social action. Gandhi did much to transform the elitist nationalism of Indian intellectuals into a mighty mass movement with social as well as political concerns. Above all, Gandhi nurtured national identity and self-respect. As Nehru summed it up, Gandhi "instilled courage and manhood in India's people; ... courage is the one sure foundation of character, he had said; without courage there is no morality, no religion, no love."[14]

Despite his best efforts, Gandhi failed to heal the widening split between Hindus and Muslims. The development of an Indian nationalism based largely on Hindu symbols and customs increasingly disturbed the Muslim minority. Tempers mounted and atrocities were committed on both sides. By the late 1930s the leaders of the Muslim League were calling for the creation of a Muslim nation in British India, a "Pakistan" or "land of the pure." As in Palestine, the rise of conflicting nationalisms in India was to lead to tragedy after World War Two.

TURMOIL IN EAST ASIA

Nationalism and modernization were well developed in Japan by 1914, due to the efforts of the Meiji reformers. Not only was Japan capable of competing politically and economically with the world's leading nations, but it had already begun building its own empire and proclaiming its special mission in Asia. China lagged far behind, but after 1912 the pace of nationalist development there began to quicken.

The Chinese nationalist movement managed to win a large measure of political independence from the imperialist West and promoted extensive modernization in the 1920s. These achievements were soon tragically undermined by internal conflict and war with an expanding Japan. Nationalism also flourished elsewhere in Asia, scoring a major victory in the Philippine islands.

THE RISE OF NATIONALIST CHINA

The Revolution of 1911–1912 that overthrew the Manchu Dynasty (page 1163) opened an era of unprecedented change for Chinese society. Before the Revolution, many progressive Chinese had realized that fundamental technological and political reforms were necessary to save the Chinese state and to meet the many-sided Western challenge. Most had hoped, however, to preserve the traditional core of Chinese civilization and culture. The fall of the two-thousand-year-old dynastic system shattered such hopes once and for all. If the emperor himself was no longer sacred, what was? Everything was open to question and to alteration.

The central figure in the revolution was a crafty old military man, Yüan Shih-k'ai. Called out of retirement to save the dynasty, Yüan betrayed the Manchus and convinced the revolutionaries that he was a Chinese Bismarck who could unite the country peacefully and prevent foreign intervention. Once elected president of the republic, however, Yüan concentrated on building his own power. He quarreled with parliament and with Sun Yat-sen (pages 1162–1163), the inspiring revolutionary leader who had built the Kuomintang, or Nationalist Party. Once again Yüan was a betrayer. In 1914, he used military force to dissolve China's parliament

and ruled as a dictator. China's first modern revolution had failed.

The extent of the failure became apparent only after Yüan's death in 1916. The central government in Peking disintegrated. For more than a decade power resided in a multitude of local military leaders, the so-called warlords. Most warlords were men of strong, flamboyant personality, capable of building armies by preying on the peasantry and of winning legal recognition from Peking. None of them proved able to establish either a new dynasty or a modern state. Their wars, taxes, and corruption created only terrible suffering.

Foreign imperialism intensified the agony of warlordism. Although China declared its neutrality in 1914, Japan aggressively seized Germany's holdings on the Shantung peninsula and forced China in 1915 to accept Japanese control of Shantung and southern Manchuria. Japan's expansion angered China's growing middle class and enraged its young patriots. On May 4th, 1919, five thousand students in Peking exploded against the decision of the Versailles Peace Conference to leave the Shantung peninsula in Japanese hands. This famous incident launched the "May Fourth Movement," which opposed both foreign domination and warlord government.

The May Fourth Movement and the anti-imperialism of Bolshevik Russia renewed the hopes of Chinese nationalists. Struggling for a foothold in southern China, Sun Yat-sen decided in 1923 to ally his Nationalist Party with the (Third) Communist International and the newly formed Chinese Communist Party. The result was the first of many "national liberation fronts," in keeping with Lenin's blueprint for (temporarily) uniting all anti-conservative, anti-imperialist forces in a common revolutionary struggle. Sun reorganized the Nationalist Party along Bolshevik lines, in an effort to develop a disciplined

party apparatus and a well-indoctrinated party army.

Sun was no communist. In his *Three Principles of the People,* elaborating on the official party ideology – Nationalism, Democracy, and People's Livelihood – nationalism remained of prime importance:

For the most part the four hundred million people of China can be spoken of as completely Han Chinese. With common habits and customs, we are completely of one race. But in the world today what position do we occupy? Compared to the other peoples of the world we have the greatest population and our civilization is four thousand years old; we should be advancing in the front rank with the nations of Europe and America. But the Chinese people have only family and clan solidarity, they

do not have national spirit. Therefore even though we have four hundred million people gathered together in one China, in reality they are just a heap of loose sand. Today we are the poorest and weakest nation in the world, and occupy the lowest position in international affairs. Other men are the carving knife and serving dish; we are the fish and the meat. Our position at this time is most perilous. If we do not earnestly espouse nationalism and weld together our four hundred million people into a strong nation, there is a danger of China's being lost and our people being destroyed. If we wish to avert this catastrophe, we must espouse nationalism and bring this national spirit to the salvation of the country.[15]

Democracy had a less exalted meaning. Sun equated it with firm rule by the Nationalists, who would promote the People's Livelihood through land reform and welfare measures. Sun was in some ways a traditional Chinese rebel and reformer, who wanted to re-establish order and protect the peasants.

Sun's plan was to use the Nationalist Party's revolutionary army to crush the war-lords and reunite China under a strong central government. When Sun unexpectedly died in 1925, this task was assumed by Chiang Kai-shek (1887–1975), the young Japanese-educated director of the party's army training school. In 1926 and 1927, Chiang led enthusiastic Nationalist armies in a highly successful attack on warlord governments in central and northern China. Preceded by teams of party propagandists, the well-disciplined Nationalist armies were welcomed by the people. In a series of complicated moves, the Nationalists consolidated their rule in 1928, and established a new capital at Nanking in central China. Foreign states recognized the Nanking government, and superficial observers believed that China was truly unified once again.

In fact, national unification was only skin-deep. China remained a vast agricultural country plagued by foreign concessions, regional differences, and a lack of modern communications. Moreover, Japan was opposed to a strong China, which could challenge Japan's stranglehold on Manchuria. Finally, the un-easy alliance between the Nationalist Party and the Chinese Communist Party had turned into a bitter, deadly rivalry. Justifiably fearful of communist subversion of the Nationalist government, encouraged by his military success and by wealthy Chinese capitalists, Chiang decided in April 1927 to liquidate his leftwing "allies" in a bloody purge. Secret agents raided communist cells without warning, and soldiers gunned down suspects on sight. Chinese communists went into hiding and vowed revenge.

CHINA'S INTELLECTUAL REVOLUTION

Nationalism was the most powerful idea in China between 1911 and 1929, but it was only one aspect of a highly complex intellectual revolution that hammered at traditional Chinese thought and practice, advocated cultural renaissance, and led China into the modern world. Two other currents in that intellectual revolution, generally known as the New Culture Movement, were particularly significant.

The New Culture Movement was founded by young Western-oriented intellectuals in Peking during the May Fourth era. These intellectuals fiercely attacked China's ancient Confucian ethics, which subordinated subjects to rulers, sons to fathers, and wives to husbands. Confucius lived in a distant feudal age, they said; his teachings were totally inappropriate to modern life. In such widely read magazines as *New Youth* and *New Tide,* the modernists provocatively advocated new and anti-Confucian virtues – individualism, democratic equality, and the critical scientific method. They also promoted the use of simple, understandable written language, a language freed from classical scholarship and literary conventions, as a means to clear thinking and mass education. China, they said, needed a whole new culture, a radically different world-view.

The most influential of these intellectuals championing liberalism was Hu Shih (1891–1962). Educated on a scholarship in the United States, Hu had studied with the educational philosopher John Dewey, whose thoroughly American pragmatism stressed compromise and practical problem solving. A master at tearing down old beliefs, the mature Hu Shih envisioned a vague and uninspiring future. The liberation and reconstruction of China was possible, he said, but it would have to occur gradually, "bit by bit, drop by drop."

MAO TSE-TUNG   Marxian theorist and champion of peasant revolution, Mao emerged as one of history's greatest guerrilla warriors. This photo shows him leading a small armed band across rugged ter- *rain in northern Shensi province, moving quickly to strike the enemy, melt away, and strike again. (Eastfoto)*

Hu personified the limitations of the Western liberal tradition in China.

The other major current growing out of the New Culture Movement was Marxian socialism. It too was Western in origin, "scientific" in approach, and materialist in its denial of religious belief and Confucian family ethics. But while liberalism and individualism reflected the bewildering range of Western thought since the Enlightenment, Marxian socialism offered Chinese intellectuals the certainty of a single all-encompassing creed. As one young communist exclaimed:

I am now able to impose order on all the ideas which I could not reconcile; I have found the key to all the problems which appeared to me self-contradictory and insoluble.[16]

Marxism was undeniably Western, and therefore modern. But it also provided a means of criticizing Western dominance, which salved Chinese pride: China's pitiful weakness was due precisely to rapacious *foreign* capitalistic imperialism. Also Marxism, as modified by Lenin and applied by the Bolsheviks, seemed to get results. For Chinese believers, it promised salvation soon. Finally, Chinese communists could and did interpret Marxism-Leninism so as to appeal to China's masses – the peasants.

Mao Tse-tung (1893–1976) in particular quickly recognized the enormous revolutionary potential of the Chinese peasantry, impoverished and oppressed by parasitic landlords. Himself a member of a prosperous, hardworking peasant family, Mao converted to

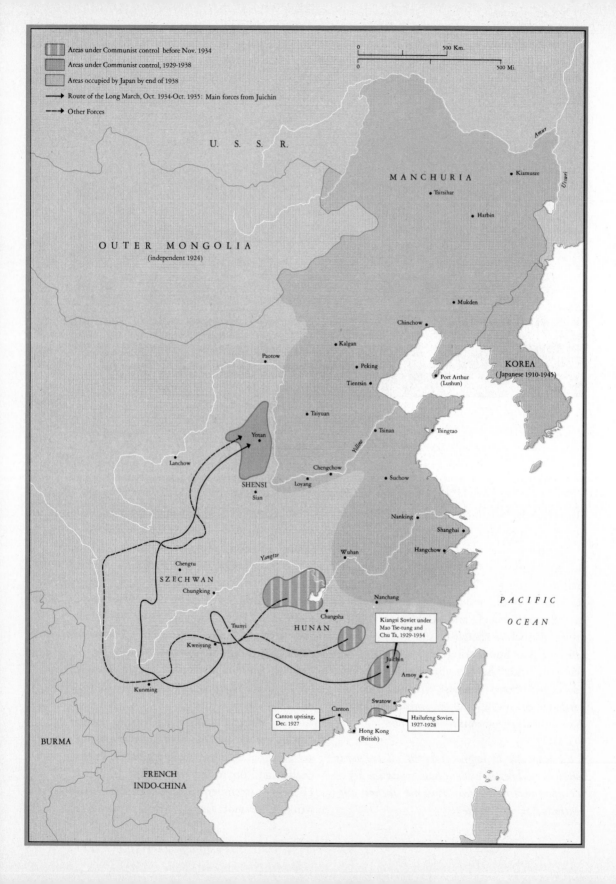

Areas under Communist control before Nov. 1934

Areas under Communist control, 1929-1938

Areas occupied by Japan by end of 1938

Route of the Long March, Oct. 1934-Oct. 1935: Main forces from Juichin

Other Forces

0   500 Km.

0   500 Mi.

U. S. S. R.

MANCHURIA

• Kiamusze

• Tsitsihar

• Harbin

OUTER MONGOLIA

(independent 1924)

• Mukden

Chinchow •

Amur

Ussuri

• Kalgan

Paotow •

• Peking

KOREA

(Japanese 1910-1945)

Port Arthur •
(Lushun)

Tientsin •

Lanchow •

Yenan •

• Taiyuan

Tsinan •

• Tsingtao

SHENSI

Yellow

Chengchow •

• Suchow

Sian •

Loyang •

Chengtu •

Yangtze

Wuhan •

Nanking •

• Shanghai

SZECHWAN

Chungking •

Nanchang •

• Hangchow

PACIFIC

Tsunyi •

Changsha •

OCEAN

Kweiyang •

HUNAN

Kiangsi Soviet under
Mao Tse-tung and
Chu Ta, 1929-1934

Juichin •

Kunming •

• Amoy

Swatow •

Canton uprising,
Dec. 1927

Canton •

Hailufeng Soviet,
1927-1928

BURMA

Hong Kong
(British)

FRENCH
INDO-CHINA

MAP 34.2 THE CHINESE COMMUNIST MOVE-
MENT AND THE WAR WITH JAPAN, 1927–
1938 *After urban uprisings ordered by Stalin
failed in 1927, Mao Tse-tung succeeded in forming a
self-governing Communist soviet in mountainous
southern China. Relentless Nationalist attacks between
1930 and 1934 finally forced the Long March to
Yenan, where the Communists were well-positioned
for guerrilla war against the Japanese.*

Marxian socialism in 1918 while working as an assistant librarian at Peking University, and began his revolutionary career as an urban labor organizer. But when in 1925 protest strikes by Chinese textile workers against their Japanese employers unexpectedly spread from the big coastal cities to rural China, Mao reconsidered the peasants. Investigating the rapid growth of radical peasant associations in Hunan province, Mao argued passionately in a famous 1927 report that

the force of the peasantry is like that of the raging winds and driving rain. It is rapidly increasing in violence. No force can stand in its way. The peasantry will tear apart all nets which bind it and hasten along the road to liberation. They will bury beneath them all forces of imperialism, militarism, corrupt officialdom, village bosses and evil gentry. Every revolutionary party, every revolutionary comrade will be subjected to their scrutiny and be accepted or rejected by them.[17]

The task of Communists was to harness the peasant hurricane and use its elemental force to destroy the existing order and take power. Mao's first experiment in peasant revolt – the Autumn Harvest Uprising of September 1927 – was no more successful than the abortive insurrections of urban workers launched by his more orthodox comrades. But Mao learned quickly. He advocated equal distribution of land and broke up his forces into small guerrilla groups. After 1928 he and his

supporters built up a self-governing Communist Soviet, centered at Juichin in southeastern China, and dug in against Nationalist attacks.

THE CHANGING CHINESE FAMILY

Confucian reverence for the family and family ties helped stabilize traditional Chinese society and gave life its meaning for many generations. The Confucian principle of subordination suffused family life – subordination of the individual to the group, the young to the old, the wife to the husband. Given in marriage by her parents at an early age, the wife owed unquestioning obedience to her husband and mother-in-law. Wealthy husbands customarily took additional wives or purchased concubines from poor families, but for women divorce and running away were both unthinkable. Women of all ages were commonly sold, and they lacked all property rights.

The Daughter of Han, a rare autobiography of a Chinese woman, as told to an American friend, offers an unforgettable glimpse of Chinese family life. Born in 1867 to poor parents in a northern city, Lao T'ai T'ai lived it all. Her footbinding was delayed to age nine, "since I loved so much to run and play." When the bandages were finally drawn tight, "my feet hurt so much that for two years I had to crawl on my knees."[18] Her arranged marriage at fourteen was a disaster: her husband was a drug addict – "in those days everyone took opium to some extent" – who grabbed everything to pay for his habit. "There was no freedom then for women," and she endured her situation until her husband sold their four-year-old daughter to buy opium. Taking her remaining baby daughter, Lao T'ai T'ai fled. She became a beggar, a cook in wealthy households, a peddler of luxury goods to wealthy cooped-up women.

The two unshakeable values that buoyed

her were a tough, fatalistic acceptance — "Only fortune that comes of itself will come. There is no use to seek for it." — and devotion to the family. Lao T'ai T'ai eventually returned home to her husband, who was "good" in those years, "but I did not miss him when he died. I had my [newborn] son and I was happy. My house was established. . . . Truly all my life I spent thinking of my family." Her devotion was reciprocated by her son and granddaughter, who cared for her well in old age.

Lao T'ai T'ai's remarkable life history encompasses both old and new Chinese attitudes toward the family. Her son moved to the city, prospered, and had only one wife. Her granddaughter eventually became a college teacher, an anti-Japanese patriot, and a determined foe of arranged marriages, admirably personifying the trend toward greater freedom and equality for Chinese women after 1911. Footbinding was outlawed and died out unlamented. Marriage for love became increasingly common, and unprecedented educational and economic opportunities opened up for women. Polygamy declined. In the short space of three generations, rising nationalism and the intellectual revolution had accomplished monumental changes in Chinese family life.

FROM LIBERALISM TO ULTRANATIONALISM IN JAPAN

The efforts of Japan's Meiji reformers (pages 1159–1160) to build a powerful nationalistic state and resist Western imperialism were spectacularly successful and deeply impressive to their fellow Asians. The Japanese, alone among non-Western peoples, had mastered modern industrial technology by 1910 and fought victorious wars against both China and Russia. World War One brought more triumphs. Japan easily seized Germany's Asian

holdings and held onto most of them as League of Nations mandates. The Japanese economy expanded enormously. Profits soared as Japan won new markets that wartime Europe could no longer supply.

In the early 1920s Japan seemed to make further progress on all fronts. Most nationalists believed Japan had a semi-divine mission to enlighten and protect Asia, but some were convinced they could achieve their goal peacefully. In 1922, Japan signed a naval arms limitation treaty with the Western powers and returned some of its control over the Shantung peninsula to China. These conciliatory moves reduced tensions in East Asia. At home, Japan seemed headed toward genuine democracy. The electorate expanded twelvefold between 1918 and 1925 as all males over twenty-five won the vote. Two-party competition was intense, and cabinet ministers were made responsible to the lower house. Japanese living standards were the highest in Asia. Literacy was universal.

But Japan's astonishing rise was accompanied by serious problems. First, Japan had a rapidly growing population and scarce natural resources. As early as the 1920s Japan was exporting manufactured goods in order to pay for imports of food and essential raw materials. Deeply enmeshed in world trade, Japan was vulnerable to every boom and bust. These conditions reinforced the widespread belief that colonies and foreign expansion were matters of life and death for Japan.

Also, rapid industrial development had created an imbalanced "dualistic" economy. The modern sector consisted of a handful of giant conglomerate firms, the so-called *zaibatsu* or "financial combine." A zaibatsu firm like Mitsubishi employed thousands of workers and owned banks, mines, steel mills, cotton factories, shipyards, and trading companies, all of which sold to one another. The zaibatsu firms had enormous economic power and dominated the other sector of the economy, which consisted of an unorganized multitude of peasant farmers and craftsmen. The result was financial oligarchy, corruption of government officials, and a weak middle class.

Third, behind the facade of party politics the old and new elites – the emperor, high government officials, big businessmen, and military leaders – were jockeying savagely for the real power. Cohesive leadership, which had played such an important role in Japan's modernization by the Meiji reformers, had ceased to exist.

By far the most serious challenge to peaceful progress, however, was fanatical nationalism. As in Europe, ultranationalism first emerged in Japan in the late nineteenth century but did not flower fully until World War One and the 1930s. Though often vague, Japan's ultranationalists shared several fundamental beliefs.

First, the ultranationalists were violently anti-Western. They rejected democracy, big business, and Marxist socialism, which they blamed for destroying the older, superior Japanese practices they wanted to restore. Reviving old myths, they stressed the emperor's godlike qualities and the samurai warrior's code of honor and obedience. Despising party politics, they assassinated moderate leaders and plotted armed uprisings to achieve their goals. Above all, the ultranationalists preached foreign expansion. Like Western imperialists with their "white man's burden," the Japanese ultranationalists thought theirs was a noble mission. "Asia for the Asians" was their self-satisfied rallying cry. As the famous ultranationalist Kita Ikki wrote in 1923:

Our seven hundred million brothers in China and India have no other path to independence than

ENTERING THE ARMY called for a solemn ceremonial send-off by fellow students in Japan. The Japanese army became a bastion of ultranationalism. (Nihon hyakuner no Kiroku, Kodansha Publishers)

that offered by our guidance and protection. . . . The noble Greece of Asian culture must complete her national reorganization on the basis of her own national polity. At the same time, let her lift the virtuous banner of an Asian league and take the leadership in a world federation which must come.[19]

The ultranationalists were noisy and violent in the 1920s, but it took the Great Depression to tip the scales decisively in their favor. The worldwide depression hit Japan like a tidal wave in 1930. Exports and wages collapsed; unemployment and raw suffering soared. Starving peasants ate the bark off trees and sold their daughters to brothels. The ultranationalists blamed the system, and people listened.

EAST ASIA, 1911–1939

1911–1912	Revolution in China overthrows Manchu dynasty and establishes republic
1915	Japan seizes German holdings in China and expands into southern Manchuria
May 4, 1919	Demonstration by Chinese students against Versailles peace conference and Japan sparks broad nationalist movement
1920s	New Cultural Movement challenges traditional Chinese values
1922	Japan signs naval agreement with Western powers
1923	Sun Yat-sen allies the Nationalist Party with Chinese Communists
	Kita Ikki advocates ultranationalism in Japan
1925–1928	Chiang Kai-shek, leader of the Nationalist Party, attacks warlord government and seeks to unify China
1927	Chiang Kai-shek purges his Communist allies
	Mao Tse-tung recognizes the revolutionary potential of the Chinese peasantry
1930–1934	Nationalists campaign continually against the Chinese Communists
1931	Mukden Incident leads to Japanese occupation of Manchuria
1932	Japan proclaims Manchuria an independent state
1934	Mao Tse-tung leads Communists on Long March to new base in northwestern China
	The Philippines gain self-governing commonwealth status from United States
1936	Japan allies with Germany in anti-Communist pact
1937	Japanese militarists launch general attack on China

JAPAN AGAINST CHINA

Among those who listened with particular care were young Japanese army officers in Manchuria. This underpopulated, resource-rich province of northeastern China, controlled by the Japanese army since its victory over Russia in 1905, seemed a particularly valuable asset in the depression. And many junior officers in Manchuria came from the peasantry and were distressed by the stories of rural suffering they heard from home. They also knew that the budget and prestige of the Japanese army had declined in the prosperous 1920s, and wanted to redress that situation.

Most worrisome of all to the young officers was the rise of Chinese nationalism. This new political force challenged the control that Japan exercised over Manchuria through Chinese warlord puppets. In response, junior officers in Manchuria, in co-operation with top generals in Tokyo, secretly manufactured an excuse for aggression in late 1931. They blew up some tracks on a Japanese-owned railroad near the city of Mukden and then quickly occupied all of Manchuria in "self-defense."

In 1932 Japan proclaimed Manchuria an independent state with a Manchu puppet as emperor. When the League of Nations condemned its aggression in Manchuria, Japan resigned in protest. Politics in Japan became increasingly chaotic. The army, though it reported directly to the emperor, was clearly an independent force subject to no outside control.

For China, the Japanese conquest of Manchuria was disastrous. After unifying most of China in 1928, the Nationalist government had won from the Western powers the right to set tariffs and other marks of sovereignty. The government had also begun to expand higher education, build railroads, and improve the banking system. Japanese aggression in Manchuria drew attention away from these modernizing efforts, which in any event had been none-too-vigorous. The Nationalist government promoted a massive boycott of Japanese goods, but lost all interest in social reform.

Above all, the Nationalist government after 1931 completely neglected land reform and the terrible poverty of the Chinese peasant. As in many backward agricultural societies, Chinese peasants paid roughly half of their crops to their landlords as rent. Ownership of land was very unequal. One careful study estimated that fully half the land was owned by a mere 4 percent of the families, usually absentee landlords living in cities. Poor peasants and farm laborers — 70 percent of the rural population — owned only one sixth of the land.

Peasants were heavily in debt and chroni-cally underfed. Eggs and meat accounted for only 2 percent of the food poor and middle peasants consumed. One contemporary Chinese economist spelled out the revolutionary implications: "It seems clear that the land problem in China today is as acute as that of eighteenth-century France or nineteenth-century Russia."[20] Mao Tse-tung certainly agreed.

Having abandoned land reform, partly because they themselves were often landowners, the Nationalists under Chiang Kai-shek devoted their energies between 1930 and 1934 to five great campaigns of encirclement and extermination against the Communists' rural power base in southeastern China. In 1934 they closed in for the kill, only to miss again. In one of the most incredible sagas of modern times, the main Communist army broke out of the Nationalist encirclement, beat off attacks, and marched 6,000 miles in twelve months to a remote region on the northwestern border. Of the 300,000 men and women who began the Long March, only about 20- to 30,000 reached the final destination. There Mao Tse-tung built up his forces once again, established a new territorial base, and won the support of local peasants by undertaking land reform.

Mao Tse-tung and his Communists gradually emerged as the most determined nationalists. Once again, the decisive factor in the eyes of ordinary Chinese was Japanese aggression. In 1937, the Japanese military and the ultra-nationalists were in command, and decided to use a minor incident near Peking as a pretext for a general attack. The Nationalist government, which had just formed a united front with the Communists in response to the demands of Chinese patriots, fought hard but could not halt the Japanese.

By late 1938, Japanese armies occupied sizeable portions of coastal China. The

JAPANESE SOLDIERS IN MANCHURIA search Chinese travelers for concealed weapons in 1931. Japanese expansion into Manchuria poisoned relations between the two peoples. (Historical Pictures Service, Inc., Chicago)

Nationalists and the Communists had retreated to the interior, both refusing to accept defeat. The determination of the Communist guerrillas equalled that of the Nationalists, and their political skill proved superior. As Europe (and the United States) edged toward World War Two in 1939, the undeclared war between China and Japan bogged down in a savage stalemate. The bloody clash on the Asian mainland was providing a spectacular example of conflicting nationalisms, convulsing China, and preparing the way for eventual Communist victory.

SOUTHEAST ASIA AND THE PHILIPPINES

The tide of nationalism was also rising in Southeast Asia. Like their counterparts in India, China, and Japan, nationalists in Southeast Asia urgently wanted genuine polit-

ical independence and freedom from foreign rule. At the same time, nationalism in Southeast Asia was part of a broader movement toward modernization and cultural renaissance. Yet even as the grandiose concepts of nationalism and modernization spread across national borders, linking the world more closely together, they were grafted onto distinct and ancient civilizations by local leaders.

In both French Indochina and the Dutch East Indies, local nationalists were inspired by events elsewhere in Asia. Japan's rise to the status of Great Power, the struggle of Gandhi and the Congress Party in India, and China's unification under the Nationalists all encouraged Vietnamese and Indonesian patriots to press their own demands. In both cases they ran up against an imperialist stone wall. In the words of one historian, "Indochina was governed by Frenchmen for Frenchmen, and the great liberal slogans of liberty, equality, and fraternity were not considered to be export goods for overseas dominions."[21] This uncompromising attitude stimulated the growth of an equally stubborn communist opposition, which emerged despite ruthless repression as the dominant anti-French force.

In the East Indies – modern Indonesia – the Dutch made some concessions after the First World War, establishing a people's council with very limited lawmaking power. But in the 1930s the Dutch cracked down hard, jailing all the important nationalist leaders. Like the French, the Dutch were determined to hold on.

In the Philippines, however, an old and well-established nationalist movement achieved success. As in colonial Latin America, the Spanish had been indefatigable missionaries in the Philippines. By the late nineteenth century 80 percent of the Filipino population was Catholic. Filipinos shared a common cultural heritage as well as a common racial origin. Education, especially for girls, was quite advanced for Southeast Asia, and in 1843 a higher percentage of people could read in the Philippines than in Spain itself. Economic development helped to create a Westernized elite, who turned first to reform and then to revolution in the 1890s. As in Egypt or Turkey, longstanding intimate contact with Western civilization created a strong nationalist movement at an early date.

Filipino nationalists were bitterly disappointed when the United States, having taken the Philippines from Spain in the Spanish-American War of 1898, failed to fulfill the universal Filipino desire for independence. The Americans convinced themselves that the Philippines were not ready, and might well be seized by Germany or Britain. As an imperialist power in the Philippines, the United States behaved somewhat better than average. Education was encouraged, as was capitalistic economic development. A popularly elected legislature was given real powers. In 1919 President Wilson even promised complete independence, though subsequent Republican administrations saw it as a distant goal.

In spite of relatively enlightened American rule, demands for independence grew. One important contributing factor was American racial attitudes. Americans treated Filipinos as inferiors, and introduced segregationist practices borrowed from the American South. One secretary of state, speaking to Filipinos who favored statehood, pulled no punches:

Gentlemen, I don't wish to suggest an invidious comparison, but statehood for Filipinos would add another serious race problem to the one we have already. The Negroes are a cancer in our body politic, a source of constant difficulty, and we wish to avoid developing another such problem.[22]

American racism made passionate nationalists of many Filipinos.

However, it was the Great Depression that had the most radical impact on the Philippines. As the United States collapsed economically, the Philippines suddenly appeared to be a liability rather than an asset. American farm groups lobbied for protection from cheap Filipino sugar, and labor unions demanded an end to Filipino immigration to protect jobs. In 1934 Congress made the Philippines a self-governing commonwealth, with independence scheduled for 1944. Sugar imports were reduced and immigration was limited to only 50 Filipinos per year.

The United States' retention of its military bases in the Philippines was denounced by some Filipino nationalists. Others were less sure. Japan was fighting in China and expanding economically into the Philippines and throughout Southeast Asia. By 1939, the greatest threat to Filipino independence appeared to come from Asia itself.

———◆———

The Asian revolt against the West began before World War One. But only after 1914 did Asian nationalisms broaden their bases and become mass movements capable of challenging Western domination effectively. These mass movements sought human dignity as well as political freedom. Generally speaking, Asian nationalists favored modernization, and adopted Western techniques and ideas even as they rejected Western rule. Everywhere Asian nationalists had to fight long and hard, though their struggle gained momentum from the relative decline of European power and confidence, the encouragement of the Soviet Union, and American calls for self-determination.

Asia's nationalisms arose out of separate historical experiences and distinct cultures. In this chapter we have seen considerable diversity on the common theme of nationalism in Turkey, the Arab world, India, China, Japan, and the Philippines. This diversity helps explain why Asian peoples also became defensive in their relations with each other while rising against Western rule. As earlier in Europe, Asian nationalists developed a strong sense of "we" and "they"; "they" included other Asians as well as Europeans. Nationalism meant freedom, modernization, and cultural renaissance, but it nonetheless proved a mixed blessing.

NOTES

1. K. M. Panikkar, *Asia and Western Dominance: A Survey of the Vasco Da Gama Epoch of Asian History,* George Allen and Unwin, London, 1959, p. 197.

2. Quoted by Henri Grimal, *La Décolonisation, 1919–1965,* Armand Colin, Paris, 1965, p. 100.

3. Quoted by Peter Mansfield, *The Ottoman Empire and Its Successors,* St. Martin's Press, New York, 1973, p. 18.

4. Harold Armstrong, *Turkey in Travail: The Birth of a New Nation,* John Lane, London, 1925, p. 75.

5. Quoted by Lord Kinross, *Atatürk: A Biography of Mustafa Kemal, Father of Modern Turkey,* William Morrow, New York, 1965, p. 181.

6. Percival Spear, *India, Pakistan, and The West,* 3rd ed., Oxford University Press, 1958, p. 67.

7. Quoted by Erik Erikson, *Gandhi's Truth: On the Origins of Militant Nonviolence,* W. W. Norton, New York, 1969, p. 225.

8. *Ibid.,* p. 105.

9. Hugh Tinker, *A New System of Slavery: The Export of Indian Labour Overseas, 1830–1920,* Oxford University Press, London, 1974.

10. Quoted by Louis Fischer, *Gandhi: His Life and Message for the World,* New American Library, New York, 1954, p. 35.

11. Quoted by Erikson, p. 225.

12. Quoted by Woodbridge Bingham, Hilary Conroy, and Frank Iklé, *A History of Asia,* 2nd ed., Allyn and Bacon, Boston, 1974, 1. 447.

13. Webb Miller, *I Found No Peace: The Journal of a Foreign Correspondent,* Simon and Schuster, New York, 1936, p. 193.

14. Quoted by Lloyd and Susanne Rudolph, *The Modernity of Tradition: Political Development in India,* Chicago University Press, Chicago, 1967, p. 248.

15. Quoted by William Theodore deBary, Wing-tsit Chan, and Burton Watson, *Sources of Chinese Tradition,* Columbia University Press, New York, 1964, pp. 768–769.

16. Quoted by John F. Fairbank, Edwin O. Reischauer, and Albert M. Craig, *East Asia: Tradition and Transformation,* Houghton Mifflin, Boston, 1973, p. 774.

17. Quoted by Benjamin I. Schwartz, *Chinese Communism and the Rise of Mao,* Harvard University Press, Cambridge, Mass., 1951, p. 74.

18. Ida Pruitt, *A Daughter of Han: The Autobiography of a Chinese Working Woman,* Yale University Press, New Haven, 1945, p. 22. Other quotations are taken, in order, from pages 83, 71, 182, 166, and 235.

19. Quoted by William Theodore deBary, Ryusaku Tsunoda, and Donald Keene, *Sources of Japanese Tradition,* Columbia University Press, New York, 1958, 2:269.

20. Quoted by Olga Lang, *Chinese Family and Society,* Yale University Press, New Haven, 1946, p. 70.

21. Bingham, Conroy, and Iklé, *A History of Asia,* 2.480.

22. Quoted by Theodore Friend, *Between Two Empires: The Ordeal of the Philippines, 1929–1946,* Yale University Press, New Haven, 1965, p. 35.

SUGGESTED READING

All of the works cited in the Notes are highly recommended. Two important general studies of nationalism and independence movements are

H. Kohn, *The Age of Nationalism: The First Era of Global History* (1962), and R. Emerson, *From Empire to Nation: The Rise to Self-Assertion of Asian and African Peoples* (1960). These may be compared with the provocative works of E. Kedourie, *Nationalism in Asia and Africa* (1970) and *England and the Middle East: The Destruction of the Ottoman Empire, 1914-1921* (1956), and a justly famous global history of the twentieth century by G. Barraclough, *An Introduction to Contemporary History* (1975). Two fine studies of the Middle East are G. Lenczowski, *The Middle East in World Affairs,* 4th ed. (1980), and S. N. Fisher, *The Middle East: A History,* 3rd ed. (1979), both of which have detailed bibliographies. On Turkey, in addition to Lord Kinross's *Atatürk* (1965), see B. Lewis, *The Emergence of Modern Turkey* (1961), and D. Kushner, *The Rise of Turkish Nationalism, 1876-1908* (1977). Peter Mansfield, *The Arab World: A Comprehensive History* (1976), and S. G. Haim, ed., *Arab Nationalism: An Anthology* (1964), provide engaging general coverage and important source materials. W. Lacqueur, *A History of Zionism* (1972), and A. Eban, *My People* (1968), discuss the Jewish homeland in Palestine. The Arab viewpoint is presented by G. Antonius, *The Arab Awakening: The Story of the Arab National Movement* (1946). R. Cottam, *Nationalism in Iran,* rev. ed. (1979), complements the classic study of D. Wilbur, *Iran: Past and Present,* 9th ed. (1981).

The historical literature on modern India is very rich. S. Wolpert, *A New History of India,* 2nd ed. (1982), is an excellent introduction, with up-to-date scholarship and detailed suggestions for further reading. Also see the handsomely illustrated volume by F. Watson, *A Concise History of India* (1975). In addition to the biographies of Gandhi by Erikson and Fischer cited in the Notes, J. Brown, *Gandhi's Rise to Power: Indian Politics, 1915-1922* (1972), and L. Gordon, *Bengal: The Nationalist Movement, 1876-1970* (1974), are major studies. Developments in the Muslim community

are considered by P. Hardy, *The Muslims of British India* (1972); B. Metcalf, *Islamic Revival in British India: Deoband, 1860-1900* (1982); and F. Robinson, *Atlas of the Islamic World Since 1500* (1982), a beautifully illustrated recent survey encompassing far more than India.

Studies of China in the twentieth century are also very numerous. I. Hsü, *The Rise of Modern China,* 2nd ed. (1975), is a comprehensive study with extensive bibliographies, which may be supplemented by the same author's *Readings in Chinese History* (1971), and the documentary collection of F. Schurmann and O. Schell, eds., *Republican China: Nationalism, War and the Rise of Communism, 1911-1949* (1967). J. Spence, *The Gate of Heavenly Peace: The Chinese and Their Revolution, 1895-1980* (1981), skillfully focuses on leading literary figures. T. Chow, *The May Fourth Movement: Intellectual Revolution in Modern China* (1960), examines a critical time period. Other important studies of China in this period include R. Hofheinz, Jr., *The Broken Wave: The Chinese Communist Peasant Movement, 1922-1928* (1977); Stuart Schram, *Mao Tse-tung* (1966); H. Schriffin, *Sun Yat-sen and the Origins of the Chinese Revolution* (1970); and L. Eastman, *The Abortive Revolution: China Under Nationalist Rule, 1927-1937* (1974). P. Ebrey, ed., *Chinese Civilization and Society: A Sourcebook* (1981), complements the classic studies of the Chinese family by Lang and Pruitt, which may be compared with M. J. Levy, *The Family Revolution in Modern China* (1949). E. Reischauer, *Japan: The Story of a Nation,* rev. ed. (1970), and P. Duus, *The Rise of Modern Japan* (1976), are excellent interpretations of the recent history of the island nation. W. Lockwood, *The Economic Development of Japan, 1868-1938* (1954), and R. Storry, *The Double Patriots: A Story of Japanese Nationalism* (1973), are valuable specialized works. For Southeast Asia, see D. G. E. Hall, *A History of South-east Asia,* 4th ed. (1981), J. Pluvier, *South-East Asia From Colonialism to Independence* (1974), and the Suggested Reading for Chapter 38.

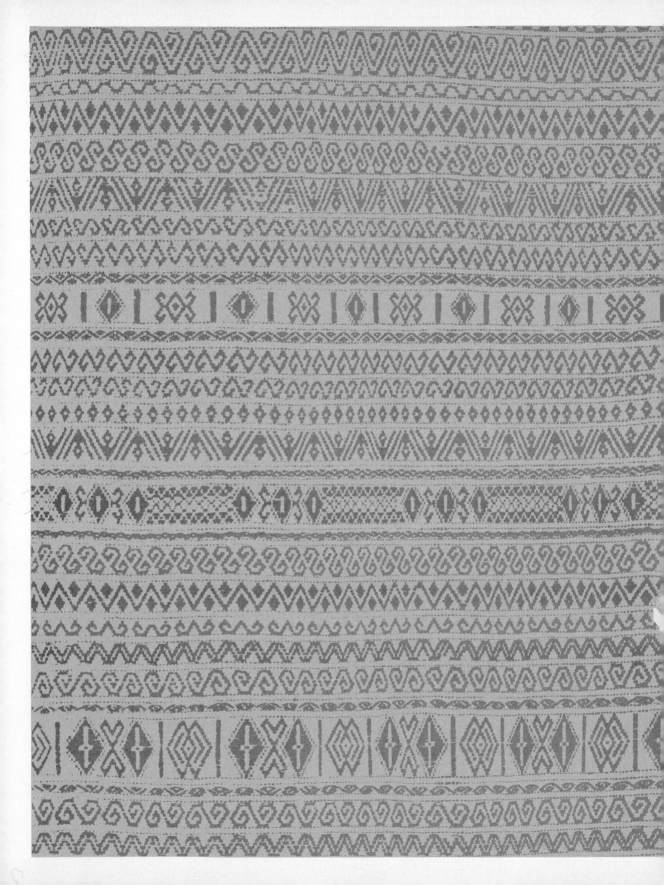

CHAPTER 35

THE AGE OF ANXIETY

WHEN ALLIED DIPLOMATS met in Paris in early 1919 with their optimistic plans for building a lasting peace, most people looked forward to happier times. They hoped that life would return to "normal." They hoped that once again life would "make sense" in the familiar prewar terms of peace, prosperity, and progress. These hopes were in vain. The Great Break – the First World War and the Russian Revolution – had mangled too many things beyond repair. Life would no longer fit neatly into the old molds.

Instead, great numbers of men and women felt themselves increasingly adrift in a strange, uncertain, and uncontrollable world. They saw themselves living in an age of anxiety, an age of continuous crisis, which lasted until at least the mid-1950s. In almost every area of human experience people went searching for ways to put meaning back into life. What did the doubts and searching mean for Western thought, art, and culture? How did political leaders try to re-establish real peace and prosperity between 1919 and 1939? And why did they fail? These are questions this chapter will try to answer.

UNCERTAINTY IN MODERN THOUGHT

A complex revolution in thought and ideas was under way before the First World War, but only small, unusual groups were aware of it. After the war, new and upsetting ideas began to spread through the entire population. Western society began to question and even abandon many cherished values and beliefs that had guided it since the eighteenth-century Enlightenment and the nineteenth-century triumph of industry, science, and evolutionary thought.

Before 1914, most people still believed in progress, reason, and the rights of the individual. Progress was a daily reality, apparent in the rising standard of living, the taming of the city, and the steady increase in popular education. Such developments also encouraged the comforting belief in the logical universe of Newtonian physics, as well as faith in the ability of a rational human mind to understand that universe through intellectual investigation. And just as there were laws of science, so were there laws of society that rational human beings could discover and then wisely act on. Finally, the rights of the individual were not just taken for granted, they were actually increasing. Well-established rights were gradually spreading to women and workers, and new "social rights" like old-age pensions were emerging. In short, before World War One most Europeans had a moderately optimistic view of the world, and with good reason.

From the 1880s on, however, a small band of serious thinkers and creative writers began to attack these well-worn optimistic ideas. These critics rejected the general faith in progress and the power of the rational human mind. One of the most influential of them, who was often ridiculed as a madman before 1914, was the German philosopher Friedrich Nietzsche (1844–1900).

Nietzsche believed that Western civilization had lost its creativity and decayed into mediocrity. Christianity's "slave morality" had glorified weakness and humility. Furthermore, human beings in the West had overstressed rational thinking at the expense of passion and emotion. Nietzsche viewed the pillars of conventional morality – reason, democracy, progress, respectability – as outworn social and psychological constructs whose influence was suffocating creativity. The only hope of revival was for a few superior individuals to free themselves from the humdrum thinking of the masses and embrace life passionately. Such individuals would become true heroes, supermen capable of leading the dumb herd of inferior men and women. Nietzsche also condemned both political democracy and greater social equality.

The growing dissatisfaction with established ideas before 1914 was apparent in other thinkers. In the 1890s, the French philosophy professor Henri Bergson (1859–1941) convinced many young people through his writing that immediate experience and intuition are as important as rational and scientific thinking for understanding reality. Indeed, according to Bergson, a religious experience or a mystical poem is often more accessible to human comprehension than a scientific law or a mathematical equation.

Another thinker who agreed about the limits of rational thinking was the French socialist Georges Sorel (1847–1922). Sorel frankly characterized Marxian socialism as an inspiring but unprovable religion rather than a rational scientific truth. Socialism would come to power, he believed, through a great, violent strike of all working people, which would miraculously shatter capitalist society. Sorel rejected democracy and believed that the masses of the new socialist society would have to be tightly controlled by a small revolutionary elite.

In the years after 1918, a growing chorus of thinkers, creative writers, and scientists echoed and enlarged on the themes first expressed by the small band of critics between 1880 and 1914. Many prophets of doom bore witness to the decline and decay of Western civilization. The experience of history's most destructive war suggested to many that human beings certainly were a pack of violent, irrational animals quite capable of tearing the individual and his or her rights to shreds.

"THE WAR, AS I SAW IT" This was the title of a series of grotesque drawings which appeared in 1920 in Simplicissimus, Germany's leading satirical magazine. Nothing shows better the terrible impact of World War One than this excellent, profoundly disturbing example of expressionist art. (Photo: Caroline Buckler)

There was growing pessimism and a general crisis of the mind. People did not know what to think. This disorientation was particularly acute in the 1930s, when the rapid rise of harsh dictatorships and the Great Depression transformed old certainties into bitter illusions.

No one expressed this state of uncertainty better than the French poet and critic Paul Valéry (1871–1945) in the early 1920s. Speaking of the "crisis of the mind," Valéry noted that Europe was looking at its future with dark foreboding:

The storm has died away, and still we are restless, uneasy, as if the storm were about to break. Almost all the affairs of men remain in a terrible uncertainty. We think of what has disappeared, and we are almost destroyed by what has been destroyed; we do not know what will be born, and we fear the future, not without reason.... Doubt and disorder are in us and with us. There is no thinking man, however shrewd or learned he may be, who can hope to dominate this anxiety, to escape from this impression of darkness.[1]

In the midst of economic, political, and social disruptions Valéry saw the "cruelly injured mind," besieged by doubts and suffering from anxieties. This was the general intellectual crisis of the twentieth century, which touched almost every field of thought. The implications of new discoveries and ideas in physics, psychology, philosophy, and literature played a central role in this crisis, disturbing "thinking people" everywhere.

THE NEW PHYSICS

Ever since the scientific revolution of the seventeenth century, scientific advances and their implications have greatly influenced the beliefs of thinking people. By the late nineteenth century, science was one of the main pillars supporting Western society's optimistic and rationalistic view of the world. The Darwinian concept of evolution had been accepted and assimilated in most intellectual circles. "Progressive minds" believed that science, unlike religion and philosophical speculation, was based on hard facts and controlled experiments. Science seemed to have achieved an unerring and almost completed picture of reality. Unchanging natural laws seemed to determine physical processes and permit useful solutions to ever more problems. All this was comforting, especially to people who no longer accepted traditional religious beliefs. And all this was challenged by the new physics.

An important first step toward the new physics was the discovery at the end of the century that atoms were not like hard, permanent little billiard balls. They were actually composed of many far smaller, fast-moving particles, such as electrons and protons. The Polish-born physicist Marie Curie (1867–1934) and her French husband discovered that radium constantly emits subatomic particles and thus does not have a constant atomic weight. Building on this and other work in radiation, the German physicist Max Planck (1858–1947) showed in 1900 that subatomic energy is emitted in uneven little spurts, which Planck called quanta, and not in a steady stream as previously believed. Planck's discovery called into question the old sharp distinction between matter and energy; the implication was that matter and energy might be different forms of the same thing. The old view of atoms as the stable, basic building blocks of nature, with a different kind of unbreakable atom for each of the ninety-two chemical elements, was badly shaken.

In 1905, the German-born Jewish genius Albert Einstein (1879–1955) went farther than the Curies and Planck in challenging Newtonian physics. His famous theory of special relativity postulated that time and space are not absolute, but relative to the viewpoint of the observer. To clarify Einstein's idea, consider a person riding on a train. From the viewpoint of an observer outside the train, the passenger's net speed is exactly the same whether the passenger is walking or sitting. From the passenger's viewpoint, walking to the restaurant car is different from sitting in a seat. The closed framework of Newtonian physics was quite limited compared to that of Einsteinian physics, which unified an apparently infinite universe with the incredibly small, fast-moving subatomic world. Moreover, Einstein's theory stated clearly that matter and energy are interchangeable and that all matter contains enormous potential energy.

The 1920s opened the "heroic age of physics," in the apt words of one of its leading pioneers, Ernest Rutherford (1871-1937). Breakthrough followed breakthrough. In 1919, Rutherford showed that the atom could be split. By 1944, seven subatomic particles had been identified, of which the most important was the neutron. The neutron's capacity to pass through other atoms allowed for even more intense experimental bombardment of matter, leading to chain reactions of unbelievable force. This was the road to the atomic bomb.

Although few nonscientists understood the revolution in physics, the implications of the new theories and discoveries, as presented by newspapers and popular writers, were disturbing to millions of men and women in the 1920s and 1930s. The new universe was strange and troubling. It lacked any absolute objective reality. Everything was "relative." Everything depended on the observer's frame of reference. Moreover, the universe was uncertain and undetermined, without stable building blocks. In 1927, the German physicist Werner Heisenberg (1901-1976) formulated the "principle of uncertainty." Heisenberg's principle postulates that because it is impossible to know the position and speed of an individual electron, it is therefore impossible to predict its behavior. Instead of Newton's dependable, rational laws, there

seemed to be only tendencies and probabilities in an extraordinarily complex and uncertain universe.

Moreover, a universe described by abstract mathematical symbols seemed to have little to do with human experience and human problems. When, for example, Max Planck was asked what science could contribute to resolving conflicts of values, his response was simple: "Science is not qualified to speak to this question." Physics, the queen of the sciences, no longer provided people easy, optimistic answers – or, for that matter, any answers at all.

FREUDIAN PSYCHOLOGY

With physics presenting an uncertain universe so unrelated to ordinary human experience, questions regarding the power and potential of the human mind assumed special significance. The findings and speculations of the leading psychologist, Sigmund Freud (page 1084), were particularly disturbing.

Before Freud, poets and mystics had probed the unconscious and irrational aspects of human behavior. But most professional, "scientific" psychologists assumed that a single, unified conscious mind processed sense experiences in a rational and logical way. Human behavior in turn was the result of rational calculation – of "thinking" – by the conscious mind. Basing his insights on the analysis of dreams and of hysteria, Freud developed a very different view of the human psyche beginning in the late 1880s.

According to Freud, human behavior is basically irrational. The key to understanding the mind is the primitive irrational unconscious, which he called the id. The unconscious is driven by sexual, aggressive, and pleasure-seeking desires and is locked in a constant battle with the other parts of the mind: the rationalizing conscious (the ego), which mediates what a person *can* do, and ingrained moral values (the superego), which tell what a person *should* do. Human behavior is a product of a fragile compromise between instinctual drives and the controls of rational thinking and moral values. Since the instinctual drives are extremely powerful, the ever-present danger for individuals and whole societies is that unacknowledged drives will overwhelm the control mechanisms in a violent, distorted way. Yet Freud also agreed with Nietzsche that the mechanisms of rational thinking and traditional moral values can be too strong. They can repress sexual desires too effectively, crippling individuals and entire peoples with guilt and neurotic fears.

Freudian psychology and clinical psychiatry had become an international movement by 1910, but only after 1918 did they receive popular attention, especially in the Protestant countries of northern Europe and in the United States. Many opponents and enthusiasts interpreted Freud as saying that the first requirement for mental health is an uninhibited sex life. Thus after the First World War, the popular interpretation of Freud reflected and encouraged the growing sexual experimentation, particularly among middle-class women. For more serious students, the psychology of Freud and his followers drastically undermined the old, easy optimism about the rational and progressive nature of the human mind.

PHILOSOPHY: LOGICAL EMPIRICISM AND EXISTENTIALISM

The intellectual crisis of the twentieth century was fully reflected in philosophy, but in two very different ways. In English-speaking countries, the main development was the acceptance of logical empiricism (or logical positivism) in university circles. In continental countries, where esoteric and remote logical empiricism has never won many converts, the primary development in philosophy was existentialism.

Logical empiricism was truly revolutionary. It quite simply rejected most of the concerns of traditional philosophy, from the existence of God to the meaning of happiness, as nonsense and hot air. This outlook began primarily with the Austrian philosopher Ludwig Wittgenstein (1889–1951), who later migrated to England, where he trained many disciples.

Wittgenstein argued in his pugnacious *Tractatus Logico-Philosophicus (Essay on Logical Philosophy)* in 1922 that philosophy is only the logical clarification of thoughts, and therefore the study of language, which expresses thoughts. The great philosophical issues of the ages – God, freedom, morality, and so on – are quite literally senseless, a great waste of time, for statements about them can neither be tested by scientific experiments nor demonstrated by the logic of mathematics. Statements about such matters reflect only the personal preferences of a given individual. As Wittgenstein put it in the famous last sentence of his work: "Of what one cannot speak, of that one must keep silent." Logical empiricism, which has remained dominant in England and the United States to this day, drastically reduced the scope of philosophical inquiry. Anxious people could find few if any answers in this direction.

Highly diverse and even contradictory, existential thinkers were loosely united in a courageous search for human and moral values in a world of terror and uncertainty. They were true voices of the age of anxiety.

Most existential thinkers in the twentieth century have been atheists. Like Nietzsche, who had already proclaimed that "God is dead," they did not believe a supreme being had established humanity's fundamental nature and given life its meaning. In the words of the famous French existentialist Jean-Paul Sartre (1905–1980), human beings simply exist: "They turn up, appear on the scene." Only after they "turn up" do they seek to define themselves. Honest human beings are terribly alone, for there is no God to help them. They are hounded by despair and the meaninglessness of life. The crisis of the existential thinker epitomized the modern intellectual crisis – the shattering of traditional beliefs in God, reason, and progress.

Existentialists did recognize that human beings, unless they kill themselves, must act. Indeed, in the words of Sartre, "man is condemned to be free." There is, therefore, the possibility – indeed, the necessity – of giving meaning to life through actions, of defining oneself through choices. To do so, individuals must become "engaged" and choose their own actions courageously, consistently, and in full awareness of their inescapable responsibility for their own behavior. In the end, existentialists argued, human beings can overcome the absurdity that existentialists saw in life.

Modern existentialism developed first in Germany in the 1920s, when the philosophers Martin Heidegger and Carl Jaspers found a sympathetic audience among disillusioned postwar university students. But it was in France during the years immediately after World War Two that existentialism came of age. The terrible conditions of the war reinforced the existential view of life and the existential approach to it. On the one hand, the armies of the German dictator Hitler had

conquered most of Europe and unleashed a hideous reign of barbarism. On the other, men and women had more than ever to define themselves by their actions. Specifically, each individual had to choose whether to join the Resistance against Hitler or to accept and even abet depraved tyranny. The writings of Sartre, who along with Albert Camus (1913–1960), was the leading French existentialist and himself active in the Resistance, became enormously influential. They offered a powerful answer to profound moral issues and the contemporary crisis.

THE REVIVAL OF CHRISTIANITY

Christianity and religion in general had been on the defensive since the late eighteenth century. The loss of faith in human reason and continuous progress led to a renewed interest in the Christian view of the world in the twentieth century. A number of thinkers and theologians began to revitalize the fundamentals of Christianity, especially after World War One. They had a powerful impact on society. Sometimes described as Christian existentialists because they shared the loneliness and despair of atheistic existentialists, they revived the tradition of Saint Augustine. They stressed human beings' sinful nature, the need for faith, and the mystery of God's forgiveness.

This development was a break with the late nineteenth century. In the years before 1914, some theologians, especially Protestant theologians, had felt the need to interpret Christian doctrine and the Bible so that they did not seem to contradict science, evolution, and common sense. Christ was therefore seen primarily as the greatest moral teacher, and the "supernatural" aspects of his divinity were strenuously played down. An important if extreme example of this tendency was the young Albert Schweitzer's *Quest of the Historical Jesus* (1906). A theologian and later a famous medical missionary and a musician of note, Schweitzer (1875–1965) argued that Christ while on earth was a completely natural man whose teachings had been only temporary rules to prepare himself and his disciples for the end of the world, which they were erroneously expecting. In short, some modern theologians were embarrassed by the miraculous, unscientific aspects of Christianity and turned away from them.

The revival of fundamental Christian belief after World War One was fed by rediscovery of the work of the nineteenth-century Danish religious philosopher Søren Kierkegaard (1813–1855), whose ideas became extremely influential. Kierkegaard had rejected formalistic religion and denounced the worldliness of the Danish Lutheran church. He had eventually resolved his personal anguish over his imperfect nature by making a total religious commitment to a remote and majestic God.

Similar ideas were brilliantly developed by the Swiss Protestant theologian Karl Barth (1886–1968), whose many influential writings after 1920 sought to recreate the religious intensity of the Reformation. For Barth, the basic fact about human beings is that they are imperfect, sinful creatures, whose reason and will are hopelessly flawed. Religious truth is therefore made known to human beings only through God's grace. People have to accept God's word and the supernatural revelation of Jesus Christ with awe, trust, and obedience. Lowly mortals should not expect to "reason out" God and his ways.

Among Catholics, the leading existential Christian thinker was Gabriel Marcel (1889–1973). Born into a cultivated French family, where his atheistic father was "gratefully

aware of all that ... art owed to Catholicism but regarded Catholic thought itself as obsolete and tainted with absurd superstitions,"[2] Marcel found in the Catholic church an answer to what he called the postwar "broken world." Catholicism and religious belief provided the hope, humanity, honesty, and piety for which he hungered. Flexible and gentle, Marcel and his countryman Jacques Maritain (1882–1973) denounced anti-Semitism and supported closer ties with non-Catholics.

After 1914, religion became much more relevant and meaningful to thinking people than it was before the war. In addition to Marcel and Maritain, many other illustrious individuals turned to religion between about 1920 and 1950. The poets T. S. Eliot and W. H. Auden, the novelists Evelyn Waugh and Aldous Huxley, the historian Arnold Toynbee, the Oxford professor C. S. Lewis, the psychoanalyst Karl Stern, and the physicist Max Planck were all either converted to religion or attracted to it for the first time. Religion, often of a despairing, existential variety, was one meaningful answer to terror and anxiety. As another famous Roman Catholic convert, the English novelist Graham Greene, explained: "One began to believe in heaven because one believed in hell."[3]

TWENTIETH-CENTURY LITERATURE

Literature articulated the general intellectual climate of pessimism, relativism, and alienation. Novelists developed new techniques to express new realities. The great nineteenth-century novelists had typically written as all-knowing narrators, describing realistic characters and their relationship to an understandable if sometimes harsh society. In the twentieth century, most major writers adopted the limited, often confused viewpoint of a single individual. Like Freud, these novelists focused their attention on the complexity and irrationality of the human mind, where feelings, memories, and desires are forever scrambled. The great French novelist Marcel Proust (1871-1922) in his semi-autobiographical *Remembrance of Things Past* (1913-1922) recalled bittersweet memories of childhood and youthful love and tried to discover their innermost meaning. To do so, Proust lived like a hermit in a soundproof Paris apartment for ten years, withdrawing from the present to dwell on the past.

Serious novelists also used the "stream-of-consciousness" technique to explore the psyche. In *Jacob's Room* (1922), Virginia Woolf (1882-1941) turned the novel into a series of internal monologues, in which ideas and emotions from different periods of time bubble up as randomly as they do from a patient on a psychoanalyst's couch. William Faulkner (1897-1963), perhaps America's greatest twentieth-century novelist, used the same technique in *The Sound and the Fury,* much of whose intense drama is confusedly seen through the eyes of an idiot. The most famous stream-of-consciousness novel – and surely the most disturbing novel of its generation – is *Ulysses,* which the Irish novelist James Joyce (1882-1941) published in 1922. Into *Ulysses'* account of an ordinary day in the life of an ordinary man, Joyce weaves an extended ironic parallel between his hero's aimless wanderings through the streets and pubs of Dublin and the adventures of Homer's hero Ulysses on his way home from Troy. Abandoning conventional grammar and blending foreign words, puns, bits of knowledge, and scraps of memory together in bewildering confusion, *Ulysses* is like modern life itself: a gigantic riddle waiting to be unraveled.

As creative writers turned their attention from society to the individual and from realism to psychological relativity, they rejected the idea of progress. Some even described "anti-utopias," nightmare visions of things to come. In 1918, an obscure German high school teacher named Oswald Spengler (1880-1936) published *Decline of the West,* which quickly became an international sensation. According to Spengler, every culture experiences a life cycle of growth and decline. Western civilization, in Spengler's opinion, was in its old age, and death was approaching, in the form of conquest by the yellow race. T. S. Eliot (1888-1965), in his famous poem *The Waste Land* (1922), depicted a world of growing desolation, although after his conversion to Anglo-Catholicism in 1927, Eliot came to hope cautiously for humanity's salvation. No such hope appeared in the work of Franz Kafka (1883-1924), whose novels *The Trial* and *The Castle,* as well as several of his greatest short stories, portray helpless individuals crushed by inexplicable hostile forces. The German-Jewish Kafka died young, at forty-one, and so did not see the world of his nightmares materialize in the Nazi state.

The Englishman George Orwell (1903-1950), however, had seen both that reality and its Stalinist counterpart by 1949 when he wrote perhaps the ultimate in anti-utopian literature: *1984.* The action is set in the future, in 1984. Big Brother – the dictator – and his totalitarian state use a new kind of language, sophisticated technology, and psychological terror to strip a weak individual of his last shred of human dignity. As the supremely self-confident chief of the Thought Police tells the tortured, broken, and framed Winston Smith: "If you want a picture of the future, imagine a boot stamping on a human face – forever."[4] A phenomenal best seller,

1984 spoke to millions of people in the closing years of the age of anxiety.

MODERN ART AND MUSIC

Throughout the twentieth century, there has been considerable unity in the arts. The "modernism" of the immediate prewar years and the 1920s is still strikingly modern. Manifestations of modernism in art, architecture, and music have of course been highly varied, just as in physics, psychology, and philosophy; yet there are resemblances, for artists, scientists, and original thinkers partake of the same culture. Creative artists rejected old forms and old values. Modernism in art and music meant constant experimentation and a search for new kinds of expression. And although many people find the modern visions of the arts strange, disturbing, and even ugly, the twentieth century, so dismal in many respects, will probably stand as one of Western civilization's great artistic eras.

ARCHITECTURE AND DESIGN

Modernism in the arts was loosely unified by a revolution in architecture. The architectural revolution not only gave the other arts striking new settings, it intended nothing less than to transform the physical framework of the urban society according to a new principle: functionalism. Buildings, like industrial products, should be useful and "functional": that is, they should serve as well as possible the purpose for which they were made. Thus, architects and designers had to work with engineers, town planners, and even sanitation experts. Moreover, they had to throw away useless ornamentation and find beauty and aesthetic pleasure in the clean lines of practical

MODERN ARCHITECTURE   Glass, steel, and cool, hard lines characterized the new international style. The Seagram Building in New York (1957) was one of Mies van der Rohe's greatest works. (Joseph E. Seagram and Sons, Inc.; photo: Ezra Stoller)

constructions and efficient machinery. The Viennese pioneer Adolf Loos (1870–1933) quite typically equated ornamentation with crime, and the Franco-Swiss genius Le Corbusier (1887–1965) insisted that "a house is a machine for living in."[5]

The United States, with its rapid urban growth and lack of rigid building traditions, pioneered in the new architecture. In the 1890s, the Chicago school of architects, led by Louis H. Sullivan (1856–1924), used cheap steel, reinforced concrete, and electric elevators to build skyscrapers and office buildings lacking almost any exterior ornamentation. In the first decade of the twentieth century, Sullivan's student Frank Lloyd Wright (1869–1959) built a series of radically new and truly modern houses featuring low lines, open interiors, and mass-produced building materials. Europeans were inspired by these efforts, and by such other American examples of practical construction as the massive, unadorned grain elevators of the Middle West, those majestic masterpieces of stark functionalism.

Around 1905, when the first really modern buildings were going up in Europe, architectural leadership shifted to the German-speaking countries and remained there until Hitler took power in 1933. In 1911, the twenty-eight-year-old Walter Gropius (1883–1969) broke sharply with the past in his design of the Fagus shoe factory at Alfeld, Germany. A clean, light elegant building of glass and iron, Gropius's new factory represented a jump right into the middle of the century.

After the First World War, the new Ger-

man republic gave Gropius the authority to merge the schools of fine and applied arts at Weimar into a single, interdisciplinary school, the Bauhaus. In spite of intense criticism from conservative politicians and university professors, the Bauhaus brought together many leading modern architects, artists, designers, and theatrical innovators, who worked as an effective, inspired team. Throwing out traditional teaching methods, they combined the study of fine art, such as painting and sculpture, with the study of applied art in the crafts of printing, weaving, and furniture making. Throughout the 1920s the Bauhaus, with its stress on functionalism and good design for everyday life, attracted enthusiastic students from all over the world. It had a great and continuing impact.

Along with Gropius, the Franco-Swiss architect and town planner Le Corbusier had a revolutionary influence on the development of modern architecture. Often drawing his inspiration from industrial forms, such as ocean liners, automobiles, and airplanes, Le Corbusier designed houses with flat roofs, open interior spaces, and clear, clean lines. His famous Savoy Villa at Poissy rested on concrete pillars and seemed to float on air. A true visionary, Le Corbusier sketched plans for a city of the future, with tall buildings surrounded by playgrounds and parks.

Another leader in the modern or "international" style was Ludwig Mies van der Rohe (1886–1969), who followed Gropius as director of the Bauhaus in 1930 and emigrated to the United States in 1937. His classic Lake Shore Apartments in Chicago, built between 1948 and 1951, symbolize the triumph of steel-frame and glass-wall modern architecture, which had grown out of Sullivan's skyscrapers and German functionalism in the great building boom after the Second World War.

MODERN PAINTING

Modern painting grew out of a revolt against French impressionism. The impressionism of Monet, Renoir, and Pissarro was, in part, a kind of "superrealism." Leaving exact copying of objects to photography, these artists sought to capture the momentary overall feeling, or impression, of light falling on a real-life scene before their eyes. By 1890, when impressionism was finally established, a few artists known as post-impressionists, or expressionists, were already striking out in new directions. After 1905, art took on an abstract, nonrepresentational character, which it has generally retained to the present.

Although individualistic in their styles, post-impressionists were united in their desire to know and depict worlds other than the visible world of fact. Like the early-nineteenth-century romantics, they wanted to portray unseen, inner worlds of emotion and imagination. Like modern novelists, they wanted to express a complicated psychological view of reality as well as an overwhelming emotional intensity. In *The Starry Night* (1889), for example, the great Dutch expressionist Vincent van Gogh (1853–1890) painted the vision of his mind's eye. Flaming cypress trees, exploding stars, and a cometlike Milky Way swirl together in one great cosmic rhythm. Paul Gauguin (1848–1903), the French stockbroker-turned-painter, pioneered in expressionist techniques, though he used them to infuse his work with tranquillity and mysticism. In 1891, he fled to the South Pacific in search of unspoiled beauty and a primitive way of life. Gauguin believed that the form and design of a picture was important in itself, and that the painter need not try to represent objects on canvas as the eye actually saw them.

Fascination with form, as opposed to light,

PICASSO: GUERNICA   *In this rich, complex work a shrieking woman falls from a burning house on the far right. On the left a woman holds a dead child, while toward the center are fragments of a warrior and a screaming horse pierced by a spear. Picasso has* *used only the mournful colors of black, white, and gray. (Pablo Picasso, Guernica [1937, May–early June]. Oil on canvas. © SPADEM, Paris/VAGA, New York, 1982)*

as characteristic of post-impressionism and expressionism. Paul Cézanne (1839–1906), who had a profound influence on twentieth-century painting, was particularly committed to form and ordered design. He told a young painter, "You must see in nature the cylinder, the sphere, and the cone."[6] As Cézanne's later work became increasingly abstract and non-representational, it also moved away from the traditional three-dimensional perspective toward the two-dimensional plane, which has characterized so much of modern art. The expressionism of a group of painters led by Henri Matisse (1869–1954) was so extreme that an exhibition of their work in Paris in 1905 prompted shocked critics to call them *les fauves*-the wild beasts. Matisse and his followers were primarily concerned not with real objects but with the arrangment of color, line, and form as an end in itself.

In 1907 a young Spaniard in Paris, Pablo Picasso (1881–1973), founded another movement – cubism. Cubism concentrated on a complex geometry of zigzagging lines and sharp-angled, overlapping planes. About three years later came the ultimate stage in the development of abstract, nonrepresentational art. Artists such as the Russian-born Wassily Kandinsky (1866–1944) turned away from nature completely. "The observer," said Kandinsky, "must learn to look at [my] pictures … as form and color combinations … as a representation of *mood* and not as a representation of *objects*."[7] On the eve of the First World War, extreme expressionism and abstract painting were developing rapidly not only in Paris but also in Russia and Germany. Modern art had become international.

In the 1920s and 1930s, the artistic movements of the prewar years were extended and consolidated. The most notable new developments were dadaism and surrealism. Dadaism attacked all accepted standards of art and behavior, delighting in outrageous conduct. Its name, from the French word *dada,* meaning "hobbyhorse," is deliberately nonsensical. A famous example of dadaism was a reproduction of Leonardo da Vinci's *Mona Lisa* in which the famous woman with the mysterious smile sports a mustache and is ridiculed with an obscene inscription. After 1924, many dadaists were attracted to surrealism, which became very influential in art in the late 1920s and 1930s. Surrealism was inspired to a great extent by Freudian psychology. Surrealists painted a fantastic world of wild dreams and complex symbols, where watches melted and giant metronomes beat time in precisely drawn but impossible, alien landscapes.

Refusing to depict ordinary visual reality, surrealist painters made powerful statements about the age of anxiety. Picasso's twenty-six-foot-long mural *Guernica* (1937) masterfully unites several powerful strands in twentieth-century art. Inspired by the Spanish Civil War, the painting commemorates the bombing of the ancient Spanish town of Guernica by fascist planes, an attack that took the lives of a thousand people – one out of every eight inhabitants – in a single night of terror. Combining the free distortion of expressionism, the overlapping planes of cubism, and the surrealist fascination with grotesque subject matter, *Guernica* is what Picasso meant it to be: an unforgettable attack on "brutality and darkness."

MODERN MUSIC

Developments in modern music were strikingly parallel to those in painting. Composers too were attracted by the emotional intensity of expressionism. The ballet *The Rite of Spring* by Igor Stravinsky (1882-1971) practically caused a riot when it was first performed in Paris in 1913 by Sergei Diaghilev's famous Russian dance company. The combination of pulsating, barbaric rhythms from the orchestra pit and an earthy representation of love-making by the dancers on the stage seemed a shocking, almost pornographic enactment of a primitive fertility rite.

After the experience of the First World War, when irrationality and violence seemed to pervade the human experience, expressionism in opera and ballet flourished. One of the most famous and powerful examples is the opera *Wozzeck* by Alban Berg (1885-1935), first performed in Berlin in 1925. Blending a half-sung, half-spoken kind of dialogue with harsh, atonal music, *Wozzeck* is a gruesome tale of a soldier driven to murder his mistress by Kafka-like inner terrors and vague suspicions of her unfaithfulness.

Some composers turned their backs on long-established musical conventions. As abstract painters arranged lines and color but did not draw identifiable objects, so modern composers arranged sounds without creating recognizable harmonies. Led by the Viennese composer Arnold Schönberg (1874-1951), they abandoned traditional harmony and tonality. The musical notes in a given piece were no longer united and organized by a key; instead they were independent and unrelated. Schönberg's twelve-tone music of the 1920s arranged all twelve notes of the scale in an abstract, mathematical pattern, or "tone row." This pattern sounded like no pattern at all to the ordinary listener and could be detected only by a highly trained eye studying the musical score. Accustomed to the harmonies of classical and romantic music, audiences generally resisted modern atonal music. Only after the Second World War did it begin to win acceptance.

Until after World War Two at the earliest, these revolutionary changes in art and music appealed mainly to a minority of "highbrows" and not to the general public. That public was primarily and enthusiastically wrapped up in movies and radio. The long-declining traditional arts and amusements of people in villages and small towns almost vanished, increasingly replaced by standardized, commercial entertainment.

Moving pictures were first shown as a popular novelty in naughty peepshows – "What the Butler Saw" – and penny arcades in the 1890s, especially in Paris. The first "movie houses" date from an experiment in Los Angeles in 1902. They quickly attracted large audiences and led to the production of short, silent action films like the eight-minute *Great Train Robbery* of 1903. American directors and businessmen then set up "movie factories," at first in the New York area and after 1910 in Los Angeles. These factories churned out two short films each week. On the eve of the First World War full-length feature films like the Italian *Quo Vadis* and the American *Birth of a Nation,* coupled with improvements in the quality of pictures, suggested the vast possibilities of screen drama.

During the First World War the United States became the dominant force in the rapidly expanding silent-film industry. In the 1920s, Mack Sennett (1884–1960) and his zany Keystone Cops specialized in short slapstick comedies noted for frantic automobile chases, custard-pie battles, and gorgeous bathing beauties. Screen stars such as Mary Pickford and Lillian Gish, Douglas Fairbanks and Rudolph Valentino became household names, with their own "fan clubs." Yet Charlie Chaplin (1889–1978), a funny little English-

man working in Hollywood, was unquestionably "The King of the Silver Screen" in the 1920s. In his enormously popular role as a lonely tramp, complete with baggy trousers, battered derby, and an awkward, shuffling walk, Chaplin symbolized "the gay spirit of laughter in a cruel, crazy world."[8] Chaplin also demonstrated that, in the hands of a genius, the new medium could combine mass entertainment and artistic accomplishment.

The early 1920s was also the great age of German films. Protected and developed during the war, the large German studios excelled in bizarre expressionist dramas, beginning with *The Cabinet of Dr. Caligari* in 1919. Unfortunately, their period of creativity was short-lived. By 1926, American money was drawing the leading German talents to Hollywood and consolidating American's international domination. Film making was big business, and European theater owners were forced to book whole blocks of American films to get the few pictures they really wanted. This system put European producers at a great disadvantage until "talkies" permitted a revival of national film industries in the 1930s, particularly in France.

Whether foreign or domestic, motion pictures became the main entertainment of the masses until after the Second World War. In Great Britain one in every four adults went to the movies twice a week in the late 1930s, and two in five went once a week. Continental countries had similar figures. The greatest appeal of motion pictures was that they offered ordinary people a temporary escape from the hard realities of everyday life. For an hour or two the moviegoer could flee the world of international tensions, uncertainty, unemployment, and personal frustrations. The appeal of escapist entertainment was especially strong during the Great Depression. Millions flocked to musical comedies featuring glittering stars

MATINEE IDOLS *Fresh and winsome, the Canadian-born Mary Pickford was affectionately known as "America's Sweetheart." Starring in sentimental romances like* Poor Little Rich Girl, Pollyanna, Little Lord Fauntleroy, *she made a fortune and reigned over Hollywood with her second husband, Douglas Fairbanks. Dark and handsome, Italian-born Rudolph Valentino was Hollywood's original "Latin lover." Shown here in his first leading role in the stirring* Four Horsemen of the Apocalypse, *the irresistible Valentino made millions of hearts beat faster until his mysterious death in 1926. (The New York Public Library Picture Collection)*

such as Ginger Rogers and Fred Astaire, and to the fanciful cartoons of Mickey Mouse and his friends.

Radio became possible with the transatlantic "wireless" communication of Guglielmo Marconi (1874–1937) in 1901 and the development of the vacuum tube in 1904, which permitted the transmission of speech and music. But only in 1920 were the first major public broadcasts of special events made in Great Britain and the United States. Lord Northcliffe, who had pioneered in journalism with the inexpensive, mass-circulation *Daily Mail,* sponsored a broadcast of "only one artist . . . the world's very best, the soprano Nellie Melba."[9] Singing from London in English, Italian, and French, Melba was heard simultaneously all over Europe on June 16, 1920. This historic event captured the public's imagination. The meteoric career of radio was launched.

Every major country quickly established national broadcasting networks. In the United States, such networks were privately owned and financed by advertising. In Great Britain, Parliament set up an independent, high-minded public corporation, the BBC, which was supported by licensing fees. Elsewhere in Europe the typical pattern was direct control by the government.

Whatever the institutional framework, radio became popular and influential. By the late 1930s, more than three out of every four households in both democratic Great Britain and dictatorial Germany had at least one cheap, mass-produced radio. In other European countries radio ownership was not quite so widespread, but the new medium was no less important.

Radio in unscrupulous hands was particularly well suited for political propaganda. Dictators like Mussolini and Hitler controlled the airwaves and could reach enormous national audiences with their frequent, dramatic speeches. In democratic countries, politicians such as President Franklin Roosevelt and Prime Minister Stanley Baldwin effectively used informal fireside chats to bolster their support.

Motion pictures also became powerful tools of indoctrination, especially in countries with dictatorial regimes. Lenin himself encouraged the development of Soviet film making, believing that the new medium was essential for the social and ideological transformation of the country. Beginning in the mid-1920s, a series of epic films, the most famous of which were directed by Sergei Eisenstein (1898–1948), brilliantly dramatized the communist view of Russian history.

In Germany, Hitler turned to a young and immensely talented woman film maker, Leni Riefenstahl (b. 1902), for a masterpiece of documentary propaganda, *The Triumph of the Will,* based on the Nazi party rally at Nuremberg in 1934. Riefenstahl combined stunning aerial photography, joyful crowds welcoming Hitler, and mass processions of young Nazi fanatics. Her film was a brilliant and all-too-powerful "documentary" of Germany's "Nazi rebirth." The new media of mass culture were clearly potentially dangerous tools of political manipulation.

THE SEARCH FOR PEACE AND POLITICAL STABILITY

The Versailles settlement had established a shaky truce, not a solid peace. Within the general context of intellectual crisis and revolutionary artistic experimentation, politicians and statesmen struggled to create a stable international order.

The pursuit of real and lasting peace proved difficult. Germany hated the Treaty of Versailles, and France was fearful and isolated. Britain was undependable, and the United States had turned its back on European problems. Eastern Europe was in ferment, and no one could predict the future of Communist Russia. Moreover, the international economic situation was poor and greatly complicated by war debts and disrupted patterns of trade. Yet for a time, from 1925 to late 1929, it appeared that peace and stability were within reach. When the subsequent collapse of the 1930s mocked these hopes, the disillusionment of liberals in the democracies was intensified.

GERMANY AND THE WESTERN POWERS

Germany was the key to lasting peace. Only under the pressure of the Allies' naval blockade and threat to extend their military occupation from the Rhineland to the rest of the country had Germany's new republican government signed the Treaty of Versailles in June 1919. To Germans of all political parties, the treaty represented a harsh, dictated peace, to be revised or repudiated as soon as possible. The treaty had neither broken nor reduced Germany, which was potentially still the strongest country in Europe. Thus, the treaty had fallen between two stools: too harsh for a peace of reconciliation, it was too soft for a peace of conquest.

Moreover, with ominous implications for the future, France and Great Britain did not see eye to eye on Germany. By the end of 1919, France wanted to stress the harsh elements in the Treaty of Versailles. Most of the war in the west had been fought on French soil, and much of rich, industrialized, northern France had been devastated. The expected costs of reconstruction were staggering, and

French politicians believed that massive reparations from Germany were a vital necessity. If the Germans had to suffer to make the payments, the French would not be overly concerned. Having compromised with President Wilson only to be betrayed by America's failure to ratify the treaty, many French leaders saw strict implementation of all provisions of the Treaty of Versailles as France's last best hope. Large reparation payments could hold Germany down indefinitely, and France would realize its goal of security.

The British soon felt differently. Prewar Germany had been Great Britain's second-best market in the entire world, and after the war a healthy, prosperous Germany appeared to be essential to the British economy. Indeed, many English people agreed with the analysis of the young English economist John Maynard Keynes (1883–1946), who eloquently denounced the Treaty of Versailles in his famous *Economic Consequences of the Peace* (1919). According to Keynes's interpretation, astronomical reparations and harsh economic measures would indeed reduce Germany to the position of an impoverished, second-rate power, but such impoverishment would increase economic hardship in all countries. Only a complete revision of the foolish treaty could save Germany – and Europe. Keynes's attack exploded like a bombshell and became very influential. It stirred deep guilt feelings about Germany in the English-speaking world, feelings that often paralyzed English and American leaders in their relations with Germany between the First and Second World Wars.

The British were also suspicious of France's army – momentarily the largest in Europe – and France's foreign policy. Ever since 1890, France had looked to Russia as a powerful ally against Germany. But with Russia hostile and socialist, and with Britain and the United States unwilling to make any firm commitments, France turned to the newly formed states of eastern Europe for diplomatic support. In 1921, France signed a mutual defense pact with Poland and associated itself closely with the so-called Little Entente, an alliance that joined Czechoslovakia, Rumania, and Yugoslavia against defeated and bitter Hungary. The British and the French were also on cool terms because of conflicts relating to their League of Nations mandates in the Middle East. In late 1920, after serving as France's brilliant ambassador to Great Britain for twenty long years, Paul Cambon mournfully wrote, "I do not believe in the possibility of a rupture but everywhere, on every point, there is disagreement, and the misfortune is that neither in Paris nor in London are they intelligent enough to reduce the disagreements to the essential points and disregard the trifles."[10]

While French and British leaders drifted in different directions, the Allied reparations commission completed its work. In April 1921, it announced that Germany had to pay the enormous sum of $35 billion over many, many years. Facing possible occupation of more of its territory, the young German republic, which had been founded in Weimar but moved back to Berlin, made its first payment in 1921. Then, in 1922, wracked by rapid inflation and political assassinations, and motivated by hostility and arrogance as well, the Weimar Republic announced its inability to pay more. It proposed a moratorium on reparations for three years, with the clear implication that thereafter reparations would either be drastically reduced or eliminated entirely.

The British were willing to accept this offer, but the French were not. Led by their tough-minded, legalistic prime minister, Raymond Poincaré, they decided they either had to call Germany's bluff or see the entire peace settlement dissolve to France's great disadvantage. So, despite strong British protests, France and its ally Belgium decided to pursue a firm policy. In early January 1923, French and Belgian armies began to occupy the Ruhr district, the heartland of industrial Germany, creating the most serious international crisis of the 1920s.

THE OCCUPATION OF THE RUHR

The strategy of Poincaré and his French supporters was simple. Since Germany would not pay reparations in hard currency or gold, France and Belgium would collect reparations in kind – coal, steel, and machinery. If forcible collection proved impossible, France would use occupation to paralyze Germany and force it to accept the Treaty of Versailles.

Strengthened by a wave of patriotism that temporarily united all political parties, the German government resisted. Believing that French armies could not operate German factories, it ordered the people of the Ruhr to stop working and start resisting – passively – the French occupation. The coal mines and steel mills of the Ruhr grew silent, leaving 10 percent of Germany's total population in need of relief. Although Americans and Britons generally denounced "French aggression," Poincaré and the French did not retreat. Their answer to passive resistance was to seal off not only the Ruhr but the entire Rhineland from the rest of Germany, permitting through only enough food to prevent starvation. They also revived plans for a separate state in the Rhineland.

By the summer of 1923, France and Germany were engaged in a great test of wills. As

"HANDS OFF THE RUHR" The French occupation
of the Ruhr to collect reparations payments raised a
storm of patriotic protest, including this anti-French
poster of 1923. (Internationaal Institut voor Sociale
Geschiedenis)

the German government had anticipated, French armies could not collect reparations from striking workers at gunpoint. But French occupation was destroying Germany and its economy. The Ruhr district, only sixty miles long and twenty-five miles wide, normally produced 80 percent of Germany's steel and coal. The rest of the German economy desperately needed this key area.

Moreover, the occupation of the Ruhr turned rapid German inflation into runaway inflation. Faced with the need to support the striking Ruhr workers and their employers, the German government began to print money to pay its bills. Prices soared. People went to the store with a big bag of paper money; they returned home with a handful of groceries. Workers were paid twice a day or more, so that they could immediately run to shops and buy something before prices went higher. Finally, in mid-November 1923, it took 4 *trillion* marks – as opposed to four marks in 1914 – to equal a single American dollar.

German money lost all value, and so did savings accounts, insurance policies, annuities, mortgages – anything with a stated fixed value. Runaway inflation brought about a social revolution. The accumulated savings of many retired and middle-class people were wiped out. The old middle-class virtues of thrift, caution, and self-reliance were cruelly mocked by catastrophic inflation. People told themselves that nothing had real value any more, not even money. The German middle and lower-middle classes felt cheated and burned with resentment. Many hated and blamed the Western governments, their own government, big business, the Jews, the workers, the communists for their misfortune. They were psychologically prepared to follow radical leaders in a moment of crisis.

In August 1923, as the mark fell and polit-

THE FRUITS OF GERMANY'S INFLATION   *In the end, currency had value only as waste paper. Here bank notes are being purchased by the bail for paper mills, along with old rags (Lumpen) and bones (Knochen). (Archiv fur Kunst u. Geschichte/Katherine Young)*

ical unrest grew throughout Germany, Gustav Stresemann assumed leadership of the government. Stresemann adopted a compromising attitude. He called off passive resistance in the Ruhr and in October agreed in principle to pay reparations, but asked for a re-examination of Germany's ability to pay. This was less than France had wanted, but Poincaré accepted Stresemann's proposal. His hard line was becoming increasingly unpopular with French citizens, and it was hated in Britain and the United States. Moreover, occupation was dreadfully expensive, and France's own currency was beginning to lose value on foreign exchange markets.

More generally, in both Germany and France power was finally passing to the moderates, who realized that continued confrontation was a destructive, no-win situation. Thus, after five long years of hostility and tension culminating in a kind of undeclared war in the Ruhr in 1923, Germany and France decided to give compromise and cooperation a try. The British, and even the Americans, were willing to help. The first step was a reasonable compromise on the reparations question.

HOPE IN FOREIGN AFFAIRS, 1924–1929

The Reparations Commission appointed an international committee of financial experts headed by an American banker, Charles G. Dawes, to reexamine reparations from a broad perspective. The committee made a series of recommendations known as the Dawes Plan (1924), which was accepted by France, Germany, and Britain. German reparations were reduced and placed on a sliding scale, like an income tax, whereby yearly payments depended on the level of German economic prosperity. The Dawes Plan also recommended large loans to Germany, loans that could come only from the United States. These loans were to help Stresemann's government put its new currency on a firm basis and promote German recovery. In short, Germany would get private loans from the United States and pay reparations to France and Britain, thus enabling those countries to repay the large sums they had borrowed from the United States during the First World War.

This circular flow of international payments was complicated and risky. For a time, though, it worked. The German republic experienced a spectacular economic recovery. By 1929, German wealth and income were 50 percent greater than in 1913. With prosperity and large, continuous inflows of American capital, Germany easily paid about $1.3 billion in reparations in 1927 and 1928, enabling France and Britain to pay the United States. In 1929, the Young Plan, named after an American businessman, further reduced German reparations and formalized the link between German reparations and French-British debts to the United States. In this way the Americans, who did not have armies but who did have money, belatedly played a part in the general economic settlement, which though far from ideal facilitated the worldwide recovery of the late 1920s.

The economic settlement was matched by a political settlement. In 1925, the leaders of Europe signed a number of agreements at Locarno, Switzerland. Stresemann, who guided German's foreign policy until his death in 1929, had suggested a treaty with France's conciliatory Aristide Briand, who had returned to office in 1924 after French voters rejected the bellicose Poincaré. By this treaty Germany and France solemnly pledged to accept their common border, and Britain agreed to fight if either country invaded the other. Stresemann also agreed to settle boundary disputes with Poland and Czechoslovakia by peaceful means, and France promised those countries military aid if they were attacked by Germany. For their efforts Stresemann and Briand shared the Nobel Peace Prize in 1926. The effect of the treaties of Locarno was far-reaching. For several years, a "spirit of Locarno" gave Europeans a sense of growing security and stability in international affairs.

Hopes were strengthened by other developments. In 1926, Germany joined the League of Nations, where Stresemann continued his "peace offensive." In 1928, fifteen countries signed the Kellogg-Briand Pact, which "condemned and renounced war as an instrument of national policy." The signing states agreed to settle international disputes peacefully. Often seen as idealistic nonsense because it made no provisions for action in case war actually occurred, the pact was nevertheless a hopeful step. It grew out of a suggestion by Briand that France and the United States renounce the possibility of war between their two countries. Briand was gently and subtly trying to draw the United States back into involvement with Europe. When Secretary of State Frank B. Kellogg proposed a multinational pact, Briand appeared close to success. Thus, the cautious optimism of the late 1920s also rested on the hope that the United States would accept its responsibilities as a great power and contribute to European stability.

HOPE IN DEMOCRATIC GOVERNMENT

Domestic politics also offered reason to hope. During the occupation of the Ruhr and the great inflation, republican government in Germany had appeared on the verge of collapse. In 1923, communists momentarily entered provincial governments, and in November an obscure nobody named Adolf Hitler leaped on a table in a beer hall in Munich and proclaimed a "national socialist revolution." But Hitler's plot was poorly organized and easily crushed, and Hitler was sentenced to prison, where he outlined his theories and program in his book *Mein Kampf* (*My Struggle*). Throughout the 1920s, Hitler's National Socialist party attracted support only from a few fanatical anti-Semites, ultranationalists, and disgruntled ex-servicemen. In 1928, his party had an insignificant twelve seats in the national parliament. Indeed, after 1923, democracy seemed to take root in Weimar Germany. A new currency was established, and the economy boomed.

The moderate businessmen who tended to dominate the various German coalition governments were convinced that economic prosperity demanded good relations with the Western powers, and they supported parliamentary government at home. Stresemann himself was a man of this class, and he was the key figure in every government until his

death in 1929. Elections were held regularly, and republican democracy appeared to have growing support among a majority of the German people.

There were, however, sharp political divisions in the country. Many unrepentant nationalists and monarchists populated the right and the army. Germany's Communists were noisy and active on the left. The Communists, directed from Moscow, reserved their greatest hatred and sharpest barbs for their cousins the Social Democrats, whom they endlessly accused of betraying the revolution. The working classes were divided politically, but most supported the nonrevolutionary but socialist Social Democrats.

The situation in France had numerous similarities to that in Germany. Communists and socialists battled for the support of the workers. After 1924, the democratically elected government rested mainly in the hands of coalitions of moderates, and business interests were well represented. France's great accomplishment was rapid rebuilding of its war-torn northern region. The expense of this undertaking led, however, to a big deficit and substantial inflation. By early 1926, the franc had fallen to 10 percent of its prewar value, causing a severe crisis. Poincaré was recalled to office, while Briand remained minister for foreign affairs. The Poincaré government proceeded to slash spending and raise taxes, restoring confidence in the economy. The franc was "saved," stabilized at about one-fifth of its prewar value. Good times prevailed until 1930.

Despite its political shortcomings, France attracted artists and writers from all over the world in the 1920s. Much of the intellectual and artistic ferment of the times flourished in Paris. As the writer Gertrude Stein (1874–1946), a leader of the large colony of American expatriates living in Paris, later recalled:

AN AMERICAN IN PARIS The young Josephine Baker suddenly became a star when she brought an exotic African eroticism to French music halls in 1925. American blacks and Africans had a powerful impact on entertainment in Europe in the 1920s and 1930s. (BBC Hulton Picture Library)

"Paris was where the twentieth century was."[11] More generally, France appealed to foreigners and the French as a harmonious combination of small businesses and family farms, of bold innovation and solid traditions.

Britain too faced challenges after 1920. The trend toward greater social equality evident during the war continued, however, helping to maintain social harmony. The great problem was unemployment. Many of Britain's best markets had been lost during the war. In June 1921 almost 2.2 million people – 23 percent of the labor force – were out of work, and throughout the 1920s unemployment remained high. Yet the state provided unemployment benefits of equal size to all those without jobs, and supplemented those payments with subsidized housing, medical aid, and increased old-age pensions. These and other measures kept living standards from seriously declining, defused class tensions, and pointed the way toward the welfare state Britain established after World War Two.

Relative social harmony was accompanied by the rise of the Labour party as an aggressive champion of the working classes and of greater social equality. Committed to socialism, the Labour party replaced the Liberal party as the main opposition to the Conservatives. The new prominence of the Labour party reflected the decline of old liberal ideals of competitive capitalism, limited government control, and individual responsibility. In 1924 and 1929, the Labour party under Ramsay MacDonald governed the country with the support of the smaller Liberal party. Yet Labour moved toward socialism gradually and democratically, so that the middle classes were not overly frightened as the working classes won new benefits.

The Conservatives under Stanley Baldwin showed the same compromising spirit on social issues. The last line of Baldwin's greatest speech in March 1925 summarized his international and domestic programs: "Give us peace in our time, O Lord." Thus, in spite of such conflicts as the 1926 strike by hard-pressed coal miners, which ended in an unsuccessful general strike, social unrest in Britain was limited in the 1920s and in the 1930s as well. In 1922, Britain granted southern, Catholic Ireland full autonomy after a bitter guerrilla war, thus removing another source of prewar friction. In summary, developments in both international relations and in the domestic politics of the leading democracies gave cause for cautious optimism in the late 1920s.

THE GREAT DEPRESSION, 1929–1939

Like the Great War, the Great Depression must be spelled with capital letters. Economic depression was nothing new. Depressions occurred throughout the nineteenth century with predictable regularity, as they recur in the form of recessions and slumps to this day. What was new about this depression was its severity and duration. It struck with ever-greater intensity from 1929 to 1933, and recovery was uneven and slow. Only with the Second World War did the depression disappear in much of the world.

The social and political consequences of prolonged economic collapse were enormous. The depression shattered the fragile optimism of political leaders in the late 1920s. Mass unemployment made insecurity a reality for millions of ordinary people, who had paid little attention to the intellectual crisis or to new directions in art and ideas. In desperation, people looked for leaders who would "do something." They were willing to support radical attempts to deal with the crisis by both democratic leaders and dictators.

THE ECONOMIC CRISIS

There is no agreement among historians and economists about why the Great Depression was so deep and lasted so long. Thus, it is best to trace the course of the great collapse before trying to identify what caused it.

Although economic activity was already declining moderately in many countries by early 1929, the crash of the stock market in the United States in October of that year really started the Great Depression. The American stock-market boom, which had seen stock prices double between early 1928 and September 1929, was built on borrowed money. Many wealthy investors, speculators, and people of modest means had bought stocks by paying only a small fraction of the total purchase price and borrowing the remainder from their stockbrokers. Such buying "on margin" was extremely dangerous. When prices started falling, the hard-pressed margin buyers either had to put up more money, which was often impossible, or sell their shares to pay off their brokers. Thus, thousands of people started selling all at once. The result was a financial panic. Countless investors and speculators were wiped out in a matter of days or weeks.

The general economic consequences were swift and severe. Stripped of their wealth and confidence, battered investors and their fellow citizens started buying fewer goods. Production began to slow down, and unemployment began to rise. Soon the entire American economy was caught in a vicious, spiraling decline.

The financial panic in the United States triggered a worldwide financial crisis, and that crisis resulted in a drastic decline in production in country after country. Throughout the 1920s, American bankers and investors had lent large amounts of capital not only to Germany but to many countries. Many of these loans were short-term, and once panic broke New York bankers began recalling them. Gold reserves thus began to flow out of European countries, particularly Germany and Austria, toward the United States. It became very hard for European businessmen to borrow money, and the panicky public began to withdraw its savings from the banks. These banking problems eventually led to the crash of the largest bank in Austria in 1931 and then to general financial chaos. The recall of private loans by American bankers also accelerated the collapse in world prices, as businessmen around the world dumped industrial goods and agricultural commodities in a frantic attempt to get cash to pay what they owed.

The financial crisis led to a general crisis of production: between 1929 and 1933, world output of goods fell by an estimated 38 percent. As this happened, each country turned inward and tried to go it alone. In 1931, for example, Britain went off the gold standard, refusing to convert bank notes into gold, and reduced the value of its money. Britain's goal was to make its goods cheaper and therefore more salable in the world market. But because more than twenty nations, including the United States in 1934, also went off the gold standard, no country gained a real advantage. Similarly, country after country followed the example of the United States when it raised protective tariffs to their highest levels ever in 1930 and tried to seal off shrinking national markets for American producers only. Within this context of fragmented and destructive economic nationalism, recovery finally began in 1933.

Although opinions differ, two factors probably best explain the relentless slide to the bottom from 1929 to early 1933. First, the international economy lacked a leadership able to maintain stability when the crisis came. Specifically, as a noted American economic historian concludes, the seriously weakened British, the traditional leaders of the world economy, "couldn't and the United States wouldn't" stabilize the international economic system in 1929.[12] The United States, which had momentarily played a positive role after the occupation of the Ruhr, cut back its in-ternational lending and erected high tariffs.

The second factor was poor national economic policy in almost every country. Governments generally cut their budgets and reduced spending when they should have run large deficits in an attempt to stimulate their economies. Since World War Two, such a "countercyclical policy," advocated by John Maynard Keynes, has become a well-established weapon against depression. But in the 1930s, Keynes's prescription was generally regarded with horror by orthodox economists.

MASS UNEMPLOYMENT

The need for large-scale government spending was tied to mass unemployment. As the financial crisis led to cuts in production, workers lost their jobs and had little money to buy goods. This led to still more cuts in production and still more unemployment, until millions were out of work. In Britain, unemployment had averaged 12 percent in the 1920s; between 1930 and 1935, it averaged more than 18 percent. Far worse was the case of the United States, where unemployment had averaged only 5 percent in the 1920s. In 1932, unemployment soared to about *one-third* of the entire labor force: 14 million people were out of work. Only by pumping new money into the economy could the government increase demand and break the vicious cycle of decline.

Along with its economic effects, mass unemployment posed a great social problem that mere numbers cannot adequately express. Millions of people lost their spirit and dignity in an apparently hopeless search for work. Homes and ways of life were disrupted in millions of personal tragedies. Young people postponed marriages they could not afford, and birthrates fell sharply. There was an increase in suicide and mental illness. Poverty or the threat of poverty became a grinding reality. In 1932, the workers of Manchester, England, appealed to their city officials – a typical appeal echoed throughout the Western world:

We tell you that thousands of people . . . are in desperate straits. We tell you that men, women, and children are going hungry. . . . We tell you that great numbers are being rendered distraught through the stress and worry of trying to exist without work. . . .

If you do not do this – if you do not provide useful work for the unemployed – what, we ask, is your alternative? Do not imagine that this colossal tragedy of unemployment is going on endlessly without some fateful catastrophe. Hungry men are angry men.[13]

Mass unemployment was a terrible time bomb preparing to explode.

THE NEW DEAL IN THE UNITED STATES

Of all the major industrial countries, only Germany was harder hit by the Great Depression, or reacted more radically to it, than the United States. Depression was so traumatic in the United States because the 1920s had been a period of complacent prosperity. The Great Depression and the response to it was a major turning point in American history.

President Herbert Hoover and his administration initially reacted to the stock-market crash and economic decline with dogged optimism and limited action. In May 1930, Hoover told a group of business and farm leaders, "I am convinced that we have now passed the worst and with continued unity of effort we shall rapidly recover." When, however, the full force of the financial crisis struck Europe in the summer of 1931 and boomeranged back to the United States, people's worst fears became reality. Banks failed; un-

MIDDLE-CLASS UNEMPLOYMENT An English office worker's unusual sandwich board poignantly summarizes the bitter despair of the unemployed in the 1930s. (BBC Hulton Picture Library)

employment soared. In 1932, industrial production fell to about 50 percent of its level in 1929. In these tragic circumstances Franklin Delano Roosevelt, a magnetic wheelchair aristocrat previously crippled by polio, won a landslide electoral victory with grand but vague promises of a "New Deal for the forgotten man."

Roosevelt's basic goal was to reform capitalism in order to preserve it. In his words,

"A frank examination of the profit system in the spring of 1933 showed it to be in collapse; but substantially everybody in the United States, in public office and out of public office, from the very rich to the very poor, was as determined as was my Administration to save it."[14] Roosevelt rejected socialism and government ownership of industry in 1933. To right the situation, he chose forceful government intervention in the economy.

In this choice Roosevelt and his advisers were greatly influenced by American experience in World War One. During the wartime emergency, the American economy had been thoroughly planned and regulated. Roosevelt and his "brain trust" of advisers adopted similar policies to restore prosperity and reduce social inequality. Roosevelt was flexible, pragmatic, and willing to experiment. Government intervention and experimentation were combined in some of the New Deal's most significant measures.

The most ambitious attempt to control and plan the economy was the National Recovery Administration (NRA), established by Congress right after Roosevelt took office. The key idea behind the NRA was to reduce competition and fix prices and wages for everyone's benefit. This goal required government, business, and labor to hammer out detailed regulations for each industry. Along with this kind of national planning in the private sector of the economy, the government believed it could sponsor enough public works projects to assure recovery. Because the NRA broke with the cherished American tradition of free competition and aroused conflicts among businessmen, consumers, and bureaucrats, it did not work well. By the time the NRA was declared unconstitutional in 1935, Roosevelt and the New Deal were already moving away from government efforts to plan and control the entire economy.

Instead, Roosevelt and his advisers attacked the key problem of mass unemployment directly. The federal government accepted the responsibility of employing directly as many people as financially possible, something Hoover had consistently rejected. Thus, when it became clear in late 1933 that the initial program of public works was too small, new agencies were created to undertake a vast range of projects.

The most famous of these was the Works Progress Administration (WPA), set up in 1935. At its peak in late 1938, this government agency employed more than 3 million individuals. One-fifth of the entire labor force worked for the WPA at some point in the 1930s. To this day thousands of public buildings, bridges, and highways built by the WPA stand as monuments to energetic government efforts to provide people with meaningful work. The WPA was enormously popular in a nation long schooled in self-reliance and the work ethic. The hope of a job with the government helped check the threat of social revolution in the United States.

Other social measures aimed in the same direction. Following the path blazed by Germany's Bismarck in the 1880s, the U.S. government in 1935 established a national social security system, with old-age pensions and unemployment benefits, to protect many workers against some of life's uncertainties. The National Labor Relations Act of 1935 gave union organizers the green light by declaring collective bargaining to be the policy of the United States. Following some bitter strikes, such as the sit-down strike at General Motors in early 1937, union membership more than doubled, from 4 million in 1935 to 9 million in 1940. In general, between 1935 and 1938 government rulings and social reforms chipped away at the privileges of the wealthy and tried to help ordinary people.

SAN FRANCISCO, 1934 Standing on the corner, waiting for something to do: this classic photograph by Dorothea Lange captures the frustration and waste of unemployment in the Depression years. (Dorothea Lange, The Oakland Museum)

Yet in spite of its undeniable accomplishments in social reform, the New Deal was only partly successful as a response to the Great Depression. At the height of the recovery, in May 1937, 7 million workers were still unemployed. The economic situation then worsened seriously in the recession of 1937 and 1938. Production fell sharply, and although unemployment never again reached the 15 million mark of 1933, it hit 11 million in 1938 and was still a staggering 10 million when war broke out in Europe in September 1939.

The New Deal never did pull the United

States out of the depression. This failure frustrated Americans then, and it is still puzzling today. Perhaps, as some have claimed, Roosevelt should have used his enormous popularity and prestige in 1933 to nationalize the banks, the railroads, and some heavy industry, so that national economic planning could have been successful. On the other hand, Roosevelt's sharp attack on big business and the wealthy after 1935 had popular appeal but also damaged business confidence and made the great capitalists uncooperative. Given the low level of profit and the underutilization of many factories, however, it is questionable whether business would have behaved much differently even if the New Deal had catered to it.

Finally, it is often argued that the New Deal did not put enough money into the economy through deficit financing. Like his predecessors in the White House, Roosevelt was attached to the ideal of the balanced budget. His largest deficit was only $4.4 billion in 1936. Compare this figure with deficits of $21.5 billion in 1942 and $57.4 billion in 1943, when the nation was prosperously engaged in total war and unemployment had vanished. By 1945, many economists concluded that the New Deal's deficit-financed public works had been too small a step in the right direction. These Keynesian views were to be very influential in postwar economic policy in Europe and America.

THE SCANDINAVIAN RESPONSE TO DEPRESSION

Of all the Western democracies, the Scandinavian countries under Socialist leadership responded most successfully to the challenge of the Great Depression. Having grown steadily in the late nineteenth century, Socialists became the largest political party in Sweden and then in Norway after the First World War. In the 1920s they passed important social reform legislation for both peasants and workers, gained practical administrative experience, and developed a unique kind of socialism. Flexible and nonrevolutionary, Scandinavian socialism grew out of a strong tradition of cooperative community action. Even before 1900, Scandinavian agricultural cooperatives had shown how individual peasant families could join together for everyone's benefit. Labor leaders and capitalists were also inclined to work together.

When the economic crisis struck in 1929, Socialist governments in Scandinavia built on this pattern of cooperative social action. Sweden in particular pioneered in the use of large-scale deficits to finance public works and thereby maintain production and employment. Scandinavian governments also increased social welfare benefits, from old-age pensions and unemployment insurance to subsidized housing and maternity allowances. All this spending required a large bureaucracy and high taxes, first on the rich and then on practically everyone. Yet both private and cooperative enterprise thrived, as did democracy. Some observers saw Scandinavia's welfare socialism as an appealing "middle way" between sick capitalism and cruel communism or fascism.

RECOVERY AND REFORM IN BRITAIN AND FRANCE

In Britain, MacDonald's Labour government and then, after 1931, the Conservative-dominated coalition government followed orthodox economic theory. The budget was balanced, but unemployed workers received barely enough welfare to live. In spite of government lethargy, the economy recovered considerably after 1932. By 1937, total production was about 20 percent higher than in 1929. In fact, for Britain the years after 1932 were actually somewhat better than the 1920s had been, quite the opposite of the situation in the United States and France.

This good but by no means brilliant performance reflected the gradual reorientation of the British economy. After going off the gold standard in 1931 and establishing protective tariffs in 1932, Britain concentrated increasingly on the national rather than the international market. The old export industries of the Industrial Revolution, such as textiles and coal, continued to decline, but the new industries like automobiles and electrical appliances grew in response to British home demand. Moreover, low interest rates encouraged a housing boom. By the end of the decade there were highly visible differences between the old, depressed industrial areas of the north and the new, growing areas of the south. These developments encouraged Britain to look inward and avoid unpleasant foreign questions.

Because France was relatively less industrialized and more isolated from the world economy, the Great Depression came late. But once the depression hit France, it stayed and stayed. Decline was steady until 1935, and the short-lived recovery never brought production or employment back up to predepression levels. Economic stagnation both reflected and heightened an ongoing political crisis. There was no stability in government. As before 1914, the French parliament was made up of many political parties, which could never cooperate for very long. In 1933, for example, five coalition cabinets formed and fell in rapid succession.

The French lost the underlying unity that had made governmental instability bearable before 1914. Fascist-type organizations agitated against parliamentary democracy and looked to Mussolini's Italy and Hitler's Germany for inspiration. In February 1934, French fascists and semifascists rioted and threatened to overturn the republic. At the same time the Communist party and many workers opposed to the existing system were looking to Stalin's Russia for guidance. The vital center of moderate republicanism was sapped from both sides.

Frightened by the growing strength of the fascists at home and abroad, the Communists, the Socialists, and the Radicals formed an alliance – the Popular Front – for the national elections of May 1936. Their clear victory reflected the trend toward extremism. The number of Communists in the parliament jumped dramatically from 10 to 72, while the Socialists, led by Léon Blum, became the strongest party in France with 146 seats. The really quite moderate Radicals slipped badly, and the conservatives lost ground to the semifascists.

In the next few months Blum's Popular Front government made the first and only real attempt to deal with the social and economic problems of the 1930s in France. Inspired by Roosevelt's New Deal, the Popular Front encouraged the union movement and launched a far-reaching program of social reform, complete with paid vacations and a forty-hour workweek. Popular with workers and the lower middle class, these measures were quickly sabotaged by rapid inflation and cries of revolution from fascists and frightened conservatives. Wealthy people sneaked their money out of the country, labor unrest grew, and France entered a severe financial crisis. Blum was forced to announce a "breathing spell" in social reform.

The fires of political dissension were also fanned by civil war in Spain. The Communists demanded that France support the Spanish republicans, while many French conservatives would gladly have joined Hitler and Mussolini in aiding the attack of Spanish fascists. Extremism grew, and France itself was within sight of civil war. Blum was forced to resign in June 1937, and the Popular Front quickly collapsed. An anxious and divided France drifted aimlessly once again, preoccupied by Hitler and German rearmament.

After the First World War, Western society entered a complex and difficult era – truly an age of anxiety. Intellectual life underwent a crisis marked by pessimism, uncertainty, and fascination with irrational forces. Rejection of old forms and ceaseless experimentation characterized art and music, while motion pictures and radio provided a new, standardized entertainment for the masses. Intellectual and artistic developments that had been confined to small avant-garde groups before 1914 gained wider currency along with the insecure state of mind they expressed.

Politics and economics were similarly disrupted. In the 1920s, statesmen groped to create an enduring peace and rebuild the prewar prosperity, and for a brief period late in the decade they even seemed to have succeeded. Then the Great Depression shattered the fragile stability. Uncertainty returned with redoubled force in the 1930s. The international economy collapsed, and unemployment struck millions. The democracies turned inward as they sought to cope with massive domestic problems and widespread disillusionment. Generally speaking, they were not very successful. The old liberal ideals of individual rights and responsibilities, elected government, and economic freedom seemed ineffective and outmoded to many, even when they managed to survive. And in many countries they were abandoned completely.

NOTES

1. P. Valéry, *Variety,* trans. Malcolm Cowley, Harcourt, Brace, New York, 1927, pp. 27–28.

2. G. Marcel, as quoted by S. Hughes, *The Obstructed Path: French Social Thought in the Years of Desperation, 1930–1960,* Harper & Row, New York, 1967, p. 82.

3. G. Greene, *Another Mexico,* Viking Press, New York, 1939, p. 3.

4. G. Orwell, *1984,* New American Library, New York, p. 220.

5. C. E. Jeanneret-Gris (Le Corbusier), *Towards a New Architecture,* J. Rodker, London, 1931, p. 15.

6. Quoted by A. H. Barr, Jr., *What Is Modern Painting?,* 9th ed., Museum of Modern Art, New York, 1966, p. 27.

7. Ibid., p. 25.

8. R. Graves and A. Hodge, *The Long Week End: A Social History of Great Britain, 1918–1939,* Macmillan, New York, 1941, p. 131.

9. Quoted by A. Briggs, *The Birth of Broadcasting,* Oxford University Press, London, 1961, 1.47.

10. Quoted by R. Butler in C. L. Mowat, ed., *The New Cambridge Modern History,* 2nd ed., Cambridge University Press, Cambridge, England, 1968, 12.229.

11. Quoted by R. J. Sontag, *A Broken World, 1919–1939,* Harper & Row, New York, 1971, p. 129.

12. C. P. Kindleberger, *The World in Depression, 1929–1939,* University of California Press, Berkeley, 1973, p. 292.

13. Quoted by S. B. Clough et al., eds., *Economic History of Europe: Twentieth Century,* Harper & Row, New York, 1968, pp. 243–245.

14. Quoted by D. Dillard, *Economic Development of the North Atlantic Community,* Prentice-Hall, Englewood Cliffs, N.J., 1967, p. 591.

SUGGESTED READING

Among general works, R. Sontag's *A Broken World, 1919–1939* (1971), and E. Wiskeman, *Europe of the Dictators, 1919–1945* (1966), are particularly recommended. The former has an excellent bibliography. A. Bullock, ed., *The Twentieth Century* (1971), is a lavish visual feast combined with penetrating essays on major developments since 1900. Crucial changes in thought before and after World War One are discussed in three rewarding intellectual histories: G. Masur, *Prophets of Yesterday* (1961); H. S. Hughes, *Consciousness and Society* (1956); and M. Biddiss, *Age of the Masses: Ideas and Society Since 1870* (1977). J. Rewald, *The History of Impressionism,* rev. ed. (1961) and *Post-Impressionism* (1956), are excellent, as are the works of A. H. Barr, Jr., cited in the Notes. P. Collaer, *A History of Modern Music* (1961), and H. R. Hitchcock, *Architecture: 19th and 20th Centuries* (1958), are good introductions, while T. Wolfe, *From Bauhaus to My House* (1981), is a lively critique of modern architecture. L. Barnett, *The Universe and Dr. Einstein* (1952), is a fascinating study of the new physics. P. Rieff, *Freud* (1956), and M. White, ed., *The Age of Analysis* (1955), open up basic questions of twentieth-century psychology and philosophy. P. Gay, *Weimar Culture* (1970), is a brilliant exploration of the many-sided artistic renaissance in Germany in the 1920s. M. Marrus, ed., *Emergence of Leisure* (1974), is a pioneering inquiry into an important aspect of mass culture. H. Daniels-Rops, *A Fight for God,* 2 vols. (1966), is a sympathetic history of the Catholic church between 1870 and 1939.

C. Maier, *Recasting Bourgeois Europe* (1975), is an ambitious comparative study of social classes and conflicts in France, Germany, and Italy after World War One. R. Wohl, *The Generation of 1914* (1979); R. Kuisel, *Capital and State in Modern France: Renovation and Economic Management* (1982); and W. McDougall, *France's Rhineland Diplomacy, 1914–1924* (1978), are three more important studies on aspects of the postwar challenge. M. Childs, *Sweden: The Middle Way* (1961), applauds Sweden's efforts at social reform. W. Neuman, *The Balance of Power in the Interwar Years, 1919–1939* (1968), perceptively examines international politics after the Locarno treaties of 1925. In addition to the contemporary works discussed in the text, the crisis of the interwar period comes alive in R. Crossman, ed., *The God That Failed* (1950), in which famous Western writers tell why they were attracted to and later repelled by communism; Ortega y Gassett's renowned *The Revolt of the Masses* (1932); and F. A. Hayek's *The Road to Serfdom* (1944), a famous warning of the dangers to democratic freedoms. In addition to C. Kindleberger's excellent study of the Great Depression cited in the Notes, there is J. Galbraith's very lively and understandable account of the stock-market collapse, *The Great Crash* (1955). Novels best portray the human tragedy of economic decline. W. Holtby, *South Riding,* and W. Greenwood, *Love on the Dole* (1933), are moving stories of the Great Depression in England; H. Fallada, *Little Man, What Now?* (1932), is the classic counterpart for Germany. Also highly recommended as commentaries on English life between the wars are R. Graves, *Goodbye to All That,* rev. ed. (1957), and G. Orwell, *The Road to Wigan Pier* (1972). Among French novelists André Gide painstakingly examines the French middle class and its values in *The Counterfeiters,* while Albert Camus, the greatest of the existential novelists, is at his unforgettable best in *The Stranger* and *The Plague.*

Chapter 36

Dictatorships and the Second World War

THE ERA OF ANXIETY and economic depression was also a time of growing strength for political dictatorship. Popularly elected governments and basic civil liberties declined drastically in Europe. On the eve of the Second World War, liberal democratic government survived only in Great Britain, France, the Low Countries, the Scandinavian nations, and neutral Switzerland. Elsewhere in Europe, various kinds of "strong men" ruled. Dictatorship seemed the wave of the future. Thus, the decline in liberal political institutions and the intellectual crisis were related elements in the general crisis of European civilization.

The era of dictatorship is a highly disturbing chapter in the history of Western civilization. The key development was not simply the resurgence of dictatorship but the rise of a new kind of tyranny – the modern totalitarian state. Modern totalitarianism reached its fullest realization in Communist Russia and Nazi Germany in the 1930s. Stalin and Hitler mobilized their peoples for enormous undertakings and ruled with unprecedented severity.

Today we want to believe that the era of totalitarian dictatorship was a terrible accident, that Stalin's slave labor camps and Hitler's gas chambers "can't happen again." But one cannot be sure: it was all very recent and very powerful. What was the nature of the twentieth-century totalitarian state? How did totalitarianism affect ordinary people, and why did it lead to another world war? These are the questions this chapter seeks to answer.

AUTHORITARIAN AND TOTALITARIAN STATES

The modern totalitarian state differed from the old-fashioned authoritarian state. Completely rejecting liberal values and drawing on the experience of total war, the totalitarian state exercised much greater control over the masses, and mobilized them for constant action. The nature of this control may be examined by comparing the old and new forms of dictatorship in a general way, before entering the strange world of Stalin's Russia and Hitler's Germany.

CONSERVATIVE AUTHORITARIANISM

The traditional form of antidemocratic government in European history has been conservative authoritarianism. Like Catherine the Great in Russia and Metternich in Austria, the leaders of such governments have tried to prevent major changes and preserve the existing social order. To do so, they have relied on obedient bureaucracies, vigilant police departments, and trustworthy armies. Popular participation in government has been forbidden or else severely limited to such natural allies as landlords, bureaucrats, and high church officials. Liberals, democrats and socialists have been persecuted as radicals and have often found themselves in jail or exile.

Yet old-fashioned authoritarian governments were limited in their power and in their objectives. Lacking modern technology and communications, they lacked the power to control many aspects of their subjects' lives. Nor did they wish to do so. Preoccupied with the goal of mere survival, these government's demands were largely limited to taxes, army recruits, and passive acceptance. As long as the people did not try to change the system, they often had considerable personal independence.

After the First World War this kind of authoritarian government revived, especially in the less-developed eastern part of Europe. There, the parliamentary regimes that had been founded on the wreckage of empires in 1918 fell one by one. By early 1938 only economically and socially advanced Czechoslovakia remained true to liberal political ideals. Conservative dictators also took over in Spain and Portugal.

There were several reasons for this development. These lands lacked a strong tradition of self-government, with its necessary restraint and compromise. Moreover, many of these new states were torn by ethnic conflicts that threatened their very existence. Dictatorship appealed to nationalists and military leaders as a way to repress such tensions and preserve national unity. Large landowners and the church were still powerful forces in these largely agrarian areas, and they often looked to dictators to save them from progressive land reform or communist agrarian upheaval. So did some members of the middle class, which was small and weak in eastern Europe. Finally, though some kind of democracy managed to stagger through the 1920s in Austria, Bulgaria, Rumania, Greece, Estonia, and Latvia, the Great Depression delivered the final blow in ·those countries by 1936.

Although some of the authoritarian regimes adopted certain Hitlerian and fascist characteristics in the 1930s, their general aims were not totalitarian. They were concerned more with maintaining the status quo than with forcing society into rapid change or war. This tradition lives on today, especially in some of the military dictatorships of Latin America.

Hungary was a good example of conservative authoritarianism. In the chaos of collapse in 1919, Béla Kun formed a Lenin-like government, but communism in Hungary was soon crushed by foreign troops, large landowners, and hostile peasants. Thereafter, a combination of great and medium-sized landowners instituted a semi-authoritarian regime, which maintained the status quo in the 1920s. Hungary had a parliament, but elections were carefully controlled. The peasants did not have the right to vote, and an upper house representing the landed aristocracy was reestablished. There was no land reform, no major social change. In the 1930s, the Hungarian government remained conservative and nationalistic. Increasingly, it was opposed by a Nazi-like fascist movement, the Arrow Cross, which demanded radical reform and totalitarian measures.

Another example of conservative authoritarianism was newly independent Poland, where democratic government was overturned in 1926 when General Joseph Pilsudski established a military dictatorship. Poland was torn by bitter party politics and sandwiched between Russia and Germany. Pilsudski silenced opposition and tried to build a strong state. His principal supporters were the army, big industrialists, and dedicated nationalists.

In Yugoslavia, King Alexander (1921–1934) proclaimed a centralized dictatorship in 1929 to prevent ethnic rivalries among Serbs, Croats, and Slovenes from tearing the country apart. An old-style authoritarian, Alexander crushed democracy, jailed separatists, and ruled through the bureaucracy.

Another example of conservative authoritarianism was Portugal, at the westernmost end of the European peninsula. Constantly shaken by military coups and uprisings after a republican revolution in 1910, very poor and backward Portugal finally got a strong dictator in Antonio de Oliveira Salazar in 1932. A devout Catholic, Salazar gave the church the strongest possible position in the country, while controlling the press and outlawing most political activity. Yet there was no attempt to mobilize the masses or to accomplish great projects. The traditional society was firmly maintained, and that was enough.

MODERN TOTALITARIANISM

Although both are dictatorships, modern totalitarianism and conservative authoritarianism differ. They may be thought of as two distinct types of political organization that in practice sometimes share certain elements.

Modern totalitarianism burst on the scene with the revolutionary total war effort of 1914–1918. The war called forth a tendency to subordinate all institutions and all classes to one supreme objective: victory. Nothing, absolutely nothing, had equal value. People were called to make ever greater sacrifices, and their personal freedom was constantly reduced by ever greater government control. As the outstanding French thinker Elie Halévy put it in 1936, the varieties of modern totalitarian tyranny – fascism, Nazism, and communism – may be thought of as "feuding brothers" with a common father, the nature of modern war.[1]

The crucial experience of World War One was carried further by Lenin and the Bolsheviks during the Russian civil war. Lenin showed how a dedicated minority could make a total effort and achieve victory over a less-determined majority. Lenin also demonstrated how institutions and human rights might be subordinated to the needs of a single group – the Communist party – and its leader, Lenin. Thus, Lenin provided a model for single-party dictatorship, and he inspired imitators.

Building on its immediate origins in World War One and the Russian civil war, modern totalitarianism reached maturity in the 1930s in Stalinist Russia and Nazi Germany. Both had several fundamental characteristics of modern totalitarianism.

Armed with modern technology and communications, the true totalitarian state began as a dictatorship exercising complete political power, but it did not stop there. Increasingly, the state took over and tried to control just as completely the economic, social, intellectual, and cultural aspects of life. Although such unlimited control could not be fully realized, the individual's freedom of action was greatly reduced. Deviation from the norm even in art or family behavior could become a crime. In theory, nothing was politically neutral, nothing was outside the scope of the state.

This grandiose vision of total state control broke decisively not only with conservative authoritarianism but also with nineteenth-century liberalism and democracy. Indeed, totalitarianism was a radical revolt against liberalism. Liberalism sought to limit the power of the state and protect the sacred rights of the individual. Moreover, liberals stood for rationality, harmony, peaceful progress, and a strong middle class. All of that disgusted totalitarians as sentimental slop. They believed in will power, preached conflict, and worshiped violence. They believed that the individual was infinitely less valuable than the state and that there were no lasting rights, only temporary rewards for loyal and effective service. Only a single powerful leader and a single party, both unrestrained by law or tradition, determined the destiny of the totalitarian state.

Unlike old-fashioned authoritarianism, modern totalitarianism was based not on elites but on the masses. As in the First World War, the totalitarian state sought and sometimes won the support and even the love of ordinary people. Modern totalitarianism built on politically alert masses, on people who had already become engaged in the political process, most notably through commitment to nationalism and socialism. Its character as a mass movement gave totalitarianism much of its elemental force.

The final shared characteristic of real totalitarian states was their boundless dynamism.

NAZI MASS RALLY, 1936 *This picture captures the spirit of modern totalitarianism. The uniformed members of the Nazi party have willingly merged themselves into a single force and await the command of the godlike leader. (Wide World Photos)*

The totalitarian society was a fully mobilized society, a society moving toward some goal. It was never content merely to survive, like an old-fashioned military dictatorship or a decaying democracy. Paradoxically, totalitarian regimes never reached their goals. Or, more precisely, as soon as one goal was achieved at the cost of enormous sacrifice, another arose at the leader's command to take its place. Thus, totalitarianism was in the end a *permanent* revolution, an *unfinished* revolution, in which rapid, profound change imposed from on high went on forever.

TOTALITARIANISM OF THE LEFT AND THE RIGHT

The two most-developed totalitarian states — Stalin's Communist Russia and Hitler's Nazi Germany — shared all the central characteristics of totalitarianism. But although those regimes may seem more alike than not, there were at least two major differences between them.

Communism as practiced in Soviet Russia grew out of Marxian socialism. Nazism in Germany grew out of extreme nationalism

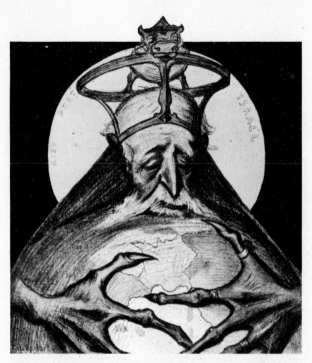

bilities for regeneration. Socialism, with its concern for social justice and human progress, is linked to the living core of Western civilization and the Judeo-Christian tradition. Stalin's communism was an ugly perversion of socialism, but even in its darkest moments it had the potential for reforming itself and creating a more humane society. Nazism, however, had no such potential. Based on the claptrap phobias of anticapitalism, anti-Semitism, and racism, its elements could be found in many a European city before the First World War. Totally negative and devoid of even perverted truth, it promised only destruction and never rebirth.

VICIOUS ANTI-SEMITISM was visible in all European countries before World War One. This 1898 French cartoon shows the Jewish banker Rothschild worshipping gold and exploiting the whole world. Jews were also denounced as revolutionary socialists intent upon destroying private property and the middle class. (Historical Pictures Service, Chicago)

STALIN'S RUSSIA

and racism. This distinction meant that private property and the middle class received very different treatment in the two states. In Soviet Russia the socialist program of the radical left was realized: all large holdings of private property were taken over by the state, and the middle class lost its wealth and status. In Germany big landowners and industrialists on the conservative right were attacked but managed to maintain their private wealth. This difference in property and class relations has led some scholars to speak of "totalitarianism of the left" – Stalinist Russia – and "totalitarianism of the right" – Nazi Germany.

More important were the differing possi-

Lenin established the basic outlines of a modern totalitarian dictatorship in Russia after the Bolshevik Revolution and during the civil war. Joseph Stalin (1879–1953) finished the job. A master of political infighting, Stalin cautiously consolidated his power and eliminated his enemies in the mid-1920s. Then in 1928, as undisputed leader of the ruling Communist party, he launched the first five-year plan – "the revolution from above," as he so aptly termed it.

The five-year plans were extremely ambitious. Often incorrectly considered a mere set of economic measures to speed up Soviet Russia's industrial development, the five-year plans actually marked the beginning of a renewed attempt to mobilize and transform Soviet society along socialist lines. The goal was to create a new way of life and to generate new attitudes and new loyalties. The means Stalin and the small Communist party elite chose were constant propaganda, enormous sacrifice, and unlimited violence and state control. Thus, the Soviet Union in the 1930s became a dynamic, modern totalitarian state.

FROM LENIN TO STALIN

By spring 1921, Lenin and the Bolsheviks had won the civil war, but they ruled a shattered and devastated land. Many farms were in ruins, and food supplies were exhausted. In southern Russia drought combined with the ravages of war to produce the worst famine in generations. By 1920, according to the government, from 50 to 90 percent of the population in seventeen provinces was starving. Industrial production also broke down completely. In 1921, for example, output of steel and cotton textiles was only about 4 percent of what it had been in 1913. The revolutionary Trotsky later wrote that "the collapse of the productive forces surpassed anything of the kind history had ever seen. The country, and the government with it, were at the very edge of the abyss."[2] The Bolsheviks had destroyed the economy as well as their foes.

In the face of economic disintegration and rioting by peasants and workers, the tough but ever-flexible Lenin changed course. In March 1921, he announced the New Economic Policy, or NEP, which re-established limited economic freedom in an attempt to rebuild agriculture and industry. During the civil war, the Communists had simply seized grain without payment. Lenin in 1921 substituted a grain tax on the country's peasant producers, who were permitted to sell their surpluses in free markets. Peasants were also encouraged to buy as many goods as they could afford from private traders and small handicraft manufacturers, both of whom were allowed to reappear. Heavy industry, railroads, and banks, however, remained wholly nationalized. Thus, NEP saw only a limited restoration of capitalism.

Lenin's New Economic Policy was shrewd and successful, from two points of view. Politically, it was a necessary but temporary compromise with Russia's overwhelming peasant majority. Flushed with victory after their revolutionary gains of 1917, the peasants would have fought to hold onto their land. With fond hopes of immediate worldwide revolution fading by 1921, Lenin realized that his government was not strong enough to take it from them. As he had accepted Germany's harsh terms at Brest-Litovsk in 1918, Lenin made a deal with the only force capable of overturning his government.

Economically, NEP brought rapid recovery. In 1926, industrial output had surpassed the level of 1913, and Russian peasants were producing almost as much grain as before the war. Counting shorter hours and increased social benefits, workers were living somewhat better than they had in the past.

As the economy recovered and the government somewhat relaxed its censorship and repression, an intense struggle for power began in the inner circles of the Communist party, for Lenin had left no chosen successor when he died in 1924. The principal contenders were the stolid Stalin and the flamboyant Trotsky.

The son of a shoemaker, Joseph Dzhugashvili – later known as Stalin – studied for the priesthood but was expelled from his theological seminary, probably for his rude rebelliousness. By 1903 he had joined the Bolsheviks. In the years before the First World War he engaged in many revolutionary activities in the Transcaucasian area of southern Russia, including a daring bank robbery to get money for the Bolsheviks. This raid gained Lenin's attention and approval. Ethnically a Georgian and not a Russian, Stalin in his early writings focused on the oppression of minority peoples in the Russian Empire.

Stalin was a good organizer but a poor speaker and writer, with no experience outside of Russia.

Leon Trotsky, a great and inspiring leader who had planned the 1917 takeover (pages 1237–1238 and then created the victorious Red Army, appeared to have all the advantages. Yet it was Stalin who succeeded Lenin. Stalin won because he was more effective at gaining the all-important support of the party, the only genuine source of power in the one-party state. Rising to general secretary of the party's Central Committee just before Lenin's first stroke in 1922, Stalin used his office to win friends and allies with jobs and promises. Stalin also won recognition as commissar of nationalities, a position that gave him the important task of governing many of Russia's minorities.

The "practical" Stalin also won because he appeared better able than the brilliant Trotsky to relate Marxist teaching to Russian realities in the 1920s. First, as commissar of nationalities, he built on Lenin's idea of granting minority groups a certain degree of freedom in culture and language while maintaining rigorous political control through carefully selected local Communists. Stalin could loudly claim, therefore, to have found a way to solve the ancient problem of ethnic demands for independence in the multinational state. And of course he did.

Second, Stalin developed a theory of "socialism in one country," which was more appealing to the majority of Communists than Trotsky's doctrine of "permanent revolution." Stalin argued that Russia had the ability to build socialism on its own. Trotsky maintained that socialism in Russia could succeed only if revolution occurred quickly throughout Europe. To many communists, Trotsky's views seemed to sell Russia short and to promise risky conflicts with capitalist countries by recklessly encouraging revolutionary movements around the world. Stalin's willingness to break with NEP and push socialism at home appealed to young militants. In short, Stalin's theory of "socialism in one country" provided many in the party with a glimmer of hope in the midst of the capitalist-appearing NEP, which they had come to detest.

With cunning skill Stalin gradually achieved absolute power between 1922 and 1927. First, he allied with Trotsky's personal enemies to crush Trotsky, who was expelled from the Soviet Union in 1929 and eventually murdered in Mexico in 1940, undoubtedly on Stalin's order. Stalin then aligned with the moderates, who wanted to go slow at home, to suppress Trotsky's radical followers. Finally, having defeated all the radicals, he turned against his allies, the moderates, and destroyed them as well. Stalin's final triumph came at the Party Congress of December 1927, which condemned all "deviation from the general party line" formulated by Stalin. The dictator was then ready to launch his "revolution from above" — the real Russian revolution for millions of ordinary citizens.

THE FIVE-YEAR PLANS

The Party Congress of 1927, which ratified Stalin's seizure of power, marked the end of the New Economic Policy and the beginning of the era of socialist five-year plans. The first five-year plan had staggering economic objectives. In just five years, total industrial output was to increase by 250 percent. Heavy industry, the preferred sector, was to grow even faster; steel production, for example, was to jump almost 300 percent. Agricultural production was slated to increase by 150 percent, and one-fifth of Russia's peasants were scheduled to give up their private plots and join

СО ЗНАМЕНЕМ ЛЕНИНА ПОБЕДИЛИ МЫ В БОЯХ ЗА ОКТЯБРЬСКУЮ РЕВОЛЮЦИЮ.
СО ЗНАМЕНЕМ ЛЕНИНА ДОБИЛИСЬ МЫ РЕШАЮЩИХ УСПЕХОВ В БОРЬБЕ ЗА ПОБЕДУ СОЦИАЛИСТИЧЕСКОГО СТРОИТЕЛЬСТВА.
С ЭТИМ ЖЕ ЗНАМЕНЕМ ПОБЕДИМ В ПРОЛЕТАРСКОЙ РЕВОЛЮЦИИ ВО ВСЕМ МИРЕ.
(Сталин. Политический отчет ЦК XVI съезду ВКП(б).)

"THE 5-YEAR PLAN IN 4 YEARS"   This typical 1930 poster shows the fatherly Stalin leading the superhuman industrialization effort against his evil foreign foes. Lukewarm supporters at home were branded as the treasonous agents of those Catholics, capitalists, social democrats, Mensheviks, Fascists, and the like, pictured on the left. (John R. Freeman)

socialist collective farms. In spite of warnings from moderate Communists that these goals were unrealistic, Stalin raised them higher as the plan got under way. By 1930, a whirlwind of economic and social change was sweeping across the country.

Stalin unleashed his "second revolution" for a variety of interrelated reasons. There were, first of all, ideological considerations. Like Lenin, Stalin and his militant supporters were deeply committed to socialism as they understood it. Since the country had recovered economically and their rule was secure, they burned to stamp out NEP's private traders, independent artisans, and few well-to-do peasants. Purely economic motivations

were also important. Although the economy had recovered, it seemed to have stalled in 1927 and 1928. A new socialist offensive seemed necessary if industry and agriculture were to grow rapidly.

Political considerations were most important. Internationally, there was the old problem remaining from prerevolutionary times of catching up with the advanced and presumably hostile capitalistic nations of the West. As Stalin said in 1931, when he pressed for ever greater speed and sacrifice: "We are fifty or a hundred years behind the advanced countries. We must make good this distance in ten years. Either we do it, or we shall go under."[3]

Domestically, there was what Communist

writers in the 1920s called the "cursed problem" – the problem of the Russian peasants. For centuries Russian peasants had wanted to own the land, and finally they had it. Sooner or later, the Communists reasoned, the peasants would become conservative little capitalists and pose a threat to the regime. Therefore, Stalin decided on a preventive war against the peasantry, in order to bring it under the absolute control of the state.

That war was collectivization – the forcible consolidation of individual peasant farms into large, state-controlled enterprises. Beginning in 1929, peasants all over the Soviet Union were ordered to give up their land and animals and to become members of collective farms, although they continued to live in their own homes. As for the kulaks, the better-off peasants, Stalin instructed party workers to "liquidate them as a class." Stripped of their land and livestock, the kulaks were generally not even permitted to join the collective farms. Many either starved or were deported to forced-labor camps for "re-education."

Since almost all peasants were in fact poor, the term *kulak* soon meant any peasant who opposed the new system. Whole villages were often attacked. One conscience-stricken colonel in the secret police confessed to a foreign journalist: "I am an old Bolshevik. I worked in the underground against the Tsar and then I fought in the Civil War. Did I do all that in order that I should now surround villages with machine-guns and order my men to fire indiscriminately into crowds of peasants? Oh, no, no!"[4]

Forced collectivization of the peasants led to economic and human disaster. Large numbers of peasants slaughtered their animals and burned their crops in sullen, hopeless protest. Between 1929 and 1933, the number of horses, cattle, sheep, and goats in the Soviet Union fell by at least one-half. Nor were the state-controlled collective farms more productive. The output of grain barely increased between 1928 and 1938, when it was almost identical to that of 1913. Communist economists had expected collectivized agriculture to pay for new factories. Instead, the state had to invest heavily in agriculture, building thousands of tractors to replace the slaughtered draft horses. Collectivized agriculture was unable to make any substantial financial contribution to Soviet industrial development in the first five-year plan. The human dimension of the tragedy was shocking. Collectivization created man-made famine in 1932–1933, and many perished. Indeed, Stalin confided to Churchill at Yalta in 1945 that 10 million people had died in the course of collectivization.

Yet collectivization was a political victory of sorts. By the end of 1932, fully 60 percent of Russian peasant families had been herded onto collective farms; by 1938, 93 percent. Regimented and indoctrinated as employees of an all-powerful state, the peasants were no longer even a potential political threat to Stalin and the Communist party. Moreover, the state was assured of grain for bread for urban workers, who were much more important politically than the peasants. Collective farmers had to meet their grain quotas first and worry about feeding themselves second. Many collectivized peasants drew much of their own food from tiny, grudgingly tolerated garden plots that they worked in their off hours. No wonder some peasants joked, with that grim humor peculiar to the totalitarian society, that the initials then used by the Communist party actually stood for "The Second Serfdom, That of the Bolsheviks."

The industrial side of the five-year plans was more successful – indeed, quite spectacular. The output of industry doubled in the first five-year plan and doubled again in the second. Soviet industry produced about four times as much in 1937 as it had in 1928. No other major country had ever achieved such rapid industrial growth. Heavy industry led the way; consumer industry grew quite slowly. Steel production – a near-obsession with Stalin, whose name fittingly meant "man of steel" in Russian – increased roughly 500 percent between 1928 and 1937. A new heavy industrial complex was built almost from scratch in western Siberia. Industrial growth also went hand in hand with urban development. Cities rose where nomadic tribes had grazed their flocks. More than 25 million people migrated to cities and industrial centers during the 1930s.

The great industrialization drive, concentrated between 1928 and 1937, was an awe-inspiring achievement purchased at a cost of enormous sacrifice. The sudden creation of dozens of new factories required a great increase in investment and a sharp decrease in consumption. Few nations had ever invested more than a sixth of their yearly net national income. Soviet planners decreed that more than a third of net income go for investment. This meant that only two-thirds of everything being produced could be consumed by the people *and* the increasingly voracious military. The money was collected from the people by means of heavy, hidden sales taxes.

There was, therefore, no improvement in the average standard of living. Indeed, the most careful studies show that the average nonfarm wage apparently purchased only about *half* as many goods in 1932 as in 1928. After 1932, real wages rose slowly, so that in 1937 workers could buy about 60 percent of what they had bought in 1928. Thus, rapid industrial development went hand in hand with an unprecedented decline in the standard of living for ordinary people.

Two other factors contributed importantly to rapid industrialization: firm labor discipline and foreign engineers. Between 1930 and 1932, trade unions lost most of their power. The government could assign workers to any job anywhere in the country, and individuals could not move without the permission of the police. When factory managers needed more hands, they called on their counterparts on the collective farms, who sent them millions of "unneeded" peasants over the years.

Foreign engineers were hired to plan and construct many of the new factories. Highly skilled American engineers, hungry for work in the depression years, were particularly important until newly trained Soviet experts began to replace them after 1932. The gigantic mills of the new Siberian steel industry were modeled on America's best. Those modern mills were eloquent testimony to the ability of Stalin's planners to harness even the skill and technology of capitalist countries to promote the surge of socialist industry.

LIFE IN STALINIST SOCIETY

The aim of Stalin's five-year plans was to create a new kind of society and human personality, as well as a strong industrial economy and a powerful army. Stalin and his helpers were good Marxian economic determinists. Once everthing was owned by the state, they believed, a socialist society and a new kind of human being would inevitably emerge. They were by no means totally successful, but they did build a new society, whose broad outlines exist to this day. For the people, life in Stalinist society had both good and bad aspects.

The most frightening aspect of Stalinist society was brutal, unrestrained police terrorism. First directed primarily against the peasants after 1929, terror was increasingly turned on leading Communists, powerful adminis-

ADULT EDUCATION   Illiteracy, especially among women, was a serious problem after the Russian Revolution. This early photo shows how adults successfully learned to read and write throughout the Soviet Union. (Sovfoto/Eastfoto)

trators, and ordinary people for no apparent reason. As one Soviet woman later recalled: "We all trembled because there was no way of getting out of it. Even a Communist himself can be caught. To avoid trouble became an exception."⁵ A climate of fear fell upon the land.

In the early 1930s, the top members of the party and government were Stalin's obedient servants, but there was some grumbling in the party. At a small gathering in November 1932 even Stalin's wife complained bitterly about the great misery of the people. Stalin showered her with insults, and she died that same night, apparently by her own hand. In late 1934, Stalin's number-two man, Sergei Kirov, was suddenly and mysteriously mur-

dered. Although Stalin himself probably ordered Kirov's murder, he used the incident to launch a reign of terror.

In August 1936, sixteen prominent old Bolsheviks confessed to all manner of plots against Stalin in spectacular public trials in Moscow. Then, in 1937, lesser party officials and newer henchmen were arrested. In addition to party members, union officials, managers, intellectuals, army officers, and countless ordinary citizens were struck down. Local units of the secret police were even ordered to arrest a certain percentage of the people in their district. In all, at least 8 million people were probably arrested.

Stalin's mass purges were truly baffling, and many explanations have been given for them. Possibly Stalin believed that the old Communists, like the peasants under NEP, were a potential threat to be wiped out in a preventive attack. Yet why did leading Communists willingly confess to crimes they could not possibly have committed? Their lives had been devoted to the party and the socialist revolution. In the words of the German novelist Arthur Koestler, they probably confessed "in order to do a last service to the Party," the party they loved even when it was wrong. Some of them were subjected to torture and psychological brainwashing. It has been argued that the purges indicate that Stalin was sadistic or insane, for his bloodbath greatly weakened the government and the army. Others see the terror as an aspect of the fully developed totalitarian state, which must by its nature always be fighting real or imaginary enemies. At the least, the mass purges were a message to the people. No one was secure. Everyone had to serve the party and its leader with redoubled devotion.

Another aspect of life in the 1930s was constant propaganda and indoctrination. Party activists lectured workers in factories and peasants on the collective farms, while newspapers, films, and radio broadcasts endlessly recounted socialist achievements and capitalist plots. Art and literature became highly political. Whereas the 1920s had seen considerable experimentation in modern art and theater, the intellectual elite were ordered by Stalin to become "engineers of human minds." Writers and artists who could effectively combine genuine creativity and political propaganda became the darlings of the regime. They often lived better than top members of the political elite. It became increasingly important for the successful writer and artist to glorify Russian nationalism. Russian history was rewritten, so that early tsars like Ivan the Terrible and Peter the Great became worthy forerunners of the greatest Russian leader of all – Stalin.

Stalin seldom appeared in public, but his presence was everywhere – in portraits, statues, books, and quotations from his "sacred" writings. Although the government persecuted religion and turned churches into "museums of atheism," the state had both an earthly religion and a high priest – Marxian socialism and Joseph Stalin.

Life was hard in Stalin's Soviet Russia. The standard of living declined substantially in the 1930s. The masses of people lived primarily on black bread and wore old, shabby clothing. There were constant shortages in the stores, although very heavily taxed vodka was always readily available. A shortage of housing was a particularly serious problem. Millions were moving into the cities, but the government built few new apartments. In 1940, there were approximately 4 people per room in every urban dwelling, as opposed to 2.7 per room in 1926. A relatively lucky family received one room for all its members, and shared both a kitchen and a toilet with others on the floor. Less fortunate workers, kulaks, and class enemies built scrap-lumber shacks or underground dugouts in shantytowns.

Life was hard, but by no means hopeless. Idealism and ideology had real appeal for many Russians, who saw themselves heroically building the world's first socialist society while capitalism crumbled in the West. This optimistic belief in the future of Soviet Russia also attracted many disillusioned Western liberals to communism in the 1930s.

On a more practical level, Soviet workers did receive some important social benefits, such as old-age pensions, free medical services, free education, and day-care centers for children. Unemployment was almost unknown. Finally, there was the possibility of personal advancement.

The key to improving one's position was

specialized skills and technical education. Rapid industrialization required massive numbers of trained experts, such as skilled workers, engineers, and plant managers. Thus, the state provided tremendous incentives to those who could serve its needs. It paid the mass of unskilled workers and collective farmers very low wages, but it dangled high salaries and many special privileges before its growing technical and managerial elite. This elite joined with the political and artistic elites in a new upper class, whose members were rich, powerful, and insecure, especially during the purges. Yet the possible gains of moving up outweighed the risks. Millions struggled bravely in universities, institutes, and night schools for the all-important specialized education. One young man summed it up: "In Soviet Russia there is no capital except education. If a person does not want to become a collective farmer or just a cleaning woman, the only means you have to get something is through education."[6]

WOMEN IN SOVIET RUSSIA

Women's lives were radically altered by Stalinist society. Marxists had traditionally believed that both capitalism and the middle-class husband exploited women. The Russian Revolution of 1917 immediately proclaimed complete equality of rights for women. In the 1920s, divorce and abortion were made very easy, and women were urged to work outside the home and liberate themselves sexually. A prominent and influential Bolshevik feminist, Alexandra Kollontai, went so far as to declare that the sexual act had no more significance than "drinking a glass of water." This observation drew a sharp rebuke from the rather prudish Lenin, who said that "no sane man would lie down to drink from a puddle in the gutter or even drink from a dirty glass."[7] After Stalin came to power, sexual and familial liberation was played down, and the most lasting changes for women involved work and education.

The changes were truly revolutionary. Young women were constantly told that they must be fully equal with men, that they could and should do anything men could do. Russian peasant women had long experienced the equality of backbreaking physical labor in the countryside, and they continued to enjoy that equality on collective farms. With the advent of the five-year plans, millions of women also began to toil in factories and on heavy construction, building dams, roads, and steel mills in summer heat and winter frost. Yet most of the opportunities open to men through education were also opened to women. Determined women pursued their studies and entered the ranks of the better-paid specialists in industry and science. Medicine practically became a woman's profession. By 1950, 75 percent of all doctors in Soviet Russia were women.

Thus Stalinist society gave women great opportunities, but demanded great sacrifices as well. The vast majority of women simply *had* to work outside the home. Wages were so low that it was almost impossible for a family or couple to live only on the husband's earnings. Moreover, the full-time workingwoman had a heavy burden of household tasks in her off-hours, for most Soviet men in the 1930s still considered the home and the children the woman's responsibility. Finally, rapid change and economic hardship led to many broken families, creating further physical, emotional, and mental strains for women. In any event, the often-neglected human resource of women was ruthlessly mobilized in Stalinist society. This too was an aspect of Soviet totalitarianism.

MUSSOLINI'S ITALY

Before turning to Hitler's Germany, it is necessary to look briefly at Mussolini's role in Italy. Like all the other emerging dictators, Mussolini hated liberalism, and he destroyed it in Italy. But that was not all. Mussolini and his supporters were the first to call themselves fascists – revolutionaries determined to create a certain kind of totalitarian state. As Mussolini's famous slogan of 1926 put it: "Everything in the state, nothing outside the state, nothing against the state." But Mussolini in power, unlike Stalin and Hitler, did not in fact create a real totalitarian state. His dictatorship was rather an instructive hybrid, a halfway house between conservative authoritarianism and modern totalitarianism.

THE SEIZURE OF POWER

Before the First World War, Italy was a liberal state moving gradually toward democracy. But there were serious problems. Much of the Italian population was still poor, and class differences were extreme. Many peasants were more attached to their villages and local interests than to the national state. Moreover, the papacy and many devout Catholics, as well as the socialists, were strongly opposed to the heirs of Cavour and Garibaldi, middle-class lawyers and politicians who ran the country largely for their own benefit.

The war worsened the political situation. Having fought on the side of the Allies almost exclusively for purposes of territorial expansion, Italian nationalists were bitterly disappointed with Italy's modest gains at Versailles. Workers and peasants also felt cheated: to win their support during the war, the government had promised social and land reform, which it did not deliver after the war.

Encouraged by the Russian Revolution of 1917, radical workers and peasants began occupying factories and seizing land in 1920. These actions scared and radicalized the property-owning classes. The Italian middle classes were already in an ugly mood, having suffered from inflation during the war. Moreover, after the war, the pope lifted his ban on participation by Catholics in Italian politics, and a strong Catholic party quickly emerged. Thus, by 1922 almost all the major groups in Italian society were opposed – though for different reasons – to the liberal parliamentary government.

Into these crosscurrents of unrest and frustration stepped the blustering, bullying Benito Mussolini (1883-1945). Son of a village schoolteacher and a poor blacksmith, Mussolini began his political career as a socialist leader and radical newspaper editor before World War One. In 1914, powerfully influenced by antiliberal cults of violent action, the young Mussolini urged that Italy join the Allies, for which he was expelled from the Italian Socialist party by its antiwar majority. Later Mussolini fought at the front and was wounded. Returning home in 1919, he organized bitter war veterans like himself into a band of "fascists" – from the Italian word for a union of forces.

At first, Mussolini's progam was a radical combination of nationalist and socialist demands, including territorial expansion, benefits for workers, and land reform for peasants. As such, it competed with the better-organized Socialist party and failed to get off the ground. When Mussolini saw that his violent verbal assaults on the rival socialists won him growing support from the frightened middle class, he shifted gears in 1920. In thought and action Mussolini was a striking example of the turbulence of the age of anxiety.

Mussolini and his growing private army of

MUSSOLINI loved to pose and show off. He was sure he had irresistible sex appeal for millions of Italian women. (National Archives, Washington)

convince themselves that they were not just opposing the "reds" but making a real revolution of their own. Many believed that they were not only destroying parliamentary government but forming a strong, dynamic movement that would help the little people against the established interests.

With the government breaking down in 1922, largely because of the chaos created by his direct-action bands, Mussolini stepped forward as the savior of order and property. Striking a conservative note in his speeches and gaining the sympathetic neutrality of army leaders, Mussolini demanded the resignation of the existing government and his own appointment by the king. In October 1922, to force matters, a large group of Fascists marched on Rome to threaten the king and force him to call on Mussolini. The threat worked. Victor Emmanuel III (1900–1946), who had no love for the old liberal politicians, asked Mussolini to form a new cabinet. Thus, after widespread violence and a threat of armed uprising, Mussolini seized power "legally." He was immediately granted dictatorial authority for one year by the king and the parliament.

THE REGIME IN ACTION

Mussolini became dictator on the strength of Italians' rejection of parliamentary government, coupled with fears of Russian-style revolution. Yet what he intended to do with his power was by no means clear until 1924. Some of his dedicated supporters pressed for a "second revolution." Mussolini's ministers, however, included old conservatives, moderates, and even two reform-minded socialists. A new electoral law was passed giving two-thirds of the representatives in the parliament to the party that won the most votes, which allowed the Fascists and their allies to win an

Black Shirts began to grow violent. Typically, a band of Fascist toughs would roar off in trucks at night and swoop down on a few isolated socialist organizers, beating them up and force-feeding them almost deadly doses of castor oil. Few people were killed, but socialist newspapers, union halls, and local socialist party headquarters were destroyed. Mussolini's toughs pushed communists and socialists out of the city governments of northern Italy.

Mussolini, a skillful politician, refused to become a puppet of frightened conservatives and capitalists. He allowed his followers to

overwhelming majority in 1923. Then, in 1924, five of Mussolini's Fascist thugs kidnapped and murdered Giacomo Matteotti, the young leader of the socialists in the parliament. In the face of this outrage, the opposition demanded that Mussolini's armed squads be dissolved and all violence be banned.

Although he may or may not have ordered Matteotti's murder, Mussolini stood at the crossroads in a severe political crisis. After some hesitation, he charged forward. Declaring his desire to "make the nation fascist," he imposed a series of repressive measures. Freedom of the press was abolished, elections were fixed, and the government ruled by decree. Mussolini arrested his political opponents, disbanded all independent labor unions, and put dedicated Fascists in control of Italy's schools. Moreover, he created a Fascist youth movement, Fascist labor unions, and many other Fascist organizations. By the end of 1926, Italy was a one-party dictatorship under Mussolini's unquestioned leadership.

Yet Mussolini did not complete the establishment of a modern totalitarian state. His Fascist party never became all-powerful. It never destroyed the old power structure, as the Communists did in Soviet Russia, or succeeded in dominating it, as the Nazis did in Germany. Membership in the Fascist party was more a sign of an Italian's respectability than a commitment to radical change. Interested primarily in personal power, Mussolini was content to compromise with the old conservative classes that controlled the army, the economy, and the state. He never tried to purge these classes or even move very vigorously against them. He controlled and propagandized labor, but left big business to regulate itself, profitably and securely. There was no land reform.

Mussolini also came to draw on the support of the Catholic church. In the Lateran Agreement of 1929 he recognized the Vatican as a tiny independent state, and he paid the church a large sum of money. The pope expressed his satisfaction and urged Italians to support Mussolini's government.

Nothing better illustrates Mussolini's unwillingness to harness everyone and everything for dynamic action than his treatment of women. He abolished divorce and told women to stay at home and produce children. To promote that goal, he decreed a special tax on bachelors in 1934. In 1938, women were limited by law to a maximum of 10 percent of the better-paying jobs in industry and government. Italian women, as women, appear not to have changed their attitudes or behavior in any important way under Fascist rule.

It is also noteworthy that Mussolini's government did not persecute Jews until late in the Second World War, when Italy was under Nazi control. Nor did Mussolini establish a truly ruthless police state. Only twenty-three political prisoners were condemned to death between 1926 and 1944. In spite of much pompous posing by the chauvinist leader, and in spite of mass meetings, salutes, and a certain copying of Hitler's aggression in foreign policy after 1933, Mussolini's Italy – though undemocratic – was never really totalitarian.

HITLER'S GERMANY

The most frightening and horrible totalitarian state was Nazi Germany. A product of Hitler's evil genius as well as Germany's social and political situation and the general attack on liberalism and rationality in the age of anxiety, Nazi Germany emerged rapidly after Hitler came to power in 1933. The Nazis quickly smashed or took over most independent organizations, mobilized the economy, and began brutally persecuting the Jewish population. From the start, all major decisions were in the hands of the aggressive dictator Adolf Hitler.

THE ROOTS OF NAZISM

Nazism grew out of many complex developments, of which the most influential were extreme nationalism and racism. These two ideas captured the mind of the young Hitler, and it was he who dominated Nazism for as long as it lasted.

Born the fourth child of a successful Austrian customs official and an indulgent mother, Adolf Hitler (1889–1945) spent his childhood happily in small towns in Austria. A good student in grade school, Hitler did poorly on reaching high school, and dropped out at age fourteen after the death of his father. After four years of unfocused loafing, Hitler finally left for Vienna to become an artist. Denied admission to the Imperial Academy of Fine Arts because he lacked talent, the dejected Hitler stayed on in Vienna. There he lived a comfortable, lazy life on his generous orphan's pension and found most of the perverted beliefs that guided his life.

In Vienna Hitler soaked up extreme German nationalism, which was particularly strong there. Austro-German nationalists, as if to compensate for their declining position in the Austro-Hungarian Empire, believed Germans to be a superior people and the natural rulers of central Europe. They often advocated union with Germany and violent expulsion of "inferior" peoples as the means of maintaining German domination of the Austro-Hungarian Empire.

Hitler was deeply impressed by Vienna's mayor Karl Lueger, whom he called "the mightiest mayor of all times." Lueger claimed to be a "Christian socialist." With the help of the Catholic trade unions, he had succeeded in winning the support of the little people of Vienna for an attack on capitalism and liberalism, which he held responsible for un-Christian behavior and excessive individualism. A master of mass politics in the urban world, Lueger showed Hitler the enormous potential of anticapitalist and antiliberal propaganda.

From Lueger and others, Hitler eagerly absorbed virulent anti-Semitism, racism, and hatred of Slavs. He was particularly inspired by the racist ravings of an ex-monk named Lanz von Liebenfels. Preaching the crudest, most exaggerated distortions of the Darwinian theory of survival, Liebenfels stressed the superiority of Germanic races, the inevitability of racial conflict, and the inferiority of the Jews. Liebenfels even anticipated the breeding and extermination policies of the Nazi state: he claimed that the master race had to multiply its numbers by means of polygamy and breeding stations, while it systematically sterilized and liquidated inferior races. Anti-Semitism and racism became Hitler's most passionate convictions, his explanation for everything. He believed inferior races – the Slavs and the Jews in particular – were responsible for Austria's woes. The Jews, he claimed, directed an international conspiracy of finance capitalism and Marxian socialism against German culture, German unity, and the German race. Hitler's belief was totally irrational, but he never doubted it.

Although he moved to Munich in 1913 to avoid being drafted into the Austrian army, the lonely Hitler greeted the outbreak of the First World War as a salvation. He later wrote in his autobiography *Mein Kampf* that, "overcome by passionate enthusiasm, I fell to my knees and thanked heaven out of an overflowing heart." The struggle and discipline of war gave life meaning, and Hitler served bravely as a dispatch carrier on the western front.

When Germany was suddenly defeated in 1918, Hitler's world was shattered. Not only was he a fanatical nationalist, but war was his reason for living. Convinced that the Jews and the Marxists had "stabbed Germany in the back," he vowed to fight on. And in the bitterness and uncertainty of postwar Germany, his wild speeches began to attract attention.

In late 1919, Hitler joined a tiny extremist group in Munich called the German Workers' party. In addition to denouncing Jews, Marxists, and democrats, the German Workers' party promised unity under a uniquely German "national socialism," which would abolish the injustices of capitalism and create a mighty "people's community." By 1921, Hitler had gained absolute control of this small but growing party. Moreover, Hitler was already a master of mass propaganda and political showmanship. Party members sported badges and uniforms, gave victory salutes, and marched like robots through the streets of Munich. But Hitler's most effective tool was the mass rally, a kind of political revival meeting. Songs, slogans, and demonstrations built up the tension until Hitler finally arrived. He then often worked his audience into a frenzy with wild, demagogic attacks on the Versailles treaty, the Jews, the war profiteers, and Germany's Weimar Republic.

Party membership multiplied tenfold after early 1922. In late 1923, when the Weimar Republic seemed on the verge of collapse, Hitler decided on an armed uprising in Munich. Inspired by Mussolini's recent easy victory, Hitler had found an ally in General Ludendorff of First World War fame. After Hitler had overthrown the Bavarian government, Ludendorff was supposed to march on Berlin with Hitler's support. The plot was poorly organized, however, and it was crushed

ADOLF HITLER   *A lonely, unsuccessful misfit before 1914, Hitler found his mission in World War One and its aftermath. He emerged as a spellbinding speaker and a master of the politics of hate and violence. (Bettmann Archive)*

by the police, backed up by the army, in less than a day. Hitler was arrested, tried, and sentenced to five years in prison. He had failed for the moment. But Nazism had been born, and it did not die.

HITLER'S ROAD TO POWER

At his trial Hitler violently denounced the Weimar Republic and skillfully presented his own program. In doing so he gained enormous publicity and attention. Moreover, he learned from his unsuccessful uprising. Hitler concluded that he had to undermine rather than overthrow the government, that he had to use its tolerant democratic framework to come to power *legally*. He forced his more violent supporters to accept his new strategy. Finally, Hitler used his brief prison term — he was released in less than a year — to dictate his autobiography, *Mein Kampf*. There, he expounded on his basic themes — "race," with

"HITLER, OUR LAST HOPE" So reads the very effective Nazi campaign poster, which is attracting attention with its gaunt and haggard faces. By 1932 almost half of all Germans, like these in Berlin, had come to agree. (Bildarchiv Preussischer Kulturbisitz)

the stress on anti-Semitism; "living space," with a sweeping vision of war and conquered territory; and the leader-dictator (the führer) with unlimited, arbitrary power. Hitler's followers had their bible.

In the years of prosperity and relative stability between 1924 and 1929, Hitler concentrated on building his National Socialist German Workers' party, or Nazi party for short. By 1928, the party had a hundred thousand highly disciplined members, and Hitler's absolute control of them was unquestioned. To appeal to the middle class, Hitler

de-emphasized the anticapitalist elements of national socialism.

The Nazis were still a small splinter group in 1928, when they received only 2.6 percent of the vote in the general elections and twelve Nazis won seats in the parliament. There, the Nazi deputies pursued the legal strategy of using democracy to destroy democracy. As Hitler's talented future minister of propaganda Joseph Goebbels (1897–1945) explained in 1928 in the party newspaper: "We become Reichstag deputies in order to paralyze the spirit of Weimar with its own aid. . . .

We come as enemies! As the wolf breaks into the sheepfold, so we come."[8]

In 1929, the Great Depression began striking down economic prosperity, one of the barriers that had kept the wolf at bay. Unemployment jumped from 1.3 million in 1929 to 5 million in 1930; that year Germany had almost as many unemployed as all the other countries of Europe combined. Industrial production fell by one-half between 1929 and 1932. By the end of 1932, an incredible 43 percent of the labor force was unemployed, and it was estimated that only one in every three union members was working full-time. No factor contributed more to Hitler's success than the economic crisis. Never very interested in economics before, Hitler began promising German voters economic as well as political and military salvation.

Hitler focused his promises on the middle and lower middle class – small businessmen, office workers, artisans, and peasants. Already disillusioned by the great inflation of 1923, these people were seized by panic as bankruptcies increased, unemployment soared, and the dreaded Communists made dramatic election gains. The middle and lower middle classes deserted the conservative and moderate parties for the Nazis in great numbers.

The Nazis also appealed strongly to German youth. Indeed, in some ways the Nazi movement was a mass movement of young Germans. Hitler himself was only forty in 1929, and he and most of his top aides were much younger than other leading German politicians. "National Socialism is the organized will of the youth," proclaimed the official Nazi slogan, and the battle cry of Gregor Strasser, a leading Nazi organizer, was, "Make way, you old ones."[9] In 1931, almost 40 percent of Nazi party members were under thirty, compared to 20 percent of Social Democrats. Two-thirds of Nazi members were

under forty. National recovery, exciting and rapid change, and personal advancement: these were the appeals of Nazism to millions of German youths.

In the election of 1930, the Nazis won 6.5 million votes and 107 seats, which made them second in strength only to the Social Democrats, the moderate socialists. The economic situation continued to deteriorate, and Hitler kept promising he would bring recovery. In 1932, the Nazi vote leaped to 14.5 million, and the Nazis became the largest party in the Reichstag.

Another reason Hitler came to power was the breakdown of democratic government as early as May 1930. Unable to gain the support of a majority in the Reichstag, Chancellor (chief minister) Heinrich Brüning convinced the president, the aging war hero General Hindenburg, to authorize rule by decree. The Weimar Republic's constitution permitted such rule in emergency situations, but the rather authoritarian, self-righteous Brüning intended to use it indefinitely. Moreover, Brüning was determined to overcome the economic crisis by cutting back government spending and ruthlessly forcing down prices and wages. Brüning's ultraorthodox policies not only intensified the economic collapse in Germany, they also convinced the lower middle classes that the country's republican leaders were stupid and corrupt. These classes were pleased rather than dismayed by Hitler's attacks on the republican system. After President Hindenburg forced Brüning to resign in May 1932, the new government headed by Franz von Papen continued to rule by decree.

The continuation of the struggle between the Social Democrats and Communists, right up until the moment Hitler took power, was another aspect of the breakdown of democratic government. The Communists foolishly refused to cooperate with the Social Demo-

1919	Treaty of Versailles
	J. M. Keynes, *Economic Consequences of the Peace*
1919–1920	U.S. Senate rejects the Treaty of Versailles
1921	Germany is billed $35 billion in reparations
1922	Mussolini seizes power in Italy
	Germany proposes a moratorium on reparations
January 1923	France and Belgium occupy the Ruhr
	Germany orders passive resistance to the occupation
October 1923	Stresemann agrees to reparations with re-examination of Germany's ability to pay
1924	Dawes Plan: German reparations reduced and put on a sliding scale; large U.S. loans to Germany recommended to promote German recovery; occupation of the Ruhr ends
	Adolf Hitler, *Mein Kampf*
1924–1929	Spectacular German economic recovery; circular flow of international funds enables sizable reparations payments
1925	Treaties of Locarno promote European security and stability
1926	Germany joins the League of Nations
1928	Kellogg-Briand Pact renounces war as an instrument of international affairs
1929	Young Plan further reduces German reparations
	Crash of U.S. stock market
1929–1933	Depths of the Great Depression

crats, even though the two parties together outnumbered the Nazis in the Reichstag, even after the elections of 1932. German Communists (and the complacent Stalin) were blinded by their ideology and their hatred of the socialists. They were certain that Hitler's rise represented the last agonies of monopoly capitalism and that a Communist revolution would quickly follow his taking power. The socialist leaders pleaded, even at the Russian embassy, for at least a temporary alliance with the Communists to block Hitler, but to no avail. Perhaps the Weimar Republic was already too far gone, but this disunity on the left was undoubtedly another nail in its coffin.

Finally, there was Hitler's skill as a politician. A master of mass propaganda and psychology, he had written in *Mein Kampf* that

1931	Japan invades Manchuria
1932	Nazis become the largest party in the Reichstag
January 1933	Hitler appointed chancellor
March 1933	Reichstag passes the Enabling Act, granting Hitler absolute dictatorial power
October 1933	Germany withdraws from the League of Nations
July 1934	Nazis murder Austrian chancellor
March 1935	Hitler announces German rearmament
June 1935	Anglo-German naval agreement
October 1935	Mussolini invades Ethiopia and receives Hitler's support
1935	Nuremburg Laws deprive Jews of all rights of citizenship
March 1936	German armies move unopposed into the demilitarized Rhineland
July 1936	Outbreak of civil war in Spain
1937	Japan invades China
	Rome-Berlin Axis
March 1938	Germany annexes Austria
September 1938	Munich Conference: Britain and France agree to German seizure of the Sudetenland from Czechoslovakia
March 1939	Germany occupies the rest of Czechoslovakia; the end of appeasement in Britain
August 1939	Russo-German nonaggression pact
September 1, 1939	Germany invades Poland
September 3, 1939	Britain and France declare war on Germany

the masses were "the driving force of the most important changes in this world" and were themselves driven by hysterical fanaticism and not by knowledge. To arouse such hysterical fanaticism, he believed that all propaganda had to be limited to a few simple, endlessly repeated slogans. Thus, in the terrible economic and political crisis, he harangued vast audiences with passionate, irrational oratory. Men moaned and women cried, seized by emotion. And many uncertain individuals, surrounded by thousands of entranced listeners, found security and a sense of belonging.

At the same time Hitler excelled at dirty, backroom politics. That, in fact, brought him to power. In 1932, he cleverly succeeded in gaining the support of key people in the army and big business. These people thought they could use Hitler for their own advantage, to get increased military spending, fat contracts, and tough measures against workers. Conservative and nationalistic politicians like Papen thought similarly. They thus accepted Hitler's demand to join the government only if he became chancellor. There would be only two other National Socialists and nine solid conservatives as ministers, and in such a coalition government, they reasoned, Hitler could be used and controlled. On January 30, 1933, Hitler was legally appointed chancellor by President Hindenburg.

THE NAZI STATE AND SOCIETY

Hitler moved rapidly and skillfully to establish an unshakable dictatorship. His first step was to continue using terror and threats to gain more power "legally." He immediately called for new elections, and applied the enormous power of the government to restrict his opponents. In the midst of a violent electoral campaign, the Reichstag building was partly destroyed by fire. Although the Nazis probably set the fire, Hitler screamed that the Communist party was responsible. On the strength of this accusation, he convinced President Hindenburg to sign dictatorial emergency acts that practically abolished freedom of speech and assembly, as well as most personal liberties.

When the Nazis won only 44 percent of the vote in the elections, Hitler immediately outlawed the Communist party and arrested its parliamentary representatives. Then, on March 23, 1933, the Nazis pushed through the Reichstag the so-called Enabling Act, which gave Hitler absolute dictatorial power for four years. Only the Social Democrats voted against this bill, for Hitler had successfully blackmailed the Center party by threatening to attack the Catholic church.

Armed with the Enabling Act, Hitler and the Nazis moved to smash or control all independent organizations. Meanwhile Hitler and his propagandists constantly proclaimed that their revolution was legal and constitutional. This stress on legality, coupled with the divide-and-conquer technique, disarmed the opposition until it was too late for effective resistance.

The systematic subjugation of independent organizations and the creation of a totalitarian state had massive repercussions. The Social Democrat and Center parties were soon dissolved, and Germany became a one-party state. Only the Nazi party was legal. Elections were farces. The Reichstag was jokingly referred to as the most expensive glee club in the country, for its only function was to sing hymns of praise to the Führer. Hitler and the Nazis took over the government bureaucracy intact, installing many Nazis in top positions. At the same time they created a series of overlapping Nazi party organizations, responsible solely to Hitler. Thus Hitler had both an established bureaucracy for normal business and a private, personal "party government" for special duties.

In the economic sphere, strikes were forbidden and labor unions were abolished, replaced by a Nazi Labor Front. Professional people – doctors and lawyers, teachers and engineers–also saw their previously independent organizations swallowed up in Nazi associations. Nor did the Nazis neglect cultural and intellectual life. Publishing houses were put under Nazi control, and universities and writers were quickly brought into line. Democratic, socialist, and "Jewish" literature was put on ever-growing blacklists. Passionate students and pitiful professors burned forbidden books in public squares. Modern art and architecture were ruthlessly prohibited. Life became violently anti-intellectual. As Hitler's cynical minister of propaganda, Joseph Goebbels, put it: "When I hear the word 'culture' I reach for my gun."[10] By 1934, a totalitarian state characterized by frightening dynamism and obedience to Hitler was already largely in place.

By 1934 only the army retained independence, and Hitler moved brutally and skillfully to establish his control there too. He realized that the army, as well as big business, was suspicious of the Nazi storm troopers (the SA), the quasi-military band of 3 million toughs in brown shirts who had fought Communists and beaten up Jews before the Nazis took power. These unruly storm troopers expected top positions in the army and even talked of a "second revolution" against capitalism. Needing the support of the army and big business, Hitler decided that the SA leaders had to be eliminated. On the night of June 30, 1934, he struck.

Hitler's elite personal guard – the SS – arrested and shot without trial roughly one thousand SA leaders and assorted political enemies. While his propagandists spread lies about SA conspiracies, the army leaders and President Hindenburg responded to the purge with congratulatory telegrams. Shortly thereafter, the army leaders swore a binding oath of "unquestioning obedience . . . to the Leader of the German State and people, Adolf Hitler." The purge of the SA was another decisive step toward unlimited totalitarian terror. The SS, the elite guard that had loyally murdered the SA leaders, grew rapidly. Under its methodical, inhuman leader Heinrich Himmler (1900–1945), the SS joined with the political police, the Gestapo, and began expanding its network of special courts and concentration camps. Nobody was safe.

From the beginning the Jews were a special object of Nazi persecution. By the end of 1934, most Jewish lawyers, doctors, professors, civil servants, and musicians had lost their jobs and right to practice their professions. In 1935, the infamous Nuremberg Laws classified as Jewish anyone having one or more Jewish grandparents and deprived Jews of all rights of citizenship. By 1938, roughly one-quarter of Germany's half-million Jews had emigrated, sacrificing almost all their property in order to leave Germany.

Following the assassination of a German diplomat in Paris by a young Jewish boy trying desperately to strike out at persecution, the attack on the Jews accelerated. A well-organized wave of violence destroyed homes, synagogues, and businesses, after which German Jews were rounded up and made to pay for the damage. It became very difficult for Jews to leave Germany. Some Germans privately opposed these outrages, but most went along or looked the other way. Although this lack of response partly reflected the individual's helplessness in the totalitarian state, it was also a sign of the great popular support Hitler's government enjoyed.

HITLER'S POPULARITY

Hitler had promised the masses economic recovery – "work and bread" – and he delivered. Breaking with Brüning's do-nothing policies, Hitler immediately launched a large public works program to pull Germany out of the depression. Work began on superhighways, offices, gigantic sports stadia, and public housing. In 1936, as Germany rearmed rapidly, government spending began to concentrate on the military. The result was that unemployment dropped steadily, from 6 million in January 1933 to about 1 million in late 1936. By 1938 there was a shortage of workers, and women eventually took many jobs previously denied to them by the antifeminist Nazis. Thus everyone had work, and between 1932 and 1938 the standard of living for the average employed worker rose by more than 20 percent. The profits of business also increased. For millions of people, economic recovery and Nazi rule went hand in hand.

For the masses of ordinary German citizens, who were not Jews, Slavs, gypsies, Jehovah's Witnesses, or Communists, Hitler's government meant greater equality and exceptional opportunities. It must be remembered that in 1933 the position of the traditional German elites – the landed aristocracy, the wealthy capitalists, and the well-educated professional classes – was still very strong. Barriers between classes were generally high. Hitler's rule introduced vast changes in this pattern. For example, stiff educational requirements, which favored the well-to-do, were greatly relaxed. The new Nazi elite was composed largely of young and poorly educated dropouts, rootless lower-middle-class people like Hitler, who rose to the top with breathtaking speed.

More generally, the Nazis, like the Russian Communists, tolerated privilege and wealth only as long as they served the needs of the party. Big business was constantly ordered around, to the point that "probably never in peacetime has an ostensibly capitalist economy been directed as non- and even anti-capitalistically as the German economy between 1933 and 1939."[11] Hitler brought about a kind of social revolution, which was enthusiastically embraced by millions of modest middle- and lower-middle-class people and even by many workers.

Hitler's extreme nationalism, which had helped him gain power, continued to appeal to Germans after 1933. Ever since the wars against Napoleon, many Germans had believed in a special mission for a superior German nation. The successes of Bismarck had furthered such feelings, and near-victory in World War One made nationalists eager for renewed expansion in the 1920s. Thus, when Hitler went from one foreign triumph to another and a great German empire seemed within reach, as we shall see, the majority of the population was delighted and praised the Führer.

By no means all Germans supported Hitler, however, and a number of German groups actively resisted him after 1933. Tens of thousands of political enemies were imprisoned, and thousands were executed. Opponents of the Nazis pursued different goals, and under totalitarian conditions they were never unified, which helps account for their ultimate lack of success. In the first years of Hitler's rule, the principal resisters were the Communists and the Social Democrats in the trade unions. But the expansion of the SS system of terror after 1935 smashed most of these leftists. A second group of opponents arose in the Catholic and Protestant churches. However, their efforts were directed primarily at preserving genuine religious life, not at overthrowing Hitler. Finally, in 1938 (and again in 1942–1943) some high-ranking army officers, who feared the consequences of Hitler's reckless aggression, plotted against him, unsuccessfully.

NAZI EXPANSION AND THE SECOND WORLD WAR

Although economic recovery and increased opportunities for social advancement won Hitler support, they were only by-products of Nazi totalitarianism. The guiding concepts of Nazism remained space and race – the territorial expansion of the superior German race. As Germany regained its economic strength and as independent organizations were

July 8, 1936

STEPPING STONES TO GLORY.

DAVID LOW was a genius of a political cartoonist and his biting criticism of appeasing leaders appeared shortly after Hitler remilitarized the Rhineland. Appeasement also appealed to millions of ordinary citizens, who wanted to avoid at any cost another great war. (Cartoon by David Low by arrangement with the Low Trustees and the London Evening Standard)

brought under control, Hitler formed alliances with other dictators and began expanding. German expansion was facilitated by the uncertain, divided, pacific Western democracies, which tried to buy off Hitler to avoid war. Yet war was inevitable, in both the west and the east, for Hitler's ambitions were essentially unlimited. On both fronts the Nazis scored enormous success until late 1942, establishing a vast empire of death and destruction.

AGGRESSION AND APPEASEMENT, 1933–1939

Hitler's tactics in international politics after 1933 strikingly resembled those he used in domestic politics between 1924 and 1933. When Hitler was weak, he righteously proclaimed that he intended to overturn the "unjust system" established by the treaties of Versailles and Locarno – but only by legal means. As he grew stronger, and as other leaders showed their willingness to compromise, he increased his demands and finally began attacking his independent neighbors (see Map 36.1).

Hitler realized that his aggressive policies had to be carefully camouflaged at first, for Germany's army was limited by the Treaty of Versailles to only a hundred thousand men. As he told a group of army commanders in February 1933, the early stages of his policy of "conquest of new living space in the East and

Germany in 1933
Remilitarized in 1936
Annexed in 1938
Satellite states, March 1939
Conquered by Germany in September 1939
Annexed by Soviet Union in September 1939

SWEDEN

ESTONIA

BALTIC SEA

•Riga

L A T V I A

•Minsk

Memel •
Annexed, March 1939

L I T H U A N I A

NORTH SEA

NETHERLANDS

Hamburg •
Bremen •

Danzig •

EAST PRUSSIA

S O V I E T

RUHR

Berlin •

Oder

Warsaw •

Brest-Litovsk •
•Pinsk

BELGIUM

Cologne •

G E R M A N Y

P O L A N D

U N I O N

RHINELAND

Rhine

Weimar •

WHITE RUSSIA

LUXEMBOURG

SAAR
Gained by plebiscite, 1935

SUDETENLAND

Prague •
BOHEMIA

C Z E C H O S L O V A K I A

SUDETENLAND

F R A N C E

Danube

Munich •

MORAVIA

S L O V A K I A

RUTHENIA

Vienna •

To Hungary,
March 1939

SWITZERLAND

A U S T R I A

Budapest •

H U N G A R Y

R U M A N I A

I T A L Y

Y U G O S L A V I A

Danube

ADRIATIC SEA

0   100   200 Km.

0   100   200 Mi.

MAP 36.1   THE GROWTH OF NAZI GERMANY,
*1933–1939 Until March 1939, Hitler brought
ethnic Germans into the Nazi state; then he turned on
the Slavic peoples he had always hated.*

its ruthless Germanization" had serious dangers. If France had real leaders, Hitler said, "it will not give us time but attack us, presumably with its eastern satellites."[12] Thus Hitler loudly proclaimed his peaceful intentions to all the world. Nevertheless, he felt strong enough to walk out of a sixty-nation disarmament conference and withdraw from the League of Nations in October 1933. Stresemann's policy of peaceful cooperation was dead; the Nazi determination to rearm was out in the open.

Following this action, which met with widespread approval at home, Hitler moved to incorporate independent Austria into a Greater Germany. Austrian Nazis climaxed an attempted overthrow by murdering the Austrian chancellor in July 1934. They were unable to take power, however, because a worried Mussolini, who had initially greeted Hitler as a fascist little brother, massed his troops on the Brenner Pass and threatened to fight. When in March 1935 Hitler established a general military draft and declared the "unequal" disarmament clauses of the Treaty of Versailles null and void, other countries appeared to understand the danger. With France taking the lead, Italy and Great Britain protested strongly and warned against future aggressive actions.

Yet the emerging united front against Hitler quickly collapsed. Of crucial importance, Britain adopted a policy of appeasement, granting Hitler everything he could reasonably want (and more) in order to avoid war. The first step was an Anglo-German naval agreement in June 1935, which broke Germany's isolation. The second step came in March 1936, when Hitler suddenly marched his armies into the demilitarized Rhineland, brazenly violating the treaties of Versailles and Locarno. This was the last good chance to stop the Nazis, for Hitler had ordered his troops to retreat if France resisted militarily. But an uncertain France would not move without British support, and the occupation of German soil by German armies seemed right and just to Britain. Its strategic position greatly improved, Germany was suddenly the strongest military power in Europe.

British appeasement, which practically dictated French policy, lasted far into 1939. It was motivated by British feelings of guilt toward Germany and the pacifism of a population still horrified by the memory of the First World War. Like many Germans, British statesmen seriously underestimated Hitler. They believed that they could use him to stop Russian communism. A leading member of Britain's government personally told Hitler in November 1937 that it was his conviction that Hitler "not only had accomplished great things in Germany itself, but that through the total destruction of Communism in his own country ... Germany rightly had to be considered as a Western bulwark against Communism."[13] Such rigid anticommunist feelings made an alliance between the Western powers and Stalin against Hitler very unlikely.

As Britain and France opted for appeasement and Russia watched all developments suspiciously, Hitler found powerful allies. In 1935, the bombastic Mussolini decided that imperial expansion was needed to revitalize fascism. From Italian colonies on the east coast of Africa he attacked the independent African kingdom of Ethiopia. The Western powers and the League of Nations piously condemned Italian aggression, which angered Mussolini, without saving Ethiopia from defeat. Hitler, who had secretly supplied Ethiopia with arms to heat up the conflict, supported Italy energetically and thereby overcame Mussolini's lingering doubts about the Nazis. The result of this cooperation was an alliance in 1936 between Italy and Germany, the so-called Rome-Berlin Axis. Japan, which had been expanding into Manchuria since 1931, quickly joined the alliance between Italy and Germany.

At the same time Germany and Italy intervened in the long, complicated Spanish Civil War, where their support eventually helped General Francisco Franco's fascist movement defeat republican Spain. Spain's only official aid came from Soviet Russia, for public opinion in Britain and especially in France was hopelessly divided on the Spanish question.

By late 1937, as he was proclaiming his peaceful intentions to the British and their gullible prime minister, Neville Chamberlain, Hitler told his generals his real plans. His "unshakable decision" was to crush Austria and Czechoslovakia at the earliest possible moment, as the first step in his long-contemplated drive to the east for "living space." By threatening Austria with invasion, Hitler forced the Austrian chancellor in March 1938 to put local Nazis in control of the government. The next day German armies moved in unopposed, and Austria became two more provinces of Greater Germany.

Simultaneously, Hitler began demanding that the pro-Nazi, German-speaking minority of western Czechoslovakia – the Sudetenland – be turned over to Germany. Yet democratic Czechoslovakia was prepared to defend itself. Moreover, France had been Czechoslovakia's ally since 1924; and if France fought, Soviet Russia was pledged to help. As war appeared inevitable – for Hitler had already told the leader of the Sudeten Germans that "we must always ask so much we cannot be satisfied" – appeasement triumphed again. In September 1938, Chamberlain flew to Germany three times in fourteen days. In these negotiations – known as the Munich Conference – to which Russia was deliberately not invited, Chamberlain and the French agreed with

Hitler that the Sudetenland should be ceded to Germany immediately. Returning to London, Chamberlain told cheering crowds that he had secured "peace with honor . . . peace for our time." Sold out by the Western powers, Czechoslovakia gave in.

Confirmed once again in his opinion of the Western democracies as weak and racially degenerate, Hitler accelerated his aggression. In a shocking violation of his solemn assurances that the Sudetenland was his last territorial demand, Hitler's armies occupied the rest of Czechoslovakia in March 1939. The effect on Western public opinion was electrifying. For the first time there was no possible rationale of self-determination for Nazi aggression, since Hitler was seizing Czechs and Slovaks as captive peoples. Thus, when Hitler used the question of German minorities in Danzig as a pretext to smash Poland, a suddenly militant Chamberlain declared that Britain and France would fight if Hitler attacked his eastern neighbor. Hitler did not take these warnings seriously, and he pressed on.

In an about-face that stunned the world, Hitler offered and Stalin signed a Russo-German nonaggression pact in August 1939, whereby each dictator promised to remain neutral if the other became involved in war. Even more startling was the attached secret protocol, which ruthlessly divided eastern Europe into German and Russian zones, "in the event of a political territorial reorganization." Although this top-secret protocol sealing the destruction of Poland and the Baltic states became known only after the war, the non-aggression pact itself was enough to make Britain and France cry treachery, for they too had been negotiating with Stalin. But Stalin had remained very distrustful of Western intentions. Moreover, Britain and France had offered him military risk without gain, while Hitler had offered territorial gain without risk. For Hitler, everything was set. He told his generals on the day of the nonaggression pact: "My only fear is that at the last moment some dirty dog will come up with a mediation plan." On September 1, 1939, German armies and warplanes smashed into Poland from three sides. Two days later, finally true to their word, Britain and France declared war on Germany. The Second World War had begun.

HITLER'S EMPIRE, 1939–1942

Using planes, tanks, and trucks in a lightning attack, Hitler's armies crushed Poland in four weeks. While Soviet Russia quickly took its part of the booty — the eastern half of Poland and the Baltic states of Lithuania, Estonia, Latvia — French and British armies dug in in the west. They expected another war of attrition and economic blockade.

In spring 1940, the lightning attack struck again. After quickly occupying Denmark, Norway, and Holland, German motorized columns broke through southern Belgium, split the Franco-British forces, and trapped the entire British army on the beaches of Dunkirk. By heroic efforts the British managed to withdraw their troops but not their equipment to England.

France was taken by the Nazis. The aging Marshal Henri-Philippe Pétain formed a new French government — the so-called Vichy government — to accept defeat, and German armies occupied most of France. By July 1940, Hitler ruled practically all of western continental Europe, and Italy and Soviet Russia were his allies. Only Britain, led by the uncompromising Winston Churchill (1874–1965), remained unconquered. Churchill proved to be one of history's greatest wartime leaders, rallying his fellow citizens with stirring speeches, infectious confidence, and bulldog determination.

Germany sought to gain control of the air, the necessary first step for a naval invasion of Britain. In the Battle of Britain up to a thousand German planes attacked British airfields and key factories in a single day, dueling with British defenders high in the skies. Losses were heavy on both sides. Then in September Hitler angrily and foolishly changed his tactics, turning from military objectives to indiscriminate bombing of British cities in an attempt to break British morale. British factories increased production of their excellent fighter planes; antiaircraft defense improved with the help of radar; and the heavily bombed people of London defiantly dug in. In September-October 1940, Britain was beating Germany three-to-one in the air war. There was no possibility of immediate German invasion of Britain.

In these circumstances the most reasonable German strategy would have been to attack Britain through the eastern Mediterranean, taking Egypt and the Suez Canal and pinching off Britain's supply of oil. Moreover, Mussolini's early defeats in Greece had drawn Hitler into the Balkans, where Germany quickly conquered Greece and Yugoslavia while forcing Hungary, Rumania and Bulgaria into alliances with Germany by April 1941. This reinforced the logic of a thrust into the eastern Mediterranean. But Hitler was not a reasonable person. His lifetime obsession with a vast east European empire for the master race irrationally dictated policy. By late 1940 he had already decided on his next move, and in June 1941 German armies suddenly attacked the Soviet Union along a vast front. With Britain still unconquered, Hitler's decision was a wild irrational gamble, epitomizing the violent, unlimited ambitions of modern totalitarianism.

Faithfully fulfilling all his obligations under the Nazi-Soviet Pact and even ignoring warnings of impending invasion, Stalin was caught off guard. Nazi armies moved like lightning across the Russian steppe. By October 1941, Leningrad was practically surrounded, Moscow beseiged, and most of the Ukraine conquered; yet the Russians did not collapse. When a severe winter struck German armies outfitted in summer uniforms, the invaders were stopped.

While Hitler's armies dramatically expanded the war in Europe, his Japanese allies did the same in Asia. Engaged in a general but undeclared war against China since 1937, Japan's rulers had increasingly come into diplomatic conflict with the Pacific Basin's other great power, the United States. When the Japanese occupied French Indochina in July 1941, the United States retaliated by cutting off sales of vital rubber, scrap iron, oil, and aviation fuel. Tension mounted further, and on December 7, 1941, Japan attacked the U.S. naval base at Pearl Harbor in Hawaii. Hitler immediately declared war on the United States, even though his treaty obligations with Japan did not require him to do so.

As Japanese forces advanced swiftly into southeast Asia after the crippling surprise attack at Pearl Harbor, Hitler and his European allies continued the two-front war against the Soviet Union and Great Britain. Not until late 1942 did the Nazis suffer their first major defeats, as we shall see in the next chapter. In the meantime Hitler ruled a vast European empire stretching from the outskirts of Moscow to the English Channel. Hitler and the top Nazi leadership began building their "New Order," and they continued their efforts until their final collapse in 1945. In doing so, they showed what Nazi victory would have meant.

Hitler's New Order was based firmly on the guiding principle of Nazi totalitarianism: racial imperialism. Within this New Order

the Nordic peoples – the Dutch, the Norwegians, and the Danes – received preferential treatment, for they were racially related to the Germans. The French, an "inferior" Latin people, occupied the middle position. They were heavily taxed to support the Nazi war effort, but were tolerated as a race. Once Nazi reverses began to mount in late 1942, however, all the occupied territories of western and northern Europe were exploited with ever-increasing intensity. Shortages and suffering afflicted millions of people.

Slavs in the conquered territories to the east were treated with harsh hatred as "subhumans." At the height of his success in 1941-1942, Hitler painted for his intimate circle the fantastic details of a vast eastern colonial empire, where the Poles, Ukranians, and Russians would be enslaved and forced to die out, while Germanic peasants resettled their abandoned lands. Himmler and the elite corps of SS volunteers struggled loyally, sometimes against the German army, to implement part of this general program even before victory was secured. In parts of Poland the SS arrested and evacuated Polish peasants to create a German "mass settlement space." Polish workers and Russian prisoners of war were transported to Germany, where they did most of the heavy labor and were systematically worked to death. The conditions of Russian slave labor in Germany were so harsh that four out of five Russian prisoners did not survive the war.

Finally, Jews were condemned to extermination, along with gypsies, Jehovah's Witnesses, and captured Communists. By 1939 German Jews had lost all their civil rights, and after the fall of Warsaw the Nazis began deporting them to Poland. There they and Jews from all over Europe were concentrated in ghettos, compelled to wear the Jewish star, and turned into slave laborers. But by 1941,

Himmler's SS was carrying out the "final solution of the Jewish question" – the murder of every single Jew. All over Hitler's empire Jews were arrested, packed like cattle onto freight trains, and dispatched to extermination camps.

There the victims were taken by force or deception to "shower rooms," which were actually gas chambers. These gas chambers, first perfected in the quiet, efficient execution of 70,000 mentally ill Germans between 1938 and 1941, permitted rapid, hideous, and thoroughly bureaucratized mass murder. For fifteen to twenty minutes there came the terrible screams and gasping sobs of men, women, and children choking to death on poison gas. Then, only silence. Special camp workers quickly tore the victims' gold teeth from their jaws and cut off their hair for use as chair stuffings. The bodies were then boiled for oil to make soap and the bones were crushed to produce fertilizers. At Auschwitz, the most infamous of the Nazi death factories, as many as 12,000 human beings were slaughtered each day. On the turbulent Russian front the SS death squads forced the Jewish population to dig giant pits, which became mass graves as the victims were lined up on the edge and cut down by machine guns. The extermination of the European

Jews was the ultimate monstrosity of Nazi racism and racial imperialism. By 1945, 6 million Jews had been murdered in cold blood.

———◆———

The tremendous practical and spiritual maladies of the age of anxiety led in many lands to the rise of dictatorships. Many of these dictatorships were variations on conservative authoritarianism, but there was also a fateful innovation – the modern totalitarian regime, most fully developed in Communist Russia and Nazi Germany. The totalitarian regimes utterly rejected the liberalism of the nineteenth century. Inspired by the lessons of total war and Lenin's one-party rule, they tried to subordinate everything to the state. Although some areas of life escaped them, state control increased to a staggering, unprecedented degree. The totalitarian regimes trampled on basic human rights with unrestrained brutality and police terror. Moreover, they were armed with the weapons of modern technology, rendering opposition almost impossible.

Both Communist Russia and Nazi Germany tried to gain the *willing* support of their populations. Monopolizing the means of expression and communication, they claimed to represent the masses and to be building new, more equal societies. Many people believed them. Both regimes also won enthusiastic supporters by offering tough, ruthless people from modest backgrounds enormous rewards for loyal and effective service. Thus these totalitarian dictatorships rested on considerable genuine popular support, as well as on police terror. This combination gave them their awesome power and dynamism. That dynamism was, however, channeled in quite different directions. Stalin and the Communist party aimed at building their kind of socialism and the new socialist personality at home. Hitler and the Nazi elite aimed at unlimited territorial and racial aggression on behalf of a master race; domestic recovery was only a means to that end. Unlimited aggression made war inevitable, first with the Western democracies and then with Germany's totalitarian neighbor. It plunged Europe into the ultimate nightmare.

NOTES

1. E. Halévy, *The Era of Tyrannies,* Doubleday, Garden City, N.Y., 1965, pp. 265–316, esp. p. 300.

2. Quoted by P. C. Roberts, " 'War Communism': A Re-examination," *Slavic Review* 29 (June 1970): 257.

3. Quoted by A. G. Mazour, *Soviet Economic Development: Operation Outstrip, 1921–1965,* Van Nostrand, Princeton, N.J., 1967, p. 130.

4. Quoted by I. Deutscher, *Stalin: A Political Biography,* 2nd ed., Oxford University Press, New York, 1967, p. 325.

5. Quoted by H. K. Geiger, *The Family in Soviet Russia,* Harvard University Press, Cambridge, 1968, p. 123.

6. Ibid., p. 156.

7. Quoted by B. Rosenthal, "Women in the Russian Revolution and After," in *Becoming Visible: Women in European History,* ed., R. Bridenthal and C. Koonz, Houghton Mifflin, Boston, 1976, p. 383.

8. Quoted by K. D. Bracher, in T. Eschenburg et al., *The Path to Dictatorship, 1918–1933,* Doubleday, Garden City, N.Y., 1966, p. 117.

9. Quoted by K. D. Bracher, *The German Dictatorship: The Origins, Structure and Effects of National Socialism,* Praeger, New York, 1970, pp. 146–147.

10. Quoted by R. Stromberg, *An Intellectual History of Modern Europe,* Appleton-Century-Crofts, New York, 1966, p. 393.

11. D. Schoenbaum, *Hitler's Social Revolution: Class and Status in Nazi Germany, 1933–1939,* Doubleday, Garden City, N.Y., 1967, p. 114.

12. Quoted by Bracher, *German Dictatorship*, p. 289.

13. Ibid., p. 306.

SUGGESTED READING

The historical literature on totalitarian dictatorships is rich and fascinating. H. Arendt, *The Origins of Totalitarianism* (1951), is a challenging interpretation. E. Weber, *Varieties of Fascism* (1964), stresses the radical social aspirations of fascist movements all across Europe. F. L. Carsten, *The Rise of Fascism*, rev. ed. (1982), and W. Laqueur, ed., *Fascism* (1976), are also recommended. On Germany, F. Stern, *The Politics of Cultural Despair* (1963), and G. Mosse, *The Crisis of German Ideology* (1964), are excellent complementary studies on the origins of Nazism. The best single work on Hitler's Germany is K. Bracher, *The German Dictatorship: The Origins, Structure and Effects of National Socialism* (1970). A Bullock's *Hitler* (1953) is a totally engrossing biography of Der Führer. In addition to *Mein Kampf, Hitler's Secret Conversations, 1941–1944* (1953) reveals the dictator's wild dreams and beliefs. Among countless special studies, E. Kogon, *The Theory and Practice of Hell* (1958), is a chilling examination of the concentration camps; M. Mayer, *They Thought They Were Free* (1955), probes the minds of ten ordinary Nazis and why they believed Hitler was their liberator; and A. Speer, *Inside the Third Reich* (1970), contains the fascinating recollections of Hitler's wizard of the armaments industry. G. Mosse, *Toward the Final Solution* (1978), is a powerful history of European racism. Jørgen Haestrup, *Europe Ablaze* (1978), is a monumental account of wartime resistance movements throughout Europe.

Richard Stites, *The Women's Liberation Movement in Russia: Feminism, Nihilism, and Bolshevism, 1860–1930* (1978); S. Fitzpatrick, *Cultural Revolution in Russia, 1928–1931* (1978); K. Geiger, *The Family in Soviet Russia* (1968); and I. Deutscher, *Stalin: A Political Biography* (1967), are all highly recommended, as is Deutscher's sympathetic three-volume study of Trotsky. S. Cohen, *Bukharin and the Bolshevik Revolution* (1973), examines the leading spokesman of moderate communism, who was destroyed by Stalin. R. Conquest, *The Great Terror* (1968), is an excellent account of Stalin's purges of the 1930s. A. Solzhenitsyn, *The Gulag Archipelago* (1974), passionately condemns Soviet police terror, which Solzhenitsyn traces back to Lenin. A. Koestler, *Darkness at Noon* (1956), is a famous fictional account of Stalin's trials of the Old Bolsheviks. R. Medvedev, *Let History Judge* (1972), is a penetrating and highly recommended history of Stalinism by a Russian dissident. Three other remarkable books are J. Scott, *Behind the Urals* (1942, 1973), the eyewitness account of an American steelworker in Russia in the 1930s; S. Alliluyeva, *Twenty Letters to a Friend* (1967), the amazing reflections of Stalin's daughter, now living in America; and M. Fainsod, *Smolensk Under Soviet Rule* (1958), a unique study based on Communist records captured first by the Germans and then by the Americans.

E. R. Tannebaum, *The Fascist Experience* (1972), is an excellent study of Italian culture and society under Mussolini. I. Silone, *Bread and Wine* (1937), is a moving novel by a famous opponent of dictatorship in Italy. Two excellent books on Spain are H. Thomas, *The Spanish Civil War* (1961), and E. Malefakis, *Agrarian Reform and Peasant Revolution in Spain* (1970). In the area of foreign relations, G. Kennan, *Russia and the West Under Lenin and Stalin* (1961), is justly famous, while A. L. Rowse, *Appeasement* (1961), powerfully denounces the policies of the appeasers. R. Paxton, *Vichy France* (1973), tells a controversial story extremely well, and J. Lukac, *The Last European War* (1976), skillfully — and infuriatingly — argues that victory by Hitler could have saved Europe from both Russian and American domination.

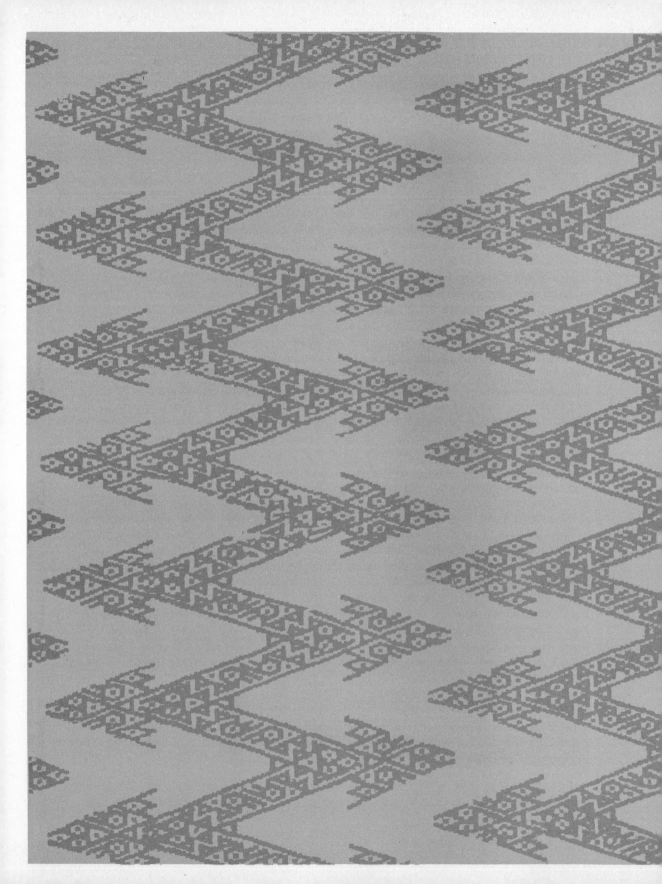

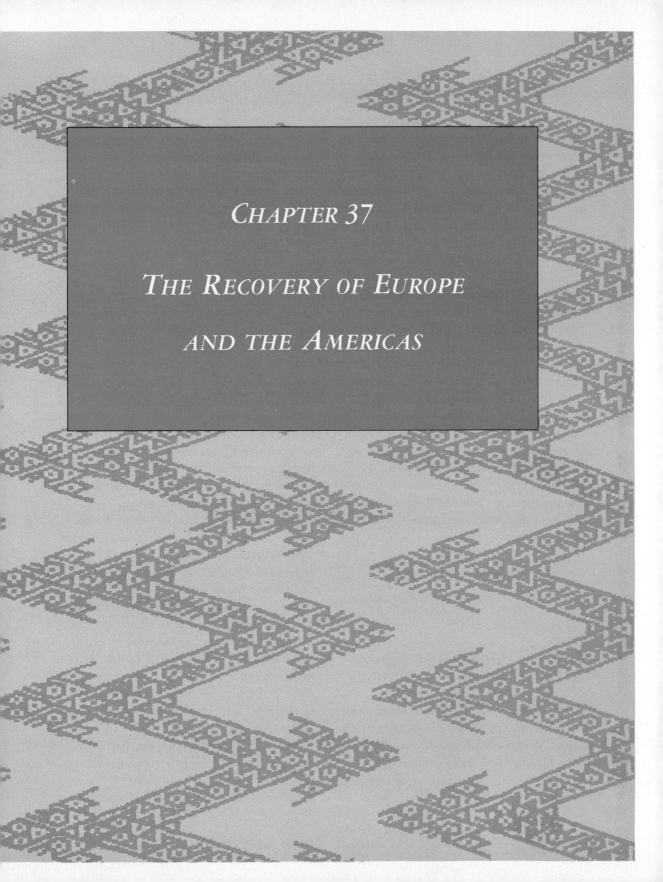

CHAPTER 37

THE RECOVERY OF EUROPE

AND THE AMERICAS

IN 1942, when Hitler's empire stretched across Europe and the Nazi "New Order" was taking shape, Western civilization was in danger of dying. A terrible, triumphant barbarism was striking at the hard-won accomplishments and uneven progress of many generations. From this low point, European society staged a truly astonishing recovery.

The Nazis and their allies were utterly defeated. Battered western Europe then experienced a great renaissance, and the western hemisphere with its strong European heritage also made exemplary progress. Soviet Russia eventually became more humane and less totalitarian. Yet there was also a tragic setback. The Grand Alliance against Hitler gave way to an apparently endless cold war, in which conflict between East and West threatened world peace and troubled domestic politics.

How and why did Europe recover from the depths of despair in one of the most extraordinary periods of rebirth in its long history? What were the causes of the cold war? How did the course of that international struggle influence domestic politics? These are some of the more important questions this chapter seeks to answer.

ALLIED VICTORY AND THE COLD WAR, 1942–1950

The recovery of Western society depended on the defeat of the Nazis and their Italian, Balkan, and Japanese allies. On this point the twenty-six allied nations, led by Britain, the United States, and Soviet Russia, were firmly agreed. The Grand Alliance – to use Winston Churchill's favorite term – functioned quite effectively in military terms to achieve this overwhelming objective. By the summer of

1943, the tide of battle had turned, and Allied victory was only a matter of time.

Yet victory was flawed. The Allies could not cooperate politically when it came to peacemaking. Motivated by different goals and hounded by misunderstandings, the United States and Soviet Russia soon found themselves at loggerheads. By the end of 1947, Europe was rigidly divided. It was West versus East in the cold war.

THE GRAND ALLIANCE

Chance, rather than choice, brought together the anti-Axis coalition. Stalin had been cooperating fully with Hitler between August 1939 and June 1941, and only the Japanese attack on Pearl Harbor in December 1941 and Hitler's immediate declaration of war had overwhelmed powerful isolationism in the United States. The Allies' first task was to try to overcome their mutual suspicions and build an unshakable alliance on the quicksand of accident. By means of two interrelated policies they succeeded.

First, President Roosevelt accepted Churchill's contention that the United States should concentrate first on defeating Hitler. Only after victory in Europe would the United States turn toward the Pacific for an all-out attack on Japan, the lesser threat. Therefore, the United States promised and sent large amounts of military aid to Britain and Russia, and American and British forces in each combat zone were tightly integrated under a single commander. America's policy of "Europe first" helped solidify the anti-Hitler coalition.

Second, within the European framework, the Americans and the British put immediate military needs first. They consistently postponed tough political questions relating to the eventual peace settlement. Thus, in December 1941 and again in May 1942, Stalin asked the United States and Britain to agree to Russia's moving its western border of 1938 further west at the expense of Poland, in effect ratifying the gains Stalin had made from his deal with Hitler in 1939.

Stalin's request ran counter to the moralistic Anglo-American Atlantic Charter of August 1941. In good Wilsonian fashion, the Atlantic Charter had called for peace without territorial expansion or secret agreements, and free elections and self-determination for all liberated nations. Stalin thus received only a military alliance and no postwar commitments in 1942. Yet the United States and Britain did not try to take advantage of Russia's precarious position in 1942, promising an invasion of continental Europe as soon as possible. They feared that hard bargaining would anger Stalin and encourage him to consider making a separate peace with Hitler.

Both sides found it advantageous to paper over their long-standing differences by stressing military operations and the total defeat of the Axis. At a conference in Casablanca, Morocco, in January 1943 to plan a massive Allied offensive, Churchill and Roosevelt adopted the principle of the "unconditional surrender" of Germany and Japan. Stalin agreed to it shortly thereafter. The policy of unconditional surrender had profound implications. It cemented the Grand Alliance together, denying Hitler any hope of dividing his foes. It probably also discouraged Germans and Japanese who might have tried to overthrow their dictators in order to make a compromise peace. And, most important, it meant that Russian and Anglo-American armies would almost certainly come together to divide all of Germany, and all of Europe, among themselves.

The military resources of the Grand Alliance were awesome. The strengths of the United States were its mighty industry, its large population, and its national unity. Even before Pearl Harbor, President Roosevelt had called America the "arsenal of democracy" and given military aid to Britain and Russia. Now the United States geared up rapidly for all-out war production, and drew heavily on a generally cooperative Latin America for resources. It not only equipped its own armies but eventually gave its allies about $50 billion of arms and equipment. Britain received by far the most, but about one-fifth of the total went to Russia in the form of badly needed trucks, planes, and munitions.

Too strong to lose and too weak to win when it stood alone, Britain too continued to make a great contribution. The British economy was totally and effectively mobilized, and the sharing of burdens through rationing and heavy taxes on war profits maintained social harmony. Moreover, as 1942 wore on, Britain could increasingly draw on the enormous physical and human resources of its empire and the United States. By early 1943, the Americans and the British combined small aircraft carriers with radar-guided bombers to rid the Atlantic of German submarines. Britain, the impregnable floating fortress, became a gigantic front-line staging area for the decisive blow to the heart of Germany.

As for Soviet Russia, so great was its strength that it might well have defeated Germany without Western help. In the face of the German advance, whole factories and whole populations were successfully evacuated to eastern Russia and Siberia. There, war production was reorganized and enormously expanded, and the Red Army was increasingly well supplied. The Red Army was also well led, for a new generation of talented military leaders quickly arose to replace those so recently purged. Most important of all, Stalin drew on the massive support and heroic determination of the Soviet people. Broad-based Russian nationalism, as opposed to narrow Communist ideology, became the powerful unifying force in what was appropriately called "the Great Patriotic War of the Fatherland."

Finally, the United States, Britain, and Soviet Russia were not alone. They had the resources of much of the world at their command. And, to a greater or lesser extent, they were aided by a growing resistance movement against the Nazis throughout Europe, even in Germany. Thus, although Ukrainian peasants often welcomed the Germans as liberators, the barbaric occupation policies of the Nazis quickly drove them to join and support behind-the-lines guerrilla forces. More generally, after Russia was invaded in June 1941, Communists throughout Europe took the lead in the underground resistance, joined by a growing number of patriots and Christians. Anti-Nazi leaders from occupied countries established governments-in-exile in London, like that of the "Free French" under the intensely proud General Charles de Gaulle. These governments gathered valuable secret information from resistance fighters and even organized armies to help defeat Hitler.

THE TIDE OF BATTLE

Barely halted at the gates of Moscow and Leningrad in 1941, the Germans renewed their Russian offensive in July 1942. This time they drove toward the southern city of Stalingrad, in an attempt to cripple communications and seize the crucial oilfields of Baku. Reaching Stalingrad, the Germans slowly occupied most of the ruined city in a month of

MAP 37.1 *WORLD WAR TWO IN EUROPE* *The map shows the extent of Hitler's empire at its height, before the battle of Stalingrad in late 1942, and the subsequent advances of the Allies until Germany surrendered on May 7, 1945.*

incredibly savage house-to-house fighting.

Then, in November 1942, Soviet armies counterattacked. They rolled over Rumanian and Italian troops to the north and south of Stalingrad, quickly closing the trap and surrounding the entire German Sixth Army of 300,000 men. The surrounded Germans were systematically destroyed, until by the end of January 1943 only 123,000 soldiers were left to surrender. Hitler, who had refused to allow a retreat, had suffered a catastrophic defeat. In the summer of 1943, the larger, better-equipped Soviet armies took the offensive and began moving forward (see Map 37.1).

In late 1942, the tide also turned in the Pacific and in North Africa. By early summer of 1942, Japan had established a great empire in east Asia. Unlike the Nazis, the Japanese made clever appeals to local nationalists, who hated European imperial domination and preferred Japan's so-called Greater Asian Co-Prosperity Sphere.

Then in the battle of the Coral Sea, in May 1942, Allied naval and air power stopped the Japanese advance and also relieved Australia from the threat of invasion. This victory was followed by the battle of Midway Island, in which American pilots sank all four of the attacking Japanese aircraft carriers and established American naval superiority in the Pacific. In August 1942, American marines attacked Guadalcanal in the Solomon Islands. Badly hampered by the policy of "Europe first" – only 15 percent of Allied resources were going to fight the war in the Pacific in early 1943 – the Americans, under General Douglas MacArthur and Admiral Chester Ni-

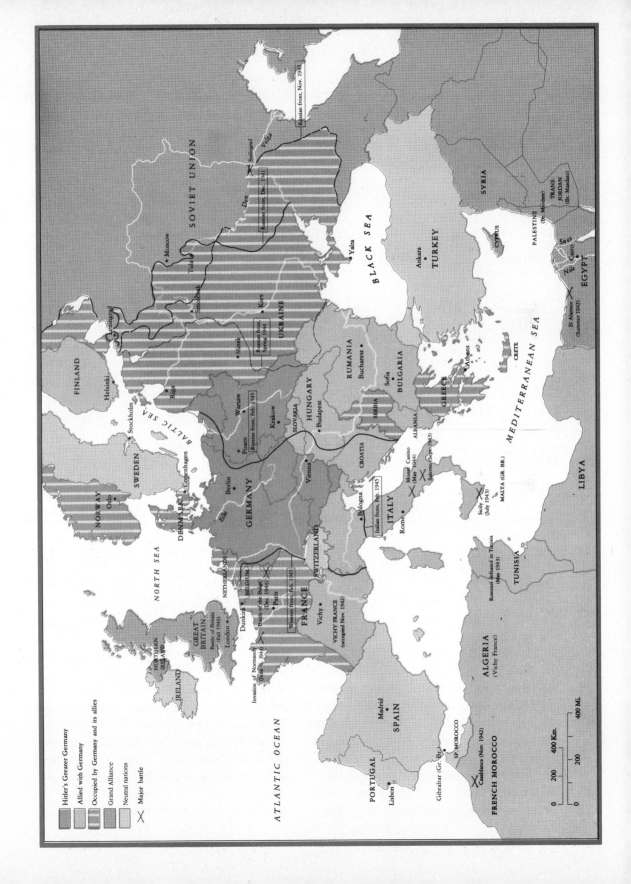

SOVIET UNION

Russian front, Nov. 1942

• Stalingrad

Volga

Don

Russian front, Dec. 1941

• Moscow

• Tula

• Smolensk

• Kiev

UKRAINE

• Minsk

Russian front, Spring 1944

BLACK SEA

• Yalta

TURKEY

• Ankara

SYRIA

CYPRUS

TRANS-JORDAN (Br. Mandate)

PALESTINE (Br. Mandate)

Suez

Cairo •

Nile

EGYPT

El Alamein (Summer 1942)

FINLAND

• Helsinki

Leningrad

BALTIC SEA

• Riga

• Stockholm

SWEDEN

• Warsaw

Russian front, Feb. 1945

• Posen

• Krakow

SLOVAKIA

HUNGARY

• Budapest

RUMANIA

• Bucharest

BULGARIA

• Sofia

SERBIA

CROATIA

ALBANIA

GREECE

• Athens

CRETE

MEDITERRANEAN SEA

LIBYA

NORWAY

• Oslo

DENMARK

• Copenhagen

Elbe

Berlin •

GERMANY

Vienna •

• Bologna

Italian front, Feb. 1945

Rome •

ITALY

Monte Casino (May 1944)

• Salerno (Sept. 1943)

Sicily (July 1943)

MALTA (GR. BR.)

NORTH SEA

NETHERLANDS

BELGIUM

Dunkirk •

Battle of the Bulge (Dec. 1944)

• Paris

Western front, Feb. 1945

SWITZERLAND

FRANCE

VICHY FRANCE (occupied Nov. 1942)

Vichy •

NORTHERN IRELAND

GREAT BRITAIN

Battle of Britain (Fall 1940)

• London

Invasion of Normandy (June 6, 1944)

IRELAND

ATLANTIC OCEAN

TUNISIA

Rommel defeated in Tunisia (May 1943)

ALGERIA (Vichy France)

Madrid •

SPAIN

PORTUGAL

• Lisbon

Gibraltar (Gr. Br.)

SP. MOROCCO

FRENCH MOROCCO

Casablanca (Nov. 1942)

Hitler's Greater Germany

Allied with Germany

Occupied by Germany and its allies

Grand Alliance

Neutral nations

Major battle

0   200   400 Km.

0   200   400 Mi.

WAR IN THE PACIFIC   *A Japanese ship burns off the coast of New Guinea as an attacking B-25 roars overhead. The lights along the shoreline are fires caused by United States bombers. (Air Force Photo)*

mitz, and the Australians nevertheless began "island hopping" toward Japan. Japanese forces were on the defensive.

In North Africa, the war had been seesawing back and forth since 1940. In May 1942, combined German and Italian armies, under the brilliant General Erwin Rommel, attacked British-occupied Egypt and the Suez Canal for the second time. After a rapid advance they were finally defeated by British forces at the battle of El Alamein, only seventy miles from Alexandria. In October, the British counterattacked in Egypt, and almost immediately

thereafter an Anglo-American force landed in Morocco and Algeria. These French possessions, which were under the control of Pétain's Vichy French government, quickly went over to the Allies.

Having driven the Axis powers from North Africa by the spring of 1943, Allied forces maintained the initiative by invading Sicily and then mainland Italy. Mussolini was deposed by a war-weary people, and the new Italian government publicly accepted unconditional surrender in September 1943. Italy, it seemed, was liberated. Yet Mussolini was rescued by German commandos in a daring raid and put at the head of a puppet government. German armies seized Rome and all of northern Italy. Fighting continued in Italy.

Indeed, bitter fighting continued in Europe for almost two years. Germany, less fully mobilized for war than Britain in 1941, applied itself to total war in 1942 and enlisted millions of prisoners of war and slave laborers from all across occupied Europe in that effort. Between early 1942 and July 1944, German war production actually *tripled*. Although British and American bombing raids killed many German civilians, they were surprisingly ineffective from a military point of view. Also, German resistance against Hitler failed. After an unsuccessful attempt on Hitler's life in July 1944, thousands of Germans were brutally liquidated by SS fanatics. Terrorized at home and frightened by the prospect of unconditional surrender, the Germans fought on with suicidal stoicism.

On June 6, 1944, American and British forces under General Dwight Eisenhower landed on the beaches of Normandy in history's greatest naval invasion. Having tricked the Germans into believing that the attack would come near the Belgian border, the Allies secured a foothold on the coast of Normandy. In a hundred dramatic days, more than 2 million men and almost a half-million vehicles pushed inland and broke through German lines. Rejecting proposals to strike straight at Berlin in a massive attack, Eisenhower moved forward cautiously on a broad front. Not until March 1945 did American troops cross the Rhine and enter Germany.

The Russians, who had been advancing steadily since July 1943, reached the outskirts of Warsaw by August 1944. For the next six months they moved southward into Rumania, Hungary, and Yugoslavia. In January 1945, Red armies again moved westward through Poland, and on April 26 they met American forces on the Elbe River. The Allies had closed their vise on Nazi Germany and overrun Europe. As Soviet forces fought their way into Berlin, Hitler committed suicide in his bunker, and on May 7 German commanders capitulated.

Three months later the United States dropped atomic bombs on Hiroshima and Nagasaki. Mass bombing of cities and civilians, one of the terrible new practices of World War Two, had ended in the final nightmare – unprecedented human destruction in a single blinding flash. The Japanese surrendered. The Second World War, which had claimed the lives of more than 50 million soldiers and civilians, was over.

THE ORIGINS OF THE COLD WAR

Total victory was not followed by genuine peace. The most powerful allies – Soviet Russia and the United States – began to quarrel as soon as the unifying threat of Nazi Germany disappeared. Though the hostility between the eastern and western superpowers was a tragic disappointment for millions of people, it was not really surprising. It grew sadly but logically out of military developments, wartime agreements, and long-standing political and ideological differences.

The conference Stalin, Roosevelt, and Churchill had held in the Iranian capital of Teheran in November 1943 was of crucial importance in determining subsequent events. There, the Big Three had jovially reaffirmed their determination to crush Germany and searched for the appropriate military strategy. Churchill, fearful of the military dangers of a direct attack and anxious to protect Britain's political interests in the eastern Mediterranean, argued that American and British forces should follow up their North African and Ital-

HIROSHIMA, AUGUST 1945 A single atomic bomb leveled 90 percent of this major city and claimed 130,000 casualties. Hiroshima has never regained its earlier prosperity. (U.S. Army Air Forces)

ian campaigns with an indirect attack on Germany through the Balkans. Roosevelt, however, agreed with Stalin that an American-British frontal assault through France would be better. This agreement was part of Roosevelt's general effort to meet Stalin's wartime demands whenever possible. As Roosevelt reportedly told his friend William Bullitt, formerly American ambassador to the Soviet Union, before the Teheran conference, "I have just a hunch that Stalin doesn't want anything but security for his country, and I think that if I give him everything I possibly can and ask nothing from him in return, *noblesse oblige,* he won't try to annex anything and will work for a world of democracy and peace."[1]

At Teheran, the Normandy invasion had

been set for the spring of 1944. Although military considerations probably largely dictated this decison, it had momentous political implications: it meant that the Russian and the American-British armies would come together in defeated Germany along a north-south line and that only Russian troops would liberate eastern Europe. Thus the basic shape of postwar Europe was already emerging. Real differences over questions like Poland were carefully ignored.

When the Big Three met again at Yalta on the Black Sea in southern Russia in February 1945, rapidly advancing Soviet armies were within one hundred miles of Berlin. The Red Army had occupied not only Poland but also Bulgaria, Rumania, Hungary, most of Yugoslavia, and much of Czechoslovakia. The temporarily stalled American-British forces had yet to cross the Rhine into Germany. Moreover, the United States was far from defeating Japan. Indeed, it was believed that the invasion and occupation of Japan would cost a million American casualties — an estimate that led to the subsequent decision to drop atomic bombs in order to save American lives. In short, Russia's position was strong and America's weak.

There was little the increasingly sick and apprehensive Roosevelt could do but double his bet on Stalin's peaceful intentions. It was agreed at Yalta that Germany would be divided into zones of occupation and would pay heavy reparations to the Soviet Union in the form of agricultural and industrial goods, though many details remained unsettled. At American insistence, Stalin agreed to declare war on Japan after Germany was defeated. He also agreed to join the proposed United Nations, which the Americans believed would help preserve peace after the war; it was founded in April 1945 in San Francisco. For Poland and eastern Europe — "that Pandora's Box of infinite troubles," according to American Secretary of State Cordell Hull — the Big Three struggled to reach an ambiguous compromise at Yalta: East European governments were to be freely elected but pro-Russian. As Churchill put it at the time, "The Poles will have their future in their own hands, with the single limitation that they must honestly follow in harmony with their allies, a policy friendly to Russia."[2]

The Yalta compromise over eastern Europe broke down almost immediately. Before the war was over, Soviet Russia demanded and obtained from the Rumanian king the appointment of an obedient Communist as prime minister. Even before the Yalta Conference, Bulgaria and Poland were in the hands of Communists, who arrived home in the baggage of the Red Army. Minor concessions to non-Communist groups thereafter did not change this situation. Elsewhere in eastern Europe, pro-Russian "coalition" governments of several parties were formed, but the key ministerial posts were reserved for Moscow-trained Communists.

At the postwar Potsdam Conference of July 1945, the long-ignored differences over eastern Europe finally surged to the fore. The compromising Roosevelt had died and been succeeded by the inflexible President Harry Truman, who demanded immediate free elections throughout eastern Europe. Stalin refused pointblank. "A freely elected government in any of these East European countries would be anti-Soviet," he admitted simply, "and that we cannot allow."[3]

Here, then, is the key to the much-debated origins of the cold war. American ideals, pumped up by the crusade against Hitler, and American politics, heavily influenced by millions of voters from eastern Europe, demanded free elections in Soviet-occupied eastern Europe. On the other hand, Stalin,

THE BIG THREE AT YALTA In 1945 a triumphant Winston Churchill, an ailing Franklin Roosevelt, and a determined Joseph Stalin met at Yalta, in southern Russia, to plan for peace. Wartime cooperation soon gave way to bitter hostility. *(National Archives, Washington)*

who had lived through two enormously destructive German invasions, wanted absolute military security from Germany and its potential eastern allies, once and for all. Suspicious by nature, he believed that only Communist states could truly be devoted allies, and he feared that free elections would result in independent and quite possibly hostile governments on his western border. Moreover, by the middle of 1945 there was no way short of war that the United States and its western allies could really influence developments in eastern Europe, and war was out of the question. Stalin was bound to have his way.

WEST VERSUS EAST

The American response to Stalin's conception of security was to "get tough." In May 1945,

Truman abruptly cut off all aid to Russia. In October, he declared that the United States would never recognize any government established by force against the free will of its people. In March 1946, former British Prime Minister Churchill ominously informed an American audience, "From Stettin in the Baltic to Trieste in the Adriatic, an iron curtain has descended across the continent." Soon emotional, moralistic denunciations of Stalin and Communist Russia re-emerged as a popular American political game. At the same time the United States demobilized with incredible speed, perhaps because, according to some historians, it felt so secure with its atomic bomb. When the war against Japan ended in September 1945, there were 12 million Americans in the armed forces; by 1947 there were only 1.5 million, as opposed to 6 million for Soviet Russia. "Getting tough" really meant "talking tough."

Stalin's agents quickly reheated the "ideological struggle against capitalist imperialism," proving as adept as the Americans at verbal abuse. Moreover, the large, well-organized Communist parties of France and Italy obediently started to uncover American plots to take over Europe, and aggressively challenged their own governments with violent criticisms and large strikes. The Soviet Union also put pressure on Iran and Turkey, and while Greek Communists battled Greek royalists, another bitter civil war raged in China. By the spring of 1947, it appeared to many Americans that Stalin wanted much more than just puppet regimes in Soviet-occupied eastern Europe. Stalin seemed determined to export communism by subversion and guerrilla warfare throughout Europe and around the world as well.

The American response to the escalating conflict was the Truman Doctrine, which was aimed at "containing" communism in areas already occupied by the Red Army. Truman told Congress in March 1947: "I believe it must be the policy of the United States to support free people who are resisting attempted subjugation by armed minorities or by outside pressure." As a first step, Truman asked Congress for large-scale military aid to Greece and Turkey. Then in June, Secretary of State George C. Marshall offered all the nations of Europe economic aid – the so-called Marshall Plan – to help them rebuild.

Stalin refused Marshall Plan assistance for all of eastern Europe. He purged the last remaining non-Communist elements from the "coalition" governments of eastern Europe and established Soviet-style, one-party Communist dictatorships. The seizure of power in Czechoslovakia in 1948 was particularly brutal and antidemocratic, greatly strengthening Western fears of limitless Communist expansion. In 1949, therefore, the United States formed an anti-Soviet military alliance of western governments, the North Atlantic Treaty Organization (NATO); in response Stalin formally united his satellites in the Warsaw Pact. Europe was divided into two hostile blocs.

In late 1949, the Communists triumphed in China, frightening and infuriating many Americans, who saw an all-powerful worldwide communist conspiracy extending even into the upper reaches of the American government. When the Russian-backed Communist forces of northern Korea invaded southern Korea in 1950, President Truman's response was swift. American-led United Nations armies intervened. The cold war had spread around the world and become very hot.

It seems clear that the rapid descent from victorious Grand Alliance to bitter cold war was intimately connected with the tragic fate of eastern Europe. When the east European

"ON A 'STRENGTH-GIVING' DIET" *This typical example of Soviet cold war "humor" from* Izvestia *in 1960 shows the revenge-seeking West German beast of Bonn, complete with U.S. knife, French fork, and British napkin, being served a Polaris missile. (Photo: Caroline Buckler)*

later began to claim the spoils of victory, a helpless but moralistic United States refused to cooperate and professed outrage. One cannot help but feel that western opposition immediately after the war came too late and probably encouraged even more aggressive measures by the always suspicious Stalin. And it helped explode the quarrel over eastern Europe into a global confrontation, which quickly became institutionalized.

THE WEST EUROPEAN RENAISSANCE

As the cold war divided Europe into two blocs, the future appeared very bleak on both sides of the Iron Curtain. Economic conditions were the worst in generations, and millions of people lived on the verge of starvation. Politically, Europe was weak and divided, a battleground for cold war ambitions. Moreover, long-cherished European empires were crumbling in the face of Asian and African nationalism. Yet Europe recovered, and the western nations led the way. In less than a generation western Europe achieved unprecedented economic prosperity and regained much of its traditional prominence in world affairs. It was an amazing rebirth — a true renaissance.

THE POSTWAR CHALLENGE

After the war, economic conditions in western Europe were terrible. Simply finding enough to eat was a real problem. Runaway inflation and black markets testified to severe shortages and hardship. The bread ration in Paris in 1946 was little more than it had been in 1942 under the Nazi occupation. Rationing

power vacuum after 1932 had lured Nazi racist imperialism, the appeasing western democracies had quite mistakenly done nothing. They had, however, had one telling insight: how, they had asked themselves, could they unite with Stalin to stop Hitler without giving Stalin great gains on his western borders? After Hitler's invasion of Soviet Russia, the western powers preferred to ignore this question and hope for the best. But when Stalin

of bread had to be introduced in Britain in 1946 for the first time. Both France and Italy produced only about half as much in 1946 as before the war. Many people believed that Europe was quite simply finished. The prominent British historian Arnold Toynbee felt that, at best, west Europeans might seek to civilize the crude but all-powerful Americans, somewhat as the ancient Greeks had civilized their Roman conquerors.

Suffering was most intense in defeated Germany. The major territorial change of the war had moved Soviet Russia's border far to the west. Poland was in turn compensated for this loss to Russia with land taken from Germany (see Map 37.2). To solidify these boundary changes, 13 million people were driven from their homes in eastern Germany (and other eastern countries) and forced to resettle in a greatly reduced Germany. In the last days of the war a captured British airman watched this "migration of a vast peasant population.... They were a pitiful sight, frozen, hungry, shoes and clothes falling apart, dragging themselves along to an unknown destination, hoping only that it might be beyond the reach of the Russian army."[4] The Russians were also seizing factories and equipment as reparations, and even tearing up railroad tracks and sending the rails to the Soviet Union. The command "Come here, woman," from a Russian soldier was the sound of terror, the prelude to rape.

In 1945 and 1946, conditions were not much better in the western zones. The western allies also treated the German population with great severity at first. By February 1946, the average daily diet of a German in the Ruhr had been reduced to two slices of bread, a pat of margarine, a spoonful of porridge, and two small potatoes. Countless Germans sold many of their possessions to American soldiers to buy food. Cigarettes replaced worthless money as currency. The winter of 1946–1947 was one of the coldest in memory, and there were widespread signs of actual starvation. By the spring of 1947, refugee-clogged, hungry, prostrate Germany was on the verge of total collapse and threatening to drag down the rest of Europe.

Yet western Europe was not finished. The Nazi occupation and the war had discredited old ideas and old leaders. All over Europe many people were willing to change and experiment in hopes of building a new and better Europe out of the rubble. New groups and new leaders were coming to the fore to guide these aspirations. Progressive Catholics and revitalized Catholic political parties – the Christian Democrats – were particularly influential.

In Italy the Christian Democrats emerged as the leading party in the first postwar elections in 1946, and in early 1948 they won an absolute majority in the parliament in a landslide victory. Their very able leader was Alcide De Gasperi, a courageous antifascist and former Vatican librarian, firmly committed to political democracy, economic reconstruction, and moderate social reform. In France too the Catholic party provided some of the best postwar leaders, like Robert Schuman. This was particularly true after January 1946, when General de Gaulle, the inspiring wartime leader of the Free French, resigned after having re-established the free and democratic Fourth Republic. Western Germany also found new and able leadership among its Catholics. In 1949, Konrad Adenauer, the former mayor of Cologne and a long-time anti-Nazi, began his long, highly successful democratic rule; the Christian Democrats became West Germany's majority party for a generation. In providing effective leadership

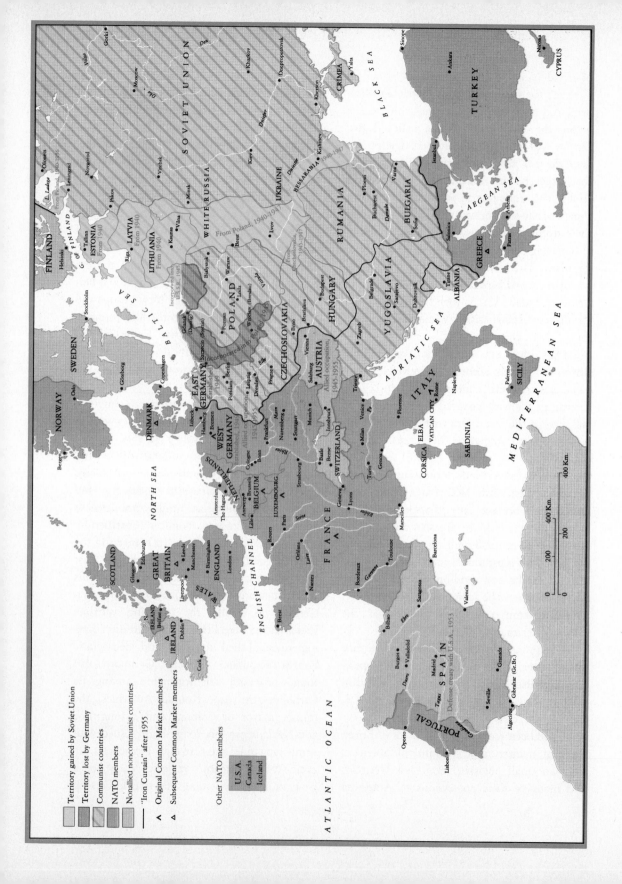

Territory gained by Soviet Union
Territory lost by Germany
Communist countries
NATO members
Nonallied noncommunist countries
"Iron Curtain" after 1955
Original Common Market members
Subsequent Common Market members

Other NATO members
U.S.A.
Canada
Iceland

ATLANTIC OCEAN

NORWAY
SWEDEN
FINLAND
G. OF FINLAND
From Finland, 1940–1956

Bergen
Oslo
Edinburgh
SCOTLAND
Glasgow
GREAT
BRITAIN
Leeds
ENGLAND
Manchester
Liverpool
Birmingham
WALES
London
IRELAND
Belfast
IRELAND
Dublin
Cork

ENGLISH CHANNEL
Brest
Rouen
Nantes
Orléans
Lille
Amsterdam
The Hague
Antwerp
Brussels
NETHERLANDS
BELGIUM
LUXEMBOURG
Paris
Seine
FRANCE
Loire
Bordeaux
Garonne
Toulouse
Lyons
Marseilles

NORTH SEA
Stockholm
Göteborg
Copenhagen
DENMARK
Lübeck
Hamburg
Bremen
WEST
GERMANY
Cologne
Bonn
Frankfurt
Nuremberg
Stuttgart
Basle
Berne
SWITZERLAND
Geneva
Rhine
Main
Munich
Innsbruck
AUSTRIA
Allied occupation
1945–1955
Salzburg

BALTIC SEA
Helsinki
Tallinn
ESTONIA
From 1940
LATVIA
From 1940
Riga
LITHUANIA
From 1940
Kaunas
Vilna
Incorporated into U.S.S.R. 1945
Gdansk (Danzig)
Szczecin (Stettin)
POLAND
Wrocław (Breslau)
Poznań
Łódź
Warsaw
EAST
GERMANY
Established 1949
Berlin
Potsdam
Leipzig
Dresden
Elbe
Prague
CZECHOSLOVAKIA
Brno
Bratislava
Vienna
From Poland, 1940–1945

SOVIET UNION
Gorki
Volga
Moscow
Don
Novgorod
Leningrad
Pskov
Vitebsk
Minsk
WHITE RUSSIA
Kiev
UKRAINE
Dnieper
Kharkov
Dnepropetrovsk
Dniester
Kherson
BESSARABIA 1940–1947
CRIMEA
Yalta
BLACK SEA
Sinope

Białystok
Brest
Lvov

HUNGARY
Budapest
Zagreb
Belgrade
YUGOSLAVIA
Sarajevo
ADRIATIC SEA
RUMANIA
Ploesti
Bucharest
Danube
Sofia
BULGARIA

Trieste
Venice
Po
ITALY
Milan
Turin
Genoa
Florence
CORSICA
ELBA
VATICAN CITY
Rome
Naples
SARDINIA
MEDITERRANEAN SEA
SICILY
Palermo

Dubrovnik
ALBANIA
Tirane
GREECE
Salonika
Athens
AEGEAN SEA
Vatna
TURKEY
Istanbul
Ankara
Nicosia
CYPRUS
Patras

SPAIN
Madrid
Valladolid
Burgos
Duero
Tagus
Valencia
Barcelona
Saragossa
Bilbao
Ebro
Seville
Granada
Gibraltar (Gr.Br.)
Algeciros
PORTUGAL
Oporto
Lisbon
Guadiana
Defense treaty with U.S.A. 1953

400 Km.
200
0
400 Km.
200
0

*MAP 37.2   EUROPE AFTER 1945   Both the So-
viet Union and Poland took land from Germany,
which was then permanently divided by the cold war.*

for their respective countries, the Christian
Democrats were inspired and united by a
common Christian and European heritage.
They steadfastly rejected totalitarianism and
narrow nationalism and placed their faith in
close cooperation.

The socialists and the communists, active
in the resistance against Hitler, also emerged
from the war with increased power and prestige, especially in France and Italy. They too
provided fresh leadership and pushed for social change and economic reform with considerable success. Thus, in the immediate
postwar years, welfare measures such as family
allowances, health insurance, and increased
public housing were enacted throughout
much of Europe. In Italy social benefits from
the state came to equal a large part of the average worker's wages. In France large banks,
insurance companies, public utilities, coal
mines, and the Renault auto company were
nationalized by the government. Britain followed the same trend. The voters threw out
Churchill and the Conservatives in 1945, and
the socialist Labour party under Clement Att-
lee moved toward establishment of the "welfare state." Many industries were nationalized,
and the government provided each citizen
with free medical service and taxed the middle
and upper classes heavily. The Labour government was also committed to providing
everyone a job and avoiding economic depression.

The massive economic aid the United
States provided under the Marshall Plan
speeded western Europe's economic recovery.
Offered to all of Europe but accepted only by
the western nations, Marshall Plan aid was
intended to create the economic prosperity on
which stable democratic societies could be
built. The plan's requirement that the participating countries coordinate their efforts for
maximum effectiveness led to the establishment of the Organization of European Economic Cooperation (OEEC). Over the next
five years the United States furnished foreign
countries roughly $22.5 billion, of which
seven-eighths was in the form of outright
gifts rather than loans. Thus America assumed its international responsibilities after
the Second World War, exercising the leadership it had shunned in the tragic years after
1919.

ECONOMIC "MIRACLES"

As Marshall Plan aid poured in, the battered
economies of western Europe began to turn
the corner in 1948. Impoverished West Germany led the way with a spectacular advance
after the western Allies permitted Adenauer's
government to reform the currency and stimulate private enterprise. Other countries were
not far behind. The outbreak of the Korean
War in 1950 further stimulated economic activity, and Europe entered a period of rapid,
sustained economic progress. By 1963, western Europe was producing more than two-
and-one-half times as much as it had before
the war. Never before had the European
economy grown so fast. For politicians and
economists, for workers and business leaders,
it was a time of astonishing, loudly proclaimed economic "miracles."

There were many reasons for western
Europe's brilliant economic performance.
American aid helped the process get off to a
fast start. Europe received equipment to repair
damaged plants and even whole new specialized factories when necessary. Thus, critical
shortages were quickly overcome. Moreover,

BERLIN DIGS OUT What was once a great newspaper building stands as a ghostly gutted-out shell in this altogether typical postwar scene from 1945. But the previously impassable street has been partially cleared of rubble and traffic has begun to move again. In the midst of ruins life refuses to die. (U.S. Army Signal Corps)

since European nations coordinated the distribution of American aid, many barriers to European trade and cooperation were quickly dropped. Aid from the United States helped, therefore, to promote both a resurgence of economic liberalism with its healthy competition and an international division of labor.

As in most of the world, economic growth became a basic objective of all west European governments, for leaders and voters were determined to avoid a return to the dangerous and demoralizing stagnation of the 1930s. Governments generally accepted Keynesian economics (page 1314) and sought to stimulate their economies, and some also adopted a number of imaginative strategies. Those in Germany and France were particularly successful and influential.

Under Minister of Economy Ludwig Erhard, a roly-poly, cigar-smoking ex-professor, postwar West Germany broke decisively with the totally regulated, straight-jacketed Nazi economy. Erhard bet on the free-market economy. He and his teachers believed not only that capitalism was more efficient but also that political and social freedom could thrive only if there were real economic freedom. Erhard's first step was to reform the currency and abolish rationing and price controls in 1948. He boldly declared, "The only ration coupon is the Mark."[5] At first profits jumped sharply, prompting businessmen to quickly employ more people and produce more. By the late 1950s, Germany had a prospering economy and full employment, a strong currency and stable prices. Germany's success aroused renewed respect for free-market capitalism and encouraged freer trade within Europe.

In France the major innovation was a new kind of planning. Under the guidance of Jean Monnet, an economic pragmatist and apostle of European unity, a planning commission set ambitious but flexible goals for the French economy. It used Marshall aid money and the nationalized banks to funnel money into key industries, several of which were state-owned. At the same time, the planning commission and the French bureaucracy encouraged private enterprise to "think big." The often-cautious French business community responded, investing heavily in new equipment and modern factories. Thus, France combined flexible planning and a "mixed" state and private economy to achieve the most rapid economic development in its long history. Throughout the 1950s and 1960s, there was hardly any unemployment in France. The average person's standard of living improved dramatically. France too was an economic "miracle."

Other factors also contributed to western Europe's economic boom. In most countries after the war, there were large numbers of men and women ready to work hard for low wages and the hope of a better future. Germany had millions of impoverished refugees, while France and Italy still had millions of poor peasants. Expanding industries in those countries thus had a great asset to draw on. More fully urbanized Britain had no such rural labor pool; this lack, along with a welfare socialism that stressed "fair shares" rather than rapid growth, helps account for its fairly poor postwar economic performance.

In 1945, impoverished Europe was still rich in the sense that it had the human skills of an advanced industrial society. Skilled workers, engineers, managers, and professionals knew what could and should be done, and they did it.

Many consumer products had been invented or perfected since the late 1920s, but few Europeans had been able to buy them during the depression and war. In 1945 the electric refrigerator, the washing machine, and the automobile were rare luxuries. There was, therefore, a great potential demand, which the economic system moved to satisfy.

Finally, ever since 1919 the nations of Europe had suffered from high tariffs and small national markets, which made for small and therefore inefficient factories. In the postwar era European countries junked many of these economic barriers and gradually created a large unified market — the Common Market. This action, which stimulated the economy, was part of the postwar search for a new European unity.

POLITICAL RECOVERY

Western Europe's political recovery was spectacular. Republics were re-established in

France, West Germany, and Italy. Constitutional monarchs were restored in Belgium, Holland, and Norway. These democratic governments took root once again and thrived. To be sure, only West Germany established a two-party system on the British-American model; states like France and Italy returned to multiparty politics and shifting parliamentary coalitions. Yet the middle-of-the road parties – primarily the Christian Democrats and the Socialists – dominated and provided continuing leadership. National self-determination was accompanied by civil liberties and great individual freedom. All of this was itself an extraordinary achievement.

Even more remarkable was the still-unfinished, still-continuing movement toward a united Europe. The Christian Democrats with their shared Catholic heritage were particularly committed to "building Europe," and other groups shared their dedication. Many Europeans believed that narrow, exaggerated nationalism had been a fundamental cause of both world wars, and that only through unity could European conflict be avoided in the future. Many west Europeans also realized how very weak their countries were in comparison with the United States and the Soviet Union, the two superpowers that had divided Europe from outside and made it into a cold war battleground. Thus, the cold war encouraged some visionaries to seek a new "European nation," a superpower capable of controlling western Europe's destiny and reasserting its influence in world affairs.

The close cooperation among European states required by the Marshall Plan led to the creation of both the OEEC and the Council of Europe in 1948. European federalists hoped that the Council of Europe would quickly evolve into a true European parliament with sovereign rights, but this did not happen.

Britain, with its empire and its "special relationship" with the United States, consistently opposed giving any real political power – any sovereignty – to the council. Many old-fashioned continental nationalists and communists felt similarly. The Council of Europe became little more than a multinational debating society.

Frustrated in the direct political approach, European federalists turned toward economics. As one of them explained, "Politics and economics are closely related. Let us try, then, for progress in economic matters. Let us suppress those obstacles of an economic nature which divide and compartmentalize the nations of Europe."[6] In this they were quite successful.

Two far-seeing French statesmen, the planner Jean Monnet and Foreign Minister Robert Schuman, courageously took the lead in 1950. The Schuman Plan called for a special international organization to control and integrate all European steel and coal production. West Germany, Italy, Belgium, the Netherlands, and Luxembourg accepted the French idea in 1952; the British would have none of it. The immediate economic goal – a single competitive market without national tariffs or quotas – was rapidly realized. By 1958, coal and steel moved as freely among the six nations of the European Coal and Steel Community as among the states of the United States. The more far-reaching political goal was to bind the six member nations so closely together economically that war among them would become unthinkable and virtually impossible. This brilliant strategy did much to reduce tragic old rivalries, particularly that of France and Germany, which practically disappeared in the postwar era.

The coal and steel community was so successful that it encouraged further technical and economic cooperation among "the Six." In 1957, the same six nations formed Euratom to pursue joint research in atomic energy. The same year they also signed the Treaty of Rome, which created the European Economic Community, generally known as the Common Market. The treaty's first goal was to reduce gradually all tariffs among the Six and create a large free-trade area. The Treaty of Rome also called for the free movement of capital and labor, and it envisioned common economic policies and institutions.

An epoch-making stride toward unity, the Common Market was a tremendous success. Tariffs were rapidly reduced, and the European economy was stimulated. Companies and regions specialized in what they did best. Western Europe was being united in a single market almost as large as that of the United States. Many medium-sized American companies rushed to Europe, for a single modern factory in, say, Belgium or southern Italy had a vast potential market of 170 million customers.

The development of the Common Market fired imaginations and encouraged hopes of rapid progress toward political as well as economic union. In the 1960s, however, these hopes were frustrated by a resurgence of more traditional nationalism. Once again, France took the lead. Mired in a bitter colonial war in Algeria, the country turned in 1958 to General de Gaulle, who established the Fifth French Republic and ruled as its president until 1969. A towering giant both literally and figuratively, de Gaulle was dedicated to reasserting France's greatness and glory. Once he had resolved the Algerian conflict, he labored to recreate a powerful, truly independent France, which would lead and even dictate to the other Common Market states. De Gaulle personified the political resurgence of

FRENCH PRESIDENT DE GAULLE welcomed the young President Kennedy to Paris in 1961. De Gaulle strongly challenged American leadership in Western Europe. (Wide World Photos)

the leading nations of western Europe, as well as declining fears of the Soviet Union in the 1960s. Viewing the United States as the main threat to genuine French (and European) independence, he withdrew all French military forces from the "American-controlled" NATO command, which had to move from Paris to Brussels. De Gaulle tried to create financial difficulties for the United States by demanding gold for the American dollars

France had accumulated. France also developed its own nuclear weapons. Within the Common Market, de Gaulle in 1963 and again in 1967 vetoed the application of the pro-American British, who were having second thoughts and wanted to join. More generally, he refused to permit the scheduled advent of majority rule within the Common Market, and he forced his partners to accept many of his views. Thus, throughout the 1960s the Common Market thrived economically, but it remained a union of revitalized sovereign states.

DECOLONIALIZATION

The postwar era saw the total collapse of colonial empires. Between 1947 and 1962, almost every colonial territory gained independence. Europe's long expansion, which had reached a high point in the late nineteenth century, was completely reversed (see Map 37.3). The spectacular collapse of Western political empires fully reflected old Europe's eclipsed power after 1945. Yet the new nations of Asia and Africa have been so deeply influenced by Western ideas and achievements that the "westernization" of the world has continued to rush forward.

Modern nationalism, with its demands for political self-determination and racial equality, spread from intellectuals to the masses in virtually every colonial territory after the First World War. Economic suffering created bitter popular resentment, and thousands of colonial subjects had been unwillingly drafted into French and British armies. Nationalist leaders stepped up their demands. By 1919, one high-ranking British official mournfully wrote: "A wave of unrest is sweeping over the Empire, as over the rest of the world. Almost every day brings some disturbance or other at our Imperial outposts."[7] The Russian Revolution

also encouraged the growth of nationalism, and Soviet Russia verbally and militarily supported nationalist independence movements.

Furthermore, European empires had been based on an enormous power differential between the rulers and the ruled, a difference that had declined almost to the vanishing point by 1945. Not only was western Europe poor and battered immediately after the war, but Japan had demonstrated that whites were not invincible. With its political power and moral authority in tatters, Europe's only choices were to give in gracefully or to wage risky wars of reconquest.

Most Europeans regarded their empires very differently after 1945 than before 1914, or even before 1939. Empire had rested on self-confidence and a sense of righteousness; Europeans had believed their superiority to be not only technical and military but spiritual and moral as well. The horrors of the Second World War and the near-destruction of Western civilization destroyed such complacent arrogance and gave opponents of imperialism the upper hand in Europe. After 1945 most Europeans were willing to let go of their colonies more or less voluntarily and to concentrate on rebuilding at home.

India played a key role in decolonialization and the end of empire. India was Britain's oldest, largest, and most lucrative nonwhite possession, and Britain had by far the largest colonial empire. Nationalist opposition to British rule coalesced after the First World War under the leadership of the British-educated lawyer Mahatma Gandhi (1869–1948), who preached nonviolent "noncooperation" against the British. Indian intellectuals effec-

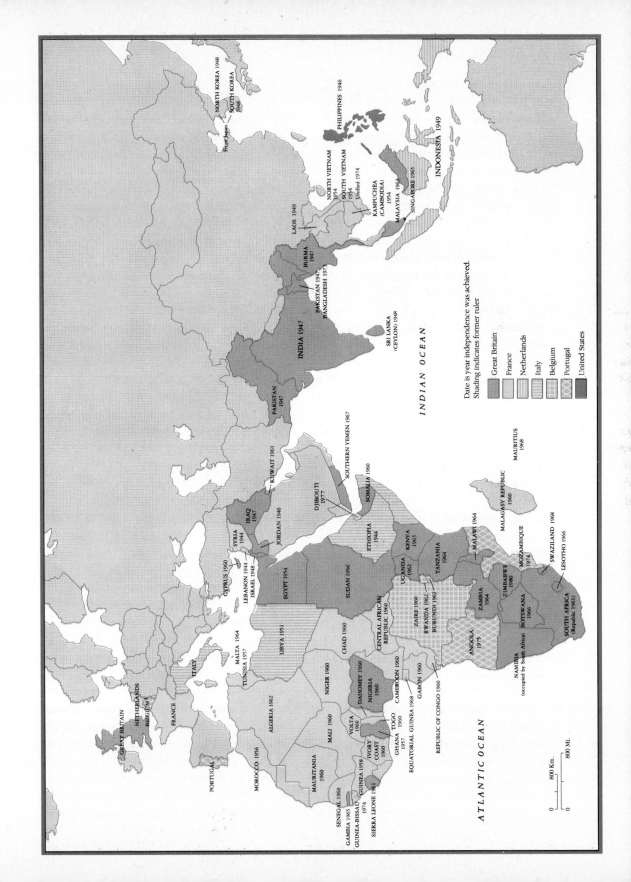

NORTH KOREA 1948
SOUTH KOREA 1948
From Japan

PHILIPPINES 1946

INDONESIA 1949

NORTH VIETNAM 1954
SOUTH VIETNAM 1954
Unified 1974
KAMPUCHEA (CAMBODIA) 1954
MALAYSIA 1963
SINGAPORE 1965

LAOS 1949

BURMA 1947

PAKISTAN 1947
BANGLADESH 1973

INDIA 1947

PAKISTAN 1947

SRI LANKA (CEYLON) 1948

INDIAN OCEAN

Date is year independence was achieved.
Shading indicates former ruler

Great Britain
France
Netherlands
Italy
Belgium
Portugal
United States

SOUTHERN YEMEN 1967

KUWAIT 1961

DJIBOUTI 1977

SOMALIA 1960

MAURITIUS 1968

IRAQ 1947

SYRIA 1944

JORDAN 1946

ETHIOPIA 1944

KENYA 1963

MALAWI 1964

CYPRUS 1960

LEBANON 1944
ISRAEL 1948

EGYPT 1954

SUDAN 1956

UGANDA 1962

TANZANIA 1964

MALAGASY REPUBLIC 1960

SWAZILAND 1968

MALTA 1964

TUNISIA 1957

ITALY

LIBYA 1951

CHAD 1960

CENTRAL AFRICAN REPUBLIC 1960

ZAIRE 1960

RWANDA 1962

BURUNDI 1962

ZAMBIA 1964

ZIMBABWE 1980

MOZAMBIQUE 1974

LESOTHO 1966

BOTSWANA 1966

SOUTH AFRICA (Republic 1961)

GREAT BRITAIN

NETHERLANDS

BELGIUM

FRANCE

MOROCCO 1956

ALGERIA 1962

NIGER 1960

CAMEROON 1960

GABON 1960

ANGOLA 1975

NAMIBIA (occupied by South Africa)

PORTUGAL

MAURITANIA 1960

MALI 1960

VOLTA 1960

DAHOMEY 1960

NIGERIA 1960

TOGO 1960

EQUATORIAL GUINEA 1968

REPUBLIC OF CONGO 1960

ATLANTIC OCEAN

SENEGAL 1960

GAMBIA 1965

GUINEA-BISSAU 1974

GUINEA 1958

SIERRA LEONE 1961

IVORY COAST 1960

GHANA 1957

0   800 Km.
0   800 Mi.

tively argued the old liberal case for equality and self-determination. In response, Britain's rulers gradually introduced political reforms and limited self-government. When the war ended, independence followed very rapidly. The new Labour government was determined to leave India: radicals and socialists had always opposed imperialism, and the heavy cost of governing India had become an intolerable financial burden. The obstacle posed by conflict between India's Hindu and Muslim populations was resolved in 1947 by creating two states, predominantly Hindu India and Muslim Pakistan.

If Indian nationalism drew on Western parliamentary liberalism, Chinese nationalism developed and triumphed in the framework of Marxist-Leninist totalitarianism. In the turbulent early 1920s, a broad alliance of nationalist forces within the Russian-supported Kuomintang – the National People's party – was dedicated to unifying China and abolishing European concessions. But in 1927 Chiang Kai-shek (1887–1975), the successor to Sun Yat-Sen (page 1162) and the leader of the Kuomintang, broke with his more radical Communist allies, headed by Mao Tse-tung.

In 1934, Mao Tse-tung (1893–1976) led his followers on an incredible five-thousand-mile march to remote northern China and dug in. Even war against the Japanese army of occupation could not force Mao and Chiang to cooperate. By late 1945, the long-standing quarrel erupted in civil war. Stalin gave Mao some aid, and the Americans gave Chiang much more. Winning the support of the peasantry by promising to expropriate the big landowners, the tougher, better-organized Communists forced the Nationalists to withdraw to the island of Taiwan in 1949.

Mao and the Communists united China's 550 million inhabitants in a strong centralized state, expelled foreigners, and began building a new society along Soviet lines, with mass arrests, forced-labor camps, and ceaseless propaganda. The peasantry was collectivized, and the inevitable five-year plans concentrated quite successfully on the expansion of heavy industry.

Most Asian countries followed the pattern of either India or China. Britain quickly gave Sri Lanka (Ceylon) and Burma independence in 1948; the Philippines became independent of the United States in 1946. The Dutch attempt to reconquer the Netherlands East Indies was unsuccessful, and in 1949 Indonesia emerged independent.

The French similarly sought to re-establish colonial rule in Indochina, but despite American aid they were defeated in 1954 by forces under the Communist and nationalist guerrilla leader Ho Chi Minh (1890–1969). At the subsequent international peace conference, French Indochina gained independence. Vietnam was divided into two hostile independent states, one communist and one anticommunist. Civil war soon broke out between the two.

In Africa, Arab nationalism was an important factor in the ending of empire. Sharing a common language and culture, Arab nationalists were also loosely united by their opposition to the colonial powers and to the migration of Jewish refugees to Palestine. The British, whose occupation policies in Palestine were condemned by Arabs and Jews, by Russians and Americans, announced their withdrawal from Palestine in 1948. The United Nations voted for the creation of two states, one Arab and one Jewish. The Arab countries immediately attacked the new Jewish nation and suffered a humiliating defeat. Thousands of Arab refugees fled Palestine.

This Arab defeat triggered a nationalist revolution in Egypt in 1952, when a young army officer named Gamal Abdel Nasser

WORKING THE LAND   China's peasants, like these girls preparing for planting, worked on state-run collective farms after the Communists abolished private ownership of land. (Magnum Photo Library © Marc Riboud Magnum)

(1918–1970) drove out the pro-Western king. In 1956 Nasser abruptly nationalized the Suez Canal, the last symbol and substance of Western power in the Middle East. Infuriated, the British and French, along with the Israelis, invaded Egypt. This was, however, to be the dying gasp of imperial power: the moralistic, anti-imperialist Americans joined with the Russians to force the British, French, and Israelis to withdraw.

The failure of the Western powers to unseat Nasser in 1956 in turn encouraged Arab nationalists in Algeria. Algeria's large French population considered Algeria an integral part

of France. It was this feeling that made the ensuing war so bitter and so atypical of decolonialization. In the end, General de Gaulle, who had returned to power as part of a movement to keep Algeria French, accepted the principle of Algerian self-determination. In 1962, after more than a century of French rule, Algeria became independent and the European population quickly fled.

In most of Africa south of the Sahara, decolonialization proceeded much more smoothly. Beginning in 1957, Britain's colonies won independence with little or no bloodshed. In 1960 the clever de Gaulle offered the leaders of French black Africa the choice of a total break with France or immediate independence within a kind of French commonwealth. Heavily dependent on France for economic aid and technology, all but one of the new states chose association with France. Throughout the 1960s and 1970s, France (and its west European partners) successfully used economic and cultural ties with former colonies, such as special trading privileges with the Common Market and heavy investment in French-based education, to maintain a powerful European presence in black Africa. Radicals charged France (and Europe generally) with "neo-colonialism," designed to perpetuate European economic domination indefinitely. In any event, enduring aid and influence in black Africa was an important manifestation of western Europe's political recovery and even of its possible emergence as a genuine superpower.

RECENT TRENDS

Events in the late 1960s and 1970s suggested that the period of unprecedented postwar recovery was finally over, and that an uncertain new era had probably begun. In 1968, a mini-revolution in France signaled the re-emergence of serious social and political conflict in western Europe and the United States after a generation of relative peace. Serious economic problems also reappeared. Most countries in the late 1960s began to suffer from rapid inflation. Governments' inability to control this inflation led to fears that the new economic orthodoxy – Keynesian economics – had not possessed the secret to permanent, stable prosperity after all.

The international monetary system, so instrumental in the postwar boom, also broke down. That system, created by the Bretton Woods Agreement of 1944, was based on the American dollar, which was supposed to be "as good as gold" since foreign governments could always exchange dollars for gold. Beginning in the 1950s, however, the United States constantly spent more abroad than it earned. By early 1971, the United States had only $11 billion in gold left in Fort Knox, and Europe had accumulated 50 billion American dollars. The result was a classic, long-overdue "run on the bank" in 1971, as holders of dollars tried to exchange their dollars for gold. President Richard Nixon was forced to stop the sale of American gold. The free-market price of gold soared, and the value of the dollar declined. The dollar, no longer "as good as gold," became just another currency, and great uncertainty arose about international trade and finance.

Furthermore, the postwar boom in Europe had been fueled by cheap oil from the Middle East. Following an Arab-Israeli war in 1973 and reflecting the desire to gain greater profit from their natural resources, the Arab states quadrupled the price of oil. This act increased inflation, worsened the worst recession since 1945, and signaled the end of an era of cheap energy.

Yet in the face of all these challenges the Common Market did not collapse. The fall of the dollar standard showed the world that western Europe was once again America's economic equal. Moreover, the Common Market continued to exert a powerful attraction. In 1973, Britain, Denmark, and Ireland finally joined; Greece, Portugal, and Spain applied for membership in 1977 and in 1981 Greece joined officially as negotiations with Portugal and Spain continued. Although a United States of Europe is still far in the future, the nations of the Common Market are cooperating more and more closely in many international undertakings and negotiations. The Common Market decided in 1977, for example, to go ahead with plans for a nuclear breeder reactor to produce electric power, and it has developed a common policy on peace in the Middle East and economic negotiations with the Third World. The movement toward European unity is still very much alive.

Democracy has remained strong in Europe, unlike much of the world, and even appears to be expanding its sway. Both Spain and Portugal scrapped their aging dictatorships in 1974 and committed themselves to building democratic governments. Greece also established parliamentary rule. More difficult to interpret is an apparent trend toward a more liberal Western communism and toward communist participation in west European governments. The large Communist parties of France and Italy have openly criticized the Soviet Union for its inattention to human rights, and both claim to be stalwart democrats worthy of trust. In Italy, the Communists have begun working with the Christian Democrats in parliament on economic and social problems. In France, Communists actually entered the cabinet after the victory of a socialist, François Mitterrand, in the presidential elections of 1981. Whether these developments signal a great "historic compromise" or merely a passing phase, only time will tell.

SOVIET EASTERN EUROPE

While western Europe surged ahead economically, regaining political independence as American influence gradually waned, eastern Europe followed a different path. Soviet Russia first tightened its grip on the "liberated" nations of eastern Europe under Stalin and then refused to let go. Economic recovery in eastern Europe proceeded, therefore, along Soviet lines, and political and social developments were largely determined by changes in the Soviet Union. Thus one must look primarily at Soviet Russia to understand the achievements and failures of east European peoples after the Second World War.

STALIN'S LAST YEARS

The unwillingness of the United States to approve of what Stalin did with territories occupied by the triumphant Red Army was at least partly responsible for the outbreak and institutionalization of the cold war. Yet Americans were not the only ones who felt disappointed and even betrayed by Stalin's postwar actions.

The Great Patriotic War of the Fatherland had fostered Russian nationalism and a relaxation of totalitarian terror. It also produced a rare but real unity between Soviet rulers and most Russian people. When an American correspondent asked a distinguished sixty-year-old Jewish scientist who had decided to leave Russia for Israel in 1972 what had been the best period in Russian history, he received a startling answer: the Second World War. The scientist explained: "At that time we all felt closer to our government than at any other time in our lives. It was not *their* country then, but *our* country. . . . It was not *their* war, but *our* war."[8] Having made such a heroic war effort, the vast majority of the Soviet people hoped in 1945 that a grateful party and government would grant greater freedom and democracy. Such hopes were soon crushed.

Even before the war ended, Stalin was moving his country back toward rigid dictatorship. As early as 1944, the leading members of the Communist party were being given a new motivating slogan: "The war on Fascism ends, the war on capitalism begins."[9] By early 1946, Stalin was publicly singing the old tune that war was inevitable as long as capitalism existed. Stalin's invention of a new foreign foe was mainly an excuse for re-establishing totalitarian measures, for the totalitarian state cannot live without enemies. Unfortunately, as the rebel Russian historian Andrei Amalrik has argued, Stalin's language at home and his actions in eastern Europe were so crudely extreme that he managed to turn an imaginary threat into a real one, as the cold war took hold.

One of Stalin's first postwar goals was to repress the millions of Soviet citizens who were outside Soviet borders when the war ended. Many had been captured by the Nazis; others were ordinary civilians who had been living abroad. Many were opposed to Stalin; some had fought for the Germans. Determined to hush up the fact that large numbers of Soviet citizens hated his regime so much that they had willingly supported the Germans and refused to go home, Stalin demanded that all these "traitors" be returned to him. At Yalta, Roosevelt and Churchill agreed, and they kept their word. American and British military commanders refused to recognize the right of political asylum under any circumstances.

Roughly 2 million people were delivered to Stalin against their will. Most were immediately arrested and sent to forced-labor camps, where about 50 percent perished. The revival of many forced-labor camps, which had accounted for roughly one-sixth of all new construction in Soviet Russia before the war, was further stimulated by large-scale purges of many people who had never left the Soviet Union, particularly in 1945 and 1946.

Culture and art were also purged. Rigid anti-Western ideological conformity was reimposed in violent campaigns led by Stalin's trusted henchman, Andrei Zhdanov. Zhdanov denounced many artists, including the composers Sergei Prokofiev and Dimitri Shostakovich and the outstanding film director Sergei Eisenstein. The great poet Anna Akhmatova was condemned as "a harlot and nun who mixes harlotry and prayer" and, like many others, driven out of the writers' union, which practically insured that her work would not be published. In 1949, Stalin launched a savage verbal attack on Soviet Jews, who were accused of being pro-Western and antisocialist.

In the political realm Stalin reasserted the Communist party's complete control of the government and his absolute mastery of the party. Five-year plans were reintroduced to cope with the enormous task of economic reconstruction. Once again heavy and military industry were given top priority, and consumer goods, housing, and still-collectivized agriculture were neglected. Everyday life was very hard: in 1952 the wages of ordinary people still bought 25 to 40 percent *less* than in 1928. In short, it was the 1930s all over again in Soviet Russia, although police terror was less intense than during that era's purges.

Stalin's prime postwar innovation was to export the Stalinist system to the countries of eastern Europe. The Communist parties of eastern Europe had established one-party states by 1948, thanks to the help of the Red Army and the Russian secret police. Rigid ideological indoctrination, attacks on religion, and a lack of civil liberties were soon facts of life. Industry was nationalized, and the middle class was stripped of its possessions. Economic life was then faithfully recast in the Stalinist mold. Forced industrialization, with five-year plans and a stress on heavy industry, lurched forward without regard for human costs. For the sake of ideological uniformity, agriculture had to be collectivized; this process went much faster in Bulgaria and Czechoslovakia than in Hungary and Poland. Finally, the satellite countries were forced to trade heavily with Soviet Russia on very unfavorable terms, as traditional economic ties with western Europe were forcibly severed.

Only Josip Tito (1892–1980), the popular resistance leader and Communist chief of Yugoslavia, was able to resist Russian economic exploitation successfully. Tito openly broke with Stalin in 1948, and, since there was no Russian army in Yugoslavia, he got away with it. Tito's successful proclamation of Communist independence led the infuriated and humiliated Stalin to purge the Communist parties of eastern Europe. Hundreds of thousands who had joined the party after the war were expelled. Popular Communist leaders who, like Tito, had led the resistance against Germany, were made to star in reruns of the great show trials of the 1930s, complete with charges of treason, unbelievable confessions, and merciless executions. Thus did history repeat itself as Stalin sought to create absolutely obedient instruments of domination in eastern Europe.

KHRUSHCHEV AND DE-STALINIZATION

In 1953, the aging Stalin finally died, and a new era slowly began in Soviet eastern Europe. Even as they struggled for power, Stalin's heirs realized that changes and reforms were necessary. There was, first of all, widespread fear and hatred of Stalin's political terrorism, which had struck both high and low with its endless purges and unjust arrests. Even Stalin's secret-police chief, Lavrenti Beria, publicly favored a relaxation of controls in an unsuccessful attempt to seize power. Beria was arrested and shot, after which the power of the secret police was curbed and many of its infamous forced-labor camps were gradually closed. Change was also necessary for economic reasons. Agriculture was in bad shape, and shortages of consumer goods were discouraging hard work and initiative. Finally, Stalin's aggressive foreign policy had led directly to an ongoing American commitment to western Europe and a strong Western alliance. Soviet Russia was isolated and contained.

On the question of just how much change should be permitted, the Communist leadership was badly split. The conservatives led by Stalin's long-time foreign minister, the stone-faced Vyacheslav Molotov, wanted to make as few changes as possible. The reformers, led by Nikita Khrushchev, argued for bold innovations. Khrushchev (1894–1971), who had joined the party as an uneducated coal miner in 1918 at twenty-four and had risen steadily to a high-level position in the 1930s, was emerging as the new ruler by 1955.

To strengthen his position and that of his fellow reformers within the party, Khrushchev launched an all-out attack on Stalin and his crimes at a closed session of the Twentieth Party Congress in 1956. In gory detail he described to the startled Communist delegates how Stalin had tortured and murdered thousands of loyal Communists, how he had trusted Hitler completely and bungled the country's defense, and how he had "supported the glorification of his own person with all conceivable methods." For hours Soviet Russia's top leader delivered an attack whose content would previously have been dismissed as "anti-Communist hysteria" in many circles throughout the Western world.

*LENIN AVENUE, VOLGOGRAD   Devastated Sta-
lingrad was completely rebuilt and then renamed
Volgograd as part of Khrushchev's de-Stalinization
campaign. Seen here are the massive apartment blocks,
the gigantic boulevard, and the stress on public transportation as opposed to private automobiles, which are
all quite characteristic of Soviet urban style. (Sovfoto/
Eastfoto)*

Khrushchev's "secret speech" was read to
Communist party meetings throughout the
country and strengthened the reform movement. The liberalization – or de-Stalinization,
as it was called in the West – of Soviet Russia
was genuine. The Communist party jealously
maintained its monopoly on political power,
but Khrushchev shook it up and brought in
new blood. The economy was made more responsive to the needs and even some of the
desires of the people, as some resources were
shifted from heavy industry and the military
toward consumer goods and agriculture. Stalinist controls over workers were relaxed,
and independent courts rather than the se-

cret police judged and punished nonpolitical
crimes.

Russia's very low standard of living finally
began to improve, and continued to rise
throughout the 1960s. By 1970, Russians
were able to buy twice as much food, three
times as much clothing, and twelve times as
many appliances as in 1950. (Even so, the
standard of living in Soviet Russia was only
about half that of the wealthier west European
countries in 1970, and well below that of east
European countries as well.)

De-Stalinization created great ferment
among writers and intellectuals, who hungered for cultural freedom. The poet Boris

Pasternak (1890–1960), who survived the Stalinist years by turning his talents to translating Shakespeare, finished his great novel, *Doctor Zhivago,* in 1956. Published in the West but not in Russia, *Doctor Zhivago* is both a literary masterpiece and a powerful challenge to communism. It tells the story of a prerevolutionary intellectual who rejects the violence and brutality of the revolution of 1917 and the Stalinist years. Even as he is destroyed, he triumphs because of his humanity and Christian spirit. Pasternak was forced by Khrushchev himself to refuse the Nobel prize in 1958 – but he was not shot. Other talented writers followed Pasternak's lead, and courageous editors let the sparks fly.

The writer Alexander Solzhenitsyn (b. 1918) created a sensation when his *One Day in the Life of Ivan Denisovich* was published in Russia in 1962. Solzhenitsyn's novel portrays in grim detail life in a Stalinist concentration camp – a life to which Solzhenitsyn himself had been unjustly condemned – and is a damning indictment of the Stalinist past.

Khrushchev also de-Stalinized Soviet foreign policy. "Peaceful coexistence" with capitalism was possible, he argued, and great wars were not inevitable. Khrushchev made positive concessions, meeting with U.S. President Dwight Eisenhower at the first summit meeting since Potsdam and agreeing in 1955 to real independence for a neutral Austria after ten long years of Allied occupation. Thus there was a relaxation of cold war tensions. At the same time Khrushchev began wooing the new nations of Asia and Africa – even if they were not communist – with promises and aid. He also proclaimed that there could be different paths to socialism, thus calling a halt to the little cold war with Tito's Yugoslavia.

De-Stalinization stimulated rebelliousness in the east European satellites. Having suf-fered in silence under Stalin, Communist reformers and the masses were quickly emboldened to seek much greater liberty and national independence. Poland took the lead in March 1956: riots there resulted in the release of more than nine thousand political prisoners, including the previously purged Wladyslaw Gomulka. Taking charge of the government, Gomulka skillfully managed to win greater autonomy for Poland while calming anti-Russian feeling.

Hungary experienced a real and very tragic revolution. Led by students and workers – the classic urban revolutionaries – the people of Budapest installed the liberal Communist reformer Imre Nagy as their new chief in October 1956. Soviet troops were forced to leave the country. One-party rule was abolished, and the new government promised free elections, freedom of expression, and massive social changes. Worst of all from the Russian point of view, Nagy declared Hungarian neutrality and renounced Hungary's military alliance with Moscow. As in 1849, the Russian answer was to invade Hungary with a large army and to crush, once again, a national, democratic revolution.

Fighting was bitter until the end, for the Hungarians hoped that the United States would fulfill its earlier propaganda promises and come to their aid. When this did not occur because of American unwillingness to risk a general war, the people of eastern Europe realized that their only hope was to strive for small domestic gains while following Russia obediently in foreign affairs. This cautious approach produced some results. In Poland, for example, the peasants were not collectivized and Catholics were allowed to practice their faith. Thus eastern Europe profited modestly from Khrushchev's policy of de-Stalinization, and could hope for still greater freedom in the future.

In October 1962, a remarkable poem entitled "Stalin's Heirs" by the popular young poet Yevgeny Yevtushenko (b. 1933) appeared in *Pravda,* the official newspaper of the Communist party and the most important one in Soviet Russia. Yevtushenko wrote:

Some of his heirs are in retirement pruning their rosebushes,
  and secretly thinking that their time will come again.
Others even attack Stalin from the rostrum but at home, at night-time, think back to bygone days. . . .[10]

Like Solzhenitsyn's novel about Stalin's concentration camps, published a month later, this very political poem was authorized by Communist party boss Khrushchev himself. It was part of his last, desperate offensive against the many well-entrenched conservative Stalinists in the party and government, who were indeed "secretly thinking their time will come again." And it did.

Within two years Khrushchev had fallen in a bloodless palace revolution. Under Leonid Brezhnev (b. 1906), Soviet Russia began a period of limited "re-Stalinization" which has not yet ended. The basic reason for this development was that Khrushchev's Communist colleagues saw de-Stalinization as a dangerous, two-sided threat. How could Khrushchev denounce the dead dictator without eventually denouncing and perhaps even arresting his still-powerful henchmen? In a heated secret debate in 1957, when the conservatives had tried without success to depose the menacing reformer, Khrushchev had pointed at two of Stalin's most devoted followers, Molotov and Kaganovich, and exclaimed: "Your hands are stained with the blood of our party leaders and of innumerable innocent Bolsheviks!" "So are yours!" Molotov and Kaganovich shouted back at him. "Yes, so are mine," Khrushchev replied. "I admit this. But during the purges I was merely carrying out your order. . . . I was not responsible. You were."[11] Moreover, the widening campaign of de-Stalinization posed a clear threat to the dictatorial authority of the party. It was producing growing, perhaps uncontrollable, criticism of the whole Communist system. The party had to tighten up while there was still time. It was clear that Khrushchev had to go.

Another reason for conservative opposition was Khrushchev's foreign policy. Although he scored some diplomatic victories, notably with Egypt and India, Khrushchev suffered a humiliating defeat in the Cuban missile crisis in 1962. Seeing a chance to change the balance of military power decisively, Khrushchev ordered missiles with nuclear warheads installed in Fidel Castro's Communist Cuba. U.S. President John F. Kennedy countered with a naval blockade of Cuba, and after a very tense diplomatic crisis, Khrushchev was forced to remove the Russian missiles in return for American pledges not to disturb Castro's regime. Khrushchev looked like a bumbling buffoon; his influence, already slipping, declined rapidly after the Cuban fiasco.

After Brezhnev and his supporters took over in 1964, they started talking cautiously of Stalin's "good points" and ignoring his crimes. Their praise of the whole Stalinist era, with its five-year plans and wartime victories, demonstrated that no real break with the past had occurred. They denounced anti-Stalinist writers such as Solzhenitsyn and sent some other liberal intellectuals to prison as a severe warning to all. The government carefully watched the tiny Russian protest movement of urban intellectuals, which had grown out of the more liberal atmosphere of de-Stalini-

zation and was calling for greater freedom. Russian leaders also launched a massive arms buildup, determined never to suffer Khrushchev's humiliation in the face of American nuclear superiority.

To eastern Europe the 1960s brought modest liberalization and more consumer goods, as well as somewhat greater national autonomy, especially in Poland and Rumania. Czechoslovakia had moved more slowly than its neighbors, but in January 1968 the reform elements in its Communist party finally triumphed. Under the new Communist leader, Anton Dubček, the government introduced major economic and political reforms. Local decision making by trade unions, managers, and consumers replaced rigid bureaucratic planning. Mindless ideological conformity gave way to exciting free expression. Enormously popular with the people, Dubček promised to build a new and profoundly democratic socialist society.

Although Dubček remembered the lesson of Hungary and constantly proclaimed military loyalty to the Warsaw Pact of Communist states, the determination of the Czech reformers to build "socialism with a human face" frightened hard-line Communists. Such a Czechoslovakia would certainly set a dangerous example for the peoples of eastern Europe and Soviet Russia, and would probably be drawn toward the democratic West. Thus 500,000 Russian and east European allied troops suddenly occupied Czechoslovakia in August 1968. The dejected Czechs made no attempt to resist. Soon unbending orthodox Communist dictators ruled once again.

Shortly thereafter, Brezhnev declared the so-called Brezhnev Doctrine, according to which Soviet Russia had the right to intervene in any socialist country whenever it saw the need. Predictably, the Russian invasion of Czechoslovakia raised a storm of protest. Many Communist parties in western Europe were harshly critical of it. None of this altered the fact that Stalin's empire was still solidly in place, and that developments in eastern Europe would continue to follow those in Soviet Russia.

The invasion of Czechoslovakia – perhaps the crucial event of the Brezhnev era – brought further re-Stalinization of Soviet Russia, though with collective rather than personal dictatorship and without uncontrolled terror. This compromise seemed to suit the leaders and most of the people. Whether westerners liked it or not, Soviet Russia appeared quite stable in the 1970s.

A rising standard of living for ordinary people contributed greatly to stability. By 1974, two-thirds of the nation's families had television sets, almost 60 percent had sewing and washing machines, and about half had some kind of refrigerator. There were still long lines and many shortages, but long-suffering Soviet consumers compared the present with the recent past and not with conditions abroad. The enduring differences between the life of the elite and the life of ordinary people also reinforced the system. Ambitious individuals still had tremendous incentive to do as the state wished, in order that they might gain access to special well-stocked stores, attend special schools, and travel abroad.

Another source of stability was that ordinary Russians remained more intensely nationalistic than almost any people in the world. The party leaders successfully identified themselves with this patriotism, stressing their role in saving the motherland during the Second World War and protecting her now from foreign foes. By playing on nationalist feelings, de-Stalinization was very easily reversed. Many ordinary Russians considered an attack on Stalin to be an attack on the great sacrifices they had willingly made for the nation. Similarly, ordinary Russians took enormous pride in their country's military power, and young men accepted an inescapable three-year hitch in the army without question. The cult of Lenin, which replaced the cult of Stalin, also had nationalistic overtones, which neutralized the general cynicism about Communist ideology.

Finally, the strength of the government was expressed in the re-Stalinization of culture and art. Free expression and protest disappeared. In 1968, when a small group of dissenters appeared in Red Square to protest the invasion of Czechoslovakia, they were arrested before they could unfurl their banners. This was to be the high point of dissent, for in the 1970s Brezhnev and company made certain that liberalism did not infect Soviet intellectuals. The slightest acts of nonconformity were severely punished, but with sophisticated, cunning methods.

Most frequently, dissidents were blacklisted

and thus rendered unable to find a decent job, since the government was the only employer. This fate was enough to keep most in line. More determined but unrenowned protesters were quietly imprisoned in jails or mental institutions. Celebrated nonconformists such as Solzhenitsyn were permanently expelled from the country. Once again Jews were persecuted as a "foreign" element, though some were eventually permitted to emigrate to Israel.

As the distinguished Russian dissident historian Roy Medvedev summed it up:

The technology of repression has become more refined in recent years. Before, repression always went much farther than necessary. Stalin killed millions of people when arresting 1000 would have enabled him to control the people. Our leaders ... found out eventually that you don't have to put people in prison or in a psychiatric hospital to silence them. There are other ways.[12]

Thus the worst aspects of Stalin's totalitarianism had been eliminated, but rule by a self-perpetuating Communist elite in the Soviet Union appeared as solid as ever throughout the 1970s.

The 1980s, however, opened on an uncertain note in the satellite empire. A spectacular resurgence of liberalism and nationalism in Poland crystallized around protests by workers and a remarkable free trade union called Solidarity. The almost-universal dissatisfaction of the Polish people with more than thirty years of communist rule, and their profound longing for "rebirth," were clear for all to see. Finally, after some major economic and cultural reforms were announced and as the power of the Polish Communist party waned and the Soviet Union demanded countermeasures, the Polish army took control of the government in December 1981. The generals imposed strict martial law, arrested thousands

of Solidarity members, and talked of revitalizing the Polish Communist party. It was widely feared in the West that the Soviet Union had once again managed to use puppets and raw force to maintain its oppressive system in eastern Europe.

THE WESTERN HEMISPHERE

One way to think of what historians used to call the New World is as a vigorous offshoot of Western civilization, an offshoot that has gradually developed its own characteristics while retaining European roots. From this perspective, one can see many illuminating parallels and divergences in the histories of Europe and the Americas. So it has been in the recent past.

Thus the western hemisphere experienced a spectacular many-sided postwar recovery, somewhat similar to that of Europe although it began earlier, especially in Latin America. Cold war conflicts also exercised a tremendous influence on domestic politics in the western hemisphere. Yet here too the timing was different, for the full force of the impact came only in the 1960s, when the cold war was assuming a secondary role in western Europe. Moreover, profound differences continued to exist between predominately English-speaking Canada and the United States, on the one hand, and Latin America on the other.

POSTWAR PROSPERITY IN THE UNITED STATES

The Second World War cured the depression in the United States and brought about the greatest boom in American history. Unemployment practically vanished as millions of new workers, half of them women, found jobs. Personal income doubled and the well-being of Americans increased dramatically. Yet the experience of the 1930s weighed heavily on people's minds, feeding fears that peace would bring renewed depression.

In fact, conversion to a peacetime economy went smoothly, marred only by a spurt of inflation accompanying the removal of government controls. Moreover, the U.S. economy continued to advance fairly steadily for a long generation. Though cold-war fears and anxieties dominated American relations with the rest of the world, the warm glow of economic prosperity soothed and satisfied at home.

This helps explain why postwar domestic politics consisted largely of modest adjustments to the status quo until the 1960s. After a flurry of unpopular postwar strikes, a conservative Republican Congress chopped away at the power of labor unions by means of the Taft-Hartley Act of 1947. But Truman's upset victory in 1948 demonstrated that Americans had no interest in undoing Roosevelt's social and economic reforms. The Congress proceeded to increase social security benefits, subsidize middle- and lower-class housing, and raise the minimum wage. These and other liberal measures extended and consolidated the New Deal. But major innovations – whether in health or civil rights – were decisively rejected, and in 1952 the Republican party and the voters turned to General Eisenhower, a national hero and self-described moderate.

The federal government's only major new undertaking during "the Eisenhower years" was the interstate highway system, a suitable symbol of the basic satisfaction of the vast majority. Some Americans feared that the United States was becoming a "blocked soci-

ety," obsessed with stability and incapable of wholesome change. This feeling contributed in 1960 to the election of the young, attractive John F. Kennedy, who promised to "get the country moving again." President Kennedy captured the popular imagination with his flair and rhetoric, revitalized the old Roosevelt coalition, and modestly expanded existing liberal legislation before he was struck down by an assassin's bullet in 1963.

THE CIVIL RIGHTS REVOLUTION

Belatedly and reluctantly, complacent postwar America experienced a genuine social revolution: after a long and sometimes bloody struggle, blacks (and their white supporters) threw off a deeply entrenched system of segregation, discrimination, and repression. This movement for civil rights advanced on several fronts. Eloquent lawyers from the National Association for the Advancement of Colored People challenged school segregation in the courts, and in 1954 won a landmark decision in the Supreme Court that "separate educational facilities are inherently unequal." While state and local governments in the south were refusing to comply, blacks were effectively challenging institutionalized inequality with bus boycotts, sit-ins, and demonstrations. As Martin Luther King told the white power structure, "We will not hate you, but we will not obey your evil laws."[13]

Blacks also used their growing political power in key northern states to gain the support of the liberal wing of the Democratic party. All these efforts culminated after the liberal landslide that elected Lyndon Johnson in 1964. The Civil Rights Act of 1964 categorically prohibited discrimination in public services and on the job. In the follow-up Voting Rights Act of 1965, the federal govern-

THE MARCH ON WASHINGTON This stunning aerial shot captures on film the dramatic climax of the civil rights struggle, the spectacular mass demonstration at the Lincoln Memorial in August 1963, which was organized by Martin Luther King and other black leaders. The march was supported by President Kennedy, who was assassinated just three months later. (Associated Press Photo)

ment firmly guaranteed all blacks the right to vote. By the 1970s, there were substantial numbers of elected black officials in all the southern states, proof positive that dramatic changes had occurred in American race relations.

Black voters and political leaders enthusiastically supported the accompanying surge of new liberal social legislation in the mid-1960s. President Johnson, reviving the New Deal approach of his early congressional years, solemnly declared "unconditional war on poverty." Congress and the administration created a host of antipoverty projects, such as the domestic peace corps, free preschools for slum children, and community-action programs. Although these programs were directed to all poor Americans – the majority of whom are white – they were also intended to extend greater equality for blacks to the realm of economics. Johnson's ambitious initiatives scored some successes, but economic disadvantages proved less easily remedied than legal and political ones.

THE TRAUMA OF VIETNAM

President Johnson wanted to go down in history as a master reformer and healer of old wounds. Instead, he opened new ones with the Vietnam war.

American involvement in Vietnam had its origins in the ideology of the cold war. From the late 1940s onward, most Americans and their leaders continued to view the world in terms of a constant struggle to stop the spread of communism. There were exceptions, to be sure, as well as lively debates over nuances and tactics. Yet anticommunism remained the basis of U.S. foreign policy on all continents. Therefore, after the defeat of the French in Indochina in 1954, when Vietnam became two hostile states, communist North Vietnam and anticommunist South Vietnam, the Eisenhower administration instinctively provided aid to the new South Vietnamese government. President Kennedy greatly increased the number of American "military advisers," to 16,000, and had the existing South Vietnamese leader deposed in 1963 when he refused to follow American directives.

Having successfully portrayed his opponent Barry Goldwater as a trigger-happy extremist in a nuclear age during the 1964 campaign, President Johnson proceeded to expand the American role in the Vietnam conflict enormously. As Johnson explained to his ambassador in Saigon, "I am not going to lose Vietnam. I am not going to be the President who saw Southeast Asia go the way China went."[14] American strategy was to "escalate" the war sufficiently to break the will of the North Vietnamese and their southern allies, but without resorting to "overkill" that might lead to war with the entire communist bloc. Thus the South received colossal U.S. military aid, American forces grew steadily to a half-million men, and the United States bombed North Vietnam with ever-greater intensity. But there was no invasion of the north, nor were essential seaborne military supplies from the Soviet Union ever disrupted. In the end, the strategy backfired. It was the Americans themselves who grew weary of the war.

The undeclared war in Vietnam, fought nightly in all its horror on American television, divided the nation. Supporters saw the war as part of a defense against communist totalitarianism in all poor countries. Critics increasingly denounced it as an immoral, unsuccessful, and unnecessary intrusion into a complex and distant civil war. There were mass protests, often led by college students.

Then in 1968, as the antiwar movement peaked, a chastened President Johnson tacitly admitted defeat: he called for negotiations with North Vietnam and announced that he would not run for re-election.

President Nixon cleverly tried to conceal this defeat by bombing heavily and extending the war to Cambodia while negotiations continued and American troops were gradually withdrawn. In January 1973, he and Henry Kissinger finally concluded a deceptive peace agreement, which allowed remaining American forces to complete their withdrawal before the civil war resumed. For two years the government of South Vietnam seemed to hold its own, but in the wake of the Watergate paralysis of government and Nixon's resignation it suddenly collapsed. After more than thirty-five years of battle, the Vietnamese communists had unified their country.

Defeat in Vietnam had a traumatic effect on the United States. Because American action in Vietnam was financed by massive deficit spending, it set off a wave of inflation, which eventually halted the expensive war on domestic poverty and even discredited all social reform. Not only did Vietnam leave a heritage of division; it also badly shook American self-confidence. Defeat and widespread denunciation left the United States uncertain about its proper role in world affairs. The long-dominant belief that the interests of the United States required an unending global struggle against the spread of communism had been gravely damaged. But by the early 1980s no alternative concept had won general support.

ECONOMIC NATIONALISM IN LATIN AMERICA

Although the countries of Latin America share a European heritage, and specifically a Spanish-Portuguese heritage, their striking differences make it difficult to generalize meaningfully about recent Latin Americcn history. Yet a growing economic nationalism seems unmistakable. As the early nineteenth century saw Spanish and Portuguese colonies win wars of political independence, recent history has been an ongoing quest for genuine economic independence through local control and industrialization. This quest has sometimes brought Latin American countries into sharp conflict with Europe and the United States, in turn encouraging a new feeling of solidarity with Africa, Asia, and Third World causes.

To understand the rise of economic nationalism, one must remember that Latin American countries developed as producers of foodstuffs and raw materials, which were exported to Europe and the United States in return for manufactured goods and capital investment. This exchange was mutually beneficial, especially in the later nineteenth century, and the countries that participated most actively, like Argentina and southern Brazil, became the wealthiest and most advanced. There was, however, a heavy price to pay. Latin America became very dependent on foreign markets, products, and investments. Industry did not develop and large landowners profited most, further enhancing their social and political power.

The old international division of labor, disrupted by the First World War but re-established in the 1920s, was finally destroyed by the Great Depression — a historical turning point as critical for Latin America as for the United States. Prices and exports of Latin American commodities collapsed as Europe and the United States drastically reduced their purchases and raised tariffs to protect domestic producers. With foreign sales plummeting,

Latin American countries could not buy industrial goods abroad. Latin America suffered the full force of the global economic crisis.

The result in the larger, more important Latin American countries was a profound shift in the direction of economic nationalism after 1930. The more popularly based governments worked to reduce foreign influence and gain control of their own economies and natural resources. They energetically promoted national industry by means of high tariffs, government grants, and even state enterprise. They favored the lower-middle and urban working classes with social benefits and higher wages in order to increase their purchasing power and gain their support. These efforts at recovery were fairly successful. By the late 1940s, the factories of Argentina, Brazil, and Chile could generally satisfy domestic consumer demand for the products of light industry. In the 1950s, some countries began moving into heavy industry. Economic nationalism and the rise of industry are particularly striking in the two largest and most influential countries, Mexico and Brazil, which together account for half the population of Latin America.

MEXICO Overthrowing the elitist, upper-class rule of the tyrant Porfiro Díaz, the spasmodic, often-chaotic Mexican Revolution of 1910 culminated in 1917 in a new constitution. This radical nationalistic document called for universal suffrage, massive land reform, benefits for labor, and strict control of foreign capital. Actual progress was quite modest until 1934, when a charismatic young Indian from a poor family, Lazaro Cárdenas, became president and dramatically revived the languishing revolution. Under Cárdenas, many large estates were divided up among small farmers or returned undivided to Indian communities.

Meanwhile, because foreign capitalists were being discouraged, Mexican businessmen built many small factories and managed to thrive. The government also championed the cause of industrial workers. In 1938, when Mexican workers became locked in a bitter dispute with British and American oil companies, Cárdenas nationalized the petroleum industry – to the astonishment of a world unaccustomed to such actions. Finally, the 1930s saw the flowering of a distinctive Mexican culture, which proudly embraced its long-despised Indian past and gloried in the modern national revolution.

In 1940 the official, semiauthoritarian party that has governed Mexico continuously since the revolution selected the first of a series of more moderate presidents. Steadfast in their radical, occasionally anti-American rhetoric, these presidents used the full power of the state to promote industrialization through a judicious mixture of public, private, and even foreign enterprise. The Mexican economy grew rapidly, at about 6 percent per year from the early 1940s to the late 1960s, with the upper and middle classes reaping the lion's share of the benefits.

BRAZIL After the fall of Brazil's monarchy in 1889, politics was largely dominated by the coffee barons and by regional rivalries. These rivalries and deteriorating economic conditions allowed a military revolt led by Getulio Vargas, governor of one of Brazil's larger states, to seize control of the federal government in 1930. Vargas, who proved to be a consummate politician, fragmented the opposition and established a mild dictatorship that lasted until 1945. Vargas's rule was generally popular, combining as it did effective economic nationalism and moderate social reform.

Somewhat like President Franklin Roosevelt in the United States, Vargas decisively

JOSÉ CLEMENTE OROZCO (1883–1949) was one of
the great and committed painters of the Mexican Revolution. Orozco believed that art should reflect the
"new order of things" and inspire the common people
— the workers and the peasants. This vibrant central
mural in the National Palace in Mexico City, one of
Orozco's many great wall paintings, depicts a brutal
Spanish conquest and a liberating revolution. (Reproduction authorized by The Instituto Nacional de
Bellas Artes)

tipped the balance of political power away from the Brazilian states to the ever-expanding federal government, which became a truly national government for the first time. Vargas and his allies also set out to industrialize Brazil and gain economic independence. While the national coffee board used mountains of surplus coffee beans to fire railroad locomotives, the government supported Brazilian manufacturers with high tariffs, generous loans, and labor peace. This probusiness policy did not prevent new social legislation: workers received shorter hours, pensions, health and accident insurance, paid vacations, and other benefits. Finally, Vargas shrewdly upheld the nationalist cause in his relations with the giant to the north. Early in the Second World War, for example, he traded U.S. military bases in Brazil for American construction of Brazil's first huge steel-making complex. By 1945, when the authoritarian Vargas fell in a bloodless military coup calling for greater political liberty, Brazil was modernizing rapidly.

Modernization continued for the next fifteen years. The economy boomed. Presidential politics were re-established, while the military kept a watchful eye for extremism among the civilian politicians. Economic nationalism was especially vigorous under the flamboyant President Kubitschek (1956–1960), a doctor of German-Czech descent. The government borrowed heavily from international bankers to promote industry and built the extravagant new capital of Brasilia in the midst of a wilderness. When Brazil's creditors demanded more conservative policies to stem inflation, Kubitschek delighted the nationalists with his firm and successful refusal. His slogan was "Fifty Years' Progress in Five," and he seemed to mean it.

The Brazilian and Mexican formula of national economic development, varying degrees of electoral competition, and social reform was shared by some other Latin American countries, notably Argentina and Chile. By the late 1950s optimism was widespread, if cautious. Economic and social progress seemed to promise less violent, more democratic politics. These expectations were profoundly shakened by the Cuban revolution.

THE CUBAN REVOLUTION

Although many aspects of the Cuban revolution are obscured by controversy, certain background conditions are clear. First, after achieving independence in 1898, Cuba was for many years virtually an American protectorate. The Cuban constitution gave the United States the legal right to intervene in Cuban affairs, a right that was frequently exercised until Roosevelt renounced it in 1934. Second, and partly because the American army had often been the real power, Cuba's political institutions were weak and its politicians were extraordinarily corrupt. Under the strongman Fulgencio Batista, an opportunistic ex-sergeant who controlled the government almost continually from 1933 to 1958, graft and outright looting were a way of life. Third, Cuba was one of Latin America's most prosperous and advanced countries by the 1950s, but its sugar-and-tourist economy was dependent on the United States. Finally, the enormous differences between rich and poor in Cuba were typical of Latin America. But Cuba also had a strong Communist party, which was highly unusual.

Fidel Castro, a magnetic leader with the gift of oratory and a flair for propaganda, managed to unify anti-Batista elements in a revolutionary front. When Castro's guerrilla forces triumphed in late 1958, the new government's goals were unclear. Castro had promised a "real" revolution but had always laughed at charges that he was a communist. As the regime consolidated its power in 1959 and 1960, it became increasingly clear that "real" meant "communist" in Castro's mind. Wealthy Cubans, who owned three-quarters of the sugar industry and many profitable businesses, fled to Miami. Soon the middle class began to follow.

Meanwhile relations with the Eisenhower administration – which had indirectly supported Castro by refusing to sell arms to Batista after March 1958 – deteriorated rapidly. Thus, in April 1961, newly elected President Kennedy went ahead with a pre-existing CIA plan to use Cuban exiles to topple Castro. But the Kennedy administration lost its nerve and abandoned the exiles as soon as they were dumped ashore at the Bay of Pigs. This doomed the invasion and the exiles were quickly captured, to be ransomed later for $60 million.

The Bay of Pigs invasion – a triumph for Castro and a humiliating, roundly criticized fiasco for the United States – had significant consequences. It freed Castro to build his version of a communist society, and he did. Political life in Cuba featured "anti-imperialism," an alliance with the Soviet bloc, the dictatorship of the party, and a vigorously promoted Castro cult. Revolutionary enthusiasm was genuine among party activists, much of Cuba's youth, and some of the masses some of the time. Prisons and emigration silenced opposition. The economy was characterized by all-pervasive state ownership, collective farms, and Soviet trade and aid. Early efforts to industrialize ran aground, and sugar production at pre-Castro levels continued to dominate the economy. Socially, the regime pursued equality and the creation of a new socialist personality. In short, revolutionary totalitarianism came to the Americas.

The failure of the United States' halfhearted effort to derail Castro heightened both hopes and fears that the Cuban revolution could spread throughout Latin America. As leftists were emboldened to try guerrilla warfare, conservatives became more rigid and suspicious of calls for change. In the United States, fear of communism aroused heightened cold-war-style interest in Latin America. Using the Organization of American States to isolate Cuba, the United States in 1961 pledged $10 billion in aid over ten years to a new hemispheric "Alliance for Progress." The Alliance was intended to promote long-term economic development and social reform, which American liberals typically assumed would immunize Latin America from the Cuban disease.

THE NEW AUTHORITARIANISM IN LATIN AMERICA

U.S. aid did contribute modestly to continued Latin America economic development in the 1960s, although population growth cancelled out two-thirds of the increase on a per capita basis. Democratic social reforms – the other half of the Alliance for Progress formula – proceeded slowly, however. Instead, the era following the Cuban revolution saw the rise of extremism and a new kind of conservative authoritarianism. By the 1980s, only four Latin American countries – Costa Rica, Venezuela, Colombia, and Mexico – retained some measure of democratic government. Brazil, Argentina, and Chile are more representative of the general trend.

Influential Brazil led the way. Intense political competition in the early 1960s prompted President João Goulart to swing to

JUAN AND EVA PERÓN Perón appealed to Argentina's workers and industrialists with his social programs and economic nationalism. His beautiful wife Eva was a consummate politician in her own right. Here they are shown parading triumphantly at Perón's presidential inauguration for another six-year term in 1952. (United Press Photo)

the left to gain fresh support. Castroism appeared to spread in the impoverished northeast, and mass meetings of leftists were answered by huge demonstrations of conservatives. Meanwhile Goulart called for radical change, proposing that the great landed estates be broken up and that Brazil's many illiterates receive the right to vote. When Goulart and his followers appeared ready to use force to implement their program, army leaders took over in 1964. The right-wing military government banned political parties and ruled by decree. It showed little sign of giving up power in the early 1980s, as Brazil industrialized rapidly and strove for status as a great power.

In Argentina, the military intervened in 1955 to oust the dictatorial populist and economic nationalist Juan Perón, but it had restored elected government. Then, worried by a Peronist revival and heartened by the Brazilian example, the army took control in 1966 and again in 1976 after a brief civilian interlude. Each military takeover was followed by an escalation of repression, and culturally and economically advanced Argentina came to resemble a genuine police state.

If events in Argentina were discouraging, Chile was tragic. Chile has a population of predominantly European origin and a long tradition of democracy and moderate reform. Thus when Salvador Allende, a doctor and the Marxist head of a coalition of Communists, Socialists, and Radicals, won a plurality of 36 percent of the vote – only 2 percent more than the runner-up nationalist – in fair elections in 1970, he was duly elected president by the Congress. Allende completed the nationalization of the American-owned copper companies – the great majority of Chileans had already embraced economic nationalism – and proceeded to socialize private industry, accelerate the breakup of landed estates, and radicalize the poor.

Marxism in action evoked a powerful backlash in Chile. The middle class fought back, and by 1973 Chile seemed headed for civil war. Then, with enormous conservative support and some U.S. backing, the traditionally impartial army struck in a well-organized coup. Allende died, probably murdered, and thousands of "leftists" were arrested, or worse, as the military imposed a harsh despotism and settled down for a long rule.

The revival of antidemocratic authoritarianism in Latin America is clearly a major development. Interpretations, however, vary widely. At one level, military government is clearly part of a determined conservative resurgence, which has at least temporarily squelched not only the Marxist and socialist challenge but most liberal and moderate reform as well. Instructed by the Cuban experience, the upper and middle classes had no intention of playing dead: if dictatorship was necessary to protect privilege and property, so

be it. Military governments effectively defended private capital and halted or reversed radical change. (Some blamed it all on Washington, the CIA, and American corporations, steadfastly ignoring the obvious decline of U.S. power, influence, and direct investment in Latin America.)

Yet some observers saw in the new military governments something more than the traditional weakness of Latin American democracy and cold-war fears of communism. They noted that military takeovers grew out of intense crises that threatened national unity as well as the upper classes. In such circumstances, the politically conscious officer corps saw the military as the only institution capable of preventing chaos in the foreseeable future.

Moreover, the new authoritarians were determined modernizers. Eager to catch up with the advanced countries, they were often deeply committed to nationalism, industrialization, technology, and even modest social progress. In a larger sense, Latin America seemed to be moving closer to Asia and Africa, where a multitude of authoritarian governments and military leaders have declared themselves best suited to meet the enormous challenges of the late twentieth century.

———◆———

The recovery of Europe and the Americas during and after World War Two is one of the most remarkable chapters in the long, uneven course of Western civilization. Although the dangerous tensions of the cold war frustrated fond hopes for a truly peaceful international order, the transition from imperialism to decolonialization proceeded rapidly, surprisingly smoothly, and without serious damage to western Europe. Instead, genuine political democracy gained unprecedented strength in the West, and economic progress quickened the pace of ongoing social and cultural transformation. Thus the tremendous promise inherent in Western society's fateful embrace of "the dual revolution," which had begun in France and England in the late eighteenth century and which had momentarily halted in the agonies of the Great Depression and the horrors of Nazi totalitarianism, was largely if perhaps only temporarily realized in the shining achievements of the postwar era.

NOTES

1. William Bullitt, "How We Won the War and Lost the Peace," *Life,* XXV (30 August 1948):94.

2. Quoted by N. Graebner, *Cold War Diplomacy, 1945-1960,* Van Nostrand, Princeton, N.J., 1962, p d17.

3. Ibid.

4. Quoted by A. Crawley, *The Spoils of War: The Rise of Western Germany Since 1945,* Bobbs-Merrill, New York, 1973, p. 10.

5. Quoted in J. Hennessy, *Economic "Miracles,"* André Deutsch, London, 1964, p. 5.

6. P. Van Zeeland, in *European Integration,* ed. C. G. Haines, Johns Hopkins Press, Baltimore, 1957, p. xi.

7. Lord Milner, quoted by R. von Albertini, "The Impact of Two World Wars on the Decline of Colonialism," *Journal of Contemporary History* 4 (January 1969):17.

8. Quoted by H. Smith, *The Russians,* Quadrangle/New York Times, New York, 1976, p. 303.

9. Quoted by D. Treadgold, *Twentieth Century Russia,* Houghton Mifflin, Boston, 5th ed., 1981 p. 442.

10. Quoted by M. Tatu, *Power in the Kremlin: From Khrushchev to Kosygin,* Viking Press, New York, 1968, p. 248.

11. Quoted by I. Deutscher, in *Soviet Society,* ed. A. Inkeles and K. Geiger, Houghton Mifflin, Boston, 1961, p.41.

12. Quoted by Smith, pp. 455-456.

13. Quoted by S. E. Morison et al., *A Concise History of the American Republic,* Oxford University Press, New York, 1977, p. 697.

14. Ibid., p. 735.

SUGGESTED READING

B. H. Liddell Hart, *The History of the Second World War* (1971), is a good overview of military developments. Three dramatic studies of special aspects of the war are A. Dallin, *German Rule in Russia, 1941-1945* (1957), which analyzes the effects of Nazi occupation policies on the Soviet population; L. Collins and D. La Pierre, *Is Paris Burning?* (1965), a best-selling account of the liberation of Paris and Hitler's plans to destroy the city; and J. Toland, *The Last 100 Days* (1966), a lively account of the end of the war. Great leaders and matchless stylists, Winston Churchill and Charles de Gaulle have both written histories of the war in the form of memoirs. Other interesting memoirs are those of Harry Truman (1958); Dwight Eisenhower, *Crusade in Europe* (1948); and Dean Acheson, *Present at the Creation* (1969), a beautifully written defense of American foreign policy in the early cold war. W. A. Williams, *The Tragedy of American Diplomacy* (1962), and G. Kolko, *The Politics of War* (1968), claim, on the contrary, that the United States was primarily responsible for the conflict with the Soviet Union. A. Fontaine, a French journalist, provides a more balanced approach in his *History of the Cold War,* 2 vols. (1968). V. Mastny's thorough investigation of Stalin's war aims, *Russia's Road to the Cold War* (1979), is highly recommended.

R. Mayne, *The Recovery of Europe, 1945-1973,* rev. ed. (1973), and N. Luxenburg, *Europe Since World War II,* rev. ed., (1979), are recommended general surveys, as are two works by W. Laqueur, *Europe*

Since Hitler (1972), and *A Continent Astray, 1970–1978* (1979). T. White, *Fire in the Ashes* (1953), is a vivid view of European resurgence and Marshall Plan aid by an outstanding journalist. Postwar economic and technological developments are carefully analyzed by D. S. Landes, *The Unbound Prometheus: Technological Change and Industrial Development in Western Europe from 1750 to the Present* (1969). A. Shonfield, *Modern Capitalism* (1965), provides an engaging, optimistic assessment of the growing importance of government investment and planning in European economic life. F. R. Willis, *France, Germany, and the New Europe, 1945–1967* (1968), is useful for postwar European diplomacy. Three outstanding works on France are J. Ardagh, *The New French Revolution* (1969), which puts the momentous social changes since 1945 in human terms; G. Wright, *Rural Revolution in France: the Peasantry in the Twentieth Century* (1964); and D. L. Hanley et al., eds., *France: Politics and Society Since 1945* (1979). R. Dahrendorf, *Society and Democracy in Germany* (1971), and H. S. Hughes, *The United States and Italy* (1968), are excellent introductions to recent German and Italian history. A. H. Halsey, *Change in British Society,* 2nd ed. (1981), is good on recent developments. H. Seton-Watson, *The East European Revolution* (1965), is a good history of the communization of eastern Europe, and S. Fischer-Galati, ed., *Eastern Europe in the Sixties* (1963), discusses major developments. P. Zinner, *National Communism and Popular Revolt in Eastern Europe* (1956) and *Revolution in Hungary* (1962), are excellent on the tragic events of 1956. H. Schwartz, *Prague's 200 Days* (1969), is an engrossing account of events in Czechoslovakia in 1968. W. Connor, *Socialism, Politics and Equality: Hierarchy and Change in Eastern Europe and the USSR* (1979), and J. Hough and M. Fainsod, *How the Soviet Union is Governed* (1978), are important general studies. A. Amalrik, *Will the Soviet Union Survive Until 1984?* (1970), is a fascinating interpretation of contemporary Soviet society and politics by a Russian who paid for his criticism with prison and exile. A. Lee, *Russian Journal* (1981), and H. Smith, *The Russians* (1976), are excellent journalistic yet comprehensive reports by perceptive American observers.

R. von Albertini, *Decolonialization* (1971), is a good history of the decline and fall of European empires. The tremendous economic problems of the newly independent countries of Asia and Africa are discussed sympathetically by B. Ward, *Rich Nations and Poor Nations* (1962), and R. Heilbroner, *The Great Ascent* (1953).

Two excellent general studies on Latin America are J. E. Fagg, *Latin America: A General History,* 3rd. ed. (1977), and R. J. Shafer, *A History of Latin America* (1978). Both books have detailed suggestions for further reading. D. Collier, ed., *The New Authoritarianism in Latin America* (1979), is an excellent introduction to contemporary political developments.

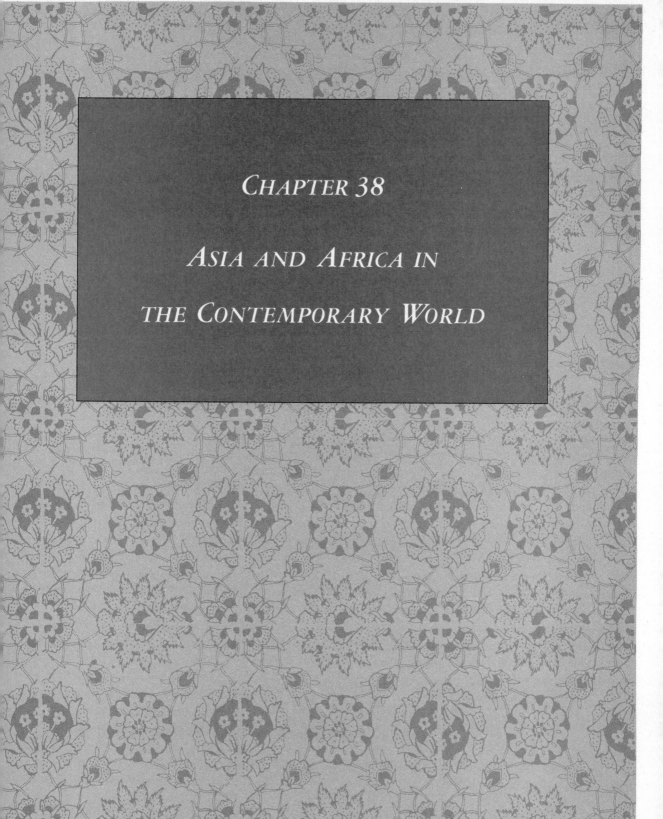

CHAPTER 38

ASIA AND AFRICA IN

THE CONTEMPORARY WORLD

WHEN FUTURE HISTORIANS look back at our era, they are likely to be particularly struck by the astonishing resurgence of Asia and Africa after World War Two. They will try to explain the astonishingly rapid rise of new or radically reorganized Asian and African countries, and their increasingly prominent role in world affairs. That is also what this chapter will try to do, though time has only partially winnowed the facts and still provides a very imperfect perspective. Here and in Chapter 40, we shall examine how the emerging nation-states are facing up to their enormous economic, social, and cultural challenges, whose solutions are proving more elusive than political strength and independence.

THE RESURGENCE OF EAST ASIA

In 1945 the two great powers of East Asia lay exhausted and devastated. Japanese aggression had sown extreme misery in China and reaped an atomic whirlwind at Hiroshima and Nagasaki. The future looked bleak. Yet both nations recovered even more spectacularly than western Europe. In the course of recovery the two countries, closely linked since the 1890s, went their separate ways. As China under Mao Tse-tung (Mao Zedong) transformed itself into a strong, self-confident communist state, Japan under American occupation turned from military expansion to democracy and astonishing economic development. Not until the 1970s would the reborn giants move somewhat closer together.

THE COMMUNIST VICTORY IN CHINA

There were many reasons for the triumph of communism in China. As a noted historian

has forcefully argued, however, "Japanese agression was . . . the most important single factor in Mao's rise to power."[1] When Japanese armies advanced rapidly in 1938 (page 1283), Chiang Kai-shek's Nationalist government moved its capital to Chungking deep in the Chinese interior. The Japanese then occupied a swath of territory five hundred miles wide in northern and central China, and the war settled into stalemate in 1939. These wartime conditions enabled the Communists, aided by their uneasy "united front" alliance with the Nationalists, to build up their strength in guerrilla bases in the countryside behind Japanese lines. Mao Tse-tung, at the peak of his creative powers, avoided pitched battles and concentrated on winning peasant support and forming a broad anti-Japanese coalition. By reducing rents, enticing intellectuals, and spreading propaganda, Mao and the Communists emerged in peasant eyes as the true patriots, the genuine nationalists. And the promise of radical redistribution of the land strongly re-enforced their appeal to poor peasants and landless laborers.

Meanwhile, the long war with Japan was exhausting the established government and its supporters. American generals were never satisfied with China's war effort, but in fact fully half of Japan's overseas armies were pinned down in China in 1945. Chiang Kai-shek's Nationalists had mobilized 14 million men and a staggering 3 million Chinese soldiers had been killed or wounded. The war created massive Chinese deficits and runaway inflation, hurting morale and ruining lives.

When Japan suddenly collapsed in August 1945, Communists and Nationalists both rushed to seize evacuated territory. Heavy fighting broke out in Manchuria. The United States, which had steadfastly supported the Nationalists during World War Two, tried unsuccessfully to work out a political com-

COMMUNIST VICTORY *Enthusiastically waving their banners, the people of Peking hail the Communist army as it triumphantly enters the Chinese capital in 1949. (Camera Press)*

promise, but civil war resumed in earnest in April 1946. At first Chiang Kai-shek's more numerous Nationalists had the upper hand. Soon the better-led, more determined Communists rallied, and by 1948 the demoralized Nationalist forces were disintegrating. In 1949 Chiang Kai-shek and 1 million mainland Chinese fled to the island of Taiwan, and Mao Tse-tung proclaimed the People's Republic of China.

Within three years the Communists had already succeeded in consolidating their rule. The Communist government seized the holdings of landlords and rich peasants — 10 percent of the farm population owned 70 to 80 percent of the land — and distributed it to 300 million poor peasants and landless laborers. This revolutionary land reform was extremely popular. Although the Chinese Communists soon began pushing the development of socialist collectives, they did so less brutally than had the Russians in the 1930s and retained genuine support in the countryside. The gradualness of collectivization reflects Mao's cautious, step-by-step consolidation of power.

Meanwhile the Communists were dealing harshly with their foes. Mao admitted in 1957 that 800,000 "class enemies" had been summarily liquidated between 1949 and 1954; the true figure is probably much higher. By means of mass arrests, forced-labor camps, and, more generally, re-education through relentless propaganda and self-criticism sessions, all visible opposition from the old ruling groups was destroyed.

RED GUARDS IN PEKING (BEIJING) *This photo of well-organized groups studying and discussing Mao's thought captures the intensity and idealism of Mao's young supporters during the Cultural Revolution.* (Eastfoto)

Finally, Mao and the Communists reunited China's 550 million inhabitants in a strong centralized state. They laid claim on a new "mandate of Heaven" and demonstrated that China was once again a great power. This was the real significance of China's Korean intervention. In 1950, when the American-led United Nations forces crossed the 38th parallel and appeared to threaten China's industrial base in Manchuria, the Chinese attacked, advanced swiftly, and fought the Americans to a bloody standstill on the Korean peninsula. This struggle against "American imperialism" mobilized the masses, and military success increased Chinese self-confidence. It was the Communists who realized many of the fondest dreams of Chinese nationalism.

MAO'S CHINA

The United States' cold war policy of isolating and denying diplomatic recognition to the People's Republic drastically reduced the westward flow of objective information about China, as did Chinese secrecy. Propaganda, both favorable and condemnatory, has tended to be wildly unrealistic. China's frequent and radical shifts in policy have bewildered even the most dedicated Western experts. Furthermore, there are fundamental differences of interpretation among China specialists: some stress China's commitment to revolutionary Marxist socialism, while others emphasize the Communists' dedication to nationalism and modernization. Finally, the Chinese themselves have begun reinterpreting their own recent history, reappraising Mao's years of power. Given all this controversy, what sense can we make of what Mao Tse-tung and the Communists did in China?

In the early 1950s Mao and the party adhered quite closely to the Soviet model. Mao and Stalin established close working relations, and the Chinese followed the Russian lead in world affairs. Alongside the gradual collectivization of agriculture, China adopted a typical Soviet five-year plan to develop large factories and heavy industry rapidly. Many Chinese plants were built by Russian specialists; Soviet economic aid was also considerable. The first five-year plan was successful, as were associated efforts to redirect higher education away from the liberal arts toward science and engineering. People remained very poor, but undeniable economic growth followed on the Communists' social revolution.

In the cultural and intellectual realms too, the Chinese followed the example of Soviet totalitarianism. Basic civil and political rights, which had been seriously curtailed by the Nationalists, were simply abolished. Temples and churches were closed; all religion was persecuted. Freedom of the press died, and the government went to incredible lengths to control information. As in the Soviet Union, ordinary telephone books were kept under lock-and-key. The big new buildings that arose looked "made in Moscow." A Soviet-style puritanism took hold; to the astonishment of "old China hands," the Communists quickly eradicated the longstanding scourges of prostitution and drug abuse, which they had long regarded as humiliating marks of exploitation and national decline. More generally, the Communists enthusiastically promoted Soviet-Marxian ideas concerning women and the family. Full equality and freedom from housework and child care became primary goals. Work in fields and factories was hailed as a proud badge of women's liberation rather than a shameful sign of poverty. It became rather easy for a woman to get a divorce, although premarital chastity remained the accepted norm.

By the mid-1950s Communist China seemed to be firmly set upon the Marxist-Leninist course of development previously perfected in Soviet Russia. There was even a brief interlude in 1957, shortly after Khrushchev launched de-Stalinization in Russia (pages 1385–1387), when Mao called upon Chinese intellectuals to cultivate "One Hundred Flowers" of free and even critical opinion. Like his Soviet counterparts, Mao soon decided that the "flowers" he had nurtured were weeds, and cut them down as he re-established uniformity of thought.

In 1958, however, Communist China began to go its own way. Mao had always stressed revolutionary free will and peasant equality. Now he proclaimed a spectacular acceleration of development, a "Great Leap Forward" in which soaring industrial growth was to be based on small-scale backyard workshops run by peasants living in gigantic self-contained communes. Creating an authentic new socialist personality was a second goal: commune members ate in common dining halls, nurseries cared for children, and fire-eating crusaders preached the evils of family ties.

The intended great leap past the Russians to socialist utopia – true communism – was an economic disaster, for frantic efforts with primitive technology often resulted only in chaos. By 1960, only China's efficient rationing system was preventing starvation. But when Khrushchev criticized Chinese policy, Mao reacted angrily and relations between the Communist giants deteriorated rapidly. Mao condemned Khrushchev and the Russians as detestable "modern revisionists" – capitalists and cowards unwilling to risk a world war certain to bring Communist revolution in the United States. The Russians abruptly cut off economic aid and withdrew their scientists who were helping China build an atomic bomb. A mood of mutual fear and hatred appeared to develop in both countries in the 1960s, as the Communist world split apart.

Mao lost influence in the party after the fiasco of the Great Leap Forward and the Sino-Soviet split, but in 1965 the old revolutionary staged a dramatic comeback. Apprehensive that China was becoming bureaucratic, capitalistic, and "revisionist" like Soviet Russia, Mao launched what he called the Great Proletarian Cultural Revolution. Its objective was to purge the party of time-serving bureaucrats and to recapture the revolutionary fervor and social equality of the Long March and his guerrilla struggle. The army and the nation's young people, especially students, responded enthusiastically. Encouraged by Mao to organize themselves into radical cadres called Red Guards, young people denounced their teachers and practiced rebellion in the name of revolution. As one Red Guard manifesto,

"Long Live the Revolutionary Rebel Spirit of the Proletariat," exulted:

Revolution is rebellion, and rebellion is the soul of Mao Tse-tung's thought. Daring to think, to speak, to act, to break through, and to make revolution – in a word, daring to rebel – is the most fundamental and most precious quality of proletarian revolutionaries; it is fundamental to the Party spirit of the Party of the proletariat! Not to rebel is revisionism, pure and simple! Revisionism has been in control of our school for seventeen years. If today we do not rise up in rebellion, when will we?

Now some of the people who were boldly opposing our rebellion have suddenly turned shy and coy, and have taken to incessant murmuring and nagging that we are too one-sided, too arrogant, too crude, and that we are going too far. All this is utter nonsense! If you are against us, please say so. Why be shy about it? Since we are bent on rebelling, the matter is no longer in your hands! Indeed we shall make the air thick with the pungent smell of gunpowder. All this talk about being "humane" and "all-sided" – let's have an end to it!

You say we are too arrogant? "Arrogant" is just what we want to be. Chairman Mao says, "And those in high positions we counted as no more than the dust." We are bent on striking down not only the reactionaries in our school, but the reactionaries all over the world. Revolutionaries take it as their task to transform the world. How can we not be "arrogant"?[2]

The Red Guard also sought to forge a new socialist spirit by purging China of all traces of "feudal" and "bourgeois" culture and thought. Some ancient monuments and works of art were destroyed in the process. Party officials, professors, and intellectuals were exiled to remote villages to purify themselves with the heavy labor of the peasant masses and to rekindle a burning devotion to the semi-divine Chairman Mao. The Red Guard attracted

enormous worldwide attention: many observers were appalled, but China's young revolutionaries inspired radical admirers around the world and served as an extreme model for the student rebellions of the late 1960s.

Although Mao and the Red Guard did succeed in mobilizing the masses, shaking up the party, and creating greater social equality, factional disputes and growing chaos enabled Mao's more moderate Communist comrades to regain much of their influence by 1969. This shift, coupled with actual fighting between China and Russia on the northern border in 1969 and not-so-secret Russian talk of atomic attack, opened the door to a spectacular if limited reconciliation between China and the United States in 1971. President Richard Nixon's pilgrimage to Peking also bespoke China's national resurgence: according to reliable reports, Nixon "felt the force of Mao" in private conversation and was "humbled and awed in a rare way" by the extraordinary heir of China's imperial tradition.[3]

Since Mao's death in 1976 and the crushing of the plot by the radical "Gang of Four," China's overriding goal appears to be economic modernization, embodied in the ongoing campaign of the Four Modernizations – agriculture, industry, science and technology, and national defense. In pursuit of such modernization, the regime has even encouraged joint ventures with foreign capitalists from Japan, Europe, and the United States. Hopes run high of finding mammoth oil deposits. Tourism has become big business. Although the Soviet Union is still considered an imperialist threat, traditional diplomatic relations have been re-established between the two countries as well as with the United States. The Chinese Communist leadership has correspondingly downplayed revolutionary Marxist purity while maintaining firm control over the population. Marxism has thus inspired a

1945	Japan surrenders
	Civil war begins in China
1946	Japan receives democratic constitution
	The Philippines gain independence
1947	Communal strife follows independence for India and Pakistan
1948	Civil war between Arabs and Jews in Palestine
1949	Korean War begins
	Mao Tse-tung (Mao Zedong) proclaims the People's Republic of China
	Indonesia under Sukarno wins independence from the Dutch
1950	China enters Korean War
	Japan begins long period of rapid economic growth
1951	Iran tries unsuccessfully to nationalize the Anglo-Iranian Oil Company
1952	American occupation of Japan officially ends
1954	Vietnamese nationalists defeat the French at Dien Bien Phu
1955	First Afro-Asian Conference of non-aligned nations meets at Bandung, Indonesia
1958	Mao Tse-tung announces the Great Leap Forward
1960	Open split between China and the Soviet Union emerges
1965	The Great Proletarian Cultural Revolution begins in China
	Growing American involvement in the Vietnamese civil war
1966	Indira Gandhi becomes Prime Minister of India
1971	President Nixon's visit to China signals improved Sino-American relations
1975	War in Vietnam ends with Communist victory
1976	China pursues modernization after Mao's death
1979	Revolution topples the shah of Iran

Chinese national revival, and that revival has in turn enabled a proud people to experiment boldly at building its own kind of socialism.

JAPAN'S AMERICAN REVOLUTION

After Japan's surrender in August 1945, American occupation forces began landing in the Tokyo-Yokohama area. Riding through what had been the very heart of industrial Japan, the combat-hardened veterans saw an eerie sight. Where mighty mills and factories had once hummed with activity, only smokestacks and giant steel safes remained standing amid miles of rubble and debris. The empty landscape manifested Japan's state of mind as it lay helpless before its conqueror.

Japan, like Nazi Germany, was formally occupied by all the Allies, but real power resided in American hands. The supreme commander was General Douglas MacArthur, the five-star hero of the Pacific, who with his advisors exercised almost absolute authority.

MacArthur and the Americans had a revolutionary plan for defeated Japan. Convinced that militaristic, anti-democratic forces were responsible for Japanese aggression and had to be destroyed, they simultaneously introduced radical reforms designed to make Japan a free democratic society along American lines. The Americans believed in their mission and in the obvious superiority of their civilization; the exhausted, demoralized Japanese, who had feared a worse fate, accepted passively. Long-suppressed liberal leaders emerged to offer crucial support and help carry the reforms forward.

Japan's sweeping American revolution began with "demilitarization" and a systematic purge. Twenty-five top government leaders and army officers were tried and convicted as war criminals by a special international tribunal; other courts sentenced hundreds to death and sent thousands to prison. Over 220,000 politicians, businessmen, and army officers were declared ineligible for office.

Many Americans wanted to try Emperor Hirohito as a war criminal, but MacArthur hesitated in the face of strong Japanese opposition. When the emperor voluntarily renounced his divinity — according to legend, the founder of the ancient imperial dynasty was the grandson of the sun goddess — MacArthur wisely decided to let him reign as a useful figurehead. According to the American-dictated constitution of 1946, the emperor was "the symbol of the State and of the people with whom resides sovereign power."

The new constitution made the government fully responsible to the Diet, whose members were popularly elected by all adults. A bill of rights granted basic civil liberties and freed all political prisoners, including communists. The constitution also abolished forever all Japanese armed forces. Japan's resurrected liberals enthusiastically supported this American move to destroy militarism.

The American occupation left Japan's powerful bureaucracy largely intact and used it to implement the fundamental social and economic reforms that were rammed through the Japanese Diet. Many had a New Deal flavor. The occupation promoted the Japanese labor movement, and the number of union workers increased fifteen-fold in three years. The occupation also introduced American-style anti-trust laws. The gigantic zaibatsu firms were broken up into many separate companies in order to encourage competition and economic democracy. The American reformers proudly "emancipated" Japanese women, granting them equality before the law. And, of lasting significance, Japan's educational system was restructured along American lines, insofar as local authorities gained greater control over local schools and access to higher education was democratized.

The occupation also imposed truly revolutionary land reform. MacArthur, often portrayed in the United States as a rigid conservative, pressured the Japanese Diet into buying up all the land owned by absentee landlords and selling it to peasants on very generous terms. This reform strengthened the small independent peasant, who became a staunch defender of postwar democracy.

The United States' efforts to remake Japan in its own image were powerful but short-lived. By 1948, when the United States began to look at the world through a cold war lens, occupation policy shifted gears. The Japanese later referred to this about-face as "the reverse course." As China went decisively communist, American leaders began to see Japan as a potential ally, not an object of social reform. The American command began purging left-wingers and rehabilitating prewar nationalists, many of whom joined the Democratic Liberal Party, which became increasingly conservative and emerged as the dominant political organization in postwar Japan. Efforts to break up the zaibatsu monopolies and encourage labor unions were quietly dropped. The United States ended the occupation in 1952. By the treaty terms, Japan regained independence and the United States retained its vast military complex in Japan. In actuality, Japan became a military protectorate, a special ally shielded, and restricted, by America's nuclear capability.

"JAPAN, INC."

Restricted to satellite status in world affairs, the Japanese people applied their extraordinary creative powers to rebuilding their country. Japan's economic recovery, like Germany's, proceeded painfully slowly immediately after the war. Beginning with the Korean War, however, the economy took off

SONY ASSEMBLY LINE *Disciplined, educated, and attentive to details, these young women make a world-famous product and epitomize the high-quality Japanese labor force. (Black Star/Eiji Miyazawa)*

and rose with spectacular speed for a whole generation. Between 1950 and 1970 the real growth rate of Japan's economy – adjusted for inflation – averaged a breathtaking 10 percent a year – almost three times that of the United States. When the occupation officially ended in 1952, Japan produced only about one third as much as France or Great Britain; by the 1970s it already produced as much as France and Great Britain combined. Per-capita production equalled that of the United States. After the Arab oil shock of 1973, the petroleum-poor Japanese did less well, though still better than most other peoples.

Japan's emergence as an economic superpower fascinated some outsiders and troubled others. While Asians and Africans looked to Japan for the secrets of successful modernization, Americans and Europeans whipped up recipes for copying Japanese success, notably Harvard professor Ezra Vogel's provocative bestseller *Japan as Number One: Lessons for America* (1979). Some of Japan's Asian neighbors again feared Japanese exploitation. And in the 1970s some Americans and Europeans began to bitterly accuse "Japan Inc." of an unholy alliance between government and business. Industries and workers hurt by Japanese "unfair competition" called upon their governments for aggressive countermeasures.

Many of the ingredients in western Europe's recovery also operated in Japan. American aid, cheap labor, and freer international trade all helped spark the process. As in western Europe, the government concentrated its energies on economic development. Japanese businessmen recognized the opportunity to replace their bombed-out plants with the latest, most efficient technology.

Japan's astonishing economic surge also seems to have had deep roots in Japanese history, culture, and national character. Restricted by geography to mountainous islands, Japan was for centuries safely isolated from invaders. By the time American and European pressure forced open its gates in the mid-nineteenth century, Japan was politically unified and culturally homogeneous. Agriculture, education, and material well-being were advanced even by European standards. Moreover, Japanese society put the needs of the group before those of the individual. When the Meiji reformers had redefined Japan's primary task as catching up with the West, they had the support of an advanced and disciplined people. Japan's modernization, even including a full share of aggressive imperialism, had been extremely rapid.

By the end of the American occupation, this tight-knit, group-centered society had reassessed its future and worked out a new national consensus. Japan's new task was to build its economy and compete efficiently in world markets. Improved living standards

emerged as a related goal after the initial successes of the 1950s. The ambitious "double-your-income" target for the 1960s was ultimately surpassed by 50 percent.

Government and big business shared leading roles in the drama of economic growth. As during the Meiji restoration, capable, respected bureaucrats directed and aided the efforts of cooperative business leaders. The government decided which industries were important, then made loans and encouraged mergers to create powerful firms in those industries. The anti-trust policy introduced by the American occupation, based on the very un-Japanese values of individualism and unrestrained competition, was scrapped.

Big business was valued and respected because it served the national goal and mirrored Japanese society. Big companies, and to a lesser extent small ones, traditionally hire workers for life immediately after they finish school. Employees are never fired and seldom laid off, and in return they are loyal and obedient. To an extent difficult for a Westerner to imagine, the business firm in Japan is a big, well-disciplined family. The workday begins with the company song; employees' social lives also revolve around the company. Wages are based on age. (Discrimination against women is severe: wages and job security are strikingly inferior.) Most unions are moderate, agreeable company unions. The social and economic distance between salaried managers and workers is slight and often breached. Efficiency, quality, and quantity are the watchwords. Management is quick to retrain employees, secure in the knowledge that they will not take their valuable new skills elsewhere. These factors, not "unfair competition," account for Japan's economic success.

Japanese society, with its inescapable stress on cooperation and compromise, has proved especially well-adapted to the challenges of modern industrial urban civilization. For example, Japan alone among industrial nations has experienced a marked decrease in crime over the last generation. In the 1970s the Japanese addressed themselves effectively to such previously neglected problems as pollution and energy resources. Highly dependent on imported resources and foreign sales, Japan also began groping for a new role in world politics. Closer relations with China, increased loans to southeast Asia, and tough trade negotiations with the United States were all features of that ongoing effort.

NEW NATIONS IN SOUTH ASIA AND THE MUSLIM WORLD

South Asia and the Muslim world have transformed themselves no less spectacularly than China and Japan. The national independence movements, which had been powerful mass campaigns since the 1930s, triumphed decisively over weakened and demoralized European imperialism after World War Two (pages 1370–1373). Between 1947 and 1962, as decolonization gathered almost irresistible strength, virtually every colonial territory won its political freedom. The complete reversal of the long process of European expansion was a turning point in world history.

The new nations of South Asia and the revitalized states of the Muslim world exhibited many variations on the dominant themes of national renaissance and modernization, especially as the struggle for political independence receded into the past.

THE INDIAN SUBCONTINENT

As we saw in Chapter 34, Mahatma Gandhi and the Indian Congress party developed the philosophy of militant nonviolence to oppose British rule of India after World War One and to lessen oppression of the Indian poor by the Indian rich. By 1929 Gandhi had succeeded in transforming the Congress party from a narrow middle-class party into a mass independence movement. Gradually and grudgingly, Britain's rulers introduced reforms culminating in limited self-government in 1937.

World War Two accelerated the drive toward independence, but also pointed it in a new direction. Humiliated that Great Britain had declared war against Germany on India's behalf without consulting them, Congress party leaders resigned their posts in the Indian government and demanded self-rule as the immediate price of political cooperation. In 1942, when Gandhi called on the British to "Quit India," threatening another civil disobedience campaign, he and the other Congress leaders were quickly arrested and jailed for the virtual duration of the war. As a result, India's wartime support for hard-pressed Britain was substantial but not always enthusiastic. Meanwhile the Congress party's prime political rival skillfully seized the opportunity to increase its influence.

That rival was the Muslim League, led by the brilliant, elegant English-educated lawyer Muhammad Ali Jinnah (1876–1948). Jinnah and the other leaders of the Muslim League feared Hindu domination of an independent Indian state led by the Congress party. Jinnah, asserting in nationalist terms the right of Muslim areas to separate from the Hindu majority, described the Muslims of India as

a nation of a hundred million, and what is more, we are a nation with our distinct culture and civilization, language, literature, arts, and architecture . . . laws and moral codes, customs and special aptitudes and ambitions. In short, we have our own distinctive outlook on life and of life.[4]

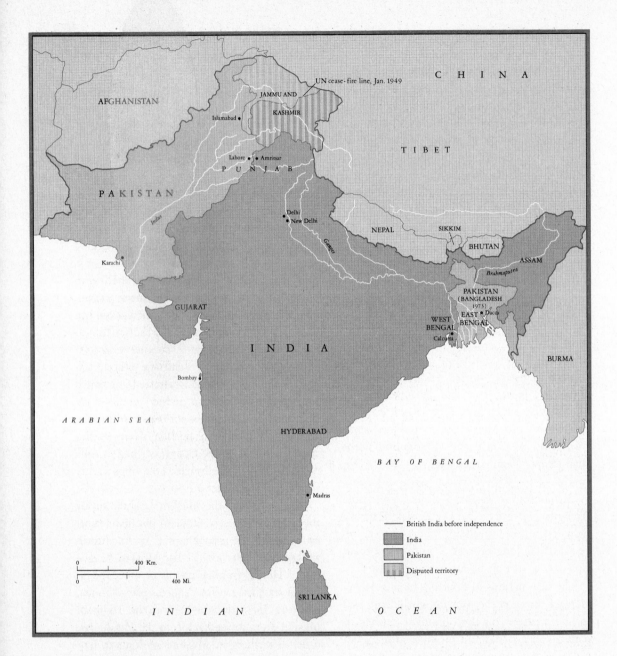

MAP 38.1 THE PARTITION OF BRITISH INDIA,
1947 Violence and fighting were most intense
where there were large Hindu and Muslim minorities
— in Kashmir, Punjab, and Bengal. The tragic result, which has occurred repeatedly throughout the
world in the twentieth century, was a forced exchange
of populations and greater homogeneity on both sides
of the border.

As Jinnah told 100,000 listeners at the Muslim League's Lahore Conference in March 1940, "If the British Government is really in earnest and sincere to secure the peace and happiness of the people of the subcontinent, the only course open to us all is to allow the major nations separate homelands by dividing India into autonomous national states."[5]

The Muslim League's insistence on the division of India appalled Gandhi. He regarded Jinnah's two-nation theory as simply untrue, and as promising the victory of hate over love. Gandhi's argument was most accurate when applied to the Bengali Muslims of northeastern India's Ganges River basin, whose language, dress, racial appearance, food, and social customs were virtually identical to those of Bengali Hindus; only in religion did they differ. The passionate debate between Jinnah and Gandhi continued unabated during the war, as millions argued whether India was one nation or two. By 1945 the subcontinent was intellectually and emotionally divided, though still momentarily held together by British rule.

When Britain's Labour government agreed to speedy independence for India after 1945 (pages 1378-1380), conflicting Hindu and Muslim nationalisms and religious hatred became the obstacles, leading to murderous clashes between the two communities in 1946. In a last attempt to preserve the subcontinent's political unity, the British proposed a federal constitution providing for extensive provincial – and thus religious and cultural – autonomy. When after some hesitation Jinnah and the Muslim League would accept nothing less than an independent Pakistan, India's last viceroy – war hero Lord Louis Mountbatten (1900–1979), Queen Victoria's great-grandson – proposed partition. Both sides accepted. At the stroke of midnight on August 14, 1947, one fifth of humanity gained political independence. As the sumptuous horse-drawn coach of the last viceroy pulled away from the final ceremony, endless cries of "Long live Mountbatten!" rose from the gigantic crowds – ringing testimony to India's residue of good feeling toward its vanquished conquerors and their splendidly peaceful departure.

Yet independence through partition was to bring tragedy. In the weeks after independence, communal strife exploded into an orgy of massacres and mass expulsions. Perhaps 100,000 Hindus and Muslims were slaughtered, and an estimated 5 million refugees from both communities fled in opposite directions to escape being hacked to death by frenzied mobs.

This wave of violence was a bitter potion for Congress leaders, who were completely powerless to stop it. "What is there to celebrate?" exclaimed Gandhi. "I see nothing but rivers of blood."[6] In January 1948, announcing yet another fast to protest Hindu persecution of Muslims in the Indian capital, and to restore "heart friendship" between the two communities, Gandhi was gunned down by a Hindu fanatic. As the Mahatma's death tragically testifies, the constructive and liberating forces of modern nationalism have frequently deteriorated into blind hatred.

After the ordeal of independence, relations between India and Pakistan – both members of the British Commonwealth – remained tense. Fighting over the disputed area of Kashmir continued until 1949, and broke out again in 1965-1966 and 1971. Like most newly independent states, Pakistan eventually adopted an authoritarian government in 1958. Unlike most, Pakistan failed to preserve its exceptionally fragile unity, which proved to be the unworkable dream of its Muslim League leaders.

Pakistan's western and eastern provinces were separated by more than a thousand miles of Indian territory, and by language, ethnic background, and social custom. They shared only the Muslim faith that had temporarily brought them together against the Hindus. The Bengalis of East Pakistan constituted a majority of the total population, but were neglected by the central government, which remained in the hands of West Pakistan's elite after Jinnah's death. In essence, East Pakistan remained a colony – of West Pakistan.

Tensions gradually came to a head in the late 1960s. Bengali leaders calling for virtual independence were charged with treason, and martial law was proclaimed in East Pakistan. In 1971 the Bengalis revolted. Despite savage repression – 10 million Bengalis fled temporarily to India, which provided some military aid – the Bengalis won their independence as the new nation of Bangladesh, the world's eighth most populous country and one of its poorest.

India was ruled for a generation after 1947 by Jawaharlal Nehru (1889–1964) and the Congress party, which introduced major social reforms. Hindu women and even young girls were granted legal equality, which included the right to vote, to seek a divorce, and to marry outside their caste. The constitution also abolished the untouchable caste, and established "ex-untouchable" quotas for university scholarships and government jobs in an effort to compensate for centuries of the most profound discrimination. In practice, attitudes toward women and untouchables evolved slowly — especially in the villages, where 85 percent of the people lived.

The Congress leadership tried with modest success to develop the country economically by means of democratic socialism. But population growth ate up much of the increase in output, and intense poverty remained the lot of most people. Poverty also encouraged widespread corruption within the bureaucracy.

The population continued to grow relentlessly about 2.4 percent per year, a rate capable of doubling India's already enormous multitude in just thirty years. Halfhearted governmental efforts to promote birth control met with indifference or hostility.

The Congress party maintained a moralizing neutrality in the cold war and sought to group the newly independent states into a "third force" of "non-aligned" nations. This effort culminated in the Afro-Asian Conference in Bandung, Indonesia, in 1955.

Nehru's daughter Indira Gandhi (b. 1917) became prime minister in 1966. Mrs. Gandhi (whose deceased husband was no relation to Mahatma Gandhi) has since dominated Indian political life with a skillful combination of charm, tact, and toughness. As it became clear that population growth was frustrating efforts to improve living standards, Mrs. Gandhi's government stepped up measures to promote family planning. Bus posters featuring smiling youngsters proclaimed that "A Happy Family is a Small Family," and doctors and nurses promoted loop rings for women, and condoms and surgical vasectomy for men. Although vasectomy is the most effective form of contraception, since it does not require continual conscientiousness, most Indian males rejected it for both psychological and religious reasons. As a doctor in a market town explained to a Western journalist:

They have mostly heard of family planning around here by now, but they are afraid. They are afraid that the sterilizing operation will destroy their male power and make them docile, like castrated animals. Mostly, they are afraid of interfering with God's will.[7]

In the face of such reluctance – and in an effort to clamp down on monumental corruption at all levels of government – Mrs. Gandhi in 1975 subverted parliamentary de-

ON THE CAMPAIGN TRAIL *Prime Minister Indira Gandhi gives the traditional sign of blessing as she travels unpretentiously through rural India, accompanied by crowds of jogging well-wishers. Indian elections are colorful and even those born into the political elite, like Mrs. Gandhi, must know how to mix with the masses. (Black Star, Stern)*

mocracy and proclaimed a state of emergency. Attacking dishonest officials, black marketeers, and tax evaders, she also threw the weight of the government behind a heavy-handed, semitotalitarian campaign of mass sterilization to reduce population growth. In some areas, poor men with very large families were rounded up and made to accept a few cents' payment to submit to a simple, almost painless irreversible vasectomy. Everywhere the pressure was intense, and 7 million men were sterilized in 1976.

Many Indian and foreign observers believed that Mrs. Gandhi's emergency measures marked the end of the parliamentary democracy and Western liberties introduced in the last phase of British rule. Instead Mrs. Gandhi – true to the British tradition – called for free elections, in which she suffered a spectacular defeat, largely because of the vastly unpopular sterilization campaign. Three years later Mrs. Gandhi won an equally stunning victory. Thus poor and overpopulated India has emerged as a maverick among the predominantly authoritarian nations of Asia and Africa in the 1970s: British-style parliamentary democracy and civil liberties have apparently sunk strong roots in the Indian soil.

SOUTHEAST ASIA

Indian independence fixed the pattern of Britain's policies in its smaller Asian possessions. Sri Lanka (Ceylon) quickly and smoothly gained independence in 1948. Malaya, however, encountered serious problems not unlike those of British India. The native Malays, an Islamic agricultural people, feared and disliked the Chinese, who had come to Malaya as poor migrant workers in the nineteenth century and stayed on to dominate the urban economy. The Malays having pressured the British into giving them the dominant voice in the federation, local Chinese communists launched an all-out guerrilla war. They were eventually defeated by the British and the Malays, and Malaya became self-governing in 1957 and independent in 1961. Yet two peoples soon meant two nations. In 1965, the largely Chinese city of Singapore was pushed out of the Malayan-dominated Federation of Malaysia. Ethnic tension continued to erupt periodically in Malaya, which still retained a large Chinese minority. The independent city-state of Singapore prospered on the hard work and inventiveness of its largely Chinese population.

The Philippine Islands had suffered enormous destruction in World War Two. The United States extended economic aid while retaining its large military bases, and then followed through on its earlier promises by granting the Philippines independence in 1946. As in Malaya, communist guerrillas tried unsuccessfully to seize power. The Philippines pursued American-style two-party competition until 1965, when President Ferdinand Marcos subverted the constitution and began his long rule as a greedy but not overly harsh dictator. Unlike most of south Asia, the Philippines – the only predominantly Christian nation in Asia – steered clear of both radical revolution and moderate reform. A tiny elite dominated the country, and the gap between rich and poor remained enormous.

The Netherlands East Indies, having successfully resisted stubborn Dutch efforts at reconquest, emerged as independent Indonesia under the nationalist leader Achmed Sukarno (1901–1970) in 1949. The populous new nation encompassed a variety of peoples, islands, and religions (Islam was predominant), and beginning in 1957 Sukarno tried to forge unity by means of his so-called "guided democracy," which rejected parliamentary democracy as politically divisive and claimed to replicate at the national level the traditional deliberation and consensus of the Indonesian village. For a time it seemed that the authoritarian, anti-Western Sukarno was in the sway of the well-organized Indonesian communists, who murdered and mutilated the seven leading army generals they kidnapped as part of an unsuccessful uprising in 1965. The army immediately retaliated, systematically slaughtering a half-million or more Indonesian communists, radicals, and noncommunist Chinese. Sukarno was forced to resign and Muslim generals ruled thereafter without any pretense of democracy.

The most bitterly destructive fighting occurred in French Indochina. The French tried to reimpose imperial rule there after the communist and nationalist guerrilla leader Ho Chi Minh (1890–1969) declared an independent republic in 1945. In spite of considerable aid from the Americans, who saw the war simply as an anticommunist struggle, the French were decisively defeated in 1954 in the battle of Dien Bien Phu. At the subsequent international peace conference, French Indochina gained independence. Laos and Cambodia became separate states; Vietnam was "temporarily" divided into two hostile sections at the 17th parallel pending elections to select a single unified government within two years.

The elections were never held and the civil war that soon broke out between the two Vietnamese governments, one communist and one anti-communist, became a very hot cold-

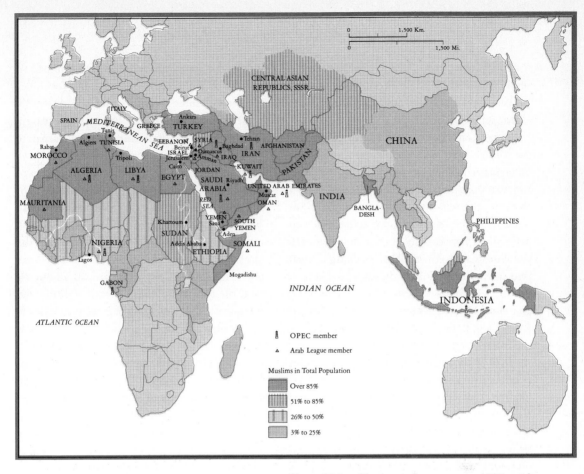

MAP 38.2 MODERN ISLAM, CA 1980 Although the Islamic heartland remains the Middle East and North Africa, Islam is growing steadily in black Africa and is the faith of heavily populated Indonesia. Compare Maps 9.3 and 25.2.

war conflict in the 1960s. The United States, as we have seen, invested tremendous military effort but fought its Vietnam War as a deeply divided country (pages 1394–1395). The tough, dedicated Communists eventually proved victorious in 1975. Thus events in Vietnam roughly recapitulated those in China, but in a long-drawn-out fashion: after a bitter civil war exacerbated by cold-war hatreds, the Communists succeeded in creating a unified Marxist nation.

THE MUSLIM WORLD

Throughout the vast arc of predominantly Islamic lands that stretches from Indonesia in Southeast Asia to Senegal in West Africa, change and bewildering internal conflict have prevailed since 1945. Everywhere, however, nationalism has remained the predominant political force. Although anti-Western and hospitable to radical social reform, nationalism in the Muslim world has remained consistently true to Islam and generally anti-communist. Cold-war conflicts and enormous oil resources have enhanced the region's global standing.

In the Arab countries of North Africa and the Middle East, with their shared but highly differentiated language and culture, nationalism has worn two faces. The practical, down-to-earth side has occupied itself with nation building within the particular states that supplanted former League of Nations mandates and European colonies. The idealistic, unrealized side is the pan-Arab dream, the dream of uniting all Arabs to recapture ancient glory and smash their enemies in the West and in Israel. Although this dream has foundered on the intense regional, ideological, and personal rivalries within the Arab world, it has contributed to political and economic alliances like the Arab League and the OPEC oil cartel.

Arab nationalists were already loosely united before World War Two in their opposition to the colonial powers and to Jewish migration to Palestine. After the French gave up their League of Nations mandates in Syria and Lebanon in 1945, having been forced by popular uprisings and British-American pressure to follow the British example, attention focused even more sharply on British-mandated Palestine. The situation was volatile. The Jews' demand that the British permit all survivors of Hitler's death camps to settle in Palestine was strenuously opposed by the Palestinian Arabs and the seven independent states of the newly founded Arab League. Murder and terrorism flourished, nurtured by bitterly conflicting Arab and Jewish nationalisms.

The British – their occupation policies in Palestine condemned by Arabs and Jews, by Russians and Americans – announced their intention to withdraw from Palestine in 1948. Initiating a pattern that was to become fa-

miliar, the insoluble problem was dumped in the lap of the United Nations. In November 1947 the United Nations General Assembly passed a non-binding resolution supporting a plan to partition Palestine into two separate states – one Arab and one Jewish. The Jews accepted but the Arabs rejected partition of Palestine, and by early 1948 an undeclared civil war raged in Palestine. The departing British looked on impartially. When the British mandate officially ended on May 14, 1948, the Jews proclaimed the state of Israel. The Arab countries immediately launched an all-out attack on the new Jewish state. Fighting for their lives, the Israelis drove off the invaders and conquered more territory; 900,000 Arab refugees fled or were expelled from old Palestine. This war left an enormous legacy of Arab bitterness toward Israel and its political allies Great Britain and the United States.

The humiliation of defeat triggered a nationalist revolution in Egypt, where a young army colonel named Gamel Abdel Nasser (1918–1970) drove out the corrupt and pro-Western king Farouk in 1952. A gifted politician and the unchallenged leader of the largest Arab state, Nasser enjoyed a powerful influence in the Middle East and throughout Asia and Africa. Perhaps his most successful and widely imitated move was radical land reform: large estates along the Nile were confiscated and divided up among peasants, without accompanying violence or drastic declines in production. Nasser, who preached the gospel of neutralism in the cold war and jailed Egyptian communists, turned for aid to the Soviet Union to demonstrate Egypt's independence. Relations with Israel and the West worsened, and in 1956 Secretary of State John Foster Dulles abruptly cancelled a U.S. offer to finance a giant new dam on the Nile, intended to promote economic development.

Nasser retaliated by immediately nationalizing the Suez Canal Company, the last remaining symbol and real substance of European power in the Middle East. Infuriated, the British and French joined forces with the Israelis and successfully invaded Egypt. This was to be the dying gasp of imperial power. Then the Americans, suddenly moralistic, reversed course and joined with the Russians – who were at that very moment crushing the Hungarian revolution – to force the British, French, and Israelis to withdraw from Egypt. This great victory for Nasser encouraged anti-Western radicalism, hopes of pan-Arab political unity, and a vague "Arab socialism." In Iraq radicals overthrew a pro-Western moderate government. In the aftermath of Suez, Egypt merged – temporarily – with Syria.

Yet the Arab world remained deeply divided. The only shared goals were opposition to Israel – war recurred in 1967 and in 1973 – and support for the right of Palestinian refugees to return to their homeland. In late 1977, after more than a generation of bitter Arab-Israeli conflict, President Anwar Sadat of Egypt tried another tack: a stunningly unexpected official visit to Israel, where his meeting with Israeli Prime Minister Menachim Begin was watched on television by millions around the world. Sadat's visit led to direct negotiations between Israel and Egypt, and a historic if limited peace settlement effectively mediated by U.S. President Jimmy Carter. Sadat's brave initiative was denounced as treason by other Arab leaders, who continued to support the uncompromisingly nationalist Palestine Liberation Organization against Israel, and who threatened to use oil as a weapon against the West. After Sadat was assassinated by Islamic fundamentalists in 1981, Egypt's relations with the Begin government deteriorated badly over the question of ever-increasing Israeli settlement on the West

GAMEL ABDEL NASSER Egypt's charismatic leader and pan-Arab visionary flashes his famous smile during an army parade in Cairo in 1955. (Bettmann Archive)

Bank – the area west of the Jordan River inhabited by Palestinian Arabs but occupied by Israel since its victories in the 1967 Six-Day War.

In the French colony of Algeria, meanwhile, Arab nationalism was emboldened by Nasser's triumph – and by the defeat of the French in Indochina. Neighboring Tunisia and Morroco, both more recently colonized, had won independence from France in 1956. But Algeria's large European population – 1 million French-speaking Europeans lived among 8 million Muslims – considered Algeria home, and an integral part of France.

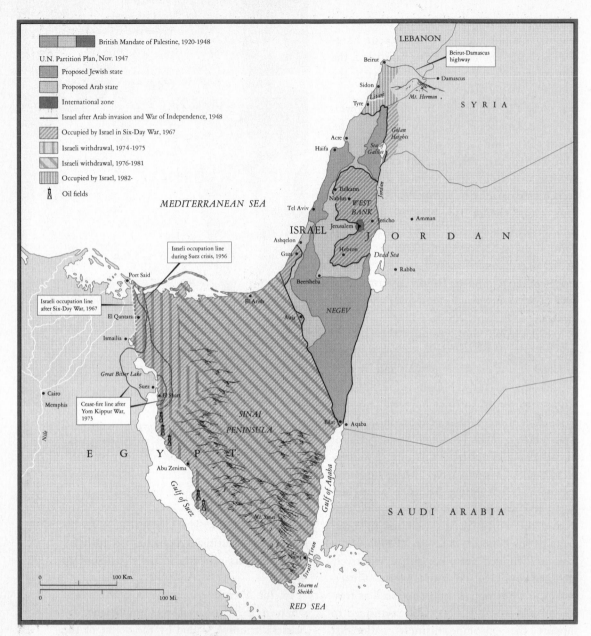

British Mandate of Palestine, 1920-1948

U.N. Partition Plan, Nov. 1947

Proposed Jewish state

Proposed Arab state

International zone

Israel after Arab invasion and War of Independence, 1948

Occupied by Israel in Six-Day War, 1967

Israeli withdrawal, 1974-1975

Israeli withdrawal, 1976-1981

Occupied by Israel, 1982-

Oil fields

MEDITERRANEAN SEA

LEBANON

Beirut

Sidon

Tyre

Acre

Haifa

Damascus

Beirut-Damascus highway

Mt. Hermon

S Y R I A

Golan Heights

Sea of Galilee

Jordan

Tulkatm

Nablus

WEST BANK

ISRAEL

Tel Aviv

Ashqelon

Gaza

Beersheba

Jerusalem

Jericho

Hebron

Amman

J O R D A N

Dead Sea

Rabba

NEGEV

Israeli occupation line during Suez crisis, 1956

Israeli occupation line after Six-Day War, 1967

Port Said

El Qantara

Ismailia

Great Bitter Lake

Suez

El Shatt

El Arish

Auja

Cairo

Memphis

Cease-fire line after Yom Kippur War, 1973

Nile

E G Y P T

Abu Zenima

Gulf of Suez

SINAI PENINSULA

Mt. Sinai

Nabq

Strait of Tiran

Sharm el Sheikh

Eilat

Aqaba

Gulf of Aqaba

S A U D I   A R A B I A

RED SEA

0   100 Km.

0   100 Mi.

MAP 38.3 PALESTINE, ISRAEL, AND THE MIDDLE EAST, 1947–1983 *Since the British mandate expired on May 14, 1948, there have been five major wars and innumerable armed clashes on what was formerly Palestine. After winning the War of Independence in 1948, Israel achieved spectacular victories in 1967 in the Six Day War, occupying the Sinai Peninsula, the Golan Heights, and the West Bank. The Yom Kippur War of 1973 eventually led to the Israeli evacuation of the Sinai and peace with Egypt, but there has been no agreement on the West Bank.*

When nationalism stirred Algerian Muslims to revolt, they found themselves confronting a solid phalanx of European settlers determined to defend their privileged position.

It was this determination that made the ensuing Algerian war so bitter and bloody. In 1958 a military coup in Algeria, resulting from the fears of the European settlers that a disillusioned, anticolonial majority of French voters would sell them out, brought General de Gaulle back to power in France. Contrary to expectations, de Gaulle accepted the principle of self-determination for Algeria in 1959, and in a national referendum the vast majority of the French population agreed. In 1962, after more than a century of French conquest, Algeria became an independent Arab state. The European population quickly fled.

Developments in the non-Arab states of Turkey and Iran testify to the diverse forms nationalism took in the Muslim world. Turkey remained basically true to Atatürk's vision of a thoroughly modernized, secularized, Europeanized state. Islam played a less influential role in daily life and thought there than in other Middle Eastern countries, and Turkey also joined NATO to protect itself from possible Russian aggression.

Iran tried again to follow Turkey's example, as it had before 1939. Once again, its success was limited. The new shah — Muhammed Reza Pahlavi, the son of Reza Shah — angered Iranian nationalists by courting Western powers and Western oil companies in the course of freeing his country from Russian influence after the war. The shah subsequently accepted the effort of the Iranian Majlis and the fiery Prime Minister Mohammed Mossaddeq in 1951 to nationalize the British-owned Anglo-Iranian Oil Company, until an effective Western boycott of Iranian oil plunged the economy into chaos. Refusing to compromise

or be dismissed, Mossaddeq forced the shah to flee to Europe in 1953. Quickly restored to his throne by loyal army officers and with the help of the American CIA, the shah set out to build a powerful modern nation to insure his rule. Iran's gigantic oil revenues provided the necessary cash. The shah undermined the power bases of the traditional politicians — big landowners and religious leaders — by means of land reform, secular education, and increased power for the central government. Modernization surged forward, but at the price of ancient values, widespread corruption, and harsh dictatorship. The result was a violent reaction against secular values, an Islamic revolution in 1978 led by religious leaders grouped around the spellbinding Ayatollah Ruholla Khomeini. The shah fled in January 1979. As rival groups struggled for power, fifty-two American diplomats were imprisoned for more than a year — a grandiose gesture of anti-Western hatred. War with neighboring Iraq for political leadership in the Persian Gulf reinforced Iran's present torment and uncertain future.

IMPERIALISM AND NATIONALISM IN BLACK AFRICA

Most of sub-Saharan Africa won political independence fairly rapidly after the war. Only Portugal's old but relatively underdeveloped African territories and white-dominated southern Africa remained beyond the reach of African nationalists by 1964. The rise of independent states in black Africa — a decisive development in world history — resulted directly from both a reaction against Western imperialism and the growth of African nationalism.

European traders had been in constant contact with Africa's coastal regions ever since the Age of Discovery. In the nineteenth century, as trade in so-called "legitimate products" like peanuts and palm oil increasingly supplanted "illegitimate" traffic in human beings, European influence continued to grow. Then came the political onslaught. After 1880 the Great Powers scrambled for territory and pushed into the interior, using overwhelming military force to mow down or intimidate African opposition and establish firm rule. By 1900, most of black Africa had been conquered – or, as Europeans preferred to say, "pacified" – and a system of imperial administration was taking shape.

Gradually but relentlessly, this imperial system transformed Africa. Generally speaking, its effect was to weaken or shatter the traditional social order and challenge accepted values. Yet this generalization must be qualified. For one thing, sub-Saharan Africa consisted of an astonishing diversity of peoples and cultures prior to the European invasion. There were, for example, over eight hundred distinct languages, and literally thousands of independent political units, ranging all the way from tiny kinship groups to large and powerful kingdoms like Ashanti of central Ghana and Ethiopia. The effects of imperialism varied accordingly.

Furthermore, the European powers themselves took rather different approaches to colonial rule. The British, for example, tended to exercise indirect rule through existing chiefs. The French believed in direct rule by appointed officials, both black and white. Finally, the number of white settlers varied greatly from region to region, which had important consequences. With these qualifications in mind, how did imperial systems generally operate in black Africa?

The self-proclaimed political goal of the French and the British – the principal foreign powers in black Africa – was to provide "good government" for their African subjects, especially after 1919. Good government meant, above all, law and order. It meant maintaining a small army and building up an African police force to put down rebellion, suppress tribal warfare, and protect life and property. More broadly, good government required a modern bureaucracy capable of taxing and governing the population. Since many African leaders and their peoples realistically chose not to resist the invader's superior force, and most others stopped fighting after experiencing crushing military defeat, the goal of law and order was widely achieved. This was a great source of satisfaction to colonial officials; it strengthened their self-confidence and convinced them that they were serving the common people, who were assumed to want only peace and security.

Colonial governments demonstrated much less interest in providing basic social services. Expenditures on education, public health, hospitals, and other social services increased after the First World War, but still remained small. Europeans feared the political implications of mass education, and typically relied instead on the modest efforts of state-subsidized mission schools. Moreover, they tried to make even their poorest colonies pay for themselves. This meant that salaries for government workers normally absorbed nearly all tax revenues.

Economically, the imperialist goal was to draw the vast untapped interior of the continent into the rapidly expanding world economy. Thus, as they completed their sometimes bloody conquest, the Europeans acted in black Africa as they had in Asia, North Africa, and Latin America. The key was railroads, from coastal trading centers to outposts hundreds of miles into the interior. Cheap, dependable

DISTRICT OFFICER ON TOUR *For many Africans, imperialism meant the local colonial official, who might be a vicious, petty tyrant or a relatively enlightened administrator. This humorous wood carving* *by Thomas Ona grows out of the rich satirical tradition upheld by the Yoruba of western Nigeria. (Berta Bascom, Berkeley)*

transportation facilitated easy shipment of raw materials out and manufactured goods in. Most African railroads were built after 1900; 5,200 miles were in operation by 1926, when attention turned to roadbuilding for trucks. Railroads and roads had two other important outcomes: troops could be moved quickly to put down any local unrest. And many African peasants began to work for wages for the first time.

Efforts to force Africa into the world economy on European terms went hand in hand with the advent of plantations and mines. The Europeans often imposed head taxes, payable in money or labor, to compel Africans to work for their white overlords. No aspect of imperialism was more disruptive and more despised by Africans than forced labor, widespread until about 1920. In some regions, however, particularly in West Africa, African peasants responded freely to the new economic opportunities by voluntarily shifting to export crops on their own farms. Overall, the result was increased production geared to the world market and a gradual decline in both traditional self-sufficient farming and nomadic herding.

In sum, the imposition of bureaucratic Western rule and the gradual growth of a world-oriented cash economy between 1900 and 1930 had a truly revolutionary impact on Africa. The experiences of two very different African countries will dramatically illustrate variations on the general pattern.

GHANA AND KENYA

Present-day Ghana, which takes its name from one of West Africa's most famous early kingdoms, had a fairly complex economy well before British armies smashed the powerful Ashanti kingdom in 1873 and established a crown colony they called the Gold Coast. Precolonial local trade was vigorous and varied, though occasionally disrupted by war and hindered by poor transportation, especially in the rainy season.

It was into this sophisticated economy that the British introduced production of cocoa beans for the world's chocolate bars. Output rose spectacularly, from a few hundred tons in the 1890s to 305,000 tons in 1936. British imperialists loved to brag about the railroads to the interior, but recent studies clearly show that independent peasants and energetic African businesspeople – many of the traders were women – were mainly responsible for the spectacular success of cocoa-bean production. Creative African entrepreneurs even went so far as to build their own roads, and they sometimes reaped big profits; in the boom of 1920, "motor cars were purchased right and left, champagne flowed freely, and expensive cigars scented the air."[8] As neighboring West African territories followed Ghana's lead, West Africa took its place in the world economy.

The Gold Coast also showed the way politically and culturally. The Westernized elite – relatively prosperous and well-educated lawyers, professionals, and journalists – and businesspeople took full advantage of opportunities provided by the fairly enlightened colonial regime. The black elite was the main presence in the limited local elections permitted by the British, for few permanent white settlers had ventured to hot and densely populated West Africa.

Across the continent in the British East African colony of Kenya, events unfolded differently. The East African peoples were more self-sufficient, less numerous, and less advanced commercially and politically. Once the British had built a strategic railroad from the coast across Kenya to Uganda, foreigners from Great Britain and India moved in to exploit the situation. Indian settlers became shopkeepers, clerks, and laborers in the towns. The British settlers, an amalgam of greedy adventurers and rich aristocrats, shared a common dream: to turn the cool, beautiful, and fertile Kenya highlands into a "white man's country" like Southern Rhodesia or the Union of South Africa. They dismissed the local population of peasant farmers as "barbarians," fit only to toil as cheap labor on their large estates and plantations. By 1929, two thousand white settlers, connected to the coast by a network of railroads, were producing a variety of crops for export.

The white settlers in Kenya manipulated the colonial government for their own interests and imposed rigorous segregation on the black (and Indian) population. Kenya's Africans thus experienced much harsher colonial rule than their fellow Africans in the Gold Coast.

THE GROWTH OF AFRICAN NATIONALISM

Western intrusion was the critical factor in the development of African nationalism, as it had been in Asia and the Middle East. Yet two things were different about Africa. Because the imperial system and Western education did not solidify in Africa until after 1900, national movements did not come of age there until after 1945. And too, Africa's multiplicity of ethnic groups, coupled with imperial boundaries that often bore no resemblance to existing ethnic boundaries, greatly compli-

RAILROAD CONSTRUCTION IN KENYA *Rail-roads opened the interior to a plantation economy and brought many more Africans into direct contact with* Europeans and Indians. (United Press International, Inc.)

cated the development of political – as distinct from cultural – nationalism. Was a modern national state to be based on ethnic tribal loyalties (as it had been in France and Germany, in China and Japan)? Was it to be founded on an all-African union of all black peoples? Or would such a state have to be built on the multitribal territories arbitrarily carved out by competing European empires? Only after 1945 did a tentative answer emerge.

A few educated West Africans in British colonies had articulated a kind of black nationalism before 1914. But the first real impetus came from the United States and the British West Indies. American blacks struggling energetically for racial justice and black self-confidence early in the twentieth century

took a renewed interest in their African origins and in the common problems of all black people. Their influence on educated Africans was great.

Of the many persons who participated in this "black nationalism" and in the "Renaissance" of American black literature in the 1920s, the most renowned was W. E. B. Du Bois (1868–1963). The first black to receive a Ph.D. from Harvard, this brilliant writer and historian was poignantly aware of his African origins and of the psychological pressures of Western culture. As Du Bois wrote in 1903 in *The Souls of Black Folk:*

It is a peculiar sensation, this double consciousness, this sense of always looking at one's self through the eyes of others, of measuring one's soul by the tape of a world that looks on in amused contempt and pity. One ever feels his two-ness – an American, a Negro: two souls, two thoughts, two unreconciled strivings, two warring ideals in one dark body, whose dogged strength alone keeps it from being torn asunder.[9]

Stirred by President Wilson's promises of self-determination, Du Bois organized pan-African congresses in Paris during the Versailles Peace Conference and in Brussels in 1921. The goals of pan-Africanists (that is, "all-Africanists") were solidarity among blacks everywhere and, eventually, a vast self-governing union of all African peoples.

The European powers were hostile, of course, but so was the tiny minority of educated blacks in the French empire. As the influential Blaise Daigne, a black politician elected to the French Parliament by the privileged African "citizens" of Senegal, told Du Bois:

We Frenchmen of Africa wish to remain French, for France has given us every liberty and accepted us without reservation along with her European children. None of us aspire to see French Africa delivered exclusively to the Africans as is demanded, though without any authority, by the American Negroes.[10]

More authoritarian than the British but less racist, French imperialists aimed to create a tiny elite of loyal "black Frenchmen" who would link the uneducated African masses to their white rulers. They were sometimes quite successful.

But educated French and British Africans experienced a strong surge of pride and cultural nationalism in the 1920s and 1930s, ignited in part by American and West Indian blacks. The Senegalese poet and political leader Léopold Senghor (b. 1906) is an outstanding example.

Senghor, a gifted interpreter of Catholicism and of the French language in his native Senegal, discovered his African heritage in the cafés and lecture halls of Paris. He and other black and white students and intellectuals marvelled at the accomplishments of American blacks in art, literature, African history, and anthropology. They listened to black musicians – jazz swept Europe by storm – and concluded that

in music American Negroes have acquired since the War a place which one can call pre-eminent; for they have impressed the entire world with their vibrating or melancholy rhythms.[11]

Senghor and his circle formulated and articulated the rich idea of *négritude,* or blackness. By blackness they meant racial pride, self-confidence, and joy in black creativity and the black spirit. The powerful cultural nationalism that grew out of the cross-fertilization of African intellectuals and blacks from the United States and the West Indies was an unexpected by-product of European imperialism.

Black consciousness also emerged in the British colonies between the world wars – especially in West Africa, which remained more advanced than East and Central Africa. The Westernized elite pressed for more equal access to government jobs, modest steps toward self-government, and an end to humiliating discrimination. This elite began to claim the right to speak for ordinary Africans, and to denounce the government-supported chiefs as Uncle Toms. Yet the great majority of well-educated British and French Africans remained moderate in their demands. They wanted to join the white man's club, not to tear it down.

The Great Depression was the decisive

1919	Du Bois organizes first pan-African congress	
1920s	Cultural nationalism grows among Africa's educated elites	
1929	Great Depression brings economic hardship and discontent	
1930–1931	Farmers in the Gold Coast organize first "cocoa hold-ups"	
1939–1945	World War Two accelerates political and economic change	
1951	Nkrumah and Convention People's Party win national elections	
1957	Nkrumah leads Ghana – former Gold Coast – to independence	
1958	De Gaulle offers commonwealth status to France's African territories; Guinea alone chooses independence	
1960	Mali and Nigeria become independent states	
1966	Ghana's Nkrumah deposed in military coup	
1967	Eastern Region secedes from Nigeria to form state of Biafra	
1975	Nigeria's military rulers permit elected civilian government	
1980	Blacks rule Zimbabwe – formerly Southern Rhodesia – after long civil war with white settlers	
1983	South Africa's whites maintain racial segregation and discrimination	

turning point in the development of African nationalism. For the first time unemployment was widespread among educated Africans, who continued to increase in number as job openings in government and the big foreign trading companies remained stable or even declined. Hostility toward well-paid white officials rose sharply. The Western-educated elite became more vocal and more political in its call for change. Some real radicals appeared.

Educated Africans ventured into new activities, often out of necessity. Especially in the towns, they supplied the leadership for many new organizations, including not only political parties and trade unions but also social clubs, native churches, and agricultural cooperatives. Radical journalists published uncompromising attacks on colonial governments in easy-to-read mass-circulation newspapers. The most spectacular of these journalists was the Nigerian Nnamdi Azikiwe, who had attended black colleges in the United States and learned his trade on an Afro-American weekly in Baltimore. The popular, flamboyant "Zik" was demanding independence for Nigeria as early as the late 1930s.

The Great Depression also produced extreme economic hardship and profound discontent among the African masses. African peasants and small businesspeople who had been drawn into the world economy, and sometimes profited from booms, now felt the agony of decade-long bust. Urban workers, many of whom were disaffiliated from their rural tribal origins, experienced a similar fate. In some areas the result was unprecedented mass protest.

The Gold Coast "cocoa holdups" of 1930–1931 and 1937–1938 are the most famous example. Cocoa completely dominated the Gold Coast's economy. As prices plummeted and cash incomes collapsed after 1929, cocoa farmers refused to sell their beans to the big British firms that fixed prices and monopolized the export trade. Instead, the farmers organized cooperatives to cut back production and sell their crops directly to European and American chocolate manufacturers. Small African traders and traditional tribal leaders largely supported the movement, which succeeded in mobilizing much of the population against the foreign companies. Many Africans saw the economic conflict in racial terms. The holdups were only partially successful, but they did force the government to establish an independent cocoa marketing board. They also demonstrated that mass organization and mass protest had come to advanced West Africa. Powerful mass-based movements for national independence could not be far behind.

ACHIEVING INDEPENDENCE WITH NEW LEADERS

The repercussions of the Second World War in black Africa greatly accelerated the changes begun in the 1930s. Mines and plantations strained to meet wartime demands. Towns mushroomed into cities, whose tin-can housing, inflation, and shortages of consumer goods created discontent and hardship. Africans had such eye-opening experiences as the curious spectacle of the British denouncing the racism of the Germans. Many African soldiers who served in India were powerfully impressed by Indian nationalism.

The attitudes of Western imperialists also changed. Both the British and the French acknowledged the need for rapid social and economic improvement in their colonies (page 1426); both began sending money and aid on a large scale for the first time. The French funneled more money into their west African colonies between 1947 and 1957 than during the entire previous half-century. The principle of self-government was written into the United Nations charter, and was now fully supported by Great Britain's postwar Labour government. As one top British official stated in 1948:

The central purpose of British colonial policy is simple. It is to guide the colonial territories to responsible government within the commonwealth in conditions that ensure to the people concerned both a fair standard of living and freedom from oppression from any quarter.[12]

Thus the key question for Great Britain's various African colonies was their rate of progress toward self-government. As usual the British, like the French, were in no rush. But a new breed of African leader was emerging, first in the British and then in the French colonies. Impatient and insistent, figures like Nkrumah, Azikiwe, and Touré were determined to gain political independence as soon as possible. These authentic spokesmen for modern African nationalism were remarkably successful: by 1964 almost all of West, East, and Central Africa had achieved statehood, usually without much bloodshed. Only the uncompromising Portuguese and the white settlers of southern Africa remained impervious to nationalist demands.

The new postwar African leaders shared three characteristics. They formed an elite by virtue of advanced European (or American) education and they had been profoundly influenced by Western thought. But compared to the interwar generation of educated Africans, they were more radical and humbler in social origin. Among them were former schoolteachers, union leaders, government clerks, and unemployed students, as well as lawyers and prize-winning poets.

Furthermore, the postwar African leaders expressed their nationalism in terms of the existing territorial governments. They accepted prevailing boundaries to avoid border disputes and to facilitate building unified modern states. Sometimes traditional tribal chiefs became their worst political enemies. Skillfully, the new leaders channeled postwar hope and discontent into support for mass political parties. These new parties in turn organized gigantic protests, and eventually came to power by winning elections held by the colonial government to choose its successor.

GHANA SHOWS THE WAY

Perhaps the most charismatic of this fascinating generation of African leaders was Kwame Nkrumah (1909–1972), under whose leadership the Gold Coast — which he rechristened Ghana — became the first independent African state to emerge from colonialism. Having begun his career as a schoolteacher in the Gold Coast, Nkrumah spent ten years studying in the United States, where he was deeply influenced by European socialists and by the Jamaican-born black leader Marcus Garvey. Garvey, convinced that blacks could never win justice in countries with white majorities, had organized a massive "Back to Africa" movement in the 1920s. He also preached "Africa for the Africans," advocating independence. Nkrumah returned to the Gold Coast immediately after the war and entered politics.

KWAME NKRUMAH This flamboyant radical leader skillfully built a mass movement to gain political independence, though he failed to create a pan-African political union. (Freelance Photographers Guild)

The time was ripe. Economic discontent erupted in rioting in February 1948; angry crowds looted European and Lebanese stores. The British, embarking on their new course, invited African proposals for constitutional reform. These proposals became the basis of the new constitution, which gave more power to Africans within the framework of (eventual) parliamentary democracy.

Meanwhile Nkrumah was building a radical mass party appealing particularly to modern elements — urban toughs, ex-servicemen, market women, union members, and cocoa farmers. Nkrumah and his party injected the joy and enthusiasm of religious revivals into their rallies and propaganda: "Self-Government Now" was their credo, secular salvation the promise.

Rejecting halfway measures — "We prefer self-government with danger to servitude in tranquillity" — Nkrumah and his Convention People's Party staged strikes and riots. Arrested, the "Deliverer of Ghana" campaigned from jail, and saw his party win a smashing victory in the national elections of 1951. Called from prison to head the transitional government, Nkrumah and his nationalist party continued to win victories in free elections, defeating both Westernized moderates and more traditional "tribal" rivals. By 1957 Nkrumah had achieved worldwide fame and influence as Ghana became the first African state to emerge from colonial control.

After Ghana's breakthrough, independence for other African colonies followed with breathtaking speed. As in Algeria, the main problem was the permanent white settlers, as distinguished from the colonial officials. Wherever white settlers were at all numerous, as in Kenya, they sought to preserve their privileged position. This white hope was fed by a substantial influx of white settlers after 1945, especially in Central Africa. Yet only in Southern Rhodesia were whites numerous enough to prevail long. Southern Rhodesian whites declared independence illegally in 1965, and held out for more than a decade until black nationalists won a long guerrilla war and renamed the country Zimbabwe. In Zambia (formerly Northern Rhodesia) and East Africa, white settlers simply lacked the numbers to challenge black nationalists or the British colonial office for long.

FRENCH-SPEAKING REGIONS

Decolonization took a somewhat different course in French-speaking Africa. As we have seen, France tried desperately after 1945 to hold onto Indochina and Algeria. Thus, although France upped its financial and technical aid to its African colonies, independence remained a dirty word until De Gaulle came to power in 1958. Seeking to head off radical nationalists, and with the crucial support of moderate black leaders, De Gaulle divided the federations of French West Africa and French Equatorial Africa into thirteen separate governments, thus creating a "French commonwealth." Plebiscites were called in each territory to ratify the new arrangement. The ballot was worded so that an affirmative vote meant continued ties with France; a *no* vote signified independence.

De Gaulle's gamble was shrewd. The educated black elite — as personified by the poet Senghor, who now led the government of Senegal — loved France and dreaded a sudden divorce. They also wanted continued French aid. France, in keeping with its ideology of assimilation, had given the vote to the educated elite in its colonies after World War Two, and about forty Africans held seats in the French parliament after 1946. Some of these impressive African politicians exercised real power and influence in metropolitan France. The Ivory Coast's Félix Houphouët-Boigny, for instance, served for a time as France's Minister of Health. For both cultural and practical reasons, therefore, French Africa's leaders tended to be moderate and in no rush for independence.

Yet political nationalism was not totally submerged. In Guinea, an inspiring young radical named Sekou Touré (b. 1922) led his people in overwhelming rejection of the new constitution. Touré had risen to prominence as a labor leader in his country's rapidly expanding mining industry; he had close ties with France's communist-dominated trade unions, and was inspired by Ghana's Nkrumah. Touré laid it out to De Gaulle, face to face:

We have to tell you bluntly, Mr. President, what the demands of the people are. . . . We have one prime and essential need: our dignity. . . . But there is no dignity without freedom. . . . We prefer freedom in poverty to opulence in slavery.[13]

De Gaulle punished Guinea as best he could. French officials and equipment were withdrawn, literally overnight, down to the last man and pencil. Guinea's total collapse was widely predicted – and devoutly hoped for in France. Yet Guinea's new government survived. Following Guinea's lead, Mali asked for independence in 1960. The other French territories quickly followed suit, though the new states retained very close ties with France.

Belgium tried belatedly to imitate De Gaulle in its enormous Congo colony, but without success. Long-time practitioners of extreme paternalism coupled with harsh, selfish rule, the Belgians had discouraged the development of an educated elite. In 1959, therefore, when following wild riots they suddenly decided to grant independence, the fabric of government simply broke down. Independence was soon followed by violent tribal conflict, civil war, and foreign intervention. The Belgian Congo was the great exception to black Africa's generally peaceful and successful transition to independence between 1957 and 1964.

BLACK AFRICA SINCE 1960

The ease with which most of black Africa achieved independence stimulated buoyant optimism in the early 1960s. While Europeans congratulated themselves on having fulfilled their "civilizing mission," Africans and sympathetic Americans anticipated even more rapid progress.

Twenty years later the outlook was different. In most former colonies, democratic government and civil liberties had given way to one-party rule or military dictatorship; Africa experienced a revival of authoritarianism comparable to that of Latin America (pages 1399–1401). Even where dictatorship did not prevail or was overturned, political conduct in Africa often seemed to slip into reverse gear. In many countries it was routine for the winners in a political power struggle to imprison, exile, or murder the losers. Corruption was widespread; politicians, army officers, and even lowly government clerks used their positions to line their pockets and reward their relatives. Corruption also plagued Asia and Latin America (and parts of North America as well), but Africa's greater poverty made the consequences particularly serious. Meanwhile the challenge of constructive economic and social development, which will be examined in Chapter 40, sometimes appeared overwhelming. As if all this were not enough, continuing white racist rule in South Africa represented a ticking time bomb for the entire continent.

Some European and American observers, surveying these conditions, have tended to write off Africa as a lost cause. Such a dismissal betrays a limited range of vision. Given the scope of their challenges, the new African countries have done rather well since independence. Nationalism, first harnessed to throw off imperialism, has served to promote some degree of unity and ongoing modernization. Fragile states have held together, and are gradually emerging as viable modern nations with their own distinct personalities.

BUILDING NATIONAL UNITY

The recent course of African history has been complex and confusing. Yet if we look first at the common legacy of imperialism, it is possible to distinguish basic patterns in the endless clatter of media reports.

The legacy of imperialism in Africa was by no means all bad. One positive outcome was a drastic reduction in the number of political units in Africa – from thousands to about forty well-defined states. These new states had functioning bureaucracies, some elected political leaders, and some modern infrastructure – that is, transportation, schools, hospitals, and the like. All the former colonies had experienced some urbanization and were tied into the world economy.

The new African states had also inherited relatively modern, diversified social structures. Tribal and religious rulers had generally lost out to a dynamic Westernized elite, whose moderate and radical wings faithfully reproduced the European political spectrum. Each new state also had the beginnings of an industrial working class (as well as a volatile urban poor population). Finally, each country inherited the cornerstone of imperial power – a tough, well-equipped army to maintain order.

Other features of the imperialist legacy have served to torment independent Africa. The disruption of traditional life caused real suffering, and resulted in fantastic post-independence expectations that could not be met. The prevailing export economies were weak, lopsided, and concentrated in foreign hands. Technical, managerial, and medical skills were in acutely short supply. Especially serious, however, was the legacy of political boundaries imposed without regard to ethnic and cultural groupings. Almost all the new states encompassed many peoples, languages, and cultures. Forging genuine national loyalty and unity in such circumstances was a formidable task.

It is within this inherited framework that black Africa's recent political development

MAP 38.4   NATIONALISM AND INDEPENDENCE IN WEST AFRICA   Most of West Africa achieved independence by 1960. Borders inherited from the colonial era were generally accepted, although the Ibo people tried unsuccessfully to break away from Nigeria in the bitter Nigerian Civil (Biafran) War.

must be understood. Great Britain and France had granted Africa democratic government in the belief that, if Africans insisted on independence, they might as well get the best. Yet Western-style democracy fared poorly. Political parties often coalesced along regional and ethnic lines, so that political competition encouraged regional conflict. Many African leaders concluded that democracy threatened national unity, and passionately believed that tough measures were needed to hold their countries together. Thus free elections and representative governments often gave way to dictators and one-party rule.

After Ghana won its independence, for instance, Nkrumah jailed without trial his main opponents – chiefs, lawyers, and intellectuals – and outlawed opposition parties. Embracing the communist and totalitarian models, Nkrumah worked to build a dynamic "revolutionary" one-party state. Nkrumah's personality, his calls for African unity, and his bitter attacks on "Western imperialists" aroused both passionate support and growing opposition. By the mid-1960s Nkrumah's grandiose economic projects had practically bankrupted Ghana, and in 1966 the army suddenly seized power while Nkrumah was visiting China. Across the continent in East Africa, Kenya and Tanzania likewise became one-party states with strong leaders.

The French-speaking countries also shifted toward one-party government to promote national unity and develop distinctive national characteristics. Mali followed Guinea into

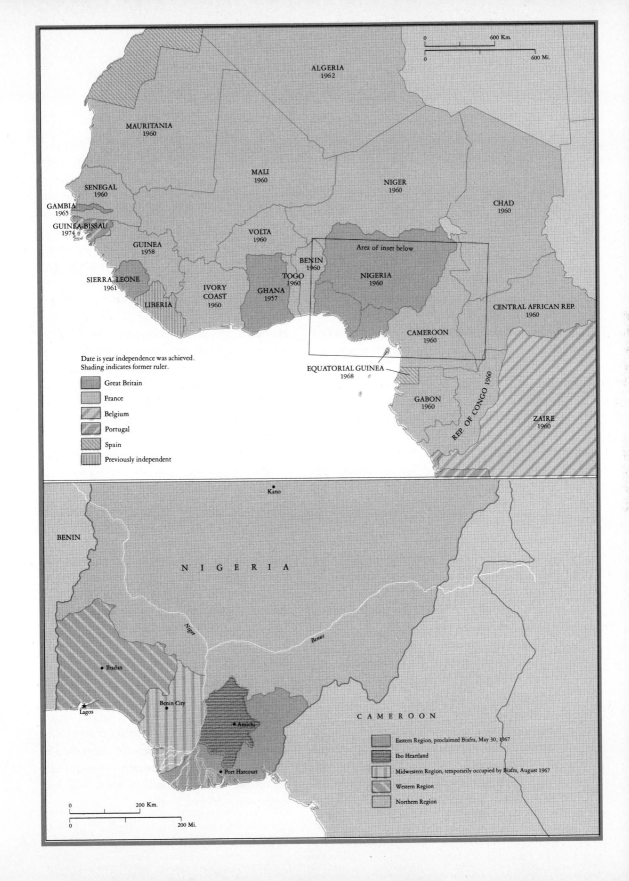

0   600 Km.

0   600 Mi.

ALGERIA
1962

MAURITANIA
1960

MALI
1960

NIGER
1960

CHAD
1960

SENEGAL
1960

GAMBIA
1965

GUINEA-BISSAU
1974

GUINEA
1958

VOLTA
1960

BENIN
1960

NIGERIA
1960

Area of inset below

SIERRA LEONE
1961

IVORY
COAST
1960

TOGO
1960

GHANA
1957

CENTRAL AFRICAN REP.
1960

LIBERIA

CAMEROON
1960

Date is year independence was achieved.
Shading indicates former ruler.

EQUATORIAL GUINEA
1968

REP. OF CONGO 1960

Great Britain

France

Belgium

Portugal

Spain

Previously independent

GABON
1960

ZAIRE
1960

Kano

BENIN

N I G E R I A

Niger

Benue

Ibadan

CAMEROON

Lagos

Benin City

Amichi

Port Harcourt

Eastern Region, proclaimed Biafra, May 30, 1967

Ibo Heartland

Midwestern Region, temporarily occupied by Biafra, August 1967

Western Region

Northern Region

0   200 Km.

0   200 Mi.

fire-eating radicalism, while Senegal and the Ivory Coast stressed moderation and close economic and cultural ties with France.

Like Nkrumah, many of the politicians at the helm of one-party states were eventually overthrown by military leaders. "The man on horseback" became a familiar figure in post-independence Africa. Between 1952, when Egypt's King Farouk was overthrown by Colonel Nasser, and 1968, Africa experienced at least seventy attempted military takeovers, twenty of which succeeded. The trend continued after 1968 with important coups in Ethiopia, Liberia, Uganda, and elsewhere. The rise of would-be Napoleons was lamented by many Western liberals and African intellectuals, who often failed to note that military rule was also widespread in Latin America, Asia, and the Near East.

As elsewhere, military rule in Africa was by nature authoritarian and undemocratic. Sometimes it placed a terrible burden on Africans; in Uganda, for instance, a crazy ex-sergeant named Idi Amin seized power, packed the army with his tribal supporters, and brutally terrorized the population for a decade. Yet military government often had redeeming qualities. Generally speaking, African military leaders were determined nationalists who managed to hold their fragile nations together. In the former Belgian Congo in the early 1960s, and in Ethiopia in the late 1970s, military governments successfully defeated separatist movements.

Equally important, military regimes were deeply committed to social and economic modernization. Drawing on a well-educated, well-organized, and highly motivated elite, they sometimes accomplished a good deal. Finally, African military leaders often believed in the ultimate goal of free, representative civilian government, which they sometimes restored after surmounting a grave national crisis. It was a question of priorities: unity came first, democracy second.

NIGERIA, AFRICA'S GIANT

The recent history of Nigeria illustrates just how difficult nation building can be. Nigeria was a name coined by the British to designate their conquests in the Niger River basin. The peoples of Nigeria encompassed many ancient kingdoms and hundreds of smaller groupings. The northern region was part of a great open plain, devoted to grazing and intensive farming; the much smaller southern region was a combination of coastal swamp and inland forest belt. Generally speaking, the peoples of the north were Muslims, while most southerners were Christians or animists. The south was dominated by two very different peoples: in the west the proud Yorubas, with a military tradition and strong, well-defined kingdom, and in the east the Ibos, with a tradition of business enterprise and independent villages.

Modern Nigeria came into being in 1914, when the British consolidated the northern and southern territories for administrative convenience. One able British governor described Nigeria in 1920 as a "collection of self-contained and mutually independent Native States, separated from one another, as many of them are, by differences of history and traditions, and by ethnological, racial, tribal, political, and religious barriers."[14] Such a land, the governor believed, could never be welded into a single homogeneous nation.

In spite of its internal divisions, Nigeria had spawned a powerful movement for national independence by 1945. The British responded receptively, and Nigeria entered into a period of intense but peaceful negotiation. In 1954, the third constitution in seven years set up the framework within which independence was achieved in 1960.

MOBILIZING IN BIAFRA   *A Biafran officer, himself only nine years old, drills a column of fresh recruits in 1969 during the Nigerian civil war. The boy* *soldiers were used for spying and sabotage, as Biafra struggled desperately against encirclement and starvation to win its independence. (Pictorial Parade)*

The key constitutional question was the relationship between the central government and the various regions. Some Nigerians, like the fiery Ibo journalist Azikiwe, wanted a strong centralized state; but the Yorubas in the west and the Muslim Hausa-Fulani leaders in the north wanted real power concentrated at the regional level. Ultimately Nigeria adopted a federal system, whereby the national government at Lagos shared power with three regional or state governments in the North, West, and East. Each region had a dominant tribe and a corresponding political party. The parties were expected to cooperate in the national parliament, and the rights of minorities were protected by law.

With a population of 55 million in 1963, "Africa's Giant" towered over the other new African nations. But after independence, Nigerians' bright hopes gradually dimmed. Ethnic rivalries made for political tensions. In 1964, minorities in the Western Region began forming their own Mid-West Region in an attempt to escape Yoruba domination. Tribal battles ensued, and in 1965 law and order broke down completely in the Western Region. At this point a group of young army officers seized power in Lagos, executing leading politicians and all officers above the rank of major. In an attempt to end the national crisis, the new Military Council imposed martial law and abolished the regional governments.

At first the young officers were popular, for the murdered politicians had been widely considered weak, corrupt, and too pro-Western. However, most of the new leaders were Ibos. The Muslim northerners had long distrusted the hardworking and clannish Ibos, who under the British had come to dominate business and the professions throughout Nigeria. Every northern town had its Ibo "strangers' district." When the Ibo-led Military Council proclaimed a highly centralized dictatorship, angry mobs in northern cities went wild. Thousands of Ibos were brutally massacred, and the panic-stricken survivors fled to their Ibo homeland. When a group of northern officers then seized the national government in a counter-coup, the traumatized Ibos revolted. Like the American south in the Civil War, the Eastern Region seceded from Nigeria in 1967 and proclaimed itself the independent state of Biafra.

The war in Biafra lasted three long years. The Ibos fought with heroic determination, believing that political independence was their only refuge from genocide. Heavily outnumbered, the Ibos were gradually surrounded. Hundreds of thousands, perhaps millions, starved to death as Biafra became another name for monumental human tragedy.

But Nigeria, like Abraham Lincoln's union, endured. The civil war entered the history books of the victors as the War for Nigerian Unity, not the War for Biafran Independence. Whatever its name, the conflict in Nigeria showed the world that Africa's "artificial" boundaries and states were remarkably durable.

Having preserved the state in the 1960s, Nigeria's military focused on building a nation in the 1970s. While the federal government held the real power, the country was divided into nineteen small, manageable states to handle local and cultural matters. The defeated Ibos were generously pardoned, not slaughtered, and Iboland was rebuilt with federal money. Modernizing investments of this kind were made possible by soaring oil revenues; Nigeria had become the world's seventh largest oil producer. In 1975, another army coup tried again to purge corruption and

sharpen the all-African diplomatic attack on South Africa. In 1979, Nigeria's military leaders were confident enough to relinquish power to an elected civilian government, and it is a good sign that elected leaders have continued to guide Africa's Giant.

The most serious recent problems have been economic, brought on by sharply falling oil revenues. In early 1983 the government suddenly expelled all illegal foreign workers, who had been welcomed during the oil boom and were now accused of taking jobs from Nigerians. In a matter of days large numbers of West Africans, led by 1.7 million Ghanaians, jammed into battered trucks and creaking ships bound for home — eloquent testimony to the effects of global recession and economic nationalism.

THE STRUGGLE IN SOUTHERN AFRICA

After the great rush toward independence, decolonization stalled. Meanwhile southern Africa remained under white rule, largely due to the numerical strength and determination of its white settlers. In Portuguese Angola and Mozambique, the white population actually increased from 70,000 to 380,000 between 1940 and the mid-1960s as white settlers established large coffee farms using forced native labor.

As economic exploitation grew, so did resentment. Nationalist liberation movements arose to wage unrelenting guerrilla warfare. After a coup overturning the long-established dictatorship in Portugal, the guerrillas managed to drive out the outnumbered settlers in 1975. Shortly thereafter, a coalition of nationalist groups also won in Zimbabwe after a long war of liberation.

This second round of decolonization in black Africa was bloodier and grimmer than the first. The third round that is taking shape

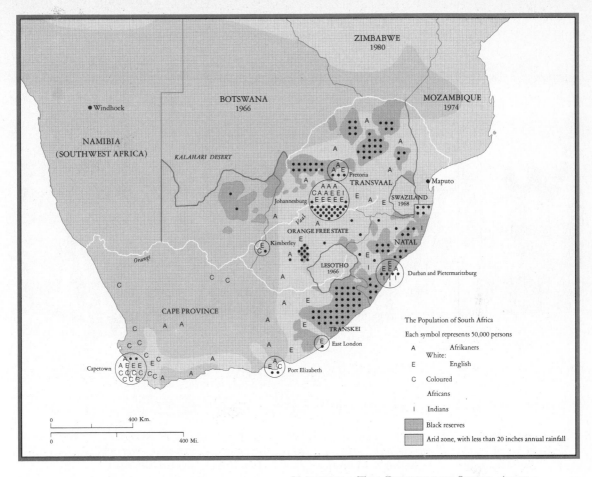

The following text labels appear on the map:

ZIMBABWE
1980

• Windhoek

BOTSWANA
1966

MOZAMBIQUE
1974

NAMIBIA
(SOUTHWEST AFRICA)

KALAHARI DESERT

• Maputo

A E
Pretoria TRANSVAAL

A A A
C A A E E I
E E E E E E

SWAZILAND
1968

Johannesburg

Vaal

ORANGE FREE STATE

E
C Kimberley

NATAL

Orange

C C

LESOTHO
1966

E
I
E A
I I
Durban and Pietermaritzburg

CAPE PROVINCE

C C
C C C
A E E E
C C C C
C C C
Capetown

C C

A A

A

E
TRANSKEI

E East London

A

E
E C Port Elizabeth

The Population of South Africa

Each symbol represents 50,000 persons

A   Afrikaners
     White:
E   English

C   Coloured

     Africans

I   Indians

▨   Black reserves

▨   Arid zone, with less than 20 inches annual rainfall

0   400 Km.

0   400 Mi.

MAP 38.5   THE REPUBLIC OF SOUTH AFRICA AND APARTHEID, CA 1960   In spite of the repressive apartheid laws, many blacks have managed to leave the reserves for South Africa's growing cities, where most Indians and coloureds already live.

in South Africa promises to be worse yet. The racial conflict in the white-ruled Republic of South Africa can be traced back in history — to the seventeenth-century Dutch settlers, complex rivalries between black tribes, settler wars of extermination and enslavement in the eighteenth and nineteenth centuries, and the surging British imperialism that resulted in the Boer War (pages 1147–1148). Although the British finally conquered the inland Dutch-settler republics, they had to compromise to avoid a long guerrilla war. Specifi-

cally, the British agreed to grant all of South Africa self-government as soon as possible, and to let its government decide which non-whites, if any, should vote. It was to be a tragic compromise.

Defeated on the battlefield, the embittered Dutch settlers known as Afrikaners elaborated a potently racist nationalism. Between 1910 — when South Africa became basically a self-governing dominion, like Canada and Australia — and 1948, the Afrikaners gradually won political power from their English-speaking

settler rivals. Since their decisive electoral victory in 1948, Afrikaner nationalists have spoken for the great majority of South African whites, who support the political leadership with varying degrees of enthusiasm.

Throughout the twentieth century the goals of Afrikaner nationalism have been remarkably consistent: white supremacy and racial segregation. In 1913, the new South African legislature passed the Native Land Act, which limited black ownership of land to native reserves encompassing a mere one-seventh of the country. Poor, overpopulated, and too small to feed themselves, the reserves have since served as a pool of cheap, temporary black labor for white farms, gold mines, and factories. A black worker – typically a young black man without a family – could leave the reserve only with special permission. In the eyes of the law, he was only a temporary migrant, who could be returned at will by his employer or the government. Thus so-called "pass laws" required every black outside the reserves to carry at all times an up-to-date pass approved by the white police. The native reserves system, combining racial segregation and indirect forced labor, has been a bulwark of white supremacy in South Africa.

Since 1948, successive Afrikaner governments have woven the somewhat haphazard early racist measures into a totalitarian fabric of racial discrimination and inequality. This system is officially known as *apartheid,* meaning separation or segregation. The population is dogmatically divided into four legally unequal racial groups – whites, blacks, Asians, and racially mixed Coloureds. Afrikaner propagandists claim to serve the interests of all racial groups by preserving separate cultures and racial purity; marriage and sexual relations between races are criminal offenses. Most observers see apartheid as a way of maintaining the lavish privileges of the white minority, who account for only one sixth of the total population.

South Africa's cities have grown rapidly, in conjunction with its emergence as the most highly industrialized country in Africa. Good jobs are reserved for whites. The whites live in luxurious modern central cities; the blacks are restricted to outlying slums plagued by poverty, crime, and white policemen. In spite of everything, these cities have produced a vibrant urban black culture, largely distinct from that of the tribal reserves. As a black journalist in Johannesburg explained in 1966:

I am supposed to be a Pondo, but I don't even know the language of that tribe. . . . I am just not a tribesman, whether I like it or not. I am, inescapably, a part of the city slums, the factory machines and our beloved shebeens [illegal bars].[15]

South Africa's harsh white supremacy has elicited many black nationalist protests since the 1920s. Black nationalists began as moderates, seeking gradual reforms. By the 1950s and early 1960s, blacks – and their Coloured, white, and Asian allies – were staging large-scale peaceful protests. These experiments in militant nonviolence were crushed by police and the army, suggesting that Gandhian civil disobedience is effective only against opponents with a developed sense of decency and fair play.

By the late 1970s, the white government had apparently destroyed the moderate nationalists. A small radical underground guerrilla movement took their place. In the short run, white privilege seemed secure, buttressed by police informers and tremendous military might – perhaps even an atomic bomb. In the long run, black nationalism seems almost certain to prevail. And because enlightened compromise on the part of the ruling whites seems unlikely, the struggle may well be viciously violent. As history has frequently shown, the longer change is blocked by unyielding repression, the more violent the eventual revolutionary upheaval.

———◆———

This chapter has examined the remarkable resurgence of Asian and African peoples after World War Two, which will almost certainly stand as a decisive turning point in world history. We have seen how the long-developing nationalist movement in China culminated in a social revolution led by the Communists, who went on to pursue innovative and fiercely independent policies that redeemed China as a Great Power in world affairs. Meanwhile Japan, defeated, demilitarized, and democratized, took a completely different path to the rank of economic superpower in a no-less-spectacular renaissance. Elsewhere – in India, Indonesia, and the Philippines – Asian peoples won their freedom and self-confidently charted independent courses. The Muslim world was also rejuvenated, most notably in Egypt under Nasser. In black Africa, a generation of nationalist leaders guided colonial territories to self-rule so successfully that by the middle 1960s only the Soviet Union still retained a large colonial empire.

The resurgence and political self-assertion of Asian and African peoples in new or revitalized states did not proceed without conflict. Serious regional and ethnic confrontations erupted, notably between Hindus and Muslims in India and between Arabs and Israelis in the Middle East. Moreover, the vestiges of Western colonialism and cold-war struggles resulted in atypical but highly destructive conflicts in Algeria, Vietnam, and Zimbabwe. The revitalized peoples of Asia and Africa continue to face tremendous economic and social challenges, as we shall see in Chapter 40. These challenges must be met if the emerging nations are to realize fully the promise of self-assertion and independence.

NOTES

1. Stuart Schram, *Mao Tse-tung,* Simon and Schuster, New York, 1966, p. 151.

2. Quoted by P. B. Ebrey, ed., *Chinese Civilization and Society: A Source Book,* The Free Press, New York, 1981, p. 393.

3. Hugh Sidey, "The Visit to Mao's House," *Life,* March 17, 1972, p. 12.

4. Quoted by Woodbridge Bingham, Hilary Conroy, and Frank Iklé, *A History of Asia,* 2nd ed., Allyn and Bacon, Boston, 1974, 2.459.

5. Quoted by Stanley Wolpert, *A New History of India,* 2nd ed., Oxford University Press, New York, 1982, p. 330.

6. Quoted by Krishan Bhata, *The Ordeal of Nationhood: A Social Study of India Since Independence, 1947-1970,* Atheneum, New York, 1971, p. 9.

7. Bernard D. Nossiter, *Soft State: A Newspaperman's Chronicle of India,* Harper and Row, New York, 1970, p. 52.

8. Quoted by G. B. Kay, ed., *The Political Economy of Colonialism in Ghana: A Collection of Documents and Statistics,* Cambridge University Press, Cambridge, 1972, p. 48.

9. W. E. B. Du Bois, *The Souls of Black Folk,* A. C. McClurg, Chicago, 1903, p. 3.

10. Quoted by Robert W. July, *A History of the African People,* 3rd ed., Charles Scribner's Sons, New York, 1980, pp. 519-520.

11. Quoted by Jacques Louis Hymans, *Léopold Sédar Senghor: An Intellectual Biography,* Edinburgh University Press, Edinburgh, 1971, p. 58.

12. Quoted by L. H. Gann and Peter Duignan, *Colonialism in Africa,* Cambridge University Press, Cambridge, 1970, 2.512.

13. Quoted by Robin Hallett, *Africa Since 1875: A Modern History,* University of Michigan Press, Ann Arbor, 1974, pp. 378-379.

14. Ibid., 345.

15. Ibid., 657.

SUGGESTED READING

Many of the works mentioned in the Suggested Reading for Chapter 34 are also valuable for considering postwar developments in Asia and the Middle East. Three other important studies on developments in China are C. Johnson, *Peasant Nationalism and Communist Power: The Emergence of Revolutionary China, 1937-1945* (1962); C. K. Yang, *The Chinese Family in the Communist Revolution* (1959); and W. L. Parish and M. K. Whyte, *Village and Family in Contemporary China* (1978). M. Meisner, *Mao's China: A History of the People's Republic* (1977), is an excellent comprehensive study and C. P. FitzGerald, *Communism Takes China: How the Revolution Went Red* (1971), is a lively illustrated account by a scholar who spent many years in China. Very recent developments are ably analyzed by I. Hsü, *China Without Mao: The Search for a New Order* (1983).

K. Kawai, *Japan's American Interlude* (1960), and R. P. Dore, *Land Reform in Japan* (1959), consider key problems of occupation policy. Three excellent and thought-provoking studies of contemporary Japanese society are E. Reischauer, *The Japanese*

(1977); F. Gibney, *Japan, the Fragile Superpower* (1977); and E. Vogel, *Japan as Number One: Lessons for America* (1979). Akira Iriye, *The Cold War in Asia: A Historical Introduction* (1974), and M. Schaller, *The United States and China in the Twentieth Century* (1979), analyze international conflicts in the postwar Pacific Basin.

F. G. Hutchins, *India's Revolution: Gandhi and the Quit India Movement* (1973), is an excellent account of wartime developments in India, which may be compared with J. Nehru, *An Autobiography* (1962), the appealing testimony of a principal architect of Indian freedom. F. Frankel, *India's Political Economy, 1947–1977* (1978), intelligently discusses the economic policies of independent India. There is a good biography of Indira Gandhi by D. Moraes (1980). For Southeast Asia there are solid general accounts by C. Dubois, *Social Forces in Southeast Asia* (1967), and R. N. Kearney, *Politics and Modernization in South and Southeast Asia* (1974). C. Cooper, *The Lost Crusade: America in Vietnam* (1972), and F. FitzGerald, *Fire in the Lake* (1973), probe the tragic war in Vietnam. Two valuable works on other Asian countries are B. Dahm, *Sukarno and the Struggle for Indonesian Independence* (1969), and T. Friend, *Between Two Empires: The Ordeal of the Philippines, 1929–1946* (1965). Recommended studies of the Middle East and Israel include a cultural investigation by R. Patai, *The Arab Mind* (1973); W. R. Polk's penetrating examination of *The United States and the Arab World,* 3rd ed. (1975); and an excellent biography of Israel's inspiring leader during its war for independence by A. Avi-Hai, *Ben Gurion, State Builder* (1974).

The studies by July and Hallett cited in the Notes are outstanding interpretations of modern Africa's rich and complex history. Both have extensive bibliographies. Important works on the colonial era include R. W. July, *The Origins of Modern African Thought* (1967); J. A. Langley, *Pan-Africanism and Nationalism in West Africa, 1900–1945: A Study in Ideology and Social Classes* (1973); R. O. Collins, *Problems in the History of Colonial Africa, 1860–1960* (1970); T. Hodgkin, *Nationalism in Colonial Africa* (1957); and the monumental investigation edited by L. H. Gann and P. Duignan, *Colonialism in Africa, 1870–1960,* 5 vols. (1969–1975). W. E. B. Du Bois, *The World and Africa* (1947), and J. Kenyatta, *Facing Mount Kenya* (1953), are powerful comments on African nationalism by the distinguished American black thinker and Kenya's foremost revolutionary and political leader. A. Hopkins, *An Economic History of West Africa* (1973), is a pioneering synthesis. C. Dewey and A. Hopkins, eds., *The Imperial Impact: Studies in the Economic History of Africa and India* (1978), is an innovative comparative study. Major works on specific countries include M. Crowder, *The Story of Nigeria,* 4th ed. (1978); P. Hill, *Migrant Cocoa Farmers in Ghana* (1963); and R. W. Johnson, *How Long Will South Africa Survive?* (1977). I. Wallerstein, *Africa, the Politics of Independence* (1961), and P. C. Lloyd, *Africa in Social Change* (1972), are useful studies on the contemporary era. F. Willett, *African Art* (1971), is a good introduction.

CHAPTER 39

LIFE IN INDUSTRIALIZED

NATIONS

WHILE EUROPE staged its astonishing political and economic recovery from the Nazi nightmare, the patterns of everyday life and the structure of Western society were changing no less rapidly and remarkably. This will come as no surprise. Thinking about modern life, one immediately thinks about the inventions and new technologies — the atomic bomb, television, computers, jet planes, contraceptive pills, to name only a few — that have so profoundly affected human existence. One also thinks of the new attitudes and demands of different groups in society, which are reflected in such phenomena as the ever-expanding role of government, the revolt of youth in the late 1960s, the women's movement, and concern about damage to the environment. Rapid social change is clearly a fact of modern life in the Western world.

It is by no means easy to make sense out of all these changes. Many "revolutions" and "crises" are merely passing fads, sensationally ballyhooed by the media today but forgotten tomorrow. Some genuinely critical developments, such as those involving the environment or the family, are complex and contradictory, making it hard to understand what is really happening, much less to explain why. In short, we are simply too close to what is going on and lack vital perspective. It is, therefore, most difficult to interpret intelligently the life we all think we know best — the life of our own times. As Voltaire once said, "The man who ventures to write contemporary history must expect to be attacked both for everything he has said and everything he has not said."[1]

Yet the historian must take a stand. How have Western society and everyday life changed since World War Two and why? What have these changes meant to people? These are the questions this chapter seeks to answer. The focus will be on three interrelated matters of particular significance: the spectacular development of science and technology, the gradual emergence of a new kind of society, and the evolving position of women and the role of the family.

SCIENCE AND TECHNOLOGY

Ever since the scientific revolution of the seventeenth century and the Industrial Revolution at the end of the eighteenth century, scientific and technical developments have powerfully influenced attitudes, society, and everyday life. Never has this influence been stronger than since about 1940. Fantastic pipedreams of science fiction a brief century ago have become realities. Submarines pass under the North Pole, and astronauts walk on the moon. Skilled surgeons replace their patients' failing arteries with plastic tubing. Millions of people around the world simultaneously watch a historic event on television. And the end is not in sight.

The reason science and technology have been so productive and influential is that for the first time in history they have been effectively joined together on a massive scale. This union of "pure theoretical" science with "applied" science or "practical" technology had already made possible striking achievements in the late nineteenth century in some select fields, most notably organic chemistry, electricity, and preventive medicine. Generally, however, the separation of science and technology still predominated in the late 1930s. Most scientists were university professors, who were little interested in such practical matters as building better machines and inventing new products. Such problems were the concern of tinkering technicians and engineers, who were to a large extent trained on the job. Their accomplishments and discoveries owed much more to careful observation and trial-and-error experimentation than to theoretical science.

During World War Two, however, scientists and technicians increasingly marched to the sound of the same drummer. Both scientific research and technical expertise began to be directed at difficult but highly practical military problems. The result was a number of spectacular breakthroughs, such as radar and the atomic bomb, that had immediate wartime applications. After the war this close cooperation between pure science and applied technology continued with equal success. Indeed, the line between science and technology became harder and harder to draw.

The consequences of the new intimate link between science and technology were enormous. Seventeenth-century propagandists for science such as Francis Bacon had predicted that scientific knowledge of nature would give human beings the power to control the physical world. With such control, they believed, it would be possible to create material abundance and genuine well-being. The successful union of science and technology created new industries and spurred rapid economic growth after 1945, making this prediction finally come true for the great majority of people in Europe and North America.

At the same time, however, the unprecedented success of science in controlling and changing the physical environment has produced unexpected and unwanted side effects. Chemical fertilizers have poisoned rivers in addition to producing bumper crops. A great good like the virtual elimination of malaria-carrying mosquitoes with DDT dramatically lowered the death rate in tropical lands, but it

LORD RUTHERFORD *The great British physicist Ernest Rutherford shows the apparatus he used to split the atom in 1919. Until World War II science was still relatively inexpensive, impractical, and independent. (Cavendish Laboratory, University of Cambridge)*

also contributed to a population explosion in those areas.

The list of such unwelcome side effects is very long. By the late 1960s, concern about the undesirable side effects of technological change had brought into being a vigorous environmental movement. In 1977, French university students were convinced that only the economic problems of inflation and unemployment were as serious for society as damage to the environment; every other problem came far behind. Fully one-third of all students said they would vote for an "ecologist candidate" for president of France. The ability of science and technology to control and alter nature has proved to be a two-edged sword, which must be wielded with great care and responsibility.

THE STIMULUS OF WORLD WAR TWO

Just before the outbreak of World War Two, a young Irish scientist and Communist named John Desmond Bernal wrote a book entitled *The Social Function of Science*. Bernal argued that the central government should be the source of funds for scientific research, and that these funds should be granted on the basis of the expected social and political benefits. Most scientists were horrified by Bernal's proposals, which were contradictory to their cherished ideals. Scientists were committed to designing their own research without any regard to its immediate usefulness. As late as 1937, the great physicist Ernest Rutherford could state that the work he and his colleagues were doing at Cambridge University in nuclear physics had no conceivable practical value for anyone and he expressed delight that such was the case. Nor did university scientists drool over government grants, since many had independent incomes to help finance their still-inexpensive equipment and experiments.

The Second World War changed this pattern. Pure science lost its impractical innocence. Most leading university scientists went to work on top-secret projects for their governments to help fight the war. The development of radar by British scientists was a particularly important outcome of this new kind of sharply focused research.

As early as 1934, the British Air Ministry set up a committee of scientists and engineers to study the problem of air defense systematically. Calculations by a leading British expert on radio waves suggested that the idea of a "death ray" so powerful it could destroy an attacking enemy aircraft was nonsense, but that detection of enemy aircraft by radio waves was theoretically possible. Radio waves emitted at intervals by a transmitter on the ground would bounce off flying aircraft, and a companion receiver on the ground would hear this echo and detect the approaching plane. Experiments went forward, and by 1939 the British had installed a very primitive radar system along the southern and eastern coasts of England.

Immediately after the outbreak of war with Germany in September 1939, the British military enlisted leading academic scientists in an all-out effort to improve the radar system. The basic problem was developing a high-powered transmitter capable of sending very short wavelengths, which could be precisely focused in a beam sweeping the sky like a searchlight. In summer 1940, British physicists made the dramatic technical breakthrough that solved this problem of short-wave transmission. The new and radically improved radar system that was quickly installed played a key role in Britain's victory in the battle for air supremacy in the fall of 1940. During the war many different types of radar were developed – for fighter planes, for bombers, for detection of submarines.

Since 1945, war-born microwave technology has generated endless applications, especially in telecommunications. Microwave transmission very conveniently carries long-distance telephone conversations, television programs, and messages to and from satellites.

The air war also greatly stimulated the development of jet aircraft and computers. Al-

ATOMIC WEAPONS were the ultimate in state-directed scientific research. In this awesome photo the mushroom cloud of an American atomic bomb rises over the Pacific island of Bikini. (Joint Army Navy Task Force)

though the first jet engines were built in the mid-1930s, large-scale government-directed research did not begin until right before the war. The challenge was to build a new kind of engine – a jet engine – capable of burning the low-grade "leftovers" of petroleum refining, thereby helping to overcome the desperate shortage of aviation fuel. The task proved extremely difficult and expensive. Only toward the end of the war did fast high-flying jet fighters become a reality. Quickly adopted for both military and peacetime purposes after the war, jet airplanes contributed to the enormous expansion of commercial aviation in the 1950s.

The problems of air defense spurred further research on electronic computers, which had barely come into existence before 1939. Computers calculated the very complex mathematical relationships between fast-moving planes and antiaircraft shells, so as to increase the likelihood of a hit.

Wartime needs led to many other major technical breakthroughs. Germany had little oil and was almost completely cut off from foreign supplies; Germany's scientists and engineers found ways to turn coal into gasoline so the German war machine did not sputter to a halt. Long ignored after petroleum became cheap and abundant in the postwar era, this wartime advance is being restudied in both Europe and North America in this era of undependable and expensive foreign oil.

The most spectacular result of directed scientific research during the war was the atomic bomb. In August 1939, Albert Einstein wrote to President Franklin Roosevelt stating that recent work in physics suggested that

it may become possible to set up a nuclear chain reaction in a large mass of uranium, by which vast amounts of power and large quantities of new radium-like elements would be generated. . . . This new phenomenon would also lead to the construction of bombs, and it is conceivable – though much less certain – that extremely powerful bombs of a new type may thus be constructed.[2]

This letter and ongoing experiments by nuclear physicists led to the top-secret Manhattan Project and the decision to build the atomic bomb.

The American government spared no expense to turn a theoretical possibility into a practical reality. A mammoth crash program went forward in several universities and special laboratories, the most important of which was the newly created laboratory at Los Alamos in the wilds of New Mexico. The Los Alamos laboratory was masterfully directed from 1942 by J. Robert Oppenheimer (1904–1967), a professor and theoretical physicist. Its sole objective was to design and build an atomic bomb. Toward that end Oppenheimer assembled a team of brilliant American and European scientists and managed to get them to cooperate effectively. After three years of intensive effort, the first atomic bomb was successfully tested in early 1945. In August 1945 two bombs were dropped on Hiroshima and Nagasaki, ending the war with Japan.

The atomic bomb showed the world both the awesome power and the heavy moral responsibilities of modern science and its high priests. As one of Oppenheimer's troubled colleagues exclaimed as he watched the first mushroom cloud rise over the American desert: "We are all sons-of-bitches now!"[3]

THE RISE OF BIG SCIENCE

The spectacular results of directed research during World War Two inspired a new model for science – Big Science. By combining theoretical work with sophisticated engineering in a large organization, Big Science can attack extremely difficult problems. Solution of these problems leads to new and better products for consumers and to new and better weapons for the military. In any event, the assumption is that almost any conceivable technical goal may be attained. Big Science is extremely expensive. Indeed, its appetite for funds is so great that it can be financed only by governments and large corporations. Thus, the ties between science and tax-paying society have grown very close.

Science has become so "big" largely because its equipment has become ever more complex and expensive. Because many advances depend directly on better instruments, the trend toward bigness goes on unabated. This trend has been particularly pronounced in atomic physics, perhaps the most prestigious and influential area of modern science. When Rutherford first "split the atom" in 1919, his equipment cost only a few dollars. In the 1930s, the price of an accelerator, or "atom smasher," reached $10,000, and the accelerators used in high-energy experiments while the atomic bomb was being built were in the $100,000 range. By 1960, however, when the west European nations pooled their resources in the European Council for Nuclear Research (CERN) to build an accelerator outside of Geneva – an accelerator with power in billions rather than millions of electron volts – the cost had jumped to $30 million.

These big accelerators have done an amazingly good job of prying apart atoms, and over two hundred different particles have been identified so far. Yet new answers produce new questions, and the logic of ever-more-sophisticated observations demands ever-more-powerful accelerators. In order to catch up with western Europe's "superCERN" accelerator, the Fermi laboratory outside of Chicago is building a comparable accelerator with a power of a trillion electron volts at a cost of $400 million dollars, with society – through the U.S. Congress – footing the bill.

Astronomers have followed physicists in the ways of Big Science. Their new eye is the radio telescope, which picks up radio emissions rather than light. The largest of these very costly radio telescopes sits atop a mountain and has a bowl a thousand feet wide to focus the radio signals from space. The receiver is suspended on cables stretched across the bowl below. Aeronautical research and development have also attained mammoth proportions. The cost of the Anglo-French *Concorde,* the first supersonic passenger airliner, has gone into the billions. The biggest area of Big Science is space research. By 1967, the U.S. National Aeronautics and Space Administration was spending $5 billion a year just for its experiments, although NASA's budget declined substantially in the 1970s.

Even ordinary science has become big and expensive by historical standards. The least costly laboratory capable of doing useful research in either pure or applied science now requires around $200,000 a year.

Populous, victorious, and wealthy, the United States took the lead in Big Science after World War Two. Between 1945 and 1965, spending on scientific research and development in the United States grew five times as fast as the national income. By 1965, fully 3 percent of all income in the United States was spent on science. While large American corporations maintained impressive research laboratories, fully three-quarters of all funds spent on scientific research and development in the United States was coming from the government by 1965. It was gener-

THE APOLLO PROGRAM   Astronauts Neil Armstrong, Michael Collins, and Edwin Aldrin, Jr., took off from Florida on July 16, 1969 in the Apollo II spacecraft. Astronaut Armstrong was the first man to set foot on the moon, four days later, on July 20. His footprint in the lunar dust brought to reality another fantasy of science fiction. The astronauts splashed down in the Pacific Ocean, and recovery was made by the U.S.S. Hornet *on July 24. (National Aeronautics and Space Administration)*

ally accepted that government should finance science heavily. One wit has pointed out that by the mid-1960s the "science policy" of the supposedly conservative Republican party in the United States was almost identical to that of the supposedly revolutionary Communist party of the Soviet Union.

One of the reasons for the similarity was that science was not demobilized in either country after the war. Indeed, scientists remained a critical part of every major military establishment and, since 1945 as during World War Two, a large portion of all scientific research has gone for "defense." Jet bombers gave way to rockets, battleships were overtaken by submarines with nuclear warheads, and spy planes were replaced with spy satellites. All such new weapons demanded breakthroughs no less remarkable than those of radar and the first atomic bomb. Roughly one-quarter of all men and women trained in science and engineering in the West — and perhaps more in the Soviet Union — have been employed full-time in the design and production of weapons to kill other men and women.

The rapid expansion of government-financed research in the United States attracted many of Europe's best scientists in the 1950s and 1960s. Thoughtful Europeans lamented this "brain drain." In his best seller *The American Challenge* (1967), the French journalist Jean-Jacques Servan-Schreiber warned that Europe was falling hopelessly behind the United States in science and technology. The only hope was to copy American patterns of research before the United States achieved an absolute stranglehold on computers, jet aircraft, atomic energy, and indeed most of the vital dynamic sectors of the late twentieth-century economy.

As the United States entered its time of troubles with the Vietnam War and began spending relatively less on scientific research, Europe did respond to the American challenge. By pooling their efforts and spending more on science and engineering, and specifically by concentrating on such projects as the *Concorde* supersonic passenger airliner and the peaceful uses of atomic energy, European countries created their own Big Science. By the late 1970s and early 1980s many European nations were devoting a substantial percentage of their income to research and development and had achieved equality with the United States in many fields of scientific endeavor (see Figure 39.1).

THE LIFE OF SCIENTISTS AND TECHNOLOGISTS

The rise of Big Science and of close ties between science and technology have greatly altered the lives of scientists. The scientific community is, first of all, much larger than ever before: of all the scientists who have ever lived, nine out of ten are alive today. The astonishing fact is that the number of scientists has been doubling every fifteen years for the past three centuries. There are, therefore, about four times as many scientists today as when the Second World War ended, just as there are a *million times* as many scientists as there were in 1670. Scientists, technologists, engineers, and medical specialists count in modern society, in part because there are so many of them.

One important consequence of the bigness of science is its high degree of specialization. With close to a hundred thousand scientific journals currently being published, no one can possibly master a broad field like physics or medicine. Instead, a field like physics is constantly dividing and subdividing into new specialties and subdisciplines. The fifty or hundred men and women who are truly abreast of the latest developments in a highly specialized field form an international "invisible college." Cooperating and competing, communicating through special journals and conferences, the leading members of these invisible colleges keep the problems of the subdiscipline under constant attack. Thus, intense specialization has undoubtedly increased the rates at which both basic knowledge is acquired and practical applications are made.

Highly specialized modern scientists and technologists must normally work as members of a team. The problems and equipment of Big Science are simply too complicated and expensive for a person to work effectively as

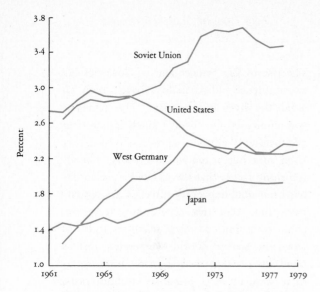

FIGURE 39.1   RESEARCH AND DEVELOPMENT
EXPENDITURES AS A PERCENTAGE OF GNP IN
THE UNITED STATES, SOVIET UNION, WEST
GERMANY, AND JAPAN, 1961–1979   *While the
United States spent less of its national income on re-
search and development after the early 1960s, Euro-
pean nations and Japan spent more. This helped
Europe and Japan narrow or even close the techno-
logical gap that had existed since the end of World
War II. (Source: Data Resources, Inc.)*

an individual researcher. The collaborative
"team" character of much of modern scientific research — members of invisible colleges
are typically the leaders of such teams — has
completely changed the work and lifestyle of
modern scientists. Old-fashioned, prewar scientists were like professional golfers — lonely
individuals who must make all the shots
themselves. Modern scientists and technologists are more like the members of American
professional football organizations. There are
owners and directors, coaches and assistant
coaches, overpaid stars and unsung heroes,
veterans and rookies, kickoff specialists and
substitutes, trainers and water boys, and even

mini-skirted beauties prancing on the side-
lines.

If this parallel seems fanciful, consider the
research group of Luis Alvarez at the high-
energy physics Radiation Laboratory of the
University of California at Berkeley in the late
1960s. This group consisted of more than two
hundred people. At the top were Alvarez and
about twenty Ph.D.s, followed by twenty
graduate research assistants and fourteen
full-time engineers. Almost fifty people were
categorized as "technical leadership" — computer programmers, equipment operators, and
so on. Finally, there were more than a hundred "technical assistants" — primarily scan-
ners who analyzed photographs showing the
tracks of particles after various collisions. A
laboratory like that of CERN outside Geneva
resembles a small city of several thousand
people — scientists, technicians, and every
kind of support personnel. A great deal of
modern science and technology goes on,
therefore, in large well-defined bureaucratic,
organizations. The individual is very often a
small cog in a great machine, a member of a
scientific army.

The advent of large-scale scientific bureaucracies has led to the emergence of a new
group, science managers and research administrators. Such managers generally have scientific backgrounds, but their main tasks are
scheduling research, managing people, and
seeking money from politicians or financial
committees of large corporations. This last
function is particularly important, for there
are limits to what even the wealthiest governments and corporations will spend for research. Competition for funds is always
intense.

Many science managers are government
bureaucrats. These managers dole out funds
and "referee" the scientific teams that are ac-

tually playing on the field. Is the *Concorde* supersonic jet too noisy to land in New York City? Does saccharin cause cancer, and should it be banned? The list of potential questions is endless. The number of such referees and the penalties they are imposing are both exploding, driven by public alarm about undesirable side effects of technological advance. More generally, the growth of the scientific bureaucracy suggests how scientists and technologists permeate the entire society and many aspects of life.

Two other changes in the lives of scientists may be noted briefly. One is the difficulty of appraising an individual's contribution to a collaborative team effort. Who deserves the real credit (or blame) for a paper coauthored by a group of twenty-five physicists? Even in a field like chemistry, which is still relatively "small" in its research techniques, more than two-thirds of all papers now have two or more authors. Questions of proper recognition within the team effort are thus very complicated and preoccupying to modern scientists.

Second and relatedly, modern science has become highly, even brutally, competitive. This competitiveness is well depicted in Nobel Prize winner James Watson's fascinating book *The Double Helix,* which tells how in 1953 Watson and an English colleague discovered the structure of DNA, the vital molecule of heredity. A brash young American Ph.D. in his twenties, Watson seemed almost obsessed by the idea that some other research team would find the solution first and thereby deprive him of the fame and fortune he desperately wanted. With so many thousands of like-minded researchers in the wealthy countries of the world, it is hardly surprising that scientific and technical knowledge rushes forward.

TOWARD A NEW SOCIETY

The prodigious expansion of science and technology has greatly affected the peoples of the Western world. By creating new products and vastly improved methods of manufacturing and farming, it has fueled rapid economic growth and rising standards of living. Moreover, especially in Europe, scientific and technological progress, combined with economic prosperity, have gone a long way toward creating a whole new society since World War Two.

This new society has been given many catchy titles. Some call it "the technocratic society," a society of highly trained specialists and experts. For others, fascinated by the great increase in personal wealth, it is "the affluent society" or "the consumer society." For those struck by the profusion of government-provided social services, it is simply "the welfare state." For still others, it is "the permissive society," where established codes of conduct no longer prevail. In fact, contemporary Western society is all of these: technocratic, affluent, welfare-oriented, and permissive. These characteristics result from changes in the class structure and indicate undeniable social progress.

THE CHANGING CLASS STRUCTURE

Since 1945, European society has become more mobile and more democratic. Old class barriers have been relaxed, and class distinctions have become fuzzier.

Changes in the structure of the middle class, directly related to the expansion of science and technology, have been particularly influential in the general drift toward a less rigid class structure. The model for the mid-

A MODERN MANAGER Despite lingering discrimination, women are increasingly found in the new middle class of salaried experts, be they in business, science, or technology. (Niépce-Rapho)

dle class in the nineteenth and early twentieth centuries was the independent, self-employed individual, who owned a business or practiced a liberal profession like law or medicine. Many businesses and professional partnerships were tightly held family firms. Marriage into such a family often provided the best opportunity for an outsider to rise to the top. Ownership of property, usually inherited property, and strong family ties were the

usual keys to wealth and standing within the middle class.

This traditional pattern, which first changed in the United States and the Soviet Union (for very different reasons) before the Second World War, has declined drastically in western Europe since 1945. A new breed of managers and experts has risen to replace traditional propertyowners as the leaders of the middle class. Within large bureaucratic corporations and government, men and women increasingly advance as individuals and on the basis of merit (and luck). Ability to serve the needs of a large organization, which usually depends on special expertise, has largely replaced inherited property and family connections in determining an individual's social position in the middle and upper middle class. Social mobility for individuals, both upward and downward, has increased. At the same time, the middle class has grown massively and has become harder to define.

There are a number of reasons for these developments. Rapid industrial and technological expansion created in large corporations and government agencies a powerful demand for technologists and managers capable of responding effectively to an ever-more-complicated world. This growing army of specialists – the backbone of the new middle class – can be led effectively only by like-minded individuals, of whom only a few at best can come from the old owning families.

Second, the old propertied middle class has lost control of many of its formerly family-owned businesses. Even very wealthy families have had to call on the general investing public for capital, and heavy inheritance taxes have forced sales of stock, further diluting family influence. Many small businesses (including family farms) simply passed out of existence, and their ex-owners joined the ranks of salaried employees. In Germany in 1950, for example, 33 percent of the labor force were self-employed and 20 percent were white-collar workers. By 1962, the percentages for these two groups were exactly reversed. Moreover, the wave of nationalization in western and eastern Europe after the Second World War automatically replaced capitalist owners with salaried managers and civil servants in state-owned companies.

Top managers and ranking civil servants represent, therefore, the model for a new middle class of salaried specialists. Well paid and highly trained, often with backgrounds in science or engineering or accounting, these experts increasingly come from all social classes, including the working class. Pragmatic and realistic, they are primarily concerned with efficiency and practical solutions to concrete problems. They tend not to be very interested in the old ideological debates about capitalism and socialism, confidently assuming that their skills are indispensable in either system or any combination of the two.

Indeed, the new middle class of experts and managers is an international class, not much different in socialist eastern Europe than in capitalist western Europe and North America. Everywhere successful managers and technocrats can pass on the opportunity for all-important advanced education to their children, but they cannot pass on the positions they have attained. Thus the new middle class, which is based largely on specialized skills and high levels of education, is more open, democratic, and insecure than the old propertied middle class.

The structure of the traditional lower classes has also become more flexible and open. There has been a massive exodus from farms and the countryside. One of the most traditional and least mobile groups in European society has drastically declined: since 1945, the number of peasants has declined by at least 50 percent in almost every European country. Meanwhile, because of rapid technological change, the industrial working class has ceased to expand, stabilizing at slightly less than one-half of the labor force in wealthy advanced countries. Job opportunities for white-collar and service employees, however, have expanded rapidly. Such employees bear a greater resemblance to the new middle class of salaried specialists than to industrial workers, who are themselves becoming better educated and more specialized. Developments within the lower classes have contributed, therefore, to the breakdown of rigid social divisions.

SOCIAL SECURITY REFORMS AND RISING AFFLUENCE

While the demands of modern technology have been breaking down rigid class divisions, European governments since 1945 have reduced class tensions with a series of social security reforms. Many of these reforms simply strengthened social security measures first pioneered in Bismarck's Germany before World War One. Unemployment and sickness benefits were increased and extended, as were retirement benefits and old-age pensions. Other programs were new.

Britain's Labour government took the lead immediately after the Second World War in establishing a comprehensive national health system; other European governments followed the British example. Depending on the system, patients either received completely free medical care or paid only a very small portion of the total cost.

Most countries also introduced family allowances – direct government grants to parents to help them raise their children. Lower-paid workers generally received the largest allowances, and the rate per child often kept increasing until the third or fourth child. These allowances helped many poor families make ends meet. Most European governments also gave maternity grants and built inexpensive public housing for low-income families and individuals. Other social welfare programs ranged from cash bonuses for getting married in Belgium and Switzerland to subsidized vacations for housewives in Sweden.

It would be wrong to think that the expansion of social security services after World War Two has provided for every human need "from cradle to grave," as early advocates of the "welfare state" hoped and critics feared. But these social reforms do provide a humane floor of well-being below which very few individuals drop in advanced countries of northern and western Europe. (Social benefits are greatest in the wealthiest nations, such as Sweden, West Germany, Britain, and less in poorer areas of southern and eastern Europe.)

These reforms have also promoted greater social and economic equality. They are expensive, and paid for in part by high taxes on the rich. In Britain, for example, where social security benefits for the population at large and taxes on the rich have both become quite high, the top 5 percent of the population received about 14 percent of national income after taxes in 1957, as opposed to fully 43 percent in 1913. Thus, extensive welfare measures have leveled society both by raising the floor and by lowering the ceiling.

The rising standard of living and the spread of standardized, mass-produced consumer goods also work to level Western society. A hundred years ago, food and drink cost roughly two-thirds of the average family's income in western and northern Europe; today it takes only about a third to two-fifths of that family's income. Consumption of traditional staples like bread and potatoes has actually declined almost everywhere in Europe since 1945, yet because incomes have risen rapidly, people eat more meat, fish, and dairy products. The long-elusive goal of adequate and good food has been attained almost universally in advanced countries.

But progress introduces new problems. Today people in Europe and North America eat too much rather than too little, giving rise to an endless proliferation of diet foods and diet fads. Another problem is that modern consumers are often remarkably ignorant of basic nutrition. They stuff themseves with candy, soft drinks, French fries, and spongy white bread, and frequently get poor value for their money. Finally, the traditional pleasures of eating good food well prepared are suffering catastrophic declines in the age of fast-food franchises and mass-produced, hopelessly standardized burgers and buns.

The phenomenal expansion of the automobile industry exemplifies even more strikingly the emergence of the "consumer society." In the United States automobile ownership was commonplace far down the social scale by the mid-1920s, whereas only the rich could generally afford cars in Europe before the Second World War. In 1948, there were only 5 million cars in western Europe, and most ordinary people dreamed at most of stepping up from a bicycle to a motorcycle. With the development of cheaper, mass-produced cars, this situation changed rapidly. By 1957, the number of cars had increased to 15 million, and automobiles had become a standard item of middle-class consumption. By 1965, the number of cars in western Europe had tripled again to 44 million, and car ownership had come well within the range of better-paid workers.

Europeans took great pleasure in the products of the "gadget revolution" as well. Like Americans, Europeans filled their houses and apartments with washing machines, vacuum cleaners, refrigerators, dishwashers, radios, TVs, and stereo sets. The purchase of these and other consumer goods has been greatly facilitated by installment purchasing, which allows people to buy on credit. Before World War Two, Europeans had rarely bought "on time." But with the expansion of social security safeguards, reducing the need to accumu-late savings for hard times, ordinary people are increasingly willing to take on debt. This change has far-reaching consequences.

Household appliances have become quite essential for most families. Middle-class women have to do much of their own housework, for young girls avoid domestic service like the plague. Moreover, more women than ever before work outside the home, and they need machines to help do house chores as quickly as possible. The power tools of "do-it-yourself" work have also become something of a necessity, for few dependable artisans are now available for household repairs.

Leisure and recreation occupies an important place in consumer societies. Indeed, with incomes rising and the workweek shrinking from roughly forty-eight hours right after the war to about forty-one hours today, leisure has become big business. In addition to ever-popular soccer matches and horse races, movies, and the more recent numbing addiction to television, individuals have at their disposal a vast range of commercialized hobbies, most of which can soak up a lot of cash. Newsstands are full of specialized magazines about everything from hunting and photography to knitting and antique collecting. Interest in "culture," as measured by attendance at concerts and exhibitions, has also increased. Even so, the commercialization of leisure through standardized manufactured products is striking.

The most astonishing leisure-time development in the consumer society has been the blossoming of mass travel and tourism. Before the Second World War travel for pleasure and relaxation was a rather aristocratic pastime. Most people had neither the time nor the money for it. But with month-long paid vacations required by law in most European countries, and widespread automobile ownership, beaches and ski resorts have become accessible to middling people and many workers. At certain times of year, hordes of Europeans surge to the sea or the mountains, and woe to the traveler who has not made arrangements well in advance. Packaged tours with cheap group flights and bargain hotel accommodations have made even distant lands easily accessible. One-fifth of West Germany's population travels abroad each year. A French company, the Club Méditerranée, has grown rich building imitation Tahitian paradises around the world. At Swedish nudist colonies on secluded west African beaches, secretaries and salesmen from Stockholm fleetingly worship the sun in the middle of the long northern winter. Truly, consumerism has come of age.

RENEWED DISCONTENT AND THE STUDENT REVOLT

For twenty years after 1945, Europeans were preoccupied with the possibilities of economic progress and consumerism. There was little social tension, and ideological conflict went out of style. In the late 1960s, however, sharp criticism and discontent re-emerged. It was a common complaint that Europeans were richer but neither happier nor better. These doubts and disappointments persist to this day.

Simmering discontent in eastern Europe is not hard to understand. The gradual improvement in the standard of living stands in naked contrast to the ongoing lack of freedom in political and intellectual life, and makes that lack of freedom all the more distasteful. It is doubtful that such dissatisfaction will produce any major improvement in the foreseeable future, given the refinement of the techniques of repression in eastern Europe,

but discontent will almost certainly continue to smolder.

The reappearance of discontent in western Europe is not so easily explained. Since the mid-1950s, west European society has been prosperous, democratic, and permissive. Yet this did not prevent hostility to the existing order from growing among some children of the new society. Radical students, in particular, rejected the materialism of their parents and claimed that the new society was repressive and badly flawed. Though these criticisms and the movements they sparked were often ridiculed by the older generation, they reflected real problems of youth, education, and a society of specialists. They deserve closer attention.

In contrast to the United States, high school and university educations in Europe were limited for centuries to a small elite. That elite consisted mainly of young men and women from the well-to-do classes, along with a sprinkling of scholarship students from humble origins. Whereas 22 percent of the American population was going on to some form of higher education in 1950, only 3 to 4 percent of west European youths were doing so. Moreover, European education was still directed toward traditional fields: literature, law, medicine, and pure science. Its basic goal was to pass on culture and pure science to an elite, and, with the exception of law and medicine, applied training for specialists was not considered very important.

After World War Two public education in western Europe began to change dramatically. Enrollments exploded. By 1960 there were at least three times as many students going to some kind of university as there had been before the war, and the number continued to rise sharply until the 1970s. Holland had ten thousand university students in 1938 and a hundred thousand in 1960. In France 14 percent of young people went to a university in 1965, as opposed to 4.5 percent in 1950. With an increase in scholarships and a growing awareness that higher education was the key to success, European universities became more democratic, opening their doors to more students from the lower middle and lower classes. Finally, in response to the prodigious expansion of science and technology, the curriculum gradually changed. All sorts of new "practical" fields – from computer science to business administration – appeared alongside the old liberal arts and sciences.

The rapid expansion of higher education created problems as well as opportunities for students. Classes were badly overcrowded, and there was little contact with professors. Competition for grades became very intense. Moreover, although more "practical" areas of study were added, they were added less quickly than many students wanted. Thus many students felt that they were not getting the kind of education they needed for the modern world and that basic university reforms were absolutely necessary. The emergence of a distinctive "youth culture" also brought students into conflict with those symbols of the older generation and parental authority – professors and school officials.

These tensions within the exploding university population came to a head in the late 1960s and early 1970s. Following in the footsteps of their American counterparts, European university students rose to challenge their university administrations and even their governments. The most far-reaching of these revolts occurred in France in 1968. It began at the stark new University of Nanterre in the gloomy industrial suburbs of Paris. Students demanded both changes in the curriculum and a real voice in running the university. The

movement spread to the hallowed halls of the medieval Sorbonne in the heart of Paris. Students occupied buildings and took over the university. This takeover led to violent clashes with police, who were ordered in to break up a demonstration that was fast becoming an uprising.

The student radicals appealed to France's industrial workers for help. Rank-and-file workers ignored the advice of their cautious union officials, and a more or less spontaneous general strike spread across France in May 1968. It seemed certain that President de Gaulle's Fifth Republic would collapse. In fact, de Gaulle stiffened, declaring he was in favor of reforms but would oppose "bedwetting." Securing the firm support of French army commanders in West Germany, he moved troops toward Paris and called for new elections. Thoroughly frightened by the protest-turned-upheaval and fearful that a successful revolution could lead only to an eventual communist takeover, the masses of France voted for a return to law and order. De Gaulle and his party scored the biggest electoral victory in modern French history. The mini-revolution collapsed. By the early 1970s student protest in France and the rest of Europe had generally subsided.

The student protest of the 1960s, which peaked in 1968 in France, was due to more than overcrowded classrooms and outdated courses. It reflected a rebirth of romantic revolutionary idealism, which repudiated the quest for ever more consumer goods as stupid and destructive. The student revolt was also inspired by the Vietnam War, which served to radicalize many students in Europe and America. These students believed that the war in Vietnam demonstrated that Western civilization was immoral and imperialistic. Finally, the students of the late 1960s were a com-

STUDENT DEMONSTRATION IN PARIS *These
rock-throwing students in the Latin Quarter of Paris
are protesting against the government. Throughout
May 1968 students often clashed with France's tough
riot police in bloody street fighting. (Wide World
Photos)*

pletely new generation: they had never known
anything but prosperity and tranquillity, and
they were bored with both.

The student revolt was also motivated by
new perceptions about the new society of
highly trained experts. Students realized that
higher specialized education was necessary for
success in life. Yet some reflective young people feared that universities would soon do
nothing but turn out docile technocrats both
to stock and to serve "the establishment."
These students also feared being locked into
unsatisfying work in large, rigid organizations
after graduation, or being rendered obsolete
and unwanted by some new technical development.

Some student intellectuals saw the class of highly trained specialists they would enter as the new exploited class in society. The remedy to this situation, they believed, was "participation" – the democratizing of decisionmaking *within* large, specialized bureaucratic organizations. Only in this way would such organizations serve real human needs and not merely exploit the individual and the environment. Thus, the often unrealistic and undisciplined student radicals tried to answer a vital question: how is our complex new society of specialized experts to be made humane and responsive?

WOMEN AND THE FAMILY

The growing emancipation of women in Europe and North America is unquestionably one of the most important developments in modern society. To be sure, there has been a good deal of semihysterical and irresponsible writing and discussion about women. Almost everyone is interested in the subject, and it lends itself well to the shallow sensationalism that characterizes so much of modern journalism. What is clear is that women today are demanding and winning new rights. Having shared fully in the postwar education revolution, women are better educated than ever before. Women are moving into areas of employment formerly closed to them. Married women in particular are much more likely to work outside the home than they were a few short years ago. Women no longer fatalistically accept childbearing and childrearing, for modern techniques of contraception have given them effective control over their bodies and the number and spacing of their offspring. In short, women are becoming more equal and independent, less confined and

stereotyped. A major transformation is in process.

The changing position of women is altering the modern family. Since the emancipation of women is far from complete, it is impossible to say at this point whether some major revolution is in process within the family. Certainly the family is evolving, but scare headlines about its impending demise are contradicted by much of the evidence. This will be apparent if we examine women's traditional role in the home and then women's new roles outside the home. We shall also look at problems of health care and old age that have special implications for women.

MARRIAGE AND MOTHERHOOD

Before the Industrial Revolution most men and women married late, and substantial numbers never married at all. Once a woman was married, though, she normally bore several children, of whom a third to a half would not survive to adulthood. Moreover, many women died in childbirth. With the growth of industry and urban society, people began to marry earlier, and fewer remained unmarried. As industrial development led to higher incomes and better diets, more children survived to adulthood, and population grew rapidly in the nineteenth century. By the late nineteenth century, contraception within marriage was spreading.

In the twentieth century, and especially since World War Two, these trends have continued. In the last thirty or forty years women have chosen to marry ever earlier. In Sweden, for example, the average age of first marriage has dropped steadily from twenty-six in the early 1940s to twenty-three in the late 1960s. Moreover, more than nine out of ten women marry at least once, usually in their early

A CONTEMPORARY FAMILY This scene sums up some important changes taking place within the family. The young father feeds and talks with the baby, while the student-mother concentrates on the education essential for successful employment. (Niépce-Rapho)

twenties. Marriage has never been more in vogue than in the contemporary era. The triumph of romantic attraction over financial calculation has been made complete, and perhaps never before have young couples expected so much emotional satisfaction from matrimony.

After marrying early, the typical woman in Europe, the United States, and Canada has her children quickly. Whereas women in the past very often had children as long as they were fertile, women in Europe and North America now have about 80 percent of their children before they are thirty. As for family size, the "baby boom" that lasted several years after 1945 made for fairly rapid population growth of 1 to 1.5 percent per year in many European countries. Since the 1960s, however, the long-term decline in birthrates has resumed. Surveys in northern and western Europe reveal that most women now believe that two instead of three children is ideal.

Women must have 2.1 children on the average if total population is to remain constant over the long term. Indeed, the number of births has fallen so sharply that total population is actually declining in four European countries. More people are dying each year than are being born in Austria, East Germany, West Germany, and Luxembourg. The United States has followed the same trend; the birthrate declined from 25 per thousand in 1957 to 15 per thousand in 1973, and has remained at about that level. Since the American death rate has remained unchanged, the rate of population growth from natural increase (that is, excluding immigration) has declined by two-thirds, from 1.5 percent to .5 percent per year in the last twenty years. The population of Africa, Asia, and Latin America is still growing very rapidly from natural increase, but that is no longer true for most European countries and countries of European ancestry.

The culmination of the trends toward early almost-universal marriage and small family size in wealthy societies has revolutionary implications for women. An examination of these implications will suggest why the emancipation of women — sooner or later — has almost assuredly been built into the structure of modern life.

The main point is that motherhood occupies a much smaller portion of a woman's life than it used to even eighty years ago. The average woman's life expectancy at birth has increased from about fifty years to about seventy-five years in this century. At the same time women are increasingly compressing childbearing into the decade between their twentieth and thirtieth birthdays, instead of bearing children until they are in their late thirties. About half of today's women, and more than half in some Western nations, have had their last baby by the age of twenty-six or twenty-seven. When the youngest child troops off to kindergarten, the mother has more than forty years of life in front of her.

This is a momentous change. Throughout history most married women have been defined to a considerable extent as mothers. Motherhood was very demanding: pregnancy followed pregnancy, and there were many children to nurse, guide, and bury. Now, however, the years devoted to having babies and caring for young children represent at most a seventh of the average woman's life. Motherhood has become a relatively short phase in most women's total life span. Perhaps a good deal of the frustration that many women feel today is due to the fact that their traditional role as mothers no longer absorbs the energies of a lifetime, and that new roles in the male-dominated world outside the family are opening up slowly.

A related revolutionary change for women is that the age-old biological link between sexual intercourse and motherhood has been severed. As everyone knows, women have gained effective control of pregnancy with oral contraceptives and intrauterine devices, and no longer have to rely on undependable males and their undependable methods. Less well known is the reason for birth control being absolutely necessary in the advanced countries today.

Women today are capable of having children for many more years than their forebears. The age of menarche — the age at which girls begin to menstruate and become fertile — has dropped from about seventeen years in the early nineteenth century to about thirteen years today. At the same time the age at onset of menopause has risen. At the beginning of the eighteenth century, menopause occurred at about age thirty-six, on average; it occurs at about fifty today. These physiological changes are poorly understood, but they are apparently due to better diets and living standards, which have also substantially increased people's height and size. In any event, modern women have of necessity separated their sexual lives from their awesome reproductive power. In doing so, women have become free to pursue sensual pleasure for its own sake. The consequences of this revolutionary development will be working themselves out for a long time.

WOMEN AT WORK

For centuries before the Industrial Revolution ordinary women were highly productive members of society. They often labored for years before marriage to accumulate the necessary dowry. Once married, women worked hard on farms and in home industries while bearing and caring for their large families. With the growth of modern industry and large cities, young women continued to work as wage earners. But once a poor woman married, she typically stopped working in a factory or a shop, struggling instead to earn money at home by practicing some low-paid craft as she looked after her children. In the middle classes, it was an extremely rare and tough-minded woman who worked outside the home for wages, although charity work was socially acceptable.

Since the beginning of the twentieth century and especially since World War Two, the situation has been changing dramatically once again. Opportunities for women of modest means to earn cash income within the home have practically disappeared. Piano teachers, novelists, and part-time typists may still work at home as independent contractors, but the ever-greater complexity of the modern wage-based economy and its sophisticated technology means that almost all would-be wage earners must turn elsewhere. Moreover, motherhood takes less and less time, so that the full-time mother-housewife has less and less economic value for families. Thus the reduction of home-centered work and child care has resulted in a sharp rise all across Europe and North America in the number of married women who are full-time wage earners.

In communist countries the trend has gone farthest. In the Soviet Union most married women work outside the home; women account for almost half of all employed persons there. In noncommunist western Europe and North America there is a good deal of variety, depending on whether married women have traditionally worked outside the home, as in France or Sweden, or stayed at home, as in Belgium and Switzerland. Nevertheless, the percentage of married women who work has risen in all countries, from a range of roughly 20 to 25 percent in 1950 to a range of 35 to 60 percent today. The trend is still upward. This rise has been particularly dramatic in the United States, where married women are twice as likely to be employed today as they were in 1952.

The dramatic growth of employment among married women is a development whose ultimate effects may be imagined only dimly. Nevertheless, it seems clear that the rising employment of married women is a powerful force in the drive for women's equality and emancipation. Take the critical matter of widespread discrimination between men and women in pay, occupation, and advancement. The young unmarried woman of seventy years ago generally accepted such injustices. She thought of them as temporary nuisances, and looked forward to marriage and motherhood for fulfillment. Today a married wage earner in her thirties has a totally different perspective. Employment is a permanent condition within which she, like her male counterpart, seeks not only income but psychological satisfaction as well. Sexism and discrimination quickly become loathsome and evoke a sense of injustice of the kind that drives revolutions and reforms. The "movement" spreads, winning converts among the young and newly awakened.

Rising employment for married women has been a factor in the decline of the birthrate (see Figure 39.2). Women who work have significantly fewer children than women of the same age who do not. Moreover, survey research shows that young women who have worked, and intend to work again, revise downward the number of children they expect to have after the first lovable but time-consuming baby is born. One reason is obvious: raising a family while holding down a full-time job is a tremendous challenge and often results in the woman being grossly overworked. The fatiguing, often frustrating multiple demands of job, motherhood, and marriage simply become more manageable with fewer children.

Another reason for the decline of the birthrate is that motherhood interrupts a woman's career. The majority of women in Western countries prefer or are forced to accept — interpretations vary — staying at home for a minimum of two or three years while their children are small. The longer the break in employment, the more a woman's career suffers. Women consistently earn less than men partly because they are employed less continuously and thus do not keep moving steadily up the bureaucratic ladders of large organizations.

Because most Western countries do little to help women in the problem of re-

Note: Data for working wives includes only women with husbands present.

FIGURE 39.2 THE DECLINE OF THE BIRTHRATE AND THE INCREASE OF WORKING WIVES IN THE UNITED STATES, 1952–1979 The challenge of working away from home has encouraged American wives to prefer fewer children and has helped lower the birthrate.

employment after their children are a little older, some women advocate the pattern of career and family typically found in communist eastern Europe. There, women are usually employed continuously until they retire. There are no career-complicating interruptions for extended mothering. Instead, a woman in a communist country receives as her right up to three months of maternity leave to care for her newborn infant and recover her strength. Then she returns to her job, leaving her baby in the care of a state-run nursery or, more frequently, a retired relative or neighbor. Some west European countries are beginning to provide well-defined maternity leaves as part of their social security systems. The United States lags far behind in this area.

What the increasing numbers of career-minded women with independent, self-assertive spirits mean for marriage and relations between the sexes is by no means clear. As we have seen, marriage remains an almost universal experience. Moreover, the decline of informal village and neighborhood socializing with the advent of the automobile and suburban living has made most wives and husbands more dependent than ever on their mates (and their children) for their emotional needs. Never has more been demanded from hearth and home.

The great increase in life expectancy for males and females has itself made marriage more stable, at least in one sense. The average couple will live together for forty years before the death of one dissolves the union, as opposed to less than twenty years together at the beginning of the century. And husbands are slowly getting the message that the old rule of leaving the dishes and diapers exclusively to wives needs rewriting, especially in two-income families.

At the same time there are contrary trends. Everywhere the divorce rate keeps moving up: it has doubled in the United States in ten years. Studies of marriage consistently show that working women are considerably more likely to get divorced than nonworking women. The independent working woman can more easily afford to leave if dissatisfied, while the no-income career housewife is practically locked into her situation.

Since the very late 1960s the marriage rate has plunged in a few advanced nations, notably Sweden, which has often led the way in social trends, and the United States. Does this decline mean only that young women and men are postponing marriage because of less

robust economic conditions? Or does it mean that marriage, after its long rise, is finally in retreat in the face of growing careerism and acceptance of new and less structured relations between (and within) the sexes? Only time will tell, but it is by no means impossible that a radical break with the past is now taking place in marriage patterns and family relationships.

HEALTH CARE AND GROWING OLD

The great increase in the number of elderly people in advanced countries is one of the major developments of our time. In 1900, a newborn female baby in western Europe could expect to live about fifty-two years and a male baby about forty-nine. In 1970, life expectancy at birth was seventy-five years for females and sixty-eight years for males. For the first time in history the vast majority of newborn infants, not just the lucky ones, will live to be senior citizens. This is certainly a great human achievement, but large numbers of elderly people also present new challenges for society, and especially for women.

One challenge that accompanies growing old for most women is several years of widowhood toward the end of life. Not only does the average woman outlive the average man by six or seven years, but the average woman marries a man two or three years her senior. The death of a spouse, which will happen far more often to women than to men, is commonly a shattering experience. During the first year after the death of a spouse, a widow or a widower in the United States is ten times more likely to die than other people in the same age group. The problems of growing old gracefully in good health, therefore, have special significance for women: their welfare depends on taking care not only of themselves

GRAY PANTHER LEADER Maggie Kuhn talks with the new Supreme Court Justice Sandra Day O'Connor at an award presentation. Senior citizens, a majority of whom are women, have formed organizations like the flamboyant Gray Panthers to assert their rights. (United Press International Photo)

but of their mates from the weaker sex as well.

Probably the most serious obstacle to preserving good health into ripe old age is that men and women vastly overestimate the powers of medical science. In the age of very sophisticated technology, they think it can do anything, especially if enough money is spent

on it. In fact, the contribution of doctors and hospitals to good health has been and will continue to be quite limited. The key to good health lies elsewhere.

One must understand first why death has struck later and later in life over the last three centuries, so that a newborn infant will live more than twice as long today as in the seventeenth century. In the first place, half of the reduction in mortality that has occurred over the last three centuries occurred before 1900. That reduction was caused in roughly equal measure by more and better food and by the control of infectious diseases borne through air and water. The mid-nineteenth-century sanitary revolution, which introduced safe water supplies, efficient sewage systems, and improved food and personal hygiene, accounted for most of the decline in infectious disease. Preventive medicine in the form of vaccinations after Pasteur's breakthrough played a welcome but quite secondary role in the decline of infectious disease before 1900.

The second half of the increase in human life expectancy has come in the twentieth century. It has largely been due to a great reduction in the rate of death during the first year of an infant's life. In 1900, between 160 and 250 of every 1,000 European children still did not reach their first birthday. Now only 10 to 30 of every 1,000 die in the first year. Mortality in early childhood also declined sharply in this century. Better care by mothers because of better knowledge, and preventive medicine in the form of vaccinations against infectious diseases, have been the key to healthier babies and small children, although pediatricians have made some contribution.

Doctors and hospitals have been able to do much less for the rest of us, however, and especially for the elderly. Medical science has made little progress in controlling the major causes of death in adults: heart disease, cancer, and stroke. An adult male in the United States who managed to reach age sixty-five in 1900 could expect to live thirteen more years; an adult male of sixty-five today may expect fifteen more years, or only two more years than his great-grandparent. To date, society has spent ever greater sums on the care of people growing old, but with only very modest results.

Modern society, oversold on the limitless possibilities of scientific progress in every domain, cannot understand the lack of improvement in the health of older people. People alternately blame the greed of the medical profession, the stinginess of government aid, and the deterioration of the environment. In fact, the individual must accept a large portion of the responsibility for illness and disease.

Ninety-nine percent of the population in advanced countries is born healthy. Having survived the old scourges of childhood because of high standards of living and preventive medicine, we are often made sick through our own bad habits. Consider the central finding of one careful five-and-a-half year study of seven thousand adults in the United States.[4] The study showed that life expectancy and health are significantly related to seven simple health habits: (1) eating three regular meals a day and avoiding snacks, (2) having breakfast every day, (3) performing moderate exercise two or three times a week, (4) sleeping seven or eight hours a night, (5) forgoing smoking, (6) maintaining moderate weight, and (7) avoiding alcohol or using it only in moderation. A forty-five-year-old man who practices three or fewer of these habits may expect to live to be sixty-seven; one who adheres to six or seven may expect to live eleven more years to age seventy-eight.

In short, a great deal of sickness, disease, premature aging, and untimely death may be prevented. One problem is teaching people how to prevent illness, for less than .5 percent of all money spent on health in the United States is spent on health education. Yet in spite of this scandalous situation the individual can learn many essential facts quite easily.

Simply practicing the seven habits mentioned above is a good start. In addition, individuals can improve their diets by eating less fat, sugar, and highly refined carbohydrates. They can eat more vegetables and foods rich in fiber, have annual checkups, and take as few drugs, legal and otherwise, as possible. The chances of growing old gracefully will be vastly improved.

———◆———

Although life in the world's industrialized nations has changed dramatically since the Second World War, it is by no means easy to interpret and evaluate what has happened. We have tried to sift the noteworthy from the trivial and the fundamental from the merely interesting by concentrating on three central developments, which are no less remarkable than the simultaneous political and economic recovery discussed in Chapter 37.

Spurred by World War Two, science and technology have raced ahead at unprecedented speed. Science has become bigger, more expensive, and more powerful than ever before, while scientific thinking and technical experts assume ever greater importance. This development contributes to the second — the growth of a more flexible and less class-conscious society, increasingly joined together by affluence and mass consumption despite periodic dissatisfaction and even upheaval. Finally, patterns of family life are experiencing major transformations. Above all, married women now have fewer children, shifting more attention to work outside the home while seeking greater equality. In so doing, women also reinforce the trend toward a more flexible class structure in Western society, and they reflect yet again the enormous influence of science, in this case on birth control methods and childhood mortality.

NOTES

1. Quoted by W. Laqueur, *Europe Since Hitler,* Penguin Books, Baltimore, 1972, p.9.

2. Quoted by J. Ziman, *The Force of Knowledge: the Scientific Dimension of Society,* Cambridge University Press, Cambridge, England, 1976, p. 128.

3. Quoted by S. Toulmin in *The Twentieth Century: A Promethean Age,* ed. A. Bullock, Thames & Hudson, London, 1971, p. 294.

4. J. Knowles, "The Responsibility of the Individual," *Daedalus* 106 (Winter 1977):61–62.

5. E. M. East, in *Scientific Monthly,* April 1931; also in *Reader's Digest* 19 (May 1931):151.

SUGGESTED READING

J. Ziman, *The Force of Knowledge: The Scientific Dimension of Society* (1976), which has an excellent bibliography, is a penetrating look at science by a leading physicist. C. P. Snow, *The Two Cultures and the Scientific Revolution,* rev. ed. (1963), explores the gap between scientists and nonscientists in a widely discussed book. A. Toffler, *Future Shock* (1970), is an interesting but exaggerated best seller, which claims that many contemporary psychological problems are due to overly rapid technical and scientific development. J. Ellul, *The Technological Society* (1964), is also highly critical of technical progress, while D. S. Landes, *The Unbound Prometheus: Technological Change and Industrial Development in Western Europe from 1750 to the Present* (1969), remains enthusiastic. Two more stimulating works on technology are J. J. Servan-Schreiber, *The World Challenge* (1981), and H. Jacoby, *The Bureaucratization of the World* (1973). T. Williams, *A Short History of Twentieth Century Technology* (1982), is a comprehensive survey of developments in all fields of applied science.

B. Barber, *Science and the Social Order* (1952), provides a good introduction to the impact of science in this century, while H. and S. Rose, *Science and Society* (1969), is a wide-ranging discussion of general issues. Three useful works treating scientific research and its practical applications are J. Jewkes et al., *The Sources of Invention,* 2nd ed. (1971); J. Langrish et al., *Wealth from Knowledge* (1972); and N. Rosenberg, ed., *The Economics of Technological Change* (1971). Science and the military are analyzed by R. Clarke, *The Science of War and Peace* (1971), and R. Reid, *Tongues of Conscience: War and the Scientist's Dilemma* (1964), is a dramatic historical account stressing moral choices. A similar theme is probed by A. Solzhenitsyn in his great novel, *The First Circle* (1968), a story of imprisoned Soviet scientists forced to develop new tools for the secret police.

D. K. Price, *The Scientific Estate* (1965), and W. O. Hagstrom, *The Scientific Community* (1965), suggest how scientists work and live. So does J. Watson, *The Double Helix* (1968), the gripping personal account of path-breaking scientific discovery, and A. Pais, *"Subtle Is the Lord": The Science and Life of Albert Einstein* (1982). A. Weinberg, *Reflections on Big Science* (1968), is a stimulating collection of essays by a renowned scholar. Finally, C. P. Snow's novel *The Search* (1958) examines the process of scientific research, as does W. Cooper's amusing story, *The Struggles of Albert Woods* (1966).

In addition to studies cited in the Suggested Reading for Chapter 37, A. Sampson, *The New Europeans* (1968), is a good guide to contemporary Western society. S. Rothman, *European Society and Politics: Britain, France, and Germany* (1976), is a valuable reference work, and S. Graubard, ed., *The New Europe?* (1963), is an important collection of articles probing declining class conflict. Two engaging books on recent intellectual developments are J. Barzun, *The House of Intellect* (1959), and R. Stromberg, *After Everything: Western Intellectual History Since 1945* (1970). L. Wylie, *Village in the Vaucluse,* rev. ed. (1964), and P. J. Hélias, *The Horse of Pride* (1980), provide fascinating pictures of life in the French village. A. Kriegel, *The French Communists* (1972) and *Eurocommunism* (1978), are also recommended. A. Touraine, *The May Movement* (1971), is sympathetic toward the French student

revolt, while the noted sociologist R. Aron, *The Elusive Revolution* (1969), is highly critical. F. Zweig, *The Worker in an Affluent Society* (1961), probes family life and economic circumstances in the British working class on the basis of extensive interviews and sees the spread of middle-class attitudes. This view is challenged by J. Goldthrope et al., *The Affluent Worker in the Class Structure* (1971). R. Dahrendorf, *Class and Class Conflict in Industrial Society* (1959), stresses the growth of the lower middle class as critical to the reducing of the polarization Marx foresaw. White-collar groups of the lower middle class receive another perceptive analysis by M. Crozier in *The Bureaucratic Phenomenon* (1964), and *The World of the Office Worker* (1971). These interpretations may be compared with that of A. Gorz, *A Strategy for Labor* (1964), and the influential works of H. Marcuse, notably *One-Dimensional Man* (1964), which argue that workers remain profoundly alienated from capitalist society in spite of mass consumerism.

Among interesting studies on specific countries not cited previously, R. E. Tyrrell, ed., *The Future That Doesn't Work* (1977), is a polemical but interesting attack on socialist policies in Britain. A. Sampson, *The New Anatomy of Britain* (1972), is a fascinating up-date of an earlier classic portrait of British society. J. Ardagh, *France in the 1980s* (1983), is another valuable examination by a veteran observer. E. Fawcett and T. Thomas, *The American Condition* (1982), is an excellent piece of reporting by two British journalists, with fine discussion of contemporary changes in family life and living patterns in the United States. W. Hollstein, *Europe in the Making* (1973), is a fervent plea to integrate Europe by a former top official of the Common Market. Three magazines, *Encounter, Commentary,* and *The Economist,* often carry interesting and intelligent articles on major social and political trends in different countries.

E. Sullerot, *Women, Society and Change* (1971), is an outstanding introduction to women's evolving role: R. Patia, ed., *Women in the Modern World* (1967), compares women's situation in many countries. Two other influential books on women and their new awareness are S. de Beauvoir, *The*

Second Sex (1962), and B. Friedan, *The Feminine Mystique* (1963). S. de Beauvoir's multivolume autobiography also makes fascinating reading. A. Rich, *On Lies, Secrets, and Silence* (1979), contains the essays of a leading feminist thinker. Two good general studies are by C. Lasch, *Haven in a Heartless World* (1977), and A. Cherlin, *Marriage, Divorce,* *Remarriage* (1981), which interpret changes in the American family. D. Burgwyn, *Marriage Without Children* (1982), is based on interviews with couples choosing this non-traditional family pattern. S. Crystal, *America's Old Age Crisis: Public Policy and the Two Worlds of Aging* (1982), examines the problems of the elderly in the United States.

CHAPTER 40

LIFE IN THE THIRD WORLD

EVERYDAY LIFE in the emerging nations of Asia and Africa changed dramatically after World War Two, as their peoples struggled to build effective nation states. Some of the changes paralleled the experiences of Europe and North America: science and modern technology altered people's lives in countless ways, and all-out industrialization to raise the standard of living profoundly affected family life and relations among social classes. Yet most observers have stressed the differences in development between the emerging nations and the industrialized world. Life remained very hard in the new nations, loosely affiliated – along with the older states of Latin America – by their common poverty and shared heritage of foreign domination. Moreover, many discerned a widening economic gap between the industrialized nations of North America and Europe, including the communist countries of eastern Europe, on the one hand and the emerging nations on the other. Some journalists have argued that the gap between North and South – that is, between rich nations and poor nations – has replaced the East-West confrontation of the Cold War and its immediate aftermath as mankind's most explosive division.

In Chapter 38 we saw something of the awe-inspiring diversity of cultures and peoples in Asia, Africa, and Latin America. This chapter will concentrate on shared problems of development and everyday life in the vast geographical expanse known collectively as the Third World. Three key questions will guide our investigation. How have the emerging nations of the Third World sought to escape from poverty, and what have been the results of their efforts? What has caused the prodigious growth of Third World cities, and what does their growth mean for their inhabitants? Finally, how do Third World thinkers and artists interpret the modern

world and the experiences of their peoples before, during and after foreign domination?

ECONOMIC AND SOCIAL CHALLENGES IN THE THIRD WORLD

Alongside the tough post-independence task of preserving political unity and building cohesive states, the emerging nations of the Third World have faced the enormous challenges of poverty, malnutrition, and disease. These scourges have weighed especially heavily on rural people, who depend on agriculture for survival and account for most of the Third World's population. Stirred by nationalism and the struggle for political freedom, peasants and landless laborers wanted the brighter future their leaders had promised them.

Most Third World leaders and their advisers in the 1950s and 1960s saw rapid industrialization and "modernization" as the answer to rural poverty and disease. Industrialization and modernization also kindled popular enthusiasm and thus promoted nation building, which in turn promised economic self-sufficiency and genuine independence. For these reasons, the leaders and peoples of the Third World in the 1950s and 1960s set themselves the massive task of building modern factories, roads, and public health services like those of Europe and North America. Their considerable success fueled rapid economic progress.

Yet social problems, complicated by surging population growth, almost dwarfed the accomplishment. Disappointments multiplied. By and large, the poorest rural people in the poorest countries gained the least from industrialization, and industrial expansion provided jobs for only a small segment even of the urban population. By the late 1960s, dissatisfaction with policies of all-out industrialization was widespread. A shift of emphasis to rural development prevailed throughout the 1970s. Different approaches proliferated as Third World nations responded to their common challenge in different ways.

DEFINING THE THIRD WORLD AND ITS POVERTY

Before considering the problems of the Third World, let us ask whether Africa, Asia, and Latin America can be validly and usefully lumped together as a single entity. Some experts prefer to speak of "the emerging nations" or "the less developed countries" – deliberately vague terms suggesting a spectrum of conditions ranging from near-hopeless poverty to moderate well-being. Others have begun to speak of a Fourth and even a Fifth World in order to distinguish among the less developed nations. Still, these countries do share important characteristics that make it valid – with reservations – to speak of them jointly.

The countries of the Third World have virtually all experienced political and/or economic domination, nationalist reaction, and a struggle for independence or autonomy. This shared past has given rise to a common consciousness, a we-are-all-victims feeling, expressed most forcefully in international relations with Europe and North America. This outlook has been nurtured by Marxists and other intellectuals and nationalists who have blamed the wealthy capitalist nations for the Third World's problems. Precisely because of their shared sense of past injustice, many influential Latin Americans identify with the Third World, despite their countries' greater affluence. The term *Third World,* widely used

by Latin American intellectuals by the late 1950s, was first coined by a French scholar to liken the peoples of Africa, Asia, and Latin America to the equally diverse but no less oppressed and humiliated French third estate before the revolution of 1789 (page 956). Later the term came into global use as a handy way of distinguishing Africa, Asia, and Latin America from the "first" and "second" worlds, the capitalist and Communist industrialized nations.

Second, most men and women in Third World countries still live in the countryside and depend on agriculture for a living. Agricultural goods and raw materials are still the primary exports. In Europe and North America, by contrast, people live mainly in cities, depending chiefly on industry and urban services for employment.

Finally, the agricultural countries of Asia, Africa, and most of Latin America are united by awareness of their common poverty. By no means everyone in the Third World is poor; some people are quite wealthy. The average standard of living, however, is low, especially compared with that of people in the wealthy industrial nations, and massive poverty remains ever-present.

It is easy to lose sight of the true dimensions of poverty in the Third World in a fog of economic statistics. In the 1950s and 1960s the United Nations and the emerging nations began collecting national income statistics; dividing those estimates by total population yields a nation's average per-capita income. These figures received enormous attention because they were stunningly low compared to those of wealthy nations. In 1960, for example, average annual income per person in all of Africa and southeast Asia was about $100. In North America it was $2500 – twenty-five times more. Journalists, politicians, and scholars often concluded that Third World

AN INDIAN FAMILY *walking barefoot across the countryside captures the human dimension of Third World poverty. Quite possibly they are landless laborers, searching for work and carrying all their meager belongings. (Black Star, Harmit Singh)*

be able to buy enough basic food, clothing and shelter in the United States would cost over $1,000 while $100 would suffice for these in India, so that someone with $1,000 in America may be worse off than someone in India with $100."[1]

National income statistics promote distorted comparisons in several ways. Basic necessities like food and clothing cost considerably less in poor countries than in rich countries. Also, the statistics on poor countries are less complete, and tend to leave out many wage-earning activities. Furthermore, fewer economic activities involve money transactions in poor countries than in rich ones, and only wage-earning work shows up consistently in national income statistics. In rich countries, only housewives do not receive money wages and thus do not show up in income statistics; there are many such "housewife" groups in the Third World.

A deeper understanding arises from considering Third World poverty in human terms, as did the postwar generation of nationalist leaders. Poverty meant, above all, not having enough to eat. Hunger and malnutrition were harsh facts of life for millions. In the poorest countries, like India, Ethiopia, and Bolivia, the average adult ate fewer than 2000 calories a day — only 85 percent of the minimal requirement. Although many poor countries fared better, none but Argentina could match the 3000 or more calories consumed in the more fortunate North. Even Third World people who consumed enough calories often suffered from the effects of unbalanced high-starch diets and inadequate protein. Severe protein deficiency stunts the brain as well as the body, and many of the poorest children grew up mentally retarded.

Poor housing — crowded, often damp and exposed to the elements — contributed significantly to the less developed world's high inci-

people were unspeakably poor and verging on mass starvation.

Such comparisons exaggerate the economic gap between the North and the South. They make a hard, sometimes desperate situation seem utterly hopeless. For example, average income per person in the United States in 1973 was about $5,000; in India it was about $100. Yet the average American was not necessarily fifty times better off than the average Indian. As an English and an Indian economist jointly point out, "Merely to survive, to

dence of chronic ill health. So too did malnutrition, scanty education and lack of such fundamentals of modern public health as adequate and safe water, sewage disposal, immunizations, prenatal care and control of communicable diseases. Infant mortality was savage, and chronic illness weakened and demoralized many adults, making them unfit for the hard labor their lives required.

Generally speaking, health status in Asia and Latin America has been better than in the new states of tropical Africa. As one authority described the situation in the early 1960s:

In the African social drama, sickness has a strong claim to being archvillain. . . . In tropical Africa, most men, women, and children are habitually unwell. Many are unwell from the day of their birth to the day of their death. . . . Most of the sick are sick of more than one disease. It is nothing unusual for a person admitted to a leprosarium to be suffering from malaria, sleeping sickness, tertiary yaws, onchoceriasis and worm infection as well as leprosy. Left to their own devices, most of the sick have no prospect of ever being not sick.[2]

The populations of poor countries were also overwhelmingly concentrated in the countryside, as small farmers and landless laborers. Rural people were often unable to read or write, and they lacked steady employment. Even with hard work, simple tools limited productivity. Basic services like safe running water were uncommon: village women around the world spent much of each day carrying water and searching for firewood or dung to use as fuel, as they must still do in many countries.

Mass poverty represented an awesome challenge to the postwar leaders of the newly emerging nations. Having raised peoples' hopes in the struggle for independence, they had to start delivering on their promises if they were to maintain trust and stay in power.

A strong commitment to modern economic and social development, already present in parts of Latin America in the 1930s, took hold in Asia and Africa in the postwar era.

THE MEDICAL REVOLUTION AND THE POPULATION EXPLOSION

Probably the most thoroughgoing success the Third World has achieved in the last thirty or forty years is its spectacular ongoing medical revolution. This achievement is underappreciated in wealthy countries, which have tended to flatter themselves with notions of Third World immaturity and helplessness.

Immediately after winning independence, the governments of emerging nations began adapting modern methods of immunology and public health. These methods were often simple, inexpensive, and extremely effective. One famous measure involved spraying with DDT in Southeast Asia, in order to control mosquitoes bearing malaria, one of the deadliest and most debilitating of tropical diseases. In Sri Lanka (formerly Ceylon), DDT spraying halved the yearly toll of deaths in the very first postwar decade — at a modest cost of $2 per person. According to the U.N.'s World Health Organization, which helped provide medical expertise to the new states, deaths from smallpox, cholera, and plague declined by more than 95 percent worldwide between 1951 and 1966.

Asian and African countries also increased the numbers of hospitals, doctors, and nurses they had inherited from the colonial past. Large African cities' biggest, most modern, and most beautiful buildings are often their hospitals. Sophisticated medical facilities have become symbols of the commitment to a better life. Critics maintain, however, that expensive medical technology is an indulgence their countries cannot afford, ill-suited to the

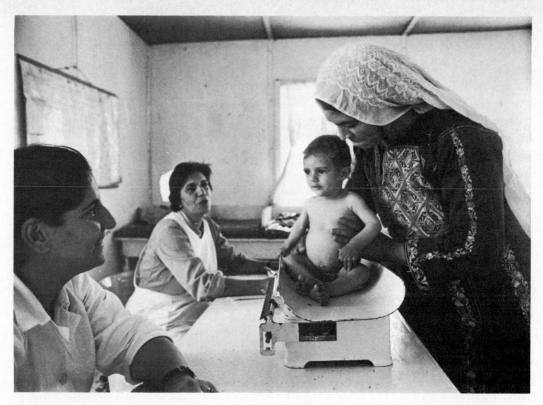

MODERN HEALTH CARE In this UN clinic for Palestinian refugees in Jordan, a baby receives the professional care that dramatically reduces infant mortality. (Stock, Boston/Owen Franken)

pressing health problems of the bulk of the population.

Such criticism has prompted a new emphasis on medical services in the countryside. Local people have been successfully trained as paramedics to staff rural outpatient clinics offering medical treatment, health education and pre- and post-natal care to the neglected rural masses. Most paramedics are women: many health problems involve childbirth and infancy, and villagers the world over consider it improper for a male to examine a woman's body.

The medical revolution has significantly lowered death rates and lengthened life expectancy in the Third World. In particular, children are increasingly likely to survive their early years, though infant mortality remains far higher than in rich countries. The average inhabitant of the Third World can now expect at birth to live about 54 years; life expectancy varies from 40 to 64 years depending on the country. In developed countries, by contrast, life expectancy at birth averages 71 years.

A much less favorable consequence of the medical revolution has been accelerated population growth. Rapid decline in the death rate was not immediately accompanied by a similar decline in the birth rate; women generally continued to bear five to seven children, as their mothers and grandmothers had. The combined populations of Asia, Africa, and Latin America, which had grown relatively modestly from 1925 to 1950, increased between 1950 and 1975 from 1,750 million to 3,000 million, as Figure 40.1 shows. Barring gigantic natural or man-made catastrophe, the population of the three continents is expected to surge to about 5,200 million in the year 2000 – an unprecedented explosion.

The population explosion in turn aroused fears of approaching famine and starvation. Thomas Malthus's gloomy late-eighteenth-century conclusion that population always tends to grow faster than food supply (page 1026) was revived and updated by "neo-Malthusian" social scientists. Such fears were exaggerated, but they did produce uneasiness in the Third World, whose leaders saw that their countries had to run fast just to maintain their already-low standards of living. They also saw that their populations consisted disproportionately of children, who had to be supported by a relatively small population of working adults. Some governments began pushing family planning and birth control to slow the growth of population.

These measures, often half-hearted, were not very successful in the 1950s and 1960s. In many countries, Islamic and Catholic religious teachings were hostile to birth control. Moreover, widespread cultural attitudes dictated that a real man keeps his wife pregnant. There were also solid economic reasons for preferring large families: farmers need plenty of children as cheap labor at planting and harvest times. And, as in Ireland before its great famine, sons and daughters were the only social security system. Since some would surely die young, a prudent couple wanted many children.

THE RACE TO INDUSTRIALIZE (1950–1970)

Many key Third World leaders, pressed on by their European, American and Soviet advisers,

Total Population

..... Africa, Asia, and Latin America

-·-·- Europe, North America, Soviet Union, and Oceania

FIGURE 40.1   THE INCREASE OF WORLD POPULATION, 1925–2000   Since the first quarter of the twentieth cntury Africa, Asia, and Latin America — the Third World — has been growing much more rapidly than industrialized Europe, North America, and the Soviet Union. Compare with Figure 31.2, p. 1142, for a long-term perspective. (Source: United Nations, Concise Report on the World Population Situation in 1970–1975 and Its Long-Range Implications, New York, 1974, p. 59.)

were convinced throughout the 1950s and most of the 1960s that all-out industrialization was the only answer to poverty and population growth. The masses, they concluded, were poor because they were imprisoned in a primitive, inefficient agricultural economy. Farm families' tiny holdings were too small for modern machinery. Big landowners exhibited more, but still limited, promise. Only modern factory industry appeared capable of creating wealth quickly enough to outrace the growth of numbers.

The two-century experience of the West, Japan, and the Soviet Union seemed to validate this faith in industrialization. Economic history became a popular subject among

Third World elites. It taught the encouraging lesson that the wealthy countries had also been agricultural and "underdeveloped" until the Industrial Revolution had lifted them out of poverty, one by one. One influential statement of this somewhat simplistic view was W. W. Rostow's *Stages of Economic Growth: A Non-Communist Manifesto* (1960). Rostow, an American economist, argued that any nation could progress through a series of well-defined stages from traditional society to American-style mass-consumption society. In that happy state, a people would be forever deaf to calls for violent upheaval and radical revolution.

Theories of modernization, particularly popular in the 1960s, assumed that all countries are following the path already taken by the industrialized nations, and that it is the task of the elite to speed the trip. Marxism, with its industrial and urban bias, preached a similar gospel. These ideas reinforced the Third World's desire to industrialize.

Nationalist leaders uniformly believed that successful industrialization requires state action and enterprise. Many were impressed by socialism in general and Stalin's forced industrialization in particular, which they saw as having won the Soviet Union international power and prominence, whatever its social costs. In Asia and Africa, furthermore, capitalists were equated with the old colonial rulers. The reasoning was practical as well as ideological: in addition to high-paying administrative jobs for political allies, modern industry meant ports, roads, schools and hospitals, as well as factories. Only the state could afford such expensive investments – as, indeed, the colonial governments had begun to realize in the twilight years of colonial rule. With the exception of the People's Republic of China, however, the new governments recognized private property and encouraged native – as

MAP 40.1   WORLD POPULATION, 1979

opposed to foreign – businessmen. The "mixed economy" – part socialist, part capitalist – became the general rule in the Third World.

Political leaders concentrated state investment in big, highly visible projects that proclaimed their independence and stimulated national pride. Enormous dams for irrigation and hydroelectric power were favored undertakings. Nasser's stupendous Aswan Dam harnessed the Nile, demonstrating that modern Egyptians could surpass even the pyramids of their ancient ancestors. The gigantic state-owned steel mill was another favorite project.

These big projects testified to the prevailing faith in expensive advanced technology and modernization along European lines. Nationalist leaders and their economic experts generally believed that rapid industrialization would depend on squeezing money for investment out of agriculture and the farm population. They measured overall success by how fast national income grew, and they tended to assume that social problems and income distribution would take care of themselves.

India, the world's most populous noncommunist country, exemplifies the general trends. After independence, Gandhi's special brand of nationalism was redirected toward economic and social rebirth through state enterprise and planning. Nehru and many Congress Party leaders believed that unregulated capitalism and free trade under British rule had deepened Indian poverty. Considering themselves democratic socialists, they introduced five-year plans, built state-owned factories and steel mills, and raised tariffs to pro-

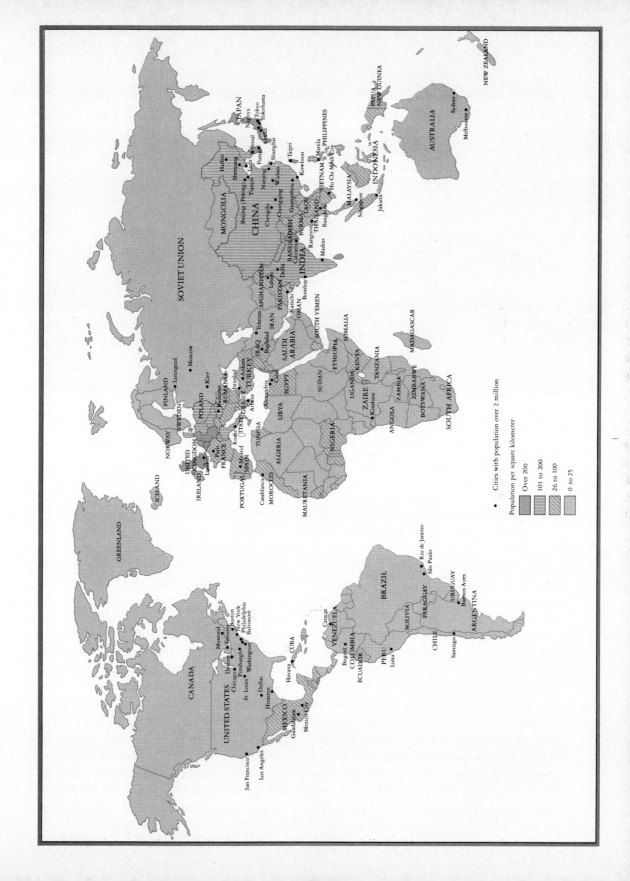

THE ASWAN DAM *Financed and built by the Soviet Union after the United States' refusal to back the project in 1956, the high dam at Aswan was Nasser's dream for Egypt's economic future. The water and the* *cheap electricity provided were supposed to make the desert bloom and to promote new industry, like that seen in the foreground. (Black Star/Ihrt-Stern)*

tect Indian manufacturers. Quite typically, they neglected agriculture, land reform, and village life.

The Third World's first great industrialization drive was in many ways a success. Industry grew faster than ever before, though from an admittedly low base in Africa and most of Asia. According to the United Nations, industry in the noncommunist developing nations grew 6.5 percent per year between 1950 and 1976. Because this growth exceeded the average annual population increase of 2.5 percent, Third World industrial production per capita grew about 4 percent per year for a long generation. The pace of industrial growth was also rapid by European and American standards: it matched the fastest rates of industrialization in the United States

before 1914, and was double that of Britain and France in the same years.

Industrial expansion also stimulated the other sectors of Third World economies. National income per capita grew about 2 percent per year in the 1950s and 1960s. This pace was far superior to the very modest increases that had occurred under colonial domination between 1900 and 1950. Future historians may well see the era after political emancipation as the era of industrial revolution in Asia and Africa.

This was particularly true of a few small countries that downgraded state leadership and achieved remarkable success by emphasizing dynamic capitalism and all-out participation in the world economy. South Korea, Taiwan, the Ivory Coast, the city-state of

Singapore, and the British colony of Hong Kong were genuine "economic miracles," industrializing rapidly and greatly improving the living standards of ordinary people.

South Korea and Taiwan were typical underdeveloped countries after World War Two – poor, small, agricultural, densely populated, and lacking in natural resources. They had also suffered from Japanese imperialism. How did these countries manage to make good?

Radical "capitalistic" land reform drew the mass of small farmers into a competitive market economy, which proved an excellent school of self-reliance and initiative. As in Japan, government cooperated with and encouraged business enterprise. Large-scale American aid also helped, and both countries threw open their arms to multinational corporations. And like Japan, both countries succeeded in preserving the fundamentals of traditional Chinese and Korean culture even as they accepted and mastered Western technology. Tough nationalist leaders maintained political stability.

Nevertheless, disillusionment with relatively rapid industrialization was spreading by the late 1960s. In the first place, the experience of a few small states like South Korea and Taiwan was quite exceptional. The countries of Asia, Africa, and Latin America did not as a whole match the "miraculous" concurrent advances of western Europe and Japan: the enormous economic gap between the rich and the poor nations had continued to widen.

Also, most Third World leaders had genuinely believed that rapid industrial development would help the rural masses. Yet careful studies showed that the main beneficiaries of industrialization were businessmen, bureaucrats, skilled workers, and urban professionals. Peasants and agricultural laborers had gained little or nothing. In fast-growing, dynamic Mexico, for instance, it was estimated that about 40 percent of the population was completely excluded from the benefits of industrialization. Moreover, the very poorest countries, such as India and Indonesia in Asia, and Ethiopia and the Sudan in Africa, were growing most slowly in per-capita terms. The industrialization prescription appeared least effective where poverty was most intense.

Finally, and perhaps most seriously, industrialization was failing to provide the sheer number of jobs needed for the sons and daughters of the population explosion. Statisticians estimated that the growth of Third World manufacturing between 1950 and 1970 provided jobs for only about one fifth of the 200 million young men and women who entered the exploding labor force in the same period. Most new enterprises employed advanced technology that required few workers. One person on a bulldozer could do the job of hundreds with shovels. For the forseeable future, most Third World people would have to remain on the farm or work in traditional handicrafts and service occupations. All-out modern industrialization had failed as a panacea.

AGRICULTURE AND VILLAGE LIFE

Since the late 1960s, the limitations of industrial development have forced Third World governments to take a renewed interest in rural people and village life. At best, this has meant giving agriculture its due and coordinating rural development with industrialization and urbanization. At worst, it has fostered a resigned "second-best" approach to the unrelenting economic and social challenge, especially in the very poorest countries. The optimistic vision of living standards approaching those of the wealthy North gives way to the pessimistic conclusion that it is only possible to ease slightly the great hardships of the rural masses.

There were other reasons for this reorientation toward agriculture and more balanced development. The extremely influential example of the People's Republic of China offered an alternative to all-out industrialization, capturing the imagination of many Asians, Africans (and Europeans) as the capitalist achievements of small Asian rivals like Taiwan and South Korea never did. As we have seen in Chapter 38, Mao and the Communists began by imitating the Soviet pattern of development, stressing heavy industry and rapid urbanization. As early as 1958, however, with the Great Leap Forward, Mao and his supporters shifted their focus back to their radical village roots. Almost unique among poor countries at that time, China made peasant agriculture and social equality its top priorities.

Despite some conspicuous failures, many observers concluded that China's concentration on agriculture had very positive consequences. Food production increased more rapidly than in most poor countries, and China became practically self-sufficient in food. The quality of village life also improved substantially as the importance of farmers was stressed. Literacy campaigns taught rural people how to read; an army of "barefoot doctors" – local peasants trained to do simple diagnosis and treatment – brought modern medicine to the Chinese countryside. The Communists also worked hard to reduce the customary gap between the rich city and the poor countryside. They set up handicraft industries in the communes and, by assigning people jobs, regulated urban migration and discouraged the "unbalanced" growth of giant industrial cities. Students and soft white-collar urban workers were periodically drafted to work in the fields.

This effort to minimize the urban-rural split was part of China's general commitment to social equality. Food was rationed and wages were relatively equal. Moreover, the Chinese consciously limited the production of consumer goods to things that almost everyone could afford, like radios and sewing machines. Similarly, the Chinese decided to rely almost exclusively on bicycles and public buses for transportation, since only a tiny elite can afford a private automobile in a poor society. China's development plan was both original and effective, even if its successes were often exaggerated and the price in personal freedom high. It is no wonder that some poor agricultural countries, especially African countries with tribal traditions of social equality, looked to China for inspiration.

More broadly, nationalist elites neglected agriculture in the 1950s because they regarded an agricultural economy as a mark of colonial servitude, which they were symbolically repudiating by embracing industrialization. Governments often established artificially low food prices, subsidizing their volatile urban supporters at the expense of the farmers. Also, the obstacles to more productive farming seemed overwhelming to unsympathetic urban elites and condescending foreign experts: farms were too small and fragmented for mechanization; peasants were too stubborn and ignorant to change their ways, and so on. Little wonder that only big farmers and some plantations received much government support.

More to the point, most honest observers were convinced that improved farm performance required land reform. Wherever large estates and absentee landlords predominated – large parts of Asia and most of Latin America, excluding Mexico, though not in black Africa

– poor peasants who had to rent land and landless laborers simply lacked the incentive to work harder. Any increased profits from larger crops went mainly to the absentee landowners.

Yet ever since the first great instance of it in the French Revolution, genuine land reform has been a profoundly radical measure, frequently bringing violence and civil war. As in Nationalist China in the 1930s, powerful landowners and their allies have generally succeeded in blocking or subverting redistribution of land to benefit the poor. Land reform, unlike industrialization, has generally been too hot for most politicians to handle.

Third World governments also neglected agriculture because feeding the masses was deceptively easy in the 1950s and early 1960s. Very poor countries received food from the United States at give-away prices, as part of a U.S. effort to dispose of its enormous grain surpluses and help American farmers. The countries of Asia, Africa, and Latin America, which had collectively produced more grain than they had consumed before 1939, began importing ever-increasing quantities after 1945 as their populations soared. Crops might fail, but starvation seemed a thing of the past. When India was urged to build up its food reserves in 1965, one top Indian official expressed a widespread attitude: "Why should we bother? Our reserves are the wheat fields of Kansas."[3]

In the short run, the Indian official was right. In 1966 and again in 1967, when the monsoon failed to deliver its life-giving rains to the Indo-Pakistan subcontinent and famine gripped the land, the United States gave India one fifth of its wheat crop. More than 60 million Indians lived exclusively on American grain. The effort required a food armada of six hundred ships, the largest fleet assembled since the Normandy invasion of 1944. The

famine was ultimately contained, and instead of millions of deaths there were only a few thousand.

This close brush with mass starvation sent a shiver down the world's spine. Complacency dissolved in the Third World; prophecies of disaster multiplied in wealthy nations. Paul Ehrlich, an American scientist, envisioned a grisly future in his polemical 1968 best-seller *The Population Bomb:*

The battle to feed all of humanity is over. In the 1970s the world will undergo famines – hundreds of millions of people are going to starve to death in spite of any crash programs embarked upon now. At this stage nothing can prevent a substantial increase in the world death rate.[4]

Other American commentators outdid each other with nightmare visions. One portrayed the earth as a crowded lifeboat in a sea of hungry poor, who would have to drown in order not to swamp the lifeboat. Another version compared truly poor countries like Bangladesh, Egypt, and Haiti to hopelessly wounded soldiers on a gory battlefield. Such victims were best left to die, so that scarce resources could be concentrated on the "walking wounded" who might yet be saved. Such crude and brutal Social Darwinism made it easy for Third World radicals to believe the worst about the rich industrialized nations.

Yet there was another face, a technological face, to the European and American interest in the Third World's food supply. Plant scientists and agricultural research stations had already set out to develop new hybrid seeds genetically engineered to suit the growing conditions of tropical agriculture. Their model was extraordinarily productive hybrid corn developed for the American Midwest in the 1940s, which had resulted in soaring yields and vast quantities of animal feed for a nation of meat-eaters. The first breakthrough

OLD AND NEW *With a fetish statue designed to frighten off evil spirits standing by, the proud owner of a two-acre plot in southern India shows a visiting expert his crop of miracle rice. As this picture suggests, the acceptance of modern technology does not necessarily require the repudiation of cultural traditions. (Woodfin Camp & Associates/Marc & Evelyne Bernheim)*

came in Mexico in the 1950s, when an American-led team supported by the Rockefeller Foundation developed new high-yielding dwarf wheats. These varieties enabled farmers to double their yields from one year to the next, though they demanded greater amounts of fertilizer and water for irrigation. Mexican wheat production soared.

Thus began the transformation of Third World agriculture – the so-called Green Revolution. In the 1960s an American-backed team of scientists in the Philippines turned their attention to rice, the Asian staff of life; they quickly developed a "miracle rice." The new hybrid also required more fertilizer and water, but yielded more and grew much faster. It permitted the revolutionary advent of year-round farming on irrigated land, making possible two, three, or even four crops a year. The brutal tropical sun of the hot dry season became an agricultural blessing for the first time. Asian scientists, financed by their governments, developed similar hybrids to meet local conditions. Increases in grain production were rapid and dramatic in some Asian countries. In gigantic India, for example, farmers upped production more than 60 percent in fifteen years. By 1980, thousands of new grain bins dotted the countryside, symbols of the agricultural revolution in India and the country's new-found ability to feed all its people.

The Green Revolution offered new hope to the Third World, but it too was no cure-all.

At first it seemed that most of its benefits flowed to the big landowners and substantial peasant farmers, who could afford the necessary investments in irrigation and fertilizer, which became much more expensive after the surge of oil prices in the 1970s. Recent Asian experience has shown, however, that even peasant families with tiny farms can gain substantially. The new techniques of year-round cropping require more work, but they enable the peasant family to squeeze more food out of its precious land. For any family lucky enough to have even three acres, the ongoing Green Revolution has been a godsend. Yet the technical revolution has shared relatively few of its benefits with the poorest classes — landless laborers, tenant farmers, and tiny landholders. Lacking even the two or three acres necessary to feed themselves with intensive effort, the very poorest groups have gained only slightly more regular employment from the Green Revolution's demand for more labor.

After early breakthroughs in Mexico, the Green Revolution's greatest successes have occurred not in Latin America but in Asia, most notably in countries with broad-based peasant ownership of land. Countries with large numbers of landless peasants and insecure tenant farmers, such as Pakistan and the Philippines, experienced less improvement than countries like South Korea and Taiwan, where land is generally peasant-owned. This helps to explain why the Green Revolution has failed to spread from Mexico throughout Latin America: as long as 3 or 4 percent of the rural population owns 60 to 80 percent of the land, which is the case in many Latin American countries, the Green Revolution will probably remain stillborn.

The same fatal equation prevails in Asian countries like Bangladesh. There an elite tenth of the population owns half the land, and the poorest half owns nothing at all. People eat less today than ten years ago, yet land reform remains a political and social minefield. As one member of a big (fifty-acre) land-owning family in Bangladesh told an American reporter in 1981: "They talk of removing property markers. It cannot happen. I will kill you if you move my property markers one inch."[5]

The Green Revolution, like the medical revolution and industrialization, represents a large but uneven step forward for the Third World. Black Africa has benefitted little from the new agricultural techniques, even though land reform has been a problem only in South Africa and Ethiopia before the revolution of 1974. Poor transportation, inadequate storage facilities, and low government-imposed agricultural prices must bear much of the blame. Also, the climatic conditions of black Africa encourage continued adherence to dry farming and root crops, whereas the Green Revolution has been almost synonymous with intensive irrigation and grain production. Throughout the Third World, therefore, relatively few of its benefits have flowed to the poorest groups — black Africans and the landless peasants of Asia and Latin America. These poor, who lack political influence and have no clear idea what needs to be done, increasingly long to escape from ill-paid, irregular work in somebody else's fields. For many of the bravest and most enterprising, life in a nearby town or city seems a way out.

THE GROWTH OF CITIES

Life in the less developed countries is marked by startling and sometimes violent contrasts. The ultra-modern has sprung up next to the traditional and the primitive; wealth for the few coexists with poverty for the many. It is

Area	1925	1950	1975	2000 (est.)	2025 (est.)
World total	21	28	39	50	63
North America	54	64	77	86	93
Europe	48	55	67	79	88
USSR	18	39	61	76	87
East Asia	10	15	30	46	63
Latin America	25	41	60	74	85
Africa	8	13	24	37	54
South Asia	9	15	23	35	51
Oceania	54	65	71	77	87

Little more than one-fifth of the world's population was urban in 1925. The urban proportion in the world total now approaches two-fifths and, according to United Nations experts, it may attain one-half by the century's end and two-thirds about 2025. The most rapid urban growth will come in the Third World, where the move to cities is still in its early stages. Thus in the next fifty years the urban populations of Europe and North America may grow by an-other two-thirds, while those of the Soviet Union and Oceania may double. But the urban population of East Asia may grow more than threefold, that of Latin America fourfold, South Asia sixfold and Africa eightfold. (Source: United Nations, Concise Report on the World Population Situation in 1970–1975 and Its Long-Range Implications, New York, 1974, p. 63.)

in the urban areas of the Third World that such contrasts are most striking. Shiny airports, international hotels and massive government buildings arise next to tar-paper slums. Like their northern counterparts, these rapidly growing cities are monuments to national independence and industrial development. Unfortunately, they are also testimonials to increasing populations and limited opportunities in the countryside. Runaway urban growth has become a distinctive feature of the Third World.

URBANIZATION IN THE THIRD WORLD

The cities of the Third World have been expanding at an astonishing pace. Many have doubled and some have even tripled in size in a single decade. The Algerian city of Algiers jumped from 300,000 to 900,000 between 1950 and 1960; Accra in Ghana, Lima in Peru, and Nairobi in Kenya grew just as fast. The less developed countries have become far more thoroughly urbanized in recent times than most people realize. In Latin America, three out of four people already live in towns and cities; in Asia and Africa, as Table 40.1 shows, one in four lives in an urban area.

This urban explosion has been so rapid that at least half of the planet's city dwellers now live in the cities of the Third World. This represents a tremendous change in a short period. As recently as 1920, three out of every four of the world's urban inhabitants were concentrated in Europe and North America.

In most Third World countries, furthermore, the largest cities have been growing fastest. Gigantic "super cities" of 2 to 10 million persons have arisen. The capital typically emerges as the all-powerful urban center, encompassing all the important elite groups and dwarfing smaller cities as well as villages. Mexico City, for example, grew from 3 million to 9 million people between 1950 and 1970, by which time it was seven times the size of the next largest Mexican city. The west European pattern of the dominant megalopolis – "Paris, the beloved monster" – has continued to spread from Latin America to Africa and Asia (though not to Asia's giants, China and India).

In the truly poor countries of Africa and Asia, moreover, the process of urbanization has really just begun. However populous the cities, the countryside still holds most of the people. If present trends continue, a city like Jakarta, the capital of Indonesia, will have 20 million people by the end of this century. Calcutta could be much larger. Such growth poses enormous questions for the future.

The urban explosion is due, first of all, to the general growth of population in the Third World. Urban residents have gained greatly from the medical revolution, but have only very gradually begun to reduce the size of their families. At the same time, the pressure of numbers in the countryside has encouraged millions to set out for the nearest city. More than half of all urban growth has been due to rural migration.

Even more than in Europe and North America in the nineteenth century, great cities are the undisputed centers of industry in the less developed countries. Half of all the industrial jobs in Mexico are concentrated in Mexico City. The same kind of extreme concentration of industry is occurring in many Third World countries. Yet careful study leads scholars to play down industrialization as a cause of urban explosion. In the words of a leading authority:

After about 1930 a new phenomenon which might be termed 'urbanization without industrialization' began to appear in the Third World. This phenomenon very rapidly acquired an inflationary character and in the early 1960s began to present most serious problems of urban employment and under-employment.[6]

In short, urban population has grown much faster than industrial employment. It is a lucky migrant who finds a real factory job.

Nevertheless, newcomers have continued to stream to the cities, pushed by hard rural conditions, pulled by urban attractions. As in early modern Europe, much migration is seasonal or temporary. Many a young person leaves home for the city to work in construction or serve as a maid, planning to return shortly with a modest nest egg. Higher wages and steadier work in the city have strongly influenced most decisions to migrate.

Yet the magnetic attraction of Third World cities is more than economic. Their attraction rests on the services and opportunities they offer, as well as changing attitudes and the urge to escape from the traditional restraints of village life. Most of the modern hospitals, secondary schools, and transportation systems in less-developed countries are in the cities. So are most banks, libraries, movie houses, and basic conveniences. Safe piped water and processed food are rare in rural areas, for instance, and village women by necessity spend much of their time carrying water and grinding grain.

The city has a special appeal for rural people who have been exposed to the seductive influence of modern education. In Africa, it is said, "the number of people who are prepared to go back to the land after more than three or four years in the classroom is infinitesimal."[7] One survey in the Ivory Coast found two out of three rural high-school graduates

SHACKS AND SKYSCRAPERS   This striking view of Caracas, Venezuela, has many counterparts throughout the Third World. Makeshift dwellings abut luxurious high-rise apartments, and the urban landscape expands with astonishing speed as newcomers pour into the city from rural areas. (Stock, Boston/ Owen Franken)

planning to move to the city; only one in ten of the illiterates expressed the same intention. Africa is not unique in this. For the young and the ambitious, the allure of the city is the excitement and opportunity of modern life. The village has taken on the curse of boredom and failure.

OVERCROWDING AND SHANTYTOWNS

Rapid population growth has placed great pressure on already-inadequate urban social services, and in many Third World cities the quality of life has deteriorated. In addition to running water, many people lack paved streets, electricity, and police and fire protection. As in the early days of England's industrial revolution, sanitation is minimal in poor sections of town. Outdoor toilets are shared by many. Raw sewage often runs in streets and streams.

Faced with a rising human tide, government officials and their well-to-do urban allies have sometimes tried to restrict internal migration to preserve the cities. Particularly in Africa, politicians have talked of sending newcomers "back to the land" in order to reduce urban unemployment, crime rates, congestion, and environmental decline. In Africa as elsewhere, these anti-migration efforts have been unsuccessful, and frustrated officials have often thrown up their hands in despair.

Surging population growth has had particularly severe consequences for housing. As in western Europe in the early nineteenth century, overcrowding has reached staggering proportions in a great many Third World cities. Old buildings are often divided and re-divided until population density reaches the absolute saturation point.

Perhaps overcrowding is best illustrated not by numbers or examples of extreme deprivation – the thousands of families in Calcutta who sleep on the sidewalks, the Hong Kong flophouses that rent beds by the hour – but by a vivid description of an older inner-city area, Singapore's Chinatown:

Chinatown . . . consists almost entirely of two or three story shop-houses. These shop-houses, originally intended to house one or two families, have been divided by a maze of interior partitions into cubicles, the majority of which are without windows and in permanent semi-darkness. Most of these cubicles are about the size of two double beds, placed side by side. In one such cubicle – dark, confined, unsanitary, and without comfort – may live a family of seven or more persons. Many of them sleep on the floor, often under the bed. Their possessions are in boxes, placed on shelves to leave the floor free for sleeping. Their food . . . is kept in tiny cupboards, which hang from the rafters. Their clothes hang on the walls, or from racks. Those who cannot even afford to rent a cubicle may live in a narrow bunk, often under the stairs.[8]

Makeshift squatter settlements are another manifestation of the urban housing problem. These shantytowns are continuously springing up, almost overnight, on the worst possible urban land. Mudflats, garbage dumps, railroad sidings, steep hills on the outskirts, even polluted waterfronts – these are the dismal sites that squatters have claimed. Typically, a group of urban poor "invades" unoccupied land and quickly throws up tents or huts. Often they are beaten off by the police, but they invade again and again until the authorities give up and a new squatter beachhead has been secured.

Squatter shantytowns have been growing much faster than more conventional urban areas in most Third World cities. In the giant Brazilian city of Rio de Janeiro, for example, the population of the shantytowns grew four times faster than the rest of the city in the 1950s and 1960s. As a result, the Third World's squatter settlements have come to house from up to two fifths of the urban population. The proportion is particularly high in Asia. Such settlements have occasionally mushroomed in American mining towns and in Europe, but never to the astonishing extent of Latin America, Asia, and Africa. The Third World has created a new urban form.

The meaning of squatter housing has been hotly debated. For a long time the "pessimists" stressed the miseries of squatter settlements – the lack of the most basic services, the pitiful one-room shacks, the hopelessness of disoriented migrants in a strange environment, the revolutionary discontent. More recently, detailed case studies have presented a more "optimistic" interpretation, stressing the vitality of the settlements and the resourcefulness of their inhabitants. Shantytowns are real neighborhoods, whose residents often share common ethnic origins and kinship ties. Active ties with the village, especially in Africa and Asia, help migrants move back and forth from city to countryside.

Moreover, the shantytowns themselves evolve, most notably in Latin America where they have existed longest. Their poor but enterprising inhabitants rely on self-help to improve their living conditions. With much sweat labor and a little hard-earned cash, a family replaces its mud walls with concrete blocks and gradually builds a real home. Or the community pressures the city to install a central water pump or build a school. Low-paid office workers in search of cheap housing may move in and continue the upgrading process.

Few members of squatter communities

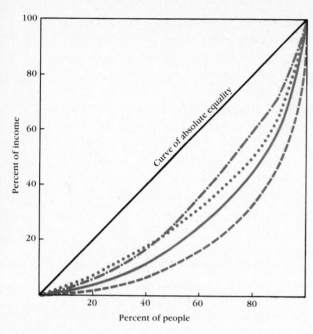

Percent of income

Curve of absolute equality

Percent of people

━━━ Third World (average of 15 countries)
‐‐‐ Brazil
•••• India
‐•‐•‐ United States (estimate)

DISTRIBUTION OF INCOME

	Richest 10%	Richest 20%	Poorest 60%	Poorest 20%
Third World average (15 countries)	38%	55%	25%	4%
Brazil	51%	67%	16%	2%
India	35%	49%	32%	7%
United States	28%[a]	41%	35%	5%

[a]Estimate; the richest 5% received 16% of income.

FIGURE 40.2 THE DISTRIBUTION OF INCOME IN THE THIRD WORLD, BRAZIL, INDIA, AND THE UNITED STATES, CA 1970 *The Lorenz curve is useful for showing the degree of economic inequality in a given country. The closer the actual distribution lies to the (theoretical) curve of absolute equality, the more nearly equal incomes are. In general, Third World countries have a high degree of income inequal-*

ity, as great as that in Europe before 1914 (see Figure 29.2, p. 1067). However, a few Third World countries, notably Taiwan and South Korea, are as equitable as the United States. Also, the United States is somewhat more equitable than most non-Communist industrialized countries (but almost identical to Canada, Great Britain, Israel, and Japan). France and West Germany are very similar to India, for example. The Communist countries appear most equitable in such comparisons, although their official data omit the tremendously valuable nonmonetary privileges of the ruling elites. (Sources: M. Todaro, Economic Development in the Third World, 2nd ed., Longman, New York, 1981, p. 128 and references cited there; U.S. Department of Commerce, Historical Statistics of the United States: Colonial Times to 1970, Part 1, Washington, D.C., GPO, 1975, p. 291.)

have been attracted to revolutionary doctrines, despite widespread fears (and hopes) to the contrary. Making a living and holding the family together are challenges enough. Indeed, one close observer describes squatters' beliefs as closely resembling those of the classic small businessman:

These beliefs can be summed up in the familiar and accepted maxims: Work hard, save your money, trust only family members (and them not too much), outwit the state, vote conservatively if possible, but always in your own economic self-interest; educate your children for their future and as old-age insurance for yourself.[9]

Thus the optimists counsel politicians to abandon their hostility to squatter settlements and help them to help themselves. The rush to the city cannot be stopped, they say. However bad life in the city is, it appears desirable to the millions of rural people who "vote with their feet." Since hard-pressed Third World governments cannot possibly provide the urban masses with subsidized housing, they must support the creativity of the "spontaneous settlement." However squalid such settlements appear, they are preferable to sleeping on sidewalks.

RICH AND POOR

Thoughtful citizens of the industrialized world must at least wonder whether their own nations are partly responsible for the Third World's poverty. Why have they inherited so much and others so little? Some theorists argue that the development of Europe and North America has caused the impoverishment of Asia, Africa, and much of Latin America. Before looking into this question in depth in Chapter 41, let us consider the truly staggering differences in well-being that Third World countries themselves contain.

Massive inequality has continued, with few exceptions, to be the reality of life in less-developed countries. Rich and poor are separated by a monumental gap, a gap that would seem intolerable to the average European or North American. Third World leaders have done little in their own backyards to reduce the inequality they so often deplore at international conferences and the United Nations.

As Third World governments have begun gathering better statistical information, it has become possible to measure the extent of inequality with some precision. (See Figure 40.2.) In most developing countries, the top 10 percent of all households receives more than one third of all national income; the top 20 percent takes from 50 to 60 percent. At the other end of the scale, the poorest 60 percent receives only a fifth to at most a third of all income; the poorest fifth gets less than 5 percent. This means that the average household in the top fifth of the population receives about *fifteen times* as much monetary income as the average household in the bottom fifth.

Such differences have been the rule in human history. If we compare Figure 40.2 with Figure 29.2 on page 1067, it is clear that the situation in the Third World today resembles that of Europe prior to World War One, before the movement toward greater equality accelerated sharply. It is noteworthy that the usual distinctions between rightist and leftist governments in the Third World, or between capitalist and socialist economies, have limited significance where shares of income are concerned. Income inequality is almost as pronounced in Mexico with its progressive, even revolutionary, tradition, as in Brazil with its rightist military rule. The fast-growing free-enterprise countries of Taiwan and South Korea exhibit substantially greater equality than socialist India (or the capitalistic Philippines).

It is in the towns and cities of the Third World that differences in wealth and well-being are most pronounced. Few rich or even middle-class people live in the countryside. Urban squatters may be better off than landless rural laborers, but they are light-years away from the luxury of the urban elite.

Consider housing. In the sober words of one careful observer, "The contrast between the opulent housing enjoyed by the tiny minority of the rich and the conditions under which the vast majority of the urban poor must live is extreme."[10] In Asia and Africa, the rich have moved into the luxurious sections previously reserved for colonial administrators and white businessmen. Particularly in Latin America, upper- and upper-middle-class people have built fine mansions in exclusive suburbs, where they live behind high walls, with many servants, protected from intruders by armed guards and fierce dogs.

A life style in the "modern" mold is almost the byword of the Third World's urban elite. From French perfume and Scotch whiskey to electronic games and the latest rock music,

A Sleek Automobile   fascinates four boys in an African village. The most ambitious youngster may already dream of acquiring power and wealth in the city. (Woodfin Camp & Assoc./Marc and Evelyne Bernheim)

imported luxuries have become the unmistakable signs of wealth and privilege. In Swahili-speaking East Africa, the common folk call them *wa Benzi* – "those who ride in a Mercedes-Benz." Even in relatively egalitarian China, the urban masses save to buy bicycles while government officials ride in chauffeur-driven state-owned limousines. The automobile has become the ultimate symbol of the urban elite.

Education also distinguishes the wealthy from the masses. Elite students often study abroad, at leading European and North American universities, or, as in Nigeria, monopolize openings in local universities. While absorbing the latest knowledge in a prestigious field like civil engineering or economics, they also absorb foreign customs and values. They master the fluent English or French that is indispensable for many top-paying jobs, especially in government. This is very important: government and politics – not business and commerce – are the high road to wealth and status in Africa, Asia, and, to a lesser extent, Latin America.

The middle classes of the Third World are still quite small relative to the total population. White-collar workers and government bureaucrats have joined the traditional ranks of merchants and professionals in the urban middle class. Their salaries, though modest, are wonderfully secure and usually carry valuable fringe benefits. Unlike recent migrants and the rural poor, white-collar workers often receive ration cards entitling them to cheap subsidized food.

An unexpected component of the urban middle classes is the modern factory proletariat, a privileged segment of the population in most poor countries. Few in number because sophisticated machines require few workers, relative to agriculture, they receive high wages for their skilled work. On the Caribbean island of Jamaica in the late 1960s, for example, aluminum workers in big, modern American-owned plants earned $60-65 a week. Meanwhile cane cutters on sugar plantations earned $3 a week, and many laborers on small farms only a dollar a week. Little wonder that modern factory workers tend to be cautious and self-satisfied in the Third World.

The great majority, the urban poor, earn precarious livings in the more traditional "bazaar economy" of petty trades and unskilled labor. Regular salaried jobs are rare and highly prized, and a complex world of tiny unregulated businesses predominates.

As in Europe a century ago, irregular armies of peddlers and pushcart operators hawk their wares and squeeze a living from commerce. West African market women, with their colorful dresses and overflowing baskets, are a classic example of this pattern. Sweat shops and home-based workers manufacture cheap goods for popular consumption. Maids, prostitutes, small-time crooks, and unemployed ex-students sell all kinds of services. This old-yet-new bazaar economy shows no signs of dying out. Indeed, it continues to grow prodigiously as migrants stream to the cities, modern industry provides few jobs, and the wide gap between rich and poor persists.

MIGRATION AND THE FAMILY

Large-scale urban migration has had a massive impact on traditional family patterns in the Third World. Particularly in Africa and Asia, the great majority of migrants to the city are young men, married and unmarried. Women tend to stay in the villages, creating a sexual imbalance in both places. There are several reasons for this pattern. Much of the movement to cities (and mines) is temporary or seasonal. At least at first, young men leave home to earn hard cash to bring back to their villages. Moreover, the cities are expensive and prospects there are uncertain. Only after a man has secured a real foothold does he marry or call for his wife and children.

Kinship and village ties help ease the rigors of temporary migration. Often a young man can go to the city rather easily because his family has close ties with friends and relatives there. Many city neighborhoods are urban versions of their residents' original villages. Networks of friendship and mutual aid help young men (and some women, especially brides) move back and forth without being overwhelmed.

For rural women, the consequences of male out-migration have been mixed. Asian and African women have long been treated as subordinates, if not inferiors, by their fathers and husbands. Now, rather suddenly, such women are finding themselves heads of households, faced with managing the farm, feeding the children, and running their own lives. In the east African country of Kenya, for instance, one third of all rural households are now headed by women.

African and Asian village women have had to become unprecedentedly self-reliant and independent. The real beginnings of more equal rights and opportunities, of women's liberation, are readily visible in Africa and Asia. The price has been high and progress uneven. Rural women often have only their children to help in the endless backbreaking labor. And their husbands, when they return, often expect their wives to revert to the old subordination.

In economically more advanced Latin America, the pattern of migration is different. Whole families migrate, very often to squatter settlements, much more commonly than in Asia and Africa. These families frequently belong to the class of landless laborers, which is generally larger in Latin America than in Africa or even Asia. Migration is also more likely to be once-and-for-all. Another difference is that women are as likely as men to move to the city. The situation in Mexico is typical:

They leave the village seeking employment, often as domestic servants. When they do not find work in the cities, they have few alternatives. If they are young, they frequently turn to prostitution; if not, they often resort to begging in the streets. Homeless peasant women, often carrying small children, roam every quarter of Mexico City.[11]

Some women also leave to escape the narrow, male dominated villages. Even so, urban migration in Latin America seems to have had less impact on traditional family patterns and on women's attitudes than in Asia and Africa. This helps explain why the women's movement has lagged behind in Latin America.

MASS CULTURE AND CONTEMPORARY THOUGHT

Ideas and beliefs have continued to change dramatically in the Third World. Education is fostering new attitudes, while mass communications relentlessly spread the sounds and viewpoints of modern life. Third-World intellectuals, in their search for the meanings of their countries' experiences, are articulating a brilliant spectrum of independent opinion in keeping with growing national diversity.

EDUCATION AND MASS COMMUNICATIONS

In their efforts to modernize and better their societies, Third-World leaders have become increasingly convinced of the critical importance of education. Meanwhile economists have begun to stress the role of "human capital" – skilled and educated workers, managers, and citizens – in the development process.

Faith in education and "book learning" has spread surprisingly rapidly to the Third World's masses, for whom education principally means jobs. Asked how their lives differ from their mothers' and grandmothers', poor and often illiterate peasant women in several countries testified to the need for an education, along with the need to earn money and have fewer children. A young African woman in Kenya explained it this way.

My mother has eleven children. She is my father's only wife. She works in the fields and grows the food we eat. She plants cabbage, spinach, and corn. She works very hard, but with so many children it is difficult to get enough food or money. All of my brothers and sisters go to school. One is already a teacher. . . .

My life is very different from my mother's. . . . Women have to get an education. Then if you get a large family and don't know how to feed it, you can find work and get some cash. That's what I will teach my children: "Get an education first."[12]

A young Asian woman on a cooperative farm in Sri Lanka, thousands of miles from Kenya, expressed a strikingly similar view:

You see, my father is a farmer: My parents lived from the land, but when my grandfather died, the land was distributed among his sons. Now my parents' portion is very small. It is not sufficient for them to exist on. . . .

*I want my children to have a firmer footing —
to have this type of life. They must learn a profession and have a better job than mine. Women in
Sri Lanka need employment. They should all have
jobs. They must be taught skills so that they can
earn a bit for their families.*[13]

As these voices suggest and Figure 40.3
verifies, young people in the Third World are
heading for schools and universities in unprecedented numbers. To be sure, general
averages obscure wide variations by country,
region, and social class. Rural people everywhere spend fewer years in school. Latin
America, in keeping with its higher incomes
and greater urbanization, has the highest percentage of students in all age groups, followed
by Asia and then by Africa. There still remains a wide education gap with the rich
countries, where more than 90 percent of both
sexes attend school through age seventeen.

Moreover, the quality of education in the
Third World is often mediocre. African and
Asian universities have tended to retain the
old colonial values, stressing law and liberal
arts at the expense of technical and vocational
training. As a result, many poor countries
find themselves with large numbers of unemployed or underemployed liberal-arts graduates. These "generalists" compete for scarce
jobs in the already-bloated government bureaucracies while less prestigious technical
jobs go begging.

A related problem is the Third World's
"brain drain": many gifted students in vital
fields like engineering and medicine end up
pursuing their careers in the rich countries of
the developed world, which need their talents
far less than their native lands. As many
Indian-trained doctors practice abroad, mainly
in advanced countries, as serve India's entire
rural population of 480 million. The threat
represented by the brain drain is one reason

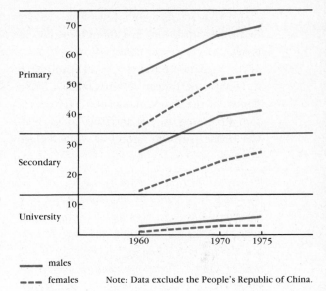

males
females   Note: Data exclude the People's Republic of China.

FIGURE 40.3 PERCENTAGE OF ALL MALES
AND FEMALES ENROLLED IN PRIMARY AND
SECONDARY SCHOOLS AND UNIVERSITIES IN THE
THIRD WORLD, 1960–1975 *(Source: United
Nations,* Concise Report on the World Population
Situation in 1970–1975 and Its Long-Range Impli-
cations, *New York, 1974, p. 28.)*

why the Third World's professional elite receives such high salaries in very poor countries.

Many observers believe that the education
drive, like its forerunner the industrialization
drive, has served the rural masses poorly. It
sometimes seems that its greatest beneficiaries
are schoolteachers, who enjoy the elite status
provided by a permanent government job. Instruction is often impractical and mind-
numbing. The children of farmers generally
learn little about agriculture, animal raising,
or practical mechanics. Instead, students may
memorize passages from ancient literary
works and religious texts, and spew back cut-
and-dried answers. No wonder children stay
away from school in droves. Village schools
succeed best at identifying the exceptional

pupils, who are then siphoned off to the city for further study and lost forever to the village.

The celebrated novelist V. S. Naipaul, born in Trinidad of Indian descent, offers a vivid glimpse of the shortcomings of village education. Returning to his ancestral India, Naipaul made surprise stops at two village schools:

We stopped first at a primary school, a small three-room brick shelter beside a banyan tree. Two brahmins [high-caste Hindus] in spotless white cotton, each washed and oiled, each with his top-lock of caste, each "drawing" 90 rupees a month, were in charge. Twenty-five children sat on the broken brick floor with their writing boards, reed pens and little pots of liquid clay. The brahmins said there were two hundred and fifty children at the school.

"But there are only twenty-five here."

"What can you do, sahib?"

Beyond the road some of the children not at school rolled in the dusty fields. Even with twenty-five children the two rooms of the school were full. In the third room, protected from sun and theft, were the teachers' bicycles, as oiled and cared for as their masters.

At the next school, a few miles down the road, the teacher was asleep in the shade of a tree. . . . His pupils sat in broken rows on strips of matting. . . . The teacher was so soundly asleep that though our jeep stopped about eight feet away from his table he did not immediately awaken. When he did — the children beginning to chant their lessons in the Indian fashion as soon as they saw us — he said he was not well. His eyes were indeed red, with illness or sleep. But redness disappeared as he came to life. He said the school had three hundred and sixty pupils; we saw only sixty.[14]

Whatever its shortcomings, formal education has spread hand in hand with another influential agent of popular instruction: mass communications. The transistor radio has penetrated the most isolated hamlets of the Third World. Governments have universally embraced radio broadcasting as a means of power, propaganda, and education. Relentlessly, the transistor propagates the outlook and attitudes of urban elites and in the process challenges old values.

Moreover, the second communications revolution — the visual one — is fast arriving even in remote villages. Television will bring the whole planet into the bars and meeting-houses of the world's villages. Judging from experience elsewhere — in remote French villages, in Eskimo communities above the Arctic circle — television will have a profound, even revolutionary impact. For one thing, the lure of the city seems certain to grow.

INTERPRETING THE EXPERIENCES OF THE EMERGING WORLD

Popular education and mass communications have compounded the influence of the Third World's writers and thinkers, its purveyors of explanations. Some intellectuals have meekly obeyed their employers, whether the Ministry of Information or a large newspaper. Others have simply embellished or reiterated some received ideology like Marxism or free-market capitalism. But some Third World intellectuals are leading the search for meanings and direction that is accompanying rapid social change and economic struggle.

Having come of age during and after the struggle for political emancipation, Third World intellectuals have been centrally preoccupied with achieving genuine independence and freedom from outside control. In a way that Europeans and North Americans often found one-sided and extreme, some Third World writers argued that real independence required a total break with the former colo-

MASS COMMUNICATIONS *An enterprising merchant in West Africa uses television to attract a crowd to a tiny shop in Dakar, Senegal. Only the man passing on the right, suggestively clad in the traditional dress of the Muslim believer, appears oblivious to the siren call of the modern age. (Stock, Boston/Philip Jon Bailey)*

nial powers and a total rejection of Western values. This was the message of Frantz Fanon (1925–1961) in his powerful study of colonial peoples, *The Wretched of the Earth,* published in 1961.

Fanon, a French-trained black psychiatrist from the Caribbean island of Martinique, was assigned to a hospital in Algeria during the bloody war for Algerian independence. He quickly came to sympathize with the guerrillas and probed deeply into the psychology of colonial revolt. According to Fanon, decolonization is always a violent and totally consuming process, whereby one "species" of men, the colonizers, is completely replaced by an absolutely different species – the colonized, the wretched of the earth. During decoloniza-

tion the colonized masses mock colonial values, "insult them, and vomit them up."

Fanon was convinced that the battle for formal independence is only the first step, and that the former imperialists remain the enemy:

The mobilization of the masses, when it arises out of the war of liberation, introduces into each man's consciousness the ideas of a common cause, of a national destiny, and of a collective history. In the same way the second phase, that of the building-up of the nation, is helped on by the existence of this cement which has been mixed with blood and anger. . . . During the colonial period the people are called upon to fight against oppression; after national liberation, they are called upon to fight against poverty, illiteracy, and underdevelopment. The struggle, they say, goes on. The people realize that life is an unending contest.

...The apotheosis of independence is transformed into the curse of independence, and the colonial power through its immense resources of coercion condemns the young nation to regression. In plain words, the colonial power says: "Since you want independence, take it and starve."

... We are not blinded by the moral reparation of national independence; nor are we fed by it. The wealth of the imperial countries is our wealth too.... Europe is literally the creation of the Third World. The wealth which smothers her is that which was stolen from the underdeveloped peoples.... So when we hear the head of a European state declare with his hand on his heart that he must come to the aid of the poor underdeveloped peoples, we do not tremble with gratitude. Quite the contrary; we say to ourselves: "It's a just reparation which will be paid to us."[15]

For Fanon, independence and national solidarity went hand in hand with outrage at the misdeeds and moral posturings of the former colonial powers. Fanon's passionate, angry work became a sacred text for radical nationalists in the 1960s.

Some more recent writers have looked beyond wholesale rejection of the industrialized powers. They too are "anti-imperialist," but they see colonial domination as only one chapter in the life of their people. Many of these writers are cultural nationalists, who apply their talents to celebrating the rich histories and cultures of their people. At the same time, they do not hesitate to criticize their own leaders and fellow citizens, with whom they are frequently dissatisfied.

The Nigerian writer Chinua Achebe (b. 1930) renders these themes with acute insight and vivid specificity in his short, moving novels. Achebe writes in English rather than his native Ibo tongue, but he writes primarily

for Africans, seeking to restore his people's self-confidence by reinterpreting the past. For Achebe, "the writer in a new nation" must first dispose of "the fundamental theme":

This theme – quite simply – is that the African people did not hear of culture for the first time from Europeans; that their societies were not mindless but frequently had a philosophy of great depth and volume and beauty, that they had poetry and above all, they had dignity. It is this dignity that many African peoples all but lost in the colonial period, and it is this that they must now regain. The worst thing that can happen to any people is the loss of their dignity and self-respect. The writer's duty is to help them regain it by showing what happened to them, what they lost.[16]

In *Things Fall Apart,* Achebe achieves his goal by bringing vividly to life the men and women of an Ibo village at the beginning of the twentieth century, with all their virtues and frailties. The hero, Okonkwo, is a mighty wrestler and hard-working, prosperous farmer, but he is stern and easily angered. Enraged at the failure of his people to reject newcomers, and especially at the white missionaries who convert his son to Christianity and provoke the slaying of the sacred python, Okonkwo kills a colonial messenger. When his act fails to spark a tribal revolt, he commits suicide. Okonkwo is destroyed by the general breakdown of tribal authority and his own intransigent recklessness. Woven into the story are the proverbs and wisdom of a sophisticated people and the beauty of a vanishing world.

In later novels, especially *A Man of the People,* Achebe portrays the post-independence disillusionment of many Third World intellectuals. The villain is Chief the Honorable Nanga, a politician with the popular touch. This "man of the people" lives in luxury, takes bribes to build expensive apartment buildings for foreigners, and flimflams the voters with celebrations and empty words. The hero, an idealistic young schoolteacher, tries to unseat Chief Nanga, with disastrous results. Beaten and hospitalized, the hero broods that the people "had become even more cynical than their leaders and were apathetic into the bargain."[17] Achebe's harsh but considered judgment is potentially applicable to many Third World nations: the rulers are corrupt and estranged from the rural masses, and the intellectuals gnash their teeth in frustration.

V. S. Naipaul, (page 1502) also describes governments from Argentina to Pakistan and beyond as marked by corruption, ineptitude, and self-deception. Another of Naipaul's recurring themes is the poignant loneliness and homelessness of uprooted people. In *The Mimic Men,* the blacks and whites, the Hindus and Chinese who populate the tiny Caribbean islands are all aliens, thrown together by "shipwreck." As one of the characters says:

V. S. NAIPAUL Having established himself as a major novelist, Naipaul has turned frequently to journalistic investigations of problems in Third World countries. His eye-witness accounts are often sharply critical. (Magnum/Ian Berry)

It was my hope [in writing] to give expression to the restlessness, the deep disorder, which the great exploration, the overthrow in three continents of established social organizations, the unnatural bringing together of peoples who could achieve fulfillment only within the security of their own societies and the landscapes hymned by their ancestors ... has brought about. The empires of our time were short-lived, but they altered the world for ever; their passing away is their least significant feature. It was my hope to sketch a subject which, fifty years hence, a great historian might pursue.... But this work will not now be written by me; I am too much a victim of that restlessness which was to have been my subject.[18]

Naipaul and Achebe, like many other talented Third World writers and intellectuals, are probing searchingly into Third World ex-

periences in pursuit of understanding and identity. This same searching goes on in other creative fields, from art and dance to architecture and social science, and seems to reflect the intellectual maturity of genuine independence.

◆

As Third World leaders and peoples threw off foreign domination after 1945 and reasserted themselves in new or revitalized states, they turned increasingly inward to attack poverty and limited economic development. The collective response was an unparalleled medical revolution and the Third World's first great industrialization drive. And the Third World displayed a rich creative diversity, its approaches to shared problems ranging from the revolutionary egalitarianism of Mao's China through the mixed economy of the majority to the market-oriented capitalism of a few small countries. Moreover, rapid urbanization, expanding educational opportunities, and greater rights for women were striking evidence of modernization and fundamental human progress. The achievement was great.

Yet so was the challenge, and results fell far short of aspirations. Deep and enduring rural poverty, overcrowded cities, enormous class differences, and the sharp criticisms of leading Third World writers mocked early hopes of quick solutions. Since the late 1960s there has been growing dissatisfaction and frustration in Third World nations. And, as we shall see, the belief grows that the Third World can meet the challenge only by reordering the entire global system and dissolving the unequal ties that bind it to the rich nations.

NOTES

1. Alasdair MacBean and V. N. Balasubramanyam, *Meeting the Third World Challenge,* St. Martin's, New York, 1976, p. 27.

2. P. J. McEwan and R. B. Sutcliffe, eds., *Modern Africa,* Thomas Y. Crowell, New York, 1965, p. 349.

3. Quoted by L. R. Brown, *Seeds of Change: The Green Revolution and Development in the 1970s,* Praeger, New York, 1970, p. 16.

4. Paul Ehrlich, *The Population Bomb,* Ballantine, New York, 1968, p. 11.

5. *Wall Street Journal,* 16 April 1981, p. 17.

6. Paul Bairoch, *The Economic Development of the Third World Since 1900,* Methuen, London, 1975, p. 144.

7. R. Dumont, *False Start in Africa,* Deutsch, London, 1966, p. 88.

8. Barrington Kaye, *Upper Nankin Street, Singapore: A Sociological Study of Households Living in a Densely Populated Area,* University of Malaya Press, Singapore, 1960, p. 2.

9. W. Mangin, "Latin American Squatter Settlements," *Latin American Research Review* 2 (1967): 84–85.

10. D. J. Dwyer, *People and Housing in Third World Cities: Perspectives on the Problem of Spontaneous Settlements,* Longman, London, 1975, p. 24.

11. Perdita Hudson, *Third World Women Speak Out: Interviews in Six Countries on Change, Development, and Basic Needs,* Praeger, New York, 1979, p. 11.

12. Hudson, *Third World Women Speak Out,* p. 22.

13. Ibid., p. 25.

14. V. S. Naipaul, *The Overcrowded Barracoon,* Knopf, New York, 1973, pp. 81–82.

15. Frantz Fanon, *The Wretched of the Earth,* Grove Press, New York, 1968, pp. 43, 93–94, 97, 102.

16. Chinua Achebe, *Morning Yet on Creation Day,* Heinemann, London, 1975, p. 81.

17. Chinua Achebe, *A Man of the People,* Heinemann, London, 1966, p. 161.

18. V. S. Naipaul, *The Mimic Men,* Macmillan, New York, 1967, p. 38.

SUGGESTED READING

P. Bairoch, *The Economic Development of the Third World Since 1900* (1975), is a valuable historical study. A. B. Mountjoy, ed., *The Third World: Problems and Perspectives* (1978), and A. MacBean and V. N. Balasubramanyam, *Meeting the Third World Challenge* (1976), are reliable, even-handed introductions to contemporary trends and policies. Two excellent recent works from a truly Third World perspective are especially recommended: E. Hermassi, *The Third World Reassessed* (1980); and M. ul Haq, *The Poverty Curtain: Choices for the Third World* (1976). The many clear and compelling works of B. Ward, notably *The Rich Nations and the Poor Nations* (1962) and *The Lopsided World* (1968), movingly convey the hopes and frustrations of sympathetic Western economists in the 1960s. Equally renowned are studies by the Swedish socialist G. Myrdal: *Asian Drama: An Inquiry Into the Poverty of Nations,* 3 vols. (1968); and *The Challenge of World Poverty: A World Anti-Poverty Program in Outline* (1970). Valuable introductions to world agriculture and population are found in various works by L. R. Brown, notably *Seeds of Change: The Green Revolution and Development in the 1970s* (1970), and *In the Human Interest: A Strategy to Stabilize World Population* (1974). R. King, *Land Reform: A World Survey* (1977), is a useful introduction to key problems.

Two valuable studies on African questions are K. Patterson, *History and Disease in Africa: An Introductory Survey and Case Studies* (1978), and P. Lloyd, ed., *The New Elites of Tropical Africa* (1966). Critical aspects of contemporary Indian economic development are carefully considered by M. Franda, *India's Rural Development: An Assessment of Alternatives* (1980), and A. G. Noble and A. K. Dutt, eds., *Indian Urbanization and Planning: Vehicles of Modernization* (1977). China's economic and social problems are skillfully placed in a broad and somewhat somber perspective by two Chinese-speaking journalists, F. Butterfield, *China: Alive in the Bitter Sea* (1982); and R. Bernstein, *From the Center of the Earth: The Search for the Truth About China* (1982).

For the prodigious growth of Third World cities, J. Abu-Lughod and R. Hay, Jr., eds., *Third World Urbanization* (1977), and the lively studies of D. J. Dwyer, *People and Housing in Third World Cities: Perspectives on the Problem of Spontaneous Settlements* (1975), and *The City in the Third World* (1974), are highly recommended. Similarly recommended is a fascinating investigation of enduring urban-rural differences by M. Lipton, *Why Poor People Stay Poor: Urban Bias in World Development* (1977), which may be complemented by C. Elliott, *Patterns of Poverty in the Third World: A Study of Social and Economic Stratification* (1975).

A good introduction to changes within families is P. Hudson, *Third World Women Speak Out: Interviews in Six Countries on Change, Development, and Basic Needs* (1979), a truly remarkable study. Other useful works on Third World women and the changes they are experiencing include L. Iglitzen and R. Ross, *Women in the World: A Comparative Study* (1976); A. de Souza, *Women in Contemporary India and South Asia* (1980); N. J. Hafkin and E. Bay, eds., *Women in Africa* (1977); and J. Ginat, *Women in Muslim Rural Society: Status and Role in Family and Community* (1982). K. Kakar, *The Inner World: A Psychoanalytic Study of Childhood and Society in India* (1978), is a fascinating interpretation of Indian dependence in family and personal relations, which is provocatively compared with the compulsive individualism of Western society.

The reader is especially encouraged to enter into the contemporary Third World with the aid of the gifted writers discussed in this chapter. F. Fanon, *The Wretched of the Earth* (1968), is a particularly strong indictment of colonialism from the 1960s. The wide-ranging work of Chinua Achebe illuminates the proud search for a viable past in his classic novel of precolonial Africa, *Things Fall Apart* (1959), and the disillusionment with unprincipled post-independence leaders in *A Man of the People* (1966). G. Moore and U. Beier, eds., *Modern Poetry from Africa* (1963), is a recommended anthology. In addition to his rich and introspective novels like *The Mimic Men* (1967), V. S. Naipaul has reported extensively on life in Third World countries. His *India: A Wounded Civilization* (1978), impressions gleaned from a trip to his family's land of origin, and *A Bend in the River* (1980), an investigation of the high price postcolonial Africa is paying for modernization, are especially original and thought-provoking. Finally, L. Heng and J. Shapiro, *Son of the Revolution* (1983), brilliantly captures the drama of Mao's China through the turbulent real-life story of a young Red Guard.

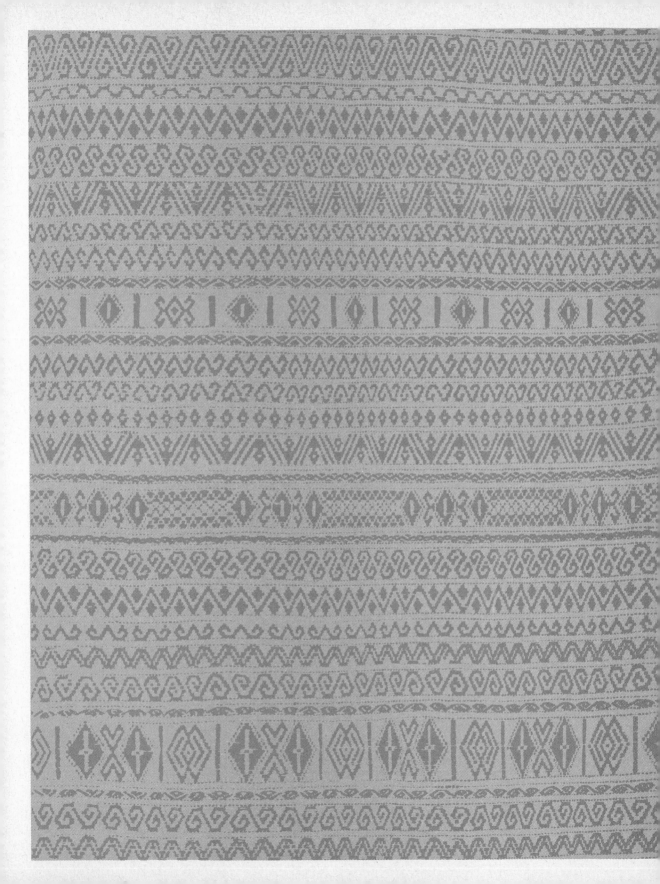

CHAPTER 41

ONE SMALL PLANET

THE IDEA OF VISITORS from elsewhere in the universe has kindled the modern imagination. Motorists swear they have seen unidentified flying objects; the alchemy of imagination even lands Captain Kirk and the crew of the *Enterprise* on our earth in our era. A best-selling author spins preposterous theories about "ancient astronauts" who landed on earth and built everything from the pyramids at Giza to the temples of the Aztecs. It is as if we earthlings, believers in the power of technology but weighed down by apparently insoluble human conflicts, yearn for some superior intelligence to decipher our little world and set it straight while there is still time.

Yet perhaps our yearning for enlightened interstellar visitors can be put to good use. We can imagine how superior intelligences, easily able to grasp our world and its complex history, would view the planet and its talented but quarrelsome human race. Surely interstellar observers would take a genuinely global perspective, free from our customary biases of creed and nation. If we try to do the same, perhaps we too can gain insight into our world's ongoing development.

From a global perspective, four questions might seem particularly important. How is the planet organized politically? How does the human race use its resources to meet its material needs? What key ideas guide its behavior? And, finally, is there hope for the planet's future?

WORLD POLITICS

Although many earthlings are deeply impressed by our recent scientific and technological achievements, highly advanced space travelers might well be less so. They might instead be astonished that accelerated technological achievement has not been matched by any corresponding change in the way the human race governs – or fails to govern – itself. Sovereign nation-states still reign supreme, as assertive and as competitive as ever, and now reinforced by ever-more-destructive weapons. The embryonic growth of an effective global political organization, of a government that could protect the world's nations from themselves, seems permanently arrested. The tension generated by powerful warlike states in a fragile and interdependent world is one of the most striking – and dangerous – characteristics of this small planet.

NATION-STATES AND THE UNITED NATIONS

The rise of the nation-state and the global triumph of nationalism has been a grand theme of modern world history. The independent territorial nation-state is clearly the fundamental principle of political organization in our times. Yet, from a global perspective we must surely question what we take for granted. Has the nation-state system, with its apparently inevitable conflicts, become a threat to life on the planet?

Some have thought so. It is one of history's ironies that nationalism has been widely condemned, especially in Europe, just as it has triumphed decisively in world politics. In *Mankind and Mother Earth* (1976), his last work, the renowned British historian Arnold Toynbee (1889–1975) poignantly expressed the post-1914 disillusionment of many European and American intellectuals. At the time of his birth, Toynbee wrote, his middle-class countrymen "supposed Earthly Paradise was just around the corner." They also assumed that the national state was "the natural, normal, rightful political unit."

Toynbee's generation of Europeans, however, lived through an era of "self-inflicted tribulation," war and genocide, largely due to their "explosive, subversive" faith in national self-determination. Toynbee borrowed a term from the ancient Greeks to explain that the spread of the western European political idea of the national state, first to eastern Europe and then to Asia and Africa, has created a fatal discrepancy —

the discrepancy between the political partition of the Oikoumenê [the habitat of the human race] into local sovereign states and the global unification of the Oikoumenê on the technological and economic planes. This misfit is the crux of mankind's present plight. Some form of global government is now needed for keeping the peace ... and for re-establishing the balance between Man and the rest of the biosphere.[1]

Similar views prevail among a small but articulate group of intellectuals and political scientists. Thus we should probably take the "unrealistic" question of world government seriously. Let us look more closely than usual at the United Nations for signs of the emergence of a global authority transcending sovereign states.

When the United Nations was founded in San Francisco in 1945, the United States was the driving force behind its creation. President Roosevelt and Democrats in the Wilsonian tradition believed that the failure of the United States to join the League of Nations had contributed tragically to the breakdown of "collective security" in the 1930s. A resurrected League would, they believed, facilitate Allied cooperation in the postwar era.

It was to be the prime purpose of the new organization "to maintain international peace and security." Primary responsibility for this awesome task was assigned to the twelve-nation Security Council. According to the U.N. charter, the Security Council had the authority to examine any international conflict, impose economic and political penalties on an aggressor, and even "take such action by air, sea, or land forces as may be necessary to restore international peace and security." In short, the Security Council had the power to police the world.

Yet this theoretical power was severely restricted in practice. China, Great Britain, France, the Soviet Union, and the United States were all made permanent members of the Security Council, and all five had to agree on any peacekeeping action. The veto power of the Big Five has been subsequently criticized for preventing the United Nations from ever regulating its most powerful members. But that was precisely the point: none of the Big Five, and certainly not the United States, was willing to surrender sovereign power to a potential world government.

Indeed, the United Nations has affirmed and reinforced the primacy of the national state in world politics. The charter directed the United Nations to pursue "friendly relations between nations based on the principle of equal rights and self-determination of peoples." Every "peace-loving" state was eligible to join and to participate in the General Assembly, the U.N.'s other main body; the General Assembly now has 153 members. Each state, whatever its size, has one voice and one vote on all resolutions. However, such resolutions become binding on states only if they are endorsed by all five of the Security Council's permanent members. The General Assembly is a world debating society, not a law-making body.

The third express purpose of the United Nations testifies to the expanded scope of governmental tasks since the late nineteenth century, as well as to global interdependence. According to its charter, the United Nations

UNITED NATIONS PEACEKEEPING FORCE IN CY-
PRUS *Men and women of the Swedish Infantry
Batallion in Cyprus move out on a military exercise in
1980. The eight-nation U.N. force in Cyprus was cre-*
*ated by the U.N. Security Council in 1964, in an at-
tempt to prevent fighting between the Greek and Turkish communities of the island republic. (United Na-
tions/ J. K. Isaac)*

is "to achieve international cooperation in solving international problems of an economic, social, cultural, or humanitarian character, and in promoting and encouraging respect for human rights and for fundamental freedom for all without distinction as to race, sex, language, or religion." This open-ended assignment is the province of a Social and Economic Council whose eighteen members are elected periodically by the General Assembly. The Council also works with such specialized affiliated agencies as the World Health Organization in Geneva and the Food and Agriculture Organization in Rome.

The scope of its original purposes helps explain the United Nations' evolution. Fond hopes of effective Allied cooperation in the Security Council soon faded as Cold War rheto-

ric and vetoes by the badly outnumbered Soviet Union began to paralyze that body. The Security Council proved somewhat more successful at quieting bloody conflicts between smaller states where the interests of the superpowers were not directly involved, such as the dispute between India and Pakistan over Kashmir, and that between Greece and Turkey over Cyprus. In 1960, it even sent military forces to re-establish order in the former Belgian Congo. This ambitious undertaking, criticized from all sides, marked the high point of Security Council peacekeeping.

With the Security Council often deadlocked, the rapidly changing General Assembly claimed ever greater authority. As decolonization picked up speed and the number of member states more than doubled, a non-aligned anti-colonial "Afro-Asian bloc" emerged. Reinforced by sympathetic Latin American countries, the bloc succeeded in organizing a coherent "Third World majority" in the General Assembly by the mid-1960s. This majority concentrated on economic and social issues, passing many fiery and fine-sounding resolutions, often directed against the former colonial powers, the United States, Israel, imperialist Portugal, and racist South Africa.

One should be cautious in drawing conclusions about the future from recent developments at the United Nations. The "Third World majority," predominantly composed of small and poor countries, clearly mistook the illusion of power at the United Nations for the substance of power in world affairs. By the 1970s, many of its resolutions were simply ignored. Meanwhile, critical international issues such as the Arab-Israeli conflict were increasingly resolved by resort to traditional diplomacy or war.

Nor did the United Nations generate much popular support around the world. Most people continued to identify with their national states, which may even provide adults with a psychological substitute for the family bonds that nurtured them in childhood. Thus nation-states continue to weave the powerful social bonds necessary for group action. As two American political scientists put it, "The nation-state may all too seldom speak the voice of reason. But it remains the only serious alternative to chaos."[2]

And yet the United Nations has also proved to be a remarkably hardy institution. It seems to be here to stay. Particularly significant is the Third World majority's successful expansion of the scope of its economic, social, and cultural mission. By the early 1980s, an alphabet soup of U.N. committees, specialized agencies, and affiliated international organiza-

tions were studying and promoting health, labor, agriculture, industrial development, and world trade, not to mention disarmament, control of narcotics, and preservation of the great whales. These U.N. agencies and affiliated organizations derived their initial authority from treaties and agreements between sovereign states, but once in operation they took on a life of their own.

Staffed by a growing international bureaucracy, U.N. agencies worked skillfully and tenaciously to consolidate their power and to serve their main constituency, the Third World majority. Without directly challenging national sovereignty, they exerted a steady pressure for more "international cooperation" in dealing with specific global issues. Partly because there were few alternatives, the world's nations sometimes went along. Thus sharp-eyed observers detected a gradual, many-sided enlargement of U.N. involvement in planetary affairs. It is not impossible that early steps toward some kind of world government are being taken.

COMPLEXITY AND VIOLENCE

In between territorial nation-states and international organizations that concentrate on specific problems there stretches a vast middle ground of alliances, blocs, partnerships, and ongoing conflicts and rivalries. It is difficult to make sense of this tangle of associations, and by the early 1980s some observers feared that the precarious world order was simply disintegrating.

One thing is clear: East-West competition is still very much alive. The mutual hostility of the two bloc leaders, the United States and the Soviet Union, had again reached Cold War intensity by the early 1980s. Many Americans were convinced that the Soviet Union

LEARNING ABOUT NUTRITION *The United Nations expert in the center is showing women with hospitalized children in Mali how to prepare meals providing maximum nourishment. (United Nations/Ray Witlin)*

had taken unfair advantage of the Nixon-Kissinger policy of détente – relaxation of tension between the two countries – in the 1970s, steadily building up its military might and pushing for gains in the Third World. Soviet actions appeared particularly menacing in the oil-rich Middle East. Having been expelled from Egypt by Anwar Sadat after the 1973 war with Israel, the Soviets sought and won toeholds in South Yemen, Somalia, and later Ethiopia. Having supported guerrilla wars against the Portuguese in Angola and Mozambique, the Soviet Union was rewarded with Marxist regimes in both countries. The spectacular 1975 airlift of 20,000 Cubans to Angola to help the new Marxist government consolidate its power rattled American nerves.

But it was in Afghanistan that Soviet actions seemed to confirm Americans' worst fears. The Soviet Union had long been interested in its Islamic neighbor (page 1265) and in April 1978 a pro-Soviet coup established a Marxist regime there. This new government soon made itself unpopular, and rebellion spread through the countryside. To preserve Communist rule, the Soviet Union in December 1979 suddenly airlifted crack troops to Kabul, the capital, and occupied Afghanistan with 100,000 men. Alarmed by the scale and precision of the Soviet invasion, many Americans feared that the Persian Gulf would be next. In response, the United States launched the largest peacetime military build-up in its history.

Even so, it was clear that neither bloc was as solid as it had been a generation earlier. China had long since broken with the Soviet Union and become an independent regional power. Poland tried to follow suit in 1980–1981; its attempt failed, but demonstrated that there are real tensions within the Warsaw Pact and COMECON, the military and economic arms of the East bloc. As for the West, serious differences on military matters surfaced within NATO (which France had long since quit), and economic quarrels recurred between the Common Market and the United States. Both bloc superpowers were apparently being restrained by their allies.

The epic struggle for political independence in Africa and Asia continued, but became a secondary issue. Black Africa pressures South Africa to give independence to Namibia, conquered by imperial Germany almost a century earlier and entrusted to South Africa as a League of Nations mandate after the First World War. Since practically all of Africa and

Asia has already won independence, that political theme has given way to a new concentration on economic relations between North and South.

One of the most striking global developments of the present era is the increasingly "multipolar" nature of world politics. Regional conflict and a fluid, complicated jockeying for regional influence are the keynotes. While the two superpowers were working to control their allies and competing for global power and influence, a number of increasingly assertive "middle powers" were arising around the world. These middle powers strove to be capable of leading or dominating their neighbors and of standing up to the world's superpowers on regional questions. The rise of middle powers reflects the fact that most of the world's countries are small and weak, with fewer than 20 million people. Only a few have the large populations, natural resources, and industrial base necessary for real power on a regional or global scale.

Striking examples are to be found in the Americas. Brazil, with more than 100 million people, vast territory and resources and one of the world's more rapidly industrializing economies, has rather suddenly emerged as South America's dominant nation-state despite recent economic difficulties. Even more striking has been the rapid rise of Mexico, with its population of over 74 million, its substantial industrial base, oil wealth, and proud nationalism. Although the world recession of the early 1980s hit hard, Mexico clearly sees itself as the natural leader of the Spanish-speaking Americas, and is openly challenging the United States for influence in the tiny states of Central America.

Strong regional powers like France and West Germany re-emerged in western Europe by the early 1960s, and in Africa and Asia a decade later. Resurgent Nigeria is unques-tionably the leading power in sub-Saharan Africa; heavily populated Egypt and much smaller Israel are regional powerhouses. Iran sought under the Shah to dominate the Persian Gulf, and it has continued to do so after the Iranian revolution, defending itself successfully in a bitter war with Iraq and challenging the conservative oligarchy in Saudi Arabia. China, India, and Japan are all regional powers; several other Asian countries, notably Indonesia, Vietnam, Pakistan, and the Philippines are determined to join them.

A high degree of competition and violent conflict characterizes the emerging multipolar political system. Conflict in the Americas and Europe has been mainly verbal, but in Africa and Asia blood has flowed freely. Of the 145 wars that have occurred worldwide between 1945 and 1979, 117 have been in the Third World. Like Germany in the Thirty Years War, some countries have been literally torn apart. Lebanon, long considered the most advanced state in the Arab world, has been practically destroyed by endless war and foreign occupation. Cambodia, invaded by American armies in 1970, then ravaged by the ultra-savage Pol Pot regime and finally occupied by Vietnamese armies, is another tragedy.

A new plague of local wars and civil conflicts has caused great suffering. Millions of refugees, like Vietnam's "boat people," fled for their lives. The war for independence in Bangladesh temporarily created over 10 million refugees, who fled into India toward Calcutta. Hungry, homeless people overwhelmed the Indian relief centers, sleeping in trees, huddling in the rain, starving to death. After the Soviet invasion of Afghanistan, fully *one-tenth* of that country's population – 1.7 million people fled. In early 1981, the United Nations commission for emergency relief counted 10 million refugees in Asia and Africa.

One of the worst refugee problems resulted from a savage war on the strategic Horn of Africa, a war that exemplifies the tragic dimensions of regional competition and violence. Both Somalia and Ethiopia – two of the world's poorest countries – had established radical pro-Soviet governments by 1977. But, predictably, nationalism was stronger than Marxist ideology: the Somalis wanted to incorporate fellow tribesmen living in Ethiopia's Ogaden region. Somalia and guerrilla armies in the Ogaden fought for four long years, but Ethiopia eventually turned the tide with Soviet arms and Cuban troops. As a result, 1.5 million refugees fled the Ogaden for Somalia, which only had 4.5 million people. The refugees, mainly women and children, lived in mass camps while their menfolk continued hit-and-run attacks in the Ogaden. Defeated and impoverished Somalia, fearing further war, opened its ports to United States naval forces in return for economic aid. Thus the new regional battles spill over into the old East-West conflict as small countries look to the contending superpowers for arms and support.

THE ARMS RACE AND NUCLEAR PROLIFERATION

Regional competition and local hot wars brought military questions once again to the forefront of world attention. The ever-rising number of military governments testifies not only to a widespread willingness to use force to crush internal opposition and maintain national unity, but also to the renewed importance of war in international relations.

Indeed, nearly every country in the world is participating in the ever-intensifying arms race. In garrison states like Israel, South Africa, and Vietnam, defense expenditures have assumed truly fantastic proportions. Uni-

fied Vietnam, having defeated the Americans and fought the Chinese to a standstill, has emerged as a modern-day Prussia or Sparta. Vietnam spends half its income on the military; its standing army of a million men is the world's third largest, after Russia and China, and one of the best. Little Vietnam, with its population of 54 million, will be a major Asian power for the foreseeable future. In both India and Brazil, there is a widespread belief that heavy defense spending is a key to economic development.

By far the most ominous aspect of the global arms race is the threat of nuclear proliferation. For a generation, nuclear weapons were concentrated in the hands of the two superpowers, who learned a grudging respect for each other. Lately, however, nuclear weapons have begun to spread, perhaps like wildfire. Some experts believe that as many as twenty countries may have their own atomic bombs in a few brief years. How has this frightening situation arisen?

Having let the atomic genie out of the bottle at Hiroshima and Nagasaki in 1945, a deeply troubled United States immediately proposed that it be recaptured through effective international control of all atomic weapons. As American representative Bernard Baruch told the first meeting of the United Nations Atomic Energy Commission in 1946:

We are here to make a choice between the quick and the dead. . . . We must elect World Peace or World Destruction. . . . [Therefore] the United States proposes the creation of an International Atomic Development Authority, to which should be entrusted all phases of the development and use of atomic energy. . . .

The Soviets, suspicious that the United States was really trying to preserve its atomic monopoly through its proposal for international control and inspection, rejected the

BOMBARDING BEIRUT, JULY 1982 War and violence regularly shake the Middle East. Here Israeli gunners shell the center of West Beirut, a possible refuge for Palestinian units. Two months later Israeli tanks and troops occupied the entire city after fierce battles with Palestinians and Muslim militia-men. (Magnum/Leonard Freed)

American idea and continued their crash program to catch up with the United States. The Soviet Union exploded its first atomic bomb in 1949. As the Cold War raged on in the 1950s, the two superpowers pressed forward with nuclear development. The United States exploded its first hydrogen bomb in 1952; within ten months the Soviet Union did the same. Further American, Soviet, and then British tests aroused intense worldwide concern about nuclear fallout. There was well-founded fear that radioactive fallout entering the food chain would cause leukemia, bone cancer, and genetic damage. Concerned scientists called for an international agreement to stop all testing of atomic bombs. Partly in response to worldwide public pressure, the United States, the Soviet Union, and Great

Britain agreed in 1958 to stop testing for three years. In 1963 these three powers signed an agreement, later signed by more than one hundred countries, banning nuclear tests in the atmosphere. A second step toward control was the 1968 Treaty on the Non-Proliferation of Nuclear Weapons, designed to halt their spread to other states. To optimists, it seemed that the nuclear arms race might yet be reversed.

Unfortunately, this has not come to pass. France and China, seeing themselves as great world powers, simply disregarded the test ban and refused to sign the non-proliferation treaty. By 1968, they too had hydrogen bombs. In 1974, India exploded an atomic device, reversing its previous commitment to nuclear arms limitations.

India's reversal was partly due to the failure of the Soviet Union and the United States to abide by the terms of the 1968 treaty on nuclear non-proliferation. According to the terms of the treaty, the nuclear powers agreed "to pursue negotiations in good faith on effective measures relating to cessation of the nuclear arms race at an early date and to nuclear disarmament, and on a treaty on general and complete disarmament under strict and effective international control." The non-nuclear states, which had seen serious efforts at disarmament by the superpowers as their payoff for promising not to go nuclear, had offered a whole series of proposals ranging from a complete test ban to a freeze or reduction on nuclear weapons before agreeing to sign the treaty.

In fact, the nuclear arms race between the Soviet Union and the United States surged ahead. According to American officials, the United States was capable in 1974 of dropping 36 bombs on each of the 218 Soviet cities with populations of 100,000 or more. The Soviet Union had 11 nuclear weapons for each American city of comparable size. The much-discussed SALT talks confined themselves to limiting the *rate* at which the Soviet Union and the United States produced more nuclear warheads. By 1980, when the second Strategic Arms Limitation Treaty failed to be ratified by the United States Senate, the superpowers appeared once again to be locked into a nuclear arms race.

Partly out of fear for their own security, many near-nuclear powers appeared poised to "go nuclear" in the early 1980s. The worldwide energy crisis of the 1970s had played a part: peaceful use of the atom to generate electric power had created as a by-product large quantities of plutonium, the raw material for bombs. Ominously, some countries were beginning to regard nuclear bombs as just an-

other weapon in the struggle for power and survival.

India, for instance, developed its atomic capability out of fear of China, which had manhandled India in a savage border war in 1962. India's nuclear blast in 1974 in turn frightened Pakistan, which has regarded India as a bitter enemy since 1947 and lost Bangladesh because of Indian armies. Pakistan's President Bhutto is reported to have said that Pakistan must have the bomb even if its people have to eat grass. By 1981, Pakistan was very close to producing nuclear weapons. It is also widely believed that both Israel and South Africa have arsenals of nuclear bombs. Israel's apparent nuclear superiority is of course profoundly distasteful to the Arabs. Hence Iraq has recently pushed hard, with help from France, to develop nuclear capability. When Israel suddenly attacked, destroying the Iraqi nuclear reactor, in June 1981, the dangers of nuclear proliferation were driven home to all.

If there are twenty or thirty nuclear powers by 1990, as some have predicted, and if regional conflicts remain so intense, will not some nation use the dreadful weapons sooner or later? And if so, is there not a danger that such a nuclear war would spread to the superpowers? And what about nuclear terrorism and blackmail? In a world full of nuclear weapons and nuclear potential, might desperate political groups, like the most radical elements of the Palestine Liberation Organization and the Irish Republican Army, steal bombs and threaten to use them? Mere airplane hijackings might seem like the good old days. And if the gap between rich and poor nations continues to widen, might not desperate states, or even regions, resort to nuclear blackmail to gain their demands? None of these ominous possibilities has yet come to pass in the early 1980s, but in a world of bitter national rivalries they make the hardheaded observer grimly apprehensive. Is the human race, as one scholar warns, "an endangered species"?[3]

GLOBAL INTERDEPENDENCE

Alongside political competition and the arms race, a contradictory phenomenon was unfolding: the nations of our small world were becoming increasingly interdependent economically and technologically. Even the great continental states with the largest land masses and populations and the richest natural resources cannot depend only on themselves. The United States requires foreign oil and the Soviet Union needs foreign grain. All countries and peoples have need of each other.

Mutual dependence in economic affairs could be interpreted as a hopeful sign for the human race. Dependence promotes peaceful cooperation and limits the scope of violence. Yet it is also clear that the existing framework of global interdependence is under attack. The poor countries of the South – the Third World – charge that the North receives far more than its rightful share from existing economic relationships. The South is demanding a new international economic order. Questions are also being raised about the role of huge, technically advanced global business enterprises – the so-called multinationals – in world development.

PRESSURE ON VITAL RESOURCES

During the postwar economic boom, which lasted until the early 1970s, the nations of the world were becoming ever more dependent on each other for vital resources. Yet resources seemed abundant, and rapid industrialization was a worldwide article of faith.

COPING WITH DISASTER   In 1979 more than half a million Cambodians were camped along the Thai-Kampuchean border. Only a massive international relief effort prevented mass starvation. (United Nations/Saw Livin)

Only those alarmed by the population explosion predicted grave shortages, and they spoke almost exclusively about food shortages in the Third World.

The situation changed suddenly in the early 1970s. Fear that the world was running out of resources was widely voiced. In a famous study aptly titled *The Limits to Growth* (1972), a group of American and European scholars argued that unlimited growth is impossible on a finite planet. By the early twenty-first century, they predicted, the ever-increasing demands of too many people and factories would exhaust the world's mineral resources and destroy the fragile biosphere with pollution.

Meanwhile Japan was importing 99 percent of its petroleum, western Europe 96 percent. When the Arab-dominated Organization of Petroleum Exporting Countries (OPEC) increased the price of crude oil *fourfold* in a single year, 1973 (page 1382), there was panic in many industrial countries. Rich countries had come to depend on the poor countries for oil and other vital mineral resources, even as poor countries had long been dependent on rich ones for capital and technology.

In much of the Third World, the pressure to grow more food for more people has led to piecemeal destruction of forests and increased soil erosion. Much of the Third World suffers from what has been called "the other energy crisis" — severe lack of firewood for cooking and heat.

A striking case is the southern edge of the Sahara desert. Population growth caused the hard-pressed peoples of this region to overgraze the land and denude the forests. As a result, the sterile sand of the Sahara has been advancing southward as much as thirty miles a year along a 3000-mile front. When famine strikes, as it has, food must be imported from North America, Australia, Argentina, the only nations that produce substantially more food than they consume.

Interdependence is also reinforced by our worldwide dependence on the air and the sea. Just as radioactive fallout has no respect for national boundaries, so pollution may sully the whole globe. Unfortunately,

the more conscious we become of various ecological stresses unfolding before us, the more we realize how little we know about the natural system and resources on which our existence depends. The frontiers of ignorance are expanding rapidly. We know little about the consequences of our actions.[4]

Deadly chemicals, including mercury, lead, and arsenic, are accumulating in the biosphere. Some fear that pollution of the oceans is leading to the contamination of its fish, one of the world's main sources of protein. Others, worried that the oceans have been overfished, fear that the significant decline in worldwide fish catch in the 1970s indicates abuse of the sea, the common heritage of mankind.

Of all the long-term pressures on resources, the growth of population is the most serious. The early 1980s, however, offer some room for cautious optimism. Population growth in the developed countries has slowed markedly or even stopped. And, of much greater importance from a global perspective, the world's poor women are beginning to bear fewer children. Small countries like Barbados, Chile, Costa Rica, South Korea, Taiwan, Tunisia, and the British colony of Hong Kong have led the way. Between 1970 and 1975, China had history's fastest five-year decline in the birth rate, from 32 births per thousand people to only 19 births per thousand.

There are several reasons why the birthrate is beginning to decline in many Third World countries. Fewer babies were dying of disease or malnutrition, which meant that fewer births were necessary to guarantee surviving children. As had happened earlier in the wealthy, industrialized nations (page 1466), better living conditions, urbanization, and more education all encouraged women to have fewer children. State-run birth control programs proved successful in some countries, particularly China. The Pill, borrowed from the West but manufactured locally, was widely used in conjunction with heavy financial penalties for those couples exceeding the birth quota, increasingly fixed at one child per couple. As in most communist countries, abortion was free and on demand.

Elsewhere – in Africa, the Muslim world, and North and South America – contraception remained very controversial in the 1970s. In North America and Europe too, heated debate on abortion was fueled by religious and feminist arguments, and secondarily by constitutional and legal issues.

Indira Gandhi's fiasco with compulsory sterilization (page 1418) suggests that, barring catastrophe, worldwide population growth will decline only gradually, as a result of billions of private decisions supplemented by government policies. This means that world population will continue to grow for a long time, as the Third World's current huge population of children form their own families. Thus the world's population – 4 billion in 1975 – will probably not stabilize until the mid-twenty-first century, when it will have reached 10 to 12 billion people. Such continued growth will put tremendous pressure on global resources.

Yet gloom is not the only possible perspective. Even with 11 billion people, the earth would be less densely populated than Europe is today, and only one fourth as densely populated as small prosperous countries like Belgium and the Netherlands, which largely feed themselves. Such countries, often overlooked in world politics, are promising models for life on a crowded planet. Moreover, the human race has exhibited considerable skill throughout its history at finding new resources and inventing new technologies. A striking example was the way that conservation, alternative energy sources, and world recession in the early 1980s at least temporarily belied gloomy prophecies about dwindling energy resources. An optimist could conclude that, at least from a quantitative and technical point of view, the adequacy of resources was a serious but by no means a completely insoluble problem.

The real key to adequate resources is probably global cooperation. Will the world's peoples work together, or will they eventually fight over resources like wild dogs over meat?

Since the late 1960s there has been dissatisfaction in Asia, Africa, and Latin America not only with the fruits of their industrialization drive but also with the world's economic system. Scholars imbued with a Third World perspective and spokesmen for the United Nations majority have declared the international system to be unjust and in need of radical change.

A brilliant Pakistani, World Bank official and member of the international bureaucratic elite, has sympathetically articulated this position:

The vastly unequal relationship between the rich and the poor nations is fast becoming the central issue of our time. The poor nations are beginning to question the basic premises of an international order which leads to ever-widening disparities between the rich and the poor countries and to a persistent denial of equality of opportunity to many poor nations. They are, in fact, arguing that in international order – just as much as within national orders – all distribution of benefits, credit, services, and decision-making becomes warped in favor of a privileged minority and that this situation cannot be changed except through fundamental institutional reforms.[5]

The subsequent Third World demand for a "new international economic order" had many causes, both distant and immediate. Critics of imperialism like J. A. Hobson (page 1155) and Third World writers on decolonization like Franz Fanon (page 1503) had long charged that the colonial powers grew rich exploiting Asia, Africa, and Latin America.

NORTH-SOUTH DIALOGUE *In late 1981 heads of state from leading nations around the world met in Cancun, Mexico, to discuss economic issues and common problems. There was little real agreement, but the* conference *was a striking example of ongoing global negotiations. How many leaders can you identify? (The White House/Michael Evans)*

Beginning in the 1950s, a number of writers, many of them Latin American Marxists, breathed new life into these ideas with their "theory of dependency." The poverty and so-called "underdevelopment" of the South, they argued, was not the starting point but the deliberate and permanent result of exploitation by the capitalist industrialized nations in the modern era. Third World countries produced cheap raw materials for wealthy industrialized countries, and were conditioned to buy their expensive manufactured goods. The prevailing economic interdependence was the unequal, unjust interdependence of dominant and subordinate, of master and peon. Declining economic aid, smug pronouncements about the overpopulation of the Third World, and the natural resentment of the poor toward the rich also fostered calls for radical restructuring of the international order.

It was the fabulously successful OPEC oil coup of 1973–1974 that ignited Third World hopes of actually achieving a new system of economic interdependence. OPEC, formed by the oil-producing nations in 1960 to acquire effective control of their oil reserves and the international oil companies that had developed them, suddenly quadrupled the price of oil. A barrel of oil that cost perhaps 20 cents to produce skyrocketed to more than $10 within a few months. The result was a massive global transfer of wealth unprecedented since the looting of Mexico and Peru by the Spanish conquistadors. Perhaps 2 percent of all the income of the rich nations was suddenly forwarded to the OPEC countries.

The Third World was euphoric. For years the developed countries had gradually reduced their economic aid. They had never seriously tried to meet the goal suggested by the U. N.

General Assembly of earmarking 1 percent of their income each year for foreign aid. In 1974, a special session of the General Assembly rammed through two radical landmark resolutions calling for the "Establishment of a New International Economic Order" and a "Program of Action" to attain it.

Among the specific demands were firm control by each country of its own natural resources, higher and more stable prices for raw materials, and equal tariff treatment for manufacturing goods from the Third World. These demands were subject to "collective bargaining," but the Third World vigorously insisted on new terms. As one sympathetic scholar observed:

There has taken place a unionization of the Third World that has marked a profound shift in international relations. It looks as if the confrontation between unions and employers that stirred capitalist societies in the nineteenth century is being reenacted, but this time on a world scale between developed and developing nations. The question this time is whether the new nations command as many assets and opportunities as did the laboring classes of capitalist nations.[6]

By the early 1980s, that profound question remains unanswered. The developing countries have negotiated some victories, notably a Common Fund under U.N. auspices to support the prices of raw materials and a limited scaling-down of their enormous debts to the industrial nations. But the North, deeply troubled by inflation and its own economic problems, is clearly a tough bargainer when it comes to basic changes.

For example, in the late 1970s, the South laid great hopes on a long, complicated conference to formulate a new Law of the Sea. The new law was to be based on the principle that the world's oceans are "a common heritage of mankind," and should be exploited only for the benefit of all nations. In practice, this was to mean that a U.N.-sponsored authority would regulate and tax use of the sea, and a global "enterprise" would even mine it. Some countries and business firms were reluctant to accept such an infringement of their economic sovereignty and scope of action. The United States withdrew from the negotiations in 1981, and in 1982 the Reagan administration and several other developed nations refused to sign the final draft of the new Law of the Sea.

Frustrated in their desire to fashion a new international economic order quickly, some Third World leaders predicted more confrontation and perhaps military conflict between North and South. Some alarmists predict that the northern industrial nations will eventually find themselves locked in a life-and-death struggle with the poor countries of Africa, Asia, and Latin America.

In considering these ominous predictions, an impartial observer is initially struck by the great gap between the richest and poorest nations. Yet closer examination hardly reveals two sharply defined economic camps, a "North" and a "South." On the contrary, there are several distinct classes of nations in terms of wealth and income, as may be seen in Map 41.1. The communist countries of eastern Europe form something of a middle-income group, as do the major oil-exporting states, which still lag behind the wealthier countries of western Europe and North America. Latin America is much better off than sub-Saharan Africa, having a number of middle-range countries to match their counterparts in highly diverse Asia.

When one adds global differences in culture, religion, politics, and historical development, the supposed clear-cut split between the rich North and the poor South breaks down further. Moreover, the solidarity of the Third

World is very fragile, resting largely on the ideological constructs of some Third World intellectuals and their supporters. As one writer put it, "in the advocacy of growth and equalization at the international level ... Third World states have astonished everybody, their enemies and their friends alike, for no one has ever believed that such a diverse congress of countries, separated by geography, geopolitics, cultural traditions, size, ideology, and a host of other factors, could ever manage to build a cohesive alliance."[7] Moreover, the success of the oil cartel has proved impossible to duplicate with less vital raw materials and more complicated issues. And the greatest differences in wealth are actually *within* many Third World countries, as we have seen (pages 1497–1499).

Thus continuing global collective bargaining seems more likely than international class (and race) war. The poorer nations will press to reduce international economic differences through taxation and welfare measures. And because global interdependence is a reality, they will gradually win concessions, as has already occurred domestically for the working classes in the wealthy nations.

The international debt crisis suggests that this is already occurring. The world economy, recovering in 1977–1978, was plunged back into severe recession by another great leap in oil prices in 1979 due to the Iranian Revolution. Growing unemployment, unbalanced budgets, and large trade deficits encouraged many Third World countries to borrow rapidly from the wealthy industrialized nations. By the middle of 1982, Third World nations – led by Mexico, Brazil, and Argentina – owed foreign banks and governments about $600 billion. Moreover, much of this staggering debt was short-term and could not possibly be repaid as it fell due.

When Mexico closed its foreign exchange markets in August 1982, unable to keep up

MAP 41.1 ESTIMATED WORLD PER CAPITA INCOME IN 1979 (*Larger Countries*)

with the payments on $80 billion of foreign debts, default and financial chaos in Mexico seemed at hand. Yet the Reagan administration, although unresponsive to Third World calls for a new international system, quickly organized a gigantic rescue operation to pump new money into Mexico and prevent default. The reason was simple: Mexico's failure to service its foreign debt would cripple or even bankrupt some of the large American banks that had lent it money. Such a failure could touch off such massive debt repudiations in the Third World and corporate losses in the industrialized countries that the whole world would be plunged into depression and even social turmoil. Thus a series of negotiations is proceeding all over the globe to reduce Third World debts, stretch out repayments far into the future, and grant desperately needed new loans. Lenders and borrowers, rich and poor, North and South are bound together in mutual dependence by the international debt crisis.

THE MULTINATIONAL CORPORATIONS

One of the most striking features of global economic interdependence has been the rapid emergence of multinational corporations in recent years. Multinationals are business firms that operate in a number of different countries and tend to adopt a global rather than national perspective. Multinational corporations are not new; the size, daring, and pervasiveness of their operations are. By 1971, the ten largest multinational corporations – the IBMs, the Royal Dutch Shell Petroleums, the General Motors – each sold more than $3 billion worth of goods annually, more than the total national incomes of four-fifths of the

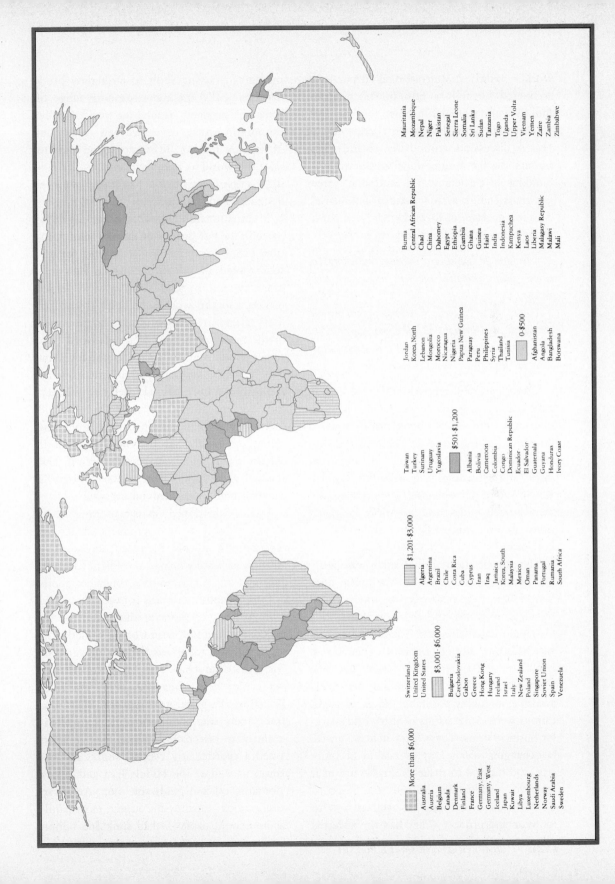

More than $6,000

Australia
Austria
Belgium
Canada
Denmark
Finland
France
Germany, East
Germany, West
Iceland
Japan
Kuwait
Luxembourg
Netherlands
Norway
Saudi Arabia
Sweden
Switzerland
United Kingdom
United States

$3,001- $6,000

Bulgaria
Czechoslovakia
Gabon
Greece
Hong Kong
Hungary
Ireland
Israel
Italy
New Zealand
Poland
Singapore
Soviet Union
Spain
Venezuela

$1,201-$3,000

Algeria
Argentina
Brazil
Chile
Costa Rica
Cuba
Cyprus
Iran
Iraq
Jamaica
Korea, South
Malaysia
Mexico
Oman
Panama
Portugal
Rumania
South Africa

$501-$1,200

Albania
Bolivia
Cameroon
Colombia
Congo
Dominican Republic
Ecuador
El Salvador
Guatemala
Guyana
Honduras
Ivory Coast
Jordan
Korea, North
Lebanon
Mongolia
Morocco
Nicaragua
Nigeria
Papua New Guinea
Paraguay
Peru
Philippines
Syria
Thailand
Tunisia
Taiwan
Turkey
Surinam
Uruguay
Yugoslavia

0-$500

Afghanistan
Angola
Bangladesh
Botswana
Burma
Central African Republic
Chad
China
Dahomey
Egypt
Ethiopia
Gambia
Ghana
Guinea
Haiti
India
Indonesia
Kampuchea
Kenya
Laos
Liberia
Malagasy Republic
Malawi
Mali
Mauritania
Mozambique
Nepal
Niger
Pakistan
Senegal
Sierra Leone
Somalia
Sri Lanka
Sudan
Tanzania
Togo
Uganda
Upper Volta
Vietnam
Yemen
Zaire
Zambia
Zimbabwe

world's countries. Multinational corporations accounted for fully a fifth of the noncommunist world's annual income.

The multinationals aroused a great deal of heated discussion around the world. Supporters saw the multinational corporations as building an efficient world economic system and transcending narrow national boundaries. As a top manager of Royal Dutch Shell put it, the multinational corporation is:

a new form of social architecture, matching the world-girding potential inherent in modern technology....

In an age when modern technology has shrunk the world, and brought us all closer together, the multinational corporation and the nation state must get used to living with each other.[8]

Critics worried precisely that the nation state was getting the worst of the new arrangement. Provocative book titles portrayed "the Frightening Angels" holding "Sovereignty at Bay," while building "Invisible Empires" and extending their nefarious "Global Reach." As usual whenever a major development attracts widespread attention, exaggerations and absurd predictions abounded on both sides.

The rise of the multinationals was partly due to the general revival of capitalism after World War Two, relatively free international economic relations, and the worldwide drive for rapid industrialization. The multinationals also had three advantages, which they put to good use. First, whereas "pure" scientific knowledge unrelated to the military was freely available, its highly profitable industrial applications were in the hands of the world's largest business firms. These firms held advanced, fast-changing technology as a kind of property, and hurried to make profitable use of it wherever they could. Second, the multinationals knew how to sell, as well as how to innovate and produce. They had the advertis-

ing and marketing skills to push their products, especially the ever-expanding range of consumer products, around the world. Finally, the multinationals developed new techniques of decision making. Managers found ways to treat the world as one big market, coordinating complex activities across many political boundaries and profiting at every point.

Multinational industrial corporations originated in the last quarter of the nineteenth century. U.S. businessmen took the lead, for reasons rooted in the nature of the American economy and society. With a vast unified market and the world's highest standard of living after 1918, U.S. businessmen pioneered in the mass production of standardized consumer goods. Many of the most famous examples – such as kerosene (John D. Rockefeller and Standard Oil), sewing machines (Singer), and farm machinery (Cyrus McCormick and International Harvester) – date from the 1880s, and others like the cheap automobile (Henry Ford), the mass retailer (Sears), and standardized food (Coca-Cola, Wrigley's chewing gum) were thriving by 1914.

Having developed mass-marketing techniques as well as new products, American corporations quickly expanded abroad. The creation of wholly-owned subsidiaries to produce and sell American-style consumer goods in foreign lands continued between the world wars. With ever more products and the attractions of the European Common Market in the late 1950s, there was the mighty surge of "the American challenge" in Europe (page 1377). Nor were other parts of the world neglected by the giant American manufacturing firms: there was continued multinational investment in raw-material production in Latin America (particularly copper, sugar, and bananas) as well as the Middle East and Africa (primarily oil and gold). By 1967, American corporations – mainly the largest, most familiar household names – had sunk $60 billion into their foreign operations. (See Figure 41.1.)

A few European companies, notably the German chemical and electrical firms, also became multinationals before 1900. Others emerged in the twentieth century. By the 1970s these European multinationals were in hot pursuit. Some, like Volkswagen and Renault (through American Motors), pushed directly into the American heartland. Big Japanese firms like Sony also rushed to go multinational in the 1960s and 1970s. While American investment was heavily concentrated in Europe and Canada, Japanese firms turned primarily to Asia for raw materials and cheap, high-quality labor. By the 1970s Japanese subsidiaries in Taiwan, Thailand, Hong Kong, and Malaysia were pouring out a torrent of transistor radios, televisions, cameras, and pocket computers. Fearful of a growing protectionist reaction in their largest foreign market, the United States, where unemployed autoworkers symbolically demolished a Japanese automobile with sledgehammers in 1979, many Japanese firms followed Sony's example and began manufacturing in the United States. The emergence of European and Japanese multinational corporations alongside their American forerunners marked the coming of age of global business in an interdependent world.

The impact of multinational corporations has been heatedly debated, especially in Third World countries. From an economic point of view, the results have been mixed. Above all, the giant firms have established advanced technology; but such technology is expensive and not always appropriate for poor countries with widespread unemployment.

The social consequences have been more striking. In brief, the multinationals have helped spread the products and values of consumer society to the elites of the Third World. Thus they have helped to create is-

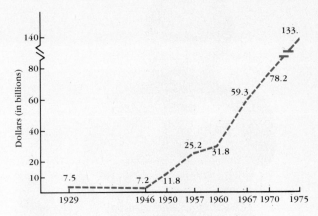

FIGURE 41.1   TOTAL INVESTMENT BY AMERICAN CORPORATIONS IN FOREIGN SUBSIDIARIES (*Source: U.S. Department of Commerce.* Survey of Current Business.)

lands of Western wealth, management, and consumer culture around the world. An advertisement for the Hilton international hotel chain catches the flavor of this social phenomenon:

After discussing the weather in hand-signal Amharic, bargaining in guide-book Turkish, and getting directions in dictionary Hebrew, it's nice to go back to a Hilton where everyone speaks your language and where holding a conference is as easy as at home.[9]

Global corporations have also used aggressive techniques of modern marketing to sell products that are not always well-suited to Third World conditions. For example, Third World mothers were urged to abandon "old-fashioned, primitive" breastfeeding (which was, ironically, making a strong comeback in rich countries) and to buy powdered-milk formulas for their babies. Yet, because mothers frequently used unsanitary bottles and contaminated water, and diluted the expensive formula to make it last longer, this "advance" tragically resulted in more infant deaths. On this and many other issues, the

SOLZHENITSYN SPEAKS   Like a prophet of old, the renowned Russian exile warns an audience at Harvard University to resist the evils of Soviet communism and Western spiritual decay. (Courtesy, Harvard University)

multinationals came into sharp conflict with host countries.

Far from helpless in such conflicts, poor countries have proved increasingly capable of exercising their sovereign rights over the past decade. Following earlier trends, many foreign mining companies, like the fabulously profitable U.S. oil companies in the Middle East, were simply nationalized. Even more importantly, Third World governments learned increasingly to make foreign manufacturing companies work within the framework of their plans and desires. Multinationals have had to share ownership with local investors, hire more local managers, provide technology on better terms, and accept a host of controls.

Moreover, governments have learned to play Americans, Europeans, and Japanese off against each other. Frustrated by such treatment, an American managing director in Malaysia pounded his desk and sputtered, "This little country and her little people need help, but they must be reasonable, otherwise we will get out of here." A Japanese manager in the same country expressed a more cooperative view: "We came here as guests, and our nation is small and needs natural resources, as well as foreign trade and investment to survive."[10] Global economic interdependence is growing, but the era when the multinational corporations "laid down the law" has passed, if it ever really existed.

PATTERNS OF THOUGHT

The renowned economist John Maynard Keynes often said that we live by our ideas and by very little else. True or not, a global perspective surely requires keen attention to patterns of collective thinking. As Keynes saw, we need to be aware of the ideas that are shaping the uncertain destiny of this small, politically fragmented, economically interdependent planet.

To be sure, human thought can be baffling in its rich profusion. Nevertheless, we can identify three distinct patterns on a global scale: the enduring strength of the modern world's secular ideologies; a vigorous revival of the world's great religions; and a search for mystical experience. The human race lives by these ideas.

SECULAR IDEOLOGIES

We have said a good deal in this book about the modern world's great secular ideologies. Almost all of these bodies of ideas, including liberalism, nationalism, and Marxian socialism as well as faith in scientific and technical progress, industrialism and democratic republicanism, took form in Europe between the eighteenth-century Enlightenment and the Revolutions of 1848. These ideologies continued to evolve with the coming of mass society in the late nineteenth century, and were carried by imperialism to the highly diverse societies of Asia and Africa. There they won converts among the local elites, who eventually conquered their imperialist masters in the twentieth century. European ideologies became worldwide ideologies, gradually outgrowing their early, specifically European character.

All this could be seen as an aspect of global interdependence. The world has come to live, in part, by shared ideas. These ideas have continued to develop in a complex global dialogue, and champions of competing views now arise from all regions. This has certainly been true of nationalist ideology, and also of Marxism. Europe, the birthplace of Marxism, has made few original intellectual contributions to Marxism since Stalin transformed it into a totalitarian ideology of forced industrialization. Since 1945, it has been Marxists from the Third World who have injected new meanings into the old ideology, notably Mao's brand of peasant-based revolution and the Marxist theory of Third World dependency (page 1407). Leftist intellectuals in Europe cheered and said "me too."

It is primarily as critics that Europeans have contributed to world Marxism. Yugoslavs have been particularly influential. After breaking with Stalin in 1948, they revived and expanded the ideas of Stalin's vanquished rival Leon Trotsky (page 1330). Trotsky had claimed that Stalin perverted socialism by introducing "state capitalism" and reactionary bureaucratic dictatorship. According to the influential Yugoslav Milovan Djilas (b. 1911)

Lenin's dedicated elite of full-time revolutionaries became Stalin's ruthless bureaucrats, "a new class" unprecedented in history. Djilas's powerful impact stemmed from his mastery of the Marxian dialectic:

The social origin of the new class lies in the proletariat just as the aristocracy arose in peasant society, and the bourgeoisie in a commercial and artisans' society. . . .

Former sons of the working class are the most steadfast members of the new class. It has always been the fate of slaves to provide for their masters the most clever and gifted representatives. In this case a new exploiting and governing class is born from the exploited class. . . .

The communists are . . . a new class.

As in other owning classes, the proof that it is a special class lies in its ownership and in its special relations to other classes. In the same way, the class to which a member belongs is indicated by the material and other privileges which ownership brings him.

As defined by Roman law, property constitutes the use, enjoyment, and disposition of material goods. The communist political bureaucracy uses, enjoys, and disposes of nationalized property.[11]

Non-Marxian criticism of communism also continued to develop, as in Jean François Revel's provocative *The Totalitarian Temptation* (1977). According to Revel, the application of the Marxist-Leninist-Maoist model, which has been adopted by many countries not strictly belonging to the communist camp, brings about phony revolution. Under the guise of supposedly progressive socialism, it builds reactionary totalitarian states of the Stalinist variety.

Old-fashioned, long-battered liberalism and democracy, which people like Revel greatly prefer, has also survived as a global ideology. In every communist country small, persecuted "human rights movements" have bravely demanded the basic liberties first set into law in the American and French revolutions. And there are always a few African and Asian intellectuals, often in exile, calling for similar rights even in the most authoritarian states.

Of the bewildering array of alternatives to the dominant secular creeds, three seem particularly noteworthy. The physicist Andrei Sakharov (b. 1921), the father of the Russian atomic bomb, who in the 1960s became a fearless leader of the human rights movement in the Soviet Union, was an eloquent spokesman for what might be called the "convergence school." According to Sakharov, humanity's best hope lay in the accelerated convergence of liberal capitalism and dictatorial communism on some middle ground of welfare capitalism and democratic socialism, like that which flourishes so successfully in the small, close-knit societies of Scandinavia, Iceland, and New Zealand. This outlook waxes and wanes in influence. But it has deep historical roots in modern society, and does not die. Meanwhile internationalists like the historian Toynbee advocated some form of world government. Many internationalists are social scientists, who characteristically believe in theoretical abstractions and technical solutions to human problems.

Finally, there has been a many-sided global reaction to the dominant faith in industrialization, consumerism, and unrestrained "modernization." The disillusionment of the Third World was matched by open resistance in the developed countries. The student revolt of the 1960s, with its vague ideology of participation, coincided with widespread nostalgia for simple, close-knit rural societies. The great Russian novelist Solzhenitsyn, caught up in the vanishing-resources doctrine of the 1970s, called on Soviet leaders to renounce Western technology and return to the earth:

Herein lies Russia's hope for winning time and winning salvation: In our vast northeastern spaces,

which over four centuries our sluggishness has prevented us from mutilating by our mistakes, we can build anew: not the senseless, voracious civilization of "progress" – no; we can set up a stable economy without pain or delay and settle people there for the first time according to the needs and principles of that economy. These spaces allow us to hope that we shall not destroy Russia in the general crisis of Western civilization.[12]

Communes sprang up in the United States and Europe in the 1960s, and there were many advocates, like E. F. Schumacher in *Small is Beautiful* (1973), of alternative technologies – like solar-heated houses to conserve nonrenewable oil – and life styles. Africa and Asia increasingly stressed "appropriate technologies," tailored to village life rather than borrowed from large-scale urban industrialized society – such as small, rugged, three-wheeled mechanical carts suited to existing country lanes, rather than large trucks requiring expensive modern highways, elaborate maintenance facilities, and large amounts of imported fuel.

Perhaps the most striking aspect of the worldwide reappraisal of industrialization was the heretical revival of Jean-Jacques Rousseau's belief in the superiority of the simple, frugal "noble savage." As Robert Heilbroner poignantly put it in 1974, in his otherwise gloomy *Inquiry into the Human Prospect:*

One element [of hope] ... is our knowledge that some human societies have existed for millennia, and that others can probably exist for future millennia, in a continuous rhythm of birth and coming of age and death, without pressing toward those dangerous ecological limits, or engendering those dangerous social tensions, that threaten present-day "advanced" societies. In our discovery of "primitive" cultures, living out their timeless histories, we may have found the single most important object lesson for future man.[13]

POPE JOHN PAUL II *The man of peace and good will arriving in Warsaw in June 1983 for a second pilgrimage to his homeland, John Paul drew vast and enthusiastic crowds, demonstrating their opposition to* an oppressive system as well as their deep-rooted Christian faith. (Gamma/Jean-Claude Francolon/ Alain Mingam/Chip Hires/François Lochan)

RELIGIOUS BELIEF: CHRISTIANITY AND ISLAM

The reaction to industrialism and consumerism was part of a broader religious response to the primacy of secular ideologies in general. The revival of Christianity among intellectuals after World War One (pages 1295–1296) was matched in the 1970s and early 1980s by a surge of popular, often fundamentalist, Christianity in many countries. Judaism and Islam were also experiencing resurgence, and Buddhism and Hinduism stopped losing ground. The continuing importance of religion in contemporary human thought – an importance that has often escaped those fascinated by secular ideology and secular history – must impress the unbiased observer.

Pope John Paul II (1978–   ) exemplifies several aspects of the worldwide Christian revival. A jet-age global evangelist, John Paul journeyed to Africa, Asia, and North and South America, inspiring enthusiastic multitudes with his warm sincerity and unfailing popular touch. John Paul's melding of a liberal social gospel with conservatism in doctrinal matters also seems to reflect the spirit of the age. Thus the pope has boldly urged a more equitable distribution of wealth in plutocratic Brazil and more civil liberties in the authoritarian Philippines, while reaffirming the church's longstanding opposition to mechanical contraception and women in the priesthood. Many of Christianity's most rapidly growing Protestant churches espouse theological fundamentalism, based on literal interpretation of the Bible.

It is also emblematic that "the Polish

AYATOLLAH KHOMEINI The apostle of Islamic regeneration and the unwavering critic of the Shah returns in triumph to Teheran from exile in February 1979. The Shah had visions of making Iran a major military power, but all his military might crumbled before the emotional appeal of Islamic revolution. (Black Star/Sipa Press-Setboun)

Pope" comes from an officially atheist Communist country. Yet after thirty-five years of Communist rule, Poland is more intensely Catholic than ever before. Lech Walesa, the courageous leader of Poland's trade union Solidarity, has said that he could never become a Communist precisely because he is a devout Roman Catholic. Poland illustrated the enduring strength of spiritual life in the face of materialistic culture and secular ideologies, of which communism is only the most openly hostile.

Finally, the attempted assassination of the pope in 1981 by a mysterious Turkish terrorist apparently connected with the Russian KGB, in an effort to undermine the Catholic Church in Poland, tragically dramatized the appeal of religious thinking. In a frightening, violent world, faith and prayer offer comfort and courage.

Islam, the religion of one seventh of the earth's people, was also experiencing a powerful resurgence by the 1970s. Like orthodox Christianity, Islam had been challenged by the self-confident secular ideologies of the West since the early nineteenth century. And although the acids of modern thought had not eaten as deeply as in Europe and North America, they had etched a seductive alternative to Islam. Moderate Muslim intellectuals advocated religious reforms; radicals wanted drastic surgery. The most famous and successful of the radicals was the twentieth-century Turkish nationalist Kemal Atatürk (pages 1261-1263), who reflected and accelerated the impact of secularism on the Muslim world.

The generation of Muslim intellectual and political leaders born in the interwar years, who reached maturity after World War Two, agreed that Islam required at least some modernizing. They accepted the attractively simple Muslim creed, "There is no god but Allah and Mohammed is his prophet," but they did not think that the laws of the Koran should be taken literally. The prohibition on lending money at interest, the social inferiority of women, even cutting off the hands of thieves and public beheading of murderers, had made sense for the Arabian peninsula in the Middle Ages. But such practices did not suit the modern age. Islam had to adapt.

These views still prevail among educated elites, and they remain dominant in Turkey and probably in Egypt. Yet throughout the Middle East they have had to bow before a revival of intense Islamic fundamentalism, the critical development of the last decade. Like some of their Christian counterparts, orthodox Muslim believers want to return to unalterable fundamentals. In taking the Koran literally, they demand that the modern world adapt to the prophet's teachings, not vice-versa. And because the masses remain deeply religious and distrustful of change, Islamic fundamentalism has aroused a heartfelt popular response.

Iran provided a spectacular manifestation of resurgent Islamic fundamentalism at the end of the 1970s. Iran's religious leaders, notably the charismatic Ayatollah Khomeini, catalyzed intense popular dissatisfaction with the Shah's all-out industrialization and heavy-handed religious reform into a successful revolution. An "Islamic Republic" was declared, to govern according to the sacred laws of the Koran. State and church were to become one. The holy men and their followers were absolutely serious: they sanctioned the stoning-to-death of prostitutes and adulterers, and proposed revising the legal code along strictly Koranic lines.

Iran's fundamentalism has been exceptionally rigid and anti-modern, partly because the country adheres to the minority Shiite version of Islam. But there is a similar movement in every Muslim country. Even where the fundamentalists are unlikely to take power, as in Indonesia or Pakistan, and where they are co-opted and neutralized, as in Saudi Arabia, they have revitalized the Muslim faith. Islamic religious thought remains vigorous and continues to win converts, especially in black Africa.

SEARCHING FOR MYSTICAL EXPERIENCE

Alongside secular ideologies and a revival of organized religion, the third strong current of intellectual attraction consists of an enormous variety of religious sects, cults, and spiritual yearnings. Some of these new outpourings welled up within one or another of the great organized religions; many more did not. Though widely divergent, these movements seemed to share a common urge toward nonrational experiences, such as meditation, spiritual mysteries and direct communication with supernatural forces.

Not that this is new. So-called "primitive" peoples have always embraced myths, visions, and continuous revelation. So too have the world's great religions, especially those of the ancient East – Taoism, Hinduism, and the Zen form of Buddhism. What is new is the receptiveness of many people in the rationalistic, scientific industrialized countries (and their disciples, the Third World elite) to ancient modes of mystical experience. Some of this interest stems from the doubt about the power of the rational human mind that blossomed after World War One. By the 1960s, it had struck deep roots in the mass culture of Europe and North America.

In this sense, the late twentieth century is reminiscent of the initial encounter of West and East in the Hellenistic Age. Then, the rationalistic, humanistic Greeks encountered the eastern mystery religions and were profoundly influenced by them. Now, various strains of mystical thought again appeared from the East and from "primitive" peoples. It could be said that the non-Western world was providing intellectual repayment for the powerful secular ideologies it had borrowed in the nineteenth century.

Reflecting upon this on-going encounter, the American social scientist Robert Heilbroner was not alone in suggesting startling implications for the future:

It is therefore possible that a post-industrial society would also turn in the direction of many pre-industrial societies — toward the exploration of inner states of experience rather than the outer world of fact and material accomplishment. Tradition and ritual, the pillars of life in virtually all societies other than those of an industrial character, would probably once again assert their ancient claims as the guide to and solace for life.[14]

Some observers see the onrush of science and technology as actually reinforcing the search for spiritual experience. Electronic communications demolish time and distance; information itself is becoming the new global environment. According to philosopher William Thompson:

Culture is full of many surprises, because culture is full of the play of opposites. And so there will be scientists and mystics in the New Age. . . . To look
at the American counterculture today, one would guess . . . that the East was about to engulf the West. But [in fact] . . . America is swallowing up and absorbing the traditional Eastern techniques of transformation, because only these are strong enough to humanize its technology. In the days before planetization, when civilization was split between East and West, there were basically two cultural directions. The Westerner went outward to level forests, conquer nations, and walk on the moon; the Easterner went inward and away from the physical into the astral and causal planes. Now . . . we can glimpse the beginnings of a new level of religious experience, neither Eastern nor Western, but planetary.[15]

The author must admit to doubts about the significance of such views. But it is just possible that the upsurge of mysticism and religious searching will exert a growing influence in the coming era, especially if disorder and economic difficulties continue to undermine the old secular faith in endless progress.

———◆———

Whatever does or does not happen, the study of world history puts the future in perspective. Future developments on this small planet will surely build on the many-layered foundations hammered out in the past. Moreover, the study of world history, of mighty struggles and fearsome challenges, of shining achievements and tragic failures, imparts a strong sense of life's essence: the process of change over time. Again the again we have seen how peoples and societies evolve, influenced by such things as ideas, human passions, and material conditions. Armed with the ability to think historically, students of history are prepared to comprehend this inexorable process of change in their own lifetimes, as the world races forward toward an uncertain destiny.

1. Arnold Toynbee, *Mankind and Mother Earth,* Oxford University Press, New York, 1976, pp. 576–577.

2. David Calleo and Benjamin Rowland, *America and the World Political Economy,* Indiana University Press, Bloomington, 1973, p. 191.

3. William Epstein, *The Last Chance: Nuclear Proliferation and Arms Control,* Free Press, New York, 1976, p. 274.

4. Lester R. Brown, *In the Human Interest: A Strategy to Stabilize World Population,* W. W. Norton, New York, 1974, p. 73.

5. Mahbub ul Haq, *The Poverty Curtain: Choices for the Third World,* Columbia University Press, New York, 1976, p. 152.

6. Elbaki Hermassi, *The Third World Reassessed,* University of California Press, Berkeley, 1980, p. 76.

7. Ibid., p. 185.

8. Quoted by Hugh Stephenson, *The Coming Clash: The Impact of Multinational Corporations on National States,* Saturday Review Press, New York, 1973, p. 60.

9. Quoted by Stephenson, *Coming Clash,* p. 65.

10. Quoted by A. R. Negandhi, *The Functioning of the Multinational Corporation: A Global Comparative Study,* Pergamon Press, New York, 1980, pp. 142.

11. Milovan Djilas, *The New Class,* Praeger, New York, 1957, pp. 41–42, 44.

12. A. I. Solzhenitsyn, *Letter to the Soviet Leaders,* Harper and Row, New York, 1974, p. 33.

13. R. L. Heilbroner, *An Inquiry into the Human Prospect,* Norton, New York, 1974, p. 141.

14. Ibid., p. 140.

15. W. I. Thompson, *Evil and World Order,* Harper and Row, New York, 1980, p. 53.

16. E. M. East, in *Scientific Monthly,* April 1931; also *Reader's Digest* 19 (May 1931): 151.

Many of the books cited in the Suggested Reading for Chapters 39 and 40 pertain to the themes of this chapter. Three helpful and stimulating studies on global politics from different viewpoints are R. Barnet, *The Lean Years: The Politics of the Age of Scarcity* (1980); F. M. Lappé and J. Collins, *Food First: Beyond the Myth of Scarcity* (1977); and S. Hoffman, *Primacy or World Order: American Foreign Policy Since the Cold War* (1978). An excellent if ominous introduction to international negotiations for the control of nuclear arms is W. Epstein, *The Last Chance: Nuclear Proliferation and Arms Control* (1976). Two clear and judicious recent studies on the evolving nuclear policies of the two great superpowers, by relatively impartial British scholars, are D. Holloway, *The Soviet Union and the Arms Race* (1983); and L. Freedman, *The Evolution of Nuclear Strategy* (1982), a history of American thinking about nuclear weapons and nuclear war. J. Hackett, *The Third World War, August 1985* (1978), is a gripping but all-too-optimistic bestselling account of limited nuclear war in the near future by a retired British general, writing "in consultation with NATO experts."

M. ul Haq, *The Poverty Curtain: Choices for the Third World* (1976), is an excellent presentation of Third World demands for a new economic order. This position is expanded in J. Tinbergen and A. J. Dolman, eds., *RIO, Reshaping the International Order: A Report to the Club of Rome* (1977); and *North-South: A Program for Survival* (1980), a report calling for increased help for the South by the blue-ribbon Independent Commission on International Development Issues, under the chairmanship of Willy Brandt. Such views do not go unchallenged, and P. T. Bauer, *Equality, The Third World, and Economic Delusion* (1981), is a vigorous defense of the industrialized nations and their wealth. J. K. Galbraith, the witty economist and former U.S. ambassador to India, argues simply and effectively that poor countries have important lessons to teach rich countries in his recent *The Voice of the Poor* (1983). Common problems and aspirations are also the

SUGGESTED READING   1535

focus of E. Laszlo et al., *Goals for Mankind* (1977). The important recent study by R. Ayres, *Banking on the Poor: The World Bank and World Poverty* (1983), shows how this international financial organization has emerged as a standard-bearer for the poorest countries. *The World Development Report,* which the World Bank publishes annually, is an outstanding source of information about current trends. Valuable studies on multinational corporations and global indebtedness include L. Solomon, *Multinational Corporations and the Emerging World Order* (1978); A. R. Negandhi, *The Functioning of the Multinational Corporation: A Global Comparative Study* (1980); R. Barnet and R. Muller, *Global Reach: The Power of the Multinational Corporations* (1975); and A. Sampson, *The Money Lenders: The People and Politics of the World Banking Crisis* (1983).

Contemporary thought is so rich and diverse that any selection must be highly arbitrary. Among works not mentioned elsewhere, E. Banfield, *The Unheavenly City Revisited* (1974), is a provocative and influential reassessment of urban problems and solutions in the United States. D. H. Meadows and D. L. Meadows, *The Limits of Growth* (1974), argues that the world will soon exhaust its natural resources. E. F. Schumacher, *Small Is Beautiful: Economics as if People Mattered* (1973), advocates conservation and a scaling-down of technology to avoid disaster. R. M. Pirsig, *Zen and the Art of Motorcycle Maintenance: An Inquiry into Values* (1976), is a stimulating exploration of the tie between modern technology and personal development.

T. R. Gurr, *Why Men Rebel* (1970), skillfully reworks the idea that revolutions occur when rising expectations are frustrated. M. Djilas, *The New Class* (1957), criticizes the ruling communist bureaucracies from a Marxist point of view, while J. Revel, *The Totalitarian Temptation* (1977), claims that many Western intellectuals have been seduced into seeing communist dictatorships as progressive socialist societies. A Sakharov, *Progress, Coexistence, and Intellectual Freedom,* rev. ed. (1970), soberly assesses the prospects for improved relations between the Soviet Union and the United States.

The Islamic revival may be approached through the sympathetic work of E. Gellner, *Muslim Society* (1981); the reservations of V. S. Naipaul, *Among the Believers: An Islamic Journey* (1981); H. Algar, ed., *Islam and Revolution: Writings and Declarations of Iman Khomeini* (1982); and J. Stempel, *Inside the Iranian Revolution* (1981).

Studies of the future are so numerous that M. Marien, *Societal Directions and Alternatives: A Critical Guide to the Literature* (1977), is a useful aid with its annotated bibliography. The many future-oriented works of the members of the Hudson Institute usually combine optimism and conservatism, as in H. Kahn et al., *The Next Two Hundred Years* (1976), and H. Kahn, *The Coming Boom* (1982). J. Lorraine, *Global Signposts to the 21st Century* (1979), and R. L. Heilbroner, *An Inquiry into the Human Prospect* (1974), are especially recommended as stimulating and intelligent studies. L. Stavrianos, *The Promise of the Coming Dark Age* (1976), is especially suited to those with cataclysmic dispositions.

NOTES ON THE ILLUSTRATIONS

Page 20 The stone pillar containing the law code of Hammurabi is in the collection of the Louvre in Paris.

Page 34 The Hittite Atarluhas from Carchemish is in the British Museum.

Page 50 Mosaic floor of the ancient Beth Alpha Synagogue in Israel.

Page 52 The relief of Assurbanipal feasting, from Nineveh, is now in the British Museum.

Page 64 Shown here is the east stairway of the apadana (audience hall) of Darius and Xerxes, with Darius' palace in the background. Achaemenid period.

Page 77 This figure is 6½ inches high, made of gold and ivory about 1600–1500 B.C.

Page 78 The Melian relief, depicting the return of Odysseus, was made of terracotta in the fifth century B.C. Greek.

Page 103 Young warrior making libation before departure. Attic red figure technique, ca 500 B.C.

Page 127 Dieties of Palmyrene in bas-relief, gypsum. Selukos Nikator crowning the Tyche of Dura.

Page 147 Terracotta vase from Mohenjo-daro. Karachi Museum.

Page 149 Terracotta idol from Harappa. New Delhi Museum.

Page 163 Bronze four-legged ritual food vessel *ting*, decorated with human faces, excavated in 1965 at Ning-hsiang, Hunan. Height 38.7 cm. Shang dynasty, fourteenth–eleventh century B.C. The Shang representations of the human face are fairly uniform in a convention probably meant to represent an enemy. The hooked flanges at the corners of this *ting* are characteristic of the latest phase of Shang and of the early Western Chou period. They occur at joints of the mould parts and make a virtue of projections sometimes produced unintentionally in casting.

Page 164 Duck-shaped vessel of Late Chou period, fifth–third century B.C.; 15 in. long by 11⅛ in. high. Brooklyn Museum, New York. It probably served as a domestic or banquet utensil. In a Chinese collector's album of the tenth century is written: "The men of old fashioned these vessels to suggest that wine drinkers should skim lightly on the surface like ducks and should not become drowned in liquor like a drunkard."

Page 175 Sketch of a graffito found in a house near the fortifications of Dura. The Parthian *clibanarius*, a knight clothed in armour from head to foot, carries a heavy spear and rides a horse protected by chain mail.

Page 184 North gate to the largest memorial mound in Sanchi, India, the oldest building in India, believed to have been erected by Ashoka in the third century B.C. The carving illustrates Buddhist writings. There are four 18-foot gateways to this mound, or tope, which is built like a big compass; the mound is 42 feet high and 103 feet in diameter.

Page 186 Bacchanalian scene (schist), Northwest India, Gandhara. Late first or early second century A.D. Stone 17 in. long by 6½ in. high.

Page 191 Jade burial suit of the Western Han dynasty, late second century B.C.; 172 cm long. Taoist lore included a belief that jade could prevent the decay of the corpse, which therefore was often furnished with small jade pieces intended to stop the nine orifices of the body. Prince Liu Sheng and his wife took this belief to great length, preparing complete suits of jade. The princess Tou Wan's consists of 2,160 tablets of jade, varying in size from 4.5 by 3.5

cm to 1.5 by 1 cm and 0.2 to 0.35 cm thick, stitched together with about 7 g of gold wire and with silk-wound iron wire.

Page 195 Pottery buildings of a farmstead, Eastern Han dynasty, first century A.D., excavated in 1951 at Cheng-chou, Honan; 76 cm high, 93 cm in diameter. The custom of placing pottery models of buildings in tombs began in the first century A.D. Plain brick-and-stucco walls topped by tiled roofs were the rule for ordinary buildings in town and country. Some farmsteads are shown within a single defensive wall. Even when no wall is present, back walls of the houses are usually without doors or windows.

Page 196 Detail of simulated Chinese village with earthenware tomb figures, Han dynasty. The village can be seen at the St. Louis Art Museum.

Page 200 Watchtower of Eastern or Later Han dynasty, A.D. 25-221. Pottery with iridescent green glaze; 47 in. high, 14¾ in. in diameter. This tomb model represents a six-story pagoda-like tower rising from a moat. Two of the floors have broad balconies, and two horsemen are riding along the edge of the moat. The tiled roofs are supported by brackets in the form of bears.

Page 224 Relief shows a school in Trier on the northern frontier of the Roman empire, about the third century A.D.

Page 233 This helmet, found in Lancashire, is now in the British Museum. The crown is embossed with combat scenes and a visor in the form of a face.

Page 268 Roman mosaic from the Bardo Museum, Tunis, illustrating a great estate.

Page 279 Vandal landowner, in a mosaic from Carthage, sixth century, in the British Museum.

Page 282 From *Vie de Saint Denis,* MS. Nov. Acq. Fr. 1098, fol. 50, in the Bibliothèque Nationale, Paris.

Page 299 Detail from Madonna enthroned with saints and angels, c. 1380-1390 by Agnolo Gaddi, a Florentine active 1369-1396. Wood.

Page 301 Emperor Justinian and his court, A.D. 546-548, in mosaic at San Vitale, Ravenna, Italy.

Page 306 *Above.* Samson destroying the temple of the Philistines, miniature from Rashid-ad-Zdin's *Universal History* (1306-1314). *Below.* Muhammed and follower fleeing from Mecca to Medina, watched by Christ, miniature from thirteenth-century Arabic manuscript. Both in the Edinburgh University Library.

Page 312 The Dome of the Rock, built in 691 by the

Caliph Omar on the site of King Solomon's and Herod's temples in Jerusalem.

Page 321 Village scene on Sanchi gateway, first century A.D.

Page 328 The galleried temple complex of Angkor Wat was constructed in the twelfth century and adorned in low relief with scenes from Hindu epics and of the royal court and army.

Page 332 Scroll of the Diamond Sutra, the Sanskrit Buddhist work *Vajraccedikā prajña pāramitā* in Chinese translation found at Tunhuang. The earliest specimen of block printing, A.D. 868. Buddha is addressing Subhiti, an aged disciple.

Page 340 After Ch'iu Ying (flourished 1622-1660), "Ch'ing Ming [Spring Festival] on the River."

Page 345 "Creation of Japan: Izanagi and Izanami Standing in Clouds and Creating Island out of Sea Water." Eitoku, late nineteenth century.

Page 348 Prince Shotoku, sixth century A.D. Artist unknown.

Page 350 Five-story pagoda, Daigo. Heian period, A.D. 951.

Page 373 The scribe Ezra rewriting the sacred records. Early eighth century, from the Codex Amiatinus (fol. 5r), Biblioteca Laurenziana, Florence.

Page 375 Upper cover of the binding of the Lindau Gospels, c. 870.

Page 377 Conant took this design from some of Walter Horn's early studies on the plan of St. Gall.

Page 379 Illustration from the North Italian Coden Paneth, MS. 28, in the Medical Library at Yale University.

Page 394 Woodcut from the Nuremberg Chronicle, 1493.

Page 400 From *Gouvernement des princes,* MS. 5062, fol. 149

Page 402 This house stands on the corner of Edmund Street in Exeter, Devon, having been moved in one piece in 1961 from its original site in the city.

Page 407 From a late fifteenth-century Flemish MS.., Douce 208, fol. 120v, The Bodleian Library, Oxford.

Page 409 Benedictine Abbey of Mont-Saint-Michel, founded in 708 in the Department of the Manche in northwestern France, a mile off the French coast in the English Channel and formerly an island at high tide. Heavily fortified.

Page 412 Pope Leo IX (left) with Warinus, Abbot of St. Arnulf of Metz, from the Bern Cod. 292, fol. 73, in the Bürgerbibliothek Bern, Switzerland.

Page 423 From MS. Sloane 2435, fol. 85, in The British Library.

Page 428 From *Piers Plowman,* MS. R.3, fol. 3v, in the Trinity College Library, Cambridge.

Page 430 Miniature from *Hours of the Virgin,* MS. ADD. 17012, fol. 6r, in The British Library.

Page 432 Detail of miniature from *Speculum Virginum* of Konrad von Hirschau, C. Inv. No. 15326, in Rheinisches Landesmuseum, Bonn.

Page 438 From MS. 93, fol. 102, Pseudo-Apuleius, Herbarium C III, 2.

Page 443 Miniature from Jean de Wavrin's *Chronique d'Angleterre,* siege of the castle of Mortagne. Flemish, late fifteenth century. MS. Roy. 14. E.IV, fol. 23r, in The British Library.

Page 445 Miniature from *Psalter of Henry VI.* French c. 1430. MS. Cotton Dom. A. XVII, fol. 122v, in The British Library.

Page 447 From St. Gregory's *Moralia in Job.* French (Citeaux), 1111 MS. 170, fol. 59r, in the Bibliothèque Publique de Dijon, France.

Page 448 Frontispiece of Moralized Bible, thirteenth century.

Page 451 From Kenneth John Conant, *Cluny: Les églises et la maison du chef d'ordre.* The Mediaeval Academy of America Publication No. 77. Cambridge, Mass., 1968.

Page 457 Presumed to be the work of Matilda, queen of William the Conqueror, the original tapestry (c. 1100) can be seen in the city of Bayeux, France. A replica is in the Victoria and Albert Museum, London.

Page 465 Aquamanile. German, twelfth or thirteenth century.

Page 468 From thirteenth-century psalter.

Page 476 Painting by Lorenzo Voltolini, eighteenth-century Veronese painter.

Page 479 Lancets with stained glass from Évron. French, fourteenth century.

Page 482 Detail of the statue of the Queen of Sheba (c. 1230) on the right portal of the north transept of Chartres Cathedral.

Page 483 Flemish, Story of Jehu, Jezebel, and the sons of Ahab, II Kings 9–10.

Page 488 Fourteenth century. From MS. Fr. 352, fol. 52v, in Bibliothèque Nationale, Paris.

Page 497 *St. Sebastian Interceding for the Plague-Stricken* by Josse Lieferinxe, in the Walters Art Gallery, Baltimore, Maryland.

Page 498 From MS. of Gilles le Msisis, *Annales,* Bib-

liothèque Royale 13076/7, fol. 16v, in the Bibliothèque Royale Albert I, Brussels.

Page 505 Episode from the battle of Crècy from Froissart's *Chronicle,* as reproduced in *Larousse Ancient and Medieval History,* p. 363.

Page 511 Florentine school, sixteenth century (c. 1530). Allegorical portrait of Dante on wood, 50 by 47½ inches.

Page 518 From Froissart's *Chronicles,* MS. Fr. 2643, fol. 125, in Bibliothèque Nationale, Paris.

Page 522 Miniature from *Roman de Fauvel,* MS. Fr. 146, fol. 34, in Bibliothèque Nationale, Paris.

Page 524 *The Four Horsemen of the Apocalypse,* woodcut c. 1498, by Albrecht Dürer, German painter and engraver (1471–1528) regarded as leader of the German Renaissance school of painting.

Page 548 A Bulom-Portuguese ivory salt cellar, sixteenth century, Sierra Leone. Formerly part of Prince Sadruddin Aga Khan's collection of African art.

Page 557 Quetzalcoatl, limestone statue of A.D. 900–1250 in San Vicente Tancuayalab, Mexico; 62¼ in. high. This life-size figure discovered in the 1840s is a classic statement of the late Huaxteca style; the precise solidity of the form is relieved by cut-out areas and delicate facial modeling; lightened by the tracery of incised surface pattern. The conical elements in the headdress identify Quetzalcoatl, the "Feathered Serpent," creator god and founder of agriculture.

Page 579 Sixteenth-century woodcut.

Page 581 Banquet scene from Boccaccio's *Decameron* by Sandro Botticelli, Italian painter (1444?–1510.)

Page 558 The original painting can be found in the Uffizi Gallery, Florence.

Page 590 Hans Memling (real name Mimmelinghe, also spelled Memline and Hemmelinck), active c. 1465–d. 1494. Tommaso Portinari (ca. 1432–1501), tempera and oil on wood, 17⅜ inches high by 13¼ inches wide. Maria Portinari (b. 1456), tempera and oil on wood, 17⅜ inches high by 13⅜ wide.

Page 592 Terracotta, School of Luca della Robbia, late fifteenth century. Della Robbia's invention of the process of making polychrome glazed terracottas led contemporaries to consider him one of the great artistic innovators. The warm humanity of this roundel (circular panel) is characteristic of della Robbia's art.

Page 596 Engraving by Johannes Stradanus (J. van der Straet), Belgian painter (1523–1605).

Page 599 Tiziano Vecellio, Italian painter, 1477–1576.

Louis Carmontelle (Louis Carrogis), French painter, engraver, and writer (1717–1806).

Page 825 Les Glaneuses by Jean François Millet (1814–1875), French genre and landscape painter of the Barbizon school. The original can be seen in the Louvre.

Page 829 Painting by Thomas Weaver engraved by William Ward and published 21 July 1812. Mezzotint 23.7 by 17.8 in.

Page 834 Colored engraving, 1746.

Page 846 Frontispiece for a map of "the most Inhabited part of Virginia containing the whole province of Maryland with part of Pensilvania, New Jersey and North Carolina drawn by Joshua Fry and Peter Jefferson in 1775," in Thomas Jeffrey's *American Atlas,* 1776, in The British Library.

Page 860 Peasant Family by Giacomo Ceruti, Italian painter active c. 1750.

Page 862 After an engraving by R. Lehman of the foundlings' home called La Rota.

Page 869 Famille de paysans, c. 1640, by Louis Le Nain, French painter (1593–1648). The original can be seen in the Louvre.

Page 875 Engraving, 1746.

Page 877 "The Remarkable Effects of Vaccination," an anonymous nineteenth-century Russian cartoon in the Clements C. Fry Collection of Medical Prints and Drawings, Yale Medical Library.

Page 890 Plaque of Oba and attendants from Nigeria (Benin). Bronze 19½ in. high.

Page 903 Sufi dance, from the *Divan* of Hafiz. Persian painting, Herar school, dated 1523. Color, gold, and silver; 7⅛ by 4 1/16 in.

Page 909 The Taj Mahal is the mausoleum in memory of Arjumand Banu Begum, called Mumtaz Mahal ("chosen one of the palace"), of which Taj Mahal is a corruption. She died in 1631. The building was begun in 1632, after plans were submitted by a council of architects. Credit for the final design is given to Usted Isa, who was either Turkish or Persian. Workmen and materials came from all over India and Central Asia. The mausoleum itself was completed by 1643, although the whole complex – consisting of the mausoleum, central garden square, mosque, and service buildings surrounded by a red sandstone wall – took much longer.

Page 913 Jahangir. Illuminated manuscript ca. 1615–1618. Borders signed by Muhammad Sadiq, mid-eighteenth century.

Page 932 Marketplace. Detail from a Japanese screen, "Pastimes and Occupations of the Twelve Months,"

Edo period. Ukiyoe school, by Hanabusa Itchō. Ink and color on paper, 11 5/16 in. by 342 in.

Page 937 Scenes from the Pleasure Quarters of Kyoto, one of a pair of six-panel folding screens of the Edo period, mid-seventeenth century. Ink, colors, and gold on paper; each panel 104.5 by 45.5 cm.

Page 954 This portrait of Louis XVI by Joseph-Siffrein Duplessis, French portrait painter (1725–1802), hangs in the Marie Antoinette Gallery at Versailles.

Page 958 This drawing by Persin de Prieur, "Premier assaut contre La Bastille," can be seen in the Musée Carnavalet, Paris.

Page 964 "Fin Tragique de Louis XVI," drawn from life by Fious; engraving by Sarcifu. Louis XVI was executed on 21 January 1793 in the Place de Louis XV, renamed the Place de la Concorde.

Page 968 "Un Comité révolutionnaire sous la Terreur," after Alexandre Évariste Fragonard, French historical painter (1780–1850).

Page 975 "Con razón o sin ella," by Francisco José de Goya y Lucientes (1746–1828), Plate 2 in *Los desastres de la guerra,* 1863. Etching. A Spanish painter, etcher, and lithographer, Goya was the chief master of the Spanish school in the eighteenth century.

Page 987 James Hargreaves (d. 1778), English inventor, weaver, and mechanic, invented the spinning jenny about 1765.

Page 991 Engraving by Henry Beighton, 1717, of the atmospheric steam engine invented about 1705 by Thomas Newcomen, English blacksmith (1663–1729).

Page 993 Honoré Daumier (1808–1879), *The Third-Class Carriage.* Oil on canvas. Daumier was both a caricaturist and a serious painter.

Page 998 The Cockerill works at Seraing, Belgium, at night. Lithograph by E. Toovey, Brussels, 1852.

Page 1006 From *Parliamentary Papers,* 1842, vol. XV.

Page 1010 "Emigrants' Arrival at Cork – A Scene on the Quay," woodcut from *Punch,* 1851.

Page 1020 "La balance politique," 1815, print in the Bibliothèque Nationale. *From left,* two Englishmen, Prussian, Metternich, Russian, Talleyrand.

Page 1023 Count Clemens von Metternich (1773–1859) by Sir Thomas Lawrence, English painter (1769–1830).

Page 1033 Eugene Delacroix (1798–1863), French painter and leader of the Romantic school.

Page 1037 Liszt am Klavier, 1840, by Josef Danhauser, German painter (1805–1845).

Page 1042 From *Punch,* 1846. The humorous weekly *Punch* – founded in 1841 by the British journalist and sociologist Henry Mayhew (1812–1887) and

photograph released 26 July 1946.

Page 1454 Astronaut Edwin E. Aldrin, Jr., leaving the lunar module. Apollo II was launched in Florida on 16 July 1969. Astronauts Neil A. Armstrong and Aldrin landed on the moon on 20 July while Michael Collins circled in the main spacecraft until rejoined by the others on 21 July. The astronauts returned to Earth on 24 July, when they were picked up in the Pacific Ocean.

Page 1464 Students in the Boulevard Saint Michel in Paris protesting the closing of the suburban Nanterre University, photographed on 3 May 1968.

INDEX

World, 1483, 1520–1521
Birth of a Nation (film), 1303
Birthrate, decline in, 1083, 1141, 1465, 1467
Bismarck, Otto von: in Revolution of 1848, 1051; in unification of Germany, 1106–1111; as chancellor of German Empire, 1117–1119; calls imperialism conference, 1148–1150; and European system of alliances, 1212–1214
Black Death, *see* Bubonic plague
Black Family in Slavery and Freedom (Gutman), 1198
Black Hand, The, 1218
Blacks: in Renaissance, 599–601; in Latin America, 1179–1185; slavery in U.S., 1192–1199; family life, 1197–1199; and civil rights movement, 1392–1393; nationalism in Africa, 1429–1430; in South Africa, 1440–1443. *See also* Slavery
Blake, William, 1002
Blanc, Louis, 1029, 1046, 1047
Blenheim, battle of, 731
Bloch, Marc, 826
Blood, Council of, 686–687
Bloodletting, 872–874
Blum, Léon, 1319–1320
Boccaccio, Giovanni, 442, 498, 586–587
Bodin, Jean, 774
Boeotia (Bo-e-she-ah), 72, 73, 77–78, 104
Boers, 1147
Boer Wars, 1147–1148, 1214–1216
Boghazköy (Bog-haz-koy), 33
Bohemia, 691–692, 693, 757–758, 1022
Boisdeffre, General, 1219
Boleyn, Anne, *see* Anne Boleyn
Bolivar, Simon, 1176–1179
Bologna, Concordat of, 682
Bologna, University of, 471
Bolsheviks, 1236–1242
Bonaparte, Louis Napoleon, *see* Napoleon III
Bonaparte, Napoleon, *see* Napoleon I
Bonhomme, Jacques, 517
Boniface, *see* St. Boniface
Boniface VIII, pope, 487–489
Book of Common Order (Knox), 653
Book of Common Prayer (Cranmer), 652
Book of the First Navigation and Discovery of the Indies (Columbus), 671
Books, first printing from movable type, 595–597
Borgia, Cesare, 610
Borgia, Rodrigo, *see* Alexander VI, pope
Borgia family, 629
Borodino, battle of, 978
Bosch, Jerome, 608
Bosnia, 1213, 1218–1219
Bossuet, Jacques, 720

Boston Tea Party, 949
Botany, beginnings in Hellenistic period, 136
Botticelli, 588
Boulton, Matthew, 990
"Bourgeois," meaning of word, 395
Bourgeoisie, in Marxian socialism, 1030
Bourges, Pragmatic Sanction of, 614, 760
Boutham, England, 401
Boxer Rebellion, 1163
Boyars, 769, 771–773
Brahe, Tycho, 791
Brahmins, 149
"Brain drain," 1501
Brandenburg, elector of, 760–762
Brassey, Thomas, 994
Brazil, 895, 1142, 1145, 1177, 1396–1400
Brazza, Pierre de, 1148
Breast-feeding, *see* Nursing of babies
Breitenfeld, battle of, 693
Brest-Litovsk, Treaty of, 1239, 1329
Brethren of the Common Life, 629
Brezhnev, Leonid, 1388–1391
Brezhnev Doctrine, 1390
Briand, Aristide, 1310, 1311
Bright, John, 1043
Britain, *see* England; Great Britain
Britain, Battle of, 1353
British College of Surgeons, 878
British East India Co., 910–914
British Empire, *see* Great Britain
British West Indies, 844
Britons, conquest by Germanic tribes, 285–286
Bronze Age, 28–29, 75–78
Brothers Karamazov, The (Dostoevsky), 1084
Brunel, Isambard Kingdom, 994
Brunelleschi, Filippo, 589, 591, 599
Bruni, Leonardo, 585
Brüning, Heinrich, 1343
Brusilov, Alexei, 1225, 1232
Bubonic plague (Black Death): spread of in 14th century, 494, 495; pathology of, 495–499; consequences of, 499; disappears, 833
Buddha, 180–182
Buddhism: beginnings in India, 180–182; in China, 186–187, 331–333; in Japan, 347–349
Bulgaria: in time of Rome, 245; independence from Ottoman Empire, 1123; in Balkan wars, 1217; in W.W. I, 1225; and 1919 peace treaty, 1246; forced into alliance with Germany, 1353; Russia occupies, 1367
Bullitt, William, 1366
Burckhardt, Jacob, 88
"Burgher," meaning of word, 395
Burgundians, 281, 613

Burke, Edmund, 962
Burlingame, Anson, 1161
Burmans, 326
Burton, Richard, 529
Bury St. Edmunds, 448
Bussy, Sir William, 516
Byblos (Bib-loss), 40–41, 42
Byron, George Gordon, 1034, 1038
Byzantine Empire: 264, 301–306; compared with Germanic West, 302–303; Justinian's law codes, 303–304; intellectual life, 304, 306
Byzantium, 270, 302

Cabal, 742
Cabinet of Dr. Caligari, The (film), 1303
Cabinet system, 743–744
Cabot, John, 675
Cabral, Pedro Alvares, 671
Caesar, Julius, 228, 231, 234–236, 243
Cairo, modernization of, 1139
Calais, 508
Calendar, 225
Caligula (Kuh-lig-u-lah), 249, 252
Callisthenes (Kuh-lis-thuh-neez), 110
Calvin, John: debt to Luther, 637; life and ideas, 643–645; influence on Knox, 653; quoted, 745; reaction to Copernican theory, 791
Calvinism: tenets of, 643–645; in France, 682–684; in Netherlands, 686; in Germany, 690–691, 694; and Puritanism, 738–739; and the Dutch, 745
Cambodia, 1420
Cambon, Paul, 1307
Cambridge University, 473
Cambyses (Kam-buy-seez), 62
Camel routes, 535–538
Campania, 208, 213
Camus, Albert, 1295
Canaan, 43
Canada, 675; developed by Colbert for French Empire, 726; British colony, 1132; immigration in, 1141, 1142
Cannae (Kan-nigh), battle of, 219
Cannon, 676–677
Canon law, 287
Canossa (Kan-no-sah), 415
Canterbury Cathedral, 481, 591
Canterbury Tales, 510, 626
Canton, foreign merchants in, 1137
Canute, 391, 457
Capital (Marx), 1125
Capitalism: medieval, 406–407; and cottage industry, 836; and Industrial Revolution, 984, 1000–1001; and foreign investment, 1135; Roosevelt's efforts to reform, 1315–1318
Capitoline Hill, 210
Caracalla (Car-ah-cal′-ah), 179, 261
Caraffa, Cardinal, 657, 660
Caravan routes, 535–538

Egypt *(Cont.)*
23–24; periods in history, 24 (chart); Old Kingdom and pharaohs, 24–28; early religion in, 25–26, 29–31; early life in, 26–28; Hyksos in, 28–29; Akhenaten and monotheism, 29–31; and Hittites, 34; early empire destroyed, 35; in decline, 40–41; Hebrews in, 42–43; defeated by Assyria, 51, 52; falls to Persian Empire, 62; influence on Thales, 100–101; Ptolemy Lagus becomes king, 112; under Ptolemies, 119, 121–122, 124–126, 135; under Rome, 261; Muslims control, 306; Napoleon's campaign in fails, 971; Europeanized, West in, 1138–1140; British in, 1148, 1150; Nasser to power in, 1380–1381; nationalism in, 1422–1423

Ehrlich, Paul, 489

Eilika, countess of Ballenstedt, 445

Einhard, 366–367, 371, 376, 585

Einstein, Albert, 1292–1293, 1410

Eiseley, Loren, 4

Eisenhower, Dwight D., 1365, 1387, 1392, 1394

Eisenstein, Dimitri, 1305

Eisenstein, Sergei, 1384

Ekkehard of Aaura, 445

El Alamein, battle of, 1364

Elba, Napoleon's escape from, 1019

Elderly, health care for, 1468–1471

Electricity, 1086

Elements of Geometry, The (Euclid), 134

Eleusinian (El-u-sin-e-ahn) mysteries, 127, 251

Elimination of Poverty, The (Louis Napoleon), 1097

Eliot, George (Mary Ann Evans), 1089

Eliot, T. S., 1296, 1297

Elizabeth, empress of Russia, 782, 811–812

Elizabeth I, queen of England: born, 649; question of birth, 650; on throne, religious policy, 652–653; dilemmas over Mary, Queen of Scots, and aid to Protestant Netherlands, 688–689; and Spanish Armada, 690; and Elizabeth Hardwick, 700; and literary achievements during reign, 706–710; reasons for success, 736

"Elizabethan Settlement" laws, 653

Emancipation Proclamation, 1196

Emigration, *see* Migrations

Emile (Rousseau), 807

Empires, *see* Imperialism

Empiric school of medicine, 137

Enabling Act, 1346

Enclosure of land, 830–831

Encomiendas (En-ko-me-ehn-dass), 885–886

Encyclopedia: The Rational Dictionary of the Sciences, the Arts, and the Crafts (Diderot and d'Alembert), 805–806, 808, 812, 874–875

Energy: and Industrial Revolution, 988–990; human requirements for, early sources of, 989–990; steam as source of, 990–992; law of conservation of, 1086; atomic, researched by Euratom, 1377; era of cheap oil ends, 1382

Engels, Friedrich, 1002, 1030

Enghein, duke of, 974

England: in Roman era, 243, 259, 261, 285; Anglo-Saxon, 285–286; Bede's history of, 286; Roman Christianity prevails at Synod of Whitby, 290; flowering of Northumbrian culture in, 372–375; recovery in, 390–391; and 11th-century trade, 404–406; development as modern state, 456–458; and medieval finances, 463–464; medieval law in, 466–470; Magna Carta signed, 469; and 13th-century dispute with papacy, 487–489; and effect of Black Death, 498–499; Hundred Years' War, 501–510; "fur-collar" crime in, 516–517; peasant revolt of 1381, 517–519; Wars of the Roses, 615; monarchy strengthened, 616–617; and Protestant Reformation, 643, 646–653; Elizabeth's dilemmas over Mary, Queen of Scots, and aid to Protestant Netherlands, 688–689; defeats Spanish Armada, 690; 1702 war with France, 730–732; James I succeeds Elizabeth, 736–737; social changes in, 737–738; rise of Puritanism, 738–739; Long Parliament and Charles I, 739; civil war, Charles executed, 740; Cromwell and the Protectorate, 740–741; restoration of monarchy, 741–742; constitutional monarchy established, 743–744; new farming system, 828–831; enclosure acts, land ownership in, 830; cottage industry, 837–839; united with Scotland, forms Great Britain, 840; Industrial Revolution in, 984–995; Continent uses industrial methods of, 995–1000; new capital/labor classes in, 1000–1008; romantic movement in, 1032–1038; effects of U.S. Civil War, 1196. *See also* Great Britain

England's Treasure by Foreign Trade (Mun), 840

Enki (Ehn-key), (Sumerian god), 12, 18

Enlightenment, 776, 799–810; scientific resolution factor in, 799; emergence of, 799–802; French philosophes, 802–806; later phase, 806–807; social setting of, 807–810; influence on absolutism, 810–818; influence on lib-

eralism, 945–946; romantic movement as revolt against, 1032

Enlil (Ehn-lil), 12, 18, 19

Ennius (Ehn-e-us), 229

Entertainment, *see* Recreation

Environment, 1447–1448

Epaminondas, 104

Ephesus, 261

Ephors (E-forz), 85

Epicureans, 129, 130

Equality, concept of, 944, 945, 1025

Era of Warring States, 164

Erasistratus (Eh-rah-sis-trat-us), 136–137

Erasmus, 597, 603, 606–607, 626, 629

Eratosthenes (Eh-rah-toss-thuh-neez), 135–136, 194

Erechtheion (Eh-reck-the-on), 93–94

Erhard, Ludwig, 1375

Ericson, Leif, 670

Eric the Red, 670

Erikson, Erik, 637

Erythrae (Air-rith-righ), 89

Escorial, 689

Eskimos, Caribou, 7

Essay Concerning Human Understanding (Locke), 802

Essay on the Principle of Population (Malthus), 1026

Essays (Montaigne), 704–706

Essenes (Eh-seens), 249

Estate agriculture, 754

Estates (orders) of French society, 955–956

Estates General of France, 615, 956

Estonia, Russian annexation of, 1353

Ethelbert, 290

Ethiopia, 550–552, 892, 1147, 1351, 1516

Etruria (E-truhr-e-ah), 213, 219

Etruscans, 208–210, 213

Euboea (U-bo-e-ah), 82, 89

Euclid, 134

Eugene, prince of Savoy, 731, 778

Eulogies of Scientists (Fontenelle), 801

Eumenes (U-men-eez), 112

Eumenides, The (Aeschylus), 95–96

Eunuchs, and Chinese bureaucracy, 919–923

Euphrates (U-frayt-eez) River, 11–15

Euratom, 1377

Euripides (U-rip-uh-deez), 96, 229

Europe: origins of culture in Near East, 4–65; civilization shaped by Hellenic Greece, 70–105; meeting of western, eastern thought, 110–138; Rome and the Roman Empire, 206–274; Greco-Roman culture spreads to, 245; barbarian invasions, 262–263; the making of, 278–286; influence of Islam on, 306, 311–313; in early Middle Ages, 360–386; recovery and reform in High Middle Ages, 390–418; life in

Lancaster, House of, 615
Land reform, 1488-1489
Language: Indo-European, 31-32; role in modern philosophy, 1294
Languedoc, 494
Laos, 1420
Lao T'ai T'ai (Lou'-Tie'-Tie'), 1279-1280
Lao Tze (Lou-dzuh), 168-169
LaRochelle, 719
La Salle, Robert, 726
Lascaris, Jonus, 584
Las Casas, Bartholomé de, 701, 702, 885, 886
Last Supper, The, 589
Lateran Agreement of 1929, 1339
Lateran Council, 467, 631, 656
Lateran Palace, 287
Lateran Synod of 1059, 413
Latifundia, 232, 259
Latin America: in 19th century, 1165-1185; revolutions against Spain, 1169-1172; racism, 1172-1173; Co-munero revolution, 1173-1175; wars of independence, 1175-1177; slavery, 1179; neocolonialism, 1180-1183; immigration, 1183-1185; U.S. inter-vention, 1206; economic nationalism, 1395-1398; new authoritarianism, 1399-1401. *See also* South America; Third World
Latin language, 273-274, 304, 376
Latium, 208, 209, 212, 213, 219
Latvia, Russian annexation of, 1353
Laud, William, 739
Law, John, 955
Law: Hammurabi's Code, 18, 19-23; Mosaic, 19, 20, 46; in ancient Greece, 74; Draco's code, 86, 152; in polis contrasted with Hellenistic cities, 116; Roman, 213-216, 224; of Germanic tribes, 283-284; beginnings of canon, 287; Roman, preserved by Byzan-tines, 303-304; Justinian's codes, 304, 470, 471, 609; medieval developments in, 397; Roman curia as court of, 417; monks studying, 449; Constitu-tions of Melfi, 465; in medieval Eu-rope, 466-473; Napoleon's civil code of 1800, 972
Law of the Sea, 1523
Law of the Twelve Tables, 216
Lawrence of Arabia, 1225, 1259
Laws, The (Plato), 102
Layard, A. H., 56
Lay investiture, 414-416
League of Armed Neutality, 950
League of Cambrai, 613
League of Nations, 1244, 1246, 1248, 1255-1256, 1511
Leakey, Louis, 4, 529-530
Leakey, Mary, 4, 529-530

Leakey, Richard, 4
Learning: revival of in Carolingian age, 372-378; effect of printing on, 596-597
Lebua Dengel, 892
Lech River, battle at, 391
Le Corbusier, 1298, 1300
Ledru-Rollin, Alexandre, 1046
Lee, Robert E., 1197
Leech Book of Bald, The, 449
Lefèvre d'Etaples, Jacques, 603
Legalism, 169
Legislative Assembly (France), 963
Legnano, battle of, 463
Le Havre, founded, 680
Leisure, *see* Recreation
Lélia (Sand), 1036
Le Nain, Louis, 727
Lenin, Vladimir Ilyich, 1236-1242, 1305, 1326, 1328, 1329
Le Nôtre, André, 723
Leo I, pope, 289
Leo III, pope, 370-371
Leo IX, pope, 412, 413
Leo X, pope, 587, 613, 615, 629, 632, 656
Leo XIII, pope, 1121
Leo Africanus, 545
Leonardo da Vinci, see da Vinci, Leo-nardo
Leopold II (of Austria), Holy Roman emperor, 777, 816
Leopold II, king of Belguim, 1148
Lepidus, 236
Leprosy, 393
Lérins, 298
Lesbos, 83
Lescot, Pierre, 680
Lespinasse, Julie de, 809
Lessons for Women (Pan Chao), 194
Le Tellier, François, 728
Leuctra, 104
Le Vau, Louis, 723
Leviathan (Hobbes), 740
Lewis, C. S., 1296
Libation Bearers, The (Aeschylus), 95
Liberalism: central ideas of, 944-945, 1025-1027; roots of, 945-946; attrac-tion of, 946-947
Liberia, 1147
Liberty, concept of, 944-945, 1025
Liberty Leading the People (Delacroix painting), 1036
Libyans, 41
Licinian-Sextian rogations, 216
Licinius (Lie-sin-e-us), 216
Liebenfels, Lanz von, 1340
Liebknecht, Karl, 1244
Liège, industrialization of, 997
Life expectancy, 1465
Life of the Emperor Augustus (Seutonius), 367

Li Lung-mien (Lee' Lung'-Myehn'), 342
"Limeys," English sailors, 868
Limits to Growth, 1519
Lincoln, Abraham, 1186, 1194-1196
Linguistics, 530
Li Po (Lee' Po'), 339-340
Lisbon, and Portuguese commerce, 671, 674
List, Friedrich, 999, 1113, 1143
Lister, Joseph, 1061-1062
Li Ssu (Lee'-Suh'), 169, 187
Liszt, Franz, 1037
Literacy: in ancient Israel, 49; among Hellenistic women, 133; under Char-lemagne, 376; in Middle Ages, 440, 471; in 17th, 18th centuries, 865
Literature: Roman, 229, 245-248; By-zantine, 304-305; Bede, *Beowulf,* 373-375; development of vernacular, 510-512; writings of Northern Re-naissance, 603-608; Montaigne, 704-706; Elizabeth, Jacobean, 706-710; French, encouraged by Ri-chelieu, 719; French classicism, 727-728; of the Enlightenment, 802-807; romantic movement in, 1034-1036; realism in, 1088-1091; 20th century, 1296-1298; Russian, 1386-1387
Lithuania, 772, 1353
Little Entente, 1307
Liu Pang (Lie-u Pang), 190
Liverpool and Manchester Railway, 992-993
Livingston, Robert, 1188
Livingstone, David, 529, 532
Livy, 210, 215, 223, 247
Lloyd George, David, 1122, 1216, 1244-1246
Locarno treaties, 1310
Locke, John, 743, 802, 946
Lodge, Henry Cabot, 1248
Loftus, W. K., 11
Logical empiricism, 1294
Lollards, 515, 647
Lombard, Peter, 475
Lombards, 281; invasion of Rome, 289; defeated by Carolingians, 366, 368
Lombardy, and unification of Italy, 1100-1102
London: 12th-century, described, 401-403; Foundling Hospital, 862; Crystal Palace exposition in, 994; filth in, 1059, *See also* Cities
London *Daily Mail,* 1216, 1305
Long Parliament, 739
Loos, Adolf, 1298
Lords, House of, *see* Parliament, English
Lorenzo the Magnificent, 587
Lorraine, 1212, 1246
Los Alamos laboratory, 1450
Lot, Ferdinand, 272-273

Lothair, Carolingian ruler, 381
Louis VI, king of France, 458-459, 478-479
Louis VII, king of France, 478-479
Louis VIII, king of France, 459, 464
Louis IX, king of France, 459, 464, 466, 486
Louis XI, king of France, 609, 615, 638
Louis XII, king of France, 613, 627
Louis XIII, king of France, 718, 720
Louis XIV, king of France, 841; as supreme example of absolutist monarch, 720; early years, personality, 721; building and use of Versailles, 722-725; economics under, 725-727; arts in reign of, 727-728; wars under, 728-732; death of, 732; provides refuge for James II, 742; hatred of Dutch, 744-745; and Peace of Utrecht, 842
Louis XV, king of France, 814-815
Louis XVI, king of France, 815; dominated by nobility, 956; accepts constitutional monarchy, 961; tries to flee, arrested, 962; imprisoned, 963; guillotined, 964-965
Louis XVIII, king of France, 1017, 1019, 1020, 1043
Louis Napoleon, see Napoleon III
Louis Philippe, king of France, 1044-1045
Louis the German, 381-382
Louis the Pious, 380-382
Louise of Savoy, 698
Louisiana, 842, 848, 1188
Louvre, 680
Lovett, William, 1072
Low Countries, see Netherlands
Loyalists, in American Revolution, 950
Loyola, Ignatius, 659-660
Lucknow Pact, 1268
Lucretia (Lu-cre-she-ah), 223-224
Luddites, 1002
Ludendorff, Erich, **1223-1224, 1228, 1341**
Lueger, Karl, 1124, 1340
Lully, Jean-Baptiste, 728
Lunéville, Treaty of, 974
Lupercalia, 195-196
Lusitania, 1224
Luther, Martin: and printing, 597; use of Lefèvre's texts, 603; early years, 631-632; launches Protestant Reformation, 632-634; his theology, 634-637; and impact of his beliefs, 635-637, 640-642; reaction to Copernican theory, 791
Lutheranism: in Scandanavia, 654; in France, 682; in Germany, 690-691, 694; supported by Richelieu, 719
Lützen, battle of, 693
Luxemburg, Rosa, 1244

Lycurgan regimen, 85-86
Lydia (Lid-de-ah), 60
Lyell, Charles, 1087
Lyons, 261
Lyrical Ballads (Wordsworth/Coleridge), 1034

MacArthur, Douglas, 1362
Macbeth (Shakespeare), 706, 709
Macaulay, Thomas, 706, 876
MacDonald, Ramsay, 1312, 1318
Macedonia: victory over Greeks, 104-105; conquests under Alexander, 110-111; after Alexander's death, 111-112; Roman conquest of, 221; Serbia takes from Ottoman Empire, 1217
Machiavelli, Niccoló: Livy's influence on, 247; despised masses, 591; life, work, 594-595; and Renaissance kings, 609-610; Borgia hero of *The Prince,* 610; on the church, 626
McKinley, William, 1206
MacMahon, Marie Edmé, 1121
Madame Bovary (Flaubert), 1089
Magellan, Ferdinand, 673
Magic "cures," 137
Magna Carta, 469
Magnetic compass, 677
Magyars, 383-385, 391, 1022, 1123-1124
Mahabharata (Ma-ha-bah'-ra-ta), 148, 154
Mahavira, Vardhamana (Ma-ha-vih-ra, Vard-ha-ma-na), 153
Mahmud (Mahk-mood), 329
Maintenon, Madame de, 726
Malaria, 393
Malaya, 1146
Mali, 542-547, 1435-1436
Malthus, Thomas, 1026, 1483
Managers, as emerging social elite, 1456-1457
Manchu dynasty, 914-929
Manchuria, 1115, 1161, 1282-1283
Mandates, 1256
Mandinke (Man-dink-uh), 542, 544
Manetho (Ma-neeth-o), 28
Manhattan Project, 1450
Manicheanism (Ma-nih-key-e-ahn-ism), 62
Manifest destiny, 1186-1190
Manila, 842
Mankind and Mother Earth, 1510
Man of the People (Achebe), 1504
Manorial system, 363, 425-427
Manuel, king of Portugal, 671
Manufacturing, see Industrial Revolution; Industry
Mao Tse-tung (Mow Tsay Tung), 1277-1279, 1283, 1380, 1406-1412
Maps, improvements in, 677

Marathas, 909-910
Marathon, battle of, 88
Marcel, Gabriel, 1296
Marchand, Jean-Baptiste, 1150
Marconi, Guglielmo, 1305
Marcos, Ferdinand, 1420
Marcus Aurelius, 254
Marduk (Mar-duke), (Babylonian god), 16, 18-19
Margaret, regent of the Netherlands, 686
Margaret of Austria, 698
Margaret of Valois, 684
Maria Theresa, queen of Austria, 811, 816, 842, 878
Maria Theresa, queen of France, 721
Marie Antoinette, queen of France, 961
Maritain, Jacques, 1296
Marius, 231
Markets: medieval, 399-400; effect of Industrial Revolution on, 993
Marne, first battle of, 1221; second battle of, 1242
Marquette, Jacques, 726
Marriage: under Hammurabi's Code, 22-23; in ancient Israel, 47-49; in ancient Athens, 100; Roman, 223-224; Muslim, Indian, 309-310, 323-325; Charlemagne decrees on, 364; in Middle Ages, 441-442; in 14th century, 519-521; in 16th, 17th centuries, 700; late, in 17th, 18th centuries, 854-855; new patterns in late 18th century, 858-859; urban in 1900, 1077-1082; black slave, 1198; modern changes in, 1463-1468. *See also* Family; Women
Marseilles, bubonic plague in, 495
Marshal, William, 441
Marshall, George C., 1369
Marshall, John, 1190
Marshall Plan for economic aid to Europe, 1369, 1373
Marsiglio of Padua, 514-515, 634
Martel, Charles, 312, 360, 362, 364
Martin, John, 1034
Martin V, pope, 515
Marx, Karl, 830, 1000, 1002; life and views of, 1030-1031; London years, 1125-1126; and Russian Revolution, 1232; doctrine studied by Lenin, 1236
Marxism, 1030-1031, 1327-1328; in China, 1277; contemporary, 1529. *See also* Communism
Mary, queen of Scots, 653, 688, 689, 698
Mary I, queen of England, 649, 650, 652, 699
Mary II (William and Mary), queen of England, 742, 743
Mary, Virgin, 435

Carthage compete for control of, 218–219; as feudal state, 464–466; medicine in, 473; Spain in, 679; and unification of Italy, 1100, 1103

Siderus Nuncius (Galileo), 793

Sieges: used by Assyrians, 53–54; engines, 134

Sieyès, Abbé, 971

Sigismund, Holy Roman emperor, 515, 899

Silesia, 842

Silk Road, 174–175, 178–179, 191

Silva, Anna da, 1103

Silver, 673–675, 696, 732, 734, 848

Simon de Montfort, 487

Simony, 410, 411, 414, 659

Sinan, Pasha, 902

Sino-Japanese War (1894–95), 1162

Sister Carrie (Dreiser), 1090

Sistine Chapel, 590, 628

Six Acts, 1041

Sixtus IV, pope, 585, 628

Sixtus V, pope, 689

Siyalk, 58–59

Skepticism: defined, 704; origins in Montaigne's writings, 704–706

Slavery: in Mesopotamia, 14; in early Egypt, 27, 29; under Hittites, 33; of Hebrews in Egypt, 43; in ancient Israel, 50; in ancient Greece, 86, 88, 98; in Hellenistic world, 122–123; in Rome, 225–227, 232, 259, 272; in medieval Europe, 424; trans-Saharan trade, 536; Muslim, 536–537; Aztec, 562; in the Renaissance, 599–602; in 15th through 18th centuries, 701–704, 734; under Ottomans, 759; Britain gains control of trade in, 842; in 18th-century Virginia, 844; transatlantic African trade, 894–898; West agrees to work to stop, 1148; in U.S., 1192–1199

Slavs: early history, 766; Viking raids on, assimilation with, 767–769; in Austrian Empire, 1022–1023

Small Is Beautiful (Schumacher), 1530

Smallpox, 834, 876–878

Smith, Adam, 1025–1026

Smolensk, Napoleon in, 978

Social Contract (Rousseau), 807

Social Darwinism, 1088, 1153

Social Function of Science, The (Bernal), 1108

Socialism: French Revolution's influence on development of, 968, 1016; utopian, 1028–1030; Marxian, 1030–1031; in French Second Republic, 1046–1047; Bismarck opposes in Germany, 1118–1119; vs. nationalism, 1124–1128; emergence in W.W. I as realistic rather than utopian, 1228; and provisional Russian government,

1235; and 1918 revolution in Germany, 1243–1244; in Scandinavia, 1318; in France, 1319–1320; Stalin's communism as perversion of, 1328; and Mussolini's early career, 1337–1338

Social science, 799, 1086–1087

Social security system: Bismarck initiates in German Empire, 1118–1119; in U.S., 1316; reforms, improvements in, 1458

Society of Jesus, *see* Jesuits

Socorro, 1174

Socrates, 91, 100, 102

Solidarity (Polish union), 1391

Solomon, 44–45, 47, 51

Solomonid dynasty, 892

Solon, 86–87

Solzhenitsyn, Alexander, 1387, 1391, 1530

Somme, battle of the, 1228

Songhay, 890

Soninke (Sohn-ink-uh), 539, 542

Sophia, archduchess of Austria, 1050

Sophists, 101–102

Sophocles, 96

Sorel, Georges, 1291

Souls of Black Folk (Du Bois), 1429–1430

Sound and the Fury, The (Faulkner), 1297

South Africa, Republic of, 1382, 1440–1443

South America: peoples and geography, 552–553; Portuguese exploration, 671; Spanish in, 673–675, 1021; immigration in, 1142–1146. *See also* Latin America; Third World

Southeast Asia: Indian culture in, 325–327; nationalism in, 1284–1285, 1419–1421. *See also* India

Southern Africa, 1440–1443

Southern Rhodesia, 1434. *See also* Zimbabwe

South German Confederation, 1021

South Korea, 1487. *See also* Korea

Soviet Union, *see* Russia

Space research, 1451

Spain: under Rome, 219, 221, 245, 261; Franks invade, 263; Visigoths in, 281; Muslims control, 306, 311–312; and the medieval *reconquista*, 484; and unification, Christianization, 617–620; Charles V inherits, 638; and explorations, 671–674; and administration of colonies, 675; economic effects of discoveries, 676; victor in Habsburg-Valois wars, start of religious wars, 679; into Low Countries, 686–688; United Provinces declare independence from, 688; Armada defeated, 690; in Thirty Years' War,

694; 17th-century decline of absolutism, 732–735; in competition for colonial empire, 841–842, 847–849; in South America, 884–886, 1169–1177; declares war on Britain, 950; Republican France declares war on, 965; rebels against Napoleon's attempt to make it French satellite, 976; grants constitution, 1021; in Africa, 1147; civil war in, 1320, 1352; dictatorship scrapped, 1383

Spanish-American War, 1151, 1206

Spanish Armada, 690

Spanish Civil War, 1320, 1352

Sparta, 72, 132; growth of, 84; social system of, 85–86; in Greek wars, 88–89; internal wars with Athens, 89–91; decline of, 103–105

Speke, John, 529

Spencer, Herbert, 1088

Spengler, Oswald, 1297

Speyer, Diet of, 634

Spice trade, 670, 678

Spinning of yarn, 986

"Spinsters," 839

Spirit of Laws, The (Montesquieu), 982

Sports, in 1900, 1075

Sri Lanka (Sree-lahnk-ah), 1419–1420, 1481

Srivijaya (Sree-vih-jah-yah) Empire, 326–327

SS (Nazi group), 1347, 1354

Ssu-ma Ch'ien (Suh-ma Kih-ehn), 187, 192, 193, 198

Stages of Economic Growth: A Non-Communist Manifesto (Rostow), 1484

Stalin, Joseph: and totalitarian Russia, 1326–1337; signs pact with Hitler, 1352; Hitler invades Russia, 1354; in W.W. II, 1360–1365; at Teheran Conference, 1365–1367; at Yalta Conference, 1367; at Potsdam Conference, 1367–1368; during postwar era, 1383–1385; attacked by Khruschchev, 1385

Stalingrad, Nazi defeat at, 1362

"Stalin's Heirs," (Yevtushenko), 1388

Stamp Act, 948–949

Standard of living: in North American colonies, 844–846; in 1900, 1066–1076; among workers after 1850, 1126; in Russia, 1335, 1386, 1390; modern, 1458

Standard Oil Co., 1200, 1203

Stanley, H. M., 529, 1128

Star Chamber, 616, 617

Starry Night, The (van Gogh painting), 1300

State: as concept under Cyrus the Great, 59; medieval origins of modern, 456–470; Machiavelli's theories on, 594–595; in the Renaissance, 609–610;